Peterson's Two-Year Colleges 2012

PETERSON'S
Publishing

About Peterson's Publishing
Peterson's Publishing provides the accurate, dependable, high-quality education content and guidance you need to succeed. No matter where you are on your academic or professional path, you can rely on Peterson's print and digital publications for the most up-to-date education exploration data, expert test-prep tools, and top-notch career success resources—everything you need to achieve your goals.

Visit us online at **www.petersonspublishing.com** and let Peterson's help you achieve your goals.

For more information, contact Peterson's Publishing, 2000 Lenox Drive, Lawrenceville, NJ 08648; 800-338-3282 Ext. 54229; or find us on the World Wide Web at www.petersonspublishing.com.

Bernadette Webster, Director of Publishing; Jill C. Schwartz, Editor; John Wells, Research Project Manager; Cathleen Fee, Research Associate; Phyllis Johnson, Software Engineer; Ray Golaszewski, Publishing Operations Manager; Linda M. Williams, Composition Manager; Karen Mount, Fulfillment Coordinator; Danielle Vreeland, Shannon White, Client Relations Representatives

ISSN 0894-9328
ISBN-13: 978-0-7689-3278-2
ISBN-10: 0-7689-3278-5

Printed in the United States of America

10 9 8 7 6 5 4 3 2 1   13 12 11

Forty-second Edition

Sustainability—Its Importance to Peterson's Publishing

What does sustainability mean to Peterson's? As a leading publisher, we are aware that our business has a direct impact on vital resources—most especially the trees that are used to make our books. Peterson's Publishing is proud that its products are certified by the Sustainable Forestry Initiative (SFI) and that all of its books are printed on paper that is 40% post-consumer waste using vegetable-based ink.

Being a part of the Sustainable Forestry Initiative (SFI) means that all of our vendors—from paper suppliers to printers—have undergone rigorous audits to demonstrate that they are maintaining a sustainable environment.

Peterson's continuously strives to find new ways to incorporate sustainability throughout all aspects of its business.

Contents

A Note from the Peterson's Editors

For nearly 50 years, Peterson's has given students and parents the most comprehensive, up-to-date information on undergraduate institutions in the United States. Peterson's researches the data published in *Peterson's Two-Year Colleges* each year. The information is furnished by the colleges and is accurate at the time of publishing.

This guide also features advice and tips on the college search and selection process, such as how to decide if a two-year college is right for you, how to approach transferring between colleges, and what's in store for adults returning to college. If you seem to be getting more, not less, anxious about choosing and getting into the right college, *Peterson's Two-Year Colleges* provides just the right help, giving you the information you need to make important college decisions and ace the admission process.

Opportunities abound for students, and this guide can help you find what you want in a number of ways:

"What You Need to Know About Two-Year Colleges" outlines the basic features and advantages of two-year colleges. "Surviving Standardized Tests" gives an overview of the common examinations students take prior to attending college. "Who's Paying for This? Financial Aid Basics" provides guidelines for financing your college education. "Frequently Asked Questions About Transferring" takes a look at the two-year college scene from the perspective of a student who is looking toward the day when he or she may pursue additional education at a four-year institution. "Returning to School: Advice for Adult Students" is an analysis of the pros and cons (mostly pros) of returning to college after already having begun a professional career. "What International Students Need to Know About Admission to U.S. Colleges and Universities" is an article written particularly for students overseas who are considering a U.S. college education. "Community Colleges and the New Green Economy" offers information on some exciting "green" programs at community colleges throughout the United States, as well as two insightful essays by Mary F. T. Spilde, President, Lane Community College and James DeHaven, V.P. of Economic and Business Development, Kalamazoo Valley Community College. Finally, "How to Use This Guide" gives details on the data in this guide: what terms mean and why they're here.

- If you already have specifics in mind, such as a particular institution or major, turn to the easy-to-use **Two-Year Colleges At-a-Glance Chart** or **Indexes**. You can look up a particular feature—location and programs offered—or use the alphabetical index and immediately find the colleges that meet your criteria.

- For information about particular colleges, turn to the **Profiles of Two-Year Colleges** section. Here, our comprehensive college profiles are arranged alphabetically by state. They provide a complete picture of need-to-know information about every accredited two-year college—from admission to graduation, including expenses, financial aid, majors, and campus safety. All the information you need to apply is placed together at the conclusion of each college **Profile**. Display ads, which appear near some of the institutions' profiles, have been provided and paid for by those colleges or universities that wished to supplement their profile data with additional information about their institution.

- In addition, two-page narrative descriptions, which appear as **College Close-Ups**, are paid for and written by college officials and offer great detail about each college. They are edited to provide a consistent format across entries for your ease of comparison.

Join the two-year college search conversation on Facebook® and Twitter™ at www.facebook.com/find.colleges and www.twitter.com/find_colleges. Peterson's Publishing is committed to providing you with the most comprehensive and reliable directories to help you unlock opportunities and realize your educational aspirations.

Peterson's publishes a full line of books—education exploration, test prep, financial aid, and career preparation. Peterson's publications can be found at high school guidance offices, college libraries and career centers, and your local bookstore and library. Peterson's books are now also available as eBooks.

We welcome any comments or suggestions you may have about this publication. Your feedback will help us make educational dreams possible for you—and others like you.

Colleges will be pleased to know that Peterson's helped you in your selection. Admissions staff members are more than happy to answer questions, address specific problems and help in any way they can. The editors at Peterson's wish you great success in your college search.

The College Admissions Process: An Overview

What You Need to Know About Two-Year Colleges

David R. Pierce

Two-year colleges—better known as community colleges—are often called "the people's colleges." With their open-door policies (admission is open to individuals with a high school diploma or its equivalent), community colleges provide access to higher education for millions of Americans who might otherwise be excluded from higher education. Community college students are diverse and of all ages, races, and economic backgrounds. While many community college students enroll full-time, an equally large number attend on a part-time basis so they can fulfill employment and family commitments as they advance their education.

Community colleges can also be referred to as either technical or junior colleges, and they may either be under public or independent control. What unites two-year colleges is that they are regionally accredited, postsecondary institutions, whose highest credential awarded is the associate degree. With few exceptions, community colleges offer a comprehensive curriculum, which includes transfer, technical, and continuing education programs.

IMPORTANT FACTORS IN A COMMUNITY COLLEGE EDUCATION

The student who attends a community college can count on receiving high-quality instruction in a supportive learning community. This setting frees the student to pursue his or her own goals, nurture special talents, explore new fields of learning, and develop the capacity for lifelong learning.

From the student's perspective, four characteristics capture the essence of community colleges:

1. They are community-based institutions that work in close partnership with high schools, community groups, and employers in extending high-quality programs at convenient times and places.

2. Community colleges are cost effective. Annual tuition and fees at public community colleges average approximately half those at public four-year colleges and less than 15 percent of private four-year institutions. In addition, since most community colleges are generally close to their students' homes, these students can also save a significant amount of money on the room, board, and transportation expenses traditionally associated with a college education.

3. They provide a caring environment, with faculty members who are expert instructors, known for excellent teaching and meeting students at the point of their individual needs, regardless of age, sex, race, current job status, or previous academic preparation. Community colleges join a strong curriculum with a broad range of counseling and career services that are intended to assist students in making the most of their educational opportunities.

4. Many offer comprehensive programs, including transfer curricula in such liberal arts programs as chemistry, psychology, and business management, that lead directly to a baccalaureate degree and career programs that prepare students for employment or assist those already employed in upgrading their skills. For those students who need to strengthen their academic skills, community colleges also offer a wide range of developmental programs in mathematics, languages, and learning skills, designed to prepare the student for success in college studies.

GETTING TO KNOW YOUR TWO-YEAR COLLEGE

The first step in determining the quality of a community college is to check the status of its accreditation. Once you have established that a community college is appropriately accredited, find out as much as you can about the programs and services it has to offer. Much of that information can be found in materials the college provides. However, the best way to learn about a college is to visit in person.

During a campus visit, be prepared to ask a lot of questions. Talk to students, faculty members, administrators, and counselors about the college and its programs, particularly those in which you have a special interest. Ask about available certificates and associate degrees. Don't be shy. Do what you can to dig below the surface. Ask college officials about the transfer rate to four-year colleges. If a college emphasizes student services, find out what particular assistance is offered, such as educational or career guidance. Colleges are eager to provide you with the information you need to make informed decisions.

COMMUNITY COLLEGES CAN SAVE YOU MONEY

If you are able to live at home while you attend college, you will certainly save money on room and board, but it does cost something to commute. Many two-year colleges offer you instruction in your own home through online learning programs or through home study courses that can save both time and money. Look into all the options, and be sure to add up all the costs of attending various colleges before deciding which is best for you.

FINANCIAL AID

Many students who attend community colleges are eligible for a range of financial aid programs, including Federal Pell Grants, Perkins and Stafford Loans, state aid, and on-campus jobs. Your high school counselor or the financial aid officer at a community college will also be able to help you. It is in your interest to apply for financial aid months in advance of the date you intend to start your college program, so find out early what assistance is available to you. While many community colleges are able to help students who make a last-minute decision to attend college, either through short-term loans or emergency grants, if you are considering entering college and think you might need financial aid, it is best to find out as much as you can as early as you can.

WORKING AND GOING TO SCHOOL

Many two-year college students maintain full-time or part-time employment while they earn their degrees. Over the years, a steadily growing number of students have chosen to attend community colleges while they fulfill family and employment responsibilities. To enable these students to balance the demands of home, work, and school, most community colleges offer classes at night and on weekends.

For the full-time student, the usual length of time it takes to obtain an associate degree is two years. However, your length of study will depend on the course load you take: the fewer credits you earn each term, the longer it will take you to earn a degree. To assist you in moving more quickly toward earning your degree, many community colleges now award credit through examination or for equivalent knowledge gained through relevant life experiences. Be certain to find out the credit options that are available to you at the college in which you are interested. You may discover that it will take less time to earn a degree than you first thought.

PREPARATION FOR TRANSFER

Studies have repeatedly shown that students who first attend a community college and then transfer to a four-year college or university do at least as well academically as the students who entered the four-year institutions as freshmen. Most community colleges have agreements with nearby four-year institutions to make transfer of credits easier. If you are thinking of transferring, be sure to meet with a counselor or faculty adviser before choosing your courses. You will want to map out a course of study with transfer in mind. Make sure you also find out the credit-transfer requirements of the four-year institution you might want to attend.

ATTENDING A TWO-YEAR COLLEGE IN ANOTHER REGION

Although many community colleges serve a specific county or district, they are committed (to the extent of their ability) to the goal of equal educational opportunity without regard to economic status, race, creed, color, sex, or national origin. Independent two-year colleges recruit from a much broader geographical area—throughout the United States and, increasingly, around the world.

Although some community colleges do provide on-campus housing for their students, most do not. However, even if on-campus housing is not available, most colleges do have housing referral services.

NEW CAREER OPPORTUNITIES

Community colleges realize that many entering students are not sure about the field in which they want to focus their studies or the career they would like to pursue. Often, students discover fields and careers they never knew existed. Community colleges have the resources to help students identify areas of career interest and to set challenging occupational goals.

Once a career goal is set, you can be confident that a community college will provide job-relevant, technical education. About half of the students who take courses for credit at community colleges do so to prepare for employment or to acquire or upgrade skills for their current job. Especially helpful in charting a career path is the assistance of a counselor or a faculty adviser, who can discuss job opportunities in your chosen field and help you map out your course of study.

In addition, since community colleges have close ties to their communities, they are in constant contact with leaders in business, industry, organized labor, and public life. Community colleges work with these individuals and their organizations to prepare students for direct entry into the world of work. For example, some community colleges have established partnerships with local businesses and industries to provide specialized training programs. Some also provide the academic portion of apprenticeship training, while others offer extensive job-shadowing and cooperative education opportunities. Be sure to examine all of the career-preparation opportunities offered by the community colleges in which you are interested.

David R. Pierce is the former President of the American Association of Community Colleges.

Surviving Standardized Tests

WHAT ARE STANDARDIZED TESTS?

Colleges and universities in the United States use tests to help evaluate applicants' readiness for admission or to place them in appropriate courses. The tests that are most frequently used by colleges are the ACT of American College Testing, Inc., and the College Board's SAT. In addition, the Educational Testing Service (ETS) offers the TOEFL test, which evaluates the English-language proficiency of nonnative speakers. The tests are offered at designated testing centers located at high schools and colleges throughout the United States and U.S. territories and at testing centers in various countries throughout the world.

Upon request, special accommodations for students with documented visual, hearing, physical, or learning disabilities are available. Examples of special accommodations include tests in Braille or large print and such aids as a reader, recorder, magnifying glass, or sign language interpreter. Additional testing time may be allowed in some instances. Contact the appropriate testing program or your guidance counselor for details on how to request special accommodations.

THE ACT

The ACT is a standardized college entrance examination that measures knowledge and skills in English, mathematics, reading, and science reasoning and the application of these skills to future academic tasks. The ACT consists of four multiple-choice tests.

Test 1: English
- 75 questions, 45 minutes
- Usage and mechanics
- Rhetorical skills

Test 2: Mathematics
- 60 questions, 60 minutes
- Pre-algebra
- Elementary algebra
- Intermediate algebra
- Coordinate geometry
- Plane geometry
- Trigonometry

Test 3: Reading
- 40 questions, 35 minutes
- Prose fiction
- Humanities
- Social studies
- Natural sciences

Test 4: Science
- 40 questions, 35 minutes
- Data representation
- Research summary
- Conflicting viewpoints

Each section is scored from 1 to 36 and is scaled for slight variations in difficulty. Students are not penalized for incorrect responses. The composite score is the average of the four scaled scores. The ACT Plus Writing includes the four multiple-choice tests and a writing test, which measures writing skills emphasized in high school English classes and in entry-level college composition courses.

To prepare for the ACT, ask your guidance counselor for a free guidebook called "Preparing for the ACT." Besides providing general test-preparation information and additional test-taking strategies, this guidebook describes the content and format of the four ACT subject area tests, summarizes test administration procedures followed at ACT test centers, and includes a practice test. Peterson's publishes *The Real ACT Prep Guide* that includes five official ACT tests.

THE SAT

The SAT measures developed critical reading and mathematical reasoning abilities as they relate to successful performance in college. It is intended to supplement the secondary school record and other information about the student in assessing readiness for college. There is one unscored, experimental section on the exam, which is used for equating and/or pretesting purposes and can cover either the mathematics or critical reading area.

Critical Reading
- 67 questions, 70 minutes
- Sentence completion
- Passage-based reading

DON'T FORGET TO . . .

❏ Take the SAT or ACT before application deadlines.

❏ Note that test registration deadlines precede test dates by about six weeks.

❏ Register to take the TOEFL test if English is not your native language and you are planning on studying at a North American college.

❏ Practice your test-taking skills with *Peterson's Master the SAT, Peterson's Ultimate ACT Tool Kit, The Real ACT Prep Guide* (published by Peterson's), *Peterson's Master TOEFL Reading Skills, Peterson's Master TOEFL Vocabulary,* and *Peterson's Master TOEFL Writing Skills*.

❏ Contact the College Board or American College Testing, Inc., in advance if you need special accommodations when taking tests.

Mathematics
- 54 questions, 70 minutes
- Multiple-choice
- Student-produced response (grid-ins)

Writing
- 49 questions plus essay, 60 minutes
- Identifying sentence errors
- Improving paragraphs
- Improving sentences
- Essay

Students receive one point for each correct response and lose a fraction of a point for each incorrect response (except for student-produced responses). These points are totaled to produce the raw scores, which are then scaled to equalize the scores for slight variations in difficulty for various editions of the test. The critical reading, writing, and mathematics scaled scores range from 200–800 per section. The total scaled score range is from 600–2400.

SAT SUBJECT TESTS

Subject Tests are required by some institutions for admission and/or placement in freshman-level courses. Each Subject Test measures one's knowledge of a specific subject and the ability to apply that knowledge. Students should check with each institution for its specific requirements. In general, students are required to take three Subject Tests (one English, one mathematics, and one of their choice).

Subject Tests are given in the following areas: biology, chemistry, Chinese, French, German, Italian, Japanese, Korean, Latin, literature, mathematics, modern Hebrew, physics, Spanish, U.S. history, and world history. These tests are 1 hour long and are primarily multiple-choice tests. Three Subject Tests may be taken on one test date.

Scored like the SAT, students gain a point for each correct answer and lose a fraction of a point for each incorrect answer. The raw scores are then converted to scaled scores that range from 200 to 800.

THE TOEFL INTERNET-BASED TEST (IBT)

The Test of English as a Foreign Language Internet-Based Test (TOEFL iBT) is designed to help assess a student's grasp of English if it is not the student's first language. Performance on the TOEFL test may help interpret scores on the critical reading sections of the SAT. The test consists of four integrated sections: speaking, listening, reading, and writing. The TOEFL iBT emphasizes integrated skills. The paper-based versions of the TOEFL will continue to be administered in certain countries where the Internet-based version has not yet been introduced. For further information, visit www.toefl.org.

WHAT OTHER TESTS SHOULD I KNOW ABOUT?

The AP Program
This program allows high school students to try college-level work and build valuable skills and study habits in the process. Subject matter is explored in more depth in AP courses than in other high school classes. A qualifying score on an AP test—which varies from school to school—can earn you college credit or advanced placement. Getting qualifying grades on enough exams can even earn you a full year's credit and sophomore standing at more than 1,500 higher-education institutions. There are more than thirty AP courses across multiple subject areas, including art history, biology, and computer science. Speak to your guidance counselor for information about your school's offerings.

College-Level Examination Program (CLEP)
The CLEP enables students to earn college credit for what they already know, whether it was learned in school, through independent study, or through other experiences outside of the classroom. More than 2,900 colleges and universities now award credit for qualifying scores on one or more of the 33 CLEP exams. The exams, which are 90 minutes in length and are primarily multiple choice, are administered at participating colleges and universities. For more information, check out the Web site at www.collegeboard.com/clep.

WHAT CAN I DO TO PREPARE FOR THESE TESTS?

Know what to expect. Get familiar with how the tests are structured, how much time is allowed, and the directions for each type of question. Get plenty of rest the night before the test and eat breakfast that morning.

There are a variety of products, from books to software to videos, available to help you prepare for most standardized tests. Find the learning style that suits you best. As for which products to buy, there are two major categories— those created by the test makers and those created by private companies. The best approach is to talk to someone who has been through the process and find out which product or products he or she recommends.

Some students report significant increases in scores after participating in coaching programs. Longer-term programs (40 hours) seem to raise scores more than short-term programs (20 hours), but beyond 40 hours, score gains are minor. Math scores appear to benefit more from coaching than critical reading scores.

Resources
There is a variety of ways to prepare for standardized tests—find a method that fits your schedule and your budget. But you should definitely prepare. Far too many students walk into these tests cold, either because they find standardized tests frightening or annoying or they just haven't found the time to study. The key is that these exams are standardized. That means these tests are largely the same from administration to administration; they always test the same concepts. They have to, or else you couldn't compare the scores of people who took the tests on different dates. The numbers or words may change, but the underlying content doesn't.

So how do you prepare? At the very least, you should review relevant material, such as math formulas and commonly used vocabulary words, and know the directions for each question type or test section. You should take at least one practice test and review your mistakes so you don't make them again on the test day. Beyond that, you know best how much preparation you need. You'll also find lots of material in libraries or bookstores to help you: books and software from the test makers and from other publishers (including Peterson's) or live courses that range from national test-preparation companies to teachers at your high school who offer classes.

Top 10 Ways Not to Take the Test

10. Cramming the night before the test.

9. Not becoming familiar with the directions before you take the test.

8. Not becoming familiar with the format of the test before you take it.

7. Not knowing how the test is graded.

6. Spending too much time on any one question.

5. Second-guessing yourself.

4. Not checking spelling, grammar, and sentence structure in essays.

3. Writing a one-paragraph essay.

2. Forgetting to take a deep breath to keep from—

1. Losing It!

Who's Paying for This?
Financial Aid Basics

A college education can be expensive—costing more than $150,000 for four years at some of the higher priced private colleges and universities. Even at the lower cost state colleges and universities, the cost of a four-year education can approach $60,000. Determining how you and your family will come up with the necessary funds to pay for your education requires planning, perseverance, and learning as much as you can about the options that are available to you. But before you get discouraged, College Board statistics show that 53 percent of full-time students attend four-year public and private colleges with tuition and fees less than $9000, while 20 percent attend colleges that have tuition and fees more than $36,000. College costs tend to be less in the western states and higher in New England.

Paying for college should not be looked at as a four-year financial commitment. For many families, paying the total cost of a student's college education out of current income and savings is usually not realistic. For families that have planned ahead and have financial savings established for higher education, the burden is a lot easier. But for most, meeting the cost of college requires the pooling of current income and assets and investing in longer-term loan options. These family resources, together with financial assistance from state, federal, and institutional sources, enable millions of students each year to attend the institution of their choice.

FINANCIAL AID PROGRAMS

There are three types of financial aid:

1. Gift-aid—Scholarships and grants are funds that do not have to be repaid.

2. Loans—Loans must be repaid, usually after graduation; the amount you have to pay back is the total you've borrowed plus any accrued interest. This is considered a source of self-help aid.

3. Student employment—Student employment is a job arranged for you by the financial aid office. This is another source of self-help aid.

The federal government has four major grant programs—the Federal Pell Grant, the Federal Supplemental Educational Opportunity Grant, Academic Competitiveness Grants (ACG), and SMART grants. ACG and SMART grants are limited to students who qualify for a Pell grant and are awarded to a select group of students. Overall, these grants are targeted to low-to-moderate income families with significant financial need. The federal government also sponsors a student employment program called the Federal Work-Study Program, which offers jobs both on and off campus, and

several loan programs, including those for students and for parents of undergraduate students.

There are two types of student loan programs: subsidized and unsubsidized. The subsidized Federal Direct Loan and the Federal Perkins Loan are need-based, government-subsidized loans. Students who borrow through these programs do not have to pay interest on the loan until after they graduate or leave school. The unsubsidized Federal Direct Loan and the Federal Direct PLUS Loan Program are not based on need, and borrowers are responsible for the interest while the student is in school. These loans are administered by different methods. Once you choose your college, the financial aid office will guide you through this process.

After you've submitted your financial aid application and you've been accepted for admission, each college will send you a letter describing your financial aid award. Most award letters show estimated college costs, how much you and your family are expected to contribute, and the amount and types of aid you have been awarded. Most students are awarded aid from a combination of sources and programs. Hence, your award is often called a financial aid "package."

SOURCES OF FINANCIAL AID

Millions of students and families apply for financial aid each year. Financial aid from all sources exceeds $143 billion per year. The largest single source of aid is the federal government, which will award more than $100 billion this year.

The next largest source of financial aid is found in the college and university community. Most of this aid is awarded to students who have a demonstrated need based on the Federal Methodology. Some institutions use a different formula, the Institutional Methodology (IM), to award their own funds in conjunction with other forms of aid. Institutional aid may be either need-based or non-need based. Aid that is not based on need is usually awarded for a student's academic performance (merit awards), specific talents or abilities, or to attract the type of students a college seeks to enroll.

Another source of financial aid is from state government. All states offer grant and/or scholarship aid, most of which is need-based. However, more and more states are offering substantial merit-based aid programs. Most state programs award aid only to students attending college in their home state.

Other sources of financial aid include:

- Private agencies
- Foundations
- Corporations
- Clubs
- Fraternal and service organizations

- Civic associations
- Unions
- Religious groups that award grants, scholarships, and low-interest loans
- Employers that provide tuition reimbursement benefits for employees and their children

More information about these different sources of aid is available from high school guidance offices, public libraries, college financial aid offices, directly from the sponsoring organizations, and on the Web at www.petersons.com and www.finaid.org.

HOW NEED-BASED FINANCIAL AID IS AWARDED

When you apply for aid, your family's financial situation is analyzed using a government-approved formula called the Federal Methodology. This formula looks at five items:

1. Demographic information of the family
2. Income of the parents
3. Assets of the parents
4. Income of the student
5. Assets of the student

This analysis determines the amount you and your family are expected to contribute toward your college expenses, called your Expected Family Contribution or EFC. If the EFC is equal to or more than the cost of attendance at a particular college, then you do not demonstrate financial need. However, even if you don't have financial need, you may still qualify for aid, as there are grants, scholarships, and loan programs that are not need-based.

If the cost of your education is greater than your EFC, then you do demonstrate financial need and qualify for assistance. The amount of your financial need that can be met varies from school to school. Some are able to meet your full need, while others can only cover a certain percentage of need. Here's the formula:

> Cost of Attendance
> − Expected Family Contribution
> = Financial Need

The EFC remains constant, but your need will vary according to the costs of attendance at a particular college. In general, the higher the tuition and fees at a particular college, the higher the cost of attendance will be. Expenses for books and supplies, room and board, transportation, and other miscellaneous items are included in the overall cost of attendance. It is important to remember that you do not have to be "needy" to qualify for financial aid. Many middle and upper-middle income families qualify for need-based financial aid.

APPLYING FOR FINANCIAL AID

Every student must complete the Free Application for Federal Student Aid (FAFSA) to be considered for financial aid. The FAFSA is available from your high school guidance office, many public libraries, colleges in your area, or directly from the U.S. Department of Education.

Students are encouraged to apply for federal student aid on the Web. The electronic version of the FAFSA can be accessed at http://www.fafsa.ed.gov. Both the student and at least one parent must apply for a federal PIN at http:// www.pin.ed.gov. The PIN serves as your electronic signature when applying for aid on the Web.

To award their own funds, some colleges require an additional application, the CSS/Financial Aid PROFILE® form. The PROFILE asks supplemental questions that some colleges and awarding agencies feel provide a more accurate assessment of the family's ability to pay for college. It is up to the college to decide whether it will use only the FAFSA or both the FAFSA and the PROFILE. PROFILE applications are available from the high school guidance office and on the Web. Both the paper application and the Web site list those colleges and programs that require the PROFILE application.

If Every College You're Applying to for Fall 2012 Requires the FAFSA

. . . then it's pretty simple: Complete the FAFSA after January 1, 2012, being certain to send it in before any college-imposed deadlines. (You are not permitted to send in the 2012–13 FAFSA before January 1, 2012.) Most college FAFSA application deadlines are in February or early March. It is easier if you have all your financial records for the previous year available, but if that is not possible, you are strongly encouraged to use estimated figures.

After you send in your FAFSA, either with the paper application or electronically, you'll receive a Student Aid Report (SAR) that includes all of the information you reported and shows your EFC. If you provided an e-mail address, the SAR is sent to you electronically; otherwise, you will receive a paper copy in the mail. Be sure to review the SAR, checking to see if the information you reported is accurately represented. If you used estimated numbers to complete the FAFSA, you may have to resubmit the SAR with any corrections to the data. The college(s) you have designated on the FAFSA will receive the information you reported and will use that data to make their decision. In many instances, the colleges to which you've applied will ask you to send copies of your and your parents' federal income tax returns for 2011, plus any other documents needed to verify the information you reported.

If a College Requires the PROFILE

Step 1: Register for the CSS/Financial Aid PROFILE in the fall of your senior year in high school. You can apply for the PROFILE online at http://profileonline.collegeboard.com/ prf/ index.jsp. Registration information with a list of the colleges that require the PROFILE is available in most high school guidance offices. There is a fee for using the Financial Aid PROFILE application ($25 for the first college and $16 for each additional college). You must pay for the service by credit card when you register. If you do not have a credit card, you will be billed. A limited number of fee waivers are automatically granted to first-time applicants based on the financial information provided on the PROFILE.

Step 2: Fill out your customized CSS/Financial Aid PROFILE. Once you register, your application will be immediately available online and will have questions which all students must complete, questions which must be completed by the student's parents (unless the student is independent and the colleges or programs selected do not require parental information), and *may* have supplemental questions needed by one or more of your schools or programs. If required, those will be found in Section Q of the application.

In addition to the PROFILE application you complete online, you may also be required to complete a Business/ Farm Supplement via traditional paper format. Completion of this form is not a part of the online process. If this form is required, instructions on how to download and print the supplemental form are provided. If your biological or adoptive parents are separated or divorced and your colleges and programs require it, your noncustodial parent may be asked to complete the Noncustodial PROFILE.

Once you complete and submit your PROFILE application, it will be processed and sent directly to your requested colleges and programs.

IF YOU DON'T QUALIFY FOR NEED-BASED AID

If you are not eligible for need-based aid, you can still find ways to lessen your burden.

Here are some suggestions:

- Search for merit scholarships. You can start at the initial stages of your application process. College merit awards are increasingly important as more and more colleges award these to students they especially want to attract. As a result, applying to a college at which your qualifications put you at the top of the entering class may give you a larger merit award. Another source of aid to look for is private scholarships that are given for special skills and talents. Additional information can be found at and at www.finaid.org.

- Seek employment during the summer and the academic year. The student employment office at your college can help you locate a school-year job. Many colleges and local businesses have vacancies remaining after they have hired students who are receiving Federal Work-Study Program financial aid.

- Borrow through the unsubsidized Federal Direct Loan program. This is generally available to all students. The terms and conditions are similar to the subsidized loans. The biggest difference is that the borrower is responsible for the interest while still in college, although the government permits students to delay paying the interest right away and add the accrued interest to the total amount owed. You must file the FAFSA to be considered.

- After you've secured what you can through scholarships, working, and borrowing, you and your parents will be expected to meet your share of the college bill (the Expected Family Contribution). Many colleges offer monthly payment plans that spread the cost over the academic year. If the monthly payments are too high, parents can borrow through the Federal Direct PLUS Loan Program, through one of the many private education loan programs available, or through home equity loans and lines of credit. Families seeking assistance in financing college expenses should inquire at the financial aid office about what programs are available at the college. Some families seek the advice of professional financial advisers and tax consultants.

Frequently Asked Questions About Transferring

Muriel M. Shishkoff

Among the students attending two-year colleges are a large number who began their higher education knowing they would eventually transfer to a four-year school to obtain their bachelor's degree. There are many reasons why students go this route. Upon graduating from high school, some simply do not have definite career goals. Although they don't want to put their education on hold, they prefer not to pay exorbitant amounts in tuition while trying to "find themselves." As the cost of a university education escalates—even in public institutions—the option of spending the freshman and sophomore years at a two-year college looks attractive to many students. Others attend a two-year college because they are unable to meet the initial entrance standards—a specified grade point average (GPA), standardized test scores, or knowledge of specific academic subjects—required by the four-year school of their choice. Many such students praise the community college system for giving them the chance to be, academically speaking, "born again." In addition, students from other countries often find that they can adapt more easily to language and cultural changes at a two-year school before transferring to a larger, more diverse four-year college.

If your plan is to attend a two-year college with the ultimate goal of transferring to a four-year school, you will be pleased to know that the increased importance of the community college route to a bachelor's degree is recognized by all segments of higher education. As a result, many two-year schools have revised their course outlines and established new courses in order to comply with the programs and curricular offerings of the universities. Institutional improvements to make transferring easier have also proliferated at both the two-and four-year levels. The generous transfer policies of the Pennsylvania, New York, and Florida state university systems, among others, reflect this attitude; these systems accept *all* credits from students who have graduated from accredited community colleges.

If you are interested in moving from a two-year college to a four-year school, the sooner you make up your mind that you are going to make the switch, the better position you will be in to transfer successfully (that is, without having wasted valuable time and credits). The ideal point at which to make such a decision is **before** you register for classes at your two-year school; a counselor can help you plan your course work with an eye toward fulfilling the requirements needed for your major course of study.

Naturally, it is not always possible to plan your transferring strategy that far in advance, but keep in mind that the key to a successful transfer is **preparation,** and preparation takes time—time to think through your objectives and time to plan the right classes to take.

As students face the prospect of transferring from a two-year to a four-year school, many thoughts and concerns about this complicated and often frustrating process race through their minds. Here are answers to the questions that are most frequently asked by transferring students.

Q Does every college and university accept transfer students?

A Most four-year institutions accept transfer students, but some do so more enthusiastically than others. Graduating from a community college is an advantage at, for example, Arizona State University and the University of Massachusetts Boston; both accept more community college transfer students than traditional freshmen. At the State University of New York at Albany, graduates of two-year transfer programs within the State University of New York System are given priority for upper-division (i.e., junior- and senior-level) vacancies.

Schools offering undergraduate work at the upper division only are especially receptive to transfer applications. On the other hand, some schools accept only a few transfer students; others refuse entrance to sophomores or those in their final year. Princeton University requires an "excellent academic record and particularly compelling reasons to transfer." Check the catalogs of several colleges for their transfer requirements before you make your final choice.

Q Do students who go directly from high school to a four-year college do better academically than transfer students from community colleges?

A On the contrary: some institutions report that transfers from two-year schools who persevere until graduation do *better* than those who started as freshmen in a four-year college.

Q Why is it so important that my two-year college be accredited?

A Four-year colleges and universities accept transfer credits only from schools formally recognized by a regional, national, or professional educational agency. This accreditation signifies that an institution or program of study meets or exceeds a minimum level of educational quality necessary for meeting stated educational objectives.

Q After enrolling at a four-year school, may I still make up necessary courses at a community college?

A Some institutions restrict credit after transfer to their own facilities. Others allow students to take a limited number of transfer courses after matriculation, depending on the subject matter. A few provide opportunities for cross-registration or dual enrollment, which means taking classes on more than one campus.

Q What do I need to do to transfer?

A First, send for your high school and college transcripts. Having chosen the school you wish to transfer to, check its admission requirements against your transcripts. If you find that you are admissible, file an application as early as possible before the deadline. Part of the process will be asking your former schools to send official transcripts to the admission office, i.e., not the copies you used in determining your admissibility.

Plan your transfer program with the head of your new department as soon as you have decided to transfer. Determine the recommended general education pattern and necessary preparation for your major. At your present school, take the courses you will need to meet transfer requirements for the new school.

Q What qualifies me for admission as a transfer student?

A Admission requirements for most four-year institutions vary. Depending on the reputation or popularity of the school and program you wish to enter, requirements may be quite selective and competitive. Usually, you will need to show satisfactory test scores, an academic record up to a certain standard, and completion of specific subject matter.

Transfer students can be eligible to enter a four-year school in a number of ways: by having been eligible for admission directly upon graduation from high school, by making up shortcomings in grades (or in subject matter not covered in high school) at a community college, or by satisfactory completion of necessary courses or credit hours at another postsecondary institution. Ordinarily, students coming from a community college or from another four-year institution must meet or exceed the receiving institution's standards for freshmen and show appropriate college-level course work taken since high school. Students who did not graduate from high school can present proof of proficiency through results on the General Educational Development (GED) test.

Q Are exceptions ever made for students who don't meet all the requirements for transfer?

A Extenuating circumstances, such as disability, low family income, refugee or veteran status, or athletic talent, may permit the special enrollment of students who would not otherwise be eligible but who demonstrate the potential for academic success. Consult the appropriate office—the Educational Opportunity Program, the disabled students' office, the athletic department, or the academic dean—to see whether an exception can be made in your case.

Q How far in advance do I need to apply for transfer?

A Some schools have a rolling admission policy, which means that they process transfer applications as they are received, all year long. With other schools, you must apply during the priority filing period, which can be up to a year before you wish to enter. Check the date with the admission office at your prospective campus.

Q Is it possible to transfer courses from several different institutions?

A Institutions ordinarily accept the courses that they consider transferable, regardless of the number of accredited schools involved. However, there is the danger of exceeding the maximum number of credit hours that can be transferred from all other schools or earned through credit by examination, extension courses, or correspondence courses. The limit placed on transfer credits varies from school to school, so read the catalog carefully to avoid taking courses you won't be able to use. To avoid duplicating courses, keep attendance at different campuses to a minimum.

Q What is involved in transferring from a semester system to a quarter or trimester system?

A In the semester system, the academic calendar is divided into two equal parts. The quarter system is more aptly named trimester, since the academic calendar is divided into three equal terms (not counting a summer session). To convert semester units into quarter units or credit hours, simply multiply the semester units by one and a half. Conversely, multiply quarter units by two thirds to come up with semester units. If you are used to a semester system of fifteen-to sixteen-week courses, the ten-week courses of the quarter system may seem to fly by.

Q Why might a course be approved for transfer credit by one four-year school but not by another?

A The beauty of postsecondary education in the United States lies in its variety. Entrance policies and graduation requirements are designed to reflect and serve each institution's mission. Because institutional policies vary so widely, schools may interpret the subject matter of a course from quite different points of view. Given that the granting of transfer credit indicates that a course is viewed as being, in effect, parallel to one offered by the receiving institution, it is easy to see how this might be the case at one university and not another.

Q Must I take a foreign language to transfer?

A Foreign language proficiency is often required for admission to a four-year institution; such proficiency also often figures in certain majors or in the general education pattern. Often, two or three years of a single language in high school will do the trick. Find out if scores received on Advanced Placement (AP) examinations, placement examinations given by the foreign language department, or SAT Subject Tests will be accepted in lieu of college course work.

Q Will the school to which I'm transferring accept pass/ no pass, pass/fail, or credit/no credit grades in lieu of letter grades?

A Usually, a limit is placed on the number of these courses you can transfer, and there may be other restrictions as well. If you want to use other-than-letter grades for the fulfillment of general education requirements or lower-division (freshman and sophomore) preparation for the major, check with the receiving institution.

Q Which is more important for transfer—my grade point average or my course completion pattern?

A Some schools believe that your past grades indicate academic potential and overshadow prior preparation for a specific degree program. Others require completion of certain introductory courses before transfer to prepare you for upper-division work in your major. In any case, appropriate course selection will cut down the time to graduation and increase your chances of making a successful transfer.

Q What happens to my credits if I change majors?

A If you change majors after admission, your transferable course credit should remain fairly intact. However, because you may need extra or different preparation for your new major, some of the courses you've taken may now be useful only as electives. The need for additional lower-level preparation may mean you're staying longer at your new school than you originally planned. On the other hand, you may already have taken courses that count toward your new major as part of the university's general education pattern.

Excerpted from *Transferring Made Easy: A Guide to Changing Colleges Successfully,* by Muriel M. Shishkoff, © 1991 by Muriel M. Shishkoff (published by Peterson's).

Returning to School: Advice for Adult Students

Sandra Cook, Ph.D.
Assistant Vice President for Academic Affairs, Enrollment Services, San Diego State University

Many adults think for a long time about returning to school without taking any action. One purpose of this article is to help the "thinkers" finally make some decisions by examining what is keeping them from action. Another purpose is to describe not only some of the difficulties and obstacles that adult students may face when returning to school but also tactics for coping with them.

If you have been thinking about going back to college, and believing that you are the only person your age contemplating college, you should know that approximately 7 million adult students are currently enrolled in higher education institutions. This number represents 50 percent of total higher education enrollments. The majority of adult students are enrolled at two-year colleges.

There are many reasons why adult students choose to attend a two-year college. Studies have shown that the three most important criteria that adult students consider when choosing a college are location, cost, and availability of the major or program desired. Most two-year colleges are public institutions that serve a geographic district, making them readily accessible to the community. Costs at most two-year colleges are far less than at other types of higher education institutions. For many students who plan to pursue a bachelor's degree, completing their first two years of college at a community college is an affordable means to that end. If you are interested in an academic program that will transfer to a four-year institution, most two-year colleges offer the "general education" courses that comprise most freshman and sophomore years. If you are interested in a vocational or technical program, two-year colleges excel in providing this type of training.

SETTING THE STAGE

There are three different "stages" in the process of adults returning to school. The first stage is uncertainty. Do I really want to go back to school? What will my friends or family think? Can I compete with those 18-year-old whiz kids? Am I too old? The second stage is choice. Once the decision to return has been made, you must choose where you will attend. There are many criteria to use in making this decision. The third stage is support. You have just added another role to your already-too-busy life. There are, however, strategies that will help you accomplish your goals—perhaps not without struggle, but with grace and humor nonetheless. Let's look at each of these stages.

UNCERTAINTY

Why are you thinking about returning to school? Is it to

- fulfill a dream that had to be delayed?
- become more educationally well-rounded?
- fill an intellectual void in your life?

These reasons focus on *personal growth*.

If you are returning to school to

- meet people and make friends
- attain and enjoy higher social status and prestige among friends, relatives, and associates
- understand/study a cultural heritage
- have a medium in which to exchange ideas

You are interested in *social and cultural opportunities*.

If you are like most adult students, you want to

- qualify for a new occupation
- enter or reenter the job market
- increase earnings potential
- qualify for a more challenging position in the same field of work

You are seeking *career growth*.

Understanding the reasons why you want to go back to school is an important step in setting your educational goals and will help you to establish some criteria for selecting a college. However, don't delay your decision because you have not been able to clearly define your motives. Many times, these aren't clear until you have already begun the process, and they may change as you move through your college experience.

Assuming you agree that additional education will benefit you, what is it that keeps you from returning to school? You may have a litany of excuses running through your mind:

- I don't have time.
- I can't afford it.
- I'm too old to learn.
- My friends will think I'm crazy.
- Teachers and students will be younger than I.

- My family can't survive without me to take care of them every minute.
- I'll be X years old when I finish.
- I'm afraid.
- I don't know what to expect.

And that is just what these are—excuses. You can make school, like anything else in your life, a priority or not. If you really want to return, you can. The more you understand your motivation for returning to school and the more you understand what excuses are keeping you from taking action, the easier your task will be.

If you think you don't have time: The best way to decide how attending class and studying can fit into your schedule is to keep track of what you do with your time each day for several weeks. Completing a standard time-management grid (each day is plotted out by the half hour) is helpful for visualizing how your time is spent. For each 3-credit-hour class you take, you will need to find 3 hours for class plus 6 to 9 hours for reading-studying-library time. This study time should be spaced evenly throughout the week, not loaded up on one day. It is not possible to learn or retain the material that way. When you examine your grid, see where there are activities that could be replaced with school and study time. You may decide to give up your bowling league or some time in front of the TV. Try not to give up sleeping, and don't cut out every moment of free time. Here are some suggestions that have come from adults who have returned to school:

- Enroll in a time-management workshop. It helps you rethink how you use your time.
- Don't think you have to take more than one course at a time. You may eventually want to work up to taking more, but consider starting with one. (It is more than you are taking now!)
- If you have a family, start assigning to them those household chores that you usually do—and don't redo what they do.
- Use your lunch hour or commuting time for reading.

If you think you cannot afford it: As mentioned earlier, two-year colleges are extremely affordable. If you cannot afford the tuition, look into the various financial aid options. Most federal and state funds are available to full- and part-time students. Loans are also available. While many people prefer not to accumulate a debt for school, these same people will think nothing of taking out a loan to buy a car. After five or six years, which is the better investment? Adult students who work should look into whether their company has a tuition-reimbursement policy. There are also private scholarships, available through foundations, service organizations, and clubs, that are focused on adult learners. Your public library, the Web, and a college financial aid adviser are three excellent sources for reference materials regarding financial aid.

If you think you are too old to learn: This is pure myth. A number of studies have shown that adult learners perform as well as, or better than, traditional-age students.

If you are afraid your friends will think you're crazy: Who cares? Maybe they will, maybe they won't. Usually, they will admire your courage and be just a little jealous of your ambition (although they'll never tell you that). Follow your dreams, not theirs.

If you are concerned because the teachers or students will be younger than you: Don't be. The age differences that may be apparent in other settings evaporate in the classroom. If anything, an adult in the classroom strikes fear into the hearts of some 18-year-olds because adults have been known to be prepared, ask questions, be truly motivated, and be there to learn!

If you think your family will have a difficult time surviving while you are in school: If you have done everything for them up to now, they might struggle. Consider this an opportunity to help them become independent and self-sufficient. Your family can only make you feel guilty if you let them. You are not abandoning them; you are becoming an educational role model. When you are happy and working toward your goals, everyone benefits. Admittedly, it sometimes takes time for them to realize this. For single parents, there are schools that offer support groups, child care, and cooperative babysitting.

If you're appalled at the thought of being X years old when you graduate in Y years: How old will you be in Y years if you don't go back to school?

If you are afraid or don't know what to expect: Know that these are natural feelings when one encounters any new situation. Adult students find that their fears usually dissipate once they begin classes. Fear of trying is usually the biggest roadblock to the reentry process.

No doubt you have dreamed up a few more reasons for not making the decision to return to school. Keep in mind that what you are doing is making up excuses, and you are using these excuses to release you from the obligation to make a decision about your life. The thought of returning to college can be scary. Anytime anyone ventures into unknown territory, there is a risk, but taking risks is a necessary component of personal and professional growth. It is your life, and you alone are responsible for making the decisions that determine its course. Education is an investment in your future.

CHOICE

Once you have decided to go back to school, your next task is to decide where to go. If your educational goals are well defined (e.g., you want to pursue a degree in order to change careers), then your task is a bit easier. But even if your educational goals are still evolving, do not defer your return. Many students who enter higher education with a specific major in mind change that major at least once.

Most students who attend a public two-year college choose the community college in the district in which they live. This is generally the closest and least expensive option if the school offers the programs you want. If you are planning to begin your education at a two-year college and then transfer to a four-year school, there are distinct advantages to choosing your four-year school early. Many community and four-year colleges have "articulation" agreements that designate what credits from the two-year school will transfer to the four-year college and how. Some four-year institutions accept an associate degree as equivalent to the freshman and sophomore years, regardless of the courses you have taken. Some four-year schools accept two-year college work only on a course-by-course basis. If you can identify which school you will transfer to, you can know in advance exactly how your two-year credits will apply, preventing an unexpected loss of credit or time.

Each institution of higher education is distinctive. Your goal in choosing a college is to come up with the best student-institution fit—matching your needs with the offerings and characteristics of the school. The first step in choosing a college is to determine what criteria are most important to you in attaining your educational goals. Location, cost, and program availability are the three main factors that influence an adult student's college choice. In considering location, don't forget that some colleges have conveniently located branch campuses. In considering cost, remember to explore your financial aid options before ruling out an institution because of its tuition. Program availability should include not only the major in which you are interested, but also whether or not classes in that major are available when you can take them.

Some additional considerations beyond location, cost, and programs are:

- Does the school have a commitment to adult students and offer appropriate services, such as child care, tutoring, and advising?

- Are classes offered at times when you can take them?

- Are there academic options for adults, such as credit for life or work experience, credit by examination (including CLEP), credit for military service, or accelerated programs?

- Is the faculty sensitive to the needs of adult learners?

Once you determine which criteria are vital in your choice of an institution, you can begin to narrow your choices. There are myriad ways for you to locate the information you desire. Many newspapers publish a "School Guide" several times a year in which colleges and universities advertise to an adult student market. In addition, schools themselves publish catalogs, class schedules, and promotional materials that contain much of the information you need, and they are yours for the asking. Many colleges sponsor information sessions and open houses that allow you to visit the campus and ask questions. An appointment with an adviser is a good way to assess the fit between you and the institution. Be sure to bring your questions with you to your interview.

SUPPORT

Once you have made the decision to return to school and have chosen the institution that best meets your needs, take some additional steps to ensure your success during your crucial first semester. Take advantage of institutional support and build some social support systems of your own. Here are some ways of doing just that:

- Plan to participate in any orientation programs. These serve the threefold purpose of providing you with a great deal of important information, familiarizing you with the campus and its facilities, and giving you the opportunity to meet and begin networking with other students.

- Take steps to deal with any academic weaknesses. Take mathematics and writing placement tests if you have reason to believe you may need some extra help in these areas. It is not uncommon for adult students to need a math refresher course or a program to help alleviate math anxiety. Ignoring a weakness won't make it go away.

- Look into adult reentry programs. Many institutions offer adults workshops focusing on ways to improve study skills, textbook reading, test-taking, and time-management skills.

- Build new support networks by joining an adult student organization, making a point of meeting other adult students through workshops, or actively seeking out a "study buddy" in each class—that invaluable friend who shares and understands your experience.

- Incorporate your new status as "student" into your family life. Doing your homework with your children at a designated "homework time" is a valuable family activity and reinforces the importance of education.

- Make sure you take a reasonable course load in your first semester. It is far better to have some extra time on your hands and to succeed magnificently than to spend the entire semester on the brink of a breakdown. Also, whenever possible, try to focus your first courses not only on requirements, but also on areas of personal interest.

- Faculty members, advisers, and student affairs personnel are there to help you during difficult times—let them assist you as often as necessary.

After completing your first semester, you will probably look back in wonder at why you thought going back to school was so imposing. Certainly, it's not without its occasional exasperations. But, as with life, keeping things in perspective and maintaining your sense of humor make the difference between just coping and succeeding brilliantly.

What International Students Need to Know About Admission to U.S. Colleges and Universities

Kitty M. Villa

There are two principles to remember about admission to a university in the United States. First, applying is almost never a one-time request for admission but an ongoing process that may involve several exchanges of information between applicant and institution. "Admission process" or "application process" means that a "yes" or "no" is usually not immediate, and requests for additional information are to be expected. To successfully manage this process, you must be prepared to send additional information when requested and then wait for replies. You need a thoughtful balance of persistence to communicate regularly and effectively with your selected universities and patience to endure what can be a very long process.

The second principle involves a marketplace analogy. The most successful applicants are alert to opportunities to create a positive impression that sets them apart from other applicants. They are able to market themselves to their target institution. Institutions are also trying to attract the highest-quality student that they can. The admissions process presents you with the opportunity to analyze your strengths and weaknesses as a student and to look for ways to present yourself in the most marketable manner.

FIRST STEP—SELECTING INSTITUTIONS

With thousands of institutions of higher education in the United States, how do you begin to narrow your choices down to the institutions that are best for you? There are many factors to consider, and you must ultimately decide which factors are most important to you.

Location

You may spend several years studying in the United States. Do you prefer an urban or rural campus? Large or small metropolitan area? If you need to live on campus, will you be unhappy at a university where most students commute from off-campus housing? How do you feel about extremely hot summers or cold winters? Eliminating institutions that do not match your preferences in terms of location will narrow your choices.

Recommendations from Friends, Professors, or Others

There are valid academic reasons to consider the recommendations of people who know you well and have firsthand knowledge about particular institutions. Friends and contacts may be able to provide you with "inside information" about the campus or its academic programs to which published sources have no access. You should carefully balance anecdotal information with your own research and your own impressions. However, current and former students, professors, and others may provide excellent information during the application process.

Your Own Academic and Career Goals

Consideration of your academic goals is more complex than it may seem at first glance. All institutions do not offer the same academic programs. The application form usually provides a definitive listing of the academic programs offered by an institution. A course catalog describes the degree program and all the courses offered. In addition to printed sources, there is a tremendous amount of institutional information available on the Web. Program descriptions, even course descriptions and course syllabi, are often available to peruse online.

You may be interested in the rankings of either the university or of a program of study. Keep in mind, however, that rankings usually assume that quality is quantifiable. Rankings are usually based on presumptions about how data relate to quality and are likely to be unproven. It is important to carefully consider the source and the criteria of any ranking information before believing and acting upon it.

Your Own Educational Background

You may be concerned about the interpretation of your educational credentials, since your country's degree nomenclature and the grading scale may differ from those in the United States. Universities use reference books about the educational systems of other countries to help them understand specific educational credentials. Generally, these credentials are interpreted by each institution; there is not a single interpretation that applies to every institution. The lack of uniformity is good news for most students, since it means that students from a wide variety of educational backgrounds can find a U.S. university that is appropriate to their needs.

To choose an appropriate institution, you can and should do an informal self-evaluation of your educational background. This self-analysis involves three important questions:

1. How Many Years of Study Have You Completed?

Completion of secondary school with at least twelve total years of education usually qualifies students to apply for undergraduate (bachelor's) degree programs. Completion of a university degree program that involves at least sixteen years of total education qualifies one to apply for admission to graduate (master's) degree programs in the United States.

2. Does the Education That You Have Completed in Your Country Provide Access to Further Study in the United States?

Consider the kind of institution where you completed your previous studies. If educational opportunities in your country are limited, it may be necessary to investigate many U.S. institutions and programs in order to find a match.

3. Are Your Previous Marks or Grades Excellent, Average, or Poor?

Your educational record influences your choice of U.S. institutions. If your grades are average or poor, it may be advisable to apply to several institutions with minimally difficult or non-competitive entrance levels.

YOU are one of the best sources of information about the level and quality of your previous studies. Awareness of your educational assets and liabilities will serve you well throughout the application process.

SECOND STEP—PLANNING AND ASSEMBLING THE APPLICATION

Planning and assembling a university application can be compared to the construction of a building. First, you must start with a solid foundation, which is the application form itself. The application, often available online as well as in paper form, usually contains a wealth of useful information, such as deadlines, fees, and degree programs available at that institution. To build a solid application, it is best to begin well in advance of the application deadline.

How to Obtain the Application Form

Application forms and links to institutional Web sites may also be available at a U.S. educational advising center associated with the American Embassy or Consulate in your country. These centers are excellent resources for international students and provide information about standardized test administration, scholarships, and other matters to students who are interested in studying in the United States. Your local U.S. Embassy or Consulate can guide you to the nearest educational advising center.

What Are the Key Components of a Complete Application?

Institutional requirements vary, but the standard components of a complete application include the following:

- Transcript
- Required standardized examination scores
- Evidence of financial support
- Letters of recommendation
- Application fee

Transcript

A complete academic record or transcript includes all courses completed, grades earned, and degrees awarded. Most universities require an official transcript to be sent directly from the school or university. In many other countries, however, the practice is to issue official transcripts and degree certificates directly to the student. If you have only one official copy of your transcript, it may be a challenge to get additional certified copies that are acceptable to U.S. universities. Some institutions will issue additional official copies for application purposes.

If your institution does not provide this service, you may have to seek an alternate source of certification. As a last resort, you may send a photocopy of your official transcript, explain that you have only one original, and ask the university for advice on how to deal with this situation.

Required Standardized Examination Scores

Arranging to take standardized examinations and earning the required scores seem to cause the most anxiety for international students.

The university application form usually indicates which examinations are required. The standardized examination required most often for undergraduate admission is the Test of English as a Foreign Language (TOEFL). Institutions may also require the SAT of undergraduate applicants. These standardized examinations are administered by the Educational Testing Service (ETS).

These examinations are offered in almost every country of the world. It is advisable to begin planning for standardized examinations at least six months prior to the application deadline of your desired institutions. Test centers fill up quickly, so it is important to register as soon as possible. Information about the examinations is available at U.S. educational advising centers associated with embassies or consulates.

Most universities require that the original test scores, not a student copy, be sent directly by the testing service. When you register for the test, be sure to indicate that the testing service should send the test scores directly to the universities.

You should begin your application process before you receive your test scores. Delaying submission of your application until the test scores arrive may cause you to miss deadlines and negatively affect the outcome of your application. If you want to know your scores in order to assess your chances of admission to an institution with rigorous admission standards, you should take the tests early.

Many universities in the United States set minimum required scores on the TOEFL or other standardized examinations. Test scores are an important factor, but most institutions also look at a number of other factors in their consideration of a candidate for admission.

For More Information

Questions about test formats, locations, dates, and registration may be addressed to:

ETS Corporate Headquarters
Rosedale Road
Princeton, New Jersey 08541
Web sites: http://www.ets.org
          http://www.ets.org/toefl/
Phone: 609-921-9000
Fax: 609-734-5410

Evidence of Financial Support

Evidence of financial support is required to issue immigration documents to admitted students. This is part of a complete application package but usually plays no role in determining admission. Most institutions make admissions decisions without regard to the source and amount of financial support.

Letters of Recommendation

Most institutions require one or more letters of recommendation. The best letters are written by former professors, employers, or others who can comment on your academic achievements or professional potential.

Some universities provide a special form for the letters of recommendation. If possible, use the forms provided. If you are applying to a large number of universities, however, or if your recommenders are not available to complete several forms, it may be necessary for you to duplicate a general recommendation letter.

Application Fee

Most universities also require an application fee, ranging from $25 to $100, which must be paid to initiate consideration of the application.

Completing the Application Form

Whether sent by mail or electronically, the application form must be neat and thoroughly filled out. Although parts of the application may not seem to apply to you or your situation, do your best to answer all the questions.

Remember that this is a process. You provide information, and your proposed university then may request clarification and further information. If you have questions, it is better to initiate the entire process by submitting the application form rather than asking questions before you apply. The university will be better able to respond to you after it has your application. Always complete as much as you can. Do not permit uncertainty about the completion of the application form to cause unnecessary delays.

THIRD STEP—DISTINGUISH YOUR APPLICATION

To distinguish your application—to market yourself successfully—is ultimately the most important part of the application process. As you select your prospective universities, begin to analyze your strengths and weaknesses as a prospective student. As you complete your application, you should strive to create a positive impression and set yourself apart from other applicants, to highlight your assets and bring these qualities to the attention of the appropriate university administrators and professors. Applying early is a very easy way to distinguish your application.

Deadline or Guideline?

The application deadline is the last date that an application for a given semester will be accepted. Often, the application will specify that all required documents and information be submitted before the deadline date. To meet the deadlines, start the application process early. This also gives you more time to take—and perhaps retake and improve—the required standardized tests.

Admissions deliberations may take several weeks or months. In the meantime, most institutions accept additional information, including improved test scores, after the posted deadline.

Even if your application is initially rejected, you may be able to provide additional information to change the decision. You can request reconsideration based on additional information, such as improved test scores, strong letters of recommendation, or information about your class rank. Applying early allows more time to improve your application. Also, some students may decide not to accept their offers of admission, leaving room for offers to students on a waiting list. Reconsideration of the admission decisions can occur well beyond the application deadline.

Think of the deadline as a guideline rather than an impermeable barrier. Many factors—the strength of the application, your research interests, the number of spaces available at the proposed institution—can override the enforcement of an application deadline. So, if you lack a test score or transcript by the official deadline, you may still be able to apply and be accepted.

Statement of Purpose

The statement of purpose is your first and perhaps best opportunity to present yourself as an excellent candidate for admission. Whether or not a personal history essay or statement of purpose is required, always include a carefully written statement of purpose with your applications. A compelling statement of purpose does not have to be lengthy, but it should include some basic components:

- Part One—Introduce yourself and describe your educational background. This is your opportunity to describe any facet of your educational experience that you wish to emphasize. Perhaps you attended a highly ranked secondary school or university in your home country. Mention the name and any noteworthy characteristics of the secondary school or university from which you graduated. Explain the grading scale used at your university. Do not forget to mention your rank in your graduating class and any honors you may have received. This is not the time to be modest.

- Part Two—Describe your current academic and career interests and goals. Think about how these will fit into those of the institution to which you are applying, and mention the reasons why you have selected that institution.

- Part Three—Describe your long-term goals. When you finish your program of study, what do you plan to do next? If you already have a job offer or a career plan, describe it. Give some thought to how you'll demonstrate that studying in the United States. will ultimately benefit others.

Use Personal Contacts When Possible

Appropriate and judicious use of your own network of contacts can be very helpful. Friends, former professors, former students of your selected institutions, and others may be willing to advise you during the application process and provide you with introductions to key administrators or professors. If suggested, you may wish to contact certain professors or administrators by mail, phone, or e-mail. A personal visit to discuss your interest in the institution may be appropriate. Whatever your choice of communication, try to make the encounter pleasant and personal. Your goal is to make a positive impression, not to rush the admission decision.

There is no single right way to be admitted to U.S. universities. The same characteristics that make the educational choice in the United States so difficult—the number of institutions and the variety of programs of study—are the same attributes that allow so many international students to find the institution that's right for them.

Kitty M. Villa is the former Assistant Director, International Office, at the University of Texas at Austin.

Community Colleges and the New Green Economy

Community colleges are a focal point for state and national efforts to create a green economy and workforce. As the United States transforms its economy into a "green" one, community colleges are leading the way—filling the need for educated technicians whose skills can cross industry lines as well as the need for technicians who are able to learn new skills as technologies evolve.

Community colleges have been at the heart of the Obama administration's recovery strategy, with $12 billion allocated over the next decade. The President recently extolled community colleges as "the unsung heroes of America's education system," essential to our country's success in the "global competition to lead in the growth of industries of the twenty-first century." With the support of state governments as well as local and, in some cases, international business partners, America's community colleges are rising to meet the demands of the new green economy.

Community colleges are training workers to work in fields such as renewable energy, energy efficiency, wind energy, green building, and sustainability. The programs are as diverse as the campuses housing them. Here is a quick look at some of the exciting "green" programs at community colleges throughout the United States.

At Mesalands Community College in Tucumcari, New Mexico, the new North American Wind Research and Training Center provides state-of-the-art facilities for research and training qualified technicians in wind energy technology. The Center includes a facility for applied research in collaboration with Sandia National Laboratories—the first-ever such partnership between a national laboratory and a community college. It also provides associate degree training for wind energy technicians, meeting the fast-growing demand for "windsmiths" in the western part of the country—jobs that pay $45,000–$60,000 per year. For more information, visit http://www.mesalands.edu/wind/default.htm.

Cape Cod Community College (CCCC) in Massachusetts has become one of the nation's leading colleges in promoting and integrating sustainability and green practices throughout all campus operations and technical training programs. Ten years ago, Cape Wind Associates, Cape Cod's first wind farm, provided $50,000 to jumpstart CCCC's wind technician program—considered a state model for community-based clean energy workforce development and education. In addition, hundreds of CCCC students have earned degrees in coastal management, solar technology, wastewater, and other careers, including cleanup of Superfund sites at an abandoned military base. Visit http://www.capecod.edu/web/guest for more information.

At Oakland Community College in Michigan, more than 350 students are enrolled in the college's Renewable Energies and Sustainable Living program and its related courses. Students gain field experience refurbishing public buildings with renewable materials, performing energy audits for the government, and working with small businesses and hospitals to reduce waste and pollution. To learn more, visit http://www.oaklandcc.edu/est/.

In 2007, Columbia Gorge Community College in Oregon became the first community college in the Pacific Northwest to offer training programs for the windpower generation industry. The college offers a one-year certificate and a two-year Associate of Applied Science (A.A.S.) degree in renewable energy technology. The Renewable Energy Technology program was designed in collaboration with industry partners from the wind energy industry and the power generation industry. Students are prepared for employment in a broad range of industries, including hydro-generation, wind-generation, automated manufacturing, and engineering technology, and the College plans to add solar array technology to this list as well. For more information, visit http://www.cgcc.cc.or.us/Academics/WindTechnologyPage.cfm.

Central Carolina Community College (CCCC) in Pittsboro, North Carolina, has been leading the way in "green" programs for more than a decade. It offered a sustainable agriculture class at its Chatham campus in 1996 and soon became the first community college in the nation to offer an Associate in Applied Science degree in sustainable agriculture and the first in North Carolina to offer an associate degree in biofuels. In addition, it was the first North Carolina community college to offer a North American Board of Certified Energy Practitioners (NABCEP)–approved solar PV panel installation course as part of its green building/renewable energy program. In 2010, CCCC added an associate degree in sustainable technology and launched its new Natural Chef culinary arts program. The College also offers an ecotourism certificate as well as certificates in other green programs. For more information about Central Carolina Community College's green programs, visit http://www.cccc.edu/green.

The Green Jobs Academy at Bucks County Community College in Pennsylvania is an exciting new venture that includes a variety of academic and private industry partners that include Gamesa, Lockheed Martin, and Dow. The Green Jobs Academy provides both long- and short-term training programs that are geared toward workers looking for new skill sets in the green and sustainability industries. Courses include Hazardous Site Remediation & Preliminary Assessments, PV Solar Design, NABCEP (*North American Board of Certified Energy Practitioners*) PV Solar Entry Level Program (40 hours), Electric Vehicle Conversion Workshop, Wind Energy Apprentice, Certified Green Supply Chain Professional, Certified Indoor Air Quality Manager, and others. For details, visit http://www.bucks.edu/academics/coned/green/index.php.

Next you'll find two essays about other green community college programs. The first essay was written by the president of Lane Community College in Eugene, Oregon, about the role Lane and other community colleges are playing in creating a workforce for the green economy. Then, read a first-hand account of the new Wind Turbine Training Program at Kalamazoo Valley Community College in Kalamazoo, Michigan—a program that has more applicants than spaces and one whose students are being hired BEFORE they even graduate. It's clear that there are exciting "green" programs at community colleges throughout the United States.

The Role of Community Colleges in Creating a Workforce for the Green Economy

by Mary F.T. Spilde, President
Lane Community College

Community colleges are expected to play a leadership role in educating and training the workforce for the green economy. Due to close connections with local and regional labor markets, colleges assure a steady supply of skilled workers by developing and adapting programs to respond to the needs of business and industry. Further, instead of waiting for employers to create job openings, many colleges are actively engaged in local economic development to help educate potential employers to grow their green business opportunities and to participate in the creation of the green economy.

As the green movement emerges there has been confusion about what constitutes a green job. It is now clear that many of the green jobs span several economic sectors such as renewable energy, construction, manufacturing, transportation and agriculture. It is predicted that there will be many middle skill jobs requiring more than a high school diploma but less than a bachelor's degree. This is precisely the unique role that community colleges play. Community colleges develop training programs, including pre-apprenticeship, that ladder the curriculum to take lower skilled workers through a relevant and sequenced course of study that provides a clear pathway to career track jobs. As noted in *Going Green: The Vital Role of Community Colleges in Building a Sustainable Future and Green Workforce*, community colleges are strategically positioned to work with employers to redefine skills and competencies needed by the green workforce and to create the framework for new and expanded green career pathways.

While there will be new occupations such as solar and wind technologists, the majority of the jobs will be in the energy management sector—retrofitting the built environment. For example, President Obama called for retrofitting more than 75 percent of federal buildings and more than 2 million homes to make them more energy-efficient. The second major area for growth will be the "greening" of existing jobs as they evolve to incorporate green practices. Both will require new knowledge, skills and abilities. For community colleges, this means developing new programs that meet newly created industry standards and adapting existing programs and courses to integrate green skills. The key is to create a new talent pool of environmentally conscious, highly skilled workers.

These two areas show remarkable promise for education and training leading to high wage/high demand jobs:

- Efficiency and energy management: There is a need for auditors and energy efficiency experts to retrofit existing buildings. Consider how much built environment we have in this country, and it's not difficult to see that this is where the vast amount of jobs are now and will be in the future.

- Greening of existing jobs: There are few currently available jobs that environmental sustainability will not impact. Whether it is jobs in construction, such as plumbers, electricians, heating and cooling technicians, painters, and building supervisors, or chefs, farmers, custodians, architects, automotive technicians and interior designers, all will need to understand how to lessen their impact on the environment.

Lane Community College offers a variety of degree and certificate programs to prepare students to enter the energy efficiency fields. Lane has offered an Energy Management program since the late 1980s—before it was hip to be green! Students in this program learn to apply basic principles of physics and analysis techniques to the description and measurement of energy in today's building systems, with the goal of evaluating and recommending alternative energy solutions that will result in greater energy efficiency and energy cost savings. Students gain a working understanding of energy systems in today's built environment and the tools to analyze and quantify energy efficiency efforts. The program began with an emphasis in residential energy efficiency/solar energy systems and has evolved to include commercial energy efficiency and renewable energy system installation technology.

The Renewable Energy Technician program is offered as a second-year option within the Energy Management program. Course work prepares students for employment designing and installing solar electric and domestic hot water systems. Renewable Energy students, along with Energy Management students, take a first-year curriculum in commercial energy efficiency giving them a solid background that includes residential energy efficiency, HVAC systems, lighting, and physics and math. In the second year, Renewable Energy students diverge from the Energy Management curriculum and take course work that starts with two courses in electricity fundamentals and one course in energy economics. In the following terms, students learn to design, install, and develop a thorough understanding of photovoltaics and domestic hot water systems.

Recent additions to Lane's offerings are Sustainability Coordinator and Water Conservation Technician degrees. Both programs were added to meet workforce demand.

Lane graduates find employment in a wide variety of disciplines and may work as facility managers, energy auditors, energy program coordinators, or control system specialists, for such diverse employers as engineering firms, public and private utilities, energy equipment companies, and departments of energy and as sustainability leaders within public and private sector organizations.

Lane Community College also provides continuing education for working professionals. The Sustainable Building Advisor (SBA) Certificate Program is a nine-month, specialized training program for working professionals. Graduate are able to advise employers or clients on strategies and tools for implementing sustainable building practices. Benefits from participating in the SBA program often include saving long-term building operating costs; improving the environmental, social, and economic viability of the region; and reducing environmental impacts and owner liability—not to mention the chance to improve one's job skills in a rapidly growing field.

The Building Operators Certificate is a professional development program created by The Northwest Energy Efficiency Council. It is offered through the Northwest Energy Education Institute at Lane. The certificate is designed for operations and maintenance staff working in public or private commercial buildings. It certifies individuals in energy and resource-efficient operation of building systems at two levels: Level I–Building System Maintenance and Level II–Equipment Troubleshooting and Maintenance.

Lane Community College constantly scans the environment to assess workforce needs and develop programs that provide highly skilled employees. Lane, like most colleges, publishes information in its catalog on workforce demand and wages so that students can make informed decisions about program choice.

Green jobs will be a large part of a healthy economy. Opportunities will abound for those who take advantage of programs with a proven record of connecting with employers and succ

Establishing a World-Class Wind Turbine Technician Academy

by James DeHaven, Vice President of Economic & Business Development

Kalamazoo Valley Community College

When Kalamazoo Valley Community College (KVCC) decided it wanted to become involved in the training of utility-grade technicians for wind-energy jobs, early on the choice was made to avoid another "me too" training course.

Our program here in Southwest Michigan, 30 miles from Lake Michigan, had to meet industry needs and industry standards.

It was also obvious from the start that the utility-grade or large wind industry had not yet adopted any uniform training standards in the United States.

Of course, these would come, but why should the college wait when European standards were solidly established and working well in Germany, France, Denmark and Great Britain?

As a result, in 2009, KVCC launched its Wind Turbine Technician Academy, the first of its kind in the United States. The noncredit academy runs 8 hours a day, five days a week, for twenty-six weeks of intense training in electricity, mechanics, wind dynamics, safety, and climbing. The college developed this program rather quickly—in eight months—to fast-track individuals into this emerging field.

KVCC based its program on the training standards forged by the Bildungszentrum fur Erneuerebare Energien (BZEE)—the Renewable Energy Education Center.

Located in Husum, Germany, and founded in 2000, the BZEE was created and supported by major wind-turbine manufacturers, component makers, and enterprises that provide operation and maintenance services.

As wind-energy production increased throughout Europe, the need for high-quality, industry-driven, international standards emerged. The BZEE has become the leading trainer for wind-turbine technicians across Europe and now in Asia.

With the exception of one college in Canada, the standards are not yet available in North America. When Kalamazoo Valley realized it could be the first college or university in the United States to offer this training program—that was enough motivation to move forward.

For the College to become certified by the BZEE, it needed to hire and send an electrical instructor and a mechanical instructor to Germany for six weeks of "train the trainer." The instructors not only had to excel in their respective fields, they also needed to be able to climb the skyscraper towers supporting megawatt-class turbines—a unique combination of skills to possess. Truly, individuals who fit this job description don't walk through the door everyday—but we found them! Amazingly, we found a top mechanical instructor who was a part-time fireman and comfortable with tall ladder rescues and a skilled electrical instructor who used to teach rappelling off the Rockies to the Marine Corps.

In addition to employing new instructors, the College needed a working utility-grade nacelle that could fit in its training lab that would be located in the KVCC Michigan Technical Education Center. So one of the instructors traveled to Denmark and purchased a 300-kilowatt turbine.

Once their own training was behind them and the turbine was on its way from the North Sea, the instructors quickly turned to crafting the curriculum necessary for our graduates to earn both an academy certificate from KVCC and a certification from the BZEE.

Promoting the innovative program to qualified potential students across the country was the next step. News releases were published throughout Michigan, and they were also picked up on the Internet. Rather quickly, KVCC found itself with more than 500 requests for applications for a program built for 16 students.

Acceptance into the academy includes a medical release, a climbing test, reading and math tests, relevant work experience, and, finally, an interview. Students in the academy's pioneer class, which graduated in spring 2010, ranged in age from their late teens to early 50s. They hailed from throughout Michigan, Indiana, Ohio, and Illinois as well as from Puerto Rico and Great Britain.

The students brought with them degrees in marketing, law, business, science, and architecture, as well as entrepreneurial experiences in several businesses, knowledge of other languages, military service, extensive travel, and electrical, computer, artistic, and technical/mechanical skills.

Kalamazoo Valley's academy has provided some high-value work experiences for the students in the form of two collaborations with industry that has allowed them to maintain and/or repair actual utility-grade turbines, including those at the 2.5 megawatt size. This hands-on experience will add to the attractiveness of the graduates in the market place. Potential employers were recently invited to an open house where they could see the lab and meet members of this pioneer class.

The College's Turbine Technician Academy has also attracted a federal grant for $550,000 to expand its program through additional equipment purchases. The plan is to erect our own climbing tower. Climbing is a vital part of any valid program, and yet wind farms cannot afford to shut turbines down just for climb-training.

When the students are asked what best distinguishes the Kalamazoo Valley program, their answers point to the experienced instructors and the working lab, which is constantly changing to offer the best training experiences to the wind students.

Industry continues to tell us that community colleges need to offer fast-track training programs of this caliber if the nation is to reach the U.S. Department of Energy's goal of 20 percent renewable energy by 2030. This would require more than 1,500 new technicians each year.

With that in mind, KVCC plans to host several BZEE orientation programs for other community colleges in order to encourage them to consider adopting the European training standards and start their own programs.

Meanwhile, applications are continuing to stream in from across the country for the next Wind Turbine Technician Academy program at Kalamazoo Valley Community College.

(A video about the program is available at www.mteckvcc.com/windtechacademy.html.)

How to Use This Guide

Peterson's *Two-Year Colleges 2012* contains a wealth of information for anyone interested in colleges offering associate degrees. This section details the criteria that institutions must meet to be included in this guide and provides information about research procedures used by Peterson's.

QUICK-REFERENCE CHART

The **Two-Year Colleges At-a-Glance Chart** is a geographically arranged table that lists colleges by name and city within the state, territory, or country in which they are located. Areas listed include the United States and its territories and other countries; the institutions in these countries are included because they are accredited by recognized U.S. accrediting bodies (see **Criteria for Inclusion** section).

The At-a-Glance chart contains basic information that enables you to compare institutions quickly according to broad characteristics such as degrees awarded, enrollment, application requirements, financial aid availability, and numbers of sports and majors offered. A dagger (†) after the institution's name indicates that an institution has an entry in the **College Close-Ups** section.

Column 1: Degrees Awarded

C= *college transfer associate degree:* the degree awarded after a "university-parallel" program, equivalent to the first two years of a bachelor's degree.

T= *terminal associate degree:* the degree resulting from a one- to three-year program providing training for a specific occupation.

B= *bachelor's degree (baccalaureate):* the degree resulting from a liberal arts, science, professional, or preprofessional program normally lasting four years, although in some cases an accelerated program can be completed in three years.

M= *master's degree:* the first graduate (postbaccalaureate) degree in the liberal arts and sciences and certain professional fields, usually requiring one to two years of full-time study.

D= *doctoral degree* (research/scholarship, professional practice, or other)

Column 2: Institutional Control

Private institutions are designated as one of the following:

Ind = *independent* (nonprofit)

I-R = *independent-religious:* nonprofit; sponsored by or affiliated with a particular religious group or having a nondenominational or interdenominational religious orientation.

Prop = *proprietary* (profit-making)

Public institutions are designated by the source of funding, as follows:

Fed = *federal*

St = *state*

Comm = *commonwealth* (Puerto Rico)

Terr = *territory* (U.S. territories)

Cou = *county*

Dist = *district:* an administrative unit of public education, often having boundaries different from units of local government.

City = *city*

St-L = *state and local:* local may refer to county, district, or city.

St-R = *state-related:* funded primarily by the state but administratively autonomous.

Column 3: Student Body

M= *men only* (100% of student body)

PM = *coed, primarily men*

W= *women only* (100% of student body)

PW = *coed, primarily women*

M/W = *coeducational*

Column 4: Undergraduate Enrollment

The figure shown represents the number of full-time and part-time students enrolled in undergraduate degree programs as of fall 2010.

Columns 5–7: Enrollment Percentages

Figures are shown for the percentages of the fall 2010 undergraduate enrollment made up of students attending part-time (column 5) and students 25 years of age or older (column 6). Also listed is the percentage of students in the last graduating class who completed a college-transfer associate program and went directly on to four-year colleges (column 7).

For columns 8 through 15, the following letter codes are used: Y = yes; N = no; R = recommended; S = for some.

Columns 8–10: Admission Policies

The information in these columns shows whether the college has an open admission policy (column 8) whereby virtually all applicants are accepted without regard to standardized test scores, grade average, or class rank; whether a high school equivalency certificate is accepted in place of a high school diploma for admission consideration (column 9); and whether a high school transcript (column 10) is required as part of the application process. In column 10, the combination of the codes R and S indicates that a high school transcript is recommended for all applicants (R) or required for some (S).

Columns 11–12: Financial Aid

These columns show which colleges offer the following types of financial aid: need-based aid (column 11) and part-time jobs (column 12), including those offered through the federal government's Federal Work-Study program.

Columns 13–15: Services and Facilities

These columns show which colleges offer the following: career counseling (column 13) on either an individual or group basis, job placement services (column 14) for individual students, and college-owned or -operated housing facilities (column 16) for noncommuting students.

Column 16: Sports

This figure indicates the number of sports that a college offers at the intramural and/or intercollegiate levels.

Column 17: Majors

This figure indicates the number of major fields of study in which a college offers degree programs.

PROFILES OF TWO-YEAR COLLEGES AND SPECIAL MESSAGES

The **Profiles of Two-Year Colleges** contain basic data in capsule form for quick review and comparison. The following outline of the **Profile** format shows the section headings and the items that each section covers. Any item that does not apply to a particular college or for which no information was supplied is omitted from that college's **Profile.** Display ads, which appear near some of the institution's profiles, have been provided and paid for by those colleges that chose to supplement their profile with additional information.

Bulleted Highlights

The bulleted highlights section features important information, for quick reference and comparison. The number of possible bulleted highlights that an ideal **Profile** would have if all questions were answered in a timely manner follow. However, not every institution provides all of the information necessary to fill out every bulleted line. In such instances, the line will not appear.

First Bullet

Institutional control: Private institutions are designated as independent (nonprofit), proprietary (profit-making), or independent, with a specific religious denomination or affiliation. Nondenominational or interdenominational religious orientation is possible and would be indicated.

Public institutions are designated by the source of funding. Designations include federal, state, province, commonwealth (Puerto Rico), territory (U.S. territories), county, district (an administrative unit of public education, often having boundaries different from units of local government), city, state and local (local may refer to county, district, or city), or state-related (funded primarily by the state but administratively autonomous).

Religious affiliation is also noted here.

Institutional type: Each institution is classified as one of the following:

> *Primarily two-year college:* Awards baccalaureate degrees, but the vast majority of students are enrolled in two-year programs.

> *Four-year college:* Awards baccalaureate degrees; may also award associate degrees; does not award graduate (postbaccalaureate) degrees.

> *Upper-level institution:* Awards baccalaureate degrees, but entering students must have at least two years of previous college-level credit; may also offer graduate degrees.

> *Comprehensive institution:* Awards baccalaureate degrees; may also award associate degrees; offers graduate degree programs, primarily at the master's, specialist's, or professional level, although one or two doctoral programs may be offered.

> *University:* Offers four years of undergraduate work plus graduate degrees through the doctorate in more than two academic or professional fields.

Founding date: If the year an institution was chartered differs from the year when instruction actually began, the earlier date is given.

System or administrative affiliation: Any coordinate institutions or system affiliations are indicated. An institution that has separate colleges or campuses for men and women but shares facilities and courses is termed a coordinate institution. A formal administrative grouping of institutions, either private or public, of which the college is a part, or the name of a single institution with which the college is administratively affiliated, is a system.

Second Bullet

Setting: Schools are designated as urban (located within a major city), suburban (a residential area within commuting distance of a major city), small-town (a small but compactly settled area not within commuting distance of a major city), or rural (a remote and sparsely populated area). The phrase *easy access to...* indicates that the campus is within an hour's drive of the nearest major metropolitan area that has a population greater than 500,000.

Third Bullet

Endowment: The total dollar value of funds and/or property donated to the institution or the multicampus educational system of which the institution is a part.

Fourth Bullet

Student body: An institution is coed (coeducational—admits men and women), primarily (80 percent or more) women, primarily men, women only, or men only.

Undergraduate students: Represents the number of full-time and part-time students enrolled in undergraduate degree programs as of fall 2010. The percentage of full-time undergraduates and the percentages of men and women are given.

Category Overviews

Undergraduates

For fall 2010, the number of full- and part-time undergraduate students is listed. This list provides the number of states and U.S. territories, including the District of Columbia and Puerto Rico (or for Canadian institutions, provinces and territories), and other countries from which undergraduates come. Percentages of undergraduates who are part-time or full-time students; transfers in; live on campus; out-of-state; Black or African American, non-Hispanic/Latino; Hispanic/Latino; Asian, non-Hispanic/Latino; Native Hawaiian or other Pacific Islander, non-Hispanic/Latino; American Indian or Alaska Native, non-Hispanic/Latino are given.

Retention: The percentage of freshmen (or, for upper-level institutions, entering students) who returned the following year for the fall term.

Freshmen

Admission: Figures are given for the number of students who applied for fall 2010 admission, the number of those who were admitted, and the number who enrolled. Freshman statistics include the average high school GPA; the percentage of freshmen who took the SAT and received critical reading, writing, and math scores above 500, above 600, and above 700; as well as the percentage of freshmen taking the ACT who received a composite score of 18 or higher.

Faculty

Total: The total number of faculty members; the percentage of full-time faculty members as of fall 2010; and the percentage of full-time faculty members who hold doctoral/first professional/ terminal degrees.

Student-faculty ratio: The school's estimate of the ratio of matriculated undergraduate students to faculty members teaching undergraduate courses.

Majors

This section lists the major fields of study offered by the college.

Academics

Calendar: Most colleges indicate one of the following: 4-1-4, 4-4-1, or a similar arrangement (two terms of equal length plus an abbreviated winter or spring term, with the numbers referring to months); semesters; trimesters; quarters; 3-3 (three courses for each of three terms); modular (the academic year is divided into small blocks of time; courses of varying lengths are assembled according to individual programs); or standard year (for most Canadian institutions).

Degrees: This names the full range of levels of certificates, diplomas, and degrees, including prebaccalaureate, graduate, and professional, that are offered by this institution:

Associate degree: Normally requires at least two but fewer than four years of full-time college work or its equivalent.

Bachelor's degree (baccalaureate): Requires at least four years but not more than five years of full-time college-level work or its equivalent. This includes all bachelor's degrees in which the normal four years of work are completed in three years and bachelor's degrees conferred in a five-year cooperative (work-study plan) program. A cooperative plan provides for alternate class attendance and employment in business, industry, or government. This allows students to combine actual work experience with their college studies.

Master's degree: Requires the successful completion of a program of study of at least the full-time equivalent of one but not more than two years of work beyond the bachelor's degree.

Doctoral degree (doctorate; research/scholarship, professional, or other): The highest degree in graduate study. The doctoral degree classification includes Doctor of Education, Doctor of Juridical Science, Doctor of Public Health, Doctor of Philosophy, Doctor of Podiatry, Doctor of Veterinary Medicine, and many more.

Post-master's certificate: Requires completion of an organized program of study of 24 credit hours beyond the master's degree but does not meet the requirements of academic degrees at the doctoral level.

Special study options: Details are next given here on study options available at each college:

Accelerated degree program: Students may earn a bachelor's degree in three academic years.

Academic remediation for entering students: Instructional courses designed for students deficient in the general competencies necessary for a regular postsecondary curriculum and educational setting.

Adult/continuing education programs: Courses offered for nontraditional students who are currently working or are returning to formal education.

Advanced placement: Credit toward a degree awarded for acceptable scores on College Board Advanced Placement (AP) tests.

Cooperative (co-op) education programs: Formal arrangements with off-campus employers allowing students to combine work and study in order to gain degree-related experience, usually extending the time required to complete a degree.

Distance learning: For-credit courses that can be accessed off-campus via cable television, the Internet, satellite, DVD, correspondence course, or other media.

Double major: A program of study in which a student concurrently completes the requirements of two majors.

English as a second language (ESL): A course of study designed specifically for students whose native language is not English.

External degree programs: A program of study in which students earn credits toward a degree through a combination of independent study, college courses, proficiency examinations, and personal experience. External degree programs require minimal or no classroom attendance.

Freshmen honors college: A separate academic program for talented freshmen.

Honors programs: Any special program for very able students offering the opportunity for educational enrichment, independent study, acceleration, or some combination of these.

Independent study: Academic work, usually undertaken outside the regular classroom structure, chosen or designed by the student with departmental approval and instructor supervision.

Internships: Any short-term, supervised work experience usually related to a student's major field, for which the student earns academic credit. The work can be full-or part-time, on or off-campus, paid or unpaid.

Off-campus study: A formal arrangement with one or more domestic institutions under which students may take courses at the other institution(s) for credit.

Part-time degree program: Students may earn a degree through part-time enrollment in regular session (daytime) classes or evening, weekend, or summer classes.

Self-designed major: Program of study based on individual interests, designed by the student with the assistance of an adviser.

Services for LD students: Special help for learning-disabled students with resolvable difficulties, such as dyslexia.

Study abroad: An arrangement by which a student completes part of the academic program studying in another country. A college may operate a campus abroad or it may have a cooperative agreement with other U.S. institutions or institutions in other countries.

Summer session for credit: Summer courses through which students may make up degree work or accelerate their program.

Tutorials: Undergraduates can arrange for special in-depth academic assignments (not for remediation)

working with faculty members one-on-one or in small groups.

ROTC: Army, Naval, or Air Force Reserve Officers' Training Corps programs offered either on campus, at a branch campus [designated by a (b)], or at a cooperating host institution [designated by (c)].

Unusual degree programs: Nontraditional programs such as a 3-2 degree program, in which three years of liberal arts study is followed by two years of study in a professional field at another institution (or in a professional division of the same institution), resulting in two bachelor's degrees or a bachelor's and a master's degree.

Student Life

Housing options: The institution's policy about whether students are permitted to live off-campus or are required to live on campus for a specified period; whether freshmen-only, coed, single-sex, cooperative, and disabled student housing options are available; whether campus housing is leased by the school and/or provided by a third party; whether freshman applicants are given priority for college housing. The phrase *college housing not available* indicates that no college-owned or -operated housing facilities are provided for undergraduates and that noncommuting students must arrange for their own accommodations.

Activities and organizations: Lists information on drama-theater groups, choral groups, marching bands, student-run campus newspapers, student-run radio stations, and social organizations (sororities, fraternities, eating clubs, etc.) and how many are represented on campus.

Campus security: Campus safety measures including 24-hour emergency response devices (telephones and alarms) and patrols by trained security personnel, student patrols, late-night transport-escort service, and controlled dormitory access (key, security card, etc.).

Student services: Information provided indicates services offered to students by the college, such as legal services, health clinics, personal-psychological counseling, and women's centers.

Athletics

Membership in one or more of the following athletic associations is indicated by initials.

NCAA: National Collegiate Athletic Association

NAIA: National Association of Intercollegiate Athletics

NCCAA: National Christian College Athletic Association

NJCAA: National Junior College Athletic Association

USCAA: United States Collegiate Athletic Association

CIS: Canadian Interuniversity Sports

The overall NCAA division in which all or most intercollegiate teams compete is designated by a roman numeral I, II, or

III. All teams that do not compete in this division are listed as exceptions.

Sports offered by the college are divided into two groups: intercollegiate (**M** or **W** following the name of each sport indicates that it is offered for men or women) and intramural. An **s** in parentheses following an **M** or **W** for an intercollegiate sport indicates that athletic scholarships (or grants-in-aid) are offered for men or women in that sport, and a c indicates a club team as opposed to a varsity team.

Standardized Tests

The most commonly required standardized tests are the ACT, SAT, and SAT Subject Tests. These and other standardized tests may be used for selective admission, as a basis for counseling or course placement, or for both purposes. This section notes if a test is used for admission or placement and whether it is required, required for some, or recommended.

In addition to the ACT and SAT, the following standardized entrance and placement examinations are referred to by their initials:

ABLE: Adult Basic Learning Examination

ACT ASSET: ACT Assessment of Skills for Successful Entry and Transfer

ACT PEP: ACT Proficiency Examination Program

CAT: California Achievement Tests

CELT: Comprehensive English Language Test

CPAt: Career Programs Assessment

CPT: Computerized Placement Test

DAT: Differential Aptitude Test

LSAT: Law School Admission Test

MAPS: Multiple Assessment Program Service

MCAT: Medical College Admission Test

MMPI: Minnesota Multiphasic Personality Inventory

OAT: Optometry Admission Test

PAA: Prueba de Aptitud Académica (Spanish-language version of the SAT)

PCAT: Pharmacy College Admission Test

PSAT/NMSQT: Preliminary SAT National Merit Scholarship Qualifying Test

SCAT: Scholastic College Aptitude Test

SRA: Scientific Research Association (administers verbal, arithmetical, and achievement tests)

TABE: Test of Adult Basic Education

TASP: Texas Academic Skills Program

TOEFL: Test of English as a Foreign Language (for international students whose native language is not English)

WPCT: Washington Pre-College Test

Costs

Costs are given for the 2011–12 academic year or for the 2010–11 academic year if 2011–12 figures were not yet available. Annual expenses may be expressed as a comprehensive fee (including full-time tuition, mandatory fees, and college room and board) or as separate figures for full-time tuition, fees, room and board, or room only. For public institutions where tuition differs according to residence, separate figures are given for area or state residents and for nonresidents. Part-time tuition is expressed in terms of a per-unit rate (per credit, per semester hour, etc.) as specified by the institution.

The tuition structure at some institutions is complex in that freshmen and sophomores may be charged a different rate from that for juniors and seniors, a professional or vocational division may have a different fee structure from the liberal arts division of the same institution, or part-time tuition may be prorated on a sliding scale according to the number of credit hours taken. Tuition and fees may vary according to academic program, campus/location, class time (day, evening, weekend), course/credit load, course level, degree level, reciprocity agreements, and student level. Room and board charges are reported as an average for one academic year and may vary according to the board plan selected, campus/location, type of housing facility, or student level. If no college-owned or -operated housing facilities are offered, the phrase *college housing not available* will appear in the Housing section of the Student Life paragraph.

Tuition payment plans that may be offered to undergraduates include tuition prepayment, installment payments, and deferred payment. A tuition prepayment plan gives a student the option of locking in the current tuition rate for the entire term of enrollment by paying the full amount in advance rather than year by year. Colleges that offer such a prepayment plan may also help the student to arrange financing.

The availability of full or partial undergraduate tuition waivers to minority students, children of alumni, employees or their children, adult students, and senior citizens may be listed.

Financial Aid

The number of Federal Work Study and/or part-time jobs and average earnings are listed. Financial aid deadlines are given as well.

Applying

Application and admission options include the following:

Early admission: Highly qualified students may matriculate before graduating from high school.

Early action plan: An admission plan that allows students to apply and be notified of an admission decision well in advance of the regular notification dates. If accepted, the candidate is not committed to enroll; students may reply to the offer under the college's regular reply policy.

Early decision plan: A plan that permits students to apply and be notified of an admission decision (and financial aid offer, if applicable) well in advance of the regular notification date. Applicants agree to accept an offer of admission and to withdraw their applications from other colleges. Candidates who are not accepted under early decision are automatically considered with the regular applicant pool, without prejudice.

Deferred entrance: The practice of permitting accepted students to postpone enrollment, usually for a period of one academic term or year.

Application fee: The fee required with an application is noted. This is typically nonrefundable, although under certain specified conditions it may be waived or returned.

Requirements: Other application requirements are grouped into three categories: required for all, required for some, and recommended. They may include an essay, standardized test scores, a high school transcript, a minimum high school grade point average (expressed as a number on a scale of 0 to 4.0, where 4.0 equals A, 3.0 equals B, etc.), letters of recommendation, an interview on campus or with local alumni, and, for certain types of schools or programs, special requirements such as a musical audition or an art portfolio.

Application deadlines and notification dates: Admission application deadlines and dates for notification of acceptance or rejection are given either as specific dates or as **rolling** and **continuous.** Rolling means that applications are processed as they are received, and qualified students are accepted as long as there are openings. Continuous means that applicants are notified of acceptance or rejection as applications are processed up until the date indicated or the actual beginning of classes. The application deadline and the notification date for transfers are given if they differ from the dates for freshmen. Early decision and early action application deadlines and notification dates are also indicated when relevant.

Admissions Contact

The name, title, and phone number of the person to contact for application information are given at the end of the Profile. The admission office address is listed in most cases. Toll-free phone numbers may also be included. The admission office fax number and e-mail address, if available, are listed, provided the school wanted them printed for use by prospective students. Finally, the URL of the institution's Web site is provided.

Additional Information

Each college that has a **College Close-Up** in the guide will have a cross-reference appended to the Profile, referring you directly to that **College Close-Up.**

COLLEGE CLOSE-UPS

These narrative descriptions provide an inside look at certain colleges, shifting the focus to a variety of other factors that should also be considered. The descriptions provide a wealth of statistics that are crucial components in the college decision-making equation—components such as tuition, financial aid, and major fields of study. Prepared exclusively by college officials, the descriptions are designed to help give students a better sense of the individuality of each institution, in terms that include campus environment, student activities, and lifestyle. Such quality-of-life intangibles can be the deciding factors in the college selection process. The absence of any college or university does not constitute an editorial decision on the part of Peterson's. In essence, these descriptions are an open forum for colleges, on a voluntary basis, to communicate their particular message to prospective college students. The colleges included have paid a fee to Peterson's to provide this information. The **College Close-Ups** are edited to provide a consistent format across entries for your ease of comparison.

INDEXES

2010–11 Changes in Institutions

Here you will find an alphabetical listing of institutions that have recently closed, merged with other institutions, or changed their name or status.

Associate Degree Programs at Two-and Four-Year Colleges

These indexes present hundreds of undergraduate fields of study that are currently offered most widely according to the colleges' responses on *Peterson's Annual Survey of Undergraduate Institutions*. The majors appear in alphabetical order, each followed by an alphabetical list of the schools that offer an associate-level program in that field. Liberal Arts and Studies indicates a general program with no specified major. The terms used for the majors are those of the U.S. Department of Education Classification of Instructional Programs (CIPs). Many institutions, however, use different terms. Readers should refer to the **College Close-Up** in this book for the school's exact terminology. In addition, although the term "major" is used in this guide, some colleges may use other terms, such as "concentration," "program of study," or "field."

SPECIAL ADVERTISING SECTION

At end of the book, don't miss the special section of ads placed by Peterson's preferred clients. Their financial support helps make it possible for Peterson's Publishing to continue to provide you with the highest-quality educational exploration, test-prep, financial aid, and career-preparation resources you need to succeed on your educational journey.

DATA COLLECTION PROCEDURES

The data contained in the **Profiles** of Two-Year Colleges and **Indexes** were researched in winter and spring 2011 through *Peterson's Annual Survey of Undergraduate Institutions.* Questionnaires were sent to the more than 1,800 colleges that meet the outlined inclusion criteria. All data included in this edition have been submitted by officials (usually admission and financial aid officers, registrars, or institutional research personnel) at the colleges themselves. All usable information received in time for publication has been included. The omission of any particular item from the **Profiles** of Two-Year Colleges and **Indexes** listing signifies either that the item is not applicable to that institution or that data were not available. Because of the comprehensive editorial review that takes place in our offices and because all material comes directly from college officials, Peterson's has every reason to believe that the information presented in this guide is accurate at the time of printing. However, students should check with a specific college or university at the time of application to verify such figures as tuition and fees, which may have changed since the publication of this volume.

CRITERIA FOR INCLUSION IN THIS BOOK

Peterson's Two-Year Colleges 2012 covers accredited institutions in the United States, U.S. territories, and other countries that award the associate degree as their most popular undergraduate offering (a few also offer bachelor's, master's, or doctoral degrees). The term two-year college is the commonly used designation for institutions that grant the associate degree, since two years is the normal duration of the traditional associate degree program. However, some programs may be completed in one year, others require three years, and, of course, part-time programs may take a considerably longer period. Therefore, "two-year college" should be understood as a conventional term that accurately describes most of the institutions included in this guide but which should not be taken literally in all cases. Also included are some non-degree-granting institutions, usually branch campuses of a multicampus system, which offer the equivalent of the first two years of a bachelor's degree, transferable to a bachelor's degree–granting institution.

To be included in this guide, an institution must have full accreditation or be a candidate for accreditation (preaccreditation) status by an institutional or specialized accrediting body recognized by the U.S. Department of Education or the Council for Higher Education Accreditation (CHEA). Institutional accrediting bodies, which review each institution as a whole, include the six regional associations of schools and colleges (Middle States, New England, North Central, Northwest, Southern, and Western), each of which is responsible for a specified portion of the United States and its territories. Other institutional accrediting bodies are national in scope and accredit specific kinds of institutions (e.g., Bible colleges, independent colleges, and rabbinical and Talmudic schools). Program registration by the New York State Board of Regents is considered to be the equivalent of institutional accreditation, since the board requires that all programs offered by an institution meet its standards before recognition is granted. This guide also includes institutions outside the United States that are accredited by these U.S. accrediting bodies. There are recognized specialized or professional accrediting bodies in more than forty different fields, each of which is authorized to accredit institutions or specific programs in its particular field. For specialized institutions that offer programs in one field only, we designate this to be the equivalent of institutional accreditation. A full explanation of the accrediting process and complete information on recognized, institutional (regional and national), and specialized accrediting bodies can be found online at www.chea.org or at www.ed.gov//admins/finaid/accred/ index.html.

Quick-Reference Chart

Two-Year Colleges At-a-Glance

This chart includes the names and locations of accredited two-year colleges in the United States and U.S. territories and shows institutions' responses to the *Peterson's Annual Survey of Undergraduate Institutions*. If an institution submitted incomplete data, one or more columns opposite the institution's name is blank. A dagger after the school name indicates that the institution has one or more entries in the *College Close-Ups* section. If a school does not appear, it did not report any of the information.

Y—Yes; N—No; R—Recommended; S—For Some

Column legend: Degrees Awarded — College Transfer Associate (C), Terminal Associate (T), Bachelor's (B), Master's (M), Doctoral (D). Institutional Control — County, District, City, State and Local, State-Related; Federal, State, Commonwealth, Territory; Independent, Independent-Religious, Proprietary. Student Body — Men, Primarily Men, Women, Primarily Women, Coed.

Institution	Location	Degrees Awarded	Institutional Control	Student Body	Undergraduate Enrollment	Percent Attending Part-Time	Percent 25 Years of Age or Older	Percent of Grads Going on to Four-Year Colleges	Open Admission	High School Equivalency Certificate Accepted	High School Transcript Required	Need-Based Aid Available	Part-Time Jobs Available	Career Counseling Services Available	Job Placement Services Available	College Housing Available	Number of Sports Available	Number of Majors Offered
UNITED STATES																		
Alabama																		
Bevill State Community College	Sumiton	C,T	St	M/W	4,556	44												
Brown Mackie College–Birmingham†	Birmingham	C,T,B	Prop	M/W														
Gadsden State Community College	Gadsden	C,T	St	M/W	7,030	39	30	19	Y	Y		Y	Y	Y	Y	Y	6	25
George C. Wallace Community College	Dothan	C,T	St	M/W	4,655	43												
H. Councill Trenholm State Technical College	Montgomery	T	St	M/W	1,758		48			Y	Y	Y		Y	Y	Y	N		20
ITT Technical Institute	Bessemer	T,B	Prop	M/W						Y			Y	Y		N		16
ITT Technical Institute	Madison	T,B	Prop	M/W												N		12
ITT Technical Institute	Mobile	T,B	Prop	M/W												N		12
Jefferson State Community College	Birmingham	C,T	St	M/W	9,644	60	37		Y	Y	S	Y	Y	Y	Y	N	3	22
J. F. Drake State Technical College	Huntsville	T	St	M/W	1,258	40												
Lawson State Community College	Birmingham	C,T	St	M/W	4,863	41	43		Y	Y	Y	Y	Y	Y	Y	Y	4	14
Lurleen B. Wallace Community College	Andalusia	C	St	M/W	1,928	40	37	0	Y	Y	Y	Y	Y	Y	Y	N	3	12
Northwest-Shoals Community College	Muscle Shoals	C	St	M/W	3,971	37	32	19	Y	Y	Y	Y	Y	Y	Y	Y	7	11
Prince Institute of Professional Studies	Montgomery	T	Prop	PW	63		68			Y	Y	Y		Y	Y	Y	N		2
Reid State Technical College	Evergreen	T	St	M/W	744	22	13		Y		Y	Y	Y	Y	Y	N		2
Southern Union State Community College	Wadley	C,T	St	M/W	4,971													
Alaska																		
Ilisagvik College	Barrow	C	St	M/W	288	86				Y	Y					Y	1	7
University of Alaska Anchorage, Kenai Peninsula College	Soldotna	C,T	St	M/W	1,934				Y	Y	Y	Y	Y			N		9
University of Alaska Anchorage, Kodiak College	Kodiak	C,T	St	M/W	540				Y	Y	S	Y		Y		N		3
University of Alaska Anchorage, Matanuska-Susitna College	Palmer	C,T	St	M/W	1,782													
Arizona																		
Arizona Western College	Yuma	C,T	St-L	M/W	8,545	67	37		Y			Y	Y	Y	Y	Y	7	55
Brown Mackie College–Phoenix†	Phoenix	T,B	Prop	M/W														10
Brown Mackie College–Tucson†	Tucson	C,T,B	Prop	M/W														15
Central Arizona College	Coolidge	C,T	Pub	M/W	7,913	62												
Chandler-Gilbert Community College	Chandler	C,T	St-L	M/W	12,296	65			Y			Y	Y	Y	Y	N	6	37
CollegeAmerica–Flagstaff	Flagstaff	T,B	Prop	M/W	300		67		Y	Y								3
Eastern Arizona College	Thatcher	C,T	St-L	M/W	6,799	65	53		Y		R	Y	Y	Y	Y	Y	10	50
Estrella Mountain Community College	Avondale	C,T	St-L	M/W	6,358	74												
GateWay Community College	Phoenix	C,T	St-L	M/W	7,346	67			Y		S	Y	Y	Y		N	5	54
Glendale Community College	Glendale	C,T	St-L	M/W	20,154	65			Y		S	Y	Y	Y	Y	N	11	32
ITT Technical Institute	Phoenix	T,B	Prop	M/W						Y		Y	Y			N		13
ITT Technical Institute	Phoenix		Prop	M/W														8
ITT Technical Institute	Tucson	T,B	Prop	M/W						Y		Y	Y			N		15
Kaplan College, Phoenix Campus	Phoenix	T	Prop	M/W														
Lamson College	Tempe	C,T	Prop	M/W	349													
Mesa Community College	Mesa	C,T	St-L	M/W	28,000		44		Y			Y	Y	Y	Y	N	11	36
Mohave Community College	Kingman	C,T	St	M/W	6,686	69	54		Y			Y	Y	Y	Y	N		34
Northland Pioneer College	Holbrook	C,T	St-L	M/W	4,636	80												
Paradise Valley Community College	Phoenix	C,T	St-L	M/W	9,951													
Phoenix College	Phoenix	C,T	Cou	M/W	13,000				Y			Y	Y	Y	Y	N	10	51
Pima Community College	Tucson	C,T	St-L	M/W	36,823	63	52		Y			Y	Y	Y		N	16	58
Pima Medical Institute	Mesa		Prop	M/W								Y				N		2
Pima Medical Institute	Mesa	T,B	Prop	M/W	958		58					S				N		6
Pima Medical Institute	Tucson	T,B	Prop	M/W	900		45			Y		S			Y	N		7
Rio Salado College	Tempe	C,T	St-L	M/W	20,865													
Scottsdale Community College	Scottsdale	C,T	St-L	M/W	11,257		30		Y			Y	Y	Y	Y	N	13	25
Tohono O'odham Community College	Sells	C,T	Pub	M/W	254	90												
Yavapai College	Prescott	C,T	St-L	M/W	8,276	77	70		Y	Y	Y	Y	Y	Y	Y	Y	5	25
Arkansas																		
Arkansas State University–Beebe	Beebe	C,T	St	M/W	4,491	42												
Arkansas State University–Mountain Home	Mountain Home	T	St	M/W	1,583	36	49		Y	Y	Y	Y	Y	Y		N		10
Cossatot Community College of the University of Arkansas	De Queen	C,T	St	M/W	1,426													
ITT Technical Institute	Little Rock	T,B	Prop	M/W						Y		Y	Y			N		13
North Arkansas College	Harrison	C,T	St-L	M/W	2,429	39												
NorthWest Arkansas Community College	Bentonville	C,T	St-L	M/W	8,006	62												
Ouachita Technical College	Malvern	C,T	St	M/W	1,610	62												
Pulaski Technical College	North Little Rock	C,T	St	M/W	10,255	53												
University of Arkansas Community College at Morrilton	Morrilton	C,T	St	M/W	2,462	35	34		Y	Y	Y	Y	Y	Y	Y	N	5	16

This chart includes the names and locations of accredited two-year colleges in the United States and U.S. territories and shows institutions' responses to the *Peterson's Annual Survey of Undergraduate Institutions*. If an institution submitted incomplete data, one or more columns opposite the institution's name is blank. A dagger after the school name indicates that the institution has one or more entries in the *College Close-Ups* section. If a school does not appear, it did not report any of the information.

Key: Y—Yes; N—No; R—Recommended; S—For Some

Column headers:
- Degrees Awarded — Bachelor's (B), Master's (M), Doctoral (D), College Transfer Associate (C), Terminal Associate (T)
- Institutional Control — County, District, City, State and Local, State-Related; Independent, Independent-Religious, Proprietary; Federal, State Commonwealth, Territory
- Student Body — Men, Primarily Men, Women, Primarily Women, Coed
- Undergraduate Enrollment
- Percent Attending Part-Time
- Percent 25 Years of Age or Older
- Percent of Grads Going on to Four-Year Colleges
- High School Equivalency Certificate Accepted
- High School Transcript Required
- Open Admissions
- Need-Based Aid Required
- Part-Time Jobs Available
- Career Counseling Available
- Job Placement Services Available
- College Housing Available
- Number of Sports Offered
- Number of Majors Offered

Institution	Location	Degrees	Control	Student Body	Undergrad Enroll.	% Part-Time	% 25+	% Grads to 4-Yr	HS Equiv.	HS Transcript	Open Adm.	Need-Based Aid	PT Jobs	Career Counsel.	Job Placement	Housing	# Sports	# Majors
California																		
Allan Hancock College	Santa Maria	C,T	St-L	M/W	10,387	71												
American Academy of Dramatic Arts	Hollywood	C	Ind	M/W	188		25		N	Y	Y		Y	Y	Y		N		1
Antelope Valley College	Lancaster	C,T	St-L	M/W	15,108	68	32		Y		Y	Y	Y	Y	Y	N	12	45
Bakersfield College	Bakersfield	C,T	St-L	M/W	15,001													
Berkeley City College	Berkeley	C,T	St-L	M/W	7,645		65		Y		R		Y	Y					21
Cambridge Career College	Yuba City	T	Prop	PW	162													
College of the Canyons	Santa Clarita	C,T	St-L	M/W	23,374		31		Y		R	Y	Y	Y	Y	N	11	50
Cuyamaca College	El Cajon	C,T	St	M/W	7,706	79												
De Anza College	Cupertino	C,T	St-L	M/W	25,191	56	52		Y	Y			Y	Y	Y	N	13	63
Deep Springs College	Deep Springs	C	Ind	M	24													
Diablo Valley College	Pleasant Hill	C,T	St-L	M/W	22,567													
East Los Angeles College	Monterey Park	C,T	St-L	M/W	31,749	75	33		Y		R	Y	Y	Y	Y	N	10	59
Fashion Careers College	San Diego	C,T	Prop	PW	91		34		N	Y	Y	Y	Y	Y	Y	N		2
FIDM/The Fashion Institute of Design & Merchandising, Los Angeles Campus†	Los Angeles	C,T,B	Prop	M/W	4,424	13	16		N	Y	Y		Y	Y	Y	Y		10
FIDM/The Fashion Institute of Design & Merchandising, Orange County Campus	Irvine	C,T	Prop	PW	372	6	8		N	Y	Y		Y	Y	Y			9
FIDM/The Fashion Institute of Design & Merchandising, San Diego Campus	San Diego	C,T	Prop	PW	292	10	10		N	Y	Y		Y	Y	Y			7
FIDM/The Fashion Institute of Design & Merchandising, San Francisco Campus	San Francisco	C,T	Prop	M/W	960	15	10		N	Y	Y		Y	Y	Y			8
Folsom Lake College	Folsom	C,T	St	M/W	9,352													
Foothill College	Los Altos Hills	C,T	St-L	M/W	18,342	80	43		Y		R	Y	Y	Y	Y	N	9	49
Golden West College	Huntington Beach	C,T	St-L	M/W	13,226		44		Y	Y	R	Y	Y	Y	Y	N	9	31
ITT Technical Institute	Anaheim	T,B	Prop	M/W									Y	Y	Y	N		14
ITT Technical Institute	Culver City		Prop	M/W														8
ITT Technical Institute	Lathrop	T,B	Prop	M/W									Y	Y	Y	N		14
ITT Technical Institute	Oakland		Prop	M/W														10
ITT Technical Institute	Oxnard	C,T,B	Prop	M/W									Y	Y	Y	N		13
ITT Technical Institute	Rancho Cordova	T,B	Prop	M/W									Y	Y	Y	N		14
ITT Technical Institute	San Bernardino	T,B	Prop	M/W									Y	Y	Y	N		14
ITT Technical Institute	San Diego	T,B	Prop	M/W									Y	Y	Y	N		13
ITT Technical Institute	San Dimas	T,B	Prop	M/W									Y	Y	Y	N		14
ITT Technical Institute	Sylmar	T,B	Prop	M/W									Y	Y	Y	N		15
ITT Technical Institute	Torrance	T,B	Prop	M/W									Y	Y	•	N		13
ITT Technical Institute	West Covina		Prop	M/W														9
Kaplan College, Bakersfield Campus	Bakersfield	T	Prop	M/W														
Kaplan College, Chula Vista Campus	Chula Vista		Prop	M/W														
Kaplan College, Fresno Campus	Clovis		Prop	M/W														
Kaplan College, Modesto Campus	Salida	T	Prop	PW														
Kaplan College, Palm Springs Campus	Palm Springs	T	Prop	M/W														
Kaplan College, Panorama City Campus	Panorama City	T	Prop	M/W														
Kaplan College, Riverside Campus	Riverside	T	Prop	M/W														
Kaplan College, Sacramento Campus	Sacramento	C,T	Prop	M/W														
Kaplan College, San Diego Campus	San Diego	T	Prop	M/W														
Kaplan College, Stockton Campus	Stockton	T	Prop	M/W														
Kaplan College, Vista Campus	Vista	T	Prop	M/W														
Los Angeles Harbor College	Wilmington	C,T	St-L	M/W	10,181	72	35		Y			Y	Y	Y	Y	N	6	23
Mendocino College	Ukiah	C,T	St-L	M/W	4,558	75	65	25	Y		Y	Y	Y	Y	Y	N	7	34
Mt. San Jacinto College	San Jacinto	C,T	St-L	M/W	17,583	64												
MTI College	Sacramento	C,T	Prop	M/W	900		62							Y	Y			3
Orange Coast College	Costa Mesa	C,T	St-L	M/W	25,316	61	32		Y			Y	Y	Y	Y	N	14	100
Pasadena City College	Pasadena	C,T	St-L	M/W	29,000													
Pima Medical Institute	Chula Vista	T,B	Prop	M/W	813		42					Y	Y	Y		N		4
Reedley College	Reedley	C	St-L	M/W	11,782	62												
San Diego City College	San Diego	C	St-L	M/W	19,497			61	Y		S		Y	Y	Y		N	16	66
San Diego Mesa College	San Diego	C	St-L	M/W	24,252													
Santa Barbara City College	Santa Barbara	T	St-L	M/W	18,092	56	29		Y	Y	R	Y	Y	Y	Y	N	10	78
Santa Rosa Junior College	Santa Rosa	C,T	St-L	M/W	25,319		54		Y			Y	Y	Y	Y	N	15	57
School of Urban Missions	Oakland	T,B	I-R	M/W	139	4												
Sierra College	Rocklin	C,T	St	M/W	19,416	72												
Solano Community College	Fairfield	C,T	St-L	M/W	10,927		46		Y	Y		Y	Y	Y	Y	N	7	47
Victor Valley College	Victorville	C,T	St	M/W														
WyoTech	Fremont	T	Prop	M/W	1,596								Y	Y	Y	N		2
Colorado																		
Colorado Mountain College	Glenwood Springs	C,T	Dist	M/W	2,465		70		Y		Y	Y	Y	Y	Y	Y	6	24
Colorado Mountain College, Alpine Campus	Steamboat Springs	C,T	Dist	M/W	1,550		30		Y		R	Y	Y	Y	Y	Y	6	21
Colorado Mountain College, Timberline Campus	Leadville	C,T	Dist	M/W	1,209		55		Y			Y	Y	Y	Y	Y	6	12
Colorado School of Trades	Lakewood	T	Prop	M/W	134			4	Y	Y								1
Front Range Community College	Westminster	C,T	St	M/W	20,092	63	43		Y			Y	Y	Y	Y	N		27
Institute of Business & Medical Careers	Fort Collins	T	Priv	M/W	302													
ITT Technical Institute	Aurora	T,B	Prop	M/W														8
ITT Technical Institute	Thornton	T,B	Prop	M/W									Y	Y	Y	N		16
Kaplan College, Denver Campus	Thornton	T	Prop	M/W														
Lamar Community College	Lamar	C,T	St	M/W	1,084	55	43		Y		Y	Y	Y	Y		Y	7	29
Northeastern Junior College	Sterling	C,T	St	M/W	2,698	66												
Otero Junior College	La Junta	C,T	St	M/W	1,660	48												

This chart includes the names and locations of accredited two-year colleges in the United States and U.S. territories and shows institutions' responses to the *Peterson's Annual Survey of Undergraduate Institutions.* If an institution submitted incomplete data, one or more columns opposite the institution's name is blank. A dagger after the school name indicates that the institution has one or more entries in the *College Close-Ups* section. If a school does not appear, it did not report any of the information.

Y—Yes; N—No; R—Recommended; S—For Some

Name	City	Degrees Awarded	Institutional Control	Student Body	Undergraduate Enrollment	% Attending Part-Time	% 25 Years or Older	% Grads to Four-Year Colleges	Open Admissions	HS Equivalency Certificate Accepted	HS Transcript Required	Need-Based Aid Available	Part-Time Jobs Available	Career Counseling Available	Job Placement Services Available	College Housing Available	Number of Sports Offered	Number of Majors Offered
Pikes Peak Community College	Colorado Springs	C,T	St	M/W	13,572													
Pima Medical Institute	Colorado Springs		Prop	M/W										Y	S	N	N	2
Pima Medical Institute	Denver	T,B	Prop	M/W	922		59							Y	Y	N	N	6
Pueblo Community College	Pueblo	C,T	St	M/W	7,736	57			Y	Y		Y	Y	Y	Y	N		32
Red Rocks Community College	Lakewood	C,T	St	M/W	9,803	65	50		Y			Y	Y	Y	Y	N	1	37
Redstone College–Denver	Broomfield	T	Prop	M/W	590													
Connecticut																		
Gateway Community College	New Haven	C,T	St	M/W	7,328	65	35		Y	Y	Y	Y	Y	Y	Y	N	4	35
Goodwin College	East Hartford	C,T,B	Prop	M/W	2,791	76	62			Y	Y	Y	Y	Y	Y	N		23
Housatonic Community College	Bridgeport	C,T	St	M/W	6,197				Y	Y	Y	Y	Y	Y	Y	N		24
Manchester Community College	Manchester	C,T	St	M/W	7,540	57			Y	Y	Y	Y	Y	Y	Y	N	4	31
Middlesex Community College	Middletown	C,T	St	M/W	2,952	60	37		Y	Y	Y	Y	Y	Y	Y	N		26
Northwestern Connecticut Community College	Winsted	C,T	St	M/W	1,711	65												
Norwalk Community College	Norwalk	C,T	St	M/W	6,740	62	37	40	Y	Y	Y	Y	Y	Y	Y	N		35
Three Rivers Community College	Norwich	C,T	St	M/W	5,161	66	45		Y	Y	R	Y	Y	Y	Y	N	2	39
Tunxis Community College	Farmington	C,T	St	M/W	4,496	58												
Delaware																		
Delaware Technical & Community College, Jack F. Owens Campus	Georgetown	C,T	St	M/W	5,031	48			Y		S	Y	Y	Y	N	4	52
Delaware Technical & Community College, Stanton/Wilmington Campus	Newark	C,T	St	M/W	7,451	56			Y		S	Y	Y	Y	N	5	64
Delaware Technical & Community College, Terry Campus	Dover	C,T	St	M/W	3,392	51			Y		S	Y	Y	Y	N	3	44
Florida																		
Brown Mackie College–Miami†	Miami	T,B	Prop	M/W														8
Chipola College	Marianna	C,T,B	St	M/W	2,274		39		Y	Y		Y	Y	Y	Y	N	4	19
College of Business and Technology	Miami	C	Prop	M/W	511		70		Y	Y	Y				Y	Y		7
College of Central Florida	Ocala	C,T,B	St-L	M/W	8,766	58	32		Y	Y	Y	Y	Y	Y	Y	N	5	19
Daytona State College	Daytona Beach	C,T,B	St	M/W	18,838	54	45	55	Y	Y	Y	Y	Y	Y	Y		12	49
Florida State College at Jacksonville	Jacksonville	C,T,B	St	M/W	28,642	64			Y	Y	Y		Y	Y	Y		11	93
Full Sail University†	Winter Park	T,B,M	Prop	PM	8,921													
Gulf Coast Community College	Panama City	C,T,B	St	M/W	7,207		38		Y		Y	Y	Y	Y	Y	N	5	29
Hillsborough Community College	Tampa	C,T	St	M/W	27,955	60	37		Y	Y	Y	Y	Y	Y	Y	Y	5	41
Indian River State College	Fort Pierce	C,T,B	St	M/W	17,511	64	48	78	Y		Y	Y	Y	Y	Y	N	7	92
ITT Technical Institute	Fort Lauderdale	T,B	Prop	M/W						Y			Y	Y		N		12
ITT Technical Institute	Fort Myers	T,B	Prop	M/W														8
ITT Technical Institute	Jacksonville	T,B	Prop	M/W						Y			Y			N		16
ITT Technical Institute	Lake Mary	T,B	Prop	M/W						Y			Y					19
ITT Technical Institute	Miami	T,B	Prop	M/W						Y			Y	Y		N		11
ITT Technical Institute	Orlando		Prop	M/W														9
ITT Technical Institute	Pinellas Park	T,B	Prop	M/W												N		14
ITT Technical Institute	Tallahassee	T,B	Prop	M/W														9
ITT Technical Institute	Tampa	T,B	Prop	M/W						Y			Y	Y		N		18
ITT Technical Institute	University Park		Prop	M/W														9
Kaplan College, Pembroke Pines	Pembroke Pines		Prop	M/W														
Lake-Sumter Community College	Leesburg	C	St-L	M/W	4,929	67	29		Y	Y	Y		Y	Y	Y	N	6	18
Miami Dade College	Miami	C,T,B	St-L	M/W	61,674	60	35		Y	Y	Y	Y	Y	Y	Y	N	8	142
Northwest Florida State College	Niceville	C,T,B	St-L	M/W	10,317													
Palm Beach State College	Lake Worth	C,T,B	St	M/W	29,534	63	33		Y	Y	Y		Y	Y	Y	N	4	67
Pasco-Hernando Community College	New Port Richey	C,T	St	M/W	11,969		35		Y	Y	Y		Y	Y	Y	N	6	19
Pensacola State College	Pensacola	C,T,B	St	M/W	11,676	61	38		Y	Y	Y		Y	Y	Y	N	16	38
Polk State College	Winter Haven	C,T,B	St	M/W	10,589	65	36		Y	Y	Y	Y	Y	Y	Y	N	7	25
Seminole State College of Florida	Sanford	C,T,B	St-L	M/W	18,028	55	43		Y		Y		Y	Y	Y	N	3	50
State College of Florida Manatee-Sarasota	Bradenton	C,T,B	St	M/W	11,232	52												
Tallahassee Community College	Tallahassee	C,T	St-L	M/W	14,739	49	26		Y	Y	Y	Y	Y	Y	Y	N	6	30
Georgia																		
Albany Technical College	Albany	T	St	M/W	4,497	34	65		Y	Y	Y					N		17
Altamaha Technical College	Jesup	T	St	M/W	1,761	60	58		Y	Y	Y					N		9
Athens Technical College	Athens	T	St	M/W	5,741	59	50		Y	Y	Y	Y		Y		N		27
Atlanta Technical College	Atlanta	T	St	M/W	5,053	47	66		Y	Y	Y			Y		N		11
Augusta Technical College	Augusta	T	St	M/W	4,864	47	57		Y	Y	Y			Y		N		24
Bainbridge College	Bainbridge	C,T	St	M/W	3,607		57			Y		S	Y	Y	Y	N	2	33
Brown Mackie College–Atlanta†	Atlanta	T	Prop	M/W														10
Central Georgia Technical College	Macon	T	St	M/W	7,902	39	61		Y	Y	Y			Y		N		27
Chattahoochee Technical College	Marietta	T	St	M/W	13,003	52	47		Y	Y	Y			Y		N		22
Columbus Technical College	Columbus	T	St	M/W	4,355	56	53		Y	Y	Y			Y		N		24
Darton College	Albany	C,T	St	M/W	5,854	51	51		Y		S	Y	Y	Y	Y	Y	14	71
DeKalb Technical College	Clarkston	T	St	M/W	4,855	55	67		Y	Y	Y			Y		N		27
Emory University, Oxford College	Oxford	C,T,B	I-R	M/W	756													
Gainesville State College	Oakwood	C,T,B	St	M/W	8,801	31												
Georgia Highlands College	Rome	C,T	St	M/W	5,226	42	26		N	Y	Y		Y	Y		N	12	40
Georgia Military College	Milledgeville	C,T	St-L	M/W	6,081	31		96	N	Y	Y		Y			Y	9	22
Georgia Northwestern Technical College	Rome	T	St	M/W	6,697	47	57		Y	Y	Y					N		13
Georgia Perimeter College	Decatur	C,T	St	M/W	24,549	53									Y		N		
Gwinnett Technical College	Lawrenceville	T	St	M/W	7,100	54	59							Y		N		27

This chart includes the names and locations of accredited two-year colleges in the United States and U.S. territories and shows institutions' responses to the *Peterson's Annual Survey of Undergraduate Institutions*. If an institution submitted incomplete data, one or more columns opposite the institution's name is blank. A dagger after the school name indicates that the institution has one or more entries in the *College Close-Ups* section. If a school does not appear, it did not report any of the information.

Column key — Degrees Awarded: College Transfer Associate (C), Terminal Associate (T), Bachelor's (B), Master's (M), Doctoral (D). Y—Yes; N—No; R—Recommended; S—For Some.

School	Location	Degrees Awarded	Institutional Control	Student Body	Undergraduate Enrollment	Percent Attending Part-Time	Percent 25 Years of Age or Older	Percent of Grads Going on to Four-Year Colleges	High School Equivalency Certificate Accepted	High School Transcript Required	Open Admissions	Need-Based Aid Available	Part-Time Jobs Available	Career Counseling Available	Job Placement Services Available	College Housing Available	Number of Sports Offered	Number of Majors Offered
Heart of Georgia Technical College	Dublin	T	St	M/W	1,817	52	49		Y	Y		Y				N		9
ITT Technical Institute	Atlanta	T,B	Prop	M/W											N	N		12
ITT Technical Institute	Duluth	T,B	Prop	M/W								Y		Y		N		14
ITT Technical Institute	Kennesaw	T,B	Prop	M/W								Y				N		14
Lanier Technical College	Oakwood	T	St	M/W	4,432	58	61		Y	Y		Y				N		21
Middle Georgia College†	Cochran	C,T,B	St	M/W	3,614	28												
Middle Georgia Technical College	Warner Robbins	T	St	M/W	4,205	36	56		Y	Y		Y		Y	Y	N		11
Moultrie Technical College	Moultrie	T	St	M/W	2,569	46	50		Y	Y		Y				N		10
North Georgia Technical College	Clarkesville	T	St	M/W	2,810	38	50		Y	Y		Y				Y		10
Ogeechee Technical College	Statesboro	T	St	M/W	2,819	42	49		Y	Y		Y				N		24
Okefenokee Technical College	Waycross	T	St	M/W	1,680	58	51		Y	Y		Y				N		11
Sandersville Technical College	Sandersville	T	St	M/W	1,028	60	53		Y	Y		Y				N		5
Savannah Technical College	Savannah	T	St	M/W	5,777	56	53		Y	Y		Y		Y		N		16
Southeastern Technical College	Vidalia	T	St	M/W	1,995	51	50		Y	Y		Y				N		13
Southern Crescent Technical College	Griffin	T	St	M/W	6,227	48	57		Y	Y		Y		Y				23
South Georgia College	Douglas	C,T	St	M/W	2,000	26												
South Georgia Technical College	Americus	T	St	M/W	2,761	37	49		Y							Y		15
Southwest Georgia Technical College	Thomasville	T	St	M/W	1,678	61	52		Y	Y		Y		Y	Y	N		11
Waycross College	Waycross	C,T	St	M/W	1,118		38			Y		Y		Y	Y	N	2	3
West Georgia Technical College	Waco	T	St	M/W	8,078	59	51		Y	Y		Y		Y	Y	N		17
Wiregrass Georgia Technical College	Valdosta	T	St	M/W	5,408	45	54		Y	Y		Y				N		15

Hawaii

School	Location	Degrees Awarded	Institutional Control	Student Body	Undergraduate Enrollment	Percent Attending Part-Time	Percent 25 Years of Age or Older	Percent of Grads Going on to Four-Year Colleges	High School Equivalency Certificate Accepted	High School Transcript Required	Open Admissions	Need-Based Aid Available	Part-Time Jobs Available	Career Counseling Available	Job Placement Services Available	College Housing Available	Number of Sports Offered	Number of Majors Offered
Hawaii Tokai International College	Honolulu	C,T	Ind	M/W	57	2		90	N	Y		Y		Y			Y	1
Honolulu Community College	Honolulu	C,T	St	M/W	4,567	64				Y			Y	Y	Y	Y	N	21
Kauai Community College	Lihue	C	St	M/W	1,345													
Leeward Community College	Pearl City	C,T	St	M/W	7,942	58	29	37	Y		S	Y	Y	Y	Y	N	3	10

Idaho

School	Location	Degrees Awarded	Institutional Control	Student Body	Undergraduate Enrollment	Percent Attending Part-Time	Percent 25 Years of Age or Older	Percent of Grads Going on to Four-Year Colleges	High School Equivalency Certificate Accepted	High School Transcript Required	Open Admissions	Need-Based Aid Available	Part-Time Jobs Available	Career Counseling Available	Job Placement Services Available	College Housing Available	Number of Sports Offered	Number of Majors Offered
Brown Mackie College–Boise†	Boise	T,B	Prop	M/W														12
ITT Technical Institute	Boise	T,B	Prop	M/W								Y		Y	Y	N		18
North Idaho College	Coeur d'Alene	C,T	St-L	M/W	5,723	40			N		S	Y	Y	Y	Y	Y	18	68

Illinois

School	Location	Degrees Awarded	Institutional Control	Student Body	Undergraduate Enrollment	Percent Attending Part-Time	Percent 25 Years of Age or Older	Percent of Grads Going on to Four-Year Colleges	High School Equivalency Certificate Accepted	High School Transcript Required	Open Admissions	Need-Based Aid Available	Part-Time Jobs Available	Career Counseling Available	Job Placement Services Available	College Housing Available	Number of Sports Offered	Number of Majors Offered
Black Hawk College	Moline	C,T	St-L	M/W	6,267	57												
City Colleges of Chicago, Harry S. Truman College	Chicago	C,T	St-L	M/W	13,174		65		Y	Y		Y	Y	Y	Y	N	1	12
City Colleges of Chicago, Malcolm X College	Chicago	C,T	St-L	M/W	6,031	58												
City Colleges of Chicago, Richard J. Daley College	Chicago	C,T	St-L	M/W	9,711	64												
College of DuPage	Glen Ellyn	C,T	St-L	M/W	27,083	61												
College of Lake County	Grayslake	C,T	Dist	M/W	18,091	69	40		Y		S	Y	Y	Y		N	9	40
Danville Area Community College	Danville	C,T	St-L	M/W	3,713	58			Y	Y	Y	Y	Y	Y		N	8	33
Elgin Community College	Elgin	C,T	St-L	M/W	12,214				Y		S		Y	Y	Y	N	8	39
Fox College	Bedford Park	T	Priv	M/W	370											N		9
Harper College	Palatine	C,T	St-L	M/W	16,060	57	28		Y	Y	Y	Y	Y			N	12	66
Highland Community College	Freeport	C,T	St-L	M/W	2,419	46	38		Y	Y	S	Y	Y	Y		N	5	53
Illinois Eastern Community Colleges, Frontier Community College	Fairfield	C,T	St-L	M/W	2,171	87	59		Y	Y	Y	Y	Y	Y	Y	N		10
Illinois Eastern Community Colleges, Lincoln Trail College	Robinson	C,T	St-L	M/W	1,062	50	45		Y	Y	Y	Y	Y	Y	Y	N	4	10
Illinois Eastern Community Colleges, Olney Central College	Olney	C,T	St-L	M/W	1,603	47	42		Y	Y	Y	Y	Y	Y	Y	N	4	14
Illinois Eastern Community Colleges, Wabash Valley College	Mount Carmel	C,T	St-L	M/W	5,584	87	40		Y	Y	Y	Y	Y	Y	Y	N	6	19
Illinois Valley Community College	Oglesby	C,T	Dist	M/W	4,529	54												
ITT Technical Institute	Burr Ridge	T,B	Prop	M/W								Y		Y	Y	N		12
ITT Technical Institute	Mount Prospect	T,B	Prop	M/W								Y		Y	Y	N		13
ITT Technical Institute	Orland Park	T,B	Prop	M/W								Y		Y	Y	N		15
John Wood Community College	Quincy	C,T	Dist	M/W	2,501	47	38	66	Y	Y	Y	Y	Y	Y	Y	N	4	28
Kankakee Community College	Kankakee	C,T	St-L	M/W	4,223	53			Y	Y	Y	Y	Y	Y	Y	N	5	40
Kaskaskia College	Centralia	C,T	St-L	M/W	5,391	57	40		Y	Y	Y	Y	Y	Y		N	9	31
Lewis and Clark Community College	Godfrey	C,T	Dist	M/W	8,179													
Lincoln Land Community College	Springfield	C,T	Dist	M/W	7,602	55	43	48	Y		R	Y	Y	Y	Y	N	6	34
McHenry County College	Crystal Lake	C,T	St-L	M/W	6,952	53	32		Y		R	Y	Y	Y	Y	N	6	24
Moraine Valley Community College	Palos Hills	C,T	St-L	M/W	17,387		31	87	Y	Y	Y	Y	Y	Y	Y	N	9	37
Morton College	Cicero	C,T	St-L	M/W			29		Y	Y		Y	Y	Y	Y	N	6	20
Northwestern College	Rosemont	C,T	Prop	M/W	1,762													
Rend Lake College	Ina	C,T	St	M/W	5,871													
Sauk Valley Community College	Dixon	C,T	Dist	M/W	2,492	49	37	78	Y		R	Y	Y	Y	Y	Y	5	50
Shawnee Community College	Ullin	C,T	St-L	M/W	3,190	70												
Solex College	Wheeling	T	Prop	M/W														
South Suburban College	South Holland	C,T	St-L	M/W	6,482		52		Y	Y	Y	Y	Y	Y		N	5	23
Triton College	River Grove	C,T	St	M/W	15,658	75												
Vet Tech Institute at Fox College	Tinley Park	T	Priv	M/W	166							Y					N	1
Waubonsee Community College	Sugar Grove	C,T	Dist	M/W	10,428	62	35		Y			Y	Y			N	10	46

Indiana

School	Location	Degrees Awarded	Institutional Control	Student Body	Undergraduate Enrollment	Percent Attending Part-Time	Percent 25 Years of Age or Older	Percent of Grads Going on to Four-Year Colleges	High School Equivalency Certificate Accepted	High School Transcript Required	Open Admissions	Need-Based Aid Available	Part-Time Jobs Available	Career Counseling Available	Job Placement Services Available	College Housing Available	Number of Sports Offered	Number of Majors Offered
Ancilla College	Donaldson	C,T	I-R	M/W	578	28	39		Y	Y		Y	Y	Y	Y	N	7	13
Brown Mackie College–Fort Wayne†	Fort Wayne	T,B	Prop	M/W														15
Brown Mackie College–Indianapolis†	Indianapolis	T,B	Prop	M/W														7

This chart includes the names and locations of accredited two-year colleges in the United States and U.S. territories and shows institutions' responses to the *Peterson's Annual Survey of Undergraduate Institutions*. If an institution submitted incomplete data, one or more columns opposite the institution's name is blank. A dagger after the school name indicates that the institution has one or more entries in the *College Close-Ups* section. If a school does not appear, it did not report any of the information.

Y—Yes; N—No; R—Recommended; S—For Some

Column key: Degrees Awarded — College Transfer Associate (C); Terminal Associate (T); Bachelor's (B), Master's (M), Doctoral (D). Institutional Control — County District City, State and Local, State-Related; Federal, State, Commonwealth, Territory; Independent, Independent-Religious, Proprietary. Student Body — Men, Primarily Men, Women, Primarily Women, Coed.

Name	Location	Degrees	Control	Student Body	Undergrad Enrollment	% Part-Time	% 25 or Older	% Grads to 4-Yr	HS Equiv Accepted	Open Admissions	HS Transcript Req	Need-Based Aid Req	Part-Time Jobs	Career Counseling	Job Placement	College Housing	Sports	Majors
Brown Mackie College–Merrillville†	Merrillville	T,B	Prop	M/W														12
Brown Mackie College–Michigan City†	Michigan City	C,T,B	Prop	M/W														13
Brown Mackie College–South Bend†	South Bend	C,T,B	Prop	PW														14
Harrison College	Anderson	T	Prop	M/W	280	78			N	Y	Y			Y	Y			10
Harrison College	Columbus	T	Prop	M/W	254	20			N	Y	Y	Y	Y	Y	Y	N		8
Harrison College	Elkhart	T,B	Prop	M/W	192													
Harrison College	Evansville	T,B	Prop	M/W	212													
Harrison College	Fort Wayne	T,B	Prop	M/W	561													
Harrison College	Indianapolis	T,B	Prop	M/W	2,668	35			N	Y	Y	Y	Y	Y	Y	N		17
Harrison College	Indianapolis	T	Prop	M/W	621	25					Y			Y	Y	N		8
Harrison College	Indianapolis		Prop	PW	458													
Harrison College	Lafayette	T,B	Prop	M/W	350	18			N	Y	Y	Y	Y	Y	Y	N		9
Harrison College	Muncie	T,B	Prop	PW	229	18			N	Y	Y	Y	Y	Y	Y	N		15
Harrison College	Terre Haute	T,B	Prop	M/W	257													
International Business College	Indianapolis	T	Priv	M/W	386						Y			Y		Y		11
ITT Technical Institute	Fort Wayne	T,B	Prop	M/W					N	Y			Y	Y		N		18
ITT Technical Institute	Indianapolis	T,B,M	Prop	M/W					N	Y			Y	Y		N		18
ITT Technical Institute	Merrillville	T,B	Prop	M/W														10
ITT Technical Institute	Newburgh	T,B	Prop	M/W					N	Y			Y	Y		N		15
Ivy Tech Community College–Bloomington	Bloomington	C,T	St	M/W	6,391	51	44		Y	Y		Y	Y	Y	Y			27
Ivy Tech Community College–Central Indiana	Indianapolis	C,T	St	M/W	22,378	65	52		Y	Y		Y	Y	Y	Y		6	42
Ivy Tech Community College–Columbus	Columbus	C,T	St	M/W	4,650	55	54		Y	Y		Y	Y	Y	Y			32
Ivy Tech Community College–East Central	Muncie	C,T	St	M/W	9,430	46	53		Y	Y		Y	Y	Y	Y			38
Ivy Tech Community College–Kokomo	Kokomo	C,T	St	M/W	5,465	53	63		Y	Y		Y	Y	Y	Y			31
Ivy Tech Community College–Lafayette	Lafayette	C,T	St	M/W	8,085	50	47		Y	Y		Y	Y	Y	Y			42
Ivy Tech Community College–North Central	South Bend	C,T	St	M/W	8,688	67	66		Y	Y		Y	Y	Y	Y			42
Ivy Tech Community College–Northeast	Fort Wayne	C,T	St	M/W	11,607	56	57		Y	Y		Y	Y	Y	Y			39
Ivy Tech Community College–Northwest	Gary	C,T	St	M/W	9,045	59	57		Y	Y		Y	Y	Y	Y			42
Ivy Tech Community College–Richmond	Richmond	C,T	St	M/W	3,913	60	67		Y	Y		Y	Y	Y	Y		1	30
Ivy Tech Community College–Southeast	Madison	C,T	St	M/W	3,024	53	53		Y	Y		Y	Y	Y	Y			18
Ivy Tech Community College–Southern Indiana	Sellersburg	C,T	St	M/W	5,133	63	58		Y	Y		Y	Y	Y	Y			31
Ivy Tech Community College–Southwest	Evansville	C,T	St	M/W	6,464	60	56		Y	Y		Y	Y	Y	Y			42
Ivy Tech Community College–Wabash Valley	Terre Haute	C,T	St	M/W	6,363	55	56		Y	Y		Y	Y	Y	Y		2	44
Kaplan College, Hammond Campus	Hammond	T	Prop	M/W														
Kaplan College, Merrillville Campus	Merrillville	T	Prop	M/W														
Kaplan College, Northwest Indianapolis Campus	Indianapolis	T	Prop	PW														
Vet Tech Institute at International Business College	Fort Wayne	T	Priv	M/W	146										Y			1
Vet Tech Institute at International Business College	Indianapolis	T	Priv	M/W	83							Y			Y			1
Vincennes University Jasper Campus	Jasper	C,T,B	St	M/W	915	50			Y	Y	Y	Y	Y	Y		N		25
Iowa																		
Brown Mackie College–Quad Cities†	Bettendorf	T	Prop	M/W														3
Des Moines Area Community College	Ankeny	C,T	St-L	M/W	22,324	60												
Hawkeye Community College	Waterloo	C,T	St-L	M/W	6,658	52	11		Y	Y	Y	Y	Y	Y	Y	N	7	33
Iowa Lakes Community College	Estherville	C,T	St-L	M/W	3,169	42												10
ITT Technical Institute	Cedar Rapids	T,B	Prop	M/W														10
ITT Technical Institute	Clive	T,B	Prop	M/W												N		11
Kaplan University, Cedar Falls	Cedar Falls	C,T,B	Prop	M/W														
Kaplan University, Cedar Rapids	Cedar Rapids	C,T,B	Prop	M/W														
Kaplan University, Council Bluffs	Council Bluffs	C,T,B	Prop	M/W														
Kaplan University, Des Moines	Urbandale	C,T,B	Prop	M/W														
Kirkwood Community College	Cedar Rapids	C,T	St-L	M/W	17,841													
Northeast Iowa Community College	Calmar	C,T	St-L	M/W	5,136	27	50		Y		R	Y	Y	Y	Y	N	9	29
North Iowa Area Community College	Mason City	C	St-L	M/W	3,744	47	23		Y	Y		Y	Y	Y	N	Y	10	40
St. Luke's College	Sioux City	T	Ind	M/W	192	28	38	49	N	Y	Y	Y	Y	N	Y			3
Southeastern Community College	West Burlington	C	St-L	M/W	3,601	42	36		Y				Y	Y		Y		6	29
Southwestern Community College	Creston	C,T	St	M/W	1,680	50												
Western Iowa Tech Community College	Sioux City	C,T	St	M/W	6,421	53	45		Y		R	Y	Y	Y	Y		7	37
Kansas																		
Allen Community College	Iola	C,T	St-L	M/W	2,277	35			Y	Y		Y	Y	Y	Y		12	67
Barton County Community College	Great Bend	C,T	St-L	M/W	4,723	78	46		Y	Y	R	Y	Y	Y	Y	Y	14	101
Brown Mackie College–Kansas City†	Lenexa	T	Prop	M/W														12
Brown Mackie College–Salina†	Salina	C,T	Prop	M/W														13
Colby Community College	Colby	C,T	St-L	M/W	1,565	52												
Cowley County Community College and Area Vocational–Technical School	Arkansas City	C,T	St-L	M/W	4,530	49	38		Y	Y		Y	Y	Y	Y	Y	10	44
Dodge City Community College	Dodge City	C,T	St-L	M/W	1,807	29			Y	Y		Y	Y	Y	Y	Y	11	70
Donnelly College	Kansas City	C,T,B	I-R	M/W	661	56												
Hesston College	Hesston	C,T	I-R	M/W	448	12	13							Y		Y	9	8
Hutchinson Community College and Area Vocational School	Hutchinson	C,T	St-L	M/W	5,453	56												
Manhattan Area Technical College	Manhattan	T	St-L	M/W	473	27												
Pratt Community College	Pratt	C,T	St-L	M/W	1,664	55	20		Y	Y	Y	Y	Y	Y	Y		11	57
Kentucky																		
Brown Mackie College–Hopkinsville†	Hopkinsville	C,T	Prop	M/W														10
Brown Mackie College–Louisville†	Louisville	T,B	Prop	M/W														16

This chart includes the names and locations of accredited two-year colleges in the United States and U.S. territories and shows institutions' responses to the *Peterson's Annual Survey of Undergraduate Institutions*. If an institution submitted incomplete data, one or more columns opposite the institution's name is blank. A dagger after the school name indicates that the institution has one or more entries in the *College Close-Ups* section. If a school does not appear, it did not report any of the information.

Degrees Awarded: College Transfer Associate (C); Terminal Associate (T); Bachelor's (B); Master's (M); Doctoral (D)

Y—Yes; N—No; R—Recommended; S—For Some

Institution	Location	Degrees Awarded	Institutional Control	Student Body	Undergraduate Enrollment	Percent Attending Part-Time	Percent 25 Years of Age or Older	Percent of Grads Going on to Four-Year Colleges	Open Admissions	High School Equivalency Certificate Accepted	High School Transcript Required	Need-Based Aid Required	Part-Time Jobs Available	Career Counseling Available	Job Placement Services Available	College Housing Available	Number of Sports Offered	Number of Majors Offered
Brown Mackie College–Northern Kentucky†	Fort Mitchell	C,T,B	Prop	M/W														12
Gateway Community and Technical College	Covington	C	St	M/W	4,799				Y	Y	Y			Y			N		14
Hazard Community and Technical College	Hazard	C,T	St	M/W	4,714	62													
Hopkinsville Community College	Hopkinsville	C,T	St	M/W	3,753	53													
ITT Technical Institute	Louisville	T,B	Prop	M/W							Y			Y	Y			N		15
Owensboro Community and Technical College	Owensboro		St	M/W	6,328	66	15		Y	Y	Y	Y		Y	Y				20
Somerset Community College	Somerset	C,T	St	M/W	8,201														
Southeast Kentucky Community and Technical College	Cumberland	C,T	St	M/W	4,959	61													
Spencerian College	Louisville	T	Prop	PW	1,155	27				Y	Y	Y		Y	Y	Y			12
Sullivan College of Technology and Design	Louisville	T,B	Prop	M/W	705	38	42	0	N	Y	Y	Y	Y	Y	Y	Y		45
West Kentucky Community and Technical College	Paducah	C,T	St	M/W	4,281	41	43		Y	Y	S	Y	Y	Y	Y	N	4	14
Louisiana																		
Blue Cliff College–Shreveport	Shreveport	T	Prop	M/W	237													
Career Technical College	Monroe	T	Prop	M/W	809	33	11		N	Y	Y			Y	Y	N		12
Elaine P. Nunez Community College	Chalmette	C,T	St	M/W	2,413	64	49		Y		S	Y	Y	Y	Y	N	2	19
ITI Technical College	Baton Rouge	T	Prop	PM	393		46		Y	Y	Y			Y	Y			7
ITT Technical Institute	Baton Rouge	T,B	Prop	M/W													N		13
ITT Technical Institute	St. Rose	T,B	Prop	M/W							Y			Y	Y		N		17
Louisiana Technical College	Baton Rouge	C	St	M/W	13,414	46													
Maine																		
Central Maine Community College	Auburn	C,T	St	M/W	2,870	52	36	27	N	Y	Y	Y	Y	Y	Y	Y	6	24
Central Maine Medical Center College of Nursing and Health Professions	Lewiston	T	Ind	M/W	200	93	76		N	Y	Y	Y			Y			2
Kaplan University	Lewiston	T	Prop	M/W														
Kaplan University	South Portland	T	Prop	M/W														
Kennebec Valley Community College	Fairfield	C,T	St	M/W	2,298	68													
Southern Maine Community College	South Portland	C,T	St	M/W	6,261	52													
York County Community College	Wells	C,T	St	M/W	1,444													
Maryland																		
Allegany College of Maryland	Cumberland	C,T	St-L	M/W	4,913													
Anne Arundel Community College	Arnold	C,T	St-L	M/W	16,741	64													
Carroll Community College	Westminster	C,T	St-L	M/W	4,108	56	30		Y		Y	Y	Y	Y	Y	N	1	25
Cecil College	North East	C	Cou	M/W	2,453	55	31		Y	Y	Y	Y	Y	Y	Y	N	7	37
College of Southern Maryland	La Plata	C,T	St-L	M/W	8,810	59													
The Community College of Baltimore County	Baltimore	C,T	Cou	M/W	26,425	66				Y	Y			Y		N	6	54
Frederick Community College	Frederick	C,T	St-L	M/W	6,233	62	50		Y			R	Y	Y	Y	N	6	43
Hagerstown Community College	Hagerstown	C,T	St-L	M/W	4,715	67	42	77	Y	Y		S	Y	Y	Y	N	12	26
Harford Community College	Bel Air	C,T	St-L	M/W	7,135	56	32	84	Y				Y	Y	Y		12	38
Howard Community College	Columbia	C,T	St-L	M/W	9,568					Y		S	Y	Y	Y		7	54
ITT Technical Institute	Owings Mills	T,B	Prop	M/W													N		12
Kaplan University, Hagerstown Campus	Hagerstown	T,B	Prop	M/W														
Montgomery College	Rockville	C,T	St-L	M/W	26,015	61	32	72	Y			R	Y	Y	Y		12	45
TESST College of Technology	Baltimore	T	Prop	M/W														
TESST College of Technology	Beltsville	T	Prop	M/W														
Wor-Wic Community College	Salisbury	C,T	St-L	M/W	4,045	68													
Massachusetts																		
Berkshire Community College	Pittsfield	C,T	St	M/W	2,275	56													
Bristol Community College	Fall River	C,T	St	M/W	8,893		43		Y	Y	Y	Y	Y	Y	Y	N	2	54
Bunker Hill Community College	Boston	C,T	St	M/W	11,009	66													
Dean College	Franklin	C,T,B	Ind	M/W	1,106	12													
Greenfield Community College	Greenfield	C,T	St	M/W	2,546	59													
Holyoke Community College	Holyoke	C,T	St	M/W	7,398	49	15		Y	Y	Y	Y		Y	Y	N	7	22
ITT Technical Institute	Norwood	T,B	Prop	M/W							Y			Y	Y		N		9
ITT Technical Institute	Woburn	T,B	Prop	M/W							Y			Y	Y				9
Massachusetts Bay Community College	Wellesley Hills	C,T	St	M/W	5,518	60	45		Y	Y		Y		Y	Y	N	9	30
Massasoit Community College	Brockton	C,T	St	M/W	7,941	54													
Mount Wachusett Community College	Gardner	C,T	St	M/W	4,761	58													
Northern Essex Community College	Haverhill	C,T	St	M/W	7,439	62	51		Y	Y	Y	Y	Y	Y	Y	N	10	58
Quinsigamond Community College	Worcester	C,T	St	M/W	8,922	53	35	45	Y	Y	Y	Y		Y	Y	N	6	44
Springfield Technical Community College	Springfield	C,T	St	M/W	6,888	56	47		Y	Y	Y	Y		Y	Y	N	9	62
Michigan																		
Alpena Community College	Alpena	C,T	St-L	M/W	2,098													
Delta College	University Center	C,T	Dist	M/W	10,899	59													
Grand Rapids Community College	Grand Rapids	C,T	Dist	M/W	17,870	58	38		Y	Y	Y	Y		Y	Y	N	14	30
ITT Technical Institute	Canton	T,B	Prop	M/W							Y			Y	Y		N		18
ITT Technical Institute	Dearborn		Prop	M/W														9
ITT Technical Institute	Swartz Creek	C,B	Prop	M/W														18
ITT Technical Institute	Troy	T,B	Prop	M/W							Y			Y	Y		N		18
ITT Technical Institute	Wyoming	T,B	Prop	M/W							Y			Y	Y		N		19
Jackson Community College	Jackson	C,T	Cou	M/W	7,870	54	47		Y	Y					Y	Y	8	26
Kalamazoo Valley Community College	Kalamazoo	C,T	St-L	M/W	11,113													
Kellogg Community College	Battle Creek	C,T	St-L	M/W	5,976	66													
Kirtland Community College	Roscommon	C,T	Dist	M/W	1,958	53	43		Y	Y		Y		Y	Y	N	3	34

This chart includes the names and locations of accredited two-year colleges in the United States and U.S. territories and shows institutions' responses to the *Peterson's Annual Survey of Undergraduate Institutions.* If an institution submitted incomplete data, one or more columns opposite the institution's name is blank. A dagger after the school name indicates that the institution has one or more entries in the *College Close-Ups* section. If a school does not appear, it did not report any of the information.

Y—Yes; N—No; R—Recommended; S—For Some

Institution	Location	Degrees Awarded	Institutional Control	Student Body	Undergrad Enrollment	% Part-Time	% 25+	% Grads to 4-Yr	HS Equiv Accepted	Open Admissions	HS Transcript Required	Need-Based Aid	Part-Time Jobs	Career Counseling	Job Placement	College Housing	Sports	Majors
Lake Michigan College	Benton Harbor	C,T	Dist	M/W	4,832	63	39	0.3	Y		Y	Y	Y	Y	Y	N	4	63
Lansing Community College	Lansing	C,T	St-L	M/W	21,123	63												
Macomb Community College	Warren	C,T	Dist	M/W	24,468	61	45		Y			Y	Y	Y	Y	N	11	72
Monroe County Community College	Monroe	C,T	Cou	M/W	4,433	61	45		Y	Y	Y		Y	Y	Y	N	2	42
Montcalm Community College	Sidney	C,T	St-L	M/W	2,117		60		Y	Y	R	Y	Y	Y	Y	N	1	23
Muskegon Community College	Muskegon	C,T	St-L	M/W	5,311	51	43		Y	Y	Y	Y	Y	Y	Y	N	8	43
Oakland Community College	Bloomfield Hills	C,T	St-L	M/W	28,939	65	49	9	Y		R	Y	Y	Y	Y	N	8	84
Southwestern Michigan College	Dowagiac	C,T	St-L	M/W	3,262	47	42		Y	Y	Y	Y	Y			Y	7	29
West Shore Community College	Scottville	C,T	Dist	M/W	1,553	58												
Minnesota																		
Alexandria Technical and Community College	Alexandria	C,T	St	M/W	2,347		28		Y	Y	Y		Y	Y	Y	N	4	52
Anoka-Ramsey Community College	Coon Rapids	C,T	St	M/W	7,679		41		Y	Y	S	Y	Y	Y	Y	N	10	22
Anoka-Ramsey Community College, Cambridge Campus	Cambridge	C,T	St	M/W	2,751		46		Y	Y	S	Y	Y	Y	Y	N	7	21
Central Lakes College	Brainerd	C,T	St	M/W	4,378		32		Y	Y	Y	Y	Y	Y	Y	N	8	30
Century College	White Bear Lake	C,T	St	M/W	10,775	53	41		Y	Y	Y	Y	Y	Y		N	9	45
Dakota County Technical College	Rosemount	C,T	St	M/W	3,672	54	46		Y	Y	S	Y	Y	Y		N	5	30
Duluth Business University	Duluth	T	Prop	PW	367		53									N		8
Hennepin Technical College	Brooklyn Park	C,T	St	M/W	13,832													
Inver Hills Community College	Inver Grove Heights	C,T	St	M/W	6,342	61	43		Y	Y	R,S	Y	Y	Y	Y	N	8	31
Itasca Community College	Grand Rapids	C,T	St	M/W	1,130													
ITT Technical Institute	Brooklyn Center		Prop	M/W														8
ITT Technical Institute	Eden Prairie	T,B	Prop	M/W														14
Lake Superior College	Duluth	C,T	St	M/W	4,366	45	29		Y		S	Y	Y	Y		N	6	38
Leech Lake Tribal College	Cass Lake	C,T	Pub	M/W	243	22												
Mesabi Range Community and Technical College	Virginia	C,T	St	M/W	1,467		37		Y	Y	Y	Y	Y	Y	Y	Y	13	16
Minneapolis Business College	Roseville	T	Priv	PW	335					Y						Y		9
Minneapolis Community and Technical College	Minneapolis	C,T	St	M/W	10,618	58												
Minnesota State College–Southeast Technical	Winona	C,T	St	M/W	2,375	40	49		Y	Y	Y	Y	Y		Y			26
Minnesota State Community and Technical College	Fergus Falls	C,T	St	M/W	6,925		34	77	Y	Y	Y	Y	Y	Y	Y	Y	14	56
Minnesota West Community and Technical College	Pipestone	C,T	St	M/W	3,464	52	43		Y	Y	Y	Y	Y	Y	Y	N	8	42
North Hennepin Community College	Brooklyn Park	C,T	St	M/W	7,456	63	44		Y	Y	R	Y	Y	Y		N	14	28
Northland Community and Technical College–Thief River Falls & East Grand Forks	Thief River Falls	C,T	St	M/W	4,135	53			Y	Y	Y	Y	Y	Y	Y	N	12	53
Northwest Technical College	Bemidji	T	St	M/W	1,419	60	40		Y	Y	Y	Y	Y	Y		Y		16
Northwest Technical Institute	Eagan	C,T	Prop	M/W	72													
Rainy River Community College	International Falls	C,T	St	M/W	342		54		Y	Y	R	Y	Y	Y	Y	Y	16	6
St. Cloud Technical & Community College	St. Cloud	C,T	St	M/W	4,883	44	15		Y	Y	Y	Y	Y	Y	Y	N	4	37
Saint Paul College–A Community & Technical College	St. Paul	C,T	St-R	M/W	5,928	59												
Mississippi																		
Antonelli College	Hattiesburg	C	Prop	M/W	354													
Antonelli College	Jackson	C,T	Prop	M/W	240													
Meridian Community College	Meridian	C,T	St-L	M/W	3,614													
Southwest Mississippi Community College	Summit	C,T	St-L	M/W	2,036	12	30		Y	Y	Y	Y	Y	Y	Y	Y	5	50
Missouri																		
Brown Mackie College–St. Louis†	Fenton	T,B	Prop	M/W														11
Crowder College	Neosho	C,T	St-L	M/W	5,219	53	12		Y	Y	Y	Y	Y	Y	Y	Y	4	35
Culinary Institute of St. Louis at Hickey College	St. Louis	T	Priv	M/W												Y		1
East Central College	Union	C,T	Dist	M/W	4,203	49												
ITT Technical Institute	Arnold	T,B	Prop	M/W						Y			Y	Y		N		17
ITT Technical Institute	Earth City	T,B	Prop	M/W					N	Y			Y	Y		N		16
ITT Technical Institute	Kansas City	T,B	Prop	M/W														12
Jefferson College	Hillsboro	C,T	St	M/W	6,192	45	25		Y	Y	Y	Y	Y	Y	Y	Y	6	18
Linn State Technical College	Linn	T	St	PM	1,176	16	18		Y	Y	Y	Y	Y	Y	Y	Y	9	23
Metropolitan Community College–Blue River	Independence	C,T	St-L	M/W	3,537	56	36		Y	Y		Y	Y	Y	Y	N	1	9
Metropolitan Community College–Business & Technology Campus	Kansas City	C,T	St-L	M/W	827		68			Y			Y	Y		N		43
Metropolitan Community College–Longview	Lee's Summit	C,T	St-L	M/W	6,539		29		Y	Y		Y	Y	Y	Y	N	5	24
Metropolitan Community College–Maple Woods	Kansas City	C,T	St-L	M/W	5,385	57	31		Y	Y		Y	Y	Y	Y	N	4	19
Metropolitan Community College–Penn Valley	Kansas City	C,T	St-L	M/W	4,956	67	59		Y	Y	Y	Y	Y	Y	Y	N	1	31
Missouri State University–West Plains	West Plains	C,T	St	M/W	2,219	39	37		Y	Y	S	Y	Y	Y	Y	Y	2	21
Saint Charles Community College	Cottleville	C,T	St	M/W	8,202	47	31		Y	Y	R,S	Y	Y	Y	Y	N	3	41
State Fair Community College	Sedalia	C,T	Dist	M/W	4,263	42												
Three Rivers Community College	Poplar Bluff	C,T	St-L	M/W	3,185	39												
Vet Tech Institute at Hickey College	St. Louis	T	Priv	M/W	125											Y		1
Wentworth Military Academy and College	Lexington	C,T	Ind	M/W	941	91	10		N	Y	Y	Y		Y		Y	10	1
Montana																		
Dawson Community College	Glendive	C,T	St-L	M/W	630	48	42		Y		Y	Y	Y	Y	Y	Y	10	14
Flathead Valley Community College	Kalispell	C,T	St-L	M/W	2,501	43												
Miles Community College	Miles City	C,T	St-L	M/W	500	25												
Montana State University–Great Falls College of Technology	Great Falls	C,T	St	M/W	1,740	48	53	74	Y	Y	Y	Y	Y		Y	N		26
The University of Montana–Helena College of Technology	Helena	C,T	St	M/W	1,500		45		Y		S	Y	Y	Y		N		16

Two-Year Colleges At-a-Glance

This chart includes the names and locations of accredited two-year colleges in the United States and U.S. territories and shows institutions' responses to the *Peterson's Annual Survey of Undergraduate Institutions*. If an institution submitted incomplete data, one or more columns opposite the institution's name is blank. A dagger after the school name indicates that the institution has one or more entries in the *College Close-Ups* section. If a school does not appear, it did not report any of the information.

Y—Yes; N—No; R—Recommended; S—For Some

College	Location	Degrees Awarded	Institutional Control	Student Body	Undergraduate Enrollment	Percent Attending Part-Time	Percent of Grads Going on to Four-Year Colleges	Percent 25 Years of Age or Older	Open Admissions	High School Equivalency Certificate Accepted	High School Transcript Required	Need-Based Aid Available	Part-Time Jobs Available	Career Counseling Available	Job Placement Services Available	College Housing Available	Number of Sports Offered	Number of Majors Offered
Nebraska																		
Central Community College–Columbus Campus	Columbus	C,T	St-L	M/W	2,619	79		44	Y	Y		Y	Y	Y	Y	Y	6	17
Central Community College–Grand Island Campus	Grand Island	C,T	St-L	M/W	3,485			44	Y	Y		Y	Y	Y	Y	Y	6	18
Central Community College–Hastings Campus	Hastings	C,T	St-L	M/W	3,069	64		44	Y	Y		Y		Y	Y	Y	6	37
Creative Center	Omaha	T,B	Prop	M/W					N	Y	Y	Y			Y	N	N	3
ITT Technical Institute	Omaha	T,B	Prop	M/W						Y			Y				N	16
Kaplan University, Lincoln	Lincoln	C,T,B	Prop	M/W														
Kaplan University, Omaha	Omaha	C,T,B	Prop	M/W														
Metropolitan Community College	Omaha	C,T	St-L	M/W	17,003	58			Y	Y	Y			Y			5	18
Mid-Plains Community College	North Platte	C,T	Dist	M/W	2,988	65	33	53	Y	Y	Y			Y		Y	5	18
Nebraska College of Technical Agriculture	Curtis	C,T	St	M/W	425	42				Y				Y	Y	Y		
Northeast Community College	Norfolk	C,T	St-L	M/W	5,377	56	57		Y		R,S	Y	Y	Y	Y	Y	8	96
Nevada																		
Career College of Northern Nevada	Sparks	T	Prop	M/W	363					Y				Y	Y	Y	5	30
Great Basin College	Elko	C,T,B	St	M/W	3,691	69	54		Y				Y	Y		N		16
ITT Technical Institute	Henderson	T,B	Prop	M/W						Y			Y	Y		N		16
ITT Technical Institute	North Las Vegas		Prop	M/W														15
Pima Medical Institute	Las Vegas	T,B	Prop	M/W	820		57			Y	S				Y	N		5
New Hampshire																		
Hesser College, Concord	Concord	C,T,B	Prop	M/W														
Hesser College, Manchester	Manchester	C,T,B	Prop	M/W														
Hesser College, Nashua	Nashua	C,T,B	Prop	M/W														
Hesser College, Portsmouth	Portsmouth	C,T,B	Prop	M/W														
Hesser College, Salem	Salem	C,T,B	Prop	M/W														
Nashua Community College	Nashua	C,T	St	M/W	2,100				Y	Y	Y	Y	Y	Y	Y	N	4	21
White Mountains Community College	Berlin	C,T	St	M/W	983	58			N	Y	Y	Y	Y	Y	Y	N		19
New Jersey																		
Burlington County College	Pemberton	C,T	Cou	M/W	10,075	45	29		Y	Y	Y	Y	Y	Y	Y	N	6	58
Camden County College†	Blackwood	C,T	St-L	M/W	15,670	46												
County College of Morris	Randolph	C,T	Cou	M/W	8,738													
Cumberland County College	Vineland	C,T	St-L	M/W	4,014													
Essex County College	Newark	C,T	Cou	M/W	13,314	41												
Mercer County Community College	Trenton	C,T	St-L	M/W	9,621	55												
Ocean County College	Toms River	C,T	Cou	M/W	10,367	44	26		Y			S	Y	Y	Y	N	12	16
Raritan Valley Community College	Branchburg	C,T	Cou	M/W	8,484	49			Y	Y	Y	Y	Y	Y	Y	N	5	57
Union County College	Cranford	C,T	St-L	M/W	12,774	49	44		Y	Y		Y	Y	Y	Y	N	6	50
New Mexico																		
Brown Mackie College–Albuquerque†	Albuquerque	T,B	Prop	M/W														12
Central New Mexico Community College	Albuquerque	C,T	St	M/W	29,948	67	54		Y			Y	Y	Y	Y	N		43
Clovis Community College	Clovis	C,T	St	M/W	4,175	76	56		Y	Y	Y	Y	Y	Y	Y	N	5	40
Doña Ana Community College	Las Cruces	C,T	St-L	M/W	9,041	65	38		Y	Y	Y		Y	Y	Y	Y		22
ITT Technical Institute	Albuquerque	T,B	Prop	M/W						Y			Y				N	16
Luna Community College	Las Vegas	C,T	St	M/W	1,789	70												20
New Mexico State University–Alamogordo	Alamogordo	C,T	St	M/W	3,944	76	47		Y		Y	Y	Y	Y	Y	N		20
New Mexico State University–Carlsbad	Carlsbad	C,T	St	M/W	1,998	71												
Pima Medical Institute	Albuquerque		Prop	M/W						Y						N		1
Pima Medical Institute	Albuquerque	T,B	Prop	M/W	716		47			Y	S	Y	Y		N			6
San Juan College	Farmington	C,T	St	M/W	8,975	66	59		Y	Y	Y	Y	Y	Y	Y	N	16	53
Santa Fe Community College	Santa Fe	C,T	St-L	M/W	4,856	66	32	45	Y		R	Y	Y	Y	Y	N		54
Southwestern Indian Polytechnic Institute	Albuquerque	C,T	Fed	M/W	635	21												
New York																		
American Academy of Dramatic Arts	New York	T	Ind	M/W	228													
The Art Institute of New York City†	New York	C,T	Prop	M/W														
ASA The College For Excellence	Brooklyn	T	Prop	M/W	6,475									Y	Y		7	8
Borough of Manhattan Community College of the City University of New York	New York	C,T	St-L	M/W	22,534	35	7		Y	Y	Y	Y	Y	Y	Y	N	5	23
Bronx Community College of the City University of New York	Bronx	C,T	St-L	M/W	10,131	41												
Broome Community College	Binghamton	C,T	St-L	M/W	6,877	32												
Bryant & Stratton College - Albany Campus	Albany	T	Prop	M/W	470	25												
Bryant & Stratton College - Amherst Campus	Clarence	T,B	Prop	M/W	474	42												
Bryant & Stratton College - Buffalo Campus	Buffalo	T,B	Prop	M/W	693	32												
Bryant & Stratton College - Greece Campus	Rochester	T	Prop	M/W	279	31												
Bryant & Stratton College - Henrietta Campus	Rochester	T	Prop	M/W	407	29												
Bryant & Stratton College - North Campus	Liverpool	T	Prop	M/W	497	33												
Bryant & Stratton College - Southtowns Campus	Orchard Park	T,B	Prop	M/W	1,206	45												
Bryant & Stratton College - Syracuse Campus	Syracuse	T	Prop	M/W	715	31												
Cayuga County Community College	Auburn	C,T	St-L	M/W	4,882		30		Y	Y	Y	Y	Y	Y	Y	Y	10	18
Corning Community College	Corning	C,T	St-L	M/W	5,396	50	25		Y	Y	Y	Y	Y	Y		N	11	47
Crouse Hospital School of Nursing	Syracuse		Ind	PW	285													
Dutchess Community College	Poughkeepsie	C,T	St-L	M/W	9,823	46		25	Y	Y	Y	Y	Y	Y	Y	N	10	41
Erie Community College	Buffalo	C,T	St-L	M/W	3,599	26												
Erie Community College, North Campus	Williamsville	C,T	St-L	M/W	6,741	33												

This chart includes the names and locations of accredited two-year colleges in the United States and U.S. territories and shows institutions' responses to the *Peterson's Annual Survey of Undergraduate Institutions*. If an institution submitted incomplete data, one or more columns opposite the institution's name is blank. A dagger after the school name indicates that the institution has one or more entries in the *College Close-Ups* section. If a school does not appear, it did not report any of the information.

Y—Yes; N—No; R—Recommended; S—For Some

Institution	Location	Degrees Awarded	Institutional Control	Student Body	Undergraduate Enrollment	Percent Attending Part-Time	Percent 25 Years of Age or Older	Percent of Grads Going on to Four-Year Colleges	Open Admissions	High School Equivalency Certificate Accepted	High School Transcript Required	Need-Based Aid Available	Part-Time Jobs Available	Career Counseling Available	Job Placement Services Available	College Housing Available	Number of Sports Offered	Number of Majors Offered
Erie Community College, South Campus	Orchard Park	C,T	St-L	M/W	4,483	38												
Everest Institute	Rochester	T	Prop	M/W	1,150													
Fashion Institute of Technology†	New York	C,T,B,M	St-L	PW	10,166	29	24		N	Y	Y	Y	Y	Y	Y	Y	7	20
Finger Lakes Community College	Canandaigua	C,T	St-L	M/W	6,699	44												
Fiorello H. LaGuardia Community College of the City University of New York	Long Island City	C,T	St-L	M/W	17,087	41	36	52	Y	Y	Y	Y	Y	Y	Y	N	8	37
Fulton-Montgomery Community College	Johnstown	C,T	St-L	M/W	2,833	34	29		Y		Y	Y	Y	Y	Y	Y	7	44
Genesee Community College	Batavia	C,T	St-L	M/W	7,208	52												
Island Drafting and Technical Institute	Amityville	C,T	Prop	M/W	131													
ITI Technical Institute	Albany	T	Prop	M/W						Y		Y	Y			N		7
ITT Technical Institute	Getzville	T	Prop	M/W						Y		Y	Y			N	N	6
ITT Technical Institute	Liverpool	T	Prop	M/W						Y		Y	Y			N	N	6
Jamestown Business College	Jamestown	T,B	Prop	M/W	386	3	56		N	Y	Y	Y		Y	Y	N	10	7
Jamestown Community College	Jamestown	C,T	St-L	M/W	3,931	29												
Jefferson Community College	Watertown	C,T	St-L	M/W	3,314	39												
Kingsborough Community College of the City University of New York	Brooklyn	C,T	St-L	M/W	18,700	40	25		Y	Y	Y	Y	Y	Y	Y	N	7	38
Long Island Business Institute	Flushing	O	Prop	PW	587	32	61	0		Y	Y			Y	Y	N		5
Mohawk Valley Community College†	Utica	C,T	St-L	M/W	7,151	33	31		Y		S	Y	Y	Y	Y		14	50
Nassau Community College	Garden City	C,T	St-L	M/W	21,952	33												
New York Career Institute	New York	T	Prop	PW	805				N	Y	Y	Y		Y	N			3
Niagara County Community College	Sanborn	C,T	St-L	M/W	7,435	37	27		Y	Y	Y	Y	Y	Y	Y		12	36
Olean Business Institute	Olean	T	Prop	M/W	87													
Onondaga Community College	Syracuse	C,T	St-L	M/W	11,755	42	29		Y	Y	Y	Y	Y	Y	Y		10	40
Phillips Beth Israel School of Nursing	New York	C,T	Ind	M/W	251	93	65		N	Y	Y	Y		Y		N		2
Plaza College	Jackson Heights	C,T,B	Prop	M/W	776													
Rockland Community College	Suffern	C,T	St-L	M/W	6,984	38												
St. Elizabeth College of Nursing	Utica	T	Ind	M/W	239	34												
St. Joseph's College of Nursing	Syracuse	T	I-R	M/W	273	39				Y	Y		Y	Y	Y			1
State University of New York College of Environmental Science & Forestry, Ranger School	Wanakena	C,T	St	PM	36			30	N	N	R	Y	Y	Y	Y		7	3
State University of New York College of Technology at Alfred	Alfred	C,T,B	St	M/W	3,717	10	15		N	Y	Y	Y	Y	Y	Y		16	10
Suffolk County Community College	Selden	C,T	St-L	M/W	28,294	33			Y	Y	Y	Y	Y	Y	Y	N	12	45
Tompkins Cortland Community College	Dryden	C,T	St-L	M/W	3,850	23	29		Y	Y	Y	Y	Y	Y	Y	Y	22	34
Ulster County Community College	Stone Ridge	C,T	St-L	M/W	3,540	50												
Westchester Community College	Valhalla	C,T	St-L	M/W	13,894	46	35		Y	Y	Y	Y	Y	Y	Y	N	11	46
Wood Tobe–Coburn School	New York	T	Priv	PW	592				N	Y		Y			N			9
North Carolina																		
Alamance Community College	Graham	C,T	St	M/W	5,512	51	44		Y	Y	Y	Y	Y	Y	Y	N	4	28
Beaufort County Community College	Washington	C,T	St	M/W	1,923				Y	Y	S	Y	Y	Y	Y	N		18
Bladen Community College	Dublin	C,T	St-L	M/W	1,736													
Blue Ridge Community College	Flat Rock	C	St-L	M/W	2,488	69												
Cape Fear Community College	Wilmington	C,T	St	M/W	9,067	54	40		Y	Y	S	Y	Y	Y	Y	N	7	33
Carolinas College of Health Sciences	Charlotte	T	Pub	M/W	436	80	57		N	Y	S	Y	Y	Y	Y			3
Carteret Community College	Morehead City	C,T	St	M/W	1,872	57												
Catawba Valley Community College	Hickory	C,T	St-L	M/W	5,504	61	42		Y	Y	Y	Y	Y	Y	Y	N	3	35
Central Carolina Community College	Sanford	C,T	St-L	M/W	5,411													
Central Piedmont Community College	Charlotte	C,T	St-L	M/W	19,364	61												
Fayetteville Technical Community College	Fayetteville	C,T	St	M/W	10,002	59	57	7	Y	Y	S	Y	Y	Y		N	7	50
Guilford Technical Community College	Jamestown	C,T	St-L	M/W	13,532	27												
ITT Technical Institute	Charlotte	T,B	Prop	M/W												N		8
ITT Technical Institute	High Point	T,B	Prop	M/W												N		7
ITT Technical Institute	Morrisville	T,B	Prop	M/W												N		7
James Sprunt Community College	Kenansville	C,T	St	M/W	1,558	49	44	1	Y	Y	Y	Y	Y	Y	Y	N	2	17
Johnston Community College	Smithfield	C,T	St	M/W	4,410	48	40		Y	Y	Y	Y	Y	Y	Y	N	4	23
King's College	Charlotte	T	Priv	M/W	648										Y	Y		9
Martin Community College	Williamston	C,T	St	M/W	755	37	49		Y	Y	Y	Y	Y	Y	Y	N		20
Montgomery Community College	Troy	C,T	St	M/W	1,039	67												
Piedmont Community College	Roxboro	C,T	St	M/W	2,874	56												
Randolph Community College	Asheboro	C,T	St	M/W	3,082	50	38	53	Y	Y	Y	Y	Y			N	2	32
Rockingham Community College	Wentworth	C,T	St	M/W	2,631	54	41		Y	Y	Y	Y	Y	Y	Y	N	7	8
Sandhills Community College	Pinehurst	C,T	St	M/W	4,571				Y	Y	Y	Y	Y	Y	Y	N	3	46
Stanly Community College	Albemarle	C,T	St	M/W	3,200													
Tri-County Community College	Murphy	C,T	St	M/W	1,353													
Wayne Community College	Goldsboro	C,T	St-L	M/W	3,585	44												
Wilson Community College	Wilson	C,T	St	M/W	2,132	50	54		Y	Y	Y	Y	Y	Y	Y	N		26
North Dakota																		
Dakota College at Bottineau	Bottineau	C,T	St	M/W	863	54	36		Y	Y	Y	Y	Y	Y	Y	Y	9	72
Lake Region State College	Devils Lake	C,T	St	M/W	1,913	73	24		Y	Y	Y	Y	Y	Y	Y	Y	7	36
North Dakota State College of Science	Wahpeton	C,T	St	M/W	2,833	40	11		Y	Y	Y	Y	Y	Y	Y	Y	8	30
Ohio																		
Antonelli College	Cincinnati	T	Prop	M/W	377													
The Art Institute of Ohio–Cincinnati	Cincinnati	C,T,B	Prop	M/W														10
ATS Institute of Technology	Highland Heights	C	Prop	M/W	353					Y	Y	Y						1

This chart includes the names and locations of accredited two-year colleges in the United States and U.S. territories and shows institutions' responses to the *Peterson's Annual Survey of Undergraduate Institutions*. If an institution submitted incomplete data, one or more columns opposite the institution's name is blank. A dagger after the school name indicates that the institution has one or more entries in the *College Close-Ups* section. If a school does not appear, it did not report any of the information.

Y—Yes; N—No; R—Recommended; S—For Some

Column key:
- **Degrees Awarded:** College Transfer Associate (C), Terminal Associate (T), State-Related Bachelor's (B), Master's (M), Doctoral (D)
- **Institutional Control:** County, District, City, State and Local; Federal, State, Commonwealth, Territory; Independent, Independent-Religious, Proprietary; State-Related
- **Student Body:** Men, Primarily Men, Women, Primarily Women, Coed
- Undergraduate Enrollment · Percent Attending Part-Time · Percent 25 Years of Age or Older · Percent of Grads Going on to Four-Year Colleges · Open Admissions · High School Equivalency Certificate Accepted · High School Transcript Required · Need-Based Aid Available · Part-Time Jobs Available · Career Counseling Services Available · Job Placement Services Available · College Housing Available · Number of Sports Offered · Number of Majors Offered

Institution	Location	Degrees	Control	Body	Enroll	%PT	%25+	%Grads	Open Adm	HS Equiv	HS Trans	Need Aid	PT Jobs	Career	Job Place	Housing	Sports	Majors
Bowling Green State University-Firelands College	Huron	C,T,B	St	M/W	2,454	45				N	Y		Y					11
Bradford School	Columbus	C,T	Priv	PW	657					N	Y		Y					14
Brown Mackie College–Akron†	Akron	T	Prop	M/W														17
Brown Mackie College–Cincinnati†	Cincinnati	T	Prop	M/W														12
Brown Mackie College–Findlay†	Findlay	T	Prop	M/W														11
Brown Mackie College–North Canton†	Canton	T	Prop	M/W														11
Bryant & Stratton College	Eastlake	C,T,B	Prop	M/W	762	36												
Bryant & Stratton College	Parma	C,T,B	Prop	M/W	528	45												
Central Ohio Technical College	Newark	T	St	M/W	4,350	49												
Cincinnati State Technical and Community College	Cincinnati	C,T	St	M/W	10,995	62	49		Y	Y	Y	Y	Y	Y	Y	N	4	64
Cleveland Institute of Electronics	Cleveland	T	Prop	PM	1,731		85			Y	Y	Y			Y			3
Columbus Culinary Institute at Bradford School	Columbus	T	Priv	M/W	241											Y		1
Cuyahoga Community College	Cleveland	C,T	St-L	M/W	30,325	60												
Davis College	Toledo	T	Prop	M/W	527	61												
Eastern Gateway Community College	Steubenville	C,T	St-L	M/W	2,209	45	26		Y	Y		S	Y	Y	Y	N	3	21
Edison State Community College	Piqua	C,T	St	M/W	3,711	61	44	74	Y	Y		S		Y	Y	N	2	38
ETI Technical College of Niles	Niles	T	Prop	M/W	421													
Harrison College	Grove City	T	Prop	M/W	99	12				Y				Y		N		9
ITT Technical Institute	Akron	T,B	Prop	M/W														8
ITT Technical Institute	Columbus	T	Prop	M/W														10
ITT Technical Institute	Dayton	T,B	Prop	M/W						N	Y					N		11
ITT Technical Institute	Hilliard	T,B	Prop	M/W														13
ITT Technical Institute	Maumee	T,B	Prop	M/W												N		10
ITT Technical Institute	Norwood	C,B	Prop	M/W								Y		Y	Y	N		16
ITT Technical Institute	Strongsville	T,B	Prop	M/W								Y		Y	Y	N		15
ITT Technical Institute	Warrensville Heights	T,B	Prop	M/W												N		12
ITT Technical Institute	Youngstown	T,B	Prop	M/W						N	Y					N		12
Kaplan College, Cincinnati Campus	Cincinnati	T	Prop	M/W														
Kaplan College, Columbus Campus	Columbus	T	Prop	M/W														
Kaplan College, Dayton Campus	Dayton	T	Prop	M/W														
Kent State University at Ashtabula	Ashtabula	C,T,B	St	M/W	2,486	45	55		Y	Y	Y	Y	Y	Y	Y	N		20
Kent State University at East Liverpool	East Liverpool	C,T,B	St	M/W	1,371	43	53		Y	Y	Y	Y	Y	Y	Y	N		10
Kent State University at Geauga	Burton	C,T,B	St	M/W	2,190	42	45		Y	Y	Y	Y	Y	Y	Y	N		11
Kent State University at Salem	Salem	C,T,B	St	M/W	1,960	31	47		Y	Y	Y	Y	Y	Y	Y	N	5	9
Kent State University at Trumbull	Warren	C,T,B	St	M/W	3,109	37	51		Y	Y	Y	Y	Y	Y	Y	N		19
Kent State University at Tuscarawas	New Philadelphia	C,B	St	M/W	2,774	40	48		Y	Y	Y	Y	Y	Y	Y	N	2	17
Lakeland Community College	Kirtland	C,T	St-L	M/W	9,406	56												
Marion Technical College	Marion	C,T	St	M/W	2,765		49		Y	Y		Y	Y	Y	Y	N	14	23
The Ohio State University Agricultural Technical Institute	Wooster	C,T	St	M/W	747													
Owens Community College	Toledo	C,T	St	M/W	19,978	57	37		Y			R	Y	Y	Y	N	12	85
School of Advertising Art	Kettering	T	Prop	M/W	116	1	3	4	N	Y	R		Y	Y	Y	N		1
Southern State Community College	Hillsboro	C,T	St	M/W	3,723	41		27	Y	Y	R	R	Y	Y	Y	N	5	17
Southwestern College of Business	Franklin	T	Prop	M/W			64		Y	Y				Y	Y			5
Stark State College of Technology	North Canton	C,T	St-L	M/W	14,830		59		Y	Y		Y	Y	Y	Y	N		49
Terra State Community College	Fremont	C,T	St	M/W	3,556	54	42		Y	Y		Y	Y	Y	Y	N	6	67
University of Cincinnati Clermont College	Batavia	C,T	St	M/W	3,713	36												
Vet Tech Institute at Bradford School	Columbus	T	Priv	M/W	175											Y		1
Virginia Marti College of Art and Design	Lakewood	T	Prop	M/W	271													
Oklahoma																		
Brown Mackie College–Oklahoma City†	Oklahoma City		Prop	M/W														11
Brown Mackie College–Tulsa†	Tulsa	T,B	Prop	M/W														11
Carl Albert State College	Poteau	C,T	St	M/W	2,363	42	35		Y			Y	Y	Y	Y	Y	6	29
Clary Sage College	Tulsa	T	Prop	PW	96		50		Y	Y		Y		Y	Y	N		3
Community Care College	Tulsa	T	Prop	PW	307		49		Y	Y	Y			Y	Y	N		13
ITT Technical Institute	Tulsa	T,B	Prop	M/W												N		14
Murray State College	Tishomingo	C,T	St	M/W	2,497		43		Y			S	Y	Y	Y	N	7	46
Oklahoma City Community College	Oklahoma City	C,T	St	M/W	14,865	61	43		Y	Y		Y	Y	Y	Y	N		46
Oklahoma State University, Oklahoma City	Oklahoma City	C,T,B	St	M/W	7,647		52		Y	Y		Y	Y	Y	Y	N		46
Oklahoma Technical College	Tulsa	T	Prop	PM	38		0		Y	Y		Y		Y	Y	N		4
Platt College	Oklahoma City	T	Prop	M/W	357		57	0	Y	Y				Y	Y	N		1
Seminole State College	Seminole	C,T	St	M/W	2,534													
Spartan College of Aeronautics and Technology	Tulsa	T,B	Prop	M	1,438													
Oregon																		
American College of Healthcare Sciences	Portland	T,M	Ind	M/W								Y		Y				1
Central Oregon Community College	Bend	C,T	Dist	M/W	6,851	52	55		Y	Y		Y	Y	Y	Y	Y	11	56
Clackamas Community College	Oregon City	C,T	Dist	M/W	8,144	61												
ITT Technical Institute	Portland	T,B	Prop	M/W								Y		Y	Y	N		19
Linn-Benton Community College	Albany	C,T	St-L	M/W	6,922	49		58	Y			S	Y	Y	Y	N	5	59
Oregon Coast Community College	Newport	C,T	Pub	M/W	535	62	54	75	Y	Y					Y	N		4
Rogue Community College	Grants Pass	C,T	St-L	M/W	5,846	54	54		Y	Y		Y		Y	Y	N	4	23
Umpqua Community College	Roseburg	C,T	St-L	M/W	2,586	47												
Pennsylvania																		
Antonelli Institute	Erdenheim	T	Prop	M/W	228		7		Y	Y		Y			Y	Y		2
The Art Institute of York–Pennsylvania	York	T,B	Prop	M/W								Y		Y				5
Bradford School	Pittsburgh	T	Priv	M/W	601							Y		Y				11

This chart includes the names and locations of accredited two-year colleges in the United States and U.S. territories and shows institutions' responses to the *Peterson's Annual Survey of Undergraduate Institutions*. If an institution submitted incomplete data, one or more columns opposite the institution's name is blank. A dagger after the school name indicates that the institution has one or more entries in the *College Close-Ups* section. If a school does not appear, it did not report any of the information.

Y—Yes; N—No; R—Recommended; S—For Some

Institution	City	Degrees Awarded	Institutional Control	Student Body	Undergraduate Enrollment	Percent Attending Part-Time	Percent 25 Years of Age or Older	Percent of Grads Going on to Four-Year Colleges	Open Admissions	High School Equivalency Certificate Accepted	High School Transcript Required	Need-Based Aid Available	Part-Time Career Jobs Available	Career Counseling Available	Job Placement Services Available	College Housing Available	Number of Sports Offered	Number of Majors Offered
Bucks County Community College	Newtown	C,T	Cou	M/W	10,800	62	34	34	Y	Y	Y		Y	Y	Y	N	8	53
Career Training Academy	Pittsburgh	T	Prop	M/W	84		54	0	N	Y	Y		Y	Y	Y			3
CHI Institute, Broomall Campus	Broomall	T	Prop	M/W														
CHI Institute, Franklin Mills Campus	Philadelphia	C,T	Prop	M/W														
Community College of Allegheny County	Pittsburgh	C,T	Cou	M/W	20,520	58												
Community College of Philadelphia	Philadelphia	C,T	St-L	M/W	39,270		53	78	Y	Y		S		Y	Y	Y	N	8	40
Consolidated School of Business	Lancaster	T	Prop	M/W	182	2												
Delaware County Community College	Media	C,T	St-L	M/W	12,237	55												
Douglas Education Center	Monessen	T	Prop	M/W	334		61	85	Y	Y	Y	Y	Y	Y	Y			0
Harcum College	Bryn Mawr	C,T	Ind	PW	1,154													
Harrisburg Area Community College	Harrisburg	C,T	St-L	M/W	23,210	62	41	43	Y			S	Y	Y	Y	N	5	86
ITT Technical Institute	Bensalem	T	Prop	M/W								Y		Y	Y	N	N	5
ITT Technical Institute	Dunmore	T	Prop	M/W														4
ITT Technical Institute	Harrisburg	T	Prop	M/W														
ITT Technical Institute	King of Prussia	T	Prop	M/W														6
ITT Technical Institute	Pittsburgh	T	Prop	M/W										Y	Y	N		6
ITT Technical Institute	Tarentum	T	Prop	M/W								Y		Y		N		7
JNA Institute of Culinary Arts	Philadelphia	T	Prop	M/W	92													1
Kaplan Career Institute, Harrisburg	Harrisburg	T	Prop	M/W														
Kaplan Career Institute, ICM Campus	Pittsburgh	C,T	Prop	M/W														
Lackawanna College	Scranton	C,T	Ind	M/W	1,387	28												
Lehigh Carbon Community College	Schnecksville	C,T	St-L	M/W	8,101	58	42	38	Y			S	Y	Y	Y	N	6	60
Montgomery County Community College	Blue Bell	C,T	Cou	M/W	13,919	54	37	72	Y	Y		S	Y	Y	Y	N	13	54
Newport Business Institute	Williamsport	T	Prop	PW	108		69		N		Y		Y	Y	Y	N		4
Northampton Community College	Bethlehem	C,T	St-L	M/W	11,328	53	38	72	Y	Y	R,S		Y	Y	Y	Y	10	61
Orleans Technical Institute	Philadelphia	C,T	Ind	M/W	676	27	58				Y		Y	Y	Y	N		1
Pennco Tech	Bristol	T	Prop	M/W	400	39	40	1	N	Y			Y	Y	Y	Y		2
Penn State Beaver	Monaca	C,T,B,M	St-R	M/W	906	24	13		N		Y	Y		Y	Y		10	118
Penn State Brandywine	Media	C,T,B	St-R	M/W	1,613	15	11		N		Y	Y		Y	Y		10	120
Penn State DuBois	DuBois	C,T,B,M	St-R	M/W	919	22	33		N		Y	Y		Y	Y		7	127
Penn State Fayette, The Eberly Campus	Uniontown	C,T,B	St-R	M/W	1,037	23	30		N		Y	Y		Y	Y		11	124
Penn State Greater Allegheny	McKeesport	C,T,B,M	St-R	M/W	768	14	10		N		Y	Y		Y	Y	Y	12	124
Penn State Hazleton	Hazleton	C,T,B,M	St-R	M/W	1,245	4	5		N		Y	Y		Y	Y	Y	8	125
Penn State Lehigh Valley	Fogelsville	C,T,B	St-R	M/W	914	23	13		N		Y	Y		Y	Y		13	119
Penn State Mont Alto	Mont Alto	C,T,B	St-R	M/W	1,252	24	21		N		Y	Y		Y	Y	Y	10	120
Penn State New Kensington	New Kensington	C,T,B,M	St-R	M/W	870	24	15		N		Y	Y		Y	Y		13	124
Penn State Schuylkill	Schuylkill Haven	C,T,B	St-R	M/W	1,034	15	15		N		Y	Y		Y	Y		8	124
Penn State Shenango	Sharon	C,T,B	St-R	M/W	714	37	55		N		Y	Y		Y	Y		7	124
Penn State Wilkes-Barre	Lehman	C,T,B	St-R	M/W	719	15	11		N		Y	Y		Y	Y		11	122
Penn State Worthington Scranton	Dunmore	C,T,B	St-R	M/W	1,386	21	21		N		Y	Y		Y	Y		10	119
Penn State York	York	C,T,B,M	St-R	M/W	1,393	32	26		N		Y	Y		Y	Y			126
Pennsylvania Highlands Community College	Johnstown	C,T	St-L	M/W	2,543		45		Y					Y	Y	N	2	23
Pennsylvania Institute of Technology	Media	C,T	Ind	M/W	1,046	12												
Pittsburgh Institute of Mortuary Science, Incorporated	Pittsburgh	C,T	Ind	M/W	193	56												
Pittsburgh Technical Institute	Oakdale	T	Prop	M/W	2,186		23		Y	Y	Y			Y	Y	Y	6	14
The Restaurant School at Walnut Hill College	Philadelphia	T,B	Prop	M/W	423		13		Y	Y	Y			Y	Y	Y		4
Triangle Tech–Greensburg School	Greensburg	T	Prop	PM	260													
Triangle Tech Inc–Bethlehem	Bethlehem	T	Prop	PM	140													
Triangle Tech, Inc.–DuBois School	DuBois	T	Prop	PM	329		48	1	N	Y	Y		Y	Y		N		4
Triangle Tech, Inc.–Erie School	Erie	C,T	Prop	PM	176													
Triangle Tech, Inc.–Sunbury School	Sunbury	T	Prop	M/W	170													
University of Pittsburgh at Titusville	Titusville	C,B	St-R	M/W	514	14	14		N		Y	Y		Y	Y	Y	11	8
Vet Tech Institute	Pittsburgh	T	Priv	M/W	345									Y		Y		1
Westmoreland County Community College	Youngwood	C,T	Cou	M/W	7,383	49	41		Y					Y	Y	N	10	45
The Williamson Free School of Mechanical Trades	Media	T	Ind	M	270		0		N	Y	Y		Y	Y	Y	Y	12	8
YTI Career Institute–York	York	T	Priv	M/W	823		31		Y	Y				Y	Y			7
Rhode Island																		
Community College of Rhode Island	Warwick	C,T	St	M/W	17,775	65	36		Y	Y			Y	Y	Y	N	10	54
New England Institute of Technology	Warwick	C,T,B,M	Ind	M/W	3,258	13				Y	Y		Y	Y	Y	N		41
South Carolina																		
Aiken Technical College	Aiken	C,T	St-L	M/W	3,128	52	42		Y	Y		Y	Y	Y	Y	N	2	20
Brown Mackie College–Greenville†	Greenville	T,B	Prop	M/W														10
Central Carolina Technical College	Sumter	C,T	St	M/W	4,382	62	51		Y	Y	Y		Y	Y	Y			14
Denmark Technical College	Denmark	C,T	St	M/W	1,033	26	28		Y	Y	Y	Y	Y	Y	Y	Y	6	8
Forrest Junior College	Anderson	C,T	Prop	M/W	94	40												
ITT Technical Institute	Columbia	T,B	Prop	M/W												N		10
ITT Technical Institute	Greenville	T,B	Prop	M/W								Y		Y		N		15
ITT Technical Institute	Myrtle Beach		Prop	M/W														7
ITT Technical Institute	North Charleston		Prop	M/W														6
Midlands Technical College	Columbia	C,T	St-L	M/W	12,078	53	41		Y		R		Y	Y	Y	N	7	46
Miller-Motte Technical College	Charleston	T	Prop	M/W	764													
Orangeburg-Calhoun Technical College	Orangeburg	C,T	St-L	M/W	3,219	52												
Spartanburg Community College	Spartanburg	C,T	St	M/W	5,871	47	40		Y				Y	Y	Y			25
Spartanburg Methodist College	Spartanburg	C,T	I-R	M/W	808	4												
Trident Technical College	Charleston	C,T	St-L	M/W	14,834	54	44		Y	Y	S		Y	Y	Y	N		39
University of South Carolina Lancaster	Lancaster	C,T	St	M/W	1,593													

This chart includes the names and locations of accredited two-year colleges in the United States and U.S. territories and shows institutions' responses to the *Peterson's Annual Survey of Undergraduate Institutions*. If an institution submitted incomplete data, one or more columns opposite the institution's name is blank. A dagger after the school name indicates that the institution has one or more entries in the *College Close-Ups* section. If a school does not appear, it did not report any of the information.

Key: Y—Yes; N—No; R—Recommended; S—For Some

Degrees Awarded: College Transfer Associate (C), Terminal Associate (T), Bachelor's (B), Master's (M), Doctoral (D)

Institution	Location	Degrees Awarded	Institutional Control	Student Body	Undergraduate Enrollment	Percent Attending Part Time	Percent 25 Years of Age or Older	Percent of Grads Going on to Four-Year Colleges	High School Equivalency Certificate Accepted	High School Transcript Required	Open Admissions	Need-Based Aid Available	Part-Time Jobs Available	Career Counseling Available	Job Placement Services Available	College Housing Available	Number of Sports Offered	Number of Majors Offered
University of South Carolina Salkehatchie	Allendale	C,T	St	M/W	965													
University of South Carolina Union	Union	C	St	M/W	500	50	33		N	Y	Y	Y	Y			N		2
South Dakota																		
Kilian Community College	Sioux Falls	C,T	Ind	M/W	390	82	64	9	Y	Y	Y	Y	Y	Y	Y	N		15
Mitchell Technical Institute	Mitchell	C,T	St	M/W	1,106		24		Y	Y	Y	Y	Y	Y	Y	Y	5	19
Sisseton-Wahpeton Community College	Sisseton	C,T	Fed	M/W	237	24												
Southeast Technical Institute	Sioux Falls	T	St	M/W	2,455	21	27		N	Y	Y	Y	Y	Y	Y	Y	3	48
Tennessee																		
Chattanooga State Community College	Chattanooga	C,T	St	M/W	9,431													
Cleveland State Community College	Cleveland	C,T	St	M/W	3,753	43	40	53	Y	Y	Y	Y	Y	Y	Y	N	8	13
Dyersburg State Community College	Dyersburg	C,T	St	M/W	3,749	49	45		Y	Y	Y	Y	Y	Y	Y	N	4	9
ITT Technical Institute	Chattanooga	T,B	Prop	M/W												N		12
ITT Technical Institute	Cordova	T,B	Prop	M/W						Y				Y	Y	N		18
ITT Technical Institute	Johnson City	T,B	Prop	M/W														10
ITT Technical Institute	Knoxville	T,B	Prop	M/W						Y				Y	Y	N		16
ITT Technical Institute	Nashville	T,B	Prop	M/W						Y				Y	Y	N		16
Jackson State Community College	Jackson	C,T	St	M/W	5,109													
John A. Gupton College	Nashville	C,T	Ind	M/W	127	19	45		N	Y		Y		Y	Y	Y		1
Kaplan Career Institute, Nashville Campus	Nashville	T	Prop	M/W														
Motlow State Community College	Tullahoma	C,T	St	M/W	5,079	46	29		Y	Y	Y	Y	Y	Y	Y	N	8	7
Nossi College of Art	Goodlettsville	C,B	Ind	M/W	660		35		N	Y	Y	Y		Y	Y	N		5
Volunteer State Community College	Gallatin	C,T	St	M/W	8,989	51	40		Y	Y	Y	Y	Y	Y	Y	N	3	17
Walters State Community College	Morristown	C,T	St	M/W	6,853	48												
Texas																		
Alvin Community College	Alvin	C,T	St-L	M/W	4,400	70												
Amarillo College	Amarillo	C,T	St-L	M/W	11,675		38		Y		Y	Y	Y	Y	Y	N	5	83
Austin Community College	Austin	C,T	St-L	M/W	44,100		41		Y	Y	Y	Y	Y	Y		N	5	90
Brown Mackie College–San Antonio†	San Antonio	C,T,B	Prop	M/W														
Central Texas College	Killeen	C,T	St-L	M/W	24,498	83												
Clarendon College	Clarendon	C,T	St-L	M/W	1,583		29		Y	Y	Y	Y	Y	Y	Y	Y	6	43
Collin County Community College District	McKinney	C,T	St-L	M/W	27,069	62	34		Y	Y	Y	Y	Y	Y	Y	N	3	49
Commonwealth Institute of Funeral Service	Houston	T	Ind	M/W	122													
Del Mar College	Corpus Christi	C,T	St-L	M/W	12,007													
Eastfield College	Mesquite	C,T	St-L	M/W	12,403	76	37		Y	Y	R	Y	Y	Y	Y	N	8	35
El Centro College	Dallas	C,T	Cou	M/W	9,245	77	52		Y	Y	S	Y	Y	Y	Y	N		37
El Paso Community College	El Paso	C,T	Cou	M/W	28,168	61												
Frank Phillips College	Borger	C,T	St-L	M/W	1,247	45	20		Y	Y	Y	Y	Y	Y	Y	Y	6	23
Hallmark College of Technology	San Antonio	T,B	Prop	M/W	356		49			Y	Y		Y	Y	Y	N		8
Hallmark Institute of Aeronautics	San Antonio	T	Priv	M/W	227		54			Y	Y	Y	Y	Y	Y	N		2
Houston Community College System	Houston	C,T	St-L	M/W	60,303	69	41		Y			S	Y	Y	Y	N		61
Howard College	Big Spring	C,T	St-L	M/W	4,103	60												
ITT Technical Institute	Arlington	T,B	Prop	M/W						Y				Y	Y	N		11
ITT Technical Institute	Austin	T,B	Prop	M/W						Y				Y	Y	N		12
ITT Technical Institute	DeSoto	T,B	Prop	M/W														9
ITT Technical Institute	Houston	T,B	Prop	M/W						Y				Y	Y	N		10
ITT Technical Institute	Houston	T,B	Prop	M/W						Y				Y	Y	N		10
ITT Technical Institute	Richardson	T,B	Prop	M/W						Y				Y	Y	N		12
ITT Technical Institute	San Antonio	T,B	Prop	M/W						Y				Y	Y	N		12
ITT Technical Institute	Waco		Prop	M/W														7
ITT Technical Institute	Webster	T,B	Prop	M/W						Y					Y	N		10
Kaplan College, Arlington	Arlington		Prop	M/W														
Kaplan College, Dallas	Dallas	T	Prop	M/W														
KD Studio	Dallas	T	Prop	M/W	177		27		Y	Y	Y	Y		Y		N		3
Kilgore College	Kilgore	C,T	St-L	M/W	6,691	52	33		Y	Y	Y	Y	Y	Y	Y	Y	6	72
Lonestar College–Cy-Fair	Cypress	C,T	St-L	M/W	18,107	73	32		Y	Y			Y		Y	N		55
Lonestar College–Kingwood	Kingwood	C,T	St-L	M/W	10,879	77	38		Y	Y			Y		Y	N	1	55
Lonestar College–Montgomery	Conroe	C,T	St-L	M/W	12,653	74	37		Y	Y			Y	Y	Y	N		61
Lonestar College–North Harris	Houston	C,T	St-L	M/W	16,356	80	39		Y	Y			Y	Y	Y	N	15	61
Lonestar College–Tomball	Tomball	C,T	St-L	M/W	11,344	80	34		Y	Y			Y	Y	Y	N		41
Lon Morris College	Jacksonville	C,T	I-R	M/W	815	8												
Mountain View College	Dallas	C,T	St-L	M/W	8,463		37		Y	Y	Y	Y	Y			N	4	13
North Central Texas College	Gainesville	C,T	St-L	M/W	9,156													
North Lake College	Irving	C,T	Cou	M/W	10,174	69												
Odessa College	Odessa	C,T	St-L	M/W	5,132													
Panola College	Carthage	C,T	St-L	M/W	2,322	55	33		Y	Y	R,S	Y	Y	Y	Y	Y	7	11
Paris Junior College	Paris	C,T	St-L	M/W	5,580	53												
Pima Medical Institute	Houston		Prop	M/W										Y		N		3
St. Philip's College	San Antonio	C,T	Dist	M/W	10,828	66	51		Y	Y	Y	Y	Y	Y	Y	N	5	64
San Jacinto College District	Pasadena	C,T	St-L	M/W	27,011	64												
South Plains College	Levelland	C,T	St-L	M/W	10,028	53												
Tarrant County College District	Fort Worth	C,T	Cou	M/W	39,596	66												
Temple College	Temple	C,T	Dist	M/W	5,659	60												
Texas State Technical College West Texas	Sweetwater	T	St	M/W	1,689	82												
Trinity Valley Community College	Athens	C,T	St-L	M/W	7,579	60	39		Y	Y	Y	Y	Y	Y	Y	Y	7	54
Tyler Junior College	Tyler	C,T	St-L	M/W	11,738	47	14		Y	Y	Y	Y	Y	Y	Y	Y	9	58

This chart includes the names and locations of accredited two-year colleges in the United States and U.S. territories and shows institutions' responses to the *Peterson's Annual Survey of Undergraduate Institutions.* If an institution submitted incomplete data, one or more columns opposite the institution's name is blank. A dagger after the school name indicates that the institution has one or more entries in the *College Close-Ups* section. If a school does not appear, it did not report any of the information.

Y—Yes; N—No; R—Recommended; S—For Some

Name	Location	Degrees Awarded	Institutional Control	Student Body	Undergrad Enrollment	% Part-Time	% 25 or Older	% Grads to 4-Yr	HS Equiv. Accepted	HS Transcript Req.	Open Admissions	Need-Based Aid	Part-Time Jobs	Career Counseling	Job Placement	College Housing	# Sports	# Majors
Vet Tech Institute of Houston	Houston	T	Priv	M/W	134											N		1
Victoria College	Victoria	C,T	Cou	M/W	4,054	66												
Wade College	Dallas	C,T,B	Prop	PW	238			31		Y	Y	Y	Y		Y	Y		4
Westwood College–Houston South Campus	Houston	T,B	Prop	M/W														
Utah																		
ITT Technical Institute	Murray	T,B	Prop	M/W							N	Y		Y	Y		N		18
LDS Business College	Salt Lake City	C,T	I-R	M/W	1,588	23												
Salt Lake Community College	Salt Lake City	C,T	St	M/W	32,947	70	37		Y			Y	Y	Y	Y		N	6	69
Snow College	Ephraim	C,T	St	M/W	4,386	34	12		Y	Y	Y	Y	Y	Y	Y		Y	14	55
Vermont																		
Community College of Vermont	Montpelier	C,T	St	M/W	7,303	50		50	Y	Y			Y	Y	Y		N		25
Landmark College†	Putney	C,T	Ind	M/W	498													
Virginia																		
Bryant & Stratton College - Richmond Campus	Richmond	T,B	Prop	M/W	572	51												
Bryant & Stratton College - Virginia Beach	Virginia Beach	T,B	Prop	M/W	595	55												
Dabney S. Lancaster Community College	Clifton Forge	C,T	St	M/W	1,437	63	25		Y		R	Y	Y	Y	Y	N	9	17
Eastern Shore Community College	Melfa	C,T	St	M/W	1,332													
Germanna Community College	Locust Grove	C,T	St	M/W	7,035	67												
ITT Technical Institute	Chantilly	T,B	Prop	M/W								Y		Y	Y		N		14
ITT Technical Institute	Norfolk	T,B	Prop	M/W								Y		Y	Y		N		18
ITT Technical Institute	Richmond	T,B	Prop	M/W								Y		Y	Y		N		17
ITT Technical Institute	Salem	T,B	Prop	M/W														9
ITT Technical Institute	Springfield	T,B	Prop	M/W							N	Y		Y	Y		N		17
John Tyler Community College	Chester	C,T	St	M/W	10,518	43	35			N	Y	Y	R	Y	Y	N	N	25
J. Sargeant Reynolds Community College	Richmond	C,T	St	M/W	12,619	44			Y	Y	R	Y	Y	Y	Y	N		26
Mountain Empire Community College	Big Stone Gap	C,T	St	M/W	3,404	32	59		Y	Y	Y	Y	Y	Y	Y	N	3	15
Patrick Henry Community College	Martinsville	C,T	St	M/W	3,501													
Paul D. Camp Community College	Franklin	C,T	St	M/W	1,579	40			Y		Y	Y	Y	Y	Y	N		10
Rappahannock Community College	Glenns	C,T	St-R	M/W	3,406	75												
Southside Virginia Community College	Alberta	C,T	St	M/W	6,353	70	49		Y		Y	Y	Y	Y	Y	N	7	15
Southwest Virginia Community College	Richlands	C,T	St	M/W	3,855	57												
Thomas Nelson Community College	Hampton	C,T	St	M/W	10,606													
Tidewater Community College	Norfolk	C,T	St	M/W	30,447													
Washington																		
The Art Institute of Seattle†	Seattle	T,B	Prop	M/W														13
Bellingham Technical College	Bellingham	C,T	St	M/W	2,864		61		Y			Y	S	Y	Y		N		25
Big Bend Community College	Moses Lake	C,T	St	M/W	2,169		40		Y			Y	S	Y	Y	Y	N	4	15
Cascadia Community College	Bothell	C,T	St	M/W	2,873	46	24		Y								N		3
Clark College	Vancouver	C,T	St	M/W	13,137	52			Y			Y	S	Y	Y	Y	N	8	37
Everett Community College	Everett	C,T	St	M/W	7,562	51												
Grays Harbor College	Aberdeen	C,T	St	M/W	2,526	37	52		Y		R	Y	Y	Y	Y	N	4	16
Green River Community College	Auburn	C,T	St	M/W	8,205													
Highline Community College	Des Moines	C,T	St	M/W	6,725	45												
ITT Technical Institute	Everett	T,B	Prop	M/W														15
ITT Technical Institute	Seattle	T,B	Prop	M/W								Y		Y	Y		N		16
ITT Technical Institute	Spokane Valley	T,B	Prop	M/W								Y		Y	Y		N		14
Lower Columbia College	Longview	C,T	St	M/W	4,290	40	55	50	Y		R	Y	Y	Y		N	5	20
North Seattle Community College	Seattle	C,T	St	M/W	6,855	70	65		Y		R	Y	Y	Y	Y	N		24
Olympic College	Bremerton	C,T,B	St	M/W	8,533	48			Y				S	Y		Y	N	9	29
Pima Medical Institute	Renton		Prop	M/W										Y		N		4
Pima Medical Institute	Seattle	T,B	Prop	M/W	357		57						S		Y		N		5
South Puget Sound Community College	Olympia	C,T	St	M/W	5,617	46												
Wenatchee Valley College	Wenatchee	C,T	St-L	M/W	3,637				Y			Y	S	Y	Y	Y	Y	13	43
Yakima Valley Community College	Yakima	C,T	St	M/W	4,479	38	36		Y				R,S	Y	Y		Y	6	38
West Virginia																		
Blue Ridge Community and Technical College	Martinsburg	C,T	St	M/W	3,936	72	25		Y	Y	Y			Y	Y		N		15
ITT Technical Institute	Huntington	T	Prop	M/W														8
Mountain State College	Parkersburg	T	Prop	M/W	166													
Potomac State College of West Virginia University	Keyser	C,T,B	St	M/W	1,836	23	13		Y	Y	Y	Y	Y	Y	Y	Y	7	53
West Virginia Junior College–Bridgeport	Bridgeport	C,T	Prop	M/W	355		40		Y	Y		Y	Y	Y	Y	Y	N		4
West Virginia Northern Community College	Wheeling	C,T	St	M/W	3,363	48	47		Y		S	Y	Y	Y	Y	N	5	22
Wisconsin																		
Blackhawk Technical College	Janesville	C,T	Dist	M/W	3,337	52	59	0	Y	Y		Y	Y	Y	Y	Y	N		23
Bryant & Stratton College	Milwaukee	C,T,B	Prop	M/W	828	44			N	Y	Y	Y	Y	Y	Y	Y	N		12
Chippewa Valley Technical College	Eau Claire	T	Dist	M/W	6,062	48	42		Y	Y		Y	Y	Y	Y	N		27
Fox Valley Technical College	Appleton	C,T	St-L	M/W	10,659	69	50		Y	Y		Y	Y	Y	Y	N	7	44
ITT Technical Institute	Green Bay	T,B	Prop	M/W								Y		Y	Y		N		17
ITT Technical Institute	Greenfield	T,B	Prop	M/W								Y		Y	Y		N		17
ITT Technical Institute	Madison	T,B	Prop	M/W														11
Lac Courte Oreilles Ojibwa Community College	Hayward	C,T	Fed	M/W	561	39												
Milwaukee Area Technical College	Milwaukee	C,T	Dist	M/W	20,215	65												

Two-Year Colleges At-a-Glance

This chart includes the names and locations of accredited two-year colleges in the United States and U.S. territories and shows institutions' responses to the *Peterson's Annual Survey of Undergraduate Institutions*. If an institution submitted incomplete data, one or more columns opposite the institution's name is blank. A dagger after the school name indicates that the institution has one or more entries in the *College Close-Ups* section. If a school does not appear, it did not report any of the information.

Key: Y—Yes; N—No; R—Recommended; S—For Some

Degrees Awarded: College Transfer Associate (C); Terminal Associate (T); Bachelor's (B), Master's (M), Doctoral (D)

Institutional Control abbreviations include: Independent; Independent-Religious; Proprietary; Federal; State; State and Local; State-Related; Commonwealth; Territory; County; District; City; Province (Prov)

Institution	City	Degrees Awarded	Institutional Control	Student Body	Undergraduate Enrollment	Percent Attending Part-Time	Percent 25 Years of Age or Older	Percent of Grads Going on to Four-Year Colleges	High School Equivalency Certificate Accepted	Open Admissions	High School Transcript Required	Need-Based Aid Available	Part-Time Jobs Available	Career Counseling Available	Job Placement Services Available	College Housing Available	Number of Sports Offered	Number of Majors Offered
Moraine Park Technical College	Fond du Lac	C,T	Dist	M/W	8,484	82	63		Y	Y	Y	Y		Y	Y	N		72
Nicolet Area Technical College	Rhinelander	C,T	St-L	M/W	1,600	75												
Southwest Wisconsin Technical College	Fennimore	T	St-L	M/W	3,409	75	35											
University of Wisconsin–Fond du Lac	Fond du Lac	C	St	M/W	779	35												
University of Wisconsin–Fox Valley	Menasha	C,T	St	M/W	1,797	42	19		N	Y	Y	Y	Y	Y		N	6	1
University of Wisconsin–Richland	Richland Center	C	St	M/W	455	39	18		Y	Y	Y	Y	Y	Y	Y	N	9	1
University of Wisconsin–Sheboygan	Sheboygan	C	St	M/W					Y	Y	Y	Y	Y	Y		N		1
University of Wisconsin–Waukesha	Waukesha	C	St	M/W	2,132	48	28		N	Y	Y	Y	Y	Y		N	9	1
Waukesha County Technical College	Pewaukee	T	St-L	M/W	8,102	69	51		Y		Y	Y	Y	Y		N		34
Wisconsin Indianhead Technical College	Shell Lake	T	Dist	M/W	3,925	56	48									N		23
Wyoming																		
Casper College	Casper	C,T	St-L	M/W	4,393	49	41	40	Y	Y		Y	Y	Y	Y	Y	Y	10	101
Central Wyoming College	Riverton	C,T	St-L	M/W	2,407	60	40	47	Y		R	Y	Y	Y	Y	Y	Y	15	62
Eastern Wyoming College	Torrington	C,T	St-L	M/W	1,391	55												
Laramie County Community College	Cheyenne	C,T	Dist	M/W	4,794	52	40	65	Y	Y	S	Y	Y	Y	Y	Y	Y	12	59
Northwest College	Powell	C,T	St-L	M/W	2,111	33	35		Y	Y	Y	Y	Y	Y	Y	Y	Y	10	61
Sheridan College	Sheridan	C,T	St-L	M/W	3,940	63	32		Y		R,S	Y	Y	Y	Y	Y	Y	9	50
Western Wyoming Community College	Rock Springs	C,T	St-L	M/W	4,120	70												
CANADA																		
Alberta																		
Southern Alberta Institute of Technology	Calgary	T,B	Prov	M/W	7,672	9			N	Y	Y					Y	7	6

Profiles
of Two-Year
Colleges

ALABAMA

Alabama Southern Community College
Monroeville, Alabama

Director of Admissions Ms. Jana S. Horton, Registrar, Alabama Southern Community College, PO Box 2000, Monroeville, AL 36461. *Phone:* 251-575-3156 Ext. 252. *E-mail:* jhorton@ascc.edu. *Web site:* http://www.ascc.edu/.

Bevill State Community College
Sumiton, Alabama

- **State-supported** 2-year, founded 1969, part of Alabama College System
- **Rural** 245-acre campus with easy access to Birmingham
- **Endowment** $142,934
- **Coed**

Undergraduates 2,544 full-time, 2,012 part-time.
Academics *Calendar:* semesters. *Degree:* certificates and associate. *Special study options:* academic remediation for entering students, adult/continuing education programs, advanced placement credit, cooperative education, honors programs, off-campus study, part-time degree program, services for LD students, summer session for credit.
Student Life *Campus security:* 24-hour emergency response devices.
Athletics Member NJCAA.
Costs (2010–11) *One-time required fee:* $40. *Tuition:* state resident $2720 full-time, $90 per credit hour part-time; nonresident $5440 full-time, $180 per credit hour part-time. Full-time tuition and fees vary according to course load. Part-time tuition and fees vary according to course load. *Required fees:* $638 full-time, $19 per credit hour part-time, $15 per year part-time. *Room and board:* $1850; room only: $1185. Room and board charges vary according to housing facility and location.
Financial Aid Of all full-time matriculated undergraduates who enrolled in 2009, 88 Federal Work-Study jobs (averaging $1807).
Applying *Options:* electronic application, early admission, deferred entrance. *Required:* high school transcript.
Freshman Application Contact Bevill State Community College, PO Box 800, Sumiton, AL 35148. *Phone:* 205-932-3221 Ext. 5101. *Web site:* http://www.bscc.edu/.

Bishop State Community College
Mobile, Alabama

Freshman Application Contact Bishop State Community College, 351 North Broad Street, Mobile, AL 36603-5898. *Phone:* 251-405-7000. *Toll-free phone:* 800-523-7235. *Web site:* http://bishop.edu/.

Brown Mackie College–Birmingham
Birmingham, Alabama

- **Proprietary** 4-year
- **Coed**

Academics *Degrees:* diplomas, associate, and bachelor's.
Freshman Application Contact Brown Mackie College–Birmingham, 105 Vulcan Road, Suite 400, Birmingham, AL 35209. *Phone:* 205-909-1500. *Toll-free phone:* 888-299-4699. *Web site:* http://www.brownmackie.edu/birmingham.

See page 360 for the College Close-Up.

Calhoun Community College
Decatur, Alabama

Freshman Application Contact Admissions Office, Calhoun Community College, PO Box 2216, Decatur, AL 35609-2216. *Phone:* 256-306-2593. *Toll-free phone:* 800-626-3628. *Fax:* 256-306-2941. *E-mail:* admissions@calhoun.edu. *Web site:* http://www.calhoun.edu/.

Central Alabama Community College
Alexander City, Alabama

Freshman Application Contact Ms. Donna Whaley, Central Alabama Community College, 1675 Cherokee Road, Alexander City, AL 35011-0699.

Phone: 256-234-6346 Ext. 6232. *Toll-free phone:* 800-643-2657 Ext. 6232. *Web site:* http://www.cacc.edu/.

Chattahoochee Valley Community College
Phenix City, Alabama

Freshman Application Contact Chattahoochee Valley Community College, 2602 College Drive, Phenix City, AL 36869-7928. *Phone:* 334-291-4929. *Toll-free phone:* 800-842-2822. *Web site:* http://www.cv.edu/.

Community College of the Air Force
Maxwell Air Force Base, Alabama

Freshman Application Contact C.M. Sgt. Robert McAlexander, Director of Admissions/Registrar, Community College of the Air Force, 130 West Maxwell Boulevard, Building 836, Maxwell Air Force Base, Maxwell AFB, AL 36112-6613. *Phone:* 334-953-6436. *Fax:* 334-953-8211. *E-mail:* ronald.hall@maxwell.af.mil. *Web site:* http://www.au.af.mil/au/ccaf/.

Enterprise State Community College
Enterprise, Alabama

Director of Admissions Mr. Gary Deas, Associate Dean of Students/Registrar, Enterprise State Community College, PO Box 1300, Enterprise, AL 36331-1300. *Phone:* 334-347-2623 Ext. 2233. *E-mail:* gdeas@eocc.edu. *Web site:* http://www.escc.edu/.

Gadsden State Community College
Gadsden, Alabama

- **State-supported** 2-year, founded 1965, part of Alabama Community College System
- **Small-town** 275-acre campus with easy access to Birmingham
- **Endowment** $2.5 million
- **Coed,** 7,030 undergraduate students, 61% full-time, 61% women, 39% men

Undergraduates 4,261 full-time, 2,769 part-time. Students come from 25 states and territories; 53 other countries; 2% are from out of state; 21% Black or African American, non-Hispanic/Latino; 3% Hispanic/Latino; 1% Asian, non-Hispanic/Latino; 0.1% Native Hawaiian or other Pacific Islander, non-Hispanic/Latino; 0.4% American Indian or Alaska Native, non-Hispanic/Latino; 1% Two or more races, non-Hispanic/Latino; 0.8% Race/ethnicity unknown; 62% transferred in; 2% live on campus. *Retention:* 69% of full-time freshmen returned.
Freshmen *Admission:* 4,484 enrolled.
Faculty *Total:* 346, 43% full-time. *Student/faculty ratio:* 17:1.
Majors Accounting technology and bookkeeping; administrative assistant and secretarial science; child-care and support services management; civil engineering technology; clinical/medical laboratory technology; communication and journalism related; computer and information sciences; court reporting; criminal justice/police science; drafting and design technology; electrical, electronic and communications engineering technology; emergency medical technology (EMT paramedic); general studies; heating, ventilation, air conditioning and refrigeration engineering technology; industrial mechanics and maintenance technology; legal assistant/paralegal; liberal arts and sciences/liberal studies; manufacturing engineering technology; mechanical engineering/mechanical technology; medical radiologic technology; registered nursing/registered nurse; sales, distribution, and marketing operations; substance abuse/addiction counseling; telecommunications technology; tool and die technology.
Academics *Calendar:* semesters. *Degree:* certificates and associate. *Special study options:* academic remediation for entering students, adult/continuing education programs, advanced placement credit, cooperative education, distance learning, English as a second language, external degree program, honors programs, internships, part-time degree program, services for LD students, study abroad, summer session for credit. *ROTC:* Army (b).
Library Meadows Library with 109,568 titles, 234 serial subscriptions, 12,030 audiovisual materials, an OPAC, a Web page.
Student Life *Housing Options:* coed. Campus housing is university owned. *Activities and Organizations:* drama/theater group, choral group, National Society of Leadership and Success, Student Government Association, Circle K, Phi Beta Kappa, International Club. *Campus security:* 24-hour patrols. *Student services:* personal/psychological counseling.

Athletics Member NJCAA. *Intercollegiate sports:* baseball M(s), basketball M(s)/W(s), cross-country running W(s), softball W(s), tennis M(s), volleyball W(s).

Costs (2010–11) *Tuition:* state resident $3924 full-time, $109 per credit hour part-time; nonresident $7164 full-time, $199 per credit hour part-time. Full-time tuition and fees vary according to reciprocity agreements. Part-time tuition and fees vary according to reciprocity agreements. *Required fees:* $684 full-time, $19 per credit hour part-time. *Room and board:* $3200. *Waivers:* minority students, adult students, senior citizens, and employees or children of employees.

Applying *Options:* early admission, deferred entrance. *Required:* high school transcript. *Application deadlines:* rolling (freshmen), rolling (transfers).

Freshman Application Contact Mrs. Jennie Dobson, Admissions and Records, Gadsden State Community College, Admissions, Allen Hall, Gadsden, AL 35902-0227. *Phone:* 256-549-8210. *Toll-free phone:* 800-226-5563. *Fax:* 256-549-8205. *E-mail:* info@gadsdenstate.edu. *Web site:* http://www.gadsdenstate.edu/.

George Corley Wallace State Community College

Selma, Alabama

Director of Admissions Ms. Sunette Newman, Registrar, George Corley Wallace State Community College, PO Box 2530, Selma, AL 36702. *Phone:* 334-876-9305. *Web site:* http://www.wccs.edu/.

George C. Wallace Community College

Dothan, Alabama

- **State-supported** 2-year, founded 1949, part of The Alabama Community College System
- **Rural** 258-acre campus
- **Coed**

Undergraduates 2,633 full-time, 2,022 part-time. 5% transferred in.

Academics *Calendar:* semesters. *Degree:* certificates, diplomas, and associate. *Special study options:* academic remediation for entering students, adult/continuing education programs, advanced placement credit, cooperative education, distance learning, English as a second language, independent study, off-campus study, part-time degree program.

Student Life *Campus security:* 24-hour patrols.

Athletics Member NJCAA.

Standardized Tests *Recommended:* SAT or ACT (for admission).

Costs (2010–11) *Tuition:* state resident $4050 full-time, $90 per credit hour part-time; nonresident $8100 full-time, $180 per credit hour part-time. Full-time tuition and fees vary according to reciprocity agreements. Part-time tuition and fees vary according to reciprocity agreements. *Required fees:* $855 full-time, $19 per credit hour part-time.

Financial Aid Of all full-time matriculated undergraduates who enrolled in 2009, 82 Federal Work-Study jobs (averaging $1975).

Applying *Options:* early admission. *Required:* high school transcript.

Freshman Application Contact Mr. Keith Saulsberry, Director, Enrollment Services/Registrar, George C. Wallace Community College, 1141 Wallace Drive, Dothan, AL 36303. *Phone:* 334-983-3521 Ext. 2470. *Toll-free phone:* 800-543-2426. *Fax:* 334-983-3600. *E-mail:* ksaulsberry@wallace.edu. *Web site:* http://www.wallace.edu/.

H. Councill Trenholm State Technical College

Montgomery, Alabama

- **State-supported** 2-year, founded 1962, part of Alabama Department of Postsecondary Education
- **Urban** 81-acre campus
- **Coed**, 1,758 undergraduate students

Undergraduates Students come from 2 states and territories; 1% are from out of state; 61% Black or African American, non-Hispanic/Latino; 1% Asian, non-Hispanic/Latino; 0.2% Native Hawaiian or other Pacific Islander, non-Hispanic/Latino; 0.5% American Indian or Alaska Native, non-Hispanic/Latino; 1% Race/ethnicity unknown. *Retention:* 55% of full-time freshmen returned.

Freshmen *Admission:* 1,048 applied, 572 admitted.

Faculty *Total:* 150, 51% full-time, 3% with terminal degrees. *Student/faculty ratio:* 10:1.

Majors Accounting technology and bookkeeping; administrative assistant and secretarial science; autobody/collision and repair technology; automotive engineering technology; child-care and support services management; computer and information sciences; culinary arts; dental assisting; diagnostic medical sonography and ultrasound technology; drafting and design technology; electrician; emergency medical technology (EMT paramedic); graphic and printing equipment operation/production; heating, ventilation, air conditioning and refrigeration engineering technology; industrial electronics technology; industrial mechanics and maintenance technology; machine tool technology; medical/clinical assistant; occupational therapist assistant; radiologic technology/science.

Academics *Calendar:* semesters. *Degree:* certificates, diplomas, and associate. *Special study options:* academic remediation for entering students, adult/continuing education programs, advanced placement credit, cooperative education, distance learning, external degree program, independent study, internships, part-time degree program, services for LD students, summer session for credit.

Library Trenholm State Learning Resources plus 1 other with 59,472 titles, 9,128 serial subscriptions, 1,054 audiovisual materials, an OPAC, a Web page.

Student Life *Housing:* college housing not available. *Activities and Organizations:* student-run newspaper, Student Government Association, College Ambassadors, Photography Club, Skills USA - VICA, Student Leadership Academy. *Campus security:* 24-hour emergency response devices and patrols, late-night transport/escort service. *Student services:* personal/psychological counseling.

Standardized Tests *Required for some:* ACT (for admission).

Costs (2010–11) *Tuition:* state resident $2700 full-time, $90 per credit hour part-time; nonresident $5400 full-time, $180 per credit hour part-time. *Required fees:* $570 full-time, $19 per credit hour part-time. *Waivers:* senior citizens and employees or children of employees.

Applying *Options:* early admission. *Required:* high school transcript. *Application deadlines:* rolling (freshmen), rolling (out-of-state freshmen), rolling (transfers).

Freshman Application Contact Mrs. Tennie McBryde, Registrar, H. Councill Trenholm State Technical College, Montgomery, AL 36108. *Phone:* 334-420-4306. *Fax:* 334-420-4201. *E-mail:* tmcbryde@trenholmstate.edu. *Web site:* http://www.trenholmstate.edu/.

ITT Technical Institute

Bessemer, Alabama

- **Proprietary** primarily 2-year, founded 1994, part of ITT Educational Services, Inc.
- **Suburban** campus
- **Coed**

Majors Business administration and management; CAD/CADD drafting/design technology; computer and information systems security; computer engineering technology; computer software and media applications related; computer software engineering; computer software technology; construction management; criminal justice/law enforcement administration; design and visual communications; electrical, electronic and communications engineering technology; game and interactive media design; legal assistant/paralegal; project management; system, networking, and LAN/WAN management; web page, digital/multimedia and information resources design.

Academics *Calendar:* quarters. *Degrees:* associate and bachelor's.

Student Life *Housing:* college housing not available. *Campus security:* 24-hour emergency response devices.

Freshman Application Contact Director of Recruitment, ITT Technical Institute, 6270 Park South Drive, Bessemer, AL 35022. *Phone:* 205-497-5700. *Toll-free phone:* 800-488-7033. *Web site:* http://www.itt-tech.edu/.

ITT Technical Institute

Madison, Alabama

- **Proprietary** primarily 2-year, part of ITT Educational Services, Inc.
- **Coed**

Majors CAD/CADD drafting/design technology; computer and information systems security; computer engineering technology; computer software engineering; computer software technology; construction management; criminal justice/law enforcement administration; design and visual communications; electrical, electronic and communications engineering technology; legal assistant/paralegal; project management; system, networking, and LAN/WAN management.

Academics *Degrees:* associate and bachelor's.

Student Life *Housing:* college housing not available.

Freshman Application Contact Director of Recruitment, ITT Technical Institute, 9238 Madison Boulevard, Suite 500, Madison, AL 35758. *Phone:* 256-542-2900. *Toll-free phone:* 877-210-4900. *Web site:* http://www.itt-tech.edu/.

ITT Technical Institute
Mobile, Alabama

- **Proprietary** primarily 2-year, part of ITT Educational Services, Inc.
- **Coed**

Majors CAD/CADD drafting/design technology; computer and information systems security; computer engineering technology; computer software engineering; computer software technology; construction management; criminal justice/law enforcement administration; design and visual communications; electrical, electronic and communications engineering technology; legal assistant/paralegal; project management; system, networking, and LAN/WAN management.

Academics *Degrees:* associate and bachelor's.

Student Life *Housing:* college housing not available.

Freshman Application Contact Director of Recruitment, ITT Technical Institute, Office Mall South, 3100 Cottage Hill Road, Building 3, Mobile, AL 36606. *Phone:* 251-472-4760. *Toll-free phone:* 877-327-1013. *Web site:* http://www.itt-tech.edu/.

James H. Faulkner State Community College
Bay Minette, Alabama

Freshman Application Contact Ms. Carmelita Mikkelsen, Director of Admissions and High School Relations, James H. Faulkner State Community College, 1900 Highway 31 South, Bay Minette, AL 36507. *Phone:* 251-580-2213. *Toll-free phone:* 800-231-3752 Ext. 2111. *Fax:* 251-580-2285. *E-mail:* cmikkelsen@faulknerstate.edu. *Web site:* http://www.faulknerstate.edu/.

Jefferson Davis Community College
Brewton, Alabama

Director of Admissions Ms. Robin Sessions, Registrar, Jefferson Davis Community College, PO Box 958, Brewton, AL 36427-0958. *Phone:* 251-867-4832. *Web site:* http://www.jdcc.edu/.

Jefferson State Community College
Birmingham, Alabama

- **State-supported** 2-year, founded 1965, part of Alabama Community College System
- **Suburban** 234-acre campus
- **Coed**, 9,644 undergraduate students, 40% full-time, 60% women, 40% men

Undergraduates 3,857 full-time, 5,787 part-time. Students come from 31 states and territories; 71 other countries; 2% are from out of state; 23% Black or African American, non-Hispanic/Latino; 2% Hispanic/Latino; 1% Asian, non-Hispanic/Latino; 0.1% Native Hawaiian or other Pacific Islander, non-Hispanic/Latino; 0.2% American Indian or Alaska Native, non-Hispanic/Latino; 2% Two or more races, non-Hispanic/Latino; 0.1% Race/ethnicity unknown; 0.9% international; 8% transferred in.

Freshmen *Admission:* 1,893 enrolled.

Faculty *Total:* 439, 31% full-time, 13% with terminal degrees. *Student/faculty ratio:* 24:1.

Majors Accounting technology and bookkeeping; administrative assistant and secretarial science; agricultural business and management; business/commerce; child-care and support services management; clinical/medical laboratory technology; computer and information sciences; construction engineering technology; criminal justice/police science; emergency medical technology (EMT paramedic); engineering technology; fire services administration; funeral service and mortuary science; general studies; hospitality administration; liberal arts and sciences/liberal studies; licensed practical/vocational nurse training; physical therapy technology; radio and television broadcasting technology; radiologic technology/science; registered nursing/registered nurse; veterinary/animal health technology.

Academics *Calendar:* semesters. *Degree:* certificates and associate. *Special study options:* academic remediation for entering students, adult/continuing education programs, advanced placement credit, distance learning, English as a second language, honors programs, independent study, internships, part-time degree program, services for LD students, summer session for credit. *ROTC:* Army (c), Air Force (c).

Library Jefferson State Libraries plus 3 others with 165,000 titles, 330 serial subscriptions, 3,349 audiovisual materials, an OPAC, a Web page.

Student Life *Housing:* college housing not available. *Activities and Organizations:* drama/theater group, student-run newspaper, radio station, choral group, Student Government Association, Phi Theta Kappa, Senior Adults, Jefferson State Ambassadors, Students in Free Enterprise (SIFE). *Campus security:* 24-hour patrols.

Athletics Member NJCAA. *Intercollegiate sports:* baseball M(s), softball W(s). *Intramural sports:* football M/W.

Costs (2011–12) *Tuition:* state resident $3690 full-time, $123 per semester hour part-time; nonresident $6450 full-time, $215 per semester hour part-time. Full-time tuition and fees vary according to course load. Part-time tuition and fees vary according to course load. *Waivers:* senior citizens and employees or children of employees.

Financial Aid Of all full-time matriculated undergraduates who enrolled in 2009, 189 Federal Work-Study jobs (averaging $1926).

Applying *Options:* electronic application, early admission, early action, deferred entrance. *Required for some:* high school transcript. *Application deadline:* rolling (freshmen). *Notification:* continuous (freshmen), continuous (transfers).

Freshman Application Contact Mrs. Lillian Owens, Director of Admissions and Retention, Jefferson State Community College, 2601 Carson Road, Birmingham, AL 35215-3098. *Phone:* 205-853-1200 Ext. 7990. *Toll-free phone:* 800-239-5900. *Fax:* 205-856-6070. *E-mail:* lowens@jeffstateonline.com. *Web site:* http://www.jeffstateonline.com/.

J. F. Drake State Technical College
Huntsville, Alabama

- **State-supported** 2-year, founded 1961, part of Alabama Department of Postsecondary Education
- **Urban** 6-acre campus
- **Coed**

Undergraduates 754 full-time, 504 part-time. Students come from 1 other state; 4% are from out of state; 23% transferred in.

Faculty *Student/faculty ratio:* 17:1.

Academics *Calendar:* semesters. *Degree:* certificates, diplomas, and associate. *Special study options:* academic remediation for entering students, cooperative education, internships, part-time degree program, services for LD students.

Student Life *Campus security:* 24-hour patrols.

Costs (2010–11) *Tuition:* state resident $2160 full-time, $90 per credit hour part-time; nonresident $4320 full-time, $180 per credit hour part-time. *Required fees:* $456 full-time, $19 per credit hour part-time.

Applying *Options:* electronic application, deferred entrance. *Required:* high school transcript.

Freshman Application Contact Mrs. Monica Sudeall, Registrar, J. F. Drake State Technical College, Huntsville, AL 35811. *Phone:* 256-539-8161. *Toll-free phone:* 888-413-7253. *Fax:* 256-551-3142. *E-mail:* sudeall@drakestate.edu. *Web site:* http://www.drakestate.edu/.

Lawson State Community College
Birmingham, Alabama

- **State-supported** 2-year, founded 1949, part of Alabama Community College System
- **Urban** 30-acre campus
- **Coed**, 4,863 undergraduate students

Undergraduates Students come from 11 states and territories; 1% are from out of state; 79% Black or African American, non-Hispanic/Latino; 1% Hispanic/Latino; 0.4% Asian, non-Hispanic/Latino; 0.1% Native Hawaiian or other Pacific Islander, non-Hispanic/Latino; 0.2% American Indian or Alaska Native, non-Hispanic/Latino; 0.4% Two or more races, non-Hispanic/Latino; 5% Race/ethnicity unknown; 0.1% international; 6% transferred in; 1% live on campus. *Retention:* 55% of full-time freshmen returned.

Freshmen *Admission:* 1,637 applied, 1,354 admitted, 1,290 enrolled.

Faculty *Total:* 218, 43% full-time. *Student/faculty ratio:* 17:1.

Majors Accounting technology and bookkeeping; administrative assistant and secretarial science; automotive engineering technology; building/construction finishing, management, and inspection related; business administration and management; child-care and support services management; computer and information sciences; criminal justice/police science; drafting and design technology; general studies; industrial electronics technology; liberal arts and sciences/liberal studies; registered nursing/registered nurse; social work.

Academics *Calendar:* semesters. *Degree:* certificates and associate. *Special study options:* academic remediation for entering students, adult/continuing education programs, cooperative education, distance learning, freshman honors college, honors programs, internships, part-time degree program, services for LD students, summer session for credit.

Library Lawson State Library with 50,859 titles, 253 serial subscriptions, an OPAC.

Student Life *Housing Options:* coed. Campus housing is university owned. *Activities and Organizations:* choral group, Student Government Association, Phi Theta Kappa, Kappa Beta Delta Honor Society, Phi Beta Lambda, Social Work Club. *Campus security:* 24-hour emergency response devices and patrols, controlled dormitory access. *Student services:* personal/psychological counseling.

Athletics Member NJCAA. *Intercollegiate sports:* baseball M, basketball M/W, volleyball W. *Intramural sports:* weight lifting M.

Costs (2011–12) *Tuition:* state resident $2790 full-time, $93 per credit hour part-time; nonresident $5580 full-time, $186 per credit hour part-time. *Required fees:* $850 full-time, $28 per credit hour part-time. *Room and board:* $4000; room only: $3000. *Payment plan:* installment. *Waivers:* senior citizens and employees or children of employees.

Financial Aid Of all full-time matriculated undergraduates who enrolled in 2009, 91 Federal Work-Study jobs (averaging $3000).

Applying *Options:* electronic application, early admission, deferred entrance. *Required:* high school transcript. *Application deadlines:* rolling (freshmen), rolling (transfers). *Notification:* continuous (freshmen), continuous (transfers).

Freshman Application Contact Mr. Jeff Shelley, Director of Admissions and Records, Lawson State Community College, 3060 Wilson Road, SW, Birmingham, AL 35221-1798. *Phone:* 205-929-6361. *Fax:* 205-923-7106. *E-mail:* jshelley@lawsonstate.edu. *Web site:* http://www.lawsonstate.edu/.

Lurleen B. Wallace Community College

Andalusia, Alabama

- **State-supported** 2-year, founded 1969, part of Alabama College System
- **Small-town** 200-acre campus
- **Endowment** $913,461
- **Coed,** 1,928 undergraduate students, 60% full-time, 66% women, 34% men

Undergraduates 1,164 full-time, 764 part-time. Students come from 7 states and territories; 4 other countries; 4% are from out of state; 23% Black or African American, non-Hispanic/Latino; 1% Hispanic/Latino; 0.3% Asian, non-Hispanic/Latino; 0.3% American Indian or Alaska Native, non-Hispanic/Latino; 0.5% Two or more races, non-Hispanic/Latino; 0.5% Race/ethnicity unknown; 0.1% international; 8% transferred in. *Retention:* 51% of full-time freshmen returned.

Freshmen *Admission:* 620 applied, 610 admitted, 493 enrolled.

Faculty *Total:* 110, 46% full-time, 5% with terminal degrees. *Student/faculty ratio:* 16:1.

Majors Accounting technology and bookkeeping; administrative assistant and secretarial science; child-care and support services management; computer and information sciences; drafting and design technology; electrician; emergency medical technology (EMT paramedic); forest technology; general studies; industrial electronics technology; liberal arts and sciences/liberal studies; registered nursing/registered nurse.

Academics *Calendar:* semesters. *Degree:* certificates, diplomas, and associate. *Special study options:* academic remediation for entering students, advanced placement credit, cooperative education, distance learning, double majors, independent study, part-time degree program, services for LD students, summer session for credit.

Library Lurleen B. Wallace Library plus 2 others with 39,862 titles, 22,432 serial subscriptions, 2,343 audiovisual materials, an OPAC, a Web page.

Student Life *Housing:* college housing not available. *Activities and Organizations:* drama/theater group, choral group, Christian Student Ministries, Civitan, Mu Alpha Theta, Phi Theta Kappa, Student Government Association. *Student services:* personal/psychological counseling.

Athletics Member NJCAA. *Intercollegiate sports:* baseball M(s), basketball M(s)/W(s), softball W(s).

Standardized Tests *Required for some:* ACT (for admission).

Costs (2011–12) *Tuition:* state resident $2760 full-time, $92 per credit hour part-time; nonresident $5520 full-time, $184 per credit hour part-time. Full-time tuition and fees vary according to course load. Part-time tuition and fees vary according to course load. *Required fees:* $570 full-time, $19 per credit hour part-time. *Waivers:* senior citizens and employees or children of employees.

Financial Aid Of all full-time matriculated undergraduates who enrolled in 2009, 70 Federal Work-Study jobs.

Applying *Required:* high school transcript. *Application deadlines:* rolling (freshmen), rolling (transfers). *Notification:* continuous until 7/15 (freshmen), continuous until 7/15 (transfers).

Freshman Application Contact Lurleen B. Wallace Community College, PO Box 1418, Andalusia, AL 36420-1418. *Phone:* 334-881-2273. *Web site:* http://www.lbwcc.edu/.

Marion Military Institute

Marion, Alabama

Director of Admissions Director of Admissions, Marion Military Institute, 1101 Washington Street, Marion, AL 36756. *Phone:* 800-664-1842 Ext. 306. *Toll-free phone:* 800-664-1842 Ext. 307. *Web site:* http://www.marionmilitary.edu/.

Northeast Alabama Community College

Rainsville, Alabama

Freshman Application Contact Northeast Alabama Community College, PO Box 159, Rainsville, AL 35986-0159. *Phone:* 256-228-6001 Ext. 325. *Web site:* http://www.nacc.edu/.

Northwest-Shoals Community College

Muscle Shoals, Alabama

- **State-supported** 2-year, founded 1963, part of Alabama Department of Postsecondary Education
- **Small-town** 210-acre campus
- **Coed,** 3,971 undergraduate students, 63% full-time, 60% women, 40% men

Undergraduates 2,497 full-time, 1,474 part-time. Students come from 6 states and territories; 3 other countries; 1% are from out of state; 12% Black or African American, non-Hispanic/Latino; 2% Hispanic/Latino; 0.2% Asian, non-Hispanic/Latino; 0.8% American Indian or Alaska Native, non-Hispanic/Latino; 0.4% Two or more races, non-Hispanic/Latino; 0.2% Race/ethnicity unknown; 0.3% international; 8% transferred in; 3% live on campus.

Freshmen *Admission:* 2,702 applied, 2,702 admitted, 981 enrolled.

Faculty *Total:* 240, 37% full-time, 4% with terminal degrees. *Student/faculty ratio:* 21:1.

Majors Administrative assistant and secretarial science; child-care and support services management; child development; computer and information sciences; criminal justice/police science; drafting and design technology; general studies; industrial electronics technology; liberal arts and sciences/liberal studies; multi/interdisciplinary studies related; registered nursing/registered nurse.

Academics *Calendar:* semesters. *Degree:* certificates, diplomas, and associate. *Special study options:* academic remediation for entering students, accelerated degree program, adult/continuing education programs, advanced placement credit, cooperative education, distance learning, honors programs, independent study, part-time degree program, services for LD students, summer session for credit.

Library Larry W. McCoy Learning Resource Center and James Glasgow Library with 106,138 titles, 215 serial subscriptions, 1,798 audiovisual materials, an OPAC.

Student Life *Housing Options:* coed. Campus housing is university owned. *Activities and Organizations:* choral group, Student Government Association, Science Club, Phi Theta Kappa, Baptist Campus Ministry, Northwest-Shoals Singers. *Campus security:* 24-hour emergency response devices and patrols. *Student services:* personal/psychological counseling.

Athletics Member NJCAA. *Intercollegiate sports:* baseball M(s), basketball M(s)/W(s), cheerleading W(s), softball W(s), volleyball W(s). *Intramural sports:* basketball M/W, softball M/W, table tennis M/W, tennis M/W, volleyball M/W.

Standardized Tests *Required:* COMPASS Placement Test for English and Math (for admission).

Costs (2011–12) *Tuition:* state resident $2760 full-time, $92 per credit hour part-time; nonresident $5520 full-time, $184 per credit hour part-time. Full-time tuition and fees vary according to program. Part-time tuition and fees vary according to program. *Required fees:* $765 full-time, $25 per credit hour part-time. *Room and board:* room only: $1800. *Waivers:* minority students, senior citizens, and employees or children of employees.

Financial Aid Of all full-time matriculated undergraduates who enrolled in 2009, 40 Federal Work-Study jobs (averaging $2715). *Financial aid deadline:* 6/1.

Applying *Options:* electronic application. *Required:* high school transcript. *Application deadlines:* rolling (freshmen), rolling (transfers). *Notification:* continuous (transfers).

Freshman Application Contact Dr. Karen Berryhill, Vice President of Student Development Services, Northwest-Shoals Community College, PO Box 2545, Muscle Shoals, AL 35662. *Phone:* 256-331-5261. *Toll-free phone:* 800-645-8967. *Fax:* 256-331-5366. *E-mail:* berryk@nwscc.edu. *Web site:* http://www.nwscc.edu/.

Prince Institute of Professional Studies

Montgomery, Alabama

- **Proprietary** 2-year, founded 1976
- **Suburban** campus
- **Coed, primarily women,** 63 undergraduate students

Undergraduates *Retention:* 100% of full-time freshmen returned.
Freshmen *Admission:* 23 applied, 23 admitted.
Faculty *Total:* 16, 25% full-time, 19% with terminal degrees. *Student/faculty ratio:* 13:1.
Majors Court reporting; legal support services related.
Academics *Calendar:* quarters. *Degree:* certificates and associate.
Library Library plus 1 other with an OPAC, a Web page.
Student Life *Housing:* college housing not available. *Student services:* personal/psychological counseling.
Costs (2011–12) *Tuition:* $2800 full-time. *Required fees:* $295 full-time. *Payment plan:* installment.
Financial Aid Of all full-time matriculated undergraduates who enrolled in 2008, 88 applied for aid, 88 were judged to have need. *Average percent of need met:* 72%. *Average financial aid package:* $3101.
Applying *Options:* electronic application. *Application fee:* $125. *Required:* high school transcript, interview. *Application deadline:* 10/1 (freshmen).
Freshman Application Contact Kellie Brescia, Director of Admissions, Prince Institute of Professional Studies, 7735 Atlanta Highway, Montgomery, AL 35117. *Phone:* 334-271-1670. *Toll-free phone:* 877-853-5569. *Fax:* 334-271-1671. *E-mail:* admissions@princeinstitute.edu. *Web site:* http://www.princeinstitute.edu/.

Reid State Technical College

Evergreen, Alabama

- **State-supported** 2-year, founded 1966, part of Alabama Community College System
- **Rural** 26-acre campus
- **Coed,** 744 undergraduate students, 78% full-time, 61% women, 39% men

Undergraduates 583 full-time, 161 part-time. Students come from 2 states and territories; 1% are from out of state.
Freshmen *Admission:* 265 applied, 265 admitted, 122 enrolled.
Faculty *Total:* 31, 77% full-time, 10% with terminal degrees. *Student/faculty ratio:* 12:1.
Majors Administrative assistant and secretarial science; electrical, electronic and communications engineering technology.
Academics *Calendar:* semesters. *Degree:* certificates, diplomas, and associate. *Special study options:* academic remediation for entering students, adult/continuing education programs, double majors, independent study, internships, part-time degree program, services for LD students, summer session for credit.
Library Edith A. Gray Library with 3,090 titles, 136 serial subscriptions, 375 audiovisual materials, a Web page.
Student Life *Housing:* college housing not available. *Activities and Organizations:* student-run newspaper, Student Government Association, Skills USA. *Campus security:* 24-hour emergency response devices, day and evening security guard. *Student services:* personal/psychological counseling.
Costs (2011–12) *Tuition:* state resident $2700 full-time; nonresident $5400 full-time. *Required fees:* $660 full-time.
Financial Aid Of all full-time matriculated undergraduates who enrolled in 2009, 35 Federal Work-Study jobs (averaging $1500).
Applying *Options:* early admission. *Required:* high school transcript. *Application deadlines:* rolling (freshmen), rolling (transfers).
Freshman Application Contact Dr. Alesia Stuart, Public Relations/Marketing/Associate Dean of Workforce Development, Reid State Technical College, Evergreen, AL 36401-0588. *Phone:* 251-578-1313 Ext. 108. *Web site:* http://www.rstc.edu/.

Remington College–Mobile Campus

Mobile, Alabama

Freshman Application Contact Remington College–Mobile Campus, 828 Downtowner Loop West, Mobile, AL 36609-5404. *Phone:* 251-343-8200. *Toll-free phone:* 800-866-0850. *Web site:* http://www.remingtoncollege.edu/.

Shelton State Community College

Tuscaloosa, Alabama

Freshman Application Contact Ms. Loretta Jones, Assistant to the Dean of Students, Shelton State Community College, 9500 Old Greensboro Road, Tuscaloosa, AL 35405. *Phone:* 205-391-2236. *Fax:* 205-391-3910. *Web site:* http://www.sheltonstate.edu/.

Snead State Community College

Boaz, Alabama

Freshman Application Contact Dr. Greg Chapman, Director of Instruction, Snead State Community College, PO Box 734, Boaz, AL 35957-0734. *Phone:* 256-840-4111. *Fax:* 256-593-7180. *E-mail:* gchapman@snead.edu. *Web site:* http://www.snead.edu/.

Southern Union State Community College

Wadley, Alabama

- **State-supported** 2-year, founded 1922, part of Alabama College System
- **Rural** campus
- **Coed**

Undergraduates 12% are from out of state. *Retention:* 58% of full-time freshmen returned.
Faculty *Student/faculty ratio:* 25:1.
Academics *Calendar:* semesters. *Degree:* certificates, diplomas, and associate. *Special study options:* academic remediation for entering students, adult/continuing education programs, advanced placement credit, distance learning, part-time degree program, summer session for credit. *ROTC:* Air Force (c).
Student Life *Campus security:* 24-hour patrols, controlled dormitory access.
Athletics Member NJCAA.
Costs (2010–11) *Tuition:* state resident $3270 full-time, $109 per credit hour part-time; nonresident $5970 full-time, $199 per credit hour part-time. Full-time tuition and fees vary according to course load. Part-time tuition and fees vary according to course load. *Room and board:* $1600.
Financial Aid Of all full-time matriculated undergraduates who enrolled in 2009, 120 Federal Work-Study jobs (averaging $1000). 30 state and other part-time jobs (averaging $800).
Applying *Options:* early admission, deferred entrance. *Required:* high school transcript.
Freshman Application Contact Admissions Office, Southern Union State Community College, PO Box 1000, Roberts Street, Wadley, AL 36276. *Phone:* 256-395-5157. *E-mail:* info@suscc.edu. *Web site:* http://www.suscc.edu/.

Wallace State Community College

Hanceville, Alabama

Director of Admissions Ms. Linda Sperling, Director of Admissions, Wallace State Community College, PO Box 2000, 801 Main Street, Hanceville, AL 35077-2000. *Phone:* 256-352-8278. *Toll-free phone:* 866-350-9722. *Web site:* http://www.wallacestate.edu/.

ALASKA

Charter College

Anchorage, Alaska

Director of Admissions Ms. Lily Sirianni, Vice President, Charter College, 2221 East Northern Lights Boulevard, Suite 120, Anchorage, AK 99508. *Phone:* 907-277-1000. *Toll-free phone:* 800-279-1008. *Web site:* http://www.chartercollege.edu/.

Ilisagvik College

Barrow, Alaska

- **State-supported** 2-year, founded 1995
- **Rural** campus
- **Coed,** 288 undergraduate students, 14% full-time, 67% women, 33% men

Undergraduates 39 full-time, 249 part-time. Students come from 3 states and territories; 3 other countries.
Freshmen *Admission:* 28 enrolled.
Faculty *Student/faculty ratio:* 6:1.
Majors African American/Black studies; American Indian/Native American studies; business administration and management; health services/allied health/health sciences; information technology; liberal arts and sciences/liberal studies; office management.

Academics *Calendar:* semesters. *Degree:* certificates, diplomas, and associate. *Special study options:* academic remediation for entering students, cooperative education, distance learning, double majors, English as a second language, independent study, internships, off-campus study, part-time degree program, services for LD students, summer session for credit.
Library Tuzzy Consortium Library with an OPAC, a Web page.
Student Life *Housing Options:* men-only, women-only. Campus housing is university owned. *Campus security:* 24-hour emergency response devices and patrols, controlled dormitory access.
Athletics *Intramural sports:* basketball M/W.
Standardized Tests *Required:* ACT ASSET (for admission).
Costs (2011–12) *Tuition:* state resident $2400 full-time, $100 per credit hour part-time; nonresident $3600 full-time, $150 per credit hour part-time. *Required fees:* $260 full-time. *Room and board:* $10,650; room only: $4050. *Payment plan:* deferred payment. *Waivers:* senior citizens and employees or children of employees.
Applying *Required:* high school transcript, minimum 2.0 GPA. *Required for some:* copy of Alaska Native Shareholder/Native American Tribal Affiliation card if native.
Freshman Application Contact Janelle Everett, Recruiter, Ilisagvik College, UIC/Narl, Barrow, AK 99723. *Phone:* 907-852-1799. *Toll-free phone:* 800-478-7337. *E-mail:* janelle.everett@ilisagvik.edu. *Web site:* http://www.ilisagvik.edu/.

University of Alaska Anchorage, Kenai Peninsula College

Soldotna, Alaska

- **State-supported** 2-year, founded 1964, part of University of Alaska System
- **Rural** 360-acre campus
- **Coed,** 1,934 undergraduate students

Majors Business administration and management; digital communication and media/multimedia; early childhood education; elementary education; emergency medical technology (EMT paramedic); human services; liberal arts and sciences/liberal studies; occupational safety and health technology; psychology.
Academics *Calendar:* semesters. *Degree:* certificates and associate. *Special study options:* academic remediation for entering students, adult/continuing education programs, advanced placement credit, cooperative education, distance learning, English as a second language, part-time degree program, services for LD students.
Library Kenai Peninsula College Library.
Student Life *Housing:* college housing not available. *Campus security:* 24-hour emergency response devices. *Student services:* health clinic.
Standardized Tests *Required:* SAT or ACT (for admission), ACT, SAT or ACCUPLACER scores (for admission).
Costs (2010–11) *Tuition:* state resident $4410 full-time, $147 per credit hour part-time; nonresident $4410 full-time, $147 per credit hour part-time. *Required fees:* $384 full-time, $14 per credit hour part-time. *Payment plan:* installment. *Waivers:* senior citizens and employees or children of employees.
Financial Aid Of all full-time matriculated undergraduates who enrolled in 2009, 50 Federal Work-Study jobs (averaging $3000). 50 state and other part-time jobs (averaging $3000).
Applying *Options:* electronic application. *Application fee:* $40. *Required:* high school transcript. *Application deadlines:* rolling (freshmen), rolling (transfers).
Freshman Application Contact Ms. Shelly Love Blatchford, Admission and Registration Coordinator, University of Alaska Anchorage, Kenai Peninsula College, 156 College Road, Soldotna, AK 99669-9798. *Phone:* 907-262-0311. *Toll-free phone:* 877-262-0330. *Web site:* http://www.kpc.alaska.edu/.

University of Alaska Anchorage, Kodiak College

Kodiak, Alaska

- **State-supported** 2-year, founded 1968, part of University of Alaska System
- **Rural** 68-acre campus
- **Coed,** 540 undergraduate students

Faculty *Total:* 40, 25% full-time. *Student/faculty ratio:* 19:1.
Majors Administrative assistant and secretarial science; business administration and management; liberal arts and sciences/liberal studies.
Academics *Calendar:* semesters. *Degree:* certificates and associate. *Special study options:* academic remediation for entering students, adult/continuing education programs, advanced placement credit, distance learning, double majors, part-time degree program.

Library Carolyn Floyd Library with 21,000 titles, 39 serial subscriptions, 2,400 audiovisual materials, an OPAC, a Web page.
Student Life *Housing:* college housing not available. *Activities and Organizations:* student-run newspaper, PHI THETA KAPPA, Student Government.
Standardized Tests *Required:* ACCUPLACER (for admission).
Costs (2010–11) *Tuition:* state resident $4410 full-time, $147 per credit part-time; nonresident $15,000 full-time, $500 per credit part-time. *Payment plan:* installment. *Waivers:* senior citizens and employees or children of employees.
Applying *Application fee:* $40. *Required for some:* high school transcript. *Application deadlines:* rolling (freshmen), rolling (out-of-state freshmen), rolling (transfers).
Freshman Application Contact University of Alaska Anchorage, Kodiak College, 117 Benny Benson Drive, Kodiak, AK 99615-6643. *Phone:* 907-486-1235. *Toll-free phone:* 800-486-7660. *Web site:* http://www.koc.alaska.edu/.

University of Alaska Anchorage, Matanuska-Susitna College

Palmer, Alaska

- **State-supported** 2-year, founded 1958, part of University of Alaska System
- **Small-town** 950-acre campus with easy access to Anchorage
- **Coed**

Undergraduates 452 full-time, 1,330 part-time. *Retention:* 55% of full-time freshmen returned.
Faculty *Student/faculty ratio:* 16:1.
Academics *Calendar:* semesters. *Degree:* certificates and associate. *Special study options:* academic remediation for entering students, adult/continuing education programs, advanced placement credit, cooperative education, distance learning, double majors, independent study, internships, off-campus study, part-time degree program, summer session for credit.
Student Life *Campus security:* 24-hour patrols.
Costs (2010–11) *Tuition:* state resident $4410 full-time, $147 per semester hour part-time; nonresident $15,000 full-time, $500 per semester hour part-time. Full-time tuition and fees vary according to course level and course load. Part-time tuition and fees vary according to course level and course load. *Required fees:* $240 full-time, $8 per semester hour part-time, $10 per term part-time.
Financial Aid Of all full-time matriculated undergraduates who enrolled in 2009, 8 Federal Work-Study jobs (averaging $3000).
Applying *Options:* electronic application. *Application fee:* $40. *Required:* high school transcript.
Freshman Application Contact Ms. Sandra Gravley, Student Services Director, University of Alaska Anchorage, Matanuska-Susitna College, PO Box 2889, Palmer, AK 99645-2889. *Phone:* 907-745-9712. *Fax:* 907-745-9747. *E-mail:* info@matsu.alaska.edu. *Web site:* http://www.matsu.alaska.edu/.

University of Alaska, Prince William Sound Community College

Valdez, Alaska

Freshman Application Contact Mr. Nathan J. Platt, Director of Student Services, University of Alaska, Prince William Sound Community College, PO Box 97, Valdez, AK 99686-0097. *Phone:* 907-834-1631. *Toll-free phone:* 800-478-8800 Ext. 1600. *E-mail:* studentservices@pwscc.edu. *Web site:* http://www.pwscc.edu/.

University of Alaska Southeast, Ketchikan Campus

Ketchikan, Alaska

Freshman Application Contact Admissions Office, University of Alaska Southeast, Ketchikan Campus, 2600 7th Avenue, Ketchikan, AK 99901-5798. *Phone:* 907-225-6177. *Toll-free phone:* 888-550-6177. *Fax:* 907-225-3895. *E-mail:* ketch.info@uas.alaska.edu. *Web site:* http://www.ketch.alaska.edu/.

University of Alaska Southeast, Sitka Campus

Sitka, Alaska

Freshman Application Contact Cynthia Rogers, Coordinator of Admissions, University of Alaska Southeast, Sitka Campus, 1332 Seward Avenue, Sitka, AK 99835-9418. *Phone:* 907-747-7705. *Toll-free phone:* 800-478-6653. *Fax:* 907-747-7793. *E-mail:* cynthia.rogers@uas.alaska.edu. *Web site:* http://www.uas.alaska.edu/.

AMERICAN SAMOA

American Samoa Community College

Pago Pago, American Samoa

Director of Admissions Sifagatogo Tuitasi, Admissions, American Samoa Community College, PO Box 2609, Pago Pago, AS 96799-2609. *Phone:* 684-699-1141. *E-mail:* admissions@amsamoa.edu. *Web site:* http://www.amsamoa.edu/.

ARIZONA

Arizona Automotive Institute

Glendale, Arizona

Director of Admissions Director of Admissions, Arizona Automotive Institute, 6829 North 46th Avenue, Glendale, AZ 85301-3597. *Phone:* 623-934-7273 Ext. 211. *Fax:* 623-937-5000. *E-mail:* info@azautoinst.com. *Web site:* http://www.aai.edu/.

Arizona College of Allied Health

Glendale, Arizona

Freshman Application Contact Admissions Department, Arizona College of Allied Health, 4425 West Olive Avenue, Suite 300, Glendale, AZ 85302-3843. *Phone:* 602-222-9300. *E-mail:* lhicks@arizonacollege.edu. *Web site:* http://www.arizonacollege.edu/.

Arizona Western College

Yuma, Arizona

- **State and locally supported** 2-year, founded 1962, part of Arizona State Community College System
- **Rural** 640-acre campus
- **Coed,** 8,545 undergraduate students, 33% full-time, 57% women, 43% men

Undergraduates 2,834 full-time, 5,711 part-time. Students come from 37 states and territories; 31 other countries; 3% are from out of state; 3% Black or African American, non-Hispanic/Latino; 57% Hispanic/Latino; 1% Asian, non-Hispanic/Latino; 0.4% Native Hawaiian or other Pacific Islander, non-Hispanic/Latino; 2% American Indian or Alaska Native, non-Hispanic/Latino; 0.1% Two or more races, non-Hispanic/Latino; 3% Race/ethnicity unknown; 9% international; 3% live on campus.

Freshmen *Admission:* 2,314 enrolled.

Faculty *Total:* 440, 25% full-time. *Student/faculty ratio:* 21:1.

Majors Accounting; agricultural business and management; agriculture; architectural technology; biology/biological sciences; business administration and management; business/commerce; carpentry; chemistry; civil engineering technology; computer and information sciences; computer graphics; construction trades related; criminal justice/law enforcement administration; crop production; data entry/microcomputer applications; dramatic/theater arts; early childhood education; electrical/electronics equipment installation and repair; elementary education; emergency medical technology (EMT paramedic); engineering; English; environmental science; fine/studio arts; fire science/firefighting; general studies; geology/earth science; health services/allied health/health sciences; heating, air conditioning, ventilation and refrigeration maintenance technology; history; hospitality administration; industrial technology; legal administrative assistant/secretary; logistics, materials, and supply chain management; marketing/marketing management; massage therapy; mass communication/media; mathematics; music; office management; parks, recreation and leisure facilities management; philosophy; physics; plumbing technology; political science and government; prenursing studies; radio and television broadcasting technology; radiologic technology/science; secondary education; social sciences; solar energy technology; Spanish; welding technology; work and family studies.

Academics *Calendar:* semesters. *Degree:* certificates and associate. *Special study options:* academic remediation for entering students, adult/continuing education programs, advanced placement credit, cooperative education, distance learning, English as a second language, honors programs, independent study, part-time degree program, services for LD students, summer session for credit.

Library Arizona Western College Library with 94,116 titles, 402 serial subscriptions, 4,486 audiovisual materials, an OPAC, a Web page.

Student Life *Housing Options:* coed. Campus housing is university owned. *Activities and Organizations:* drama/theater group, student-run newspaper, radio and television station, choral group, Student Government Association, Spirit Squad, Dance Team, Students in Free Enterprise (SIFE), International Students Team, national fraternities, national sororities. *Campus security:* 24-hour emergency response devices and patrols, student patrols, late-night transport/escort service. *Student services:* health clinic, personal/psychological counseling.

Athletics Member NJCAA. *Intercollegiate sports:* baseball M(s), basketball M(s)/W(s), football M(s), soccer M(s), softball W(s), volleyball W(s). *Intramural sports:* cheerleading M(c)/W(c).

Standardized Tests *Required for some:* SAT or ACT (for admission).

Costs (2010–11) *Tuition:* state resident $1440 full-time, $60 per credit hour part-time; nonresident $6000 full-time, $66 per credit hour part-time. Full-time tuition and fees vary according to course load. Part-time tuition and fees vary according to course load. *Room and board:* $5400; room only: $2030. Room and board charges vary according to board plan. *Payment plan:* installment. *Waivers:* senior citizens and employees or children of employees.

Financial Aid Of all full-time matriculated undergraduates who enrolled in 2009, 350 Federal Work-Study jobs (averaging $1500). 100 state and other part-time jobs (averaging $1800).

Applying *Options:* electronic application, early admission, deferred entrance. *Application deadlines:* rolling (freshmen), rolling (out-of-state freshmen), rolling (transfers).

Freshman Application Contact Amy Pignatore, Director of Admissions/Registrar, Arizona Western College, PO Box 929, Yuma, AZ 85366. *Phone:* 928-317-7600. *Toll-free phone:* 888-293-0392. *Fax:* 928-344-7712. *E-mail:* amy.pignatore@azwestern.edu. *Web site:* http://www.azwestern.edu/.

Brown Mackie College–Phoenix

Phoenix, Arizona

- **Proprietary** primarily 2-year, part of Education Management Corporation
- **Coed**

Majors Accounting technology and bookkeeping; business administration and management; criminal justice/law enforcement administration; health services administration; information technology; legal assistant/paralegal; legal studies; medical/clinical assistant; occupational therapist assistant; surgical technology.

Academics *Degrees:* diplomas, associate, and bachelor's.

Costs (2010–11) *Tuition:* Tuition varies by program. Students should contact Brown Mackie College for tuition information.

Freshman Application Contact Brown Mackie College–Phoenix, 13430 North Black Canyon Highway, Suite 190, Phoenix, AZ 85029. *Phone:* 602-337-3044. *Toll-free phone:* 866-824-4793. *Web site:* http://www.brownmackie.edu/phoenix/.

See page 392 for the College Close-Up.

Brown Mackie College–Tucson

Tucson, Arizona

- **Proprietary** primarily 2-year, founded 1972, part of Education Management Corporation
- **Suburban** campus
- **Coed**

Majors Accounting; accounting technology and bookkeeping; athletic training; biomedical technology; business administration and management; computer and information systems security; criminal justice/law enforcement administration; early childhood education; health/health-care administration; information technology; legal assistant/paralegal; legal studies; medical/clinical assistant; occupational therapist assistant; surgical technology.

Academics *Degrees:* diplomas, associate, and bachelor's.

Costs (2010–11) *Tuition:* Tuition varies by program. Students should contact Brown Mackie College for tuition information.

Freshman Application Contact Brown Mackie College–Tucson, 4585 East Speedway, Suite 204, Tucson, AZ 85712. *Phone:* 520-319-3300. *Web site:* http://www.brownmackie.edu/tucson/.

See page 404 for the College Close-Up.

The Bryman School of Arizona

Phoenix, Arizona

Freshman Application Contact Admissions Office, The Bryman School of Arizona, 2250 West Peoria Avenue, Phoenix, AZ 85029. *Phone:* 602-274-4300. *Toll-free phone:* 800-729-4819. *Fax:* 602-248-9087. *Web site:* http://www.brymanschool.edu/.

Carrington College - Mesa
Mesa, Arizona

Director of Admissions Valentina Colmone, Campus Director, Carrington College - Mesa, 630 West Southern Avenue, Mesa, AZ 85210. *Phone:* 480-212-1600. *E-mail:* vcolmone@apollocollege.edu. *Web site:* http://carrington.edu/.

Carrington College - Phoenix
Phoenix, Arizona

Director of Admissions Admissions Director, Carrington College - Phoenix, 8503 North 27th Avenue, Phoenix, AZ 85051. *Phone:* 602-324-5505. *Web site:* http://carrington.edu/home.

Carrington College - Phoenix Westside
Phoenix, Arizona

Director of Admissions Cindy Nestor, Admissions, Carrington College - Phoenix Westside, 2701 West Bethany Home Road, Phoenix, AZ 85017. *Phone:* 602-433-1222. *Fax:* 602-433-1222. *E-mail:* cnestor@apollocollege.com. *Web site:* http://carrington.edu/home.

Carrington College - Tucson
Tucson, Arizona

Director of Admissions Mr. Dennis C. Wilson, Executive Director, Carrington College - Tucson, 3550 North Oracle Road, Tucson, AZ 85705. *Phone:* 520-888-5885. *Fax:* 520-887-3005. *E-mail:* dwilson@apollo.edu. *Web site:* http://carrington.edu/.

Central Arizona College
Coolidge, Arizona

- **Public** 2-year, founded 1961
- **Rural** 850-acre campus with easy access to Phoenix
- **Coed**

Undergraduates 2,976 full-time, 4,937 part-time. Students come from 4 other countries; 17% live on campus.
Faculty *Student/faculty ratio:* 14:1.
Academics *Calendar:* semesters. *Degree:* certificates and associate. *Special study options:* academic remediation for entering students, adult/continuing education programs, distance learning, honors programs, independent study, internships, part-time degree program, services for LD students, student-designed majors, study abroad, summer session for credit.
Student Life *Campus security:* 24-hour emergency response devices and patrols, late-night transport/escort service.
Athletics Member NJCAA.
Costs (2010–11) *Tuition:* state resident $1560 full-time, $65 per credit hour part-time; nonresident $6936 full-time, $130 per credit hour part-time. Full-time tuition and fees vary according to course level, course load, program, reciprocity agreements, and student level. Part-time tuition and fees vary according to course level, course load, program, and student level. *Room and board:* $4612. Room and board charges vary according to housing facility and location.
Financial Aid Of all full-time matriculated undergraduates who enrolled in 2009, 68 Federal Work-Study jobs (averaging $1310).
Applying *Options:* electronic application, early admission, deferred entrance.
Freshman Application Contact Dr. James Moore, Dean of Records and Admissions, Central Arizona College, 8470 North Overfield Road, Coolidge, AZ 85128. *Phone:* 520-494-5261. *Toll-free phone:* 800-237-9814. *Fax:* 520-426-5083. *E-mail:* james.moore@centralaz.edu. *Web site:* http://www.centralaz.edu/.

Chandler-Gilbert Community College
Chandler, Arizona

- **State and locally supported** 2-year, founded 1985, part of Maricopa County Community College District System
- **Rural** 80-acre campus with easy access to Phoenix
- **Coed,** 12,296 undergraduate students, 35% full-time, 53% women, 47% men

Undergraduates 4,284 full-time, 8,012 part-time. Students come from 32 states and territories; 6% are from out of state; 2% transferred in. *Retention:* 60% of full-time freshmen returned.

Freshmen *Admission:* 2,341 enrolled.
Faculty *Student/faculty ratio:* 25:1.
Majors Accounting; accounting technology and bookkeeping; airline pilot and flight crew; business administration and management; business administration, management and operations related; business/commerce; business, management, and marketing related; computer and information sciences; computer and information sciences and support services related; computer programming; computer programming (vendor/product certification); computer systems analysis; computer systems networking and telecommunications; criminal justice/safety; data entry/microcomputer applications; data modeling/warehousing and database administration; dietetic technology; dietitian assistant; dramatic/theater arts; electromechanical technology; elementary education; fine/studio arts; general studies; information technology; kinesiology and exercise science; liberal arts and sciences and humanities related; liberal arts and sciences/liberal studies; lineworker; massage therapy; mechanic and repair technologies related; music management; organizational behavior; physical sciences; psychology; registered nursing/registered nurse; social work; visual and performing arts.
Academics *Calendar:* semesters. *Degree:* certificates, diplomas, and associate. *Special study options:* academic remediation for entering students, advanced placement credit, English as a second language, freshman honors college, honors programs, part-time degree program, summer session for credit.
Library Chandler-Gilbert Community College Library with an OPAC.
Student Life *Housing:* college housing not available. *Activities and Organizations:* student-run newspaper, choral group. *Campus security:* 24-hour emergency response devices and patrols, late-night transport/escort service. *Student services:* personal/psychological counseling.
Athletics Member NJCAA. *Intercollegiate sports:* baseball M, basketball M/W, golf M/W, soccer M/W, softball W, volleyball W.
Costs (2010–11) *Tuition:* area resident $1704 full-time, $71 per credit hour part-time; state resident $7488 full-time, $96 per credit hour part-time; nonresident $7488 full-time, $96 per credit hour part-time. Full-time tuition and fees vary according to reciprocity agreements. Part-time tuition and fees vary according to reciprocity agreements. *Required fees:* $30 full-time, $15 per term part-time. *Payment plans:* installment, deferred payment. *Waivers:* employees or children of employees.
Applying *Options:* electronic application.
Freshman Application Contact Ryan Cain, Coordinator of Enrollment Services, Chandler-Gilbert Community College, 2626 East Pecos Road, Chandler, AZ 85225-2479. *Phone:* 480-732-7044. *E-mail:* ryan.cain@cgcmail.maricopa.edu. *Web site:* http://www.cgc.maricopa.edu/.

Cochise College
Sierra Vista, Arizona

Freshman Application Contact Ms. Debbie Quick, Director of Admissions and Records, Cochise College, 901 North Colombo Avenue, Sierra Vista, AZ 85635-2317. *Phone:* 520-515-5412. *Toll-free phone:* 800-593-9567. *Fax:* 520-515-4006. *E-mail:* quickd@cochise.edu. *Web site:* http://www.cochise.edu/.

Coconino Community College
Flagstaff, Arizona

Freshman Application Contact Miss Veronica Hipolito, Director of Student Services, Coconino Community College, 2800 South Lone Tree Road, Flagstaff, AZ 86001. *Phone:* 928-226-4334 Ext. 4334. *Toll-free phone:* 800-350-7122. *Fax:* 928-226-4114. *E-mail:* veronica.hipolito@coconino.edu. *Web site:* http://www.coconino.edu/.

CollegeAmerica–Flagstaff
Flagstaff, Arizona

- **Proprietary** primarily 2-year
- **Coed,** 300 undergraduate students

Undergraduates *Retention:* 60% of full-time freshmen returned.
Faculty *Student/faculty ratio:* 33:1.
Majors Computer systems networking and telecommunications; health/healthcare administration; medical/health management and clinical assistant.
Academics *Degrees:* associate and bachelor's.
Freshman Application Contact CollegeAmerica–Flagstaff, 3012 East Route 66, Flagstaff, AZ 86004. *Phone:* 928-213-6060. *Toll-free phone:* 800-622-2894. *Web site:* http://www.collegeamerica.edu/.

Diné College
Tsaile, Arizona

Freshman Application Contact Mrs. Louise Litzin, Registrar, Diné College, PO Box 67, Tsaile, AZ 86556. *Phone:* 928-724-6633. *Fax:* 928-724-3349. *E-mail:* louise@dinecollege.edu. *Web site:* http://www.dinecollege.edu/.

Eastern Arizona College
Thatcher, Arizona

- **State and locally supported** 2-year, founded 1888, part of Arizona State Community College System.
- **Small-town** campus
- **Endowment** $3.2 million
- **Coed,** 6,799 undergraduate students, 35% full-time, 56% women, 44% men

Undergraduates 2,381 full-time, 4,418 part-time. Students come from 31 states and territories; 20 other countries; 4% are from out of state; 3% Black or African American, non-Hispanic/Latino; 20% Hispanic/Latino; 1% Asian, non-Hispanic/Latino; 0.1% Native Hawaiian or other Pacific Islander, non-Hispanic/Latino; 8% American Indian or Alaska Native, non-Hispanic/Latino; 0.4% Two or more races, non-Hispanic/Latino; 3% Race/ethnicity unknown; 0.6% international; 3% transferred in; 5% live on campus. *Retention:* 74% of full-time freshmen returned.

Freshmen *Admission:* 1,636 applied, 1,636 admitted, 1,636 enrolled.

Faculty *Total:* 276, 32% full-time, 10% with terminal degrees. *Student/faculty ratio:* 11:1.

Majors Agribusiness; agriculture; anthropology; art; art teacher education; automobile/automotive mechanics technology; biology/biological sciences; business administration and management; business, management, and marketing related; business operations support and secretarial services related; business teacher education; chemistry; child-care provision; civil engineering technology; commercial and advertising art; corrections; criminal justice/law enforcement administration; criminal justice/police science; data entry/microcomputer applications; drafting and design technology; dramatic/theater arts; elementary education; emergency medical technology (EMT paramedic); English; entrepreneurship; foreign languages and literatures; forestry; geology/earth science; health and physical education/fitness; health/medical preparatory programs related; history; information science/studies; liberal arts and sciences/liberal studies; machine shop technology; management information systems and services related; mathematics; mining technology; music; physics; political science and government; pre-law studies; premedical studies; prepharmacy studies; psychology; registered nursing/registered nurse; secondary education; sociology; technology/industrial arts teacher education; welding technology; wildlife biology.

Academics *Calendar:* semesters. *Degree:* certificates and associate. *Special study options:* academic remediation for entering students, adult/continuing education programs, advanced placement credit, cooperative education, distance learning, double majors, independent study, internships, part-time degree program, services for LD students, study abroad, summer session for credit.

Library Alumni Library with an OPAC, a Web page.

Student Life *Housing Options:* men-only, women-only. Campus housing is university owned. *Activities and Organizations:* drama/theater group, choral group, marching band, Latter-Day Saints Student Association, Criminal Justice Student Association, Multicultural Council, Phi Theta Kappa, Mark Allen Dorm Club. *Campus security:* 24-hour emergency response devices, late-night transport/escort service, controlled dormitory access, 20-hour patrols by trained security personnel. *Student services:* personal/psychological counseling.

Athletics Member NJCAA. *Intercollegiate sports:* baseball M(s), basketball M(s)/W(s), football M(s), golf M/W, softball W(s), volleyball W(s). *Intramural sports:* basketball M/W, racquetball M/W, swimming and diving M/W, table tennis M/W, tennis M/W, volleyball M/W.

Costs (2010–11) *Tuition:* state resident $1520 full-time, $85 per credit hour part-time; nonresident $8120 full-time, $140 per credit hour part-time. *Required fees:* $58 per credit hour part-time, $140 per term part-time. *Room and board:* $5075; room only: $2690. Room and board charges vary according to board plan and housing facility. *Waivers:* senior citizens and employees or children of employees.

Financial Aid Of all full-time matriculated undergraduates who enrolled in 2008, 1,976 applied for aid, 1,719 were judged to have need, 64 had their need fully met. In 2008, 400 non-need-based awards were made. *Average percent of need met:* 49%. *Average financial aid package:* $4598. *Average need-based gift aid:* $4491. *Average non-need-based aid:* $2057.

Applying *Options:* electronic application, early admission, deferred entrance. *Recommended:* high school transcript. *Application deadlines:* rolling (freshmen), rolling (transfers). *Notification:* continuous (freshmen).

Freshman Application Contact Erline Norton, Records Assistant, Eastern Arizona College, 615 North Stadium Avenue, Thatcher, AZ 85552-0769.

Phone: 928-428-8250. *Toll-free phone:* 800-678-3808. *Fax:* 928-428-2578. *E-mail:* admissions@eac.edu. *Web site:* http://www.eac.edu/.

Estrella Mountain Community College
Avondale, Arizona

- **State and locally supported** 2-year, founded 1992, part of Maricopa County Community College District System
- **Urban** campus with easy access to Phoenix
- **Coed**

Undergraduates 1,631 full-time, 4,727 part-time.

Faculty *Student/faculty ratio:* 22:1.

Academics *Calendar:* semesters. *Degree:* certificates and associate. *Special study options:* academic remediation for entering students, adult/continuing education programs, advanced placement credit, cooperative education, distance learning, English as a second language, honors programs, independent study, part-time degree program, services for LD students, summer session for credit. *ROTC:* Air Force (c).

Student Life *Campus security:* 24-hour emergency response devices and patrols, late-night transport/escort service.

Costs (2010–11) *Tuition:* area resident $1704 full-time, $71 per credit hour part-time; state resident $7488 full-time, $312 per credit hour part-time, nonresident $7488 full-time, $312 per credit hour part-time. *Required fees:* $30 full-time, $15 per term part-time.

Applying *Options:* electronic application.

Freshman Application Contact Estrella Mountain Community College, 3000 North Dysart Road, Avondale, AZ 85392. *Phone:* 623-935-8812. *Web site:* http://www.emc.maricopa.edu/.

Everest College
Phoenix, Arizona

Freshman Application Contact Mr. Jim Askins, Director of Admissions, Everest College, 10400 North 25th Avenue, Suite 190, Phoenix, AZ 85021. *Phone:* 602-942-4141. *Fax:* 602-943-0960. *E-mail:* jaskins@cci.edu. *Web site:* http://www.everest.edu/.

GateWay Community College
Phoenix, Arizona

- **State and locally supported** 2-year, founded 1968, part of Maricopa County Community College District System, administratively affiliated with GateWay Community College
- **Urban** 20-acre campus
- **Coed,** 7,346 undergraduate students

Undergraduates 214 full-time, 444 part-time.

Freshmen *Admission:* 658 applied, 658 admitted, 658 enrolled.

Faculty *Total:* 326, 33% full-time. *Student/faculty ratio:* 16:1.

Majors Accounting; accounting and computer science; accounting technology and bookkeeping; administrative assistant and secretarial science; aeronautical/aerospace engineering technology; automobile/automotive mechanics technology; biotechnology; business administration and management; business administration, management and operations related; business automation/technology/data entry; business/commerce; cabinetmaking and millwork; carpentry; clinical laboratory science/medical technology; computer and information sciences; computer systems networking and telecommunications; construction/heavy equipment/earthmoving equipment operation; court reporting; diagnostic medical sonography and ultrasound technology; electrician; electromechanical technology; elementary education; energy management and systems technology; general studies; health and medical administrative services related; health/health-care administration; heating, air conditioning, ventilation and refrigeration maintenance technology; heating, ventilation, air conditioning and refrigeration engineering technology; industrial and product design; ironworking; liberal arts and sciences/liberal studies; lineworker; management information systems; manufacturing engineering technology; marketing/marketing management; masonry; medical radiologic technology; medical transcription; nuclear medical technology; occupational safety and health technology; organizational behavior; painting and wall covering; personal and culinary services related; physical sciences; physical therapy technology; pipefitting and sprinkler fitting; plumbing technology; radiologic technology/science; registered nursing/registered nurse; respiratory care therapy; sheet metal technology; surgical technology; water quality and wastewater treatment management and recycling technology; web page, digital/multimedia and information resources design.

Academics *Calendar:* semesters. *Degree:* certificates, diplomas, and associate. *Special study options:* academic remediation for entering students, accelerated degree program, adult/continuing education programs, advanced placement credit, cooperative education, distance learning, double majors, English as a second language, freshman honors college, honors programs, independent study, internships, off-campus study, part-time degree program, services for LD students, study abroad, summer session for credit. *ROTC:* Army (c), Air Force (c).

Library GateWay Library with an OPAC.

Student Life *Housing:* college housing not available. *Campus security:* 24-hour emergency response devices and patrols, student patrols, late-night transport/escort service. *Student services:* personal/psychological counseling, women's center.

Athletics Member NJCAA. *Intercollegiate sports:* baseball M, cross-country running M/W, golf M/W, soccer M/W, softball W.

Costs (2010–11) *Tuition:* area resident $2130 full-time; state resident $9360 full-time; nonresident $9360 full-time. Full-time tuition and fees vary according to program and reciprocity agreements. Part-time tuition and fees vary according to program and reciprocity agreements. *Required fees:* $30 full-time. *Payment plans:* installment, deferred payment. *Waivers:* employees or children of employees.

Applying *Options:* electronic application, early admission, deferred entrance. *Required for some:* high school transcript, interview. *Application deadlines:* rolling (freshmen), rolling (transfers). *Notification:* continuous (freshmen), continuous (transfers).

Freshman Application Contact Director of Admissions and Records, GateWay Community College, 108 North 40th Street, Phoenix, AZ 85034. *Phone:* 602-286-8200. *Fax:* 602-286-8200. *E-mail:* enroll@gatewaycc.edu. *Web site:* http://www.gatewaycc.edu/.

Glendale Community College
Glendale, Arizona

- **State and locally supported** 2-year, founded 1965, part of Maricopa County Community College District System
- **Suburban** 222-acre campus with easy access to Phoenix
- **Endowment** $1.2 million
- **Coed,** 20,154 undergraduate students, 35% full-time, 54% women, 46% men

Undergraduates 7,126 full-time, 13,028 part-time. Students come from 51 states and territories; 92 other countries; 8% are from out of state; 7% transferred in. *Retention:* 64% of full-time freshmen returned.

Freshmen *Admission:* 3,423 enrolled.

Faculty *Student/faculty ratio:* 24:1.

Majors Accounting technology and bookkeeping; administrative assistant and secretarial science; architectural drafting and CAD/CADD; automobile/automotive mechanics technology; behavioral sciences; biotechnology; business administration and management; business/commerce; CAD/CADD drafting/design technology; cinematography and film/video production; commercial and advertising art; computer and information sciences; computer and information systems analysis; computer systems networking and telecommunications; criminal justice/safety; data entry/microcomputer applications; early childhood education; educational leadership and administration; emergency medical technology (EMT paramedic); engineering technology; family and community services; fire science/firefighting; graphic design; homeland security, law enforcement, firefighting and protective services related; kinesiology and exercise science; marketing/marketing management; music management; public relations/image management; recording arts technology; registered nursing/registered nurse; web page, digital/multimedia and information resources design.

Academics *Calendar:* semesters. *Degree:* certificates and associate. *Special study options:* academic remediation for entering students, adult/continuing education programs, advanced placement credit, cooperative education, distance learning, double majors, English as a second language, freshman honors college, honors programs, internships, off-campus study, part-time degree program, services for LD students, study abroad, summer session for credit. *ROTC:* Army (c), Air Force (c).

Library Library/Media Center plus 1 other with 97,768 titles, 30,094 serial subscriptions, 6,032 audiovisual materials, an OPAC, a Web page.

Student Life *Housing:* college housing not available. *Activities and Organizations:* drama/theater group, student-run newspaper, choral group, marching band, Phi Theta Kappa, M.E.Ch.A. (Movimiento Estudiantil Chicano de Aztlan), Associated Student Government, Biotechnology Club, Compass. *Campus security:* 24-hour patrols, student patrols, late-night transport/escort service. *Student services:* personal/psychological counseling, legal services.

Athletics Member NJCAA. *Intercollegiate sports:* baseball M(s), basketball M(s)/W(s), cross-country running M(s)/W(s), football M(s), golf M(s), soccer M(s)/W(s), softball W(s), tennis M(s)/W(s), track and field M(s)/W(s), volleyball W(s). *Intramural sports:* golf M, racquetball M/W, softball W, tennis M/W, volleyball W.

Costs (2011–12) *Tuition:* state resident $71 per semester hour part-time; nonresident $96 per semester hour part-time. Full-time tuition and fees vary according to program and reciprocity agreements. Part-time tuition and fees vary according to course load, program, and reciprocity agreements. *Required*

fees: $15 per term part-time. *Payment plan:* installment. *Waivers:* employees or children of employees.

Financial Aid Of all full-time matriculated undergraduates who enrolled in 2009, 350 Federal Work-Study jobs (averaging $1700).

Applying *Options:* electronic application. *Required for some:* high school transcript. *Application deadlines:* 8/20 (freshmen), 8/20 (transfers). *Notification:* continuous until 8/20 (freshmen), continuous until 8/20 (transfers).

Freshman Application Contact Ms. Mary Blackwell, Dean of Enrollment Services, Glendale Community College, 6000 West Olive Avenue, Glendale, AZ 85302. *Phone:* 623-435-3305. *Fax:* 623-845-3303. *E-mail:* info@gc.maricopa.edu. *Web site:* http://www.gc.maricopa.edu/.

High-Tech Institute
Phoenix, Arizona

Freshman Application Contact Mr. Glen Husband, Vice President of Admissions, High-Tech Institute, 1515 East Indian School Road, Phoenix, AZ 85014-4901. *Phone:* 602-279-9700. *Web site:* http://www.high-techinstitute.com/.

ITT Technical Institute
Phoenix, Arizona

- **Proprietary** primarily 2-year, founded 1972, part of ITT Educational Services, Inc.
- **Urban** campus
- **Coed**

Majors CAD/CADD drafting/design technology; computer and information systems security; computer engineering technology; computer software engineering; computer software technology; construction management; criminal justice/law enforcement administration; design and visual communications; electrical, electronic and communications engineering technology; legal assistant/paralegal; project management; registered nursing/registered nurse; system, networking, and LAN/WAN management.

Academics *Calendar:* quarters. *Degrees:* associate and bachelor's.

Student Life *Housing:* college housing not available.

Financial Aid Of all full-time matriculated undergraduates who enrolled in 2009, 10 Federal Work-Study jobs (averaging $4000).

Freshman Application Contact Director of Recruitment, ITT Technical Institute, 10220 North 25th Avenue, Suite 100, Phoenix, AZ 85021. *Phone:* 602-749-7900. *Toll-free phone:* 877-221-1132. *Web site:* http://www.itt-tech.edu/.

ITT Technical Institute
Phoenix, Arizona

- **Proprietary** 2-year, part of ITT Educational Services, Inc.
- **Coed**

Majors CAD/CADD drafting/design technology; computer and information systems security; computer engineering technology; criminal justice/law enforcement administration; electrical, electronic and communications engineering technology; legal assistant/paralegal; project management; system, networking, and LAN/WAN management.

Academics *Calendar:* quarters.

Freshman Application Contact Director of Recruitment, ITT Technical Institute, 1840 N. 95th Avenue, Suite 132, Phoenix, AZ 85037. *Phone:* 623-474-7900. *Toll-free phone:* 800-210-1178. *Web site:* http://www.itt-tech.edu/.

ITT Technical Institute
Tucson, Arizona

- **Proprietary** primarily 2-year, founded 1984, part of ITT Educational Services, Inc.
- **Urban** campus
- **Coed**

Majors CAD/CADD drafting/design technology; computer and information systems security; computer engineering technology; computer software and media applications related; computer software engineering; computer software technology; construction management; criminal justice/law enforcement administration; design and visual communications; electrical, electronic and communications engineering technology; game and interactive media design; legal assistant/paralegal; project management; system, networking, and LAN/WAN management; web page, digital/multimedia and information resources design.

Academics *Calendar:* quarters. *Degrees:* associate and bachelor's.

Student Life *Housing:* college housing not available.

Freshman Application Contact Director of Recruitment, ITT Technical Institute, 1455 West River Road, Tucson, AZ 85704. *Phone:* 520-408-7488. *Toll-free phone:* 800-870-9730. *Web site:* http://www.itt-tech.edu/.

Kaplan College, Phoenix Campus

Phoenix, Arizona

- **Proprietary** 2-year, founded 1972
- **Coed**

Academics *Calendar:* continuous. *Degree:* diplomas and associate.
Freshman Application Contact Kaplan College, Phoenix Campus, 13610 North Black Canyon Highway, Suite 104, Phoenix, AZ 85029. *Phone:* 602-548-1955. *Toll-free phone:* 877-548-1955. *Web site:* http://www.kc-phoenix.com/.

Lamson College

Tempe, Arizona

- **Proprietary** 2-year, founded 1889, part of National Career Education, Inc.
- **Urban** campus with easy access to Phoenix
- **Coed**

Academics *Calendar:* quarters. *Degree:* diplomas and associate. *Special study options:* academic remediation for entering students, adult/continuing education programs, English as a second language, internships, summer session for credit.
Student Life *Campus security:* 24-hour patrols.
Standardized Tests *Required:* Wonderlic aptitude test (for admission).
Applying *Application fee:* $25. *Required:* high school transcript, interview.
Freshman Application Contact Lamson College, 875 West Elliot Road, Suite 206, Tempe, AZ 85284. *Phone:* 480-898-7000. *Toll-free phone:* 800-898-7017. *Web site:* http://www.lamsoncollege.com/.

Mesa Community College

Mesa, Arizona

- **State and locally supported** 2-year, founded 1965, part of Maricopa County Community College District System
- **Urban** 160-acre campus with easy access to Phoenix
- **Coed,** 28,000 undergraduate students

Undergraduates Students come from 18 states and territories; 4% are from out of state.
Freshmen *Average high school GPA:* 2.
Faculty *Total:* 1,065, 25% full-time.
Majors Accounting; administrative assistant and secretarial science; agricultural business and management; agricultural mechanization; agronomy and crop science; art; automobile/automotive mechanics technology; biology/biological sciences; business administration and management; child development; criminal justice/law enforcement administration; data processing and data processing technology; drafting and design technology; electrical, electronic and communications engineering technology; engineering technology; family and consumer sciences/human sciences; fashion merchandising; finance; fire science/firefighting; heavy equipment maintenance technology; horticultural science; industrial technology; insurance; interior design; liberal arts and sciences/liberal studies; library and information science; marketing/marketing management; mathematics; medical administrative assistant and medical secretary; music; ornamental horticulture; pre-engineering; quality control technology; real estate; registered nursing/registered nurse; teacher assistant/aide.
Academics *Calendar:* semesters. *Degree:* certificates and associate. *Special study options:* academic remediation for entering students, adult/continuing education programs, advanced placement credit, cooperative education, distance learning, English as a second language, freshman honors college, honors programs, independent study, off-campus study, part-time degree program, services for LD students, student-designed majors, study abroad, summer session for credit. *ROTC:* Army (c), Air Force (c).
Library Information Commons with 56,224 titles, 794 serial subscriptions, an OPAC, a Web page.
Student Life *Housing:* college housing not available. *Activities and Organizations:* drama/theater group, student-run newspaper, radio station, choral group, MECHA, International Student Association, American Indian Association, Asian/Pacific Islander Club. *Campus security:* 24-hour emergency response devices and patrols, student patrols. *Student services:* personal/psychological counseling, legal services.
Athletics Member NJCAA. *Intercollegiate sports:* baseball M, basketball M/W, cross-country running M, football M, golf M/W, soccer M/W, softball W, tennis M/W, track and field M/W, volleyball W, wrestling M. *Intramural sports:* basketball M/W, cross-country running M, football M/W, tennis M/W, track and field M/W, volleyball M/W, wrestling M/W.

Costs (2010–11) *Tuition:* area resident $1704 full-time, $71 per credit hour part-time; state resident $6720 full-time, $96 per credit hour part-time; nonresident $7488 full-time, $96 per credit hour part-time. Full-time tuition and fees vary according to course load and reciprocity agreements. Part-time tuition and fees vary according to course load and reciprocity agreements. *Payment plan:* installment. *Waivers:* employees or children of employees.
Applying *Options:* electronic application, early admission, deferred entrance. *Application deadlines:* 8/22 (freshmen), 8/22 (transfers). *Notification:* continuous (freshmen).
Freshman Application Contact Ms. Kathleen Perales, Manager, Recruitment, Mesa Community College, 1833 West Southern Avenue, Mesa, AZ 85202-4866. *Phone:* 480-461-7751. *Fax:* 480-654-7379. *E-mail:* admissions@mc.maricopa.edu. *Web site:* http://www.mesacc.edu/.

Mohave Community College

Kingman, Arizona

- **State-supported** 2-year, founded 1971
- **Small-town** 160-acre campus
- **Coed,** 6,686 undergraduate students, 31% full-time, 63% women, 37% men

Undergraduates 2,058 full-time, 4,628 part-time. Students come from 16 states and territories; 5% are from out of state; 1% Black or African American, non-Hispanic/Latino; 15% Hispanic/Latino; 2% Asian, non-Hispanic/Latino; 0.4% Native Hawaiian or other Pacific Islander, non-Hispanic/Latino; 2% American Indian or Alaska Native, non-Hispanic/Latino; 0.9% Two or more races, non-Hispanic/Latino; 2% Race/ethnicity unknown.
Freshmen *Admission:* 1,303 enrolled.
Faculty *Total:* 367, 19% full-time, 10% with terminal degrees. *Student/faculty ratio:* 21:1.
Majors Accounting; art; automobile/automotive mechanics technology; building/construction finishing, management, and inspection related; business administration and management; computer and information sciences related; computer programming (specific applications); computer science; criminal justice/police science; culinary arts; dental assisting; dental hygiene; drafting and design technology; education; emergency medical technology (EMT paramedic); English; fire science/firefighting; heating, air conditioning, ventilation and refrigeration maintenance technology; history; information technology; legal assistant/paralegal; liberal arts and sciences/liberal studies; mathematics; medical/clinical assistant; personal and culinary services related; pharmacy technician; physical therapy technology; psychology; registered nursing/registered nurse; sociology; substance abuse/addiction counseling; surgical technology; truck and bus driver/commercial vehicle operation/instruction; welding technology.
Academics *Calendar:* semesters. *Degree:* certificates and associate. *Special study options:* academic remediation for entering students, adult/continuing education programs, cooperative education, distance learning, English as a second language, independent study, part-time degree program, summer session for credit.
Library Mohave Community College Library with 45,849 titles, 476 serial subscriptions, an OPAC, a Web page.
Student Life *Housing:* college housing not available. *Activities and Organizations:* Art Club, Phi Theta Kappa, Computer Club (MC4), Science Club, student government. *Campus security:* late-night transport/escort service.
Costs (2010–11) *Tuition:* state resident $2070 full-time, $69 per credit hour part-time; nonresident $6210 full-time, $207 per credit hour part-time. Full-time tuition and fees vary according to program. Part-time tuition and fees vary according to program. *Required fees:* $240 full-time, $8 per credit part-time. *Payment plans:* installment, deferred payment. *Waivers:* employees or children of employees.
Applying *Options:* early admission, deferred entrance. *Application deadlines:* rolling (freshmen), rolling (transfers). *Notification:* continuous (freshmen), continuous (transfers).
Freshman Application Contact Ms. Jann Woods, Dean of Student Services, Mohave Community College, 1971 Jagerson Ave, Kingman, AZ 86409. *Phone:* 928-757-0803. *Toll-free phone:* 888-664-2832. *Fax:* 928-757-0808. *E-mail:* jwoods@mohave.edu. *Web site:* http://www.mohave.edu/.

Northland Pioneer College

Holbrook, Arizona

- **State and locally supported** 2-year, founded 1974, part of Arizona State Community College System
- **Rural** 50-acre campus
- **Coed**

Undergraduates 946 full-time, 3,690 part-time. Students come from 17 states and territories; 3 other countries; 0.9% transferred in.
Faculty *Student/faculty ratio:* 17:1.

Academics *Calendar:* semesters. *Degree:* certificates and associate. *Special study options:* advanced placement credit, cooperative education, distance learning, double majors, English as a second language, freshman honors college, honors programs, independent study, internships, part-time degree program, services for LD students, summer session for credit.

Student Life *Campus security:* evening security.

Costs (2010–11) *Tuition:* state resident $1344 full-time, $56 per credit hour part-time; nonresident $6480 full-time, $95 per credit hour part-time. *Required fees:* $35 full-time, $35 per term part-time. *Payment plans:* installment, deferred payment.

Financial Aid Of all full-time matriculated undergraduates who enrolled in 2009, 80 Federal Work-Study jobs (averaging $4000).

Applying *Options:* early admission.

Freshman Application Contact Ms. Suzette Willis, Coordinator of Admissions, Northland Pioneer College, PO Box 610, Holbrook, AZ 86025. *Phone:* 928-536-6271. *Toll-free phone:* 800-266-7845. *Fax:* 928-536-6212. *Web site:* http://www.npc.edu/.

Paradise Valley Community College
Phoenix, Arizona

- **State and locally supported** 2-year, founded 1985, part of Maricopa County Community College District System
- **Urban** campus
- **Coed**

Undergraduates 3,043 full-time, 6,908 part-time. 4% are from out of state.

Academics *Calendar:* semesters. *Degree:* certificates and associate. *Special study options:* academic remediation for entering students, accelerated degree program, adult/continuing education programs, advanced placement credit, cooperative education, distance learning, English as a second language, honors programs, independent study, internships, off-campus study, part-time degree program, services for LD students, study abroad, summer session for credit. *ROTC:* Army (c).

Student Life *Campus security:* 24-hour emergency response devices and patrols, late-night transport/escort service.

Athletics Member NJCAA.

Costs (2010–11) *Tuition:* area resident $2130 full-time, $71 per credit hour part-time; state resident $9360 full-time, $312 per credit hour part-time; nonresident $9360 full-time, $312 per credit hour part-time. Full-time tuition and fees vary according to course load and reciprocity agreements. Part-time tuition and fees vary according to course load and reciprocity agreements. *Required fees:* $30 full-time.

Financial Aid Of all full-time matriculated undergraduates who enrolled in 2009, 50 Federal Work-Study jobs (averaging $2500).

Applying *Options:* early admission.

Freshman Application Contact Paradise Valley Community College, 18401 North 32nd Street, Phoenix, AZ 85032-1200. *Phone:* 602-787-7020. *Web site:* http://www.pvc.maricopa.edu/.

The Paralegal Institute, Inc.
Phoenix, Arizona

Freshman Application Contact Patricia Yancy, Director of Admissions, The Paralegal Institute, Inc., 2933 West Indian School Road, Drawer 11408, Phoenix, AZ 85061-1408. *Phone:* 602-212-0501. *Toll-free phone:* 800-354-1254. *Fax:* 602-212-0502. *E-mail:* paralegalinst@mindspring.com. *Web site:* http://www.theparalegalinstitute.edu/.

Phoenix College
Phoenix, Arizona

- **County-supported** 2-year, founded 1920, part of Maricopa County Community College District System
- **Urban** 52-acre campus
- **Coed,** 13,000 undergraduate students, 26% full-time, 62% women, 38% men

Undergraduates 3,375 full-time, 9,625 part-time. 12% Black or African American, non-Hispanic/Latino; 35% Hispanic/Latino; 3% Asian, non-Hispanic/Latino; 0.1% Native Hawaiian or other Pacific Islander, non-Hispanic/Latino; 4% American Indian or Alaska Native, non-Hispanic/Latino; 12% Race/ethnicity unknown; 0.5% international.

Faculty *Total:* 654, 23% full-time. *Student/faculty ratio:* 20:1.

Majors Accounting; architectural drafting and CAD/CADD; art; banking and financial support services; building/home/construction inspection; business administration and management; business/commerce; child-care and support services management; civil engineering technology; clinical/medical laboratory technology; commercial and advertising art; commercial photography; computer and information sciences; computer graphics; computer systems analysis; criminal justice/safety; culinary arts; dental assisting; dental hygiene;

dramatic/theater arts; elementary education; family and community services; family and consumer sciences/human sciences; fashion/apparel design; fashion merchandising; fine/studio arts; fire science/firefighting; food service systems administration; forensic science and technology; general studies; graphic design; health information/medical records technology; histologic technology/histotechnologist; interior design; journalism; legal assistant/paralegal; liberal arts and sciences/liberal studies; marketing/marketing management; massage therapy; medical/clinical assistant; medical office management; music management; natural sciences; parks, recreation and leisure; physical sciences; recording arts technology; registered nursing/registered nurse; sign language interpretation and translation; surveying technology; visual and performing arts; web page, digital/multimedia and information resources design.

Academics *Calendar:* semesters. *Degree:* certificates, diplomas, and associate. *Special study options:* academic remediation for entering students, adult/continuing education programs, advanced placement credit, cooperative education, distance learning, English as a second language, freshman honors college, honors programs, independent study, internships, off-campus study, part-time degree program, services for LD students, study abroad, summer session for credit. *ROTC:* Army (c), Navy (c), Air Force (c).

Library Fannin Library with 83,000 titles, 394 serial subscriptions.

Student Life *Housing:* college housing not available. *Activities and Organizations:* drama/theater group, student-run radio station, choral group, Black Student Union, NASA (Native American Club), International Club, MECHA (Mexican Club), ALE (Asociacion Latina Estudiantil). *Campus security:* 24-hour emergency response devices, student patrols, late-night transport/escort service. *Student services:* personal/psychological counseling.

Athletics Member NCAA, NJCAA. All NCAA Division II. *Intercollegiate sports:* baseball M(s), basketball M(s)/W(s), cross-country running M(s)/W(s), football M(s), golf M(s)/W(s), soccer M/W, softball W(s), tennis M(s)/W(s), track and field M(s)/W(s), volleyball W(s).

Costs (2011–12) *Tuition:* area resident $1704 full-time, $71 per credit hour part-time; state resident $6720 full-time, $280 per credit hour part-time; nonresident $7488 full-time, $312 per credit hour part-time. Full-time tuition and fees vary according to reciprocity agreements. Part-time tuition and fees vary according to course load and reciprocity agreements. *Required fees:* $30 full-time, $15 per term part-time. *Payment plan:* installment. *Waivers:* employees or children of employees.

Financial Aid Of all full-time matriculated undergraduates who enrolled in 2009, 220 Federal Work-Study jobs (averaging $4800).

Applying *Options:* electronic application, early admission, deferred entrance. *Application deadlines:* rolling (freshmen), rolling (out-of-state freshmen), rolling (transfers). *Notification:* continuous (freshmen), continuous (out-of-state freshmen), continuous (transfers).

Freshman Application Contact Ms. Kathleen French, Director of Admissions, Registration, and Records, Phoenix College, 1202 West Thomas Road, Phoenix, AZ 85013. *Phone:* 602-285-7503. *Fax:* 602-285-7813. *E-mail:* kathy.french@pcmail.maricopa.edu. *Web site:* http://www.pc.maricopa.edu/.

Pima Community College
Tucson, Arizona

- **State and locally supported** 2-year, founded 1966
- **Urban** 486-acre campus with easy access to Tucson, Arizona
- **Endowment** $4.1 million
- **Coed,** 36,823 undergraduate students, 37% full-time, 55% women, 45% men

Undergraduates 13,700 full-time, 23,123 part-time. Students come from 31 states and territories; 31 other countries; 4% are from out of state; 4% Black or African American, non-Hispanic/Latino; 34% Hispanic/Latino; 2% Asian, non-Hispanic/Latino; 0.2% Native Hawaiian or other Pacific Islander, non-Hispanic/Latino; 3% American Indian or Alaska Native, non-Hispanic/Latino; 2% Two or more races, non-Hispanic/Latino; 13% Race/ethnicity unknown; 2% international; 6% transferred in. *Retention:* 66% of full-time freshmen returned.

Freshmen *Admission:* 4,633 enrolled.

Faculty *Total:* 1,566, 20% full-time. *Student/faculty ratio:* 29:1.

Majors Accounting; administrative assistant and secretarial science; aircraft powerplant technology; American Indian/Native American studies; animation, interactive technology, video graphics and special effects; anthropology; architectural drafting and CAD/CADD; automobile/automotive mechanics technology; building/property maintenance; business administration and management; cinematography and film/video production; clinical/medical laboratory assistant; clinical/medical laboratory science and allied professions related; clinical/medical laboratory technology; clinical/medical social work; computer engineering technology; computer systems analysis; computer systems networking and telecommunications; criminal justice/police science; criminal justice/safety; dental hygiene; dental laboratory technology; design and visual communications; early childhood education; electrical, electronic and communications engineering technology; elementary education; fashion merchandising;

fire science/firefighting; general studies; health and medical administrative services related; health/health-care administration; histologic technician; homeland security, law enforcement, firefighting and protective services related; hospitality administration; industrial electronics technology; industrial production technologies related; industrial technology; language interpretation and translation; laser and optical technology; legal assistant/paralegal; liberal arts and sciences/liberal studies; machine shop technology; massage therapy; medical radiologic technology; mining and petroleum technologies related; music; pharmacy technician; political science and government; radio and television; radiologic technology/science; registered nursing/registered nurse; respiratory care therapy; restaurant, culinary, and catering management; sign language interpretation and translation; sociology; veterinary/animal health technology; visual and performing arts; welding technology.

Academics *Calendar:* semesters. *Degrees:* certificates, diplomas, associate, and postbachelor's certificates. *Special study options:* academic remediation for entering students, accelerated degree program, adult/continuing education programs, advanced placement credit, cooperative education, distance learning, double majors, English as a second language, honors programs, independent study, internships, off-campus study, part-time degree program, services for LD students, student-designed majors, summer session for credit. *ROTC:* Army (c), Navy (c), Air Force (c).

Library Pima College Library with 276,548 titles, 788 serial subscriptions, 21,434 audiovisual materials, an OPAC, a Web page.

Student Life *Housing:* college housing not available. *Activities and Organizations:* drama/theater group, student-run newspaper, choral group, Student Social Services Organization, Spanish Language Club, Student Nurses Association at Pima, Gay-Straight Student Alliance (GSA), Pima Photography Club, national fraternities. *Campus security:* 24-hour emergency response devices and patrols, late-night transport/escort service. *Student services:* health clinic.

Athletics Member NJCAA. *Intercollegiate sports:* baseball M(s), basketball M(s)/W(s), cheerleading W, cross-country running M(s)/W(s), football M(s), golf M(s)/W(s), soccer M(s)/W(s), softball W(s), tennis M(s)/W(s), track and field M(s)/W(s), volleyball W(s). *Intramural sports:* badminton M/W, basketball M/W, cross-country running M/W, equestrian sports M(c)/W(c), football M, golf M/W, ice hockey M(c), racquetball M/W, tennis M/W, track and field M/W, volleyball M/W, wrestling M(c).

Costs (2011–12) *Tuition:* state resident $1755 full-time, $54 per credit hour part-time; nonresident $8820 full-time, $90 per credit hour part-time. Full-time tuition and fees vary according to course load and program. Part-time tuition and fees vary according to course load and program. *Required fees:* $155 full-time, $5 per credit hour part-time, $10 per term part-time. *Payment plans:* installment, deferred payment. *Waivers:* employees or children of employees.

Applying *Options:* electronic application. *Application deadlines:* rolling (freshmen), rolling (out-of-state freshmen), rolling (transfers).

Freshman Application Contact Michael Tulino, Director of Admissions and Registrar, Pima Community College, 4905B East Broadway Boulevard, Tucson, AZ 85709-1120. *Phone:* 520-206-4640. *Fax:* 520-206-4790. *E-mail:* mtulino@pima.edu. *Web site:* http://www.pima.edu/.

Pima Medical Institute

Mesa, Arizona

- **Proprietary** 2-year
- **Urban** campus
- **Coed**

Majors Health/health-care administration; veterinary/animal health technology.

Academics *Special study options:* cooperative education, distance learning, internships.

Student Life *Housing:* college housing not available.

Standardized Tests *Required:* Wonderlic Scholastic Level Exam (for admission).

Applying *Required:* high school transcript, interview.

Freshman Application Contact Pima Medical Institute, 2160 S. Power Road, Mesa, AZ 85209. *Phone:* 480-898-9898. *Web site:* http://www.pmi.edu/.

Pima Medical Institute

Mesa, Arizona

- **Proprietary** primarily 2-year, founded 1985, part of Vocational Training Institutes, Inc.
- **Urban** campus
- **Coed,** 958 undergraduate students

Majors Health/health-care administration; occupational therapist assistant; physical therapy technology; radiologic technology/science; registered nursing/registered nurse; respiratory therapy technician.

Academics *Calendar:* modular. *Degrees:* certificates, associate, and bachelor's. *Special study options:* distance learning.

Library E-Global.

Student Life *Housing:* college housing not available.

Standardized Tests *Required:* Wonderlic aptitude test (for admission).

Applying *Required:* interview. *Required for some:* high school transcript.

Freshman Application Contact Admissions Office, Pima Medical Institute, 957 South Dobson Road, Mesa, AZ 85202. *Phone:* 480-644-0267 Ext. 225. *Toll-free phone:* 888-898-9048. *Web site:* http://www.pmi.edu/.

Pima Medical Institute

Tucson, Arizona

- **Proprietary** primarily 2-year, founded 1972, part of Vocational Training Institutes, Inc.
- **Urban** campus
- **Coed,** 900 undergraduate students

Majors Health/health-care administration; occupational therapist assistant; physical therapy technology; radiologic technology/science; registered nursing/registered nurse; respiratory therapy technician; veterinary/animal health technology.

Academics *Calendar:* modular. *Degrees:* certificates, associate, and bachelor's. *Special study options:* academic remediation for entering students, accelerated degree program, adult/continuing education programs, cooperative education, distance learning, internships.

Library E-Global with an OPAC, a Web page.

Student Life *Housing:* college housing not available.

Standardized Tests *Required:* Wonderlic Scholastic Level Exam (for admission).

Applying *Options:* early admission. *Required:* interview. *Required for some:* high school transcript.

Freshman Application Contact Admissions Office, Pima Medical Institute, 3350 East Grant Road, Tucson, AZ 85716. *Phone:* 520-326-1600 Ext. 5112. *Toll-free phone:* 888-898-9048. *Web site:* http://www.pmi.edu/.

The Refrigeration School

Phoenix, Arizona

Freshman Application Contact Ms. Heather Haskell, The Refrigeration School, 4210 East Washington Street. *Phone:* 602-275-7133. *Toll-free phone:* 800-993-8999. *Fax:* 602-267-4811. *E-mail:* heather@rsiaz.edu. *Web site:* http://www.refrigerationschool.com/.

Rio Salado College

Tempe, Arizona

- **State and locally supported** 2-year, founded 1978, part of Maricopa County Community College District System
- **Urban** campus
- **Coed**

Undergraduates Students come from 44 states and territories; 38 other countries; 4% are from out of state.

Faculty *Student/faculty ratio:* 25:1.

Academics *Calendar:* semesters. *Degree:* certificates and associate. *Special study options:* academic remediation for entering students, accelerated degree program, adult/continuing education programs, advanced placement credit, cooperative education, distance learning, double majors, English as a second language, external degree program, honors programs, independent study, internships, part-time degree program, services for LD students, summer session for credit.

Student Life *Campus security:* 24-hour emergency response devices, late-night transport/escort service.

Costs (2010–11) *Tuition:* area resident $1704 full-time, $71 per credit hour part-time; state resident $7488 full-time, $312 per credit hour part-time; nonresident $7488 full-time, $312 per credit hour part-time. Full-time tuition and fees vary according to course load, program, and reciprocity agreements. Part-time tuition and fees vary according to course load and reciprocity agreements. *Required fees:* $30 full-time. *Payment plans:* installment, deferred payment.

Applying *Options:* electronic application, early admission, deferred entrance.

Freshman Application Contact Laurel Redman, Director, Instruction Support Services and Student Development, Rio Salado College, 2323 West 14th Street, Tempe 85281. *Phone:* 480-517-8563. *Toll-free phone:* 800-729-1197. *Fax:* 480-517-8199. *E-mail:* admission@riomail.maricopa.edu. *Web site:* http://www.rio.maricopa.edu/.

Scottsdale Community College

Scottsdale, Arizona

- **State and locally supported** 2-year, founded 1969, part of Maricopa County Community College District System
- **Urban** 160-acre campus with easy access to Phoenix
- **Coed**, 11,257 undergraduate students

Undergraduates Students come from 53 states and territories; 74 other countries; 3% are from out of state; 4% Black or African American, non-Hispanic/Latino; 13% Hispanic/Latino; 2% Asian, non-Hispanic/Latino; 0.2% Native Hawaiian or other Pacific Islander, non-Hispanic/Latino; 4% American Indian or Alaska Native, non-Hispanic/Latino; 1% Two or more races, non-Hispanic/Latino; 7% Race/ethnicity unknown; 1% international.

Faculty *Total:* 689, 23% full-time, 13% with terminal degrees. *Student/faculty ratio:* 18:1.

Majors Accounting; administrative assistant and secretarial science; business administration and management; criminal justice/law enforcement administration; culinary arts; dramatic/theater arts; electrical, electronic and communications engineering technology; emergency medical technology (EMT paramedic); environmental design/architecture; equestrian studies; fashion merchandising; finance; fire science/firefighting; hospitality administration; hotel/motel administration; information science/studies; interior design; kindergarten/preschool education; mathematics; medical administrative assistant and medical secretary; photography; public administration; real estate; registered nursing/registered nurse; special products marketing.

Academics *Calendar:* semesters. *Degree:* certificates, diplomas, and associate. *Special study options:* academic remediation for entering students, adult/continuing education programs, advanced placement credit, cooperative education, English as a second language, honors programs, internships, off-campus study, part-time degree program, services for LD students, study abroad, summer session for credit.

Library Scottsdale Community College Library with an OPAC, a Web page.

Student Life *Housing:* college housing not available. *Activities and Organizations:* drama/theater group, student-run newspaper, radio station, choral group, Student Leadership Forum, International Community Club, Phi Theta Kappa, Music Industry Club, SCC ASID-Interior Design group. *Campus security:* 24-hour emergency response devices and patrols, student patrols, late-night transport/escort service, 24-hour automatic surveillance cameras. *Student services:* personal/psychological counseling.

Athletics Member NCAA, NJCAA. All NCAA Division II. *Intercollegiate sports:* baseball M, basketball M/W, cross-country running M/W, football M, golf M/W, soccer M/W, softball W, tennis M/W, track and field M/W, volleyball W. *Intramural sports:* archery M/W, badminton M/W, basketball M/W, racquetball M/W, track and field M/W, volleyball M/W.

Costs (2011–12) *Tuition:* area resident $2130 full-time; state resident $9360 full-time; nonresident $9360 full-time. *Required fees:* $30 full-time. *Payment plan:* deferred payment. *Waivers:* employees or children of employees.

Financial Aid Of all full-time matriculated undergraduates who enrolled in 2009, 75 Federal Work-Study jobs (averaging $2000). *Financial aid deadline:* 7/15.

Applying *Options:* electronic application, early admission. *Application deadline:* rolling (freshmen). *Notification:* continuous (freshmen).

Freshman Application Contact Ms. Fran Watkins, Director of Admissions and Records, Scottsdale Community College, 9000 East Chaparral Road, Scottsdale, AZ 85256. *Phone:* 480-423-6133. *Fax:* 480-423-6200. *E-mail:* fran.watkins@sccmail.maricopa.edu. *Web site:* http://www.scottsdalecc.edu/.

Scottsdale Culinary Institute

Scottsdale, Arizona

Director of Admissions Scottsdale Culinary Institute, 8100 East Camelback Road, Suite 1001, Scottsdale, AZ 85251-3940. *Toll-free phone:* 800-848-2433. *Web site:* http://www.scichefs.com/.

Sessions College for Professional Design

Tempe, Arizona

Freshman Application Contact Admissions, Sessions College for Professional Design, 398 South Mlll Avenue, Suite 300, Tempe, AZ 85281. *Phone:* 480-212-1704. *Toll-free phone:* 800-258-4115. *E-mail:* admissions@sessions.edu. *Web site:* http://www.sessions.edu/.

South Mountain Community College

Phoenix, Arizona

Director of Admissions Dean of Enrollment Services, South Mountain Community College, 7050 South Twenty-fourth Street, Phoenix, AZ 85040. *Phone:* 602-243-8120. *Web site:* http://www.southmountaincc.edu/.

Southwest Institute of Healing Arts

Tempe, Arizona

Director of Admissions Katie Yearous, Student Advisor, Southwest Institute of Healing Arts, 1100 East Apache Boulevard, Tempe, AZ 85281. *Phone:* 480-994-9244. *Toll-free phone:* 888-504-9106. *E-mail:* joannl@swiha.net. *Web site:* http://www.swiha.org/.

Tohono O'odham Community College

Sells, Arizona

- **Public** 2-year, founded 1998
- **Rural** 10-acre campus
- **Endowment** $138,720
- **Coed**

Undergraduates 25 full-time, 229 part-time. Students come from 1 other state. *Retention:* 100% of full-time freshmen returned.

Faculty *Student/faculty ratio:* 4:1.

Academics *Calendar:* semesters. *Degree:* certificates, diplomas, and associate. *Special study options:* academic remediation for entering students, adult/continuing education programs, cooperative education, distance learning, double majors, part-time degree program, services for LD students, summer session for credit.

Costs (2010–11) *Tuition:* state resident $1008 full-time, $42 per credit hour part-time; nonresident $5064 full-time, $72 per credit hour part-time. Full-time tuition and fees vary according to course load. Part-time tuition and fees vary according to course load.

Applying *Application fee:* $25. *Required:* high school transcript.

Freshman Application Contact Admissions, Tohono O'odham Community College, PO Box 3129, Sells, AZ 85634. *Phone:* 520-383-8401. *E-mail:* info@tocc.cc.az.us. *Web site:* http://www.tocc.cc.az.us/.

Universal Technical Institute

Avondale, Arizona

Freshman Application Contact Director of Admission, Universal Technical Institute, 10695 West Pierce Street, Avondale, AZ 85323. *Phone:* 623-245-4600. *Toll-free phone:* 800-859-1202. *Fax:* 623-245-4601. *Web site:* http://www.uti.edu/.

Yavapai College

Prescott, Arizona

- **State and locally supported** 2-year, founded 1966, part of Arizona State Community College System
- **Small-town** 100-acre campus
- **Coed**, 8,276 undergraduate students, 23% full-time, 59% women, 41% men

Undergraduates 1,917 full-time, 6,359 part-time. Students come from 30 states and territories; 18% are from out of state; 5% live on campus.

Freshmen *Admission:* 1,098 enrolled.

Faculty *Total:* 404, 28% full-time. *Student/faculty ratio:* 15:1.

Majors Accounting; administrative assistant and secretarial science; agribusiness; agricultural business and management; agriculture; aquaculture; architectural drafting and CAD/CADD; automobile/automotive mechanics technology; business administration and management; commercial and advertising art; construction engineering technology; criminal justice/police science; education related; equestrian studies; film/cinema/video studies; fine arts related; fire science/firefighting; graphic design; gunsmithing; horse husbandry/equine science and management; information science/studies; legal administrative assistant/secretary; legal assistant/paralegal; liberal arts and sciences/liberal studies; registered nursing/registered nurse.

Academics *Calendar:* semesters. *Degree:* certificates and associate. *Special study options:* academic remediation for entering students, adult/continuing education programs, advanced placement credit, cooperative education, distance learning, English as a second language, honors programs, independent study, internships, off-campus study, part-time degree program, services for LD students, summer session for credit. *ROTC:* Army (c), Air Force (c).

Library Yavapai College Library with 81,144 titles, 1,091 serial subscriptions, an OPAC, a Web page.

Student Life *Housing Options:* coed. Campus housing is university owned. *Activities and Organizations:* drama/theater group, student-run newspaper, choral group, Re-Entry Club, Student Nurses Association, Native American Club, International Club, VICA (Vocational Industrial Clubs of America). *Campus security:* 24-hour emergency response devices and patrols, student patrols, late-night transport/escort service, controlled dormitory access. *Student services:* health clinic, personal/psychological counseling, women's center.

Athletics Member NJCAA. *Intercollegiate sports:* baseball M(s), soccer M(s), softball W(s), volleyball W(s).

Costs (2011–12) *Tuition:* state resident $1488 full-time; nonresident $8158 full-time. *Room and board:* $5020.

Financial Aid Of all full-time matriculated undergraduates who enrolled in 2009, 100 Federal Work-Study jobs (averaging $2000).

Applying *Options:* early admission, deferred entrance. *Required:* high school transcript. *Required for some:* essay or personal statement. *Application deadlines:* rolling (freshmen), rolling (transfers).

Freshman Application Contact Mrs. Sheila Jarrell, Admissions, Registration, and Records Manager, Yavapai College, 1100 East Sheldon Street, Prescott, AZ 86301-3297. *Phone:* 928-776-2107. *Toll-free phone:* 800-922-6787. *Fax:* 928-776-2151. *E-mail:* registration@yc.edu. *Web site:* http://www.yc.edu/.

ARKANSAS

Arkansas Northeastern College

Blytheville, Arkansas

Freshman Application Contact Mrs. Leslie Wells, Admissions Counselor, Arkansas Northeastern College, PO Box 1109, Blytheville, AR 72316. *Phone:* 870-762-1020 Ext. 1118. *Fax:* 870-763-1654. *E-mail:* lwells@anc.edu. *Web site:* http://www.anc.edu/.

Arkansas State University–Beebe

Beebe, Arkansas

- **State-supported** 2-year, founded 1927, part of Arkansas State University System
- **Small-town** 320-acre campus with easy access to Memphis
- **Coed**

Undergraduates 2,601 full-time, 1,890 part-time. Students come from 20 states and territories; 1% are from out of state; 6% transferred in; 12% live on campus. *Retention:* 64% of full-time freshmen returned.

Faculty *Student/faculty ratio:* 30:1.

Academics *Calendar:* semesters. *Degree:* certificates and associate. *Special study options:* academic remediation for entering students, adult/continuing education programs, advanced placement credit, distance learning, honors programs, part-time degree program, summer session for credit. *ROTC:* Army (b).

Student Life *Campus security:* 24-hour emergency response devices and patrols.

Costs (2010–11) *Tuition:* state resident $2136 full-time; nonresident $3480 full-time. Full-time tuition and fees vary according to course load. Part-time tuition and fees vary according to course load. *Room and board:* $3144.

Financial Aid Of all full-time matriculated undergraduates who enrolled in 2009, 16 Federal Work-Study jobs (averaging $1800). 112 state and other part-time jobs (averaging $750).

Applying *Options:* electronic application, deferred entrance. *Required:* high school transcript.

Freshman Application Contact Mr. Ronald Hudson, Coordinator of Student Recruitment, Arkansas State University–Beebe, PO Box 1000, Beebe, AR 72012. *Phone:* 501-882-8860. *Toll-free phone:* 800-632-9985. *E-mail:* rdhudson@asub.edu. *Web site:* http://www.asub.edu/.

Arkansas State University–Mountain Home

Mountain Home, Arkansas

- **State-supported** 2-year, founded 2000, part of Arkansas State University System
- **Small-town** 136-acre campus
- **Endowment** $3.3 million
- **Coed,** 1,583 undergraduate students, 64% full-time, 63% women, 37% men

Undergraduates 1,021 full-time, 562 part-time. Students come from 19 states and territories; 7% are from out of state; 7% transferred in. *Retention:* 65% of full-time freshmen returned.

Freshmen *Admission:* 601 applied, 389 admitted, 252 enrolled. *Average high school GPA:* 2.79.

Faculty *Total:* 80, 60% full-time, 19% with terminal degrees. *Student/faculty ratio:* 20:1.

Majors Administrative assistant and secretarial science; business/commerce; criminal justice/law enforcement administration; emergency medical technology (EMT paramedic); forensic science and technology; funeral service and mortuary science; information science/studies; liberal arts and sciences/liberal studies; middle school education; respiratory care therapy.

Academics *Calendar:* semesters. *Degree:* certificates and associate. *Special study options:* academic remediation for entering students, advanced placement credit, cooperative education, distance learning, independent study, part-time degree program, services for LD students, summer session for credit. *ROTC:* Army (b).

Library Norma Wood Library with 33,573 titles, 15,360 serial subscriptions, 2,212 audiovisual materials, an OPAC, a Web page.

Student Life *Housing:* college housing not available. *Activities and Organizations:* Phi Theta Kappa, Circle K, Criminal Justice Club, Mortuary Science Club, Student Ambassadors. *Campus security:* during operation hours security is present and available as needed.

Standardized Tests *Recommended:* SAT or ACT (for admission), COMPASS, ASSET.

Costs (2010–11) *Tuition:* state resident $2400 full-time, $80 per credit hour part-time; nonresident $4050 full-time, $135 per credit hour part-time. Full-time tuition and fees vary according to course load. Part-time tuition and fees vary according to course load. *Required fees:* $510 full-time, $17 per credit hour part-time. *Payment plan:* installment. *Waivers:* children of alumni, senior citizens, and employees or children of employees.

Applying *Options:* electronic application. *Required:* high school transcript. *Recommended:* placement scores, GED scores accepted. *Notification:* continuous (freshmen).

Freshman Application Contact Ms. Delba PArrish, Admissions Coordinator, Arkansas State University–Mountain Home, 1600 South College Street, Mountain Home, AR 72653. *Phone:* 870-508-6180. *Fax:* 870-508-6287. *E-mail:* dparrish@asumh.edu. *Web site:* http://www.asumh.edu/.

Arkansas State University–Newport

Newport, Arkansas

Director of Admissions Robert Summers, Director of Admissions/Registrar, Arkansas State University–Newport, 7648 Victory Boulevard, Newport, AR 72112. *Phone:* 870-512-7800. *Toll-free phone:* 800-976-1676. *Fax:* 870-512-7825. *E-mail:* robert.summers@asun.edu. *Web site:* http://www.asun.edu/.

Black River Technical College

Pocahontas, Arkansas

Director of Admissions Director of Admissions, Black River Technical College, 1410 Highway 304 East, Pocahontas, AR 72455. *Phone:* 870-892-4565. *Toll-free phone:* 800-919-3086. *Web site:* http://www.blackrivertech.edu/.

Cossatot Community College of the University of Arkansas

De Queen, Arkansas

- **State-supported** 2-year, founded 1991, part of University of Arkansas System
- **Rural** 30-acre campus
- **Endowment** $108,167
- **Coed**

Undergraduates Students come from 4 states and territories; 2% are from out of state.

Faculty *Student/faculty ratio:* 12:1.

Academics *Calendar:* semesters. *Degree:* certificates and associate. *Special study options:* academic remediation for entering students, accelerated degree program, adult/continuing education programs, advanced placement credit, cooperative education, distance learning, double majors, independent study, internships, off-campus study, part-time degree program, services for LD students, summer session for credit.

Costs (2010–11) *Tuition:* area resident $1500 full-time, $50 per credit hour part-time; state resident $1800 full-time, $60 per credit hour part-time; nonresident $4500 full-time, $150 per credit hour part-time. Full-time tuition and fees vary according to course load and program. Part-time tuition and fees vary according to course load and program. *Required fees:* $280 full-time, $5 per credit hour part-time, $65 per term part-time.

Financial Aid Of all full-time matriculated undergraduates who enrolled in 2009, 14 Federal Work-Study jobs (averaging $2700).

Applying *Options:* electronic application. *Recommended:* high school transcript.

Freshman Application Contact Cossatot Community College of the University of Arkansas, DeQueen, AR 71832. *Phone:* 870-584-4471. *Toll-free phone:* 800-844-4471. *Web site:* http://www.cccua.edu/.

Crowley's Ridge College

Paragould, Arkansas

Freshman Application Contact Amanda Drake, Director of Admissions, Crowley's Ridge College, 100 College Drive, Paragould, AR 72450-9731. *Phone:* 870-236-6901. *Toll-free phone:* 800-264-1096. *Fax:* 870-236-7748. *E-mail:* njoneshi@crc.pioneer.paragould.ar.us. *Web site:* http://www.crc.edu/.

East Arkansas Community College

Forrest City, Arkansas

Freshman Application Contact Ms. DeAnna Adams, Director of Enrollment Management/Institutional Research, East Arkansas Community College, 1700 Newcastle Road, Forrest City, AR 72335-2204. *Phone:* 870-633-4480. *Toll-free phone:* 877-797-3222. *Fax:* 870-633-3840. *E-mail:* dadams@eacc.edu. *Web site:* http://www.eacc.edu/.

ITT Technical Institute

Little Rock, Arkansas

- **Proprietary** primarily 2-year, founded 1993, part of ITT Educational Services, Inc.
- **Urban** campus
- **Coed**

Majors CAD/CADD drafting/design technology; computer and information systems security; computer engineering technology; computer software engineering; computer software technology; construction management; criminal justice/law enforcement administration; design and visual communications; electrical, electronic and communications engineering technology; game and interactive media design; legal assistant/paralegal; project management; system, networking, and LAN/WAN management.

Academics *Calendar:* quarters. *Degrees:* associate and bachelor's.

Student Life *Housing:* college housing not available.

Freshman Application Contact Director of Recruitment, ITT Technical Institute, 4520 South University Avenue, Little Rock, AR 72204. *Phone:* 501-565-5550. *Toll-free phone:* 800-359-4429. *Web site:* http://www.itt-tech.edu/.

Mid-South Community College

West Memphis, Arkansas

Freshman Application Contact Jeremy Reece, Director of Admissions, Mid-South Community College, 2000 West Broadway, West Memphis, AR 72301. *Phone:* 870-733-6786. *Fax:* 870-733-6719. *E-mail:* jreece@midsouthcc.edu. *Web site:* http://www.midsouthcc.edu/.

National Park Community College

Hot Springs, Arkansas

Director of Admissions Dr. Allen B. Moody, Director of Institutional Services/Registrar, National Park Community College, 101 College Drive, Hot Springs, AR 71913. *Phone:* 501-760-4222. *Toll-free phone:* 800-760-1825. *E-mail:* bmoody@npcc.edu. *Web site:* http://www.npcc.edu/.

North Arkansas College

Harrison, Arkansas

- **State and locally supported** 2-year, founded 1974
- **Small-town** 40-acre campus
- **Coed**
- 100% of applicants were admitted

Undergraduates 1,491 full-time, 938 part-time. Students come from 1 other country; 2% are from out of state; 10% transferred in. *Retention:* 50% of full-time freshmen returned.

Faculty *Student/faculty ratio:* 19:1.

Academics *Calendar:* semesters. *Degree:* certificates and associate. *Special study options:* academic remediation for entering students, adult/continuing education programs, advanced placement credit, distance learning, freshman honors college, honors programs, independent study, internships, part-time degree program, services for LD students, summer session for credit.

Student Life *Campus security:* 24-hour emergency response devices.

Athletics Member NJCAA.

Costs (2010–11) *Tuition:* area resident $1770 full-time, $59 per credit hour part-time; state resident $2430 full-time, $81 per credit hour part-time; nonresident $4560 full-time, $152 per credit hour part-time. Full-time tuition and fees vary according to course load. Part-time tuition and fees vary according to course load. *Required fees:* $150 full-time, $5 per credit hour part-time.

Applying *Options:* deferred entrance. *Required for some:* high school transcript.

Freshman Application Contact Mrs. Charla Jennings, Director of Admissions, North Arkansas College, 1515 Pioneer Drive, Harrison, AR 72601. *Phone:* 870-391-3221. *Toll-free phone:* 800-679-6622. *Fax:* 870-391-3339. *E-mail:* charlam@northark.edu. *Web site:* http://www.northark.edu/.

NorthWest Arkansas Community College

Bentonville, Arkansas

- **State and locally supported** 2-year, founded 1989
- **Urban** 77-acre campus
- **Coed**
- 100% of applicants were admitted

Undergraduates 3,034 full-time, 4,972 part-time. Students come from 21 states and territories; 2% are from out of state; 13% transferred in. *Retention:* 57% of full-time freshmen returned.

Faculty *Student/faculty ratio:* 20:1.

Academics *Calendar:* semesters. *Degree:* certificates and associate. *Special study options:* academic remediation for entering students, accelerated degree program, adult/continuing education programs, advanced placement credit, cooperative education, distance learning, double majors, English as a second language, honors programs, independent study, internships, part-time degree program, services for LD students, student-designed majors, summer session for credit. *ROTC:* Army (c), Air Force (c).

Student Life *Campus security:* 24-hour emergency response devices and patrols.

Costs (2010–11) *Tuition:* area resident $2100 full-time, $70 per credit hour part-time; state resident $3300 full-time, $110 per credit hour part-time; nonresident $4650 full-time, $155 per credit hour part-time. *Required fees:* $512 full-time, $14 per credit hour part-time, $50 per term part-time.

Applying *Options:* electronic application. *Application fee:* $10. *Required:* high school transcript.

Freshman Application Contact NorthWest Arkansas Community College, One College Drive, Bentonville, AR 72712. *Phone:* 479-636-9222. *Toll-free phone:* 800-995-6922. *Fax:* 479-619-4116. *E-mail:* admissions@nwacc.edu. *Web site:* http://www.nwacc.edu/.

Ouachita Technical College

Malvern, Arkansas

- **State-supported** 2-year, founded 1972
- **Small-town** 11-acre campus
- **Coed**

Undergraduates 605 full-time, 1,005 part-time.

Faculty *Student/faculty ratio:* 16:1.

Academics *Calendar:* semesters. *Degree:* certificates and associate. *Special study options:* academic remediation for entering students, accelerated degree program, advanced placement credit, cooperative education, distance learning, double majors, independent study, internships, part-time degree program, services for LD students, summer session for credit.

Student Life *Campus security:* 24-hour patrols.

Standardized Tests *Recommended:* SAT or ACT (for admission), ACT COMPASS or ASSET.

Costs (2010–11) *Tuition:* state resident $1800 full-time, $60 per credit hour part-time; nonresident $3600 full-time, $120 per credit hour part-time. Full-time tuition and fees vary according to program. Part-time tuition and fees vary according to program. No tuition increase for student's term of enrollment. *Required fees:* $450 full-time, $15 per credit hour part-time.
Financial Aid Of all full-time matriculated undergraduates who enrolled in 2009, 18 Federal Work-Study jobs (averaging $2400).
Applying *Options:* electronic application, early admission, deferred entrance. *Required:* high school transcript.
Freshman Application Contact Kathy Lazenby, Counselor, Ouachita Technical College, One College Circle, Malvern, AR 72104. *Phone:* 501-337-5000 Ext. 1103. *Toll-free phone:* 800-337-0266. *Fax:* 501-337-9382. *E-mail:* vkesterson@otcweb.edu. *Web site:* http://www.otcweb.edu/.

Ozarka College
Melbourne, Arkansas

Freshman Application Contact Ms. Zeda Wilkerson, Director of Admissions, Ozarka College, PO Box 10, Melbourne, AR 72556. *Phone:* 870-368-7371 Ext. 2028. *Toll-free phone:* 800-821-4335. *E-mail:* zwilkerson@ozarka.edu. *Web site:* http://www.ozarka.edu/.

Phillips Community College of the University of Arkansas
Helena, Arkansas

Director of Admissions Mr. Lynn Boone, Registrar, Phillips Community College of the University of Arkansas, PO Box 785, Helena, AR 72342-0785. *Phone:* 870-338-6474. *Web site:* http://www.pccua.edu/.

Pulaski Technical College
North Little Rock, Arkansas

- **State-supported** 2-year, founded 1945
- **Urban** 40-acre campus with easy access to Little Rock
- **Coed**

Undergraduates 4,856 full-time, 5,399 part-time. Students come from 5 states and territories; 1% are from out of state; 6% transferred in.
Faculty *Student/faculty ratio:* 25:1.
Academics *Calendar:* semesters. *Degree:* certificates and associate. *Special study options:* academic remediation for entering students, advanced placement credit, distance learning, part-time degree program, services for LD students, summer session for credit.
Student Life *Campus security:* certified law enforcement personnel 7 am to 11 pm.
Costs (2010–11) *Tuition:* state resident $1968 full-time, $82 per credit hour part-time; nonresident $3240 full-time, $135 per credit hour part-time. Full-time tuition and fees vary according to course load. *Required fees:* $290 full-time, $10 per credit hour part-time, $25 per term part-time.
Applying *Options:* electronic application. *Required:* high school transcript.
Freshman Application Contact Mr. Clark Atkins, Director of Admissions, Pulaski Technical College, 3000 West Scenic Drive, North Little Rock, AR 72118. *Phone:* 501-812-2734. *Fax:* 501-812-2316. *E-mail:* catkins@pulaskitech.edu. *Web site:* http://www.pulaskitech.edu/.

Remington College–Little Rock Campus
Little Rock, Arkansas

Director of Admissions Brian Maggio, Director of·Recruitment, Remington College–Little Rock Campus, 19 Remington Drive, Little Rock, AR 72204. *Phone:* 501-312-0007. *Fax:* 501-225-3819. *E-mail:* brian.maggio@remingtoncollege.edu. *Web site:* http://www.remingtoncollege.edu/.

Rich Mountain Community College
Mena, Arkansas

Director of Admissions Dr. Steve Rook, Dean of Students, Rich Mountain Community College, 1100 College Drive, Mena, AR 71953. *Phone:* 479-394-7622 Ext. 1400. *Web site:* http://www.rmcc.edu/.

South Arkansas Community College
El Dorado, Arkansas

Freshman Application Contact Mr. Dean Inman, Director of Enrollment Services, South Arkansas Community College, PO Box 7010, El Dorado, AR 71731-7010. *Phone:* 870-864-7142. *Toll-free phone:* 800-955-2289 Ext. 142.

Fax: 870-864-7109. *E-mail:* dinman@southark.edu. *Web site:* http://www.southark.edu/.

Southeast Arkansas College
Pine Bluff, Arkansas

Freshman Application Contact Ms. Barbara Dunn, Coordinator of Admissions and Enrollment Management, Southeast Arkansas College, 1900 Hazel Street, Pine Bluff, AR 71603. *Phone:* 870-543-5957. *Toll-free phone:* 888-SEARK TC. *Fax:* 870-543-5956. *E-mail:* bdunn@seark.edu. *Web site:* http://www.seark.edu/.

Southern Arkansas University Tech
Camden, Arkansas

Freshman Application Contact Mrs. Beverly Ellis, Admissions Analyst, Southern Arkansas University Tech, PO Box 3499, Camden, AR 71711-1599. *Phone:* 870-574-4558. *Fax:* 870-574-4478. *E-mail:* bellis@sautech.edu. *Web site:* http://www.sautech.edu/.

University of Arkansas Community College at Batesville
Batesville, Arkansas

Freshman Application Contact Ms. Sharon Gage, Admissions Coordinator, University of Arkansas Community College at Batesville, PO Box 3350, Batesville, AR 72503. *Phone:* 870-612-2042. *Toll-free phone:* 800-508-7878. *Fax:* 870-612-2129. *E-mail:* sgage@uaccb.edu. *Web site:* http://www.uaccb.edu/.

University of Arkansas Community College at Hope
Hope, Arkansas

Freshman Application Contact University of Arkansas Community College at Hope, PO Box 140, Hope, AR 71802. *Phone:* 870-772-8174. *Web site:* http://www.uacch.edu/.

University of Arkansas Community College at Morrilton
Morrilton, Arkansas

- **State-supported** 2-year, founded 1961, part of University of Arkansas System
- **Rural** 70-acre campus
- **Coed,** 2,462 undergraduate students, 65% full-time, 61% women, 39% men

Undergraduates 1,590 full-time, 872 part-time. Students come from 2 states and territories; 8% Black or African American, non-Hispanic/Latino; 4% Hispanic/Latino; 0.4% Asian, non-Hispanic/Latino; 0.5% American Indian or Alaska Native, non-Hispanic/Latino; 4% Two or more races, non-Hispanic/Latino; 9% transferred in.
Freshmen *Admission:* 1,610 applied, 1,040 admitted, 694 enrolled. *Average high school GPA:* 2.83. *Test scores:* ACT scores over 18: 72%; ACT scores over 24: 17%.
Faculty *Total:* 118, 58% full-time, 6% with terminal degrees. *Student/faculty ratio:* 19:1.
Majors Autobody/collision and repair technology; automobile/automotive mechanics technology; business/commerce; child development; commercial and advertising art; computer technology/computer systems technology; criminal justice/law enforcement administration; drafting and design technology; education (multiple levels); forensic science and technology; general studies; heating, air conditioning, ventilation and refrigeration maintenance technology; liberal arts and sciences/liberal studies; petroleum technology; registered nursing/registered nurse; surveying technology.
Academics *Calendar:* semesters. *Degree:* certificates and associate. *Special study options:* academic remediation for entering students, advanced placement credit, distance learning, double majors, internships, part-time degree program, services for LD students, summer session for credit.
Library E. Allen Gordon Library with 18,820 titles, 73 serial subscriptions, 1,681 audiovisual materials, an OPAC, a Web page.
Student Life *Housing:* college housing not available. *Activities and Organizations:* drama/theater group, choral group, Student Government Association, Phi Beta Lambda, Student Practical Nurses Organization, Computer Information Systems Club, Early Childhood Development Organization. *Campus*

security: 24-hour emergency response devices, campus alert system. *Student services:* personal/psychological counseling.

Athletics Member NJCAA. *Intramural sports:* basketball M/W, football M/W, table tennis M/W, ultimate Frisbee M/W, volleyball M/W.

Costs (2010–11) *Tuition:* area resident $2190 full-time, $73 per credit hour part-time; state resident $2400 full-time, $80 per credit hour part-time; nonresident $3510 full-time, $117 per credit hour part-time. Full-time tuition and fees vary according to course load and program. Part-time tuition and fees vary according to course load and program. *Required fees:* $630 full-time, $20 per credit hour part-time, $15 per term part-time. *Payment plan:* installment. *Waivers:* senior citizens and employees or children of employees.

Financial Aid Of all full-time matriculated undergraduates who enrolled in 2009, 1,335 applied for aid, 1,172 were judged to have need, 150 had their need fully met. 22 Federal Work-Study jobs (averaging $2119). In 2009, 94 non-need-based awards were made. *Average percent of need met:* 54%. *Average financial aid package:* $4419. *Average need-based loan:* $1759. *Average need-based gift aid:* $4034. *Average non-need-based aid:* $2016. *Financial aid deadline:* 7/1.

Applying *Options:* electronic application, early admission, deferred entrance. *Required:* high school transcript. *Required for some:* immunization records and prior college transcript(s). *Application deadlines:* rolling (freshmen), rolling (transfers). *Notification:* continuous (freshmen), continuous (transfers).

Freshman Application Contact Ms. Rachel Mullins, Coordinator of Recruitment, University of Arkansas Community College at Morrilton, 1537 University Boulevard, Morrilton, AR 72110. *Phone:* 501-977-2174. *Toll-free phone:* 800-264-1094. *Fax:* 501-977-2123. *E-mail:* mullins@uaccm.edu. *Web site:* http://www.uaccm.edu/.

CALIFORNIA

Academy of Couture Art

West Hollywood, California

Admissions Office Contact Academy of Couture Art, Pacific Design Center, 8687 Melrose Avenue, Suite G520, West Hollywood, CA 90069. *Web site:* http://www.academyofcoutureart.com/.

Allan Hancock College

Santa Maria, California

- **State and locally supported** 2-year, founded 1920
- **Small-town** 120-acre campus
- **Endowment** $1.1 million
- **Coed**

Undergraduates 2,996 full-time, 7,391 part-time. Students come from 27 states and territories; 12 other countries.

Faculty *Student/faculty ratio:* 17:1.

Academics *Calendar:* semesters. *Degree:* certificates and associate. *Special study options:* adult/continuing education programs, advanced placement credit, cooperative education, distance learning, English as a second language, part-time degree program, services for LD students, study abroad, summer session for credit.

Student Life *Campus security:* 24-hour emergency response devices and patrols, student patrols, late-night transport/escort service.

Costs (2010–11) *Tuition:* state resident $0 full-time; nonresident $5700 full-time, $190 per unit part-time. Full-time tuition and fees vary according to course load. Part-time tuition and fees vary according to course load. *Required fees:* $846 full-time, $27 per unit part-time, $18 per term part-time.

Financial Aid Of all full-time matriculated undergraduates who enrolled in 2009, 250 Federal Work-Study jobs (averaging $3000).

Applying *Options:* electronic application.

Freshman Application Contact Ms. Adela Esquivel Swinson, Director of Admissions and Records, Allan Hancock College, 800 South College Drive, Santa Maria, CA 93454-6399. *Phone:* 805-922-6966 Ext. 3272. *Toll-free phone:* 866-342-5242. *Fax:* 805-922-3477. *Web site:* http://www.hancockcollege.edu/.

American Academy of Dramatic Arts

Hollywood, California

- **Independent** 2-year, founded 1974
- **Suburban** 4-acre campus with easy access to Los Angeles
- **Endowment** $1.7 million
- **Coed,** 188 undergraduate students, 100% full-time, 56% women, 44% men

Undergraduates 188 full-time. Students come from 37 states and territories; 15 other countries; 59% are from out of state; 7% Black or African American, non-Hispanic/Latino; 11% Hispanic/Latino; 2% Asian, non-Hispanic/Latino; 0.5% American Indian or Alaska Native, non-Hispanic/Latino; 9% Two or more races, non-Hispanic/Latino; 5% Race/ethnicity unknown; 20% international.

Freshmen *Admission:* 419 applied, 91 admitted, 91 enrolled.

Faculty *Total:* 41, 22% full-time. *Student/faculty ratio:* 12:1.

Majors Dramatic/theater arts.

Academics *Calendar:* continuous. *Degree:* certificates, diplomas, and associate. *Special study options:* internships.

Library Bryn Morgan Library with 12,500 titles, 6 serial subscriptions, 1,500 audiovisual materials.

Student Life *Housing:* college housing not available. *Campus security:* 24-hour emergency response devices, 8-hour patrols by trained security personnel.

Costs (2011–12) *Tuition:* $29,900 full-time. *Required fees:* $600 full-time. *Payment plan:* installment.

Financial Aid Of all full-time matriculated undergraduates who enrolled in 2009, 15 Federal Work-Study jobs (averaging $2000).

Applying *Options:* deferred entrance. *Application fee:* $50. *Required:* essay or personal statement, high school transcript, 2 letters of recommendation, interview, audition. *Recommended:* minimum 2.0 GPA. *Application deadlines:* rolling (freshmen), rolling (transfers). *Notification:* continuous (freshmen), continuous (transfers).

Freshman Application Contact American Academy of Dramatic Arts, 1336 North La Brea Avenue, Hollywood, CA 90028. *Phone:* 323-464-2777. *Toll-free phone:* 800-222-2867. *Web site:* http://www.aada.org/.

American Career College

Anaheim, California

Director of Admissions Susan Pailet, Senior Executive Director of Admission, American Career College, 1200 North Magnolia Avenue, Anaheim, CA 92801. *Phone:* 714-952-9066. *Toll-free phone:* 888-844-6522. *E-mail:* info@americancareer.com. *Web site:* http://www.americancareer.com/.

American Career College

Los Angeles, California

Director of Admissions Tamra Adams, Director of Admissions, American Career College, 4021 Rosewood Avenue, Los Angeles, CA 90004-2932. *Phone:* 323-668-7555. *Toll-free phone:* 888-844-6522. *E-mail:* info@americancareer.com. *Web site:* http://www.americancareer.com/.

American Career College

Ontario, California

Director of Admissions Juan Tellez, Director of Admissions, American Career College, 3130 East Sedona Court, Ontario, CA 91764. *Phone:* 951-739-0788. *Toll-free phone:* 888-844-6522. *E-mail:* info@americancareer.com. *Web site:* http://www.americancareer.com/.

American River College

Sacramento, California

Freshman Application Contact American River College, 4700 College Oak Drive, Sacramento, CA 95841-4286. *Phone:* 916-484-8171. *Web site:* http://www.arc.losrios.edu/.

Antelope Valley College
Lancaster, California

- **State and locally supported** 2-year, founded 1929, part of California Community College System
- **Suburban** 135-acre campus with easy access to Los Angeles
- **Endowment** $299,569
- **Coed,** 15,108 undergraduate students, 32% full-time, 60% women, 40% men

Undergraduates 4,802 full-time, 10,306 part-time. Students come from 7 states and territories; 1% are from out of state; 16% transferred in. *Retention:* 68% of full-time freshmen returned.
Freshmen *Admission:* 2,830 applied, 2,830 admitted, 2,830 enrolled.
Faculty *Total:* 618, 32% full-time. *Student/faculty ratio:* 45:1.
Majors Administrative assistant and secretarial science; aircraft powerplant technology; airframe mechanics and aircraft maintenance technology; apparel and textiles; autobody/collision and repair technology; automobile/automotive mechanics technology; avionics maintenance technology; biology/biological sciences; business administration and management; business/commerce; childcare and support services management; child development; cinematography and film/video production; computer and information sciences; computer graphics; computer programming; construction engineering technology; corrections; criminal justice/law enforcement administration; criminal justice/police science; data processing and data processing technology; drafting and design technology; electrical, electronic and communications engineering technology; engineering; engineering technology; family and consumer sciences/home economics teacher education; fiber, textile and weaving arts; fire prevention and safety technology; foods, nutrition, and wellness; health and physical education/fitness; heating, air conditioning, ventilation and refrigeration maintenance technology; interior design; liberal arts and sciences/liberal studies; marketing/marketing management; mathematics; medical administrative assistant and medical secretary; music; ornamental horticulture; photography; physical sciences; real estate; registered nursing/registered nurse; teacher assistant/aide; welding technology; work and family studies.
Academics *Calendar:* semesters. *Degree:* certificates and associate. *Special study options:* academic remediation for entering students, adult/continuing education programs, advanced placement credit, cooperative education, distance learning, English as a second language, honors programs, independent study, part-time degree program; services for LD students, student-designed majors, summer session for credit. *ROTC:* Air Force (c).
Library Antelope Valley College Library with 43,000 titles, 175 serial subscriptions, an OPAC.
Student Life *Housing:* college housing not available. *Activities and Organizations:* drama/theater group, student-run newspaper, choral group. *Campus security:* 24-hour emergency response devices and patrols, late-night transport/escort service. *Student services:* personal/psychological counseling.
Athletics *Intercollegiate sports:* baseball M, basketball M/W, cross-country running M/W, football M, golf M/W, soccer W, softball W, tennis W, track and field M/W, volleyball W. *Intramural sports:* basketball M/W, golf M/W, swimming and diving M/W, tennis M/W, volleyball M/W, weight lifting M/W.
Costs (2010–11) *Tuition:* state resident $0 full-time; nonresident $4710 full-time, $157 per unit part-time. Full-time tuition and fees vary according to course load. Part-time tuition and fees vary according to course load. *Required fees:* $780 full-time, $26 per unit part-time.
Applying *Options:* electronic application, early admission. *Required:* high school transcript. *Recommended:* assessment. *Application deadlines:* rolling (freshmen), rolling (transfers). *Notification:* continuous (freshmen), continuous (transfers).
Freshman Application Contact Welcome Center, Antelope Valley College, 3041 West Avenue K, Lancaster, CA 93536-5426. *Phone:* 661-722-6331. *Web site:* http://www.avc.edu/.

Applied Professional Training, Inc.
Carlsbad, California

Director of Admissions Monica Hoffman, Director of Admissions/Registrar, Applied Professional Training, Inc., 5751 Palmer Way, Suite D, PO Box 131717, Carlsbad, CA 92013. *Phone:* 800-431-8488. *Toll-free phone:* 800-431-8488. *Fax:* 888-431-8588. *E-mail:* aptc@aptc.com. *Web site:* http://www.aptc.edu/.

Aviation & Electronic Schools of America
Colfax, California

Freshman Application Contact Admissions Office, Aviation & Electronic Schools of America, 111 South Railroad Street, PO Box 1810, Colfax, CA 95713-1810. *Phone:* 530-346-6792. *Toll-free phone:* 800-345-2742. *Fax:* 530-346-8466. *E-mail:* aesa@aesa.com. *Web site:* http://www.aesa.com/.

Bakersfield College
Bakersfield, California

- **State and locally supported** 2-year, founded 1913, part of California Community College System
- **Urban** 175-acre campus
- **Coed**

Academics *Calendar:* semesters. *Degree:* associate. *Special study options:* academic remediation for entering students, accelerated degree program, adult/continuing education programs, advanced placement credit, cooperative education, English as a second language, internships, part-time degree program, services for LD students, summer session for credit.
Student Life *Campus security:* 24-hour patrols, late-night transport/escort service.
Financial Aid Of all full-time matriculated undergraduates who enrolled in 2009, 300 Federal Work-Study jobs (averaging $2500). 15 state and other part-time jobs (averaging $2500).
Freshman Application Contact Bakersfield College, 1801 Panorama Drive, Bakersfield, CA 93305-1299. *Phone:* 661-395-4301. *Web site:* http://www.bakersfieldcollege.edu/.

Barstow College
Barstow, California

Director of Admissions Heather Caldon, Manager of Admissions and Records, Barstow College, 2700 Barstow Road, Barstow, CA 92311-6699. *Phone:* 760-252-2411 Ext. 7236. *Fax:* 760-252-6754. *E-mail:* hcaldon@barstow.edu. *Web site:* http://www.barstow.edu/.

Berkeley City College
Berkeley, California

- **State and locally supported** 2-year, founded 1974, part of California Community College System, administratively affiliated with Peralta Community College District
- **Urban** campus with easy access to San Francisco
- **Coed,** 7,645 undergraduate students

Undergraduates 1% are from out of state; 18% Black or African American, non-Hispanic/Latino; 12% Hispanic/Latino; 16% Asian, non-Hispanic/Latino; 0.5% Native Hawaiian or other Pacific Islander, non-Hispanic/Latino; 0.5% American Indian or Alaska Native, non-Hispanic/Latino; 3% Two or more races, non-Hispanic/Latino; 31% Race/ethnicity unknown.
Freshmen *Admission:* 6,245 applied, 6,245 admitted.
Faculty *Total:* 180, 27% full-time. *Student/faculty ratio:* 35:1.
Majors Accounting; art; biology/biotechnology laboratory technician; business administration and management; business/commerce; computer and information sciences; computer and information sciences related; computer and information systems security; computer graphics; computer software and media applications related; creative writing; data entry/microcomputer applications related; English; fine/studio arts; general studies; liberal arts and sciences/liberal studies; medical administrative assistant and medical secretary; office management; Spanish; web page, digital/multimedia and information resources design; writing.
Academics *Calendar:* semesters. *Degree:* certificates and associate. *Special study options:* academic remediation for entering students, adult/continuing education programs, cooperative education, distance learning, double majors, English as a second language, independent study, internships, off-campus study, part-time degree program, services for LD students, student-designed majors, study abroad, summer session for credit.
Library Susan A. Duncan Library plus 1 other with an OPAC, a Web page.
Student Life *Housing:* college housing not available. *Activities and Organizations:* choral group, Civic Engagement Club, Global Studies Club, Indigenous Student Alliance, The National Society of Leadership and Success, The Digital Arts Club (DAC). *Campus security:* 24-hour patrols. *Student services:* health clinic, personal/psychological counseling.
Costs (2011–12) *Tuition:* state resident $0 full-time; nonresident $6616 full-time, $225 per unit part-time. Full-time tuition and fees vary according to class time, course load, and program. Part-time tuition and fees vary according to class time and course load. *Required fees:* $780 full-time, $26 per unit part-time, $68 per term part-time. *Waivers:* minority students, children of alumni, adult students, senior citizens, and employees or children of employees.
Financial Aid Of all full-time matriculated undergraduates who enrolled in 2009, 34 Federal Work-Study jobs (averaging $3000).
Applying *Options:* electronic application, early admission, deferred entrance. *Recommended:* high school transcript. *Application deadlines:* rolling (fresh-

men), rolling (out-of-state freshmen), rolling (transfers). *Notification:* continuous (freshmen), continuous (out-of-state freshmen), continuous (transfers).
Freshman Application Contact Dr. May Kuang-chi Chen, Vice President of Student Services, Berkeley City College, 2050 Center Street, Berkeley, CA 94704. *Phone:* 510-981-2820. *Fax:* 510-841-7333. *E-mail:* mrivas@peralta.edu. *Web site:* http://www.berkeleycitycollege.edu/.

Bryan College
Gold River, California
Freshman Application Contact Bryan College, 2317 Gold Meadow Way, Gold River, CA 95670. *Phone:* 916-649-2400. *Toll-free phone:* 866-649-2400. *Web site:* http://www.bryancollege.edu/.

Butte College
Oroville, California
Freshman Application Contact Ms. Nancy Jenson, Registrar, Butte College, 3536 Butte Campus Drive, Oroville, CA 95965-8399. *Phone:* 530-895-2361. *Web site:* http://www.butte.edu/.

Cabrillo College
Aptos, California
Freshman Application Contact Tama Bolton, Director of Admissions and Records, Cabrillo College, 6500 Soquel Drive, Aptos, CA 95003-3194. *Phone:* 831-477-3548. *Fax:* 831-479-5782. *E-mail:* tabolton@cabrillo.edu. *Web site:* http://www.cabrillo.edu/.

California Culinary Academy
San Francisco, California
Director of Admissions Ms. Nancy Seyfert, Vice President of Admissions, California Culinary Academy, 625 Polk Street, San Francisco, CA 94102-3368. *Phone:* 800-229-2433 Ext. 275. *Toll-free phone:* 800-229-2433 (in-state); 800-BAYCHEF (out-of-state). *Web site:* http://www.baychef.com/.

Cambridge Career College
Yuba City, California
- **Proprietary** 2-year
- **Suburban** campus with easy access to Sacramento
- **Coed, primarily women**
Undergraduates 162 full-time. *Retention:* 89% of full-time freshmen returned.
Academics *Degree:* certificates and associate.
Applying *Application fee:* $100. *Required:* high school transcript, interview.
Freshman Application Contact Admissions Office, Cambridge Career College, 990-A Klamath Lane, Yuba City, CA 95993. *Phone:* 530-674-9199. *Fax:* 530-671-7319. *Web site:* http://cambridge.edu/.

Canada College
Redwood City, California
Freshman Application Contact Canada College, 4200 Farm Hill Boulevard, Redwood City, CA 94061-1099. *Phone:* 650-306-3125. *Web site:* http://www.canadacollege.edu/.

Carrington College California - Pleasant Hill
Pleasant Hill, California
Admissions Office Contact Carrington College California - Pleasant Hill, 380 Civic Drive, Suite 300, Pleasant Hill, CA 94523. *Web site:* http://carrington.edu/.

Carrington College California - San Jose
San Jose, California
Director of Admissions Admissions Director, Carrington College California - San Jose, 6201 San Ignacio Avenue, San Jose, CA 95119. *Phone:* 408-360-0840. *Web site:* http://carrington.edu/.

Carrington College California - San Leandro
San Leandro, California
Admissions Office Contact Carrington College California - San Leandro, 15555 East 14th Street, Suite 500, San Leandro, CA 94578. *Web site:* http://carrington.edu/.

Carrington College of California - Antioch
Antioch, California
Freshman Application Contact Admissions Director, Carrington College of California - Antioch, 2157 Country Hills Drive, Antioch, CA 94509. *Phone:* 925-522-7777. *Web site:* http://carrington.edu/.

Carrington College of California - Citrus Heights
Citrus Heights, California
Admissions Office Contact Carrington College of California - Citrus Heights, 7301 Greenback Lane, Suite A, Citrus Heights, CA 95621. *Web site:* http://carrington.edu/.

Carrington College of California - Emeryville
Emeryville, California
Freshman Application Contact Admissions Office, Carrington College of California - Emeryville, 6001 Shellmound Street, Suite 145, Emeryville, CA 94608. *Phone:* 510-601-0133. *Fax:* 510-623-9822. *Web site:* http://carrington.edu/.

Carrington College of California - Sacramento
Sacramento, California
Admissions Office Contact Carrington College of California - Sacramento, 8909 Folsom Boulevard, Sacramento, CA 95826. *Web site:* http://carrington.edu/.

Cerritos College
Norwalk, California
Director of Admissions Ms. Stephanie Murguia, Director of Admissions and Records, Cerritos College, 11110 Alondra Boulevard, Norwalk, CA 90650-6298. *Phone:* 562-860-2451. *E-mail:* smurguia@cerritos.edu. *Web site:* http://www.cerritos.edu/.

Cerro Coso Community College
Ridgecrest, California
Freshman Application Contact Mrs. Heather Ootash, Counseling/Matriculation Coordinator, Cerro Coso Community College, 3000 College Heights Boulevard, Ridgecrest, CA 93555. *Phone:* 760-384-6291. *Fax:* 760-375-4776. *E-mail:* hostash@cerrocoso.edu. *Web site:* http://www.cerrocoso.edu/.

Chabot College
Hayward, California
Director of Admissions Ms. Judy Young, Director of Admissions and Records, Chabot College, 25555 Hesperian Boulevard, Hayward, CA 94545-5001. *Phone:* 510-723-6700. *Web site:* http://www.chabotcollege.edu/.

Chaffey College
Rancho Cucamonga, California
Freshman Application Contact Erlinda Martinez, Coordinator of Admissions, Chaffey College, 5885 Haven Avenue, Rancho Cucamonga, CA 91737-3002. *Phone:* 909-652-6610. *E-mail:* erlinda.martinez@chaffey.edu. *Web site:* http://www.chaffey.edu/.

Citrus College
Glendora, California

Freshman Application Contact Admissions and Records, Citrus College, Glendora, CA 91741-1899. *Phone:* 626-914-8511. *Fax:* 626-914-8613. *E-mail:* admissions@citruscollege.edu. *Web site:* http://www.citruscollege.edu/.

City College of San Francisco
San Francisco, California

Freshman Application Contact Ms. Mary Lou Leyba-Frank, Dean of Admissions and Records, City College of San Francisco, 50 Phelan Avenue, San Francisco, CA 94112-1821. *Phone:* 415-239-3291. *Fax:* 415-239-3936. *E-mail:* mleyba@ccsf.edu. *Web site:* http://www.ccsf.edu/.

Coastline Community College
Fountain Valley, California

Freshman Application Contact Jennifer McDonald, Director of Admissions and Records, Coastline Community College, 11460 Warner Avenue, Fountain Valley, CA 92708-2597. *Phone:* 714-241-6163. *Web site:* http://coastline.cccd.edu/.

Coleman University
San Marcos, California

Director of Admissions Senior Admissions Officer, Coleman University, 1284 West San Marcos Boulevard, San Marcos, CA 92078. *Phone:* 760-747-3990. *Fax:* 760-752-9808. *Web site:* http://www.coleman.edu/.

College of Alameda
Alameda, California

Freshman Application Contact College of Alameda, 555 Ralph Appezzato Memorial Parkway, Alameda, CA 94501-2109. *Phone:* 510-748-2204. *Web site:* http://alameda.peralta.edu/.

College of Marin
Kentfield, California

Freshman Application Contact College of Marin, 835 College Avenue, Kentfield, CA 94904. *Phone:* 415-485-9414. *Web site:* http://www.marin.edu/.

College of San Mateo
San Mateo, California

Director of Admissions Mr. Henry Villareal, Dean of Admissions and Records, College of San Mateo, 1700 West Hillsdale Boulevard, San Mateo, CA 94402-3784. *Phone:* 650-574-6590. *E-mail:* csmadmission@smccd.edu. *Web site:* http://www.collegeofsanmateo.edu/.

College of the Canyons
Santa Clarita, California

- **State and locally supported** 2-year, founded 1969, part of California Community College System
- **Suburban** 224-acre campus with easy access to Los Angeles
- **Coed,** 23,374 undergraduate students

Undergraduates 2% are from out of state; 6% Black or African American, non-Hispanic/Latino; 35% Hispanic/Latino; 9% Asian, non-Hispanic/Latino; 0.6% American Indian or Alaska Native, non-Hispanic/Latino; 2% Race/ethnicity unknown; 0.5% international. *Retention:* 64% of full-time freshmen returned.

Faculty *Total:* 617, 27% full-time. *Student/faculty ratio:* 28:1.

Majors Accounting technology and bookkeeping; administrative assistant and secretarial science; animation, interactive technology, video graphics and special effects; architectural drafting and CAD/CADD; art; athletic training; automobile/automotive mechanics technology; biological and physical sciences; building/construction site management; business administration and management; child-care provision; computer science; computer systems networking and telecommunications; criminal justice/police science; dramatic/theater arts; English; fire prevention and safety technology; French; graphic design; health and physical education/fitness; history; hospitality administration; hotel/motel administration; humanities; interior design; journalism; landscaping and groundskeeping; legal assistant/paralegal; liberal arts and sciences/liberal stud-

ies; library and archives assisting; manufacturing engineering technology; mathematics; music; parks, recreation and leisure; photography; pre-engineering; psychology; radio and television; real estate; registered nursing/registered nurse; restaurant, culinary, and catering management; sales, distribution, and marketing operations; sign language interpretation and translation; small business administration; social sciences; sociology; Spanish; surveying technology; water quality and wastewater treatment management and recycling technology; welding technology.

Academics *Calendar:* semesters. *Degree:* certificates and associate. *Special study options:* academic remediation for entering students, adult/continuing education programs, advanced placement credit, cooperative education, distance learning, double majors, English as a second language, honors programs, independent study, internships, off-campus study, part-time degree program, services for LD students, study abroad, summer session for credit.

Library College of the Canyons Library with 58,528 titles, 146 serial subscriptions, 7,760 audiovisual materials, an OPAC, a Web page.

Student Life *Housing:* college housing not available. *Activities and Organizations:* drama/theater group, choral group, Alpha Gamma Sigma, Biology Club, Future Educators Club, Phi Theta Kappa, Psychology Club. *Campus security:* 24-hour emergency response devices, late-night transport/escort service. *Student services:* health clinic, personal/psychological counseling, women's center.

Athletics *Intercollegiate sports:* baseball M, basketball M/W, cross-country running M/W, football M, golf M/W, ice hockey M(c), soccer M/W, softball W, swimming and diving M/W, track and field M/W, volleyball W.

Costs (2011–12) *Tuition:* state resident $670 full-time, $26 per unit part-time; nonresident $4366 full-time, $154 per unit part-time. *Required fees:* $28 full-time, $46 per year part-time.

Applying *Options:* electronic application, early admission. *Recommended:* high school transcript. *Application deadlines:* rolling (freshmen), rolling (transfers). *Notification:* continuous (freshmen), continuous (transfers).

Freshman Application Contact Ms. Jasmine Ruys, Director, Admissions and Records and Online Services, College of the Canyons, 26455 Rockwell Canyon Road, Santa Clarita, CA 91355. *Phone:* 661-362-3280. *Toll-free phone:* 888-206-7827. *Fax:* 661-254-7996. *E-mail:* jasmine.ruys@canyons.edu. *Web site:* http://www.canyons.edu/.

College of the Desert
Palm Desert, California

Freshman Application Contact College of the Desert, 43-500 Monterey Avenue, Palm Desert, CA 92260-9305. *Phone:* 760-346-8041 Ext. 7441. *Web site:* http://www.collegeofthedesert.edu/.

See next page for display and page 410 for the College Close-Up.

College of the Redwoods
Eureka, California

Freshman Application Contact Director of Enrollment Management, College of the Redwoods, 7351 Tompkins Hill Road, Eureka, CA 95501-9300. *Phone:* 707-476-4100. *Toll-free phone:* 800-641-0400. *Fax:* 707-476-4400. *Web site:* http://www.redwoods.edu/.

College of the Sequoias
Visalia, California

Freshman Application Contact Ms. Lisa Hott, Director for Admissions, College of the Sequoias, 915 South Mooney Boulevard, Visalia, CA 93277-2234. *Phone:* 559-737-4844. *Fax:* 559-737-4820. *Web site:* http://www.cos.edu/.

College of the Siskiyous
Weed, California

Freshman Application Contact Recruitment and Admissions, College of the Siskiyous, 800 College Avenue, Weed, CA 96094-2899. *Phone:* 530-938-5555. *Toll-free phone:* 888-397-4339. *E-mail:* admissions-weed@siskyous.edu. *Web site:* http://www.siskiyous.edu/.

Columbia College
Sonora, California

Freshman Application Contact Admissions Office, Columbia College, 11600 Columbia College Drive, Sonora, CA 95370. *Phone:* 209-588-5231. *Fax:* 209-588-5337. *E-mail:* ccadmissions@yosemite.edu. *Web site:* http://www.gocolumbia.edu/.

Community Christian College

Redlands, California

Freshman Application Contact Enrique D. Melendez, Assistant Director of Admissions, Community Christian College, 251 Tennessee Street, Redlands, CA 92373. *Phone:* 909-222-9556. *Fax:* 909-335-9101. *E-mail:* emelendez@cccollege.edu. *Web site:* http://www.cccollege.edu/.

Concorde Career College

Garden Grove, California

Freshman Application Contact Chris Becker, Director, Concorde Career College, 12951 Euclid Street, Suite 101, Garden Grove, CA 92840. *Phone:* 714-703-1900. *Fax:* 714-530-4737. *E-mail:* cbecker@concorde.edu. *Web site:* http://www.concorde.edu/.

Concorde Career College

North Hollywood, California

Freshman Application Contact Madeline Volker, Director, Concorde Career College, 12412 Victory Boulevard, North Hollywood, CA 91606. *Phone:* 818-766-8151. *Fax:* 818-766-1587. *E-mail:* mvolker@concorde.edu. *Web site:* http://www.concorde.edu/.

Contra Costa College

San Pablo, California

Freshman Application Contact Admissions and Records Office, Contra Costa College, San Pablo, CA 94806. *Phone:* 510-235-7800 Ext. 7500. *Fax:* 510-412-0769. *E-mail:* A&R@contracosta.edu. *Web site:* http://www.contracosta.edu/.

Copper Mountain College

Joshua Tree, California

Freshman Application Contact Dr. Laraine Turk, Associate Dean of Student Services, Copper Mountain College, 6162 Rotary Way, Joshua Tree, CA 92252. *Phone:* 760-366-5290. *Web site:* http://www.cmccd.edu/.

Cosumnes River College

Sacramento, California

Freshman Application Contact Admissions and Records, Cosumnes River College, 8401 Center Parkway, Sacramento, CA 95823-5799. *Phone:* 916-691-7411. *Web site:* http://www.crc.losrios.edu/.

Crafton Hills College

Yucaipa, California

Director of Admissions Larry Aycock, Admissions and Records Coordinator, Crafton Hills College, 11711 Sand Canyon Road, Yucaipa, CA 92399-1799. *Phone:* 909-389-3663. *E-mail:* laycock@craftonhills.edu. *Web site:* http://www.craftonhills.edu/.

Cuesta College

San Luis Obispo, California

Freshman Application Contact Cuesta College, PO Box 8106, San Luis Obispo, CA 93403-8106. *Phone:* 805-546-3130 Ext. 2262. *Web site:* http://www.cuesta.edu/.

Cuyamaca College

El Cajon, California

- **State-supported** 2-year, founded 1978, part of Grossmont-Cuyamaca Community College District
- **Suburban** 165-acre campus with easy access to San Diego
- **Coed**

Undergraduates 1,636 full-time, 6,070 part-time. Students come from 8 other countries.

Academics *Calendar:* semesters. *Degree:* certificates, diplomas, and associate. *Special study options:* academic remediation for entering students, adult/continuing education programs, advanced placement credit, cooperative education, distance learning, double majors, English as a second language, honors programs, internships, off-campus study, part-time degree program, services for LD students, student-designed majors, study abroad, summer session for credit. *ROTC:* Army (c), Air Force (c).

Student Life *Campus security:* 24-hour emergency response devices and patrols, late-night transport/escort service.

Costs (2010–11) *Tuition:* state resident $0 full-time; nonresident $5700 full-time, $190 per unit part-time. Full-time tuition and fees vary according to course load. Part-time tuition and fees vary according to course load. *Required fees:* $820 full-time, $26 per unit part-time, $20 per term part-time.

Financial Aid Of all full-time matriculated undergraduates who enrolled in 2009, 42 Federal Work-Study jobs (averaging $2700). 51 state and other part-time jobs (averaging $1100).

Applying *Options:* electronic application, early admission.

Freshman Application Contact Ms. Susan Topham, Dean of Admissions and Records, Cuyamaca College, 900 Rancho San Diego Parkway, El Cajon, CA 92019-4304. *Phone:* 619-660-4302. *Fax:* 619-660-4575. *E-mail:* susan.topham@gcccd.edu. *Web site:* http://www.cuyamaca.net/.

Cypress College

Cypress, California

Freshman Application Contact Admissions Office, Cypress College, 9200 Valley View, Cypress, CA 90630-5897. *Phone:* 714-484-7346. *Fax:* 714-484-7446. *E-mail:* admissions@cypresscollege.edu. *Web site:* http://www.cypresscollege.edu/.

De Anza College

Cupertino, California

- **State and locally supported** 2-year, founded 1967, part of California Community College System
- **Suburban** 112-acre campus with easy access to San Francisco and San Jose
- **Coed,** 25,191 undergraduate students, 44% full-time, 50% women, 50% men

Undergraduates 11,139 full-time, 14,052 part-time. 3% Black or African American, non-Hispanic/Latino; 12% Hispanic/Latino; 33% Asian, non-Hispanic/Latino; 0.6% Native Hawaiian or other Pacific Islander, non-Hispanic/Latino; 0.5% American Indian or Alaska Native, non-Hispanic/Latino; 9% Two or more races, non-Hispanic/Latino; 13% Race/ethnicity unknown.

Freshmen *Admission:* 4,320 enrolled.

Faculty *Total:* 794, 38% full-time. *Student/faculty ratio:* 36:1.

Majors Accounting; administrative assistant and secretarial science; art; art history, criticism and conservation; automobile/automotive mechanics technology; behavioral sciences; biology/biological sciences; business administration and management; business machine repair; ceramic arts and ceramics; child development; commercial and advertising art; computer graphics; computer programming; computer science; construction engineering technology; corrections; criminal justice/law enforcement administration; criminal justice/police science; developmental and child psychology; drafting/design engineering technologies related; dramatic/theater arts; drawing; economics; engineering; engineering technology; English; environmental studies; film/cinema/video studies; history; humanities; industrial technology; information science/studies; international relations and affairs; journalism; legal assistant/paralegal; liberal arts and sciences/liberal studies; licensed practical/vocational nurse training; machine tool technology; marketing/marketing management; mass communication/media; mathematics; medical/clinical assistant; music; philosophy; photography; physical education teaching and coaching; physical therapy; physics; political science and government; pre-engineering; printmaking; professional, technical, business, and scientific writing; psychology; purchasing, procurement/acquisitions and contracts management; radio and television; real estate; registered nursing/registered nurse; rhetoric and composition; sculpture; social sciences; sociology; Spanish.

Academics *Calendar:* quarters. *Degree:* certificates, diplomas, and associate. *Special study options:* academic remediation for entering students, adult/continuing education programs, advanced placement credit, cooperative edu-

cation, distance learning, English as a second language, external degree program, honors programs, independent study, internships, part-time degree program, services for LD students, student-designed majors, study abroad, summer session for credit. *ROTC:* Army (c), Air Force (c).

Library A. Robert DeHart Learning Center with 80,000 titles, 927 serial subscriptions.

Student Life *Housing:* college housing not available. *Activities and Organizations:* drama/theater group, student-run newspaper, choral group, Student Nurses Association, Phi Theta Kappa, Automotive Club, Vietnamese Club, Filipino Club. *Campus security:* 24-hour emergency response devices, student patrols, late-night transport/escort service. *Student services:* health clinic, personal/psychological counseling, legal services.

Athletics Member NCAA. All Division II. *Intercollegiate sports:* baseball M, basketball M/W, cross-country running M/W, football M, golf M/W, soccer M/W, softball W, swimming and diving M/W, tennis M/W, track and field M/W, volleyball M/W, water polo M. *Intramural sports:* badminton M/W, basketball M, soccer M/W, swimming and diving M/W, volleyball M/W.

Costs (2011–12) *Tuition:* state resident $765 full-time; nonresident $6120 full-time. *Required fees:* $113 full-time. *Payment plan:* installment. *Waivers:* minority students and adult students.

Applying *Options:* early admission. *Application fee:* $22. *Application deadlines:* rolling (freshmen), rolling (transfers). *Notification:* continuous (freshmen), continuous (transfers).

Freshman Application Contact De Anza College, 21250 Stevens Creek Boulevard, Cupertino, CA 95014-5793. *Phone:* 408-864-8292. *Web site:* http://www.deanza.fhda.edu/.

Deep Springs College

Deep Springs, California

- **Independent** 2-year, founded 1917
- **Rural** 3000-acre campus
- **Endowment** $10.6 million
- **Men only**

Undergraduates 24 full-time. Students come from 13 states and territories; 1 other country; 80% are from out of state; 100% live on campus. *Retention:* 92% of full-time freshmen returned.

Faculty *Student/faculty ratio:* 4:1.

Academics *Calendar:* 6 seven-week terms. *Degree:* associate. *Special study options:* accelerated degree program, cooperative education, freshman honors college, honors programs, independent study, internships, student-designed majors, summer session for credit.

Standardized Tests *Required:* SAT and SAT Subject Tests or ACT (for admission).

Applying *Required:* essay or personal statement, high school transcript, interview.

Freshman Application Contact David Neidorf, President, Deep Springs College, HC 72, Box 45001, Dyer, NV 89010-9803. *Phone:* 760-872-2000. *Fax:* 760-872-4466. *E-mail:* apcom@deepsprings.edu. *Web site:* http://www.deepsprings.edu/.

Diablo Valley College

Pleasant Hill, California

- **State and locally supported** 2-year, founded 1949, part of Contra Costa Community College District
- **Suburban** 100-acre campus with easy access to San Francisco
- **Coed**

Undergraduates 7,340 full-time, 15,227 part-time. Students come from 16 states and territories; 68 other countries; 0.2% are from out of state. *Retention:* 61% of full-time freshmen returned.

Faculty *Student/faculty ratio:* 17:1.

Academics *Calendar:* semesters. *Degree:* certificates and associate. *Special study options:* academic remediation for entering students, adult/continuing education programs, advanced placement credit, cooperative education, part-time degree program, services for LD students, student-designed majors, study abroad, summer session for credit. *ROTC:* Air Force (c).

Student Life *Campus security:* 24-hour emergency response devices and patrols, student patrols.

Costs (2010–11) *Tuition:* state resident $0 full-time; nonresident $4440 full-time, $185 per unit part-time. *Required fees:* $634 full-time, $26 per unit part-time.

Financial Aid *Financial aid deadline:* 5/23.

Applying *Options:* early admission. *Recommended:* high school transcript.

Freshman Application Contact Ileana Dorn, Director of Admissions and Records, Diablo Valley College, Pleasant Hill, CA 94523-1529. *Phone:* 925-685-1230 Ext. 2330. *Fax:* 925-609-8085. *E-mail:* idorn@dvc.edu. *Web site:* http://www.dvc.edu/.

East Los Angeles College

Monterey Park, California

- **State and locally supported** 2-year, founded 1945, part of Los Angeles Community College District System
- **Urban** 84-acre campus with easy access to Los Angeles
- **Coed,** 31,749 undergraduate students, 25% full-time, 56% women, 44% men

Undergraduates 8,063 full-time, 23,686 part-time. Students come from 17 states and territories; 0.1% are from out of state; 11% transferred in.

Freshmen *Admission:* 2,765 enrolled.

Faculty *Total:* 829, 28% full-time, 15% with terminal degrees.

Majors Accounting; administrative assistant and secretarial science; anthropology; architectural engineering technology; art; Asian studies; automobile/automotive mechanics technology; biology/biological sciences; business administration and management; chemistry; child development; civil engineering technology; computer engineering technology; computer programming; counselor education/school counseling and guidance; criminal justice/law enforcement administration; criminal justice/police science; data processing and data processing technology; developmental and child psychology; drafting and design technology; dramatic/theater arts; electrical, electronic and communications engineering technology; emergency medical technology (EMT paramedic); engineering; English; environmental studies; family and consumer sciences/human sciences; finance; fire science/firefighting; French; geography; geology/earth science; health information/medical records administration; Hispanic-American, Puerto Rican, and Mexican-American/Chicano studies; history; Japanese; journalism; legal administrative assistant/secretary; liberal arts and sciences/liberal studies; marketing/marketing management; mathematics; medical administrative assistant and medical secretary; medical/clinical assistant; music; philosophy; photography; physical education teaching and coaching; political science and government; pre-engineering; psychology; public administration; real estate; registered nursing/registered nurse; respiratory care therapy; rhetoric and composition; social work; sociology; Spanish; trade and industrial teacher education.

Academics *Calendar:* semesters. *Degree:* certificates and associate. *Special study options:* academic remediation for entering students, accelerated degree program, adult/continuing education programs, advanced placement credit, cooperative education, distance learning, double majors, English as a second language, freshman honors college, honors programs, independent study, internships, off-campus study, part-time degree program, services for LD students, student-designed majors, study abroad, summer session for credit.

Library ELAC Helen Miller Bailey Library plus 2 others with 102,000 titles, 228 serial subscriptions, an OPAC, a Web page.

Student Life *Housing:* college housing not available. *Activities and Organizations:* drama/theater group, student-run newspaper, choral group, marching band, Administration of Justice, American Society of Engineers and Architects, Society of Hispanic Professional Engineers, MENTE, Asian Student Intercultural Association (A.S.I.A) and the International Student Club, Chicano/Community for Creative Medicine, Science Associations, Advocates and Educators for Young Children, Child Development Club. *Campus security:* 24-hour emergency response devices and patrols, late-night transport/escort service, Los Angeles County Sheriff Sub-station. *Student services:* health clinic, personal/psychological counseling.

Athletics *Intercollegiate sports:* baseball M, basketball M/W, cheerleading W, cross-country running M/W, football M, soccer M/W, softball W, track and field M/W, volleyball W, wrestling M.

Standardized Tests *Required:* mathematics and English placement tests, international students require TOEFL score of 450, CBT score 133, IBT score 45 or higher (for admission).

Costs (2011–12) *Tuition:* state resident $1080 full-time, $36 per unit part-time; nonresident $6270 full-time, $209 per unit part-time. No tuition increase for student's term of enrollment. *Required fees:* $22 full-time, $36 per unit part-time.

Financial Aid Of all full-time matriculated undergraduates who enrolled in 2009, 189 Federal Work-Study jobs (averaging $3000).

Applying *Options:* electronic application, early admission. *Recommended:* high school transcript, English and mathematics placement test. *Application deadline:* rolling (freshmen). *Notification:* continuous until 9/2 (freshmen).

Freshman Application Contact Mr. Jeremy Allred, Associate Dean of Admissions, East Los Angeles College, 1301 Avenida Cesar Chavez, Monterey Park, CA 91754. *Phone:* 323-265-8801. *Fax:* 323-265-8688. *E-mail:* allredjp@elac.edu. *Web site:* http://www.elac.edu/.

El Camino College

Torrance, California

Director of Admissions Mr. William Mulrooney, Director of Admissions, El Camino College, 16007 Crenshaw Boulevard, Torrance, CA 90506-0001.

Phone: 310-660-3418. *Toll-free phone:* 866-ELCAMINO. *Fax:* 310-660-6779. *E-mail:* wmulrooney@elcamino.edu. *Web site:* http://www.elcamino.edu/.

Empire College

Santa Rosa, California

Freshman Application Contact Ms. Dahnja Barker, Admissions Officer, Empire College, 3035 Cleveland Avenue, Santa Rosa, CA 95403. *Phone:* 707-546-4000. *Web site:* http://www.empcol.edu.

Everest College

City of Industry, California

Freshman Application Contact Admissions Office, Everest College, 12801 Crossroads Parkway South, City of Industry, CA 91746. *Phone:* 562-908-2500. *Toll-free phone:* 888-741-4270. *Fax:* 562-908-7656. *Web site:* http://www.everest.edu/.

Everest College

Ontario, California

Freshman Application Contact Admissions Office, Everest College, 1819 South Excise Avenue, Ontario, CA 91761. *Phone:* 909-484-4311. *Fax:* 909-484-1162. *Web site:* http://www.everest.edu/campus/ontario/.

Everest College

Rancho Cucamonga, California

Admissions Office Contact Everest College, 9616 Archibald Avenue, Suite 100, Rancho Cucamonga, CA 91730. *Web site:* http://www.everest-college.com/.

Evergreen Valley College

San Jose, California

Freshman Application Contact Evergreen Valley College, 3095 Yerba Buena Road, San Jose, CA 95135-1598. *Phone:* 408-270-6423. *Web site:* http://www.evc.edu/.

Fashion Careers College

San Diego, California

- **Proprietary** 2-year, founded 1979
- **Urban** campus with easy access to San Diego
- **Coed, primarily women,** 91 undergraduate students, 100% full-time, 88% women, 12% men

Undergraduates 91 full-time. Students come from 18 states and territories; 2 other countries; 20% are from out of state.

Freshmen *Admission:* 28 enrolled.

Faculty *Total:* 9, 11% full-time.

Majors Fashion/apparel design; fashion merchandising.

Academics *Calendar:* quarters. *Degree:* certificates and associate. *Special study options:* adult/continuing education programs, cooperative education, distance learning, double majors, internships.

Library Fashion Careers of California Library with 800 titles, 14 serial subscriptions, 175 audiovisual materials.

Student Life *Housing:* college housing not available. *Campus security:* 24-hour emergency response devices.

Standardized Tests *Required:* Wonderlic aptitude test (for admission).

Costs (2011–12) *Tuition:* $19,900 full-time. Full-time tuition and fees vary according to class time, course load, degree level, and program. *Required fees:* $525 full-time. *Payment plan:* installment.

Financial Aid Of all full-time matriculated undergraduates who enrolled in 2009, 10 Federal Work-Study jobs (averaging $1760).

Applying *Options:* electronic application. *Application fee:* $25. *Required:* essay or personal statement, high school transcript, interview. *Application deadlines:* rolling (freshmen), rolling (out-of-state freshmen), rolling (transfers). *Notification:* continuous (freshmen), continuous (out-of-state freshmen), continuous (transfers).

Freshman Application Contact Ms. Ronny Catarcio, Admissions Advisory, Fashion Careers College, 1923 Morena Boulevard, San Diego, CA 92110. *Phone:* 619-275-4700 Ext. 328. *Toll-free phone:* 888-FCCC999. *Fax:* 619-275-0635. *E-mail:* ronny@fashioncareerscollege.com. *Web site:* http://www.fashioncareerscollege.com/.

Feather River College
Quincy, California

Freshman Application Contact Leslie Mikesell, Interim Director of Admissions and Records, Feather River College, 570 Golden Eagle Avenue, Quincy, CA 95971-9124. *Phone:* 530-283-0202 Ext. 600. *Toll-free phone:* 800-442-9799 Ext. 286. *E-mail:* lmikesell@frc.edu. *Web site:* http://www.frc.edu/.

FIDM/The Fashion Institute of Design & Merchandising, Los Angeles Campus
Los Angeles, California

- **Proprietary** primarily 2-year, founded 1969, part of The Fashion Institute of Design and Merchandising/FIDM
- **Urban** campus
- **Coed,** 4,424 undergraduate students, 87% full-time, 88% women, 12% men

Undergraduates 3,849 full-time, 575 part-time. Students come from 45 states and territories; 10 other countries; 37% are from out of state; 18% transferred in. *Retention:* 91% of full-time freshmen returned.
Freshmen *Admission:* 1,720 applied, 1,151 admitted, 846 enrolled. *Average high school GPA:* 2.75.
Faculty *Total:* 366, 19% full-time. *Student/faculty ratio:* 16:1.
Majors Apparel and accessories marketing; apparel and textiles; business administration and management; commercial and advertising art; consumer merchandising/retailing management; design and visual communications; fashion/apparel design; fashion merchandising; interior design; metal and jewelry arts.
Academics *Calendar:* quarters. *Degrees:* associate and bachelor's (also includes Orange County Campus). *Special study options:* academic remediation for entering students, adult/continuing education programs, advanced placement credit, cooperative education, distance learning, English as a second language, independent study, internships, part-time degree program, services for LD students, study abroad, summer session for credit.
Library FIDM Los Angeles Campus Library with 24,564 titles, 280 serial subscriptions, 5,298 audiovisual materials, an OPAC.
Student Life *Activities and Organizations:* student-run newspaper, ASID (student chapter), Design Council, Phi Theta Kappa Honor Society, Student Council, MODE. *Campus security:* 24-hour emergency response devices and patrols, late-night transport/escort service. *Student services:* personal/psychological counseling.
Standardized Tests *Recommended:* SAT or ACT (for admission).
Costs (2010–11) *Tuition:* $27,635 full-time. Full-time tuition and fees vary according to program. Part-time tuition and fees vary according to program. No tuition increase for student's term of enrollment. *Required fees:* $525 full-time. *Payment plans:* tuition prepayment, installment. *Waivers:* employees or children of employees.
Financial Aid Of all full-time matriculated undergraduates who enrolled in 2009, 88 Federal Work-Study jobs (averaging $2935).
Applying *Options:* electronic application, deferred entrance. *Application fee:* $225. *Required:* essay or personal statement, high school transcript, minimum 2.0 GPA, 3 letters of recommendation, interview, major-determined project. *Application deadlines:* rolling (freshmen), rolling (out-of-state freshmen), rolling (transfers).
Freshman Application Contact Ms. Susan Aronson, Director of Admissions, FIDM/The Fashion Institute of Design & Merchandising, Los Angeles Campus, Los Angeles, CA 90015. *Phone:* 213-624-1201. *Toll-free phone:* 800-624-1200. *Fax:* 213-624-4799. *E-mail:* saronson@fidm.com. *Web site:* http://www.fidm.edu/.

See page 414 for the College Close-Up.

FIDM/The Fashion Institute of Design & Merchandising, Orange County Campus
Irvine, California

- **Proprietary** 2-year, founded 1981, part of The Fashion Institute of Design and Merchandising/FIDM
- **Coed, primarily women,** 372 undergraduate students, 94% full-time, 87% women, 13% men

Undergraduates 351 full-time, 21 part-time. Students come from 15 states and territories; 2 other countries; 13% are from out of state; 3% Black or African American, non-Hispanic/Latino; 31% Hispanic/Latino; 15% Asian, non-Hispanic/Latino; 3% Native Hawaiian or other Pacific Islander, non-Hispanic/Latino; 1% American Indian or Alaska Native, non-Hispanic/Latino; 1% Two or more races, non-Hispanic/Latino; 7% Race/ethnicity unknown; 3% international; 28% transferred in. *Retention:* 67% of full-time freshmen returned.
Freshmen *Admission:* 473 applied, 333 admitted, 203 enrolled. *Average high school GPA:* 2.75.
Faculty *Total:* 33, 24% full-time. *Student/faculty ratio:* 17:1.
Majors Apparel and textiles; commercial and advertising art; consumer merchandising/retailing management; fashion/apparel design; fashion merchandising; fiber, textile and weaving arts; industrial technology; interior design; marketing/marketing management.
Academics *Calendar:* quarters. *Degree:* associate. *Special study options:* academic remediation for entering students, adult/continuing education programs, advanced placement credit, cooperative education, distance learning, English as a second language, independent study, internships, part-time degree program, services for LD students, study abroad, summer session for credit.
Library FIDM Orange County Campus Library with 24,755 titles, 266 serial subscriptions, 1,983 audiovisual materials.
Student Life *Activities and Organizations:* student-run newspaper, ASID (student chapter), Design Council, Association of Manufacturing Students. *Campus security:* 24-hour emergency response devices and patrols, late-night transport/escort service. *Student services:* personal/psychological counseling.
Applying *Options:* deferred entrance. *Application fee:* $225. *Required:* essay or personal statement, high school transcript, minimum 2.0 GPA, 3 letters of recommendation, interview, entrance requirement project. *Application deadlines:* rolling (freshmen), rolling (out-of-state freshmen), rolling (transfers). *Notification:* continuous (freshmen), continuous (out-of-state freshmen), continuous (transfers).
Freshman Application Contact Admissions, FIDM/The Fashion Institute of Design & Merchandising, Orange County Campus, 17590 Gillette Avenue, Irvine, CA 92614-5610. *Phone:* 949-851-6200. *Toll-free phone:* 888-974-3436. *Fax:* 949-851-6808. *Web site:* http://www.fidm.com/.

FIDM/The Fashion Institute of Design & Merchandising, San Diego Campus
San Diego, California

- **Proprietary** 2-year, founded 1985, part of The Fashion Institute of Design and Merchandising/FIDM
- **Urban** campus
- **Coed, primarily women,** 292 undergraduate students, 90% full-time, 90% women, 10% men

Undergraduates 264 full-time, 28 part-time. Students come from 10 states and territories; 2 other countries; 4% are from out of state; 4% Black or African American, non-Hispanic/Latino; 30% Hispanic/Latino; 10% Asian, non-Hispanic/Latino; 2% Native Hawaiian or other Pacific Islander, non-Hispanic/Latino; 0.7% American Indian or Alaska Native, non-Hispanic/Latino; 3% Two or more races, non-Hispanic/Latino; 7% Race/ethnicity unknown; 2% international; 30% transferred in. *Retention:* 50% of full-time freshmen returned.
Freshmen *Admission:* 251 applied, 174 admitted, 94 enrolled. *Average high school GPA:* 2.75. *Test scores:* ACT scores over 18: 100%; ACT scores over 24: 40%; ACT scores over 30: 10%.
Faculty *Total:* 24, 8% full-time. *Student/faculty ratio:* 21:1.
Majors Apparel and accessories marketing; commercial and advertising art; consumer merchandising/retailing management; design and visual communications; fashion/apparel design; fashion merchandising; interior design.
Academics *Calendar:* quarters. *Degree:* associate. *Special study options:* academic remediation for entering students, adult/continuing education programs, advanced placement credit, cooperative education, distance learning, English as a second language, independent study, internships, part-time degree program, services for LD students, study abroad, summer session for credit.
Library FIDM San Diego Campus Library with 4,777 titles, 143 serial subscriptions, 1,808 audiovisual materials, an OPAC.
Student Life *Activities and Organizations:* Student Council, Phi Theta Kappa. *Campus security:* 24-hour emergency response devices and patrols. *Student services:* personal/psychological counseling.
Standardized Tests *Recommended:* SAT or ACT (for admission).
Costs (2010–11) *Tuition:* $27,635 full-time. Full-time tuition and fees vary according to program. Part-time tuition and fees vary according to program. No tuition increase for student's term of enrollment. *Required fees:* $525 full-time. *Payment plans:* tuition prepayment, installment. *Waivers:* employees or children of employees.
Applying *Options:* electronic application, deferred entrance. *Application fee:* $225. *Required:* essay or personal statement, high school transcript, minimum 2.0 GPA, 3 letters of recommendation, interview, major-determined project. *Application deadlines:* rolling (freshmen), rolling (out-of-state freshmen), rolling (transfers).
Freshman Application Contact Ms. Susan Aronson, Director of Admissions, FIDM/The Fashion Institute of Design & Merchandising, San Diego Campus,

San Diego, CA 92101. *Phone:* 213-624-1200 Ext. 5400. *Toll-free phone:* 800-243-3436. *Fax:* 619-232-4322. *E-mail:* info@fidm.com. *Web site:* http://www.fidm.com/.

FIDM/The Fashion Institute of Design & Merchandising, San Francisco Campus

San Francisco, California

- **Proprietary** 2-year, founded 1973, part of The Fashion Institute of Design and Merchandising/FIDM
- **Urban** campus
- **Coed,** 960 undergraduate students, 85% full-time, 90% women, 10% men

Undergraduates 815 full-time, 145 part-time. Students come from 13 states and territories; 3 other countries; 8% are from out of state; 6% Black or African American, non-Hispanic/Latino; 20% Hispanic/Latino; 15% Asian, non-Hispanic/Latino; 2% Native Hawaiian or other Pacific Islander, non-Hispanic/Latino; 0.2% American Indian or Alaska Native, non-Hispanic/Latino; 5% Two or more races, non-Hispanic/Latino; 9% Race/ethnicity unknown; 5% international; 25% transferred in. *Retention:* 67% of full-time freshmen returned.

Freshmen *Admission:* 434 applied, 302 admitted, 206 enrolled. *Average high school GPA:* 2.75. *Test scores:* ACT scores over 18: 100%; ACT scores over 24: 40%; ACT scores over 30: 10%.

Faculty *Total:* 77, 13% full-time. *Student/faculty ratio:* 20:1.

Majors Apparel and accessories marketing; apparel and textiles; commercial and advertising art; consumer merchandising/retailing management; design and visual communications; fashion/apparel design; fashion merchandising; interior design.

Academics *Calendar:* quarters. *Degree:* associate. *Special study options:* academic remediation for entering students, adult/continuing education programs, advanced placement credit, cooperative education, distance learning, English as a second language, honors programs, independent study, internships, off-campus study, part-time degree program, services for LD students, study abroad, summer session for credit.

Library FIDM San Francisco Library with 6,928 titles, 281 serial subscriptions, 2,287 audiovisual materials, an OPAC.

Student Life *Housing:* college housing not available. *Activities and Organizations:* ASID (student chapter), Student Council, Premiere Marketing Group, Phi Theta Kappa. *Campus security:* 24-hour emergency response devices and patrols. *Student services:* personal/psychological counseling.

Standardized Tests *Recommended:* SAT or ACT (for admission).

Costs (2010–11) *Tuition:* $27,635 full-time. Full-time tuition and fees vary according to program. Part-time tuition and fees vary according to program. No tuition increase for student's term of enrollment. *Required fees:* $525 full-time. *Payment plan:* tuition prepayment. *Waivers:* employees or children of employees.

Applying *Options:* electronic application, deferred entrance. *Application fee:* $225. *Required:* essay or personal statement, high school transcript, 3 letters of recommendation, interview, major-determined project. *Application deadlines:* rolling (freshmen), rolling (out-of-state freshmen), rolling (transfers).

Freshman Application Contact Ms. Susan Aronson, Director of Admissions, FIDM/The Fashion Institute of Design & Merchandising, San Francisco Campus, San Francisco, CA 94108. *Phone:* 213-624-1201. *Toll-free phone:* 800-711-7175. *Fax:* 415-296-7299. *E-mail:* info@fidm.com. *Web site:* http://www.fidm.edu/.

Folsom Lake College

Folsom, California

- **State-supported** 2-year, founded 2004, part of Los Rios Community College District System
- **Suburban** campus with easy access to Sacramento
- **Coed**

Faculty *Student/faculty ratio:* 32:1.

Academics *Degree:* certificates, diplomas, and associate. *Special study options:* academic remediation for entering students, advanced placement credit, cooperative education, distance learning, English as a second language, independent study, internships, services for LD students, study abroad, summer session for credit.

Student Life *Campus security:* 24-hour emergency response devices and patrols, late-night transport/escort service.

Costs (2010–11) *Tuition:* state resident $0 full-time; nonresident $4560 full-time, $190 per unit part-time. Full-time tuition and fees vary according to course load. Part-time tuition and fees vary according to course load. *Required fees:* $624 full-time, $26 per unit part-time.

Applying *Options:* electronic application. *Recommended:* high school transcript.

Freshman Application Contact Admissions Office, Folsom Lake College, 10 College Parkway, Folsom, CA 95630. *Phone:* 916-608-6500. *Web site:* http://www.flc.losrios.edu/.

Foothill College

Los Altos Hills, California

- **State and locally supported** 2-year, founded 1958, part of Foothill-DeAnza Community College District
- **Suburban** 122-acre campus with easy access to San Jose
- **Endowment** $15.0 million
- **Coed,** 18,342 undergraduate students, 20% full-time, 51% women, 49% men

Undergraduates 3,728 full-time, 14,614 part-time. Students come from 16 states and territories; 74 other countries; 7% are from out of state; 25% transferred in.

Freshmen *Admission:* 5,697 applied, 5,697 admitted, 1,266 enrolled.

Faculty *Total:* 633, 32% full-time. *Student/faculty ratio:* 34:1.

Majors Accounting; American studies; anthropology; art; art history, criticism and conservation; athletic training; avionics maintenance technology; biology/biological sciences; biology/biotechnology laboratory technician; business administration and management; chemistry; child development; classics and classical languages; comparative literature; creative writing; dental assisting; dental hygiene; diagnostic medical sonography and ultrasound technology; economics; electrical, electronic and communications engineering technology; emergency medical technology (EMT paramedic); English; fine/studio arts; history; international business/trade/commerce; landscape architecture; legal studies; linguistics; mathematics; medical radiologic technology; music; ornamental horticulture; philosophy; photography; physical education teaching and coaching; physician assistant; physics; plant nursery management; political science and government; psychology; radio and television; radiologic technology/science; real estate; respiratory care therapy; social sciences; sociology; Spanish; veterinary/animal health technology; women's studies.

Academics *Calendar:* quarters. *Degree:* certificates and associate. *Special study options:* academic remediation for entering students, accelerated degree program, adult/continuing education programs, advanced placement credit, cooperative education, distance learning, English as a second language, honors programs, independent study, internships, off-campus study, part-time degree program, services for LD students, student-designed majors, study abroad, summer session for credit. *ROTC:* Army (c), Air Force (c).

Library Hubert H. Semans Library with 70,000 titles, 450 serial subscriptions, 5,150 audiovisual materials, an OPAC, a Web page.

Student Life *Housing:* college housing not available. *Activities and Organizations:* drama/theater group, student-run newspaper, radio station, choral group. *Campus security:* 24-hour emergency response devices and patrols, late-night transport/escort service. *Student services:* health clinic, personal/psychological counseling, legal services.

Athletics Member NJCAA. *Intercollegiate sports:* basketball M/W, football M, golf M, soccer M/W, softball W, swimming and diving M/W, tennis M, volleyball M, water polo W.

Costs (2011–12) *Tuition:* state resident $612 full-time, $17 per unit part-time; nonresident $4284 full-time, $19 per unit part-time. Full-time tuition and fees vary according to course load. Part-time tuition and fees vary according to course load. *Required fees:* $42 per term part-time. *Waivers:* employees or children of employees.

Financial Aid Of all full-time matriculated undergraduates who enrolled in 2009, 80 Federal Work-Study jobs (averaging $1300). 210 state and other part-time jobs.

Applying *Options:* electronic application. *Recommended:* high school transcript. *Application deadlines:* 9/15 (freshmen), rolling (transfers). *Notification:* continuous (freshmen), continuous (transfers).

Freshman Application Contact Ms. Shawna Aced, Registrar, Foothill College, Admissions and Records, 12345 El Monte Road, Los Altos Hills, CA 94022. *Phone:* 650-949-7771. *E-mail:* acedshawna@hda.edu. *Web site:* http://www.foothill.edu/.

Fresno City College

Fresno, California

Freshman Application Contact Office Assistant, Fresno City College, 1101 East University Avenue, Fresno, CA 93741-0002. *Phone:* 559-442-4600 Ext. 8604. *Fax:* 559-237-4232. *E-mail:* fcc.admissions@fresnocitycollege.edu. *Web site:* http://www.fresnocitycollege.edu/.

Fullerton College
Fullerton, California

Director of Admissions Mr. Albert Abutin, Dean of Admissions and Records, Fullerton College, 321 East Chapman Avenue, Fullerton, CA 92832-2095. *Phone:* 714-992-7076. *Fax:* 714-992-9903. *E-mail:* aabutin@fullcoll.edu. *Web site:* http://www.fullcoll.edu/.

Gavilan College
Gilroy, California

Freshman Application Contact Gavilan College, 5055 Santa Teresa Boulevard, Gilroy, CA 95020-9599. *Phone:* 408-848-4754. *Web site:* http://www.gavilan.edu/.

Glendale Community College
Glendale, California

Freshman Application Contact Ms. Sharon Combs, Dean, Admissions, and Records, Glendale Community College, 1500 North Verdugo Road, Glendale, CA 91208. *Phone:* 818-240-1000 Ext. 5910. *E-mail:* scombs@glendale.edu. *Web site:* http://www.glendale.edu/.

Golden West College
Huntington Beach, California

- **State and locally supported** 2-year, founded 1966, part of Coast Community College District System
- **Suburban** 122-acre campus with easy access to Los Angeles
- **Endowment** $880,684
- **Coed,** 13,226 undergraduate students, 32% full-time, 54% women, 46% men

Undergraduates 4,291 full-time, 8,935 part-time. Students come from 28 other countries.

Faculty *Total:* 455, 32% full-time. *Student/faculty ratio:* 34:1.

Majors Accounting; administrative assistant and secretarial science; architectural engineering technology; art; automobile/automotive mechanics technology; biological and physical sciences; biology/biological sciences; business administration and management; commercial and advertising art; consumer merchandising/retailing management; cosmetology; criminal justice/law enforcement administration; criminal justice/police science; drafting and design technology; electrical, electronic and communications engineering technology; engineering technology; graphic and printing equipment operation/production; humanities; journalism; legal administrative assistant/secretary; liberal arts and sciences/liberal studies; marketing/marketing management; mathematics; music; natural sciences; ornamental horticulture; physical sciences; radio and television; real estate; registered nursing/registered nurse; sign language interpretation and translation.

Academics *Calendar:* semesters (summer session). *Degree:* certificates and associate. *Special study options:* academic remediation for entering students, adult/continuing education programs, advanced placement credit, cooperative education, distance learning, English as a second language, external degree program, honors programs, independent study, internships, part-time degree program, services for LD students, student-designed majors, study abroad, summer session for credit. *ROTC:* Air Force (c).

Library Golden West College Library plus 1 other with 95,000 titles, 410 serial subscriptions, an OPAC, a Web page.

Student Life *Housing:* college housing not available. *Activities and Organizations:* drama/theater group, student-run newspaper, choral group. *Campus security:* 24-hour emergency response devices and patrols, late-night transport/escort service. *Student services:* health clinic, personal/psychological counseling, legal services.

Athletics Member NJCAA. *Intercollegiate sports:* baseball M, cross-country running M/W, football M, soccer M/W, softball W, swimming and diving M/W, track and field M/W, volleyball M/W, water polo M/W.

Costs (2010–11) *Tuition:* state resident $0 full-time; nonresident $4940 full-time, $190 per unit part-time. *Required fees:* $738 full-time, $26 per unit part-time, $31 per term part-time.

Applying *Options:* early admission. *Required for some:* essay or personal statement. *Recommended:* high school transcript. *Application deadlines:* rolling (freshmen), rolling (transfers). *Notification:* continuous (freshmen), continuous (transfers).

Freshman Application Contact Golden West College, PO Box 2748, 15744 Golden West Street, Huntington Beach, CA 92647-2748. *Phone:* 714-892-7711 Ext. 58196. *Web site:* http://www.goldenwestcollege.edu/.

Golf Academy of America
Carlsbad, California

Director of Admissions Ms. Deborah Wells, Admissions Coordinator, Golf Academy of America, 1950 Camino Vida Roble, Suite 125, Carlsbad, CA 92008. *Phone:* 760-414-1501. *Toll-free phone:* 800-342-7342. *E-mail:* sdga@sdgagolf.com. *Web site:* http://www.golfacademy.edu/.

Grossmont College
El Cajon, California

Freshman Application Contact Admissions Office, Grossmont College, 8800 Grossmont College Drive, El Cajon, CA 92020-1799. *Phone:* 619-644-7186. *Web site:* http://www.grossmont.edu/.

Hartnell College
Salinas, California

Director of Admissions Director of Admissions, Hartnell College, 411 Central Avenue, Salinas, CA 93901. *Phone:* 831-755-6711. *Fax:* 831-759-6014. *Web site:* http://www.hartnell.edu/.

Heald College–Concord
Concord, California

Freshman Application Contact Director of Admissions, Heald College–Concord, 5130 Commercial Circle, Concord, CA 94520. *Phone:* 925-288-5800. *Toll-free phone:* 800-755-3550. *Fax:* 925-288-5896. *E-mail:* concordinfo@heald.edu. *Web site:* http://www.heald.edu/.

Heald College–Fresno
Fresno, California

Freshman Application Contact Director of Admissions, Heald College–Fresno, 255 West Bullard Avenue, Fresno, CA 93704-1706. *Phone:* 559-438-4222. *Toll-free phone:* 800-755-3550. *Fax:* 559-438-0948. *E-mail:* fresnoinfo@heald.edu. *Web site:* http://www.heald.edu/.

Heald College–Hayward
Hayward, California

Freshman Application Contact Director of Admissions, Heald College–Hayward, 25500 Industrial Boulevard, Hayward, CA 94545. *Phone:* 510-783-2100. *Toll-free phone:* 800-755-3550. *Fax:* 510-783-3287. *E-mail:* harwardinfo@heald.edu. *Web site:* http://www.heald.edu/.

Heald College–Rancho Cordova
Rancho Cordova, California

Freshman Application Contact Director of Admissions, Heald College–Rancho Cordova, 2910 Prospect Park Drive, Rancho Cordova, CA 95670-6005. *Phone:* 916-638-1616. *Toll-free phone:* 800-755-3550. *Fax:* 916-638-1580. *E-mail:* ranchocordovainfo@heald.edu. *Web site:* http://www.heald.edu/.

Heald College–Roseville
Roseville, California

Freshman Application Contact Director of Admissions, Heald College–Roseville, 7 Sierra Gate Plaza, Roseville, CA 95678. *Phone:* 916-789-8600. *Toll-free phone:* 800-755-3550. *Fax:* 916-789-8606. *E-mail:* rosevilleinfo@heald.edu. *Web site:* http://www.heald.edu/.

Heald College–Salinas
Salinas, California

Freshman Application Contact Director of Admissions, Heald College–Salinas, 1450 North Main Street, Salinas, CA 93906. *Phone:* 831-443-1700. *Toll-free phone:* 800-755-3550. *Fax:* 831-443-1050. *E-mail:* salinasinfo@heald.edu. *Web site:* http://www.heald.edu/.

Heald College–San Francisco
San Francisco, California

Freshman Application Contact Director of Admissions, Heald College–San Francisco, 350 Mission Street, San Francisco, CA 94105. *Phone:* 415-808-

3000. *Toll-free phone:* 800-755-3550. *Fax:* 415-808-3005. *E-mail:* sanfranciscoinfo@heald.edu. *Web site:* http://www.heald.edu/.

Heald College–San Jose
Milpitas, California

Freshman Application Contact Director of Admissions, Heald College–San Jose, 341 Great Mall Parkway, Milpitas, CA 95035. *Phone:* 408-934-4900. *Toll-free phone:* 800-755-3550. *Fax:* 408-934-7777. *E-mail:* sanjoseinfo@heald.edu. *Web site:* http://www.heald.edu/.

Heald College–Stockton
Stockton, California

Freshman Application Contact Director of Admissions, Heald College–Stockton, 1605 East March Lane, Stockton, CA 95210. *Phone:* 209-473-5200. *Toll-free phone:* 800-755-3550. *Fax:* 209-477-2739. *E-mail:* stocktoninfo@heald.edu. *Web site:* http://www.heald.edu/.

High-Tech Institute
Sacramento, California

Freshman Application Contact Admissions Office, High-Tech Institute, 9738 Lincoln Village Drive, Suite 100, Sacramento, CA 95827. *Phone:* 916-929-9700. *Toll-free phone:* 800-322-4128. *Web site:* http://www.high-techinstitute.com/.

Imperial Valley College
Imperial, California

Director of Admissions Dawn Chun, Associate Dean of Admissions and Records, Imperial Valley College, 380 East Aten Road, PO Box 158, Imperial, CA 92251-0158. *Phone:* 760-352-8320 Ext. 200. *Web site:* http://www.imperial.edu/.

Irvine Valley College
Irvine, California

Director of Admissions Mr. John Edwards, Director of Admissions, Records, and Enrollment Services, Irvine Valley College, 5500 Irvine Center Drive, Irvine, CA 92618. *Phone:* 949-451-5416. *Web site:* http://www.ivc.edu/.

ITT Technical Institute
Anaheim, California

- **Proprietary** primarily 2-year, founded 1982, part of ITT Educational Services, Inc.
- **Suburban** campus
- **Coed**

Majors Business administration and management; CAD/CADD drafting/design technology; computer and information systems security; computer engineering technology; computer systems networking and telecommunications; construction management; criminal justice/law enforcement administration; design and visual communications; electrical, electronic and communications engineering technology; game and interactive media design; health information/medical records technology; legal assistant/paralegal; project management; system, networking, and LAN/WAN management.
Academics *Calendar:* quarters. *Degrees:* associate and bachelor's.
Student Life *Housing:* college housing not available.
Financial Aid Of all full-time matriculated undergraduates who enrolled in 2009, 20 Federal Work-Study jobs (averaging $5000).
Freshman Application Contact Director of Recruitment, ITT Technical Institute, 4000 West Metropolitan Drive, Suite 100, Anaheim, CA 92801-9938. *Phone:* 714-941-2400. *Web site:* http://www.itt-tech.edu/.

ITT Technical Institute
Culver City, California

- **Proprietary** 2-year, part of ITT Educational Services, Inc.
- **Coed**

Majors CAD/CADD drafting/design technology; computer and information systems security; computer engineering technology; criminal justice/law enforcement administration; electrical, electronic and communications engineering technology; legal assistant/paralegal; project management; system, networking, and LAN/WAN management.
Academics *Calendar:* quarters.

Freshman Application Contact Director of Recruitment, ITT Technical Institute, 6101 W. Centinela Avenue, Culver City, CA 90230. *Phone:* 310-417-5800. *Toll-free phone:* 800-215-6151. *Web site:* http://www.itt-tech.edu/.

ITT Technical Institute
Lathrop, California

- **Proprietary** primarily 2-year, founded 1997, part of ITT Educational Services, Inc.
- **Coed**

Majors Business administration and management; CAD/CADD drafting/design technology; computer and information systems security; computer engineering technology; computer systems networking and telecommunications; construction management; criminal justice/law enforcement administration; design and visual communications; electrical, electronic and communications engineering technology; game and interactive media design; legal assistant/paralegal; project management; system, networking, and LAN/WAN management; web page, digital/multimedia and information resources design.
Academics *Calendar:* quarters. *Degrees:* associate and bachelor's.
Student Life *Housing:* college housing not available.
Freshman Application Contact Director of Recruitment, ITT Technical Institute, 16916 South Harlan Road, Lathrop, CA 95330. *Phone:* 209-858-0077. *Toll-free phone:* 800-346-1786. *Web site:* http://www.itt-tech.edu/.

ITT Technical Institute
Oakland, California

- **Proprietary** 2-year, part of ITT Educational Services, Inc.
- **Coed**

Majors CAD/CADD drafting/design technology; computer and information systems security; computer engineering technology; computer software engineering; computer software technology; criminal justice/law enforcement administration; electrical, electronic and communications engineering technology; legal assistant/paralegal; project management; system, networking, and LAN/WAN management.
Academics *Calendar:* quarters.
Freshman Application Contact Director of Recruitment, ITT Technical Institute, 7901 Oakport Street, Suite 3000, Oakland, CA 94621. *Phone:* 510-553-2800. *Toll-free phone:* 877-442-5833. *Web site:* http://www.itt-tech.edu/.

ITT Technical Institute
Oxnard, California

- **Proprietary** primarily 2-year, founded 1993, part of ITT Educational Services, Inc.
- **Urban** campus
- **Coed**

Majors CAD/CADD drafting/design technology; computer and information systems security; computer engineering technology; construction management; criminal justice/law enforcement administration; design and visual communications; electrical, electronic and communications engineering technology; game and interactive media design; health information/medical records technology; information technology project management; legal assistant/paralegal; project management; system, networking, and LAN/WAN management.
Academics *Calendar:* quarters. *Degrees:* associate and bachelor's.
Student Life *Housing:* college housing not available.
Freshman Application Contact Director of Recruitment, ITT Technical Institute, 2051 Solar Drive, Suite 150, Oxnard, CA 93036. *Phone:* 805-988-0143. *Toll-free phone:* 800-530-1582. *Web site:* http://www.itt-tech.edu/.

ITT Technical Institute
Rancho Cordova, California

- **Proprietary** primarily 2-year, founded 1954, part of ITT Educational Services, Inc.
- **Urban** campus
- **Coed**

Majors Business administration and management; CAD/CADD drafting/design technology; computer and information systems security; computer engineering technology; computer systems networking and telecommunications; construction management; criminal justice/law enforcement administration; design and visual communications; electrical, electronic and communications engineering technology; game and interactive media design; legal assistant/paralegal; project management; system, networking, and LAN/WAN management; web page, digital/multimedia and information resources design.

Academics *Calendar:* quarters. *Degrees:* associate and bachelor's.

Student Life *Housing:* college housing not available.

Freshman Application Contact Director of Recruitment, ITT Technical Institute, 10863 Gold Center Drive, Rancho Cordova, CA 95670-6034. *Phone:* 916-851-3900. *Toll-free phone:* 800-488-8466. *Web site:* http://www.itt-tech.edu/.

ITT Technical Institute

San Bernardino, California

- **Proprietary** primarily 2-year, founded 1987, part of ITT Educational Services, Inc.
- **Urban** campus
- **Coed**

Majors Business administration and management; CAD/CADD drafting/design technology; computer and information systems security; computer engineering technology; construction management; criminal justice/law enforcement administration; design and visual communications; electrical, electronic and communications engineering technology; game and interactive media design; health information/medical records technology; legal assistant/paralegal; project management; system, networking, and LAN/WAN management; web page, digital/multimedia and information resources design.

Academics *Calendar:* quarters. *Degrees:* associate and bachelor's.

Student Life *Housing:* college housing not available.

Freshman Application Contact Director of Recruitment, ITT Technical Institute, 670 East Carnegie Drive, San Bernardino, CA 92408. *Phone:* 909-806-4600. *Toll-free phone:* 800-888-3801. *Web site:* http://www.itt-tech.edu/.

ITT Technical Institute

San Diego, California

- **Proprietary** primarily 2-year, founded 1981, part of ITT Educational Services, Inc.
- **Suburban** campus
- **Coed**

Majors Business administration and management; CAD/CADD drafting/design technology; computer and information systems security; computer engineering technology; construction management; criminal justice/law enforcement administration; design and visual communications; electrical, electronic and communications engineering technology; game and interactive media design; legal assistant/paralegal; project management; system, networking, and LAN/WAN management; web page, digital/multimedia and information resources design.

Academics *Calendar:* quarters. *Degrees:* associate and bachelor's.

Student Life *Housing:* college housing not available.

Freshman Application Contact Director of Recruitment, ITT Technical Institute, 9680 Granite Ridge Drive, San Diego, CA 92123. *Phone:* 858-571-8500. *Toll-free phone:* 800-883-0380. *Web site:* http://www.itt-tech.edu/.

ITT Technical Institute

San Dimas, California

- **Proprietary** primarily 2-year, founded 1982, part of ITT Educational Services, Inc.
- **Suburban** campus
- **Coed**

Majors Business administration and management; CAD/CADD drafting/design technology; computer and information systems security; computer engineering technology; construction management; criminal justice/law enforcement administration; design and visual communications; electrical, electronic and communications engineering technology; game and interactive media design; health information/medical records technology; legal assistant/paralegal; project management; system, networking, and LAN/WAN management; web page, digital/multimedia and information resources design.

Academics *Calendar:* quarters. *Degrees:* associate and bachelor's.

Student Life *Housing:* college housing not available.

Financial Aid Of all full-time matriculated undergraduates who enrolled in 2009, 20 Federal Work-Study jobs (averaging $4500).

Freshman Application Contact Director of Recruitment, ITT Technical Institute, 650 West Cienega Avenue, San Dimas, CA 91773. *Phone:* 909-971-2300. *Toll-free phone:* 800-414-6522. *Web site:* http://www.itt-tech.edu/.

ITT Technical Institute

Sylmar, California

- **Proprietary** primarily 2-year, founded 1982, part of ITT Educational Services, Inc.
- **Urban** campus
- **Coed**

Majors Business administration and management; CAD/CADD drafting/design technology; computer and information systems security; computer engineering technology; computer systems networking and telecommunications; construction management; criminal justice/law enforcement administration; design and visual communications; electrical, electronic and communications engineering technology; game and interactive media design; health information/medical records technology; legal assistant/paralegal; project management; system, networking, and LAN/WAN management; web page, digital/multimedia and information resources design.

Academics *Calendar:* quarters. *Degrees:* associate and bachelor's.

Student Life *Housing:* college housing not available.

Freshman Application Contact Director of Recruitment, ITT Technical Institute, 12669 Encinitas Avenue, Sylmar, CA 91342-3664. *Phone:* 818-364-5151. *Toll-free phone:* 800-363-2086. *Web site:* http://www.itt-tech.edu/.

ITT Technical Institute

Torrance, California

- **Proprietary** primarily 2-year, founded 1987, part of ITT Educational Services, Inc.
- **Urban** campus
- **Coed**

Majors Business administration and management; CAD/CADD drafting/design technology; computer and information systems security; computer engineering technology; construction management; criminal justice/law enforcement administration; design and visual communications; electrical, electronic and communications engineering technology; game and interactive media design; health information/medical records technology; legal assistant/paralegal; project management; system, networking, and LAN/WAN management.

Academics *Calendar:* quarters. *Degrees:* associate and bachelor's.

Student Life *Housing:* college housing not available.

Financial Aid Of all full-time matriculated undergraduates who enrolled in 2009, 6 Federal Work-Study jobs (averaging $4000).

Freshman Application Contact Director of Recruitment, ITT Technical Institute, 20050 South Vermont Avenue, Torrance, CA 90502. *Phone:* 310-380-1555. *Web site:* http://www.itt-tech.edu/.

ITT Technical Institute

West Covina, California

- **Proprietary** 2-year, part of ITT Educational Services, Inc.
- **Coed**

Majors CAD/CADD drafting/design technology; computer and information systems security; computer engineering technology; criminal justice/law enforcement administration; design and visual communications; electrical, electronic and communications engineering technology; legal assistant/paralegal; project management; system, networking, and LAN/WAN management.

Academics *Calendar:* quarters.

Freshman Application Contact Director of Recruitment, ITT Technical Institute, 1530 W. Cameron Avenue, West Covina, CA 91790. *Phone:* 626-813-3681. *Toll-free phone:* 877-480-2766. *Web site:* http://www.itt-tech.edu/.

Kaplan College, Bakersfield Campus

Bakersfield, California

- **Proprietary** 2-year
- **Coed**

Academics *Degree:* certificates, diplomas, and associate.

Freshman Application Contact Kaplan College, Bakersfield Campus, 1914 Wible Road, Bakersfield, CA 93304. *Phone:* 661-836-6300. *Web site:* http://www.kc-bakersfield.com/.

Kaplan College, Chula Vista Campus

Chula Vista, California

- **Proprietary** 2-year
- **Coed**

Freshman Application Contact Kaplan College, Chula Vista Campus, 555 Broadway, Chula Vista, CA 91910. *Phone:* 877-473-3052. *Toll-free phone:* 887-473-3052. *Web site:* http://www.kc-chulavista.com/.

Kaplan College, Fresno Campus
Clovis, California
- Proprietary 2-year
- Coed

Freshman Application Contact Kaplan College, Fresno Campus, 44 Shaw Avenue, Rodeo Plaza Shopping Center, Clovis, CA 93612. *Phone:* 559-325-5100. *Toll-free phone:* 800-526-0256. *Web site:* http://www.kc-fresno.com/.

Kaplan College, Modesto Campus
Salida, California
- Proprietary 2-year
- Coed, primarily women

Academics *Calendar:* semesters. *Degree:* diplomas and associate.
Freshman Application Contact Kaplan College, Modesto Campus, 5172 Kiernan Court, Salida, CA 95368. *Phone:* 209-543-7000. *Toll-free phone:* 800-526-0256. *Web site:* http://www.kc-modesto.com/.

Kaplan College, Palm Springs Campus
Palm Springs, California
- Proprietary 2-year
- Coed

Academics *Degree:* diplomas and associate.
Freshman Application Contact Kaplan College, Palm Springs Campus, 2475 East Tahquitz Canyon Way, Palm Springs, CA 92262. *Phone:* 760-778-3540. *Web site:* http://www.kc-palmsprings.com/.

Kaplan College, Panorama City Campus
Panorama City, California
- Proprietary 2-year, founded 1996
- Coed

Academics *Degree:* diplomas and associate.
Freshman Application Contact Kaplan College, Panorama City Campus, 14355 Roscoe Boulevard, Panorama City, CA 91402. *Phone:* 818-672-3005. *Toll-free phone:* 800-526-0256. *Web site:* http://www.kc-panoramacity.com/.

Kaplan College, Riverside Campus
Riverside, California
- Proprietary 2-year
- Coed

Academics *Degree:* diplomas and associate.
Freshman Application Contact Kaplan College, Riverside Campus, 4040 Vine Street, Riverside, CA 92507. *Phone:* 951-276-1704. *Web site:* http://www.kc-riverside.com/.

Kaplan College, Sacramento Campus
Sacramento, California
- Proprietary 2-year
- Coed

Academics *Calendar:* semesters. *Degree:* diplomas and associate.
Freshman Application Contact Kaplan College, Sacramento Campus, 4330 Watt Avenue, Suite 400, Sacramento, CA 95821. *Phone:* 916-649-8168. *Toll-free phone:* 800-526-0256. *Web site:* http://www.kc-sacramento.com/.

Kaplan College, San Diego Campus
San Diego, California
- Proprietary 2-year, founded 1976
- Urban campus
- Coed

Academics *Calendar:* semesters. *Degrees:* certificates, diplomas, and associate (also includes Vista campus).
Freshman Application Contact Kaplan College, San Diego Campus, 9055 Balboa Avenue, San Diego, CA 92123. *Phone:* 858-279-4500. *Toll-free phone:* 800-526-0256. *Web site:* http://www.kc-sandiego.com/.

Kaplan College, Stockton Campus
Stockton, California
- Proprietary 2-year
- Coed

Academics *Degree:* diplomas and associate.
Freshman Application Contact Kaplan College, Stockton Campus, 722 West March Lane, Stockton, CA 95207. *Phone:* 209-954-4208. *Web site:* http://www.kc-stockton.com/.

Kaplan College, Vista Campus
Vista, California
- Proprietary 2-year
- Coed

Academics *Degree:* diplomas and associate.
Freshman Application Contact Kaplan College, Vista Campus, 2022 University Drive, Vista, CA 92083. *Phone:* 760-630-1555. *Web site:* http://www.kc-vista.com/.

Lake Tahoe Community College
South Lake Tahoe, California
Freshman Application Contact Office of Admissions and Records, Lake Tahoe Community College, One College Drive, South Lake Tahoe, CA 96150. *Phone:* 530-541-4660 Ext. 211. *Fax:* 530-541-7852. *E-mail:* admissions@ltcc.edu. *Web site:* http://www.ltcc.edu/.

Laney College
Oakland, California
Freshman Application Contact Mrs. Barbara Simmons, District Admissions Officer, Laney College, 900 Fallon Street, Oakland, CA 94607-4893. *Phone:* 510-466-7369. *Web site:* http://www.peralta.cc.ca.us/.

Las Positas College
Livermore, California
Director of Admissions Mrs. Sylvia R. Rodriguez, Director of Admissions and Records, Las Positas College, 3000 Campus Hill Drive, Livermore, CA 94551. *Phone:* 925-373-4942. *Web site:* http://www.laspositascollege.edu/.

Lassen Community College District
Susanville, California
Freshman Application Contact Mr. Chris J. Alberico, Registrar, Lassen Community College District, Highway 139, PO Box 3000, Susanville, CA 96130. *Phone:* 530-257-6181. *Web site:* http://www.lassencollege.edu/.

Le Cordon Bleu College of Culinary Arts in Los Angeles
Pasadena, California
Director of Admissions Nora Sandoval, Registrar, Le Cordon Bleu College of Culinary Arts in Los Angeles, 521 East Green Street, Pasadena, CA 91101. *Phone:* 626-229-1300. *Fax:* 626-204-3905. *E-mail:* nsandoval@la.chefs.edu. *Web site:* http://www.chefs.edu/Los-Angeles.

Long Beach City College
Long Beach, California
Director of Admissions Mr. Ross Miyashiro, Dean of Admissions and Records, Long Beach City College, 4901 East Carson Street, Long Beach, CA 90808-1780. *Phone:* 562-938-4130. *Web site:* http://www.lbcc.edu/.

Los Angeles City College
Los Angeles, California
Freshman Application Contact Elaine Geismar, Director of Student Assistance Center, Los Angeles City College, 855 North Vermont Avenue, Los Angeles, CA 90029-3590. *Phone:* 323-953-4340. *Web site:* http://www.lacitycollege.edu/.

Los Angeles County College of Nursing and Allied Health
Los Angeles, California

Freshman Application Contact Admissions Office, Los Angeles County College of Nursing and Allied Health, 1237 North Mission Road, Los Angeles, CA 90033. *Phone:* 323-226-4911. *Web site:* http://www.dhs.co.la.ca.us/wps/portal/collegeofnursing/.

Los Angeles Harbor College
Wilmington, California

- **State and locally supported** 2-year, founded 1949, part of Los Angeles Community College District System
- **Suburban** 80-acre campus with easy access to Los Angeles
- **Coed,** 10,181 undergraduate students, 28% full-time, 61% women, 39% men

Undergraduates 2,812 full-time, 7,369 part-time. Students come from 14 states and territories; 15 other countries.
Freshmen *Admission.* 1,526 enrolled. *Average high school GPA:* 2.5.
Faculty *Total:* 484, 23% full-time. *Student/faculty ratio:* 43:1.
Majors Accounting; administrative assistant and secretarial science; architectural engineering technology; automobile/automotive mechanics technology; biology/biological sciences; business administration and management; computer engineering technology; criminal justice/police science; data processing and data processing technology; developmental and child psychology; drafting and design technology; electrical, electronic and communications engineering technology; electromechanical technology; engineering technology; fire science/firefighting; information science/studies; legal administrative assistant/secretary; liberal arts and sciences/liberal studies; medical administrative assistant and medical secretary; physics; pre-engineering; real estate; registered nursing/registered nurse.
Academics *Calendar:* semesters. *Degree:* certificates and associate. *Special study options:* academic remediation for entering students, accelerated degree program, adult/continuing education programs, advanced placement credit, cooperative education, distance learning, double majors, English as a second language, freshman honors college, honors programs, independent study, off-campus study, part-time degree program, services for LD students, study abroad, summer session for credit.
Library Harbor College Library with 89,768 titles, 21 serial subscriptions, 35 audiovisual materials, an OPAC, a Web page.
Student Life *Housing:* college housing not available. *Activities and Organizations:* drama/theater group, student-run newspaper, television station, choral group, Alpha Gamma Sigma, EOP&S, Creando Un Nuevo Futuro, Psychology Club, Honors Transfer Program. *Campus security:* 24-hour emergency response devices and patrols, late-night transport/escort service. *Student services:* health clinic, personal/psychological counseling, legal services.
Athletics *Intercollegiate sports:* baseball M, basketball M, football M, soccer M/W, softball W, volleyball W.
Costs (2011–12) *Tuition:* state resident $0 full-time; nonresident $5088 full-time, $212 per unit part-time. *Required fees:* $646 full-time, $26 per unit part-time, $22 per year part-time.
Financial Aid Of all full-time matriculated undergraduates who enrolled in 2009, 100 Federal Work-Study jobs (averaging $1800).
Applying *Options:* electronic application, early admission, deferred entrance. *Application deadlines:* 9/3 (freshmen), 9/3 (out-of-state freshmen), 9/3 (transfers).
Freshman Application Contact Los Angeles Harbor College, 1111 Figueroa Place, Wilmington, CA 90744-2397. *Phone:* 310-233-4091. *Web site:* http://www.lahc.edu/.

Los Angeles Mission College
Sylmar, California

Freshman Application Contact Ms. Angela Merrill, Admissions Supervisor, Los Angeles Mission College, 13356 Eldridge Avenue, Sylmar, CA 91342-3245. *Phone:* 818-364-7658. *Web site:* http://www.lamission.edu/.

Los Angeles Pierce College
Woodland Hills, California

Director of Admissions Ms. Shelley L. Gerstl, Dean of Admissions and Records, Los Angeles Pierce College, 6201 Winnetka Avenue, Woodland Hills, CA 91371-0001. *Phone:* 818-719-6448. *Web site:* http://www.piercecollege.edu/.

Los Angeles Southwest College
Los Angeles, California

Director of Admissions Dan W. Walden, Dean of Academic Affairs, Los Angeles Southwest College, 1600 West Imperial Highway, Los Angeles, CA 90047-4810. *Phone:* 323-242-5511. *Web site:* http://www.lasc.edu/.

Los Angeles Trade-Technical College
Los Angeles, California

Director of Admissions Dr. Raul Cardoza, Los Angeles Trade-Technical College, 400 West Washington Boulevard, Los Angeles, CA 90015-4108. *Phone:* 213-763-5301. *E-mail:* CardozaRJ@lattc.edu. *Web site:* http://www.lattc.edu/.

Los Angeles Valley College
Van Nuys, California

Director of Admissions Mr. Florentino Manzano, Associate Dean, Los Angeles Valley College, 5800 Fulton Avenue, Van Nuys, CA 91401-4096. *Phone:* 818-947-2353. *E-mail:* manzanf@lavc.edu. *Web site:* http://www.lavc.cc.ca.us/.

Los Medanos College
Pittsburg, California

Freshman Application Contact Ms. Gail Newman, Director of Admissions and Records, Los Medanos College, 2700 East Leland Road, Pittsburg, CA 94565-5197. *Phone:* 925-439-2181 Ext. 7500. *Web site:* http://www.losmedanos.net/.

Mendocino College
Ukiah, California

- **State and locally supported** 2-year, founded 1973, part of California Community College System
- **Rural** 127-acre campus
- **Coed,** 4,558 undergraduate students, 25% full-time, 62% women, 38% men

Undergraduates 1,143 full-time, 3,415 part-time. Students come from 16 states and territories; 2 other countries; 0.2% transferred in.
Freshmen *Admission:* 661 applied, 661 admitted, 354 enrolled.
Faculty *Total:* 305, 16% full-time, 3% with terminal degrees. *Student/faculty ratio:* 16:1.
Majors Accounting; administrative assistant and secretarial science; agriculture; art; automobile/automotive mechanics technology; biology/biological sciences; business administration and management; chemistry; child development; criminal justice/law enforcement administration; criminal justice/police science; data processing and data processing technology; developmental and child psychology; dramatic/theater arts; English; fiber, textile and weaving arts; finance; French; health professions related; human services; information science/studies; kindergarten/preschool education; liberal arts and sciences/liberal studies; mathematics; music; ornamental horticulture; physical education teaching and coaching; physical sciences; psychology; real estate; rhetoric and composition; social sciences; Spanish; substance abuse/addiction counseling.
Academics *Calendar:* semesters. *Degree:* certificates and associate. *Special study options:* academic remediation for entering students, adult/continuing education programs, advanced placement credit, cooperative education, distance learning, English as a second language, honors programs, independent study, internships, part-time degree program, services for LD students, summer session for credit.
Library Lowery Library with 27,441 titles, 275 serial subscriptions, a Web page.
Student Life *Housing:* college housing not available. *Activities and Organizations:* drama/theater group, student-run radio station, choral group. *Campus security:* late-night transport/escort service, security patrols 6 pm to 10 pm.
Athletics Member NJCAA. *Intercollegiate sports:* baseball M, basketball M/W, football M, soccer W, volleyball W. *Intramural sports:* table tennis M/W, tennis M/W.
Costs (2010–11) *Tuition:* state resident $0 full-time; nonresident $5700 full-time, $190 per unit part-time. Full-time tuition and fees vary according to course load. Part-time tuition and fees vary according to course load. *Required fees:* $780 full-time, $26 per unit part-time.
Financial Aid *Financial aid deadline:* 5/20.
Applying *Options:* electronic application, early admission, deferred entrance. *Required:* high school transcript. *Application deadlines:* rolling (freshmen), rolling (transfers). *Notification:* continuous (freshmen), continuous (transfers).

Freshman Application Contact Mendocino College, 1000 Hensley Creek Road, Ukiah, CA 95482-0300. *Phone:* 707-468-3103. *Web site:* http://www.mendocino.edu/.

Merced College
Merced, California

Freshman Application Contact Ms. Cherie Davis, Associate Registrar, Merced College, 3600 M Street, Merced, CA 95348-2898. *Phone:* 209-384-6188. *Fax:* 209-384-6339. *Web site:* http://www.mccd.edu/.

Merritt College
Oakland, California

Freshman Application Contact Ms. Barbara Simmons, District Admissions Officer, Merritt College, 12500 Campus Drive, Oakland, CA 94619-3196. *Phone:* 510-466-7369. *E-mail:* hperdue@peralta.cc.ca.us. *Web site:* http://www.merritt.edu/.

MiraCosta College
Oceanside, California

Freshman Application Contact Director of Admissions, MiraCosta College, One Barnard Drive, Oceanside, CA 92056-3899. *Phone:* 760-795-6620. *Toll-free phone:* 888-201-8480. *E-mail:* admissions@miracosta.edu. *Web site:* http://www.miracosta.edu/.

Mission College
Santa Clara, California

Director of Admissions Daniel Sanidad, Dean of Student Services, Mission College, 3000 Mission College Boulevard, Santa Clara, CA 95054-1897. *Phone:* 408-855-5139. *Web site:* http://www.missioncollege.org/.

Modesto Junior College
Modesto, California

Freshman Application Contact Ms. Susie Agostini, Dean of Matriculation, Admissions, and Records, Modesto Junior College, 435 College Avenue, Modesto, CA 95350. *Phone:* 209-575-6470. *Fax:* 209-575-6859. *E-mail:* mjcadmissions@mail.yosemite.cc.ca.us. *Web site:* http://www.mjc.edu/.

Monterey Peninsula College
Monterey, California

Director of Admissions Ms. Vera Coleman, Registrar, Monterey Peninsula College, 980 Fremont Street, Monterey, CA 93940-4799. *Phone:* 831-646-4007. *E-mail:* vcoleman@mpc.edu. *Web site:* http://www.mpc.edu/.

Moorpark College
Moorpark, California

Freshman Application Contact Ms. Katherine Colborn, Registrar, Moorpark College, 7075 Campus Road, Moorpark, CA 93021-2899. *Phone:* 805-378-1415. *Web site:* http://www.moorparkcollege.edu/.

Mt. San Antonio College
Walnut, California

Freshman Application Contact Dr. George Bradshaw, Dean of Enrollment Management, Mt. San Antonio College, Walnut, CA 91789. *Phone:* 909-594-5611 Ext. 4505. *Toll-free phone:* 800-672-2463 Ext. 4415. *Web site:* http://www.mtsac.edu/.

Mt. San Jacinto College
San Jacinto, California

- **State and locally supported** 2-year, founded 1963, part of California Community College System
- **Suburban** 180-acre campus with easy access to San Diego
- **Coed**

Undergraduates 6,356 full-time, 11,227 part-time.
Academics *Calendar:* semesters. *Degree:* certificates, diplomas, and associate. *Special study options:* academic remediation for entering students, adult/continuing education programs, advanced placement credit, distance learning, double majors, English as a second language, honors programs, off-campus study, part-time degree program, services for LD students, study abroad, summer session for credit.
Student Life *Campus security:* part-time trained security personnel.
Costs (2010–11) *Tuition:* state resident $0 full-time; nonresident $5730 full-time, $191 per unit part-time. *Required fees:* $780 full-time, $26 per unit part-time.
Financial Aid Of all full-time matriculated undergraduates who enrolled in 2009, 109 Federal Work-Study jobs (averaging $1114). 125 state and other part-time jobs (averaging $1000).
Applying *Options:* early admission. *Recommended:* high school transcript.
Freshman Application Contact Mt. San Jacinto College, 1499 North State Street, San Jacinto, CA 92583-2399. *Phone:* 951-639-5212. *Toll-free phone:* 800-624-5561 Ext. 1410. *Web site:* http://www.msjc.edu/.

MTI College
Sacramento, California

- **Proprietary** 2-year, founded 1965
- **Suburban** 5-acre campus with easy access to Sacramento
- **Coed,** 900 undergraduate students
- 62% of applicants were admitted

Freshmen *Admission:* 629 applied, 390 admitted.
Faculty *Student/faculty ratio:* 15:1.
Majors Business administration and management; legal assistant/paralegal; system, networking, and LAN/WAN management.
Academics *Calendar:* continuous. *Degree:* diplomas and associate.
Standardized Tests *Required:* MTI Assessment (for admission).
Financial Aid Of all full-time matriculated undergraduates who enrolled in 2009, 35 Federal Work-Study jobs (averaging $1722).
Applying *Application fee:* $50. *Required:* interview.
Freshman Application Contact Director of Admissions, MTI College, 5221 Madison Avenue, Sacramento, CA 95841. *Phone:* 916-339-1500. *Fax:* 916-339-0305. *Web site:* http://www.mticollege.edu/.

Napa Valley College
Napa, California

Director of Admissions Mr. Oscar De Haro, Vice President of Student Services, Napa Valley College, 2277 Napa-Vallejo Highway, Napa, CA 94558-6236. *Phone:* 707-253-3000. *E-mail:* odeharo@napavalley.edu. *Web site:* http://www.napavalley.edu/.

New York Film Academy
Los Angeles, California

Freshman Application Contact Admissions Office, New York Film Academy, 3801 Barham Boulevard, Los Angeles, CA 90068. *Phone:* 818-733-2600. *Fax:* 818-733-4074. *E-mail:* studios@nyfa.edu. *Web site:* http://www.nyfa.com/.

Ohlone College
Fremont, California

Freshman Application Contact Christopher Williamson, Director of Admissions and Records, Ohlone College, 43600 Mission Boulevard, Fremont, CA 94539-5884. *Phone:* 510-659-6518. *Fax:* 510-659-7321. *E-mail:* cwilliamson@ohlone.edu. *Web site:* http://www.ohlone.edu/.

Orange Coast College
Costa Mesa, California

- **State and locally supported** 2-year, founded 1947, part of Coast Community College District System
- **Suburban** 162-acre campus with easy access to Los Angeles
- **Endowment** $10.0 million
- **Coed,** 25,316 undergraduate students, 39% full-time, 49% women, 51% men

Undergraduates 9,797 full-time, 15,519 part-time. Students come from 52 states and territories; 69 other countries; 3% are from out of state; 2% Black or African American, non-Hispanic/Latino; 22% Hispanic/Latino; 22% Asian, non-Hispanic/Latino; 0.7% Native Hawaiian or other Pacific Islander, non-Hispanic/Latino; 0.5% American Indian or Alaska Native, non-Hispanic/Latino; 2% Two or more races, non-Hispanic/Latino; 6% Race/ethnicity unknown; 3% international; 8% transferred in. *Retention:* 79% of full-time freshmen returned.
Freshmen *Admission:* 5,326 enrolled.
Faculty *Total:* 759, 31% full-time. *Student/faculty ratio:* 36:1.

Majors Accounting; administrative assistant and secretarial science; aeronautics/aviation/aerospace science and technology; airline pilot and flight crew; anthropology; architectural engineering technology; art; athletic training; avionics maintenance technology; behavioral sciences; biology/biological sciences; building/home/construction inspection; business administration and management; cardiovascular technology; chemistry; child-care and support services management; child-care provision; cinematography and film/video production; clinical laboratory science/medical technology; commercial and advertising art; communications technology; computer engineering technology; computer graphics; computer programming; computer programming (specific applications); computer typography and composition equipment operation; construction engineering technology; culinary arts; dance; data entry/microcomputer applications related; data processing and data processing technology; dental hygiene; dietetics; drafting and design technology; dramatic/theater arts; economics; electrical and power transmission installation; electrical, electronic and communications engineering technology; electrical/electronics equipment installation and repair; emergency medical technology (EMT paramedic); engineering; English; family and consumer economics related; family and consumer sciences/human sciences; fashion merchandising; film/cinema/video studies; food science; foods, nutrition, and wellness; food technology and processing; French; geography; geology/earth science; German; health professions related; heating, air conditioning, ventilation and refrigeration maintenance technology; history; horticultural science; hotel/motel administration; housing and human environments; human development and family studies; humanities; industrial and product design; industrial radiologic technology; information science/studies; interior design; journalism; kindergarten/preschool education; kinesiology and exercise science; legal administrative assistant/secretary; liberal arts and sciences/liberal studies; machine shop technology; machine tool technology; marine maintenance and ship repair technology; marketing/marketing management; mass communication/media; mathematics; medical administrative assistant and medical secretary; medical/clinical assistant; music; musical instrument fabrication and repair; music management; natural sciences; nuclear medical technology; ornamental horticulture; philosophy; photography; physical education teaching and coaching; physics; political science and government; religious studies; respiratory care therapy; restaurant, culinary, and catering management; retailing; selling skills and sales; social sciences; sociology; Spanish; special products marketing; welding technology; word processing.

Academics *Calendar:* semesters plus summer session. *Degree:* certificates and associate. *Special study options:* academic remediation for entering students, adult/continuing education programs, advanced placement credit, cooperative education, distance learning, double majors, English as a second language, external degree program, freshman honors college, honors programs, internships, off-campus study, part-time degree program, services for LD students, student-designed majors, study abroad, summer session for credit. *ROTC:* Army (c), Air Force (c).

Library Library with 105,892 titles, 216 serial subscriptions, 3,299 audiovisual materials, an OPAC, a Web page.

Student Life *Housing:* college housing not available. *Activities and Organizations:* drama/theater group, student-run newspaper, choral group, Circle K, Vietnamese Student Association, Doctors of Tomorrow, Sierra Club, Christian Students at OCC. *Campus security:* 24-hour emergency response devices and patrols, student patrols, late-night transport/escort service. *Student services:* health clinic, personal/psychological counseling, legal services.

Athletics *Intercollegiate sports:* baseball M, basketball M/W, bowling M(c)/W(c), crew M/W, cross-country running M/W, football M, golf M/W, soccer M/W, softball W, swimming and diving M/W, tennis M/W, track and field M/W, volleyball W, water polo M/W.

Costs (2011–12) *Tuition:* state resident $780 full-time, $26 per unit part-time; nonresident $6390 full-time, $187 per unit part-time. *Required fees:* $902 full-time, $26 per unit part-time.

Financial Aid Of all full-time matriculated undergraduates who enrolled in 2009, 108 Federal Work-Study jobs (averaging $3000). *Financial aid deadline:* 5/28.

Applying *Options:* electronic application. *Application deadlines:* rolling (freshmen), rolling (transfers). *Notification:* continuous (freshmen), continuous (transfers).

Freshman Application Contact Dean of Enrollment Services, Orange Coast College, 2701 Fairview Road, Costa Mesa, CA 92926. *Phone:* 714-432-5788. *Fax:* 714-432-5072. *Web site:* http://www.orangecoastcollege.com/.

Oxnard College
Oxnard, California

Freshman Application Contact Ms. Susan Cabral, Registrar, Oxnard College, 4000 South Rose Avenue, Oxnard, CA 93033-6699. *Phone:* 805-986-5843. *Fax:* 805-986-5943. *E-mail:* scabral@vcccd.edu. *Web site:* http://www.oxnardcollege.edu/.

Palomar College
San Marcos, California

Freshman Application Contact Mr. Herman Lee, Director of Enrollment Services, Palomar College, 1140 West Mission Road, San Marcos, CA 92069-1487. *Phone:* 760-744-1150 Ext. 2171. *Fax:* 760-744-2932. *E-mail:* admissions@palomar.edu. *Web site:* http://www.palomar.edu/.

Palo Verde College
Blythe, California

Freshman Application Contact Diana Rodriguez, Vice President of Student Services, Palo Verde College, 1 College Drive, Blythe, CA 92225. *Phone:* 760-921-5428. *Fax:* 760-921-3608. *E-mail:* diana.rodriguez@paloverde.edu. *Web site:* http://www.paloverde.edu/.

Pasadena City College
Pasadena, California

- **State and locally supported** 2-year, founded 1924, part of California Community College System
- **Urban** 55-acre campus with easy access to Los Angeles
- **Coed**

Undergraduates 29,000 full-time.
Faculty *Student/faculty ratio:* 20:1.
Academics *Calendar:* semesters. *Degree:* certificates and associate. *Special study options:* academic remediation for entering students, adult/continuing education programs, advanced placement credit, English as a second language, honors programs, part-time degree program, services for LD students, student-designed majors, study abroad, summer session for credit.
Student Life *Campus security:* 24-hour emergency response devices and patrols, late-night transport/escort service, cadet patrols.
Costs (2010–11) *Tuition:* state resident $0 full-time; nonresident $6540 full-time, $218 per unit part-time. Full-time tuition and fees vary according to course load. Part-time tuition and fees vary according to course load. *Required fees:* $844 full-time, $26 per unit part-time, $24 per term part-time.
Freshman Application Contact Pasadena City College, 1570 East Colorado Boulevard, Pasadena, CA 91106-2041. *Phone:* 626-585-7805. *Fax:* 626-585-7915. *Web site:* http://www.pasadena.edu/.

Pima Medical Institute
Chula Vista, California

- **Proprietary** primarily 2-year, founded 1998, administratively affiliated with Vocational Training Institutes, Inc
- **Urban** campus
- **Coed,** 813 undergraduate students

Majors Health/health-care administration; radiologic technology/science; respiratory therapy technician; veterinary/animal health technology.
Academics *Calendar:* modular. *Degrees:* certificates, associate, and bachelor's. *Special study options:* cooperative education, distance learning, internships.
Library E-Global.
Student Life *Housing:* college housing not available.
Standardized Tests *Required:* Wonderlic Scholastic Level Exam (for admission).
Applying *Required:* high school transcript, interview.
Freshman Application Contact Admissions Office, Pima Medical Institute, 780 Bay Boulevard, Suite 101, Chula Vista, CA 91910. *Phone:* 619-425-3200. *Toll-free phone:* 888-898-9048. *Web site:* http://www.pmi.edu/.

Platt College
Cerritos, California

Freshman Application Contact Ms. Ilene Holt, Dean of Student Services, Platt College, 10900 East 183rd Street, Suite 290, Cerritos, CA 90703-5342. *Phone:* 562-809-5100. *Toll-free phone:* 800-807-5288. *Web site:* http://www.platt.edu/.

Platt College
Huntington Beach, California

Director of Admissions Ms. Lisa Rhodes, President, Platt College, 7755 Center Avenue, Suite 600, Huntington Beach, CA 92647. *Phone:* 949-833-2300 Ext. 222. *Toll-free phone:* 888-866-6697 Ext. 230. *Web site:* http://www.plattcollege.edu/.

Platt College
Ontario, California

Director of Admissions Ms. Jennifer Abandonato, Director of Admissions, Platt College, 3700 Inland Empire Boulevard, Suite 400, Ontario, CA 91764. *Phone:* 909-941-9410. *Toll-free phone:* 888-866-6697. *Web site:* http://www.plattcollege.edu/.

Platt College–Los Angeles
Alhambra, California

Director of Admissions Mr. Detroit Whiteside, Director of Admissions, Platt College–Los Angeles, 1000 South Fremont A9W, Alhambra, CA 91803. *Phone:* 323-258-8050. *Toll-free phone:* 888-866-6697. *Web site:* http://www.plattcollege.edu/.

Porterville College
Porterville, California

Director of Admissions Ms. Judy Pope, Director of Admissions and Records/Registrar, Porterville College, 100 East College Avenue, Porterville, CA 93257-6058. *Phone:* 559-791-2222. *Web site:* http://www.pc.cc.ca.us/.

Professional Golfers Career College
Temecula, California

Freshman Application Contact Mr. Mark Bland, Director of Admissions, Professional Golfers Career College, 26109 Ynez Road, Temecula, CA 92591. *Phone:* 951-719-2994. *Toll-free phone:* 800-877-4380. *Fax:* 951-719-1643. *E-mail:* Mark@golfcollege.edu. *Web site:* http://www.golfcollege.edu/.

Reedley College
Reedley, California

- **State and locally supported** 2-year, founded 1926, part of State Center Community College District System
- **Rural** 350-acre campus
- **Coed**

Undergraduates 4,423 full-time, 7,359 part-time. Students come from 15 states and territories; 1% are from out of state.
Faculty *Student/faculty ratio:* 14:1.
Academics *Calendar:* semesters. *Degree:* certificates, diplomas, and associate. *Special study options:* academic remediation for entering students, adult/continuing education programs, advanced placement credit, cooperative education, distance learning, English as a second language, freshman honors college, honors programs, independent study, part-time degree program, services for LD students, study abroad, summer session for credit. *ROTC:* Air Force (c).
Student Life *Campus security:* 24-hour emergency response devices, late-night transport/escort service, 24-hour on-campus police dispatcher.
Costs (2010–11) *Tuition:* state resident $0 full-time; nonresident $5700 full-time. Full-time tuition and fees vary according to program. Part-time tuition and fees vary according to program. *Required fees:* $1496 full-time. *Room and board:* $2502; room only: $1402. Room and board charges vary according to board plan.
Applying *Required:* high school transcript.
Freshman Application Contact Admissions and Records Office, Reedley College, 995 North Reed Avenue, Reedley, CA 93654. *Phone:* 559-638-0323. *Fax:* 559-637-2523. *Web site:* http://www.reedleycollege.edu/.

Rio Hondo College
Whittier, California

Director of Admissions Ms. Judy G. Pearson, Director of Admissions and Records, Rio Hondo College, 3600 Workman Mill Road, Whittier, CA 90601-1699. *Phone:* 562-692-0921 Ext. 3153. *Web site:* http://www.riohondo.edu/.

Riverside Community College District
Riverside, California

Freshman Application Contact Ms. Lorraine Anderson, District Dean of Admissions and Records, Riverside Community College District, Riverside, CA 92506. *Phone:* 951-222-8600. *Fax:* 951-222-8037. *E-mail:* admissions@rcc.edu. *Web site:* http://www.rcc.edu/.

Sacramento City College
Sacramento, California

Director of Admissions Mr. Sam T. Sandusky, Dean, Student Services, Sacramento City College, 3835 Freeport Boulevard, Sacramento, CA 95822-1386. *Phone:* 916-558-2438. *Web site:* http://www.scc.losrios.edu/.

Saddleback College
Mission Viejo, California

Freshman Application Contact Admissions Office, Saddleback College, 28000 Marguerite Parkway, Mission Viejo, CA 92692. *Phone:* 949-582-4555. *Fax:* 949-347-8315. *E-mail:* earaiza@saddleback.edu. *Web site:* http://www.saddleback.edu/.

Sage College
Moreno Valley, California

Admissions Office Contact Sage College, 12125 Day Street, Building L, Moreno Valley, CA 92557-6720. *Toll-free phone:* 888-781-2727. *Web site:* http://www.sagecollege.edu/.

The Salvation Army College for Officer Training at Crestmont
Rancho Palos Verdes, California

Freshman Application Contact Capt. Kevin Jackson, Director of Curriculum, The Salvation Army College for Officer Training at Crestmont, 30840 Hawthorne Boulevard, Rancho Palos Verdes, CA 90275. *Phone:* 310-544-6442. *Fax:* 310-265-6520. *Web site:* http://www.crestmont.edu/.

San Bernardino Valley College
San Bernardino, California

Director of Admissions Ms. Helena Johnson, Director of Admissions and Records, San Bernardino Valley College, 701 South Mount Vernon Avenue, San Bernardino, CA 92410-2748. *Phone:* 909-384-4401. *Web site:* http://www.valleycollege.edu/.

San Diego City College
San Diego, California

- **State and locally supported** 2-year, founded 1914, part of San Diego Community College District System
- **Urban** 60-acre campus with easy access to San Diego and Tijuana
- **Endowment** $166,270
- **Coed,** 19,497 undergraduate students

Undergraduates 14% Black or African American, non-Hispanic/Latino; 38% Hispanic/Latino; 9% Asian, non-Hispanic/Latino; 0.6% Native Hawaiian or other Pacific Islander, non-Hispanic/Latino; 0.8% American Indian or Alaska Native, non-Hispanic/Latino; 10% Race/ethnicity unknown.
Faculty *Total:* 663, 22% full-time, 19% with terminal degrees. *Student/faculty ratio:* 35:1.
Majors Accounting; administrative assistant and secretarial science; African American/Black studies; anthropology; art; artificial intelligence; automobile/automotive mechanics technology; behavioral sciences; biology/biological sciences; business administration and management; carpentry; commercial and advertising art; computer engineering technology; consumer services and advocacy; cosmetology; court reporting; data processing and data processing technology; developmental and child psychology; drafting and design technology; dramatic/theater arts; electrical, electronic and communications engineering technology; emergency medical technology (EMT paramedic); engineering technology; English; environmental engineering technology; fashion merchandising; finance; graphic and printing equipment operation/production; Hispanic-American, Puerto Rican, and Mexican-American/Chicano studies; hospitality administration; industrial technology; insurance; interior design; journalism; labor and industrial relations; Latin American studies; legal administrative assistant/secretary; legal assistant/paralegal; liberal arts and sciences/liberal studies; licensed practical/vocational nurse training; machine tool technology; marketing/marketing management; mathematics; modern languages; music; occupational safety and health technology; parks, recreation and leisure; photography; physical education teaching and coaching; physical sciences; political science and government; pre-engineering; psychology; radio and television; real estate; registered nursing/registered nurse; rhetoric and composition; social sciences; social work; sociology; special products marketing; teacher assistant/aide; telecommunications technology; tourism and travel

services management; transportation and materials moving related; welding technology.

Academics *Calendar:* semesters. *Degree:* certificates and associate. *Special study options:* academic remediation for entering students, adult/continuing education programs, cooperative education, distance learning, English as a second language, external degree program, honors programs, independent study, off-campus study, part-time degree program, services for LD students, student-designed majors, summer session for credit. *ROTC:* Air Force (c).

Library San Diego City College Library with 88,000 titles, 191 serial subscriptions, 950 audiovisual materials, an OPAC.

Student Life *Housing:* college housing not available. *Activities and Organizations:* drama/theater group, student-run newspaper, radio station, choral group, Alpha Gamma Sigma, Association of United Latin American Students, MECHA, Afrikan Student Union, Student Nurses Association. *Campus security:* 24-hour emergency response devices and patrols, late-night transport/escort service. *Student services:* health clinic, personal/psychological counseling.

Athletics *Intercollegiate sports:* baseball M, basketball M/W, cross-country running M/W, football M, golf M/W, soccer M/W, softball W, tennis M/W, track and field M/W, volleyball M/W. *Intramural sports:* archery M/W, badminton M/W, baseball M, basketball M/W, bowling M/W, racquetball M/W, soccer M/W, softball W, swimming and diving M/W, tennis M/W, track and field M/W, volleyball M/W, weight lifting M/W.

Costs (2011–12) *One-time required fee:* $50. *Tuition:* state resident $780 full-time; nonresident $6480 full-time. *Required fees:* $50 full-time.

Financial Aid Of all full-time matriculated undergraduates who enrolled in 2009, 90 Federal Work-Study jobs (averaging $3844). 19 state and other part-time jobs (averaging $2530).

Applying *Options:* electronic application. *Required for some:* high school transcript. *Application deadlines:* rolling (freshmen), rolling (transfers).

Freshman Application Contact Ms. Lou Humphries, Registrar/Supervisor of Admissions, Records, Evaluations and Veterans, San Diego City College, 1313 Park Boulevard, San Diego, CA 92101-4787. *Phone:* 619-388-3474. *Fax:* 619-388-3505. *E-mail:* lhumphri@sdccd.edu. *Web site:* http://www.sdcity.edu/.

San Diego Mesa College
San Diego, California

- **State and locally supported** 2-year, founded 1964, part of San Diego Community College District System
- **Suburban** 104-acre campus
- **Coed**

Undergraduates 24,252 full-time.

Academics *Calendar:* semesters. *Degree:* certificates, diplomas, and associate. *Special study options:* academic remediation for entering students, adult/continuing education programs, English as a second language, external degree program, honors programs, independent study, part-time degree program, services for LD students, summer session for credit.

Student Life *Campus security:* 24-hour emergency response devices and patrols, late-night transport/escort service.

Costs (2010–11) *Tuition:* state resident $0 full-time; nonresident $4560 full-time, $190 per unit part-time. Full-time tuition and fees vary according to course load and program. Part-time tuition and fees vary according to course load and program. *Required fees:* $660 full-time, $26 per unit part-time, $18 per term part-time.

Financial Aid Of all full-time matriculated undergraduates who enrolled in 2009, 115 Federal Work-Study jobs (averaging $5000). *Financial aid deadline:* 6/30.

Applying *Options:* electronic application, early admission.

Freshman Application Contact Ms. Cheri Sawyer, Admissions Supervisor, San Diego Mesa College, 7250 Mesa College Drive, San Diego, CA 92111. *Phone:* 619-388-2686. *Fax:* 619-388-2960. *E-mail:* csawyer@sdccd.edu. *Web site:* http://www.sdmesa.edu/.

San Diego Miramar College
San Diego, California

Freshman Application Contact Ms. Dana Andras, Admissions Supervisor, San Diego Miramar College, 10440 Black Mountain Road, San Diego, CA 92126-2999. *Phone:* 619-536-7854. *E-mail:* dmaxwell@sdccd.cc.ca.us. *Web site:* http://www.sdmiramar.edu/.

San Joaquin Delta College
Stockton, California

Freshman Application Contact Ms. Catherine Mooney, Registrar, San Joaquin Delta College, 5151 Pacific Avenue, Stockton, CA 95207. *Phone:*

209-954-5635. *Fax:* 209-954-5769. *E-mail:* admissions@deltacollege.edu. *Web site:* http://www.deltacollege.edu/.

San Joaquin Valley College
Bakersfield, California

Freshman Application Contact Enrollment Services Director, San Joaquin Valley College, 201 New Stine Road, Bakersfield, CA 93309. *Phone:* 661-834-0126. *Toll-free phone:* 866-544-7898. *Fax:* 661-834-8124. *E-mail:* admissions@sjvc.edu. *Web site:* http://www.sjvc.edu/.

San Joaquin Valley College
Visalia, California

Freshman Application Contact Enrollment Services Director, San Joaquin Valley College, 8400 West Mineral King Boulevard, Visalia, CA 93291. *Phone:* 559-651-2500. *Fax:* 559-734-9048. *E-mail:* admissions@sjvc.edu. *Web site:* http://www.sjvc.edu/.

San Joaquin Valley College–Fresno Aviation Campus
Fresno, California

Freshman Application Contact Enrollment Services Coordinator, San Joaquin Valley College–Fresno Aviation Campus, 4985 East Anderson Avenue, Fresno, CA 93727. *Phone:* 559-453-0123. *Fax:* 599-453-0133. *E-mail:* admissions@sjvc.edu. *Web site:* http://www.sjvc.edu/.

San Joaquin Valley College–Online
Visalia, California

Freshman Application Contact Enrollment Services Director, San Joaquin Valley College–Online, 801 S. Akers Street, Suite 150, Visalia, CA 93277. *E-mail:* admissions@sjvc.edu. *Web site:* http://www.sjvc.edu/campus/SJVC_Online/.

San Jose City College
San Jose, California

Freshman Application Contact Mr. Carlo Santos, Director of Admissions/Registrar, San Jose City College, 2100 Moorpark Avenue, San Jose, CA 95128-2799. *Phone:* 408-288-3707. *Fax:* 408-298-1935. *Web site:* http://www.sjcc.edu/.

Santa Ana College
Santa Ana, California

Freshman Application Contact Mrs. Christie Steward, Admissions Clerk, Santa Ana College, 1530 West 17th Street, Santa Ana, CA 92706-3398. *Phone:* 714-564-6053. *Web site:* http://www.sac.edu/.

Santa Barbara City College
Santa Barbara, California

- **State and locally supported** 2-year, founded 1908, part of California Community College System
- **Small-town** 65-acre campus
- **Endowment** $21.1 million
- **Coed,** 18,092 undergraduate students, 44% full-time, 53% women, 47% men

Undergraduates 7,952 full-time, 10,140 part-time. Students come from 46 states and territories; 66 other countries; 6% are from out of state; 3% Black or African American, non-Hispanic/Latino; 29% Hispanic/Latino; 3% Asian, non-Hispanic/Latino; 1% Native Hawaiian or other Pacific Islander, non-Hispanic/Latino; 0.7% American Indian or Alaska Native, non-Hispanic/Latino; 4% Two or more races, non-Hispanic/Latino; 3% Race/ethnicity unknown; 10% international; 5% transferred in.

Freshmen *Admission:* 4,448 applied, 4,448 admitted, 2,098 enrolled.

Faculty *Total:* 806, 33% full-time. *Student/faculty ratio:* 27:1.

Majors Accounting; acting; administrative assistant and secretarial science; African American/Black studies; American Indian/Native American studies; anthropology; applied horticulture/horticulture operations; art history, criticism and conservation; athletic training; automobile/automotive mechanics technology; biology/biological sciences; biomedical technology; biotechnology; business administration and management; chemistry; child-care and support services management; commercial and advertising art; computer engineering; computer science; cosmetology; criminal justice/law enforcement administration; culinary arts related; drafting and design technology; dramatic/theater arts; economics; electrical, electronic and communications engineering technology; electrical/electronics equipment installation and repair; engineering; engineering technology; English; environmental/environmental health engineering; environmental studies; film/cinema/video studies; finance; fine/studio arts; food service systems administration; French; geography; geology/earth science; health information/medical records technology; Hispanic-American, Puerto Rican, and Mexican-American/Chicano studies; history; hotel/motel administration; industrial engineering; industrial technology; information science/studies; information technology; institutional food workers; interior design; international relations and affairs; kindergarten/preschool education; kinesiology and exercise science; landscaping and groundskeeping; legal studies; liberal arts and sciences/liberal studies; licensed practical/vocational nurse training; marine maintenance and ship repair technology; marketing/marketing management; mathematics; medical radiologic technology; music; network and system administration; ornamental horticulture; parks, recreation and leisure; philosophy; physical education teaching and coaching; physics; political science and government; psychology; real estate; registered nursing/registered nurse; sales, distribution, and marketing operations; selling skills and sales; sociology; Spanish; speech communication and rhetoric; theater design and technology; therapeutic recreation.

Academics *Calendar:* semesters. *Degree:* certificates and associate. *Special study options:* academic remediation for entering students, adult/continuing education programs, advanced placement credit, cooperative education, distance learning, double majors, English as a second language, honors programs, independent study, internships, part-time degree program, services for LD students, study abroad, summer session for credit. *ROTC:* Army (c).

Library Eli Luria Library with 140,471 titles, 976 serial subscriptions, 57 audiovisual materials, an OPAC, a Web page.

Student Life *Housing:* college housing not available. *Activities and Organizations:* choral group, IDEAS, Video Game Club, Glee Club, Marketing Club, Project H.O.P.E. *Campus security:* 24-hour emergency response devices and patrols, late-night transport/escort service. *Student services:* health clinic, personal/psychological counseling.

Athletics *Intercollegiate sports:* baseball M, basketball M/W, cross-country running M/W, football M, golf M/W, soccer M/W, softball W, tennis M/W, track and field M/W, volleyball W.

Costs (2011–12) *Tuition:* nonresident $210 per unit part-time. Full-time tuition and fees vary according to course load. Part-time tuition and fees vary according to course load. *Required fees:* $36 per unit part-time, $43 per term part-time. *Payment plan:* deferred payment. *Waivers:* employees or children of employees.

Financial Aid Of all full-time matriculated undergraduates who enrolled in 2009, 151 Federal Work-Study jobs (averaging $5400).

Applying *Options:* electronic application, early admission. *Recommended:* high school transcript. *Application deadlines:* 8/19 (freshmen), 8/19 (transfers). *Notification:* continuous (freshmen), continuous (transfers).

Freshman Application Contact Ms. Allison Curtis, Director of Admissions and Records, Santa Barbara City College, Santa Barbara, CA 93109. *Phone:* 805-965-0581 Ext. 2352. *Fax:* 805-962-0497. *E-mail:* admissions@sbcc.edu. *Web site:* http://www.sbcc.edu/.

Santa Monica College
Santa Monica, California

Director of Admissions Ms. Teresita Rodriguez, Dean of Enrollment Services, Santa Monica College, 1900 Pico Boulevard, Santa Monica, CA 90405-1628. *Phone:* 310-434-4774. *Web site:* http://www.smc.edu/.

Santa Rosa Junior College
Santa Rosa, California

- **State and locally supported** 2-year, founded 1918, part of California Community College System
- **Urban** 93-acre campus with easy access to San Francisco
- **Endowment** $25.0 million
- **Coed,** 25,319 undergraduate students, 35% full-time, 56% women, 44% men

Undergraduates 8,801 full-time, 16,518 part-time. Students come from 40 other countries; 2% are from out of state; 2% Black or African American, non-Hispanic/Latino; 17% Hispanic/Latino; 3% Asian, non-Hispanic/Latino; 1% Native Hawaiian or other Pacific Islander, non-Hispanic/Latino; 0.8% American Indian or Alaska Native, non-Hispanic/Latino; 6% Two or more races, non-Hispanic/Latino; 18% Race/ethnicity unknown.

Freshmen *Admission:* 5,001 applied, 5,001 admitted.

Faculty *Total:* 1,371, 22% full-time, 13% with terminal degrees. *Student/faculty ratio:* 22:1.

Majors Agricultural business and management; agricultural mechanization; agriculture; animal sciences; anthropology; architecture; architecture related;

art; art history, criticism and conservation; automobile/automotive mechanics technology; behavioral sciences; biology/biological sciences; business administration and management; chemistry; child development; civil engineering; computer science; criminal justice/law enforcement administration; culinary arts; dance; dental hygiene; diesel mechanics technology; dramatic/theater arts; economics; electrical, electronic and communications engineering technology; emergency medical technology (EMT paramedic); English; environmental studies; ethnic, cultural minority, gender, and group studies related; fashion and fabric consulting; fashion/apparel design; fashion merchandising; fire science/firefighting; floriculture/floristry management; graphic design; health and physical education related; history; horse husbandry/equine science and management; humanities; human services; interior design; landscape architecture; Latin American studies; licensed practical/vocational nurse training; mathematics; natural resources/conservation; natural resources management and policy; philosophy; physics; political science and government; precision production trades; pre-pharmacy studies; psychology; registered nursing/registered nurse; social sciences; surveying engineering; women's studies.

Academics *Calendar:* semesters. *Degree:* certificates and associate. *Special study options:* academic remediation for entering students, adult/continuing education programs, advanced placement credit, cooperative education, distance learning, English as a second language, independent study, internships, off-campus study, part-time degree program, services for LD students, study abroad, summer session for credit.

Library Plover Library with 129,197 titles, 356 serial subscriptions, 13,951 audiovisual materials, an OPAC, a Web page.

Student Life *Housing:* college housing not available. *Activities and Organizations:* drama/theater group, student-run newspaper, choral group, AG Ambassadors, MECHA, Alpha Gamma Sigma, Phi Theta Kappa, Puente. *Campus security:* 24-hour emergency response devices and patrols. *Student services:* health clinic, personal/psychological counseling.

Athletics Member NJCAA. *Intercollegiate sports:* baseball M, basketball M/W, cross-country running M/W, football M, golf M, ice hockey M(c), rugby M(c), soccer M/W, softball W, swimming and diving M/W, tennis M/W, track and field M/W, volleyball W, water polo M/W, wrestling M.

Costs (2011–12) *One-time required fee:* $34. *Tuition:* state resident $0 full-time; nonresident $5088 full-time, $212 per unit part-time. Full-time tuition and fees vary according to course load. Part-time tuition and fees vary according to course load. *Required fees:* $624 full-time, $26 per unit part-time. *Payment plans:* installment, deferred payment.

Financial Aid Of all full-time matriculated undergraduates who enrolled in 2008, 135 Federal Work-Study jobs (averaging $2210). 43 state and other part-time jobs (averaging $7396).

Applying *Options:* electronic application, early admission. *Application deadlines:* rolling (freshmen), rolling (out-of-state freshmen), rolling (transfers). *Notification:* continuous (freshmen), continuous (out-of-state freshmen), continuous (transfers).

Freshman Application Contact Ms. Diane Traversi, Director of Enrollment Services, Santa Rosa Junior College, 1501 Mendocino Avenue, Santa Rosa, CA 95401. *Phone:* 707-527-4510. *Fax:* 707-527-4798. *E-mail:* admininfo@santarosa.edu. *Web site:* http://www.santarosa.edu/.

Santiago Canyon College
Orange, California

Freshman Application Contact Denise Pennock, Admissions and Records, Santiago Canyon College, 8045 East Chapman Avenue, Orange, CA 92869. *Phone:* 714-564-4000. *Web site:* http://www.sccollege.edu/.

School of Urban Missions
Oakland, California

- **Independent interdenominational** primarily 2-year, founded 1991
- **Coed**
- **59%** of applicants were admitted

Undergraduates 133 full-time, 6 part-time. 45% transferred in.

Faculty *Student/faculty ratio:* 11:1.

Academics *Calendar:* trimesters. *Degrees:* associate and bachelor's. *Special study options:* distance learning.

Costs (2010–11) *Tuition:* $7800 full-time, $260 per credit hour part-time. Full-time tuition and fees vary according to program. Part-time tuition and fees vary according to program. *Required fees:* $105 full-time. *Room only:* Room and board charges vary according to housing facility.

Applying *Options:* deferred entrance. *Application fee:* $25. *Required:* essay or personal statement, 2 letters of recommendation, interview, pastoral recommendation.

Freshman Application Contact Admissions, School of Urban Missions, 735 105th Avenue, Oakland, CA 94603. *Phone:* 510-567-6174. *Toll-free phone:* 800-385-6364. *Fax:* 510-568-1024. *Web site:* http://www.sum.edu/.

Shasta College
Redding, California

Director of Admissions Dr. Kevin O'Rorke, Dean of Enrollment Services, Shasta College, PO Box 496006, 11555 Old Oregon Trail, Redding, CA 96049-6006. *Phone:* 530-242-7669. *Web site:* http://www.shastacollege.edu/.

Sierra College
Rocklin, California

- **State-supported** 2-year, founded 1936, part of California Community College System
- **Suburban** 327-acre campus with easy access to Sacramento
- **Coed**

Undergraduates 5,355 full-time, 14,061 part-time. 1% are from out of state; 4% transferred in; 1% live on campus.
Faculty *Student/faculty ratio:* 25:1.
Academics *Calendar:* semesters. *Degree:* certificates and associate. *Special study options:* academic remediation for entering students, accelerated degree program, advanced placement credit, distance learning, double majors, English as a second language, honors programs, independent study, internships, off-campus study, part-time degree program, services for LD students, study abroad, summer session for credit.
Student Life *Campus security:* 24-hour emergency response devices and patrols, late-night transport/escort service.
Costs (2011–12) *Tuition:* state resident $0 full-time; nonresident $5904 full-time, $210 per unit part-time. *Required fees:* $1080 full-time, $36 per unit part-time.
Financial Aid Of all full-time matriculated undergraduates who enrolled in 2009, 150 Federal Work-Study jobs (averaging $2340).
Applying *Options:* electronic application, early admission.
Freshman Application Contact Sierra College, 5000 Rocklin Road, Rocklin, CA 95677-3397. *Phone:* 916-660-7341. *Web site:* http://www.sierracollege.edu/.

Skyline College
San Bruno, California

Freshman Application Contact Terry Stats, Admissions Office, Skyline College, 3300 College Drive, San Bruno, CA 94066-1698. *Phone:* 650-738-4251. *E-mail:* stats@smccd.net. *Web site:* http://skylinecollege.net/.

Solano Community College
Fairfield, California

- **State and locally supported** 2-year, founded 1945, part of California Community College System
- **Suburban** 192-acre campus with easy access to Sacramento and San Francisco
- **Coed**, 10,927 undergraduate students

Undergraduates Students come from 43 states and territories; 6 other countries; 1% are from out of state.
Freshmen *Admission:* 10,927 applied.
Faculty *Total:* 374, 39% full-time. *Student/faculty ratio:* 27:1.
Majors Accounting; African American/Black studies; African studies; airframe mechanics and aircraft maintenance technology; art; automobile/automotive mechanics technology; avionics maintenance technology; biological and physical sciences; biology/biological sciences; business administration and management; business machine repair; chemistry; commercial and advertising art; computer programming; cosmetology; criminal justice/law enforcement administration; drafting and design technology; electrical, electronic and communications engineering technology; English; family and consumer sciences/human sciences; fashion merchandising; finance; fire science/firefighting; French; German; Hispanic-American, Puerto Rican, and Mexican-American/Chicano studies; history; journalism; kindergarten/preschool education; legal administrative assistant/secretary; liberal arts and sciences/liberal studies; machine tool technology; marketing/marketing management; mathematics; music; ornamental horticulture; photography; physical education teaching and coaching; physics; political science and government; psychology; public administration; registered nursing/registered nurse; social sciences; Spanish; telecommunications technology; welding technology.
Academics *Calendar:* semesters. *Degree:* certificates, diplomas, and associate. *Special study options:* academic remediation for entering students, adult/continuing education programs, advanced placement credit, cooperative education, distance learning, double majors, English as a second language, honors programs, independent study, off-campus study, part-time degree program, services for LD students, study abroad, summer session for credit.
Library Solano Community College Library with 32,000 titles.

Student Life *Housing:* college housing not available. *Activities and Organizations:* drama/theater group, student-run newspaper, choral group, national fraternities. *Campus security:* 24-hour patrols, student patrols, late-night transport/escort service. *Student services:* health clinic, personal/psychological counseling.
Athletics *Intercollegiate sports:* baseball M, basketball M/W, football M, softball W, swimming and diving M/W, volleyball W, water polo M/W.
Costs (2011–12) *One-time required fee:* $13. *Tuition:* state resident $764 full-time, $26 per unit part-time; nonresident $5700 full-time, $197 per unit part-time. Full-time tuition and fees vary according to course load. Part-time tuition and fees vary according to course load. *Required fees:* $26 per unit part-time.
Financial Aid Of all full-time matriculated undergraduates who enrolled in 2009, 125 Federal Work-Study jobs (averaging $2000). 30 state and other part-time jobs (averaging $2000).
Applying *Options:* electronic application, early admission, deferred entrance. *Application deadlines:* rolling (freshmen), rolling (transfers).
Freshman Application Contact Solano Community College, 4000 Suisun Valley Road, Fairfield, CA 94534. *Phone:* 707-864-7000 Ext. 4313. *Web site:* http://www.solano.edu/.

South Coast College
Orange, California

Director of Admissions South Coast College, 2011 West Chapman Avenue, Orange, CA 92868. *Toll-free phone:* 800-337-8366. *Web site:* http://www.southcoastcollege.com/.

Southwestern College
Chula Vista, California

Freshman Application Contact Director of Admissions and Records, Southwestern College, 900 Otay Lakes Road, Chula Vista, CA 91910-7299. *Phone:* 619-421-6700 Ext. 5215. *Fax:* 619-482-6489. *Web site:* http://www.swc.edu/.

Stanbridge College
Irvine, California

Admissions Office Contact Stanbridge College, 2041 Business Center Drive, Irvine, CA 92612. *Web site:* http://www.stanbridge.edu/.

Taft College
Taft, California

Freshman Application Contact Harold Russell III, Director of Financial Aid and Admissions, Taft College, 29 Emmons Park Drive, Taft, CA 93268-2317. *Phone:* 661-763-7763. *Fax:* 661-763-7758. *E-mail:* hrussell@taft.org. *Web site:* http://www.taftcollege.edu/.

Unitek College
Fremont, California

Admissions Office Contact Unitek College, 4670 Auto Mall Parkway, Fremont, CA 94538. *Web site:* http://www.unitekcollege.edu/.

Ventura College
Ventura, California

Freshman Application Contact Ms. Susan Bricker, Registrar, Ventura College, 4667 Telegraph Road, Ventura, CA 93003-3899. *Phone:* 805-654-6456. *Fax:* 805-654-6357. *E-mail:* sbricker@vcccd.net. *Web site:* http://www.venturacollege.edu/.

Victor Valley College
Victorville, California

- **State-supported** 2-year, founded 1961, part of California Community College System
- **Small-town** 253-acre campus with easy access to Los Angeles
- **Coed**

Undergraduates 2% are from out of state. *Retention:* 63% of full-time freshmen returned.
Faculty *Student/faculty ratio:* 28:1.
Academics *Calendar:* semesters. *Degree:* certificates, diplomas, and associate. *Special study options:* academic remediation for entering students, accelerated degree program, advanced placement credit, cooperative education, distance learning, double majors, English as a second language, honors pro-

grams, independent study, internships, off-campus study, part-time degree program, services for LD students, study abroad, summer session for credit.
Student Life *Campus security:* 24-hour emergency response devices and patrols, late-night transport/escort service, part-time trained security personnel.
Athletics Member NCAA, NJCAA.
Costs (2010–11) *Tuition:* state resident $0 full-time; nonresident $4392 full-time, $183 per unit part-time. *Required fees:* $624 full-time, $26 per unit part-time.
Financial Aid *Average need-based loan:* $6168. *Average need-based gift aid:* $3707.
Freshman Application Contact Ms. Greta Moon, Director of Admissions and Records (Interim), Victor Valley College, 18422 Bear Valley Road, Victorville, CA 92395. *Phone:* 760-245-4271. *Fax:* 760-843-7707. *E-mail:* moong@vvc.edu. *Web site:* http://www.vvc.edu/.

West Hills Community College
Coalinga, California

Freshman Application Contact Sandra Dagnino, West Hills Community College, 300 Cherry Lane, Coalinga, CA 93210-1399. *Phone:* 559-934-3203. *Toll-free phone:* 800-266-1114. *Fax:* 559-934-2830. *E-mail:* sandradagnino@westhillscollege.com. *Web site:* http://www.westhillscollege.com/.

West Los Angeles College
Culver City, California

Director of Admissions Mr. Len Isaksen, Director of Admissions, West Los Angeles College, 9000 Overland Avenue, Culver City, CA 90230-3519. *Phone:* 310-287-4255. *Web site:* http://www.lacolleges.net/.

West Valley College
Saratoga, California

Freshman Application Contact Ms. Barbara Ogilvie, Supervisor, Admissions and Records, West Valley College, 14000 Fruitvale Avenue, Saratoga, CA 95070-5698. *Phone:* 408-741-4630. *E-mail:* barbara_ogilvie@westvalley.edu. *Web site:* http://www.westvalley.edu/.

Woodland Community College
Woodland, California

Admissions Office Contact Woodland Community College, 2300 East Gibson Road, Woodland, CA 95776. *Web site:* http://www.yccd.edu/woodland/.

WyoTech
Fremont, California

- **Proprietary** 2-year, founded 1966, administratively affiliated with Corinthian Colleges, Inc
- **Urban** campus
- **Coed,** 1,596 undergraduate students
- 80% of applicants were admitted

Freshmen *Admission:* 560 applied, 446 admitted.
Faculty *Total:* 92, 87% full-time. *Student/faculty ratio:* 25:1.
Majors Automobile/automotive mechanics technology; automotive engineering technology.
Academics *Calendar:* continuous. *Degree:* certificates, diplomas, and associate. *Special study options:* academic remediation for entering students.
Library Learning Resource Center with 1,000 audiovisual materials.
Student Life *Housing:* college housing not available. *Campus security:* security personnel.
Freshman Application Contact Admissions Department, WyoTech, 200 Whitney Place, Fremont, CA 94539-7663. *Phone:* 510-580-3507. *Toll-free phone:* 800-248-8585. *Fax:* 510-490-8599. *Web site:* http://www.wyotech.edu/.

WyoTech
West Sacramento, California

Freshman Application Contact Admissions Office, WyoTech, 980 Riverside Parkway, West Sacramento, CA 95605-1507. *Phone:* 916-376-8888. *Toll-free phone:* 888-577-7559. *Fax:* 916-617-2059. *Web site:* http://www.wyotech.com/.

WyoTech Long Beach
Long Beach, California

Freshman Application Contact Admissions Office, WyoTech Long Beach, 2161 Technology Place, Long Beach, CA 90810. *Phone:* 562-624-9530. *Fax:* 562-437-8111. *Web site:* http://www.wyotech.edu/campus/long_beach.

Yuba College
Marysville, California

Director of Admissions Dr. David Farrell, Dean of Student Development, Yuba College, 2088 North Beale Road, Marysville, CA 95901-7699. *Phone:* 530-741-6705. *Web site:* http://www.yccd.edu/.

COLORADO

Aims Community College
Greeley, Colorado

Freshman Application Contact Ms. Susie Gallardo, Admissions Technician, Aims Community College, Box 69, 5401 West 20th Street, Greeley, CO 80632-0069. *Phone:* 970-330-8008 Ext. 6624. *E-mail:* wgreen@chiron.aims.edu. *Web site:* http://www.aims.edu/.

Anthem College Aurora
Aurora, Colorado

Director of Admissions Amy Marshall, Director of Admissions, Anthem College Aurora, 350 Blackhawk Street, Aurora, CO 80011. *Phone:* 720-859-7900. *Toll-free phone:* 800-322-4132. *Web site:* http://www.anthem.edu/locations/anthem-college-aurora/.

Arapahoe Community College
Littleton, Colorado

Freshman Application Contact Arapahoe Community College, 5900 South Santa Fe Drive, PO Box 9002, Littleton, CO 80160-9002. *Phone:* 303-797-5621. *Web site:* http://www.arapahoe.edu/.

Bel–Rea Institute of Animal Technology
Denver, Colorado

Director of Admissions Ms. Paulette Kaufman, Director, Bel–Rea Institute of Animal Technology, 1681 South Dayton Street, Denver, CO 80247. *Phone:* 303-751-8700. *Toll-free phone:* 800-950-8001. *E-mail:* admissions@bel-rea.com. *Web site:* http://www.bel-rea.com/.

Boulder College of Massage Therapy
Boulder, Colorado

Freshman Application Contact Admissions Office, Boulder College of Massage Therapy, 6255 Longbow Drive, Boulder, CO 80301. *Phone:* 303-530-2100. *Toll-free phone:* 800-442-5131. *Fax:* 303-530-2204. *E-mail:* admissions@bcmt.org. *Web site:* http://www.bcmt.org/.

CollegeAmerica–Colorado Springs
Colorado Springs, Colorado

Freshman Application Contact CollegeAmerica–Colorado Springs, 3645 Citadel Drive South, Colorado Springs, CO 80909. *Phone:* 719-637-0600. *Web site:* http://www.collegeamerica.edu/.

CollegeAmerica–Denver
Denver, Colorado

Freshman Application Contact Admissions Office, CollegeAmerica–Denver, 1385 South Colorado Boulevard, Denver, CO 80222. *Phone:* 303-300-8740. *Web site:* http://www.collegeamerica.com/.

CollegeAmerica–Fort Collins
Fort Collins, Colorado
Director of Admissions Ms. Anna DiTorrice-Mull, Director of Admissions, CollegeAmerica–Fort Collins, 4601 South Mason Street, Fort Collins, CO 80525-3740. *Phone:* 970-223-6060 Ext. 8002. *Toll-free phone:* 800-97-SKILLS. *Web site:* http://www.collegeamerica.edu/.

Colorado Mountain College
Glenwood Springs, Colorado
- **District-supported** 2-year, founded 1965, part of Colorado Mountain College District System
- **Rural** 680-acre campus
- **Coed,** 2,465 undergraduate students

Undergraduates 44% live on campus.
Freshmen *Average high school GPA:* 2.4.
Faculty *Total:* 28. *Student/faculty ratio:* 12:1.
Majors Accounting; behavioral sciences; biological and physical sciences; biology/biological sciences; business administration and management; commercial and advertising art; computer and information sciences and support services related; computer engineering technology; computer systems networking and telecommunications; criminal justice/law enforcement administration; data entry/microcomputer applications related; dramatic/theater arts; English; humanities; liberal arts and sciences/liberal studies; licensed practical/vocational nurse training; mathematics; natural sciences; photography; psychology; registered nursing/registered nurse; social sciences; therapeutic recreation; veterinary/animal health technology.
Academics *Calendar:* semesters. *Degree:* certificates and associate. *Special study options:* academic remediation for entering students, adult/continuing education programs, advanced placement credit, cooperative education, distance learning, double majors, English as a second language, honors programs, independent study, internships, part-time degree program, services for LD students, study abroad, summer session for credit.
Library Quigley Library with 36,000 titles, 186 serial subscriptions, an OPAC, a Web page.
Student Life *Housing:* on-campus residence required for freshman year. *Options:* coed, disabled students. Campus housing is university owned. Freshman applicants given priority for college housing. *Activities and Organizations:* drama/theater group, student-run newspaper, student government, Outdoor activities, World Awareness Society, Peer Mentors, Student Activities Board. *Campus security:* 24-hour emergency response devices, student patrols, controlled dormitory access. *Student services:* health clinic, personal/psychological counseling.
Athletics Member NJCAA. *Intramural sports:* basketball M/W, rock climbing M/W, skiing (cross-country) M/W, skiing (downhill) M/W, ultimate Frisbee M/W, volleyball M/W.
Standardized Tests *Recommended:* SAT or ACT (for admission).
Costs (2010–11) *Tuition:* area resident $1470 full-time, $49 per credit hour part-time; state resident $2460 full-time, $82 per credit hour part-time; nonresident $7680 full-time, $256 per credit hour part-time. Full-time tuition and fees vary according to course load. Part-time tuition and fees vary according to course load. *Required fees:* $180 full-time. *Room and board:* $7680; room only: $4040. Room and board charges vary according to board plan. *Payment plan:* installment. *Waivers:* senior citizens and employees or children of employees.
Applying *Options:* electronic application, early admission, deferred entrance. *Required:* high school transcript. *Application deadlines:* rolling (freshmen), rolling (out-of-state freshmen), rolling (transfers).
Freshman Application Contact Vicky Butler, Admissions Assistant, Colorado Mountain College, 3000 CR 114, Glenwood Springs, CO 81601. *Phone:* 970-947-8276. *Toll-free phone:* 800-621-8559. *E-mail:* Vvalentine@coloradomtn.edu. *Web site:* http://www.coloradomtn.edu/.

Colorado Mountain College, Alpine Campus
Steamboat Springs, Colorado
- **District-supported** 2-year, founded 1965, part of Colorado Mountain College District System
- **Small-town** 10-acre campus
- **Coed,** 1,550 undergraduate students

Undergraduates 44% live on campus.
Freshmen *Average high school GPA:* 2.4.
Faculty *Total:* 25. *Student/faculty ratio:* 12:1.
Majors Accounting; behavioral sciences; biological and physical sciences; biology/biological sciences; business administration and management; computer engineering technology; consumer merchandising/retailing management; data entry/microcomputer applications related; English; fine/studio arts; geology/earth science; hospitality administration; hotel/motel administration; humanities; liberal arts and sciences/liberal studies; marketing/marketing management; mathematics; parks, recreation and leisure facilities management; physical sciences; pre-engineering; social sciences.
Academics *Calendar:* semesters. *Degree:* certificates and associate. *Special study options:* academic remediation for entering students, adult/continuing education programs, advanced placement credit, cooperative education, distance learning, double majors, English as a second language, honors programs, independent study, internships, off-campus study, part-time degree program, services for LD students, study abroad, summer session for credit.
Library Main Library plus 1 other with 17,000 titles, 192 serial subscriptions, an OPAC, a Web page.
Student Life *Housing:* on-campus residence required for freshman year. *Options:* coed, disabled students. Campus housing is university owned. *Activities and Organizations:* student-run newspaper, student government, Forensics Team, Ski Club, International Club, Phi Theta Kappa. *Campus security:* 24-hour emergency response devices, student patrols, controlled dormitory access. *Student services:* health clinic, personal/psychological counseling.
Athletics Member NJCAA. *Intercollegiate sports:* skiing (downhill) M/W. *Intramural sports:* basketball M/W, skiing (cross-country) M/W, skiing (downhill) M/W, soccer M/W, ultimate Frisbee M/W, volleyball M/W.
Standardized Tests *Recommended:* SAT or ACT (for admission).
Costs (2010–11) *Tuition:* area resident $1470 full-time, $49 per credit hour part-time; state resident $2460 full-time, $82 per credit hour part-time; nonresident $7680 full-time, $256 per credit hour part-time. Full-time tuition and fees vary according to course load. Part-time tuition and fees vary according to course load. *Required fees:* $180 full-time. *Room and board:* $7680; room only: $4040. Room and board charges vary according to board plan. *Payment plan:* installment. *Waivers:* senior citizens and employees or children of employees.
Financial Aid Of all full-time matriculated undergraduates who enrolled in 2009, 40 Federal Work-Study jobs (averaging $1173). 62 state and other part-time jobs (averaging $1060).
Applying *Options:* electronic application, early admission, deferred entrance. *Recommended:* high school transcript. *Application deadlines:* rolling (freshmen), rolling (out-of-state freshmen), rolling (transfers).
Freshman Application Contact Ms. Stephanie Fletcher, Admissions Assistant, Colorado Mountain College, Alpine Campus, 1330 Bob Adams Drive, Steamboat Springs, CO 80487. *Phone:* 970-870-4417 Ext. 4417. *Toll-free phone:* 800-621-8559. *E-mail:* stephaniefletcher@coloradomtn.edu. *Web site:* http://www.coloradomtn.edu/.

Colorado Mountain College, Timberline Campus
Leadville, Colorado
- **District-supported** 2-year, founded 1965, part of Colorado Mountain College District System
- **Rural** 200-acre campus
- **Coed,** 1,209 undergraduate students

Undergraduates 30% live on campus.
Freshmen *Average high school GPA:* 2.4.
Faculty *Total:* 16. *Student/faculty ratio:* 12:1.
Majors Accounting; business/commerce; corrections; criminal justice/law enforcement administration; early childhood education; environmental studies; general studies; historic preservation and conservation; land use planning and management; liberal arts and sciences/liberal studies; parks, recreation and leisure; parks, recreation and leisure facilities management.
Academics *Calendar:* semesters. *Degree:* certificates and associate. *Special study options:* academic remediation for entering students, adult/continuing education programs, advanced placement credit, cooperative education, distance learning, double majors, English as a second language, honors programs, independent study, internships, part-time degree program, services for LD students, study abroad, summer session for credit.
Library 25,000 titles, 185 serial subscriptions, an OPAC, a Web page.
Student Life *Housing:* on-campus residence required for freshman year. *Options:* coed, disabled students. Freshman applicants given priority for college housing. *Activities and Organizations:* Environmental Club, Outdoor Club, Student Activities Board. *Campus security:* 24-hour emergency response devices, student patrols, controlled dormitory access. *Student services:* health clinic, personal/psychological counseling.
Athletics *Intramural sports:* basketball M, rock climbing M/W, skiing (cross-country) M/W, skiing (downhill) M/W, soccer M/W, volleyball M/W.
Standardized Tests *Recommended:* SAT or ACT (for admission).
Costs (2010–11) *Tuition:* area resident $1470 full-time, $49 per credit hour part-time; state resident $2460 full-time, $82 per credit hour part-time; nonresident $7680 full-time, $256 per credit hour part-time. Full-time tuition and fees vary according to course load. Part-time tuition and fees vary according to

course load. *Required fees:* $180 full-time. *Room and board:* $7680. Room and board charges vary according to board plan. *Payment plan:* installment. *Waivers:* senior citizens and employees or children of employees.

Applying *Options:* electronic application, early admission, deferred entrance. *Required:* high school transcript. *Application deadlines:* rolling (freshmen), rolling (out-of-state freshmen), rolling (transfers).

Freshman Application Contact Ms. Mary Laing, Admissions Assistant, Colorado Mountain College, Timberline Campus, 901South Highway 24, Leadville, CO 80461. *Phone:* 719-486-4292. *Toll-free phone:* 800-621-8559. *E-mail:* joinus@coloradomtn.edu. *Web site:* http://www.coloradomtn.edu/.

Colorado Northwestern Community College

Rangely, Colorado

Director of Admissions Mr. Gene Bilodeau, Registrar, Colorado Northwestern Community College, 500 Kennedy Drive, Rangely, CO 81648-3598. *Phone:* 970-824-1103. *Toll-free phone:* 970-675-3221 Ext. 218 (in-state); 800-562-1105 Ext. 218 (out-of-state). *E-mail:* gene.bilodeau@cncc.edu. *Web site:* http://www.cncc.edu/.

Colorado School of Healing Arts

Lakewood, Colorado

Freshman Application Contact Colorado School of Healing Arts, 7655 West Mississippi Avenue, Suite 100, Lakewood, CO 80220. *Phone:* 303-986-2320. *Toll-free phone:* 800-233-7114. *Fax:* 303-980-6594. *Web site:* http://www.csha.net/.

Colorado School of Trades

Lakewood, Colorado

- **Proprietary** 2-year, founded 1947
- **Suburban** campus
- **Coed,** 134 undergraduate students, 100% full-time, 1% women, 99% men
- 87% of applicants were admitted

Undergraduates 134 full-time. 88% are from out of state.
Freshmen *Admission:* 174 applied, 152 admitted, 30 enrolled.
Faculty *Total:* 10. *Student/faculty ratio:* 12:1.
Majors Gunsmithing.
Academics *Degree:* associate.
Costs (2011–12) *One-time required fee:* $161. *Tuition:* $18,900 full-time. No tuition increase for student's term of enrollment. *Payment plan:* installment.
Applying *Application fee:* $25. *Required:* essay or personal statement, high school transcript, interview.
Freshman Application Contact Colorado School of Trades, 1575 Hoyt Street, Lakewood, CO 80215-2996. *Toll-free phone:* 800-234-4594. *Web site:* http://www.schooloftrades.com/.

Community College of Aurora

Aurora, Colorado

Freshman Application Contact Community College of Aurora, 16000 East Centre Tech Parkway, Aurora, CO 80011-9036. *Phone:* 303-360-4701. *Web site:* http://www.ccaurora.edu/.

Community College of Denver

Denver, Colorado

Freshman Application Contact Mr. Michael Rusk, Dean of Students, Community College of Denver, PO Box 173363, Campus Box 201, Denver, CO 80127-3363. *Phone:* 303-556-6325. *Fax:* 303-556-2431. *E-mail:* enrollment_services@ccd.edu. *Web site:* http://www.ccd.edu/.

Denver Academy of Court Reporting

Westminster, Colorado

Director of Admissions Director of Admissions, Denver Academy of Court Reporting, 9051 Harlan Street, Unit 20, Westminster, CO 80031. *Phone:* 303-427-5292. *Toll-free phone:* 800-574-2087. *Web site:* http://www.denveracademy.edu/.

Everest College

Aurora, Colorado

Freshman Application Contact Everest College, 14280 East Jewell Avenue, Suite 100, Aurora, CO 80014. *Phone:* 303-745-6244. *Web site:* http://www.everest.edu/.

Everest College

Colorado Springs, Colorado

Director of Admissions Director of Admissions, Everest College, 1815 Jet Wing Drive, Colorado Springs, CO 80916. *Phone:* 719-630-6580. *Toll-free phone:* 888-741-4271. *Fax:* 719-638-6818. *Web site:* http://www.everest.edu/.

Everest College

Denver, Colorado

Freshman Application Contact Admissions Office, Everest College, 9065 Grant Street, Denver, CO 80229-4339. *Phone:* 303-457-2757. *Fax:* 303-457-4030. *Web site:* http://www.everest.edu/.

Front Range Community College

Westminster, Colorado

- **State-supported** 2-year, founded 1968, part of Community Colleges of Colorado System
- **Suburban** 90-acre campus with easy access to Denver
- **Endowment** $294,302
- **Coed,** 20,092 undergraduate students, 37% full-time, 57% women, 43% men

Undergraduates 7,445 full-time, 12,647 part-time. Students come from 44 states and territories; 26 other countries; 2% are from out of state; 2% Black or African American, non-Hispanic/Latino; 13% Hispanic/Latino; 3% Asian, non-Hispanic/Latino; 0.4% Native Hawaiian or other Pacific Islander, non-Hispanic/Latino; 0.9% American Indian or Alaska Native, non-Hispanic/Latino; 1% Two or more races, non-Hispanic/Latino; 10% Race/ethnicity unknown; 1% international; 9% transferred in. *Retention:* 43% of full-time freshmen returned.
Freshmen *Admission:* 8,187 applied, 8,187 admitted, 3,634 enrolled.
Faculty *Total:* 1,118, 19% full-time. *Student/faculty ratio:* 23:1.
Majors Accounting technology and bookkeeping; animal health; animation, interactive technology, video graphics and special effects; applied horticulture/horticulture operations; architectural engineering technology; automobile/automotive mechanics technology; CAD/CADD drafting/design technology; dietitian assistant; early childhood education; electrical, electronic and communications engineering technology; emergency medical technology (EMT paramedic); general studies; health information/medical records technology; heating, ventilation, air conditioning and refrigeration engineering technology; hospitality administration; interior design; legal assistant/paralegal; liberal arts and sciences and humanities related; liberal arts and sciences/liberal studies; masonry; medical office assistant; registered nursing/registered nurse; science technologies related; sign language interpretation and translation; veterinary/animal health technology; welding technology; wildlife, fish and wildlands science and management.
Academics *Calendar:* semesters. *Degree:* certificates and associate. *Special study options:* academic remediation for entering students, advanced placement credit, cooperative education, distance learning, double majors, English as a second language, freshman honors college, honors programs, independent study, internships, off-campus study, part-time degree program, services for LD students, student-designed majors, study abroad, summer session for credit. *ROTC:* Army (c), Air Force (c).
Library College Hill Library with an OPAC, a Web page.
Student Life *Housing:* college housing not available. *Activities and Organizations:* drama/theater group, student-run newspaper, Student Government Association, Student Colorado Registry of Interpreters for the Deaf, Students in Free Enterprise (SIFE), Gay Straight Alliance, Recycling Club. *Campus security:* 24-hour patrols, late-night transport/escort service. *Student services:* personal/psychological counseling.
Costs (2010–11) *Tuition:* state resident $2310 full-time, $96 per credit hour part-time; nonresident $9926 full-time, $414 per credit hour part-time. Full-time tuition and fees vary according to location and program. Part-time tuition and fees vary according to location and program. *Required fees:* $241 full-time, $241 per year part-time, $11 per term part-time. *Waivers:* employees or children of employees.
Financial Aid Of all full-time matriculated undergraduates who enrolled in 2009, 165 Federal Work-Study jobs (averaging $1316). 277 state and other part-time jobs (averaging $1635).
Applying *Options:* electronic application, early admission, deferred entrance. *Application deadlines:* rolling (freshmen), rolling (out-of-state freshmen), roll-

ing (transfers). *Notification:* continuous (freshmen), continuous (out-of-state freshmen), continuous (transfers).
Freshman Application Contact Ms. Yolanda Espinoza, Registrar, Front Range Community College, Westminster, CO 80031. *Phone:* 303-404-5000. *Fax:* 303-439-2614. *E-mail:* yolanda.espinoza@frontrange.edu. *Web site:* http://frcc.cc.co.us/.

Heritage College
Denver, Colorado
Freshman Application Contact Admissions Office, Heritage College, 12 Lakeside Lane, Denver, CO 80212-7413. *Web site:* http://www.heritage-education.com/.

Institute of Business & Medical Careers
Fort Collins, Colorado
- **Private** 2-year, founded 1987, administratively affiliated with Institute of Business and Medical Careers- Greeley, Colorado and Cheyenne, Wyoming
- **Suburban** campus with easy access to Denver
- **Coed**
- 100% of applicants were admitted

Undergraduates 302 full-time. Students come from 1 other state; 2% are from out of state. *Retention:* 69% of full-time freshmen returned.
Faculty *Student/faculty ratio:* 14:1.
Academics *Calendar:* continuous. *Degree:* certificates, diplomas, and associate. *Special study options:* accelerated degree program, cooperative education, honors programs, internships.
Costs (2010–11) *One-time required fee:* $75. *Tuition:* $10,800 full-time, $300 per credit hour part-time. Full-time tuition and fees vary according to course load and program. Part-time tuition and fees vary according to course load and program. No tuition increase for student's term of enrollment. *Payment plans:* tuition prepayment, installment.
Financial Aid Of all full-time matriculated undergraduates who enrolled in 2008, 822 applied for aid, 775 were judged to have need, 658 had their need fully met. 28 Federal Work-Study jobs (averaging $2262). *Average percent of need met:* 70. *Average financial aid package:* $7500. *Average need-based loan:* $3500. *Average need-based gift aid:* $3205.
Applying *Application fee:* $75. *Required:* high school transcript, interview.
Freshman Application Contact Mr. Kevin McNeil, Regional Director of Admissions, Institute of Business & Medical Careers, 3842 South Mason Street, Fort Collins, CO 80525. *Phone:* 970-223-2669 Ext. 1105. *Toll-free phone:* 800-495-2669. *E-mail:* kmcneil@ibmc.edu. *Web site:* http://www.ibmc.edu/.

IntelliTec College
Colorado Springs, Colorado
Director of Admissions Director of Admissions, IntelliTec College, 2315 East Pikes Peak Avenue, Colorado Springs, CO 80909-6030. *Phone:* 719-632-7626. *Toll-free phone:* 800-748-2282. *Web site:* http://www.intelliteccollege.edu/.

IntelliTec College
Grand Junction, Colorado
Freshman Application Contact Admissions, IntelliTec College, 772 Horizon Drive, Grand Junction, CO 81506. *Phone:* 970-245-8101. *Fax:* 970-243-8074. *Web site:* http://www.intelliteccollege.edu/.

IntelliTec Medical Institute
Colorado Springs, Colorado
Director of Admissions Michelle Squibb, Admissions Representative, IntelliTec Medical Institute, 2345 North Academy Boulevard, Colorado Springs, CO 80909. *Phone:* 719-596-7400. *Web site:* http://www.intelliteccollege.edu/.

ITT Technical Institute
Aurora, Colorado
- **Proprietary** primarily 2-year
- **Coed**

Majors CAD/CADD drafting/design technology; communications technology; computer and information systems security; computer engineering tech-

nology; criminal justice/law enforcement administration; design and visual communications; legal assistant/paralegal; system, networking, and LAN/WAN management.
Academics *Degrees:* associate and bachelor's.
Freshman Application Contact Director of Recruitment, ITT Technical Institute, 12500 East Iliff Avenue, Suite 100, Aurora, CO 80014. *Phone:* 303-695-6317. *Web site:* http://www.itt-tech.edu/.

ITT Technical Institute
Thornton, Colorado
- **Proprietary** primarily 2-year, founded 1984, part of ITT Educational Services, Inc.
- **Suburban** campus
- **Coed**

Majors CAD/CADD drafting/design technology; communications technology; computer and information systems security; computer engineering technology; computer software and media applications related; computer software engineering; computer software technology; construction management; criminal justice/law enforcement administration; design and visual communications; electrical, electronic and communications engineering technology; legal assistant/paralegal; project management; system, networking, and LAN/WAN management; web/multimedia management and webmaster; web page, digital/multimedia and information resources design.
Academics *Calendar:* quarters. *Degrees:* associate and bachelor's.
Student Life *Housing:* college housing not available.
Freshman Application Contact Director of Recruitment, ITT Technical Institute, 500 East 84th Avenue, Suite B12, Thornton, CO 80229. *Phone:* 303-288-4488. *Toll-free phone:* 800-395-4488. *Web site:* http://www.itt-tech.edu/.

Kaplan College, Denver Campus
Thornton, Colorado
- **Proprietary** 2-year, founded 1977
- **Coed**

Academics *Calendar:* continuous. *Degree:* certificates, diplomas, and associate.
Freshman Application Contact Kaplan College, Denver Campus, 500 East 84th Avenue, Suite W-200, Thornton, CO 80229. *Phone:* 303-295-0550. *Web site:* http://www.kc-denver.com/.

Lamar Community College
Lamar, Colorado
- **State-supported** 2-year, founded 1937, part of Colorado Community College and Occupational Education System
- **Small-town** 125-acre campus
- **Endowment** $136,000
- **Coed,** 1,084 undergraduate students, 45% full-time, 58% women, 42% men

Undergraduates 485 full-time, 599 part-time. Students come from 28 states and territories; 4 other countries; 16% are from out of state; 4% transferred in; 20% live on campus.
Freshmen *Admission:* 517 applied, 517 admitted, 330 enrolled.
Faculty *Total:* 50, 36% full-time. *Student/faculty ratio:* 15:1.
Majors Accounting; agricultural business and management; agriculture; agronomy and crop science; animal sciences; animal training; biological and physical sciences; biology/biological sciences; business administration and management; computer programming; computer science; computer typography and composition equipment operation; construction trades; cosmetology; criminal justice/safety; data processing and data processing technology; emergency medical technology (EMT paramedic); entrepreneurship; equestrian studies; farm and ranch management; history; information science/studies; liberal arts and sciences/liberal studies; licensed practical/vocational nurse training; management information systems; marketing/marketing management; medical office computer specialist; pre-engineering; registered nursing/registered nurse.
Academics *Calendar:* semesters. *Degree:* certificates, diplomas, and associate. *Special study options:* academic remediation for entering students, adult/continuing education programs, advanced placement credit, cooperative education, distance learning, double majors, English as a second language, independent study, internships, part-time degree program, services for LD students, student-designed majors, summer session for credit.
Library Learning Resources Center with 27,729 titles, 172 serial subscriptions, an OPAC.
Student Life *Housing:* on-campus residence required for freshman year. *Options:* coed. Campus housing is university owned. *Campus security:* 24-hour emergency response devices and patrols, student patrols, late-night trans-

port/escort service, controlled dormitory access. *Student services:* health clinic, personal/psychological counseling.

Athletics Member NJCAA. *Intercollegiate sports:* baseball M(s), basketball M(s)/W(s), equestrian sports M(s)/W(s), golf M(s), soccer M(c), softball W(s), volleyball W(s).

Costs (2010–11) *Tuition:* state resident $2888 full-time, $96 per credit hour part-time; nonresident $5723 full-time, $191 per credit hour part-time. Full-time tuition and fees vary according to course load, program, and reciprocity agreements. Part-time tuition and fees vary according to course load, program, and reciprocity agreements. *Required fees:* $394 full-time, $11 per credit hour part-time, $11 per term part-time. *Room and board:* $5294; room only: $1504. *Payment plan:* installment. *Waivers:* employees or children of employees.

Financial Aid Of all full-time matriculated undergraduates who enrolled in 2009, 32 Federal Work-Study jobs (averaging $1000). 89 state and other part-time jobs (averaging $1000).

Applying *Options:* electronic application, early admission. *Application deadlines:* 9/16 (freshmen), 9/16 (transfers).

Freshman Application Contact Director of Admissions, Lamar Community College, 2401 South Main Street, Lamar, CO 81052-3999. *Phone:* 719-336-1592. *Toll-free phone:* 800-968-6920. *E-mail:* admissions@lamarcc.edu. *Web site:* http://www.lamarcc.edu/.

Lincoln Technical Institute

Denver, Colorado

Director of Admissions Jennifer Hash, Assistant Director of Admissions, Lincoln Technical Institute, 460 South Lipan Street, Denver, CO 80223-2025. *Phone:* 800-347-3232 Ext. 43032. *Toll-free phone:* 800-347-3232. *Web site:* http://www.lincolnedu.com/campus/denver-co/.

Morgan Community College

Fort Morgan, Colorado

Freshman Application Contact Ms. Kim Maxwell, Morgan Community College, 920 Barlow Road, Fort Morgan, CO 80701-4399. *Phone:* 970-542-3111. *Toll-free phone:* 800-622-0216. *Fax:* 970-867-6608. *E-mail:* kim.maxwell@morgancc.edu. *Web site:* http://www.morgancc.edu/.

Northeastern Junior College

Sterling, Colorado

- **State-supported** 2-year, founded 1941, part of Colorado Community College and Occupational Education System
- **Small-town** 65-acre campus
- **Endowment** $5.4 million
- **Coed**

Undergraduates 910 full-time, 1,788 part-time. Students come from 21 states and territories; 8 other countries; 6% are from out of state; 2% transferred in; 44% live on campus. *Retention:* 56% of full-time freshmen returned.

Faculty *Student/faculty ratio:* 36:1.

Academics *Calendar:* semesters. *Degree:* certificates and associate. *Special study options:* academic remediation for entering students, accelerated degree program, adult/continuing education programs, advanced placement credit, cooperative education, distance learning, double majors, English as a second language, honors programs, independent study, internships, part-time degree program, services for LD students, summer session for credit.

Student Life *Campus security:* 24-hour emergency response devices, late-night transport/escort service, controlled dormitory access.

Athletics Member NCAA, NJCAA. All NCAA Division I.

Costs (2010–11) *Tuition:* state resident $2310 full-time, $96 per credit hour part-time; nonresident $7940 full-time, $331 per credit hour part-time. Full-time tuition and fees vary according to course load. Part-time tuition and fees vary according to course load. *Required fees:* $571 full-time, $10 per semester hour part-time, $11 per term part-time. *Room and board:* $5840; room only: $2658. Room and board charges vary according to board plan and housing facility.

Applying *Options:* electronic application, early admission, deferred entrance. *Required:* high school transcript.

Freshman Application Contact Andy Long, Director of Admissions, Northeastern Junior College, 100 College Avenue, Sterling, CO 80751-2399. *Phone:* 970-521-7000. *Toll-free phone:* 800-626-4637. *E-mail:* andy.long@njc.edu. *Web site:* http://www.njc.edu/.

Otero Junior College

La Junta, Colorado

- **State-supported** 2-year, founded 1941, part of Colorado Community College and Occupational Education System
- **Rural** 50-acre campus
- **Coed**

Undergraduates 870 full-time, 790 part-time. 17% live on campus.

Academics *Calendar:* semesters. *Degree:* certificates and associate. *Special study options:* academic remediation for entering students, adult/continuing education programs, advanced placement credit, distance learning, external degree program, internships, part-time degree program, summer session for credit.

Student Life *Campus security:* 24-hour patrols, late-night transport/escort service.

Athletics Member NJCAA.

Costs (2010–11) *Tuition:* state resident $2310 full-time; nonresident $4578 full-time. *Required fees:* $206 full-time. *Room and board:* $5354. Room and board charges vary according to board plan and housing facility. *Payment plans:* installment, deferred payment.

Financial Aid Of all full-time matriculated undergraduates who enrolled in 2009, 30 Federal Work-Study jobs (averaging $2000). 100 state and other part-time jobs (averaging $2000).

Applying *Options:* electronic application, early admission. *Recommended:* high school transcript.

Freshman Application Contact Mr. Jeff Paolucci, Vice President for Student Services, Otero Junior College, 1802 Colorado Avenue, La Junta, CO 81050-3415. *Phone:* 719-384-6833. *Fax:* 719-384-6933. *E-mail:* jan.schiro@ojc.edu. *Web site:* http://www.ojc.edu/.

Pikes Peak Community College

Colorado Springs, Colorado

- **State-supported** 2-year, founded 1968, part of Colorado Community College and Occupational Education System
- **Urban** 287-acre campus with easy access to Denver
- **Coed**

Academics *Calendar:* semesters. *Degree:* certificates and associate. *Special study options:* academic remediation for entering students, adult/continuing education programs, advanced placement credit, cooperative education, distance learning, double majors, English as a second language, independent study, internships, part-time degree program, services for LD students, summer session for credit. *ROTC:* Army (c).

Student Life *Campus security:* 24-hour emergency response devices and patrols, late-night transport/escort service.

Costs (2010–11) *Tuition:* state resident $2888 full-time, $96 per credit hour part-time; nonresident $12,408 full-time, $414 per credit hour part-time. Full-time tuition and fees vary according to course load. Part-time tuition and fees vary according to course load.

Financial Aid Of all full-time matriculated undergraduates who enrolled in 2009, 168 Federal Work-Study jobs (averaging $1225). 327 state and other part-time jobs (averaging $1791).

Applying *Required for some:* high school transcript.

Freshman Application Contact Pikes Peak Community College, 5675 South Academy Boulevard, Colorado Springs, CO 80906-5498. *Phone:* 719-540-7041. *Toll-free phone:* 866-411-7722. *Web site:* http://www.ppcc.edu/.

Pima Medical Institute

Colorado Springs, Colorado

- **Proprietary** 2-year
- **Urban** campus
- **Coed**

Majors Health/health-care administration; veterinary/animal health technology.

Academics *Special study options:* cooperative education, distance learning, internships.

Student Life *Housing:* college housing not available.

Standardized Tests *Required:* Wonderlic Scholastic Level Exam (for admission).

Applying *Required:* high school transcript, interview.

Freshman Application Contact Pima Medical Institute, 3770 Citadel Drive North, Colorado Springs, CO 80909. *Phone:* 719-482-7462. *Web site:* http://www.pmi.edu/.

Pima Medical Institute

Denver, Colorado

- **Proprietary** primarily 2-year, founded 1988, part of Vocational Training Institutes, Inc.
- **Urban** campus
- **Coed,** 922 undergraduate students

Majors Health/health-care administration; occupational therapist assistant; ophthalmic technology; physical therapy technology; radiologic technology/science; respiratory therapy technician.

Academics *Calendar:* modular. *Degrees:* certificates, associate, and bachelor's. *Special study options:* academic remediation for entering students, cooperative education, distance learning, internships.

Library E-Global.

Student Life *Housing:* college housing not available.

Standardized Tests *Required:* Wonderlic Scholastic Level Exam (for admission).

Applying *Required:* interview. *Required for some:* high school transcript.

Freshman Application Contact Admissions Office, Pima Medical Institute, 1701 West 72nd Avenue, Suite 130, Denver, CO 80221. *Phone:* 303-426-1800. *Toll-free phone:* 888-898-9048. *Web site:* http://www.pmi.edu/.

Platt College

Aurora, Colorado

Freshman Application Contact Admissions Office, Platt College, 3100 South Parker Road, Suite 200, Aurora, CO 80014-3141. *Phone:* 303-369-5151. *Web site:* http://www.plattcolorado.edu/.

Pueblo Community College

Pueblo, Colorado

- **State-supported** 2-year, founded 1933, part of Colorado Community College System
- **Urban** 35-acre campus
- **Endowment** $1.1 million
- **Coed,** 7,736 undergraduate students, 39% full-time, 65% women, 35% men

Undergraduates 3,054 full-time, 4,682 part-time. Students come from 24 states and territories; 6 other countries; 1% are from out of state; 3% Black or African American, non-Hispanic/Latino; 31% Hispanic/Latino; 1% Asian, non-Hispanic/Latino; 3% American Indian or Alaska Native, non-Hispanic/Latino; 7% Race/ethnicity unknown. *Retention:* 59% of full-time freshmen returned.

Freshmen *Admission:* 2,833 applied, 2,833 admitted.

Faculty *Total:* 427, 26% full-time. *Student/faculty ratio:* 19:1.

Majors Accounting technology and bookkeeping; animation, interactive technology, video graphics and special effects; autobody/collision and repair technology; automobile/automotive mechanics technology; business administration and management; child development; communications technology; computer/information technology services administration related; cosmetology; criminal justice/law enforcement administration; dental assisting; dental hygiene; diagnostic medical sonography and ultrasound technology; electrical, electronic and communications engineering technology; emergency medical technology (EMT paramedic); energy management and systems technology; engineering technology; fire science/firefighting; general studies; hospitality and recreation marketing; liberal arts and sciences and humanities related; liberal arts and sciences/liberal studies; library and archives assisting; machine shop technology; occupational therapist assistant; physical therapy technology; radiologic technology/science; registered nursing/registered nurse; respiratory care therapy; science technologies related; web page, digital/multimedia and information resources design; welding technology.

Academics *Calendar:* semesters. *Degree:* certificates and associate. *Special study options:* academic remediation for entering students, accelerated degree program, advanced placement credit, cooperative education, distance learning, double majors, English as a second language, honors programs, independent study, internships, part-time degree program, services for LD students, summer session for credit.

Library The Library with 38,719 titles, 8,586 serial subscriptions, 15,870 audiovisual materials, an OPAC.

Student Life *Housing:* college housing not available. *Activities and Organizations:* drama/theater group, choral group, Phi Theta Kappa, Welding Club, Culinary Arts Club, Performing Arts Club, Art Club. *Campus security:* 24-hour emergency response devices, late-night transport/escort service. *Student services:* personal/psychological counseling.

Costs (2010–11) *One-time required fee:* $10. *Tuition:* state resident $2888 full-time, $88 per credit hour part-time; nonresident $12,408 full-time, $394 per credit hour part-time. Full-time tuition and fees vary according to course load, location, and program. Part-time tuition and fees vary according to course load, location, and program. *Required fees:* $511 full-time, $12 per credit hour part-time, $44 per term part-time. *Payment plan:* installment. *Waivers:* senior citizens.

Financial Aid Of all full-time matriculated undergraduates who enrolled in 2009, 2,291 applied for aid, 2,115 were judged to have need, 45 had their need fully met. 145 Federal Work-Study jobs (averaging $3750). 150 state and other part-time jobs (averaging $3750). In 2009, 75 non-need-based awards were made. *Average percent of need met:* 70%. *Average financial aid package:* $4750. *Average need-based loan:* $3245. *Average need-based gift aid:* $3000. *Average non-need-based aid:* $1200. *Average indebtedness upon graduation:* $15,000.

Applying *Options:* electronic application, early admission, deferred entrance. *Application deadlines:* rolling (freshmen), rolling (out-of-state freshmen), rolling (transfers). *Notification:* continuous until 9/1 (freshmen), continuous until 9/1 (out-of-state freshmen), continuous until 9/1 (transfers).

Freshman Application Contact Ms. Barbara Benedict, Assistant Director of Admissions and Records, Pueblo Community College, 900 West Orman Avenue, Pueblo, CO 81004. *Phone:* 719-549-3039. *Toll-free phone:* 800-642-6017. *Fax:* 719-549-3012. *Web site:* http://www.pueblocc.edu/.

Red Rocks Community College

Lakewood, Colorado

- **State-supported** 2-year, founded 1969, part of Colorado Community College and Occupational Education System
- **Urban** 120-acre campus with easy access to Denver
- **Coed,** 9,803 undergraduate students, 35% full-time, 50% women, 50% men

Undergraduates 3,444 full-time, 6,359 part-time. Students come from 42 states and territories; 14 other countries; 4% are from out of state; 9% transferred in. *Retention:* 57% of full-time freshmen returned.

Freshmen *Admission:* 4,525 applied, 4,525 admitted, 1,943 enrolled.

Faculty *Total:* 558, 15% full-time. *Student/faculty ratio:* 23:1.

Majors Animation, interactive technology, video graphics and special effects; art; biology/biological sciences; biotechnology; business administration and management; chemistry; cinematography and film/video production; communication sciences and disorders; computer science; criminal justice/law enforcement administration; dramatic/theater arts; economics; elementary education; engineering; English; French; general studies; geology/earth science; German; graphic design; history; humanities; kindergarten/preschool education; liberal arts and sciences/liberal studies; mass communication/media; mathematics; music performance; parks, recreation and leisure; philosophy; physical education teaching and coaching; physics; political science and government; psychology; secondary education; sociology; Spanish; speech communication and rhetoric.

Academics *Calendar:* semesters. *Degree:* certificates and associate. *Special study options:* academic remediation for entering students, adult/continuing education programs, cooperative education, distance learning, English as a second language, honors programs, off-campus study, part-time degree program, services for LD students, study abroad, summer session for credit. *ROTC:* Army (c), Air Force (c).

Library Marvin Buckels Library with 39,012 titles, 50 serial subscriptions, 3,815 audiovisual materials, an OPAC, a Web page.

Student Life *Housing:* college housing not available. *Activities and Organizations:* drama/theater group. *Campus security:* 24-hour emergency response devices and patrols. *Student services:* personal/psychological counseling.

Athletics *Intramural sports:* volleyball M/W.

Costs (2010–11) *Tuition:* state resident $2888 full-time, $96 per credit hour part-time; nonresident $12,408 full-time, $414 per credit hour part-time. Full-time tuition and fees vary according to program and reciprocity agreements. Part-time tuition and fees vary according to program and reciprocity agreements. *Required fees:* $316 full-time, $9 per credit hour part-time, $11 per term part-time. *Payment plans:* installment, deferred payment. *Waivers:* employees or children of employees.

Financial Aid Of all full-time matriculated undergraduates who enrolled in 2009, 21 Federal Work-Study jobs (averaging $5000). 95 state and other part-time jobs (averaging $5000).

Applying *Options:* electronic application, early admission. *Application deadlines:* rolling (freshmen), rolling (out-of-state freshmen), rolling (transfers). *Notification:* continuous (freshmen), continuous (out-of-state freshmen), continuous (transfers).

Freshman Application Contact Admissions Office, Red Rocks Community College, 13300 West 6th Avenue, Lakewood, CO 80228-1255. *Phone:* 303-914-6360. *Fax:* 303-914-6919. *E-mail:* admissions@rrcc.edu. *Web site:* http://www.rrcc.edu/.

Redstone College–Denver

Broomfield, Colorado

- **Proprietary** 2-year, founded 1965
- **Coed**

Academics *Calendar:* continuous. *Degree:* certificates, diplomas, and associate.

Financial Aid Of all full-time matriculated undergraduates who enrolled in 2009, 20 Federal Work-Study jobs.

Freshman Application Contact Redstone College–Denver, 10851 West 120th Avenue, Broomfield, CO 80021. *Phone:* 303-466-7383. *Toll-free phone:* 877-801-1025. *Web site:* http://www.redstone.edu/.

Remington College–Colorado Springs Campus

Colorado Springs, Colorado

Freshman Application Contact Remington College–Colorado Springs Campus, 6050 Erin Park Drive, #250, Colorado Springs, CO 80918. *Phone:* 719-532-1234 Ext. 202. *Web site:* http://www.remingtoncollege.edu/.

Trinidad State Junior College

Trinidad, Colorado

Freshman Application Contact Dr. Sandra Veltri, Vice President of Student/Academic Affairs, Trinidad State Junior College, 600 Prospect Street, Trinidad, CO 81082. *Phone:* 719-846-5559. *Toll-free phone:* 800-621-8752. *Fax:* 719-846-5620. *E-mail:* sandy.veltri@trinidadstate.edu. *Web site:* http://www.trinidadstate.edu/.

CONNECTICUT

Asnuntuck Community College

Enfield, Connecticut

Freshman Application Contact Timothy St. James, Director of Admissions, Asnuntuck Community College, 170 Elm Street, Enfield, CT 06082-3800. *Phone:* 860-253-3087. *Toll-free phone:* 800-501-3967. *Fax:* 860-253-3014. *E-mail:* tstjames@acc.commnet.edu. *Web site:* http://www.acc.commnet.edu/.

Capital Community College

Hartford, Connecticut

Freshman Application Contact Ms. Jackie Phillips, Director of the Welcome and Advising Center, Capital Community College, 950 Main Street, Hartford, CT 06103. *Phone:* 860-906-5078. *Toll-free phone:* 800-894-6126. *E-mail:* jphillips@ccc.commnet.edu. *Web site:* http://www.ccc.commnet.edu/.

Gateway Community College

New Haven, Connecticut

- **State-supported** 2-year, founded 1992, part of Connecticut Community–Technical College System
- **Urban** 5-acre campus with easy access to New York City
- **Coed,** 7,328 undergraduate students, 35% full-time, 60% women, 40% men

Undergraduates 2,553 full-time, 4,775 part-time.

Freshmen *Admission:* 3,773 applied, 3,763 admitted, 1,390 enrolled.

Faculty *Total:* 407, 21% full-time, 4% with terminal degrees. *Student/faculty ratio:* 9:1.

Majors Accounting; automobile/automotive mechanics technology; avionics maintenance technology; biomedical technology; business administration and management; computer and information sciences related; computer engineering related; computer engineering technology; computer graphics; computer typography and composition equipment operation; consumer merchandising/retailing management; data entry/microcomputer applications; data processing and data processing technology; dietetics; electrical, electronic and communications engineering technology; engineering-related technologies; engineering technology; fashion merchandising; fire science/firefighting; gerontology; hotel/motel administration; human services; industrial radiologic technology; industrial technology; kindergarten/preschool education; legal administrative assistant/secretary; liberal arts and sciences/liberal studies; mechanical engineering/mechanical technology; medical administrative assistant and medical secretary; mental health counseling; nuclear medical technology; registered nursing/registered nurse; special products marketing; substance abuse/addiction counseling; word processing.

Academics *Calendar:* semesters. *Degree:* certificates and associate. *Special study options:* academic remediation for entering students, adult/continuing education programs, advanced placement credit, distance learning, English as a second language, external degree program, independent study, internships, off-campus study, part-time degree program, services for LD students, summer session for credit.

Library Gateway Community College Library plus 2 others with 46,090 titles, 275 serial subscriptions, 3,121 audiovisual materials, an OPAC, a Web page.

Student Life *Housing:* college housing not available. *Activities and Organizations:* drama/theater group, student-run newspaper. *Campus security:* late-night transport/escort service. *Student services:* personal/psychological counseling, women's center.

Athletics Member NJCAA. *Intercollegiate sports:* baseball M, basketball M/W, soccer M, softball W.

Costs (2011–12) *Tuition:* state resident $3096 full-time, $129 per credit part-time; nonresident $9288 full-time, $387 per credit part-time. *Required fees:* $394 full-time. *Payment plan:* installment. *Waivers:* senior citizens and employees or children of employees.

Financial Aid Of all full-time matriculated undergraduates who enrolled in 2009, 42 Federal Work-Study jobs (averaging $3399). 14 state and other part-time jobs (averaging $840).

Applying *Options:* early admission, deferred entrance. *Application fee:* $20. *Required:* high school transcript. *Required for some:* essay or personal statement, interview. *Application deadlines:* 9/1 (freshmen), 9/1 (transfers). *Notification:* continuous until 9/1 (freshmen), continuous until 9/1 (transfers).

Freshman Application Contact Ms. Kim Shea, Director of Admissions, Gateway Community College, New Haven, CT 06511. *Phone:* 203-789-7043. *Toll-free phone:* 800-390-7723. *Fax:* 203-285-2018. *E-mail:* gateway_ctc@commnet.edu. *Web site:* http://www.gwcc.commnet.edu/.

Goodwin College

East Hartford, Connecticut

- **Proprietary** primarily 2-year, founded 1999
- **Urban** 660-acre campus with easy access to Hartford
- **Coed,** 2,791 undergraduate students, 24% full-time, 84% women, 16% men

Undergraduates 670 full-time, 2,121 part-time. 1% are from out of state; 18% transferred in. *Retention:* 38% of full-time freshmen returned.

Freshmen *Admission:* 918 applied, 918 admitted, 455 enrolled.

Faculty *Total:* 225, 21% full-time, 18% with terminal degrees. *Student/faculty ratio:* 13:1.

Majors Accounting technology and bookkeeping; business administration and management; business/commerce; child-care and support services management; child development; criminal justice/law enforcement administration; entrepreneurship; environmental studies; health services/allied health/health sciences; homeland security; homeland security, law enforcement, firefighting and protective services related; human resources management; human services; liberal arts and sciences/liberal studies; medical administrative assistant and medical secretary; medical/clinical assistant; medical insurance coding; medical insurance/medical billing; nonprofit management; occupational therapist assistant; office management; registered nursing/registered nurse; respiratory care therapy.

Academics *Calendar:* semesters. *Degrees:* certificates, associate, and bachelor's. *Special study options:* academic remediation for entering students, adult/continuing education programs, advanced placement credit, distance learning, double majors, English as a second language, internships, off-campus study, part-time degree program, services for LD students, summer session for credit.

Library Goodwin College Library with an OPAC.

Student Life *Housing:* college housing not available. *Activities and Organizations:* student-run newspaper, choral group. *Campus security:* 24-hour emergency response devices, evening security patrolman. *Student services:* personal/psychological counseling.

Costs (2010–11) *Tuition:* $18,000 full-time, $560 per credit hour part-time. Full-time tuition and fees vary according to course load and program. Part-time tuition and fees vary according to course load and program. *Required fees:* $500 full-time. *Payment plan:* installment. *Waivers:* employees or children of employees.

Financial Aid Of all full-time matriculated undergraduates who enrolled in 2008, 510 applied for aid, 505 were judged to have need. *Average percent of need met:* 24%. *Average financial aid package:* $8473. *Average need-based loan:* $3567. *Average need-based gift aid:* $6835.

Applying *Options:* electronic application, early admission, early decision, early action, deferred entrance. *Application fee:* $50. *Required:* essay or personal statement, high school transcript, minimum 2.0 GPA, medical exam. *Recommended:* 2 letters of recommendation, interview. *Application deadlines:* rolling (freshmen), rolling (transfers), 6/1 (early action). *Early decision* *deadline:* 3/1. *Notification:* continuous (freshmen), continuous (transfers), 3/15 (early decision), 6/15 (early action).

Freshman Application Contact Mr. Nicholas Lentino, Director of Admissions, Goodwin College, One Riverside Drive, East Hartford, CT 06118. *Phone:* 860-727-6765. *Toll-free phone:* 800-889-3282. *Fax:* 860-291-9550. *E-mail:* nlantino@goodwin.edu. *Web site:* http://www.goodwin.edu/.

Housatonic Community College

Bridgeport, Connecticut

- **State-supported** 2-year, founded 1965, part of Connecticut Community–Technical College System
- **Urban** 4-acre campus with easy access to New York City
- **Coed,** 6,197 undergraduate students

Undergraduates 28% Black or African American, non-Hispanic/Latino; 24% Hispanic/Latino; 3% Asian, non-Hispanic/Latino; 0.1% Native Hawaiian or other Pacific Islander, non-Hispanic/Latino; 0.2% American Indian or Alaska Native, non-Hispanic/Latino; 1% Two or more races, non-Hispanic/Latino; 4% Race/ethnicity unknown.

Faculty *Total:* 391, 18% full-time. *Student/faculty ratio:* 14:1.

Majors Accounting; administrative assistant and secretarial science; art; avionics maintenance technology; business administration and management; child development; clinical/medical laboratory technology; commercial and advertising art; computer typography and composition equipment operation; criminal justice/law enforcement administration; data processing and data processing technology; environmental studies; humanities; human services; journalism; liberal arts and sciences/liberal studies; mathematics; mental health counseling; physical therapy; pre-engineering; public administration; registered nursing/registered nurse; social sciences; substance abuse/addiction counseling.

Academics *Calendar:* semesters. *Degree:* certificates and associate. *Special study options:* academic remediation for entering students, adult/continuing education programs, advanced placement credit, cooperative education, distance learning, double majors, English as a second language, honors programs, independent study, internships, part-time degree program, services for LD students, summer session for credit. *ROTC:* Army (c). *Unusual degree programs:* nursing with Bridgeport Hospital.

Library Housatonic Community College Library with 30,000 titles, 300 serial subscriptions, an OPAC, a Web page.

Student Life *Housing:* college housing not available. *Activities and Organizations:* drama/theater group, student-run newspaper, Student Senate, Association of Latin American Students, Community Action Network, Drama Club. *Campus security:* 24-hour emergency response devices, late-night transport/escort service. *Student services:* health clinic, personal/psychological counseling, women's center.

Costs (2010–11) *Tuition:* state resident $3024 full-time, $126 per credit hour part-time; nonresident $9796 full-time, $378 per credit hour part-time. Full-time tuition and fees vary according to course load and program. Part-time tuition and fees vary according to course load and program. Part-time mandatory fees differ depending upon course load. *Required fees:* $382 full-time. *Payment plans:* installment, deferred payment. *Waivers:* senior citizens and employees or children of employees.

Financial Aid Of all full-time matriculated undergraduates who enrolled in 2009, 70 Federal Work-Study jobs (averaging $2850).

Applying *Options:* electronic application, deferred entrance. *Application fee:* $20. *Required:* high school transcript. *Required for some:* interview. *Application deadlines:* rolling (freshmen), rolling (transfers). *Notification:* continuous (freshmen), continuous (transfers).

Freshman Application Contact Ms. Delores Y. Curtis, Director of Admissions, Housatonic Community College, 900 Lafayette Boulevard, Bridgeport, CT 06604-4704. *Phone:* 203-332-5102. *Web site:* http://www.hctc.commnet.edu/.

Lincoln College of New England

Suffield, Connecticut

Freshman Application Contact Director of Admissions, Lincoln College of New England, 1760 Mapleton Avenue, Suffield, CT 06078. *Phone:* 860-628-4751. *Toll-free phone:* 800-825-0087. *E-mail:* admissions@lincolncollegene.edu. *Web site:* http://www.lincolncollegene.edu/.

Manchester Community College

Manchester, Connecticut

- **State-supported** 2-year, founded 1963, part of Connecticut Community–Technical College System
- **Small-town** 160-acre campus with easy access to Hartford
- **Coed,** 7,540 undergraduate students, 43% full-time, 53% women, 47% men

Undergraduates 3,213 full-time, 4,327 part-time. 13% Black or African American, non-Hispanic/Latino; 13% Hispanic/Latino; 4% Asian, non-Hispanic/Latino; 0.2% Native Hawaiian or other Pacific Islander, non-Hispanic/Latino; 0.1% American Indian or Alaska Native, non-Hispanic/Latino; 2% Two or more races, non-Hispanic/Latino; 9% Race/ethnicity unknown; 0.6% international; 12% transferred in. *Retention:* 60% of full-time freshmen returned.

Freshmen *Admission:* 2,802 applied, 2,788 admitted, 1,610 enrolled.

Faculty *Total:* 494, 22% full-time, 5% with terminal degrees. *Student/faculty ratio:* 20:1.

Majors Accounting; administrative assistant and secretarial science; business administration and management; clinical/medical laboratory technology; commercial and advertising art; criminal justice/law enforcement administration; dramatic/theater arts; engineering science; fine/studio arts; general studies; hotel/motel administration; human services; industrial engineering; industrial technology; information science/studies; journalism; kindergarten/preschool education; legal administrative assistant/secretary; legal assistant/paralegal; liberal arts and sciences/liberal studies; management information systems; marketing/marketing management; medical administrative assistant and medical secretary; music; occupational therapist assistant; physical therapy technology; respiratory care therapy; social work; speech communication and rhetoric; surgical technology; teacher assistant/aide.

Academics *Calendar:* semesters. *Degree:* certificates and associate. *Special study options:* academic remediation for entering students, adult/continuing education programs, cooperative education, distance learning, double majors, English as a second language, independent study, internships, off-campus study, part-time degree program, services for LD students, student-designed majors, summer session for credit.

Student Life *Housing:* college housing not available. *Activities and Organizations:* drama/theater group, student-run newspaper, choral group. *Student services:* women's center.

Athletics Member NJCAA. *Intercollegiate sports:* baseball M, basketball M/W, soccer M/W, softball W.

Costs (2011–12) *Tuition:* state resident $3096 full-time; nonresident $9288 full-time. *Required fees:* $394 full-time. *Payment plan:* installment. *Waivers:* senior citizens and employees or children of employees.

Financial Aid Of all full-time matriculated undergraduates who enrolled in 2009, 80 Federal Work-Study jobs (averaging $2000). 45 state and other part-time jobs (averaging $2000).

Applying *Options:* electronic application. *Application fee:* $20. *Required:* high school transcript. *Application deadlines:* rolling (freshmen), rolling (transfers). *Notification:* continuous (freshmen), continuous (transfers).

Freshman Application Contact Director of Admissions, Manchester Community College, PO Box 1046, Manchester, CT 06045-1046. *Phone:* 860-512-3210. *Fax:* 860-512-3221. *Web site:* http://www.mcc.commnet.edu/.

Middlesex Community College

Middletown, Connecticut

- **State-supported** 2-year, founded 1966, part of Connecticut Community–Technical College System
- **Suburban** 38-acre campus with easy access to Hartford
- **Endowment** $287,691
- **Coed,** 2,952 undergraduate students, 40% full-time, 58% women, 42% men

Undergraduates 1,186 full-time, 1,766 part-time. Students come from 6 states and territories; 10 other countries; 1% are from out of state; 9% transferred in. *Retention:* 54% of full-time freshmen returned.

Freshmen *Admission:* 993 applied, 606 enrolled.

Faculty *Total:* 147, 30% full-time, 20% with terminal degrees. *Student/faculty ratio:* 22:1.

Majors Accounting; administrative assistant and secretarial science; biological and physical sciences; biology/biotechnology laboratory technician; broadcast journalism; business administration and management; commercial and advertising art; computer programming; criminal justice/police science; engineering science; engineering technology; environmental studies; fine/studio arts; human services; industrial radiologic technology; intermedia/multimedia; legal administrative assistant/secretary; liberal arts and sciences/liberal studies; marketing/marketing management; mass communication/media; medical administrative assistant and medical secretary; medical radiologic technology;

mental health counseling; ophthalmic laboratory technology; pre-engineering; substance abuse/addiction counseling.

Academics *Calendar:* semesters. *Degree:* certificates and associate. *Special study options:* academic remediation for entering students, adult/continuing education programs, advanced placement credit, cooperative education, distance learning, double majors, English as a second language, honors programs, independent study, internships, off-campus study, part-time degree program, services for LD students, summer session for credit.

Library Jean Burr Smith Library with 70,773 titles, 32,235 serial subscriptions, 2,285 audiovisual materials, an OPAC, a Web page.

Student Life *Housing:* college housing not available. *Activities and Organizations:* drama/theater group, student-run newspaper, Phi Theta Kappa, Human Services Association, Peace and Justice Club, Poetry Club, International Student Club. *Campus security:* 24-hour emergency response devices and patrols.

Standardized Tests *Required:* CPT (for admissión).

Costs (2011–12) *Tuition:* state resident $3096 full-time, $129 per credit part-time; nonresident $9288 full-time, $387 per credit part-time. Full-time tuition and fees vary according to course load, degree level, and program. Part-time tuition and fees vary according to course load, degree level, and program. *Required fees:* $394 full-time, $79 per course part-time. *Payment plan:* installment. *Waivers:* employees or children of employees.

Financial Aid Of all full-time matriculated undergraduates who enrolled in 2009, 50 Federal Work-Study jobs (averaging $5000). 2 state and other part-time jobs (averaging $5000).

Applying *Options:* electronic application, early admission, deferred entrance. *Application fee:* $20. *Required:* high school transcript. *Application deadlines:* rolling (freshmen), rolling (transfers).

Freshman Application Contact Mensimah Shabazz, Director of Admissions, Middlesex Community College, Middletown, CT 06457-4889. *Phone:* 860-343-5742. *Fax:* 860-344-3055. *E-mail:* mshabazz@mxcc.commnet.edu. *Web site:* http://www.mxcc.commnet.edu/.

Naugatuck Valley Community College

Waterbury, Connecticut

Freshman Application Contact Ms. Lucretia Sveda, Director of Enrollment Services, Naugatuck Valley Community College, Waterbury, CT 06708. *Phone:* 203-575-8016. *Fax:* 203-596-8766. *E-mail:* lsveda@nvcc.commnet.edu. *Web site:* http://www.nvcc.commnet.edu/.

Northwestern Connecticut Community College

Winsted, Connecticut

- **State-supported** 2-year, founded 1965, part of Connecticut Community–Technical College System
- **Small-town** 5-acre campus with easy access to Hartford
- **Coed**

Undergraduates 591 full-time, 1,120 part-time. Students come from 5 states and territories; 1% are from out of state; 8% transferred in. *Retention:* 63% of full-time freshmen returned.

Academics *Calendar:* semesters. *Degree:* certificates and associate. *Special study options:* academic remediation for entering students, adult/continuing education programs, advanced placement credit, cooperative education, distance learning, double majors, English as a second language, independent study, internships, part-time degree program, services for LD students, summer session for credit.

Student Life *Campus security:* evening security patrols.

Costs (2010–11) *Tuition:* state resident $3024 full-time, $126 per credit hour part-time; nonresident $9072 full-time, $378 per credit hour part-time. Full-time tuition and fees vary according to reciprocity agreements. Part-time tuition and fees vary according to course load and reciprocity agreements. *Required fees:* $382 full-time, $65 per credit hour part-time, $185 per term part-time.

Applying *Options:* deferred entrance. *Application fee:* $20.

Freshman Application Contact Admissions Office, Northwestern Connecticut Community College, Park Place East, Winsted, CT 06098-1798. *Phone:* 860-738-6330. *Fax:* 860-738-6437. *E-mail:* admissions@nwcc.commnet.edu. *Web site:* http://www.nwcc.commnet.edu/.

Norwalk Community College

Norwalk, Connecticut

- **State-supported** 2-year, founded 1961, part of Connecticut Community–Technical College System
- **Suburban** 30-acre campus with easy access to New York City
- **Endowment** $16.7 million
- **Coed,** 6,740 undergraduate students, 38% full-time, 59% women, 41% men

Undergraduates 2,531 full-time, 4,209 part-time. Students come from 9 states and territories; 44 other countries; 4% are from out of state; 6% transferred in.

Freshmen *Admission:* 3,949 applied, 852 enrolled.

Faculty *Total:* 455, 24% full-time. *Student/faculty ratio:* 18:1.

Majors Accounting; administrative assistant and secretarial science; architectural engineering technology; art; business administration and management; commercial and advertising art; computer and information systems security; computer systems networking and telecommunications; construction engineering technology; criminal justice/law enforcement administration; early childhood education; engineering science; finance; fine/studio arts; fire science/firefighting; general studies; graphic design; hotel/motel administration; human services; information science/studies; information technology; interior design; kinesiology and exercise science; legal assistant/paralegal; liberal arts and sciences/liberal studies; marketing/marketing management; medical office management; parks, recreation and leisure; psychology; registered nursing/registered nurse; respiratory care therapy; restaurant/food services management; speech communication and rhetoric; web page, digital/multimedia and information resources design; women's studies.

Academics *Calendar:* semesters. *Degree:* certificates and associate. *Special study options:* academic remediation for entering students, adult/continuing education programs, advanced placement credit, cooperative education, distance learning, English as a second language, freshman honors college, honors programs, independent study, internships, part-time degree program, services for LD students, summer session for credit.

Library Everett I. L. Baker Library with 60,433 titles, 191 serial subscriptions, 5,719 audiovisual materials, an OPAC, a Web page.

Student Life *Housing:* college housing not available. *Activities and Organizations:* student-run newspaper, choral group, Student World Assembly, Archaeology Club, Literature Club, Art Club, Phi Theta Kappa. *Campus security:* late-night transport/escort service, all buildings are secured each evening; there are foot patrols and vehicle patrols by security from 8am to 11pm. *Student services:* personal/psychological counseling, women's center.

Costs (2011–12) *Tuition:* state resident $6980 full-time, $129 per credit part-time; nonresident $20,860 full-time, $387 per credit part-time. Full-time tuition and fees vary according to course load and program. Part-time tuition and fees vary according to course load and program. *Required fees:* $800 full-time, $70 per term part-time. *Payment plan:* installment. *Waivers:* senior citizens and employees or children of employees.

Financial Aid Of all full-time matriculated undergraduates who enrolled in 2009, 42 Federal Work-Study jobs (averaging $2581). 60 state and other part-time jobs (averaging $2046).

Applying *Options:* electronic application, deferred entrance. *Application fee:* $20. *Required:* high school transcript. *Application deadlines:* rolling (freshmen), rolling (transfers). *Notification:* continuous (freshmen), continuous (transfers).

Freshman Application Contact Mr. Curtis Antrum, Admissions Counselor, Norwalk Community College, 188 Richards Avenue, Norwalk, CT 06854-1655. *Phone:* 203-857-7060. *Toll-free phone:* 888-462-6282. *Fax:* 203-857-3335. *E-mail:* admissions@ncc.commnet.edu. *Web site:* http://www.ncc.commnet.edu/.

Quinebaug Valley Community College

Danielson, Connecticut

Freshman Application Contact Dr. Toni Moumouris, Director of Admissions, Quinebaug Valley Community College, 742 Upper Maple Street, Danielson, CT 06239. *Phone:* 860-774-1130 Ext. 318. *Fax:* 860-774-7768. *E-mail:* qu_isd@commnet.edu. *Web site:* http://www.qvcc.commnet.edu/.

St. Vincent's College

Bridgeport, Connecticut

Freshman Application Contact Mr. Joseph Marrone, Director of Admissions and Recruitment Marketing, St. Vincent's College, 2800 Main Street, Bridgeport, CT 06606-4292. *Phone:* 203-576-5515. *Toll-free phone:* 800-873-1013. *Fax:* 203-576-5893. *E-mail:* jmarrone@stvincentscollege.edu. *Web site:* http://www.stvincentscollege.edu/.

Three Rivers Community College
Norwich, Connecticut

- **State-supported** 2-year, founded 1963, part of Connecticut Community–Technical College System
- **Suburban** 40-acre campus with easy access to Hartford
- **Coed,** 5,161 undergraduate students, 34% full-time, 58% women, 42% men

Undergraduates 1,741 full-time, 3,420 part-time. 1% are from out of state.
Freshmen *Admission:* 1,101 enrolled.
Faculty *Total:* 234, 33% full-time, 4% with terminal degrees. *Student/faculty ratio:* 22:1.
Majors Accounting; administrative assistant and secretarial science; architectural engineering technology; avionics maintenance technology; business administration and management; civil engineering technology; computer engineering technology; computer programming; consumer merchandising/retailing management; corrections; criminal justice/law enforcement administration; data processing and data processing technology; drafting and design technology; dramatic/theater arts; electrical, electronic and communications engineering technology; engineering; engineering science; engineering technology; environmental engineering technology; fire science/firefighting; hospitality administration, hotel/motel administration; human services; hydrology and water resources science; industrial technology; kindergarten/preschool education; laser and optical technology; legal administrative assistant/secretary; liberal arts and sciences/liberal studies; marketing/marketing management; mechanical engineering/mechanical technology; nuclear/nuclear power technology; pre-engineering; professional, technical, business, and scientific writing; public administration; registered nursing/registered nurse; special products marketing; substance abuse/addiction counseling; tourism and travel services management.
Academics *Calendar:* semesters. *Degrees:* certificates and associate (engineering technology programs are offered on the Thames Valley Campus; liberal arts, transfer and career programs are offered on the Mohegan Campus). *Special study options:* academic remediation for entering students, adult/continuing education programs, advanced placement credit, cooperative education, distance learning, double majors, English as a second language, independent study, internships, part-time degree program, student-designed majors, study abroad, summer session for credit.
Library Three Rivers Community College Learning Resource Center plus 1 other with an OPAC.
Student Life *Housing:* college housing not available. *Activities and Organizations:* drama/theater group, student-run newspaper, national fraternities. *Campus security:* 24-hour emergency response devices, late-night transport/escort service, 14 hour patrols by trained security personnel. *Student services:* personal/psychological counseling.
Athletics *Intramural sports:* baseball M(c)/W(c), golf M(c)/W(c).
Costs (2010–11) *Tuition:* state resident $3024 full-time, $126 per credit hour part-time; nonresident $9796 full-time, $378 per credit hour part-time. *Required fees:* $382 full-time, $65 per credit hour part-time, $191 per term part-time. *Payment plan:* installment. *Waivers:* senior citizens and employees or children of employees.
Financial Aid Of all full-time matriculated undergraduates who enrolled in 2009, 40 Federal Work-Study jobs (averaging $3000). 80 state and other part-time jobs (averaging $3000).
Applying *Options:* electronic application, early admission, deferred entrance. *Application fee:* $20. *Required for some:* minimum 3.0 GPA. *Recommended:* high school transcript. *Application deadlines:* rolling (freshmen), rolling (transfers). *Notification:* continuous (freshmen), continuous (transfers).
Freshman Application Contact Ms. Aida Garcia, Admissions and Recruitment Counselor, Three Rivers Community College, 574 New London Turnpike, Norwich, CT 06360. *Phone:* 860-383-5268. *Fax:* 860-885-1684. *E-mail:* admissions@trcc.commnet.edu. *Web site:* http://www.trcc.commnet.edu/.

Tunxis Community College
Farmington, Connecticut

- **State-supported** 2-year, founded 1969, part of Connecticut Community–Technical College System
- **Suburban** 12-acre campus with easy access to Hartford
- **Coed**

Undergraduates 1,874 full-time, 2,622 part-time. Students come from 6 states and territories; 2% are from out of state. *Retention:* 59% of full-time freshmen returned.
Faculty *Student/faculty ratio:* 19:1.
Academics *Calendar:* semesters. *Degree:* certificates and associate. *Special study options:* academic remediation for entering students, adult/continuing education programs, cooperative education, distance learning, double majors, English as a second language, honors programs, independent study, internships, part-time degree program, services for LD students, summer session for credit.
Student Life *Campus security:* 24-hour emergency response devices.
Costs (2010–11) *Tuition:* state resident $3024 full-time, $126 per credit hour part-time; nonresident $9072 full-time, $189 per credit hour part-time. *Required fees:* $382 full-time.
Applying *Options:* deferred entrance. *Application fee:* $20. *Required:* high school transcript.
Freshman Application Contact Mr. Peter McCluskey, Director of Admissions, Tunxis Community College, 271 Scott Swamp Road, Farmington, CT 06032. *Phone:* 860-255-3550. *Fax:* 860-255-3559. *E-mail:* pmccluskey@txcc.commnet.edu. *Web site:* http://www.tunxis.commnet.edu/.

DELAWARE

Delaware College of Art and Design
Wilmington, Delaware

Freshman Application Contact Ms. Allison Gullo, Delaware College of Art and Design, 600 North Market Street, Wilmington, DE 19801. *Phone:* 302-622-8867 Ext. 111. *Fax:* 302-622-8870. *E-mail:* agullo@dcad.edu. *Web site:* http://www.dcad.edu/.

Delaware Technical & Community College, Jack F. Owens Campus
Georgetown, Delaware

- **State-supported** 2-year, founded 1967, part of Delaware Technical and Community College System
- **Small-town** 120-acre campus
- **Coed,** 5,031 undergraduate students, 52% full-time, 65% women, 35% men

Undergraduates 2,593 full-time, 2,438 part-time. 18% Black or African American, non-Hispanic/Latino; 5% Hispanic/Latino; 1% Asian, non-Hispanic/Latino; 0.1% Native Hawaiian or other Pacific Islander, non-Hispanic/Latino; 0.3% American Indian or Alaska Native, non-Hispanic/Latino; 2% Two or more races, non-Hispanic/Latino; 0.7% Race/ethnicity unknown; 3% international. *Retention:* 59% of full-time freshmen returned.
Freshmen *Admission:* 926 enrolled.
Faculty *Total:* 348, 35% full-time.
Majors Accounting; aeronautical/aerospace engineering technology; agricultural business and management; agricultural production; applied horticulture/horticulture operations; architectural engineering technology; automobile/automotive mechanics technology; biology/biological sciences; biology/biotechnology laboratory technician; business automation/technology/data entry; business/commerce; civil engineering technology; clinical/medical laboratory assistant; computer and information sciences; computer technology/computer systems technology; construction management; criminal justice/law enforcement administration; criminal justice/police science; customer service support/call center/teleservice operation; diagnostic medical sonography and ultrasound technology; drafting and design technology; early childhood education; e-commerce; education (multiple levels); electrical, electronic and communications engineering technology; elementary education; emergency medical technology (EMT paramedic); energy management and systems technology; entrepreneurship; heating, air conditioning, ventilation and refrigeration maintenance technology; human services; kindergarten/preschool education; legal administrative assistant/secretary; licensed practical/vocational nurse training; management information systems; marketing/marketing management; mathematics teacher education; mechanical drafting and CAD/CADD; medical/clinical assistant; middle school education; nuclear engineering technology; occupational therapist assistant; office management; physical therapy technology; poultry science; radiologic technology/science; registered nursing/registered nurse; respiratory therapy technician; surveying technology; turf and turfgrass management; veterinary/animal health technology; water quality and wastewater treatment management and recycling technology.
Academics *Calendar:* semesters. *Degree:* certificates, diplomas, and associate. *Special study options:* academic remediation for entering students, advanced placement credit, cooperative education, distance learning, double majors, English as a second language, internships, part-time degree program, services for LD students, study abroad, summer session for credit.
Library Stephen J. Betze Library with 62,663 titles, 514 serial subscriptions, an OPAC, a Web page.
Student Life *Housing:* college housing not available. *Activities and Organizations:* student-run radio station. *Campus security:* 24-hour emergency response devices, late-night transport/escort service.

Athletics Member NJCAA. *Intercollegiate sports:* baseball M(s), golf M, softball W(s). *Intramural sports:* football M/W.
Costs (2010–11) *Tuition:* state resident $2598 full-time, $108 per credit hour part-time; nonresident $6496 full-time, $271 per credit hour part-time. *Required fees:* $516 full-time, $7 per credit hour part-time, $25 per term part-time. *Payment plan:* deferred payment. *Waivers:* senior citizens and employees or children of employees.
Financial Aid Of all full-time matriculated undergraduates who enrolled in 2009, 250 Federal Work-Study jobs (averaging $2000).
Applying *Options:* electronic application, early admission, deferred entrance. *Application fee:* $10. *Required for some:* high school transcript. *Application deadlines:* rolling (freshmen), rolling (transfers). *Notification:* continuous (freshmen), continuous (transfers).
Freshman Application Contact Ms. Claire McDonald, Admissions Counselor, Delaware Technical & Community College, Jack F. Owens Campus, PO Box 610, Georgetown, DE 19947. *Phone:* 302-856-5400. *Fax:* 302-856-9461. *Web site:* http://www.dtcc.edu/.

Delaware Technical & Community College, Stanton/Wilmington Campus
Newark, Delaware

- **State-supported** 2-year, founded 1968, part of Delaware Technical and Community College System
- **Urban** campus with easy access to Philadelphia
- **Coed,** 7,451 undergraduate students, 44% full-time, 59% women, 41% men

Undergraduates 3,294 full-time, 4,157 part-time. 26% Black or African American, non-Hispanic/Latino; 7% Hispanic/Latino; 3% Asian, non-Hispanic/Latino; 0.1% Native Hawaiian or other Pacific Islander, non-Hispanic/Latino; 0.3% American Indian or Alaska Native, non-Hispanic/Latino; 2% Two or more races, non-Hispanic/Latino; 2% Race/ethnicity unknown; 2% international. *Retention:* 55% of full-time freshmen returned.
Freshmen *Admission:* 1,343 enrolled.
Faculty *Total:* 532, 34% full-time.
Majors Accounting; agricultural business and management; architectural engineering technology; automobile/automotive mechanics technology; biology/biological sciences; biology/biotechnology laboratory technician; business administration and management; business automation/technology/data entry; business/commerce; CAD/CADD drafting/design technology; cardiovascular technology; chemical technology; civil drafting and CAD/CADD; computer and information sciences; computer engineering technology; computer systems networking and telecommunications; construction management; criminal justice/law enforcement administration; criminal justice/police science; culinary arts; customer service management; customer service support/call center/teleservice operation; dental hygiene; diagnostic medical sonography and ultrasound technology; drafting and design technology; early childhood education; education (multiple levels); electrical, electronic and communications engineering technology; electrocardiograph technology; elementary education; emergency care attendant (EMT ambulance); emergency medical technology (EMT paramedic); energy management and systems technology; engineering/industrial management; fire prevention and safety technology; fire science/firefighting; fire services administration; heating, ventilation, air conditioning and refrigeration engineering technology; histologic technology/histotechnologist; hotel/motel administration; human services; kindergarten/preschool education; kinesiology and exercise science; management information systems; management science; manufacturing engineering technology; marketing/marketing management; mathematics teacher education; mechanical engineering/mechanical technology; medical/clinical assistant; middle school education; nuclear engineering technology; nuclear medical technology; occupational therapist assistant; office management; operations research; physical therapy technology; radiologic technology/science; registered nursing/registered nurse; respiratory therapy technician; restaurant, culinary, and catering management; science technologies related; substance abuse/addiction counseling; surveying technology.
Academics *Calendar:* semesters. *Degree:* certificates, diplomas, and associate. *Special study options:* academic remediation for entering students, advanced placement credit, cooperative education, distance learning, double majors, English as a second language, internships, part-time degree program, services for LD students, study abroad, summer session for credit. *ROTC:* Air Force (c).
Library Stanton Campus Library and John Eugene Derrickson Memorial Library with 74,259 titles, 793 serial subscriptions, an OPAC, a Web page.
Student Life *Housing:* college housing not available. *Campus security:* 24-hour emergency response devices, late-night transport/escort service. *Student services:* personal/psychological counseling, women's center.
Athletics Member NJCAA. *Intercollegiate sports:* basketball M(s)/W(s), soccer M(s), softball W(s). *Intramural sports:* basketball M/W, football M/W, softball W, volleyball M/W.

Costs (2010–11) *Tuition:* state resident $2598 full-time, $108 per credit hour part-time; nonresident $6496 full-time, $271 per credit hour part-time. *Required fees:* $516 full-time, $7 per credit hour part-time, $25 per term part-time. *Payment plan:* deferred payment. *Waivers:* senior citizens and employees or children of employees.
Applying *Options:* electronic application, early admission, deferred entrance. *Application fee:* $10. *Required for some:* high school transcript. *Application deadlines:* rolling (freshmen), rolling (transfers). *Notification:* continuous (freshmen), continuous (transfers).
Freshman Application Contact Ms. Rebecca Bailey, Admissions Coordinator, Wilmington, Delaware Technical & Community College, Stanton/Wilmington Campus, 333 Shipley Street, Wilmington, DE 19713. *Phone:* 302-571-5343. *Fax:* 302-577-2548. *Web site:* http://www.dtcc.edu/.

Delaware Technical & Community College, Terry Campus
Dover, Delaware

- **State-supported** 2-year, founded 1972, part of Delaware Technical and Community College System
- **Small-town** 70-acre campus with easy access to Philadelphia
- **Coed,** 3,392 undergraduate students, 49% full-time, 64% women, 36% men

Undergraduates 1,675 full-time, 1,717 part-time. 29% Black or African American, non-Hispanic/Latino; 4% Hispanic/Latino; 2% Asian, non-Hispanic/Latino; 0.2% Native Hawaiian or other Pacific Islander, non-Hispanic/Latino; 0.4% American Indian or Alaska Native, non-Hispanic/Latino; 2% Two or more races, non-Hispanic/Latino; 2% Race/ethnicity unknown; 2% international. *Retention:* 54% of full-time freshmen returned.
Freshmen *Admission:* 683 enrolled.
Faculty *Total:* 241, 35% full-time.
Majors Accounting; agricultural business and management; architectural engineering technology; bilingual and multilingual education; biomedical technology; business administration and management; business automation/technology/data entry; business/commerce; civil engineering technology; commercial and advertising art; computer and information sciences; computer engineering technology; computer systems networking and telecommunications; computer technology/computer systems technology; construction management; criminal justice/law enforcement administration; criminal justice/police science; culinary arts; digital communication and media/multimedia; drafting and design technology; early childhood education; e-commerce; education (multiple levels); electrical, electronic and communications engineering technology; electromechanical technology; elementary education; emergency medical technology (EMT paramedic); energy management and systems technology; entrepreneurship; hotel/motel administration; human resources management; human services; interior design; kindergarten/preschool education; legal administrative assistant/secretary; management information systems; marketing/marketing management; mathematics teacher education; medical/clinical assistant; middle school education; office management; photography; registered nursing/registered nurse; substance abuse/addiction counseling.
Academics *Calendar:* semesters. *Degree:* certificates, diplomas, and associate. *Special study options:* academic remediation for entering students, advanced placement credit, cooperative education, distance learning, double majors, English as a second language, internships, part-time degree program, services for LD students, study abroad, summer session for credit.
Library 15,327 titles, 245 serial subscriptions, an OPAC.
Student Life *Housing:* college housing not available. *Activities and Organizations:* marching band. *Campus security:* 24-hour emergency response devices, late-night transport/escort service.
Athletics Member NJCAA. *Intercollegiate sports:* lacrosse M(s), soccer M(s)/W(s), softball W(s).
Costs (2010–11) *Tuition:* state resident $2598 full-time, $108 per credit hour part-time; nonresident $6496 full-time, $271 per credit hour part-time. *Required fees:* $516 full-time, $7 per credit hour part-time, $25 per term part-time. *Payment plan:* deferred payment. *Waivers:* senior citizens and employees or children of employees.
Financial Aid Of all full-time matriculated undergraduates who enrolled in 2009, 50 Federal Work-Study jobs (averaging $1500).
Applying *Options:* electronic application, early admission, deferred entrance. *Application fee:* $10. *Required for some:* high school transcript. *Application deadlines:* rolling (freshmen), rolling (transfers). *Notification:* continuous (freshmen), continuous (transfers).
Freshman Application Contact Mrs. Maria Harris, Admissions Officer, Delaware Technical & Community College, Terry Campus, 100 Campus Drive, Dover, DE 19904. *Phone:* 302-857-1020. *Fax:* 302-857-1296. *E-mail:* mharris@outland.dtcc.edu. *Web site:* http://www.dtcc.edu/terry/.

FLORIDA

Angley College
Deland, Florida

Freshman Application Contact Admissions Office, Angley College, 230 North Woodland Boulevard, Suite 310, Deland, FL 32720. *Phone:* 877-483-3635. *Toll-free phone:* 866-483-3635. *Fax:* 866-507-0524. *E-mail:* admissions@angley.edu. *Web site:* http://www.angley.edu/.

ATI Career Training Center
Fort Lauderdale, Florida

Director of Admissions Director of Admissions, ATI Career Training Center, 2880 NW 62nd Street, Fort Lauderdale, FL 33309-9731. *Phone:* 954-973-4760. *Web site:* http://www.aticareertraining.edu/.

ATI College of Health
Miami, Florida

Director of Admissions Admissions, ATI College of Health, 1395 NW 167th Street, Suite 200, Miami, FL 33169-5742. *Phone:* 305-628-1000. *Fax:* 305-628-1461. *E-mail:* admissions@atienterprises.edu. *Web site:* http://www.aticareertraining.edu/.

Brevard Community College
Cocoa, Florida

Freshman Application Contact Ms. Stephanie Burnette, Registrar, Brevard Community College, Cocoa, FL 32922-6597. *Phone:* 321-433-7271. *Fax:* 321-433-7172. *E-mail:* cocoaadmissions@brevardcc.edu. *Web site:* http://www.brevardcc.edu/.

Broward College
Fort Lauderdale, Florida

Freshman Application Contact Willie J. Alexander, Associate Vice President for Student Affairs/College Registrar, Broward College, 225 East Las Olas Boulevard, Fort Lauderdale, FL 33301. *Phone:* 954-201-7471. *Fax:* 954-201-7466. *E-mail:* walexand@broward.edu. *Web site:* http://www.broward.edu/.

Brown Mackie College–Miami
Miami, Florida

- **Proprietary** primarily 2-year, part of Education Management Corporation
- **Coed**

Majors Accounting technology and bookkeeping; business administration and management; criminal justice/law enforcement administration; early childhood education; health/health-care administration; information technology; legal assistant/paralegal; medical/clinical assistant.

Academics *Degrees:* diplomas, associate, and bachelor's.

Costs (2010–11) *Tuition:* Tuition varies by program. Students should contact Brown Mackie College for tuition information.

Freshman Application Contact Brown Mackie College–Miami, One Herald Plaza, Miami, FL 33132. *Phone:* 305-341-6600. *Toll-free phone:* 866-505-0335. *Web site:* http://www.brownmackie.edu/miami/.

See page 382 for the College Close-Up.

Central Florida Institute
Palm Harbor, Florida

Director of Admissions Carol Bruno, Director of Admissions, Central Florida Institute, 30522 US Highway 19 North, Suite 300, Palm Harbor, FL 34684. *Phone:* 727-786-4707. *Web site:* http://www.cfinstitute.com/.

Centura Institute
Orlando, Florida

Director of Admissions John DiBenedetto, Director of Admissions, Centura Institute, 6359 Edgewater Drive, Orlando, FL 32810. *Phone:* 407-275-9696. *Toll-free phone:* 877-604-2121. *Fax:* 407-275-4499. *E-mail:* admcircorl@centura.edu. *Web site:* http://www.centurainstitute.edu/.

Chipola College
Marianna, Florida

- **State-supported** primarily 2-year, founded 1947
- **Rural** 105-acre campus
- **Coed**, 2,274 undergraduate students, 47% full-time, 61% women, 39% men

Undergraduates 1,073 full-time, 1,201 part-time. Students come from 11 states and territories; 3 other countries; 6% are from out of state; 17% Black or African American, non-Hispanic/Latino; 2% Hispanic/Latino; 0.7% Asian, non-Hispanic/Latino; 0.8% American Indian or Alaska Native, non-Hispanic/Latino; 10% transferred in.

Freshmen *Admission:* 226 enrolled. *Average high school GPA:* 2.5. *Test scores:* SAT critical reading scores over 500: 16%; SAT math scores over 500: 36%; ACT scores over 18: 81%; SAT critical reading scores over 600: 4%; SAT math scores over 600: 12%; ACT scores over 24: 25%; ACT scores over 30: 3%.

Faculty *Total:* 154, 28% full-time, 12% with terminal degrees. *Student/faculty ratio:* 24:1.

Majors Accounting; agriculture; agronomy and crop science; art; biological and physical sciences; business administration and management; clinical laboratory science/medical technology; computer and information sciences related; computer science; education; finance; liberal arts and sciences/liberal studies; mass communication/media; mathematics teacher education; pre-engineering; registered nursing/registered nurse; science teacher education; secondary education; social work.

Academics *Calendar:* semesters. *Degrees:* certificates, associate, and bachelor's. *Special study options:* academic remediation for entering students, adult/continuing education programs, advanced placement credit, distance learning, honors programs, independent study, part-time degree program, services for LD students, summer session for credit.

Library Chipola Library with 37,740 titles, 226 serial subscriptions.

Student Life *Housing:* college housing not available. *Activities and Organizations:* drama/theater group, student-run newspaper, choral group, Drama/Theater Group. *Campus security:* night security personnel.

Athletics Member NJCAA. *Intercollegiate sports:* baseball M(s), basketball M(s)/W(s), softball W(s).

Costs (2011–12) *Tuition:* state resident $2790 full-time, $93 per semester hour part-time; nonresident $7950 full-time, $265 per semester hour part-time. Full-time tuition and fees vary according to degree level. Part-time tuition and fees vary according to degree level. *Required fees:* $40 full-time. *Waivers:* employees or children of employees.

Applying *Options:* early admission. *Required:* high school transcript. *Application deadlines:* rolling (freshmen), rolling (transfers). *Notification:* continuous (freshmen), continuous (transfers).

Freshman Application Contact Mrs. Kathy L. Rehberg, Registrar, Chipola College, 3094 Indian Circle, Marianna, FL 32446-3065. *Phone:* 850-718-2233. *Fax:* 850-718-2287. *E-mail:* rehbergk@chipola.edu. *Web site:* http://www.chipola.edu/.

City College
Casselberry, Florida

Director of Admissions Ms. Kimberly Bowden, Director of Admissions, City College, 853 Semoran Boulevard, Suite 200, Casselberry, FL 32707-5342. *Phone:* 352-335-4000. *Fax:* 352-335-4303. *E-mail:* kbowden@citycollege.edu. *Web site:* http://www.citycollegeorlando.edu/.

City College
Fort Lauderdale, Florida

Freshman Application Contact City College, 2000 West Commercial Boulevard, Suite 200, Fort Lauderdale, FL 33309. *Phone:* 954-492-5353. *Web site:* http://www.citycollege.edu/.

City College
Gainesville, Florida

Freshman Application Contact Admissions Office, City College, 7001 Northwest 4th Boulevard, Gainesville, FL 32607. *Phone:* 352-335-4000. *Web site:* http://www.citycollege.edu/.

City College
Miami, Florida

Freshman Application Contact Admissions Office, City College, 9300 South Dadeland Boulevard, Suite PH, Miami, FL 33156. *Phone:* 305-666-9242. *Fax:* 305-666-9243. *Web site:* http://www.citycollege.edu/.

College of Business and Technology
Miami, Florida

- **Proprietary** 2-year, founded 1988
- **Coed,** 511 undergraduate students, 100% full-time, 34% women, 66% men

Undergraduates 511 full-time. Students come from 7 states and territories; 8% Black or African American, non-Hispanic/Latino; 86% Hispanic/Latino; 0.2% Native Hawaiian or other Pacific Islander, non-Hispanic/Latino; 1% American Indian or Alaska Native, non-Hispanic/Latino; 2% Two or more races, non-Hispanic/Latino; 0.4% Race/ethnicity unknown; 6% transferred in.
Freshmen *Admission:* 591 applied, 511 admitted, 511 enrolled. *Average high school GPA:* 2.8.
Faculty *Total:* 28, 43% full-time, 100% with terminal degrees. *Student/faculty ratio:* 15:1.
Majors Accounting; business administration and management; computer graphics; computer systems networking and telecommunications; heating, air conditioning, ventilation and refrigeration maintenance technology; medical/clinical assistant; system, networking, and LAN/WAN management.
Academics *Calendar:* semesters. *Degree:* certificates, diplomas, and associate. *Special study options:* academic remediation for entering students, accelerated degree program, adult/continuing education programs, advanced placement credit, cooperative education, distance learning, double majors, English as a second language, honors programs, independent study, internships, off-campus study, part-time degree program, services for LD students, summer session for credit.
Library The Bill Clinton Library plus 1 other with 700,000 titles, 200,000 serial subscriptions, 1,200 audiovisual materials, an OPAC, a Web page.
Student Life *Housing Options:* Campus housing is provided by a third party. *Activities and Organizations:* student-run newspaper.
Costs (2010–11) *Tuition:* $12,420 full-time, $414 per credit part-time. *Waivers:* employees or children of employees.
Applying *Options:* electronic application. *Application fee:* $25. *Required:* essay or personal statement, high school transcript, minimum 2.6 GPA, 2 letters of recommendation, interview.
Freshman Application Contact Ms. Ivis Delgado, Admissions Representative, College of Business and Technology, 8230 West Flagler Street, Miami, FL 33144. *Phone:* 305-273-4499 Ext. 2204. *Fax:* 305-485-4411. *E-mail:* admissions@cbt.edu. *Web site:* http://www.cbt.edu/.

College of Central Florida
Ocala, Florida

- **State and locally supported** primarily 2-year, founded 1957, part of Florida Community College System
- **Small-town** 139-acre campus
- **Endowment** $40.1 million
- **Coed,** 8,766 undergraduate students, 42% full-time, 62% women, 38% men

Undergraduates 3,666 full-time, 5,100 part-time.
Freshmen *Admission:* 1,345 enrolled. *Test scores:* ACT scores over 18: 77%; ACT scores over 24: 29%; ACT scores over 30: 5%.
Faculty *Total:* 611, 21% full-time, 10% with terminal degrees. *Student/faculty ratio:* 18:1.
Majors Accounting technology and bookkeeping; automobile/automotive mechanics technology; business/commerce; drafting and design technology; early childhood education; emergency medical technology (EMT paramedic); fire science/firefighting; health information/medical records technology; human services; information technology; landscaping and groundskeeping; liberal arts and sciences/liberal studies; marketing/marketing management; office management; parks, recreation and leisure; physical therapy technology; registered nursing/registered nurse; restaurant, culinary, and catering management; veterinary/animal health technology.
Academics *Calendar:* semesters. *Degrees:* certificates, diplomas, associate, and bachelor's. *Special study options:* academic remediation for entering students, adult/continuing education programs, advanced placement credit, cooperative education, distance learning, English as a second language, freshman honors college, honors programs, independent study, internships, part-time degree program, services for LD students, summer session for credit.
Library Learning Resources Center plus 1 other with 60,558 titles, 412 serial subscriptions, 6,244 audiovisual materials, an OPAC, a Web page.
Student Life *Housing:* college housing not available. *Activities and Organizations:* drama/theater group, student-run newspaper, choral group, Student Activities Board, African-American Student Union, ROC (Realizing Our Cause), Gay Straight Alliance, Musagettas. *Campus security:* 24-hour emergency response devices and patrols, student patrols, late-night transport/escort service. *Student services:* personal/psychological counseling.
Athletics Member NJCAA. *Intercollegiate sports:* baseball M(s), basketball M(s)/W(s), softball W(s), tennis W(s), volleyball W(s).

Standardized Tests *Recommended:* SAT (for admission), ACT (for admission), SAT or ACT (for admission), SAT and SAT Subject Tests or ACT (for admission), SAT Subject Tests (for admission).
Costs (2011–12) *Tuition:* state resident $2106 full-time, $91 per credit hour part-time; nonresident $9688 full-time, $344 per credit hour part-time. Full-time tuition and fees vary according to course level, degree level, and program. Part-time tuition and fees vary according to course level, degree level, and program. *Required fees:* $632 full-time, $21 per credit hour part-time. *Waivers:* employees or children of employees.
Financial Aid Of all full-time matriculated undergraduates who enrolled in 2009, 85 Federal Work-Study jobs (averaging $1505).
Applying *Options:* early admission. *Application fee:* $30. *Required:* high school transcript. *Application deadlines:* rolling (freshmen), rolling (transfers). *Notification:* continuous (freshmen), continuous (transfers).
Freshman Application Contact Ms. Devona Sewell, Registrar, Admission and Records, College of Central Florida, 3001 SW College Road, Ocala, FL 34474. *Phone:* 352-237-2111 Ext. 1398. *Fax:* 352-873-5882. *E-mail:* sewelld@cf.edu. *Web site:* http://www.cf.edu/.

Daytona State College
Daytona Beach, Florida

- **State-supported** primarily 2-year, founded 1958, part of Florida Community College System
- **Suburban** 100-acre campus with easy access to Orlando
- **Coed,** 18,838 undergraduate students, 46% full-time, 61% women, 39% men

Undergraduates 8,605 full-time, 10,233 part-time. Students come from 51 states and territories; 52 other countries; 9% are from out of state; 16% Black or African American, non-Hispanic/Latino; 10% Hispanic/Latino; 2% Asian, non-Hispanic/Latino; 0.5% American Indian or Alaska Native, non-Hispanic/Latino; 0.4% Two or more races, non-Hispanic/Latino; 1% Race/ethnicity unknown; 0.4% international; 3% transferred in. *Retention:* 81% of full-time freshmen returned.
Freshmen *Admission:* 2,523 enrolled.
Faculty *Total:* 1,138, 30% full-time, 59% with terminal degrees. *Student/faculty ratio:* 22:1.
Majors Accounting; administrative assistant and secretarial science; architectural engineering technology; automobile/automotive mechanics technology; biology teacher education; business administration and management; child development; communications technology; computer and information sciences related; computer engineering related; computer graphics; computer/information technology services administration related; computer programming; computer programming (specific applications); computer science; computer systems networking and telecommunications; criminal justice/law enforcement administration; criminal justice/police science; culinary arts; dental hygiene; drafting and design technology; electrical, electronic and communications engineering technology; elementary education; emergency medical technology (EMT paramedic); fire science/firefighting; health information/medical records administration; hospitality administration; hotel/motel administration; human services; industrial radiologic technology; industrial technology; information technology; interior design; kindergarten/preschool education; legal assistant/paralegal; machine shop technology; mathematics teacher education; medical administrative assistant and medical secretary; occupational therapist assistant; photographic and film/video technology; physical therapy; plastics and polymer engineering technology; radio and television; registered nursing/registered nurse; respiratory care therapy; robotics technology; secondary education; special education–early childhood; tourism and travel services management.
Academics *Calendar:* semesters. *Degrees:* certificates, diplomas, associate, bachelor's, and postbachelor's certificates. *Special study options:* academic remediation for entering students, adult/continuing education programs, advanced placement credit, cooperative education, distance learning, double majors, English as a second language, external degree program, freshman honors college, honors programs, independent study, internships, off-campus study, part-time degree program, services for LD students, study abroad, summer session for credit. *ROTC:* Army (c), Air Force (c).
Library Mary Karl Memorial Library plus 1 other with 91,000 titles, 700 serial subscriptions, 5,000 audiovisual materials, an OPAC, a Web page.
Student Life *Housing:* college housing not available. *Activities and Organizations:* drama/theater group, student-run newspaper, choral group, Florida Student Nursing Association, Phi Theta Kappa, Mu Rho Chapter, Student Government Association, Campus Crusade for Christ, Student Paralegal Association, national fraternities, national sororities. *Campus security:* 24-hour emergency response devices and patrols, late-night transport/escort service. *Student services:* personal/psychological counseling, women's center.
Athletics Member NJCAA. *Intercollegiate sports:* baseball M(s), basketball M(s)/W(s), golf W(s), softball W(s), swimming and diving M(s)/W(s). *Intramural sports:* basketball M/W, cheerleading M/W, football M/W, golf M/W, racquetball M/W, soccer M/W, table tennis M/W, tennis M/W, volleyball M/W.

Costs (2011–12) *Tuition:* state resident $2847 full-time, $95 per credit hour part-time; nonresident $10,737 full-time, $358 per credit hour part-time. Full-time tuition and fees vary according to course level, course load, degree level, and program. Part-time tuition and fees vary according to course level, course load, degree level, and program. *Required fees:* $60 full-time, $30 per term part-time. *Payment plan:* deferred payment. *Waivers:* employees or children of employees.

Financial Aid Of all full-time matriculated undergraduates who enrolled in 2009, 193 Federal Work-Study jobs (averaging $1542).

Applying *Options:* electronic application, early admission, deferred entrance. *Required:* high school transcript. *Application deadlines:* rolling (freshmen), rolling (transfers). *Notification:* continuous (freshmen), continuous (transfers).

Freshman Application Contact Mrs. Karen Sanders, Director of Admissions and Recruitment, Daytona State College, 1200 International Speedway Boulevard, Daytona Beach, FL 32114. *Phone:* 386-506-3050. *E-mail:* sanderk@daytonastate.edu. *Web site:* http://www.daytonastate.edu/.

Edison State College

Fort Myers, Florida

Freshman Application Contact Ms. Pat Armstrong, Admissions Specialist, Edison State College, 8099 College Parkway, Fort Myers, FL 33919. *Phone:* 239-489-9360 Ext. 1360. *Toll-free phone:* 800-749-2ECC. *E-mail:* registrar@edison.edu. *Web site:* http://www.edison.edu/.

Everest Institute

Fort Lauderdale, Florida

Freshman Application Contact Admissions Office, Everest Institute, 1040 Bayview Drive, Fort Lauderdale, FL 33304. *Phone:* 954-630-0066. *Toll-free phone:* 888-741-4270. *Web site:* http://www.everest.edu/.

Everest Institute

Hialeah, Florida

Director of Admissions Director of Admissions, Everest Institute, 530 West 49th Street, Hialeah, FL 33012. *Phone:* 305-558-9500. *Toll-free phone:* 888-741-4270. *Fax:* 305-558-4419. *Web site:* http://www.everest.edu/.

Everest Institute

Miami, Florida

Director of Admissions Director of Admissions, Everest Institute, 111 Northwest 183rd Street, Second Floor, Miami, FL 33169. *Phone:* 305-949-9500. *Web site:* http://www.everest.edu/.

Everest Institute

Miami, Florida

Freshman Application Contact Director of Admissions, Everest Institute, 9020 Southwest 137th Avenue, Miami, FL 33186. *Phone:* 305-386-9900. *Fax:* 305-388-1740. *Web site:* http://www.everest.edu/.

Everest University

Orange Park, Florida

Freshman Application Contact Admissions Office, Everest University, 805 Wells Road, Orange Park, FL 32073. *Phone:* 904-264-9122. *Web site:* http://www.everest.edu/.

Florida Career College

Miami, Florida

Director of Admissions Mr. David Knobel, President, Florida Career College, 1321 Southwest 107 Avenue, Suite 201B, Miami, FL 33174. *Phone:* 305-553-6065. *Web site:* http://www.careercollege.edu/.

Florida College of Natural Health

Bradenton, Florida

Freshman Application Contact Admissions Office, Florida College of Natural Health, 616 67th Street Circle East, Bradenton, FL 34208. *Phone:* 941-744-1244. *Toll-free phone:* 800-966-7117. *Fax:* 941-744-1242. *Web site:* http://www.fcnh.com/.

Florida College of Natural Health

Maitland, Florida

Freshman Application Contact Admissions Office, Florida College of Natural Health, 2600 Lake Lucien Drive, Suite 140, Maitland, FL 32751. *Phone:* 407-261-0319. *Toll-free phone:* 800-393-7337. *Web site:* http://www.fcnh.com/.

Florida College of Natural Health

Miami, Florida

Director of Admissions Admissions Coordinator, Florida College of Natural Health, 7925 Northwest 12th Street, Suite 201, Miami, FL 33126. *Phone:* 305-597-9599. *Toll-free phone:* 800-599-9599. *Fax:* 305-597-9110. *Web site:* http://www.fcnh.com/.

Florida College of Natural Health

Pompano Beach, Florida

Freshman Application Contact Admissions Office, Florida College of Natural Health, 2001 West Sample Road, Suite 100, Pompano Beach, FL 33064. *Phone:* 954-975-6400. *Toll-free phone:* 800-541-9299. *Web site:* http://www.fcnh.com/.

Florida Gateway College

Lake City, Florida

Freshman Application Contact Florida Gateway College, Lake City, FL 32025-8703. *Fax:* 386-755-1521. *E-mail:* admissions@mail.lakecity.cc.fl.us. *Web site:* http://www.fgc.edu/.

Florida Keys Community College

Key West, Florida

Director of Admissions Ms. Cheryl A. Malsheimer, Director of Admissions and Records, Florida Keys Community College, 5901 College Road, Key West, FL 33040-4397. *Phone:* 305-296-9081 Ext. 201. *Web site:* http://www.fkcc.edu/.

The Florida School of Midwifery

Gainseville, Florida

Freshman Application Contact Admissions Office, The Florida School of Midwifery, PO Box 5505, Gainseville, FL 32627-5505. *Phone:* 352-338-0766. *Fax:* 352-338-2013. *E-mail:* info@midwiferyschool.org. *Web site:* http://www.midwiferyschool.org/.

Florida State College at Jacksonville

Jacksonville, Florida

- **State-supported** primarily 2-year, founded 1963, part of Florida Community College System
- **Urban** 825-acre campus
- **Endowment** $28.8 million
- **Coed**, 28,642 undergraduate students, 36% full-time, 59% women, 41% men

Undergraduates 10,206 full-time, 18,436 part-time. 10% are from out of state; 7% transferred in.

Freshmen *Admission:* 8,562 applied, 4,148 admitted, 3,233 enrolled.

Faculty *Total:* 918, 43% full-time, 23% with terminal degrees. *Student/faculty ratio:* 37:1.

Majors Accounting; administrative assistant and secretarial science; aircraft powerplant technology; airframe mechanics and aircraft maintenance technology; airline pilot and flight crew; architectural drafting and CAD/CADD; architectural engineering technology; autobody/collision and repair technology; automobile/automotive mechanics technology; aviation/airway management; banking and financial support services; biomedical technology; business administration and management; business administration, management and operations related; child-care and support services management; child-care provision; civil engineering technology; commercial and advertising art; computer and information sciences; computer and information sciences and support services related; computer and information sciences related; computer and information systems security; computer engineering technology; computer graphics; computer hardware engineering; computer/information technology services administration related; computer programming; computer programming related; computer programming (specific applications); computer programming (vendor/product certification); computer software and media applications related; computer software engineering; computer systems analysis; computer systems networking and telecommunications; construction engineering technology; criminal justice/law enforcement administration; criminal justice/police science; culinary arts; data entry/microcomputer applications; data entry/microcomputer applications related; data modeling/warehousing and database administration; dental hygiene; design and visual communications; diagnostic medical sonography and ultrasound technology; dietetics; dietitian assistant; drafting and design technology; early childhood education; electrical, electronic and communications engineering technology; emergency medical technology (EMT paramedic); engineering technology; fashion merchandising; fire prevention and safety technology; fire science/firefighting; fire services administration; food service systems administration; health information/medical records administration; homeland security, law enforcement, firefighting and protective services related; hospitality administration; hospitality and recreation marketing; hotel/motel administration; human services; information science/studies; information technology; instrumentation technology; insurance; interior design; legal assistant/paralegal; liberal arts and sciences/liberal studies; machine shop technology; marketing/marketing management; masonry; medical office management; medical radiologic technology; network and system administration; nuclear/nuclear power technology; office management; office occupations and clerical services; physical therapy technology; printmaking; real estate; registered nursing/registered nurse; respiratory care therapy; retailing; sign language interpretation and translation; substance abuse/addiction counseling; theater design and technology; tourism and travel services marketing; visual and performing arts related; water quality and wastewater treatment management and recycling technology; web/multimedia management and webmaster; web page, digital/multimedia and information resources design; word processing.

Academics *Calendar:* semesters. *Degrees:* certificates, diplomas, associate, and bachelor's. *Special study options:* academic remediation for entering students, accelerated degree program, adult/continuing education programs, advanced placement credit, cooperative education, distance learning, double majors, English as a second language, honors programs, independent study, internships, off-campus study, part-time degree program, services for LD students, study abroad, summer session for credit. *ROTC:* Navy (c).

Library Florida State College at Jacksonville Library and Learning Commons plus 7 others with 211,361 titles, 3,299 serial subscriptions, 21,541 audiovisual materials, an OPAC, a Web page.

Student Life *Activities and Organizations:* drama/theater group, student-run newspaper, radio and television station, choral group, Phi Theta Kappa, Troupe de Kent, Forensic Team, Brain Bowl Team, International Student Association. *Campus security:* 24-hour emergency response devices and patrols, late-night transport/escort service. *Student services:* personal/psychological counseling, women's center.

Athletics Member NJCAA. *Intercollegiate sports:* baseball M(s), basketball M(s)/W(s), softball W(s), tennis W(s), volleyball W(s). *Intramural sports:* badminton M/W, basketball M/W, bowling M/W, football M/W, golf M/W, soccer M/W, softball M/W, table tennis M/W, tennis M/W, volleyball M/W.

Costs (2010–11) *Tuition:* state resident $2211 full-time, $92 per credit hour part-time; nonresident $8464 full-time, $353 per credit hour part-time. Full-time tuition and fees vary according to degree level and program. Part-time tuition and fees vary according to degree level and program. *Required fees:* $240 full-time. *Payment plan:* installment. *Waivers:* employees or children of employees.

Applying *Options:* electronic application, early admission, deferred entrance. *Application fee:* $25. *Required:* high school transcript. *Application deadlines:* rolling (freshmen), rolling (out-of-state freshmen), rolling (transfers).

Freshman Application Contact Dr. Peter Biegel, AVP, Enrollment Management, Florida State College at Jacksonville, 501 West State Street, Jacksonville, FL 32202. *Phone:* 904-632-3131. *Fax:* 904-632-5105. *E-mail:* pbiegel@fscj.edu. *Web site:* http://www.fscj.edu/.

Florida Technical College

Auburndale, Florida

Director of Admissions Mr. Charles Owens, Admissions Office, Florida Technical College, 298 Havendale Boulevard, Auburndale, FL 33823. *Phone:* 863-967-8822. *Web site:* http://www.flatech.edu/.

Florida Technical College

DeLand, Florida

Freshman Application Contact Mr. Bill Atkinson, Director, Florida Technical College, 1450 South Woodland Boulevard, 3rd Floor, DeLand, FL 32720. *Phone:* 386-734-3303. *Fax:* 386-734-5150. *Web site:* http://www.flatech.edu/.

Florida Technical College

Orlando, Florida

Director of Admissions Ms. Jeanette E. Muschlitz, Director of Admissions, Florida Technical College, 12689 Challenger Parkway, Orlando, FL 32826. *Phone:* 407-678-5600. *Web site:* http://www.flatech.edu/.

Fortis College

Tampa, Florida

Freshman Application Contact Admissions Office, Fortis College, 3910 US Highway 301 North, Suite 200, Tampa, FL 33619-1259. *Phone:* 813-620-1446. *Fax:* 813-620-1641. *Web site:* http://www.fortis.edu/tampa-florida.php.

Fortis College

Winter Park, Florida

Freshman Application Contact Admissions Office, Fortis College, 1573 West Fairbanks Avenue, Suite 100, Winter Park, FL 32789. *Phone:* 407-843-3984. *Toll-free phone:* 855-4FORTIS. *Fax:* 407-843-9828. *Web site:* http://www.fortis.edu/.

Full Sail University

Winter Park, Florida

- **Proprietary** comprehensive, founded 1979
- **Suburban** 190-acre campus with easy access to Orlando
- **Coed, primarily men**

Undergraduates Students come from 50 states and territories; 40 other countries; 70% are from out of state. *Retention:* 84% of 2008 full-time freshmen returned.

Faculty *Student/faculty ratio:* 8:1.

Academics *Calendar:* modular. *Degrees:* associate, bachelor's, and master's. *Special study options:* academic remediation for entering students, cooperative education, internships, services for LD students, summer session for credit.

Student Life *Campus security:* 24-hour patrols.

Financial Aid Of all full-time matriculated undergraduates who enrolled in 2008, 7,337 applied for aid, 6,925 were judged to have need. 475 Federal Work-Study jobs (averaging $1380). In 2008, 1291. *Average financial aid package:* $7921. *Average need-based gift aid:* $4212. *Average non-need-based aid:* $3572. *Average indebtedness upon graduation:* $63,978.

Applying *Options:* electronic application. *Application fee:* $150. *Required:* high school transcript. *Required for some:* minimum "A" average in Algebra II.

Freshman Application Contact Ms. Mary Beth Plank, Director of Admissions, Full Sail University, 3300 University Boulevard, Winter Park, FL 32792-7437. *Phone:* 407-679-6333. *Toll-free phone:* 800-226-7625. *E-mail:* admissions@fullsail.com. *Web site:* http://www.fullsail.edu/.

See page 416 for the College Close-Up.

Gulf Coast Community College

Panama City, Florida

- **State-supported** primarily 2-year, founded 1957
- **Suburban** 80-acre campus
- **Coed,** 7,207 undergraduate students

Majors Accounting technology and bookkeeping; business administration and management; child-care provision; cinematography and film/video production; civil engineering technology; computer programming (specific applications); computer technology/computer systems technology; construction engineering technology; criminal justice/law enforcement administration; dental hygiene; diagnostic medical sonography and ultrasound technology; drafting and design technology; electrical, electronic and communications engineering technology; electrician; electromechanical and instrumentation and maintenance technologies related; emergency medical technology (EMT paramedic); executive assistant/executive secretary; fire prevention and safety technology; hospitality administration; legal assistant/paralegal; liberal arts and sciences/liberal studies; management information systems and services related; medical radiologic technology; physical therapy technology; psychiatric/mental health services technology; radio and television; registered nursing/registered nurse; respiratory care therapy; restaurant, culinary, and catering management.

Academics *Calendar:* semesters. *Degrees:* certificates, associate, and bachelor's. *Special study options:* academic remediation for entering students, accelerated degree program, adult/continuing education programs, advanced placement credit, cooperative education, distance learning, double majors, English as a second language, external degree program, honors programs, independent study, off-campus study, part-time degree program, services for LD students, summer session for credit.

Library Gulf Coast Community College Library with 117,901 titles, 124 serial subscriptions, 5,204 audiovisual materials, an OPAC, a Web page.

Student Life *Housing:* college housing not available. *Activities and Organizations:* drama/theater group, student-run newspaper, radio station, choral group. *Campus security:* patrols by trained security personnel during campus hours. *Student services:* personal/psychological counseling.

Athletics Member NJCAA. *Intercollegiate sports:* baseball M(s), basketball M(s)/W(s), cheerleading M(s)/W(s), softball W(s), volleyball W(s). *Intramural sports:* basketball M/W, volleyball M/W.

Costs (2010–11) *Tuition:* state resident $2025 full-time, $68 per credit hour part-time; nonresident $8176 full-time, $273 per credit hour part-time. *Required fees:* $607 full-time, $20 per credit hour part-time.

Financial Aid Of all full-time matriculated undergraduates who enrolled in 2009, 145 Federal Work-Study jobs (averaging $3200). 60 state and other part-time jobs (averaging $2600).

Applying *Options:* electronic application, early admission, deferred entrance. *Required:* high school transcript. *Application deadlines:* rolling (freshmen), rolling (transfers). *Notification:* continuous (freshmen).

Freshman Application Contact Mrs. Jackie Kuczenski, Administrative Secretary of Admissions, Gulf Coast Community College, 5230 West Highway 98, Panama City, FL 32401-1058. *Phone:* 850-769-1551 Ext. 4892. *Toll-free phone:* 800-311-3628. *Fax:* 850-913-3308. *Web site:* http://www.gulfcoast.edu/.

High-Tech Institute
Orlando, Florida

Freshman Application Contact Admissions Office, High-Tech Institute, 3710 Maguire Boulevard, Orlando, FL 32803. *Toll-free phone:* 866-326-1985. *Web site:* http://www.high-techinstitute.com/.

Hillsborough Community College
Tampa, Florida

- **State-supported** 2-year, founded 1968, part of Florida Community College System
- **Urban** campus
- **Coed,** 27,955 undergraduate students, 40% full-time, 58% women, 42% men

Undergraduates 11,271 full-time, 16,684 part-time. Students come from 36 states and territories; 121 other countries; 0.9% are from out of state; 13% transferred in.

Freshmen *Admission:* 4,542 enrolled.

Faculty *Total:* 1,288, 22% full-time, 13% with terminal degrees.

Majors Accounting technology and bookkeeping; aquaculture; architectural engineering technology; biomedical technology; biotechnology; building/construction site management; business administration and management; childcare and support services management; cinematography and film/video production; computer/information technology services administration related; computer programming (specific applications); computer systems analysis; computer technology/computer systems technology; criminal justice/law enforcement administration; dental hygiene; diagnostic medical sonography and ultrasound technology; dietitian assistant; electrical, electronic and communications engineering technology; emergency medical technology (EMT paramedic); engineering technology; environmental control technologies related; executive assistant/executive secretary; fire prevention and safety technology; hospitality administration; landscaping and groundskeeping; legal assistant/paralegal; liberal arts and sciences/liberal studies; management information systems; management information systems and services related; medical radiologic technology; nuclear medical technology; operations management; opticianry; optometric technician; psychiatric/mental health services technology; registered nursing/registered nurse; respiratory care therapy; restaurant, culinary, and catering management; restaurant/food services management; special education–individuals with hearing impairments; veterinary/animal health technology.

Academics *Calendar:* semesters. *Degree:* certificates and associate. *Special study options:* academic remediation for entering students, advanced placement credit, cooperative education, distance learning, English as a second language, honors programs, off-campus study, part-time degree program, services for LD students, summer session for credit. *ROTC:* Army (c), Air Force (c).

Library Main Library plus 4 others with 170,615 titles, 1,283 serial subscriptions, 50,000 audiovisual materials, an OPAC, a Web page.

Student Life *Housing Options:* Campus housing is provided by a third party. *Activities and Organizations:* drama/theater group, student-run newspaper, radio station, choral group, Student Government Association, Student Nursing Association, Phi Theta Kappa, International Students, Radiography Club. *Campus security:* 24-hour emergency response devices and patrols, late-night transport/escort service, emergency call box locations. *Student services:* personal/psychological counseling.

Athletics Member NJCAA. *Intercollegiate sports:* baseball M(s), basketball M(s)/W(s), softball W(s), tennis W(s), volleyball W(s).

Standardized Tests *Required:* Florida College Placement Test (CPT) (for admission).

Costs (2010–11) *Tuition:* state resident $2264 full-time, $94 per credit hour part-time; nonresident $8271 full-time, $345 per credit hour part-time. *Payment plan:* installment. *Waivers:* senior citizens.

Applying *Options:* electronic application, early admission. *Application fee:* $20. *Required:* high school transcript. *Application deadlines:* 8/10 (freshmen), 8/10 (out-of-state freshmen), 8/10 (transfers). *Notification:* continuous (freshmen), continuous (out-of-state freshmen), continuous (transfers).

Freshman Application Contact Mr. Edwin Olmo, Enrollment and Student Success Officer, Hillsborough Community College, PO Box 31127, Tampa, FL 33631-3127. *Phone:* 813-253-7032. *E-mail:* eolmo2@hccfl.edu. *Web site:* http://www.hccfl.edu/.

Indian River State College
Fort Pierce, Florida

- **State-supported** primarily 2-year, founded 1960, part of Florida Community College System
- **Small-town** 133-acre campus
- **Coed,** 17,511 undergraduate students, 36% full-time, 61% women, 39% men

Undergraduates 6,233 full-time, 11,278 part-time. Students come from 31 states and territories; 127 other countries; 15% are from out of state; 17% Black or African American, non-Hispanic/Latino; 13% Hispanic/Latino; 2% Asian, non-Hispanic/Latino; 0.1% Native Hawaiian or other Pacific Islander, non-Hispanic/Latino; 0.3% American Indian or Alaska Native, non-Hispanic/Latino; 0.6% Two or more races, non-Hispanic/Latino; 3% Race/ethnicity unknown; 0.9% international; 119% transferred in.

Freshmen *Admission:* 2,133 enrolled. *Average high school GPA:* 2.86.

Faculty *Total:* 843, 24% full-time, 14% with terminal degrees. *Student/faculty ratio:* 24:1.

Majors Accounting; administrative assistant and secretarial science; agricultural business and management; airline pilot and flight crew; anthropology; apparel and textiles; architectural drafting and CAD/CADD; art teacher education; automobile/automotive mechanics technology; banking and financial support services; biology/biological sciences; biology teacher education; business administration and management; carpentry; chemistry; child development; civil engineering technology; clinical/medical laboratory technology; computer engineering technology; computer programming; computer science; computer typography and composition equipment operation; consumer merchandising/retailing management; corrections; cosmetology; criminal justice/law enforcement administration; criminal justice/police science; criminal justice/safety; culinary arts; dental hygiene; drafting and design technology; dramatic/theater arts; economics; education; electrical, electronic and communications engineering technology; emergency medical technology (EMT paramedic); engineering; engineering technology; English; family and consumer sciences/human sciences; fashion merchandising; finance; fire science/firefighting; foods, nutrition, and wellness; forestry; French; health/health-care administration; health information/medical records administration; heating, air conditioning, ventilation and refrigeration maintenance technology; history; hotel/motel administration; humanities; human services; hydrology and water resources science; industrial radiologic technology; information science/studies; interior design; journalism; kindergarten/preschool education; language interpretation and translation; legal assistant/paralegal; liberal arts and sciences/liberal studies; library and information science; licensed practical/vocational nurse training; marine science/merchant marine officer; marketing/marketing management; mathematics; mathematics teacher education; medical administrative assistant and medical secretary; music; organizational behavior; pharmacy; philosophy; physical education teaching and coaching; physical therapy; physical therapy technology; physics; political science and government; pre-engineering; psychology; registered nursing/registered nurse; respiratory care therapy; rhetoric and composition; science teacher education; social sciences; social work; sociology; Spanish; special education; special products marketing; surveying technology; teacher assistant/aide.

Academics *Calendar:* semesters. *Degrees:* certificates, diplomas, associate, and bachelor's. *Special study options:* academic remediation for entering students, adult/continuing education programs, advanced placement credit, distance learning, English as a second language, independent study, part-time degree program, services for LD students, summer session for credit.

Library Charles S. Miley Learning Resource Center with 136,522 titles, 200 serial subscriptions, 6,052 audiovisual materials, an OPAC, a Web page.

Student Life *Housing:* college housing not available. *Activities and Organizations:* drama/theater group, choral group. *Campus security:* 24-hour emergency response devices and patrols. *Student services:* health clinic, personal/psychological counseling, women's center.

Athletics Member NJCAA. *Intercollegiate sports:* baseball M(s), basketball M(s)/W(s), softball W(s), swimming and diving M(s)/W(s), volleyball W(s).

Intramural sports: basketball M/W, racquetball M/W, soccer M, volleyball M/W.

Costs (2010–11) *Tuition:* state resident $2208 full-time, $92 per credit part-time; nonresident $8424 full-time, $351 per credit part-time. Full-time tuition and fees vary according to course load and degree level. Part-time tuition and fees vary according to course load and degree level. *Payment plans:* installment, deferred payment.

Applying *Options:* early admission, deferred entrance. *Required:* high school transcript. *Application deadlines:* rolling (freshmen), rolling (transfers). *Notification:* continuous (freshmen), continuous (transfers).

Freshman Application Contact Mr. Steven Payne, Dean of Educational Services, Indian River State College, 3209 Virginia Avenue, Fort Pierce, FL 34981-5596. *Phone:* 772-462-7805. *E-mail:* spayne@ircc.edu. *Web site:* http://www.irsc.edu/.

ITT Technical Institute
Fort Lauderdale, Florida

- **Proprietary** primarily 2-year, founded 1991, part of ITT Educational Services, Inc.
- **Suburban** campus
- **Coed**

Majors CAD/CADD drafting/design technology; computer and information systems security; computer engineering technology; construction management; criminal justice/law enforcement administration; design and visual communications; electrical, electronic and communications engineering technology; health information/medical records technology; legal assistant/paralegal; project management; registered nursing/registered nurse; system, networking, and LAN/WAN management.

Academics *Calendar:* quarters. *Degrees:* associate and bachelor's.

Student Life *Housing:* college housing not available.

Freshman Application Contact Director of Recruitment, ITT Technical Institute, 3401 South University Drive, Fort Lauderdale, FL 33328-2021. *Phone:* 954-476-9300. *Toll-free phone:* 800-488-7797. *Web site:* http://www.itt-tech.edu/.

ITT Technical Institute
Fort Myers, Florida

- **Proprietary** primarily 2-year
- **Coed**

Majors CAD/CADD drafting/design technology; computer and information systems security; computer engineering technology; construction management; criminal justice/law enforcement administration; electrical, electronic and communications engineering technology; legal assistant/paralegal; system, networking, and LAN/WAN management.

Academics *Degrees:* associate and bachelor's.

Freshman Application Contact Director of Recruitment, ITT Technical Institute, 13500 Powers Court, Suite 100, Fort Myers, FL 33912. *Phone:* 239-603-8700. *Toll-free phone:* 877-485-5313. *Web site:* http://www.itt-tech.edu/.

ITT Technical Institute
Jacksonville, Florida

- **Proprietary** primarily 2-year, founded 1991, part of ITT Educational Services, Inc.
- **Urban** campus
- **Coed**

Majors CAD/CADD drafting/design technology; computer and information systems security; computer engineering technology; computer software and media applications related; computer software engineering; computer software technology; construction management; criminal justice/law enforcement administration; design and visual communications; electrical, electronic and communications engineering technology; legal assistant/paralegal; project management; registered nursing/registered nurse; system, networking, and LAN/WAN management; web/multimedia management and webmaster; web page, digital/multimedia and information resources design.

Academics *Calendar:* quarters. *Degrees:* associate and bachelor's.

Student Life *Housing:* college housing not available.

Financial Aid Of all full-time matriculated undergraduates who enrolled in 2009, 5 Federal Work-Study jobs.

Freshman Application Contact Director of Recruitment, ITT Technical Institute, 7011 A.C. Skinner Parkway, Jacksonville, FL 32256. *Phone:* 904-573-9100. *Toll-free phone:* 800-318-1264. *Web site:* http://www.itt-tech.edu/.

ITT Technical Institute
Lake Mary, Florida

- **Proprietary** primarily 2-year, founded 1989, part of ITT Educational Services, Inc.
- **Suburban** campus
- **Coed**

Majors CAD/CADD drafting/design technology; computer and information systems security; computer engineering technology; computer software and media applications related; computer software engineering; computer software technology; computer systems networking and telecommunications; construction management; criminal justice/law enforcement administration; design and visual communications; electrical, electronic and communications engineering technology; game and interactive media design; health information/medical records technology; legal assistant/paralegal; project management; registered nursing/registered nurse; system, networking, and LAN/WAN management; web/multimedia management and webmaster; web page, digital/multimedia and information resources design.

Academics *Calendar:* quarters. *Degrees:* associate and bachelor's.

Freshman Application Contact Director of Recruitment, ITT Technical Institute, 1400 South International Parkway, Lake Mary, FL 32746. *Phone:* 407-660-2900. *Toll-free phone:* 866-489-8441. *Fax:* 407-660-2566. *Web site:* http://www.itt-tech.edu/.

ITT Technical Institute
Miami, Florida

- **Proprietary** primarily 2-year, founded 1996, part of ITT Educational Services, Inc.
- **Coed**

Majors CAD/CADD drafting/design technology; computer and information systems security; computer engineering technology; construction management; criminal justice/law enforcement administration; design and visual communications; electrical, electronic and communications engineering technology; health information/medical records technology; legal assistant/paralegal; project management; system, networking, and LAN/WAN management.

Academics *Calendar:* quarters. *Degrees:* associate and bachelor's.

Student Life *Housing:* college housing not available.

Freshman Application Contact Director of Recruitment, ITT Technical Institute, 7955 NW 12th Street, Suite 119, Miami, FL 33126. *Phone:* 305-477-3080. *Toll-free phone:* 877-216-8352. *Web site:* http://www.itt-tech.edu/.

ITT Technical Institute
Orlando, Florida

- **Proprietary** 2-year, part of ITT Educational Services, Inc.
- **Coed**

Majors CAD/CADD drafting/design technology; computer and information systems security; computer engineering technology; criminal justice/law enforcement administration; design and visual communications; electrical, electronic and communications engineering technology; legal assistant/paralegal; project management; system, networking, and LAN/WAN management.

Academics *Calendar:* quarters.

Freshman Application Contact Director of Recruitment, ITT Technical Institute, 8301 Southpark Circle, Suite 100, Orlando, FL 32819. *Phone:* 407-371-6000. *Toll-free phone:* 877-201-4367. *Web site:* http://www.itt-tech.edu/.

ITT Technical Institute
Pinellas Park, Florida

- **Proprietary** primarily 2-year, part of ITT Educational Services, Inc.
- **Coed**

Majors CAD/CADD drafting/design technology; computer and information systems security; computer engineering technology; computer software and media applications related; computer software engineering; computer software technology; construction management; criminal justice/law enforcement administration; design and visual communications; legal assistant/paralegal; project management; system, networking, and LAN/WAN management; web/multimedia management and webmaster; web page, digital/multimedia and information resources design.

Academics *Degrees:* associate and bachelor's.

Student Life *Housing:* college housing not available.

Freshman Application Contact Director of Recruitment, ITT Technical Institute, 877 Executive Center Drive W, Suite 100, Pinellas Park, FL 33781-2658. *Phone:* 727-209-4700. *Toll-free phone:* 866-488-5084. *Web site:* http://www.itt-tech.edu/.

ITT Technical Institute
Tallahassee, Florida

- **Proprietary** primarily 2-year
- **Coed**

Majors CAD/CADD drafting/design technology; computer and information systems security; computer engineering technology; computer software and media applications related; construction management; criminal justice/law enforcement administration; electrical, electronic and communications engineering technology; system, networking, and LAN/WAN management; web/multimedia management and webmaster.

Academics *Degrees:* associate and bachelor's.

Freshman Application Contact Director of Recruitment, ITT Technical Institute, 2639 North Monroe Street, Building A, Suite 100, Tallahassee, FL 32303. *Phone:* 850-422-6300. *Toll-free phone:* 877-230-3559. *Web site:* http://www.itt-tech.edu/.

ITT Technical Institute
Tampa, Florida

- **Proprietary** primarily 2-year, founded 1981, part of ITT Educational Services, Inc.
- **Suburban** campus
- **Coed**

Majors CAD/CADD drafting/design technology; computer and information systems security; computer engineering technology; computer software and media applications related; computer software engineering; computer software technology; construction management; criminal justice/law enforcement administration; design and visual communications; electrical, electronic and communications engineering technology; game and interactive media design; health information/medical records technology; legal assistant/paralegal; project management; registered nursing/registered nurse; system, networking, and LAN/WAN management; web/multimedia management and webmaster; web page, digital/multimedia and information resources design.

Academics *Calendar:* quarters. *Degrees:* associate and bachelor's.

Student Life *Housing:* college housing not available.

Freshman Application Contact Director of Recruitment, ITT Technical Institute, 4809 Memorial Highway, Tampa, FL 33634-7151. *Phone:* 813-885-2244. *Toll-free phone:* 800-825-2831. *Web site:* http://www.itt-tech.edu/.

ITT Technical Institute
University Park, Florida

- **Proprietary** 2-year, part of ITT Educational Services, Inc.
- **Coed**

Majors CAD/CADD drafting/design technology; computer and information systems security; computer engineering technology; criminal justice/law enforcement administration; design and visual communications; electrical, electronic and communications engineering technology; legal assistant/paralegal; project management; system, networking, and LAN/WAN management.

Academics *Calendar:* quarters.

Freshman Application Contact Director of Recruitment, ITT Technical Institute, 8039 Cooper Creek Boulvevard, University Park, FL 34201. *Phone:* 941-309-9200. *Toll-free phone:* 800-342-8684. *Web site:* http://www.itt-tech.edu/.

Kaplan College, Pembroke Pines
Pembroke Pines, Florida

- **Proprietary** 2-year
- **Coed**

Freshman Application Contact Kaplan College, Pembroke Pines, 10131 Pines Boulevard, Pembroke Pines, FL 33026. *Phone:* 954-885-3500. *Web site:* http://www.kc-pembrokepines.com/.

Keiser Career College–Greenacres
Greenacres, Florida

Freshman Application Contact Admissions Office, Keiser Career College–Greenacres, 6812 Forest Hill Boulevard, Suite D-1, Greenacres, FL 33413. *Web site:* http://www.keisercareer.edu/kcc2009/ga_campus.htm.

Key College
Dania, Florida

Director of Admissions Mr. Ronald H. Dooley, President and Director of Admissions, Key College, 225 East Dania Beach Boulevard, Dania, FL 33004.

Phone: 954-581-2223 Ext. 23. *Toll-free phone:* 800-581-8292. *Web site:* http://www.keycollege.edu/.

Lake-Sumter Community College
Leesburg, Florida

- **State and locally supported** 2-year, founded 1962, part of Florida College System
- **Suburban** 112-acre campus with easy access to Orlando
- **Endowment** $3.9 million
- **Coed,** 4,929 undergraduate students, 33% full-time, 62% women, 38% men

Undergraduates 1,641 full-time, 3,288 part-time. 1% are from out of state; 5% transferred in.

Freshmen *Admission:* 1,353 applied, 1,353 admitted, 728 enrolled.

Faculty *Total:* 428, 20% full-time, 15% with terminal degrees. *Student/faculty ratio:* 17:1.

Majors Business administration and management; child-care provision; commercial and advertising art; computer and information sciences related; computer science; computer technology/computer systems technology; criminal justice/law enforcement administration; early childhood education; electrical, electronic and communications engineering technology; emergency medical technology (EMT paramedic); fire science/firefighting; health information/medical records administration; legal assistant/paralegal; liberal arts and sciences/liberal studies; mathematics; office management; registered nursing/registered nurse; sport and fitness administration/management.

Academics *Calendar:* semesters. *Degree:* certificates, diplomas, and associate. *Special study options:* academic remediation for entering students, adult/continuing education programs, advanced placement credit, cooperative education, distance learning, double majors, independent study, internships, off-campus study, part-time degree program, services for LD students, summer session for credit.

Library Lake-Sumter Community College Library with 82,023 titles, 167 serial subscriptions, 1,761 audiovisual materials, an OPAC, a Web page.

Student Life *Housing:* college housing not available. *Activities and Organizations:* drama/theater group, student-run newspaper, choral group, Phi Theta Kappa, Student Government Association, Theatre Arts Society, Nursing Student's Association, Safire. *Campus security:* 24-hour emergency response devices. *Student services:* women's center.

Athletics Member NJCAA. *Intercollegiate sports:* baseball M(s), softball W(s), volleyball W(s). *Intramural sports:* basketball M/W, golf M/W, table tennis M/W, volleyball W.

Costs (2010–11) *Tuition:* state resident $2760 full-time, $92 per credit hour part-time; nonresident $10,542 full-time, $351 per credit hour part-time. Full-time tuition and fees vary according to course load. Part-time tuition and fees vary according to course load. *Required fees:* $2556 full-time. *Payment plans:* installment, deferred payment. *Waivers:* employees or children of employees.

Financial Aid Of all full-time matriculated undergraduates who enrolled in 2009, 420 applied for aid, 420 were judged to have need. 39 Federal Work-Study jobs (averaging $1701). In 2009, 95 non-need-based awards were made. *Average financial aid package:* $3166. *Average need-based gift aid:* $1912. *Average non-need-based aid:* $770.

Applying *Options:* electronic application. *Application fee:* $25. *Required:* high school transcript. *Application deadlines:* rolling (freshmen), rolling (transfers). *Notification:* continuous (freshmen), continuous (transfers).

Freshman Application Contact Ms. Bonnie Yanick, Enrollment Specialist, Lake-Sumter Community College, 9501 U.S. Highway 441, Leesburg, FL 34788-8751. *Phone:* 352-365-3561. *Fax:* 352-365-3553. *E-mail:* admissinquiry@lscc.edu. *Web site:* http://www.lscc.edu/.

Le Cordon Bleu College of Culinary Arts, Miami
Miramar, Florida

Freshman Application Contact Admissions Office, Le Cordon Bleu College of Culinary Arts, Miami, 3221 Enterprise Way, Miramar, FL 33025. *Phone:* 954-628-4000. *Toll-free phone:* 888-569-3222. *Web site:* http://www.miamiculinary.com/.

Lincoln College of Technology
West Palm Beach, Florida

Director of Admissions Mr. Kevin Cassidy, Director of Admissions, Lincoln College of Technology, 2410 Metro Centre Boulevard, West Palm Beach, FL 33407. *Phone:* 561-842-8324 Ext. 117. *Toll-free phone:* 800-826-9986. *Fax:* 561-842-9503. *Web site:* http://www.lincolnedu.com/.

MedVance Institute

Atlantis, Florida

Director of Admissions Campus Director, MedVance Institute, 170 JFK Drive, Atlantis, FL 33462. *Phone:* 561-304-3466. *Toll-free phone:* 877-606-3382. *Fax:* 561-304-3471. *Web site:* http://www.medvance.edu/.

Miami Dade College

Miami, Florida

- **State and locally supported** primarily 2-year, founded 1960, part of Florida Community College System
- **Urban** campus
- **Endowment** $147.9 million
- **Coed,** 61,674 undergraduate students, 40% full-time, 59% women, 41% men

Undergraduates 24,875 full-time, 36,799 part-time. Students come from 41 states and territories; 189 other countries; 1% are from out of state; 17% Black or African American, non-Hispanic/Latino; 69% Hispanic/Latino; 1% Asian, non-Hispanic/Latino; 0.1% Native Hawaiian or other Pacific Islander, non-Hispanic/Latino; 0.1% American Indian or Alaska Native, non-Hispanic/Latino; 0.2% Two or more races, non-Hispanic/Latino; 2% Race/ethnicity unknown; 2% international; 2% transferred in.

Freshmen *Admission:* 12,501 applied, 12,501 admitted, 12,501 enrolled.

Faculty *Total:* 2,340, 28% full-time, 19% with terminal degrees. *Student/faculty ratio:* 31:1.

Majors Accounting technology and bookkeeping; administrative assistant and secretarial science; aeronautics/aviation/aerospace science and technology; agriculture; airline pilot and flight crew; air traffic control; American studies; anthropology; architectural drafting and CAD/CADD; architectural engineering technology; art; Asian studies; audiology and speech-language pathology; aviation/airway management; behavioral sciences; biology/biological sciences; biology teacher education; biomedical technology; biotechnology; business administration and management; business administration, management and operations related; chemistry; chemistry teacher education; child development; cinematography and film/video production; civil engineering technology; clinical/medical laboratory technology; commercial and advertising art; comparative literature; computer engineering technology; computer graphics; computer programming; computer science; computer software technology; computer technology/computer systems technology; construction engineering technology; cooking and related culinary arts; court reporting; criminal justice/law enforcement administration; criminal justice/police science; culinary arts; dance; data processing and data processing technology; dental hygiene; diagnostic medical sonography and ultrasound technology; dietetics; dietetic technology; drafting and design technology; dramatic/theater arts; economics; education; education related; electrical and electronic engineering technologies related; electrical, electronic and communications engineering technology; elementary education; emergency medical technology (EMT paramedic); engineering; engineering related; engineering technology; English; environmental engineering technology; finance; fire science/firefighting; food science; forestry; French; funeral service and mortuary science; general studies; geology/earth science; German; health information/medical records administration; health/medical preparatory programs related; health professions related; health services/allied health/health sciences; heating, air conditioning, ventilation and refrigeration maintenance technology; heating, ventilation, air conditioning and refrigeration engineering technology; histologic technician; history; homeland security, law enforcement, firefighting and protective services related; horticultural science; hospitality administration; humanities; human services; industrial technology; information science/studies; interior design; international relations and affairs; Italian; journalism; kindergarten/preschool education; landscaping and groundskeeping; Latin American studies; legal administrative assistant/secretary; legal assistant/paralegal; management information systems; marketing/marketing management; mass communication/media; mathematics; mathematics teacher education; medical/clinical assistant; middle school education; music; music performance; music teacher education; natural sciences; nonprofit management; nuclear medical technology; ophthalmic technology; ornamental horticulture; parks, recreation and leisure; philosophy; photographic and film/video technology; photography; physical education teaching and coaching; physical sciences; physical therapy technology; physics; physics teacher education; plant nursery management; political science and government; Portuguese; pre-engineering; psychology; public administration; radio and television; radio and television broadcasting technology; radiologic technology/science; recording arts technology; registered nursing/registered nurse; respiratory care therapy; respiratory therapy technician; science teacher education; sign language interpretation and translation; social sciences; social work; sociology; Spanish; special education; substance abuse/addiction counseling; teacher assistant/aide; telecommunications technology; tourism and travel services management.

Academics *Calendar:* 16-16-6-6. *Degrees:* certificates, associate, and bachelor's. *Special study options:* academic remediation for entering students, accelerated degree program, adult/continuing education programs, advanced placement credit, cooperative education, distance learning, English as a second language, freshman honors college, honors programs, independent study, internships, off-campus study, part-time degree program, services for LD students, study abroad, summer session for credit. *ROTC:* Army (c), Air Force (c).

Library Main Library plus 8 others with 363,432 titles, 3,824 serial subscriptions, 30,991 audiovisual materials, an OPAC, a Web page.

Student Life *Housing:* college housing not available. *Activities and Organizations:* drama/theater group, student-run newspaper, radio and television station, choral group, national fraternities. *Campus security:* 24-hour patrols. *Student services:* personal/psychological counseling.

Athletics Member NJCAA. *Intercollegiate sports:* baseball M(s), basketball M(s)/W(s), softball W(s), volleyball W(s). *Intramural sports:* basketball M/W, racquetball M/W, soccer M/W, softball M/W, tennis M/W, volleyball M/W, weight lifting M/W.

Costs (2010–11) *One-time required fee:* $20. *Tuition:* state resident $2190 full-time, $95 per credit hour part-time; nonresident $10,370 full-time, $346 per credit hour part-time. Full-time tuition and fees vary according to course load. Part-time tuition and fees vary according to course load. *Waivers:* employees or children of employees.

Financial Aid Of all full-time matriculated undergraduates who enrolled in 2009, 800 Federal Work-Study jobs (averaging $5000). 125 state and other part-time jobs (averaging $5000).

Applying *Options:* electronic application, early admission. *Application fee:* $30. *Required:* high school transcript. *Required for some:* some programs such as Honors College have additional admissions requirements. *Application deadlines:* rolling (freshmen), rolling (transfers). *Notification:* continuous (freshmen), continuous (out-of-state freshmen), continuous (transfers).

Freshman Application Contact Ms. Dulce Beltran, College Registrar, Miami Dade College, 11011 SW 104th Street, Miami, FL 33176. *Phone:* 305-237-2103. *Fax:* 305-237-2964. *E-mail:* dbeltran@mdc.edu. *Web site:* http://www.mdc.edu/.

North Florida Community College

Madison, Florida

Freshman Application Contact Mr. Bobby Scott, North Florida Community College, 325 Northwest Turner Davis Drive, Madison, FL 32340. *Phone:* 850-973-9450. *Fax:* 850-973-1697. *Web site:* http://www.nfcc.edu/.

Northwest Florida State College

Niceville, Florida

- **State and locally supported** primarily 2-year, founded 1963, part of Florida Community College System
- **Small-town** 264-acre campus
- **Endowment** $28.6 million
- **Coed**

Undergraduates Students come from 18 states and territories.

Faculty *Student/faculty ratio:* 15:1.

Academics *Calendar:* semesters plus summer sessions. *Degrees:* certificates, associate, and bachelor's. *Special study options:* academic remediation for entering students, accelerated degree program, adult/continuing education programs, advanced placement credit, distance learning, English as a second language, independent study, part-time degree program, services for LD students, summer session for credit. *ROTC:* Army (b).

Student Life *Campus security:* 24-hour patrols.

Athletics Member NJCAA.

Standardized Tests *Required for some:* ACT, SAT I, ACT ASSET, MAPS, or Florida College Entry Placement Test are used for placement not admission.

Costs (2010–11) *Tuition:* state resident $2568 full-time, $85 per credit hour part-time; nonresident $11,511 full-time, $335 per credit hour part-time. Full-time tuition and fees vary according to course load, degree level, and reciprocity agreements. Part-time tuition and fees vary according to course load, degree level, and reciprocity agreements. *Required fees:* $15 per credit hour part-time. *Payment plans:* tuition prepayment, installment, deferred payment.

Financial Aid Of all full-time matriculated undergraduates who enrolled in 2009, 81 Federal Work-Study jobs (averaging $1500). 11 state and other part-time jobs (averaging $1460).

Applying *Options:* electronic application. *Required:* high school transcript.

Freshman Application Contact Ms. Christine Bishop, Registrar/Division Director Enrollment Services, Northwest Florida State College, 100 College Boulevard, Niceville, FL 32578. *Phone:* 850-729-5373. *Fax:* 850-729-5323. *E-mail:* registrar@nwfsc.edu. *Web site:* http://www.nwfsc.edu/.

Orlando Culinary Academy
Orlando, Florida

Admissions Office Contact Orlando Culinary Academy, 8511 Commodity Circle, Suite 100, Orlando, FL 32819. *Toll-free phone:* 888-793-3222. *Web site:* http://www.orlandoculinary.com/.

Palm Beach State College
Lake Worth, Florida

- **State-supported** primarily 2-year, founded 1933, part of Florida State College System
- **Urban** 150-acre campus with easy access to West Palm Beach
- **Endowment** $23.0 million
- **Coed,** 29,534 undergraduate students, 37% full-time, 58% women, 42% men

Undergraduates 10,913 full-time, 18,621 part-time. Students come from 49 states and territories; 146 other countries; 5% are from out of state; 5% transferred in.
Freshmen *Admission:* 5,127 applied, 5,127 admitted, 5,127 enrolled.
Faculty *Total:* 1,473, 19% full-time, 16% with terminal degrees. *Student/faculty ratio:* 43:1.
Majors Accounting; administrative assistant and secretarial science; airline pilot and flight crew; apparel and textiles; art; art history, criticism and conservation; biology/biological sciences; botany/plant biology; building/construction finishing, management, and inspection related; business administration and management; ceramic arts and ceramics; chemistry; commercial and advertising art; comparative literature; computer and information sciences and support services related; computer programming; computer programming (specific applications); computer science; criminal justice/law enforcement administration; criminal justice/police science; data processing and data processing technology; dental hygiene; drafting and design technology; dramatic/theater arts; economics; education; electrical, electronic and communications engineering technology; elementary education; English; family and consumer sciences/human sciences; fashion/apparel design; fashion merchandising; finance; fire science/firefighting; foods, nutrition, and wellness; health teacher education; history; hotel/motel administration; industrial radiologic technology; interior design; journalism; kindergarten/preschool education; legal administrative assistant/secretary; liberal arts and sciences/liberal studies; marketing/marketing management; mass communication/media; mathematics; music; network and system administration; occupational therapy; philosophy; photography; physical education teaching and coaching; physical sciences; physical therapy; political science and government; pre-engineering; psychology; registered nursing/registered nurse; religious studies; social sciences; social work; special products marketing; surveying technology; web page, digital/multimedia and information resources design; word processing; zoology/animal biology.
Academics *Calendar:* semesters. *Degrees:* certificates, diplomas, associate, and bachelor's. *Special study options:* academic remediation for entering students, adult/continuing education programs, advanced placement credit, cooperative education, distance learning, double majors, English as a second language, freshman honors college, honors programs, independent study, internships, off-campus study, part-time degree program, services for LD students, student-designed majors, study abroad, summer session for credit.
Library Harold C. Manor Library plus 3 others with 151,000 titles, 1,474 serial subscriptions, an OPAC, a Web page.
Student Life *Housing:* college housing not available. *Activities and Organizations:* drama/theater group, student-run newspaper, choral group, student government, Phi Theta Kappa, Students for International Understanding, Black Student Union, Drama Club, national fraternities. *Campus security:* 24-hour emergency response devices and patrols. *Student services:* health clinic, women's center.
Athletics Member NJCAA. *Intercollegiate sports:* baseball M(s), basketball M(s)/W(s), softball W(s), volleyball W(s).
Standardized Tests *Recommended:* SAT and SAT Subject Tests or ACT (for admission).
Costs (2010–11) *One-time required fee:* $20. *Tuition:* state resident $2138 full-time, $89 per credit hour part-time; nonresident $7752 full-time, $323 per credit hour part-time. Full-time tuition and fees vary according to course level, course load, and student level. Part-time tuition and fees vary according to course level, course load, and student level. *Required fees:* $10 full-time, $10 per term part-time. *Waivers:* employees or children of employees.
Applying *Options:* electronic application, early admission, deferred entrance. *Application fee:* $20. *Application deadlines:* 8/20 (freshmen), 8/20 (transfers). *Notification:* continuous until 8/20 (freshmen), continuous until 8/20 (transfers).
Freshman Application Contact Ms. Anne Guiler, Coordinator of Distance Learning, Palm Beach State College, Lake Worth, FL 33461. *Phone:* 561-868-3032. *Fax:* 561-868-3584. *E-mail:* enrollmt@palmbeachstate.edu. *Web site:* http://www.palmbeachstate.edu/.

Pasco-Hernando Community College
New Port Richey, Florida

- **State-supported** 2-year, founded 1972, part of Florida Community College System
- **Suburban** 142-acre campus with easy access to Tampa
- **Endowment** $20.3 million
- **Coed,** 11,969 undergraduate students

Undergraduates 1% are from out of state.
Faculty *Total:* 396, 28% full-time. *Student/faculty ratio:* 26:1.
Majors Business administration and management; computer programming related; computer programming (specific applications); computer systems networking and telecommunications; computer technology/computer systems technology; criminal justice/law enforcement administration; dental hygiene; drafting and design technology; e-commerce; emergency medical technology (EMT paramedic); human services; information technology; legal assistant/paralegal; liberal arts and sciences/liberal studies; marketing/marketing management; physical therapy technology; radiologic technology/science; registered nursing/registered nurse; web page, digital/multimedia and information resources design.
Academics *Calendar:* semesters. *Degree:* certificates, diplomas, and associate. *Special study options:* academic remediation for entering students, accelerated degree program, adult/continuing education programs, advanced placement credit, cooperative education, distance learning, double majors, honors programs, independent study, internships, off-campus study, part-time degree program, services for LD students, study abroad, summer session for credit. *ROTC:* Army (c).
Library Alric Pottberg Library plus 3 others with 85,853 titles, 356 serial subscriptions, 4,016 audiovisual materials, an OPAC, a Web page.
Student Life *Housing:* college housing not available. *Activities and Organizations:* drama/theater group, choral group, Student Government Association, Phi Theta Kappa, Phi Beta Lambda, Human Services, PHCC Cares. *Campus security:* 24-hour patrols. *Student services:* personal/psychological counseling.
Athletics *Intercollegiate sports:* baseball M(s), basketball M(s), cross-country running W(s), softball W(s), volleyball W(s). *Intramural sports:* cheerleading M/W.
Standardized Tests *Recommended:* SAT and SAT Subject Tests or ACT (for admission), CPT.
Costs (2010–11) *Tuition:* state resident $88 per credit part-time; nonresident $334 per credit part-time. *Payment plans:* installment, deferred payment.
Financial Aid Of all full-time matriculated undergraduates who enrolled in 2009, 83 Federal Work-Study jobs (averaging $3201).
Applying *Options:* electronic application. *Application fee:* $25. *Required:* high school transcript. *Application deadlines:* rolling (freshmen), rolling (transfers). *Notification:* continuous (freshmen), continuous (transfers).
Freshman Application Contact Ms. Debra Bullard, Director of Admissions and Student Records, Pasco-Hernando Community College, New Port Richey, FL 34654-5199. *Phone:* 727-816-3261. *Fax:* 727-816-3389. *E-mail:* bullard@phcc.edu. *Web site:* http://www.phcc.edu/.

Pensacola State College
Pensacola, Florida

- **State-supported** primarily 2-year, founded 1948, part of Florida Community College System
- **Urban** 160-acre campus
- **Coed,** 11,676 undergraduate students, 39% full-time, 61% women, 39% men

Undergraduates 4,600 full-time, 7,076 part-time. Students come from 25 states and territories; 1% are from out of state; 5% transferred in.
Freshmen *Admission:* 1,360 enrolled.
Faculty *Total:* 196, 100% full-time, 18% with terminal degrees. *Student/faculty ratio:* 25:1.
Majors Accounting technology and bookkeeping; animal sciences related; automobile/automotive mechanics technology; business administration and management; business administration, management and operations related; child-care provision; cinematography and film/video production; civil engineering technology; commercial and advertising art; computer and information sciences related; computer programming (specific applications); computer systems analysis; construction engineering technology; criminal justice/law enforcement administration; dental hygiene; diagnostic medical sonography and ultrasound technology; dietetics; drafting and design technology; education; electrical, electronic and communications engineering technology; emergency medical technology (EMT paramedic); executive assistant/executive secretary; fire prevention and safety technology; forest technology; health/health-care administration; health information/medical records administration; hospitality administration; landscaping and groundskeeping; legal assistant/paralegal; liberal arts and sciences/liberal studies; management information

systems and services related; manufacturing engineering technology; medical radiologic technology; operations management; photographic and film/video technology; physical therapy technology; registered nursing/registered nurse; restaurant, culinary, and catering management.

Academics *Calendar:* semesters. *Degrees:* certificates, diplomas, associate, and bachelor's. *Special study options:* academic remediation for entering students, adult/continuing education programs, advanced placement credit, cooperative education, distance learning, double majors, external degree program, honors programs, independent study, part-time degree program, services for LD students, summer session for credit. *ROTC:* Army (b).

Library Learning Resource Center plus 2 others.

Student Life *Housing:* college housing not available. *Activities and Organizations:* drama/theater group, student-run newspaper, choral group. *Campus security:* 24-hour emergency response devices and patrols, student patrols, late-night transport/escort service. *Student services:* health clinic, personal/psychological counseling.

Athletics Member NJCAA. *Intercollegiate sports:* baseball M(s), basketball M(s)/W(s), softball W(s), volleyball W. *Intramural sports:* archery M/W, badminton M/W, basketball M/W, bowling M/W, cross-country running M/W, gymnastics M/W, racquetball M/W, sailing M/W, swimming and diving M/W, tennis M/W, track and field M/W, volleyball M/W, weight lifting M/W, wrestling M.

Costs (2010–11) *One-time required fee:* $30. *Tuition:* state resident $2179 full-time; nonresident $8213 full-time. Full-time tuition and fees vary according to degree level. Part-time tuition and fees vary according to degree level. *Waivers:* senior citizens and employees or children of employees.

Financial Aid Of all full-time matriculated undergraduates who enrolled in 2009, 120 Federal Work-Study jobs (averaging $3000).

Applying *Options:* early admission. *Application fee:* $30. *Required:* high school transcript. *Application deadlines:* 8/30 (freshmen), 8/30 (transfers). *Notification:* continuous until 8/30 (freshmen), continuous until 8/30 (transfers).

Freshman Application Contact Ms. Martha Caughey, Registrar, Pensacola State College, 1000 College Boulevard, Pensacola, FL 32504-8998. *Phone:* 850-484-1600. *Fax:* 850-484-1829. *Web site:* http://www.pensacolastate.edu/.

Polk State College
Winter Haven, Florida

- **State-supported** primarily 2-year, founded 1964, part of Florida Community College System
- **Suburban** 98-acre campus with easy access to Orlando and Tampa
- **Endowment** $13.4 million
- **Coed,** 10,589 undergraduate students, 35% full-time, 63% women, 37% men

Undergraduates 3,739 full-time, 6,850 part-time. Students come from 15 states and territories; 63 other countries; 1% are from out of state; 4% transferred in. *Retention:* 67% of full-time freshmen returned.

Freshmen *Admission:* 1,503 enrolled. *Test scores:* SAT math scores over 500: 53%; SAT math scores over 600: 5%; SAT math scores over 700: 1%.

Faculty *Total:* 721, 25% full-time, 10% with terminal degrees. *Student/faculty ratio:* 17:1.

Majors Accounting technology and bookkeeping; business administration and management; business administration, management and operations related; cardiovascular technology; child development; corrections; criminal justice/law enforcement administration; data processing and data processing technology; diagnostic medical sonography and ultrasound technology; electrical and power transmission installation; emergency medical technology (EMT paramedic); finance; fire science/firefighting; health information/medical records administration; information science/studies; liberal arts and sciences/liberal studies; marketing/marketing management; medical administrative assistant and medical secretary; occupational therapist assistant; physical therapy technology; pre-engineering; radiologic technology/science; registered nursing/registered nurse; respiratory care therapy; transportation/mobility management.

Academics *Calendar:* semesters 16-16-6-6. *Degrees:* certificates, associate, and bachelor's. *Special study options:* academic remediation for entering students, accelerated degree program, adult/continuing education programs, advanced placement credit, cooperative education, distance learning, double majors, English as a second language, honors programs, independent study, off-campus study, part-time degree program, services for LD students, student-designed majors, study abroad, summer session for credit. *ROTC:* Army (c).

Library Polk State College Library with 169,777 titles, 342 serial subscriptions, 6,269 audiovisual materials, an OPAC, a Web page.

Student Life *Housing:* college housing not available. *Activities and Organizations:* drama/theater group, choral group. *Campus security:* 24-hour emergency response devices and patrols. *Student services:* personal/psychological counseling.

Athletics Member NJCAA. *Intercollegiate sports:* baseball M(s), basketball M(s), soccer W(s), softball W(s), volleyball W(s). *Intramural sports:* basketball M/W, bowling M/W, football M/W, volleyball M/W.

Costs (2010–11) *Tuition:* state resident $2819 full-time, $94 per credit hour part-time; nonresident $10,443 full-time, $348 per credit hour part-time. Full-time tuition and fees vary according to course load and degree level. Part-time tuition and fees vary according to course load and degree level. Tuition for Upper Division in-state $3,184 full-time, $106.13 per credit hour part-time; nonresident $15,968 full-time, $532.26 per credit hour part-time. *Waivers:* employees or children of employees.

Applying *Options:* electronic application, early admission, deferred entrance. *Required:* high school transcript. *Application deadlines:* rolling (freshmen), rolling (transfers). *Notification:* continuous (freshmen), continuous (transfers).

Freshman Application Contact Polk State College, 999 Avenue H, NE, Winter Haven, FL 33881-4299. *Phone:* 863-297-1010 Ext. 5016. *Web site:* http://www.polk.edu/.

Rasmussen College Fort Myers
Fort Myers, Florida

Director of Admissions Admissions Director, Rasmussen College Fort Myers, 9160 Forum Corporate Parkway, Suite 100, Fort Myers, FL 33905. *Phone:* 239-477-2100. *Toll-free phone:* 866-344-0229. *Fax:* 239-477-2101. *Web site:* http://www.rasmussen.edu/.

Rasmussen College Ocala
Ocala, Florida

Freshman Application Contact Admissions Office, Rasmussen College Ocala, 2221 Southwest 19th Avenue Road, Ocala, FL 34471. *Phone:* 352-629-1941. *Toll-free phone:* 877-593-2783. *Web site:* http://www.rasmussen.edu/.

Rasmussen College Pasco County
Holiday, Florida

Director of Admissions Ms. Claire L. Walker, Senior Admissions Representative, Rasmussen College Pasco County, 2127 Grand Boulevard, Holiday, FL 34690. *Phone:* 727-942-0069. *Toll-free phone:* 888-729-7247. *Web site:* http://www.rasmussen.edu/.

Remington College–Largo Campus
Largo, Florida

Director of Admissions Kathy McCabe, Director of Recruitment, Remington College–Largo Campus, 8550 Ulmerton Road, Largo, FL 33771. *Phone:* 727-532-1999. *Toll-free phone:* 888-900-2343. *Fax:* 727-530-7710. *E-mail:* kathy.mccabe@remingtoncollege.edu. *Web site:* http://www.remingtoncollege.edu/.

Remington College–Tampa Campus
Tampa, Florida

Freshman Application Contact Remington College–Tampa Campus, 2410 East Busch Boulevard, Tampa, FL 33612-8410. *Phone:* 813-932-0701. *Toll-free phone:* 800-992-4850. *Web site:* http://www.remingtoncollege.edu/.

St. Johns River Community College
Palatka, Florida

Director of Admissions Dean of Admissions and Records, St. Johns River Community College, 5001 Saint Johns Avenue, Palatka, FL 32177-3897. *Phone:* 386-312-4032. *Fax:* 386-312-4289. *Web site:* http://www.sjrcc.edu/.

Sanford-Brown Institute
Fort Lauderdale, Florida

Director of Admissions Scott Nelowet, Sanford-Brown Institute, 1201 West Cypress Creek Road, Fort Lauderdale, FL 33309. *Phone:* 904-363-6221. *Fax:* 904-363-6824. *E-mail:* snelowet@sbjacksonville.com. *Web site:* http://www.sbftlauderdale.com/.

Sanford-Brown Institute
Jacksonville, Florida

Freshman Application Contact Denise Neal, Assistant Director of Admissions, Sanford-Brown Institute, 10255 Fortune Parkway, Suite 501. *Phone:* 904-380-2912. *Fax:* 904-363-6824. *E-mail:* dneal@sbjacksonville.com. *Web site:* http://www.sbjacksonville.com/.

Sanford-Brown Institute
Tampa, Florida

Admissions Office Contact Sanford-Brown Institute, 5701 East Hillsborough Avenue, Tampa, FL 33610. *Toll-free phone:* 888-450-0333. *Web site:* http://www.sbtampa.com/.

Seminole State College of Florida
Sanford, Florida

- **State and locally supported** primarily 2-year, founded 1966
- **Small-town** 200-acre campus with easy access to Orlando
- **Endowment** $6.2 million
- **Coed,** 18,028 undergraduate students, 45% full-time, 59% women, 41% men

Undergraduates 8,098 full-time, 9,930 part-time. Students come from 82 other countries; 0.2% are from out of state; 18% Black or African American, non-Hispanic/Latino; 19% Hispanic/Latino; 3% Asian, non-Hispanic/Latino; 0.2% Native Hawaiian or other Pacific Islander, non-Hispanic/Latino; 0.4% American Indian or Alaska Native, non-Hispanic/Latino; 1% Two or more races, non-Hispanic/Latino; 3% Race/ethnicity unknown; 2% international; 3% transferred in.
Freshmen *Admission:* 5,533 applied, 5,533 admitted, 3,010 enrolled.
Faculty *Total:* 784, 30% full-time, 12% with terminal degrees. *Student/faculty ratio:* 28:1.
Majors Accounting; administrative assistant and secretarial science; architectural engineering technology; automobile/automotive mechanics technology; banking and financial support services; building/construction finishing, management, and inspection related; business administration and management; child development; civil engineering technology; computer and information sciences and support services related; computer and information sciences related; computer and information systems security; computer engineering related; computer engineering technology; computer graphics; computer hardware engineering; computer/information technology services administration related; computer programming; computer programming related; computer programming (specific applications); computer programming (vendor/product certification); computer software and media applications related; computer software engineering; computer systems networking and telecommunications; construction engineering technology; criminal justice/law enforcement administration; data entry/microcomputer applications; data entry/microcomputer applications related; data modeling/warehousing and database administration; data processing and data processing technology; drafting and design technology; electrical, electronic and communications engineering technology; emergency medical technology (EMT paramedic); finance; fire science/firefighting; industrial technology; information science/studies; information technology; interior design; legal assistant/paralegal; liberal arts and sciences/liberal studies; marketing/marketing management; network and system administration; physical therapy; registered nursing/registered nurse; respiratory care therapy; telecommunications technology; web/multimedia management and webmaster; web page, digital/multimedia and information resources design; word processing.
Academics *Calendar:* semesters. *Degrees:* certificates, diplomas, associate, and bachelor's. *Special study options:* academic remediation for entering students, accelerated degree program, adult/continuing education programs, advanced placement credit, cooperative education, distance learning, double majors, English as a second language, external degree program, honors programs, independent study, internships, part-time degree program, services for LD students, study abroad, summer session for credit. *ROTC:* Army (b).
Library Seminole State College Library - SLM plus 6 others with 120,137 titles, 411 serial subscriptions, 7,403 audiovisual materials, an OPAC, a Web page.
Student Life *Housing:* college housing not available. *Activities and Organizations:* drama/theater group, student-run newspaper, choral group, Phi Beta Lambda, Phi Theta Kappa, Student Government Association, Sigma Phi Gamma, Hispanic Student Association. *Campus security:* 24-hour emergency response devices and patrols. *Student services:* personal/psychological counseling.
Athletics Member NJCAA. *Intercollegiate sports:* baseball M(s), golf W(s), softball W(s).
Standardized Tests *Required:* CPT (for admission). *Recommended:* ACT (for admission).
Costs (2011–12) *Tuition:* state resident $2904 full-time, $97 per credit hour part-time; nonresident $10,607 full-time, $354 per credit hour part-time. Full-time tuition and fees vary according to degree level and program. Part-time tuition and fees vary according to degree level and program. *Required fees:* $714 full-time, $24 per credit hour part-time. *Payment plan:* deferred payment. *Waivers:* senior citizens and employees or children of employees.
Applying *Options:* electronic application, early admission, deferred entrance. *Required:* high school transcript, minimum 2.0 GPA. *Application deadlines:* rolling (freshmen), rolling (transfers). *Notification:* continuous (freshmen), continuous (transfers).
Freshman Application Contact Ms. Pamela Mennechey, Director of Admissions, Seminole State College of Florida, Sanford, FL 32773-6199. *Phone:* 407-708-2050. *Fax:* 407-708-2395. *E-mail:* admissions@scc-fl.edu. *Web site:* http://www.seminolestate.edu/.

South Florida Community College
Avon Park, Florida

Director of Admissions Ms. Annie Alexander-Harvey, Dean of Student Services, South Florida Community College, 600 West College Drive, Avon Park, FL 33825-9356. *Phone:* 863-453-6661 Ext. 7107. *Web site:* http://www.sfcc.cc.fl.us/.

Southwest Florida College
Tampa, Florida

Director of Admissions Admissions, Southwest Florida College, 3910 Riga Boulevard, Tampa, FL 33619. *Phone:* 813-630-4401. *Toll-free phone:* 877-493-5147. *Web site:* http://www.swfc.edu/.

State College of Florida Manatee-Sarasota
Bradenton, Florida

- **State-supported** primarily 2-year, founded 1957, part of Florida Community College System
- **Suburban** 100-acre campus with easy access to Tampa-St. Petersburg
- **Coed**

Undergraduates 5,419 full-time, 5,813 part-time. Students come from 29 states and territories; 43 other countries; 2% are from out of state; 5% transferred in. *Retention:* 63% of full-time freshmen returned.
Academics *Calendar:* semesters. *Degrees:* certificates, associate, and bachelor's. *Special study options:* academic remediation for entering students, advanced placement credit, cooperative education, distance learning, English as a second language, honors programs, independent study, part-time degree program, services for LD students, summer session for credit.
Student Life *Campus security:* 24-hour emergency response devices and patrols, late-night transport/escort service.
Athletics Member NJCAA.
Costs (2010–11) *Tuition:* state resident $2847 full-time, $95 per hour part-time; nonresident $10,737 full-time, $358 per hour part-time.
Financial Aid Of all full-time matriculated undergraduates who enrolled in 2009, 82 Federal Work-Study jobs (averaging $2800). *Financial aid deadline:* 8/15.
Applying *Options:* early admission. *Required:* high school transcript.
Freshman Application Contact Ms. MariLynn Lewy, AVP, Student Services, State College of Florida Manatee-Sarasota, Bradenton, FL 34206. *Phone:* 941-752-5384. *Fax:* 941-727-6380. *E-mail:* lewym@scf.edu. *Web site:* http://www.scf.edu/.

Tallahassee Community College
Tallahassee, Florida

- **State and locally supported** 2-year, founded 1966, part of Florida Community College System
- **Suburban** 258-acre campus
- **Endowment** $6.9 million
- **Coed,** 14,739 undergraduate students, 51% full-time, 55% women, 45% men

Undergraduates 7,500 full-time, 7,239 part-time. Students come from 43 states and territories; 106 other countries; 5% are from out of state; 35% Black or African American, non-Hispanic/Latino; 8% Hispanic/Latino; 1% Asian, non-Hispanic/Latino; 0.1% Native Hawaiian or other Pacific Islander, non-Hispanic/Latino; 0.3% American Indian or Alaska Native, non-Hispanic/Latino; 2% Two or more races, non-Hispanic/Latino; 3% Race/ethnicity unknown; 0.8% international; 25% transferred in. *Retention:* 56% of full-time freshmen returned.
Freshmen *Admission:* 3,416 enrolled.
Faculty *Total:* 906, 19% full-time, 16% with terminal degrees. *Student/faculty ratio:* 25:1.
Majors Accounting technology and bookkeeping; administrative assistant and secretarial science; business administration and management; civil engineering technology; computer and information sciences; computer graphics; computer programming; computer programming (specific applications); computer systems networking and telecommunications; construction engineering technology; criminal justice/law enforcement administration; data processing and data

processing technology; dental hygiene; emergency medical technology (EMT paramedic); engineering; film/cinema/video studies; finance; health information/medical records technology; kindergarten/preschool education; legal administrative assistant/secretary; legal assistant/paralegal; liberal arts and sciences/liberal studies; management information systems; marketing/marketing management; network and system administration; parks, recreation and leisure; public administration; registered nursing/registered nurse; respiratory care therapy; word processing.

Academics *Calendar:* semesters. *Degree:* certificates and associate. *Special study options:* academic remediation for entering students, accelerated degree program, adult/continuing education programs, advanced placement credit, distance learning, English as a second language, external degree program, honors programs, independent study, off-campus study, part-time degree program, services for LD students, study abroad, summer session for credit. *ROTC:* Army (c), Navy (c), Air Force (c).

Library Tallahassee Community College Library with 236,009 titles, 14,459 serial subscriptions, 4,576 audiovisual materials, an OPAC.

Student Life *Housing:* college housing not available. *Activities and Organizations:* drama/theater group, student-run newspaper, choral group, Student Government Association, International Student Organization, Phi Theta Kappa, Model United Nations, Honors Council. *Campus security:* 24-hour emergency response devices and patrols, late-night transport/escort service. *Student services:* personal/psychological counseling.

Athletics Member NJCAA. *Intercollegiate sports:* baseball M(s), basketball M(s)/W(s), softball W(s). *Intramural sports:* basketball M/W, football M/W, soccer M/W, softball M/W, volleyball M/W.

Costs (2010–11) *Tuition:* state resident $2232 full-time, $86 per credit hour part-time; nonresident $7887 full-time, $303 per credit hour part-time. Full-time tuition and fees vary according to course load. Part-time tuition and fees vary according to course load. *Payment plan:* installment. *Waivers:* employees or children of employees.

Financial Aid Of all full-time matriculated undergraduates who enrolled in 2008, 265 Federal Work-Study jobs (averaging $2395).

Applying *Options:* electronic application, early admission, deferred entrance. *Required:* high school transcript. *Application deadlines:* 8/1 (freshmen), 8/1 (transfers).

Freshman Application Contact Student Success Center, Tallahassee Community College, 444 Appleyard Drive, Tallahassee, FL 32304-2895. *Phone:* 850-201-8555. *E-mail:* admissions@tcc.fl.edu. *Web site:* http://www.tcc.fl.edu/.

Valencia Community College
Orlando, Florida

Freshman Application Contact Dr. Renee Simpson, Assistant Vice President of Admissions and Records, Valencia Community College, Orlando, FL 32802-3028. *Phone:* 407-582-1511. *Fax:* 407-582-1866. *E-mail:* rsimpson@valenciacc.edu. *Web site:* http://www.valencia.cc.fl.us/.

GEORGIA

Albany Technical College
Albany, Georgia

- **State-supported** 2-year, founded 1961, part of Technical College System of Georgia
- **Coed,** 4,497 undergraduate students, 66% full-time, 61% women, 39% men

Undergraduates 2,965 full-time, 1,532 part-time. 0.3% are from out of state; 75% Black or African American, non-Hispanic/Latino; 0.5% Hispanic/Latino; 0.4% Asian, non-Hispanic/Latino; 0.1% Native Hawaiian or other Pacific Islander, non-Hispanic/Latino; 0.2% American Indian or Alaska Native, non-Hispanic/Latino; 0.9% Two or more races, non-Hispanic/Latino; 0.3% Race/ethnicity unknown. *Retention:* 59% of full-time freshmen returned.

Freshmen *Admission:* 731 enrolled.

Majors Accounting; adult development and aging; child development; computer and information sciences; corrections and criminal justice related; culinary arts; drafting and design technology; electrical and electronic engineering technologies related; forest technology; hotel/motel administration; human development and family studies related; industrial technology; manufacturing engineering technology; marketing/marketing management; medical radiologic technology; pharmacy technician; tourism and travel services management.

Academics *Calendar:* quarters. *Degree:* certificates, diplomas, and associate. *Special study options:* distance learning.

Library Albany Technical College Library and Media Center.

Student Life *Housing:* college housing not available.

Costs (2010–11) *Tuition:* state resident $2025 full-time, $45 per credit hour part-time; nonresident $4050 full-time, $90 per credit hour part-time. Full-time tuition and fees vary according to program. *Required fees:* $243 full-time.

Applying *Options:* early admission. *Application fee:* $15. *Required:* high school transcript.

Freshman Application Contact Albany Technical College, 1704 South Slappey Boulevard, Albany, GA 31701. *Phone:* 229-430-3520. *Web site:* http://www.albanytech.edu/.

Altamaha Technical College
Jesup, Georgia

- **State-supported** 2-year, part of Technical College System of Georgia
- **Coed,** 1,761 undergraduate students, 40% full-time, 50% women, 50% men

Undergraduates 702 full-time, 1,059 part-time. 32% Black or African American, non-Hispanic/Latino; 1% Hispanic/Latino; 0.4% Asian, non-Hispanic/Latino; 0.4% Native Hawaiian or other Pacific Islander, non-Hispanic/Latino; 0.3% American Indian or Alaska Native, non-Hispanic/Latino; 2% Race/ethnicity unknown. *Retention:* 59% of full-time freshmen returned.

Freshmen *Admission:* 450 enrolled.

Majors Administrative assistant and secretarial science; child development; computer programming; computer systems networking and telecommunications; criminal justice/safety; information science/studies; machine tool technology; manufacturing engineering technology; marketing/marketing management.

Academics *Calendar:* quarters. *Degree:* certificates, diplomas, and associate. *Special study options:* distance learning.

Student Life *Housing:* college housing not available.

Costs (2010–11) *Tuition:* state resident $2025 full-time, $45 per credit hour part-time; nonresident $4050 full-time, $90 per credit hour part-time. *Required fees:* $243 full-time.

Applying *Options:* early admission. *Application fee:* $15. *Required:* high school transcript.

Freshman Application Contact Altamaha Technical College, 1777 West Cherry Street, Jesup, GA 31545. *Phone:* 912-427-1958. *Web site:* http://www.altamahatech.edu/.

Andrew College
Cuthbert, Georgia

Freshman Application Contact Ms. Bridget Kurkowski, Director of Admission, Andrew College, 413 College Street, Cuthbert, GA 39840. *Phone:* 229-732-5986. *Toll-free phone:* 800-664-9250. *Fax:* 229-732-2176. *E-mail:* admissions@andrewcollege.edu. *Web site:* http://www.andrewcollege.edu/.

Athens Technical College
Athens, Georgia

- **State-supported** 2-year, founded 1958, part of Technical College System of Georgia
- **Suburban** 41-acre campus with easy access to Atlanta
- **Coed,** 5,741 undergraduate students, 41% full-time, 66% women, 34% men

Undergraduates 2,327 full-time, 3,414 part-time. 0.1% are from out of state; 23% Black or African American, non-Hispanic/Latino; 3% Hispanic/Latino; 6% Asian, non-Hispanic/Latino; 0.3% American Indian or Alaska Native, non-Hispanic/Latino; 0.2% Two or more races, non-Hispanic/Latino; 4% Race/ethnicity unknown. *Retention:* 56% of full-time freshmen returned.

Freshmen *Admission:* 798 enrolled.

Majors Accounting; administrative assistant and secretarial science; biology/biotechnology laboratory technician; child development; clinical laboratory science/medical technology; communications technology; computer programming; computer systems networking and telecommunications; criminal justice/law enforcement administration; dental assisting; dental hygiene; diagnostic medical sonography and ultrasound technology; electrical, electronic and communications engineering technology; emergency medical technology (EMT paramedic); hotel/motel administration; information science/studies; legal assistant/paralegal; licensed practical/vocational nurse training; logistics, materials, and supply chain management; marketing/marketing management; medical radiologic technology; physical therapy; registered nursing/registered nurse; respiratory care therapy; surgical technology; tourism and travel services management; veterinary/animal health technology.

Academics *Calendar:* quarters. *Degree:* certificates, diplomas, and associate. *Special study options:* distance learning.

Student Life *Housing:* college housing not available.

Costs (2010–11) *Tuition:* state resident $2025 full-time, $45 per credit hour part-time; nonresident $4050 full-time, $90 per credit hour part-time. *Required fees:* $243 full-time.

Financial Aid Of all full-time matriculated undergraduates who enrolled in 2009, 34 Federal Work-Study jobs (averaging $3090).
Applying *Options:* early admission. *Application fee:* $26. *Required:* high school transcript.
Freshman Application Contact Athens Technical College, 800 US Highway 29 North, Athens, GA 30601-1500. *Phone:* 706-355-5008. *Web site:* http://www.athenstech.edu/.

Atlanta Metropolitan College
Atlanta, Georgia

Freshman Application Contact Ms. Audrey Reid, Director, Office of Admissions, Atlanta Metropolitan College, 1630 Metropolitan Parkway, SW, Atlanta, GA 30310-4498. *Phone:* 404-756-4004. *Fax:* 404-756-4407. *E-mail:* admissions@atlm.edu. *Web site:* http://www.atlm.edu/.

Atlanta Technical College
Atlanta, Georgia

- **State-supported** 2-year, founded 1945, part of Technical College System of Georgia
- **Coed,** 5,053 undergraduate students, 53% full-time, 58% women, 42% men

Undergraduates 2,659 full-time, 2,394 part-time. 0.2% are from out of state; 94% Black or African American, non-Hispanic/Latino; 0.8% Hispanic/Latino; 0.9% Asian, non-Hispanic/Latino; 0.1% American Indian or Alaska Native, non-Hispanic/Latino; 1% Race/ethnicity unknown. *Retention:* 52% of full-time freshmen returned.
Freshmen *Admission:* 891 enrolled.
Majors Accounting; child development; computer programming; culinary arts; dental hygiene; health information/medical records technology; hotel/motel administration; information technology; legal assistant/paralegal; marketing/marketing management; tourism and travel services management.
Academics *Calendar:* quarters. *Degree:* certificates, diplomas, and associate. *Special study options:* distance learning, study abroad.
Student Life *Housing:* college housing not available.
Costs (2010–11) *Tuition:* state resident $2025 full-time, $45 per credit hour part-time; nonresident $4050 full-time, $90 per credit hour part-time. Full-time tuition and fees vary according to program. Part-time tuition and fees vary according to program. *Required fees:* $246 full-time.
Applying *Options:* early admission. *Application fee:* $25. *Required:* high school transcript.
Freshman Application Contact Atlanta Technical College, 1560 Metropolitan Parkway, SW, Atlanta, GA 30310. *Phone:* 404-225-4455. *Web site:* http://www.atlantatech.org/.

Augusta Technical College
Augusta, Georgia

- **State-supported** 2-year, founded 1961, part of Technical College System of Georgia
- **Urban** 70-acre campus
- **Coed,** 4,864 undergraduate students, 53% full-time, 62% women, 38% men

Undergraduates 2,558 full-time, 2,306 part-time. 2% are from out of state; 53% Black or African American, non-Hispanic/Latino; 2% Hispanic/Latino; 1% Asian, non-Hispanic/Latino; 0.5% American Indian or Alaska Native, non-Hispanic/Latino; 2% Race/ethnicity unknown. *Retention:* 50% of full-time freshmen returned.
Freshmen *Admission:* 928 enrolled.
Majors Accounting; administrative assistant and secretarial science; biotechnology; business administration and management; cardiovascular technology; child development; computer programming; computer systems networking and telecommunications; criminal justice/safety; culinary arts; e-commerce; electrical, electronic and communications engineering technology; emergency medical technology (EMT paramedic); fire science/firefighting; information science/studies; marketing/marketing management; mechanical engineering/mechanical technology; medical radiologic technology; occupational therapist assistant; parks, recreation and leisure facilities management; pharmacy technician; respiratory care therapy; respiratory therapy technician; surgical technology.
Academics *Calendar:* quarters. *Degree:* certificates, diplomas, and associate. *Special study options:* distance learning, study abroad.
Library Information Technology Center.
Student Life *Housing:* college housing not available.
Costs (2010–11) *Tuition:* state resident $2025 full-time, $45 per credit hour part-time; nonresident $4050 full-time, $90 per credit hour part-time. Full-time tuition and fees vary according to program. Part-time tuition and fees vary according to program. *Required fees:* $255 full-time.

Applying *Options:* early admission. *Application fee:* $20. *Required:* high school transcript.
Freshman Application Contact Augusta Technical College, 3200 Augusta Tech Drive, Augusta, GA 30906. *Phone:* 706-771-4150. *Web site:* http://www.augustatech.edu/.

Bainbridge College
Bainbridge, Georgia

- **State-supported** 2-year, founded 1972, part of University System of Georgia
- **Small-town** 160-acre campus
- **Coed,** 3,607 undergraduate students, 56% full-time, 70% women, 30% men

Undergraduates 2,020 full-time, 1,587 part-time. Students come from 3 states and territories; 1% are from out of state.
Freshmen *Admission:* 972 applied, 750 admitted.
Faculty *Total:* 201, 35% full-time, 18% with terminal degrees.
Majors Accounting; administrative assistant and secretarial science; agriculture; art; biology/biological sciences; business administration and management; business teacher education; chemistry; criminal justice/law enforcement administration; data processing and data processing technology; drafting and design technology; dramatic/theater arts; education; electrical, electronic and communications engineering technology; elementary education; English; family and consumer sciences/human sciences; forestry; health teacher education; history; information science/studies; journalism; kindergarten/preschool education; liberal arts and sciences/liberal studies; licensed practical/vocational nurse training; marketing/marketing management; mathematics; political science and government; psychology; registered nursing/registered nurse; rhetoric and composition; sociology; welding technology.
Academics *Calendar:* semesters. *Degree:* certificates and associate. *Special study options:* academic remediation for entering students, adult/continuing education programs, advanced placement credit, distance learning, double majors, independent study, part-time degree program, services for LD students, study abroad, summer session for credit.
Library Bainbridge College Library with 42,399 titles, 90 serial subscriptions, 2,873 audiovisual materials, an OPAC.
Student Life *Housing:* college housing not available. *Activities and Organizations:* drama/theater group, Canoe Club, Alpha Beta Gamma, Circle K, Sigma Kappa Delta, Student Government Association. *Campus security:* 24-hour patrols.
Athletics *Intramural sports:* table tennis M/W, volleyball M/W.
Standardized Tests *Required for some:* SAT or ACT (for admission), ACT COMPASS.
Costs (2010–11) *Tuition:* state resident $1920 full-time, $80 per credit hour part-time; nonresident $7680 full-time, $320 per credit hour part-time. Full-time tuition and fees vary according to course load. Part-time tuition and fees vary according to course load. No tuition increase for student's term of enrollment. *Required fees:* $688 full-time, $344 per term part-time. *Waivers:* senior citizens.
Applying *Options:* electronic application, early admission. *Required for some:* high school transcript, minimum 1.8 GPA, 3 letters of recommendation, interview, immunizations/waivers, medical records and criminal. *Application deadlines:* rolling (freshmen), rolling (transfers). *Notification:* continuous (freshmen), continuous (transfers).
Freshman Application Contact Mrs. Connie Snyder, Director of Admissions and Records, Bainbridge College, 2500 East Shotwell Street, Bainbridge, GA 39819. *Phone:* 229-248-2504. *Fax:* 229-248-2525. *E-mail:* csnyder@bainbridge.edu. *Web site:* http://www.bainbridge.edu/.

Brown Mackie College–Atlanta
Atlanta, Georgia

- **Proprietary** 2-year, part of Education Management Corporation
- **Urban** campus
- **Coed**

Majors Accounting technology and bookkeeping; business administration and management; criminal justice/law enforcement administration; early childhood education; health/health-care administration; legal assistant/paralegal; medical/clinical assistant; occupational therapist assistant; pharmacy technician; surgical technology.
Academics *Degree:* diplomas and associate.
Costs (2010–11) *Tuition:* Tuition varies by program. Students should contact Brown Mackie College for tuition information.
Freshman Application Contact Brown Mackie College–Atlanta, 4370 Peachtree Road, NE, Atlanta, GA 30319. *Phone:* 404-799-4500. *Web site:* http://www.brownmackie.edu/atlanta/.

See page 358 for the College Close-Up.

Central Georgia Technical College
Macon, Georgia

- **State-supported** 2-year, founded 1966, part of Technical College System of Georgia
- **Suburban** campus
- **Coed,** 7,902 undergraduate students, 61% full-time, 66% women, 34% men

Undergraduates 4,799 full-time, 3,103 part-time. 0.1% are from out of state; 64% Black or African American, non-Hispanic/Latino; 0.3% Hispanic/Latino; 0.8% Asian, non-Hispanic/Latino; 0.3% Native Hawaiian or other Pacific Islander, non-Hispanic/Latino; 0.3% American Indian or Alaska Native, non-Hispanic/Latino; 0.6% Two or more races, non-Hispanic/Latino; 0.7% Race/ethnicity unknown. *Retention:* 55% of full-time freshmen returned.

Freshmen *Admission:* 1,571 enrolled.

Majors Accounting; administrative assistant and secretarial science; adult development and aging; banking and financial support services; business administration and management; cabinetmaking and millwork; cardiovascular technology; carpentry; child-care and support services management; child development; clinical/medical laboratory technology; computer programming; computer systems networking and telecommunications; criminal justice/safety; dental hygiene; drafting and design technology; e-commerce; electrical, electronic and communications engineering technology; hotel/motel administration; industrial technology; information science/studies; legal assistant/paralegal; marketing/marketing management; medical radiologic technology; tourism and travel services management; veterinary/animal health technology; web page, digital/multimedia and information resources design.

Academics *Calendar:* quarters. *Degree:* certificates, diplomas, and associate. *Special study options:* distance learning.

Student Life *Housing:* college housing not available.

Costs (2010–11) *Tuition:* state resident $2025 full-time, $45 per credit hour part-time; nonresident $4050 full-time, $90 per credit hour part-time. *Required fees:* $243 full-time.

Financial Aid Of all full-time matriculated undergraduates who enrolled in 2009, 175 Federal Work-Study jobs (averaging $2000). *Financial aid deadline:* 9/1.

Applying *Options:* early admission. *Application fee:* $20. *Required:* high school transcript.

Freshman Application Contact Central Georgia Technical College, 3300 Macon Tech Drive, Macon, GA 31206. *Phone:* 478-757-3408. *Web site:* http://www.centralgatech.edu/.

Chattahoochee Technical College
Marietta, Georgia

- **State-supported** 2-year, founded 1961, part of Technical College System of Georgia
- **Suburban** campus with easy access to Atlanta
- **Coed,** 13,003 undergraduate students, 48% full-time, 60% women, 40% men

Undergraduates 6,224 full-time, 6,779 part-time. 0.5% are from out of state; 34% Black or African American, non-Hispanic/Latino; 3% Hispanic/Latino; 2% Asian, non-Hispanic/Latino; 0.4% Native Hawaiian or other Pacific Islander, non-Hispanic/Latino; 0.4% American Indian or Alaska Native, non-Hispanic/Latino; 1% Two or more races, non-Hispanic/Latino; 2% Race/ethnicity unknown; 0.3% international. *Retention:* 51% of full-time freshmen returned.

Freshmen *Admission:* 1,857 enrolled.

Majors Accounting; administrative assistant and secretarial science; automobile/automotive mechanics technology; biomedical technology; business administration and management; child development; civil engineering technology; computer and information systems security; computer programming; computer systems networking and telecommunications; criminal justice/safety; culinary arts; drafting and design technology; electrical, electronic and communications engineering technology; fire science/firefighting; horticultural science; information science/studies; logistics, materials, and supply chain management; marketing/marketing management; medical radiologic technology; parks, recreation and leisure facilities management; web page, digital/multimedia and information resources design.

Academics *Calendar:* quarters. *Degree:* certificates, diplomas, and associate. *Special study options:* distance learning.

Student Life *Housing:* college housing not available.

Costs (2010–11) *Tuition:* state resident $2025 full-time, $45 per credit hour part-time; nonresident $4050 full-time, $90 per credit hour part-time. *Required fees:* $264 full-time.

Financial Aid Of all full-time matriculated undergraduates who enrolled in 2009, 40 Federal Work-Study jobs (averaging $2500).

Applying *Options:* early admission. *Application fee:* $15. *Required:* high school transcript.

Freshman Application Contact Chattahoochee Technical College, 980 South Cobb Drive, SE, Marietta, GA 30060. *Phone:* 770-528-4581. *Web site:* http://www.chattahoocheetech.edu/.

Columbus Technical College
Columbus, Georgia

- **State-supported** 2-year, founded 1961, part of Technical College System of Georgia
- **Urban** campus with easy access to Atlanta
- **Coed,** 4,355 undergraduate students, 44% full-time, 67% women, 33% men

Undergraduates 1,912 full-time, 2,443 part-time. 14% are from out of state; 45% Black or African American, non-Hispanic/Latino; 3% Hispanic/Latino; 2% Asian, non-Hispanic/Latino; 0.2% Native Hawaiian or other Pacific Islander, non-Hispanic/Latino; 0.6% American Indian or Alaska Native, non-Hispanic/Latino; 0.9% Two or more races, non-Hispanic/Latino; 3% Race/ethnicity unknown; 0.1% international. *Retention:* 42% of full-time freshmen returned.

Freshmen *Admission:* 789 enrolled.

Majors Accounting; administrative assistant and secretarial science; automobile/automotive mechanics technology; child development; computer engineering related; computer systems networking and telecommunications; dental hygiene; diagnostic medical sonography and ultrasound technology; drafting and design technology; electrical, electronic and communications engineering technology; emergency medical technology (EMT paramedic); health information/medical records technology; horticultural science; industrial technology; information science/studies; machine tool technology; mechanical engineering/mechanical technology; medical office management; medical radiologic technology; pharmacy technician; registered nursing/registered nurse; respiratory therapy technician; surgical technology; web page, digital/multimedia and information resources design.

Academics *Calendar:* quarters. *Degree:* certificates, diplomas, and associate. *Special study options:* distance learning.

Library Columbus Technical College Library.

Student Life *Housing:* college housing not available.

Costs (2010–11) *Tuition:* state resident $2025 full-time, $45 per credit hour part-time; nonresident $4050 full-time, $90 per credit hour part-time. *Required fees:* $243 full-time.

Financial Aid Of all full-time matriculated undergraduates who enrolled in 2009, 6 Federal Work-Study jobs (averaging $2000).

Applying *Options:* early admission. *Application fee:* $15. *Required:* high school transcript.

Freshman Application Contact Columbus Technical College, 928 Manchester Expressway, Columbus, GA 31904-6572. *Phone:* 706-649-1901. *Web site:* http://www.columbustech.edu/.

Darton College
Albany, Georgia

- **State-supported** 2-year, founded 1965, part of University System of Georgia
- **Urban** 185-acre campus
- **Endowment** $978,169
- **Coed,** 5,854 undergraduate students, 49% full-time, 69% women, 31% men

Undergraduates 2,874 full-time, 2,980 part-time. Students come from 24 states and territories; 46 other countries; 7% are from out of state; 42% Black or African American, non-Hispanic/Latino; 1% Hispanic/Latino; 0.9% Asian, non-Hispanic/Latino; 0.2% American Indian or Alaska Native, non-Hispanic/Latino; 0.3% Two or more races, non-Hispanic/Latino; 0.8% Race/ethnicity unknown; 1% international; 10% transferred in. *Retention:* 45% of full-time freshmen returned.

Freshmen *Admission:* 1,464 enrolled. *Average high school GPA:* 2.73. *Test scores:* SAT critical reading scores over 500: 31%; SAT math scores over 500: 28%; ACT scores over 18: 44%; SAT critical reading scores over 600: 7%; SAT math scores over 600: 4%; ACT scores over 24: 8%; SAT critical reading scores over 700: 1%.

Faculty *Total:* 282, 43% full-time. *Student/faculty ratio:* 21:1.

Majors Accounting; administrative assistant and secretarial science; agriculture; anthropology; art; art teacher education; behavioral aspects of health; biological and biomedical sciences related; biology/biological sciences; business administration and management; business teacher education; cardiovascular technology; chemistry; clinical laboratory science/medical technology; computer and information sciences; computer and information sciences and support services related; computer science; computer support specialist; criminal justice/law enforcement administration; dance; dental hygiene; diagnostic medical sonography and ultrasound technology; drama and dance teacher education; dramatic/theater arts; economics; emergency medical technology (EMT paramedic); engineering technology; English; English/language arts teacher education; environmental studies; foreign languages and literatures; forensic science and technology; forestry; general studies; geography; health and physical education/fitness; health information/medical records administration; health information/medical records technology; health/medical preparatory programs related; histologic technician; history; history teacher education; journalism; licensed practical/vocational nurse training; mathematics; mathematics teacher education; middle school education; music; music teacher education; nuclear medical technology; occupational therapist assistant; office occupations and clerical services; philosophy; physical therapy technology; physics; political science and government; pre-dentistry studies; pre-engineering; pre-law studies; premedical studies; pre-pharmacy studies; pre-veterinary studies; psychology; registered nursing/registered nurse; respiratory care therapy; science teacher education; social work; sociology; special education; speech teacher education; trade and industrial teacher education.

Academics *Calendar:* semesters. *Degrees:* certificates, associate, and post-bachelor's certificates. *Special study options:* academic remediation for entering students, accelerated degree program, adult/continuing education programs, advanced placement credit, cooperative education, distance learning, double majors, English as a second language, honors programs, independent study, off-campus study, part-time degree program, services for LD students, student-designed majors, study abroad, summer session for credit. *ROTC:* Army (c).

Library Weatherbee Learning Resources Center with 100,248 titles, 263 serial subscriptions, 5,182 audiovisual materials, an OPAC, a Web page.

Student Life *Housing Options:* coed. Campus housing is university owned. *Activities and Organizations:* drama/theater group, choral group, Cultural Exchange Club, Democratic, Independent, & Republican Team (D.I.R.T.), Human Services Club, Outdoor Adventure Club (OAC), Music Club. *Campus security:* 24-hour emergency response devices and patrols, student patrols, late-night transport/escort service, controlled dormitory access. *Student services:* personal/psychological counseling.

Athletics Member NJCAA. *Intercollegiate sports:* baseball M(s), basketball W(s), cross-country running M(s)/W(s), golf M(s), soccer M(s)/W(s), softball W(s), swimming and diving M(s)/W(s), wrestling M. *Intramural sports:* badminton M/W, basketball M/W, bowling M/W, football M, racquetball M/W, table tennis M, volleyball M/W.

Standardized Tests *Required:* non-traditional students must take the COMPASS test (for admission). *Required for some:* SAT or ACT (for admission), SAT Subject Tests (for admission). *Recommended:* SAT or ACT (for admission), SAT Subject Tests (for admission).

Costs (2010–11) *Tuition:* state resident $1920 full-time, $80 per credit hour part-time; nonresident $7440 full-time, $310 per credit hour part-time. Part-time tuition and fees vary according to course load. $2398 of 15 credits/semester in-state; $9276 if 15 credits/semester out-of-state. *Required fees:* $794 full-time, $397 per term part-time. *Room and board:* $6712. Room and board charges vary according to board plan and housing facility. *Waivers:* senior citizens and employees or children of employees.

Financial Aid Of all full-time matriculated undergraduates who enrolled in 2009, 60 Federal Work-Study jobs.

Applying *Options:* electronic application, deferred entrance. *Application fee:* $20. *Required:* minimum 2.0 GPA, proof of immunization. *Required for some:* high school transcript. *Application deadlines:* 7/20 (freshmen), 7/20 (transfers). *Notification:* continuous until 7/27 (freshmen), continuous until 7/27 (transfers).

Freshman Application Contact Darton College, 2400 Gillionville Road, Albany, GA 31707-3098. *Phone:* 229-430-6740. *Web site:* http://www.darton.edu/.

DeKalb Technical College
Clarkston, Georgia

- **State-supported** 2-year, founded 1961, part of Technical College System of Georgia
- **Suburban** 17-acre campus with easy access to Atlanta
- **Coed,** 4,855 undergraduate students, 45% full-time, 62% women, 38% men

Undergraduates 2,202 full-time, 2,653 part-time. 0.3% are from out of state; 76% Black or African American, non-Hispanic/Latino; 1% Hispanic/Latino; 3% Asian, non-Hispanic/Latino; 0.2% Native Hawaiian or other Pacific Islander, non-Hispanic/Latino; 0.3% American Indian or Alaska Native, non-Hispanic/Latino; 1% Two or more races, non-Hispanic/Latino; 0.9% Race/ethnicity unknown. *Retention:* 46% of full-time freshmen returned.

Freshmen *Admission:* 760 enrolled.

Majors Accounting; administrative assistant and secretarial science; automobile/automotive mechanics technology; business/commerce; clinical/medical laboratory technology; computer engineering technology; computer programming; computer systems networking and telecommunications; criminal justice/

safety; drafting and design technology; electrical, electronic and communications engineering technology; electromechanical technology; engineering technology; heating, ventilation, air conditioning and refrigeration engineering technology; industrial technology; information science/studies; instrumentation technology; legal administrative assistant/secretary; legal assistant/paralegal; machine tool technology; marketing/marketing management; medical/clinical assistant; operations management; ophthalmic laboratory technology; opticianry; surgical technology; telecommunications technology.

Academics *Calendar:* quarters. *Degree:* certificates, diplomas, and associate. *Special study options:* distance learning.

Student Life *Housing:* college housing not available.

Costs (2010–11) *Tuition:* state resident $2025 full-time, $45 per credit hour part-time; nonresident $4050 full-time, $90 per credit hour part-time. *Required fees:* $291 full-time.

Financial Aid Of all full-time matriculated undergraduates who enrolled in 2009, 7,200 applied for aid, 7,100 were judged to have need. 145 Federal Work-Study jobs (averaging $4000). *Average financial aid package:* $4500. *Average need-based gift aid:* $4500.

Applying *Options:* early admission. *Application fee:* $20. *Required:* high school transcript.

Freshman Application Contact DeKalb Technical College, 495 North Indian Creek Drive, Clarkston, GA 30021-2397. *Phone:* 404-297-9522 Ext. 1229. *Web site:* http://www.dekalbtech.edu/.

East Georgia College
Swainsboro, Georgia

Freshman Application Contact East Georgia College, 131 College Circle, Swainsboro, GA 30401-2699. *Phone:* 478-289-2017. *Web site:* http://www.ega.edu/.

Emory University, Oxford College
Oxford, Georgia

- **Independent Methodist** primarily 2-year, founded 1836, administratively affiliated with Emory University
- **Small-town** 150-acre campus with easy access to Atlanta
- **Endowment** $26.0 million
- **Coed**

Undergraduates 755 full-time, 1 part-time. Students come from 36 states and territories; 16 other countries; 62% are from out of state; 95% live on campus. *Retention:* 89% of full-time freshmen returned.

Faculty *Student/faculty ratio:* 10:1.

Academics *Calendar:* semesters. *Degrees:* associate and bachelor's. *Special study options:* advanced placement credit, double majors, independent study, internships, off-campus study, services for LD students, study abroad, summer session for credit. *Unusual degree programs:* 3-2 engineering with Georgia Institute of Technology.

Student Life *Campus security:* 24-hour emergency response devices and patrols, student patrols, late-night transport/escort service, controlled dormitory access.

Athletics Member NJCAA.

Standardized Tests *Required:* SAT or ACT (for admission). *Required for some:* SAT Subject Tests (for admission).

Costs (2010–11) *Comprehensive fee:* $42,734 includes full-time tuition ($32,800), mandatory fees ($462), and room and board ($9472). Full-time tuition and fees vary according to course load. Part-time tuition: $1000 per credit hour. Part-time tuition and fees vary according to course load. *Room and board:* college room only: $6522. Room and board charges vary according to board plan.

Financial Aid Of all full-time matriculated undergraduates who enrolled in 2009, 225 Federal Work-Study jobs (averaging $1600).

Applying *Options:* electronic application, early admission, early action, deferred entrance. *Application fee:* $50. *Required:* essay or personal statement, high school transcript, 1 letter of recommendation. *Required for some:* interview. *Recommended:* minimum 3.0 GPA, 2 letters of recommendation.

Freshman Application Contact Emory University, Oxford College, 100 Hamill Street, PO Box 1328, Oxford, GA 30054. *Phone:* 770-784-8328. *Toll-free phone:* 800-723-8328. *Web site:* http://oxford.emory.edu/.

Everest Institute
Atlanta, Georgia

Freshman Application Contact Admissions Office, Everest Institute, 1706 Northeast Expressway, Atlanta, GA 30329. *Phone:* 404-327-8787. *Toll-free phone:* 888-741-4270. *Web site:* http://www.everest.edu/.

Gainesville State College

Oakwood, Georgia

- **State-supported** primarily 2-year, founded 1964, part of University System of Georgia
- **Small-town** 220-acre campus with easy access to Atlanta
- **Coed**

Undergraduates 6,068 full-time, 2,733 part-time. Students come from 17 states and territories; 72 other countries; 1% are from out of state; 7% transferred in.

Faculty *Student/faculty ratio:* 26:1.

Academics *Calendar:* semesters. *Degrees:* associate and bachelor's. *Special study options:* academic remediation for entering students, adult/continuing education programs, advanced placement credit, distance learning, double majors, English as a second language, honors programs, internships, off-campus study, part-time degree program, services for LD students, study abroad, summer session for credit. *ROTC:* Army (c), Air Force (c).

Student Life *Campus security:* 24-hour emergency response devices and patrols.

Standardized Tests *Recommended:* SAT or ACT (for admission).

Costs (2010–11) *Tuition:* state resident $2160 full-time, $90 per credit hour part-time; nonresident $8160 full-time, $340 per credit hour part-time. *Required fees:* $554 full-time, $484 per year part-time.

Financial Aid Of all full-time matriculated undergraduates who enrolled in 2009, 58 Federal Work-Study jobs (averaging $2308).

Applying *Options:* electronic application, early admission. *Application fee:* $35. *Required:* high school transcript.

Freshman Application Contact Mr. Mack Palmour, Director of Admissions, Gainesville State College, PO Box 1358, Gainesville, GA 30503. *Phone:* 678-717-3641. *Fax:* 678-717-3751. *E-mail:* admissions@gsc.edu. *Web site:* http://www.gsc.edu/.

Georgia Highlands College

Rome, Georgia

- **State-supported** 2-year, founded 1970, part of University System of Georgia
- **Suburban** 226-acre campus with easy access to Atlanta
- **Endowment** $1.2 million
- **Coed,** 5,226 undergraduate students, 58% full-time, 62% women, 38% men

Undergraduates 3,056 full-time, 2,170 part-time. Students come from 40 states and territories; 39 other countries; 0.5% are from out of state; 13% Black or African American, non-Hispanic/Latino; 6% Hispanic/Latino; 2% Asian, non-Hispanic/Latino; 0.1% Native Hawaiian or other Pacific Islander, non-Hispanic/Latino; 0.3% American Indian or Alaska Native, non-Hispanic/Latino; 2% Two or more races, non-Hispanic/Latino; 0.6% Race/ethnicity unknown; 6% transferred in. *Retention:* 60% of full-time freshmen returned.

Freshmen *Admission:* 2,081 applied, 1,616 admitted, 1,190 enrolled. *Average high school GPA:* 2.7.

Faculty *Total:* 241, 56% full-time, 27% with terminal degrees. *Student/faculty ratio:* 22:1.

Majors Accounting; agriculture; art; automobile/automotive mechanics technology; biological and physical sciences; business administration and management; clinical laboratory science/medical technology; computer programming; criminal justice/police science; criminal justice/safety; dental hygiene; economics; electrical, electronic and communications engineering technology; emergency medical technology (EMT paramedic); English; foreign languages and literatures; forestry; geology/earth science; history; horticultural science; hotel/motel administration; human services; information science/studies; journalism; kindergarten/preschool education; legal assistant/paralegal; liberal arts and sciences/liberal studies; marketing/marketing management; occupational therapy; philosophy; physical therapy; physical therapy technology; physician assistant; political science and government; psychology; radiologic technology/science; registered nursing/registered nurse; respiratory care therapy; secondary education; sociology.

Academics *Calendar:* semesters. *Degree:* associate. *Special study options:* academic remediation for entering students, advanced placement credit, cooperative education, distance learning, double majors, honors programs, independent study, part-time degree program, services for LD students, study abroad, summer session for credit.

Library Georgia Highlands Library plus 2 others with 70,302 titles, 248 serial subscriptions, 7,185 audiovisual materials, an OPAC, a Web page.

Student Life *Housing:* college housing not available. *Activities and Organizations:* drama/theater group, student-run newspaper, Highlands Association of Nursing Students, Green Highlands, Black Awareness Society, Political Science Association, Phi Theta Kappa. *Campus security:* 24-hour emergency response devices and patrols, emergency phone/email alert system. *Student services:* personal/psychological counseling.

Athletics *Intramural sports:* basketball M/W, bowling M/W, football M/W, golf M/W, sailing M/W, soccer M/W, softball M/W, table tennis M/W, tennis M/W, ultimate Frisbee M/W, volleyball M/W, weight lifting M/W.

Costs (2011–12) *Tuition:* state resident $2554 full-time, $80 per credit hour part-time; nonresident $8074 full-time, $310 per credit hour part-time. Full-time tuition and fees vary according to course load. Part-time tuition and fees vary according to course load. *Required fees:* $734 full-time, $347 per term part-time. *Waivers:* senior citizens.

Financial Aid Of all full-time matriculated undergraduates who enrolled in 2009, 50 Federal Work-Study jobs (averaging $3500).

Applying *Options:* electronic application, deferred entrance. *Application fee:* $20. *Required:* high school transcript, minimum 2.0 GPA. *Required for some:* minimum 2.2 GPA. *Application deadlines:* rolling (freshmen), rolling (out-of-state freshmen), rolling (transfers). *Notification:* continuous (freshmen), continuous (out-of-state freshmen), continuous (transfers).

Freshman Application Contact Mr. Todd Jones, Director of Admissions, Georgia Highlands College, 3175 Cedartown Highway, Rome, GA 30161. *Phone:* 706-295-6339. *Toll-free phone:* 800-332-2406. *Fax:* 706-295-6610. *E-mail:* tjones@highlands.edu. *Web site:* http://www.highlands.edu/.

Georgia Military College

Milledgeville, Georgia

- **State and locally supported** 2-year, founded 1879
- **Small-town** 40-acre campus
- **Endowment** $9.4 million
- **Coed,** 6,081 undergraduate students, 69% full-time, 61% women, 39% men

Undergraduates 4,198 full-time, 1,883 part-time. Students come from 33 states and territories; 5% are from out of state; 42% Black or African American, non-Hispanic/Latino; 3% Hispanic/Latino; 1% Asian, non-Hispanic/Latino; 0.4% American Indian or Alaska Native, non-Hispanic/Latino; 2% Two or more races, non-Hispanic/Latino; 2% Race/ethnicity unknown; 37% transferred in. *Retention:* 48% of full-time freshmen returned.

Freshmen *Admission:* 1,619 applied, 1,619 admitted, 1,390 enrolled. *Average high school GPA:* 2.39.

Faculty *Total:* 423, 25% full-time, 5% with terminal degrees. *Student/faculty ratio:* 14:1.

Majors Army ROTC/military science; biology/biological sciences; business administration and management; criminal justice/law enforcement administration; early childhood education; education; general studies; health services/allied health/health sciences; health teacher education; history; homeland security, law enforcement, firefighting and protective services related; human development and family studies; information technology; international relations and affairs; legal assistant/paralegal; logistics, materials, and supply chain management; mass communication/media; prenursing studies; psychology; public health education and promotion; secondary education; social sciences.

Academics *Calendar:* quarters. *Degree:* associate. *Special study options:* academic remediation for entering students, advanced placement credit, cooperative education, distance learning, double majors, external degree program, independent study, off-campus study, part-time degree program, services for LD students, study abroad, summer session for credit. *ROTC:* Army (b).

Library Sibley-Cone Library with 57,000 titles, 27,500 serial subscriptions, 1,700 audiovisual materials, an OPAC, a Web page.

Student Life *Housing:* on-campus residence required through sophomore year. *Options:* coed. Campus housing is university owned. *Activities and Organizations:* drama/theater group, student-run newspaper, choral group, Student Government Association, Alpha Phi Omega (community service organization), Drama Club, Book Club, Biology Club. *Campus security:* 24-hour emergency response devices and patrols, controlled dormitory access. *Student services:* health clinic.

Athletics Member NJCAA. *Intercollegiate sports:* football M(s), riflery M(s)/W(s). *Intramural sports:* basketball M, cross-country running M/W, football M, golf M, soccer M/W, tennis M/W, track and field M/W, volleyball M/W.

Standardized Tests *Required for some:* SAT or ACT (for admission). *Recommended:* SAT or ACT (for admission).

Costs (2010–11) *One-time required fee:* $900. *Tuition:* state resident $12,750 full-time, $110 per quarter hour part-time. Full-time tuition and fees vary according to location. Part-time tuition and fees vary according to course load and location. *Required fees:* $897 full-time, $17 per quarter hour part-time, $25 per term part-time. *Room and board:* $6150. *Payment plan:* installment. *Waivers:* senior citizens and employees or children of employees.

Financial Aid Of all full-time matriculated undergraduates who enrolled in 2009, 50 Federal Work-Study jobs (averaging $1421).

Applying *Options:* electronic application, early admission, deferred entrance. *Application fee:* $35. *Required:* high school transcript. *Application deadlines:* rolling (freshmen), rolling (transfers).

Freshman Application Contact Georgia Military College, 201 East Greene Street, Old Capitol Building, Milledgeville, GA 31061-3398. *Phone:* 478-

387-4948. *Toll-free phone:* 800-342-0413. *Web site:* http://www.gmc.cc.ga.us/.

Georgia Northwestern Technical College
Rome, Georgia

- **State-supported** 2-year, founded 1962, part of Technical College System of Georgia
- **Coed,** 6,697 undergraduate students, 53% full-time, 64% women, 36% men

Undergraduates 3,555 full-time, 3,142 part-time. 0.9% are from out of state; 11% Black or African American, non-Hispanic/Latino; 2% Hispanic/Latino; 0.5% Asian, non-Hispanic/Latino; 0.3% American Indian or Alaska Native, non-Hispanic/Latino; 2% Two or more races, non-Hispanic/Latino. *Retention:* 57% of full-time freshmen returned.
Freshmen *Admission:* 1,018 enrolled.
Majors Accounting; child development; computer programming; criminal justice/safety; environmental engineering technology; fire science/firefighting; information science/studies; legal assistant/paralegal; marketing/marketing management; medical office management; respiratory therapy technician; surgical technology; web page, digital/multimedia and information resources design.
Academics *Calendar:* quarters. *Degree:* certificates, diplomas, and associate. *Special study options:* distance learning.
Student Life *Housing:* college housing not available.
Costs (2010–11) *Tuition:* state resident $2025 full-time, $45 per credit hour part-time; nonresident $4050 full-time, $90 per credit hour part-time. *Required fees:* $243 full-time.
Applying *Options:* early admission. *Application fee:* $20. *Required:* high school transcript.
Freshman Application Contact Georgia Northwestern Technical College, One Maurice Culberson Drive, Rome, GA 30161. *Phone:* 706-295-6933. *Web site:* http://www.gntc.edu/.

Georgia Perimeter College
Decatur, Georgia

- **State-supported** 2-year, founded 1964, part of University System of Georgia
- **Suburban** 100-acre campus with easy access to Atlanta
- **Coed**

Undergraduates 11,522 full-time, 13,027 part-time. 10% are from out of state; 5% transferred in.
Faculty *Student/faculty ratio:* 24:1.
Academics *Calendar:* semesters. *Degree:* certificates and associate. *Special study options:* academic remediation for entering students, adult/continuing education programs, advanced placement credit, distance learning, English as a second language, honors programs, part-time degree program, services for LD students, study abroad, summer session for credit. *ROTC:* Army (c).
Student Life *Campus security:* 24-hour emergency response devices and patrols, late-night transport/escort service.
Athletics Member NJCAA.
Standardized Tests *Recommended:* SAT or ACT (for admission).
Financial Aid Of all full-time matriculated undergraduates who enrolled in 2009, 218 Federal Work-Study jobs (averaging $3000).
Applying *Options:* electronic application, early admission. *Application fee:* $20. *Required:* high school transcript.
Freshman Application Contact Georgia Perimeter College, 3251 Panthersville Road, Decatur, GA 30034-3897. *Phone:* 678-891-3250. *Toll-free phone:* 888-696-2780. *Web site:* http://www.gpc.edu/.

Gordon College
Barnesville, Georgia

Freshman Application Contact Gordon College, 419 College Drive, Barnesville, GA 30204-1762. *Phone:* 678-359-5021. *Toll-free phone:* 800-282-6504. *Web site:* http://www.gdn.edu/.

Gupton-Jones College of Funeral Service
Decatur, Georgia

Freshman Application Contact Ms. Beverly Wheaton, Registrar, Gupton-Jones College of Funeral Service, 5141 Snapfinger Woods Drive, Decatur, GA 30035-4022. *Phone:* 770-593-2257. *Toll-free phone:* 800-848-5352. *Web site:* http://www.gupton-jones.edu/.

Gwinnett Technical College
Lawrenceville, Georgia

- **State-supported** 2-year, founded 1984, part of Technical College System of Georgia
- **Suburban** 93-acre campus with easy access to Atlanta
- **Coed,** 7,100 undergraduate students, 46% full-time, 60% women, 40% men

Undergraduates 3,285 full-time, 3,815 part-time. 0.1% are from out of state; 35% Black or African American, non-Hispanic/Latino; 5% Hispanic/Latino; 7% Asian, non-Hispanic/Latino; 0.2% Native Hawaiian or other Pacific Islander, non-Hispanic/Latino; 0.4% American Indian or Alaska Native, non-Hispanic/Latino; 2% Two or more races, non-Hispanic/Latino; 3% Race/ethnicity unknown. *Retention:* 54% of full-time freshmen returned.
Freshmen *Admission:* 830 enrolled.
Majors Accounting; administrative assistant and secretarial science; automobile/automotive mechanics technology; building/construction finishing, management, and inspection related; business administration and management; computer programming; computer science; computer systems networking and telecommunications; drafting and design technology; electrical, electronic and communications engineering technology; emergency medical technology (EMT paramedic); horticultural science; hotel/motel administration; information science/studies; interior design; machine tool technology; management information systems; marketing/marketing management; medical/clinical assistant; medical radiologic technology; ornamental horticulture; photography; physical therapy; physical therapy technology; respiratory care therapy; tourism and travel services management; veterinary/animal health technology.
Academics *Calendar:* quarters. *Degree:* certificates, diplomas, and associate. *Special study options:* distance learning.
Library Gwinnett Technical Institute Media Center.
Student Life *Housing:* college housing not available.
Costs (2010–11) *Tuition:* state resident $2025 full-time, $45 per credit hour part-time; nonresident $4050 full-time, $90 per credit hour part-time. *Required fees:* $309 full-time.
Financial Aid Of all full-time matriculated undergraduates who enrolled in 2009, 20 Federal Work-Study jobs (averaging $2100).
Applying *Options:* early admission. *Application fee:* $20. *Required:* high school transcript.
Freshman Application Contact Gwinnett Technical College, 5150 Sugarloaf Parkway, Lawrenceville, GA 30043-5702. *Phone:* 678-762-7580 Ext. 434. *Web site:* http://www.gwinnetttech.edu/.

Heart of Georgia Technical College
Dublin, Georgia

- **State-supported** 2-year, founded 1984, part of Technical College System of Georgia
- **Small-town** campus with easy access to Atlanta
- **Coed,** 1,817 undergraduate students, 48% full-time, 58% women, 42% men

Undergraduates 875 full-time, 942 part-time. 44% Black or African American, non-Hispanic/Latino; 0.3% Hispanic/Latino; 0.1% Asian, non-Hispanic/Latino; 0.3% Native Hawaiian or other Pacific Islander, non-Hispanic/Latino; 0.2% American Indian or Alaska Native, non-Hispanic/Latino; 0.3% Two or more races, non-Hispanic/Latino; 0.7% Race/ethnicity unknown. *Retention:* 54% of full-time freshmen returned.
Freshmen *Admission:* 264 enrolled.
Majors Business, management, and marketing related; child development; criminal justice/safety; electrical, electronic and communications engineering technology; health information/medical records technology; machine tool technology; marketing/marketing management; medical radiologic technology; respiratory therapy technician.
Academics *Calendar:* quarters. *Degree:* certificates, diplomas, and associate. *Special study options:* distance learning.
Student Life *Housing:* college housing not available.
Costs (2010–11) *Tuition:* state resident $2025 full-time, $45 per credit hour part-time; nonresident $4050 full-time, $90 per credit hour part-time. *Required fees:* $255 full-time.
Applying *Options:* early admission. *Application fee:* $15. *Required:* high school transcript.
Freshman Application Contact Heart of Georgia Technical College, 560 Pinehill Road, Dublin, GA 31021. *Phone:* 478-274-7837. *Web site:* http://www.heartofgatech.edu/.

High-Tech Institute
Marietta, Georgia

Director of Admissions Frank Webster, Office Manager, High-Tech Institute, 1090 Northchase Parkway, Suite 150, Marietta, GA 30067. *Phone:* 770-988-

9877. *Toll-free phone:* 800-987-0110. *Fax:* 770-988-8824. *E-mail:* ckusema@hightechschools.com. *Web site:* http://www.high-techinstitute.com/.

Interactive College of Technology
Chamblee, Georgia

Freshman Application Contact Director of Admissions, Interactive College of Technology, 5303 New Peachtree Road, Chamblee, GA 30341. *Phone:* 770-216-2960. *Toll-free phone:* 800-447-2011. *Fax:* 770-216-2988. *Web site:* http://www.ict-ils.edu/.

ITT Technical Institute
Atlanta, Georgia

- **Proprietary** primarily 2-year, part of ITT Educational Services, Inc.
- **Coed**

Majors CAD/CADD drafting/design technology; computer and information systems security; computer engineering technology; computer software engineering; computer software technology; construction management; criminal justice/law enforcement administration; design and visual communications; electrical, electronic and communications engineering technology; legal assistant/paralegal; project management; system, networking, and LAN/WAN management.
Academics *Degrees:* associate and bachelor's.
Student Life *Housing:* college housing not available.
Freshman Application Contact Director of Recruitment, ITT Technical Institute, 485 Oak Place, Suite 800, Atlanta, GA 30349. *Phone:* 404-765-4600. *Toll-free phone:* 877-488-6102. *Web site:* http://www.itt-tech.edu/.

ITT Technical Institute
Duluth, Georgia

- **Proprietary** primarily 2-year, founded 2003, part of ITT Educational Services, Inc.
- **Coed**

Majors CAD/CADD drafting/design technology; computer and information systems security; computer engineering technology; computer software engineering; computer software technology; construction management; criminal justice/law enforcement administration; design and visual communications; electrical, electronic and communications engineering technology; game and interactive media design; legal assistant/paralegal; project management; system, networking, and LAN/WAN management; web page, digital/multimedia and information resources design.
Academics *Calendar:* quarters. *Degrees:* associate and bachelor's.
Student Life *Housing:* college housing not available.
Freshman Application Contact Director of Recruitment, ITT Technical Institute, 10700 Abbotts Bridge Road, Duluth, GA 30097. *Phone:* 678-957-8510. *Toll-free phone:* 866-489-8818. *Web site:* http://www.itt-tech.edu/.

ITT Technical Institute
Kennesaw, Georgia

- **Proprietary** primarily 2-year, founded 2004, part of ITT Educational Services, Inc.
- **Coed**

Majors CAD/CADD drafting/design technology; computer and information systems security; computer engineering technology; computer software engineering; computer software technology; construction management; criminal justice/law enforcement administration; design and visual communications; electrical, electronic and communications engineering technology; game and interactive media design; legal assistant/paralegal; project management; system, networking, and LAN/WAN management; web page, digital/multimedia and information resources design.
Academics *Calendar:* quarters. *Degrees:* associate and bachelor's.
Freshman Application Contact Director of Recruitment, ITT Technical Institute, 2065 ITT Tech Way, Kennesaw, GA 30144. *Phone:* 770-426-2300. *Toll-free phone:* 877-231-6415. *Web site:* http://www.itt-tech.edu/.

Lanier Technical College
Oakwood, Georgia

- **State-supported** 2-year, founded 1964, part of Technical College System of Georgia
- **Coed**, 4,432 undergraduate students, 42% full-time, 64% women, 36% men

Undergraduates 1,865 full-time, 2,567 part-time. 10% Black or African American, non-Hispanic/Latino; 5% Hispanic/Latino; 2% Asian, non-His-panic/Latino; 0.2% Native Hawaiian or other Pacific Islander, non-Hispanic/Latino; 0.6% American Indian or Alaska Native, non-Hispanic/Latino; 0.4% Two or more races, non-Hispanic/Latino; 1% Race/ethnicity unknown. *Retention:* 59% of full-time freshmen returned.
Freshmen *Admission:* 757 enrolled.
Majors Accounting; administrative assistant and secretarial science; banking and financial support services; child development; computer and information systems security; computer programming; computer science; computer systems networking and telecommunications; criminal justice/safety; drafting and design technology; electrical, electronic and communications engineering technology; fire science/firefighting; health professions related; industrial technology; information science/studies; interior design; marketing/marketing management; medical radiologic technology; occupational safety and health technology; surgical technology; web page, digital/multimedia and information resources design.
Academics *Calendar:* quarters. *Degree:* certificates, diplomas, and associate. *Special study options:* distance learning.
Student Life *Housing:* college housing not available.
Costs (2010–11) *Tuition:* state resident $2025 full-time, $45 per credit hour part-time; nonresident $4050 full-time, $90 per credit hour part-time. *Required fees:* $270 full-time.
Applying *Options:* early admission. *Application fee:* $20. *Required:* high school transcript.
Freshman Application Contact Lanier Technical College, 2990 Landrum Education Drive, PO Box 58, Oakwood, GA 30566. *Phone:* 770-531-6332. *Web site:* http://www.laniertech.edu/.

Le Cordon Bleu College of Culinary Arts, Atlanta
Tucker, Georgia

Freshman Application Contact Admissions Office, Le Cordon Bleu College of Culinary Arts, Atlanta, 1957 Lakeside Parkway, Tucker, GA 30084. *Toll-free phone:* 888-549-8222. *Web site:* http://www.atlantaculinary.com/.

Middle Georgia College
Cochran, Georgia

- **State-supported** primarily 2-year, founded 1884, part of University System of Georgia
- **Small-town** 165-acre campus
- **Endowment** $847,031
- **Coed**

Undergraduates 2,586 full-time, 1,028 part-time. Students come from 36 states and territories; 31 other countries; 4% are from out of state; 7% transferred in; 35% live on campus. *Retention:* 63% of full-time freshmen returned.
Faculty *Student/faculty ratio:* 22:1.
Academics *Calendar:* semesters. *Degrees:* certificates, associate, and bachelor's. *Special study options:* academic remediation for entering students, accelerated degree program, advanced placement credit, cooperative education, distance learning, double majors, honors programs, internships, part-time degree program, student-designed majors, study abroad, summer session for credit.
Student Life *Campus security:* 24-hour emergency response devices and patrols, late-night transport/escort service, controlled dormitory access, patrols by police officers.
Athletics Member NJCAA.
Standardized Tests *Required for some:* SAT or ACT (for admission). *Recommended:* SAT or ACT (for admission).
Costs (2010–11) *Tuition:* state resident $2694 full-time, $90 per credit hour part-time; nonresident $10,176 full-time, $340 per credit hour part-time. Full-time tuition and fees vary according to course load and program. Part-time tuition and fees vary according to course load and program. *Required fees:* $574 full-time. *Room and board:* $6980. Room and board charges vary according to board plan and housing facility.
Financial Aid Of all full-time matriculated undergraduates who enrolled in 2009, 91 Federal Work-Study jobs (averaging $692).
Applying *Options:* electronic application, early admission, deferred entrance. *Application fee:* $20. *Required:* high school transcript, minimum 2.0 GPA. *Required for some:* essay or personal statement, minimum 3.5 GPA, 3 letters of recommendation, interview.
Freshman Application Contact Ms. Jennifer Brannon, Director of Admissions, Middle Georgia College, 1100 2nd Street, Southeast, Cochran, GA 31014. *Phone:* 478-934-3103. *Fax:* 478-934-3403. *E-mail:* admissions@mgc.edu. *Web site:* http://www.mgc.edu/.

See next page for Display and page 422 for the College Close-Up.

Middle Georgia Technical College

Warner Robbins, Georgia

- **State-supported** 2-year, founded 1973, part of Technical College System of Georgia

- **Coed,** 4,205 undergraduate students, 64% full-time, 52% women, 48% men

Undergraduates 2,696 full-time, 1,509 part-time. 2% are from out of state; 38% Black or African American, non-Hispanic/Latino; 2% Hispanic/Latino; 1% Asian, non-Hispanic/Latino; 0.2% Native Hawaiian or other Pacific Islander, non-Hispanic/Latino; 0.4% American Indian or Alaska Native, non-Hispanic/Latino; 1% Two or more races, non-Hispanic/Latino; 3% Race/ethnicity unknown. *Retention:* 50% of full-time freshmen returned.

Freshmen *Admission:* 970 enrolled.

Majors Accounting; administrative assistant and secretarial science; airframe mechanics and aircraft maintenance technology; child development; computer systems networking and telecommunications; dental hygiene; drafting and design technology; information science/studies; marketing/marketing management; medical radiologic technology; web page, digital/multimedia and information resources design.

Academics *Calendar:* quarters. *Degree:* certificates, diplomas, and associate. *Special study options:* distance learning.

Student Life *Housing:* college housing not available.

Costs (2010–11) *Tuition:* state resident $2025 full-time, $45 per credit hour part-time; nonresident $4050 full-time, $90 per credit hour part-time. *Required fees:* $243 full-time.

Applying *Options:* early admission. *Application fee:* $20. *Required:* high school transcript.

Freshman Application Contact Middle Georgia Technical College, 80 Cohen Walker Drive, Warner Robbins, GA 31088. *Phone:* 478-988-6800 Ext. 4023. *Toll-free phone:* 800-474-1031. *Web site:* http://www.middlegatech.edu/.

Moultrie Technical College

Moultrie, Georgia

- **State-supported** 2-year, founded 1964, part of Technical College System of Georgia

- **Coed,** 2,569 undergraduate students, 54% full-time, 63% women, 37% men

Undergraduates 1,391 full-time, 1,178 part-time. 38% Black or African American, non-Hispanic/Latino; 3% Hispanic/Latino; 0.4% Asian, non-Hispanic/Latino; 0.1% American Indian or Alaska Native, non-Hispanic/Latino; 0.4% Two or more races, non-Hispanic/Latino; 0.6% Race/ethnicity unknown. *Retention:* 54% of full-time freshmen returned.

Freshmen *Admission:* 416 enrolled.

Majors Accounting; administrative assistant and secretarial science; child development; civil engineering technology; computer systems networking and telecommunications; criminal justice/safety; electrical, electronic and communications engineering technology; information science/studies; marketing/marketing management; web page, digital/multimedia and information resources design.

Academics *Calendar:* quarters. *Degree:* certificates, diplomas, and associate. *Special study options:* distance learning.

Student Life *Housing:* college housing not available.

Costs (2010–11) *Tuition:* state resident $2025 full-time, $45 per credit hour part-time; nonresident $4050 full-time, $90 per credit hour part-time. *Required fees:* $243 full-time.

Applying *Options:* early admission. *Application fee:* $20. *Required:* high school transcript.

Freshman Application Contact Moultrie Technical College, 800 Veterans Parkway North, Moultrie, GA 31788. *Phone:* 229-217-4144. *Web site:* http://www.moultrietech.edu/.

North Georgia Technical College
Clarkesville, Georgia

- **State-supported** 2-year, founded 1943, part of Technical College System of Georgia
- **Coed,** 2,810 undergraduate students, 62% full-time, 59% women, 41% men

Undergraduates 1,739 full-time, 1,071 part-time. 2% are from out of state; 6% Black or African American, non-Hispanic/Latino; 2% Hispanic/Latino; 0.9% Asian, non-Hispanic/Latino; 0.5% American Indian or Alaska Native, non-Hispanic/Latino; 0.7% Two or more races, non-Hispanic/Latino; 0.5% Race/ethnicity unknown. *Retention:* 54% of full-time freshmen returned.
Freshmen *Admission:* 687 enrolled.
Majors Administrative assistant and secretarial science; computer systems networking and telecommunications; criminal justice/safety; culinary arts; heating, ventilation, air conditioning and refrigeration engineering technology; horticultural science; industrial technology; parks, recreation and leisure facilities management; turf and turfgrass management; web page, digital/multimedia and information resources design.
Academics *Calendar:* quarters. *Degree:* certificates, diplomas, and associate. *Special study options:* distance learning.
Student Life *Housing Options:* coed. Campus housing is university owned.
Costs (2010–11) *Tuition:* state resident $2025 full-time, $45 per credit hour part-time; nonresident $4050 full-time, $90 per credit hour part-time. *Required fees:* $270 full-time.
Applying *Options:* early admission. *Application fee:* $15. *Required:* high school transcript.
Freshman Application Contact North Georgia Technical College, 1500 Georgia Highway 197, North, PO Box 65, Clarkesville, GA 30523. *Phone:* 706-754-7724. *Web site:* http://www.northgatech.edu/.

Ogeechee Technical College
Statesboro, Georgia

- **State-supported** 2-year, founded 1989, part of Technical College System of Georgia
- **Small-town** campus
- **Coed,** 2,819 undergraduate students, 58% full-time, 66% women, 34% men

Undergraduates 1,625 full-time, 1,194 part-time. 1% are from out of state; 37% Black or African American, non-Hispanic/Latino; 0.5% Hispanic/Latino; 0.5% Asian, non-Hispanic/Latino; 0.1% Native Hawaiian or other Pacific Islander, non-Hispanic/Latino; 0.2% American Indian or Alaska Native, non-Hispanic/Latino; 1% Two or more races, non-Hispanic/Latino; 0.9% Race/ethnicity unknown. *Retention:* 55% of full-time freshmen returned.
Freshmen *Admission:* 510 enrolled.
Majors Accounting; administrative assistant and secretarial science; agribusiness; automobile/automotive mechanics technology; banking and financial support services; child development; computer systems networking and telecommunications; construction trades; culinary arts; dental hygiene; forest technology; funeral service and mortuary science; health information/medical records technology; hotel/motel administration; information science/studies; interior design; legal assistant/paralegal; marketing/marketing management; opticianry; tourism and travel services management; veterinary/animal health technology; water quality and wastewater treatment management and recycling technology; wildlife, fish and wildlands science and management; wood science and wood products/pulp and paper technology.
Academics *Calendar:* quarters. *Degree:* certificates, diplomas, and associate. *Special study options:* distance learning.
Student Life *Housing:* college housing not available.
Costs (2010–11) *Tuition:* state resident $2025 full-time, $45 per credit hour part-time; nonresident $4050 full-time, $90 per credit hour part-time. *Required fees:* $258 full-time.
Applying *Options:* early admission. *Application fee:* $15. *Required:* high school transcript.
Freshman Application Contact Ogeechee Technical College, One Joe Kennedy Boulevard, Statesboro, GA 30458. *Phone:* 912-871-1600. *Toll-free phone:* 800-646-1316. *Web site:* http://www.ogeecheetech.edu/.

Okefenokee Technical College
Waycross, Georgia

- **State-supported** 2-year, part of Technical College System of Georgia
- **Small-town** campus
- **Coed,** 1,680 undergraduate students, 42% full-time, 64% women, 36% men

Undergraduates 711 full-time, 969 part-time. 27% Black or African American, non-Hispanic/Latino; 1% Hispanic/Latino; 0.5% Asian, non-Hispanic/Latino; 0.6% American Indian or Alaska Native, non-Hispanic/Latino; 0.4%

Two or more races, non-Hispanic/Latino; 0.2% Race/ethnicity unknown. *Retention:* 47% of full-time freshmen returned.
Freshmen *Admission:* 371 enrolled.
Majors Administrative assistant and secretarial science; child development; clinical/medical laboratory technology; computer systems networking and telecommunications; computer technology/computer systems technology; criminal justice/police science; forest technology; information science/studies; occupational safety and health technology; respiratory therapy technician; surgical technology.
Academics *Calendar:* quarters. *Degree:* certificates, diplomas, and associate. *Special study options:* distance learning.
Student Life *Housing:* college housing not available.
Costs (2010–11) *Tuition:* state resident $2025 full-time, $45 per credit hour part-time; nonresident $4050 full-time, $90 per credit hour part-time. *Required fees:* $243 full-time.
Applying *Options:* early admission. *Application fee:* $15. *Required:* high school transcript.
Freshman Application Contact Okefenokee Technical College, 1701 Carswell Avenue, Waycross, GA 31503. *Phone:* 912-338-5251. *Web site:* http://www.okefenokeetech.edu/.

Sandersville Technical College
Sandersville, Georgia

- **State-supported** 2-year, part of Technical College System of Georgia
- **Coed,** 1,028 undergraduate students, 40% full-time, 55% women, 45% men

Undergraduates 414 full-time, 614 part-time. 62% Black or African American, non-Hispanic/Latino; 0.1% Hispanic/Latino; 0.5% Asian, non-Hispanic/Latino; 0.3% American Indian or Alaska Native, non-Hispanic/Latino; 0.3% Two or more races, non-Hispanic/Latino; 1% Race/ethnicity unknown. *Retention:* 65% of full-time freshmen returned.
Freshmen *Admission:* 211 enrolled.
Majors Accounting; administrative assistant and secretarial science; child development; computer systems networking and telecommunications; information science/studies.
Academics *Calendar:* quarters. *Degree:* certificates, diplomas, and associate. *Special study options:* distance learning.
Student Life *Housing:* college housing not available.
Costs (2010–11) *Tuition:* state resident $2025 full-time, $45 per credit hour part-time; nonresident $4050 full-time, $90 per credit hour part-time. *Required fees:* $243 full-time.
Applying *Options:* early admission. *Application fee:* $25. *Required:* high school transcript.
Freshman Application Contact Sandersville Technical College, 1189 Deepstep Road, Sandersville, GA 31082. *Phone:* 478-553-2065. *Web site:* http://www.sandersvilletech.edu/.

Savannah River College
Augusta, Georgia

Admissions Office Contact Savannah River College, 2528 Center West Parkway, Augusta, GA 30909. *Web site:* http://www.savannahrivercollege.edu/.

Savannah Technical College
Savannah, Georgia

- **State-supported** 2-year, founded 1929, part of Technical College System of Georgia
- **Urban** 15-acre campus
- **Coed,** 5,777 undergraduate students, 44% full-time, 67% women, 33% men

Undergraduates 2,558 full-time, 3,219 part-time. 1% are from out of state; 52% Black or African American, non-Hispanic/Latino; 3% Hispanic/Latino; 2% Asian, non-Hispanic/Latino; 0.3% Native Hawaiian or other Pacific Islander, non-Hispanic/Latino; 0.4% American Indian or Alaska Native, non-Hispanic/Latino; 3% Two or more races, non-Hispanic/Latino; 0.6% Race/ethnicity unknown; 0.1% international. *Retention:* 48% of full-time freshmen returned.
Freshmen *Admission:* 1,156 enrolled.
Majors Accounting; administrative assistant and secretarial science; automobile/automotive mechanics technology; child development; computer systems networking and telecommunications; criminal justice/safety; culinary arts; electrical, electronic and communications engineering technology; fire science/firefighting; heating, ventilation, air conditioning and refrigeration engineering technology; hotel/motel administration; industrial technology; information technology; marketing/marketing management; surgical technology; tourism and travel services management.

Academics *Calendar:* quarters. *Degree:* certificates, diplomas, and associate. *Special study options:* distance learning.
Student Life *Housing:* college housing not available.
Costs (2010–11) *Tuition:* state resident $2025 full-time, $45 per credit hour part-time; nonresident $4050 full-time, $90 per credit hour part-time. *Required fees:* $243 full-time.
Applying *Options:* early admission. *Application fee:* $15. *Required:* high school transcript.
Freshman Application Contact Savannah Technical College, 5717 White Bluff Road, Savannah, GA 31405. *Phone:* 912-443-5711. *Toll-free phone:* 800-769-6362. *Web site:* http://www.savannahtech.edu/.

Southeastern Technical College
Vidalia, Georgia

- **State-supported** 2-year, founded 1989, part of Technical College System of Georgia
- **Coed,** 1,995 undergraduate students, 49% full-time, 71% women, 29% men

Undergraduates 985 full-time, 1,010 part-time. 36% Black or African American, non-Hispanic/Latino; 3% Hispanic/Latino; 0.2% Asian, non-Hispanic/Latino; 0.1% Native Hawaiian or other Pacific Islander, non-Hispanic/Latino; 0.2% American Indian or Alaska Native, non-Hispanic/Latino; 0.3% Race/ethnicity unknown. *Retention:* 55% of full-time freshmen returned.
Freshmen *Admission:* 249 enrolled.
Majors Accounting; administrative assistant and secretarial science; child development; computer systems networking and telecommunications; criminal justice/safety; dental hygiene; design and visual communications; electrical, electronic and communications engineering technology; information science/studies; marketing/marketing management; medical radiologic technology; respiratory therapy technician; web page, digital/multimedia and information resources design.
Academics *Calendar:* quarters. *Degree:* certificates, diplomas, and associate. *Special study options:* distance learning.
Student Life *Housing:* college housing not available.
Costs (2010–11) *Tuition:* state resident $2025 full-time, $45 per credit hour part-time; nonresident $4050 full-time, $90 per credit hour part-time. *Required fees:* $243 full-time.
Applying *Options:* early admission. *Application fee:* $25. *Required:* high school transcript.
Freshman Application Contact Southeastern Technical College, 3001 East First Street, Vidalia, GA 30474. *Phone:* 912-538-3121. *Web site:* http://www.southeasterntech.edu/.

Southern Crescent Technical College
Griffin, Georgia

- **State-supported** 2-year, founded 1965, part of Technical College System of Georgia
- **Small-town** 10-acre campus with easy access to Atlanta
- **Coed,** 6,227 undergraduate students, 52% full-time, 67% women, 33% men

Undergraduates 3,222 full-time, 3,005 part-time. 0.1% are from out of state; 42% Black or African American, non-Hispanic/Latino; 1% Hispanic/Latino; 1% Asian, non-Hispanic/Latino; 0.1% Native Hawaiian or other Pacific Islander, non-Hispanic/Latino; 0.2% American Indian or Alaska Native, non-Hispanic/Latino; 2% Two or more races, non-Hispanic/Latino; 0.6% Race/ethnicity unknown. *Retention:* 47% of full-time freshmen returned.
Freshmen *Admission:* 847 enrolled.
Majors Accounting; administrative assistant and secretarial science; automobile/automotive mechanics technology; business administration and management; child development; computer and information systems security; computer programming; computer systems networking and telecommunications; criminal justice/safety; drafting and design technology; electrical, electronic and communications engineering technology; emergency medical technology (EMT paramedic); heating, ventilation, air conditioning and refrigeration engineering technology; horticultural science; industrial technology; legal assistant/paralegal; manufacturing engineering technology; marketing/marketing management; medical radiologic technology; pharmacy technician; respiratory therapy technician; surgical technology; web page, digital/multimedia and information resources design.
Academics *Calendar:* quarters. *Degree:* certificates, diplomas, and associate. *Special study options:* distance learning.
Library Griffin Technical College Library.
Costs (2010–11) *Tuition:* state resident $2025 full-time, $45 per credit hour part-time; nonresident $4050 full-time, $90 per credit hour part-time. *Required fees:* $243 full-time.
Applying *Options:* early admission. *Application fee:* $20. *Required:* high school transcript.

Freshman Application Contact Southern Crescent Technical College, 501 Varsity Road, Griffin, GA 30223. *Phone:* 770-646-6160. *Web site:* http://www.sctech.edu/.

South Georgia College
Douglas, Georgia

- **State-supported** 2-year, founded 1906, part of University System of Georgia
- **Small-town** 250-acre campus
- **Endowment** $153,798
- **Coed**

Undergraduates 1,487 full-time, 513 part-time. Students come from 13 states and territories; 2% are from out of state; 6% transferred in.
Faculty *Student/faculty ratio:* 27:1.
Academics *Calendar:* semesters. *Degree:* certificates and associate. *Special study options:* academic remediation for entering students, adult/continuing education programs, advanced placement credit, part-time degree program, services for LD students, study abroad, summer session for credit.
Student Life *Campus security:* 24-hour emergency response devices and patrols, controlled dormitory access.
Athletics Member NJCAA.
Costs (2010–11) *Tuition:* state resident $2398 full-time, $80 per credit hour part-time; nonresident $9276 full-time, $310 per credit hour part-time. *Required fees:* $760 full-time, $760 per term part-time. *Room and board:* $6850; room only: $4250. Room and board charges vary according to board plan.
Applying *Options:* electronic application, early admission, deferred entrance. *Application fee:* $20. *Required:* high school transcript.
Freshman Application Contact South Georgia College, 100 West College Park Drive, Douglas, GA 31533-5098. *Phone:* 912-260-4419. *Toll-free phone:* 800-342-6364. *Web site:* http://www.sgc.edu/.

South Georgia Technical College
Americus, Georgia

- **State-supported** 2-year, founded 1948, part of Technical College System of Georgia
- **Coed,** 2,761 undergraduate students, 63% full-time, 54% women, 46% men

Undergraduates 1,729 full-time, 1,032 part-time. 2% are from out of state; 60% Black or African American, non-Hispanic/Latino; 0.8% Hispanic/Latino; 0.3% Asian, non-Hispanic/Latino; 0.1% American Indian or Alaska Native, non-Hispanic/Latino; 1% Race/ethnicity unknown. *Retention:* 52% of full-time freshmen returned.
Freshmen *Admission:* 738 enrolled.
Majors Accounting; administrative assistant and secretarial science; child development; computer systems networking and telecommunications; criminal justice/safety; culinary arts; drafting and design technology; electrical, electronic and communications engineering technology; heating, ventilation, air conditioning and refrigeration engineering technology; horticultural science; industrial technology; information science/studies; legal assistant/paralegal; manufacturing engineering technology; marketing/marketing management.
Academics *Calendar:* quarters. *Degree:* certificates, diplomas, and associate. *Special study options:* distance learning.
Student Life *Housing Options:* men-only, women-only. Campus housing is university owned.
Costs (2010–11) *Tuition:* state resident $2025 full-time, $45 per credit hour part-time; nonresident $4050 full-time, $90 per credit hour part-time. *Required fees:* $270 full-time.
Applying *Options:* early admission. *Application fee:* $15. *Required:* high school transcript.
Freshman Application Contact South Georgia Technical College, 900 South Georgia Tech Parkway, Americus, GA 31709. *Phone:* 229-931-2299. *Web site:* http://www.southgatech.edu/.

Southwest Georgia Technical College
Thomasville, Georgia

- **State-supported** 2-year, founded 1963, part of Technical College System of Georgia
- **Coed,** 1,678 undergraduate students, 39% full-time, 67% women, 33% men

Undergraduates 648 full-time, 1,030 part-time. 1% are from out of state; 36% Black or African American, non-Hispanic/Latino; 1% Hispanic/Latino; 0.6% Asian, non-Hispanic/Latino; 0.5% American Indian or Alaska Native, non-Hispanic/Latino; 0.2% Two or more races, non-Hispanic/Latino; 0.7% Race/ethnicity unknown. *Retention:* 50% of full-time freshmen returned.
Freshmen *Admission:* 249 enrolled.

Majors Accounting; administrative assistant and secretarial science; agricultural mechanization; child development; computer systems networking and telecommunications; criminal justice/safety; information science/studies; medical radiologic technology; registered nursing/registered nurse; respiratory care therapy; surgical technology.

Academics *Calendar:* quarters. *Degree:* certificates, diplomas, and associate. *Special study options:* distance learning.

Student Life *Housing:* college housing not available.

Costs (2010–11) *Tuition:* state resident $2025 full-time, $45 per credit hour part-time; nonresident $4050 full-time, $90 per credit hour part-time. *Required fees:* $243 full-time.

Applying *Options:* electronic application, early admission. *Application fee:* $15. *Required:* high school transcript.

Freshman Application Contact Southwest Georgia Technical College, 15689 US 19 North, Thomasville, GA 31792. *Phone:* 229-225-5089. *Web site:* http://www.southwestgatech.edu/.

Waycross College

Waycross, Georgia

- **State-supported** 2-year, founded 1976, part of University System of Georgia
- **Small-town** 150-acre campus
- **Coed**, 1,118 undergraduate students

Undergraduates 3% are from out of state. *Retention:* 58% of full-time freshmen returned.

Freshmen *Admission:* 1,118 applied, 1,118 admitted.

Faculty *Student/faculty ratio:* 19:1.

Majors Health professions related; liberal arts and sciences/liberal studies; precision production related.

Academics *Calendar:* semesters. *Degree:* certificates and associate. *Special study options:* academic remediation for entering students, adult/continuing education programs, advanced placement credit, distance learning, off-campus study, part-time degree program, study abroad, summer session for credit.

Library Waycross College Library.

Student Life *Housing:* college housing not available. *Campus security:* late-night transport/escort service, security guards.

Athletics Member NJCAA. *Intercollegiate sports:* basketball M(s), softball W(s).

Standardized Tests *Recommended:* SAT or ACT (for admission).

Costs (2010–11) *Tuition:* state resident $2398 full-time, $80 per hour part-time; nonresident $9276 full-time, $310 per hour part-time. Full-time tuition and fees vary according to course load. Part-time tuition and fees vary according to course load. *Required fees:* $3 per hour part-time. *Waivers:* senior citizens.

Financial Aid Of all full-time matriculated undergraduates who enrolled in 2009, 20 Federal Work-Study jobs (averaging $2000).

Applying *Options:* electronic application, early admission, deferred entrance. *Application fee:* $20. *Required:* high school transcript. *Application deadlines:* rolling (freshmen), rolling (transfers). *Notification:* continuous (freshmen), continuous (transfers).

Freshman Application Contact Waycross College, 2001 South Georgia Parkway, Waycross, GA 31503-9248. *Phone:* 912-449-7600. *Web site:* http://www.waycross.edu/.

West Georgia Technical College

Waco, Georgia

- **State-supported** 2-year, founded 1966, part of Technical College System of Georgia
- **Coed**, 8,078 undergraduate students, 41% full-time, 69% women, 31% men

Undergraduates 3,308 full-time, 4,770 part-time. 3% are from out of state; 29% Black or African American, non-Hispanic/Latino; 2% Hispanic/Latino; 0.9% Asian, non-Hispanic/Latino; 0.1% Native Hawaiian or other Pacific Islander, non-Hispanic/Latino; 0.4% American Indian or Alaska Native, non-Hispanic/Latino; 0.1% Two or more races, non-Hispanic/Latino; 3% Race/ethnicity unknown. *Retention:* 51% of full-time freshmen returned.

Freshmen *Admission:* 1,138 enrolled.

Majors Accounting; administrative assistant and secretarial science; automobile/automotive mechanics technology; child development; computer systems networking and telecommunications; criminal justice/safety; electrical, electronic and communications engineering technology; fire science/firefighting; health information/medical records technology; industrial technology; information science/studies; marketing/marketing management; medical radiologic technology; pharmacy technician; plastics and polymer engineering technology; social work; web page, digital/multimedia and information resources design.

Academics *Calendar:* quarters. *Degree:* certificates, diplomas, and associate. *Special study options:* distance learning.

Student Life *Housing:* college housing not available.

Costs (2010–11) *Tuition:* state resident $2025 full-time, $45 per credit hour part-time; nonresident $4050 full-time, $90 per credit hour part-time. *Required fees:* $255 full-time.

Financial Aid Of all full-time matriculated undergraduates who enrolled in 2009, 68 Federal Work-Study jobs (averaging $800).

Applying *Options:* early admission. *Application fee:* $20. *Required:* high school transcript.

Freshman Application Contact West Georgia Technical College, 176 Murphy Campus Boulevard, Waco, GA 30182. *Phone:* 770-537-5719. *Web site:* http://www.westgatech.edu/.

Wiregrass Georgia Technical College

Valdosta, Georgia

- **State-supported** 2-year, founded 1963, part of Technical College System of Georgia
- **Suburban** 18-acre campus
- **Coed**, 5,408 undergraduate students, 55% full-time, 66% women, 34% men

Undergraduates 2,951 full-time, 2,457 part-time. 1% are from out of state; 39% Black or African American, non-Hispanic/Latino; 2% Hispanic/Latino; 0.6% Asian, non-Hispanic/Latino; 0.2% Native Hawaiian or other Pacific Islander, non-Hispanic/Latino; 0.2% American Indian or Alaska Native, non-Hispanic/Latino; 0.5% Two or more races, non-Hispanic/Latino; 3% Race/ethnicity unknown. *Retention:* 46% of full-time freshmen returned.

Freshmen *Admission:* 673 enrolled.

Majors Accounting; administrative assistant and secretarial science; banking and financial support services; child development; computer and information systems security; computer programming; computer systems networking and telecommunications; criminal justice/safety; drafting and design technology; e-commerce; fire science/firefighting; machine tool technology; marketing/marketing management; medical radiologic technology; web page, digital/multimedia and information resources design.

Academics *Calendar:* quarters. *Degree:* certificates, diplomas, and associate. *Special study options:* distance learning.

Student Life *Housing:* college housing not available.

Costs (2010–11) *Tuition:* state resident $2025 full-time, $45 per credit hour part-time; nonresident $4050 full-time, $90 per credit hour part-time. *Required fees:* $276 full-time.

Applying *Options:* early admission. *Application fee:* $20. *Required:* high school transcript.

Freshman Application Contact Wiregrass Georgia Technical College, 4089 Val Tech Road, Valdosta, GA 31602. *Phone:* 229-468-2278. *Web site:* http://www.wiregrass.edu/.

GUAM

Guam Community College

Barrigada, Guam

Freshman Application Contact Mr. Patrick L. Clymer, Registrar, Guam Community College, PO Box 23069, Sesame Street, Barrigada, GU 96921. *Phone:* 671-735-5561. *Fax:* 671-735-5531. *E-mail:* patrick.clymer@guamcc.edu. *Web site:* http://www.guamcc.net/.

HAWAII

Hawaii Community College

Hilo, Hawaii

Director of Admissions Mrs. Tammy M. Tanaka, Admissions Specialist, Hawaii Community College, 200 West Kawili Street, Hilo, HI 96720-4091. *Phone:* 808-974-7661. *Web site:* http://www.hawcc.hawaii.edu/.

Hawaii Tokai International College
Honolulu, Hawaii

- **Independent** 2-year, founded 1992, part of Tokai University Educational System (Japan)
- **Urban** campus
- **Coed,** 57 undergraduate students, 98% full-time, 54% women, 46% men

Undergraduates 56 full-time, 1 part-time. Students come from 3 states and territories; 3 other countries; 26% Race/ethnicity unknown; 74% international; 60% live on campus. *Retention:* 88% of full-time freshmen returned.

Freshmen *Admission:* 13 applied, 13 admitted, 13 enrolled. *Average high school GPA:* 3.

Faculty *Total:* 17, 35% full-time, 35% with terminal degrees. *Student/faculty ratio:* 4:1.

Majors Liberal arts and sciences/liberal studies.

Academics *Calendar:* quarters. *Degree:* certificates, diplomas, and associate. *Special study options:* English as a second language, part-time degree program, study abroad, summer session for credit.

Library The Learning Center with 7,000 titles, 35 serial subscriptions, 500 audiovisual materials, an OPAC.

Student Life *Housing Options:* Campus housing is university owned. *Activities and Organizations:* Running Club, Kendo Club, Music Club, Baseball Club, Phi Theta Kappa International Honor Society, Student Government. *Campus security:* 24-hour patrols. *Student services:* personal/psychological counseling.

Standardized Tests *Required for some:* TOEFL score of 450 PBT for international students.

Costs (2011–12) *Tuition:* $400 per credit hour part-time. Full-time tuition and fees vary according to course load and program. Part-time tuition and fees vary according to course load and program. *Required fees:* $140 per term part-time. *Room only:* Room and board charges vary according to board plan. *Payment plan:* installment. *Waivers:* employees or children of employees.

Applying *Options:* deferred entrance. *Application fee:* $50. *Required:* essay or personal statement, high school transcript, minimum 2.5 GPA. *Required for some:* interview. *Recommended:* 1 letter of recommendation. *Application deadlines:* rolling (freshmen), rolling (out-of-state freshmen), rolling (transfers). *Notification:* continuous (freshmen), continuous (out-of-state freshmen), continuous (transfers).

Freshman Application Contact Ms. Morna Dexter, Director, Student Services, Hawaii Tokai International College, 2241 Kapiolani Boulevard, Honolulu, HI 96826. *Phone:* 808-983-4187. *Fax:* 808-983-4173. *E-mail:* studentservices@tokai.edu. *Web site:* http://www.hawaiitokai.edu/.

Heald College–Honolulu
Honolulu, Hawaii

Freshman Application Contact Director of Admissions, Heald College–Honolulu, 1500 Kapiolani Boulevard, Honolulu, HI 96814. *Phone:* 808-955-1500. *Toll-free phone:* 800-755-3550. *Fax:* 808-955-6964. *E-mail:* honoluluinfo@heald.edu. *Web site:* http://www.heald.edu/.

Honolulu Community College
Honolulu, Hawaii

- **State-supported** 2-year, founded 1920, part of University of Hawaii System
- **Urban** 20-acre campus
- **Coed,** 4,567 undergraduate students, 36% full-time, 44% women, 56% men

Undergraduates 1,640 full-time, 2,927 part-time. Students come from 32 states and territories; 16 other countries; 2% are from out of state; 10% transferred in. *Retention:* 55% of full-time freshmen returned.

Freshmen *Admission:* 812 enrolled.

Faculty *Total:* 205, 63% full-time.

Majors Architectural engineering technology; automobile/automotive mechanics technology; avionics maintenance technology; carpentry; commercial and advertising art; community organization and advocacy; cosmetology; criminal justice/police science; drafting and design technology; electrical, electronic and communications engineering technology; engineering technology; fashion/apparel design; fire science/firefighting; food technology and processing; heating, air conditioning, ventilation and refrigeration maintenance technology; human services; kindergarten/preschool education; liberal arts and sciences/liberal studies; marine maintenance and ship repair technology; occupational safety and health technology; welding technology.

Academics *Calendar:* semesters. *Degree:* certificates and associate. *Special study options:* academic remediation for entering students, accelerated degree program, advanced placement credit, cooperative education, distance learning, English as a second language, internships, part-time degree program, services

for LD students, student-designed majors, summer session for credit. *ROTC:* Army (c), Air Force (c).

Library Honolulu Community College Library plus 1 other with 54,902 titles, 1,280 serial subscriptions, 858 audiovisual materials, an OPAC, a Web page.

Student Life *Housing:* college housing not available. *Activities and Organizations:* student-run newspaper, Phi Theta Kappa, Hui 'Oiwi, Fashion Society. *Campus security:* 24-hour emergency response devices. *Student services:* health clinic, personal/psychological counseling.

Standardized Tests *Required for some:* TOEFL required for international applicants.

Costs (2010–11) *Tuition:* state resident $2142 full-time, $88 per credit hour part-time; nonresident $6774 full-time, $281 per credit hour part-time. Full-time tuition and fees vary according to course load. Part-time tuition and fees vary according to course load. *Required fees:* $30 full-time, $1 per credit hour part-time, $10 per term part-time. *Payment plan:* installment. *Waivers:* employees or children of employees.

Financial Aid Of all full-time matriculated undergraduates who enrolled in 2009, 30 Federal Work-Study jobs (averaging $1600).

Applying *Options:* early admission. *Application deadlines:* 8/15 (freshmen), 8/15 (transfers). *Notification:* continuous until 8/15 (freshmen), continuous until 8/15 (transfers).

Freshman Application Contact Ms. Grace Funai, Admissions Office, Honolulu Community College, 874 Dillingham Boulevard, Honolulu, HI 96817. *Phone:* 808-845-9129. *E-mail:* honcc@hawaii.edu. *Web site:* http://www.honolulu.hawaii.edu/.

Kapiolani Community College
Honolulu, Hawaii

Freshman Application Contact Kapiolani Community College, 4303 Diamond Head Road, Honolulu, HI 96816-4421. *Phone:* 808-734-9555. *Web site:* http://kapiolani.hawaii.edu/page/home.

Kauai Community College
Lihue, Hawaii

- **State-supported** 2-year, founded 1965, part of University of Hawaii System
- **Small-town** 100-acre campus
- **Coed**

Academics *Calendar:* semesters. *Degree:* certificates and associate. *Special study options:* accelerated degree program, advanced placement credit, cooperative education, distance learning, English as a second language, internships, part-time degree program, services for LD students, summer session for credit.

Student Life *Campus security:* student patrols, 6-hour evening patrols by trained security personnel.

Costs (2010–11) *Tuition:* state resident $2640 full-time, $88 per credit part-time; nonresident $8430 full-time, $281 per credit part-time. Full-time tuition and fees vary according to course load. Part-time tuition and fees vary according to course load. *Required fees:* $30 per term part-time.

Financial Aid Of all full-time matriculated undergraduates who enrolled in 2009, 10 Federal Work-Study jobs (averaging $3000). 30 state and other part-time jobs (averaging $3000).

Applying *Options:* early admission. *Required for some:* high school transcript. *Recommended:* high school transcript.

Freshman Application Contact Mr. Leighton Oride, Admissions Officer and Registrar, Kauai Community College, 3-1901 Kaumualii Highway, Lihue, HI 96766. *Phone:* 808-245-8225. *Fax:* 808-245-8297. *E-mail:* arkauai@hawaii.edu. *Web site:* http://kauai.hawaii.edu/.

Leeward Community College
Pearl City, Hawaii

- **State-supported** 2-year, founded 1968, part of University of Hawaii System
- **Suburban** 49-acre campus with easy access to Honolulu
- **Coed,** 7,942 undergraduate students, 42% full-time, 60% women, 40% men

Undergraduates 3,296 full-time, 4,646 part-time. Students come from 31 states and territories; 13 other countries; 0.8% are from out of state; 2% Black or African American, non-Hispanic/Latino; 11% Hispanic/Latino; 37% Asian, non-Hispanic/Latino; 12% Native Hawaiian or other Pacific Islander, non-Hispanic/Latino; 0.3% American Indian or Alaska Native, non-Hispanic/Latino; 26% Two or more races, non-Hispanic/Latino; 1% Race/ethnicity unknown; 0.5% international; 7% transferred in. *Retention:* 65% of full-time freshmen returned.

Freshmen *Admission:* 2,013 applied, 2,013 admitted, 1,404 enrolled.

Faculty *Total:* 283, 63% full-time. *Student/faculty ratio:* 23:1.

Majors Accounting; administrative assistant and secretarial science; automobile/automotive mechanics technology; business administration and management; computer and information sciences; cooking and related culinary arts; desktop publishing and digital imaging design; education (specific levels and methods) related; liberal arts and sciences/liberal studies; radio and television broadcasting technology.

Academics *Calendar:* semesters. *Degree:* certificates and associate. *Special study options:* academic remediation for entering students, advanced placement credit, cooperative education, distance learning, English as a second language, honors programs, independent study, internships, off-campus study, part-time degree program, services for LD students, study abroad, summer session for credit. *ROTC:* Air Force (c).

Library 66,000 titles, 147 serial subscriptions, 1,062 audiovisual materials, an OPAC, a Web page.

Student Life *Housing:* college housing not available. *Activities and Organizations:* drama/theater group, student-run newspaper, choral group, Soccer Club, Japan Circle, Future Teachers Club, Leeward Campus Crusade For Christ, 4n Tongues (Hip Hop). *Campus security:* 24-hour emergency response devices and patrols, late-night transport/escort service. *Student services:* health clinic, personal/psychological counseling.

Athletics *Intramural sports:* soccer M/W, tennis M/W, volleyball M/W.

Costs (2011–12) *One-time required fee:* $25. *Tuition:* state resident $2328 full-time, $97 per credit part-time; nonresident $6960 full-time, $290 per credit part-time. Full-time tuition and fees vary according to course load. Part-time tuition and fees vary according to course load. *Required fees:* $45 full-time, $1 per credit part-time, $18 per term part-time. *Payment plan:* installment.

Applying *Options:* electronic application, early admission. *Application fee:* $25. *Required for some:* high school transcript. *Application deadlines:* 7/15 (freshmen), 7/15 (out-of-state freshmen), 7/15 (transfers), 7/15 (early action). *Early decision deadline:* 7/15 (for plan 1), 7/15 (for plan 2). *Notification:* continuous (freshmen), continuous (out-of-state freshmen), continuous (transfers).

Freshman Application Contact Ms. Anna Donald, Office Assistant, Leeward Community College, 96-045 Ala Ike, Pearl City, HI 96782-3393. *Phone:* 808-455-0642. *Web site:* http://www.lcc.hawaii.edu/.

Maui Community College
Kahului, Hawaii

Freshman Application Contact Mr. Stephen Kameda, Director of Admissions and Records, Maui Community College, 310 Kaahumanu Avenue, Kahului, HI 96732. *Phone:* 808-984-3267. *Toll-free phone:* 800-479-6692. *Fax:* 808-242-9618. *E-mail:* kameda@hawaii.edu. *Web site:* http://maui.hawaii.edu/.

Remington College–Honolulu Campus
Honolulu, Hawaii

Director of Admissions Louis LaMair, Director of Recruitment, Remington College–Honolulu Campus, 1111 Bishop Street, Suite 400, Honolulu, HI 96813. *Phone:* 808-942-1000. *Fax:* 808-533-3064. *E-mail:* louis.lamair@remingtoncollege.edu. *Web site:* http://www.remingtoncollege.edu/.

Windward Community College
Kaneohe, Hawaii

Director of Admissions Geri Imai, Registrar, Windward Community College, 45-720 Keaahala Road, Kaneohe, HI 96744-3528. *Phone:* 808-235-7430. *E-mail:* gerii@hawaii.edu. *Web site:* http://www.wcc.hawaii.edu/.

IDAHO

Brown Mackie College–Boise
Boise, Idaho

- **Proprietary** primarily 2-year, part of Education Management Corporation
- **Coed**

Majors Accounting technology and bookkeeping; business administration and management; criminal justice/law enforcement administration; health/healthcare administration; information technology; legal assistant/paralegal; legal studies; medical/clinical assistant; occupational therapist assistant; office management; surgical technology; veterinary/animal health technology.

Academics *Degrees:* diplomas, associate, and bachelor's.

Costs (2010–11) *Tuition:* Tuition varies by program. Students should contact Brown Mackie College for tuition information.

Freshman Application Contact Brown Mackie College–Boise, 9050 West Overland Road, Suite 100, Boise, ID 83709. *Phone:* 208-321-8800. *Web site:* http://www.brownmackie.edu/boise/.

See page 362 for the College Close-Up.

Carrington College - Boise
Boise, Idaho

Director of Admissions Director of Admissions, Carrington College - Boise, 1122 North Liberty Street, Boise, ID 83704. *Phone:* 208-377-8080 Ext. 35. *Web site:* http://carrington.edu/.

College of Southern Idaho
Twin Falls, Idaho

Freshman Application Contact Director of Admissions, Registration, and Records, College of Southern Idaho, PO Box 1238, Twin Falls, ID 83303-1238. *Phone:* 208-732-6232. *Toll-free phone:* 800-680-0274. *Fax:* 208-736-3014. *Web site:* http://www.csi.edu/.

Eastern Idaho Technical College
Idaho Falls, Idaho

Freshman Application Contact Dr. Steve Albiston, Dean of Students, Eastern Idaho Technical College, 1600 South 25th East, Idaho Falls, ID 83404. *Phone:* 208-524-3000 Ext. 3366. *Toll-free phone:* 800-662-0261 Ext. 3371. *Fax:* 208-525-7026. *E-mail:* steven.albiston@my.eitc.edu. *Web site:* http://www.eitc.edu/.

ITT Technical Institute
Boise, Idaho

- **Proprietary** primarily 2-year, founded 1906, part of ITT Educational Services, Inc.
- **Urban** campus
- **Coed**

Majors CAD/CADD drafting/design technology; communications technology; computer and information systems security; computer engineering technology; computer software and media applications related; computer software engineering; construction management; criminal justice/law enforcement administration; design and visual communications; electrical, electronic and communications engineering technology; game and interactive media design; health information/medical records technology; legal assistant/paralegal; project management; registered nursing/registered nurse; system, networking, and LAN/WAN management; web/multimedia management and webmaster; web page, digital/multimedia and information resources design.

Academics *Calendar:* quarters. *Degrees:* associate and bachelor's.

Student Life *Housing:* college housing not available.

Financial Aid Of all full-time matriculated undergraduates who enrolled in 2009, 9 Federal Work-Study jobs (averaging $5500).

Freshman Application Contact Director of Recruitment, ITT Technical Institute, 12302 West Explorer Drive, Boise, ID 83713. *Phone:* 208-322-8844. *Toll-free phone:* 800-666-4888. *Fax:* 208-322-0173. *Web site:* http://www.itt-tech.edu/.

North Idaho College
Coeur d'Alene, Idaho

- **State and locally supported** 2-year, founded 1933
- **Small-town** 42-acre campus
- **Coed,** 5,723 undergraduate students, 60% full-time, 59% women, 41% men

Undergraduates 3,437 full-time, 2,286 part-time. 0.9% Black or African American, non-Hispanic/Latino; 3% Hispanic/Latino; 1% Asian, non-Hispanic/Latino; 0.3% Native Hawaiian or other Pacific Islander, non-Hispanic/Latino; 2% American Indian or Alaska Native, non-Hispanic/Latino; 8% Two or more races, non-Hispanic/Latino.

Freshmen *Admission:* 2,684 applied, 1,565 admitted, 1,224 enrolled.

Faculty *Total:* 447, 36% full-time, 8% with terminal degrees. *Student/faculty ratio:* 17:1.

Majors Administrative assistant and secretarial science; agriculture; American Indian/Native American studies; anthropology; art; astronomy; athletic training; automobile/automotive mechanics technology; biological and physical sciences; biology/biological sciences; botany/plant biology; business administration and management; business teacher education; carpentry; chemistry; clinical laboratory science/medical technology; commercial and advertising art; computer and information sciences and support services related; computer and information sciences related; computer programming; computer science; criminal justice/law enforcement administration; criminal justice/police science; culinary arts; developmental and child psychology; drafting and design technology; dramatic/theater arts; education; electrical, electronic and communications engineering technology; elementary education; engineering; English; environmental health; fishing and fisheries sciences and management; forestry; French; geology/earth science; German; health/health-care administration; heating, air conditioning, ventilation and refrigeration maintenance technology; heavy equipment maintenance technology; history; hospitality administration; human services; journalism; legal administrative assistant/secretary; legal assistant/paralegal; liberal arts and sciences/liberal studies; licensed practical/vocational nurse training; machine tool technology; marine maintenance and ship repair technology; mass communication/media; mathematics; medical administrative assistant and medical secretary; music; music teacher education; physical sciences; physics; political science and government; psychology; registered nursing/registered nurse; social sciences; sociology; Spanish; welding technology; wildlife biology; wildlife, fish and wildlands science and management; zoology/animal biology.

Academics *Calendar:* semesters. *Degree:* certificates and associate. *Special study options:* academic remediation for entering students, adult/continuing education programs, advanced placement credit, cooperative education, distance learning, English as a second language, independent study, internships, off-campus study, part-time degree program, services for LD students, summer session for credit. *ROTC:* Army (c).

Library Molstead Library Computer Center with 60,893 titles, 751 serial subscriptions, an OPAC, a Web page.

Student Life *Housing Options:* coed. Campus housing is university owned. *Activities and Organizations:* drama/theater group, student-run newspaper, choral group, Ski Club, Fusion, Baptist student ministries, Journalism Club, Phi Theta Kappa. *Campus security:* 24-hour emergency response devices and patrols, late-night transport/escort service. *Student services:* health clinic, personal/psychological counseling, women's center, legal services.

Athletics Member NJCAA. *Intercollegiate sports:* basketball M(s)/W(s), cheerleading M(s)/W(s), soccer M(s)/W(s), softball W(s), volleyball W(s), wrestling M(s). *Intramural sports:* basketball M/W, bowling M/W, cheerleading M/W, crew M(c)/W(c), cross-country running M(c)/W(c), football M/W, golf M/W, racquetball M/W, sailing M(c)/W(c), skiing (cross-country) M(c)/W(c), skiing (downhill) M(c)/W(c), soccer M(c)/W(c), softball M/W, table tennis M/W, tennis M/W, track and field M(c)/W(c), volleyball M/W.

Costs (2010–11) *Tuition:* area resident $1608 full-time, $67 per credit hour part-time; state resident $2808 full-time, $108 per credit hour part-time; nonresident $6160 full-time, $257 per credit hour part-time. *Required fees:* $1050 full-time. *Room and board:* $6000.

Financial Aid Of all full-time matriculated undergraduates who enrolled in 2009, 142 Federal Work-Study jobs (averaging $1425). 106 state and other part-time jobs (averaging $1327).

Applying *Options:* electronic application, early admission, deferred entrance. *Application fee:* $25. *Required for some:* essay or personal statement, high school transcript, county residency certificate. *Application deadlines:* 8/20 (freshmen), 8/20 (transfers).

Freshman Application Contact North Idaho College, 1000 West Garden Avenue, Coeur d Alene, ID 83814-2199. *Phone:* 208-769-3303. *Toll-free phone:* 877-404-4536 Ext. 3311. *E-mail:* admit@nic.edu. *Web site:* http://www.nic.edu/.

ILLINOIS

Benedictine University at Springfield
Springfield, Illinois

Freshman Application Contact Kevin Hinkle, Associate Director of Admissions, Benedictine University at Springfield, 1500 North Fifth Street, Springfield, IL 62702. *Phone:* 217-525-1420 Ext. 321. *Toll-free phone:* 800-635-7289. *Fax:* 217-525-1497. *E-mail:* khinkle@sci.edu. *Web site:* http://www1.ben.edu/springfield/.

Black Hawk College
Moline, Illinois

- **State and locally supported** 2-year, founded 1946, part of Black Hawk College District System
- **Urban** 161-acre campus
- **Coed**

Undergraduates 2,715 full-time, 3,552 part-time. Students come from 14 states and territories; 9 other countries; 6% are from out of state; 3% transferred in.

Faculty *Student/faculty ratio:* 19:1.

Academics *Calendar:* semesters. *Degree:* certificates and associate. *Special study options:* academic remediation for entering students, accelerated degree program, adult/continuing education programs, advanced placement credit, cooperative education, distance learning, English as a second language, independent study, internships, off-campus study, part-time degree program, services for LD students, study abroad, summer session for credit.

Student Life *Campus security:* 24-hour patrols.

Athletics Member NJCAA.

Costs (2010–11) *Tuition:* area resident $2550 full-time, $85 per credit hour part-time; state resident $5790 full-time, $193 per credit hour part-time; nonresident $5790 full-time, $193 per credit hour part-time. *Required fees:* $285 full-time, $10 per credit hour part-time.

Financial Aid Of all full-time matriculated undergraduates who enrolled in 2009, 157 Federal Work-Study jobs (averaging $1437). 176 state and other part-time jobs (averaging $1023).

Applying *Options:* electronic application, early admission, deferred entrance. *Recommended:* high school transcript.

Freshman Application Contact Ms. Vashti Berry, College Recruiter, Black Hawk College, 6600-34th Avenue, Moline, IL 61265. *Phone:* 309-796-5341. *E-mail:* berryv@bhc.edu. *Web site:* http://www.bhc.edu/.

Carl Sandburg College
Galesburg, Illinois

Director of Admissions Ms. Carol Kreider, Dean of Student Support Services, Carl Sandburg College, 2400 Tom L. Wilson Boulevard, Galesburg, IL 61401-9576. *Phone:* 309-341-5234. *Web site:* http://www.sandburg.edu/.

City Colleges of Chicago, Harold Washington College
Chicago, Illinois

Freshman Application Contact Admissions Office, City Colleges of Chicago, Harold Washington College, 30 East Lake Street, Chicago, IL 60601-2449. *Phone:* 312-553-6010. *Web site:* http://hwashington.ccc.edu/.

City Colleges of Chicago, Harry S. Truman College
Chicago, Illinois

- **State and locally supported** 2-year, founded 1956, part of City Colleges of Chicago
- **Urban** 5-acre campus
- **Coed**, 13,174 undergraduate students

Faculty *Student/faculty ratio:* 34:1.

Majors Accounting; automobile/automotive mechanics technology; biological and physical sciences; business administration and management; child-care provision; computer systems networking and telecommunications; criminal justice/safety; general studies; information technology; liberal arts and sciences/liberal studies; mechanical drafting and CAD/CADD; registered nursing/registered nurse.

Academics *Calendar:* semesters. *Degree:* certificates, diplomas, and associate. *Special study options:* academic remediation for entering students, adult/continuing education programs, advanced placement credit, cooperative education, distance learning, English as a second language, honors programs, internships, part-time degree program, services for LD students, summer session for credit.

Student Life *Housing:* college housing not available. *Activities and Organizations:* drama/theater group. *Campus security:* 24-hour patrols, late-night transport/escort service. *Student services:* personal/psychological counseling.

Athletics Member NJCAA. *Intercollegiate sports:* basketball M.

Costs (2010–11) *Tuition:* $87 per credit hour part-time; state resident $209 per credit hour part-time; nonresident $260 per credit hour part-time. Full-time tuition and fees vary according to program. Part-time tuition and fees vary according to program. *Required fees:* $80 per term part-time. *Payment plans:* installment, deferred payment. *Waivers:* senior citizens and employees or children of employees.

Financial Aid Of all full-time matriculated undergraduates who enrolled in 2009, 150 Federal Work-Study jobs (averaging $3000).

Applying *Options:* early admission, deferred entrance. *Application deadlines:* rolling (freshmen), rolling (transfers). *Notification:* continuous until 9/8 (freshmen), continuous until 9/8 (transfers).

Freshman Application Contact City Colleges of Chicago, Harry S. Truman College, 1145 West Wilson Avenue, Chicago, IL 60640-5616. *Phone:* 773-907-4000 Ext. 1112. *Web site:* http://www.trumancollege.edu/.

City Colleges of Chicago, Kennedy-King College

Chicago, Illinois

Freshman Application Contact Admissions Office, City Colleges of Chicago, Kennedy-King College, 6301 South Halstead Street, Chicago, IL 60621. *Phone:* 773-602-5062. *Fax:* 773-602-5055. *Web site:* http://kennedyking.ccc.edu/.

City Colleges of Chicago, Malcolm X College

Chicago, Illinois

- **State and locally supported** 2-year, founded 1911, part of City Colleges of Chicago
- **Urban** 20-acre campus
- **Coed**

Undergraduates 2,522 full-time, 3,509 part-time.
Faculty *Student/faculty ratio:* 25:1.
Academics *Calendar:* semesters. *Degree:* certificates and associate. *Special study options:* academic remediation for entering students, adult/continuing education programs, advanced placement credit, cooperative education, distance learning, English as a second language, part-time degree program, services for LD students, summer session for credit.
Student Life *Campus security:* 24-hour emergency response devices and patrols.
Athletics Member NJCAA.
Costs (2010–11) *Tuition:* area resident $2088 full-time, $87 per credit hour part-time; state resident $5007 full-time, $209 per credit hour part-time; nonresident $6232 full-time, $260 per credit hour part-time. Full-time tuition and fees vary according to program. Part-time tuition and fees vary according to program. *Required fees:* $400 full-time, $80 per term part-time.
Financial Aid Of all full-time matriculated undergraduates who enrolled in 2009, 200 Federal Work-Study jobs (averaging $2500).
Applying *Options:* electronic application. *Required:* high school transcript, minimum 2.0 GPA. *Required for some:* essay or personal statement, interview.
Freshman Application Contact Ms. Kimberly Hollingsworth, Dean of Student Services, City Colleges of Chicago, Malcolm X College, 1900 West Van Buren Street, Chicago, IL 60612-3145. *Phone:* 312-850-7120. *Fax:* 312-850-7119. *E-mail:* khollingsworth@ccc.edu. *Web site:* http://malcolmx.ccc.edu/.

City Colleges of Chicago, Olive-Harvey College

Chicago, Illinois

Freshman Application Contact City Colleges of Chicago, Olive-Harvey College, 10001 South Woodlawn Avenue, Chicago, IL 60628-1645. *Phone:* 773-291-6362. *Web site:* http://oliveharvey.ccc.edu/.

City Colleges of Chicago, Richard J. Daley College

Chicago, Illinois

- **State and locally supported** 2-year, founded 1960, part of City Colleges of Chicago
- **Urban** 25-acre campus
- **Coed**

Undergraduates 3,507 full-time, 6,204 part-time. Students come from 2 states and territories. *Retention:* 52% of full-time freshmen returned.
Faculty *Student/faculty ratio:* 44:1.
Academics *Calendar:* semesters. *Degree:* certificates and associate. *Special study options:* academic remediation for entering students, adult/continuing education programs, advanced placement credit, distance learning, English as a second language, honors programs, off-campus study, part-time degree program, services for LD students, study abroad, summer session for credit. *ROTC:* Air Force (c).
Student Life *Campus security:* 24-hour emergency response devices and patrols.
Athletics Member NJCAA.
Costs (2010–11) *Tuition:* area resident $2370 full-time; state resident $7775 full-time; nonresident $9257 full-time. Full-time tuition and fees vary according to course load. Part-time tuition and fees vary according to course load. *Required fees:* $350 full-time. *Payment plans:* installment, deferred payment.
Financial Aid Of all full-time matriculated undergraduates who enrolled in 2009, 250 Federal Work-Study jobs (averaging $2500).

Applying *Options:* early admission, deferred entrance. *Required:* high school transcript. *Required for some:* essay or personal statement. *Recommended:* interview.
Freshman Application Contact City Colleges of Chicago, Richard J. Daley College, 7500 South Pulaski Road, Chicago, IL 60652-1242. *Phone:* 773-838-7606. *Web site:* http://daley.ccc.edu/.

City Colleges of Chicago, Wilbur Wright College

Chicago, Illinois

Freshman Application Contact Ms. Amy Aiello, Assistant Dean of Student Services, City Colleges of Chicago, Wilbur Wright College, Chicago, IL 60634. *Phone:* 773-481-8207. *Fax:* 773-481-8185. *E-mail:* aaiello@ccc.edu. *Web site:* http://wright.ccc.edu/.

College of DuPage

Glen Ellyn, Illinois

- **State and locally supported** 2-year, founded 1967
- **Suburban** 297-acre campus with easy access to Chicago
- **Coed**

Undergraduates 10,591 full-time, 16,492 part-time. Students come from 11 states and territories; 3% transferred in. *Retention:* 66% of full-time freshmen returned.
Faculty *Student/faculty ratio:* 24:1.
Academics *Calendar:* semesters. *Degree:* certificates and associate. *Special study options:* academic remediation for entering students, accelerated degree program, adult/continuing education programs, advanced placement credit, cooperative education, distance learning, double majors, English as a second language, external degree program, honors programs, independent study, internships, off-campus study, part-time degree program, services for LD students, student-designed majors, study abroad, summer session for credit.
Student Life *Campus security:* 24-hour emergency response devices and patrols, student patrols, late-night transport/escort service.
Athletics Member NJCAA.
Costs (2010–11) *Tuition:* area resident $3870 full-time, $129 per credit hour part-time; state resident $9480 full-time, $316 per credit hour part-time; nonresident $11,580 full-time, $386 per credit hour part-time.
Financial Aid Of all full-time matriculated undergraduates who enrolled in 2009, 424 Federal Work-Study jobs (averaging $4135).
Applying *Options:* early admission, deferred entrance. *Application fee:* $20.
Freshman Application Contact Amy Hauenstein, Coordinator of Admission Services, College of DuPage, SRC 2048, 45 Fawell Boulevard, Glen Ellyn, IL 60137-6599. *Phone:* 630-942-2442. *Fax:* 630-790-2686. *E-mail:* hauenstein@cod.edu. *Web site:* http://www.cod.edu/.

College of Lake County

Grayslake, Illinois

- **District-supported** 2-year, founded 1967, part of Illinois Community College Board
- **Suburban** 226-acre campus with easy access to Chicago and Milwaukee
- **Coed,** 18,091 undergraduate students, 31% full-time, 56% women, 44% men

Undergraduates 5,679 full-time, 12,412 part-time. Students come from 31 other countries; 1% are from out of state.
Freshmen *Admission:* 2,027 admitted, 2,027 enrolled.
Faculty *Total:* 976, 21% full-time, 14% with terminal degrees. *Student/faculty ratio:* 19:1.
Majors Accounting technology and bookkeeping; administrative assistant and secretarial science; architectural drafting and CAD/CADD; art; automobile/automotive mechanics technology; biological and physical sciences; business administration and management; business automation/technology/data entry; chemical technology; child-care provision; civil engineering technology; computer installation and repair technology; computer programming (specific applications); computer systems networking and telecommunications; construction engineering technology; criminal justice/police science; dental hygiene; electrical, electronic and communications engineering technology; electrician; engineering; fire prevention and safety technology; heating, air conditioning, ventilation and refrigeration maintenance technology; industrial mechanics and maintenance technology; landscaping and groundskeeping; liberal arts and sciences/liberal studies; machine shop technology; mechanical engineering/mechanical technology; medical office management; medical radiologic technology; music; music teacher education; natural resources management and policy; ornamental horticulture; professional, technical, business, and scientific writing; registered nursing/registered nurse; restaurant, culinary,

and catering management; selling skills and sales; social work; substance abuse/addiction counseling; turf and turfgrass management.

Academics *Calendar:* semesters. *Degree:* certificates and associate. *Special study options:* academic remediation for entering students, adult/continuing education programs, advanced placement credit, cooperative education, distance learning, double majors, English as a second language, honors programs, independent study, internships, off-campus study, part-time degree program, services for LD students, student-designed majors, study abroad, summer session for credit.

Library College of Lake County Library plus 1 other with 106,842 titles, 766 serial subscriptions, an OPAC, a Web page.

Student Life *Housing:* college housing not available. *Activities and Organizations:* drama/theater group, student-run newspaper, radio station, choral group, Latino Alliance, Asian Student Alliance, Pride Alliance, Black Student Union, International Club. *Campus security:* 24-hour emergency response devices and patrols, late-night transport/escort service. *Student services:* health clinic, personal/psychological counseling, women's center.

Athletics Member NJCAA. *Intercollegiate sports:* baseball M(s), basketball M(s)/W(s), cross-country running M(s)/W(s), golf M(s), soccer M(s)/W(s), softball W(s), tennis M(s)/W(s), volleyball W(s). *Intramural sports:* cheerleading W, golf M/W.

Costs (2011–12) *Tuition:* area resident $2160 full-time, $90 per credit hour part-time; state resident $5520 full-time, $230 per credit hour part-time; nonresident $7440 full-time, $310 per credit hour part-time. *Required fees:* $384 full-time, $16 per credit hour part-time. *Payment plan:* installment. *Waivers:* senior citizens and employees or children of employees.

Financial Aid Of all full-time matriculated undergraduates who enrolled in 2009, 98 Federal Work-Study jobs (averaging $1311).

Applying *Options:* electronic application, early admission, deferred entrance. *Required for some:* high school transcript, interview. *Application deadlines:* rolling (freshmen), rolling (transfers). *Notification:* continuous (freshmen), continuous (transfers).

Freshman Application Contact Director, Student Recruitment, College of Lake County, Grayslake, IL 60030-1198. *Phone:* 847-543-2383. *Fax:* 847-543-3061. *Web site:* http://www.clcillinois.edu/.

The College of Office Technology
Chicago, Illinois

Director of Admissions Mr. William Bolton, Director of Admissions, The College of Office Technology, 1520 West Division Street, Chicago, IL 60622. *Phone:* 773-278-0042. *Toll-free phone:* 800-953-6161. *E-mail:* bbolton@cot.edu. *Web site:* http://www.cotedu.com/.

Danville Area Community College
Danville, Illinois

- **State and locally supported** 2-year, founded 1946, part of Illinois Community College Board
- **Small-town** 50-acre campus
- **Coed,** 3,713 undergraduate students, 42% full-time, 56% women, 44% men

Undergraduates 1,564 full-time, 2,149 part-time. 7% are from out of state; 5% transferred in.

Freshmen *Admission:* 711 enrolled.

Faculty *Total:* 150, 37% full-time, 5% with terminal degrees. *Student/faculty ratio:* 26:1.

Majors Accounting technology and bookkeeping; agricultural business and management; automobile/automotive mechanics technology; business automation/technology/data entry; CAD/CADD drafting/design technology; childcare provision; computer programming; computer programming (specific applications); computer systems networking and telecommunications; construction engineering technology; corrections; criminal justice/police science; data processing and data processing technology; engineering; executive assistant/executive secretary; fire science/firefighting; floriculture/floristry management; general studies; health information/medical records technology; industrial electronics technology; industrial mechanics and maintenance technology; juvenile corrections; landscaping and groundskeeping; liberal arts and sciences/liberal studies; manufacturing engineering technology; mechanical engineering/mechanical technology; medical administrative assistant and medical secretary; office occupations and clerical services; radiologic technology/science; registered nursing/registered nurse; selling skills and sales; teacher assistant/aide; turf and turfgrass management.

Academics *Calendar:* semesters. *Degree:* certificates and associate. *Special study options:* academic remediation for entering students, adult/continuing education programs, advanced placement credit, cooperative education, distance learning, double majors, English as a second language, independent study, internships, part-time degree program, services for LD students, summer session for credit.

Library Library with 50,000 titles, 2,487 audiovisual materials, an OPAC.

Student Life *Housing:* college housing not available. *Activities and Organizations:* choral group. *Campus security:* 24-hour patrols. *Student services:* personal/psychological counseling.

Athletics Member NJCAA. *Intercollegiate sports:* baseball M(s), basketball M(s)/W(s), cheerleading W(s), cross-country running M(s)/W(s), golf M(s), soccer M(s), softball W(s), volleyball W(s).

Costs (2010–11) *Tuition:* area resident $2670 full-time, $89 per credit hour part-time; state resident $5250 full-time, $175 per credit hour part-time; nonresident $5250 full-time, $175 per credit hour part-time. Full-time tuition and fees vary according to program. Part-time tuition and fees vary according to program. *Required fees:* $360 full-time, $12 per credit hour part-time. *Payment plan:* installment. *Waivers:* senior citizens and employees or children of employees.

Financial Aid Of all full-time matriculated undergraduates who enrolled in 2008, 60 Federal Work-Study jobs (averaging $2500). 113 state and other part-time jobs (averaging $4500).

Applying *Options:* early admission, deferred entrance. *Required:* high school transcript. *Application deadlines:* rolling (freshmen), rolling (transfers).

Freshman Application Contact Danville Area Community College, 2000 East Main Street, Danville, IL 61832-5199. *Phone:* 217-443-8803. *Web site:* http://www.dacc.edu.

Elgin Community College
Elgin, Illinois

- **State and locally supported** 2-year, founded 1949, part of Illinois Community College Board
- **Suburban** 145-acre campus with easy access to Chicago
- **Coed,** 12,214 undergraduate students

Freshmen *Admission:* 1,254 admitted.

Majors Accounting; administrative assistant and secretarial science; automobile/automotive mechanics technology; baking and pastry arts; biological and physical sciences; business administration and management; child-care provision; clinical/medical laboratory technology; computer systems networking and telecommunications; criminal justice/police science; culinary arts; data entry/microcomputer applications; design and visual communications; electrical, electronic and communications engineering technology; engineering; entrepreneurship; executive assistant/executive secretary; fine/studio arts; general studies; graphic design; heating, air conditioning, ventilation and refrigeration maintenance technology; hotel/motel administration; kinesiology and exercise science; legal administrative assistant/secretary; legal assistant/paralegal; liberal arts and sciences/liberal studies; machine tool technology; manufacturing engineering technology; marketing/marketing management; medical transcription; music; physical therapy technology; radiologic technology/science; registered nursing/registered nurse; restaurant, culinary, and catering management; retailing; social work; web page, digital/multimedia and information resources design; welding technology.

Academics *Calendar:* semesters. *Degree:* certificates, diplomas, and associate. *Special study options:* academic remediation for entering students, accelerated degree program, adult/continuing education programs, advanced placement credit, cooperative education, distance learning, double majors, English as a second language, honors programs, independent study, internships, off-campus study, part-time degree program, services for LD students, student-designed majors, study abroad, summer session for credit.

Library Renner Learning Resource Center with an OPAC, a Web page.

Student Life *Housing:* college housing not available. *Activities and Organizations:* drama/theater group, student-run newspaper, choral group, Phi Theta Kappa Honor Society, Organization of Latin American Students, Asian Filipino Club, Amnesty International, Student Government. *Campus security:* grounds are patrolled Sunday-Saturday 7am-11pm during the academic year. *Student services:* personal/psychological counseling.

Athletics Member NJCAA. *Intercollegiate sports:* baseball M(s), basketball M(s)/W(s), cross-country running M(s)/W(s), golf M(s), soccer M(s)/W(s), softball W(s), tennis M(s)/W(s), volleyball W(s).

Costs (2011–12) *Tuition:* area resident $2970 full-time, $99 per credit hour part-time; state resident $10,081 full-time, $336 per credit hour part-time; nonresident $13,358 full-time, $445 per credit hour part-time. Full-time tuition and fees vary according to program. Part-time tuition and fees vary according to program. *Required fees:* $10 full-time. *Payment plan:* installment. *Waivers:* senior citizens and employees or children of employees.

Applying *Options:* electronic application, early admission. *Required for some:* high school transcript, some academic programs have additional departmental admission requirements that students must meet. *Application deadlines:* rolling (freshmen), rolling (transfers). *Notification:* continuous (freshmen), continuous (transfers).

Freshman Application Contact Admissions, Recruitment, and Student Life, Elgin Community College, 1700 Spartan Drive, Elgin, IL 60123. *Phone:* 847-214-7414. *E-mail:* admissions@elgin.edu. *Web site:* http://www.elgin.edu/.

Fox College

Bedford Park, Illinois

- **Private** 2-year, founded 1932
- **Suburban** campus
- **Coed,** 370 undergraduate students
- 58% of applicants were admitted

Freshmen *Admission:* 1,127 applied, 656 admitted.

Majors Accounting and business/management; administrative assistant and secretarial science; business administration and management; graphic design; medical/clinical assistant; physical therapy technology; retailing; tourism and travel services management; veterinary/animal health technology.

Academics *Degree:* diplomas and associate. *Special study options:* accelerated degree program, internships.

Student Life *Housing:* college housing not available.

Freshman Application Contact Admissions Office, Fox College, 6640 South Cicero, Bedford Park, IL 60638. *Phone:* 708-444-4500. *Web site:* http://www.foxcollege.edu/.

Gem City College

Quincy, Illinois

Director of Admissions Admissions Director, Gem City College, PO Box 179, Quincy, IL 62301. *Phone:* 217-222-0391. *Web site:* http://www.gemcitycollege.com/.

Harper College

Palatine, Illinois

- **State and locally supported** 2-year, founded 1965, part of Illinois Community College Board
- **Suburban** 200-acre campus with easy access to Chicago
- **Endowment** $2.6 million
- **Coed,** 16,060 undergraduate students, 43% full-time, 56% women, 44% men

Undergraduates 6,964 full-time, 9,096 part-time. Students come from 9 states and territories; 1% are from out of state; 6% Black or African American, non-Hispanic/Latino; 12% Hispanic/Latino; 12% Asian, non-Hispanic/Latino; 0.2% American Indian or Alaska Native, non-Hispanic/Latino; 7% Race/ethnicity unknown; 0.6% international; 8% transferred in. *Retention:* 55% of full-time freshmen returned.

Freshmen *Admission:* 6,243 applied, 6,783 admitted, 1,902 enrolled. *Test scores:* ACT scores over 18: 74%; ACT scores over 24: 24%; ACT scores over 30: 4%.

Faculty *Total:* 888, 23% full-time. *Student/faculty ratio:* 23:1.

Majors Accounting; administrative assistant and secretarial science; architectural drafting and CAD/CADD; architectural engineering technology; art; banking and financial support services; biology/biological sciences; business administration and management; cardiovascular technology; chemistry; child-care provision; computer and information sciences; computer programming; computer programming (specific applications); computer science; criminal justice/law enforcement administration; cyber/computer forensics and counterterrorism; dental hygiene; diagnostic medical sonography and ultrasound technology; dietetics; dietetic technology; early childhood education; electrical, electronic and communications engineering technology; elementary education; emergency medical technology (EMT paramedic); engineering; English; environmental studies; fashion and fabric consulting; fashion/apparel design; fashion merchandising; finance; fine/studio arts; fire science/firefighting; food service systems administration; health teacher education; heating, air conditioning, ventilation and refrigeration maintenance technology; history; homeland security; hospitality administration; humanities; human services; interior design; international business/trade/commerce; legal administrative assistant/secretary; legal assistant/paralegal; liberal arts and sciences/liberal studies; marketing/marketing management; mathematics; medical administrative assistant and medical secretary; medical/clinical assistant; music; nanotechnology; philosophy; physical education teaching and coaching; physical sciences; psychology; public relations, advertising, and applied communication related; radiologic technology/science; registered nursing/registered nurse; sales, distribution, and marketing operations; small business administration; sociology and anthropology; speech communication and rhetoric; theater/theater arts management; web page, digital/multimedia and information resources design.

Academics *Calendar:* semesters. *Degree:* certificates and associate. *Special study options:* academic remediation for entering students, accelerated degree program, adult/continuing education programs, advanced placement credit, cooperative education, distance learning, English as a second language, honors programs, independent study, internships, part-time degree program, services for LD students, study abroad, summer session for credit.

Library Harper College Library with 151,731 titles, 238 serial subscriptions, 10,664 audiovisual materials, an OPAC, a Web page.

Student Life *Housing:* college housing not available. *Activities and Organizations:* drama/theater group, student-run newspaper, radio station, choral group, Student Radio Station, Program Board, Student Senate, Nursing Club, Phi Theta Kappa. *Campus security:* 24-hour emergency response devices and patrols, late-night transport/escort service. *Student services:* health clinic, personal/psychological counseling, women's center, legal services.

Athletics Member NJCAA. *Intercollegiate sports:* baseball M, basketball M/W, cross-country running M/W, football M, soccer M/W, softball W, track and field M/W, volleyball W, wrestling M. *Intramural sports:* baseball M, basketball M, football M, racquetball M/W, softball M/W, table tennis M/W, tennis M/W, volleyball M/W.

Costs (2010–11) *Tuition:* area resident $2364 full-time, $99 per credit hour part-time; state resident $8532 full-time, $356 per credit hour part-time; nonresident $10,344 full-time, $431 per credit hour part-time. Full-time tuition and fees vary according to course load. Part-time tuition and fees vary according to course load. *Required fees:* $14 per credit hour part-time, $36 per term part-time. *Payment plan:* installment. *Waivers:* senior citizens and employees or children of employees.

Financial Aid Of all full-time matriculated undergraduates who enrolled in 2009, 85 Federal Work-Study jobs (averaging $1210).

Applying *Options:* electronic application, early admission, deferred entrance. *Application fee:* $25. *Required:* high school transcript. *Application deadlines:* rolling (freshmen), rolling (transfers). *Notification:* continuous (freshmen), continuous (transfers).

Freshman Application Contact Admissions Office, Harper College, 1200 West Algonquin Road, Palatine, IL 60067. *Phone:* 847-925-6700. *Fax:* 847-925-6044. *E-mail:* admissions@harpercollege.edu. *Web site:* http://goforward.harpercollege.edu/.

Heartland Community College

Normal, Illinois

Freshman Application Contact Ms. Candace Brownlee, Director of Student Recruitment, Heartland Community College, 1500 West Raab Road, Normal, IL 61761. *Phone:* 309-268-8041. *Fax:* 309-268-7992. *E-mail:* candace.brownlee@heartland.edu. *Web site:* http://www.heartland.edu/.

Highland Community College

Freeport, Illinois

- **State and locally supported** 2-year, founded 1962, part of Illinois Community College Board
- **Rural** 240-acre campus
- **Coed,** 2,419 undergraduate students, 54% full-time, 61% women, 39% men

Undergraduates 1,315 full-time, 1,104 part-time. 4% are from out of state; 4% transferred in.

Freshmen *Admission:* 604 applied, 604 admitted, 532 enrolled. *Test scores:* ACT scores over 18: 72%; ACT scores over 24: 23%; ACT scores over 30: 1%.

Faculty *Total:* 195, 23% full-time, 5% with terminal degrees. *Student/faculty ratio:* 18:1.

Majors Accounting; administrative assistant and secretarial science; agricultural business and management; agricultural mechanization; art; autobody/collision and repair technology; automobile/automotive mechanics technology; biological and physical sciences; business administration and management; chemistry; child-care and support services management; child-care provision; child development; commercial and advertising art; computer and information sciences and support services related; computer and information sciences related; computer programming (specific applications); computer science; data processing and data processing technology; drafting and design technology; dramatic/theater arts; education; electrical, electronic and communications engineering technology; engineering; engineering science; engineering technology; general studies; geology/earth science; graphic design; health information/medical records technology; heavy equipment maintenance technology; history; human services; information technology; kindergarten/preschool education; liberal arts and sciences/liberal studies; marketing/marketing management; mathematics; mathematics teacher education; mechanical engineering/mechanical technology; medical/clinical assistant; music teacher education; physical sciences; physics; political science and government; pre-engineering; psychology; registered nursing/registered nurse; sociology; special education; speech teacher education; teacher assistant/aide; web page, digital/multimedia and information resources design.

Academics *Calendar:* semesters. *Degree:* certificates and associate. *Special study options:* academic remediation for entering students, adult/continuing education programs, advanced placement credit, cooperative education, distance learning, English as a second language, external degree program, honors programs, independent study, internships, part-time degree program, services for LD students, student-designed majors, summer session for credit.

Library Clarence Mitchell Libarary with 71 serial subscriptions, 6,843 audio-visual materials, an OPAC, a Web page.

Student Life *Housing:* college housing not available. *Activities and Organizations:* drama/theater group, student-run newspaper, choral group, Phi Theta Kappa, Royal Scots, Prairie Wind, intramurals, Collegiate Choir. *Campus security:* 24-hour emergency response devices and patrols. *Student services:* personal/psychological counseling.

Athletics Member NJCAA. *Intercollegiate sports:* baseball M(s), basketball M(s)/W(s), golf M(s)/W(s), softball W(s), volleyball W(s). *Intramural sports:* basketball M/W, volleyball M/W.

Costs (2010–11) *Tuition:* area resident $2820 full-time, $94 per credit hour part-time; state resident $4470 full-time, $149 per credit hour part-time; nonresident $4710 full-time, $157 per credit hour part-time. Full-time tuition and fees vary according to program and reciprocity agreements. Part-time tuition and fees vary according to program and reciprocity agreements. *Required fees:* $270 full-time, $9 per credit hour part-time. *Payment plans:* installment, deferred payment. *Waivers:* minority students, senior citizens, and employees or children of employees.

Financial Aid Of all full-time matriculated undergraduates who enrolled in 2008, 897 applied for aid, 792 were judged to have need. 61 Federal Work-Study jobs (averaging $1318). In 2008, 57 non-need-based awards were made. *Average percent of need met:* 35%. *Average financial aid package:* $5922. *Average need-based loan:* $2873. *Average need-based gift aid:* $4708. *Average non-need-based aid:* $3238.

Applying *Options:* electronic application, early admission, deferred entrance. *Required for some:* high school transcript. *Application deadlines:* rolling (freshmen), rolling (transfers).

Freshman Application Contact Mr. Jeremy Bradt, Director, Enrollment and Records, Highland Community College, 2998 West Pearl City Road, Freeport, IL 61032. *Phone:* 815-235-6121 Ext. 3486. *Fax:* 815-235-6130. *E-mail:* jeremy.bradt@highland.edu. *Web site:* http://www.highland.edu/.

Illinois Central College

East Peoria, Illinois

Freshman Application Contact Illinois Central College, One College Drive, East Peoria, IL 61635-0001. *Phone:* 309-694-5784. *Toll-free phone:* 800-422-2293. *Web site:* http://www.icc.edu/.

Illinois Eastern Community Colleges, Frontier Community College

Fairfield, Illinois

- **State and locally supported** 2-year, founded 1976, part of Illinois Eastern Community College System
- **Rural** 8-acre campus
- **Coed,** 2,171 undergraduate students, 13% full-time, 61% women, 39% men

Undergraduates 288 full-time, 1,883 part-time. 1% are from out of state.
Freshmen *Admission:* 28 enrolled.
Faculty *Total:* 205, 3% full-time. *Student/faculty ratio:* 16:1.
Majors Administrative assistant and secretarial science; automobile/automotive mechanics technology; biological and physical sciences; business automation/technology/data entry; corrections; general studies; information technology; liberal arts and sciences/liberal studies; quality control technology; registered nursing/registered nurse.
Academics *Calendar:* semesters. *Degree:* certificates and associate. *Special study options:* academic remediation for entering students, adult/continuing education programs, advanced placement credit, cooperative education, distance learning, double majors, English as a second language, external degree program, independent study, part-time degree program, services for LD students, student-designed majors, summer session for credit.
Library 19,244 titles, 96 serial subscriptions, 2,659 audiovisual materials.
Student Life *Housing:* college housing not available.
Costs (2011–12) *Tuition:* area resident $2272 full-time, $71 per semester hour part-time; state resident $6338 full-time, $197 per semester hour part-time; nonresident $8581 full-time, $268 per semester hour part-time. *Required fees:* $490 full-time, $15 per semester hour part-time, $5 per term part-time. *Waivers:* senior citizens and employees or children of employees.
Applying *Options:* early admission, deferred entrance. *Required:* high school transcript. *Application deadlines:* rolling (freshmen), rolling (transfers). *Notification:* continuous (freshmen), continuous (transfers).
Freshman Application Contact Ms. Mary Atkins, Coordinator of Registration and Records, Illinois Eastern Community Colleges, Frontier Community College, Frontier Drive, Fairfield, IL 62837. *Phone:* 618-842-3711 Ext. 4111. *Fax:* 618-842-6340. *E-mail:* atkinsm@iecc.edu. *Web site:* http://www.iecc.edu/fcc/.

Illinois Eastern Community Colleges, Lincoln Trail College

Robinson, Illinois

- **State and locally supported** 2-year, founded 1969, part of Illinois Eastern Community College System
- **Rural** 120-acre campus
- **Coed,** 1,062 undergraduate students, 50% full-time, 58% women, 42% men

Undergraduates 531 full-time, 531 part-time. 2% are from out of state.
Freshmen *Admission:* 82 enrolled.
Faculty *Total:* 92, 23% full-time. *Student/faculty ratio:* 19:1.
Majors Biological and physical sciences; business automation/technology/data entry; corrections; general studies; health information/medical records administration; liberal arts and sciences/liberal studies; mechanical engineering/mechanical technology; quality control technology; teacher assistant/aide; telecommunications technology.
Academics *Calendar:* semesters. *Degree:* certificates and associate. *Special study options:* academic remediation for entering students, adult/continuing education programs, advanced placement credit, cooperative education, distance learning, double majors, English as a second language, external degree program, independent study, internships, part-time degree program, services for LD students, student-designed majors, summer session for credit.
Library Eagleton Learning Resource Center plus 1 other with 15,563 titles, 34 serial subscriptions, 652 audiovisual materials.
Student Life *Housing:* college housing not available. *Activities and Organizations:* drama/theater group, choral group, national fraternities.
Athletics Member NJCAA. *Intercollegiate sports:* baseball M(s), basketball M(s)/W(s), softball W(s), volleyball W(s). *Intramural sports:* baseball M, basketball M, softball W, volleyball M/W.
Costs (2011–12) *Tuition:* area resident $2272 full-time, $71 per semester hour part-time; state resident $6338 full-time, $197 per semester hour part-time; nonresident $8581 full-time, $268 per semester hour part-time. *Required fees:* $490 full-time, $15 per semester hour part-time, $5 per term part-time. *Waivers:* senior citizens and employees or children of employees.
Applying *Options:* early admission, deferred entrance. *Required:* high school transcript. *Application deadlines:* rolling (freshmen), rolling (transfers). *Notification:* continuous (freshmen), continuous (transfers).
Freshman Application Contact Ms. Becky Mikeworth, Director of Admissions, Illinois Eastern Community Colleges, Lincoln Trail College, 11220 State Highway 1, Robinson, IL 62454. *Phone:* 618-544-8657 Ext. 1137. *Fax:* 618-544-7423. *E-mail:* mikeworthb@iecc.edu. *Web site:* http://www.iecc.edu/ltc/.

Illinois Eastern Community Colleges, Olney Central College

Olney, Illinois

- **State and locally supported** 2-year, founded 1962, part of Illinois Eastern Community College System
- **Rural** 128-acre campus
- **Coed,** 1,603 undergraduate students, 53% full-time, 64% women, 36% men

Undergraduates 848 full-time, 755 part-time. 1% are from out of state.
Freshmen *Admission:* 73 enrolled.
Faculty *Total:* 125, 39% full-time. *Student/faculty ratio:* 17:1.
Majors Accounting; administrative assistant and secretarial science; autobody/collision and repair technology; automobile/automotive mechanics technology; biological and physical sciences; business automation/technology/data entry; corrections; criminal justice/police science; general studies; industrial mechanics and maintenance technology; liberal arts and sciences/liberal studies; medical administrative assistant and medical secretary; medical radiologic technology; registered nursing/registered nurse.
Academics *Calendar:* semesters. *Degree:* certificates and associate. *Special study options:* academic remediation for entering students, adult/continuing education programs, advanced placement credit, cooperative education, distance learning, double majors, English as a second language, external degree program, independent study, internships, part-time degree program, services for LD students, student-designed majors, summer session for credit.
Library Anderson Learning Resources Center plus 1 other with 21,020 titles, 22 serial subscriptions, 1,156 audiovisual materials.
Student Life *Housing:* college housing not available. *Activities and Organizations:* drama/theater group, student-run newspaper, choral group.
Athletics Member NJCAA. *Intercollegiate sports:* baseball M(s), basketball M(s)/W(s), softball W(s), volleyball W(s). *Intramural sports:* baseball M, basketball M/W, softball W.
Costs (2011–12) *Tuition:* area resident $2272 full-time, $71 per semester hour part-time; state resident $6338 full-time, $197 per semester hour part-time;

nonresident $8581 full-time, $268 per semester hour part-time. *Required fees:* $490 full-time, $15 per semester hour part-time, $5 per term part-time. *Waivers:* senior citizens and employees or children of employees.

Applying *Options:* early admission, deferred entrance. *Required:* high school transcript. *Application deadlines:* rolling (freshmen), rolling (transfers). *Notification:* continuous (freshmen), continuous (transfers).

Freshman Application Contact Ms. Chris Webber, Assistant Dean for Student Services, Illinois Eastern Community Colleges, Olney Central College, 305 North West Street, Olney, IL 62450. *Phone:* 618-395-7777 Ext. 2005. *Fax:* 618-392-5212. *E-mail:* webberc@iecc.edu. *Web site:* http://www.iecc.edu/occ/.

Illinois Eastern Community Colleges, Wabash Valley College
Mount Carmel, Illinois

- **State and locally supported** 2-year, founded 1960, part of Illinois Eastern Community College System
- **Rural** 40-acre campus
- **Coed,** 5,584 undergraduate students, 13% full-time, 29% women, 71% men

Undergraduates 741 full-time, 4,843 part-time. 4% are from out of state.
Freshmen *Admission:* 99 enrolled.
Faculty *Total:* 150, 26% full-time. *Student/faculty ratio:* 38:1.
Majors Administrative assistant and secretarial science; agricultural business and management; agricultural production; biological and physical sciences; business administration and management; business automation/technology/ data entry; child development; corrections; diesel mechanics technology; electrical, electronic and communications engineering technology; energy management and systems technology; general studies; industrial technology; liberal arts and sciences/liberal studies; machine tool technology; manufacturing engineering technology; mining technology; radio and television; social work.
Academics *Calendar:* semesters. *Degree:* certificates and associate. *Special study options:* academic remediation for entering students, adult/continuing education programs, advanced placement credit, cooperative education, distance learning, double majors, English as a second language, external degree program, independent study, internships, part-time degree program, services for LD students, student-designed majors, summer session for credit.
Library Bauer Media Center plus 1 other with 32,811 titles, 21,649 serial subscriptions, 1,480 audiovisual materials.
Student Life *Housing:* college housing not available. *Activities and Organizations:* drama/theater group, student-run newspaper, radio and television station, choral group.
Athletics Member NJCAA. *Intercollegiate sports:* baseball M(s), basketball M(s)/W(s), softball W(s), tennis M, volleyball W(s). *Intramural sports:* baseball M, basketball M/W, cross-country running M/W, softball W, volleyball M/W.
Costs (2011–12) *Tuition:* area resident $2272 full-time, $71 per semester hour part-time; state resident $6338 full-time, $197 per semester hour part-time; nonresident $8581 full-time, $268 per semester hour part-time. *Required fees:* $490 full-time, $15 per semester hour part-time, $5 per term part-time. *Waivers:* senior citizens and employees or children of employees.
Applying *Options:* early admission, deferred entrance. *Required:* high school transcript. *Application deadlines:* rolling (freshmen), rolling (transfers). *Notification:* continuous (freshmen), continuous (transfers).
Freshman Application Contact Mrs. Diana Spear, Assistant Dean for Student Services, Illinois Eastern Community Colleges, Wabash Valley College, 2200 College Drive, Mt. Carmel, IL 62863. *Phone:* 618-262-8641 Ext. 3101. *Fax:* 618-262-8641. *E-mail:* speard@iecc.edu. *Web site:* http://www.iecc.edu/wvc/

Illinois Valley Community College
Oglesby, Illinois

- **District-supported** 2-year, founded 1924, part of Illinois Community College Board
- **Rural** 410-acre campus with easy access to Chicago
- **Endowment** $3.2 million
- **Coed**

Undergraduates 2,082 full-time, 2,447 part-time. Students come from 3 states and territories; 0.1% are from out of state; 36% transferred in. *Retention:* 62% of full-time freshmen returned.
Academics *Calendar:* semesters. *Degree:* certificates and associate. *Special study options:* academic remediation for entering students, adult/continuing education programs, advanced placement credit, distance learning, English as a second language, honors programs, independent study, internships, off-campus

study, part-time degree program, services for LD students, student-designed majors, study abroad, summer session for credit.
Student Life *Campus security:* 24-hour patrols.
Standardized Tests *Recommended:* ACT (for admission).
Costs (2010–11) *Tuition:* area resident $2188 full-time, $68 per credit hour part-time; state resident $7879 full-time, $246 per credit hour part-time; nonresident $8943 full-time, $279 per credit hour part-time. *Required fees:* $2434 full-time, $7 per credit hour part-time, $5 per term part-time.
Financial Aid Of all full-time matriculated undergraduates who enrolled in 2009, 81 Federal Work-Study jobs (averaging $955).
Applying *Options:* electronic application, early admission, deferred entrance. *Required:* high school transcript.
Freshman Application Contact Ms. Tracy Morris, Director of Admissions and Records, Illinois Valley Community College, Oglesby, IL 61348. *Phone:* 815-224-0437. *Fax:* 815-224-3033. *E-mail:* tracy_morris@ivcc.edu. *Web site:* http://www.ivcc.edu/.

ITT Technical Institute
Burr Ridge, Illinois

- **Proprietary** primarily 2-year, founded 1998, part of ITT Educational Services, Inc.
- **Coed**

Majors CAD/CADD drafting/design technology; computer and information systems security; computer engineering technology; computer software engineering; computer software technology; construction management; criminal justice/law enforcement administration; design and visual communications; electrical, electronic and communications engineering technology; legal assistant/paralegal; project management; system, networking, and LAN/WAN management.
Academics *Calendar:* quarters. *Degrees:* associate and bachelor's.
Student Life *Housing:* college housing not available.
Freshman Application Contact Director of Recruitment, ITT Technical Institute, 800 Jorie Boulevard, Suite 100, Burr Ridge, IL 60527. *Phone:* 630-472-7000. *Toll-free phone:* 877-488-0001. *Web site:* http://www.itt-tech.edu/.

ITT Technical Institute
Mount Prospect, Illinois

- **Proprietary** primarily 2-year, founded 1986, part of ITT Educational Services, Inc.
- **Suburban** campus
- **Coed**

Majors CAD/CADD drafting/design technology; computer and information systems security; computer engineering technology; computer software engineering; computer software technology; construction management; criminal justice/law enforcement administration; design and visual communications; electrical, electronic and communications engineering technology; legal assistant/paralegal; project management; system, networking, and LAN/WAN management; web page, digital/multimedia and information resources design.
Academics *Calendar:* quarters. *Degrees:* associate and bachelor's.
Student Life *Housing:* college housing not available.
Freshman Application Contact Director of Recruitment, ITT Technical Institute, 1401 Feehanville Drive, Mount Prospect, IL 60056. *Phone:* 847-375-8800. *Web site:* http://www.itt-tech.edu/.

ITT Technical Institute
Orland Park, Illinois

- **Proprietary** primarily 2-year, founded 1993, part of ITT Educational Services, Inc.
- **Suburban** campus
- **Coed**

Majors CAD/CADD drafting/design technology; computer and information systems security; computer engineering technology; computer software engineering; computer software technology; construction management; criminal justice/law enforcement administration; design and visual communications; electrical, electronic and communications engineering technology; information technology project management; legal assistant/paralegal; project management; registered nursing/registered nurse; system, networking, and LAN/WAN management; web page, digital/multimedia and information resources design.
Academics *Calendar:* quarters. *Degrees:* associate and bachelor's.
Student Life *Housing:* college housing not available.
Financial Aid Of all full-time matriculated undergraduates who enrolled in 2009, 6 Federal Work-Study jobs (averaging $4000).
Freshman Application Contact Director of Recruitment, ITT Technical Institute, 11551 184th Place, Orland Park, IL 60467. *Phone:* 708-326-3200. *Web site:* http://www.itt-tech.edu/.

John A. Logan College
Carterville, Illinois

Director of Admissions Mr. Terry Crain, Dean of Student Services, John A. Logan College, 700 Logan College Road, Carterville, IL 62918-9900. *Phone:* 618-985-3741 Ext. 8382. *Fax:* 618-985-4433. *E-mail:* terrycrain@jalc.edu. *Web site:* http://www.jalc.edu/.

John Wood Community College
Quincy, Illinois

- **District-supported** 2-year, founded 1974, part of Illinois Community College Board
- **Small-town** campus
- **Coed,** 2,501 undergraduate students, 53% full-time, 58% women, 42% men

Undergraduates 1,318 full-time, 1,183 part-time. Students come from 19 states and territories; 1 other country; 9% are from out of state; 10% transferred in.

Freshmen *Admission:* 812 applied, 782 admitted, 610 enrolled. *Average high school GPA:* 2.89. *Test scores:* ACT scores over 18: 65%; ACT scores over 24: 16%; ACT scores over 30: 1%.

Faculty *Total:* 277, 18% full-time, 5% with terminal degrees. *Student/faculty ratio:* 14:1.

Majors Accounting; administrative assistant and secretarial science; agricultural business and management; animal sciences; applied horticulture/horticulture operations; biological and physical sciences; business administration and management; CAD/CADD drafting/design technology; carpentry; child-care provision; clinical/medical laboratory technology; criminal justice/police science; electrician; emergency medical technology (EMT paramedic); executive assistant/executive secretary; fire science/firefighting; general studies; graphic design; legal administrative assistant/secretary; liberal arts and sciences/liberal studies; management information systems; manufacturing engineering technology; medical staff services technology; office management; radiologic technology/science; registered nursing, nursing administration, nursing research and clinical nursing related; restaurant, culinary, and catering management; selling skills and sales.

Academics *Calendar:* semesters. *Degree:* certificates and associate. *Special study options:* academic remediation for entering students, accelerated degree program, adult/continuing education programs, advanced placement credit, cooperative education, English as a second language, external degree program, independent study, internships, off-campus study, part-time degree program, services for LD students, student-designed majors, study abroad, summer session for credit.

Library Academic Support Center with 18,000 titles, 160 serial subscriptions, 2,000 audiovisual materials, an OPAC, a Web page.

Student Life *Housing:* college housing not available. *Activities and Organizations:* choral group. *Campus security:* 24-hour emergency response devices, late-night transport/escort service, campus police department, 911-enhanced phone system.

Athletics Member NJCAA. *Intercollegiate sports:* baseball M(s), basketball M(s)/W(s), softball W(s). *Intramural sports:* basketball M/W, volleyball M/W.

Standardized Tests *Recommended:* ACT (for admission).

Costs (2010–11) *Tuition:* area resident $3510 full-time, $117 per credit hour part-time; state resident $6810 full-time, $227 per credit hour part-time; nonresident $6810 full-time, $227 per credit hour part-time. Full-time tuition and fees vary according to program and reciprocity agreements. Part-time tuition and fees vary according to program and reciprocity agreements. *Required fees:* $300 full-time, $10 per credit hour part-time. *Payment plan:* installment. *Waivers:* employees or children of employees.

Applying *Options:* electronic application, early admission. *Required:* high school transcript. *Application deadlines:* rolling (freshmen), rolling (out-of-state freshmen), rolling (transfers). *Notification:* continuous (freshmen), continuous (out-of-state freshmen), continuous (transfers).

Freshman Application Contact Mr. Lee Wibbell, Director of Admissions, John Wood Community College, Quincy, IL 62305-8736. *Phone:* 217-641-4339. *Fax:* 217-224-4208. *E-mail:* admissions@jwcc.edu. *Web site:* http://www.jwcc.edu/.

Joliet Junior College
Joliet, Illinois

Freshman Application Contact Ms. Jennifer Kloberdanz, Director of Admissions and Recruitment, Joliet Junior College, 1215 Houbolt Road, Joliet, IL 60431. *Phone:* 815-729-9020 Ext. 2414. *E-mail:* admission@jjc.edu. *Web site:* http://www.jjc.edu/.

Kankakee Community College
Kankakee, Illinois

- **State and locally supported** 2-year, founded 1966, part of Illinois Community College Board
- **Small-town** 178-acre campus with easy access to Chicago
- **Endowment** $2.2 million
- **Coed,** 4,223 undergraduate students, 47% full-time, 61% women, 39% men

Undergraduates 1,974 full-time, 2,249 part-time. Students come from 5 other countries.

Freshmen *Admission:* 381 enrolled.

Faculty *Total:* 204, 34% full-time.

Majors Accounting; administrative assistant and secretarial science; agriculture; applied horticulture/horticulture operations; automobile/automotive mechanics technology; avionics maintenance technology; biological and physical sciences; business/commerce; business, management, and marketing related; child development; clinical/medical laboratory technology; construction management; criminal justice/law enforcement administration; drafting and design technology; electrical, electronic and communications engineering technology; elementary education; emergency medical technology (EMT paramedic); engineering; fine/studio arts; general studies; graphic design; heating, air conditioning, ventilation and refrigeration maintenance technology; horticultural science; industrial radiologic technology; information science/studies; legal assistant/paralegal; machine tool technology; marketing/marketing management; mathematics teacher education; medical office assistant; physical therapy technology; psychology; radiologic technology/science; registered nursing/registered nurse; respiratory care therapy; secondary education; special education; teacher assistant/aide; visual and performing arts related; welding technology.

Academics *Calendar:* semesters. *Degrees:* certificates, diplomas, and associate (also offers continuing education program with significant enrollment not reflected in profile). *Special study options:* academic remediation for entering students, advanced placement credit, distance learning, English as a second language, honors programs, independent study, internships, off-campus study, part-time degree program, services for LD students, student-designed majors, study abroad, summer session for credit. *ROTC:* Army (c).

Library Kankakee Community College Learning Resource Center with 42,861 titles, 140 serial subscriptions, 4,475 audiovisual materials, an OPAC, a Web page.

Student Life *Housing:* college housing not available. *Activities and Organizations:* drama/theater group, Student Advisory Council, Brother to Brother, Phi Theta Kappa, Political Science Involved, Rotaract. *Campus security:* 24-hour patrols, late-night transport/escort service.

Athletics Member NJCAA. *Intercollegiate sports:* baseball M(s), basketball M(s)/W(s), soccer M, softball W(s), volleyball W(s). *Intramural sports:* basketball M.

Costs (2011–12) *Tuition:* area resident $2670 full-time; state resident $4608 full-time; nonresident $12,930 full-time. *Required fees:* $300 full-time. *Payment plan:* installment. *Waivers:* senior citizens and employees or children of employees.

Financial Aid Of all full-time matriculated undergraduates who enrolled in 2009, 70 Federal Work-Study jobs (averaging $1100). *Financial aid deadline:* 10/1.

Applying *Options:* electronic application, early admission. *Required:* high school transcript. *Application deadlines:* rolling (freshmen), rolling (transfers). *Notification:* continuous (freshmen), continuous (transfers).

Freshman Application Contact Ms. Michelle Driscoll, Kankakee Community College, 100 College Drive, Kankakee, IL 60901. *Phone:* 815-802-8520. *Fax:* 815-802-8521. *E-mail:* mdriscoll@kcc.edu. *Web site:* http://www.kcc.edu/.

Kaskaskia College
Centralia, Illinois

- **State and locally supported** 2-year, founded 1966, part of Illinois Community College Board
- **Rural** 195-acre campus with easy access to St. Louis
- **Endowment** $4.0 million
- **Coed,** 5,391 undergraduate students, 43% full-time, 60% women, 40% men

Undergraduates 2,322 full-time, 3,069 part-time. Students come from 4 states and territories; 3 other countries; 1% are from out of state; 6% Black or African American, non-Hispanic/Latino; 1% Hispanic/Latino; 0.4% Asian, non-Hispanic/Latino; 0.1% Native Hawaiian or other Pacific Islander, non-Hispanic/Latino; 0.3% American Indian or Alaska Native, non-Hispanic/Latino; 0.3% Race/ethnicity unknown; 0.4% international; 32% transferred in.

Freshmen *Admission:* 894 applied, 894 admitted, 894 enrolled.

Faculty *Total:* 231, 32% full-time, 5% with terminal degrees. *Student/faculty ratio:* 26:1.

Majors Accounting; agriculture; architectural drafting and CAD/CADD; autobody/collision and repair technology; automobile/automotive mechanics technology; biological and physical sciences; business automation/technology/data entry; business/commerce; carpentry; child-care provision; clinical/medical laboratory technology; criminal justice/law enforcement administration; culinary arts; electrical, electronic and communications engineering technology; emergency medical technology (EMT paramedic); executive assistant/executive secretary; general studies; health information/medical records technology; industrial mechanics and maintenance technology; information science/studies; juvenile corrections; liberal arts and sciences/liberal studies; mathematics teacher education; network and system administration; occupational therapist assistant; physical therapy technology; radiologic technology/science; registered nursing/registered nurse; respiratory care therapy; teacher assistant/aide; veterinary/animal health technology.

Academics *Calendar:* semesters. *Degree:* certificates and associate. *Special study options:* academic remediation for entering students, accelerated degree program, adult/continuing education programs, cooperative education, distance learning, double majors, English as a second language, honors programs, independent study, internships, off-campus study, part-time degree program, services for LD students, study abroad, summer session for credit.

Library Kaskaskia College Library with 18,270 titles, 89 serial subscriptions, 641 audiovisual materials, an OPAC, a Web page.

Student Life *Housing:* college housing not available. *Activities and Organizations:* drama/theater group, student-run newspaper, choral group, Phi Theta Kappa, Administration of Justice, Student Radiology Club, Cosmetology Club, Vocal Music Club. *Campus security:* 24-hour emergency response devices and patrols, late-night transport/escort service. *Student services:* personal/psychological counseling.

Athletics Member NJCAA. *Intercollegiate sports:* baseball M(s), basketball M(s)/W(s), cheerleading M(s)/W(s), cross-country running M(s)/W(s), golf M(s)/W(s), soccer M(s)/W(s), softball W(s), tennis M(s), volleyball W(s).

Standardized Tests *Recommended:* ACT (for admission).

Costs (2010–11) *Tuition:* area resident $2464 full-time, $77 per credit hour part-time; state resident $4800 full-time, $150 per credit hour part-time; nonresident $10,880 full-time, $340 per credit hour part-time. Full-time tuition and fees vary according to program. Part-time tuition and fees vary according to program. *Required fees:* $352 full-time, $11 per credit hour part-time. *Payment plan:* installment. *Waivers:* senior citizens and employees or children of employees.

Applying *Options:* early admission, deferred entrance. *Required:* high school transcript. *Required for some:* interview. *Application deadlines:* rolling (freshmen), rolling (transfers). *Notification:* continuous (freshmen), continuous (transfers).

Freshman Application Contact Jan Ripperda, Manager of Records and Registration, Kaskaskia College, 27210 College Road, Centralia, IL 62801. *Phone:* 618-545-3041. *Toll-free phone:* 800-642-0859. *Fax:* 618-532-1990. *E-mail:* jripperda@kaskaskia.edu. *Web site:* http://www.kaskaskia.edu/.

Kishwaukee College

Malta, Illinois

Freshman Application Contact Ms. Sally Misciasci, Admission Analyst, Kishwaukee College, 21193 Malta Road, Malta, IL 60150. *Phone:* 815-825-2086 Ext. 400. *Web site:* http://www.kishwaukeecollege.edu/.

Lake Land College

Mattoon, Illinois

Freshman Application Contact Mr. Jon VanDyke, Dean of Admission Services, Lake Land College, Mattoon, IL 61938-9366. *Phone:* 217-234-5378. *Toll-free phone:* 800-252-4121. *E-mail:* admissions@lakeland.cc.il.us. *Web site:* http://www.lakelandcollege.edu/.

Le Cordon Bleu College of Culinary Arts in Chicago

Chicago, Illinois

Freshman Application Contact Mr. Matthew Verratti, Vice President of Admissions and Marketing, Le Cordon Bleu College of Culinary Arts in Chicago, 361 West Chestnut, Chicago, IL 60610. *Phone:* 312-873-2064. *Toll-free phone:* 877-828-7772. *Fax:* 312-798-2903. *E-mail:* mverratti@chicnet.org. *Web site:* http://www.chefs.edu/chicago/.

Lewis and Clark Community College

Godfrey, Illinois

- **District-supported** 2-year, founded 1970, part of Illinois Community College Board
- **Small-town** 275-acre campus with easy access to St. Louis
- **Coed**

Academics *Calendar:* semesters. *Degree:* certificates and associate. *Special study options:* academic remediation for entering students, adult/continuing education programs, advanced placement credit, cooperative education, distance learning, double majors, English as a second language, independent study, internships, off-campus study, part-time degree program, services for LD students, summer session for credit. *ROTC:* Army (b).

Student Life *Campus security:* 24-hour emergency response devices and patrols.

Athletics Member NJCAA.

Costs (2010–11) *Tuition:* area resident $2088 full-time, $87 per credit hour part-time; state resident $6264 full-time, $261 per credit hour part-time; nonresident $8352 full-time, $348 per credit hour part-time. *Required fees:* $408 full-time, $17 per credit hour part-time.

Applying *Options:* early admission, deferred entrance. *Required for some:* interview. *Recommended:* high school transcript.

Freshman Application Contact Lewis and Clark Community College, 5800 Godfrey Road, Godfrey, IL 62035-2466. *Phone:* 618-468-5100. *Toll-free phone:* 800-500-LCCC. *Web site:* http://www.lc.edu/.

Lincoln College

Lincoln, Illinois

Director of Admissions Gretchen Bree, Director of Admissions, Lincoln College, 300 Keokuk Street, Lincoln, IL 62656-1699. *Phone:* 217-732-3155 Ext. 256. *Toll-free phone:* 800-569-0556. *E-mail:* gbree@lincolncollege.edu. *Web site:* http://www.lincolncollege.edu/.

Lincoln Land Community College

Springfield, Illinois

- **District-supported** 2-year, founded 1967, part of Illinois Community College Board
- **Suburban** 441-acre campus with easy access to St. Louis
- **Endowment** $2.2 million
- **Coed,** 7,602 undergraduate students, 45% full-time, 58% women, 42% men

Undergraduates 3,401 full-time, 4,201 part-time. Students come from 16 states and territories; 1% are from out of state; 1% transferred in. *Retention:* 40% of full-time freshmen returned.

Freshmen *Admission:* 1,196 enrolled. *Average high school GPA:* 3.18. *Test scores:* ACT scores over 18: 69%; ACT scores over 24: 20%; ACT scores over 30: 2%.

Faculty *Total:* 358, 36% full-time, 33% with terminal degrees. *Student/faculty ratio:* 23:1.

Majors Accounting; administrative assistant and secretarial science; agricultural production; airframe mechanics and aircraft maintenance technology; architectural drafting and CAD/CADD; autobody/collision and repair technology; automobile/automotive mechanics technology; aviation/airway management; biological and physical sciences; building/property maintenance; business automation/technology/data entry; business/commerce; child-care provision; computer programming; computer programming (specific applications); computer systems networking and telecommunications; construction engineering technology; criminal justice/police science; electrical, electronic and communications engineering technology; engineering; fine/studio arts; fire science/firefighting; general studies; graphic design; industrial electronics technology; landscaping and groundskeeping; legal administrative assistant/secretary; liberal arts and sciences/liberal studies; medical office assistant; music; occupational therapist assistant; radiologic technology/science; registered nursing/registered nurse; teacher assistant/aide.

Academics *Calendar:* semesters. *Degree:* certificates and associate. *Special study options:* academic remediation for entering students, accelerated degree program, adult/continuing education programs, advanced placement credit, distance learning, English as a second language, external degree program, honors programs, independent study, internships, off-campus study, part-time degree program, services for LD students, study abroad, summer session for credit.

Library Learning Resource Center with 65,000 titles, 10,000 serial subscriptions, an OPAC, a Web page.

Student Life *Housing:* college housing not available. *Activities and Organizations:* drama/theater group, student-run newspaper, choral group, Student Senate, Phi Theta Kappa, Model Illinois Government, student newspaper, Madrigals. *Campus security:* 24-hour emergency response devices and patrols, late-night transport/escort service. *Student services:* health clinic, personal/psychological counseling.

Athletics Member NJCAA. *Intercollegiate sports:* baseball M(s), basketball M(s)/W(s), soccer M(s), softball W(s), volleyball W(s). *Intramural sports:* basketball M/W, cheerleading W, volleyball W.

Costs (2010–11) *Tuition:* area resident $2490 full-time, $83 per credit hour part-time; state resident $4980 full-time, $166 per credit hour part-time; nonresident $7470 full-time, $249 per credit hour part-time. Full-time tuition and fees vary according to program. Part-time tuition and fees vary according to program. *Required fees:* $330 full-time, $11 per credit hour part-time. *Payment plans:* installment, deferred payment. *Waivers:* senior citizens and employees or children of employees.

Applying *Options:* electronic application, early admission, deferred entrance. *Recommended:* high school transcript. *Application deadlines:* rolling (freshmen), rolling (transfers). *Notification:* continuous (freshmen), continuous (transfers).

Freshman Application Contact Mr. Ron Gregoire, Executive Director of Admissions and Records, Lincoln Land Community College, 5250 Shepherd Road, PO Box 19256, Springfield, IL 62794-9256. *Phone:* 217-786-2243. *Toll-free phone:* 800-727-4161 Ext. 298. *Fax:* 217-786-2492. *E-mail:* ron.gregoire@llcc.edu. *Web site:* http://www.llcc.edu/.

MacCormac College
Chicago, Illinois

Director of Admissions Mr. David Grassi, Director of Admissions, MacCormac College, 506 South Wabash Avenue, Chicago, IL 60605-1667. *Phone:* 312-922-1884 Ext. 102. *Web site:* http://www.maccormac.edu/.

McHenry County College
Crystal Lake, Illinois

- **State and locally supported** 2-year, founded 1967, part of Illinois Community College Board
- **Suburban** 109-acre campus with easy access to Chicago
- **Coed,** 6,952 undergraduate students, 47% full-time, 56% women, 44% men

Undergraduates 3,265 full-time, 3,687 part-time. 0.1% are from out of state; 1% Black or African American, non-Hispanic/Latino; 10% Hispanic/Latino; 2% Asian, non-Hispanic/Latino; 0.3% American Indian or Alaska Native, non-Hispanic/Latino; 2% international.

Freshmen *Admission:* 2,654 applied, 2,654 admitted, 1,647 enrolled. *Average high school GPA:* 2.25.

Faculty *Total:* 365, 26% full-time. *Student/faculty ratio:* 23:1.

Majors Accounting; administrative assistant and secretarial science; animation, interactive technology, video graphics and special effects; applied horticulture/horticulture operations; automobile/automotive mechanics technology; biological and physical sciences; building/home/construction inspection; business administration and management; child-care provision; computer and information systems security; criminal justice/police science; electrical, electronic and communications engineering technology; emergency medical technology (EMT paramedic); engineering; fine/studio arts; fire science/firefighting; general studies; health and physical education/fitness; information technology; liberal arts and sciences/liberal studies; music; operations management; registered nursing/registered nurse; selling skills and sales.

Academics *Calendar:* semesters. *Degree:* certificates and associate. *Special study options:* academic remediation for entering students, accelerated degree program, adult/continuing education programs, advanced placement credit, cooperative education, distance learning, English as a second language, honors programs, independent study, internships, part-time degree program, services for LD students, study abroad, summer session for credit.

Library McHenry County College Library with 40,000 titles, 330 serial subscriptions, 6,000 audiovisual materials, an OPAC, a Web page.

Student Life *Housing:* college housing not available. *Activities and Organizations:* drama/theater group, student-run newspaper, choral group, Phi Theta Kappa, Student Senate, Equality Club, Writer's Block, Latinos Unidos. *Campus security:* 24-hour emergency response devices and patrols, late-night transport/escort service. *Student services:* personal/psychological counseling.

Athletics Member NJCAA. *Intercollegiate sports:* baseball M(s), basketball M(s)/W(s), soccer M(s), softball W(s), tennis M(s)/W(s), volleyball W(s).

Costs (2011–12) *Tuition:* area resident $2460 full-time, $82 per credit hour part-time; state resident $7766 full-time, $259 per credit hour part-time; nonresident $9491 full-time, $316 per credit hour part-time. Full-time tuition and fees vary according to course load. Part-time tuition and fees vary according to course load. *Required fees:* $284 full-time, $9 per credit hour part-time, $7 per credit hour part-time. *Payment plan:* installment. *Waivers:* employees or children of employees.

Financial Aid Of all full-time matriculated undergraduates who enrolled in 2009, 200 Federal Work-Study jobs (averaging $3700). 130 state and other part-time jobs (averaging $2000).

Applying *Options:* electronic application, early admission, deferred entrance. *Application fee:* $15. *Recommended:* high school transcript. *Application deadlines:* rolling (freshmen), rolling (out-of-state freshmen), rolling (transfers). *Notification:* continuous (freshmen), continuous (out-of-state freshmen), continuous (transfers).

Freshman Application Contact Fran DuWaldt, Enrollment Processor, McHenry County College, 8900 US Highway 14, Crystal Lake, IL 60012-2761. *Phone:* 815-455-8588. *E-mail:* admissions@mchenry.edu. *Web site:* http://www.mchenry.edu/.

Moraine Valley Community College
Palos Hills, Illinois

- **State and locally supported** 2-year, founded 1967, part of Illinois Community College Board
- **Suburban** 294-acre campus with easy access to Chicago
- **Endowment** $13.6 million
- **Coed,** 17,387 undergraduate students, 44% full-time, 54% women, 46% men

Undergraduates 7,736 full-time, 9,651 part-time. Students come from 7 states and territories; 42 other countries; 10% Black or African American, non-Hispanic/Latino; 13% Hispanic/Latino; 2% Asian, non-Hispanic/Latino; 0.2% American Indian or Alaska Native, non-Hispanic/Latino; 0.3% Two or more races, non-Hispanic/Latino; 8% Race/ethnicity unknown; 2% international; 3% transferred in. *Retention:* 65% of full-time freshmen returned.

Freshmen *Admission:* 4,798 applied, 4,798 admitted, 1,296 enrolled. *Test scores:* ACT scores over 18: 74%; ACT scores over 24: 16%; ACT scores over 30: 1%.

Faculty *Total:* 812, 22% full-time, 7% with terminal degrees. *Student/faculty ratio:* 28:1.

Majors Administrative assistant and secretarial science; automobile/automotive mechanics technology; biological and physical sciences; business administration and management; business/commerce; child-care provision; computer and information systems security; criminal justice/police science; emergency medical technology (EMT paramedic); fire prevention and safety technology; fire science/firefighting; graphic design; health aides/attendants/orderlies related; health information/medical records technology; heating, air conditioning, ventilation and refrigeration maintenance technology; human resources management; industrial electronics technology; instrumentation technology; liberal arts and sciences/liberal studies; management information systems; mathematics teacher education; mechanical engineering/mechanical technology; parks, recreation and leisure facilities management; radiologic technology/science; registered nursing/registered nurse; respiratory care therapy; restaurant, culinary, and catering management; retailing; science teacher education; small business administration; special education; substance abuse/addiction counseling; system, networking, and LAN/WAN management; teacher assistant/aide; tourism and travel services management; visual and performing arts; web/multimedia management and webmaster.

Academics *Calendar:* semesters. *Degree:* certificates and associate. *Special study options:* academic remediation for entering students, accelerated degree program, adult/continuing education programs, advanced placement credit, cooperative education, distance learning, double majors, English as a second language, honors programs, independent study, internships, off-campus study, part-time degree program, services for LD students, study abroad, summer session for credit.

Library Library with 71,111 titles, 410 serial subscriptions, 19,282 audiovisual materials, an OPAC, a Web page.

Student Life *Housing:* college housing not available. *Activities and Organizations:* drama/theater group, student-run newspaper, choral group, student newspaper, Speech Team, Alliance of Latin American Students, Phi Theta Kappa, Arab Student Union. *Campus security:* 24-hour emergency response devices and patrols, late-night transport/escort service, safety and security programs. *Student services:* personal/psychological counseling, women's center.

Athletics Member NJCAA. *Intercollegiate sports:* baseball M(s), basketball M(s)/W(s), cross-country running M(s)/W(s), golf M(s), soccer M(s)/W(s), softball W, tennis M(s)/W(s), volleyball W(s). *Intramural sports:* badminton M/W, basketball M/W, softball W, volleyball W.

Costs (2011–12) *Tuition:* $100 per credit hour part-time; state resident $247 per credit hour part-time; nonresident $289 per credit hour part-time. *Required fees:* $5 per credit hour part-time, $3 per term part-time. *Payment plan:* installment. *Waivers:* senior citizens and employees or children of employees.

Financial Aid Of all full-time matriculated undergraduates who enrolled in 2009, 84 Federal Work-Study jobs (averaging $2500). 260 state and other part-time jobs (averaging $2200).

Applying *Options:* electronic application, early admission, deferred entrance. *Required:* high school transcript. *Application deadlines:* rolling (freshmen), rolling (transfers). *Notification:* continuous (freshmen), continuous (transfers).

Freshman Application Contact Ms. Claudia Roselli, Director, Admissions and Recruitment, Moraine Valley Community College, 9000 West College Parkway, Palos Hills, IL 60465-0937. *Phone:* 708-974-5357. *Fax:* 708-974-0681. *E-mail:* roselli@morainevalley.edu. *Web site:* http://www.morainevalley.edu/.

Morrison Institute of Technology
Morrison, Illinois

Freshman Application Contact Mrs. Tammy Pruis, Admission Secretary, Morrison Institute of Technology, 701 Portland Avenue, Morrison, IL 61270. *Phone:* 815-772-7218. *Fax:* 815-772-7584. *E-mail:* admissions@morrison.tec.il.us. *Web site:* http://www.morrison.tec.il.us/.

Morton College
Cicero, Illinois

- **State and locally supported** 2-year, founded 1924, part of Illinois Community College Board
- **Suburban** 25-acre campus with easy access to Chicago
- **Coed**

Undergraduates Students come from 7 states and territories; 8 other countries; 0.6% are from out of state; 5% Black or African American, non-Hispanic/Latino; 74% Hispanic/Latino; 1% Asian, non-Hispanic/Latino; 0.1% Native Hawaiian or other Pacific Islander, non-Hispanic/Latino; 8% Race/ethnicity unknown; 0.1% international. *Retention:* 57% of full-time freshmen returned.
Freshmen *Admission:* 412 applied, 412 admitted.
Faculty *Total:* 270, 19% full-time, 11% with terminal degrees. *Student/faculty ratio:* 23:1.
Majors Accounting; administrative assistant and secretarial science; art; automobile/automotive mechanics technology; biological and physical sciences; business administration and management; criminal justice/police science; data processing and data processing technology; drafting and design technology; finance; fine/studio arts; heating, air conditioning, ventilation and refrigeration maintenance technology; legal administrative assistant/secretary; liberal arts and sciences/liberal studies; marketing/marketing management; medical administrative assistant and medical secretary; music; physical therapy; real estate; registered nursing/registered nurse.
Academics *Calendar:* semesters. *Degree:* certificates and associate. *Special study options:* academic remediation for entering students, adult/continuing education programs, advanced placement credit, distance learning, English as a second language, internships, part-time degree program, services for LD students, student-designed majors, summer session for credit.
Library Learning Resource Center with 55,000 titles, 327 serial subscriptions, an OPAC, a Web page.
Student Life *Housing:* college housing not available. *Activities and Organizations:* drama/theater group, student-run newspaper, Morton Ambassador Program, Campus Activities Board, Student Government Association, Nursing Club. *Campus security:* 24-hour patrols, security cameras.
Athletics Member NJCAA. *Intercollegiate sports:* baseball M(s), basketball M(s)/W(s), cross-country running M(s)/W(s), soccer M/W(s), softball W(s), volleyball W(s).
Costs (2011–12) *Tuition:* area resident $2528 full-time, $79 per credit hour part-time; state resident $6624 full-time, $207 per credit hour part-time; nonresident $8672 full-time, $271 per credit hour part-time. *Required fees:* $468 full-time, $14 per credit hour part-time, $10 per term part-time. *Payment plan:* deferred payment. *Waivers:* employees or children of employees.
Financial Aid Of all full-time matriculated undergraduates who enrolled in 2009, 15 Federal Work-Study jobs (averaging $2000).
Applying *Application fee:* $10. *Application deadlines:* rolling (freshmen), rolling (transfers).
Freshman Application Contact Morton College, 3801 South Central Avenue, Cicero, IL 60804-4398. *Phone:* 708-656-8000 Ext. 401. *Web site:* http://www.morton.edu/.

Northwestern College
Rosemont, Illinois

- **Proprietary** 2-year, founded 1902
- **Urban** 3-acre campus
- **Coed**

Undergraduates 706 full-time, 1,056 part-time.
Academics *Calendar:* quarters. *Degrees:* certificates and associate (profile includes branch campuses in Bridgeview and Naperville, IL). *Special study options:* academic remediation for entering students, cooperative education,

double majors, honors programs, independent study, internships, part-time degree program, summer session for credit.
Standardized Tests *Required:* SAT or ACT (for admission).
Applying *Application fee:* $25. *Required:* high school transcript.
Freshman Application Contact Northwestern College, 9700 West Higgins Road, Suite 750, Rosemont, IL 60018. *Phone:* 773-481-3730. *Toll-free phone:* 800-396-5613. *Web site:* http://www.northwesterncollege.edu/.

Oakton Community College
Des Plaines, Illinois

Freshman Application Contact Mr. Dale Cohen, Admissions Specialist, Oakton Community College, 1600 East Golf Road, Des Plaines, IL 60016-1268. *Phone:* 847-635-1703. *Fax:* 847-635-1890. *E-mail:* dcohen@oakton.edu. *Web site:* http://www.oakton.edu/.

Parkland College
Champaign, Illinois

Freshman Application Contact Admissions Representative, Parkland College, Champaign, IL 61821-1899. *Phone:* 217-351-2482. *Toll-free phone:* 800-346-8089. *Fax:* 217-351-2640. *E-mail:* mhenry@parkland.edu. *Web site:* http://www.parkland.edu/.

Prairie State College
Chicago Heights, Illinois

Freshman Application Contact Jaime Miller, Director of Admissions, Prairie State College, 202 South Halsted Street, Chicago Heights, IL 60411. *Phone:* 708-709-3513. *E-mail:* jmmiller@prairiestate.edu. *Web site:* http://www.prairiestate.edu/.

Rasmussen College Aurora
Aurora, Illinois

Admissions Office Contact Rasmussen College Aurora, 2363 Sequoia Drive, Aurora, IL 60506. *Toll-free phone:* 877-888-4110. *Web site:* http://www.rasmussen.edu/.

Rasmussen College Rockford, Illinois
Rockford, Illinois

Admissions Office Contact Rasmussen College Rockford, Illinois, 6000 East State Street, Fourth Floor, Rockford, IL 61108-2513. *Toll-free phone:* 877-533-5825. *Web site:* http://www.rasmussen.edu/.

Rend Lake College
Ina, Illinois

- **State-supported** 2-year, founded 1967, part of Illinois Community College Board
- **Rural** 350-acre campus
- **Coed**

Academics *Calendar:* semesters. *Degree:* certificates and associate. *Special study options:* academic remediation for entering students, adult/continuing education programs, advanced placement credit, cooperative education, distance learning, honors programs, independent study, internships, off-campus study, part-time degree program, services for LD students, summer session for credit.
Student Life *Campus security:* 24-hour emergency response devices and patrols, late-night transport/escort service.
Athletics Member NJCAA.
Costs (2010–11) *Tuition:* area resident $2720 full-time, $85 per credit hour part-time; state resident $3888 full-time, $122 per credit hour part-time; nonresident $4800 full-time, $150 per credit hour part-time. Full-time tuition and fees vary according to course load and reciprocity agreements. Part-time tuition and fees vary according to course load and reciprocity agreements. *Required fees:* $96 full-time, $3 per credit hour part-time.
Financial Aid Of all full-time matriculated undergraduates who enrolled in 2009, 133 Federal Work-Study jobs (averaging $1000). 174 state and other part-time jobs (averaging $940).
Applying *Options:* electronic application, deferred entrance. *Required:* high school transcript.
Freshman Application Contact Mr. Jason Swann, Recruiter, Rend Lake College, 468 North Ken Gray Parkway, Ina, IL 62846-9801. *Phone:* 618-437-5321 Ext. 1265. *Toll-free phone:* 800-369-5321. *Fax:* 618-437-5677. *E-mail:* swannj@rlc.edu. *Web site:* http://www.rlc.edu/.

Richland Community College

Decatur, Illinois

Freshman Application Contact Ms. JoAnn Wirey, Director of Admissions and Records, Richland Community College, Decatur, IL 62521. *Phone:* 217-875-7200 Ext. 284. *Fax:* 217-875-7783. *E-mail:* jwirey@richland.edu. *Web site:* http://www.richland.edu/.

Rockford Career College

Rockford, Illinois

Director of Admissions Ms. Barbara Holliman, Director of Admissions, Rockford Career College, 1130 South Alpine Road, Suite 100, Rockford, IL 61108. *Phone:* 815-965-8616 Ext. 16. *Web site:* http://www.rockfordcareercollege.edu/.

Rock Valley College

Rockford, Illinois

Freshman Application Contact Rock Valley College, 3301 North Mulford Road, Rockford, IL 61114-5699. *Phone:* 815-921-4283. *Toll-free phone:* 800-973-7821. *Web site:* http://www.rockvalleycollege.edu/.

Sauk Valley Community College

Dixon, Illinois

- **District-supported** 2-year, founded 1965, part of Illinois Community College Board
- **Rural** 165-acre campus
- **Endowment** $1.1 million
- **Coed,** 2,492 undergraduate students, 51% full-time, 60% women, 40% men

Undergraduates 1,269 full-time, 1,223 part-time.
Freshmen *Admission:* 585 applied, 585 admitted, 298 enrolled.
Faculty *Total:* 144, 30% full-time, 8% with terminal degrees. *Student/faculty ratio:* 22:1.
Majors Accounting; administrative assistant and secretarial science; architecture; art; athletic training; biology/biological sciences; business administration and management; chemistry; computer and information sciences related; corrections; criminal justice/law enforcement administration; criminal justice/police science; dramatic/theater arts; early childhood education; economics; education; electrical, electronic and communications engineering technology; elementary education; English; French; heating, air conditioning, ventilation and refrigeration maintenance technology; history; human services; industrial radiologic technology; legal administrative assistant/secretary; liberal arts and sciences/liberal studies; marketing/marketing management; mathematics; mechanical engineering/mechanical technology; medical office assistant; music; occupational therapy; physical education teaching and coaching; physical therapy; physics; political science and government; pre-dentistry studies; premedical studies; pre-pharmacy studies; pre-veterinary studies; psychology; public administration and social service professions related; registered nursing/registered nurse; rhetoric and composition; secondary education; social work; sociology; Spanish; special education; speech communication and rhetoric.
Academics *Calendar:* semesters. *Degree:* certificates and associate. *Special study options:* academic remediation for entering students, accelerated degree program, adult/continuing education programs, cooperative education, distance learning, English as a second language, honors programs, independent study, internships, off-campus study, part-time degree program, services for LD students, student-designed majors, summer session for credit.
Library Learning Resource Center plus 1 other with 55,000 titles, 268 serial subscriptions, an OPAC.
Student Life *Housing Options:* coed, disabled students. Campus housing is provided by a third party. *Activities and Organizations:* drama/theater group, choral group. *Campus security:* 24-hour emergency response devices and patrols, late-night transport/escort service. *Student services:* personal/psychological counseling.
Athletics Member NJCAA. *Intercollegiate sports:* baseball M(s), basketball M(s)/W(s), cross-country running M(s)/W(s), softball W(s), tennis M(s)/W(s). *Intramural sports:* basketball M/W.
Standardized Tests *Recommended:* ACT (for admission).
Costs (2010–11) *Tuition:* area resident $3168 full-time, $99 per credit hour part-time; state resident $8160 full-time, $255 per credit hour part-time; non-resident $9248 full-time, $289 per credit hour part-time. Full-time tuition and fees vary according to course load. Part-time tuition and fees vary according to course load. *Room and board:* $6228. Room and board charges vary according

to housing facility. *Payment plan:* installment. *Waivers:* senior citizens and employees or children of employees.
Financial Aid Of all full-time matriculated undergraduates who enrolled in 2008, 961 applied for aid, 837 were judged to have need, 40 had their need fully met. In 2008, 19 non-need-based awards were made. *Average percent of need met:* 47%. *Average financial aid package:* $4425. *Average need-based loan:* $2243. *Average need-based gift aid:* $4745. *Average non-need-based aid:* $2631.
Applying *Options:* electronic application, early admission, deferred entrance. *Recommended:* high school transcript. *Application deadlines:* rolling (freshmen), rolling (transfers). *Notification:* continuous (freshmen), continuous (transfers).
Freshman Application Contact Sauk Valley Community College, 173 Illinois Route 2, Dixon, IL 61021. *Phone:* 815-288-5511 Ext. 378. *Web site:* http://www.svcc.edu/.

Shawnee Community College

Ullin, Illinois

- **State and locally supported** 2-year, founded 1967, part of Illinois Community College Board
- **Rural** 163-acre campus
- **Coed**

Undergraduates 942 full-time, 2,248 part-time. Students come from 6 states and territories; 2 other countries; 4% are from out of state.
Faculty *Student/faculty ratio:* 20:1.
Academics *Calendar:* semesters. *Degree:* certificates and associate. *Special study options:* academic remediation for entering students, accelerated degree program, adult/continuing education programs, advanced placement credit, distance learning, double majors, English as a second language, external degree program, independent study, internships, off-campus study, part-time degree program, services for LD students, summer session for credit.
Student Life *Campus security:* 24-hour patrols.
Athletics Member NJCAA.
Standardized Tests *Required for some:* ACT (for admission). *Recommended:* ACT (for admission).
Costs (2010–11) *Tuition:* area resident $2610 full-time, $87 per credit hour part-time; state resident $3930 full-time, $131 per credit hour part-time; non-resident $4350 full-time, $145 per credit hour part-time. Full-time tuition and fees vary according to program and reciprocity agreements. Part-time tuition and fees vary according to program and reciprocity agreements.
Financial Aid Of all full-time matriculated undergraduates who enrolled in 2009, 60 Federal Work-Study jobs (averaging $2000). 50 state and other part-time jobs (averaging $2000).
Applying *Options:* electronic application, early admission, deferred entrance. *Required:* high school transcript.
Freshman Application Contact Mrs. Erin King, Recruiter/Advisor, Shawnee Community College, 8364 Shawnee College Road, Ullin, IL 62992. *Phone:* 618-634-3200. *Toll-free phone:* 800-481-2242. *Fax:* 618-634-3300. *E-mail:* erink@shawneecc.edu. *Web site:* http://www.shawneecc.edu/.

Solex College

Wheeling, Illinois

- **Proprietary** 2-year, administratively affiliated with The School of Massage Therapy at SOLEX
- **Suburban** campus with easy access to Chicago
- **Coed**

Academics *Degree:* certificates and associate. *Special study options:* adult/continuing education programs, English as a second language, internships, off-campus study, part-time degree program, summer session for credit.
Standardized Tests *Required:* SAT or ACT (for admission).
Applying *Options:* electronic application. *Application fee:* $150. *Required:* high school transcript.
Freshman Application Contact Solex College, 350 East Dundee Road, Wheeling, IL 60090. *Web site:* http://www.solex.edu/.

Southeastern Illinois College

Harrisburg, Illinois

Freshman Application Contact Dr. David Nudo, Director of Counseling, Southeastern Illinois College, 3575 College Road, Harrisburg, IL 62946-4925. *Phone:* 618-252-5400 Ext. 2430. *Toll-free phone:* 866-338-2742. *Web site:* http://www.sic.edu/.

South Suburban College

South Holland, Illinois

- **State and locally supported** 2-year, founded 1927, part of Illinois Community College Board
- **Suburban** campus with easy access to Chicago
- **Coed,** 6,482 undergraduate students, 36% full-time, 71% women, 29% men

Undergraduates 2,358 full-time, 4,124 part-time. 6% are from out of state; 67% Black or African American, non-Hispanic/Latino; 2% Hispanic/Latino; 0.8% Asian, non-Hispanic/Latino; 6% Native Hawaiian or other Pacific Islander, non-Hispanic/Latino; 0.3% American Indian or Alaska Native, non-Hispanic/Latino; 0.3% Two or more races, non-Hispanic/Latino; 2% Race/ethnicity unknown; 3% international. *Retention:* 58% of full-time freshmen returned.

Freshmen *Admission:* 873 applied, 873 admitted. *Average high school GPA:* 2.33.

Faculty *Total:* 763, 37% full-time. *Student/faculty ratio:* 22:1.

Majors Accounting; accounting technology and bookkeeping; architectural drafting and CAD/CADD; biological and physical sciences; building/home/construction inspection; CAD/CADD drafting/design technology; child-care provision; construction engineering technology; court reporting; criminal justice/safety; electrical, electronic and communications engineering technology; executive assistant/executive secretary; fine/studio arts; information technology; kinesiology and exercise science; legal assistant/paralegal; liberal arts and sciences/liberal studies; nursing administration; occupational therapist assistant; office management; radiologic technology/science; small business administration; social work.

Academics *Calendar:* semesters. *Degree:* certificates and associate. *Special study options:* academic remediation for entering students, adult/continuing education programs, advanced placement credit, cooperative education, distance learning, English as a second language, honors programs, internships, off-campus study, part-time degree program, services for LD students, study abroad, summer session for credit.

Library South Suburban College Library with 32,066 titles, 142 serial subscriptions, an OPAC, a Web page.

Student Life *Housing:* college housing not available. *Activities and Organizations:* drama/theater group, choral group. *Campus security:* 24-hour emergency response devices and patrols.

Athletics Member NJCAA. *Intercollegiate sports:* baseball M, basketball M/W, soccer M/W, softball W, volleyball W.

Costs (2011–12) *Tuition:* area resident $2710 full-time, $100 per credit hour part-time; state resident $8340 full-time, $278 per credit hour part-time; nonresident $9700 full-time, $333 per credit hour part-time. Full-time tuition and fees vary according to course load and reciprocity agreements. Part-time tuition and fees vary according to course load and reciprocity agreements. *Required fees:* $414 full-time. *Payment plan:* installment. *Waivers:* senior citizens and employees or children of employees.

Financial Aid Of all full-time matriculated undergraduates who enrolled in 2009, 121 Federal Work-Study jobs (averaging $1750).

Applying *Options:* early admission, deferred entrance. *Required:* high school transcript. *Required for some:* essay or personal statement. *Recommended:* essay or personal statement, minimum 2.0 GPA. *Application deadlines:* rolling (freshmen), rolling (transfers). *Notification:* continuous (freshmen), continuous (transfers).

Freshman Application Contact Tiffane Jones, Admissions, South Suburban College, 15800 South State Street, South Holland, IL 60473-1270. *Phone:* 708-596-2000 Ext. 2158. *E-mail:* admissionsquestions@ssc.edu. *Web site:* http://www.ssc.edu/.

Southwestern Illinois College

Belleville, Illinois

Freshman Application Contact Mike Leiker, Director of Admissions, Southwestern Illinois College, 2500 Carlyle Road, Belleville, IL 62221-5899. *Phone:* 618-235-2700 Ext. 5400. *Toll-free phone:* 800-222-5131. *Fax:* 618-277-0631. *Web site:* http://www.southwestern.cc.il.us/.

Spoon River College

Canton, Illinois

Freshman Application Contact Ms. Missy Wilkinson, Director of Admissions and Records, Spoon River College, 23235 North County 22, Canton, IL 61520-9801. *Phone:* 309-649-6305. *Toll-free phone:* 800-334-7337. *Fax:* 309-649-6235. *E-mail:* info@spoonrivercollege.edu. *Web site:* http://www.src.edu/.

Taylor Business Institute

Chicago, Illinois

Director of Admissions Mr. Rashed Jahangir, Taylor Business Institute, 318 West Adams, Chicago, IL 60606. *Web site:* http://www.tbiil.edu/.

Triton College

River Grove, Illinois

- **State-supported** 2-year, founded 1964, part of Illinois Community College Board
- **Suburban** 100-acre campus with easy access to Chicago
- **Coed**

Undergraduates 3,893 full-time, 11,765 part-time. *Retention:* 56% of full-time freshmen returned.

Faculty *Student/faculty ratio:* 24:1.

Academics *Calendar:* semesters. *Degree:* certificates and associate. *Special study options:* academic remediation for entering students, adult/continuing education programs, advanced placement credit, cooperative education, distance learning, English as a second language, freshman honors college, honors programs, internships, part-time degree program, student-designed majors, summer session for credit.

Student Life *Campus security:* 24-hour emergency response devices and patrols.

Athletics Member NJCAA.

Costs (2010–11) *Tuition:* area resident $2640 full-time, $88 per credit hour part-time; state resident $6966 full-time, $232 per credit hour part-time; nonresident $8736 full-time, $291 per credit hour part-time. *Required fees:* $240 full-time, $5 per credit hour part-time, $30 per term part-time.

Financial Aid Of all full-time matriculated undergraduates who enrolled in 2009, 250 Federal Work-Study jobs (averaging $2000).

Applying *Options:* deferred entrance. *Application fee:* $10. *Required:* high school transcript.

Freshman Application Contact Ms. Mary-Rita Moore, Dean of Admissions, Triton College, 2000 Fifth Avenue, River Grove, IL 60171. *Phone:* 708-456-0300 Ext. 3679. *Toll-free phone:* 800-942-7404. *Fax:* 708-583-3162. *E-mail:* mpatrice@triton.edu. *Web site:* http://www.triton.edu/.

Vet Tech Institute at Fox College

Tinley Park, Illinois

- **Private** 2-year, founded 2006
- **Suburban** campus
- **Coed,** 166 undergraduate students
- 52% of applicants were admitted

Freshmen *Admission:* 551 applied, 287 admitted.

Majors Veterinary/animal health technology.

Academics *Degree:* associate. *Special study options:* accelerated degree program, internships.

Student Life *Housing:* college housing not available.

Freshman Application Contact Admissions Office, Vet Tech Institute at Fox College, 18020 South Oak Park Avenue, Tinley Park, IL 60477. *Phone:* 888-884-3694. *Web site:* http://www.vettechinstitute.edu/chicago.

Waubonsee Community College

Sugar Grove, Illinois

- **District-supported** 2-year, founded 1966, part of Illinois Community College Board
- **Small-town** 243-acre campus with easy access to Chicago
- **Endowment** $1.1 million
- **Coed,** 10,428 undergraduate students, 38% full-time, 57% women, 43% men

Undergraduates 3,927 full-time, 6,501 part-time. Students come from 12 states and territories; 8% Black or African American, non-Hispanic/Latino; 22% Hispanic/Latino; 2% Asian, non-Hispanic/Latino; 0.3% American Indian or Alaska Native, non-Hispanic/Latino; 3% transferred in. *Retention:* 65% of full-time freshmen returned.

Freshmen *Admission:* 1,883 applied, 1,883 admitted, 1,375 enrolled.

Faculty *Total:* 713, 16% full-time, 8% with terminal degrees. *Student/faculty ratio:* 18:1.

Majors Accounting; administrative assistant and secretarial science; autobody/collision and repair technology; automobile/automotive mechanics technology; biological and physical sciences; business administration and management; business automation/technology/data entry; CAD/CADD drafting/design technology; child-care provision; community health services counseling; computer programming; construction management; criminal justice/police science; education (multiple levels); electrical, electronic and communications engineering technology; electrician; emergency care attendant (EMT ambulance); engineering; executive assistant/executive secretary; fine/studio arts; fire science/firefighting; general studies; graphic design; health and physical education/fitness; health information/medical records technology; heating, air conditioning, ventilation and refrigeration maintenance technology; human resources management; industrial mechanics and maintenance technology; industrial technology; liberal arts and sciences/liberal studies; library and archives assisting; logistics, materials, and supply chain management; massage therapy; mathematics teacher education; music teacher education; radio and television broadcasting technology; registered nursing/registered nurse; retailing; sign language interpretation and translation; small business administration; social work; special education; system, networking, and LAN/WAN management; teacher assistant/aide; web page, digital/multimedia and information resources design; welding technology.

Academics *Calendar:* semesters. *Degree:* certificates and associate. *Special study options:* academic remediation for entering students, accelerated degree program, advanced placement credit, distance learning, English as a second language, honors programs, independent study, internships, part-time degree program, services for LD students, study abroad, summer session for credit. *ROTC:* Army (c).

Library Todd Library with 76,581 titles, 433 serial subscriptions, 2,990 audiovisual materials, an OPAC, a Web page.

Student Life *Housing:* college housing not available. *Activities and Organizations:* drama/theater group, student-run newspaper, choral group, Phi Theta Kappa, Otaku Gamers Society, Waubonsee Student Education Association (WSEA), Business Club, Latinos Unidos. *Campus security:* 24-hour emergency response devices and patrols, late-night transport/escort service.

Athletics Member NJCAA. *Intercollegiate sports:* baseball M, basketball M(s)/W(s), cross-country running M(s)/W(s), golf M(s), soccer M/W(s), softball M(s), tennis M(s)/W(s), volleyball W(s), wrestling M. *Intramural sports:* basketball M/W, table tennis M/W, volleyball M/W.

Costs (2011–12) *Tuition:* area resident $2790 full-time, $93 per semester hour part-time; state resident $7932 full-time, $265 per semester hour part-time; nonresident $8698 full-time, $290 per semester hour part-time. Full-time tuition and fees vary according to course load and reciprocity agreements. Part-time tuition and fees vary according to course load and reciprocity agreements. *Required fees:* $150 full-time, $5 per semester hour part-time. *Payment plan:* installment. *Waivers:* senior citizens and employees or children of employees.

Financial Aid Of all full-time matriculated undergraduates who enrolled in 2009, 23 Federal Work-Study jobs (averaging $2000).

Applying *Application deadlines:* rolling (freshmen), rolling (transfers). *Notification:* continuous (freshmen), continuous (transfers).

Freshman Application Contact Joy Sanders, Admissions Manager, Waubonsee Community College, Route 47 at Waubonsee Drive, Sugar Grove, IL 60554. *Phone:* 630-466-7900 Ext. 5756. *Fax:* 630-466-6663. *E-mail:* admissions@waubonsee.edu. *Web site:* http://www.waubonsee.edu/.

Worsham College of Mortuary Science

Wheeling, Illinois

Director of Admissions President, Worsham College of Mortuary Science, 495 Northgate Parkway, Wheeling, IL 60090-2646. *Phone:* 847-808-8444. *Web site:* http://www.worshamcollege.com/.

INDIANA

Ancilla College

Donaldson, Indiana

- **Independent Roman Catholic** 2-year, founded 1937
- **Rural** 63-acre campus with easy access to Chicago
- **Endowment** $3.1 million
- **Coed,** 578 undergraduate students, 72% full-time, 69% women, 31% men

Undergraduates 419 full-time, 159 part-time. Students come from 4 states and territories; 4 other countries; 10% are from out of state; 7% Black or African American, non-Hispanic/Latino; 6% Hispanic/Latino; 0.7% Asian, non-Hispanic/Latino; 0.5% American Indian or Alaska Native, non-Hispanic/Latino; 0.5% Two or more races, non-Hispanic/Latino; 0.9% Race/ethnicity unknown; 0.7% international; 10% transferred in. *Retention:* 45% of full-time freshmen returned.

Freshmen *Admission:* 470 applied, 376 admitted, 187 enrolled. *Average high school GPA:* 2.38. *Test scores:* SAT critical reading scores over 500: 13%; SAT math scores over 500: 23%; ACT scores over 18: 41%; SAT critical reading scores over 600: 2%; ACT scores over 24: 1%.

Faculty *Total:* 47, 40% full-time, 15% with terminal degrees. *Student/faculty ratio:* 20:1.

Majors Behavioral sciences; biological and physical sciences; biology/biological sciences; business administration and management; criminal justice/safety; early childhood education; elementary education; general studies; health services/allied health/health sciences; history; mass communication/media; registered nursing/registered nurse; secondary education.

Academics *Calendar:* semesters. *Degree:* certificates and associate. *Special study options:* academic remediation for entering students, accelerated degree program, adult/continuing education programs, advanced placement credit, cooperative education, double majors, independent study, internships, part-time degree program, services for LD students, student-designed majors, summer session for credit.

Library Ball Library with 27,859 titles, 152 serial subscriptions, 1,499 audiovisual materials, an OPAC, a Web page.

Student Life *Housing:* college housing not available. *Activities and Organizations:* student-run newspaper, Student Senate, Student Nursing Organization, Ancilla Student Ambassadors, Phi Theta Kappa. *Campus security:* 24-hour patrols, late-night transport/escort service. *Student services:* personal/psychological counseling.

Athletics Member NJCAA. *Intercollegiate sports:* baseball M(s), basketball M(s)/W(s), cheerleading M(s)/W(s), golf M(s)/W(s), soccer M(s), softball W(s), volleyball W(s).

Standardized Tests *Required for some:* SAT or ACT (for admission). *Recommended:* SAT or ACT (for admission).

Costs (2010–11) *Tuition:* $13,050 full-time, $435 per credit hour part-time. Full-time tuition and fees vary according to course load and program. Part-time tuition and fees vary according to course load and program. *Required fees:* $230 full-time, $55 per term part-time. *Payment plan:* installment. *Waivers:* employees or children of employees.

Financial Aid Of all full-time matriculated undergraduates who enrolled in 2009, 28 Federal Work-Study jobs (averaging $1820). 16 state and other part-time jobs (averaging $1000). *Financial aid deadline:* 3/1.

Applying *Options:* electronic application. *Required:* high school transcript. *Application deadlines:* rolling (freshmen), rolling (transfers).

Freshman Application Contact Mr. Tony Booker, Director of Admissions, Ancilla College, 9601 Union Road, Donaldson, IN 46513. *Phone:* 574-936-8898 Ext. 330. *Toll-free phone:* 866-262-4552 Ext. 350. *Fax:* 574-935-1773. *E-mail:* admissions@ancilla.edu. *Web site:* http://www.ancilla.edu/.

Aviation Institute of Maintenance–Indianapolis

Indianapolis, Indiana

Freshman Application Contact Admissions Office, Aviation Institute of Maintenance–Indianapolis, 7251 West McCarty Street, Indianapolis, IN 46241. *Toll-free phone:* 888-349-5387. *Web site:* http://www.aviationmaintenance.edu/.

Brown Mackie College–Fort Wayne

Fort Wayne, Indiana

- **Proprietary** primarily 2-year, part of Education Management Corporation
- **Coed**

Majors Accounting technology and bookkeeping; athletic training; biomedical technology; business administration and management; computer software technology; criminal justice/law enforcement administration; dietetic technology; health/health-care administration; legal assistant/paralegal; legal studies; medical/clinical assistant; occupational therapist assistant; office management; physical therapy technology; surgical technology.

Academics *Calendar:* quarters. *Degrees:* certificates, diplomas, associate, and bachelor's.

Costs (2010–11) *Tuition:* Tuition varies by program. Students should contact Brown Mackie College for tuition information.

Freshman Application Contact Brown Mackie College–Fort Wayne, 3000 East Coliseum Boulevard, Fort Wayne, IN 46805. *Phone:* 260-484-4400. *Toll-free phone:* 866-433-2289. *Web site:* http://www.brownmackie.edu/fortwayne/.

See page 368 for the College Close-Up.

Brown Mackie College–Indianapolis
Indianapolis, Indiana

- **Proprietary** primarily 2-year, part of Education Management Corporation
- **Coed**

Majors Business administration and management; criminal justice/law enforcement administration; health/health-care administration; legal assistant/paralegal; legal studies; medical/clinical assistant; occupational therapist assistant.

Academics *Degrees:* certificates, diplomas, associate, and bachelor's.

Costs (2010–11) *Tuition:* Tuition varies by program. Students should contact Brown Mackie College for tuition information.

Freshman Application Contact Brown Mackie College–Indianapolis, 1200 North Meridian Street, Suite 100, Indianapolis, IN 46204. *Phone:* 317-554-8301. *Toll-free phone:* 866-255-0279. *Web site:* http://www.brownmackie.edu/indianapolis/.

See page 374 for the College Close-Up.

Brown Mackie College–Merrillville
Merrillville, Indiana

- **Proprietary** primarily 2-year, founded 1890, part of Education Management Corporation
- **Small-town** campus
- **Coed**

Majors Accounting technology and bookkeeping; business administration and management; computer software technology; criminal justice/law enforcement administration; gerontology; health/health-care administration; legal assistant/paralegal; legal studies; medical/clinical assistant; medical office management; occupational therapist assistant; surgical technology.

Academics *Calendar:* quarters. *Degrees:* certificates, diplomas, associate, and bachelor's.

Costs (2010–11) *Tuition:* Tuition varies by program. Students should contact Brown Mackie College for tuition information.

Freshman Application Contact Brown Mackie College–Merrillville, 1000 East 80th Place, Suite 205S, Merrillville, IN 46410. *Phone:* 219-769-3321. *Toll-free phone:* 800-258-3321. *Web site:* http://www.brownmackie.edu/merrillville/.

See page 380 for the College Close-Up.

Brown Mackie College–Michigan City
Michigan City, Indiana

- **Proprietary** primarily 2-year, part of Education Management Corporation
- **Rural** campus
- **Coed**

Majors Accounting technology and bookkeeping; business administration and management; computer software technology; criminal justice/law enforcement administration; early childhood education; health/health-care administration; legal assistant/paralegal; legal studies; massage therapy; medical/clinical assistant; medical office management; surgical technology; veterinary/animal health technology.

Academics *Calendar:* quarters. *Degrees:* certificates, diplomas, associate, and bachelor's.

Costs (2010–11) *Tuition:* Tuition varies by program. Students should contact Brown Mackie College for tuition information.

Freshman Application Contact Brown Mackie College–Michigan City, 325 East US Highway 20, Michigan City, IN 46360. *Phone:* 219-877-3100. *Toll-free phone:* 800-519-2416. *Web site:* http://www.brownmackie.edu/michigancity/.

See page 384 for the College Close-Up.

Brown Mackie College–South Bend
South Bend, Indiana

- **Proprietary** primarily 2-year, founded 1882, part of Education Management Corporation
- **Urban** campus
- **Coed, primarily women**

Majors Accounting technology and bookkeeping; business administration and management; computer software technology; criminal justice/law enforcement administration; early childhood education; health/health-care administration; information technology; legal assistant/paralegal; legal studies; massage therapy; medical/clinical assistant; occupational therapist assistant; physical therapy technology; veterinary/animal health technology.

Academics *Calendar:* quarters. *Degrees:* certificates, associate, and bachelor's.

Costs (2010–11) *Tuition:* Tuition varies by program. Students should contact Brown Mackie College for tuition information.

Freshman Application Contact Brown Mackie College–South Bend, 3454 Douglas Road, South Bend, IN 46635. *Phone:* 574-237-0774. *Toll-free phone:* 800-743-2447. *Web site:* http://www.brownmackie.edu/southbend/.

See page 402 for the College Close-Up.

College of Court Reporting
Hobart, Indiana

Freshman Application Contact Ms. Nicky Rodriquez, Director of Admissions, College of Court Reporting, 111 West Tenth Street, Suite 111, Hobart, IN 46342. *Phone:* 219-942-1459 Ext. 222. *Toll-free phone:* 866-294-3974. *Fax:* 219-942-1631. *E-mail:* nrodriquez@ccr.edu. *Web site:* http://www.ccr.edu/.

Harrison College
Anderson, Indiana

- **Proprietary** 2-year, founded 1902
- **Small-town** campus with easy access to Indianapolis
- **Coed,** 280 undergraduate students, 22% full-time, 84% women, 16% men

Undergraduates 62 full-time, 218 part-time. 14% Black or African American, non-Hispanic/Latino; 0.4% American Indian or Alaska Native, non-Hispanic/Latino; 0.4% Two or more races, non-Hispanic/Latino; 22% transferred in. *Retention:* 50% of full-time freshmen returned.

Freshmen *Admission:* 46 applied, 33 enrolled.

Faculty *Student/faculty ratio:* 16:1.

Majors Accounting; administrative assistant and secretarial science; banking and financial support services; business administration and management; criminal justice/law enforcement administration; health information/medical records technology; human resources management; marketing/marketing management; medical/clinical assistant; medical insurance coding.

Academics *Calendar:* quarters. *Degree:* certificates, diplomas, and associate. *Special study options:* adult/continuing education programs, cooperative education, distance learning, double majors, independent study, internships, part-time degree program.

Library Main Library plus 1 other.

Standardized Tests *Required:* Wonderlic Scholastic Level Exam (SLE) (for admission).

Applying *Options:* electronic application, early admission. *Application fee:* $50. *Required:* high school transcript, interview. *Application deadlines:* rolling (freshmen), rolling (transfers). *Notification:* continuous (freshmen), continuous (transfers).

Freshman Application Contact Mr. Kynan Simison, Director of Admissions, Harrison College, 140 East 53rd Street, Anderson, IN 46013. *Phone:* 765-644-7514. *Toll-free phone:* 888-544-4422. *Fax:* 765-664-5724. *E-mail:* kynan.simison@harrison.edu. *Web site:* http://www.harrison.edu/.

Harrison College
Columbus, Indiana

- **Proprietary** 2-year
- **Rural** campus
- **Coed,** 254 undergraduate students, 80% full-time, 89% women, 11% men
- **100%** of applicants were admitted

Undergraduates 203 full-time, 51 part-time. 1% Black or African American, non-Hispanic/Latino; 2% Hispanic/Latino; 0.4% Race/ethnicity unknown; 15% transferred in. *Retention:* 40% of full-time freshmen returned.

Freshmen *Admission:* 33 applied, 33 admitted, 32 enrolled.

Faculty *Student/faculty ratio:* 15:1.

Majors Accounting; administrative assistant and secretarial science; banking and financial support services; business administration and management; health information/medical records technology; marketing/marketing management; medical/clinical assistant; medical insurance coding.

Academics *Calendar:* quarters. *Degree:* certificates, diplomas, and associate. *Special study options:* adult/continuing education programs, cooperative education, distance learning, double majors, independent study, internships, part-time degree program.

Library Main Library plus 1 other.

Student Life *Housing:* college housing not available.

Standardized Tests *Required:* Wonderlic Scholastic Level Exam (SLE) (for admission).

Applying *Options:* electronic application. *Application fee:* $50. *Required:* high school transcript, interview. *Application deadlines:* rolling (freshmen),

rolling (out-of-state freshmen), rolling (transfers). *Notification:* continuous (freshmen), continuous (out-of-state freshmen), continuous (transfers).
Freshman Application Contact Ms. Gina Pate, Director of Admissions, Harrison College, 2222 Poshard Drive, Columbus, IN 47203. *Phone:* 812-379-9000. *Toll-free phone:* 888-544-4422. *Fax:* 812-375-0414. *E-mail:* gina.pate@harrison.edu. *Web site:* http://www.harrison.edu/.

Harrison College
Elkhart, Indiana
- **Proprietary** primarily 2-year
- **Coed**

Faculty *Student/faculty ratio:* 25:1.
Academics *Calendar:* quarters. *Degrees:* certificates, diplomas, associate, and bachelor's.
Standardized Tests *Required:* Wonderlic Scholastic Level Exam (SLE) (for admission).
Applying *Application fee:* $50. *Required:* high school transcript, interview.
Freshman Application Contact Matt Brady, Director of Admissions, Harrison College, 56075 Parkway Avenue, Elkhart, IN 46516. *Phone:* 574-522-0397. *Toll-free phone:* 888-544-4422. *E-mail:* matt.brady@harrison.edu. *Web site:* http://www.harrison.edu/.

Harrison College
Evansville, Indiana
- **Proprietary** primarily 2-year
- **Urban** campus
- **Coed**

Faculty *Student/faculty ratio:* 15:1.
Academics *Calendar:* quarters. *Degrees:* certificates, diplomas, associate, and bachelor's. *Special study options:* adult/continuing education programs, cooperative education, distance learning, double majors, independent study, internships, part-time degree program.
Standardized Tests *Required:* Wonderlic Scholastic Level Exam (SLE) (for admission).
Applying *Options:* electronic application. *Application fee:* $50. *Required:* high school transcript, interview.
Freshman Application Contact Mr. Bryan Barber, Harrison College, 4601 Theater Drive, Evansville, IN 47715. *Phone:* 812-476-6000. *Toll-free phone:* 888-544-4422. *Fax:* 812-471-8576. *E-mail:* bryan.barber@harrison.edu. *Web site:* http://www.harrison.edu/.

Harrison College
Fort Wayne, Indiana
- **Proprietary** primarily 2-year
- **Urban** campus
- **Coed**

Faculty *Student/faculty ratio:* 15:1.
Academics *Calendar:* quarters. *Degrees:* certificates, diplomas, associate, and bachelor's. *Special study options:* adult/continuing education programs, cooperative education, distance learning, double majors, independent study, internships, part-time degree program.
Standardized Tests *Required:* Wonderlic Scholastic Level Exam (SLE) (for admission).
Applying *Options:* electronic application. *Application fee:* $50. *Required:* high school transcript, interview.
Freshman Application Contact Mr. Matt Wallace, Associate Director of Admissions, Harrison College, 6413 North Clinton Street, Fort Wayne, IN 46825. *Phone:* 260-471-7667. *Toll-free phone:* 888-544-4422. *Fax:* 260-471-6918. *E-mail:* matt.wallace@harrison.edu. *Web site:* http://www.harrison.edu/

Harrison College
Indianapolis, Indiana
- **Proprietary** primarily 2-year, founded 1902
- **Urban** 1-acre campus with easy access to Indianapolis
- **Coed,** 2,668 undergraduate students, 65% full-time, 75% women, 25% men

Undergraduates 1,740 full-time, 928 part-time. Students come from 32 states and territories; 1 other country; 17% Black or African American, non-Hispanic/Latino; 2% Hispanic/Latino; 0.5% Asian, non-Hispanic/Latino; 0.3% American Indian or Alaska Native, non-Hispanic/Latino; 0.6% Two or more races, non-Hispanic/Latino; 36% Race/ethnicity unknown; 12% transferred in. *Retention:* 44% of full-time freshmen returned.

Freshmen *Admission:* 622 applied, 484 admitted, 387 enrolled.
Faculty *Student/faculty ratio:* 16:1.
Majors Accounting; administrative assistant and secretarial science; baking and pastry arts; business administration and management; computer systems networking and telecommunications; computer technology/computer systems technology; criminal justice/safety; culinary arts; fashion merchandising; finance; health/health-care administration; hotel/motel administration; human resources management; information technology; management information systems and services related; marketing/marketing management; medical/clinical assistant.
Academics *Calendar:* quarters. *Degrees:* certificates, diplomas, associate, and bachelor's. *Special study options:* adult/continuing education programs, cooperative education, distance learning, double majors, internships, part-time degree program, summer session for credit.
Student Life *Housing:* college housing not available. *Activities and Organizations:* Student Advisory Board, Student Ambassadors, Phi Beta Lambda. *Campus security:* 24-hour patrols.
Standardized Tests *Required:* Wonderlic Scholastic Level Exam (SLE) (for admission).
Applying *Options:* electronic application. *Application fee:* $50. *Required:* high school transcript, interview. *Application deadlines:* rolling (freshmen), rolling (transfers). *Notification:* continuous (freshmen), continuous (transfers).
Freshman Application Contact Mr. Ted Lukomski, Director of Admissions, Harrison College, 550 East Washington Street, Indianapolis, IN 46204. *Phone:* 317-264-5656. *Toll-free phone:* 888-544-4422. *Fax:* 317-264-5650. *E-mail:* ted.lukomski@ibcschools.edu. *Web site:* http://www.harrison.edu/.

Harrison College
Indianapolis, Indiana
- **Proprietary** 2-year
- **Urban** campus
- **Coed,** 321 undergraduate students, 75% full-time, 86% women, 14% men

Undergraduates 241 full-time, 80 part-time. 6% Black or African American, non-Hispanic/Latino; 1% Hispanic/Latino; 0.3% Native Hawaiian or other Pacific Islander, non-Hispanic/Latino; 2% Two or more races, non-Hispanic/Latino; 10% Race/ethnicity unknown; 10% transferred in. *Retention:* 58% of full-time freshmen returned.
Freshmen *Admission:* 99 applied, 54 admitted, 53 enrolled.
Faculty *Total:* 14. *Student/faculty ratio:* 13:1.
Majors Computer and information sciences; veterinary/animal health technology.
Academics *Calendar:* quarters. *Degree:* certificates, diplomas, and associate. *Special study options:* adult/continuing education programs.
Student Life *Housing:* college housing not available.
Standardized Tests *Required:* Wonderlic Scholastic Level Exam (for admission).
Applying *Application fee:* $50. *Required:* high school transcript, interview. *Application deadlines:* rolling (freshmen), rolling (out-of-state freshmen), rolling (transfers). *Notification:* continuous (freshmen), continuous (out-of-state freshmen), continuous (transfers).
Freshman Application Contact Mr. Matt Stein, Director of Admissions, Harrison College, 6300 Technology Center Drive, Indianapolis, IN 46278. *Phone:* 317-873-6500. *Toll-free phone:* 888-544-4422. *Fax:* 317-733-6266. *E-mail:* matthew.stein@harrison.edu. *Web site:* http://www.harrison.edu/.

Harrison College
Indianapolis, Indiana
- **Proprietary** 2-year
- **Urban** campus
- **Coed, primarily women**

Faculty *Student/faculty ratio:* 15:1.
Academics *Calendar:* quarters. *Degree:* certificates, diplomas, and associate. *Special study options:* adult/continuing education programs, cooperative education, distance learning, double majors, independent study, internships, part-time degree program.
Standardized Tests *Required:* Wonderlic Scholastic Level Exam (SLE), TEAS Exam for Associate Degree in Nursing (for admission).
Applying *Options:* electronic application. *Application fee:* $50. *Required:* high school transcript, interview.
Freshman Application Contact Jan Carter, Director of Admissions, Harrison College, 8150 Brookville Road, Indianapolis, IN 46239. *Phone:* 317-375-8000. *Toll-free phone:* 888-544-4422. *Fax:* 317-351-1871. *E-mail:* jan.carter@harrison.edu. *Web site:* http://www.harrison.edu/.

Harrison College
Lafayette, Indiana

- **Proprietary** primarily 2-year
- **Small-town** campus
- **Coed,** 350 undergraduate students, 82% full-time, 85% women, 15% men

Undergraduates 286 full-time, 64 part-time. 5% Black or African American, non-Hispanic/Latino; 6% Hispanic/Latino; 0.6% Asian, non-Hispanic/Latino; 0.3% Native Hawaiian or other Pacific Islander, non-Hispanic/Latino; 0.3% American Indian or Alaska Native, non-Hispanic/Latino; 1% Two or more races, non-Hispanic/Latino; 17% transferred in. *Retention:* 45% of full-time freshmen returned.

Freshmen *Admission:* 32 applied, 32 admitted, 32 enrolled.

Faculty *Student/faculty ratio:* 15:1.

Majors Accounting; administrative assistant and secretarial science; banking and financial support services; business administration and management; health information/medical records technology; human resources management; marketing/marketing management; medical/clinical assistant; medical insurance coding.

Academics *Calendar:* quarters. *Degrees:* certificates, diplomas, associate, and bachelor's. *Special study options:* adult/continuing education programs, cooperative education, distance learning, double majors, independent study, internships, part-time degree program.

Library Main Library plus 1 other.

Student Life *Housing:* college housing not available.

Standardized Tests *Required:* Wonderlic Scholastic Level Exam (SLE) (for admission).

Applying *Options:* electronic application. *Application fee:* $50. *Required:* high school transcript, interview. *Application deadlines:* rolling (freshmen), rolling (out-of-state freshmen), rolling (transfers). *Notification:* continuous (freshmen), continuous (out-of-state freshmen), continuous (transfers).

Freshman Application Contact Ms. Stacy Golleher, Associate Director of Admissions, Harrison College, 4705 Meijer Court, Lafayette, IN 47905. *Phone:* 765-447-9550. *Toll-free phone:* 888-544-4422. *Fax:* 765-447-0868. *E-mail:* stacy.golleher@harrison.edu. *Web site:* http://www.harrison.edu/.

Harrison College
Muncie, Indiana

- **Proprietary** primarily 2-year
- **Small-town** campus
- **Coed, primarily women,** 229 undergraduate students, 82% full-time, 78% women, 22% men

Undergraduates 187 full-time, 42 part-time. 12% Black or African American, non-Hispanic/Latino; 2% Two or more races, non-Hispanic/Latino. *Retention:* 52% of full-time freshmen returned.

Freshmen *Admission:* 117 enrolled.

Faculty *Student/faculty ratio:* 16:1.

Majors Accounting; administrative assistant and secretarial science; business administration and management; business administration, management and operations related; computer and information sciences and support services related; computer technology/computer systems technology; criminal justice/safety; finance; health/health-care administration; health information/medical records technology; human resources management; information technology; management information systems and services related; marketing/marketing management; medical/clinical assistant.

Academics *Calendar:* quarters. *Degrees:* certificates, diplomas, associate, and bachelor's. *Special study options:* adult/continuing education programs, cooperative education, distance learning, double majors, independent study, part-time degree program.

Library Main Library plus 1 other.

Student Life *Housing:* college housing not available. *Activities and Organizations:* Phi Beta Lambda.

Standardized Tests *Required:* Wonderlic Scholastic Level Exam (SLE) (for admission).

Applying *Options:* electronic application. *Application fee:* $50. *Required:* high school transcript, interview. *Application deadlines:* rolling (freshmen), rolling (transfers). *Notification:* continuous (freshmen), continuous (transfers).

Freshman Application Contact Mr. Jeremy Linder, Associate Director of Admissions, Harrison College, Muncie, IN 47303. *Phone:* 765-288-8681. *Toll-free phone:* 888-544-4422. *Fax:* 765-288-8797. *E-mail:* Jeremy.linder@harrison.edu. *Web site:* http://www.harrison.edu/.

Harrison College
Terre Haute, Indiana

- **Proprietary** primarily 2-year, founded 1902
- **Small-town** campus
- **Coed**

Faculty *Student/faculty ratio:* 15:1.

Academics *Calendar:* quarters. *Degrees:* certificates, diplomas, associate, and bachelor's. *Special study options:* adult/continuing education programs, cooperative education, distance learning, double majors, independent study, internships, part-time degree program.

Standardized Tests *Required:* Wonderlic Scholastic Level Exam (SLE) (for admission).

Applying *Options:* electronic application. *Application fee:* $50. *Required:* high school transcript, interview.

Freshman Application Contact Sarah Stultz, Associate Director of Admissions, Harrison College, 1378 South State Road 46, Terre Haute, IN 47803. *Phone:* 812-877-2100. *Toll-free phone:* 888-544-4422. *Fax:* 812-877-4440. *E-mail:* sarah.stultz@harrison.edu. *Web site:* http://www.harrison.edu/.

International Business College
Indianapolis, Indiana

- **Private** 2-year, founded 1889
- **Suburban** campus
- **Coed,** 386 undergraduate students
- 76% of applicants were admitted

Freshmen *Admission:* 1,006 applied, 766 admitted.

Majors Accounting and business/management; business administration and management; computer programming; dental assisting; graphic design; legal administrative assistant/secretary; legal assistant/paralegal; medical/clinical assistant; system, networking, and LAN/WAN management; tourism and travel services management; veterinary/animal health technology.

Academics *Calendar:* semesters. *Degree:* diplomas and associate. *Special study options:* accelerated degree program, internships.

Freshman Application Contact Admissions Office, International Business College, 7205 Shadeland Station, Indianapolis, IN 46256. *Phone:* 317-813-2300. *Toll-free phone:* 800-589-6500. *Web site:* http://www.ibcindianapolis.edu/.

ITT Technical Institute
Fort Wayne, Indiana

- **Proprietary** primarily 2-year, founded 1967, part of ITT Educational Services, Inc.
- **Coed**

Majors Business administration and management; CAD/CADD drafting/design technology; computer and information systems security; computer engineering technology; computer software and media applications related; computer software engineering; computer software technology; computer systems networking and telecommunications; construction management; criminal justice/law enforcement administration; design and visual communications; electrical, electronic and communications engineering technology; game and interactive media design; industrial technology; legal assistant/paralegal; project management; registered nursing/registered nurse; system, networking, and LAN/WAN management.

Academics *Calendar:* quarters. *Degrees:* associate and bachelor's.

Student Life *Housing:* college housing not available.

Freshman Application Contact Director of Recruitment, ITT Technical Institute, 2810 Dupont Commerce Court, Fort Wayne, IN 46825. *Phone:* 260-497-6200. *Toll-free phone:* 800-866-4488. *Fax:* 260-497-6299. *Web site:* http://www.itt-tech.edu/.

ITT Technical Institute
Indianapolis, Indiana

- **Proprietary** founded 1966, part of ITT Educational Services, Inc.
- **Suburban** campus
- **Coed**

Majors Accounting technology and bookkeeping; CAD/CADD drafting/design technology; computer and information systems security; computer engineering technology; computer software and media applications related; computer software engineering; computer software technology; construction management; criminal justice/law enforcement administration; design and visual communications; electrical, electronic and communications engineering technology; game and interactive media design; health information/medical records technology; industrial technology; legal assistant/paralegal; project

management; registered nursing/registered nurse; system, networking, and LAN/WAN management.
Academics *Calendar:* quarters. *Degrees:* diplomas, associate, bachelor's, and master's.
Student Life *Housing:* college housing not available.
Freshman Application Contact Director of Recruitment, ITT Technical Institute, 9511 Angola Court, Indianapolis, IN 46268-1119. *Phone:* 317-875-8640. *Toll-free phone:* 800-937-4488. *Web site:* http://www.itt-tech.edu/.

ITT Technical Institute
Merrillville, Indiana

- **Proprietary** primarily 2-year
- **Coed**

Majors CAD/CADD drafting/design technology; computer and information systems security; computer engineering technology; construction management; criminal justice/law enforcement administration; electrical, electronic and communications engineering technology; legal assistant/paralegal; project management; registered nursing/registered nurse; system, networking, and LAN/WAN management.
Academics *Degrees:* associate and bachelor's.
Freshman Application Contact Director of Recruitment, ITT Technical Institute, 8488 Georgia Street, Merrillville, IN 46410. *Phone:* 219-738-6100. *Toll-free phone:* 877-418-8134. *Web site:* http://www.itt-tech.edu/.

ITT Technical Institute
Newburgh, Indiana

- **Proprietary** primarily 2-year, founded 1966, part of ITT Educational Services, Inc.
- **Coed**

Majors CAD/CADD drafting/design technology; computer and information systems security; computer engineering technology; computer software and media applications related; computer software engineering; computer software technology; construction management; criminal justice/law enforcement administration; design and visual communications; game and interactive media design; industrial technology; legal assistant/paralegal; project management; registered nursing/registered nurse; system, networking, and LAN/WAN management.
Academics *Calendar:* quarters. *Degrees:* associate and bachelor's.
Student Life *Housing:* college housing not available.
Freshman Application Contact Director of Recruitment, ITT Technical Institute, 10999 Stahl Road, Newburgh, IN 47630-7430. *Phone:* 812-858-1600. *Toll-free phone:* 800-832-4488. *Web site:* http://www.itt-tech.edu/.

Ivy Tech Community College–Bloomington
Bloomington, Indiana

- **State-supported** 2-year, founded 2001, part of Ivy Tech Community College System
- **Coed,** 6,391 undergraduate students, 49% full-time, 57% women, 43% men

Undergraduates 3,108 full-time, 3,283 part-time. 6% transferred in. *Retention:* 50% of full-time freshmen returned.
Freshmen *Admission:* 2,141 applied, 2,141 admitted, 1,381 enrolled.
Faculty *Total:* 351, 19% full-time. *Student/faculty ratio:* 25:1.
Majors Accounting technology and bookkeeping; building/property maintenance; business administration and management; business automation/technology/data entry; cabinetmaking and millwork; child-care and support services management; computer and information sciences; criminal justice/safety; early childhood education; electrical, electronic and communications engineering technology; electrician; emergency medical technology (EMT paramedic); executive assistant/executive secretary; general studies; heating, air conditioning, ventilation and refrigeration maintenance technology; human services; industrial technology; legal assistant/paralegal; liberal arts and sciences/liberal studies; library and archives assisting; machine tool technology; mechanic and repair technologies related; mechanics and repair; pipefitting and sprinkler fitting; psychiatric/mental health services technology; registered nursing/registered nurse; tool and die technology.
Academics *Calendar:* semesters. *Degree:* certificates and associate. *Special study options:* academic remediation for entering students, adult/continuing education programs, advanced placement credit, distance learning, external degree program, internships, part-time degree program, services for LD students, summer session for credit.
Library 5,516 titles, 97 serial subscriptions, 1,281 audiovisual materials, an OPAC, a Web page.

Student Life *Activities and Organizations:* student government, Phi Theta Kappa. *Campus security:* late-night transport/escort service.
Costs (2010–11) *Tuition:* state resident $3137 full-time, $105 per credit hour part-time; nonresident $6641 full-time, $221 per credit hour part-time. *Required fees:* $120 full-time, $60 per term part-time. *Payment plans:* installment, deferred payment. *Waivers:* senior citizens and employees or children of employees.
Financial Aid Of all full-time matriculated undergraduates who enrolled in 2009, 51 Federal Work-Study jobs (averaging $3259).
Applying *Options:* electronic application, deferred entrance. *Required:* high school transcript. *Required for some:* interview. *Application deadlines:* rolling (freshmen), rolling (transfers). *Notification:* continuous (freshmen), continuous (transfers).
Freshman Application Contact Mr. Neil Frederick, Assistant Director of Admissions, Ivy Tech Community College–Bloomington, 200 Daniels Way, Bloomington, IN 47404. *Phone:* 812-330-6026. *Fax:* 812-332-8147. *E-mail:* nfrederi@ivytech.edu. *Web site:* http://www.ivytech.edu/.

Ivy Tech Community College–Central Indiana
Indianapolis, Indiana

- **State-supported** 2-year, founded 1963, part of Ivy Tech Community College System
- **Urban** 10-acre campus
- **Coed,** 22,378 undergraduate students, 35% full-time, 59% women, 41% men

Undergraduates 7,912 full-time, 14,466 part-time. 1% are from out of state; 5% transferred in. *Retention:* 54% of full-time freshmen returned.
Freshmen *Admission:* 3,609 enrolled.
Faculty *Total:* 838, 20% full-time. *Student/faculty ratio:* 32:1.
Majors Accounting technology and bookkeeping; automobile/automotive mechanics technology; biotechnology; building/property maintenance; business administration and management; business automation/technology/data entry; cabinetmaking and millwork; carpentry; child-care and support services management; child development; computer and information sciences; criminal justice/safety; design and visual communications; drafting and design technology; early childhood education; electrical, electronic and communications engineering technology; electrician; executive assistant/executive secretary; general studies; heating, air conditioning, ventilation and refrigeration maintenance technology; hospitality administration related; human services; industrial production technologies related; industrial technology; legal assistant/paralegal; liberal arts and sciences/liberal studies; machine shop technology; machine tool technology; masonry; mechanics and repair; medical/clinical assistant; medical radiologic technology; occupational safety and health technology; occupational therapist assistant; painting and wall covering; pipefitting and sprinkler fitting; psychiatric/mental health services technology; registered nursing/registered nurse; respiratory care therapy; sheet metal technology; surgical technology; tool and die technology.
Academics *Calendar:* semesters. *Degree:* certificates and associate. *Special study options:* academic remediation for entering students, adult/continuing education programs, advanced placement credit, cooperative education, distance learning, English as a second language, internships, off-campus study, part-time degree program, services for LD students, summer session for credit.
Library 20,247 titles, 138 serial subscriptions, 2,135 audiovisual materials, an OPAC, a Web page.
Student Life *Housing:* college housing not available. *Activities and Organizations:* student-run newspaper, student government, Phi Theta Kappa, Human Services Club, Administrative Office Assistants Club, Radiology Club. *Campus security:* 24-hour emergency response devices and patrols, late-night transport/escort service. *Student services:* personal/psychological counseling.
Athletics *Intramural sports:* baseball M, basketball M/W, cheerleading W, golf M/W, softball W, volleyball M/W.
Costs (2010–11) *Tuition:* state resident $3136 full-time, $105 per credit hour part-time; nonresident $6640 full-time, $221 per credit hour part-time. *Required fees:* $120 full-time, $60 per term part-time. *Payment plans:* installment, deferred payment. *Waivers:* senior citizens and employees or children of employees.
Financial Aid Of all full-time matriculated undergraduates who enrolled in 2009, 92 Federal Work-Study jobs (averaging $3766).
Applying *Options:* electronic application, early admission, deferred entrance. *Required:* high school transcript. *Required for some:* interview. *Application deadlines:* rolling (freshmen), rolling (transfers). *Notification:* continuous (freshmen), continuous (transfers).
Freshman Application Contact Ms. Tracy Funk, Director of Admissions, Ivy Tech Community College–Central Indiana, 50 West Fall Creek Parkway North Drive, Indianapolis, IN 46208-4777. *Phone:* 317-921-4371. *Toll-free phone:* 888-IVYLINE. *Fax:* 317-917-5919. *E-mail:* tfunk@ivytech.edu. *Web site:* http://www.ivytech.edu/.

Ivy Tech Community College–Columbus

Columbus, Indiana

- **State-supported** 2-year, founded 1963, part of Ivy Tech Community College System
- **Small-town** campus with easy access to Indianapolis
- **Coed,** 4,650 undergraduate students, 45% full-time, 69% women, 31% men

Undergraduates 2,092 full-time, 2,558 part-time. 5% transferred in. *Retention:* 51% of full-time freshmen returned.

Freshmen *Admission:* 864 enrolled.

Faculty *Total:* 271, 21% full-time. *Student/faculty ratio:* 23:1.

Majors Accounting technology and bookkeeping; automobile/automotive mechanics technology; building/property maintenance; business administration and management; business automation/technology/data entry; cabinet-making and millwork; child-care and support services management; computer and information sciences; design and visual communications; drafting and design technology; early childhood education; electrical and power transmission installation; electrical, electronic and communications engineering technology; executive assistant/executive secretary; general studies; heating, air conditioning, ventilation and refrigeration maintenance technology; human services; industrial technology; legal assistant/paralegal; liberal arts and sciences/liberal studies; library and archives assisting; machine tool technology; masonry; mechanic and repair technologies related; mechanics and repair; medical/clinical assistant; medical radiologic technology; pipefitting and sprinkler fitting; psychiatric/mental health services technology; robotics technology; surgical technology; tool and die technology.

Academics *Calendar:* semesters. *Degree:* certificates and associate. *Special study options:* academic remediation for entering students, adult/continuing education programs, advaneed placement credit, distance learning, internships, part-time degree program, services for LD students, summer session for credit.

Library 7,855 titles, 13,382 serial subscriptions, 989 audiovisual materials, an OPAC, a Web page.

Student Life *Housing:* college housing not available. *Activities and Organizations:* student government, Phi Theta Kappa, LPN Club. *Campus security:* late-night transport/escort service, trained evening security personnel, escort service.

Costs (2010–11) *Tuition:* state resident $3136 full-time, $105 per credit hour part-time; nonresident $6640 full-time, $221 per credit hour part-time. *Required fees:* $120 full-time, $60 per term part-time. *Payment plans:* installment, deferred payment. *Waivers:* senior citizens and employees or children of employees.

Financial Aid Of all full-time matriculated undergraduates who enrolled in 2009, 26 Federal Work-Study jobs (averaging $1694).

Applying *Options:* electronic application, early admission, deferred entrance. *Required:* high school transcript. *Required for some:* interview. *Application deadlines:* rolling (freshmen), rolling (transfers). *Notification:* continuous (freshmen), continuous (transfers).

Freshman Application Contact Mr. Neil Bagadiong, Assistant Director of Student Affairs, Ivy Tech Community College–Columbus, 4475 Central Avenue, Columbus, IN 47203-1868. *Phone:* 812-374-5129. *Toll-free phone:* 800-922-4838. *Fax:* 812-372-0331. *E-mail:* nbagadio@ivytech.edu. *Web site:* http://www.ivytech.edu/.

Ivy Tech Community College–East Central

Muncie, Indiana

- **State-supported** 2-year, founded 1968, part of Ivy Tech Community College System
- **Suburban** 15-acre campus with easy access to Indianapolis
- **Coed,** 9,430 undergraduate students, 54% full-time, 63% women, 37% men

Undergraduates 5,060 full-time, 4,370 part-time. 4% transferred in. *Retention:* 52% of full-time freshmen returned.

Freshmen *Admission:* 2,189 enrolled.

Faculty *Total:* 553, 19% full-time. *Student/faculty ratio:* 25:1.

Majors Accounting technology and bookkeeping; automobile/automotive mechanics technology; building/property maintenance; business administration and management; business automation/technology/data entry; cabinet-making and millwork; carpentry; child-care and support services management; computer and information sciences; construction trades; construction trades related; criminal justice/safety; early childhood education; electrical, electronic and communications engineering technology; electrician; executive assistant/executive secretary; general studies; heating, air conditioning, ventilation and refrigeration maintenance technology; hospitality administration; hospitality administration related; human services; industrial mechanics and maintenance technology; industrial production technologies related; industrial technology; legal assistant/paralegal; liberal arts and sciences/liberal studies; library and archives assisting; machine tool technology; masonry; medical/clinical assistant; medical radiologic technology; painting and wall covering; physical therapy technology; pipefitting and sprinkler fitting; psychiatric/mental health services technology; registered nursing/registered nurse; surgical technology; tool and die technology.

Academics *Calendar:* semesters. *Degree:* certificates and associate. *Special study options:* academic remediation for entering students, adult/continuing education programs, advanced placement credit, distance learning, internships, part-time degree program, services for LD students.

Library 5,779 titles, 145 serial subscriptions, 6,266 audiovisual materials, an OPAC, a Web page.

Student Life *Housing:* college housing not available. *Activities and Organizations:* Business Professionals of America, Skills USA - VICA, student government, Phi Theta Kappa, Human Services Club.

Costs (2010–11) *Tuition:* state resident $3136 full-time, $105 per credit hour part-time; nonresident $6640 full-time, $231 per credit hour part-time. *Required fees:* $120 full-time, $60 per term part-time. *Payment plans:* installment, deferred payment. *Waivers:* senior citizens and employees or children of employees.

Financial Aid Of all full-time matriculated undergraduates who enrolled in 2009, 65 Federal Work-Study jobs (averaging $2666).

Applying *Options:* electronic application, early admission, deferred entrance. *Required:* high school transcript. *Required for some:* interview. *Application deadlines:* rolling (freshmen), rolling (transfers). *Notification:* continuous (freshmen), continuous (transfers).

Freshman Application Contact Ms. Mary Lewellen, Ivy Tech Community College–East Central, 4301 South Cowan Road, Muncie, IN 47302-9448. *Phone:* 765-289-2291 Ext. 391. *Toll-free phone:* 800-589-8324. *Fax:* 765-289-2292. *E-mail:* mlewelle@ivytech.edu. *Web site:* http://www.ivytech.edu/.

Ivy Tech Community College–Kokomo

Kokomo, Indiana

- **State-supported** 2-year, founded 1968, part of Ivy Tech Community College System
- **Small-town** 20-acre campus with easy access to Indianapolis
- **Coed,** 5,465 undergraduate students, 47% full-time, 64% women, 36% men

Undergraduates 2,592 full-time, 2,873 part-time. 3% transferred in. *Retention:* 58% of full-time freshmen returned.

Freshmen *Admission:* 1,012 enrolled.

Faculty *Total:* 324, 23% full-time. *Student/faculty ratio:* 22:1.

Majors Accounting technology and bookkeeping; automobile/automotive mechanics technology; building/property maintenance; business administration and management; business automation/technology/data entry; cabinet-making and millwork; child-care and support services management; computer and information sciences; construction trades related; criminal justice/safety; drafting and design technology; early childhood education; electrical, electronic and communications engineering technology; electrician; emergency medical technology (EMT paramedic); executive assistant/executive secretary; general studies; heating, air conditioning, ventilation and refrigeration maintenance technology; human services; industrial technology; legal assistant/paralegal; liberal arts and sciences/liberal studies; library and archives assisting; machine tool technology; mechanic and repair technologies related; mechanics and repair; medical/clinical assistant; pipefitting and sprinkler fitting; psychiatric/mental health services technology; surgical technology; tool and die technology.

Academics *Calendar:* semesters. *Degree:* certificates and associate. *Special study options:* academic remediation for entering students, adult/continuing education programs, advanced placement credit, distance learning, internships, part-time degree program, services for LD students, summer session for credit.

Library 5,177 titles, 99 serial subscriptions, 772 audiovisual materials, an OPAC, a Web page.

Student Life *Housing:* college housing not available. *Activities and Organizations:* student-run newspaper, student government, Collegiate Secretaries International, Licensed Practical Nursing Club, Phi Theta Kappa. *Campus security:* 24-hour emergency response devices, late-night transport/escort service. *Student services:* personal/psychological counseling.

Costs (2010–11) *Tuition:* state resident $3136 full-time, $105 per credit hour part-time; nonresident $6640 full-time, $221 per credit hour part-time. *Required fees:* $120 full-time, $60 per term part-time. *Payment plans:* installment, deferred payment. *Waivers:* senior citizens and employees or children of employees.

Financial Aid Of all full-time matriculated undergraduates who enrolled in 2009, 45 Federal Work-Study jobs (averaging $1829).

Applying *Options:* electronic application, early admission. *Required:* high school transcript. *Required for some:* interview. *Application deadlines:* rolling (freshmen), rolling (transfers). *Notification:* continuous (freshmen), continuous (transfers).

Freshman Application Contact Ms. Suzanne Dillman, Director of Admissions, Ivy Tech Community College–Kokomo, 1815 East Morgan Street, Kokomo, IN 46903-1373. *Phone:* 765-459-0561 Ext. 318. *Toll-free phone:* 800-459-0561. *Fax:* 765-454-5111. *E-mail:* sdillman@ivytech.edu. *Web site:* http://www.ivytech.edu/.

Ivy Tech Community College–Lafayette
Lafayette, Indiana

- **State-supported** 2-year, founded 1968, part of Ivy Tech Community College System
- **Suburban** campus with easy access to Indianapolis
- **Coed,** 8,085 undergraduate students, 50% full-time, 56% women, 44% men

Undergraduates 4,042 full-time, 4,043 part-time. 5% transferred in. *Retention:* 52% of full-time freshmen returned.
Freshmen *Admission:* 1,610 enrolled.
Faculty *Total:* 433, 23% full-time. *Student/faculty ratio:* 25:1.
Majors Accounting; accounting technology and bookkeeping; automobile/automotive mechanics technology; biotechnology; building/property maintenance; business administration and management; business automation/technology/data entry; cabinetmaking and millwork; carpentry; child-care and support services management; computer and information sciences; drafting and design technology; early childhood education; electrical, electronic and communications engineering technology; electrician; executive assistant/executive secretary; general studies; heating, air conditioning, ventilation and refrigeration maintenance technology; human services; industrial production technologies related; industrial technology; ironworking; legal assistant/paralegal; liberal arts and sciences/liberal studies; library and archives assisting; lineworker; machine tool technology; masonry; mechanic and repair technologies related; mechanics and repair; medical/clinical assistant; painting and wall covering; pipefitting and sprinkler fitting; psychiatric/mental health services technology; quality control and safety technologies related; quality control technology; registered nursing/registered nurse; respiratory care therapy; robotics technology; sheet metal technology; surgical technology; tool and die technology.
Academics *Calendar:* semesters. *Degree:* certificates and associate. *Special study options:* academic remediation for entering students, advanced placement credit, distance learning, internships, part-time degree program, services for LD students, summer session for credit.
Library 8,043 titles, 200 serial subscriptions, 2,234 audiovisual materials, an OPAC, a Web page.
Student Life *Housing:* college housing not available. *Activities and Organizations:* student-run newspaper, student government, Phi Theta Kappa, LPN Club, Accounting Club; Student Computer Technology Association. *Student services:* personal/psychological counseling.
Costs (2010–11) *Tuition:* state resident $3136 full-time, $105 per credit hour part-time; nonresident $6640 full-time, $221 per credit hour part-time. *Required fees:* $120 full-time, $60 per term part-time. *Payment plans:* installment, deferred payment. *Waivers:* senior citizens and employees or children of employees.
Financial Aid Of all full-time matriculated undergraduates who enrolled in 2009, 65 Federal Work-Study jobs (averaging $2222). 1 state and other part-time job (averaging $2436).
Applying *Options:* electronic application. *Required:* high school transcript. *Required for some:* interview. *Application deadlines:* rolling (freshmen), rolling (transfers). *Notification:* continuous (freshmen), continuous (transfers).
Freshman Application Contact Ms. Judy Doppelfeld, Director of Admissions, Ivy Tech Community College–Lafayette, 3101 South Creasy Lane, PO Box 6299, Lafayette, IN 47903. *Phone:* 765-269-5116. *Toll-free phone:* 800-669-4882. *Fax:* 765-772-9293. *E-mail:* jdopplef@ivytech.edu. *Web site:* http://www.ivytech.edu/.

Ivy Tech Community College–North Central
South Bend, Indiana

- **State-supported** 2-year, founded 1968, part of Ivy Tech Community College System
- **Suburban** 4-acre campus
- **Coed,** 8,688 undergraduate students, 33% full-time, 62% women, 38% men

Undergraduates 2,887 full-time, 5,801 part-time. 1% are from out of state; 6% transferred in. *Retention:* 55% of full-time freshmen returned.

Freshmen *Admission:* 1,402 enrolled.
Faculty *Total:* 414, 23% full-time. *Student/faculty ratio:* 23:1.
Majors Accounting technology and bookkeeping; automobile/automotive mechanics technology; biotechnology; building/property maintenance; business administration and management; business automation/technology/data entry; cabinetmaking and millwork; carpentry; child-care and support services management; clinical/medical laboratory technology; computer and information sciences; criminal justice/safety; design and visual communications; early childhood education; educational/instructional technology; electrical, electronic and communications engineering technology; electrician; emergency medical technology (EMT paramedic); executive assistant/executive secretary; general studies; heating, air conditioning, ventilation and refrigeration maintenance technology; hospitality administration; human services; industrial production technologies related; industrial technology; interior design; ironworking; legal assistant/paralegal; liberal arts and sciences/liberal studies; library and archives assisting; machine tool technology; masonry; mechanic and repair technologies related; mechanics and repair; medical/clinical assistant; painting and wall covering; pipefitting and sprinkler fitting; registered nursing/registered nurse; robotics technology; sheet metal technology; telecommunications technology; tool and die technology.
Academics *Calendar:* semesters. *Degree:* certificates and associate. *Special study options:* academic remediation for entering students, adult/continuing education programs, advanced placement credit, distance learning, English as a second language, internships, off-campus study, part-time degree program, services for LD students, summer session for credit.
Library 6,246 titles, 90 serial subscriptions, 689 audiovisual materials, an OPAC, a Web page.
Student Life *Housing:* college housing not available. *Activities and Organizations:* Phi Theta Kappa, student government, LPN Club. *Campus security:* 24-hour emergency response devices and patrols, late-night transport/escort service, security during open hours. *Student services:* personal/psychological counseling, women's center.
Costs (2010–11) *Tuition:* state resident $3136 full-time, $105 per credit hour part-time; nonresident $6640 full-time, $221 per credit hour part-time. *Required fees:* $120 full-time, $60 per term part-time. *Payment plans:* installment, deferred payment. *Waivers:* senior citizens and employees or children of employees.
Financial Aid Of all full-time matriculated undergraduates who enrolled in 2009, 100 Federal Work-Study jobs (averaging $1538).
Applying *Options:* electronic application, early admission, deferred entrance. *Required:* high school transcript. *Required for some:* interview. *Application deadlines:* rolling (freshmen), rolling (transfers). *Notification:* continuous (freshmen), continuous (transfers).
Freshman Application Contact Ms. Pam Decker, Director of Admissions, Ivy Tech Community College–North Central, 220 Dean Johnson Boulevard, South Bend, IN 46601-3415. *Phone:* 574-289-7001. *Fax:* 574-236-7177. *E-mail:* pdecker@ivytech.edu. *Web site:* http://www.ivytech.edu/.

Ivy Tech Community College–Northeast
Fort Wayne, Indiana

- **State-supported** 2-year, founded 1969, part of Ivy Tech Community College System
- **Urban** 22-acre campus
- **Coed,** 11,607 undergraduate students, 44% full-time, 60% women, 40% men

Undergraduates 5,077 full-time, 6,530 part-time. 1% are from out of state; 6% transferred in. *Retention:* 49% of full-time freshmen returned.
Freshmen *Admission:* 2,401 enrolled.
Faculty *Total:* 551, 22% full-time. *Student/faculty ratio:* 27:1.
Majors Accounting technology and bookkeeping; automobile/automotive mechanics technology; building/property maintenance; business administration and management; business automation/technology/data entry; cabinetmaking and millwork; child-care and support services management; computer and information sciences; construction trades; construction trades related; drafting and design technology; early childhood education; electrical, electronic and communications engineering technology; electrician; executive assistant/executive secretary; general studies; heating, air conditioning, ventilation and refrigeration maintenance technology; hospitality administration; hospitality administration related; human services; industrial production technologies related; industrial technology; ironworking; legal assistant/paralegal; liberal arts and sciences/liberal studies; library and archives assisting; machine tool technology; masonry; massage therapy; mechanics and repair; medical/clinical assistant; occupational safety and health technology; painting and wall covering; pipefitting and sprinkler fitting; psychiatric/mental health services technology; respiratory care therapy; robotics technology; sheet metal technology; tool and die technology.

Academics *Calendar:* semesters. *Degree:* certificates and associate. *Special study options:* adult/continuing education programs, advanced placement credit, distance learning, English as a second language, internships, part-time degree program, services for LD students, summer session for credit.
Library 18,389 titles, 110 serial subscriptions, 3,397 audiovisual materials, an OPAC, a Web page.
Student Life *Housing:* college housing not available. *Activities and Organizations:* student-run newspaper, student government, LPN Club, Phi Theta Kappa. *Campus security:* 24-hour emergency response devices and patrols, late-night transport/escort service.
Costs (2010–11) *Tuition:* state resident $3136 full-time, $105 per credit hour part-time; nonresident $6640 full-time, $221 per credit hour part-time. *Required fees:* $120 full-time, $60 per term part-time. *Payment plans:* installment, deferred payment. *Waivers:* senior citizens and employees or children of employees.
Financial Aid Of all full-time matriculated undergraduates who enrolled in 2009, 40 Federal Work-Study jobs (averaging $4041).
Applying *Options:* early admission. *Required:* high school transcript. *Required for some:* interview. *Application deadlines:* rolling (freshmen), rolling (transfers). *Notification:* continuous (freshmen), continuous (transfers).
Freshman Application Contact Mr. Steve Scheer, Director of Admissions, Ivy Tech Community College–Northeast, 3800 North Anthony Boulevard, Ft. Wayne, IN 46805-1489. *Phone:* 260-480-4221. *Toll-free phone:* 800-859-4882. *Fax:* 260-480-2053. *E-mail:* sscheer@ivytech.edu. *Web site:* http://www.ivytech.edu/.

Ivy Tech Community College–Northwest

Gary, Indiana

- **State-supported** 2-year, founded 1963, part of Ivy Tech Community College System
- **Urban** 13-acre campus with easy access to Chicago
- **Coed,** 9,045 undergraduate students, 41% full-time, 63% women, 37% men

Undergraduates 3,743 full-time, 5,302 part-time. 6% transferred in. *Retention:* 48% of full-time freshmen returned.
Freshmen *Admission:* 1,932 enrolled.
Faculty *Total:* 411, 28% full-time. *Student/faculty ratio:* 25:1.
Majors Accounting technology and bookkeeping; automobile/automotive mechanics technology; building/construction finishing, management, and inspection related; building/property maintenance; business administration and management; business automation/technology/data entry; cabinetmaking and millwork; carpentry; child-care and support services management; computer and information sciences; construction trades; criminal justice/safety; drafting and design technology; early childhood education; electrical, electronic and communications engineering technology; electrician; executive assistant/executive secretary; funeral service and mortuary science; general studies; heating, air conditioning, ventilation and refrigeration maintenance technology; hospitality administration; human services; industrial technology; ironworking; legal assistant/paralegal; liberal arts and sciences/liberal studies; library and archives assisting; machine tool technology; masonry; mechanic and repair technologies related; mechanics and repair; medical/clinical assistant; occupational safety and health technology; painting and wall covering; pipefitting and sprinkler fitting; psychiatric/mental health services technology; registered nursing/registered nurse; respiratory care therapy; sheet metal technology; surgical technology; telecommunications technology; tool and die technology.
Academics *Calendar:* semesters. *Degree:* certificates and associate. *Special study options:* academic remediation for entering students, adult/continuing education programs, advanced placement credit, distance learning, internships, part-time degree program, services for LD students, summer session for credit.
Library 13,805 titles, 160 serial subscriptions, 4,295 audiovisual materials, an OPAC, a Web page.
Student Life *Housing:* college housing not available. *Activities and Organizations:* Phi Theta Kappa, LPN Club, Computer Club, student government, Business Club. *Campus security:* 24-hour emergency response devices, late-night transport/escort service.
Costs (2010–11) *Tuition:* state resident $3136 full-time, $105 per credit hour part-time; nonresident $6640 full-time, $221 per credit hour part-time. *Required fees:* $120 full-time, $60 per term part-time.
Financial Aid Of all full-time matriculated undergraduates who enrolled in 2009, 74 Federal Work-Study jobs (averaging $2131).
Applying *Options:* electronic application, deferred entrance. *Required:* high school transcript. *Required for some:* interview. *Application deadlines:* rolling (freshmen), rolling (transfers). *Notification:* continuous (freshmen), continuous (transfers).
Freshman Application Contact Ms. Twilla Lewis, Associate Dean of Student Affairs, Ivy Tech Community College–Northwest, 1440 East 35th Avenue, Gary, IN 46409-499. *Phone:* 219-981-1111 Ext. 2273. *Toll-free phone:* 800-

843-4882. *Fax:* 219-981-4415. *E-mail:* tlewis@ivytech.edu. *Web site:* http://www.ivytech.edu/.

Ivy Tech Community College–Richmond

Richmond, Indiana

- **State-supported** 2-year, founded 1963, part of Ivy Tech Community College System
- **Small-town** 23-acre campus with easy access to Indianapolis
- **Coed,** 3,913 undergraduate students, 40% full-time, 66% women, 34% men

Undergraduates 1,546 full-time, 2,367 part-time. 3% transferred in. *Retention:* 56% of full-time freshmen returned.
Freshmen *Admission:* 603 enrolled.
Faculty *Total:* 197, 21% full-time. *Student/faculty ratio:* 25:1.
Majors Accounting technology and bookkeeping; automobile/automotive mechanics technology; building/property maintenance; business administration and management; business automation/technology/data entry; cabinetmaking and millwork; child-care and support services management; computer and information sciences; construction trades; construction trades related; early childhood education; electrical, electronic and communications engineering technology; electrician; executive assistant/executive secretary; general studies; heating, air conditioning, ventilation and refrigeration maintenance technology; human services; industrial production technologies related; industrial technology; legal assistant/paralegal; liberal arts and sciences/liberal studies; library and archives assisting; machine tool technology; mechanics and repair; medical/clinical assistant; pipefitting and sprinkler fitting; psychiatric/mental health services technology; registered nursing/registered nurse; robotics technology; tool and die technology.
Academics *Calendar:* semesters. *Degree:* certificates and associate. *Special study options:* academic remediation for entering students, adult/continuing education programs, advanced placement credit, distance learning, independent study, internships, off-campus study, part-time degree program, services for LD students, summer session for credit.
Student Life *Housing:* college housing not available. *Activities and Organizations:* student-run newspaper, student government, Phi Theta Kappa, LPN Club, CATS 2000, Business Professionals of America. *Campus security:* 24-hour emergency response devices, late-night transport/escort service. *Student services:* personal/psychological counseling.
Athletics *Intramural sports:* softball M/W.
Costs (2010–11) *Tuition:* state resident $3136 full-time, $105 per credit hour part-time; nonresident $6640 full-time, $221 per credit hour part-time. *Required fees:* $120 full-time, $60 per term part-time. *Payment plans:* installment, deferred payment. *Waivers:* senior citizens and employees or children of employees.
Financial Aid Of all full-time matriculated undergraduates who enrolled in 2009, 14 Federal Work-Study jobs (averaging $3106). 1 state and other part-time job (averaging $3380).
Applying *Options:* electronic application, early admission. *Required:* high school transcript. *Required for some:* interview. *Application deadlines:* rolling (freshmen), rolling (transfers). *Notification:* continuous (freshmen), continuous (transfers).
Freshman Application Contact Mr. Jeff Plasterer, Director of Admissions, Ivy Tech Community College–Richmond, 2325 Chester Boulevard, Richmond, IN 47374-1298. *Phone:* 765-966-2656 Ext. 1212. *Toll-free phone:* 800-659-4562. *Fax:* 765-962-8741. *E-mail:* jplaster@ivytech.edu. *Web site:* http://www.ivytech.edu/richmond/.

Ivy Tech Community College–Southeast

Madison, Indiana

- **State-supported** 2-year, founded 1963, part of Ivy Tech Community College System
- **Small-town** 5-acre campus with easy access to Louisville
- **Coed,** 3,024 undergraduate students, 47% full-time, 69% women, 31% men

Undergraduates 1,422 full-time, 1,602 part-time. 4% transferred in. *Retention:* 61% of full-time freshmen returned.
Freshmen *Admission:* 527 enrolled.
Faculty *Total:* 179, 25% full-time. *Student/faculty ratio:* 21:1.
Majors Accounting technology and bookkeeping; business administration and management; business automation/technology/data entry; child-care and support services management; computer and information sciences; early childhood education; electrical, electronic and communications engineering technology; executive assistant/executive secretary; general studies; human services; industrial technology; legal assistant/paralegal; liberal arts and sci-

ences/liberal studies; library and archives assisting; licensed practical/vocational nurse training; medical/clinical assistant; psychiatric/mental health services technology; registered nursing/registered nurse:

Academics *Calendar:* semesters. *Degree:* certificates and associate. *Special study options:* academic remediation for entering students, advanced placement credit, distance learning, internships, part-time degree program, services for LD students, summer session for credit.

Library 9,027 titles, 14,299 serial subscriptions, 1,341 audiovisual materials, an OPAC, a Web page.

Student Life *Housing:* college housing not available. *Activities and Organizations:* student government, Phi Theta Kappa, LPN Club. *Campus security:* 24-hour emergency response devices.

Costs (2010–11) *Tuition:* state resident $3136 full-time, $105 per credit hour part-time; nonresident $6640 full-time, $221 per credit hour part-time. *Required fees:* $120 full-time, $60 per term part-time. *Payment plans:* installment, deferred payment. *Waivers:* senior citizens and employees or children of employees.

Financial Aid Of all full-time matriculated undergraduates who enrolled in 2009, 26 Federal Work-Study jobs (averaging $1696).

Applying *Options:* electronic application. *Required:* high school transcript. *Required for some:* interview. *Application deadlines:* rolling (freshmen), rolling (transfers). *Notification:* continuous (freshmen), continuous (transfers).

Freshman Application Contact Ms. Cindy Hutcherson, Assistant Director of Admission/Career Counselor, Ivy Tech Community College–Southeast, 590 Ivy Tech Drive, Madison, IN 47250-1881. *Phone:* 812-265-2580 Ext. 4142. *Toll-free phone:* 800-403-2190. *Fax:* 812-265-4028. *E-mail:* chutcher@ivytech.edu. *Web site:* http://www.ivytech.edu/.

Ivy Tech Community College– Southern Indiana

Sellersburg, Indiana

- **State-supported** 2-year, founded 1968, part of Ivy Tech Community College System
- **Small-town** 63-acre campus with easy access to Louisville
- **Coed,** 5,133 undergraduate students, 37% full-time, 57% women, 43% men

Undergraduates 1,879 full-time, 3,254 part-time. 6% transferred in. *Retention:* 51% of full-time freshmen returned.

Freshmen *Admission:* 1,140 enrolled.

Faculty *Total:* 238, 23% full-time. *Student/faculty ratio:* 25:1.

Majors Accounting technology and bookkeeping; automobile/automotive mechanics technology; building/property maintenance; business administration and management; business automation/technology/data entry; cabinetmaking and millwork; carpentry; child-care and support services management; computer and information sciences; design and visual communications; early childhood education; electrical, electronic and communications engineering technology; electrician; executive assistant/executive secretary; general studies; heating, air conditioning, ventilation and refrigeration maintenance technology; human services; industrial technology; legal assistant/paralegal; liberal arts and sciences/liberal studies; library and archives assisting; machine tool technology; masonry; mechanics and repair; medical/clinical assistant; pipefitting and sprinkler fitting; psychiatric/mental health services technology; registered nursing/registered nurse; respiratory care therapy; sheet metal technology; tool and die technology.

Academics *Calendar:* semesters. *Degree:* certificates and associate. *Special study options:* academic remediation for entering students, adult/continuing education programs, advanced placement credit, cooperative education, distance learning, internships, part-time degree program, services for LD students, summer session for credit.

Library 7,634 titles, 66 serial subscriptions, 648 audiovisual materials, an OPAC, a Web page.

Student Life *Housing:* college housing not available. *Activities and Organizations:* Phi Theta Kappa, Practical Nursing Club, Medical Assistant Club, Accounting Club, student government. *Campus security:* late-night transport/escort service.

Costs (2010–11) *Tuition:* state resident $105 per credit hour part-time; nonresident $221 per credit hour part-time. *Required fees:* $60 per term part-time.

Financial Aid Of all full-time matriculated undergraduates who enrolled in 2009, 20 Federal Work-Study jobs (averaging $5007). 1 state and other part-time job (averaging $6080).

Applying *Options:* electronic application, early admission, deferred entrance. *Required:* high school transcript. *Required for some:* interview. *Application deadlines:* rolling (freshmen), rolling (transfers). *Notification:* continuous (freshmen), continuous (transfers).

Freshman Application Contact Ms. Mindy Steinberg, Director of Admissions, Ivy Tech Community College–Southern Indiana, 8204 Highway 311, Sellersburg, IN 47172-1897. *Phone:* 812-246-3301. *Toll-free phone:*

800-321-9021. *Fax:* 812-246-9905. *E-mail:* msteinbe@ivytech.edu. *Web site:* http://www.ivytech.edu/.

Ivy Tech Community College– Southwest

Evansville, Indiana

- **State-supported** 2-year, founded 1963, part of Ivy Tech Community College System
- **Suburban** 15-acre campus
- **Coed,** 6,464 undergraduate students, 40% full-time, 56% women, 44% men

Undergraduates 2,589 full-time, 3,875 part-time. 5% transferred in. *Retention:* 52% of full-time freshmen returned.

Freshmen *Admission:* 1,119 enrolled.

Faculty *Total:* 364, 22% full-time. *Student/faculty ratio:* 22:1.

Majors Accounting technology and bookkeeping; automobile/automotive mechanics technology; boilermaking; building/property maintenance; business administration and management; business automation/technology/data entry; cabinetmaking and millwork; carpentry; child-care and support services management; computer and information sciences; construction/heavy equipment/earthmoving equipment operation; criminal justice/safety; design and visual communications; early childhood education; electrical, electronic and communications engineering technology; electrician; emergency medical technology (EMT paramedic); executive assistant/executive secretary; general studies; graphic design; heating, air conditioning, ventilation and refrigeration maintenance technology; human services; industrial production technologies related; industrial technology; interior design; ironworking; legal assistant/paralegal; liberal arts and sciences/liberal studies; library and archives assisting; machine tool technology; masonry; mechanic and repair technologies related; mechanics and repair; medical/clinical assistant; painting and wall covering; pipefitting and sprinkler fitting; psychiatric/mental health services technology; registered nursing/registered nurse; robotics technology; sheet metal technology; surgical technology; tool and die technology.

Academics *Calendar:* semesters. *Degree:* certificates and associate. *Special study options:* academic remediation for entering students, advanced placement credit, cooperative education, distance learning, independent study, internships, part-time degree program, services for LD students, summer session for credit.

Library 7,082 titles, 107 serial subscriptions, 1,755 audiovisual materials, an OPAC, a Web page.

Student Life *Housing:* college housing not available. *Activities and Organizations:* student government, Phi Theta Kappa, LPN Club, National Association of Industrial Technology, Design Club. *Campus security:* late-night transport/escort service.

Costs (2010–11) *Tuition:* state resident $3136 full-time, $105 per credit hour part-time; nonresident $6640 full-time, $221 per credit hour part-time. *Required fees:* $120 full-time, $60 per term part-time. *Payment plans:* installment, deferred payment. *Waivers:* senior citizens and employees or children of employees.

Financial Aid Of all full-time matriculated undergraduates who enrolled in 2009, 65 Federal Work-Study jobs (averaging $2264).

Applying *Options:* electronic application, early admission, deferred entrance. *Required:* high school transcript. *Required for some:* interview. *Application deadlines:* rolling (freshmen), rolling (transfers). *Notification:* continuous (freshmen), continuous (transfers).

Freshman Application Contact Ms. Denise Johnson-Kincade, Director of Admissions, Ivy Tech Community College–Southwest, 3501 First Avenue, Evansville, IN 47710-3398. *Phone:* 812-429-1430. *Fax:* 812-429-9878. *E-mail:* ajohnson@ivytech.edu. *Web site:* http://www.ivytech.edu/.

Ivy Tech Community College–Wabash Valley

Terre Haute, Indiana

- **State-supported** 2-year, founded 1966, part of Ivy Tech Community College System
- **Suburban** 55-acre campus with easy access to Indianapolis
- **Coed,** 6,363 undergraduate students, 45% full-time, 58% women, 42% men

Undergraduates 2,878 full-time, 3,485 part-time. 2% are from out of state; 6% transferred in. *Retention:* 51% of full-time freshmen returned.

Freshmen *Admission:* 1,058 enrolled.

Faculty *Total:* 299, 29% full-time. *Student/faculty ratio:* 25:1.

Majors Accounting technology and bookkeeping; airframe mechanics and aircraft maintenance technology; allied health diagnostic, intervention, and treatment professions related; automobile/automotive mechanics technology; building/property maintenance; business administration and management; cabinetmaking and millwork; carpentry; child-care and support services management; clinical/medical laboratory technology; computer and information sciences; construction/heavy equipment/earthmoving equipment operation; criminal justice/safety; design and visual communications; early childhood education; electrical, electronic and communications engineering technology; electrician; emergency medical technology (EMT paramedic); executive assistant/executive secretary; general studies; heating, air conditioning, ventilation and refrigeration maintenance technology; human services; industrial production technologies related; industrial technology; ironworking; legal assistant/paralegal; liberal arts and sciences/liberal studies; library and archives assisting; machine tool technology; masonry; mechanics and repair; medical/clinical assistant; medical radiologic technology; occupational safety and health technology; office management; painting and wall covering; pipefitting and sprinkler fitting; psychiatric/mental health services technology; quality control and safety technologies related; registered nursing/registered nurse; robotics technology; sheet metal technology; surgical technology; tool and die technology.

Academics *Calendar:* semesters. *Degree:* certificates and associate. *Special study options:* academic remediation for entering students, adult/continuing education programs, advanced placement credit, distance learning, internships, part-time degree program, services for LD students, summer session for credit.

Library 4,403 titles, 77 serial subscriptions, 406 audiovisual materials, an OPAC, a Web page.

Student Life *Housing:* college housing not available. *Activities and Organizations:* student government, Phi Theta Kappa, LPN Club, National Association of Industrial Technology. *Campus security:* 24-hour emergency response devices. *Student services:* personal/psychological counseling, women's center.

Athletics *Intramural sports:* basketball M/W, volleyball M/W.

Costs (2010–11) *Tuition:* state resident $3136 full-time, $105 per credit hour part-time; nonresident $6640 full-time, $221 per credit hour part-time. *Required fees:* $120 full-time, $60 per term part-time. *Payment plans:* installment, deferred payment. *Waivers:* senior citizens and employees or children of employees.

Financial Aid Of all full-time matriculated undergraduates who enrolled in 2009, 51 Federal Work-Study jobs (averaging $2110). 1 state and other part-time job (averaging $2963).

Applying *Options:* electronic application, early admission, deferred entrance. *Required:* high school transcript. *Required for some:* interview. *Application deadlines:* rolling (freshmen), rolling (transfers). *Notification:* continuous (freshmen), continuous (transfers).

Freshman Application Contact Mr. Michael Fisher, Director of Admissions, Ivy Tech Community College–Wabash Valley, 7999 U.S. Highway 41 South, Terre Haute, IN 47802-4898. *Phone:* 812-298-2300. *Toll-free phone:* 800-377-4882. *Fax:* 812-298-2291. *E-mail:* mfisher@ivytech.edu. *Web site:* http://www.ivytech.edu/.

Kaplan College, Hammond Campus
Hammond, Indiana

- **Proprietary** 2-year, founded 1962
- **Suburban** campus
- **Coed**

Academics *Calendar:* quarters. *Degree:* certificates, diplomas, and associate.

Freshman Application Contact Kaplan College, Hammond Campus, 7833 Indianapolis Boulevard, Hammond, IN 46324. *Phone:* 219-844-0100. *Web site:* http://www.kc-hammond.com/.

Kaplan College, Merrillville Campus
Merrillville, Indiana

- **Proprietary** 2-year, founded 1968
- **Coed**

Academics *Degree:* certificates, diplomas, and associate.

Freshman Application Contact Kaplan College, Merrillville Campus, 3803 East Lincoln Highway, Merrillville, IN 46410. *Phone:* 219-947-8400. *Web site:* http://www.kc-merrillville.com/.

Kaplan College, Northwest Indianapolis Campus
Indianapolis, Indiana

- **Proprietary** 2-year
- **Coed, primarily women**

Academics *Degree:* diplomas and associate.

Freshman Application Contact Kaplan College, Northwest Indianapolis Campus, 7302 Woodland Drive, Indianapolis, IN 46278. *Phone:* 317-299-6001. *Toll-free phone:* 800-849-4995. *Web site:* http://www.kc-indy.com/.

Lincoln Technical Institute
Indianapolis, Indiana

Director of Admissions Ms. Cindy Ryan, Director of Admissions, Lincoln Technical Institute, 7225 Winton Drive, Building 128, Indianapolis, IN 46268. *Phone:* 317-632-5553. *Toll-free phone:* 800-554-4465. *Web site:* http://www.lincolnedu.com/.

Mid-America College of Funeral Service
Jeffersonville, Indiana

Freshman Application Contact Mr. Richard Nelson, Dean of Students, Mid-America College of Funeral Service, 3111 Hamburg Pike, Jeffersonville, IN 47130-9630. *Phone:* 812-288-8878. *Toll-free phone:* 800-221-6158. *Fax:* 812-288-5942. *E-mail:* macfs@mindspring.com. *Web site:* http://www.mid-america.edu/.

Vet Tech Institute at International Business College
Fort Wayne, Indiana

- **Private** 2-year, founded 2005
- **Suburban** campus
- **Coed,** 146 undergraduate students
- 49% of applicants were admitted

Freshmen *Admission:* 346 applied, 170 admitted.

Majors Veterinary/animal health technology.

Academics *Degree:* associate. *Special study options:* accelerated degree program, internships.

Freshman Application Contact Admissions Office, Vet Tech Institute at International Business College, 5699 Coventry Lane, Fort Wayne, IN 46804. *Phone:* 800-589-6363. *Toll-free phone:* 800-589-6363. *Web site:* http://www.vettechinstitute.edu/.

Vet Tech Institute at International Business College
Indianapolis, Indiana

- **Private** 2-year, founded 2007
- **Suburban** campus
- **Coed,** 83 undergraduate students
- 53% of applicants were admitted

Freshmen *Admission:* 363 applied, 191 admitted.

Majors Veterinary/animal health technology.

Academics *Degree:* associate. *Special study options:* accelerated degree program, internships.

Freshman Application Contact Admissions Office, Vet Tech Institute at International Business College, 7205 Shadeland Station, Indianapolis, IN 46256. *Phone:* 800-589-6500. *Toll-free phone:* 800-589-6500. *Web site:* http://www.vettechinstitute.edu/indianapolis.

Vincennes University
Vincennes, Indiana

Director of Admissions Christian Blome, Director of Admissions, Vincennes University, 1002 North First Street, Vincennes, IN 47591-5202. *Phone:* 800-742-9198. *Toll-free phone:* 800-742-9198. *E-mail:* cblome@vinu.edu. *Web site:* http://www.vinu.edu/.

Vincennes University Jasper Campus
Jasper, Indiana

- **State-supported** primarily 2-year, founded 1970, part of Vincennes University
- **Small-town** 140-acre campus
- **Coed,** 915 undergraduate students

Undergraduates Students come from 1 other state; 1 other country.

Faculty *Total:* 51, 39% full-time. *Student/faculty ratio:* 16:1.

Majors Accounting; administrative assistant and secretarial science; behavioral sciences; business administration and management; business teacher education; computer programming; computer programming related; computer systems networking and telecommunications; criminal justice/police science; drafting and design technology; education; education (multiple levels); elementary education; finance; furniture design and manufacturing; industrial technology; legal administrative assistant/secretary; liberal arts and sciences/liberal studies; management information systems; medical administrative assistant and medical secretary; psychology; social sciences; social work; sociology; word processing.

Academics *Calendar:* semesters. *Degrees:* certificates, associate, and bachelor's. *Special study options:* academic remediation for entering students, adult/continuing education programs, advanced placement credit, distance learning, part-time degree program, summer session for credit.

Library Vincennes University Jasper Library with 14,000 titles, 180 serial subscriptions, an OPAC.

Student Life *Housing:* college housing not available. *Activities and Organizations:* student-run newspaper. *Student services:* personal/psychological counseling.

Costs (2010–11) *Tuition:* state resident $4326 full-time; nonresident $10,508 full-time. *Required fees:* $208 full-time. *Payment plan:* installment. *Waivers:* senior citizens and employees or children of employees.

Financial Aid Of all full-time matriculated undergraduates who enrolled in 2009, 3 Federal Work-Study jobs (averaging $3200).

Applying *Application fee:* $20. *Required:* high school transcript. *Application deadlines:* rolling (freshmen), rolling (transfers).

Freshman Application Contact Ms. Louann Gilbert, Admissions Director, Vincennes University Jasper Campus, 850 College Avenue, Jasper, IN 47546-9393. *Phone:* 812-482-3030. *Toll-free phone:* 800-809-VUJC. *Fax:* 812-481-5960. *E-mail:* lagilbert@vinu.edu. *Web site:* http://vujc.vinu.edu/.

IOWA

Brown Mackie College–Quad Cities
Bettendorf, Iowa

- **Proprietary** 2-year, part of Education Management Corporation
- **Coed**

Majors Accounting technology and bookkeeping; business administration and management; medical/clinical assistant.

Academics *Degree:* diplomas and associate.

Costs (2010–11) *Tuition:* Tuition varies by program. Students should contact Brown Mackie College for tuition information.

Freshman Application Contact Brown Mackie College–Quad Cities, 2119 East Kimberly Road, Bettendorf, IA 52722. *Phone:* 309-762-2100. *Toll-free phone:* 888-420-1652. *Web site:* http://www.brownmackie.edu/quad-cities/.

See page 394 for the College Close-Up.

Clinton Community College
Clinton, Iowa

Freshman Application Contact Mr. Gary Mohr, Executive Director of Enrollment Management and Marketing, Clinton Community College, 1000 Lincoln Boulevard, Clinton, IA 52732-6299. *Phone:* 563-336-3322. *Fax:* 563-336-3350. *E-mail:* gmohr@eicc.edu. *Web site:* http://www.eicc.edu/ccc/.

Des Moines Area Community College
Ankeny, Iowa

- **State and locally supported** 2-year, founded 1966, part of Iowa Area Community Colleges System
- **Small-town** 362-acre campus
- **Endowment** $11.1 million
- **Coed**

Undergraduates 8,947 full-time, 13,377 part-time. Students come from 43 states and territories; 69 other countries. *Retention:* 58% of full-time freshmen returned.

Faculty *Student/faculty ratio:* 33:1.

Academics *Calendar:* semesters. *Degrees:* certificates, diplomas, and associate (profile also includes information from the Boone, Carroll, Des Moines, and Newton campuses). *Special study options:* academic remediation for entering students, adult/continuing education programs, advanced placement credit, cooperative education, distance learning, English as a second language, honors programs, off-campus study, part-time degree program, services for LD students, student-designed majors, summer session for credit.

Student Life *Campus security:* 24-hour emergency response devices and patrols, late-night transport/escort service.

Athletics Member NJCAA.

Standardized Tests *Required for some:* SAT or ACT (for admission), ACT, COMPASS.

Costs (2010–11) *Tuition:* state resident $3750 full-time, $125 per credit hour part-time; nonresident $7500 full-time, $125 per credit hour part-time. Full-time tuition and fees vary according to course load and reciprocity agreements. Part-time tuition and fees vary according to course load and reciprocity agreements. *Room and board:* Room and board charges vary according to location.

Financial Aid Of all full-time matriculated undergraduates who enrolled in 2009, 377 Federal Work-Study jobs (averaging $1055).

Applying *Options:* electronic application, early admission, deferred entrance. *Required for some:* high school transcript, interview.

Freshman Application Contact Mr. Michael Lentsch, Director of Enrollment Management, Des Moines Area Community College, 2006 South Ankeny Boulevard, Ankeny, IA 50021-8995. *Phone:* 515-964-6216. *Toll-free phone:* 800-362-2127. *Fax:* 515-964-6391. *E-mail:* mjleutsch@dmacc.edu. *Web site:* http://www.dmacc.edu/.

Ellsworth Community College
Iowa Falls, Iowa

Director of Admissions Mrs. Nancy Walters, Registrar, Ellsworth Community College, 1100 College Avenue, Iowa Falls, IA 50126-1199. *Phone:* 641-648-4611. *Toll-free phone:* 800-ECC-9235. *Web site:* http://www.iavalley.cc.ia.us/ecc/.

Hawkeye Community College
Waterloo, Iowa

- **State and locally supported** 2-year, founded 1966
- **Rural** 320-acre campus
- **Endowment** $1.2 million
- **Coed,** 6,658 undergraduate students, 48% full-time, 56% women, 44% men

Undergraduates 3,181 full-time, 3,477 part-time. Students come from 7 states and territories; 6 other countries; 1% are from out of state; 15% transferred in. *Retention:* 63% of full-time freshmen returned.

Freshmen *Admission:* 3,877 applied, 2,877 admitted, 1,517 enrolled. *Test scores:* ACT scores over 18: 49%; ACT scores over 24: 13%; ACT scores over 30: 2%.

Faculty *Total:* 341, 34% full-time, 7% with terminal degrees. *Student/faculty ratio:* 23:1.

Majors Accounting; agricultural/farm supplies retailing and wholesaling; agricultural power machinery operation; animal/livestock husbandry and production; applied horticulture/horticulture operations; architectural drafting and CAD/CADD; autobody/collision and repair technology; automobile/automotive mechanics technology; child-care provision; civil engineering technology; clinical/medical laboratory technology; commercial photography; computer and information sciences; computer systems networking and telecommunications; criminal justice/police science; dental hygiene; diesel mechanics technology; electrical, electronic and communications engineering technology; executive assistant/executive secretary; graphic communications; human resources management; interior design; liberal arts and sciences/liberal studies; machine tool technology; manufacturing engineering technology; medical administrative assistant and medical secretary; multi/interdisciplinary studies related; natural resources management and policy; registered nursing/registered nurse; respiratory care therapy; sales, distribution, and marketing operations; tool and die technology; web page, digital/multimedia and information resources design.

Academics *Calendar:* semesters. *Degree:* certificates, diplomas, and associate. *Special study options:* academic remediation for entering students, adult/continuing education programs, advanced placement credit, cooperative education, distance learning, English as a second language, external degree program, part-time degree program, services for LD students, study abroad, summer session for credit. *ROTC:* Army (c).

Library Hawkeye Community College Library with 105,073 titles, 249 serial subscriptions, 2,995 audiovisual materials, an OPAC, a Web page.

Student Life *Housing:* college housing not available. *Activities and Organizations:* Student Senate, Phi Theta Kappa, Student Ambassadors, All Ag/Horticulture, IAAP. *Campus security:* 24-hour patrols. *Student services:* health clinic, personal/psychological counseling, women's center.

Athletics *Intramural sports:* basketball M/W, bowling M/W, cross-country running M/W, golf M/W, soccer M/W, softball M/W, volleyball M/W.

Standardized Tests *Required for some:* ACT (for admission).

Costs (2010–11) *Tuition:* state resident $3584 full-time, $128 per credit hour part-time; nonresident $4284 full-time, $153 per credit hour part-time. Full-time tuition and fees vary according to course load and program. Part-time tuition and fees vary according to course load and program. *Required fees:* $168 full-time, $6 per credit hour part-time. *Payment plans:* installment, deferred payment. *Waivers:* employees or children of employees.

Applying *Options:* electronic application, deferred entrance. *Required:* high school transcript. *Application deadlines:* rolling (freshmen), rolling (out-of-state freshmen), rolling (transfers). *Notification:* continuous (freshmen), continuous (out-of-state freshmen), continuous (transfers).

Freshman Application Contact Ms. Holly Grimm-See, Associate Director, Admissions and Recruitment, Hawkeye Community College, PO Box 8015, Waterloo, IA 50704-8015. *Phone:* 319-296-4277. *Toll-free phone:* 800-670-4769. *Fax:* 319-296-2505. *E-mail:* holly.grimm-see@hawkeyecollege.edu. *Web site:* http://www.hawkeyecollege.edu/.

Indian Hills Community College
Ottumwa, Iowa

Freshman Application Contact Mrs. Jane Sapp, Admissions Officer, Indian Hills Community College, 525 Grandview Avenue, Building #1, Ottumwa, IA 52501-1398. *Phone:* 641-683-5155. *Toll-free phone:* 800-726-2585. *Web site:* http://www.ihcc.cc.ia.us/.

Iowa Central Community College
Fort Dodge, Iowa

Freshman Application Contact Mrs. Deb Bahis, Coordinator of Admissions, Iowa Central Community College, 330 Avenue M, Fort Dodge, IA 50501-5798. *Phone:* 515-576-0099 Ext. 2402. *Toll-free phone:* 800-362-2793. *Fax:* 515-576-7724. *E-mail:* bahls@iowacentral.com. *Web site:* http://www.iccc.cc.ia.us/.

Iowa Lakes Community College
Estherville, Iowa

- **State and locally supported** 2-year, founded 1967, part of Iowa Community College System
- **Small-town** 20-acre campus
- **Endowment** $1.7 million
- **Coed**

Undergraduates 1,839 full-time, 1,330 part-time. Students come from 34 states and territories; 7 other countries; 35% live on campus. *Retention:* 59% of full-time freshmen returned.
Faculty *Student/faculty ratio:* 24:1.
Academics *Calendar:* semesters. *Degree:* certificates, diplomas, and associate. *Special study options:* academic remediation for entering students, accelerated degree program, adult/continuing education programs, advanced placement credit, cooperative education, distance learning, English as a second language, external degree program, honors programs, independent study, internships, part-time degree program, services for LD students, summer session for credit.
Student Life *Campus security:* 24-hour emergency response devices, student patrols.
Athletics Member NJCAA.
Costs (2010–11) *Tuition:* state resident $4320 full-time, $135 per credit hour part-time; nonresident $4384 full-time, $137 per credit hour part-time. Full-time tuition and fees vary according to course load, program, and reciprocity agreements. Part-time tuition and fees vary according to course load, program, and reciprocity agreements. *Required fees:* $556 full-time, $30 per credit hour part-time. *Room and board:* $4900. Room and board charges vary according to housing facility and location.
Financial Aid Of all full-time matriculated undergraduates who enrolled in 2009, 210 Federal Work-Study jobs (averaging $800).
Applying *Options:* electronic application. *Required:* high school transcript. *Required for some:* interview.
Freshman Application Contact Ms. Anne Stansbury Johnson, Assistant Director Admissions, Iowa Lakes Community College, 3200 College Drive, Emmetsburg, IA 50536. *Phone:* 712-852-5254. *Toll-free phone:* 800-521-5054. *Fax:* 712-852-2152. *E-mail:* info@iowalakes.edu. *Web site:* http://www.iowalakes.edu/.

Iowa Western Community College
Council Bluffs, Iowa

Freshman Application Contact Ms. Tori Christie, Director of Admissions, Iowa Western Community College, 2700 College Road, Box 4-C, Council Bluffs, IA 51502. *Phone:* 712-325-3288. *Toll-free phone:* 800-432-5852. *E-mail:* admissions@iwcc.edu. *Web site:* http://www.iwcc.edu/.

ITT Technical Institute
Cedar Rapids, Iowa

- **Proprietary** primarily 2-year
- **Coed**

Majors CAD/CADD drafting/design technology; computer and information systems security; computer engineering technology; computer software engineering; computer software technology; construction management; criminal justice/law enforcement administration; legal assistant/paralegal; project management; system, networking, and LAN/WAN management.
Academics *Degrees:* associate and bachelor's.
Freshman Application Contact Director of Recruitment, ITT Technical Institute, 3735 Queen Court SW, Cedar Rapids, IA 52404. *Phone:* 319-297-3400. *Toll-free phone:* 877-320-4625. *Web site:* http://www.itt-tech.edu/.

ITT Technical Institute
Clive, Iowa

- **Proprietary** primarily 2-year, part of ITT Educational Services, Inc.
- **Coed**

Majors CAD/CADD drafting/design technology; computer and information systems security; computer engineering technology; computer software engineering; computer software technology; construction management; criminal justice/law enforcement administration; electrical, electronic and communications engineering technology; legal assistant/paralegal; project management; system, networking, and LAN/WAN management.
Academics *Degrees:* associate and bachelor's.
Student Life *Housing:* college housing not available.
Freshman Application Contact Director of Recruitment, ITT Technical Institute, 1860 Northwest 118th Street, Suite 110, Clive, IA 50325. *Phone:* 515-327-5500. *Toll-free phone:* 877-526-7312. *Web site:* http://www.itt-tech.edu/.

Kaplan University, Cedar Falls
Cedar Falls, Iowa

- **Proprietary** primarily 2-year, founded 2000
- **Coed**

Academics *Calendar:* quarters. *Degrees:* certificates, diplomas, associate, and bachelor's.
Freshman Application Contact Kaplan University, Cedar Falls, 7009 Nordic Drive, Cedar Falls, IA 50613. *Phone:* 319-277-0220. *Toll-free phone:* 800-728-1220. *Web site:* http://www.cedarfalls.kaplanuniversity.edu/.

Kaplan University, Cedar Rapids
Cedar Rapids, Iowa

- **Proprietary** primarily 2-year, founded 1900, administratively affiliated with Kaplan University - Davenport Campus
- **Suburban** campus
- **Coed**

Academics *Calendar:* quarters. *Degrees:* certificates, diplomas, associate, and bachelor's (branch locations in Des Moines, Mason City, and Cedar Falls with significant enrollment not reflected in profile).
Financial Aid Of all full-time matriculated undergraduates who enrolled in 2009, 10 Federal Work-Study jobs (averaging $889). 3 state and other part-time jobs (averaging $1885).
Freshman Application Contact Kaplan University, Cedar Rapids, 3165 Edgewood Parkway, SW, Cedar Rapids, IA 52404. *Phone:* 319-363-0481. *Toll-free phone:* 800-728-0481. *Web site:* http://www.cedarrapids.kaplanuniversity.edu/.

Kaplan University, Council Bluffs
Council Bluffs, Iowa

- **Proprietary** primarily 2-year, founded 2004
- **Coed**

Academics *Degrees:* certificates, associate, and bachelor's.
Standardized Tests *Required:* Wonderlic aptitude test (for admission).
Freshman Application Contact Kaplan University, Council Bluffs, 1751 Madison Avenue, Council Bluffs, IA 51503. *Phone:* 712-328-4212. *Toll-free phone:* 800-518-4212. *Web site:* http://www.councilbluffs.kaplanuniversity.edu/.

Kaplan University, Des Moines
Urbandale, Iowa

- **Proprietary** primarily 2-year
- **Coed**

Academics *Degrees:* certificates, diplomas, associate, and bachelor's.
Freshman Application Contact Kaplan University, Des Moines, 4655 121st Street, Urbandale, IA 50323. *Phone:* 515-727-2100. *Web site:* http://www.desmoines.kaplanuniversity.edu/.

Kirkwood Community College
Cedar Rapids, Iowa

- **State and locally supported** 2-year, founded 1966, part of Iowa Department of Education Division of Community Colleges
- **Suburban** 630-acre campus
- **Endowment** $16.0 million
- **Coed**

Undergraduates 9,715 full-time, 8,126 part-time. Students come from 37 states and territories; 94 other countries; 3% are from out of state.
Faculty *Student/faculty ratio:* 24:1.
Academics *Calendar:* semesters. *Degree:* certificates, diplomas, and associate. *Special study options:* academic remediation for entering students, accelerated degree program, adult/continuing education programs, advanced placement credit, cooperative education, distance learning, English as a second language, external degree program, honors programs, independent study, internships, off-campus study, part-time degree program, services for LD students, student-designed majors, summer session for credit.
Student Life *Campus security:* 24-hour emergency response devices and patrols.
Athletics Member NJCAA.
Costs (2010–11) *Tuition:* state resident $3330 full-time; nonresident $4080 full-time.
Applying *Options:* electronic application, early admission. *Required:* high school transcript.
Freshman Application Contact Kirkwood Community College, PO Box 2068, Cedar Rapids, IA 52406-2068. *Phone:* 319-398-5517. *Toll-free phone:* 800-332-2055. *Web site:* http://www.kirkwood.cc.ia.us/.

Marshalltown Community College
Marshalltown, Iowa

Freshman Application Contact Ms. Deana Inman, Director of Admissions, Marshalltown Community College, 3700 South Center Street, Marshalltown, IA 50158-4760. *Phone:* 641-752-7106. *Toll-free phone:* 866-622-4748. *Fax:* 641-752-8149. *Web site:* http://www.marshalltowncommunitycollege.com/.

Muscatine Community College
Muscatine, Iowa

Freshman Application Contact Gary Mohr, Executive Director of Enrollment Management and Marketing, Muscatine Community College, 152 Colorado Street, Muscatine, IA 52761-5396. *Phone:* 563-336-3322. *Toll-free phone:* 800-351-4669. *Fax:* 563-336-3350. *E-mail:* gmohr@eicc.edu. *Web site:* http://www.eicc.edu/.

Northeast Iowa Community College
Calmar, Iowa

- **State and locally supported** 2-year, founded 1966, part of Iowa Area Community Colleges System
- **Rural** 210-acre campus
- **Endowment** $558,880
- **Coed**, 5,136 undergraduate students, 49% full-time, 61% women, 39% men

Undergraduates 2,511 full-time, 2,625 part-time. Students come from 23 states and territories; 4 other countries; 10% are from out of state; 2% Black or African American, non-Hispanic/Latino; 1% Hispanic/Latino; 0.2% Asian, non-Hispanic/Latino; 0.1% American Indian or Alaska Native, non-Hispanic/Latino; 1% Two or more races, non-Hispanic/Latino; 4% Race/ethnicity unknown; 0.1% international; 40% transferred in. *Retention:* 57% of full-time freshmen returned.
Freshmen *Admission:* 1,718 applied, 1,142 admitted, 744 enrolled. *Average high school GPA:* 2.7.
Faculty *Total:* 281, 41% full-time, 3% with terminal degrees. *Student/faculty ratio:* 17:1.
Majors Accounting; administrative assistant and secretarial science; agribusiness; agricultural and food products processing; agricultural power machinery operation; agricultural production; automobile/automotive mechanics technology; business administration and management; business automation/technology/data entry; clinical/medical laboratory technology; computer programming (specific applications); construction trades; cosmetology; crop production; dairy husbandry and production; desktop publishing and digital imaging design; electrical, electronic and communications engineering technology; electrician; emergency medical technology (EMT paramedic); energy management and systems technology; fire science/firefighting; health information/medical records technology; liberal arts and sciences/liberal studies; plumbing technology; radiologic technology/science; registered nursing/registered nurse; respiratory care therapy; sales, distribution, and marketing operations; social work.
Academics *Calendar:* semesters. *Degree:* certificates, diplomas, and associate. *Special study options:* academic remediation for entering students, adult/continuing education programs, advanced placement credit, cooperative education, distance learning, double majors, honors programs, internships, off-campus study, part-time degree program, services for LD students, summer session for credit.
Library Wilder Resource Center & Burton Payne Library plus 2 others with 44,835 titles, 341 serial subscriptions, 7,326 audiovisual materials, an OPAC, a Web page.
Student Life *Housing:* college housing not available. *Activities and Organizations:* student-run newspaper, national fraternities, national sororities. *Campus security:* security personnel on weeknights. *Student services:* personal/psychological counseling.
Athletics *Intramural sports:* basketball M/W, bowling M/W, football M/W, golf M/W, skiing (downhill) M/W, swimming and diving M/W, table tennis M/W, tennis M/W, volleyball M/W.
Costs (2010–11) *Tuition:* state resident $4384 full-time, $136 per credit hour part-time; nonresident $4384 full-time, $136 per credit hour part-time. Full-time tuition and fees vary according to course load. Part-time tuition and fees vary according to course load. *Required fees:* $416 full-time, $13 per credit hour part-time. *Payment plan:* installment. *Waivers:* senior citizens and employees or children of employees.
Financial Aid Of all full-time matriculated undergraduates who enrolled in 2009, 154 Federal Work-Study jobs (averaging $1248). 45 state and other part-time jobs (averaging $980).
Applying *Options:* electronic application. *Recommended:* high school transcript. *Application deadlines:* rolling (freshmen), rolling (out-of-state freshmen), rolling (transfers). *Notification:* continuous (freshmen), continuous (out-of-state freshmen), continuous (transfers).
Freshman Application Contact Ms. Brynn McConnell, Admissions Representative, Northeast Iowa Community College, Calmar, IA 52132. *Phone:* 563-562-3263 Ext. 307. *Toll-free phone:* 800-728-CALMAR. *Fax:* 563-562-4369. *E-mail:* mcconnellb@nicc.edu. *Web site:* http://www.nicc.edu/.

North Iowa Area Community College
Mason City, Iowa

- **State and locally supported** 2-year, founded 1918, part of Iowa Community College System
- **Rural** 320-acre campus
- **Coed**, 3,744 undergraduate students, 53% full-time, 55% women, 45% men

Undergraduates 1,994 full-time, 1,750 part-time. 23% are from out of state; 3% Black or African American, non-Hispanic/Latino; 3% Hispanic/Latino; 1% Asian, non-Hispanic/Latino; 0.4% American Indian or Alaska Native, non-Hispanic/Latino; 0.6% Two or more races, non-Hispanic/Latino; 3% Race/ethnicity unknown; 0.8% international; 9% live on campus.
Freshmen *Admission:* 2,045 applied, 2,045 admitted, 812 enrolled.
Faculty *Total:* 256, 33% full-time, 7% with terminal degrees. *Student/faculty ratio:* 17:1.
Majors Accounting; accounting technology and bookkeeping; administrative assistant and secretarial science; agricultural economics; agricultural/farm supplies retailing and wholesaling; agricultural production; automobile/automotive mechanics technology; business administration and management; carpentry; clinical/medical laboratory technology; computer systems networking and telecommunications; criminal justice/police science; desktop publishing and digital imaging design; early childhood education; electrical, electronic and communications engineering technology; emergency medical technology (EMT paramedic); entrepreneurship; fire prevention and safety technology; health and medical administrative services related; heating, air conditioning, ventilation and refrigeration maintenance technology; hospitality administration; insurance; legal administrative assistant/secretary; liberal arts and sciences/liberal studies; licensed practical/vocational nurse training; manufacturing engineering technology; mechanical drafting and CAD/CADD; medical administrative assistant and medical secretary; medical/clinical assistant; multi/interdisciplinary studies related; network and system administration; nursing assistant/aide and patient care assistant/aide; physical education teaching and coaching; physical therapy technology; registered nursing/registered nurse; sales, distribution, and marketing operations; sport and fitness administration/management; tool and die technology; web page, digital/multimedia and information resources design; welding technology.
Academics *Calendar:* semesters. *Degree:* certificates, diplomas, and associate. *Special study options:* academic remediation for entering students, advanced placement credit, cooperative education, distance learning, English as a second language, external degree program, honors programs, internships, part-time degree program, services for LD students, student-designed majors, study abroad, summer session for credit.

Library North Iowa Area Community College Library with 29,540 titles, 413 serial subscriptions, 7,773 audiovisual materials, an OPAC, a Web page.
Student Life *Housing Options:* coed. Campus housing is university owned. *Activities and Organizations:* drama/theater group, student-run newspaper, choral group, Student Senate, intramurals, band/orchestra. *Campus security:* 24-hour emergency response devices. *Student services:* health clinic, personal/psychological counseling.
Athletics Member NJCAA. *Intercollegiate sports:* baseball M(s), basketball M(s)/W(s), cross-country running M(s)/W(s), golf M(s)/W(s), soccer M(s), softball W(s), track and field M(s)/W(s), volleyball W(s), wrestling M(s). *Intramural sports:* cheerleading W.
Costs (2010–11) *Tuition:* state resident $3490 full-time, $116 per semester hour part-time; nonresident $5236 full-time, $174 per semester hour part-time. Full-time tuition and fees vary according to course load. Part-time tuition and fees vary according to course load. *Required fees:* $422 full-time, $14 per semester hour part-time. *Room and board:* $4950. Room and board charges vary according to housing facility. *Payment plan:* installment. *Waivers:* senior citizens and employees or children of employees.
Financial Aid Of all full-time matriculated undergraduates who enrolled in 2009, 125 Federal Work-Study jobs (averaging $2000). 4 state and other part-time jobs (averaging $2000).
Applying *Options:* electronic application. *Application deadlines:* rolling (freshmen), rolling (transfers). *Notification:* continuous (freshmen), continuous (transfers).
Freshman Application Contact Ms. Rachel McGuire, Director of Admissions, North Iowa Area Community College, 500 College Drive, Mason City, IA 50401. *Phone:* 641-422-4104. *Toll-free phone:* 888-GO NIACC Ext. 4245. *Fax:* 641-422-4385. *E-mail:* request@niacc.edu. *Web site:* http://www.niacc.edu/.

Northwest Iowa Community College

Sheldon, Iowa

Director of Admissions Ms. Lisa Story, Director of Enrollment Management, Northwest Iowa Community College, 603 West Park Street, Sheldon, IA 51201-1046. *Phone:* 712-324-5061 Ext. 115. *Toll-free phone:* 800-352-4907. *E-mail:* lstory@nwicc.edu. *Web site:* http://www.nwicc.edu/.

St. Luke's College

Sioux City, Iowa

- **Independent** 2-year, founded 1967, part of St. Luke's Regional Medical Center
- **Rural** 3-acre campus with easy access to Omaha
- **Endowment** $1.1 million
- **Coed,** 192 undergraduate students, 72% full-time, 91% women, 9% men

Undergraduates 138 full-time, 54 part-time. Students come from 16 states and territories; 1 other country; 38% are from out of state; 1% Black or African American, non-Hispanic/Latino; 3% Hispanic/Latino; 3% Asian, non-Hispanic/Latino; 2% American Indian or Alaska Native, non-Hispanic/Latino; 20% transferred in. *Retention:* 100% of full-time freshmen returned.
Freshmen *Admission:* 173 applied, 76 admitted, 3 enrolled. *Average high school GPA:* 2.86. *Test scores:* ACT scores over 18: 84%; ACT scores over 24: 21%; ACT scores over 30: 1%.
Faculty *Total:* 32, 59% full-time, 13% with terminal degrees. *Student/faculty ratio:* 8:1.
Majors Radiologic technology/science; registered nursing/registered nurse; respiratory care therapy.
Academics *Calendar:* semesters. *Degree:* certificates and associate. *Special study options:* advanced placement credit, cooperative education, summer session for credit.
Library St. Luke's College with 2,355 titles, 70 serial subscriptions, 180 audiovisual materials, an OPAC, a Web page.
Student Life *Housing:* college housing not available. *Campus security:* 24-hour emergency response devices and patrols, late-night transport/escort service. *Student services:* health clinic, personal/psychological counseling.
Standardized Tests *Required:* SAT or ACT (for admission).
Costs (2011–12) *Tuition:* $15,300 full-time, $425 per quarter hour part-time. Full-time tuition and fees vary according to course load, degree level, and program. Part-time tuition and fees vary according to course load and degree level. *Required fees:* $1025 full-time, $600 per year part-time. *Payment plans:* installment, deferred payment. *Waivers:* employees or children of employees.
Financial Aid Of all full-time matriculated undergraduates who enrolled in 2009, 133 applied for aid, 133 were judged to have need, 20 had their need fully met. 8 Federal Work-Study jobs (averaging $1125). 1 state and other part-time job (averaging $1000). *Average percent of need met:* 80%. *Average financial aid package:* $8639. *Average need-based loan:* $4238. *Average need-based gift aid:* $5727. *Average indebtedness upon graduation:* $16,493.

Applying *Options:* electronic application. *Application fee:* $50. *Required:* essay or personal statement, high school transcript, minimum 2.5 GPA, interview. *Application deadline:* 8/1 (freshmen). *Notification:* continuous (transfers).
Freshman Application Contact Ms. Sherry McCarthy, Admissions Coordinator, St. Luke's College, 2720 Stone Park Boulevard, Sioux City, IA 51104. *Phone:* 712-279-3149. *Toll-free phone:* 800-352-4660 Ext. 3149. *Fax:* 712-233-8017. *E-mail:* mccartsj@stlukes.org. *Web site:* http://stlukescollege.edu/.

Scott Community College

Bettendorf, Iowa

Freshman Application Contact Mr. Gary Mohr, Executive Director of Enrollment Management and Marketing, Scott Community College, 500 Belmont Road, Bettendorf, IA 52722-6804. *Phone:* 563-336-3322. *Toll-free phone:* 800-895-0811. *Fax:* 563-336-3350. *E-mail:* gmohr@eicc.edu. *Web site:* http://www.eicc.edu/scc/.

Southeastern Community College

West Burlington, Iowa

- **State and locally supported** 2-year, founded 1968, part of Iowa Department of Education Division of Community Colleges
- **Small-town** 160-acre campus
- **Coed,** 3,601 undergraduate students, 58% full-time, 61% women, 39% men

Undergraduates 2,092 full-time, 1,509 part-time. 13% are from out of state; 4% Black or African American, non-Hispanic/Latino; 3% Hispanic/Latino; 0.7% Asian, non-Hispanic/Latino; 0.2% Native Hawaiian or other Pacific Islander, non-Hispanic/Latino; 0.6% American Indian or Alaska Native, non-Hispanic/Latino; 0.8% Two or more races, non-Hispanic/Latino; 4% Race/ethnicity unknown; 0.7% international; 2% live on campus.
Freshmen *Admission:* 886 applied, 526 admitted, 460 enrolled. *Test scores:* ACT scores over 18: 66%; ACT scores over 24: 15%; ACT scores over 30: 1%.
Faculty *Total:* 192, 42% full-time, 5% with terminal degrees. *Student/faculty ratio:* 17:1.
Majors Accounting; administrative assistant and secretarial science; agricultural business and management; agronomy and crop science; artificial intelligence; automobile/automotive mechanics technology; biomedical technology; business administration and management; child development; computer programming; construction engineering technology; cosmetology; criminal justice/law enforcement administration; drafting and design technology; electrical, electronic and communications engineering technology; emergency medical technology (EMT paramedic); engineering related; industrial radiologic technology; information science/studies; liberal arts and sciences/liberal studies; licensed practical/vocational nurse training; machine tool technology; mechanical engineering/mechanical technology; medical/clinical assistant; registered nursing/registered nurse; respiratory care therapy; substance abuse/addiction counseling; trade and industrial teacher education; welding technology.
Academics *Calendar:* semesters. *Degree:* certificates, diplomas, and associate. *Special study options:* academic remediation for entering students, adult/continuing education programs, advanced placement credit, cooperative education, distance learning, English as a second language, independent study, internships, part-time degree program, services for LD students, student-designed majors, summer session for credit.
Library Yohe Memorial Library.
Student Life *Housing Options:* coed, men-only, disabled students. Campus housing is university owned. *Activities and Organizations:* drama/theater group, student-run newspaper, choral group. *Campus security:* controlled dormitory access, night patrols by trained security personnel.
Athletics Member NJCAA. *Intercollegiate sports:* baseball M(s), basketball M(s), softball W(s), volleyball W(s). *Intramural sports:* basketball M, bowling M/W, softball M/W, volleyball M/W, weight lifting M/W.
Costs (2010–11) *Tuition:* state resident $3780 full-time, $126 per credit hour part-time; nonresident $3930 full-time, $131 per credit hour part-time.
Financial Aid Of all full-time matriculated undergraduates who enrolled in 2008, 1,568 applied for aid, 1,409 were judged to have need. In 2008, 34 non-need-based awards were made. *Average financial aid package:* $7692. *Average need-based loan:* $3054. *Average need-based gift aid:* $5601. *Average non-need-based aid:* $1044.
Applying *Options:* early admission, deferred entrance. *Application deadlines:* rolling (freshmen), rolling (transfers). *Notification:* continuous (freshmen).
Freshman Application Contact Ms. Stacy White, Admissions, Southeastern Community College, 1500 West Agency Road, West Burlington, IA 52655-0180. *Phone:* 319-752-2731 Ext. 8137. *Toll-free phone:* 866-722-4692. *E-mail:* admoff@scciowa.edu. *Web site:* http://www.scciowa.edu

Southwestern Community College

Creston, Iowa

- **State-supported** 2-year, founded 1966, part of Iowa Department of Education Division of Community Colleges
- **Rural** 420-acre campus
- **Coed**

Undergraduates 839 full-time, 841 part-time. Students come from 21 states and territories; 2 other countries; 5% are from out of state; 6% transferred in; 3% live on campus. *Retention:* 57% of full-time freshmen returned.
Faculty *Student/faculty ratio:* 13:1.
Academics *Calendar:* semesters. *Degree:* certificates, diplomas, and associate. *Special study options:* academic remediation for entering students, adult/continuing education programs, advanced placement credit, distance learning, double majors, part-time degree program, summer session for credit.
Student Life *Campus security:* 24-hour emergency response devices and patrols, controlled dormitory access.
Athletics Member NJCAA.
Standardized Tests *Required for some:* SAT or ACT (for admission), ACT COMPASS.
Costs (2010–11) *Tuition:* state resident $4020 full-time, $116 per credit hour part-time; nonresident $4635 full-time, $143 per credit hour part-time. Full-time tuition and fees vary according to course load and program. Part-time tuition and fees vary according to course load and program. *Required fees:* $360 full-time, $12 per credit hour part-time. *Room and board:* $4900. Room and board charges vary according to housing facility.
Financial Aid Of all full-time matriculated undergraduates who enrolled in 2009, 84 Federal Work-Study jobs (averaging $1075). 42 state and other part-time jobs (averaging $1080).
Applying *Options:* electronic application, early admission. *Required:* high school transcript.
Freshman Application Contact Ms. Lisa Carstens, Admissions Coordinator, Southwestern Community College, 1501 West Townline Street, Creston, IA 50801. *Phone:* 641-782-7081 Ext. 453. *Toll-free phone:* 800-247-4023. *Fax:* 641-782-3312. *E-mail:* carstens@swcciowa.edu. *Web site:* http://www.swcciowa.edu/.

Vatterott College

Des Moines, Iowa

Freshman Application Contact Mr. Henry Franken, Co-Director, Vatterott College, 7000 Fleur Drive, Suite 290, Des Moines, IA 50321. *Phone:* 515-309-9000. *Toll-free phone:* 800-353-7264. *Fax:* 515-309-0366. *Web site:* http://www.vatterott-college.edu/.

Western Iowa Tech Community College

Sioux City, Iowa

- **State-supported** 2-year, founded 1966, part of Iowa Department of Education Division of Community Colleges
- **Suburban** 143-acre campus
- **Endowment** $950,452
- **Coed,** 6,421 undergraduate students, 47% full-time, 57% women, 43% men

Undergraduates 3,042 full-time, 3,379 part-time. Students come from 23 states and territories; 7 other countries; 16% are from out of state; 6% transferred in; 2% live on campus.
Freshmen *Admission:* 821 enrolled. *Average high school GPA:* 2.63. *Test scores:* ACT scores over 18: 66%; ACT scores over 24: 21%; ACT scores over 30: 1%.
Faculty *Total:* 360, 21% full-time, 3% with terminal degrees. *Student/faculty ratio:* 25:1.
Majors Accounting; administrative assistant and secretarial science; agricultural/farm supplies retailing and wholesaling; autobody/collision and repair technology; automobile/automotive mechanics technology; biomedical technology; business administration and management; business automation/technology/data entry; carpentry; child-care and support services management; child-care provision; clinical/medical laboratory technology; criminal justice/law enforcement administration; criminal justice/police science; dental hygiene; electrical, electronic and communications engineering technology; emergency medical technology (EMT paramedic); executive assistant/executive secretary; fire science/firefighting; human resources management; industrial mechanics and maintenance technology; interior design; legal administrative assistant/secretary; liberal arts and sciences/liberal studies; machine tool technology; medical administrative assistant and medical secretary; multi/interdisciplinary studies related; musical instrument fabrication and repair; nursing assistant/aide and patient care assistant/aide; occupational therapist assistant; physical therapy technology; registered nursing/registered nurse; sales, distribution, and marketing operations; securities services administration; surgical technology; tool and die technology; turf and turfgrass management.
Academics *Calendar:* semesters. *Degree:* certificates, diplomas, and associate. *Special study options:* academic remediation for entering students, accelerated degree program, adult/continuing education programs, advanced placement credit, cooperative education, distance learning, double majors, English as a second language, honors programs, independent study, internships, off-campus study, part-time degree program, services for LD students, summer session for credit.
Library Western Iowa Tech Community College Library Services with 28,439 titles, 218 serial subscriptions, 11,852 audiovisual materials, an OPAC, a Web page.
Student Life *Activities and Organizations:* drama/theater group, Student Senate, Phi Theta Kappa, Diversity Club. *Campus security:* 24-hour emergency response devices and patrols. *Student services:* personal/psychological counseling.
Athletics *Intramural sports:* basketball M/W, bowling M/W, football M/W, soccer M/W, softball W, volleyball M/W, wrestling M/W.
Costs (2010–11) *Tuition:* state resident $3204 full-time, $118 per credit hour part-time; nonresident $3564 full-time, $133 per credit hour part-time. *Required fees:* $16 per credit hour part-time. *Room and board:* $4977. Room and board charges vary according to housing facility. *Payment plan:* installment.
Financial Aid Of all full-time matriculated undergraduates who enrolled in 2009, 148 Federal Work-Study jobs (averaging $1000). 2 state and other part-time jobs (averaging $2500).
Applying *Options:* electronic application, early admission, deferred entrance. *Recommended:* high school transcript. *Application deadlines:* rolling (freshmen), rolling (transfers). *Notification:* continuous (freshmen), continuous (transfers).
Freshman Application Contact Lora Vanderzwaag, Director of Admissions, Western Iowa Tech Community College, 4647 Stone Avenue, PO Box 5199, Sioux City, IA 51102-5199. *Phone:* 712-274-6400. *Toll-free phone:* 800-352-4649 Ext. 6403. *Fax:* 712-274-6441. *Web site:* http://www.witcc.edu/.

KANSAS

Allen Community College

Iola, Kansas

- **State and locally supported** 2-year, founded 1923, part of Kansas State Board of Regents
- **Small-town** 88-acre campus
- **Coed,** 2,277 undergraduate students

Undergraduates Students come from 20 states and territories; 8 other countries; 9% are from out of state; 4% Black or African American, non-Hispanic/Latino; 4% Hispanic/Latino; 0.8% Asian, non-Hispanic/Latino; 0.8% Native Hawaiian or other Pacific Islander, non-Hispanic/Latino; 2% American Indian or Alaska Native, non-Hispanic/Latino; 0.6% international. *Retention:* 56% of full-time freshmen returned.
Freshmen *Average high school GPA:* 2.97.
Faculty *Total:* 155, 23% full-time. *Student/faculty ratio:* 17:1.
Majors Accounting; administrative assistant and secretarial science; agricultural production; architecture; art; athletic training; banking and financial support services; biology/biological sciences; business administration and management; business/commerce; business teacher education; chemistry; child development; computer science; computer systems networking and telecommunications; criminal justice/law enforcement administration; data processing and data processing technology; drafting and design technology; dramatic/theater arts; economics; electrical and electronics engineering; electrical, electronic and communications engineering technology; elementary education; emergency medical technology (EMT paramedic); engineering; engineering technology; equestrian studies; family and consumer sciences/human sciences; farm and ranch management; forestry; funeral service and mortuary science; general studies; geography; health aide; health and physical education/fitness; history; home health aide/home attendant; hospital and health-care facilities administration; humanities; industrial technology; information science/studies; journalism; language interpretation and translation; library and information science; mathematics; music; nuclear/nuclear power technology; nursing assistant/aide and patient care assistant/aide; parks, recreation and leisure facilities management; philosophy; physical therapy; physics; political science and government; pre-dentistry studies; pre-law studies; pre-medical studies; pre-pharmacy studies; pre-veterinary studies; psychology; religious studies; rhetoric and composition; secondary education; social work;

sociology; technology/industrial arts teacher education; wood science and wood products/pulp and paper technology; writing.

Academics *Calendar:* semesters. *Degree:* certificates and associate. *Special study options:* academic remediation for entering students, adult/continuing education programs, cooperative education, distance learning, English as a second language, independent study, internships, part-time degree program, services for LD students, student-designed majors, summer session for credit.

Library Learning Resource Center plus 1 other with 49,416 titles, 159 serial subscriptions, an OPAC.

Student Life *Housing Options:* coed, men-only, women-only. Campus housing is university owned. *Activities and Organizations:* drama/theater group, choral group, intramurals, Student Senate, Biology Club, Theatre, Phi Theta Kappa. *Student services:* personal/psychological counseling.

Athletics Member NJCAA. *Intercollegiate sports:* baseball M(s), basketball M(s)/W(s), cheerleading M(s)/W(s), cross-country running M(s)/W(s), golf M(s), soccer M(s)/W(s), softball W(s), track and field M(s)/W(s), volleyball W(s). *Intramural sports:* basketball M/W, football M/W, soccer M/W, softball M/W, table tennis M/W, tennis M/W, volleyball M/W.

Standardized Tests *Required:* SAT or ACT (for admission).

Costs (2011–12) *Tuition:* state resident $1410 full-time, $47 per hour part-time; nonresident $1410 full-time, $47 per hour part-time. Full-time tuition and fees vary according to course load. Part-time tuition and fees vary according to course load. *Required fees:* $540 full-time, $18 per hour part-time. *Room and board:* $4300; room only: $3600. Room and board charges vary according to housing facility. *Waivers:* employees or children of employees.

Financial Aid Of all full-time matriculated undergraduates who enrolled in 2008, 510 applied for aid, 411 were judged to have need, 384 had their need fully met. 40 Federal Work-Study jobs (averaging $2600). 112 state and other part-time jobs (averaging $2600). In 2008, 22 non-need-based awards were made. *Average percent of need met:* 80%. *Average financial aid package:* $4738. *Average need-based loan:* $2482. *Average need-based gift aid:* $3257. *Average non-need-based aid:* $1241.

Applying *Options:* electronic application, early admission, deferred entrance. *Required:* high school transcript. *Application deadlines:* 8/24 (freshmen), 8/24 (transfers). *Notification:* continuous (freshmen), continuous (transfers).

Freshman Application Contact Mr. Rebecca Bilderback, Director of Admissions, Allen Community College, 1801 North Cottonwood, Iola, KS 66749. *Phone:* 620-365-5116 Ext. 267. *Fax:* 620-365-7406. *E-mail:* bilderback@allencc.edu. *Web site:* http://www.allencc.edu/.

Barton County Community College
Great Bend, Kansas

- **State and locally supported** 2-year, founded 1969, part of Kansas Board of Regents
- **Rural** 140-acre campus
- **Endowment** $4.4 million
- **Coed,** 4,723 undergraduate students, 22% full-time, 44% women, 56% men

Undergraduates 1,028 full-time, 3,695 part-time. Students come from 49 states and territories; 23 other countries; 7% are from out of state; 4% transferred in; 8% live on campus.

Freshmen *Admission:* 395 enrolled. *Average high school GPA:* 3.03. *Test scores:* ACT scores over 18: 72%; ACT scores over 24: 17%; ACT scores over 30: 1%.

Faculty *Total:* 196, 35% full-time, 3% with terminal degrees. *Student/faculty ratio:* 23:1.

Majors Accounting; administrative assistant and secretarial science; agricultural business and management; agriculture; anthropology; architecture; art; athletic training; automobile/automotive mechanics technology; banking and financial support services; biology/biological sciences; business administration and management; chemistry; child-care and support services management; chiropractic assistant; clinical/medical laboratory technology; computer/information technology services administration related; computer programming (specific applications); computer science; computer systems networking and telecommunications; corrections; criminal justice/police science; crop production; cytotechnology; dance; dental hygiene; dietitian assistant; dramatic/theater arts; early childhood education; economics; elementary education; emergency care attendant (EMT ambulance); emergency medical technology (EMT paramedic); engineering technology; English; financial planning and services; fire science/firefighting; forestry; funeral service and mortuary science; general studies; geology/earth science; graphic design; hazardous materials management and waste technology; health aides/attendants/orderlies related; health and medical administrative services related; health information/medical records administration; history; home health aide/home attendant; homeland security, law enforcement, firefighting and protective services related; human resources management; human resources management and ser-

vices related; industrial production technologies related; information science/studies; journalism; kinesiology and exercise science; liberal arts and sciences/liberal studies; licensed practical/vocational nurse training; livestock management; logistics, materials, and supply chain management; marketing/marketing management; mathematics; medical administrative assistant and medical secretary; medical/clinical assistant; medical insurance coding; medical office assistant; medical transcription; medication aide; military studies; modern languages; music; nursing assistant/aide and patient care assistant/aide; occupational therapy; optometric technician; pharmacy; pharmacy technician; philosophy; phlebotomy technology; physical education teaching and coaching; physical sciences; physical therapy; physical therapy technology; physician assistant; physics; political science and government; pre-dentistry studies; pre-engineering; pre-law studies; premedical studies; pre-veterinary studies; psychology; public administration; radiologic technology/science; registered nursing/registered nurse; religious studies; respiratory care therapy; secondary education; social work; sociology; speech communication and rhetoric; sport and fitness administration/management; wildlife, fish and wildlands science and management.

Academics *Calendar:* semesters. *Degree:* certificates and associate. *Special study options:* academic remediation for entering students, accelerated degree program, adult/continuing education programs, advanced placement credit, cooperative education, distance learning, double majors, English as a second language, external degree program, honors programs, independent study, internships, part-time degree program, services for LD students, summer session for credit.

Library Barton County Community College Library with 42,502 titles, 12,384 serial subscriptions, 457 audiovisual materials, an OPAC, a Web page.

Student Life *Housing Options:* coed, disabled students. Campus housing is university owned. Freshman campus housing is guaranteed. *Activities and Organizations:* drama/theater group, student-run newspaper, choral group, Danceline, Business Professionals, Psychology Club, Agriculture Club, Cougarettes. *Campus security:* 24-hour emergency response devices and patrols. *Student services:* health clinic, personal/psychological counseling.

Athletics Member NJCAA. *Intercollegiate sports:* baseball M(s), basketball M(s)/W(s), cheerleading M(s)/W(s), cross-country running M(s)/W(s), golf M(s)/W(s), soccer M(s)/W(s), softball W(s), tennis M(s)/W(s), track and field M(s)/W(s), volleyball W(s). *Intramural sports:* basketball M/W, bowling M/W, football M/W, golf M/W, softball M/W, swimming and diving M/W, table tennis M/W, tennis M/W, track and field M/W, volleyball M/W.

Costs (2010–11) *Tuition:* state resident $1620 full-time, $54 per credit hour part-time; nonresident $2550 full-time, $85 per credit hour part-time. Full-time tuition and fees vary according to course load. Part-time tuition and fees vary according to course load. *Required fees:* $900 full-time, $30 per credit hour part-time. *Room and board:* $4600. Room and board charges vary according to board plan. *Payment plans:* installment, deferred payment. *Waivers:* senior citizens and employees or children of employees.

Financial Aid Of all full-time matriculated undergraduates who enrolled in 2009, 102 Federal Work-Study jobs (averaging $2400).

Applying *Options:* electronic application, early admission. *Recommended:* high school transcript. *Application deadlines:* rolling (freshmen), rolling (transfers).

Freshman Application Contact Mr. Todd Moore, Director of Admissions and Promotions, Barton County Community College, 245 Northeast 30th Road, Great Bend, KS 67530. *Phone:* 620-792-9241. *Toll-free phone:* 800-722-6842. *Fax:* 620-786-1160. *E-mail:* admissions@bartonccc.edu. *Web site:* http://www.bartonccc.edu/.

Brown Mackie College–Kansas City
Lenexa, Kansas

- **Proprietary** 2-year, founded 1892, part of Education Management Corporation
- **Suburban** campus
- **Coed**

Majors Accounting technology and bookkeeping; athletic training; business administration and management; CAD/CADD drafting/design technology; criminal justice/law enforcement administration; health/health-care administration; legal assistant/paralegal; licensed practical/vocational nurse training; medical/clinical assistant; occupational therapist assistant; office management; veterinary/animal health technology.

Academics *Calendar:* quarters. *Degree:* certificates, diplomas, and associate.

Costs (2010–11) *Tuition:* Tuition varies by program. Students should contact Brown Mackie College for tuition information.

Freshman Application Contact Brown Mackie College–Kansas City, 9705 Lenexa Drive, Lenexa, KS 66215. *Phone:* 913-768-1900. *Toll-free phone:* 800-635-9101. *Web site:* http://www.brownmackie.edu/kansascity/.

See page 376 for the College Close-Up.

Brown Mackie College–Salina

Salina, Kansas

- **Proprietary** 2-year, founded 1892, part of Education Management Corporation
- **Small-town** campus
- **Coed**

Majors Accounting technology and bookkeeping; athletic training; business administration and management; CAD/CADD drafting/design technology; computer systems networking and telecommunications; criminal justice/law enforcement administration; general studies; health/health-care administration; legal assistant/paralegal; licensed practical/vocational nurse training; medical/clinical assistant; occupational therapist assistant; office management.

Academics *Calendar:* modular. *Degree:* certificates, diplomas, and associate.

Costs (2010–11) *Tuition:* Tuition varies by program. Students should contact Brown Mackie College for tuition information.

Freshman Application Contact Brown Mackie College–Salina, 2106 South 9th Street, Salina, KS 67401-2810. *Phone:* 785-825-5422. *Toll-free phone:* 800-365-0433. *Web site:* http://www.brownmackie.edu/salina/.

See page 398 for the College Close-Up.

Butler Community College

El Dorado, Kansas

Freshman Application Contact Mr. Glenn Lygrisse, Interim Director of Enrollment Management, Butler Community College, 901 South Haverhill Road, El Dorado, KS 67042. *Phone:* 316-321-2222. *Fax:* 316-322-3109. *E-mail:* admissions@butlercc.edu. *Web site:* http://www.butlercc.edu/.

Cloud County Community College

Concordia, Kansas

Director of Admissions Kim Reynolds, Director of Admissions, Cloud County Community College, 2221 Campus Drive, PO Box 1002, Concordia, KS 66901-1002. *Phone:* 785-243-1435 Ext. 214. *Toll-free phone:* 800-729-5101. *Web site:* http://www.cloud.edu/.

Coffeyville Community College

Coffeyville, Kansas

Freshman Application Contact Stacia Meek, Admissions Counselor/Marketing Event Coordinator, Coffeyville Community College, 400 West 11th Street, Coffeyville, KS 67337-5063. *Phone:* 620-252-7100. *Toll-free phone:* 877-51RAVEN. *E-mail:* staciam@coffeyville.edu. *Web site:* http://www.coffeyville.edu/.

Colby Community College

Colby, Kansas

- **State and locally supported** 2-year, founded 1964, part of Kansas State Board of Education
- **Small-town** 80-acre campus
- **Endowment** $3.4 million
- **Coed**

Undergraduates 759 full-time, 806 part-time. Students come from 15 states and territories; 5 other countries; 30% are from out of state; 6% transferred in; 30% live on campus.

Faculty *Student/faculty ratio:* 11:1.

Academics *Calendar:* semesters. *Degree:* certificates, diplomas, and associate. *Special study options:* academic remediation for entering students, adult/continuing education programs, advanced placement credit, cooperative education, distance learning, double majors, honors programs, internships, part-time degree program, services for LD students, student-designed majors, summer session for credit.

Student Life *Campus security:* 24-hour emergency response devices and patrols.

Athletics Member NJCAA.

Standardized Tests *Recommended:* SAT or ACT (for admission).

Costs (2010–11) *Tuition:* state resident $1664 full-time, $52 per credit hour part-time; nonresident $3104 full-time, $97 per credit hour part-time. Full-time tuition and fees vary according to course load and program. Part-time tuition and fees vary according to course load and program. *Required fees:* $1152 full-time, $36 per credit hour part-time. *Room and board:* $4690. Room and board charges vary according to housing facility.

Financial Aid Of all full-time matriculated undergraduates who enrolled in 2009, 95 Federal Work-Study jobs (averaging $1500). 30 state and other part-time jobs (averaging $2000).

Applying *Options:* electronic application, early admission, deferred entrance. *Required:* high school transcript. *Required for some:* interview.

Freshman Application Contact Ms. Nikol Nolan, Admissions Director, Colby Community College, Colby, KS 67701-4099. *Phone:* 785-462-3984 Ext. 5496. *Toll-free phone:* 888-634-9350 Ext. 690. *Fax:* 785-460-4691. *E-mail:* admissions@colbycc.edu. *Web site:* http://www.colbycc.edu/.

Cowley County Community College and Area Vocational–Technical School

Arkansas City, Kansas

- **State and locally supported** 2-year, founded 1922, part of Kansas State Board of Education
- **Small-town** 19-acre campus
- **Endowment** $3.5 million
- **Coed,** 4,530 undergraduate students, 51% full-time, 61% women, 39% men

Undergraduates 2,307 full-time, 2,223 part-time. Students come from 26 states and territories; 30 other countries; 7% are from out of state; 9% live on campus.

Freshmen *Admission:* 577 applied, 577 admitted, 577 enrolled. *Average high school GPA:* 3.06. *Test scores:* ACT scores over 18: 89%; ACT scores over 24: 29%; ACT scores over 30: 1%.

Faculty *Total:* 244, 20% full-time, 0.4% with terminal degrees. *Student/faculty ratio:* 27:1.

Majors Accounting; administrative assistant and secretarial science; agriculture; art; automobile/automotive mechanics technology; biology/biological sciences; business administration and management; chemistry; child-care and support services management; child development; computer and information sciences; computer and information systems security; computer graphics; computer programming (specific applications); computer science; cosmetology; criminal justice/law enforcement administration; criminal justice/police science; dietetics and clinical nutrition services related; drafting and design technology; dramatic/theater arts; education; electromechanical and instrumentation and maintenance technologies related; elementary education; emergency medical technology (EMT paramedic); engineering technology; entrepreneurship; forensic science and technology; hotel/motel administration; industrial radiologic technology; journalism; legal administrative assistant/secretary; liberal arts and sciences/liberal studies; machine tool technology; marketing/marketing management; medical insurance coding; medical transcription; music; physical and biological anthropology; pre-engineering; religious studies; social work; technology/industrial arts teacher education; welding technology.

Academics *Calendar:* semesters. *Degree:* certificates, diplomas, and associate. *Special study options:* academic remediation for entering students, accelerated degree program, adult/continuing education programs, advanced placement credit, cooperative education, distance learning, external degree program, independent study, off-campus study, part-time degree program, services for LD students, summer session for credit.

Library Renn Memorial Library with 27,000 titles, 12,000 serial subscriptions, 1,000 audiovisual materials, an OPAC, a Web page.

Student Life *Housing Options:* coed, men-only, women-only. Campus housing is university owned. *Activities and Organizations:* drama/theater group, student-run newspaper, choral group, Academic Civic Engagement through Services (ACES), Peers Advocating for Wellness (PAWS), Phi Theta Kappa, Student Government Association, Phi Beta Lambda. *Campus security:* 24-hour emergency response devices and patrols, late-night transport/escort service, controlled dormitory access, residence hall entrances are locked at night. *Student services:* health clinic, personal/psychological counseling.

Athletics Member NJCAA. *Intercollegiate sports:* baseball M(s), basketball M(s)/W(s), cross-country running M(s)/W(s), soccer M(s)/W(s), softball W(s), tennis M(s)/W(s), track and field M(s)/W(s), volleyball W(s). *Intramural sports:* basketball M/W, bowling M/W, football M, softball M/W, tennis M/W, volleyball M/W.

Standardized Tests *Recommended:* ACT (for admission).

Costs (2010–11) *Tuition:* area resident $1504 full-time, $47 per credit hour part-time; state resident $1824 full-time, $57 per credit hour part-time; nonresident $3328 full-time, $104 per credit hour part-time. *Required fees:* $800 full-time, $25 per credit hour part-time. *Room and board:* $4425. Room and board charges vary according to board plan. *Payment plan:* installment. *Waivers:* employees or children of employees.

Financial Aid Of all full-time matriculated undergraduates who enrolled in 2009, 50 Federal Work-Study jobs (averaging $1500). 75 state and other part-time jobs (averaging $2000).

Applying *Options:* electronic application, early admission. *Required:* high school transcript. *Application deadlines:* rolling (freshmen), rolling (transfers).

Freshman Application Contact Mr. Ben Schears, Executive Director of Enrollment and Outreach Services, Cowley County Community College and Area Vocational–Technical School, PO Box 1147, Arkansas City, KS 67005. *Phone:* 620-441-5368. *Toll-free phone:* 800-593-CCCC. *Fax:* 620-441-5350. *E-mail:* admissions@cowley.edu. *Web site:* http://www.cowley.edu/.

Dodge City Community College
Dodge City, Kansas

- **State and locally supported** 2-year, founded 1935, part of Kansas State Board of Education
- **Small-town** 143-acre campus
- **Coed,** 1,807 undergraduate students, 100% full-time, 55% women, 45% men

Undergraduates 1,807 full-time. Students come from 24 states and territories; 10% are from out of state; 20% live on campus.

Faculty *Total:* 163, 34% full-time. *Student/faculty ratio:* 18:1.

Majors Accounting; administrative assistant and secretarial science; agricultural business and management; agricultural economics; agricultural mechanization; agronomy and crop science; animal sciences; art; athletic training; automobile/automotive mechanics technology; behavioral sciences; biological and physical sciences; biology/biological sciences; broadcast journalism; business administration and management; chemistry; child development; clinical laboratory science/medical technology; communications technology; computer programming; computer science; construction engineering technology; cosmetology; criminal justice/law enforcement administration; data processing and data processing technology; dramatic/theater arts; education; electrical, electronic and communications engineering technology; elementary education; engineering; engineering technology; English; equestrian studies; farm and ranch management; finance; fire science/firefighting; forestry; health information/medical records administration; history; humanities; hydrology and water resources science; industrial technology; information science/studies; journalism; legal administrative assistant/secretary; liberal arts and sciences/liberal studies; licensed practical/vocational nurse training; marketing/marketing management; mass communication/media; mathematics; medical administrative assistant and medical secretary; music; music teacher education; physical education teaching and coaching; physical sciences; physical therapy; physics; political science and government; pre-engineering; pre-pharmacy studies; psychology; radio and television; real estate; registered nursing/registered nurse; respiratory care therapy; rhetoric and composition; social sciences; social work; welding technology; wildlife biology.

Academics *Calendar:* semesters. *Degree:* certificates and associate. *Special study options:* academic remediation for entering students, adult/continuing education programs, advanced placement credit, cooperative education, English as a second language, external degree program, internships, part-time degree program, student-designed majors, summer session for credit.

Library Learning Resource Center with 30,000 titles, 225 serial subscriptions.

Student Life *Housing Options:* coed. Campus housing is university owned. *Activities and Organizations:* drama/theater group, student-run newspaper, radio station, choral group. *Student services:* health clinic, personal/psychological counseling.

Athletics Member NJCAA. *Intercollegiate sports:* baseball M(s), basketball M(s)/W(s), cross-country running M(s)/W(s), equestrian sports M/W, football M(s), golf M(s), softball W(s), volleyball W(s). *Intramural sports:* basketball M/W, bowling M/W, football M, golf M, racquetball M/W, volleyball M/W, weight lifting M/W.

Costs (2010–11) *Tuition:* state resident $2080 full-time, $65 per credit hour part-time; nonresident $2400 full-time, $75 per credit hour part-time. *Required fees:* $200 full-time, $50 per term part-time. *Room and board:* $4502.

Applying *Options:* electronic application, early admission, deferred entrance. *Required:* high school transcript. *Application deadlines:* rolling (freshmen), rolling (transfers). *Notification:* continuous (freshmen), continuous (transfers).

Freshman Application Contact Dodge City Community College, 2501 North 14th Avenue, Dodge City, KS 67801-2399. *Phone:* 620-225-1321. *Web site:* http://www.dc3.edu/.

Donnelly College
Kansas City, Kansas

- **Independent Roman Catholic** primarily 2-year, founded 1949
- **Urban** 4-acre campus
- **Coed**

Undergraduates 291 full-time, 370 part-time. Students come from 2 states and territories; 42 other countries; 15% are from out of state; 2% transferred in; 2% live on campus. *Retention:* 48% of full-time freshmen returned.

Faculty *Student/faculty ratio:* 16:1.

Academics *Calendar:* semesters. *Degrees:* certificates, associate, and bachelor's. *Special study options:* academic remediation for entering students,

advanced placement credit, distance learning, double majors, English as a second language, external degree program, independent study, internships, part-time degree program, services for LD students, summer session for credit.

Student Life *Campus security:* 24-hour emergency response devices.

Costs (2010–11) *Comprehensive fee:* $11,760 includes full-time tuition ($5910), mandatory fees ($40), and room and board ($5810). Full-time tuition and fees vary according to course level, course load, degree level, program, and student level. Part-time tuition and fees vary according to course level, degree level, program, and student level. *Room and board:* college room only: $3680.

Applying *Options:* electronic application, early admission, deferred entrance. *Recommended:* high school transcript.

Freshman Application Contact Mr. Edward Marquez, Director of Admissions, Donnelly College, 608 North 18th Street, Kansas City, KS 66102. *Phone:* 913-621-8713. *Fax:* 913-621-8719. *E-mail:* admissions@donnelly.edu. *Web site:* http://www.donnelly.edu/.

Flint Hills Technical College
Emporia, Kansas

Freshman Application Contact Admissions Office, Flint Hills Technical College, 3301 West 18th Avenue, Emporia, KS 66801. *Phone:* 620-341-1325. *Toll-free phone:* 800-711-6947. *Web site:* http://www.fhtc.net/.

Fort Scott Community College
Fort Scott, Kansas

Director of Admissions Mrs. Mert Barrows, Director of Admissions, Fort Scott Community College, 2108 South Horton, Fort Scott, KS 66701. *Phone:* 620-223-2700 Ext. 353. *Toll-free phone:* 800-874-3722. *Web site:* http://www.fortscott.edu/.

Garden City Community College
Garden City, Kansas

Freshman Application Contact Office of Admissions, Garden City Community College, 801 Campus Drive, Garden City, KS 67846. *Phone:* 620-276-9531. *Fax:* 620-276-9650. *E-mail:* admissions@gcccks.edu. *Web site:* http://www.gcccks.edu/.

Hesston College
Hesston, Kansas

- **Independent Mennonite** 2-year, founded 1909
- **Small-town** 50-acre campus with easy access to Wichita
- **Coed,** 448 undergraduate students, 88% full-time, 58% women, 42% men

Undergraduates 396 full-time, 52 part-time. Students come from 30 states and territories; 11 other countries; 45% are from out of state; 6% Black or African American, non-Hispanic/Latino; 5% Hispanic/Latino; 0.9% Asian, non-Hispanic/Latino; 0.2% Native Hawaiian or other Pacific Islander, non-Hispanic/Latino; 2% American Indian or Alaska Native, non-Hispanic/Latino; 2% Two or more races, non-Hispanic/Latino; 1% Race/ethnicity unknown; 8% international; 9% transferred in; 73% live on campus. *Retention:* 78% of full-time freshmen returned.

Freshmen *Admission:* 844 applied, 236 enrolled. *Average high school GPA:* 3.25. *Test scores:* SAT critical reading scores over 500: 48%; SAT math scores over 500: 52%; SAT writing scores over 500: 28%; ACT scores over 18: 75%; SAT critical reading scores over 600: 12%; SAT math scores over 600: 14%; SAT writing scores over 600: 8%; ACT scores over 24: 27%; ACT scores over 30: 2%.

Faculty *Total:* 51, 67% full-time, 18% with terminal degrees. *Student/faculty ratio:* 12:1.

Majors Aeronautics/aviation/aerospace science and technology; biblical studies; business administration and management; computer/information technology services administration related; kindergarten/preschool education; liberal arts and sciences/liberal studies; pastoral studies/counseling; registered nursing/registered nurse.

Academics *Calendar:* semesters. *Degree:* associate. *Special study options:* academic remediation for entering students, advanced placement credit, cooperative education, double majors, English as a second language, independent study, internships, part-time degree program, services for LD students, summer session for credit.

Library Mary Miller Library with 35,000 titles, 234 serial subscriptions, 2,670 audiovisual materials, an OPAC, a Web page.

Student Life *Housing:* on-campus residence required through sophomore year. *Options:* men-only, women-only. Campus housing is university owned. Freshman campus housing is guaranteed. *Activities and Organizations:* drama/theater group, student-run newspaper, choral group, Peace and Service Club, intramural sports, Ministry Assistants. *Campus security:* 24-hour emergency response devices, controlled dormitory access. *Student services:* personal/psychological counseling.

Athletics Member NJCAA. *Intercollegiate sports:* baseball M(s), basketball M(s)/W(s), cross-country running M(s)/W(s), soccer M(s)/W(s), softball W(s), tennis M(s)/W(s), volleyball W(s). *Intramural sports:* basketball M/W, golf M(c)/W(c), soccer M/W, ultimate Frisbee M/W, volleyball M/W.

Standardized Tests *Required:* SAT or ACT (for admission).

Costs (2011–12) *Comprehensive fee:* $28,818 includes full-time tuition ($21,312), mandatory fees ($340), and room and board ($7166). Full-time tuition and fees vary according to program. Part-time tuition: $888 per hour. Part-time tuition and fees vary according to course load and program. *Required fees:* $85 per term part-time. *Payment plan:* installment. *Waivers:* senior citizens and employees or children of employees.

Financial Aid Of all full-time matriculated undergraduates who enrolled in 2009, 120 Federal Work-Study jobs (averaging $800).

Applying *Options:* electronic application, early admission, deferred entrance. *Application fee:* $15. *Required:* high school transcript, 2 letters of recommendation. *Required for some:* interview. *Application deadlines:* rolling (freshmen), rolling (transfers).

Freshman Application Contact Joel Kauffman, Vice President of Admissions, Hesston College, Hesston, KS 67062. *Phone:* 620-327-8222. *Toll-free phone:* 800-995-2757. *Fax:* 620-327-8300. *E-mail:* admissions@hesston.edu. *Web site:* http://www.hesston.edu/.

Highland Community College

Highland, Kansas

Director of Admissions Ms. Cheryl Rasmussen, Vice President of Student Services, Highland Community College, 606 West Main Street, Highland, KS 66035. *Phone:* 785-442-6020. *Fax:* 785-442-6106. *Web site:* http://www.highlandcc.edu/.

Hutchinson Community College and Area Vocational School

Hutchinson, Kansas

- **State and locally supported** 2-year, founded 1928, part of Kansas Board of Regents
- **Small-town** 47-acre campus
- **Coed**

Undergraduates 2,415 full-time, 3,038 part-time. Students come from 41 states and territories; 5 other countries; 6% are from out of state; 8% transferred in; 7% live on campus. *Retention:* 64% of full-time freshmen returned.

Faculty *Student/faculty ratio:* 18:1.

Academics *Calendar:* semesters. *Degree:* certificates and associate. *Special study options:* academic remediation for entering students, adult/continuing education programs, advanced placement credit, cooperative education, distance learning, double majors, English as a second language, honors programs, independent study, internships, part-time degree program, services for LD students, student-designed majors, summer session for credit. *ROTC:* Army (c).

Student Life *Campus security:* 24-hour emergency response devices and patrols, student patrols, late-night transport/escort service, controlled dormitory access.

Athletics Member NJCAA.

Costs (2010–11) *Tuition:* state resident $1984 full-time, $62 per credit hour part-time; nonresident $3072 full-time, $96 per credit hour part-time. *Required fees:* $544 full-time, $17 per credit hour part-time. *Room and board:* $4920. Room and board charges vary according to board plan.

Applying *Options:* electronic application, early admission, deferred entrance. *Required for some:* interview. *Recommended:* high school transcript.

Freshman Application Contact Mr. Corbin Strobel, Director of Admissions, Hutchinson Community College and Area Vocational School, 1300 North Plum, Hutchinson, KS 67501. *Phone:* 620-665-3536. *Toll-free phone:* 800-289-3501 Ext. 3536. *Fax:* 620-665-3301. *E-mail:* strobelc@hutchcc.edu. *Web site:* http://www.hutchcc.edu/.

Independence Community College

Independence, Kansas

Freshman Application Contact Ms. Sally A. Ciufulescu, Director of Admissions, Independence Community College, Brookside Drive and College Avenue, PO Box 708, Independence, KS 67301-0708. *Phone:* 620-332-5400. *Toll-free phone:* 800-842-6063. *Fax:* 620-331-0946. *E-mail:* sciufulescu@indycc.edu. *Web site:* http://www.indycc.edu/.

Johnson County Community College

Overland Park, Kansas

Director of Admissions Dr. Charles J. Carlsen, President, Johnson County Community College, 12345 College Boulevard, Overland Park, KS 66210-1299. *Phone:* 913-469-8500 Ext. 3806. *Web site:* http://www.johnco.cc.ks.us/

Kansas City Kansas Community College

Kansas City, Kansas

Freshman Application Contact Dr. Denise McDowell, Dean of Enrollment Management/Registrar, Kansas City Kansas Community College, Admissions Office, 7250 State Avenue, Kansas City, KS 66112. *Phone:* 913-288-7694. *Fax:* 913-288-7648. *E-mail:* dmcdowell@kckcc.edu. *Web site:* http://www.kckcc.edu/.

Labette Community College

Parsons, Kansas

Freshman Application Contact Ms. Tammy Fuentez, Director of Admission, Labette Community College, 200 South 14th Street, Parsons, KS 67357-4299. *Phone:* 620-421-6700. *Toll-free phone:* 888-522-3883. *Fax:* 620-421-0180. *Web site:* http://www.labette.edu/.

Manhattan Area Technical College

Manhattan, Kansas

- **State and locally supported** 2-year, founded 1965
- **Suburban** 19-acre campus
- **Coed**

Undergraduates 343 full-time, 130 part-time. 23% transferred in.

Faculty *Student/faculty ratio:* 11:1.

Academics *Calendar:* semesters. *Degree:* certificates, diplomas, and associate.

Costs (2010–11) *Tuition:* state resident $2580 full-time, $86 per credit part-time; nonresident $2580 full-time, $86 per credit part-time. Full-time tuition and fees vary according to program. Part-time tuition and fees vary according to program.

Applying *Application fee:* $40. *Required for some:* high school transcript. *Recommended:* high school transcript.

Freshman Application Contact Mr. Rick Smith, Coordinator of Admissions and Recruitment, Manhattan Area Technical College, 3136 Dickens Avenue, Manhattan, KS 66503. *Phone:* 785-587-2800 Ext. 104. *Toll-free phone:* 800-352-7575. *Fax:* 913-587-2804. *Web site:* http://www.matc.net/.

National American University

Overland Park, Kansas

Freshman Application Contact Admissions Office, National American University, 10310 Mastin, Overland Park, KS 66212. *Web site:* http://www.national.edu/.

Neosho County Community College

Chanute, Kansas

Freshman Application Contact Ms. Lisa Last, Dean of Student Development, Neosho County Community College, 800 West 14th Street, Chanute, KS 66720. *Phone:* 620-431-2820 Ext. 213. *Toll-free phone:* 800-729-6222. *Fax:* 620-431-0082. *E-mail:* llast@neosho.edu. *Web site:* http://www.neosho.edu/.

North Central Kansas Technical College

Beloit, Kansas

Freshman Application Contact Ms. Judy Heidrick, Director of Admissions, North Central Kansas Technical College, PO Box 507, 3033 US Highway 24, Beloit, KS 67420. *Toll-free phone:* 800-658-4655. *E-mail:* jheidrick@ncktc.tec.ks.us. *Web site:* http://www.ncktc.edu/.

Northeast Kansas Technical Center of Highland Community College

Atchison, Kansas

Admissions Office Contact Northeast Kansas Technical Center of Highland Community College, 1501 West Riley Street, Atchison, KS 66002. *Toll-free phone:* 800-567-4890. *Web site:* http://www.nektc.net/.

Northwest Kansas Technical College

Goodland, Kansas

Admissions Office Contact Northwest Kansas Technical College, PO Box 668, 1209 Harrison Street, Goodland, KS 67735. *Toll-free phone:* 800-316-4127. *Web site:* http://www.nwktc.edu/.

Pratt Community College

Pratt, Kansas

- **State and locally supported** 2-year, founded 1938, part of Kansas State Board of Education
- **Rural** 80-acre campus with easy access to Wichita
- **Endowment** $3.0 million
- **Coed,** 1,664 undergraduate students, 45% full-time, 54% women, 46% men

Undergraduates 751 full-time, 913 part-time. Students come from 32 states and territories; 14 other countries; 14% are from out of state; 8% transferred in; 35% live on campus. *Retention:* 60% of full-time freshmen returned.

Freshmen *Admission:* 308 enrolled.

Faculty *Total:* 45, 4% with terminal degrees. *Student/faculty ratio:* 15:1.

Majors Accounting; administrative assistant and secretarial science; agricultural business and management; agricultural economics; agricultural mechanization; agricultural teacher education; agriculture; animal/livestock husbandry and production; animal sciences; art; art teacher education; athletic training; automobile/automotive mechanics technology; biological and physical sciences; biology/biological sciences; business administration and management; business teacher education; chemistry; child development; commercial and advertising art; comparative literature; computer and information sciences and support services related; computer systems networking and telecommunications; computer typography and composition equipment operation; counselor education/school counseling and guidance; data entry/microcomputer applications; data entry/microcomputer applications related; design and applied arts related; education (multiple levels); elementary education; energy management and systems technology; English; family and consumer sciences/human sciences; farm and ranch management; fine/studio arts; health teacher education; history; humanities; human services; kindergarten/preschool education; liberal arts and sciences/liberal studies; mass communication/media; mathematics; music; physical education teaching and coaching; pre-engineering; psychology; registered nursing/registered nurse; rhetoric and composition; social sciences; social work; sociology; speech teacher education; trade and industrial teacher education; welding technology; wildlife biology; word processing.

Academics *Calendar:* semesters. *Degree:* certificates and associate. *Special study options:* academic remediation for entering students, adult/continuing education programs, advanced placement credit, cooperative education, distance learning, internships, part-time degree program, summer session for credit.

Library The Linda Hunt Memorial Library with 28,700 titles, 78 serial subscriptions, 1,849 audiovisual materials, an OPAC, a Web page.

Student Life *Housing:* on-campus residence required through sophomore year. *Options:* coed, men-only, women-only. Campus housing is university owned. *Activities and Organizations:* drama/theater group, student-run newspaper, choral group, Phi Theta Kappa, Rotaract, Christian Challenge, Block and Bridle, Kappa Beta Delta. *Campus security:* 24-hour patrols, late-night transport/escort service, controlled dormitory access. *Student services:* health clinic, personal/psychological counseling.

Athletics Member NJCAA. *Intercollegiate sports:* baseball M(s), basketball M(s)/W(s), cheerleading W(s), cross-country running M(s)/W(s), soccer M(s)/W(s), softball W(s), track and field M(s)/W(s), volleyball W(s), wrestling M(s). *Intramural sports:* basketball M/W, softball M/W, table tennis M/W, volleyball M/W, weight lifting M/W.

Standardized Tests *Required for some:* ASSET.

Costs (2011–12) *Tuition:* state resident $1666 full-time, $49 per credit hour part-time; nonresident $1870 full-time, $55 per credit hour part-time. Full-time tuition and fees vary according to program. Part-time tuition and fees vary according to program. *Required fees:* $32 per credit hour part-time. *Room and board:* $5772. Room and board charges vary according to board plan and housing facility. *Payment plan:* installment. *Waivers:* employees or children of employees.

Financial Aid Of all full-time matriculated undergraduates who enrolled in 2009, 77 Federal Work-Study jobs (averaging $800). 25 state and other part-time jobs (averaging $800). *Financial aid deadline:* 8/1.

Applying *Options:* electronic application, early admission. *Required:* high school transcript. *Application deadlines:* rolling (freshmen), rolling (transfers).

Freshman Application Contact Ms. Theresa Ziehr, Office Assistant, Student Services, Pratt Community College, 348 Northeast State Road 61, Pratt, KS 67124. *Phone:* 620-450-2217. *Toll-free phone:* 800-794-3091. *Fax:* 620-672-5288. *E-mail:* theresaz@prattcc.edu. *Web site:* http://www.prattcc.edu/.

Seward County Community College

Liberal, Kansas

Director of Admissions Dr. Gerald Harris, Dean of Student Services, Seward County Community College, PO Box 1137, Liberal, KS 67905-1137. *Phone:* 620-624-1951 Ext. 617. *Toll-free phone:* 800-373-9951 Ext. 710. *Web site:* http://www.sccc.edu/.

Wichita Area Technical College

Wichita, Kansas

Freshman Application Contact Ms. Jessica Ross, Dean, Enrollment Management, Wichita Area Technical College, Wichita, KS 67211-2099. *Phone:* 316-677-9400. *Fax:* 316-677-9555. *E-mail:* info@watc.edu. *Web site:* http://www.wichitatech.com/.

KENTUCKY

Ashland Community and Technical College

Ashland, Kentucky

Freshman Application Contact Ashland Community and Technical College, 1400 College Drive, Ashland, KY 41101-3683. *Phone:* 606-326-2008. *Toll-free phone:* 800-370-7191. *Web site:* http://www.ashland.kctcs.edu/.

ATA College

Louisville, Kentucky

Freshman Application Contact Admissions Office, ATA College, 10180 Linn Station Road, Suite A200, Louisville, KY 40223. *Phone:* 502-371-8330. *Fax:* 502-371-8598. *Web site:* http://www.ata.edu/.

Beckfield College

Florence, Kentucky

Freshman Application Contact Mrs. Leah Boerger, Director of Admissions, Beckfield College, 16 Spiral Drive, Florence, KY 41042. *Phone:* 859-371-9393. *E-mail:* lboerger@beckfield.edu. *Web site:* http://www.beckfield.edu/.

Big Sandy Community and Technical College

Prestonsburg, Kentucky

Director of Admissions Jimmy Wright, Director of Admissions, Big Sandy Community and Technical College, One Bert T. Combs Drive, Prestonsburg, KY 41653-1815. *Phone:* 606-886-3863. *Toll-free phone:* 888-641-4132. *E-mail:* jimmy.wright@kctcs.edu. *Web site:* http://www.bigsandy.kctcs.edu/.

Bluegrass Community and Technical College

Lexington, Kentucky

Freshman Application Contact Mrs. Shelbie Hugle, Director of Admission Services, Bluegrass Community and Technical College, 470 Cooper Drive, Lexington, KY 40506. *Phone:* 859-246-6216. *Toll-free phone:* 866-744-4872 Ext. 5111. *E-mail:* shelbie.hugle@kctcs.edu. *Web site:* http://www.bluegrass.kctcs.edu/.

Bowling Green Technical College

Bowling Green, Kentucky

Director of Admissions Mark Garrett, Chief Student Affairs Officer, Bowling Green Technical College, 1845 Loop Drive, Bowling Green, KY 42101. *Phone:* 270-901-1114. *Toll-free phone:* 800-790.0990. *Web site:* http://www.bowlinggreen.kctcs.edu/.

Brown Mackie College–Hopkinsville

Hopkinsville, Kentucky

- **Proprietary** 2-year, part of Education Management Corporation
- **Small-town** campus
- **Coed**

Majors Accounting technology and bookkeeping; business administration and management; computer programming; computer programming (specific applications); computer software technology; criminal justice/law enforcement administration; legal assistant/paralegal; medical/clinical assistant; medical office management; occupational therapist assistant.

Academics *Calendar:* quarters. *Degree:* diplomas and associate.

Costs (2010–11) *Tuition:* Tuition varies by program. Students should contact Brown Mackie College for tuition information.

Freshman Application Contact Brown Mackie College–Hopkinsville, 4001 Fort Cambell Boulevard, Hopkinsville, KY 42240. *Phone:* 270-886-1302. *Toll-free phone:* 800-359-4753. *Web site:* http://www.brownmackie.edu/Hopkinsville/.

See page 372 for the College Close-Up.

Brown Mackie College–Louisville

Louisville, Kentucky

- **Proprietary** primarily 2-year, founded 1972, part of Education Management Corporation
- **Suburban** campus
- **Coed**

Majors Accounting technology and bookkeeping; biomedical technology; business administration and management; computer systems networking and telecommunications; criminal justice/law enforcement administration; early childhood education; electrical, electronic and communications engineering technology; graphic design; health/health-care administration; legal assistant/paralegal; legal studies; medical/clinical assistant; occupational therapist assistant; pharmacy technician; surgical technology; veterinary/animal health technology.

Academics *Calendar:* quarters. *Degrees:* certificates, diplomas, associate, and bachelor's.

Costs (2010–11) *Tuition:* Tuition varies by program. Students should contact Brown Mackie College for tuition information.

Freshman Application Contact Brown Mackie College–Louisville, 3605 Fern Valley Road, Louisville, KY 40219. *Phone:* 502-968-7191. *Toll-free phone:* 800-999-7387. *Web site:* http://www.brownmackie.edu/louisville/.

See page 378 for the College Close-Up.

Brown Mackie College–Northern Kentucky

Fort Mitchell, Kentucky

- **Proprietary** primarily 2-year, founded 1927, part of Education Management Corporation
- **Suburban** campus
- **Coed**

Majors Accounting technology and bookkeeping; business administration and management; CAD/CADD drafting/design technology; computer software technology; criminal justice/law enforcement administration; health/health-care administration; information technology; legal assistant/paralegal; medical/clinical assistant; occupational therapist assistant; pharmacy technician; surgical technology.

Academics *Calendar:* quarters. *Degrees:* certificates, diplomas, associate, and bachelor's.

Costs (2010–11) *Tuition:* Tuition varies by program. Students should contact Brown Mackie College for tuition information.

Freshman Application Contact Brown Mackie College–Northern Kentucky, 309 Buttermilk Pike, Fort Mitchell, KY 41017-2191. *Phone:* 859-341-5627. *Toll-free phone:* 800-888-1445. *Web site:* http://www.brownmackie.edu/northernkentucky/.

See page 388 for the College Close-Up.

Daymar College

Bellevue, Kentucky

Freshman Application Contact Cathy Baird, Director of Admissions, Daymar College, 119 Fairfield Avenue, Bellevue, KY 41073. *Phone:* 859-291-0800. *Toll-free phone:* 877-258-7796. *Fax:* 859-491-7500. *Web site:* http://www.daymarcollege.edu/.

Daymar College

Bowling Green, Kentucky

Freshman Application Contact Mrs. Traci Henderson, Admissions Director, Daymar College, 2421 Fitzgerald Industrial Drive, Bowling Green, KY 42101. *Phone:* 270-843-6750. *Toll-free phone:* 877-258-7796. *E-mail:* thenderson@daymarcollege.edu. *Web site:* http://www.daymarcollege.edu/.

Daymar College

Louisville, Kentucky

Director of Admissions Mr. Patrick Carney, Director of Admissions, Daymar College, 4400 Breckenridge Lane, Suite 415, Louisville, KY 40218. *Web site:* http://www.daymarcollege.edu/.

Daymar College

Owensboro, Kentucky

Freshman Application Contact Ms. Vickie McDougal, Director of Admissions, Daymar College, 3361 Buckland Square, Owensboro, KY 42301. *Phone:* 270-926-4040. *Toll-free phone:* 800-960-4090. *Fax:* 270-685-4090. *E-mail:* info@daymarcollege.edu. *Web site:* http://www.daymarcollege.edu/.

Daymar College

Paducah, Kentucky

Freshman Application Contact Daymar College, 509 South 30th Street, Paducah, KY 42001. *Phone:* 270-444-9950. *Toll-free phone:* 877-258-7796. *Web site:* http://www.daymarcollege.edu/.

Elizabethtown Community and Technical College

Elizabethtown, Kentucky

Freshman Application Contact Elizabethtown Community and Technical College, 620 College Street Road, Elizabethtown, KY 42701. *Phone:* 270-706-8800. *Toll-free phone:* 877-246-2322. *Web site:* http://www.elizabethtown.kctcs.edu/.

Gateway Community and Technical College

Covington, Kentucky

- **State-supported** 2-year, founded 1961, part of Kentucky Community and Technical College System
- **Suburban** campus with easy access to Cincinnati
- **Coed**, 4,799 undergraduate students

Undergraduates 10% Black or African American, non-Hispanic/Latino; 2% Hispanic/Latino; 0.4% Asian, non-Hispanic/Latino; 0.2% Native Hawaiian or other Pacific Islander, non-Hispanic/Latino; 0.3% American Indian or Alaska Native, non-Hispanic/Latino; 1% Two or more races, non-Hispanic/Latino; 1% Race/ethnicity unknown.

Freshmen *Average high school GPA:* 2.55.

Faculty *Total:* 259, 32% full-time. *Student/faculty ratio:* 19:1.

Majors Accounting technology and bookkeeping; business administration and management; CAD/CADD drafting/design technology; criminal justice/law enforcement administration; early childhood education; engineering technology; fire science/firefighting; general studies; health professions related; industrial technology; information technology; manufacturing engineering technology; office occupations and clerical services; registered nursing/registered nurse.

Academics *Calendar:* semesters. *Degree:* certificates, diplomas, and associate. *Special study options:* academic remediation for entering students, cooperative education, distance learning, internships, part-time degree program, services for LD students, summer session for credit.

Library Main Library plus 3 others.

Student Life *Housing:* college housing not available. *Activities and Organizations:* Multi-Cultural Student Organization, Student Government Association,

Speech Team, American Criminal Justice Association, Phi Theta Kappa. *Student services:* personal/psychological counseling.
Standardized Tests *Required:* ACT or ACT COMPASS (for admission).
Costs (2010–11) *Tuition:* state resident $3120 full-time, $130 per credit part-time; nonresident $10,680 full-time, $445 per credit part-time. Full-time tuition and fees vary according to course load and location. Part-time tuition and fees vary according to course load and location. *Payment plan:* installment. *Waivers:* senior citizens and employees or children of employees.
Applying *Options:* electronic application, early admission. *Required:* high school transcript. *Application deadlines:* rolling (freshmen), rolling (out-of-state freshmen), rolling (transfers). *Notification:* continuous (freshmen), continuous (out-of-state freshmen), continuous (transfers).
Freshman Application Contact Gateway Community and Technical College, 1025 Amsterdam Road, Covington, KY 41011. *Phone:* 859-442-4176. *E-mail:* andre.washington@kctcs.edu. *Web site:* http://www.gateway.kctcs.edu/.

Hazard Community and Technical College
Hazard, Kentucky

- **State-supported** 2-year, founded 1968, part of Kentucky Community and Technical College System
- **Rural** 34-acre campus
- **Coed**

Undergraduates 1,806 full-time, 2,908 part-time. 2% are from out of state.
Faculty *Student/faculty ratio:* 25:1.
Academics *Calendar:* semesters. *Degree:* certificates, diplomas, and associate. *Special study options:* cooperative education, distance learning, honors programs, independent study.
Costs (2010–11) *Tuition:* state resident $3120 full-time, $130 per credit hour part-time; nonresident $10,680 full-time, $445 per credit hour part-time. *Payment plans:* installment, deferred payment.
Applying *Options:* early admission. *Required:* high school transcript.
Freshman Application Contact Director of Admissions, Hazard Community and Technical College, 1 Community College Drive, Hazard, KY 41701-2403. *Phone:* 606-487-3102. *Toll-free phone:* 800-246-7521. *Web site:* http://www.hazard.kctcs.edu/.

Henderson Community College
Henderson, Kentucky

Freshman Application Contact Ms. Teresa Hamiton, Admissions Counselor, Henderson Community College, 2660 South Green Street, Henderson, KY 42420-4623. *Phone:* 270-827-1867 Ext. 354. *Web site:* http://www.henderson.kctcs.edu/.

Hopkinsville Community College
Hopkinsville, Kentucky

- **State-supported** 2-year, founded 1965, part of Kentucky Community and Technical College System
- **Small-town** 69-acre campus with easy access to Nashville
- **Coed**

Undergraduates 1,771 full-time, 1,982 part-time. Students come from 7 states and territories; 31% are from out of state; 8% transferred in. *Retention:* 55% of full-time freshmen returned.
Faculty *Student/faculty ratio:* 25:1.
Academics *Calendar:* semesters. *Degree:* certificates, diplomas, and associate. *Special study options:* academic remediation for entering students, advanced placement credit, cooperative education, distance learning, honors programs, independent study, part-time degree program, services for LD students, summer session for credit.
Student Life *Campus security:* 24-hour emergency response devices, late-night transport/escort service, security provided by trained security personnel during hours of normal operation.
Costs (2010–11) *Tuition:* state resident $3380 full-time, $130 per credit hour part-time; nonresident $11,570 full-time, $445 per credit hour part-time. Full-time tuition and fees vary according to reciprocity agreements. Part-time tuition and fees vary according to reciprocity agreements.
Financial Aid Of all full-time matriculated undergraduates who enrolled in 2009, 30 Federal Work-Study jobs (averaging $1500). *Financial aid deadline:* 6/30.
Applying *Options:* electronic application, deferred entrance. *Recommended:* high school transcript.
Freshman Application Contact Ms. Janet Level, Student Records, Hopkinsville Community College, Room 135, English Education Center, 202 Bastogne Avenue, Fort Campbell, KY. *Phone:* 270-707-3918. *Fax:* 270-707-3973. *E-mail:* janet.level@kctcs.edu. *Web site:* http://hopkinsville.kctcs.edu/.

ITT Technical Institute
Louisville, Kentucky

- **Proprietary** primarily 2-year, founded 1993, part of ITT Educational Services, Inc.
- **Suburban** campus
- **Coed**

Majors CAD/CADD drafting/design technology; computer and information systems security; computer engineering technology; computer software and media applications related; computer software engineering; computer software technology; construction management; criminal justice/law enforcement administration; design and visual communications; electrical, electronic and communications engineering technology; game and interactive media design; legal assistant/paralegal; project management; registered nursing/registered nurse; system, networking, and LAN/WAN management.
Academics *Calendar:* quarters. *Degrees:* associate and bachelor's.
Student Life *Housing:* college housing not available.
Freshman Application Contact Director of Recruitment, ITT Technical Institute, 9500 Ormsby Station Road, Suite 100, Louisville, KY 40223. *Phone:* 502-327-7424. *Toll-free phone:* 888-790-7427. *Web site:* http://www.itt-tech.edu/.

Jefferson Community and Technical College
Louisville, Kentucky

Freshman Application Contact Ms. Melanie Vaughan-Cooke, Admissions Coordinator, Jefferson Community and Technical College, Louisville, KY 40202. *Phone:* 502-213-4000. *Fax:* 502-213-2540. *Web site:* http://www.jefferson.kctcs.edu/.

Madisonville Community College
Madisonville, Kentucky

Director of Admissions Mr. Jay Parent, Registrar, Madisonville Community College, 2000 College Drive, Madisonville, KY 42431-9185. *Phone:* 270-821-2250. *Web site:* http://www.madcc.kctcs.edu/.

Maysville Community and Technical College
Maysville, Kentucky

Director of Admissions Ms. Patee Massie, Registrar, Maysville Community and Technical College, 1755 US 68, Maysville, KY 41056. *Phone:* 606-759-7141. *Fax:* 606-759-5818. *E-mail:* ccsmayrg@ukcc.uky.edu. *Web site:* http://www.maysville.kctcs.edu/.

Maysville Community and Technical College
Morehead, Kentucky

Director of Admissions Patee Massie, Registrar, Maysville Community and Technical College, 609 Viking Drive, Morehead, KY 40351. *Phone:* 606-759-7141 Ext. 66184. *Web site:* http://www.maysville.kctcs.edu/.

National College
Danville, Kentucky

Director of Admissions James McGuire, Campus Director, National College, 115 East Lexington Avenue, Danville, KY 40422. *Phone:* 859-236-6991. *Toll-free phone:* 800-664-1886. *Web site:* http://www.national-college.edu/.

National College
Florence, Kentucky

Director of Admissions Mr. Terry Kovacs, Campus Director, National College, 7627 Ewing Boulevard, Florence, KY 41042. *Phone:* 859-525-6510. *Toll-free phone:* 800-664-1886. *Web site:* http://www.national-college.edu/.

National College
Lexington, Kentucky

Director of Admissions Kim Thomasson, Campus Director, National College, 2376 Sir Barton Way, Lexington, KY 40509. *Phone:* 859-253-0621. *Toll-free phone:* 800-664-1886. *Web site:* http://www.national-college.edu/.

National College

Louisville, Kentucky

Director of Admissions Vincent C. Tinebra, Campus Director, National College, 3950 Dixie Highway, Louisville, KY 40216. *Phone:* 502-447-7634. *Toll-free phone:* 800-664-1886. *Web site:* http://www.national-college.edu/.

National College

Pikeville, Kentucky

Director of Admissions Tammy Riley, Campus Director, National College, 288 South Mayo Trail, Suite 2, Pikeville, KY 41501. *Phone:* 606-478-7200. *Toll-free phone:* 800-664-1886. *Web site:* http://www.national-college.edu/.

National College

Richmond, Kentucky

Director of Admissions Ms. Keeley Gadd, Campus Director, National College, 139 South Killarney Lane, Richmond, KY 40475. *Phone:* 859-623-8956. *Toll-free phone:* 800-664-1886. *Web site:* http://www.national-college.edu/.

Owensboro Community and Technical College

Owensboro, Kentucky

- **State-supported** 2-year, founded 1986, part of Kentucky Community and Technical College System
- **Suburban** 102-acre campus
- **Coed,** 6,328 undergraduate students, 34% full-time, 55% women, 45% men

Undergraduates 2,136 full-time, 4,192 part-time. Students come from 7 states and territories; 2% are from out of state.

Freshmen *Admission:* 703 enrolled.

Faculty *Total:* 212, 46% full-time, 9% with terminal degrees. *Student/faculty ratio:* 28:1.

Majors Agriculture; business administration and management; computer and information sciences; computer/information technology services administration related; criminal justice/police science; data entry/microcomputer applications; diagnostic medical sonography and ultrasound technology; electrical, electronic and communications engineering technology; executive assistant/executive secretary; fire science/firefighting; human services; information technology; kindergarten/preschool education; liberal arts and sciences/liberal studies; medical radiologic technology; network and system administration; precision production trades; registered nursing/registered nurse; social work; word processing.

Academics *Calendar:* semesters. *Degree:* certificates, diplomas, and associate. *Special study options:* academic remediation for entering students, adult/continuing education programs, advanced placement credit, cooperative education, distance learning, double majors, English as a second language, external degree program, honors programs, independent study, off-campus study, part-time degree program, services for LD students, student-designed majors, study abroad, summer session for credit.

Library Learning Resource Center with 25,600 titles, 24,614 serial subscriptions, an OPAC, a Web page.

Student Life *Activities and Organizations:* drama/theater group, student-run newspaper, radio and television station, choral group, Student Government Association. *Campus security:* 24-hour emergency response devices, late-night transport/escort service.

Standardized Tests *Recommended:* SAT or ACT (for admission).

Costs (2011–12) *Tuition:* state resident $3900 full-time, $130 per credit hour part-time; nonresident $13,350 full-time, $445 per credit hour part-time. Full-time tuition and fees vary according to reciprocity agreements. Part-time tuition and fees vary according to reciprocity agreements. *Payment plan:* installment. *Waivers:* senior citizens and employees or children of employees.

Financial Aid Of all full-time matriculated undergraduates who enrolled in 2009, 34 Federal Work-Study jobs (averaging $5120). *Financial aid deadline:* 4/1.

Applying *Options:* electronic application. *Required:* high school transcript. *Application deadlines:* rolling (freshmen), rolling (transfers). *Notification:* continuous (freshmen), continuous (transfers).

Freshman Application Contact Ms. Barbara Tipmore, Admissions Counselor, Owensboro Community and Technical College, 4800 New Hartford Road, Owensboro, KY 42303. *Phone:* 270-686-4530. *Toll-free phone:* 866-755-6282. *E-mail:* barb.tipmore@kctcs.edu. *Web site:* http://www.octc.kctcs.edu/.

St. Catharine College

St. Catharine, Kentucky

Director of Admissions Ms. Amy C. Carrico, Director of Admissions, St. Catharine College, 2735 Bardstown Road, St. Catharine, KY 40061-9499. *Phone:* 859-336-5082. *Toll-free phone:* 800-599-2000 Ext. 1227. *Web site:* http://www.sccky.edu/.

Somerset Community College

Somerset, Kentucky

- **State-supported** 2-year, founded 1965, part of Kentucky Community and Technical College System
- **Small-town** 70-acre campus
- **Coed**

Undergraduates *Retention:* 59% of full-time freshmen returned.

Faculty *Student/faculty ratio:* 23:1.

Academics *Calendar:* semesters. *Degree:* certificates, diplomas, and associate. *Special study options:* academic remediation for entering students, adult/continuing education programs, advanced placement credit, distance learning, part-time degree program, summer session for credit.

Costs (2010–11) *Tuition:* state resident $3900 full time, $130 per credit hour part-time; nonresident $13,350 full-time, $445 per credit hour part-time.

Applying *Options:* electronic application, early admission. *Required:* high school transcript.

Freshman Application Contact Director of Admission, Somerset Community College, 808 Monticello Street, Somerset, KY 42501-2973. *Phone:* 606-451-6630. *Toll-free phone:* 877-629-9722. *E-mail:* somerset-admissions@kctcs.edu. *Web site:* http://www.somerset.kctcs.edu/.

Southeast Kentucky Community and Technical College

Cumberland, Kentucky

- **State-supported** 2-year, founded 1960, part of Kentucky Community and Technical College System
- **Rural** 150-acre campus
- **Coed**

Undergraduates 1,943 full-time, 3,016 part-time. Students come from 10 states and territories; 1 other country; 5% are from out of state; 1% transferred in. *Retention:* 65% of full-time freshmen returned.

Faculty *Student/faculty ratio:* 19:1.

Academics *Calendar:* semesters. *Degree:* certificates, diplomas, and associate. *Special study options:* academic remediation for entering students, accelerated degree program, adult/continuing education programs, advanced placement credit, distance learning, independent study, part-time degree program, study abroad, summer session for credit.

Standardized Tests *Recommended:* ACT (for admission).

Costs (2010–11) *Tuition:* state resident $3900 full-time, $130 per credit hour part-time; nonresident $13,000 full-time, $430 per credit hour part-time. Full-time tuition and fees vary according to reciprocity agreements. Part-time tuition and fees vary according to reciprocity agreements. *Required fees:* $144 full-time.

Financial Aid Of all full-time matriculated undergraduates who enrolled in 2009, 90 Federal Work-Study jobs (averaging $635).

Applying *Required:* high school transcript.

Freshman Application Contact Southeast Kentucky Community and Technical College, 700 College Road, Cumberland, KY 40823-1099. *Phone:* 606-589-2145 Ext. 13018. *Toll-free phone:* 888-274-SECC Ext. 2108. *Web site:* http://www.soucc.kctcs.net/.

Southwestern College of Business

Florence, Kentucky

Freshman Application Contact Director of Admission, Southwestern College of Business, 8095 Connector Drive, Florence, KY 41042. *Phone:* 859-282-9999. *Web site:* http://www.swcollege.net/.

Spencerian College

Louisville, Kentucky

- **Proprietary** 2-year, founded 1892, administratively affiliated with The Sullivan University System
- **Urban** 10-acre campus
- **Coed, primarily women,** 1,155 undergraduate students, 73% full-time, 86% women, 14% men

Undergraduates 843 full-time, 312 part-time. 16% Black or African American, non-Hispanic/Latino; 2% Hispanic/Latino; 0.7% Asian, non-Hispanic/Latino; 0.3% Native Hawaiian or other Pacific Islander, non-Hispanic/Latino; 0.8% American Indian or Alaska Native, non-Hispanic/Latino; 11% Two or more races, non-Hispanic/Latino; 5% Race/ethnicity unknown; 1% live on campus.

Freshmen *Admission:* 266 admitted, 266 enrolled.

Faculty *Total:* 124, 52% full-time, 5% with terminal degrees. *Student/faculty ratio:* 14:1.

Majors Accounting; accounting and business/management; business administration and management; cardiovascular technology; clinical laboratory science/medical technology; massage therapy; medical insurance/medical billing; medical office management; medical radiologic technology; radiologic technology/science; registered nursing/registered nurse; surgical technology.

Academics *Calendar:* quarters. *Degree:* certificates, diplomas, and associate. *Special study options:* distance learning, internships, summer session for credit.

Library Spencerian College Learning Resource Center with 1,650 titles, 31,000 serial subscriptions, 277 audiovisual materials, an OPAC, a Web page.

Student Life *Housing Options:* coed. *Activities and Organizations:* Student Activities Board. *Campus security:* 24-hour emergency response devices, late-night transport/escort service.

Costs (2010–11) *Comprehensive fee:* $25,135 includes full-time tuition ($15,420), mandatory fees ($2170), and room and board ($7545). Full-time tuition and fees vary according to class time and program. Part-time tuition: $260 per credit hour. Part-time tuition and fees vary according to class time and program. No tuition increase for student's term of enrollment. *Required fees:* $50 per course part-time. *Room and board:* college room only: $5355. *Payment plan:* installment. *Waivers:* employees or children of employees.

Applying *Application fee:* $100. *Required:* high school transcript, interview. *Required for some:* essay or personal statement. *Notification:* continuous (freshmen), continuous (out-of-state freshmen), continuous (transfers).

Freshman Application Contact Spencerian College, 4627 Dixie Highway, Louisville, KY 40216. *Phone:* 502-447-1000 Ext. 7808. *Toll-free phone:* 800-264-1799. *Web site:* http://www.spencerian.edu/.

Spencerian College–Lexington

Lexington, Kentucky

Freshman Application Contact Spencerian College–Lexington, 1575 Winchester Road, Lexington, KY 40505. *Phone:* 859-223-9608 Ext. 5430. *Toll-free phone:* 800-456-3253. *Web site:* http://www.spencerian.edu/.

Sullivan College of Technology and Design

Louisville, Kentucky

- **Proprietary** primarily 2-year, founded 1961, part of The Sullivan University System, Inc.
- **Suburban** 10-acre campus with easy access to Louisville
- **Coed,** 705 undergraduate students, 62% full-time, 30% women, 70% men

Undergraduates 440 full-time, 265 part-time. Students come from 8 states and territories; 7 other countries; 11% are from out of state; 18% Black or African American, non-Hispanic/Latino; 3% Hispanic/Latino; 0.9% Asian, non-Hispanic/Latino; 0.3% Native Hawaiian or other Pacific Islander, non-Hispanic/Latino; 0.3% American Indian or Alaska Native, non-Hispanic/Latino; 6% Two or more races, non-Hispanic/Latino; 6% transferred in; 3% live on campus. *Retention:* 86% of full-time freshmen returned.

Freshmen *Admission:* 323 applied, 184 admitted, 181 enrolled.

Faculty *Total:* 82, 40% full-time. *Student/faculty ratio:* 11:1.

Majors Animation, interactive technology, video graphics and special effects; architectural drafting and CAD/CADD; architectural engineering technology; architecture related; artificial intelligence; CAD/CADD drafting/design technology; civil drafting and CAD/CADD; computer and information sciences; computer and information sciences and support services related; computer and information systems security; computer engineering technology; computer graphics; computer hardware engineering; computer hardware technology; computer installation and repair technology; computer programming (vendor/product certification); computer systems networking and telecommunications; computer technology/computer systems technology; desktop publishing and digital imaging design; digital communication and media/multimedia; drafting and design technology; drafting/design engineering technologies related; electrical and electronic engineering technologies related; electrical, electronic and communications engineering technology; electrical/electronics equipment installation and repair; electrical/electronics maintenance and repair technology related; electromechanical and instrumentation and maintenance technologies related; engineering technologies and engineering related; engineering technology; graphic and printing equipment operation/production; graphic communications; graphic communications related; graphic design; heating, ventilation, air conditioning and refrigeration engineering technology; housing and human environments; industrial electronics technology; industrial mechanics and maintenance technology; information technology; interior design; manufacturing engineering technology; mechanical drafting and CAD/CADD; mechanical engineering/mechanical technology; network and system administration; robotics technology; web page, digital/multimedia and information resources design.

Academics *Calendar:* quarters. *Degrees:* certificates, diplomas, associate, and bachelor's. *Special study options:* academic remediation for entering students, accelerated degree program, adult/continuing education programs, advanced placement credit, double majors, independent study, internships, part-time degree program, services for LD students, summer session for credit.

Library Sullivan College of Technology and Design Library with 2,836 titles, 68 serial subscriptions, 356 audiovisual materials, an OPAC, a Web page.

Student Life *Housing Options:* coed. Campus housing is university owned and leased by the school. Freshman campus housing is guaranteed. *Activities and Organizations:* ASID, IIDA, ADDA, ADFED, Skills USA. *Campus security:* late-night transport/escort service, controlled dormitory access, telephone alarm device during hours school is open; patrols by trained security personnel while classes are in session.

Standardized Tests *Required:* Career Performance Assessment Test (CPAt) or ACT or SAT scores in place of CPAt results (for admission). *Recommended:* SAT or ACT (for admission).

Costs (2010–11) *One-time required fee:* $100. *Comprehensive fee:* $25,600 includes full-time tuition ($16,425), mandatory fees ($850), and room and board ($8325). Full-time tuition and fees vary according to course load, degree level, and program. Part-time tuition: $445 per credit hour. Part-time tuition and fees vary according to course load, degree level, and program. No tuition increase for student's term of enrollment. *Required fees:* $50 per course part-time. *Room and board:* college room only: $5355. Room and board charges vary according to board plan and housing facility. *Payment plan:* installment. *Waivers:* employees or children of employees.

Applying *Options:* deferred entrance. *Application fee:* $100. *Required:* high school transcript, interview. *Recommended:* minimum 2.0 GPA. *Application deadlines:* rolling (freshmen), rolling (out-of-state freshmen), rolling (transfers). *Notification:* continuous (freshmen), continuous (out-of-state freshmen), continuous (transfers).

Freshman Application Contact Mr. Aamer Z. Chauhdri, Director of Admissions, Sullivan College of Technology and Design, 3901 Atkinson Square Drive, Louisville, KY 40218. *Phone:* 502-456-6509 Ext. 8220. *Toll-free phone:* 800-884-6528. *Fax:* 502-456-2341. *E-mail:* achauhdri@sctd.edu. *Web site:* http://www.sctd.edu/.

West Kentucky Community and Technical College

Paducah, Kentucky

- **State-supported** 2-year, founded 1932, part of Kentucky Community and Technical College System
- **Small-town** 117-acre campus
- **Coed,** 4,281 undergraduate students, 59% full-time, 65% women, 35% men

Undergraduates 2,532 full-time, 1,749 part-time. Students come from 14 states and territories; 1 other country; 5% are from out of state; 8% Black or African American, non-Hispanic/Latino; 2% Hispanic/Latino; 0.6% Asian, non-Hispanic/Latino; 0.1% Native Hawaiian or other Pacific Islander, non-Hispanic/Latino; 0.4% American Indian or Alaska Native, non-Hispanic/Latino; 1% Two or more races, non-Hispanic/Latino; 2% Race/ethnicity unknown; 24% transferred in. *Retention:* 64% of full-time freshmen returned.

Freshmen *Admission:* 841 enrolled. *Test scores:* ACT scores over 18: 91%; ACT scores over 24: 37%; ACT scores over 30: 7%.

Faculty *Total:* 369, 36% full-time. *Student/faculty ratio:* 15:1.

Majors Accounting; business administration and management; computer and information sciences; court reporting; criminal justice/law enforcement administration; culinary arts; diagnostic medical sonography and ultrasound technology; electrician; fire science/firefighting; machine shop technology; physical therapy technology; registered nursing/registered nurse; respiratory care therapy; surgical technology.

Academics *Calendar:* semesters. *Degree:* certificates, diplomas, and associate. *Special study options:* academic remediation for entering students, adult/continuing education programs, cooperative education, distance learning, English as a second language, honors programs, independent study, internships, part-time degree program, study abroad.

Library WKCTC Matheson Library with 74,676 titles, 155 serial subscriptions, 5,043 audiovisual materials, an OPAC, a Web page.

Student Life *Housing:* college housing not available. *Activities and Organizations:* drama/theater group, choral group. *Campus security:* late-night transport/escort service, 14-hour patrols by trained security personnel.

Athletics *Intramural sports:* basketball M/W, golf M/W, soccer M/W, volleyball M/W.

Standardized Tests *Required:* SAT or ACT (for admission). *Recommended:* ACT (for admission).

Costs (2010–11) *Tuition:* state resident $3900 full-time, $130 per credit hour part-time; nonresident $13,350 full-time, $445 per credit hour part-time. *Waivers:* senior citizens and employees or children of employees.

Financial Aid Of all full-time matriculated undergraduates who enrolled in 2009, 50 Federal Work-Study jobs (averaging $1650).

Applying *Options:* early admission. *Required for some:* high school transcript. *Application deadlines:* rolling (freshmen), rolling (transfers).

Freshman Application Contact Mr. Jerry Anderson, Admissions Counselor, West Kentucky Community and Technical College, 4810 Alben Barkley Drive, Paducah, KY 42002-7380. *Phone:* 270-554-3266. *E-mail:* jerry.anderson@kctcs.edu. *Web site:* http://www.westkentucky.kctcs.edu/.

LOUISIANA

Baton Rouge Community College

Baton Rouge, Louisiana

Director of Admissions Nancy Clay, Interim Executive Director for Enrollment Services, Baton Rouge Community College, 5310 Florida Boulevard, Baton Rouge, LA 70806. *Phone:* 225-216-8700. *Toll-free phone:* 800-601-4558. *Web site:* http://www.mybrcc.edu/.

Baton Rouge School of Computers

Baton Rouge, Louisiana

Freshman Application Contact Admissions Office, Baton Rouge School of Computers, 10425 Plaza Americana, Baton Rouge, LA 70816. *Phone:* 225-923-2524. *Fax:* 225-923-2979. *E-mail:* admissions@brsc.net. *Web site:* http://www.brsc.edu/.

Blue Cliff College–Lafayette

Lafayette, Louisiana

Freshman Application Contact Admissions Office, Blue Cliff College–Lafayette, 100 Asma Boulevard, Suite 350, Lafayette, LA 70508-3862. *Toll-free phone:* 800-514-2609. *Web site:* http://www.bluecliffcollege.com/.

Blue Cliff College–Shreveport

Shreveport, Louisiana

- **Proprietary** 2-year
- **Urban** campus
- **Coed**

Faculty *Student/faculty ratio:* 12:1.

Academics *Degree:* certificates and associate. *Special study options:* part-time degree program, summer session for credit.

Applying *Required:* interview. *Required for some:* high school transcript.

Freshman Application Contact Blue Cliff College–Shreveport, 8731 Park Plaza Drive, Shreveport, LA 71105. *Toll-free phone:* 800-516-6597. *Web site:* http://www.bluecliffcollege.com/.

Bossier Parish Community College

Bossier City, Louisiana

Freshman Application Contact Ms. Ann Jampole, Director of Admissions, Bossier Parish Community College, 2719 Airline Drive North, Bossier City, LA 71111-5801. *Phone:* 318-678-6166. *Fax:* 318-742-8664. *Web site:* http://www.bpcc.edu/.

Camelot College

Baton Rouge, Louisiana

Freshman Application Contact Camelot College, 2618 Wooddale Boulevard, Suite A, Baton Rouge, LA 70805. *Phone:* 225-928-3005. *Toll-free phone:* 800-470-3320. *Web site:* http://www.camelotcollege.com/.

Cameron College

New Orleans, Louisiana

Admissions Office Contact Cameron College, 2740 Canal Street, New Orleans, LA 70119. *Web site:* http://www.cameroncollege.com/.

Career Technical College

Monroe, Louisiana

- **Proprietary** 2-year, founded 1985, part of Delta Career Education Corporation
- **Small-town** campus with easy access to Shreveport
- **Coed,** 809 undergraduate students, 67% full-time, 75% women, 25% men

Undergraduates 546 full-time, 263 part-time. Students come from 3 states and territories; 1% are from out of state; 9% transferred in. *Retention:* 90% of full-time freshmen returned.

Freshmen *Admission:* 809 enrolled. *Average high school GPA:* 2.5.

Faculty *Total:* 39, 59% full-time, 23% with terminal degrees. *Student/faculty ratio:* 22:1.

Majors Administrative assistant and secretarial science; business administration and management; computer and information sciences and support services related; corrections and criminal justice related; legal administrative assistant/secretary; management science; massage therapy; medical/clinical assistant; medical office management; radiologic technology/science; respiratory therapy technician; surgical technology.

Academics *Calendar:* quarters. *Degree:* diplomas and associate. *Special study options:* academic remediation for entering students, advanced placement credit, cooperative education, double majors, independent study, internships.

Library Jones E-Library.

Student Life *Housing:* college housing not available. *Activities and Organizations:* student-run newspaper, MAC Club, Scrub Club, Ambassadors, Rad Tech Club, Resp Therapy Club. *Campus security:* 24-hour emergency response devices, late-night transport/escort service, Evening Security Guard.

Standardized Tests *Required:* SLE-Wonderlic Scholastic Level Exam; Math Proficiency Exam; English Proficiency Exam (for admission).

Costs (2011–12) *Tuition:* $237 per credit part-time. Full-time tuition and fees vary according to program. Part-time tuition and fees vary according to program. No tuition increase for student's term of enrollment. *Required fees:* $237 per credit part-time. *Payment plans:* tuition prepayment, installment. *Waivers:* employees or children of employees.

Applying *Options:* deferred entrance. *Application fee:* $40. *Required:* high school transcript, interview. *Notification:* continuous (freshmen), continuous (out-of-state freshmen), continuous (transfers).

Freshman Application Contact Mrs. Susan Boudreaux, Admissions Office, Career Technical College, 2319 Louisville Avenue, Monroe, LA 71201. *Phone:* 318-323-2889. *Toll-free phone:* 800-923-1947. *Fax:* 318-324-9883. *E-mail:* susan.boudreaux@careertc.edu. *Web site:* http://www.careertc.edu/.

Delgado Community College

New Orleans, Louisiana

Freshman Application Contact Ms. Gwen Boute, Director of Admissions, Delgado Community College, 501 City Park Avenue, New Orleans, LA 70119-4399. *Phone:* 504-671-5010. *Fax:* 504-483-1895. *E-mail:* enroll@dcc.edu. *Web site:* http://www.dcc.edu/.

Delta College of Arts and Technology

Baton Rouge, Louisiana

Freshman Application Contact Ms. Beulah Laverghe-Brown, Admissions Director, Delta College of Arts and Technology, 7380 Exchange Place, Baton Rouge, LA 70806-3851. *Phone:* 225-928-7770. *Fax:* 225-927-9096. *E-mail:* bbrown@deltacollege.com. *Web site:* http://www.deltacollege.com/.

Delta School of Business & Technology
Lake Charles, Louisiana

Freshman Application Contact Jeffery Tibodeaux, Director of Admissions, Delta School of Business & Technology, 517 Broad Street, Lake Charles, LA 70601. *Phone:* 337-439-5765. *Web site:* http://www.deltatech.edu/.

Elaine P. Nunez Community College
Chalmette, Louisiana

- **State-supported** 2-year, founded 1992, part of Louisiana Community and Technical College System
- **Suburban** 20-acre campus with easy access to New Orleans
- **Endowment** $1.2 million
- **Coed,** 2,413 undergraduate students, 36% full-time, 67% women, 33% men

Undergraduates 879 full-time, 1,534 part-time. 14% transferred in. *Retention:* 59% of full-time freshmen returned.
Freshmen *Admission:* 253 enrolled. *Average high school GPA:* 2.47.
Faculty *Total:* 83, 49% full-time. *Student/faculty ratio:* 25:1.
Majors Administrative assistant and secretarial science; business/commerce; carpentry; child-care provision; culinary arts; education; emergency medical technology (EMT paramedic); general studies; health information/medical records administration; heating, air conditioning, ventilation and refrigeration maintenance technology; industrial technology; information science/studies; kindergarten/preschool education; legal assistant/paralegal; liberal arts and sciences and humanities related; liberal arts and sciences/liberal studies; medical office management; nursing assistant/aide and patient care assistant/aide; welding technology.
Academics *Calendar:* semesters. *Degree:* certificates, diplomas, and associate. *Special study options:* academic remediation for entering students, adult/continuing education programs, advanced placement credit, cooperative education, distance learning, double majors, independent study, internships, off-campus study, part-time degree program, services for LD students, student-designed majors, summer session for credit.
Library Nunez Community College Library with 72,500 titles, 2,500 serial subscriptions, 3,128 audiovisual materials, an OPAC, a Web page.
Student Life *Housing:* college housing not available. *Activities and Organizations:* drama/theater group, student-run newspaper, Nunez Environmental Team, national fraternities. *Campus security:* 24-hour emergency response devices, late-night transport/escort service, security cameras. *Student services:* personal/psychological counseling.
Athletics *Intramural sports:* basketball M, football M/W.
Standardized Tests *Recommended:* ACT (for admission).
Costs (2010–11) *Tuition:* state resident $2078 full-time; nonresident $4598 full-time. Part-time tuition and fees vary according to course load. *Required fees:* $400 full-time. *Payment plan:* installment. *Waivers:* senior citizens and employees or children of employees.
Financial Aid Of all full-time matriculated undergraduates who enrolled in 2009, 70 Federal Work-Study jobs (averaging $1452).
Applying *Options:* early admission, deferred entrance. *Application fee:* $10. *Required for some:* high school transcript. *Application deadlines:* rolling (freshmen), rolling (transfers).
Freshman Application Contact Mrs. Becky Maillet, Elaine P. Nunez Community College, 3710 Paris Road, Chalmette, LA 70043. *Phone:* 504-278-6477. *E-mail:* bmaillet@nunez.edu. *Web site:* http://www.nunez.edu/.

Gretna Career College
Gretna, Louisiana

Freshman Application Contact Admissions Office, Gretna Career College, 1415 Whitney Avenue, Gretna, LA 70053-5835. *Phone:* 504-366-5409. *Fax:* 504-365-1004. *Web site:* http://www.gretnacareercollege.com/.

ITI Technical College
Baton Rouge, Louisiana

- **Proprietary** 2-year, founded 1973
- **Suburban** 10-acre campus
- **Coed, primarily men,** 393 undergraduate students, 100% full-time, 18% women, 82% men

Undergraduates 393 full-time. Students come from 3 states and territories; 1% are from out of state. *Retention:* 72% of full-time freshmen returned.
Freshmen *Admission:* 435 applied, 371 admitted, 75 enrolled.
Faculty *Total:* 51, 47% full-time, 49% with terminal degrees. *Student/faculty ratio:* 15:1.

Majors Chemical technology; computer technology/computer systems technology; drafting and design technology; electrical, electronic and communications engineering technology; information technology; instrumentation technology; office occupations and clerical services.
Academics *Calendar:* continuous. *Degree:* certificates and associate. *Special study options:* internships.
Library ITI Technical College Library with 1,260 titles.
Student Life *Campus security:* Electronic alarm devices are activated during non-business hours and security cameras monitor campus 24 hours.
Costs (2010–11) *Tuition:* Full-time tuition and fees vary according to program. No tuition increase for student's term of enrollment. Tuition and fees vary depending upon program; please contact school directly for costs. *Payment plan:* installment.
Applying *Required:* high school transcript, interview.
Freshman Application Contact Mrs. Marcia Stevens, Admissions Director, ITI Technical College, 13944 Airline Highway, Baton Rouge, LA 70817. *Phone:* 225-752-4230 Ext. 261. *Toll-free phone:* 800-467-4484. *Fax:* 225-756-0903. *E-mail:* mstevens@iticollege.edu. *Web site:* http://www.iticollege.edu/.

ITT Technical Institute
Baton Rouge, Louisiana

- **Proprietary** primarily 2-year
- **Coed**

Majors CAD/CADD drafting/design technology; communications technology; computer and information systems security; computer engineering technology; computer software and media applications related; construction management; criminal justice/law enforcement administration; design and visual communications; electrical, electronic and communications engineering technology; legal assistant/paralegal; project management; system, networking, and LAN/WAN management; web/multimedia management and webmaster.
Academics *Degrees:* associate and bachelor's.
Student Life *Housing:* college housing not available.
Freshman Application Contact Director of Recruitment, ITT Technical Institute, 14111 Airline Highway, Suite 101, Baton Rouge, LA 70817. *Phone:* 225-754-5800. *Toll-free phone:* 800-295-8485. *Web site:* http://www.itt-tech.edu/.

ITT Technical Institute
St. Rose, Louisiana

- **Proprietary** primarily 2-year, founded 1998, part of ITT Educational Services, Inc.
- **Coed**

Majors CAD/CADD drafting/design technology; communications technology; computer and information systems security; computer engineering technology; computer software and media applications related; computer software engineering; computer software technology; construction management; criminal justice/law enforcement administration; design and visual communications; electrical, electronic and communications engineering technology; game and interactive media design; legal assistant/paralegal; project management; system, networking, and LAN/WAN management; web/multimedia management and webmaster; web page, digital/multimedia and information resources design.
Academics *Calendar:* quarters. *Degrees:* associate and bachelor's.
Student Life *Housing:* college housing not available.
Freshman Application Contact Director of Recruitment, ITT Technical Institute, 140 James Drive East, St. Rose, LA 70087. *Phone:* 504-463-0338. *Toll-free phone:* 866-463-0338. *Web site:* http://www.itt-tech.edu/.

Louisiana State University at Alexandria
Alexandria, Louisiana

Freshman Application Contact Ms. Shelly Kieffer, Director of Admissions and Recruiting, Louisiana State University at Alexandria, 8100 Highway 71 South, Alexandria, LA 71302-9121. *Phone:* 318-473-6424. *Toll-free phone:* 888-473-6417. *Fax:* 318-473-6418. *E-mail:* admissions@lsua.edu. *Web site:* http://www.lsua.edu/.

Louisiana State University at Eunice
Eunice, Louisiana

Freshman Application Contact Ms. Gracie Guillory, Director of Financial Aid, Louisiana State University at Eunice, PO Box 1129, Eunice, LA 70535-

1129. *Phone:* 337-550-1282. *Toll-free phone:* 888-367-5783. *Web site:* http://www.lsue.edu/.

Louisiana Technical College

Baton Rouge, Louisiana

- **State-supported** 2-year, founded 1930, part of Louisiana Community and Technical College System
- **Urban** campus
- **Endowment** $286,936
- **Coed**

Undergraduates 7,264 full-time, 6,150 part-time. 1% are from out of state.
Faculty *Student/faculty ratio:* 10:1.
Academics *Degree:* certificates, diplomas, and associate.
Standardized Tests *Required:* COMPASS (for admission).
Costs (2010–11) *Tuition:* state resident $908 full-time, $30 per credit part-time; nonresident $1860 full-time, $62 per credit part-time. *Required fees:* $420 full-time, $14 per credit part-time.
Applying *Application fee:* $5. *Required:* high school transcript.
Freshman Application Contact Ms. Amber Aguillard, Admissions Officer, Louisiana Technical College, 3250 North Acadian Thruway, East, Baton Rouge, LA 70805. *Phone:* 225-359-9263. *Toll-free phone:* 800-351-7611. *Fax:* 225-359-9354. *E-mail:* aaguillard@ltc.edu. *Web site:* http://region2.ltc.edu/.

Louisiana Technical College–Florida Parishes Campus

Greensburg, Louisiana

Director of Admissions Mrs. Sharon G. Hornsby, Campus Dean, Louisiana Technical College–Florida Parishes Campus, PO Box 1300, Greensburg, LA 70441. *Phone:* 225-222-4251. *Toll-free phone:* 800-827-9750. *Web site:* http://www.ltc.edu/.

Louisiana Technical College–Northeast Louisiana Campus

Winnsboro, Louisiana

Director of Admissions Admissions Office, Louisiana Technical College–Northeast Louisiana Campus, 1710 Warren Street, Winnsboro, LA 71295. *Phone:* 318-435-2163. *Toll-free phone:* 800-320-6133. *Web site:* http://www.ltc.edu/.

Louisiana Technical College–Young Memorial Campus

Morgan City, Louisiana

Director of Admissions Ms. Melanie Henry, Admissions Office, Louisiana Technical College–Young Memorial Campus, 900 Youngs Road, Morgan City, LA 70381. *Phone:* 504-380-2436. *Fax:* 504-380-2440. *Web site:* http://www.ltc.edu/.

MedVance Institute

Baton Rouge, Louisiana

Director of Admissions Ms. Sheri Kirley, Associate Director of Admissions, MedVance Institute, 9255 Interline Avenue, Baton Rouge, LA 70809. *Phone:* 225-248-1015. *Web site:* http://www.medvance.org/.

Remington College–Baton Rouge Campus

Baton Rouge, Louisiana

Director of Admissions Monica Butler-Johnson, Director of Recruitment, Remington College–Baton Rouge Campus, 10551 Coursey Boulevard, Baton Rouge, LA 70816. *Phone:* 225-236-3200. *Fax:* 225-922-3250. *E-mail:* monica.johnson@remingtoncollege.edu. *Web site:* http://www.remingtoncollege.edu/.

Remington College–Lafayette Campus

Lafayette, Louisiana

Freshman Application Contact Remington College–Lafayette Campus, 303 Rue Louis XIV, Lafayette, LA 70508. *Phone:* 337-981-4010. *Toll-free phone:* 800-736-2687. *Web site:* http://www.remingtoncollege.edu/.

Remington College–Shreveport

Shreveport, Louisiana

Freshman Application Contact Marc Wright, Remington College–Shreveport, 2106 Bert Kouns Industrial Loop, Shreveport, LA 71118. *Phone:* 318-671-4000. *Web site:* http://www.remingtoncollege.edu/shreveport/.

River Parishes Community College

Sorrento, Louisiana

Director of Admissions Ms. Allison Dauzat, Dean of Students and Enrollment Management, River Parishes Community College, PO Box 310, Sorrento, LA 70778. *Phone:* 225-675-8270. *Fax:* 225-675-5478. *E-mail:* adauzat@rpcc.cc.la.us. *Web site:* http://www.rpcc.edu/.

Southern University at Shreveport

Shreveport, Louisiana

Freshman Application Contact Ms. Juanita Johnson, Acting Admissions Records Technician, Southern University at Shreveport, 3050 Martin Luther King, Jr. Drive, Shreveport, LA 71107. *Phone:* 318-674-3342. *Toll-free phone:* 800-458-1472 Ext. 342. *Web site:* http://www.susla.edu/.

MAINE

Beal College

Bangor, Maine

Freshman Application Contact Admissions Assistant, Beal College, 99 Farm Road, Bangor, ME 04401. *Phone:* 207-947-4591. *Toll-free phone:* 800-660-7351. *Fax:* 207-947-0208. *E-mail:* admissions@bealcollege.edu. *Web site:* http://www.bealcollege.edu/.

Central Maine Community College

Auburn, Maine

- **State-supported** 2-year, founded 1964, part of Maine Community College System
- **Small-town** 135-acre campus
- **Endowment** $525,621
- **Coed**, 2,870 undergraduate students, 48% full-time, 52% women, 48% men

Undergraduates 1,367 full-time, 1,503 part-time. Students come from 11 states and territories; 2% are from out of state; 5% transferred in; 8% live on campus.
Freshmen *Admission:* 2,335 applied, 887 admitted, 702 enrolled. *Test scores:* SAT critical reading scores over 500: 22%; SAT math scores over 500: 22%; SAT writing scores over 500: 18%; SAT critical reading scores over 600: 3%; SAT math scores over 600: 3%; SAT writing scores over 600: 3%; SAT writing scores over 700: 1%.
Faculty *Total:* 215, 26% full-time, 1% with terminal degrees. *Student/faculty ratio:* 17:1.
Majors Accounting technology and bookkeeping; administrative assistant and secretarial science; architectural engineering technology; automobile/automotive mechanics technology; business administration and management; child development; clinical/medical laboratory technology; communications systems installation and repair technology; computer installation and repair technology; construction engineering technology; construction trades related; criminal justice/law enforcement administration; electromechanical technology; graphic and printing equipment operation/production; human services; liberal arts and sciences/liberal studies; licensed practical/vocational nurse training; machine tool technology; medical/clinical assistant; multi/interdisciplinary studies related; occupational safety and health technology; registered nursing/registered nurse; teacher assistant/aide; vehicle maintenance and repair technologies related.
Academics *Calendar:* semesters. *Degree:* certificates, diplomas, and associate. *Special study options:* academic remediation for entering students, adult/

continuing education programs, advanced placement credit, cooperative education, distance learning, double majors, English as a second language, independent study, internships, part-time degree program, services for LD students, summer session for credit.

Library Central Maine Community College Library with 15,914 titles, 200 serial subscriptions, 2 audiovisual materials, an OPAC, a Web page.

Student Life *Housing Options:* coed, men-only, women-only. Campus housing is university owned. Freshman applicants given priority for college housing. *Activities and Organizations:* drama/theater group. *Campus security:* 24-hour emergency response devices, controlled dormitory access, night patrols by police. *Student services:* health clinic, personal/psychological counseling.

Athletics Member USCAA. *Intercollegiate sports:* baseball M, basketball M/W, golf M, soccer M/W, softball W, volleyball M/W.

Standardized Tests *Recommended:* SAT (for admission).

Costs (2010–11) *One-time required fee:* $185. *Tuition:* state resident $2520 full-time, $84 per credit hour part-time; nonresident $5040 full-time, $168 per credit hour part-time. Full-time tuition and fees vary according to course load and program. Part-time tuition and fees vary according to course load and program. *Required fees:* $744 full-time, $16 per credit hour part-time. *Room and board:* $8586; room only: $4150. Room and board charges vary according to housing facility. *Payment plan:* installment. *Waivers:* employees or children of employees.

Financial Aid Of all full-time matriculated undergraduates who enrolled in 2009, 89 Federal Work-Study jobs (averaging $1200). *Financial aid deadline:* 8/1.

Applying *Options:* electronic application, deferred entrance. *Application fee:* $20. *Required:* high school transcript. *Application deadlines:* rolling (freshmen), rolling (transfers). *Notification:* continuous (freshmen), continuous (transfers).

Freshman Application Contact Ms. Joan Nichols, Admissions Assistant, Central Maine Community College, 1250 Turner Street, Auburn, ME 04210. *Phone:* 207-755-5273. *Toll-free phone:* 800-891-2002. *Fax:* 207-755-5493. *E-mail:* enroll@cmcc.edu. *Web site:* http://www.cmcc.edu/.

Central Maine Medical Center College of Nursing and Health Professions
Lewiston, Maine

- **Independent** 2-year, founded 1891
- **Urban** campus
- **Coed,** 200 undergraduate students, 7% full-time, 86% women, 15% men

Undergraduates 14 full-time, 186 part-time. Students come from 2 states and territories; 1% are from out of state; 5% live on campus.

Freshmen *Admission:* 3 enrolled. *Test scores:* SAT critical reading scores over 500: 59%; SAT math scores over 500: 67%; SAT critical reading scores over 600: 21%; SAT math scores over 600: 21%.

Faculty *Total:* 20, 80% full-time, 15% with terminal degrees. *Student/faculty ratio:* 10:1.

Majors Radiologic technology/science; registered nursing/registered nurse.

Academics *Calendar:* semesters. *Degree:* associate. *Special study options:* advanced placement credit, off-campus study, services for LD students, summer session for credit.

Library Gerrish True Health Sciences Library plus 1 other with 1,975 titles, 339 serial subscriptions, an OPAC, a Web page.

Student Life *Housing Options:* coed. Campus housing is university owned. *Activities and Organizations:* Student Communication Council, student government, Student Nurses Association. *Campus security:* 24-hour emergency response devices and patrols, late-night transport/escort service, controlled dormitory access. *Student services:* health clinic, personal/psychological counseling.

Standardized Tests *Required:* SAT or ACT (for admission), Kaplan Entrance Exam (for admission).

Costs (2011–12) *Tuition:* $7245 full-time, $210 per credit hour part-time. *Required fees:* $1630 full-time. *Room only:* $1900. Room and board charges vary according to housing facility.

Financial Aid Of all full-time matriculated undergraduates who enrolled in 2009, 5 applied for aid, 4 were judged to have need. *Average financial aid package:* $17,200. *Average need-based loan:* $4000. *Average need-based gift aid:* $7700.

Applying *Options:* electronic application. *Application fee:* $40. *Required:* essay or personal statement, high school transcript, entrance exam; SAT/ACT or 12 college credits. *Application deadline:* 2/15 (freshmen). *Notification:* 3/15 (freshmen).

Freshman Application Contact Ms. Dagmar Jenison, Assistant Registrar, Central Maine Medical Center College of Nursing and Health Professions, 70 Middle Street, Lewiston, ME 04240. *Phone:* 207-795-2843. *Fax:* 207-795-2849. *E-mail:* jenisod@cmhc.org. *Web site:* http://www.cmmcson.edu/.

Eastern Maine Community College
Bangor, Maine

Freshman Application Contact Mr. W. Gregory Swett, Director of Admissions, Eastern Maine Community College, 354 Hogan Road, Bangor, ME 04401. *Phone:* 207-974-4680. *Toll-free phone:* 800-286-9357. *Fax:* 207-974-4683. *E-mail:* admissions@emcc.edu. *Web site:* http://www.emcc.edu/.

Kaplan University
Lewiston, Maine

- **Proprietary** 2-year
- **Coed**

Academics *Degree:* certificates and associate.

Freshman Application Contact Kaplan University, 475 Lisbon Street, Lewiston, ME 04240. *Phone:* 207-333-3300. *Web site:* http://www.kaplanuniversity.edu/.

Kaplan University
South Portland, Maine

- **Proprietary** 2-year, founded 1966
- **Urban** campus
- **Coed**

Academics *Calendar:* modular. *Degree:* certificates and associate.

Financial Aid Of all full-time matriculated undergraduates who enrolled in 2009, 25 Federal Work-Study jobs (averaging $3000).

Freshman Application Contact Kaplan University, 265 Western Avenue, South Portland, ME 04106. *Phone:* 207-774-6126. *Toll-free phone:* 800-639-3110 Ext. 240 (in-state); 800-639-3110 Ext. 242 (out-of-state). *Web site:* http://www.kaplanuniversity.edu/.

Kennebec Valley Community College
Fairfield, Maine

- **State-supported** 2-year, founded 1970, part of Maine Community College System
- **Small-town** 61-acre campus
- **Endowment** $246,029
- **Coed**

Undergraduates 730 full-time, 1,568 part-time. Students come from 3 states and territories; 1% are from out of state; 9% transferred in.

Academics *Calendar:* semesters. *Degree:* certificates, diplomas, and associate. *Special study options:* academic remediation for entering students, accelerated degree program, adult/continuing education programs, advanced placement credit, distance learning, external degree program, independent study, internships, part-time degree program, services for LD students, summer session for credit.

Student Life *Campus security:* evening security patrol.

Standardized Tests *Required for some:* HESI nursing exam, HOBET for Allied Health programs, ACCUPLACER. *Recommended:* SAT or ACT (for admission).

Costs (2010–11) *One-time required fee:* $30. *Tuition:* state resident $2520 full-time, $84 per credit hour part-time; nonresident $5040 full-time, $168 per credit hour part-time. *Required fees:* $840 full-time, $3 per credit hour part-time.

Financial Aid Of all full-time matriculated undergraduates who enrolled in 2009, 34 Federal Work-Study jobs (averaging $1207).

Applying *Options:* electronic application, deferred entrance. *Application fee:* $20. *Required:* essay or personal statement, high school transcript. *Required for some:* interview.

Freshman Application Contact Mr. Jim Bourgoin, Director of Admissions, Kennebec Valley Community College, Fairfield, ME 04937-1367. *Phone:* 207-453-5035. *Toll-free phone:* 800-528-5882 Ext. 5035. *Fax:* 207-453-5011. *E-mail:* admissions@kvcc.me.edu. *Web site:* http://www.kvcc.me.edu/.

Northern Maine Community College
Presque Isle, Maine

Freshman Application Contact Ms. Nancy Gagnon, Admissions Secretary, Northern Maine Community College, 33 Edgemont Drive, Presque Isle, ME 04769-2016. *Phone:* 207-768-2785. *Toll-free phone:* 800-535-6682. *Fax:* 207-768-2848. *E-mail:* ngagnon@nmcc.edu. *Web site:* http://www.nmcc.edu/

Southern Maine Community College
South Portland, Maine

- **State-supported** 2-year, founded 1946, part of Maine Community College System
- **Small-town** 80-acre campus
- **Coed**

Undergraduates 2,993 full-time, 3,268 part-time. Students come from 28 states and territories; 58 other countries; 4% are from out of state; 10% transferred in; 5% live on campus. *Retention:* 49% of full-time freshmen returned.
Faculty *Student/faculty ratio:* 19:1.
Academics *Calendar:* semesters. *Degree:* certificates, diplomas, and associate. *Special study options:* academic remediation for entering students, advanced placement credit, distance learning, double majors, English as a second language, honors programs, internships, off-campus study, part-time degree program, services for LD students, study abroad, summer session for credit.
Student Life *Campus security:* 24-hour emergency response devices and patrols, student patrols, late-night transport/escort service, controlled dormitory access.
Standardized Tests *Recommended:* SAT or ACT (for admission), ACCUPLACER.
Costs (2010–11) *Tuition:* state resident $2520 full-time, $84 per credit hour part-time; nonresident $5040 full-time, $168 per credit hour part-time. Full-time tuition and fees vary according to course load, program, and reciprocity agreements. Part-time tuition and fees vary according to course load, program, and reciprocity agreements. *Required fees:* $875 full-time, $28 per credit hour part-time, $25 per term part-time. *Room and board:* $8226.
Financial Aid Of all full-time matriculated undergraduates who enrolled in 2009, 130 Federal Work-Study jobs (averaging $1500).
Applying *Options:* electronic application. *Application fee:* $20. *Required:* high school transcript or proof of high school graduation.
Freshman Application Contact Staci Grasky, Associate Dean for Enrollment Services, Southern Maine Community College, 2 Fort Road, South, Portland, ME 04106. *Phone:* 207-741-5515. *Toll-free phone:* 877-282-2182. *Fax:* 207-741-5760. *E-mail:* sgrasky@smccme.edu. *Web site:* http://www.smccme.edu/

Washington County Community College
Calais, Maine

Director of Admissions Mr. Kent Lyons, Admissions Counselor, Washington County Community College, One College Drive, Calais, ME 04619. *Phone:* 207-454-1000. *Toll-free phone:* 800-210-6932 Ext. 41049. *Web site:* http://www.wccc.me.edu/.

York County Community College
Wells, Maine

- **State-supported** 2-year, founded 1994, part of Maine Community College System
- **Small-town** 84-acre campus with easy access to Boston
- **Coed**

Undergraduates Students come from 3 states and territories; 3 other countries; 2% are from out of state.
Faculty *Student/faculty ratio:* 15:1.
Academics *Calendar:* semesters. *Degree:* certificates and associate. *Special study options:* academic remediation for entering students, accelerated degree program, adult/continuing education programs, advanced placement credit, cooperative education, distance learning, internships, part-time degree program, services for LD students, summer session for credit.
Student Life *Campus security:* 24-hour emergency response devices, late-night transport/escort service.
Costs (2010–11) *Tuition:* state resident $84 per credit hour part-time; nonresident $168 per credit hour part-time. Full-time tuition and fees vary according to course load and program. Part-time tuition and fees vary according to course load and program. *Required fees:* $75 per course part-time.
Financial Aid Of all full-time matriculated undergraduates who enrolled in 2009, 512 applied for aid, 441 were judged to have need, 23 had their need fully met. 26 Federal Work-Study jobs (averaging $1200). In 2009, 8. *Average percent of need met:* 52. *Average financial aid package:* $6359. *Average need-based loan:* $2926. *Average need-based gift aid:* $5131. *Average non-need-based aid:* $687.
Applying *Options:* electronic application. *Application fee:* $20. *Required:* high school transcript, interview.

Freshman Application Contact York County Community College, 112 College Drive, Wells, ME 04090. *Phone:* 207-646-9282 Ext. 311. *Toll-free phone:* 800-580-3820. *Web site:* http://www.yccc.edu/.

MARSHALL ISLANDS

College of the Marshall Islands
Majuro, Marshall Islands, Marshall Islands

Freshman Application Contact Ms. Rosita Capelle, Director of Admissions and Records, College of the Marshall Islands, PO Box 1258, Majuro MH96960. *Phone:* 692-625-6823. *Fax:* 692-625-7203. *E-mail:* cmiadmissions@cmi.edu. *Web site:* http://www.cmi.edu/.

MARYLAND

Allegany College of Maryland
Cumberland, Maryland

- **State and locally supported** 2-year, founded 1961, part of Maryland State Community Colleges System
- **Small-town** 311-acre campus
- **Coed**

Undergraduates 7% live on campus.
Faculty *Student/faculty ratio:* 16:1.
Academics *Calendar:* semesters. *Degree:* certificates and associate. *Special study options:* academic remediation for entering students, adult/continuing education programs, advanced placement credit, distance learning, double majors, English as a second language, honors programs, independent study, internships, part-time degree program, summer session for credit. *ROTC:* Army (c).
Student Life *Campus security:* 24-hour emergency response devices and patrols, late-night transport/escort service.
Athletics Member NJCAA.
Standardized Tests *Required for some:* ACT (for admission).
Costs (2010–11) *Tuition:* area resident $3060 full-time; state resident $5700 full-time; nonresident $6840 full-time. Full-time tuition and fees vary according to course load and location. Part-time tuition and fees vary according to course load and location. *Required fees:* $206 full-time. *Room and board:* Room and board charges vary according to housing facility. *Payment plans:* installment, deferred payment.
Financial Aid Of all full-time matriculated undergraduates who enrolled in 2009, 188 Federal Work-Study jobs (averaging $1360).
Applying *Options:* electronic application, early admission. *Required:* high school transcript.
Freshman Application Contact Ms. Cathy Nolan, Director of Admissions and Registration, Allegany College of Maryland, Cumberland, MD 21502. *Phone:* 301-784-5000 Ext. 5202. *Fax:* 301-784-5220. *E-mail:* cnolan@allegany.edu. *Web site:* http://www.allegany.edu/.

Anne Arundel Community College
Arnold, Maryland

- **State and locally supported** 2-year, founded 1961
- **Suburban** 230-acre campus with easy access to Baltimore and Washington, DC
- **Coed**

Undergraduates 5,957 full-time, 10,784 part-time. Students come from 19 states and territories. *Retention:* 58% of full-time freshmen returned.
Faculty *Student/faculty ratio:* 18:1.
Academics *Calendar:* semesters. *Degree:* certificates and associate. *Special study options:* academic remediation for entering students, accelerated degree program, adult/continuing education programs, advanced placement credit, cooperative education, distance learning, English as a second language, freshman honors college, honors programs, independent study, internships, part-time degree program, services for LD students, summer session for credit. *ROTC:* Army (c), Air Force (c).
Student Life *Campus security:* 24-hour emergency response devices and patrols, student patrols, late-night transport/escort service.
Athletics Member NJCAA.
Costs (2010–11) *Tuition:* area resident $3010 full-time, $88 per credit hour part-time; state resident $5440 full-time, $169 per credit hour part-time; nonresident $9340 full-time, $299 per credit hour part-time. Full-time tuition and

fees vary according to course load. Part-time tuition and fees vary according to course load. *Required fees:* $370 full-time, $11 per credit hour part-time, $20 per term part-time.

Financial Aid Of all full-time matriculated undergraduates who enrolled in 2009, 104 Federal Work-Study jobs (averaging $1900). 55 state and other part-time jobs (averaging $1740).

Applying *Options:* early admission, deferred entrance.

Freshman Application Contact Mr. Thomas McGinn, Director of Enrollment Development and Admissions, Anne Arundel Community College, 101 College Parkway, Arnold, MD 21012-1895. *Phone:* 410-777-2240. *Fax:* 410-777-2246. *E-mail:* 4info@aacc.edu. *Web site:* http://www.aacc.edu/.

Baltimore City Community College
Baltimore, Maryland

Freshman Application Contact Baltimore City Community College, 2901 Liberty Heights Avenue, Baltimore, MD 21215-7893. *Phone:* 410-462-8311. *Toll-free phone:* 888-203-1261. *Web site:* http://www.bccc.edu/.

Carroll Community College
Westminster, Maryland

- **State and locally supported** 2-year, founded 1993, part of Maryland Higher Education Commission
- **Suburban** 80-acre campus with easy access to Baltimore
- **Endowment** $3.2 million
- **Coed,** 4,108 undergraduate students, 44% full-time, 62% women, 38% men

Undergraduates 1,793 full-time, 2,315 part-time. Students come from 7 states and territories; 6 other countries; 2% are from out of state; 4% Black or African American, non-Hispanic/Latino; 2% Hispanic/Latino; 0.8% Asian, non-Hispanic/Latino; 0.1% Native Hawaiian or other Pacific Islander, non-Hispanic/Latino; 0.4% American Indian or Alaska Native, non-Hispanic/Latino; 0.4% Two or more races, non-Hispanic/Latino; 2% Race/ethnicity unknown; 0.3% international; 10% transferred in.

Freshmen *Admission:* 954 applied, 954 admitted, 954 enrolled.

Faculty *Total:* 277, 26% full-time, 3% with terminal degrees. *Student/faculty ratio:* 18:1.

Majors Accounting; administrative assistant and secretarial science; architectural drafting and CAD/CADD; art; business administration and management; child-care and support services management; computer and information sciences; computer graphics; criminal justice/police science; education (multiple levels); emergency care attendant (EMT ambulance); forensic science and technology; general studies; health information/medical records technology; health professions related; kindergarten/preschool education; kinesiology and exercise science; legal studies; liberal arts and sciences/liberal studies; management information systems; music; physical therapy technology; psychology; registered nursing/registered nurse; theater design and technology.

Academics *Calendar:* semesters plus winter session. *Degree:* certificates and associate. *Special study options:* academic remediation for entering students, advanced placement credit, distance learning, English as a second language, honors programs, independent study, internships, part-time degree program, services for LD students, summer session for credit.

Library Random House Learning Resources Center with 101,743 titles, 215 serial subscriptions, 3,814 audiovisual materials, an OPAC, a Web page.

Student Life *Housing:* college housing not available. *Activities and Organizations:* drama/theater group, choral group, Student Government Organization, Carroll Community Chorus, Campus Activities Board, Green Team, Academic Communities (Creativity, Education, Great Ideas, Health and Wellness). *Campus security:* 24-hour emergency response devices, late-night transport/escort service.

Athletics *Intramural sports:* soccer M/W.

Costs (2010–11) *Tuition:* area resident $3624 full-time, $121 per credit hour part-time; state resident $5244 full-time, $175 per credit hour part-time; non-resident $7368 full-time, $246 per credit hour part-time. *Payment plan:* deferred payment. *Waivers:* senior citizens and employees or children of employees.

Applying *Required:* high school transcript. *Application deadlines:* rolling (freshmen), rolling (out-of-state freshmen), rolling (transfers). *Notification:* continuous (freshmen), continuous (out-of-state freshmen), continuous (transfers).

Freshman Application Contact Ms. Candace Edwards, Director of Admissions, Carroll Community College, 1601 Washington Road, Westminster, MD 21157. *Phone:* 410-386-8405. *Toll-free phone:* 888-221-9748. *Fax:* 410-386-8446. *E-mail:* cedwards@carrollcc.edu. *Web site:* http://www.carrollcc.edu/.

Cecil College
North East, Maryland

- **County-supported** 2-year, founded 1968
- **Small-town** 105-acre campus with easy access to Baltimore
- **Endowment** $3.3 million
- **Coed,** 2,453 undergraduate students, 45% full-time, 62% women, 38% men

Undergraduates 1,104 full-time, 1,349 part-time. Students come from 6 states and territories; 12 other countries; 7% are from out of state; 8% Black or African American, non-Hispanic/Latino; 3% Hispanic/Latino; 0.8% Asian, non-Hispanic/Latino; 0.4% American Indian or Alaska Native, non-Hispanic/Latino; 2% Two or more races, non-Hispanic/Latino; 1% Race/ethnicity unknown; 0.4% international; 0.1% transferred in.

Freshmen *Admission:* 697 applied, 697 admitted, 697 enrolled.

Faculty *Total:* 251, 18% full-time, 5% with terminal degrees. *Student/faculty ratio:* 13:1.

Majors Accounting technology and bookkeeping; biology/biological sciences; business administration and management; business administration, management and operations related; business/commerce; business/corporate communications; child-care and support services management; commercial photography; computer and information sciences; computer programming; computer programming (specific applications); criminal justice/police science; data processing and data processing technology; education; elementary education; emergency medical technology (EMT paramedic); fire science/firefighting; general studies; graphic design; health services/allied health/health sciences; horse husbandry/equine science and management; information science/studies; information technology; kindergarten/preschool education; liberal arts and sciences/liberal studies; logistics, materials, and supply chain management; management information systems; marketing/marketing management; mathematics; photography; physical sciences; physics; public relations/image management; registered nursing/registered nurse; transportation and materials moving related; transportation/mobility management; web page, digital/multimedia and information resources design.

Academics *Calendar:* semesters. *Degree:* certificates and associate. *Special study options:* academic remediation for entering students, accelerated degree program, adult/continuing education programs, advanced placement credit, cooperative education, distance learning, double majors, English as a second language, independent study, internships, off-campus study, part-time degree program, services for LD students, summer session for credit.

Library Cecil County Veterans Memorial Library with 38,140 titles, 225 serial subscriptions, 1,220 audiovisual materials, an OPAC, a Web page.

Student Life *Housing:* college housing not available. *Activities and Organizations:* drama/theater group, Student Government, Non-traditional Student Organization, Student Nurses Association, national fraternities. *Campus security:* 24-hour emergency response devices, late-night transport/escort service. *Student services:* personal/psychological counseling, women's center.

Athletics Member NJCAA. *Intercollegiate sports:* baseball M(s), basketball M(s)/W(s), cheerleading W, soccer W(s), softball W(s), tennis W(s), volleyball W(s).

Costs (2010–11) *Tuition:* area resident $2700 full-time, $90 per credit hour part-time; state resident $5400 full-time, $180 per credit hour part-time; non-resident $6750 full-time, $225 per credit hour part-time. *Required fees:* $362 full-time. *Payment plan:* deferred payment. *Waivers:* senior citizens and employees or children of employees.

Applying *Options:* electronic application, early admission, deferred entrance. *Required:* high school transcript. *Application deadlines:* rolling (freshmen), rolling (out-of-state freshmen), rolling (transfers). *Notification:* continuous (freshmen), continuous (out-of-state freshmen), continuous (transfers).

Freshman Application Contact Dr. Diane Lane, Cecil College, One Seahawk Drive, North East, MD 21901-1999. *Phone:* 410-287-1002. *Fax:* 410-287-1001. *E-mail:* dlane@cecil.edu. *Web site:* http://www.cecil.edu/.

Chesapeake College
Wye Mills, Maryland

Freshman Application Contact Randy Holliday, Director of Student Recruitment and Outreach, Chesapeake College, PO Box 8, Wye Mills, MD 21679-0008. *Phone:* 410-822-5400. *Fax:* 410-827-5875. *E-mail:* rholliday@chesapeake.edu. *Web site:* http://www.chesapeake.edu/.

College of Southern Maryland
La Plata, Maryland

- **State and locally supported** 2-year, founded 1958
- **Rural** 175-acre campus with easy access to Washington, DC
- **Coed**

Undergraduates 3,595 full-time, 5,215 part-time. 4% transferred in.

Academics *Calendar:* semesters. *Degree:* certificates and associate. *Special study options:* academic remediation for entering students, accelerated degree program, adult/continuing education programs, advanced placement credit, cooperative education, distance learning, honors programs, internships, part-time degree program, services for LD students, study abroad, summer session for credit.

Student Life *Campus security:* 24-hour emergency response devices and patrols.

Athletics Member NJCAA.

Costs (2010–11) *Tuition:* area resident $3874 full-time, $105 per credit hour part-time; state resident $6753 full-time, $183 per credit hour part-time; non-resident $8745 full-time, $237 per credit hour part-time. Full-time tuition and fees vary according to course load. Part-time tuition and fees vary according to course load.

Financial Aid Of all full-time matriculated undergraduates who enrolled in 2009, 25 Federal Work-Study jobs (averaging $1200).

Applying *Options:* electronic application, early admission, deferred entrance. *Recommended:* high school transcript.

Freshman Application Contact Information Center Coordinator, College of Southern Maryland, PO Box 910, La Plata, MD 20646-0910. *Phone:* 301-934-7520 Ext. 7765. *Toll-free phone:* 800-933-9177. *Fax:* 301-934-7698. *E-mail:* info@csmd.edu. *Web site:* http://www.csmd.edu/.

The Community College of Baltimore County

Baltimore, Maryland

- **County-supported** 2-year, founded 1957
- **Suburban** 350-acre campus
- **Coed,** 26,425 undergraduate students, 34% full-time, 62% women, 38% men

Undergraduates 9,038 full-time, 17,387 part-time. 37% Black or African American, non-Hispanic/Latino; 3% Hispanic/Latino; 5% Asian, non-Hispanic/Latino; 0.2% Native Hawaiian or other Pacific Islander, non-Hispanic/Latino; 0.5% American Indian or Alaska Native, non-Hispanic/Latino; 2% Two or more races, non-Hispanic/Latino; 3% Race/ethnicity unknown.

Freshmen *Admission:* 5,030 enrolled.

Faculty *Total:* 1,320, 31% full-time, 8% with terminal degrees.

Majors Accounting technology and bookkeeping; administrative assistant and secretarial science; aeronautics/aviation/aerospace science and technology; architectural drafting and CAD/CADD; autobody/collision and repair technology; automobile/automotive mechanics technology; building/construction finishing, management, and inspection related; building/construction site management; business administration and management; business administration, management and operations related; business/commerce; chemistry teacher education; child-care and support services management; child-care provision; commercial and advertising art; computer and information sciences; computer systems networking and telecommunications; criminal justice/police science; dental hygiene; diesel mechanics technology; early childhood education; education; electrical, electronic and communications engineering technology; elementary education; emergency medical technology (EMT paramedic); engineering; engineering technologies and engineering related; funeral service and mortuary science; geography; hotel/motel administration; hydraulics and fluid power technology; labor and industrial relations; legal assistant/paralegal; liberal arts and sciences and humanities related; liberal arts and sciences/liberal studies; management information systems; mathematics teacher education; medical administrative assistant and medical secretary; medical informatics; medical radiologic technology; multi/interdisciplinary studies related; occupational safety and health technology; occupational therapy; parks, recreation and leisure; physician assistant; physics teacher education; psychiatric/mental health services technology; respiratory care therapy; science technologies related; sign language interpretation and translation; Spanish language teacher education; substance abuse/addiction counseling; veterinary/animal health technology; visual and performing arts.

Academics *Calendar:* semesters. *Degree:* certificates and associate. *Special study options:* academic remediation for entering students, advanced placement credit, cooperative education, distance learning, English as a second language, honors programs, independent study, internships, off-campus study, services for LD students, study abroad, summer session for credit.

Student Life *Housing:* college housing not available. *Campus security:* 24-hour emergency response devices and patrols, late-night transport/escort service.

Athletics Member NJCAA. *Intercollegiate sports:* baseball M(s), basketball M(s)/W(s), lacrosse M(s)/W(s), soccer M(s)/W(s), softball W(s), volleyball W(s).

Standardized Tests *Recommended:* SAT or ACT (for admission).

Costs (2010–11) *Tuition:* area resident $3000 full-time; state resident $5730 full-time; nonresident $8580 full-time. *Required fees:* $402 full-time. *Payment plan:* installment. *Waivers:* employees or children of employees.

Applying *Required:* high school transcript. *Application deadlines:* rolling (freshmen), rolling (out-of-state freshmen), rolling (transfers).

Freshman Application Contact Ms. Diane Drake, Director of Admissions, The Community College of Baltimore County, 7201 Rossville Boulevard, Baltimore, MD 21228. *Phone:* 443-840-4392. *E-mail:* ddrake@ccbcmd.edu. *Web site:* http://www.ccbcmd.edu/.

Frederick Community College

Frederick, Maryland

- **State and locally supported** 2-year, founded 1957
- **Small-town** 100-acre campus with easy access to Baltimore and Washington, DC
- **Endowment** $4.0 million
- **Coed,** 6,233 undergraduate students, 38% full-time, 59% women, 41% men

Undergraduates 2,359 full-time, 3,874 part-time. 1% are from out of state. *Retention:* 45% of full-time freshmen returned.

Freshmen *Admission:* 1,573 enrolled.

Faculty *Total:* 522, 19% full-time. *Student/faculty ratio:* 12:1.

Majors Accounting; art; biology/biological sciences; building/construction finishing, management, and inspection related; business administration and management; chemistry; child development; computer engineering technology; computer science; criminal justice/law enforcement administration; data processing and data processing technology; drafting and design technology; education; electrical, electronic and communications engineering technology; elementary education; emergency medical technology (EMT paramedic); engineering; English; finance; fire science/firefighting; general studies; human services; information technology; international business/trade/commerce; kindergarten/preschool education; legal administrative assistant/secretary; legal assistant/paralegal; liberal arts and sciences/liberal studies; marketing/marketing management; mass communication/media; mathematics; mathematics teacher education; medical administrative assistant and medical secretary; music teacher education; nuclear medical technology; physical education teaching and coaching; physical sciences; political science and government; psychology; registered nursing/registered nurse; respiratory care therapy; Spanish language teacher education; surgical technology.

Academics *Calendar:* semesters. *Degree:* certificates and associate. *Special study options:* academic remediation for entering students, adult/continuing education programs, advanced placement credit, cooperative education, distance learning, English as a second language, freshman honors college, honors programs, independent study, internships, off-campus study, part-time degree program, services for LD students, study abroad, summer session for credit. *ROTC:* Army (c).

Library FCC Library with 40,000 titles, 5,150 serial subscriptions, an OPAC, a Web page.

Student Life *Housing:* college housing not available. *Activities and Organizations:* drama/theater group, student-run newspaper. *Campus security:* 24-hour emergency response devices and patrols, late-night transport/escort service. *Student services:* personal/psychological counseling, women's center.

Athletics Member NJCAA. *Intercollegiate sports:* baseball M, basketball M/W, golf M/W, soccer M/W, softball W, volleyball W.

Costs (2010–11) *Tuition:* area resident $3090 full-time, $103 per credit hour part-time; state resident $6690 full-time, $223 per credit hour part-time; nonresident $9090 full-time, $303 per credit hour part-time. *Required fees:* $750 full-time, $17 per credit hour part-time, $50 per term part-time. *Payment plan:* deferred payment. *Waivers:* senior citizens and employees or children of employees.

Financial Aid Of all full-time matriculated undergraduates who enrolled in 2009, 25 Federal Work-Study jobs (averaging $1368). 14 state and other part-time jobs (averaging $2715).

Applying *Options:* electronic application. *Recommended:* high school transcript. *Application deadlines:* rolling (freshmen), rolling (transfers). *Notification:* continuous (freshmen), continuous (transfers).

Freshman Application Contact Ms. Lisa A. Freel, Director of Admissions, Frederick Community College, 7932 Opossumtown Pike, Frederick, MD 21702. *Phone:* 301-846-2468. *Fax:* 301-624-2799. *E-mail:* admissions@frederick.edu. *Web site:* http://www.frederick.edu/.

Hagerstown Community College

Hagerstown, Maryland

- **State and locally supported** 2-year, founded 1946
- **Suburban** 319-acre campus with easy access to Baltimore and Washington, DC
- **Coed,** 4,715 undergraduate students, 33% full-time, 62% women, 38% men

Undergraduates 1,544 full-time, 3,171 part-time. Students come from 8 states and territories; 21% are from out of state; 9% transferred in. *Retention:* 63% of full-time freshmen returned.

Freshmen *Admission:* 1,045 enrolled.

Faculty *Total:* 273, 28% full-time, 5% with terminal degrees. *Student/faculty ratio:* 18:1.

Majors Accounting technology and bookkeeping; animation, interactive technology, video graphics and special effects; biology/biotechnology laboratory technician; business administration and management; business/commerce; child-care and support services management; commercial and advertising art; computer and information sciences; criminal justice/police science; early childhood education; education; electromechanical technology; elementary education; emergency medical technology (EMT paramedic); engineering; health information/medical records administration; industrial technology; liberal arts and sciences and humanities related; liberal arts and sciences/liberal studies; management information systems; mechanical engineering/mechanical technology; medical radiologic technology; psychiatric/mental health services technology; registered nursing/registered nurse; transportation/mobility management; web page, digital/multimedia and information resources design.

Academics *Calendar:* semesters. *Degree:* certificates and associate. *Special study options:* academic remediation for entering students, accelerated degree program, adult/continuing education programs, advanced placement credit, cooperative education, distance learning, English as a second language, honors programs, independent study, internships, off-campus study, part-time degree program, services for LD students, student-designed majors, summer session for credit.

Library William Brish Library with 45,705 titles, 228 serial subscriptions, an OPAC, a Web page.

Student Life *Housing:* college housing not available. *Activities and Organizations:* drama/theater group, student-run newspaper, choral group, Phi Theta Kappa, Robinwood Players Theater Club, Association of Nursing Students, Radiography Club, Art and Design Club. *Campus security:* 24-hour patrols, student patrols. *Student services:* health clinic, personal/psychological counseling.

Athletics Member NJCAA. *Intercollegiate sports:* baseball M(s), basketball M(s)/W(s), cross-country running M(s)/W(s), golf M/W, soccer M(s)/W, softball W(s), track and field M(s)/W(s), volleyball W(s). *Intramural sports:* cheerleading M/W, golf M/W, lacrosse M/W, table tennis M/W, tennis M/W.

Costs (2010–11) *Tuition:* area resident $3000 full-time, $100 per credit hour part-time; state resident $4680 full-time, $156 per credit hour part-time; non-resident $6180 full-time, $206 per credit hour part-time. *Required fees:* $320 full-time, $9 per credit hour part-time, $25 per term part-time. *Payment plan:* installment. *Waivers:* senior citizens and employees or children of employees.

Financial Aid Of all full-time matriculated undergraduates who enrolled in 2009, 27 Federal Work-Study jobs (averaging $2955).

Applying *Options:* electronic application. *Required for some:* high school transcript, selective admissions for RN, LPN, EMT, and radiography programs. *Application deadlines:* rolling (freshmen), rolling (transfers). *Notification:* continuous (freshmen), continuous (out-of-state freshmen), continuous (transfers).

Freshman Application Contact Dr. Daniel Bock, Assistant Director, Admissions, Records and Registration, Hagerstown Community College, 11400 Robinwood Drive, Hagerstown, MD 21742-6514. *Phone:* 301-790-2800 Ext. 335. *Fax:* 301-791-9165. *E-mail:* debock@hagerstowncc.edu. *Web site:* http://www.hagerstowncc.edu/.

Harford Community College

Bel Air, Maryland

- **State and locally supported** 2-year, founded 1957
- **Small-town** 331-acre campus with easy access to Baltimore
- **Coed,** 7,135 undergraduate students, 44% full-time, 60% women, 40% men

Undergraduates 3,122 full-time, 4,013 part-time.

Freshmen *Admission:* 1,361 enrolled.

Faculty *Total:* 396, 24% full-time, 5% with terminal degrees. *Student/faculty ratio:* 23:1.

Majors Accounting; accounting technology and bookkeeping; applied horticulture/horticulture operations; business administration and management; business/commerce; CAD/CADD drafting/design technology; chemistry teacher education; commercial photography; communications technologies and support services related; computer and information sciences; computer and information systems security; criminal justice/police science; design and visual communications; early childhood education; education; electroneurodiagnostic/electroencephalographic technology; elementary education; engineering; engineering technologies and engineering related; environmental studies; industrial production technologies related; interior design; legal assistant/paralegal; legal studies; liberal arts and sciences and humanities related; liberal arts and sciences/liberal studies; management information systems; massage therapy; mathematics teacher education; medical/clinical assistant; multi/interdisciplinary studies related; physics teacher education; psychiatric/mental health services technology; registered nursing/registered nurse; science technologies related; substance abuse/addiction counseling; theater design and technology; visual and performing arts.

Academics *Calendar:* semesters. *Degree:* certificates, diplomas, and associate. *Special study options:* academic remediation for entering students, adult/continuing education programs, advanced placement credit, cooperative education, distance learning, double majors, English as a second language, honors programs, independent study, internships, part-time degree program, services for LD students, student-designed majors, study abroad, summer session for credit.

Library Harford Community College Library with 58,454 titles, 128 serial subscriptions, 3,617 audiovisual materials, an OPAC, a Web page.

Student Life *Activities and Organizations:* drama/theater group, student-run newspaper, radio station, choral group, Student Association, Paralegal Club, Multi-National Students Association, Student Nurses Association, Gamers Guild. *Campus security:* 24-hour patrols, late-night transport/escort service. *Student services:* personal/psychological counseling.

Athletics Member NJCAA. *Intercollegiate sports:* baseball M(s), basketball M(s)/W(s), cheerleading M(c)/W(c), cross-country running M(c)/W(c), golf M(s), lacrosse M(s)/W(s), soccer M(s)/W(s), softball W(s), tennis M/W, volleyball W(s). *Intramural sports:* badminton M/W, basketball M/W, football M/W, soccer M/W, softball M/W, tennis M/W, volleyball M/W.

Costs (2011–12) *Tuition:* area resident $2755 full-time, $82 per credit hour part-time; state resident $5215 full-time, $164 per credit hour part-time; non-resident $7675 full-time, $246 per credit hour part-time. *Required fees:* $300 full-time. *Waivers:* senior citizens and employees or children of employees.

Financial Aid Of all full-time matriculated undergraduates who enrolled in 2009, 55 Federal Work-Study jobs (averaging $1800).

Applying *Options:* electronic application. *Application deadlines:* rolling (freshmen), rolling (transfers). *Notification:* continuous (transfers).

Freshman Application Contact Ms. Donna Strasavich, Enrollment Specialist, Harford Community College, 401 Thomas Run Road, Bel Air, MD 21015-1698. *Phone:* 443-412-2311. *Fax:* 443-412-2169. *E-mail:* sendinfo@harford.edu. *Web site:* http://www.harford.edu/.

Howard Community College

Columbia, Maryland

- **State and locally supported** 2-year, founded 1966
- **Suburban** 122-acre campus with easy access to Baltimore and Washington, DC
- **Coed,** 9,568 undergraduate students

Undergraduates 13% Black or African American, non-Hispanic/Latino; 7% Hispanic/Latino; 13% Asian, non-Hispanic/Latino; 0.2% Native Hawaiian or other Pacific Islander, non-Hispanic/Latino; 0.4% American Indian or Alaska Native, non-Hispanic/Latino; 2% Two or more races, non-Hispanic/Latino; 3% Race/ethnicity unknown. *Retention:* 64% of full-time freshmen returned.

Faculty *Total:* 673, 23% full-time. *Student/faculty ratio:* 19:1.

Majors Accounting; administrative assistant and secretarial science; architecture; art; biological and physical sciences; biomedical technology; biotechnology; business administration and management; cardiovascular technology; child development; clinical laboratory science/medical technology; computer and information sciences related; computer graphics; computer/information technology services administration related; computer science; computer systems networking and telecommunications; consumer merchandising/retailing management; criminal justice/law enforcement administration; data entry/microcomputer applications; design and applied arts related; dramatic/theater arts; electrical, electronic and communications engineering technology; elementary education; emergency medical technology (EMT paramedic); engineering; environmental studies; fashion merchandising; financial planning and services; general studies; health teacher education; information science/studies; information technology; kindergarten/preschool education; legal administrative assistant/secretary; liberal arts and sciences/liberal studies; licensed practical/vocational nurse training; medical administrative assistant and medical secretary; music; nuclear medical technology; office management; photography; physical sciences; pre-dentistry studies; premedical studies; pre-pharmacy studies; pre-veterinary studies; psychology; registered nursing/registered nurse; secondary education; social sciences; sport and fitness administration/management; substance abuse/addiction counseling; telecommunications technology; theater design and technology.

Academics *Calendar:* semesters. *Degree:* certificates and associate. *Special study options:* academic remediation for entering students, adult/continuing education programs, advanced placement credit, cooperative education, distance learning, double majors, English as a second language, external degree program, freshman honors college, honors programs, off-campus study, part-time degree program, services for LD students, study abroad, summer session for credit.

Library Howard Community College Library with 45,707 titles, 39,910 serial subscriptions, 2,636 audiovisual materials, an OPAC, a Web page.

Student Life *Housing:* college housing not available. *Activities and Organizations:* drama/theater group, student-run newspaper, choral group, Phi Theta Kappa, Nursing Club, Black Leadership Organization, student newspaper, Student Government Association. *Campus security:* 24-hour emergency response devices and patrols, late-night transport/escort service. *Student services:* personal/psychological counseling.

Athletics Member NJCAA. *Intercollegiate sports:* basketball M/W, cross-country running M/W, lacrosse M/W, soccer M/W, track and field M/W, volleyball W. *Intramural sports:* basketball M/W, lacrosse M, softball W.

Standardized Tests *Required for some:* SAT or ACT (for admission).

Costs (2010–11) *Tuition:* area resident $3480 full-time, $116 per credit hour part-time; state resident $5970 full-time, $199 per credit hour part-time; non-resident $7320 full-time, $244 per credit hour part-time. *Required fees:* $648 full-time, $19 per credit hour part-time. *Payment plan:* installment. *Waivers:* senior citizens and employees or children of employees.

Applying *Options:* electronic application, early admission, deferred entrance. *Application fee:* $25. *Required for some:* essay or personal statement, high school transcript, 2 letters of recommendation. *Application deadlines:* rolling (freshmen), rolling (out-of-state freshmen), rolling (transfers). *Notification:* continuous (freshmen), continuous (out-of-state freshmen), continuous (transfers).

Freshman Application Contact Ms. Christy Thomson, Assistant Director of Admissions, Howard Community College, Columbia, MD 21044-3197. *Phone:* 443-518-4599. *Fax:* 443-518-4589. *E-mail:* hsinfo@howardcc.edu. *Web site:* http://www.howardcc.edu/.

ITT Technical Institute

Owings Mills, Maryland

- **Proprietary** primarily 2-year, founded 2005
- **Coed**

Majors CAD/CADD drafting/design technology; computer and information systems security; computer engineering technology; computer software and media applications related; computer systems networking and telecommunications; construction management; design and visual communications; electrical, electronic and communications engineering technology; game and interactive media design; information technology project management; system, networking, and LAN/WAN management; web page, digital/multimedia and information resources design.

Academics *Calendar:* quarters. *Degrees:* associate and bachelor's.

Student Life *Housing:* college housing not available.

Freshman Application Contact Director of Recruitment, ITT Technical Institute, 11301 Red Run Boulevard, Owings Mills, MD 21117. *Phone:* 443-394-7115. *Toll-free phone:* 877-411-6782. *Web site:* http://www.itt-tech.edu/.

Kaplan University, Hagerstown Campus

Hagerstown, Maryland

- **Proprietary** primarily 2-year, founded 1938, administratively affiliated with Kaplan Higher Education
- **Small-town** 8-acre campus
- **Coed**

Undergraduates 3% live on campus.

Academics *Calendar:* quarters. *Degrees:* certificates, diplomas, associate, and bachelor's.

Financial Aid Of all full-time matriculated undergraduates who enrolled in 2009, 21 Federal Work-Study jobs (averaging $1343).

Freshman Application Contact Kaplan University, Hagerstown Campus, 18618 Crestwood Drive, Hagerstown, MD 21742-2797. *Phone:* 301-739-2680 Ext. 217. *Toll-free phone:* 800-422-2670. *Web site:* http://www.ku-hagerstown.com/.

Montgomery College

Rockville, Maryland

- **State and locally supported** 2-year, founded 1946
- **Suburban** 333-acre campus with easy access to Washington, DC
- **Endowment** $15.5 million
- **Coed,** 26,015 undergraduate students, 39% full-time, 54% women, 46% men

Undergraduates 10,056 full-time, 15,959 part-time. Students come from 30 states and territories; 174 other countries; 4% are from out of state; 25% Black or African American, non-Hispanic/Latino; 18% Hispanic/Latino; 13% Asian, non-Hispanic/Latino; 0.4% Native Hawaiian or other Pacific Islander, non-Hispanic/Latino; 0.3% American Indian or Alaska Native, non-Hispanic/Latino; 1% Two or more races, non-Hispanic/Latino; 7% international; 5% transferred in.

Freshmen *Admission:* 8,878 applied, 8,878 admitted, 3,859 enrolled.

Faculty *Total:* 1,309, 40% full-time, 29% with terminal degrees. *Student/faculty ratio:* 20:1.

Majors Accounting technology and bookkeeping; animation, interactive technology, video graphics and special effects; applied horticulture/horticulture operations; architectural drafting and CAD/CADD; art; automobile/automotive mechanics technology; biology/biotechnology laboratory technician; building/construction finishing, management, and inspection related; business/commerce; chemistry teacher education; child-care provision; commercial and advertising art; commercial photography; communications technologies and support services related; computer and information sciences; computer and information systems security; computer technology/computer systems technology; criminal justice/police science; crisis/emergency/disaster management; data entry/microcomputer applications; diagnostic medical sonography and ultrasound technology; early childhood education; elementary education; engineering; English/language arts teacher education; fire prevention and safety technology; geography; graphic and printing equipment operation/production; health information/medical records technology; hotel/motel administration; interior design; legal assistant/paralegal; liberal arts and sciences and humanities related; liberal arts and sciences/liberal studies; management information systems and services related; mathematics teacher education; medical radiologic technology; physical therapy technology; physics teacher education; psychiatric/mental health services technology; registered nursing/registered nurse; sign language interpretation and translation; Spanish language teacher education; speech communication and rhetoric; surgical technology.

Academics *Calendar:* semesters. *Degree:* certificates and associate. *Special study options:* academic remediation for entering students, accelerated degree program, adult/continuing education programs, advanced placement credit, cooperative education, distance learning, double majors, English as a second language, external degree program, honors programs, independent study, internships, off-campus study, part-time degree program, services for LD students, study abroad, summer session for credit. *ROTC:* Air Force (c).

Library Montgomery College Libraries plus 1 other with 365,096 titles, 46,797 serial subscriptions, 20,812 audiovisual materials, an OPAC, a Web page.

Student Life *Activities and Organizations:* drama/theater group, student-run newspaper, choral group. *Campus security:* 24-hour emergency response devices and patrols, late-night transport/escort service. *Student services:* personal/psychological counseling, women's center.

Athletics Member NJCAA. *Intercollegiate sports:* baseball M, basketball M/W, cross-country running M/W, golf M, lacrosse M, soccer M/W, softball W, tennis M/W, track and field M/W, volleyball M/W. *Intramural sports:* baseball M, basketball M/W, bowling M/W, cheerleading W, cross-country running M/W, golf M/W, lacrosse M, soccer M/W, softball W, tennis M/W, track and field M/W, volleyball M/W.

Costs (2011–12) *One-time required fee:* $25. *Tuition:* area resident $3300 full-time, $110 per credit hour part-time; state resident $6750 full-time, $225 per credit hour part-time; nonresident $9240 full-time, $308 per credit hour part-time. Full-time tuition and fees vary according to course load. Part-time tuition and fees vary according to course load. *Required fees:* $1080 full-time, $36 per credit hour part-time. *Payment plans:* installment, deferred payment. *Waivers:* senior citizens and employees or children of employees.

Applying *Options:* electronic application, early admission, deferred entrance. *Application fee:* $25. *Recommended:* high school transcript, interview. *Application deadlines:* rolling (freshmen), rolling (out-of-state freshmen), rolling (transfers). *Notification:* continuous (freshmen), continuous (out-of-state freshmen), continuous (transfers).

Freshman Application Contact Montgomery College, 51 Mannakee Street, Rockville, MD 20850. *Phone:* 240-567-5034. *Web site:* http://www.montgomerycollege.edu/.

Prince George's Community College

Largo, Maryland

Freshman Application Contact Ms. Vera Bagley, Director of Admissions and Records, Prince George's Community College, 301 Largo Road, Largo, MD 20774-2199. *Phone:* 301-322-0801. *Fax:* 301-322-0119. *E-mail:* enrollmentservices@pgcc.edu. *Web site:* http://www.pgcc.edu/.

TESST College of Technology

Baltimore, Maryland

- **Proprietary** 2-year, founded 1956
- **Coed**

Academics *Calendar:* quarters. *Degree:* certificates and associate.
Freshman Application Contact TESST College of Technology, 1520 South Caton Avenue, Baltimore, MD 21227. *Phone:* 410-644-6400. *Toll-free phone:* 800-833-0209. *Web site:* http://www.tesst.com/.

TESST College of Technology

Beltsville, Maryland

- **Proprietary** 2-year, founded 1967
- **Coed**

Academics *Calendar:* quarters. *Degree:* certificates and associate.
Applying *Application fee:* $20.
Freshman Application Contact TESST College of Technology, 4600 Powder Mill Road, Beltsville, MD 20705. *Phone:* 301-937-8448. *Toll-free phone:* 800-833-0209. *Web site:* http://www.tesst.com/.

TESST College of Technology

Towson, Maryland

Freshman Application Contact TESST College of Technology, 803 Glen Eagles Court, Towson, MD 21286. *Phone:* 410-296-5350. *Toll-free phone:* 800-48-TESST. *Web site:* http://www.tesst.com/.

Wor-Wic Community College

Salisbury, Maryland

- **State and locally supported** 2-year, founded 1976
- **Small-town** 202-acre campus
- **Endowment** $5.5 million
- **Coed**

Undergraduates 1,290 full-time, 2,755 part-time. Students come from 11 states and territories; 2% are from out of state; 7% transferred in.
Faculty *Student/faculty ratio:* 21:1.
Academics *Calendar:* semesters. *Degree:* certificates and associate. *Special study options:* academic remediation for entering students, accelerated degree program, adult/continuing education programs, advanced placement credit, distance learning, double majors, English as a second language, honors programs, independent study, internships, part-time degree program, services for LD students, summer session for credit.
Student Life *Campus security:* 24-hour emergency response devices, late-night transport/escort service, patrols by trained security personnel 9 am to midnight.
Standardized Tests *Required for some:* ACT (for admission).
Costs (2010–11) *Tuition:* area resident $2670 full-time, $89 per credit hour part-time; state resident $5910 full-time, $197 per credit hour part-time; non-resident $7290 full-time, $243 per credit hour part-time. *Required fees:* $228 full-time, $7 per credit hour part-time, $15 per term part-time.
Applying *Options:* early admission. *Recommended:* high school transcript.
Freshman Application Contact Mr. Richard Webster, Director of Admissions, Wor-Wic Community College, 32000 Campus Drive, Salisbury, MD 21804. *Phone:* 410-334-2895. *Fax:* 410-334-2954. *E-mail:* admissions@worwic.edu. *Web site:* http://www.worwic.edu/.

MASSACHUSETTS

Bay State College

Boston, Massachusetts

Freshman Application Contact Kim Olds, Director of Admissions, Bay State College, 122 Commonwealth Avenue, MA 02116. *Phone:* 617-217-9115.

Toll-free phone: 800-81-LEARN. *Fax:* 617-536-1735. *E-mail:* admissions@baystate.edu. *Web site:* http://www.baystate.edu/.

See page 352 for the College Close-Up.

Benjamin Franklin Institute of Technology

Boston, Massachusetts

Freshman Application Contact Ms. Brittainy Johnson, Associate Director of Admissions, Benjamin Franklin Institute of Technology, Boston, MA 02116. *Phone:* 617-423-4630 Ext. 122. *Fax:* 617-482-3706. *E-mail:* bjohnson@bfit.edu. *Web site:* http://www.bfit.edu/.

Berkshire Community College

Pittsfield, Massachusetts

- **State-supported** 2-year, founded 1960, part of Massachusetts Public Higher Education System
- **Rural** 100-acre campus
- **Endowment** $4.4 million
- **Coed**

Undergraduates 996 full-time, 1,279 part-time. Students come from 4 states and territories; 21 other countries; 4% are from out of state; 6% transferred in.
Faculty *Student/faculty ratio:* 15:1.
Academics *Calendar:* semesters. *Degree:* certificates and associate. *Special study options:* academic remediation for entering students, accelerated degree program, adult/continuing education programs, advanced placement credit, cooperative education, distance learning, double majors, English as a second language, honors programs, independent study, internships, off-campus study, part-time degree program, services for LD students, summer session for credit.
Student Life *Campus security:* 24-hour emergency response devices and patrols, late-night transport/escort service.
Athletics Member NJCAA.
Costs (2010–11) *One-time required fee:* $10. *Tuition:* state resident $624 full-time, $26 per credit part-time; nonresident $6240 full-time, $260 per credit part-time. Full-time tuition and fees vary according to course load, degree level, program, and reciprocity agreements. Part-time tuition and fees vary according to course load, degree level, program, and reciprocity agreements. *Required fees:* $3528 full-time, $147 per credit part-time.
Financial Aid Of all full-time matriculated undergraduates who enrolled in 2009, 80 Federal Work-Study jobs (averaging $1600).
Applying *Options:* deferred entrance. *Application fee:* $10. *Required:* high school transcript. *Recommended:* interview.
Freshman Application Contact Ms. Tina Schettini, Enrollment Services, Berkshire Community College, 1350 West Street, Pittsfield, MA 01201-5786. *Phone:* 413-236-1635. *Toll-free phone:* 800-816-1233 Ext. 242. *Fax:* 413-496-9511. *E-mail:* tschetti@berkshirecc.edu. *Web site:* http://www.berkshirecc.edu/.

Bristol Community College

Fall River, Massachusetts

- **State-supported** 2-year, founded 1965, part of Massachusetts Community College System
- **Urban** 105-acre campus with easy access to Boston
- **Endowment** $3.9 million
- **Coed,** 8,893 undergraduate students

Undergraduates Students come from 10 states and territories; 21 other countries; 9% are from out of state; 6% Black or African American, non-Hispanic/Latino; 5% Hispanic/Latino; 2% Asian, non-Hispanic/Latino; 0.6% American Indian or Alaska Native, non-Hispanic/Latino; 15% Race/ethnicity unknown; 0.3% international.
Faculty *Total:* 415, 25% full-time.
Majors Accounting; banking and financial support services; business administration and management; business operations support and secretarial services related; clinical/medical laboratory technology; communication disorders sciences and services related; communications systems installation and repair technology; computer and information sciences; computer and information sciences related; computer programming; computer science; computer systems analysis; cooking and related culinary arts; cosmetology and personal grooming arts related; criminal justice/safety; culinary arts related; data processing and data processing technology; dental hygiene; design and visual communications; dramatic/theater arts and stagecraft related; electromechanical technology; engineering; engineering related; engineering science; engineering technologies and engineering related; entrepreneurship; environmental/environmental health engineering; finance and financial management services related; fine/studio arts; fire science/firefighting; general studies; graphic design; humanities; industrial production technologies related; information sci-

ence/studies; intermedia/multimedia; kindergarten/preschool education; legal assistant/paralegal; liberal arts and sciences/liberal studies; management information systems; manufacturing engineering; marketing/marketing management; mathematics and statistics related; mechanical engineering; medical administrative assistant and medical secretary; occupational therapist assistant; real estate; receptionist; registered nursing/registered nurse; small business administration; social sciences; social work; speech communication and rhetoric; structural engineering.

Academics *Calendar:* semesters. *Degree:* certificates and associate. *Special study options:* academic remediation for entering students, adult/continuing education programs, cooperative education, distance learning, English as a second language, honors programs, independent study, internships, off-campus study, part-time degree program, services for LD students, student-designed majors, summer session for credit.

Library Learning Resources Center with 65,000 titles, 380 serial subscriptions, an OPAC, a Web page.

Student Life *Housing:* college housing not available. *Activities and Organizations:* drama/theater group, student-run newspaper, International Club, MASS/PIRG WaterWatch, Criminal Justice Society, Students in Free Enterprise (SIFE), Portuguese Club. *Campus security:* 24-hour emergency response devices and patrols, student patrols, late-night transport/escort service. *Student services:* health clinic, personal/psychological counseling, women's center.

Athletics Member NJCAA. *Intramural sports:* basketball M/W, soccer M/W.

Costs (2011–12) *Tuition:* state resident $576 full-time; nonresident $5520 full-time. Full-time tuition and fees vary according to course load. Part-time tuition and fees vary according to course load. *Required fees:* $3102 full-time, $146 per credit hour part-time. *Payment plan:* installment. *Waivers:* senior citizens and employees or children of employees.

Financial Aid Of all full-time matriculated undergraduates who enrolled in 2009, 205 Federal Work-Study jobs (averaging $1627). 65 state and other part-time jobs (averaging $1478).

Applying *Application fee:* $10. *Required:* high school transcript. *Notification:* continuous (freshmen), continuous (transfers).

Freshman Application Contact Mr. Rodney S. Clark, Dean of Admissions, Bristol Community College, 777 Elsbree Street, Fall River, MA 02720. *Phone:* 508-678-2811 Ext. 2177. *Fax:* 508-730-3265. *E-mail:* rodney.clark@bristolcc.edu. *Web site:* http://www.bristolcc.edu/.

Bunker Hill Community College
Boston, Massachusetts

- **State-supported** 2-year, founded 1973
- **Urban** 21-acre campus
- **Endowment** $1.6 million
- **Coed**

Undergraduates 3,767 full-time, 7,242 part-time. Students come from 78 other countries; 7% transferred in.

Faculty *Student/faculty ratio:* 19:1.

Academics *Calendar:* semesters. *Degree:* certificates and associate. *Special study options:* academic remediation for entering students, advanced placement credit, cooperative education, distance learning, English as a second language, external degree program, honors programs, independent study, internships, part-time degree program, services for LD students, study abroad, summer session for credit.

Student Life *Campus security:* 24-hour emergency response devices and patrols, late-night transport/escort service.

Athletics Member NJCAA.

Costs (2010–11) *Tuition:* state resident $576 full-time, $24 per credit part-time; nonresident $5520 full-time, $230 per credit part-time. Full-time tuition and fees vary according to course load. Part-time tuition and fees vary according to course load. *Required fees:* $2568 full-time, $107 per credit part-time.

Financial Aid Of all full-time matriculated undergraduates who enrolled in 2009, 135 Federal Work-Study jobs (averaging $2376).

Applying *Options:* deferred entrance. *Application fee:* $10. *Required:* high school transcript.

Freshman Application Contact Mr. David Gomes, Director of Admissions, Bunker Hill Community College, 250 New Rutherford Avenue, Boston, MA 02129. *Phone:* 617-228-2346. *Fax:* 617-228-2082. *Web site:* http://www.bhcc.mass.edu/.

Cape Cod Community College
West Barnstable, Massachusetts

Freshman Application Contact Director of Admissions, Cape Cod Community College, 2240 Iyannough Road, West Barnstable, MA 02668-1599. *Phone:* 508-362-2131 Ext. 4311. *Toll-free phone:* 877-846-3672. *Fax:*

508-375-4089. *E-mail:* admiss@capecod.edu. *Web site:* http://www.capecod.edu/.

Dean College
Franklin, Massachusetts

- **Independent** primarily 2-year, founded 1865
- **Small-town** 100-acre campus with easy access to Boston and Providence
- **Endowment** $22.8 million
- **Coed**

Undergraduates 975 full-time, 131 part-time. Students come from 23 states and territories; 131 other countries; 48% are from out of state; 4% transferred in; 88% live on campus. *Retention:* 62% of full-time freshmen returned.

Faculty *Student/faculty ratio:* 19:1.

Academics *Calendar:* semesters. *Degrees:* certificates, associate, and bachelor's. *Special study options:* academic remediation for entering students, accelerated degree program, adult/continuing education programs, advanced placement credit, English as a second language, freshman honors college, honors programs, independent study, internships, off-campus study, part-time degree program, services for LD students, student-designed majors, summer session for credit.

Student Life *Campus security:* 24-hour emergency response devices and patrols, late-night transport/escort service, controlled dormitory access.

Athletics Member NJCAA.

Standardized Tests *Required:* SAT or ACT (for admission).

Costs (2010–11) *Comprehensive fee:* $41,582 includes full-time tuition ($29,140) and room and board ($12,442). Full-time tuition and fees vary according to program. Part-time tuition: $780 per course. Part-time tuition and fees vary according to program. *Room and board:* college room only: $7868.

Applying *Options:* electronic application, deferred entrance. *Application fee:* $35. *Required:* essay or personal statement, high school transcript. *Recommended:* minimum 2.0 GPA, interview.

Freshman Application Contact Mr. James Fowler, Dean College, 99 Main Street, Franklin, MA 02038. *Phone:* 508-541-1547. *Toll-free phone:* 877-TRY-DEAN. *Fax:* 508-541-8726. *E-mail:* jfowler@dean.edu. *Web site:* http://www.dean.edu/.

FINE Mortuary College, LLC
Norwood, Massachusetts

Freshman Application Contact Dean Marsha Wise, Admissions Office, FINE Mortuary College, LLC, 150 Kerry Place, Norwood, MA 02062. *Phone:* 781-762-1211. *Fax:* 781-762-7177. *E-mail:* mwise@fine-ne.com. *Web site:* http://www.fine-ne.com/.

Greenfield Community College
Greenfield, Massachusetts

- **State-supported** 2-year, founded 1962, part of Commonwealth of Massachusetts Department of Higher Education
- **Small-town** 120-acre campus
- **Coed**

Undergraduates 1,045 full-time, 1,501 part-time. Students come from 5 states and territories; 7 other countries; 5% are from out of state; 9% transferred in. *Retention:* 59% of full-time freshmen returned.

Academics *Calendar:* semesters. *Degree:* certificates and associate. *Special study options:* academic remediation for entering students, adult/continuing education programs, advanced placement credit, cooperative education, distance learning, double majors, English as a second language, honors programs, independent study, internships, part-time degree program, services for LD students, summer session for credit.

Student Life *Campus security:* 24-hour emergency response devices and patrols, late-night transport/escort service.

Standardized Tests *Required for some:* Psychological Corporation Practical Nursing Entrance Examination.

Costs (2010–11) *Tuition:* state resident $624 full-time, $26 per credit hour part-time; nonresident $6744 full-time, $281 per credit hour part-time. Full-time tuition and fees vary according to class time, course load, and program. Part-time tuition and fees vary according to class time, course load, and program. *Required fees:* $3686 full-time, $210 per credit hour part-time, $20 per term part-time.

Applying *Options:* electronic application. *Application fee:* $10. *Required for some:* high school transcript, interview.

Freshman Application Contact Mr. Herbert Hentz, Assistant Director of Admission, Greenfield Community College, 1 College Drive, Greenfield, MA 01301-9739. *Phone:* 413-775-1000. *Fax:* 413-773-5129. *E-mail:* admission@gcc.mass.edu. *Web site:* http://www.gcc.mass.edu/.

Holyoke Community College
Holyoke, Massachusetts

- **State-supported** 2-year, founded 1946, part of Massachusetts Public Higher Education System
- **Small-town** 135-acre campus
- **Endowment** $7.3 million
- **Coed,** 7,398 undergraduate students, 51% full-time, 62% women, 38% men

Undergraduates 3,775 full-time, 3,623 part-time. Students come from 7 states and territories; 1% are from out of state; 6% Black or African American, non-Hispanic/Latino; 19% Hispanic/Latino; 2% Asian, non-Hispanic/Latino; 0.1% Native Hawaiian or other Pacific Islander, non-Hispanic/Latino; 0.3% American Indian or Alaska Native, non-Hispanic/Latino; 1% Two or more races, non-Hispanic/Latino; 2% Race/ethnicity unknown; 0.3% international; 7% transferred in.

Freshmen *Admission:* 1,742 admitted, 1,747 enrolled.

Faculty *Total:* 523, 25% full-time, 19% with terminal degrees. *Student/faculty ratio:* 19:1.

Majors Accounting technology and bookkeeping; administrative assistant and secretarial science; art; business administration and management; child-care and support services management; computer programming (specific applications); criminal justice/safety; engineering; environmental control technologies related; geography; health and physical education/fitness; hospitality administration related; liberal arts and sciences and humanities related; liberal arts and sciences/liberal studies; medical radiologic technology; music; opticianry; registered nursing/registered nurse; retailing; social work; sport and fitness administration/management; veterinary/animal health technology.

Academics *Calendar:* semesters. *Degree:* certificates and associate. *Special study options:* academic remediation for entering students, adult/continuing education programs, advanced placement credit, cooperative education, distance learning, double majors, English as a second language, external degree program, honors programs, independent study, internships, off-campus study, part-time degree program, services for LD students, student-designed majors, study abroad, summer session for credit. *ROTC:* Army (c), Air Force (c).

Library Elaine Marieb Library with 88,149 titles, 29,599 serial subscriptions, 9,327 audiovisual materials, an OPAC, a Web page.

Student Life *Housing:* college housing not available. *Activities and Organizations:* drama/theater group, student-run newspaper, radio station, Drama Club, Japanese Anime Club, Student Senate, LISA Club, STRIVE. *Campus security:* 24-hour emergency response devices and patrols, late-night transport/escort service. *Student services:* health clinic, personal/psychological counseling, women's center.

Athletics Member NJCAA. *Intercollegiate sports:* baseball M, basketball M/W, golf M/W, skiing (downhill) M(c)/W(c), soccer M/W, softball W, volleyball W.

Costs (2011–12) *Tuition:* state resident $576 full-time, $129 per credit part-time; nonresident $5520 full-time, $335 per credit part-time. Full-time tuition and fees vary according to course load. Part-time tuition and fees vary according to course load. *Required fees:* $2700 full-time, $90 per term part-time. *Payment plan:* installment. *Waivers:* senior citizens and employees or children of employees.

Applying *Options:* early admission, deferred entrance. *Required:* high school transcript. *Recommended:* interview. *Application deadlines:* rolling (freshmen), rolling (transfers). *Notification:* continuous (freshmen), continuous (transfers).

Freshman Application Contact Ms. Marcia Rosbury-Henne, Director of Admissions and Transfer Affairs, Holyoke Community College, Admission Office, Holyoke, MA 01040. *Phone:* 413-552-2000. *Toll-free phone:* 888-530-8855. *Fax:* 413-552-2045. *E-mail:* admissions@hcc.edu. *Web site:* http://www.hcc.edu/.

ITT Technical Institute
Norwood, Massachusetts

- **Proprietary** primarily 2-year, founded 1990, part of ITT Educational Services, Inc.
- **Suburban** campus
- **Coed**

Majors CAD/CADD drafting/design technology; computer and information systems security; computer engineering technology; computer software and media applications related; electrical, electronic and communications engineering technology; game and interactive media design; system, networking, and LAN/WAN management; web/multimedia management and webmaster; web page, digital/multimedia and information resources design.

Academics *Calendar:* quarters. *Degrees:* associate and bachelor's.

Student Life *Housing:* college housing not available.

Freshman Application Contact Director of Recruitment, ITT Technical Institute, 333 Providence Highway, Norwood, MA 02062. *Phone:* 781-278-7200. *Toll-free phone:* 800-879-8324. *Web site:* http://www.itt-tech.edu/.

ITT Technical Institute
Woburn, Massachusetts

- **Proprietary** primarily 2-year, founded 2000, part of ITT Educational Services, Inc.
- **Coed**

Majors CAD/CADD drafting/design technology; computer and information systems security; computer engineering technology; computer software and media applications related; electrical, electronic and communications engineering technology; game and interactive media design; system, networking, and LAN/WAN management; web/multimedia management and webmaster; web page, digital/multimedia and information resources design.

Academics *Calendar:* quarters. *Degrees:* associate and bachelor's.

Student Life *Housing:* college housing not available.

Freshman Application Contact Director of Recruitment, ITT Technical Institute, 200 Ballardvale Stree, Suite 200, Woburn, MA 01801. *Phone:* 978-658-2636. *Toll-free phone:* 800-430-5097. *Web site:* http://www.itt-tech.edu/.

Labouré College
Boston, Massachusetts

Director of Admissions Ms. Gina M. Morrissette, Director of Admissions, Labouré College, 2120 Dorchester Avenue, Boston, MA 02124-5698. *Phone:* 617-296-8300. *Web site:* http://www.laboure.edu/.

Marian Court College
Swampscott, Massachusetts

Director of Admissions Bryan Boppert, Director of Admissions, Marian Court College, 35 Little's Point Road, Swampscott, MA 01907-2840. *Phone:* 781-309-5230. *Fax:* 781-309-5286. *Web site:* http://www.mariancourt.edu/.

Massachusetts Bay Community College
Wellesley Hills, Massachusetts

- **State-supported** 2-year, founded 1961
- **Suburban** 84-acre campus with easy access to Boston
- **Coed,** 5,518 undergraduate students, 40% full-time, 58% women, 42% men

Undergraduates 2,204 full-time, 3,314 part-time. Students come from 12 states and territories; 97 other countries; 8% are from out of state; 25% transferred in. *Retention:* 54% of full-time freshmen returned.

Freshmen *Admission:* 2,247 applied, 2,236 admitted, 1,276 enrolled.

Faculty *Total:* 343, 23% full-time. *Student/faculty ratio:* 19:1.

Majors Accounting; automotive engineering technology; biological and physical sciences; biology/biotechnology laboratory technician; business administration and management; business/commerce; chemical technology; child-care and support services management; computer and information sciences; computer engineering technology; computer science; criminal justice/law enforcement administration; drafting and design technology; engineering technology; environmental engineering technology; forensic science and technology; general studies; hospitality administration; human services; information science/studies; international relations and affairs; legal assistant/paralegal; liberal arts and sciences/liberal studies; mechanical engineering/mechanical technology; medical radiologic technology; physical therapy technology; registered nursing/registered nurse; respiratory care therapy; social sciences; speech communication and rhetoric.

Academics *Calendar:* semesters. *Degree:* certificates and associate. *Special study options:* academic remediation for entering students, adult/continuing education programs, advanced placement credit, cooperative education, distance learning, honors programs, internships, part-time degree program, services for LD students, summer session for credit.

Library Perkins Library with 51,429 titles, 280 serial subscriptions, 4,780 audiovisual materials, an OPAC, a Web page.

Student Life *Housing:* college housing not available. *Activities and Organizations:* drama/theater group, student-run newspaper, Student Government Association, Latino Student Organization, New World Society Club, Mass Bay Players, Student Occupational Therapy Association. *Campus security:* 24-hour emergency response devices and patrols. *Student services:* health clinic, personal/psychological counseling.

Athletics Member NJCAA. *Intercollegiate sports:* baseball M, basketball M/W, cross-country running M/W, golf M/W, soccer M/W, softball W, tennis M/W, volleyball W. *Intramural sports:* ice hockey M, soccer M/W.

Costs (2010–11) *Tuition:* state resident $3704 full-time, $24 per credit hour part-time; nonresident $8648 full-time, $230 per credit hour part-time. Full-time tuition and fees vary according to program and reciprocity agreements. Part-time tuition and fees vary according to program and reciprocity agreements. *Required fees:* $127 per credit hour part-time, $40 per term part-time. *Payment plan:* installment. *Waivers:* senior citizens and employees or children of employees.
Financial Aid Of all full-time matriculated undergraduates who enrolled in 2009, 59 Federal Work-Study jobs (averaging $1840).
Applying *Options:* electronic application, deferred entrance. *Application fee:* $20. *Application deadlines:* rolling (freshmen), rolling (transfers). *Notification:* continuous (freshmen), continuous (transfers).
Freshman Application Contact Ms. Donna Raposa, Director of Admissions, Massachusetts Bay Community College, 50 Oakland Street, Wellesley Hills, MA 02481. *Phone:* 781-239-2500. *Fax:* 781-239-1047. *E-mail:* info@massbay.edu. *Web site:* http://www.massbay.edu/.

Massasoit Community College
Brockton, Massachusetts

- **State-supported** 2-year, founded 1966
- **Suburban** 100-acre campus with easy access to Boston
- **Coed**

Undergraduates 3,631 full-time, 4,310 part-time. Students come from 13 states and territories; 6 other countries; 1% are from out of state; 6% transferred in.
Academics *Calendar:* semesters. *Degree:* certificates and associate. *Special study options:* academic remediation for entering students, accelerated degree program, adult/continuing education programs, cooperative education, distance learning, English as a second language, independent study, internships, off-campus study, part-time degree program, services for LD students, summer session for credit.
Student Life *Campus security:* 24-hour patrols.
Athletics Member NJCAA.
Costs (2010–11) *Tuition:* state resident $576 full-time, $24 per credit hour part-time; nonresident $5520 full-time, $230 per credit hour part-time. Full-time tuition and fees vary according to program. Part-time tuition and fees vary according to program. *Required fees:* $2976 full-time, $124 per credit hour part-time. *Payment plans:* installment, deferred payment.
Financial Aid Of all full-time matriculated undergraduates who enrolled in 2009, 45 Federal Work-Study jobs (averaging $3200).
Freshman Application Contact Michelle Hughes, Director of Admissions, Massasoit Community College, 1 Massasoit Boulevard, Brockton, MA 02302-3996. *Phone:* 508-588-9100. *Toll-free phone:* 800-CAREERS. *Web site:* http://www.massasoit.mass.edu/.

Middlesex Community College
Bedford, Massachusetts

Director of Admissions Ms. Laurie Dimitrov, Director, Admissions and Recruitment, Middlesex Community College, Springs Road, Bedford, MA 01730-1655. *Phone:* 978-656-3207. *Toll-free phone:* 800-818-3434. *E-mail:* orellanad@middlesex.cc.ma.us. *Web site:* http://www.middlesex.mass.edu/.

Mount Wachusett Community College
Gardner, Massachusetts

- **State-supported** 2-year, founded 1963, part of Massachusetts Public Higher Education System
- **Small-town** 270-acre campus with easy access to Boston
- **Endowment** $3.9 million
- **Coed**

Undergraduates 1,987 full-time, 2,774 part-time. Students come from 12 states and territories; 21 other countries; 5% are from out of state; 6% transferred in. *Retention:* 56% of full-time freshmen returned.
Faculty *Student/faculty ratio:* 24:1.
Academics *Calendar:* semesters. *Degree:* certificates and associate. *Special study options:* academic remediation for entering students, accelerated degree program, adult/continuing education programs, advanced placement credit, cooperative education, distance learning, double majors, English as a second language, honors programs, independent study, internships, part-time degree program, services for LD students, study abroad, summer session for credit.
Student Life *Campus security:* 24-hour emergency response devices and patrols.
Standardized Tests *Required for some:* SAT (for admission). *Recommended:* SAT (for admission), ACT (for admission), SAT or ACT (for admission), SAT and SAT Subject Tests or ACT (for admission), SAT Subject Tests (for admission).

Costs (2010–11) *Tuition:* state resident $750 full-time, $25 per credit hour part-time; nonresident $6900 full-time, $230 per credit hour part-time. Full-time tuition and fees vary according to program and reciprocity agreements. Part-time tuition and fees vary according to program and reciprocity agreements. *Required fees:* $4800 full-time, $155 per credit hour part-time, $75 per term part-time.
Financial Aid Of all full-time matriculated undergraduates who enrolled in 2009, 47 Federal Work-Study jobs (averaging $2228).
Applying *Options:* electronic application, early admission. *Application fee:* $10. *Required:* high school transcript. *Required for some:* 2 letters of recommendation. *Recommended:* interview.
Freshman Application Contact Mr. John D. Walsh, Director of Admissions, Mount Wachusett Community College, 444 Green Street, Gardner, MA 01440-1000. *Phone:* 978-632-6600 Ext. 110. *Fax:* 978-630-9554. *E-mail:* admissions@mwcc.mass.edu. *Web site:* http://www.mwcc.mass.edu/.

Northern Essex Community College
Haverhill, Massachusetts

- **State-supported** 2-year, founded 1960
- **Suburban** 106-acre campus with easy access to Boston
- **Endowment** $3.2 million
- **Coed,** 7,439 undergraduate students, 38% full-time, 62% women, 38% men

Undergraduates 2,834 full-time, 4,605 part-time. Students come from 7 states and territories; 18% are from out of state; 5% transferred in. *Retention:* 59% of full-time freshmen returned.
Freshmen *Admission:* 3,347 applied, 3,164 admitted, 1,358 enrolled.
Faculty *Total:* 532, 20% full-time. *Student/faculty ratio:* 22:1.
Majors Accounting; administrative assistant and secretarial science; biological and physical sciences; business administration and management; business teacher education; civil engineering technology; commercial and advertising art; computer and information sciences; computer engineering technology; computer graphics; computer programming; computer programming related; computer programming (specific applications); computer science; computer systems networking and telecommunications; computer typography and composition equipment operation; criminal justice/law enforcement administration; dance; data processing and data processing technology; dental assisting; dramatic/theater arts; education; electrical, electronic and communications engineering technology; elementary education; engineering science; finance; general studies; health information/medical records administration; history; hotel/motel administration; human services; industrial radiologic technology; international relations and affairs; journalism; kindergarten/preschool education; legal assistant/paralegal; liberal arts and sciences/liberal studies; machine tool technology; marketing/marketing management; materials science; medical administrative assistant and medical secretary; medical transcription; mental health counseling; music; parks, recreation and leisure; physical education teaching and coaching; political science and government; radiologic technology/science; real estate; registered nursing/registered nurse; respiratory care therapy; respiratory therapy technician; sign language interpretation and translation; telecommunications technology; tourism and travel services management; web/multimedia management and webmaster; web page, digital/multimedia and information resources design; women's studies.
Academics *Calendar:* semesters. *Degree:* certificates and associate. *Special study options:* academic remediation for entering students, adult/continuing education programs, advanced placement credit, cooperative education, distance learning, double majors, English as a second language, freshman honors college, honors programs, independent study, internships, off-campus study, part-time degree program, services for LD students, study abroad, summer session for credit. *ROTC:* Air Force (c).
Library Bentley Library with 61,120 titles, 598 serial subscriptions, an OPAC.
Student Life *Housing:* college housing not available. *Activities and Organizations:* drama/theater group, student-run newspaper. *Campus security:* 24-hour emergency response devices and patrols. *Student services:* health clinic, personal/psychological counseling, women's center.
Athletics Member NJCAA. *Intercollegiate sports:* baseball M, basketball M/W, cross-country running M/W, volleyball M/W. *Intramural sports:* basketball M/W, cross-country running M/W, football M/W, golf M/W, racquetball M/W, skiing (cross-country) M/W, skiing (downhill) M/W, weight lifting M/W.
Standardized Tests *Required:* Psychological Corporation Aptitude Test for Practical Nursing (for admission).
Costs (2010–11) *Tuition:* state resident $600 full-time, $25 per credit hour part-time; nonresident $6384 full-time, $266 per credit hour part-time. *Required fees:* $2784 full-time, $116 per credit hour part-time. *Payment plan:* installment. *Waivers:* employees or children of employees.
Financial Aid Of all full-time matriculated undergraduates who enrolled in 2009, 74 Federal Work-Study jobs (averaging $1759).
Applying *Options:* early admission. *Application fee:* $25. *Required:* high school transcript. *Application deadlines:* rolling (freshmen), rolling (transfers). *Notification:* continuous (freshmen), continuous (transfers).

Freshman Application Contact Ms. Nora Sheridan, Director of Admissions, Northern Essex Community College, Haverhill, MA 01830. *Phone:* 978-556-3616. *Toll-free phone:* 800-NECC-123. *Fax:* 978-556-3155. *Web site:* http://www.necc.mass.edu/.

North Shore Community College
Danvers, Massachusetts

Freshman Application Contact Dr. Joanne Light, Dean of Enrollment Services, North Shore Community College, Danvers, MA 01923. *Phone:* 978-762-4000 Ext. 4337. *Fax:* 978-762-4015. *E-mail:* info@northshore.edu. *Web site:* http://www.northshore.edu/.

Quincy College
Quincy, Massachusetts

Freshman Application Contact Paula Smith, Dean, Enrollment Services, Quincy College, 34 Coddington Street, Quincy, MA 02169-4522. *Phone:* 617-984-1700. *Toll-free phone:* 800-698-1700. *Fax:* 617-984-1779. *E-mail:* psmith@quincycollege.edu. *Web site:* http://www.quincycollege.edu/.

Quinsigamond Community College
Worcester, Massachusetts

- **State-supported** 2-year, founded 1963, part of Massachusetts System of Higher Education
- **Urban** 57-acre campus with easy access to Boston
- **Endowment** $373,092
- **Coed,** 8,922 undergraduate students, 47% full-time, 56% women, 44% men

Undergraduates 4,195 full-time, 4,727 part-time. Students come from 10 states and territories; 32 other countries; 1% are from out of state; 6% transferred in. *Retention:* 59% of full-time freshmen returned.
Freshmen *Admission:* 4,063 applied, 4,063 admitted, 1,866 enrolled.
Faculty *Total:* 546, 23% full-time, 12% with terminal degrees. *Student/faculty ratio:* 21:1.
Majors Accounting; administrative assistant and secretarial science; alternative and complementary medicine related; art; automobile/automotive mechanics technology; business administration and management; business/commerce; civil engineering technology; commercial and advertising art; community organization and advocacy; computer engineering technology; computer graphics; computer programming; computer programming (specific applications); computer systems analysis; computer technology/computer systems technology; consumer merchandising/retailing management; criminal justice/law enforcement administration; criminal justice/police science; data processing and data processing technology; dental hygiene; dental services and allied professions related; electrical, electronic and communications engineering technology; electromechanical technology; emergency medical technology (EMT paramedic); executive assistant/executive secretary; fire science/firefighting; fire services administration; general studies; hospitality administration; hotel/motel administration; human services; information science/studies; kindergarten/preschool education; liberal arts and sciences/liberal studies; manufacturing engineering technology; medical office assistant; medical radiologic technology; occupational therapist assistant; registered nursing/registered nurse; respiratory care therapy; restaurant/food services management; telecommunications technology; web page, digital/multimedia and information resources design.
Academics *Calendar:* semesters. *Degree:* certificates and associate. *Special study options:* academic remediation for entering students, accelerated degree program, adult/continuing education programs, advanced placement credit, cooperative education, distance learning, double majors, English as a second language, honors programs, independent study, internships, off-campus study, part-time degree program, services for LD students, summer session for credit. *ROTC:* Army (c).
Library Alden Library with 60,000 titles, 225 serial subscriptions, 2,800 audiovisual materials, an OPAC, a Web page.
Student Life *Housing:* college housing not available. *Activities and Organizations:* drama/theater group, student-run newspaper, Phi Theta Kappa, academic-related clubs, Student Senate, Chess Club, Business Club. *Campus security:* 24-hour emergency response devices and patrols, late-night transport/escort service. *Student services:* personal/psychological counseling.
Athletics Member NJCAA. *Intercollegiate sports:* baseball M, basketball M/W, softball W. *Intramural sports:* basketball M/W, soccer M/W, ultimate Frisbee M/W, volleyball M/W.
Costs (2011–12) *Tuition:* state resident $576 full-time, $24 per credit hour part-time; nonresident $5520 full-time, $230 per credit hour part-time. Full-time tuition and fees vary according to course load and program. Part-time tuition and fees vary according to course load and program. *Required fees:* $3656 full-time, $134 per credit hour part-time, $235 per term part-time. *Pay-*

ment plan: installment. *Waivers:* senior citizens and employees or children of employees.
Applying *Options:* electronic application. *Application fee:* $20. *Required:* high school transcript. *Required for some:* interview. *Application deadlines:* rolling (freshmen), rolling (out-of-state freshmen), rolling (transfers), *Notification:* continuous (freshmen), continuous (out-of-state freshmen), continuous (transfers).
Freshman Application Contact Quinsigamond Community College, 670 West Boylston Street, Worcester, MA 01606-2092. *Phone:* 508-854-4260. *Web site:* http://www.qcc.edu/.

Roxbury Community College
Roxbury Crossing, Massachusetts

Director of Admissions Mr. Milton Samuels, Director, Admissions, Roxbury Community College, 1234 Columbus Avenue, Roxbury Crossing, MA 02120-3400. *Phone:* 617-541-5310. *Web site:* http://www.rcc.mass.edu/.

Springfield Technical Community College
Springfield, Massachusetts

- **State-supported** 2-year, founded 1967
- **Urban** 34-acre campus
- **Endowment** $4.8 million
- **Coed,** 6,888 undergraduate students, 44% full-time, 57% women, 43% men

Undergraduates 3,045 full-time, 3,843 part-time. Students come from 8 states and territories; 3% are from out of state; 15% Black or African American, non-Hispanic/Latino; 20% Hispanic/Latino; 2% Asian, non-Hispanic/Latino; 0.6% American Indian or Alaska Native, non-Hispanic/Latino; 0.6% Two or more races, non-Hispanic/Latino; 8% Race/ethnicity unknown; 1% international; 8% transferred in.
Freshmen *Admission:* 3,199 applied, 2,790 admitted, 1,349 enrolled.
Faculty *Total:* 402, 37% full-time. *Student/faculty ratio:* 18:1.
Majors Accounting; administrative assistant and secretarial science; animation, interactive technology, video graphics and special effects; automotive engineering technology; biology/biological sciences; biotechnology; building/construction finishing, management, and inspection related; business administration and management; business/commerce; chemistry; civil engineering technology; clinical/medical laboratory technology; commercial and advertising art; commercial photography; computer and information systems security; computer engineering technology; computer programming (specific applications); computer science; criminal justice/police science; data processing and data processing technology; dental hygiene; diagnostic medical sonography and ultrasound technology; early childhood education; electrical, electronic and communications engineering technology; electromechanical technology; elementary education; engineering; entrepreneurship; executive assistant/executive secretary; finance; fine/studio arts; fire prevention and safety technology; fire science/firefighting; general studies; heating, ventilation, air conditioning and refrigeration engineering technology; landscaping and groundskeeping; laser and optical technology; liberal arts and sciences/liberal studies; marketing/marketing management; massage therapy; mathematics; mechanical engineering/mechanical technology; medical administrative assistant and medical secretary; medical/clinical assistant; medical insurance coding; network and system administration; nuclear medical technology; occupational therapist assistant; physical therapy technology; physics; premedical studies; radio and television broadcasting technology; radiologic technology/science; recording arts technology; registered nursing/registered nurse; respiratory care therapy; secondary education; small business administration; sport and fitness administration/management; surgical technology; telecommunications technology; web page, digital/multimedia and information resources design.
Academics *Calendar:* semesters. *Degree:* certificates and associate. *Special study options:* academic remediation for entering students, adult/continuing education programs, advanced placement credit, cooperative education, distance learning, English as a second language, honors programs, independent study, internships, off-campus study, part-time degree program, services for LD students, summer session for credit.
Library Springfield Technical Community College Library with 57,119 titles, 230 serial subscriptions, 1,600 audiovisual materials, an OPAC, a Web page.
Student Life *Housing:* college housing not available. *Activities and Organizations:* Phi Theta Kappa, Landscape Design Club, Dental Hygiene Club, Clinical Lab Science Club, Physical Therapist Assistant Club. *Campus security:* 24-hour emergency response devices and patrols, late-night transport/escort service. *Student services:* health clinic, personal/psychological counseling.
Athletics Member NJCAA. *Intercollegiate sports:* basketball M/W, golf M, lacrosse W, soccer M/W, wrestling M. *Intramural sports:* basketball M/W, cross-country running M/W, golf M/W, skiing (cross-country) M/W, volleyball M/W, weight lifting M/W.

Standardized Tests *Required for some:* SAT (for admission).

Costs (2010–11) *Tuition:* state resident $750 full-time, $25 per credit part-time; nonresident $7260 full-time, $242 per credit part-time. Full-time tuition and fees vary according to reciprocity agreements. Part-time tuition and fees vary according to reciprocity agreements. No tuition increase for student's term of enrollment. *Required fees:* $3636 full-time, $114 per credit part-time, $108 per term part-time. *Payment plan:* installment. *Waivers:* senior citizens and employees or children of employees.

Financial Aid Of all full-time matriculated undergraduates who enrolled in 2009, 124 Federal Work-Study jobs (averaging $2400).

Applying *Options:* electronic application. *Application fee:* $10. *Required:* high school transcript. *Required for some:* interview. *Application deadlines:* rolling (freshmen), rolling (transfers).

Freshman Application Contact Mr. Ray Blair, Springfield Technical Community College, Springfield, MA 01105. *Phone:* 413-781-7822 Ext. 4868. *E-mail:* rblair@stcc.edu. *Web site:* http://www.stcc.edu/.

Urban College of Boston

Boston, Massachusetts

Director of Admissions Dr. Henry J. Johnson, Director of Enrollment Services/Registrar, Urban College of Boston, 178 Tremont Street, Boston, MA 02111. *Phone:* 617-348-6353. *Web site:* http://www.urbancollegeofboston.org/.

MICHIGAN

Alpena Community College

Alpena, Michigan

- **State and locally supported** 2-year, founded 1952
- **Small-town** 700-acre campus
- **Endowment** $3.3 million
- **Coed**

Undergraduates Students come from 4 states and territories; 2% live on campus. *Retention:* 55% of full-time freshmen returned.
Faculty *Student/faculty ratio:* 17:1.
Academics *Calendar:* semesters. *Degree:* certificates and associate. *Special study options:* academic remediation for entering students, advanced placement credit, distance learning, double majors, internships, part-time degree program, services for LD students, summer session for credit.
Student Life *Campus security:* 24-hour emergency response devices.
Athletics Member NJCAA.
Costs (2010–11) *Tuition:* area resident $2760 full-time, $92 per contact hour part-time; state resident $4140 full-time, $138 per contact hour part-time; nonresident $4740 full-time, $184 per contact hour part-time. *Required fees:* $500 full-time, $16 per contact hour part-time. *Room and board:* room only: $3000.
Financial Aid Of all full-time matriculated undergraduates who enrolled in 2009, 80 Federal Work-Study jobs (averaging $1200). 20 state and other part-time jobs (averaging $800).
Applying *Options:* electronic application, early admission, deferred entrance. *Required:* high school transcript.
Freshman Application Contact Mr. Mike Kollien, Director of Admissions, Alpena Community College, 665 Johnson, Alpena, MI 49707. *Phone:* 989-358-7339. *Toll-free phone:* 888-468-6222. *Fax:* 989-358-7540. *E-mail:* kollienm@alpenacc.edu. *Web site:* http://www.alpenacc.edu/.

Bay de Noc Community College

Escanaba, Michigan

Freshman Application Contact Bay de Noc Community College, 2001 North Lincoln Road, Escanaba, MI 49829-2511. *Phone:* 906-786-5802 Ext. 1276. *Toll-free phone:* 800-221-2001 Ext. 1276. *Web site:* http://www.baydenoc.cc.mi.us/.

Bay Mills Community College

Brimley, Michigan

Freshman Application Contact Ms. Elaine Lehre, Admissions Officer, Bay Mills Community College, 12214 West Lakeshore Drive, Brimley, MI 49715. *Phone:* 906-248-3354. *Toll-free phone:* 800-844-BMCC. *Fax:* 906-248-3351. *Web site:* http://www.bmcc.edu/.

Delta College

University Center, Michigan

- **District-supported** 2-year, founded 1961
- **Rural** 640-acre campus
- **Endowment** $12.0 million
- **Coed**

Undergraduates 4,499 full-time, 6,400 part-time. Students come from 2 states and territories; 22 other countries; 4% transferred in.
Faculty *Student/faculty ratio:* 20:1.
Academics *Calendar:* semesters. *Degree:* certificates and associate. *Special study options:* academic remediation for entering students, adult/continuing education programs, advanced placement credit, cooperative education, distance learning, double majors, external degree program, freshman honors college, honors programs, independent study, internships, off-campus study, part-time degree program, services for LD students, student-designed majors, study abroad, summer session for credit.
Student Life *Campus security:* 24-hour emergency response devices and patrols, student patrols, late-night transport/escort service.
Athletics Member NJCAA.
Costs (2010–11) *Tuition:* area resident $1968 full-time, $82 per credit hour part-time; state resident $2976 full-time, $124 per credit hour part-time; nonresident $4320 full-time, $180 per credit hour part-time. Full-time tuition and fees vary according to course load. Part-time tuition and fees vary according to course load. *Required fees:* $360 full-time, $30 per term part-time.
Financial Aid Of all full-time matriculated undergraduates who enrolled in 2009, 115 Federal Work-Study jobs (averaging $2307). 67 state and other part-time jobs (averaging $2214).
Applying *Options:* electronic application, early admission, deferred entrance. *Application fee:* $20. *Required for some:* essay or personal statement. *Recommended:* high school transcript.
Freshman Application Contact Mr. Gary Brasseur, Associate Director of Admissions, Delta College, 1961 Delta Road, University Center, MI 48710. *Phone:* 989-686-9590. *Toll-free phone:* 800-285-1705. *Fax:* 989-667-2202. *E-mail:* admit@delta.edu. *Web site:* http://www.delta.edu/.

Glen Oaks Community College

Centreville, Michigan

Freshman Application Contact Ms. Beverly M. Andrews, Director of Admissions/Registrar, Glen Oaks Community College, 62249 Shimmel Road, Centreville, MI 49032-9719. *Phone:* 269-467-9945 Ext. 248. *Toll-free phone:* 888-994-7818. *Web site:* http://www.glenoaks.edu/.

Gogebic Community College

Ironwood, Michigan

Freshman Application Contact Ms. Jeanne Graham, Director of Admissions, Gogebic Community College, E4946 Jackson Road, Ironwood, MI 49938. *Phone:* 906-932-4231 Ext. 306. *Toll-free phone:* 800-682-5910 Ext. 207. *Fax:* 906-932-2339. *E-mail:* jeanneg@gogebic.edu. *Web site:* http://www.gogebic.edu/.

Grand Rapids Community College

Grand Rapids, Michigan

- **District-supported** 2-year, founded 1914, part of Michigan Department of Education
- **Urban** 35-acre campus
- **Coed,** 17,870 undergraduate students, 42% full-time, 52% women, 48% men

Undergraduates 7,584 full-time, 10,286 part-time. Students come from 8 states and territories; 24 other countries; 1% are from out of state; 13% Black or African American, non-Hispanic/Latino; 7% Hispanic/Latino; 3% Asian, non-Hispanic/Latino; 1% American Indian or Alaska Native, non-Hispanic/Latino; 3% Race/ethnicity unknown; 5% transferred in.
Freshmen *Admission:* 12,046 applied, 8,548 admitted, 3,871 enrolled. *Average high school GPA:* 2.52.
Faculty *Total:* 213, 100% full-time, 14% with terminal degrees. *Student/faculty ratio:* 52:1.
Majors Administrative assistant and secretarial science; architectural engineering technology; art; automobile/automotive mechanics technology; business administration and management; computer engineering technology; computer programming; computer science; corrections; criminal justice/law enforcement administration; criminal justice/police science; culinary arts; dental hygiene; drafting and design technology; electrical, electronic and communications engineering technology; fashion merchandising; forestry; geology/earth science; heating, air conditioning, ventilation and refrigeration maintenance technology; industrial technology; legal administrative assistant/secre-

tary; liberal arts and sciences/liberal studies; licensed practical/vocational nurse training; mass communication/media; medical administrative assistant and medical secretary; music; plastics and polymer engineering technology; quality control technology; registered nursing/registered nurse; welding technology.

Academics *Calendar:* semesters. *Degree:* certificates and associate. *Special study options:* academic remediation for entering students, adult/continuing education programs, advanced placement credit, cooperative education, distance learning, English as a second language, honors programs, independent study, off-campus study, part-time degree program, services for LD students, study abroad, summer session for credit.

Library Arthur Andrews Memorial Library plus 1 other with an OPAC, a Web page.

Student Life *Housing:* college housing not available. *Activities and Organizations:* drama/theater group, student-run newspaper, choral group, Student Congress, Phi Theta Kappa, Hispanic Student Organization, Asian Student Organization, Service Learning Advisory Board, national fraternities, national sororities. *Campus security:* 24-hour emergency response devices, late-night transport/escort service. *Student services:* personal/psychological counseling.

Athletics Member NJCAA. *Intercollegiate sports:* baseball M, basketball M(s)/W(s), football M(s), golf M(s), softball W(s), swimming and diving M(s)/W(s), tennis M(s)/W(s), track and field M(s), volleyball W(s), wrestling M(s). *Intramural sports:* badminton M/W, basketball M/W, skiing (cross-country) M/W, skiing (downhill) M/W, soccer M/W, swimming and diving M/W, tennis M/W, volleyball M/W.

Standardized Tests *Required for some:* ACT ASSET. *Recommended:* SAT or ACT (for admission).

Costs (2011–12) *Tuition:* area resident $2685 full-time, $90 per contact hour part-time; state resident $5880 full-time, $196 per contact hour part-time; non-resident $8790 full-time, $293 per contact hour part-time. Full-time tuition and fees vary according to course load. Part-time tuition and fees vary according to course load. *Required fees:* $240 full-time, $5 per contact hour part-time, $30 per term part-time. *Payment plan:* installment. *Waivers:* employees or children of employees.

Financial Aid Of all full-time matriculated undergraduates who enrolled in 2008, 6,142 applied for aid, 4,896 were judged to have need, 1,012 had their need fully met. In 2008, 96 non-need-based awards were made. *Average financial aid package:* $4850. *Average need-based loan:* $2764. *Average need-based gift aid:* $3984. *Average non-need-based aid:* $1051.

Applying *Options:* early admission, deferred entrance. *Application fee:* $20. *Required:* high school transcript. *Application deadline:* 8/30 (freshmen). *Notification:* continuous (freshmen), continuous (transfers).

Freshman Application Contact Ms. Diane Patrick, Director of Admissions, Grand Rapids Community College, Grand Rapids, MI 49503-3201. *Phone:* 616-234-4100. *Fax:* 616-234-4005. *E-mail:* dpatrick@grcc.edu. *Web site:* http://www.grcc.edu/.

Henry Ford Community College

Dearborn, Michigan

Freshman Application Contact Admissions Office, Henry Ford Community College, 5101 Evergreen Road, Dearborn, MI 48128-1495. *Phone:* 313-845-6403. *Toll-free phone:* 800-585-HFCC. *Fax:* 313-845-6464. *E-mail:* enroll@hfcc.edu. *Web site:* http://www.hfcc.edu/.

ITT Technical Institute

Canton, Michigan

- **Proprietary** primarily 2-year, founded 2002, part of ITT Educational Services, Inc.
- **Coed**

Majors Business administration and management; CAD/CADD drafting/design technology; communications technology; computer and information systems security; computer engineering technology; computer software and media applications related; computer software engineering; computer software technology; criminal justice/law enforcement administration; design and visual communications; electrical, electronic and communications engineering technology; game and interactive media design; legal assistant/paralegal; project management; registered nursing/registered nurse; system, networking, and LAN/WAN management; web/multimedia management and webmaster; web page, digital/multimedia and information resources design.

Academics *Calendar:* quarters. *Degrees:* associate and bachelor's.

Student Life *Housing:* college housing not available.

Freshman Application Contact Director of Recruitment, ITT Technical Institute, 1905 South Haggerty Road, Canton, MI 48188-2025. *Phone:* 784-397-7800. *Toll-free phone:* 800-247-4477. *Web site:* http://www.itt-tech.edu/.

ITT Technical Institute

Dearborn, Michigan

- **Proprietary** 2-year, part of ITT Educational Services, Inc.
- **Coed**

Majors CAD/CADD drafting/design technology; communications technology; computer and information systems security; computer engineering technology; criminal justice/law enforcement administration; electrical, electronic and communications engineering technology; legal assistant/paralegal; project management; system, networking, and LAN/WAN management.

Academics *Calendar:* quarters.

Freshman Application Contact Director of Recruitment, ITT Technical Institute, 19855 W. Outer Drive, Suite L10W, Dearborn, MI 48124. *Phone:* 313-278-5208. *Toll-free phone:* 800-605-0801. *Web site:* http://www.itt-tech.edu/.

ITT Technical Institute

Swartz Creek, Michigan

- **Proprietary** primarily 2-year, founded 2005, part of ITT Educational Services, Inc.
- **Coed**

Majors CAD/CADD drafting/design technology; communications technology; computer and information systems security; computer engineering technology; computer software and media applications related; computer software engineering; computer software technology; construction management; criminal justice/law enforcement administration; design and visual communications; electrical, electronic and communications engineering technology; game and interactive media design; information technology project management; legal assistant/paralegal; project management; system, networking, and LAN/WAN management; web/multimedia management and webmaster; web page, digital/multimedia and information resources design.

Academics *Calendar:* quarters. *Degrees:* associate and bachelor's.

Freshman Application Contact Director of Recruitment, ITT Technical Institute, 6359 Miller Road, Swartz Creek, MI 48473. *Phone:* 810-628-2500. *Toll-free phone:* 800-514-6564. *Web site:* http://www.itt-tech.edu/.

ITT Technical Institute

Troy, Michigan

- **Proprietary** primarily 2-year, founded 1987, part of ITT Educational Services, Inc.
- **Coed**

Majors Business administration and management; CAD/CADD drafting/design technology; communications technology; computer and information systems security; computer engineering technology; computer software and media applications related; computer software engineering; computer software technology; construction management; criminal justice/law enforcement administration; design and visual communications; electrical, electronic and communications engineering technology; game and interactive media design; legal assistant/paralegal; project management; system, networking, and LAN/WAN management; web/multimedia management and webmaster; web page, digital/multimedia and information resources design.

Academics *Calendar:* quarters. *Degrees:* associate and bachelor's.

Student Life *Housing:* college housing not available.

Freshman Application Contact Director of Recruitment, ITT Technical Institute, 1522 East Big Beaver Road, Troy, MI 48083-1905. *Phone:* 248-524-1800. *Toll-free phone:* 800-832-6817. *Fax:* 248-524-1965. *Web site:* http://www.itt-tech.edu/.

ITT Technical Institute

Wyoming, Michigan

- **Proprietary** primarily 2-year, part of ITT Educational Services, Inc.
- **Coed**

Majors Business administration and management; CAD/CADD drafting/design technology; communications technology; computer and information systems security; computer engineering technology; computer software and media applications related; computer software engineering; computer software technology; construction management; criminal justice/law enforcement administration; design and visual communications; electrical, electronic and communications engineering technology; game and interactive media design; information technology project management; legal assistant/paralegal; project management; system, networking, and LAN/WAN management; web/multimedia management and webmaster; web page, digital/multimedia and information resources design.

Academics *Calendar:* quarters. *Degrees:* associate and bachelor's.

Student Life *Housing:* college housing not available.

Freshman Application Contact Director of Recruitment, ITT Technical Institute, 1980 Metro Court SW, Wyoming, MI 49519. *Phone:* 616-406-1200. *Toll-free phone:* 800-632-4676. *Web site:* http://www.itt-tech.edu/.

Jackson Community College
Jackson, Michigan

- **County-supported** 2-year, founded 1928
- **Suburban** 580-acre campus with easy access to Detroit
- **Coed,** 7,870 undergraduate students, 46% full-time, 61% women, 39% men

Undergraduates 3,583 full-time, 4,287 part-time. 1% are from out of state; 8% Black or African American, non-Hispanic/Latino; 4% Hispanic/Latino; 0.7% Asian, non-Hispanic/Latino; 0.1% Native Hawaiian or other Pacific Islander, non-Hispanic/Latino; 0.8% American Indian or Alaska Native, non-Hispanic/Latino; 1% Two or more races, non-Hispanic/Latino; 5% Race/ethnicity unknown; 0.2% international; 2% live on campus. *Retention:* 56% of full-time freshmen returned.
Freshmen *Admission:* 1,695 enrolled.
Faculty *Total:* 457, 21% full-time. *Student/faculty ratio:* 23:1.
Majors Accounting and finance; administrative assistant and secretarial science; airline pilot and flight crew; automobile/automotive mechanics technology; business administration and management; computer and information sciences and support services related; construction trades related; corrections; criminal justice/law enforcement administration; data processing and data processing technology; diagnostic medical sonography and ultrasound technology; early childhood education; electrical, electronic and communications engineering technology; emergency medical technology (EMT paramedic); executive assistant/executive secretary; general studies; graphic design; heating, ventilation, air conditioning and refrigeration engineering technology; liberal arts and sciences/liberal studies; licensed practical/vocational nurse training; marketing/marketing management; medical/clinical assistant; medical insurance/medical billing; medical radiologic technology; medical transcription; registered nursing/registered nurse.
Academics *Calendar:* semesters. *Degree:* certificates and associate. *Special study options:* academic remediation for entering students, accelerated degree program, adult/continuing education programs, advanced placement credit, cooperative education, distance learning, English as a second language, external degree program, independent study, internships, part-time degree program, services for LD students, summer session for credit. *ROTC:* Army (c).
Library Atkinson Learning Resources Center plus 1 other with an OPAC, a Web page.
Student Life *Housing Options:* coed. Campus housing is university owned. *Activities and Organizations:* drama/theater group, choral group. *Campus security:* 24-hour emergency response devices and patrols, student patrols, late-night transport/escort service, controlled dormitory access. *Student services:* personal/psychological counseling.
Athletics Member NJCAA. *Intercollegiate sports:* baseball M(s), basketball M(s)/W(s), cross-country running M(s)/W(s), golf M(s)/W(s), ice hockey M(c), soccer M(s)/W(s), softball W(s), volleyball W(s).
Costs (2010–11) *Tuition:* area resident $2280 full-time, $95 per contact hour part-time; state resident $3216 full-time, $134 per contact hour part-time; nonresident $4584 full-time, $191 per contact hour part-time. Full-time tuition and fees vary according to course load. Part-time tuition and fees vary according to course load. *Required fees:* $840 full-time, $30 per contact hour part-time. *Room and board:* room only: $5940. *Payment plan:* deferred payment. *Waivers:* senior citizens and employees or children of employees.
Applying *Options:* electronic application, early admission. *Application deadlines:* rolling (freshmen), rolling (transfers). *Notification:* continuous (freshmen), continuous (transfers).
Freshman Application Contact Ms. Julie Hand, Assistant Dean of Enrollment Services, Jackson Community College, 2111 Emmons Road, Jackson, MI 49201. *Phone:* 517-796-8425. *Toll-free phone:* 888-522-7344. *Fax:* 517-796-8631. *E-mail:* admissions@jccmi.edu. *Web site:* http://www.jccmi.edu/.

Kalamazoo Valley Community College
Kalamazoo, Michigan

- **State and locally supported** 2-year, founded 1966
- **Suburban** 187-acre campus
- **Coed**

Undergraduates 1% are from out of state.
Academics *Calendar:* semesters. *Degree:* certificates and associate. *Special study options:* academic remediation for entering students, advanced placement credit, cooperative education, distance learning, English as a second language, honors programs, independent study, internships, off-campus study, part-time degree program, services for LD students, student-designed majors, summer session for credit. *ROTC:* Army (c).

Student Life *Campus security:* 24-hour emergency response devices and patrols.
Athletics Member NJCAA.
Standardized Tests *Required:* ACT (for admission).
Costs (2010–11) *Tuition:* area resident $1836 full-time, $77 per credit hour part-time; state resident $3024 full-time, $126 per credit hour part-time; nonresident $4080 full-time, $170 per credit hour part-time.
Financial Aid Of all full-time matriculated undergraduates who enrolled in 2008, 65 Federal Work-Study jobs (averaging $2552).
Applying *Required:* high school transcript.
Freshman Application Contact Kalamazoo Valley Community College, PO Box 4070, Kalamazoo, MI 49003-4070. *Phone:* 269-488-4207. *Web site:* http://www.kvcc.edu/.

Kellogg Community College
Battle Creek, Michigan

- **State and locally supported** 2-year, founded 1956, part of Michigan Department of Education
- **Urban** 120-acre campus
- **Coed**

Undergraduates 2,053 full-time, 3,923 part-time.
Faculty *Student/faculty ratio:* 23:1.
Academics *Calendar:* semesters. *Degree:* certificates and associate. *Special study options:* academic remediation for entering students, accelerated degree program, adult/continuing education programs, advanced placement credit, cooperative education, distance learning, double majors, English as a second language, freshman honors college, honors programs, independent study, internships, off-campus study, part-time degree program, services for LD students, summer session for credit.
Student Life *Campus security:* 24-hour emergency response devices and patrols, late-night transport/escort service.
Athletics Member NJCAA.
Standardized Tests *Required for some:* ACT (for admission), SAT or ACT (for admission).
Costs (2010–11) *Tuition:* area resident $2295 full-time, $77 per credit hour part-time; state resident $3720 full-time, $124 per credit hour part-time; nonresident $5325 full-time, $178 per credit hour part-time. *Required fees:* $210 full-time, $7 per credit hour part-time.
Financial Aid Of all full-time matriculated undergraduates who enrolled in 2009, 41 Federal Work-Study jobs (averaging $2251). 43 state and other part-time jobs (averaging $2058).
Applying *Options:* electronic application, early admission. *Required for some:* high school transcript, minimum 2.0 GPA.
Freshman Application Contact Ms. Denise Newman, Director of Enrollment Services, Kellogg Community College, 450 North Avenue, Battle Creek, MI 49017. *Phone:* 269-965-3931 Ext. 2620. *Fax:* 269-965-4133. *E-mail:* harriss@kellogg.edu. *Web site:* http://www.kellogg.edu/.

Keweenaw Bay Ojibwa Community College
Baraga, Michigan

Freshman Application Contact Megan Shanahan, Admissions Officer, Keweenaw Bay Ojibwa Community College, 111 Beartown Road, Baraga, MI 49908. *Phone:* 909-353-4600. *E-mail:* megan@kbocc.org. *Web site:* http://www.kbocc.org/.

Kirtland Community College
Roscommon, Michigan

- **District-supported** 2-year, founded 1966, part of Michigan Department of Energy, Labor and Economic Growth - Community Colleges Service Unit
- **Rural** 180-acre campus
- **Coed,** 1,958 undergraduate students, 47% full-time, 61% women, 39% men

Undergraduates 913 full-time, 1,045 part-time. Students come from 4 states and territories; 1 other country; 1% Black or African American, non-Hispanic/Latino; 0.9% Hispanic/Latino; 0.4% Asian, non-Hispanic/Latino; 0.2% Native Hawaiian or other Pacific Islander, non-Hispanic/Latino; 1% American Indian or Alaska Native, non-Hispanic/Latino; 2% Race/ethnicity unknown; 0.2% international.
Freshmen *Admission:* 1,176 applied, 1,176 admitted, 275 enrolled. *Test scores:* ACT scores over 18: 66%; ACT scores over 24: 6%; ACT scores over 30: 1%.
Faculty *Total:* 142, 27% full-time. *Student/faculty ratio:* 19:1.

Majors Administrative assistant and secretarial science; art; automobile/automotive mechanics technology; biological and physical sciences; business administration and management; cardiovascular technology; carpentry; computer systems analysis; corrections; cosmetology; creative writing; criminal justice/law enforcement administration; drafting and design technology; education (multiple levels); electrical, electronic and communications engineering technology; fire services administration; general studies; graphic design; heating, air conditioning, ventilation and refrigeration maintenance technology; industrial and product design; industrial technology; information science/studies; legal administrative assistant/secretary; liberal arts and sciences/liberal studies; licensed practical/vocational nurse training; management information systems; medical administrative assistant and medical secretary; nail technician and manicurist; registered nursing/registered nurse; small engine mechanics and repair technology; surgical technology; teacher assistant/aide; web/multimedia management and webmaster; welding technology.

Academics *Calendar:* semesters. *Degree:* certificates and associate. *Special study options:* academic remediation for entering students, adult/continuing education programs, advanced placement credit, cooperative education, distance learning, English as a second language, honors programs, independent study, internships, part-time degree program, summer session for credit.

Library Kirtland Community College Library with 35,000 titles, 347 serial subscriptions, an OPAC.

Student Life *Housing:* college housing not available. *Activities and Organizations:* student-run newspaper. *Campus security:* student patrols, late-night transport/escort service, campus warning siren, uniformed armed police officers. *Student services:* personal/psychological counseling.

Athletics Member NJCAA. *Intercollegiate sports:* basketball M(s)/W(s), cross-country running M(s)/W(s), golf M(s)/W(s).

Standardized Tests *Recommended:* ACT (for admission).

Costs (2011–12) *Tuition:* area resident $2445 full-time; state resident $4470 full-time; nonresident $5520 full-time. *Required fees:* $270 full-time. *Payment plan:* installment. *Waivers:* minority students, senior citizens, and employees or children of employees.

Financial Aid Of all full-time matriculated undergraduates who enrolled in 2009, 50 Federal Work-Study jobs (averaging $1253). 28 state and other part-time jobs (averaging $1647).

Applying *Options:* electronic application. *Application deadlines:* rolling (freshmen), rolling (transfers). *Notification:* continuous until 8/22 (freshmen), continuous until 8/22 (transfers).

Freshman Application Contact Ms. Michelle Vyskocil, Dean of Student Services, Kirtland Community College, 10775 North Saint Helen Road, Roscommon, MI 48653. *Phone:* 989-275-5000 Ext. 248. *Fax:* 989-275-6789. *E-mail:* registrar@kirtland.edu. *Web site:* http://www.kirtland.edu/.

Lake Michigan College
Benton Harbor, Michigan

- **District-supported** 2-year, founded 1946, part of Michigan Department of Education
- **Small-town** 260-acre campus
- **Endowment** $8.1 million
- **Coed,** 4,832 undergraduate students, 37% full-time, 59% women, 41% men

Undergraduates 1,792 full-time, 3,040 part-time. Students come from 6 states and territories; 47 other countries; 2% are from out of state; 6% transferred in. *Retention:* 56% of full-time freshmen returned.

Freshmen *Admission:* 1,768 applied, 1,693 admitted, 813 enrolled. *Average high school GPA:* 2.79.

Faculty *Total:* 329, 17% full-time, 9% with terminal degrees. *Student/faculty ratio:* 19:1.

Majors Accounting; administrative assistant and secretarial science; applied horticulture/horticulture operations; art; athletic training; biology/biological sciences; business administration and management; chemistry; computer and information sciences; corrections; criminal justice/law enforcement administration; dental assisting; drafting and design technology; dramatic/theater arts; early childhood education; elementary education; emergency medical technology (EMT paramedic); English; environmental science; foreign languages and literatures; general studies; geography; geology/earth science; graphic design; health and physical education/fitness; history; hospitality administration; humanities; industrial technology; landscaping and groundskeeping; legal administrative assistant/secretary; liberal arts and sciences/liberal studies; machine tool technology; manufacturing engineering; marketing/marketing management; mass communication/media; mathematics; medical administrative assistant and medical secretary; medical radiologic technology; mortuary science and embalming; music; nuclear/nuclear power technology; philosophy; physical sciences; physical therapy; physician assistant; physics; political science and government; precision production related; pre-dentistry studies; pre-engineering; pre-law studies; premedical studies; pre-pharmacy studies; pre-veterinary studies; psychology; radiologic technology/science; registered nursing/registered nurse; secondary education; social work; sociology; turf and turfgrass management; viticulture and enology.

Academics *Calendar:* semesters. *Degree:* certificates and associate. *Special study options:* academic remediation for entering students, adult/continuing education programs, cooperative education, distance learning, English as a second language, honors programs, independent study, part-time degree program, services for LD students, student-designed majors, summer session for credit.

Library William Hessel Library with 93,587 titles, 16,865 serial subscriptions, 3,651 audiovisual materials, an OPAC, a Web page.

Student Life *Housing:* college housing not available. *Activities and Organizations:* drama/theater group, choral group, Soccer Club, Phi Theta Kappa, Gamers Guild, Student Nursing Association, Movie Club. *Campus security:* 24-hour emergency response devices, contracted campus security force.

Athletics Member NJCAA. *Intercollegiate sports:* baseball M(s), basketball M(s)/W(s), softball W(s), volleyball W(s).

Costs (2011–12) *Tuition:* area resident $2310 full-time, $77 per contact hour part-time; state resident $3420 full-time, $114 per contact hour part-time; nonresident $4470 full-time, $149 per contact hour part-time. *Required fees:* $960 full-time, $32 per contact hour part-time. *Payment plan:* installment. *Waivers:* senior citizens and employees or children of employees.

Applying *Options:* electronic application. *Required:* high school transcript. *Required for some:* interview. *Application deadlines:* rolling (freshmen), rolling (transfers). *Notification:* continuous (freshmen), continuous (transfers).

Freshman Application Contact Mr. Louis Thomas, Lead Admissions Specialist, Lake Michigan College, 2755 East Napier Avenue, Benton Harbor, MI 49022-1899. *Phone:* 269-927-6584. *Toll-free phone:* 800-252-1LMC. *Fax:* 269-927-6718. *E-mail:* thomas@lakemichigancollege.edu. *Web site:* http://www.lakemichigancollege.edu/.

Lansing Community College
Lansing, Michigan

- **State and locally supported** 2-year, founded 1957, part of Michigan Department of Education
- **Urban** 28-acre campus
- **Endowment** $5.2 million
- **Coed**

Undergraduates 7,815 full-time, 13,308 part-time. Students come from 18 states and territories; 27 other countries; 1% are from out of state.

Faculty *Student/faculty ratio:* 14:1.

Academics *Calendar:* semesters. *Degrees:* certificates, associate, and post-bachelor's certificates. *Special study options:* academic remediation for entering students, adult/continuing education programs, advanced placement credit, cooperative education, distance learning, double majors, English as a second language, external degree program, honors programs, independent study, internships, part-time degree program, services for LD students, study abroad, summer session for credit. *ROTC:* Army (c), Air Force (c).

Student Life *Campus security:* 24-hour emergency response devices and patrols, student patrols, late-night transport/escort service.

Athletics Member NJCAA.

Costs (2010–11) *Tuition:* area resident $2280 full-time, $76 per credit hour part-time; state resident $4200 full-time, $140 per credit hour part-time; nonresident $6300 full-time, $210 per credit hour part-time. *Required fees:* $50 full-time, $25 per term part-time.

Financial Aid Of all full-time matriculated undergraduates who enrolled in 2009, 125 Federal Work-Study jobs (averaging $2636). 122 state and other part-time jobs (averaging $2563).

Applying *Options:* electronic application, early admission, deferred entrance. *Required for some:* essay or personal statement, high school transcript, 2 letters of recommendation, interview.

Freshman Application Contact Ms. Tammy Grossbauer, Director of Admissions/Registrar, Lansing Community College, PO Box 40010, Lansing, MI 48901-7210. *Phone:* 517-483-9886. *Toll-free phone:* 800-644-4LCC. *Fax:* 517-483-1170. *E-mail:* grossbt@lcc.edu. *Web site:* http://www.lcc.edu/.

Macomb Community College
Warren, Michigan

- **District-supported** 2-year, founded 1954, part of Michigan Public Community College System
- **Suburban** 384-acre campus with easy access to Detroit
- **Endowment** $12.3 million
- **Coed,** 24,468 undergraduate students, 39% full-time, 51% women, 49% men

Undergraduates 9,583 full-time, 14,885 part-time. Students come from 5 states and territories. *Retention:* 70% of full-time freshmen returned.

Freshmen *Admission:* 1,412 enrolled.

Faculty *Total:* 1,148, 19% full-time, 9% with terminal degrees. *Student/faculty ratio:* 24:1.

Majors Accounting; administrative assistant and secretarial science; agriculture; architectural drafting and CAD/CADD; automobile/automotive mechanics technology; automotive engineering technology; biology/biological sciences; business administration and management; business automation/technology/data entry; business/commerce; cabinetmaking and millwork; chemistry; child-care and support services management; civil engineering technology; commercial and advertising art; computer programming; computer programming (specific applications); construction engineering technology; criminal justice/law enforcement administration; criminal justice/police science; culinary arts; drafting and design technology; drafting/design engineering technologies related; electrical, electronic and communications engineering technology; electrical/electronics equipment installation and repair; electromechanical technology; emergency medical technology (EMT paramedic); energy management and systems technology; engineering related; finance; fire prevention and safety technology; forensic science and technology; general studies; graphic and printing equipment operation/production; heating, air conditioning, ventilation and refrigeration maintenance technology; heating, ventilation, air conditioning and refrigeration engineering technology; industrial mechanics and maintenance technology; industrial technology; international/global studies; legal assistant/paralegal; legal studies; liberal arts and sciences/liberal studies; machine tool technology; manufacturing engineering technology; marketing/marketing management; mathematics; mechanical drafting and CAD/CADD; mechanical engineering/mechanical technology; mechanic and repair technologies related; medical/clinical assistant; mental health counseling; metallurgical technology; music performance; occupational therapist assistant; operations management; physical therapy technology; plastics and polymer engineering technology; plumbing technology; pre-engineering; quality control and safety technologies related; quality control technology; registered nursing/registered nurse; respiratory care therapy; robotics technology; sheet metal technology; social psychology; speech communication and rhetoric; surgical technology; surveying technology; tool and die technology; veterinary/animal health technology; welding technology.

Academics *Calendar:* semesters. *Degree:* certificates and associate. *Special study options:* academic remediation for entering students, adult/continuing education programs, advanced placement credit, cooperative education, English as a second language, honors programs, internships, off-campus study, part-time degree program, services for LD students, student-designed majors, summer session for credit.

Library Library of South Campus, Library of Center Campus with 159,226 titles, 4,240 serial subscriptions, an OPAC.

Student Life *Housing:* college housing not available. *Activities and Organizations:* drama/theater group, Phi Beta Kappa, Adventure Unlimited, Alpha Rho Rho, SADD. *Campus security:* 24-hour emergency response devices and patrols, late-night transport/escort service, security phones in parking lots, surveillance cameras. *Student services:* health clinic, personal/psychological counseling.

Athletics Member NJCAA. *Intercollegiate sports:* baseball M(s), basketball M(s), cross-country running M(s)/W(s), soccer M(s), softball W(s), track and field M(s)/W(s), volleyball W(s). *Intramural sports:* baseball M, basketball M, bowling M/W, cross-country running M/W, football M/W, skiing (cross-country) M/W, skiing (downhill) M/W, volleyball M/W.

Costs (2010–11) *Tuition:* area resident $2480 full-time, $80 per credit hour part-time; state resident $3782 full-time, $122 per credit hour part-time; nonresident $4929 full-time, $159 per credit hour part-time. Full-time tuition and fees vary according to course load. Part-time tuition and fees vary according to course load. *Required fees:* $100 full-time, $50 per term part-time. *Waivers:* senior citizens and employees or children of employees.

Applying *Options:* early admission, deferred entrance. *Application deadlines:* rolling (freshmen), rolling (transfers).

Freshman Application Contact Mr. Brian Bouwman, Coordinator of Admissions and Transfer Credit, Macomb Community College, G312, 14500 East 12 Mile Road, Warren, MI 48088-3896. *Phone:* 586-445-7246. *Toll-free phone:* 866-622-6624. *Fax:* 586-445-7140. *E-mail:* stevensr@macomb.edu. *Web site:* http://www.macomb.edu/.

Mid Michigan Community College

Harrison, Michigan

Freshman Application Contact Tena Diamond, Admissions Specialist, Mid Michigan Community College, 1375 South Clare Avenue, Harrison, MI 48625-9447. *Phone:* 989-386-6661. *E-mail:* apply@midmich.edu. *Web site:* http://www.midmich.edu/.

Monroe County Community College

Monroe, Michigan

- **County-supported** 2-year, founded 1964, part of Michigan Department of Education
- **Small-town** 150-acre campus with easy access to Detroit and Toledo
- **Coed,** 4,433 undergraduate students, 39% full-time, 59% women, 41% men

Undergraduates 1,712 full-time, 2,721 part-time. Students come from 1 other country; 4% are from out of state; 5% transferred in.
Freshmen *Admission:* 1,700 applied, 1,698 admitted, 769 enrolled. *Average high school GPA:* 2.5.
Faculty *Total:* 201, 27% full-time.
Majors Accounting; administrative assistant and secretarial science; architectural engineering technology; art; biology/biological sciences; business administration and management; child development; clinical laboratory science/medical technology; computer and information sciences related; computer engineering technology; computer graphics; computer programming (specific applications); criminal justice/police science; criminal justice/safety; culinary arts; data processing and data processing technology; drafting and design technology; electrical, electronic and communications engineering technology; elementary education; English; finance; funeral service and mortuary science; industrial technology; information technology; journalism; legal administrative assistant/secretary; liberal arts and sciences/liberal studies; marketing/marketing management; mass communication/media; mathematics; medical administrative assistant and medical secretary; physical therapy; pre-engineering; psychology; registered nursing/registered nurse; respiratory care therapy; rhetoric and composition; social work; web/multimedia management and webmaster; web page, digital/multimedia and information resources design; welding technology; word processing.

Academics *Calendar:* semesters. *Degree:* certificates and associate. *Special study options:* academic remediation for entering students, advanced placement credit, independent study, part-time degree program, services for LD students, summer session for credit.

Library Campbell Learning Resource Center with 47,352 titles, 321 serial subscriptions, an OPAC.

Student Life *Housing:* college housing not available. *Activities and Organizations:* drama/theater group, student-run newspaper, choral group, student government, Society of Auto Engineers, Oasis, Nursing Students Organization. *Campus security:* police patrols during open hours.

Athletics *Intramural sports:* soccer M/W, volleyball M/W.

Standardized Tests *Required:* ACT ASSET, ACT COMPASS (for admission). *Required for some:* ACT (for admission). *Recommended:* ACT (for admission).

Costs (2010–11) *Tuition:* area resident $1728 full-time, $72 per contact hour part-time; state resident $2976 full-time, $124 per contact hour part-time; nonresident $3312 full-time, $138 per contact hour part-time. *Required fees:* $62 full-time, $6 per contact hour part-time, $25 per term part-time. *Payment plan:* installment. *Waivers:* senior citizens and employees or children of employees.

Applying *Options:* early admission, deferred entrance. *Application fee:* $25. *Required:* high school transcript. *Application deadline:* rolling (transfers). *Notification:* continuous (freshmen), continuous (transfers).

Freshman Application Contact Mr. Mark V. Hall, Director of Admissions and Guidance Services, Monroe County Community College, 1555 South Raisinville Road, Monroe, MI 48161. *Phone:* 734-384-4261. *Toll-free phone:* 877-YES MCCC. *Fax:* 734-242-9711. *E-mail:* mhall@monroeccc.edu. *Web site:* http://www.monroeccc.edu/.

Montcalm Community College

Sidney, Michigan

- **State and locally supported** 2-year, founded 1965, part of Michigan Department of Education
- **Rural** 240-acre campus with easy access to Grand Rapids
- **Endowment** $3.9 million
- **Coed,** 2,117 undergraduate students, 40% full-time, 66% women, 34% men

Undergraduates 855 full-time, 1,262 part-time. 0.6% Black or African American, non-Hispanic/Latino; 0.5% American Indian or Alaska Native, non-Hispanic/Latino; 2% Two or more races, non-Hispanic/Latino; 7% Race/ethnicity unknown; 0.3% international.
Freshmen *Admission:* 869 applied, 869 admitted. *Average high school GPA:* 2.28. *Test scores:* ACT scores over 18: 74%; ACT scores over 24: 15%.
Faculty *Total:* 179, 19% full-time, 7% with terminal degrees. *Student/faculty ratio:* 21:1.
Majors Accounting; administrative assistant and secretarial science; automobile/automotive mechanics technology; business administration and management; child-care and support services management; child-care provision; computer installation and repair technology; corrections; cosmetology; crimi-

nal justice/law enforcement administration; data processing and data processing technology; drafting and design technology; electrical, electronic and communications engineering technology; emergency medical technology (EMT paramedic); entrepreneurship; general studies; industrial engineering; industrial technology; liberal arts and sciences/liberal studies; medical administrative assistant and medical secretary; registered nursing/registered nurse; teacher assistant/aide; welding technology.

Academics *Calendar:* semesters. *Degree:* certificates and associate. *Special study options:* academic remediation for entering students, adult/continuing education programs, advanced placement credit, cooperative education, distance learning, double majors, independent study, internships, off-campus study, part-time degree program, services for LD students, study abroad, summer session for credit.

Library Montcalm Community College Library with 29,848 titles, 3,670 serial subscriptions, an OPAC, a Web page.

Student Life *Housing:* college housing not available. *Activities and Organizations:* drama/theater group, student-run newspaper, choral group, Nursing Club, Native American Club, Phi Theta Kappa, Business Club, Judo Club. *Student services:* personal/psychological counseling.

Athletics *Intramural sports:* volleyball M/W.

Costs (2010–11) *Tuition:* area resident $2370 full-time; state resident $4380 full-time; nonresident $6510 full-time. Full-time tuition and fees vary according to course load. Part-time tuition and fees vary according to course load. *Required fees:* $270 full-time. *Payment plan:* installment. *Waivers:* senior citizens and employees or children of employees.

Financial Aid Of all full-time matriculated undergraduates who enrolled in 2009, 57 Federal Work-Study jobs (averaging $2000).

Applying *Options:* electronic application, early admission, deferred entrance. *Recommended:* high school transcript. *Application deadlines:* rolling (freshmen), rolling (transfers). *Notification:* continuous (freshmen), continuous (transfers).

Freshman Application Contact Ms. Debra Alexander, Associate Dean of Student Services, Montcalm Community College, 2800 College Drive, SW, Sidney, MI 48885. *Phone:* 989-328-1276. *Toll-free phone:* 877-328-2111. *E-mail:* admissions@montcalm.edu. *Web site:* http://www.montcalm.edu/.

Mott Community College
Flint, Michigan

Freshman Application Contact Ms. Delores Deen, Executive Dean of Student Services, Mott Community College, 1401 East Court Street, Flint, MI 48503. *Phone:* 810-762-0315. *Toll-free phone:* 800-852-8614. *Fax:* 810-232-9442. *Web site:* http://www.mcc.edu/.

Muskegon Community College
Muskegon, Michigan

- **State and locally supported** 2-year, founded 1926, part of Michigan Department of Education
- **Small-town** 112-acre campus with easy access to Grand Rapids
- **Coed,** 5,311 undergraduate students, 49% full-time, 52% women, 48% men

Undergraduates 2,601 full-time, 2,710 part-time.

Freshmen *Admission:* 3,834 applied, 1,571 admitted, 773 enrolled.

Faculty *Total:* 218, 45% full-time. *Student/faculty ratio:* 20:1.

Majors Accounting; administrative assistant and secretarial science; advertising; anthropology; applied mathematics; art; art history, criticism and conservation; art teacher education; automobile/automotive mechanics technology; biology/biotechnology laboratory technician; biomedical technology; business administration and management; business machine repair; chemical engineering; child development; commercial and advertising art; criminal justice/law enforcement administration; data processing and data processing technology; design and applied arts related; developmental and child psychology; drafting and design technology; economics; education; electrical, electronic and communications engineering technology; electromechanical technology; elementary education; engineering technology; finance; hospitality administration; hospitality and recreation marketing; hotel/motel administration; industrial technology; information science/studies; legal administrative assistant/secretary; liberal arts and sciences/liberal studies; machine tool technology; marketing/marketing management; medical administrative assistant and medical secretary; parks, recreation and leisure; registered nursing/registered nurse; special products marketing; transportation and materials moving related; welding technology.

Academics *Calendar:* semesters. *Degree:* associate. *Special study options:* academic remediation for entering students, adult/continuing education programs, cooperative education, honors programs, part-time degree program, student-designed majors, summer session for credit.

Library Hendrik Meijer and Technology Center with 48,597 titles, 450 serial subscriptions.

Student Life *Housing:* college housing not available. *Activities and Organizations:* drama/theater group, student-run newspaper, choral group, Respiratory Therapy, Hispanic Student Organization, Black Student Alliance, International Club, Rotaract. *Campus security:* 24-hour emergency response devices, on-campus security officer. *Student services:* personal/psychological counseling.

Athletics Member NJCAA. *Intercollegiate sports:* baseball M, basketball M(s)/W(s), golf M/W, softball W, tennis M/W, volleyball W(s), wrestling M. *Intramural sports:* basketball M/W, skiing (downhill) M(c)/W(c).

Costs (2011–12) *Tuition:* area resident $2310 full-time, $77 per credit part-time; state resident $4050 full-time, $135 per credit part-time; nonresident $5550 full-time, $185 per credit part-time. *Payment plan:* deferred payment.

Financial Aid Of all full-time matriculated undergraduates who enrolled in 2009, 250 Federal Work-Study jobs (averaging $2500). 50 state and other part-time jobs (averaging $2500).

Applying *Options:* electronic application, early admission, deferred entrance. *Required:* high school transcript. *Application deadlines:* rolling (freshmen), rolling (transfers). *Notification:* continuous (freshmen), continuous (transfers).

Freshman Application Contact Ms. Darlene Peklar, Enrollment Generalist, Muskegon Community College, 221 South Quarterline Road, Muskegon, MI 49442-1493. *Phone:* 231-777-0366. *E-mail:* Dalene.Peklar@muskegoncc.edu. *Web site:* http://www.muskegoncc.edu/.

North Central Michigan College
Petoskey, Michigan

Director of Admissions Ms. Julieanne Tobin, Director of Enrollment Management, North Central Michigan College, 1515 Howard Street, Petoskey, MI 49770-8717. *Phone:* 231-439-6511. *Toll-free phone:* 888-298-6605. *E-mail:* jtobin@ncmich.edu. *Web site:* http://www.ncmich.edu/.

Northwestern Michigan College
Traverse City, Michigan

Freshman Application Contact Mr. James Bensley, Coordinator of Admissions, Northwestern Michigan College, 1701 East Front Street, Traverse City, MI 49686-3061. *Phone:* 231-995-1034. *Toll-free phone:* 800-748-0566. *Fax:* 616-955-1339. *E-mail:* welcome@nmc.edu. *Web site:* http://www.nmc.edu/.

Oakland Community College
Bloomfield Hills, Michigan

- **State and locally supported** 2-year, founded 1964
- **Suburban** 540-acre campus with easy access to Detroit
- **Endowment** $998,105
- **Coed,** 28,939 undergraduate students, 35% full-time, 56% women, 44% men

Undergraduates 10,183 full-time, 18,756 part-time. Students come from 8 states and territories; 51 other countries; 0.1% are from out of state; 16% Black or African American, non-Hispanic/Latino; 2% Hispanic/Latino; 2% Asian, non-Hispanic/Latino; 0.4% American Indian or Alaska Native, non-Hispanic/Latino; 0.1% Two or more races, non-Hispanic/Latino; 31% Race/ethnicity unknown; 5% international. *Retention:* 49% of full-time freshmen returned.

Freshmen *Admission:* 9,660 applied, 9,660 admitted, 3,428 enrolled.

Faculty *Total:* 1,264, 20% full-time. *Student/faculty ratio:* 28:1.

Majors Accounting and business/management; accounting technology and bookkeeping; architectural engineering technology; business administration and management; business automation/technology/data entry; carpentry; ceramic arts and ceramics; child-care and support services management; community health services counseling; computer and information sciences and support services related; computer and information systems security; computer hardware technology; computer/information technology services administration related; computer programming; computer systems analysis; computer technology/computer systems technology; construction management; corrections; cosmetology; court reporting; criminalistics and criminal science; criminal justice/police science; culinary arts; data processing and data processing technology; dental hygiene; diagnostic medical sonography and ultrasound technology; drafting and design technology; dramatic/theater arts; electrical, electronic and communications engineering technology; electrician; electromechanical technology; emergency medical technology (EMT paramedic); engineering; entrepreneurship; fire science/firefighting; general studies; graphic design; health/health-care administration; health professions related; heating, ventilation, air conditioning and refrigeration engineering technology; histologic technology/histotechnologist; hotel/motel administration; industrial technology; information technology; interior design; international business/trade/commerce; kinesiology and exercise science; landscape architecture; landscaping and groundskeeping; legal assistant/paralegal; liberal arts and sciences/liberal studies; library and archives assisting; machine tool technology; manufacturing engineering technology; massage therapy; mechanical drafting and CAD/CADD; mechanics and repair; medical/clinical assistant; medical radiologic technology; medical transcription; medium/heavy vehicle and truck technology; music performance; music theory and composition; nuclear medical technology; occupational therapist assistant; pharmacy technician; photographic and film/video technology; photography; pipefitting and sprinkler fitting; precision metal working related; radio and television broadcasting technology; registered nursing/registered nurse; respiratory care therapy; restaurant/food services management; robotics technology; salon/beauty salon management; sheet metal technology; sign language interpretation and translation; surgical technology; tool and die technology; veterinary/animal health technology; voice and opera; welding technology; woodworking related.

Academics *Calendar:* semesters. *Degree:* certificates and associate. *Special study options:* academic remediation for entering students, adult/continuing education programs, advanced placement credit, cooperative education, distance learning, English as a second language, internships, off-campus study, part-time degree program, services for LD students, study abroad, summer session for credit.

Library Main Library plus 5 others with 229,160 titles, 1,209 serial subscriptions, 7,196 audiovisual materials, an OPAC, a Web page.

Student Life *Housing:* college housing not available. *Activities and Organizations:* drama/theater group, choral group, Phi Theta Kappa, International Student Organization, organizations related to student majors, Gamers, student government. *Campus security:* 24-hour emergency response devices, late-night transport/escort service. *Student services:* personal/psychological counseling, women's center.

Athletics Member NJCAA. *Intercollegiate sports:* basketball M(s)/W(s), cross-country running M(s)/W(s), golf M(s), soccer M(c), softball W(s), tennis W(s), track and field M(s)(c)/W(s)(c), volleyball W(s).

Costs (2010–11) *Tuition:* area resident $2001 full-time, $67 per credit hour part-time; state resident $3387 full-time, $113 per credit hour part-time; nonresident $4752 full-time, $158 per credit hour part-time. Full-time tuition and fees vary according to course load. Part-time tuition and fees vary according to course load. *Required fees:* $70 full-time, $35 per term part-time. *Waivers:* senior citizens and employees or children of employees.

Financial Aid Of all full-time matriculated undergraduates who enrolled in 2009, 3,844 applied for aid, 3,294 were judged to have need, 67 had their need fully met. 202 Federal Work-Study jobs (averaging $4190). In 2009, 30 non-need-based awards were made. *Average percent of need met:* 44%. *Average financial aid package:* $4467. *Average need-based loan:* $1576. *Average need-based gift aid:* $4685. *Average non-need-based aid:* $1330.

Applying *Options:* electronic application, deferred entrance. *Recommended:* high school transcript, interview. *Application deadlines:* rolling (freshmen), rolling (transfers). *Notification:* continuous (freshmen), continuous (transfers).

Freshman Application Contact Dr. Maurice McCall, Registrar and Director of Enrollment Services, Oakland Community College, 2480 Opdyke Road, Bloomfield Hills, MI 48304-2266. *Phone:* 248-341-2186. *Fax:* 248-341-2099. *E-mail:* mhmccall@oaklandcc.edu. *Web site:* http://www.oaklandcc.edu/.

Saginaw Chippewa Tribal College

Mount Pleasant, Michigan

Freshman Application Contact Ms. Tracy Reed, Admissions Officer/Registrar/Financial Aid, Saginaw Chippewa Tribal College, 2274 Enterprise Drive, Mount Pleasant, MI 48858. *Phone:* 989-775-4123. *Fax:* 989-775-4528. *E-mail:* treed@sagchip.org. *Web site:* http://www.sagchip.edu/.

St. Clair County Community College

Port Huron, Michigan

Director of Admissions Mr. Pete Lacey, Director of Admissions and Records, St. Clair County Community College, 323 Erie Street, PO Box 5015, Port Huron, MI 48061-5015. *Phone:* 810-989-5552. *Toll-free phone:* 800-553-2427. *Web site:* http://www.sc4.edu/.

Schoolcraft College

Livonia, Michigan

Freshman Application Contact Ms. Cheryl Hagen, Dean of Student Services, Schoolcraft College, 18600 Haggerty Road, Livonia, MI 48152-2696. *Phone:* 734-462-4426. *Fax:* 734-462-4553. *E-mail:* admissions@schoolcraft.edu. *Web site:* http://www.schoolcraft.edu/.

Southwestern Michigan College

Dowagiac, Michigan

- **State and locally supported** 2-year, founded 1964
- **Rural** 240-acre campus
- **Coed,** 3,262 undergraduate students, 53% full-time, 60% women, 40% men

Undergraduates 1,726 full-time, 1,536 part-time. Students come from 4 states and territories; 18 other countries; 9% are from out of state; 8% Black or African American, non-Hispanic/Latino; 2% Hispanic/Latino; 0.5% Asian, non-Hispanic/Latino; 0.1% Native Hawaiian or other Pacific Islander, non-Hispanic/Latino; 1% American Indian or Alaska Native, non-Hispanic/Latino; 2% Two or more races, non-Hispanic/Latino; 6% Race/ethnicity unknown; 1% international; 42% transferred in; 8% live on campus. *Retention:* 62% of full-time freshmen returned.

Freshmen *Admission:* 806 applied, 806 admitted, 806 enrolled.

Faculty *Total:* 166, 35% full-time, 27% with terminal degrees. *Student/faculty ratio:* 24:1.

Majors Accounting technology and bookkeeping; automobile/automotive mechanics technology; business administration and management; computer programming; computer support specialist; computer systems networking and telecommunications; drafting and design technology; early childhood education; electrical, electronic and communications engineering technology; emergency medical technology (EMT paramedic); engineering technology; executive assistant/executive secretary; fire science/firefighting; general studies; graphic and printing equipment operation/production; health information/medical records technology; industrial mechanics and maintenance technology; industrial production technologies related; liberal arts and sciences/liberal studies; machine tool technology; medical/clinical assistant; prenursing studies; professional, technical, business, and scientific writing; registered nursing/registered nurse; social work; teacher assistant/aide; theater design and technology; tool and die technology; welding technology.

Academics *Calendar:* semesters. *Degree:* certificates and associate. *Special study options:* academic remediation for entering students, accelerated degree program, adult/continuing education programs, advanced placement credit, cooperative education, distance learning, double majors, English as a second language, independent study, internships, part-time degree program, services for LD students, student-designed majors, summer session for credit.

Library Fred L. Mathews Library with 37,260 titles, 12,209 serial subscriptions, 2,526 audiovisual materials, an OPAC, a Web page.

Student Life *Housing Options:* coed. Campus housing is university owned. *Activities and Organizations:* drama/theater group, choral group, Dionysus Drama Club, Synergy Dance Club, SMC Community of Veterans, Alpha Kappa Omega, SMC Green Club. *Campus security:* 24-hour emergency response devices and patrols, controlled dormitory access, day and evening police patrols.

Athletics *Intramural sports:* basketball M/W, football M/W, golf M/W, racquetball M/W, rock climbing M/W, soccer M/W, softball M/W.

Costs (2010–11) *Tuition:* area resident $2438 full-time, $94 per contact hour part-time; state resident $3133 full-time, $121 per contact hour part-time; nonresident $3406 full-time, $131 per contact hour part-time. *Required fees:* $832 full-time, $32 per contact hour part-time. *Room and board:* $7353; room only: $5150. *Payment plan:* installment. *Waivers:* employees or children of employees.

Financial Aid Of all full-time matriculated undergraduates who enrolled in 2009, 125 Federal Work-Study jobs (averaging $1000). 75 state and other part-time jobs (averaging $1000).

Applying *Options:* electronic application, deferred entrance. *Required:* high school transcript. *Required for some:* interview. *Application deadlines:* rolling (freshmen), rolling (transfers). *Notification:* continuous until 9/10 (freshmen), continuous until 9/10 (transfers).

Freshman Application Contact Dr. Margaret Hay, Dean of Students and Academic Support, Southwestern Michigan College, Dowagiac, MI 49047. *Phone:* 269-782-1000 Ext. 1306. *Toll-free phone:* 800-456-8675. *Fax:* 269-782-1331. *E-mail:* mhay@swmich.edu. *Web site:* http://www.swmich.edu/.

Washtenaw Community College

Ann Arbor, Michigan

Freshman Application Contact Washtenaw Community College, 4800 East Huron River Drive, PO Box D-1, Ann Arbor, MI 48106. *Phone:* 734-973-3315. *Web site:* http://www.wccnet.edu/.

Wayne County Community College District

Detroit, Michigan

Freshman Application Contact Office of Enrollment Management and Student Services, Wayne County Community College District, 801 West Fort

Street, Detroit, MI 48226-9975. *Phone:* 313-496-2634. *E-mail:* caafjh@wcccd.edu. *Web site:* http://www.wcccd.edu/.

West Shore Community College
Scottville, Michigan

- **District-supported** 2-year, founded 1967, part of Michigan Department of Education
- **Rural** 375-acre campus
- **Coed**

Undergraduates Students come from 1 other state; 3% transferred in.

Academics *Calendar:* semesters. *Degree:* certificates and associate. *Special study options:* academic remediation for entering students, adult/continuing education programs, advanced placement credit, cooperative education, distance learning, independent study, internships, off-campus study, part-time degree program, services for LD students, student-designed majors, summer session for credit.

Student Life *Campus security:* 24-hour emergency response devices and patrols.

Costs (2010–11) *Tuition:* area resident $2280 full-time, $76 per contact hour part-time; state resident $3990 full-time, $133 per contact hour part-time; nonresident $5340 full-time, $178 per contact hour part-time. Full-time tuition and fees vary according to course load and program. *Required fees:* $206 full-time, $4 per contact hour part-time, $40 per term part-time.

Financial Aid Of all full-time matriculated undergraduates who enrolled in 2009, 80 Federal Work-Study jobs (averaging $3000). 40 state and other part-time jobs (averaging $3000).

Applying *Options:* early admission, deferred entrance. *Application fee:* $15. *Required:* high school transcript.

Freshman Application Contact Wendy Fought, Director of Admissions, West Shore Community College, PO Box 277, 3000 North Stiles Road, Scottville, MI 49454-0277. *Phone:* 231-843-5503. *Fax:* 231-845-3944. *E-mail:* admissions@westshore.edu. *Web site:* http://www.westshore.edu/.

MICRONESIA

College of Micronesia–FSM
Kolonia Pohnpei, Federated States of Micronesia, Micronesia

Freshman Application Contact Rita Hinga, Student Services Specialist, College of Micronesia–FSM, PO Box 159, Kolonia Pohnpei, FM 96941-0159, Micronesia. *Phone:* 691-320-3795 Ext. 15. *E-mail:* rhinga@comfsm.fm. *Web site:* http://www.comfsm.fm/.

MINNESOTA

Alexandria Technical and Community College
Alexandria, Minnesota

- **State-supported** 2-year, founded 1961, part of Minnesota State Colleges and Universities System
- **Small-town** 106-acre campus
- **Coed**, 2,347 undergraduate students, 67% full-time, 48% women, 52% men

Undergraduates 1,580 full-time, 767 part-time. Students come from 18 states and territories; 4% are from out of state.

Freshmen *Admission:* 2,012 applied, 1,367 admitted.

Faculty *Total:* 109, 65% full-time, 4% with terminal degrees. *Student/faculty ratio:* 19:1.

Majors Accounting; administrative assistant and secretarial science; banking and financial support services; building/construction site management; business administration and management; carpentry; child-care and support services management; child-care provision; clinical/medical laboratory technology; commercial and advertising art; computer and information sciences; computer and information systems security; computer systems networking and telecommunications; criminal justice/police science; customer service management; diesel mechanics technology; energy management and systems technology; farm and ranch management; fashion merchandising; geographic information science and cartography; health and physical education/fitness; hospitality administration; human services; industrial mechanics and mainte-

nance technology; interior design; legal administrative assistant/secretary; legal assistant/paralegal; liberal arts and sciences/liberal studies; licensed practical/vocational nurse training; machine tool technology; manufacturing engineering technology; marine maintenance and ship repair technology; marketing/marketing management; masonry; mechanical drafting and CAD/CADD; medical administrative assistant and medical secretary; medical insurance coding; medical reception; medical transcription; multi/interdisciplinary studies related; nursing assistant/aide and patient care assistant/aide; office management; office occupations and clerical services; operations management; phlebotomy technology; receptionist; registered nursing/registered nurse; selling skills and sales; small engine mechanics and repair technology; truck and bus driver/commercial vehicle operation/instruction; web page, digital/multimedia and information resources design; welding technology.

Academics *Calendar:* semesters. *Degree:* certificates, diplomas, and associate. *Special study options:* academic remediation for entering students, advanced placement credit, distance learning, double majors, independent study, internships, part-time degree program, services for LD students, student-designed majors, summer session for credit.

Library Learning Resource Center with 26,769 titles, 102 serial subscriptions, 1,378 audiovisual materials, an OPAC, a Web page.

Student Life *Housing:* college housing not available. *Activities and Organizations:* choral group, Skills USA, Business Professionals of America, Delta Epsilon Chi, Student Senate, Phi Theta Kappa. *Campus security:* student patrols, late-night transport/escort service, security cameras inside and outside. *Student services:* personal/psychological counseling.

Athletics *Intramural sports:* basketball M/W, football M/W, softball M/W, volleyball M/W.

Costs (2010–11) *Tuition:* state resident $4958 full-time, $146 per credit part-time; nonresident $4958 full-time, $146 per credit part-time. *Required fees:* $588 full-time, $18 per credit part-time. *Payment plan:* installment. *Waivers:* senior citizens and employees or children of employees.

Financial Aid Of all full-time matriculated undergraduates who enrolled in 2009, 94 Federal Work-Study jobs (averaging $1871).

Applying *Options:* electronic application, early admission, deferred entrance. *Application fee:* $20. *Required:* high school transcript, interview. *Application deadlines:* rolling (freshmen), rolling (out-of-state freshmen), rolling (transfers). *Notification:* continuous (freshmen), continuous (out-of-state freshmen), continuous (transfers).

Freshman Application Contact Janet Dropik, Admissions Receptionist, Alexandria Technical and Community College, 1601 Jefferson Street, Alexandria, MN 56308. *Phone:* 320-762-4520. *Toll-free phone:* 888-234-1222. *Fax:* 320-762-4603. *E-mail:* admissionsrep@alextech.edu. *Web site:* http://www.alextech.edu/.

Anoka-Ramsey Community College
Coon Rapids, Minnesota

- **State-supported** 2-year, founded 1965, part of Minnesota State Colleges and Universities System
- **Suburban** 100-acre campus with easy access to Minneapolis-St. Paul
- **Coed**, 7,679 undergraduate students

Undergraduates 3% are from out of state; 9% Black or African American, non-Hispanic/Latino; 1% Hispanic/Latino; 4% Asian, non-Hispanic/Latino; 0.1% Native Hawaiian or other Pacific Islander, non-Hispanic/Latino; 1% American Indian or Alaska Native, non-Hispanic/Latino; 1% Race/ethnicity unknown; 0.3% international. *Retention:* 44% of full-time freshmen returned.

Freshmen *Admission:* 3,103 applied, 2,816 admitted.

Faculty *Total:* 270, 39% full-time. *Student/faculty ratio:* 29:1.

Majors Accounting; accounting technology and bookkeeping; alternative and complementary medical support services related; bioengineering and biomedical engineering; biology/biological sciences; biology/biotechnology laboratory technician; business administration and management; business/commerce; community health and preventive medicine; computer science; computer systems networking and telecommunications; dramatic/theater arts; environmental science; fine/studio arts; human resources management; liberal arts and sciences/liberal studies; marketing/marketing management; multi/interdisciplinary studies related; music; physical therapy technology; pre-engineering; registered nursing/registered nurse.

Academics *Calendar:* semesters. *Degree:* certificates and associate. *Special study options:* academic remediation for entering students, accelerated degree program, advanced placement credit, cooperative education, distance learning, double majors, honors programs, independent study, internships, off-campus study, part-time degree program, services for LD students, study abroad, summer session for credit. *ROTC:* Air Force (c).

Library Coon Rapids Campus Library with 42,327 titles, 225 serial subscriptions, 1,415 audiovisual materials, an OPAC, a Web page.

Student Life *Housing:* college housing not available. *Activities and Organizations:* drama/theater group, student-run newspaper, choral group, student government, Phi Theta Kappa, Multicultural Club, CRU (Campus Christian group), Salmagundi (student newspaper). *Campus security:* 24-hour emergency response devices, late-night transport/escort service. *Student services:* personal/psychological counseling.

Athletics Member NJCAA. *Intercollegiate sports:* baseball M, basketball M/W, soccer M/W, softball W, volleyball W. *Intramural sports:* basketball M/W, bowling M/W, football M/W, golf M/W, ice hockey M/W, soccer M/W, softball M/W, tennis M/W, volleyball M/W.

Costs (2010–11) *Tuition:* state resident $3919 full-time, $131 per credit part-time; nonresident $3919 full-time, $131 per credit part-time. Full-time tuition and fees vary according to course load and program. Part-time tuition and fees vary according to course load and program. *Required fees:* $568 full-time, $21 per credit part-time. *Payment plans:* installment, deferred payment. *Waivers:* senior citizens and employees or children of employees.

Financial Aid Of all full-time matriculated undergraduates who enrolled in 2009, 111 Federal Work-Study jobs (averaging $4000). 151 state and other part-time jobs (averaging $4000).

Applying *Options:* electronic application, early admission, deferred entrance. *Application fee:* $20. *Required for some:* high school transcript. *Application deadlines:* rolling (freshmen), rolling (out-of-state freshmen), rolling (transfers). *Notification:* continuous (freshmen), continuous (out-of-state freshmen), continuous (transfers).

Freshman Application Contact Admissions Department, Anoka-Ramsey Community College, 11200 Mississippi Boulevard, NW, Coon Rapids, MN 55433-3470. *Phone:* 763-433-1300. *Fax:* 763-433-1521. *E-mail:* admissions@anokaramsey.edu. *Web site:* http://www.anokaramsey.edu/.

Anoka-Ramsey Community College, Cambridge Campus
Cambridge, Minnesota

- **State-supported** 2-year, founded 1965, part of Minnesota State Colleges and Universities System
- **Small-town** campus
- **Coed,** 2,751 undergraduate students

Undergraduates 2% are from out of state; 2% Black or African American, non-Hispanic/Latino; 0.8% Hispanic/Latino; 1% Asian, non-Hispanic/Latino; 0.3% Native Hawaiian or other Pacific Islander, non-Hispanic/Latino; 1% American Indian or Alaska Native, non-Hispanic/Latino; 1% Race/ethnicity unknown; 0.3% international. *Retention:* 48% of full-time freshmen returned.

Freshmen *Admission:* 708 applied, 632 admitted.

Faculty *Total:* 65, 46% full-time. *Student/faculty ratio:* 32:1.

Majors Accounting; accounting technology and bookkeeping; alternative and complementary medical support services related; bioengineering and biomedical engineering; biology/biological sciences; biology/biotechnology laboratory technician; business administration and management; business/commerce; community health and preventive medicine; computer science; computer systems networking and telecommunications; dramatic/theater arts; environmental science; fine/studio arts; human resources management; liberal arts and sciences/liberal studies; marketing/marketing management; multi/interdisciplinary studies related; music; pre-engineering; registered nursing/registered nurse.

Academics *Calendar:* semesters. *Degree:* certificates and associate. *Special study options:* academic remediation for entering students, accelerated degree program, advanced placement credit, cooperative education, distance learning, double majors, honors programs, independent study, internships, off-campus study, part-time degree program, services for LD students, study abroad, summer session for credit. *ROTC:* Air Force (c).

Library Cambridge Campus Library with 26,475 titles, 136 serial subscriptions, 1,613 audiovisual materials, an OPAC, a Web page.

Student Life *Housing:* college housing not available. *Activities and Organizations:* drama/theater group, student-run newspaper, choral group. *Campus security:* 24-hour emergency response devices, late-night transport/escort service. *Student services:* personal/psychological counseling.

Athletics Member NJCAA. *Intercollegiate sports:* baseball M, basketball M/W, soccer M/W, softball W, volleyball W. *Intramural sports:* bowling M/W, golf M/W, volleyball M/W.

Costs (2010–11) *Tuition:* state resident $3919 full-time, $131 per credit part-time; nonresident $3919 full-time, $131 per credit part-time. Full-time tuition and fees vary according to course load and program. Part-time tuition and fees vary according to course load and program. *Required fees:* $568 full-time, $21 per credit part-time. *Payment plans:* installment, deferred payment. *Waivers:* senior citizens and employees or children of employees.

Applying *Options:* electronic application, early admission, deferred entrance. *Application fee:* $20. *Required for some:* high school transcript. *Application deadlines:* rolling (freshmen), rolling (out-of-state freshmen), rolling (transfers). *Notification:* continuous (freshmen), continuous (out-of-state freshmen), continuous (transfers).

Freshman Application Contact Admissions Department, Anoka-Ramsey Community College, Cambridge Campus, 300 Spirit River Drive South, Cambridge, MN 55008-5706. *Phone:* 763-433-1300. *Fax:* 763-433-1841. *E-mail:* admissions@anokaramsey.edu. *Web site:* http://www.anokaramsey.edu/.

Anoka Technical College
Anoka, Minnesota

Director of Admissions Mr. Robert Hoenie, Director of Admissions, Anoka Technical College, 1355 West Highway 10, Anoka, MN 55303. *Phone:* 763-576-4746. *E-mail:* info@anokatech.edu. *Web site:* http://www.anokatech.edu/

Brown College
Mendota Heights, Minnesota

Freshman Application Contact Mr. Mark Fredrichs, Registrar, Brown College, 1440 Northland Drive, Mendota Heights, MN 55120. *Phone:* 651-905-3400. *Toll-free phone:* 800-6BROWN6. *Fax:* 651-905-3550. *Web site:* http://www.browncollege.edu/.

Central Lakes College
Brainerd, Minnesota

- **State-supported** 2-year, founded 1938, part of Minnesota State Colleges and Universities System
- **Small-town** campus
- **Endowment** $3.4 million
- **Coed,** 4,378 undergraduate students, 57% full-time, 57% women, 43% men

Undergraduates 2,517 full-time, 1,861 part-time. Students come from 12 states and territories; 0.3% are from out of state; 2% Black or African American, non-Hispanic/Latino; 0.8% Hispanic/Latino; 0.9% Asian, non-Hispanic/Latino; 0.1% Native Hawaiian or other Pacific Islander, non-Hispanic/Latino; 3% American Indian or Alaska Native, non-Hispanic/Latino; 0.2% Race/ethnicity unknown.

Faculty *Total:* 155, 58% full-time. *Student/faculty ratio:* 20:1.

Majors Accounting; administrative assistant and secretarial science; applied horticulture/horticulture operations; business administration and management; child-care and support services management; commercial and advertising art; computer systems networking and telecommunications; computer technology/computer systems technology; conservation biology; criminalistics and criminal science; criminal justice/police science; criminal justice/safety; developmental and child psychology; diesel mechanics technology; engineering; horticultural science; industrial electronics technology; industrial engineering; kindergarten/preschool education; legal administrative assistant/secretary; liberal arts and sciences/liberal studies; machine tool technology; marketing/marketing management; mechanical drafting and CAD/CADD; medical administrative assistant and medical secretary; natural resources/conservation; photographic and film/video technology; registered nursing/registered nurse; robotics technology; welding technology.

Academics *Calendar:* semesters. *Degree:* certificates, diplomas, and associate. *Special study options:* academic remediation for entering students, advanced placement credit, distance learning, English as a second language, external degree program, independent study, internships, off-campus study, part-time degree program, services for LD students, summer session for credit.

Library Learning Resource Center with 16,052 titles, 286 serial subscriptions, an OPAC, a Web page.

Student Life *Housing:* college housing not available. *Activities and Organizations:* drama/theater group, student-run newspaper, choral group. *Campus security:* 24-hour emergency response devices and patrols, student patrols, late-night transport/escort service. *Student services:* personal/psychological counseling.

Athletics Member NJCAA. *Intercollegiate sports:* baseball M, basketball M/W, football M, golf M/W, softball W, volleyball W. *Intramural sports:* basketball M/W, bowling M/W, football M, golf M/W, softball M/W, tennis M/W, volleyball M/W.

Costs (2010–11) *Tuition:* state resident $4322 full-time, $144 per credit part-time; nonresident $4322 full-time, $144 per credit part-time. Full-time tuition and fees vary according to course load and program. Part-time tuition and fees vary according to course load and program. *Required fees:* $605 full-time, $20 per credit part-time. *Payment plan:* installment. *Waivers:* senior citizens and employees or children of employees.

Applying *Options:* electronic application, deferred entrance. *Application fee:* $20. *Required:* high school transcript. *Application deadlines:* rolling (freshmen), rolling (out-of-state freshmen), rolling (transfers).

Freshman Application Contact Ms. Rose Tretter, Central Lakes College, 501 West College Drive, Brainerd, MN 56401-3904. *Phone:* 218-855-8036. *Toll-free phone:* 800-933-0346 Ext. 2586. *Fax:* 218-855-8220. *E-mail:* cdaniels@clcmn.edu. *Web site:* http://www.clcmn.edu/.

Century College

White Bear Lake, Minnesota

- **State-supported** 2-year, founded 1970, part of Minnesota State Colleges and Universities System

- **Suburban** 150-acre campus with easy access to Minneapolis-St. Paul

- **Coed,** 10,775 undergraduate students, 47% full-time, 55% women, 45% men

Undergraduates 5,019 full-time, 5,756 part-time. Students come from 40 states and territories; 56 other countries; 7% are from out of state; 11% Black or African American, non-Hispanic/Latino; 3% Hispanic/Latino; 15% Asian, non-Hispanic/Latino; 0.2% Native Hawaiian or other Pacific Islander, non-Hispanic/Latino; 1% American Indian or Alaska Native, non-Hispanic/Latino; 2% Race/ethnicity unknown; 1% international; 37% transferred in.

Freshmen *Admission:* 3,542 applied, 3,542 admitted, 1,734 enrolled.

Majors Accounting; administrative assistant and secretarial science; autobody/collision and repair technology; automobile/automotive mechanics technology; building/property maintenance; business administration and management; CAD/CADD drafting/design technology; computer and information sciences; computer and information systems security; computer science; computer systems networking and telecommunications; computer technology/computer systems technology; cosmetology; criminalistics and criminal science; criminal justice/police science; criminal justice/safety; dental assisting; dental hygiene; digital communication and media/multimedia; education (multiple levels); emergency medical technology (EMT paramedic); energy management and systems technology; engineering; greenhouse management; heating, air conditioning, ventilation and refrigeration maintenance technology; homeland security, law enforcement, firefighting and protective services related; horticultural science; human services; interior design; landscaping and groundskeeping; language interpretation and translation; liberal arts and sciences/liberal studies; marketing/marketing management; medical administrative assistant and medical secretary; music; nail technician and manicurist; network and system administration; nursing assistant/aide and patient care assistant/aide; office occupations and clerical services; orthotics/prosthetics; radiologic technology/science; registered nursing/registered nurse; sport and fitness administration/management; substance abuse/addiction counseling; teacher assistant/aide.

Academics *Calendar:* semesters. *Degree:* certificates, diplomas, and associate. *Special study options:* academic remediation for entering students, advanced placement credit, distance learning, double majors, English as a second language, honors programs, internships, part-time degree program, services for LD students, study abroad, summer session for credit. *ROTC:* Air Force (c).

Library Century College Library with 67,602 titles, 338 serial subscriptions, 5,221 audiovisual materials, an OPAC, a Web page.

Student Life *Housing:* college housing not available. *Activities and Organizations:* drama/theater group, student-run newspaper, choral group, Asian Student Association, Intercultural Club, Student Senate, Phi Theta Kappa, Planning Activities Committee. *Campus security:* late-night transport/escort service, day patrols. *Student services:* personal/psychological counseling.

Athletics Member NJCAA. *Intercollegiate sports:* baseball M, golf M/W, soccer M/W, softball W. *Intramural sports:* badminton M/W, basketball M/W, bowling M/W, golf M/W, soccer M/W, softball M/W, table tennis M/W, volleyball M/W.

Costs (2010–11) *Tuition:* state resident $4467 full-time, $149 per credit hour part-time; nonresident $4467 full-time, $149 per credit hour part-time. Full-time tuition and fees vary according to course load, program, and reciprocity agreements. Part-time tuition and fees vary according to course load, program, and reciprocity agreements. *Required fees:* $557 full-time, $19 per credit hour part-time. *Payment plan:* installment. *Waivers:* senior citizens and employees or children of employees.

Financial Aid Of all full-time matriculated undergraduates who enrolled in 2009, 81 Federal Work-Study jobs (averaging $2763). 85 state and other part-time jobs (averaging $2646).

Applying *Options:* electronic application, deferred entrance. *Application fee:* $20. *Required:* high school transcript. *Application deadlines:* rolling (freshmen), rolling (transfers).

Freshman Application Contact Ms. Christine Paulos, Admissions Director, Century College, 3300 Century Avenue North, White Bear Lake, MN 55110. *Phone:* 651-779-2619. *Toll-free phone:* 800-228-1978. *Fax:* 651-773-1796. *E-mail:* admissions@century.edu. *Web site:* http://www.century.edu/.

Dakota County Technical College

Rosemount, Minnesota

- **State-supported** 2-year, founded 1970, part of Minnesota State Colleges and Universities System

- **Suburban** 100-acre campus with easy access to Minneapolis-St. Paul

- **Endowment** $3.2 million

- **Coed,** 3,672 undergraduate students, 46% full-time, 40% women, 60% men

Undergraduates 1,690 full-time, 1,982 part-time. Students come from 8 states and territories; 28 other countries; 3% are from out of state; 17% transferred in.

Freshmen *Admission:* 3,672 enrolled.

Faculty *Total:* 141, 66% full-time. *Student/faculty ratio:* 30:1.

Majors Accounting; autobody/collision and repair technology; automobile/automotive mechanics technology; biomedical technology; business administration and management; child-care provision; commercial and advertising art; computer programming; computer systems networking and telecommunications; dental assisting; electrician; energy management and systems technology; executive assistant/executive secretary; graphic design; heavy equipment maintenance technology; interior design; kinesiology and exercise science; landscaping and groundskeeping; legal administrative assistant/secretary; lineworker; manufacturing engineering technology; marketing/marketing management; masonry; medical administrative assistant and medical secretary; medical/clinical assistant; medium/heavy vehicle and truck technology; photography; real estate; tourism and travel services management; web page, digital/multimedia and information resources design.

Academics *Calendar:* semesters. *Degree:* certificates, diplomas, and associate. *Special study options:* academic remediation for entering students, cooperative education, distance learning, double majors, English as a second language, independent study, internships, part-time degree program, services for LD students, student-designed majors, summer session for credit.

Library DCTC Library with 27,292 titles, 130 serial subscriptions, 1,097 audiovisual materials, an OPAC, a Web page.

Student Life *Housing:* college housing not available. *Activities and Organizations:* Phi Theta Kappa International Honor Society, SkillsUSA Minnesota, Multicultural Student Leadership Association, Veterans Club, Automotive Club. *Campus security:* 24-hour emergency response devices, late-night transport/escort service. *Student services:* personal/psychological counseling.

Athletics Member NJCAA. *Intercollegiate sports:* baseball M, basketball M, soccer M/W, softball W, volleyball W.

Costs (2011–12) *Tuition:* state resident $4680 full-time; nonresident $4680 full-time. Full-time tuition and fees vary according to program. Part-time tuition and fees vary according to program. *Required fees:* $630 full-time. *Payment plans:* installment, deferred payment. *Waivers:* senior citizens and employees or children of employees.

Applying *Options:* electronic application. *Application fee:* $20. *Required for some:* high school transcript. *Application deadlines:* rolling (freshmen), rolling (out-of-state freshmen), rolling (transfers).

Freshman Application Contact Mr. Patrick Lair, Admissions Director, Dakota County Technical College, 1300 East 145th Street, Rosemount, MN 55068. *Phone:* 651-423-8399. *Toll-free phone:* 877-YES-DCTC Ext. 302 (in-state); 877-YES-DCTC (out-of-state). *Fax:* 651-423-8775. *E-mail:* admissions@dctc.mnscu.edu. *Web site:* http://www.dctc.edu/.

Duluth Business University

Duluth, Minnesota

- **Proprietary** 2-year, founded 1891
- **Urban** 2-acre campus
- **Coed, primarily women,** 367 undergraduate students

Freshmen *Admission:* 278 applied.

Majors Accounting technology and bookkeeping; business administration and management; commercial and advertising art; health information/medical records technology; massage therapy; medical/clinical assistant; phlebotomy technology; veterinary/animal health technology.

Academics *Calendar:* quarters. *Degree:* diplomas and associate.

Student Life *Housing:* college housing not available.

Costs (2010–11) *Tuition:* $16,800 full-time, $350 per credit hour part-time. Full-time tuition and fees vary according to program. Part-time tuition and fees vary according to program. *Required fees:* $600 full-time, $300 per year part-time. *Payment plan:* installment.

Applying *Application fee:* $35.

Freshman Application Contact Mr. Mark Traux, Director of Admissions, Duluth Business University, 4724 Mike Colalillo Drive, Duluth, MN 55807. *Phone:* 218-722-4000. *Toll-free phone:* 800-777-8406. *Fax:* 218-628-2127. *E-mail:* markt@dbumn.edu. *Web site:* http://www.dbumn.edu/.

Minnesota

Dunwoody College of Technology
Minneapolis, Minnesota

Freshman Application Contact Shaun Manning, Director of Admissions, Dunwoody College of Technology, 818 Dunwoody Boulevard, Minneapolis, MN 55403. *Phone:* 612-374-5800 Ext. 8110. *Toll-free phone:* 800-292-4625. *E-mail:* smanning@dunwoody.edu. *Web site:* http://www.dunwoody.edu/.

Fond du Lac Tribal and Community College
Cloquet, Minnesota

Freshman Application Contact Kathie Jubie, Admissions Representative, Fond du Lac Tribal and Community College, 2101 14th Street, Cloquet, MN 55720. *Phone:* 218-879-0808. *Toll-free phone:* 800-657-3712. *E-mail:* admissions@fdltcc.edu. *Web site:* http://www.fdltcc.edu/.

Hennepin Technical College
Brooklyn Park, Minnesota

- **State-supported** 2-year, founded 1972, part of Minnesota State Colleges and Universities System
- **Suburban** 100-acre campus with easy access to Minneapolis-St. Paul
- **Coed**

Faculty *Student/faculty ratio:* 25:1.
Academics *Calendar:* semesters. *Degree:* certificates, diplomas, and associate. *Special study options:* academic remediation for entering students, adult/continuing education programs, advanced placement credit, cooperative education, distance learning, double majors, English as a second language, honors programs, independent study, internships, services for LD students, student-designed majors, summer session for credit.
Student Life *Campus security:* late-night transport/escort service, security service.
Costs (2010–11) *Tuition:* state resident $4321 full-time; nonresident $4321 full-time, $144 per credit part-time. *Required fees:* $308 full-time, $10 per credit part-time.
Financial Aid Of all full-time matriculated undergraduates who enrolled in 2009, 72 Federal Work-Study jobs (averaging $3000).
Applying *Options:* electronic application. *Application fee:* $20. *Recommended:* high school transcript.
Freshman Application Contact Hennepin Technical College, 9000 Brooklyn Boulevard, Brooklyn Park, MN 55445. *Phone:* 763-488-2415. *Toll-free phone:* 800-345-4655. *Web site:* http://www.hennepintech.edu/.

Herzing University
Minneapolis, Minnesota

Freshman Application Contact Ms. Shelly Larson, Director of Admissions, Herzing University, 5700 West Broadway, Minneapolis, MN 55428. *Phone:* 763-231-3155. *Fax:* 763-535-9205. *E-mail:* info@mpls.herzing.edu. *Web site:* http://www.herzing.edu/.

Hibbing Community College
Hibbing, Minnesota

Freshman Application Contact Admissions, Hibbing Community College, 1515 East 25th Street, Hibbing, MN 55746. *Phone:* 218-262-7200. *Toll-free phone:* 800-224-4HCC. *Fax:* 218-262-6717. *E-mail:* admissions@hibbing.edu. *Web site:* http://www.hcc.mnscu.edu/.

High-Tech Institute
St. Louis Park, Minnesota

Freshman Application Contact Admissions Office, High-Tech Institute, 5100 Gamble Drive, St. Louis Park, MN 55416. *Toll-free phone:* 888-324-9700. *Web site:* http://www.high-techinstitute.com/.

Inver Hills Community College
Inver Grove Heights, Minnesota

- **State-supported** 2-year, founded 1969, part of Minnesota State Colleges and Universities System
- **Suburban** 100-acre campus with easy access to Minneapolis-St. Paul
- **Coed,** 6,342 undergraduate students, 39% full-time, 60% women, 40% men

Undergraduates 2,502 full-time, 3,840 part-time. Students come from 19 states and territories; 2% are from out of state; 11% Black or African American, non-Hispanic/Latino; 5% Hispanic/Latino; 6% Asian, non-Hispanic/Latino; 0.3% Native Hawaiian or other Pacific Islander, non-Hispanic/Latino; 1% American Indian or Alaska Native, non-Hispanic/Latino; 2% Race/ethnicity unknown; 0.6% international; 5% transferred in.
Freshmen *Admission:* 1,000 applied, 977 admitted, 907 enrolled.
Faculty *Total:* 226, 46% full-time.
Majors Accounting; airline pilot and flight crew; aviation/airway management; biology/biological sciences; building/construction finishing, management, and inspection related; building/construction site management; building/home/construction inspection; business administration and management; business/commerce; computer and information sciences and support services related; computer programming; computer programming (specific applications); computer programming (vendor/product certification); computer science; computer systems networking and telecommunications; computer technology/computer systems technology; criminal justice/police science; criminal justice/safety; education; emergency medical technology (EMT paramedic); fine/studio arts; health/health-care administration; human services; legal administrative assistant/secretary; legal assistant/paralegal; liberal arts and sciences/liberal studies; medical administrative assistant and medical secretary; multi/interdisciplinary studies related; network and system administration; physical education teaching and coaching; registered nursing/registered nurse.
Academics *Calendar:* semesters. *Degree:* certificates and associate. *Special study options:* academic remediation for entering students, accelerated degree program, advanced placement credit, cooperative education, distance learning, English as a second language, external degree program, honors programs, independent study, internships, off-campus study, part-time degree program, services for LD students, summer session for credit. *ROTC:* Army (c), Air Force (c).
Library 42,073 titles, 300 serial subscriptions, an OPAC, a Web page.
Student Life *Housing:* college housing not available. *Activities and Organizations:* drama/theater group, choral group, VIBE, Student Senate, Health Service Student Association, Phi Theta Kappa, Nursing Club. *Campus security:* late-night transport/escort service, evening police patrol. *Student services:* health clinic, personal/psychological counseling.
Athletics *Intramural sports:* bowling M/W, football M/W, ice hockey M/W, softball M/W, table tennis M/W, tennis M/W, ultimate Frisbee M/W, volleyball M/W.
Costs (2010–11) *Tuition:* state resident $3582 full-time, $149 per credit hour part-time; nonresident $3582 full-time, $149 per credit hour part-time. Full-time tuition and fees vary according to course load, location, program, and reciprocity agreements. Part-time tuition and fees vary according to course load, location, program, and reciprocity agreements. *Required fees:* $390 full-time, $16 per credit hour part-time. *Payment plan:* installment. *Waivers:* senior citizens and employees or children of employees.
Financial Aid Of all full-time matriculated undergraduates who enrolled in 2009, 3,600 applied for aid, 3,250 were judged to have need. 175 Federal Work-Study jobs (averaging $2300). 153 state and other part-time jobs (averaging $2300). *Average percent of need met:* 48%. *Average financial aid package:* $4300. *Average need-based loan:* $4200. *Average need-based gift aid:* $3800.
Applying *Options:* electronic application. *Application fee:* $20. *Required for some:* high school transcript. *Recommended:* high school transcript. *Application deadlines:* 8/15 (freshmen), rolling (transfers). *Notification:* continuous (freshmen), continuous (transfers).
Freshman Application Contact Mr. Casey Carmody, Admissions Representative, Inver Hills Community College, 2500 East 80th Street, Inver Grove Heights, MN 55076-3224. *Phone:* 651-450-3589. *Fax:* 651-450-3677. *E-mail:* admissions@inverhills.edu. *Web site:* http://www.inverhills.edu/.

Itasca Community College
Grand Rapids, Minnesota

- **State-supported** 2-year, founded 1922, part of Minnesota State Colleges and Universities System
- **Rural** 24-acre campus
- **Endowment** $3.9 million
- **Coed**

Undergraduates 879 full-time, 251 part-time. Students come from 2 other countries; 4% are from out of state; 10% live on campus. *Retention:* 53% of full-time freshmen returned.
Faculty *Student/faculty ratio:* 15:1.
Academics *Calendar:* semesters. *Degree:* certificates, diplomas, and associate. *Special study options:* academic remediation for entering students, adult/continuing education programs, advanced placement credit, cooperative education, double majors, independent study, internships, off-campus study, part-time degree program, services for LD students, study abroad, summer session for credit.

Student Life *Campus security:* student patrols, late-night transport/escort service, controlled dormitory access, evening patrols by trained security personnel.

Athletics Member NJCAA.

Costs (2010–11) *Tuition:* state resident $4280 full-time, $143 per credit part-time; nonresident $5465 full-time, $182 per credit part-time. Full-time tuition and fees vary according to course load and program. Part-time tuition and fees vary according to program. *Required fees:* $572 full-time, $19 per credit part-time. *Room and board:* $5972. Room and board charges vary according to board plan and housing facility.

Applying *Options:* electronic application. *Application fee:* $20. *Required:* high school transcript. *Required for some:* 3 letters of recommendation.

Freshman Application Contact Ms. Candace Perry, Director of Enrollment Services, Itasca Community College, Grand Rapids, MN 55744. *Phone:* 218-322-2340. *Toll-free phone:* 800-996-6422 Ext. 4464. *Fax:* 218-327-4350. *E-mail:* iccinfo@itascacc.edu. *Web site:* http://www.itascacc.edu/.

ITT Technical Institute

Brooklyn Center, Minnesota

- **Proprietary** 2-year, part of ITT Educational Services, Inc.
- **Coed**

Majors CAD/CADD drafting/design technology; computer and information systems security; computer engineering technology; criminal justice/law enforcement administration; electrical, electronic and communications engineering technology; legal assistant/paralegal; project management; system, networking, and LAN/WAN management.

Academics *Calendar:* quarters.

Freshman Application Contact Director of Recruitment, ITT Technical Institute, 6120 Earle Brown Drive, Suite 100, Brooklyn Center, MN 55430. *Phone:* 763-549-5900. *Toll-free phone:* 800-216-8883. *Web site:* http://www.itt-tech.edu/.

ITT Technical Institute

Eden Prairie, Minnesota

- **Proprietary** primarily 2-year, founded 2003, part of ITT Educational Services, Inc.
- **Coed**

Majors CAD/CADD drafting/design technology; computer and information systems security; computer engineering technology; computer software and media applications related; computer software engineering; computer software technology; criminal justice/law enforcement administration; design and visual communications; electrical, electronic and communications engineering technology; game and interactive media design; legal assistant/paralegal; project management; system, networking, and LAN/WAN management; web page, digital/multimedia and information resources design.

Academics *Calendar:* quarters. *Degrees:* associate and bachelor's.

Freshman Application Contact Director of Recruitment, ITT Technical Institute, 8911 Columbine Road, Eden Prairie, MN 55347. *Phone:* 952-914-5300. *Toll-free phone:* 888-488-9646. *Web site:* http://www.itt-tech.edu/.

Lake Superior College

Duluth, Minnesota

- **State-supported** 2-year, founded 1995, part of Minnesota State Colleges and Universities System
- **Urban** 105-acre campus
- **Endowment** $476,618
- **Coed**, 4,366 undergraduate students, 55% full-time, 58% women, 42% men

Undergraduates 2,380 full-time, 1,986 part-time. Students come from 29 states and territories; 3 other countries; 9% are from out of state; 39% transferred in. *Retention:* 56% of full-time freshmen returned.

Freshmen *Admission:* 2,319 applied, 2,319 admitted, 641 enrolled.

Faculty *Total:* 280, 38% full-time. *Student/faculty ratio:* 13:1.

Majors Accounting; administrative assistant and secretarial science; airframe mechanics and aircraft maintenance technology; airline pilot and flight crew; architectural drafting and CAD/CADD; automobile/automotive mechanics technology; aviation/airway management; business administration and management; CAD/CADD drafting/design technology; carpentry; civil engineering technology; computer and information sciences; computer hardware technology; computer programming; computer systems networking and tele-

communications; computer technology/computer systems technology; data modeling/warehousing and database administration; dental hygiene; electrical, electronic and communications engineering technology; electrician; fine/studio arts; fire prevention and safety technology; legal administrative assistant/secretary; legal assistant/paralegal; liberal arts and sciences/liberal studies; machine tool technology; management information systems; mechanical drafting and CAD/CADD; medical administrative assistant and medical secretary; occupational therapist assistant; physical therapy technology; radiologic technology/science; registered nursing/registered nurse; respiratory care therapy; selling skills and sales; surgical technology; telecommunications technology; welding technology.

Academics *Calendar:* semesters. *Degree:* certificates, diplomas, and associate. *Special study options:* academic remediation for entering students, advanced placement credit, distance learning, double majors, English as a second language, independent study, internships, part-time degree program, services for LD students, summer session for credit.

Library Harold P. Erickson Library with 2,869 titles, 100 serial subscriptions, 280 audiovisual materials, an OPAC, a Web page.

Student Life *Housing:* college housing not available. *Activities and Organizations:* Business Professionals of America, Gus Gus Players, Art Club, All Nations, Phi Theta Kappa. *Campus security:* late-night transport/escort service, 15-hour patrols by trained security personnel. *Student services:* health clinic, personal/psychological counseling, women's center.

Athletics *Intramural sports:* baseball M/W, basketball M/W, field hockey M/W, ice hockey M/W, softball M/W, volleyball M/W.

Costs (2011–12) *Tuition:* state resident $3984 full-time, $133 per credit part-time; nonresident $8169 full-time, $272 per credit part-time. Full-time tuition and fees vary according to course load and reciprocity agreements. Part-time tuition and fees vary according to course load and reciprocity agreements. *Required fees:* $624 full-time, $21 per credit part-time. *Payment plans:* installment, deferred payment. *Waivers:* senior citizens and employees or children of employees.

Financial Aid Of all full-time matriculated undergraduates who enrolled in 2009, 100 Federal Work-Study jobs (averaging $2380). 100 state and other part-time jobs (averaging $2380).

Applying *Options:* early admission, deferred entrance. *Application fee:* $20. *Required for some:* high school transcript. *Application deadlines:* rolling (freshmen), rolling (transfers). *Notification:* continuous (freshmen), continuous (transfers).

Freshman Application Contact Ms. Melissa Leno, Director of Admissions, Lake Superior College, 2101 Trinity Road, Duluth, MN 55811. *Phone:* 218-723-4895. *Toll-free phone:* 800-432-2884. *Fax:* 218-733-5945. *E-mail:* enroll@lsc.edu. *Web site:* http://www.lsc.edu/.

Le Cordon Bleu College of Culinary Arts

Saint Paul, Minnesota

Freshman Application Contact Admissions Office, Le Cordon Bleu College of Culinary Arts, 1315 Mendota Heights Road, Saint Paul, MN 55120. *Phone:* 651-675-4700. *Toll-free phone:* 888-348-5222. *Web site:* http://www.twincitiesculinary.com/.

Leech Lake Tribal College

Cass Lake, Minnesota

- **Public** 2-year, founded 1992
- **Rural** campus
- **Coed**

Undergraduates 190 full-time, 53 part-time. Students come from 1 other state.

Faculty *Student/faculty ratio:* 16:1.

Academics *Calendar:* semesters. *Degree:* certificates, diplomas, and associate. *Special study options:* academic remediation for entering students, advanced placement credit, double majors, independent study, internships, part-time degree program, services for LD students, summer session for credit.

Costs (2010–11) *Tuition:* state resident $4200 full-time. *Required fees:* $230 full-time. *Payment plans:* installment, deferred payment.

Applying *Application fee:* $15. *Required:* high school transcript.

Freshman Application Contact Ms. Shelly Braford, Recruiter, Leech Lake Tribal College, PO Box 180, 6945 Littlewolf Road NW, Cass Lake, MN 56633. *Phone:* 218-335-4200 Ext. 4270. *Fax:* 218-335-4217. *E-mail:* shelly.braford@lltc.edu. *Web site:* http://www.lltc.edu/.

Mesabi Range Community and Technical College

Virginia, Minnesota

- **State-supported** 2-year, founded 1918, part of Minnesota State Colleges and Universities System
- **Small-town** 30-acre campus
- **Coed,** 1,467 undergraduate students

Undergraduates Students come from 6 states and territories; 2 other countries; 4% are from out of state; 10% live on campus.

Faculty *Total:* 89. *Student/faculty ratio:* 24:1.

Majors Administrative assistant and secretarial science; business/commerce; computer graphics; computer/information technology services administration related; computer programming related; computer programming (specific applications); computer software and media applications related; computer systems networking and telecommunications; electrical/electronics equipment installation and repair; human services; information technology; instrumentation technology; liberal arts and sciences/liberal studies; pre-engineering; substance abuse/addiction counseling; web page, digital/multimedia and information resources design.

Academics *Calendar:* semesters. *Degree:* certificates, diplomas, and associate. *Special study options:* academic remediation for entering students, adult/continuing education programs, advanced placement credit, cooperative education, independent study, internships, off-campus study, part-time degree program, services for LD students, student-designed majors, study abroad, summer session for credit.

Library Mesabi Library with 23,000 titles, 167 serial subscriptions.

Student Life *Housing Options:* coed. Campus housing is provided by a third party. *Activities and Organizations:* drama/theater group, student-run newspaper, choral group, Student Senate, Human Services Club, Native American Club, Student Life Club, Black Awareness Club. *Campus security:* late-night transport/escort service. *Student services:* personal/psychological counseling.

Athletics Member NJCAA. *Intercollegiate sports:* baseball M, basketball M/W, football M, softball W, volleyball W. *Intramural sports:* badminton M/W, basketball M/W, bowling M/W, field hockey M/W, football M/W, golf M/W, ice hockey M/W, skiing (cross-country) M/W, skiing (downhill) M/W, tennis M/W, volleyball M/W.

Costs (2010–11) *Tuition:* state resident $4280 full-time, $143 per credit hour part-time; nonresident $5122 full-time, $171 per credit hour part-time. *Required fees:* $564 full-time, $19 per credit hour part-time. *Room and board:* room only: $3894. *Payment plan:* installment. *Waivers:* senior citizens.

Financial Aid Of all full-time matriculated undergraduates who enrolled in 2009, 117 Federal Work-Study jobs (averaging $1610). 77 state and other part-time jobs (averaging $1470).

Applying *Options:* early admission, deferred entrance. *Application fee:* $20. *Required:* high school transcript. *Application deadlines:* rolling (freshmen), rolling (transfers). *Notification:* continuous (freshmen), continuous (transfers).

Freshman Application Contact Ms. Brenda Kochevar, Enrollment Services Director, Mesabi Range Community and Technical College, Virginia, MN 55792. *Phone:* 218-749-0314. *Toll-free phone:* 800-657-3860. *Fax:* 218-749-0318. *E-mail:* b.kochevar@mr.mnscu.edu. *Web site:* http://www.mesabirange.edu/.

Minneapolis Business College

Roseville, Minnesota

- **Private** 2-year, founded 1874
- **Suburban** campus with easy access to Minneapolis-St. Paul
- **Coed, primarily women,** 335 undergraduate students
- 87% of applicants were admitted

Freshmen *Admission:* 815 applied, 711 admitted.

Majors Accounting and business/management; business administration and management; computer programming; graphic design; legal administrative assistant/secretary; legal assistant/paralegal; medical/clinical assistant; system, networking, and LAN/WAN management; tourism and travel services management.

Academics *Degree:* diplomas and associate. *Special study options:* accelerated degree program, internships.

Freshman Application Contact Admissions Office, Minneapolis Business College, 1711 West County Road B, Roseville, MN 55113. *Phone:* 651-636-7406. *Toll-free phone:* 800-279-5200. *Web site:* http://www.minneapolisbusinesscollege.edu/.

Minneapolis Community and Technical College

Minneapolis, Minnesota

- **State-supported** 2-year, founded 1965, part of Minnesota State Colleges and Universities System
- **Urban** 22-acre campus
- **Coed**

Undergraduates 4,477 full-time, 6,141 part-time.

Academics *Calendar:* semesters. *Degree:* certificates, diplomas, and associate. *Special study options:* academic remediation for entering students, adult/continuing education programs, advanced placement credit, distance learning, English as a second language, honors programs, independent study, internships, off-campus study, part-time degree program, services for LD students, student-designed majors, study abroad, summer session for credit.

Student Life *Campus security:* 24-hour emergency response devices, late-night transport/escort service.

Costs (2010–11) *Tuition:* state resident $4305 full-time, $144 per credit hour part-time; nonresident $4305 full-time, $144 per credit hour part-time. Full-time tuition and fees vary according to program and reciprocity agreements. Part-time tuition and fees vary according to program and reciprocity agreements. *Required fees:* $669 full-time, $22 per credit hour part-time.

Applying *Options:* electronic application, early admission, deferred entrance. *Application fee:* $20. *Required:* high school transcript.

Freshman Application Contact Minneapolis Community and Technical College, 1501 Hennepin Avenue, Minneapolis, MN 55403. *Phone:* 612-659-6200. *Toll-free phone:* 800-247-0911. *E-mail:* admissions.office@minneapolis.edu. *Web site:* http://www.mctc.mnscu.edu/.

Minnesota School of Business–Brooklyn Center

Brooklyn Center, Minnesota

Freshman Application Contact Mr. Bruce Christman, Director of Admissions, Minnesota School of Business–Brooklyn Center, Brooklyn Center, MN 55430. *Phone:* 763-585-7777. *Fax:* 763-566-7030. *Web site:* http://www.msbcollege.edu/.

Minnesota School of Business–Plymouth

Minneapolis, Minnesota

Freshman Application Contact Minnesota School of Business–Plymouth, Plymouth, MN 55447. *Phone:* 763-476-2000. *Fax:* 763-476-1000. *Web site:* http://www.msbcollege.edu/.

Minnesota School of Business–Richfield

Richfield, Minnesota

Freshman Application Contact Ms. Patricia Murray, Director of Admissions, Minnesota School of Business–Richfield, Richfield, MN 55430. *Phone:* 612-861-2000 Ext. 720. *Toll-free phone:* 800-752-4223. *Fax:* 612-861-5548. *E-mail:* pmurray@msbcollege.com. *Web site:* http://www.msbcollege.edu/.

Minnesota School of Business–St. Cloud

Waite Park, Minnesota

Freshman Application Contact Ms. Candi Janssen, Director of Admissions, Minnesota School of Business–St. Cloud, Waite Park, MN 56387. *Phone:* 320-257-2000. *Toll-free phone:* 866-403-3333. *Fax:* 320-257-0131. *E-mail:* cjanssen@msbcollege.edu. *Web site:* http://www.msbcollege.edu/.

Minnesota School of Business–Shakopee

Shakopee, Minnesota

Freshman Application Contact Ms. Gretchen Seifert, Director of Admissions, Minnesota School of Business–Shakopee, Shakopee, MN 55379. *Phone:* 952-516-7015. *Toll-free phone:* 866-766-1200. *Fax:* 952-345-1201. *Web site:* http://www.msbcollege.edu/.

Minnesota State College–Southeast Technical

Winona, Minnesota

- **State-supported** 2-year, founded 1992, part of Minnesota State Colleges and Universities System
- **Small-town** 132-acre campus with easy access to Minneapolis-St. Paul
- **Coed,** 2,375 undergraduate students, 60% full-time, 60% women, 40% men

Undergraduates 1,436 full-time, 939 part-time. 28% are from out of state; 4% Black or African American, non-Hispanic/Latino; 1% Hispanic/Latino; 2% Asian, non-Hispanic/Latino; 0.1% Native Hawaiian or other Pacific Islander, non-Hispanic/Latino; 1% American Indian or Alaska Native, non-Hispanic/Latino; 0.4% Race/ethnicity unknown; 0.4% international.

Freshmen *Admission:* 696 enrolled.

Faculty *Total:* 120, 48% full-time. *Student/faculty ratio:* 22:1.

Majors Accounting; accounting technology and bookkeeping; administrative assistant and secretarial science; autobody/collision and repair technology; biomedical technology; business administration and management; CAD/CADD drafting/design technology; carpentry; child-care and support services management; computer programming; computer systems networking and telecommunications; computer technology/computer systems technology; cosmetology; criminal justice/safety; electrical, electronic and communications engineering technology; heating, air conditioning, ventilation and refrigeration maintenance technology; industrial mechanics and maintenance technology; legal administrative assistant/secretary; massage therapy; medical administrative assistant and medical secretary; multi/interdisciplinary studies related; radiologic technology/science; registered nursing/registered nurse; retailing; selling skills and sales; web page, digital/multimedia and information resources design.

Academics *Calendar:* semesters. *Degree:* certificates, diplomas, and associate. *Special study options:* distance learning, double majors, internships.

Library Learning Resource Center.

Student Life *Housing Options:* cooperative. *Activities and Organizations:* Student Senate, Business Professionals of America, Skills USA, Delta Epsilon Chi (DEX). *Campus security:* 24-hour emergency response devices, late-night transport/escort service.

Costs (2010–11) *Tuition:* state resident $5076 full-time, $152 per credit hour part-time; nonresident $5076 full-time, $152 per credit hour part-time. *Required fees:* $417 full-time. *Room and board:* $6412. *Payment plan:* installment. *Waivers:* senior citizens and employees or children of employees.

Financial Aid Of all full-time matriculated undergraduates who enrolled in 2008, 49 Federal Work-Study jobs (averaging $2930). 41 state and other part-time jobs (averaging $3239).

Applying *Options:* electronic application. *Application fee:* $20. *Required:* high school transcript. *Recommended:* interview. *Application deadlines:* rolling (freshmen), rolling (out-of-state freshmen), rolling (transfers). *Notification:* continuous (freshmen), continuous (out-of-state freshmen), continuous (transfers).

Freshman Application Contact Admissions, SE Technical, Minnesota State College–Southeast Technical, 1250 Homer Road, PO Box 409, Winona, MN 55987. *Phone:* 877-853-8324. *Toll-free phone:* 800-372-8164. *Fax:* 507-453-2715. *E-mail:* enrollmentservices@southeastmn.edu. *Web site:* http://www.southeastmn.edu/.

Minnesota State Community and Technical College

Fergus Falls, Minnesota

- **State-supported** 2-year, founded 1960, part of Minnesota State Colleges and Universities System
- **Rural** campus
- **Coed,** 6,925 undergraduate students

Undergraduates 4% Black or African American, non-Hispanic/Latino; 1% Hispanic/Latino; 1% Asian, non-Hispanic/Latino; 0.2% Native Hawaiian or other Pacific Islander, non-Hispanic/Latino; 3% American Indian or Alaska Native, non-Hispanic/Latino; 4% Race/ethnicity unknown; 2% live on campus.

Faculty *Total:* 456, 42% full-time, 5% with terminal degrees. *Student/faculty ratio:* 18:1.

Majors Accounting; administrative assistant and secretarial science; agricultural and food products processing; architectural drafting and CAD/CADD; art; autobody/collision and repair technology; automotive engineering technology; biochemistry and molecular biology; biology/biological sciences; building/construction site management; business administration and management; business automation/technology/data entry; carpentry; civil engineering technology; clinical/medical laboratory assistant; clinical/medical laboratory technology; computer and information systems security; computer engineering technology; computer programming; computer systems networking and telecommunications; computer technology/computer systems technology; cooking and related culinary arts; cosmetology; criminal justice/safety; dental assisting; dental hygiene; diesel mechanics technology; electrical and electronic engineering technologies related; electrical, electronic and communications engineering technology; environmental studies; fashion merchandising; financial planning and services; fire services administration; graphic design; health information/medical records technology; heating, ventilation, air conditioning and refrigeration engineering technology; horse husbandry/equine science and management; human resources management; legal administrative assistant/secretary; legal assistant/paralegal; liberal arts and sciences/liberal studies; licensed practical/vocational nurse training; lineworker; manufacturing engineering technology; marine maintenance and ship repair technology; marketing/marketing management; mechanical drafting and CAD/CADD; medical administrative assistant and medical secretary; merchandising, sales, and marketing operations related (general); music; pharmacy technician; plumbing technology; radiologic technology/science; registered nursing/registered nurse; telecommunications technology; web page, digital/multimedia and information resources design.

Academics *Calendar:* semesters. *Degree:* certificates, diplomas, and associate. *Special study options:* academic remediation for entering students, accelerated degree program, advanced placement credit, cooperative education, distance learning, double majors, English as a second language, freshman honors college, honors programs, independent study, internships, off-campus study, part-time degree program, services for LD students, study abroad, summer session for credit.

Library Minnesota State Community and Technical College - Fergus Falls Library plus 4 others with an OPAC.

Student Life *Housing Options:* coed. Campus housing is university owned. *Activities and Organizations:* drama/theater group, choral group, Student Senate, Students In Free Enterprise (SIFE), Phi Theta Kappa, Business Professionals of America, Skills USA - VICA. *Campus security:* 24-hour emergency response devices, late-night transport/escort service, security for special events. *Student services:* personal/psychological counseling, women's center.

Athletics Member NJCAA. *Intercollegiate sports:* baseball M, basketball M/W, football M, golf M/W, softball W, volleyball W. *Intramural sports:* badminton M/W, basketball M/W, bowling M/W, football M/W, golf M/W, skiing (cross-country) M/W, skiing (downhill) M/W, soccer M/W, softball M/W, table tennis M/W, tennis M/W, volleyball M/W, weight lifting M/W.

Costs (2010–11) *Tuition:* state resident $4734 full-time, $148 per credit hour part-time; nonresident $4734 full-time, $148 per credit hour part-time. Full-time tuition and fees vary according to location and program. Part-time tuition and fees vary according to location and program. *Required fees:* $615 full-time, $22 per credit hour part-time. *Room and board:* $6724; room only: $3350. Room and board charges vary according to board plan and housing facility. *Waivers:* senior citizens and employees or children of employees.

Financial Aid *Financial aid deadline:* 7/1.

Applying *Options:* electronic application, early admission, deferred entrance. *Application fee:* $20. *Required:* high school transcript. *Application deadlines:* rolling (freshmen), rolling (out-of-state freshmen), rolling (transfers). *Notification:* continuous (freshmen), continuous (out-of-state freshmen), continuous (transfers).

Freshman Application Contact Ms. Carrie Brimhall, Dean of Enrollment Management, Minnesota State Community and Technical College, Fergus Falls, MN 56537-1009. *Phone:* 218-736-1528. *Toll-free phone:* 888-MY-MSCTC. *E-mail:* carrie.brimhall@minnesota.edu. *Web site:* http://www.minnesota.edu/.

Minnesota West Community and Technical College

Pipestone, Minnesota

- **State-supported** 2-year, founded 1967, part of Minnesota State Colleges and Universities System
- **Rural** campus
- **Coed,** 3,464 undergraduate students, 48% full-time, 54% women, 46% men

Undergraduates 1,659 full-time, 1,805 part-time. Students come from 30 states and territories; 2 other countries; 10% are from out of state; 8% transferred in. *Retention:* 63% of full-time freshmen returned.

Freshmen *Admission:* 2,568 applied, 1,751 admitted, 527 enrolled. *Average high school GPA:* 2.58.

Faculty *Total:* 95, 88% full-time. *Student/faculty ratio:* 13:1.

Majors Accounting; administrative assistant and secretarial science; agribusiness; agricultural and food products processing; agricultural/farm supplies retailing and wholesaling; agricultural production; agriculture; agronomy and crop science; automobile/automotive mechanics technology; biology/biotechnology laboratory technician; business administration and management; business/commerce; child-care and support services management; clinical/medical laboratory technology; computer and information systems security; computer engineering technology; computer science; computer systems networking and telecommunications; computer technology/computer systems technology; criminal justice/police science; dental assisting; diesel mechanics technology; electrical and power transmission installation; electrical and power transmission installation related; electrician; energy management and systems technology; heating, air conditioning, ventilation and refrigeration maintenance technology; hospital and health-care facilities administration; human services; hydraulics and fluid power technology; information technology; liberal arts and sciences and humanities related; liberal arts and sciences/liberal studies; lineworker; manufacturing engineering technology; medical administrative assistant and medical secretary; medical/clinical assistant; medical insurance coding; plumbing technology; radiologic technology/science; registered nursing/registered nurse; robotics technology.

Academics *Calendar:* semesters. *Degrees:* certificates, diplomas, and associate (profile contains information from Canby, Granite Falls, Jackson, and Worthington campuses). *Special study options:* academic remediation for entering students, advanced placement credit, cooperative education, distance learning, double majors, external degree program, honors programs, independent study, internships, part-time degree program, services for LD students, summer session for credit.

Library Library and Academic Resource Center plus 4 others with 44,078 titles, 213 serial subscriptions, 4,253 audiovisual materials, an OPAC, a Web page.

Student Life *Housing:* college housing not available. *Activities and Organizations:* choral group.

Athletics Member NJCAA. *Intercollegiate sports:* baseball M, basketball M/W, cheerleading W, football M, golf M/W, softball W, volleyball W, wrestling M. *Intramural sports:* softball M/W, volleyball M/W.

Costs (2010–11) *Tuition:* state resident $4990 full-time, $156 per credit hour part-time; nonresident $4990 full-time, $156 per credit hour part-time. Full-time tuition and fees vary according to reciprocity agreements. Part-time tuition and fees vary according to reciprocity agreements. *Required fees:* $508 full-time, $16 per credit hour part-time. *Payment plan:* installment. *Waivers:* senior citizens and employees or children of employees.

Applying *Options:* electronic application. *Application fee:* $20. *Required:* high school transcript. *Application deadlines:* rolling (freshmen), rolling (transfers).

Freshman Application Contact Ms. Crystal Strouth, College Registrar, Minnesota West Community and Technical College, 1450 Collegeway, Worthington, MN 56187. *Phone:* 507-372-3451. *Toll-free phone:* 800-658-2330. *Fax:* 507-372-5803. *E-mail:* crystal.strouth@mnwest.edu. *Web site:* http://www.mnwest.edu/.

National American University
Bloomington, Minnesota

Freshman Application Contact Ms. Jennifer Michaelson, Admissions Assistant, National American University, 321 Kansas City Street, Rapid City, SD 57201. *Phone:* 605-394-4827. *Toll-free phone:* 800-209-0490. *E-mail:* jmichaelson@national.edu. *Web site:* http://www.national.edu/.

National American University
Brooklyn Center, Minnesota

Freshman Application Contact Admissions Office, National American University, 6120 Earle Brown Drive, Suite 100, Brooklyn Center, MN 55430. *Web site:* http://www.national.edu/.

Normandale Community College
Bloomington, Minnesota

Freshman Application Contact Admissions Office, Normandale Community College, Normandy Community College, 9700 France Avenue South, Bloomington, MN 55431. *Phone:* 952-487-8201. *Toll-free phone:* 866-880-8740. *Fax:* 952-487-8230. *E-mail:* information@normandale.edu. *Web site:* http://www.normandale.edu/.

North Hennepin Community College
Brooklyn Park, Minnesota

- **State-supported** 2-year, founded 1966, part of Minnesota State Colleges and Universities System
- **Suburban** 80-acre campus
- **Endowment** $682,674
- **Coed,** 7,456 undergraduate students, 38% full-time, 57% women, 43% men

Undergraduates 2,796 full-time, 4,660 part-time. Students come from 11 states and territories; 58 other countries; 0.3% are from out of state; 20% Black

or African American, non-Hispanic/Latino; 2% Hispanic/Latino; 12% Asian, non-Hispanic/Latino; 0.2% Native Hawaiian or other Pacific Islander, non-Hispanic/Latino; 1% American Indian or Alaska Native, non-Hispanic/Latino; 2% Race/ethnicity unknown; 1% international; 13% transferred in. *Retention:* 56% of full-time freshmen returned.

Freshmen *Admission:* 1,372 applied, 1,372 admitted, 1,314 enrolled.

Faculty *Total:* 248, 42% full-time, 6% with terminal degrees. *Student/faculty ratio:* 30:1.

Majors Accounting; biology/biological sciences; building/construction site management; building/home/construction inspection; business administration and management; chemistry; clinical/medical laboratory technology; computer science; construction management; criminal justice/law enforcement administration; criminal justice/police science; criminal justice/safety; engineering; finance; fine/studio arts; graphic design; histologic technology/histotechnologist; history; legal assistant/paralegal; liberal arts and sciences/liberal studies; management information systems; marketing/marketing management; mathematics; multi/interdisciplinary studies related; physical education teaching and coaching; pre-engineering; registered nursing/registered nurse; small business administration.

Academics *Calendar:* semesters. *Degree:* certificates and associate. *Special study options:* academic remediation for entering students, accelerated degree program, adult/continuing education programs, advanced placement credit, distance learning, double majors, English as a second language, external degree program, honors programs, independent study, internships, off-campus study, part-time degree program, services for LD students, student-designed majors, study abroad, summer session for credit. *ROTC:* Army (c), Navy (c), Air Force (c).

Library Learning Resource Center with 52,849 titles, 8,000 serial subscriptions, 3,244 audiovisual materials, an OPAC, a Web page.

Student Life *Housing:* college housing not available. *Activities and Organizations:* drama/theater group, choral group, Muslim Student Association, Phi Theta Kappa, Student Anime Game Club, Multicultural Club. *Campus security:* 24-hour emergency response devices, student patrols, late-night transport/escort service. *Student services:* personal/psychological counseling.

Athletics *Intramural sports:* badminton M/W, basketball M/W, bowling M/W, cross-country running M/W, football M/W, golf M/W, ice hockey M/W, rock climbing M/W, soccer M/W, softball M/W, table tennis M/W, tennis M/W, volleyball M/W, weight lifting M/W.

Costs (2010–11) *Tuition:* state resident $3623 full-time, $151 per credit hour part-time; nonresident $3623 full-time, $151 per credit hour part-time. Full-time tuition and fees vary according to course load, location, and program. Part-time tuition and fees vary according to course load, location, and program. *Required fees:* $348 full-time, $15 per credit hour part-time. *Payment plan:* installment. *Waivers:* senior citizens and employees or children of employees.

Financial Aid Of all full-time matriculated undergraduates who enrolled in 2008, 100 Federal Work-Study jobs, 100 state and other part-time jobs.

Applying *Options:* electronic application, early admission, deferred entrance. *Application fee:* $20. *Recommended:* high school transcript. *Application deadlines:* rolling (freshmen), rolling (transfers). *Notification:* continuous (freshmen), continuous (transfers).

Freshman Application Contact Ms. Alison Leintz, Admissions Specialist, North Hennepin Community College, 7411 85th Ave N., Brooklyn Park, MN 55445. *Phone:* 763-424-0722. *Toll-free phone:* 800-818-0395. *Fax:* 763-424-0929. *E-mail:* aleintz@nhcc.edu. *Web site:* http://www.nhcc.edu/.

Northland Community and Technical College—Thief River Falls & East Grand Forks
Thief River Falls, Minnesota

- **State-supported** 2-year, founded 1965, part of Minnesota State Colleges and Universities System
- **Small-town** 239-acre campus
- **Coed,** 4,135 undergraduate students, 47% full-time, 57% women, 43% men

Undergraduates 1,946 full-time, 2,189 part-time. Students come from 19 states and territories; 1 other country; 45% are from out of state; 10% transferred in.

Freshmen *Admission:* 1,569 applied, 1,569 admitted, 608 enrolled.

Faculty *Total:* 233, 54% full-time. *Student/faculty ratio:* 21:1.

Majors Accounting; administrative assistant and secretarial science; aeronautics/aviation/aerospace science and technology; architectural engineering technology; autobody/collision and repair technology; automobile/automotive mechanics technology; aviation/airway management; business administration and management; cardiovascular technology; carpentry; child-care provision; child development; computer and information sciences and support services related; computer and information sciences related; computer graphics; computer science; computer software and media applications related; consumer merchandising/retailing management; criminal justice/law enforcement administration; criminal justice/police science; criminology; data entry/microcomputer applications; data entry/microcomputer applications related; data modeling/warehousing and database administration; drafting and design technology; electrical, electronic and communications engineering technology; emergency medical technology (EMT paramedic); entrepreneurship; farm and ranch management; fire prevention and safety technology; heating, air conditioning, ventilation and refrigeration maintenance technology; industrial electronics technology; information technology; liberal arts and sciences/liberal studies; licensed practical/vocational nurse training; manufacturing engineering technology; marketing/marketing management; massage therapy; mass communication/media; medical administrative assistant and medical secretary; network and system administration; occupational therapist assistant; pharmacy technician; physical therapy technology; plumbing technology; radiologic technology/science; registered nursing/registered nurse; respiratory care therapy; surgical technology; web/multimedia management and webmaster; web page, digital/multimedia and information resources design; welding technology; word processing.

Academics *Calendar:* semesters. *Degree:* certificates, diplomas, and associate. *Special study options:* academic remediation for entering students, adult/continuing education programs, advanced placement credit, distance learning, double majors, internships, off-campus study, part-time degree program, services for LD students, summer session for credit.

Library Northland Comm & Tech College Library plus 1 other with 42,588 titles, 166 serial subscriptions, 3,411 audiovisual materials, an OPAC, a Web page.

Student Life *Housing:* college housing not available. *Activities and Organizations:* student-run radio station, choral group, Student Senate, Nursing, African Student Association, Martial Arts, PAMA. *Campus security:* student patrols, late-night transport/escort service. *Student services:* personal/psychological counseling, women's center.

Athletics Member NJCAA. *Intercollegiate sports:* baseball M, basketball M/W, football M, softball W, volleyball W. *Intramural sports:* basketball M/W, bowling M/W, golf M/W, ice hockey M/W, racquetball M/W, rock climbing M/W, soccer M/W, softball M/W, volleyball M/W, weight lifting M/W.

Costs (2010–11) *Tuition:* state resident $4576 full-time, $153 per credit hour part-time; nonresident $4576 full-time, $153 per credit hour part-time. Full-time tuition and fees vary according to course load and program. Part-time tuition and fees vary according to course load and program. *Required fees:* $522 full-time, $17 per credit hour part-time. *Payment plan:* installment. *Waivers:* senior citizens and employees or children of employees.

Financial Aid Of all full-time matriculated undergraduates who enrolled in 2009, 75 Federal Work-Study jobs (averaging $2500). 40 state and other part-time jobs (averaging $2500).

Applying *Options:* electronic application, early admission, deferred entrance. *Application fee:* $20. *Required:* high school transcript. *Application deadlines:* 8/26 (freshmen), 8/26 (out-of-state freshmen), 8/26 (transfers). *Notification:* continuous (freshmen), continuous (out-of-state freshmen), continuous (transfers).

Freshman Application Contact Mr. Eugene Klinke, Director of Enrollment Management and Multicultural Services, Northland Community and Technical College–Thief River Falls & East Grand Forks, 1101 Highway One East, Thief River Falls, MN 56701. *Phone:* 218-683-8554. *Toll-free phone:* 800-959-6282. *Fax:* 218-683-8980. *E-mail:* eugene.klinke@northlandcollege.edu. *Web site:* http://www.northlandcollege.edu/.

Northwest Technical College

Bemidji, Minnesota

- **State-supported** 2-year, founded 1993, part of Minnesota State Colleges and Universities System, administratively affiliated with Bemidji State University
- **Small-town** campus
- **Endowment** $306,205
- **Coed,** 1,419 undergraduate students, 40% full-time, 67% women, 33% men

Undergraduates 568 full-time, 851 part-time. Students come from 22 states and territories; 4 other countries; 15% are from out of state; 2% Black or African American, non-Hispanic/Latino; 0.9% Hispanic/Latino; 1% Asian, non-Hispanic/Latino; 0.3% Native Hawaiian or other Pacific Islander, non-Hispanic/Latino; 9% American Indian or Alaska Native, non-Hispanic/Latino; 0.7% Race/ethnicity unknown; 0.2% international; 11% transferred in; 5% live on campus.

Freshmen *Admission:* 281 applied, 281 admitted, 194 enrolled.

Faculty *Total:* 67, 51% full-time. *Student/faculty ratio:* 19:1.

Majors Accounting; administrative assistant and secretarial science; automobile/automotive mechanics technology; business administration and management; child-care and support services management; computer systems networking and telecommunications; dental assisting; energy management and systems technology; engine machinist; industrial safety technology; industrial

technology; licensed practical/vocational nurse training; manufacturing engineering technology; medical administrative assistant and medical secretary; registered nursing/registered nurse; sales, distribution, and marketing operations.

Academics *Calendar:* semesters. *Degree:* certificates, diplomas, and associate. *Special study options:* academic remediation for entering students, advanced placement credit, cooperative education, distance learning, double majors, external degree program, independent study, internships, off-campus study, part-time degree program, services for LD students, student-designed majors, summer session for credit.

Library Northwest Technical College Learning Enrichment Center with 4,577 titles, 46 serial subscriptions, 804 audiovisual materials, an OPAC, a Web page.

Student Life *Housing Options:* coed. Campus housing is provided by a third party. *Activities and Organizations:* drama/theater group, choral group, campus government, Phi Theta Kappa. *Campus security:* student patrols, late-night transport/escort service. *Student services:* health clinic, personal/psychological counseling.

Costs (2011–12) *Tuition:* state resident $4800 full-time, $160 per credit part-time; nonresident $4800 full-time, $160 per credit part-time. Full-time tuition and fees vary according to program. Part-time tuition and fees vary according to program. *Required fees:* $282 full-time, $57 per credit part-time. *Room and board:* $6480; room only: $4380. Room and board charges vary according to board plan. *Payment plan:* installment. *Waivers:* senior citizens and employees or children of employees.

Financial Aid Of all full-time matriculated undergraduates who enrolled in 2009, 20 Federal Work-Study jobs (averaging $1500). 10 state and other part-time jobs (averaging $1500).

Applying *Options:* electronic application. *Application fee:* $20. *Required:* high school transcript. *Application deadlines:* rolling (freshmen), rolling (out-of-state freshmen), rolling (transfers). *Notification:* continuous (freshmen), continuous (out-of-state freshmen), continuous (transfers).

Freshman Application Contact Ms. Kari Kantack-Miller, Diversity and Enrollment Representative, Northwest Technical College, 905 Grant Avenue, Southeast, Bemidji, MN 56601. *Phone:* 218-333-6645. *Toll-free phone:* 800-942-8324. *Fax:* 218-333-6694. *E-mail:* kari.kantack@ntcmn.edu. *Web site:* http://www.ntcmn.edu/.

Northwest Technical Institute

Eagan, Minnesota

- **Proprietary** 2-year, founded 1957
- **Suburban** 2-acre campus with easy access to Minneapolis-St. Paul
- **Coed**

Academics *Calendar:* semesters. *Degree:* associate. *Special study options:* honors programs, independent study.

Student Life *Campus security:* 24-hour emergency response devices and patrols, late-night transport/escort service.

Costs (2010–11) *Tuition:* $15,850 full-time. No tuition increase for student's term of enrollment. *Payment plans:* tuition prepayment, installment.

Applying *Application fee:* $25. *Required:* high school transcript, interview.

Freshman Application Contact Northwest Technical Institute, 950 Blue Gentian Road, Suite 500, Eagan, MN 55121. *Phone:* 952-944-0080 Ext. 103. *Toll-free phone:* 800-443-4223. *Web site:* http://www.nti.edu/.

Pine Technical College

Pine City, Minnesota

Freshman Application Contact Pine Technical College, 900 4th Street SE, Pine City, MN 55063. *Phone:* 320-629-5100. *Toll-free phone:* 800-521-7463. *Web site:* http://www.pinetech.edu/.

Rainy River Community College

International Falls, Minnesota

- **State-supported** 2-year, founded 1967, part of Minnesota State Colleges and Universities System
- **Small-town** 80-acre campus
- **Coed,** 342 undergraduate students, 83% full-time, 63% women, 37% men

Undergraduates 284 full-time, 58 part-time. 15% Black or African American, non-Hispanic/Latino; 0.9% Hispanic/Latino; 1% Asian, non-Hispanic/Latino; 8% American Indian or Alaska Native, non-Hispanic/Latino; 6% international.

Faculty *Total:* 21, 52% full-time. *Student/faculty ratio:* 15:1.

Majors Administrative assistant and secretarial science; biological and physical sciences; business administration and management; liberal arts and sciences/liberal studies; pre-engineering; real estate.

Academics *Calendar:* semesters. *Degree:* certificates, diplomas, and associate. *Special study options:* academic remediation for entering students, adult/

continuing education programs, advanced placement credit, cooperative education, honors programs, independent study, internships, part-time degree program, services for LD students, summer session for credit.

Library Rainy River Community College Library with 20,000 titles, an OPAC.

Student Life *Housing Options:* disabled students. Campus housing is university owned. *Activities and Organizations:* drama/theater group, Anishinaabe Student Coalition, Student Senate, Black Student Association. *Campus security:* 24-hour emergency response devices, late-night transport/escort service, controlled dormitory access. *Student services:* personal/psychological counseling.

Athletics Member NJCAA. *Intercollegiate sports:* basketball M/W, ice hockey W, softball W, volleyball W. *Intramural sports:* archery M/W, badminton M/W, baseball M, bowling M/W, cheerleading M/W, cross-country running M/W, ice hockey M, skiing (cross-country) M/W, skiing (downhill) M/W, swimming and diving M/W, table tennis M/W, tennis M/W, volleyball M/W, weight lifting M/W.

Costs (2011–12) *Tuition:* state resident $4280 full-time; nonresident $5465 full-time. Full-time tuition and fees vary according to program and reciprocity agreements. Part-time tuition and fees vary according to program and reciprocity agreements. *Required fees:* $594 full-time. *Room and board:* Room and board charges vary according to housing facility. *Payment plan:* installment. *Waivers:* employees or children of employees.

Applying *Options:* electronic application, early admission, deferred entrance. *Application fee:* $20. *Recommended:* high school transcript. *Application deadlines:* rolling (freshmen), rolling (out-of-state freshmen), rolling (transfers). *Notification:* continuous (freshmen), continuous (transfers).

Freshman Application Contact Ms. Berta Hagen, Registrar, Rainy River Community College, 1501 Highway 71, International Falls, MN 56649. *Phone:* 218-285-2207. *Toll-free phone:* 800-456-3996. *Fax:* 218-285-2314. *E-mail:* bhagen@rrcc.mnscu.edu. *Web site:* http://www.rrcc.mnscu.edu/.

Rasmussen College Brooklyn Park

Brooklyn Park, Minnesota

Admissions Office Contact Rasmussen College Brooklyn Park, 8301 93rd Avenue North, Brooklyn Park, MN 55445-1512. *Toll-free phone:* 877-495-4500. *Web site:* http://www.rasmussen.cdu/.

Rasmussen College Eagan

Eagan, Minnesota

Director of Admissions Ms. Jacinda Miller, Admissions Coordinator, Rasmussen College Eagan, 3500 Federal Drive, Eagan, MN 55122-1346. *Phone:* 651-687-9000. *Toll-free phone:* 800-852-6367. *Web site:* http://www.rasmussen.edu/.

Rasmussen College Eden Prairie

Eden Prairie, Minnesota

Freshman Application Contact Director of Admissions, Rasmussen College Eden Prairie, 7905 Golden Triangle Drive, Suite100, Eden Prairie, MN 55344. *Phone:* 952-545-2000. *Toll-free phone:* 800-852-0929. *Fax:* 952-545-7038. *Web site:* http://www.rasmussen.edu/.

Rasmussen College Lake Elmo/ Woodbury

Lake Elmo, Minnesota

Admissions Office Contact Rasmussen College Lake Elmo/Woodbury, 8565 Eagle Point Circle, Lake Elmo, MN 55042. *Toll-free phone:* 888-813-2358. *Web site:* http://www.rasmussen.edu/.

Rasmussen College Mankato

Mankato, Minnesota

Freshman Application Contact Ms. Kathy Clifford, Director of Admissions, Rasmussen College Mankato, 501 Holly Lane, Mankato, MN 56001-6803. *Phone:* 507-625-6556. *Toll-free phone:* 800-657-6767. *Fax:* 507-625-6557. *E-mail:* rascoll@ic.mankato.mn.us. *Web site:* http://www.rasmussen.edu/.

Rasmussen College Moorhead

Moorhead, Minnesota

Admissions Office Contact Rasmussen College Moorhead, 1250 29th Avenue South, Moorhead, MN 56560. *Toll-free phone:* 866-562-2758. *Web site:* http://www.rasmussen.edu/.

Rasmussen College St. Cloud

St. Cloud, Minnesota

Freshman Application Contact Ms. Andrea Peters, Director of Admissions, Rasmussen College St. Cloud, 226 Park Avenue South, St. Cloud, MN 56301-3713. *Phone:* 320-251-5600. *Toll-free phone:* 800-852-0460. *Fax:* 320-251-3702. *E-mail:* admstc@rasmussen.edu. *Web site:* http://www.rasmussen.edu/.

Ridgewater College

Willmar, Minnesota

Freshman Application Contact Ms. Linda Barron, Admissions Assistant, Ridgewater College, PO Box 1097, Willmar, MN 56201-1097. *Phone:* 320-222-5976. *Toll-free phone:* 800-722-1151 Ext. 2906. *E-mail:* linda.barron@ridgewater.edu. *Web site:* http://www.ridgewater.edu/.

Riverland Community College

Austin, Minnesota

Freshman Application Contact Ms. Renee Njos, Admission Secretary, Riverland Community College, Austin, MN 55912. *Phone:* 507-433-0820. *Toll-free phone:* 800-247-5039. *Fax:* 507-433-0515. *E-mail:* admissions@riverland.edu. *Web site:* http://www.riverland.edu/.

Rochester Community and Technical College

Rochester, Minnesota

Director of Admissions Mr. Troy Tynsky, Director of Admissions, Rochester Community and Technical College, 851 30th Avenue, SE, Rochester, MN 55904-4999. *Phone:* 507-280-3509. *Web site:* http://www.rctc.edu/.

St. Cloud Technical & Community College

St. Cloud, Minnesota

- **State-supported** 2-year, founded 1948, part of Minnesota State Colleges and Universities System
- **Urban** 35-acre campus with easy access to Minneapolis-St. Paul
- **Coed,** 4,883 undergraduate students, 56% full-time, 52% women, 48% men

Undergraduates 2,742 full-time, 2,141 part-time. Students come from 15 states and territories; 3 other countries; 1% are from out of state; 36% transferred in.

Freshmen *Admission:* 1,984 applied, 1,924 admitted, 1,092 enrolled. *Average high school GPA:* 3.16.

Faculty *Total:* 214, 49% full-time, 7% with terminal degrees. *Student/faculty ratio:* 23:1.

Majors Accounting; advertising; architectural drafting and CAD/CADD; autobody/collision and repair technology; automobile/automotive mechanics technology; banking and financial support services; business administration and management; cardiovascular technology; carpentry; child-care and support services management; civil engineering technology; computer programming; computer programming (specific applications); computer systems networking and telecommunications; dental assisting; dental hygiene; diagnostic medical sonography and ultrasound technology; electrical and power transmission installation; electrical, electronic and communications engineering technology; emergency medical technology (EMT paramedic); executive assistant/executive secretary; health information/medical records technology; heating, air conditioning, ventilation and refrigeration maintenance technology; instrumentation technology; legal administrative assistant/secretary; licensed practical/vocational nurse training; machine tool technology; mechanical drafting and CAD/CADD; medium/heavy vehicle and truck technology; plumbing technology; registered nursing/registered nurse; sales, distribution, and marketing operations; surgical technology; teacher assistant/aide; water quality and wastewater treatment management and recycling technology; web page, digital/multimedia and information resources design; welding technology.

Academics *Calendar:* semesters. *Degree:* certificates, diplomas, and associate. *Special study options:* academic remediation for entering students, adult/continuing education programs, advanced placement credit, cooperative education, distance learning, English as a second language, independent study, internships, part-time degree program, services for LD students, summer session for credit.

Library Learning Resource Center plus 1 other with 10,000 titles, 600 serial subscriptions, an OPAC, a Web page.

Student Life *Housing:* college housing not available. *Activities and Organizations:* drama/theater group, student-run newspaper, Student Senate, Distributive Education Club of America, Business Professionals of America, Child and Adult Care Education, Central Minnesota Builders Association. *Campus security:* late-night transport/escort service. *Student services:* personal/psychological counseling, women's center.

Athletics Member NJCAA. *Intercollegiate sports:* baseball M, basketball M/W, softball W, volleyball W. *Intramural sports:* volleyball M/W.

Costs (2010–11) *Tuition:* state resident $4404 full-time, $147 per credit part-time; nonresident $4404 full-time, $147 per credit part-time. Full-time tuition and fees vary according to course load and program. Part-time tuition and fees vary according to course load and program. *Required fees:* $518 full-time, $17 per credit part-time. *Payment plan:* installment. *Waivers:* senior citizens and employees or children of employees.

Financial Aid Of all full-time matriculated undergraduates who enrolled in 2008, 38 Federal Work-Study jobs (averaging $4000). 50 state and other part-time jobs (averaging $4000).

Applying *Options:* electronic application, early admission, deferred entrance. *Application fee:* $20. *Required:* high school transcript. *Required for some:* essay or personal statement, interview. *Application deadlines:* rolling (freshmen), rolling (transfers). *Notification:* continuous until 8/1 (freshmen), continuous until 8/1 (transfers).

Freshman Application Contact Ms. Jodi Elness, Admissions Office, St. Cloud Technical & Community College, 1540 Northway Drive, St. Cloud, MN 56303. *Phone:* 320-308-5089. *Toll-free phone:* 800-222-1009. *Fax:* 320-308-5981. *E-mail:* jelness@sctcc.edu. *Web site:* http://www.sctcc.edu/.

Saint Paul College–A Community & Technical College

St. Paul, Minnesota

- **State-related** 2-year, founded 1919, part of Minnesota State Colleges and Universities System
- **Urban** campus
- **Coed**

Undergraduates 2,454 full-time, 3,474 part-time. 8% are from out of state; 13% transferred in.

Faculty *Student/faculty ratio:* 18:1.

Academics *Calendar:* semesters. *Degree:* certificates, diplomas, and associate. *Special study options:* academic remediation for entering students, adult/continuing education programs, distance learning, English as a second language, honors programs, internships, off-campus study, part-time degree program, summer session for credit.

Student Life *Campus security:* late-night transport/escort service.

Standardized Tests *Required:* ACCUPLACER (for admission).

Costs (2010–11) *Tuition:* state resident $4402 full-time, $147 per credit hour part-time; nonresident $4402 full-time, $147 per credit hour part-time. Full-time tuition and fees vary according to program. Part-time tuition and fees vary according to program. *Required fees:* $362 full-time, $12 per credit hour part-time. *Payment plans:* installment, deferred payment.

Financial Aid Of all full-time matriculated undergraduates who enrolled in 2009, 48 Federal Work-Study jobs (averaging $2500). 94 state and other part-time jobs (averaging $2500).

Applying *Options:* electronic application, early admission. *Application fee:* $20. *Required for some:* high school transcript, interview.

Freshman Application Contact Ms. Sarah Carrico, Saint Paul College–A Community & Technical College, 235 Marshall Avenue, Saint Paul, MN 55102. *Phone:* 651-846-1424. *Toll-free phone:* 800-227-6029. *Fax:* 651-846-1703. *E-mail:* admissions@saintpaul.edu. *Web site:* http://www.saintpaul.edu/.

South Central College

North Mankato, Minnesota

Freshman Application Contact Ms. Beverly Herda, Director of Admissions, South Central College, 1920 Lee Boulevard, North Mankato, MN 56003. *Phone:* 507-389-7334. *Fax:* 507-388-9951. *Web site:* http://southcentral.edu/.

Vermilion Community College

Ely, Minnesota

Freshman Application Contact Mr. Todd Heiman, Director of Enrollment Services, Vermilion Community College, 1900 East Camp Street, Ely, MN 55731-1996. *Phone:* 218-365-7224. *Toll-free phone:* 800-657-3608. *Web site:* http://www.vcc.edu/.

MISSISSIPPI

Antonelli College

Hattiesburg, Mississippi

- **Proprietary** 2-year
- **Coed**

Academics *Calendar:* quarters. *Degree:* certificates and associate.

Applying *Application fee:* $75.

Freshman Application Contact Mrs. Karen Gautreau, Director, Antonelli College, 1500 North 31st Avenue, Hattiesburg, MS 39401. *Phone:* 601-583-4100. *Fax:* 601-583-0839. *E-mail:* admissionsh@antonellicollege.edu. *Web site:* http://antonellicollege.edu/.

Antonelli College

Jackson, Mississippi

- **Proprietary** 2-year
- **Coed**

Academics *Calendar:* quarters. *Degree:* diplomas and associate.

Applying *Application fee:* $75.

Freshman Application Contact Antonelli College, 2323 Lakeland Drive, Jackson, MS 39232. *Phone:* 601-362-9991. *Web site:* http://www.antonellicollege.edu/.

Coahoma Community College

Clarksdale, Mississippi

Freshman Application Contact Mrs. Wanda Holmes, Director of Admissions and Records, Coahoma Community College, Clarksdale, MS 38614-9799. *Phone:* 662-621-4205. *Toll-free phone:* 800-844-1222. *Web site:* http://www.ccc.cc.ms.us/.

Copiah-Lincoln Community College

Wesson, Mississippi

Freshman Application Contact Julia Parker, Director of Distance Learning, Copiah-Lincoln Community College, PO Box 371, Wesson, MS 39191-0457. *Phone:* 601-643-8619. *Fax:* 601-643-8222. *E-mail:* julia.parker@colin.edu. *Web site:* http://www.colin.edu/.

Copiah-Lincoln Community College– Natchez Campus

Natchez, Mississippi

Freshman Application Contact Copiah-Lincoln Community College–Natchez Campus, 11 Co-Lin Circle, Natchez, MS 39120-8446. *Phone:* 601-442-9111 Ext. 224. *Web site:* http://www.colin.edu/.

East Central Community College

Decatur, Mississippi

Director of Admissions Ms. Donna Luke, Director of Admissions, Records, and Research, East Central Community College, PO Box 129, Decatur, MS 39327-0129. *Phone:* 601-635-2111 Ext. 206. *Toll-free phone:* 877-462-3222. *Web site:* http://www.eccc.cc.ms.us/.

East Mississippi Community College

Scooba, Mississippi

Director of Admissions Ms. Melinda Sciple, Admissions Officer, East Mississippi Community College, PO Box 158, Scooba, MS 39358-0158. *Phone:* 662-476-5041. *Web site:* http://www.eastms.edu/.

Hinds Community College

Raymond, Mississippi

Director of Admissions Ms. Ginger Turner, Director of Admissions and Records, Hinds Community College, PO Box 1100, Raymond, MS 39154-1100. *Phone:* 601-857-3280. *Toll-free phone:* 800-HINDSCC. *Fax:* 601-857-3539. *Web site:* http://www.hindscc.edu/.

Holmes Community College

Goodman, Mississippi

Director of Admissions Dr. Lynn Wright, Dean of Admissions and Records, Holmes Community College, PO Box 369, Goodman, MS 39079-0369. *Phone:* 601-472-2312 Ext. 1023. *Web site:* http://www.holmescc.edu/.

Itawamba Community College

Fulton, Mississippi

Freshman Application Contact Mr. Larry Boggs, Director of Student Recruitment and Scholarships, Itawamba Community College, 602 West Hill Street, Fulton, MS 38843. *Phone:* 601-862-8252. *E-mail:* laboggs@iccms.edu. *Web site:* http://www.icc.cc.ms.us/.

Jones County Junior College

Ellisville, Mississippi

Director of Admissions Mrs. Dianne Speed, Director of Admissions and Records, Jones County Junior College, 900 South Court Street, Ellisville, MS 39437-3901. *Phone:* 601-477-4025. *Web site:* http://www.jcjc.edu/.

Meridian Community College

Meridian, Mississippi

- **State and locally supported** 2-year, founded 1937, part of Mississippi State Board for Community and Junior Colleges
- **Small-town** 62-acre campus
- **Endowment** $6.3 million
- **Coed**

Undergraduates 2,651 full-time, 963 part-time. Students come from 16 states and territories; 3% are from out of state; 12% live on campus. *Retention:* 51% of full-time freshmen returned.

Faculty *Student/faculty ratio:* 18:1.

Academics *Calendar:* semesters. *Degree:* certificates and associate. *Special study options:* academic remediation for entering students, adult/continuing education programs, advanced placement credit, cooperative education, distance learning, English as a second language, external degree program, independent study, part-time degree program, services for LD students, summer session for credit.

Student Life *Campus security:* 24-hour patrols, student patrols.

Athletics Member NJCAA.

Standardized Tests *Recommended:* ACT (for admission).

Costs (2010–11) *Tuition:* state resident $2000 full-time, $100 per semester hour part-time; nonresident $3380 full-time, $157 per semester hour part-time. Full-time tuition and fees vary according to course load and program. Part-time tuition and fees vary according to course load and program. *Required fees:* $190 full-time. *Room and board:* $3100. Room and board charges vary according to board plan.

Applying *Options:* early admission. *Required:* high school transcript, minimum 2.0 GPA. *Required for some:* essay or personal statement.

Freshman Application Contact Ms. Angela Payne, Director of Admissions, Meridian Community College, 910 Highway 19 North, Meridian, MS 39307. *Phone:* 601-484-8357. *Toll-free phone:* 800-622-8731. *E-mail:* apayne@meridiancc.edu. *Web site:* http://www.meridiancc.edu/.

Mississippi Delta Community College

Moorhead, Mississippi

Director of Admissions Mr. Joseph F. Ray Jr., Vice President of Admissions, Mississippi Delta Community College, PO Box 668, Highway 3 and Cherry Street, Moorhead, MS 38761-0668. *Phone:* 662-246-6308. *Web site:* http://www.msdelta.edu/.

Mississippi Gulf Coast Community College

Perkinston, Mississippi

Freshman Application Contact Mr. Ladd Taylor, Director of Admissions, Mississippi Gulf Coast Community College, Perkinston, MS 39573. *Phone:* 601-928-6264. *Fax:* 601-928-6299. *E-mail:* ladd.taylor@mgccc.edu. *Web site:* http://www.mgccc.edu/.

Northeast Mississippi Community College

Booneville, Mississippi

Freshman Application Contact Office of Enrollment Services, Northeast Mississippi Community College, 101 Cunningham Boulevard, Booneville, MS 38829. *Phone:* 662-720-7239. *Toll-free phone:* 800-555-2154. *E-mail:* admitme@nemcc.edu. *Web site:* http://www.nemcc.edu/.

Northwest Mississippi Community College

Senatobia, Mississippi

Director of Admissions Ms. Deanna Ferguson, Director of Admissions and Recruiting, Northwest Mississippi Community College, 4975 Highway 51 North, Senatobia, MS 38668-1701. *Phone:* 662-562-3222. *Web site:* http://www.northwestms.edu/.

Pearl River Community College

Poplarville, Mississippi

Freshman Application Contact Mr. J. Dow Ford, Director of Admissions, Pearl River Community College, 101 Highway 11 North, Poplarville, MS 39470. *Phone:* 601-403-1000. *Toll-free phone:* 877-772-2338. *E-mail:* dford@prcc.edu. *Web site:* http://www.prcc.edu/.

Southwest Mississippi Community College

Summit, Mississippi

- **State and locally supported** 2-year, founded 1918, part of Mississippi State Board for Community and Junior Colleges
- **Rural** 701-acre campus
- **Coed,** 2,036 undergraduate students, 88% full-time, 63% women, 37% men

Undergraduates 1,789 full-time, 247 part-time. Students come from 8 states and territories; 1 other country; 10% are from out of state; 67% transferred in; 35% live on campus. *Retention:* 65% of full-time freshmen returned.

Freshmen *Admission:* 598 enrolled.

Faculty *Total:* 90, 79% full-time. *Student/faculty ratio:* 24:1.

Majors Accounting; administrative assistant and secretarial science; advertising; automobile/automotive mechanics technology; biological and physical sciences; biology/biological sciences; business administration and management; business teacher education; carpentry; chemistry; computer programming related; computer science; computer systems networking and telecommunications; construction engineering technology; cosmetology; diesel mechanics technology; early childhood education; education; electrical, electronic and communications engineering technology; elementary education; emergency medical technology (EMT paramedic); engineering; English; fashion merchandising; finance; health information/medical records technology; health professions related; heating, air conditioning, ventilation and refrigeration maintenance technology; history; humanities; information technology; legal administrative assistant/secretary; liberal arts and sciences/liberal studies; licensed practical/vocational nurse training; marketing/marketing management; massage therapy; medical insurance/medical billing; music; music teacher education; network and system administration; nursing assistant/aide and patient care assistant/aide; occupational safety and health technology; petroleum technology; physical education teaching and coaching; physical sciences; registered nursing/registered nurse; social sciences; web/multimedia management and webmaster; welding technology; well drilling.

Academics *Calendar:* semesters. *Degree:* certificates and associate. *Special study options:* academic remediation for entering students, adult/continuing education programs, advanced placement credit, distance learning, part-time degree program, summer session for credit.

Library Library Learning Resources Center (LLRC) with 34,000 titles, 150 serial subscriptions, an OPAC.

Student Life *Housing Options:* men-only, women-only. Campus housing is university owned. *Activities and Organizations:* student-run newspaper, choral group, marching band. *Campus security:* 24-hour patrols.

Athletics Member NJCAA. *Intercollegiate sports:* baseball M(s), basketball M(s)/W(s), football M(s), soccer M(s)/W(s), softball W(s). *Intramural sports:* basketball M/W.

Costs (2010–11) *Tuition:* state resident $1950 full-time, $100 per credit hour part-time; nonresident $4650 full-time, $215 per credit hour part-time. Full-time tuition and fees vary according to class time. Part-time tuition and fees vary according to class time and course load. *Required fees:* $140 full-time, $70 per term part-time. *Room and board:* $2730. Room and board charges vary according to board plan. *Payment plan:* deferred payment. *Waivers:* senior citizens.

Financial Aid Of all full-time matriculated undergraduates who enrolled in 2009, 85 Federal Work-Study jobs (averaging $698). 6 state and other part-time jobs (averaging $550).

Applying *Required:* high school transcript. *Application deadlines:* 8/1 (freshmen), 8/1 (out-of-state freshmen), 8/1 (transfers).

Freshman Application Contact Mr. Matthew Calhoun, Vice President of Admissions and Records, Southwest Mississippi Community College, 1156 College Drive, Summit, MS 39666. *Phone:* 601-276-2001. *Fax:* 601-276-3888. *E-mail:* mattc@smcc.edu. *Web site:* http://www.smcc.cc.ms.us/.

Virginia College at Jackson

Jackson, Mississippi

Director of Admissions Director of Admissions, Virginia College at Jackson, 5360 I-55 North, Jackson, MS 39211. *Phone:* 601-977-0960. *Toll-free phone:* 866-623-6765. *Web site:* http://www.vc.edu/.

MISSOURI

Allied College

Maryland Heights, Missouri

Freshman Application Contact Admissions Office, Allied College, 13723 Riverport Drive, Maryland Heights, MO 63043. *Phone:* 314-595-3400. *Toll-free phone:* 888-393-9320. *Web site:* http://www.hightechinstitute.edu/.

American College of Technology

Saint Joseph, Missouri

Director of Admissions Richard Lingle, Lead Admission Coordinator, American College of Technology, 2300 Frederick Avenue, Saint Joseph, MO 64506. *Phone:* 800-908-9329 Ext. 13. *Toll-free phone:* 800-908-9329. *E-mail:* ricahrd@acot.edu. *Web site:* http://www.acot.edu/.

Aviation Institute of Maintenance–Kansas City

Kansas City, Missouri

Freshman Application Contact Aviation Institute of Maintenance–Kansas City, 4100 Raytown Road, Kansas City, MO 64129. *Phone:* 816-753-9920. *Fax:* 816-753-9941. *Web site:* http://www.aviationmaintenance.edu/aviation-kansascity.asp.

Brown Mackie College–St. Louis

Fenton, Missouri

- **Proprietary** primarily 2-year, part of Education Management Corporation
- **Coed**

Majors Accounting technology and bookkeeping; business administration and management; criminal justice/law enforcement administration; health/healthcare administration; information technology; legal assistant/paralegal; legal studies; medical/clinical assistant; office management; pharmacy technician; surgical technology.

Academics *Degrees:* diplomas, associate, and bachelor's.

Costs (2010–11) *Tuition:* Tuition varies by program. Students should contact Brown Mackie College for tuition information.

Freshman Application Contact Brown Mackie College–St. Louis, #2 Soccer Park Road, Fenton, MO 63026. *Phone:* 636-651-3290. *Web site:* http://www.brownmackie.edu/st-louis/.

See page 396 for the College Close-Up.

Concorde Career College

Kansas City, Missouri

Freshman Application Contact Deborah Crow, Director, Concorde Career College, 3239 Broadway, Kansas City, MO 64111-2407. *Phone:* 816-531-5223. *Fax:* 816-756-3231. *E-mail:* dcrow@concorde.edu. *Web site:* http://www.concorde.edu/.

Cottey College

Nevada, Missouri

Freshman Application Contact Ms. Judi Steege, Director of Admission, Cottey College, 1000 West Austin Boulevard, Nevada, MO 64772. *Phone:* 417-667-8181. *Toll-free phone:* 888-526-8839. *Fax:* 417-667-8103. *E-mail:* enrollmgt@cottey.edu. *Web site:* http://www.cottey.edu/.

Crowder College

Neosho, Missouri

- **State and locally supported** 2-year, founded 1963, part of Missouri Coordinating Board for Higher Education
- **Rural** 608-acre campus
- **Coed,** 5,219 undergraduate students, 47% full-time, 63% women, 37% men

Undergraduates 2,479 full-time, 2,740 part-time. Students come from 19 states and territories; 25 other countries; 4% are from out of state; 0.8% transferred in; 10% live on campus.

Freshmen *Admission:* 1,103 enrolled.

Faculty *Total:* 436, 19% full-time, 7% with terminal degrees. *Student/faculty ratio:* 12:1.

Majors Administrative assistant and secretarial science; agribusiness; agriculture; art; biology/biological sciences; business administration and management; business automation/technology/data entry; computer systems networking and telecommunications; construction engineering technology; drafting and design technology; dramatic/theater arts; education; electrical, electronic and communications engineering technology; elementary education; environmental engineering technology; environmental health; executive assistant/executive secretary; farm and ranch management; fire science/firefighting; general studies; industrial technology; legal administrative assistant/secretary; liberal arts and sciences/liberal studies; mass communication/media; mathematics; mathematics and computer science; medical administrative assistant and medical secretary; music; physical education teaching and coaching; physical sciences; poultry science; pre-engineering; psychology; public relations/image management; registered nursing/registered nurse.

Academics *Calendar:* semesters. *Degree:* certificates and associate. *Special study options:* academic remediation for entering students, adult/continuing education programs, advanced placement credit, cooperative education, English as a second language, freshman honors college, honors programs, independent study, part-time degree program, student-designed majors, study abroad, summer session for credit.

Library Bill & Margot Lee Library with 42,019 titles, 183 serial subscriptions, 6,330 audiovisual materials, an OPAC, a Web page.

Student Life *Housing Options:* men-only, women-only. Campus housing is university owned. *Activities and Organizations:* drama/theater group, student-run newspaper, choral group, Phi Theta Kappa, Students in Free Enterprise (SIFE), Baptist Student Union, Student Senate, Student Ambassadors. *Campus security:* 24-hour patrols. *Student services:* personal/psychological counseling.

Athletics Member NJCAA. *Intercollegiate sports:* baseball M(s), basketball W(s), soccer M(s).

Costs (2011–12) *Tuition:* area resident $2040 full-time, $68 per credit hour part-time; state resident $2850 full-time, $95 per credit hour part-time; nonresident $3690 full-time, $123 per credit hour part-time. *Required fees:* $340 full-time. *Room and board:* $3870. *Payment plan:* installment. *Waivers:* senior citizens and employees or children of employees.

Financial Aid Of all full-time matriculated undergraduates who enrolled in 2009, 150 Federal Work-Study jobs (averaging $1000).

Applying *Application fee:* $25. *Required:* high school transcript. *Application deadlines:* rolling (freshmen), rolling (transfers). *Notification:* continuous (freshmen).

Freshman Application Contact Mr. Jim Riggs, Admissions Coordinator, Crowder College, Neosho, MO 64850. *Phone:* 417-451-3223 Ext. 5466. *Toll-free phone:* 866-238-7788. *Fax:* 417-455-5731. *E-mail:* jimriggs@crowder.edu. *Web site:* http://www.crowder.edu/.

Culinary Institute of St. Louis at Hickey College

St. Louis, Missouri

- **Private** 2-year, founded 2009
- **Suburban** campus
- **Coed**

Majors Culinary arts.

Academics *Degree:* associate.

Freshman Application Contact Admissions Office, Culinary Institute of St. Louis at Hickey College, 2700 North Lindbergh Boulevard, St. Louis, MO

63114. *Phone:* 314-434-2212. *Toll-free phone:* 877-226-CHEF. *Web site:* http://www.ci-stl.com/.

East Central College
Union, Missouri

- **District-supported** 2-year, founded 1959
- **Rural** 207-acre campus with easy access to St. Louis
- **Endowment** $2.5 million
- **Coed**

Undergraduates 2,137 full-time, 2,066 part-time. Students come from 6 states and territories; 2 other countries. *Retention:* 61% of full-time freshmen returned.
Faculty *Student/faculty ratio:* 22:1.
Academics *Calendar:* semesters. *Degree:* certificates and associate. *Special study options:* academic remediation for entering students, adult/continuing education programs, advanced placement credit, distance learning, English as a second language, honors programs, independent study, internships, off-campus study, part-time degree program, services for LD students, study abroad, summer session for credit.
Student Life *Campus security:* 24-hour emergency response devices, late-night transport/escort service.
Athletics Member NJCAA.
Costs (2010–11) *Tuition:* area resident $1464 full-time, $61 per credit hour part-time; state resident $2088 full-time, $87 per credit hour part-time; nonresident $3144 full-time, $131 per credit hour part-time. Full-time tuition and fees vary according to program. Part-time tuition and fees vary according to program. *Required fees:* $240 full-time, $10 per credit hour part-time. *Payment plans:* installment, deferred payment.
Financial Aid Of all full-time matriculated undergraduates who enrolled in 2009, 35 Federal Work-Study jobs (averaging $1500). 35 state and other part-time jobs (averaging $1500).
Applying *Options:* early admission, deferred entrance. *Required:* high school transcript.
Freshman Application Contact Miss Megen Poynter, Admissions Coordinator, East Central College, 1964 Prarie Dell Road, Union, MO 63084. *Phone:* 636-584-6564. *Fax:* 636-584-7347. *E-mail:* poyntcrm@eastcentral.edu. *Web site:* http://www.eastcentral.edu/.

Everest College
Springfield, Missouri

Freshman Application Contact Admissions Office, Everest College, 1010 West Sunshine, Springfield, MO 65807-2488. *Phone:* 417-864-7220. *Fax:* 417-864-5697. *Web site:* http://www.everest.edu/campus/springfield/.

Heritage College
Kansas City, Missouri

Freshman Application Contact Admissions Office, Heritage College, 1200 East 104th Street, Suite 300, Kansas City, MO 64131. *Phone:* 816-942-5474. *Toll-free phone:* 888-334-7339. *E-mail:* info@heritage-education.com. *Web site:* http://www.heritage-education.com/.

High-Tech Institute
Kansas City, Missouri

Freshman Application Contact Admissions Office, High-Tech Institute, 9001 State Line Road, Kansas City, MO 64114. *Phone:* 816-444-4300. *Toll-free phone:* 866-296-2110. *Fax:* 816-444-4494. *Web site:* http://www.high-techinstitute.com/.

IHM Health Studies Center
St. Louis, Missouri

Freshman Application Contact Admissions Director, IHM Health Studies Center, 2500 Abbott Place, St. Louis, MO 63143. *Phone:* 314-768-1234. *Fax:* 314-768-1595. *E-mail:* info@ihmhealthstudies.edu. *Web site:* http://www.ihmhealthstudies.com/.

ITT Technical Institute
Arnold, Missouri

- **Proprietary** primarily 2-year, founded 1997, part of ITT Educational Services, Inc.
- **Coed**

Majors Business administration and management; CAD/CADD drafting/design technology; computer and information systems security; computer engineering technology; computer software and media applications related; computer software engineering; computer software technology; construction management; criminal justice/law enforcement administration; design and visual communications; electrical, electronic and communications engineering technology; information technology project management; legal assistant/paralegal; project management; system, networking, and LAN/WAN management; web/multimedia management and webmaster; web page, digital/multimedia and information resources design.
Academics *Calendar:* quarters. *Degrees:* associate and bachelor's.
Student Life *Housing:* college housing not available.
Freshman Application Contact Director of Recruitment, ITT Technical Institute, 1930 Meyer Drury Drive, Arnold, MO 63010. *Phone:* 636-464-6600. *Toll-free phone:* 888-488-1082. *Web site:* http://www.itt-tech.edu/.

ITT Technical Institute
Earth City, Missouri

- **Proprietary** primarily 2-year, founded 1936, part of ITT Educational Services, Inc.
- **Suburban** campus
- **Coed**

Majors CAD/CADD drafting/design technology; computer and information systems security; computer engineering technology; computer software and media applications related; computer software engineering; computer software technology; construction management; criminal justice/law enforcement administration; design and visual communications; electrical, electronic and communications engineering technology; game and interactive media design; legal assistant/paralegal; project management; registered nursing/registered nurse; system, networking, and LAN/WAN management; web page, digital/multimedia and information resources design.
Academics *Calendar:* quarters. *Degrees:* associate and bachelor's.
Student Life *Housing:* college housing not available.
Freshman Application Contact Director of Recruitment, ITT Technical Institute, 3640 Corporate Trail Drive, Earth City, MO 63045. *Phone:* 314-298-7800. *Toll-free phone:* 800-235-5488. *Web site:* http://www.itt-tech.edu/.

ITT Technical Institute
Kansas City, Missouri

- **Proprietary** primarily 2-year, founded 2004, part of ITT Educational Services, Inc.
- **Coed**

Majors CAD/CADD drafting/design technology; computer and information systems security; computer engineering technology; computer software engineering; computer software technology; construction management; criminal justice/law enforcement administration; design and visual communications; electrical, electronic and communications engineering technology; legal assistant/paralegal; project management; system, networking, and LAN/WAN management.
Academics *Calendar:* quarters. *Degrees:* associate and bachelor's.
Freshman Application Contact Director of Recruitment, ITT Technical Institute, 9150 East 41st Terrace, Kansas City, MO 64133. *Phone:* 816-276-1400. *Toll-free phone:* 877-488-1442. *Web site:* http://www.itt-tech.edu/.

Jefferson College
Hillsboro, Missouri

- **State-supported** 2-year, founded 1963
- **Rural** 480-acre campus with easy access to St. Louis
- **Coed,** 6,192 undergraduate students, 55% full-time, 59% women, 41% men

Undergraduates 3,429 full-time, 2,763 part-time. 12% are from out of state; 2% Black or African American, non-Hispanic/Latino; 0.6% Hispanic/Latino; 0.5% Asian, non-Hispanic/Latino; 0.1% Native Hawaiian or other Pacific Islander, non-Hispanic/Latino; 0.5% American Indian or Alaska Native, non-Hispanic/Latino; 3% Race/ethnicity unknown; 0.3% international.
Freshmen *Admission:* 1,527 enrolled.
Faculty *Total:* 374, 24% full-time, 7% with terminal degrees.
Majors Administrative assistant and secretarial science; automobile/automotive mechanics technology; business administration and management; CAD/CADD drafting/design technology; child-care and support services management; computer systems networking and telecommunications; criminal justice/law enforcement administration; criminal justice/police science; culinary arts; early childhood education; engineering; information technology; legal administrative assistant/secretary; liberal arts and sciences/liberal studies; licensed practical/vocational nurse training; registered nursing/registered nurse; veterinary/animal health technology; welding technology.
Academics *Calendar:* semesters. *Degree:* certificates, diplomas, and associate. *Special study options:* academic remediation for entering students, adult/

continuing education programs, advanced placement credit, distance learning, English as a second language, freshman honors college, honors programs, internships, off-campus study, part-time degree program, services for LD students, summer session for credit.

Library Jefferson College Library plus 1 other with 71,817 titles, 62 serial subscriptions, 2,166 audiovisual materials, an OPAC, a Web page.

Student Life *Housing Options:* coed. Campus housing is university owned. *Activities and Organizations:* drama/theater group, student-run newspaper, television station, choral group, Student Senate, Nursing associations, Baptist Student Unit, Phi Beta Lambda, Phi Theta Kappa, national sororities. *Campus security:* 24-hour patrols. *Student services:* personal/psychological counseling.

Athletics Member NJCAA. *Intercollegiate sports:* baseball M(s), basketball W(s), cheerleading M(s)/W(s), soccer M(s), softball W(s), volleyball W(s).

Costs (2011–12) *One-time required fee:* $25. *Tuition:* area resident $2550 full-time, $85 per credit hour part-time; state resident $3840 full-time, $128 per credit hour part-time; nonresident $5100 full-time, $170 per credit hour part-time. Full-time tuition and fees vary according to program. Part-time tuition and fees vary according to program. *Room and board:* $5794. Room and board charges vary according to housing facility. *Payment plan:* installment. *Waivers:* senior citizens and employees or children of employees.

Financial Aid Of all full-time matriculated undergraduates who enrolled in 2008, 2,567 applied for aid, 1,872 were judged to have need, 78 had their need fully met. 99 Federal Work-Study jobs (averaging $962). 112 state and other part-time jobs (averaging $1106). In 2008, 177 non-need-based awards were made. *Average percent of need met:* 57%. *Average financial aid package:* $5178. *Average need-based loan:* $2985. *Average need-based gift aid:* $2532. *Average non-need-based aid:* $1514.

Applying *Options:* electronic application, early admission. *Application fee:* $25. *Required:* high school transcript. *Application deadlines:* rolling (freshmen), rolling (transfers).

Freshman Application Contact Ms. Julie Fraser, Director of Admissions and Financial Aid, Jefferson College, 1000 Viking Drive, Hillsboro, MO 63050-2441. *Phone:* 636-797-3000. *Fax:* 636-789-5103. *E-mail:* admissions@ jeffco.edu. *Web site:* http://www.jeffco.edu/.

Linn State Technical College
Linn, Missouri

- **State-supported** 2-year, founded 1961
- **Rural** 249-acre campus
- **Endowment** $104,288
- **Coed, primarily men,** 1,176 undergraduate students, 84% full-time, 11% women, 89% men
- **65%** of applicants were admitted

Undergraduates 986 full-time, 190 part-time. Students come from 5 states and territories; 3% are from out of state; 2% Black or African American, non-Hispanic/Latino; 0.3% Hispanic/Latino; 0.4% Asian, non-Hispanic/Latino; 0.1% Native Hawaiian or other Pacific Islander, non-Hispanic/Latino; 0.6% American Indian or Alaska Native, non-Hispanic/Latino; 1% Race/ethnicity unknown; 9% transferred in; 15% live on campus. *Retention:* 81% of full-time freshmen returned.

Freshmen *Admission:* 1,085 applied, 705 admitted, 451 enrolled. *Average high school GPA:* 2.92.

Faculty *Total:* 89, 93% full-time. *Student/faculty ratio:* 15:1.

Majors Aircraft powerplant technology; airframe mechanics and aircraft maintenance technology; autobody/collision and repair technology; automobile/automotive mechanics technology; civil engineering technology; computer programming; computer systems networking and telecommunications; drafting and design technology; electrical, electronic and communications engineering technology; electrical/electronics equipment installation and repair; electrician; heating, air conditioning, ventilation and refrigeration maintenance technology; heavy equipment maintenance technology; lineworker; machine tool technology; management information systems; manufacturing engineering technology; medium/heavy vehicle and truck technology; motorcycle maintenance and repair technology; nuclear/nuclear power technology; physical therapy technology; turf and turfgrass management; welding technology.

Academics *Calendar:* semesters. *Degree:* certificates and associate. *Special study options:* academic remediation for entering students, accelerated degree program, adult/continuing education programs, advanced placement credit, cooperative education, distance learning, double majors, independent study, internships, off-campus study, part-time degree program, services for LD students, summer session for credit. *ROTC:* Army (c).

Library Linn State Technical College Library with 14,984 titles, 126 serial subscriptions, 1,931 audiovisual materials, an OPAC, a Web page.

Student Life *Housing Options:* coed, men-only, women-only, disabled students. Campus housing is university owned. *Activities and Organizations:* Skills USA, Phi Theta Kappa, Student Government Association, Aviation Club, Electricity Club. *Campus security:* 24-hour emergency response

devices, student patrols, controlled dormitory access, indoor and outdoor surveillance cameras. *Student services:* personal/psychological counseling.

Athletics *Intramural sports:* archery M/W, basketball M/W, bowling M/W, football M/W, golf M/W, riflery M/W, softball M/W, table tennis M/W, volleyball M/W.

Standardized Tests *Required:* COMPASS (for admission). *Required for some:* ACT (for admission).

Costs (2010–11) *Tuition:* state resident $4380 full-time, $146 per credit hour part-time; nonresident $8760 full-time, $292 per credit hour part-time. Full-time tuition and fees vary according to course load. Part-time tuition and fees vary according to course load. *Required fees:* $990 full-time, $33 per credit hour part-time. *Room and board:* $3530; room only: $3030. Room and board charges vary according to board plan. *Payment plan:* installment. *Waivers:* employees or children of employees.

Financial Aid Of all full-time matriculated undergraduates who enrolled in 2009, 70 Federal Work-Study jobs (averaging $769).

Applying *Options:* electronic application. *Required:* high school transcript. *Required for some:* essay or personal statement, interview, some require high school attendance, mechanical test. *Application deadlines:* rolling (freshmen), rolling (out-of-state freshmen), rolling (transfers). *Notification:* continuous (freshmen), continuous (out-of-state freshmen), continuous (transfers).

Freshman Application Contact Linn State Technical College, One Technology Drive, Linn, MO 65051-9606. *Phone:* 573-897-5196. *Toll-free phone:* 800-743-TECH. *Web site:* http://www.linnstate.edu/.

Metro Business College
Cape Girardeau, Missouri

Director of Admissions Ms. Kyla Evans, Admissions Director, Metro Business College, 1732 North Kingshighway, Cape Girardeau, MO 63701. *Phone:* 573-334-9181. *Fax:* 573-334-0617. *Web site:* http://www.metrobusinesscollege.edu/.

Metro Business College
Jefferson City, Missouri

Freshman Application Contact Ms. Cheri Chockley, Campus Director, Metro Business College, 1407 Southwest Boulevard, Jefferson City, MO 65109. *Phone:* 573-635-6600. *Toll-free phone:* 888-43-METRO. *Fax:* 573-635-6999. *E-mail:* cheri@metrobusinesscollege.edu. *Web site:* http://www.metrobusinesscollege.edu/.

Metro Business College
Rolla, Missouri

Freshman Application Contact Admissions Office, Metro Business College, 1202 East Highway 72, Rolla, MO 65401. *Phone:* 573-364-8464. *Toll-free phone:* 888-43-METRO. *Fax:* 573-364-8077. *E-mail:* inforolla@ metrobusinesscollege.edu. *Web site:* http://www.metrobusinesscollege.edu/.

Metropolitan Community College–Blue River
Independence, Missouri

- **State and locally supported** 2-year, founded 1997, part of Metropolitan Community Colleges System
- **Suburban** campus with easy access to Kansas City
- **Endowment** $3.3 million
- **Coed,** 3,537 undergraduate students, 44% full-time, 59% women, 41% men

Undergraduates 1,551 full-time, 1,986 part-time. Students come from 6 states and territories; 5% transferred in. *Retention:* 54% of full-time freshmen returned.

Freshmen *Admission:* 853 applied, 853 admitted, 853 enrolled.

Faculty *Total:* 246, 16% full-time, 9% with terminal degrees. *Student/faculty ratio:* 20:1.

Majors Accounting technology and bookkeeping; administrative assistant and secretarial science; business administration and management; computer and information sciences related; computer science; criminal justice/police science; fire science/firefighting; information science/studies; liberal arts and sciences/liberal studies.

Academics *Calendar:* semesters. *Degree:* certificates and associate. *Special study options:* academic remediation for entering students, accelerated degree program, adult/continuing education programs, advanced placement credit, cooperative education, distance learning, English as a second language, honors programs, independent study, internships, off-campus study, part-time degree program, study abroad.

Library Blue River Community College Library with 10,312 titles, 66 serial subscriptions, an OPAC, a Web page.

Student Life *Housing:* college housing not available. *Activities and Organizations:* choral group. *Campus security:* 24-hour emergency response devices and patrols.

Athletics Member NJCAA. *Intercollegiate sports:* soccer M/W.

Costs (2011–12) *Tuition:* area resident $2310 full-time, $77 per credit hour part-time; state resident $4230 full-time, $141 per credit hour part-time; nonresident $5700 full-time, $190 per credit hour part-time. Full-time tuition and fees vary according to class time, course load, location, program, and reciprocity agreements. Part-time tuition and fees vary according to class time, course load, location, program, and reciprocity agreements. *Required fees:* $150 full-time. *Payment plan:* installment. *Waivers:* senior citizens and employees or children of employees.

Applying *Options:* early admission, deferred entrance. *Application deadlines:* rolling (freshmen), rolling (transfers).

Freshman Application Contact Dr. Jon Burke, Dean of Student Development, Metropolitan Community College–Blue River, Independence, MO 64057. *Phone:* 816-604-6118. *Fax:* 816-655-6014. *Web site:* http://www.mcckc.edu/.

Metropolitan Community College–Business & Technology Campus
Kansas City, Missouri

- **State and locally supported** 2-year, founded 1995, part of Metropolitan Community Colleges System
- **Urban** 23-acre campus
- **Endowment** $3.3 million
- **Coed,** 827 undergraduate students, 33% full-time, 12% women, 88% men
- **100% of applicants were admitted**

Undergraduates 275 full-time, 552 part-time. Students come from 1 other state; 2% are from out of state; 11% Black or African American, non-Hispanic/Latino; 5% Hispanic/Latino; 1% Asian, non-Hispanic/Latino; 0.5% Native Hawaiian or other Pacific Islander, non-Hispanic/Latino; 0.5% American Indian or Alaska Native, non-Hispanic/Latino; 5% Two or more races, non-Hispanic/Latino; 3% Race/ethnicity unknown. *Retention:* 29% of full-time freshmen returned.

Freshmen *Admission:* 179 applied, 179 admitted.

Faculty *Total:* 94, 16% full-time, 1% with terminal degrees. *Student/faculty ratio:* 11:1.

Majors Accounting; accounting technology and bookkeeping; artificial intelligence; building/construction site management; business administration and management; business/commerce; carpentry; computer and information sciences; computer and information sciences and support services related; computer and information sciences related; computer and information systems security; computer graphics; computer/information technology services administration related; computer programming; computer programming related; computer programming (specific applications); computer programming (vendor/product certification); computer science; computer software and media applications related; computer systems analysis; computer systems networking and telecommunications; data entry/microcomputer applications; data entry/microcomputer applications related; data modeling/warehousing and database administration; data processing and data processing technology; drafting and design technology; electrical, electronic and communications engineering technology; engineering; engineering-related technologies; environmental engineering technology; glazier; information science/studies; information technology; liberal arts and sciences/liberal studies; machine shop technology; management information systems and services related; masonry; network and system administration; quality control technology; system, networking, and LAN/WAN management; web/multimedia management and webmaster; web page, digital/multimedia and information resources design; word processing.

Academics *Calendar:* semesters. *Degree:* certificates and associate.

Library Learning Resource Center/Library with an OPAC.

Student Life *Housing:* college housing not available. *Campus security:* 24-hour patrols, late-night transport/escort service.

Costs (2011–12) *Tuition:* area resident $2310 full-time, $77 per credit hour part-time; state resident $4230 full-time, $141 per credit hour part-time; nonresident $5700 full-time, $190 per credit hour part-time. Full-time tuition and fees vary according to program and reciprocity agreements. Part-time tuition and fees vary according to program and reciprocity agreements. *Required fees:* $150 full-time. *Payment plan:* installment. *Waivers:* senior citizens and employees or children of employees.

Applying *Application deadlines:* rolling (freshmen), rolling (transfers).

Freshman Application Contact Mr. Tom Wheeler, Dean of Instruction, Metropolitan Community College–Business & Technology Campus, Kansas

City, MO 64120. *Phone:* 816-604-5240. *Toll-free phone:* 800-841-7158. *Web site:* http://www.mcckc.edu/.

Metropolitan Community College–Longview
Lee's Summit, Missouri

- **State and locally supported** 2-year, founded 1969, part of Metropolitan Community Colleges System
- **Suburban** 147-acre campus with easy access to Kansas City
- **Endowment** $3.3 million
- **Coed,** 6,539 undergraduate students, 46% full-time, 57% women, 43% men

Undergraduates 2,993 full-time, 3,546 part-time. Students come from 6 states and territories. *Retention:* 53% of full-time freshmen returned.

Freshmen *Admission:* 1,396 applied, 1,396 admitted.

Faculty *Total:* 303, 28% full-time, 32% with terminal degrees. *Student/faculty ratio:* 26:1.

Majors Accounting; administrative assistant and secretarial science; agricultural mechanization; automobile/automotive mechanics technology; biological and physical sciences; biology/biological sciences; business administration and management; chemistry; computer and information sciences related; computer programming; computer science; computer typography and composition equipment operation; corrections; criminal justice/law enforcement administration; criminal justice/police science; data processing and data processing technology; engineering; heavy equipment maintenance technology; human services; legal administrative assistant/secretary; liberal arts and sciences/liberal studies; marketing/marketing management; medical administrative assistant and medical secretary; pre-engineering.

Academics *Calendar:* semesters. *Degree:* certificates and associate. *Special study options:* academic remediation for entering students, accelerated degree program, adult/continuing education programs, advanced placement credit, cooperative education, distance learning, English as a second language, honors programs, independent study, internships, off-campus study, part-time degree program, study abroad.

Library Longview Community College Library with 56,266 titles, 288 serial subscriptions, an OPAC, a Web page.

Student Life *Housing:* college housing not available. *Activities and Organizations:* drama/theater group, student-run newspaper, choral group, student newspaper, student government, Phi Theta Kappa, Longview Mighty Voices Choir, Longview Broadcasting Network, national fraternities. *Campus security:* 24-hour patrols. *Student services:* personal/psychological counseling.

Athletics Member NJCAA. *Intercollegiate sports:* baseball M(s), cross-country running W(s), volleyball W(s). *Intramural sports:* basketball M/W, swimming and diving M/W, volleyball M/W.

Costs (2011–12) *Tuition:* area resident $2310 full-time, $77 per credit hour part-time; state resident $4230 full-time, $141 per credit hour part-time; nonresident $5700 full-time, $190 per credit hour part-time. Full-time tuition and fees vary according to reciprocity agreements. Part-time tuition and fees vary according to reciprocity agreements. *Required fees:* $150 full-time. *Payment plan:* installment. *Waivers:* senior citizens and employees or children of employees.

Applying *Options:* early admission, deferred entrance. *Application deadlines:* rolling (freshmen), rolling (transfers).

Freshman Application Contact Ms. Janet Cline, Dean of Student Development, Metropolitan Community College–Longview, 500 Southwest Longview Road, Lee's Summit, MO 64081-2105. *Phone:* 816-604-2249. *Fax:* 816-672-2040. *E-mail:* janet.cline@mcckc.edu. *Web site:* http://www.mcckc.edu/.

Metropolitan Community College–Maple Woods
Kansas City, Missouri

- **State and locally supported** 2-year, founded 1969, part of Metropolitan Community Colleges System
- **Suburban** 205-acre campus
- **Coed,** 5,385 undergraduate students, 43% full-time, 59% women, 41% men

Undergraduates 2,317 full-time, 3,068 part-time. Students come from 7 states and territories; 2 other countries; 7% transferred in. *Retention:* 50% of full-time freshmen returned.

Freshmen *Admission:* 1,272 applied, 1,272 admitted, 1,272 enrolled.

Faculty *Total:* 262, 20% full-time, 29% with terminal degrees. *Student/faculty ratio:* 27:1.

Majors Accounting; administrative assistant and secretarial science; avionics maintenance technology; biological and physical sciences; biology/biological sciences; business administration and management; chemistry; computer and information sciences related; computer programming; computer science; criminal justice/law enforcement administration; criminal justice/police science; data processing and data processing technology; legal administrative assistant/secretary; liberal arts and sciences/liberal studies; marketing/marketing management; medical administrative assistant and medical secretary; pre-engineering; veterinary/animal health technology.

Academics *Calendar:* semesters. *Degree:* certificates and associate. *Special study options:* academic remediation for entering students, accelerated degree program, adult/continuing education programs, advanced placement credit, cooperative education, distance learning, English as a second language, honors programs, internships, off-campus study, part-time degree program, services for LD students, summer session for credit.

Library Maple Woods Community College Library with 32,906 titles, 250 serial subscriptions, an OPAC.

Student Life *Housing:* college housing not available. *Activities and Organizations:* drama/theater group, student-run newspaper, choral group, Student Activities Council, Art Club, Friends of All Cultures, Phi Theta Kappa, Engineering Club, national fraternities. *Campus security:* 24-hour patrols, late-night transport/escort service. *Student services:* personal/psychological counseling.

Athletics Member NJCAA. *Intercollegiate sports:* baseball M(s), soccer M/W, softball W(s). *Intramural sports:* softball M/W, volleyball M/W.

Costs (2011–12) *Tuition:* area resident $2310 full-time, $77 per credit hour part-time; state resident $4230 full-time, $141 per credit hour part-time; nonresident $5700 full-time, $190 per credit hour part-time. Full-time tuition and fees vary according to reciprocity agreements. Part-time tuition and fees vary according to reciprocity agreements. *Required fees:* $150 full-time. *Payment plan:* installment. *Waivers:* senior citizens and employees or children of employees.

Applying *Options:* early admission, deferred entrance. *Application deadlines:* rolling (freshmen), rolling (transfers). *Notification:* continuous (freshmen), continuous (transfers).

Freshman Application Contact Ms. Shelli Allen, Dean of Student Development and Enrollment Management, Metropolitan Community College–Maple Woods, 2601 Northeast Barry Road, Kansas City, MO 64156-1299. *Phone:* 816-604-3175. *Fax:* 816-437-3351. *Web site:* http://www.mcckc.edu/.

Metropolitan Community College– Penn Valley

Kansas City, Missouri

- **State and locally supported** 2-year, founded 1969, part of Metropolitan Community Colleges System
- **Urban** 25-acre campus
- **Endowment** $3.3 million
- **Coed,** 4,956 undergraduate students, 33% full-time, 70% women, 30% men

Undergraduates 1,628 full-time, 3,328 part-time. Students come from 6 states and territories; 44 other countries; 2% are from out of state; 7% transferred in. *Retention:* 45% of full-time freshmen returned.

Freshmen *Admission:* 886 applied, 886 admitted, 886 enrolled.

Faculty *Total:* 304, 33% full-time, 28% with terminal degrees. *Student/faculty ratio:* 16:1.

Majors Accounting; administrative assistant and secretarial science; biological and physical sciences; biology/biological sciences; business administration and management; chemistry; child-care provision; commercial and advertising art; computer and information sciences related; computer science; corrections; criminal justice/law enforcement administration; criminal justice/police science; data processing and data processing technology; emergency medical technology (EMT paramedic); engineering; family and consumer sciences/human sciences; fashion/apparel design; fashion merchandising; health information/medical records administration; kindergarten/preschool education; legal administrative assistant/secretary; legal assistant/paralegal; liberal arts and sciences/liberal studies; marketing/marketing management; medical administrative assistant and medical secretary; occupational therapy; physical therapy; registered nursing/registered nurse; respiratory care therapy; special products marketing.

Academics *Calendar:* semesters. *Degree:* certificates and associate. *Special study options:* academic remediation for entering students, accelerated degree program, adult/continuing education programs, advanced placement credit, cooperative education, distance learning, English as a second language, honors programs, independent study, internships, off-campus study, part-time degree program, study abroad.

Library Penn Valley Community College Library with 91,428 titles, 89,242 serial subscriptions, an OPAC.

Student Life *Housing:* college housing not available. *Activities and Organizations:* drama/theater group, student-run newspaper, choral group, Black Student Association, Los Americanos, Phi Theta Kappa, Fashion Club, national

fraternities. *Campus security:* 24-hour patrols. *Student services:* personal/psychological counseling.

Athletics Member NJCAA. *Intercollegiate sports:* basketball M(s)/W(s).

Costs (2011–12) *Tuition:* area resident $2310 full-time, $77 per credit hour part-time; state resident $4230 full-time, $141 per credit hour part-time; nonresident $5700 full-time, $190 per credit hour part-time. Full-time tuition and fees vary according to reciprocity agreements. Part-time tuition and fees vary according to reciprocity agreements. *Required fees:* $150 full-time. *Payment plan:* installment. *Waivers:* senior citizens and employees or children of employees.

Applying *Options:* early admission. *Required:* high school transcript. *Application deadlines:* rolling (freshmen), rolling (transfers).

Freshman Application Contact Ms. Lisa Minis, Dean of Student Services, Metropolitan Community College–Penn Valley, 3201 Southwest Trafficway, Kansas City, MO 64111. *Phone:* 816-604-4101. *Fax:* 816-759-4478. *Web site:* http://www.mcckc.edu/.

Midwest Institute

Earth City, Missouri

Freshman Application Contact Admissions Office, Midwest Institute, 4260 Shoreline Drive, Earth City, MO 63045. *Phone:* 314-344-4440. *Toll-free phone:* 800-695-5550. *Fax:* 314-344-0495. *Web site:* http://www.midwestinstitute.com/.

Midwest Institute

Kirkwood, Missouri

Freshman Application Contact Admissions Office, Midwest Institute, 10910 Manchester Road, Kirkwood, MO 63122. *Web site:* http://www.midwestinstitute.com/.

Mineral Area College

Park Hills, Missouri

Freshman Application Contact Linda Huffman, Registrar, Mineral Area College, PO Box 1000, Park Hills, MO 63601-1000. *Phone:* 573-518-2130. *Fax:* 573-518-2166. *E-mail:* lhuffman@mineralarea.edu. *Web site:* http://www.mineralarea.edu/.

Missouri College

St. Louis, Missouri

Director of Admissions Mr. Doug Brinker, Admissions Director, Missouri College, 10121 Manchester Road, St. Louis, MO 63122-1583. *Phone:* 314-821-7700. *Fax:* 314-821-0891. *Web site:* http://www.mocollege.com/.

Missouri State University–West Plains

West Plains, Missouri

- **State-supported** 2-year, founded 1963, part of Missouri State University
- **Small-town** 20-acre campus
- **Endowment** $2.0 million
- **Coed,** 2,219 undergraduate students, 61% full-time, 60% women, 40% men

Undergraduates 1,360 full-time, 859 part-time. Students come from 26 states and territories; 6 other countries; 3% are from out of state; 2% transferred in; 6% live on campus. *Retention:* 56% of full-time freshmen returned.

Freshmen *Admission:* 1,010 applied, 743 admitted, 596 enrolled. *Average high school GPA:* 3.13. *Test scores:* ACT scores over 18: 60%; ACT scores over 24: 15%.

Faculty *Total:* 114, 29% full-time, 14% with terminal degrees. *Student/faculty ratio:* 27:1.

Majors Accounting; agriculture; business administration and management; business/commerce; child-care and support services management; computer and information sciences related; computer graphics; computer programming (specific applications); criminal justice/law enforcement administration; criminal justice/police science; engineering; entrepreneurship; food science; general studies; horticultural science; industrial technology; information technology; legal assistant/paralegal; management information systems and services related; registered nursing/registered nurse; respiratory therapy technician.

Academics *Calendar:* semesters. *Degree:* certificates and associate. *Special study options:* academic remediation for entering students, advanced placement credit, cooperative education, distance learning, honors programs, internships, off-campus study, part-time degree program, services for LD students, study abroad, summer session for credit.

Library Garnett Library with 50,717 titles, 142 serial subscriptions, 1,236 audiovisual materials, an OPAC, a Web page.

Student Life *Housing Options:* men-only, women-only. Campus housing is university owned. *Activities and Organizations:* Student Government Association, Chi Alpha, Adult Students in Higher Education, Lambda Lambda Lambda, Programming Board. *Campus security:* late-night transport/escort service, access only with key. *Student services:* health clinic, personal/psychological counseling.

Athletics Member NJCAA. *Intercollegiate sports:* basketball M(s), volleyball W(s).

Costs (2011–12) *Tuition:* state resident $3210 full-time, $107 per credit part-time; nonresident $6410 full-time, $214 per credit part-time. Full-time tuition and fees vary according to course load, location, and program. Part-time tuition and fees vary according to course load and location. *Required fees:* $294 full-time, $5 per credit part-time, $72 per year part-time. *Room and board:* $5116. Room and board charges vary according to board plan. *Payment plan:* deferred payment. *Waivers:* senior citizens and employees or children of employees.

Financial Aid Of all full-time matriculated undergraduates who enrolled in 2009, 63 Federal Work-Study jobs (averaging $2000).

Applying *Options:* electronic application. *Application fee:* $15. *Required for some:* high school transcript. *Application deadlines:* 8/20 (freshmen), 8/20 (out-of-state freshmen), 8/20 (transfers). *Notification:* continuous (freshmen), continuous (out-of-state freshmen), continuous (transfers).

Freshman Application Contact Ms. Melissa Jett, Coordinator of Admissions, Missouri State University–West Plains, 128 Garfield, West Plains, MO 65775. *Phone:* 417-255-7955. *Fax:* 417-255-7959. *E-mail:* melissajett@missouristate.edu. *Web site:* http://wp.missouristate.edu/.

Moberly Area Community College
Moberly, Missouri

Freshman Application Contact Dr. James Grant, Dean of Student Services, Moberly Area Community College, Moberly, MO 65270-1304. *Phone:* 660-263-4110 Ext. 235. *Toll-free phone:* 800-622-2070 Ext. 270. *Fax:* 660-263-2406. *E-mail:* info@macc.edu. *Web site:* http://www.macc.edu/.

North Central Missouri College
Trenton, Missouri

Freshman Application Contact Megan Goodin, Admissions Assistant, North Central Missouri College, Trenton, MO 64683. *Phone:* 660-359-3948 Ext. 1410. *Toll-free phone:* 800-880-6180 Ext. 401. *E-mail:* megoodin@mail.ncmissouri.edu. *Web site:* http://www.ncmissouri.edu/.

Ozarks Technical Community College
Springfield, Missouri

Director of Admissions Mr. Jeff Jochems, Dean of Student Development, Ozarks Technical Community College, PO Box 5958, 1001 East Chestnut Expressway, Springfield, MO 65801. *Phone:* 417-895-7136. *Web site:* http://www.otc.edu/.

Pinnacle Career Institute
Kansas City, Missouri

Director of Admissions Ms. Ruth Matous, Director of Admissions, Pinnacle Career Institute, 1001 East 101st Terrace, Suite 325, Kansas City, MO 64131. *Phone:* 816-331-5700 Ext. 212. *Toll-free phone:* 800-614-0900. *Web site:* http://www.pcitraining.edu/.

Ranken Technical College
St. Louis, Missouri

Director of Admissions Ms. Elizabeth Keserauskis, Director of Admissions, Ranken Technical College, 4431 Finney Avenue, St. Louis, MO 63113. *Phone:* 314-371-0233 Ext. 4811. *Toll-free phone:* 866-4RANKEN. *Web site:* http://www.ranken.edu/.

Saint Charles Community College
Cottleville, Missouri

- **State-supported** 2-year, founded 1986, part of Missouri Coordinating Board for Higher Education
- **Suburban** 234-acre campus with easy access to St. Louis
- **Coed,** 8,202 undergraduate students, 53% full-time, 57% women, 43% men

Undergraduates 4,313 full-time, 3,889 part-time. Students come from 11 states and territories; 20 other countries; 5% transferred in. *Retention:* 64% of full-time freshmen returned.

Freshmen *Admission:* 2,874 applied, 2,817 admitted, 1,789 enrolled.

Faculty *Total:* 420, 23% full-time, 9% with terminal degrees. *Student/faculty ratio:* 25:1.

Majors Accounting technology and bookkeeping; biology/biological sciences; chemistry; child-care provision; civil engineering; commercial and advertising art; criminal justice/police science; drafting and design technology; dramatic/theater arts; economics; education; education (specific subject areas) related; emergency medical technology (EMT paramedic); engineering; English; fire science/firefighting; foreign languages and literatures; French; general studies; health information/medical records technology; history; human services; industrial technology; liberal arts and sciences/liberal studies; licensed practical/vocational nurse training; marketing/marketing management; massage therapy; mathematics; mechanical engineering; medical administrative assistant and medical secretary; music history, literature, and theory; occupational therapist assistant; philosophy; political science and government; precision production related; psychology; registered nursing/registered nurse; social work; sociology; Spanish; teacher assistant/aide.

Academics *Calendar:* semesters. *Degree:* certificates and associate. *Special study options:* academic remediation for entering students, adult/continuing education programs, advanced placement credit, cooperative education, distance learning, double majors, English as a second language, independent study, internships, part-time degree program, services for LD students, study abroad, summer session for credit.

Library Paul and Helen Schnare Library with 94,931 titles, 278 serial subscriptions, 8,108 audiovisual materials, an OPAC, a Web page.

Student Life *Housing:* college housing not available. *Activities and Organizations:* drama/theater group, student-run newspaper, choral group, Phi Theta Kappa, Student Nurse Organization, Student Ambassadors, Outdoors Crew, Roller Hockey. *Campus security:* 24-hour emergency response devices and patrols, late-night transport/escort service, campus police officers on duty during normal operating hours. *Student services:* personal/psychological counseling.

Athletics Member NJCAA. *Intercollegiate sports:* baseball M(s), soccer M(s)/W(s), softball W(s).

Costs (2011–12) *Tuition:* area resident $1920 full-time, $80 per credit hour part-time; state resident $2832 full-time, $118 per credit hour part-time; nonresident $4200 full-time, $175 per credit hour part-time. *Payment plan:* installment. *Waivers:* senior citizens and employees or children of employees.

Applying *Options:* electronic application, early admission, deferred entrance. *Required for some:* high school transcript, minimum 2.5 GPA. *Recommended:* high school transcript. *Application deadlines:* rolling (freshmen), rolling (out-of-state freshmen), rolling (transfers). *Notification:* continuous (freshmen), continuous (out-of-state freshmen), continuous (transfers).

Freshman Application Contact Ms. Kathy Brockgreitens-Gober, Director of Admissions/Registrar/Financial Assistance, Saint Charles Community College, 4601 Mid Rivers Mall Drive, Cottleville, MO 63376-0975. *Phone:* 636-922-8229. *Fax:* 636-922-8236. *E-mail:* regist@stchas.edu. *Web site:* http://www.stchas.edu/.

St. Louis College of Health Careers
St. Louis, Missouri

Freshman Application Contact Admissions Office, St. Louis College of Health Careers, 909 South Taylor Avenue, St. Louis, MO 63110-1511. *Phone:* 314-652-0300. *Toll-free phone:* 866-529-7380. *Fax:* 314-652-4825. *Web site:* http://www.slchc.com/.

St. Louis Community College at Florissant Valley
St. Louis, Missouri

Freshman Application Contact Ms. Brenda Davenport, Manager of Admissions and Registration, St. Louis Community College at Florissant Valley, 3400 Pershall Road, St. Louis, MO 63135-1499. *Phone:* 314-513-4248. *Fax:* 314-513-4724. *Web site:* http://www.stlcc.edu/.

St. Louis Community College at Forest Park
St. Louis, Missouri

Freshman Application Contact Director of Admissions, St. Louis Community College at Forest Park, 5600 Oakland Avenue, St. Louis, MO 63110-1316. *Phone:* 314-644-9129. *Fax:* 314-644-9375. *E-mail:* fp_admissions@stlcc.edu. *Web site:* http://www.stlcc.edu/.

St. Louis Community College at Meramec

Kirkwood, Missouri

Freshman Application Contact Director of Admissions, St. Louis Community College at Meramec, 11333 Big Bend Boulevard, Kirkwood, MO 63122-5720. *Phone:* 314-984-7601. *Fax:* 314-984-7051. *E-mail:* mc-admissions@stlcc.edu. *Web site:* http://www.stlcc.edu/.

Sanford-Brown College

Fenton, Missouri

Director of Admissions Ms. Judy Wilga, Director of Admissions, Sanford-Brown College, 1203 Smizer Mill Road, Fenton, MO 63026. *Phone:* 636-349-4900 Ext. 102. *Toll-free phone:* 800-456-7222. *Fax:* 636-349-9170. *Web site:* http://www.sanford-brown.edu/.

Sanford-Brown College

Hazelwood, Missouri

Director of Admissions Sherri Bremer, Director of Admissions, Sanford-Brown College, 75 Village Square, Hazelwood, MO 63042. *Phone:* 314-731-5200 Ext. 201. *Web site:* http://www.sanford-brown.edu/.

Sanford-Brown College

St. Peters, Missouri

Director of Admissions Karl J. Petersen, Executive Director, Sanford-Brown College, 100 Richmond Center Boulevard, St. Peters, MO 63376. *Phone:* 636-949-2620. *Toll-free phone:* 888-793-2433. *Fax:* 636-949-5081. *E-mail:* karl.peterson@wix.net. *Web site:* http://www.sanford-brown.edu/.

Southeast Missouri Hospital College of Nursing and Health Sciences

Cape Girardeau, Missouri

Director of Admissions Tonya L. Buttry, President, Southeast Missouri Hospital College of Nursing and Health Sciences, 2001 William Street, Cape Girardeau, MO 63701. *Phone:* 534-334-6825. *E-mail:* tbuttry@sehosp.org. *Web site:* http://www.southeastmissourihospitalcollege.edu/.

State Fair Community College

Sedalia, Missouri

- **District-supported** 2-year, founded 1966, part of Missouri Coordinating Board for Higher Education
- **Small-town** 128-acre campus
- **Endowment** $6.5 million
- **Coed**

Undergraduates 2,455 full-time, 1,808 part-time. Students come from 19 states and territories; 1% are from out of state; 5% transferred in; 3% live on campus. *Retention:* 61% of full-time freshmen returned.
Faculty *Student/faculty ratio:* 21:1.
Academics *Calendar:* semesters. *Degree:* certificates and associate. *Special study options:* academic remediation for entering students, adult/continuing education programs, advanced placement credit, distance learning, English as a second language, internships, off-campus study, part-time degree program, services for LD students, summer session for credit. *ROTC:* Army (b).
Student Life *Campus security:* controlled dormitory access, security during evening class hours.
Athletics Member NJCAA.
Costs (2010–11) *Tuition:* area resident $2040 full-time, $68 per credit hour part-time; state resident $2880 full-time, $96 per credit hour part-time; nonresident $4560 full-time, $152 per credit hour part-time. Full-time tuition and fees vary according to location and program. Part-time tuition and fees vary according to location and program. *Required fees:* $420 full-time, $14 per credit hour part-time. *Room and board:* $4350.
Financial Aid Of all full-time matriculated undergraduates who enrolled in 2009, 85 Federal Work-Study jobs (averaging $1616).
Applying *Options:* electronic application. *Application fee:* $25. *Required:* high school transcript.
Freshman Application Contact State Fair Community College, 3201 West 16th Street, Sedalia, MO 65301-2199. *Phone:* 660-596-7221. *Toll-free phone:* 877-311-7322 Ext. 217 (in-state); 877-311-7322 (out-of-state). *Web site:* http://www.sfccmo.edu/.

Three Rivers Community College

Poplar Bluff, Missouri

- **State and locally supported** 2-year, founded 1966, part of Missouri Coordinating Board for Higher Education
- **Rural** 70-acre campus
- **Endowment** $678,633
- **Coed**

Undergraduates 1,942 full-time, 1,243 part-time. Students come from 13 states and territories; 4% are from out of state; 0.1% transferred in; 5% live on campus.
Faculty *Student/faculty ratio:* 23:1.
Academics *Calendar:* semesters. *Degree:* certificates and associate. *Special study options:* academic remediation for entering students, accelerated degree program, adult/continuing education programs, advanced placement credit, distance learning, double majors, English as a second language, external degree program, honors programs, independent study, internships, part-time degree program, services for LD students, summer session for credit.
Student Life *Campus security:* 24-hour patrols.
Athletics Member NJCAA.
Costs (2010–11) *Tuition:* area resident $2010 full-time, $67 per credit hour part-time; state resident $3210 full-time, $107 per credit hour part-time; non-resident $4020 full-time, $134 per credit hour part-time. *Required fees:* $605 full-time, $14 per credit hour part-time. *Room and board:* room only: $3324. *Payment plans:* installment, deferred payment.
Applying *Options:* early admission. *Application fee:* $20. *Required:* high school transcript.
Freshman Application Contact Ms. Marcia Fields, Director of Admissions and Recruiting, Three Rivers Community College, Poplar Bluff, MO 63901. *Phone:* 573-840-9675. *Toll-free phone:* 877-TRY-TRCC Ext. 605 (in-state); 877-TRY-TRCC (out-of-state). *E-mail:* trytrcc@trcc.edu. *Web site:* http://www.trcc.edu/.

Vatterott College

Kansas City, Missouri

Admissions Office Contact Vatterott College, 8955 East 38th Terrace, Kansas City, MO 64129. *Toll-free phone:* 866-314-6454 (in-state); 877-201-4420 (out-of-state). *Web site:* http://www.vatterott-college.edu/.

Vatterott College

O'Fallon, Missouri

Director of Admissions Gertrude Bogan-Jones, Director of Admissions, Vatterott College, 927 East Terra Lane, O'Fallon, MO 63366. *Phone:* 636-978-7488. *Toll-free phone:* 888-766-3601. *Fax:* 636-978-5121. *E-mail:* ofallon@vatterott-college.edu. *Web site:* http://www.vatterott-college.edu/.

Vatterott College

St. Ann, Missouri

Director of Admissions Ann Farajallah, Director of Admissions, Vatterott College, 3925 Industrial Drive, St. Ann, MO 63074-1807. *Phone:* 314-264-1020. *Toll-free phone:* 866-314-6454. *Web site:* http://www.vatterott-college.edu/.

Vatterott College

St. Joseph, Missouri

Director of Admissions Director of Admissions, Vatterott College, 3131 Frederick Avenue, St. Joseph, MO 64506. *Phone:* 816-364-5399. *Toll-free phone:* 800-282-5327. *Fax:* 816-364-1593. *Web site:* http://www.vatterott-college.edu/.

Vatterott College

Sunset Hills, Missouri

Director of Admissions Director of Admission, Vatterott College, 12970 Maurer Industrial Drive, St. Louis, MO 63127. *Phone:* 314-843-4200. *Fax:* 314-843-1709. *Web site:* http://www.vatterott-college.edu/.

Vatterott College

Springfield, Missouri

Freshman Application Contact Mr. Scott Lester, Director of Admissions, Vatterott College, 1258 East Trafficway Street, Springfield, MO 65802. *Phone:* 417-831-8116. *Toll-free phone:* 800-766-5829. *Fax:* 417-831-5099.

E-mail: springfield@vatterott-college.edu. *Web site:* http://www.vatterott-college.edu/.

Vet Tech Institute at Hickey College

St. Louis, Missouri

- **Private** 2-year, founded 2007
- **Suburban** campus
- **Coed,** 125 undergraduate students
- 49% of applicants were admitted

Freshmen *Admission:* 588 applied, 290 admitted.

Majors Veterinary/animal health technology.

Academics *Degree:* associate. *Special study options:* accelerated degree program, internships.

Freshman Application Contact Admissions Office, Vet Tech Institute at Hickey College, 2780 North Lindbergh Boulevard, St. Louis, MO 63114. *Phone:* 888-884-1459. *Web site:* http://www.vettechinstitute.edu/.

Wentworth Military Academy and College

Lexington, Missouri

- **Independent** 2-year, founded 1880
- **Small-town** 130-acre campus with easy access to Kansas City
- **Coed,** 941 undergraduate students, 9% full-time, 49% women, 51% men

Undergraduates 84 full-time, 857 part-time. Students come from 22 states and territories; 4 other countries; 43% are from out of state; 2% Black or African American, non-Hispanic/Latino; 2% Hispanic/Latino; 1% Asian, non-Hispanic/Latino; 1% Native Hawaiian or other Pacific Islander, non-Hispanic/Latino; 0.4% American Indian or Alaska Native, non-Hispanic/Latino; 1% Two or more races, non-Hispanic/Latino; 1% Race/ethnicity unknown; 2% international; 0.1% transferred in. *Retention:* 88% of full-time freshmen returned.

Freshmen *Admission:* 456 applied, 456 admitted, 92 enrolled. *Average high school GPA:* 2.88. *Test scores:* SAT critical reading scores over 500: 33%; SAT math scores over 500: 73%; SAT math scores over 600: 33%.

Faculty *Total:* 63, 30% full-time, 8% with terminal degrees. *Student/faculty ratio:* 10:1.

Majors Liberal arts and sciences/liberal studies.

Academics *Calendar:* semesters. *Degree:* diplomas and associate. *Special study options:* academic remediation for entering students, adult/continuing education programs, advanced placement credit, distance learning, English as a second language, part-time degree program, student-designed majors, summer session for credit. *ROTC:* Army (b).

Library Sellers-Coombs Library with 18,890 titles, 49 serial subscriptions, 919 audiovisual materials, a Web page.

Student Life *Housing Options:* men-only, women-only. Campus housing is university owned. *Activities and Organizations:* choral group, marching band. *Campus security:* 24-hour emergency response devices and patrols. *Student services:* health clinic, personal/psychological counseling.

Athletics Member NJCAA. *Intercollegiate sports:* basketball M, cross-country running M/W, soccer M, track and field M/W, volleyball W, wrestling M. *Intramural sports:* archery M/W, riflery M/W, swimming and diving M/W, weight lifting W.

Standardized Tests *Required for some:* SAT or ACT (for admission). *Recommended:* SAT or ACT (for admission).

Costs (2011–12) *Comprehensive fee:* $29,700. Full-time tuition and fees vary according to course load and program. Part-time tuition: $180 per credit. Part-time tuition and fees vary according to course load and program. *Payment plan:* installment. *Waivers:* employees or children of employees.

Applying *Application fee:* $100. *Required:* high school transcript. *Application deadlines:* 9/1 (freshmen), 9/1 (out-of-state freshmen), 9/1 (transfers). *Notification:* continuous until 9/1 (freshmen), continuous until 9/1 (out-of-state freshmen), continuous until 9/1 (transfers).

Freshman Application Contact Capt. Mike Bellis, College Admissions Director, Wentworth Military Academy and College, 1880 Washington Avenue, Lexington, MO 64067. *Phone:* 660-259-2221 Ext. 1351. *Fax:* 660-259-2677. *E-mail:* admissions@wma.edu. *Web site:* http://www.wma.edu.

MONTANA

Blackfeet Community College

Browning, Montana

Freshman Application Contact Ms. Deana M. McNabb, Registrar and Admissions Officer, Blackfeet Community College, PO Box 819, Browning, MT 59417-0819. *Phone:* 406-338-5421. *Toll-free phone:* 800-549-7457. *Fax:* 406-338-3272. *Web site:* http://www.bfcc.org/.

Chief Dull Knife College

Lame Deer, Montana

Freshman Application Contact Director of Admissions, Chief Dull Knife College, PO Box 98, 1 College Drive, Lame Deer, MT 59043-0098. *Phone:* 406-477-6215. *Web site:* http://www.cdkc.edu/.

Dawson Community College

Glendive, Montana

- **State and locally supported** 2-year, founded 1940, part of Montana University System
- **Rural** 300-acre campus
- **Endowment** $344,944
- **Coed,** 630 undergraduate students, 52% full-time, 59% women, 41% men

Undergraduates 328 full-time, 302 part-time.

Freshmen *Admission:* 153 enrolled.

Faculty *Total:* 32, 91% full-time. *Student/faculty ratio:* 20:1.

Majors Administrative assistant and secretarial science; agricultural business and management; agricultural power machinery operation; business/commerce; child-care provision; clinical/medical social work; community psychology; computer and information sciences; computer and information sciences related; criminal justice/police science; liberal arts and sciences/liberal studies; music; substance abuse/addiction counseling; welding technology.

Academics *Calendar:* semesters. *Degree:* certificates and associate. *Special study options:* academic remediation for entering students, adult/continuing education programs, distance learning, independent study, internships, part-time degree program, services for LD students, summer session for credit.

Library Jane Carey Memorial Library with 18,870 titles, 1,112 audiovisual materials, an OPAC, a Web page.

Student Life *Housing Options:* coed. Campus housing is university owned. *Activities and Organizations:* drama/theater group, choral group, Phi Theta Kappa, Associated Student Body, Rodeo Club, Law Enforcement Club, Campus Corp. *Campus security:* 24-hour emergency response devices.

Athletics Member NJCAA. *Intercollegiate sports:* baseball M, basketball M(s)/W(s), equestrian sports M(s)/W(s), softball W. *Intramural sports:* basketball M/W, bowling M/W, golf M/W, racquetball M/W, softball M/W, table tennis M/W, tennis M/W, volleyball M/W.

Costs (2011–12) *Tuition:* area resident $1566 full-time, $52 per credit part-time; state resident $2673 full-time, $89 per credit part-time; nonresident $7329 full-time, $178 per credit part-time. *Required fees:* $1290 full-time, $43 per hour part-time. *Room and board:* $3300. *Waivers:* senior citizens and employees or children of employees.

Financial Aid Of all full-time matriculated undergraduates who enrolled in 2009, 45 Federal Work-Study jobs (averaging $1500). 17 state and other part-time jobs (averaging $1500).

Applying *Options:* deferred entrance. *Application fee:* $30. *Required:* high school transcript. *Application deadlines:* rolling (freshmen), rolling (transfers). *Notification:* continuous (freshmen), continuous (transfers).

Freshman Application Contact Dawson Community College, 300 College Drive, PO Box 421, Glendive, MT 59330-0421. *Phone:* 406-377-3396 Ext. 410. *Toll-free phone:* 800-821-8320. *Web site:* http://www.dawson.edu/.

Flathead Valley Community College

Kalispell, Montana

- **State and locally supported** 2-year, founded 1967, part of Montana University System
- **Small-town** 209-acre campus
- **Endowment** $2.5 million
- **Coed**

Undergraduates 1,430 full-time, 1,071 part-time. Students come from 34 states and territories; 4 other countries; 4% are from out of state; 7% transferred in. *Retention:* 56% of full-time freshmen returned.

Faculty *Student/faculty ratio:* 18:1.

Academics *Calendar:* semesters. *Degree:* certificates and associate. *Special study options:* academic remediation for entering students, adult/continuing education programs, advanced placement credit, cooperative education, distance learning, double majors, English as a second language, honors programs, independent study, internships, part-time degree program, services for LD students, study abroad, summer session for credit.

Costs (2010–11) *Tuition:* area resident $2660 full-time, $95 per credit part-time; state resident $4032 full-time, $114 per credit part-time; nonresident $9800 full-time, $350 per credit part-time. Part-time tuition and fees vary according to course load. *Required fees:* $924 full-time, $33 per credit part-time.

Applying *Options:* early admission, deferred entrance. *Application fee:* $15. *Required:* high school transcript.

Freshman Application Contact Ms. Marlene C. Stoltz, Admissions/Graduation Coordinator, Flathead Valley Community College, 777 Grandview Drive, Kalispell, MT 59901-2622. *Phone:* 406-756-3846. *Toll-free phone:* 800-313-3822. *E-mail:* mstoltz@fvcc.cc.mt.us. *Web site:* http://www.fvcc.edu/.

Fort Belknap College
Harlem, Montana

Director of Admissions Ms. Dixie Brockie, Registrar and Admissions Officer, Fort Belknap College, PO Box 159, Harlem, MT 59526-0159. *Phone:* 406-353-2607 Ext. 233. *Fax:* 406-353-2898. *E-mail:* dbrockie@mail.fbcc.edu. *Web site:* http://www.fbcc.edu/.

Fort Peck Community College
Poplar, Montana

Director of Admissions Mr. Robert McAnally, Vice President for Student Services, Fort Peck Community College, PO Box 398, Poplar, MT 59255-0398. *Phone:* 406-768-6329. *Web site:* http://www.fpcc.edu/.

Little Big Horn College
Crow Agency, Montana

Freshman Application Contact Ms. Ann Bullis, Dean of Student Services, Little Big Horn College, Box 370, 1 Forest Lane, Crow Agency, MT 59022-0370. *Phone:* 406-638-2228 Ext. 50. *Web site:* http://www.lbhc.cc.mt.us/.

Miles Community College
Miles City, Montana

- **State and locally supported** 2-year, founded 1939, part of Montana University System
- **Small-town** 8-acre campus
- **Coed**

Undergraduates 376 full-time, 124 part-time. Students come from 16 states and territories; 8 other countries; 10% are from out of state; 8% transferred in; 32% live on campus.

Faculty *Student/faculty ratio:* 14:1.

Academics *Calendar:* semesters. *Degree:* certificates and associate. *Special study options:* academic remediation for entering students, accelerated degree program, adult/continuing education programs, advanced placement credit, cooperative education, distance learning, double majors, English as a second language, honors programs, independent study, internships, part-time degree program, services for LD students, summer session for credit.

Student Life *Campus security:* 24-hour emergency response devices.

Athletics Member NJCAA.

Costs (2010–11) *Tuition:* area resident $2130 full-time, $71 per credit hour part-time; state resident $3000 full-time, $100 per credit hour part-time; nonresident $5790 full-time, $193 per credit hour part-time. Full-time tuition and fees vary according to reciprocity agreements. Part-time tuition and fees vary according to reciprocity agreements. *Required fees:* $1290 full-time, $43 per credit hour part-time. *Room and board:* $4200; room only: $2250. Room and board charges vary according to board plan and housing facility. *Payment plans:* installment, deferred payment.

Financial Aid Of all full-time matriculated undergraduates who enrolled in 2009, 25 Federal Work-Study jobs (averaging $1400). 22 state and other part-time jobs (averaging $1300).

Applying *Options:* electronic application, early admission, deferred entrance. *Application fee:* $30. *Required:* high school transcript.

Freshman Application Contact Mr. Jake Samuelson, Admissions Representative, Miles Community College, 2715 Dickinson Street, Miles City, MT 59301. *Phone:* 406-874-6178. *Toll-free phone:* 800-541-9281. *E-mail:* samuelsonj@milescc.edu. *Web site:* http://www.milescc.edu/.

Montana State University–Great Falls College of Technology
Great Falls, Montana

- **State-supported** 2-year, founded 1969, part of Montana University System
- **Small-town** 40-acre campus
- **Endowment** $11,300
- **Coed,** 1,740 undergraduate students, 52% full-time, 70% women, 30% men

Undergraduates 907 full-time, 833 part-time. Students come from 22 states and territories; 1 other country; 3% are from out of state; 2% Black or African American, non-Hispanic/Latino; 3% Hispanic/Latino; 2% Asian, non-Hispanic/Latino; 7% American Indian or Alaska Native, non-Hispanic/Latino; 6% Race/ethnicity unknown; 0.1% international; 8% transferred in. *Retention:* 48% of full-time freshmen returned.

Freshmen *Admission:* 444 applied, 437 admitted, 277 enrolled. *Average high school GPA:* 2.79.

Faculty *Total:* 143, 29% full-time, 8% with terminal degrees. *Student/faculty ratio:* 15:1.

Majors Accounting technology and bookkeeping; autobody/collision and repair technology; business administration and management; carpentry; computer systems networking and telecommunications; dental hygiene; dietetic technology; emergency medical technology (EMT paramedic); energy management and systems technology; entrepreneurship; fire science/firefighting; graphic design; health information/medical records technology; information technology; interior design; liberal arts and sciences and humanities related; licensed practical/vocational nurse training; medical/clinical assistant; medical insurance coding; medical transcription; physical therapy technology; radiologic technology/science; respiratory care therapy; surgical technology; web page, digital/multimedia and information resources design; welding technology.

Academics *Calendar:* semesters. *Degree:* certificates and associate. *Special study options:* academic remediation for entering students, advanced placement credit, distance learning, double majors, English as a second language, independent study, internships, off-campus study, part-time degree program, services for LD students, summer session for credit.

Library Weaver Library with 9,157 titles, 39,123 serial subscriptions, 1,052 audiovisual materials, an OPAC, a Web page.

Student Life *Housing:* college housing not available. *Activities and Organizations:* The Associated Students of Montana State University - Great Falls (ASMSUGF), Native American Students. *Campus security:* 24-hour emergency response devices.

Costs (2010–11) *Tuition:* state resident $3025 full-time, $104 per credit hour part-time; nonresident $9277 full-time, $364 per credit hour part-time. Full-time tuition and fees vary according to course load and program. Part-time tuition and fees vary according to course load and program. *Required fees:* $529 full-time, $67 per credit hour part-time. *Payment plan:* deferred payment. *Waivers:* minority students, senior citizens, and employees or children of employees.

Financial Aid Of all full-time matriculated undergraduates who enrolled in 2009, 48 Federal Work-Study jobs (averaging $2000). 13 state and other part-time jobs (averaging $2000).

Applying *Options:* early admission. *Application fee:* $30. *Required:* high school transcript, proof of immunization. *Application deadlines:* rolling (freshmen), rolling (out-of-state freshmen), rolling (transfers).

Freshman Application Contact Ms. Dana Freshly, Admissions, Montana State University–Great Falls College of Technology, 2100 16th Avenue South, Great Falls, MT 59405. *Phone:* 406-771-4300. *Toll-free phone:* 800-446-2698. *Fax:* 406-771-4329. *E-mail:* dfreshly@msugf.edu. *Web site:* http://www.msugf.edu/.

Salish Kootenai College
Pablo, Montana

Freshman Application Contact Ms. Jackie Moran, Admissions Officer, Salish Kootenai College, PO Box 70, Pablo, MT 59855-0117. *Phone:* 406-275-4866. *Fax:* 406-275-4810. *E-mail:* jackie_moran@skc.edu. *Web site:* http://www.skc.edu/.

Stone Child College
Box Elder, Montana

Director of Admissions Mr. Ted Whitford, Director of Admissions/Registrar, Stone Child College, RR1, Box 1082, Box Elder, MT 59521. *Phone:* 406-395-4313 Ext. 110. *E-mail:* uanet337@quest.ocsc.montana.edu. *Web site:* http://www.stonechild.edu/.

The University of Montana–Helena College of Technology
Helena, Montana

- **State-supported** 2-year, founded 1939, part of Montana University System
- **Small-town** campus
- **Coed,** 1,500 undergraduate students

Undergraduates Students come from 8 states and territories; 1% are from out of state; 0.5% Black or African American, non-Hispanic/Latino; 2% Hispanic/Latino; 1% Asian, non-Hispanic/Latino; 5% American Indian or Alaska Native, non-Hispanic/Latino; 8% Race/ethnicity unknown.

Freshmen *Admission:* 458 applied, 323 admitted.

Faculty *Total:* 100, 65% full-time. *Student/faculty ratio:* 14:1.

Majors Accounting technology and bookkeeping; airframe mechanics and aircraft maintenance technology; automobile/automotive mechanics technology; business automation/technology/data entry; carpentry; computer programming; diesel mechanics technology; executive assistant/executive secretary; fire science/firefighting; general studies; legal administrative assistant/secretary; licensed practical/vocational nurse training; machine tool technology; medical administrative assistant and medical secretary; office occupations and clerical services; welding technology.

Academics *Calendar:* semesters. *Degree:* certificates and associate. *Special study options:* academic remediation for entering students, adult/continuing education programs, distance learning, part-time degree program, services for LD students, summer session for credit.

Library UM-Helena Library with 95,845 titles, 38,794 serial subscriptions, 6,219 audiovisual materials, an OPAC, a Web page.

Student Life *Housing:* college housing not available. *Activities and Organizations:* Student Senate, Circle K, College Christian Fellowship. *Student services:* personal/psychological counseling.

Costs (2011–12) *Tuition:* state resident $3041 full-time, $98 per credit hour part-time; nonresident $8066 full-time, $205 per credit hour part-time. Full-time tuition and fees vary according to course load and reciprocity agreements. Part-time tuition and fees vary according to course load and reciprocity agreements. *Required fees:* $69 per credit hour part-time. *Payment plan:* installment. *Waivers:* minority students, senior citizens, and employees or children of employees.

Financial Aid Of all full-time matriculated undergraduates who enrolled in 2008, 445 applied for aid, 334 were judged to have need. 42 Federal Work-Study jobs (averaging $1549). 22 state and other part-time jobs (averaging $1476). In 2008, 37 non-need-based awards were made. *Average financial aid package:* $6368. *Average need-based loan:* $3428. *Average need-based gift aid:* $3111. *Average non-need-based aid:* $1769. *Average indebtedness upon graduation:* $14,068.

Applying *Options:* electronic application, early admission, deferred entrance. *Application fee:* $30. *Required for some:* high school transcript. *Application deadlines:* rolling (freshmen), rolling (transfers).

Freshman Application Contact Mr. Kendall May, Admissions Representative/Recruiter, The University of Montana–Helena College of Technology, 1115 North Roberts Street, Helena, MT 59601. *Phone:* 406-444-5436. *Toll-free phone:* 800-241-4882. *E-mail:* kendall.may@umhelena.edu. *Web site:* http://www.umhelena.edu/.

NEBRASKA

Central Community College–Columbus Campus
Columbus, Nebraska

- **State and locally supported** 2-year, founded 1968, part of Central Community College
- **Small-town** 90-acre campus
- **Coed,** 2,619 undergraduate students, 21% full-time, 63% women, 37% men

Undergraduates 560 full-time, 2,059 part-time. Students come from 36 states and territories; 18 other countries; 4% are from out of state; 2% Black or African American, non-Hispanic/Latino; 12% Hispanic/Latino; 0.6% Asian, non-Hispanic/Latino; 0.2% Native Hawaiian or other Pacific Islander, non-Hispanic/Latino; 0.7% American Indian or Alaska Native, non-Hispanic/Latino; 0.9% Two or more races, non-Hispanic/Latino; 4% Race/ethnicity unknown; 5% transferred in; 17% live on campus.

Freshmen *Admission:* 366 enrolled.

Faculty *Total:* 88, 45% full-time, 8% with terminal degrees.

Majors Administrative assistant and secretarial science; agricultural business and management; automobile/automotive mechanics technology; business administration and management; child-care and support services management; commercial and advertising art; computer and information sciences; criminal justice/safety; drafting and design technology; electrical, electronic and communications engineering technology; liberal arts and sciences/liberal studies; licensed practical/vocational nurse training; machine tool technology; marketing/marketing management; medical/clinical assistant; quality control technology; welding technology.

Academics *Calendar:* semesters plus six-week summer session. *Degree:* certificates, diplomas, and associate. *Special study options:* academic remediation for entering students, accelerated degree program, adult/continuing education programs, advanced placement credit, cooperative education, distance learning, English as a second language, external degree program, independent study, internships, off-campus study, part-time degree program, services for LD students, student-designed majors, summer session for credit.

Library Learning Resources Center with 22,000 titles, 118 serial subscriptions, an OPAC.

Student Life *Housing Options:* coed. Campus housing is university owned. *Activities and Organizations:* drama/theater group, choral group, Phi Theta Kappa, Drama Club, Art Club, Cantari, Chorale. *Campus security:* 24-hour emergency response devices and patrols, controlled dormitory access, night security. *Student services:* personal/psychological counseling, women's center.

Athletics Member NJCAA. *Intercollegiate sports:* basketball M(s), golf M(s), softball W(s), volleyball W(s). *Intramural sports:* basketball M/W, football M, softball M/W, table tennis M/W, volleyball M/W.

Costs (2011–12) *Tuition:* state resident $1872 full-time, $78 per credit part-time; nonresident $2208 full-time, $117 per credit part-time. *Required fees:* $192 full-time. *Room and board:* Room and board charges vary according to board plan. *Payment plan:* deferred payment. *Waivers:* employees or children of employees.

Applying *Options:* electronic application, early admission. *Required:* high school transcript. *Required for some:* 3 letters of recommendation, interview. *Application deadlines:* rolling (freshmen), rolling (transfers). *Notification:* continuous (freshmen), continuous (transfers).

Freshman Application Contact Ms. Erica Leffler, Admissions/Recruiting Coordinator, Central Community College–Columbus Campus, PO Box 1027, Columbus, NE 68602-1027. *Phone:* 402-562-1296. *Toll-free phone:* 800-642-1083. *Fax:* 402-562-1201. *E-mail:* eleffler@cccneb.edu. *Web site:* http://www.cccneb.edu/.

Central Community College–Grand Island Campus
Grand Island, Nebraska

- **State and locally supported** 2-year, founded 1976, part of Central Community College
- **Small-town** 64-acre campus
- **Coed,** 3,485 undergraduate students, 13% full-time, 66% women, 34% men

Undergraduates 439 full-time, 3,046 part-time. Students come from 36 states and territories; 18 other countries; 4% are from out of state; 2% Black or African American, non-Hispanic/Latino; 12% Hispanic/Latino; 0.7% Asian, non-Hispanic/Latino; 0.5% American Indian or Alaska Native, non-Hispanic/Latino; 0.5% Two or more races, non-Hispanic/Latino; 4% Race/ethnicity unknown; 26% transferred in; 10% live on campus.

Freshmen *Admission:* 153 enrolled.

Faculty *Total:* 112, 41% full-time, 7% with terminal degrees. *Student/faculty ratio:* 15:1.

Majors Administrative assistant and secretarial science; automobile/automotive mechanics technology; business administration and management; child-care and support services management; child development; clinical/medical social work; computer and information sciences; criminal justice/safety; drafting and design technology; electrical, electronic and communications engineering technology; heating, air conditioning, ventilation and refrigeration maintenance technology; legal assistant/paralegal; liberal arts and sciences/liberal studies; licensed practical/vocational nurse training; medical/clinical assistant; network and system administration; registered nursing/registered nurse; welding technology.

Academics *Calendar:* semesters plus six-week summer session. *Degree:* certificates, diplomas, and associate. *Special study options:* academic remediation for entering students, accelerated degree program, adult/continuing education programs, advanced placement credit, cooperative education, distance learning, English as a second language, external degree program, independent study, internships, off-campus study, part-time degree program, services for LD students, student-designed majors, summer session for credit.

Library Central Community College–Grand Island Campus Library with 5,700 titles, 94 serial subscriptions, an OPAC, a Web page.

Student Life *Housing Options:* coed. Campus housing is provided by a third party. Freshman applicants given priority for college housing. *Activities and Organizations:* Mid-Nebraska Users of Computers, Student Activities Organization, intramurals, TRIO, Phi Theta Kappa. *Student services:* personal/psychological counseling.

Athletics *Intramural sports:* bowling M/W, softball M/W, table tennis M/W, volleyball M/W.

Costs (2011–12) *Tuition:* state resident $1872 full-time, $78 per credit part-time; nonresident $2808 full-time, $117 per credit part-time. *Required fees:* $192 full-time, $8 per credit part-time. *Payment plan:* deferred payment. *Waivers:* employees or children of employees.

Applying *Options:* electronic application, early admission. *Required:* high school transcript. *Required for some:* 3 letters of recommendation, interview. *Application deadlines:* rolling (freshmen), rolling (transfers). *Notification:* continuous (freshmen), continuous (transfers).

Freshman Application Contact Michelle Lubken, Admissions Director, Central Community College–Grand Island Campus, PO Box 4903, Grand Island, NE 68802-4903. *Phone:* 308-398-7406 Ext. 406. *Toll-free phone:* 800-652-9177. *Fax:* 308-398-7398. *E-mail:* mlubken@cccneb.edu. *Web site:* http://www.cccneb.edu/.

Central Community College–Hastings Campus

Hastings, Nebraska

- **State and locally supported** 2-year, founded 1966, part of Central Community College
- **Small-town** 600-acre campus
- **Coed,** 3,069 undergraduate students, 36% full-time, 57% women, 43% men

Undergraduates 1,100 full-time, 1,969 part-time. Students come from 36 states and territories; 18 other countries; 4% are from out of state; 1% Black or African American, non-Hispanic/Latino; 7% Hispanic/Latino; 0.9% Asian, non-Hispanic/Latino; 0.4% American Indian or Alaska Native, non-Hispanic/Latino; 0.8% Two or more races, non-Hispanic/Latino; 8% Race/ethnicity unknown; 5% transferred in; 26% live on campus.

Freshmen *Admission:* 526 enrolled.

Faculty *Total:* 91, 69% full-time, 9% with terminal degrees. *Student/faculty ratio:* 15:1.

Majors Administrative assistant and secretarial science; agricultural business and management; applied horticulture/horticulture operations; autobody/collision and repair technology; automobile/automotive mechanics technology; building/construction finishing, management, and inspection related; business administration and management; child-care and support services management; child development; clinical/medical laboratory technology; clinical/medical social work; commercial and advertising art; construction engineering technology; criminal justice/safety; dental assisting; dental hygiene; diesel mechanics technology; drafting and design technology; electrical, electronic and communications engineering technology; electrician; graphic and printing equipment operation/production; health information/medical records technology; heating, air conditioning, ventilation and refrigeration maintenance technology; hotel/motel administration; industrial mechanics and maintenance technology; industrial technology; liberal arts and sciences/liberal studies; library and archives assisting; logistics, materials, and supply chain management; machine tool technology; medical/clinical assistant; quality control technology; radio and television broadcasting technology; restaurant, culinary, and catering management; truck and bus driver/commercial vehicle operation/instruction; vehicle and vehicle parts and accessories marketing; welding technology.

Academics *Calendar:* semesters plus six-week summer session. *Degree:* certificates, diplomas, and associate. *Special study options:* academic remediation for entering students, accelerated degree program, adult/continuing education programs, advanced placement credit, cooperative education, distance learning, English as a second language, external degree program, independent study, internships, off-campus study, part-time degree program, services for LD students, student-designed majors, summer session for credit.

Library Nuckolls Library with 4,025 titles, 52 serial subscriptions, an OPAC.

Student Life *Housing Options:* coed, men-only, women-only. Campus housing is university owned. *Activities and Organizations:* student-run radio station, Student Senate, Central Dormitory Council, Judicial Board, Seeds and Soils, Young Farmers and Ranchers. *Campus security:* 24-hour emergency response devices and patrols, controlled dormitory access. *Student services:* personal/psychological counseling, women's center.

Athletics *Intramural sports:* basketball M/W, bowling M/W, golf M/W, softball M/W, volleyball M/W, weight lifting M/W.

Costs (2011–12) *Tuition:* state resident $1872 full-time, $78 per credit part-time; nonresident $2808 full-time, $117 per credit part-time. *Required fees:* $192 full-time. *Room and board:* Room and board charges vary according to

board plan. *Payment plan:* deferred payment. *Waivers:* employees or children of employees.

Financial Aid Of all full-time matriculated undergraduates who enrolled in 2009, 70 Federal Work-Study jobs (averaging $1200). 12 state and other part-time jobs (averaging $1250).

Applying *Options:* electronic application, early admission. *Required:* high school transcript. *Required for some:* 3 letters of recommendation, interview. *Application deadlines:* rolling (freshmen), rolling (transfers). *Notification:* continuous (freshmen), continuous (transfers).

Freshman Application Contact Mr. Robert Glenn, Admissions and Recruiting Director, Central Community College–Hastings Campus, PO Box 1024, East Highway 6, Hastings, NE 68902-1024. *Phone:* 402-461-2428. *Toll-free phone:* 800-742-7872. *E-mail:* rglenn@ccneb.edu. *Web site:* http://www.cccneb.edu/.

Creative Center

Omaha, Nebraska

- **Proprietary** primarily 2-year, founded 1993
- **Urban** 2-acre campus
- **Coed**

Faculty *Total:* 16, 25% full-time. *Student/faculty ratio:* 19:1.

Majors Computer graphics; design and visual communications; illustration.

Academics *Calendar:* semesters. *Degrees:* associate and bachelor's. *Special study options:* distance learning, part-time degree program, services for LD students.

Library Student Library plus 1 other.

Student Life *Housing:* college housing not available.

Costs (2011–12) *Tuition:* $23,600 full-time. Full-time tuition and fees vary according to course load and student level. Part-time tuition and fees vary according to course load and student level.

Applying *Application fee:* $100. *Required:* essay or personal statement, high school transcript, 1 letter of recommendation, interview, portfolio. *Application deadlines:* rolling (freshmen), rolling (out-of-state freshmen), rolling (transfers). *Notification:* continuous (freshmen), continuous (out-of-state freshmen), continuous (transfers).

Freshman Application Contact Mr. Richard Caldwell, Director of Admissions, Creative Center, 10850 Emmet Street, Omaha, NE 68164. *Phone:* 402-898-1000 Ext. 216. *Toll-free phone:* 888-898-1789. *Fax:* 402-898-1301. *E-mail:* admission@creativecenter.edu. *Web site:* http://www.creativecenter.edu/.

ITT Technical Institute

Omaha, Nebraska

- **Proprietary** primarily 2-year, founded 1991, part of ITT Educational Services, Inc.
- **Urban** campus
- **Coed**

Majors CAD/CADD drafting/design technology; computer and information systems security; computer engineering technology; computer software engineering; computer software technology; computer systems networking and telecommunications; construction management; criminal justice/law enforcement administration; design and visual communications; electrical, electronic and communications engineering technology; game and interactive media design; legal assistant/paralegal; project management; registered nursing/registered nurse; system, networking, and LAN/WAN management; web page, digital/multimedia and information resources design.

Academics *Calendar:* quarters. *Degrees:* associate and bachelor's.

Student Life *Housing:* college housing not available.

Freshman Application Contact Director of Recruitment, ITT Technical Institute, 9814 M Street, Omaha, NE 68127-2056. *Phone:* 402-331-2900. *Toll-free phone:* 800-677-9260. *Web site:* http://www.itt-tech.edu/.

Kaplan University, Lincoln

Lincoln, Nebraska

- **Proprietary** primarily 2-year, founded 1884
- **Urban** campus
- **Coed**

Academics *Calendar:* quarters. *Degrees:* certificates, diplomas, associate, and bachelor's.

Freshman Application Contact Kaplan University, Lincoln, 1821 K Street, Lincoln, NE 68501-2826. *Phone:* 402-474-5315. *Web site:* http://www.lincoln.kaplanuniversity.edu/.

Kaplan University, Omaha

Omaha, Nebraska

- **Proprietary** primarily 2-year, founded 1891
- **Urban** campus
- **Coed**

Academics *Calendar:* quarters. *Degrees:* certificates, diplomas, associate, and bachelor's.

Freshman Application Contact Kaplan University, Omaha, 5425 North 103rd Street, Omaha, NE 68134. *Phone:* 402-572-8500. *Toll-free phone:* 800-642-1456. *Web site:* http://www.omaha.kaplanuniversity.edu/.

Little Priest Tribal College

Winnebago, Nebraska

Director of Admissions Ms. Karen Kemling, Director of Admissions and Records, Little Priest Tribal College, PO Box 270, Winnebago, NE 68071. *Phone:* 402-878-2380. *Web site:* http://www.littlepriest.edu/.

Metropolitan Community College

Omaha, Nebraska

- **State and locally supported** 2-year, founded 1974, part of Nebraska Coordinating Commission for Postsecondary Education
- **Urban** 172-acre campus
- **Endowment** $1.4 million
- **Coed**

Undergraduates 7,095 full-time, 9,908 part-time. Students come from 31 states and territories; 3% are from out of state; 17% transferred in. *Retention:* 50% of full-time freshmen returned.

Faculty *Student/faculty ratio:* 16:1.

Academics *Calendar:* quarters. *Degree:* certificates, diplomas, and associate. *Special study options:* academic remediation for entering students, adult/continuing education programs, advanced placement credit, cooperative education, distance learning, English as a second language, independent study, internships, part-time degree program, services for LD students, summer session for credit. *ROTC:* Army (c).

Student Life *Campus security:* 24-hour emergency response devices and patrols, late-night transport/escort service, controlled dormitory access, security on duty 9 pm to 6 am.

Costs (2010–11) *Tuition:* state resident $2160 full-time, $48 per credit hour part-time; nonresident $3218 full-time, $72 per credit hour part-time. Full-time tuition and fees vary according to course load. Part-time tuition and fees vary according to course load. *Required fees:* $225 full-time, $5 per credit hour part-time. *Room and board:* $4740.

Applying *Options:* early admission. *Recommended:* high school transcript.

Freshman Application Contact Ms. Maria Vazquez, Associate Vice President for Student Affairs, Metropolitan Community College, PO Box 3777, Omaha, NE 69103-0777. *Phone:* 402-457-2430. *Toll-free phone:* 800-228-9553. *Fax:* 402-457-2238. *E-mail:* mvazquez@mccncb.cdu. *Web site:* http://www.mccneb.edu/.

Mid-Plains Community College

North Platte, Nebraska

- **District-supported** 2-year, founded 1973
- **Small-town** campus
- **Coed,** 2,988 undergraduate students, 35% full-time, 51% women, 49% men

Undergraduates 1,057 full-time, 1,931 part-time. Students come from 32 states and territories; 3 other countries; 9% are from out of state; 0.1% transferred in; 8% live on campus. *Retention:* 44% of full-time freshmen returned.

Freshmen *Admission:* 415 applied, 415 admitted, 415 enrolled.

Faculty *Total:* 313, 21% full-time, 2% with terminal degrees. *Student/faculty ratio:* 11:1.

Majors Administrative assistant and secretarial science; autobody/collision and repair technology; automobile/automotive mechanics technology; building/construction finishing, management, and inspection related; business administration and management; clinical/medical laboratory technology; commercial and advertising art; computer and information sciences; construction engineering technology; dental assisting; diesel mechanics technology; fire science/firefighting; heating, air conditioning, ventilation and refrigeration maintenance technology; liberal arts and sciences/liberal studies; licensed practical/vocational nurse training; registered nursing/registered nurse; transportation and materials moving related; welding technology.

Academics *Calendar:* semesters. *Degree:* certificates, diplomas, and associate. *Special study options:* academic remediation for entering students, adult/continuing education programs, advanced placement credit, cooperative education, distance learning, English as a second language, external degree program, independent study, internships, part-time degree program, summer session for credit.

Library McDonald-Belton L R C plus 1 other with 65,352 titles, 4,697 serial subscriptions, 3,455 audiovisual materials, an OPAC, a Web page.

Student Life *Housing Options:* coed, disabled students. Campus housing is university owned. *Activities and Organizations:* drama/theater group, student-run newspaper, choral group, Student Senate, Phi Theta Kappa, Phi Beta Lambda, Intercollegiate Athletics, MPCC Student Nurses Association. *Campus security:* controlled dormitory access, patrols by trained security personnel.

Athletics Member NJCAA. *Intercollegiate sports:* baseball M(s), basketball M(s)/W(s), golf M(s), softball W(s), volleyball W(s). *Intramural sports:* baseball M, basketball M/W, softball W, volleyball W.

Standardized Tests *Required for some:* COMPASS. *Recommended:* ACT (for admission).

Costs (2011–12) *Tuition:* state resident $2100 full-time, $70 per credit hour part-time; nonresident $2730 full-time, $91 per credit hour part-time. *Required fees:* $450 full-time, $15 per credit hour part-time. *Room and board:* $4700. Room and board charges vary according to board plan, housing facility, and location. *Waivers:* senior citizens and employees or children of employees.

Applying *Options:* electronic application. *Required:* high school transcript. *Required for some:* interview. *Application deadlines:* rolling (freshmen), rolling (transfers). *Notification:* continuous (freshmen), continuous (transfers).

Freshman Application Contact Ms. Sherry Mihel, Advisor, Mid-Plains Community College, 1101 Halligan Drive, North Platte, NE 69101. *Phone:* 308-535-3710. *Toll-free phone:* 800-658-4308 (in-state); 800-658-4348 (out-of-state). *Fax:* 308-534-5767. *E-mail:* mihels@mpcc.edu. *Web site:* http://www.mpcc.edu/.

Myotherapy Institute

Lincoln, Nebraska

Freshman Application Contact Admissions Office, Myotherapy Institute, 6020 South 58th Street, Lincoln, NE 68516. *Phone:* 402-421-7410. *Toll-free phone:* 800-896-3363. *Web site:* http://www.myotherapy.edu/.

Nebraska College of Technical Agriculture

Curtis, Nebraska

- **State-supported** 2-year, founded 1965, part of University of Nebraska System, administratively affiliated with Institute of Agriculture and Natural Resources - University of Nebraska
- **Rural** 634-acre campus
- **Coed**

Undergraduates 246 full-time, 179 part-time. Students come from 10 states and territories; 45% live on campus. *Retention:* 64% of full-time freshmen returned.

Faculty *Student/faculty ratio:* 13:1.

Academics *Calendar:* 8-week modular system. *Degree:* certificates and associate. *Special study options:* academic remediation for entering students, adult/continuing education programs, distance learning, double majors, external degree program, independent study, internships, part-time degree program, study abroad.

Student Life *Campus security:* 24-hour emergency response devices, controlled dormitory access, night security.

Athletics Member USCAA.

Standardized Tests *Required:* ACT (for admission).

Costs (2010–11) *Tuition:* state resident $3015 full-time, $107 per credit hour part-time; nonresident $6023 full-time, $213 per credit hour part-time. *Required fees:* $628 full-time. *Room and board:* $4580; room only: $2100. Room and board charges vary according to board plan.

Applying *Options:* early admission. *Application fee:* $25. *Required:* high school transcript. *Recommended:* interview.

Freshman Application Contact Kevin Martin, Assistant Admissions Coordinator, Nebraska College of Technical Agriculture, 404 East 7th Street, Curtis, NE 69025, NE 69025. *Phone:* 308-367-4124. *Toll-free phone:* 800-3CURTIS. *Web site:* http://www.ncta.unl.edu/.

Nebraska Indian Community College

Macy, Nebraska

Director of Admissions Ms. Theresa Henry, Admission Counselor, Nebraska Indian Community College, PO Box 428, Macy, NE 68039-0428. *Phone:* 402-837-5078. *Toll-free phone:* 888-843-6432 Ext. 14. *Web site:* http://www.thenicc.edu/.

Northeast Community College

Norfolk, Nebraska

- **State and locally supported** 2-year, founded 1973, part of Nebraska Coordinating Commission for Postsecondary Education

- **Small-town** 205-acre campus

- **Coed,** 5,377 undergraduate students, 44% full-time, 46% women, 54% men

Undergraduates 2,343 full-time, 3,034 part-time. 6% are from out of state; 2% Black or African American, non-Hispanic/Latino; 9% Hispanic/Latino; 0.3% Asian, non-Hispanic/Latino; 1% American Indian or Alaska Native, non-Hispanic/Latino; 0.5% Two or more races, non-Hispanic/Latino; 3% Race/ethnicity unknown; 1% international; 5% transferred in; 6% live on campus. *Retention:* 65% of full-time freshmen returned.

Freshmen *Admission:* 1,644 applied, 1,644 admitted, 985 enrolled.

Faculty *Total:* 381, 30% full-time, 26% with terminal degrees. *Student/faculty ratio:* 16:1.

Majors Accounting; administrative assistant and secretarial science; agribusiness; agricultural mechanics and equipment technology; agricultural mechanization; agriculture; agriculture and agriculture operations related; agronomy and crop science; animal sciences; applied horticulture/horticultural business services related; applied horticulture/horticulture operations; architectural drafting and CAD/CADD; art; autobody/collision and repair technology; automobile/automotive mechanics technology; banking and financial support services; biological and biomedical sciences related; biology/biological sciences; building/construction finishing, management, and inspection related; business administration and management; business operations support and secretarial services related; chemistry; computer and information sciences; computer and information sciences and support services related; computer programming; computer programming (specific applications); computer science; corrections; criminal justice/police science; crop production; culinary arts; dairy science; diesel mechanics technology; dramatic/theater arts; early childhood education; education; electrician; electromechanical technology; elementary education; emergency medical technology (EMT paramedic); energy management and systems technology; engineering; English; entrepreneurship; farm and ranch management; finance and financial management services related; food service systems administration; general studies; graphic design; health aide; health and medical administrative services related; health and physical education/fitness; health/medical preparatory programs related; heating, air conditioning, ventilation and refrigeration maintenance technology; industrial mechanics and maintenance technology; international business/trade/commerce; journalism; legal administrative assistant/secretary; liberal arts and sciences/liberal studies; library and archives assisting; licensed practical/vocational nurse training; lineworker; livestock management; marketing/marketing management; mass communication/media; mathematics; medical administrative assistant and medical secretary; medical insurance coding; medical radiologic technology; medium/heavy vehicle and truck technology; merchandising; music management; music performance; music teacher education; office management; office occupations and clerical services; physical therapy technology; physics; predentistry studies; pre-engineering; pre-law studies; premedical studies; prenursing studies; pre-pharmacy studies; pre-veterinary studies; psychology; radio and television broadcasting technology; real estate; recording arts technology; registered nursing/registered nurse; rhetoric and composition; secondary education; social sciences; surgical technology; veterinary/animal health technology; welding technology.

Academics *Calendar:* semesters. *Degree:* certificates, diplomas, and associate. *Special study options:* academic remediation for entering students, adult/continuing education programs, advanced placement credit, cooperative education, distance learning, double majors, English as a second language, internships, off-campus study, part-time degree program, services for LD students, summer session for credit.

Library Library Resource Center plus 1 other with an OPAC, a Web page.

Student Life *Housing Options:* disabled students. Campus housing is university owned. *Activities and Organizations:* drama/theater group, student-run newspaper, radio and television station, choral group. *Campus security:* 24-hour patrols, controlled dormitory access. *Student services:* personal/psychological counseling.

Athletics Member NJCAA. *Intercollegiate sports:* basketball M(s)/W(s), cheerleading W(s). *Intramural sports:* basketball M/W, bowling M/W, football M/W, soccer M/W, softball M/W, table tennis M/W, volleyball M/W.

Costs (2010–11) *Tuition:* state resident $2170 full-time, $70 per credit hour part-time; nonresident $2713 full-time, $88 per credit hour part-time. *Required fees:* $442 full-time. *Room and board:* $5884; room only: $2940. Room and board charges vary according to board plan and housing facility. *Payment plan:* installment. *Waivers:* employees or children of employees.

Financial Aid Of all full-time matriculated undergraduates who enrolled in 2008, 1,745 applied for aid, 1,424 were judged to have need, 236 had their need fully met. 89 Federal Work-Study jobs (averaging $1001). In 2008, 50 non-need-based awards were made. *Average percent of need met:* 57%. *Average financial aid package:* $6059. *Average need-based loan:* $2834. *Average need-based gift aid:* $3903. *Average non-need-based aid:* $999. *Average indebtedness upon graduation:* $10,725.

Applying *Options:* electronic application, early admission. *Required for some:* high school transcript, minimum 2.0 GPA, 3 letters of recommendation, interview. *Recommended:* high school transcript. *Application deadlines:* rolling (freshmen), rolling (out-of-state freshmen), rolling (transfers). *Notification:* continuous (freshmen), continuous (out-of-state freshmen), continuous (transfers).

Freshman Application Contact Maureen Baker, Dean of Students, Northeast Community College, 801 East Benjamin Avenue, PO Box 469, Norfolk, NE 68702-0469. *Phone:* 402-844-7258. *Toll-free phone:* 800-348-9033 Ext. 7260. *Fax:* 402-844-7403. *E-mail:* admission@northeast.edu. *Web site:* http://www.northeast.edu/.

Omaha School of Massage Therapy and Healthcare of Herzing University

Omaha, Nebraska

Admissions Office Contact Omaha School of Massage Therapy and Healthcare of Herzing University, 9748 Park Drive, Omaha, NE 68127. *Web site:* http://www.osmhc.com/.

Southeast Community College, Beatrice Campus

Beatrice, Nebraska

Freshman Application Contact Admissions Office, Southeast Community College, Beatrice Campus, 4771 West Scott Road, Beatrice, NE 68310. *Phone:* 402-228-3468. *Toll-free phone:* 800-233-5027. *Fax:* 402-228-2218. *Web site:* http://www.southeast.edu/.

Southeast Community College, Lincoln Campus

Lincoln, Nebraska

Freshman Application Contact Admissions Office, Southeast Community College, Lincoln Campus, 8800 O Street, Lincoln, NE 68520-1299. *Phone:* 402-471-3333. *Toll-free phone:* 800-642-4075. *Fax:* 402-437-2404. *Web site:* http://www.southeast.edu/.

Southeast Community College, Milford Campus

Milford, Nebraska

Freshman Application Contact Admissions Office, Southeast Community College, Milford Campus, 600 State Street, Milford, NE 68405. *Phone:* 402-761-2131. *Toll-free phone:* 800-933-7223. *Fax:* 402-761-2324. *Web site:* http://www.southeast.edu/.

Vatterott College

Omaha, Nebraska

Freshman Application Contact Admissions Office, Vatterott College, 5318 South 136th Street, Omaha, NE 68137. *Phone:* 402-891-9411. *Fax:* 402-891-9413. *Web site:* http://www.vatterott-college.edu/.

Western Nebraska Community College

Sidney, Nebraska

Director of Admissions Mr. Troy Archuleta, Admissions and Recruitment Director, Western Nebraska Community College, 371 College Drive, Sidney, NE 69162. *Phone:* 308-635-6015. *Toll-free phone:* 800-222-9682 (in-state); 800-348-4435 (out-of-state). *E-mail:* rhovey@wncc.net. *Web site:* http://www.wncc.net/.

NEVADA

Career College of Northern Nevada
Sparks, Nevada

- **Proprietary** 2-year, founded 1984
- **Urban** 1-acre campus
- **Coed**

Undergraduates 363 full-time. Students come from 3 states and territories; 2 other countries; 3% are from out of state. *Retention:* 51% of full-time freshmen returned.

Faculty *Student/faculty ratio:* 20:1.

Academics *Calendar:* quarters six-week terms. *Degree:* diplomas and associate. *Special study options:* academic remediation for entering students, accelerated degree program, cooperative education, double majors, internships, summer session for credit.

Student Life *Campus security:* 24-hour emergency response devices.

Financial Aid Of all full-time matriculated undergraduates who enrolled in 2009, 6 Federal Work-Study jobs (averaging $3000).

Applying *Application fee:* $25. *Required:* essay or personal statement, high school transcript, interview.

Freshman Application Contact Ms. Laura Goldhammer, Director of Admissions, Career College of Northern Nevada, 1421 Pullman Drive, Sparks, NV 89434. *Phone:* 775-856-2266 Ext. 11. *Fax:* 775-856-0935. *E-mail:* lgoldhammer@ccnn4u.com. *Web site:* http://www.ccnn.edu/.

Carrington College - Las Vegas
Las Vegas, Nevada

Admissions Office Contact Carrington College - Las Vegas, 5740 South Eastern Avenue, Las Vegas, NV 89119. *Web site:* http://carrington.edu/.

Carrington College - Reno
Reno, Nevada

Admissions Office Contact Carrington College - Reno, 5580 Kietzke Lane, Reno, NV 89511. *Web site:* http://carrington.edu/.

College of Southern Nevada
North Las Vegas, Nevada

Freshman Application Contact Admissions and Records, College of Southern Nevada, 3200 East Cheyenne Avenue, North Las Vegas, NV 89030-4296. *Phone:* 702-651-4060. *Web site:* http://www.csn.edu/.

Everest College
Henderson, Nevada

Admissions Office Contact Everest College, 170 North Stephanie Street, 1st Floor, Henderson, NV 89074. *Web site:* http://www.everest.edu/campus/henderson/.

Great Basin College
Elko, Nevada

- **State-supported** primarily 2-year, founded 1967, part of University and Community College System of Nevada
- **Small-town** 45-acre campus
- **Endowment** $187,761
- **Coed,** 3,691 undergraduate students, 31% full-time, 66% women, 34% men

Undergraduates 1,141 full-time, 2,550 part-time. Students come from 13 states and territories; 3% are from out of state; 5% live on campus. *Retention:* 77% of full-time freshmen returned.

Freshmen *Admission:* 558 admitted, 558 enrolled.

Faculty *Total:* 241, 27% full-time. *Student/faculty ratio:* 15:1.

Majors Anthropology; art; business administration and management; business/commerce; chemistry; criminal justice/safety; data processing and data processing technology; diesel mechanics technology; electrical, electronic and communications engineering technology; elementary education; English; geology/earth science; history; industrial technology; interdisciplinary studies; kindergarten/preschool education; management science; mathematics; natural resources management and policy related; office management; operations management; physics; psychology; registered nursing/registered nurse; secondary education; social sciences; social work; sociology; surveying technology; welding technology.

Academics *Calendar:* semesters. *Degrees:* certificates, associate, bachelor's, and postbachelor's certificates. *Special study options:* academic remediation for entering students, accelerated degree program, adult/continuing education programs, cooperative education, distance learning, double majors, English as a second language, external degree program, independent study, part-time degree program, services for LD students, summer session for credit.

Library Learning Resource Center with 113,341 titles, 142 serial subscriptions, 1,852 audiovisual materials, an OPAC.

Student Life *Housing Options:* coed, disabled students. Campus housing is university owned. *Activities and Organizations:* Student Nurses Organization, Housing Central, Skills USA, Agriculture Student Organization, Colleges Against Cancer. *Campus security:* late-night transport/escort service, evening patrols by trained security personnel. *Student services:* personal/psychological counseling.

Athletics *Intramural sports:* badminton M/W, basketball M/W, rock climbing M/W, volleyball M/W, weight lifting M/W.

Costs (2011–12) *Tuition:* state resident $2243 full-time, $69 per credit hour part-time; nonresident $8590 full-time, $227 per credit hour part-time. Full-time tuition and fees vary according to course level. Part-time tuition and fees vary according to course level. *Required fees:* $165 full-time, $6 per credit hour part-time. *Room and board:* room only: $2299. Room and board charges vary according to housing facility. *Payment plan:* deferred payment. *Waivers:* senior citizens and employees or children of employees.

Financial Aid Of all full-time matriculated undergraduates who enrolled in 2009, 35 Federal Work-Study jobs (averaging $1000). 50 state and other part-time jobs (averaging $1800).

Applying *Options:* electronic application, early admission, deferred entrance. *Application fee:* $10. *Application deadlines:* rolling (freshmen), rolling (out-of-state freshmen), rolling (transfers). *Notification:* continuous (freshmen), continuous (out-of-state freshmen), continuous (transfers).

Freshman Application Contact Ms. Janice King, Director of Admissions and Registrar, Great Basin College, 1500 College Parkway, Elko, NV 89801-3348. *Phone:* 775-753-2361. *Fax:* 775-753-2311. *E-mail:* janicek@gwmail.gbcnv.edu. *Web site:* http://www.gbcnv.edu/.

High-Tech Institute
Las Vegas, Nevada

Freshman Application Contact Admissions Office, High-Tech Institute, 2320 South Rancho Drive, Las Vegas, NV 89102. *Phone:* 702-385-6700. *Toll-free phone:* 866-385-6700. *Web site:* http://www.high-techinstitute.com/.

ITT Technical Institute
Henderson, Nevada

- **Proprietary** primarily 2-year, founded 1997, part of ITT Educational Services, Inc.
- **Coed**

Majors CAD/CADD drafting/design technology; computer and information systems security; computer engineering technology; computer software and media applications related; computer software engineering; computer software technology; construction management; criminal justice/law enforcement administration; design and visual communications; electrical, electronic and communications engineering technology; game and interactive media design; legal assistant/paralegal; project management; registered nursing/registered nurse; system, networking, and LAN/WAN management; web page, digital/multimedia and information resources design.

Academics *Degrees:* associate and bachelor's.

Student Life *Housing:* college housing not available.

Financial Aid Of all full-time matriculated undergraduates who enrolled in 2009, 6 Federal Work-Study jobs (averaging $5000).

Freshman Application Contact Director of Recruitment, ITT Technical Institute, 168 North Gibson Road, Henderson, NV 89014. *Phone:* 702-558-5404. *Toll-free phone:* 800-488-8459. *Web site:* http://www.itt-tech.edu/.

ITT Technical Institute
North Las Vegas, Nevada

- **Proprietary** 2-year, part of ITT Educational Services, Inc.
- **Coed**

Majors CAD/CADD drafting/design technology; computer and information systems security; computer engineering technology; computer software and media applications related; computer software engineering; computer software technology; construction management; criminal justice/law enforcement administration; design and visual communications; electrical, electronic and communications engineering technology; game and interactive media design; legal assistant/paralegal; project management; system, networking, and LAN/WAN management; web page, digital/multimedia and information resources design.

Academics *Calendar:* quarters.
Freshman Application Contact Director of Recruitment, ITT Technical Institute, 3825 W. Cheyenne Avenue, Suite 600, North Las Vegas, NV 89032. *Phone:* 702-240-0967. *Toll-free phone:* 877-832-8442. *Web site:* http://www.itt-tech.edu/.

Kaplan College–Las Vegas Campus

Las Vegas, Nevada

Freshman Application Contact Admissions Office, Kaplan College–Las Vegas Campus, 3535 West Sahara Avenue, Las Vegas, NV 89102. *Toll-free phone:* 888-727-7863. *Web site:* http://las-vegas.kaplancollege.com/.

Le Cordon Bleu College of Culinary Arts, Las Vegas

Las Vegas, Nevada

Freshman Application Contact Admissions Office, Le Cordon Bleu College of Culinary Arts, Las Vegas, 1451 Center Crossing Road, Las Vegas, NV 89144. *Toll-free phone:* 888-551-8222. *Web site:* http://www.vegasculinary.com/.

Pima Medical Institute

Las Vegas, Nevada

- **Proprietary** primarily 2-year, founded 2003, part of Vocational Training Institutes, Inc.
- **Urban** campus
- **Coed,** 820 undergraduate students

Majors Health/health-care administration; physical therapy technology; radiologic technology/science; respiratory therapy technician; veterinary/animal health technology.
Academics *Calendar:* modular. *Degrees:* certificates, associate, and bachelor's. *Special study options:* advanced placement credit, distance learning, internships.
Library E-Global.
Student Life *Housing:* college housing not available.
Standardized Tests *Required:* Wonderlic Scholastic Level Exam (for admission).
Applying *Required:* interview. *Required for some:* essay or personal statement, high school transcript.
Freshman Application Contact Admissions Office, Pima Medical Institute, 3333 East Flamingo Road, Las Vegas, NV 89121. *Phone:* 702-458-9650 Ext. 202. *Toll-free phone:* 800-477-PIMA. *Web site:* http://www.pmi.edu/.

Truckee Meadows Community College

Reno, Nevada

Director of Admissions Mr. Dave Harbeck, Director of Admissions and Records, Truckee Meadows Community College, 7000 Dandini Boulevard, Reno, NV 89512-3901. *Phone:* 775-674-7623. *Fax:* 775-673-7028. *E-mail:* dharbeck@tmcc.edu. *Web site:* http://www.tmcc.edu/.

Western Nevada College

Carson City, Nevada

Freshman Application Contact Admissions and Records, Western Nevada College, 2201 West College Parkway, Carson City, NV 89703. *Phone:* 775-445-2377. *Fax:* 775-445-3147. *E-mail:* wncc_aro@wncc.edu. *Web site:* http://www.wnc.edu/.

NEW HAMPSHIRE

Great Bay Community College

Portsmouth, New Hampshire

Freshman Application Contact Matt Thornton, Admissions Coordinator, Great Bay Community College, 320 Corporate Drive, Portsmouth, NH 03801.

Phone: 603-427-7605. *Toll-free phone:* 800-522-1194. *E-mail:* askgreatbay@ccsnh.edu. *Web site:* http://www.greatbay.edu/.

Hesser College, Concord

Concord, New Hampshire

- **Proprietary** primarily 2-year
- **Coed**

Academics *Degrees:* certificates, diplomas, associate, and bachelor's.
Freshman Application Contact Hesser College, Concord, 25 Hall Street, Suite 104, Concord, NH 03301. *Phone:* 603-225-9200. *Web site:* http://www.concord.hesser.edu/.

Hesser College, Manchester

Manchester, New Hampshire

- **Proprietary** primarily 2-year, founded 1900
- **Urban** campus
- **Coed**

Academics *Calendar:* semesters. *Degrees:* certificates, diplomas, associate, and bachelor's.
Financial Aid Of all full-time matriculated undergraduates who enrolled in 2009, 700 Federal Work-Study jobs (averaging $1000).
Freshman Application Contact Hesser College, Manchester, 3 Sundial Avenue, Manchester, NH 03103. *Phone:* 603-668-6660. *Web site:* http://www.manchester.hesser.edu/.

Hesser College, Nashua

Nashua, New Hampshire

- **Proprietary** primarily 2-year
- **Coed**

Academics *Degrees:* certificates, diplomas, associate, and bachelor's.
Freshman Application Contact Hesser College, Nashua, 410 Amherst Street, Nashua, NH 03063. *Phone:* 603-883-0404. *Web site:* http://www.nashua.hesser.edu/.

Hesser College, Portsmouth

Portsmouth, New Hampshire

- **Proprietary** primarily 2-year
- **Coed**

Academics *Degrees:* certificates, diplomas, associate, and bachelor's.
Freshman Application Contact Hesser College, Portsmouth, 170 Commerce Way, Portsmouth, NH 03801. *Phone:* 603-436-5300. *Web site:* http://www.portsmouth.hesser.edu/.

Hesser College, Salem

Salem, New Hampshire

- **Proprietary** primarily 2-year
- **Coed**

Academics *Degrees:* certificates, diplomas, associate, and bachelor's.
Freshman Application Contact Hesser College, Salem, 11 Manor Parkway, Salem, NH 03079. *Phone:* 603-898-3480. *Web site:* http://www.salem.hesser.edu/.

Lakes Region Community College

Laconia, New Hampshire

Director of Admissions Wayne Fraser, Director of Admissions, Lakes Region Community College, 379 Belmont Road, Laconia, NH 03246. *Phone:* 603-524-3207 Ext. 766. *Toll-free phone:* 800-357-2992. *E-mail:* wfraser@ccsnh.edu. *Web site:* http://www.lrcc.edu/.

Manchester Community College

Manchester, New Hampshire

Freshman Application Contact Ms. Jacquie Poirier, Coordinator of Admissions, Manchester Community College, 1066 Front Street, Manchester, NH 03102-8518. *Phone:* 603-668-6706 Ext. 283. *E-mail:* jpoirier@nhctc.edu. *Web site:* http://www.manchestercommunitycollege.edu/.

Nashua Community College
Nashua, New Hampshire

- **State-supported** 2-year, founded 1967, part of Community College System of New Hampshire
- **Urban** 66-acre campus with easy access to Boston
- **Coed,** 2,100 undergraduate students, 45% full-time, 51% women, 49% men

Undergraduates 950 full-time, 1,150 part-time.
Faculty *Total:* 108, 39% full-time.
Majors Accounting; airframe mechanics and aircraft maintenance technology; autobody/collision and repair technology; automobile/automotive mechanics technology; business administration and management; child development; computer and information sciences; computer engineering technology; computer science; data processing and data processing technology; drafting and design technology; electrical, electronic and communications engineering technology; electromechanical technology; engineering technology; general studies; human services; kindergarten/preschool education; legal assistant/paralegal; liberal arts and sciences/liberal studies; machine tool technology; social work.
Academics *Calendar:* semesters. *Degree:* certificates and associate. *Special study options:* academic remediation for entering students, adult/continuing education programs, cooperative education, distance learning, English as a second language, internships, part-time degree program, services for LD students, student-designed majors, summer session for credit.
Library Walter B. Peterson Library and Media Center with 22,000 titles, 250 serial subscriptions, an OPAC.
Student Life *Housing:* college housing not available. *Activities and Organizations:* drama/theater group, student-run newspaper, Student Senate, Phi Theta Kappa, AmeriCorp, Paralegal Club, Athletics. *Campus security:* 24-hour emergency response devices, late-night transport/escort service. *Student services:* personal/psychological counseling.
Athletics *Intercollegiate sports:* soccer M/W. *Intramural sports:* skiing (cross-country) M/W, skiing (downhill) M/W, soccer M/W, weight lifting M/W.
Costs (2010–11) *Tuition:* state resident $4680 full-time, $195 per credit hour part-time; nonresident $10,680 full-time, $445 per credit hour part-time. Full-time tuition and fees vary according to class time. Part-time tuition and fees vary according to class time. *Required fees:* $384 full-time, $16 per credit hour part-time. *Payment plan:* installment. *Waivers:* senior citizens and employees or children of employees.
Financial Aid Of all full-time matriculated undergraduates who enrolled in 2009, 35 Federal Work-Study jobs (averaging $1000).
Applying *Options:* deferred entrance. *Application fee:* $20. *Required:* high school transcript, interview. *Required for some:* TEAS testing for prenursing. *Application deadlines:* rolling (freshmen), rolling (transfers). *Notification:* continuous (freshmen), continuous (transfers).
Freshman Application Contact Ms. Patricia Goodman, Vice President of Student Services, Nashua Community College, Nashua, NH 03063. *Phone:* 603-882-6923 Ext. 1529. *Fax:* 603-882-8690. *E-mail:* pgoodman@ccsnh.edu. *Web site:* http://www.nashuacc.edu/.

NHTI, Concord's Community College
Concord, New Hampshire

Freshman Application Contact Mr. Francis P. Meyer, Director of Admissions, NHTI, Concord's Community College, 31 College Drive, Concord, NH 03301-7412. *Phone:* 603-271-7131. *Toll-free phone:* 800-247-0179. *E-mail:* fmeyer@nhctc.edu. *Web site:* http://www.nhti.edu/.

River Valley Community College
Claremont, New Hampshire

Director of Admissions Charles Kusselow, Director of Admissions, River Valley Community College, 1 College Drive, Claremont, NH 03743. *Phone:* 603-542-7744 Ext. 5322. *Toll-free phone:* 800-837-0658. *Fax:* 603-543-1844. *E-mail:* ckusselow@ccsnh.edu. *Web site:* http://www.rivervalley.edu/.

White Mountains Community College
Berlin, New Hampshire

- **State-supported** 2-year, founded 1966, part of Community College System of New Hampshire
- **Rural** 325-acre campus
- **Coed,** 983 undergraduate students, 42% full-time, 63% women, 37% men

Undergraduates 417 full-time, 566 part-time. Students come from 4 states and territories; 4% are from out of state.
Freshmen *Admission:* 198 enrolled.
Faculty *Total:* 253, 11% full-time, 0.4% with terminal degrees.
Majors Accounting; administrative assistant and secretarial science; automobile/automotive mechanics technology; baking and pastry arts; business administration and management; computer and information sciences; computer engineering technology; criminal justice/safety; culinary arts; diesel mechanics technology; early childhood education; environmental studies; general studies; geographic information science and cartography; human services; liberal arts and sciences/liberal studies; medical office assistant; registered nursing/registered nurse; surveying technology.
Academics *Calendar:* semesters. *Degree:* certificates, diplomas, and associate. *Special study options:* academic remediation for entering students, adult/continuing education programs, advanced placement credit, distance learning, double majors, external degree program, independent study, internships, part-time degree program, services for LD students, summer session for credit.
Library Fortier Library with 18,000 titles, 85 serial subscriptions, 350 audiovisual materials, an OPAC.
Student Life *Housing:* college housing not available. *Activities and Organizations:* Student Senate.
Standardized Tests *Required:* ACCUPLACER Placement Test (for admission).
Costs (2011–12) *Tuition:* state resident $5850 full-time, $195 per credit part-time; nonresident $13,350 full-time, $445 per credit part-time. *Required fees:* $540 full-time, $18 per credit part-time. *Payment plan:* deferred payment. *Waivers:* senior citizens and employees or children of employees.
Applying *Options:* electronic application. *Application fee:* $20. *Required:* high school transcript, placement test. *Required for some:* essay or personal statement. *Application deadlines:* rolling (freshmen), rolling (transfers). *Notification:* continuous (freshmen), continuous (transfers).
Freshman Application Contact Ms. Jamie Rivard, Program Assistant, White Mountains Community College, 2020 Riverside Drive, Berlin, NH 03570. *Phone:* 603-752-1113 Ext. 3000. *Toll-free phone:* 800-445-4525. *Fax:* 603-752-6335. *E-mail:* jrivard@ccsnh.edu. *Web site:* http://www.wmcc.edu/.

NEW JERSEY

Assumption College for Sisters
Mendham, New Jersey

Freshman Application Contact Sr. Gerardine Tantsits, Academic Dean/Registrar, Assumption College for Sisters, 350 Bernardsville Road, Mendham, NJ 07945-2923. *Phone:* 973-543-6528 Ext. 228. *Fax:* 973-543-1738. *E-mail:* deanregistrar@acs350.org. *Web site:* http://www.acs350.org/.

Atlantic Cape Community College
Mays Landing, New Jersey

Freshman Application Contact Mrs. Linda McLeod, Assistant Director, Admissions and College Recruitment, Atlantic Cape Community College, 5100 Black Horse Pike, Mays Landing, NJ 08330-2699. *Phone:* 609-343-5009. *Toll-free phone:* 800-645-CHIEF. *Fax:* 609-343-4921. *E-mail:* accadmit@atlantic.edu. *Web site:* http://www.atlantic.edu/.

Bergen Community College
Paramus, New Jersey

Freshman Application Contact Admissions Office, Bergen Community College, 400 Paramus Road, Paramus, NJ 07652-1595. *Phone:* 201-447-7195. *E-mail:* admsoffice@bergen.edu. *Web site:* http://www.bergen.edu/.

Berkeley College
Woodland Park, New Jersey

Freshman Application Contact Berkeley College, 44 Rifle Camp Road, Woodland Park, NJ 07424-3353. *Phone:* 973-278-5400. *Toll-free phone:* 800-446-5400. *Web site:* http://www.berkeleycollege.edu/.

Brookdale Community College
Lincroft, New Jersey

Director of Admissions Ms. Kim Toomey, Registrar, Brookdale Community College, 765 Newman Springs Road, Lincroft, NJ 07738-1597. *Phone:* 732-224-2268. *Web site:* http://www.brookdalecc.edu/.

Burlington County College

Pemberton, New Jersey

- **County-supported** 2-year, founded 1966
- **Suburban** 225-acre campus with easy access to Philadelphia
- **Coed,** 10,075 undergraduate students, 55% full-time, 58% women, 42% men

Undergraduates 5,566 full-time, 4,509 part-time. Students come from 17 states and territories; 1% are from out of state; 7% transferred in. *Retention:* 63% of full-time freshmen returned.

Freshmen *Admission:* 5,666 applied, 5,666 admitted, 2,289 enrolled.

Faculty *Total:* 615, 9% full-time. *Student/faculty ratio:* 30:1.

Majors Accounting; agribusiness; American Sign Language (ASL); animation, interactive technology, video graphics and special effects; art; automotive engineering technology; biological and physical sciences; biology/biological sciences; biotechnology; business administration and management; chemical engineering; chemistry; commercial and advertising art; communication disorders sciences and services related; computer graphics; computer science; construction engineering technology; criminal justice/police science; dental hygiene; drafting and design technology; dramatic/theater arts; education; electrical, electronic and communications engineering technology; engineering; engineering technologies and engineering related; English; environmental science; fashion/apparel design; fire science/firefighting; food service systems administration; geological and earth sciences/geosciences related; graphic and printing equipment operation/production; graphic design; health information/medical records technology; health services/allied health/health sciences; history; hospitality administration; human services; information technology; international/global studies; journalism; legal assistant/paralegal; liberal arts and sciences/liberal studies; management information systems; mathematics; medical radiologic technology; music; philosophy; physics; psychology; registered nursing/registered nurse; respiratory care therapy; restaurant/food services management; retailing; sales, distribution, and marketing operations; sign language interpretation and translation; social sciences; sociology.

Academics *Calendar:* semesters plus 2 summer terms. *Degree:* certificates and associate. *Special study options:* academic remediation for entering students, adult/continuing education programs, advanced placement credit, cooperative education, distance learning, double majors, English as a second language, honors programs, independent study, internships, part-time degree program, services for LD students, summer session for credit.

Library Burlington County College Library plus 1 other with 92,400 titles, 1,750 serial subscriptions, an OPAC, a Web page.

Student Life *Housing:* college housing not available. *Activities and Organizations:* drama/theater group, student-run radio station, choral group, Student Government Association, Phi Theta Kappa, Creative Writing Guild. *Campus security:* 24-hour emergency response devices and patrols, late-night transport/escort service, electronic entrances to buildings and rooms, surveillance cameras. *Student services:* health clinic, personal/psychological counseling.

Athletics Member NJCAA. *Intercollegiate sports:* baseball M(s), basketball M(s)/W(s), golf M/W, soccer M/W, softball W. *Intramural sports:* archery M.

Costs (2011–12) *Tuition:* area resident $2760 full-time, $92 per credit part-time; state resident $3240 full-time, $108 per credit hour part-time; nonresident $5190 full-time, $173 per credit hour part-time. Full-time tuition and fees vary according to course load. Part-time tuition and fees vary according to course load. *Required fees:* $855 full-time, $29 per credit part-time. *Waivers:* employees or children of employees.

Financial Aid Of all full-time matriculated undergraduates who enrolled in 2009, 100 Federal Work-Study jobs (averaging $1200). 100 state and other part-time jobs (averaging $2000).

Applying *Options:* electronic application, early admission, deferred entrance. *Application fee:* $20. *Required:* high school transcript. *Application deadlines:* rolling (freshmen), rolling (transfers). *Notification:* continuous (freshmen), continuous (transfers).

Freshman Application Contact Burlington County College, 601 Pemberton Browns Mills Road, Pemberton, NJ 08068. *Phone:* 609-894-9311 Ext. 1200. *Web site:* http://www.bcc.edu/.

Camden County College

Blackwood, New Jersey

- **State and locally supported** 2-year, founded 1967, part of New Jersey Commission on Higher Education
- **Suburban** 320-acre campus with easy access to Philadelphia
- **Coed**

Undergraduates 8,529 full-time, 7,141 part-time. Students come from 9 states and territories. *Retention:* 67% of full-time freshmen returned.

Academics *Calendar:* semesters. *Degree:* certificates and associate. *Special study options:* academic remediation for entering students, adult/continuing education programs, cooperative education, distance learning, double majors, English as a second language, external degree program, freshman honors college, honors programs, independent study, internships, off-campus study, part-time degree program, services for LD students, study abroad, summer session for credit.

Student Life *Campus security:* 24-hour emergency response devices.

Athletics Member NJCAA.

Costs (2010–11) *Tuition:* area resident $2880 full-time, $96 per credit part-time; state resident $3000 full-time, $100 per credit part-time; nonresident $3000 full-time, $100 per credit part-time. Full-time tuition and fees vary according to course load. Part-time tuition and fees vary according to course load. *Required fees:* $846 full-time, $28 per credit part-time, $3 per term part-time.

Financial Aid Of all full-time matriculated undergraduates who enrolled in 2009, 117 Federal Work-Study jobs (averaging $1126).

Applying *Options:* early admission. *Required for some:* high school transcript.

Freshman Application Contact Donald Delaney, Outreach Coordinator, School and Community Academic Programs, Camden County College, PO Box 200, Blackwood, NJ 08012-0200. *Phone:* 856 227 7200 Ext. 4371. *Toll free phone:* 888-228-2466. *Fax:* 856-374-4916. *E-mail:* ddelaney@camdencc.edu. *Web site:* http://www.camdencc.edu/.

See page 208 for Display and page 408 for the College Close-Up.

County College of Morris

Randolph, New Jersey

- **County-supported** 2-year, founded 1966, part of New Jersey Commission on Higher Education
- **Suburban** 218-acre campus with easy access to New York City
- **Coed**

Undergraduates 5,076 full-time, 3,662 part-time.

Academics *Calendar:* semesters. *Degree:* certificates and associate.

Athletics Member NJCAA.

Costs (2010–11) *Tuition:* area resident $3300 full-time, $110 per credit part-time; state resident $6600 full-time, $220 per credit part-time; nonresident $9330 full-time, $311 per credit part-time. *Required fees:* $645 full-time, $17 per credit part-time, $15 per course part-time.

Financial Aid Of all full-time matriculated undergraduates who enrolled in 2009, 588 Federal Work-Study jobs (averaging $1947).

Applying *Application fee:* $30. *Required:* high school transcript.

Freshman Application Contact County College of Morris, 214 Center Grove Road, Randolph, NJ 07869-2086. *Phone:* 973-328-5100. *Toll-free phone:* 888-226-8001. *Web site:* http://www.ccm.edu/.

Cumberland County College

Vineland, New Jersey

- **State and locally supported** 2-year, founded 1963, part of New Jersey Commission on Higher Education
- **Small-town** 100-acre campus with easy access to Philadelphia
- **Coed**

Undergraduates 2,365 full-time, 1,649 part-time.

Faculty *Student/faculty ratio:* 14:1.

Academics *Calendar:* semesters. *Degree:* certificates and associate. *Special study options:* academic remediation for entering students, advanced placement credit, cooperative education, distance learning, double majors, English as a second language, honors programs, part-time degree program, services for LD students, summer session for credit.

Student Life *Campus security:* 24-hour emergency response devices, late-night transport/escort service.

Athletics Member NJCAA.

Costs (2010–11) *Tuition:* area resident $2970 full-time, $99 per credit hour part-time; state resident $5940 full-time, $198 per credit hour part-time; nonresident $11,880 full-time, $396 per credit hour part-time. *Required fees:* $870 full-time, $29 per credit hour part-time.

Financial Aid Of all full-time matriculated undergraduates who enrolled in 2009, 100 Federal Work-Study jobs (averaging $500). 100 state and other part-time jobs (averaging $600).

Applying *Options:* electronic application, early admission, deferred entrance. *Application fee:* $25. *Required:* high school transcript.

Freshman Application Contact Ms. Anne Daly-Eimer, Director of Admissions and Registration, Cumberland County College, PO Box 1500, College Drive, Vineland, NJ 08362. *Phone:* 856-691-8986. *Web site:* http://www.cccnj.edu/.

Essex County College

Newark, New Jersey

- **County-supported** 2-year, founded 1966, part of New Jersey Commission on Higher Education
- **Urban** 22-acre campus with easy access to New York City
- **Coed**

Undergraduates 7,915 full-time, 5,399 part-time. Students come from 9 states and territories; 69 other countries; 1% are from out of state; 2% transferred in. *Retention:* 55% of full-time freshmen returned.

Faculty *Student/faculty ratio:* 29:1.

Academics *Calendar:* semesters. *Degree:* certificates and associate. *Special study options:* academic remediation for entering students, accelerated degree program, adult/continuing education programs, advanced placement credit, cooperative education, distance learning, double majors, English as a second language, independent study, internships, off-campus study, part-time degree program, services for LD students, summer session for credit. *ROTC:* Army (c).

Student Life *Campus security:* 24-hour emergency response devices and patrols.

Athletics Member NJCAA.

Costs (2010–11) *Tuition:* area resident $3255 full-time, $109 per credit hour part-time; state resident $6510 full-time, $217 per credit hour part-time; nonresident $6510 full-time, $217 per credit hour part-time. *Required fees:* $975 full-time, $33 per credit hour part-time.

Financial Aid Of all full-time matriculated undergraduates who enrolled in 2008, 256 Federal Work-Study jobs (averaging $2488).

Applying *Options:* electronic application, deferred entrance. *Application fee:* $25. *Required:* high school transcript.

Freshman Application Contact Ms. Marva Mack, Director of Admissions, Essex County College, 303 University Avenue, Newark, NJ 07102. *Phone:* 973-877-3119. *Fax:* 973-623-6449. *Web site:* http://www.essex.edu/.

Gloucester County College

Sewell, New Jersey

Freshman Application Contact Ms. Judy Atkinson, Registrar/Admissions, Gloucester County College, 1400 Tanyard Road, Sewell, NJ 08080. *Phone:* 856-415-2209. *E-mail:* jatkinso@gccnj.edu. *Web site:* http://www.gccnj.edu/.

Hudson County Community College

Jersey City, New Jersey

Director of Admissions Mr. Robert Martin, Assistant Dean of Admissions, Hudson County Community College, 25 Journal Square, Jersey City, NJ 07306. *Phone:* 201-714-2115. *Fax:* 201-714-2136. *E-mail:* martin@hccc.edu. *Web site:* http://www.hccc.edu/.

Mercer County Community College

Trenton, New Jersey

- **State and locally supported** 2-year, founded 1966
- **Suburban** 292-acre campus with easy access to New York City and Philadelphia
- **Coed**

Undergraduates 4,372 full-time, 5,249 part-time. Students come from 5 states and territories; 91 other countries; 7% are from out of state; 3% transferred in. *Retention:* 68% of full-time freshmen returned.

Faculty *Student/faculty ratio:* 22:1.

Academics *Calendar:* semesters. *Degree:* certificates and associate. *Special study options:* academic remediation for entering students, accelerated degree program, adult/continuing education programs, advanced placement credit, cooperative education, distance learning, double majors, English as a second language, external degree program, independent study, internships, part-time degree program, services for LD students, student-designed majors, summer session for credit. *ROTC:* Army (c), Air Force (c).

Student Life *Campus security:* 24-hour emergency response devices and patrols.

Athletics Member NJCAA.

Costs (2010–11) *Tuition:* area resident $2460 full-time, $103 per credit hour part-time; state resident $3480 full-time, $145 per credit hour part-time; nonresident $5520 full-time, $230 per credit hour part-time. Full-time tuition and fees vary according to program and reciprocity agreements. Part-time tuition and fees vary according to program and reciprocity agreements. *Required fees:* $613 full-time, $25 per credit hour part-time, $25 per term part-time.

Financial Aid Of all full-time matriculated undergraduates who enrolled in 2009, 100 Federal Work-Study jobs (averaging $1500). 12 state and other part-time jobs (averaging $1500).

Applying *Options:* electronic application, deferred entrance. *Required:* high school transcript. *Recommended:* interview.

Freshman Application Contact Dr. L. Campbell, Dean for Student and Academic Services, Mercer County Community College, 1200 Old Trenton Road, PO Box B, Trenton, NJ 08690-1004. *Phone:* 609-586-4800 Ext. 3222. *Toll-free phone:* 800-392-MCCC. *Fax:* 609-586-6944. *E-mail:* admiss@ mccc.edu. *Web site:* http://www.mccc.edu/.

Middlesex County College

Edison, New Jersey

Director of Admissions Mr. Peter W. Rice, Director of Admissions and Recruitment, Middlesex County College, 2600 Woodbridge Avenue, PO Box 3050, Edison, NJ 08818-3050. *Phone:* 732-906-4243. *Web site:* http://www.middlesexcc.edu/.

Ocean County College

Toms River, New Jersey

- **County-supported** 2-year, founded 1964, part of New Jersey Commission on Higher Education
- **Small-town** 275-acre campus with easy access to Philadelphia
- **Coed,** 10,367 undergraduate students, 56% full-time, 57% women, 43% men

Undergraduates 5,775 full-time, 4,592 part-time. Students come from 25 states and territories; 2 other countries; 1% are from out of state; 3% transferred in. *Retention:* 73% of full-time freshmen returned.

Freshmen *Admission:* 3,772 applied, 2,686 admitted, 2,686 enrolled.

Faculty *Total:* 536, 20% full-time. *Student/faculty ratio:* 29:1.

Majors Administrative assistant and secretarial science; broadcast journalism; business administration and management; business/commerce; communications technologies and support services related; computer and information sciences; criminal justice/police science; engineering; engineering technologies and engineering related; environmental science; fire prevention and safety technology; general studies; human services; liberal arts and sciences/liberal studies; registered nursing/registered nurse; sign language interpretation and translation.

Academics *Calendar:* semesters. *Degree:* certificates, diplomas, and associate. *Special study options:* academic remediation for entering students, accelerated degree program, adult/continuing education programs, advanced placement credit, cooperative education, distance learning, English as a second language, honors programs, independent study, internships, part-time degree program, services for LD students, study abroad, summer session for credit.

Library Ocean County College Library with 102,082 titles, 399 serial subscriptions, 4,825 audiovisual materials, an OPAC, a Web page.

Student Life *Housing:* college housing not available. *Activities and Organizations:* drama/theater group, student-run newspaper, radio and television station, choral group, Phi Theta Kappa, ASOCC - Student Government, Student Nurses Organization, NJ STARS Club, Phi Beta Lambda. *Campus security:* 24-hour emergency response devices and patrols, late-night transport/escort service. *Student services:* personal/psychological counseling.

Athletics Member NJCAA. *Intercollegiate sports:* baseball M, basketball M/W, cross-country running M/W, golf M/W, soccer M/W, softball W, swimming and diving M/W, tennis M/W. *Intramural sports:* basketball M/W, cheerleading M(c)/W(c), ice hockey M, sailing M(c)/W(c), soccer M/W, softball W, volleyball M/W.

Costs (2011–12) *Tuition:* area resident $2820 full-time, $94 per credit part-time; state resident $3780 full-time, $126 per credit part-time; nonresident $6180 full-time, $206 per credit part-time. Full-time tuition and fees vary according to program. Part-time tuition and fees vary according to program. *Required fees:* $890 full-time, $28 per credit part-time, $20 per term part-time. *Payment plan:* installment. *Waivers:* senior citizens and employees or children of employees.

Financial Aid Of all full-time matriculated undergraduates who enrolled in 2009, 76 Federal Work-Study jobs (averaging $1300). 45 state and other part-time jobs (averaging $850).

Applying *Options:* electronic application, early admission, deferred entrance. *Required for some:* high school transcript. *Application deadlines:* rolling (freshmen), rolling (out-of-state freshmen), rolling (transfers). *Notification:* continuous (freshmen), continuous (out-of-state freshmen), continuous (transfers).

Freshman Application Contact Ocean County College, College Drive, PO Box 2001, Toms River, NJ 08754-2001. *Phone:* 732-255-0304 Ext. 2423. *Web site:* http://www.ocean.edu/.

Passaic County Community College

Paterson, New Jersey

Freshman Application Contact Mr. Patrick Noonan, Director of Admissions, Passaic County Community College, One College Boulevard, Paterson, NJ 07505-1179. *Phone:* 973-684-6304. *Web site:* http://www.pccc.cc.nj.us/.

Raritan Valley Community College

Branchburg, New Jersey

- **County-supported** 2-year, founded 1965
- **Small-town** 225-acre campus with easy access to New York City and Philadelphia
- **Endowment** $1.1 million
- **Coed,** 8,484 undergraduate students, 51% full-time, 53% women, 47% men

Undergraduates 4,325 full-time, 4,159 part-time. Students come from 20 states and territories; 1% are from out of state; 10% Black or African American, non-Hispanic/Latino; 13% Hispanic/Latino; 5% Asian, non-Hispanic/Latino; 0.2% Native Hawaiian or other Pacific Islander, non-Hispanic/Latino; 0.2% American Indian or Alaska Native, non-Hispanic/Latino; 1% Two or more races, non-Hispanic/Latino; 7% Race/ethnicity unknown; 2% international; 9% transferred in.

Freshmen *Admission:* 2,575 applied, 2,459 admitted, 1,634 enrolled.

Faculty *Total:* 499, 23% full-time. *Student/faculty ratio:* 24:1.

Majors Accounting related; accounting technology and bookkeeping; administrative assistant and secretarial science; animation, interactive technology, video graphics and special effects; automotive engineering technology; biotechnology; business administration and management; business/commerce; chemical technology; child-care provision; cinematography and film/video production; communication and media related; computer and information sciences and support services related; computer programming (vendor/product certification); computer systems networking and telecommunications; construction engineering technology; corrections; criminal justice/law enforcement administration; criminal justice/police science; critical incident response/special police operations; dance; dental assisting; dental hygiene; design and applied arts related; diesel mechanics technology; digital communication and media/multimedia; engineering science; engineering technologies and engineering related; English; financial planning and services; fine/studio arts; health and physical education/fitness; health information/medical records technology; health services/allied health/health sciences; heating, ventilation, air conditioning and refrigeration engineering technology; information technology; interior design; international business/trade/commerce; kindergarten/preschool education; kinesiology and exercise science; legal assistant/paralegal; liberal arts and sciences/liberal studies; lineworker; management information systems; manufacturing engineering technology; marketing/marketing management; medical/clinical assistant; meeting and event planning; multi/interdisciplinary studies related; music; opticianry; optometric technician; registered nursing/registered nurse; respiratory care therapy; restaurant, culinary, and catering management; small business administration; web page; digital/multimedia and information resources design.

Academics *Calendar:* semesters. *Degree:* certificates and associate. *Special study options:* academic remediation for entering students, adult/continuing education programs, advanced placement credit, cooperative education, distance learning, double majors, English as a second language, honors programs, independent study, internships, off-campus study, part-time degree program, services for LD students, summer session for credit. *ROTC:* Army (c), Air Force (c).

Library Evelyn S. Field Library with 91,595 titles, 24,596 serial subscriptions, 2,566 audiovisual materials, an OPAC, a Web page.

Student Life *Housing:* college housing not available. *Activities and Organizations:* drama/theater group, student-run newspaper, radio station, choral group, Phi Theta Kappa, Orgullo Latino, Student Nurses Association, Business Club/SIFE, Game Development club. *Campus security:* 24-hour emergency response devices and patrols, late-night transport/escort service, 24-hour outdoor and indoor surveillance cameras; 24-hr mobile patrols; 24-hr communication center. *Student services:* personal/psychological counseling, women's center.

Athletics Member NJCAA. *Intercollegiate sports:* baseball M, basketball M/W, soccer M/W, softball W. *Intramural sports:* golf M/W.

Costs (2010–11) *Tuition:* area resident $2970 full-time, $99 per credit hour part-time; state resident $3270 full-time, $109 per credit hour part-time; nonresident $3270 full-time, $109 per credit hour part-time. Full-time tuition and fees vary according to course load and program. Part-time tuition and fees vary according to course load and program. *Required fees:* $870 full-time, $22 per credit hour part-time, $80 per term part-time. *Payment plan:* installment. *Waivers:* senior citizens and employees or children of employees.

Financial Aid Of all full-time matriculated undergraduates who enrolled in 2009, 12 Federal Work-Study jobs (averaging $2500).

Applying *Options:* electronic application, early admission. *Application fee:* $25. *Required:* high school transcript. *Application deadlines:* rolling (freshmen), rolling (transfers).
Freshman Application Contact Mr. Daniel Palubniak, Registrar, Enrollment Services, Raritan Valley Community College, PO Box 3300, Somerville, NJ 08876-1265. *Phone:* 908-526-1200 Ext. 8206. *Fax:* 908-704-3442. *E-mail:* dpalubni@raritanval.edu. *Web site:* http://www.raritanval.edu/.

Salem Community College
Carneys Point, New Jersey

Freshman Application Contact Lynn Fishlock, Director of Enrollment and Transfer Services, Salem Community College, 460 Hollywood Avenue, Carneys Point, NJ 08069. *Phone:* 856-351-2701. *Fax:* 856-299-9193. *E-mail:* info@salemcc.edu. *Web site:* http://www.salemcc.edu/.

Sussex County Community College
Newton, New Jersey

Freshman Application Contact Mr. James Donohue, Director of Admissions and Registrar, Sussex County Community College, 1 College Hill Road, Newton, NJ 07860. *Phone:* 973-300-2219. *Fax:* 973-579-5226. *E-mail:* jdonohue@sussex.edu. *Web site:* http://www.sussex.edu/.

Union County College
Cranford, New Jersey

- **State and locally supported** 2-year, founded 1933, part of New Jersey Commission on Higher Education
- **Urban** 48-acre campus with easy access to New York City
- **Endowment** $8.5 million
- **Coed,** 12,774 undergraduate students, 51% full-time, 64% women, 36% men

Undergraduates 6,482 full-time, 6,292 part-time. Students come from 11 states and territories; 77 other countries; 3% are from out of state; 26% Black or African American, non-Hispanic/Latino; 29% Hispanic/Latino; 3% Asian, non-Hispanic/Latino; 0.3% Native Hawaiian or other Pacific Islander, non-Hispanic/Latino; 0.6% American Indian or Alaska Native, non-Hispanic/Latino; 16% Race/ethnicity unknown; 2% international; 4% transferred in. *Retention:* 54% of full-time freshmen returned.
Freshmen *Admission:* 6,367 applied, 5,241 admitted, 2,802 enrolled.
Faculty *Total:* 528, 35% full-time, 28% with terminal degrees. *Student/faculty ratio:* 32:1.
Majors Accounting technology and bookkeeping; allied health diagnostic, intervention, and treatment professions related; American Sign Language (ASL); American Sign Language related; animation, interactive technology, video graphics and special effects; automobile/automotive mechanics technology; biology/biological sciences; business administration and management; business/commerce; chemistry; civil engineering technology; computer and information sciences and support services related; computer science; criminal justice/law enforcement administration; criminal justice/police science; customer service support/call center/teleservice operation; dental assisting; dental hygiene; diagnostic medical sonography and ultrasound technology; electromechanical technology; emergency medical technology (EMT paramedic); engineering; fire prevention and safety technology; hospitality administration; hotel/motel administration; human services; information science/studies; information technology; language interpretation and translation; legal assistant/paralegal; liberal arts and sciences/liberal studies; licensed practical/vocational nurse training; management information systems; manufacturing engineering technology; marketing/marketing management; mass communication/media; mathematics; mechanical engineering/mechanical technology; medical radiologic technology; nuclear medical technology; physical therapy technology; radiologic technology/science; recording arts technology; registered nursing/registered nurse; rehabilitation and therapeutic professions related; respiratory care therapy; security and loss prevention; sign language interpretation and translation; sport and fitness administration/management; telecommunications technology.
Academics *Calendar:* semesters. *Degree:* certificates, diplomas, and associate. *Special study options:* academic remediation for entering students, accelerated degree program, adult/continuing education programs, advanced placement credit, distance learning, English as a second language, honors programs, independent study, internships, off-campus study, part-time degree program, services for LD students, student-designed majors, summer session for credit. *ROTC:* Air Force (c).
Library MacKay Library plus 2 others with 137,731 titles, 20,938 serial subscriptions, 3,610 audiovisual materials, an OPAC, a Web page.
Student Life *Housing:* college housing not available. *Activities and Organizations:* drama/theater group, student-run newspaper, radio and television station, SIGN, Business Management Club, Art Society, La Sociedad Hispanica

de UCC, Architecture Club. *Campus security:* 24-hour emergency response devices and patrols, late-night transport/escort service. *Student services:* personal/psychological counseling.
Athletics Member NJCAA. *Intercollegiate sports:* baseball M, basketball M/W(s), golf M/W, soccer M, volleyball W. *Intramural sports:* cheerleading W.
Costs (2011–12) *Tuition:* area resident $2616 full-time, $109 per credit part-time; state resident $5232 full-time, $218 per credit part-time; nonresident $5232 full-time, $218 per credit part-time. Full-time tuition and fees vary according to course load. Part-time tuition and fees vary according to course load. *Required fees:* $889 full-time, $33 per credit part-time. *Payment plan:* deferred payment. *Waivers:* senior citizens and employees or children of employees.
Financial Aid Of all full-time matriculated undergraduates who enrolled in 2009, 150 Federal Work-Study jobs (averaging $1700).
Applying *Options:* electronic application, early admission, deferred entrance. *Application fee:* $35. *Required:* high school transcript. *Required for some:* interview. *Application deadlines:* rolling (freshmen), rolling (transfers). *Notification:* continuous (freshmen), continuous (transfers).
Freshman Application Contact Ms. Jo Ann Davis-Wayne, Director of Admissions, Records, and Registration, Union County College, Cranford, NJ 07016. *Phone:* 908-709-7127. *Fax:* 908-709-7125. *E-mail:* davis@ucc.edu. *Web site:* http://www.ucc.edu/.

Warren County Community College
Washington, New Jersey

Freshman Application Contact Shannon Horwath, Associate Director of Admissions, Warren County Community College, 475 Route 57 West, Washington, NJ 07882-9605. *Phone:* 908-835-2300. *E-mail:* shorwath@warren.edu. *Web site:* http://www.warren.edu/.

NEW MEXICO

Brown Mackie College–Albuquerque
Albuquerque, New Mexico

- **Proprietary** primarily 2-year, part of Education Management Corporation
- **Coed**

Majors Accounting technology and bookkeeping; architectural drafting and CAD/CADD; business administration and management; criminal justice/law enforcement administration; health/health-care administration; information technology; legal assistant/paralegal; legal studies; medical/clinical assistant; occupational therapist assistant; pharmacy technician; veterinary/animal health technology.
Academics *Degrees:* associate and bachelor's.
Costs (2010–11) *Tuition:* Tuition varies by program. Students should contact Brown Mackie College for tuition information.
Freshman Application Contact Brown Mackie College–Albuquerque, 10500 Cooper Avenue NE, Albuquerque, NM 87123. *Phone:* 505-559-5200. *Toll-free phone:* 877-271-3488. *Web site:* http://www.brownmackie.edu/.

See page 356 for the College Close-Up.

Carrington College - Albuquerque
Albuquerque, New Mexico

Admissions Office Contact Carrington College - Albuquerque, 1001 Menaul Boulevard NE, Albuquerque, NM 87107. *Web site:* http://carrington.edu/.

Central New Mexico Community College
Albuquerque, New Mexico

- **State-supported** 2-year, founded 1965
- **Urban** 60-acre campus
- **Endowment** $892,730
- **Coed,** 29,948 undergraduate students, 33% full-time, 56% women, 44% men

Undergraduates 9,818 full-time, 20,130 part-time. Students come from 31 states and territories; 5% transferred in. *Retention:* 58% of full-time freshmen returned.
Freshmen *Admission:* 7,591 applied, 7,591 admitted, 4,158 enrolled.
Faculty *Total:* 1,224, 26% full-time, 33% with terminal degrees. *Student/faculty ratio:* 27:1.

Majors Accounting; administrative assistant and secretarial science; agriculture; architectural drafting and CAD/CADD; art; automotive engineering technology; banking and financial support services; biotechnology; building/construction finishing, management, and inspection related; business administration and management; child-care and support services management; clinical/medical laboratory technology; computer systems analysis; construction trades related; cosmetology; criminal justice/safety; culinary arts; data processing and data processing technology; diagnostic medical sonography and ultrasound technology; electrical, electronic and communications engineering technology; electrical/electronics drafting and CAD/CADD; elementary education; engineering; environmental/environmental health engineering; executive assistant/executive secretary; fire prevention and safety technology; general studies; health information/medical records administration; hospitality administration; information science/studies; international business/trade/commerce; laser and optical technology; legal assistant/paralegal; liberal arts and sciences/liberal studies; manufacturing engineering technology; medical radiologic technology; parks, recreation and leisure; registered nursing/registered nurse; respiratory care therapy; surveying technology; technology/industrial arts teacher education; vehicle maintenance and repair technologies related; veterinary/animal health technology.

Academics *Calendar:* trimesters. *Degree:* certificates and associate. *Special study options:* academic remediation for entering students, adult/continuing education programs, advanced placement credit, cooperative education, distance learning, double majors, English as a second language, internships, part-time degree program, services for LD students, summer session for credit. *ROTC:* Army (c), Navy (c), Air Force (c).

Library Main Campus Library plus 1 other with 75,167 titles, 622 serial subscriptions, an OPAC, a Web page.

Student Life *Housing:* college housing not available. *Activities and Organizations:* student-run newspaper, Skills USA, Native American Student Club, ESL Club, GED Club, Artworks. *Campus security:* 24-hour emergency response devices and patrols, late-night transport/escort service. *Student services:* health clinic, personal/psychological counseling.

Costs (2010–11) *Tuition:* state resident $1584 full-time, $44 per credit hour part-time; nonresident $7968 full-time, $218 per credit hour part-time. Full-time tuition and fees vary according to course load. Part-time tuition and fees vary according to course load. *Required fees:* $120 full-time, $43 per term part-time. *Payment plan:* installment. *Waivers:* senior citizens.

Financial Aid Of all full-time matriculated undergraduates who enrolled in 2009, 175 Federal Work-Study jobs (averaging $6000). 225 state and other part-time jobs (averaging $6000).

Applying *Options:* electronic application. *Application deadlines:* rolling (freshmen), rolling (out-of-state freshmen), rolling (transfers). *Notification:* continuous (freshmen), continuous (out-of-state freshmen), continuous (transfers).

Freshman Application Contact Ms. Jane Campbell, Director, Enrollment Services, Central New Mexico Community College, Albuquerque, NM 87106. *Phone:* 505-224-3160. *Fax:* 505-224-3237. *Web site:* http://www.cnm.edu/.

Clovis Community College

Clovis, New Mexico

- **State-supported** 2-year, founded 1990
- **Small-town** 25-acre campus
- **Endowment** $740,423
- **Coed,** 4,175 undergraduate students, 24% full-time, 64% women, 36% men

Undergraduates 995 full-time, 3,180 part-time. Students come from 37 states and territories; 14% are from out of state; 8% transferred in. *Retention:* 43% of full-time freshmen returned.

Freshmen *Admission:* 513 applied, 513 admitted, 483 enrolled.

Faculty *Total:* 182, 29% full-time, 5% with terminal degrees. *Student/faculty ratio:* 21:1.

Majors Administrative assistant and secretarial science; automation engineer technology; automobile/automotive mechanics technology; business administration and management; commercial and advertising art; computer and information sciences; cosmetology; criminal justice/police science; early childhood education; education; electrician; emergency care attendant (EMT ambulance); executive assistant/executive secretary; fine/studio arts; fire science/firefighting; general studies; health and physical education/fitness; heating, air conditioning, ventilation and refrigeration maintenance technology; industrial mechanics and maintenance technology; information technology; information technology project management; legal administrative assistant/secretary; legal assistant/paralegal; legal support services related; liberal arts and sciences/liberal studies; library and archives assisting; licensed practical/vocational nurse training; management information systems; medical/clinical assistant; network and system administration; office management; office occupations and clerical services; pre-engineering; psychology; radiologist assistant; registered nursing/registered nurse; sign language interpretation and translation; teacher assistant/aide; web/multimedia management and webmaster; welding technology.

Academics *Calendar:* semesters. *Degree:* certificates and associate. *Special study options:* academic remediation for entering students, adult/continuing education programs, advanced placement credit, cooperative education, distance learning, double majors, English as a second language, independent study, internships, part-time degree program, services for LD students, summer session for credit.

Library Clovis Community College Library and Learning Resources Center with 52,000 titles, 370 serial subscriptions, an OPAC.

Student Life *Housing:* college housing not available. *Activities and Organizations:* drama/theater group, choral group, Student Senate, Student Nursing Association, Black Advisory Council, Hispanic Advisory Council, student ambassadors. *Campus security:* student patrols, late-night transport/escort service. *Student services:* personal/psychological counseling.

Athletics *Intramural sports:* basketball M/W, cross-country running M/W, racquetball M/W, tennis M/W, volleyball M/W.

Applying *Required:* high school transcript. *Required for some:* interview. *Application deadlines:* rolling (freshmen), rolling (transfers). *Notification:* continuous (freshmen), continuous (transfers).

Freshman Application Contact Ms. Rosie Corrie, Director of Admissions and Records/Registrar, Clovis Community College, Clovis, NM 88101-8381. *Phone:* 575-769-4962. *Fax:* 575-769-4190. *E-mail:* admissions@clovis.edu. *Web site:* http://www.clovis.edu/.

Doña Ana Community College

Las Cruces, New Mexico

- **State and locally supported** 2-year, founded 1973, part of New Mexico State University System
- **Urban** 15-acre campus with easy access to El Paso
- **Endowment** $18,682
- **Coed,** 9,041 undergraduate students, 35% full-time, 56% women, 44% men

Undergraduates 3,179 full-time, 5,862 part-time. Students come from 14 states and territories; 1 other country; 12% are from out of state; 3% Black or African American, non-Hispanic/Latino; 65% Hispanic/Latino; 1% Asian, non-Hispanic/Latino; 2% American Indian or Alaska Native, non-Hispanic/Latino; 5% Race/ethnicity unknown; 2% international; 2% transferred in. *Retention:* 85% of full-time freshmen returned.

Freshmen *Admission:* 556 applied, 2,058 enrolled.

Faculty *Total:* 344. *Student/faculty ratio:* 21:1.

Majors Administrative assistant and secretarial science; architectural engineering technology; automobile/automotive mechanics technology; business administration and management; computer engineering technology; computer typography and composition equipment operation; consumer merchandising/retailing management; drafting and design technology; electrical, electronic and communications engineering technology; emergency medical technology (EMT paramedic); fashion merchandising; finance; fire science/firefighting; heating, air conditioning, ventilation and refrigeration maintenance technology; hospitality administration; hydrology and water resources science; industrial radiologic technology; legal assistant/paralegal; library and information science; registered nursing/registered nurse; respiratory care therapy; welding technology.

Academics *Calendar:* semesters. *Degree:* certificates and associate. *Special study options:* academic remediation for entering students, adult/continuing education programs, advanced placement credit, cooperative education, distance learning, English as a second language, freshman honors college, honors programs, internships, part-time degree program, services for LD students, summer session for credit. *ROTC:* Army (c), Air Force (c).

Library Library/Media Center with 17,140 titles, 213 serial subscriptions, an OPAC.

Student Life *Housing Options:* coed. Campus housing is university owned. *Activities and Organizations:* drama/theater group, student-run newspaper, radio and television station, choral group, marching band, national fraternities, national sororities. *Campus security:* 24-hour emergency response devices and patrols, late-night transport/escort service, controlled dormitory access. *Student services:* health clinic, personal/psychological counseling, women's center, legal services.

Standardized Tests *Recommended:* ACT, ACT ASSET, or ACT COMPASS.

Costs (2010–11) *Tuition:* area resident $1368 full-time, $57 per credit hour part-time; state resident $1632 full-time, $68 per credit hour part-time; nonresident $4056 full-time, $169 per credit hour part-time. Full-time tuition and fees vary according to course load and program. Part-time tuition and fees vary according to course load and program. *Room and board:* $8924; room only: $5739. Room and board charges vary according to board plan and housing facility. *Payment plan:* installment. *Waivers:* employees or children of employees.

Financial Aid Of all full-time matriculated undergraduates who enrolled in 2009, 15 Federal Work-Study jobs (averaging $2800). 106 state and other part-time jobs (averaging $2800). *Financial aid deadline:* 6/30.

Applying *Options:* electronic application, deferred entrance. *Application fee:* $20. *Required:* high school transcript. *Application deadline:* rolling (freshmen).

Freshman Application Contact Mrs. Ricci Montes, Admissions Advisor, Doña Ana Community College, MSC-3DA, Box 30001, 3400 South Espina Street, Las Cruces, NM 88003-8001. *Phone:* 575-527-7683.* *Toll-free phone:* 800-903-7503. *Fax:* 575-527-7515. *Web site:* http://dabcc-www.nmsu.edu/.

Eastern New Mexico University–Roswell
Roswell, New Mexico

Freshman Application Contact Eastern New Mexico University–Roswell, PO Box 6000, Roswell, NM 88202-6000. *Phone:* 505-624-7142. *Toll-free phone:* 800-243-6687. *Web site:* http://www.enmu.edu/.

Institute of American Indian Arts
Santa Fe, New Mexico

Director of Admissions Myra Garro, Manager of Enrollment and Admissions, Institute of American Indian Arts, 83 Avan Nu Po Road, Santa Fe, NM 87508. *Phone:* 505-424-2328. *Web site:* http://www.iaia.edu/.

ITT Technical Institute
Albuquerque, New Mexico

- **Proprietary** primarily 2-year, founded 1989, part of ITT Educational Services, Inc.
- **Coed**

Majors CAD/CADD drafting/design technology; computer and information systems security; computer engineering technology; computer software and media applications related; computer software engineering; computer software technology; construction management; criminal justice/law enforcement administration; design and visual communications; electrical, electronic and communications engineering technology; health information/medical records technology; legal assistant/paralegal; project management; registered nursing/registered nurse; system, networking, and LAN/WAN management; web/multimedia management and webmaster.

Academics *Calendar:* quarters. *Degrees:* associate and bachelor's.

Student Life *Housing:* college housing not available.

Freshman Application Contact Director of Recruitment, ITT Technical Institute, 5100 Masthead Street, NE, Albuquerque, NM 87109. *Phone:* 505-828-1114. *Toll-free phone:* 800-636-1114. *Web site:* http://www.itt-tech.edu/.

Luna Community College
Las Vegas, New Mexico

- **State-supported** 2-year
- **Small-town** 25-acre campus
- **Coed**

Undergraduates 544 full-time, 1,245 part-time. Students come from 6 states and territories; 1% are from out of state; 1% transferred in. *Retention:* 38% of full-time freshmen returned.

Academics *Calendar:* semesters. *Degree:* certificates, diplomas, and associate. *Special study options:* academic remediation for entering students, cooperative education, distance learning, honors programs, independent study, part-time degree program.

Costs (2010–11) *Tuition:* area resident $768 full-time, $32 per credit part-time; state resident $960 full-time, $40 per credit part-time; nonresident $1896 full-time, $79 per credit part-time. Full-time tuition and fees vary according to program and reciprocity agreements. Part-time tuition and fees vary according to program and reciprocity agreements. *Required fees:* $46 full-time, $23 per term part-time.

Applying *Options:* electronic application. *Required:* high school transcript.

Freshman Application Contact Ms. Henrietta Griego, Director of Admissions, Recruitment, and Retention, Luna Community College, PO Box 1510, Las Vegas, NM 87701. *Phone:* 505-454-2020. *Toll-free phone:* 800-588-7232 Ext. 1202. *Fax:* 505-454-2588. *E-mail:* hgriego@luna.cc.nm.us. *Web site:* http://www.luna.edu/.

Mesalands Community College
Tucumcari, New Mexico

Director of Admissions Mr. Ken Brashear, Director of Enrollment Management, Mesalands Community College, 911 South Tenth Street, Tucumcari, NM 88401. *Phone:* 505-461-4413. *Web site:* http://www.mesalands.edu/.

National American University
Rio Rancho, New Mexico

Freshman Application Contact Admissions Office, National American University, 1601 Rio Rancho, Suite 200, Rio Rancho, NM 87124. *Web site:* http://www.national.edu/.

Navajo Technical College
Crownpoint, New Mexico

Director of Admissions Director of Admission, Navajo Technical College, PO Box 849, Crownpoint, NM 87313. *Phone:* 505-786-4100. *Web site:* http://www.navajotech.edu/.

New Mexico Junior College
Hobbs, New Mexico

Director of Admissions Mr. Robert Bensing, Dean of Enrollment Management, New Mexico Junior College, 5317 Lovington Highway, Hobbs, NM 88240-9123. *Phone:* 505-392-5092. *Toll-free phone:* 800-657-6260. *Web site:* http://www.nmjc.edu/.

New Mexico Military Institute
Roswell, New Mexico

Freshman Application Contact New Mexico Military Institute, Roswell, NM 88201-5173. *Phone:* 505-624-8050. *Toll-free phone:* 800-421-5376. *Fax:* 505-624-8058. *E-mail:* admissions@nmmi.edu. *Web site:* http://www.nmmi.edu/.

New Mexico State University–Alamogordo
Alamogordo, New Mexico

- **State-supported** 2-year, founded 1958, part of New Mexico State University System
- **Small-town** 540-acre campus
- **Endowment** $88,381
- **Coed,** 3,944 undergraduate students, 24% full-time, 65% women, 35% men

Undergraduates 937 full-time, 3,007 part-time. Students come from 28 states and territories; 15% are from out of state; 5% transferred in. *Retention:* 60% of full-time freshmen returned.

Freshmen *Admission:* 394 applied, 394 admitted, 394 enrolled. *Average high school GPA:* 2.76.

Faculty *Total:* 146, 34% full-time. *Student/faculty ratio:* 24:1.

Majors Administrative assistant and secretarial science; animation, interactive technology, video graphics and special effects; biomedical technology; business/commerce; computer programming; criminal justice/safety; early childhood education; education; electrical, electronic and communications engineering technology; electrician; ethnic, cultural minority, gender, and group studies related; fine/studio arts; general studies; graphic design; human services; information technology; legal assistant/paralegal; liberal arts and sciences and humanities related; office occupations and clerical services; registered nursing/registered nurse.

Academics *Calendar:* semesters. *Degree:* certificates and associate. *Special study options:* academic remediation for entering students, adult/continuing education programs, advanced placement credit, distance learning, double majors, honors programs, independent study, internships, off-campus study, part-time degree program, services for LD students, study abroad, summer session for credit.

Library David H. Townsend Library with 50,000 titles, 350 serial subscriptions, an OPAC, a Web page.

Student Life *Housing:* college housing not available. *Activities and Organizations:* drama/theater group, choral group, Student Government, Advocates for Children and Education, Phi Theta Kappa, Social Science Club, Student Veterans of America-Alamogordo. *Campus security:* 24-hour emergency response devices.

Costs (2011–12) *Tuition:* area resident $1824 full-time, $72 per credit hour part-time; state resident $2160 full-time, $86 per credit hour part-time; nonresident $4872 full-time, $199 per credit hour part-time. Full-time tuition and fees vary according to course load. *Required fees:* $96 full-time, $4 per credit hour part-time. *Payment plans:* installment, deferred payment. *Waivers:* senior citizens and employees or children of employees.

Financial Aid Of all full-time matriculated undergraduates who enrolled in 2009, 10 Federal Work-Study jobs (averaging $3300). 60 state and other part-time jobs (averaging $3300). *Financial aid deadline:* 5/1.

Applying *Options:* electronic application, early admission, deferred entrance. *Application fee:* $15. *Required:* high school transcript, minimum 2.0 GPA. *Application deadlines:* rolling (freshmen), rolling (out-of-state freshmen), rolling (transfers). *Notification:* continuous (freshmen), continuous (out-of-state freshmen), continuous (transfers).

Freshman Application Contact Ms. Bobi McDonald, Coordinator of Admissions and Records, New Mexico State University–Alamogordo, 2400 North Scenic Drive, Alamogordo, NM 88311-0477. *Phone:* 505-439-3700. *E-mail:* advisor@nmsua.nmsu.edu. *Web site:* http://nmsua.edu/.

New Mexico State University–Carlsbad

Carlsbad, New Mexico

- **State-supported** 2-year, founded 1950, part of New Mexico State University System
- **Small-town** 40-acre campus
- **Coed**

Undergraduates 583 full-time, 1,415 part-time. Students come from 20 states and territories; 0.6% are from out of state; 5% transferred in. *Retention:* 41% of full-time freshmen returned.

Academics *Calendar:* semesters. *Degree:* certificates, diplomas, and associate. *Special study options:* academic remediation for entering students, adult/continuing education programs, advanced placement credit, cooperative education, distance learning, double majors, English as a second language, honors programs, independent study, internships, part-time degree program, services for LD students, student-designed majors, summer session for credit.

Student Life *Campus security:* 24-hour emergency response devices, late-night transport/escort service.

Costs (2010–11) *One-time required fee:* $20. *Tuition:* area resident $864 full-time, $36 per credit hour part-time; state resident $1320 full-time, $55 per credit hour part-time; nonresident $2712 full-time, $113 per credit hour part-time.

Financial Aid Of all full-time matriculated undergraduates who enrolled in 2009, 5 Federal Work-Study jobs (averaging $2300). 29 state and other part-time jobs (averaging $3000).

Applying *Options:* electronic application, early admission. *Application fee:* $20. *Required for some:* high school transcript.

Freshman Application Contact Ms. Everal Shannon, Records Specialist, New Mexico State University–Carlsbad, 1500 University Drive, Carlsbad, NM 88220. *Phone:* 575-234-9222. *Fax:* 575-885-4951. *E-mail:* eshannon@nmsu.edu. *Web site:* http://www.cavern.nmsu.edu/.

New Mexico State University–Grants

Grants, New Mexico

Director of Admissions Ms. Irene Lutz, Campus Student Services Officer, New Mexico State University–Grants, 1500 3rd Street, Grants, NM 87020-2025. *Phone:* 505-287-7981. *Web site:* http://grants.nmsu.edu/.

Northern New Mexico College

Espanola, New Mexico

Freshman Application Contact Mr. Mike L. Costello, Registrar, Northern New Mexico College, 921 Paseo de Onate, Espanola, NM 87532. *Phone:* 505-747-2193. *Fax:* 505-747-2191. *E-mail:* dms@nnmc.edu. *Web site:* http://www.nnmc.edu/.

Pima Medical Institute

Albuquerque, New Mexico

- **Proprietary** 2-year
- **Urban** campus
- **Coed**

Majors Health/health-care administration.

Academics *Special study options:* cooperative education, distance learning, internships.

Student Life *Housing:* college housing not available.

Standardized Tests *Required:* Wonderlic Scholastic Level Exam (for admission).

Applying *Required:* high school transcript, interview.

Freshman Application Contact Pima Medical Institute, 2305 San Pedro NE, Suite D, Albuquerque, NM 87110. *Phone:* 505-816-0556. *Web site:* http://www.pmi.edu/.

Pima Medical Institute

Albuquerque, New Mexico

- **Proprietary** primarily 2-year, founded 1985, part of Vocational Training Institutes, Inc.
- **Urban** campus
- **Coed,** 716 undergraduate students

Majors Dental hygiene; health/health-care administration; physical therapy technology; radiologic technology/science; registered nursing/registered nurse; respiratory therapy technician.

Academics *Calendar:* modular. *Degrees:* certificates, associate, and bachelor's. *Special study options:* academic remediation for entering students, cooperative education, distance learning, internships, services for LD students.

Library E-Global.

Student Life *Housing:* college housing not available.

Standardized Tests *Required:* Wonderlic Scholastic Level Exam (for admission).

Financial Aid Of all full-time matriculated undergraduates who enrolled in 2009, 6 Federal Work-Study jobs.

Applying *Options:* early admission. *Required:* interview. *Required for some:* high school transcript.

Freshman Application Contact Admissions Office, Pima Medical Institute, 4400 Cutler Avenue NE, Albuquerque, NM 87110. *Phone:* 505-881-1234. *Toll-free phone:* 888-898-9048. *Fax:* 505-881-5329. *Web site:* http://www.pmi.edu/.

San Juan College

Farmington, New Mexico

- **State-supported** 2-year, founded 1958, part of New Mexico Higher Education Department
- **Small-town** 698-acre campus
- **Endowment** $9.8 million
- **Coed,** 8,975 undergraduate students, 34% full-time, 48% women, 52% men

Undergraduates 3,090 full-time, 5,885 part-time. Students come from 49 states and territories; 21 other countries; 18% are from out of state; 1% Black or African American, non-Hispanic/Latino; 14% Hispanic/Latino; 0.7% Asian, non-Hispanic/Latino; 0.1% Native Hawaiian or other Pacific Islander, non-Hispanic/Latino; 33% American Indian or Alaska Native, non-Hispanic/Latino; 0.4% Two or more races, non-Hispanic/Latino; 4% Race/ethnicity unknown; 0.3% international; 2% transferred in.

Freshmen *Admission:* 2,884 applied, 2,884 admitted, 1,215 enrolled.

Faculty *Total:* 432, 33% full-time. *Student/faculty ratio:* 24:1.

Majors Accounting technology and bookkeeping; autobody/collision and repair technology; automobile/automotive mechanics technology; biology/biological sciences; business administration and management; carpentry; chemistry; child-care provision; clinical/medical laboratory technology; commercial and advertising art; cosmetology; criminal justice/police science; criminal justice/safety; data processing and data processing technology; dental hygiene; diesel mechanics technology; drafting and design technology; electrical, electronic and communications engineering technology; elementary education; emergency medical technology (EMT paramedic); engineering; fire science/firefighting; general studies; geography; geology/earth science; health and physical education/fitness; health information/medical records technology; industrial mechanics and maintenance technology; industrial technology; instrumentation technology; landscaping and groundskeeping; legal assistant/paralegal; liberal arts and sciences/liberal studies; machine shop technology; mathematics; occupational safety and health technology; parks, recreation and leisure; physical sciences; physical therapy technology; physics; premedical studies; psychology; public administration; registered nursing/registered nurse; respiratory care therapy; secondary education; social work; solar energy technology; special education; surgical technology; theater design and technology; veterinary/animal health technology; welding technology.

Academics *Calendar:* semesters. *Degree:* certificates, diplomas, and associate. *Special study options:* academic remediation for entering students, adult/continuing education programs, advanced placement credit, cooperative education, distance learning, English as a second language, honors programs, independent study, internships, part-time degree program, services for LD students, summer session for credit.

Library San Juan College Library with 91,010 titles, 256 serial subscriptions, 2,651 audiovisual materials, an OPAC, a Web page.

Student Life *Housing:* college housing not available. *Activities and Organizations:* drama/theater group, student-run newspaper, radio station, choral group, national fraternities, national sororities. *Campus security:* 24-hour emergency response devices and patrols, late-night transport/escort service. *Student services:* personal/psychological counseling.

Athletics *Intramural sports:* archery M/W, badminton M/W, basketball M/W, bowling M/W, cross-country running M/W, football M/W, golf M/W, racquetball M/W, rock climbing M/W, skiing (cross-country) M/W, skiing (downhill) M/W, soccer M/W, softball M/W, table tennis M/W, tennis M/W, volleyball M/W.

Costs (2011–12) *Tuition:* state resident $1110 full-time; nonresident $2730 full-time. Full-time tuition and fees vary according to reciprocity agreements. *Required fees:* $180 full-time. *Payment plans:* tuition prepayment, installment. *Waivers:* senior citizens and employees or children of employees.

Financial Aid Of all full-time matriculated undergraduates who enrolled in 2009, 150 Federal Work-Study jobs (averaging $2500). 175 state and other part-time jobs (averaging $2500).

Applying *Options:* electronic application, early admission, deferred entrance. *Required:* high school transcript. *Application deadlines:* rolling (freshmen), rolling (transfers). *Notification:* continuous (freshmen), continuous (transfers).

Freshman Application Contact Skylar Maston, Enrollment Services Coordinator, San Juan College, Farmington, NM 87402. *Phone:* 505-566-3300. *E-mail:* mastons@sanjuancollege.edu. *Web site:* http://www.sanjuancollege.edu/.

Santa Fe Community College

Santa Fe, New Mexico

- **State and locally supported** 2-year, founded 1983
- **Suburban** 366-acre campus with easy access to Albuquerque
- **Coed,** 4,856 undergraduate students, 34% full-time, 62% women, 38% men

Undergraduates 1,668 full-time, 3,188 part-time. Students come from 50 states and territories; 17 other countries; 11% are from out of state. *Retention:* 56% of full-time freshmen returned.

Freshmen *Admission:* 550 enrolled.

Faculty *Total:* 338, 20% full-time. *Student/faculty ratio:* 17:1.

Majors Accounting; administrative assistant and secretarial science; architectural drafting and CAD/CADD; art; art history, criticism and conservation; banking and financial support services; behavioral sciences; biology/biological sciences; business administration and management; ceramic arts and ceramics; cinematography and film/video production; commercial photography; computer and information sciences; computer programming; construction engineering technology; creative writing; criminal justice/police science; criminal justice/safety; culinary arts; dental assisting; design and visual communications; drafting and design technology; education; electrical, electronic and communications engineering technology; engineering; entrepreneurship; environmental studies; ethnic, cultural minority, gender, and group studies related; fashion/apparel design; film/cinema/video studies; fine and studio arts management; general studies; health and physical education/fitness; humanities; interior design; intermedia/multimedia; kindergarten/preschool education; legal assistant/paralegal; metal and jewelry arts; parks, recreation and leisure; photography; physical sciences; printmaking; psychology; radio and television broadcasting technology; registered nursing/registered nurse; respiratory care therapy; sculpture; sign language interpretation and translation; social work; Spanish; surveying technology; water quality and wastewater treatment management and recycling technology; woodworking.

Academics *Calendar:* semesters. *Degree:* certificates and associate. *Special study options:* academic remediation for entering students, adult/continuing education programs, advanced placement credit, cooperative education, distance learning, double majors, English as a second language, external degree program, honors programs, independent study, internships, part-time degree program, services for LD students, summer session for credit.

Library Learning Resource Center with 155,000 titles, 7,820 serial subscriptions, 4,350 audiovisual materials, an OPAC, a Web page.

Student Life *Housing:* college housing not available. *Activities and Organizations:* drama/theater group, choral group, Student Ambassadors, Student Government Association, The Clay Club, The Ping-Pong Club, Phi Theta Kappa. *Campus security:* 24-hour emergency response devices and patrols, late-night transport/escort service. *Student services:* personal/psychological counseling.

Costs (2011–12) *Tuition:* area resident $1080 full-time, $36 per credit hour part-time; state resident $1410 full-time, $47 per credit hour part-time; nonresident $2550 full-time, $85 per credit hour part-time. Full-time tuition and fees vary according to reciprocity agreements. Part-time tuition and fees vary according to reciprocity agreements. *Required fees:* $144 full-time, $5 per credit hour part-time. *Payment plan:* deferred payment. *Waivers:* senior citizens and employees or children of employees.

Applying *Options:* electronic application, early admission, deferred entrance. *Recommended:* high school transcript. *Application deadlines:* rolling (freshmen), rolling (transfers). *Notification:* continuous (freshmen), continuous (transfers).

Freshman Application Contact Ms. Rebecca Estrada, Director of Recruitment, Santa Fe Community College, 6401 Richards Ave, Santa Fe, NM 87508. *Phone:* 505-428-1604. *Fax:* 505-428-1468. *E-mail:* rebecca.estrada@sfcc.edu. *Web site:* http://www.sfcc.edu/.

Southwestern Indian Polytechnic Institute

Albuquerque, New Mexico

- **Federally supported** 2-year, founded 1971
- **Suburban** 144-acre campus
- **Coed**

Undergraduates 502 full-time, 133 part-time. Students come from 33 states and territories; 60% live on campus.

Faculty *Student/faculty ratio:* 15:1.

Academics *Calendar:* trimesters. *Degree:* certificates and associate. *Special study options:* academic remediation for entering students, advanced placement credit, cooperative education, distance learning, double majors, internships, part-time degree program, services for LD students, summer session for credit.

Student Life *Campus security:* 24-hour emergency response devices and patrols, late-night transport/escort service.

Costs (2010–11) *Tuition:* state resident $675 full-time, $150 per term part-time; nonresident $675 full-time, $150 per term part-time. Full-time tuition and fees vary according to course load. Part-time tuition and fees vary according to course load. Students attending SIPI are required to be registered member of federally recognized Indian Tribes. *Room and board:* $165.

Financial Aid Of all full-time matriculated undergraduates who enrolled in 2009, 25 Federal Work-Study jobs (averaging $300). 37 state and other part-time jobs (averaging $400). *Financial aid deadline:* 10/1.

Applying *Required:* high school transcript, Certificate of Indian Blood .

Freshman Application Contact Southwestern Indian Polytechnic Institute, 9169 Coors, NW, Box 10146, Albuquerque, NM 87184-0146. *Phone:* 505-346-2324. *Toll-free phone:* 800-586-7474. *Web site:* http://www.sipi.edu/.

University of New Mexico–Los Alamos Branch

Los Alamos, New Mexico

Freshman Application Contact Mrs. Irene K. Martinez, Enrollment Representative, University of New Mexico–Los Alamos Branch, 4000 University Drive, Los Alamos, NM 87544-2233. *Phone:* 505-662-0332. *Toll-free phone:* 800-894-5919. *E-mail:* L65130@unm.edu. *Web site:* http://www.la.unm.edu/.

University of New Mexico–Taos

Taos, New Mexico

Director of Admissions Vickie Alvarez, Student Enrollment Associate, University of New Mexico–Taos, 115 Civic Plaza Drive, Taos, NM 87571. *Phone:* 575-737-6425. *Toll-free phone:* 575-737-6000. *E-mail:* valvarez@unm.edu. *Web site:* http://taos.unm.edu/.

University of New Mexico–Valencia Campus

Los Lunas, New Mexico

Director of Admissions Richard M. Hulett, Director of Admissions and Recruitment, University of New Mexico–Valencia Campus, 280 La Entrada, Los Lunas, NM 87031-7633. *Phone:* 505-277-2446. *E-mail:* mhulett@unm.edu. *Web site:* http://www.unm.edu/~unmvc/.

NEW YORK

Adirondack Community College

Queensbury, New York

Freshman Application Contact Office of Admissions, Adirondack Community College, 640 Bay Road, Queensbury, NY 12804. *Phone:* 518-743-2264. *Fax:* 518-743-2200. *Web site:* http://www.sunyacc.edu/.

American Academy McAllister Institute of Funeral Service

New York, New York

Freshman Application Contact Mr. Norman Provost, Registrar, American Academy McAllister Institute of Funeral Service, 450 West 56th Street, New

York, NY 10019-3602. *Phone:* 212-757-1190. *Toll-free phone:* 866-932-2264. *Web site:* http://www.funeraleducation.org/.

American Academy of Dramatic Arts
New York, New York

- **Independent** 2-year, founded 1884
- **Urban** campus
- **Endowment** $4.6 million
- **Coed**

Undergraduates 228 full-time. Students come from 33 states and territories; 19 other countries; 87% are from out of state.
Faculty *Student/faculty ratio:* 14:1.
Academics *Calendar:* continuous. *Degree:* certificates and associate.
Student Life *Campus security:* 24-hour emergency response devices, trained security guard during hours of operation.
Costs (2010–11) *Tuition:* $28,620 full-time. Full-time tuition and fees vary according to student level. *Required fees:* $600 full-time.
Financial Aid Of all full-time matriculated undergraduates who enrolled in 2009, 197 applied for aid, 114 were judged to have need. 49 Federal Work-Study jobs (averaging $878). 50 state and other part-time jobs (averaging $1200). In 2009, 61. *Average percent of need met:* 55. *Average financial aid package:* $17,000. *Average need-based loan:* $4500. *Average need-based gift aid:* $8000. *Average non-need-based aid:* $8000. *Average indebtedness upon graduation:* $20,000. *Financial aid deadline:* 5/15.
Applying *Options:* deferred entrance. *Application fee:* $50. *Required:* essay or personal statement, high school transcript, minimum 2.0 GPA, 2 letters of recommendation, interview, audition.
Freshman Application Contact Ms. Karen Higginbotham, Director of Admissions, American Academy of Dramatic Arts, 120 Madison Avenue, New York, NY 10016. *Phone:* 212-686-9244 Ext. 315. *Toll-free phone:* 800-463-8990. *Fax:* 212-696-1284. *E-mail:* admissions-ny@aada.org. *Web site:* http://www.aada.org/.

The Art Institute of New York City
New York, New York

- **Proprietary** 2-year, founded 1980, part of Education Management Corporation
- **Urban** campus
- **Coed**

Majors Cinematography and film/video production; fashion/apparel design; graphic design; interior design; web page, digital/multimedia and information resources design.
Academics *Calendar:* quarters. *Degree:* certificates, diplomas, and associate.
Costs (2010–11) *Tuition:* Tuition cost varies by program. Prospective students should contact the school for current tuition costs. Other charges include a starting kit for all first-quarter students. Kits vary in price, depending on the program of study.
Freshman Application Contact The Art Institute of New York City, 11 Beach Street, New York, NY 10013. *Phone:* 212-226-5500. *Toll-free phone:* 800-654-2433. *Web site:* http://www.artinstitutes.edu/newyork/.

See page 348 for the College Close-Up.

ASA The College For Excellence
Brooklyn, New York

- **Proprietary** 2-year, founded 1985
- **Urban** campus with easy access to New York City
- **Coed,** 6,475 undergraduate students

Freshmen *Admission:* 3,368 applied.
Majors Accounting; business automation/technology/data entry; computer and information systems security; criminal justice/law enforcement administration; health information/medical records technology; medical/clinical assistant; medical office management; pharmacy technician.
Academics *Calendar:* semesters. *Degree:* certificates and associate. *Special study options:* academic remediation for entering students, accelerated degree program, advanced placement credit, cooperative education, distance learning, English as a second language, internships, part-time degree program.
Athletics Member NJCAA. *Intercollegiate sports:* baseball M(s), basketball M(s)/W(s), football M(s), soccer M(s), tennis M(s)/W(s). *Intramural sports:* basketball M/W, softball M/W, volleyball M/W.
Costs (2011–12) *Tuition:* $12,094 full-time.
Applying *Options:* electronic application. *Application fee:* $25. *Required:* high school transcript, interview.
Freshman Application Contact Admissions Office, ASA The College For Excellence, 81 Willoughby Street, Brooklyn, NY 11201. *Phone:* 718-522-9073. *Web site:* http://www.asa.edu/.

Berkeley College–New York City Campus
New York, New York

Freshman Application Contact Berkeley College–New York City Campus, 3 East 43rd Street, New York, NY 10017-4604. *Phone:* 212-986-4343. *Toll-free phone:* 800-446-5400. *Web site:* http://www.berkeleycollege.edu/.

Berkeley College–Westchester Campus
White Plains, New York

Freshman Application Contact Director of Admissions, Berkeley College–Westchester Campus, White Plains, NY 10601. *Phone:* 914-694-1122. *Toll-free phone:* 800-446-5400. *Fax:* 914-328-9469. *E-mail:* info@berkeleycollege.edu. *Web site:* http://www.berkeleycollege.edu/.

Borough of Manhattan Community College of the City University of New York
New York, New York

- **State and locally supported** 2-year, founded 1963, part of City University of New York System
- **Urban** 5-acre campus
- **Coed,** 22,534 undergraduate students, 65% full-time, 59% women, 41% men

Undergraduates 14,658 full-time, 7,876 part-time. 1% are from out of state; 31% Black or African American, non-Hispanic/Latino; 37% Hispanic/Latino; 11% Asian, non-Hispanic/Latino; 0.2% American Indian or Alaska Native, non-Hispanic/Latino; 7% international; 2% transferred in.
Freshmen *Admission:* 20,368 admitted, 5,176 enrolled. *Test scores:* SAT critical reading scores over 500: 10%; SAT math scores over 500: 11%; SAT writing scores over 500: 7%; SAT critical reading scores over 600: 1%; SAT math scores over 600: 1%; SAT writing scores over 600: 1%.
Faculty *Total:* 1,337, 30% full-time, 32% with terminal degrees. *Student/faculty ratio:* 24:1.
Majors Accounting technology and bookkeeping; administrative assistant and secretarial science; business administration and management; community organization and advocacy; computer and information sciences; computer science; computer systems networking and telecommunications; criminal justice/police science; emergency medical technology (EMT paramedic); engineering; English; forensic science and technology; health information/medical records technology; liberal arts and sciences/liberal studies; mathematics; physical sciences; radio and television broadcasting technology; registered nursing/registered nurse; respiratory therapy technician; small business administration; teacher assistant/aide; visual and performing arts; web page, digital/multimedia and information resources design.
Academics *Calendar:* semesters. *Degree:* certificates and associate. *Special study options:* academic remediation for entering students, adult/continuing education programs, advanced placement credit, cooperative education, distance learning, English as a second language, honors programs, independent study, internships, off-campus study, part-time degree program, services for LD students, study abroad, summer session for credit.
Library A. Philip Randolph Library with 111,966 titles, 253 serial subscriptions, an OPAC, a Web page.
Student Life *Housing:* college housing not available. *Activities and Organizations:* drama/theater group, student-run newspaper, choral group. *Campus security:* 24-hour patrols. *Student services:* health clinic, personal/psychological counseling, women's center.
Athletics Member NJCAA. *Intercollegiate sports:* baseball M, basketball M/W, soccer M/W, swimming and diving M/W, volleyball W.
Standardized Tests *Recommended:* SAT or ACT (for admission).
Costs (2011–12) *Tuition:* $3150 per year part-time; nonresident $6300 per year part-time. Full-time tuition and fees vary according to course load. Part-time tuition and fees vary according to course load. *Payment plan:* installment. *Waivers:* senior citizens and employees or children of employees.
Applying *Options:* electronic application, deferred entrance. *Application fee:* $65. *Required:* high school transcript. *Application deadlines:* rolling (freshmen), rolling (transfers). *Notification:* continuous (freshmen), continuous (transfers).
Freshman Application Contact Dr. Eugenio Barrios, Director of Enrollment Management, Borough of Manhattan Community College of the City University of New York, 199 Chambers Street, Room S-300, New York, NY 10007. *Phone:* 212-220-1265. *Fax:* 212-220-2366. *E-mail:* admissions@bmcc.cuny.edu. *Web site:* http://www.bmcc.cuny.edu/.

Bramson ORT College
Forest Hills, New York

Freshman Application Contact Admissions Office, Bramson ORT College, 69-30 Austin Street, Forest Hills, NY 11375-4239. *Phone:* 718-261-5800. *Fax:* 718-575-5119. *E-mail:* admissions@bramsonort.edu. *Web site:* http://www.bramsonort.edu/.

Bronx Community College of the City University of New York
Bronx, New York

- **State and locally supported** 2-year, founded 1959, part of City University of New York System
- **Urban** 50-acre campus with easy access to New York City
- **Endowment** $469,572
- **Coed**

Undergraduates 6,013 full-time, 4,118 part-time. Students come from 119 other countries; 8% are from out of state; 10% transferred in. *Retention:* 65% of full-time freshmen returned.
Faculty *Student/faculty ratio:* 28:1.
Academics *Calendar:* semesters. *Degree:* certificates and associate. *Special study options:* academic remediation for entering students, accelerated degree program, adult/continuing education programs, advanced placement credit, cooperative education, distance learning, double majors, English as a second language, honors programs, independent study, internships, off-campus study, part-time degree program, services for LD students, study abroad, summer session for credit.
Student Life *Campus security:* 24-hour emergency response devices and patrols, late-night transport/escort service, a free shuttle bus service provides evening students with transportation from campus to several subway and bus lines between 5pm-11pm.
Athletics Member NJCAA.
Standardized Tests *Recommended:* SAT or ACT (for admission).
Costs (2010–11) *Tuition:* state resident $3150 full-time, $135 per credit hour part-time; nonresident $5040 full-time, $210 per credit hour part-time. Full-time tuition and fees vary according to course load. Part-time tuition and fees vary according to course load. *Required fees:* $354 full-time.
Applying *Options:* early admission. *Application fee:* $65. *Required:* high school transcript, copy of accredited high school diploma or GED scores.
Freshman Application Contact Ms. Alba N. Cancetty, Admissions Officer, Bronx Community College of the City University of New York, 2155 University Avenue, Bronx, NY 10453. *Phone:* 718-289-5888. *E-mail:* admission@bcc.cuny.edu. *Web site:* http://www.bcc.cuny.edu/.

Broome Community College
Binghamton, New York

- **State and locally supported** 2-year, founded 1946, part of State University of New York System
- **Suburban** 223-acre campus
- **Endowment** $1.3 million
- **Coed**

Undergraduates 4,655 full-time, 2,222 part-time. Students come from 26 states and territories; 43 other countries; 1% are from out of state; 6% transferred in.
Academics *Calendar:* semesters. *Degree:* certificates and associate. *Special study options:* academic remediation for entering students, adult/continuing education programs, advanced placement credit, distance learning, English as a second language, external degree program, honors programs, independent study, internships, off-campus study, part-time degree program, services for LD students, student-designed majors, study abroad, summer session for credit.
Student Life *Campus security:* 24-hour emergency response devices and patrols.
Athletics Member NJCAA.
Costs (2010–11) *One-time required fee:* $80. *Tuition:* state resident $3464 full-time, $145 per credit hour part-time; nonresident $6928 full-time, $290 per credit hour part-time. Full-time tuition and fees vary according to course load. Part-time tuition and fees vary according to course load. *Required fees:* $334 full-time, $8 per credit hour part-time.
Financial Aid Of all full-time matriculated undergraduates who enrolled in 2009, 186 Federal Work-Study jobs (averaging $1140).
Applying *Options:* electronic application, early admission. *Required:* high school transcript. *Required for some:* interview.
Freshman Application Contact Ms. Jenae Norris, Director of Admissions, Broome Community College, PO Box 1017, Upper Front Street, Binghamton,

NY 13902. *Phone:* 607-778-5001. *Fax:* 607-778-5394. *E-mail:* admissions@sunybroome.edu. *Web site:* http://www.sunybroome.edu/.

Bryant & Stratton College - Albany Campus
Albany, New York

- **Proprietary** 2-year, founded 1857, part of Bryant and Stratton College, Inc.
- **Suburban** campus
- **Coed**

Undergraduates 354 full-time, 116 part-time. Students come from 1 other state. *Retention:* 45% of full-time freshmen returned.
Academics *Calendar:* semesters. *Degree:* associate. *Special study options:* academic remediation for entering students, distance learning, double majors, independent study, internships, part-time degree program, services for LD students, summer session for credit.
Student Life *Campus security:* 24-hour emergency response devices.
Standardized Tests *Required:* CPAt, ACCUPLACER (for admission). *Recommended:* SAT or ACT (for admission).
Financial Aid Of all full-time matriculated undergraduates who enrolled in 2009, 41 Federal Work-Study jobs (averaging $1343).
Applying *Options:* deferred entrance. *Required:* high school transcript, interview, entrance and placement evaluations.
Freshman Application Contact Mr. Robert Ferrell, Director of Admissions, Bryant & Stratton College - Albany Campus, 1259 Central Avenue, Albany, NY 12205. *Phone:* 518-437-1802 Ext. 205. *Fax:* 518-437-1048. *Web site:* http://www.bryantstratton.edu/.

Bryant & Stratton College - Amherst Campus
Clarence, New York

- **Proprietary** primarily 2-year, founded 1977
- **Suburban** 5-acre campus with easy access to Buffalo
- **Coed**

Undergraduates 277 full-time, 197 part-time. Students come from 1 other state; 9% transferred in.
Academics *Calendar:* trimesters. *Degrees:* associate and bachelor's. *Special study options:* academic remediation for entering students, adult/continuing education programs, advanced placement credit, distance learning, internships, part-time degree program, services for LD students, summer session for credit.
Standardized Tests *Required:* TABE, CPAt or ACCUPLACER (for admission). *Recommended:* SAT or ACT (for admission).
Applying *Options:* electronic application, early admission. *Required:* high school transcript, interview, entrance evaluation and placement evaluation. *Required for some:* essay or personal statement.
Freshman Application Contact Mr. Brian K. Dioguardi, Director of Admissions, Bryant & Stratton College - Amherst Campus, Audubon Business Center, 40 Hazelwood Drive, Amherst, NY 14228. *Phone:* 716-691-0012. *Fax:* 716-691-0012. *E-mail:* bkdioguardi@bryantstratton.edu. *Web site:* http://www.bryantstratton.edu/.

Bryant & Stratton College - Buffalo Campus
Buffalo, New York

- **Proprietary** primarily 2-year, founded 1854
- **Urban** campus
- **Coed**
- 75% of applicants were admitted

Undergraduates 473 full-time, 220 part-time. Students come from 1 other state; 7% transferred in.
Academics *Calendar:* trimesters. *Degrees:* associate and bachelor's. *Special study options:* academic remediation for entering students, adult/continuing education programs, advanced placement credit, distance learning, internships, part-time degree program, services for LD students, summer session for credit.
Standardized Tests *Required:* TABE, CPAt or ACCUPLACER (for admission). *Recommended:* SAT or ACT (for admission).
Applying *Options:* electronic application, early admission. *Required:* high school transcript, interview, entrance and placement evaluation. *Required for some:* essay or personal statement.
Freshman Application Contact Mr. Philip J. Struebel, Director of Admissions, Bryant & Stratton College - Buffalo Campus, 465 Main Street, Suite 400, Buffalo, NY 14203. *Phone:* 716-884-9120. *Fax:* 716-884-0091.

E-mail: pjstruebel@bryantstratton.edu.
Web site: http://www.bryantstratton.edu/.

Bryant & Stratton College - Greece Campus

Rochester, New York

- **Proprietary** 2-year, founded 1973, part of Bryant and Stratton College, Inc.
- **Suburban** campus
- **Coed**

Undergraduates 192 full-time, 87 part-time. Students come from 1 other state; 4% transferred in.
Faculty *Student/faculty ratio:* 10:1.
Academics *Calendar:* semesters. *Degree:* associate. *Special study options:* academic remediation for entering students, adult/continuing education programs, advanced placement credit, distance learning, independent study, internships, part-time degree program, services for LD students, summer session for credit.
Student Life *Campus security:* 24-hour emergency response devices, late-night transport/escort service.
Standardized Tests *Required:* CPAt (for admission). *Recommended:* SAT or ACT (for admission).
Financial Aid Of all full-time matriculated undergraduates who enrolled in 2009, 40 Federal Work-Study jobs (averaging $600).
Applying *Options:* electronic application, deferred entrance. *Required:* high school transcript, interview, entrance evaluation and placement evaluation.
Freshman Application Contact Bryant & Stratton College - Greece Campus, 150 Bellwood Drive, Rochester, NY 14606. *Phone:* 585-720-0660. *Web site:* http://www.bryantstratton.edu/.

Bryant & Stratton College - Henrietta Campus

Rochester, New York

- **Proprietary** 2-year, founded 1985, part of Bryant and Stratton College, Inc.
- **Urban** 1-acre campus
- **Coed**

Undergraduates 288 full-time, 119 part-time. Students come from 1 other state; 7% transferred in.
Faculty *Student/faculty ratio:* 10:1.
Academics *Calendar:* semesters. *Degree:* associate. *Special study options:* academic remediation for entering students, adult/continuing education programs, advanced placement credit, distance learning, independent study, internships, part-time degree program, services for LD students, summer session for credit.
Student Life *Campus security:* late-night transport/escort service.
Standardized Tests *Required:* CPAt (for admission). *Recommended:* SAT or ACT (for admission).
Financial Aid Of all full-time matriculated undergraduates who enrolled in 2009, 44 Federal Work-Study jobs (averaging $630).
Applying *Options:* electronic application, deferred entrance. *Required:* high school transcript, interview, entrance evaluation and placement evaluation. *Recommended:* minimum 2.0 GPA.
Freshman Application Contact Bryant & Stratton College - Henrietta Campus, 1225 Jefferson Road, Rochester, NY 14623-3136. *Phone:* 585-292-5627 Ext. 101. *Web site:* http://www.bryantstratton.edu/.

Bryant & Stratton College - North Campus

Liverpool, New York

- **Proprietary** 2-year, founded 1983, part of Bryant and Stratton Business Institute, Inc.
- **Suburban** 1-acre campus with easy access to Syracuse
- **Coed**

Undergraduates 333 full-time, 164 part-time.
Faculty *Student/faculty ratio:* 9:1.
Academics *Calendar:* semesters. *Degree:* diplomas and associate. *Special study options:* academic remediation for entering students, adult/continuing education programs, advanced placement credit, cooperative education, distance learning, double majors, independent study, internships, part-time degree program, services for LD students, summer session for credit.
Student Life *Campus security:* 24-hour emergency response devices.
Standardized Tests *Required:* TABE, CPAt (for admission).

Applying *Options:* deferred entrance. *Application fee:* $25. *Required:* high school transcript, interview, entrance evaluation and placement evaluation. *Recommended:* minimum 2.0 GPA.
Freshman Application Contact Ms. Heather Macnik, Director of Admissions, Bryant & Stratton College - North Campus, 8687 Carling Road, Liverpool, NY 13090-1315. *Phone:* 315-652-6500. *Web site:* http://www.bryantstratton.edu/.

Bryant & Stratton College - Southtowns Campus

Orchard Park, New York

- **Proprietary** primarily 2-year, founded 1989
- **Suburban** campus with easy access to Buffalo
- **Coed**

Undergraduates 663 full-time, 543 part-time. Students come from 27 states and territories; 1 other country; 60% are from out of state; 11% transferred in.
Academics *Calendar:* trimesters. *Degrees:* associate and bachelor's. *Special study options:* academic remediation for entering students, adult/continuing education programs, advanced placement credit, distance learning, internships, part-time degree program, services for LD students, summer session for credit.
Standardized Tests *Required:* TABE, CPAt or ACCUPLACER (for admission). *Recommended:* SAT or ACT (for admission).
Applying *Options:* electronic application, early admission. *Required:* high school transcript, interview, entrance and placement evaluations. *Required for some:* essay or personal statement.
Freshman Application Contact Bryant & Stratton College - Southtowns Campus, 200 Redtail, Orchard Park, NY 14127. *Phone:* 716-677-9500. *Web site:* http://www.bryantstratton.edu/.

Bryant & Stratton College - Syracuse Campus

Syracuse, New York

- **Proprietary** 2-year, founded 1854, part of Bryant and Stratton Business Institute, Inc.
- **Urban** 1-acre campus
- **Coed**

Undergraduates 494 full-time, 221 part-time. Students come from 2 states and territories; 2 other countries; 1% are from out of state; 6% transferred in; 12% live on campus. *Retention:* 38% of full-time freshmen returned.
Faculty *Student/faculty ratio:* 13:1.
Academics *Calendar:* semesters. *Degree:* associate. *Special study options:* academic remediation for entering students, cooperative education, distance learning, double majors, internships, part-time degree program, services for LD students, summer session for credit.
Student Life *Campus security:* 24-hour emergency response devices and patrols, controlled dormitory access.
Athletics Member NJCAA.
Standardized Tests *Required:* CPAt (for admission). *Recommended:* SAT or ACT (for admission).
Applying *Required:* high school transcript, interview, entrance, placement evaluations.
Freshman Application Contact Ms. Dawn Rajkowski, Director of High School Enrollments, Bryant & Stratton College - Syracuse Campus, 953 James Street, Syracuse, NY 13203-2502. *Phone:* 315-472-6603 Ext. 248. *Fax:* 315-474-4383. *Web site:* http://www.bryantstratton.edu/.

Business Informatics Center, Inc.

Valley Stream, New York

Freshman Application Contact Admissions Office, Business Informatics Center, Inc., 134 South Central Avenue, Valley Stream, NY 11580-5431. *Phone:* 516-561-0050. *Fax:* 516-561-0074. *E-mail:* info@thecollegeforbusiness.com. *Web site:* http://www.thecollegeforbusiness.com/.

Cayuga County Community College

Auburn, New York

- **State and locally supported** 2-year, founded 1953, part of State University of New York System
- **Small-town** 50-acre campus with easy access to Rochester and Syracuse
- **Endowment** $666,198
- **Coed,** 4,882 undergraduate students

Undergraduates 2% Black or African American, non-Hispanic/Latino; 1% Hispanic/Latino; 0.5% Asian, non-Hispanic/Latino; 0.5% American Indian or Alaska Native, non-Hispanic/Latino; 1% Two or more races, non-Hispanic/

Latino; 23% Race/ethnicity unknown. *Retention:* 47% of full-time freshmen returned.

Freshmen *Admission:* 740 applied, 704 admitted.

Faculty *Total:* 262, 23% full-time.

Majors Accounting technology and bookkeeping; art; business administration and management; child-care and support services management; communication and journalism related; communications systems installation and repair technology; computer and information sciences; computer and information sciences and support services related; corrections; criminal justice/police science; drafting and design technology; electrical, electronic and communications engineering technology; geography; humanities; information science/studies; liberal arts and sciences/liberal studies; mechanical engineering; registered nursing/registered nurse.

Academics *Calendar:* semesters. *Degree:* certificates and associate. *Special study options:* academic remediation for entering students, accelerated degree program, adult/continuing education programs, advanced placement credit, cooperative education, distance learning, double majors, honors programs, independent study, internships, off-campus study, part-time degree program, services for LD students, study abroad, summer session for credit.

Library Norman F. Bourke Memorial Library plus 2 others with 85,000 titles, 250 serial subscriptions, 8,930 audiovisual materials, an OPAC, a Web page.

Student Life *Housing Options:* coed. Campus housing is provided by a third party. *Activities and Organizations:* drama/theater group, student-run newspaper, radio and television station, choral group, Student Activity Board, Student Government, Criminal Justice Club, Tutor Club, Early Childhood Club. *Campus security:* security from 8 am to 9 pm. *Student services:* health clinic.

Athletics Member NJCAA. *Intercollegiate sports:* basketball M/W, bowling M/W, golf M, lacrosse M/W, soccer M/W, volleyball W. *Intramural sports:* basketball M/W, racquetball M/W, skiing (cross-country) M/W, soccer M/W, softball M/W, tennis M/W, volleyball M/W.

Standardized Tests *Required for some:* SAT or ACT (for admission).

Costs (2011–12) *Tuition:* state resident $3560 full-time, $140 per credit hour part-time; nonresident $7120 full-time, $280 per credit hour part-time. Full-time tuition and fees vary according to class time, course load, location, and program. Part-time tuition and fees vary according to class time, course load, location, and program. *Required fees:* $674 full-time, $7 per credit part-time. *Payment plan:* installment. *Waivers:* senior citizens and employees or children of employees.

Financial Aid Of all full-time matriculated undergraduates who enrolled in 2009, 150 Federal Work-Study jobs (averaging $2000). 200 state and other part-time jobs (averaging $1000).

Applying *Options:* electronic application, deferred entrance. *Required:* high school transcript. *Required for some:* interview. *Application deadlines:* rolling (freshmen), rolling (transfers). *Notification:* continuous (freshmen), continuous (transfers).

Freshman Application Contact Cayuga County Community College, 197 Franklin Street, Auburn, NY 13021-3099. *Phone:* 315-255-1743 Ext. 2244. *Web site:* http://www.cayuga-cc.edu/.

Clinton Community College

Plattsburgh, New York

Director of Admissions Mrs. Karen L. Burnam, Director of Admissions and Financial Aid, Clinton Community College, 136 Clinton Point Drive, Plattsburgh, NY 12901-9573. *Phone:* 518-562-4170. *Toll-free phone:* 800-552-1160. *Web site:* http://clintoncc.suny.edu/.

Cochran School of Nursing

Yonkers, New York

Freshman Application Contact Cochran School of Nursing, 967 North Broadway, Yonkers, NY 10701. *Phone:* 914-964-4606. *Web site:* http://www.cochranschoolofnursing.us/.

The College of Westchester

White Plains, New York

Freshman Application Contact Mr. Dale T. Smith, Vice President, The College of Westchester, 325 Central Avenue, PO Box 710, White Plains, NY 10602. *Phone:* 914-948-4442 Ext. 311. *Toll-free phone:* 800-333-4924 Ext. 318. *Fax:* 914-948-5441. *E-mail:* admissions@cw.edu. *Web site:* http://www.cw.edu/.

Columbia-Greene Community College

Hudson, New York

Freshman Application Contact Christine Pepitone, Director of Admissions, Columbia-Greene Community College, 4400 Route 23, Hudson, NY 12534-0327. *Phone:* 518-828-4181 Ext. 3388. *E-mail:* christine.pepitone@sunycgcc.edu. *Web site:* http://www.sunycgcc.edu/.

Corning Community College

Corning, New York

- **State and locally supported** 2-year, founded 1956, part of State University of New York System
- **Rural** 500-acre campus
- **Endowment** $3.1 million
- **Coed,** 5,396 undergraduate students, 50% full-time, 57% women, 43% men

Undergraduates 2,708 full-time, 2,688 part-time. Students come from 7 states and territories; 30 other countries; 6% are from out of state; 4% transferred in. *Retention:* 58% of full-time freshmen returned.

Freshmen *Admission:* 2,554 applied, 2,517 admitted, 949 enrolled.

Faculty *Total:* 313, 32% full-time, 38% with terminal degrees. *Student/faculty ratio:* 21:1.

Majors Accounting; administrative assistant and secretarial science; auto-body/collision and repair technology; automobile/automotive mechanics technology; automotive engineering technology; biological and physical sciences; business administration and management; chemical technology; child-care provision; computer and information sciences; computer and information sciences related; computer graphics; computer/information technology services administration related; computer programming; computer programming related; computer science; computer systems networking and telecommunications; computer technology/computer systems technology; corrections and criminal justice related; criminal justice/law enforcement administration; drafting and design technology; education related; electrical, electronic and communications engineering technology; elementary education; emergency medical technology (EMT paramedic); environmental science; fine/studio arts; fire science/firefighting; general studies; health and physical education/fitness; hospitality administration related; humanities; human services; industrial technology; information technology; liberal arts and sciences/liberal studies; machine shop technology; machine tool technology; mathematics; mechanical engineering/mechanical technology; optical sciences; outdoor education; pre-engineering; registered nursing/registered nurse; social sciences; substance abuse/addiction counseling; word processing.

Academics *Calendar:* semesters. *Degree:* certificates and associate. *Special study options:* academic remediation for entering students, accelerated degree program, adult/continuing education programs, advanced placement credit, cooperative education, distance learning, double majors, honors programs, independent study, internships, off-campus study, part-time degree program, services for LD students, student-designed majors, study abroad, summer session for credit. *ROTC:* Army (c), Navy (c), Air Force (c).

Library Arthur A. Houghton, Jr. Library with 53,438 titles, 24,350 serial subscriptions, 755 audiovisual materials, an OPAC, a Web page.

Student Life *Housing:* college housing not available. *Activities and Organizations:* drama/theater group, student-run newspaper, radio station, choral group, Student Association, WCEB radio station, Muse of Fire theatre group, Activities Programming Committee, Nursing Society. *Campus security:* 24-hour emergency response devices and patrols, late-night transport/escort service. *Student services:* health clinic, personal/psychological counseling.

Athletics Member NJCAA. *Intercollegiate sports:* baseball M, basketball M/W, bowling M/W, golf M/W, soccer M/W, softball W, volleyball W. *Intramural sports:* badminton M/W, basketball M/W, bowling M/W, cross-country running M/W, golf M/W, soccer M/W, softball M/W, table tennis M/W, volleyball M/W, weight lifting M/W.

Costs (2011–12) *Tuition:* state resident $4106 full-time; nonresident $8676 full-time. Part-time tuition and fees vary according to course load. *Payment plan:* installment. *Waivers:* senior citizens and employees or children of employees.

Financial Aid Of all full-time matriculated undergraduates who enrolled in 2009, 264 Federal Work-Study jobs (averaging $1128).

Applying *Options:* electronic application, early admission. *Application fee:* $25. *Required:* high school transcript. *Required for some:* interview. *Application deadlines:* rolling (freshmen), rolling (transfers). *Notification:* continuous (freshmen), continuous (transfers).

Freshman Application Contact Corning Community College, One Academic Drive, Corning, NY 14830-3297. *Phone:* 607-962-9427. *Toll-free phone:* 800-358-7171 Ext. 220. *Web site:* http://www.corning-cc.edu/.

Crouse Hospital School of Nursing
Syracuse, New York

- **Independent** 2-year, founded 1913
- **Urban** campus
- **Coed, primarily women**

Undergraduates Students come from 2 states and territories; 1% are from out of state.
Academics *Calendar:* semesters. *Degree:* associate. *Special study options:* academic remediation for entering students, advanced placement credit, part-time degree program, services for LD students.
Student Life *Campus security:* 24-hour emergency response devices and patrols, late-night transport/escort service, controlled dormitory access.
Standardized Tests *Required for some:* SAT or ACT (for admission). *Recommended:* SAT or ACT (for admission).
Costs (2010–11) *Tuition:* $8136 full-time, $245 per credit hour part-time. Full-time tuition and fees vary according to course load. Part-time tuition and fees vary according to course load. *Required fees:* $850 full-time, $990 per term part-time. *Room only:* $3500.
Financial Aid Of all full-time matriculated undergraduates who enrolled in 2008, 121 applied for aid, 121 were judged to have need. *Average percent of need met:* 66. *Average financial aid package:* $4677. *Average need-based loan:* $3324. *Average need-based gift aid:* $2141. *Average indebtedness upon graduation:* $2896.
Applying *Options:* deferred entrance. *Application fee:* $30. *Required:* high school transcript, minimum 2.5 GPA, 2 letters of recommendation.
Freshman Application Contact Ms. Amy Graham, Enrollment Management Supervisor, Crouse Hospital School of Nursing, 736 Irving Avenue, Syracuse, NY 13210. *Phone:* 315-470-7481. *Fax:* 315-470-7925. *E-mail:* amygraham@crouse.org. *Web site:* http://www.crouse.org/nursing/.

Dorothea Hopfer School of Nursing at The Mount Vernon Hospital
Mount Vernon, New York

Director of Admissions Sandra Farrior, Coordinator of Student Services, Dorothea Hopfer School of Nursing at The Mount Vernon Hospital, 53 Valentine Street, Mount Vernon, NY 10550. *Phone:* 914-361-6472. *E-mail:* hopferadmissions@sshsw.org. *Web site:* http://www.ssmc.org/.

Dutchess Community College
Poughkeepsie, New York

- **State and locally supported** 2-year, founded 1957, part of State University of New York System
- **Suburban** 130-acre campus with easy access to New York City
- **Coed,** 9,823 undergraduate students, 54% full-time, 55% women, 45% men

Undergraduates 5,274 full-time, 4,549 part-time. 3% transferred in.
Freshmen *Admission:* 2,266 enrolled. *Average high school GPA:* 2.53.
Faculty *Total:* 489, 26% full-time, 7% with terminal degrees.
Majors Accounting; administrative assistant and secretarial science; architectural engineering technology; biological and physical sciences; business administration and management; child development; clinical/medical laboratory technology; commercial and advertising art; computer and information sciences; computer science; construction engineering technology; consumer merchandising/retailing management; criminal justice/law enforcement administration; criminal justice/safety; dietetics; electrical and electronics engineering; electrical, electronic and communications engineering technology; electromechanical technology; elementary education; emergency medical technology (EMT paramedic); engineering science; foods, nutrition, and wellness; humanities; information science/studies; kindergarten/preschool education; legal assistant/paralegal; liberal arts and sciences/liberal studies; mass communication/media; mathematics; medical/clinical assistant; mental health counseling; parks, recreation and leisure; physical therapy technology; psychiatric/mental health services technology; registered nursing/registered nurse; science teacher education; social sciences; special products marketing; speech communication and rhetoric; telecommunications technology; tourism and travel services management.
Academics *Calendar:* semesters. *Degree:* certificates and associate. *Special study options:* academic remediation for entering students, adult/continuing education programs, advanced placement credit, English as a second language, freshman honors college, honors programs, internships, off-campus study, part-time degree program, summer session for credit.
Library Dutchess Library with 85,975 titles, 244 serial subscriptions, an OPAC, a Web page.
Student Life *Housing:* college housing not available. *Activities and Organizations:* drama/theater group, student-run newspaper, radio station, choral group.

Campus security: 24-hour emergency response devices and patrols, late-night transport/escort service. *Student services:* health clinic, personal/psychological counseling.
Athletics Member NJCAA. *Intercollegiate sports:* baseball M, basketball M/W, bowling M/W, golf M, soccer M/W, softball W, tennis M/W, volleyball W. *Intramural sports:* badminton M/W, basketball M/W, football M, soccer M/W, tennis M/W, volleyball M/W.
Costs (2011–12) *Tuition:* state resident $2900 full-time; nonresident $5800 full-time. *Required fees:* $417 full-time.
Applying *Options:* early admission, deferred entrance. *Required:* high school transcript. *Application deadlines:* rolling (freshmen), rolling (transfers). *Notification:* continuous (freshmen), continuous (transfers).
Freshman Application Contact Dutchess Community College, 53 Pendell Road, Poughkeepsie, NY 12601-1595. *Phone:* 845-431-8010. *Toll-free phone:* 800-763-3933. *Web site:* http://www.sunydutchess.edu/.

Ellis Hospital School of Nursing
Schenectady, New York

Freshman Application Contact Marilyn Stapleton, Director of School, Ellis Hospital School of Nursing, 1101 Nott Street, Schenectady, NY 12308. *Phone:* 518-243-4471. *Fax:* 518-243-4470. *E-mail:* stapletonm@ellishospital.org. *Web site:* http://www.ellismedicine.org/school/.

Elmira Business Institute
Elmira, New York

Freshman Application Contact Admissions Director, Elmira Business Institute, Elmira, NY 14901. *Phone:* 607-733-7178. *Toll-free phone:* 800-843-1812. *E-mail:* info@ebi-college.com. *Web site:* http://www.ebi-college.com/.

Erie Community College
Buffalo, New York

- **State and locally supported** 2-year, founded 1971, part of State University of New York System
- **Urban** 1-acre campus
- **Coed**

Undergraduates 2,646 full-time, 953 part-time. Students come from 18 states and territories; 2 other countries; 1% are from out of state; 3% transferred in.
Faculty *Student/faculty ratio:* 18:1.
Academics *Calendar:* semesters. *Degree:* certificates, diplomas, and associate. *Special study options:* academic remediation for entering students, adult/continuing education programs, advanced placement credit, cooperative education, distance learning, double majors, English as a second language, honors programs, independent study, internships, part-time degree program, services for LD students, student-designed majors, study abroad, summer session for credit. *ROTC:* Army (c).
Student Life *Campus security:* 24-hour emergency response devices and patrols, late-night transport/escort service.
Athletics Member NJCAA.
Costs (2010–11) *One-time required fee:* $50. *Tuition:* area resident $3300 full-time, $138 per credit hour part-time; state resident $6600 full-time, $276 per credit hour part-time; nonresident $6600 full-time, $276 per credit hour part-time. *Required fees:* $390 full-time, $5 per credit hour part-time, $60 per term part-time.
Applying *Options:* electronic application. *Application fee:* $25. *Required:* high school transcript. *Required for some:* interview.
Freshman Application Contact Erie Community College, 121 Ellicott Street, Buffalo, NY 14203-2698. *Phone:* 716-851-1155. *Fax:* 716-270-2821. *Web site:* http://www.ecc.edu/.

Erie Community College, North Campus
Williamsville, New York

- **State and locally supported** 2-year, founded 1946, part of State University of New York System
- **Suburban** 120-acre campus with easy access to Buffalo
- **Coed**

Undergraduates 4,502 full-time, 2,239 part-time. Students come from 25 states and territories; 17 other countries; 0.6% are from out of state; 5% transferred in.
Faculty *Student/faculty ratio:* 18:1.
Academics *Calendar:* semesters plus summer sessions, winter intersession. *Degree:* certificates, diplomas, and associate. *Special study options:* academic remediation for entering students, adult/continuing education programs,

advanced placement credit, cooperative education, distance learning, double majors, English as a second language, honors programs, independent study, internships, part-time degree program, services for LD students, student-designed majors, study abroad, summer session for credit. *ROTC:* Army (c).
Student Life *Campus security:* 24-hour emergency response devices and patrols, late-night transport/escort service.
Athletics Member NJCAA.
Costs (2010–11) *One-time required fee:* $50. *Tuition:* area resident $3300 full-time, $138 per credit hour part-time; state resident $6600 full-time, $276 per credit hour part-time; nonresident $6600 full-time, $276 per credit hour part-time. *Required fees:* $390 full-time, $5 per credit hour part-time, $60 per term part-time.
Applying *Options:* electronic application. *Application fee:* $25. *Required:* high school transcript. *Required for some:* interview.
Freshman Application Contact Erie Community College, North Campus, 6205 Main Street, Williamsville, NY 14221-7095. *Phone:* 716-851-1455. *Fax:* 716-270-2961. *Web site:* http://www.ecc.edu/.

Erie Community College, South Campus

Orchard Park, New York

- **State and locally supported** 2-year, founded 1974, part of State University of New York System
- **Suburban** 110-acre campus with easy access to Buffalo
- **Coed**

Undergraduates 2,801 full-time, 1,682 part-time. Students come from 19 states and territories; 4 other countries; 2% are from out of state; 4% transferred in.
Faculty *Student/faculty ratio:* 18:1.
Academics *Calendar:* semesters plus summer sessions, winter intersession. *Degree:* certificates, diplomas, and associate. *Special study options:* academic remediation for entering students, adult/continuing education programs, advanced placement credit, cooperative education, distance learning, double majors, English as a second language, honors programs, independent study, internships, part-time degree program, services for LD students, student-designed majors, study abroad, summer session for credit. *ROTC:* Army (c).
Student Life *Campus security:* 24-hour emergency response devices and patrols, late-night transport/escort service.
Athletics Member NJCAA.
Costs (2010–11) *One-time required fee:* $50. *Tuition:* area resident $3300 full-time, $138 per credit hour part-time; state resident $6600 full-time, $276 per credit hour part-time; nonresident $6600 full-time, $276 per credit hour part-time. *Required fees:* $390 full-time, $5 per credit hour part-time, $60 per term part-time.
Applying *Options:* electronic application. *Application fee:* $25. *Required:* high school transcript. *Required for some:* interview.
Freshman Application Contact Erie Community College, South Campus, 4041 Southwestern Boulevard, Orchard Park, NY 14127-2199. *Phone:* 716-851-1655. *Fax:* 716-851-1687. *Web site:* http://www.ecc.edu/.

Eugenio María de Hostos Community College of the City University of New York

Bronx, New York

Freshman Application Contact Mr. Roland Velez, Director of Admissions, Eugenio María de Hostos Community College of the City University of New York, 120 149th Street, Bronx, NY 10451. *Phone:* 718-319-7968. *Fax:* 718-319-7919. *E-mail:* admissions@hostos.cuny.edu. *Web site:* http://www.hostos.cuny.edu/.

Everest Institute

Rochester, New York

- **Proprietary** 2-year, founded 1863, part of Corinthian Colleges, Inc.
- **Suburban** 2-acre campus
- **Coed**

Undergraduates *Retention:* 64% of full-time freshmen returned.
Faculty *Student/faculty ratio:* 16:1.
Academics *Calendar:* quarters. *Degree:* certificates, diplomas, and associate. *Special study options:* adult/continuing education programs, advanced placement credit, cooperative education, distance learning, part-time degree program, summer session for credit.

Standardized Tests *Required for some:* CPAt for those with High School Diploma or GED; COMPASS or Asset for applicants without a High School Diploma or GED.
Applying *Options:* early admission, deferred entrance. *Required:* high school transcript, interview.
Freshman Application Contact Deanna Pfluke, Director of Admissions, Everest Institute, 1630 Portland Avenue, Rochester, NY 14621. *Phone:* 585-266-0430. *Fax:* 585-266-8243. *Web site:* http://www.everest.edu/campus/rochester/.

Fashion Institute of Technology

New York, New York

- **State and locally supported** comprehensive, founded 1944, part of State University of New York System
- **Urban** 5-acre campus
- **Endowment** $24.3 million
- **Coed, primarily women,** 10,166 undergraduate students, 71% full-time, 85% women, 15% men

Undergraduates 7,210 full-time, 2,956 part-time. Students come from 48 states and territories; 68 other countries; 29% are from out of state; 8% transferred in; 26% live on campus. *Retention:* 87% of 2008 full-time freshmen returned.
Freshmen *Admission:* 4,263 applied, 1,669 admitted, 1,070 enrolled. *Average high school GPA:* 3.4.
Faculty *Total:* 1,016, 25% full-time. *Student/faculty ratio:* 17:1.
Majors Advertising; animation, interactive technology, video graphics and special effects; apparel and textile manufacturing; commercial and advertising art; commercial photography; entrepreneurial and small business related; fashion/apparel design; fashion merchandising; fashion modeling; fine and studio arts management; fine/studio arts; graphic design; illustration; industrial and product design; interior design; international marketing; marketing research; merchandising, sales, and marketing operations related (specialized); metal and jewelry arts; special products marketing.
Academics *Calendar:* semesters. *Degrees:* certificates, associate, bachelor's, and master's. *Special study options:* academic remediation for entering students, adult/continuing education programs, advanced placement credit, distance learning, English as a second language, honors programs, internships, part-time degree program, services for LD students, study abroad, summer session for credit.
Library Gladys Marcus Library.
Student Life *Housing Options:* coed, women-only. Campus housing is university owned and is provided by a third party. Freshman applicants given priority for college housing. *Activities and Organizations:* drama/theater group, student-run newspaper, radio and television station, choral group, FITSA/Student Government, Merchandising Society/Style Shop, Delta Epilson Chi: Promoting Leadership in Marketing, Merchandising, and Advertising, PRSSA: Public Relations Student Society of America, Student Ambassadors. *Campus security:* 24-hour emergency response devices and patrols, late-night transport/escort service, controlled dormitory access. *Student services:* health clinic, personal/psychological counseling.
Athletics Member NJCAA. *Intercollegiate sports:* basketball M, cheerleading W, cross-country running M/W, swimming and diving M/W, table tennis M/W, tennis W, volleyball W. *Intramural sports:* basketball M/W, table tennis M/W, tennis M/W, volleyball M/W.
Costs (2010–11) *Tuition:* state resident $5168 full-time, $215 per credit hour part-time; nonresident $13,550 full-time, $564 per credit hour part-time. Full-time tuition and fees vary according to degree level. Part-time tuition and fees vary according to degree level. *Required fees:* $500 full-time. *Room and board:* $11,700. Room and board charges vary according to board plan and housing facility. *Payment plan:* installment. *Waivers:* employees or children of employees.
Financial Aid Of all full-time matriculated undergraduates who enrolled in 2008, 4,507 applied for aid, 3,512 were judged to have need, 459 had their need fully met. 553 Federal Work-Study jobs (averaging $1479). In 2008, 170 non-need-based awards were made. *Average percent of need met:* 63%. *Average financial aid package:* $11,305. *Average need-based loan:* $4298. *Average need-based gift aid:* $5355. *Average non-need-based aid:* $1676. *Average indebtedness upon graduation:* $24,143.
Applying *Options:* electronic application. *Application fee:* $40. *Required:* essay or personal statement, high school transcript. *Required for some:* portfolio for art and design programs. *Application deadlines:* 2/1 (freshmen), 2/1 (transfers). *Notification:* continuous (freshmen), continuous (transfers).
Freshman Application Contact Ms. Laura Arbrogast, Director of Admissions, Fashion Institute of Technology, Seventh Avenue at 27th Street, New York, NY 10001-5992. *Phone:* 212-217-3760. *Toll-free phone:* 800-GOTOFIT. *Fax:* 212-217-3761. *E-mail:* fitinfo@fitnyc.edu. *Web site:* http://www.fitnyc.edu/.

See next page for Display and page 412 for the College Close-Up.

Finger Lakes Community College

Canandaigua, New York

- **State and locally supported** 2-year, founded 1965, part of State University of New York System
- **Small-town** 300-acre campus with easy access to Rochester
- **Coed**

Undergraduates 3,750 full-time, 2,949 part-time. Students come from 12 states and territories; 2 other countries; 0.3% are from out of state; 4% transferred in.

Faculty *Student/faculty ratio:* 20:1.

Academics *Calendar:* semesters. *Degree:* certificates and associate. *Special study options:* academic remediation for entering students, advanced placement credit, distance learning, English as a second language, honors programs, internships, off-campus study, part-time degree program, services for LD students, summer session for credit. *ROTC:* Army (c).

Student Life *Campus security:* 24-hour emergency response devices and patrols, late-night transport/escort service.

Athletics Member NJCAA.

Costs (2010–11) *Tuition:* state resident $3328 full-time, $126 per credit hour part-time; nonresident $6656 full-time, $252 per credit hour part-time. Full-time tuition and fees vary according to course load. Part-time tuition and fees vary according to course load. *Required fees:* $410 full-time, $12 per credit hour part-time.

Financial Aid Of all full-time matriculated undergraduates who enrolled in 2009, 200 Federal Work-Study jobs (averaging $2200). 100 state and other part-time jobs (averaging $2200).

Applying *Options:* electronic application, early admission, deferred entrance. *Required:* high school transcript. *Recommended:* interview.

Freshman Application Contact Ms. Bonnie B. Ritts, Director of Admissions, Finger Lakes Community College, 3325 Marvin Sands Drive, Canandaigua, NY 14424-8395. *Phone:* 585-394-3500 Ext. 7278. *Fax:* 585-394-5005. *E-mail:* admissions@flcc.edu. *Web site:* http://www.flcc.edu/.

Fiorello H. LaGuardia Community College of the City University of New York

Long Island City, New York

- **State and locally supported** 2-year, founded 1970, part of City University of New York System
- **Urban** 6-acre campus
- **Coed,** 17,087 undergraduate students, 59% full-time, 59% women, 41% men

Undergraduates 10,040 full-time, 7,047 part-time. Students come from 21 states and territories; 152 other countries; 2% are from out of state; 15% Black or African American, non-Hispanic/Latino; 36% Hispanic/Latino; 15% Asian, non-Hispanic/Latino; 0.3% Native Hawaiian or other Pacific Islander, non-Hispanic/Latino; 0.5% American Indian or Alaska Native, non-Hispanic/Latino; 16% Race/ethnicity unknown; 7% international; 12% transferred in.

Freshmen *Admission:* 6,943 applied, 6,943 admitted, 3,239 enrolled.

Faculty *Total:* 984, 30% full-time, 24% with terminal degrees. *Student/faculty ratio:* 24:1.

Majors Accounting technology and bookkeeping; administrative assistant and secretarial science; adult development and aging; biology/biological sciences; business administration and management; civil engineering; commercial photography; computer and information sciences and support services related; computer installation and repair technology; computer programming; computer science; data entry/microcomputer applications; dietetic technology; electrical and electronics engineering; emergency medical technology (EMT paramedic); engineering science; environmental science; funeral service and mortuary science; gerontology; industrial and product design; information science/studies; legal assistant/paralegal; liberal arts and sciences/liberal studies; licensed practical/vocational nurse training; mechanical engineering; occupational therapist assistant; photographic and film/video technology; physical therapy technology; psychiatric/mental health services technology; registered nursing/registered nurse; restaurant/food services management; Spanish; speech communication and rhetoric; teacher assistant/aide; tourism and travel services management; veterinary/animal health technology; visual and performing arts.

Academics *Calendar:* enhanced semester. *Degree:* certificates and associate. *Special study options:* academic remediation for entering students, accelerated degree program, adult/continuing education programs, advanced placement credit, cooperative education, distance learning, double majors, English as a second language, honors programs, independent study, internships, off-campus study, part-time degree program, services for LD students, student-designed majors, study abroad, summer session for credit.
Library Fiorello H. LaGuardia Community College Library Media Resources Center plus 1 other with 312,040 titles, 546 serial subscriptions, 3,363 audiovisual materials, an OPAC, a Web page.
Student Life *Housing:* college housing not available. *Activities and Organizations:* drama/theater group, student-run newspaper, radio station, Bangladesh Student Association, Christian Club, Chinese Club, Web Radio, Black Student Union. *Campus security:* 24-hour emergency response devices and patrols, late-night transport/escort service. *Student services:* health clinic, personal/psychological counseling, women's center, legal services.
Athletics *Intramural sports:* basketball M/W, bowling M/W, football M, soccer M/W, softball M/W, swimming and diving M/W, table tennis M/W, volleyball M/W.
Costs (2010–11) *Tuition:* state resident $3150 full-time, $135 per credit hour part-time; nonresident $6300 full-time, $210 per credit hour part-time. *Required fees:* $342 full-time, $86 per term part-time. *Payment plan:* installment. *Waivers:* senior citizens and employees or children of employees.
Financial Aid Of all full-time matriculated undergraduates who enrolled in 2009, 7,674 applied for aid, 7,208 were judged to have need, 118 had their need fully met. 343 Federal Work-Study jobs (averaging $650). *Average percent of need met:* 51%. *Average financial aid package:* $6079. *Average need-based loan:* $4319. *Average need-based gift aid:* $4743.
Applying *Options:* electronic application, early admission, deferred entrance. *Application fee:* $65. *Required:* high school transcript. *Application deadlines:* rolling (freshmen), rolling (transfers). *Notification:* continuous (freshmen), continuous (transfers).
Freshman Application Contact Ms. LaVora Desvigne, Director of Admissions, Fiorello H. LaGuardia Community College of the City University of New York, RM-147, 31-10 Thomson Avenue, Long Island City, NY 11101. *Phone:* 718-482-5114. *Fax:* 718-482-5112. *E-mail:* admissions@lagcc.cuny.edu. *Web site:* http://www.lagcc.cuny.edu/.

Fulton-Montgomery Community College
Johnstown, New York

- **State and locally supported** 2-year, founded 1964, part of State University of New York System
- **Rural** 195-acre campus
- **Endowment** $1.7 million
- **Coed,** 2,833 undergraduate students, 66% full-time, 58% women, 42% men

Undergraduates 1,863 full-time, 970 part-time. Students come from 6 states and territories; 18 other countries; 1% are from out of state; 4% transferred in. *Retention:* 56% of full-time freshmen returned.
Freshmen *Admission:* 727 enrolled.
Faculty *Total:* 145, 37% full-time. *Student/faculty ratio:* 24:1.
Majors Accounting; administrative assistant and secretarial science; art; automobile/automotive mechanics technology; behavioral sciences; biological and physical sciences; biology/biological sciences; business administration and management; carpentry; commercial and advertising art; computer engineering technology; computer science; computer typography and composition equipment operation; construction engineering technology; criminal justice/law enforcement administration; data processing and data processing technology; developmental and child psychology; dramatic/theater arts; electrical, electronic and communications engineering technology; elementary education; engineering science; English; environmental studies; finance; fine/studio arts; graphic and printing equipment operation/production; health teacher education; history; humanities; human services; information science/studies; kindergarten/preschool education; legal administrative assistant/secretary; liberal arts and sciences/liberal studies; mass communication/media; mathematics; medical administrative assistant and medical secretary; natural resources/conservation; physical education teaching and coaching; physical sciences; psychology; registered nursing/registered nurse; social sciences; teacher assistant/aide.
Academics *Calendar:* semesters plus winter session. *Degree:* certificates and associate. *Special study options:* academic remediation for entering students, accelerated degree program, adult/continuing education programs, advanced placement credit, cooperative education, distance learning, double majors, English as a second language, external degree program, honors programs, independent study, internships, off-campus study, part-time degree program, services for LD students, student-designed majors, study abroad, summer session for credit.
Library Evans Library with an OPAC, a Web page.

Student Life *Housing Options:* Campus housing is university owned and is provided by a third party. *Activities and Organizations:* drama/theater group, student-run newspaper, choral group. *Campus security:* weekend and night security. *Student services:* personal/psychological counseling.
Athletics Member NJCAA. *Intercollegiate sports:* baseball M, basketball M/W, soccer M/W, softball W, volleyball W. *Intramural sports:* baseball M, basketball M/W, skiing (cross-country) M(c)/W(c), skiing (downhill) M(c)/W(c), volleyball M/W.
Costs (2011–12) *Tuition:* state resident $3194 full-time; nonresident $6388 full-time. Part-time tuition and fees vary according to course load. *Required fees:* $544 full-time. *Room and board:* $7320; room only: $5830. *Payment plans:* installment, deferred payment. *Waivers:* senior citizens and employees or children of employees.
Financial Aid Of all full-time matriculated undergraduates who enrolled in 2009, 87 Federal Work-Study jobs (averaging $1500).
Applying *Options:* electronic application, early admission, deferred entrance. *Required:* high school transcript. *Application deadlines:* 9/10 (freshmen), 9/10 (transfers). *Notification:* continuous (freshmen), continuous (transfers).
Freshman Application Contact Fulton-Montgomery Community College, 2805 State Highway 67, Johnstown, NY 12095-3790. *Phone:* 518-762-4651 Ext. 8301. *Web site:* http://www.fmcc.suny.edu/.

Genesee Community College
Batavia, New York

- **State and locally supported** 2-year, founded 1966, part of State University of New York System
- **Small-town** 256-acre campus with easy access to Buffalo and Rochester
- **Endowment** $1.9 million
- **Coed**

Undergraduates 3,452 full-time, 3,756 part-time. Students come from 18 states and territories; 27 other countries; 2% are from out of state; 6% transferred in.
Faculty *Student/faculty ratio:* 18:1.
Academics *Calendar:* semesters. *Degree:* certificates and associate. *Special study options:* academic remediation for entering students, adult/continuing education programs, advanced placement credit, cooperative education, distance learning, double majors, honors programs, independent study, internships, part-time degree program, services for LD students, summer session for credit.
Student Life *Campus security:* 24-hour emergency response devices and patrols, student patrols, late-night transport/escort service.
Athletics Member NJCAA.
Standardized Tests *Recommended:* ACT (for admission).
Costs (2010–11) *Tuition:* state resident $3720 full-time, $140 per credit hour part-time; nonresident $4320 full-time, $160 per credit hour part-time. Full-time tuition and fees vary according to course load. Part-time tuition and fees vary according to course load. *Required fees:* $320 full-time, $24 per credit hour part-time. *Room and board:* room only: $5400. Room and board charges vary according to board plan and housing facility.
Financial Aid Of all full-time matriculated undergraduates who enrolled in 2008, 2,826 applied for aid, 2,520 were judged to have need, 980 had their need fully met. 145 Federal Work-Study jobs (averaging $1090). 68 state and other part-time jobs (averaging $1895). *Average percent of need met:* 68. *Average financial aid package:* $4320. *Average need-based loan:* $3300. *Average need-based gift aid:* $2975. *Average indebtedness upon graduation:* $8750.
Applying *Options:* electronic application. *Required:* high school transcript. *Required for some:* 1 letter of recommendation.
Freshman Application Contact Mrs. Tanya Lane-Martin, Director of Admissions, Genesee Community College, Batavia, NY 14020. *Phone:* 585-343-0055 Ext. 6413. *Toll-free phone:* 800-CALL GCC. *Fax:* 585-345-6892. *E-mail:* tmlanemartin@genesee.edu. *Web site:* http://www.genesee.edu/.

Helene Fuld College of Nursing of North General Hospital
New York, New York

Freshman Application Contact Helene Fuld College of Nursing of North General Hospital, 24 East 120th Street, New York, NY 10035. *Phone:* 212-616-7271. *Web site:* http://www.helenefuld.edu/.

Herkimer County Community College
Herkimer, New York

Director of Admissions Mr. Scott J. Hughes, Associate Dean for Enrollment Management, Herkimer County Community College, Reservoir Road,

Herkimer, NY 13350. *Phone:* 315-866-0300 Ext. 278. *Toll-free phone:* 888-464-4222 Ext. 8278. *Web site:* http://www.herkimer.edu/.

Hudson Valley Community College
Troy, New York

Freshman Application Contact Ms. Marie Claire Bauer, Director of Admissions, Hudson Valley Community College, 80 Vandenburgh Avenue, Troy, NY 12180-6096. *Phone:* 518-629-7309. *Toll-free phone:* 877-325-HVCC. *Web site:* http://www.hvcc.edu/.

Institute of Design and Construction
Brooklyn, New York

Director of Admissions Mr. Kevin Giannetti, Director of Admissions, Institute of Design and Construction, 141 Willoughby Street, Brooklyn, NY 11201-5317. *Phone:* 718-855-3661. *Web site:* http://www.idcbrooklyn.org/.

Island Drafting and Technical Institute
Amityville, New York

- **Proprietary** 2-year, founded 1957
- **Suburban** campus with easy access to New York City
- **Coed**

Undergraduates 131 full-time. Students come from 1 other state.
Faculty *Student/faculty ratio:* 15:1.
Academics *Calendar:* semesters. *Degree:* certificates, diplomas, and associate. *Special study options:* accelerated degree program, adult/continuing education programs, summer session for credit.
Costs (2010–11) *Tuition:* $14,850 full-time, $495 per credit hour part-time. No tuition increase for student's term of enrollment.
Applying *Options:* early admission. *Application fee:* $25. *Required:* interview. *Recommended:* high school transcript.
Freshman Application Contact Jaimie Laudicina, Director of Enrollment Services, Island Drafting and Technical Institute, Island Drafting and Technical Institute, 128 Broadway, Amityville, NY 11701. *Phone:* 631-691-8733. *Fax:* 631-691-8738. *E-mail:* info@idti.edu. *Web site:* http://www.idti.edu/.

ITT Technical Institute
Albany, New York

- **Proprietary** 2-year, founded 1998, part of ITT Educational Services, Inc.
- **Coed**

Majors CAD/CADD drafting/design technology; computer engineering technology; computer software and media applications related; design and visual communications; system, networking, and LAN/WAN management; web/multimedia management and webmaster; web page, digital/multimedia and information resources design.
Academics *Calendar:* quarters. *Degree:* associate.
Student Life *Housing:* college housing not available.
Freshman Application Contact Director of Recruitment, ITT Technical Institute, 13 Airline Drive, Albany, NY 12205. *Phone:* 518-452-9300. *Toll-free phone:* 800-489-1191. *Web site:* http://www.itt-tech.edu/.

ITT Technical Institute
Getzville, New York

- **Proprietary** 2-year, part of ITT Educational Services, Inc.
- **Coed**

Majors CAD/CADD drafting/design technology; computer engineering technology; computer software and media applications related; design and visual communications; system, networking, and LAN/WAN management; web page, digital/multimedia and information resources design.
Academics *Degree:* associate.
Student Life *Housing:* college housing not available.
Freshman Application Contact Director of Recruitment, ITT Technical Institute, 2295 Millersport Highway, PO Box 327, Getzville, NY 14068. *Phone:* 716-689-2200. *Toll-free phone:* 800-469-7593. *Web site:* http://www.itt-tech.edu/.

ITT Technical Institute
Liverpool, New York

- **Proprietary** 2-year, founded 1998, part of ITT Educational Services, Inc.
- **Coed**

Majors CAD/CADD drafting/design technology; computer engineering technology; computer software and media applications related; design and visual communications; system, networking, and LAN/WAN management; web page, digital/multimedia and information resources design.
Academics *Calendar:* semesters. *Degree:* associate.
Student Life *Housing:* college housing not available.
Freshman Application Contact Director of Recruitment, ITT Technical Institute, 235 Greenfield Parkway, Liverpool, NY 13088. *Phone:* 315-461-8000. *Toll-free phone:* 877-488-0011. *Web site:* http://www.itt-tech.edu/.

Jamestown Business College
Jamestown, New York

- **Proprietary** primarily 2-year, founded 1886
- **Small-town** 1-acre campus
- **Coed,** 386 undergraduate students, 97% full-time, 73% women, 27% men

Undergraduates 375 full-time, 11 part-time. Students come from 2 states and territories; 9% are from out of state; 13% transferred in.
Freshmen *Admission:* 113 applied, 101 admitted, 78 enrolled.
Faculty *Total:* 25, 32% full-time. *Student/faculty ratio:* 28:1.
Majors Accounting; administrative assistant and secretarial science; business administration and management; computer and information sciences; legal administrative assistant/secretary; marketing/marketing management; medical administrative assistant and medical secretary.
Academics *Calendar:* quarters. *Degrees:* certificates, associate, and bachelor's. *Special study options:* academic remediation for entering students, advanced placement credit, double majors, internships, part-time degree program, summer session for credit.
Library James Prendergast Library with 279,270 titles, 372 serial subscriptions, an OPAC, a Web page.
Student Life *Housing:* college housing not available. *Campus security:* 24-hour emergency response devices.
Athletics *Intramural sports:* basketball M(c)/W(c), bowling M(c)/W(c), racquetball M(c)/W(c), skiing (cross-country) M(c)/W(c), skiing (downhill) M(c)/W(c), softball M(c)/W(c), swimming and diving M(c)/W(c), table tennis M(c)/W(c), volleyball M(c)/W(c), weight lifting M(c)/W(c).
Costs (2011–12) *One-time required fee:* $25. *Tuition:* $10,200 full-time, $283 per credit hour part-time. *Required fees:* $900 full-time, $150 per term part-time.
Applying *Application fee:* $25. *Required:* essay or personal statement, high school transcript, interview. *Application deadlines:* rolling (freshmen), rolling (transfers).
Freshman Application Contact Mrs. Brenda Salemme, Director of Admissions and Placement, Jamestown Business College, 7 Fairmount Avenue, Box 429, Jamestown, NY 14702-0429. *Phone:* 716-664-5100. *Fax:* 716-664-3144. *E-mail:* admissions@jbcny.org. *Web site:* http://www.jbcny.org/.

Jamestown Community College
Jamestown, New York

- **State and locally supported** 2-year, founded 1950, part of State University of New York System
- **Small-town** 107-acre campus
- **Endowment** $6.4 million
- **Coed**

Undergraduates 2,807 full-time, 1,124 part-time. Students come from 13 states and territories; 9% are from out of state; 6% transferred in.
Faculty *Student/faculty ratio:* 18:1.
Academics *Calendar:* semesters. *Degree:* certificates and associate. *Special study options:* academic remediation for entering students, adult/continuing education programs, advanced placement credit, cooperative education, distance learning, honors programs, independent study, internships, off-campus study, part-time degree program, services for LD students, study abroad, summer session for credit.
Athletics Member NJCAA.
Costs (2010–11) *Tuition:* state resident $3720 full-time, $156 per credit hour part-time; nonresident $7440 full-time, $281 per credit hour part-time. Full-time tuition and fees vary according to course load and program. Part-time tuition and fees vary according to course load and program. *Required fees:* $460 full-time. *Room and board:* room only: $5300. Room and board charges vary according to board plan.
Financial Aid Of all full-time matriculated undergraduates who enrolled in 2009, 85 Federal Work-Study jobs (averaging $1500). 85 state and other part-time jobs (averaging $1300).
Applying *Options:* electronic application, deferred entrance. *Required:* high school transcript. *Required for some:* standardized test scores used for placement.
Freshman Application Contact Ms. Wendy Present, Director of Admissions and Recruitment, Jamestown Community College, 525 Falconer Street, PO

Box 20, Jamestown, NY 14702-0020. *Phone:* 716-338-1001. *Toll-free phone:* 800-388-8557. *Fax:* 716-338-1450. *E-mail:* admissions@mail.sunyjcc.edu. *Web site:* http://www.sunyjcc.edu/.

Jefferson Community College
Watertown, New York

- **State and locally supported** 2-year, founded 1961, part of State University of New York System
- **Small-town** 90-acre campus with easy access to Syracuse
- **Coed**

Undergraduates 2,024 full-time, 1,290 part-time. Students come from 9 states and territories; 3 other countries.

Faculty *Student/faculty ratio:* 18:1.

Academics *Calendar:* semesters. *Degree:* certificates and associate. *Special study options:* academic remediation for entering students, advanced placement credit, cooperative education, distance learning, double majors, honors programs, independent study, internships, part-time degree program, services for LD students, student-designed majors, summer session for credit.

Student Life *Campus security:* 24-hour emergency response devices and patrols.

Athletics Member NJCAA.

Standardized Tests *Recommended:* SAT or ACT (for admission).

Costs (2010–11) *Tuition:* state resident $3480 full-time, $145 per credit hour part-time; nonresident $5424 full-time, $226 per credit hour part-time. Full-time tuition and fees vary according to course load, program, and reciprocity agreements. Part-time tuition and fees vary according to course load, program, and reciprocity agreements. *Required fees:* $378 full-time, $15 per credit hour part-time.

Financial Aid Of all full-time matriculated undergraduates who enrolled in 2009, 1,748 applied for aid. 98 Federal Work-Study jobs (averaging $1093).

Applying *Options:* electronic application, early admission, deferred entrance. *Required:* high school transcript. *Required for some:* interview.

Freshman Application Contact Ms. Rosanne N. Weir, Director of Admissions, Jefferson Community College, 1220 Coffeen Street, Watertown, NY 13601. *Phone:* 315-786-2277. *Fax:* 315-786-2459. *E-mail:* admissions@sunyjefferson.edu. *Web site:* http://www.sunyjefferson.edu/.

Kingsborough Community College of the City University of New York
Brooklyn, New York

- **State and locally supported** 2-year, founded 1963, part of City University of New York System
- **Urban** 72-acre campus with easy access to New York City
- **Coed,** 18,700 undergraduate students, 60% full-time, 56% women, 44% men

Undergraduates 11,232 full-time, 7,468 part-time. Students come from 10 states and territories; 136 other countries; 1% are from out of state; 8% transferred in. *Retention:* 68% of full-time freshmen returned.

Freshmen *Admission:* 2,933 enrolled. *Average high school GPA:* 2.7.

Faculty *Total:* 983, 35% full-time, 29% with terminal degrees. *Student/faculty ratio:* 25:1.

Majors Accounting; administrative assistant and secretarial science; art; biology/biological sciences; broadcast journalism; business administration and management; chemistry; commercial and advertising art; community health services counseling; computer and information sciences; computer science; data processing and data processing technology; design and applied arts related; dramatic/theater arts; early childhood education; education; elementary education; engineering science; fashion merchandising; health and physical education related; human services; journalism; labor and industrial relations; liberal arts and sciences/liberal studies; marine maintenance and ship repair technology; marketing/marketing management; mathematics; mental health counseling; music; parks, recreation and leisure; physical therapy; physical therapy technology; physics; psychiatric/mental health services technology; registered nursing/registered nurse; sport and fitness administration/management; teacher assistant/aide; tourism and travel services management.

Academics *Calendar:* semesters. *Degree:* associate. *Special study options:* academic remediation for entering students, adult/continuing education programs, advanced placement credit, distance learning, English as a second language, honors programs, independent study, internships, off-campus study, part-time degree program, services for LD students, summer session for credit.

Library Robert J. Kibbee Library with 185,912 titles, 458 serial subscriptions, an OPAC.

Student Life *Housing:* college housing not available. *Activities and Organizations:* drama/theater group, student-run newspaper, radio station, choral group,

Peer Advisors, Caribbean Club, DECA. *Campus security:* 24-hour emergency response devices and patrols. *Student services:* health clinic, personal/psychological counseling, women's center.

Athletics Member NJCAA. *Intercollegiate sports:* baseball M, basketball M/W, soccer M, softball W, tennis M/W, track and field M/W, volleyball W. *Intramural sports:* baseball M, basketball M/W, soccer M, softball W, tennis M/W, track and field M/W, volleyball W.

Costs (2011–12) *Tuition:* state resident $3225 full-time; nonresident $6300 full-time. *Required fees:* $350 full-time. *Payment plan:* installment. *Waivers:* senior citizens.

Applying *Application fee:* $65. *Required:* high school transcript. *Application deadlines:* 8/15 (freshmen), rolling (transfers).

Freshman Application Contact Mr. Robert Ingenito, Director of Admissions Information Center, Kingsborough Community College of the City University of New York, 2001 Oriental Boulevard, Brooklyn, NY 11235. *Phone:* 718-368-4600. *Fax:* 718-368-5356. *E-mail:* info@kbcc.cuny.edu. *Web site:* http://www.kbcc.cuny.edu/.

Long Island Business Institute
Flushing, New York

- **Proprietary** 2-year, founded 1968
- **Urban** campus with easy access to New York City
- **Coed, primarily women,** 587 undergraduate students, 68% full-time, 76% women, 24% men

Undergraduates 398 full-time, 189 part-time. Students come from 2 states and territories; 31 other countries; 12% Black or African American, non-Hispanic/Latino; 16% Hispanic/Latino; 43% Asian, non-Hispanic/Latino; 0.9% Two or more races, non-Hispanic/Latino; 0.4% Race/ethnicity unknown; 2% international; 3% transferred in.

Freshmen *Admission:* 160 applied, 144 admitted, 141 enrolled.

Faculty *Total:* 91, 23% full-time, 2% with terminal degrees. *Student/faculty ratio:* 19:1.

Majors Accounting; business administration and management; court reporting; homeland security; medical office management.

Academics *Calendar:* semesters. *Degrees:* certificates, diplomas, and associate (information provided for Commack and Flushing campuses). *Special study options:* academic remediation for entering students, adult/continuing education programs, advanced placement credit, cooperative education, English as a second language, honors programs, independent study, part-time degree program, summer session for credit.

Library Flushing Main Campus Library, Commack Branch Campus Library with 4,700 titles, 69 serial subscriptions, 799 audiovisual materials, an OPAC, a Web page.

Student Life *Housing:* college housing not available. *Activities and Organizations:* Small Business Club, Web Design Club, Investment Club, Court Reporting Alumni Association. *Campus security:* 24-hour emergency response devices.

Standardized Tests *Required:* ASSET, CELSA (for admission).

Costs (2011–12) *Tuition:* $13,299 full-time, $375 per credit part-time. *Required fees:* $600 full-time. *Payment plans:* installment, deferred payment.

Applying *Application fee:* $55. *Required:* essay or personal statement, high school transcript, interview. *Application deadlines:* rolling (freshmen), rolling (transfers).

Freshman Application Contact Mr. Robert Nazar, Director of Admissions, Long Island Business Institute, 136-18 39th Avenue, Flushing, NY 11354. *Phone:* 718-939-5100. *Fax:* 718-939-9235. *E-mail:* rnazar@libi.edu. *Web site:* http://www.libi.edu/.

Long Island College Hospital School of Nursing
Brooklyn, New York

Freshman Application Contact Ms. Barbara Evans, Admissions Assistant, Long Island College Hospital School of Nursing, 350 Henry Street, 7th Floor, Brooklyn, NY 11201. *Phone:* 718-780-1071. *Fax:* 718-780-1936. *E-mail:* bevans@chpnet.org. *Web site:* http://www.futurenurselich.org/.

Memorial Hospital School of Nursing
Albany, New York

Freshman Application Contact Admissions Office, Memorial Hospital School of Nursing, 600 Northern Boulevard, Albany, NY 12204. *Web site:* http://www.nehealth.com/son/.

Mildred Elley School
Albany, New York

Director of Admissions Mr. Michael Cahalan, Enrollment Manager, Mildred Elley School, 855 Central Avenue, Albany, NY 12206. *Phone:* 518-786-3171 Ext. 227. *Toll-free phone:* 800-622-6327. *Web site:* http://www.mildred-elley.edu/.

Mohawk Valley Community College
Utica, New York

- **State and locally supported** 2-year, founded 1946, part of State University of New York System
- **Suburban** 80-acre campus
- **Endowment** $3.5 million
- **Coed,** 7,151 undergraduate students, 67% full-time, 55% women, 45% men

Undergraduates 4,759 full-time, 2,392 part-time. Students come from 17 states and territories; 22 other countries; 9% Black or African American, non-Hispanic/Latino; 6% Hispanic/Latino; 2% Asian, non-Hispanic/Latino; 0.2% Native Hawaiian or other Pacific Islander, non-Hispanic/Latino; 0.5% American Indian or Alaska Native, non-Hispanic/Latino; 2% Two or more races, non-Hispanic/Latino; 0.3% Race/ethnicity unknown; 1% international; 5% transferred in; 7% live on campus.

Freshmen *Admission:* 4,479 applied, 4,214 admitted, 1,744 enrolled. *Average high school GPA:* 2.7.

Faculty *Total:* 383, 38% full-time, 24% with terminal degrees. *Student/faculty ratio:* 23:1.

Majors Accounting technology and bookkeeping; administrative assistant and secretarial science; advertising; airframe mechanics and aircraft maintenance technology; art; banking and financial support services; building/property maintenance; business administration and management; chemical technology; civil engineering technology; commercial and advertising art; commercial photography; communications systems installation and repair technology; community organization and advocacy; computer and information sciences; computer and information sciences and support services related; computer programming; criminal justice/law enforcement administration; design and applied arts related; drafting and design technology; dramatic/theater arts; electrical and electronic engineering technologies related; electrical, electronic and communications engineering technology; electrical/electronics maintenance and repair technology related; elementary education; emergency medical technology (EMT paramedic); engineering; entrepreneurship; fire services administration; food service systems administration; heating, ventilation, air conditioning and refrigeration engineering technology; hotel/motel administration; humanities; industrial production technologies related; liberal arts and sciences and humanities related; liberal arts and sciences/liberal studies; management information systems and services related; mechanical engineering/mechanical technology; medical/clinical assistant; medical radiologic technology; nutrition sciences; parks, recreation and leisure facilities management; public administration; registered nursing/registered nurse; respiratory care therapy; restaurant, culinary, and catering management; secondary education; sign language interpretation and translation; substance abuse/addiction counseling; surveying technology.

Academics *Calendar:* semesters. *Degree:* certificates and associate. *Special study options:* academic remediation for entering students, advanced placement credit, distance learning, double majors, English as a second language, honors programs, independent study, internships, off-campus study, part-time degree program, services for LD students, student-designed majors, summer session for credit. *ROTC:* Army (c).

Library Mohawk Valley Community College Library plus 1 other with 118,529 titles, 39,749 serial subscriptions, 8,890 audiovisual materials, an OPAC, a Web page.

Student Life *Housing Options:* coed, men-only, women-only, disabled students. Campus housing is provided by a third party. Freshman applicants given priority for college housing. *Activities and Organizations:* drama/theater group, student-run newspaper, choral group, Student Congress, Student Nurses Organization (SNO), Black Student Union, Ski Club, Returning Adult Student Association (RASA). *Campus security:* 24-hour emergency response devices and patrols, late-night transport/escort service, controlled dormitory access. *Student services:* health clinic, personal/psychological counseling.

Athletics Member NJCAA. *Intercollegiate sports:* baseball M, basketball M/W, bowling M/W, cross-country running M/W, golf M/W, ice hockey M, lacrosse M/W, soccer M/W, softball W, tennis M/W, track and field M/W, volleyball W. *Intramural sports:* basketball M/W, racquetball M/W, soccer M/W, tennis M/W, volleyball M/W, weight lifting M/W.

Costs (2010–11) *Tuition:* state resident $3400 full-time, $120 per credit hour part-time; nonresident $6800 full-time, $240 per credit hour part-time. *Required fees:* $470 full-time, $5 per credit hour part-time, $35 per term part-time. *Room and board:* $8260; room only: $5020. Room and board charges vary according to board plan. *Payment plan:* installment. *Waivers:* senior citizens and employees or children of employees.

Financial Aid Of all full-time matriculated undergraduates who enrolled in 2009, 229 Federal Work-Study jobs (averaging $1750).

Applying *Options:* electronic application, deferred entrance. *Required for some:* high school transcript. *Recommended:* interview. *Application deadlines:* rolling (freshmen), rolling (out-of-state freshmen), rolling (transfers). *Notification:* continuous (freshmen), continuous (out-of-state freshmen), continuous (transfers).

Freshman Application Contact Mrs. Sandra Fiebiger, Data Processing Clerk, Admissions, Mohawk Valley Community College, Utica, NY 13501. *Phone:* 315-792-5640. *Toll-free phone:* 800-SEE-MVCC. *Fax:* 315-792-5527. *E-mail:* sandra.fiebiger@mvcc.edu. *Web site:* http://www.mvcc.edu/.

See page 226 for Display and page 424 for the College Close-Up.

Monroe Community College
Rochester, New York

Freshman Application Contact Mr. Andrew Freeman, Director of Admissions, Monroe Community College, 1000 East Henrietta Road, Rochester, NY 14623-5780. *Phone:* 585-292-2231. *Fax:* 585-292-3860. *E-mail:* admissions@monroecc.edu. *Web site:* http://www.monroecc.edu/.

Nassau Community College
Garden City, New York

- **State and locally supported** 2-year, founded 1959, part of State University of New York System
- **Suburban** 225-acre campus with easy access to New York City
- **Coed**

Undergraduates 14,702 full-time, 7,250 part-time. Students come from 19 states and territories; 69 other countries; 0.3% are from out of state; 7% transferred in. *Retention:* 32% of full-time freshmen returned.

Faculty *Student/faculty ratio:* 18:1.

Academics *Calendar:* semesters. *Degree:* certificates and associate. *Special study options:* academic remediation for entering students, adult/continuing education programs, advanced placement credit, cooperative education, distance learning, English as a second language, honors programs, internships, off-campus study, part-time degree program, services for LD students, summer session for credit.

Student Life *Campus security:* 24-hour emergency response devices and patrols, late-night transport/escort service.

Athletics Member NJCAA.

Standardized Tests *Recommended:* SAT or ACT (for admission).

Costs (2010–11) *Tuition:* area resident $3732 full-time, $156 per credit part-time; state resident $7464 full-time, $312 per credit part-time; nonresident $7464 full-time, $312 per credit part-time. *Required fees:* $280 full-time, $15 per term part-time, $15 per term part-time.

Financial Aid Of all full-time matriculated undergraduates who enrolled in 2009, 400 Federal Work-Study jobs (averaging $3000).

Applying *Options:* electronic application, deferred entrance. *Application fee:* $40. *Required:* high school transcript. *Required for some:* minimum 3.0 GPA, interview. *Recommended:* minimum 2.0 GPA.

Freshman Application Contact Mr. Craig Wright, Vice President of Enrollment Management, Nassau Community College, Garden City, NY 11530. *Phone:* 516-572-7345. *E-mail:* admissions@sunynassau.edu. *Web site:* http://www.ncc.edu/.

New York Career Institute
New York, New York

- **Proprietary** 2-year, founded 1942
- **Urban** campus
- **Coed, primarily women,** 805 undergraduate students, 59% full-time, 91% women, 9% men

Undergraduates 475 full-time, 330 part-time.

Faculty *Total:* 47, 19% full-time.

Majors Court reporting; legal assistant/paralegal; medical office assistant.

Academics *Calendar:* trimesters (semesters for evening division). *Degree:* associate. *Special study options:* academic remediation for entering students, advanced placement credit, cooperative education, internships, part-time degree program, summer session for credit.

Library 5,010 titles, 23 serial subscriptions.

Student Life *Housing:* college housing not available. *Activities and Organizations:* student-run newspaper.

Standardized Tests *Required:* CPAt (for admission).

Applying *Application fee:* $50. *Required:* high school transcript, interview. *Application deadlines:* 9/21 (freshmen), 9/21 (transfers). *Notification:* continuous (freshmen), continuous (transfers).

Freshman Application Contact Mr. Larry Stieglitz, Director of Admissions, New York Career Institute, 11 Park Place, New York, NY 10007. *Phone:* 212-962-0002 Ext. 115. *Fax:* 212-385-7574. *E-mail:* lstieglitz@nyci.edu. *Web site:* http://www.nyci.com/.

New York College of Health Professions
Syosset, New York

Director of Admissions Ms. Mary Rodas, Associate Director of Admissions, New York College of Health Professions, 6801 Jericho Turnpike, Syosset, NY 11791-4413. *Toll-free phone:* 800-922-7337 Ext. 351. *E-mail:* rdodas@nycollege.edu. *Web site:* http://www.nycollege.edu/.

Niagara County Community College
Sanborn, New York

- **State and locally supported** 2-year, founded 1962, part of State University of New York System
- **Rural** 287-acre campus with easy access to Buffalo
- **Endowment** $2.9 million
- **Coed,** 7,435 undergraduate students, 63% full-time, 56% women, 44% men

Undergraduates 4,697 full-time, 2,738 part-time. Students come from 16 states and territories; 5 other countries; 1% are from out of state; 4% transferred in; 4% live on campus.

Freshmen *Admission:* 4,809 applied, 4,809 admitted, 1,778 enrolled. *Average high school GPA:* 2.48.

Faculty *Total:* 391, 29% full-time, 16% with terminal degrees. *Student/faculty ratio:* 17:1.

Majors Accounting; administrative assistant and secretarial science; animal sciences; biological and physical sciences; business administration and management; chemical technology; computer science; consumer merchandising/retailing management; criminal justice/law enforcement administration; culinary arts; design and applied arts related; drafting and design technology; drafting/design engineering technologies related; dramatic/theater arts; fine/studio arts; general studies; hospitality administration; humanities; human services; information science/studies; liberal arts and sciences/liberal studies; mass communication/media; mathematics; medical/clinical assistant; medical radiologic technology; music; natural resources/conservation; occupational health and industrial hygiene; parks, recreation and leisure; physical education teaching and coaching; physical therapy technology; registered nursing/registered nurse; social sciences; sport and fitness administration/management; surgical technology; web page, digital/multimedia and information resources design.

Academics *Calendar:* semesters. *Degree:* certificates and associate. *Special study options:* academic remediation for entering students, adult/continuing education programs, advanced placement credit, cooperative education, double majors, honors programs, independent study, internships, off-campus study, part-time degree program, services for LD students, student-designed majors, study abroad, summer session for credit. *ROTC:* Army (c).

Library Henrietta G. Lewis Library with 98,908 titles, 333 serial subscriptions, 5,513 audiovisual materials, an OPAC, a Web page.

Student Life *Housing Options:* coed. Campus housing is provided by a third party. *Activities and Organizations:* drama/theater group, student-run newspaper, radio station, choral group, student radio station, Student Nurses Association, Phi Theta Kappa, Alpha Beta Gamma, Physical Education Club. *Campus security:* 24-hour emergency response devices and patrols, student patrols, late-night transport/escort service. *Student services:* health clinic, personal/psychological counseling.

Athletics Member NJCAA. *Intercollegiate sports:* baseball M, basketball M(s)/W(s), golf M/W, lacrosse M/W, soccer M/W, softball W, wrestling M(s). *Intramural sports:* basketball M/W, racquetball M/W, skiing (cross-country) M(c)/W(c), soccer M/W, swimming and diving M/W, tennis M/W, volleyball W.

Costs (2011–12) *Tuition:* state resident $3480 full-time, $145 per credit hour part-time; nonresident $6960 full-time, $290 per credit hour part-time. Full-time tuition and fees vary according to course load and program. Part-time tuition and fees vary according to course load and program. *Required fees:* $320 full-time. *Payment plan:* installment. *Waivers:* senior citizens and employees or children of employees.

Financial Aid Of all full-time matriculated undergraduates who enrolled in 2009, 4,021 applied for aid, 4,021 were judged to have need. 203 Federal Work-Study jobs (averaging $2210). 91 state and other part-time jobs (averaging $590). *Average financial aid package:* $3312. *Average need-based loan:* $4715. *Average need-based gift aid:* $1485.

Applying *Options:* electronic application, early admission. *Required:* high school transcript. *Required for some:* minimum 2.0 GPA. *Notification:* continuous until 8/31 (freshmen), continuous until 8/31 (transfers).

Freshman Application Contact Ms. Kathy Saunders, Director of Enrollment Services, Niagara County Community College, 3111 Saunders Settlement Road, Sanborn, NY 14132. *Phone:* 716-614-6200. *Fax:* 716-614-6820. *E-mail:* admissions@niagaracc.suny.edu. *Web site:* http://www.niagaracc.suny.edu/.

North Country Community College
Saranac Lake, New York

Freshman Application Contact Enrollment Management Assistant, North Country Community College, 23 Santanoni Avenue, PO Box 89, Saranac Lake, NY 12983-0089. *Phone:* 518-891-2915 Ext. 686. *Toll-free phone:* 888-TRY-NCCC Ext. 233. *Fax:* 518-891-0898. *E-mail:* info@nccc.edu. *Web site:* http://www.nccc.edu/.

Olean Business Institute
Olean, New York

- **Proprietary** 2-year, founded 1961
- **Small-town** campus
- **Coed**

Academics *Calendar:* semesters. *Degree:* diplomas and associate. *Special study options:* double majors, internships, part-time degree program, summer session for credit.

Student Life *Campus security:* 24-hour emergency response devices, late-night transport/escort service.

Applying *Application fee:* $25. *Required:* high school transcript. *Required for some:* essay or personal statement, interview.

Freshman Application Contact Olean Business Institute, 301 North Union Street, Olean, NY 14760-2691. *Phone:* 716-372-7978. *Web site:* http://www.obi.edu/.

Onondaga Community College
Syracuse, New York

- **State and locally supported** 2-year, founded 1962, part of State University of New York System
- **Suburban** 194-acre campus
- **Endowment** $5.6 million
- **Coed,** 11,755 undergraduate students, 58% full-time, 52% women, 48% men

Undergraduates 6,836 full-time, 4,919 part-time. Students come from 13 states and territories; 27 other countries; 0.3% are from out of state; 12% Black or African American, non-Hispanic/Latino; 4% Hispanic/Latino; 2% Asian, non-Hispanic/Latino; 2% American Indian or Alaska Native, non-Hispanic/Latino; 1% Two or more races, non-Hispanic/Latino; 7% Race/ethnicity unknown; 0.5% international; 6% transferred in; 5% live on campus. *Retention:* 56% of full-time freshmen returned.

Freshmen *Admission:* 7,852 applied, 5,447 admitted, 1,994 enrolled.

Faculty *Total:* 647, 26% full-time. *Student/faculty ratio:* 26:1.

Majors Accounting; accounting technology and bookkeeping; architectural engineering technology; architectural technology; art; automobile/automotive mechanics technology; business administration and management; business/commerce; computer engineering technology; computer science; computer systems networking and telecommunications; computer typography and composition equipment operation; construction engineering technology; criminal justice/law enforcement administration; criminal justice/police science; design and applied arts related; education (multiple levels); electrical and electronic engineering technologies related; electrical, electronic and communications engineering technology; engineering science; environmental engineering technology; fire prevention and safety technology; general studies; health information/medical records technology; health professions related; homeland security, law enforcement, firefighting and protective services related; hospitality administration; humanities; interior design; liberal arts and sciences and humanities related; mechanical engineering/mechanical technology; music; parks, recreation and leisure; photography; physical therapy technology; public administration and social service professions related; radio and television; registered nursing/registered nurse; respiratory care therapy; speech communication and rhetoric.

Academics *Calendar:* semesters. *Degree:* certificates, diplomas, and associate. *Special study options:* academic remediation for entering students, accelerated degree program, adult/continuing education programs, advanced placement credit, cooperative education, distance learning, English as a second language, external degree program, honors programs, internships, part-time

degree program, services for LD students, study abroad, summer session for credit. *ROTC:* Air Force (c).

Library Sidney B. Coulter Library with 91,037 titles, 244 serial subscriptions, 14,834 audiovisual materials, an OPAC, a Web page.

Student Life *Housing Options:* coed. Campus housing is provided by a third party. *Activities and Organizations:* drama/theater group, student-run newspaper, radio station, choral group. *Campus security:* 24-hour emergency response devices and patrols, controlled dormitory access. *Student services:* health clinic, personal/psychological counseling.

Athletics Member NJCAA. *Intercollegiate sports:* baseball M, basketball M/W, lacrosse M/W, soccer M/W, softball W, tennis M/W, volleyball W. *Intramural sports:* basketball M/W, golf M/W, skiing (downhill) M/W, swimming and diving M/W, tennis M/W, volleyball M/W.

Costs (2011–12) *Tuition:* area resident $3784 full-time, $151 per credit hour part-time; state resident $7568 full-time, $302 per credit hour part-time; nonresident $7568 full-time, $302 per credit hour part-time. Full-time tuition and fees vary according to program. Part-time tuition and fees vary according to course load and program. *Required fees:* $460 full-time, $96 per term part-time. *Room and board:* room only: $5832. Room and board charges vary according to board plan. *Payment plan:* installment. *Waivers:* senior citizens and employees or children of employees.

Financial Aid Of all full-time matriculated undergraduates who enrolled in 2008, 5,402 applied for aid, 4,623 were judged to have need, 70 had their need fully met. 102 Federal Work-Study jobs (averaging $2762). *Average percent of need met:* 51%. *Average financial aid package:* $5742. *Average need-based loan:* $2894. *Average need-based gift aid:* $4536.

Applying *Options:* electronic application. *Required:* high school transcript. Some programs require specific prerequisite courses and/or tests to be admitted directly to the program. An alternate program is offered. *Required for some:* minimum 2.0 GPA; interview. *Application deadlines:* 8/13 (freshmen), 8/13 (transfers). *Notification:* continuous (freshmen), continuous (transfers).

Freshman Application Contact Mrs. Katherine Perry, Director of Admissions, Onondaga Community College, 4585 West Seneca Turnpike, Syracuse, NY 13215. *Phone:* 315-488-2602. *Fax:* 315-488-2107. *E-mail:* admissions@sunyocc.edu. *Web site:* http://www.sunyocc.edu/.

Orange County Community College
Middletown, New York

Freshman Application Contact Michael Roe, Director of Admissions and Recruitment, Orange County Community College, 115 South Street, Middletown, NY 10940. *Phone:* 845-341-4205. *Fax:* 845-343-1228. *E-mail:* apply@sunyorange.edu. *Web site:* http://www.sunyorange.edu/.

Phillips Beth Israel School of Nursing
New York, New York

- **Independent** 2-year, founded 1904
- **Urban** campus
- **Endowment** $1.2 million
- **Coed,** 251 undergraduate students, 7% full-time, 77% women, 23% men

Undergraduates 17 full-time, 234 part-time. Students come from 9 states and territories; 6 other countries; 15% are from out of state; 23% Black or African American, non-Hispanic/Latino; 9% Hispanic/Latino; 14% Asian, non-Hispanic/Latino; 4% Native Hawaiian or other Pacific Islander, non-Hispanic/Latino; 40% transferred in. *Retention:* 84% of full-time freshmen returned.

Freshmen *Admission:* 145 applied, 12 admitted, 7 enrolled. *Average high school GPA:* 2.9. *Test scores:* SAT critical reading scores over 500: 100%; SAT math scores over 500: 100%.

Faculty *Total:* 25, 40% full-time, 32% with terminal degrees. *Student/faculty ratio:* 10:1.

Majors Health professions related; registered nursing/registered nurse.

Academics *Calendar:* semesters. *Degree:* associate. *Special study options:* academic remediation for entering students, advanced placement credit, cooperative education, distance learning, honors programs, off-campus study, part-time degree program, services for LD students, summer session for credit.

Library Phillips Health Science Library with 12,000 titles, 950 serial subscriptions, an OPAC.

Student Life *Housing:* college housing not available. *Activities and Organizations:* student-run newspaper, choral group, Student Government Organization, National Student Nurses Association. *Campus security:* 24-hour emergency response devices. *Student services:* health clinic, personal/psychological counseling.

Standardized Tests *Required:* nursing exam (for admission). *Recommended:* SAT (for admission).

Costs (2011–12) *Tuition:* $16,400 full-time, $400 per credit part-time. Full-time tuition and fees vary according to course load. Part-time tuition and fees vary according to course load. *Required fees:* $2590 full-time. *Payment plan:* installment. *Waivers:* employees or children of employees.

Financial Aid *Financial aid deadline:* 6/1.

Applying *Options:* deferred entrance. *Application fee:* $50. *Required:* essay or personal statement, high school transcript, minimum 2.5 GPA, 2 letters of recommendation, interview, entrance exam. *Application deadlines:* 4/1 (freshmen), 4/1 (transfers). *Notification:* continuous (freshmen), continuous (transfers).

Freshman Application Contact Mrs. Bernice Pass-Stern, Assistant Dean, Phillips Beth Israel School of Nursing, 776 Sixth Avenue, 4th Floor, New York, NY 10010-6354. *Phone:* 212-614-6176. *Fax:* 212-614-6109. *E-mail:* bstern@chpnet.org. *Web site:* http://www.futurenursebi.org/.

Plaza College

Jackson Heights, New York

- **Proprietary** primarily 2-year, founded 1916
- **Urban** campus with easy access to New York City
- **Coed**

Academics *Calendar:* semesters. *Degrees:* associate and bachelor's. *Special study options:* academic remediation for entering students, English as a second language, internships, services for LD students, summer session for credit.

Student Life *Campus security:* 24-hour emergency response devices.

Standardized Tests *Required:* CPAt (for admission).

Costs (2010–11) *One-time required fee:* $100. *Tuition:* $9900 full-time. Full-time tuition and fees vary according to program. Part-time tuition and fees vary according to course load and program. *Required fees:* $1450 full-time.

Applying *Options:* electronic application. *Application fee:* $100. *Required:* essay or personal statement, interview, placement test.

Freshman Application Contact Dean Rose Ann Black, Dean of Administration, Plaza College, 74-09 37th Avenue, Jackson Heights, NY 11372. *Phone:* 718-779-1430. *Toll-free phone:* 877-752-9233. *E-mail:* info@plazacollege.edu. *Web site:* http://www.plazacollege.edu/.

Queensborough Community College of the City University of New York

Bayside, New York

Freshman Application Contact Ms. Ann Tullio, Director of Registration, Queensborough Community College of the City University of New York, 222-05 56th Avenue, Bayside, NY 11364. *Phone:* 718-631-6307. *Fax:* 718-281-5189. *Web site:* http://www.qcc.cuny.edu/.

Rockland Community College

Suffern, New York

- **State and locally supported** 2-year, founded 1959, part of State University of New York System
- **Suburban** 150-acre campus with easy access to New York City
- **Coed**

Undergraduates 4,314 full-time, 2,670 part-time. 2% are from out of state; 7% transferred in. *Retention:* 69% of full-time freshmen returned.

Academics *Calendar:* semesters. *Degree:* certificates and associate. *Special study options:* academic remediation for entering students, adult/continuing education programs, advanced placement credit, cooperative education, distance learning, double majors, English as a second language, honors programs, independent study, internships, part-time degree program, services for LD students, student-designed majors, study abroad, summer session for credit.

Student Life *Campus security:* 24-hour emergency response devices and patrols, student patrols, late-night transport/escort service.

Athletics Member NJCAA.

Costs (2010–11) *Tuition:* state resident $3515 full-time, $146 per credit hour part-time; nonresident $7030 full-time, $292 per credit hour part-time. Full-time tuition and fees vary according to course load and program. Part-time tuition and fees vary according to course load and program. *Required fees:* $293 full-time. *Payment plans:* installment, deferred payment.

Financial Aid Of all full-time matriculated undergraduates who enrolled in 2008, 60 Federal Work-Study jobs (averaging $2213). *Average need-based loan:* $3781. *Average need-based gift aid:* $3523.

Applying *Options:* early admission, deferred entrance. *Required:* high school transcript.

Freshman Application Contact Rockland Community College, 145 College Road, Suffern, NY 10901-3699. *Phone:* 845-574-4237. *Toll-free phone:* 800-722-7666. *Web site:* http://www.sunyrockland.edu/.

St. Elizabeth College of Nursing

Utica, New York

- **Independent** 2-year, founded 1904, administratively affiliated with St. Elizabeth Medical Center
- **Small-town** campus with easy access to Syracuse
- **Coed**
- 45% of applicants were admitted

Undergraduates 157 full-time, 82 part-time. Students come from 5 states and territories; 4 other countries; 2% are from out of state; 42% transferred in. *Retention:* 56% of full-time freshmen returned.

Faculty *Student/faculty ratio:* 10:1.

Academics *Calendar:* semesters. *Degree:* associate. *Special study options:* accelerated degree program, distance learning, off-campus study, part-time degree program, services for LD students, summer session for credit.

Student Life *Campus security:* 24-hour patrols.

Standardized Tests *Recommended:* SAT or ACT (for admission).

Costs (2010–11) *Tuition:* $11,530 full-time, $325 per credit hour part-time. Full-time tuition and fees vary according to course load, program, and student level. Part-time tuition and fees vary according to course load, program, and student level. *Required fees:* $950 full-time, $475 per term part-time.

Applying *Application fee:* $65. *Required:* essay or personal statement, high school transcript, 2 letters of recommendation. *Recommended:* minimum 2.5 GPA.

Freshman Application Contact St. Elizabeth College of Nursing, 2215 Genesee Street, Utica, NY 13501. *Phone:* 315-798-8253. *Web site:* http://www.secon.edu/.

St. Joseph's College of Nursing

Syracuse, New York

- **Independent religious** 2-year, founded 1898
- **Urban** campus
- **Coed,** 273 undergraduate students, 61% full-time, 91% women, 9% men

Undergraduates 166 full-time, 107 part-time. Students come from 2 states and territories; 25% live on campus.

Freshmen *Admission:* 42 applied, 23 admitted, 10 enrolled. *Average high school GPA:* 3. *Test scores:* SAT critical reading scores over 500: 56%; SAT math scores over 500: 50%; ACT scores over 18: 100%; ACT scores over 24: 1%.

Faculty *Total:* 29, 55% full-time. *Student/faculty ratio:* 9:1.

Majors Registered nursing/registered nurse.

Academics *Calendar:* semesters. *Degree:* associate. *Special study options:* academic remediation for entering students, adult/continuing education programs, advanced placement credit, cooperative education, internships, part-time degree program, services for LD students.

Library St. Joseph's Hospital Health Center School of Nursing Library with 4,500 titles, 230 serial subscriptions, 500 audiovisual materials, an OPAC.

Student Life *Housing Options:* coed. Campus housing is university owned. Freshman applicants given priority for college housing. *Activities and Organizations:* New York State Student Nurse's Association, Syracuse Area Black Nurses Association, Student Body Organization. *Campus security:* 24-hour patrols. *Student services:* health clinic, personal/psychological counseling, legal services.

Standardized Tests *Required:* SAT or ACT (for admission).

Costs (2011–12) *Tuition:* $16,245 full-time, $465 per credit hour part-time. Full-time tuition and fees vary according to course load. Part-time tuition and fees vary according to course load. *Required fees:* $200 full-time. *Room only:* $4200. *Payment plan:* installment. *Waivers:* employees or children of employees.

Applying *Options:* deferred entrance. *Application fee:* $50. *Required:* essay or personal statement, high school transcript, minimum 3.0 GPA, 2 letters of recommendation, interview.

Freshman Application Contact Ms. Rhonda Reader, Assistant Dean for Admissions, St. Joseph's College of Nursing, 206 Prospect Avenue, Syracuse, NY 13203. *Phone:* 315-448-5040. *Fax:* 315-448-5745. *E-mail:* collegeofnursing@sjhsyr.org. *Web site:* http://www.sjhsyr.org/nursing/.

St. Paul's School of Nursing

Flushing, New York

Director of Admissions Nancy Wolinski, Chairperson of Admissions, St. Paul's School of Nursing, 30-50 Whitestone Expressway, Suite 400, Flushing, NY 11354. *Phone:* 718-357-0500 Ext. 131. *E-mail:* nwolinski@svcmcny.org. *Web site:* http://www.stpaulsschoolofnursing.com/.

Samaritan Hospital School of Nursing

Troy, New York

Director of Admissions Ms. Jennifer Marrone, Student Services Coordinator, Samaritan Hospital School of Nursing, 2215 Burdett Avenue, Troy, NY 12180. *Phone:* 518-271-3734. *Fax:* 518-271-3303. *E-mail:* marronej@nehealth.com. *Web site:* http://www.nehealth.com/.

Schenectady County Community College

Schenectady, New York

Freshman Application Contact Mr. David Sampson, Director of Admissions, Schenectady County Community College, 78 Washington Avenue, Schenectady, NY 12305-2294. *Phone:* 518-381-1370. *E-mail:* sampsodg@gw.sunysccc.edu. *Web site:* http://www.sunysccc.edu/.

Simmons Institute of Funeral Service

Syracuse, New York

Freshman Application Contact Ms. Vera Wightman, Director of Admissions, Simmons Institute of Funeral Service, 1828 South Avenue, Syracuse, NY 13207. *Phone:* 315-475-5142. *Toll-free phone:* 800-727-3536. *Fax:* 315-475-3817. *E-mail:* admissions@simmonsinstitute.com. *Web site:* http://www.simmonsinstitute.com/.

State University of New York College of Environmental Science & Forestry, Ranger School

Wanakena, New York

- **State-supported** 2-year, founded 1912
- **Rural** 2800-acre campus
- **Coed, primarily men,** 36 undergraduate students, 100% full-time, 17% women, 83% men

Undergraduates 36 full-time. 97% transferred in; 100% live on campus.
Freshmen *Admission:* 1 enrolled.
Faculty *Total:* 6, 100% full-time, 17% with terminal degrees. *Student/faculty ratio:* 6:1.
Majors Forest technology; natural resources/conservation; surveying technology.
Academics *Calendar:* semesters. *Degrees:* associate (The associate degrees offered at The Ranger School campus of SUNY-ESF are 1 + 1 programs enrolling students for the second year of study after they complete their first-year requirements at SUNY-ESF's Syracuse campus or the college of their choice). *Special study options:* advanced placement credit, distance learning.
Library Ranger School Library with 1,500 titles, 60 serial subscriptions, an OPAC.
Student Life *Housing Options:* coed. Campus housing is university owned. *Campus security:* 24-hour emergency response devices. *Student services:* health clinic, personal/psychological counseling, legal services.
Athletics *Intramural sports:* basketball M/W, ice hockey M/W, skiing (cross-country) M/W, skiing (downhill) M/W, softball M/W, volleyball M/W, weight lifting M/W.
Standardized Tests *Required:* SAT or ACT (for admission).
Costs (2011–12) *Tuition:* state resident $4970 full-time, $207 per credit hour part-time; nonresident $13,380 full-time, $558 per credit hour part-time. Full-time tuition and fees vary according to location. Part-time tuition and fees vary according to location. *Room and board:* $10,020. Room and board charges vary according to housing facility. *Payment plan:* installment.
Financial Aid Of all full-time matriculated undergraduates who enrolled in 2009, 43 applied for aid, 40 were judged to have need, 36 had their need fully met. 5 Federal Work-Study jobs (averaging $1801). In 2009, 2 non-need-based awards were made. *Average percent of need met:* 90%. *Average financial aid package:* $10,051. *Average need-based loan:* $4260. *Average need-based gift aid:* $7749. *Average non-need-based aid:* $2250.
Applying *Options:* electronic application, deferred entrance. *Application fee:* $50. *Required:* minimum 2.0 GPA. *Recommended:* essay or personal statement, high school transcript, minimum 2.5 GPA, interview. *Application deadlines:* rolling (freshmen), rolling (transfers), 11/15 (early action).
Freshman Application Contact Ms. Susan Sanford, Director of Admissions, State University of New York College of Environmental Science & Forestry, Ranger School, Syracuse, NY 13210-2779. *Phone:* 315-470-6600. *Toll-free phone:* 800-777-7373. *Fax:* 315-470-6933. *E-mail:* esfinfo@esf.edu. *Web site:* http://www.esf.edu/rangerschool/default.asp.

State University of New York College of Technology at Alfred

Alfred, New York

- **State-supported** primarily 2-year, founded 1908, part of The State University of New York System
- **Rural** 1084-acre campus
- **Endowment** $3.1 million
- **Coed,** 3,717 undergraduate students, 90% full-time, 37% women, 63% men

Undergraduates 3,359 full-time, 358 part-time. Students come from 35 states and territories; 19 other countries; 9% Black or African American, non-Hispanic/Latino; 5% Hispanic/Latino; 3% Asian, non-Hispanic/Latino; 0.1% Native Hawaiian or other Pacific Islander, non-Hispanic/Latino; 0.2% American Indian or Alaska Native, non-Hispanic/Latino; 2% Two or more races, non-Hispanic/Latino; 0.7% Race/ethnicity unknown; 8% transferred in; 74% live on campus. *Retention:* 85% of full-time freshmen returned.
Freshmen *Admission:* 5,386 applied, 2,852 admitted, 1,285 enrolled. *Average high school GPA:* 2.8.
Faculty *Total:* 206, 77% full-time. *Student/faculty ratio:* 20:1.
Majors Automobile/automotive mechanics technology; business administration and management; computer/information technology services administration related; construction engineering technology; court reporting; electromechanical technology; liberal arts and sciences/liberal studies; mechanical engineering/mechanical technology; social sciences; welding technology.
Academics *Calendar:* semesters. *Degrees:* certificates, associate, and bachelor's. *Special study options:* academic remediation for entering students, adult/continuing education programs, advanced placement credit, cooperative education, distance learning, double majors, English as a second language, honors programs, independent study, internships, off-campus study, part-time degree program, services for LD students, student-designed majors, study abroad, summer session for credit. *ROTC:* Army (c).
Library Walter C. Hinkle Memorial Library plus 1 other with 69,648 titles, 61,503 serial subscriptions, 4,048 audiovisual materials, an OPAC, a Web page.
Student Life *Housing Options:* coed, men-only, women-only, disabled students. Campus housing is university owned. Freshman campus housing is guaranteed. *Activities and Organizations:* drama/theater group, student-run newspaper, radio station, choral group, Outdoor Recreation Club, International Club, intramural sports, Sustainability Club, Student Senate, national fraternities, national sororities. *Campus security:* 24-hour emergency response devices and patrols, late-night transport/escort service, controlled dormitory access, residence hall entrance guards. *Student services:* health clinic, personal/psychological counseling.
Athletics Member NJCAA. *Intercollegiate sports:* baseball M, basketball M/W, cross-country running M/W, football M(s), lacrosse M, soccer M/W, softball W, swimming and diving M/W, track and field M/W, volleyball W, wrestling M. *Intramural sports:* basketball M/W, football M/W, golf M/W, ice hockey M(c), rock climbing M/W, soccer M/W, softball M/W, tennis M/W, ultimate Frisbee M/W, volleyball M/W.
Standardized Tests *Required for some:* SAT or ACT (for admission). *Recommended:* SAT or ACT (for admission).
Costs (2011–12) *Tuition:* state resident $4970 full-time, $207 per credit part-time; nonresident $9100 full-time, $379 per credit part-time. Full-time tuition and fees vary according to course load and degree level. Part-time tuition and fees vary according to course load and degree level. *Required fees:* $1248 full-time, $121 per credit hour part-time, $5 per term part-time. *Room and board:* $9690; room only: $5600. Room and board charges vary according to board plan and housing facility. *Payment plan:* installment. *Waivers:* employees or children of employees.
Financial Aid Of all full-time matriculated undergraduates who enrolled in 2009, 3,097 applied for aid, 2,727 were judged to have need, 230 had their need fully met. 283 Federal Work-Study jobs (averaging $1210). In 2009, 470 non-need-based awards were made. *Average percent of need met:* 72%. *Average financial aid package:* $12,584. *Average need-based loan:* $6226. *Average need-based gift aid:* $4515. *Average non-need-based aid:* $1886. *Average indebtedness upon graduation:* $29,741.
Applying *Options:* electronic application. *Application fee:* $40. *Required:* high school transcript, minimum 2.0 GPA. *Recommended:* essay or personal statement, interview. *Application deadlines:* rolling (freshmen), rolling (out-of-state freshmen), rolling (transfers). *Notification:* continuous (freshmen), continuous (out-of-state freshmen), continuous (transfers).
Freshman Application Contact Mrs. Deborah Goodrich, Associate Vice President for Enrollment Management, State University of New York College of Technology at Alfred, Huntington Administration Building, 10 Upper College Drive, Alfred, NY 14802. *Phone:* 607-587-4215. *Toll-free phone:* 800-4-ALFRED. *Fax:* 607-587-4299. *E-mail:* admissions@alfredstate.edu. *Web site:* http://www.alfredstate.edu/.

Suffolk County Community College

Selden, New York

- **State and locally supported** 2-year, founded 1959, part of State University of New York System
- **Small-town** 500-acre campus with easy access to New York City
- **Coed,** 28,294 undergraduate students, 49% full-time, 54% women, 46% men

Undergraduates 13,853 full-time, 14,441 part-time. Students come from 14 states and territories; 1% are from out of state.

Freshmen *Average high school GPA:* 2.5. *Test scores:* SAT critical reading scores over 500: 36%; SAT math scores over 500: 38%; ACT scores over 18: 30%; SAT critical reading scores over 600: 8%; SAT math scores over 600: 8%; ACT scores over 24: 4%; SAT critical reading scores over 700: 1%.

Faculty *Student/faculty ratio:* 18:1.

Majors Accounting; art; automobile/automotive mechanics technology; biological and physical sciences; biology/biological sciences; business administration and management; chemistry; child development; civil engineering technology; communications systems installation and repair technology; computer and information sciences and support services related; computer programming; computer science; construction engineering technology; consumer merchandising/retailing management; criminal justice/law enforcement administration; criminal justice/police science; culinary arts; data processing and data processing technology; dietetics; drafting and design technology; dramatic/theater arts; electrical, electronic and communications engineering technology; engineering; engineering science; English; humanities; human services; information science/studies; information technology; interior design; journalism; kindergarten/preschool education; legal assistant/paralegal; liberal arts and sciences/liberal studies; marketing/marketing management; mathematics; music; photographic and film/video technology; physical therapy; registered nursing/registered nurse; sign language interpretation and translation; social sciences; substance abuse/addiction counseling; women's studies.

Academics *Calendar:* semesters. *Degree:* certificates, diplomas, and associate. *Special study options:* academic remediation for entering students, adult/continuing education programs, advanced placement credit, cooperative education, distance learning, English as a second language, freshman honors college, honors programs, independent study, internships, off-campus study, part-time degree program, services for LD students, study abroad, summer session for credit. *ROTC:* Army (c).

Library an OPAC, a Web page.

Student Life *Housing:* college housing not available. *Activities and Organizations:* drama/theater group, student-run newspaper, choral group. *Campus security:* 24-hour emergency response devices and patrols. *Student services:* personal/psychological counseling.

Athletics Member NJCAA. *Intercollegiate sports:* baseball M, basketball M/W, bowling M/W, cross-country running M/W, golf M/W, lacrosse M, soccer M, softball W, swimming and diving M/W, tennis M/W, track and field M/W, volleyball W.

Costs (2010–11) *Tuition:* area resident $3776 full-time, $158 per credit hour part-time; state resident $7552 full-time, $316 per credit hour part-time; nonresident $7552 full-time, $316 per credit hour part-time. *Required fees:* $420 full-time, $104 per term part-time. *Payment plan:* installment.

Financial Aid Of all full-time matriculated undergraduates who enrolled in 2009, 109 Federal Work-Study jobs (averaging $1377).

Applying *Options:* electronic application, deferred entrance. *Application fee:* $35. *Required:* high school transcript. *Required for some:* interview. *Application deadlines:* rolling (freshmen), rolling (transfers). *Notification:* continuous (freshmen), continuous (transfers).

Freshman Application Contact Suffolk County Community College, 533 College Road, Selden, NY 11784-2899. *Phone:* 631-451-4000. *Web site:* http://www.sunysuffolk.edu/.

Sullivan County Community College

Loch Sheldrake, New York

Freshman Application Contact Ms. Sari Rosenheck, Director of Admissions and Registration Services, Sullivan County Community College, 112 College Road, Loch Sheldrake, NY 12759. *Phone:* 845-434-5750 Ext. 4200. *Toll-free phone:* 800-577-5243. *Fax:* 845-434-4806. *E-mail:* sarir@sullivan.suny.edu. *Web site:* http://www.sullivan.suny.edu/.

TCI–The College of Technology

New York, New York

Freshman Application Contact Director of Admission, TCI–The College of Technology, 320 West 31st Street, New York, NY 10001-2705. *Phone:* 212-594-4000. *Toll-free phone:* 800-878-8246. *E-mail:* admissions@tcicollege.edu. *Web site:* http://www.tciedu.com/.

Tompkins Cortland Community College

Dryden, New York

- **State and locally supported** 2-year, founded 1968, part of State University of New York System
- **Rural** 250-acre campus with easy access to Syracuse
- **Endowment** $8.0 million
- **Coed,** 3,850 undergraduate students, 77% full-time, 55% women, 45% men

Undergraduates 2,968 full-time, 882 part-time. Students come from 19 states and territories; 26 other countries; 1% are from out of state; 8% Black or African American, non-Hispanic/Latino; 6% Hispanic/Latino; 1% Asian, non-Hispanic/Latino; 0.1% Native Hawaiian or other Pacific Islander, non-Hispanic/Latino; 0.5% American Indian or Alaska Native, non-Hispanic/Latino; 2% Two or more races, non-Hispanic/Latino; 0.1% Race/ethnicity unknown; 2% international; 10% transferred in; 21% live on campus.

Freshmen *Admission:* 1,122 enrolled.

Faculty *Total:* 324, 22% full-time, 15% with terminal degrees. *Student/faculty ratio:* 19:1.

Majors Accounting technology and bookkeeping; administrative assistant and secretarial science; biotechnology; business administration and management; business, management, and marketing related; child-care and support services management; commercial and advertising art; community organization and advocacy; computer and information sciences; computer and information sciences and support services related; construction trades related; creative writing; criminal justice/law enforcement administration; early childhood education; electrical, electronic and communications engineering technology; engineering; forensic science and technology; hotel/motel administration; humanities; information science/studies; international business/trade/commerce; kindergarten/preschool education; legal assistant/paralegal; liberal arts and sciences/liberal studies; natural resources/conservation; parks, recreation and leisure facilities management; parks, recreation, leisure, and fitness studies related; photography; radio and television broadcasting technology; registered nursing/registered nurse; speech communication and rhetoric; sport and fitness administration/management; substance abuse/addiction counseling; web/multimedia management and webmaster.

Academics *Calendar:* semesters. *Degree:* certificates and associate. *Special study options:* academic remediation for entering students, adult/continuing education programs, advanced placement credit, cooperative education, distance learning, double majors, English as a second language, honors programs, independent study, internships, off-campus study, part-time degree program, services for LD students, study abroad, summer session for credit.

Library Gerald A. Barry Memorial Library plus 1 other with 65,386 titles, 200 serial subscriptions, 3,445 audiovisual materials, an OPAC, a Web page.

Student Life *Housing Options:* coed. Campus housing is provided by a third party. *Activities and Organizations:* drama/theater group, College Entertainment Board, Sport Management Club, Nursing Club, Media Club, Writer's Guild. *Campus security:* 24-hour patrols, late-night transport/escort service, controlled dormitory access, armed peace officers. *Student services:* health clinic, personal/psychological counseling.

Athletics Member NJCAA. *Intercollegiate sports:* baseball M, basketball M/W, golf M/W, lacrosse M, soccer M/W, softball W, volleyball W. *Intramural sports:* archery M/W, badminton M/W, basketball M/W, bowling M/W, football M/W, golf M/W, lacrosse M/W, racquetball M/W, skiing (cross-country) M/W, skiing (downhill) M/W, soccer M/W, softball M/W, squash M/W, swimming and diving M/W, table tennis M/W, tennis M/W, ultimate Frisbee M/W, volleyball M/W, water polo M/W, weight lifting M/W, wrestling M/W.

Costs (2010–11) *Tuition:* state resident $3760 full-time, $139 per credit hour part-time; nonresident $7820 full-time, $288 per credit hour part-time. Part-time tuition and fees vary according to course load. *Required fees:* $626 full-time, $25 per credit hour part-time, $10 per term part-time. *Room and board:* $7950. Room and board charges vary according to board plan and housing facility. *Payment plans:* installment, deferred payment. *Waivers:* employees or children of employees.

Financial Aid Of all full-time matriculated undergraduates who enrolled in 2009, 150 Federal Work-Study jobs (averaging $1000). 150 state and other part-time jobs (averaging $1000).

Applying *Options:* electronic application, early admission, deferred entrance. *Application fee:* $15. *Required:* high school transcript. *Required for some:* essay or personal statement, interview. *Application deadlines:* rolling (freshmen), rolling (out-of-state freshmen), rolling (transfers). *Notification:* continuous (freshmen), continuous (out-of-state freshmen), continuous (transfers).

Freshman Application Contact Mr. Sandy Drumluk, Director of Admissions, Tompkins Cortland Community College, 170 North Street, PO Box 139, Dryden, NY 13053-0139. *Phone:* 607-844-6580. *Toll-free phone:* 888-567-8211. *Fax:* 607-844-6538. *E-mail:* admissions@tc3.edu. *Web site:* http://www.TC3.edu/.

Trocaire College
Buffalo, New York

Freshman Application Contact Mrs. Theresa Horner, Director of Records, Trocaire College, 360 Choate Avenue, Buffalo, NY 14220-2094. *Phone:* 716-827-2459. *Fax:* 716-828-6107. *E-mail:* info@trocaire.edu. *Web site:* http://www.trocaire.edu/.

Ulster County Community College
Stone Ridge, New York

- **State and locally supported** 2-year, founded 1961, part of State University of New York System
- **Rural** 165-acre campus
- **Endowment** $4.9 million
- **Coed**

Undergraduates 1,759 full-time, 1,781 part-time. Students come from 10 states and territories; 8 other countries; 6% transferred in.
Faculty *Student/faculty ratio:* 19:1.
Academics *Calendar:* semesters. *Degree:* certificates, diplomas, and associate. *Special study options:* academic remediation for entering students, adult/continuing education programs, advanced placement credit, cooperative education, distance learning, double majors, English as a second language, honors programs, independent study, internships, off-campus study, part-time degree program, services for LD students, student-designed majors, study abroad, summer session for credit.
Student Life *Campus security:* 24-hour emergency response devices and patrols.
Athletics Member NJCAA.
Costs (2010–11) *Tuition:* state resident $3820 full-time, $140 per credit hour part-time; nonresident $7640 full-time, $280 per credit hour part-time. *Required fees:* $500 full-time, $45 per course part-time, $19 per term part-time. *Payment plans:* installment, deferred payment.
Financial Aid Of all full-time matriculated undergraduates who enrolled in 2009, 45 Federal Work-Study jobs (averaging $1000).
Applying *Options:* electronic application, early admission, deferred entrance. *Required:* high school transcript.
Freshman Application Contact Admissions Office, Ulster County Community College, 491 Cottekill Road, Stone Ridge, NY 12484. *Phone:* 845-687-5022. *Toll-free phone:* 800-724-0833. *E-mail:* admissionsoffice@sunyulster.edu. *Web site:* http://www.sunyulster.edu/.

Utica School of Commerce
Utica, New York

Freshman Application Contact Senior Admissions Coordinator, Utica School of Commerce, 201 Bleecker Street, Utica, NY 13501-2280. *Phone:* 315-733-2300. *Toll-free phone:* 800-321-4USC. *Fax:* 315-733-9281. *Web site:* http://www.uscny.edu/.

Westchester Community College
Valhalla, New York

- **State and locally supported** 2-year, founded 1946, part of State University of New York System
- **Suburban** 218-acre campus with easy access to New York City
- **Coed,** 13,894 undergraduate students, 54% full-time, 54% women, 46% men

Undergraduates 7,549 full-time, 6,345 part-time. Students come from 12 states and territories; 57 other countries; 0.5% are from out of state; 9% transferred in.
Freshmen *Admission:* 5,530 applied, 5,530 admitted, 2,613 enrolled.
Faculty *Total:* 524, 32% full-time. *Student/faculty ratio:* 18:1.
Majors Accounting; administrative assistant and secretarial science; apparel and textile manufacturing; business administration and management; child development; civil engineering technology; clinical laboratory science/medical technology; clinical/medical laboratory technology; community organization and advocacy; computer and information sciences; computer and information sciences and support services related; computer and information sciences related; computer and information systems security; computer science; computer systems networking and telecommunications; consumer merchandising/retailing management; corrections; culinary arts; dance; data processing and data processing technology; design and applied arts related; dietetics; education (multiple levels); electrical, electronic and communications engineering technology; emergency medical technology (EMT paramedic); engineering science; engineering technology; environmental control technologies related; film/video and photographic arts related; finance; fine/studio arts; food technology and processing; humanities; information science/studies; international business/trade/commerce; legal assistant/paralegal; liberal arts and sciences/liberal studies; marketing/marketing management; mass communication/media; mechanical engineering/mechanical technology; public administration; registered nursing/registered nurse; respiratory care therapy; social sciences; substance abuse/addiction counseling; veterinary/animal health technology.
Academics *Calendar:* semesters. *Degree:* certificates and associate. *Special study options:* academic remediation for entering students, adult/continuing education programs, advanced placement credit, cooperative education, distance learning, double majors, English as a second language, honors programs, independent study, internships, off-campus study, part-time degree program, services for LD students, student-designed majors, study abroad, summer session for credit.
Library Harold L. Drimmer Library plus 1 other with 128,720 titles, 395 serial subscriptions, 7,745 audiovisual materials, an OPAC, a Web page.
Student Life *Housing:* college housing not available. *Activities and Organizations:* drama/theater group, student-run newspaper, radio station, choral group, Deca Fashion Retail, Future Educators, Respiratory Club, Black Student Union, Diversity Action. *Campus security:* 24-hour emergency response devices and patrols, late-night transport/escort service. *Student services:* health clinic, personal/psychological counseling, women's center.
Athletics Member NJCAA. *Intercollegiate sports:* baseball M, basketball M/W, bowling M/W, golf M, soccer M, softball W, volleyball W. *Intramural sports:* badminton M/W, basketball M/W, softball M/W, swimming and diving M/W, tennis M/W, volleyball M/W, weight lifting M/W.
Costs (2011–12) *Tuition:* state resident $3850 full-time, $161 per credit hour part-time; nonresident $9626 full-time, $403 per credit hour part-time. *Required fees:* $363 full-time, $83 per term part-time.
Financial Aid Of all full-time matriculated undergraduates who enrolled in 2009, 200 Federal Work-Study jobs (averaging $1000).
Applying *Options:* early admission. *Application fee:* $25. *Required:* high school transcript. *Recommended:* interview. *Application deadlines:* rolling (freshmen), rolling (transfers). *Notification:* continuous until 2/2 (freshmen), continuous (transfers).
Freshman Application Contact Ms. Gloria Leon, Director of Admissions, Westchester Community College, 75 Grasslands Road, Administration Building, Valhalla, NY 10595-1698. *Phone:* 914-606-6735. *Fax:* 914-606-6540. *E-mail:* admissions@sunywcc.edu. *Web site:* http://www.sunywcc.edu/.

Wood Tobe–Coburn School
New York, New York

- **Private** 2-year, founded 1879, part of Bradford Schools, Inc.
- **Urban** campus
- **Coed, primarily women,** 592 undergraduate students
- 83% of applicants were admitted

Freshmen *Admission:* 1,162 applied, 970 admitted.
Majors Accounting and business/management; business administration and management; computer programming; fashion/apparel design; fashion merchandising; graphic design; medical/clinical assistant; system, networking, and LAN/WAN management; tourism and travel services management.
Academics *Calendar:* semesters. *Degree:* diplomas and associate. *Special study options:* accelerated degree program, internships.
Student Life *Housing:* college housing not available.
Freshman Application Contact Admissions Office, Wood Tobe–Coburn School, 8 East 40th Street, New York, NY 10016. *Phone:* 212-686-9040. *Toll-free phone:* 800-394-9663. *Web site:* http://www.woodtobecoburn.edu/.

NORTH CAROLINA

Alamance Community College
Graham, North Carolina

- **State-supported** 2-year, founded 1959, part of North Carolina Community College System
- **Small-town** 48-acre campus
- **Endowment** $2.9 million
- **Coed,** 5,512 undergraduate students, 49% full-time, 65% women, 35% men

Undergraduates 2,710 full-time, 2,802 part-time. Students come from 6 states and territories; 1% are from out of state; 20% transferred in.
Freshmen *Admission:* 701 applied, 701 admitted, 701 enrolled. *Average high school GPA:* 2.
Faculty *Total:* 435, 26% full-time, 3% with terminal degrees. *Student/faculty ratio:* 12:1.
Majors Accounting technology and bookkeeping; animal sciences; applied horticulture/horticulture operations; automobile/automotive mechanics tech-

nology; banking and financial support services; biotechnology; business administration and management; carpentry; clinical/medical laboratory technology; commercial and advertising art; criminal justice/safety; culinary arts; electrical, electronic and communications engineering technology; executive assistant/executive secretary; heating, ventilation, air conditioning and refrigeration engineering technology; information science/studies; kindergarten/preschool education; legal administrative assistant/secretary; liberal arts and sciences/liberal studies; machine tool technology; mechanical engineering/mechanical technology; medical administrative assistant and medical secretary; medical/clinical assistant; office occupations and clerical services; registered nursing/registered nurse; retailing; teacher assistant/aide; welding technology.

Academics *Calendar:* semesters. *Degree:* certificates, diplomas, and associate. *Special study options:* academic remediation for entering students, adult/continuing education programs, cooperative education, distance learning, double majors, English as a second language, independent study, off-campus study, part-time degree program, services for LD students, summer session for credit.

Library Learning Resources Center with 22,114 titles, 185 serial subscriptions, an OPAC, a Web page.

Student Life *Housing:* college housing not available. *Campus security:* 24-hour emergency response devices and patrols, student patrols, late-night transport/escort service. *Student services:* personal/psychological counseling.

Athletics *Intramural sports:* basketball M/W, bowling M/W, tennis M/W, volleyball M/W.

Costs (2010–11) *Tuition:* state resident $1808 full-time, $57 per credit hour part-time; nonresident $7952 full-time, $249 per credit hour part-time. Full-time tuition and fees vary according to course load. Part-time tuition and fees vary according to course load. *Required fees:* $30 full-time, $16 per term part-time. *Waivers:* senior citizens.

Financial Aid Of all full-time matriculated undergraduates who enrolled in 2009, 4,000 applied for aid, 3,000 were judged to have need. 200 Federal Work-Study jobs. *Average percent of need met:* 30%. *Average financial aid package:* $4500. *Average need-based gift aid:* $4500. *Average indebtedness upon graduation:* $2500.

Applying *Options:* electronic application. *Required:* high school transcript. *Application deadlines:* rolling (freshmen), rolling (transfers). *Notification:* continuous (freshmen), continuous (transfers).

Freshman Application Contact Ms. Elizabeth Brehler, Director for Enrollment Management, Alamance Community College, Graham, NC 27253-8000. *Phone:* 336-506-4120. *Fax:* 336-506-4264. *E-mail:* brehlere@alamancecc.edu. *Web site:* http://www.alamancecc.edu/.

Asheville-Buncombe Technical Community College
Asheville, North Carolina

Freshman Application Contact Asheville-Buncombe Technical Community College, 340 Victoria Road, Asheville, NC 28801-4897. *Phone:* 828-254-1921 Ext. 7520. *Web site:* http://www.abtech.edu/.

Beaufort County Community College
Washington, North Carolina

- **State-supported** 2-year, founded 1967, part of North Carolina Community College System
- **Coed,** 1,923 undergraduate students

Undergraduates 35% Black or African American, non-Hispanic/Latino; 2% Hispanic/Latino; 0.1% Asian, non-Hispanic/Latino; 0.3% American Indian or Alaska Native, non-Hispanic/Latino; 2% Race/ethnicity unknown.

Freshmen *Admission:* 999 applied, 999 admitted.

Majors Accounting; administrative assistant and secretarial science; automobile/automotive mechanics technology; business administration and management; clinical/medical laboratory technology; computer programming; criminal justice/law enforcement administration; criminal justice/police science; drafting and design technology; electrical, electronic and communications engineering technology; heavy equipment maintenance technology; information science/studies; kindergarten/preschool education; liberal arts and sciences/liberal studies; mechanical engineering/mechanical technology; medical office management; registered nursing/registered nurse; welding technology.

Academics *Calendar:* semesters. *Degree:* certificates, diplomas, and associate. *Special study options:* academic remediation for entering students, advanced placement credit, cooperative education, distance learning, English as a second language, part-time degree program, services for LD students, summer session for credit.

Library Beaufort Community College Library with 25,734 titles, 214 serial subscriptions, an OPAC, a Web page.

Student Life *Housing:* college housing not available. *Activities and Organizations:* Student Government Association, Gamma Beta Phi, BECANS-Nursing. *Campus security:* 24-hour emergency response devices and patrols, late-night transport/escort service. *Student services:* personal/psychological counseling.

Standardized Tests *Required:* ACCUPLACER, COMPASS, Asset (for admission). *Recommended:* SAT or ACT (for admission).

Costs (2010–11) *Tuition:* state resident $1808 full-time, $57 per credit hour part-time; nonresident $7952 full-time, $249 per credit hour part-time. Part-time tuition and fees vary according to course load. *Required fees:* $64 full-time, $2 per credit hour part-time. *Waivers:* senior citizens and employees or children of employees.

Applying *Options:* electronic application. *Required for some:* high school transcript. *Application deadlines:* rolling (freshmen), rolling (out-of-state freshmen), rolling (transfers). *Notification:* continuous (freshmen), continuous (out-of-state freshmen), continuous (transfers).

Freshman Application Contact Mr. Gary Burbage, Director of Admissions, Beaufort County Community College, PO Box 1069, 5337 US Highway 264 East, Washington, NC 27889-1069. *Phone:* 252-940-6233. *Fax:* 252-940-6393. *E-mail:* garyb@beaufortccc.edu. *Web site:* http://www.beaufortccc.edu/

Bladen Community College
Dublin, North Carolina

- **State and locally supported** 2-year, founded 1967, part of North Carolina Community College System
- **Rural** 45-acre campus
- **Endowment** $72,151
- **Coed**

Undergraduates Students come from 3 states and territories. *Retention:* 35% of full-time freshmen returned.

Academics *Calendar:* semesters. *Degree:* certificates, diplomas, and associate. *Special study options:* academic remediation for entering students, adult/continuing education programs, advanced placement credit, distance learning, double majors, independent study, part-time degree program, services for LD students, summer session for credit.

Student Life *Campus security:* 14-hour patrols.

Standardized Tests *Required:* ACT COMPASS (for admission). *Recommended:* SAT or ACT (for admission).

Costs (2010–11) *Tuition:* state resident $1356 full-time, $57 per credit hour part-time; nonresident $5964 full-time, $249 per credit hour part-time. Full-time tuition and fees vary according to course load. Part-time tuition and fees vary according to course load. *Required fees:* $83 full-time, $28 per term part-time.

Financial Aid Of all full-time matriculated undergraduates who enrolled in 2008, 36 Federal Work-Study jobs (averaging $1278).

Applying *Options:* electronic application, deferred entrance. *Required:* high school transcript.

Freshman Application Contact Ms. Andrea Fisher, Enrollment Specialist, Bladen Community College, PO Box 266, Dublin, NC 28332. *Phone:* 910-879-5593. *Fax:* 910-879-5564. *E-mail:* acarterfisher@bladencc.edu. *Web site:* http://www.bladen.cc.nc.us/.

Blue Ridge Community College
Flat Rock, North Carolina

- **State and locally supported** 2-year, founded 1969, part of North Carolina Community College System
- **Small-town** 109-acre campus
- **Coed**

Undergraduates 766 full-time, 1,722 part-time. Students come from 6 states and territories; 1% are from out of state.

Academics *Calendar:* semesters. *Degree:* certificates, diplomas, and associate. *Special study options:* academic remediation for entering students, adult/continuing education programs, advanced placement credit, cooperative education, distance learning, double majors, English as a second language, internships, part-time degree program, services for LD students, summer session for credit.

Student Life *Campus security:* sheriff's deputy during class hours.

Athletics Member NJCAA.

Costs (2010–11) *Tuition:* state resident $1808 full-time, $57 per credit hour part-time; nonresident $7952 full-time, $249 per credit hour part-time. *Required fees:* $82 full-time, $33 per term part-time.

Financial Aid Of all full-time matriculated undergraduates who enrolled in 2009, 35 Federal Work-Study jobs (averaging $1920). 34 state and other part-time jobs (averaging $1920).

Applying *Options:* early admission. *Required:* high school transcript.

Freshman Application Contact Blue Ridge Community College, 180 West Campus Drive, Flat Rock, NC 28731. *Phone:* 828-694-1810. *Web site:* http://www.blueridge.edu/.

Brunswick Community College
Supply, North Carolina

Freshman Application Contact Admissions Counselor, Brunswick Community College, 50 College Road, PO Box 30, Supply, NC 28462-0030. *Phone:* 910-755-7300. *Toll-free phone:* 800-754-1050 Ext. 324. *Fax:* 910-754-9609. *E-mail:* admissions@brunswickcc.edu. *Web site:* http://www.brunswickcc.edu/.

Caldwell Community College and Technical Institute
Hudson, North Carolina

Freshman Application Contact Carolyn Woodard, Director of Enrollment Management Services, Caldwell Community College and Technical Institute, 2855 Hickory Boulevard, Hudson, NC 28638. *Phone:* 828-726-2703. *Fax:* 828-726-2709. *E-mail:* cwoodard@cccti.edu. *Web site:* http://www.cccti.edu/.

Cape Fear Community College
Wilmington, North Carolina

- **State-supported** 2-year, founded 1959, part of North Carolina Community College System
- **Urban** 150-acre campus
- **Endowment** $4.0 million
- **Coed,** 9,067 undergraduate students, 46% full-time, 53% women, 47% men

Undergraduates 4,143 full-time, 4,924 part-time. Students come from 42 states and territories; 11% are from out of state; 15% Black or African American, non-Hispanic/Latino; 3% Hispanic/Latino; 1% Asian, non-Hispanic/Latino; 0.8% American Indian or Alaska Native, non-Hispanic/Latino; 4% Race/ethnicity unknown; 8% transferred in.
Freshmen *Admission:* 7,638 applied, 4,185 admitted, 1,393 enrolled.
Faculty *Total:* 474, 54% full-time. *Student/faculty ratio:* 18:1.
Majors Accounting technology and bookkeeping; architectural engineering technology; automobile/automotive mechanics technology; building/property maintenance; business administration and management; chemical technology; cinematography and film/video production; computer systems networking and telecommunications; computer technology/computer systems technology; criminal justice/police science; culinary arts; dental hygiene; diagnostic medical sonography and ultrasound technology; early childhood education; electrical, electronic and communications engineering technology; electrical/electronics equipment installation and repair; electromechanical and instrumentation and maintenance technologies related; executive assistant/executive secretary; hotel/motel administration; instrumentation technology; interior design; landscaping and groundskeeping; legal assistant/paralegal; liberal arts and sciences/liberal studies; machine shop technology; marine maintenance and ship repair technology; mechanical engineering/mechanical technology; medical office management; medical radiologic technology; nuclear/nuclear power technology; occupational therapist assistant; registered nursing/registered nurse; surgical technology.
Academics *Calendar:* semesters. *Degree:* certificates, diplomas, and associate. *Special study options:* academic remediation for entering students, adult/continuing education programs, advanced placement credit, cooperative education, distance learning, double majors, English as a second language, independent study, off-campus study, part-time degree program, services for LD students, summer session for credit.
Library Cape Fear Community College Library with 47,352 titles, 581 serial subscriptions, 7,175 audiovisual materials, an OPAC, a Web page.
Student Life *Housing:* college housing not available. *Activities and Organizations:* student-run newspaper, choral group, Nursing Club, Dental Hygiene Club, Pineapple Guild, Phi Theta Kappa, Occupational Therapy. *Campus security:* 24-hour emergency response devices and patrols, late-night transport/escort service, armed police officer. *Student services:* personal/psychological counseling.
Athletics Member NJCAA. *Intercollegiate sports:* basketball M, cheerleading M/W, golf M/W, soccer M/W, volleyball M/W. *Intramural sports:* softball M/W, tennis M/W.
Costs (2010–11) *Tuition:* state resident $1806 full-time, $57 per credit part-time; nonresident $7952 full-time, $249 per credit part-time. Full-time tuition and fees vary according to course load. Part-time tuition and fees vary according to course load. *Required fees:* $137 full-time. *Payment plan:* deferred payment. *Waivers:* senior citizens and employees or children of employees.

Financial Aid Of all full-time matriculated undergraduates who enrolled in 2009, 102 Federal Work-Study jobs (averaging $1598).
Applying *Options:* electronic application, early admission. *Required for some:* high school transcript, interview, placement testing. *Application deadlines:* 8/15 (freshmen), rolling (transfers). *Notification:* continuous (freshmen), continuous (transfers).
Freshman Application Contact Ms. Linda Kasyan, Director of Enrollment Management, Cape Fear Community College, 411 North Front Street, Wilmington, NC 28401-3993. *Phone:* 910-362-7054. *Toll-free phone:* 910-362-7557. *Fax:* 910-362-7080. *E-mail:* admissions@cfcc.edu. *Web site:* http://www.cfcc.edu/.

Carolinas College of Health Sciences
Charlotte, North Carolina

- **Public** 2-year, founded 1990
- **Urban** 3-acre campus with easy access to Charlotte
- **Endowment** $1.5 million
- **Coed,** 436 undergraduate students, 20% full-time, 84% women, 16% men

Undergraduates 87 full-time, 349 part-time. Students come from 3 states and territories; 10% are from out of state; 11% Black or African American, non-Hispanic/Latino; 3% Hispanic/Latino; 2% Asian, non-Hispanic/Latino; 0.5% Native Hawaiian or other Pacific Islander, non-Hispanic/Latino; 1% American Indian or Alaska Native, non-Hispanic/Latino; 0.7% Two or more races, non-Hispanic/Latino; 3% Race/ethnicity unknown; 67% transferred in.
Freshmen *Admission:* 50 applied, 3 admitted, 3 enrolled. *Average high school GPA:* 3.39.
Faculty *Total:* 71, 37% full-time. *Student/faculty ratio:* 6:1.
Majors Medical radiologic technology; radiologic technology/science; registered nursing/registered nurse.
Academics *Calendar:* semesters. *Degree:* certificates, diplomas, and associate. *Special study options:* advanced placement credit, distance learning, independent study, services for LD students, summer session for credit.
Library AHEC Library with 9,810 titles, 503 serial subscriptions, an OPAC, a Web page.
Student Life *Housing Options:* Campus housing is provided by a third party. *Campus security:* 24-hour emergency response devices and patrols, late-night transport/escort service. *Student services:* health clinic, personal/psychological counseling.
Standardized Tests *Required for some:* SAT or ACT (for admission).
Costs (2011–12) *Tuition:* $9075 full-time, $275 per credit part-time. Full-time tuition and fees vary according to course load and program. Part-time tuition and fees vary according to course load and program. *Required fees:* $655 full-time, $125 per term part-time. *Waivers:* employees or children of employees.
Financial Aid Of all full-time matriculated undergraduates who enrolled in 2008, 5 Federal Work-Study jobs (averaging $5500).
Applying *Options:* electronic application. *Application fee:* $50. *Required for some:* high school transcript, minimum 2.5 GPA, interview. *Recommended:* minimum 2.5 GPA. *Application deadline:* 2/5 (freshmen). *Notification:* 3/15 (freshmen).
Freshman Application Contact Ms. Nicki Sabourin, Admissions Representative, Carolinas College of Health Sciences, 1200 Blythe Boulevard, Charlotte, NC 28203. *Phone:* 704-355-5043. *Fax:* 704-355-9336. *E-mail:* cchsinformation@carolinashealthcare.org. *Web site:* http://www.carolinascollege.edu/.

Carteret Community College
Morehead City, North Carolina

- **State-supported** 2-year, founded 1963, part of North Carolina Community College System
- **Small-town** 25-acre campus
- **Coed**

Undergraduates 804 full-time, 1,068 part-time. Students come from 27 states and territories; 2 other countries; 8% transferred in. *Retention:* 52% of full-time freshmen returned.
Faculty *Student/faculty ratio:* 9:1.
Academics *Calendar:* semesters. *Degree:* certificates, diplomas, and associate. *Special study options:* academic remediation for entering students, adult/continuing education programs, cooperative education, distance learning, double majors, internships, part-time degree program, services for LD students, summer session for credit.
Student Life *Campus security:* late-night transport/escort service, security service from 7 am until 11:30 pm.
Standardized Tests *Recommended:* SAT or ACT (for admission).
Costs (2010–11) *Tuition:* state resident $1356 full-time, $57 per credit hour part-time; nonresident $5964 full-time, $249 per credit hour part-time. Full-

time tuition and fees vary according to course load and program. *Required fees:* $63 full-time, $19 per term part-time.
Applying *Options:* electronic application. *Required:* high school transcript. *Required for some:* interview.
Freshman Application Contact Ms. Margie Ward, Admissions Officer, Carteret Community College, 3505 Arendell Street, Morehead City, NC 28557-2989. *Phone:* 252-222-6155. *Fax:* 252-222-6265. *E-mail:* admissions@carteret.edu. *Web site:* http://www.carteret.edu/.

Catawba Valley Community College
Hickory, North Carolina

- **State and locally supported** 2-year, founded 1960, part of North Carolina Community College System
- **Small-town** 50-acre campus with easy access to Charlotte
- **Endowment** $1.2 million
- **Coed,** 5,504 undergraduate students, 39% full-time, 57% women, 43% men

Undergraduates 2,171 full-time, 3,333 part-time. Students come from 7 states and territories; 1 other country; 1% are from out of state; 26% transferred in.
Freshmen *Admission:* 2,133 applied, 2,057 admitted, 928 enrolled. *Average high school GPA:* 2.9.
Faculty *Total:* 533, 29% full-time. *Student/faculty ratio:* 12:1.
Majors Accounting technology and bookkeeping; applied horticulture/horticulture operations; architectural engineering technology; automobile/automotive mechanics technology; banking and financial support services; business administration and management; commercial and advertising art; computer engineering technology; computer programming; computer systems networking and telecommunications; criminal justice/safety; customer service management; cyber/computer forensics and counterterrorism; dental hygiene; early childhood education; e-commerce; electrical, electronic and communications engineering technology; electromechanical and instrumentation and maintenance technologies related; electroneurodiagnostic/electroencephalographic technology; emergency medical technology (EMT paramedic); fire prevention and safety technology; forensic science and technology; general studies; health information/medical records technology; industrial engineering; information technology; liberal arts and sciences/liberal studies; medical office management; medical radiologic technology; office management; photographic and film/video technology; polysomnography; registered nursing/registered nurse; respiratory care therapy; turf and turfgrass management.
Academics *Calendar:* semesters. *Degree:* certificates, diplomas, and associate. *Special study options:* academic remediation for entering students, adult/continuing education programs, advanced placement credit, cooperative education, distance learning, double majors, English as a second language, independent study, part-time degree program, services for LD students, student-designed majors, summer session for credit.
Library Learning Resource Center with 25,000 titles, 610 serial subscriptions, 700 audiovisual materials, an OPAC, a Web page.
Student Life *Housing:* college housing not available. *Activities and Organizations:* drama/theater group, choral group, Circle K, Phi Theta Kappa, ASIA (Hmong Club), Rotoract, Catawba Valley Outing Club. *Campus security:* 24-hour patrols. *Student services:* personal/psychological counseling.
Athletics Member NJCAA. *Intercollegiate sports:* baseball M, basketball M/W, volleyball W.
Standardized Tests *Required:* Applicants must take the COMPASS test series (for admission).
Costs (2010–11) *Tuition:* state resident $1356 full-time, $57 per credit hour part-time; nonresident $5964 full-time, $249 per credit hour part-time. Part-time tuition and fees vary according to course load. *Required fees:* $87 full-time, $5 per credit hour part-time, $11 per term part-time. *Payment plan:* installment. *Waivers:* senior citizens and employees or children of employees.
Applying *Options:* electronic application, early admission, deferred entrance. *Required:* high school transcript. *Application deadlines:* rolling (freshmen), rolling (out-of-state freshmen), rolling (transfers). *Notification:* continuous (freshmen), continuous (out-of-state freshmen), continuous (transfers).
Freshman Application Contact Catawba Valley Community College, 2550 Highway 70 SE, Hickory, NC 28602-9699. *Phone:* 828-327-7000 Ext. 4618. *Web site:* http://www.cvcc.edu/.

Central Carolina Community College
Sanford, North Carolina

- **State and locally supported** 2-year, founded 1962, part of North Carolina Community College System
- **Small-town** 41-acre campus
- **Endowment** $2.0 million
- **Coed**

Undergraduates 5,411 full-time. Students come from 36 states and territories; 6% are from out of state.

Faculty *Student/faculty ratio:* 10:1.
Academics *Calendar:* semesters. *Degree:* certificates, diplomas, and associate. *Special study options:* academic remediation for entering students, adult/continuing education programs, advanced placement credit, distance learning, double majors, English as a second language, independent study, internships, part-time degree program, services for LD students, summer session for credit.
Student Life *Campus security:* 24-hour emergency response devices and patrols, student patrols, patrols by trained security personnel during operating hours.
Athletics Member NJCAA.
Costs (2010–11) *Tuition:* state resident $1783 full-time; nonresident $7543 full-time. Full-time tuition and fees vary according to course load. Part-time tuition and fees vary according to course load.
Financial Aid Of all full-time matriculated undergraduates who enrolled in 2009, 70 Federal Work-Study jobs (averaging $1361). *Financial aid deadline:* 5/4.
Applying *Options:* electronic application, early admission, deferred entrance. *Required:* high school transcript.
Freshman Application Contact Ms. Michelle Wheeler, Registrar, Central Carolina Community College, 1105 Kelly Drive, Sanford, NC 27330-9000. *Phone:* 919-718-7239. *Toll-free phone:* 800-682-8353 Ext. 7300. *Fax:* 919-718-7380. *Web site:* http://www.cccc.edu/.

Central Piedmont Community College
Charlotte, North Carolina

- **State and locally supported** 2-year, founded 1963, part of North Carolina Community College System
- **Urban** 37-acre campus
- **Endowment** $16.7 million
- **Coed**

Undergraduates 7,630 full-time, 11,734 part-time. Students come from 13 states and territories; 117 other countries; 3% are from out of state; 11% transferred in.
Academics *Calendar:* semesters. *Degree:* certificates, diplomas, and associate. *Special study options:* academic remediation for entering students, accelerated degree program, advanced placement credit, cooperative education, distance learning, English as a second language, honors programs, off-campus study, part-time degree program, services for LD students, student-designed majors, summer session for credit.
Student Life *Campus security:* 24-hour emergency response devices and patrols.
Athletics Member NJCAA.
Costs (2010–11) *Tuition:* state resident $1695 full-time, $57 per credit hour part-time; nonresident $7455 full-time, $249 per credit hour part-time. *Required fees:* $216 full-time, $1 per credit hour part-time, $60 per term part-time.
Financial Aid Of all full-time matriculated undergraduates who enrolled in 2009, 99 Federal Work-Study jobs (averaging $2988).
Applying *Required:* high school transcript.
Freshman Application Contact Ms. Linda McComb, Associate Dean, Central Piedmont Community College, PO Box 35009, Charlotte, NC 28235-5009. *Phone:* 704-330-6784. *Fax:* 704-330-6136. *Web site:* http://www.cpcc.edu/.

Cleveland Community College
Shelby, North Carolina

Freshman Application Contact Cleveland Community College, 137 South Post Road, Shelby, NC 28152. *Phone:* 704-484-6073. *Web site:* http://www.clevelandcommunitycollege.edu/.

Coastal Carolina Community College
Jacksonville, North Carolina

Freshman Application Contact Ms. Heather Calihan, Counseling Coordinator, Coastal Carolina Community College, Jacksonville, NC 28546. *Phone:* 910-938-6241. *Fax:* 910-455-2767. *E-mail:* calihanh@coastal.cc.nc.us. *Web site:* http://www.coastalcarolina.edu/.

College of The Albemarle
Elizabeth City, North Carolina

Freshman Application Contact Mr. Kenny Krentz, Director of Admissions and International Students, College of The Albemarle, PO Box 2327, Elizabeth City, NC 27906-2327. *Phone:* 252-335-0821. *Fax:* 252-335-2011. *E-mail:* kkrentz@albemarle.edu. *Web site:* http://www.albemarle.edu/.

Craven Community College

New Bern, North Carolina

Freshman Application Contact Ms. Millicent Fulford, Recruiter, Craven Community College, 800 College Court, New Bern, NC 28562-4984. *Phone:* 252-638-7232. *Web site:* http://www.craven.cc.nc.us/.

Davidson County Community College

Lexington, North Carolina

Freshman Application Contact Davidson County Community College, PO Box 1287, Lexington, NC 27293-1287. *Phone:* 336-249-8186 Ext. 6715. *Fax:* 336-224-0240. *E-mail:* admissions@davidsonccc.edu. *Web site:* http://www.davidsonccc.edu/.

Durham Technical Community College

Durham, North Carolina

Director of Admissions Ms. Penny Augustine, Director of Admissions and Testing, Durham Technical Community College, 1637 Lawson Street, Durham, NC 27703-5023. *Phone:* 919-686-3619. *Web site:* http://www.durhamtech.edu/.

ECPI College of Technology

Greensboro, North Carolina

Admissions Office Contact ECPI College of Technology, 7802 Airport Center Drive, Greensboro, NC 27409. *Toll-free phone:* 866-708-6170. *Web site:* http://www.ecpi.edu/.

Edgecombe Community College

Tarboro, North Carolina

Freshman Application Contact Ms. Jackie Heath, Admissions Officer, Edgecombe Community College, 2009 West Wilson Street, Tarboro, NC 27886-9399. *Phone:* 252-823-5166 Ext. 254. *Web site:* http://www.edgecombe.edu/.

Fayetteville Technical Community College

Fayetteville, North Carolina

- **State-supported** 2-year, founded 1961, part of North Carolina Community College System
- **Suburban** 209-acre campus with easy access to Raleigh
- **Endowment** $15,184
- **Coed,** 10,002 undergraduate students, 41% full-time, 67% women, 33% men

Undergraduates 4,130 full-time, 5,872 part-time. Students come from 41 states and territories; 35 other countries; 21% are from out of state; 44% Black or African American, non-Hispanic/Latino; 8% Hispanic/Latino; 0.6% Asian, non-Hispanic/Latino; 0.2% Native Hawaiian or other Pacific Islander, non-Hispanic/Latino; 3% American Indian or Alaska Native, non-Hispanic/Latino; 1% Two or more races, non-Hispanic/Latino; 5% Race/ethnicity unknown; 0.3% international; 20% transferred in.

Freshmen *Admission:* 4,136 applied, 4,136 admitted, 1,436 enrolled. *Average high school GPA:* 2.68.

Faculty *Total:* 795, 40% full-time. *Student/faculty ratio:* 13:1.

Majors Accounting; applied horticulture/horticulture operations; architectural engineering technology; automobile/automotive mechanics technology; banking and financial support services; building/construction finishing, management, and inspection related; business administration and management; civil engineering technology; commercial and advertising art; computer and information systems security; computer programming; computer systems networking and telecommunications; corrections and criminal justice related; criminal justice/safety; crisis/emergency/disaster management; culinary arts; dental hygiene; early childhood education; e-commerce; electrical, electronic and communications engineering technology; electrician; elementary education; emergency medical technology (EMT paramedic); fire prevention and safety technology; forensic science and technology; funeral service and mortuary science; game and interactive media design; heating, air conditioning, ventilation and refrigeration maintenance technology; hotel, motel, and restaurant management; human resources management; information science/studies; information technology; legal assistant/paralegal; liberal arts and sciences and humanities related; liberal arts and sciences/liberal studies; machine shop technology; marketing/marketing management; medical office management;

nuclear medical technology; office management; operations management; pharmacy technician; physical therapy technology; public administration; radiologic technology/science; registered nursing/registered nurse; respiratory care therapy; speech-language pathology assistant; surgical technology; surveying technology.

Academics *Calendar:* semesters. *Degree:* certificates, diplomas, and associate. *Special study options:* academic remediation for entering students, adult/continuing education programs, advanced placement credit, cooperative education, distance learning, double majors, English as a second language, independent study, internships, off-campus study, part-time degree program, services for LD students, summer session for credit.

Library Paul H. Thompson Library plus 1 other with 68,496 titles, 326 serial subscriptions, 5,669 audiovisual materials, an OPAC, a Web page.

Student Life *Housing:* college housing not available. *Activities and Organizations:* Parents for Higher Education, Early Childhood Club, Phi Beta Lambda, Association of Nursing Students, African/American Heritage Club. *Campus security:* 24-hour emergency response devices and patrols, late-night transport/escort service, campus-wide emergency notification system. *Student services:* personal/psychological counseling.

Athletics *Intramural sports:* basketball M/W, bowling M/W, football M/W, golf M/W, softball M/W, tennis M/W, volleyball M/W.

Standardized Tests *Required:* ACCUPLACER is required or ACT and SAT scores in lieu of ACCUPLACER if the scores are no more than 5 years old or ASSET and COMPASS scores are also accepted if they are no more than 3 years old (for admission).

Costs (2010–11) *One-time required fee:* $25. *Tuition:* state resident $1808 full-time, $57 per credit hour part-time; nonresident $7952 full-time, $249 per credit hour part-time. Full-time tuition and fees vary according to course load. Part-time tuition and fees vary according to course load. *Required fees:* $90 full-time, $45 per term part-time. *Payment plan:* installment. *Waivers:* senior citizens and employees or children of employees.

Financial Aid Of all full-time matriculated undergraduates who enrolled in 2009, 75 Federal Work-Study jobs (averaging $2000). *Financial aid deadline:* 6/1.

Applying *Options:* electronic application. *Required for some:* essay or personal statement, high school transcript, interview. *Application deadlines:* rolling (freshmen), rolling (out-of-state freshmen), rolling (transfers). *Notification:* continuous (freshmen), continuous (out-of-state freshmen), continuous (transfers).

Freshman Application Contact Mr. Harper Shackelford, Dean of Enrollment Management, Fayetteville Technical Community College, 2201 Hull Road, Fayetteville, NC 28303. *Phone:* 910-678-8413. *Fax:* 910-678-0085. *E-mail:* shackelh@faytechcc.edu. *Web site:* http://www.faytechcc.edu/.

Forsyth Technical Community College

Winston-Salem, North Carolina

Freshman Application Contact Admissions Office, Forsyth Technical Community College, 2100 Silas Creek Parkway, Winston-Salem, NC 27103-5197. *Phone:* 336-734-7556. *E-mail:* admissions@forsythtech.edu. *Web site:* http://www.forsythtech.edu/.

Gaston College

Dallas, North Carolina

Freshman Application Contact Terry Basier, Director of Enrollment Management and Admissions, Gaston College, 201 Highway 321 South, Dallas, NC 28034. *Phone:* 704-922-6214. *Fax:* 704-922-6443. *Web site:* http://www.gaston.edu/.

Guilford Technical Community College

Jamestown, North Carolina

- **State and locally supported** 2-year, founded 1958, part of North Carolina Community College System
- **Suburban** 158-acre campus
- **Endowment** $2.7 million
- **Coed**

Undergraduates 9,930 full-time, 3,602 part-time. Students come from 22 states and territories; 100 other countries; 0.7% are from out of state; 29% transferred in. *Retention:* 58% of full-time freshmen returned.

Faculty *Student/faculty ratio:* 21:1.

Academics *Calendar:* semesters. *Degree:* certificates, diplomas, and associate. *Special study options:* academic remediation for entering students, adult/continuing education programs, advanced placement credit, cooperative education, distance learning, double majors, English as a second language, external degree program, independent study, internships, off-campus study, part-time degree program, services for LD students, student-designed majors, summer session for credit. *ROTC:* Army (c), Air Force (c).

Student Life *Campus security:* 24-hour emergency response devices and patrols, late-night transport/escort service.

Athletics Member NJCAA.

Costs (2010–11) *Tuition:* state resident $1808 full-time, $57 per credit hour part-time; nonresident $7952 full-time, $249 per credit hour part-time. Full-time tuition and fees vary according to course load and program. Part-time tuition and fees vary according to course load and program. *Required fees:* $173 full-time, $45 per term part-time.

Applying *Options:* electronic application, early admission, deferred entrance. *Required:* high school transcript. *Required for some:* interview.

Freshman Application Contact Guilford Technical Community College, PO Box 309, Jamestown, NC 27282-0309. *Phone:* 336-334-4822 Ext. 2901. *Web site:* http://www.gtcc.edu/.

Halifax Community College

Weldon, North Carolina

Director of Admissions Mrs. Scottie Dickens, Director of Admissions, Halifax Community College, PO Drawer 809, Weldon, NC 27890-0809. *Phone:* 252-536-7220. *Web site:* http://www.hcc.cc.nc.us/.

Haywood Community College

Clyde, North Carolina

Director of Admissions Ms. Debbie Rowland, Coordinator of Admissions, Haywood Community College, 185 Freedlander Drive, Clyde, NC 28721-9453. *Phone:* 828-627-4505. *Web site:* http://www.haywood.edu/.

Isothermal Community College

Spindale, North Carolina

Freshman Application Contact Ms. Vickie Searcy, Enrollment Management Office, Isothermal Community College, PO Box 804, Spindale, NC 28160-0804. *Phone:* 828-286-3636 Ext. 251. *Fax:* 828-286-8109. *E-mail:* vsearcy@isothermal.edu. *Web site:* http://www.isothermal.edu/.

ITT Technical Institute

Charlotte, North Carolina

- **Proprietary** primarily 2-year
- **Coed**

Majors CAD/CADD drafting/design technology; computer and information systems security; computer engineering technology; construction management; criminal justice/law enforcement administration; electrical, electronic and communications engineering technology; system, networking, and LAN/WAN management; web page, digital/multimedia and information resources design.

Academics *Degrees:* associate and bachelor's.

Student Life *Housing:* college housing not available.

Freshman Application Contact Director of Recruitment, ITT Technical Institute, 4135 Southstream Boulevard, Suite 200, Charlotte, NC 28217. *Phone:* 704-423-3100. *Toll-free phone:* 800-488-0173. *Web site:* http://www.itt-tech.edu/.

ITT Technical Institute

High Point, North Carolina

- **Proprietary** primarily 2-year, founded 2007, part of ITT Educational Services, Inc.
- **Coed**

Majors CAD/CADD drafting/design technology; computer and information systems security; computer engineering technology; construction management; criminal justice/law enforcement administration; electrical, electronic and communications engineering technology; system, networking, and LAN/WAN management.

Academics *Calendar:* quarters. *Degrees:* associate and bachelor's.

Student Life *Housing:* college housing not available.

Freshman Application Contact Director of Recruitment, ITT Technical Institute, 4050 Piedmont Parkway, Suite 110, High Point, NC 27265. *Phone:* 336-819-5900. *Toll-free phone:* 877-536-5231. *Web site:* http://www.itt-tech.edu/.

ITT Technical Institute

Morrisville, North Carolina

- **Proprietary** primarily 2-year, part of ITT Educational Services, Inc.
- **Coed**

Majors CAD/CADD drafting/design technology; computer and information systems security; computer engineering technology; construction management; criminal justice/law enforcement administration; electrical, electronic and communications engineering technology; system, networking, and LAN/WAN management.

Academics *Degrees:* associate and bachelor's.

Student Life *Housing:* college housing not available.

Freshman Application Contact Director of Recruitment, ITT Technical Institute, 5520 Dillard Drive, Suite 100, Morrisville, NC 27560. *Phone:* 919-233-2520. *Toll-free phone:* 877-203-5533. *Web site:* http://www.itt-tech.edu/.

James Sprunt Community College

Kenansville, North Carolina

- **State-supported** 2-year, founded 1964, part of North Carolina Community College System
- **Rural** 51-acre campus
- **Endowment** $1.0 million
- **Coed,** 1,558 undergraduate students, 51% full-time, 70% women, 30% men

Undergraduates 790 full-time, 768 part-time. Students come from 3 states and territories; 1% are from out of state; 47% Black or African American, non-Hispanic/Latino; 4% Hispanic/Latino; 0.2% Asian, non-Hispanic/Latino; 0.2% Native Hawaiian or other Pacific Islander, non-Hispanic/Latino; 0.3% American Indian or Alaska Native, non-Hispanic/Latino; 0.7% Two or more races, non-Hispanic/Latino; 0.7% Race/ethnicity unknown; 20% transferred in.

Freshmen *Admission:* 569 applied, 302 admitted, 222 enrolled.

Faculty *Total:* 138, 42% full-time, 4% with terminal degrees.

Majors Accounting; agribusiness; animal sciences; business administration and management; child development; commercial and advertising art; criminal justice/safety; early childhood education; elementary education; general studies; information technology; institutional food workers; liberal arts and sciences and humanities related; liberal arts and sciences/liberal studies; medical/clinical assistant; registered nursing/registered nurse; viticulture and enology.

Academics *Calendar:* semesters. *Degree:* certificates, diplomas, and associate. *Special study options:* academic remediation for entering students, accelerated degree program, advanced placement credit, cooperative education, distance learning, double majors, English as a second language, independent study, internships, part-time degree program, services for LD students, summer session for credit.

Library James Sprunt Community College Library with 27,471 titles, 134 serial subscriptions, 621 audiovisual materials, an OPAC.

Student Life *Housing:* college housing not available. *Activities and Organizations:* student-run newspaper, Student Nurses Association, Art Club, Alumni Association, National Technical-Vocational Honor Society, Phi Theta Kappa, national sororities. *Campus security:* day, evening and Saturday trained security personnel. *Student services:* personal/psychological counseling.

Athletics *Intercollegiate sports:* softball M/W, volleyball M/W.

Costs (2011–12) *Tuition:* state resident $1808 full-time, $57 per semester hour part-time; nonresident $7952 full-time, $249 per semester hour part-time. Full-time tuition and fees vary according to course load. Part-time tuition and fees vary according to course load. *Required fees:* $70 full-time, $35 per term part-time. *Waivers:* senior citizens and employees or children of employees.

Financial Aid Of all full-time matriculated undergraduates who enrolled in 2009, 35 Federal Work-Study jobs (averaging $1057).

Applying *Options:* electronic application. *Required:* high school transcript. *Application deadlines:* rolling (freshmen), rolling (transfers). *Notification:* continuous (freshmen), continuous (transfers).

Freshman Application Contact Ms. Lea Matthews, Admissions Specialist, James Sprunt Community College, Highway 11 South, 133 James Sprunt Drive, Kenansville, NC 28349. *Phone:* 910-296-6078. *Fax:* 910-296-1222. *E-mail:* lmatthews@jamessprunt.edu. *Web site:* http://www.jamessprunt.com/.

Johnston Community College

Smithfield, North Carolina

- **State-supported** 2-year, founded 1969, part of North Carolina Community College System
- **Rural** 100-acre campus
- **Coed,** 4,410 undergraduate students, 52% full-time, 63% women, 37% men

Undergraduates 2,283 full-time, 2,127 part-time.

Freshmen *Admission:* 1,028 enrolled.

Faculty *Total:* 385, 37% full-time. *Student/faculty ratio:* 14:1.

Majors Accounting; accounting technology and bookkeeping; administrative assistant and secretarial science; business administration and management; commercial and advertising art; computer programming; criminal justice/police science; diesel mechanics technology; early childhood education; electrical, electronic and communications engineering technology; heating, air conditioning, ventilation and refrigeration maintenance technology; kindergarten/preschool education; landscaping and groundskeeping; legal assistant/paralegal; liberal arts and sciences/liberal studies; machine shop technology; machine tool technology; medical administrative assistant and medical secretary; medical/clinical assistant; medical office management; medical radiologic technology; office management; registered nursing/registered nurse.

Academics *Calendar:* semesters. *Degree:* certificates, diplomas, and associate. *Special study options:* academic remediation for entering students, adult/continuing education programs, advanced placement credit, cooperative education, distance learning, double majors, honors programs, independent study, part-time degree program, services for LD students, summer session for credit.

Library Johnston Community College Library plus 1 other with 33,094 titles, 197 serial subscriptions, an OPAC, a Web page.

Student Life *Housing:* college housing not available. *Activities and Organizations:* choral group. *Campus security:* 24-hour patrols. *Student services:* personal/psychological counseling.

Athletics Member NJCAA. *Intercollegiate sports:* golf M/W, softball M/W, volleyball M/W. *Intramural sports:* basketball M/W.

Standardized Tests *Required:* ACCUPLACER (for admission). *Recommended:* SAT or ACT (for admission).

Costs (2010–11) *Tuition:* state resident $1808 full-time, $57 per credit hour part-time; nonresident $7952 full-time, $249 per credit hour part-time. Full-time tuition and fees vary according to course load. Part-time tuition and fees vary according to course load. *Required fees:* $97 full-time. *Waivers:* senior citizens and employees or children of employees.

Financial Aid Of all full-time matriculated undergraduates who enrolled in 2009, 35 Federal Work-Study jobs (averaging $1853).

Applying *Options:* electronic application. *Required:* high school transcript, interview. *Application deadlines:* rolling (freshmen), rolling (transfers). *Notification:* continuous (freshmen), continuous (transfers).

Freshman Application Contact Dr. Pamela J. Harrell, Vice President of Student Services, Johnston Community College, Smithfield, NC 27577-2350. *Phone:* 919-209-2048. *Fax:* 919-989-7862. *E-mail:* pjharrell@johnstoncc.edu. *Web site:* http://www.johnstoncc.edu/.

King's College

Charlotte, North Carolina

- **Private** 2-year, founded 1901
- **Suburban** campus
- **Coed,** 648 undergraduate students
- 76% of applicants were admitted

Freshmen *Admission:* 1,279 applied, 974 admitted.

Majors Accounting and business/management; business administration and management; computer programming; graphic design; legal administrative assistant/secretary; legal assistant/paralegal; medical/clinical assistant; system, networking, and LAN/WAN management; tourism and travel services management.

Academics *Calendar:* quarters. *Degree:* diplomas and associate. *Special study options:* accelerated degree program, internships.

Freshman Application Contact Admissions Office, King's College, 322 Lamar Avenue, Charlotte, NC 28204-2436. *Phone:* 704-372-0266. *Toll-free phone:* 800-768-2255. *Web site:* http://www.kingscollegecharlotte.edu/.

Lenoir Community College

Kinston, North Carolina

Freshman Application Contact Ms. Tammy Buck, Director of Enrollment Management, Lenoir Community College, PO Box 188, Kinston, NC 28502-0188. *Phone:* 252-527-6223 Ext. 309. *Fax:* 252-526-5112. *E-mail:* tbuck@lenoircc.edu. *Web site:* http://www.lenoircc.edu/.

Living Arts College

Raleigh, North Carolina

Freshman Application Contact Wayne Moseley, Admissions, Living Arts College, 3000 Wakefield Crossing Drive, Raleigh, NC 27614. *Phone:* 919-488-5912. *Toll-free phone:* 800-288-7442. *Fax:* 919-488-8490. *E-mail:* wmoseley@hdigi.com. *Web site:* http://www.higherdigital.com/.

Louisburg College

Louisburg, North Carolina

Freshman Application Contact Mr. Jim Schlimmer, Vice President for Enrollment Management, Louisburg College, 501 North Main Street, Louisburg, NC 27549-2399. *Phone:* 919-497-3233. *Toll-free phone:* 800-775-0208. *Fax:* 919-496-1788. *E-mail:* admissions@louisburg.edu. *Web site:* http://www.louisburg.edu/.

Martin Community College

Williamston, North Carolina

- **State-supported** 2-year, founded 1968, part of North Carolina Community College System
- **Rural** 65-acre campus
- **Endowment** $32,015
- **Coed,** 755 undergraduate students, 63% full-time, 66% women, 34% men

Undergraduates 475 full-time, 280 part-time. Students come from 1 other state; 0.8% are from out of state; 47% Black or African American, non-Hispanic/Latino; 0.3% Hispanic/Latino; 0.3% Asian, non-Hispanic/Latino; 0.3% American Indian or Alaska Native, non-Hispanic/Latino; 13% Race/ethnicity unknown; 27% transferred in.

Freshmen *Admission:* 208 enrolled.

Faculty *Total:* 78, 28% full-time. *Student/faculty ratio:* 10:1.

Majors Accounting; administrative assistant and secretarial science; automobile/automotive mechanics technology; business administration and management; cosmetology; dietitian assistant; electrical and power transmission installation related; electromechanical technology; equestrian studies; general studies; heating, air conditioning, ventilation and refrigeration maintenance technology; heating, ventilation, air conditioning and refrigeration engineering technology; information science/studies; liberal arts and sciences and humanities related; liberal arts and sciences/liberal studies; management information systems; management information systems and services related; medical administrative assistant and medical secretary; medical/clinical assistant; physical therapy technology.

Academics *Calendar:* semesters. *Degree:* certificates, diplomas, and associate. *Special study options:* academic remediation for entering students, advanced placement credit, distance learning, English as a second language, independent study, internships, off-campus study, part-time degree program, services for LD students, summer session for credit.

Library Martin Community College Learning Resources Center with 36,443 titles, 215 serial subscriptions, 10,809 audiovisual materials, an OPAC.

Student Life *Housing:* college housing not available. *Activities and Organizations:* Phi Theta Kappa, Student Government Association, Alpha Beta Gamma, Physical Therapy Club, Equine Club. *Campus security:* 24-hour emergency response devices, part-time patrols by trained security personnel. *Student services:* personal/psychological counseling.

Costs (2010–11) *Tuition:* state resident $1808 full-time, $57 per credit hour part-time; nonresident $7952 full-time, $249 per credit hour part-time. *Waivers:* employees or children of employees.

Financial Aid Of all full-time matriculated undergraduates who enrolled in 2009, 30 Federal Work-Study jobs (averaging $1200).

Applying *Options:* electronic application. *Required:* high school transcript. *Required for some:* interview. *Application deadlines:* rolling (freshmen), rolling (transfers). *Notification:* continuous until 8/17 (freshmen), continuous until 8/17 (transfers).

Freshman Application Contact Martin Community College, 1161 Kehukee Park Road, Williamston, NC 27892. *Phone:* 252-792-1521 Ext. 243. *Web site:* http://www.martin.cc.nc.us/.

Mayland Community College

Spruce Pine, North Carolina

Director of Admissions Ms. Cathy Morrison, Director of Admissions, Mayland Community College, PO Box 547, Spruce Pine, NC 28777-0547. *Phone:* 828-765-7351 Ext. 224. *Web site:* http://www.mayland.edu/.

McDowell Technical Community College

Marion, North Carolina

Freshman Application Contact Mr. Rick L. Wilson, Director of Admissions, McDowell Technical Community College, 54 College Drive, Marion, NC 28752. *Phone:* 828-652-0632. *Fax:* 828-652-1014. *E-mail:* rickw@mcdowelltech.edu. *Web site:* http://www.mcdowelltech.edu/.

Mitchell Community College
Statesville, North Carolina

Freshman Application Contact Mr. Doug Rhoney, Counselor, Mitchell Community College, 500 West Broad, Statesville, NC 28677-5293. *Phone:* 704-878-3280. *Web site:* http://www.mitchellcc.edu/.

Montgomery Community College
Troy, North Carolina

- **State-supported** 2-year, founded 1967, part of North Carolina Community College System
- **Rural** 159-acre campus
- **Coed**

Undergraduates 346 full-time, 693 part-time.

Academics *Calendar:* semesters. *Degree:* certificates, diplomas, and associate. *Special study options:* academic remediation for entering students, advanced placement credit, cooperative education, distance learning, English as a second language, part-time degree program, services for LD students, summer session for credit.

Costs (2010–11) *Tuition:* state resident $1808 full-time, $57 per credit hour part-time; nonresident $7652 full-time, $249 per credit hour part-time. Full-time tuition and fees vary according to course load. Part-time tuition and fees vary according to course load. *Required fees:* $65 full-time, $33 per term part-time.

Financial Aid Of all full-time matriculated undergraduates who enrolled in 2009, 24 Federal Work-Study jobs (averaging $500).

Applying *Options:* early admission, deferred entrance. *Required:* high school transcript.

Freshman Application Contact Montgomery Community College, 1011 Page Street, Troy, NC 27371. *Phone:* 910-576-6222 Ext. 240. *Toll-free phone:* 800-839-6222. *Web site:* http://www.montgomery.edu/.

Nash Community College
Rocky Mount, North Carolina

Freshman Application Contact Ms. Dorothy Gardner, Admissions Officer, Nash Community College, PO Box 7488, Rocky Mount, NC 27804. *Phone:* 252-451-8300. *E-mail:* dgardner@nashcc.edu. *Web site:* http://www.nash.cc.nc.us/.

Pamlico Community College
Grantsboro, North Carolina

Director of Admissions Mr. Floyd H. Hardison, Admissions Counselor, Pamlico Community College, PO Box 185, Grantsboro, NC 28529-0185. *Phone:* 252-249-1851 Ext. 28. *Web site:* http://www.pamlico.cc.nc.us/.

Piedmont Community College
Roxboro, North Carolina

- **State-supported** 2-year, founded 1970, part of North Carolina Community College System
- **Small-town** 178-acre campus
- **Coed**

Undergraduates 1,251 full-time, 1,623 part-time. Students come from 3 states and territories; 4 other countries.

Academics *Calendar:* semesters. *Degree:* certificates, diplomas, and associate. *Special study options:* academic remediation for entering students, adult/continuing education programs, advanced placement credit, cooperative education, English as a second language, off-campus study, part-time degree program, summer session for credit.

Student Life *Campus security:* security guard during certain evening and weekend hours.

Costs (2010–11) *Tuition:* state resident $1851 full-time, $57 per credit hour part-time; nonresident $7995 full-time, $249 per credit hour part-time. *Required fees:* $43 full-time, $21 per term part-time.

Financial Aid Of all full-time matriculated undergraduates who enrolled in 2009, 30 Federal Work-Study jobs (averaging $1500).

Applying *Options:* electronic application, early admission, deferred entrance. *Required for some:* high school transcript.

Freshman Application Contact Piedmont Community College, PO Box 1197, Roxboro, NC 27573-1197. *Phone:* 336-599-1181 Ext. 219. *Web site:* http://www.piedmont.cc.nc.us/.

Pitt Community College
Greenville, North Carolina

Freshman Application Contact Ms. Bev Webster, Interim Coordinator of Counseling, Pitt Community College, PO Drawer 7007, Greenville, NC 27835-7007. *Phone:* 252-493-7217. *Fax:* 252-321-4612. *E-mail:* pittadm@pcc.pitt.cc.nc.us. *Web site:* http://www.pittcc.edu/.

Randolph Community College
Asheboro, North Carolina

- **State-supported** 2-year, founded 1962, part of North Carolina Community College System
- **Small-town** 35-acre campus with easy access to Greensboro, Winston-Salem, High Point
- **Endowment** $8.4 million
- **Coed**, 3,082 undergraduate students, 50% full-time, 64% women, 36% men

Undergraduates 1,541 full-time, 1,541 part-time. Students come from 4 states and territories; 13 other countries; 1% are from out of state; 8% Black or African American, non-Hispanic/Latino; 5% Hispanic/Latino; 0.8% Asian, non-Hispanic/Latino; 0.1% Native Hawaiian or other Pacific Islander, non-Hispanic/Latino; 0.4% American Indian or Alaska Native, non-Hispanic/Latino; 19% Race/ethnicity unknown; 16% transferred in. *Retention:* 63% of full-time freshmen returned.

Freshmen *Admission:* 2,219 applied, 2,219 admitted, 435 enrolled. *Average high school GPA:* 2.8.

Faculty *Total:* 357, 25% full-time. *Student/faculty ratio:* 18:1.

Majors Accounting; autobody/collision and repair technology; automobile/automotive mechanics technology; biology/biotechnology laboratory technician; business administration and management; commercial and advertising art; commercial photography; computer systems networking and telecommunications; cosmetology; criminal justice/safety; early childhood education; electrician; electromechanical and instrumentation and maintenance technologies related; entrepreneurship; funeral service and mortuary science; industrial electronics technology; information technology; interior design; liberal arts and sciences and humanities related; liberal arts and sciences/liberal studies; logistics, materials, and supply chain management; machine shop technology; medical/clinical assistant; medical office management; office management; photographic and film/video technology; photojournalism; physical therapy technology; pre-engineering; prenursing studies; radiologic technology/science; registered nursing/registered nurse.

Academics *Calendar:* semesters. *Degree:* certificates, diplomas, and associate. *Special study options:* academic remediation for entering students, adult/continuing education programs, advanced placement credit, cooperative education, distance learning, double majors, English as a second language, independent study, internships, off-campus study, part-time degree program, services for LD students, summer session for credit.

Library R. Alton Cox Learning Resources Center with 39,374 titles, 24,926 serial subscriptions, 9,908 audiovisual materials, an OPAC, a Web page.

Student Life *Housing:* college housing not available. *Activities and Organizations:* Student Government Association, Phi Theta Kappa, Student Nurse Association, Phi Beta Lambda, Campus Crusaders. *Campus security:* 24-hour emergency response devices, security officer during open hours. *Student services:* personal/psychological counseling.

Athletics *Intramural sports:* basketball M/W, volleyball M/W.

Costs (2011–12) *Tuition:* state resident $1808 full-time, $57 per credit part-time; nonresident $7952 full-time, $249 per credit part-time. *Required fees:* $88 full-time, $3 per credit part-time. *Payment plan:* installment. *Waivers:* senior citizens.

Applying *Options:* electronic application, deferred entrance. *Required:* high school transcript. *Application deadlines:* rolling (freshmen), rolling (transfers). *Notification:* continuous (freshmen), continuous (transfers).

Freshman Application Contact Ms. Brandi F. Hagerman, Director of Enrollment Management/Registrar, Randolph Community College, PO Box 1009, Asheboro, NC 27204-1009. *Phone:* 336-633-0213. *Fax:* 336-629-9547. *E-mail:* bhagerman@randolph.edu. *Web site:* http://www.randolph.edu/.

Richmond Community College
Hamlet, North Carolina

Freshman Application Contact Daphne Stancil, Director of Admissions/Registrar, Richmond Community College, PO Box 1189, Hamlet, NC 28345-1189. *Phone:* 910-410-1732. *Fax:* 910-582-7102. *E-mail:* daphnes@richmondcc.edu. *Web site:* http://www.richmondcc.edu/.

Roanoke-Chowan Community College

Ahoskie, North Carolina

Director of Admissions Miss Sandra Copeland, Director, Counseling Services, Roanoke-Chowan Community College, 109 Community College Road, Ahoskie, NC 27910. *Phone:* 252-862-1225. *Web site:* http://www.roanokechowan.edu/.

Robeson Community College

Lumberton, North Carolina

Freshman Application Contact Ms. Judy Revels, Director of Admissions, Robeson Community College, PO Box 1420, 5160 Fayetteville Road, Lumberton, NC 28359-1420. *Phone:* 910-618-5680 Ext. 251. *Web site:* http://www.robeson.cc.nc.us/.

Rockingham Community College

Wentworth, North Carolina

- **State-supported** 2-year, founded 1964, part of North Carolina Community College System
- **Rural** 257-acre campus
- **Coed,** 2,631 undergraduate students, 46% full-time, 63% women, 37% men

Undergraduates 1,216 full-time, 1,415 part-time. Students come from 10 states and territories; 8 other countries; 1% are from out of state; 25% Black or African American, non-Hispanic/Latino; 2% Hispanic/Latino; 0.5% Asian, non-Hispanic/Latino; 0.1% Native Hawaiian or other Pacific Islander, non-Hispanic/Latino; 0.6% American Indian or Alaska Native, non-Hispanic/Latino; 0.7% Two or more races, non-Hispanic/Latino; 1% Race/ethnicity unknown; 0.1% international; 18% transferred in.
Freshmen *Admission:* 485 enrolled.
Faculty *Total:* 113, 60% full-time, 9% with terminal degrees. *Student/faculty ratio:* 18:1.
Majors Accounting; business administration and management; criminal justice/police science; electromechanical technology; liberal arts and sciences/liberal studies; medical administrative assistant and medical secretary; registered nursing/registered nurse; respiratory care therapy.
Academics *Calendar:* semesters. *Degree:* certificates, diplomas, and associate. *Special study options:* academic remediation for entering students, adult/continuing education programs, advanced placement credit, cooperative education, part-time degree program, student-designed majors, summer session for credit.
Library Gerald B. James Library with 43,044 titles, 374 serial subscriptions, 3,990 audiovisual materials, an OPAC, a Web page.
Student Life *Housing:* college housing not available. *Activities and Organizations:* student-run newspaper. *Student services:* personal/psychological counseling.
Athletics Member NJCAA. *Intercollegiate sports:* baseball M, basketball M, golf M, volleyball W. *Intramural sports:* cheerleading W, table tennis M/W, tennis M/W, volleyball M/W.
Costs (2010–11) *Tuition:* state resident $1600 full-time, $50 per credit hour part-time; nonresident $7722 full-time, $241 per credit hour part-time. Full-time tuition and fees vary according to course load. Part-time tuition and fees vary according to course load. *Required fees:* $96 full-time. *Payment plan:* installment.
Financial Aid Of all full-time matriculated undergraduates who enrolled in 2009, 37 Federal Work-Study jobs (averaging $2300).
Applying *Options:* electronic application, early admission, deferred entrance. *Application deadlines:* rolling (freshmen), rolling (transfers). *Notification:* continuous (freshmen), continuous (transfers).
Freshman Application Contact Mrs. Leigh Tysor, Director of Enrollment Services, Rockingham Community College, PO Box 38, Wentworth, NC 27375-0038. *Phone:* 336-342-4261 Ext. 2114. *Fax:* 336-342-1809. *E-mail:* admissions@rockinghamcc.edu. *Web site:* http://www.rockinghamcc.edu/.

Rowan-Cabarrus Community College

Salisbury, North Carolina

Freshman Application Contact Mrs. Gail Cummins, Director of Admissions and Recruitment, Rowan-Cabarrus Community College, PO Box 1595, Salisbury, NC 28145-1595. *Phone:* 704-637-0760. *Fax:* 704-633-6804. *Web site:* http://www.rowancabarrus.edu/.

Sampson Community College

Clinton, North Carolina

Director of Admissions Mr. William R. Jordan, Director of Admissions, Sampson Community College, PO Box 318, 1801 Sunset Avenue, Highway 24 West, Clinton, NC 28329-0318. *Phone:* 910-592-8084 Ext. 2022. *Web site:* http://www.sampsoncc.edu/.

Sandhills Community College

Pinehurst, North Carolina

- **State-supported** 2-year, founded 1963, part of North Carolina Community College System
- **Small-town** 240-acre campus
- **Endowment** $10.7 million
- **Coed,** 4,571 undergraduate students

Faculty *Total:* 409, 35% full-time. *Student/faculty ratio:* 13:1.
Majors Accounting; administrative assistant and secretarial science; architectural engineering technology; art; art teacher education; automobile/automotive mechanics technology; biological and physical sciences; business administration and management; business, management, and marketing related; child development; civil engineering technology; clinical/medical laboratory technology; computer engineering related; computer engineering technology; computer/information technology services administration related; computer programming; computer programming (specific applications); cosmetology; criminal justice/law enforcement administration; criminal justice/police science; culinary arts; fine/studio arts; gerontology; hotel/motel administration; human services; information science/studies; kindergarten/preschool education; landscaping and groundskeeping; liberal arts and sciences/liberal studies; licensed practical/vocational nurse training; mathematics; medical administrative assistant and medical secretary; mental health counseling; music; music teacher education; nursing assistant/aide and patient care assistant/aide; pre-engineering; radiologic technology/science; registered nursing/registered nurse; respiratory care therapy; science teacher education; substance abuse/addiction counseling; surgical technology; surveying technology; turf and turfgrass management; web/multimedia management and webmaster.
Academics *Calendar:* semesters. *Degree:* certificates, diplomas, and associate. *Special study options:* academic remediation for entering students, advanced placement credit, cooperative education, distance learning, double majors, English as a second language, independent study, internships, off-campus study, part-time degree program, services for LD students, summer session for credit.
Library Boyd Library with 76,080 titles, 286 serial subscriptions, 2,317 audiovisual materials, an OPAC, a Web page.
Student Life *Housing:* college housing not available. *Activities and Organizations:* drama/theater group, student-run newspaper, choral group, marching band, Rotaract (Service Club - College Affiliate of Rotary International), Student Government Association, Outdoors Club, New Beginning Gospel Choir, Revolutionary Gamers Club. *Campus security:* 24-hour emergency response devices, security on duty until 12 am. *Student services:* personal/psychological counseling.
Athletics Member NJCAA. *Intercollegiate sports:* basketball M, golf M/W, volleyball W.
Costs (2010–11) *Tuition:* state resident $1695 full-time, $57 per credit hour part-time; nonresident $7455 full-time, $249 per credit hour part-time. Full-time tuition and fees vary according to location and program. Part-time tuition and fees vary according to location and program. *Required fees:* $97 full-time, $49 per term part-time. *Payment plan:* installment. *Waivers:* senior citizens and employees or children of employees.
Applying *Options:* electronic application, deferred entrance. *Required:* high school transcript. *Application deadlines:* rolling (freshmen), rolling (transfers). *Notification:* continuous (freshmen), continuous (transfers).
Freshman Application Contact Mr. Isai Robledo, Recruiter, Sandhills Community College, 3395 Airport Road, Pinehurst, NC 28374-8299. *Phone:* 910-246-5365. *Toll-free phone:* 800-338-3944. *Fax:* 910-695-3981. *E-mail:* robledoi@sandhills.edu. *Web site:* http://www.sandhills.edu/.

South College–Asheville

Asheville, North Carolina

Freshman Application Contact Director of Admissions, South College–Asheville, 1567 Patton Avenue, Asheville, NC 28806. *Phone:* 828-277-5521. *Fax:* 828-277-6151. *Web site:* http://www.southcollegenc.edu.

Southeastern Community College

Whiteville, North Carolina

Freshman Application Contact Ms. Sylvia Tart, Registrar, Southeastern Community College, PO Box 151, Whiteville, NC 28472. *Phone:* 910-642-

7141 Ext. 249. *Fax:* 910-642-5658. *E-mail:* start@sccnc.edu. *Web site:* http://www.sccnc.edu/.

South Piedmont Community College
Polkton, North Carolina

Freshman Application Contact Ms. Jeania Martin, Admissions Coordinator, South Piedmont Community College, PO Box 126, Polkton, NC 28135-0126. *Phone:* 704-272-7635. *Toll-free phone:* 800-766-0319. *E-mail:* abaucom@vnet.net. *Web site:* http://www.spcc.edu/.

Southwestern Community College
Sylva, North Carolina

Freshman Application Contact Mr. Delos Monteith, Institutional Research and Planning Officer, Southwestern Community College, 447 College Drive, Sylva, NC 28779. *Phone:* 828-586-4091 Ext. 236. *Toll-free phone:* 800-447-4091. *Fax:* 828-586-3129. *E-mail:* delos@southwesterncc.edu. *Web site:* http://www.southwesterncc.edu/.

Stanly Community College
Albemarle, North Carolina

- **State-supported** 2-year, founded 1971, part of North Carolina Community College System
- **Small-town** 150-acre campus with easy access to Charlotte
- **Coed**

Undergraduates Students come from 13 states and territories; 3 other countries; 3% are from out of state.
Faculty *Student/faculty ratio:* 9:1.
Academics *Calendar:* semesters. *Degree:* certificates, diplomas, and associate. *Special study options:* academic remediation for entering students, adult/continuing education programs, advanced placement credit, cooperative education, distance learning, double majors, English as a second language, independent study, internships, part-time degree program, services for LD students, study abroad, summer session for credit.
Student Life *Campus security:* 24-hour emergency response devices and patrols, late-night transport/escort service.
Costs (2010–11) *Tuition:* state resident $1695 full-time, $57 per credit part-time; nonresident $7455 full-time, $249 per credit part-time. *Required fees:* $121 full-time, $61 per term part-time.
Financial Aid Of all full-time matriculated undergraduates who enrolled in 2009, 20 Federal Work-Study jobs (averaging $1800).
Applying *Options:* electronic application, early admission, deferred entrance. *Required:* high school transcript.
Freshman Application Contact Mrs. Denise B. Ross, Associate Dean, Admissions, Stanly Community College, 141 College Drive, Albemarle, NC 28001. *Phone:* 704-982-0121 Ext. 264. *Fax:* 704-982-0255. *E-mail:* dross7926@stanly.edu. *Web site:* http://www.stanly.edu/.

Surry Community College
Dobson, North Carolina

Freshman Application Contact Renita Hazelwood, Director of Admissions, Surry Community College, 630 South Main Street, Dobson, NC 27017. *Phone:* 336-386-3392. *Fax:* 336-386-3690. *E-mail:* hazelwoodr@surry.edu. *Web site:* http://www.surry.edu/.

Tri-County Community College
Murphy, North Carolina

- **State-supported** 2-year, founded 1964, part of North Carolina Community College System
- **Rural** 40-acre campus
- **Coed**

Faculty *Student/faculty ratio:* 21:1.
Academics *Calendar:* semesters. *Degree:* certificates, diplomas, and associate. *Special study options:* academic remediation for entering students, adult/continuing education programs, distance learning, double majors, internships, part-time degree program, study abroad, summer session for credit.
Costs (2010–11) *Tuition:* state resident $1404 full-time, $57 per credit hour part-time; nonresident $5964 full-time, $278 per credit hour part-time. *Required fees:* $29 full-time.
Financial Aid Of all full-time matriculated undergraduates who enrolled in 2009, 11 Federal Work-Study jobs.
Applying *Required:* high school transcript.
Freshman Application Contact Dr. Jason Chambers, Director of Student Services and Admissions, Tri-County Community College, 21 Campus Circle,

Murphy, NC 28906-7919. *Phone:* 828-837-6810. *Fax:* 828-837-3266. *E-mail:* jchambers@tricountycc.edu. *Web site:* http://www.tricountycc.edu/.

Vance-Granville Community College
Henderson, North Carolina

Freshman Application Contact Ms. Kathy Kutl, Admissions Officer, Vance-Granville Community College, PO Box 917, State Road 1126, Henderson, NC 27536. *Phone:* 252-492-2061 Ext. 3265. *Fax:* 252-430-0460. *Web site:* http://www.vgcc.edu/.

Wake Technical Community College
Raleigh, North Carolina

Director of Admissions Ms. Susan Bloomfield, Director of Admissions, Wake Technical Community College, 9101 Fayetteville Road, Raleigh, NC 27603-5696. *Phone:* 919-866-5452. *E-mail:* srbloomfield@waketech.edu. *Web site:* http://www.waketech.edu/.

Wayne Community College
Goldsboro, North Carolina

- **State and locally supported** 2-year, founded 1957, part of North Carolina Community College System
- **Small-town** 125-acre campus
- **Endowment** $92,210
- **Coed**

Undergraduates 2,008 full-time, 1,577 part-time. Students come from 47 states and territories; 16% are from out of state; 19% transferred in.
Faculty *Student/faculty ratio:* 20:1.
Academics *Calendar:* semesters. *Degree:* certificates, diplomas, and associate. *Special study options:* academic remediation for entering students, adult/continuing education programs, advanced placement credit, cooperative education, distance learning, double majors, English as a second language, external degree program, honors programs, part-time degree program, services for LD students, summer session for credit.
Student Life *Campus security:* 24-hour emergency response devices and patrols, student patrols.
Costs (2010–11) *Tuition:* state resident $1808 full-time, $57 per credit hour part-time; nonresident $7952 full-time, $249 per credit hour part-time.
Financial Aid Of all full-time matriculated undergraduates who enrolled in 2009, 100 Federal Work-Study jobs (averaging $2000).
Applying *Options:* electronic application, deferred entrance. *Required:* high school transcript, interview.
Freshman Application Contact Ms. Jennifer Parker, Associate/Director of Admissions and Records, Wayne Community College, PO Box 8002, Goldsboro, NC 27533. *Phone:* 919-735-5151 Ext. 6721. *Fax:* 919-736-9425. *E-mail:* jbparker@waynecc.edu. *Web site:* http://www.waynecc.edu/.

Western Piedmont Community College
Morganton, North Carolina

Freshman Application Contact Susan Williams, Director of Admissions, Western Piedmont Community College, 1001 Burkemont Avenue, Morganton, NC 28655-4511. *Phone:* 828-438-6051. *Fax:* 828-438-6065. *E-mail:* swilliams@wpcc.edu. *Web site:* http://www.wpcc.edu/.

Wilkes Community College
Wilkesboro, North Carolina

Freshman Application Contact Mr. Mac Warren, Director of Admissions, Wilkes Community College, PO Box 120, Wilkesboro, NC 28697. *Phone:* 336-838-6141. *Fax:* 336-838-6547. *E-mail:* mac.warren@wilkescc.edu. *Web site:* http://www.wilkescc.edu/.

Wilson Community College
Wilson, North Carolina

- **State-supported** 2-year, founded 1958, part of North Carolina Community College System
- **Small-town** 35-acre campus
- **Endowment** $837,821
- **Coed**, 2,132 undergraduate students, 50% full-time, 67% women, 33% men

Undergraduates 1,075 full-time, 1,057 part-time. Students come from 1 other state; 48% Black or African American, non-Hispanic/Latino; 3% Hispanic/

Latino; 0.7% Asian, non-Hispanic/Latino; 0.1% Native Hawaiian or other Pacific Islander, non-Hispanic/Latino; 0.8% American Indian or Alaska Native, non-Hispanic/Latino; 0.1% Two or more races, non-Hispanic/Latino; 2% Race/ethnicity unknown; 13% transferred in.
Freshmen *Admission:* 1,628 applied, 930 admitted, 415 enrolled.
Faculty *Total:* 104, 49% full-time, 3% with terminal degrees. *Student/faculty ratio:* 12:1.
Majors Accounting; biology/biotechnology laboratory technician; business administration and management; computer and information systems security; computer systems networking and telecommunications; criminal justice/safety; early childhood education; electrician; elementary education; fire prevention and safety technology; fire science/firefighting; game and interactive media design; general studies; heating, air conditioning, ventilation and refrigeration maintenance technology; industrial technology; information technology; legal assistant/paralegal; liberal arts and sciences and humanities related; liberal arts and sciences/liberal studies; mechanical engineering/mechanical technology; medical office management; office management; registered nursing/registered nurse; sign language interpretation and translation; special education; surgical technology.
Academics *Calendar:* semesters. *Degree:* certificates, diplomas, and associate. *Special study options:* academic remediation for entering students, advanced placement credit, cooperative education, distance learning, double majors, English as a second language, independent study, internships, part-time degree program, services for LD students, summer session for credit.
Library 38,466 titles, an OPAC.
Student Life *Housing:* college housing not available. *Campus security:* 11-hour patrols by trained security personnel.
Costs (2010–11) *Tuition:* state resident $1808 full-time, $57 per credit hour part-time; nonresident $7952 full-time, $249 per credit hour part-time. *Required fees:* $99 full-time, $1 per credit hour part-time, $28 per term part-time.
Financial Aid Of all full-time matriculated undergraduates who enrolled in 2009, 65 Federal Work-Study jobs (averaging $1500).
Applying *Options:* electronic application, deferred entrance. *Required:* high school transcript. *Application deadlines:* rolling (freshmen), rolling (transfers). *Notification:* continuous (freshmen), continuous (transfers).
Freshman Application Contact Mrs. Maegan Williams, Admissions Technician, Wilson Community College, Wilson, NC 27893-0305. *Phone:* 252-246-1275. *Fax:* 252-243-7148. *E-mail:* mwilliams@wilsoncc.edu. *Web site:* http://www.wilsoncc.edu/.

NORTH DAKOTA

Bismarck State College
Bismarck, North Dakota

Freshman Application Contact Greg Sturm, Dean of Admissions and Enrollment Services, Bismarck State College, PO Box 5587, Bismarck, ND 58506-5587. *Phone:* 701-224-5426. *Toll-free phone:* 800-445-5073. *Fax:* 701-224-5643. *E-mail:* gregory.sturm@bsc.nodak.edu. *Web site:* http://www.bismarckstate.edu/.

Cankdeska Cikana Community College
Fort Totten, North Dakota

Director of Admissions Mr. Ermen Brown Jr., Registrar, Cankdeska Cikana Community College, PO Box 269, Fort Totten, ND 58335-0269. *Phone:* 701-766-1342. *Toll-free phone:* 888-783-1463. *Web site:* http://www.littlehoop.edu/.

Dakota College at Bottineau
Bottineau, North Dakota

- **State-supported** 2-year, founded 1906, part of North Dakota University System
- **Rural** 35-acre campus
- **Coed,** 863 undergraduate students, 46% full-time, 52% women, 48% men

Undergraduates 399 full-time, 464 part-time. Students come from 37 states and territories; 1 other country; 15% are from out of state; 5% Black or African American, non-Hispanic/Latino; 2% Hispanic/Latino; 1% Asian, non-Hispanic/Latino; 0.1% Native Hawaiian or other Pacific Islander, non-Hispanic/Latino; 4% American Indian or Alaska Native, non-Hispanic/Latino; 1% Two

or more races, non-Hispanic/Latino; 16% Race/ethnicity unknown; 3% international.
Freshmen *Admission:* 221 enrolled.
Faculty *Total:* 77, 35% full-time, 6% with terminal degrees. *Student/faculty ratio:* 18:1.
Majors Accounting; accounting related; accounting technology and book-keeping; administrative assistant and secretarial science; adult development and aging; advertising; agriculture; applied horticulture/horticultural business services related; applied horticulture/horticulture operations; biology/biological sciences; business administration and management; business automation/technology/data entry; chemistry; child-care and support services management; child-care provision; computer and information sciences; computer and information sciences and support services related; computer software and media applications related; computer technology/computer systems technology; crop production; education; entrepreneurial and small business related; environmental engineering technology; executive assistant/executive secretary; fishing and fisheries sciences and management; floriculture/floristry management; general studies; greenhouse management; health and physical education/fitness; health services/allied health/health sciences; history; horticultural science; hospitality and recreation marketing; humanities; information science/studies; information technology; landscaping and groundskeeping; liberal arts and sciences and humanities related; liberal arts and sciences/liberal studies; licensed practical/vocational nurse training; marketing/marketing management; marketing related; mathematics; medical administrative assistant and medical secretary; medical/clinical assistant; medical insurance coding; medical office assistant; medical transcription; natural resources/conservation; network and system administration; office management; office occupations and clerical services; ornamental horticulture; parks, recreation and leisure; parks, recreation and leisure facilities management; parks, recreation, leisure, and fitness studies related; physical sciences; physical sciences related; pre-medical studies; prenursing studies; pre-veterinary studies; psychology; receptionist; registered nursing/registered nurse; science technologies related; small business administration; social sciences; teacher assistant/aide; turf and turf-grass management; urban forestry; wildlife, fish and wildlands science and management; zoology/animal biology.
Academics *Calendar:* semesters. *Degree:* certificates, diplomas, and associate. *Special study options:* academic remediation for entering students, advanced placement credit, cooperative education, distance learning, double majors, off-campus study, part-time degree program, services for LD students, summer session for credit.
Library Dakota College at Bottineau Library plus 1 other with 46,294 titles, 174 serial subscriptions, an OPAC, a Web page.
Student Life *Housing:* on-campus residence required through sophomore year. *Options:* men-only, women-only. Campus housing is university owned. Freshman campus housing is guaranteed. *Activities and Organizations:* drama/theater group, student-run newspaper, Student Senate, Wildlife Club/Horticulture Club, Snowboarding Club, Phi Theta Kappa, Delta Epsilon Chi. *Campus security:* controlled dormitory access, Security cameras. *Student services:* health clinic, personal/psychological counseling.
Athletics Member NJCAA. *Intercollegiate sports:* baseball M(s), basketball M(s)/W(s), football M(s), ice hockey M(s), softball W(s), volleyball W(s). *Intramural sports:* archery M/W, badminton M/W, basketball M/W, skiing (downhill) M/W, volleyball M/W.
Standardized Tests *Required:* ACT (for admission).
Costs (2010–11) *Tuition:* state resident $3857 full-time; nonresident $5417 full-time. Full-time tuition and fees vary according to location and reciprocity agreements. Part-time tuition and fees vary according to course load, location, and reciprocity agreements. *Required fees:* $183 per credit hour part-time. *Room and board:* $4476. Room and board charges vary according to gender, housing facility, and location. *Waivers:* minority students and employees or children of employees.
Financial Aid Of all full-time matriculated undergraduates who enrolled in 2009, 50 Federal Work-Study jobs (averaging $1100).
Applying *Options:* electronic application, early admission, deferred entrance. *Application fee:* $35. *Required:* high school transcript, immunization records. *Application deadlines:* rolling (freshmen), rolling (out-of-state freshmen), rolling (transfers).
Freshman Application Contact Mrs. Luann Soland, Admissions Counselor, Dakota College at Bottineau, 105 Simrall Boulevard, Bottineau, ND 58318. *Phone:* 701-228-5487. *Toll-free phone:* 800-542-6866. *Fax:* 701-228-5499. *E-mail:* jancy.brisson@dakotacollege.edu. *Web site:* http://www.dakotacollege.edu/.

Fort Berthold Community College
New Town, North Dakota

Freshman Application Contact Office of Admissions, Fort Berthold Community College, PO Box 490, 220 8th Avenue North, New Town, ND 58763-0490. *Phone:* 701-627-4738 Ext. 295.

Lake Region State College

Devils Lake, North Dakota

- **State-supported** 2-year, founded 1941, part of North Dakota University System
- **Small-town** 120-acre campus
- **Coed,** 1,913 undergraduate students, 27% full-time, 57% women, 43% men

Undergraduates 524 full-time, 1,389 part-time. Students come from 31 states and territories; 10 other countries; 11% are from out of state; 4% transferred in; 20% live on campus. *Retention:* 45% of full-time freshmen returned.

Freshmen *Admission:* 317 enrolled.

Faculty *Total:* 154, 27% full-time, 11% with terminal degrees. *Student/faculty ratio:* 12:1.

Majors Accounting; accounting technology and bookkeeping; administrative assistant and secretarial science; agricultural business and management; automobile/automotive mechanics technology; avionics maintenance technology; business administration and management; child-care and support services management; child-care provision; computer and information sciences; computer programming (specific applications); computer programming (vendor/product certification); computer science; computer systems networking and telecommunications; criminal justice/police science; electrical and electronic engineering technologies related; electrical and electronics engineering; electrical/electronics equipment installation and repair; executive assistant/executive secretary; fashion merchandising; information technology; legal administrative assistant/secretary; legal assistant/paralegal; liberal arts and sciences/liberal studies; licensed practical/vocational nurse training; management information systems; marketing research; medical administrative assistant and medical secretary; multi/interdisciplinary studies related; nursing assistant/aide and patient care assistant/aide; office management; office occupations and clerical services; pathologist assistant; sales, distribution, and marketing operations; sign language interpretation and translation; small business administration.

Academics *Calendar:* semesters. *Degree:* certificates, diplomas, and associate. *Special study options:* academic remediation for entering students, adult/continuing education programs, cooperative education, distance learning, double majors, English as a second language, freshman honors college, honors programs, internships, part-time degree program, summer session for credit.

Library Paul Hoghaug Library with 60,000 titles, 200 serial subscriptions, 2,000 audiovisual materials, an OPAC.

Student Life *Housing Options:* men-only, women-only. Campus housing is university owned. *Activities and Organizations:* drama/theater group, DECA, drama, SOTA (Students Other than Average), Student Senate, Computer Club. *Campus security:* 24-hour emergency response devices, controlled dormitory access. *Student services:* personal/psychological counseling.

Athletics Member NJCAA. *Intercollegiate sports:* basketball M(s)/W(s). *Intramural sports:* basketball M/W, football M/W, golf M/W, ice hockey M/W, softball M/W, table tennis M/W, volleyball M/W.

Standardized Tests *Required:* SAT or ACT (for admission), COMPASS (for admission).

Costs (2010–11) *Tuition:* state resident $3065 full-time, $128 per credit hour part-time; nonresident $3065 full-time, $128 per credit hour part-time. Full-time tuition and fees vary according to course load, location, and program. Part-time tuition and fees vary according to location and program. *Required fees:* $843 full-time, $28 per credit hour part-time. *Room and board:* $4900; room only: $1860. Room and board charges vary according to board plan and housing facility. *Payment plan:* installment. *Waivers:* minority students.

Financial Aid Of all full-time matriculated undergraduates who enrolled in 2009, 398 applied for aid, 331 were judged to have need, 326 had their need fully met. 33 Federal Work-Study jobs (averaging $1503). In 2009, 172 non-need-based awards were made. *Average percent of need met:* 70%. *Average financial aid package:* $7300. *Average need-based loan:* $2836. *Average need-based gift aid:* $4584. *Average non-need-based aid:* $599.

Applying *Options:* electronic application. *Application fee:* $35. *Required:* high school transcript, immunizations, transcripts. *Required for some:* interview. *Application deadlines:* rolling (freshmen), rolling (transfers). *Notification:* continuous (freshmen), continuous (transfers).

Freshman Application Contact Ms. Kelsey Walters, Administrative Assistant, Admissions Office, Lake Region State College, 1801 College Drive North, Devils Lake, ND 58301. *Phone:* 701-662-1514. *Toll-free phone:* 800-443-1313 Ext. 514. *Fax:* 701-662-1581. *E-mail:* kelsey.walters@lrsc.edu. *Web site:* http://www.lrsc.edu/.

North Dakota State College of Science

Wahpeton, North Dakota

- **State-supported** 2-year, founded 1903, part of North Dakota University System
- **Rural** 125-acre campus
- **Endowment** $9.3 million
- **Coed,** 2,833 undergraduate students, 60% full-time, 45% women, 55% men

Undergraduates 1,703 full-time, 1,130 part-time. Students come from 33 states and territories; 10 other countries; 40% are from out of state; 4% Black or African American, non-Hispanic/Latino; 0.4% Hispanic/Latino; 0.5% Asian, non-Hispanic/Latino; 2% American Indian or Alaska Native, non-Hispanic/Latino; 0.3% Two or more races, non-Hispanic/Latino; 1% international; 66% live on campus. *Retention:* 70% of full-time freshmen returned.

Freshmen *Admission:* 861 applied, 696 admitted, 655 enrolled. *Average high school GPA:* 2.73.

Faculty *Total:* 256, 43% full-time, 5% with terminal degrees. *Student/faculty ratio:* 13:1.

Majors Agricultural business and management; architectural engineering technology; autobody/collision and repair technology; automobile/automotive mechanics technology; building/construction site management; business/commerce; civil engineering technology; computer programming (specific applications); construction engineering technology; culinary arts; dental assisting; dental hygiene; diesel mechanics technology; electrical and electronic engineering technologies related; emergency medical technology (EMT paramedic); engineering technologies and engineering related; health information/medical records technology; heating, air conditioning, ventilation and refrigeration maintenance technology; heating, ventilation, air conditioning and refrigeration engineering technology; liberal arts and sciences/liberal studies; licensed practical/vocational nurse training; machine tool technology; multi/interdisciplinary studies related; occupational therapist assistant; pharmacy technician; psychiatric/mental health services technology; science technologies related; small engine mechanics and repair technology; vehicle maintenance and repair technologies related; welding technology.

Academics *Calendar:* semesters. *Degree:* certificates, diplomas, and associate. *Special study options:* academic remediation for entering students, adult/continuing education programs, cooperative education, distance learning, double majors, English as a second language, independent study, internships, part-time degree program, services for LD students, student-designed majors, summer session for credit.

Library Mildred Johnson Library with 78,876 titles, 242 serial subscriptions, 4,046 audiovisual materials, an OPAC, a Web page.

Student Life *Housing:* on-campus residence required for freshman year. *Options:* coed, men-only, women-only. Campus housing is university owned. Freshman campus housing is guaranteed. *Activities and Organizations:* drama/theater group, choral group, marching band, music, Drama Club, Inter-Varsity Christian Fellowship, Cultural Diversity, Habitat for Humanity. *Campus security:* 24-hour emergency response devices and patrols, student patrols, late-night transport/escort service, controlled dormitory access. *Student services:* health clinic, personal/psychological counseling, legal services.

Athletics Member NJCAA. *Intercollegiate sports:* basketball M(s)/W(s), football M(s), softball W, volleyball W(s). *Intramural sports:* baseball M, basketball M/W, cheerleading W, field hockey M/W, football M, racquetball M/W, softball M/W, volleyball M/W.

Standardized Tests *Required:* ACT (for admission).

Costs (2010–11) *Tuition:* state resident $4173 full-time; nonresident $10,171 full-time. Full-time tuition and fees vary according to program. Part-time tuition and fees vary according to program. *Room and board:* $5728. Room and board charges vary according to board plan. *Payment plan:* installment. *Waivers:* minority students, children of alumni, and employees or children of employees.

Financial Aid Of all full-time matriculated undergraduates who enrolled in 2008, 1,245 applied for aid, 925 were judged to have need, 904 had their need fully met. *Average percent of need met:* 62%. *Average financial aid package:* $7164. *Average need-based loan:* $3791. *Average need-based gift aid:* $3121.

Applying *Options:* electronic application, early admission. *Application fee:* $35. *Required:* high school transcript. *Application deadlines:* rolling (freshmen), rolling (out-of-state freshmen), rolling (transfers). *Notification:* continuous (freshmen), continuous (out-of-state freshmen), continuous (transfers).

Freshman Application Contact Ms. Karen Reilly, Director of Enrollment Services, North Dakota State College of Science, 800 North 6th Street, Wahpeton, ND 58076. *Phone:* 701-671-2189. *Toll-free phone:* 800-342-4325 Ext. 2202. *Fax:* 701-671-2332. *Web site:* http://www.ndscs.nodak.edu/.

Rasmussen College Bismarck

Bismarck, North Dakota

Admissions Office Contact Rasmussen College Bismarck, 1701 East Century Avenue, Bismarck, ND 58503. *Toll-free phone:* 877-530-9600. *Web site:* http://www.rasmussen.edu/.

Rasmussen College Fargo

Fargo, North Dakota

Freshman Application Contact Ms. Elizabeth Largent, Director, Rasmussen College Fargo, 4012 19th Avenue, SW, Fargo, ND 58103. *Phone:* 701-277-3889. *Toll-free phone:* 800-817-0009. *Fax:* 701-277-5604. *Web site:* http://www.rasmussen.edu/.

Sitting Bull College

Fort Yates, North Dakota

Director of Admissions Ms. Melody Silk, Director of Registration and Admissions, Sitting Bull College, 1341 92nd Street, Fort Yates, ND 58538-9701. *Phone:* 701-854-3864. *Fax:* 701-854-3403. *E-mail:* melodys@sbcl.edu. *Web site:* http://www.sittingbull.edu/.

Turtle Mountain Community College

Belcourt, North Dakota

Director of Admissions Ms. Joni LaFontaine, Admissions/Records Officer, Turtle Mountain Community College, Box 340, Belcourt, ND 58316-0340. *Phone:* 701-477-5605 Ext. 217. *E-mail:* jlafontaine@tm.edu. *Web site:* http://www.turtle-mountain.cc.nd.us/.

United Tribes Technical College

Bismarck, North Dakota

Freshman Application Contact Ms. Vivian Gillette, Director of Admissions, United Tribes Technical College, Bismarck, ND 58504. *Phone:* 701-255-3285 Ext. 1334. *Fax:* 701-530-0640. *E-mail:* vgillette@uttc.edu. *Web site:* http://www.uttc.edu/.

Williston State College

Williston, North Dakota

Freshman Application Contact Ms. Jan Solem, Director for Admission and Records, Williston State College, PO Box 1326, Williston, ND 58802-1326. *Phone:* 701-774-4554. *Toll-free phone:* 888-863-9455. *Fax:* 701-774-4211. *E-mail:* wsc.admission@wsc.nodak.edu. *Web site:* http://www.wsc.nodak.edu/.

NORTHERN MARIANA ISLANDS

Northern Marianas College

Saipan, Northern Mariana Islands

Freshman Application Contact Ms. Leilani M. Basa-Alam, Admission Specialist, Northern Marianas College, PO Box 501250, Saipan, MP 96950-1250. *Phone:* 670-234-3690 Ext. 1539. *Fax:* 670-235-4967. *E-mail:* leilanib@nmcnet.edu. *Web site:* http://www.nmcnet.edu/.

OHIO

Academy of Court Reporting

Akron, Ohio

Freshman Application Contact Admissions, Academy of Court Reporting, 2930 West Market Street, Akron, OH 44333. *Phone:* 330-867-4030. *Toll-free phone:* 866-323-0540. *Fax:* 330-867-3432. *E-mail:* careeradvocate@miamijacobs.edu. *Web site:* http://www.acr.edu/.

Academy of Court Reporting

Cleveland, Ohio

Freshman Application Contact Director of Admissions, Academy of Court Reporting, 2044 Euclid Avenue, Cleveland, OH 44115. *Phone:* 216-861-3222. *Fax:* 216-861-4517. *Web site:* http://www.acr.edu/.

Akron Institute of Herzing University

Akron, Ohio

Admissions Office Contact Akron Institute of Herzing University, 1600 South Arlington Street, Suite 100, Akron, OH 44306. *Toll-free phone:* 800-311-0512. *Web site:* http://www.akroninstitute.com/.

Antonelli College

Cincinnati, Ohio

- **Proprietary** 2-year, founded 1947
- **Urban** campus
- **Coed**

Academics *Calendar:* quarters. *Degree:* diplomas and associate. *Special study options:* honors programs, internships, part-time degree program, summer session for credit.

Student Life *Campus security:* 24-hour emergency response devices, security personnel while classes are in session.

Applying *Options:* early admission, deferred entrance. *Application fee:* $100. *Required:* high school transcript, interview. *Required for some:* art portfolio.

Freshman Application Contact Antonelli College, 124 East Seventh Street, Cincinnati, OH 45202. *Phone:* 513-241-4338. *Toll-free phone:* 800-505-4338. *Web site:* http://www.antonellicollege.edu/.

The Art Institute of Cincinnati

Cincinnati, Ohio

Director of Admissions Director of Admissions, The Art Institute of Cincinnati, 1171 East Kemper Road, Cincinnati, OH 45246. *Phone:* 513-751-1206. *Fax:* 513-751-1209. *Web site:* http://www.aic-arts.edu/.

The Art Institute of Ohio–Cincinnati

Cincinnati, Ohio

- **Proprietary** primarily 2-year, part of Education Management Corporation
- **Urban** campus
- **Coed**

Majors Advertising; animation, interactive technology, video graphics and special effects; cinematography and film/video production; culinary arts; design and visual communications; fashion merchandising; graphic design; interior design; restaurant, culinary, and catering management; web page, digital/multimedia and information resources design.

Academics *Calendar:* continuous. *Degrees:* diplomas, associate, and bachelor's.

Costs (2010–11) *Tuition:* Tuition cost varies by program. Prospective students should contact the school for current tuition costs. Other charges include a starting kit for all first-quarter students. Kits vary in price, depending on the program of study.

Freshman Application Contact The Art Institute of Ohio–Cincinnati, 8845 Governors Hill Drive, Cincinnati, OH 45249-3317. *Phone:* 513-833-2400. *Toll-free phone:* 866-613-5184. *Web site:* http://www.artinstitutes.edu/cincinnati/.

ATS Institute of Technology

Highland Heights, Ohio

- **Proprietary** 2-year
- **Suburban** campus with easy access to Cleveland
- **Coed**, 353 undergraduate students

Majors Licensed practical/vocational nurse training.

Academics *Degree:* diplomas and associate. *Special study options:* academic remediation for entering students, accelerated degree program, advanced placement credit, English as a second language, external degree program, part-time degree program. *Unusual degree programs:* nursing.

Library ATS Library plus 1 other.

Student Life *Campus security:* security guard. *Student services:* personal/psychological counseling.

Standardized Tests *Required:* Entrance exam called PSB (Psychological Service Bureau) is required for all entering students except for those applying for Bridge program (for admission).

Costs (2011–12) *Tuition:* $40,000 full-time. Full-time tuition and fees vary according to course load, degree level, and program. Part-time tuition and fees vary according to course load and program. *Payment plan:* installment.

Applying *Application fee:* $30. *Required:* high school transcript, minimum 2.5 GPA, interview, complete background check and physical evaluation. *Required for some:* essay or personal statement, .

Freshman Application Contact Admissions Office, ATS Institute of Technology, 325 Alpha Park, Highland Heights, OH 44143. *Phone:* 440-449-1700 Ext. 103. *E-mail:* info@atsinstitute.edu. *Web site:* http://www.atsinstitute.edu/.

Belmont Technical College

St. Clairsville, Ohio

Director of Admissions Michael Sterling, Director of Recruitment, Belmont Technical College, 120 Fox Shannon Place, St. Clairsville, OH 43950-9735. *Phone:* 740-695-9500 Ext. 1563. *Toll-free phone:* 800-423-1188. *E-mail:* msterling@btc.edu. *Web site:* http://www.btc.edu/.

Bowling Green State University-Firelands College

Huron, Ohio

- **State-supported** primarily 2-year, founded 1968, part of Bowling Green State University System
- **Rural** 216-acre campus with easy access to Cleveland and Toledo
- **Endowment** $2.0 million
- **Coed**

Undergraduates 1,352 full-time, 1,102 part-time. Students come from 4 states and territories; 6% transferred in.

Faculty *Student/faculty ratio:* 18:1.

Academics *Calendar:* semesters. *Degrees:* certificates, associate, and bachelor's (also offers some upper-level and graduate courses). *Special study options:* academic remediation for entering students, adult/continuing education programs, advanced placement credit, distance learning, double majors, independent study, internships, part-time degree program, services for LD students, student-designed majors, summer session for credit. *ROTC:* Army (c), Air Force (c).

Student Life *Campus security:* 24-hour emergency response devices, late-night transport/escort service, patrols by trained security personnel.

Costs (2010–11) *Tuition:* state resident $4308 full-time, $2154 per year part-time; nonresident $11,616 full-time, $5814 per year part-time. Full-time tuition and fees vary according to course load and location. Part-time tuition and fees vary according to course load and location. *Required fees:* $220 full-time, $118 per year part-time. *Payment plans:* tuition prepayment, installment.

Applying *Options:* electronic application, early admission, deferred entrance. *Application fee:* $40. *Required:* high school transcript.

Freshman Application Contact Debralee Divers, Director of Admissions and Financial Aid, Bowling Green State University-Firelands College, One University Drive, Huron, OH 44839-9791. *Phone:* 419-433-5560. *Toll-free phone:* 800-322-4787. *Fax:* 419-372-0604. *E-mail:* divers@bgsu.edu. *Web site:* http://www.firelands.bgsu.edu/.

Bradford School

Columbus, Ohio

- **Private** 2-year, founded 1911
- **Suburban** campus
- **Coed, primarily women,** 657 undergraduate students
- 52% of applicants were admitted

Freshmen *Admission:* 2,120 applied, 1,094 admitted.

Majors Accounting and business/management; business administration and management; computer programming; culinary arts; graphic design; legal administrative assistant/secretary; legal assistant/paralegal; medical/clinical assistant; system, networking, and LAN/WAN management; tourism and travel services management; veterinary/animal health technology.

Academics *Calendar:* semesters. *Degree:* diplomas and associate. *Special study options:* accelerated degree program, independent study.

Freshman Application Contact Admissions Office, Bradford School, 2469 Stelzer Road, Columbus, OH 43219. *Phone:* 614-416-6200. *Toll-free phone:* 800-678-7981. *Web site:* http://www.bradfordschoolcolumbus.edu/.

Brown Mackie College–Akron

Akron, Ohio

- **Proprietary** 2-year, founded 1968, part of Education Management Corporation
- **Suburban** campus
- **Coed**

Majors Accounting technology and bookkeeping; business administration and management; criminal justice/law enforcement administration; data modeling/warehousing and database administration; early childhood education; health/health-care administration; information technology; legal assistant/paralegal; medical/clinical assistant; occupational therapist assistant; office management; pharmacy technician; surgical technology; veterinary/animal health technology.

Academics *Calendar:* quarters. *Degree:* certificates, diplomas, and associate.

Costs (2010–11) *Tuition:* Tuition varies by program. Students should contact Brown Mackie College for tuition information.

Freshman Application Contact Brown Mackie College–Akron, 755 White Pond Drive, Suite 101, Akron, OH 44320. *Phone:* 330-869-3600. *Web site:* http://www.brownmackie.edu/akron/.

See page 354 for the College Close-Up.

Brown Mackie College–Cincinnati

Cincinnati, Ohio

- **Proprietary** 2-year, founded 1927, part of Education Management Corporation
- **Suburban** campus
- **Coed**

Majors Accounting technology and bookkeeping; audiovisual communications technologies related; biomedical technology; business administration and management; computer systems networking and telecommunications; criminal justice/law enforcement administration; data modeling/warehousing and database administration; early childhood education; electrical, electronic and communications engineering technology; health/health-care administration; information technology; legal assistant/paralegal; medical/clinical assistant; office management; pharmacy technician; surgical technology; veterinary/animal health technology.

Academics *Calendar:* quarters. *Degree:* certificates, diplomas, and associate.

Costs (2010–11) *Tuition:* Tuition varies by program. Students should contact Brown Mackie College for tuition information.

Freshman Application Contact Brown Mackie College–Cincinnati, 1011 Glendale-Milford Road, Cincinnati, OH 45215. *Phone:* 513-771-2424. *Toll-free phone:* 800-888-1445. *Web site:* http://www.brownmackie.edu/cincinnati/

See page 364 for the College Close-Up.

Brown Mackie College–Findlay

Findlay, Ohio

- **Proprietary** 2-year, founded 1929, part of Education Management Corporation
- **Rural** campus
- **Coed**

Majors Accounting technology and bookkeeping; business administration and management; criminal justice/law enforcement administration; early childhood education; health/health-care administration; legal assistant/paralegal; medical/clinical assistant; occupational therapist assistant; office management; pharmacy technician; surgical technology; veterinary/animal health technology.

Academics *Calendar:* continuous. *Degree:* diplomas and associate.

Costs (2010–11) *Tuition:* Tuition varies by program. Students should contact Brown Mackie College for tuition information.

Freshman Application Contact Brown Mackie College–Findlay, 1700 Fostoria Avenue, Suite 100, Findlay, OH 45840. *Phone:* 419-423-2211. *Toll-free phone:* 800-842-3687. *Web site:* http://www.brownmackie.edu/findlay/.

See page 366 for the College Close-Up.

Brown Mackie College–North Canton

Canton, Ohio

- **Proprietary** 2-year, founded 1929, part of Education Management Corporation
- **Suburban** campus
- **Coed**

Majors Accounting technology and bookkeeping; business administration and management; CAD/CADD drafting/design technology; computer systems networking and telecommunications; criminal justice/law enforcement administration; health/health-care administration; legal assistant/paralegal; medical/clinical assistant; pharmacy technician; surgical technology; veterinary/animal health technology.

Academics *Calendar:* quarters. *Degree:* diplomas and associate.

Costs (2010–11) *Tuition:* Tuition varies by program. Students should contact Brown Mackie College for tuition information.

Freshman Application Contact Brown Mackie College–North Canton, 4300 Munson Street NW, Canton, OH 44718-3674. *Phone:* 330-494-1214. *Web site:* http://www.brownmackie.edu/northcanton/.

See page 386 for the College Close-Up.

Bryant & Stratton College

Eastlake, Ohio

- **Proprietary** primarily 2-year, founded 1987, part of Bryant and Stratton College, Inc.
- **Suburban** campus with easy access to Cleveland
- **Coed**

Undergraduates 490 full-time, 272 part-time. Students come from 1 other state; 1% transferred in. *Retention:* 28% of full-time freshmen returned.

Faculty *Student/faculty ratio:* 12:1.

Academics *Calendar:* semesters. *Degrees:* associate and bachelor's. *Special study options:* academic remediation for entering students, advanced placement credit, distance learning, independent study, internships, part-time degree program, summer session for credit.

Student Life *Campus security:* 24-hour emergency response devices, late-night transport/escort service.

Standardized Tests *Required:* CPAt (for admission). *Recommended:* SAT or ACT (for admission).

Financial Aid Of all full-time matriculated undergraduates who enrolled in 2009, 12 Federal Work-Study jobs (averaging $2800).

Applying *Options:* deferred entrance. *Application fee:* $35. *Required:* high school transcript, interview, entrance evaluation and placement evaluation. *Required for some:* essay or personal statement. *Recommended:* minimum 2.0 GPA.

Freshman Application Contact Ms. Melanie Pettit, Director of Admissions, Bryant & Stratton College, 35350 Curtis Boulevard, Eastlake, OH 44095. *Phone:* 440-510-1112. *Web site:* http://www.bryantstratton.edu/.

Bryant & Stratton College

Parma, Ohio

- **Proprietary** primarily 2-year, founded 1981, part of Bryant and Stratton College, Inc.
- **Suburban** 4-acre campus with easy access to Cleveland
- **Coed**

Undergraduates 288 full-time, 240 part-time. Students come from 1 other state. *Retention:* 60% of full-time freshmen returned.

Faculty *Student/faculty ratio:* 12:1.

Academics *Calendar:* semesters. *Degrees:* associate and bachelor's. *Special study options:* academic remediation for entering students, cooperative education, distance learning, double majors, independent study, internships, part-time degree program, summer session for credit.

Student Life *Campus security:* 24-hour emergency response devices.

Standardized Tests *Required:* CPAt (for admission). *Recommended:* SAT or ACT (for admission).

Applying *Options:* deferred entrance. *Required:* high school transcript, interview, entrance evaluation and placement evaluation.

Freshman Application Contact Bryant & Stratton College, 12955 Snow Road, Parma, OH 44130-1013. *Phone:* 216-265-3151. *Toll-free phone:* 800-327-3151. *Web site:* http://www.bryantstratton.edu/.

Central Ohio Technical College

Newark, Ohio

- **State-supported** 2-year, founded 1971, part of Ohio Board of Regents
- **Small-town** 155-acre campus with easy access to Columbus
- **Endowment** $1.7 million
- **Coed**

Undergraduates 2,213 full-time, 2,137 part-time. Students come from 3 states and territories; 1% are from out of state; 6% transferred in. *Retention:* 51% of full-time freshmen returned.

Faculty *Student/faculty ratio:* 22:1.

Academics *Calendar:* quarters. *Degree:* certificates and associate. *Special study options:* academic remediation for entering students, accelerated degree program, adult/continuing education programs, advanced placement credit, cooperative education, distance learning, double majors, English as a second

language, internships, off-campus study, part-time degree program, services for LD students, summer session for credit.

Student Life *Campus security:* 24-hour emergency response devices and patrols, student patrols, late-night transport/escort service.

Costs (2010–11) *Tuition:* state resident $3852 full-time, $107 per credit hour part-time; nonresident $6552 full-time, $182 per credit hour part-time.

Financial Aid Of all full-time matriculated undergraduates who enrolled in 2009, 43 Federal Work-Study jobs (averaging $4000).

Applying *Options:* electronic application, early admission, deferred entrance. *Application fee:* $20. *Required:* high school transcript.

Freshman Application Contact Mr. John K. Merrin, Admissions Representative, Central Ohio Technical College, 1179 University Drive, Newark, OH 43055-1767. *Phone:* 740-366-9222. *Toll-free phone:* 800-9NEWARK. *Fax:* 740-366-5047. *E-mail:* jmerrin@cotc.edu. *Web site:* http://www.cotc.edu/.

Chatfield College

St. Martin, Ohio

Freshman Application Contact Chatfield College, 20918 State Route 251, St. Martin, OH 45118-9705. *Phone:* 513-875-3344 Ext. 137. *Web site:* http://www.chatfield.edu/.

The Christ College of Nursing and Health Sciences

Cincinnati, Ohio

Freshman Application Contact Mr. Bradley Jackson, Admissions, The Christ College of Nursing and Health Sciences, 2139 Auburn Avenue, Cincinnati, OH 45219. *Phone:* 513-585-0016. *E-mail:* bradley.jackson@thechristcollege.edu. *Web site:* http://www.thechristcollege.edu/.

Cincinnati State Technical and Community College

Cincinnati, Ohio

- **State-supported** 2-year, founded 1966, part of Ohio Board of Regents
- **Urban** 46-acre campus
- **Coed**, 10,995 undergraduate students, 38% full-time, 53% women, 47% men

Undergraduates 4,206 full-time, 6,789 part-time. Students come from 8 states and territories; 76 other countries; 10% are from out of state; 27% Black or African American, non-Hispanic/Latino; 1% Hispanic/Latino; 1% Asian, non-Hispanic/Latino; 0.9% American Indian or Alaska Native, non-Hispanic/Latino; 1% Two or more races, non-Hispanic/Latino; 6% Race/ethnicity unknown; 1% international. *Retention:* 51% of full-time freshmen returned.

Freshmen *Admission:* 2,515 enrolled.

Faculty *Total:* 724, 26% full-time. *Student/faculty ratio:* 18:1.

Majors Accounting; administrative assistant and secretarial science; aeronautical/aerospace engineering technology; allied health and medical assisting services related; applied horticulture/horticultural business services related; architectural engineering technology; automotive engineering technology; biomedical technology; business administration and management; business, management, and marketing related; chemical technology; child-care provision; cinematography and film/video production; civil engineering technology; clinical/medical laboratory technology; commercial and advertising art; computer and information sciences; computer engineering technology; computer programming; computer programming (specific applications); criminal justice/police science; culinary arts; diagnostic medical sonography and ultrasound technology; dietetics; electrical and electronic engineering technologies related; electrical, electronic and communications engineering technology; electromechanical technology; emergency medical technology (EMT paramedic); entrepreneurship; environmental engineering technology; executive assistant/executive secretary; fire science/firefighting; general studies; health information/medical records technology; health professions related; heating, ventilation, air conditioning and refrigeration engineering technology; hotel/motel administration; information science/studies; international business/trade/commerce; landscaping and groundskeeping; laser and optical technology; liberal arts and sciences/liberal studies; management information systems; marketing/marketing management; mechanical engineering/mechanical technology; mechanic and repair technologies related; medical/clinical assistant; occupational therapist assistant; office management; parks, recreation, leisure, and fitness studies related; plastics and polymer engineering technology; professional, technical, business, and scientific writing; purchasing, procurement/acquisitions and contracts management; real estate; registered nursing/registered nurse; respiratory care therapy; restaurant, culinary, and catering management; science technologies related; security and loss prevention; sign language interpretation and translation; surgical technology; surveying technology; telecommunications technology; turf and turfgrass management.

Academics *Calendar:* 5 ten-week terms. *Degree:* certificates and associate. *Special study options:* academic remediation for entering students, advanced placement credit, cooperative education, distance learning, double majors, English as a second language, honors programs, independent study, internships, off-campus study, part-time degree program, services for LD students, student-designed majors, summer session for credit.

Library Johnnie Mae Berry Library plus 1 other with 39,802 titles, 309 serial subscriptions, 3,570 audiovisual materials, an OPAC, a Web page.

Student Life *Housing:* college housing not available. *Activities and Organizations:* drama/theater group, student government, Nursing Student Association, Phi Theta Kappa, American Society of Civil Engineers, Students in Free Enterprise (SIFE). *Campus security:* 24-hour emergency response devices and patrols, late-night transport/escort service. *Student services:* personal/psychological counseling.

Athletics Member NJCAA. *Intercollegiate sports:* basketball M/W, golf M/W, soccer M/W. *Intramural sports:* cheerleading W.

Costs (2011–12) *One-time required fee:* $10. *Tuition:* state resident $4128 full-time, $86 per credit hour part-time; nonresident $8256 full-time, $172 per credit hour part-time. *Required fees:* $258 full-time, $6 per credit hour part-time, $31 per term part-time. *Waivers:* employees or children of employees.

Financial Aid Of all full-time matriculated undergraduates who enrolled in 2009, 100 Federal Work-Study jobs (averaging $3500).

Applying *Options:* electronic application. *Required:* high school transcript. *Application deadlines:* rolling (freshmen), rolling (transfers). *Notification:* continuous (freshmen).

Freshman Application Contact Ms. Gabriele Boeckermann, Director of Admission, Cincinnati State Technical and Community College, Cincinnati, OH 45223-2690. *Phone:* 513-569-1550. *Fax:* 513-569-1562. *E-mail:* adm@cincinnatistate.edu. *Web site:* http://www.cincinnatistate.edu/.

Clark State Community College

Springfield, Ohio

Freshman Application Contact Admissions Office, Clark State Community College, PO Box 570, Springfield, OH 45501-0570. *Phone:* 937-328-3858. *Fax:* 937-328-6133. *E-mail:* admissions@clarkstate.edu. *Web site:* http://www.clarkstate.edu/.

Cleveland Institute of Electronics

Cleveland, Ohio

- **Proprietary** 2-year, founded 1934
- **Coed, primarily men,** 1,731 undergraduate students

Undergraduates Students come from 52 states and territories; 70 other countries; 97% are from out of state.

Faculty *Total:* 8, 50% full-time, 13% with terminal degrees.

Majors Computer/information technology services administration related; computer software engineering; electrical, electronic and communications engineering technology.

Academics *Calendar:* continuous. *Degrees:* diplomas and associate (offers only external degree programs conducted through home study). *Special study options:* accelerated degree program, adult/continuing education programs, distance learning, external degree program, independent study, part-time degree program.

Library 5,000 titles, 38 serial subscriptions.

Costs (2011–12) *Tuition:* $1885 per term part-time. No tuition increase for student's term of enrollment. *Payment plans:* tuition prepayment, installment.

Applying *Options:* electronic application, early admission. *Required:* high school transcript. *Application deadlines:* rolling (freshmen), rolling (out-of-state freshmen), rolling (transfers). *Notification:* continuous (freshmen), continuous (out-of-state freshmen), continuous (transfers).

Freshman Application Contact Mr. Scott Katzenmeyer, Registrar, Cleveland Institute of Electronics, Cleveland, OH 44114. *Phone:* 216-781-9400. *Toll-free phone:* 800-243-6446. *Fax:* 216-781-0331. *E-mail:* instruct@cie-wc.edu. *Web site:* http://www.cie-wc.edu/.

Columbus Culinary Institute at Bradford School

Columbus, Ohio

- **Private** 2-year, founded 2006
- **Suburban** campus
- **Coed,** 241 undergraduate students
- 53% of applicants were admitted

Freshmen *Admission:* 1,028 applied, 546 admitted.

Majors Culinary arts.

Academics *Calendar:* semesters. *Degree:* associate.

Freshman Application Contact Admissions Office, Columbus Culinary Institute at Bradford School, 2435 Stelzer Road, Columbus, OH 43219. *Phone:* 614-944-4200. *Toll-free phone:* 800-678-7981. *Web site:* http://www.columbusculinary.com/.

Columbus State Community College

Columbus, Ohio

Freshman Application Contact Ms. Tari Blaney, Director of Admissions, Columbus State Community College, Box 1609, Columbus, OH 43216-1609. *Phone:* 614-287-2669. *Toll-free phone:* 800-621-6407 Ext. 2669. *Fax:* 614-287-6019. *E-mail:* tblaney@cscc.edu. *Web site:* http://www.cscc.edu/.

Cuyahoga Community College

Cleveland, Ohio

- **State and locally supported** 2-year, founded 1963
- **Urban** campus
- **Endowment** $22.5 million
- **Coed**

Undergraduates 12,120 full-time, 18,205 part-time. Students come from 32 states and territories; 27 other countries; 1% are from out of state; 4% transferred in. *Retention:* 48% of full-time freshmen returned.

Faculty *Student/faculty ratio:* 18:1.

Academics *Calendar:* semesters. *Degree:* certificates and associate. *Special study options:* adult/continuing education programs, advanced placement credit, cooperative education, distance learning, English as a second language, external degree program, independent study, part-time degree program, services for LD students, summer session for credit.

Student Life *Campus security:* 24-hour emergency response devices and patrols, late-night transport/escort service.

Athletics Member NJCAA.

Costs (2010–11) *Tuition:* area resident $2537 full-time, $85 per credit hour part-time; state resident $3354 full-time, $112 per credit hour part-time; nonresident $6868 full-time, $229 per credit hour part-time. *Payment plans:* installment, deferred payment.

Financial Aid Of all full-time matriculated undergraduates who enrolled in 2009, 802 Federal Work-Study jobs (averaging $3300).

Applying *Options:* early admission, deferred entrance. *Required for some:* high school transcript.

Freshman Application Contact Mr. Kevin McDaniel, Director of Admissions and Records, Cuyahoga Community College, Cleveland, OH 44115. *Phone:* 216-987-4030. *Toll-free phone:* 800-954-8742. *Fax:* 216-696-2567. *Web site:* http://www.tri-c.edu/.

Davis College

Toledo, Ohio

- **Proprietary** 2-year, founded 1858
- **Urban** 1-acre campus with easy access to Detroit
- **Coed**

Undergraduates 207 full-time, 320 part-time. Students come from 2 states and territories; 3% are from out of state; 16% transferred in.

Faculty *Student/faculty ratio:* 15:1.

Academics *Calendar:* quarters. *Degree:* diplomas and associate. *Special study options:* academic remediation for entering students, adult/continuing education programs, advanced placement credit, distance learning, internships, part-time degree program, summer session for credit.

Student Life *Campus security:* 24-hour emergency response devices, security cameras for parking lot.

Standardized Tests *Required:* CPAt (for admission).

Costs (2010–11) *Tuition:* $9036 full-time, $251 per credit hour part-time. *Required fees:* $480 full-time.

Financial Aid Of all full-time matriculated undergraduates who enrolled in 2009, 10 Federal Work-Study jobs (averaging $3500).

Applying *Options:* electronic application, early admission, deferred entrance. *Application fee:* $30. *Required:* high school transcript, interview.

Freshman Application Contact Ms. Dana Stern, Davis College, 4747 Monroe Street, Toledo, OH 43623-4307. *Phone:* 419-473-2700. *Toll-free phone:* 800-477-7021. *Fax:* 419-473-2472. *E-mail:* dstern@daviscollege.edu. *Web site:* http://daviscollege.edu/.

Daymar College

Chillicothe, Ohio

Freshman Application Contact Admissions Office, Daymar College, 1410 Industrial Drive, Chillicothe, OH 45601. *Phone:* 740-774-6300. *Toll-free* *phone:* 877-258-7796. *Fax:* 740-774-6317. *Web site:* http://www.daymarcollege.edu/.

Daymar College
Jackson, Ohio

Freshman Application Contact Admissions Office, Daymar College, 504 McCarty Lane, Jackson, OH 45640. *Phone:* 740-286-1554. *Toll-free phone:* 877-258-7796. *Fax:* 740-774-6317. *Web site:* http://www.daymarcollege.edu/

Daymar College
Lancaster, Ohio

Freshman Application Contact Holly Hankinson, Admissions Office, Daymar College, 1579 Victor Road, NW, Lancaster, OH 43130. *Phone:* 740-687-6126. *Toll-free phone:* 877-258-7796. *E-mail:* hhankinson@daymarcollege.edu. *Web site:* http://www.daymarcollege.edu/.

Daymar College
New Boston, Ohio

Freshman Application Contact Mike Bell, Admissions Representative, Daymar College, 3879 Rhodes Avenue, New Boston, OH 45662. *Phone:* 740-456-4124. *Toll-free phone:* 877-258-7796. *Web site:* http://www.daymarcollege.edu/.

Eastern Gateway Community College
Steubenville, Ohio

- **State and locally supported** 2-year, founded 1966, part of Ohio Board of Regents
- **Small-town** 83-acre campus with easy access to Pittsburgh
- **Coed,** 2,209 undergraduate students, 55% full-time, 60% women, 40% men

Undergraduates 1,219 full-time, 990 part-time. 10% are from out of state.
Freshmen *Admission:* 1,400 applied, 1,400 admitted, 509 enrolled.
Faculty *Student/faculty ratio:* 16:1.
Majors Accounting; administrative assistant and secretarial science; business administration and management; child-care and support services management; computer engineering related; corrections; criminal justice/police science; data processing and data processing technology; dental assisting; drafting and design technology; electrical, electronic and communications engineering technology; emergency medical technology (EMT paramedic); industrial radiologic technology; industrial technology; legal administrative assistant/secretary; licensed practical/vocational nurse training; mechanical engineering/mechanical technology; medical administrative assistant and medical secretary; medical/clinical assistant; real estate; respiratory care therapy.
Academics *Calendar:* semesters. *Degree:* certificates and associate. *Special study options:* academic remediation for entering students, accelerated degree program, adult/continuing education programs, cooperative education, distance learning, double majors, part-time degree program, services for LD students, summer session for credit.
Library Eastern Gateway Community College Library with an OPAC.
Student Life *Housing:* college housing not available. *Activities and Organizations:* Student Senate, Phi Theta Kappa. *Campus security:* 24-hour emergency response devices, day and evening security.
Athletics *Intercollegiate sports:* basketball M/W. *Intramural sports:* basketball M/W, football M/W, softball M/W.
Standardized Tests *Required for some:* SAT or ACT (for admission).
Costs (2010–11) *Tuition:* area resident $2790 full-time, $93 per credit part-time; state resident $2970 full-time, $99 per credit part-time; nonresident $3780 full-time, $126 per credit part-time. Full-time tuition and fees vary according to reciprocity agreements. Part-time tuition and fees vary according to reciprocity agreements. *Waivers:* senior citizens and employees or children of employees.
Financial Aid Of all full-time matriculated undergraduates who enrolled in 2009, 30 Federal Work-Study jobs (averaging $1500).
Applying *Options:* electronic application, early admission, deferred entrance. *Application fee:* $20. *Required for some:* high school transcript. *Notification:* continuous (freshmen), continuous (out-of-state freshmen), continuous (transfers).
Freshman Application Contact Mrs. Kristen Taylor, Director of Admissions, Eastern Gateway Community College, 4000 Sunset Boulevard, Steubenville,

OH 43952. *Phone:* 740-264-5591 Ext. 142. *Toll-free phone:* 800-68-COLLEGE Ext. 142. *Fax:* 740-266-2944. *E-mail:* kltaylor@egcc.edu. *Web site:* http://www.egcc.edu/.

Edison State Community College
Piqua, Ohio

- **State-supported** 2-year, founded 1973, part of Ohio Board of Regents
- **Small-town** 130-acre campus with easy access to Cincinnati and Dayton
- **Endowment** $2.1 million
- **Coed,** 3,711 undergraduate students, 39% full-time, 65% women, 35% men

Undergraduates 1,463 full-time, 2,248 part-time. Students come from 2 states and territories; 3 other countries; 1% are from out of state; 2% Black or African American, non-Hispanic/Latino; 1% Hispanic/Latino; 0.8% Asian, non-Hispanic/Latino; 0.6% American Indian or Alaska Native, non-Hispanic/Latino; 0.7% Two or more races, non-Hispanic/Latino; 2% Race/ethnicity unknown; 0.2% international; 3% transferred in. *Retention:* 55% of full-time freshmen returned.
Freshmen *Admission:* 1,336 applied, 1,336 admitted, 801 enrolled. *Average high school GPA:* 2.78. *Test scores:* ACT scores over 18: 78%; ACT scores over 24: 20%; ACT scores over 30: 1%.
Faculty *Total:* 256, 21% full-time, 7% with terminal degrees. *Student/faculty ratio:* 18:1.
Majors Accounting; art; business administration and management; child development; clinical/medical laboratory technology; commercial and advertising art; computer and information sciences; computer and information systems security; computer programming; computer systems networking and telecommunications; criminal justice/police science; dramatic/theater arts; education; electrical, electronic and communications engineering technology; electromechanical technology; executive assistant/executive secretary; human resources management; industrial technology; information technology; legal administrative assistant/secretary; legal assistant/paralegal; liberal arts and sciences/liberal studies; logistics, materials, and supply chain management; marketing/marketing management; mechanical drafting and CAD/CADD; mechanical engineering/mechanical technology; medical administrative assistant and medical secretary; medical/clinical assistant; medium/heavy vehicle and truck technology; physical therapy technology; pre-engineering; prenursing studies; real estate; registered nursing/registered nurse; sales, distribution, and marketing operations; social work; speech communication and rhetoric; web page, digital/multimedia and information resources design.
Academics *Calendar:* semesters. *Degree:* certificates and associate. *Special study options:* academic remediation for entering students, accelerated degree program, adult/continuing education programs, advanced placement credit, distance learning, double majors, English as a second language, honors programs, independent study, internships, off-campus study, part-time degree program, services for LD students, student-designed majors, summer session for credit.
Library Edison Community College Library with 29,851 titles, 542 serial subscriptions, 2,424 audiovisual materials, an OPAC, a Web page.
Student Life *Housing:* college housing not available. *Activities and Organizations:* drama/theater group, Campus Crusade for Christ, Student Ambassadors, Edison Stagelight Players, Writers Club, Edison Photo Society. *Campus security:* late-night transport/escort service, 18-hour patrols by trained security personnel. *Student services:* health clinic, personal/psychological counseling.
Athletics Member NJCAA. *Intercollegiate sports:* basketball M(s)/W(s), volleyball W(s).
Standardized Tests *Required:* ACT ASSET, ACT COMPASS (for admission).
Costs (2010–11) *One-time required fee:* $20. *Tuition:* state resident $3690 full-time, $123 per credit hour part-time; nonresident $6900 full-time, $230 per credit hour part-time. Full-time tuition and fees vary according to course load, program, and reciprocity agreements. Part-time tuition and fees vary according to course load, program, and reciprocity agreements. *Required fees:* $15 full-time. *Payment plans:* installment, deferred payment. *Waivers:* senior citizens and employees or children of employees.
Financial Aid Of all full-time matriculated undergraduates who enrolled in 2009, 42 Federal Work-Study jobs (averaging $3000).
Applying *Options:* electronic application. *Application fee:* $20. *Required:* high school transcript. *Application deadlines:* rolling (freshmen), rolling (transfers).
Freshman Application Contact Ms. Velina Bogart, Coordinator, Edison State Community College, 1973 Edison Drive, Piqua, OH 45356. *Phone:* 937-778-7854. *Toll-free phone:* 800-922-3722. *Fax:* 937-778-4692. *E-mail:* vbogart@edisonohio.edu. *Web site:* http://www.edisonohio.edu/.

ETI Technical College of Niles

Niles, Ohio

- **Proprietary** 2-year, founded 1989
- **Small-town** campus with easy access to Cleveland and Pittsburgh
- **Coed**

Undergraduates Students come from 2 states and territories; 10% are from out of state.

Faculty *Student/faculty ratio:* 22:1.

Academics *Calendar:* semesters. *Degree:* diplomas and associate. *Special study options:* academic remediation for entering students, adult/continuing education programs, advanced placement credit, part-time degree program, services for LD students.

Student Life *Campus security:* 24-hour emergency response devices.

Standardized Tests *Recommended:* SAT (for admission), ACT (for admission).

Costs (2010–11) *Tuition:* $7320 full-time, $305 per credit hour part-time. Full-time tuition and fees vary according to course load and program. Part-time tuition and fees vary according to course load and program. *Required fees:* $350 full-time, $150 per term part-time.

Financial Aid Of all full-time matriculated undergraduates who enrolled in 2008, 475 applied for aid, 370 were judged to have need, 450 had their need fully met. *Average percent of need met:* 100. *Average financial aid package:* $15,250. *Average need-based loan:* $3500. *Average need-based gift aid:* $5750.

Applying *Options:* early admission, deferred entrance. *Application fee:* $50. *Required:* high school transcript, interview.

Freshman Application Contact Ms. Diane Marsteller, Director of Admissions, ETI Technical College of Niles, 2076 Youngstown-Warren Road, Niles, OH 44446-4398. *Phone:* 330-652-9919. *Fax:* 330-652-4399. *Web site:* http://www.eti-college.com/.

Fortis College

Centerville, Ohio

Freshman Application Contact Fortis College, 555 East Alex Bell Road, Centerville, OH 45459. *Phone:* 937-433-3410. *Toll-free phone:* 800-837-7387. *Web site:* http://www.retstechcenter.com/.

Fortis College Cuyahoga Falls

Cuyahoga Falls, Ohio

Freshman Application Contact Admissions Office, Fortis College Cuyahoga Falls, 2545 Bailey Road, Cuyahoga Falls, OH 44221. *Phone:* 330-923-9959. *Fax:* 330-923-0886. *Web site:* http://www.fortis.edu/cuyahoga-falls-ohio.php.

Fortis College–Ravenna

Ravenna, Ohio

Freshman Application Contact Admissions Office, Fortis College–Ravenna, 653 Enterprise Parkway, Ravenna, OH 44266. *Toll-free phone:* 800-794-2856. *Web site:* http://www.fortis.edu/.

Gallipolis Career College

Gallipolis, Ohio

Freshman Application Contact Mr. Jack Henson, Director of Admissions, Gallipolis Career College, 1176 Jackson Pike, Suite 312, Gallipolis, OH 45631. *Phone:* 740-446-4367. *Toll-free phone:* 800-214-0452. *Fax:* 740-446-4124. *E-mail:* admissions@gallipoliscareercollege.com. *Web site:* http://www.gallipoliscareercollege.com/.

Good Samaritan College of Nursing and Health Science

Cincinnati, Ohio

Freshman Application Contact Admissions Office, Good Samaritan College of Nursing and Health Science, 375 Dixmyth Avenue, Cincinnati, OH 45220. *Phone:* 513-862-2743. *Fax:* 513-862-3572. *Web site:* http://www.gscollege.edu/.

Harrison College

Grove City, Ohio

- **Proprietary** 2-year
- **Coed,** 99 undergraduate students, 88% full-time, 83% women, 17% men

Undergraduates 87 full-time, 12 part-time. 6% Black or African American, non-Hispanic/Latino; 3% Hispanic/Latino; 1% Asian, non-Hispanic/Latino; 1% Two or more races, non-Hispanic/Latino; 4% Race/ethnicity unknown; 15% transferred in. *Retention:* 69% of full-time freshmen returned.

Freshmen *Admission:* 45 applied, 45 admitted, 16 enrolled.

Majors Accounting; administrative assistant and secretarial science; business administration and management; criminal justice/law enforcement administration; finance; human resources management; marketing/marketing management; medical/clinical assistant; medical insurance/medical billing.

Academics *Calendar:* quarters. *Degree:* associate.

Library Main Library plus 1 other.

Student Life *Housing:* college housing not available.

Standardized Tests *Required:* Wonderlic Scholastic Level Exam (SLE) (for admission).

Applying *Options:* electronic application. *Application fee:* $50. *Required:* high school transcript, interview. *Application deadlines:* rolling (freshmen), rolling (transfers). *Notification:* continuous (freshmen), continuous (transfers).

Freshman Application Contact Mark Jones, Harrison College, 3880 Jackpot Road, Grove City, OH 43123. *Phone:* 614-539-8800. *Toll-free phone:* 888-544-4422. *E-mail:* mark.jones@harrison.edu. *Web site:* http://www.harrison.edu/.

Herzing University

Toledo, Ohio

Admissions Office Contact Herzing University, 5212 Hill Avenue, Toledo, OH 43615. *Web site:* http://www.herzing.edu/toledo.

Hocking College

Nelsonville, Ohio

Director of Admissions Ms. Lyn Hull, Director of Admissions, Hocking College, 3301 Hocking Parkway, Nelsonville, OH 45764-9588. *Phone:* 740-753-3591 Ext. 2803. *Toll-free phone:* 877-462-5464. *E-mail:* hull_lyn@hocking.edu. *Web site:* http://www.hocking.edu/.

Hondros College

Westerville, Ohio

Director of Admissions Ms. Carol Thomas, Operations Manager, Hondros College, 4140 Executive Parkway, Westerville, OH 43081-3855. *Phone:* 614-508-7244. *Toll-free phone:* 800-783-0095. *Web site:* http://www.hondroscollege.com/.

International College of Broadcasting

Dayton, Ohio

Director of Admissions Mr. Aan McIntosh, Director of Admissions, International College of Broadcasting, 6 South Smithville Road, Dayton, OH 45431-1833. *Phone:* 937-258-8251. *Fax:* 937-258-8714. *Web site:* http://www.icbcollege.com/.

ITT Technical Institute

Akron, Ohio

- **Proprietary** primarily 2-year
- **Coed**

Majors CAD/CADD drafting/design technology; computer and information systems security; computer engineering technology; construction management; criminal justice/law enforcement administration; electrical, electronic and communications engineering technology; legal assistant/paralegal; system, networking, and LAN/WAN management.

Academics *Degrees:* associate and bachelor's.

Freshman Application Contact ITT Technical Institute, 3428 West Market Street, Akron, OH 44333. *Phone:* 330-865-8600. *Toll-free phone:* 877-818-0154. *Web site:* http://www.itt-tech.edu/.

ITT Technical Institute
Columbus, Ohio
- **Proprietary** 2-year, part of ITT Educational Services, Inc.
- **Coed**

Majors CAD/CADD drafting/design technology; computer and information systems security; computer engineering technology; computer software technology; construction management; criminal justice/law enforcement administration; design and visual communications; electrical, electronic and communications engineering technology; legal assistant/paralegal; system, networking, and LAN/WAN management.

Academics *Calendar:* quarters. *Degree:* associate.

Freshman Application Contact Director of Recruitment, ITT Technical Institute, 4717 Hilton Corporate Drive, Columbus, OH 43232. *Phone:* 614-868-2000. *Toll-free phone:* 877-233-8864. *Web site:* http://www.itt-tech.edu/.

ITT Technical Institute
Dayton, Ohio
- **Proprietary** primarily 2-year, founded 1935, part of ITT Educational Services, Inc.
- **Suburban** campus
- **Coed**

Majors Architectural drafting and CAD/CADD; business administration and management; CAD/CADD drafting/design technology; computer and information systems security; computer engineering technology; computer software technology; construction management; criminal justice/law enforcement administration; design and visual communications; legal assistant/paralegal; system, networking, and LAN/WAN management.

Academics *Calendar:* quarters. *Degrees:* associate and bachelor's.

Student Life *Housing:* college housing not available.

Freshman Application Contact Director of Recruitment, ITT Technical Institute, 3325 Stop 8 Road, Dayton, OH 45414. *Phone:* 937-264-7700. *Toll-free phone:* 800-568-3241. *Web site:* http://www.itt-tech.edu/.

ITT Technical Institute
Hilliard, Ohio
- **Proprietary** primarily 2-year, founded 2003, part of ITT Educational Services, Inc.
- **Coed**

Majors Business administration and management; CAD/CADD drafting/design technology; computer and information systems security; computer engineering technology; computer software technology; construction management; criminal justice/law enforcement administration; design and visual communications; electrical, electronic and communications engineering technology; legal assistant/paralegal; registered nursing/registered nurse; system, networking, and LAN/WAN management; web page, digital/multimedia and information resources design.

Academics *Calendar:* quarters. *Degrees:* associate and bachelor's.

Freshman Application Contact Director of Recruitment, ITT Technical Institute, 3781 Park Mill Run Drive, Hilliard, OH 43026. *Phone:* 614-771-4888. *Toll-free phone:* 888-483-4888. *Web site:* http://www.itt-tech.edu/.

ITT Technical Institute
Maumee, Ohio
- **Proprietary** primarily 2-year
- **Coed**

Majors CAD/CADD drafting/design technology; computer and information systems security; computer engineering technology; computer software technology; construction management; criminal justice/law enforcement administration; design and visual communications; electrical, electronic and communications engineering technology; legal assistant/paralegal; system, networking, and LAN/WAN management.

Academics *Degrees:* associate and bachelor's.

Student Life *Housing:* college housing not available.

Freshman Application Contact Director of Recruitment, ITT Technical Institute, 1656 Henthorne Drive, Suite B, Maumee, OH 43537. *Phone:* 419-861-6500. *Toll-free phone:* 877-205-4639. *Web site:* http://www.itt-tech.edu/.

ITT Technical Institute
Norwood, Ohio
- **Proprietary** primarily 2-year, founded 1995, part of ITT Educational Services, Inc.
- **Coed**

Majors Accounting technology and bookkeeping; business administration and management; CAD/CADD drafting/design technology; computer and information systems security; computer engineering technology; computer software and media applications related; computer software technology; construction management; criminal justice/law enforcement administration; design and visual communications; electrical, electronic and communications engineering technology; legal assistant/paralegal; registered nursing/registered nurse; system, networking, and LAN/WAN management; web/multimedia management and webmaster; web page, digital/multimedia and information resources design.

Academics *Calendar:* quarters. *Degrees:* associate and bachelor's.

Student Life *Housing:* college housing not available.

Freshman Application Contact Director of Recruitment, ITT Technical Institute, 4750 Wesley Avenue, Norwood, OH 45212. *Phone:* 513-531-8300. *Toll-free phone:* 800-314-8324. *Web site:* http://www.itt-tech.edu/.

ITT Technical Institute
Strongsville, Ohio
- **Proprietary** primarily 2-year, founded 1994, part of ITT Educational Services, Inc.
- **Coed**

Majors Accounting technology and bookkeeping; business administration and management; CAD/CADD drafting/design technology; computer and information systems security; computer engineering technology; computer software and media applications related; computer software technology; construction management; criminal justice/law enforcement administration; design and visual communications; electrical, electronic and communications engineering technology; legal assistant/paralegal; system, networking, and LAN/WAN management; web/multimedia management and webmaster; web page, digital/multimedia and information resources design.

Academics *Calendar:* quarters. *Degrees:* associate and bachelor's.

Student Life *Housing:* college housing not available.

Freshman Application Contact Director of Recruitment, ITT Technical Institute, 14955 Sprague Road, Strongsville, OH 44136. *Phone:* 440-234-9091. *Toll-free phone:* 800-331-1488. *Web site:* http://www.itt-tech.edu/.

ITT Technical Institute
Warrensville Heights, Ohio
- **Proprietary** primarily 2-year, founded 2005
- **Coed**

Majors Business administration and management; CAD/CADD drafting/design technology; computer and information systems security; computer engineering technology; computer software technology; construction management; criminal justice/law enforcement administration; design and visual communications; electrical, electronic and communications engineering technology; legal assistant/paralegal; system, networking, and LAN/WAN management; web page, digital/multimedia and information resources design.

Academics *Calendar:* quarters. *Degrees:* associate and bachelor's.

Student Life *Housing:* college housing not available.

Freshman Application Contact Director of Recruitment, ITT Technical Institute, 4700 Richmond Road, Warrensville Heights, OH 44128. *Phone:* 216-896-6500. *Toll-free phone:* 800-741-3494. *Web site:* http://www.itt-tech.edu/.

ITT Technical Institute
Youngstown, Ohio
- **Proprietary** primarily 2-year, founded 1967, part of ITT Educational Services, Inc.
- **Suburban** campus
- **Coed**

Majors Business administration and management; CAD/CADD drafting/design technology; computer and information systems security; computer engineering technology; computer software and media applications related; computer software technology; construction management; criminal justice/law enforcement administration; design and visual communications; electrical, electronic and communications engineering technology; legal assistant/paralegal; system, networking, and LAN/WAN management.

Academics *Calendar:* quarters. *Degrees:* associate and bachelor's.

Student Life *Housing:* college housing not available.

Financial Aid Of all full-time matriculated undergraduates who enrolled in 2009, 5 Federal Work-Study jobs (averaging $3979).

Freshman Application Contact Director of Recruitment, ITT Technical Institute, 1030 North Meridian Road, Youngstown, OH 44509-4098. *Phone:* 330-270-1600. *Toll-free phone:* 800-832-5001. *Web site:* http://www.itt-tech.edu/.

James A. Rhodes State College
Lima, Ohio

Freshman Application Contact Mr. Scot Lingrell, Director, Student Advising and Development, James A. Rhodes State College, 4240 Campus Drive, Lima, OH 45804-3597. *Phone:* 419-995-8050. *E-mail:* peterl@ltc.tec.oh.us. *Web site:* http://www.rhodesstate.edu/.

Kaplan College, Cincinnati Campus
Cincinnati, Ohio

- **Proprietary** 2-year
- **Coed**

Academics *Degree:* diplomas and associate.
Freshman Application Contact Kaplan College, Cincinnati Campus, 801 Linn Street, Cincinnati, OH 45203. *Phone:* 513-421-9900. *Web site:* http://www.kc-cincy.com/.

Kaplan College, Columbus Campus
Columbus, Ohio

- **Proprietary** 2-year
- **Coed**

Academics *Degree:* diplomas and associate.
Freshman Application Contact Kaplan College, Columbus Campus, 2745 Winchester Pike, Columbus, OH 43232. *Phone:* 614-456-4600. *Web site:* http://www.kc-columbus.com/.

Kaplan College, Dayton Campus
Dayton, Ohio

- **Proprietary** 2-year, founded 1971
- **Urban** campus
- **Coed**

Academics *Calendar:* quarters. *Degree:* diplomas and associate.
Freshman Application Contact Kaplan College, Dayton Campus, 2800 East River Road, Dayton, OH 45439. *Phone:* 937-294-6155. *Toll-free phone:* 800-932-9698. *Web site:* http://www.kc-dayton.com/.

Kent State University at Ashtabula
Ashtabula, Ohio

- **State-supported** primarily 2-year, founded 1958, part of Kent State University System
- **Small-town** 120-acre campus with easy access to Cleveland
- **Coed,** 2,486 undergraduate students, 55% full-time, 65% women, 35% men

Undergraduates 1,360 full-time, 1,126 part-time. Students come from 5 states and territories; 2% are from out of state; 7% Black or African American, non-Hispanic/Latino; 3% Hispanic/Latino; 0.5% Asian, non-Hispanic/Latino; 0.6% American Indian or Alaska Native, non-Hispanic/Latino; 1% Two or more races, non-Hispanic/Latino; 3% Race/ethnicity unknown; 9% transferred in. *Retention:* 59% of full-time freshmen returned.
Freshmen *Admission:* 613 applied, 601 admitted, 456 enrolled. *Average high school GPA:* 2.73. *Test scores:* ACT scores over 18: 71%; ACT scores over 24: 18%.
Faculty *Total:* 119, 45% full-time. *Student/faculty ratio:* 20:1.
Majors Accounting; administrative assistant and secretarial science; business administration and management; computer engineering technology; criminal justice/police science; electrical, electronic and communications engineering technology; engineering technology; environmental studies; finance; human services; industrial technology; kindergarten/preschool education; legal administrative assistant/secretary; liberal arts and sciences/liberal studies; marketing/marketing management; materials science; mechanical engineering/mechanical technology; physical therapy; real estate; registered nursing/registered nurse.
Academics *Calendar:* semesters. *Degrees:* certificates, associate, and bachelor's (also offers some upper-level and graduate courses). *Special study options:* academic remediation for entering students, advanced placement credit, distance learning, double majors, English as a second language, freshman honors college, honors programs, internships, part-time degree program,

services for LD students, student-designed majors, study abroad, summer session for credit. *ROTC:* Army (c), Air Force (c).
Library 51,884 titles, 225 serial subscriptions.
Student Life *Housing:* college housing not available. *Activities and Organizations:* drama/theater group, student-run newspaper, student government, student veterans association, Student Nurses Association, Student Occupational Therapy Association (SOTA), Media Club. *Campus security:* 24-hour emergency response devices.
Standardized Tests *Required for some:* SAT or ACT (for admission). *Recommended:* SAT or ACT (for admission).
Costs (2010–11) *Tuition:* state resident $5110 full-time, $233 per credit hour part-time; nonresident $13,070 full-time, $595 per credit hour part-time. Full-time tuition and fees vary according to course level and course load. Part-time tuition and fees vary according to course level and course load. *Payment plans:* installment, deferred payment. *Waivers:* senior citizens and employees or children of employees.
Financial Aid Of all full-time matriculated undergraduates who enrolled in 2009, 1,037 applied for aid, 990 were judged to have need, 261 had their need fully met. In 2009, 3 non-need-based awards were made. *Average percent of need met:* 49%. *Average financial aid package:* $8074. *Average need-based loan:* $3587. *Average need-based gift aid:* $5295. *Average non-need-based aid:* $833.
Applying *Options:* early admission, deferred entrance. *Application fee:* $30. *Required:* high school transcript. *Application deadlines:* 8/1 (freshmen), 7/15 (out-of-state freshmen), 7/15 (transfers). *Notification:* continuous until 8/1 (freshmen), continuous until 7/15 (out-of-state freshmen), continuous until 7/15 (transfers).
Freshman Application Contact Kent State University at Ashtabula, 3300 Lake Road West, Ashtabula, OH 44004-2299. *Phone:* 440-964-4217. *Web site:* http://www.ashtabula.kent.edu/.

Kent State University at East Liverpool
East Liverpool, Ohio

- **State-supported** primarily 2-year, founded 1967, part of Kent State University System
- **Small-town** 4-acre campus with easy access to Pittsburgh
- **Coed,** 1,371 undergraduate students, 57% full-time, 69% women, 31% men

Undergraduates 785 full-time, 586 part-time. Students come from 7 states and territories; 5% are from out of state; 6% transferred in. *Retention:* 63% of full-time freshmen returned.
Freshmen *Admission:* 229 applied, 226 admitted, 158 enrolled. *Average high school GPA:* 2.75. *Test scores:* ACT scores over 18: 71%; ACT scores over 24: 17%.
Faculty *Total:* 76, 37% full-time. *Student/faculty ratio:* 17:1.
Majors Accounting; business administration and management; computer and information sciences related; computer engineering technology; criminal justice/law enforcement administration; legal administrative assistant/secretary; liberal arts and sciences/liberal studies; occupational therapy; physical therapy; registered nursing/registered nurse.
Academics *Calendar:* semesters. *Degrees:* certificates, associate, and bachelor's (also offers some upper-level and graduate courses). *Special study options:* academic remediation for entering students, accelerated degree program, adult/continuing education programs, advanced placement credit, distance learning, double majors, English as a second language, freshman honors college, honors programs, internships, part-time degree program, services for LD students, student-designed majors, study abroad, summer session for credit. *ROTC:* Army (c), Air Force (c).
Library Blair Memorial Library with 31,320 titles, 135 serial subscriptions, an OPAC, a Web page.
Student Life *Housing:* college housing not available. *Activities and Organizations:* student-run newspaper, Student Senate, Student Nurses Association, Alpha Beta Gamma, Occupational Therapist Assistant Club, Physical Therapist Assistant Club. *Campus security:* student patrols, late-night transport/escort service.
Standardized Tests *Required for some:* SAT or ACT (for admission). *Recommended:* SAT or ACT (for admission).
Costs (2010–11) *Tuition:* state resident $5110 full-time, $233 per credit hour part-time; nonresident $13,070 full-time, $595 per credit hour part-time. Full-time tuition and fees vary according to course level and course load. Part-time tuition and fees vary according to course level and course load. *Payment plans:* installment, deferred payment. *Waivers:* senior citizens and employees or children of employees.
Financial Aid Of all full-time matriculated undergraduates who enrolled in 2009, 476 applied for aid, 459 were judged to have need, 94 had their need fully met. In 2009, 2 non-need-based awards were made. *Average percent of need met:* 47%. *Average financial aid package:* $8079. *Average need-based*

loan: $3501. *Average need-based gift aid:* $5194. *Average non-need-based aid:* $1000.

Applying *Options:* early admission, deferred entrance. *Application fee:* $30. *Required:* high school transcript. *Application deadlines:* rolling (freshmen), rolling (transfers). *Notification:* continuous until 9/1 (freshmen), continuous until 9/1 (transfers).

Freshman Application Contact Melissa Ace, Director of Enrollment Management and Student Services, Kent State University at East Liverpool, 400 East 4th Street, East Liverpool, OH 43920-3497. *Phone:* 330-382-7462. *E-mail:* mpeter22@kent.edu. *Web site:* http://www.eliv.kent.edu/.

Kent State University at Geauga

Burton, Ohio

- **State-supported** founded 1964, part of Kent State University System

- **Rural** 87-acre campus with easy access to Cleveland

- **Coed,** 2,190 undergraduate students, 58% full-time, 65% women, 35% men

Undergraduates 1,272 full-time, 918 part-time. Students come from 10 states and territories; 7 other countries; 1% are from out of state; 9% Black or African American, non-Hispanic/Latino; 1% Hispanic/Latino; 2% Asian, non-Hispanic/Latino; 0.4% American Indian or Alaska Native, non-Hispanic/Latino; 0.7% Two or more races, non-Hispanic/Latino; 3% Race/ethnicity unknown; 0.3% international; 5% transferred in. *Retention:* 72% of full-time freshmen returned.

Freshmen *Admission:* 232 enrolled. *Average high school GPA:* 2.49. *Test scores:* SAT critical reading scores over 500: 35%; SAT math scores over 500: 31%; SAT writing scores over 500: 20%; SAT critical reading scores over 600: 8%; SAT math scores over 600: 8%; SAT writing scores over 600: 5%.

Faculty *Total:* 116, 26% full-time. *Student/faculty ratio:* 18:1.

Majors Accounting technology and bookkeeping; applied horticulture/horticulture operations; business administration and management; emergency medical technology (EMT paramedic); general studies; industrial technology; information technology; liberal arts and sciences/liberal studies; nursing science; physical sciences; science technologies related.

Academics *Calendar:* semesters. *Degrees:* certificates, associate, and bachelor's. *Special study options:* academic remediation for entering students, advanced placement credit, distance learning, double majors, English as a second language, freshman honors college, honors programs, independent study, internships, part-time degree program, services for LD students, student-designed majors, study abroad, summer session for credit. *ROTC:* Army (c), Air Force (c).

Library Kent State University Library with 8,300 titles, 6,600 serial subscriptions, an OPAC, a Web page.

Student Life *Housing:* college housing not available. *Activities and Organizations:* Student Ambassadors, Campus Crusade for Christ, Gaia Society. *Campus security:* 24-hour emergency response devices.

Standardized Tests *Required for some:* SAT or ACT (for admission). *Recommended:* SAT or ACT (for admission).

Costs (2010–11) *Tuition:* state resident $5110 full-time, $233 per credit hour part-time; nonresident $13,070 full-time, $595 per credit hour part-time. Full-time tuition and fees vary according to course level and course load. Part-time tuition and fees vary according to course level and course load. *Payment plans:* installment, deferred payment. *Waivers:* senior citizens and employees or children of employees.

Financial Aid Of all full-time matriculated undergraduates who enrolled in 2009, 487 applied for aid, 447 were judged to have need, 138 had their need fully met. In 2009, 3 non-need-based awards were made. *Average percent of need met:* 48%. *Average financial aid package:* $7450. *Average need-based loan:* $3744. *Average need-based gift aid:* $4581. *Average non-need-based aid:* $398.

Applying *Options:* electronic application, deferred entrance. *Application fee:* $30. *Required:* high school transcript. *Application deadlines:* rolling (freshmen), rolling (transfers). *Notification:* continuous (freshmen), continuous (transfers).

Freshman Application Contact Thomas Hoiles, Kent State University at Geauga, 14111 Claridon-Troy Road, Burton, OH 44021. *Phone:* 440-834-4187. *Fax:* 440-834-8846. *E-mail:* thoiles@kent.edu. *Web site:* http://www.geauga.kent.edu/.

Kent State University at Salem

Salem, Ohio

- **State-supported** primarily 2-year, founded 1966, part of Kent State University System
- **Rural** 98-acre campus
- **Coed,** 1,960 undergraduate students, 69% full-time, 69% women, 31% men

Undergraduates 1,361 full-time, 599 part-time. Students come from 2 states and territories; 7 other countries; 2% are from out of state; 3% Black or African American, non-Hispanic/Latino; 1% Hispanic/Latino; 0.4% Asian, non-Hispanic/Latino; 0.7% American Indian or Alaska Native, non-Hispanic/Latino; 0.5% Two or more races, non-Hispanic/Latino; 2% Race/ethnicity unknown; 0.1% international; 8% transferred in. *Retention:* 57% of full-time freshmen returned.

Freshmen *Admission:* 412 applied, 398 admitted, 261 enrolled. *Average high school GPA:* 2.79. *Test scores:* SAT writing scores over 500: 100%; ACT scores over 18: 69%; ACT scores over 24: 17%; ACT scores over 30: 1%.

Faculty *Total:* 123, 36% full-time. *Student/faculty ratio:* 18:1.

Majors Administrative assistant and secretarial science; allied health diagnostic, intervention, and treatment professions related; applied horticulture/horticulture operations; business/commerce; computer programming (specific applications); education; industrial technology; liberal arts and sciences/liberal studies; medical radiologic technology.

Academics *Calendar:* semesters. *Degrees:* associate and bachelor's (also offers some upper-level and graduate courses). *Special study options:* academic remediation for entering students, adult/continuing education programs, advanced placement credit, distance learning, double majors, freshman honors college, honors programs, internships, part-time degree program, services for LD students, study abroad, summer session for credit. *ROTC:* Army (c), Air Force (c).

Library 19,000 titles, 163 serial subscriptions, 158 audiovisual materials, an OPAC, a Web page.

Student Life *Housing:* college housing not available. *Activities and Organizations:* Honors Club, Human Services Technology Club, Radiologic Technology Club, Student Government Organization, Students for Professional Nursing. *Campus security:* 24-hour emergency response devices, late-night transport/escort service. *Student services:* women's center.

Athletics *Intramural sports:* basketball M/W, skiing (downhill) M/W, table tennis M/W, tennis M/W, volleyball M/W.

Standardized Tests *Required for some:* SAT or ACT (for admission). *Recommended:* SAT or ACT (for admission).

Costs (2010–11) *Tuition:* state resident $5110 full-time, $233 per credit hour part-time; nonresident $13,070 full-time, $595 per credit hour part-time. Full-time tuition and fees vary according to course level and course load. Part-time tuition and fees vary according to course level and course load. *Payment plans:* installment, deferred payment. *Waivers:* senior citizens and employees or children of employees.

Financial Aid Of all full-time matriculated undergraduates who enrolled in 2009, 943 applied for aid, 894 were judged to have need, 225 had their need fully met. In 2009, 9 non-need-based awards were made. *Average percent of need met:* 49%. *Average financial aid package:* $7981. *Average need-based loan:* $3643. *Average need-based gift aid:* $5125. *Average non-need-based aid:* $581.

Applying *Options:* electronic application, early admission, deferred entrance. *Application fee:* $30. *Required:* high school transcript. *Required for some:* essay or personal statement. *Application deadlines:* rolling (freshmen), rolling (transfers).

Freshman Application Contact Mrs. Judy Heisler, Admissions Secretary, Kent State University at Salem, 2491 State Route 45 South, Salem, OH 44460-9412. *Phone:* 330-332-0361 Ext. 74201. *E-mail:* ask-us@salem.kent.edu. *Web site:* http://www.salem.kent.edu/.

Kent State University at Trumbull

Warren, Ohio

- **State-supported** primarily 2-year, founded 1954, part of Kent State University System
- **Suburban** 200-acre campus with easy access to Cleveland
- **Coed,** 3,109 undergraduate students, 63% full-time, 63% women, 37% men

Undergraduates 1,945 full-time, 1,164 part-time. Students come from 5 states and territories; 5 other countries; 1% are from out of state; 14% Black or African American, non-Hispanic/Latino; 2% Hispanic/Latino; 0.8% Asian, non-Hispanic/Latino; 0.1% Native Hawaiian or other Pacific Islander, non-Hispanic/Latino; 0.3% American Indian or Alaska Native, non-Hispanic/Latino; 0.8% Two or more races, non-Hispanic/Latino; 3% Race/ethnicity unknown; 0.1% international; 7% transferred in. *Retention:* 64% of full-time freshmen returned.

Freshmen *Admission:* 561 applied, 553 admitted, 455 enrolled. *Average high school GPA:* 2.56. *Test scores:* SAT math scores over 500: 100%; ACT scores over 18: 68%; SAT math scores over 600: 100%; ACT scores over 24: 12%.

Faculty *Total:* 127, 45% full-time. *Student/faculty ratio:* 24:1.

Majors Accounting technology and bookkeeping; automobile/automotive mechanics technology; business administration and management; computer engineering technology; computer/information technology services administration related; computer technology/computer systems technology; criminal justice/safety; electrical, electronic and communications engineering technology; English; environmental engineering technology; general studies; industrial technology; legal assistant/paralegal; liberal arts and sciences/liberal studies; manufacturing engineering; mechanical engineering/mechanical technology; nursing science; speech communication and rhetoric; systems engineering.

Academics *Calendar:* semesters. *Degrees:* certificates, associate, and bachelor's (also offers some upper-level and graduate courses). *Special study options:* academic remediation for entering students, adult/continuing education programs, advanced placement credit, cooperative education, distance learning, double majors, English as a second language, freshman honors college, honors programs, independent study, internships, part-time degree program, services for LD students, student-designed majors, study abroad, summer session for credit. *ROTC:* Army (c), Air Force (c).

Library Trumbull Campus Library with 65,951 titles, 759 serial subscriptions, an OPAC, a Web page.

Student Life *Housing:* college housing not available. *Activities and Organizations:* drama/theater group, National Student Nurses Association, Spot On Improv Group, Amnesty International, Campus Crusade for Christ. *Campus security:* 24-hour emergency response devices, late-night transport/escort service, patrols by trained security personnel during open hours. *Student services:* personal/psychological counseling.

Standardized Tests *Required for some:* SAT or ACT (for admission). *Recommended:* SAT or ACT (for admission).

Costs (2010–11) *Tuition:* state resident $5110 full-time, $233 per credit hour part-time; nonresident $13,070 full-time, $595 per credit hour part-time. Full-time tuition and fees vary according to course level, course load, and location. Part-time tuition and fees vary according to course level, course load, and location. *Payment plans:* installment, deferred payment. *Waivers:* senior citizens and employees or children of employees.

Financial Aid Of all full-time matriculated undergraduates who enrolled in 2009, 1,294 applied for aid, 1,235 were judged to have need, 313 had their need fully met. In 2009, 4 non-need-based awards were made. *Average percent of need met:* 48%. *Average financial aid package:* $8015. *Average need-based loan:* $3575. *Average need-based gift aid:* $5087. *Average non-need-based aid:* $1995.

Applying *Options:* deferred entrance. *Application fee:* $30. *Required:* high school transcript. *Application deadlines:* rolling (freshmen), rolling (transfers). *Notification:* continuous until 8/30 (freshmen), continuous until 8/30 (transfers).

Freshman Application Contact Kent State University at Trumbull, Warren, OH 44483. *Phone:* 330-675-8935. *Web site:* http://www.trumbull.kent.edu/.

Kent State University at Tuscarawas
New Philadelphia, Ohio

- **State-supported** primarily 2-year, founded 1962, part of Kent State University System
- **Small-town** 172-acre campus with easy access to Cleveland
- **Coed,** 2,774 undergraduate students, 60% full-time, 58% women, 42% men

Undergraduates 1,659 full-time, 1,115 part-time. Students come from 4 states and territories; 3 other countries; 1% are from out of state; 2% Black or African American, non-Hispanic/Latino; 1% Hispanic/Latino; 0.5% Asian, non-Hispanic/Latino; 0.1% American Indian or Alaska Native, non-Hispanic/Latino; 0.7% Two or more races, non-Hispanic/Latino; 3% Race/ethnicity unknown; 0.1% international; 8% transferred in. *Retention:* 66% of full-time freshmen returned.

Freshmen *Admission:* 672 applied, 647 admitted, 515 enrolled. *Average high school GPA:* 2.74. *Test scores:* ACT scores over 18: 76%; ACT scores over 24: 17%; ACT scores over 30: 1%.

Faculty *Total:* 135, 37% full-time. *Student/faculty ratio:* 23:1.

Majors Accounting; administrative assistant and secretarial science; animation, interactive technology, video graphics and special effects; business administration and management; communications technology; computer engineering technology; criminal justice/police science; early childhood education; electrical, electronic and communications engineering technology; engineering technology; environmental studies; industrial technology; liberal arts and sciences/liberal studies; mechanical engineering/mechanical technology; plastics and polymer engineering technology; registered nursing/registered nurse; veterinary/animal health technology.

Academics *Calendar:* semesters. *Degrees:* certificates, associate, and bachelor's (also offers some upper-level and graduate courses). *Special study options:* academic remediation for entering students, accelerated degree program, adult/continuing education programs, advanced placement credit, distance learning, double majors, freshman honors college, honors programs, independent study, internships, part-time degree program, services for LD students, student-designed majors, summer session for credit. *ROTC:* Army (c), Air Force (c).

Library Tuscarawas Campus Library with 63,880 titles, 208 serial subscriptions, 1,179 audiovisual materials, an OPAC, a Web page.

Student Life *Housing:* college housing not available. *Activities and Organizations:* choral group, Society of Mechanical Engineers, IEEE, Imagineers, Criminal Justice Club, Salt and Light.

Athletics *Intramural sports:* basketball M/W, volleyball M/W.

Standardized Tests *Required for some:* SAT or ACT (for admission). *Recommended:* SAT or ACT (for admission).

Costs (2010–11) *Tuition:* state resident $5110 full-time, $233 per credit hour part-time; nonresident $13,070 full-time, $595 per credit hour part-time. Full-time tuition and fees vary according to course level and course load. Part-time tuition and fees vary according to course level and course load. *Payment plans:* installment, deferred payment. *Waivers:* senior citizens and employees or children of employees.

Financial Aid Of all full-time matriculated undergraduates who enrolled in 2009, 1,257 applied for aid, 1,197 were judged to have need, 177 had their need fully met. In 2009, 15 non-need-based awards were made. *Average percent of need met:* 49%. *Average financial aid package:* $7855. *Average need-based loan:* $3483. *Average need-based gift aid:* $5030. *Average non-need-based aid:* $1125.

Applying *Options:* electronic application, early admission, deferred entrance. *Application fee:* $30. *Required:* high school transcript. *Application deadlines:* 9/1 (freshmen), 9/1 (transfers). *Notification:* continuous (freshmen), continuous (transfers).

Freshman Application Contact Mrs. Laurie R. Donley, Director of Enrollment Management and Student Services, Kent State University at Tuscarawas, 330 University Drive Northeast, New Philadelphia, OH 44663-9403. *Phone:* 330-339-3391 Ext. 47425. *Fax:* 330-339-3321. *E-mail:* ldonley@kent.edu. *Web site:* http://www.tusc.kent.edu/.

Lakeland Community College
Kirtland, Ohio

- **State and locally supported** 2-year, founded 1967, part of Ohio Board of Regents
- **Suburban** 380-acre campus with easy access to Cleveland
- **Endowment** $354,142
- **Coed**

Undergraduates 4,151 full-time, 5,255 part-time. 4% transferred in.

Faculty *Student/faculty ratio:* 20:1.

Academics *Calendar:* semesters. *Degree:* certificates and associate. *Special study options:* academic remediation for entering students, adult/continuing education programs, advanced placement credit, cooperative education, distance learning, English as a second language, external degree program, independent study, internships, off-campus study, part-time degree program, services for LD students, study abroad, summer session for credit.

Student Life *Campus security:* 24-hour emergency response devices and patrols, student patrols, late-night transport/escort service.

Athletics Member NJCAA.

Costs (2010–11) *Tuition:* area resident $2888 full-time, $96 per credit hour part-time; state resident $3537 full-time, $118 per credit hour part-time; nonresident $7569 full-time, $252 per credit hour part-time. Full-time tuition and fees vary according to course load. Part-time tuition and fees vary according to course load. *Required fees:* $29 full-time, $14 per term part-time.

Financial Aid Of all full-time matriculated undergraduates who enrolled in 2008, 60 Federal Work-Study jobs.

Applying *Options:* electronic application, early admission, deferred entrance. *Application fee:* $15. *Required:* high school transcript.

Freshman Application Contact Lakeland Community College, 7700 Clocktower Drive, Kirtland, OH 44094-5198. *Phone:* 440-525-7230. *Toll-free phone:* 800-589-8520. *Web site:* http://www.lakeland.cc.oh.us/.

Lorain County Community College
Elyria, Ohio

Director of Admissions Ms. Thalia Fountain, Interim Director of Enrollment Services, Lorain County Community College, 1005 Abbe Road, North, Elyria, OH 44035. *Phone:* 440-366-7683. *Toll-free phone:* 800-995-5222 Ext. 4032. *Fax:* 440-366-4150. *Web site:* http://www.loraincc.edu/.

Marion Technical College
Marion, Ohio

- **State-supported** 2-year, founded 1971, part of University System of Ohio
- **Small-town** 180-acre campus with easy access to Columbus
- **Coed,** 2,765 undergraduate students

Undergraduates 5% Black or African American, non-Hispanic/Latino; 1% Hispanic/Latino; 0.5% Asian, non-Hispanic/Latino; 0.2% American Indian or Alaska Native, non-Hispanic/Latino; 2% Race/ethnicity unknown. *Retention:* 57% of full-time freshmen returned.

Faculty *Total:* 185, 19% full-time. *Student/faculty ratio:* 18:1.

Majors Accounting; administrative assistant and secretarial science; business administration and management; clinical/medical laboratory technology; computer programming (vendor/product certification); computer software and media applications related; computer systems networking and telecommunications; drafting and design technology; electrical, electronic and communications engineering technology; engineering technology; finance; human services; industrial technology; information technology; legal assistant/paralegal; marketing/marketing management; mechanical engineering/mechanical technology; medical administrative assistant and medical secretary; physical therapy technology; radiologic technology/science; registered nursing/registered nurse; social work; telecommunications technology.

Academics *Calendar:* quarters. *Degree:* certificates and associate. *Special study options:* academic remediation for entering students, accelerated degree program, adult/continuing education programs, advanced placement credit, cooperative education, distance learning, double majors, independent study, internships, off-campus study, part-time degree program, services for LD students, student-designed majors, summer session for credit.

Library Marion Campus Library with 52,000 titles, 251 serial subscriptions, 1,582 audiovisual materials, an OPAC, a Web page.

Student Life *Housing:* college housing not available. *Activities and Organizations:* drama/theater group, choral group, outdoor pursuits, Young Republicans, Environmental Group, Economics and Business Club, Psychology Club. *Student services:* personal/psychological counseling.

Athletics *Intercollegiate sports:* basketball M/W, golf M/W, rugby M, softball W, volleyball W. *Intramural sports:* badminton M/W, basketball M/W, bowling M/W, football M, golf M, racquetball M/W, rock climbing M/W, rugby M/W, skiing (cross-country) M/W, skiing (downhill) M/W, soccer M/W, table tennis M/W, volleyball M/W.

Standardized Tests *Required:* COMPASS or ACT (for admission). *Required for some:* ACT (for admission).

Costs (2010–11) *Tuition:* state resident $3852 full-time, $107 per credit hour part-time; nonresident $5760 full-time, $160 per credit hour part-time. Full-time tuition and fees vary according to course load, program, and reciprocity agreements. Part-time tuition and fees vary according to course load, program, and reciprocity agreements. *Required fees:* $150 full-time. *Payment plan:* deferred payment. *Waivers:* senior citizens and employees or children of employees.

Financial Aid Of all full-time matriculated undergraduates who enrolled in 2009, 28 Federal Work-Study jobs (averaging $1200), 45 state and other part-time jobs (averaging $1000).

Applying *Options:* electronic application, early admission, deferred entrance. *Application fee:* $20. *Required:* high school transcript. *Required for some:* minimum 2.5 GPA, some programs are Limited Enrollment Programs with specific admission criteria. *Recommended:* interview. *Application deadlines:* rolling (freshmen), rolling (out-of-state freshmen), rolling (transfers). *Notification:* continuous (freshmen), continuous (out-of-state freshmen), continuous (transfers).

Freshman Application Contact Mr. Joel Liles, Dean of Enrollment Services, Marion Technical College, 1467 Mount Vernon Avenue, Marion, OH 43302. *Phone:* 740-389-4636 Ext. 249. *Fax:* 740-389-6136. *E-mail:* enroll@mtc.edu. *Web site:* http://www.mtc.edu/.

Miami–Jacobs College
Dayton, Ohio

Director of Admissions Mary Percell, Vice President of Information Services, Miami–Jacobs College, PO Box 1433, Dayton, OH 45401-1433. *Phone:* 937-461-5174 Ext. 118. *Web site:* http://www.miamijacobs.edu/.

Miami University–Middletown Campus
Middletown, Ohio

Freshman Application Contact Diane Cantonwine, Assistant Director of Admission and Financial Aid, Miami University–Middletown Campus, 4200 East University Boulevard, Middletown, OH 45042-3497. *Phone:* 513-727-

3346. *Toll-free phone:* 866-426-4643. *Fax:* 513-727-3223. *E-mail:* cantondm@muohio.edu. *Web site:* http://www.mid.muohio.edu/.

North Central State College
Mansfield, Ohio

Freshman Application Contact Ms. Nikia L. Fletcher, Director of Admissions, North Central State College, 2441 Kenwood Circle, PO Box 698, Mansfield, OH 44901-0698. *Phone:* 419-755-4813. *Toll-free phone:* 888-755-4899. *E-mail:* nfletcher@ncstatecollege.edu. *Web site:* http://www.ncstatecollege.edu/.

Northwest State Community College
Archbold, Ohio

Director of Admissions Mr. Jeffrey Ferezan, Dean of Student Success and Advocacy Center, Northwest State Community College, 22-600 State Route 34, Archbold, OH 43502-9542. *Phone:* 419-267-1213. *Web site:* http://www.northweststate.edu/.

Ohio Business College
Lorain, Ohio

Director of Admissions Mr. Jim Unger, Admissions Director, Ohio Business College, 1907 North Ridge Road, Lorain, OH 44055. *Toll-free phone:* 888-514-3126. *Web site:* http://www.ohiobusinesscollege.com/.

Ohio Business College
Sandusky, Ohio

Freshman Application Contact Ohio Business College, 5202 Timber Commons Drive, Sandusky, OH 44870. *Phone:* 419-627-8345. *Toll-free phone:* 888-627-8345. *Web site:* http://www.ohiobusinesscollege.com/.

Ohio College of Massotherapy
Akron, Ohio

Director of Admissions Mr. John Atkins, Director of Admissions and Marketing, Ohio College of Massotherapy, 225 Heritage Woods Drive, Akron, OH 44321. *Phone:* 330-665-1084 Ext. 11. *Toll-free phone:* 888-888-4325. *E-mail:* johna@ocm.edu. *Web site:* http://www.ocm.edu/.

The Ohio State University Agricultural Technical Institute
Wooster, Ohio

- **State-supported** 2-year, founded 1971, part of Ohio State University System
- **Small-town** campus with easy access to Cleveland and Columbus
- **Endowment** $2.2 million
- **Coed**

Undergraduates 747 full-time. Students come from 13 states and territories; 2 other countries; 2% are from out of state; 7% transferred in. *Retention:* 68% of full-time freshmen returned.

Faculty *Student/faculty ratio:* 16:1.

Academics *Calendar:* quarters. *Degree:* certificates, diplomas, and associate. *Special study options:* academic remediation for entering students, accelerated degree program, adult/continuing education programs, advanced placement credit, cooperative education, distance learning, double majors, independent study, internships, part-time degree program, services for LD students, student-designed majors, study abroad, summer session for credit. *ROTC:* Army (c), Navy (c), Air Force (c).

Student Life *Campus security:* 24-hour emergency response devices and patrols, controlled dormitory access.

Standardized Tests *Required for some:* SAT or ACT (for admission).

Costs (2010–11) *Tuition:* state resident $6300 full-time; nonresident $20,484 full-time. Full-time tuition and fees vary according to course load. Part-time tuition and fees vary according to course load. *Room and board:* $7035; room only: $5865. Room and board charges vary according to board plan.

Applying *Options:* electronic application. *Application fee:* $40. *Required:* high school transcript.

Freshman Application Contact Ms. Sarah Elvey, Admissions Counselor, The Ohio State University Agricultural Technical Institute, 1328 Dover Road, Wooster, OH 44691. *Phone:* 330-287-1228. *Toll-free phone:* 800-647-8283 Ext. 1327. *Fax:* 330-287-1333. *E-mail:* elvey.3@osu.edu. *Web site:* http://www.ati.osu.edu/.

Ohio Technical College

Cleveland, Ohio

Director of Admissions Mr. Marc Brenner, President, Ohio Technical College, 1374 East 51st Street, Cleveland, OH 44103. *Phone:* 216-881-1700. *Toll-free phone:* 800-322-7000. *Fax:* 216-881-9145. *E-mail:* ohioauto@aol.com. *Web site:* http://www.ohiotechnicalcollege.com/.

Ohio Valley College of Technology

East Liverpool, Ohio

Freshman Application Contact Mr. Scott S. Rogers, Director, Ohio Valley College of Technology, 16808 St. Clair Avenue, PO Box 7000, East Liverpool, OH 43920. *Phone:* 330-385-1070. *Toll-free phone:* 877-777-8451. *Web site:* http://www.ovct.edu/.

Owens Community College

Toledo, Ohio

- **State-supported** 2-year, founded 1966
- **Suburban** 420-acre campus with easy access to Detroit
- **Endowment** $1.2 million
- **Coed,** 19,978 undergraduate students, 43% full-time, 50% women, 50% men

Undergraduates 8,616 full-time, 11,362 part-time. Students come from 21 states and territories; 32 other countries; 3% are from out of state; 0.7% transferred in.

Freshmen *Admission:* 8,553 applied, 8,553 admitted, 3,304 enrolled. *Average high school GPA:* 2.43. *Test scores:* SAT critical reading scores over 500: 23%; SAT math scores over 500: 24%; SAT writing scores over 500: 14%; ACT scores over 18: 58%; SAT critical reading scores over 600: 7%; SAT math scores over 600: 7%; ACT scores over 24: 8%.

Faculty *Total:* 1,313, 16% full-time, 9% with terminal degrees. *Student/faculty ratio:* 22:1.

Majors Accounting technology and bookkeeping; African American/Black studies; agricultural business and management; agricultural mechanization; architectural drafting and CAD/CADD; architectural engineering technology; automotive engineering technology; banking and financial support services; biology/biological sciences; biomedical technology; biotechnology; business administration and management; business/commerce; Canadian studies; chemistry; commercial and advertising art; commercial photography; communications technology; computer engineering technology; computer programming (specific applications); construction engineering technology; corrections; creative writing; criminal justice/law enforcement administration; criminal justice/police science; dental hygiene; desktop publishing and digital imaging design; diagnostic medical sonography and ultrasound technology; dietetics; dramatic/theater arts; early childhood education; education; education (multiple levels); electrical, electronic and communications engineering technology; electromechanical technology; engineering; English; environmental engineering technology; executive assistant/executive secretary; fine and studio arts management; fire prevention and safety technology; fire science/firefighting; foreign languages and literatures; general studies; health/health-care administration; health information/medical records technology; history; hydraulics and fluid power technology; industrial technology; information technology; interior design; international business/trade/commerce; landscaping and groundskeeping; licensed practical/vocational nurse training; manufacturing engineering technology; massage therapy; mathematics; mechanical engineering/mechanical technology; medical administrative assistant and medical secretary; medical/health management and clinical assistant; medical radiologic technology; music history, literature, and theory; music management; music performance; nuclear medical technology; occupational therapist assistant; office management; operations management; physical therapy technology; psychology; public administration; quality control technology; radiologic technology/science; registered nursing/registered nurse; restaurant/food services management; sales, distribution, and marketing operations; security and loss prevention; social work; sociology; speech communication and rhetoric; surgical technology; surveying technology; tool and die technology; welding technology; women's studies.

Academics *Calendar:* semesters. *Degree:* certificates and associate. *Special study options:* academic remediation for entering students, accelerated degree program, adult/continuing education programs, advanced placement credit, cooperative education, distance learning, double majors, English as a second language, external degree program, freshman honors college, honors programs, independent study, internships, part-time degree program, services for LD students, summer session for credit. *ROTC:* Army (c), Air Force (c).

Library Owens Community College Library plus 1 other with 36,770 titles, 9,612 serial subscriptions, 13,470 audiovisual materials, an OPAC, a Web page.

Student Life *Housing:* college housing not available. *Activities and Organizations:* drama/theater group, student-run newspaper, choral group, Student Government, Black Student Union, Gay-Straight Alliance, International Student Union, Computer Club. *Campus security:* 24-hour emergency response devices and patrols, student patrols, classroom doors that lock from the inside; campus alert system.

Athletics Member NJCAA. *Intercollegiate sports:* baseball M, basketball M(s)/W(s), cheerleading W, golf M/W, soccer M, softball W, volleyball W. *Intramural sports:* basketball M/W, bowling M/W, football M, golf M/W, softball M/W, table tennis M/W, tennis M/W, volleyball M/W, weight lifting M/W.

Costs (2010–11) *Tuition:* state resident $3250 full-time, $116 per credit hour part-time; nonresident $6510 full-time, $248 per credit hour part-time. Full-time tuition and fees vary according to course load and reciprocity agreements. Part-time tuition and fees vary according to course load and reciprocity agreements. *Required fees:* $454 full-time, $454 per term part-time. *Payment plans:* installment, deferred payment. *Waivers:* senior citizens and employees or children of employees.

Applying *Options:* electronic application, early admission. *Required for some:* minimum 2.0 GPA, interview. *Recommended:* high school transcript. *Application deadlines:* rolling (freshmen), rolling (out-of-state freshmen), rolling (transfers). *Notification:* continuous (freshmen), continuous (out-of-state freshmen), continuous (transfers).

Freshman Application Contact Ms. Jennifer Irelan, Director, Enrollment Services, Owens Community College, Toledo, OH 43699. *Phone:* 567-661-7188. *Toll-free phone:* 800-GO-OWENS. *E-mail:* jennifer_irelan@owens.edu. *Web site:* http://www.owens.edu/.

Professional Skills Institute

Toledo, Ohio

Director of Admissions Ms. Hope Finch, Director of Marketing, Professional Skills Institute, 20 Arco Drive, Toledo, OH 43607. *Phone:* 419-531-9610. *Web site:* http://www.proskills.com/.

Remington College–Cleveland Campus

Cleveland, Ohio

Director of Admissions Director of Recruitment, Remington College–Cleveland Campus, 14445 Broadway Avenue, Cleveland, OH 44125. *Phone:* 216-475-7520. *Fax:* 216-475-6055. *Web site:* http://www.remingtoncollege.edu/.

Remington College–Cleveland West Campus

North Olmstead, Ohio

Freshman Application Contact Remington College–Cleveland West Campus, 26350 Brookpark Road, North Olmstead, OH 44070. *Phone:* 440-777-2560. *Web site:* http://www.remingtoncollege.edu/.

Rosedale Bible College

Irwin, Ohio

Director of Admissions Mr. John Showalter, Director of Enrollment Services, Rosedale Bible College, 2270 Rosedale Road, Irwin, OH 43029-9501. *Phone:* 740-857-1311. *Fax:* 740-857-1577. *E-mail:* pweber@rosedale.edu. *Web site:* http://www.rosedalebible.org/.

School of Advertising Art

Kettering, Ohio

- **Proprietary** 2-year, founded 1983
- **Suburban** 5-acre campus with easy access to Columbus
- **Coed,** 116 undergraduate students, 73% women, 27% men

Undergraduates 116 full-time. Students come from 3 states and territories; 2% are from out of state; 2% Black or African American, non-Hispanic/Latino; 2% Hispanic/Latino; 0.9% Native Hawaiian or other Pacific Islander, non-Hispanic/Latino; 4% Race/ethnicity unknown. *Retention:* 86% of full-time freshmen returned.

Freshmen *Admission:* 263 applied, 165 admitted, 63 enrolled.

Faculty *Total:* 9, 89% full-time. *Student/faculty ratio:* 14:1.

Majors Commercial and advertising art.

Academics *Calendar:* trimesters. *Degree:* diplomas and associate.

Library SAA Library with 590 titles, 26 serial subscriptions, an OPAC, a Web page.

Student Life *Housing:* college housing not available. *Student services:* personal/psychological counseling.

Costs (2011–12) *One-time required fee:* $100. *Tuition:* $21,960 full-time. *Required fees:* $1443 full-time. *Payment plan:* installment. *Waivers:* employees or children of employees.

Applying *Options:* electronic application. *Required:* high school transcript, minimum 2.0 GPA, interview. *Required for some:* essay or personal statement, 2 letters of recommendation.

Freshman Application Contact Ms. Abigail Heaney, Admissions, School of Advertising Art, 1725 East David Road, Kettering, OH 45440. *Phone:* 937-294-0592. *Toll-free phone:* 877-300-9866. *Fax:* 937-294-5869. *E-mail:* Abbie@saa.edu. *Web site:* http://www.saa.edu/.

Sinclair Community College

Dayton, Ohio

Freshman Application Contact Ms. Sara Smith, Director and Systems Manager, Outreach Services, Sinclair Community College, 444 West Third Street, Dayton, OH 45402-1460. *Phone:* 937-512-3060. *Toll-free phone:* 800-315-3000. *Fax:* 937-512-2393. *E-mail:* ssmith@sinclair.edu. *Web site:* http://www.sinclair.edu/.

Southern State Community College

Hillsboro, Ohio

- **State-supported** 2-year, founded 1975
- **Rural** 60-acre campus
- **Endowment** $1.8 million
- **Coed,** 3,723 undergraduate students, 59% full-time, 69% women, 31% men

Undergraduates 2,206 full-time, 1,517 part-time.

Freshmen *Admission:* 1,793 applied, 1,793 admitted, 649 enrolled.

Faculty *Total:* 198, 29% full-time, 9% with terminal degrees. *Student/faculty ratio:* 26:1.

Majors Accounting technology and bookkeeping; agricultural production; business/commerce; computer programming (specific applications); computer technology/computer systems technology; corrections; criminal justice/law enforcement administration; drafting and design technology; emergency medical technology (EMT paramedic); executive assistant/executive secretary; human services; kindergarten/preschool education; liberal arts and sciences/liberal studies; medical/clinical assistant; real estate; registered nursing/registered nurse; respiratory care therapy.

Academics *Calendar:* quarters. *Degree:* certificates and associate. *Special study options:* academic remediation for entering students, advanced placement credit, cooperative education, distance learning, double majors, independent study, internships, off-campus study, part-time degree program, services for LD students, student-designed majors, summer session for credit.

Library Learning Resources Center plus 3 others with 60,550 titles, 225 serial subscriptions, 3,225 audiovisual materials, an OPAC, a Web page.

Student Life *Housing:* college housing not available. *Activities and Organizations:* drama/theater group, choral group, Student Government Association, Drama Club. *Student services:* personal/psychological counseling.

Athletics Member USCAA. *Intercollegiate sports:* baseball M(c), basketball M(s)/W(s), soccer M(s), softball W(s), volleyball W(s).

Costs (2011–12) *Tuition:* state resident $3633 full-time; nonresident $6933 full-time. Full-time tuition and fees vary according to course load. Part-time tuition and fees vary according to course load. *Payment plan:* deferred payment. *Waivers:* senior citizens and employees or children of employees.

Financial Aid Of all full-time matriculated undergraduates who enrolled in 2009, 3,500 applied for aid, 2,785 were judged to have need, 2,745 had their need fully met. 21 Federal Work-Study jobs (averaging $1182). In 2009, 1240 non-need-based awards were made. *Average percent of need met:* 84%. *Average financial aid package:* $3000. *Average need-based loan:* $1001. *Average need-based gift aid:* $1547. *Average non-need-based aid:* $1167.

Applying *Options:* electronic application, early admission, deferred entrance. *Recommended:* high school transcript. *Application deadlines:* rolling (freshmen), rolling (transfers). *Notification:* continuous (freshmen), continuous (transfers).

Freshman Application Contact Ms. Wendy Johnson, Director of Admissions, Southern State Community College, Hillsboro, OH 45133. *Phone:* 937-393-3431 Ext. 2720. *Toll-free phone:* 800-628-7722. *Fax:* 937-393-6682. *E-mail:* wjohnson@sscc.edu. *Web site:* http://www.sscc.edu/.

Southwestern College of Business

Cincinnati, Ohio

Freshman Application Contact Director of Admission, Southwestern College of Business, 149 Northland Boulevard, Cincinnati, OH 45246-1122.

Phone: 513-874-0432. *Fax:* 513-874-1330. *Web site:* http://www.swcollege.net/.

Southwestern College of Business

Cincinnati, Ohio

Freshman Application Contact Admissions Director, Southwestern College of Business, 632 Vine Street, Suite 200, Cincinnati, OH 45202-4304. *Phone:* 513-421-3212. *Fax:* 513-421-8325. *Web site:* http://www.swcollege.net/.

Southwestern College of Business

Dayton, Ohio

Director of Admissions William Furlong, Director of Admissions, Southwestern College of Business, 111 West First Street, Dayton, OH 45402-3003. *Phone:* 937-224-0061. *Web site:* http://www.swcollege.net/.

Southwestern College of Business

Franklin, Ohio

- **Proprietary** 2-year, founded 1981
- **Suburban** campus with easy access to Cincinnati and Dayton
- **Coed**

Undergraduates Students come from 1 other state. *Retention:* 57% of full-time freshmen returned.

Majors Administrative assistant and secretarial science; business administration and management; clinical/medical laboratory science and allied professions related; computer and information sciences and support services related; criminal justice/law enforcement administration.

Academics *Calendar:* quarters. *Degree:* certificates, diplomas, and associate. *Special study options:* cooperative education, independent study.

Costs (2010–11) *Tuition:* $11,100 full-time. Full-time tuition and fees vary according to class time, course level, course load, degree level, location, program, reciprocity agreements, and student level. *Required fees:* $100 full-time. *Payment plan:* installment.

Applying *Required:* high school transcript, interview. *Application deadline:* rolling (freshmen). *Notification:* continuous (freshmen).

Freshman Application Contact Admissions Director, Southwestern College of Business, 201 East Second Street, Franklin, OH 45005. *Phone:* 937-746-6633. *Fax:* 937-746-6754. *Web site:* http://www.swcollege.net/.

Stark State College of Technology

North Canton, Ohio

- **State and locally supported** 2-year, founded 1970, part of Ohio Board of Regents
- **Suburban** 34-acre campus with easy access to Cleveland
- **Endowment** $2.1 million
- **Coed,** 14,830 undergraduate students

Undergraduates Students come from 28 states and territories; 0.5% are from out of state; 18% Black or African American, non-Hispanic/Latino; 0.8% Hispanic/Latino; 0.6% Asian, non-Hispanic/Latino; 0.1% Native Hawaiian or other Pacific Islander, non-Hispanic/Latino; 0.5% American Indian or Alaska Native, non-Hispanic/Latino; 2% Two or more races, non-Hispanic/Latino; 6% Race/ethnicity unknown. *Retention:* 5% of full-time freshmen returned.

Freshmen *Test scores:* ACT scores over 18: 60%; ACT scores over 24: 8%; ACT scores over 30: 1%.

Faculty *Total:* 740, 24% full-time. *Student/faculty ratio:* 20:1.

Majors Accounting; administrative assistant and secretarial science; architectural engineering technology; automobile/automotive mechanics technology; biomedical technology; business administration and management; child development; civil engineering technology; clinical/medical laboratory technology; computer and information sciences and support services related; computer and information sciences related; computer engineering related; computer hardware engineering; computer/information technology services administration related; computer programming; computer programming related; computer programming (specific applications); computer programming (vendor/product certification); computer software and media applications related; computer software engineering; computer systems networking and telecommunications; consumer merchandising/retailing management; court reporting; data entry/microcomputer applications; data entry/microcomputer applications related; dental hygiene; drafting and design technology; environmental studies; finance; fire science/firefighting; food technology and processing; health information/medical records administration; human services; industrial technology; information technology; international business/trade/commerce; legal administrative assistant/secretary; marketing/marketing management; mechanical engineering/mechanical technology; medical/clinical assistant; occupational therapy; operations management; physical therapy; registered nursing/registered nurse; respiratory care therapy; surveying technology; web/multimedia management and webmaster; web page, digital/multimedia and information resources design; word processing.

Academics *Calendar:* semesters. *Degree:* certificates and associate. *Special study options:* academic remediation for entering students, adult/continuing education programs, distance learning, external degree program, independent study, off-campus study, part-time degree program, services for LD students, student-designed majors, summer session for credit.

Library Learning Resource Center plus 1 other with 82,728 titles, 23,331 serial subscriptions, an OPAC.

Student Life *Housing:* college housing not available. *Activities and Organizations:* student-run newspaper, Phi Theta Kappa, Business Student Club, Institute of Management Accountants, Stark State College Association of Medical Assistants, Student Health Information Management Association. *Campus security:* 24-hour emergency response devices, late-night transport/escort service. *Student services:* personal/psychological counseling.

Standardized Tests *Recommended:* SAT or ACT (for admission).

Costs (2010–11) *Tuition:* state resident $4073 full-time, $136 per credit hour part-time; nonresident $6323 full-time, $211 per credit hour part-time. Full-time tuition and fees vary according to course load and program. Part-time tuition and fees vary according to program. *Payment plan:* installment. *Waivers:* senior citizens and employees or children of employees.

Financial Aid Of all full-time matriculated undergraduates who enrolled in 2009, 194 Federal Work-Study jobs (averaging $2383).

Applying *Options:* electronic application, early admission, deferred entrance. *Application fee:* $65. *Required:* high school transcript. *Application deadlines:* rolling (freshmen), rolling (transfers).

Freshman Application Contact Mr. Wallace Hoffer, Dean of Student Services, Stark State College of Technology, 6200 Frank Road, NW, Canton, OH 44720. *Phone:* 330-966-5450. *Toll-free phone:* 800-797-8275. *Fax·* 330-497-6313. *E-mail:* info@starkstate.edu. *Web site:* http://www.starkstate.edu/.

Stautzenberger College
Maumee, Ohio

Director of Admissions Ms. Karen Fitzgerald, Director of Admissions and Marketing, Stautzenberger College, 1796 Indian Wood Circle, Maumee, OH 43537. *Phone:* 419-866-0261. *Toll-free phone:* 800-552-5099. *Fax:* 419-867-9821. *E-mail:* klfitzgerald@stautzenberger.com. *Web site:* http://www.stautzen.com/.

Terra State Community College
Fremont, Ohio

- **State-supported** 2-year, founded 1968, part of Ohio Board of Regents
- **Small-town** 100-acre campus with easy access to Toledo
- **Coed,** 3,556 undergraduate students, 46% full-time, 56% women, 44% men

Undergraduates 1,621 full-time, 1,935 part-time. Students come from 4 states and territories; 2 other countries; 0.2% are from out of state; 21% transferred in. *Retention:* 43% of full-time freshmen returned.

Freshmen *Admission:* 690 enrolled.

Faculty *Total:* 217, 21% full-time, 5% with terminal degrees. *Student/faculty ratio:* 21:1.

Majors Accounting; agricultural business and management; animation, interactive technology, video graphics and special effects; architectural engineering technology; art history, criticism and conservation; automotive engineering technology; banking and financial support services; biological and physical sciences; biology/biological sciences; business administration and management; business/commerce; chemistry; commercial and advertising art; computer and information sciences; computer programming; computer systems networking and telecommunications; criminal justice/police science; data processing and data processing technology; desktop publishing and digital imaging design; economics; education; electrical and electronic engineering technologies related; electrical, electronic and communications engineering technology; engineering; English; executive assistant/executive secretary; fine/studio arts; general studies; health/health-care administration; health information/medical records administration; health information/medical records technology; health professions related; heating, ventilation, air conditioning and refrigeration engineering technology; history; hospitality administration; humanities; kindergarten/preschool education; language interpretation and translation; liberal arts and sciences/liberal studies; manufacturing engineering technology; marketing/marketing management; mathematics; mechanical engineering/mechanical technology; mechanical engineering technologies related; medical administrative assistant and medical secretary; medical/clinical assistant; medical/health management and clinical assistant; medical insurance coding; medical office assistant; music; music management; music performance; music related; nuclear/nuclear power technology; operations management; physics; plastics and polymer engineering technology; psychology; real estate; registered nursing/registered nurse; robotics technology; sheet metal technology; social sciences; social work; teaching assistants/aides related; web page, digital/multimedia and information resources design; welding technology.

Academics *Calendar:* semesters. *Degree:* certificates, diplomas, and associate. *Special study options:* academic remediation for entering students, adult/continuing education programs, advanced placement credit, cooperative education, distance learning, double majors, independent study, internships, off-campus study, part-time degree program, services for LD students, student-designed majors, summer session for credit.

Library Learning Resource Center with 22,675 titles, 383 serial subscriptions, an OPAC, a Web page.

Student Life *Housing:* college housing not available. *Activities and Organizations:* choral group, Phi Theta Kappa, Student Activities Club, Society of Plastic Engineers, Koinonia, Student Senate. *Campus security:* 24-hour emergency response devices. *Student services:* personal/psychological counseling, legal services.

Athletics *Intramural sports:* basketball M/W, bowling M/W, football M, golf M/W, table tennis M/W, volleyball M/W.

Costs (2010–11) *Tuition:* state resident $2769 full-time, $115 per semester hour part-time; nonresident $4523 full-time, $188 per semester hour part-time. Full-time tuition and fees vary according to course load. Part-time tuition and fees vary according to course load. *Required fees:* $307 full-time, $13 per semester hour part-time. *Payment plan:* installment. *Waivers:* senior citizens and employees or children of employees.

Financial Aid Of all full-time matriculated undergraduates who enrolled in 2009, 57 Federal Work-Study jobs (averaging $1450).

Applying *Options:* electronic application, early admission, deferred entrance. *Required:* high school transcript. *Application deadlines:* rolling (freshmen), rolling (transfers).

Freshman Application Contact Mr. Heath Martin, Director of Admissions and Enrollment Services, Terra State Community College, 2830 Napoleon Road, Fremont, OH 43420. *Phone:* 419-559-2350. *Toll-free phone:* 800-334-3886. *Fax:* 419-559-2352. *E-mail:* hmartin01@terra.edu. *Web site:* http://www.terra.edu/.

Trumbull Business College
Warren, Ohio

Director of Admissions Admissions Office, Trumbull Business College, 3200 Ridge Road, Warren, OH 44484. *Phone:* 330-369-6792. *Toll-free phone:* 330-369-3200. *E-mail:* admissions@tbc-trumbullbusiness.com. *Web site:* http://www.tbc-trumbullbusiness.com/.

The University of Akron–Wayne College
Orrville, Ohio

Freshman Application Contact Ms. Alicia Broadus, Student Services Counselor, The University of Akron–Wayne College, Orrville, OH 44667. *Phone:* 800-221-8308 Ext. 8901. *Toll-free phone:* 800-221-8308 Ext. 8900. *Fax:* 330-684-8989. *E-mail:* wayneadmissions@uakron.edu. *Web site:* http://www.wayne.uakron.edu/.

University of Cincinnati Clermont College
Batavia, Ohio

- **State-supported** 2-year, founded 1972, part of University of Cincinnati System
- **Rural** 91-acre campus with easy access to Cincinnati
- **Endowment** $338,141
- **Coed**

Undergraduates 2,391 full-time, 1,322 part-time. Students come from 16 states and territories; 21% are from out of state.

Faculty *Student/faculty ratio:* 20:1.

Academics *Calendar:* quarters. *Degrees:* certificates, associate, and postbachelor's certificates. *Special study options:* academic remediation for entering students, adult/continuing education programs, advanced placement credit, cooperative education, distance learning, double majors, honors programs, independent study, internships, off-campus study, part-time degree program, services for LD students, student-designed majors, study abroad, summer session for credit. *ROTC:* Air Force (c).

Student Life *Campus security:* 24-hour emergency response devices, Implementing 24-hour patrols by trained security personnel in spring or summer 2010.

Costs (2010–11) *Tuition:* state resident $4182 full-time, $116 per credit hour part-time; nonresident $11,034 full-time, $306 per credit hour part-time. Full-time tuition and fees vary according to course load, program, and reciprocity agreements. Part-time tuition and fees vary according to course load, program, and reciprocity agreements. *Required fees:* $681 full-time, $20 per credit hour part-time.

Applying *Options:* electronic application, deferred entrance. *Application fee:* $50. *Required:* high school transcript.

Freshman Application Contact Mrs. Jamie Adkins, Records Management Officer, University of Cincinnati Clermont College, 4200 Clermont College Drive, Batavia, OH 45103. *Phone:* 513-732-5294. *Fax:* 513-732-5303. *E-mail:* jamie.adkins@uc.edu. *Web site:* http://www.ucclermont.edu/.

University of Cincinnati Raymond Walters College
Cincinnati, Ohio

Freshman Application Contact Leigh Schlegal, Admission Counselor, University of Cincinnati Raymond Walters College, 9555 Plainfield Road, Cincinnati, OH 45236-1007. *Phone:* 513-745-5783. *Fax:* 513-745-5768. *Web site:* http://www.rwc.uc.edu/.

University of Northwestern Ohio
Lima, Ohio

Freshman Application Contact Mr. Dan Klopp, Vice President for Enrollment Management, University of Northwestern Ohio, 1441 North Cable Road, Lima, OH 45805-1498. *Phone:* 419-227-3141. *Fax:* 419-229-6926. *E-mail:* klopp_d@unoh.edu. *Web site:* http://www.unoh.edu/.

Vatterott College
Broadview Heights, Ohio

Director of Admissions Mr. Jack Chalk, Director of Admissions, Vatterott College, 5025 East Royalton Road, Broadview Heights, OH 44147. *Phone:* 440-526-1660. *Toll-free phone:* 866-314-6454. *Web site:* http://www.vatterott-college.edu/.

Vet Tech Institute at Bradford School
Columbus, Ohio

- **Private** 2-year, founded 2005
- **Suburban** campus
- **Coed,** 175 undergraduate students
- 39% of applicants were admitted

Freshmen *Admission:* 636 applied, 246 admitted.

Majors Veterinary/animal health technology.

Academics *Degree:* associate. *Special study options:* accelerated degree program, internships.

Freshman Application Contact Admissions Office, Vet Tech Institute at Bradford School, 2469 Stelzer Road, Columbus, OH 43219. *Phone:* 800-678-7981. *Toll-free phone:* 800-678-7981. *Web site:* http://www.vettechinstitute.edu/.

Virginia Marti College of Art and Design
Lakewood, Ohio

- **Proprietary** 2-year, founded 1966
- **Urban** campus with easy access to Cleveland
- **Coed**

Undergraduates *Retention:* 62% of full-time freshmen returned.

Faculty *Student/faculty ratio:* 12:1.

Academics *Calendar:* quarters. *Degree:* certificates and associate. *Special study options:* academic remediation for entering students, adult/continuing education programs, internships, part-time degree program, summer session for credit.

Student Life *Campus security:* 24-hour emergency response devices.

Standardized Tests *Required:* CAPS (for admission).

Applying *Options:* electronic application, early admission, deferred entrance. *Application fee:* $50. *Required:* essay or personal statement, high school transcript, minimum 2.0 GPA, 1 letter of recommendation, interview. *Required for some:* Entrance Evaluation Test.

Freshman Application Contact Virginia Marti College of Art and Design, 11724 Detroit Avenue, PO Box 580, Lakewood, OH 44107-3002. *Phone:* 216-221-8584 Ext. 106. *Web site:* http://www.vmcad.edu/.

Washington State Community College
Marietta, Ohio

Freshman Application Contact Ms. Rebecca Peroni, Director of Admissions, Washington State Community College, 110 Coligate Drive, Marietta, OH 45750. *Phone:* 740-374-8716. *Fax:* 740-376-0257. *E-mail:* rperoni@wscc.edu. *Web site:* http://www.wscc.edu/.

Wright State University, Lake Campus
Celina, Ohio

Freshman Application Contact Sandra Gilbert, Student Services Officer, Wright State University, Lake Campus, 7600 State Route 703, Celina, OH 45822-2921. *Phone:* 419-586-0324. *Toll-free phone:* 800-237-1477. *Fax:* 419-586-0358. *Web site:* http://www.wright.edu/lake/.

Zane State College
Zanesville, Ohio

Director of Admissions Mr. Paul Young, Director of Admissions, Zane State College, 1555 Newark Road, Zanesville, OH 43701-2626. *Phone:* 740-454-2501 Ext. 1225. *Toll-free phone:* 704-454-2501 (in-state); 800-686-8324 Ext. 1225 (out-of-state). *E-mail:* pyoung@zanestate.edu. *Web site:* http://www.zanestate.edu/.

OKLAHOMA

Brown Mackie College–Oklahoma City
Oklahoma City, Oklahoma

- **Proprietary** 2-year, part of Education Management Corporation
- **Coed**

Admissions Office Contact Brown Mackie College–Oklahoma City, 7101 Northwest Expressway, Suite 800, Oklahoma City, OK 73132. *Toll-free phone:* 888-229-3280. *Web site:* http://www.brownmackie.edu/oklahoma-city/

See page 390 for the College Close-Up.

Brown Mackie College–Tulsa
Tulsa, Oklahoma

- **Proprietary** primarily 2-year, part of Education Management Corporation
- **Coed**

Majors Accounting technology and bookkeeping; business administration and management; criminal justice/law enforcement administration; health services administration; information technology; legal assistant/paralegal; legal studies; medical/clinical assistant; occupational therapist assistant; office management; surgical technology.

Academics *Degrees:* diplomas, associate, and bachelor's.

Costs (2010–11) *Tuition:* Tuition varies by program. Students should contact Brown Mackie College for tuition information.

Freshman Application Contact Brown Mackie College–Tulsa, 4608 South Garnett, Suite 110, Tulsa, OK 74146. *Phone:* 918-628-3700. *Toll-free phone:* 888-794-8411. *Web site:* http://www.brownmackie.edu/tulsa/.

See page 406 for the College Close-Up.

Carl Albert State College
Poteau, Oklahoma

- **State-supported** 2-year, founded 1934, part of Oklahoma State Regents for Higher Education
- **Small-town** 78-acre campus
- **Endowment** $5.7 million
- **Coed,** 2,363 undergraduate students, 58% full-time, 66% women, 34% men

Undergraduates 1,369 full-time, 994 part-time. Students come from 16 states and territories; 9 other countries.

Freshmen *Admission:* 601 enrolled.

Faculty *Total:* 154, 33% full-time, 2% with terminal degrees. *Student/faculty ratio:* 16:1.

Majors Biology/biological sciences; business administration and management; business/commerce; child development; computer and information sciences; elementary education; engineering; engineering technologies and engineering related; English; film/cinema/video studies; fine arts related; foods, nutrition, and wellness; health professions related; health services/allied health/health sciences; hotel/motel administration; journalism; management information systems; mathematics; music related; physical education teaching and coaching; physical sciences; physical therapy technology; pre-law studies; radiologic technology/science; registered nursing/registered nurse; rhetoric and composition; secondary education; social sciences; telecommunications technology.

Academics *Calendar:* semesters. *Degree:* certificates and associate. *Special study options:* academic remediation for entering students, adult/continuing education programs, cooperative education, part-time degree program.

Library Joe E. White Library with 27,200 titles, 1,350 serial subscriptions, an OPAC.

Student Life *Housing Options:* Campus housing is university owned. *Activities and Organizations:* drama/theater group, student-run newspaper, radio station, choral group, Student Government Association, Phi Theta Kappa, Baptist Student Union, BACCHUS, Student Physical Therapist Assistant Association. *Campus security:* security guards. *Student services:* health clinic, personal/psychological counseling.

Athletics Member NJCAA. *Intercollegiate sports:* baseball M, basketball M(s)/W(s), softball M. *Intramural sports:* tennis M/W, volleyball M/W, weight lifting M.

Costs (2010–11) *Tuition:* state resident $1248 full-time, $52 per credit hour part-time; nonresident $3648 full-time, $152 per credit hour part-time. Full-time tuition and fees vary according to course load. Part-time tuition and fees vary according to course load. *Required fees:* $648 full-time, $27 per credit hour part-time. *Room and board:* Room and board charges vary according to board plan. *Payment plan:* installment. *Waivers:* senior citizens and employees or children of employees.

Financial Aid Of all full-time matriculated undergraduates who enrolled in 2009, 136 Federal Work-Study jobs (averaging $1761).

Applying *Required:* high school transcript. *Application deadlines:* 8/13 (freshmen), 8/15 (transfers). *Notification:* continuous (freshmen), continuous (transfers).

Freshman Application Contact Dawn Webster, Admission Clerk, Carl Albert State College, 1507 South McKenna, Poteau, OK 74953-5208. *Phone:* 918-647-1300. *Fax:* 918-647-1306. *E-mail:* dwebster@carlalbert.edu. *Web site:* http://www.carlalbert.edu/.

Clary Sage College
Tulsa, Oklahoma

- **Proprietary** 2-year, part of Dental Directions, Inc.
- **Urban** 6-acre campus
- **Coed, primarily women,** 96 undergraduate students, 100% full-time, 100% women

Undergraduates 96 full-time. Students come from 2 states and territories.

Faculty *Total:* 21, 95% full-time. *Student/faculty ratio:* 16:1.

Majors Cosmetology; fashion/apparel design; interior design.

Academics *Degree:* diplomas and associate. *Special study options:* adult/continuing education programs, distance learning, part-time degree program.

Student Life *Housing:* college housing not available. *Activities and Organizations:* Student Ambassadors. *Campus security:* security guard during hours of operation. *Student services:* personal/psychological counseling.

Costs (2011–12) *Tuition:* $16,275 full-time. Full-time tuition and fees vary according to class time, course level, course load, degree level, location, program, and reciprocity agreements. Part-time tuition and fees vary according to class time, course level, location, and reciprocity agreements. *Required fees:* $2478 full-time. *Payment plans:* tuition prepayment, installment. *Waivers:* employees or children of employees.

Applying *Options:* electronic application. *Application fee:* $100. *Required:* essay or personal statement, high school transcript, interview. *Application deadlines:* rolling (freshmen), rolling (out-of-state freshmen), rolling (transfers). *Notification:* continuous (freshmen), continuous (out-of-state freshmen), continuous (transfers).

Freshman Application Contact Ms. Teresa L. Knox, Chief Executive Officer, Clary Sage College, 4242 South Sheridan, Tulsa, OK 74145. *Phone:* 918-610-0027 Ext. 2005. *E-mail:* tknox@communitycarecollege.edu. *Web site:* http://www.clarysagecollege.com/.

Community Care College
Tulsa, Oklahoma

- **Proprietary** 2-year, founded 1995, part of Dental Directions, Inc.
- **Urban** 6-acre campus
- **Coed, primarily women,** 307 undergraduate students, 100% full-time, 94% women, 6% men

Undergraduates 307 full-time. Students come from 6 states and territories; 7% are from out of state; 26% Black or African American, non-Hispanic/Latino; 6% Hispanic/Latino; 2% Asian, non-Hispanic/Latino; 12% American Indian or Alaska Native, non-Hispanic/Latino; 9% Race/ethnicity unknown.

Freshmen *Admission:* 84 enrolled.

Faculty *Total:* 30, 100% full-time. *Student/faculty ratio:* 21:1.

Majors Adult and continuing education; business administration, management and operations related; dental assisting; early childhood education; health and physical education/fitness; health/health-care administration; legal assistant/paralegal; massage therapy; medical/clinical assistant; medical insurance coding; pharmacy technician; surgical technology; veterinary/animal health technology.

Academics *Calendar:* continuous. *Degree:* diplomas and associate. *Special study options:* adult/continuing education programs, distance learning, independent study, internships, services for LD students.

Student Life *Housing:* college housing not available. *Activities and Organizations:* Student Ambassadors. *Campus security:* campus security personnel are available during school hours. *Student services:* personal/psychological counseling.

Costs (2011–12) *Tuition:* $19,049 full-time. Full-time tuition and fees vary according to class time, course level, course load, degree level, location, program, and reciprocity agreements. Part-time tuition and fees vary according to class time, course level, location, and reciprocity agreements. *Required fees:* $2492 full-time. *Payment plans:* tuition prepayment, installment. *Waivers:* employees or children of employees.

Applying *Options:* electronic application. *Application fee:* $100. *Required:* essay or personal statement, high school transcript, interview. *Application deadlines:* rolling (freshmen), rolling (out-of-state freshmen). *Notification:* continuous (freshmen), continuous (out-of-state freshmen).

Freshman Application Contact Ms. Teresa L. Knox, Chief Executive Officer, Community Care College, 4242 South Sheridan, Tulsa, OK 74145. *Phone:* 918-610-0027 Ext. 2005. *Fax:* 918-610-0029. *E-mail:* tknox@communitycarecollege.edu. *Web site:* http://www.communitycarecollege.edu/.

Connors State College
Warner, Oklahoma

Freshman Application Contact Ms. Sonya Baker, Registrar, Connors State College, Route 1 Box 1000, Warner, OK 74469-9700. *Phone:* 918-463-6233. *Web site:* http://www.connorsstate.edu/.

Eastern Oklahoma State College
Wilburton, Oklahoma

Freshman Application Contact Ms. Leah McLaughlin, Director of Admissions, Eastern Oklahoma State College, 1301 West Main, Wilburton, OK 74578-4999. *Phone:* 918-465-1811. *Fax:* 918-465-2431. *E-mail:* lmiller@eosc.edu. *Web site:* http://www.eosc.edu/.

Heritage College
Oklahoma City, Oklahoma

Freshman Application Contact Admissions Office, Heritage College, 7100 I-35 Services Road, Suite 7118, Oklahoma City, OK 73149. *Phone:* 405-631-3399. *Toll-free phone:* 888-334-7339. *E-mail:* info@heritage-education.com. *Web site:* http://www.heritage-education.com/campus_oklahoma.htm.

ITT Technical Institute
Tulsa, Oklahoma

- **Proprietary** primarily 2-year, founded 2005
- **Coed**

Majors CAD/CADD drafting/design technology; communications technology; computer and information systems security; computer engineering technology; computer software engineering; computer software technology; construction management; criminal justice/law enforcement administration; design and visual communications; electrical, electronic and communications engineering technology; legal assistant/paralegal; project management; registered nursing/registered nurse; system, networking, and LAN/WAN management.

Academics *Calendar:* quarters. *Degrees:* associate and bachelor's.

Student Life *Housing:* college housing not available.
Freshman Application Contact Director of Recruitment, ITT Technical Institute, 8421 East 61st Street, Suite U, Tulsa, OK 74133. *Phone:* 918-615-3900. *Toll-free phone:* 800-514-6535. *Web site:* http://www.itt-tech.edu/.

Murray State College
Tishomingo, Oklahoma

- **State-supported** 2-year, founded 1908, part of Oklahoma State Regents for Higher Education
- **Rural** 120-acre campus
- **Coed**

Undergraduates 1,291 full-time, 1,206 part-time. Students come from 20 states and territories; 13 other countries; 3% are from out of state; 6% live on campus.
Faculty *Student/faculty ratio:* 27:1.
Academics *Calendar:* semesters. *Degree:* associate. *Special study options:* academic remediation for entering students, advanced placement credit, distance learning, honors programs, internships, part-time degree program, services for LD students, summer session for credit.
Student Life *Campus security:* 24-hour patrols.
Athletics Member NJCAA.
Standardized Tests *Required:* SAT or ACT (for admission).
Costs (2010–11) *Tuition:* state resident $2580 full-time, $86 per credit hour part-time; nonresident $6390 full-time, $213 per credit hour part-time. *Room and board:* $6000. Room and board charges vary according to board plan.
Financial Aid Of all full-time matriculated undergraduates who enrolled in 2009, 68 Federal Work-Study jobs (averaging $3354). 20 state and other part-time jobs (averaging $2516).
Applying *Options:* electronic application, early admission. *Required:* high school transcript.
Freshman Application Contact Murray State College, One Murray Campus, Tishomingo, OK 73460-3130. *Phone:* 580-371-2371. *Web site:* http://www.mscok.edu/.

Northeastern Oklahoma Agricultural and Mechanical College
Miami, Oklahoma

Freshman Application Contact Amy Ishmael, Vice President for Enrollment Management, Northeastern Oklahoma Agricultural and Mechanical College, 200 1 Street, NE, Miami, OK 74354-6434. *Phone:* 918-540-6212. *Toll-free phone:* 800-464-6636. *Fax:* 918-540-6946. *E-mail:* neoadmission@neo.edu. *Web site:* http://www.neo.edu/.

Northern Oklahoma College
Tonkawa, Oklahoma

Freshman Application Contact Ms. Sheri Snyder, Director of College Relations, Northern Oklahoma College, 1220 East Grand Avenue, PO Box 310, Tonkawa, OK 74653-0310. *Phone:* 580-628-6290. *Toll-free phone:* 800-429-5715. *Web site:* http://www.north-ok.edu/.

Oklahoma City Community College
Oklahoma City, Oklahoma

- **State-supported** 2-year, founded 1969, part of Oklahoma State Regents for Higher Education
- **Urban** 143-acre campus
- **Endowment** $266,740
- **Coed,** 14,865 undergraduate students, 39% full-time, 58% women, 42% men

Undergraduates 5,845 full-time, 9,020 part-time. Students come from 23 states and territories; 43 other countries; 4% are from out of state; 11% Black or African American, non-Hispanic/Latino; 9% Hispanic/Latino; 6% Asian, non-Hispanic/Latino; 0.3% Native Hawaiian or other Pacific Islander, non-Hispanic/Latino; 6% American Indian or Alaska Native, non-Hispanic/Latino; 1% Two or more races, non-Hispanic/Latino; 10% Race/ethnicity unknown; 0.7% international.
Freshmen *Admission:* 5,465 applied, 2,803 enrolled. *Test scores:* ACT scores over 18: 70%; ACT scores over 24: 16%.
Faculty *Total:* 640, 23% full-time, 8% with terminal degrees. *Student/faculty ratio:* 28:1.
Majors Accounting; airframe mechanics and aircraft maintenance technology; American government and politics; art; automobile/automotive mechanics technology; avionics maintenance technology; biology/biological sciences; biomedical technology; biotechnology; broadcast journalism; business administration and management; chemistry; child development; commercial and

advertising art; comparative literature; computer engineering technology; computer science; design and applied arts related; design and visual communications; drafting and design technology; dramatic/theater arts; electrical, electronic and communications engineering technology; emergency medical technology (EMT paramedic); finance; fine/studio arts; foreign languages and literatures; health information/medical records administration; history; humanities; insurance; liberal arts and sciences/liberal studies; mass communication/media; mathematics; modern languages; music; occupational therapy; philosophy; physical therapy; physics; political science and government; pre-engineering; psychology; registered nursing/registered nurse; respiratory care therapy; sociology; surgical technology.
Academics *Calendar:* semesters. *Degree:* certificates and associate. *Special study options:* academic remediation for entering students, accelerated degree program, advanced placement credit, cooperative education, distance learning, double majors, English as a second language, honors programs, independent study, internships, part-time degree program, services for LD students, student-designed majors, summer session for credit.
Library Keith Leftwich Memorial Library with 85,940 titles, 557 serial subscriptions, 16,563 audiovisual materials, an OPAC, a Web page.
Student Life *Housing:* college housing not available. *Activities and Organizations:* drama/theater group, student-run newspaper, choral group, Health Professions Association, Black Student Association, Nursing Student Association, Hispanic Organization Promoting Education (H.O.P.E), Phi Theta Kappa (Honorary). *Campus security:* 24-hour emergency response devices and patrols, late-night transport/escort service. *Student services:* personal/psychological counseling.
Athletics *Intramural sports:* basketball M/W, bowling M/W, football M/W, rock climbing M/W, soccer M(c)/W(c), volleyball M/W, weight lifting M/W.
Standardized Tests *Required for some:* ACT (for admission). *Recommended:* SAT or ACT (for admission).
Costs (2011–12) *One-time required fee:* $25. *Tuition:* state resident $1564 full-time, $65 per credit hour part-time; nonresident $5106 full-time, $213 per credit hour part-time. Full-time tuition and fees vary according to class time, course level, and program. Part-time tuition and fees vary according to class time, course level, and program. *Required fees:* $563 full-time, $23 per credit hour part-time. *Payment plan:* installment. *Waivers:* senior citizens and employees or children of employees.
Financial Aid Of all full-time matriculated undergraduates who enrolled in 2009, 4,062 applied for aid, 3,608 were judged to have need, 1,576 had their need fully met. 315 Federal Work-Study jobs (averaging $4800). 240 state and other part-time jobs (averaging $2502). In 2009, 321 non-need-based awards were made. *Average percent of need met:* 70%. *Average financial aid package:* $7351. *Average need-based loan:* $2801. *Average need-based gift aid:* $4769. *Average non-need-based aid:* $589.
Applying *Options:* electronic application. *Application fee:* $25. *Required for some:* high school transcript. *Application deadlines:* rolling (freshmen), rolling (out-of-state freshmen), rolling (transfers). *Notification:* continuous (freshmen), continuous (out-of-state freshmen), continuous (transfers).
Freshman Application Contact Mr. Jon Horinek, Director of Recruitment and Admissions, Oklahoma City Community College, 7777 South May Avenue, Oklahoma City, OK 73159. *Phone:* 405-682-7743. *Fax:* 405-682-7817. *E-mail:* jhorinek@occc.edu. *Web site:* http://www.occc.edu/.

Oklahoma State University Institute of Technology
Okmulgee, Oklahoma

Freshman Application Contact Mary Graves, Director, Admissions, Oklahoma State University Institute of Technology, 1801 East Fourth Street, Okmulgee, OK 74447-3901. *Phone:* 918-293-5298. *Toll-free phone:* 800-722-4471. *Fax:* 918-293-4643. *E-mail:* mary.r.graves@okstate.edu. *Web site:* http://www.osuit.edu/.

Oklahoma State University, Oklahoma City
Oklahoma City, Oklahoma

- **State-supported** primarily 2-year, founded 1961, part of Oklahoma State University
- **Urban** 110-acre campus
- **Coed,** 7,647 undergraduate students

Undergraduates Students come from 9 states and territories; 8 other countries; 1% are from out of state. *Retention:* 36% of full-time freshmen returned.
Freshmen *Admission:* 1,082 applied, 1,082 admitted.
Faculty *Total:* 381, 22% full-time. *Student/faculty ratio:* 20:1.
Majors Accounting; American Sign Language (ASL); architectural engineering technology; art; building/home/construction inspection; business administration and management; civil engineering technology; construction

engineering technology; construction management; construction trades; criminal justice/police science; drafting and design technology; early childhood education; economics; electrical and power transmission installation; electrical, electronic and communications engineering technology; electrocardiograph technology; emergency medical technology (EMT paramedic); engineering technology; fire prevention and safety technology; fire science/firefighting; general studies; health/health-care administration; history; horticultural science; humanities; human services; illustration; information science/studies; information technology; language interpretation and translation; occupational safety and health technology; physics; pre-engineering; prenursing studies; professional, technical, business, and scientific writing; psychology; public administration and social service professions related; radiologic technology/science; registered nursing/registered nurse; sign language interpretation and translation; substance abuse/addiction counseling; surveying technology; turf and turfgrass management; veterinary/animal health technology; web page, digital/multimedia and information resources design.

Academics *Calendar:* semesters. *Degrees:* certificates, associate, and bachelor's. *Special study options:* academic remediation for entering students, advanced placement credit, cooperative education, distance learning, double majors, honors programs, independent study, part-time degree program, services for LD students, study abroad, summer session for credit.

Library Oklahoma State University-Oklahoma City Campus Library with 12,278 titles, 265 serial subscriptions, an OPAC, a Web page.

Student Life *Housing:* college housing not available. *Activities and Organizations:* Phi Theta Kappa, Deaf/Hearing Social Club, American Criminal Justice Association, Horticulture Club, Vet-Tech Club. *Campus security:* 24-hour patrols, late-night transport/escort service.

Costs (2010–11) *Tuition:* state resident $2889 full-time, $100 per credit hour part-time; nonresident $7749 full-time, $269 per credit hour part-time. Full-time tuition and fees vary according to course level, degree level, and program. Part-time tuition and fees vary according to course level, degree level, and program. No tuition increase for student's term of enrollment. *Required fees:* $30 full-time, $11 per credit hour part-time. *Payment plan:* installment. *Waivers:* senior citizens and employees or children of employees.

Applying *Options:* electronic application, early admission. *Required:* high school transcript. *Application deadlines:* rolling (freshmen), rolling (transfers). *Notification:* continuous (freshmen), continuous (transfers).

Freshman Application Contact Kyle Williams, Director, Enrollment Management, Oklahoma State University, Oklahoma City, 900 North Portland, AD202, Oklahoma City, OK 73107. *Phone:* 405-945-9152. *E-mail:* wilkylw@osuokc.edu. *Web site:* http://www.osuokc.edu/.

Oklahoma Technical College
Tulsa, Oklahoma

- **Proprietary** 2-year, part of Dental Directions, Inc.
- **Urban** 9-acre campus
- **Coed, primarily men,** 38 undergraduate students, 100% full-time, 3% women, 97% men

Undergraduates 38 full-time. Students come from 2 states and territories; 16% Black or African American, non-Hispanic/Latino; 5% Hispanic/Latino; 3% Asian, non-Hispanic/Latino; 5% American Indian or Alaska Native, non-Hispanic/Latino; 5% Two or more races, non-Hispanic/Latino; 8% Race/ethnicity unknown.

Faculty *Total:* 13, 100% full-time. *Student/faculty ratio:* 9:1.

Majors Automobile/automotive mechanics technology; barbering; diesel mechanics technology; welding technology.

Academics *Degree:* diplomas and associate. *Special study options:* adult/continuing education programs, distance learning, internships, services for LD students.

Student Life *Housing:* college housing not available. *Activities and Organizations:* Student Ambassadors. *Campus security:* campus security available during school hours. *Student services:* personal/psychological counseling.

Costs (2011–12) *Tuition:* $26,486 full-time. Full-time tuition and fees vary according to degree level, location, and program. Part-time tuition and fees vary according to degree level, location, and program. *Required fees:* $1027 full-time. *Payment plans:* tuition prepayment, installment. *Waivers:* employees or children of employees.

Applying *Options:* electronic application. *Application fee:* $100. *Required:* essay or personal statement, high school transcript, interview. *Required for some:* valid Oklahoma driver's license. *Application deadlines:* rolling (freshmen), rolling (out-of-state freshmen), rolling (transfers). *Notification:* continuous (freshmen), continuous (out-of-state freshmen), continuous (transfers).

Freshman Application Contact Ms. Teresa L. Knox, Chief Executive Officer, Oklahoma Technical College, 4242 South Sheridan, Tulsa, OK 74145. *Phone:* 918-610-0027 Ext. 2005. *Fax:* 918-610-0029. *E-mail:* tknox@communitycarecollege.edu. *Web site:* http://www.oklahomatechnicalcollege.com/.

Platt College
Moore, Oklahoma

Admissions Office Contact Platt College, 201 North Eastern Avenue, Moore, OK 73160. *Web site:* http://plattcollege.org/campuses/moore-campus/.

Platt College
Oklahoma City, Oklahoma

- **Proprietary** 2-year, founded 1979
- **Urban** campus with easy access to Oklahoma City
- **Coed,** 357 undergraduate students, 100% full-time, 90% women, 10% men

Undergraduates 357 full-time. 30% Black or African American, non-Hispanic/Latino; 13% Hispanic/Latino; 2% Asian, non-Hispanic/Latino; 5% American Indian or Alaska Native, non-Hispanic/Latino.

Freshmen *Admission:* 225 enrolled.

Faculty *Total:* 27, 59% full-time. *Student/faculty ratio:* 60:1.

Majors Licensed practical/vocational nurse training.

Academics *Calendar:* continuous. *Degree:* diplomas and associate. *Special study options:* academic remediation for entering students, internships, part-time degree program.

Library Platt College Learning Resource Center with an OPAC.

Student Life *Housing:* college housing not available. *Campus security:* 24-hour emergency response devices, security officer for evening and Saturday classes.

Applying *Application fee:* $100.

Freshman Application Contact Ms. Kim Lamb, Director of Admissions, Platt College, 309 South Ann Arbor, Oklahoma City, OK 73128. *Phone:* 405-946-7799. *Fax:* 405-943-2150. *E-mail:* klamb@plattcollege.org. *Web site:* http://www.plattcolleges.edu.

Platt College
Tulsa, Oklahoma

Director of Admissions Mrs. Susan Rone, Director, Platt College, 3801 South Sheridan Road, Tulsa, OK 74145-111. *Phone:* 918-663-9000. *Fax:* 918-622-1240. *E-mail:* susanr@plattcollege.org. *Web site:* http://www.plattcollege.org/

Redlands Community College
El Reno, Oklahoma

Director of Admissions Ms. Tricia Hobson, Director, Enrollment Management, Redlands Community College, 1300 South Country Club Road, El Reno, OK 73036-5304. *Phone:* 405-262-2552 Ext. 1263. *Toll-free phone:* 866-415-6367. *Fax:* 405-422-1239. *E-mail:* hobsont@redlandscc.edu. *Web site:* http://www.redlandscc.edu/.

Rose State College
Midwest City, Oklahoma

Freshman Application Contact Ms. Mechelle Aitson-Roessler, Registrar and Director of Admissions, Rose State College, 6420 Southeast 15th Street, Midwest City, OK 73110-2799. *Phone:* 405-733-7308. *Toll-free phone:* 866-621-0987. *Fax:* 405-736-0203. *E-mail:* maitson@ms.rose.cc.ok.us. *Web site:* http://www.rose.edu/.

Seminole State College
Seminole, Oklahoma

- **State-supported** 2-year, founded 1931, part of Oklahoma State Regents for Higher Education
- **Small-town** 40-acre campus with easy access to Oklahoma City
- **Coed**

Undergraduates Students come from 13 states and territories; 5 other countries; 2% are from out of state; 8% live on campus.

Faculty *Student/faculty ratio:* 25:1.

Academics *Calendar:* semesters. *Degree:* diplomas and associate. *Special study options:* academic remediation for entering students, accelerated degree program, adult/continuing education programs, advanced placement credit, cooperative education, distance learning, honors programs, independent study, off-campus study, part-time degree program, services for LD students, summer session for credit.

Student Life *Campus security:* 24-hour patrols, student patrols, late-night transport/escort service, controlled dormitory access.

Athletics Member NJCAA.

Standardized Tests *Recommended:* ACT (for admission).

Costs (2010–11) *Tuition:* state resident $1877 full-time, $63 per credit hour part-time; nonresident $5897 full-time, $197 per credit hour part-time. *Required fees:* $1124 full-time, $37 per credit hour part-time. *Room and board:* Room and board charges vary according to location. *Payment plans:* installment, deferred payment.
Applying *Options:* early admission, deferred entrance. *Application fee:* $15. *Required:* high school transcript.
Freshman Application Contact Mr. Chris Lindley, Director of Enrollment Management, Seminole State College, PO Box 351, 2701 Boren Boulevard, Seminole, OK 74818-0351. *Phone:* 405-382-9272. *Fax:* 405-382-9524. *E-mail:* lindley_c@ssc.cc.ok.us. *Web site:* http://www.ssc.cc.ok.us/.

Southwestern Oklahoma State University at Sayre
Sayre, Oklahoma

Freshman Application Contact Ms. Kim Seymour, Registrar, Southwestern Oklahoma State University at Sayre, 409 East Mississippi Avenue, Sayre, OK 73662. *Phone:* 580-928-5533 Ext. 101. *Fax:* 580-928-1140. *E-mail:* kim.seymour@swosu.edu. *Web site:* http://www.swosu.edu/sayre/.

Spartan College of Aeronautics and Technology
Tulsa, Oklahoma

- **Proprietary** primarily 2-year, founded 1928
- **Urban** 26-acre campus
- **Men only**

Undergraduates 1,438 full-time. 76% are from out of state; 0.2% transferred in. *Retention:* 66% of full-time freshmen returned.
Faculty *Student/faculty ratio:* 14:1.
Academics *Calendar:* calendar terms. *Degrees:* certificates, diplomas, associate, and bachelor's. *Special study options:* cooperative education, honors programs, independent study.
Financial Aid Of all full-time matriculated undergraduates who enrolled in 2009, 23 Federal Work-Study jobs (averaging $4341).
Applying *Application fee:* $100. *Required:* high school transcript. *Recommended:* interview.
Freshman Application Contact Mr. Mark Fowler, Vice President of Student Records and Finance, Spartan College of Aeronautics and Technology, 8820 East Pine Street, PO Box 582833, Tulsa, OK 74158-2833. *Phone:* 918-836-6886. *Toll-free phone:* 800-331-1204 (in-state); 800-331-124 (out-of-state). *Web site:* http://www.spartan.edu/.

Tulsa Community College
Tulsa, Oklahoma

Freshman Application Contact Ms. Leanne Brewer, Director of Admissions and Records, Tulsa Community College, 6111 East Skelly Drive, Tulsa, OK 74135. *Phone:* 918-595-7811. *Fax:* 918-595-7910. *E-mail:* lbrewer@tulsacc.edu. *Web site:* http://www.tulsacc.edu/.

Tulsa Welding School
Tulsa, Oklahoma

Freshman Application Contact Mrs. Debbie Renee Burke, Vice President/Executive Director, Tulsa Welding School, 2545 East 11th Street, Tulsa, OK 74104. *Phone:* 918-587-6789 Ext. 2258. *Toll-free phone:* 800-WELD-PRO. *Fax:* 918-295-6812. *E-mail:* dburke@twsweld.com. *Web site:* http://www.weldingschool.com/.

Vatterott College
Oklahoma City, Oklahoma

Freshman Application Contact Mr. Mark Hybers, Director of Admissions, Vatterott College, Oklahoma City, OK 73127. *Phone:* 405-945-0088 Ext. 4416. *Toll-free phone:* 888-948-0088. *Fax:* 405-945-0788. *E-mail:* mark.hybers@vatterott-college.edu. *Web site:* http://www.vatterott-college.edu/.

Vatterott College
Tulsa, Oklahoma

Freshman Application Contact Mr. Terry Queeno, Campus Director, Vatterott College, 4343 South 118th East Avenue, Suite A, Tulsa, OK 74146. *Phone:* 918-836-6656. *Toll-free phone:* 888-857-4016. *Fax:* 918-836-9698.

E-mail: tulsa@vatterott-college.edu. *Web site:* http://www.vatterott-college.edu/.

Western Oklahoma State College
Altus, Oklahoma

Freshman Application Contact Dr. Larry W. Paxton, Director of Academic Services, Western Oklahoma State College, 2801 North Main, Altus, OK 73521. *Phone:* 580-477-7720. *Fax:* 580-477-7723. *E-mail:* larry.paxton@wosc.edu. *Web site:* http://www.wosc.edu/.

OREGON

American College of Healthcare Sciences
Portland, Oregon

- **Urban** campus
- **Coed**

Undergraduates Students come from 50 states and territories; 63 other countries. *Retention:* 92% of full-time freshmen returned.
Majors Alternative and complementary medicine related.
Academics *Degrees:* certificates, diplomas, associate, master's, and postbachelor's certificates.
Costs (2010–11) *One-time required fee:* $200. *Tuition:* $255 per credit part-time.
Applying *Application fee:* $35. *Required:* essay or personal statement, high school transcript, standardized test scores, recommendation from Admissions Committee. *Required for some:* interview. *Application deadlines:* rolling (freshmen), rolling (transfers).
Freshman Application Contact ACHS Admissions, American College of Healthcare Sciences, 5940 SW Hood Avenue, Portland, OR 97239. *Phone:* 503-244-0726. *Toll-free phone:* 800-487-8839. *Fax:* 503-244-0727. *E-mail:* achs@achs.edu. *Web site:* http://www.achs.edu/.

Blue Mountain Community College
Pendleton, Oregon

Director of Admissions Ms. Theresa Bosworth, Director of Admissions, Blue Mountain Community College, 2411 Northwest Carden Avenue, PO Box 100, Pendleton, OR 97801-1000. *Phone:* 541-278-5774. *E-mail:* tbosworth@bluecc.edu. *Web site:* http://www.bluecc.edu/.

Carrington College - Portland
Portland, Oregon

Freshman Application Contact Admissions Office, Carrington College - Portland, 2004 Lloyd Center, 3rd Floor, Portland, OR 97232. *Phone:* 503-761-6100. *Web site:* http://carrington.edu/.

Central Oregon Community College
Bend, Oregon

- **District-supported** 2-year, founded 1949, part of Oregon Community College Association
- **Small-town** 193-acre campus
- **Endowment** $10.0 million
- **Coed,** 6,851 undergraduate students, 48% full-time, 54% women, 46% men

Undergraduates 3,289 full-time, 3,562 part-time. Students come from 10 states and territories; 6% are from out of state; 0.6% Black or African American, non-Hispanic/Latino; 6% Hispanic/Latino; 1% Asian, non-Hispanic/Latino; 0.3% Native Hawaiian or other Pacific Islander, non-Hispanic/Latino; 3% American Indian or Alaska Native, non-Hispanic/Latino; 0.2% Two or more races, non-Hispanic/Latino; 7% Race/ethnicity unknown; 7% transferred in; 2% live on campus. *Retention:* 57% of full-time freshmen returned.
Freshmen *Admission:* 1,625 applied, 1,625 admitted, 1,006 enrolled.
Faculty *Total:* 283, 39% full-time. *Student/faculty ratio:* 27:1.
Majors Accounting; administrative assistant and secretarial science; airline pilot and flight crew; art; automobile/automotive mechanics technology; biological and physical sciences; biology/biological sciences; business administration and management; CAD/CADD drafting/design technology; child-care and support services management; computer and information sciences related; computer science; computer systems networking and telecommunications; cooking and related culinary arts; customer service management; dental assist-

ing; dietetics; drafting and design technology; early childhood education; education; electrical, electronic and communications engineering technology; emergency medical technology (EMT paramedic); engineering; fire science/firefighting; fishing and fisheries sciences and management; foreign languages and literatures; forestry; forest technology; health and physical education/fitness; health information/medical records technology; hotel/motel administration; humanities; industrial technology; kinesiology and exercise science; liberal arts and sciences/liberal studies; licensed practical/vocational nurse training; management information systems; manufacturing engineering technology; marketing/marketing management; massage therapy; mathematics; medical/clinical assistant; natural resources/conservation; physical sciences; physical therapy; polymer/plastics engineering; pre-law studies; premedical studies; pre-pharmacy studies; radiologic technology/science; registered nursing/registered nurse; retailing; social sciences; speech communication and rhetoric; sport and fitness administration/management; substance abuse/addiction counseling.

Academics *Calendar:* quarters. *Degree:* certificates and associate. *Special study options:* academic remediation for entering students, cooperative education, distance learning, double majors, English as a second language, independent study, internships, part-time degree program, student-designed majors, study abroad, summer session for credit. *ROTC:* Army (c).

Library COCC Library plus 1 other with 76,421 titles, 329 serial subscriptions, 3,570 audiovisual materials, an OPAC, a Web page.

Student Life *Housing Options:* coed. Campus housing is university owned. *Activities and Organizations:* drama/theater group, student-run newspaper, choral group, club sports, student newspaper, Criminal Justice Club, Aviation Club. *Campus security:* 24-hour emergency response devices and patrols, late-night transport/escort service. *Student services:* personal/psychological counseling.

Athletics *Intercollegiate sports:* golf M/W. *Intramural sports:* baseball M, basketball M/W, cross-country running M/W, football M, skiing (cross-country) M/W, skiing (downhill) M/W, soccer M/W, track and field M/W, volleyball M/W, weight lifting M/W.

Costs (2010–11) *Tuition:* area resident $3150 full-time, $70 per credit part-time; state resident $4320 full-time, $96 per credit part-time; nonresident $8775 full-time, $195 per credit part-time. *Required fees:* $123 full-time. *Room and board:* $7920. *Payment plan:* installment. *Waivers:* employees or children of employees.

Financial Aid Of all full-time matriculated undergraduates who enrolled in 2009, 725 Federal Work-Study jobs (averaging $2130).

Applying *Options:* electronic application. *Application fee:* $25. *Application deadlines:* rolling (freshmen), rolling (transfers). *Notification:* continuous (freshmen), continuous (transfers).

Freshman Application Contact Central Oregon Community College, 2600 Northwest College Way, Bend, OR 97701-5998. *Phone:* 541-383-7500. *Web site:* http://www.cocc.edu/.

Chemeketa Community College

Salem, Oregon

Freshman Application Contact Chemeketa Community College, 4000 Lancaster Drive NE, P.O. Box 14007, Salem, OR 97309. *Phone:* 503-399-5001. *Web site:* http://www.chemeketa.edu/.

Clackamas Community College

Oregon City, Oregon

- **District-supported** 2-year, founded 1966
- **Suburban** 175-acre campus with easy access to Portland
- **Endowment** $9.7 million
- **Coed**

Undergraduates 3,205 full-time, 4,939 part-time. Students come from 21 states and territories; 16 other countries; 1% are from out of state; 41% transferred in. *Retention:* 91% of full-time freshmen returned.

Faculty *Student/faculty ratio:* 14:1.

Academics *Calendar:* quarters. *Degree:* certificates, diplomas, and associate. *Special study options:* academic remediation for entering students, accelerated degree program, adult/continuing education programs, advanced placement credit, cooperative education, distance learning, double majors, English as a second language, honors programs, independent study, internships, part-time degree program, services for LD students, study abroad, summer session for credit.

Student Life *Campus security:* 24-hour emergency response devices and patrols, student patrols, late-night transport/escort service.

Athletics Member NJCAA.

Costs (2010–11) *Tuition:* state resident $3552 full-time, $74 per credit hour part-time; nonresident $10,512 full-time, $219 per credit hour part-time. *Required fees:* $5 per credit hour part-time.

Financial Aid Of all full-time matriculated undergraduates who enrolled in 2009, 115 Federal Work-Study jobs (averaging $1330).

Applying *Options:* early admission.

Freshman Application Contact Ms. Tara Sprehe, Registrar, Clackamas Community College, 19600 South Molalla Avenue, Oregon City, OR 97045. *Phone:* 503-657-6958 Ext. 2742. *Fax:* 503-650-6654. *E-mail:* pattyw@clackamas.edu. *Web site:* http://www.clackamas.edu/.

Clatsop Community College

Astoria, Oregon

Freshman Application Contact Ms. Kristen Lee, Director, Enrollment Services, Clatsop Community College, 1653 Jerome Avenue, Astoria, OR 97103. *Phone:* 503-338-2326. *Toll-free phone:* 866-252-8767. *Fax:* 503-325-5738. *E-mail:* admissions@clatsopcc.edu. *Web site:* http://www.clatsopcc.edu/.

Columbia Gorge Community College

The Dalles, Oregon

Director of Admissions Ms. Karen Carter, Chief Student Services Officer, Columbia Gorge Community College, 400 East Scenic Drive, The Dalles, OR 97058. *Phone:* 541-506-6011. *E-mail:* kcarter@cgcc.cc.or.us. *Web site:* http://www.cgcc.cc.or.us/.

Everest College

Portland, Oregon

Freshman Application Contact Admissions Office, Everest College, 425 Southwest Washington Street, Portland, OR 97204. *Phone:* 503-222-3225. *Fax:* 503-228-6926. *Web site:* http://www.everest.edu/.

Heald College–Portland

Portland, Oregon

Freshman Application Contact Director of Admissions, Heald College–Portland, 625 SW Broadway, 4th Floor, Portland, OR 97205. *Phone:* 503-229-0492. *Toll-free phone:* 800-755-3550. *Fax:* 503-229-0498. *E-mail:* portlandinfo@heald.edu. *Web site:* http://www.heald.edu/.

ITT Technical Institute

Portland, Oregon

- **Proprietary** primarily 2-year, founded 1971, part of ITT Educational Services, Inc.
- **Urban** campus
- **Coed**

Majors CAD/CADD drafting/design technology; computer and information systems security; computer engineering technology; computer software and media applications related; computer software engineering; computer software technology; computer systems networking and telecommunications; construction management; criminal justice/law enforcement administration; design and visual communications; electrical, electronic and communications engineering technology; game and interactive media design; industrial technology; legal assistant/paralegal; project management; registered nursing/registered nurse; system, networking, and LAN/WAN management; web/multimedia management and webmaster; web page, digital/multimedia and information resources design.

Academics *Calendar:* quarters. *Degrees:* associate and bachelor's.

Student Life *Housing:* college housing not available.

Financial Aid Of all full-time matriculated undergraduates who enrolled in 2009, 15 Federal Work-Study jobs (averaging $5000).

Freshman Application Contact Director of Recruitment, ITT Technical Institute, 9500 Northeast Cascades Parkway, Portland, OR 97220. *Phone:* 503-255-6500. *Toll-free phone:* 800-234-5488. *Web site:* http://www.itt-tech.edu/.

Klamath Community College

Klamath Falls, Oregon

Freshman Application Contact Admissions Office, Klamath Community College, 7390 South 6th Street, Klamath Falls, OR 97603. *Phone:* 541-882-3521. *Web site:* http://www.klamathcc.edu/.

Lane Community College

Eugene, Oregon

Director of Admissions Ms. Helen Garrett, Director of Admissions/Registrar, Lane Community College, 4000 East 30th Avenue, Eugene, OR 97405-0640. *Phone:* 541-747-4501 Ext. 2686. *Web site:* http://www.lanecc.edu/.

Le Cordon Bleu College of Culinary Arts in Portland

Portland, Oregon

Admissions Office Contact Le Cordon Bleu College of Culinary Arts in Portland, 921 Southwest Morrison Street, Suite 400, Portland, OR 97205. *Toll-free phone:* 888-891-6222. *Web site:* http://www.wci.edu/.

Linn-Benton Community College

Albany, Oregon

- **State and locally supported** 2-year, founded 1966
- **Small-town** 104-acre campus
- **Coed,** 6,922 undergraduate students, 51% full-time, 50% women, 50% men

Undergraduates 3,556 full-time, 3,366 part-time. 2% Black or African American, non-Hispanic/Latino; 6% Hispanic/Latino; 1% Asian, non-Hispanic/Latino; 1% American Indian or Alaska Native, non-Hispanic/Latino; 6% Two or more races, non-Hispanic/Latino; 0.1% Race/ethnicity unknown; 0.3% international.
Freshmen *Admission:* 2,772 applied, 2,523 enrolled.
Faculty *Total:* 510, 31% full-time. *Student/faculty ratio:* 20:1.
Majors Accounting; administrative assistant and secretarial science; agricultural business and management; agricultural teacher education; agriculture; animal sciences; art; automobile/automotive mechanics technology; biological and physical sciences; biology/biological sciences; business administration and management; chemistry; child-care and support services management; civil engineering technology; commercial and advertising art; computer and information sciences; computer and information sciences and support services related; computer programming (specific applications); criminal justice/police science; criminal justice/safety; culinary arts; culinary arts related; dairy husbandry and production; desktop publishing and digital imaging design; diesel mechanics technology; drafting and design technology; dramatic/theater arts; economics; education; elementary education; engineering; English; family and consumer sciences/human sciences; foreign languages and literatures; graphic communications related; horse husbandry/equine science and management; horticultural science; industrial technology; juvenile corrections; legal administrative assistant/secretary; liberal arts and sciences/liberal studies; machine tool technology; mathematics; medical administrative assistant and medical secretary; medical/clinical assistant; metallurgical technology; multi/interdisciplinary studies related; network and system administration; physical education teaching and coaching; physical sciences; physics; pre-engineering; professional, technical, business, and scientific writing; registered nursing/registered nurse; restaurant, culinary, and catering management; rhetoric and composition; teacher assistant/aide; water quality and wastewater treatment management and recycling technology; welding technology.
Academics *Calendar:* quarters. *Degree:* certificates and associate. *Special study options:* academic remediation for entering students, adult/continuing education programs, advanced placement credit, cooperative education, distance learning, English as a second language, independent study, internships, part-time degree program, services for LD students, student-designed majors, study abroad, summer session for credit. *ROTC:* Army (c), Air Force (c).
Library Linn-Benton Community College Library with 42,561 titles, 91 serial subscriptions, 8,758 audiovisual materials, an OPAC, a Web page.
Student Life *Housing:* college housing not available. *Activities and Organizations:* drama/theater group, student-run newspaper, choral group, EBOP Club, Multicultural Club, Campus Family Co-op, Horticulture Club, Collegiate Secretary Club. *Campus security:* 24-hour emergency response devices and patrols, student patrols, late-night transport/escort service. *Student services:* personal/psychological counseling.
Athletics *Intercollegiate sports:* baseball M(s), basketball M(s)/W(s), volleyball W(s). *Intramural sports:* basketball M/W, tennis M/W, ultimate Frisbee M/W, volleyball M/W.
Costs (2011–12) *Tuition:* state resident $3360 full-time, $84 per credit part-time; nonresident $7120 full-time, $178 per credit part-time.
Financial Aid Of all full-time matriculated undergraduates who enrolled in 2009, 290 Federal Work-Study jobs (averaging $1800).
Applying *Options:* electronic application, deferred entrance. *Application fee:* $30. *Required for some:* high school transcript. *Application deadlines:* rolling (freshmen), rolling (transfers).
Freshman Application Contact Ms. Christine Baker, Outreach Coordinator, Linn-Benton Community College, 6500 Pacific Boulevard, SW, Albany, OR

97321. *Phone:* 541-917-4813. *Fax:* 541-917-4838. *E-mail:* admissions@linnbenton.edu. *Web site:* http://www.linnbenton.edu/.

Mt. Hood Community College

Gresham, Oregon

Director of Admissions Dr. Craig Kolins, Associate Vice President of Enrollment Services, Mt. Hood Community College, 26000 Southeast Stark Street, Gresham, OR 97030-3300. *Phone:* 503-491-7265. *Web site:* http://www.mhcc.cc.or.us/.

Oregon Coast Community College

Newport, Oregon

- **Public** 2-year, founded 1987, administratively affiliated with Clatsop Community College
- **Small-town** 24-acre campus
- **Coed,** 535 undergraduate students, 38% full-time, 63% women, 37% men

Undergraduates 204 full-time, 331 part-time. Students come from 4 states and territories; 1% are from out of state; 0.9% Black or African American, non-Hispanic/Latino; 7% Hispanic/Latino; 2% Asian, non-Hispanic/Latino; 0.9% Native Hawaiian or other Pacific Islander, non-Hispanic/Latino; 2% American Indian or Alaska Native, non-Hispanic/Latino; 4% Two or more races, non-Hispanic/Latino; 2% Race/ethnicity unknown. *Retention:* 29% of full-time freshmen returned.
Freshmen *Admission:* 151 enrolled.
Faculty *Total:* 49, 20% full-time, 29% with terminal degrees. *Student/faculty ratio:* 14:1.
Majors General studies; liberal arts and sciences/liberal studies; marine biology and biological oceanography; registered nursing/registered nurse.
Academics *Calendar:* quarters. *Degree:* certificates and associate. *Special study options:* academic remediation for entering students, cooperative education, distance learning, English as a second language, honors programs, internships, part-time degree program, services for LD students, summer session for credit.
Library Oregon Coast Community College Library with 10,455 titles, 50 serial subscriptions, 1,537 audiovisual materials, an OPAC, a Web page.
Student Life *Housing:* college housing not available.
Standardized Tests *Required for some:* Nursing Entrance Exam.
Costs (2010–11) *Tuition:* state resident $2844 full-time, $79 per credit part-time; nonresident $6192 full-time, $172 per credit part-time. Full-time tuition and fees vary according to program. Part-time tuition and fees vary according to program. *Required fees:* $252 full-time, $7 per credit part-time. *Payment plan:* deferred payment. *Waivers:* employees or children of employees.
Freshman Application Contact Student Services, Oregon Coast Community College, 400 SE College Way, Newport, OR 97366. *Phone:* 541-265-2283. *Fax:* 541-265-3820. *E-mail:* webinfo@occc.cc.or.us. *Web site:* http://www.oregoncoastcc.org.

Portland Community College

Portland, Oregon

Freshman Application Contact PCC Admissions and Registration Office, Portland Community College, PO Box 19000, Portland, OR 97280. *Phone:* 503-977-8888. *Web site:* http://www.pcc.edu/.

Rogue Community College

Grants Pass, Oregon

- **State and locally supported** 2-year, founded 1970
- **Rural** 84-acre campus
- **Endowment** $5.4 million
- **Coed,** 5,846 undergraduate students, 46% full-time, 56% women, 44% men

Undergraduates 2,702 full-time, 3,144 part-time. Students come from 29 states and territories; 1 other country; 2% are from out of state; 65% transferred in.
Freshmen *Admission:* 935 enrolled.
Faculty *Total:* 386, 21% full-time. *Student/faculty ratio:* 21:1.
Majors Accounting technology and bookkeeping; automobile/automotive mechanics technology; business administration and management; business/commerce; child-care and support services management; computer software technology; construction engineering technology; construction trades; criminal justice/police science; diesel mechanics technology; electrical and power transmission installation; electrical, electronic and communications engineering technology; emergency medical technology (EMT paramedic); fire prevention and safety technology; general studies; liberal arts and sciences/liberal

studies; manufacturing engineering technology; marketing/marketing management; mechanics and repair; medical office computer specialist; registered nursing/registered nurse; social work; welding technology.

Academics *Calendar:* quarters. *Degree:* certificates, diplomas, and associate. *Special study options:* academic remediation for entering students, adult/continuing education programs, advanced placement credit, cooperative education, distance learning, double majors, English as a second language, independent study, internships, part-time degree program, services for LD students, study abroad, summer session for credit.

Library Rogue Community College Library with 33,000 titles, 275 serial subscriptions, an OPAC.

Student Life *Housing:* college housing not available. *Activities and Organizations:* drama/theater group, student-run newspaper, choral group. *Campus security:* 24-hour emergency response devices and patrols, late-night transport/escort service. *Student services:* personal/psychological counseling, women's center.

Athletics *Intramural sports:* basketball M/W, soccer M/W, tennis M/W, volleyball M/W.

Costs (2010–11) *Tuition:* state resident $2700 full-time, $75 per credit hour part-time; nonresident $3276 full-time, $91 per credit hour part-time. *Required fees:* $294 full-time, $98 per term part-time. *Payment plan:* installment. *Waivers:* employees or children of employees.

Financial Aid Of all full-time matriculated undergraduates who enrolled in 2009, 2,044 applied for aid, 1,812 were judged to have need, 83 had their need fully met. 80 Federal Work-Study jobs (averaging $2419). In 2009, 47 non-need-based awards were made. *Average percent of need met:* 75%. *Average financial aid package:* $8988. *Average need-based loan:* $3526. *Average need-based gift aid:* $5420. *Average non-need-based aid:* $1233.

Applying *Options:* electronic application, early admission. *Application deadlines:* rolling (freshmen), rolling (out-of-state freshmen), rolling (transfers).

Freshman Application Contact Ms. Claudia Sullivan, Director of Enrollment Services, Rogue Community College, 3345 Redwood Highway, Grants Pass, OR 97527-9298. *Phone:* 541-956-7176. *Fax:* 541-471-3585. *E-mail:* csullivan@roguecc.edu. *Web site:* http://www.roguecc.edu/.

Southwestern Oregon Community College

Coos Bay, Oregon

Freshman Application Contact Miss Lela Wells, Southwestern Oregon Community College, Student First Stop, 1988 Newmark Avenue, Coos Bay, OR 97420. *Phone:* 541-888-7611. *Toll-free phone:* 800-962-2838. *E-mail:* lwells@socc.edu. *Web site:* http://www.socc.edu/.

Tillamook Bay Community College

Tillamook, Oregon

Freshman Application Contact Lori Gates, Tillamook Bay Community College, 4301 Third Street, Tillamook, OR 97141. *Phone:* 503-842-8222. *Fax:* 503-842-2214. *E-mail:* gates@tillamookbay.cc. *Web site:* http://www.tbcc.cc.or.us/.

Treasure Valley Community College

Ontario, Oregon

Freshman Application Contact Ms. Candace Bell, Office of Admissions and Student Services, Treasure Valley Community College, 650 College Boulevard, Ontario, OR 97914. *Phone:* 541-881-8822 Ext. 239. *Fax:* 541-881-2721. *E-mail:* clbell@tvcc.cc. *Web site:* http://www.tvcc.cc.or.us/.

Umpqua Community College

Roseburg, Oregon

- **State and locally supported** 2-year, founded 1964
- **Rural** 100-acre campus
- **Endowment** $6.1 million
- **Coed**

Undergraduates 1,376 full-time, 1,210 part-time. Students come from 4 states and territories; 4 other countries; 60% transferred in.

Faculty *Student/faculty ratio:* 23:1.

Academics *Calendar:* quarters. *Degree:* certificates and associate. *Special study options:* academic remediation for entering students, accelerated degree program, adult/continuing education programs, advanced placement credit, cooperative education, distance learning, English as a second language, honors programs, independent study, internships, part-time degree program, services for LD students, study abroad, summer session for credit.

Student Life *Campus security:* 24-hour emergency response devices and patrols.

Costs (2010–11) *Tuition:* state resident $3630 full-time, $69 per credit hour part-time; nonresident $8910 full-time, $193 per credit hour part-time. *Required fees:* $300 full-time, $7 per credit hour part-time, $15 per term part-time.

Financial Aid Of all full-time matriculated undergraduates who enrolled in 2009, 120 Federal Work-Study jobs (averaging $3000).

Applying *Options:* early admission, deferred entrance. *Application fee:* $25. *Recommended:* high school transcript.

Freshman Application Contact Mr. Ted Swagerty, Recruiter, Umpqua Community College, PO Box 967, Roseburg, OR 97470-0226. *Phone:* 541-440-4600 Ext. 7661. *Fax:* 541-440-4612. *E-mail:* Ted.Swagerty@umpqua.edu. *Web site:* http://www.umpqua.edu/.

PENNSYLVANIA

Antonelli Institute

Erdenheim, Pennsylvania

- **Proprietary** 2-year, founded 1938
- **Suburban** 15-acre campus with easy access to Philadelphia
- **Coed,** 228 undergraduate students

Undergraduates 29% are from out of state. *Retention:* 78% of full-time freshmen returned.

Majors Commercial and advertising art; photography.

Academics *Calendar:* semesters. *Degree:* associate. *Special study options:* adult/continuing education programs.

Financial Aid Of all full-time matriculated undergraduates who enrolled in 2009, 5 Federal Work-Study jobs (averaging $2000).

Freshman Application Contact Admissions Office, Antonelli Institute, 300 Montgomery Avenue, Erdenheim, PA 19038. *Phone:* 800-722-7871. *Toll-free phone:* 800-722-7871. *Web site:* http://www.antonelli.edu/.

The Art Institute of York–Pennsylvania

York, Pennsylvania

- **Proprietary** primarily 2-year, founded 1952, part of Education Management Corporation
- **Suburban** campus
- **Coed**

Majors Animation, interactive technology, video graphics and special effects; consumer merchandising/retailing management; graphic design; interior design; web page, digital/multimedia and information resources design.

Academics *Calendar:* quarters. *Degrees:* associate and bachelor's.

Costs (2010–11) *Tuition:* Tuition cost varies by program. Prospective students should contact the school for current tuition costs. Other charges include a starting kit for all first-quarter students. Kits vary in price, depending on the program of study.

Freshman Application Contact The Art Institute of York–Pennsylvania, 1409 Williams Road, York, PA 17402-9012. *Phone:* 717-755-2300. *Toll-free phone:* 800-864-7725. *Web site:* http://www.artinstitutes.edu/york/.

Berks Technical Institute

Wyomissing, Pennsylvania

Freshman Application Contact Mr. Allan Brussolo, Academic Dean, Berks Technical Institute, 2205 Ridgewood Road, Wyomissing, PA 19610-1168. *Phone:* 610-372-1722. *Toll-free phone:* 800-284-4672 (in-state); 800-821-4662 (out-of-state). *Fax:* 610-376-4684. *E-mail:* abrussolo@berks.edu. *Web site:* http://www.berkstech.com/.

Bidwell Training Center

Pittsburgh, Pennsylvania

Freshman Application Contact Admissions Office, Bidwell Training Center, 1815 Metropolitan Street, Pittsburgh, PA 15233. *Phone:* 412-322-1773. *Toll-free phone:* 800-516-1800. *E-mail:* admissions@mcg-btc.org. *Web site:* http://www.bidwell-training.org/.

Bradford School
Pittsburgh, Pennsylvania

- **Private** 2-year, founded 1968
- **Urban** campus
- **Coed,** 601 undergraduate students
- 89% of applicants were admitted

Freshmen *Admission:* 1,016 applied, 908 admitted.

Majors Accounting and business/management; business administration and management; computer programming; dental assisting; graphic design; legal administrative assistant/secretary; legal assistant/paralegal; medical/clinical assistant; merchandising; system, networking, and LAN/WAN management; tourism and travel services management.

Academics *Degree:* diplomas and associate. *Special study options:* accelerated degree program.

Freshman Application Contact Admissions Office, Bradford School, 125 West Station Square Drive, Pittsburgh, PA 15219. *Phone:* 412-391-6710. *Toll-free phone:* 800-391-6810. *Web site:* http://www.bradfordpittsburgh.edu/.

Bucks County Community College
Newtown, Pennsylvania

- **County-supported** 2-year, founded 1964
- **Suburban** 200-acre campus with easy access to Philadelphia
- **Endowment** $3.8 million
- **Coed,** 10,800 undergraduate students, 38% full-time, 56% women, 44% men

Undergraduates 4,124 full-time, 6,676 part-time. Students come from 16 states and territories; 33 other countries; 0.7% are from out of state; 4% Black or African American, non-Hispanic/Latino; 4% Hispanic/Latino; 2% Asian, non-Hispanic/Latino; 0.1% Native Hawaiian or other Pacific Islander, non-Hispanic/Latino; 0.6% American Indian or Alaska Native, non-Hispanic/Latino; 0.7% Two or more races, non-Hispanic/Latino; 16% Race/ethnicity unknown; 0.6% international; 75% transferred in. *Retention:* 61% of full-time freshmen returned.

Freshmen *Admission:* 5,363 applied, 5,247 admitted, 2,579 enrolled.

Faculty *Total:* 632, 28% full-time. *Student/faculty ratio:* 25:1.

Majors Accounting; American studies; art; biology/biological sciences; business administration and management; chemistry; child-care provision; cinematography and film/video production; commercial and advertising art; computer and information sciences; computer and information sciences related; computer engineering technology; computer/information technology services administration related; computer programming; computer programming related; computer programming (specific applications); computer science; consumer merchandising/retailing management; corrections; criminal justice/law enforcement administration; criminal justice/police science; culinary arts; dramatic/theater arts; education; engineering; environmental studies; food service systems administration; health professions related; health teacher education; historic preservation and conservation; hospitality administration; hotel/motel administration; humanities; information science/studies; information technology; journalism; kindergarten/preschool education; legal assistant/paralegal; liberal arts and sciences/liberal studies; marketing/marketing management; mass communication/media; mathematics; medical/clinical assistant; music; physical education teaching and coaching; psychology; radio and television; registered nursing/registered nurse; social sciences; social work; sport and fitness administration/management; visual and performing arts; woodworking.

Academics *Calendar:* semesters. *Degree:* certificates and associate. *Special study options:* academic remediation for entering students, adult/continuing education programs, advanced placement credit, cooperative education, distance learning, English as a second language, external degree program, independent study, internships, part-time degree program, services for LD students, student-designed majors, summer session for credit.

Library Bucks County Community College Library with 146,215 titles, 290 serial subscriptions, 2,738 audiovisual materials, an OPAC, a Web page.

Student Life *Housing:* college housing not available. *Activities and Organizations:* drama/theater group, student-run newspaper, television station, choral group, Phi Theta Kappa, Inter-Varsity Christian Fellowship, Drama Club, Habitat for Humanity, Future Teachers Organization. *Campus security:* 24-hour emergency response devices and patrols, late-night transport/escort service. *Student services:* personal/psychological counseling, women's center.

Athletics Member NJCAA. *Intercollegiate sports:* baseball M, basketball M, equestrian sports M/W, golf M/W, soccer M/W, tennis M/W, volleyball W. *Intramural sports:* basketball M/W, soccer M/W, softball M/W, tennis M/W, volleyball W.

Costs (2010–11) *Tuition:* area resident $3150 full-time, $105 per credit hour part-time; state resident $6300 full-time, $210 per credit hour part-time; nonresident $9450 full-time, $315 per credit hour part-time. Full-time tuition and fees vary according to course load and reciprocity agreements. Part-time tuition and fees vary according to course load and reciprocity agreements. *Required fees:* $854 full-time, $26 per credit hour part-time, $28 per term part-time. *Payment plans:* installment, deferred payment. *Waivers:* senior citizens and employees or children of employees.

Financial Aid Of all full-time matriculated undergraduates who enrolled in 2008, 175 Federal Work-Study jobs (averaging $2023).

Applying *Options:* electronic application, early admission. *Required:* high school transcript. *Required for some:* essay or personal statement, interview.

Freshman Application Contact Ms. Marlene Barlow, Director of Admissions, Bucks County Community College, Newtown, PA 18940. *Phone:* 215-968-8137. *Fax:* 215-968-8110. *E-mail:* barlowm@bucks.edu. *Web site:* http://www.bucks.edu/.

Butler County Community College
Butler, Pennsylvania

Freshman Application Contact Ms. Patricia Bajuszik, Director of Admissions, Butler County Community College, College Drive, PO Box 1205, Butler, PA 16003-1203. *Phone:* 724-287-8711 Ext. 344. *Toll-free phone:* 888-826-2829. *Fax:* 724-287-4961. *E-mail:* pattie.bajoszik@bc3.edu. *Web site:* http://www.bc3.edu/.

Cambria-Rowe Business College
Indiana, Pennsylvania

Freshman Application Contact Mrs. Stacey Bell-Leger, Representative at Indiana Campus, Cambria-Rowe Business College, 422 South 13th Street, Indiana, PA 15701. *Phone:* 724-483-0222. *Fax:* 724-463-7246. *E-mail:* sbell-leger@crbc.net. *Web site:* http://www.crbc.net/.

Cambria-Rowe Business College
Johnstown, Pennsylvania

Freshman Application Contact Mrs. Amanda Artim, Director of Admissions, Cambria-Rowe Business College, 221 Central Avenue, Johnstown, PA 15902-2494. *Phone:* 814-536-5168. *Toll-free phone:* 800-NEWCAREER. *Fax:* 814-536-5160. *E-mail:* admissions@crbc.net. *Web site:* http://www.crbc.net/.

Career Training Academy
Monroeville, Pennsylvania

Freshman Application Contact Career Training Academy, 4314 Old William Penn Highway, Suite 103, Monroeville, PA 15146. *Phone:* 412-372-3900. *Web site:* http://www.careerta.edu/.

Career Training Academy
New Kensington, Pennsylvania

Freshman Application Contact Career Training Academy, 950 Fifth Avenue, New Kensington, PA 15068-6301. *Phone:* 724-337-1000. *Web site:* http://www.careerta.com/.

Career Training Academy
Pittsburgh, Pennsylvania

- **Proprietary** 2-year
- **Suburban** campus with easy access to Pittsburgh
- **Coed,** 84 undergraduate students, 100% full-time, 92% women, 8% men

Undergraduates 84 full-time. Students come from 1 other state; 10% Black or African American, non-Hispanic/Latino.

Freshmen *Admission:* 10 enrolled.

Faculty *Total:* 10, 70% full-time, 10% with terminal degrees. *Student/faculty ratio:* 9:1.

Majors Massage therapy; medical/clinical assistant; medical insurance coding.

Academics *Calendar:* continuous. *Degree:* diplomas and associate. *Special study options:* academic remediation for entering students, advanced placement credit, cooperative education, internships.

Costs (2011–12) *Tuition:* $11,280 full-time.

Applying *Application fee:* $30. *Required:* essay or personal statement, high school transcript, interview. *Application deadlines:* rolling (freshmen), rolling (out-of-state freshmen).

Freshman Application Contact Jamie Vignone, Career Training Academy, 1500 Northway Mall, Suite 200, Pittsburgh, PA 15237. *Phone:* 412-367-4000. *Fax:* 412-369-7223. *E-mail:* admission3@careerta.edu. *Web site:* http://www.careerta.edu/.

CHI Institute, Broomall Campus
Broomall, Pennsylvania

- **Proprietary** 2-year, founded 1958
- **Small-town** campus
- **Coed**

Academics *Calendar:* quarters. *Degree:* diplomas and associate.
Freshman Application Contact CHI Institute, Broomall Campus, 1991 Sproul Road, Suite 42, Broomall, PA 19008. *Phone:* 610-353-3300. *Web site:* http://www.chitraining.com/.

CHI Institute, Franklin Mills Campus
Philadelphia, Pennsylvania

- **Proprietary** 2-year, founded 1981
- **Suburban** campus
- **Coed**

Academics *Calendar:* quarters. *Degree:* certificates, diplomas, and associate.
Financial Aid Of all full-time matriculated undergraduates who enrolled in 2009, 30 Federal Work-Study jobs (averaging $2050).
Freshman Application Contact CHI Institute, Franklin Mills Campus, 177 Franklin Mills Boulevard, Philadelphia, PA 19154. *Phone:* 215-612-6600. *Toll-free phone:* 800-336-7696. *Web site:* http://www.chitraining.com/.

Commonwealth Technical Institute
Johnstown, Pennsylvania

Freshman Application Contact Ms. Rebecca Halza, Admissions Supervisor, Commonwealth Technical Institute, Hiram G. Andrews Center, 727 Goucher Street, Johnstown, PA 15905. *Phone:* 814-255-8200. *Toll-free phone:* 800-762-4211 Ext. 8237. *Fax:* 814-255-8283. *E-mail:* rhalza@state.pa.us. *Web site:* http://www.hgac.org/.

Community College of Allegheny County
Pittsburgh, Pennsylvania

- **County-supported** 2-year, founded 1966
- **Urban** 242-acre campus
- **Coed**

Undergraduates 8,525 full-time, 11,995 part-time. 1% are from out of state.
Faculty *Student/faculty ratio:* 17:1.
Academics *Calendar:* semesters. *Degree:* certificates, diplomas, and associate. *Special study options:* academic remediation for entering students, advanced placement credit, cooperative education, distance learning, English as a second language, independent study, internships, off-campus study, part-time degree program, services for LD students, summer session for credit.
Student Life *Campus security:* 24-hour emergency response devices and patrols, late-night transport/escort service.
Athletics Member NJCAA.
Costs (2010–11) *Tuition:* $85 per credit hour part-time; state resident $171 per credit hour part-time; nonresident $256 per credit hour part-time. Full-time tuition and fees vary according to program. Part-time tuition and fees vary according to program.
Applying *Recommended:* high school transcript.
Freshman Application Contact Admissions, Community College of Allegheny County, 800 Allegheny Avenue, Pittsburgh, PA 15233. *Phone:* 412-237-2511. *Web site:* http://www.ccac.edu/.

Community College of Beaver County
Monaca, Pennsylvania

Freshman Application Contact Enrollment Management, Community College of Beaver County, One Campus Drive, Monaca, PA 15061-2588. *Phone:* 724-480-3500. *Toll-free phone:* 800-335-0222. *E-mail:* admissions@ccbc.edu. *Web site:* http://www.ccbc.edu/.

Community College of Philadelphia
Philadelphia, Pennsylvania

- **State and locally supported** 2-year, founded 1964
- **Urban** 14-acre campus
- **Coed,** 39,270 undergraduate students

Undergraduates Students come from 50 other countries.
Faculty *Total:* 1,132, 35% full-time.
Majors Accounting; architectural engineering technology; art; automobile/automotive mechanics technology; business administration and management; chemical technology; clinical/medical laboratory technology; computer science; construction engineering technology; criminal justice/law enforcement administration; culinary arts; dental hygiene; drafting and design technology; education; engineering; engineering technology; facilities planning and management; finance; fire science/firefighting; forensic science and technology; health information/medical records administration; health professions related; hotel/motel administration; human services; industrial radiologic technology; international business/trade/commerce; kindergarten/preschool education; legal assistant/paralegal; liberal arts and sciences/liberal studies; marketing/marketing management; medical administrative assistant and medical secretary; medical/clinical assistant; mental health counseling; music; photography; pre-engineering; recording arts technology; registered nursing/registered nurse; respiratory care therapy; sign language interpretation and translation.
Academics *Calendar:* semesters. *Degree:* certificates, diplomas, and associate. *Special study options:* academic remediation for entering students, accelerated degree program, adult/continuing education programs, advanced placement credit, cooperative education, distance learning, English as a second language, external degree program, honors programs, independent study, internships, off-campus study, part-time degree program, services for LD students, student-designed majors, study abroad, summer session for credit. *ROTC:* Army (c).
Library Main Campus Library plus 2 others with 110,000 titles, 420 serial subscriptions, an OPAC, a Web page.
Student Life *Housing:* college housing not available. *Activities and Organizations:* drama/theater group, student-run newspaper, choral group, Philadelphia L.E.A.D.S, Phi Theta Kappa, Student Government Association, Vanguard Student Newspaper, Fundraising Club. *Campus security:* 24-hour emergency response devices and patrols, phone/alert systems in classrooms/buildings. *Student services:* personal/psychological counseling, women's center.
Athletics *Intercollegiate sports:* baseball M, basketball M/W, cross-country running M/W, soccer M, softball W, tennis M/W, track and field M/W, volleyball M/W. *Intramural sports:* basketball M/W, soccer M/W, tennis M/W, track and field M/W, volleyball M/W.
Costs (2010–11) *Tuition:* area resident $4410 full-time, $128 per credit hour part-time; state resident $6144 full-time, $256 per credit hour part-time; nonresident $11,910 full-time, $384 per credit hour part-time. Full-time tuition and fees vary according to program. Part-time tuition and fees vary according to program. *Payment plan:* installment. *Waivers:* senior citizens and employees or children of employees.
Applying *Options:* electronic application, early admission, deferred entrance. *Application fee:* $20. *Required for some:* high school transcript, allied health and nursing programs have specific entry requirements. *Application deadlines:* rolling (freshmen), rolling (transfers). *Notification:* continuous (freshmen), continuous (transfers).
Freshman Application Contact Community College of Philadelphia, 1700 Spring Garden Street, Philadelphia, PA 19130-3991. *Phone:* 215-751-8010. *Web site:* http://www.ccp.edu/.

Consolidated School of Business
Lancaster, Pennsylvania

- **Proprietary** 2-year, founded 1986
- **Suburban** 4-acre campus with easy access to Philadelphia
- **Coed**

Undergraduates 179 full-time, 3 part-time. Students come from 2 states and territories; 1% are from out of state.
Faculty *Student/faculty ratio:* 15:1.
Academics *Calendar:* continuous. *Degree:* diplomas and associate. *Special study options:* accelerated degree program, honors programs, independent study, internships, part-time degree program, services for LD students, student-designed majors.
Costs (2010–11) *Tuition:* $26,500 full-time, $350 per credit hour part-time. Full-time tuition and fees vary according to course load and program. Part-time tuition and fees vary according to course load and program. No tuition increase for student's term of enrollment. *Required fees:* $3750 full-time. *Payment plans:* installment, deferred payment.
Applying *Options:* electronic application. *Required:* high school transcript, interview.
Freshman Application Contact Ms. Libby Paul, Admissions Representative, Consolidated School of Business, 2124 Ambassador Circle, Lancaster, PA 17603. *Phone:* 717-394-6211. *Toll-free phone:* 800-541-8298. *Fax:* 717-394-6213. *E-mail:* lpaul@csb.edu. *Web site:* http://www.csb.edu/.

Consolidated School of Business
York, Pennsylvania

Freshman Application Contact Ms. Sandra Swanger, Admissions Representative, Consolidated School of Business, 1605 Clugston Road, York, PA 17404. *Phone:* 717-764-9550. *Toll-free phone:* 800-520-0691. *Fax:* 717-764-9469. *E-mail:* sswanger@csb.edu. *Web site:* http://www.csb.edu/.

Dean Institute of Technology
Pittsburgh, Pennsylvania

Director of Admissions Mr. Richard D. Ali, Admissions Director, Dean Institute of Technology, 1501 West Liberty Avenue, Pittsburgh, PA 15226-1103. *Phone:* 412-531-4433. *Web site:* http://www.deantech.edu/.

Delaware County Community College
Media, Pennsylvania

- **State and locally supported** 2-year, founded 1967
- **Suburban** 123-acre campus with easy access to Philadelphia
- **Endowment** $3.8 million
- **Coed**

Undergraduates 5,557 full-time, 6,680 part-time. Students come from 9 states and territories; 53 other countries; 1% are from out of state; 9% transferred in. *Retention:* 61% of full-time freshmen returned.
Faculty *Student/faculty ratio:* 24:1.
Academics *Calendar:* semesters. *Degree:* certificates and associate. *Special study options:* academic remediation for entering students, adult/continuing education programs, advanced placement credit, cooperative education, distance learning, double majors, English as a second language, independent study, internships, part-time degree program, services for LD students, student-designed majors, summer session for credit.
Student Life *Campus security:* 24-hour emergency response devices and patrols, late-night transport/escort service.
Athletics Member NJCAA.
Costs (2010–11) *One-time required fee:* $50. *Tuition:* area resident $2328 full-time, $97 per credit hour part-time; state resident $4656 full-time, $194 per credit hour part-time; nonresident $6984 full-time, $291 per credit hour part-time. Full-time tuition and fees vary according to course load. Part-time tuition and fees vary according to course load. *Required fees:* $928 full-time, $37 per credit hour part-time, $20 per term part-time.
Financial Aid Of all full-time matriculated undergraduates who enrolled in 2009, 95 Federal Work-Study jobs (averaging $900).
Applying *Options:* early admission. *Application fee:* $25. *Required:* high school transcript.
Freshman Application Contact Ms. Hope Diehl, Director of Admissions and Enrollment Services, Delaware County Community College, 901 South Media Line Road, Media, PA 19063-1094. *Phone:* 610-359-5050. *Toll-free phone:* 800-872-1102 (in-state); 800-543-0146 (out-of-state). *Fax:* 610-723-1530. *E-mail:* admiss@dccc.edu. *Web site:* http://www.dccc.edu/.

Douglas Education Center
Monessen, Pennsylvania

- **Proprietary** 2-year, founded 1904
- **Small-town** campus with easy access to Pittsburgh
- **Coed,** 334 undergraduate students, 100% full-time, 66% women, 34% men

Undergraduates 334 full-time. Students come from 49 states and territories; 4 other countries; 32% are from out of state; 4% Black or African American, non-Hispanic/Latino; 4% Hispanic/Latino; 0.6% Asian, non-Hispanic/Latino; 0.6% Native Hawaiian or other Pacific Islander, non-Hispanic/Latino; 0.6% American Indian or Alaska Native, non-Hispanic/Latino; 1% Two or more races, non-Hispanic/Latino; 1% Race/ethnicity unknown; 1% international. *Retention:* 87% of full-time freshmen returned.
Freshmen *Admission:* 104 enrolled.
Faculty *Total:* 37, 35% full-time. *Student/faculty ratio:* 16:1.
Majors Art; business administration and management; cosmetology; design and visual communications; film/cinema/video studies; graphic design; illustration; medical/clinical assistant; medical office management.
Academics *Degree:* diplomas and associate. *Special study options:* advanced placement credit.
Library Douglas Education Center Library / Learning Resource Center plus 2 others with 126 serial subscriptions, 820 audiovisual materials, an OPAC.
Student Life *Campus security:* 24-hour emergency response devices.
Standardized Tests *Required:* Wonderlic aptitude test (for admission).
Financial Aid Of all full-time matriculated undergraduates who enrolled in 2009, 5 Federal Work-Study jobs (averaging $2500).
Applying *Application fee:* $50. *Required:* high school transcript, interview. *Application deadlines:* rolling (freshmen), rolling (out-of-state freshmen), rolling (transfers). *Notification:* continuous (freshmen), continuous (out-of-state freshmen), continuous (transfers).
Freshman Application Contact Ms. Sherry Lee Walters, Director of Enrollment Services, Douglas Education Center, 130 Seventh Street, Monessen, PA 15062. *Phone:* 724-684-3684 Ext. 2181. *Web site:* http://www.dec.edu/.

DuBois Business College
DuBois, Pennsylvania

Director of Admissions Mrs. Lisa Doty, Director of Admissions, DuBois Business College, 1 Beaver Drive, DuBois, PA 15801-2401. *Phone:* 814-371-6920. *Toll-free phone:* 800-692-6213. *Fax:* 814-371-3947. *E-mail:* dotylj@dbcollege.com. *Web site:* http://www.dbcollege.com/.

Erie Business Center, Main
Erie, Pennsylvania

Freshman Application Contact Erie Business Center, Main, 246 West Ninth Street, Erie, PA 16501-1392. *Phone:* 814-456-7504. *Toll-free phone:* 800-352-3743. *Web site:* http://www.eriebc.edu/.

Erie Business Center, South
New Castle, Pennsylvania

Freshman Application Contact Erie Business Center, South, 170 Cascade Galleria, New Castle, PA 16101-3950. *Phone:* 724-658-9066. *Toll-free phone:* 800-722-6227. *E-mail:* admissions@eriebcs.com. *Web site:* http://www.eriebc.edu/.

Erie Institute of Technology
Erie, Pennsylvania

Freshman Application Contact Erie Institute of Technology, 940 Millcreek Mall, Erie, PA 16565. *Phone:* 814-868-9900. *Toll-free phone:* 866-868-3743. *Web site:* http://www.erieit.edu/.

Everest Institute
Pittsburgh, Pennsylvania

Director of Admissions Director of Admissions, Everest Institute, 100 Forbes Avenue, Suite 1200, Pittsburgh, PA 15222. *Phone:* 412-261-4520. *Toll-free phone:* 888-279-3314. *Fax:* 412-261-4546. *Web site:* http://www.everest.edu/.

Fortis Institute
Forty Fort, Pennsylvania

Freshman Application Contact Admissions Office, Fortis Institute, 166 Slocum Street, Forty Fort, PA 18704. *Phone:* 570-288-8400. *Web site:* http://www.fortis.edu/.

Harcum College
Bryn Mawr, Pennsylvania

- **Independent** 2-year, founded 1915
- **Suburban** 12-acre campus with easy access to Philadelphia
- **Coed, primarily women**

Undergraduates 20% live on campus. *Retention:* 64% of full-time freshmen returned.
Faculty *Student/faculty ratio:* 12:1.
Academics *Calendar:* semesters. *Degree:* certificates and associate. *Special study options:* academic remediation for entering students, accelerated degree program, adult/continuing education programs, advanced placement credit, distance learning, English as a second language, honors programs, independent study, internships, off-campus study, part-time degree program, services for LD students, summer session for credit.
Student Life *Campus security:* 24-hour emergency response devices and patrols, late-night transport/escort service, controlled dormitory access.
Athletics Member NJCAA.
Standardized Tests *Recommended:* SAT or ACT (for admission).
Costs (2010–11) *One-time required fee:* $100. *Comprehensive fee:* $27,020 includes full-time tuition ($18,600), mandatory fees ($220), and room and board ($8200). Full-time tuition and fees vary according to course load and program. Part-time tuition: $595 per credit hour. Part-time tuition and fees vary according to course load.
Financial Aid Of all full-time matriculated undergraduates who enrolled in 2009, 703 applied for aid, 675 were judged to have need, 17 had their need fully met. 160 Federal Work-Study jobs (averaging $1500). *Average percent of need met:* 51. *Average financial aid package:* $13,662. *Average need-based loan:* $3876. *Average need-based gift aid:* $10,390. *Average indebtedness upon graduation:* $17,641. *Financial aid deadline:* 5/1.
Applying *Options:* electronic application, deferred entrance. *Application fee:* $50. *Required:* high school transcript, minimum 2.0 GPA. *Required for some:* 1 letter of recommendation, interview. *Recommended:* essay or personal statement.

Freshman Application Contact Office of Enrollment Management, Harcum College, 750 Montgomery Avenue, Bryn Mawr, PA 19010-3476. *Phone:* 610-526-6050. *Toll-free phone:* 800-345-2600. *E-mail:* enroll@harcum.edu. *Web site:* http://www.harcum.edu/.

Harrisburg Area Community College

Harrisburg, Pennsylvania

- **State and locally supported** 2-year, founded 1964
- **Urban** 212-acre campus
- **Endowment** $25.9 million
- **Coed,** 23,210 undergraduate students, 38% full-time, 63% women, 37% men

Undergraduates 8,783 full-time, 14,427 part-time. Students come from 10 states and territories; 58 other countries; 1% are from out of state; 7% transferred in.

Freshmen *Admission:* 10,716 applied, 10,469 admitted, 2,220 enrolled.

Faculty *Total:* 1,159, 31% full-time, 7% with terminal degrees. *Student/faculty ratio:* 22:1.

Majors Accounting and business/management; accounting technology and bookkeeping; administrative assistant and secretarial science; agribusiness; architectural engineering technology; architecture; art; automobile/automotive mechanics technology; banking and financial support services; biology/biological sciences; building/home/construction inspection; business administration and management; business/commerce; cabinetmaking and millwork; cardiovascular technology; chemistry; civil engineering technology; clinical/medical laboratory technology; computer and information sciences; computer and information systems security; computer installation and repair technology; computer science; computer systems networking and telecommunications; construction engineering technology; construction trades; court reporting; crafts, folk art and artisanry; criminalistics and criminal science; criminal justice/law enforcement administration; criminal justice/police science; culinary arts; dental hygiene; design and visual communications; diagnostic medical sonography and ultrasound technology; dietetics; dietetics and clinical nutrition services related; dramatic/theater arts; early childhood education; electrical, electronic and communications engineering technology; electrician; emergency medical technology (EMT paramedic); engineering; engineering technologies and engineering related; environmental science; environmental studies; fire science/firefighting; food service systems administration; general studies; geographic information science and cartography; graphic design; health/health-care administration; health services administration; heating, air conditioning, ventilation and refrigeration maintenance technology; hospitality administration; hotel/motel administration; human services; industrial mechanics and maintenance technology; international relations and affairs; landscaping and groundskeeping; legal assistant/paralegal; lineworker; management information systems and services related; mass communication/media; mathematics; mechanical engineering/mechanical technology; medical/clinical assistant; music management; nuclear medical technology; photography; physical sciences; psychology; radiologic technology/science; real estate; registered nursing/registered nurse; respiratory care therapy; retailing; sales, distribution, and marketing operations; secondary education; small business administration; social sciences; social work; surgical technology; tourism and travel services management; visual and performing arts; viticulture and enology; web page, digital/multimedia and information resources design.

Academics *Calendar:* semesters. *Degree:* certificates, diplomas, and associate. *Special study options:* academic remediation for entering students, adult/continuing education programs, advanced placement credit, distance learning, double majors, English as a second language, honors programs, independent study, internships, part-time degree program, services for LD students, student-designed majors, study abroad, summer session for credit. *ROTC:* Army (b).

Library McCormick Library plus 6 others with 155,069 titles, 855 serial subscriptions, 8,449 audiovisual materials, an OPAC, a Web page.

Student Life *Housing:* college housing not available. *Activities and Organizations:* drama/theater group, student-run newspaper, Student Government Association, Phi Theta Kappa, African American Student Association, Mosiaco Club, Fourth Estate. *Campus security:* 24-hour emergency response devices and patrols, late-night transport/escort service.

Athletics *Intercollegiate sports:* basketball M/W, soccer M, tennis M/W. *Intramural sports:* basketball M/W, soccer M/W, swimming and diving M/W, tennis M/W, volleyball M/W.

Costs (2010–11) *One-time required fee:* $35. *Tuition:* area resident $3195 full-time, $107 per credit hour part-time; state resident $5490 full-time, $183 per credit hour part-time; nonresident $8235 full-time, $275 per credit hour part-time. Full-time tuition and fees vary according to location and program. Part-time tuition and fees vary according to location and program. *Required fees:* $525 full-time, $23 per credit hour part-time. *Payment plan:* installment. *Waivers:* senior citizens and employees or children of employees.

Applying *Options:* electronic application, early admission, deferred entrance. *Application fee:* $35. *Required for some:* high school transcript, 1 letter of recommendation, interview. *Application deadlines:* rolling (freshmen), rolling (transfers).

Freshman Application Contact Mrs. Vanita L. Cowan, Administrative Clerk, Admissions, Harrisburg Area Community College, Harrisburg, PA 17110. *Phone:* 717-780-2694. *Toll-free phone:* 800-ABC-HACC. *Fax:* 717-231-7674. *E-mail:* admit@hacc.edu. *Web site:* http://www.hacc.edu/.

Hussian School of Art

Philadelphia, Pennsylvania

Freshman Application Contact Director of Admissions, Hussian School of Art, The Bourse, Suite 300, 111 South Independence Mall East, Philadelphia, PA 19106. *Phone:* 215-574-9600. *Fax:* 215-574-9800. *E-mail:* info@hussianart.edu. *Web site:* http://www.hussianart.edu/.

ITT Technical Institute

Bensalem, Pennsylvania

- **Proprietary** 2-year, founded 2000, part of ITT Educational Services, Inc.
- **Coed**

Majors CAD/CADD drafting/design technology; computer engineering technology; criminal justice/law enforcement administration; system, networking, and LAN/WAN management; web page, digital/multimedia and information resources design.

Academics *Calendar:* quarters. *Degree:* diplomas and associate.

Student Life *Housing:* college housing not available.

Freshman Application Contact Director of Recruitment, ITT Technical Institute, 3330 Tillman Drive, Bensalem, PA 19020. *Phone:* 215-244-8871. *Toll-free phone:* 866-488-8324. *Web site:* http://www.itt-tech.edu/.

ITT Technical Institute

Dunmore, Pennsylvania

- **Proprietary** 2-year, part of ITT Educational Services, Inc.
- **Coed**

Majors CAD/CADD drafting/design technology; computer engineering technology; criminal justice/law enforcement administration; system, networking, and LAN/WAN management.

Academics *Calendar:* quarters. *Degree:* diplomas and associate.

Freshman Application Contact ITT Technical Institute, 1000 Meade Street, Dunmore, PA 18512. *Phone:* 570-330-0600. *Toll-free phone:* 800-774-9791. *Web site:* http://www.itt-tech.edu/.

ITT Technical Institute

Harrisburg, Pennsylvania

- **Proprietary** 2-year, part of ITT Educational Services, Inc.
- **Coed**

Majors CAD/CADD drafting/design technology; computer engineering technology; computer software and media applications related; criminal justice/law enforcement administration; system, networking, and LAN/WAN management; web page, digital/multimedia and information resources design.

Academics *Degree:* diplomas and associate.

Freshman Application Contact Director of Recruitment, ITT Technical Institute, 449 Eisenhower Boulevard, Suite 100, Harrisburg, PA 17111. *Phone:* 717-565-1700. *Toll-free phone:* 800-847-4756. *Web site:* http://www.itt-tech.edu/.

ITT Technical Institute

King of Prussia, Pennsylvania

- **Proprietary** 2-year, founded 2002, part of ITT Educational Services, Inc.
- **Coed**

Majors CAD/CADD drafting/design technology; computer engineering technology; criminal justice/law enforcement administration; system, networking, and LAN/WAN management; web page, digital/multimedia and information resources design.

Academics *Calendar:* quarters. *Degree:* diplomas and associate.

Freshman Application Contact Director of Recruitment, ITT Technical Institute, 760 Moore Road, King of Prussia, PA 19406-1212. *Phone:* 610-491-8004. *Toll-free phone:* 866-902-8324. *Web site:* http://www.itt-tech.edu/.

ITT Technical Institute
Pittsburgh, Pennsylvania

- **Proprietary** 2-year, part of ITT Educational Services, Inc.
- **Coed**

Majors CAD/CADD drafting/design technology; computer engineering technology; computer software and media applications related; criminal justice/law enforcement administration; system, networking, and LAN/WAN management; web page, digital/multimedia and information resources design.

Academics *Calendar:* quarters. *Degree:* diplomas and associate.

Student Life *Housing:* college housing not available.

Freshman Application Contact Director of Recruitment, ITT Technical Institute, 10 Parkway Center, Pittsburgh, PA 15220-3801. *Phone:* 412-937-9150. *Toll-free phone:* 800-353-8324. *Web site:* http://www.itt-tech.edu/.

ITT Technical Institute
Tarentum, Pennsylvania

- **Proprietary** 2-year, part of ITT Educational Services, Inc.
- **Coed**

Majors CAD/CADD drafting/design technology; computer engineering technology; computer software and media applications related; criminal justice/law enforcement administration; system, networking, and LAN/WAN management; web/multimedia management and webmaster; web page, digital/multimedia and information resources design.

Academics *Calendar:* quarters. *Degree:* diplomas and associate.

Student Life *Housing:* college housing not available.

Freshman Application Contact Director of Recruitment, ITT Technical Institute, 100 Pittsburgh Mills Circle, Suite 100, Tarentum, PA 15084. *Phone:* 724-274-1400. *Toll-free phone:* 800-488-0121. *Web site:* http://www.itt-tech.edu/.

JNA Institute of Culinary Arts
Philadelphia, Pennsylvania

- **Proprietary** 2-year, founded 1988
- **Urban** campus with easy access to Philadelphia
- **Coed,** 92 undergraduate students, 100% full-time, 49% women, 51% men

Undergraduates 92 full-time. 65% Black or African American, non-Hispanic/Latino; 4% Hispanic/Latino; 2% Asian, non-Hispanic/Latino. *Retention:* 52% of full-time freshmen returned.

Freshmen *Admission:* 40 enrolled.

Majors Restaurant, culinary, and catering management.

Academics *Calendar:* continuous. *Degree:* associate.

Costs (2010–11) *Tuition:* $10,000 full-time. Full-time tuition and fees vary according to program. No tuition increase for student's term of enrollment. *Payment plans:* installment, deferred payment. *Waivers:* children of alumni.

Freshman Application Contact Admissions Office, JNA Institute of Culinary Arts, 1212 South Broad Street, Philadelphia, PA 19146. *Web site:* http://www.culinaryarts.com/.

Johnson College
Scranton, Pennsylvania

Freshman Application Contact Ms. Melissa Ide, Director of Enrollment Management, Johnson College, 3427 North Main Avenue, Scranton, PA 18508. *Phone:* 570-702-8910. *Toll-free phone:* 800-2-WE-WORK Ext. 125. *Fax:* 570-348-2181. *E-mail:* admit@johnson.edu. *Web site:* http://www.johnson.edu/.

Kaplan Career Institute, Harrisburg
Harrisburg, Pennsylvania

- **Proprietary** 2-year, founded 1918
- **Suburban** campus
- **Coed**

Academics *Calendar:* quarters. *Degree:* certificates, diplomas, and associate.

Freshman Application Contact Kaplan Career Institute, Harrisburg, 5650 Derry Street, Harrisburg, PA 17111-3518. *Phone:* 717-558-1300. *Toll-free phone:* 800-431-1995. *Web site:* http://harrisburg.kaplancareerinstitute.com/.

Kaplan Career Institute, ICM Campus
Pittsburgh, Pennsylvania

- **Proprietary** 2-year, founded 1963
- **Urban** campus
- **Coed**

Academics *Calendar:* continuous. *Degree:* diplomas and associate.

Freshman Application Contact Kaplan Career Institute, ICM Campus, 10 Wood Street, Pittsburgh, PA 15222-1977. *Phone:* 412-261-2647. *Toll-free phone:* 800-441-5222. *Web site:* http://www.kci-pittsburgh.com/.

Keystone Technical Institute
Harrisburg, Pennsylvania

Freshman Application Contact Tom Bogush, Director of Admissions, Keystone Technical Institute, 2301 Academy Drive, Harrisburg, PA 17112. *Phone:* 717-545-4747. *Toll-free phone:* 800-400-3322. *Fax:* 717-901-9090. *E-mail:* info@acadcampus.com. *Web site:* http://www.kti.edu.

Lackawanna College
Scranton, Pennsylvania

- **Independent** 2-year, founded 1894
- **Urban** 4-acre campus
- **Endowment** $1.9 million
- **Coed**

Undergraduates 999 full-time, 388 part-time. Students come from 13 states and territories; 10% are from out of state; 10% transferred in; 17% live on campus. *Retention:* 34% of full-time freshmen returned.

Faculty *Student/faculty ratio:* 13:1.

Academics *Calendar:* semesters. *Degree:* certificates, diplomas, and associate. *Special study options:* academic remediation for entering students, adult/continuing education programs, cooperative education, double majors, English as a second language, internships, part-time degree program, services for LD students, summer session for credit. *ROTC:* Army (c), Air Force (c).

Student Life *Campus security:* 24-hour emergency response devices and patrols, late-night transport/escort service, controlled dormitory access, patrols by college liaison staff.

Athletics Member NJCAA.

Standardized Tests *Recommended:* SAT (for admission), ACT (for admission), SAT or ACT (for admission).

Costs (2010–11) *Comprehensive fee:* $18,660 includes full-time tuition ($11,300), mandatory fees ($160), and room and board ($7200). Full-time tuition and fees vary according to course load. Part-time tuition: $385 per credit hour. Part-time tuition and fees vary according to course load. *Required fees:* $55 per term part-time. *Payment plans:* installment, deferred payment.

Financial Aid Of all full-time matriculated undergraduates who enrolled in 2009, 1,040 applied for aid, 956 were judged to have need, 27 had their need fully met. 91 Federal Work-Study jobs (averaging $875). In 2009, 4. *Average percent of need met:* 55. *Average financial aid package:* $9780. *Average need-based loan:* $3704. *Average need-based gift aid:* $6651. *Average non-need-based aid:* $1912. *Average indebtedness upon graduation:* $16,680.

Applying *Options:* electronic application, early admission, deferred entrance. *Application fee:* $30. *Required:* high school transcript, interview.

Freshman Application Contact Ms. Stacey Muchal, Associate Director of Admissions, Lackawanna College, 501 Vine Street, Scranton, PA 18509. *Phone:* 570-961-7868. *Toll-free phone:* 877-346-3552. *Fax:* 570-961-7843. *E-mail:* muchals@lackawanna.edu. *Web site:* http://www.lackawanna.edu/.

Lancaster General College of Nursing & Health Sciences
Lancaster, Pennsylvania

Freshman Application Contact Admissions Office, Lancaster General College of Nursing & Health Sciences, 410 North Lime Street, Lancaster, PA 17602. *Web site:* http://www.lancastergeneralcollege.edu/content/.

Lansdale School of Business
North Wales, Pennsylvania

Director of Admissions Ms. Marianne H. Johnson, Director of Admissions, Lansdale School of Business, 201 Church Road, North Wales, PA 19454-4148. *Phone:* 215-699-5700 Ext. 112. *Fax:* 215-699-8770. *E-mail:* mjohnson@lsb.edu. *Web site:* http://www.lsb.edu/.

Laurel Business Institute
Uniontown, Pennsylvania

Freshman Application Contact Mrs. Lisa Dolan, Laurel Business Institute, 11 East Penn Street, PO Box 877, Uniontown, PA 15401. *Phone:* 724-439-4900 Ext. 158. *Fax:* 724-439-3607. *E-mail:* ldolan@laurel.edu. *Web site:* http://www.laurel.edu/.

Laurel Technical Institute
Meadville, Pennsylvania

Freshman Application Contact Admissions Officer, Laurel Technical Institute, 628 Arch Street, Suite B105, Meadville, PA 16335. *Phone:* 814-724-0700. *Fax:* 814-724-2777. *E-mail:* lti.admission@laurel.edu. *Web site:* http://www.laurel.edu/lti/.

Laurel Technical Institute
Sharon, Pennsylvania

Freshman Application Contact Irene Lewis, Laurel Technical Institute, 335 Boyd Drive, Sharon, PA 16146. *Phone:* 724-983-0700. *Toll-free phone:* 800-289-2069. *Fax:* 724-983-8355. *E-mail:* info@biop.edu. *Web site:* http://www.laurel.edu/lti/.

Le Cordon Bleu Institute of Culinary Arts in Pittsburgh
Pittsburgh, Pennsylvania

Freshman Application Contact Ms. Juliette Mariani, Dean of Students, Le Cordon Bleu Institute of Culinary Arts in Pittsburgh, 717 Liberty Avenue, 19th Floor, Pittsburgh, PA 15222. *Phone:* 412-566-2433. *Toll-free phone:* 800-432-2433. *Fax:* 412-566-2434. *Web site:* http://www.chefs.edu/Pittsburgh.

Lehigh Carbon Community College
Schnecksville, Pennsylvania

- **State and locally supported** 2-year, founded 1967
- **Suburban** 254-acre campus with easy access to Philadelphia
- **Endowment** $2.0 million
- **Coed,** 8,101 undergraduate students, 42% full-time, 61% women, 39% men

Undergraduates 3,365 full-time, 4,736 part-time. Students come from 10 states and territories; 15 other countries; 2% are from out of state; 56% transferred in. *Retention:* 56% of full-time freshmen returned.
Freshmen *Admission:* 4,144 applied, 4,144 admitted, 1,541 enrolled.
Faculty *Total:* 550, 16% full-time, 3% with terminal degrees. *Student/faculty ratio:* 20:1.
Majors Accounting technology and bookkeeping; aeronautics/aviation/aerospace science and technology; airline pilot and flight crew; animation, interactive technology, video graphics and special effects; art; biology/biological sciences; biotechnology; building/construction site management; business administration and management; chemical technology; computer and information sciences; computer and information systems security; computer engineering technology; computer programming; computer systems analysis; computer systems networking and telecommunications; construction trades; criminal justice/law enforcement administration; criminal justice/safety; drafting and design technology; early childhood education; education; electrical, electronic and communications engineering technology; engineering; fashion/apparel design; general studies; graphic design; health information/medical records technology; heating, air conditioning, ventilation and refrigeration maintenance technology; horticultural science; humanities; human resources management; human services; industrial electronics technology; information science/studies; interior design; legal assistant/paralegal; liberal arts and sciences/liberal studies; logistics, materials, and supply chain management; manufacturing engineering technology; mathematics; mechanical engineering/mechanical technology; medical/clinical assistant; nanotechnology; occupational therapist assistant; operations management; physical sciences; physical therapy technology; psychology; radio and television broadcasting technology; recording arts technology; registered nursing/registered nurse; resort management; social sciences; special education; speech communication and rhetoric; sport and fitness administration/management; teacher assistant/aide; veterinary/animal health technology; web page, digital/multimedia and information resources design.
Academics *Calendar:* semesters. *Degree:* certificates, diplomas, and associate. *Special study options:* academic remediation for entering students, adult/continuing education programs, advanced placement credit, cooperative education, distance learning, English as a second language, external degree program, honors programs, independent study, internships, part-time degree program, services for LD students, summer session for credit. *ROTC:* Army (c).
Library Rothrock Library with 91,756 titles, 374 serial subscriptions, 5,281 audiovisual materials, an OPAC, a Web page.
Student Life *Housing:* college housing not available. *Activities and Organizations:* drama/theater group, student-run radio station, choral group, Phi Theta Kappa, STEP Student Association, Students in Free Enterprise (SIFE), Student Government Association, WXLV 90.3FM college radio station. *Campus security:* 24-hour emergency response devices. *Student services:* personal/psychological counseling.
Athletics *Intercollegiate sports:* baseball M, basketball M/W, golf M/W, soccer M, softball W, volleyball W. *Intramural sports:* volleyball M.
Standardized Tests *Required for some:* TEAS (for those applying to Nursing Program).
Costs (2010–11) *Tuition:* area resident $2640 full-time, $88 per credit part-time; state resident $5550 full-time, $185 per credit part-time; nonresident $8460 full-time, $282 per credit part-time. *Required fees:* $480 full-time, $16 per credit part-time. *Payment plan:* installment. *Waivers:* senior citizens and employees or children of employees.
Applying *Options:* electronic application. *Required for some:* essay or personal statement, high school transcript, interview. *Application deadlines:* rolling (freshmen), rolling (out-of-state freshmen), rolling (transfers). *Notification:* continuous (freshmen), continuous (out-of-state freshmen), continuous (transfers).
Freshman Application Contact Ms. Mary Theresa Taglang, Associate Dean of Admissions and Strategic Outreach, Lehigh Carbon Community College, Schnecksville, PA 18078. *Phone:* 610-799-1575. *Fax:* 610-799-1527. *E-mail:* tellme@lccc.edu. *Web site:* http://www.lccc.edu/.

Lincoln Technical Institute
Allentown, Pennsylvania

Freshman Application Contact Admissions Office, Lincoln Technical Institute, 5151 Tilghman Street, Allentown, PA 18104-3298. *Phone:* 610-398-5301. *Web site:* http://www.lincolnedu.com/.

Lincoln Technical Institute
Philadelphia, Pennsylvania

Director of Admissions Mr. James Kuntz, Executive Director, Lincoln Technical Institute, 9191 Torresdale Avenue, Philadelphia, PA 19136-1595. *Phone:* 215-335-0800. *Toll-free phone:* 800-238-8381. *Fax:* 215-335-1443. *E-mail:* jkuntz@lincolntech.com. *Web site:* http://www.lincolnedu.com/.

Lincoln Technical Institute
Plymouth Meeting, Pennsylvania

Freshman Application Contact Admissions Office, Lincoln Technical Institute, 1 Plymouth Meeting, # 300, Plymouth Meeting, PA 19462-1326. *Web site:* http://www.lincolnedu.com/.

Luzerne County Community College
Nanticoke, Pennsylvania

Freshman Application Contact Mr. Francis Curry, Director of Admissions, Luzerne County Community College, 1333 South Prospect Street, Nanticoke, PA 18634-9804. *Phone:* 570-740-0337. *Toll-free phone:* 800-377-5222 Ext. 337. *Fax:* 570-740-0238. *E-mail:* admissions@luzerne.edu. *Web site:* http://www.luzerne.edu/.

Manor College
Jenkintown, Pennsylvania

Director of Admissions I. Jerry Czenstuch, Vice President of Enrollment Management, Manor College, 700 Fox Chase Road, Jenkintown, PA 19046. *Phone:* 215-884-2216. *E-mail:* ftadmiss@manor.edu. *Web site:* http://www.manor.edu/.

See next page for Display and page 420 for the College Close-Up.

McCann School of Business & Technology
Pottsville, Pennsylvania

Freshman Application Contact Ms. Linda Walinsky, Director, Pottsville Campus, McCann School of Business & Technology, 2650 Woodglen Road, Pottsville, PA 17901. *Phone:* 570-622-7622. *Toll-free phone:* 888-622-2664. *Fax:* 570-622-7770. *Web site:* http://www.mccannschool.com/.

Mercyhurst North East
North East, Pennsylvania

Director of Admissions Travis Lindahl, Director of Admissions, Mercyhurst North East, 16 West Division Street, North East, PA 16428. *Phone:* 814-725-6217. *Toll-free phone:* 866-846-6042. *Fax:* 814-725-6251. *E-mail:* neadmiss@mercyhurst.edu. *Web site:* http://northeast.mercyhurst.edu/.

Metropolitan Career Center
Philadelphia, Pennsylvania

Freshman Application Contact Admissions Office, Metropolitan Career Center, 100 South Broad Street, Suite 830, Philadelphia, PA 19110. *Phone:* 215-568-7861. *Web site:* http://www.careersinit.org/.

Montgomery County Community College
Blue Bell, Pennsylvania

- **County-supported** 2-year, founded 1964
- **Suburban** 186-acre campus with easy access to Philadelphia
- **Coed,** 13,919 undergraduate students, 46% full-time, 57% women, 43% men

Undergraduates 6,342 full-time, 7,577 part-time. Students come from 16 states and territories; 105 other countries; 1% are from out of state; 13% Black or African American, non-Hispanic/Latino; 5% Hispanic/Latino; 5% Asian, non-Hispanic/Latino; 0.2% Native Hawaiian or other Pacific Islander, non-Hispanic/Latino; 0.2% American Indian or Alaska Native, non-Hispanic/Latino; 1% Two or more races, non-Hispanic/Latino; 9% Race/ethnicity unknown; 2% international; 2% transferred in. *Retention:* 61% of full-time freshmen returned.

Freshmen *Admission:* 7,983 applied, 7,983 admitted, 4,570 enrolled.

Faculty *Total:* 749, 26% full-time. *Student/faculty ratio:* 23:1.

Majors Accounting; accounting technology and bookkeeping; administrative assistant and secretarial science; architectural drafting and CAD/CADD; art; automotive engineering technology; baking and pastry arts; biology/biological sciences; biotechnology; business administration and management; business/commerce; business/corporate communications; CAD/CADD drafting/design technology; child-care and support services management; clinical/medical laboratory technology; commercial and advertising art; communications technologies and support services related; computer and information sciences; computer programming; computer systems networking and telecommunications; criminal justice/police science; culinary arts; dental hygiene; electrical, electronic and communications engineering technology; electromechanical technology; elementary education; engineering science; engineering technologies and engineering related; environmental science; fire prevention and safety technology; hospitality and recreation marketing; humanities; information science/studies; liberal arts and sciences/liberal studies; management information systems and services related; mathematics; mechanical drafting and CAD/CADD; mechanical engineering/mechanical technology; medical/clinical assistant; medical radiologic technology; physical education teaching and coaching; physical sciences; psychiatric/mental health services technology; radio, television, and digital communication related; real estate; recording arts technology; registered nursing/registered nurse; sales, distribution, and marketing operations; secondary education; social sciences; speech communication and rhetoric; surgical technology; teacher assistant/aide; tourism and travel services marketing.

Academics *Calendar:* semesters. *Degree:* certificates and associate. *Special study options:* academic remediation for entering students, accelerated degree program, adult/continuing education programs, advanced placement credit, cooperative education, distance learning, English as a second language, honors programs, independent study, internships, part-time degree program, services for LD students, student-designed majors, study abroad, summer session for credit.

Library The Brendlinger Library/Branch Library Pottstown Campus plus 1 other with 72,398 titles, 415 serial subscriptions, 31,055 audiovisual materials, an OPAC, a Web page.

Student Life *Housing:* college housing not available. *Activities and Organizations:* drama/theater group, student-run newspaper, radio and television station, choral group, student government, Thrive (Christian Fellowship), radio station, Drama Club, African - American Student League. *Campus security:* 24-hour emergency response devices and patrols, late-night transport/escort service, bicycle patrol. *Student services:* health clinic, personal/psychological counseling.

Athletics Member NJCAA. *Intercollegiate sports:* baseball M, basketball M/W, soccer M/W, softball W, volleyball W. *Intramural sports:* badminton M/W, basketball M/W, bowling M/W, cross-country running M/W, football M, racquetball M/W, soccer M/W, table tennis M/W, tennis M/W, volleyball M/W, weight lifting M/W.

Costs (2010–11) *Tuition:* area resident $2880 full-time, $96 per credit hour part-time; state resident $6060 full-time, $192 per credit hour part-time; non-resident $9240 full-time, $288 per credit hour part-time. *Required fees:* $630 full-time, $21 per credit hour part-time. *Payment plan:* deferred payment. *Waivers:* senior citizens and employees or children of employees.

Financial Aid Of all full-time matriculated undergraduates who enrolled in 2009, 60 Federal Work-Study jobs (averaging $2500).

Applying *Options:* electronic application, early admission, deferred entrance. *Application fee:* $25. *Required:* high school transcript. *Required for some:* interview. *Application deadline:* rolling (transfers). *Notification:* continuous (freshmen), continuous (transfers).

Freshman Application Contact Ms. Penny Sawyer, Director of Admissions and Recruitment, Montgomery County Community College, Blue Bell, PA 19422. *Phone:* 215-641-6551. *Fax:* 215-619-7188. *E-mail:* admrec@admin.mc3.edu. *Web site:* http://www.mc3.edu/.

New Castle School of Trades
Pulaski, Pennsylvania

Freshman Application Contact Mr. James Catheline, Admissions Director, New Castle School of Trades, New Castle Youngstown Road, Route 422 RD1, Pulaski, PA 16143-9721. *Phone:* 724-964-8811. *Toll-free phone:* 800-837-8299 Ext. 12. *Web site:* http://www.ncstrades.com/.

Newport Business Institute
Lower Burrell, Pennsylvania

Freshman Application Contact Admissions Coordinator, Newport Business Institute, Lower Burrell, PA 15068. *Phone:* 724-339-7542. *Toll-free phone:* 800-752-7695. *Fax:* 724-339-2950. *E-mail:* admissions@newportbusiness.com. *Web site:* http://www.nbi.edu/.

Newport Business Institute
Williamsport, Pennsylvania

- **Proprietary** 2-year, founded 1955
- **Small-town** campus
- **Coed, primarily women,** 108 undergraduate students, 100% full-time, 92% women, 8% men

Undergraduates 108 full-time. 18% Black or African American, non-Hispanic/Latino; 0.9% Hispanic/Latino; 16% transferred in.
Freshmen *Admission:* 23 applied, 23 admitted, 20 enrolled.
Faculty *Total:* 26, 23% full-time. *Student/faculty ratio:* 9:1.
Majors Administrative assistant and secretarial science; business administration and management; legal administrative assistant/secretary; medical administrative assistant and medical secretary.
Academics *Calendar:* quarters. *Degree:* associate. *Special study options:* distance learning, internships, part-time degree program, summer session for credit.
Student Life *Housing:* college housing not available. *Activities and Organizations:* Student Council.
Financial Aid *Financial aid deadline:* 8/1.
Applying *Options:* electronic application, deferred entrance. *Application fee:* $25. *Required:* high school transcript, interview. *Application deadlines:* rolling (freshmen), rolling (transfers).
Freshman Application Contact Ms. Ashley Wall, Admissions Representative, Newport Business Institute, 941 West Third Street, Williamsport, PA 17701. *Phone:* 570-326-2869. *Toll-free phone:* 800-962-6971. *Fax:* 570-326-2136. *E-mail:* admissions2_NBI@Comcast.net. *Web site:* http://www.nbi.edu/.

Northampton Community College
Bethlehem, Pennsylvania

- **State and locally supported** 2-year, founded 1967
- **Suburban** 165-acre campus with easy access to Philadelphia
- **Endowment** $23.9 million
- **Coed,** 11,328 undergraduate students, 47% full-time, 59% women, 41% men

Undergraduates 5,319 full-time, 6,009 part-time. Students come from 26 states and territories; 43 other countries; 2% are from out of state; 10% Black or African American, non-Hispanic/Latino; 15% Hispanic/Latino; 2% Asian, non-Hispanic/Latino; 0.2% Native Hawaiian or other Pacific Islander, non-Hispanic/Latino; 0.6% American Indian or Alaska Native, non-Hispanic/Latino; 0.3% Two or more races, non-Hispanic/Latino; 3% Race/ethnicity unknown; 0.9% international; 9% transferred in; 2% live on campus.
Freshmen *Admission:* 4,659 applied, 4,659 admitted, 2,470 enrolled.
Faculty *Total:* 744, 17% full-time, 23% with terminal degrees. *Student/faculty ratio:* 22:1.
Majors Accounting technology and bookkeeping; acting; administrative assistant and secretarial science; architectural engineering technology; athletic training; automobile/automotive mechanics technology; biology/biological sciences; biotechnology; business administration and management; business/commerce; CAD/CADD drafting/design technology; chemical technology; chemistry; computer and information systems security; computer installation and repair technology; computer programming; computer science; computer systems networking and telecommunications; construction management; criminal justice/safety; culinary arts; dental hygiene; diagnostic medical sonography and ultrasound technology; early childhood education; electrical, electronic and communications engineering technology; electrician; electro-mechanical technology; engineering; fine/studio arts; fire science/firefighting; fire services administration; funeral service and mortuary science; general studies; graphic design; heating, air conditioning, ventilation and refrigeration maintenance technology; hotel/motel administration; industrial electronics technology; interior design; journalism; legal administrative assistant/secretary; legal assistant/paralegal; liberal arts and sciences and humanities related; liberal arts and sciences/liberal studies; marketing/marketing management; mathematics; medical administrative assistant and medical secretary; middle school education; physics; quality control technology; radio and television broadcasting technology; radiologic technology/science; registered nursing/registered nurse; restaurant/food services management; secondary education; social work; speech communication and rhetoric; sport and fitness administration/management; surgical technology; teacher assistant/aide; veterinary/animal health technology; web page, digital/multimedia and information resources design.
Academics *Calendar:* semesters. *Degree:* certificates, diplomas, and associate. *Special study options:* academic remediation for entering students, adult/continuing education programs, advanced placement credit, distance learning, English as a second language, honors programs, independent study, internships, off-campus study, part-time degree program, services for LD students, student-designed majors, study abroad, summer session for credit.
Library Paul & Harriet Mack Library with 89,396 titles, 258 serial subscriptions, 4,994 audiovisual materials, an OPAC, a Web page.
Student Life *Housing Options:* coed. Campus housing is university owned. *Activities and Organizations:* drama/theater group, student-run newspaper, radio station, choral group, Phi Theta Kappa, Student Senate, Acta Non Verba, Dental Hygiene Club, Hispanic American Cultural Club. *Campus security:* 24-hour emergency response devices and patrols, controlled dormitory access. *Student services:* health clinic, personal/psychological counseling.
Athletics Member NJCAA. *Intercollegiate sports:* baseball M, basketball M/W, bowling M/W, golf M/W, soccer M, softball W, tennis M/W, volleyball W. *Intramural sports:* basketball M/W, cheerleading M(c)/W(c), soccer M/W, volleyball M/W, wrestling M(c).
Costs (2010–11) *Tuition:* area resident $2370 full-time, $79 per credit hour part-time; state resident $4740 full-time, $158 per credit hour part-time; non-resident $7110 full-time, $237 per credit hour part-time. Full-time tuition and fees vary according to course load. Part-time tuition and fees vary according to course load. *Required fees:* $900 full-time, $30 per credit hour part-time. *Room and board:* $7066; room only: $4080. Room and board charges vary according to board plan and housing facility. *Payment plan:* installment. *Waivers:* senior citizens and employees or children of employees.
Financial Aid Of all full-time matriculated undergraduates who enrolled in 2009, 2,443 applied for aid, 1,832 were judged to have need, 696 had their need fully met. 230 Federal Work-Study jobs (averaging $1175). 100 state and other part-time jobs (averaging $1933). *Average percent of need met:* 80%.
Applying *Options:* electronic application, deferred entrance. *Application fee:* $25. *Required for some:* high school transcript, minimum 2.5 GPA, interview, interview required: rad, veterinary, and surgical technologies. *Recommended:* high school transcript. *Application deadlines:* rolling (freshmen), rolling (out-of-state freshmen), rolling (transfers). *Notification:* continuous (freshmen), continuous (out-of-state freshmen), continuous (transfers).
Freshman Application Contact Mr. James McCarthy, Director of Admissions, Northampton Community College, 3835 Green Pond Road, Bethlehem, PA 18020-7599. *Phone:* 610-861-5506. *Fax:* 610-861-5551. *E-mail:* jrmccarthy@northampton.edu. *Web site:* http://www.northampton.edu/.

North Central Industrial Technical Education Center
Ridgway, Pennsylvania

Director of Admissions Lugene Inzana, Director, North Central Industrial Technical Education Center, 653 Montmorenci Avenue, Ridgway, PA 15853.

Phone: 814-772-1012. *Toll-free phone:* 800-242-5872. *Fax:* 814-772-1554. *E-mail:* linzana@ncentral.com. *Web site:* http://web2.ncentral.com/itec/.

Oakbridge Academy of Arts
Lower Burrell, Pennsylvania

Freshman Application Contact Matthew Belferman, Admissions Coordinator, Oakbridge Academy of Arts, 1250 Greensburg Road, Lower Burrell, PA 15068. *Phone:* 724-335-5336. *Toll-free phone:* 800-734-5601. *E-mail:* mbelferman@oaa.edu. *Web site:* http://oaa.edu/.

Orleans Technical Institute
Philadelphia, Pennsylvania

- **Independent** 2-year
- **Urban** campus with easy access to Philadelphia
- **Coed,** 676 undergraduate students, 73% full-time, 26% women, 74% men

Undergraduates 492 full-time, 184 part-time. Students come from 3 states and territories; 5% are from out of state; 50% Black or African American, non-Hispanic/Latino; 12% Hispanic/Latino; 3% Asian, non-Hispanic/Latino; 0.1% Native Hawaiian or other Pacific Islander, non-Hispanic/Latino; 0.1% American Indian or Alaska Native, non-Hispanic/Latino; 0.3% Two or more races, non-Hispanic/Latino; 0.3% Race/ethnicity unknown; 1% transferred in.
Freshmen *Admission:* 395 applied, 273 admitted, 211 enrolled.
Faculty *Total:* 54, 50% full-time. *Student/faculty ratio:* 15:1.
Majors Court reporting.
Academics *Calendar:* trimesters. *Degree:* diplomas and associate. *Special study options:* academic remediation for entering students, cooperative education, internships, part-time degree program, summer session for credit.
Library Orleans Technical Institute Library and Learning Resource Center plus 1 other with 592 titles, 25 serial subscriptions, 7 audiovisual materials, an OPAC, a Web page.
Student Life *Housing:* college housing not available. *Campus security:* 24-hour emergency response devices.
Standardized Tests *Required:* Wonderlic (for admission).
Costs (2011–12) *Tuition:* $9320 full-time. Full-time tuition and fees vary according to class time, degree level, and program. Part-time tuition and fees vary according to class time, degree level, and program. *Required fees:* $860 full-time. *Payment plan:* installment.
Financial Aid Of all full-time matriculated undergraduates who enrolled in 2009, 5 Federal Work-Study jobs (averaging $4800). *Financial aid deadline:* 8/1.
Applying *Options:* electronic application. *Application fee:* $125. *Required:* high school transcript, interview. *Application deadlines:* rolling (freshmen), rolling (transfers).
Freshman Application Contact Mrs. Kathleen Beloin, Admissions Secretary, Orleans Technical Institute, 2770 Red Lion Road, Philadelphia, PA 19114. *Phone:* 215-728-4700. *Fax:* 215-745-1689. *E-mail:* beloik@jevs.org. *Web site:* http://www.orleanstech.edu/.

Pace Institute
Reading, Pennsylvania

Director of Admissions Mr. Ed Levandowski, Director of Enrollment Management, Pace Institute, 606 Court Street, Reading, PA 19601. *Phone:* 610-375-1212. *Fax:* 610-375-1924. *Web site:* http://www.paceinstitute.com/.

Penn Commercial Business and Technical School
Washington, Pennsylvania

Director of Admissions Mr. Michael John Joyce, Director of Admissions, Penn Commercial Business and Technical School, 242 Oak Spring Road, Washington, PA 15301. *Phone:* 724-222-5330 Ext. 1. *E-mail:* mjoyce@penn-commercial.com. *Web site:* http://www.penncommercial.net/.

Pennco Tech
Bristol, Pennsylvania

- **Proprietary** 2-year, founded 1961, part of Pennco Institutes, Inc.
- **Suburban** 7-acre campus with easy access to Philadelphia
- **Coed,** 400 undergraduate students, 61% full-time, 20% women, 80% men

Undergraduates 245 full-time, 155 part-time. Students come from 3 states and territories; 5% are from out of state; 1% transferred in; 3% live on campus.
Freshmen *Admission:* 229 applied, 79 enrolled.

Faculty *Total:* 28, 82% full-time. *Student/faculty ratio:* 14:1.
Majors Autobody/collision and repair technology; vehicle maintenance and repair technologies related.
Academics *Calendar:* modular. *Degree:* certificates, diplomas, and associate. *Special study options:* academic remediation for entering students, adult/continuing education programs, advanced placement credit, double majors.
Library Resource Center with 6,000 titles, 30 serial subscriptions, a Web page.
Student Life *Housing Options:* men-only. Campus housing is university owned. *Campus security:* 24-hour emergency response devices, controlled dormitory access.
Standardized Tests *Required for some:* SAT and SAT Subject Tests or ACT (for admission), IBM Aptitude Test.
Costs (2011–12) *Tuition:* $21,500 full-time, $5000 per course part-time. Full-time tuition and fees vary according to class time and program. Part-time tuition and fees vary according to class time and program. *Room only:* $3000. *Payment plan:* installment. *Waivers:* employees or children of employees.
Applying *Application fee:* $100. *Required:* interview. *Required for some:* essay or personal statement. *Application deadlines:* rolling (freshmen), rolling (transfers).
Director of Admissions Mr. Glenn Slater, Corporate Director of Admissions and Marketing, Pennco Tech, 3815 Otter Street, Bristol, PA 19007-3696. *Phone:* 215-785-0111. *Fax:* 215-785-1945. *E-mail:* admissions@penncotech.com. *Web site:* http://www.penncotech.com/.

Penn State Beaver
Monaca, Pennsylvania

- **State-related** primarily 2-year, founded 1964, part of Pennsylvania State University
- **Small-town** 91-acre campus with easy access to Pittsburgh
- **Coed,** 906 undergraduate students, 76% full-time, 48% women, 52% men

Undergraduates 690 full-time, 216 part-time. 7% are from out of state; 9% Black or African American, non-Hispanic/Latino; 2% Hispanic/Latino; 2% Asian, non-Hispanic/Latino; 0.1% American Indian or Alaska Native, non-Hispanic/Latino; 2% Two or more races, non-Hispanic/Latino; 2% Race/ethnicity unknown; 0.3% international; 5% transferred in; 20% live on campus. *Retention:* 67% of full-time freshmen returned.
Freshmen *Admission:* 454 applied, 271 enrolled. *Average high school GPA:* 2.92. *Test scores:* SAT critical reading scores over 500: 38%; SAT math scores over 500: 49%; SAT writing scores over 500: 30%; SAT critical reading scores over 600: 4%; SAT math scores over 600: 12%; SAT writing scores over 600: 4%.
Faculty *Total:* 64, 52% full-time, 41% with terminal degrees. *Student/faculty ratio:* 18:1.
Majors Accounting; acting; actuarial science; adult and continuing education administration; advertising; aerospace, aeronautical and astronautical/space engineering; African American/Black studies; agribusiness; agricultural and extension education; agricultural business and management related; agricultural engineering; agricultural mechanization; agriculture; agronomy and crop science; animal sciences; animal sciences related; anthropology; applied economics; archeology; architectural engineering; art; art history, criticism and conservation; art teacher education; Asian studies (East); astronomy; atmospheric sciences and meteorology; biochemistry; bioengineering and biomedical engineering; biological and biomedical sciences related; biological and physical sciences; biology/biological sciences; biology/biotechnology laboratory technician; business administration and management; business/commerce; business/managerial economics; chemical engineering; chemistry; civil engineering; classics and classical languages; communication and journalism related; communication sciences and disorders; comparative literature; computer and information sciences; computer engineering; criminal justice/law enforcement administration; economics; electrical and electronics engineering; elementary education; engineering science; English; environmental/environmental health engineering; film/cinema/video studies; finance; food science; foreign language teacher education; forest sciences and biology; forest technology; French; geography; geological and earth sciences/geosciences related; geology/earth science; German; graphic design; health/health-care administration; history; horticultural science; hospitality administration related; human development and family studies; human nutrition; industrial engineering; information science/studies; international relations and affairs; Italian; Japanese; Jewish/Judaic studies; journalism; kinesiology and exercise science; labor and industrial relations; landscaping and groundskeeping; Latin American studies; liberal arts and sciences/liberal studies; logistics, materials, and supply chain management; management information systems; marketing/marketing management; materials science; mathematics; mechanical engineering; medical microbiology and bacteriology; medieval and Renaissance studies; mining and mineral engineering; music; natural resources and conservation related; natural resources/conservation; nuclear engineering; organizational behavior; parks, recreation and leisure facilities management; petroleum engi-

neering; philosophy; physics; political science and government; premedical studies; psychology; registered nursing/registered nurse; rehabilitation and therapeutic professions related; religious studies; Russian; secondary education; sociology; soil science and agronomy; Spanish; special education; speech communication and rhetoric; statistics; theater design and technology; toxicology; turf and turfgrass management; visual and performing arts; women's studies.

Academics *Calendar:* semesters. *Degrees:* associate, bachelor's, and master's. *Special study options:* academic remediation for entering students, adult/continuing education programs, advanced placement credit, distance learning, double majors, English as a second language, honors programs, independent study, internships, services for LD students, study abroad, summer session for credit.

Student Life *Housing Options:* coed. Campus housing is university owned. Freshman campus housing is guaranteed. *Activities and Organizations:* drama/theater group, student-run newspaper, radio station. *Campus security:* 24-hour patrols, controlled dormitory access. *Student services:* health clinic, personal/psychological counseling.

Athletics Member NJCAA. *Intercollegiate sports:* baseball M, basketball M, softball M/W, volleyball W. *Intramural sports:* basketball M/W, cheerleading M(c)/W(c), cross-country running M/W, football M, golf M/W, soccer M/W, softball M/W, table tennis M/W.

Standardized Tests *Required:* SAT or ACT (for admission).

Costs (2010–11) *Tuition:* state resident $11,892 full-time, $481 per credit part-time; nonresident $18,148 full-time, $756 per credit part-time. Full-time tuition and fees vary according to course level, degree level, location, program, and student level. Part-time tuition and fees vary according to course level, course load, degree level, location, program, and student level. *Required fees:* $838 full-time. *Room and board:* $8370; room only: $4540. Room and board charges vary according to board plan, housing facility, and location. *Payment plans:* installment, deferred payment. *Waivers:* employees or children of employees.

Financial Aid Of all full-time matriculated undergraduates who enrolled in 2008, 573 applied for aid, 473 were judged to have need, 32 had their need fully met. In 2008, 48 non-need-based awards were made. *Average percent of need met:* 61%. *Average financial aid package:* $10,069. *Average need-based loan:* $3936. *Average need-based gift aid:* $6603. *Average non-need-based aid:* $2040. *Average indebtedness upon graduation:* $31,135.

Applying *Options:* electronic application, early admission, deferred entrance. *Application fee:* $50. *Required:* high school transcript. *Required for some:* interview. *Recommended:* essay or personal statement. *Application deadlines:* rolling (freshmen), rolling (transfers). *Notification:* continuous (freshmen), continuous (transfers).

Freshman Application Contact Admissions Office, Penn State Beaver, 100 University Drive, Monaca, PA 15061. *Phone:* 724-773-3800. *Fax:* 724-773-3658. *E-mail:* br-admissions@psu.edu. *Web site:* http://www.br.psu.edu/.

Penn State Brandywine
Media, Pennsylvania

- **State-related** primarily 2-year, founded 1966, part of Pennsylvania State University
- **Small-town** 87-acre campus with easy access to Philadelphia
- **Coed,** 1,613 undergraduate students, 85% full-time, 42% women, 58% men

Undergraduates 1,376 full-time, 237 part-time. 5% are from out of state; 12% Black or African American, non-Hispanic/Latino; 4% Hispanic/Latino; 6% Asian, non-Hispanic/Latino; 2% Two or more races, non-Hispanic/Latino; 3% Race/ethnicity unknown; 0.3% international; 3% transferred in. *Retention:* 73% of full-time freshmen returned.

Freshmen *Admission:* 761 applied, 390 enrolled. *Average high school GPA:* 2.91. *Test scores:* SAT critical reading scores over 500: 36%; SAT math scores over 500: 50%; SAT writing scores over 500: 33%; SAT critical reading scores over 600: 6%; SAT math scores over 600: 14%; SAT writing scores over 600: 5%; SAT critical reading scores over 700: 1%; SAT math scores over 700: 2%.

Faculty *Total:* 129, 47% full-time, 43% with terminal degrees. *Student/faculty ratio:* 17:1.

Majors Accounting; acting; actuarial science; adult and continuing education administration; advertising; aerospace, aeronautical and astronautical/space engineering; African American/Black studies; agribusiness; agricultural and extension education; agricultural business and management related; agricultural engineering; agricultural mechanization; agriculture; agronomy and crop science; American studies; animal sciences; animal sciences related; anthropology; applied economics; archeology; architectural engineering; art; art history, criticism and conservation; art teacher education; Asian studies (East); astronomy; atmospheric sciences and meteorology; biochemistry; bioengineering and biomedical engineering; biological and biomedical sciences related; biological and physical sciences; biology/biological sciences; biology/biotechnology laboratory technician; business administration and management; business/commerce; business/managerial economics; chemical engineering;

chemistry; civil engineering; classics and classical languages; communication and journalism related; communication sciences and disorders; comparative literature; computer and information sciences; computer engineering; criminal justice/law enforcement administration; economics; electrical and electronics engineering; electrical, electronic and communications engineering technology; elementary education; engineering science; English; environmental/environmental health engineering; film/cinema/video studies; finance; food science; foreign language teacher education; forest sciences and biology; forest technology; French; geography; geological and earth sciences/geosciences related; geology/earth science; German; graphic design; health/health-care administration; history; horticultural science; hospitality administration related; human development and family studies; human nutrition; industrial engineering; information science/studies; international relations and affairs; Italian; Japanese; Jewish/Judaic studies; journalism; kinesiology and exercise science; labor and industrial relations; landscape architecture; landscaping and groundskeeping; Latin American studies; liberal arts and sciences/liberal studies; logistics, materials, and supply chain management; management information systems; marketing/marketing management; materials science; mathematics; mechanical engineering; medical microbiology and bacteriology; medieval and Renaissance studies; mining and mineral engineering; music; natural resources and conservation related; natural resources/conservation; nuclear engineering; organizational behavior; parks, recreation and leisure facilities management; petroleum engineering; philosophy; physics; political science and government; premedical studies; psychology; registered nursing/registered nurse; rehabilitation and therapeutic professions related; religious studies; Russian; secondary education; sociology; soil science and agronomy; Spanish; special education; speech communication and rhetoric; statistics; theater design and technology; turf and turfgrass management; visual and performing arts; women's studies.

Academics *Calendar:* semesters. *Degrees:* certificates, associate, and bachelor's. *Special study options:* academic remediation for entering students, adult/continuing education programs, advanced placement credit, distance learning, double majors, English as a second language, honors programs, independent study, internships, services for LD students, study abroad, summer session for credit. *ROTC:* Army (c), Air Force (c).

Student Life *Housing:* college housing not available. *Activities and Organizations:* student-run newspaper, choral group. *Campus security:* late-night transport/escort service, part-time trained security personnel. *Student services:* health clinic, personal/psychological counseling, women's center.

Athletics Member NJCAA. *Intercollegiate sports:* baseball M, basketball M/W, soccer M/W, tennis M/W, volleyball W. *Intramural sports:* basketball M/W, cheerleading M(c)/W(c), golf M/W, ice hockey M(c)/W(c), lacrosse M/W, soccer M/W, softball W(c), tennis M/W, volleyball M(c)/W.

Standardized Tests *Required:* SAT or ACT (for admission).

Costs (2010–11) *Tuition:* state resident $11,892 full-time, $481 per credit part-time; nonresident $18,148 full-time, $756 per credit part-time. Full-time tuition and fees vary according to course level, degree level, location, program, and student level. Part-time tuition and fees vary according to course level, course load, degree level, location, program, and student level. *Required fees:* $838 full-time. *Payment plans:* installment, deferred payment. *Waivers:* employees or children of employees.

Financial Aid Of all full-time matriculated undergraduates who enrolled in 2008, 1,003 applied for aid, 750 were judged to have need, 33 had their need fully met. In 2008, 116 non-need-based awards were made. *Average percent of need met:* 58%. *Average financial aid package:* $9078. *Average need-based loan:* $3921. *Average need-based gift aid:* $6280. *Average non-need-based aid:* $2367. *Average indebtedness upon graduation:* $31,135.

Applying *Options:* electronic application, early admission, deferred entrance. *Application fee:* $50. *Required:* high school transcript. *Required for some:* interview. *Recommended:* essay or personal statement. *Application deadlines:* rolling (freshmen), rolling (transfers). *Notification:* continuous (freshmen), continuous (transfers).

Freshman Application Contact Admissions Office, Penn State Brandywine, 25 Yearsley Mill Road, Media, PA 19063-5596. *Phone:* 610-892-1200. *Fax:* 610-892-1320. *E-mail:* bwadmissions@psu.edu. *Web site:* http://www.brandywine.psu.edu/.

Penn State DuBois
DuBois, Pennsylvania

- **State-related** primarily 2-year, founded 1935, part of Pennsylvania State University
- **Small-town** 20-acre campus
- **Coed,** 919 undergraduate students, 78% full-time, 52% women, 48% men

Undergraduates 721 full-time, 198 part-time. 2% are from out of state; 0.9% Black or African American, non-Hispanic/Latino; 2% Hispanic/Latino; 0.3% Asian, non-Hispanic/Latino; 0.9% Two or more races, non-Hispanic/Latino; 1% Race/ethnicity unknown; 0.3% international; 3% transferred in. *Retention:* 73% of full-time freshmen returned.

Freshmen *Admission:* 313 applied, 207 enrolled. *Average high school GPA:* 2.9. *Test scores:* SAT critical reading scores over 500: 25%; SAT math scores over 500: 32%; SAT writing scores over 500: 24%; SAT critical reading scores over 600: 4%; SAT math scores over 600: 8%; SAT writing scores over 600: 2%.

Faculty *Total:* 87, 53% full-time, 43% with terminal degrees. *Student/faculty ratio:* 13:1.

Majors Accounting; acting; actuarial science; adult and continuing education administration; advertising; aerospace, aeronautical and astronautical/space engineering; African American/Black studies; agribusiness; agricultural and extension education; agricultural business and management related; agricultural engineering; agricultural mechanization; agriculture; agronomy and crop science; animal sciences; animal sciences related; anthropology; applied economics; archeology; architectural engineering; art; art history, criticism and conservation; art teacher education; Asian studies (East); astronomy; atmospheric sciences and meteorology; biochemistry; bioengineering and biomedical engineering; biological and biomedical sciences related; biological and physical sciences; biology/biological sciences; biology/biotechnology laboratory technician; biomedical technology; business administration and management; business/commerce; business/managerial economics; chemical engineering; chemistry; civil engineering; classics and classical languages; clinical/medical laboratory technology; communication and journalism related; communication sciences and disorders; comparative literature; computer and information sciences; computer engineering; criminal justice/law enforcement administration; economics; electrical and electronics engineering; electrical, electronic and communications engineering technology; elementary education; engineering science; English; environmental/environmental health engineering; film/cinema/video studies; finance; food science; foreign language teacher education; forest sciences and biology; forest technology; French; geography; geological and earth sciences/geosciences related; geology/earth science; German; graphic design; health/health-care administration; history; horticultural science; hospitality administration related; human development and family studies; human nutrition; industrial engineering; information science/studies; international business/trade/commerce; international relations and affairs; Italian; Japanese; Jewish/Judaic studies; journalism; kinesiology and exercise science; labor and industrial relations; landscaping and groundskeeping; Latin American studies; liberal arts and sciences/liberal studies; management information systems; marketing/marketing management; materials science; mathematics; mechanical engineering; mechanical engineering/mechanical technology; medical microbiology and bacteriology; medieval and Renaissance studies; metallurgical technology; mining and mineral engineering; music; natural resources and conservation related; natural resources/conservation; nuclear engineering; occupational therapist assistant; organizational behavior; parks, recreation and leisure facilities management; petroleum engineering; philosophy; physical therapy technology; physics; political science and government; premedical studies; psychology; registered nursing/registered nurse; rehabilitation and therapeutic professions related; religious studies; Russian; secondary education; sociology; soil science and agronomy; Spanish; special education; speech communication and rhetoric; statistics; telecommunications technology; theater design and technology; toxicology; turf and turfgrass management; visual and performing arts; wildlife, fish and wildlands science and management; women's studies.

Academics *Calendar:* semesters. *Degrees:* associate, bachelor's, and master's. *Special study options:* academic remediation for entering students, accelerated degree program, adult/continuing education programs, advanced placement credit, distance learning, double majors, honors programs, independent study, internships, services for LD students, student-designed majors, study abroad, summer session for credit.

Student Life *Housing:* college housing not available. *Activities and Organizations:* drama/theater group, student-run newspaper, choral group. *Student services:* health clinic, personal/psychological counseling, women's center.

Athletics Member NJCAA. *Intercollegiate sports:* basketball M, cross-country running M/W, golf M/W, volleyball W. *Intramural sports:* basketball M/W, football M, soccer M/W, table tennis M/W, volleyball M/W.

Standardized Tests *Required:* SAT or ACT (for admission).

Costs (2010–11) *Tuition:* state resident $11,892 full-time, $481 per credit part-time; nonresident $18,148 full-time, $756 per credit part-time. Full-time tuition and fees vary according to course level, degree level, location, program, and student level. Part-time tuition and fees vary according to course level, course load, degree level, location, program, and student level. *Required fees:* $704 full-time. *Payment plans:* installment, deferred payment. *Waivers:* employees or children of employees.

Financial Aid Of all full-time matriculated undergraduates who enrolled in 2008, 642 applied for aid, 586 were judged to have need, 29 had their need fully met. In 2008, 4 non-need-based awards were made. *Average percent of need met:* 61%. *Average financial aid package:* $10,851. *Average need-based loan:* $3821. *Average need-based gift aid:* $6569. *Average non-need-based aid:* $2000. *Average indebtedness upon graduation:* $31,135.

Applying *Options:* electronic application, early admission, deferred entrance. *Application fee:* $50. *Required:* high school transcript. *Required for some:*

interview. *Recommended:* essay or personal statement. *Application deadlines:* rolling (freshmen), rolling (transfers). *Notification:* continuous (freshmen), continuous (transfers).

Freshman Application Contact Admissions Office, Penn State DuBois, College Place, DuBois, PA 15801-3199. *Phone:* 814-375-4720. *Toll-free phone:* 800-346-7627. *Fax:* 814-375-4784. *E-mail:* duboisinfo@psi.edu. *Web site:* http://www.ds.psu.edu/.

Penn State Fayette, The Eberly Campus
Uniontown, Pennsylvania

- **State-related** primarily 2-year, founded 1934, part of Pennsylvania State University
- **Small-town** 92-acre campus
- **Coed,** 1,037 undergraduate students, 77% full-time, 59% women, 41% men

Undergraduates 802 full-time, 235 part-time. 3% are from out of state; 5% Black or African American, non-Hispanic/Latino; 1% Hispanic/Latino; 0.5% Asian, non-Hispanic/Latino; 0.2% American Indian or Alaska Native, non-Hispanic/Latino; 0.9% Two or more races, non-Hispanic/Latino; 3% Race/ethnicity unknown; 0.9% international; 5% transferred in. *Retention:* 77% of full-time freshmen returned.

Freshmen *Admission:* 458 applied, 248 enrolled. *Average high school GPA:* 3.04. *Test scores:* SAT critical reading scores over 500: 28%; SAT math scores over 500: 37%; SAT writing scores over 500: 22%; SAT critical reading scores over 600: 6%; SAT math scores over 600: 8%; SAT writing scores over 600: 5%; SAT critical reading scores over 700: 1%; SAT math scores over 700: 1%; SAT writing scores over 700: 1%.

Faculty *Total:* 92, 61% full-time, 38% with terminal degrees. *Student/faculty ratio:* 13:1.

Majors Accounting; acting; actuarial science; adult and continuing education administration; advertising; aerospace, aeronautical and astronautical/space engineering; African American/Black studies; agribusiness; agricultural and extension education; agricultural business and management related; agricultural engineering; agricultural mechanization; agriculture; agronomy and crop science; animal sciences; animal sciences related; anthropology; applied economics; archeology; architectural engineering; architectural engineering technology; art; art history, criticism and conservation; art teacher education; Asian studies (East); astronomy; atmospheric sciences and meteorology; biochemistry; bioengineering and biomedical engineering; biological and biomedical sciences related; biological and physical sciences; biology/biological sciences; biology/biotechnology laboratory technician; biomedical technology; business administration and management; business/commerce; business/managerial economics; chemical engineering; chemistry; civil engineering; classics and classical languages; communication and journalism related; communication sciences and disorders; comparative literature; computer and information sciences; computer engineering; criminal justice/law enforcement administration; criminal justice/safety; economics; electrical and electronics engineering; electrical, electronic and communications engineering technology; elementary education; engineering science; English; environmental/environmental health engineering; film/cinema/video studies; finance; food science; foreign language teacher education; forest sciences and biology; forest technology; French; geography; geological and earth sciences/geosciences related; geology/earth science; German; graphic design; health/health-care administration; history; horticultural science; hospitality administration related; human development and family studies; human nutrition; industrial engineering; information science/studies; international relations and affairs; Italian; Japanese; Jewish/Judaic studies; journalism; kinesiology and exercise science; labor and industrial relations; landscaping and groundskeeping; Latin American studies; liberal arts and sciences/liberal studies; logistics, materials, and supply chain management; management information systems; manufacturing engineering; marketing/marketing management; materials science; mathematics; mechanical engineering; medical microbiology and bacteriology; medieval and Renaissance studies; metallurgical technology; mining and mineral engineering; natural resources and conservation related; natural resources/conservation; nuclear engineering; organizational behavior; parks, recreation and leisure facilities management; petroleum engineering; philosophy; physics; political science and government; premedical studies; psychology; registered nursing/registered nurse; rehabilitation and therapeutic professions related; religious studies; Russian; secondary education; sociology; soil science and agronomy; Spanish; special education; speech communication and rhetoric; statistics; telecommunications technology; theater design and technology; toxicology; turf and turfgrass management; visual and performing arts; women's studies.

Academics *Calendar:* semesters. *Degrees:* associate and bachelor's. *Special study options:* academic remediation for entering students, accelerated degree program, adult/continuing education programs, advanced placement credit, distance learning, double majors, honors programs, independent study, internships, services for LD students, student-designed majors, study abroad, summer session for credit.

Student Life *Housing:* college housing not available. *Activities and Organizations:* drama/theater group. *Campus security:* student patrols, 8-hour patrols by trained security personnel. *Student services:* health clinic, personal/psychological counseling.

Athletics Member NJCAA. *Intercollegiate sports:* baseball M, basketball M, softball W, volleyball W. *Intramural sports:* badminton M/W, basketball M/W, cheerleading M(c)/W(c), equestrian sports M(c)/W(c), football M/W, golf M(c)/W(c), softball M/W, tennis M/W, volleyball M/W, weight lifting M/W.

Standardized Tests *Required:* SAT or ACT (for admission).

Costs (2010–11) *Tuition:* state resident $11,892 full-time, $481 per credit part-time; nonresident $18,148 full-time, $756 per credit part-time. Full-time tuition and fees vary according to course level, degree level, location, program, and student level. Part-time tuition and fees vary according to course level, course load, degree level, location, program, and student level. *Required fees:* $724 full-time. *Payment plans:* installment, deferred payment. *Waivers:* employees or children of employees.

Financial Aid Of all full-time matriculated undergraduates who enrolled in 2008, 677 applied for aid, 615 were judged to have need, 36 had their need fully met. In 2008, 23 non-need-based awards were made. *Average percent of need met:* 60%. *Average financial aid package:* $10,051. *Average need-based loan:* $3893. *Average need-based gift aid:* $6339. *Average non-need-based aid:* $2304. *Average indebtedness upon graduation:* $31,135.

Applying *Options:* electronic application, early admission, deferred entrance. *Application fee:* $50. *Required:* high school transcript. *Required for some:* interview. *Recommended:* essay or personal statement. *Application deadlines:* rolling (freshmen), rolling (transfers). *Notification:* continuous (freshmen), continuous (transfers).

Freshman Application Contact Admissions Office, Penn State Fayette, The Eberly Campus, 1 University Drive, PO Box 519, Uniontown, PA 15401-0519. *Phone:* 724-430-4130. *Toll-free phone:* 877-568-4130. *Fax:* 724-430-4175. *E-mail:* feadm@psu.edu. *Web site:* http://www.fe.psu.edu/.

Penn State Greater Allegheny

McKeesport, Pennsylvania

- **State-related** primarily 2-year, founded 1947, part of Pennsylvania State University
- **Small-town** 40-acre campus with easy access to Pittsburgh
- **Coed,** 768 undergraduate students, 86% full-time, 45% women, 55% men

Undergraduates 657 full-time, 111 part-time. 9% are from out of state; 28% Black or African American, non-Hispanic/Latino; 2% Hispanic/Latino; 3% Asian, non-Hispanic/Latino; 0.1% Native Hawaiian or other Pacific Islander, non-Hispanic/Latino; 0.1% American Indian or Alaska Native, non-Hispanic/Latino; 3% Two or more races, non-Hispanic/Latino; 2% Race/ethnicity unknown; 2% international; 3% transferred in; 27% live on campus. *Retention:* 69% of full-time freshmen returned.

Freshmen *Admission:* 569 applied, 279 enrolled. *Average high school GPA:* 2.8. *Test scores:* SAT critical reading scores over 500: 24%; SAT math scores over 500: 30%; SAT writing scores over 500: 21%; SAT critical reading scores over 600: 5%; SAT math scores over 600: 6%; SAT writing scores over 600: 4%; SAT math scores over 700: 1%.

Faculty *Total:* 63, 57% full-time, 49% with terminal degrees. *Student/faculty ratio:* 15:1.

Majors Accounting; acting; actuarial science; adult and continuing education administration; advertising; aerospace, aeronautical and astronautical/space engineering; African American/Black studies; agribusiness; agricultural and extension education; agricultural business and management related; agricultural engineering; agricultural mechanization; agriculture; agronomy and crop science; animal sciences; animal sciences related; anthropology; applied economics; archeology; architectural engineering; art; art history, criticism and conservation; art teacher education; Asian studies (East); astronomy; atmospheric sciences and meteorology; biochemistry; bioengineering and biomedical engineering; biological and biomedical sciences related; biological and physical sciences; biology/biological sciences; biology/biotechnology laboratory technician; business administration and management; business/commerce; business/managerial economics; chemical engineering; chemistry; civil engineering; classics and classical languages; communication and journalism related; communication sciences and disorders; comparative literature; computer and information sciences; computer engineering; criminal justice/law enforcement administration; economics; electrical and electronics engineering; elementary education; engineering science; English; environmental/environmental health engineering; film/cinema/video studies; finance; food science; foreign language teacher education; forest sciences and biology; forest technology; French; geography; geological and earth sciences/geosciences related; geology/earth science; German; graphic design; health/health-care administration; history; horticultural science; hospitality administration related; human development and family studies; human nutrition; industrial engineering;

information science/studies; international relations and affairs; Italian; Japanese; Jewish/Judaic studies; journalism; kinesiology and exercise science; labor and industrial relations; landscaping and groundskeeping; Latin American studies; liberal arts and sciences/liberal studies; logistics, materials, and supply chain management; management information systems; manufacturing engineering; marketing/marketing management; materials science; mathematics; mechanical engineering; medical microbiology and bacteriology; medieval and Renaissance studies; mining and mineral engineering; music; natural resources and conservation related; natural resources/conservation; nuclear engineering; organizational behavior; parks, recreation and leisure facilities management; petroleum engineering; philosophy; physics; political science and government; premedical studies; psychology; registered nursing/registered nurse; rehabilitation and therapeutic professions related; religious studies; Russian; secondary education; sociology; soil science and agronomy; Spanish; special education; speech communication and rhetoric; statistics; theater design and technology; toxicology; turf and turfgrass management; visual and performing arts; women's studies.

Academics *Calendar:* semesters. *Degrees:* certificates, associate, bachelor's, and master's. *Special study options:* academic remediation for entering students, adult/continuing education programs, advanced placement credit, distance learning, double majors, English as a second language, honors programs, independent study, internships, services for LD students, student-designed majors, study abroad, summer session for credit.

Student Life *Housing Options:* coed, disabled students. Campus housing is university owned. Freshman campus housing is guaranteed. *Activities and Organizations:* drama/theater group, student-run newspaper, radio and television station, choral group. *Campus security:* 24-hour patrols, controlled dormitory access. *Student services:* health clinic, personal/psychological counseling, women's center.

Athletics Member NJCAA. *Intercollegiate sports:* baseball M, basketball M, softball W, volleyball W. *Intramural sports:* basketball M/W, cheerleading M(c)/W(c), football M/W, ice hockey M(c), racquetball M/W, skiing (cross-country) M(c)/W(c), skiing (downhill) M(c)/W(c), soccer M(c)/W(c), softball M/W, tennis M/W, volleyball M/W.

Standardized Tests *Required:* SAT or ACT (for admission).

Costs (2010–11) *Tuition:* state resident $11,892 full-time, $481 per credit part-time; nonresident $18,148 full-time, $756 per credit part-time. Full-time tuition and fees vary according to course level, degree level, location, program, and student level. Part-time tuition and fees vary according to course level, course load, degree level, location, program, and student level. *Required fees:* $838 full-time. *Room and board:* $8370; room only: $4540. Room and board charges vary according to board plan, housing facility, and location. *Payment plans:* installment, deferred payment. *Waivers:* employees or children of employees.

Financial Aid Of all full-time matriculated undergraduates who enrolled in 2008, 544 applied for aid, 481 were judged to have need, 10 had their need fully met. In 2008, 27 non-need-based awards were made. *Average percent of need met:* 62%. *Average financial aid package:* $11,087. *Average need-based loan:* $3817. *Average need-based gift aid:* $7344. *Average non-need-based aid:* $3515. *Average indebtedness upon graduation:* $31,135.

Applying *Options:* electronic application, early admission, deferred entrance. *Application fee:* $50. *Required:* high school transcript. *Required for some:* interview. *Recommended:* essay or personal statement. *Application deadlines:* rolling (freshmen), rolling (transfers). *Notification:* continuous (freshmen), continuous (transfers).

Freshman Application Contact Admissions Office, Penn State Greater Allegheny, 4000 University Drive, McKeesport, PA 15132-7698. *Phone:* 412-675-9010. *Fax:* 412-675-9046. *E-mail:* psuga@psu.edu. *Web site:* http://www.ga.psu.edu/.

Penn State Hazleton

Hazleton, Pennsylvania

- **State-related** primarily 2-year, founded 1934, part of Pennsylvania State University
- **Small-town** 98-acre campus
- **Coed,** 1,245 undergraduate students, 96% full-time, 43% women, 57% men

Undergraduates 1,191 full-time, 54 part-time. 28% are from out of state; 3% transferred in; 38% live on campus. *Retention:* 79% of full-time freshmen returned.

Freshmen *Admission:* 1,514 applied, 564 enrolled. *Average high school GPA:* 2.81. *Test scores:* SAT critical reading scores over 500: 34%; SAT math scores over 500: 38%; SAT writing scores over 500: 29%; SAT critical reading scores over 600: 4%; SAT math scores over 600: 11%; SAT writing scores over 600: 5%; SAT math scores over 700: 1%.

Faculty *Total:* 85, 64% full-time, 45% with terminal degrees. *Student/faculty ratio:* 19:1.

Majors Accounting; acting; actuarial science; adult and continuing education administration; advertising; aerospace, aeronautical and astronautical/space engineering; African American/Black studies; agribusiness; agricultural and extension education; agricultural business and management related; agricultural engineering; agricultural mechanization; agriculture; agronomy and crop science; animal sciences; animal sciences related; anthropology; applied economics; archeology; architectural engineering; art; art history, criticism and conservation; art teacher education; Asian studies (East); astronomy; atmospheric sciences and meteorology; biochemistry; bioengineering and biomedical engineering; biological and biomedical sciences related; biological and physical sciences; biology/biological sciences; biology/biotechnology laboratory technician; biomedical technology; business administration and management; business/commerce; business/managerial economics; chemical engineering; chemistry; civil engineering; classics and classical languages; clinical/medical laboratory technology; communication and journalism related; communication sciences and disorders; comparative literature; computer and information sciences; computer engineering; criminal justice/law enforcement administration; economics; electrical and electronics engineering; electrical, electronic and communications engineering technology; elementary education; engineering science; English; environmental/environmental health engineering; film/cinema/video studies; finance; food science; forest sciences and biology; forest technology; French; geography; geological and earth sciences/geosciences related; geology/earth science; German; graphic design; health/health-care administration; history; horticultural science; hospitality administration related; human development and family studies; human nutrition; industrial engineering; information science/studies; international relations and affairs; Italian; Japanese; Jewish/Judaic studies; journalism; kinesiology and exercise science; labor and industrial relations; landscaping and groundskeeping; Latin American studies; liberal arts and sciences/liberal studies; logistics, materials, and supply chain management; management information systems; manufacturing engineering; marketing/marketing management; materials science; mathematics; mechanical engineering; mechanical engineering/mechanical technology; medical microbiology and bacteriology; medieval and Renaissance studies; metallurgical technology; mining and mineral engineering; music; natural resources and conservation related; natural resources/conservation; nuclear engineering; organizational behavior; parks, recreation and leisure facilities management; petroleum engineering; philosophy; physical therapy technology; physics; political science and government; premedical studies; psychology; registered nursing/registered nurse; rehabilitation and therapeutic professions related; religious studies; Russian; secondary education; sociology; soil science and agronomy; Spanish; special education; speech communication and rhetoric; statistics; telecommunications technology; theater design and technology; toxicology; turf and turfgrass management; visual and performing arts; women's studies.

Academics *Calendar:* semesters. *Degrees:* associate, bachelor's, and master's. *Special study options:* academic remediation for entering students, accelerated degree program, adult/continuing education programs, advanced placement credit, distance learning, double majors, English as a second language, honors programs, independent study, internships, services for LD students, student-designed majors, study abroad, summer session for credit. *ROTC:* Army (b), Air Force (c).

Student Life *Housing Options:* coed. Campus housing is university owned. Freshman campus housing is guaranteed. *Activities and Organizations:* drama/theater group, student-run newspaper, radio station, choral group. *Campus security:* 24-hour patrols, late-night transport/escort service, controlled dormitory access. *Student services:* health clinic, personal/psychological counseling, women's center, legal services.

Athletics Member NJCAA. *Intercollegiate sports:* baseball M, basketball M/W, cheerleading M/W, soccer M, softball W(s), tennis M/W, volleyball M/W. *Intramural sports:* basketball M/W, skiing (downhill) M(c)/W(c), soccer M/W, volleyball M/W.

Standardized Tests *Required:* SAT or ACT (for admission).

Costs (2010–11) *Tuition:* state resident $11,892 full-time, $481 per credit part-time; nonresident $18,148 full-time, $756 per credit part-time. Full-time tuition and fees vary according to course level, degree level, location, program, and student level. Part-time tuition and fees vary according to course level, course load, degree level, location, program, and student level. *Required fees:* $786 full-time. *Room and board:* $8370; room only: $4540. Room and board charges vary according to board plan, housing facility, and location. *Payment plans:* installment, deferred payment. *Waivers:* employees or children of employees.

Financial Aid Of all full-time matriculated undergraduates who enrolled in 2008, 1,031 applied for aid, 886 were judged to have need, 30 had their need fully met. In 2008, 93 non-need-based awards were made. *Average percent of need met:* 55%. *Average financial aid package:* $9388. *Average need-based loan:* $3692. *Average need-based gift aid:* $6639. *Average non-need-based aid:* $2689. *Average indebtedness upon graduation:* $31,135.

Applying *Options:* electronic application, early admission, deferred entrance. *Application fee:* $50. *Required:* high school transcript. *Required for some:* interview. *Recommended:* essay or personal statement. *Application deadlines:* rolling (freshmen), rolling (transfers). *Notification:* continuous (freshmen), continuous (transfers).

Freshman Application Contact Admissions Office, Penn State Hazleton, Hazleton, PA 18202-1291. *Phone:* 570-450-3142. *Toll-free phone:* 800-279-8495. *Fax:* 570-450-3182. *E-mail:* admissions-hn@psu.edu. *Web site:* http://www.hn.psu.edu/.

Penn State Lehigh Valley
Fogelsville, Pennsylvania

- **State-related** primarily 2-year, founded 1912, part of Pennsylvania State University
- **Small-town** 42-acre campus
- **Coed,** 914 undergraduate students, 77% full-time, 46% women, 54% men

Undergraduates 707 full-time, 207 part-time. 4% are from out of state; 3% Black or African American, non-Hispanic/Latino; 13% Hispanic/Latino; 7% Asian, non-Hispanic/Latino; 0.1% Native Hawaiian or other Pacific Islander, non-Hispanic/Latino; 0.4% American Indian or Alaska Native, non-Hispanic/Latino; 2% Two or more races, non-Hispanic/Latino; 3% Race/ethnicity unknown; 0.1% international; 7% transferred in. *Retention:* 72% of full-time freshmen returned.

Freshmen *Admission:* 483 applied, 279 enrolled. *Average high school GPA:* 2.89. *Test scores:* SAT critical reading scores over 500: 45%; SAT math scores over 500: 54%; SAT writing scores over 500: 37%; SAT critical reading scores over 600: 14%; SAT math scores over 600: 19%; SAT writing scores over 600: 6%; SAT critical reading scores over 700: 2%; SAT math scores over 700: 2%.

Faculty *Total:* 92, 36% full-time, 39% with terminal degrees. *Student/faculty ratio:* 15:1.

Majors Accounting; acting; actuarial science; adult and continuing education administration; advertising; aerospace, aeronautical and astronautical/space engineering; African American/Black studies; agribusiness; agricultural and extension education; agricultural business and management related; agricultural engineering; agricultural mechanization; agriculture; American studies; animal sciences; animal sciences related; anthropology; applied economics; archeology; architectural engineering; art; art history, criticism and conservation; art teacher education; Asian studies (East); astronomy; atmospheric sciences and meteorology; biochemistry; bioengineering and biomedical engineering; biological and biomedical sciences related; biological and physical sciences; biology/biological sciences; biology/biotechnology laboratory technician; business/commerce; business/managerial economics; chemical engineering; chemistry; civil engineering; classics and classical languages; communication and journalism related; communication sciences and disorders; comparative literature; computer and information sciences; computer engineering; criminal justice/law enforcement administration; economics; electrical and electronics engineering; elementary education; engineering science; English; environmental/environmental health engineering; film/cinema/video studies; finance; food science; foreign languages and literatures; forest sciences and biology; forest technology; French; geography; geological and earth sciences/geosciences related; geology/earth science; German; graphic design; health/health-care administration; history; horticultural science; hospitality administration related; human development and family studies; human nutrition; industrial engineering; information science/studies; international business/trade/commerce; international relations and affairs; Italian; Japanese; Jewish/Judaic studies; journalism; kinesiology and exercise science; labor and industrial relations; landscape architecture; landscaping and groundskeeping; Latin American studies; liberal arts and sciences/liberal studies; logistics, materials, and supply chain management; management information systems; management sciences and quantitative methods related; marketing/marketing management; materials science; mathematics; mechanical engineering; medical microbiology and bacteriology; medieval and Renaissance studies; mining and mineral engineering; natural resources and conservation related; natural resources/conservation; nuclear engineering; organizational behavior; parks, recreation and leisure facilities management; petroleum engineering; philosophy; physics; political science and government; premedical studies; professional, technical, business, and scientific writing; psychology; registered nursing/registered nurse; rehabilitation and therapeutic professions related; religious studies; Russian; secondary education; sociology; soil science and agronomy; Spanish; special education; speech communication and rhetoric; statistics; theater design and technology; turf and turfgrass management; visual and performing arts; women's studies.

Academics *Calendar:* semesters. *Degrees:* associate and bachelor's (enrollment figures include students enrolled at The Graduate School at Penn State who are taking courses at this location). *Special study options:* academic remediation for entering students, accelerated degree program, adult/continuing education programs, advanced placement credit, cooperative education, distance learning, honors programs, independent study, internships, services for LD students, study abroad, summer session for credit. *ROTC:* Army (c).

Student Life *Housing:* college housing not available. *Activities and Organizations:* drama/theater group, student-run newspaper.

Athletics Member NJCAA. *Intercollegiate sports:* baseball M, basketball M/W, bowling M(c)/W(c), cheerleading M/W, cross-country running M/W, football M(c), golf M(c)/W(c), ice hockey M(c)/W(c), skiing (downhill) M(c)/W(c), soccer M(c)/W, tennis M/W, volleyball M(c)/W. *Intramural sports:* badminton M/W, basketball M/W, football M/W, golf M/W, soccer M/W, volleyball M/W.

Standardized Tests *Required:* SAT or ACT (for admission).

Costs (2010–11) *Tuition:* state resident $11,892 full-time, $481 per credit part-time; nonresident $18,148 full-time, $756 per credit part-time. Full-time tuition and fees vary according to course level, degree level, location, program, and student level. Part-time tuition and fees vary according to course level, course load, degree level, location, program, and student level. *Required fees:* $828 full-time. *Payment plans:* installment, deferred payment. *Waivers:* employees or children of employees.

Financial Aid Of all full-time matriculated undergraduates who enrolled in 2008, 478 applied for aid, 382 were judged to have need, 13 had their need fully met. In 2008, 40 non-need-based awards were made. *Average percent of need met:* 58%. *Average financial aid package:* $9147. *Average need-based loan:* $3877. *Average need-based gift aid:* $6720. *Average non-need-based aid:* $2129. *Average indebtedness upon graduation:* $31,135.

Applying *Options:* electronic application, early admission, deferred entrance. *Application fee:* $50. *Required:* high school transcript. *Application deadlines:* rolling (freshmen), rolling (transfers). *Notification:* continuous (freshmen), continuous (transfers).

Freshman Application Contact Admissions Office, Penn State Lehigh Valley, 2809 Saucon Valley Road, Fogelsville, PA 18051-9999. *Phone:* 610-285-5000. *Fax:* 610-285-5220. *E-mail:* admissions-lv@psu.edu. *Web site:* http://www.lv.psu.edu/.

Penn State Mont Alto

Mont Alto, Pennsylvania

- **State-related** primarily 2-year, founded 1929, part of Pennsylvania State University
- **Small-town** 64-acre campus
- **Coed**, 1,252 undergraduate students, 76% full-time, 58% women, 42% men

Undergraduates 957 full-time, 295 part-time. 17% are from out of state; 12% Black or African American, non-Hispanic/Latino; 4% Hispanic/Latino; 1% Asian, non-Hispanic/Latino; 0.1% Native Hawaiian or other Pacific Islander, non-Hispanic/Latino; 0.3% American Indian or Alaska Native, non-Hispanic/Latino; 2% Two or more races, non-Hispanic/Latino; 2% Race/ethnicity unknown; 0.4% international; 6% transferred in; 34% live on campus. *Retention:* 79% of full-time freshmen returned.

Freshmen *Admission:* 595 applied, 417 enrolled. *Average high school GPA:* 2.9. *Test scores:* SAT critical reading scores over 500: 37%; SAT math scores over 500: 41%; SAT writing scores over 500: 29%; SAT critical reading scores over 600: 7%; SAT math scores over 600: 9%; SAT writing scores over 600: 3%; SAT critical reading scores over 700: 1%; SAT math scores over 700: 1%; SAT writing scores over 700: 1%.

Faculty *Total:* 121, 48% full-time, 35% with terminal degrees. *Student/faculty ratio:* 13:1.

Majors Accounting; acting; actuarial science; adult and continuing education administration; advertising; aerospace, aeronautical and astronautical/space engineering; African American/Black studies; agribusiness; agricultural and extension education; agricultural business and management related; agricultural engineering; agricultural mechanization; agriculture; agronomy and crop science; animal sciences; animal sciences related; anthropology; applied economics; archeology; architectural engineering; art; art history, criticism and conservation; art teacher education; Asian studies (East); astronomy; atmospheric sciences and meteorology; biochemistry; bioengineering and biomedical engineering; biological and biomedical sciences related; biological and physical sciences; biology/biological sciences; biology/biotechnology laboratory technician; business administration and management; business/commerce; business/managerial economics; chemical engineering; chemistry; civil engineering; classics and classical languages; communication and journalism related; communication sciences and disorders; comparative literature; computer and information sciences; computer engineering; criminal justice/law enforcement administration; economics; electrical and electronics engineering; elementary education; engineering science; English; environmental/environmental health engineering; film/cinema/video studies; finance; food science; foreign language teacher education; forest sciences and biology; forest technology; French; geography; geological and earth sciences/geosciences related; geology/earth science; German; graphic design; health/health-care administration; history; horticultural science; hospitality administration related; human development and family studies; human nutrition; industrial engineering; information science/studies; international relations and affairs; Italian; Japanese; Jewish/Judaic studies; journalism; kinesiology and exercise science; labor and industrial relations; landscaping and groundskeeping; Latin American studies; liberal arts and sciences/liberal studies; management information systems; marketing/marketing management; materials science; mathematics; mechanical engineering; medical microbiology and bacteriology; medieval

and Renaissance studies; mining and mineral engineering; music; natural resources and conservation related; natural resources/conservation; nuclear engineering; occupational therapist assistant; occupational therapy; organizational behavior; parks, recreation and leisure facilities management; petroleum engineering; philosophy; physical therapy technology; physics; political science and government; premedical studies; psychology; registered nursing/registered nurse; rehabilitation and therapeutic professions related; religious studies; Russian; secondary education; sociology; soil science and agronomy; Spanish; special education; speech communication and rhetoric; statistics; theater design and technology; toxicology; turf and turfgrass management; visual and performing arts; women's studies.

Academics *Calendar:* semesters. *Degrees:* associate and bachelor's. *Special study options:* academic remediation for entering students, accelerated degree program, adult/continuing education programs, advanced placement credit, distance learning, double majors, honors programs, independent study, internships, services for LD students, study abroad, summer session for credit. *ROTC:* Army (c).

Student Life *Housing Options:* coed, disabled students. Campus housing is university owned. Freshman campus housing is guaranteed. *Activities and Organizations:* drama/theater group, student-run newspaper. *Campus security:* 24-hour patrols, controlled dormitory access. *Student services:* health clinic, women's center.

Athletics Member NJCAA. *Intercollegiate sports:* basketball M/W, cheerleading M/W, cross-country running M/W, golf M/W, soccer M/W, softball W, tennis M/W, volleyball W. *Intramural sports:* badminton M/W, basketball M/W, cheerleading M(c)/W(c), racquetball M/W, soccer M/W, softball W, volleyball M/W.

Standardized Tests *Required:* SAT or ACT (for admission).

Costs (2010–11) *Tuition:* state resident $11,892 full-time, $481 per credit part-time; nonresident $18,148 full-time, $756 per credit part-time. Full-time tuition and fees vary according to course level, degree level, location, program, and student level. Part-time tuition and fees vary according to course level, course load, degree level, location, program, and student level. *Required fees:* $838 full-time. *Room and board:* $8370; room only: $4540. Room and board charges vary according to board plan, housing facility, and location. *Payment plans:* installment, deferred payment. *Waivers:* employees or children of employees.

Financial Aid Of all full-time matriculated undergraduates who enrolled in 2008, 774 applied for aid, 651 were judged to have need, 34 had their need fully met. In 2008, 47 non-need-based awards were made. *Average percent of need met:* 58%. *Average financial aid package:* $9783. *Average need-based loan:* $3768. *Average need-based gift aid:* $6075. *Average non-need-based aid:* $3204. *Average indebtedness upon graduation:* $31,135.

Applying *Options:* electronic application, early admission, deferred entrance. *Application fee:* $50. *Required:* high school transcript. *Required for some:* interview. *Recommended:* essay or personal statement. *Application deadlines:* rolling (freshmen), rolling (transfers). *Notification:* continuous (freshmen), continuous (transfers).

Freshman Application Contact Admissions Office, Penn State Mont Alto, 1 Campus Drive, Mont Alto, PA 17237-9703. *Phone:* 717-749-6130. *Toll-free phone:* 800-392-6173. *Fax:* 717-749-6132. *E-mail:* psuma@psu.edu. *Web site:* http://www.ma.psu.edu/.

Penn State New Kensington

New Kensington, Pennsylvania

- **State-related** primarily 2-year, founded 1958, part of Pennsylvania State University
- **Small-town** 71-acre campus with easy access to Pittsburgh
- **Coed**, 870 undergraduate students, 76% full-time, 40% women, 60% men

Undergraduates 657 full-time, 213 part-time. 17% are from out of state; 4% Black or African American, non-Hispanic/Latino; 1% Hispanic/Latino; 0.3% Asian, non-Hispanic/Latino; 0.1% American Indian or Alaska Native, non-Hispanic/Latino; 2% Two or more races, non-Hispanic/Latino; 2% Race/ethnicity unknown; 0.1% international; 5% transferred in; 29% live on campus. *Retention:* 75% of full-time freshmen returned.

Freshmen *Admission:* 552 applied, 226 enrolled. *Average high school GPA:* 2.68. *Test scores:* SAT critical reading scores over 500: 22%; SAT math scores over 500: 27%; SAT writing scores over 500: 18%; SAT critical reading scores over 600: 6%; SAT math scores over 600: 5%; SAT writing scores over 600: 4%; SAT critical reading scores over 700: 1%; SAT math scores over 700: 1%.

Faculty *Total:* 77, 57% full-time, 49% with terminal degrees. *Student/faculty ratio:* 17:1.

Majors Accounting; acting; actuarial science; adult and continuing education administration; advertising; aerospace, aeronautical and astronautical/space engineering; African American/Black studies; agribusiness; agricultural and extension education; agricultural business and management related; agricultural engineering; agricultural mechanization; agriculture; agronomy and crop science; animal sciences; animal sciences related; anthropology; applied economics; archeology; architectural engineering; art; art history, criticism and conservation; art teacher education; Asian studies (East); astronomy; atmospheric sciences and meteorology; biochemistry; bioengineering and biomedical engineering; biological and biomedical sciences related; biological and physical sciences; biology/biological sciences; biology/biotechnology laboratory technician; biomedical technology; business administration and management; business/commerce; business/managerial economics; chemical engineering; chemistry; civil engineering; classics and classical languages; communication and journalism related; communication sciences and disorders; comparative literature; computer and information sciences; computer engineering; computer engineering technology; criminal justice/law enforcement administration; economics; electrical and electronics engineering; electrical, electronic and communications engineering technology; elementary education; engineering science; English; environmental/environmental health engineering; film/cinema/video studies; finance; food science; forest sciences and biology; forest technology; French; geography; geological and earth sciences/geosciences related; geology/earth science; German; graphic design; health/health-care administration; history; horticultural science; hospitality administration related; human development and family studies; human nutrition; industrial engineering; information science/studies; international relations and affairs; Italian; Japanese; Jewish/Judaic studies; journalism; kinesiology and exercise science; labor and industrial relations; landscaping and groundskeeping; Latin American studies; liberal arts and sciences/liberal studies; logistics, materials, and supply chain management; management information systems; marketing/marketing management; materials science; mathematics; mechanical engineering; mechanical engineering/mechanical technology; medical microbiology and bacteriology; medical radiologic technology; medieval and Renaissance studies; metallurgical technology; mining and mineral engineering; music; natural resources and conservation related; natural resources/conservation; nuclear engineering; organizational behavior; parks, recreation and leisure facilities management; petroleum engineering; philosophy; physics; political science and government; premedical studies; psychology; registered nursing/registered nurse; rehabilitation and therapeutic professions related; religious studies; Russian; secondary education; sociology; soil science and agronomy; Spanish; special education; speech communication and rhetoric; statistics; telecommunications technology; theater design and technology; toxicology; turf and turfgrass management; visual and performing arts; women's studies.

Academics *Calendar:* semesters. *Degrees:* associate, bachelor's, and master's. *Special study options:* academic remediation for entering students, adult/continuing education programs, advanced placement credit, distance learning, double majors, honors programs, independent study, internships, services for LD students, study abroad, summer session for credit.

Student Life *Housing Options:* disabled students. *Activities and Organizations:* drama/theater group, student-run newspaper, choral group. *Campus security:* part-time trained security personnel. *Student services:* health clinic, women's center.

Athletics Member NJCAA. *Intercollegiate sports:* baseball M, basketball M/W, cheerleading M/W, golf M/W, softball W, volleyball W. *Intramural sports:* badminton M/W, basketball M/W, bowling M/W, cheerleading M(c)/W(c), football M/W, ice hockey M(c)/W(c), racquetball M/W, skiing (downhill) M(c)/W(c), soccer M/W, softball W, volleyball M/W.

Standardized Tests *Required:* SAT or ACT (for admission).

Costs (2010–11) *Tuition:* state resident $11,892 full-time, $481 per credit part-time; nonresident $18,148 full-time, $756 per credit part-time. Full-time tuition and fees vary according to course level, degree level, location, program, and student level. Part-time tuition and fees vary according to course level, course load, degree level, location, program, and student level. *Required fees:* $786 full-time. *Payment plans:* installment, deferred payment. *Waivers:* employees or children of employees.

Financial Aid Of all full-time matriculated undergraduates who enrolled in 2008, 776 applied for aid, 720 were judged to have need, 30 had their need fully met. In 2008, 15 non-need-based awards were made. *Average percent of need met:* 58%. *Average financial aid package:* $10,943. *Average need-based loan:* $3996. *Average need-based gift aid:* $7125. *Average non-need-based aid:* $2132. *Average indebtedness upon graduation:* $31,135.

Applying *Options:* electronic application, early admission, deferred entrance. *Application fee:* $50. *Required:* high school transcript. *Required for some:* interview. *Recommended:* essay or personal statement. *Application deadlines:* rolling (freshmen), rolling (transfers). *Notification:* continuous (freshmen), continuous (transfers).

Freshman Application Contact Admissions Office, Penn State New Kensington, 3550 Seventh Street Road, New Kensington, PA 15068. *Phone:* 724-334-5466. *Toll-free phone:* 888-968-7297. *Fax:* 724-334-6111. *E-mail:* nkadmissions@psu.edu. *Web site:* http://www.nk.psu.edu/.

Penn State Schuylkill
Schuylkill Haven, Pennsylvania

- **State-related** primarily 2-year, founded 1934, part of Pennsylvania State University
- **Small-town** 42-acre campus
- **Coed,** 1,034 undergraduate students, 85% full-time, 55% women, 45% men

Undergraduates 876 full-time, 158 part-time. 17% are from out of state; 29% Black or African American, non-Hispanic/Latino; 6% Hispanic/Latino; 3% Asian, non-Hispanic/Latino; 0.2% American Indian or Alaska Native, non-Hispanic/Latino; 2% Two or more races, non-Hispanic/Latino; 3% Race/ethnicity unknown; 0.5% international; 4% transferred in; 29% live on campus. *Retention:* 74% of full-time freshmen returned.
Freshmen *Admission:* 552 applied, 388 enrolled. *Average high school GPA:* 2.68. *Test scores:* SAT critical reading scores over 500: 20%; SAT math scores over 500: 21%; SAT writing scores over 500: 18%; SAT critical reading scores over 600: 4%; SAT math scores over 600: 3%; SAT writing scores over 600: 2%; SAT critical reading scores over 700: 1%.
Faculty *Total:* 77, 57% full-time, 49% with terminal degrees. *Student/faculty ratio:* 17:1.
Majors Accounting; acting; actuarial science; adult and continuing education administration; advertising; aerospace, aeronautical and astronautical/space engineering; African American/Black studies; agribusiness; agricultural and extension education; agricultural business and management related; agricultural engineering; agricultural mechanization; agriculture; American studies; animal sciences; animal sciences related; anthropology; applied economics; archeology; architectural engineering; art; art history, criticism and conservation; art teacher education; Asian studies (East); astronomy; atmospheric sciences and meteorology; biochemistry; bioengineering and biomedical engineering; biological and biomedical sciences related; biological and physical sciences; biology/biological sciences; biology/biotechnology laboratory technician; biomedical technology; business/commerce; business/managerial economics; chemical engineering; chemistry; civil engineering; classics and classical languages; clinical/medical laboratory technology; communication and journalism related; communication sciences and disorders; comparative literature; computer and information sciences; computer engineering; criminal justice/law enforcement administration; criminal justice/safety; economics; electrical and electronics engineering; electrical, electronic and communications engineering technology; elementary education; engineering science; English; environmental/environmental health engineering; film/cinema/video studies; finance; food science; forest sciences and biology; forest technology; French; geography; geological and earth sciences/geosciences related; geology/earth science; German; graphic design; health/health-care administration; history; horticultural science; hospitality administration related; human development and family studies; human nutrition; industrial engineering; information science/studies; international business/trade/commerce; international relations and affairs; Italian; Japanese; Jewish/Judaic studies; journalism; kinesiology and exercise science; labor and industrial relations; landscape architecture; landscaping and groundskeeping; Latin American studies; liberal arts and sciences/liberal studies; logistics, materials, and supply chain management; management information systems; management sciences and quantitative methods related; marketing/marketing management; materials science; mathematics; mechanical engineering; medical microbiology and bacteriology; medical radiologic technology; medieval and Renaissance studies; metallurgical technology; mining and mineral engineering; natural resources and conservation related; natural resources/conservation; nuclear engineering; organizational behavior; parks, recreation and leisure facilities management; petroleum engineering; philosophy; physics; political science and government; premedical studies; psychology; registered nursing/registered nurse; rehabilitation and therapeutic professions related; religious studies; Russian; secondary education; sociology; soil science and agronomy; Spanish; special education; speech communication and rhetoric; statistics; telecommunications technology; theater design and technology; turf and turfgrass management; visual and performing arts; women's studies.
Academics *Calendar:* semesters. *Degrees:* certificates, associate, and bachelor's (bachelor's degree programs completed at the Harrisburg campus). *Special study options:* academic remediation for entering students, accelerated degree program, adult/continuing education programs, advanced placement credit, cooperative education, distance learning, double majors, honors programs, independent study, internships, services for LD students, student-designed majors, study abroad, summer session for credit.
Student Life *Housing Options:* disabled students. Campus housing is provided by a third party. Freshman campus housing is guaranteed. *Activities and Organizations:* drama/theater group, student-run newspaper, choral group. *Campus security:* 24-hour patrols, controlled dormitory access.
Athletics Member NJCAA. *Intercollegiate sports:* basketball M, cross-country running M/W, golf M, soccer M, softball W, volleyball W. *Intramural sports:* basketball M/W, football M, soccer M/W, softball M/W, table tennis M/W, volleyball M/W.

Standardized Tests *Required:* SAT or ACT (for admission).

Costs (2010–11) *Tuition:* state resident $11,892 full-time, $481 per credit part-time; nonresident $18,148 full-time, $756 per credit part-time. Full-time tuition and fees vary according to course level, degree level, location, program, and student level. Part-time tuition and fees vary according to course level, course load, degree level, location, program, and student level. *Required fees:* $734 full-time. *Payment plans:* installment, deferred payment. *Waivers:* employees or children of employees.

Financial Aid Of all full-time matriculated undergraduates who enrolled in 2008, 776 applied for aid, 720 were judged to have need, 30 had their need fully met. In 2008, 15 non-need-based awards were made. *Average percent of need met:* 58%. *Average financial aid package:* $10,943. *Average need-based loan:* $3996. *Average need-based gift aid:* $7125. *Average non-need-based aid:* $2132. *Average indebtedness upon graduation:* $31,135.

Applying *Options:* electronic application, early admission, deferred entrance. *Application fee:* $50. *Required:* high school transcript. *Application deadlines:* rolling (freshmen), rolling (transfers). *Notification:* continuous (freshmen), continuous (transfers).

Freshman Application Contact Admissions Office, Penn State Schuylkill, 200 University Drive, Schuylkill Haven, PA 17972-2208. *Phone:* 570-385-6252. *Fax:* 570-385-6272. *E-mail:* sl-admissions@psu.edu. *Web site:* http://www.sl.psu.edu/.

Penn State Shenango
Sharon, Pennsylvania

- **State-related** primarily 2-year, founded 1965, part of Pennsylvania State University
- **Small-town** 14-acre campus
- **Coed,** 714 undergraduate students, 63% full-time, 63% women, 37% men

Undergraduates 450 full-time, 264 part-time. 17% are from out of state; 8% Black or African American, non-Hispanic/Latino; 2% Hispanic/Latino; 0.7% Asian, non-Hispanic/Latino; 0.2% American Indian or Alaska Native, non-Hispanic/Latino; 0.8% Two or more races, non-Hispanic/Latino; 3% Race/ethnicity unknown; 0.2% international; 5% transferred in. *Retention:* 58% of full-time freshmen returned.

Freshmen *Admission:* 217 applied, 108 enrolled. *Average high school GPA:* 2.83. *Test scores:* SAT critical reading scores over 500: 22%; SAT math scores over 500: 25%; SAT writing scores over 500: 10%; SAT critical reading scores over 600: 1%; SAT math scores over 600: 4%; SAT math scores over 700: 3%.

Faculty *Total:* 71, 42% full-time, 34% with terminal degrees. *Student/faculty ratio:* 12:1.

Majors Accounting; acting; actuarial science; adult and continuing education administration; advertising; aerospace, aeronautical and astronautical/space engineering; African American/Black studies; agribusiness; agricultural and extension education; agricultural business and management related; agricultural engineering; agricultural mechanization; agriculture; agronomy and crop science; animal sciences; animal sciences related; anthropology; applied economics; archeology; architectural engineering; art; art history, criticism and conservation; art teacher education; Asian studies (East); astronomy; atmospheric sciences and meteorology; biochemistry; bioengineering and biomedical engineering; biological and biomedical sciences related; biological and physical sciences; biology/biological sciences; biology/biotechnology laboratory technician; biomedical technology; business administration and management; business/commerce; business/managerial economics; chemical engineering; chemistry; civil engineering; classics and classical languages; communication and journalism related; communication sciences and disorders; comparative literature; computer and information sciences; computer engineering; criminal justice/law enforcement administration; economics; electrical and electronics engineering; electrical, electronic and communications engineering technology; elementary education; engineering science; English; environmental/environmental health engineering; film/cinema/video studies; finance; food science; foreign language teacher education; forest sciences and biology; forest technology; French; geography; geological and earth sciences/geosciences related; geology/earth science; German; graphic design; health/health-care administration; history; horticultural science; hospitality administration related; human development and family studies; human nutrition; industrial engineering; information science/studies; international relations and affairs; Italian; Japanese; Jewish/Judaic studies; journalism; kinesiology and exercise science; labor and industrial relations; landscaping and groundskeeping; Latin American studies; liberal arts and sciences/liberal studies; logistics, materials, and supply chain management; management information systems; marketing/marketing management; materials science; mathematics; mechanical engineering; mechanical engineering/mechanical technology; medical microbiology and bacteriology; medieval and Renaissance studies; metallurgical technology; mining and mineral engineering; music; natural resources and conservation related; natural resources/conservation; nuclear engineering; organizational behavior; parks, recreation and leisure facilities management; petroleum engineering; philosophy; physical therapy technology; physics;

political science and government; premedical studies; psychology; registered nursing/registered nurse; rehabilitation and therapeutic professions related; religious studies; Russian; secondary education; sociology; soil science and agronomy; Spanish; special education; speech communication and rhetoric; statistics; telecommunications technology; theater design and technology; toxicology; turf and turfgrass management; visual and performing arts; women's studies.

Academics *Calendar:* semesters. *Degrees:* certificates, associate, and bachelor's. *Special study options:* academic remediation for entering students, accelerated degree program, adult/continuing education programs, advanced placement credit, distance learning, double majors, honors programs, independent study, internships, services for LD students, student-designed majors, study abroad, summer session for credit.

Student Life *Housing:* college housing not available. *Activities and Organizations:* choral group. *Campus security:* part-time trained security personnel. *Student services:* health clinic, women's center.

Athletics *Intramural sports:* basketball M(c)/W, bowling M/W, football M(c), golf M/W, softball M/W, tennis M/W, volleyball M/W.

Standardized Tests *Required:* SAT or ACT (for admission).

Costs (2010–11) *Tuition:* state resident $11,892 full-time, $481 per credit part-time; nonresident $18,148 full-time, $756 per credit part-time. Full-time tuition and fees vary according to course level, degree level, location, program, and student level. Part-time tuition and fees vary according to course level, course load, degree level, location, program, and student level. *Required fees:* $630 full-time. *Payment plans:* installment, deferred payment. *Waivers:* employees or children of employees.

Financial Aid Of all full-time matriculated undergraduates who enrolled in 2008, 438 applied for aid, 410 were judged to have need, 18 had their need fully met. In 2008, 10 non-need-based awards were made. *Average percent of need met:* 56%. *Average financial aid package:* $10,771. *Average need-based loan:* $3779. *Average need-based gift aid:* $6548. *Average non-need-based aid:* $2569. *Average indebtedness upon graduation:* $31,135.

Applying *Options:* electronic application, early admission, deferred entrance. *Application fee:* $50. *Required:* high school transcript. *Required for some:* interview. *Recommended:* essay or personal statement. *Application deadlines:* rolling (freshmen), rolling (transfers). *Notification:* continuous (freshmen), continuous (transfers).

Freshman Application Contact Admissions Office, Penn State Shenango, 147 Shenango Avenue, Sharon, PA 16146-1537. *Phone:* 724-983-2803. *Fax:* 724-983-2820. *E-mail:* psushenango@psu.edu. *Web site:* http://www.shenango.psu.edu/.

Penn State Wilkes-Barre
Lehman, Pennsylvania

- **State-related** primarily 2-year, founded 1916, part of Pennsylvania State University
- **Rural** 156-acre campus
- **Coed,** 719 undergraduate students, 85% full-time, 30% women, 70% men

Undergraduates 609 full-time, 110 part-time. 5% are from out of state; 4% Black or African American, non-Hispanic/Latino; 3% Hispanic/Latino; 2% Asian, non-Hispanic/Latino; 0.2% American Indian or Alaska Native, non-Hispanic/Latino; 1% Two or more races, non-Hispanic/Latino; 1% Race/ethnicity unknown; 0.2% international; 3% transferred in. *Retention:* 80% of full-time freshmen returned.

Freshmen *Admission:* 333 applied, 208 enrolled. *Average high school GPA:* 2.91. *Test scores:* SAT critical reading scores over 500: 40%; SAT math scores over 500: 39%; SAT writing scores over 500: 29%; SAT critical reading scores over 600: 6%; SAT math scores over 600: 12%; SAT writing scores over 600: 3%; SAT critical reading scores over 700: 1%; SAT math scores over 700: 1%.

Faculty *Total:* 63, 57% full-time, 44% with terminal degrees. *Student/faculty ratio:* 15:1.

Majors Accounting; acting; actuarial science; adult and continuing education administration; advertising; aerospace, aeronautical and astronautical/space engineering; African American/Black studies; agribusiness; agricultural and extension education; agricultural business and management related; agricultural engineering; agricultural mechanization; agriculture; agronomy and crop science; animal sciences; animal sciences related; anthropology; applied economics; archeology; architectural engineering; art; art history, criticism and conservation; art teacher education; astronomy; atmospheric sciences and meteorology; biochemistry; bioengineering and biomedical engineering; biological and biomedical sciences related; biological and physical sciences; biology/biological sciences; biology/biotechnology laboratory technician; business administration and management; business/commerce; business/managerial economics; chemical engineering; chemistry; civil engineering; classics and classical languages; communication and journalism related; communication sciences and disorders; comparative literature; computer and information sciences; computer engineering; criminal justice/law enforcement administration; criminal justice/safety; economics; electrical and electronics engineering; electrical, electronic and communications engineering technology; elementary education; engineering science; English; environmental/environmental health engineering; film/cinema/video studies; finance; food science; forest sciences and biology; forest technology; French; geography; geological and earth sciences/geosciences related; geology/earth science; German; graphic design; health/health-care administration; history; horticultural science; hospitality administration related; human development and family studies; human nutrition; industrial engineering; information science/studies; international relations and affairs; Italian; Japanese; Jewish/Judaic studies; journalism; kinesiology and exercise science; labor and industrial relations; landscape architecture; landscaping and groundskeeping; Latin American studies; liberal arts and sciences/liberal studies; management information systems; manufacturing engineering; marketing/marketing management; materials science; mathematics; mechanical engineering; medical microbiology and bacteriology; medieval and Renaissance studies; metallurgical technology; mining and mineral engineering; music; natural resources and conservation related; natural resources/conservation; nuclear engineering; organizational behavior; parks, recreation and leisure facilities management; petroleum engineering; philosophy; physics; political science and government; premedical studies; psychology; registered nursing/registered nurse; rehabilitation and therapeutic professions related; religious studies; Russian; secondary education; sociology; soil science and agronomy; Spanish; special education; speech communication and rhetoric; statistics; surveying technology; telecommunications technology; theater design and technology; toxicology; turf and turfgrass management; visual and performing arts; women's studies.

Academics *Calendar:* semesters. *Degrees:* certificates, associate, and bachelor's (enrollment figures include students enrolled at The Graduate School at Penn State who are taking courses at this location). *Special study options:* academic remediation for entering students, accelerated degree program, adult/continuing education programs, advanced placement credit, distance learning, double majors, honors programs, independent study, internships, services for LD students, student-designed majors, study abroad, summer session for credit. *ROTC:* Army (c), Air Force (c).

Student Life *Housing:* college housing not available. *Activities and Organizations:* student-run newspaper, radio station. *Campus security:* part-time trained security personnel. *Student services:* health clinic, personal/psychological counseling.

Athletics Member NJCAA. *Intercollegiate sports:* baseball M, basketball M, cross-country running M/W, golf M/W, soccer M/W, volleyball W. *Intramural sports:* basketball M/W, bowling M(c)/W(c), cheerleading M(c)/W(c), football M, racquetball M/W, softball W, volleyball M(c)/W.

Standardized Tests *Required:* SAT or ACT (for admission).

Costs (2010–11) *Tuition:* state resident $11,892 full-time, $481 per credit part-time; nonresident $18,148 full-time, $756 per credit part-time. Full-time tuition and fees vary according to course level, degree level, location, program, and student level. Part-time tuition and fees vary according to course level, course load, degree level, location, program, and student level. *Required fees:* $724 full-time. *Payment plans:* installment, deferred payment. *Waivers:* employees or children of employees.

Financial Aid Of all full-time matriculated undergraduates who enrolled in 2008, 495 applied for aid, 408 were judged to have need, 16 had their need fully met. In 2008, 40 non-need-based awards were made. *Average percent of need met:* 59%. *Average financial aid package:* $9495. *Average need-based loan:* $3920. *Average need-based gift aid:* $6367. *Average non-need-based aid:* $2415. *Average indebtedness upon graduation:* $31,135.

Applying *Options:* electronic application, early admission, deferred entrance. *Application fee:* $50. *Required:* high school transcript. *Required for some:* interview. *Recommended:* essay or personal statement. *Application deadlines:* rolling (freshmen), rolling (transfers). *Notification:* continuous (freshmen), continuous (transfers).

Freshman Application Contact Admissions Office, Penn State Wilkes-Barre, PO PSU, Lehman, PA 18627-0217. *Phone:* 570-675-9238. *Toll-free phone:* 800-966-6613. *Fax:* 570-675-9113. *E-mail:* wbadmissions@psu.edu. *Web site:* http://www.wb.psu.edu/.

Penn State Worthington Scranton

Dunmore, Pennsylvania

- **State-related** primarily 2-year, founded 1923, part of Pennsylvania State University
- **Small-town** 43-acre campus
- **Coed,** 1,386 undergraduate students, 79% full-time, 52% women, 48% men

Undergraduates 1,096 full-time, 290 part-time. 2% are from out of state; 2% Black or African American, non-Hispanic/Latino; 4% Hispanic/Latino; 3% Asian, non-Hispanic/Latino; 0.1% American Indian or Alaska Native, non-Hispanic/Latino; 2% Two or more races, non-Hispanic/Latino; 3% Race/ethnicity unknown; 0.2% international; 5% transferred in. *Retention:* 69% of full-time freshmen returned.

Freshmen *Admission:* 587 applied, 362 enrolled. *Average high school GPA:* 2.83. *Test scores:* SAT critical reading scores over 500: 33%; SAT math scores over 500: 38%; SAT writing scores over 500: 28%; SAT critical reading scores over 600: 5%; SAT math scores over 600: 12%; SAT writing scores over 600: 5%; SAT critical reading scores over 700: 1%; SAT writing scores over 700: 1%.

Faculty *Total:* 103, 54% full-time, 39% with terminal degrees. *Student/faculty ratio:* 17:1.

Majors Accounting; acting; actuarial science; adult and continuing education administration; advertising; aerospace, aeronautical and astronautical/space engineering; African American/Black studies; agribusiness; agricultural and extension education; agricultural business and management related; agricultural engineering; agricultural mechanization; agriculture; agronomy and crop science; American studies; animal sciences; animal sciences related; anthropology; applied economics; archeology; architectural engineering; architectural engineering technology; art; art history, criticism and conservation; art teacher education; Asian studies (East); astronomy; atmospheric sciences and meteorology; biochemistry; bioengineering and biomedical engineering; biological and biomedical sciences related; biological and physical sciences; biology/biological sciences; biology/biotechnology laboratory technician; business administration and management; business/commerce; business/managerial economics; chemical engineering; chemistry; civil engineering; classics and classical languages; communication and journalism related; communication sciences and disorders; comparative literature; computer and information sciences; computer engineering; criminal justice/law enforcement administration; economics; electrical and electronics engineering; electrical, electronic and communications engineering technology; elementary education; engineering science; English; environmental/environmental health engineering; film/cinema/video studies; finance; food science; foreign language teacher education; forest sciences and biology; forest technology; French; geography; geological and earth sciences/geosciences related; geology/earth science; German; graphic design; health/health-care administration; history; horticultural science; hospitality administration related; human development and family studies; human nutrition; industrial engineering; information science/studies; international relations and affairs; Italian; Japanese; Jewish/Judaic studies; journalism; kinesiology and exercise science; labor and industrial relations; landscaping and groundskeeping; Latin American studies; liberal arts and sciences/liberal studies; management information systems; marketing/marketing management; materials science; mathematics; mechanical engineering; medical microbiology and bacteriology; medieval and Renaissance studies; mining and mineral engineering; music; natural resources and conservation related; natural resources/conservation; nuclear engineering; organizational behavior; parks, recreation and leisure facilities management; petroleum engineering; philosophy; physics; political science and government; premedical studies; psychology; registered nursing/registered nurse; rehabilitation and therapeutic professions related; religious studies; Russian; secondary education; sociology; soil science and agronomy; Spanish; special education; speech communication and rhetoric; statistics; theater design and technology; turf and turfgrass management; visual and performing arts; women's studies.

Academics *Calendar:* semesters. *Degrees:* certificates, associate, and bachelor's. *Special study options:* academic remediation for entering students, accelerated degree program, adult/continuing education programs, advanced placement credit, cooperative education, distance learning, double majors, honors programs, independent study, internships, services for LD students, study abroad, summer session for credit. *ROTC:* Army (c), Air Force (c).

Student Life *Housing:* college housing not available. *Activities and Organizations:* drama/theater group, student-run newspaper, choral group. *Campus security:* part-time trained security personnel. *Student services:* health clinic, personal/psychological counseling, women's center.

Athletics Member NJCAA. *Intercollegiate sports:* baseball M, basketball M/W, cheerleading M/W, cross-country running M/W, soccer M, softball W, volleyball W. *Intramural sports:* basketball M/W, bowling M(c)/W(c), skiing (downhill) M(c)/W(c), soccer M/W, softball M/W, volleyball M/W(c), weight lifting M(c)/W(c).

Standardized Tests *Required:* SAT or ACT (for admission).

Costs (2010–11) *Tuition:* state resident $11,892 full-time, $481 per credit part-time; nonresident $18,148 full-time, $756 per credit part-time. Full-time tuition and fees vary according to course level, degree level, location, program, and student level. Part-time tuition and fees vary according to course level, course load, degree level, location, program, and student level. *Required fees:* $704 full-time. *Payment plans:* installment, deferred payment. *Waivers:* employees or children of employees.

Financial Aid Of all full-time matriculated undergraduates who enrolled in 2008, 904 applied for aid, 760 were judged to have need, 26 had their need fully met. In 2008, 54 non-need-based awards were made. *Average percent of need met:* 59%. *Average financial aid package:* $9067. *Average need-based loan:* $3888. *Average need-based gift aid:* $6009. *Average non-need-based aid:* $2838. *Average indebtedness upon graduation:* $31,135.

Applying *Options:* electronic application, early admission, deferred entrance. *Application fee:* $50. *Required:* high school transcript. *Required for some:*

interview. *Recommended:* essay or personal statement. *Application deadlines:* rolling (freshmen), rolling (transfers). *Notification:* continuous (freshmen), continuous (transfers).

Freshman Application Contact Admissions Office, Penn State Worthington Scranton, 120 Ridge View Drive, Dunmore, PA 18512-1699. *Phone:* 570-963-2500. *Fax:* 570-963-2524. *E-mail:* wsadmissions@psu.edu. *Web site:* http://www.sn.psu.edu/.

Penn State York

York, Pennsylvania

- **State-related** primarily 2-year, founded 1926, part of Pennsylvania State University
- **Suburban** 53-acre campus
- **Coed,** 1,393 undergraduate students, 68% full-time, 43% women, 57% men

Undergraduates 948 full-time, 445 part-time. 7% are from out of state; 7% Black or African American, non-Hispanic/Latino; 6% Hispanic/Latino; 5% Asian, non-Hispanic/Latino; 0.1% Native Hawaiian or other Pacific Islander, non-Hispanic/Latino; 0.2% American Indian or Alaska Native, non-Hispanic/Latino; 2% Two or more races, non-Hispanic/Latino; 2% Race/ethnicity unknown; 4% international; 4% transferred in. *Retention:* 76% of full-time freshmen returned.

Freshmen *Admission:* 678 applied, 325 enrolled. *Average high school GPA:* 2.85. *Test scores:* SAT critical reading scores over 500: 38%; SAT math scores over 500: 53%; SAT writing scores over 500: 32%; SAT critical reading scores over 600: 9%; SAT math scores over 600: 17%; SAT writing scores over 600: 6%; SAT math scores over 700: 2%.

Faculty *Total:* 112, 53% full-time, 42% with terminal degrees. *Student/faculty ratio:* 15:1.

Majors Accounting; acting; actuarial science; adult and continuing education administration; advertising; aerospace, aeronautical and astronautical/space engineering; African American/Black studies; agribusiness; agricultural and extension education; agricultural business and management related; agricultural engineering; agricultural mechanization; agriculture; agronomy and crop science; American studies; animal sciences; animal sciences related; anthropology; applied economics; archeology; architectural engineering; art; art history, criticism and conservation; art teacher education; Asian studies (East); astronomy; atmospheric sciences and meteorology; biochemistry; bioengineering and biomedical engineering; biological and biomedical sciences related; biological and physical sciences; biology/biological sciences; biology/biotechnology laboratory technician; biomedical technology; business administration and management; business/commerce; business/managerial economics; chemical engineering; chemistry; civil engineering; classics and classical languages; communication and journalism related; communication sciences and disorders; comparative literature; computer and information sciences; computer engineering; criminal justice/law enforcement administration; economics; electrical and electronics engineering; electrical, electronic and communications engineering technology; elementary education; engineering science; English; environmental/environmental health engineering; film/cinema/video studies; finance; food science; foreign language teacher education; forest sciences and biology; forest technology; French; geography; geological and earth sciences/geosciences related; geology/earth science; German; graphic design; health/health-care administration; history; horticultural science; hospitality administration related; human development and family studies; human nutrition; industrial engineering; industrial technology; information science/studies; international relations and affairs; Italian; Japanese; Jewish/Judaic studies; journalism; kinesiology and exercise science; labor and industrial relations; landscaping and groundskeeping; Latin American studies; liberal arts and sciences/liberal studies; logistics, materials, and supply chain management; management information systems; manufacturing engineering; marketing/marketing management; materials science; mathematics; mechanical engineering; mechanical engineering/mechanical technology; medical microbiology and bacteriology; medieval and Renaissance studies; metallurgical technology; mining and mineral engineering; music; natural resources and conservation related; natural resources/conservation; nuclear engineering; organizational behavior; parks, recreation and leisure facilities management; petroleum engineering; philosophy; physics; political science and government; premedical studies; psychology; registered nursing/registered nurse; rehabilitation and therapeutic professions related; religious studies; Russian; secondary education; sociology; soil science and agronomy; Spanish; special education; speech communication and rhetoric; statistics; telecommunications technology; theater design and technology; toxicology; turf and turfgrass management; visual and performing arts; women's studies.

Academics *Calendar:* semesters. *Degrees:* certificates, associate, bachelor's, and master's (also offers up to 2 years of most bachelor's degree programs offered at University Park campus). *Special study options:* academic remediation for entering students, accelerated degree program, adult/continuing education programs, advanced placement credit, distance learning, double majors, English as a second language, honors programs, independent study, intern-

ships, services for LD students, student-designed majors, study abroad, summer session for credit.

Student Life *Housing:* college housing not available. *Activities and Organizations:* drama/theater group, student-run newspaper. *Campus security:* part-time trained security personnel. *Student services:* health clinic, personal/psychological counseling, women's center.

Athletics Member NJCAA.

Standardized Tests *Required:* SAT or ACT (for admission).

Costs (2010–11) *Tuition:* state resident $11,892 full-time, $481 per credit part-time; nonresident $18,148 full-time, $756 per credit part-time. Full-time tuition and fees vary according to course level, degree level, location, program, and student level. Part-time tuition and fees vary according to course level, course load, degree level, location, program, and student level. *Required fees:* $704 full-time. *Payment plans:* installment, deferred payment. *Waivers:* employees or children of employees.

Financial Aid Of all full-time matriculated undergraduates who enrolled in 2008, 758 applied for aid, 597 were judged to have need, 33 had their need fully met. In 2008, 59 non-need-based awards were made. *Average percent of need met:* 58%. *Average financial aid package:* $9160. *Average need-based loan:* $3819. *Average need-based gift aid:* $5905. *Average non-need-based aid:* $2670. *Average indebtedness upon graduation:* $31,135.

Applying *Options:* electronic application, early admission, deferred entrance. *Application fee:* $50. *Required:* high school transcript. *Required for some:* interview. *Recommended:* essay or personal statement. *Application deadlines:* rolling (freshmen), rolling (transfers). *Notification:* continuous (freshmen), continuous (transfers).

Freshman Application Contact Admissions Office, Penn State York, 1031 Edgecomb Avenue, York, PA 17403-3398. *Phone:* 717-771-4040. *Toll-free phone:* 800-778-6227. *Fax:* 717-771-4005. *E-mail:* ykadmissions@psu.edu. *Web site:* http://www.yk.psu.edu/.

Pennsylvania Highlands Community College

Johnstown, Pennsylvania

- **State and locally supported** 2-year, founded 1994
- **Small-town** campus
- **Coed,** 2,543 undergraduate students, 38% full-time, 57% women, 43% men

Undergraduates 955 full-time, 1,588 part-time. Students come from 4 states and territories; 2% are from out of state. *Retention:* 34% of full-time freshmen returned.

Faculty *Student/faculty ratio:* 13:1.

Majors Accounting; banking and financial support services; computer and information sciences; computer and information sciences and support services related; computer/information technology services administration related; computer programming; computer programming related; computer programming (specific applications); construction engineering technology; consumer merchandising/retailing management; court reporting; electrical, electronic and communications engineering technology; environmental engineering technology; general studies; geography; health/health-care administration; heating, ventilation, air conditioning and refrigeration engineering technology; hospitality administration; human services; industrial technology; liberal arts and sciences/liberal studies; network and system administration; web/multimedia management and webmaster.

Academics *Calendar:* semesters. *Degree:* certificates, diplomas, and associate. *Special study options:* academic remediation for entering students, adult/continuing education programs, advanced placement credit, cooperative education, distance learning, honors programs, independent study, internships, part-time degree program, services for LD students.

Library Pennsylvania Highlands Community College Main Library plus 1 other with an OPAC, a Web page.

Student Life *Housing:* college housing not available.

Athletics Member NJCAA. *Intercollegiate sports:* basketball M, volleyball W.

Costs (2011–12) *Tuition:* area resident $3800 full-time, $95 per credit part-time; state resident $6730 full-time, $192 per credit part-time; nonresident $9450 full-time, $282 per credit part-time. Full-time tuition and fees vary according to course load and reciprocity agreements. Part-time tuition and fees vary according to course load and reciprocity agreements. *Required fees:* $950 full-time, $30 per credit part-time. *Payment plan:* installment. *Waivers:* employees or children of employees.

Financial Aid Of all full-time matriculated undergraduates who enrolled in 2009, 25 Federal Work-Study jobs (averaging $2500).

Applying *Application fee:* $20.

Freshman Application Contact Mr. Jeff Maul, Admissions Officer, Pennsylvania Highlands Community College, 101 Community College Way, Johnstown, PA 15904. *Phone:* 814-262-6431. *E-mail:* jmaul@pennhighlands.edu. *Web site:* http://www.pennhighlands.edu/.

Pennsylvania Institute of Technology

Media, Pennsylvania

- **Independent** 2-year, founded 1953
- **Small-town** 12-acre campus with easy access to Philadelphia
- **Coed**

Undergraduates 923 full-time, 123 part-time. *Retention:* 45% of full-time freshmen returned.

Faculty *Student/faculty ratio:* 22:1.

Academics *Calendar:* semesters. *Degree:* certificates and associate. *Special study options:* academic remediation for entering students, adult/continuing education programs, advanced placement credit, cooperative education, part-time degree program, summer session for credit.

Student Life *Campus security:* 24-hour emergency response devices.

Costs (2010–11) *Tuition:* $9900 full-time, $330 per credit part-time. Full-time tuition and fees vary according to course load, degree level, and program. Part-time tuition and fees vary according to course load, degree level, and program. *Required fees:* $900 full-time, $30 per credit part-time.

Financial Aid Of all full-time matriculated undergraduates who enrolled in 2009, 15 Federal Work-Study jobs (averaging $1025). *Financial aid deadline:* 8/1.

Applying *Options:* electronic application, deferred entrance. *Application fee:* $25. *Required:* high school transcript, interview. *Required for some:* 2 letters of recommendation. *Recommended:* essay or personal statement.

Freshman Application Contact Ms. Angela Cassetta, Dean of Enrollment Management, Pennsylvania Institute of Technology, 800 Manchester Avenue, Media, PA 19063-4036. *Phone:* 610-892-1550 Ext. 1553. *Toll-free phone:* 800-422-0025. *Fax:* 610-892-1510. *E-mail:* info@pit.edu. *Web site:* http://www.pit.edu/.

Pennsylvania School of Business

Allentown, Pennsylvania

Freshman Application Contact Mr. Bill Barber, Director, Pennsylvania School of Business, 406 West Hamilton Street, Allentown, PA 18101. *Phone:* 610-841-3333. *Fax:* 610-841-3334. *E-mail:* wbarber@pennschoolofbusiness.edu. *Web site:* http://www.psb.edu/.

Pittsburgh Institute of Aeronautics

Pittsburgh, Pennsylvania

Freshman Application Contact Mr. Vincent J. Mezza, Director of Admissions, Pittsburgh Institute of Aeronautics, PO Box 10897, Pittsburgh, PA 15236-0897. *Phone:* 412-346-2100. *Toll-free phone:* 800-444-1440. *Fax:* 412-466-5013. *E-mail:* admissions@pia.edu. *Web site:* http://www.pia.edu/.

Pittsburgh Institute of Mortuary Science, Incorporated

Pittsburgh, Pennsylvania

- **Independent** 2-year, founded 1939
- **Urban** campus
- **Coed**

Undergraduates 85 full-time, 108 part-time. Students come from 12 states and territories; 1 other country; 37% are from out of state.

Faculty *Student/faculty ratio:* 13:1.

Academics *Calendar:* trimesters. *Degree:* diplomas and associate. *Special study options:* academic remediation for entering students, adult/continuing education programs, distance learning, part-time degree program, services for LD students.

Student Life *Campus security:* 24-hour emergency response devices.

Applying *Options:* electronic application. *Application fee:* $40. *Required:* essay or personal statement, high school transcript, minimum 2.0 GPA, 2 letters of recommendation, interview, immunizations.

Freshman Application Contact Ms. Karen Rocco, Registrar, Pittsburgh Institute of Mortuary Science, Incorporated, 5808 Baum Boulevard, Pittsburgh, PA 15206-3706. *Phone:* 412-362-8500 Ext. 105. *Toll-free phone:* 800-933-5808. *Fax:* 412-362-1684. *E-mail:* pims5808@aol.com. *Web site:* http://www.pims.edu/.

Pittsburgh Technical Institute

Oakdale, Pennsylvania

- **Proprietary** 2-year, founded 1946
- **Suburban** 180-acre campus with easy access to Pittsburgh
- **Coed**, 2,186 undergraduate students, 100% full-time, 37% women, 63% men
- 86% of applicants were admitted

Undergraduates 2,186 full-time. Students come from 20 states and territories; 15% are from out of state; 5% Black or African American, non-Hispanic/Latino; 0.9% Hispanic/Latino; 0.3% Asian, non-Hispanic/Latino; 0.2% Native Hawaiian or other Pacific Islander, non-Hispanic/Latino; 0.4% American Indian or Alaska Native, non-Hispanic/Latino; 2% Two or more races, non-Hispanic/Latino; 30% Race/ethnicity unknown; 10% transferred in; 40% live on campus.

Freshmen *Admission:* 1,605 applied, 1,385 admitted, 794 enrolled. *Average high school GPA:* 2.59.

Faculty *Total:* 134, 59% full-time. *Student/faculty ratio:* 23:1.

Majors Architectural drafting and CAD/CADD; business administration and management; computer graphics; computer programming; computer technology/computer systems technology; electrical, electronic and communications engineering technology; electrical/electronics equipment installation and repair; homeland security, law enforcement, firefighting and protective services related; hotel/motel administration; mechanical drafting and CAD/CADD; medical/health management and clinical assistant; medical office assistant; surgical technology; web page, digital/multimedia and information resources design.

Academics *Calendar:* quarters. *Degree:* certificates and associate. *Special study options:* academic remediation for entering students, advanced placement credit, cooperative education, distance learning, double majors, internships, services for LD students.

Library Library Resource Center with 10,776 titles, 164 serial subscriptions, 2,036 audiovisual materials, an OPAC.

Student Life *Housing Options:* coed. Campus housing is university owned and leased by the school. Freshman campus housing is guaranteed. *Activities and Organizations:* drama/theater group, American Society of Travel Agents (ASTA), MEDICS Club, Alpha Beta Gamma (ABG), Drama Club, Campus Crusade. *Campus security:* 24-hour emergency response devices and patrols, controlled dormitory access. *Student services:* personal/psychological counseling.

Athletics *Intramural sports:* basketball M/W, cross-country running M/W, soccer M/W, softball M/W, ultimate Frisbee M/W, volleyball M/W.

Costs (2011–12) *Tuition:* $14,983 full-time. Full-time tuition and fees vary according to program. No tuition increase for student's term of enrollment. *Room only:* $6075. Room and board charges vary according to housing facility. *Payment plans:* installment, deferred payment. *Waivers:* children of alumni and employees or children of employees.

Applying *Options:* electronic application, deferred entrance. *Required:* high school transcript, interview. *Required for some:* essay or personal statement, 1 letter of recommendation, certain programs require a criminal background check; surgical technology requires a dexterity test; some programs require applicants to be in top 50-80% of class; Practical Nursing requires entrance exam. *Recommended:* interview. *Application deadlines:* rolling (freshmen), rolling (out-of-state freshmen), rolling (transfers). *Notification:* continuous (freshmen), continuous (out-of-state freshmen), continuous (transfers).

Freshman Application Contact Ms. Nancy Goodlin, Admissions Office Assistant, Pittsburgh Technical Institute, 1111 McKee Road, Oakdale, PA 15071. *Phone:* 412-809-5100. *Toll-free phone:* 800-784-9675. *Fax:* 412-809-5351. *E-mail:* goodlin.nancy@pti.edu. *Web site:* http://www.pti.edu/.

Prism Career Institute

Upper Darby, Pennsylvania

Director of Admissions Ms. Dina Gentile, Director, Prism Career Institute, 6800 Market Street, Upper Darby, PA 19082. *Phone:* 610-789-6700. *Toll-free phone:* 888-252-8608. *Fax:* 610-789-5208. *E-mail:* dgentile@pjaschool.com. *Web site:* http://www.prismcareerinstitute.edu/.

Reading Area Community College

Reading, Pennsylvania

Director of Admissions Ms. Maria Mitchell, Associate Vice President of Enrollment Management and Student Services, Reading Area Community College, PO Box 1706, Reading, PA 19603-1706. *Phone:* 610-607-6224. *Toll-free phone:* 800-626-1665. *E-mail:* mmitchell@racc.edu. *Web site:* http://www.racc.edu/.

The Restaurant School at Walnut Hill College

Philadelphia, Pennsylvania

- **Proprietary** primarily 2-year, founded 1974
- **Urban** 2-acre campus
- **Coed,** 423 undergraduate students, 100% full-time, 47% women, 53% men
- 97% of applicants were admitted

Undergraduates 423 full-time. Students come from 2 other countries; 33% are from out of state; 17% Black or African American, non-Hispanic/Latino; 5% Hispanic/Latino; 2% Asian, non-Hispanic/Latino; 0.5% Two or more races, non-Hispanic/Latino; 30% Race/ethnicity unknown; 9% transferred in. *Retention:* 64% of full-time freshmen returned.
Freshmen *Admission:* 174 applied, 168 admitted, 212 enrolled.
Faculty *Total:* 19, 95% full-time. *Student/faculty ratio:* 22:1.
Majors Baking and pastry arts; culinary arts; hotel/motel administration; restaurant/food services management.
Academics *Calendar:* quarters. *Degrees:* associate and bachelor's. *Special study options:* internships, part-time degree program.
Library Alumni Resource Center with a Web page.
Student Life *Housing Options:* coed. Campus housing is leased by the school. *Activities and Organizations:* Wine Club, Book Club, Coffee & Tea Club, Craft Club, Flair Bartending. *Campus security:* 24-hour emergency response devices and patrols, student patrols, controlled dormitory access.
Standardized Tests *Recommended:* SAT or ACT (for admission).
Costs (2011–12) *One-time required fee:* $200. *Tuition:* $17,850 full-time. *Required fees:* $3300 full-time. *Room only:* $4500. Room and board charges vary according to housing facility. *Payment plans:* installment, deferred payment.
Applying *Options:* electronic application, early admission, early decision, deferred entrance. *Application fee:* $50. *Required:* essay or personal statement, high school transcript, 2 letters of recommendation, interview. *Required for some:* entrance exam. *Recommended:* minimum 2.0 GPA. *Application deadline:* rolling (freshmen).
Freshman Application Contact Miss Toni Morelli, Director of Admissions, The Restaurant School at Walnut Hill College, 4207 Walnut Street, Philadelphia, PA 19104-3518. *Phone:* 267-295-2353. *Toll-free phone:* 877-925-6884 Ext. 3011. *Fax:* 215-222-4219. *E-mail:* tmorelli@walnuthillcollege.edu. *Web site:* http://www.walnuthillcollege.edu/.

Rosedale Technical Institute

Pittsburgh, Pennsylvania

Freshman Application Contact Ms. Debbie Bier, Director of Admissions, Rosedale Technical Institute, 215 Beecham Drive, Suite 2, Pittsburgh, PA 15205-9791. *Phone:* 412-521-6200. *Toll-free phone:* 800-521-6262. *Fax:* 412-521-2520. *E-mail:* admissions@rosedaletech.org. *Web site:* http://www.rosedaletech.org/.

Sanford-Brown Institute–Monroeville

Pittsburgh, Pennsylvania

Director of Admissions Timothy Babyok, Director of Admission, Sanford-Brown Institute–Monroeville, Penn Center East, 777 Penn Center Boulevard, Building 7, Pittsburgh, PA 15235. *Phone:* 412-373-6400. *Toll-free phone:* 80-622-1394 (in-state); 800-622-1394 (out-of-state). *Fax:* 412-374-0863. *Web site:* http://www.monroeville.sanfordbrown.edu/.

Sanford-Brown Institute–Pittsburgh

Pittsburgh, Pennsylvania

Director of Admissions Mr. Bruce E. Jones, Director of Admission, Sanford-Brown Institute–Pittsburgh, 421 Seventh Avenue, Pittsburgh, PA 15219-1907. *Phone:* 412-281-7083 Ext. 114. *Toll-free phone:* 800-333-6607. *Web site:* http://www.sanfordbrown.edu/.

South Hills School of Business & Technology

Altoona, Pennsylvania

Freshman Application Contact Ms. Holly J. Emerick, Director of Admissions, South Hills School of Business & Technology, 508 58th Street, Altoona, PA 16602. *Phone:* 814-944-6134. *Fax:* 814-944-4684. *E-mail:* hemerick@southhills.edu. *Web site:* http://www.southhills.edu/.

South Hills School of Business & Technology

State College, Pennsylvania

Freshman Application Contact Ms. Diane M. Brown, Director of Admissions, South Hills School of Business & Technology, 480 Waupelani Drive, State College, PA 16801-4516. *Phone:* 814-234-7755 Ext. 2020. *Toll-free phone:* 888-282-7427 Ext. 2020. *Fax:* 814-234-0926. *E-mail:* admissions@southhills.edu. *Web site:* http://www.southhills.edu/.

Thaddeus Stevens College of Technology

Lancaster, Pennsylvania

Director of Admissions Ms. Erin Kate Nelsen, Director of Enrollment, Thaddeus Stevens College of Technology, 750 East King Street, Lancaster, PA 17602-3198. *Phone:* 717-299-7772. *Toll-free phone:* 800-842-3832. *Web site:* http://www.stevenscollege.edu/.

Triangle Tech–Greensburg School

Greensburg, Pennsylvania

- **Proprietary** 2-year, founded 1944, part of Triangle Tech Group, Inc.
- **Small-town** 1-acre campus with easy access to Pittsburgh
- **Coed, primarily men**

Undergraduates 260 full-time. Students come from 1 other state.
Faculty *Student/faculty ratio:* 12:1.
Academics *Calendar:* semesters. *Degree:* diplomas and associate. *Special study options:* academic remediation for entering students, adult/continuing education programs, advanced placement credit, summer session for credit.
Costs (2010–11) *Tuition:* $14,558 full-time. *Required fees:* $308 full-time.
Applying *Options:* deferred entrance. *Application fee:* $75. *Required:* high school transcript, interview.
Freshman Application Contact Mr. John Mazzarese, Vice President of Admissions, Triangle Tech–Greensburg School, 222 East Pittsburgh Street, Greensburg, PA 15601. *Phone:* 412-359-1000. *Toll-free phone:* 800-874-8324. *Web site:* http://www.triangle-tech.com/.

Triangle Tech Inc–Bethlehem

Bethlehem, Pennsylvania

- **Proprietary** 2 year
- **Urban** campus
- **Coed, primarily men**

Undergraduates 140 full-time. Students come from 2 states and territories; 11% are from out of state; 4% transferred in.
Faculty *Student/faculty ratio:* 15:1.
Academics *Degree:* associate.
Standardized Tests *Required:* TABE test for student advising (for admission).
Costs (2010–11) *Tuition:* $14,558 full-time, $404 per credit part-time. *Required fees:* $276 full-time.
Applying *Required:* high school transcript, interview, high school diploma or GED, tour of school.
Freshman Application Contact Triangle Tech Inc–Bethlehem, Lehigh Valley Industrial Park IV, 31 South Commerce Way, Bethlehem, PA 18017. *Web site:* http://www.triangle-tech.edu/.

Triangle Tech, Inc.–DuBois School

DuBois, Pennsylvania

- **Proprietary** 2-year, founded 1944, part of Triangle Tech Group, Inc.
- **Small-town** 5-acre campus
- **Coed, primarily men,** 329 undergraduate students, 100% full-time, 3% women, 97% men

Undergraduates 329 full-time. Students come from 2 states and territories; 1 other country.
Freshmen *Admission:* 246 applied, 246 admitted, 137 enrolled. *Average high school GPA:* 2.
Faculty *Total:* 21, 100% full-time. *Student/faculty ratio:* 15:1.
Majors Carpentry; drafting and design technology; electrical, electronic and communications engineering technology; welding technology.
Academics *Calendar:* semesters. *Degree:* diplomas and associate. *Special study options:* academic remediation for entering students, advanced placement credit, off-campus study.
Library Library Resource Center with 1,200 titles, 15 serial subscriptions, 60 audiovisual materials.

Student Life *Housing:* college housing not available. *Activities and Organizations:* Student Council.

Costs (2010–11) *Tuition:* $14,558 full-time. *Required fees:* $387 full-time. *Payment plan:* installment. *Waivers:* employees or children of employees.

Applying *Options:* deferred entrance. *Required:* high school transcript, minimum 2.0 GPA, interview. *Application deadlines:* rolling (freshmen), rolling (transfers).

Freshman Application Contact Terry Kucic, Director of Admissions, Triangle Tech, Inc.–DuBois School, PO Box 551, DuBois, PA 15801. *Phone:* 814-371-2090. *Toll-free phone:* 800-874-8324. *Fax:* 814-371-9227. *E-mail:* tkucic@triangle-tech.com. *Web site:* http://www.triangle-tech.edu/.

Triangle Tech, Inc.–Erie School

Erie, Pennsylvania

- **Proprietary** 2-year, founded 1976, part of Triangle Tech Group, Inc.
- **Urban** 1-acre campus
- **Coed, primarily men**

Undergraduates 176 full-time. Students come from 3 states and territories; 10% are from out of state.

Faculty *Student/faculty ratio:* 12:1.

Academics *Calendar:* semesters. *Degree:* associate. *Special study options:* academic remediation for entering students, advanced placement credit, services for LD students.

Student Life *Campus security:* 24-hour emergency response devices.

Costs (2010–11) *Tuition:* $14,558 full-time, $404 per credit part-time. *Required fees:* $318 full-time.

Financial Aid Of all full-time matriculated undergraduates who enrolled in 2009, 5 Federal Work-Study jobs (averaging $2000).

Applying *Options:* deferred entrance. *Application fee:* $75. *Required:* high school transcript, interview.

Freshman Application Contact Admissions Representative, Triangle Tech, Inc.–Erie School, 2000 Liberty Street, Erie, PA 16502-2594. *Phone:* 814-453-6016. *Toll-free phone:* 800-874-8324 (in-state); 800-TRI-TECH (out-of-state). *Web site:* http://www.triangle-tech.com/.

Triangle Tech, Inc.–Pittsburgh School

Pittsburgh, Pennsylvania

Freshman Application Contact Director of Admissions, Triangle Tech, Inc.–Pittsburgh School, 1940 Perrysville Avenue, Pittsburgh, PA 15214-3897. *Phone:* 412-359-1000. *Toll-free phone:* 800-874-8324. *Fax:* 412-359-1012. *E-mail:* info@triangle-tech.edu. *Web site:* http://www.triangle-tech.edu/.

Triangle Tech, Inc.–Sunbury School

Sunbury, Pennsylvania

- **Proprietary** 2-year
- **Rural** 4-acre campus
- **Coed**
- 100% of applicants were admitted

Undergraduates 170 full-time. Students come from 2 states and territories. *Retention:* 75% of full-time freshmen returned.

Faculty *Student/faculty ratio:* 12:1.

Academics *Calendar:* semesters. *Degree:* associate. *Special study options:* advanced placement credit, cooperative education.

Applying *Required:* high school transcript.

Freshman Application Contact Triangle Tech, Inc.–Sunbury School, 191 Performance Road, Sunbury, PA 17801. *Phone:* 412-359-1000. *Web site:* http://www.triangle-tech.edu/.

Tri-State Business Institute

Erie, Pennsylvania

Director of Admissions Guy M. Euliano, President, Tri-State Business Institute, 5757 West 26th Street, Erie, PA 16506. *Phone:* 814-838-7673. *Fax:* 814-838-8642. *E-mail:* geuliano@tsbi.org. *Web site:* http://www.tsbi.edu/.

University of Pittsburgh at Titusville

Titusville, Pennsylvania

- **State-related** primarily 2-year, founded 1963, part of University of Pittsburgh System
- **Small-town** 10-acre campus
- **Endowment** $850,000
- **Coed,** 514 undergraduate students, 86% full-time, 63% women, 37% men

Undergraduates 442 full-time, 72 part-time. Students come from 15 states and territories; 8% are from out of state; 19% Black or African American, non-Hispanic/Latino; 2% Hispanic/Latino; 2% Asian, non-Hispanic/Latino; 0.2% American Indian or Alaska Native, non-Hispanic/Latino; 3% Two or more races, non-Hispanic/Latino; 3% Race/ethnicity unknown; 8% transferred in; 55% live on campus.

Freshmen *Admission:* 183 enrolled. *Average high school GPA:* 3.02. *Test scores:* SAT critical reading scores over 500: 21%; SAT math scores over 500: 27%; SAT writing scores over 500: 23%; ACT scores over 18: 67%; SAT critical reading scores over 600: 4%; SAT math scores over 600: 4%; SAT writing scores over 600: 4%; ACT scores over 24: 10%; SAT math scores over 700: 1%; ACT scores over 30: 3%.

Majors Accounting; business/commerce; human services; liberal arts and sciences/liberal studies; management information systems; natural sciences; physical therapy technology; registered nursing/registered nurse.

Academics *Calendar:* semesters. *Degrees:* certificates, associate, and bachelor's. *Special study options:* academic remediation for entering students, advanced placement credit, distance learning, internships, part-time degree program, study abroad, summer session for credit.

Library Haskell Memorial Library with 49,256 titles, 126 serial subscriptions, an OPAC.

Student Life *Housing:* on-campus residence required through sophomore year. *Options:* coed, disabled students. Campus housing is university owned. Freshman campus housing is guaranteed. *Activities and Organizations:* drama/theater group, Phi Theta Kappa, Weight Club, SAB, Students in Free Enterprise (SIFE), Diversity Club. *Campus security:* 24-hour emergency response devices and patrols, controlled dormitory access. *Student services:* health clinic, personal/psychological counseling.

Athletics Member NJCAA. *Intercollegiate sports:* basketball M(s)/W(s). *Intramural sports:* badminton M/W, basketball M/W, bowling M/W, football M/W, golf M/W, racquetball M/W, softball M/W, table tennis M/W, tennis M/W, volleyball M/W, weight lifting M/W.

Standardized Tests *Required:* SAT or ACT (for admission). *Recommended:* SAT (for admission).

Costs (2010–11) *Tuition:* state resident $9942 full-time, $414 per credit part-time; nonresident $18,778 full-time, $782 per credit part-time. Full-time tuition and fees vary according to program. Part-time tuition and fees vary according to program. *Required fees:* $780 full-time, $128 per term part-time. *Room and board:* $8556. Room and board charges vary according to board plan. *Payment plan:* installment.

Financial Aid Of all full-time matriculated undergraduates who enrolled in 2008, 429 applied for aid, 408 were judged to have need, 23 had their need fully met. In 2008, 10 non-need-based awards were made. *Average percent of need met:* 80%. *Average financial aid package:* $15,305. *Average need-based loan:* $9451. *Average need-based gift aid:* $1992. *Average non-need-based aid:* $39,059.

Applying *Options:* electronic application, early admission, deferred entrance. *Application fee:* $45. *Required:* high school transcript, minimum 2.0 GPA. *Required for some:* essay or personal statement, 1 letter of recommendation. *Recommended:* interview. *Application deadlines:* rolling (freshmen), rolling (transfers). *Notification:* continuous (freshmen).

Freshman Application Contact Mr. John R. Mumford, Executive Director of Enrollment Management, University of Pittsburgh at Titusville, PO Box 287, Titusville, PA 16354. *Phone:* 814-827-4409. *Toll-free phone:* 888-878-0462. *Fax:* 814-827-4519. *E-mail:* uptadm@pitt.edu. *Web site:* http://www.upt.pitt.edu/.

Valley Forge Military College

Wayne, Pennsylvania

Freshman Application Contact Maj. Greg Potts, Dean of Enrollment Management, Valley Forge Military College, 1001 Eagle Road, Wayne, PA 19087-3695. *Phone:* 610-989-1300. *Toll-free phone:* 800-234-8362. *Fax:* 610-688-1545. *E-mail:* admissions@vfmac.edu. *Web site:* http://www.vfmac.edu/.

See page 426 for the College Close-Up.

Vet Tech Institute
Pittsburgh, Pennsylvania

- **Private** 2-year, founded 1958
- **Urban** campus
- **Coed,** 345 undergraduate students
- **61%** of applicants were admitted

Freshmen *Admission:* 528 applied, 323 admitted.

Majors Veterinary/animal health technology.

Academics *Calendar:* quarters. *Degree:* associate. *Special study options:* accelerated degree program, internships, summer session for credit.

Freshman Application Contact Admissions Office, Vet Tech Institute, 125 7th Street, Pittsburgh, PA 15222-3400. *Phone:* 412-391-7021. *Web site:* http://www.vettechinstitute.edu/.

Westmoreland County Community College
Youngwood, Pennsylvania

- **County-supported** 2-year, founded 1970
- **Rural** 85-acre campus with easy access to Pittsburgh
- **Endowment** $435,469
- **Coed,** 7,383 undergraduate students, 51% full-time, 63% women, 37% men

Undergraduates 3,784 full-time, 3,599 part-time. Students come from 6 states and territories; 0.3% are from out of state; 4% Black or African American, non-Hispanic/Latino; 1% Hispanic/Latino; 0.5% Asian, non-Hispanic/Latino; 0.3% American Indian or Alaska Native, non-Hispanic/Latino; 24% transferred in. *Retention:* 59% of full-time freshmen returned.

Freshmen *Admission:* 3,272 applied, 3,272 admitted, 2,056 enrolled.

Faculty *Total:* 537, 17% full-time. *Student/faculty ratio:* 19:1.

Majors Accounting technology and bookkeeping; applied horticulture/horticulture operations; architectural drafting and CAD/CADD; baking and pastry arts; banking and financial support services; biology/biotechnology laboratory technician; business administration and management; chemical technology; child-care provision; computer and information systems security; computer engineering technology; computer programming; computer systems networking and telecommunications; criminal justice/safety; culinary arts; dental hygiene; dietetic technology; early childhood education; electrical, electronic and communications engineering technology; executive assistant/executive secretary; fire prevention and safety technology; fire science/firefighting; floriculture/floristry management; health and medical administrative services related; heating, air conditioning, ventilation and refrigeration maintenance technology; human resources management; human services; industrial mechanics and maintenance technology; legal assistant/paralegal; liberal arts and sciences/liberal studies; machine shop technology; machine tool technology; manufacturing engineering technology; marketing/marketing management; mechanical drafting and CAD/CADD; mechanical engineering/mechanical technology; photographic and film/video technology; radiologic technology/science; real estate; registered nursing/registered nurse; restaurant, culinary, and catering management; tourism and travel services management; turf and turfgrass management; web page, digital/multimedia and information resources design; welding technology.

Academics *Calendar:* semesters. *Degree:* certificates, diplomas, and associate. *Special study options:* academic remediation for entering students, adult/continuing education programs, advanced placement credit, cooperative education, distance learning, double majors, English as a second language, honors programs, independent study, internships, off-campus study, part-time degree program, services for LD students, summer session for credit.

Library Westmoreland County Community College Learning Resources Center with 64,000 titles, 250 serial subscriptions, 3,500 audiovisual materials, an OPAC, a Web page.

Student Life *Housing:* college housing not available. *Activities and Organizations:* drama/theater group, choral group, Phi Theta Kappa, Sigma Alpha Pi Leadership Society, Criminal Justice Fraternity, Early Childhood Education Club, SADAA/SADHA. *Campus security:* 24-hour emergency response devices and patrols, late-night transport/escort service. *Student services:* personal/psychological counseling.

Athletics Member NJCAA. *Intercollegiate sports:* baseball M, basketball M/W, bowling M/W, cross-country running M/W, golf M/W, softball W, volleyball W. *Intramural sports:* basketball M/W, bowling M/W, golf M/W, skiing (downhill) M/W, table tennis M/W, volleyball M/W, weight lifting M/W.

Costs (2010–11) *Tuition:* area resident $2280 full-time, $76 per credit hour part-time; state resident $4560 full-time, $152 per credit hour part-time; nonresident $6840 full-time, $228 per credit hour part-time. *Required fees:* $20 per credit hour part-time. *Waivers:* senior citizens and employees or children of employees.

Applying *Options:* electronic application, early admission. *Application fee:* $10. *Application deadlines:* rolling (freshmen), rolling (transfers). *Notification:* continuous (freshmen), continuous (transfers).

Freshman Application Contact Mr. Andrew Colosimo, Admissions Coordinator, Westmoreland County Community College, 145 Pavillon Lane, Youngwood, PA 15697. *Phone:* 724-925-4064. *Toll-free phone:* 800-262-2103. *Fax:* 724-925-5802. *E-mail:* admission@wccc.edu. *Web site:* http://www.wccc.edu/.

The Williamson Free School of Mechanical Trades
Media, Pennsylvania

- **Independent** 2-year, founded 1888
- **Small-town** 222-acre campus with easy access to Philadelphia
- **Men only,** 270 undergraduate students, 100% full-time

Undergraduates 270 full-time. Students come from 7 states and territories; 15% are from out of state; 100% live on campus.

Freshmen *Admission:* 412 applied, 100 admitted, 100 enrolled. *Average high school GPA:* 2.5.

Faculty *Total:* 29. *Student/faculty ratio:* 12:1.

Majors Carpentry; construction engineering technology; electrical, electronic and communications engineering technology; energy management and systems technology; horticultural science; landscaping and groundskeeping; machine tool technology; turf and turfgrass management.

Academics *Calendar:* semesters. *Degree:* diplomas and associate. *Special study options:* academic remediation for entering students, independent study, off-campus study.

Library Shrigley Library plus 3 others with 1,600 titles, 70 serial subscriptions.

Student Life *Housing Options:* men-only. Freshman campus housing is guaranteed. *Activities and Organizations:* student-run newspaper, choral group, Campus Crusade for Christ, Skills USA. *Campus security:* evening patrols, gate security. *Student services:* health clinic, personal/psychological counseling.

Athletics Member NJCAA. *Intercollegiate sports:* baseball M, basketball M, cross-country running M, football M, lacrosse M, soccer M, tennis M, wrestling M. *Intramural sports:* archery M, basketball M, table tennis M, volleyball M, weight lifting M.

Standardized Tests *Required:* Armed Services Vocational Aptitude Battery (for admission).

Applying *Required:* essay or personal statement, high school transcript, minimum 2.0 GPA, interview, average performance or better on the Armed Services Vocational Aptitude Battery (ASVAB). *Required for some:* 3 letters of recommendation. *Application deadline:* 2/28 (freshmen).

Freshman Application Contact Mr. Jay Merillat, Dean of Enrollments, The Williamson Free School of Mechanical Trades, 106 South New Middletown Road, Media, PA 19063. *Phone:* 610-566-1776 Ext. 235. *E-mail:* jmerillat@williamson.edu. *Web site:* http://www.williamson.edu/.

WyoTech
Blairsville, Pennsylvania

Freshman Application Contact Mr. Tim Smyers, WyoTech, 500 Innovation Drive, Blairsville, PA 15717. *Phone:* 724-459-2311. *Toll-free phone:* 800-822-8253. *Fax:* 724-459-6499. *E-mail:* tsmyers@wyotech.edu. *Web site:* http://www.wyotech.com/.

Yorktowne Business Institute
York, Pennsylvania

Director of Admissions Director of Admissions, Yorktowne Business Institute, West Seventh Avenue, York, PA 17404. *Phone:* 717-846-5000. *Toll-free phone:* 800-840-1004. *Web site:* http://www.ybi.edu/.

YTI Career Institute–York
York, Pennsylvania

- **Private** 2-year, founded 1967, part of York Technical Institute, LLC
- **Suburban** campus with easy access to Harrisburg
- **Coed,** 823 undergraduate students, 100% full-time, 33% women, 67% men

Undergraduates 823 full-time. Students come from 5 states and territories; 10% are from out of state.

Freshmen *Admission:* 790 enrolled.

Faculty *Total:* 69, 70% full-time. *Student/faculty ratio:* 18:1.

Majors Accounting; business administration and management; CAD/CADD drafting/design technology; computer and information sciences and support services related; electrical, electronic and communications engineering technology; medical/clinical assistant; parks, recreation and leisure facilities management.

Academics *Calendar:* continuous. *Degree:* diplomas and associate. *Special study options:* academic remediation for entering students, advanced placement credit, cooperative education, internships.

Student Life *Student services:* personal/psychological counseling.

Standardized Tests *Required:* ACT COMPASS (for admission).

Costs (2010–11) *Tuition:* $27,195 full-time. Full-time tuition and fees vary according to location and program. *Payment plan:* installment. *Waivers:* employees or children of employees.

Applying *Application fee:* $50. *Required:* high school transcript, minimum 2.0 GPA, interview. *Recommended:* admissions test.

Freshman Application Contact YTI Career Institute–York, 1405 Williams Road, York, PA 17402-9017. *Phone:* 717-757-1100 Ext. 318. *Toll-free phone:* 800-229-9675 (in-state); 800-227-9675 (out-of-state). *Web site:* http://www.yti.edu/.

PUERTO RICO

Centro de Estudios Multidisciplinarios
Rio Piedras, Puerto Rico

Director of Admissions Admissions Department, Centro de Estudios Multidisciplinarios, Calle 13 #1206, Ext. San Agustin, Rio Piedras, PR 00926. *Phone:* 787-765-4210 Ext. 115. *Toll-free phone:* 877-779CDEM. *Web site:* http://www.cempr.edu/.

Colegio Universitario de San Juan
San Juan, Puerto Rico

Freshman Application Contact Colegio Universitario de San Juan, Jose R. Oliver Street, Hato Rey, PR 00918. *Phone:* 787-250-7111 Ext. 2227. *Web site:* http://www.cunisanjuan.edu/.

Huertas Junior College
Caguas, Puerto Rico

Director of Admissions Mrs. Barbara Hassim López, Director of Admissions, Huertas Junior College, PO Box 8429, Caguas, PR 00726. *Phone:* 787-743-1242. *Fax:* 787-743-0203. *E-mail:* huertas@huertas.org. *Web site:* http://www.huertas.edu/.

Humacao Community College
Humacao, Puerto Rico

Director of Admissions Ms. Xiomara Sanchez, Director of Admissions, Humacao Community College, PO Box 9139, Humacao, PR 00792. *Phone:* 787-852-2525.

Instituto Comercial de Puerto Rico Junior College
San Juan, Puerto Rico

Freshman Application Contact Admissions Office, Instituto Comercial de Puerto Rico Junior College, 558 Munoz Rivera Avenue, PO Box 190304, San Juan, PR 00919-0304. *Phone:* 787-753-6335. *Web site:* http://www.icprjc.edu/.

Puerto Rico Technical Junior College
San Juan, Puerto Rico

Director of Admissions Admissions Department, Puerto Rico Technical Junior College, 703 Ponce De Leon Avenue, Hato Rey, San Juan, PR 00917. *Phone:* 787-751-0628 Ext. 28.

Ramírez College of Business and Technology
San Juan, Puerto Rico

Director of Admissions Mr. Arnaldo Castro, Director of Admissions, Ramírez College of Business and Technology, Avenue Ponce de Leon #70, San Juan, PR 00918. *Phone:* 787-763-3120. *E-mail:* ramirezcollege@prtc.net. *Web site:* http://www.galeon.com/ramirezcollege/.

Universidad Central del Caribe
Bayamón, Puerto Rico

Director of Admissions Admissions Department, Universidad Central del Caribe, PO Box 60-327, Bayamón, PR 00960-6032. *Phone:* 787-740-1611. *Toll-free phone:* 809-616-1616. *Web site:* http://www.uccaribe.edu/.

University of Puerto Rico at Carolina
Carolina, Puerto Rico

Director of Admissions Ms. Celia Mendez, Admissions Officer, University of Puerto Rico at Carolina, PO Box 4800, Carolina, PR 00984-4800. *Phone:* 787-757-1485. *Web site:* http://uprc.edu/.

RHODE ISLAND

Community College of Rhode Island
Warwick, Rhode Island

- **State-supported** 2-year, founded 1964
- **Suburban** 205-acre campus with easy access to Boston
- **Coed,** 17,775 undergraduate students, 35% full-time, 59% women, 41% men

Undergraduates 6,231 full-time, 11,544 part-time. Students come from 18 states and territories; 4% are from out of state; 8% Black or African American, non-Hispanic/Latino; 13% Hispanic/Latino; 3% Asian, non-Hispanic/Latino; 0.6% American Indian or Alaska Native, non-Hispanic/Latino; 0.5% Two or more races, non-Hispanic/Latino; 9% Race/ethnicity unknown.

Freshmen *Admission:* 7,664 applied, 7,643 admitted, 3,646 enrolled.

Faculty *Total:* 821, 39% full-time. *Student/faculty ratio:* 21:1.

Majors Accounting; administrative assistant and secretarial science; adult development and aging; art; banking and financial support services; biological and physical sciences; biotechnology; business administration and management; business/commerce; chemical technology; clinical/medical laboratory technology; computer and information sciences; computer engineering technology; computer hardware technology; computer programming; computer programming (specific applications); computer systems networking and telecommunications; criminal justice/police science; customer service management; dental hygiene; diagnostic medical sonography and ultrasound technology; dramatic/theater arts; early childhood education; electrical, electronic and communications engineering technology; engineering; engineering technologies and engineering related; fire science/firefighting; general studies; histologic technician; jazz/jazz studies; kindergarten/preschool education; legal administrative assistant/secretary; legal assistant/paralegal; liberal arts and sciences/liberal studies; licensed practical/vocational nurse training; marketing/marketing management; massage therapy; mechanical engineering/mechanical technology; medical administrative assistant and medical secretary; mental health counseling; music; occupational therapist assistant; opticianry; physical therapy technology; radiologic technology/science; registered nursing/registered nurse; respiratory care therapy; social work; special education; substance abuse/addiction counseling; surveying engineering; telecommunications technology; theater design and technology; web/multimedia management and webmaster.

Academics *Calendar:* semesters. *Degree:* certificates, diplomas, and associate. *Special study options:* academic remediation for entering students, adult/continuing education programs, advanced placement credit, cooperative education, distance learning, double majors, English as a second language, external degree program, honors programs, independent study, internships, off-campus study, part-time degree program, services for LD students, study abroad, summer session for credit. *ROTC:* Army (c).

Library Community College of Rhode Island Learning Resources Center plus 3 others with an OPAC, a Web page.

Student Life *Housing:* college housing not available. *Activities and Organizations:* drama/theater group, choral group, Distributive Education Clubs of America, Theater group - Players, Skills USA, Phi Theta Kappa, student government. *Campus security:* 24-hour emergency response devices and patrols. *Student services:* health clinic, personal/psychological counseling.

Athletics Member NJCAA. *Intercollegiate sports:* baseball M(s), basketball M(s)/W(s), cross-country running M/W, golf M/W, soccer M(s)/W(s), softball W(s), tennis M/W, track and field M/W, volleyball W(s). *Intramural sports:* basketball M/W, cross-country running M/W, volleyball M/W, water polo M/W.

Costs (2010–11) *Tuition:* state resident $3356 full-time, $153 per credit hour part-time; nonresident $9496 full-time, $454 per credit hour part-time. Part-time tuition and fees vary according to course load. *Required fees:* $11 per credit hour part-time, $17 per term part-time. *Payment plans:* installment, deferred payment. *Waivers:* senior citizens and employees or children of employees.

Financial Aid Of all full-time matriculated undergraduates who enrolled in 2009, 500 Federal Work-Study jobs (averaging $2500).

Applying *Options:* deferred entrance. *Application fee:* $20. *Application deadlines:* rolling (freshmen), rolling (transfers). *Notification:* continuous (freshmen).

Freshman Application Contact Community College of Rhode Island, Flanagan Campus, 1762 Louisquisset Pike, Lincoln, RI 02865-4585. *Phone:* 401-333-7490. *Fax:* 401-333-7122. *E-mail:* webadmission@ccri.edu. *Web site:* http://www.ccri.edu/.

New England Institute of Technology

Warwick, Rhode Island

- **Independent** primarily 2-year, founded 1940
- **Suburban** 10-acre campus with easy access to Boston
- **Coed,** 3,258 undergraduate students, 87% full-time, 23% women, 77% men

Undergraduates 2,829 full-time, 429 part-time. Students come from 10 states and territories; 22 other countries; 7% Black or African American, non-Hispanic/Latino; 7% Hispanic/Latino; 2% Asian, non-Hispanic/Latino; 0.6% American Indian or Alaska Native, non-Hispanic/Latino; 0.5% Two or more races, non-Hispanic/Latino; 13% Race/ethnicity unknown; 3% international.

Freshmen *Admission:* 596 enrolled.

Faculty *Total:* 310, 36% full-time, 10% with terminal degrees.

Majors Airline pilot and flight crew; animation, interactive technology, video graphics and special effects; architectural engineering technology; autobody/collision and repair technology; automobile/automotive mechanics technology; business administration and management; business/commerce; carpentry; cinematography and film/video production; computer and information sciences; computer engineering; computer programming; computer science; computer systems analysis; computer technology/computer systems technology; construction engineering technology; criminal justice/law enforcement administration; desktop publishing and digital imaging design; drafting and design technology; electrical and electronics engineering; electrical, electronic and communications engineering technology; electrical/electronics equipment installation and repair; graphic and printing equipment operation/production; graphic communications; heating, air conditioning, ventilation and refrigeration maintenance technology; industrial technology; information technology; interior design; manufacturing engineering; manufacturing engineering technology; marine maintenance and ship repair technology; mechanical engineering; medical/clinical assistant; occupational therapist assistant; physical therapy technology; pipefitting and sprinkler fitting; radio and television broadcasting technology; recording arts technology; registered nursing/registered nurse; surgical technology; web page, digital/multimedia and information resources design.

Academics *Calendar:* quarters. *Degrees:* associate, bachelor's, and master's. *Special study options:* academic remediation for entering students, adult/continuing education programs, advanced placement credit, distance learning, English as a second language, internships, part-time degree program, services for LD students, summer session for credit.

Library Library with 48,701 titles, 16,491 serial subscriptions, 1,470 audiovisual materials, an OPAC, a Web page.

Student Life *Housing:* college housing not available. *Campus security:* security personnel during open hours. *Student services:* personal/psychological counseling.

Costs (2011–12) *Tuition:* $18,825 full-time, $430 per credit hour part-time. Full-time tuition and fees vary according to degree level and program. Part-time tuition and fees vary according to degree level and program. No tuition increase for student's term of enrollment. *Required fees:* $890 full-time. *Payment plans:* tuition prepayment, installment. *Waivers:* employees or children of employees.

Financial Aid Of all full-time matriculated undergraduates who enrolled in 2009, 250 Federal Work-Study jobs (averaging $2290).

Applying *Options:* early admission, deferred entrance. *Application fee:* $25. *Required:* high school transcript, interview, basic skills testing, Ronald P. Carver reading test used for placement. Portfolio recommended for drafting program. *Application deadlines:* rolling (freshmen), rolling (transfers).

Freshman Application Contact Mr. Mark Blondin, Director of Admissions, New England Institute of Technology, 2500 Post Road, Warwick, RI 02886-2244. *Phone:* 401-739-5000. *Fax:* 401-738-5122. *E-mail:* neit@ids.net. *Web site:* http://www.neit.edu/.

Aiken Technical College

Aiken, South Carolina

- **State and locally supported** 2-year, founded 1972, part of South Carolina State Board for Technical and Comprehensive Education
- **Rural** 88-acre campus
- **Endowment** $4.1 million
- **Coed,** 3,128 undergraduate students, 48% full-time, 64% women, 36% men

Undergraduates 1,504 full-time; 1,624 part-time. 8% are from out of state; 32% Black or African American, non-Hispanic/Latino; 2% Hispanic/Latino; 0.9% Asian, non-Hispanic/Latino; 0.4% Native Hawaiian or other Pacific Islander, non-Hispanic/Latino; 0.5% American Indian or Alaska Native, non-Hispanic/Latino; 2% Race/ethnicity unknown; 0.1% international; 9% transferred in. *Retention:* 49% of full-time freshmen returned.

Freshmen *Admission:* 1,722 applied, 881 admitted, 698 enrolled.

Faculty *Total:* 232, 24% full-time. *Student/faculty ratio:* 18:1.

Majors Accounting; administrative assistant and secretarial science; automobile/automotive mechanics technology; child-care and support services management; computer engineering technology; computer programming; computer systems networking and telecommunications; criminal justice/law enforcement administration; data processing and data processing technology; early childhood education; electrical, electronic and communications engineering technology; industrial mechanics and maintenance technology; liberal arts and sciences/liberal studies; management science; marketing related; medical radiologic technology; multi/interdisciplinary studies related; radiation protection/health physics technology; registered nursing/registered nurse; sales, distribution, and marketing operations.

Academics *Calendar:* semesters. *Degree:* certificates, diplomas, and associate. *Special study options:* academic remediation for entering students, advanced placement credit, cooperative education, internships, off-campus study, part-time degree program, services for LD students, summer session for credit.

Library Aiken Technical College Library with 62,235 titles, 165 serial subscriptions, an OPAC, a Web page.

Student Life *Housing:* college housing not available. *Campus security:* 24-hour emergency response devices and patrols, late-night transport/escort service. *Student services:* personal/psychological counseling.

Athletics Member NJCAA. *Intercollegiate sports:* basketball M, softball W.

Costs (2011–12) *Tuition:* area resident $3416 full-time, $143 per credit hour part-time; state resident $3776 full-time, $158 per credit hour part-time; nonresident $9600 full-time, $400 per credit hour part-time. Full-time tuition and fees vary according to course load and reciprocity agreements. Part-time tuition and fees vary according to course load and reciprocity agreements. *Required fees:* $290 full-time, $15 per credit hour part-time, $85 per term part-time. *Payment plan:* installment.

Financial Aid Of all full-time matriculated undergraduates who enrolled in 2009, 48 Federal Work-Study jobs (averaging $3000).

Applying *Options:* electronic application, deferred entrance. *Required:* high school transcript. *Required for some:* essay or personal statement. *Application deadlines:* rolling (freshmen), rolling (transfers). *Notification:* continuous (freshmen).

Freshman Application Contact Aiken Technical College, PO Drawer 696, Aiken, SC 29802-0696. *Phone:* 803-593-9231 Ext. 1584. *Web site:* http://www.atc.edu/.

Brown Mackie College–Greenville

Greenville, South Carolina

- **Proprietary** primarily 2-year, part of Education Management Corporation
- **Coed**

Majors Accounting technology and bookkeeping; business administration and management; criminal justice/law enforcement administration; health/healthcare administration; information technology; legal assistant/paralegal; legal studies; medical/clinical assistant; office management; surgical technology.

Academics *Degrees:* certificates, associate, and bachelor's.

Costs (2010–11) *Tuition:* Tuition varies by program. Students should contact Brown Mackie College for tuition information.

Freshman Application Contact Brown Mackie College–Greenville, Two Liberty Square, 75 Beattie Place, Suite 100, Greenville, SC 29601. *Phone:* 864-239-5300. *Toll-free phone:* 877-479-8465. *Web site:* http://www.brownmackie.edu/greenville/.

See page 370 for the College Close-Up.

Central Carolina Technical College

Sumter, South Carolina

- **State-supported** 2-year, founded 1963, part of South Carolina State Board for Technical and Comprehensive Education
- **Small-town** 70-acre campus
- **Endowment** $1.2 million
- **Coed,** 4,382 undergraduate students, 38% full-time, 69% women, 31% men

Undergraduates 1,674 full-time, 2,708 part-time. Students come from 3 states and territories; 1% are from out of state; 50% Black or African American, non-Hispanic/Latino; 2% Hispanic/Latino; 1% Asian, non-Hispanic/Latino; 0.2% Two or more races, non-Hispanic/Latino; 4% Race/ethnicity unknown; 7% transferred in.

Freshmen *Admission:* 867 enrolled.

Faculty *Total:* 229, 40% full-time. *Student/faculty ratio:* 20:1.

Majors Accounting; administrative assistant and secretarial science; business administration and management; child-care and support services management; criminal justice/safety; data processing and data processing technology; environmental control technologies related; industrial electronics technology; legal assistant/paralegal; liberal arts and sciences/liberal studies; natural resources management and policy; registered nursing/registered nurse; sales, distribution, and marketing operations; surgical technology.

Academics *Calendar:* semesters. *Degree:* certificates, diplomas, and associate. *Special study options:* academic remediation for entering students, adult/continuing education programs, advanced placement credit, cooperative education, distance learning, external degree program, independent study, internships, part-time degree program, services for LD students, summer session for credit.

Library Central Carolina Technical College Library with 28,395 titles, 127 serial subscriptions, an OPAC, a Web page.

Student Life *Housing:* college housing not available. *Activities and Organizations:* Creative Arts Society, Phi Theta Kappa, Computer Club, National Student Nurses Association (local chapter), Natural Resources Management Club. *Campus security:* 24-hour emergency response devices, student patrols, security patrols parking lots and halls during working hours and off-duty Sumter officers are deployed on main campus during peak hours. *Student services:* personal/psychological counseling.

Standardized Tests *Required:* COMPASS/ASSET (for admission). *Required for some:* SAT (for admission), ACT (for admission), SAT or ACT (for admission).

Costs (2010–11) *Tuition:* area resident $3180 full-time, $133 per credit hour part-time; state resident $3740 full-time, $156 per credit hour part-time; non-resident $5672 full-time, $237 per credit hour part-time. *Required fees:* $200 full-time. *Payment plan:* deferred payment. *Waivers:* senior citizens and employees or children of employees.

Applying *Options:* electronic application. *Required:* high school transcript. *Application deadlines:* rolling (freshmen), rolling (transfers).

Freshman Application Contact Ms. Barbara Wright, Director of Admissions and Counseling, Central Carolina Technical College, 506 North Guignard Drive, Sumter, SC 29150. *Phone:* 803-778-6695. *Toll-free phone:* 800-221-8711 Ext. 455. *Fax:* 803-778-6696. *E-mail:* wrightb@cctech.edu. *Web site:* http://www.cctech.edu/.

Clinton Junior College

Rock Hill, South Carolina

Director of Admissions Robert M. Copeland, Vice President for Student Affairs, Clinton Junior College, PO Box 968, 1029 Crawford Road, Rock Hill, SC 29730. *Phone:* 803-327-7402. *Toll-free phone:* 877-837-9645. *Fax:* 803-327-3261. *E-mail:* rcopeland@clintonjrcollege.org. *Web site:* http://www.clintonjuniorcollege.edu/.

Denmark Technical College

Denmark, South Carolina

- **State-supported** 2-year, founded 1948, part of South Carolina State Board for Technical and Comprehensive Education
- **Rural** 53-acre campus
- **Coed,** 1,033 undergraduate students, 74% full-time, 56% women, 44% men

Undergraduates 767 full-time, 266 part-time. 5% are from out of state; 96% Black or African American, non-Hispanic/Latino; 0.1% Hispanic/Latino; 0.3% Asian, non-Hispanic/Latino; 0.1% American Indian or Alaska Native, non-Hispanic/Latino; 0.2% Race/ethnicity unknown; 2% transferred in. *Retention:* 32% of full-time freshmen returned.

Freshmen *Admission:* 386 enrolled.

Faculty *Total:* 46, 76% full-time. *Student/faculty ratio:* 21:1.

Majors Administrative assistant and secretarial science; automobile/automotive mechanics technology; business administration and management; computer and information sciences; criminal justice/law enforcement administration; engineering technology; human services; kindergarten/pre-school education.

Academics *Calendar:* semesters. *Degree:* certificates, diplomas, and associate. *Special study options:* academic remediation for entering students, adult/continuing education programs, advanced placement credit, cooperative education, distance learning, independent study, internships, off-campus study, part-time degree program, summer session for credit.

Library Denmark Technical College Learning Resources Center with 18,728 titles, 195 serial subscriptions, 802 audiovisual materials, an OPAC.

Student Life *Housing Options:* men-only, women-only. Campus housing is university owned. Freshman applicants given priority for college housing. *Activities and Organizations:* choral group, Student Government Association, DTC Choir, athletics, Phi Theta Kappa Internal Honor Society, Esquire Club (men & women). *Campus security:* 24-hour patrols, late-night transport/escort service, 24 hour emergency contact line/alarm devices. *Student services:* health clinic, personal/psychological counseling.

Athletics Member NJCAA. *Intercollegiate sports:* basketball M/W, cheerleading W. *Intramural sports:* baseball M, basketball M/W, softball W, tennis M/W, volleyball M/W.

Standardized Tests *Required:* ACT, ASSET, and COMPASS (for admission). *Recommended:* SAT or ACT (for admission).

Costs (2010–11) *Tuition:* state resident $2590 full-time, $95 per credit hour part-time; nonresident $4870 full-time, $190 per credit hour part-time. Full-time tuition and fees vary according to course load. Part-time tuition and fees vary according to course load. No tuition increase for student's term of enrollment. *Room and board:* $3566; room only: $1762. *Payment plan:* installment. *Waivers:* senior citizens.

Financial Aid Of all full-time matriculated undergraduates who enrolled in 2009, 250 Federal Work-Study jobs (averaging $2000).

Applying *Options:* early admission, deferred entrance. *Application fee:* $10. *Required:* high school transcript. *Application deadlines:* rolling (freshmen), rolling (out-of-state freshmen), rolling (transfers).

Freshman Application Contact Mrs. Tonya Thomas, Dean of Enrollment Management, Denmark Technical College, PO Box 327, 1126 Solomon Blatt Boulevard, Denmark, SC 29042. *Phone:* 803-793-5182. *Fax:* 803-793-5942. *E-mail:* thomast@denmarktech.edu. *Web site:* http://www.denmarktech.edu/.

ECPI College of Technology

Charleston, South Carolina

Admissions Office Contact ECPI College of Technology, 7410 Northside Drive, Suite 100, Charleston, SC 29420. *Toll-free phone:* 866-708-6166. *Web site:* http://www.ecpi.edu/.

ECPI College of Technology

Columbia, South Carolina

Admissions Office Contact ECPI College of Technology, 250 Berryhill Road, #300, Columbia, SC 29210. *Toll-free phone:* 866-708-6168 (in-state); 866-708-6768 (out-of-state). *Web site:* http://www.ecpi.edu/.

ECPI College of Technology

Greenville, South Carolina

Admissions Office Contact ECPI College of Technology, 1001 Keys Drive, #100, Greenville, SC 29615. *Toll-free phone:* 866-708-6171. *Web site:* http://www.ecpi.edu/.

Florence-Darlington Technical College

Florence, South Carolina

Director of Admissions Shelley Fortin, Vice President for Enrollment Management and Student Services, Florence-Darlington Technical College, 2715 West Lucas Street, PO Box 100548, Florence, SC 29501-0548. *Phone:* 843-661-8111 Ext. 117. *Toll-free phone:* 800-228-5745. *E-mail:* shelley.fortin@fdtc.edu. *Web site:* http://www.fdtc.edu/.

Forrest Junior College

Anderson, South Carolina

- **Proprietary** 2-year, founded 1946
- **Rural** 3-acre campus
- **Coed**

Undergraduates 56 full-time, 38 part-time. Students come from 2 states and territories; 1% are from out of state; 10% transferred in.
Faculty *Student/faculty ratio:* 5:1.
Academics *Calendar:* quarters. *Degree:* certificates, diplomas, and associate. *Special study options:* advanced placement credit, cooperative education, distance learning, double majors, independent study, internships, part-time degree program, summer session for credit.
Student Life *Campus security:* 24-hour emergency response devices, late-night transport/escort service.
Standardized Tests *Required:* Gates-McGinnity (for admission).
Costs (2010–11) *Tuition:* $8820 full-time, $245 per credit hour part-time. *Required fees:* $150 full-time, $245 per credit hour part-time.
Financial Aid Of all full-time matriculated undergraduates who enrolled in 2008, 94 applied for aid, 87 were judged to have need.
Applying *Options:* electronic application, deferred entrance. *Application fee:* $50. *Required:* essay or personal statement, high school transcript, minimum 2.0 GPA, interview. *Recommended:* minimum 2.5 GPA.
Freshman Application Contact Ms. Janie Turmon, Admissions and Placement Coordinator/Representative, Forrest Junior College, 601 East River Street, Anderson, SC 29624. *Phone:* 864-225-7653 Ext. 210. *Fax:* 864-261-7471. *E-mail:* janieturmon@forrestcollege.com. *Web site:* http://www.forrestcollege.edu/.

Greenville Technical College

Greenville, South Carolina

Director of Admissions Carolyn Watkins, Dean of Admissions, Greenville Technical College, PO Box 5616, Greenville, SC 29606-5616. *Phone:* 864-250-8287. *E-mail:* carolyn.watkins@gvltec.edu. *Web site:* http://www.gvltec.com/.

Horry-Georgetown Technical College

Conway, South Carolina

Freshman Application Contact Mr. George Swindoll, Vice President for Enrollment, Development, and Registration, Horry-Georgetown Technical College, 2050 Highway 502 East, PO Box 261966, Conway, SC 29528-6066. *Phone:* 843-349-5277. *Fax:* 843-349-7501. *E-mail:* george.swindoll@hgtc.edu. *Web site:* http://www.hgtc.edu/.

ITT Technical Institute

Columbia, South Carolina

- **Proprietary** primarily 2-year, part of ITT Educational Services, Inc.
- **Coed**

Majors CAD/CADD drafting/design technology; computer and information systems security; computer engineering technology; computer software and media applications related; construction management; criminal justice/law enforcement administration; design and visual communications; system, networking, and LAN/WAN management; web/multimedia management and webmaster; web page, digital/multimedia and information resources design.
Academics *Degrees:* associate and bachelor's.
Student Life *Housing:* college housing not available.
Freshman Application Contact Director of Recruitment, ITT Technical Institute, 1628 Browning Road, Suite 180, Columbia, SC 29210. *Phone:* 803-216-6000. *Toll-free phone:* 800-242-5158. *Web site:* http://www.itt-tech.edu/.

ITT Technical Institute

Greenville, South Carolina

- **Proprietary** primarily 2-year, founded 1992, part of ITT Educational Services, Inc.
- **Coed**

Majors CAD/CADD drafting/design technology; computer and information systems security; computer engineering technology; computer software and media applications related; computer software technology; construction management; criminal justice/law enforcement administration; design and visual communications; electrical, electronic and communications engineering technology; game and interactive media design; legal assistant/paralegal; project management; system, networking, and LAN/WAN management; web/multimedia management and webmaster; web page, digital/multimedia and information resources design.

Academics *Calendar:* quarters. *Degrees:* associate and bachelor's.
Student Life *Housing:* college housing not available.
Financial Aid Of all full-time matriculated undergraduates who enrolled in 2009, 3 Federal Work-Study jobs.
Freshman Application Contact Director of Recruitment, ITT Technical Institute, 6 Independence Pointe, Greenville, SC 29615. *Phone:* 864-288-0777. *Toll-free phone:* 800-932-4488. *Web site:* http://www.itt-tech.edu/.

ITT Technical Institute

Myrtle Beach, South Carolina

- **Proprietary** 2-year, part of ITT Educational Services, Inc.
- **Coed**

Majors CAD/CADD drafting/design technology; computer and information systems security; computer engineering technology; construction management; electrical, electronic and communications engineering technology; legal assistant/paralegal; system, networking, and LAN/WAN management.
Academics *Calendar:* quarters.
Freshman Application Contact Director of Recruitment, ITT Technical Institute, 9654 N. Kings Highway, Suite 101, Myrtle Beach, SC 29572. *Phone:* 843-497-7820. *Toll-free phone:* 877-316-7054. *Web site:* http://www.itt-tech.edu/.

ITT Technical Institute

North Charleston, South Carolina

- **Proprietary** 2-year, part of ITT Educational Services, Inc.
- **Coed**

Majors CAD/CADD drafting/design technology; computer and information systems security; computer engineering technology; construction management; legal assistant/paralegal; system, networking, and LAN/WAN management.
Academics *Calendar:* quarters.
Freshman Application Contact Director of Recruitment, ITT Technical Institute, 2431 W. Aviation Avenue, North Charleston, SC 29406. *Phone:* 843-745-5700. *Toll-free phone:* 877-291-0900. *Web site:* http://www.itt-tech.edu/.

Midlands Technical College

Columbia, South Carolina

- **State and locally supported** 2-year, founded 1974, part of South Carolina State Board for Technical and Comprehensive Education
- **Suburban** 113-acre campus
- **Endowment** $5.1 million
- **Coed,** 12,078 undergraduate students, 47% full-time, 61% women, 39% men

Undergraduates 5,697 full-time, 6,381 part-time. Students come from 30 states and territories; 3% are from out of state; 35% Black or African American, non-Hispanic/Latino; 2% Hispanic/Latino; 2% Asian, non-Hispanic/Latino; 0.5% American Indian or Alaska Native, non-Hispanic/Latino; 0.2% Two or more races, non-Hispanic/Latino; 4% Race/ethnicity unknown; 0.0% international; 10% transferred in.
Freshmen *Admission:* 5,753 applied, 3,763 admitted, 2,282 enrolled.
Faculty *Total:* 733, 29% full-time, 12% with terminal degrees. *Student/faculty ratio:* 20:1.
Majors Accounting; administrative assistant and secretarial science; architectural engineering technology; automobile/automotive mechanics technology; business administration and management; business/commerce; child-care provision; civil engineering technology; clinical/medical laboratory technology; commercial and advertising art; computer and information sciences and support services related; computer installation and repair technology; computer systems networking and telecommunications; construction engineering technology; court reporting; criminal justice/safety; data processing and data processing technology; dental assisting; dental hygiene; electrical, electronic and communications engineering technology; engineering technology; gerontology; health information/medical records technology; health professions related; heating, air conditioning, ventilation and refrigeration maintenance technology; industrial electronics technology; industrial mechanics and maintenance technology; legal assistant/paralegal; liberal arts and sciences/liberal studies; licensed practical/vocational nurse training; mechanical drafting and CAD/CADD; mechanical engineering/mechanical technology; medical/clinical assistant; medical radiologic technology; multi/interdisciplinary studies related; nuclear medical technology; occupational therapist assistant; pharmacy technician; physical therapy technology; precision production related; precision production trades; registered nursing/registered nurse; respiratory care therapy; sales, distribution, and marketing operations; surgical technology; youth services.
Academics *Calendar:* semesters. *Degree:* certificates, diplomas, and associate. *Special study options:* academic remediation for entering students, adult/

continuing education programs, advanced placement credit, cooperative education, distance learning, double majors, English as a second language, internships, part-time degree program, services for LD students, student-designed majors, summer session for credit.

Library Midlands Technical College Library with 98,507 titles, 423 serial subscriptions, 2,114 audiovisual materials, an OPAC, a Web page.

Student Life *Housing:* college housing not available. *Activities and Organizations:* drama/theater group, student-run newspaper. *Campus security:* 24-hour emergency response devices and patrols, late-night transport/escort service.

Athletics *Intramural sports:* basketball M, bowling M/W, equestrian sports M/W, football M, softball M/W, ultimate Frisbee M/W, volleyball M/W.

Standardized Tests *Required for some:* ACT ASSET. *Recommended:* SAT or ACT (for admission).

Costs (2010–11) *One-time required fee:* $25. *Tuition:* area resident $3480 full-time, $145 per credit hour part-time; state resident $4344 full-time, $181 per credit hour part-time; nonresident $10,440 full-time, $435 per credit hour part-time. Full-time tuition and fees vary according to course load. Part-time tuition and fees vary according to course load. *Required fees:* $200 full-time, $100 per term part-time. *Payment plan:* installment. *Waivers:* senior citizens and employees or children of employees.

Financial Aid Of all full-time matriculated undergraduates who enrolled in 2009, 138 Federal Work-Study jobs (averaging $2496).

Applying *Options:* electronic application, early admission, deferred entrance. *Application fee:* $35. *Required for some:* interview. *Recommended:* high school transcript. *Application deadlines:* rolling (freshmen), rolling (transfers). *Notification:* continuous (freshmen), continuous (transfers).

Freshman Application Contact Ms. Sylvia Littlejohn, Director of Admissions, Midlands Technical College, PO Box 2408, Columbia, SC 29202. *Phone:* 803-738-8324. *Fax:* 803-790-7524. *E-mail:* admissions@midlandstech.edu. *Web site:* http://www.midlandstech.edu/.

Miller-Motte Technical College
Charleston, South Carolina

- **Proprietary** 2-year, founded 2000, part of Delta Career Education Corporation
- **Urban** campus
- **Coed**

Academics *Calendar:* quarters. *Degree:* certificates, diplomas, and associate. *Special study options:* distance learning, part-time degree program.

Standardized Tests *Required:* Wonderlic (for admission).

Costs (2010–11) *Tuition:* $11,750 full-time. Full-time tuition and fees vary according to course load and program. Part-time tuition and fees vary according to course load and program. No tuition increase for student's term of enrollment. *Required fees:* $575 full-time.

Applying *Application fee:* $35. *Required:* high school transcript, interview.

Freshman Application Contact Ms. Elaine Cue, Campus President, Miller-Motte Technical College, 8085 Rivers Avenue, Suite E, Charleston, SC 29406. *Phone:* 843-574-0101. *Toll-free phone:* 877-617-4740. *Fax:* 843-266-3424. *E-mail:* juliasc@miller-mott.net. *Web site:* http://www.miller-motte.com/.

Northeastern Technical College
Cheraw, South Carolina

Freshman Application Contact Mrs. Mary K. Newton, Dean of Students, Northeastern Technical College, PO Drawer 1007, Cheraw, SC 29520-1007. *Phone:* 843-921-6935. *Fax:* 843-921-1476. *E-mail:* mpace@netc.edu. *Web site:* http://www.netc.edu/.

Orangeburg-Calhoun Technical College
Orangeburg, South Carolina

- **State and locally supported** 2-year, founded 1968, part of State Board for Technical and Comprehensive Education, South Carolina
- **Small-town** 100-acre campus with easy access to Columbia
- **Coed**

Undergraduates 1,538 full-time, 1,681 part-time. Students come from 11 states and territories; 1 other country.

Faculty *Student/faculty ratio:* 20:1.

Academics *Calendar:* semesters. *Degree:* certificates, diplomas, and associate. *Special study options:* academic remediation for entering students, adult/continuing education programs, advanced placement credit, cooperative education, distance learning, independent study, internships, part-time degree pro-

gram, services for LD students, student-designed majors, summer session for credit.

Student Life *Campus security:* 24-hour emergency response devices and patrols.

Costs (2010–11) *Tuition:* area resident $1717 full-time, $141 per credit hour part-time; state resident $2125 full-time, $175 per credit hour part-time; nonresident $3109 full-time, $257 per credit hour part-time.

Applying *Application fee:* $15. *Required:* high school transcript. *Required for some:* interview.

Freshman Application Contact Mr. Dana Rickards, Director of Recruitment, Orangeburg-Calhoun Technical College, 3250 St Matthews Road, NE, Orangeburg, SC 29118-8299. *Phone:* 803-535-1219. *Toll-free phone:* 800-813-6519. *Web site:* http://www.octech.edu/.

Piedmont Technical College
Greenwood, South Carolina

Director of Admissions Mr. Steve Coleman, Director of Admissions, Piedmont Technical College, 620 North Emerald Road, PO Box 1467, Greenwood, SC 29648-1467. *Phone:* 864-941-8603. *Toll-free phone:* 800-868-5528. *Web site:* http://www.ptc.edu/.

Spartanburg Community College
Spartanburg, South Carolina

- **State-supported** 2-year, founded 1961, part of South Carolina State Board for Technical and Comprehensive Education
- **Suburban** 104-acre campus with easy access to Charlotte
- **Coed**, 5,871 undergraduate students, 53% full-time, 63% women, 37% men

Undergraduates 3,133 full-time, 2,738 part-time. Students come from 14 states and territories; 5 other countries; 2% are from out of state; 20% Black or African American, non-Hispanic/Latino; 2% Hispanic/Latino; 2% Asian, non-Hispanic/Latino; 0.2% American Indian or Alaska Native, non-Hispanic/Latino; 0.9% Two or more races, non-Hispanic/Latino; 29% Race/ethnicity unknown; 28% transferred in. *Retention:* 57% of full-time freshmen returned.

Freshmen *Admission:* 3,946 applied, 2,237 admitted, 1,277 enrolled.

Faculty *Total:* 365, 30% full-time. *Student/faculty ratio:* 16:1.

Majors Accounting; administrative assistant and secretarial science; applied horticulture/horticulture operations; automobile/automotive mechanics technology; business administration and management; clinical/medical laboratory technology; computer and information sciences; data processing and data processing technology; drafting and design technology; electrical, electronic and communications engineering technology; engineering technology; heating, air conditioning, ventilation and refrigeration maintenance technology; horticultural science; industrial electronics technology; liberal arts and sciences/liberal studies; machine tool technology; marketing/marketing management; mechanical drafting and CAD/CADD; mechanical engineering/mechanical technology; medical radiologic technology; multi/interdisciplinary studies related; radiation protection/health physics technology; registered nursing/registered nurse; respiratory care therapy; sales, distribution, and marketing operations.

Academics *Calendar:* semesters condensed semesters plus summer sessions. *Degree:* certificates, diplomas, and associate. *Special study options:* academic remediation for entering students, adult/continuing education programs, advanced placement credit, cooperative education, distance learning, English as a second language, part-time degree program, services for LD students, summer session for credit.

Library Spartanburg Community College Library with 40,078 titles, 295 serial subscriptions, an OPAC, a Web page.

Student Life *Housing:* college housing not available. *Activities and Organizations:* drama/theater group, student-run newspaper. *Campus security:* 24-hour emergency response devices and patrols. *Student services:* personal/psychological counseling, women's center.

Standardized Tests *Required for some:* SAT or ACT (for admission).

Costs (2011–12) *Tuition:* area resident $3536 full-time, $148 per credit hour part-time; state resident $4384 full-time, $183 per credit hour part-time; nonresident $7298 full-time, $305 per credit hour part-time. Full-time tuition and fees vary according to course load. *Required fees:* $40 full-time, $20 per term part-time. *Payment plan:* installment. *Waivers:* senior citizens.

Applying *Options:* electronic application, early admission. *Application fee:* $25. *Required:* high school transcript, interview, high school diploma, GED or equivalent. *Application deadlines:* rolling (freshmen), rolling (transfers). *Notification:* continuous (freshmen), continuous (transfers).

Freshman Application Contact Kathy Jo Lancaster, Admissions Counselor, Spartanburg Community College, PO Box 4386, Spartanburg, SC 29305. *Phone:* 864-592-4815. *Toll-free phone:* 866-591-3700. *Fax:* 864-592-4564. *E-mail:* admissions@stcsc.edu. *Web site:* http://www.sccsc.edu/.

Spartanburg Methodist College
Spartanburg, South Carolina

- **Independent Methodist** 2-year, founded 1911
- **Urban** 110-acre campus with easy access to Charlotte
- **Endowment** $14.2 million
- **Coed**

Undergraduates 775 full-time, 33 part-time. Students come from 8 states and territories; 1 other country; 6% are from out of state; 4% transferred in; 68% live on campus.
Faculty *Student/faculty ratio:* 18:1.
Academics *Calendar:* semesters. *Degree:* associate. *Special study options:* academic remediation for entering students, advanced placement credit, English as a second language, honors programs, independent study, part-time degree program, services for LD students, summer session for credit.
Student Life *Campus security:* 24-hour emergency response devices and patrols, student patrols, late-night transport/escort service, controlled dormitory access.
Athletics Member NJCAA.
Standardized Tests *Required:* SAT or ACT (for admission).
Costs (2010–11) *One-time required fee:* $150. *Comprehensive fee:* $20,984 includes full-time tuition ($13,359), mandatory fees ($225), and room and board ($7400). Full-time tuition and fees vary according to course load. Part-time tuition: $361 per semester hour. Part-time tuition and fees vary according to course load. *Payment plans:* installment, deferred payment.
Financial Aid Of all full-time matriculated undergraduates who enrolled in 2009, 80 Federal Work-Study jobs (averaging $1600). 90 state and other part-time jobs (averaging $1600). *Financial aid deadline:* 8/30.
Applying *Options:* electronic application, deferred admission. *Application fee:* $20. *Required:* essay or personal statement, high school transcript, minimum 2.0 GPA, rank in upper 75% of high school class. *Required for some:* interview. *Recommended:* interview.
Freshman Application Contact Daniel L. Philbeck, Vice President for Enrollment Management, Spartanburg Methodist College, 1000 Powell Mill Road, Spartanburg, SC 29301-5899. *Phone:* 864-587-4223. *Toll-free phone:* 800-772-7286. *Fax:* 864-587-4355. *E-mail:* admiss@smcsc.edu. *Web site:* http://www.smcsc.edu/.

Technical College of the Lowcountry
Beaufort, South Carolina

Freshman Application Contact Rhonda Cole, Admissions Services Manager, Technical College of the Lowcountry, 921 Ribaut Road, PO Box 1288, Beaufort, SC 29901-1288. *Phone:* 843-525-8229. *Fax:* 843-525-8285. *E-mail:* rcole@tcl.edu. *Web site:* http://www.tclonline.org/.

Tri-County Technical College
Pendleton, South Carolina

Director of Admissions Renae Frazier, Director, Recruitment and Admissions, Tri-County Technical College, PO Box 587, 7900 Highway 76, Pendleton, SC 29670-0587. *Phone:* 864-646-1550. *Fax:* 864-646-1890. *E-mail:* infocent@tctc.edu. *Web site:* http://www.tctc.edu/.

Trident Technical College
Charleston, South Carolina

- **State and locally supported** 2-year, founded 1964, part of South Carolina State Board for Technical and Comprehensive Education
- **Urban** campus
- **Coed,** 14,834 undergraduate students, 46% full-time, 63% women, 37% men

Undergraduates 6,856 full-time, 7,978 part-time. 4% are from out of state.
Freshmen *Admission:* 2,850 admitted, 2,850 enrolled.
Faculty *Total:* 803, 38% full-time. *Student/faculty ratio:* 22:1.
Majors Accounting; administrative assistant and secretarial science; airframe mechanics and aircraft maintenance technology; automobile/automotive mechanics technology; biological and physical sciences; business administration and management; child-care provision; civil engineering technology; clinical/medical laboratory technology; commercial and advertising art; computer engineering technology; computer graphics; computer/information technology services administration related; computer programming (specific applications); computer systems networking and telecommunications; criminal justice/law enforcement administration; culinary arts; dental hygiene; electrical, electronic and communications engineering technology; engineering technology; horticultural science; hotel/motel administration; human services; industrial technology; legal assistant/paralegal; legal studies; liberal arts and sciences/liberal studies; machine tool technology; marketing/marketing management; mechanical engineering/mechanical technology; medical administrative assistant and medical secretary; occupational therapy; physical therapy; registered nursing/registered nurse; respiratory care therapy; telecommunications technology; veterinary/animal health technology; web/multimedia management and webmaster; web page, digital/multimedia and information resources design.
Academics *Calendar:* semesters. *Degree:* certificates, diplomas, and associate. *Special study options:* academic remediation for entering students, advanced placement credit, cooperative education, distance learning, double majors, English as a second language, part-time degree program, services for LD students, summer session for credit.
Library Learning Resources Center plus 3 others with 135,345 titles, 785 serial subscriptions, 12,486 audiovisual materials, an OPAC, a Web page.
Student Life *Housing:* college housing not available. *Activities and Organizations:* drama/theater group, student-run newspaper, radio station, Phi Theta Kappa, Lex Artis Paralegal Society, Hospitality and Culinary Student Association, Partnership for Change in Communities and Families, Society of Student Leaders. *Campus security:* 24-hour emergency response devices and patrols, late-night transport/escort service. *Student services:* personal/psychological counseling.
Costs (2011–12) *Tuition:* area resident $3530 full-time, $144 per credit hour part-time; state resident $3916 full-time, $160 per credit hour part-time; nonresident $6582 full-time, $275 per credit hour part-time. Full-time tuition and fees vary according to course load. Part-time tuition and fees vary according to course load. *Required fees:* $50 full-time, $5 per credit hour part-time. *Payment plan:* installment. *Waivers:* senior citizens and employees or children of employees.
Applying *Options:* electronic application, early admission. *Application fee:* $30. *Required for some:* high school transcript. *Application deadlines:* 8/9 (freshmen), 8/9 (transfers). *Notification:* continuous (freshmen), continuous (transfers).
Freshman Application Contact Ms. Clara Martin, Admissions Director, Trident Technical College, Charleston, SC 29423-8067. *Phone:* 843-574-6326. *Fax:* 843-574-6109. *E-mail:* Clara.Martin@tridenttech.edu. *Web site:* http://www.tridenttech.edu/.

University of South Carolina Lancaster
Lancaster, South Carolina

- **State-supported** 2-year, founded 1959, part of University of South Carolina System
- **Small-town** 17-acre campus with easy access to Charlotte
- **Coed**

Undergraduates 794 full-time, 799 part-time. Students come from 10 states and territories; 2 other countries; 1% are from out of state.
Faculty *Student/faculty ratio:* 14:1.
Academics *Calendar:* semesters. *Degree:* associate. *Special study options:* academic remediation for entering students, advanced placement credit, distance learning, honors programs, independent study, internships, part-time degree program, services for LD students.
Athletics Member NJCAA.
Standardized Tests *Required:* SAT or ACT (for admission).
Costs (2010–11) *One-time required fee:* $50. *Tuition:* state resident $5496 full-time, $229 per credit hour part-time; nonresident $13,752 full-time, $573 per credit hour part-time. Full-time tuition and fees vary according to student level. Part-time tuition and fees vary according to student level. *Required fees:* $482 full-time, $15 per credit hour part-time.
Applying *Options:* electronic application, early admission. *Application fee:* $40. *Required:* high school transcript.
Freshman Application Contact Susan Vinson, Admissions Counselor, University of South Carolina Lancaster, PO Box 889, Lancaster, SC 29721. *Phone:* 803-313-7000. *Fax:* 803-313-7116. *E-mail:* vinsons@mailbox.sc.edu. *Web site:* http://usclancaster.sc.edu/.

University of South Carolina Salkehatchie
Allendale, South Carolina

- **State-supported** 2-year, founded 1965, part of University of South Carolina System
- **Rural** 95-acre campus
- **Coed**

Undergraduates 6% are from out of state. *Retention:* 45% of full-time freshmen returned.
Faculty *Student/faculty ratio:* 16:1.
Academics *Calendar:* semesters. *Degree:* associate. *Special study options:* academic remediation for entering students, adult/continuing education programs, advanced placement credit, distance learning, part-time degree program, summer session for credit.

Student Life *Campus security:* 24-hour emergency response devices.

Athletics Member NJCAA.

Standardized Tests *Required:* SAT or ACT (for admission).

Costs (2010–11) *Tuition:* state resident $6870 full-time, $229 per credit part-time; nonresident $17,190 full-time, $573 per credit part-time. Full-time tuition and fees vary according to student level. Part-time tuition and fees vary according to student level. *Payment plans:* installment, deferred payment.

Applying *Options:* electronic application. *Application fee:* $40. *Required:* high school transcript, minimum 2.0 GPA.

Freshman Application Contact Ms. Carmen Brown, Admissions Coordinator, University of South Carolina Salkehatchie, PO Box 617, Allendale, SC 29810. *Phone:* 803-584-3446. *Toll-free phone:* 800-922-5500. *Fax:* 803-584-3884. *E-mail:* cdbrown@mailbox.sc.edu. *Web site:* http://uscsalkehatchie.sc.edu/.

University of South Carolina Sumter

Sumter, South Carolina

Freshman Application Contact Mr. Keith Britton, Director of Admissions, University of South Carolina Sumter, 200 Miller Road, Sumter, SC 29150-2498. *Phone:* 803-938-3882. *Fax:* 803-938-3901. *E-mail:* kbritton@usc.sumter.edu. *Web site:* http://www.uscsumter.edu/.

University of South Carolina Union

Union, South Carolina

- **State-supported** 2-year, founded 1965, part of University of South Carolina System
- **Small-town** campus with easy access to Charlotte
- **Coed,** 500 undergraduate students, 50% full-time, 60% women, 40% men

Undergraduates 250 full-time, 250 part-time.

Freshmen *Admission:* 400 enrolled. *Average high school GPA:* 3.

Faculty *Total:* 25, 48% full-time. *Student/faculty ratio:* 14:1.

Majors Biological and physical sciences; liberal arts and sciences/liberal studies.

Academics *Calendar:* semesters. *Degree:* associate. *Special study options:* part-time degree program.

Student Life *Housing:* college housing not available. *Activities and Organizations:* drama/theater group, student-run newspaper, choral group.

Standardized Tests *Required:* SAT or ACT (for admission).

Costs (2011–12) *Tuition:* state resident $2850 full-time; nonresident $4850 full-time.

Financial Aid Of all full-time matriculated undergraduates who enrolled in 2009, 16 Federal Work-Study jobs (averaging $3400).

Applying *Application fee:* $40. *Required:* high school transcript. *Application deadline:* rolling (freshmen).

Freshman Application Contact Mr. Terry Young, Director of Enrollment Services, University of South Carolina Union, PO Drawer 729, Union, SC 29379-0729. *Phone:* 864-429-8728. *E-mail:* tyoung@gwm.sc.edu. *Web site:* http://uscunion.sc.edu/.

Williamsburg Technical College

Kingstree, South Carolina

Freshman Application Contact Williamsburg Technical College, 601 Martin Luther King, Jr Avenue, Kingstree, SC 29556-4197. *Phone:* 843-355-4162. *Toll-free phone:* 800-768-2021. *Web site:* http://www.wiltech.edu/.

York Technical College

Rock Hill, South Carolina

Freshman Application Contact Mr. Kenny Aldridge, Admissions Department Manager, York Technical College, Rock Hill, SC 29730. *Phone:* 803-327-8008. *Toll-free phone:* 800-922-8324. *Fax:* 803-981-7237. *E-mail:* kaldridge@yorktech.com. *Web site:* http://www.yorktech.com/.

SOUTH DAKOTA

Kilian Community College

Sioux Falls, South Dakota

- **Independent** 2-year, founded 1977
- **Urban** 2-acre campus
- **Coed,** 390 undergraduate students, 18% full-time, 69% women, 31% men

Undergraduates 71 full-time, 319 part-time. Students come from 3 states and territories; 6% are from out of state; 10% transferred in.

Freshmen *Admission:* 54 enrolled.

Faculty *Total:* 52, 10% full-time, 13% with terminal degrees. *Student/faculty ratio:* 11:1.

Majors Accounting; American Indian/Native American studies; business administration and management; counseling psychology; criminal justice/law enforcement administration; education; financial planning and services; history; information technology; liberal arts and sciences/liberal studies; medical office management; psychology; social work; sociology; substance abuse/addiction counseling.

Academics *Calendar:* trimesters. *Degree:* certificates and associate. *Special study options:* academic remediation for entering students, distance learning, double majors, English as a second language, independent study, part-time degree program, services for LD students, summer session for credit.

Library Sioux Falls Public Library with 78,000 titles, 395 serial subscriptions, an OPAC, a Web page.

Student Life *Housing:* college housing not available. *Activities and Organizations:* Phi Theta Kappa, Students in Free Enterprise (SIFE), Student Leadership. *Campus security:* late-night transport/escort service. *Student services:* personal/psychological counseling.

Costs (2010–11) *Tuition:* $9072 full-time, $252 per credit hour part-time. *Required fees:* $300 full-time, $100 per term part-time. *Payment plan:* installment. *Waivers:* senior citizens and employees or children of employees.

Applying *Options:* electronic application, deferred entrance. *Application fee:* $25. *Required:* high school transcript. *Application deadlines:* rolling (freshmen), rolling (out-of-state freshmen), rolling (transfers).

Freshman Application Contact Ms. Mary Klockman, Director of Admissions, Kilian Community College, 300 East 6th Street, Sioux Falls, SD 57103. *Phone:* 605-221-3100. *Toll-free phone:* 800-888-1147. *Fax:* 605-336-2606. *E-mail:* info@killian.edu. *Web site:* http://www.kilian.edu/.

Lake Area Technical Institute

Watertown, South Dakota

Director of Admissions Ms. Debra Shephard, Assistant Director, Lake Area Technical Institute, 230 11th Street, NE, Watertown, SD 57201. *Phone:* 605-882-5284. *Toll-free phone:* 800-657-4344. *E-mail:* latiinfo@lati.tec.sd.us. *Web site:* http://www.lakeareatech.edu/.

Mitchell Technical Institute

Mitchell, South Dakota

- **State-supported** 2-year, founded 1968
- **Rural** 90-acre campus
- **Coed,** 1,106 undergraduate students, 85% full-time, 29% women, 71% men

Undergraduates 939 full-time, 167 part-time. Students come from 11 states and territories; 9% are from out of state; 1% Black or African American, non-Hispanic/Latino; 1% Native Hawaiian or other Pacific Islander, non-Hispanic/Latino; 2% American Indian or Alaska Native, non-Hispanic/Latino; 0.1% Race/ethnicity unknown; 8% live on campus. *Retention:* 81% of full-time freshmen returned.

Freshmen *Admission:* 1,339 applied, 641 admitted.

Faculty *Total:* 61, 93% full-time. *Student/faculty ratio:* 18:1.

Majors Accounting and business/management; business automation/technology/data entry; carpentry; clinical/medical laboratory technology; computer science; construction trades related; culinary arts; electrical, electronic and communications engineering technology; electrician; energy management and systems technology; heating, air conditioning, ventilation and refrigeration maintenance technology; lineworker; medical/clinical assistant; medical radiologic technology; precision systems maintenance and repair technologies related; radiologic technology/science; small engine mechanics and repair technology; speech-language pathology; telecommunications technology.

Academics *Calendar:* semesters. *Degree:* certificates, diplomas, and associate. *Special study options:* academic remediation for entering students, advanced placement credit, cooperative education, distance learning, internships, part-time degree program, services for LD students, summer session for credit.

Library Instructional Services Center with 100 serial subscriptions, an OPAC.

Student Life *Housing Options:* coed. Campus housing is provided by a third party. *Activities and Organizations:* Student Representative Board, Skills USA, Post-Secondary Agricultural Students, Rodeo Club, Student Veterans Organization. *Student services:* personal/psychological counseling.

Athletics *Intercollegiate sports:* equestrian sports M/W. *Intramural sports:* basketball M/W, riflery M/W, softball M/W, volleyball M/W.

Standardized Tests *Required for some:* COMPASS. *Recommended:* ACT (for admission).

Costs (2010–11) *Tuition:* state resident $3240 full-time, $90 per credit hour part-time; nonresident $3240 full-time. Full-time tuition and fees vary according to course load and program. Part-time tuition and fees vary according to course load and program. *Required fees:* $3000 full-time, $49 per credit hour part-time, $49 per credit hour part-time. *Waivers:* employees or children of employees.

Financial Aid Of all full-time matriculated undergraduates who enrolled in 2009, 52 Federal Work-Study jobs (averaging $1375).

Applying *Options:* electronic application. *Application fee:* $60. *Required:* high school transcript. *Required for some:* essay or personal statement, interview. *Recommended:* minimum 2.0 GPA. *Application deadlines:* rolling (freshmen), rolling (out-of-state freshmen), rolling (transfers). *Notification:* continuous (freshmen), continuous (out-of-state freshmen), continuous (transfers).

Freshman Application Contact Mr. Clayton Deuter, Director of Admissions, Mitchell Technical Institute, 1800 East Spruce Street, Mitchell, SD 57301. *Phone:* 605-995-3025. *Toll-free phone:* 800-952-0042. *Fax:* 605-995-3067. *E-mail:* clayton.deuter@mitchelltech.edu. *Web site:* http://www.mitchelltech.edu/.

National American University

Ellsworth AFB, South Dakota

Freshman Application Contact Admissions Office, National American University, 1000 Ellsworth Street, Suite 2400B, Ellsworth AFB, SD 57706. *Web site:* http://www.national.edu/.

Sisseton-Wahpeton Community College

Sisseton, South Dakota

- **Federally supported** 2-year, founded 1979
- **Rural** 2-acre campus
- **Coed**

Undergraduates 181 full-time, 56 part-time. 2% are from out of state; 0.4% transferred in.

Faculty *Student/faculty ratio:* 10:1.

Academics *Calendar:* semesters. *Degree:* certificates and associate. *Special study options:* academic remediation for entering students, adult/continuing education programs, cooperative education, double majors, internships, off-campus study, part-time degree program, summer session for credit.

Student Life *Campus security:* 24-hour emergency response devices.

Standardized Tests *Required:* COMPASS test (for admission).

Costs (2010–11) *Tuition:* state resident $3300 full-time, $110 per credit hour part-time; nonresident $3300 full-time, $110 per credit hour part-time. Full-time tuition and fees vary according to course load and program. Part-time tuition and fees vary according to course load and program. No tuition increase for student's term of enrollment. *Room and board:* $6000.

Financial Aid Of all full-time matriculated undergraduates who enrolled in 2009, 5 Federal Work-Study jobs (averaging $1200).

Applying *Required:* high school transcript. *Required for some:* Certificate of Indian Blood for enrolled tribal members. *Recommended:* minimum 2.0 GPA, interview.

Freshman Application Contact Sisseton-Wahpeton Community College, Old Agency Box 689, Sisseton, SD 57262. *Phone:* 605-698-3966 Ext. 1180. *Web site:* http://www.swc.tc/.

Southeast Technical Institute

Sioux Falls, South Dakota

- **State-supported** 2-year, founded 1968
- **Urban** 168-acre campus
- **Endowment** $468,959
- **Coed,** 2,455 undergraduate students, 79% full-time, 47% women, 53% men

Undergraduates 1,940 full-time, 515 part-time. Students come from 7 states and territories; 9% are from out of state; 1% Black or African American, non-

Hispanic/Latino; 3% Hispanic/Latino; 0.6% Asian, non-Hispanic/Latino; 2% American Indian or Alaska Native, non-Hispanic/Latino; 1% Two or more races, non-Hispanic/Latino; 12% Race/ethnicity unknown; 15% transferred in; 8% live on campus. *Retention:* 68% of full-time freshmen returned.

Freshmen *Admission:* 3,119 applied, 1,324 admitted, 592 enrolled. *Average high school GPA:* 2.73.

Faculty *Total:* 180, 46% full-time, 3% with terminal degrees. *Student/faculty ratio:* 18:1.

Majors Accounting; animation, interactive technology, video graphics and special effects; applied horticulture/horticulture operations; architectural engineering technology; autobody/collision and repair technology; automobile/automotive mechanics technology; banking and financial support services; biomedical technology; building/construction finishing, management, and inspection related; business administration and management; cardiovascular technology; child-care and support services management; child-care provision; civil engineering technology; clinical/medical laboratory science and allied professions related; clinical/medical laboratory technology; commercial and advertising art; computer and information sciences and support services related; computer and information systems security; computer/information technology services administration related; computer installation and repair technology; computer programming; computer programming related; computer software engineering; computer systems networking and telecommunications; computer technology/computer systems technology; criminal justice/police science; desktop publishing and digital imaging design; diagnostic medical sonography and ultrasound technology; diesel mechanics technology; electrical, electronic and communications engineering technology; electrical/electronics equipment installation and repair; electromechanical technology; finance; health unit coordinator/ward clerk; heating, air conditioning, ventilation and refrigeration maintenance technology; horticultural science; industrial technology; licensed practical/vocational nurse training; machine shop technology; machine tool technology; marketing/marketing management; mechanical engineering/mechanical technology; merchandising, sales, and marketing operations related (general); nuclear medical technology; office occupations and clerical services; surgical technology; turf and turfgrass management.

Academics *Calendar:* semesters. *Degree:* certificates, diplomas, and associate. *Special study options:* academic remediation for entering students, accelerated degree program, advanced placement credit, distance learning, double majors, independent study, internships, part-time degree program, services for LD students, summer session for credit.

Library Southeast Library with 10,643 titles, 158 serial subscriptions, an OPAC, a Web page.

Student Life *Housing Options:* coed. Campus housing is provided by a third party. *Activities and Organizations:* VICA (Vocational Industrial Clubs of America), American Landscape Contractors Association. *Campus security:* 24-hour emergency response devices and patrols, late-night transport/escort service. *Student services:* personal/psychological counseling.

Athletics *Intramural sports:* basketball M/W, bowling M/W, volleyball M/W.

Standardized Tests *Recommended:* ACT (for admission).

Costs (2010–11) *Tuition:* state resident $2700 full-time, $90 per credit part-time; nonresident $2700 full-time, $90 per credit part-time. *Required fees:* $1807 full-time, $60 per credit hour part-time. *Room and board:* room only: $4600. *Payment plan:* installment.

Financial Aid Of all full-time matriculated undergraduates who enrolled in 2009, 35 Federal Work-Study jobs (averaging $2550).

Applying *Options:* electronic application. *Required:* high school transcript, minimum 2.2 GPA. *Required for some:* interview, background check and drug testing. *Application deadlines:* rolling (freshmen), rolling (out-of-state freshmen), rolling (transfers). *Notification:* continuous (freshmen), continuous (out-of-state freshmen), continuous (transfers).

Freshman Application Contact Mr. Scott Dorman, Recruiter, Southeast Technical Institute, Sioux Falls, SD 57107. *Phone:* 605-367-4458. *Toll-free phone:* 800-247-0789. *Fax:* 605-367-8305. *E-mail:* scott.dorman@southeasttech.edu. *Web site:* http://www.southeasttech.edu/.

Western Dakota Technical Institute

Rapid City, South Dakota

Freshman Application Contact Jill Elder, Western Dakota Technical Institute, 800 Mickelson Drive, Rapid City, SD 57703. *Phone:* 605-718-2411. *Toll-free phone:* 800-544-8765. *Fax:* 605-394-2204. *E-mail:* jill.elder@wdt.edu. *Web site:* http://www.westerndakotatech.org/.

TENNESSEE

Chattanooga College–Medical, Dental and Technical Careers

Chattanooga, Tennessee

Director of Admissions Toney McFadden, Admission Director, Chattanooga College–Medical, Dental and Technical Careers, 3805 Brainerd Road, Chattanooga, TN 37411-3798. *Phone:* 423-624-0077. *Fax:* 423-624-1575. *Web site:* http://www.ecpconline.com/.

Chattanooga State Community College

Chattanooga, Tennessee

- **State-supported** 2-year, founded 1965, part of Tennessee Board of Regents
- **Urban** 100-acre campus
- **Endowment** $5.6 million
- **Coed**

Undergraduates 4,412 full-time, 5,019 part-time. Students come from 30 states and territories; 11 other countries; 9% are from out of state.
Faculty *Student/faculty ratio:* 19:1.
Academics *Calendar:* semesters. *Degree:* certificates, diplomas, and associate. *Special study options:* academic remediation for entering students, accelerated degree program, adult/continuing education programs, advanced placement credit, cooperative education, distance learning, double majors, external degree program, honors programs, independent study, internships, part-time degree program, services for LD students, summer session for credit.
Student Life *Campus security:* 24-hour emergency response devices and patrols, late-night transport/escort service.
Athletics Member NJCAA.
Costs (2010–11) *Tuition:* state resident $3127 full-time, $118 per credit hour part-time; nonresident $11,983 full-time, $369 per credit hour part-time. *Required fees:* $295 full-time.
Applying *Options:* electronic application, early admission, deferred entrance. *Application fee:* $15. *Required for some:* high school transcript, interview. *Recommended:* high school transcript.
Freshman Application Contact Ms. Diane Norris, Director of Admissions, Chattanooga State Community College, 4501 Amnicola Highway, Chattanooga, TN 37406. *Phone:* 423-697-4401 Ext. 3107. *Fax:* 423-697-4709. *E-mail:* diane.norris@chattanoogastate.edu. *Web site:* http://www.chattanoogastate.edu/.

Cleveland State Community College

Cleveland, Tennessee

- **State-supported** 2-year, founded 1967, part of Tennessee Board of Regents
- **Suburban** 83-acre campus
- **Endowment** $5.3 million
- **Coed**, 3,753 undergraduate students, 57% full-time, 59% women, 41% men

Undergraduates 2,132 full-time, 1,621 part-time. Students come from 11 states and territories; 3 other countries; 1% are from out of state; 16% transferred in.
Freshmen *Admission:* 1,041 applied, 666 enrolled. *Average high school GPA:* 3.08. *Test scores:* ACT scores over 18: 73%; ACT scores over 24: 11%.
Faculty *Total:* 194, 37% full-time, 13% with terminal degrees. *Student/faculty ratio:* 14:1.
Majors Administrative assistant and secretarial science; business administration and management; child development; community organization and advocacy; criminal justice/police science; general studies; industrial technology; kindergarten/preschool education; liberal arts and sciences and humanities related; liberal arts and sciences/liberal studies; public administration and social service professions related; registered nursing/registered nurse; science technologies related.
Academics *Calendar:* semesters. *Degree:* certificates and associate. *Special study options:* academic remediation for entering students, adult/continuing education programs, advanced placement credit, cooperative education, distance learning, double majors, external degree program, honors programs, independent study, internships, off-campus study, part-time degree program, services for LD students, summer session for credit.
Library Cleveland State Community College Library with 147,405 titles, 831 serial subscriptions, 9,142 audiovisual materials, an OPAC, a Web page.

Student Life *Housing:* college housing not available. *Activities and Organizations:* student-run newspaper, choral group, Human Services/Social Work, Computer Aided Design, Phi Theta Kappa, Student Nursing Association, Early Childhood Education. *Campus security:* 24-hour emergency response devices and patrols. *Student services:* personal/psychological counseling.
Athletics Member NJCAA. *Intercollegiate sports:* baseball M(s), basketball M(s)/W(s), softball W(s). *Intramural sports:* archery M/W, basketball M/W, bowling M/W, cheerleading M(c)/W(c), softball W, table tennis M/W, volleyball M/W.
Costs (2010–11) *Tuition:* state resident $3209 full-time, $118 per credit hour part-time; nonresident $12,395 full-time, $487 per credit hour part-time. Full-time tuition and fees vary according to course load. *Required fees:* $269 full-time, $14 per credit hour part-time. *Payment plan:* deferred payment. *Waivers:* senior citizens and employees or children of employees.
Financial Aid Of all full-time matriculated undergraduates who enrolled in 2009, 52 Federal Work-Study jobs (averaging $1025).
Applying *Options:* electronic application, early admission, deferred entrance. *Application fee:* $10. *Required:* high school transcript. *Application deadlines:* rolling (freshmen), rolling (transfers). *Notification:* continuous (freshmen), continuous (transfers).
Freshman Application Contact Ms. Midge Burnette, Director of Admissions and Records, Cleveland State Community College, Cleveland, TN 37320-3570. *Phone:* 423-472-7141 Ext. 212. *Toll-free phone:* 800-604-2722. *Fax:* 423-478-6255. *E-mail:* mburnette@clevelandstatecc.edu. *Web site:* http://www.clevelandstatecc.edu/.

Columbia State Community College

Columbia, Tennessee

Freshman Application Contact Mr. Joey Scruggs, Coordinator of Recruitment, Columbia State Community College, PO Box 1315, Columbia, TN 38402-1315. *Phone:* 931-540-2540. *E-mail:* scruggs@coscc.cc.tn.us. *Web site:* http://www.columbiastate.edu/.

Concorde Career College

Memphis, Tennessee

Freshman Application Contact Dee Vickers, Director, Concorde Career College, 5100 Poplar Avenue, Suite 132, Memphis, TN 38137. *Phone:* 901-761-9494. *Fax:* 901-761-3293. *E-mail:* dvickers@concorde.edu. *Web site:* http://www.concorde.edu/.

Daymar Institute

Nashville, Tennessee

Director of Admissions Admissions Office, Daymar Institute, 340 Plus Park Boulevard, Nashville, TN 37217. *Phone:* 615-361-7555. *Fax:* 615-367-2736. *Web site:* http://www.daymarinstitute.edu/.

Dyersburg State Community College

Dyersburg, Tennessee

- **State-supported** 2-year, founded 1969, part of Tennessee Board of Regents
- **Small-town** 100-acre campus with easy access to Memphis
- **Endowment** $4.5 million
- **Coed**, 3,749 undergraduate students, 51% full-time, 69% women, 31% men

Undergraduates 1,927 full-time, 1,822 part-time. Students come from 4 states and territories; 1 other country; 2% are from out of state; 6% transferred in. *Retention:* 53% of full-time freshmen returned.
Freshmen *Admission:* 1,657 applied, 1,657 admitted, 902 enrolled. *Average high school GPA:* 2:36. *Test scores:* ACT scores over 18: 55%; ACT scores over 24: 5%.
Faculty *Total:* 205, 28% full-time, 13% with terminal degrees. *Student/faculty ratio:* 17:1.
Majors Business administration and management; child development; computer/information technology services administration related; criminal justice/police science; electrical, electronic and communications engineering technology; emergency medical technology (EMT paramedic); health information/medical records technology; liberal arts and sciences/liberal studies; registered nursing/registered nurse.
Academics *Calendar:* semesters. *Degree:* certificates and associate. *Special study options:* academic remediation for entering students, adult/continuing education programs, advanced placement credit, distance learning, double majors, honors programs, independent study, part-time degree program, services for LD students, summer session for credit.
Library Learning Resource Center with 40,693 titles, 87 serial subscriptions, 2,274 audiovisual materials, an OPAC, a Web page.

Student Life *Housing:* college housing not available. *Activities and Organizations:* drama/theater group, choral group, student government, Phi Theta Kappa, Minority Association for Successful Students, Video Club, Psychology Club. *Campus security:* 24-hour patrols. *Student services:* personal/psychological counseling.

Athletics Member NJCAA. *Intercollegiate sports:* baseball M(s), basketball M(s)/W(s), cheerleading W(s), softball W(s).

Standardized Tests *Required:* SAT or ACT (for admission).

Costs (2011–12) *Tuition:* state resident $2832 full-time, $118 per credit hour part-time; nonresident $11,959 full-time, $369 per credit hour part-time. Part-time tuition and fees vary according to course load. *Required fees:* $271 full-time, $24 per credit hour part-time, $13 per term part-time. *Payment plan:* deferred payment. *Waivers:* senior citizens and employees or children of employees.

Financial Aid Of all full-time matriculated undergraduates who enrolled in 2008, 56 Federal Work-Study jobs (averaging $1760). 92 state and other part-time jobs (averaging $1419).

Applying *Options:* early admission. *Application fee:* $10. *Required:* high school transcript. *Application deadlines:* rolling (freshmen), rolling (transfers). *Notification:* continuous (freshmen), continuous (transfers).

Freshman Application Contact Ms. Jordan Willis, Admissions Counselor, Dyersburg State Community College, Dyersburg, TN 38024. *Phone:* 731-286-3324. *Fax:* 731-286-3325. *E-mail:* willis@dscc.edu. *Web site:* http://www.dscc.edu/.

Fountainhead College of Technology

Knoxville, Tennessee

Freshman Application Contact Director of Administration, Fountainhead College of Technology, 3203 Tazewell Pike, Knoxville, TN 37918-2530. *Phone:* 865-688-9422. *Toll-free phone:* 888-218-7335. *Fax:* 865-688-2419. *Web site:* http://www.fountainheadcollege.edu/.

High-Tech Institute

Memphis, Tennessee

Freshman Application Contact Admissions Office, High-Tech Institute, 5865 Shelby Oaks Circle, Suite 100, Memphis, TN 38134. *Toll-free phone:* 866-269-7251. *Web site:* http://www.high-techinstitute.com/.

High-Tech Institute

Nashville, Tennessee

Freshman Application Contact Admissions Office, High-Tech Institute, 560 Royal Parkway, Nashville, TN 37214. *Phone:* 615-902-9705. *Toll-free phone:* 888-616-6549. *Web site:* http://www.high-techinstitute.com/.

ITT Technical Institute

Chattanooga, Tennessee

- **Proprietary** primarily 2-year, part of ITT Educational Services, Inc.
- **Coed**

Majors CAD/CADD drafting/design technology; computer and information systems security; computer engineering technology; computer software engineering; computer software technology; construction management; criminal justice/law enforcement administration; design and visual communications; electrical, electronic and communications engineering technology; legal assistant/paralegal; project management; system, networking, and LAN/WAN management.

Academics *Degrees:* associate and bachelor's.

Student Life *Housing:* college housing not available.

Freshman Application Contact Director of Recruitment, ITT Technical Institute, 5600 Brainerd Road, Suite G-1, Chattanooga, TN 37411. *Phone:* 423-510-6800. *Toll-free phone:* 877-474-8312. *Web site:* http://www.itt-tech.edu/.

ITT Technical Institute

Cordova, Tennessee

- **Proprietary** primarily 2-year, founded 1994, part of ITT Educational Services, Inc.
- **Suburban** campus
- **Coed**

Majors Accounting technology and bookkeeping; business administration and management; CAD/CADD drafting/design technology; computer and informa-

tion systems security; computer engineering technology; computer software and media applications related; computer software engineering; computer software technology; computer systems networking and telecommunications; construction management; criminal justice/law enforcement administration; design and visual communications; electrical, electronic and communications engineering technology; game and interactive media design; legal assistant/paralegal; project management; system, networking, and LAN/WAN management; web page, digital/multimedia and information resources design.

Academics *Calendar:* quarters. *Degrees:* associate and bachelor's.

Student Life *Housing:* college housing not available.

Freshman Application Contact Director of Recruitment, ITT Technical Institute, 7260 Goodlett Farms Parkway, Cordova, TN 38016. *Phone:* 901-381-0200. *Toll-free phone:* 866-444-5141. *Web site:* http://www.itt-tech.edu/.

ITT Technical Institute

Johnson City, Tennessee

- **Proprietary** primarily 2-year
- **Coed**

Majors CAD/CADD drafting/design technology; computer and information systems security; computer engineering technology; computer software engineering; computer software technology; construction management; electrical, electronic and communications engineering technology; legal assistant/paralegal; project management; system, networking, and LAN/WAN management.

Academics *Degrees:* associate and bachelor's.

Freshman Application Contact Director of Recruitment, ITT Technical Institute, 4721 Lake Park Drive, Suite 100, Johnson City, TN 37615. *Phone:* 423-952-4400. *Toll-free phone:* 877-301-9691. *Web site:* http://www.itt-tech.edu/.

ITT Technical Institute

Knoxville, Tennessee

- **Proprietary** primarily 2-year, founded 1988, part of ITT Educational Services, Inc.
- **Suburban** campus
- **Coed**

Majors CAD/CADD drafting/design technology; computer and information systems security; computer engineering technology; computer software and media applications related; computer software engineering; computer software technology; computer systems networking and telecommunications; construction management; criminal justice/law enforcement administration; design and visual communications; electrical, electronic and communications engineering technology; game and interactive media design; information technology project management; legal assistant/paralegal; project management; system, networking, and LAN/WAN management.

Academics *Calendar:* quarters. *Degrees:* associate and bachelor's.

Student Life *Housing:* college housing not available.

Freshman Application Contact Director of Recruitment, ITT Technical Institute, 10208 Technology Drive, Knoxville, TN 37932. *Phone:* 865-671-2800. *Toll-free phone:* 800-671-2801. *Web site:* http://www.itt-tech.edu/.

ITT Technical Institute

Nashville, Tennessee

- **Proprietary** primarily 2-year, founded 1984, part of ITT Educational Services, Inc.
- **Urban** campus
- **Coed**

Majors CAD/CADD drafting/design technology; computer and information systems security; computer engineering technology; computer software and media applications related; computer software engineering; computer software technology; computer systems networking and telecommunications; construction management; criminal justice/law enforcement administration; design and visual communications; electrical, electronic and communications engineering technology; game and interactive media design; legal assistant/paralegal; project management; system, networking, and LAN/WAN management; web page, digital/multimedia and information resources design.

Academics *Calendar:* quarters. *Degrees:* associate and bachelor's.

Student Life *Housing:* college housing not available.

Freshman Application Contact Director of Recruitment, ITT Technical Institute, 2845 Elm Hill Pike, Nashville, TN 37214. *Phone:* 615-889-8700. *Toll-free phone:* 800-331-8386. *Web site:* http://www.itt-tech.edu/.

Jackson State Community College
Jackson, Tennessee

- **State-supported** 2-year, founded 1967, part of Tennessee Board of Regents
- **Suburban** 97-acre campus with easy access to Memphis
- **Endowment** $800,579
- **Coed**

Undergraduates Students come from 7 states and territories; 3 other countries. *Retention:* 49% of full-time freshmen returned.

Faculty *Student/faculty ratio:* 21:1.

Academics *Calendar:* semesters. *Degree:* certificates, diplomas, and associate. *Special study options:* academic remediation for entering students, adult/continuing education programs, advanced placement credit, cooperative education, distance learning, external degree program, honors programs, independent study, internships, off-campus study, part-time degree program, services for LD students, summer session for credit. *ROTC:* Army (b).

Student Life *Campus security:* 24-hour patrols, late-night transport/escort service, field camera surveillance.

Athletics Member NJCAA.

Standardized Tests *Required:* SAT or ACT (for admission), COMPASS (for admission). *Recommended:* ACT (for admission).

Costs (2010–11) *One-time required fee:* $10. *Tuition:* state resident $3193 full-time, $118 per credit hour part-time; nonresident $12,126 full-time, $487 per credit hour part-time. Full-time tuition and fees vary according to course load. Part-time tuition and fees vary according to course load. *Required fees:* $253 full-time, $9 per credit hour part-time, $14 per term part-time.

Financial Aid Of all full-time matriculated undergraduates who enrolled in 2009, 30 Federal Work-Study jobs (averaging $3000). 10 state and other part-time jobs (averaging $3000).

Applying *Options:* electronic application. *Application fee:* $10. *Required for some:* high school transcript.

Freshman Application Contact Ms. Andrea Winchester, Director of Admissions, Jackson State Community College, 2046 North Parkway, Jackson, TN 38301-3797. *Phone:* 731-425-8844 Ext. 484. *Toll-free phone:* 800-355-5722. *Fax:* 731-425-9559. *E-mail:* awinchester@jscc.edu. *Web site:* http://www.jscc.edu/.

John A. Gupton College
Nashville, Tennessee

- **Independent** 2-year, founded 1946
- **Urban** 1-acre campus with easy access to Nashville
- **Endowment** $60,000
- **Coed,** 127 undergraduate students, 81% full-time, 54% women, 46% men

Undergraduates 103 full-time, 24 part-time. Students come from 11 states and territories; 15% are from out of state; 24% Black or African American, non-Hispanic/Latino; 0.8% Hispanic/Latino; 0.8% Native Hawaiian or other Pacific Islander, non-Hispanic/Latino; 47% transferred in; 11% live on campus.

Freshmen *Admission:* 97 applied, 64 admitted, 47 enrolled.

Faculty *Total:* 13, 15% full-time. *Student/faculty ratio:* 8:1.

Majors Funeral service and mortuary science.

Academics *Calendar:* semesters. *Degree:* diplomas and associate. *Special study options:* part-time degree program.

Library Memorial Library with 4,000 titles, 54 serial subscriptions, a Web page.

Student Life *Housing Options:* coed. Campus housing is university owned. *Campus security:* controlled dormitory access, day patrols.

Standardized Tests *Required:* ACT (for admission).

Costs (2011–12) *Tuition:* $9248 full-time, $289 per semester hour part-time. Full-time tuition and fees vary according to course load. Part-time tuition and fees vary according to course load. *Required fees:* $70 full-time. *Room only:* $3600. *Payment plan:* installment.

Financial Aid *Financial aid deadline:* 6/1.

Applying *Options:* deferred entrance. *Application fee:* $20. *Required:* essay or personal statement, high school transcript, 2 letters of recommendation. *Application deadlines:* rolling (freshmen), rolling (transfers).

Freshman Application Contact John A. Gupton College, 1616 Church Street, Nashville, TN 37203-2920. *Phone:* 615-327-3927. *Web site:* http://www.guptoncollege.edu/.

Kaplan Career Institute, Nashville Campus
Nashville, Tennessee

- **Proprietary** 2-year, founded 1981
- **Coed**

Academics *Degree:* certificates, diplomas, and associate.

Freshman Application Contact Kaplan Career Institute, Nashville Campus, 750 Envious Lane, Nashville, TN 37217. *Phone:* 615-269-9900. *Toll-free phone:* 800-336-4457. *Web site:* http://www.kci-nashville.com/.

MedVance Institute
Cookeville, Tennessee

Director of Admissions Ms. Sharon Mellott, Director of Admissions, MedVance Institute, 1025 Highway 111, Cookeville, TN 38501. *Phone:* 931-526-3660. *Toll-free phone:* 800-259-3659 (in-state); 800-256-9085 (out-of-state). *Web site:* http://www.medvance.edu/.

Mid-America Baptist Theological Seminary
Cordova, Tennessee

Freshman Application Contact Mr. Duffy Guyton, Director of Admissions, Mid-America Baptist Theological Seminary, PO Box 2350, Cordova, TN 38016. *Phone:* 901-751-8453 Ext. 3066. *Toll-free phone:* 800-968-4508. *Fax:* 901-751-8454. *E-mail:* info@mabts.edu. *Web site:* http://www.mabts.edu/.

Miller-Motte Technical College
Clarksville, Tennessee

Director of Admissions Ms. Lisa Teague, Director of Admissions, Miller-Motte Technical College, 1820 Business Park Drive, Clarksville, TN 37040. *Phone:* 800-558-0071. *E-mail:* lisateague@hotmail.com. *Web site:* http://www.miller-motte.com/.

Motlow State Community College
Tullahoma, Tennessee

- **State-supported** 2-year, founded 1969, part of Tennessee Board of Regents
- **Rural** 187-acre campus with easy access to Nashville
- **Endowment** $3.5 million
- **Coed,** 5,079 undergraduate students, 54% full-time, 62% women, 38% men

Undergraduates 2,760 full-time, 2,319 part-time. Students come from 15 states and territories; 5 other countries; 1% are from out of state; 7% transferred in.

Freshmen *Admission:* 5,319 applied, 1,659 admitted, 1,311 enrolled. *Average high school GPA:* 2.87.

Faculty *Total:* 278, 31% full-time, 12% with terminal degrees. *Student/faculty ratio:* 25:1.

Majors Business administration and management; education; general studies; liberal arts and sciences/liberal studies; registered nursing/registered nurse; special education–early childhood; web page, digital/multimedia and information resources design.

Academics *Calendar:* semesters. *Degree:* certificates and associate. *Special study options:* academic remediation for entering students, accelerated degree program, adult/continuing education programs, advanced placement credit, cooperative education, distance learning, double majors, honors programs, independent study, part-time degree program, services for LD students, study abroad, summer session for credit.

Library Crouch Library with 116,049 titles, 211 serial subscriptions, 4,111 audiovisual materials, an OPAC, a Web page.

Student Life *Housing:* college housing not available. *Activities and Organizations:* drama/theater group, choral group, PTK Club, Communication Club, Student Government Association, Art Club, Baptist Student Union. *Campus security:* 24-hour patrols, late-night transport/escort service. *Student services:* personal/psychological counseling.

Athletics Member NJCAA. *Intercollegiate sports:* baseball M(s), basketball M(s)/W(s), softball W(s). *Intramural sports:* badminton M/W, basketball M/W, bowling M/W, golf M/W, tennis M/W, volleyball M/W.

Costs (2010–11) *Tuition:* state resident $2832 full-time, $118 per credit hour part-time; nonresident $8856 full-time, $369 per credit hour part-time. *Required fees:* $271 full-time. *Payment plans:* installment, deferred payment. *Waivers:* senior citizens and employees or children of employees.

Financial Aid Of all full-time matriculated undergraduates who enrolled in 2008, 38 Federal Work-Study jobs (averaging $1858).

Applying *Options:* electronic application, early admission, deferred entrance. *Application fee:* $10. *Required:* high school transcript. *Application deadlines:* 8/13 (freshmen), 8/13 (transfers). *Notification:* continuous (freshmen), continuous (transfers).

Freshman Application Contact Ms. Sheri Mason, Assistant Director of Student Services, Motlow State Community College, Lynchburg, TN 37352-8500. *Phone:* 931-393-1764. *Toll-free phone:* 800-654-4877. *Fax:* 931-393-1681. *E-mail:* lmonks@mscc.edu. *Web site:* http://www.mscc.cc.tn.us/.

Nashville Auto Diesel College

Nashville, Tennessee

Freshman Application Contact Ms. Peggie Werrbach, Director of Admissions, Nashville Auto Diesel College, 1524 Gallatin Road, Nashville, TN 37206. *Phone:* 615-226-3990 Ext. 8465. *Toll-free phone:* 800-228-NADC. *Fax:* 615-262-8466. *E-mail:* wpruitt@nadcedu.com. *Web site:* http://www.nadcedu.com/.

Nashville State Technical Community College

Nashville, Tennessee

Freshman Application Contact Mr. Beth Mahan, Coordinator of Recruitment, Nashville State Technical Community College, 120 White Bridge Road, Nashville, TN 37209-4515. *Phone:* 615-353-3214. *Toll-free phone:* 800-272-7363. *E-mail:* beth.mahan@nscc.edu. *Web site:* http://www.nscc.edu/.

National College

Bristol, Tennessee

Freshman Application Contact National College, 1328 Highway 11 West, Bristol, TN 37620. *Phone:* 423-878-4440. *Web site:* http://www.national-college.edu/.

National College

Knoxville, Tennessee

Director of Admissions Frank Alvey, Campus Director, National College, 8415 Kingston Pike, Knoxville, TN 37919. *Phone:* 865-539-2011. *Toll-free phone:* 800-664-1886. *Fax:* 865-539-2049. *Web site:* http://www.national-college.edu/.

National College

Nashville, Tennessee

Director of Admissions Jerry Lafferty, Campus Director, National College, 5042 Linbar Drive, Suite 200, Nashville, TN 37211. *Phone:* 615-333-3344. *Toll-free phone:* 800-664-1886. *Web site:* http://www.national-college.edu/.

North Central Institute

Clarksville, Tennessee

Freshman Application Contact Dale Wood, Director of Admissions, North Central Institute, 168 Jack Miller Boulevard, Clarksville, TN 37042. *Phone:* 931-431-9700. *Fax:* 931-431-9771. *E-mail:* admissions@nci.edu. *Web site:* http://www.nci.edu/.

Northeast State Technical Community College

Blountville, Tennessee

Freshman Application Contact Dr. Jon P. Harr, Vice President for Student Affairs, Northeast State Technical Community College, PO Box 246, Blountville, TN 37617. *Phone:* 423-323-0231. *Toll-free phone:* 800-836-7822. *Fax:* 423-323-0240. *E-mail:* jpharr@northeaststate.edu. *Web site:* http://www.northeaststate.edu/.

Nossi College of Art

Goodlettsville, Tennessee

- **Independent** primarily 2-year
- **Urban** 10-acre campus with easy access to Nashville
- **Coed,** 660 undergraduate students, 100% full-time, 55% women, 45% men
- 63% of applicants were admitted

Undergraduates 660 full-time. Students come from 10 states and territories; 1 other country; 10% are from out of state; 16% Black or African American, non-Hispanic/Latino; 2% Hispanic/Latino; 0.8% Asian, non-Hispanic/Latino; 1% Race/ethnicity unknown. *Retention:* 75% of full-time freshmen returned.

Freshmen *Admission:* 210 applied, 133 admitted.

Faculty *Total:* 37, 16% full-time. *Student/faculty ratio:* 10:1.

Majors Commercial and advertising art; commercial photography; film/video and photographic arts related; graphic design; illustration.

Academics *Calendar:* semesters. *Degrees:* associate and bachelor's. *Special study options:* independent study, internships, services for LD students, summer session for credit.

Library Learning Resource Center with an OPAC.

Student Life *Housing:* college housing not available. *Activities and Organizations:* national fraternities. *Campus security:* campus has a gated entrance, all doors are kept locked.

Costs (2011–12) *Tuition:* $14,100 full-time, $4700 per term part-time. Full-time tuition and fees vary according to course load, degree level, and program. Part-time tuition and fees vary according to course load, degree level, and program. No tuition increase for student's term of enrollment. *Payment plan:* installment.

Applying *Options:* electronic application, early admission. *Application fee:* $100. *Required:* essay or personal statement, high school transcript, interview, portfolio of work is required for Associate or Bachelor of Graphic Art and Design program and the Bachelor of Illustration program.

Freshman Application Contact Ms. Mary Alexander, Admissions Director, Nossi College of Art, 590 Cheron Road, Madison, TN 37115. *Phone:* 615-514-2787 (ARTS). *Toll-free phone:* 877-860-1601. *Fax:* 615-514-2788. *E-mail:* admissions@nossi.edu. *Web site:* http://www.nossi.edu/.

Pellissippi State Technical Community College

Knoxville, Tennessee

Freshman Application Contact Director of Admissions and Records, Pellissippi State Technical Community College, PO Box 22990, Knoxville, TN 37933-0990. *Phone:* 865-694-6400. *Fax:* 865-539-7217. *Web site:* http://www.pstcc.edu/.

Remington College–Memphis Campus

Memphis, Tennessee

Director of Admissions Randal Hayes, Director of Recruitment, Remington College–Memphis Campus, 2731 Nonconnah Boulevard, Memphis, TN 38132-2131. *Phone:* 901-345-1000. *Fax:* 901-396-8310. *E-mail:* randal.hayes@remingtoncollege.edu. *Web site:* http://www.remingtoncollege.edu/.

Remington College–Nashville Campus

Nashville, Tennessee

Director of Admissions Mr. Frank Vivelo, Campus President, Remington College–Nashville Campus, 441 Donelson Pike, Suite 150, Nashville, TN 37214. *Phone:* 615-889-5520. *Fax:* 615-889-5528. *E-mail:* frank.vivelo@remingtoncollege.edu. *Web site:* http://www.remingtoncollege.edu/.

Roane State Community College

Harriman, Tennessee

Freshman Application Contact Admissions Office, Roane State Community College, 276 Patton Lane, Harriman, TN 37748. *Phone:* 865-882-4523. *Toll-free phone:* 800-343-9104. *E-mail:* admissions@roanestate.edu. *Web site:* http://www.roanestate.edu/.

Southwest Tennessee Community College

Memphis, Tennessee

Freshman Application Contact Ms. Cindy Meziere, Assistant Director of Recruiting, Southwest Tennessee Community College, PO Box 780, Memphis, TN 38103-0780. *Phone:* 901-333-4195. *Toll-free phone:* 877-717-STCC. *Fax:* 901-333-4473. *E-mail:* cmeziere@southwest.tn.edu. *Web site:* http://www.southwest.tn.edu/.

Vatterott College

Memphis, Tennessee

Admissions Office Contact Vatterott College, 2655 Dividend Drive, Memphis, TN 38132. *Toll-free phone:* 866-314-6454. *Web site:* http://www.vatterott-college.edu/.

Volunteer State Community College

Gallatin, Tennessee

- **State-supported** 2-year, founded 1970, part of Tennessee Board of Regents
- **Suburban** 100-acre campus with easy access to Nashville
- **Coed,** 8,989 undergraduate students, 49% full-time, 62% women, 38% men

Undergraduates 4,402 full-time, 4,587 part-time. Students come from 9 states and territories; 12 other countries; 0.9% are from out of state; 10% Black or African American, non-Hispanic/Latino; 3% Hispanic/Latino; 1% Asian, non-Hispanic/Latino; 0.1% Native Hawaiian or other Pacific Islander, non-Hispanic/Latino; 0.4% American Indian or Alaska Native, non-Hispanic/Latino; 1% Two or more races, non-Hispanic/Latino; 1% Race/ethnicity unknown; 0.5% international; 7% transferred in.
Freshmen *Admission:* 2,310 applied, 2,310 admitted, 1,664 enrolled. *Average high school GPA:* 2.91. *Test scores:* ACT scores over 18: 64%; ACT scores over 24: 12%.
Faculty *Total:* 382, 39% full-time, 8% with terminal degrees. *Student/faculty ratio:* 26:1.
Majors Business administration and management; child development; clinical/medical laboratory technology; community organization and advocacy; criminal justice/police science; education; fire science/firefighting; general studies; health information/medical records technology; health professions related; legal assistant/paralegal; liberal arts and sciences/liberal studies; medical radiologic technology; ophthalmic technology; physical therapy technology; respiratory care therapy; web page, digital/multimedia and information resources design.
Academics *Calendar:* semesters. *Degree:* certificates and associate. *Special study options:* academic remediation for entering students, accelerated degree program, adult/continuing education programs, advanced placement credit, distance learning, double majors, English as a second language, honors programs, independent study, internships, part-time degree program, services for LD students, study abroad, summer session for credit.
Library Thigpen Learning Resource Center with 53,098 titles, 180 serial subscriptions, 3,525 audiovisual materials, an OPAC, a Web page.
Student Life *Housing:* college housing not available. *Activities and Organizations:* drama/theater group, student-run newspaper, radio station, choral group, Gamma Beta Phi, Returning Woman's Organization, Phi Theta Kappa, Student Government Association, The Settler. *Campus security:* 24-hour emergency response devices and patrols, late-night transport/escort service. *Student services:* health clinic, personal/psychological counseling.
Athletics Member NJCAA. *Intercollegiate sports:* baseball M(s), basketball M(s)/W(s), softball W(s). *Intramural sports:* basketball M/W.
Standardized Tests *Required for some:* SAT or ACT (for admission).
Costs (2010–11) *Tuition:* state resident $2832 full-time, $118 per credit hour part-time; nonresident $11,688 full-time, $487 per credit hour part-time. Full-time tuition and fees vary according to course load. Part-time tuition and fees vary according to course load. *Required fees:* $269 full-time, $9 per credit hour part-time, $22 per term part-time. *Payment plan:* deferred payment. *Waivers:* senior citizens and employees or children of employees.
Financial Aid Of all full-time matriculated undergraduates who enrolled in 2008, 3,494 applied for aid, 2,598 were judged to have need, 166 had their need fully met. 25 Federal Work-Study jobs (averaging $2127). In 2008, 74 non-need-based awards were made. *Average percent of need met:* 50%. *Average financial aid package:* $5869. *Average need-based loan:* $2855. *Average need-based gift aid:* $4879. *Average non-need-based aid:* $2218.
Applying *Options:* electronic application, early admission, deferred entrance. *Application fee:* $10. *Required:* high school transcript. *Required for some:* essay or personal statement, minimum 2.0 GPA. *Application deadlines:* 8/28

(freshmen), 8/28 (transfers). *Notification:* continuous (freshmen), continuous (transfers).
Freshman Application Contact Mr. Tim Amyx, Director of Admissions, Volunteer State Community College, 1480 Nashville Pike, Gallatin, TN 37066-3188. *Phone:* 615-452-8600 Ext. 3614. *Toll-free phone:* 888-335-8722. *Fax:* 615-230-4875. *E-mail:* admissions@volstate.edu. *Web site:* http://www.volstate.edu/.

Walters State Community College

Morristown, Tennessee

- **State-supported** 2-year, founded 1970, part of Tennessee Board of Regents
- **Small-town** 100-acre campus
- **Endowment** $7.6 million
- **Coed**

Undergraduates 3,591 full-time, 3,262 part-time. Students come from 11 states and territories; 9 other countries; 0.6% are from out of state; 5% transferred in. *Retention:* 58% of full-time freshmen returned.
Faculty *Student/faculty ratio:* 22:1.
Academics *Calendar:* semesters. *Degree:* certificates and associate. *Special study options:* academic remediation for entering students, accelerated degree program, adult/continuing education programs, advanced placement credit, distance learning, freshman honors college, honors programs, part-time degree program, summer session for credit. *ROTC:* Army (c).
Student Life *Campus security:* 24-hour emergency response devices and patrols, late-night transport/escort service.
Athletics Member NJCAA.
Standardized Tests *Required:* SAT or ACT (for admission).
Costs (2010–11) *Tuition:* state resident $2832 full-time, $118 per semester hour part-time; nonresident $11,668 full-time, $487 per semester hour part-time. *Required fees:* $269 full-time, $16 per semester hour part-time, $20 per year part-time.
Applying *Options:* early admission. *Application fee:* $10. *Required:* high school transcript.
Freshman Application Contact Mr. Michael Campbell, Assistant Vice President for Student Affairs, Walters State Community College, 500 South Davy Crockett Parkway, Morristown, TN 37813-6899. *Phone:* 423-585-2682. *Toll-free phone:* 800-225-4770. *Fax:* 423-585-6876. *E-mail:* mike.campbell@ws.edu. *Web site:* http://www.ws.edu/.

TEXAS

The Academy of Health Care Professions

Houston, Texas

Freshman Application Contact Admissions Office, The Academy of Health Care Professions, 240 Northwest Mall Boulevard, Houston, TX 77092. *Phone:* 713-425-3100. *Toll-free phone:* 800-487-6728. *Fax:* 713-425-3193. *Web site:* http://www.academyofhealth.com/.

Alvin Community College

Alvin, Texas

- **State and locally supported** 2-year, founded 1949
- **Suburban** 114-acre campus with easy access to Houston
- **Coed**

Undergraduates 1,325 full-time, 3,075 part-time.
Faculty *Student/faculty ratio:* 17:1.
Academics *Calendar:* semesters. *Degree:* certificates, diplomas, and associate. *Special study options:* academic remediation for entering students, accelerated degree program, adult/continuing education programs, advanced placement credit, distance learning, double majors, English as a second language, honors programs, independent study, internships, part-time degree program, services for LD students, student-designed majors, study abroad, summer session for credit.
Student Life *Campus security:* 24-hour patrols, late-night transport/escort service.
Athletics Member NJCAA.
Costs (2010–11) *Tuition:* area resident $1080 full-time, $37 per credit hour part-time; state resident $2160 full-time, $72 per credit hour part-time; nonresident $3900 full-time, $130 per credit hour part-time. Full-time tuition and fees vary according to program. Part-time tuition and fees vary according to program. *Required fees:* $396 full-time.

Financial Aid Of all full-time matriculated undergraduates who enrolled in 2009, 65 Federal Work-Study jobs (averaging $3300). 3 state and other part-time jobs (averaging $3000).

Applying *Options:* electronic application. *Required for some:* high school transcript.

Freshman Application Contact Alvin Community College, 3110 Mustang Road, Alvin, TX 77511-4898. *Phone:* 281-756-3531. *Web site:* http://www.alvincollege.edu/.

Amarillo College

Amarillo, Texas

- **State and locally supported** 2-year, founded 1929
- **Urban** 1542-acre campus
- **Endowment** $27.8 million
- **Coed,** 11,675 undergraduate students, 35% full-time, 61% women, 39% men

Undergraduates 4,069 full-time, 7,606 part-time. 4% Black or African American, non-Hispanic/Latino; 30% Hispanic/Latino; 2% Asian, non-Hispanic/Latino; 1% American Indian or Alaska Native, non-Hispanic/Latino; 2% Race/ethnicity unknown.

Faculty *Total:* 480, 47% full-time, 8% with terminal degrees.

Majors Accounting; administrative assistant and secretarial science; airframe mechanics and aircraft maintenance technology; architectural engineering technology; art; automobile/automotive mechanics technology; behavioral sciences; biblical studies; biology/biological sciences; broadcast journalism; business administration and management; business teacher education; chemical technology; chemistry; child development; clinical laboratory science/medical technology; commercial and advertising art; computer engineering technology; computer programming; computer science; computer systems analysis; corrections; criminal justice/law enforcement administration; criminal justice/police science; dental hygiene; drafting and design technology; dramatic/theater arts; electrical, electronic and communications engineering technology; elementary education; emergency medical technology (EMT paramedic); engineering; English; environmental health; fine/studio arts; fire science/firefighting; funeral service and mortuary science; general studies; geology/earth science; health information/medical records administration; heating, air conditioning, ventilation and refrigeration maintenance technology; heavy equipment maintenance technology; history; industrial radiologic technology; information science/studies; instrumentation technology; interior design; journalism; laser and optical technology; legal administrative assistant/secretary; liberal arts and sciences/liberal studies; licensed practical/vocational nurse training; machine tool technology; mass communication/media; mathematics; medical administrative assistant and medical secretary; modern languages; music; music teacher education; natural sciences; nuclear medical technology; occupational therapy; photography; physical education teaching and coaching; physical sciences; physical therapy; physics; pre-engineering; pre-pharmacy studies; psychology; public relations/image management; radio and television; radiologic technology/science; real estate; registered nursing/registered nurse; religious studies; respiratory care therapy; rhetoric and composition; social sciences; social work; substance abuse/addiction counseling; telecommunications technology; tourism and travel services management; visual and performing arts.

Academics *Calendar:* semesters. *Degree:* certificates and associate. *Special study options:* academic remediation for entering students, adult/continuing education programs, advanced placement credit, cooperative education, distance learning, English as a second language, freshman honors college, honors programs, part-time degree program, services for LD students, summer session for credit.

Library Lynn Library Learning Center plus 2 others with 62,076 titles, 22,000 serial subscriptions, an OPAC, a Web page.

Student Life *Housing:* college housing not available. *Activities and Organizations:* drama/theater group, student-run newspaper, radio station, choral group, Student Government Association, College Republicans. *Campus security:* 24-hour patrols, late-night transport/escort service.

Athletics *Intramural sports:* basketball M/W, soccer M/W, softball M/W, tennis M/W, volleyball M/W.

Costs (2010–11) *Tuition:* area resident $1506 full-time, $63 per semester hour part-time; state resident $2034 full-time, $85 per semester hour part-time; nonresident $2994 full-time, $125 per semester hour part-time. Full-time tuition and fees vary according to course load. Part-time tuition and fees vary according to course load. *Payment plan:* installment. *Waivers:* senior citizens and employees or children of employees.

Financial Aid Of all full-time matriculated undergraduates who enrolled in 2009, 100 Federal Work-Study jobs (averaging $3000).

Applying *Options:* early admission, deferred entrance. *Required:* high school transcript. *Notification:* continuous (freshmen), continuous (transfers).

Freshman Application Contact Amarillo College, PO Box 447, Amarillo, TX 79178-0001. *Phone:* 806-371-5000. *Fax:* 806-371-5497. *E-mail:* askac@actx.edu. *Web site:* http://www.actx.edu/.

Angelina College

Lufkin, Texas

Freshman Application Contact Angelina College, PO Box 1768, Lufkin, TX 75902-1768. *Phone:* 936-633-5213. *Web site:* http://www.angelina.cc.tx.us/.

ATI Technical Training Center

Dallas, Texas

Freshman Application Contact Admissions Office, ATI Technical Training Center, 6627 Maple Avenue, Dallas, TX 75235. *Phone:* 214-352-2222. *Web site:* http://www.aticareertraining.edu/.

Austin Community College

Austin, Texas

- **State and locally supported** 2-year, founded 1972
- **Urban** campus with easy access to Austin
- **Endowment** $1.8 million
- **Coed,** 44,100 undergraduate students, 26% full-time, 56% women, 44% men

Undergraduates 11,519 full-time, 32,581 part-time.

Faculty *Total:* 1,962, 28% full-time. *Student/faculty ratio:* 20:1.

Majors Accounting technology and bookkeeping; administrative assistant and secretarial science; animation, interactive technology, video graphics and special effects; anthropology; art; automobile/automotive mechanics technology; banking and financial support services; biology/biological sciences; biology/biotechnology laboratory technician; business administration and management; business/commerce; carpentry; chemistry; child development; clinical/medical laboratory technology; commercial and advertising art; commercial photography; computer and information sciences; computer programming; computer systems networking and telecommunications; corrections; creative writing; criminal justice/police science; culinary arts; dance; dental hygiene; diagnostic medical sonography and ultrasound technology; drafting and design technology; dramatic/theater arts; early childhood education; economics; electrical, electronic and communications engineering technology; emergency medical technology (EMT paramedic); engineering; environmental engineering technology; fire prevention and safety technology; foreign languages and literatures; French; general studies; geographic information science and cartography; geography; geology/earth science; German; health and physical education/fitness; health information/medical records technology; health teacher education; heating, ventilation, air conditioning and refrigeration engineering technology; history; hospitality administration; human services; international business/trade/commerce; Japanese; journalism; Latin; legal assistant/paralegal; marketing/marketing management; mathematics; middle school education; music; music management; occupational therapist assistant; philosophy; physical sciences; physical therapy technology; physics; political science and government; pre-dentistry studies; premedical studies; pre-pharmacy studies; pre-veterinary studies; professional, technical, business, and scientific writing; psychology; radio and television; radiologic technology/science; real estate; registered nursing/registered nurse; rhetoric and composition; Russian; secondary education; sign language interpretation and translation; social work; sociology; Spanish; substance abuse/addiction counseling; surgical technology; surveying technology; therapeutic recreation; watchmaking and jewelrymaking; welding technology; writing.

Academics *Calendar:* semesters. *Degree:* certificates and associate. *Special study options:* academic remediation for entering students, accelerated degree program, adult/continuing education programs, advanced placement credit, cooperative education, distance learning, English as a second language, honors programs, independent study, internships, part-time degree program, services for LD students, summer session for credit. *ROTC:* Army (c), Air Force (c).

Library Main Library plus 7 others with 177,423 titles, 46,327 serial subscriptions, 16,595 audiovisual materials, an OPAC, a Web page.

Student Life *Housing:* college housing not available. *Activities and Organizations:* student-run newspaper, Student Government Association, Physical Therapist Assistant Club, African Student Association, ASL Friends United. *Student services:* personal/psychological counseling.

Athletics *Intramural sports:* basketball M/W, bowling M/W, golf M/W, soccer M/W, volleyball W.

Costs (2010–11) *Tuition:* area resident $1260 full-time; state resident $4500 full-time; nonresident $8640 full-time. Full-time tuition and fees vary according to course load. Part-time tuition and fees vary according to course load. *Required fees:* $480 full-time. *Payment plan:* installment. *Waivers:* senior citizens and employees or children of employees.

Financial Aid Of all full-time matriculated undergraduates who enrolled in 2009, 6,557 applied for aid, 5,346 were judged to have need. 365 Federal Work-Study jobs (averaging $3310). 54 state and other part-time jobs (averaging $2613). *Average need-based loan:* $1758. *Average need-based gift aid:* $2576.

Applying *Options:* electronic application. *Required:* high school transcript. *Application deadlines:* rolling (freshmen), rolling (transfers).
Freshman Application Contact Ms. Linda Kluck, Director, Admissions and Records, Austin Community College, 5930 Middle Fiskville Road, Austin, TX 78752. *Phone:* 512-223-7503. *Fax:* 512-223-7665. *E-mail:* admission@austincc.edu. *Web site:* http://www.austincc.edu/.

Blinn College
Brenham, Texas

Freshman Application Contact Mrs. Stephanie Wehring, Coordinator, Recruitment and Admissions, Blinn College, 902 College Avenue, Brenham, TX 77833-4049. *Phone:* 979-830-4152. *Fax:* 979-830-4110. *E-mail:* recruit@blinn.edu. *Web site:* http://www.blinn.edu/.

Brazosport College
Lake Jackson, Texas

Freshman Application Contact Brazosport College, 500 College Drive, Lake Jackson, TX 77566-3199. *Phone:* 979-230-3020. *Web site:* http://www.brazosport.edu/.

Brookhaven College
Farmers Branch, Texas

Freshman Application Contact Admissions Office, Brookhaven College, 3939 Valley View Lane, Farmers Branch, TX 75244-4997. *Phone:* 972-860-4883. *Fax:* 972-860-4886. *E-mail:* bhcinfo@dcccd.edu. *Web site:* http://www.brookhavencollege.edu/.

Brown Mackie College–San Antonio
San Antonio, Texas

- **Proprietary** 4-year
- **Coed**

Academics *Degrees:* associate and bachelor's.
Director of Admissions Director of Admissions, Brown Mackie College–San Antonio, 4715 Fredericksburg Road, Suite 100, San Antonio, TX 78229. *Phone:* 210-428-2210. *Toll-free phone:* 877-460-1714. *Web site:* http://www.brownmackie.edu/san-antonio.

See page 400 for the College Close-Up.

Cedar Valley College
Lancaster, Texas

Freshman Application Contact Admissions Office, Cedar Valley College, Lancaster, TX 75134-3799. *Phone:* 972-860-8206. *Fax:* 972-860-8207. *Web site:* http://www.cedarvalleycollege.edu/.

Center for Advanced Legal Studies
Houston, Texas

Freshman Application Contact Mr. James Scheffer, Center for Advanced Legal Studies, 3910 Kirby, Suite 200, Houston, TX 77098. *Phone:* 713-529-2778. *Fax:* 713-523-2715. *E-mail:* james.scheffer@paralegal.edu. *Web site:* http://www.paralegal.edu/.

Central Texas College
Killeen, Texas

- **State and locally supported** 2-year, founded 1967
- **Suburban** 500-acre campus with easy access to Austin
- **Endowment** $3.5 million
- **Coed**

Undergraduates 4,163 full-time, 20,335 part-time. Students come from 50 states and territories; 38 other countries; 19% are from out of state; 7% transferred in; 1% live on campus. *Retention:* 58% of full-time freshmen returned.
Faculty *Student/faculty ratio:* 11:1.
Academics *Calendar:* semesters. *Degree:* certificates and associate. *Special study options:* academic remediation for entering students, accelerated degree program, adult/continuing education programs, advanced placement credit, distance learning, English as a second language, external degree program, internships, part-time degree program, services for LD students, student-designed majors, summer session for credit. *ROTC:* Army (b).
Student Life *Campus security:* 24-hour emergency response devices and patrols.

Costs (2010–11) *Tuition:* area resident $1530 full-time, $51 per credit hour part-time; state resident $1920 full-time, $64 per credit hour part-time; nonresident $4500 full-time, $150 per credit hour part-time. Full-time tuition and fees vary according to course load, location, and program. Part-time tuition and fees vary according to course load, location, and program. *Room and board:* $3630.
Financial Aid Of all full-time matriculated undergraduates who enrolled in 2009, 68 Federal Work-Study jobs (averaging $3658).
Applying *Options:* electronic application, early admission, deferred entrance. *Required:* high school transcript, minimum 2.0 GPA.
Freshman Application Contact Admissions Office, Central Texas College, PO Box 1800, Killeen, TX 76540-1800. *Phone:* 254-526-1696. *Toll-free phone:* 800-792-3348 Ext. 1696. *Fax:* 254-526-1545. *E-mail:* admrec@ctcd.edu. *Web site:* http://www.ctcd.edu/.

Cisco College
Cisco, Texas

Freshman Application Contact Mr. Olin O. Odom III, Dean of Admission/Registrar, Cisco College, 101 College Heights, Cisco, TX 76437-9321. *Phone:* 254-442-2567 Ext. 5130. *E-mail:* oodom@cjc.edu. *Web site:* http://www.cisco.edu/.

Clarendon College
Clarendon, Texas

- **State and locally supported** 2-year, founded 1898
- **Rural** 109-acre campus
- **Endowment** $2.1 million
- **Coed,** 1,583 undergraduate students

Undergraduates Students come from 14 states and territories; 2 other countries; 4% are from out of state; 21% live on campus.
Freshmen *Admission:* 498 applied, 498 admitted.
Faculty *Total:* 94, 38% full-time, 6% with terminal degrees. *Student/faculty ratio:* 19:1.
Majors Accounting; agribusiness; agricultural economics; agriculture; architecture; art; behavioral sciences; biology/biological sciences; business administration and management; chemistry; computer and information sciences; dramatic/theater arts; economics; education; electromechanical technology; elementary education; engineering; English; environmental science; farm and ranch management; finance; general studies; health services/allied health/health sciences; history; horse husbandry/equine science and management; kinesiology and exercise science; liberal arts and sciences/liberal studies; marketing/marketing management; mass communication/media; mathematics; music; physical education teaching and coaching; physical therapy; pre-dentistry studies; pre-law studies; premedical studies; psychology; registered nursing/registered nurse; rhetoric and composition; secondary education; social sciences; social work related; sociology.
Academics *Calendar:* semesters. *Degree:* certificates and associate. *Special study options:* academic remediation for entering students, adult/continuing education programs, advanced placement credit, distance learning, double majors, English as a second language, independent study, part-time degree program, services for LD students, summer session for credit.
Library Vera Dial Dickey Library plus 1 other with 21,027 titles, 10,588 serial subscriptions, 448 audiovisual materials, an OPAC, a Web page.
Student Life *Housing:* on-campus residence required through sophomore year. *Options:* coed, men-only, women-only. Campus housing is university owned. *Activities and Organizations:* drama/theater group, choral group. *Campus security:* 8-hour patrols by trained security personnel, Emergency notification system through text messaging.
Athletics Member NJCAA. *Intercollegiate sports:* baseball M(s), basketball M(s)/W(s), cheerleading M(s)/W(s), cross-country running M(s)/W(s), softball W(s), volleyball W(s). *Intramural sports:* basketball M/W, volleyball M/W.
Costs (2010–11) *Tuition:* area resident $1260 full-time; state resident $1830 full-time, $42 per credit hour part-time; nonresident $2760 full-time, $73 per credit hour part-time. *Required fees:* $1230 full-time, $41 per credit hour part-time. *Room and board:* $4156; room only: $1350. *Payment plan:* installment. *Waivers:* senior citizens.
Financial Aid Of all full-time matriculated undergraduates who enrolled in 2009, 47 Federal Work-Study jobs (averaging $575). 12 state and other part-time jobs (averaging $485).
Applying *Options:* electronic application, early admission. *Required:* high school transcript. *Required for some:* interview. *Application deadlines:* rolling (freshmen), rolling (out-of-state freshmen), rolling (transfers). *Notification:* continuous (freshmen), continuous (out-of-state freshmen), continuous (transfers).
Freshman Application Contact Ms. Martha Smith, Admissions Director, Clarendon College, PO Box 968, Clarendon, TX 79226. *Phone:* 806-874-3571 Ext. 106. *Toll-free phone:* 800-687-9737. *Fax:* 806-874-3201. *E-mail:*

martha.smith@clarendoncollege.edu.
Web site: http://www.clarendoncollege.edu/.

Coastal Bend College
Beeville, Texas

Freshman Application Contact Ms. Alicia Ulloa, Director of Admissions/Registrar, Coastal Bend College, Beeville, TX 78102-2197. *Phone:* 361-354-2245. *Fax:* 361-354-2254. *E-mail:* register@coastalbend.edu. *Web site:* http://www.coastalbend.edu/.

College of the Mainland
Texas City, Texas

Freshman Application Contact Ms. Kelly Musick, Registrar/Director of Admissions, College of the Mainland, 1200 Amburn Road, Texas City, TX 77591. *Phone:* 409-938-1211 Ext. 469. *Toll-free phone:* 888-258-8859 Ext. 264. *Fax:* 409-938-3126. *E-mail:* sem@com.edu. *Web site:* http://www.com.edu/.

Collin County Community College District
McKinney, Texas

- **State and locally supported** 2-year, founded 1985
- **Suburban** 333-acre campus with easy access to Dallas-Fort Worth
- **Endowment** $4.2 million
- **Coed,** 27,069 undergraduate students, 38% full-time, 57% women, 43% men

Undergraduates 10,216 full-time, 16,853 part-time. Students come from 48 states and territories; 109 other countries; 6% are from out of state; 11% Black or African American, non-Hispanic/Latino; 14% Hispanic/Latino; 8% Asian, non-Hispanic/Latino; 0.1% Native Hawaiian or other Pacific Islander, non-Hispanic/Latino; 0.6% American Indian or Alaska Native, non-Hispanic/Latino; 1% Two or more races, non-Hispanic/Latino; 3% Race/ethnicity unknown; 4% international; 12% transferred in. *Retention:* 62% of full-time freshmen returned.
Freshmen *Admission:* 5,132 applied, 5,132 admitted, 5,132 enrolled.
Faculty *Total:* 1,161, 30% full-time, 24% with terminal degrees. *Student/faculty ratio:* 26:1.
Majors Administrative assistant and secretarial science; animation, interactive technology, video graphics and special effects; biology/biotechnology laboratory technician; business administration and management; business automation/technology/data entry; child-care provision; child development; commercial and advertising art; computer and information sciences; computer and information systems security; computer programming; computer systems networking and telecommunications; criminal justice/police science; culinary arts; dental hygiene; drafting and design technology; early childhood education; educational/instructional technology; electrical, electronic and communications engineering technology; electrical/electronics drafting and CAD/CADD; electrical/electronics equipment installation and repair; emergency medical technology (EMT paramedic); engineering technology; environmental engineering technology; fire prevention and safety technology; fire science/firefighting; general studies; health information/medical records technology; Hispanic-American, Puerto Rican, and Mexican-American/Chicano studies; hospitality administration; interior design; kindergarten/preschool education; legal assistant/paralegal; liberal arts and sciences/liberal studies; medical transcription; middle school education; music; music management; real estate; recording arts technology; registered nursing/registered nurse; respiratory care therapy; sales, distribution, and marketing operations; secondary education; sign language interpretation and translation; speech communication and rhetoric; surgical technology; telecommunications technology; web page, digital/multimedia and information resources design.
Academics *Calendar:* semesters. *Degree:* certificates and associate. *Special study options:* academic remediation for entering students, adult/continuing education programs, advanced placement credit, cooperative education, distance learning, English as a second language, honors programs, internships, part-time degree program, services for LD students, summer session for credit. *ROTC:* Air Force (c).
Library Spring Creek Library, Preston Ridge Library, Central Park Library plus 3 others with 178,212 titles, 888 serial subscriptions, 32,095 audiovisual materials, an OPAC, a Web page.
Student Life *Housing:* college housing not available. *Activities and Organizations:* drama/theater group, choral group, student government, Phi Theta Kappa, Baptist Student Ministry, National Society of Leadership Success, Political Science Club. *Campus security:* 24-hour emergency response devices and patrols, late-night transport/escort service. *Student services:* personal/psychological counseling.

Athletics Member NJCAA. *Intercollegiate sports:* basketball M(s)/W(s), tennis M(s)/W(s), volleyball W(s).
Standardized Tests *Required:* COMPASS (for admission).
Costs (2011–12) *Tuition:* area resident $810 full-time, $27 per semester hour part-time; state resident $1680 full-time, $56 per semester hour part-time; nonresident $3300 full-time, $111 per semester hour part-time. *Required fees:* $214 full-time, $7 per semester hour part-time. *Payment plan:* installment. *Waivers:* senior citizens and employees or children of employees.
Financial Aid Of all full-time matriculated undergraduates who enrolled in 2008, 3,737 applied for aid, 2,818 were judged to have need, 21 had their need fully met. In 2008, 169 non-need-based awards were made. *Average percent of need met:* 51%. *Average financial aid package:* $5170. *Average need-based loan:* $3082. *Average need-based gift aid:* $4663. *Average non-need-based aid:* $618. *Average indebtedness upon graduation:* $4547.
Applying *Options:* electronic application. *Required:* high school transcript. *Application deadlines:* rolling (freshmen), rolling (out-of-state freshmen), rolling (transfers). *Notification:* continuous (freshmen), continuous (out-of-state freshmen), continuous (transfers).
Freshman Application Contact Mr. Todd Fields, Registrar, Collin County Community College District, 2800 East Spring Creek Parkway, Plano, TX 75074. *Phone:* 972-881-5174. *Fax:* 972-881-5175. *E-mail:* tfields@collin.edu. *Web site:* http://www.collin.edu/.

Commonwealth Institute of Funeral Service
Houston, Texas

- **Independent** 2-year, founded 1988
- **Urban** campus with easy access to Houston
- **Coed**

Academics *Calendar:* quarters. *Degree:* certificates and associate. *Special study options:* adult/continuing education programs, external degree program.
Student Life *Campus security:* 24-hour emergency response devices, daytime trained security personnel.
Standardized Tests *Required for some:* Wonderlic aptitude test or THEA. *Recommended:* SAT or ACT (for admission).
Costs (2010–11) *Comprehensive fee:* $22,800 includes full-time tuition ($12,800), mandatory fees ($100), and room and board ($9900). Full-time tuition and fees vary according to course load and program. Part-time tuition and fees vary according to course load and program.
Applying *Application fee:* $50. *Required:* high school transcript.
Freshman Application Contact Ms. Patricia Moreno, Registrar, Commonwealth Institute of Funeral Service, 415 Barren Springs Drive, Houston, TX 77090. *Phone:* 281-873-0262. *Toll-free phone:* 800-628-1580. *Fax:* 281-873-5232. *E-mail:* p.moreno@commonwealth.edu. *Web site:* http://www.commonwealth.edu/.

Computer Career Center
El Paso, Texas

Director of Admissions Ms. Sarah Hernandez, Registrar, Computer Career Center, 6101 Montana Avenue, El Paso, TX 79925. *Phone:* 915-779-8031. *Web site:* http://www.computercareercenter.com/.

Court Reporting Institute of Dallas
Dallas, Texas

Director of Admissions Ms. Debra Smith-Armstrong, Director of Admissions, Court Reporting Institute of Dallas, 8585 North Stemmons Freeway, Suite 200 North, Dallas, TX 75247. *Phone:* 214-350-9722 Ext. 227. *Toll-free phone:* 800-880-9722. *Web site:* http://www.crid.com/.

Court Reporting Institute of Houston
Houston, Texas

Freshman Application Contact Admissions Office, Court Reporting Institute of Houston, 13101 Northwest Freeway, Suite 100, Houston, TX 77040. *Phone:* 713-996-8300. *Toll-free phone:* 866-996-8300. *Web site:* http://www.crid.com/.

Culinary Institute Alain & Marie LeNotre
Houston, Texas

Freshman Application Contact Admissions Office, Culinary Institute Alain & Marie LeNotre, 7070 Allensby, Houston, TX 77022-4322. *Phone:* 713-358-

5070. *Toll-free phone:* 888-LENOTRE.
Web site: http://www.culinaryinstitute.edu/.

Dallas Institute of Funeral Service
Dallas, Texas

Freshman Application Contact Director of Admissions, Dallas Institute of Funeral Service, 3909 South Buckner Boulevard, Dallas, TX 75227. *Phone:* 214-388-5466. *Toll-free phone:* 800-235-5444. *Fax:* 214-388-0316. *E-mail:* difs@dallasinstitute.edu. *Web site:* http://www.dallasinstitute.edu/.

Del Mar College
Corpus Christi, Texas

- **State and locally supported** 2-year, founded 1935
- **Urban** 159-acre campus
- **Coed**

Undergraduates 3,722 full-time, 8,285 part-time. Students come from 43 states and territories; 57 other countries; 1% are from out of state.
Faculty *Student/faculty ratio:* 18:1.
Academics *Calendar:* semesters. *Degree:* certificates and associate. *Special study options:* academic remediation for entering students, accelerated degree program, adult/continuing education programs, advanced placement credit, cooperative education, distance learning, double majors, English as a second language, freshman honors college, honors programs, internships, off-campus study, part-time degree program, services for LD students, summer session for credit. *ROTC:* Army (b).
Student Life *Campus security:* 24-hour emergency response devices and patrols.
Financial Aid Of all full-time matriculated undergraduates who enrolled in 2009, 259 Federal Work-Study jobs (averaging $960). 449 state and other part-time jobs (averaging $1082).
Applying *Options:* electronic application, early admission, deferred entrance. *Required:* high school transcript.
Freshman Application Contact Ms. Frances P. Jordan, Director of Admissions and Registrar, Del Mar College, 101 Baldwin, Corpus Christi, TX 78404. *Phone:* 361-698-1255. *Toll-free phone:* 800-652-3357. *Fax:* 361-698-1595. *E-mail:* fjordan@delmar.edu. *Web site:* http://www.delmar.edu/.

Eastfield College
Mesquite, Texas

- **State and locally supported** 2-year, founded 1970, part of Dallas County Community College District System
- **Suburban** 244-acre campus with easy access to Dallas-Fort Worth
- **Coed,** 12,403 undergraduate students, 24% full-time, 58% women, 42% men

Undergraduates 3,026 full-time, 9,377 part-time. Students come from 7 states and territories; 26 other countries; 0.6% are from out of state; 2% transferred in.
Freshmen *Admission:* 3,200 applied, 3,200 admitted, 1,173 enrolled.
Faculty *Total:* 564, 21% full-time. *Student/faculty ratio:* 24:1.
Majors Accounting; autobody/collision and repair technology; automobile/automotive mechanics technology; business administration and management; business/commerce; child-care and support services management; computer and information sciences related; computer engineering technology; computer hardware engineering; computer/information technology services administration related; computer programming; computer programming related; computer systems networking and telecommunications; criminal justice/safety; data entry/microcomputer applications; data processing and data processing technology; drafting and design technology; e-commerce; education; electrical, electronic and communications engineering technology; electrical/electronics drafting and CAD/CADD; executive assistant/executive secretary; graphic and printing equipment operation/production; heating, air conditioning, ventilation and refrigeration maintenance technology; legal administrative assistant/secretary; liberal arts and sciences/liberal studies; multi/interdisciplinary studies related; music; network and system administration; psychiatric/mental health services technology; sign language interpretation and translation; social work; speech communication and rhetoric; substance abuse/addiction counseling; word processing.
Academics *Calendar:* semesters. *Degree:* certificates and associate. *Special study options:* academic remediation for entering students, adult/continuing education programs, advanced placement credit, cooperative education, distance learning, English as a second language, honors programs, part-time degree program, services for LD students, summer session for credit.
Library Eastfield College Learning Resource Center with 66,988 titles, 415 serial subscriptions, 2,620 audiovisual materials, an OPAC, a Web page.
Student Life *Housing:* college housing not available. *Activities and Organizations:* drama/theater group, student-run newspaper, choral group, LULAC,

Rodeo Club, Phi Theta Kappa, Rising Star, Communications Club. *Campus security:* 24-hour emergency response devices and patrols. *Student services:* health clinic, personal/psychological counseling, women's center.
Athletics Member NJCAA. *Intercollegiate sports:* baseball M, basketball M, golf M, soccer W, tennis M/W, volleyball M/W. *Intramural sports:* basketball M, football M, softball M/W, volleyball M/W.
Costs (2010–11) *Tuition:* area resident $1230 full-time, $41 per credit part-time; state resident $2280 full-time, $76 per credit part-time; nonresident $3630 full-time, $121 per credit part-time. Full-time tuition and fees vary according to course load. Part-time tuition and fees vary according to course load. *Payment plan:* installment. *Waivers:* senior citizens.
Applying *Options:* early admission, deferred entrance. *Recommended:* high school transcript. *Application deadlines:* rolling (freshmen), rolling (transfers). *Notification:* continuous (freshmen), continuous (transfers).
Freshman Application Contact Ms. Glynis Miller, Director of Admissions/Registrar, Eastfield College, 3737 Motley Drive, Mesquite, TX 75150-2099. *Phone:* 972-860-7010. *Fax:* 972-860-8306. *E-mail:* efc@dcccd.edu. *Web site:* http://www.efc.dcccd.edu/.

El Centro College
Dallas, Texas

- **County-supported** 2-year, founded 1966, part of Dallas County Community College District System
- **Urban** 2-acre campus
- **Coed,** 9,245 undergraduate students, 23% full-time, 68% women, 32% men

Undergraduates 2,107 full-time, 7,138 part-time. Students come from 22 states and territories; 6 other countries; 0.3% are from out of state; 33% Black or African American, non-Hispanic/Latino; 34% Hispanic/Latino; 4% Asian, non-Hispanic/Latino; 0.6% American Indian or Alaska Native, non-Hispanic/Latino; 3% Race/ethnicity unknown; 0.1% international; 99% transferred in. *Retention:* 46% of full-time freshmen returned.
Freshmen *Admission:* 1,439 applied, 1,439 admitted, 1,112 enrolled.
Faculty *Total:* 454, 28% full-time, 10% with terminal degrees. *Student/faculty ratio:* 16:1.
Majors Accounting; apparel and accessories marketing; baking and pastry arts; biotechnology; business administration and management; business automation/technology/data entry; business/commerce; cardiovascular technology; clinical/medical laboratory technology; computer and information systems security; computer/information technology services administration related; computer programming; computer science; culinary arts; data processing and data processing technology; diagnostic medical sonography and ultrasound technology; emergency medical technology (EMT paramedic); executive assistant/executive secretary; fashion/apparel design; health information/medical records administration; information science/studies; interior design; legal administrative assistant/secretary; legal assistant/paralegal; licensed practical/vocational nurse training; medical/clinical assistant; medical radiologic technology; medical transcription; office occupations and clerical services; peace studies and conflict resolution; radiologic technology/science; registered nursing/registered nurse; respiratory care therapy; special products marketing; surgical technology; teacher assistant/aide; web page, digital/multimedia and information resources design.
Academics *Calendar:* semesters. *Degree:* certificates and associate. *Special study options:* academic remediation for entering students, adult/continuing education programs, advanced placement credit, cooperative education, distance learning, double majors, English as a second language, freshman honors college, honors programs, internships, part-time degree program, services for LD students, summer session for credit. *ROTC:* Army (c).
Library El Centro College Library with 77,902 titles, 224 serial subscriptions, 585 audiovisual materials, an OPAC, a Web page.
Student Life *Housing:* college housing not available. *Activities and Organizations:* choral group, Phi Theta Kappa, student government, Paralegal Student Association, El Centro Computer Society, Conflict Resolution Society. *Campus security:* 24-hour emergency response devices and patrols, late-night transport/escort service. *Student services:* health clinic, personal/psychological counseling.
Costs (2011–12) *Tuition:* area resident $1230 full-time, $45 per credit hour part-time; state resident $2280 full-time, $83 per credit hour part-time; nonresident $3630 full-time, $132 per credit hour part-time. Full-time tuition and fees vary according to class time and program. Part-time tuition and fees vary according to class time and program. *Payment plans:* installment, deferred payment. *Waivers:* senior citizens and employees or children of employees.
Applying *Options:* electronic application, early admission. *Required for some:* high school transcript, 1 letter of recommendation. *Application deadlines:* rolling (freshmen), rolling (transfers).
Freshman Application Contact Ms. Rebecca Garza, Director of Admissions and Registrar, El Centro College, Dallas, TX 75202. *Phone:* 214-860-2618. *Fax:* 214-860-2233. *E-mail:* rgarza@dcccd.edu. *Web site:* http://www.ecc.dcccd.edu/.

El Paso Community College

El Paso, Texas

- **County-supported** 2-year, founded 1969
- **Urban** campus
- **Coed**

Undergraduates 10,943 full-time, 17,225 part-time.

Academics *Calendar:* semesters. *Degree:* certificates and associate. *Special study options:* academic remediation for entering students, adult/continuing education programs, advanced placement credit, cooperative education, distance learning, English as a second language, external degree program, honors programs, internships, off-campus study, part-time degree program, services for LD students, summer session for credit. *ROTC:* Army (c).

Student Life *Campus security:* 24-hour patrols, late-night transport/escort service.

Athletics Member NJCAA.

Costs (2010–11) *Tuition:* state resident $1428 full-time, $60 per hour part-time; nonresident $1980 full-time, $83 per hour part-time. Full-time tuition and fees vary according to course load. Part-time tuition and fees vary according to course load. *Required fees:* $240 full-time, $10 per hour part-time.

Financial Aid Of all full-time matriculated undergraduates who enrolled in 2009, 750 Federal Work-Study jobs (averaging $1800). 50 state and other part-time jobs (averaging $1800).

Applying *Options:* early admission, deferred entrance. *Application fee:* $10.

Freshman Application Contact Daryle Hendry, Director of Admissions, El Paso Community College, PO Box 20500, El Paso, TX 79998-0500. *Phone:* 915-831-2580. *E-mail:* daryleh@epcc.edu. *Web site:* http://www.epcc.edu/.

Everest College

Arlington, Texas

Freshman Application Contact Admissions Office, Everest College, 300 Six Flags Drive, Suite 200, Arlington, TX 76011. *Phone:* 817-652-7790. *Fax:* 817-649-6033. *Web site:* http://www.everest.edu/.

Everest College

Dallas, Texas

Freshman Application Contact Admissions Office, Everest College, 6060 North Central Expressway, Suite 101, Dallas, TX 75206-5209. *Phone:* 214-234-4850. *Fax:* 214-696-6208. *Web site:* http://www.everest.edu/.

Everest College

Fort Worth, Texas

Freshman Application Contact Admissions Office, Everest College, 5237 North Riverside Drive, Suite 100, Fort Worth, TX 76137. *Phone:* 817-838-3000. *Fax:* 817-838-2040. *Web site:* http://www.everest.edu/.

Frank Phillips College

Borger, Texas

- **State and locally supported** 2-year, founded 1948
- **Small-town** 60-acre campus
- **Endowment** $919,464
- **Coed,** 1,247 undergraduate students, 55% full-time, 54% women, 46% men

Undergraduates 686 full-time, 561 part-time. Students come from 15 states and territories; 6 other countries; 10% are from out of state; 6% transferred in; 20% live on campus. *Retention:* 52% of full-time freshmen returned.

Freshmen *Admission:* 217 enrolled.

Faculty *Total:* 75, 47% full-time, 8% with terminal degrees. *Student/faculty ratio:* 18:1.

Majors Accounting; administrative assistant and secretarial science; agricultural business and management; animal/livestock husbandry and production; biology/biological sciences; business administration and management; business/commerce; chemistry; computer and information systems security; elementary education; English; farm and ranch management; general studies; history; industrial technology; liberal arts and sciences/liberal studies; mathematics; physics; psychology; secondary education; sociology; system, networking, and LAN/WAN management; visual and performing arts.

Academics *Calendar:* semesters. *Degree:* certificates and associate. *Special study options:* academic remediation for entering students, accelerated degree program, adult/continuing education programs, advanced placement credit, cooperative education, distance learning, honors programs, internships, part-time degree program, services for LD students, summer session for credit.

Library James W. Dillard Library with 45,631 titles, 14,360 serial subscriptions, 1,143 audiovisual materials, an OPAC.

Student Life *Housing Options:* coed, men-only, women-only. Campus housing is university owned. *Activities and Organizations:* choral group. *Campus security:* 24-hour emergency response devices and patrols, controlled dormitory access. *Student services:* personal/psychological counseling.

Athletics Member NJCAA. *Intercollegiate sports:* baseball M(s), basketball M(s)/W(s), golf M, softball W, volleyball W(s). *Intramural sports:* basketball M/W, racquetball M/W, volleyball M/W.

Costs (2011–12) *Tuition:* area resident $864 full-time, $36 per hour part-time; state resident $1416 full-time, $59 per hour part-time; nonresident $1562 full-time, $66 per hour part-time. Full-time tuition and fees vary according to program. Part-time tuition and fees vary according to course load and program. *Required fees:* $1216 full-time, $44 per hour part-time, $80 per hour part-time. *Room and board:* $4220. Room and board charges vary according to housing facility. *Payment plan:* installment. *Waivers:* employees or children of employees.

Financial Aid Of all full-time matriculated undergraduates who enrolled in 2009, 24 Federal Work-Study jobs (averaging $5200). 6 state and other part-time jobs (averaging $4800). *Financial aid deadline:* 8/31.

Applying *Options:* electronic application, early admission, deferred entrance. *Required:* high school transcript. *Application deadline:* 8/25 (freshmen). *Notification:* continuous until 8/25 (freshmen).

Freshman Application Contact Ms. Michele Stevens, Director of Enrollment Management, Frank Phillips College, PO Box 5118, Borger, TX 79008-5118. *Phone:* 806-457-4200 Ext. 707. *Toll-free phone:* 800-687-2056. *Fax:* 806-457-4225. *E-mail:* mstevens@fpctx.edu. *Web site:* http://www.fpctx.edu/.

Galveston College

Galveston, Texas

Freshman Application Contact Galveston College, 4015 Avenue Q, Galveston, TX 77550-7496. *Phone:* 409-944-1234. *Web site:* http://www.gc.edu/.

Grayson County College

Denison, Texas

Freshman Application Contact Tana Adams, Lead Enrollment Advisor, Grayson County College, 6101 Grayson Drive, Denison, TX 75020-8299. *Phone:* 903-463-8627. *E-mail:* hallt@grayson.edu. *Web site:* http://www.grayson.edu/.

Hallmark College of Technology

San Antonio, Texas

- **Proprietary** primarily 2-year, founded 1969, administratively affiliated with Hallmark College of Aeronautics
- **Suburban** 3-acre campus
- **Coed,** 356 undergraduate students, 100% full-time, 55% women, 45% men

Undergraduates 356 full-time. Students come from 1 other state.

Freshmen *Admission:* 356 enrolled.

Faculty *Total:* 43, 47% full-time, 7% with terminal degrees. *Student/faculty ratio:* 8:1.

Majors Airframe mechanics and aircraft maintenance technology; business automation/technology/data entry; computer systems networking and telecommunications; data processing and data processing technology; electrical, electronic and communications engineering technology; medical administrative assistant and medical secretary; medical/clinical assistant; medical insurance coding.

Academics *Calendar:* continuous. *Degrees:* certificates, associate, and bachelor's. *Special study options:* accelerated degree program, internships.

Library Randall K. Williams Learning Resource Center plus 1 other.

Student Life *Housing:* college housing not available. *Activities and Organizations:* Alpha Beta Kappa Honor Society. *Campus security:* 24-hour emergency response devices.

Standardized Tests *Required:* Wonderlic aptitude test (for admission).

Applying *Application fee:* $110. *Required:* high school transcript, interview, tour. *Required for some:* essay or personal statement. *Application deadlines:* rolling (freshmen), rolling (transfers). *Notification:* continuous (freshmen), continuous (transfers).

Freshman Application Contact Hallmark College of Technology, 10401 IH 10 West, San Antonio, TX 78230. *Phone:* 210-690-9000 Ext. 212. *Toll-free phone:* 800-880-6600. *Web site:* http://www.hallmarkcollege.edu/.

Hallmark Institute of Aeronautics

San Antonio, Texas

- **Private** 2-year, administratively affiliated with Hallmark College of Technology
- **Urban** 2-acre campus
- **Coed,** 227 undergraduate students, 100% full-time, 8% women, 92% men

Undergraduates 227 full-time. Students come from 1 other state; 10% Black or African American, non-Hispanic/Latino; 49% Hispanic/Latino; 1% Asian, non-Hispanic/Latino; 0.4% Native Hawaiian or other Pacific Islander, non-Hispanic/Latino; 3% Two or more races, non-Hispanic/Latino; 0.4% Race/ethnicity unknown.

Freshmen *Admission:* 193 enrolled.

Faculty *Total:* 17, 100% full-time. *Student/faculty ratio:* 17:1.

Majors Aircraft powerplant technology; airframe mechanics and aircraft maintenance technology.

Academics *Calendar:* continuous. *Degree:* diplomas and associate. *Special study options:* academic remediation for entering students.

Library (Virtual Library) plus 1 other.

Student Life *Housing:* college housing not available. *Activities and Organizations:* Alpha Beta Kappa. *Campus security:* 24-hour emergency response devices and patrols.

Costs (2010–11) *One-time required fee:* $205. *Tuition:* $29,872 full-time. Full-time tuition and fees vary according to program. No tuition increase for student's term of enrollment. Tuition varies by program: Combined AAS Airframe and Powerplant Technology is $29,872; AAS-Airframe Technology, $18,711; AAS-Powerplant Technology, $19,602; Aviation Technician Diploma, $26,727; Airframe Technician Diploma, $16,038; Powerplant Technician Diploma, $16, 929. Tuition, books equipment, supplies are included. The Registration fee for all students is $110 and a Security Fee is charged for all students in the amount of $95. *Payment plans:* installment, deferred payment. *Waivers:* employees or children of employees.

Applying *Application fee:* $110. *Required:* high school transcript, interview, assessment, tour, background check. *Application deadlines:* rolling (freshmen), rolling (transfers). *Notification:* continuous (freshmen), continuous (transfers).

Freshman Application Contact Hallmark Institute of Aeronautics, 8901 Wetmore Road, San Antonio, TX 78216. *Phone:* 210-826-1000 Ext. 106. *Toll-free phone:* 888-656-9300. *Web site:* http://www.hallmarkcollege.edu/programs-school-of-aeronautics.aspx/.

Hill College of the Hill Junior College District

Hillsboro, Texas

Freshman Application Contact Ms. Diane Harvey, Director of Admissions/Registrar, Hill College of the Hill Junior College District, 112 Lamar Drive, Hillsboro, TX 76645. *Phone:* 254-582-2555. *Fax:* 254-582-7591. *E-mail:* diharvey@hill-college.cc.tx.us. *Web site:* http://www.hillcollege.edu/.

Houston Community College System

Houston, Texas

- **State and locally supported** 2-year, founded 1971
- **Urban** campus
- **Coed,** 60,303 undergraduate students, 31% full-time, 59% women, 41% men

Undergraduates 18,824 full-time, 41,479 part-time. 10% are from out of state; 28% Black or African American, non-Hispanic/Latino; 30% Hispanic/Latino; 10% Asian, non-Hispanic/Latino; 0.3% Native Hawaiian or other Pacific Islander, non-Hispanic/Latino; 0.2% American Indian or Alaska Native, non-Hispanic/Latino; 1% Two or more races, non-Hispanic/Latino; 0.9% Race/ethnicity unknown; 11% international; 7% transferred in.

Freshmen *Admission:* 9,672 enrolled.

Faculty *Total:* 3,644, 23% full-time, 15% with terminal degrees. *Student/faculty ratio:* 25:1.

Majors Accounting; animation, interactive technology, video graphics and special effects; applied horticulture/horticulture operations; automobile/automotive mechanics technology; banking and financial support services; biology/biotechnology laboratory technician; business administration and management; business automation/technology/data entry; business/corporate communications; cardiovascular technology; chemical technology; child development; cinematography and film/video production; clinical/medical laboratory science and allied professions related; clinical/medical laboratory technology; commercial photography; computer engineering technology; computer programming; computer programming (specific applications); computer systems networking and telecommunications; construction engineering technology; cosmetology; court reporting; criminal justice/police science; culinary arts; desktop publishing and digital imaging design; drafting and design technology; emergency medical technology (EMT paramedic); fashion/apparel design; fashion merchandising; fire prevention and safety technology; geographic information science and cartography; graphic and printing equipment operation/production; health and physical education/fitness; health information/medical records technology; histologic technician; hotel/motel administration; instrumentation technology; interior design; international business/trade/commerce; legal assistant/paralegal; logistics, materials, and supply chain management; manufacturing engineering technology; marketing/marketing management; music management; music performance; music theory and composition; network and system administration; nuclear medical technology; occupational therapist assistant; physical therapy technology; psychiatric/mental health services technology; public administration; radio and television broadcasting technology; radiologic technology/science; real estate; registered nursing/registered nurse; respiratory care therapy; sign language interpretation and translation; tourism and travel services management; turf and turfgrass management.

Academics *Calendar:* semesters. *Degree:* certificates and associate. *Special study options:* academic remediation for entering students, adult/continuing education programs, advanced placement credit, cooperative education, distance learning, English as a second language, honors programs, independent study, internships, part-time degree program, services for LD students, study abroad, summer session for credit. *ROTC:* Army (c), Air Force (c).

Library an OPAC, a Web page.

Student Life *Housing:* college housing not available. *Activities and Organizations:* drama/theater group, student-run newspaper, television station. *Campus security:* 24-hour emergency response devices and patrols, late-night transport/escort service. *Student services:* personal/psychological counseling.

Costs (2010–11) *Tuition:* area resident $1704 full-time, $82 per credit hour part-time; state resident $3534 full-time, $147 per credit hour part-time; nonresident $4224 full-time, $300 per credit hour part-time. Full-time tuition and fees vary according to course load. Part-time tuition and fees vary according to course load. *Required fees:* $6 per term part-time.

Applying *Required for some:* high school transcript, interview. *Application deadline:* rolling (freshmen). *Notification:* continuous (transfers).

Freshman Application Contact Ms. Mary Lemburg, Registrar, Houston Community College System, 3100 Main Street, PO Box 667517, Houston, TX 77266-7517. *Phone:* 713-718-8500. *Fax:* 713-718-2111. *Web site:* http://www.hccs.edu/.

Howard College

Big Spring, Texas

- **State and locally supported** 2-year, founded 1945, part of Howard County Junior College District System
- **Small-town** 120-acre campus
- **Endowment** $1.2 million
- **Coed**

Undergraduates 1,636 full-time, 2,467 part-time. 8% live on campus. *Retention:* 54% of full-time freshmen returned.

Faculty *Student/faculty ratio:* 14:1.

Academics *Calendar:* semesters. *Degree:* certificates and associate. *Special study options:* academic remediation for entering students, adult/continuing education programs, advanced placement credit, cooperative education, distance learning, English as a second language, independent study, internships, part-time degree program, services for LD students, summer session for credit.

Student Life *Campus security:* 24-hour emergency response devices and patrols.

Athletics Member NJCAA.

Costs (2010–11) *Tuition:* area resident $1472 full-time, $40 per hour part-time; state resident $1820 full-time, $52 per hour part-time; nonresident $2388 full-time, $74 per hour part-time. Full-time tuition and fees vary according to course load and location. Part-time tuition and fees vary according to course load and location. *Required fees:* $212 full-time, $176 per term part-time. *Room and board:* $3971; room only: $1300. *Payment plans:* installment, deferred payment.

Applying *Options:* electronic application, early admission. *Required:* high school transcript.

Freshman Application Contact Ms. TaNeal Richardson, Assistant Registrar, Howard College, 1001 Birdwell Lane, Big Spring, TX 79720-3702. *Phone:* 432-264-5105. *Toll-free phone:* 866-HC-HAWKS. *Fax:* 432-264-5604. *E-mail:* trichardson@howardcollege.edu. *Web site:* http://www.howardcollege.edu/.

ITT Technical Institute
Arlington, Texas

- **Proprietary** primarily 2-year, founded 1982, part of ITT Educational Services, Inc.
- **Suburban** campus
- **Coed**

Majors CAD/CADD drafting/design technology; computer and information systems security; computer engineering technology; computer software and media applications related; computer software technology; construction management; design and visual communications; electrical, electronic and communications engineering technology; legal assistant/paralegal; project management; system, networking, and LAN/WAN management.

Academics *Calendar:* quarters. *Degrees:* associate and bachelor's.

Student Life *Housing:* college housing not available.

Freshman Application Contact Director of Recruitment, ITT Technical Institute, 551 Ryan Plaza Drive, Arlington, TX 76011. *Phone:* 817-794-5100. *Toll-free phone:* 888-288-4950. *Fax:* 817-275-8446. *Web site:* http://www.itt-tech.edu/.

ITT Technical Institute
Austin, Texas

- **Proprietary** primarily 2-year, founded 1985, part of ITT Educational Services, Inc.
- **Urban** campus
- **Coed**

Majors Accounting technology and bookkeeping; CAD/CADD drafting/design technology; computer and information systems security; computer engineering technology; computer software technology; construction management; design and visual communications; electrical, electronic and communications engineering technology; legal assistant/paralegal; project management; system, networking, and LAN/WAN management; web page, digital/multimedia and information resources design.

Academics *Calendar:* quarters. *Degrees:* associate and bachelor's.

Student Life *Housing:* college housing not available.

Financial Aid Of all full-time matriculated undergraduates who enrolled in 2009, 1 Federal Work-Study job.

Freshman Application Contact Director of Recruitment, ITT Technical Institute, 6330 Highway 290 East, Austin, TX 78723. *Phone:* 512-467-6800. *Toll-free phone:* 800-431-0677. *Fax:* 512-467-6677. *Web site:* http://www.itt-tech.edu/.

ITT Technical Institute
DeSoto, Texas

- **Proprietary** primarily 2-year
- **Coed**

Majors CAD/CADD drafting/design technology; computer and information systems security; computer engineering technology; computer software technology; construction management; design and visual communications; electrical, electronic and communications engineering technology; legal assistant/paralegal; system, networking, and LAN/WAN management.

Academics *Degrees:* associate and bachelor's.

Freshman Application Contact Director of Recruitment, ITT Technical Institute, 921 West Belt Line Road, Suite 181, DeSoto, TX 75115. *Phone:* 972-274-8600. *Toll-free phone:* 877-854-5728. *Web site:* http://www.itt-tech.edu/.

ITT Technical Institute
Houston, Texas

- **Proprietary** primarily 2-year, founded 1985, part of ITT Educational Services, Inc.
- **Suburban** campus
- **Coed**

Majors CAD/CADD drafting/design technology; computer and information systems security; computer engineering technology; computer software technology; construction management; design and visual communications; electrical, electronic and communications engineering technology; legal assistant/paralegal; project management; system, networking, and LAN/WAN management.

Academics *Calendar:* quarters. *Degrees:* associate and bachelor's.

Student Life *Housing:* college housing not available.

Freshman Application Contact Director of Recruitment, ITT Technical Institute, 15651 North Freeway, Houston, TX 77090. *Phone:* 281-873-0512. *Toll-free phone:* 800-879-6486. *Web site:* http://www.itt-tech.edu/.

ITT Technical Institute
Houston, Texas

- **Proprietary** primarily 2-year, founded 1983, part of ITT Educational Services, Inc.
- **Urban** campus
- **Coed**

Majors CAD/CADD drafting/design technology; computer and information systems security; computer engineering technology; computer software technology; construction management; design and visual communications; electrical, electronic and communications engineering technology; legal assistant/paralegal; project management; system, networking, and LAN/WAN management.

Academics *Calendar:* quarters. *Degrees:* associate and bachelor's.

Student Life *Housing:* college housing not available.

Freshman Application Contact Director of Recruitment, ITT Technical Institute, 2950 South Gessner, Houston, TX 77063-3751. *Phone:* 713-952-2294. *Toll-free phone:* 800-235-4787. *Web site:* http://www.itt-tech.edu/.

ITT Technical Institute
Richardson, Texas

- **Proprietary** primarily 2-year, founded 1989, part of ITT Educational Services, Inc.
- **Suburban** campus
- **Coed**

Majors Accounting technology and bookkeeping; CAD/CADD drafting/design technology; computer and information systems security; computer engineering technology; computer software and media applications related; computer software technology; construction management; design and visual communications; electrical, electronic and communications engineering technology; legal assistant/paralegal; project management; system, networking, and LAN/WAN management.

Academics *Calendar:* quarters. *Degrees:* associate and bachelor's.

Student Life *Housing:* college housing not available.

Financial Aid Of all full-time matriculated undergraduates who enrolled in 2009, 5 Federal Work-Study jobs (averaging $5000).

Director of Admissions Director of Recruitment, ITT Technical Institute, 2101 Waterview Parkway, Richardson, TX 75080. *Phone:* 972-690-9100. *Toll-free phone:* 888-488-5761. *Web site:* http://www.itt-tech.edu/.

ITT Technical Institute
San Antonio, Texas

- **Proprietary** primarily 2-year, founded 1988, part of ITT Educational Services, Inc.
- **Urban** campus
- **Coed**

Majors Accounting technology and bookkeeping; CAD/CADD drafting/design technology; computer and information systems security; computer engineering technology; computer software technology; construction management; design and visual communications; electrical, electronic and communications engineering technology; legal assistant/paralegal; project management; system, networking, and LAN/WAN management; web page, digital/multimedia and information resources design.

Academics *Calendar:* quarters. *Degrees:* associate and bachelor's.

Student Life *Housing:* college housing not available.

Freshman Application Contact Director of Recruitment, ITT Technical Institute, 5700 Northwest Parkway, San Antonio, TX 78249-3303. *Phone:* 210-694-4612. *Toll-free phone:* 800-880-0570. *Web site:* http://www.itt-tech.edu/.

ITT Technical Institute
Waco, Texas

- **Proprietary** 2-year, part of ITT Educational Services, Inc.
- **Coed**

Majors CAD/CADD drafting/design technology; computer and information systems security; computer engineering technology; electrical, electronic and communications engineering technology; legal assistant/paralegal; project management; system, networking, and LAN/WAN management.

Academics *Calendar:* quarters.

Freshman Application Contact Director of Recruitment, ITT Technical Institute, 3700 S. Jack Kultgen Expressway, Suite 100, Waco, TX 76706. *Phone:* 254-881-2200. *Toll-free phone:* 877-201-7143. *Web site:* http://www.itt-tech.edu/.

ITT Technical Institute

Webster, Texas

- **Proprietary** primarily 2-year, founded 1995, part of ITT Educational Services, Inc.
- **Coed**

Majors CAD/CADD drafting/design technology; computer and information systems security; computer engineering technology; computer software technology; construction management; design and visual communications; electrical, electronic and communications engineering technology; legal assistant/paralegal; project management; system, networking, and LAN/WAN management.

Academics *Calendar:* quarters. *Degrees:* associate and bachelor's.

Student Life *Housing:* college housing not available.

Freshman Application Contact Director of Recruitment, ITT Technical Institute, 1001 Magnolia Avenue, Webster, TX 77598. *Phone:* 281-316-4700. *Toll-free phone:* 888-488-9347. *Web site:* http://www.itt-tech.edu/.

Jacksonville College

Jacksonville, Texas

Freshman Application Contact Danny Morris, Director of Admissions, Jacksonville College, 105 B.J. Albritton Drive, Jacksonville, TX 75766. *Phone:* 903-589-7110. *Toll-free phone:* 800-256-8522. *E-mail:* admissions@jacksonville-college.org. *Web site:* http://www.jacksonville-college.edu/.

Kaplan College, Arlington

Arlington, Texas

- **Proprietary** 2-year
- **Coed**

Freshman Application Contact Kaplan College, Arlington, 2241 South Watson Road, Arlington, TX 76010. *Phone:* 866-249-2074. *Toll-free phone:* 866-249-2074. *Web site:* http://www.kc-arlington.com/.

Kaplan College, Dallas

Dallas, Texas

- **Proprietary** 2-year, founded 1987
- **Coed**

Academics *Degree:* diplomas and associate.

Freshman Application Contact Kaplan College, Dallas, 12005 Ford Road, Suite 100, Dallas, TX 75234. *Phone:* 972-385-1446. *Toll-free phone:* 800-525-1446. *Web site:* http://www.kc-dallas.com/.

KD Studio

Dallas, Texas

- **Proprietary** 2-year, founded 1979
- **Urban** campus
- **Coed**, 177 undergraduate students

Undergraduates 9% are from out of state; 46% Black or African American, non-Hispanic/Latino; 18% Hispanic/Latino; 2% Asian, non-Hispanic/Latino. *Retention:* 69% of full-time freshmen returned.

Freshmen *Admission:* 21 applied, 21 admitted.

Faculty *Total:* 28, 100% full-time, 4% with terminal degrees. *Student/faculty ratio:* 6:1.

Majors Acting; film/cinema/video studies; musical theater.

Academics *Calendar:* semesters. *Degree:* associate. *Special study options:* cooperative education.

Library KD Studio Library with 800 titles, 15 serial subscriptions.

Student Life *Housing:* college housing not available. *Activities and Organizations:* drama/theater group, Student Council. *Campus security:* 24-hour emergency response devices and patrols.

Costs (2011–12) *Tuition:* $12,860 full-time, $348 per credit part-time. Full-time tuition and fees vary according to program. No tuition increase for student's term of enrollment. *Required fees:* $200 full-time, $200 per year part-time. *Payment plan:* installment.

Applying *Options:* deferred entrance. *Application fee:* $100. *Required:* essay or personal statement, high school transcript, interview, Audition. *Application deadlines:* rolling (freshmen), rolling (transfers).

Freshman Application Contact Mr. T. A. Taylor, Director of Education, KD Studio, 2600 Stemmons Freeway, Suite 117, Dallas, TX 75207. *Phone:* 214-638-0484. *Fax:* 214-630-5140. *E-mail:* tataylor@kdstudio.com. *Web site:* http://www.kdstudio.com/.

Kilgore College

Kilgore, Texas

- **State and locally supported** 2-year, founded 1935
- **Small-town** 35-acre campus with easy access to Dallas-Fort Worth
- **Coed,** 6,691 undergraduate students, 48% full-time, 62% women, 38% men

Undergraduates 3,197 full-time, 3,494 part-time. Students come from 25 states and territories; 37 other countries; 1% are from out of state; 6% transferred in; 7% live on campus. *Retention:* 55% of full-time freshmen returned.

Freshmen *Admission:* 1,368 enrolled.

Faculty *Total:* 281, 49% full-time, 8% with terminal degrees. *Student/faculty ratio:* 22:1.

Majors Accounting technology and bookkeeping; aerospace, aeronautical and astronautical/space engineering; agriculture; architecture; art; autobody/collision and repair technology; automobile/automotive mechanics technology; biological and physical sciences; business administration and management; business/commerce; chemical engineering; chemistry; child-care and support services management; child-care provision; civil engineering; clinical/medical laboratory technology; commercial and advertising art; commercial photography; computer and information sciences; computer installation and repair technology; computer programming; computer systems networking and telecommunications; corrections; court reporting; criminal justice/law enforcement administration; dance; diesel mechanics technology; drafting and design technology; dramatic/theater arts; electrical, electronic and communications engineering technology; elementary education; emergency medical technology (EMT paramedic); English; executive assistant/executive secretary; fashion merchandising; forestry; general studies; geology/earth science; health teacher education; heating, air conditioning, ventilation and refrigeration maintenance technology; journalism; legal assistant/paralegal; management information systems; mathematics; mechanical engineering; medical radiologic technology; metallurgical technology; multi/interdisciplinary studies related; music; occupational safety and health technology; occupational therapist assistant; operations management; petroleum engineering; physical education teaching and coaching; physical therapy; physical therapy technology; physics; pre-dentistry studies; pre-law studies; premedical studies; pre-pharmacy studies; pre-veterinary studies; psychology; radiologic technology/science; registered nursing/registered nurse; religious studies; rhetoric and composition; social sciences; surgical technology; trade and industrial teacher education; web/multimedia management and webmaster; welding technology.

Academics *Calendar:* semesters. *Degree:* certificates and associate. *Special study options:* academic remediation for entering students, adult/continuing education programs, advanced placement credit, cooperative education, distance learning, English as a second language, internships, part-time degree program, services for LD students, student-designed majors, summer session for credit.

Library Randolph C. Watson Library plus 1 other with 65,000 titles, 6,679 serial subscriptions, 13,351 audiovisual materials, an OPAC, a Web page.

Student Life *Housing Options:* coed, men-only, women-only. Campus housing is university owned. *Activities and Organizations:* drama/theater group, student-run newspaper, choral group, marching band. *Campus security:* 24-hour emergency response devices and patrols. *Student services:* personal/psychological counseling.

Athletics Member NJCAA. *Intercollegiate sports:* basketball M(s)/W(s), cheerleading M(s)/W(s), football M(s). *Intramural sports:* basketball M/W, football M/W, racquetball M/W, tennis M/W, volleyball M/W.

Costs (2010–11) *Tuition:* area resident $600 full-time, $25 per semester hour part-time; state resident $1920 full-time, $80 per semester hour part-time; nonresident $2880 full-time, $120 per semester hour part-time. *Required fees:* $576 full-time, $24 per semester hour part-time. *Room and board:* $3980. Room and board charges vary according to board plan and housing facility. *Payment plan:* installment. *Waivers:* senior citizens and employees or children of employees.

Financial Aid Of all full-time matriculated undergraduates who enrolled in 2009, 80 Federal Work-Study jobs (averaging $2500). *Financial aid deadline:* 6/1.

Applying *Options:* electronic application, early admission. *Required:* high school transcript. *Required for some:* interview. *Application deadlines:* rolling (freshmen), rolling (out-of-state freshmen), rolling (transfers).

Freshman Application Contact Ms. Jeanna Centers, Admissions Specialist, Kilgore College, 1100 Broadway Boulevard, Kilgore, TX 75662-3299. *Phone:* 903-983-8202. *Fax:* 903-983-8607. *E-mail:* register@kilgore.cc.tx.us. *Web site:* http://www.kilgore.edu/.

Lamar Institute of Technology

Beaumont, Texas

Freshman Application Contact Admissions Office, Lamar Institute of Technology, 855 East Lavaca, Beaumont, TX 77705. *Phone:* 409-880-8354. *Toll-free phone:* 800-950-6989. *Web site:* http://www.lit.edu/.

Lamar State College–Orange

Orange, Texas

Freshman Application Contact Kerry Olson, Director of Admissions and Financial Aid, Lamar State College–Orange, 410 Front Street, Orange, TX 77632. *Phone:* 409-882-3362. *Fax:* 409-882-3374. *Web site:* http://www.lsco.edu/.

Lamar State College–Port Arthur

Port Arthur, Texas

Freshman Application Contact Ms. Connie Nicholas, Registrar, Lamar State College–Port Arthur, PO Box 310, Port Arthur, TX 77641-0310. *Phone:* 409-984-6165. *Toll-free phone:* 800-477-5872. *Fax:* 409-984-6025. *E-mail:* nichoca@lamarpa.edu. *Web site:* http://www.lamarpa.edu/.

Laredo Community College

Laredo, Texas

Freshman Application Contact Ms. Josie Soliz, Admissions Records Supervisor, Laredo Community College, Laredo, TX 78040-4395. *Phone:* 956-721-5177. *Fax:* 956-721-5493. *Web site:* http://www.laredo.edu/.

Lee College

Baytown, Texas

Director of Admissions Ms. Becki Griffith, Registrar, Lee College, PO Box 818, Baytown, TX 77522-0818. *Phone:* 281-425-6399. *Toll-free phone:* 800-621-8724. *E-mail:* bgriffit@lee.edu. *Web site:* http://www.lee.edu/.

Lonestar College–Cy-Fair

Cypress, Texas

- **State and locally supported** 2-year, founded 2002, part of Lone Star College System
- **Suburban** campus with easy access to Houston
- **Coed,** 18,107 undergraduate students, 27% full-time, 58% women, 42% men

Undergraduates 4,855 full-time, 13,252 part-time. Students come from 19 states and territories; 68 other countries; 1% are from out of state; 0.4% Black or African American, non-Hispanic/Latino; 13% Hispanic/Latino; 10% Asian, non-Hispanic/Latino; 0.4% American Indian or Alaska Native, non-Hispanic/Latino; 9% Race/ethnicity unknown; 0.6% international.

Freshmen *Admission:* 5,127 applied, 5,127 admitted, 5,127 enrolled.

Faculty *Total:* 2,020, 33% full-time, 14% with terminal degrees. *Student/faculty ratio:* 8:1.

Majors Accounting; agricultural business and management; animation, interactive technology, video graphics and special effects; anthropology; architecture; art; biology/biological sciences; business administration and management; chemistry; computer and information sciences; computer science; criminal justice/law enforcement administration; dance; design and visual communications; diagnostic medical sonography and ultrasound technology; dramatic/theater arts; economics; education; electrical, electronic and communications engineering technology; emergency medical technology (EMT paramedic); engineering; English; finance; fire science/firefighting; foreign languages and literatures; geography; geology/earth science; health information/medical records technology; history; humanities; industrial technology; information technology; interdisciplinary studies; kinesiology and exercise science; language interpretation and translation; logistics, materials, and supply chain management; management science; marketing/marketing management; mathematics; medical radiologic technology; metallurgical technology; music; office occupations and clerical services; philosophy; physics; political science and government; psychology; radiation protection/health physics technology; registered nursing/registered nurse; religious studies; rhetoric and composition; social sciences; sociology; speech communication and rhetoric; welding technology.

Academics *Calendar:* semesters. *Degree:* certificates, diplomas, and associate. *Special study options:* academic remediation for entering students, accelerated degree program, adult/continuing education programs, advanced placement credit, cooperative education, distance learning, double majors, English as a second language, honors programs, independent study, internships, part-time degree program, services for LD students, study abroad, summer session for credit.

Library an OPAC, a Web page.

Student Life *Housing:* college housing not available. *Activities and Organizations:* drama/theater group, choral group. *Campus security:* 24-hour emer-

gency response devices and patrols, late-night transport/escort service. *Student services:* personal/psychological counseling.

Costs (2010–11) *Tuition:* area resident $912 full-time, $38 per credit hour part-time; state resident $2592 full-time, $108 per credit hour part-time; nonresident $2952 full-time, $123 per credit hour part-time. Full-time tuition and fees vary according to course load. Part-time tuition and fees vary according to course load. *Required fees:* $288 full-time, $11 per credit hour part-time, $12 per term part-time. *Payment plan:* installment. *Waivers:* employees or children of employees.

Applying *Options:* electronic application, early admission.

Freshman Application Contact Admissions Office, Lonestar College–Cy-Fair, 9191 Barker Cypress Road, Cypress, TX 77433-1383. *Phone:* 281-290-3200. *E-mail:* cfc.info@lonestar.edu. *Web site:* http://www.lonestar.edu/cyfair.

Lonestar College–Kingwood

Kingwood, Texas

- **State and locally supported** 2-year, founded 1984, part of Lone Star College System
- **Suburban** 264-acre campus with easy access to Houston
- **Coed,** 10,879 undergraduate students, 23% full-time, 64% women, 36% men

Undergraduates 2,459 full-time, 8,420 part-time. Students come from 14 states and territories; 37 other countries; 1% are from out of state; 14% Black or African American, non-Hispanic/Latino; 20% Hispanic/Latino; 4% Asian, non-Hispanic/Latino; 0.5% American Indian or Alaska Native, non-Hispanic/Latino; 8% Race/ethnicity unknown; 0.7% international.

Freshmen *Admission:* 2,729 applied, 2,729 admitted, 2,729 enrolled.

Faculty *Total:* 1,232, 38% full-time, 8% with terminal degrees. *Student/faculty ratio:* 7:1.

Majors Accounting; administrative assistant and secretarial science; animation, interactive technology, video graphics and special effects; anthropology; architecture; art; astronomy; biology/biological sciences; business administration and management; chemistry; computer and information sciences; computer engineering technology; computer graphics; computer science; computer typography and composition equipment operation; cosmetology; criminal justice/law enforcement administration; dental hygiene; design and visual communications; dramatic/theater arts; economics; education; engineering; English; facilities planning and management; finance; foreign languages and literatures; geography; geology/earth science; health information/medical records technology; heating, air conditioning, ventilation and refrigeration maintenance technology; history; humanities; human services; information science/studies; interdisciplinary studies; interior design; kinesiology and exercise science; licensed practical/vocational nurse training; marketing/marketing management; mathematics; medical radiologic technology; music; occupational therapy; philosophy; physics; political science and government; psychology; registered nursing/registered nurse; respiratory care therapy; rhetoric and composition; social sciences; sociology; visual and performing arts; welding technology.

Academics *Calendar:* semesters. *Degree:* certificates and associate. *Special study options:* academic remediation for entering students, accelerated degree program, adult/continuing education programs, advanced placement credit, cooperative education, distance learning, double majors, English as a second language, honors programs, independent study, internships, part-time degree program, services for LD students, study abroad, summer session for credit.

Library Lone Star College-Kingwood Library with an OPAC, a Web page.

Student Life *Housing:* college housing not available. *Activities and Organizations:* drama/theater group, student-run television station, choral group. *Campus security:* 24-hour emergency response devices and patrols, late-night transport/escort service. *Student services:* personal/psychological counseling.

Athletics *Intramural sports:* baseball M.

Costs (2010–11) *Tuition:* area resident $912 full-time, $38 per credit hour part-time; state resident $2592 full-time, $108 per credit hour part-time; nonresident $2952 full-time, $123 per credit hour part-time. Full-time tuition and fees vary according to course load. Part-time tuition and fees vary according to course load. *Required fees:* $288 full-time, $11 per credit hour part-time, $12 per term part-time. *Payment plan:* installment. *Waivers:* employees or children of employees.

Financial Aid Of all full-time matriculated undergraduates who enrolled in 2009, 28 Federal Work-Study jobs, 6 state and other part-time jobs. *Financial aid deadline:* 4/1.

Applying *Options:* electronic application, early admission. *Application deadlines:* rolling (freshmen), rolling (transfers).

Freshman Application Contact Admissions Office, Lonestar College–Kingwood, 20000 Kingwood Drive, Kingwood, TX 77339. *Phone:* 281-312-1525. *Fax:* 281-312-1477. *E-mail:* kingwoodadvising@lonestar.edu. *Web site:* http://www.lonestar.edu/kingwood.htm.

Lonestar College–Montgomery

Conroe, Texas

- **State and locally supported** 2-year, founded 1995, part of Lone Star College System
- **Suburban** campus with easy access to Houston
- **Coed,** 12,653 undergraduate students, 26% full-time, 61% women, 39% men

Undergraduates 3,331 full-time, 9,322 part-time. Students come from 25 states and territories; 48 other countries; 2% are from out of state; 9% Black or African American, non-Hispanic/Latino; 20% Hispanic/Latino; 4% Asian, non-Hispanic/Latino; 0.6% American Indian or Alaska Native, non-Hispanic/Latino; 4% Race/ethnicity unknown; 0.6% international.
Freshmen *Admission:* 3,267 applied, 3,267 admitted, 3,267 enrolled.
Faculty *Total:* 1,416, 38% full-time, 14% with terminal degrees. *Student/faculty ratio:* 8:1.
Majors Accounting and business/management; administrative assistant and secretarial science; animation, interactive technology, video graphics and special effects; anthropology; architecture; art; astronomy; audiovisual communications technologies related; automobile/automotive mechanics technology; biology/biological sciences; biology/biotechnology laboratory technician; business administration and management; CAD/CADD drafting/design technology; chemistry; computer and information systems security; computer programming; computer science; computer software technology; computer systems networking and telecommunications; criminal justice/law enforcement administration; design and visual communications; drafting/design engineering technologies related; dramatic/theater arts; economics; education; emergency medical technology (EMT paramedic); engineering; English; finance; fire science/firefighting; foreign languages and literatures; geology/earth science; health information/medical records technology; heating, air conditioning, ventilation and refrigeration maintenance technology; history; humanities; human services; information technology; interdisciplinary studies; kinesiology and exercise science; land use planning and management; marketing/marketing management; mathematics; medical radiologic technology; music; philosophy; physical therapy technology; physics; political science and government; psychology; radiation protection/health physics technology; registered nursing/registered nurse; religious studies; rhetoric and composition; robotics technology; social work; sociology; system, networking, and LAN/WAN management; web/multimedia management and webmaster; web page, digital/multimedia and information resources design; welding technology.
Academics *Calendar:* semesters. *Degree:* certificates and associate. *Special study options:* academic remediation for entering students, adult/continuing education programs, advanced placement credit, cooperative education, distance learning, double majors, English as a second language, honors programs, independent study, internships, part-time degree program, services for LD students, study abroad, summer session for credit.
Library Library/Learning Resources Center with an OPAC, a Web page.
Student Life *Housing:* college housing not available. *Activities and Organizations:* drama/theater group, student-run newspaper, choral group, Campus Crusade for Christ, Criminal Justice Club, Phi Theta Kappa, Latino-American Student Association, African-American Cultural Awareness. *Campus security:* 24-hour emergency response devices and patrols, late-night transport/escort service. *Student services:* personal/psychological counseling.
Costs (2010–11) *Tuition:* area resident $912 full-time, $38 per credit hour part-time; state resident $2592 full-time, $108 per credit hour part-time; nonresident $2952 full-time, $123 per credit hour part-time. Full-time tuition and fees vary according to course load. Part-time tuition and fees vary according to course load. *Required fees:* $288 full-time, $11 per credit hour part-time, $12 per term part-time. *Payment plan:* installment. *Waivers:* employees or children of employees.
Financial Aid Of all full-time matriculated undergraduates who enrolled in 2009, 25 Federal Work-Study jobs (averaging $2500). 4 state and other part-time jobs.
Applying *Options:* electronic application, early admission. *Application deadlines:* rolling (freshmen), rolling (transfers).
Freshman Application Contact Lonestar College–Montgomery, 3200 College Park Drive, Conroe, TX 77384. *Phone:* 936-273-7236. *Web site:* http://www.lonestar.edu/montgomery.

Lonestar College–North Harris

Houston, Texas

- **State and locally supported** 2-year, founded 1972, part of Lone Star College System
- **Suburban** campus with easy access to Houston
- **Coed,** 16,356 undergraduate students, 20% full-time, 62% women, 38% men

Undergraduates 3,232 full-time, 13,124 part-time. Students come from 16 states and territories; 59 other countries; 0.9% are from out of state; 27% Black or African American, non-Hispanic/Latino; 34% Hispanic/Latino; 7% Asian, non-Hispanic/Latino; 0.3% American Indian or Alaska Native, non-Hispanic/Latino; 7% Race/ethnicity unknown; 1% international.
Freshmen *Admission:* 4,169 applied, 4,169 admitted, 4,169 enrolled.
Faculty *Total:* 1,713, 42% full-time, 11% with terminal degrees. *Student/faculty ratio:* 7:1.
Majors Accounting; administrative assistant and secretarial science; animation, interactive technology, video graphics and special effects; anthropology; architecture; art; automobile/automotive mechanics technology; aviation/airway management; biology/biological sciences; business administration and management; CAD/CADD drafting/design technology; chemistry; computer and information sciences; computer science; cosmetology; criminal justice/law enforcement administration; dance; design and visual communications; drafting and design technology; dramatic/theater arts; economics; education; electrical, electronic and communications engineering technology; emergency medical technology (EMT paramedic); engineering; English; finance; foreign languages and literatures; geography; geology/earth science; health information/medical records technology; heating, air conditioning, ventilation and refrigeration maintenance technology; history; hospitality administration; human services; information science/studies; interdisciplinary studies; journalism; kinesiology and exercise science; language interpretation and translation; legal administrative assistant/secretary; legal studies; liberal arts and sciences/liberal studies; management information systems; marketing/marketing management; mathematics; music; pharmacy technician; philosophy; photography; physical education teaching and coaching; physics; political science and government; pre-engineering; psychology; registered nursing/registered nurse; religious studies; respiratory care therapy; rhetoric and composition; sociology; welding technology.
Academics *Calendar:* semesters. *Degree:* certificates and associate. *Special study options:* academic remediation for entering students, adult/continuing education programs, advanced placement credit, cooperative education, distance learning, double majors, English as a second language, honors programs, independent study, internships, part-time degree program, services for LD students, study abroad, summer session for credit.
Library an OPAC, a Web page.
Student Life *Activities and Organizations:* drama/theater group, student-run newspaper, choral group, Student Government Association, Phi Theta Kappa, Ambassadors, honors student organizations, Soccer Club. *Campus security:* 24-hour emergency response devices and patrols, late-night transport/escort service. *Student services:* personal/psychological counseling, women's center.
Athletics *Intramural sports:* badminton M/W, baseball M/W, basketball M/W, bowling M/W, football M/W, golf M/W, gymnastics M/W, racquetball M/W, soccer M/W, softball M/W, table tennis M/W, tennis M/W, track and field M/W, volleyball M/W, weight lifting M/W.
Costs (2010–11) *Tuition:* area resident $912 full-time, $38 per credit hour part-time; state resident $2592 full-time, $108 per credit hour part-time; nonresident $2952 full-time, $123 per credit hour part-time. Full-time tuition and fees vary according to course load. Part-time tuition and fees vary according to course load. *Required fees:* $288 full-time, $11 per credit hour part-time, $12 per term part-time. *Payment plan:* installment. *Waivers:* employees or children of employees.
Applying *Options:* electronic application, early admission. *Application deadlines:* rolling (freshmen), rolling (transfers).
Freshman Application Contact Admissions Office, Lonestar College–North Harris, 2700 W. W. Thorne Drive, Houston, TX 77073-3499. *Phone:* 281-618-5410. *E-mail:* nhcounselor@lonestar.edu. *Web site:* http://www.lonestar.edu/northharris.

Lonestar College–Tomball

Tomball, Texas

- **State and locally supported** 2-year, founded 1988, part of Lone Star College System
- **Suburban** campus with easy access to Houston
- **Coed,** 11,344 undergraduate students, 20% full-time, 60% women, 40% men

Undergraduates 2,267 full-time, 9,077 part-time. Students come from 12 states and territories; 51 other countries; 1% are from out of state; 11% Black or African American, non-Hispanic/Latino; 21% Hispanic/Latino; 7% Asian, non-Hispanic/Latino; 0.6% American Indian or Alaska Native, non-Hispanic/Latino; 4% Race/ethnicity unknown; 0.8% international.
Freshmen *Admission:* 3,014 applied, 3,014 admitted, 3,014 enrolled.
Faculty *Total:* 1,092, 43% full-time, 15% with terminal degrees. *Student/faculty ratio:* 8:1.
Majors Accounting; administrative assistant and secretarial science; animation, interactive technology, video graphics and special effects; art; biology/biological sciences; business administration and management; chemistry; computer and information sciences; computer programming; computer science; criminal justice/law enforcement administration; dance; dramatic/theater arts; economics; education; electrical, electronic and communications engineering

technology; engineering; English; finance; foreign languages and literatures; geography; geology/earth science; health information/medical records technology; history; humanities; interdisciplinary studies; kinesiology and exercise science; marketing/marketing management; mathematics; music; occupational therapy; pharmacy technician; philosophy; physics; political science and government; registered nursing/registered nurse; religious studies; rhetoric and composition; sociology; system, networking, and LAN/WAN management; veterinary/animal health technology.

Academics *Calendar:* semesters. *Degree:* certificates and associate. *Special study options:* academic remediation for entering students, adult/continuing education programs, advanced placement credit, cooperative education, distance learning, double majors, English as a second language, honors programs, independent study, internships, part-time degree program, services for LD students, study abroad, summer session for credit.

Library an OPAC, a Web page.

Student Life *Housing:* college housing not available. *Activities and Organizations:* drama/theater group, student-run newspaper, choral group, Phi Theta Kappa, Occupational Therapy OTA, Veterinary Technicians Student Organization, STARS, Student Nurses Association. *Campus security:* 24-hour emergency response devices and patrols, late-night transport/escort service, trained security personnel during open hours. *Student services:* personal/psychological counseling.

Costs (2010–11) *Tuition.* area resident $912 full-time, $38 per credit hour part-time; state resident $2592 full-time, $108 per credit hour part-time; nonresident $2952 full-time, $123 per credit hour part-time. Full-time tuition and fees vary according to course load. Part-time tuition and fees vary according to course load. *Required fees:* $288 full-time, $11 per credit hour part-time, $12 per term part-time. *Payment plan:* installment. *Waivers:* employees or children of employees.

Financial Aid Of all full-time matriculated undergraduates who enrolled in 2009, 34 Federal Work-Study jobs (averaging $3000).

Applying *Options:* electronic application, early admission. *Application deadlines:* rolling (freshmen), rolling (transfers).

Freshman Application Contact Admissions Office, Lonestar College–Tomball, 30555 Tomball Parkway, Tomball, TX 77375-4036. *Phone:* 281-351-3310. *E-mail:* tcinfo@lonestar.edu. *Web site:* http://www.lonestar.edu/tomball.

Lon Morris College
Jacksonville, Texas

- **Independent United Methodist** 2-year, founded 1854
- **Small-town** 76-acre campus
- **Endowment** $20.1 million
- **Coed**

Undergraduates 747 full-time, 68 part-time. Students come from 15 states and territories; 4% are from out of state; 2% transferred in; 76% live on campus. *Retention:* 53% of full-time freshmen returned.

Faculty *Student/faculty ratio:* 15:1.

Academics *Calendar:* semesters. *Degree:* associate. *Special study options:* academic remediation for entering students, advanced placement credit, distance learning, English as a second language, independent study, part-time degree program, services for LD students, study abroad, summer session for credit.

Student Life *Campus security:* 24-hour emergency response devices and patrols, late-night transport/escort service, controlled dormitory access.

Athletics Member NJCAA.

Standardized Tests *Recommended:* SAT (for admission), ACT (for admission), SAT or ACT (for admission).

Costs (2010–11) *Comprehensive fee:* $19,830 includes full-time tuition ($12,000), mandatory fees ($1500), and room and board ($6330). *Room and board:* college room only: $3000.

Financial Aid Of all full-time matriculated undergraduates who enrolled in 2009, 63 Federal Work-Study jobs (averaging $1300). 9 state and other part-time jobs (averaging $2500).

Applying *Options:* electronic application, deferred entrance. *Application fee:* $35. *Required:* essay or personal statement, high school transcript.

Freshman Application Contact Mr. Rafael Gonzalez, Director of Enrollment Management, Lon Morris College, 800 College Avenue, Jacksonville, TX 75766. *Phone:* 903-589-4059. *Toll-free phone:* 800-259-5753. *Web site:* http://www.lonmorris.edu/.

McLennan Community College
Waco, Texas

Freshman Application Contact Dr. Vivian G. Jefferson, Director, Admissions and Recruitment, McLennan Community College, 1400 College Drive, Waco, TX 76708. *Phone:* 254-299-8689. *Fax:* 254-299-8694. *E-mail:* vjefferson@mclennan.edu. *Web site:* http://www.mclennan.edu/.

Mountain View College
Dallas, Texas

- **State and locally supported** 2-year, founded 1970, part of Dallas County Community College District System
- **Urban** 200-acre campus
- **Coed,** 8,463 undergraduate students

Undergraduates 27% Black or African American, non-Hispanic/Latino; 50% Hispanic/Latino; 5% Asian, non-Hispanic/Latino; 0.4% American Indian or Alaska Native, non-Hispanic/Latino; 2% Race/ethnicity unknown; 0.3% international. *Retention:* 45% of full-time freshmen returned.

Faculty *Total:* 377, 20% full-time. *Student/faculty ratio:* 27:1.

Majors Accounting; airline pilot and flight crew; aviation/airway management; business administration and management; computer systems networking and telecommunications; criminal justice/safety; drafting and design technology; education; electrical, electronic and communications engineering technology; liberal arts and sciences/liberal studies; music; speech communication and rhetoric; welding technology.

Academics *Calendar:* semesters. *Degree:* certificates and associate. *Special study options:* academic remediation for entering students, adult/continuing education programs, advanced placement credit, cooperative education, distance learning, double majors, English as a second language, external degree program, freshman honors college, honors programs, independent study, internships, part-time degree program, services for LD students, summer session for credit.

Student Life *Housing:* college housing not available. *Activities and Organizations:* drama/theater group, choral group. *Campus security:* 24-hour patrols, late-night transport/escort service. *Student services:* health clinic, personal/psychological counseling.

Athletics Member NJCAA. *Intercollegiate sports:* baseball M, basketball M/W, soccer M/W, volleyball W.

Costs (2010–11) *Tuition:* area resident $984 full-time, $41 per credit part-time; state resident $1824 full-time, $76 per credit part-time; nonresident $2904 full-time, $121 per credit part-time. *Payment plan:* installment. *Waivers:* senior citizens and employees or children of employees.

Financial Aid Of all full-time matriculated undergraduates who enrolled in 2009, 145 Federal Work-Study jobs (averaging $2700).

Applying *Options:* electronic application, early admission, deferred entrance. *Required:* high school transcript. *Application deadlines:* rolling (freshmen), rolling (transfers). *Notification:* continuous (freshmen), continuous (transfers).

Freshman Application Contact Ms. Glenda Hall, Director of Admissions, Mountain View College, 4849 West Illinois Avenue, Dallas, TX 75211-6599. *Phone:* 214-860-8666. *Fax:* 214-860-8570. *E-mail:* ghall@dcccd.edu. *Web site:* http://www.mountainviewcollege.edu/.

Navarro College
Corsicana, Texas

Freshman Application Contact David Edwards, Registrar, Navarro College, 3200 West 7th Avenue, Corsicana, TX 75110-4899. *Phone:* 903-875-7348. *Toll-free phone:* 800-NAVARRO (in-state); 800-628-2776 (out-of-state). *Fax:* 903-875-7353. *E-mail:* david.edwards@navarrocollege.edu. *Web site:* http://www.navarrocollege.edu/.

North Central Texas College
Gainesville, Texas

- **State and locally supported** 2-year, founded 1924
- **Suburban** 132-acre campus with easy access to Dallas-Fort Worth
- **Endowment** $4.3 million
- **Coed**

Undergraduates Students come from 14 states and territories; 21 other countries; 5% are from out of state; 1% live on campus. *Retention:* 68% of full-time freshmen returned.

Faculty *Student/faculty ratio:* 25:1.

Academics *Calendar:* semesters. *Degree:* certificates, diplomas, and associate. *Special study options:* academic remediation for entering students, adult/continuing education programs, advanced placement credit, cooperative education, distance learning, internships, part-time degree program, services for LD students, summer session for credit. *ROTC:* Army (c).

Student Life *Campus security:* late-night transport/escort service, controlled dormitory access, cameras added to campus.

Athletics Member NJCAA.

Costs (2010–11) *Tuition:* area resident $1080 full-time, $36 per credit hour part-time; state resident $2100 full-time, $70 per credit hour part-time; nonresident $3480 full-time, $116 per credit hour part-time. *Required fees:* $300 full-time, $10 per credit hour part-time. *Room and board:* Room and board charges vary according to housing facility. *Payment plans:* installment, deferred payment.

Financial Aid Of all full-time matriculated undergraduates who enrolled in 2009, 108 Federal Work-Study jobs (averaging $1253). 29 state and other part-time jobs (averaging $392).

Applying *Options:* electronic application, early admission. *Required:* high school transcript.

Freshman Application Contact Melinda Carroll, Director of Admissions/ Registrar, North Central Texas College, 1525 West California, Gainesville, TX 76240-4699. *Phone:* 940-668-7731. *Fax:* 940-668-7075. *E-mail:* mcarroll@ nctc.edu. *Web site:* http://www.nctc.edu/.

Northeast Texas Community College
Mount Pleasant, Texas

Freshman Application Contact Ms. Sherry Keys, Director of Admissions, Northeast Texas Community College, PO Box 1307, Mount Pleasant, TX 75456-1307. *Phone:* 903-572-1911 Ext. 263. *Web site:* http://www.ntcc.edu/.

North Lake College
Irving, Texas

- **County-supported** 2-year, founded 1977, part of Dallas County Community College District System
- **Suburban** 250-acre campus with easy access to Dallas-Fort Worth
- **Coed**

Undergraduates 3,171 full-time, 7,003 part-time. Students come from 18 states and territories; 23 other countries; 9% are from out of state; 8% transferred in. *Retention:* 55% of full-time freshmen returned.

Faculty *Student/faculty ratio:* 21:1.

Academics *Calendar:* semesters. *Degree:* certificates and associate. *Special study options:* academic remediation for entering students, accelerated degree program, adult/continuing education programs, advanced placement credit, cooperative education, distance learning, double majors, English as a second language, external degree program, independent study, internships, off-campus study, part-time degree program, services for LD students, study abroad, summer session for credit.

Student Life *Campus security:* 24-hour emergency response devices, student patrols, late-night transport/escort service.

Athletics Member NJCAA.

Costs (2010–11) *Tuition:* area resident $1230 full-time, $41 per credit hour part-time; state resident $2280 full-time, $76 per credit hour part-time; nonresident $3630 full-time, $121 per credit hour part-time.

Applying *Options:* electronic application, early admission. *Recommended:* high school transcript.

Freshman Application Contact Admissions/Registration Office (A405), North Lake College, 5001 North MacArthur Boulevard, Irving, TX 75038. *Phone:* 972-273-3183. *Web site:* http://www.northlakecollege.edu/.

Northwest Vista College
San Antonio, Texas

Freshman Application Contact Dr. Elaine Lang, Interim Director of Enrollment Management, Northwest Vista College, 3535 North Ellison Drive, San Antonio, TX 78251. *Phone:* 210-348-2016. *E-mail:* elang@accd.edu. *Web site:* http://www.alamo.edu/nvc/.

Odessa College
Odessa, Texas

- **State and locally supported** 2-year, founded 1946
- **Urban** 87-acre campus
- **Endowment** $813,199
- **Coed**

Undergraduates 1,475 full-time, 3,657 part-time. Students come from 20 states and territories; 2% are from out of state; 4% live on campus. *Retention:* 44% of full-time freshmen returned.

Faculty *Student/faculty ratio:* 19:1.

Academics *Calendar:* semesters. *Degree:* certificates and associate. *Special study options:* academic remediation for entering students, adult/continuing education programs, advanced placement credit, cooperative education, distance learning, independent study, internships, part-time degree program, services for LD students, summer session for credit.

Student Life *Campus security:* 24-hour emergency response devices and patrols, late-night transport/escort service, controlled dormitory access.

Athletics Member NJCAA.

Costs (2010–11) *Tuition:* area resident $1560 full-time, $156 per course part-time; state resident $2310 full-time, $231 per course part-time; nonresident $3360 full-time, $456 per course part-time. Full-time tuition and fees vary according to course load. Part-time tuition and fees vary according to course load. *Required fees:* $330 full-time, $33 per course part-time. *Room and board:* $4011.

Financial Aid Of all full-time matriculated undergraduates who enrolled in 2009, 59 Federal Work-Study jobs (averaging $1527). 8 state and other part-time jobs (averaging $1904).

Applying *Options:* electronic application, early admission, deferred entrance.

Freshman Application Contact Ms. Tracy Hilliard, Associate Director, Admissions, Odessa College, 201 West University Avenue, Odessa, TX 79764. *Phone:* 432-335-6816. *Fax:* 432-335-6303. *E-mail:* thilliard@odessa.edu. *Web site:* http://www.odessa.edu/.

Palo Alto College
San Antonio, Texas

Freshman Application Contact Ms. Rachel Montejano, Director of Enrollment Management, Palo Alto College, 1400 West Villaret Boulevard, San Antonio, TX 78224. *Phone:* 210-921-5279. *Fax:* 210-921-5310. *E-mail:* pacar@accd.edu. *Web site:* http://www.alamo.edu/pac/.

Panola College
Carthage, Texas

- **State and locally supported** 2-year, founded 1947
- **Small-town** 35-acre campus
- **Endowment** $1.8 million
- **Coed,** 2,322 undergraduate students, 45% full-time, 69% women, 31% men

Undergraduates 1,049 full-time, 1,273 part-time. Students come from 28 states and territories; 15 other countries; 9% are from out of state; 20% Black or African American, non-Hispanic/Latino; 6% Hispanic/Latino; 0.7% Asian, non-Hispanic/Latino; 0.7% American Indian or Alaska Native, non-Hispanic/Latino; 0.5% Two or more races, non-Hispanic/Latino; 1% international; 12% transferred in; 10% live on campus. *Retention:* 46% of full-time freshmen returned.

Freshmen *Admission:* 397 admitted, 397 enrolled.

Faculty *Total:* 139, 45% full-time, 5% with terminal degrees. *Student/faculty ratio:* 18:1.

Majors Administrative assistant and secretarial science; business automation/ technology/data entry; general studies; health information/medical records technology; industrial technology; information science/studies; middle school education; multi/interdisciplinary studies related; occupational therapist assistant; registered nursing/registered nurse; secondary education.

Academics *Calendar:* semesters. *Degree:* certificates and associate. *Special study options:* academic remediation for entering students, advanced placement credit, cooperative education, distance learning, English as a second language, part-time degree program, services for LD students, summer session for credit.

Library M. P. Baker Library with 118,779 titles, 32,073 serial subscriptions, 4,801 audiovisual materials, an OPAC, a Web page.

Student Life *Housing Options:* coed. Campus housing is university owned. *Activities and Organizations:* drama/theater group, student-run newspaper, choral group, Student Government Organization, Student Occupational Therapy Assistant Club, Baptist Student Union, Texas Nursing Student Association, Phi Theta Kappa. *Campus security:* controlled dormitory access.

Athletics Member NCAA, NJCAA. *Intercollegiate sports:* baseball M(s), basketball M(s)/W(s), volleyball W(s). *Intramural sports:* basketball M/W, football M/W, racquetball M/W, table tennis M/W, volleyball M/W, weight lifting M/W.

Costs (2010–11) *Tuition:* area resident $600 full-time, $61 per semester hour part-time; state resident $1464 full-time, $97 per semester hour part-time; nonresident $2088 full-time, $123 per semester hour part-time. *Required fees:* $864 full-time. *Room and board:* $4455. Room and board charges vary according to housing facility. *Payment plan:* deferred payment. *Waivers:* employees or children of employees.

Applying *Options:* electronic application, early admission. *Required for some:* high school transcript. *Recommended:* high school transcript. *Application deadlines:* rolling (freshmen), rolling (transfers). *Notification:* continuous (freshmen), continuous (transfers).

Freshman Application Contact Mr. Jeremy Dorman, Registrar/Director of Admissions, Panola College, 1109 West Panola Street, Carthage, TX 75633-2397. *Phone:* 903-693-2009. *Fax:* 903-693-2031. *E-mail:* bsimpson@ panola.edu. *Web site:* http://www.panola.edu/.

Paris Junior College
Paris, Texas

- State and locally supported 2-year, founded 1924
- Rural 54-acre campus
- Endowment $9.5 million
- Coed

Undergraduates 2,649 full-time, 2,931 part-time. Students come from 29 states and territories; 5 other countries; 3% are from out of state; 50% transferred in; 4% live on campus. *Retention:* 53% of full-time freshmen returned. **Faculty** *Student/faculty ratio:* 25:1.

Academics *Calendar:* semesters. *Degree:* certificates, diplomas, and associate. *Special study options:* academic remediation for entering students, adult/continuing education programs, advanced placement credit, cooperative education, distance learning, English as a second language, external degree program, part-time degree program, services for LD students, summer session for credit.

Student Life *Campus security:* 24-hour emergency response devices and patrols, late-night transport/escort service.

Athletics Member NJCAA.

Costs (2010–11) *Tuition:* area resident $936 full-time, $39 per credit hour part-time; state resident $1680 full-time, $70 per credit hour part-time; nonresident $2664 full-time, $111 per credit hour part-time. Full-time tuition and fees vary according to course load. Part-time tuition and fees vary according to course load. *Required fees:* $228 full-time. *Room and board:* $3400. Room and board charges vary according to board plan and housing facility.

Financial Aid Of all full-time matriculated undergraduates who enrolled in 2009, 60 Federal Work-Study jobs (averaging $3800).

Applying *Options:* electronic application, early admission. *Required:* high school transcript.

Freshman Application Contact Paris Junior College, 2400 Clarksville Street, Paris, TX 75460-6298. *Phone:* 903-782-0425. *Toll-free phone:* 800-232-5804. *Web site:* http://www.parisjc.edu/.

Pima Medical Institute
Houston, Texas

- Proprietary 2-year
- Urban campus
- Coed

Majors Health/health-care administration; radiologic technology/science; respiratory therapy technician.

Academics *Special study options:* cooperative education, distance learning, internships.

Student Life *Housing:* college housing not available.

Standardized Tests *Required:* Wonderlic Scholastic Level Exam (for admission).

Applying *Required:* high school transcript, interview.

Freshman Application Contact Christopher Luebke, Corporate Director of Admissions, Pima Medical Institute, 2160 South Power Road, Mesa, AZ 85209. *Phone:* 480-610-6063. *E-mail:* cluebke@pmi.edu. *Web site:* http://www.pmi.edu/.

Ranger College
Ranger, Texas

Freshman Application Contact Dr. Jim Davis, Dean of Students, Ranger College, 1100 College Circle, Ranger, TX 76470. *Phone:* 254-647-3234 Ext. 110. *Web site:* http://www.ranger.cc.tx.us/.

Remington College–Dallas Campus
Garland, Texas

Director of Admissions Ms. Shonda Wisenhunt, Remington College–Dallas Campus, 1800 Eastgate Drive, Garland, TX 75041. *Phone:* 972-686-7878. *Fax:* 972-686-5116. *E-mail:* shonda.wisenhunt@remingtoncollege.edu. *Web site:* http://www.remingtoncollege.edu/.

Remington College–Fort Worth Campus
Fort Worth, Texas

Director of Admissions Marcia Kline, Director of Recruitment, Remington College–Fort Worth Campus, 300 East Loop 820, Fort Worth, TX 76112. *Phone:* 817-451-0017. *Toll-free phone:* 800-336-6668. *Fax:* 817-496-1257. *E-mail:* marcia.kline@remingtoncollege.edu. *Web site:* http://www.remingtoncollege.edu/.

Remington College–Houston Campus
Houston, Texas

Director of Admissions Kevin Wilkinson, Director of Recruitment, Remington College–Houston Campus, 3110 Hayes Road, Suite 380, Houston, TX 77082. *Phone:* 281-899-1240. *Fax:* 281-597-8466. *E-mail:* kevin.wilkinson@remingtoncollege.edu. *Web site:* http://www.remingtoncollege.edu/houston/.

Remington College–Houston Southeast
Webster, Texas

Director of Admissions Lori Minor, Director of Recruitment, Remington College–Houston Southeast, 20985 Interstate 45 South, Webster, TX 77598. *Phone:* 281-554-1700. *Fax:* 281-554-1765. *E-mail:* lori.minor@remingtoncollege.edu. *Web site:* http://www.remingtoncollege.edu/houstonsoutheast/.

Remington College–North Houston Campus
Houston, Texas

Director of Admissions Edmund Flores, Director of Recruitment, Remington College–North Houston Campus, 11310 Greens Crossing Boulevard, Suite 300, Houston, TX 77067. *Phone:* 281-885-4450. *Fax:* 281-875-9964. *E-mail:* edmund.flores@remingtoncollege.edu. *Web site:* http://www.remingtoncollege.edu/.

Richland College
Dallas, Texas

Freshman Application Contact Ms. Carol McKinney, Department Assistant, Richland College, 12800 Abrams Road, Dallas, TX 75243-2199. *Phone:* 972-238-6100. *Web site:* http://www.rlc.dcccd.edu/.

St. Philip's College
San Antonio, Texas

- District-supported 2-year, founded 1898, part of Alamo Community College District System
- Urban 68-acre campus with easy access to San Antonio
- Coed, 10,828 undergraduate students, 34% full-time, 56% women, 44% men

Undergraduates 3,714 full-time, 7,114 part-time. Students come from 45 states and territories; 11 other countries; 1% are from out of state; 10% transferred in.

Freshmen *Admission:* 1,622 enrolled.

Faculty *Total:* 547, 42% full-time, 8% with terminal degrees. *Student/faculty ratio:* 18:1.

Majors Accounting; administrative assistant and secretarial science; aircraft powerplant technology; airframe mechanics and aircraft maintenance technology; art; autobody/collision and repair technology; automobile/automotive mechanics technology; biology/biological sciences; biomedical technology; building/construction finishing, management, and inspection related; business administration and management; CAD/CADD drafting/design technology; chemistry; clinical/medical laboratory technology; computer and information systems security; computer systems networking and telecommunications; computer technology/computer systems technology; construction engineering technology; criminal justice/law enforcement administration; culinary arts; data entry/microcomputer applications; diesel mechanics technology; dramatic/theater arts; dramatic/theater arts and stagecraft related; early childhood education; e-commerce; economics; education; electrical/electronics equipment installation and repair; electromechanical technology; English; environmental science; geology/earth science; health information/medical records technology; heating, air conditioning, ventilation and refrigeration maintenance technology; history; hotel/motel administration; kinesiology and exercise science; legal administrative assistant/secretary; liberal arts and sciences/liberal studies; mathematics; medical administrative assistant and medical secretary; medical radiologic technology; music; occupational therapist assistant; philosophy; physical therapy technology; political science and government; pre-dentistry studies; pre-engineering; pre-law studies; premedical studies; prenursing studies; pre-pharmacy studies; psychology; respiratory care therapy; restaurant/food services management; rhetoric and composition; social work; sociology; Spanish; system, networking, and LAN/WAN management; teacher assistant/aide; welding technology.

Academics *Calendar:* semesters. *Degree:* certificates, diplomas, and associate. *Special study options:* academic remediation for entering students, adult/continuing education programs, advanced placement credit, cooperative education, distance learning, double majors, English as a second language, honors programs, independent study, internships, off-campus study, part-time degree program, services for LD students, study abroad, summer session for credit. *ROTC:* Army (c).

Library Learning Resource Center plus 1 other with 114,386 titles, 58,757 serial subscriptions, 12,043 audiovisual materials, an OPAC, a Web page.

Student Life *Housing:* college housing not available. *Activities and Organizations:* drama/theater group, student-run newspaper, choral group, Phi Theta Kappa, Respiratory Therapy Club, Anime, Diagnostic Medical Sonography. *Campus security:* 24-hour emergency response devices and patrols, late-night transport/escort service. *Student services:* health clinic, women's center.

Athletics *Intramural sports:* basketball M/W, cheerleading M/W, table tennis M/W, volleyball M/W, weight lifting M/W.

Costs (2010–11) *Tuition:* area resident $1605 full-time, $53 per credit hour part-time; state resident $3210 full-time, $107 per credit hour part-time; nonresident $6420 full-time, $214 per credit hour part-time. *Required fees:* $284 full-time, $142 per term part-time. *Payment plan:* installment. *Waivers:* senior citizens and employees or children of employees.

Applying *Options:* electronic application, early admission. *Required:* high school transcript. *Application deadlines:* rolling (freshmen), rolling (transfers). *Notification:* continuous (freshmen), continuous (transfers).

Freshman Application Contact Ms. Penelope Velasco, Associate Director, Residency and Reports, St. Philip's College, 1801 Martin Luther King Drive, San Antonio, TX 78203-2098. *Phone:* 210-486-2283. *Fax:* 210-486-2103. *E-mail:* pvelasco@alamo.edu. *Web site:* http://www.alamo.edu/spc/.

San Antonio College
San Antonio, Texas

Director of Admissions Mr. J. Martin Ortega, Director of Admissions and Records, San Antonio College, 1300 San Pedro Avenue, San Antonio, TX 78212-4299. *Phone:* 210-733-2582. *Toll-free phone:* 800-944-7575. *Web site:* http://www.alamo.edu/sac/sacmain/sac.htm.

San Jacinto College District
Pasadena, Texas

- **State and locally supported** 2-year, founded 1961
- **Suburban** 445-acre campus with easy access to Houston
- **Endowment** $2.2 million
- **Coed**

Undergraduates 9,689 full-time, 17,322 part-time. Students come from 40 states and territories; 92 other countries; 4% are from out of state; 47% transferred in.

Faculty *Student/faculty ratio:* 24:1.

Academics *Calendar:* semesters. *Degree:* certificates and associate. *Special study options:* academic remediation for entering students, accelerated degree program, adult/continuing education programs, advanced placement credit, cooperative education, distance learning, double majors, English as a second language, honors programs, part-time degree program, services for LD students, student-designed majors, study abroad, summer session for credit. *ROTC:* Army (c), Air Force (c).

Student Life *Campus security:* 24-hour emergency response devices and patrols, late-night transport/escort service.

Athletics Member NJCAA.

Costs (2010–11) *Tuition:* area resident $1486 full-time, $38 per credit hour part-time; state resident $2286 full-time, $63 per credit hour part-time; nonresident $3886 full-time, $113 per credit hour part-time. Full-time tuition and fees vary according to course load. Part-time tuition and fees vary according to course load. *Required fees:* $260 full-time, $130 per term part-time.

Applying *Options:* electronic application, early admission. *Required:* high school transcript. *Required for some:* interview.

Freshman Application Contact San Jacinto College District, 4624 Fairmont Parkway, Pasadena, TX 77504-3323. *Phone:* 281-998-6150. *Web site:* http://www.sanjac.edu/.

South Plains College
Levelland, Texas

- **State and locally supported** 2-year, founded 1958
- **Small-town** 177-acre campus
- **Endowment** $3.0 million
- **Coed**

Undergraduates 4,704 full-time, 5,324 part-time. Students come from 21 states and territories; 8 other countries; 4% are from out of state; 9% transferred in; 10% live on campus. *Retention:* 45% of full-time freshmen returned.

Faculty *Student/faculty ratio:* 20:1.

Academics *Calendar:* semesters. *Degree:* certificates and associate. *Special study options:* academic remediation for entering students, accelerated degree program, adult/continuing education programs, advanced placement credit, distance learning, double majors, internships, off-campus study, part-time degree program, services for LD students, study abroad, summer session for credit. *ROTC:* Army (c), Air Force (c).

Student Life *Campus security:* 24-hour emergency response devices and patrols, controlled dormitory access.

Athletics Member NJCAA.

Standardized Tests *Recommended:* ACT (for admission), SAT Subject Tests (for admission).

Costs (2010–11) *Tuition:* area resident $1484 full-time, $26 per credit hour part-time; state resident $2012 full-time, $48 per credit hour part-time; nonresident $2396 full-time, $64 per credit hour part-time. Full-time tuition and fees vary according to class time, course load, location, and program. Part-time tuition and fees vary according to class time, course load, location, and program. *Required fees:* $1442 full-time, $68 per credit hour part-time, $79 per term part-time. *Room and board:* $3100. Room and board charges vary according to housing facility.

Financial Aid Of all full-time matriculated undergraduates who enrolled in 2009, 80 Federal Work-Study jobs (averaging $2000). 22 state and other part-time jobs (averaging $2000).

Applying *Options:* electronic application, early admission. *Required:* high school transcript.

Freshman Application Contact Mrs. Andrea Rangel, Dean of Admissions and Records, South Plains College, 1401 College Avenue, Levelland, TX 78336. *Phone:* 806-894-9611 Ext. 2370. *Fax:* 806-897-3167. *E-mail:* arangel@southplainscollege.edu. *Web site:* http://www.southplainscollege.edu/.

South Texas College
McAllen, Texas

Freshman Application Contact Mr. Matthew Hebbard, Director of Enrollment Services and Registrar, South Texas College, 3201 West Pecan, McAllen, TX 78501. *Phone:* 956-872-2147. *Toll-free phone:* 800-742-7822. *E-mail:* mshebbar@southtexascollege.edu. *Web site:* http://www.southtexascollege.edu/.

Southwest Institute of Technology
Austin, Texas

Freshman Application Contact Director of Admissions, Southwest Institute of Technology, 5424 Highway 290 West, Suite 200, Austin, TX 78735-8800. *Phone:* 512-892-2640. *Fax:* 512-892-1045. *Web site:* http://www.swse.net/.

Southwest Texas Junior College
Uvalde, Texas

Director of Admissions Mr. Joe C. Barker, Dean of Admissions and Student Services, Southwest Texas Junior College, 2401 Garner Field Road, Uvalde, TX 78801-6297. *Phone:* 830-278-4401 Ext. 7284. *Web site:* http://www.swtjc.net/.

Tarrant County College District
Fort Worth, Texas

- **County-supported** 2-year, founded 1967
- **Urban** 667-acre campus
- **Endowment** $1.5 million
- **Coed**

Undergraduates 13,623 full-time, 25,973 part-time. Students come from 37 states and territories.

Faculty *Student/faculty ratio:* 23:1.

Academics *Calendar:* semesters. *Degree:* certificates and associate. *Special study options:* academic remediation for entering students, adult/continuing education programs, advanced placement credit, distance learning, English as a second language, honors programs, part-time degree program, services for LD students, summer session for credit. *ROTC:* Army (c), Air Force (c).

Student Life *Campus security:* 24-hour emergency response devices and patrols.

Costs (2010–11) *Tuition:* area resident $1200 full-time, $50 per credit hour part-time; state resident $1752 full-time, $73 per credit hour part-time; nonresident $3960 full-time, $165 per credit hour part-time. Full-time tuition and fees vary according to program. Part-time tuition and fees vary according to program.

Financial Aid Of all full-time matriculated undergraduates who enrolled in 2009, 372 Federal Work-Study jobs (averaging $1325). 39 state and other part-time jobs (averaging $927).

Applying *Options:* early admission.

Freshman Application Contact Dr. Billy Roessler, Director of Records and Reports, Tarrant County College District, 1500 Houston Street, Fort Worth, TX 76102-6599. *Phone:* 817-515-5026. *E-mail:* billy.roessler@tccd.edu. *Web site:* http://www.tccd.edu/.

Temple College

Temple, Texas

- **District-supported** 2-year, founded 1926
- **Suburban** 106-acre campus with easy access to Austin
- **Endowment** $638,964
- **Coed**

Undergraduates 2,250 full-time, 3,409 part-time. Students come from 30 states and territories; 9 other countries; 2% are from out of state; 7% transferred in.

Faculty *Student/faculty ratio:* 19:1.

Academics *Calendar:* semesters. *Degree:* certificates and associate. *Special study options:* academic remediation for entering students, adult/continuing education programs, advanced placement credit, cooperative education, distance learning, English as a second language, internships, off-campus study, part-time degree program, services for LD students, study abroad, summer session for credit.

Student Life *Campus security:* 24-hour emergency response devices and patrols.

Athletics Member NJCAA.

Standardized Tests *Required:* (for admission).

Costs (2010–11) *Tuition:* area resident $2400 full-time, $80 per semester hour part-time; state resident $3900 full-time, $130 per semester hour part-time; nonresident $5880 full-time, $196 per semester hour part-time. Full-time tuition and fees vary according to course load and program. Part-time tuition and fees vary according to course load and program. *Required fees:* $150 full-time, $24 per course part-time, $24 per term part-time. *Room and board:* $7309.

Financial Aid Of all full-time matriculated undergraduates who enrolled in 2008, 116 Federal Work-Study jobs (averaging $2007). 67 state and other part-time jobs (averaging $1119).

Applying *Options:* electronic application, early admission. *Required for some:* high school transcript. *Recommended:* high school transcript.

Freshman Application Contact Ms. Carey Rose, Director of Admissions and Records, Temple College, 2600 South First Street, Temple, TX 76504. *Phone:* 254-298-8303. *Toll-free phone:* 800-460-4636. *E-mail:* carey.rose@templejc.edu. *Web site:* http://www.templejc.edu/.

Texarkana College

Texarkana, Texas

Freshman Application Contact Mr. Van Miller, Director of Admissions, Texarkana College, 2500 North Robison Road, Texarkana, TX 75599-0001. *Phone:* 903-838-4541. *Fax:* 903-832-5030. *E-mail:* vmiller@texarkanacollege.edu. *Web site:* http://www.texarkanacollege.edu/.

Texas Culinary Academy

Austin, Texas

Director of Admissions Paula Paulette, Vice President of Marketing and Admissions, Texas Culinary Academy, 3110 Esperanza Crossing, Suite 100, Austin, TX 78758. *Phone:* 512-837-2665. *Toll-free phone:* 888-553-2433. *E-mail:* ppaulette@txca.com. *Web site:* http://www.txca.com/.

Texas Southmost College

Brownsville, Texas

Freshman Application Contact New Student Relations, Texas Southmost College, 80 Fort Brown, Brownsville, TX 78520-4991. *Phone:* 956-882-8860. *Toll-free phone:* 877-882-8721. *Fax:* 956-882-8959. *Web site:* http://www.utb.edu/.

Texas State Technical College Harlingen

Harlingen, Texas

Director of Admissions Mrs. Blanca Guerra, Director of Admissions and Records, Texas State Technical College Harlingen, 1902 North Loop 499, Harlingen, TX 78550-3697. *Phone:* 956-364-4100. *Toll-free phone:* 800-852-

8784. *Fax:* 956-364-5117. *E-mail:* blanca.guerra@harlingen.tstc.edu. *Web site:* http://www.harlingen.tstc.edu/.

Texas State Technical College–Marshall

Marshall, Texas

Director of Admissions Pat Robbins, Registrar, Texas State Technical College–Marshall, 2650 East End Boulevard South, Marshall, TX 75671. *Phone:* 903-935-1010. *Toll-free phone:* 888-382-8782. *Fax:* 903-923-3282. *E-mail:* Pat.Robbins@marshall.tstc.edu. *Web site:* http://www.marshall.tstc.edu/.

Texas State Technical College Waco

Waco, Texas

Freshman Application Contact Mr. Marcus Balch, Director, Recruiting Services, Texas State Technical College Waco, 3801 Campus Drive, Waco, TX 76705. *Phone:* 254-867-2026. *Toll-free phone:* 800-792-8784 Ext. 2362. *Fax:* 254-867-3827. *E-mail:* marcus.balch@tstc.edu. *Web site:* http://waco.tstc.edu/.

Texas State Technical College West Texas

Sweetwater, Texas

- **State-supported** 2-year, founded 1970, part of Texas State Technical College System
- **Small-town** 115-acre campus
- **Endowment** $100,429
- **Coed**

Undergraduates 299 full-time, 1,390 part-time. Students come from 18 states and territories; 3% are from out of state; 10% transferred in; 14% live on campus.

Faculty *Student/faculty ratio:* 7:1.

Academics *Calendar:* semesters. *Degree:* certificates and associate. *Special study options:* academic remediation for entering students, adult/continuing education programs, advanced placement credit, cooperative education, distance learning, internships, part-time degree program, services for LD students, summer session for credit.

Student Life *Campus security:* 24-hour patrols.

Standardized Tests *Required:* ACCUPLACER primarily; also accept THEA, TASP, SAT and ACTTHEA (for admission).

Costs (2010–11) *Tuition:* state resident $2412 full-time, $67 per semester hour part-time; nonresident $6768 full-time, $188 per semester hour part-time. *Required fees:* $1224 full-time, $37 per semester hour part-time. *Room and board:* $6900; room only: $3775. Room and board charges vary according to board plan and housing facility.

Financial Aid Of all full-time matriculated undergraduates who enrolled in 2009, 127 Federal Work-Study jobs (averaging $1350).

Applying *Options:* electronic application, early admission, deferred entrance. *Required:* high school transcript.

Freshman Application Contact Ms. Maria Aguirre-Acuna, Texas State Technical College West Texas, 300 Homer K Taylor Drive, Sweetwater, TX 79556-4108. *Phone:* 325-235-7349. *Toll-free phone:* 800-592-8784. *Fax:* 325-235-7443. *E-mail:* maria.aquirre@sweetwater.tstc.edu. *Web site:* http://www.westtexas.tstc.edu/.

Trinity Valley Community College

Athens, Texas

- **State and locally supported** 2-year, founded 1946
- **Rural** 65-acre campus with easy access to Dallas-Fort Worth
- **Endowment** $2.9 million
- **Coed**, 7,579 undergraduate students, 40% full-time, 62% women, 38% men

Undergraduates 3,035 full-time, 4,544 part-time. Students come from 27 states and territories; 11 other countries; 1% are from out of state; 12% live on campus.

Freshmen *Admission:* 855 enrolled.

Faculty *Total:* 255, 54% full-time, 3% with terminal degrees. *Student/faculty ratio:* 26:1.

Majors Accounting; agricultural teacher education; animal sciences; art; automobile/automotive mechanics technology; biology/biological sciences; business administration and management; business teacher education; chemistry; child development; computer science; corrections; cosmetology; criminal justice/law enforcement administration; criminal justice/police science; dance;

data processing and data processing technology; developmental and child psychology; drafting and design technology; dramatic/theater arts; education; elementary education; emergency medical technology (EMT paramedic); English; farm and ranch management; fashion merchandising; finance; geology/earth science; heating, air conditioning, ventilation and refrigeration maintenance technology; history; horticultural science; insurance; journalism; kindergarten/preschool education; legal administrative assistant/secretary; liberal arts and sciences/liberal studies; licensed practical/vocational nurse training; marketing/marketing management; mathematics; music; physical education teaching and coaching; physical sciences; political science and government; pre-engineering; psychology; range science and management; real estate; registered nursing/registered nurse; religious studies; rhetoric and composition; sociology; Spanish; surgical technology; welding technology.

Academics *Calendar:* semesters. *Degree:* certificates, diplomas, and associate. *Special study options:* academic remediation for entering students, adult/continuing education programs, advanced placement credit, cooperative education, distance learning, double majors, English as a second language, honors programs, independent study, internships, part-time degree program, services for LD students, summer session for credit.

Library Ginger Murchison Learning Resource Center plus 3 others with 54,940 titles, 257 serial subscriptions, 1,954 audiovisual materials, an OPAC, a Web page.

Student Life *Housing Options:* men-only, women-only. Campus housing is university owned. *Activities and Organizations:* drama/theater group, student-run newspaper, choral group, marching band, Student Senate, Phi Theta Kappa, Delta Epsilon Chi. *Campus security:* 24-hour emergency response devices and patrols, controlled dormitory access. *Student services:* personal/psychological counseling.

Athletics Member NJCAA. *Intercollegiate sports:* basketball M(s)/W(s), cheerleading M(s)/W(s), football M(s), softball W(s), volleyball W(s). *Intramural sports:* baseball M/W, basketball M/W, football M, table tennis M/W, volleyball M/W.

Costs (2011–12) *Tuition:* area resident $1920 full-time, $30 per semester hour part-time; state resident $3360 full-time, $78 per semester hour part-time; nonresident $4200 full-time, $106 per semester hour part-time. Full-time tuition and fees vary according to course load. Part-time tuition and fees vary according to course load. *Required fees:* $34 per semester hour part-time. *Room and board:* $4000. Room and board charges vary according to board plan. *Payment plan:* installment. *Waivers:* employees or children of employees.

Financial Aid Of all full-time matriculated undergraduates who enrolled in 2009, 80 Federal Work-Study jobs (averaging $1544). 40 state and other part-time jobs (averaging $1544).

Applying *Options:* electronic application, early admission. *Required:* high school transcript. *Application deadlines:* rolling (freshmen), rolling (transfers). *Notification:* continuous (freshmen), continuous (transfers).

Freshman Application Contact Dr. Colette Hilliard, Dean of Enrollment Management and Registrar, Trinity Valley Community College, 100 Cardinal Drive, Athens, TX 75751. *Phone:* 903-675-6209 Ext. 209. *Web site:* http://www.tvcc.edu/.

Tyler Junior College

Tyler, Texas

- **State and locally supported** 2-year, founded 1926
- **Suburban** 85-acre campus
- **Coed,** 11,738 undergraduate students, 53% full-time, 59% women, 41% men

Undergraduates 6,234 full-time, 5,504 part-time. Students come from 36 states and territories; 25 other countries; 1% are from out of state; 23% Black or African American, non-Hispanic/Latino; 11% Hispanic/Latino; 2% Asian, non-Hispanic/Latino; 0.5% American Indian or Alaska Native, non-Hispanic/Latino; 1% Race/ethnicity unknown; 1% international; 9% transferred in; 9% live on campus. *Retention:* 45% of full-time freshmen returned.

Freshmen *Admission:* 6,830 applied, 6,830 admitted, 2,826 enrolled. *Average high school GPA:* 3.07.

Faculty *Total:* 538, 50% full-time. *Student/faculty ratio:* 22:1.

Majors Accounting; administrative assistant and secretarial science; agriculture; art; automobile/automotive mechanics technology; behavioral sciences; biology/biological sciences; business administration and management; chemistry; child development; clinical/medical laboratory technology; commercial and advertising art; computer and information sciences; computer and information sciences related; computer engineering technology; computer graphics; computer programming related; computer science; computer systems networking and telecommunications; criminal justice/law enforcement administration; criminal justice/police science; dance; data entry/microcomputer applications; dental hygiene; dramatic/theater arts; economics; emergency medical technology (EMT paramedic); engineering; environmental science; family and con-

sumer sciences/human sciences; fire science/firefighting; geology/earth science; health/health-care administration; health information/medical records technology; horticultural science; industrial radiologic technology; information technology; legal administrative assistant/secretary; liberal arts and sciences/liberal studies; licensed practical/vocational nurse training; mathematics; medical administrative assistant and medical secretary; modern languages; optometric technician; photography; physical education teaching and coaching; physics; political science and government; psychology; registered nursing/registered nurse; respiratory care therapy; sign language interpretation and translation; social sciences; speech communication and rhetoric; substance abuse/addiction counseling; surgical technology; surveying technology; welding technology.

Academics *Calendar:* semesters. *Degree:* certificates and associate. *Special study options:* academic remediation for entering students, accelerated degree program, adult/continuing education programs, advanced placement credit, distance learning, English as a second language, freshman honors college, honors programs, part-time degree program, services for LD students, summer session for credit.

Library Vaughn Library and Learning Resource Center with 569 serial subscriptions, 64,776 audiovisual materials, an OPAC.

Student Life *Housing Options:* men-only, women-only. Campus housing is university owned. *Activities and Organizations:* drama/theater group, student-run newspaper, choral group, marching band, student government, religious affiliation clubs, Phi Theta Kappa, national fraternities, national sororities. *Campus security:* 24-hour patrols, controlled dormitory access. *Student services:* health clinic, personal/psychological counseling.

Athletics Member NJCAA. *Intercollegiate sports:* baseball M, basketball M(s)/W(s), football M(s), golf M/W, soccer M(s)/W(s), tennis M(s)/W(s), volleyball W(s). *Intramural sports:* basketball M/W, racquetball M/W, volleyball M/W, weight lifting M/W.

Costs (2011–12) *Tuition:* area resident $672 full-time, $28 per credit hour part-time; state resident $1704 full-time, $71 per credit hour part-time; nonresident $2184 full-time, $91 per credit hour part-time. *Required fees:* $948 full-time, $36 per credit hour part-time, $80 per term part-time. *Room and board:* $2530. Room and board charges vary according to housing facility. *Payment plan:* installment. *Waivers:* senior citizens.

Financial Aid Of all full-time matriculated undergraduates who enrolled in 2008, 8,023 applied for aid. 37 Federal Work-Study jobs, 23 state and other part-time jobs.

Applying *Options:* early admission. *Required:* high school transcript. *Application deadlines:* rolling (freshmen), rolling (transfers).

Freshman Application Contact Ms. Janna Chancey, Director of Enrollment Management, Tyler Junior College, PO Box 9020, Tyler, TX 75711-9020. *Phone:* 903-510-3325. *Toll-free phone:* 800-687-5680. *E-mail:* jcha@tjc.edu. *Web site:* http://www.tjc.edu/.

Universal Technical Institute

Houston, Texas

Director of Admissions Director of Admissions, Universal Technical Institute, 721 Lockhaven Drive, Houston, TX 77073-5598. *Phone:* 281-443-6262. *Toll-free phone:* 800-325-0354. *Fax:* 281-443-0610. *Web site:* http://www.uti.edu/.

Vernon College

Vernon, Texas

Director of Admissions Mr. Joe Hite, Dean of Admissions/Registrar, Vernon College, 4400 College Drive, Vernon, TX 76384-4092. *Phone:* 940-552-6291 Ext. 2204. *Web site:* http://www.vernoncollege.edu/.

Vet Tech Institute of Houston

Houston, Texas

- **Private** 2-year, founded 1958
- **Suburban** campus
- **Coed,** 134 undergraduate students
- **63%** of applicants were admitted

Freshmen *Admission:* 610 applied, 385 admitted.

Majors Veterinary/animal health technology.

Academics *Degree:* associate. *Special study options:* accelerated degree program, internships.

Student Life *Housing:* college housing not available.

Freshman Application Contact Admissions Office, Vet Tech Institute of Houston, 4669 Southwest Freeway, Suite 100, Houston, TX 77027. *Phone:* 888-884-1468. *Web site:* http://www.vettechinstitute.edu/.

Victoria College
Victoria, Texas

- **County-supported** 2-year, founded 1925
- **Urban** 80-acre campus
- **Endowment** $2.3 million
- **Coed**

Undergraduates 1,362 full-time, 2,692 part-time. Students come from 12 states and territories; 15 other countries; 0.6% are from out of state; 66% transferred in.
Faculty *Student/faculty ratio:* 18:1.
Academics *Calendar:* semesters. *Degree:* certificates and associate. *Special study options:* academic remediation for entering students, adult/continuing education programs, advanced placement credit, distance learning, part-time degree program, services for LD students, summer session for credit.
Student Life *Campus security:* 24-hour emergency response devices.
Costs (2010–11) *Tuition:* area resident $1020 full-time, $34 per semester hour part-time; state resident $2370 full-time, $79 per semester hour part-time; nonresident $3000 full-time, $100 per semester hour part-time. Full-time tuition and fees vary according to course load and location. Part-time tuition and fees vary according to course load and location. *Required fees:* $1110 full-time, $37 per semester hour part-time.
Applying *Required:* high school transcript.
Freshman Application Contact Ms. Lavern Dentler, Registrar, Victoria College, 2200 East Red River, Victoria, TX 77901-4494. *Phone:* 361-573-3291. *Toll-free phone:* 877-843-4369. *Fax:* 361-582-2525. *E-mail:* registrar@victoriacollege.edu. *Web site:* http://www.victoriacollege.edu/.

Virginia College at Austin
Austin, Texas

Admissions Office Contact Virginia College at Austin, 6301 East Highway 290, Austin, TX 78723. *Toll-free phone:* 866-314-6324. *Web site:* http://www.vc.edu/.

Wade College
Dallas, Texas

- **Proprietary** primarily 2-year, founded 1965
- **Urban** 175-acre campus
- **Coed, primarily women,** 238 undergraduate students

Undergraduates 5% are from out of state. *Retention:* 49% of full-time freshmen returned.
Faculty *Total:* 18, 50% full-time, 11% with terminal degrees. *Student/faculty ratio:* 15:1.
Majors Fashion/apparel design; graphic design; interior design; merchandising, sales, and marketing operations related (specialized).
Academics *Calendar:* trimesters. *Degrees:* associate and bachelor's. *Special study options:* academic remediation for entering students, advanced placement credit, double majors, part-time degree program, summer session for credit.
Library College Library with 4,782 titles, 109 serial subscriptions, 147 audiovisual materials, an OPAC, a Web page.
Student Life *Housing Options:* coed, men-only, women-only. Campus housing is leased by the school and is provided by a third party. *Activities and Organizations:* Merchandising Design Student Association. *Campus security:* 24-hour emergency response devices and patrols, late-night transport/escort service, controlled dormitory access.
Costs (2010–11) *One-time required fee:* $125. *Tuition:* $10,900 full-time, $1265 per course part-time. Full-time tuition and fees vary according to course load and degree level. Part-time tuition and fees vary according to course load and degree level. No tuition increase for student's term of enrollment. *Required fees:* $1050 full-time. *Room only:* $4400. *Payment plan:* installment.
Applying *Options:* electronic application. *Required:* high school transcript, interview. *Application deadlines:* rolling (freshmen), rolling (transfers).
Freshman Application Contact Wade College, INFOMart, 1950 Stemmons Freeway, Suite 4080, LB 562, Dallas, TX 75207. *Phone:* 214-637-3530. *Toll-free phone:* 800-624-4850. *Web site:* http://www.wadecollege.edu/.

Weatherford College
Weatherford, Texas

Freshman Application Contact Mr. Ralph Willingham, Director of Admissions, Weatherford College, 225 College Park Drive, Weatherford, TX 76086-5699. *Phone:* 817-598-6248. *Toll-free phone:* 800-287-5471 Ext. 248. *Fax:* 817-598-6205. *E-mail:* willingham@wc.edu. *Web site:* http://www.wc.edu/.

Western Technical College
El Paso, Texas

Freshman Application Contact Laura Pena, Director of Admissions, Western Technical College, 9451 Diana, El Paso, TX 79930-2610. *Phone:* 915-566-9621. *Toll-free phone:* 800-201-9232. *E-mail:* lpena@westerntech.edu. *Web site:* http://www.westerntech.edu/.

Western Technical College
El Paso, Texas

Freshman Application Contact Mr. Bill Terrell, Chief Admissions Officer, Western Technical College, 9624 Plaza Circle, El Paso, TX 79927. *Phone:* 915-532-3737 Ext. 117. *Fax:* 915-532-6946. *E-mail:* bterrell@wtc-ep.edu. *Web site:* http://www.westerntech.edu/.

Western Texas College
Snyder, Texas

Director of Admissions Dr. Jim Clifton, Dean of Student Services, Western Texas College, 6200 College Avenue, Snyder, TX 79549. *Phone:* 325-573-8511 Ext. 204. *Toll-free phone:* 888-GO-TO-WTC. *E-mail:* jclifton@wtc.cc.tx.us. *Web site:* http://www.wtc.edu/.

Westwood College–Houston South Campus
Houston, Texas

- **Proprietary** primarily 2-year, founded 2003
- **Coed**

Academics *Calendar:* continuous. *Degrees:* diplomas, associate, and bachelor's.
Freshman Application Contact Westwood College–Houston South Campus, 7322 Southwest Freeway #110, Houston, TX 77074. *Phone:* 713-777-4779. *Toll-free phone:* 888-227-4260. *Web site:* http://www.westwood.edu/.

Wharton County Junior College
Wharton, Texas

Freshman Application Contact Mr. Albert Barnes, Dean of Admissions and Registration, Wharton County Junior College, 911 Boling Highway, Wharton, TX 77488-3298. *Phone:* 979-532-6381. *E-mail:* albertb@wcjc.edu. *Web site:* http://www.wcjc.edu/.

UTAH

Everest College
West Valley City, Utah

Director of Admissions Director of Admissions, Everest College, 3280 West 3500 South, West Valley City, UT 84119. *Phone:* 801-840-4800. *Toll-free phone:* 888-741-4271. *Fax:* 801-969-0828. *Web site:* http://www.everest.edu/.

ITT Technical Institute
Murray, Utah

- **Proprietary** primarily 2-year, founded 1984, part of ITT Educational Services, Inc.
- **Suburban** campus
- **Coed**

Majors CAD/CADD drafting/design technology; communications technology; computer and information systems security; computer engineering technology; computer software and media applications related; computer software engineering; computer software technology; construction management; criminal justice/law enforcement administration; design and visual communications; electrical, electronic and communications engineering technology; game and interactive media design; graphic design; legal assistant/paralegal; project management; system, networking, and LAN/WAN management; web/multimedia management and webmaster; web page, digital/multimedia and information resources design.
Academics *Calendar:* quarters. *Degrees:* associate and bachelor's.
Student Life *Housing:* college housing not available.

Freshman Application Contact Director of Recruitment, ITT Technical Institute, 920 West Levoy Drive, Murray, UT 84123-2500. *Phone:* 801-263-3313. *Toll-free phone:* 800-365-2136. *Web site:* http://www.itt-tech.edu/.

LDS Business College
Salt Lake City, Utah

- **Independent** 2-year, founded 1886, affiliated with The Church of Jesus Christ of Latter-day Saints, part of Latter-day Saints Church Educational System
- **Urban** 2-acre campus with easy access to Salt Lake City
- **Coed**

Undergraduates 1,218 full-time, 370 part-time. Students come from 47 states and territories; 64 other countries; 48% are from out of state; 54% transferred in.

Faculty *Student/faculty ratio:* 20:1.

Academics *Calendar:* semesters. *Degree:* certificates and associate. *Special study options:* academic remediation for entering students, adult/continuing education programs, advanced placement credit, internships, part-time degree program, services for LD students, summer session for credit. *ROTC:* Army (c), Air Force (c).

Student Life *Campus security:* 24-hour emergency response devices and patrols.

Standardized Tests *Recommended:* SAT or ACT (for admission).

Costs (2010–11) *Tuition:* $2900 full-time, $121 per credit hour part-time. Full-time tuition and fees vary according to course load. Part-time tuition and fees vary according to course load. Students who are not members of the LDS Church pay $5,800 per year.

Financial Aid *Average need-based gift aid:* $3797.

Applying *Options:* electronic application, deferred entrance. *Application fee:* $35. *Required:* essay or personal statement, high school transcript, interview.

Freshman Application Contact Miss Dawn Fellows, Assistant Director of Admissions, LDS Business College, 95 North 300 West, Salt Lake City, UT 84101-3500. *Phone:* 801-524-8146. *Toll-free phone:* 800-999-5767. *Fax:* 801-524-1900. *E-mail:* DFellows@ldsbc.edu. *Web site:* http://www.ldsbc.edu/.

Provo College
Provo, Utah

Director of Admissions Mr. Gordon Peters, College Director, Provo College, 1450 West 820 North, Provo, UT 84601. *Phone:* 801-375-1861. *Toll-free phone:* 877- 777-5886. *Fax:* 801-375-9728. *E-mail:* gordonp@provocollege.org. *Web site:* http://www.provocollege.edu/.

Salt Lake Community College
Salt Lake City, Utah

- **State-supported** 2-year, founded 1948, part of Utah System of Higher Education
- **Urban** 114-acre campus with easy access to Salt Lake City
- **Endowment** $818,597
- **Coed**, 32,947 undergraduate students, 30% full-time, 51% women, 49% men

Undergraduates 9,944 full-time, 23,003 part-time. 3% transferred in.

Freshmen *Admission:* 3,858 applied, 3,858 admitted, 3,858 enrolled.

Faculty *Total:* 1,529, 23% full-time. *Student/faculty ratio:* 23:1.

Majors Accounting technology and bookkeeping; airline pilot and flight crew; architectural engineering technology; autobody/collision and repair technology; avionics maintenance technology; biology/biological sciences; biology/biotechnology laboratory technician; building/construction finishing, management, and inspection related; business administration and management; chemistry; clinical/medical laboratory technology; computer and information sciences; computer science; cosmetology; criminal justice/law enforcement administration; culinary arts; dental hygiene; design and visual communications; diesel mechanics technology; drafting and design technology; economics; electrical, electronic and communications engineering technology; engineering; engineering technology; English; entrepreneurship; environmental engineering technology; finance; general studies; geology/earth science; graphic design; health professions related; heating, air conditioning, ventilation and refrigeration maintenance technology; history; human development and family studies; humanities; industrial radiologic technology; information science/studies; information technology; instrumentation technology; international/global studies; international relations and affairs; kinesiology and exercise science; legal assistant/paralegal; marketing/marketing management; mass communication/media; medical/clinical assistant; medical radiologic technology; music; occupational therapist assistant; photographic and film/video technology; physical sciences; physical therapy technology; physics; political science and government; psychology; public health related; quality control

technology; radio and television broadcasting technology; registered nursing/registered nurse; sign language interpretation and translation; social work; sociology; speech communication and rhetoric; sport and fitness administration/management; surveying technology; teacher assistant/aide; telecommunications technology; welding technology.

Academics *Calendar:* semesters. *Degree:* certificates, diplomas, and associate. *Special study options:* academic remediation for entering students, advanced placement credit, cooperative education, distance learning, double majors, English as a second language, internships, part-time degree program, services for LD students, student-designed majors, study abroad, summer session for credit. *ROTC:* Army (c), Air Force (c).

Library Markosian Library plus 2 others with 159,705 titles, 24,117 serial subscriptions, 21,203 audiovisual materials, an OPAC, a Web page.

Student Life *Housing:* college housing not available. *Activities and Organizations:* drama/theater group, student-run newspaper, radio and television station, choral group, marching band. *Campus security:* 24-hour emergency response devices and patrols, late-night transport/escort service. *Student services:* health clinic, personal/psychological counseling.

Athletics Member NJCAA. *Intercollegiate sports:* baseball M(s), basketball M(s)/W(s), cheerleading M(s)/W(s), soccer M(c)/W(c), softball W(s), volleyball W(s).

Costs (2010–11) *Tuition:* state resident $2520 full-time, $105 per credit hour part-time; nonresident $8760 full-time, $365 per credit hour part-time. *Required fees:* $412 full-time, $23 per credit hour part-time. *Payment plan:* installment. *Waivers:* senior citizens and employees or children of employees.

Financial Aid Of all full-time matriculated undergraduates who enrolled in 2009, 132 Federal Work-Study jobs (averaging $2567).

Applying *Options:* electronic application, early admission. *Application fee:* $40. *Application deadlines:* rolling (freshmen), rolling (transfers).

Freshman Application Contact Ms. Kathy Thompson, Salt Lake Community College, Salt Lake City, UT 84130. *Phone:* 801-957-4485. *E-mail:* kathy.thompson@slcc.edu. *Web site:* http://www.slcc.edu/.

Snow College
Ephraim, Utah

- **State-supported** 2-year, founded 1888, part of Utah System of Higher Education
- **Rural** 50-acre campus
- **Endowment** $6.2 million
- **Coed**, 4,386 undergraduate students, 66% full-time, 54% women, 46% men

Undergraduates 2,876 full-time, 1,510 part-time. Students come from 34 states and territories; 12 other countries; 8% are from out of state; 0.9% Black or African American, non-Hispanic/Latino; 3% Hispanic/Latino; 0.3% Asian, non-Hispanic/Latino; 2% Native Hawaiian or other Pacific Islander, non-Hispanic/Latino; 1% American Indian or Alaska Native, non-Hispanic/Latino; 0.6% Two or more races, non-Hispanic/Latino; 2% Race/ethnicity unknown; 2% international; 2% transferred in. *Retention:* 48% of full-time freshmen returned.

Freshmen *Admission:* 2,397 applied, 2,397 admitted, 1,434 enrolled. *Average high school GPA:* 3.3. *Test scores:* ACT scores over 18: 73%; ACT scores over 24: 22%; ACT scores over 30: 2%.

Faculty *Total:* 269, 42% full-time, 6% with terminal degrees. *Student/faculty ratio:* 20:1.

Majors Accounting; administrative assistant and secretarial science; agricultural business and management; agriculture; animal sciences; art; automobile/automotive mechanics technology; biology/biological sciences; botany/plant biology; building/construction finishing, management, and inspection related; business administration and management; business teacher education; chemistry; child development; computer science; construction engineering technology; criminal justice/law enforcement administration; dance; dramatic/theater arts; economics; education; elementary education; family and community services; family and consumer sciences/human sciences; farm and ranch management; foods, nutrition, and wellness; forestry; French; geography; geology/earth science; history; humanities; information science/studies; Japanese; kindergarten/preschool education; liberal arts and sciences/liberal studies; mass communication/media; mathematics; music; music history, literature, and theory; music teacher education; philosophy; physical education teaching and coaching; physical sciences; physics; political science and government; pre-engineering; range science and management; science teacher education; sociology; soil science and agronomy; Spanish; trade and industrial teacher education; voice and opera; zoology/animal biology.

Academics *Calendar:* semesters. *Degree:* certificates, diplomas, and associate. *Special study options:* academic remediation for entering students, adult/continuing education programs, advanced placement credit, cooperative education, English as a second language, external degree program, honors programs, independent study, part-time degree program, services for LD students, summer session for credit.

Library Lucy Phillips Library with 51,352 titles, 201 serial subscriptions, 6,676 audiovisual materials, an OPAC, a Web page.

Student Life *Housing Options:* coed. Campus housing is university owned. *Activities and Organizations:* drama/theater group, student-run newspaper, radio station, choral group, Phi Beta Lambda, Latter-Day Saints Singers, International Student Society, BAAD Club (Alcohol and Drug Prevention), Dead Cats Society (Life Science Club). *Campus security:* 24-hour emergency response devices and patrols, student patrols, late-night transport/escort service. *Student services:* health clinic, personal/psychological counseling.

Athletics Member NJCAA. *Intercollegiate sports:* basketball M(s)/W(s), football M(s), softball W(s), volleyball W(s). *Intramural sports:* badminton M/W, basketball M/W, bowling M/W, football M/W, golf M/W, lacrosse M/W, racquetball M/W, soccer M/W, softball M/W, tennis M/W, ultimate Frisbee M/W, volleyball M/W, water polo M/W, wrestling M.

Standardized Tests *Recommended:* SAT or ACT (for admission).

Costs (2011–12) *Tuition:* state resident $2520 full-time, $150 per credit part-time; nonresident $9196 full-time, $600 per credit part-time. Full-time tuition and fees vary according to course load. Part-time tuition and fees vary according to course load. *Required fees:* $390 full-time, $30 per credit hour part-time. *Room and board:* $5000. Room and board charges vary according to board plan, housing facility, and location. *Payment plan:* installment. *Waivers:* employees or children of employees.

Financial Aid Of all full-time matriculated undergraduates who enrolled in 2009, 302 Federal Work-Study jobs (averaging $1017).

Applying *Options:* electronic application, early admission. *Application fee:* $30. *Required:* high school transcript. *Application deadlines:* 6/15 (freshmen), 6/1 (transfers). *Notification:* continuous (freshmen), continuous (transfers).

Freshman Application Contact Ms. Lorie Parry, Admissions Advisor, Snow College, 150 East College Avenue, Ephraim, UT 84627. *Phone:* 435-283-7144. *Fax:* 435-283-7157. *E-mail:* snowcollege@snow.edu. *Web site:* http://www.snow.edu/.

Utah State University–College of Eastern Utah

Price, Utah

Freshman Application Contact Mr. Todd Olsen, Director of Admissions and Scholarships, Utah State University–College of Eastern Utah, 451 East 400 North, Price, UT 84501. *Phone:* 435-613-5217. *Fax:* 435-613-5814. *E-mail:* todd.olsen@ceu.edu. *Web site:* http://www.ceu.edu/.

VERMONT

Community College of Vermont

Montpelier, Vermont

- **State-supported** 2-year, founded 1970, part of Vermont State Colleges System
- **Rural** campus
- **Coed,** 7,303 undergraduate students, 18% full-time, 68% women, 32% men

Undergraduates 1,316 full-time, 5,987 part-time. Students come from 18 states and territories; 3% are from out of state; 3% Black or African American, non-Hispanic/Latino; 2% Hispanic/Latino; 2% Asian, non-Hispanic/Latino; 0.1% Native Hawaiian or other Pacific Islander, non-Hispanic/Latino; 2% American Indian or Alaska Native, non-Hispanic/Latino; 1% Two or more races, non-Hispanic/Latino; 8% Race/ethnicity unknown.

Freshmen *Admission:* 904 applied, 904 admitted.

Faculty *Total:* 891, 23% with terminal degrees. *Student/faculty ratio:* 13:1.

Majors Accounting; administrative assistant and secretarial science; art; business administration and management; CAD/CADD drafting/design technology; child development; community organization and advocacy; computer and information sciences; computer science; computer systems networking and telecommunications; criminal justice/law enforcement administration; data entry/microcomputer applications; developmental and child psychology; digital communication and media/multimedia; early childhood education; education; environmental science; graphic design; hospitality administration; human services; industrial technology; information technology; liberal arts and sciences/liberal studies; social sciences; teacher assistant/aide.

Academics *Calendar:* semesters. *Degree:* certificates, diplomas, and associate. *Special study options:* academic remediation for entering students, accelerated degree program, adult/continuing education programs, advanced placement credit, cooperative education, distance learning, double majors, English as a second language, external degree program, independent study,

internships, part-time degree program, services for LD students, student-designed majors, study abroad, summer session for credit.

Library Hartness Library plus 1 other with 59,000 titles, 36,500 serial subscriptions, 6,200 audiovisual materials, an OPAC, a Web page.

Student Life *Housing:* college housing not available.

Costs (2010–11) *Tuition:* state resident $6150 full-time, $205 per credit hour part-time; nonresident $12,300 full-time, $410 per credit hour part-time. *Required fees:* $150 full-time, $50 per term part-time. *Payment plan:* installment. *Waivers:* senior citizens and employees or children of employees.

Financial Aid Of all full-time matriculated undergraduates who enrolled in 2009, 84 Federal Work-Study jobs (averaging $2000).

Applying *Options:* electronic application. *Application deadlines:* rolling (freshmen), rolling (out-of-state freshmen), rolling (transfers). *Notification:* continuous (freshmen), continuous (out-of-state freshmen), continuous (transfers).

Freshman Application Contact Community College of Vermont, PO Box 489, Montpelier, VT 05601. *Phone:* 802-654-0505. *Web site:* http://www.ccv.edu/.

Landmark College

Putney, Vermont

- **Independent** 2-year, founded 1983
- **Small-town** 125-acre campus
- **Endowment** $9.9 million
- **Coed**

Undergraduates 498 full-time. Students come from 36 states and territories; 11 other countries; 94% are from out of state; 17% transferred in; 95% live on campus.

Faculty *Student/faculty ratio:* 6:1.

Academics *Calendar:* semesters. *Degree:* associate. *Special study options:* academic remediation for entering students, advanced placement credit, services for LD students, study abroad, summer session for credit.

Student Life *Campus security:* 24-hour emergency response devices and patrols, controlled dormitory access.

Standardized Tests *Required:* Wechsler Adult Intelligence Scale III and Nelson Denny Reading Test (for admission).

Costs (2010–11) *Comprehensive fee:* $56,500 includes full-time tuition ($47,500), mandatory fees ($500), and room and board ($8500). *Room and board:* college room only: $4400. Room and board charges vary according to board plan and housing facility.

Financial Aid Of all full-time matriculated undergraduates who enrolled in 2009, 341 applied for aid, 243 were judged to have need, 3 had their need fully met. 85 Federal Work-Study jobs (averaging $1000). 3 state and other part-time jobs (averaging $1000). In 2009, 18. *Average percent of need met:* 45. *Average financial aid package:* $26,000. *Average need-based loan:* $4500. *Average need-based gift aid:* $21,000. *Average non-need-based aid:* $7800. *Average indebtedness upon graduation:* $6100.

Applying *Options:* electronic application, deferred entrance. *Application fee:* $75. *Required:* essay or personal statement, high school transcript, 2 letters of recommendation, interview, diagnosis of LD and/or ADHD and cognitive testing.

Freshman Application Contact Admissions Main Desk, Landmark College, Putney, VT 05346. *Phone:* 802-387-6718. *Fax:* 802-387-6868. *E-mail:* admissions@landmark.edu. *Web site:* http://www.landmark.edu/.

See page 418 for the College Close-Up.

New England Culinary Institute

Montpelier, Vermont

Freshman Application Contact Jan Knutsen, Vice President of Enrollment, New England Culinary Institute, 56 College Street, Montpelier, VT 05602-3115. *Toll-free phone:* 877-223-6324. *Fax:* 802-225-3280. *E-mail:* janknutsen@neci.edu. *Web site:* http://www.neci.edu/.

VIRGINIA

ACT College

Arlington, Virginia

Freshman Application Contact Admissions Office, ACT College, 1100 Wilson Boulevard, Arlington, VA 22209. *Phone:* 703-527-6660. *Toll-free phone:* 866-950-7979. *E-mail:* info@actcollege.edu. *Web site:* http://www.healthtraining.com/.

Advanced Technology Institute

Virginia Beach, Virginia

Freshman Application Contact Admissions Office, Advanced Technology Institute, 5700 Southern Boulevard, Suite 100, Virginia Beach, VA 23462. *Phone:* 757-490-1241. *Web site:* http://www.auto.edu/.

Aviation Institute of Maintenance–Chesapeake

Chesapeake, Virginia

Freshman Application Contact Aviation Institute of Maintenance–Chesapeake, 2211 South Military Highway, Chesapeake, VA 23320. *Phone:* 757-363-2121. *Fax:* 757-363-2044. *Web site:* http://www.aviationmaintenance.edu/aviation-norfolk.asp.

Aviation Institute of Maintenance–Manassas

Manassas, Virginia

Freshman Application Contact Aviation Institute of Maintenance–Manassas, 9821 Godwin Drive, Manassas, VA 20110. *Phone:* 703-257-5515. *Toll-free phone:* 888-349-5387- (in-state); 888-349-5387 (out-of-state). *Fax:* 703-257-5523. *Web site:* http://www.aviationmaintenance.edu/aviation-washington-dc.asp.

Blue Ridge Community College

Weyers Cave, Virginia

Freshman Application Contact Blue Ridge Community College, PO Box 80, Weyers Cave, VA 24486-0080. *Phone:* 540-453-2217. *Toll-free phone:* 888-750-2722. *Web site:* http://www.brcc.edu/.

Bryant & Stratton College - Richmond Campus

Richmond, Virginia

- **Proprietary** primarily 2-year, founded 1952, part of Bryant and Stratton Business Institute, Inc.
- **Suburban** campus
- **Coed**

Undergraduates 280 full-time, 292 part-time. Students come from 1 other state; 7% transferred in.
Faculty *Student/faculty ratio:* 10:1.
Academics *Calendar:* semesters. *Degrees:* associate and bachelor's. *Special study options:* academic remediation for entering students, adult/continuing education programs, advanced placement credit, distance learning, double majors, independent study, internships, part-time degree program, summer session for credit.
Student Life *Campus security:* late-night transport/escort service.
Standardized Tests *Required:* TABE, CPAt (for admission). *Recommended:* SAT or ACT (for admission).
Applying *Options:* deferred entrance. *Required:* high school transcript, interview, entrance evaluation and placement evaluation.
Freshman Application Contact Mr. David K. Mayle, Director of Admissions, Bryant & Stratton College - Richmond Campus, 8141 Hull Street Road, Richmond, VA 23235-6411. *Phone:* 804-745-2444. *Fax:* 804-745-6884. *E-mail:* tlawson@bryanstratton.edu. *Web site:* http://www.bryantstratton.edu/.

Bryant & Stratton College - Virginia Beach

Virginia Beach, Virginia

- **Proprietary** primarily 2-year, founded 1952, part of Bryant and Stratton Business Institute, Inc.
- **Suburban** campus
- **Coed**

Undergraduates 267 full-time, 328 part-time. Students come from 2 states and territories; 1% are from out of state; 10% transferred in.

Faculty *Student/faculty ratio:* 12:1.
Academics *Calendar:* semesters. *Degrees:* associate and bachelor's. *Special study options:* academic remediation for entering students, adult/continuing education programs, advanced placement credit, double majors, independent study, internships, part-time degree program, services for LD students, summer session for credit.
Student Life *Campus security:* 24-hour emergency response devices, late-night transport/escort service.
Standardized Tests *Required:* CPAt (for admission).
Financial Aid Of all full-time matriculated undergraduates who enrolled in 2009, 30 Federal Work-Study jobs (averaging $5000).
Applying *Options:* electronic application. *Application fee:* $35. *Required:* essay or personal statement, high school transcript, interview.
Freshman Application Contact Bryant & Stratton College - Virginia Beach, 301 Centre Pointe Drive, Virginia Beach, VA 23462-4417. *Phone:* 757-499-7900 Ext. 173. *Web site:* http://www.bryantstratton.edu/.

Central Virginia Community College

Lynchburg, Virginia

Freshman Application Contact Admissions Office, Central Virginia Community College, 3506 Wards Road, Lynchburg, VA 24502-2498. *Phone:* 434-832-7633. *Toll-free phone:* 800-562-3060. *Fax:* 434-832-7793. *Web site:* http://www.cvcc.vccs.edu/.

Centura College

Chesapeake, Virginia

Director of Admissions Director of Admissions, Centura College, 932 Ventures Way, Chesapeake, VA 23320. *Phone:* 757-549-2121. *Fax:* 575-549-1196. *Web site:* http://www.centuracollege.com/.

Centura College

Newport News, Virginia

Director of Admissions Victoria Whitehead, Director of Admissions, Centura College, 616 Denbigh Boulevard, Newport News, VA 23608. *Phone:* 757-874-2121. *Fax:* 757-874-3857. *E-mail:* admdircpen@centura.edu. *Web site:* http://www.centuracollege.edu/.

Centura College

Norfolk, Virginia

Director of Admissions Director of Admissions, Centura College, 7020 North Military Highway, Norfolk, VA 23518. *Phone:* 757-853-2121. *Fax:* 757-852-9017. *Web site:* http://www.centuracollege.edu/.

Centura College

Richmond, Virginia

Director of Admissions Terry Gates, Director of Admissions, Centura College, 7001 West Broad Street, Richmond, VA 23294. *Phone:* 804-672-2300. *Fax:* 804-672-3338. *Web site:* http://www.centuracollege.edu/.

Centura College

Richmond, Virginia

Freshman Application Contact Admissions Office, Centura College, 7914 Midlothian Turnpike, Richmond, VA 23235-5230. *Phone:* 804-330-0111. *Toll-free phone:* 877-575-5627. *Fax:* 804-330-3809. *Web site:* http://www.centuracollege.edu/.

Centura College

Virginia Beach, Virginia

Freshman Application Contact Admissions Office, Centura College, 2697 Dean Drive, Suite 100, Virginia Beach, VA 23452. *Phone:* 757-340-2121. *Toll-free phone:* 877-575-5627. *Fax:* 757-340-9704. *Web site:* http://www.centuracollege.edu/.

Dabney S. Lancaster Community College

Clifton Forge, Virginia

- **State-supported** 2-year, founded 1964, part of Virginia Community College System
- **Rural** 117-acre campus
- **Endowment** $3.3 million
- **Coed,** 1,437 undergraduate students, 37% full-time, 60% women, 40% men

Undergraduates 527 full-time, 910 part-time. Students come from 5 states and territories; 6% are from out of state; 24% transferred in.
Freshmen *Admission:* 91 enrolled.
Faculty *Total:* 95, 22% full-time. *Student/faculty ratio:* 15:1.
Majors Administrative assistant and secretarial science; biological and physical sciences; business administration and management; computer programming; criminal justice/law enforcement administration; data processing and data processing technology; drafting and design technology; drafting/design engineering technologies related; education; electrical, electronic and communications engineering technology; forest technology; information science/studies; legal administrative assistant/secretary; liberal arts and sciences/liberal studies; medical administrative assistant and medical secretary; registered nursing/registered nurse; wood science and wood products/pulp and paper technology.
Academics *Calendar:* semesters. *Degree:* certificates, diplomas, and associate. *Special study options:* academic remediation for entering students, adult/continuing education programs, advanced placement credit, cooperative education, distance learning, honors programs, independent study, internships, part-time degree program, services for LD students, study abroad, summer session for credit.
Library Scott Hall plus 1 other with 37,716 titles, 376 serial subscriptions, an OPAC, a Web page.
Student Life *Housing:* college housing not available. *Activities and Organizations:* drama/theater group. *Campus security:* 24-hour emergency response devices. *Student services:* personal/psychological counseling.
Athletics *Intercollegiate sports:* basketball M. *Intramural sports:* basketball M/W, bowling M/W, equestrian sports M/W, football M/W, golf M/W, skiing (downhill) M/W, soccer M/W, tennis M/W, volleyball M/W.
Costs (2011–12) *Tuition:* state resident $2424 full-time, $110 per credit hour part-time; nonresident $7070 full-time, $303 per credit hour part-time. Full-time tuition and fees vary according to reciprocity agreements. Part-time tuition and fees vary according to reciprocity agreements. *Required fees:* $156 full-time. *Payment plan:* installment. *Waivers:* senior citizens.
Applying *Options:* electronic application, early admission, deferred entrance. *Recommended:* high school transcript, interview. *Application deadlines:* rolling (freshmen), rolling (out-of-state freshmen), rolling (transfers). *Notification:* continuous (freshmen), continuous (out-of-state freshmen), continuous (transfers).
Freshman Application Contact Ms. Kathy Nicely, Registration Specialist, Dabney S. Lancaster Community College, Scott Hall, Clifton Forge, VA 24422. *Phone:* 540-863-2841. *Fax:* 540-863-2915. *E-mail:* knicely@dslcc.edu. *Web site:* http://www.dslcc.edu/.

Danville Community College

Danville, Virginia

Freshman Application Contact Cathy Pulliam, Coordinator of Student Recruitment and Enrollment, Danville Community College, 1008 South Main Street, Danville, VA 24541-4088. *Phone:* 434-797-8538. *Toll-free phone:* 800-560-4291. *E-mail:* cpulliam@dcc.vccs.edu. *Web site:* http://www.dcc.vccs.edu/.

Eastern Shore Community College

Melfa, Virginia

- **State-supported** 2-year, founded 1971, part of Virginia Community College System
- **Rural** 117-acre campus with easy access to Hampton Roads/Virginia Beach Norfolk
- **Coed**

Undergraduates 229 full-time, 1,103 part-time. Students come from 3 states and territories; 2% are from out of state.
Faculty *Student/faculty ratio:* 13:1.
Academics *Calendar:* semesters. *Degree:* certificates and associate. *Special study options:* academic remediation for entering students, adult/continuing education programs, distance learning, English as a second language, honors programs, off-campus study, part-time degree program, services for LD students, summer session for credit.

Student Life *Campus security:* night security guard.
Standardized Tests *Required:* COMPASS (for admission).
Costs (2010–11) *Tuition:* state resident $3030 full-time, $101 per credit hour part-time; nonresident $8388 full-time, $280 per credit hour part-time. Full-time tuition and fees vary according to course load. Part-time tuition and fees vary according to course load. *Required fees:* $225 full-time, $8 per credit hour part-time.
Financial Aid Of all full-time matriculated undergraduates who enrolled in 2009, 11 Federal Work-Study jobs.
Applying *Options:* electronic application. *Required:* high school transcript, high school diploma.
Freshman Application Contact P. Bryan Smith, Dean of Student Services, Eastern Shore Community College, 29300 Lankford Highway, Melfa, VA 23410. *Phone:* 757-789-1732. *Toll-free phone:* 877-871-8455. *Fax:* 757-789-1737. *E-mail:* bsmith@es.vccs.edu. *Web site:* http://www.es.vccs.edu/.

ECPI College of Technology

Richmond, Virginia

Freshman Application Contact Director, ECPI College of Technology, 800 Moorefield Park Drive, Richmond, VA 23236. *Phone:* 804-330-5533. *Toll-free phone:* 800-986-1200. *Fax:* 804-330-5577. *E-mail:* agerard@ecpi.edu. *Web site:* http://www.ecpi.edu/.

Everest College

Arlington, Virginia

Freshman Application Contact Director of Admissions, Everest College, 801 North Quincy Street, Suite 500, Arlington, VA 22203. *Phone:* 703-248-8887. *Fax:* 703-351-2202. *Web site:* http://www.everest.edu/.

Germanna Community College

Locust Grove, Virginia

- **State-supported** 2-year, founded 1970, part of Virginia Community College System
- **Suburban** 100-acre campus with easy access to Washington, DC
- **Coed**

Undergraduates 2,296 full-time, 4,739 part-time.
Faculty *Student/faculty ratio:* 19:1.
Academics *Calendar:* semesters. *Degree:* certificates and associate. *Special study options:* academic remediation for entering students, advanced placement credit, distance learning, double majors, English as a second language, independent study, off-campus study, part-time degree program, services for LD students, study abroad, summer session for credit.
Student Life *Campus security:* 24-hour patrols.
Costs (2010–11) *Tuition:* state resident $3030 full-time, $101 per credit hour part-time; nonresident $7488 full-time, $295 per credit hour part-time. Full-time tuition and fees vary according to course load. Part-time tuition and fees vary according to course load. *Required fees:* $262 full-time, $9 per credit hour part-time. *Payment plans:* installment, deferred payment.
Financial Aid Of all full-time matriculated undergraduates who enrolled in 2009, 31 Federal Work-Study jobs (averaging $1212). 14 state and other part-time jobs (averaging $1667).
Applying *Options:* electronic application, early admission. *Required for some:* high school transcript.
Freshman Application Contact Ms. Rita Dunston, Registrar, Germanna Community College, 10000 Germanna Point Drive, Fredericksburg, VA 22408. *Phone:* 540-891-3020. *Fax:* 540-891-3092. *Web site:* http://www.gcc.vccs.edu/.

ITT Technical Institute

Chantilly, Virginia

- **Proprietary** primarily 2-year, founded 2002, part of ITT Educational Services, Inc.
- **Coed**

Majors CAD/CADD drafting/design technology; communications technology; computer and information systems security; computer engineering technology; computer software and media applications related; construction management; criminal justice/law enforcement administration; design and visual communications; electrical, electronic and communications engineering technology; legal assistant/paralegal; project management; system, networking, and LAN/WAN management; web/multimedia management and webmaster; web page, digital/multimedia and information resources design.
Academics *Calendar:* quarters. *Degrees:* associate and bachelor's.
Student Life *Housing:* college housing not available.
Freshman Application Contact Director of Recruitment, ITT Technical Institute, 14420 Abermarle Point Place, Suite 100, Chantilly, VA 20151.

Phone: 703-263-2541. *Toll-free phone:* 888-895-8324. *Web site:* http://www.itt-tech.edu/.

ITT Technical Institute

Norfolk, Virginia

- **Proprietary** primarily 2-year, founded 1988, part of ITT Educational Services, Inc.
- **Suburban** campus
- **Coed**

Majors Business administration and management; CAD/CADD drafting/design technology; communications technology; computer and information systems security; computer engineering technology; computer software and media applications related; construction management; criminal justice/law enforcement administration; design and visual communications; electrical, electronic and communications engineering technology; game and interactive media design; information technology project management; legal assistant/paralegal; project management; registered nursing/registered nurse; system, networking, and LAN/WAN management; web/multimedia management and webmaster; web page, digital/multimedia and information resources design.
Academics *Calendar:* quarters. *Degrees:* associate and bachelor's.
Student Life *Housing:* college housing not available.
Financial Aid Of all full-time matriculated undergraduates who enrolled in 2009, 3 Federal Work-Study jobs (averaging $5000).
Freshman Application Contact Director of Recruitment, ITT Technical Institute, 863 Glenrock Road, Suite 100, Norfolk, VA 23502-3701. *Phone:* 757-466-1260. *Toll-free phone:* 888-253-8324. *Web site:* http://www.itt-tech.edu/.

ITT Technical Institute

Richmond, Virginia

- **Proprietary** primarily 2-year, founded 1999, part of ITT Educational Services, Inc.
- **Coed**

Majors Business administration and management; CAD/CADD drafting/design technology; communications technology; computer and information systems security; computer engineering technology; computer software and media applications related; computer software technology; construction management; criminal justice/law enforcement administration; design and visual communications; electrical, electronic and communications engineering technology; game and interactive media design; legal assistant/paralegal; project management; system, networking, and LAN/WAN management; web/multimedia management and webmaster; web page, digital/multimedia and information resources design.
Academics *Calendar:* quarters. *Degrees:* associate and bachelor's.
Student Life *Housing:* college housing not available.
Freshman Application Contact Director of Recruitment, ITT Technical Institute, 300 Gateway Centre Parkway, Richmond, VA 23235. *Phone:* 804-330-4992. *Toll-free phone:* 888-330-4888. *Web site:* http://www.itt-tech.edu/.

ITT Technical Institute

Salem, Virginia

- **Proprietary** primarily 2-year
- **Coed**

Majors CAD/CADD drafting/design technology; communications technology; computer and information systems security; computer engineering technology; construction management; criminal justice/law enforcement administration; electrical, electronic and communications engineering technology; legal assistant/paralegal; system, networking, and LAN/WAN management.
Academics *Degrees:* associate and bachelor's.
Freshman Application Contact Director of Recruitment, ITT Technical Institute, 2159 Apperson Drive, Salem, VA 24153. *Phone:* 540-989-2500. *Toll-free phone:* 877-208-6132. *Web site:* http://www.itt-tech.edu/.

ITT Technical Institute

Springfield, Virginia

- **Proprietary** primarily 2-year, founded 2002, part of ITT Educational Services, Inc.
- **Coed**

Majors CAD/CADD drafting/design technology; communications technology; computer and information systems security; computer engineering technology; computer software and media applications related; computer software engineering; computer software technology; construction management; criminal justice/law enforcement administration; design and visual communica-

tions; electrical, electronic and communications engineering technology; game and interactive media design; legal assistant/paralegal; project management; system, networking, and LAN/WAN management; web/multimedia management and webmaster; web page, digital/multimedia and information resources design.
Academics *Calendar:* quarters. *Degrees:* associate and bachelor's.
Student Life *Housing:* college housing not available.
Freshman Application Contact Director of Recruitment, ITT Technical Institute, 7300 Boston Boulevard, Springfield, VA 22153. *Phone:* 703-440-9535. *Toll-free phone:* 866-817-8324. *Web site:* http://www.itt-tech.edu/.

John Tyler Community College

Chester, Virginia

- **State-supported** 2-year, founded 1967, part of Virginia Community College System
- **Suburban** 160-acre campus with easy access to Richmond
- **Endowment** $2.1 million
- **Coed,** 10,518 undergraduate students, 29% full-time, 59% women, 41% men

Undergraduates 3,096 full-time, 7,422 part-time. Students come from 7 states and territories; 3 other countries; 1% are from out of state. *Retention:* 53% of full-time freshmen returned.
Faculty *Total:* 495, 19% full-time, 18% with terminal degrees. *Student/faculty ratio:* 25:1.
Majors Accounting related; administrative assistant and secretarial science; architectural engineering technology; architectural technology; business administration and management; business administration, management and operations related; business/commerce; child-care provision; computer and information sciences; criminal justice/law enforcement administration; electrical and electronics engineering; engineering; engineering technology; funeral service and mortuary science; general studies; human services; industrial electronics technology; liberal arts and sciences/liberal studies; management information systems; mechanical engineering/mechanical technology; mechanical engineering technologies related; mental and social health services and allied professions related; quality control and safety technologies related; registered nursing/registered nurse; visual and performing arts related.
Academics *Calendar:* semesters. *Degree:* certificates and associate. *Special study options:* academic remediation for entering students, adult/continuing education programs, advanced placement credit, distance learning, external degree program, honors programs, off-campus study, part-time degree program, services for LD students, study abroad, summer session for credit. *ROTC:* Army (c).
Library John Tyler Community College Learning Resource and Technology Center with 49,393 titles, 179 serial subscriptions, an OPAC, a Web page.
Student Life *Housing:* college housing not available. *Activities and Organizations:* drama/theater group, choral group, Phi Theta Kappa -TauRho, Phi Theta Kappa - BOO, Art Club, Elements of Life Club, Funeral Services Club. *Campus security:* 24-hour emergency response devices and patrols.
Costs (2010–11) *Tuition:* state resident $2580 full-time, $101 per credit hour part-time; nonresident $7226 full-time, $295 per credit hour part-time. Full-time tuition and fees vary according to course load. Part-time tuition and fees vary according to course load. *Required fees:* $50 full-time, $7 per credit hour part-time, $25 per term part-time. *Payment plan:* installment. *Waivers:* senior citizens.
Applying *Options:* early admission, deferred entrance. *Recommended:* high school transcript. *Application deadline:* rolling (freshmen). *Notification:* continuous (freshmen).
Freshman Application Contact Ms. Joy James, Director of Admission, John Tyler Community College, Chester, VA 23831. *Phone:* 804-706-5214. *Toll-free phone:* 800-552-3490. *Fax:* 804-796-4362. *Web site:* http://www.jtcc.edu/.

J. Sargeant Reynolds Community College

Richmond, Virginia

- **State-supported** 2-year, founded 1972, part of Virginia Community College System
- **Suburban** 207-acre campus
- **Coed,** 12,619 undergraduate students

Majors Administrative assistant and secretarial science; agricultural business and management; biological and physical sciences; business administration and management; business/commerce; clinical/medical laboratory technology; computer and information sciences; dental laboratory technology; electrical and electronic engineering technologies related; emergency medical technology (EMT paramedic); engineering; engineering technologies and engineering related; homeland security, law enforcement, firefighting and protective services related; industrial technology; liberal arts and sciences/liberal studies; management information systems; mental and social health services and allied professions related; occupational therapist assistant; optometric technician; public administration and social service professions related; registered nursing/registered nurse; respiratory care therapy; social sciences; special education; vehicle maintenance and repair technologies related; visual and performing arts related.

Academics *Calendar:* semesters. *Degree:* certificates and associate. *Special study options:* academic remediation for entering students, adult/continuing education programs, advanced placement credit, distance learning, English as a second language, independent study, internships, off-campus study, part-time degree program, services for LD students, summer session for credit.

Library J. Sargeant Reynolds Community College Library plus 3 others with 101,858 titles, 45,875 serial subscriptions, 2,483 audiovisual materials, an OPAC, a Web page.

Student Life *Housing:* college housing not available. *Activities and Organizations:* drama/theater group. *Campus security:* 24-hour emergency response devices and patrols, late-night transport/escort service, security during open hours. *Student services:* personal/psychological counseling.

Costs (2011–12) *Tuition:* state resident $118 per credit hour part-time; nonresident $311 per credit hour part-time. Full-time tuition and fees vary according to course load. Part-time tuition and fees vary according to course load. *Payment plan:* installment. *Waivers:* senior citizens.

Financial Aid Of all full-time matriculated undergraduates who enrolled in 2008, 14,628 applied for aid, 11,184 were judged to have need. 64 Federal Work-Study jobs (averaging $2600). In 2008, 121 non-need-based awards were made. *Average percent of need met:* 49%. *Average financial aid package:* $6950. *Average need-based loan:* $2792. *Average need-based gift aid:* $3400. *Average non-need-based aid:* $891. *Average indebtedness upon graduation:* $3891.

Applying *Options:* electronic application. *Required:* high school transcript. *Required for some:* interview. *Application deadlines:* rolling (freshmen), rolling (transfers). *Notification:* continuous (freshmen), continuous (transfers).

Freshman Application Contact Ms. Karen Pettis-Walden, Director of Admissions and Records, J. Sargeant Reynolds Community College, PO Box 85622, Richmond, VA 23285-5622. *Phone:* 804-523-5029. *Fax:* 804-371-3650. *E-mail:* kpettis-walden@reynolds.edu. *Web site:* http://www.reynolds.edu/.

Lord Fairfax Community College
Middletown, Virginia

Freshman Application Contact Karen Bucher, Director of Enrollment Management, Lord Fairfax Community College, 173 Skirmisher Lane, Middletown, VA 22645. *Phone:* 540-868-7132. *Toll-free phone:* 800-906-LFCC. *Fax:* 540-868-7005. *E-mail:* kbucher@lfcc.edu. *Web site:* http://www.lfcc.edu/.

Mountain Empire Community College
Big Stone Gap, Virginia

- **State-supported** 2-year, founded 1972, part of Virginia Community College System
- **Rural** campus
- **Coed,** 3,404 undergraduate students, 47% full-time, 62% women, 38% men

Undergraduates 1,606 full-time, 1,798 part-time. Students come from 10 states and territories; 3% are from out of state; 2% Black or African American, non-Hispanic/Latino; 0.3% Hispanic/Latino; 0.3% Asian, non-Hispanic/Latino; 0.2% American Indian or Alaska Native, non-Hispanic/Latino; 0.2% Race/ethnicity unknown. *Retention:* 48% of full-time freshmen returned.

Faculty *Total:* 202, 20% full-time.

Majors Accounting related; business administration, management and operations related; business operations support and secretarial services related; CAD/CADD drafting/design technology; corrections; criminal justice/law enforcement administration; electrical, electronic and communications engineering technology; emergency medical technology (EMT paramedic); industrial production technologies related; industrial technology; legal assistant/paralegal; liberal arts and sciences/liberal studies; natural resources/conservation; registered nursing/registered nurse; respiratory care therapy.

Academics *Calendar:* semesters. *Degree:* certificates and associate. *Special study options:* academic remediation for entering students, adult/continuing education programs, advanced placement credit, cooperative education, distance learning, double majors, external degree program, independent study, internships, part-time degree program, student-designed majors, summer session for credit.

Library Wampler Library with 44,136 titles, 148 serial subscriptions, an OPAC, a Web page.

Student Life *Housing:* college housing not available. *Activities and Organizations:* drama/theater group, Phi Theta Kappa, Healing Hands, Rho Nu (SNAV), Students in Free Enterprise (SIFE), Merits. *Campus security:* 24-hour emergency response devices and patrols. *Student services:* personal/psychological counseling.

Athletics *Intramural sports:* basketball M/W, football M/W, volleyball M/W.

Costs (2010–11) *Tuition:* state resident $2652 full-time, $111 per credit hour part-time; nonresident $7268 full-time, $304 per credit hour part-time. *Payment plan:* installment. *Waivers:* senior citizens.

Financial Aid Of all full-time matriculated undergraduates who enrolled in 2009, 150 Federal Work-Study jobs (averaging $1200). 30 state and other part-time jobs (averaging $650).

Applying *Options:* electronic application, early admission, deferred entrance. *Required:* high school transcript. *Required for some:* minimum 2.0 GPA. *Application deadlines:* rolling (freshmen), rolling (transfers). *Notification:* continuous (freshmen), continuous (transfers).

Freshman Application Contact Mountain Empire Community College, 3441 Mountain Empire Road, Big Stone Gap, VA 24219. *Phone:* 276-523-2400 Ext. 219. *Web site:* http://www.mecc.edu/.

National College
Bluefield, Virginia

Freshman Application Contact National College, 100 Logan Street, PO Box 629, Bluefield, VA 24605-1405. *Phone:* 276-326-3621. *Toll-free phone:* 800-664-1886. *Web site:* http://www.national-college.edu/.

National College
Charlottesville, Virginia

Director of Admissions Kimberly Moore, Campus Director, National College, 1819 Emmet Street, Charlottesville, VA 22901. *Phone:* 434-295-0136. *Toll-free phone:* 800-664-1886. *Fax:* 434-979-8061. *Web site:* http://www.national-college.edu/.

National College
Danville, Virginia

Freshman Application Contact Admissions Office, National College, 734 Main Street, Danville, VA 24541-1819. *Phone:* 434-793-6822. *Toll-free phone:* 800-664-1886. *Web site:* http://www.national-college.edu/.

National College
Harrisonburg, Virginia

Director of Admissions Jack Evey, Campus Director, National College, 51 B Burgess Road, Harrisonburg, VA 22801-9709. *Phone:* 540-432-0943. *Toll-free phone:* 800-664-1886. *Web site:* http://www.national-college.edu/.

National College
Lynchburg, Virginia

Freshman Application Contact Admissions Representative, National College, 104 Candlewood Court, Lynchburg, VA 24502-2653. *Phone:* 804-239-3500. *Toll-free phone:* 800-664-1886. *Web site:* http://www.national-college.edu/.

National College
Martinsville, Virginia

Director of Admissions Mr. John Scott, Campus Director, National College, 10 Church Street, PO Box 232, Martinsville, VA 24114. *Phone:* 276-632-5621. *Toll-free phone:* 800-664-1886 (in-state); 800-664-1866 (out-of-state). *Web site:* http://www.national-college.edu/.

National College
Salem, Virginia

Freshman Application Contact Director of Admissions, National College, 1813 East Main Street, Salem, VA 24153. *Phone:* 540-986-1800. *Toll-free phone:* 800-664-1886. *Fax:* 540-444-4198. *Web site:* http://www.national-college.edu/.

New River Community College
Dublin, Virginia

Freshman Application Contact Ms. Margaret G. Taylor, Director of Student Services, New River Community College, PO Box 1127, Dublin, VA 24084-

1127. *Phone:* 540-674-3600. *Fax:* 540-674-3644. *E-mail:* nrtaylm@nr.edu. *Web site:* http://www.nr.edu/.

Northern Virginia Community College
Annandale, Virginia

Director of Admissions Dr. Max L. Bassett, Dean of Academic and Student Services, Northern Virginia Community College, 4001 Wakefield Chapel Road, Annandale, VA 22003-3796. *Phone:* 703-323-3195. *Web site:* http://www.nvcc.edu/.

Patrick Henry Community College
Martinsville, Virginia

- **State-supported** 2-year, founded 1962, part of Virginia Community College System
- **Rural** 137-acre campus
- **Coed**

Undergraduates 3,501 full-time. Students come from 4 states and territories. *Retention:* 49% of full-time freshmen returned.

Academics *Calendar:* semesters. *Degree:* associate. *Special study options:* academic remediation for entering students, adult/continuing education programs, advanced placement credit, cooperative education, distance learning, independent study, internships, part-time degree program, services for LD students, summer session for credit.

Student Life *Campus security:* 24-hour emergency response devices and patrols, late-night transport/escort service.

Athletics Member NJCAA.

Costs (2010–11) *Tuition:* state resident $2472 full-time, $103 per credit hour part-time; nonresident $6710 full-time, $280 per credit hour part-time. Full-time tuition and fees vary according to course load. Part-time tuition and fees vary according to course load. *Required fees:* $200 full-time, $9 per credit hour part-time.

Financial Aid Of all full-time matriculated undergraduates who enrolled in 2009, 41 Federal Work-Study jobs (averaging $2000).

Applying *Options:* electronic application, early admission, deferred entrance. *Required:* high school transcript.

Freshman Application Contact Mr. Travis Tisdale, Coordinator, Admissions and Records, Patrick Henry Community College, Martinsville, VA 24115. *Phone:* 276-656-0311. *Toll-free phone:* 800-232-7997. *Fax:* 276-656-0352. *Web site:* http://www.ph.vccs.edu/.

Paul D. Camp Community College
Franklin, Virginia

- **State-supported** 2-year, founded 1971, part of Virginia Community College System
- **Small-town** 99-acre campus
- **Endowment** $500,000
- **Coed,** 1,579 undergraduate students, 27% full-time, 68% women, 32% men

Undergraduates 426 full-time, 1,153 part-time. Students come from 2 states and territories; 2 other countries; 0.5% are from out of state; 38% Black or African American, non-Hispanic/Latino; 4% Race/ethnicity unknown. *Retention:* 66% of full-time freshmen returned.

Freshmen *Admission:* 597 applied, 597 admitted. *Average high school GPA:* 2.2.

Faculty *Total:* 109, 17% full-time. *Student/faculty ratio:* 17:1.

Majors Administrative assistant and secretarial science; business administration and management; computer technology/computer systems technology; criminal justice/law enforcement administration; data processing and data processing technology; early childhood education; education; industrial technology; liberal arts and sciences/liberal studies; registered nursing/registered nurse.

Academics *Calendar:* semesters. *Degree:* certificates and associate. *Special study options:* academic remediation for entering students, adult/continuing education programs, advanced placement credit, cooperative education, distance learning, honors programs, independent study, internships, off-campus study, part-time degree program, summer session for credit.

Library Paul D. Camp Community College Library with 22,000 titles, 200 serial subscriptions, an OPAC.

Student Life *Housing:* college housing not available. *Activities and Organizations:* student-run newspaper, African-American History Club, Phi Beta Lambda, Phi Theta Kappa, Student Government Association, Student Newspaper. *Campus security:* late-night transport/escort service.

Costs (2011–12) *Tuition:* state resident $2624 full-time, $109 per credit part-time; nonresident $7772 full-time, $302 per credit part-time. Full-time tuition and fees vary according to course load. Part-time tuition and fees vary accord-

ing to course load. *Payment plan:* tuition prepayment. *Waivers:* senior citizens.

Financial Aid Of all full-time matriculated undergraduates who enrolled in 2009, 30 Federal Work-Study jobs (averaging $2000).

Applying *Options:* electronic application, deferred entrance. *Required:* high school transcript. *Application deadlines:* rolling (freshmen), rolling (transfers). *Notification:* continuous (freshmen), continuous (transfers).

Freshman Application Contact Dr. Joe Edenfield, Director of Admissions and Records, Paul D. Camp Community College, PO Box 737, 100 North College Drive, Franklin, VA 23851-0737. *Phone:* 757-569-6744. *E-mail:* jedenfield@pdc.edu. *Web site:* http://www.pc.vccs.edu/.

Piedmont Virginia Community College
Charlottesville, Virginia

Freshman Application Contact Ms. Mary Lee Walsh, Dean of Student Services, Piedmont Virginia Community College, 501 College Drive, Charlottesville, VA 22902-7589. *Phone:* 434-961-6540. *Fax:* 434-961-5425. *E-mail:* mwalsh@pvcc.edu. *Web site:* http://www.pvcc.edu/.

Rappahannock Community College
Glenns, Virginia

- **State-related** 2-year, founded 1970, part of Virginia Community College System
- **Rural** 217-acre campus
- **Coed**

Undergraduates 837 full-time, 2,569 part-time.

Academics *Calendar:* semesters. *Degree:* certificates, diplomas, and associate. *Special study options:* academic remediation for entering students, adult/continuing education programs, distance learning, internships, off-campus study, part-time degree program, summer session for credit.

Student Life *Campus security:* 24-hour emergency response devices.

Costs (2010–11) *Tuition:* state resident $2424 full-time, $101 per credit hour part-time; nonresident $6710 full-time, $280 per credit hour part-time. Full-time tuition and fees vary according to course load. Part-time tuition and fees vary according to course load. *Required fees:* $209 full-time, $9 per credit hour part-time.

Financial Aid Of all full-time matriculated undergraduates who enrolled in 2009, 40 Federal Work-Study jobs (averaging $1015).

Applying *Options:* early admission.

Freshman Application Contact Ms. Wilnet Willis, Admissions and Records Officer, Rappahannock Community College, Glenns Campus, PO Box 287, Glenns, VA 23149-0287. *Phone:* 804-758-6742. *Toll-free phone:* 800-836-9381. *Web site:* http://www.rappahannock.edu/.

Richard Bland College of The College of William and Mary
Petersburg, Virginia

Freshman Application Contact Office of Admissions, Richard Bland College of The College of William and Mary, 11301 Johnson Road, Petersburg, VA 23805-7100. *Phone:* 804-862-6249. *Web site:* http://www.rbc.edu/.

Southside Virginia Community College
Alberta, Virginia

- **State-supported** 2-year, founded 1970, part of Virginia Community College System
- **Rural** 207-acre campus
- **Endowment** $1.3 million
- **Coed,** 6,353 undergraduate students, 30% full-time, 62% women, 38% men

Undergraduates 1,924 full-time, 4,429 part-time. Students come from 5 states and territories; 0.1% are from out of state.

Freshmen *Admission:* 438 applied, 438 admitted, 387 enrolled.

Faculty *Total:* 290, 25% full-time, 6% with terminal degrees. *Student/faculty ratio:* 17:1.

Majors Administrative assistant and secretarial science; biological and physical sciences; business administration and management; criminal justice/law enforcement administration; education; electrical, electronic and communications engineering technology; emergency care attendant (EMT ambulance); fire science/firefighting; general studies; human services; information science/

studies; information technology; liberal arts and sciences/liberal studies; registered nursing/registered nurse; respiratory care therapy.
Academics *Calendar:* semesters. *Degree:* certificates, diplomas, and associate. *Special study options:* academic remediation for entering students, advanced placement credit, distance learning, honors programs, off-campus study, part-time degree program, services for LD students, study abroad, summer session for credit. *ROTC:* Army (c).
Library Julian M. Howell Library plus 1 other with 28,752 titles, 122 serial subscriptions, 2,678 audiovisual materials, an OPAC, a Web page.
Student Life *Housing:* college housing not available. *Activities and Organizations:* choral group, Student Forum, Phi Theta Kappa, Phi Beta Lambda, Alpha Delta Omega.
Athletics *Intramural sports:* baseball M(c), basketball M(c), cheerleading M(c)/W(c), softball M(c)/W(c), table tennis M(c)/W(c), tennis M(c)/W(c), volleyball M/W.
Costs (2010–11) *Tuition:* state resident $3030 full-time, $101 per credit hour part-time; nonresident $8388 full-time, $280 per credit hour part-time. Full-time tuition and fees vary according to course load. Part-time tuition and fees vary according to course load. *Required fees:* $270 full-time, $9 per credit hour part-time. *Payment plan:* installment. *Waivers:* senior citizens.
Applying *Options:* electronic application, deferred entrance. *Required:* high school transcript, interview. *Application deadlines:* rolling (freshmen), rolling (transfers). *Notification:* continuous (freshmen), continuous (transfers).
Freshman Application Contact Mr. Brent Richey, Dean of Enrollment Management, Southside Virginia Community College, 109 Campus Drive, Alberta, VA 23821. *Phone:* 434-949-1012. *Fax:* 434-949-7863. *E-mail:* rhina.jones@sv.vccs.edu. *Web site:* http://www.southside.edu/.

Southwest Virginia Community College
Richlands, Virginia

- **State-supported** 2-year, founded 1968, part of Virginia Community College System
- **Rural** 100-acre campus
- **Endowment** $8.3 million
- **Coed**

Undergraduates 1,648 full-time, 2,207 part-time. Students come from 5 states and territories; 1% are from out of state; 4% transferred in. *Retention:* 56% of full-time freshmen returned.
Faculty *Student/faculty ratio:* 20:1.
Academics *Calendar:* semesters. *Degree:* certificates, diplomas, and associate. *Special study options:* academic remediation for entering students, adult/continuing education programs, advanced placement credit, distance learning, double majors, honors programs, internships, part-time degree program, summer session for credit.
Student Life *Campus security:* 24-hour emergency response devices and patrols, student patrols, heavily saturated camera system.
Standardized Tests *Required:* ASSET or COMPASS (for admission).
Costs (2010–11) *Tuition:* state resident $2260 full-time, $95 per credit hour part-time; nonresident $6398 full-time, $267 per credit hour part-time. *Required fees:* $168 full-time, $7 per credit hour part-time, $17 per term part-time.
Financial Aid Of all full-time matriculated undergraduates who enrolled in 2009, 150 Federal Work-Study jobs (averaging $1140).
Applying *Options:* electronic application, early admission, deferred entrance. *Required:* high school transcript, interview.
Freshman Application Contact Mr. Jim Farris, Director of Admissions, Records, and Counseling, Southwest Virginia Community College, Box SVCC, Richlands, VA 24641. *Phone:* 276-964-7300. *Toll-free phone:* 800-822-7822. *Fax:* 276-964-7716. *Web site:* http://www.sw.edu/.

TESST College of Technology
Alexandria, Virginia

Director of Admissions Mr. Bob Somers, Director, TESST College of Technology, 6315 Bren Mar Drive, Alexandria, VA 22312-6342. *Phone:* 703-548-4800. *Toll-free phone:* 800-833-0209. *Fax:* 703-683-2765. *E-mail:* tesstal@erols.com. *Web site:* http://www.tesst.com/.

Thomas Nelson Community College
Hampton, Virginia

- **State-supported** 2-year, founded 1968, part of Virginia Community College System
- **Suburban** 85-acre campus with easy access to Virginia Beach
- **Coed**

Faculty *Student/faculty ratio:* 22:1.

Academics *Calendar:* semesters. *Degree:* certificates, diplomas, and associate. *Special study options:* academic remediation for entering students, accelerated degree program, adult/continuing education programs, advanced placement credit, cooperative education, distance learning, English as a second language, external degree program, honors programs, internships, off-campus study, part-time degree program, services for LD students, summer session for credit.
Student Life *Campus security:* 24-hour emergency response devices and patrols, late-night transport/escort service.
Costs (2010–11) *Tuition:* state resident $3030 full-time, $101 per credit hour part-time; nonresident $8388 full-time, $280 per credit hour part-time. *Required fees:* $232 full-time, $7 per credit hour part-time, $19 per term part-time.
Financial Aid Of all full-time matriculated undergraduates who enrolled in 2009, 110 Federal Work-Study jobs (averaging $3000).
Applying *Options:* electronic application, early admission, deferred entrance. *Required for some:* interview. *Recommended:* high school transcript.
Freshman Application Contact Ms. Jerri Newson, Admissions Office Manager, Thomas Nelson Community College, PO Box 9407, Hampton, VA 23670-0407. *Phone:* 757-825-2800. *Fax:* 757-825-2763. *E-mail:* admissions@tncc.edu. *Web site:* http://www.tncc.edu/.

Tidewater Community College
Norfolk, Virginia

- **State-supported** 2-year, founded 1968, part of Virginia Community College System
- **Suburban** 520-acre campus
- **Endowment** $7.1 million
- **Coed**

Undergraduates 12,101 full-time, 18,346 part-time. Students come from 53 states and territories; 10% are from out of state.
Faculty *Student/faculty ratio:* 29:1.
Academics *Calendar:* semesters. *Degree:* certificates, diplomas, and associate. *Special study options:* academic remediation for entering students, accelerated degree program, adult/continuing education programs, advanced placement credit, cooperative education, distance learning, English as a second language, honors programs, independent study, internships, off-campus study, part-time degree program, services for LD students, summer session for credit.
Student Life *Campus security:* 24-hour patrols.
Costs (2010–11) *Tuition:* state resident $2424 full-time, $101 per credit hour part-time; nonresident $6710 full-time, $280 per credit hour part-time. *Required fees:* $788 full-time, $33 per credit hour part-time.
Financial Aid Of all full-time matriculated undergraduates who enrolled in 2009, 64 Federal Work-Study jobs (averaging $2000).
Applying *Options:* early admission, deferred entrance.
Freshman Application Contact Kellie Sorey PhD, Registrar, Tidewater Community College, Norfolk, VA 23510. *Phone:* 757-822-1900. *E-mail:* CentralRecords@tcc.edu. *Web site:* http://www.tcc.edu/.

Virginia Highlands Community College
Abingdon, Virginia

Freshman Application Contact Karen Cheers, Acting Director of Admissions, Records, and Financial Aid, Virginia Highlands Community College, PO Box 828, 100 VHCC Drive Abingdon, Abingdon, VA 24212. *Phone:* 276-739-2490. *Toll-free phone:* 877-207-6115. *E-mail:* kcheers@vhcc.edu. *Web site:* http://www.vhcc.edu/.

Virginia Western Community College
Roanoke, Virginia

Freshman Application Contact Admissions Office, Virginia Western Community College, PO Box 14007, Roanoke, VA 24038. *Phone:* 540-857-7231. *Web site:* http://www.virginiawestern.edu/.

Wytheville Community College
Wytheville, Virginia

Director of Admissions Ms. Sabrina Terry, Registrar, Wytheville Community College, 1000 East Main Street, Wytheville, VA 24382-3308. *Phone:* 276-223-4755. *Toll-free phone:* 800-468-1195. *E-mail:* wcdixxs@wcc.vccs.edu. *Web site:* http://www.wcc.vccs.edu/.

WASHINGTON

The Art Institute of Seattle

Seattle, Washington

- **Proprietary** primarily 2-year, founded 1982, part of Education Management Corporation
- **Urban** campus
- **Coed**

Majors Animation, interactive technology, video graphics and special effects; baking and pastry arts; cinematography and film/video production; culinary arts; fashion/apparel design; fashion merchandising; graphic design; industrial and product design; interior design; photography; recording arts technology; restaurant, culinary, and catering management; web page, digital/multimedia and information resources design.

Academics *Calendar:* quarters. *Degrees:* diplomas, associate, and bachelor's.

Costs (2010–11) *Tuition:* Tuition cost varies by program. Prospective students should contact the school for current tuition costs. Other charges include a starting kit for all first-quarter students. Kits vary in price, depending on the program of study.

Freshman Application Contact The Art Institute of Seattle, 2323 Elliott Avenue, Seattle, WA 98121-1642. *Phone:* 206-448-6600. *Toll-free phone:* 800-275-2471. *Web site:* http://www.artinstitutes.edu/seattle/.

See page 350 for the College Close-Up.

Bates Technical College

Tacoma, Washington

Director of Admissions Director of Admissions, Bates Technical College, 1101 South Yakima Avenue, Tacoma, WA 98405-4895. *Phone:* 253-680-7000. *Toll-free phone:* 800-562-7099. *E-mail:* registration@bates.ctc.edu. *Web site:* http://www.bates.ctc.edu/.

Bellevue College

Bellevue, Washington

Freshman Application Contact Morenika Jacobs, Associate Dean of Enrollment Services, Bellevue College, 3000 Landerholm Circle, SE, Bellevue, WA 98007-6484. *Phone:* 425-564-2205. *Fax:* 425-564-4065. *Web site:* http://www.bcc.ctc.edu/.

Bellingham Technical College

Bellingham, Washington

- **State-supported** 2-year, founded 1957, part of Washington State Board for Community and Technical Colleges (SBCTC)
- **Suburban** 21-acre campus with easy access to Vancouver, British Columbia, Canada
- **Coed,** 2,864 undergraduate students

Faculty *Total:* 189, 67% full-time. *Student/faculty ratio:* 24:1.

Majors Accounting technology and bookkeeping; autobody/collision and repair technology; automobile/automotive mechanics technology; building/property maintenance; civil engineering technology; communications systems installation and repair technology; computer systems networking and telecommunications; culinary arts; data entry/microcomputer applications; diesel mechanics technology; electrician; executive assistant/executive secretary; fishing and fisheries sciences and management; heating, air conditioning, ventilation and refrigeration maintenance technology; heavy/industrial equipment maintenance technologies related; industrial mechanics and maintenance technology; instrumentation technology; legal assistant/paralegal; machine tool technology; marketing/marketing management; medical radiologic technology; registered nursing/registered nurse; surgical technology; surveying technology; welding technology.

Academics *Degree:* certificates and associate. *Special study options:* academic remediation for entering students, distance learning, English as a second language, internships, part-time degree program, services for LD students, summer session for credit.

Library Information Technology Resource Center with an OPAC, a Web page.

Student Life *Housing:* college housing not available. *Student services:* personal/psychological counseling.

Standardized Tests *Required:* Accuplacer entrance exam or waiver (for admission).

Costs (2011–12) *Tuition:* state resident $4050 full-time, $82 per credit part-time; nonresident $5468 full-time, $110 per credit part-time. Full-time tuition and fees vary according to course load and program. Part-time tuition and fees vary according to course load and program. *Required fees:* $600 full-time, $50 per course part-time.

Financial Aid Of all full-time matriculated undergraduates who enrolled in 2009, 40 state and other part-time jobs (averaging $2300).

Applying *Options:* early admission, deferred entrance. *Required for some:* high school transcript, some programs have prerequisites. *Application deadlines:* rolling (freshmen), rolling (out-of-state freshmen), rolling (transfers).

Freshman Application Contact Bellingham Technical College, 3028 Lindbergh Avenue, Bellingham, WA 98225. *Phone:* 360-752-8324. *Web site:* http://www.btc.ctc.edu/.

Big Bend Community College

Moses Lake, Washington

- **State-supported** 2-year, founded 1962
- **Small-town** 159-acre campus
- **Coed,** 2,169 undergraduate students, 69% full-time, 59% women, 41% men

Undergraduates 1,497 full-time, 672 part-time. 4% are from out of state; 2% Black or African American, non-Hispanic/Latino; 29% Hispanic/Latino; 1% Asian, non-Hispanic/Latino; 1% American Indian or Alaska Native, non-Hispanic/Latino; 6% Race/ethnicity unknown; 0.1% international; 5% live on campus.

Faculty *Student/faculty ratio:* 20:1.

Majors Accounting technology and bookkeeping; airline pilot and flight crew; automobile/automotive mechanics technology; avionics maintenance technology; computer support specialist; early childhood education; industrial electronics technology; industrial mechanics and maintenance technology; liberal arts and sciences/liberal studies; licensed practical/vocational nurse training; medical/clinical assistant; medical office management; office management; registered nursing/registered nurse; welding technology.

Academics *Calendar:* quarters. *Degree:* certificates and associate. *Special study options:* academic remediation for entering students, advanced placement credit, cooperative education, distance learning, part-time degree program, services for LD students, summer session for credit.

Library Big Bend Community College Library with 41,900 titles, 3,700 serial subscriptions, 3,150 audiovisual materials, an OPAC, a Web page.

Student Life *Housing Options:* coed. Campus housing is university owned. *Activities and Organizations:* choral group. *Campus security:* 24-hour emergency response devices, student patrols. *Student services:* personal/psychological counseling.

Athletics *Intercollegiate sports:* baseball M, basketball M/W, softball W, volleyball W.

Costs (2010–11) *Tuition:* state resident $87 per credit part-time; nonresident $273 per credit part-time. *Required fees:* $3 per credit part-time. *Payment plan:* installment. *Waivers:* senior citizens.

Financial Aid Of all full-time matriculated undergraduates who enrolled in 2009, 47 Federal Work-Study jobs (averaging $1831). 118 state and other part-time jobs (averaging $1743).

Applying *Options:* electronic application, early admission, deferred entrance. *Application fee:* $30. *Required for some:* high school transcript. *Application deadlines:* rolling (freshmen), rolling (transfers). *Notification:* continuous (freshmen), continuous (transfers).

Freshman Application Contact Candis Lacher, Associate Vice President of Student Services, Big Bend Community College, 7662 Chanute Street, Moses Lake, WA 98837. *Phone:* 509-793-2061. *Toll-free phone:* 877-745-1212. *Fax:* 509-793-6243. *E-mail:* admissions@bigbend.edu. *Web site:* http://www.bigbend.edu/.

Carrington College - Spokane

Spokane, Washington

Director of Admissions Deanna Baker, Campus Director, Carrington College - Spokane, 10102 East Knox Avenue, Suite 200, Spokane, WA 99206. *Phone:* 509-532-8888. *Fax:* 509-533-5983. *Web site:* http://carrington.edu/.

Cascadia Community College

Bothell, Washington

- **State-supported** 2-year, founded 1999
- **Suburban** 128-acre campus
- **Coed,** 2,873 undergraduate students, 54% full-time, 49% women, 51% men

Undergraduates 1,542 full-time, 1,331 part-time. Students come from 2 states and territories; 7 other countries; 1% are from out of state; 0.9% Black or African American, non-Hispanic/Latino; 7% Hispanic/Latino; 6% Asian, non-Hispanic/Latino; 0.3% Native Hawaiian or other Pacific Islander, non-Hispanic/Latino; 0.3% American Indian or Alaska Native, non-Hispanic/Latino; 6% Two or more races, non-Hispanic/Latino; 11% Race/ethnicity unknown; 1% international; 23% transferred in.

Freshmen *Admission:* 398 enrolled.

Faculty *Total:* 143, 26% full-time. *Student/faculty ratio:* 21:1.
Majors Liberal arts and sciences and humanities related; liberal arts and sciences/liberal studies; science technologies related.
Academics *Calendar:* quarters. *Degree:* certificates and associate. *Special study options:* academic remediation for entering students, accelerated degree program, adult/continuing education programs, advanced placement credit, cooperative education, distance learning, English as a second language, independent study, internships, off-campus study, part-time degree program, services for LD students, study abroad, summer session for credit.
Library UWB/CCC Campus Library with 73,749 titles, 850 serial subscriptions, 6,100 audiovisual materials, an OPAC, a Web page.
Student Life *Housing:* college housing not available. *Campus security:* 24-hour emergency response devices, late-night transport/escort service.
Costs (2010–11) *Tuition:* state resident $3135 full-time, $87 per credit hour part-time; nonresident $8370 full-time, $259 per credit hour part-time. *Required fees:* $156 full-time, $53 per term part-time. *Waivers:* senior citizens and employees or children of employees.
Applying *Options:* electronic application. *Application deadlines:* rolling (freshmen), rolling (out-of-state freshmen), rolling (transfers). *Notification:* continuous (freshmen), continuous (out-of-state freshmen), continuous (transfers).
Freshman Application Contact Ms. Erin Blakeney, Dean for Student Success, Cascadia Community College, 18345 Campus Way, NE, Bothell, WA 98011. *Phone:* 425-352-8000. *Fax:* 425-352-8137. *E-mail:* admissions@cascadia.ctc.edu. *Web site:* http://www.cascadia.edu/.

Centralia College
Centralia, Washington

Freshman Application Contact Admissions Office, Centralia College, Centralia, WA 98531. *Phone:* 360-736-9391 Ext. 221. *Fax:* 360-330-7503. *E-mail:* admissions@centralia.edu. *Web site:* http://www.centralia.edu/.

Clark College
Vancouver, Washington

- **State-supported** 2-year, founded 1933, part of Washington State Board for Community and Technical Colleges
- **Urban** 101-acre campus with easy access to Portland
- **Coed,** 13,137 undergraduate students, 48% full-time, 57% women, 43% men

Undergraduates 6,314 full-time, 6,823 part-time. 3% Black or African American, non-Hispanic/Latino; 6% Hispanic/Latino; 4% Asian, non-Hispanic/Latino; 0.3% Native Hawaiian or other Pacific Islander, non-Hispanic/Latino; 1% American Indian or Alaska Native, non-Hispanic/Latino; 5% Two or more races, non-Hispanic/Latino; 5% Race/ethnicity unknown; 0.6% international; 24% transferred in. *Retention:* 58% of full-time freshmen returned.
Freshmen *Admission:* 8,352 applied, 8,352 admitted, 876 enrolled.
Faculty *Total:* 757, 30% full-time, 11% with terminal degrees. *Student/faculty ratio:* 21:1.
Majors Accounting technology and bookkeeping; applied horticulture/horticulture operations; automobile/automotive mechanics technology; baking and pastry arts; business administration and management; business automation/technology/data entry; computer programming; computer systems networking and telecommunications; construction engineering technology; culinary arts; data entry/microcomputer applications; dental hygiene; diesel mechanics technology; early childhood education; electrical, electronic and communications engineering technology; emergency medical technology (EMT paramedic); executive assistant/executive secretary; graphic communications; human resources management; landscaping and groundskeeping; legal administrative assistant/secretary; legal assistant/paralegal; liberal arts and sciences/liberal studies; machine tool technology; manufacturing engineering technology; medical administrative assistant and medical secretary; medical/clinical assistant; radiologic technology/science; registered nursing/registered nurse; retailing; selling skills and sales; sport and fitness administration/management; substance abuse/addiction counseling; surveying technology; telecommunications technology; web/multimedia management and webmaster; welding technology.
Academics *Calendar:* quarters. *Degree:* certificates, diplomas, and associate. *Special study options:* academic remediation for entering students, accelerated degree program, adult/continuing education programs, advanced placement credit, cooperative education, distance learning, English as a second language, independent study, internships, part-time degree program, services for LD students, study abroad, summer session for credit. *ROTC:* Army (c), Air Force (c).
Library Lewis D. Cannell Library with an OPAC, a Web page.
Student Life *Housing:* college housing not available. *Activities and Organizations:* drama/theater group, student-run newspaper, choral group. *Campus security:* 24-hour patrols, late-night transport/escort service, security staff during hours of operation. *Student services:* health clinic, personal/psychological counseling, legal services.
Athletics *Intercollegiate sports:* baseball M, basketball M(s)/W(s), cross-country running M(s)/W(s), fencing M(c)/W(c), soccer M(s)/W(s), softball W, track and field M(s)/W(s), volleyball W(s). *Intramural sports:* basketball M/W, fencing M/W, soccer M/W, softball M/W, volleyball M/W.
Costs (2011–12) *Tuition:* state resident $3377 full-time, $93 per credit hour part-time; nonresident $8612 full-time, $265 per credit hour part-time. Full-time tuition and fees vary according to course load and reciprocity agreements. Part-time tuition and fees vary according to course load and reciprocity agreements. *Payment plan:* installment. *Waivers:* senior citizens and employees or children of employees.
Applying *Options:* electronic application, early admission, deferred entrance. *Application fee:* $20. *Required for some:* high school transcript, interview. *Application deadlines:* 7/30 (freshmen), 7/30 (transfers). *Notification:* continuous (freshmen), continuous (transfers).
Freshman Application Contact Ms. Sheryl Anderson, Director of Admissions, Clark College, Vancover, WA 98663. *Phone:* 360-992-2308. *Fax:* 360-992-2867. *E-mail:* admissions@clark.edu. *Web site:* http://www.clark.edu/.

Clover Park Technical College
Lakewood, Washington

Director of Admissions Ms. Judy Richardson, Registrar, Clover Park Technical College, 4500 Steilacoom Boulevard, SW, Lakewood, WA 98499. *Phone:* 253-589-5570. *Web site:* http://www.cptc.edu/.

Columbia Basin College
Pasco, Washington

Freshman Application Contact Admissions Department, Columbia Basin College, 2600 North 20th Avenue, Pasco, WA 99301-3397. *Phone:* 509-542-4524. *Fax:* 509-544-2023. *E-mail:* admissions@columbiabasin.edu. *Web site:* http://www.columbiabasin.edu/.

Edmonds Community College
Lynnwood, Washington

Freshman Application Contact Ms. Nancy Froemming, Enrollment Services Office Manager, Edmonds Community College, 20000 68th Avenue West, Lynwood, WA 98036-5999. *Phone:* 425-640-1853. *Fax:* 425-640-1159. *E-mail:* nanci.froemming@edcc.edu. *Web site:* http://www.edcc.edu/.

Everest College
Vancouver, Washington

Director of Admissions Ms. Renee Schiffhauer, Director of Admissions, Everest College, 120 Northeast 136th Avenue, Suite 130, Vancouver, WA 98684. *Phone:* 360-254-3282. *Fax:* 360-254-3035. *E-mail:* rschiffhauer@cci.edu. *Web site:* http://www.everest.edu/.

Everett Community College
Everett, Washington

- **State-supported** 2-year, founded 1941, part of Washington State Board for Community and Technical Colleges
- **Suburban** 22-acre campus with easy access to Seattle
- **Coed**

Undergraduates 3,707 full-time, 3,855 part-time. Students come from 24 other countries; 3% are from out of state; 3% transferred in. *Retention:* 46% of full-time freshmen returned.
Faculty *Student/faculty ratio:* 24:1.
Academics *Calendar:* quarters. *Degree:* certificates, diplomas, and associate. *Special study options:* academic remediation for entering students, adult/continuing education programs, advanced placement credit, cooperative education, distance learning, English as a second language, independent study, internships, part-time degree program, services for LD students, study abroad, summer session for credit.
Student Life *Campus security:* 24-hour emergency response devices and patrols, late-night transport/escort service.
Athletics Member NJCAA.
Standardized Tests *Required:* ACT ASSET, ACT COMPASS (for admission).
Costs (2010–11) *Tuition:* $87 per credit part-time; state resident $3135 full-time, $140 per credit part-time; nonresident $4744 full-time, $259 per credit part-time. Full-time tuition and fees vary according to course load. Part-time tuition and fees vary according to course load. *Required fees:* $105 full-time.

Applying *Options:* electronic application, early admission, deferred entrance. *Recommended:* high school transcript.

Freshman Application Contact Ms. Linda Baca, Entry Services Manager, Everett Community College, 2000 Tower Street, Everett, WA 98201-1327. *Phone:* 425-388-9219. *Fax:* 425-388-9173. *E-mail:* admissions@everettcc.edu. *Web site:* http://www.everettcc.edu/.

Grays Harbor College
Aberdeen, Washington

- **State-supported** 2-year, founded 1930, part of Washington State Board for Community and Technical Colleges
- **Small-town** 125-acre campus
- **Endowment** $8.3 million
- **Coed,** 2,526 undergraduate students, 63% full-time, 50% women, 50% men

Undergraduates 1,589 full-time, 937 part-time. Students come from 11 states and territories; 1 other country; 0.8% are from out of state; 3% Black or African American, non-Hispanic/Latino; 4% Hispanic/Latino; 2% Asian, non-Hispanic/Latino; 0.1% Native Hawaiian or other Pacific Islander, non-Hispanic/Latino; 4% American Indian or Alaska Native, non-Hispanic/Latino; 6% Two or more races, non-Hispanic/Latino; 2% Race/ethnicity unknown; 0.1% international; 17% transferred in. *Retention:* 57% of full-time freshmen returned.

Freshmen *Admission:* 201 enrolled.

Faculty *Total:* 132, 46% full-time, 100% with terminal degrees. *Student/faculty ratio:* 19:1.

Majors Accounting technology and bookkeeping; automobile/automotive mechanics technology; business administration and management; carpentry; child-care and support services management; criminal justice/police science; diesel mechanics technology; general studies; human services; industrial technology; information science/studies; liberal arts and sciences/liberal studies; natural resources/conservation; office management; registered nursing/registered nurse; welding technology.

Academics *Calendar:* quarters. *Degree:* certificates, diplomas, and associate. *Special study options:* academic remediation for entering students, accelerated degree program, adult/continuing education programs, advanced placement credit, cooperative education, distance learning, double majors, English as a second language, external degree program, honors programs, independent study, internships, part-time degree program, services for LD students, study abroad, summer session for credit.

Library Spellman Library with 40,000 titles, 240 serial subscriptions, an OPAC, a Web page.

Student Life *Housing:* college housing not available. *Activities and Organizations:* drama/theater group, student-run newspaper, choral group, Phi Theta Kappa, TYEE, Student Nurses Association, Human Services Student Association, Student Council. *Campus security:* 24-hour emergency response devices, late-night transport/escort service. *Student services:* personal/psychological counseling, women's center.

Athletics *Intercollegiate sports:* baseball M(s), basketball M(s)/W(s), golf M(s)/W(s), softball W(s).

Costs (2011–12) *Tuition:* state resident $3118 full-time, $87 per credit hour part-time; nonresident $3534 full-time, $259 per credit hour part-time. *Required fees:* $275 full-time, $8 per contact hour part-time.

Financial Aid Of all full-time matriculated undergraduates who enrolled in 2008, 47 Federal Work-Study jobs (averaging $1298). 166 state and other part-time jobs (averaging $1673). *Average financial aid package:* $5270.

Applying *Options:* electronic application, early admission. *Recommended:* high school transcript. *Application deadlines:* rolling (freshmen), 9/1 (transfers). *Notification:* continuous (freshmen), continuous (transfers).

Freshman Application Contact Ms. Brenda Dell, Admissions Officer, Grays Harbor College, 1620 Edward P Smith Drive, Aberdeen, WA 98520-7599. *Phone:* 360-532-9020 Ext. 4026. *Toll-free phone:* 800-562-4830. *Web site:* http://www.ghc.ctc.edu/.

Green River Community College
Auburn, Washington

- **State-supported** 2-year, founded 1965, part of Washington State Board for Community and Technical Colleges
- **Small-town** 168-acre campus with easy access to Seattle
- **Coed**

Undergraduates 5,056 full-time, 3,149 part-time. Students come from 41 other countries. *Retention:* 61% of full-time freshmen returned.

Faculty *Student/faculty ratio:* 23:1.

Academics *Calendar:* quarters. *Degree:* certificates, diplomas, and associate. *Special study options:* academic remediation for entering students, adult/continuing education programs, advanced placement credit, cooperative education, distance learning, English as a second language, internships, off-campus study, part-time degree program, services for LD students, study abroad, summer session for credit.

Student Life *Campus security:* 24-hour emergency response devices and patrols, student patrols, late-night transport/escort service.

Athletics Member NJCAA.

Costs (2010–11) *Tuition:* state resident $2925 full-time, $81 per credit hour part-time; nonresident $3345 full-time, $94 per credit hour part-time. Full-time tuition and fees vary according to course load. Part-time tuition and fees vary according to course load. *Required fees:* $398 full-time, $12 per credit hour part-time, $120 per term part-time.

Financial Aid Of all full-time matriculated undergraduates who enrolled in 2009, 137 Federal Work-Study jobs (averaging $2224). 186 state and other part-time jobs (averaging $1164).

Applying *Options:* electronic application, early admission, deferred entrance. *Required for some:* high school transcript.

Freshman Application Contact Ms. Peggy Morgan, Program Support Supervisor, Green River Community College, 12401 Southeast 320th Street, Auburn, WA 98092-3699. *Phone:* 253-833-9111. *Fax:* 253-288-3454. *Web site:* http://www.greenriver.edu/.

Highline Community College
Des Moines, Washington

- **State-supported** 2-year, founded 1961, part of Washington State Board for Community and Technical Colleges
- **Suburban** 81-acre campus with easy access to Seattle
- **Endowment** $1.4 million
- **Coed**

Undergraduates 3,722 full-time, 3,003 part-time. Students come from 6 states and territories; 50 other countries; 1% are from out of state; 49% transferred in. *Retention:* 59% of full-time freshmen returned.

Faculty *Student/faculty ratio:* 22:1.

Academics *Calendar:* quarters. *Degree:* certificates, diplomas, and associate. *Special study options:* academic remediation for entering students, advanced placement credit, cooperative education, distance learning, English as a second language, freshman honors college, honors programs, independent study, internships, off-campus study, part-time degree program, services for LD students, student-designed majors, study abroad, summer session for credit. *ROTC:* Army (c), Air Force (c).

Student Life *Campus security:* 24-hour emergency response devices and patrols, late-night transport/escort service.

Athletics Member NJCAA.

Costs (2010–11) *Tuition:* $87 per credit part-time; state resident $3135 full-time, $100 per credit part-time; nonresident $3534 full-time, $259 per credit part-time. Full-time tuition and fees vary according to course load. Part-time tuition and fees vary according to course load. *Required fees:* $75 full-time, $87 per credit part-time, $75 per term part-time.

Applying *Options:* electronic application. *Application fee:* $26.

Freshman Application Contact Ms. Laura Westergard, Director of Admissions, Highline Community College, 2400 South 240th Street, Des Moines, WA 98198-9800. *Phone:* 206-878-3710 Ext. 9800. *Web site:* http://www.highline.edu/.

ITT Technical Institute
Everett, Washington

- **Proprietary** primarily 2-year, part of ITT Educational Services, Inc.
- **Coed**

Majors CAD/CADD drafting/design technology; computer and information systems security; computer engineering technology; computer software engineering; computer software technology; construction management; criminal justice/law enforcement administration; design and visual communications; electrical, electronic and communications engineering technology; game and interactive media design; legal assistant/paralegal; project management; system, networking, and LAN/WAN management; web/multimedia management and webmaster; web page, digital/multimedia and information resources design.

Academics *Degrees:* associate and bachelor's.

Freshman Application Contact Director of Recruitment, ITT Technical Institute, 1615 75th Street SW, Everett, WA 98203. *Phone:* 425-583-0200. *Toll-free phone:* 800-272-3791. *Web site:* http://www.itt-tech.edu/.

ITT Technical Institute
Seattle, Washington

- **Proprietary** primarily 2-year, founded 1932, part of ITT Educational Services, Inc.
- **Urban** campus
- **Coed**

Majors CAD/CADD drafting/design technology; computer and information systems security; computer engineering technology; computer software and media applications related; computer software engineering; computer software technology; construction management; criminal justice/law enforcement administration; design and visual communications; electrical, electronic and communications engineering technology; game and interactive media design; legal assistant/paralegal; project management; system, networking, and LAN/WAN management; web/multimedia management and webmaster; web page, digital/multimedia and information resources design.

Academics *Calendar:* quarters. *Degrees:* associate and bachelor's.

Student Life *Housing:* college housing not available.

Freshman Application Contact Director of Recruitment, ITT Technical Institute, 12720 Gateway Drive, Suite 100, Seattle, WA 98168-3333. *Phone:* 206-244-3300. *Toll-free phone:* 800-422-2029. *Web site:* http://www.itt-tech.edu/.

ITT Technical Institute
Spokane Valley, Washington

- **Proprietary** primarily 2-year, founded 1985, part of ITT Educational Services, Inc.
- **Suburban** campus
- **Coed**

Majors CAD/CADD drafting/design technology; communications technology; computer and information systems security; computer engineering technology; construction management; criminal justice/law enforcement administration; design and visual communications; electrical, electronic and communications engineering technology; game and interactive media design; legal assistant/paralegal; project management; system, networking, and LAN/WAN management; web/multimedia management and webmaster; web page, digital/multimedia and information resources design.

Academics *Calendar:* quarters. *Degrees:* associate and bachelor's.

Student Life *Housing:* college housing not available.

Freshman Application Contact Director of Recruitment, ITT Technical Institute, 13518 East Indiana Avenue, Spokane Valley, WA 99212-2682. *Phone:* 509-926-2900. *Toll-free phone:* 800-777-8324. *Web site:* http://www.itt-tech.edu/.

Lake Washington Technical College
Kirkland, Washington

Freshman Application Contact Shawn Miller, Registrar Enrollment Services, Lake Washington Technical College, 11605 132nd Avenue NE, Kirkland, WA 98034-8506. *Phone:* 425-739-8104. *E-mail:* info@lwtc.edu. *Web site:* http://www.lwtc.edu/.

Lower Columbia College
Longview, Washington

- **State-supported** 2-year, founded 1934, part of Washington State Board for Community and Technical Colleges
- **Rural** 39-acre campus with easy access to Portland
- **Endowment** $7.5 million
- **Coed,** 4,290 undergraduate students, 60% full-time, 63% women, 37% men

Undergraduates 2,579 full-time, 1,711 part-time. Students come from 13 states and territories; 2 other countries; 2% are from out of state; 6% transferred in. *Retention:* 65% of full-time freshmen returned.

Freshmen *Admission:* 373 enrolled.

Faculty *Total:* 222, 31% full-time. *Student/faculty ratio:* 24:1.

Majors Accounting; accounting technology and bookkeeping; administrative assistant and secretarial science; automobile/automotive mechanics technology; business administration and management; criminal justice/law enforcement administration; data entry/microcomputer applications; diesel mechanics technology; early childhood education; fire science/firefighting; industrial mechanics and maintenance technology; instrumentation technology; legal administrative assistant/secretary; liberal arts and sciences/liberal studies; machine tool technology; medical administrative assistant and medical secretary; medical/clinical assistant; registered nursing/registered nurse; substance abuse/addiction counseling; welding technology.

Academics *Calendar:* quarters. *Degree:* certificates, diplomas, and associate. *Special study options:* academic remediation for entering students, advanced placement credit, cooperative education, distance learning, English as a second language, independent study, internships, part-time degree program, services for LD students, student-designed majors, summer session for credit.

Library Alan Thompson Library plus 1 other with 38,380 titles, 140 serial subscriptions, 4,711 audiovisual materials, an OPAC, a Web page.

Student Life *Housing:* college housing not available. *Activities and Organizations:* drama/theater group, choral group, Multicultural Students Club, Drama Club, Symphonic Band, Forensic, Concert Choir. *Campus security:* 24-hour emergency response devices and patrols. *Student services:* personal/psychological counseling.

Athletics *Intercollegiate sports:* baseball M(s), basketball M(s)/W(s), soccer W(s), softball W(s), volleyball W(s).

Costs (2010–11) *One-time required fee:* $17. *Tuition:* state resident $3405 full-time, $95 per credit part-time; nonresident $4170 full-time, $118 per credit part-time. Full-time tuition and fees vary according to course load and reciprocity agreements. Part-time tuition and fees vary according to course load and reciprocity agreements. *Required fees:* $293 full-time, $7 per credit part-time. *Payment plan:* deferred payment. *Waivers:* senior citizens and employees or children of employees.

Financial Aid Of all full-time matriculated undergraduates who enrolled in 2009, 440 Federal Work-Study jobs (averaging $708). 447 state and other part-time jobs (averaging $2415).

Applying *Options:* electronic application. *Application fee:* $14. *Recommended:* high school transcript. *Application deadlines:* rolling (freshmen); rolling (transfers). *Notification:* continuous (freshmen).

Freshman Application Contact Ms. Lynn Lawrence, Director of Registration, Lower Columbia College, 1600 Maple Street, Longview, WA 98632. *Phone:* 360-442-2371. *Fax:* 360-442-2379. *E-mail:* registration@lowercolumbia.edu. *Web site:* http://www.lowercolumbia.edu.

North Seattle Community College
Seattle, Washington

- **State-supported** 2-year, founded 1970, part of Seattle Community College District
- **Urban** 65-acre campus
- **Endowment** $4.4 million
- **Coed,** 6,855 undergraduate students, 30% full-time, 60% women, 40% men

Undergraduates 2,086 full-time, 4,769 part-time. Students come from 50 states and territories; 39 other countries; 5% are from out of state; 8% Black or African American, non-Hispanic/Latino; 0.4% Hispanic/Latino; 11% Asian, non-Hispanic/Latino; 1% Native Hawaiian or other Pacific Islander, non-Hispanic/Latino; 0.9% American Indian or Alaska Native, non-Hispanic/Latino; 9% Two or more races, non-Hispanic/Latino; 18% Race/ethnicity unknown; 22% transferred in.

Freshmen *Admission:* 5,726 applied, 5,726 admitted, 783 enrolled.

Faculty *Total:* 317, 32% full-time, 15% with terminal degrees. *Student/faculty ratio:* 20:1.

Majors Accounting technology and bookkeeping; administrative assistant and secretarial science; allied health and medical assisting services related; architectural drafting and CAD/CADD; art; biomedical technology; business/corporate communications; civil drafting and CAD/CADD; communications systems installation and repair technology; computer and information systems security; computer systems networking and telecommunications; early childhood education; electrical, electronic and communications engineering technology; heating, air conditioning, ventilation and refrigeration maintenance technology; liberal arts and sciences/liberal studies; licensed practical/vocational nurse training; mechanical drafting and CAD/CADD; medical/clinical assistant; music; pharmacy technician; real estate; registered nursing/registered nurse; telecommunications technology; watchmaking and jewelrymaking.

Academics *Calendar:* quarters. *Degree:* certificates, diplomas, and associate. *Special study options:* academic remediation for entering students, adult/continuing education programs, advanced placement credit, cooperative education, distance learning, English as a second language, external degree program, independent study, internships, part-time degree program, services for LD students, study abroad, summer session for credit. *ROTC:* Army (c).

Library North Seattle Community College Library with 52,496 titles, 594 serial subscriptions, an OPAC, a Web page.

Student Life *Housing:* college housing not available. *Activities and Organizations:* drama/theater group, choral group, Muslim Students Association, Indonesian Community Club, Literary Guild, Phi Theta Kappa, Vietnamese Student Association. *Campus security:* 24-hour emergency response devices, late-night transport/escort service, patrols by security. *Student services:* personal/psychological counseling, women's center.

Athletics *Intercollegiate sports:* basketball M/W. *Intramural sports:* basketball M/W.

Costs (2010–11) *Tuition:* state resident $3132 full-time, $87 per credit part-time; nonresident $8288 full-time, $259 per credit part-time. Full-time tuition and fees vary according to course load. Part-time tuition and fees vary according to course load. *Payment plan:* deferred payment. *Waivers:* senior citizens and employees or children of employees.
Applying *Options:* electronic application, early admission, deferred entrance. *Required:* high school transcript. *Required for some:* essay or personal statement, English/Math Placement Test. *Application deadlines:* rolling (freshmen), rolling (transfers). *Notification:* continuous until 9/24 (freshmen), continuous until 9/24 (transfers).
Freshman Application Contact Ms. Betsy Abts, Registrar, North Seattle Community College, Seattle, WA 98103-3599. *Phone:* 206-527-3663. *Fax:* 206-527-3671. *E-mail:* arrc@sccd.ctc.edu. *Web site:* http://www.northseattle.edu/.

Northwest Aviation College
Auburn, Washington

Freshman Application Contact Mr. Shawn Pratt, Assistant Director of Education, Northwest Aviation College, 506 23rd NE, Auburn, WA 98002. *Phone:* 253-854-4960. *Toll-free phone:* 800-246-4960. *Fax:* 253-931-0768. *E-mail:* spratt@afsmac.com. *Web site:* http://www.afsnac.com/.

Northwest Indian College
Bellingham, Washington

Freshman Application Contact Office of Admissions, Northwest Indian College, 2522 Kwina Road, Bellingham, WA 98226. *Phone:* 360-676-2772. *Toll-free phone:* 866-676-2772. *Fax:* 360-392-4333. *E-mail:* admissions@nwic.edu. *Web site:* http://www.nwic.edu/.

Northwest School of Wooden Boatbuilding
Port Hadlock, Washington

Director of Admissions Student Services Coordinator, Northwest School of Wooden Boatbuilding, 42 North Water Street, Port Hadlock, WA 98339. *Phone:* 360-385-4948. *Fax:* 360-385-5089. *E-mail:* info@nwboatschool.org. *Web site:* http://www.nwboatschool.org/.

Olympic College
Bremerton, Washington

- **State-supported** primarily 2-year, founded 1946, part of Washington State Board for Community and Technical Colleges
- **Suburban** 33-acre campus with easy access to Seattle
- **Coed,** 8,533 undergraduate students

Undergraduates 4% Black or African American, non-Hispanic/Latino; 6% Hispanic/Latino; 8% Asian, non-Hispanic/Latino; 2% American Indian or Alaska Native, non-Hispanic/Latino; 0.6% international.
Freshmen *Admission:* 805 applied, 805 admitted.
Faculty *Total:* 459, 26% full-time. *Student/faculty ratio:* 28:1.
Majors Accounting technology and bookkeeping; administrative assistant and secretarial science; animation, interactive technology, video graphics and special effects; automobile/automotive mechanics technology; building/construction finishing, management, and inspection related; business administration and management; computer programming; computer systems networking and telecommunications; cosmetology; criminal justice/police science; culinary arts; drafting and design technology; early childhood education; electrical, electronic and communications engineering technology; electrician; fire science/firefighting; hospitality administration; industrial technology; legal administrative assistant/secretary; marine maintenance and ship repair technology; medical/clinical assistant; natural resources/conservation; organizational leadership; physical therapy technology; plumbing technology; registered nursing/registered nurse; substance abuse/addiction counseling; teacher assistant/aide; welding technology.
Academics *Calendar:* quarters. *Degrees:* certificates, diplomas, associate, and bachelor's. *Special study options:* academic remediation for entering students, adult/continuing education programs, advanced placement credit, cooperative education, distance learning, English as a second language, honors programs, independent study, off-campus study, part-time degree program, services for LD students, summer session for credit.
Library Haselwood Library with 60,000 titles, 541 serial subscriptions, an OPAC, a Web page.
Student Life *Housing:* college housing not available. *Activities and Organizations:* drama/theater group, student-run newspaper, choral group, Phi Theta Kappa, International Student Club, Oceans (Nursing), ASOC, ASAD. *Campus security:* 24-hour emergency response devices and patrols, student patrols,

late-night transport/escort service. *Student services:* personal/psychological counseling, women's center.
Athletics *Intercollegiate sports:* baseball M(s), basketball M(s)/W(s), cross-country running M/W, golf M/W, soccer M(s)/W(s), softball W(s), volleyball W(s). *Intramural sports:* basketball M/W, table tennis M/W, volleyball M/W, weight lifting M/W.
Costs (2010–11) *Tuition:* state resident $3135 full-time, $87 per quarter hour part-time; nonresident $3536 full-time, $100 per quarter hour part-time. Full-time tuition and fees vary according to course level, course load, and degree level. Part-time tuition and fees vary according to course level, course load, and degree level. *Required fees:* $240 full-time, $5 per credit hour part-time, $65 per term part-time. *Payment plan:* installment. *Waivers:* senior citizens.
Financial Aid Of all full-time matriculated undergraduates who enrolled in 2009, 105 Federal Work-Study jobs (averaging $2380). 31 state and other part-time jobs (averaging $2880).
Applying *Options:* electronic application, early admission, deferred entrance. *Required for some:* high school transcript. *Application deadlines:* rolling (freshmen), rolling (transfers). *Notification:* continuous (freshmen), continuous (transfers).
Freshman Application Contact Ms. Jennifer Fyllingness, Director of Admissions and Outreach, Olympic College, 1600 Chester Avenue, Bremerton, WA 98337-1699. *Phone:* 360-475-7128. *Toll-free phone:* 800-259-6718. *Fax:* 360-475-7202. *E-mail:* jfyllingness@olympic.edu. *Web site:* http://www.olympic.edu/.

Peninsula College
Port Angeles, Washington

Freshman Application Contact Ms. Pauline Marvin, Peninsula College, 1502 East Lauridsen Boulevard, Port Angeles, WA 98362. *Phone:* 360-417-6596. *Fax:* 360-457-8100. *E-mail:* admissions@pcadmin.ctc.edu. *Web site:* http://www.pc.ctc.edu/.

Pierce College at Puyallup
Puyallup, Washington

Director of Admissions Ms. Cindy Burbank, Director of Admissions, Pierce College at Puyallup, 1601 39th Avenue Southeast, Puyallup, WA 98374-2222. *Phone:* 253-964-6686. *Web site:* http://www.pierce.ctc.edu/.

Pima Medical Institute
Renton, Washington

- **Proprietary** 2-year
- **Urban** campus
- **Coed**

Majors Health/health-care administration; occupational therapist assistant; respiratory therapy technician; veterinary/animal health technology.
Academics *Special study options:* cooperative education, distance learning, internships.
Student Life *Housing:* college housing not available.
Standardized Tests *Required:* Wonderlic Scholastic Level Exam (for admission).
Applying *Required:* high school transcript, interview.
Freshman Application Contact Pima Medical Institute, 555 S. Renton Village Place, Renton, WA 98057. *Phone:* 425-228-9600. *Web site:* http://www.pmi.edu/.

Pima Medical Institute
Seattle, Washington

- **Proprietary** primarily 2-year, founded 1989, part of Vocational Training Institutes, Inc.
- **Urban** campus
- **Coed,** 357 undergraduate students

Majors Dental hygiene; health/health-care administration; physical therapy technology; radiologic technology/science; veterinary/animal health technology.
Academics *Calendar:* modular. *Degrees:* certificates, associate, and bachelor's. *Special study options:* distance learning.
Library E-Global.
Student Life *Housing:* college housing not available.
Standardized Tests *Required:* Wonderlic aptitude test (for admission).
Applying *Required:* interview. *Required for some:* high school transcript.
Freshman Application Contact Admissions Office, Pima Medical Institute, 9709 Third Avenue NE, Suite 400, Seattle, WA 98115. *Phone:* 206-322-6100. *Toll-free phone:* 888-898-9048. *Web site:* http://www.pmi.edu/.

Renton Technical College

Renton, Washington

Director of Admissions Becky Riverman, Vice President for Student Services, Renton Technical College, 3000 NE Fourth Street, Renton, WA 98056. *Phone:* 425-235-2463. *Web site:* http://www.rtc.edu/.

Seattle Central Community College

Seattle, Washington

Freshman Application Contact Admissions Office, Seattle Central Community College, 1701 Broadway, Seattle, WA 98122-2400. *Phone:* 206-587-5450. *Web site:* http://www.seattlecentral.edu/.

Shoreline Community College

Shoreline, Washington

Director of Admissions Mr. Chris Linebarger, Director, Recruiting and Enrollment Services, Shoreline Community College, 16101 Greenwood Avenue North, Shoreline, WA 98133-5696. *Phone:* 206-546-4581. *Web site:* http://www.shore.ctc.edu/.

Skagit Valley College

Mount Vernon, Washington

Freshman Application Contact Ms. Karen Marie Bade, Admissions and Recruitment Coordinator, Skagit Valley College, 2405 College Way, Mount Vernon, WA 98273-5899. *Phone:* 360-416-7620. *E-mail:* karenmarie.bade@skagit.edu. *Web site:* http://www.skagit.edu/.

South Puget Sound Community College

Olympia, Washington

- **State-supported** 2-year, founded 1970, part of Washington State Board for Community and Technical Colleges
- **Suburban** 102-acre campus with easy access to Seattle
- **Coed**

Undergraduates 3,014 full-time, 2,603 part-time. Students come from 11 states and territories; 10 other countries; 2% are from out of state; 3% transferred in. *Retention:* 56% of full-time freshmen returned.
Faculty *Student/faculty ratio:* 22:1.
Academics *Calendar:* quarters. *Degree:* certificates, diplomas, and associate. *Special study options:* academic remediation for entering students, adult/continuing education programs, advanced placement credit, cooperative education, English as a second language, internships, part-time degree program, services for LD students, study abroad, summer session for credit. *ROTC:* Army (c).
Student Life *Campus security:* 24-hour emergency response devices and patrols, late-night transport/escort service.
Costs (2010–11) *Tuition:* state resident $2913 full-time, $84 per credit hour part-time; nonresident $3390 full-time, $102 per credit hour part-time. Full-time tuition and fees vary according to course load. Part-time tuition and fees vary according to course load. *Required fees:* $113 full-time.
Financial Aid Of all full-time matriculated undergraduates who enrolled in 2009, 42 Federal Work-Study jobs (averaging $3150). 14 state and other part-time jobs (averaging $4400). *Financial aid deadline:* 6/29.
Applying *Options:* electronic application, early admission, deferred entrance. **Freshman Application Contact** Ms. Lyn Sharp, South Puget Sound Community College, 2011 Mottman Road, SW, Olympia, WA 98512-6292. *Phone:* 360-754-7711 Ext. 5237. *E-mail:* lsharp@spcc.ctc.edu. *Web site:* http://www.spscc.ctc.edu/.

South Seattle Community College

Seattle, Washington

Director of Admissions Ms. Kim Manderbach, Dean of Student Services/Registration, South Seattle Community College, 6000 16th Avenue, SW, Seattle, WA 98106-1499. *Phone:* 206-764-5378. *Fax:* 206-764-7947. *E-mail:* kimmanderb@sccd.ctc.edu. *Web site:* http://southseattle.edu/.

Spokane Community College

Spokane, Washington

Freshman Application Contact Ms. Brenda Burns, Researcher, District Institutional Research, Spokane Community College, Spokane, WA 99217-5399. *Phone:* 509-434-5242. *Toll-free phone:* 800-248-5644. *Fax:* 509-434-5249. *E-mail:* mlee@ccs.spokane.edu.
Web site: http://www.scc.spokane.edu/.

Spokane Falls Community College

Spokane, Washington

Freshman Application Contact Admissions Office, Spokane Falls Community College, Admissions MS 3011, 3410 West Fort George Wright Drive, Spokane, WA 99224. *Phone:* 509-533-3401. *Toll-free phone:* 888-509-7944. *Fax:* 509-533-3852. *Web site:* http://www.spokanefalls.edu/.

Tacoma Community College

Tacoma, Washington

Freshman Application Contact Enrollment Services, Tacoma Community College, 6501 South 19th Street, Tacoma, WA 98466. *Phone:* 253-566-5325. *Fax:* 253-566-6034. *Web site:* http://www.tacomacc.edu/.

Walla Walla Community College

Walla Walla, Washington

Freshman Application Contact Walla Walla Community College, 500 Tausick Way, Walla Walla, WA 99362-9267. *Phone:* 509-522-2500. *Toll-free phone:* 877-992-9922. *Web site:* http://www.wwcc.edu/home/.

Wenatchee Valley College

Wenatchee, Washington

- **State and locally supported** 2-year, founded 1939, part of Washington State Board for Community and Technical Colleges
- **Rural** 56-acre campus
- **Coed**, 3,637 undergraduate students

Majors Accounting; accounting technology and bookkeeping; administrative assistant and secretarial science; agricultural mechanization; agricultural production; athletic training; automobile/automotive mechanics technology; biology/biological sciences; business administration and management; carpentry; chemistry; clinical/medical laboratory assistant; clinical/medical laboratory technology; commercial and advertising art; computer systems networking and telecommunications; design and applied arts related; early childhood education; economics; education; fire science/firefighting; heating, air conditioning, ventilation and refrigeration maintenance technology; history; industrial electronics technology; industrial radiologic technology; kindergarten/preschool education; legal administrative assistant/secretary; liberal arts and sciences/liberal studies; licensed practical/vocational nurse training; mathematics; medical administrative assistant and medical secretary; medical/clinical assistant; music; music teacher education; office management; parks, recreation and leisure; physical education teaching and coaching; physical sciences; pre-engineering; radiologic technology/science; registered nursing/registered nurse; sociology; substance abuse/addiction counseling; trade and industrial teacher education.
Academics *Calendar:* quarters. *Degree:* certificates, diplomas, and associate. *Special study options:* academic remediation for entering students, adult/continuing education programs, advanced placement credit, cooperative education, distance learning, English as a second language, external degree program, independent study, part-time degree program, services for LD students, summer session for credit.
Library John Brown Library plus 1 other with 32,000 titles, 220 serial subscriptions, an OPAC, a Web page.
Student Life *Housing Options:* coed. Campus housing is university owned. *Activities and Organizations:* drama/theater group, student-run newspaper, choral group. *Campus security:* 24-hour patrols, evening and late night security patrols.
Athletics *Intercollegiate sports:* baseball M, basketball M(s)/W(s), soccer M/W, softball W(s). *Intramural sports:* badminton M/W, basketball M/W, football M/W, golf M/W, racquetball M/W, skiing (cross-country) M/W, skiing (downhill) M/W, tennis M/W, volleyball M/W, weight lifting M/W.
Costs (2010–11) *Tuition:* state resident $2090 full-time, $87 per credit part-time; nonresident $2357 full-time, $100 per credit part-time. Full-time tuition and fees vary according to course load. *Required fees:* $89 full-time, $4 per credit part-time. *Payment plan:* installment. *Waivers:* senior citizens and employees or children of employees.
Applying *Options:* electronic application, early admission, deferred entrance. *Required for some:* high school transcript. *Application deadline:* rolling (freshmen).
Freshman Application Contact Ms. Cecilia Escobedo, Registrar/Admissions Coordinator, Wenatchee Valley College, 1300 Fifth Street, Wenatchee, WA 98801-1799. *Phone:* 509-682-6836. *E-mail:* cescobedo@wvc.edu. *Web site:* http://www.wvc.edu/.

Whatcom Community College

Bellingham, Washington

Freshman Application Contact Entry and Advising Center, Whatcom Community College, 237 West Kellogg Road, Bellingham, WA 98226-8003. *Phone:* 360-676-2170. *Fax:* 360-676-2171. *E-mail:* admit@whatcom.ctc.edu. *Web site:* http://www.whatcom.ctc.edu/.

Yakima Valley Community College

Yakima, Washington

- **State-supported** 2-year, founded 1928, part of Washington State Board for Community and Technical Colleges
- **Small-town** 20-acre campus
- **Coed,** 4,479 undergraduate students, 62% full-time, 65% women, 35% men

Undergraduates 2,786 full-time, 1,693 part-time. 1% live on campus.

Freshmen *Admission:* 496 applied, 496 admitted, 448 enrolled.

Faculty *Total:* 319, 33% full-time, 13% with terminal degrees. *Student/faculty ratio:* 20:1.

Majors Accounting; administrative assistant and secretarial science; agricultural business and management; agricultural mechanization; agricultural production related; agriculture; agronomy and crop science; animal sciences; automobile/automotive mechanics technology; broadcast journalism; business administration and management; child development; civil engineering technology; computer engineering technology; computer graphics; computer science; criminal justice/law enforcement administration; criminal justice/police science; dental hygiene; electrical, electronic and communications engineering technology; family and consumer economics related; hotel/motel administration; industrial radiologic technology; industrial technology; instrumentation technology; kindergarten/preschool education; legal administrative assistant/secretary; liberal arts and sciences/liberal studies; management information systems; marketing/marketing management; medical administrative assistant and medical secretary; occupational therapy; pre-engineering; registered nursing/registered nurse; special products marketing; substance abuse/addiction counseling; tourism and travel services management; veterinary/animal health technology.

Academics *Calendar:* quarters. *Degree:* certificates and associate. *Special study options:* academic remediation for entering students, adult/continuing education programs, advanced placement credit, cooperative education, distance learning, English as a second language, internships, part-time degree program, services for LD students, summer session for credit.

Library Raymond Library with 44,715 titles, 21,056 serial subscriptions, 3,709 audiovisual materials, an OPAC.

Student Life *Housing Options:* coed. Campus housing is university owned. *Activities and Organizations:* drama/theater group, choral group. *Campus security:* 24-hour emergency response devices, student patrols, late-night transport/escort service, controlled dormitory access. *Student services:* personal/psychological counseling.

Athletics Member NJCAA. *Intercollegiate sports:* baseball M(s), basketball M(s)/W(s), soccer W, softball W(s), volleyball W(s), wrestling M(s). *Intramural sports:* basketball M/W, volleyball W, wrestling M.

Standardized Tests *Required:* ACT COMPASS (for admission).

Costs (2010–11) *Tuition:* state resident $3135 full-time, $87 per credit hour part-time; nonresident $3535 full-time, $100 per credit hour part-time. Full-time tuition and fees vary according to course load. Part-time tuition and fees vary according to course load. *Required fees:* $308 full-time, $8 per credit hour part-time. *Room and board:* room only: $3150. Room and board charges vary according to housing facility. *Payment plans:* installment, deferred payment. *Waivers:* senior citizens and employees or children of employees.

Financial Aid Of all full-time matriculated undergraduates who enrolled in 2009, 133 Federal Work-Study jobs (averaging $1164). 156 state and other part-time jobs (averaging $2083).

Applying *Application fee:* $20. *Required:* placement testing. *Required for some:* high school transcript, interview. *Recommended:* high school transcript. *Application deadlines:* 8/12 (freshmen), 9/12 (transfers). *Notification:* continuous until 9/12 (freshmen), continuous until 9/12 (transfers).

Freshman Application Contact Denise Anderson, Registrar and Director for Enrollment Services, Yakima Valley Community College, PO Box 1647, Yakima, WA 98907-1647. *Phone:* 509-574-4702. *Fax:* 509-574-6879. *E-mail:* admis@yvcc.edu. *Web site:* http://www.yvcc.edu/.

WEST VIRGINIA

Blue Ridge Community and Technical College

Martinsburg, West Virginia

- **State-supported** 2-year, founded 1974
- **Small-town** campus
- **Coed,** 3,936 undergraduate students, 28% full-time, 59% women, 41% men

Undergraduates 1,097 full-time, 2,839 part-time. 6% are from out of state; 0.2% transferred in. *Retention:* 60% of full-time freshmen returned.

Freshmen *Admission:* 478 enrolled. *Test scores:* SAT critical reading scores over 500: 45%; ACT scores over 18: 34%; SAT critical reading scores over 600: 10%; ACT scores over 24: 1%.

Faculty *Total:* 106, 47% full-time. *Student/faculty ratio:* 29:1.

Majors Automobile/automotive mechanics technology; business, management, and marketing related; criminal justice/safety; culinary arts; design and visual communications; electromechanical technology; emergency medical technology (EMT paramedic); fashion merchandising; fire science/firefighting; general studies; heating, air conditioning, ventilation and refrigeration maintenance technology; information technology; legal assistant/paralegal; office occupations and clerical services; quality control and safety technologies related.

Academics *Degree:* certificates and associate. *Special study options:* academic remediation for entering students, accelerated degree program, adult/continuing education programs, advanced placement credit, double majors, English as a second language, independent study, internships, part-time degree program, services for LD students.

Library Martinsburg Public Library.

Student Life *Housing:* college housing not available. *Activities and Organizations:* national fraternities. *Campus security:* late-night transport/escort service. *Student services:* personal/psychological counseling.

Standardized Tests *Recommended:* SAT and SAT Subject Tests or ACT (for admission).

Costs (2010–11) *Tuition:* state resident $3072 full-time, $128 per credit hour part-time; nonresident $5520 full-time, $230 per credit hour part-time. Full-time tuition and fees vary according to course load and program. Part-time tuition and fees vary according to course load and program. *Waivers:* senior citizens and employees or children of employees.

Applying *Options:* deferred entrance. *Application fee:* $25. *Required:* high school transcript. *Required for some:* interview.

Freshman Application Contact Brenda K. Neal, Director of Access, Blue Ridge Community and Technical College, 400 West Stephen Street, Martinsburg, WV 25401. *Phone:* 304-260-4380 Ext. 2109. *Fax:* 304-260-4376. *E-mail:* bneal@blueridgectc.edu. *Web site:* http://www.blueridgectc.edu/.

Community & Technical College at West Virginia University Institute of Technology

Montgomery, West Virginia

Director of Admissions Ms. Lisa Graham, Director of Admissions, Community & Technical College at West Virginia University Institute of Technology, 405 Fayette Pike, Montgomery, WV 25136. *Phone:* 304-442-3167. *Toll-free phone:* 888-554-8324. *Web site:* http://ctc.wvutech.edu/.

Eastern West Virginia Community and Technical College

Moorefield, West Virginia

Freshman Application Contact Learner Support Services, Eastern West Virginia Community and Technical College, HC 65 Box 402, Moorefield, WV 26836. *Phone:* 304-434-8000. *Toll-free phone:* 877-982-2322. *Fax:* 304-434-7000. *E-mail:* askeast@eastern.wvnet.edu. *Web site:* http://www.eastern.wvnet.edu/.

Everest Institute

Cross Lanes, West Virginia

Freshman Application Contact Director of Admissions, Everest Institute, 5514 Big Tyler Road, Cross Lanes, WV 25313-1390. *Phone:* 304-776-6290. *Toll-free phone:* 888-741-4271. *Fax:* 304-776-6262. *Web site:* http://www.everest.edu/.

Huntington Junior College
Huntington, West Virginia

Director of Admissions Mr. James Garrett, Educational Services Director, Huntington Junior College, 900 Fifth Avenue, Huntington, WV 25701-2004. *Phone:* 304-697-7550. *Web site:* http://www.huntingtonjuniorcollege.com/.

ITT Technical Institute
Huntington, West Virginia

- **Proprietary** 2-year, part of ITT Educational Services, Inc.
- **Coed**

Majors CAD/CADD drafting/design technology; computer engineering technology; computer software technology; criminal justice/law enforcement administration; design and visual communications; legal assistant/paralegal; registered nursing/registered nurse; system, networking, and LAN/WAN management.

Academics *Calendar:* quarters. *Degree:* associate.

Freshman Application Contact Director of Recruitment, ITT Technical Institute, 5183 US Route 60, Building 1, Suite 40, Huntington, WV 25705. *Phone:* 304-733-8700. *Toll-free phone:* 800-224-4695. *Web site:* http://www.itt-tech.edu/.

Kanawha Valley Community and Technical College
Institute, West Virginia

Freshman Application Contact Mr. Bryce Casto, Vice President, Student Affairs, Kanawha Valley Community and Technical College, 333 Sullivan Hall. *Phone:* 304-766-3140. *Toll-free phone:* 800-987-2112. *Fax:* 304-766-4158. *E-mail:* castosb@wvstateu.edu. *Web site:* http://www.wvsctc.edu/.

Mountain State College
Parkersburg, West Virginia

- **Proprietary** 2-year, founded 1888
- **Small-town** campus
- **Coed**

Undergraduates 166 full-time. Students come from 2 states and territories; 4% transferred in. *Retention:* 70% of full-time freshmen returned.

Faculty *Student/faculty ratio:* 17:1.

Academics *Calendar:* quarters. *Degree:* diplomas and associate. *Special study options:* distance learning, double majors, honors programs, independent study, internships, part-time degree program.

Standardized Tests *Required:* CPAt (for admission).

Costs (2010–11) *One-time required fee:* $1035. *Tuition:* $8100 full-time. Full-time tuition and fees vary according to class time. Part-time tuition and fees vary according to class time. No tuition increase for student's term of enrollment.

Applying *Required:* interview.

Freshman Application Contact Ms. Judith Sutton, President, Mountain State College, 1508 Spring Street, Parkersburg, WV 26101-3993. *Phone:* 304-485-5487. *Toll-free phone:* 800-841-0201. *Fax:* 304-485-3524. *E-mail:* jsutton@msc.edu. *Web site:* http://www.msc.edu/.

Mountwest Community & Technical College
Huntington, West Virginia

Freshman Application Contact Dr. Tammy Johnson, Admissions Director, Mountwest Community & Technical College, 1 John Marshall Drive, Huntington, WV 25755. *Phone:* 304-696-3160. *Toll-free phone:* 800-642-3499. *Fax:* 304-696-3135. *E-mail:* admissions@marshall.edu. *Web site:* http://www.mctc.edu/.

New River Community and Technical College
Beckley, West Virginia

Director of Admissions Dr. Allen B. Withers, Vice President, Student Services, New River Community and Technical College, 167 Dye Drive, Beckley, WV 25801. *Phone:* 304-929-5011. *E-mail:* awithers@newriver.edu. *Web site:* http://www.newriver.edu/.

Pierpont Community & Technical College
Fairmont, West Virginia

Freshman Application Contact Mr. Steve Leadman, Director of Admissions and Recruiting, Pierpont Community & Technical College, 1201 Locust Avenue, Fairmont, WV 26554. *Phone:* 304-367-4892. *Toll-free phone:* 800-641-5678. *Fax:* 304-367-4789. *Web site:* http://www.pierpont.edu/.

Potomac State College of West Virginia University
Keyser, West Virginia

- **State-supported** primarily 2-year, founded 1901, part of West Virginia Higher Education Policy Commission
- **Small-town** 18-acre campus
- **Coed,** 1,836 undergraduate students, 77% full-time, 51% women, 49% men

Undergraduates 1,415 full-time, 421 part-time. Students come from 18 states and territories; 3 other countries; 29% are from out of state; 14% Black or African American, non-Hispanic/Latino; 3% Hispanic/Latino; 0.7% Asian, non-Hispanic/Latino; 0.2% Native Hawaiian or other Pacific Islander, non-Hispanic/Latino; 1% American Indian or Alaska Native, non-Hispanic/Latino; 0.3% Two or more races, non-Hispanic/Latino; 2% Race/ethnicity unknown; 0.3% international; 4% transferred in. *Retention:* 50% of full-time freshmen returned.

Freshmen *Admission:* 1,006 admitted, 710 enrolled. *Average high school GPA:* 2.78. *Test scores:* SAT critical reading scores over 500: 17%; SAT math scores over 500: 15%; ACT scores over 18: 63%; SAT critical reading scores over 600: 3%; SAT math scores over 600: 2%; ACT scores over 24: 16%; ACT scores over 30: 1%.

Faculty *Total:* 100, 41% full-time, 15% with terminal degrees. *Student/faculty ratio:* 25:1.

Majors Accounting; administrative assistant and secretarial science; agricultural business and management; agricultural economics; agricultural mechanization; agricultural teacher education; agriculture; agriculture and agriculture operations related; agronomy and crop science; animal sciences; biological and physical sciences; biology/biological sciences; business administration and management; business/managerial economics; chemistry; civil engineering technology; computer and information sciences related; computer engineering technology; computer programming; computer programming (specific applications); computer science; computer systems networking and telecommunications; criminal justice/safety; data processing and data processing technology; economics; education; electrical, electronic and communications engineering technology; elementary education; engineering; English; forestry; forest technology; geology/earth science; history; horticultural science; hospitality administration; information technology; journalism; kindergarten/preschool education; liberal arts and sciences/liberal studies; mathematics; mechanical engineering/mechanical technology; medical administrative assistant and medical secretary; network and system administration; parks, recreation and leisure facilities management; physical education teaching and coaching; political science and government; pre-engineering; psychology; social work; sociology; wildlife, fish and wildlands science and management; wood science and wood products/pulp and paper technology.

Academics *Calendar:* semesters. *Degrees:* certificates, associate, and bachelor's. *Special study options:* academic remediation for entering students, adult/continuing education programs, advanced placement credit, distance learning, double majors, honors programs, independent study, internships, part-time degree program, services for LD students, study abroad, summer session for credit.

Library Mary F. Shipper Library with 44,197 titles, 304 serial subscriptions, 23,395 audiovisual materials, an OPAC, a Web page.

Student Life *Housing:* on-campus residence required for freshman year. *Options:* coed. Campus housing is university owned. Freshman applicants given priority for college housing. *Activities and Organizations:* drama/theater group, student-run newspaper, choral group, Community Chorus, Circle K, Agriculture and Forestry Club, Business Club. *Campus security:* 24-hour patrols, late-night transport/escort service, controlled dormitory access. *Student services:* health clinic, personal/psychological counseling.

Athletics Member NJCAA. *Intercollegiate sports:* baseball M(s), basketball M(s)/W(s), golf M(s)/W(s), soccer M/W, softball W(s), volleyball W(s). *Intramural sports:* basketball M/W, football M/W, volleyball M/W.

Standardized Tests *Required for some:* SAT or ACT (for admission).

Costs (2010–11) *Tuition:* state resident $2280 full-time, $95 per credit hour part-time; nonresident $8140 full-time, $340 per credit hour part-time. Part-time tuition and fees vary according to course load. *Required fees:* $606 full-time, $26 per credit hour part-time.

Financial Aid Of all full-time matriculated undergraduates who enrolled in 2009, 70 Federal Work-Study jobs (averaging $1300).

Applying *Options:* electronic application, early admission. *Required:* high school transcript. *Application deadlines:* rolling (freshmen), rolling (transfers).

Freshman Application Contact Ms. Beth Little, Director of Enrollment Services, Potomac State College of West Virginia University, 75 Arnold Street, Keyser, WV 26726. *Phone:* 304-788-6820. *Toll-free phone:* 800-262-7332 Ext. 6820. *Fax:* 304-788-6939. *E-mail:* go2psc@mail.wvu.edu. *Web site:* http://www.potomacstatecollege.edu/.

Southern West Virginia Community and Technical College

Mount Gay, West Virginia

Freshman Application Contact Mr. Roy Simmons, Registrar, Southern West Virginia Community and Technical College, PO Box 2900, Mt. Gay, WV 25637. *Phone:* 304-792-7160 Ext. 120. *Fax:* 304-792-7096. *E-mail:* admissions@southern.wvnet.edu. *Web site:* http://southernwv.edu/.

Valley College of Technology

Martinsburg, West Virginia

Freshman Application Contact Ms. Gail Kennedy, Admissions Director, Valley College of Technology, 287 Aikens Center, Martinsburg, WV 25404. *Phone:* 304-263-0878. *Fax:* 304-263-2413. *E-mail:* gkennedy@vct.edu. *Web site:* http://www.vct.edu/.

West Virginia Business College

Nutter Fort, West Virginia

Director of Admissions Robert Wright, Campus Director, West Virginia Business College, 116 Pennsylvania Avenue, Nutter Fort, WV 26301. *Phone:* 304-624-7695. *E-mail:* info@wvbc.edu. *Web site:* http://www.wvbc.edu/.

West Virginia Business College

Wheeling, West Virginia

Freshman Application Contact Ms. Karen D. Shaw, Director, West Virginia Business College, 1052 Main Street, Wheeling, WV 26003. *Phone:* 304-232-0361. *Fax:* 304-232-0363. *E-mail:* wvbcwheeling@stratuswave.net. *Web site:* http://www.wvbc.edu/.

West Virginia Junior College

Charleston, West Virginia

Freshman Application Contact West Virginia Junior College, 1000 Virginia Street East, Charleston, WV 25301-2817. *Phone:* 304-345-2820. *Toll-free phone:* 800-924-5208. *Web site:* http://www.wvjc.edu/.

West Virginia Junior College

Morgantown, West Virginia

Freshman Application Contact Admissions Office, West Virginia Junior College, 148 Willey Street, Morgantown, WV 26505-5521. *Phone:* 304-296-8282. *Web site:* http://www.wvjcmorgantown.edu/.

West Virginia Junior College– Bridgeport

Bridgeport, West Virginia

- **Proprietary** 2-year, founded 1922, administratively affiliated with West Virginia Junior College-Charleston, WV (Main Campus)
- **Small-town** 3-acre campus with easy access to Pittsburgh, PA
- **Coed,** 355 undergraduate students, 100% full-time, 76% women, 24% men

Undergraduates 355 full-time. Students come from 5 states and territories; 1% Black or African American, non-Hispanic/Latino. *Retention:* 73% of full-time freshmen returned.

Freshmen *Average high school GPA:* 2.5.

Faculty *Total:* 19, 37% full-time, 100% with terminal degrees. *Student/faculty ratio:* 16:1.

Majors Computer technology/computer systems technology; medical administrative assistant and medical secretary; medical/clinical assistant; web/multimedia management and webmaster.

Academics *Calendar:* quarters. *Degree:* associate. *Special study options:* cooperative education, distance learning, internships, summer session for credit.

Library WVJC Resource Center plus 1 other.

Student Life *Housing:* college housing not available. *Activities and Organizations:* Medical Assisting Club, FBLA (Business students), Computer Club, Dental Assisting Club, Pharmacy Tech Club. *Campus security:* 24-hour emergency response devices.

Financial Aid Of all full-time matriculated undergraduates who enrolled in 2009, 10 Federal Work-Study jobs.

Applying *Options:* electronic application. *Required:* essay or personal statement, minimum 2.0 GPA, interview. *Application deadline:* rolling (freshmen). *Notification:* continuous (freshmen).

Freshman Application Contact Ms. Chasity Duarte, Admissions Office, West Virginia Junior College–Bridgeport, 176 Thompson Drive, Bridgeport, WV 26330. *Phone:* 304-842-4007 Ext. 108. *Toll-free phone:* 800-470-5627. *Fax:* 304-842-8191. *E-mail:* admissions@wvjcinfo.net. *Web site:* http://www.wvjcinfo.net/.

West Virginia Northern Community College

Wheeling, West Virginia

- **State-supported** 2-year, founded 1972
- **Small-town** campus with easy access to Pittsburgh
- **Endowment** $484,389
- **Coed,** 3,363 undergraduate students, 52% full-time, 68% women, 32% men

Undergraduates 1,762 full-time, 1,601 part-time. Students come from 15 states and territories; 21% are from out of state; 11% transferred in.

Freshmen *Admission:* 575 enrolled. *Average high school GPA:* 2.8. *Test scores:* SAT critical reading scores over 500: 28%; SAT math scores over 500: 11%; ACT scores over 18: 60%; SAT critical reading scores over 600: 6%; SAT math scores over 600: 6%; ACT scores over 24: 7%.

Faculty *Total:* 208, 30% full-time. *Student/faculty ratio:* 14:1.

Majors Administrative assistant and secretarial science; business/commerce; computer programming; criminal justice/police science; culinary arts; executive assistant/executive secretary; general studies; health information/medical records technology; heating, air conditioning, ventilation and refrigeration maintenance technology; hospitality administration; information technology; legal assistant/paralegal; liberal arts and sciences and humanities related; liberal arts and sciences/liberal studies; medical/clinical assistant; medical radiologic technology; multi/interdisciplinary studies related; registered nursing/registered nurse; respiratory care therapy; science technologies related; social work; surgical technology.

Academics *Calendar:* semesters. *Degree:* certificates and associate. *Special study options:* academic remediation for entering students, accelerated degree program, adult/continuing education programs, advanced placement credit, distance learning, double majors, honors programs, internships, part-time degree program, student-designed majors, summer session for credit.

Library Wheeling B and O Campus Library plus 2 others with 36,650 titles, 188 serial subscriptions, 3,495 audiovisual materials, an OPAC, a Web page.

Student Life *Housing:* college housing not available. *Activities and Organizations:* student-run newspaper, Community Outreach Opportunity Program (COOP). *Campus security:* security personnel during evening and night classes.

Athletics *Intramural sports:* basketball M/W, bowling M/W, golf M/W, softball M/W, volleyball M/W.

Standardized Tests *Recommended:* SAT or ACT (for admission).

Costs (2011–12) *Tuition:* state resident $1968 full-time, $82 per credit hour part-time; nonresident $6480 full-time, $270 per credit hour part-time. Full-time tuition and fees vary according to course load and program. Part-time tuition and fees vary according to course load and program. *Required fees:* $490 full-time, $15 per credit hour part-time, $15 per term part-time. *Payment plan:* installment. *Waivers:* adult students, senior citizens, and employees or children of employees.

Applying *Options:* electronic application, early admission, deferred entrance. *Required for some:* high school transcript. *Application deadlines:* rolling (freshmen), rolling (transfers).

Freshman Application Contact Mr. Richard McCray, Assistant Director of Admissions, West Virginia Northern Community College, 1704 Market Street, Wheeling, WV 26003. *Phone:* 304-214-8838. *E-mail:* rmccray@northern.wvnet.edu. *Web site:* http://www.wvncc.edu/.

West Virginia University at Parkersburg

Parkersburg, West Virginia

Freshman Application Contact Christine Post, Associate Dean of Enrollment Management, West Virginia University at Parkersburg, 300 Campus Drive, Parkersburg, WV 26104. *Phone:* 304-424-8223 Ext. 223. *Toll-free phone:* 800-WVA-WVUP. *Fax:* 304-424-8332. *E-mail:* christine.post@mail.wvu.edu. *Web site:* http://www.wvup.edu/.

WISCONSIN

Blackhawk Technical College

Janesville, Wisconsin

- **District-supported** 2-year, founded 1968, part of Wisconsin Technical College System
- **Rural** 84-acre campus
- **Coed,** 3,337 undergraduate students, 48% full-time, 61% women, 39% men

Undergraduates 1,586 full-time, 1,751 part-time. Students come from 3 states and territories; 1% are from out of state; 6% Black or African American, non-Hispanic/Latino; 7% Hispanic/Latino; 0.7% Asian, non-Hispanic/Latino; 0.5% American Indian or Alaska Native, non-Hispanic/Latino; 0.8% Two or more races, non-Hispanic/Latino; 28% Race/ethnicity unknown. *Retention:* 83% of full-time freshmen returned.

Freshmen *Admission:* 695 enrolled.

Faculty *Total:* 388, 28% full-time, 0.8% with terminal degrees. *Student/faculty ratio:* 17:1.

Majors Accounting; administrative assistant and secretarial science; business administration and management; clinical/medical laboratory technology; computer and information systems security; computer systems networking and telecommunications; criminal justice/police science; culinary arts; drafting/design engineering technologies related; early childhood education; electromechanical technology; fire science/firefighting; heating, air conditioning, ventilation and refrigeration maintenance technology; industrial engineering; industrial technology; legal administrative assistant/secretary; management science; marketing/marketing management; medical administrative assistant and medical secretary; physical therapy; radiologic technology/science; registered nursing/registered nurse; web/multimedia management and webmaster.

Academics *Calendar:* semesters. *Degree:* associate. *Special study options:* academic remediation for entering students, accelerated degree program, adult/continuing education programs, advanced placement credit, cooperative education, distance learning, English as a second language, external degree program, independent study, internships, part-time degree program, services for LD students, student-designed majors, summer session for credit.

Library Blackhawk Technical College Library plus 2 others with 101,024 titles, 300 serial subscriptions, 5,889 audiovisual materials, an OPAC.

Student Life *Housing:* college housing not available. *Activities and Organizations:* student-run newspaper, Student Government, Association of Information Technology Professionals, Criminal Justice, Epicurean Club, Phi Theta Kappa Honor Society. *Campus security:* student patrols. *Student services:* personal/psychological counseling, women's center.

Costs (2010–11) *Tuition:* state resident $113 per credit part-time; nonresident $166 per credit part-time. Full-time tuition and fees vary according to course load. Part-time tuition and fees vary according to course load. *Required fees:* $5 per credit part-time. *Payment plan:* deferred payment. *Waivers:* senior citizens.

Financial Aid Of all full-time matriculated undergraduates who enrolled in 2009, 33 Federal Work-Study jobs (averaging $1150).

Applying *Options:* electronic application. *Application fee:* $30. *Required:* high school transcript. *Application deadlines:* rolling (freshmen), rolling (transfers). *Notification:* continuous (freshmen), continuous (transfers).

Freshman Application Contact Blackhawk Technical College, PO Box 5009, Janesville, WI 53547-5009. *Phone:* 608-757-7713. *Toll-free phone:* 800-472-0024. *Web site:* http://www.blackhawk.edu/.

Bryant & Stratton College

Milwaukee, Wisconsin

- **Proprietary** primarily 2-year, founded 1863, part of Bryant and Stratton College, Inc.
- **Urban** campus
- **Coed,** 828 undergraduate students, 56% full-time, 84% women, 16% men

Undergraduates 460 full-time, 368 part-time. Students come from 1 other state; 33% transferred in. *Retention:* 70% of full-time freshmen returned.

Freshmen *Admission:* 433 applied, 387 admitted, 385 enrolled.

Faculty *Total:* 102, 19% full-time. *Student/faculty ratio:* 13:1.

Majors Accounting; administrative assistant and secretarial science; business/commerce; commercial and advertising art; computer and information systems security; criminal justice/law enforcement administration; design and visual communications; financial planning and services; human resources management and services related; legal assistant/paralegal; medical/clinical assistant; system, networking, and LAN/WAN management.

Academics *Calendar:* semesters. *Degrees:* associate and bachelor's. *Special study options:* academic remediation for entering students, adult/continuing education programs, advanced placement credit, cooperative education, distance learning, double majors, independent study, internships, part-time degree program, summer session for credit.

Library Bryant and Stratton College Library plus 1 other with 120 serial subscriptions, 100 audiovisual materials.

Student Life *Housing:* college housing not available. *Activities and Organizations:* student-run newspaper, Phi Beta Lambda, Association of Information Technology Professionals, Allied Health Association, Institute of Management Accountants, Student Advisory Board. *Campus security:* 24-hour emergency response devices and patrols.

Standardized Tests *Required:* CPAt; ACCUPLACER (for admission). *Recommended:* SAT or ACT (for admission).

Applying *Options:* electronic application. *Required:* high school transcript, interview, entrance and placement evaluations. *Application deadlines:* rolling (freshmen), rolling (transfers). *Notification:* continuous (freshmen), continuous (transfers).

Freshman Application Contact Mr. Dan Basile, Director of Admissions, Bryant & Stratton College, 310 West Wisconsin Avenue, Suite 500 East, Milwaukee, WI 53203-2214. *Phone:* 414-276-5200. *Web site:* http://www.bryantstratton.edu/.

Chippewa Valley Technical College

Eau Claire, Wisconsin

- **District-supported** 2-year, founded 1912, part of Wisconsin Technical College System
- **Urban** 160-acre campus
- **Coed,** 6,062 undergraduate students, 52% full-time, 56% women, 44% men

Undergraduates 3,122 full-time, 2,940 part-time. 2% are from out of state; 3% transferred in.

Freshmen *Admission:* 2,306 enrolled.

Faculty *Total:* 514, 44% full-time, 6% with terminal degrees.

Majors Accounting; administrative assistant and secretarial science; agricultural business and management related; applied horticulture/horticultural business services related; business administration and management; civil engineering technology; clinical/medical laboratory technology; computer programming; computer systems networking and telecommunications; criminal justice/police science; dental hygiene; diagnostic medical sonography and ultrasound technology; early childhood education; electromechanical technology; emergency medical technology (EMT paramedic); health information/medical records technology; heating, ventilation, air conditioning and refrigeration engineering technology; legal assistant/paralegal; marketing/marketing management; medical radiologic technology; multi/interdisciplinary studies related; nanotechnology; operations management; physical therapy technology; registered nursing/registered nurse; respiratory care therapy; substance abuse/addiction counseling.

Academics *Calendar:* semesters. *Degree:* certificates, diplomas, and associate. *Special study options:* academic remediation for entering students, accelerated degree program, adult/continuing education programs, advanced placement credit, cooperative education, distance learning, double majors, English as a second language, independent study, internships, part-time degree program, services for LD students, summer session for credit.

Library The Learning Center with an OPAC, a Web page.

Student Life *Housing:* college housing not available. *Activities and Organizations:* Collegiate DECA. *Campus security:* 24-hour emergency response devices, late-night transport/escort service, security cameras. *Student services:* health clinic, personal/psychological counseling.

Costs (2010–11) *Tuition:* state resident $106 per credit hour part-time; nonresident $159 per credit hour part-time. Full-time tuition and fees vary according to course load and program. Part-time tuition and fees vary according to course load and program. *Required fees:* $6 per credit hour part-time. *Payment plans:* installment, deferred payment. *Waivers:* senior citizens.

Financial Aid Of all full-time matriculated undergraduates who enrolled in 2009, 218 Federal Work-Study jobs (averaging $875).

Applying *Options:* electronic application, early admission, deferred entrance. *Application fee:* $30. *Required:* high school transcript. *Required for some:* interview. *Application deadlines:* rolling (freshmen), rolling (transfers). *Notification:* continuous (freshmen), continuous (transfers).

Freshman Application Contact Admissions Office, Chippewa Valley Technical College, 620 West Clairemont Avenue, Eau Claire, WI 54701-6162. *Phone:* 715-833-6200. *Toll-free phone:* 800-547-2882. *Fax:* 715-833-6470. *E-mail:* infocenter@cvtc.edu. *Web site:* http://www.cvtc.edu/.

College of Menominee Nation
Keshena, Wisconsin

Director of Admissions Tessa James, Admissions Coordinator, College of Menominee Nation, PO Box 1179, Keshena, WI 54135. *Phone:* 715-799-5600 Ext. 3053. *Toll-free phone:* 800-567-2344. *E-mail:* tjames@menominee.edu. *Web site:* http://www.menominee.edu/.

Fox Valley Technical College
Appleton, Wisconsin

- **State and locally supported** 2-year, founded 1967, part of Wisconsin Technical College System
- **Suburban** 100-acre campus
- **Endowment** $1.6 million
- **Coed,** 10,659 undergraduate students, 31% full-time, 49% women, 51% men

Undergraduates 3,342 full-time, 7,317 part-time. Students come from 11 states and territories; 14 other countries; 0.8% are from out of state; 2% Black or African American, non-Hispanic/Latino; 3% Hispanic/Latino; 3% Asian, non-Hispanic/Latino; 0.1% Native Hawaiian or other Pacific Islander, non-Hispanic/Latino; 1% American Indian or Alaska Native, non-Hispanic/Latino; 0.2% Two or more races, non-Hispanic/Latino; 5% Race/ethnicity unknown; 0.3% international.

Freshmen *Admission:* 1,035 enrolled.

Faculty *Total:* 938, 33% full-time. *Student/faculty ratio:* 11:1.

Majors Accounting; administrative assistant and secretarial science; agricultural/farm supplies retailing and wholesaling; agricultural mechanization; airline pilot and flight crew; autobody/collision and repair technology; automobile/automotive mechanics technology; avionics maintenance technology; banking and financial support services; business administration and management; computer engineering technology; computer programming; computer systems analysis; computer systems networking and telecommunications; criminal justice/police science; dental hygiene; early childhood education; electrical, electronic and communications engineering technology; electromechanical technology; emergency medical technology (EMT paramedic); environmental control technologies related; fire prevention and safety technology; forensic science and technology; graphic and printing equipment operation/production; graphic communications; heavy equipment maintenance technology; hospitality administration; human resources management; instrumentation technology; interior design; manufacturing engineering technology; marketing/marketing management; mechanical drafting and CAD/CADD; medical office management; multi/interdisciplinary studies related; natural resources/conservation; occupational therapist assistant; operations management; registered nursing/registered nurse; restaurant, culinary, and catering management; substance abuse/addiction counseling; web/multimedia management and webmaster; welding technology; wildland/forest firefighting and investigation.

Academics *Calendar:* semesters. *Degree:* certificates, diplomas, and associate. *Special study options:* academic remediation for entering students, accelerated degree program, advanced placement credit, cooperative education, distance learning, double majors, English as a second language, independent study, internships, off-campus study, part-time degree program, services for LD students, student-designed majors, study abroad, summer session for credit.

Library William M. Sirek Educational Resource Center plus 1 other with 52,172 titles, 205 serial subscriptions, 6,049 audiovisual materials, an OPAC, a Web page.

Student Life *Housing:* college housing not available. *Activities and Organizations:* student-run newspaper, Student Government Association, Phi Theta Kappa, Culinary Arts, Student Nurses, Post Secondary Agribusiness. *Campus security:* 24-hour emergency response devices, late-night transport/escort service, 16-hour patrols by trained security personnel. *Student services:* health clinic, personal/psychological counseling.

Athletics *Intercollegiate sports:* basketball M/W, volleyball W. *Intramural sports:* basketball M/W, football M/W, soccer M/W, softball M/W, table tennis M/W, volleyball M/W, weight lifting M/W.

Costs (2011–12) *Tuition:* state resident $3180 full-time, $122 per credit part-time; nonresident $4770 full-time, $175 per credit part-time. *Payment plan:* installment.

Applying *Options:* electronic application, early admission, deferred entrance. *Application fee:* $30. *Required:* high school transcript. *Application deadlines:* rolling (freshmen), rolling (transfers).

Freshman Application Contact Admissions Center, Fox Valley Technical College, 1825 North Bluemound Drive, PO Box 2277, Appleton, WI 54912-2277. *Phone:* 920-735-5643. *Toll-free phone:* 800-735-3882. *Fax:* 920-735-2582. *Web site:* http://www.fvtc.edu/.

Gateway Technical College
Kenosha, Wisconsin

Freshman Application Contact Admissions, Gateway Technical College, 3520 30th Avenue, Kenosha, WI 53144-1690. *Phone:* 262-564-2300. *Fax:* 262-564-2301. *E-mail:* admissions@gtc.edu. *Web site:* http://www.gtc.edu/.

ITT Technical Institute
Green Bay, Wisconsin

- **Proprietary** primarily 2-year, founded 2000, part of ITT Educational Services, Inc.
- **Coed**

Majors Business administration and management; CAD/CADD drafting/design technology; computer and information systems security; computer engineering technology; computer software and media applications related; computer software engineering; computer software technology; construction management; criminal justice/law enforcement administration; design and visual communications; electrical, electronic and communications engineering technology; game and interactive media design; information technology project management; legal assistant/paralegal; project management; system, networking, and LAN/WAN management; web page, digital/multimedia and information resources design.

Academics *Calendar:* quarters. *Degrees:* associate and bachelor's.

Student Life *Housing:* college housing not available.

Freshman Application Contact Director of Recruitment, ITT Technical Institute, 470 Security Boulevard, Green Bay, WI 54313. *Phone:* 920-662-9000. *Toll-free phone:* 888-884-3626. *Fax:* 920-662-9384. *Web site:* http://www.itt-tech.edu/.

ITT Technical Institute
Greenfield, Wisconsin

- **Proprietary** primarily 2-year, founded 1968, part of ITT Educational Services, Inc.
- **Suburban** campus
- **Coed**

Majors Business administration and management; CAD/CADD drafting/design technology; computer and information systems security; computer engineering technology; computer software and media applications related; computer software engineering; computer software technology; construction management; criminal justice/law enforcement administration; design and visual communications; electrical, electronic and communications engineering technology; game and interactive media design; information technology project management; legal assistant/paralegal; project management; system, networking, and LAN/WAN management; web page, digital/multimedia and information resources design.

Academics *Calendar:* quarters. *Degrees:* associate and bachelor's.

Student Life *Housing:* college housing not available.

Freshman Application Contact Director of Recruitment, ITT Technical Institute, 6300 West Layton Avenue, Greenfield, WI 53220-4612. *Phone:* 414-282-9494. *Web site:* http://www.itt-tech.edu/.

ITT Technical Institute
Madison, Wisconsin

- **Proprietary** primarily 2-year, part of ITT Educational Services, Inc.
- **Coed**

Majors CAD/CADD drafting/design technology; computer and information systems security; computer engineering technology; computer software engineering; computer software technology; construction management; criminal justice/law enforcement administration; electrical, electronic and communications engineering technology; legal assistant/paralegal; project management; system, networking, and LAN/WAN management.

Academics *Degrees:* associate and bachelor's.

Freshman Application Contact Director of Recruitment, ITT Technical Institute, 2450 Rimrock Road, Suite 100, Madison, WI 53713. *Phone:* 608-288-6301. *Toll-free phone:* 877-628-5960. *Web site:* http://www.itt-tech.edu/.

Lac Courte Oreilles Ojibwa Community College
Hayward, Wisconsin

- **Federally supported** 2-year, founded 1982
- **Rural** 2-acre campus
- **Endowment** $2.3 million
- **Coed**

Undergraduates 341 full-time, 220 part-time. 6% transferred in.

Faculty *Student/faculty ratio:* 15:1.

Academics *Calendar:* semesters. *Degree:* certificates and associate. *Special study options:* academic remediation for entering students, adult/continuing education programs, distance learning, double majors, external degree program, honors programs, independent study, internships, part-time degree program, services for LD students.

Student Life *Campus security:* 24-hour emergency response devices.

Standardized Tests *Required:* ACT COMPASS (for admission).

Costs (2010–11) *Tuition:* state resident $3840 full-time, $160 per credit part-time. Full-time tuition and fees vary according to class time, course level, course load, degree level, location, program, reciprocity agreements, and student level. Part-time tuition and fees vary according to class time, course level, course load, degree level, location, program, reciprocity agreements, and student level.

Financial Aid Of all full-time matriculated undergraduates who enrolled in 2009, 15 Federal Work-Study jobs (averaging $1400).

Applying *Options:* early admission. *Application fee:* $10. *Required:* high school transcript.

Freshman Application Contact Ms. Annette Wiggins, Registrar, Lac Courte Oreilles Ojibwa Community College, 13466 West Trepania Road, Hayward, WI 54843-2181. *Phone:* 715-634-4790 Ext. 104. *Toll-free phone:* 888-526-6221. *Web site:* http://www.lco.edu/.

Lakeshore Technical College
Cleveland, Wisconsin

Freshman Application Contact Lakeshore Technical College, 1290 North Avenue, Cleveland, WI 53015. *Phone:* 920-693-1339. *Toll-free phone:* 888-GO TO LTC. *Fax:* 920-693-3561. *Web site:* http://www.gotoltc.com/.

Madison Area Technical College
Madison, Wisconsin

Director of Admissions Ms. Maureen Menendez, Interim Admissions Administrator, Madison Area Technical College, 3550 Anderson Street, Madison, WI 53704-2599. *Phone:* 608-246-6212. *Toll-free phone:* 800-322-6282. *Web site:* http://www.matcmadison.edu/matc/.

Madison Media Institute
Madison, Wisconsin

Freshman Application Contact Mr. Chris K. Hutchings, President/Director, Madison Media Institute, 2702 Agriculture Drive, Madison, WI 53718. *Phone:* 608-237-8301. *Toll-free phone:* 800-236-4997. *Web site:* http://www.madisonmedia.edu/.

Mid-State Technical College
Wisconsin Rapids, Wisconsin

Freshman Application Contact Ms. Carole Prochnow, Admissions Assistant, Mid-State Technical College, 500 32nd Street North, Wisconsin Rapids, WI 54494-5599. *Phone:* 715-422-5444. *Toll-free phone:* 888-575-6782. *Web site:* http://www.mstc.edu/.

Milwaukee Area Technical College
Milwaukee, Wisconsin

- **District-supported** 2-year, founded 1912, part of Wisconsin Technical College System
- **Urban** campus
- **Coed**

Undergraduates 7,048 full-time, 13,167 part-time. Students come from 16 states and territories; 50 other countries; 1% are from out of state; 16% transferred in. *Retention:* 47% of full-time freshmen returned.

Faculty *Student/faculty ratio:* 14:1.

Academics *Calendar:* semesters. *Degree:* certificates, diplomas, and associate. *Special study options:* academic remediation for entering students, accelerated degree program, adult/continuing education programs, advanced placement credit, cooperative education, distance learning, double majors, English as a second language, external degree program, freshman honors college, honors programs, independent study, internships, off-campus study, part-time degree program, services for LD students, student-designed majors, study abroad, summer session for credit.

Student Life *Campus security:* 24-hour emergency response devices and patrols, student patrols, late-night transport/escort service.

Athletics Member NJCAA.

Standardized Tests *Required:* ACCUPLACER (for admission).

Costs (2010–11) *Tuition:* state resident $3042 full-time, $113 per credit hour part-time; nonresident $7292 full-time, $164 per credit hour part-time. Full-time tuition and fees vary according to course level and degree level. Part-time tuition and fees vary according to course level and degree level. *Required fees:* $395 full-time. *Payment plans:* installment, deferred payment.

Financial Aid Of all full-time matriculated undergraduates who enrolled in 2009, 300 Federal Work-Study jobs (averaging $3900).

Applying *Options:* electronic application. *Application fee:* $30. *Required:* high school transcript.

Freshman Application Contact Sarah Adams, Director, Enrollment Services, Milwaukee Area Technical College, 700 West State Street, Milwaukee, WI 53233-1443. *Phone:* 414-297-6595. *Fax:* 414-297-7800. *E-mail:* adamss4@matc.edu. *Web site:* http://www.matc.edu/.

Moraine Park Technical College
Fond du Lac, Wisconsin

- **District-supported** 2-year, founded 1967, part of Wisconsin Technical College System
- **Small-town** 40-acre campus with easy access to Milwaukee
- **Coed,** 8,484 undergraduate students, 18% full-time, 64% women, 36% men

Undergraduates 1,512 full-time, 6,972 part-time. 2% Black or African American, non-Hispanic/Latino; 1% Hispanic/Latino; 0.6% Asian, non-Hispanic/Latino; 0.1% Native Hawaiian or other Pacific Islander, non-Hispanic/Latino; 0.6% American Indian or Alaska Native, non-Hispanic/Latino; 0.7% Two or more races, non-Hispanic/Latino; 1% Race/ethnicity unknown.

Freshmen *Admission:* 868 enrolled.

Faculty *Total:* 356, 40% full-time. *Student/faculty ratio:* 15:1.

Majors Accounting; accounting technology and bookkeeping; administrative assistant and secretarial science; automobile/automotive mechanics technology; automotive engineering technology; blasting; business administration and management; carpentry; child-care provision; chiropractic assistant; civil engineering technology; clinical/medical laboratory technology; computer and information sciences and support services related; computer numerically controlled (CNC) machinist technology; computer programming related; computer systems networking and telecommunications; corrections; court reporting; data modeling/warehousing and database administration; early childhood education; electrician; electromechanical technology; emergency medical technology (EMT paramedic); food preparation; graphic communications; graphic design; hair styling and hair design; health information/medical records technology; heating, air conditioning, ventilation and refrigeration maintenance technology; heating, ventilation, air conditioning and refrigeration engineering technology; hotel/motel administration; human resources management; industrial electronics technology; industrial mechanics and maintenance technology; industrial production technologies related; industrial technology; legal administrative assistant/secretary; legal assistant/paralegal; licensed practical/vocational nurse training; lineworker; machine shop technology; marketing/marketing management; mechanical drafting and CAD/CADD; mechanical engineering technologies related; mechatronics, robotics, and automation engineering; medical/clinical assistant; medical insurance coding; medical office assistant; medical radiologic technology; medical transcription; merchandising, sales, and marketing operations related (general); metal fabricator; multi/interdisciplinary studies related; nursing assistant/aide and patient care assistant/aide; office occupations and clerical services; operations management; pharmacy technician; pipefitting and sprinkler fitting; plumbing technology; printing management; registered nursing/registered nurse; respiratory care therapy; restaurant, culinary, and catering management; structural engineering; substance abuse/addiction counseling; surgical technology; teacher assistant/aide; tool and die technology; veterinary/animal health technology; water quality and wastewater treatment management and recycling technology; web page, digital/multimedia and information resources design; welding technology.

Academics *Calendar:* semesters. *Degree:* certificates, diplomas, and associate. *Special study options:* academic remediation for entering students, accelerated degree program, adult/continuing education programs, advanced placement credit, distance learning, English as a second language, external degree program, independent study, internships, part-time degree program, services for LD students, summer session for credit.

Library Moraine Park Technical College Library/Learning Resource Center with 41,737 titles, 280 serial subscriptions, 11,438 audiovisual materials, an OPAC, a Web page.

Student Life *Housing:* college housing not available. *Campus security:* 24-hour emergency response devices. *Student services:* personal/psychological counseling.

Standardized Tests *Required:* ACT, ACCUPLACER OR COMPASS (for admission). *Required for some:* ACT (for admission).

Costs (2010–11) *Tuition:* state resident $3180 full-time, $106 per credit hour part-time; nonresident $4770 full-time, $159 per credit hour part-time. Full-time tuition and fees vary according to program. Part-time tuition and fees vary according to program. *Required fees:* $174 full-time, $6 per credit hour part-time. *Payment plan:* deferred payment. *Waivers:* senior citizens.

Applying *Options:* electronic application, deferred entrance. *Application fee:* $30. *Required:* high school transcript, placement test. *Required for some:* interview. *Application deadlines:* rolling (freshmen), rolling (out-of-state freshmen), rolling (transfers). *Notification:* continuous (freshmen), continuous (out-of-state freshmen), continuous (transfers).

Freshman Application Contact Ms. Karen Jarvis, Student Services, Moraine Park Technical College, 235 North National Avenue, Fond du Lac, WI 54935. *Phone:* 920-924-3200. *Toll-free phone:* 800-472-4554. *Fax:* 920-924-3421. *E-mail:* kjarvis@morainepark.edu. *Web site:* http://www.morainepark.edu/.

Nicolet Area Technical College
Rhinelander, Wisconsin

- **State and locally supported** 2-year, founded 1968, part of Wisconsin Technical College System
- **Rural** 280-acre campus
- **Coed**

Undergraduates Students come from 8 states and territories; 4 other countries; 1% are from out of state.

Faculty *Student/faculty ratio:* 16:1.

Academics *Calendar:* semesters. *Degree:* certificates, diplomas, and associate. *Special study options:* academic remediation for entering students, adult/continuing education programs, advanced placement credit, cooperative education, distance learning, double majors, English as a second language, independent study, internships, part-time degree program, services for LD students, study abroad, summer session for credit.

Student Life *Campus security:* 24-hour emergency response devices, student patrols.

Athletics Member NJCAA.

Standardized Tests *Required:* ACCUPLACER Testing or ACT (for admission). *Recommended:* ACT (for admission).

Costs (2010–11) *Tuition:* state resident $3180 full-time, $106 per credit part-time; nonresident $4770 full-time, $159 per credit part-time. Full-time tuition and fees vary according to course level and reciprocity agreements. Part-time tuition and fees vary according to course level and reciprocity agreements. *Required fees:* $159 full-time, $5 per credit part-time.

Applying *Options:* electronic application, early admission. *Application fee:* $30. *Required:* high school transcript.

Freshman Application Contact Ms. Susan Kordula, Director of Admissions, Nicolet Area Technical College, PO Box 518, Rhinelander, WI 54501. *Phone:* 715-365-4451. *Toll-free phone:* 800-544-3039 Ext. 4451. *E-mail:* inquire@nicoletcollege.edu. *Web site:* http://www.nicoletcollege.edu/.

Northcentral Technical College
Wausau, Wisconsin

Director of Admissions Ms. Carolyn Michalski, Team Leader, Student Services, Northcentral Technical College, 1000 West Campus Drive, Wausau, WI 54401-1899. *Phone:* 715-675-3331 Ext. 4285. *Web site:* http://www.ntc.edu/.

Northeast Wisconsin Technical College
Green Bay, Wisconsin

Freshman Application Contact Christine Lemerande, Program Enrollment Supervisor, Northeast Wisconsin Technical College, 2740 W Mason Street, PO Box 19042, Green Bay, WI 54307-9042. *Phone:* 920-498-5444. *Toll-free phone:* 888-385-6982. *Fax:* 920-498-6882. *Web site:* http://www.nwtc.edu/.

Rasmussen College Green Bay
Green Bay, Wisconsin

Admissions Office Contact Rasmussen College Green Bay, 940 South Taylor Street, Suite 100, Green Bay, WI 54303. *Toll-free phone:* 888-201-9144. *Web site:* http://www.rasmussen.edu/.

Southwest Wisconsin Technical College
Fennimore, Wisconsin

- **State and locally supported** 2-year, founded 1967, part of Wisconsin Technical College System
- **Rural** 53-acre campus
- **Coed**

Undergraduates 852 full-time, 2,557 part-time. Students come from 5 states and territories; 1% transferred in; 3% live on campus. *Retention:* 71% of full-time freshmen returned.

Faculty *Student/faculty ratio:* 18:1.

Academics *Calendar:* semesters. *Degree:* certificates, diplomas, and associate. *Special study options:* academic remediation for entering students, advanced placement credit, distance learning, double majors, English as a second language, independent study, internships, off-campus study, part-time degree program, services for LD students, student-designed majors, summer session for credit.

Student Life *Campus security:* 24-hour emergency response devices.

Athletics Member NJCAA.

Standardized Tests *Required for some:* TABE and the HESI (nursing students only) for admissions decisions.

Costs (2010–11) *Tuition:* state resident $3042 full-time, $101 per credit part-time; nonresident $4563 full-time, $152 per credit part-time. Full-time tuition and fees vary according to course load, degree level, program, and reciprocity agreements. Part-time tuition and fees vary according to course load, degree level, program, and reciprocity agreements. *Required fees:* $278 full-time. *Room and board:* $6137; room only: $3000. Room and board charges vary according to housing facility. *Payment plans:* installment, deferred payment.

Applying *Options:* electronic application, early admission. *Application fee:* $30. *Required:* high school transcript, interview.

Freshman Application Contact Student Services, Southwest Wisconsin Technical College, 1800 Bronson Boulevard, Fennimore, WI 53809-9778. *Phone:* 608-822-2354. *Toll-free phone:* 800-362-3322. *Fax:* 608-822-6019. *E-mail:* student-services@swtc.edu. *Web site:* http://www.swtc.edu/.

University of Wisconsin–Baraboo/Sauk County
Baraboo, Wisconsin

Freshman Application Contact Ms. Jan Gerlach, Assistant Director of Student Services, University of Wisconsin–Baraboo/Sauk County, Baraboo, WI 53913-1015. *Phone:* 608-355-5270. *E-mail:* booinfo@uwc.edu. *Web site:* http://www.baraboo.uwc.edu/.

University of Wisconsin–Barron County
Rice Lake, Wisconsin

Freshman Application Contact Assistant Dean for Student Services, University of Wisconsin–Barron County, 1800 College Drive, Rice Lake, WI 54868-2497. *Phone:* 715-234-8024. *Fax:* 715-234-8024. *Web site:* http://www.barron.uwc.edu/.

University of Wisconsin–Fond du Lac
Fond du Lac, Wisconsin

- **State-supported** 2-year, founded 1968, part of University of Wisconsin System
- **Small-town** 182-acre campus with easy access to Milwaukee
- **Coed**

Undergraduates 506 full-time, 273 part-time. Students come from 3 states and territories; 1% are from out of state; 4% transferred in. *Retention:* 58% of full-time freshmen returned.

Faculty *Student/faculty ratio:* 19:1.

Academics *Calendar:* semesters. *Degree:* associate. *Special study options:* academic remediation for entering students, accelerated degree program, adult/continuing education programs, advanced placement credit, cooperative education, distance learning, independent study, off-campus study, part-time degree program, services for LD students, study abroad, summer session for credit.

Student Life *Campus security:* 24-hour emergency response devices.

Athletics Member NJCAA.

Standardized Tests *Required:* SAT or ACT (for admission).

Costs (2010–11) *Tuition:* state resident $4268 full-time, $178 per credit part-time; nonresident $11,589 full-time, $483 per credit part-time. Full-time tuition and fees vary according to reciprocity agreements. Part-time tuition and fees vary according to reciprocity agreements. *Required fees:* $337 full-time, $14 per credit hour part-time.

Financial Aid Of all full-time matriculated undergraduates who enrolled in 2008, 38 Federal Work-Study jobs (averaging $2100).

Applying *Options:* electronic application. *Application fee:* $35. *Required:* high school transcript.

Freshman Application Contact University of Wisconsin–Fond du Lac, 400 University Drive, Fond du Lac, WI 54935. *Phone:* 920-929-1122. *Web site:* http://www.fdl.uwc.edu/.

University of Wisconsin–Fox Valley
Menasha, Wisconsin

- **State-supported** 2-year, founded 1933, part of University of Wisconsin System
- **Urban** 33-acre campus
- **Coed,** 1,797 undergraduate students, 58% full-time, 52% women, 48% men

Undergraduates 1,037 full-time, 760 part-time. Students come from 3 states and territories; 4 other countries; 1% are from out of state.

Freshmen *Admission:* 1,166 enrolled. *Average high school GPA:* 2.5.

Faculty *Total:* 91, 34% full-time. *Student/faculty ratio:* 20:1.

Majors Liberal arts and sciences/liberal studies.

Academics *Calendar:* semesters. *Degree:* certificates and associate. *Special study options:* academic remediation for entering students, accelerated degree program, adult/continuing education programs, advanced placement credit, cooperative education, distance learning, honors programs, independent study, off-campus study, part-time degree program, services for LD students, study abroad, summer session for credit.

Library UW Fox Library with 29,000 titles, 230 serial subscriptions, an OPAC, a Web page.

Student Life *Housing:* college housing not available. *Activities and Organizations:* drama/theater group, student-run newspaper, radio and television station, choral group, Business Club, Education Club, Earth Science Club, Computer Science Club, Political Science Club. *Campus security:* 24-hour emergency response devices, late-night transport/escort service. *Student services:* personal/psychological counseling.

Athletics Member NJCAA. *Intercollegiate sports:* basketball M/W, golf M/W, soccer M/W, tennis M/W, volleyball M/W. *Intramural sports:* basketball M/W, volleyball M/W, wrestling M(c).

Standardized Tests *Required:* ACT (for admission).

Costs (2010–11) *Tuition:* state resident $4268 full-time, $189 per credit part-time; nonresident $11,251 full-time, $480 per credit part-time. Full-time tuition and fees vary according to course load and reciprocity agreements. Part-time tuition and fees vary according to course load and reciprocity agreements. *Required fees:* $264 full-time, $11 per credit part-time. *Payment plans:* installment, deferred payment. *Waivers:* minority students and senior citizens.

Applying *Options:* electronic application, early admission. *Application fee:* $44. *Required:* essay or personal statement, high school transcript. *Application deadlines:* rolling (freshmen), rolling (out-of-state freshmen), rolling (transfers). *Notification:* continuous (freshmen), continuous (transfers).

Freshman Application Contact University of Wisconsin–Fox Valley, 1478 Midway Road, Menasha, WI 54952. *Phone:* 920-832-2620. *Toll-free phone:* 888-INFOUWC. *Web site:* http://www.uwfox.uwc.edu/.

University of Wisconsin–Manitowoc
Manitowoc, Wisconsin

Freshman Application Contact Dr. Christopher Lewis, Assistant Campus Dean for Student Services, University of Wisconsin–Manitowoc, 705 Viebahn Street, Manitowoc, WI 54220-6699. *Phone:* 920-683-4707. *Fax:* 920-683-4776. *E-mail:* christopher.lewis@uwc.edu. *Web site:* http://www.manitowoc.uwc.edu/.

University of Wisconsin–Marathon County
Wausau, Wisconsin

Freshman Application Contact Dr. Nolan Beck, Director of Student Services, University of Wisconsin–Marathon County, 518 South Seventh Avenue, Wausau, WI 54401-5396. *Phone:* 715-261-6238. *Toll-free phone:* 888-367-8962. *Fax:* 715-848-3568. *Web site:* http://www.uwmc.uwc.edu/.

University of Wisconsin–Marinette
Marinette, Wisconsin

Freshman Application Contact Ms. Cynthia M. Bailey, Assistant Campus Dean for Student Services, University of Wisconsin–Marinette, 750 West Bay Shore, Marinette, WI 54143-4299. *Phone:* 715-735-4301. *E-mail:* cynthia.bailey@uwc.edu. *Web site:* http://www.uwc.edu/.

University of Wisconsin–Marshfield/Wood County
Marshfield, Wisconsin

Freshman Application Contact Mr. Jeff Meece, Director of Student Services, University of Wisconsin–Marshfield/Wood County, 2000 West 5th Street, Marshfield, WI 54449. *Phone:* 715-389-6500. *Fax:* 715-384-1718. *Web site:* http://marshfield.uwc.edu/.

University of Wisconsin–Richland
Richland Center, Wisconsin

- **State-supported** 2-year, founded 1967, part of University of Wisconsin System
- **Rural** 135-acre campus
- **Coed,** 455 undergraduate students, 61% full-time, 49% women, 51% men

Undergraduates 279 full-time, 176 part-time. *Retention:* 55% of full-time freshmen returned.

Freshmen *Admission:* 455 enrolled.

Faculty *Total:* 36, 42% full-time, 47% with terminal degrees. *Student/faculty ratio:* 18:1.

Majors Biological and physical sciences; liberal arts and sciences/liberal studies.

Academics *Calendar:* semesters. *Degree:* associate. *Special study options:* academic remediation for entering students, adult/continuing education programs, advanced placement credit, distance learning, external degree program, independent study, off-campus study, part-time degree program, services for LD students, study abroad, summer session for credit.

Library Miller Memorial Library with 40,000 titles, 200 serial subscriptions, an OPAC, a Web page.

Student Life *Housing Options:* coed. Campus housing is provided by a third party. *Activities and Organizations:* drama/theater group, Student Senate, International Club, Campus Ambassadors, Educators of the Future-Student WEA, Natural Resources Club. *Student services:* personal/psychological counseling.

Athletics *Intercollegiate sports:* basketball M/W, volleyball W. *Intramural sports:* badminton M/W, basketball M/W, football M/W, golf M/W, racquetball M/W, swimming and diving M/W, table tennis M/W, tennis M/W, volleyball M/W.

Standardized Tests *Required:* SAT or ACT (for admission). *Recommended:* ACT (for admission).

Costs (2010–11) *Tuition:* state resident $4750 full-time, $198 per credit part-time; nonresident $11,252 full-time, $489 per credit part-time. Full-time tuition and fees vary according to reciprocity agreements. Part-time tuition and fees vary according to reciprocity agreements. *Required fees:* $479 full-time. *Room and board:* room only: $3300. Room and board charges vary according to board plan. *Payment plan:* installment. *Waivers:* senior citizens.

Financial Aid Of all full-time matriculated undergraduates who enrolled in 2008, 52 Federal Work-Study jobs (averaging $2100).

Applying *Options:* electronic application. *Application fee:* $44. *Required:* high school transcript. *Required for some:* interview. *Application deadlines:* rolling (freshmen), 9/1 (transfers). *Notification:* continuous until 9/1 (freshmen), continuous until 9/1 (transfers).

Freshman Application Contact Mr. John D. Poole, Assistant Campus Dean, University of Wisconsin–Richland, 1200 Highway 14 West, Richland Center, WI 53581. *Phone:* 608-647-8422. *Fax:* 608-647-2275. *E-mail:* john.poole@uwc.edu. *Web site:* http://richland.uwc.edu/.

University of Wisconsin–Rock County
Janesville, Wisconsin

Freshman Application Contact University of Wisconsin–Rock County, 2909 Kellogg Avenue, Janesville, WI 53546-5699. *Phone:* 608-758-6523. *Toll-free phone:* 888-INFO-UWC. *Web site:* http://rock.uwc.edu/.

University of Wisconsin–Sheboygan
Sheboygan, Wisconsin

- **State-supported** 2-year, founded 1933, part of University of Wisconsin System
- **Small-town** 75-acre campus with easy access to Milwaukee
- **Coed**

Majors Liberal arts and sciences/liberal studies.

Academics *Calendar:* semesters. *Degree:* associate. *Special study options:* academic remediation for entering students, adult/continuing education programs, advanced placement credit, distance learning, English as a second language, independent study, off-campus study, part-time degree program, services for LD students, summer session for credit.

Library Battig Memorial Library.

Student Life *Housing:* college housing not available. *Campus security:* 24-hour patrols by city police.

Costs (2010–11) *Tuition:* state resident $4547 full-time; nonresident $11,530 full-time. Full-time tuition and fees vary according to reciprocity agreements. Part-time tuition and fees vary according to reciprocity agreements. *Payment plan:* installment.

Financial Aid Of all full-time matriculated undergraduates who enrolled in 2008, 30 Federal Work-Study jobs (averaging $2100).

Applying *Options:* electronic application. *Application fee:* $44. *Required:* high school transcript. *Required for some:* interview. *Application deadlines:* rolling (freshmen), rolling (transfers).

Freshman Application Contact University of Wisconsin–Sheboygan, One University Drive, Sheboygan, WI 53081-4789. *Phone:* 920-459-6633. *Web site:* http://www.sheboygan.uwc.edu/.

University of Wisconsin–Washington County
West Bend, Wisconsin

Freshman Application Contact Mr. Dan Cebrario, Associate Director of Student Services, University of Wisconsin–Washington County, Student Services Office, 400 University Drive, West Bend, WI 53095. *Phone:* 262-335-5201. *Fax:* 262-335-5220. *E-mail:* dan.cibrario@uwc.edu. *Web site:* http://www.washington.uwc.edu/.

University of Wisconsin–Waukesha
Waukesha, Wisconsin

- **State-supported** 2-year, founded 1966, part of University of Wisconsin System
- **Suburban** 86-acre campus with easy access to Milwaukee
- **Coed,** 2,132 undergraduate students, 52% full-time, 48% women, 52% men

Undergraduates 1,099 full-time, 1,033 part-time. Students come from 2 other countries; 1% are from out of state; 8% transferred in.

Freshmen *Admission:* 1,391 enrolled.

Faculty *Total:* 91, 66% full-time, 49% with terminal degrees. *Student/faculty ratio:* 23:1.

Majors Liberal arts and sciences/liberal studies.

Academics *Calendar:* semesters. *Degree:* associate. *Special study options:* academic remediation for entering students, advanced placement credit, distance learning, honors programs, internships, off-campus study, part-time degree program, services for LD students, study abroad, summer session for credit.

Library University of Wisconsin-Waukesha Library plus 1 other with 61,000 titles, 300 serial subscriptions.

Student Life *Housing:* college housing not available. *Activities and Organizations:* drama/theater group, student-run newspaper, choral group, Student Government, Student Activities Committee, Campus Crusade, Phi Theta Kappa, Circle K. *Campus security:* part-time patrols by trained security personnel. *Student services:* personal/psychological counseling.

Athletics Member NJCAA. *Intercollegiate sports:* basketball M/W, golf M/W, soccer M/W, tennis M/W, volleyball W. *Intramural sports:* basketball M, bowling M/W, football M/W, skiing (downhill) M/W, table tennis M/W, volleyball M(c).

Standardized Tests *Required:* SAT or ACT (for admission).

Costs (2011–12) *Tuition:* state resident $4576 full-time, $192 per credit hour part-time; nonresident $11,559 full-time, $483 per credit hour part-time. Full-time tuition and fees vary according to course load and reciprocity agreements. Part-time tuition and fees vary according to course load and reciprocity agreements. *Payment plan:* installment. *Waivers:* senior citizens.

Financial Aid Of all full-time matriculated undergraduates who enrolled in 2008, 63 Federal Work-Study jobs (averaging $2100).

Applying *Options:* electronic application, early admission, deferred entrance. *Application fee:* $44. *Required:* high school transcript. *Required for some:* interview. *Recommended:* essay or personal statement, admission interview may be recommended. *Application deadline:* rolling (freshmen). *Notification:* continuous (freshmen).

Freshman Application Contact Ms. Deb Kusick, Admissions Specialist, University of Wisconsin–Waukesha, 1500 North University Drive, Waukesha, WI 53188-2799. *Phone:* 262-521-5200. *Fax:* 262-521-5530. *E-mail:* deborah.kusick@uwc.edu. *Web site:* http://www.waukesha.uwc.edu/.

Waukesha County Technical College
Pewaukee, Wisconsin

- **State and locally supported** 2-year, founded 1923, part of Wisconsin Technical College System
- **Suburban** 137-acre campus with easy access to Milwaukee
- **Coed,** 8,102 undergraduate students, 31% full-time, 52% women, 48% men

Undergraduates 2,527 full-time, 5,575 part-time. 4% Black or African American, non-Hispanic/Latino; 12% Hispanic/Latino; 1% Asian, non-Hispanic/Latino; 0.1% Native Hawaiian or other Pacific Islander, non-Hispanic/Latino; 0.5% American Indian or Alaska Native, non-Hispanic/Latino; 14% Race/ethnicity unknown.

Freshmen *Admission:* 715 enrolled.

Faculty *Total:* 885, 21% full-time.

Majors Accounting; administrative assistant and secretarial science; architectural drafting and CAD/CADD; autobody/collision and repair technology; automobile/automotive mechanics technology; computer and information sciences and support services related; computer installation and repair technology; computer programming; computer systems analysis; computer systems networking and telecommunications; criminal justice/police science; dental hygiene; early childhood education; electrical, electronic and communications engineering technology; electrical/electronics drafting and CAD/CADD; electromechanical and instrumentation and maintenance technologies related; financial planning and services; fire prevention and safety technology; graphic communications; graphic design; hospitality administration; interior design; manufacturing engineering technology; marketing/marketing management; mechanical drafting and CAD/CADD; mental and social health services and allied professions related; multi/interdisciplinary studies related; operations management; registered nursing/registered nurse; restaurant, culinary, and catering management; retailing; surgical technology; teacher assistant/aide; telecommunications technology.

Academics *Calendar:* semesters. *Degree:* certificates, diplomas, and associate. *Special study options:* academic remediation for entering students, adult/continuing education programs, advanced placement credit, cooperative education, distance learning, English as a second language, part-time degree program, services for LD students, student-designed majors, summer session for credit.

Student Life *Housing:* college housing not available. *Campus security:* patrols by police officers 8 am to 10 pm.

Costs (2010–11) *Tuition:* state resident $3180 full-time, $106 per credit hour part-time; nonresident $4770 full-time, $159 per credit hour part-time. Full-time tuition and fees vary according to program. Part-time tuition and fees vary according to program. *Required fees:* $191 full-time, $6 per credit hour part-time. *Payment plans:* installment, deferred payment. *Waivers:* senior citizens.

Financial Aid Of all full-time matriculated undergraduates who enrolled in 2009, 34 Federal Work-Study jobs (averaging $2500). 100 state and other part-time jobs (averaging $2000).

Applying *Application fee:* $30. *Required:* high school transcript. *Required for some:* interview. *Application deadlines:* rolling (freshmen), rolling (transfers).

Freshman Application Contact Waukesha County Technical College, 800 Main Street, Pewaukee, WI 53072-4601. *Phone:* 262-691-5464. *Toll-free phone:* 888-892-WCTC. *Web site:* http://www.wctc.edu/.

Western Technical College

La Crosse, Wisconsin

Freshman Application Contact Ms. Jane Wells, Manager of Admissions, Registration, and Records, Western Technical College, PO Box 908, La Crosse, WI 54602-0908. *Phone:* 608-785-9158. *Toll-free phone:* 800-322-9982 (in-state); 800-248-9982 (out-of-state). *Fax:* 608-785-9094. *E-mail:* mildes@wwtc.edu. *Web site:* http://www.westerntc.edu/.

Wisconsin Indianhead Technical College

Shell Lake, Wisconsin

- **District-supported** 2-year, founded 1912, part of Wisconsin Technical College System
- **Urban** 113-acre campus
- **Endowment** $2.3 million
- **Coed,** 3,925 undergraduate students, 44% full-time, 59% women, 41% men

Undergraduates 1,724 full-time, 2,201 part-time. Students come from 11 states and territories; 7% are from out of state. *Retention:* 66% of full-time freshmen returned.

Freshmen *Admission:* 826 enrolled.

Faculty *Total:* 581, 26% full-time. *Student/faculty ratio:* 10:1.

Majors Accounting; administrative assistant and secretarial science; architectural engineering technology; business administration and management; computer installation and repair technology; computer systems networking and telecommunications; corrections; court reporting; criminal justice/police science; early childhood education; emergency medical technology (EMT paramedic); energy management and systems technology; finance; heating, ventilation, air conditioning and refrigeration engineering technology; marketing/marketing management; mechanical drafting and CAD/CADD; medical administrative assistant and medical secretary; mental and social health services and allied professions related; multi/interdisciplinary studies related; occupational therapist assistant; operations management; registered nursing/registered nurse; web page, digital/multimedia and information resources design.

Academics *Calendar:* semesters. *Degree:* certificates, diplomas, and associate.

Student Life *Housing:* college housing not available. *Student services:* health clinic.

Costs (2010–11) *Tuition:* state resident $3392 full-time, $106 per credit part-time; nonresident $5088 full-time, $159 per credit part-time. Full-time tuition and fees vary according to course level, course load, degree level, program, and reciprocity agreements. Part-time tuition and fees vary according to course level, course load, degree level, program, and reciprocity agreements. *Required fees:* $128 full-time, $4 per course part-time. *Payment plan:* installment.

Applying *Options:* electronic application. *Application fee:* $30. *Application deadline:* rolling (freshmen).

Freshman Application Contact Mr. Steve Bitzer, Vice President, Student Affairs and Campus Administrator, Wisconsin Indianhead Technical College, 2100 Beaser Avenue, Ashland, WI 54806. *Phone:* 715-468-2815 Ext. 3149. *Toll-free phone:* 800-243-9482. *Fax:* 715-468-2819. *E-mail:* Steve.Bitzer@witc.edu. *Web site:* http://www.witc.edu/.

WYOMING

Casper College

Casper, Wyoming

- **State and locally supported** 2-year, founded 1945, part of Wyoming Community College Commission
- **Small-town** 200-acre campus
- **Coed,** 4,393 undergraduate students, 51% full-time, 58% women, 42% men

Undergraduates 2,223 full-time, 2,170 part-time. Students come from 39 states and territories; 21 other countries; 8% are from out of state; 1% Black or African American, non-Hispanic/Latino; 4% Hispanic/Latino; 0.5% Asian, non-Hispanic/Latino; 0.2% Native Hawaiian or other Pacific Islander, non-Hispanic/Latino; 1% American Indian or Alaska Native, non-Hispanic/Latino; 0.6% Race/ethnicity unknown; 1% international; 3% transferred in; 15% live on campus. *Retention:* 62% of full-time freshmen returned.

Freshmen *Admission:* 1,172 applied, 1,172 admitted, 789 enrolled. *Average high school GPA:* 3. *Test scores:* SAT critical reading scores over 500: 36%; SAT math scores over 500: 28%; SAT writing scores over 500: 18%; ACT scores over 18: 74%; SAT math scores over 600: 11%; ACT scores over 24: 18%; ACT scores over 30: 1%.

Faculty *Total:* 251, 60% full-time, 17% with terminal degrees. *Student/faculty ratio:* 16:1.

Majors Accounting; accounting technology and bookkeeping; acting; administrative assistant and secretarial science; agricultural business and management; agriculture; airline pilot and flight crew; animal sciences; anthropology; art; art teacher education; athletic training; autobody/collision and repair technology; automobile/automotive mechanics technology; biology/biological sciences; business administration and management; business automation/technology/data entry; chemistry; clinical laboratory science/medical technology; computer programming; construction management; construction trades; criminal justice/law enforcement administration; crisis/emergency/disaster management; dance; diesel mechanics technology; drafting and design technology; economics; electrical, electronic and communications engineering technology; elementary education; emergency medical technology (EMT paramedic); energy management and systems technology; engineering; English; entrepreneurship; environmental science; fine/studio arts; fire science/firefighting; foreign languages and literatures; forensic science and technology; general studies; geographic information science and cartography; geology/earth science; graphic design; health aide; history; hospitality administration; industrial mechanics and maintenance technology; international relations and affairs; kindergarten/preschool education; legal assistant/paralegal; liberal arts and sciences/liberal studies; machine tool technology; management information systems; manufacturing engineering technology; marketing/marketing management; mathematics; mining technology; museum studies; music; musical theater; music performance; music teacher education; nutrition sciences; occupational therapist assistant; pharmacy technician; phlebotomy technology; photography; physical education teaching and coaching; physics; political science and government; pre-dentistry studies; pre-law studies; premedical studies; pre-occupational therapy; pre-optometry; pre-pharmacy studies; pre-physical therapy; pre-veterinary studies; psychology; radiologic technology/science; range science and management; registered nursing/registered nurse; respiratory care therapy; retailing; robotics technology; social studies teacher education; social work; sociology; speech communication and rhetoric; statistics related; substance abuse/addiction counseling; teacher assistant/aide; technology/industrial arts teacher education; theater design and technology; water quality and wastewater treatment management and recycling technology; web/multimedia management and webmaster; web page, digital/multimedia and information resources design; welding technology; wildlife, fish and wildlands science and management; women's studies.

Academics *Calendar:* semesters. *Degree:* certificates and associate. *Special study options:* academic remediation for entering students, accelerated degree program, advanced placement credit, cooperative education, distance learning, English as a second language, honors programs, independent study, internships, off-campus study, part-time degree program, services for LD students, summer session for credit.

Library Goodstein Library with 124,000 titles, 385 serial subscriptions, an OPAC, a Web page.

Student Life *Housing Options:* coed. Campus housing is university owned. *Activities and Organizations:* drama/theater group, student-run newspaper, choral group, Student Senate, Student Activities Board, Agriculture Club, Theater Club, Phi Theta Kappa. *Campus security:* 24-hour patrols, late-night transport/escort service. *Student services:* health clinic, personal/psychological counseling.

Athletics Member NCAA, NJCAA. All NCAA Division I. *Intercollegiate sports:* basketball M(s)/W(s), equestrian sports M/W, volleyball W(s). *Intramural sports:* basketball M/W, bowling M/W, football M/W, golf M/W, racquetball M/W, soccer M/W, softball M/W, tennis M/W.

Costs (2010–11) *Tuition:* state resident $1632 full-time, $68 per semester hour part-time; nonresident $4896 full-time, $204 per semester hour part-time. Part-time tuition and fees vary according to course load. *Required fees:* $216 full-time, $9 per semester hour part-time. *Room and board:* $4650. Room and board charges vary according to board plan and housing facility. *Payment plan:* installment. *Waivers:* senior citizens and employees or children of employees.

Financial Aid Of all full-time matriculated undergraduates who enrolled in 2009, 80 Federal Work-Study jobs (averaging $2000).

Applying *Options:* electronic application, early admission. *Required:* high school transcript. *Application deadlines:* 8/15 (freshmen), 8/15 (transfers). *Notification:* continuous until 8/15 (freshmen), continuous until 8/15 (transfers).

Freshman Application Contact Mrs. Kyla Foltz, Admissions Coordinator, Casper College, 125 College Drive, Casper, WY 82601. *Phone:* 307-268-2111. *Toll-free phone:* 800-442-2963. *Fax:* 307-268-2611. *E-mail:* kfoltz@caspercollege.edu. *Web site:* http://www.caspercollege.edu/.

Central Wyoming College

Riverton, Wyoming

- **State and locally supported** 2-year, founded 1966, part of Wyoming Community College Commission
- **Small-town** 200-acre campus
- **Endowment** $9.6 million
- **Coed,** 2,407 undergraduate students, 40% full-time, 59% women, 41% men

Undergraduates 954 full-time, 1,453 part-time. Students come from 47 states and territories; 12 other countries; 13% are from out of state; 0.9% Black or African American, non-Hispanic/Latino; 5% Hispanic/Latino; 0.4% Asian, non-Hispanic/Latino; 0.3% Native Hawaiian or other Pacific Islander, non-Hispanic/Latino; 13% American Indian or Alaska Native, non-Hispanic/Latino; 2% Two or more races, non-Hispanic/Latino; 2% Race/ethnicity unknown; 1% international; 7% transferred in; 8% live on campus. *Retention:* 53% of full-time freshmen returned.

Freshmen *Admission:* 522 applied, 522 admitted, 424 enrolled. *Average high school GPA:* 2.97. *Test scores:* SAT critical reading scores over 500: 43%; SAT math scores over 500: 57%; ACT scores over 18: 65%; SAT critical reading scores over 600: 21%; SAT math scores over 600: 7%; ACT scores over 24: 16%; ACT scores over 30: 1%.

Faculty *Total:* 200, 52% full-time, 28% with terminal degrees. *Student/faculty ratio:* 11:1.

Majors Accounting; accounting technology and bookkeeping; acting; administrative assistant and secretarial science; agricultural and domestic animal services related; agricultural business and management; American Indian/Native American studies; area studies related; art; athletic training; automobile/automotive mechanics technology; biology/biological sciences; business administration and management; business automation/technology/data entry; business/commerce; carpentry; child-care and support services management; commercial photography; computer science; computer technology/computer systems technology; criminal justice/law enforcement administration; culinary arts; customer service support/call center/teleservice operation; dental assisting; dramatic/theater arts; early childhood education; elementary education; emergency medical technology (EMT paramedic); engineering; English; environmental/environmental health engineering; environmental science; equestrian studies; fire science/firefighting; general studies; geology/earth science; graphic design; health services/allied health/health sciences; homeland security, law enforcement, firefighting and protective services related; hotel/motel administration; international/global studies; manufacturing engineering; mathematics; medical office assistant; music; occupational safety and health technology; office occupations and clerical services; parks, recreation and leisure; parks, recreation and leisure facilities management; physical sciences; pre-law studies; psychology; radio and television; range science and management; registered nursing/registered nurse; rehabilitation and therapeutic professions related; secondary education; selling skills and sales; social sciences; teacher assistant/aide; theater design and technology; welding technology.

Academics *Calendar:* semesters. *Degree:* certificates, diplomas, and associate. *Special study options:* academic remediation for entering students, adult/continuing education programs, advanced placement credit, cooperative education, distance learning, double majors, English as a second language, honors programs, independent study, off-campus study, part-time degree program, services for LD students, summer session for credit.

Library Central Wyoming College Library with 54,974 titles, 2,940 serial subscriptions, 1,450 audiovisual materials, an OPAC, a Web page.

Student Life *Housing Options:* coed. Campus housing is university owned. *Activities and Organizations:* drama/theater group, student-run radio and television station, choral group, Multi-Cultural Club, La Vida Nueva Club, Fellowship of College Christians, Quality Leaders, Science Club. *Campus security:* 24-hour emergency response devices, late-night transport/escort service, controlled dormitory access. *Student services:* personal/psychological counseling.

Athletics Member NJCAA. *Intercollegiate sports:* basketball M(s)/W(s), equestrian sports M(s)/W(s), volleyball W(s). *Intramural sports:* badminton M/W, basketball M/W, football M/W, rock climbing M/W, skiing (cross-country) M/W, skiing (downhill) M/W, soccer M/W, softball M/W, swimming and diving M/W, table tennis M/W, tennis M/W, ultimate Frisbee M/W, volleyball M/W, weight lifting M/W.

Costs (2011–12) *Tuition:* state resident $1704 full-time, $71 per credit part-time; nonresident $5112 full-time, $213 per credit part-time. Full-time tuition and fees vary according to course load, program, and reciprocity agreements. Part-time tuition and fees vary according to course load, program, and reciprocity agreements. *Required fees:* $504 full-time, $21 per credit part-time. *Room and board:* $4275; room only: $2075. Room and board charges vary according to board plan and housing facility. *Payment plans:* installment, deferred payment. *Waivers:* senior citizens and employees or children of employees.

Financial Aid Of all full-time matriculated undergraduates who enrolled in 2009, 596 applied for aid, 516 were judged to have need. 57 Federal Work-Study jobs (averaging $1954). *Financial aid deadline:* 6/30.

Applying *Options:* electronic application, early admission, deferred entrance. *Recommended:* high school transcript. *Application deadlines:* rolling (freshmen), rolling (out-of-state freshmen), rolling (transfers).

Freshman Application Contact Mrs. Brenda Barlow, Admissions Assistant, Central Wyoming College, 2660 Peck Avenue, Riverton, WY 82501-2273. *Phone:* 307-855-2119. *Toll-free phone:* 800-735-8418 Ext. 2119. *Fax:* 307-855-2093. *E-mail:* admit@cwc.edu. *Web site:* http://www.cwc.edu/.

Eastern Wyoming College

Torrington, Wyoming

- **State and locally supported** 2-year, founded 1948, part of Wyoming Community College Commission
- **Rural** 40-acre campus
- **Coed**

Undergraduates 624 full-time, 767 part-time.

Faculty *Student/faculty ratio:* 14:1.

Academics *Calendar:* semesters. *Degree:* certificates, diplomas, and associate. *Special study options:* academic remediation for entering students, accelerated degree program, adult/continuing education programs, advanced placement credit, cooperative education, distance learning, English as a second language, honors programs, independent study, internships, part-time degree program, services for LD students, student-designed majors, summer session for credit.

Student Life *Campus security:* 24-hour emergency response devices, controlled dormitory access.

Athletics Member NJCAA.

Costs (2010–11) *Tuition:* state resident $1632 full-time, $68 per credit hour part-time; nonresident $4896 full-time, $204 per credit hour part-time. Full-time tuition and fees vary according to location. Part-time tuition and fees vary according to location. *Required fees:* $384 full-time, $16 per credit hour part-time. *Room and board:* $3806. Room and board charges vary according to housing facility.

Financial Aid Of all full-time matriculated undergraduates who enrolled in 2009, 100 Federal Work-Study jobs (averaging $700). 60 state and other part-time jobs (averaging $700).

Applying *Options:* electronic application, early admission. *Recommended:* high school transcript.

Freshman Application Contact Dr. Rex Cogdill, Vice President for Students Services, Eastern Wyoming College, 3200 West C Street, Torrington, WY 82240. *Phone:* 307-532-8257. *Toll-free phone:* 800-658-3195. *Fax:* 307-532-8222. *E-mail:* rex.cogdill@ewc.wy.edu. *Web site:* http://www.ewc.wy.edu/.

Laramie County Community College

Cheyenne, Wyoming

- **District-supported** 2-year, founded 1968, part of Wyoming Community College Commission
- **Small-town** 271-acre campus
- **Endowment** $14.5 million
- **Coed,** 4,794 undergraduate students, 48% full-time, 60% women, 40% men

Undergraduates 2,299 full-time, 2,495 part-time. Students come from 36 states and territories; 26 other countries; 14% are from out of state; 3% Black or African American, non-Hispanic/Latino; 8% Hispanic/Latino; 0.3% Asian, non-Hispanic/Latino; 0.1% Native Hawaiian or other Pacific Islander, non-Hispanic/Latino; 0.9% American Indian or Alaska Native, non-Hispanic/Latino; 0.1% Two or more races, non-Hispanic/Latino; 4% Race/ethnicity unknown; 2% international; 5% transferred in; 6% live on campus. *Retention:* 56% of full-time freshmen returned.

Freshmen *Admission:* 1,482 applied, 1,482 admitted, 409 enrolled. *Average high school GPA:* 2.89. *Test scores:* ACT scores over 18: 68%; ACT scores over 24: 16%; ACT scores over 30: 1%.

Faculty *Total:* 373, 24% full-time, 4% with terminal degrees. *Student/faculty ratio:* 17:1.

Majors Accounting; agribusiness; agricultural business technology; agricultural production; agriculture; anthropology; art; autobody/collision and repair technology; automobile/automotive mechanics technology; biological and physical sciences; biology/biological sciences; business administration and management; business/commerce; chemistry; computer programming; computer science; corrections; criminal justice/law enforcement administration; dental hygiene; diagnostic medical sonography and ultrasound technology; diesel mechanics technology; digital communication and media/multimedia; drafting and design technology; early childhood education; economics; education; emergency medical technology (EMT paramedic); energy management and systems technology; engineering; English; entrepreneurship; equestrian studies; fire science/firefighting; heating, air conditioning, ventilation and refrigeration maintenance technology; history; homeland security, law enforcement, firefighting and protective services related; humanities; human services; legal assistant/paralegal; mass communication/media; mathematics; multi/interdisciplinary studies related; music; physical education teaching and coaching; physical therapy technology; political science and government; pre-law studies; pre-pharmacy studies; psychology; public administration; radiologic technology/science; registered nursing/registered nurse; religious studies; social sciences; sociology; Spanish; speech communication and rhetoric; surgical technology; wildlife, fish and wildlands science and management.

Academics *Calendar:* semesters. *Degree:* certificates and associate. *Special study options:* academic remediation for entering students, adult/continuing education programs, advanced placement credit, cooperative education, distance learning, double majors, English as a second language, honors programs, independent study, internships, off-campus study, part-time degree program, services for LD students, summer session for credit. *ROTC:* Army (c), Air Force (c).

Library Ludden Library plus 1 other with 57,385 titles, 198 serial subscriptions, 5,580 audiovisual materials, an OPAC, a Web page.

Student Life *Housing Options:* coed. Campus housing is university owned. *Activities and Organizations:* drama/theater group, student-run newspaper, choral group. *Campus security:* 24-hour emergency response devices and patrols, late-night transport/escort service, controlled dormitory access. *Student services:* personal/psychological counseling.

Athletics Member NJCAA. *Intercollegiate sports:* basketball M(s), cheerleading M(s)/W(s), equestrian sports M(s)/W(s), soccer M(s)/W(s), volleyball W(s). *Intramural sports:* basketball M/W, equestrian sports M/W, golf M/W, racquetball M/W, rock climbing M/W, skiing (cross-country) M/W, soccer M/W, softball M/W, table tennis M/W, ultimate Frisbee M/W, volleyball M/W.

Costs (2010–11) *One-time required fee:* $20. *Tuition:* state resident $1632 full-time, $68 per credit hour part-time; nonresident $4896 full-time, $204 per credit hour part-time. Part-time tuition and fees vary according to course load. *Required fees:* $840 full-time, $35 per credit hour part-time. *Room and board:* $7140; room only: $4527. Room and board charges vary according to board plan and housing facility. *Payment plan:* installment. *Waivers:* senior citizens and employees or children of employees.

Applying *Options:* electronic application, deferred entrance. *Application fee:* $20. *Required for some:* high school transcript, interview. *Application deadlines:* rolling (freshmen), rolling (out-of-state freshmen), rolling (transfers). *Notification:* continuous (freshmen), continuous (out-of-state freshmen), continuous (transfers).

Freshman Application Contact Ms. Holly Allison, Director of Admissions, Laramie County Community College, 1400 East College Drive, Cheyenne, WY 82007. *Phone:* 307-778-1117. *Toll-free phone:* 800-522-2993 Ext. 1357. *Fax:* 307-778-1360. *E-mail:* learnmore@lccc.wy.edu. *Web site:* http://www.lccc.wy.edu/.

Northwest College
Powell, Wyoming

- **State and locally supported** 2-year, founded 1946, part of Wyoming Community College Commission
- **Rural** 124-acre campus
- **Endowment** $6.1 million
- **Coed,** 2,111 undergraduate students, 67% full-time, 59% women, 41% men

Undergraduates 1,411 full-time, 700 part-time. Students come from 35 states and territories; 20 other countries; 24% are from out of state; 6% transferred in. *Retention:* 58% of full-time freshmen returned.

Freshmen *Admission:* 550 enrolled.

Faculty *Total:* 154, 51% full-time. *Student/faculty ratio:* 16:1.

Majors Accounting; administrative assistant and secretarial science; agribusiness; agricultural communication/journalism; agricultural production; agricultural teacher education; animal sciences; anthropology; archeology; art; athletic training; biology/biological sciences; broadcast journalism; business administration and management; business/commerce; CAD/CADD drafting/design technology; chemistry; cinematography and film/video production; commercial and advertising art; commercial photography; criminal justice/law enforcement administration; crop production; desktop publishing and digital imaging design; electrician; elementary education; engineering; English; equestrian studies; farm and ranch management; French; general studies; graphic and printing equipment operation/production; health and physical education/fitness; health/medical preparatory programs related; health services/allied health/health sciences; history; journalism; kindergarten/preschool education; liberal arts and sciences/liberal studies; mathematics; music; natural resources management and policy; occupational safety and health technology; parks, recreation and leisure; physics; playwriting and screenwriting; political science and government; pre-pharmacy studies; psychology; radio and television; radio, television, and digital communication related; range science and management; registered nursing/registered nurse; secondary education; social

sciences; sociology; Spanish; speech communication and rhetoric; veterinary/animal health technology; visual and performing arts related; welding technology.

Academics *Calendar:* semesters. *Degree:* certificates and associate. *Special study options:* academic remediation for entering students, adult/continuing education programs, advanced placement credit, cooperative education, distance learning, double majors, English as a second language, external degree program, independent study, internships, part-time degree program, services for LD students, study abroad, summer session for credit.

Library John Taggart Hinckley Library with 50,349 titles, 44,908 serial subscriptions, 93,586 audiovisual materials, an OPAC, a Web page.

Student Life *Housing:* on-campus residence required for freshman year. *Options:* coed, women-only, disabled students. Campus housing is university owned. Freshman campus housing is guaranteed. *Activities and Organizations:* drama/theater group, student-run newspaper, radio and television station, choral group. *Campus security:* 24-hour emergency response devices and patrols, late-night transport/escort service, controlled dormitory access. *Student services:* health clinic, personal/psychological counseling.

Athletics Member NJCAA. *Intercollegiate sports:* basketball M(s)/W(s), equestrian sports M(s)/W(s), soccer M(s)/W(s), volleyball W(s), wrestling M(s). *Intramural sports:* basketball M/W, football M/W, golf M/W, racquetball M/W, softball M/W, tennis M/W, volleyball M/W.

Standardized Tests *Recommended:* SAT or ACT (for admission), ACT COMPASS.

Costs (2010–11) *Tuition:* state resident $1632 full-time, $68 per credit hour part-time; nonresident $4896 full-time, $204 per credit hour part-time. Full-time tuition and fees vary according to course load, location, and program. Part-time tuition and fees vary according to course load, location, and program. *Required fees:* $614 full-time, $21 per credit hour part-time. *Room and board:* $4202; room only: $1890. Room and board charges vary according to board plan and housing facility. *Payment plan:* installment. *Waivers:* children of alumni, senior citizens, and employees or children of employees.

Financial Aid Of all full-time matriculated undergraduates who enrolled in 2009, 115 Federal Work-Study jobs (averaging $2700). 215 state and other part-time jobs (averaging $2700).

Applying *Options:* electronic application. *Required:* high school transcript. *Required for some:* minimum 2.0 GPA. *Recommended:* minimum 2.0 GPA. *Application deadlines:* rolling (freshmen), rolling (out-of-state freshmen), rolling (transfers). *Notification:* continuous (freshmen), continuous (out-of-state freshmen), continuous (transfers).

Freshman Application Contact Mr. West Hernandez, Admissions Manager, Northwest College, 231 West 6th Street, Orendorff Building 1, Powell, WY 82435-1898. *Phone:* 307-754-6103. *Toll-free phone:* 800-560-4692. *Fax:* 307-754-6249. *E-mail:* west.hernandez@northwestcollege.edu. *Web site:* http://www.northwestcollege.edu/.

Sheridan College
Sheridan, Wyoming

- **State and locally supported** 2-year, founded 1948, part of Wyoming Community College Commission
- **Small-town** 124-acre campus
- **Endowment** $17.5 million
- **Coed,** 3,940 undergraduate students, 37% full-time, 48% women, 52% men

Undergraduates 1,447 full-time, 2,493 part-time. Students come from 29 states and territories; 12 other countries; 18% are from out of state; 4% transferred in; 12% live on campus.

Freshmen *Admission:* 586 admitted, 586 enrolled.

Faculty *Total:* 168, 54% full-time, 11% with terminal degrees. *Student/faculty ratio:* 21:1.

Majors Administrative assistant and secretarial science; agricultural business and management; agriculture; agriculture and agriculture operations related; art; biological and physical sciences; biology/biological sciences; building construction technology; business/commerce; CAD/CADD drafting/design technology; communication and journalism related; computer and information sciences; computer and information systems security; criminal justice/safety; culinary arts; dental hygiene; diesel mechanics technology; dramatic/theater arts; early childhood education; electrical and electronic engineering technologies related; elementary education; engineering; English; environmental engineering technology; foreign languages and literatures; general studies; health and physical education/fitness; health services/allied health/health sciences; history; horticultural science; hospitality administration; information science/studies; kinesiology and exercise science; machine tool technology; massage therapy; mathematics; mining technology; multi/interdisciplinary studies related; music; precision production related; psychology; range science and management; registered nursing/registered nurse; secondary education; social sciences; surveying technology; teacher assistant/aide; turf and turfgrass management; web/multimedia management and webmaster; welding technology.

Academics *Calendar:* semesters. *Degree:* certificates and associate. *Special study options:* academic remediation for entering students, advanced placement credit, cooperative education, distance learning, double majors, English as a second language, independent study, internships, off-campus study, part-time degree program, services for LD students, summer session for credit.

Library Griffith Memorial Library plus 1 other with 34,589 titles, 108 serial subscriptions, 6,869 audiovisual materials, an OPAC, a Web page.

Student Life *Housing Options:* coed, women-only, disabled students. Campus housing is university owned. *Activities and Organizations:* drama/theater group, student-run newspaper, choral group, student government, Phi Theta Kappa, Art Club, Nursing Club, Police Science Club. *Campus security:* 24-hour emergency response devices, student patrols, controlled dormitory access, night patrols by certified officers. *Student services:* personal/psychological counseling, legal services.

Athletics Member NJCAA. *Intercollegiate sports:* basketball M(s)/W(s), cross-country running M(s)/W(s), volleyball W(s). *Intramural sports:* basketball M/W, bowling M/W, soccer M/W, softball M/W, table tennis M/W, tennis M/W, ultimate Frisbee M/W, volleyball M/W.

Costs (2011–12) *Tuition:* state resident $1704 full-time, $71 per credit hour part-time; nonresident $5112 full-time, $213 per credit hour part-time. Full-time tuition and fees vary according to course load, location, program, and reciprocity agreements. Part-time tuition and fees vary according to course load, location, program, and reciprocity agreements. *Required fees:* $690 full-time, $23 per credit hour part-time. *Room and board:* $4900. Room and board charges vary according to board plan, housing facility, and location. *Payment plan:* installment. *Waivers:* senior citizens and employees or children of employees.

Financial Aid Of all full-time matriculated undergraduates who enrolled in 2009, 92 Federal Work-Study jobs (averaging $1798).

Applying *Options:* electronic application, early admission, deferred entrance. *Required for some:* high school transcript. *Recommended:* high school transcript. *Application deadlines:* rolling (freshmen), rolling (transfers). *Notification:* continuous (freshmen), continuous (transfers).

Freshman Application Contact Mr. Zane Garstad, Director of Enrollment Services, Sheridan College, PO Box 1500, Sheridan, WY 82801-1500. *Phone:* 307-674-6446 Ext. 2002. *Toll-free phone:* 800-913-9139 Ext. 2002. *Fax:* 307-674-7205. *E-mail:* admissions@sheridan.edu. *Web site:* http://www.sheridan.edu/.

Western Wyoming Community College

Rock Springs, Wyoming

- **State and locally supported** 2-year, founded 1959
- **Small-town** 342-acre campus
- **Endowment** $9.3 million
- **Coed**

Undergraduates 1,242 full-time, 2,878 part-time. 11% live on campus.

Faculty *Student/faculty ratio:* 18:1.

Academics *Calendar:* semesters. *Degree:* certificates, diplomas, and associate. *Special study options:* academic remediation for entering students, adult/continuing education programs, advanced placement credit, cooperative education, distance learning, double majors, English as a second language, honors programs, independent study, internships, part-time degree program, services for LD students, summer session for credit.

Student Life *Campus security:* 24-hour emergency response devices and patrols, late-night transport/escort service, controlled dormitory access, patrols by trained security personnel from 4 pm to 8 am, 24-hour patrols on weekends and holidays.

Athletics Member NJCAA.

Costs (2010–11) *Tuition:* $84 per credit hour part-time; state resident $1994 full-time, $118 per credit hour part-time; nonresident $5258 full-time, $220 per credit hour part-time. Full-time tuition and fees vary according to reciprocity agreements. Part-time tuition and fees vary according to course load and reciprocity agreements. *Room and board:* $3870; room only: $2072. Room and board charges vary according to board plan and housing facility.

Financial Aid Of all full-time matriculated undergraduates who enrolled in 2009, 20 Federal Work-Study jobs (averaging $1500).

Applying *Options:* electronic application, early admission, deferred entrance. *Required:* high school transcript.

Freshman Application Contact Director of Admissions, Western Wyoming Community College, PO Box 428, Rock Springs, WY 82902-0428. *Phone:* 307-382-1647382-1647. *Toll-free phone:* 800-226-1181. *Fax:* 307-382-1636382-1636. *E-mail:* admissions@wwcc.wy.eduadmissions@wwcc.wy.edu. *Web site:* http://www.wwcc.wy.edu/.

WyoTech

Laramie, Wyoming

Director of Admissions Director of Admissions, WyoTech, 4373 North Third Street, Laramie, WY 82072-9519. *Phone:* 307-742-3776. *Toll-free phone:* 800-521-7158. *Fax:* 307-721-4854. *Web site:* http://www.wyotech.com/.

CANADA

CANADA

Southern Alberta Institute of Technology

Calgary, Alberta, Canada

- **Province-supported** primarily 2-year, founded 1916
- **Urban** 96-acre campus
- **Coed,** 7,672 undergraduate students, 91% full-time, 42% women, 58% men

Undergraduates 6,954 full-time, 718 part-time.

Faculty *Total:* 962.

Majors Business administration and management; business administration, management and operations related; construction management; geography related; information science/studies; petroleum engineering.

Academics *Calendar:* trimesters. *Degrees:* certificates, diplomas, associate, and bachelor's. *Special study options:* cooperative education, distance learning, independent study, internships, off-campus study, services for LD students.

Library SAIT Library with 135,000 titles, 100 serial subscriptions, an OPAC, a Web page.

Student Life *Housing Options:* coed, disabled students. Campus housing is university owned. *Activities and Organizations:* drama/theater group, student-run newspaper, radio and television station, SAIT Petroleum Society, Business Student's Association, Global Passport, Environmental Technology Students Organization, Civil Engineering Technology Concrete Toboggan. *Campus security:* 24-hour emergency response devices and patrols, late-night transport/escort service. *Student services:* health clinic, personal/psychological counseling.

Athletics *Intercollegiate sports:* basketball M(s)/W(s), cross-country running M/W, ice hockey M(s)/W(s), soccer M(s)/W(s), volleyball M(s)/W(s). *Intramural sports:* basketball M/W, football M/W, ice hockey M/W, soccer M/W, softball M/W, volleyball M/W.

Applying *Options:* electronic application, early admission, early decision. *Application fee:* $50 Canadian dollars. *Required:* high school transcript. *Required for some:* essay or personal statement, interview. *Application deadlines:* rolling (freshmen), rolling (out-of-state freshmen), rolling (transfers).

Freshman Application Contact Southern Alberta Institute of Technology, 1301 16th Avenue NW, Calgary, AB T2M 0L4, Canada. *Phone:* 403-284-8857. *Toll-free phone:* 877-284-SAIT. *Web site:* http://www.sait.ca/.

INTERNATIONAL

MEXICO

Westhill University
Sante Fe, Mexico

Freshman Application Contact Admissions, Westhill University, 56 Domingo Garcia Ramos, Zona Escolar, Prados de la Montana I, 05610 Sante Fe, Cuajimalpa, Mexico. *Phone:* 52-55 5292-1121. *Toll-free phone:* 877-403-4535. *E-mail:* admissions@westhill.edu.mx. *Web site:* http://www.westhill.edu.mx/.

PALAU

Palau Community College
Koror, Palau

Freshman Application Contact Ms. Dahlia Katosang, Director of Admissions and Financial Aid, Palau Community College, PO Box 9, Koror, PW 96940-0009. *Phone:* 680-488-2471 Ext. 233. *Fax:* 680-488-4468. *E-mail:* dahliapcc@palaunet.com. *Web site:* http://www.palau.edu/.

College
Close-Ups

THE ART INSTITUTE OF NEW YORK CITY
NEW YORK, NEW YORK

A focused education from The Art Institute of New York City can help students turn their creative energy into a powerful tool that can make a difference in the world. Students are part of a collaborative and supportive community, where experienced instructors provide the guidance and skills needed to pursue a career in the creative economy.

The school's programs in the areas of design, media arts, and fashion give students the opportunity to learn by using professional-grade technology and build a portfolio of work to show potential employers after graduation.

The Art Institute of New York City is accredited by the Accrediting Council for Independent Colleges and Schools (ACICS) to award associate degrees. ACICS is listed as a nationally recognized accrediting agency by the United States Department of Education and is recognized by the Council for Higher Education Accreditation. ACICS can be contacted at 750 First Street NE, Suite 980, Washington, D.C. 20002; phone: 202-336-6780.

The Art Institute of New York City has received permission to operate from the State of New York Board of Regents, State Education Department, 89 Washington Avenue, 5 North Mezzanine, Albany, New York 12234; phone: 518-474-2593.

Academic Programs

No matter which course of study a student may choose, the professionals at The Art Institute of New York City will guide, support, and help each student as their talents evolve on their journey of personal and professional transformation. Students studying design learn to fine-tune their visual thinking and problem-solving skills, as they create everything from logos to TV ads. Programs in the area of media arts focus on utilizing technology to deliver information and entertainment, while students studying fashion learn to design clothes for the runway or run a retail shop.

Associate degree programs are offered in digital filmmaking, fashion design, fashion merchandising and marketing, graphic design, interior design, and Web design and interactive media.

Costs

Tuition costs vary by program. Prospective students should contact the school for current tuition costs. Other charges include a starting kit for all first-quarter students. Kits vary in price, depending on the program of study.

Financial Aid

Financial aid is available for those who qualify. Students who require financial assistance should first complete and submit a Free Application for Federal Student Aid (FAFSA) and meet with a financial aid officer.

Faculty

Faculty members are experienced professionals who create a learning environment that is similar to the professional world students will face after graduation. Instructors are focused on helping students develop the skills they need to transform their creative potential into marketable skills.

Student Body Profile

Students come to The Art Institute of New York City from throughout the United States and abroad. The student population includes recent high school graduates, transfer students, and those who have left a previous employment situation to study and train for a new career. Students are creative, competitive, and open to new ideas. They place great value on an education that prepares them for an exciting entry-level position in the arts.

Student Activities

There are several events for students throughout the year that celebrate culture, health, and holidays. The Student Activities Office also provides shape-up and wellness programs for students, along with The Art Institute of New York City Celebrates Women program. Students are offered many opportunities to volunteer throughout the year. Culinary students work at various events throughout the city as well as open-house programs at the school.

Facilities and Resources

The Art Institute of New York City provides a learning environment with professional-grade technology applicable to each student's course of study. Students have the opportunity to build a portfolio of work that shows potential employers that they are trained to use the software, hardware, or equipment utilized within the industry. Depending upon the course of study, students are immersed in a creative environment—from classrooms to computer labs to studios—focused on relevant, hands-on education designed to prepare students for the real world. The school contains computer labs, drawing studios, a student bookstore, and an art gallery.

Location

The Art Institute of New York City is located in the SoHo/Tribeca district of New York City. Manhattan is a hub of contemporary style, and New York City provides a wealth of opportunities for students to explore their creative side. Broadway plays, art museums, music halls, and professional sports teams are just some of the many entertainment options available to students who make the Big Apple their home.

Admission Requirements

Applicants must complete an application form and write a 150-word essay to apply for admission to The Art Institute of New York City. A personal interview with an admissions representative is required. Applicants must provide official high school transcripts, proof of successful completion of the General Educational Development (GED) test, or transcripts from any college previously attended. There is a $50 application fee.

For the most recent information regarding admission requirements, please refer to the current academic catalog.

Application and Information

To obtain an application or make arrangements for an interview or tour of the school, prospective students should contact:

The Art Institute of New York City
11 Beach Street
New York, New York 10013

Phone: 212-226-5500
        800-654-2433 (toll-free)

Fax: 212-966-0706

Web site: http://www.artinstitutes.edu/newyork

The Art Institute of Atlanta; The Art Institute of Atlanta–Decatur[1]; The Art Institute of Austin[2]; The Art Institute of California–Hollywood; The Art Institute of California–Inland Empire; The Art Institute of California–Los Angeles; The Art Institute of California–Orange County; The Art Institute of California–Sacramento; The Art Institute of California–San Diego; The Art Institute of California–San Francisco; The Art Institute of California–Sunnyvale; The Art Institute of Charleston[1]; The Art Institute of Charlotte; The Art Institute of Colorado; The Art Institute of Dallas[3]; The Art Institute of Fort Lauderdale; The Art Institute of Fort Worth[3]; The Art Institute of Houston; The Art Institute of Houston–North[2]; The Art Institute of Indianapolis[4]; The Art Institute of Jacksonville[5]; The Art Institute of Las Vegas; The Art Institute of Michigan; The Art Institute of New York City; The Art Institute of Ohio–Cincinnati[6]; The Art Institute of Philadelphia; The Art Institute of Phoenix; The Art Institute of Pittsburgh; The Art Institute of Portland; The Art Institute of Raleigh–Durham; The Art Institute of Salt Lake City; The Art Institute of San Antonio[2];The Art Institute of Seattle; The Art Institute of Tampa[5]; The Art Institute of Tennessee–Nashville[1]; The Art Institute of Tucson; The Art Institute of Vancouver; The Art Institute of Virginia Beach[1,7]; The Art Institute of Washington[1,7]; The Art Institute of Washington–Northern Virginia[1,7]; The Art Institute of Wisconsin; The Art Institute of York–Pennsylvania; The Art Institutes International–Kansas City; The Art Institutes International Minnesota; The Illinois Institute of Art–Chicago; The Illinois Institute of Art–Schaumburg; The Illinois Institute of Art–Tinley Park; Miami International University of Art & Design; The New England Institute of Art.

[1]A branch of The Art Institute of Atlanta
[2]A branch of The Art Institute of Houston
[3]A campus of South University
[4]The Art Institute of Indianapolis is regulated by the Indiana Commission on Proprietary Education, 302 West Washington Street, Room E201, Indianapolis, Indiana 46204, AC-0080
[5]A branch of Miami International University of Art & Design
[6]The Art Institute of Ohio–Cincinnati, 8845 Governors Hill Drive, Suite 100, Cincinnati, Ohio 45249-3317, OH Reg. #04-01-1698B
[7]Certified by the State Council of Higher Education to operate in Virginia

THE ART INSTITUTE OF SEATTLE
SEATTLE, WASHINGTON

The Art Institute of Seattle®
CREATE TOMORROW

A focused education from The Art Institute of Seattle can help students turn their creative energy into a powerful tool that can make a difference in the world. Students are part of a collaborative and supportive community, where experienced instructors provide the guidance and skills needed to pursue a career in the creative economy.

The school's programs in the areas of design, media arts, fashion, and culinary give students the opportunity to learn by using professional-grade technology and build a portfolio of work to show potential employers after graduation.

The Art Institute of Seattle is accredited by the Northwest Commission on Colleges and Universities (NWCCU), an institutional accrediting body recognized by the United States Department of Education.

The Art Institute of Seattle is licensed under Chapter 28c.10RCW; inquiries or complaints regarding this or any other private vocational school may be made to the Workforce Training and Education Coordinating Board, 128 10th Avenue SW, P.O. Box 43105, Olympia, Washington 98504-3105; phone: 360-753-5662.

The associate of applied arts in culinary arts degree program is accredited by the Accrediting Commission of the American Culinary Federation Education Foundation.

The interior design program leading to the Bachelor of Fine Arts degree is accredited by the Council for Interior Design Accreditation, 206 Grandville Avenue, Suite 350, Grand Rapids, Michigan 49503, www.accredit-id.org.

Academic Programs

No matter which course of study a student may choose, the professionals at The Art Institute of Seattle will guide, support, and help each student as their talents evolve on their journey of personal and professional transformation. Students studying design learn to fine-tune their visual thinking and problem-solving skills, as they create everything from logos to TV ads. Programs in the area of media arts focus on utilizing technology to deliver information and entertainment, while students studying fashion learn to design clothes for the runway or run a retail shop. Culinary programs focus on the fundamental techniques while exposing students to a full menu of international cuisines and management techniques.

Associate degrees are available in animation art and design, audio production, baking and pastry, culinary arts, fashion design, fashion marketing, graphic design, industrial design technology, interior design, photography, video production, and Web design and interactive media.

Bachelor's degree programs are available in audio design technology, culinary arts management, digital filmmaking and video production, fashion design, fashion marketing, game art and design, graphic design, industrial design, interior design, media arts and animation, photography, and Web design and interactive media.

Diploma programs are offered in baking and pastry, digital design, residential design, and the art of cooking.

The Art Institute of Seattle operates on a year-round, quarterly basis. Each quarter totals eleven weeks. Bachelor's degree programs are twelve quarters in length.

Costs

Tuition cost varies by program. Prospective students should contact the school for current tuition costs. Other charges include a starting kit for all first-quarter students. Kits vary in price, depending on the program of study.

Financial Aid

Financial aid is available for those who qualify. Students who require financial assistance should first complete and submit a Free Application for Federal Student Aid (FAFSA) and meet with a financial aid officer.

Faculty

Faculty members are experienced professionals who create a learning environment that is similar to the professional world students will face after graduation. Instructors are focused on helping students develop the skills they need to transform their creative potential into marketable skills.

Student Body Profile

Students come to The Art Institute of Seattle from throughout the United States and abroad. The student population includes recent high school graduates, transfer students, and those who have left a previous employment situation to study and train for a new career. Students are creative, competitive, and open to new ideas. They place great value on an education that prepares them for an exciting entry-level position in the arts.

Student Activities

The Art Institute of Seattle places high importance on student life, both inside and outside the classroom. The school provides an environment that encourages involvement in a wide variety of activities, including clubs and organizations, community service opportunities, and various committees designed to enhance the quality of student life. Numerous all-school programs and events are planned throughout the year to meet students' needs.

Facilities and Resources

The Art Institute of Seattle provides a learning environment with professional-grade technology applicable to each student's course of study. Students have the opportunity to build a portfolio of work that shows potential employers that they are trained to use the software, hardware, or equipment utilized within the industry. Depending upon the course of study, students are immersed in a creative environment—from classrooms to computer labs to studios—focused on relevant, hands-on education designed to prepare students for the real world.

The urban campus that comprises three facilities. The school houses classrooms, audio and video studios, a student store, student lounges, copy centers, a gallery, a woodshop, a sculpture room, fashion display windows, a resource center, a technology center, and culinary facilities. The Art Institute of Seattle is also home to a public student-run restaurant.

Location

The Art Institute of Seattle is located in the city's Belltown district. Founded by Native Americans and traders, the city has retained respect for its different cultures and customs. People from all over the world come to study, work, and live in this city that is known for its friendly people and beautiful natural surroundings.

World-class companies, such as Microsoft, Boeing, Starbucks, Amazon.com, and Nordstrom, make their global headquarters in Seattle. As a gateway to the Pacific Rim, Seattle is a crossroads where creativity, technology, and business meet.

Admission Requirements

A student seeking admission to The Art Institute of Seattle is required to interview with an admissions representative (in person or over the phone). Applicants are required to have a high school diploma or a General Educational Development (GED) certificate and to submit an admissions application and an essay describing how an education at The Art Institute of Seattle may help the student to achieve career goals. For advanced placement, additional information, including college transcripts, letters of recommendation, or portfolio work, may be required. Students may apply for admission online.

The Art Institute of Seattle follows a rolling admissions schedule. Students are encouraged to apply for their chosen quarter early so that they may take advantage of orientation activities. Students may also apply until the actual start date for any given quarter, depending on space availability. There is a $50 application fee.

For the most recent information regarding admission requirements, please refer to the current academic catalog.

Application and Information

To obtain an application, make arrangements for an interview, or tour the school, prospective students should contact:

The Art Institute of Seattle
2323 Elliott Avenue
Seattle, Washington 98121-1642
Phone: 206-448-6600
          800-275-2471 (toll-free)
Fax: 206-269-0275
Web site: http://www.artinstitutes.edu/seattle

The Art Institute of Atlanta; The Art Institute of Atlanta–Decatur[1]; The Art Institute of Austin[2]; The Art Institute of California–Hollywood; The Art Institute of California–Inland Empire; The Art Institute of California–Los Angeles; The Art Institute of California–Orange County; The Art Institute of California–Sacramento; The Art Institute of California–San Diego; The Art Institute of California–San Francisco; The Art Institute of California–Sunnyvale; The Art Institute of Charleston[1]; The Art Institute of Charlotte; The Art Institute of Colorado; The Art Institute of Dallas[3]; The Art Institute of Fort Lauderdale; The Art Institute of Fort Worth[3]; The Art Institute of Houston; The Art Institute of Houston–North[2]; The Art Institute of Indianapolis[4]; The Art Institute of Jacksonville[5]; The Art Institute of Las Vegas; The Art Institute of Michigan; The Art Institute of New York City; The Art Institute of Ohio–Cincinnati[6]; The Art Institute of Philadelphia; The Art Institute of Phoenix; The Art Institute of Pittsburgh; The Art Institute of Portland; The Art Institute of Raleigh–Durham; The Art Institute of Salt Lake City; The Art Institute of San Antonio[2];The Art Institute of Seattle; The Art Institute of Tampa[5]; The Art Institute of Tennessee–Nashville[1]; The Art Institute of Tucson; The Art Institute of Vancouver; The Art Institute of Virginia Beach[1,7]; The Art Institute of Washington[1,7]; The Art Institute of Washington–Northern Virginia[1,7]; The Art Institute of Wisconsin; The Art Institute of York–Pennsylvania; The Art Institutes International–Kansas City; The Art Institutes International Minnesota; The Illinois Institute of Art–Chicago; The Illinois Institute of Art–Schaumburg; The Illinois Institute of Art–Tinley Park; Miami International University of Art & Design; The New England Institute of Art.

[1]A branch of The Art Institute of Atlanta
[2]A branch of The Art Institute of Houston
[3]A campus of South University
[4]The Art Institute of Indianapolis is regulated by the Indiana Commission on Proprietary Education, 302 West Washington Street, Room E201, Indianapolis, Indiana 46204, AC-0080
[5]A branch of Miami International University of Art & Design
[6]The Art Institute of Ohio–Cincinnati, 8845 Governors Hill Drive, Suite 100, Cincinnati, Ohio 45249-3317, OH Reg. #04-01-1698B
[7]Certified by the State Council of Higher Education to operate in Virginia

BAY STATE COLLEGE
BOSTON, MASSACHUSETTS

The College and Its Mission

Founded in 1946, Bay State College is a private, independent, coeducational institution located in Boston's historic Back Bay. Since its founding, Bay State College has been preparing graduates for outstanding careers and continued education.

Bay State College is a small, private college focused on passionate students who want to turn their interests into a rewarding career. The College offers associate and bachelor's degrees in a number of rewarding fields. Everyone at Bay State—from admissions counselors and professors to the career services team—helps to assist, guide, and advise students, from the moment they apply and throughout their careers. Located in Boston's Back Bay, the College offers the city of Boston as a campus, small classes, and one-on-one attention. For students seeking a career in one of the professions offered by Bay State, a degree program at the College could be a strong first step on their career path.

The College offers associate degrees and bachelor's degrees. The educational experience offered through the variety of programs prepares students to excel in the careers of their choice. Personalized attention is the cornerstone of a Bay State College education. Through the transformative power of its core values of quality, respect, and support, Bay State College has been able to assist students with setting and achieving goals that prepare them for careers and continued education.

Recognizing that one of the most important aspects of college is life outside the classroom, the Office of Student Affairs seeks to provide services from orientation through graduation and beyond. Special events throughout the year include a fashion show and a host of events produced by the Entertainment Management Association. Students also enjoy professional sports teams such as the Boston Celtics and Boston Red Sox.

Bay State College's campus experience can be whatever the student chooses it to be. It's not the typical college campus—its residence halls are actually brownstones along Boston's trendy Commonwealth Avenue and Bay State's quad could be Boston Common, the banks of the Charles River by the Esplanade, or Copley Square. That's the advantage of being located in Boston's Back Bay, which is also the safest neighborhood in the city. Campus activities can also be as varied as the students' interests. Students can relax at a favorite coffee shop, bike along the Charles River, ice skate on the Frog Pond, check out the city's nightlife, or take in a baseball game at Fenway Park.

Bay State College is accredited by the New England Association of Schools and Colleges, is authorized to award the Associate in Science, Associate in Applied Science, and three Bachelor of Science degrees by the Commonwealth of Massachusetts. Bay State is a member of several professional educational associations. Its medical assisting program is accredited by the Accrediting Bureau of Health Education Schools (ABHES). The physical therapist assistant program is accredited by the Commission on Accreditation in Physical Therapy Education (CAPTE) of the American Physical Therapy Association (APTA).

Academic Programs

Bay State College operates on a semester calendar. The fall semester runs from early September to late December. The spring semester runs from late January until mid-May. A satellite campus is located in Middleborough, Massachusetts.

Bachelor's degrees are offered in criminal justice, entertainment management, fashion merchandising, and management.

Associate degrees are offered in business administration, criminal justice, early childhood education, entertainment management (with a concentration in audio production), fashion design, fashion merchandising, health studies, marketing, medical assisting, nursing, physical therapist assistant studies, retail business management, and hospitality management.

Bay State College also offers courses on-ground and online to working adults in its Evening & Online Division. The courses are offered in eight-week sessions and allow more flexibility for students who must balance work and family commitments while pursuing their education.

Bay State College continually reviews, enhances, and adds new programs to help graduates remain industry-current in their respective fields.

Off-Campus Programs

Many students cite Bay State's internship program as a turning point for them. Bay State internships allow students to gain hands-on experience and spend time working in their chosen fields. These valuable opportunities can give students an advantage when they apply for positions after they have completed school.

Bay State's Boston location allows the College to offer internships at many well-known companies and organizations. Students are able to apply what they've learned in the classroom and do meaningful work in their field of study. In addition, they build working relationships with people in their chosen profession. For more information on internships, prospective students may contact Tom Corrigan, Director of Career Services, at 617-217-9000.

Costs

Tuition for 2010–12 for full-time students is $21,930, based on 30 credits per year ($731 per credit). However, many students choose to take 24 credits, which is also considered full-time enrollment, bringing the cost to $17,544 per year. Evening students pay $270 per credit. Room and board are $11,800 per year, the application fee is $40, a student services fee is $375, and the student activity fee is $50. The cost of books and additional fees vary by major. A residence hall security deposit of $300 and a technology fee of $250 are required of all resident students.

The fall tuition payment due date is July 1; the spring tuition payment is due December 1.

Financial Aid

Each student works with a personal advocate to thoroughly explain financial options and guide them through the financial aid application process. Many options are available: aid, grants and scholarships, federal programs, and private loans. Bay State College's Financial Aid Department and tuition planners can help students determine what aid may apply. Approximately 85 percent of students receive some form of financial assistance. Bay State College requires a completed Free Application for Federal Student Aid (FAFSA) form and signed federal tax forms. The College's institutional financial aid priority deadline is March 15. Financial aid is granted on a rolling basis.

Faculty

There are 72 faculty members, many holding advanced degrees and several holding doctoral degrees. The student-faculty ratio is 20:1.

Student Body Profile

There are approximately 1,100 students in degree programs in both the Day and Evening Divisions.

Student Activities

Bay State College students participate in a multitude of activities offered by the College through existing student organizations. Students also have the opportunity to create clubs and organizations that meet their interests. Existing organizations include the Student

Government Association, Entertainment Management Association, Justice Society, the Criminal Justice Society, DEX, and the Early Childhood Education Club. Students also produce an annual talent show as well as an annual fashion show that showcases the original designs of the students in the College's fashion design program. A literary magazine is also published annually and features the work of students throughout the College.

Facilities and Resources

Advisement/Counseling: Trained staff members assist students in selecting courses and programs of study to satisfy their educational objectives. A counseling center is available to provide mental and physical health referrals to all Bay State College students in need of such services. Referral networks are extensive, within a wide range of geographic areas, and provide access to a variety of public and private health agencies.

Specialized Services: The Office of Academic Development at Bay State College is designed to meet and support the various academic needs of the student body and serve as a resource for supplemental instruction, academic plans, learning accommodations, and other types of support. The Office of Academic Development operates on the belief that all students can achieve success in their courses by accessing support services and creating individual academic plans.

The Center for Learning and Academic Success (CLAS) at Bay State College is a key component available to help students achieve academic success. Students come to CLAS to get support in specific subject areas as well as study skills such as note-taking, reading comprehension, writing research papers, time management, and coping with exam anxiety. They utilize CLAS to develop study plans and strategies that positively impact their grades in all subjects. Students can also take advantage of the tutoring and seminars CLAS offers. CLAS's goal is to ensure that students are provided with exceptional academic support in all areas of study.

Career Planning/Placement: For many college students, the transition from student life to professional life is filled with questions and uncharted realities. But Bay State College's Career Services Department offers students their own personal career advancement team. The Career Services Department can help students learn to write a resume and cover letter, use social networks, practice interviewing skills, find the right job opportunity, and learn other career-related functions. Bay State College even provides each student with a Professionalism Grade, which lets future employers know they have what it takes to start contributing on day one. The Career Services Department at Bay State College is determined to see each student succeed and offers valuable instruction that will serve students throughout their professional careers.

Library and Audiovisual Services: The library is staffed with trained librarians who are available to guide students in their research process. The library's resources include 7,500 books, eighty-five periodical subscriptions, and a dramatically increased reach through its online library resource databases that include ProQuest, InfoTrac, and LexisNexis. In addition, the library provides computer access and study space for students. The library catalog and databases are accessible from any Internet-ready terminal.

First-Year Experience: The First-Year Experience (FYE) is a 1-credit course that is required of all first-year students and takes place during the first three days that students are on campus. FYE combines social activities with an academic syllabus that is designed to ease the transition into the college experience. Through FYE, students have the opportunity to connect with their academic advisers as well as with other students in their academic programs. At the conclusion of FYE, students are on the road to mapping out their personal action plan for success. The plan, designed by students, guided by academic advisers, and revisited each semester, helps students set, monitor, and achieve academic and life goals. It also builds the preparation for lifelong accomplishment.

Location

Located in the historic city of Boston, Massachusetts, and surrounded by dozens of colleges and universities, Bay State College is an ideal setting in which to pursue a college degree. Tree-lined streets around the school are mirrored in the skyscrapers of the Back Bay. The College is located within walking distance of several major league sport franchises, concert halls, museums, the Freedom Train, Boston Symphony Hall, the Boston Public Library, and the Boston Public Garden. World-class shopping and major cultural and sporting events help make college life an experience that students will always remember. The College is accessible by the MBTA and commuter rail and bus, and is near Boston Logan International Airport.

Admission Requirements

An applicant to Bay State College must be a high school graduate, a current high school student working toward graduation, or a recipient of a GED certificate. The Office of Admissions requires that applicants to the associate degree programs have a minimum of a 2.0 GPA (on a 4.0 scale); if available, applicants may submit SAT and/or ACT scores. Applicants to bachelor's degree programs must have a minimum 2.3 GPA (on a 4.0 scale) and must also submit SAT or ACT scores.

International applicants must also submit high school transcripts translated to English with an explanation of the grading system, financial documentation, and a minimum TOEFL score of 500 on the paper-based exam or 173 on the computer-based exam if English is not their native language.

The physical therapist assistant studies program requires a minimum 2.7 GPA (on a 4.0 scale) and the Evening Division has different or additional admission requirements. For more information about these programs, interested students should visit the Web site at http://www.baystate.edu.

A personal interview is required for all prospective students—parents are encouraged to attend. Applicants must receive the recommendation of a Bay State College Admissions Officer.

Application and Information

Applications are accepted on a rolling basis. A $40 fee is required at the time of application.

Students are responsible for arranging for their official high school transcripts, test scores, and letters of recommendation to be submitted to Bay State College.

The Bay State College Admissions Office notifies applicants of a decision within one week of receipt of the transcript and other required documents. When a student is accepted to Bay State College, there is a $100 nonrefundable tuition deposit required to ensure a place in the class; the deposit is credited toward the tuition fee. Deposits are due within thirty days of acceptance. Once a student is accepted, a Bay State College representative creates a personalized financial plan that provides payment options for a Bay State College education.

Applications should be submitted to:

Admissions Office
Bay State College
122 Commonwealth Avenue
Boston, Massachusetts 02116

Phone: 800-81-LEARN (53276)
Fax: 617-249-0400 (eFax)
E-mail: admissions@baystate.edu
Web site: http://www.baystate.edu
　　　　http://www.facebook.com/baystatecollege
　　　　http://twitter.com/baystatecollege

BROWN MACKIE COLLEGE–AKRON
AKRON, OHIO

The College and Its Mission

Brown Mackie College–Akron is one of over twenty-five locations in the Brown Mackie College family of schools (http://www.brownmackie.edu), which is dedicated to providing educational programs that prepare students to pursue entry-level positions in a competitive, rapidly changing workplace. Brown Mackie College schools offer bachelor's degree, associate degree, certificate, and diploma programs in health sciences, business, information technology, legal studies, and design to over 20,000 students in the Midwest, Southeast, Southwest, and Western United States.

The College was founded in Cincinnati, Ohio, in February 1927, as a traditional business college. In March 1980, the College added a branch campus in Akron, Ohio. The College outgrew this space and relocated to its current address in January 2007.

Brown Mackie College–Akron is accredited by the Accrediting Council for Independent Colleges and Schools (ACICS) to award associate degrees and diplomas. The Accrediting Council for Independent Colleges and Schools is listed as a nationally recognized accrediting agency by the United States Department of Education and is recognized by the Council for Higher Education Accreditation. ACICS can be contacted at 750 First Street NE, Suite 980, Washington, D.C. 20002; phone: 202-336-6780.

Brown Mackie College–Akron is licensed by the Ohio State Board of Career Colleges and Schools, 35 East Gay Street, Suite 403, Columbus, Ohio 43215 (Ohio registration #03-09-1685T).

The surgical technology program is accredited by the Commission on Accreditation of Allied Health Education Programs (www.caahep.org) upon the recommendation of the Accreditation Review Council on Education in Surgical Technology and Surgical Assisting (ARC/STSA). The Commission on Accreditation of Allied Health Education Programs is located at 1361 Park Street Clearwater, Florida 33756; phone: 727-210-2350; www.caahep.org.

The occupational therapy assistant program is accredited by the Accreditation Council for Occupational Therapy Education (ACOTE) of the American Occupational Therapy Association (AOTA), located at 4720 Montgomery Lane, P.O. Box 31220, Bethesda, Maryland 20824; phone: 301-652-AOTA.

The College is a nonresidential, smoke-free institution.

Academic Programs

Brown Mackie College–Akron provides higher education to traditional and nontraditional students through associate degree and diploma programs that can assist them in enhancing their career opportunities, broadening their perspec-

tives through appropriate general education courses, thinking independently and critically, and improving problem-solving abilities.

Each College quarter comprises twelve weeks. Associate degree programs require a minimum of eight quarters to complete. Programs are offered on a year-round basis, providing students with the ability to work uninterrupted toward their degree. The College offers all programs in a unique One Course a Month format. This schedule allows students to focus studies on only one course for four weeks and has proven convenient for students with multiple obligations such as jobs and family.

Associate Degree Programs: The Associate of Applied Business degree is awarded in accounting technology, business management, criminal justice, office management, and paralegal. The Associate of Applied Science degree is awarded in computer networking and applications, database technology, early childhood education, health care administration, information technology, medical assisting, occupational therapy assistant, pharmacy technology, surgical technology, and veterinary technology.

Diploma Programs: The College also offers diploma programs in accounting, business, criminal justice, medical assistant, medical coding and billing, paralegal assistant, and practical nursing.

Costs

Tuition for the 2010–11 academic year was $285 per credit hour, and $15 per credit hour for general fees. Tuition for the practical nursing program was $350 per credit hour, and $25 per credit hour for general fees. Tuition for the surgical technology program was $330 per credit hour, and $15 per credit hour for general fees. Tuition for the occupational therapy assistant program was $350 per credit hour, and $15 per credit hour for general fees. The cost of textbooks and other instructional materials varies by program.

Financial Aid

Financial aid is available to those who qualify. The College maintains a full-time staff of financial aid professionals to assist qualified students in obtaining financial assistance. The College participates in several student aid programs. Forms of financial aid available through federal resources include the Federal Pell Grant Program, Federal Supplemental Educational Opportunity Grant (FSEOG) Program, Federal Work-Study Program, Federal Stafford Student Loan Program (subsidized and unsubsidized), and the Federal PLUS Loan Program. Eligible students may also apply for veterans' educational benefits. Students with physical or mental disabilities that are a handicap to employment may be eligible for training services through the state Agency for Vocational

Rehabilitation. For further information, students should contact the College's Student Financial Services Office.

Each year, the College makes available scholarships of up to $1000 each to qualifying seniors from area high schools. Only one scholarship is awarded per high school. In order to qualify, a senior must be graduating from a participating high school, have maintained a cumulative grade point average of at least 2.0, and submitted a brief essay. The student's extracurricular activities and community service are also considered. These scholarships are available only to students enrolling in one of the College's degree programs. Students awarded the scholarship must enroll at Brown Mackie College–Akron between June and September immediately following their high school graduation. Applications for these scholarships can be obtained from the guidance departments of participating high schools. These applications must be completed and returned to the College by March 31.

Faculty

There are 20 full-time and 39 part-time faculty members. The student-faculty ratio is 17:1.

Facilities and Resources

Brown Mackie College–Akron provides media presentation rooms for special instructional needs, libraries that provide instructional resources and academic support for both faculty members and students, and qualified and experienced faculty members who are committed to the academic and technical preparation of their students. The College is nonresidential; students who are unable to commute daily from their homes may request assistance from the Office of Admissions in locating off-campus housing. The College is accessible by public transportation and provides ample parking, available at no charge.

Location

The College is located at 755 White Pond Drive in Akron, Ohio. For added convenience, the College also operates learning sites at 809 White Pond Drive and 388 South Main Street in Akron.

Admission Requirements

Each applicant for admission is assigned an Assistant Director of Admissions who directs the applicant through the steps of the admissions process, providing information on curriculum, policies, procedures, and services and assisting the applicant in setting necessary appointments and interviews.

To qualify for admission, each applicant must provide documentation of graduation from an accredited high school or from a state-approved secondary education curriculum or provide official documentation of high school graduation equivalency. All transcripts become the property of the College. Admission to the College is based upon the applicant meeting the stated requirements, a review of the applicant's previous education records, and a review of the applicant's career interests. If previous academic records indicate that the College's education and training programs would not benefit the applicant, the College reserves the right to advise the applicant not to enroll. Special requirements for enrollment into certain programs are discussed in the descriptions of those programs.

For the most recent information regarding admission requirements, please refer to the current academic catalog.

Application and Information

Applicants must complete and submit an application form along with documentation of graduation from an accredited high school or state-approved secondary education curriculum, or applicants must provide official documentation of high school graduation equivalency. For additional information, prospective students should contact:

Senior Director of Admissions
Brown Mackie College–Akron
755 White Pond Drive
Akron, Ohio 44320

Phone: 330-869-3600
Fax: 330-869-3650
E-mail: bmcakadm@brownmackie.edu
Web site: http://www.brownmackie.edu/Akron

BROWN MACKIE COLLEGE– ALBUQUERQUE
ALBUQUERQUE, NEW MEXICO

The College and Its Mission

Brown Mackie College–Albuquerque is one of over twenty-five locations in the Brown Mackie College family of schools (www.brownmackie.edu), which is dedicated to providing educational programs that prepare students to pursue entry-level positions in a competitive, rapidly changing workplace. Brown Mackie College schools offer bachelor's degree, associate degree, certificate, and diploma programs in health sciences, business, information technology, legal studies, and design to over 20,000 students in the Midwest, Southeast, Southwest, and Western United States.

Brown Mackie College was originally founded and approved by the Board of Trustees of Kansas Wesleyan College in Salina, Kansas on July 30, 1892. In 1938, the College was incorporated as the Brown Mackie School of Business under the ownership of Perry E. Brown and A. B. Mackie, former instructors at Kansas Wesleyan University in Salina, Kansas. Their last names formed the name of Brown Mackie. By January 1975, with improvements in curricula and higher degree-granting status, the Brown Mackie School of Business became Brown Mackie College.

Brown Mackie College–Albuquerque is accredited by the Accrediting Council for Independent Colleges and Schools to award bachelor's degrees, associate degrees, and diplomas. The Accrediting Council for Independent Colleges and Schools is listed as a nationally recognized accrediting agency by the United States Department of Education and is recognized by the Council for Higher Education Accreditation. ACICS can be contacted at 750 First Street NE, Suite 980, Washington, D.C. 20002; phone: 202-336-6780.

The occupational therapy assistant program has applied for accreditation by the Accreditation Council for Occupational Therapy Education (ACOTE) of the American Occupational Therapy Association (AOTA), located at 4720 Montgomery Lane, P.O. Box 31220, Bethesda, Maryland 20824; phone: 301-652-AOTA.

Academic Programs

Brown Mackie College–Albuquerque provides higher education to traditional and nontraditional students through bachelor's degree, associate degree and diploma programs that assist in enhancing their career opportunities, broadening their perspectives through appropriate general education courses, thinking independently and critically, and improving problem-solving abilities.

The College strives to develop within its students the desire for lifelong and continued education.

Each College quarter comprises twelve weeks. Bachelor's degree programs require a minimum of sixteen quarters to complete. Associate degree programs require a minimum of eight quarters to complete. Programs are offered on a year-round basis, providing students with the ability to work uninterrupted toward completion of their programs. The College offers all programs in a unique One Course a Month format. This allows students to focus studies on only one course for four weeks. This schedule has proven convenient for students with multiple obligations such as jobs and family.

Bachelor's Degree Programs: The Bachelor of Science degree is awarded in business administration, criminal justice, health care management, and legal studies.

Associate Degree Programs: The Associate of Applied Science degree is awarded in accounting technology, architectural design and drafting technology, business management, criminal justice, health care administration, information technology, medical assisting, occupational therapy assistant, paralegal, pharmacy technology, surgical technology, and veterinary technology.

Diploma Programs: The College offers diploma programs in accounting, business, criminal justice, medical assistant, and paralegal assistant.

Costs

Tuition in the 2010–11 academic year for most bachelor's and associate degrees and certificate programs was $295 per credit hour; fees were $20 per credit hour. Tuition for the occupational therapy assistant program was $325 per credit hour; fees were $20 per credit hour. Tuition for the surgical technology program was $310 per credit hour; fees were $20 per credit hour. The cost of textbooks and other instructional materials varies by program.

Financial Aid

Financial aid is available for those who qualify. The College maintains a full-time staff of financial aid professionals to assist qualified students in obtaining the financial assistance they require to meet their educational expenses. Available resources include federal and state aid, student loans from private lenders, and Federal Work-Study opportunities, both on and off College premises.

Each year, the College makes available scholarships of $1000 each to qualifying seniors from area high schools. No more than one scholarship is awarded per high school. In order to qualify, a senior must have graduated from a participating high school, must have maintained a cumulative grade point average of at least 2.0, and submitted a brief essay. The student's extracurricular activities and community service are also considered. These scholarships are available only to students enrolling in one of the College's degree programs. Students awarded the scholarship must enroll at Brown Mackie College–Albuquerque between June and September immediately following their high school graduation. Applications for these scholarships can be obtained from the guidance departments of participating high schools. These applications must be completed and returned to the College by March 31.

Faculty

Experienced faculty members provide academic support and are committed to the academic and technical preparation of their students. The College has both full-time and part-time instructors, with a student-faculty ratio of 15:1.

Facilities and Resources

Brown Mackie College–Albuquerque is housed in a modern facility with more than 35,000 square feet of space for its programs. The College is equipped with multiple computer labs, with over 100 computers. High-speed access to the Internet and other online resources are available to students and faculty. Multimedia classrooms are outfitted with overhead projectors, VCR/DVD players, and computers.

The campus is nonresidential; public transportation and ample parking at no cost are available. The campus is a smoke-free facility.

Location

Brown Mackie College–Albuquerque is conveniently located at 10500 Copper Avenue NE in Albuquerque, New Mexico. The College has a generous parking area and is easily accessible by public transportation.

Admission Requirements

Each applicant for admission is assigned an Assistant Director of Admissions who directs the applicant through the steps of the admissions process. They provide information on curriculum, policies, procedures, and services and assist the applicant in setting necessary appointments and interviews.

To qualify for admission, each applicant must provide documentation of graduation from an accredited high school, or from a state-approved secondary education curriculum, or provide official documentation of high school graduation equivalency. All transcripts become the property of the College. Admission to the College is based on the applicant meeting the stated requirements, a review of the applicant's previous educational records, and a review of the applicant's career interests. If previous academic records indicate the College's education and training programs would not benefit the applicant, the College reserves the right to advise the applicant not to enroll. Special requirements for enrollment into certain programs are discussed in the descriptions of those programs.

For the most recent information regarding admission requirements, prospective students should refer to the current academic catalog.

Application and Information

Applicants must complete and submit an application form, along with documentation of graduation from an accredited high school or state-approved secondary education curriculum or official documentation of high school graduation equivalency.

For additional information, prospective students should contact:

Director of Admissions
Brown Mackie College–Albuquerque
10500 Copper Avenue
Albuquerque, New Mexico 87123
Phone: 505-559-5200
      877-271-3488 (toll-free)
Fax: 505-559-5222
E-mail: bmcalbadm@brownmackie.edu
Web site: http://www.brownmackie.edu/Albuquerque

BROWN MACKIE COLLEGE–ATLANTA

ATLANTA, GEORGIA

The College and Its Mission

Brown Mackie College–Atlanta is one of over twenty-five locations in the Brown Mackie College family of schools (http://www.brownmackie.edu), which is dedicated to providing educational programs that prepare students to pursue entry-level positions in a competitive, rapidly changing workplace. Brown Mackie College schools offer bachelor's degree, associate degree, certificate, and diploma programs in health sciences, business, information technology, legal studies, and design to over 20,000 students in the Midwest, Southeast, Southwest, and Western United States.

Brown Mackie College–Atlanta is accredited by the Accrediting Council for Independent Colleges and Schools (ACICS) to award associate degrees and diplomas. The Accrediting Council for Independent Colleges and Schools is listed as a nationally recognized accrediting agency by the United States Department of Education and is recognized by the Council for Higher Education Accreditation. ACICS can be contacted at 750 First Street NE, Suite 980, Washington, D.C. 20002; phone: 202-336-6780.

The occupational therapy assistant program is accredited by the Accreditation Council for Occupational Therapy Education (ACOTE) of the American Occupational Therapy Association (AOTA), located at 4720 Montgomery Lane, P.O. Box 31220, Bethesda, Maryland 20824; phone: 301-652-AOTA.

The Brown Mackie College–Atlanta Associate of Applied Science in surgical technology program is accredited by the Accrediting Bureau of Health Education Schools (http://www.abhes.org).

The College is a nonresidential, smoke-free institution.

Academic Programs

Brown Mackie College–Atlanta provides higher education to traditional and nontraditional students through associate degree and diploma programs that can assist students in enhancing their career opportunities, broadening their perspectives through appropriate general education courses, thinking independently and critically, and improving problem-solving abilities. The College strives to develop within its students the desire for lifelong and continued education.

Each College quarter comprises twelve weeks. Associate degree programs require a minimum of eight quarters to complete. Programs are offered on a year-round basis, providing students with the ability to work uninterrupted toward their degrees. The College offers all programs in a unique One Course a Month format. This schedule allows students to focus studies on only one course for four weeks and has proven convenient for students with multiple obligations such as jobs and family.

Associate Degree Programs The Associate of Applied Business degree is awarded in accounting technology, business management, criminal justice, and paralegal. The Associate of Applied Science degree is awarded in early childhood education, health care administration, medical assisting, occupational therapy assistant, pharmacy technology, and surgical technology.

Diploma Programs The College also offers diploma programs in accounting, business, criminal justice, medical assistant, and paralegal assistant.

Costs

Tuition for the 2010–11 academic year was $336 per credit hour and $15 per credit hour for general fees. Tuition for the occupational therapy assistant program was $350 per credit hour and $15 per credit hour for general fees. Tuition for the surgical technology program was $330 per credit hour and $15 per credit hour for general fees. The cost of textbooks and other instructional materials varies by program.

Financial Aid

Financial aid is available to those who qualify. The College maintains a full-time staff of financial aid professionals to assist qualified students in obtaining financial assistance. The College participates in several student aid programs. Forms of financial aid available through federal resources include the Federal Pell Grant Program, Federal Supplemental Educational Opportunity Grant (FSEOG) Program, Federal Work-Study Program, Federal Perkins Loan Program, Federal Stafford Student Loan Program (subsidized and unsubsidized), and the Federal PLUS Loan Program. Eligible students may also apply for state awards and veterans' educational benefits. Students with physical or mental disabilities that are a handicap to employment may be eligible for training services through the state Agency for Vocational Rehabilitation. For further information, students should contact the College's Student Financial Services Office.

Faculty

There are 4 full-time and 5 part-time faculty members. The average student-faculty ratio is 19:1. Each student has a faculty and student adviser.

Facilities and Resources

The College comprises administrative offices, faculty and student lounges, a reception area, and spacious classrooms and laboratories. Instructional equipment includes personal computers, LANs, printers, and transcribers. The library provides support for the academic programs through volumes covering a broad range of subjects, as well as through Internet access. Vehicle parking is provided for both students and staff members.

Location

Brown Mackie College–Atlanta is located at 4370 Peachtree Road NE in Atlanta, Georgia, which is easily accessible from I-285 and the MARTA Brookhaven rail station.

Admission Requirements

Each applicant for admission is assigned an Assistant Director of Admissions who directs the applicant through the steps of the admissions process, providing information on curriculum, policies, procedures, and services and assisting the applicant in setting necessary appointments and interviews.

To qualify for admission, each applicant must provide documentation of graduation from an accredited high school or from a state-approved secondary education curriculum or provide official documentation of high school graduation equivalency. All transcripts become the property of the College. Admission to the College is based upon the applicant meeting the stated requirements, a review of the applicant's previous education records, and a review of the applicant's career interests. If previous academic records indicate that the College's education and training programs would not benefit the applicant, the College reserves the right to advise the applicant not to enroll. Special requirements for enrollment into certain programs are discussed in the descriptions of those programs.

For the most recent information regarding admission requirements, please refer to the current academic catalog.

Application and Information

Applicants must complete and submit an application form along with documentation of graduation from an accredited high school or state-approved secondary education curriculum, or applicants must provide official documentation of high school graduation equivalency.

For additional information, prospective students should contact:

Director of Admissions
Brown Mackie College–Atlanta
4370 Peachtree Road NE
Atlanta, Georgia 30319
Phone: 404-799-4500
       877-479-8419 (toll-free)
Fax: 404-799-4522
E-mail: bmcatadm@brownmackie.edu
Web site: http://www.brownmackie.edu/Atlanta

BROWN MACKIE COLLEGE–BIRMINGHAM

BIRMINGHAM, ALABAMA

The College and Its Mission

Brown Mackie College–Birmingham is one of over twenty-five locations in the Brown Mackie College family of schools (www.brownmackie.edu), which is dedicated to providing educational programs that prepare students to pursue entry-level positions in a competitive, rapidly changing workplace. Brown Mackie College schools offer bachelor's degree, associate degree, certificate, and diploma programs in health sciences, business, information technology, legal studies, and design to over 20,000 students in the Midwest, Southeast, Southwest, and Western United States.

Brown Mackie College was originally founded and approved by the Board of Trustees of Kansas Wesleyan College in Salina, Kansas on July 30, 1892. In 1938 the College was incorporated as the Brown Mackie School of Business under the ownership of Perry E. Brown and A. B. Mackie, former instructors at Kansas Wesleyan University in Salina, Kansas. Their last names formed the name of Brown Mackie. By January 1975, with improvements in curricula and higher degree-granting status, the Brown Mackie School of Business became Brown Mackie College.

Brown Mackie College–Birmingham is accredited by the Accrediting Council for Independent Colleges and Schools (ACICS) to award bachelor's degrees, associate degrees, and diplomas. ACICS is listed as a nationally recognized accrediting agency by the United States Department of Education and is recognized by the Council for Higher Education Accreditation. ACICS can be contacted at 750 First Street NE, Suite 980, Washington, D.C. 20002; phone: 202-336-6780.

Academic Programs

Brown Mackie College–Birmingham provides higher education to traditional and nontraditional students through bachelor's degree, associate degree, and diploma programs that assist in enhancing their career opportunities, broadening their perspectives through appropriate general education courses, thinking independently and critically, and improving problem-solving abilities. The College strives to develop within its students the desire for lifelong and continued education.

Each College quarter comprises twelve weeks. Bachelor's degree programs require a minimum of sixteen quarters to complete. Associate degree programs require a minimum of eight quarters to complete. Programs are offered on a year-round basis, providing students with the ability to work uninterrupted toward completion of their programs. The College offers all programs in a unique One Course a Month format. This allows students to focus studies on only one course for four weeks. This schedule has proven convenient for students with multiple obligations such as jobs and family.

Bachelor's Degree Programs: The Bachelor of Science degree is awarded in business administration, health care management, and legal studies.

Associate Degree Programs: The Associate of Science degree is awarded in accounting technology, architectural design and drafting technology, biomedical equipment technology, business management, graphic design, health care administration, information technology, medical assisting, paralegal, and surgical technology.

Diploma Programs: The College offers diploma programs in accounting, business, dental assistant, healthcare administrative specialist, medical assistant, and paralegal assistant.

Costs

Tuition in the 2010–11 academic year for bachelor's and associate degree and certificate programs was $295 per credit hour; fees were $15 per credit hour. Tuition for the surgical technology program was $330 per credit hour; fees were $15 per credit hour. The cost of textbooks and other instructional materials varies by program.

Financial Aid

Financial aid is available for those who qualify. The College maintains a full-time staff of financial aid professionals to assist qualified students in obtaining the financial assistance they require to meet their educational expenses. Available resources include federal and state aid, student loans from private lenders, and Federal Work-Study opportunities, both on and off College premises.

Each year, the College makes available scholarships of $1000 each to qualifying seniors from area high schools. No more than one scholarship is awarded per high school. In order to qualify, a senior must have graduated from a participating high school, maintained a cumulative grade point average of at least 2.0, and submitted a brief essay. The student's extracurricular activities and community service are also considered. These scholarships are available only to students enrolling in one of the College's degree programs. Students awarded the scholarship must enroll at Brown Mackie College–Birmingham between June and September immediately following their high school graduation. Applications for these scholarships can be obtained from the guidance departments of participating high schools. These applications must be completed and returned to the College by March 31.

Faculty

Experienced faculty members provide academic support and are committed to the academic and technical preparation of their students. The College has both full-time and part-time instructors, with a student-faculty ratio of 15:1.

Facilities and Resources

A modern facility, Brown Mackie College–Birmingham offers approximately 35,000 square feet of classroom, computer and allied health labs, library, and office space. The College is equipped with multiple computer labs, housing over 100 computers. High-speed access to the Internet and other online resources are available to students and faculty. Multimedia classrooms are outfitted with overhead projectors, VCR/DVD players, and computers.

The campus is nonresidential; public transportation and ample parking at no cost are available. The campus is a smoke-free facility.

Location

Brown Mackie College–Birmingham is conveniently located at 105 Vulcan Road in Birmingham, Alabama. The College has a generous parking area and is easily accessible by public transportation.

Admission Requirements

Each applicant for admission is assigned an Assistant Director of Admissions who directs the applicant through the steps of the admissions process. They provide information on curriculum, policies, procedures, and services and assist the applicant in setting necessary appointments and interviews. To qualify for admission, each applicant must provide documentation of graduation from an accredited high school or from a state-approved secondary education curriculum or provide official documentation of high school graduation equivalency. All transcripts become the property of the College. Admission to the College is based on the applicant meeting the stated requirements, a review of the applicant's previous educational records, and a review of the applicant's career interests. If previous academic records indicate the College's education and training programs would not benefit the applicant, the College reserves the right to advise the applicant not to enroll. Special requirements for enrollment into certain programs are discussed in the descriptions of those programs.

For the most recent information regarding admission requirements, prospective students should refer to the current academic catalog.

Application and Information

Applicants must complete and submit an application form along with documentation of graduation from an accredited high school or state-approved secondary education curriculum, or official documentation of high school graduation equivalency.

For additional information, prospective students should contact:

Director of Admissions
Brown Mackie College–Birmingham
105 Vulcan Road, Suite 100
Birmingham, Alabama 35209
Phone: 205-909-1500
      888-299-4699 (toll-free)
Fax: 205-909-1588
E-mail: bmbirmadm@brownmackie.edu
Web site: http://www.brownmackie.edu/Birmingham

BROWN MACKIE COLLEGE–BOISE

BOISE, IDAHO

The College and Its Mission

Brown Mackie College–Boise is one of over twenty-five locations in the Brown Mackie College family of schools (www.brownmackie.edu), which is dedicated to providing educational programs that prepare students to pursue entry-level positions in a competitive, rapidly changing workplace. Brown Mackie College schools offer bachelor's degree, associate degree, certificate, and diploma programs in health sciences, business, information technology, legal studies, and design to over 20,000 students in the Midwest, Southeast, Southwest, and Western United States.

Brown Mackie College–Boise is accredited by the Accrediting Council for Independent Colleges and Schools (ACICS) to award bachelor's degrees, associate degrees, and diplomas. The Accrediting Council for Independent Colleges and Schools is listed as a nationally recognized accrediting agency by the United States Department of Education and is recognized by the Council for Higher Education Accreditation. ACICS can be contacted at 750 First Street NE, Suite 980, Washington, D.C. 20002; phone: 202-336-6780.

The occupational therapy assistant program is accredited by the Accreditation Council for Occupational Therapy Education (ACOTE) of the American Occupational Therapy Association (AOTA), located at 4720 Montgomery Lane, P.O. Box 31220, Bethesda, Maryland 20824-1220; phone: 301-652-2682.

The Associate of Applied Science in veterinary technology program at Brown Mackie College–Boise is accredited by the American Veterinary Medical Association (AVMA) as a program for educating veterinary technicians. The American Veterinary Medical Association can be contacted at 1931 North Meacham Road, Suite 100, Schaumburg, Illinois, 60173-4360; phone: 800-248-2862 (toll-free).

Academic Programs

Brown Mackie College–Boise provides higher education to traditional and nontraditional students through bachelor's degree, associate degree, and diploma programs that assist in enhancing their career opportunities, broadening their perspectives through appropriate general education courses, thinking independently and critically, and improving problem-solving abilities.

Each College quarter comprises twelve weeks. Bachelor's degree programs require a minimum of sixteen quarters to complete. Associate degree programs require a minimum of eight quarters to complete. Programs are offered on a year-round basis, providing students with the opportunity to work uninterrupted toward completion of their programs. The College offers all programs in a unique One Course a Month format. This allows students to focus studies on only one course for four weeks. This schedule has proven convenient for students with multiple obligations such as jobs and family.

Bachelor's Degree Programs: The Bachelor of Science degree is awarded in business administration, criminal justice, health care management, and legal studies.

Associate Degree Programs: The Associate of Science degree is awarded in accounting technology, bioscience laboratory technology, business management, criminal justice, health care administration, information technology, medical assisting, paralegal, and surgical technology.

The Associate of Applied Science degree is awarded in architectural design and drafting technology, occupational therapy assistant, and veterinary technology.

Diploma Programs: The College offers a diploma program in accounting, business, criminal justice, medical assistant, and paralegal assistant.

Costs

Tuition for programs in the 2010–11 academic year was $295 per credit hour with a $15 per credit hour general fee applied to instructional costs for activities and services. The cost of textbooks and other instructional materials varies by program. Tuition for the occupational therapy assistant courses was $390 per credit hour with a $15 per credit fee applied to instructional costs for activities and services. Tuition for the surgical technology program was $330 per credit hour with a $15 per credit fee applied to instructional costs for activities and services.

Financial Aid

Financial aid is available for those who qualify. The College maintains a full-time staff of financial aid professionals to assist qualified students in obtaining financial assistance. The College participates in several student aid programs. Forms of financial aid available through federal resources include the Federal Pell Grant Program, Federal Supplemental Educational Opportunity Grant (FSEOG) Program, Federal Work-Study Program, Federal Perkins Loan Program, Federal Stafford Student Loan Program (subsidized and unsubsidized), and the Federal PLUS Loan Program.

Each year, the College makes available President's Scholarships of $1000 each to qualifying seniors from area high schools. No more than one scholarship is awarded per high school. In order to qualify, a senior must be graduating from a participating high school, must be maintaining a cumulative grade point average of at least 2.0, and must submit a brief essay. The student's extracurricular activities and community service are also considered. The President's Scholarship is available only to students enrolling in one of the College's degree programs. Students awarded the scholarship must enroll at Brown Mackie College–Boise between June and September immediately following their high school graduation. Applications for these scholarships can be obtained from the guidance departments of participating high schools. These applications must be completed and returned to the College by March 31.

Faculty

There are 17 full-time and 34 part-time faculty members at the College. The average student-faculty ratio is 15:1. Each student is assigned a department chair as an adviser.

Facilities and Resources

Opened in 2008, this modern facility offers more than 40,000 square feet of tastefully decorated classrooms, laboratories, and office space designed to specifications of the College for its business, medical, and technical programs. Instructional equipment is comparable to current technology used in business and industry today. Modern classrooms for special instructional needs offer multimedia capabilities with surround sound and overhead projectors accessible through computer, DVD, or VHS. Internet access and instructional resources are available at the College's library. Experienced faculty members provide academic support and are committed to the academic and technical preparation of their students.

The campus is nonresidential. The College has a generous parking area and is easily accessible by public transportation.

Location

Brown Mackie College–Boise is conveniently located at 9050 West Overland Road in Boise, Idaho.

Admission Requirements

Each applicant for admission is assigned an Assistant Director of Admissions who directs the applicant through the steps of the admissions process. They provide information on curriculum, policies, procedures, and services, and assist the applicant in setting necessary appointments and interviews.

To qualify for admission, each applicant must provide documentation of graduation from an accredited high school or from a state-approved secondary education curriculum or provide official documentation of high school graduation equivalency. All transcripts become the property of the College.

As part of the admission process, students are given an assessment of academic skills. Although the results of this assessment do not determine eligibility for admission, they provide the College with a means of determining the need for academic support as well as a means by which the College can evaluate the effectiveness of its educational programs. All new students are required to complete this assessment, which is readministered at the end of the student's program so results may be compared with those of the initial administration.

In addition to the College's general admission requirements, applicants enrolling in the occupational therapy assistant program must document one of the following: a high school cumulative grade point average of at least 2.5, a score on the GED examination of at least 57 (557 if taken on or after January 15, 2002), or completion of 12 quarter-credit hours or 8 semester-credit hours of collegiate course work with a grade point average of at least 2.5. Credit hours may not include Professional Development (CF 1100), the Brown Mackie College–Boise course. Students entering the program must also have completed a biology course with a grade of at least a C (or an average of at least 2.0 on a 4.0 scale).

For the most recent information regarding admission requirements, prospective students should refer to the current academic catalog.

Application and Information

Applicants must complete and submit an application form, along with documentation of graduation from an accredited high school or state-approved secondary education curriculum or official documentation of high school graduation equivalency.

For additional information, prospective students should contact:

Director of Admissions
Brown Mackie College–Boise
9050 West Overland Road
Boise, Idaho 83709
Phone: 208-321-8800
      888-810-9286 (toll-free)
Fax: 208-375-3249
E-mail: bmcboiadm@brownmackie.edu
Web site: http://www.brownmackie.edu/Boise

BROWN MACKIE COLLEGE–CINCINNATI

CINCINNATI, OHIO

The College and Its Mission

Brown Mackie College–Cincinnati is one of over twenty-five locations in the Brown Mackie College family of schools (www.brownmackie.edu), which is dedicated to providing educational programs that prepare students to pursue entry-level positions in a competitive, rapidly changing workplace. Brown Mackie College schools offer bachelor's degree, associate degree, certificate, and diploma programs in health sciences, business, information technology, legal studies, and design to over 20,000 students in the Midwest, Southeast, Southwest, and Western United States.

The College was founded in February 1927 as Southern Ohio Business College. In 1978, the College's main location was relocated from downtown Cincinnati to the Bond Hill–Roselawn area and in 1995 to its current location at 1011 Glendale-Milford Road in the community of Woodlawn.

Brown Mackie College–Cincinnati is accredited by the Accrediting Council for Independent Colleges and Schools (ACICS) to award associate degrees, certificates, and diplomas. The Accrediting Council for Independent Colleges and Schools is listed as a nationally recognized accrediting agency by the United States Department of Education and is recognized by the Council for Higher Education Accreditation. ACICS can be contacted at 750 First Street NE, Suite 980, Washington, D.C. 20002; phone: 202-336-6780.

The Brown Mackie College–Cincinnati Associate of Applied Science degree in surgical technology is accredited by the Commission on Accreditation of Allied Health Education Programs (www.caahep.org), upon the recommendation of the Accreditation Review Committee on Education in Surgical Technology. Commission on Accreditation of Allied Health Education Programs is located at 1361 Park Street Clearwater, Florida 33756; phone: 727-210-2350.

The Brown Mackie College–Cincinnati veterinary technology program has provisional programmatic accreditation granted by the American Veterinary Medical Association (AVMA) through the Committee on Veterinary Technician Education and Activities (CVTEA).

The College is licensed by the Ohio State Board of Career Colleges and Schools, 35 East Gay Street, Suite 403, Columbus, Ohio 43215-3138; phone: 614-466-2752. (Ohio registration #03-09-1686T).

The College is regulated by the Indiana Commission on Proprietary Education, 302 West Washington Street, Room E201, Indianapolis, Indiana 46204; phone: 800-227-5695 (toll-free) or 317-232-1320. (Indiana advertising code: AC0150).

The College is nonresidential and smoke free.

Academic Programs

Brown Mackie College–Cincinnati provides higher education to traditional and nontraditional students through associate degree, diploma, and certificate programs that can assist them in enhancing their career opportunities, broadening their perspectives through appropriate general education courses, thinking independently and critically, and improving problem-solving abilities. The College strives to develop within its students the desire for lifelong and continued education.

Each College quarter comprises twelve weeks. Associate degree programs require a minimum of eight quarters to complete. Programs are offered on a year-round basis, providing students with the ability to work uninterrupted toward their degrees. The College offers all programs in a unique One Course a Month format. This schedule allows students to focus studies on only one course for four weeks and has proven convenient for students with multiple obligations such as jobs and family.

Associate Degree Programs: The Associate of Applied Business degree is awarded in accounting technology, business management, computer networking and applications, criminal justice, information technology, office management, and paralegal. The Associate of Applied Science degree is awarded in architectural design and drafting technology, audio/video production, biomedical equipment technology, early childhood education, health care administration, medical assisting, pharmacy technology, surgical technology, and veterinary technology.

Diploma Programs: The College offers diploma programs in accounting, audio/video technician, business, criminal justice, medical assistant, paralegal assistant, and practical nursing.

Certificate Program: The College offers a certificate program in computer networking.

Costs

Tuition for the 2010–11 academic year was $285 per credit hour and $15 per credit hour for general fees. Tuition for the practical nursing program was $350 per credit hour and $25 per credit hour for general fees. Tuition for the surgical technology program was $330 per credit hour and $15 per credit hour for general fees. The cost of textbooks and other instructional materials varies by program.

Financial Aid

Financial aid is available to those who qualify. The College maintains a full-time staff of financial aid professionals to assist qualified students in obtaining financial assistance. The College participates in several student aid programs. Forms of financial aid available to qualified students through federal resources include the Federal Pell Grant Program, Federal Supplemental Educational Opportunity Grant (FSEOG) Program, Federal Work-Study Program, Federal Perkins Loan Program, Federal Stafford Student Loan Program (subsidized and unsubsidized), and the Federal PLUS Loan Program. Eligible students may apply for state awards, such as veterans' educational benefits. Students with physical or mental disabilities that are a handicap to employment may be eligible for training services through the state Agency for Vocational Rehabilitation. For further information, students should contact the College's Student Financial Services Office.

Each year, the College makes available President's Scholarships of up to $1000 each to qualifying seniors from area high schools. No more than one scholarship is awarded per high school. In order to qualify, a senior must be graduating from a participating high school, have maintained a cumulative grade point average of at least 2.0, and submitted a brief essay. The student's extracurricular activities and community service are also considered. The President's Scholarship is available only to students enrolling in one of the College's degree programs. Students awarded the scholarship must enroll at Brown Mackie College–Cincinnati between June and September immediately following their high school graduation. Applications for these scholarships can be obtained from the guidance departments of participating high schools. These applications must be completed and returned to the College by March 31.

The Education Foundation was established in 2000 to offer scholarship support to students interested in continuing their education at one of the postsecondary, career-focused schools in the EDMC system. The number and amount of the awards can vary depending on the funds available. Scholarship applications are considered every quarter. At Brown Mackie College–Cincinnati, applicants must be currently enrolled in an associate degree program and in their fourth quarter or higher (but no further than their second-to-last quarter) at the time of application. Awards are made based on academic performance and potential, as well as financial need.

Faculty

There are 40 full-time and 90 part-time faculty members. The average student-faculty ratio is 20:1. Each student has a faculty and student adviser.

Academic Facilities

Brown Mackie College–Cincinnati consists of more than 57,000 square feet of classroom, laboratory, and office space at the main campus and more than 28,000 square feet at the learning site. Both sites are designed to specifications of the College for its business, computer, medical, and creative programs.

Location

Brown Mackie College–Cincinnati is located in the Woodlawn section of Cincinnati, Ohio. The College is accessible by public transportation and provides parking at no cost. For added convenience, the College also holds classes at the Norwood Learning Site at 4805 Montgomery Road in Norwood, Ohio.

Admission Requirements

Each applicant for admission is assigned an Assistant Director of Admissions, who directs the applicant through the steps of the admissions process, providing information on curriculum, policies, procedures, and services and assisting the applicant in setting necessary appointments and interviews.

To qualify for admission, each applicant must provide documentation of graduation from an accredited high school or from a state-approved secondary education curriculum or provide official documentation of high school graduation equivalency. All transcripts become the property of the College. Admission to the College is based on the applicant meeting the stated requirements, a review of the applicant's previous educational records, and a review of the applicant's career interests. If previous academic records indicate that the College's education and training programs would not benefit the applicant, the College reserves the right to advise the applicant not to enroll. Special requirements for enrollment into certain programs are discussed in the descriptions of those programs.

For the most recent information regarding admission requirements, please refer to the current academic catalog.

Application and Information

Applicants must complete and submit an application form, along with documentation of graduation from an accredited high school or state-approved secondary education curriculum or official documentation of high school graduation equivalency.

For additional information, prospective students should contact:

Senior Director of Admissions
Brown Mackie College–Cincinnati
1011 Glendale-Milford Road
Cincinnati, Ohio 45215
Phone: 512-771-2424
      800-888-1445 (toll-free)
Fax: 513-771-3413
E-mail: bmcciadm@brownmackie.edu
Web site: http://www.brownmackie.edu/Cincinnati

BROWN MACKIE COLLEGE–FINDLAY

FINDLAY, OHIO

The College and Its Mission

Brown Mackie College–Findlay is one of over twenty-five locations in the Brown Mackie College family of schools (www.brownmackie.edu), which is dedicated to providing educational programs that prepare students to pursue entry-level positions in a competitive, rapidly changing workplace. Brown Mackie College schools offer bachelor's degree, associate degree, certificate, and diploma programs in health sciences, business, information technology, legal studies, and design to over 20,000 students in the Midwest, Southeast, Southwest, and Western United States.

Brown Mackie College–Findlay was founded in 1926 by William H. Stautzenberger to provide solid business education at a reasonable cost. In 1960, the College was acquired by George R. Hawes, who served as its president until 1969. The College changed its name from Southern Ohio College–Findlay in 2001 to AEC Southern Ohio College; it was changed again to Brown Mackie College–Findlay in November 2004.

Brown Mackie College–Findlay is accredited by the Accrediting Council for Independent Colleges and Schools (ACICS) to award associate degrees and diplomas. ACICS is listed as a nationally recognized accrediting agency by the U.S. Department of Education. Its accreditation of degree-granting institutions is recognized by the Council for Higher Education Accreditation. ACICS can be contacted at 750 First Street NE, Suite 980, Washington, D.C. 20002; phone: 202-336-6780.

The occupational therapy assistant program is accredited by the Accreditation Council for Occupational Therapy Education (ACOTE) of the American Occupational Therapy Association (AOTA), located at 4720 Montgomery Lane, P.O. Box 31220, Bethesda, Maryland 20824-1220; phone: 301-652-AOTA.

The Brown Mackie College–Findlay Associate of Applied Science degree in surgical technology is accredited by the Commission on Accreditation of Allied Health Education Programs (www.caahep.org) upon the recommendation of the Accreditation Review Committee on Education in Surgical Technology of the Commission on Accreditation of Allied Health Education Programs, 1361 Park Street Clearwater, Florida 33756; phone: 727-210-2350.

The veterinary technology program has provisional programmatic accreditation granted by the American Veterinary Medical Association (AVMA) through the Committee on Veterinary Technician Education and Activities (CVTEA).

The College is licensed by the Ohio State Board of Career Colleges and Schools, 35 East Gay Street, Suite 403, Columbus, Ohio 43215-3138; phone: 614-466-2752. (Ohio registration #03-09-1687T).

Brown Mackie College–Findlay is a nonresidential, smoke-free institution. Although the College does not offer residential housing, students who are unable to commute daily from their homes may request assistance from the Admissions Office in locating housing. Ample parking is available at no additional cost.

Academic Programs

Brown Mackie College–Findlay provides higher education to traditional and nontraditional students through associate degree and diploma programs that can assist them in enhancing their career opportunities, broadening their perspectives through appropriate general education courses, thinking independently and critically, and improving problem-solving abilities. The College strives to develop within its students the desire for lifelong and continued education.

Each College quarter comprises twelve weeks. Associate degree programs require a minimum of eight quarters to complete. Programs are offered on a year-round basis, providing students with the ability to work uninterrupted toward completion of their programs. The College offers all programs in a unique One Course a Month format. This schedule allows students to focus studies on only one course for four weeks and has proven convenient for students with multiple obligations such as jobs and family.

Associate Degree Programs: The Associate of Applied Business degree is awarded in accounting technology, business management, criminal justice, and paralegal. The Associate of Applied Science degree is awarded in architectural design and drafting technology, health care administration, medical assisting, occupational therapy assistant, pharmacy technology, surgical technology, and veterinary technology.

Diploma Programs: In addition to the associate degree programs, the College offers diploma programs in business, computer software applications, criminal justice, dental assisting, medical assistant, paralegal assistant, and practical nursing.

Costs

Tuition for programs in the 2010–11 academic year was $285 per credit hour, with a $15 per credit hour general fee. Tuition for the practical nursing diploma program was $350 per credit hour, with a $25 per credit hour general fee. Tuition for the occupational therapy assistant program was $350 per credit hour, with a $15 per credit hour general fee. Tuition for the surgical technology program was $330 per credit hour, with a $15 per credit hour general fee. The length of the program determines total cost. The cost of textbooks and other instructional materials varies by program.

Financial Aid

Financial aid is available to those who qualify. The College maintains a full-time staff of financial aid professionals to assist qualified students in obtaining financial assistance. The College participates in several student aid programs. Forms of financial aid available through federal resources include the Federal Pell Grant Program, Federal Supplemental Educational Opportunity

Grant (FSEOG) Program, Federal Work-Study Program, Federal Perkins Loan Program, Federal Stafford Student Loan Program (subsidized and unsubsidized), and the Federal PLUS Loan Program. Eligible students may apply for state awards, such as the Ohio Instructional Grant (OIG), and veterans' educational benefits. Students with physical or mental disabilities that are a handicap to employment may be eligible for training services through the state Agency for Vocational Rehabilitation. For further information, students should contact the College's Student Financial Services Office.

Each year, the College makes available President's Scholarships of up to $1000 each to qualifying seniors from area high schools. No more than one scholarship is awarded per high school. In order to qualify, a senior must be graduating from a participating high school, have maintained a cumulative grade point average of at least 2.0, and submitted a brief essay. The student's extracurricular activities and community service are also considered. The President's Scholarship is available only to students enrolling in one of the College's degree programs. Students awarded the scholarship must enroll at Brown Mackie College–Findlay between June and September immediately following their high school graduation. Applications for these scholarships can be obtained from the guidance departments of participating high schools. These applications must be completed and returned to the College by March 31.

Faculty

There are 27 full-time and 90 part-time adjunct instructors at the College. The average student-faculty ratio is 14:1. Each student is assigned a faculty adviser.

Academic Facilities

The College has more than 50,000 square feet of academic classrooms, laboratories, and offices. The facility includes seven networked computer labs, a criminal justice lab, a surgical technology lab, a pharmacy technology lab, two veterinary technology labs, four nursing labs, and a medical assisting lab. The labs provide students with hands-on opportunities to apply knowledge and skills learned in the classroom.

Location

Located at 1700 Fostoria Avenue, Suite 100, in Findlay, Ohio, the College is easily accessible from Interstate 75.

Admission Requirements

Each applicant for admission is assigned an Assistant Director of Admissions, who directs the applicant through the steps of the admissions process, providing information on curriculum, policies, procedures, and services and assisting the applicant in setting necessary appointments and interviews.

To qualify for admission, each applicant must provide documentation of graduation from an accredited high school or from a state-approved secondary education curriculum or provide official documentation of high school graduation equivalency. All transcripts become the property of the College. Admission to the College is based upon the applicant meeting the stated requirements, a review of the applicant's previous educational records, and a review of the applicant's career interests. If previous academic records indicate that the College's education and training programs would not benefit the applicant, the College reserves the right to advise the applicant not to enroll. Special requirements for enrollment into certain programs are discussed in the descriptions of those programs.

For the most recent information regarding admission requirements, please refer to the current academic catalog.

Application and Information

Applicants must complete and submit an application form, along with documentation of graduation from an accredited high school or state-approved secondary education curriculum or official documentation of high school graduation equivalency.

For additional information, prospective students should contact:

Director of Admissions
Brown Mackie College–Findlay
1700 Fostoria Avenue, Suite 100
Findlay, Ohio 45840
Phone: 419-423-2211
      800-842-3687 (toll-free)
Fax: 419-423-0725
E-mail: bmcfiadm@brownmackie.edu
Web site: http://www.brownmackie.edu/Findlay

BROWN MACKIE COLLEGE–FORT WAYNE

FORT WAYNE, INDIANA

The College and Its Mission

Brown Mackie College–Fort Wayne is one of over twenty-five locations in the Brown Mackie College family of schools (www.brownmackie.edu), which is dedicated to providing educational programs that prepare students to pursue entry-level positions in a competitive, rapidly changing workplace. Brown Mackie College schools offer bachelor's degree, associate degree, certificate, and diploma programs in health sciences, business, information technology, legal studies, and design to over 20,000 students in the Midwest, Southeast, Southwest, and Western United States.

Brown Mackie College–Fort Wayne is one of the oldest institutions of its kind in the country and the oldest in the state of Indiana. Established in 1882 as the South Bend Commercial College, the school later changed its name to Michiana College. In 1930, the College was incorporated under the laws of the state of Indiana and was authorized to confer associate degrees and certificates in business. In 1992, the College in South Bend added a branch location in Fort Wayne. In 2004, Michiana College changed its name to Brown Mackie College–Fort Wayne.

Brown Mackie College–Fort Wayne is owned and operated by Education Management Corporation (EDMC), 210 Sixth Avenue, 33rd Floor, Pittsburgh, Pennsylvania 15222-2603. EDMC has been in business for over forty years and is one of the largest providers of private post-secondary education in North America with eighty-nine campus locations in twenty-eight states and Canada.

Brown Mackie College–Fort Wayne is accredited by the Accrediting Council for Independent Colleges and Schools (ACICS) to award bachelor's degrees, associate degrees, diplomas, and certificates. ACICS is listed as a nationally recognized accrediting agency by the United States Department of Education and is recognized by the Council for Higher Education Accreditation. ACICS can be contacted at 750 First Street NE, Suite 980, Washington, D.C. 20002-4241; phone: 202-336-6780.

The occupational therapy assistant program is accredited by the Accreditation Council for Occupational Therapy Education (ACOTE) of the American Occupational Therapy Association (AOTA), 4720 Montgomery Lane, P.O. Box 31220, Bethesda, Maryland 20824-1220; phone: 301-652-2682. In order to practice as occupational therapy assistants, graduates must pass the certification examination for the certified occupational therapy assistant. Application for such examination is arranged through the National Board for Certification in Occupational Therapy, Inc. (NBCOT). Graduates may request application materials and the candidate handbook from NBCOT or apply online. For further information, graduates should contact NBCOT, 800 South Frederick Avenue, Suite 200, Gaithersburg, Maryland 20877-4150; phone: 301-990-7979; www.nbcot.org. To practice as an occupational therapy assistant in Indiana, a graduate must be certified by the state. Graduates may apply for a temporary permit to work between graduation and successful completion of certification examination. For information on application procedures for either a temporary permit or permanent state endorsement, graduates should contact the Occupational Therapy Committee, Health Professions Bureau, Indiana Government Center South, 402 West Washington Street, Room 041, Indianapolis, Indiana 46204; phone: 317-232-2960; e-mail: hbp6@hpb.state.in.us; www.in.gov/hpb/boards/otc/.

The College's diploma program in practical nursing is accredited by the Indiana State Board of Nursing, 402 West Washington Street, Room W066, Indianapolis, Indiana 46204; phone: 317-234-2043. Graduates are eligible to complete two applications: the National Council Licensure Examination (NCLEX) and the Indiana

licensure application. Indiana applications for licensure by examination must be completed by each candidate and be submitted to the Health Professions Bureau. Registration with NCLEX must be completed according to the instructions in the NCLEX Candidate Bulletin. Both the Indiana licensure application and the NCLEX registration process must be completed before eligibility to take the examination can be granted by the Indiana Board of Nursing. Graduates may obtain further information by contacting the Indiana State Board of Nursing, 402 West Washington Street, Room W066, Indianapolis, Indiana 46204; phone: 317-234-2043; www.ai.org/hpb.

The surgical technology program is accredited by the Accrediting Bureau of Health Education Schools (ABHES). Graduates of this program are eligible at their option to sit for the surgical technologist certification examination. Graduates who pass this examination are awarded the Certified Surgical Technologist (CST) credential. A CST must be recertified every four years through continuing education or reexamination. Further information can be obtained by contacting the Surgical Technology Program Director or by contacting the ABHES, 7777 Leesburg Pike, Suite 314 North, Falls Church, Virginia 22043; phone: 703-917-9503; www.abhes.org.

The College is licensed and regulated by the Indiana Commission on Proprietary Education, 302 West Washington Street, Room E201, Indianapolis, Indiana 46204; phone: 800-227-5695 (toll-free) or 317-232-1320. (Indiana advertising code: AC-0109).

Academic Programs

Brown Mackie College–Fort Wayne provides higher education to traditional and nontraditional students through bachelor's degree, associate degree, diploma, and certificate programs that assist them in enhancing their career opportunities, broadening their perspectives through appropriate general education courses, thinking independently and critically, and improving problem-solving abilities. The College strives to develop within its students the desire for lifelong and continued education.

Each College quarter comprises twelve weeks. Bachelor's degree programs require a minimum of sixteen quarters to complete. Associate degree programs require a minimum of eight quarters to complete. Programs are offered on a year-round basis, providing students with the ability to work uninterrupted toward their degrees. The College offers all programs in a unique One Course a Month format. This allows students to focus studies on only one course for four weeks. This schedule has proven convenient for students with multiple obligations such as jobs and family.

Bachelor's Degree Programs: The Bachelor of Science degree is awarded in business administration, criminal justice, health care management, and legal studies.

Associate Degree Programs: The Associate of Science degree is awarded in accounting technology, business management, criminal justice, health care administration, medical assisting, office management, paralegal, and surgical technology.

The Associate of Applied Science degree is awarded in biomedical equipment technology, dietetics technology, health and fitness training, health and therapeutic massage, nursing, occupational therapy assistant, physical therapist assistant, and veterinary technology.

Diploma Program: A diploma is awarded in practical nursing.

Certificate Programs: The College offers certificate programs in accounting, business, criminal justice, fitness trainer, medical assistant, and paralegal assistant.

Costs

Tuition in the 2010–11 academic year was $285 per credit hour with fees of $15 per credit hour for all programs except nursing, practical nursing, surgical technology, personal fitness training, occupational therapy assistant, and physical therapist assistant. The cost of textbooks and other instructional materials varies by program. For the nursing program, tuition was $390 per credit hour; fees were $25 per credit hour. For the practical nursing program, tuition was $350 per credit hour; fees were $25 per credit hour. For the surgical technology program, tuition was $330 per credit hour; fees were $15. Tuition for the personal fitness training programs was $295 per credit hour; fees were $25 per credit hour. Textbook expenses are estimated at $400 for the first term, $600 for the second term, and $100 for the third, fourth, and fifth terms. For certain courses in the occupational therapy assistant and physical therapist assistant programs, tuition was $350 per credit hour; fees were $15 per credit hour. Textbook expenses are estimated at $370 per quarter for the first six terms and $460 for the seventh term.

Financial Aid

The College maintains a full-time staff of financial aid professionals to assist qualified students in obtaining financial assistance. The College participates in several student aid programs. Forms of financial aid available through federal resources include the Federal Pell Grant Program, Federal Supplemental Educational Opportunity Grant (FSEOG) Program, Federal Work-Study Program, Federal Perkins Loan Program, Federal Stafford Student Loan Program (subsidized and unsubsidized), and the Federal PLUS Loan Program. Eligible students may apply for Indiana state awards, such as the Frank O'Bannon Grant Program (formerly the Indiana State Grant Program), the Higher Education Award, and Twenty-First Century Scholarships for high school students; the Core 40 awards; and veterans' educational benefits. For further information, students should contact the College Student Financial Services Office.

Each year, the College makes available President's Scholarships of $1000 each to qualifying seniors from area high schools. No more than one scholarship is awarded per high school. In order to qualify, a senior must have graduated from a participating high school, maintained a cumulative grade point average of at least 2.0, and submitted a brief essay. The student's extracurricular activities and community service are also considered. The President's Scholarship is available only to students enrolling in one of the College's degree programs. Students awarded the scholarship must enroll at Brown Mackie College–Fort Wayne between June and September immediately following their high school graduation. Applications for these scholarships can be obtained from the guidance departments of participating high schools. These applications must be completed and returned to the College by March 31.

Faculty

The College has 45 full-time and 80 part-time instructors, with a student-faculty ratio of 15:1. Each student is assigned a faculty adviser.

Facilities and Resources

In 2005, the campus relocated to a 75,000-square-foot facility at 3000 East Coliseum Boulevard. Record enrollment allowed the institution to triple in size in less than one year. The three-story building offers a modern, professional environment for study. Ten classrooms are outfitted as "classrooms of the future," with an instructor workstation, full multimedia capabilities, a surround sound system, and projection screen that can be accessed by computer, DVD, or VHS equipment. The Brown Mackie College–Fort Wayne facility includes a criminal justice lab, surgical technology labs, medical labs, computer labs, and occupational and physical therapy labs, as well as a library and bookstore. The labs provide students with hands-on opportunities to apply knowledge and skills learned in the classroom. Students are welcome to use the labs when those facilities are not in use for scheduled classes.

The College is nonresidential. The College facility is accessible by public transportation. Ample parking is provided at no additional charge. The campus is a smoke-free facility.

Location

Brown Mackie College–Fort Wayne is located at 3000 East Coliseum Boulevard in Fort Wayne, Indiana. For added convenience, the College also operates a learning site at 2135 South Hannah Drive in Fort Wayne.

Admission Requirements

Each applicant for admission is assigned an Assistant Director of Admissions, who directs the applicant through the steps of the admissions process, providing information on curriculum, policies, procedures, and services and assisting the applicant in setting necessary appointments and interviews.

To qualify for admission, each applicant must provide documentation of graduation from an accredited high school or from a state-approved secondary education curriculum or provide official documentation of high school graduation equivalency. All transcripts become the property of the College. Admission to the College is based on the applicant meeting the stated requirements, a review of the applicant's previous educational records, and a review of the applicant's career interests. If previous academic records indicate the College's education and training programs would not benefit the applicant, the College reserves the right to advise the applicant not to enroll. Special requirements for enrollment into certain programs are discussed in the descriptions of those programs.

In addition to the College's general admission requirements, applicants enrolling in the practical nursing program must document the following, which must be completed and a record of proof must appear in the student's file prior to the start of the nursing fundamentals course. No student will be admitted to a clinical agency unless all paperwork is completed. This paperwork is a requirement of all contracted agencies. This paperwork includes records of (1) a complete physical, current to within six months of admission; (2) a two-step Mantoux test that is kept current throughout schooling; (3) a hepatitis B vaccination or signed refusal; (4) up-to-date immunizations, including tetanus and rubella; (5) a record of current CPR certification that is maintained throughout the student's clinical experience; and (6) hospitalization insurance or a signed waiver.

Application and Information

Applicants must complete and submit an application form along with documentation of graduation from an accredited high school or state-approved secondary education curriculum, or official documentation of high school graduation equivalency.

For additional information, prospective students should contact:

Director of Admissions
Brown Mackie College–Fort Wayne
3000 East Coliseum Boulevard
Fort Wayne, Indiana 46805
Phone: 260-484-4400
      866-433-2289 (toll-free)
Fax: 260-484-2678
E-mail: bmcfwaadm@brownmackie.edu
Web site: http://www.brownmackie.edu/FortWayne

BROWN MACKIE COLLEGE–GREENVILLE

GREENVILLE, SOUTH CAROLINA

The College and Its Mission

Brown Mackie College–Greenville is one of over twenty-five locations in the Brown Mackie College family of schools (www.brownmackie.edu), which is dedicated to providing educational programs that prepare students to pursue entry-level positions in a competitive, rapidly changing workplace. Brown Mackie College schools offer bachelor's degree, associate degree, and certificate programs in health sciences, business, information technology, and legal studies to over 20,000 students in the Midwest, Southeast, Southwest, and Western United States.

Brown Mackie College was originally founded and approved by the Board of Trustees of Kansas Wesleyan College in Salina, Kansas on July 30, 1892. In 1938, the College was incorporated as The Brown Mackie School of Business under the ownership of Perry E. Brown and A. B. Mackie, former instructors at Kansas Wesleyan University in Salina, Kansas. Their last names formed the name of Brown Mackie. By January 1975, with improvements in curricula and higher degree-granting status, The Brown Mackie School of Business became Brown Mackie College.

Brown Mackie College–Greenville is accredited by the Accrediting Council for Independent Colleges and Schools (ACICS) to award certificates, associate degrees, and bachelor's degrees. ACICS is listed as a nationally recognized accrediting agency by the United States Department of Education and is recognized by the Council for Higher Education Accreditation. ACICS can be contacted at 750 First Street NE, Suite 980, Washington, D.C. 20002; phone: 202-336-6780.

The occupational therapy assistant program has applied for accreditation by the Accreditation Council for Occupational Therapy Education (ACOTE) of the American Occupational Therapy Association (AOTA), located at 4720 Montgomery Lane, P.O. Box 31220, Bethesda, Maryland 20824; phone: 301-652-AOTA.

Academic Programs

Brown Mackie College–Greenville provides higher education to traditional and nontraditional students through bachelor's degree, associate degree, and certificate programs that assist in enhancing their career opportunities, broadening their perspectives through appropriate general education courses, thinking independently and critically, and improving problem-solving abilities. The College strives to develop within its students the desire for lifelong and continued education.

Each College quarter comprises twelve weeks. Bachelor's degree programs require a minimum of sixteen quarters to complete. Associate degree programs require a minimum of eight quarters to complete. Programs are offered on a year-round basis, providing students with the ability to work uninterrupted toward completion of their degrees. The College offers all programs in a unique One Course a Month format. This allows students to focus studies on only one course for four weeks. This schedule has proven convenient for students with multiple obligations such as jobs and family.

Bachelor's Degree Programs: The Bachelor of Science degree is awarded in business administration, criminal justice, health care management, and legal studies.

Associate Degree Programs: The Associate of Applied Science degree is awarded in accounting technology, business management, criminal justice, health care administration, information technology, medical assisting, occupational therapy assistant, office management, paralegal, and surgical technology.

Certificate Programs: The certificate is awarded in accounting, business, criminal justice, medical assistant, and paralegal assistant.

Costs

Tuition in the 2010–11 academic year for most bachelor's and associate degrees and certificates was $285 per credit hour; fees were $15 per credit hour. Tuition for the occupational therapy assistant program was $350 per credit hour; fees were $15 per credit hour. Tuition for the surgical technology program was $330 per credit hour; fees were $15 per credit hour. The cost of textbooks and other instructional expenses varies by program.

Financial Aid

Financial aid is available for those who qualify. The College maintains a full-time staff of financial aid professionals to assist qualified students in obtaining the financial assistance they require to meet their educational expenses. Available resources include federal and state aid, student loans from private lenders, and Federal Work-Study opportunities, both on and off college premises.

Each year, the College makes available President's Scholarships of $1000 each to qualifying seniors from area high schools. No more than one scholarship is awarded per high school. In order to qualify, a senior must have graduated from a participating high school, maintained a cumulative grade point average of at least 2.0, and submitted a brief essay. The student's extracurricular activities and community service are also considered. The President's Scholarship is available only to students enrolling in one of the College's degree programs. Students awarded the scholarship must enroll at Brown Mackie College–Greenville between June and September immediately following their high school graduation. Applications for these scholarships can be obtained from the guidance departments of participating high schools. These applications must be completed and returned to the College by March 31.

Faculty

Experienced faculty members provide academic support and are committed to the academic and technical preparation of their students. The College has 9 full-time and 30 part-time instructors, with a student-faculty ratio of 24:1. Each student is assigned a faculty adviser.

Facilities and Resources

A modern facility, Brown Mackie College–Greenville offers more than 40,000 square feet of educational space. The College is equipped with multiple computer labs housing over 100 computers; high-speed access to the Internet and other online resources are available for students and faculty. Multimedia classrooms are outfitted with overhead projectors, VCR/DVD players, and computers.

The campus is nonresidential. The College has a generous parking area and is easily accessible by public transportation. The campus is a smoke-free facility.

Location

Brown Mackie College–Greenville is conveniently located at Two Liberty Square, 75 Beattie Place, Suite 100, in Greenville, South Carolina.

Admission Requirements

Each applicant for admission is assigned an Assistant Director of Admissions who directs the applicant through the steps of the admissions process. They provide information on curriculum, policies, procedures, and services and assist the applicant in setting necessary appointments and interviews.

To qualify for admission, each applicant must provide documentation of graduation from an accredited high school or a state-approved secondary education curriculum, or provide official documentation of high school graduation equivalency. All transcripts become the property of the College. Admission to the College is based on the applicant meeting the stated requirements, a review of the applicant's previous educational records, and a review of the applicant's career interests. If previous academic records indicate the College's education and training programs would not benefit the applicant, the College reserves the right to advise the applicant not to enroll. Special requirements for enrollment into certain programs are discussed in the descriptions of those programs.

For the most recent information regarding admission requirements, prospective students should refer to the current academic catalog.

Application and Information

Applicants must complete and submit an application form along with documentation of graduation from an accredited high school or state-approved secondary education curriculum or official documentation of high school graduation equivalency.

For additional information, prospective students should contact:

Director of Admissions
Brown Mackie College–Greenville
Two Liberty Square
75 Beattie Place, Suite 100
Greenville, South Carolina 29601
Phone: 864-239-5300
877-479-8465 (toll-free)
Fax: 864-232-4094
E-mail: bmcgrweb@brownmackie.edu
Web site: http://www.brownmackie.edu/greenville

BROWN MACKIE COLLEGE–HOPKINSVILLE

HOPKINSVILLE, KENTUCKY

BROWN MACKIE COLLEGE
HOPKINSVILLE™

The College and Its Mission

Brown Mackie College–Hopkinsville is one of over twenty-five locations in the Brown Mackie College family of schools (www.brownmackie.edu), which is dedicated to providing educational programs that prepare students to pursue entry-level positions in a competitive, rapidly changing workplace. Brown Mackie College schools offer bachelor's degree, associate degree, certificate, and diploma programs in health sciences, business, information technology, legal studies, and design to over 20,000 students in the Midwest, Southeast, Southwest, and Western United States.

Brown Mackie College–Hopkinsville is accredited by the Accrediting Council for Independent Colleges and Schools (ACICS) to award associate degrees and diplomas. ACICS is listed as a nationally recognized accrediting agency by the United States Department of Education and is recognized by the Council for Higher Education Accreditation. ACICS can be contacted at 750 First Street NE, Suite 980, Washington, D.C. 20002; phone: 202-336-6780.

The occupational therapy assistant program is accredited by the Accreditation Council for Occupational Therapy Education (ACOTE) of the American Occupational Therapy Association (AOTA), located at 4720 Montgomery Lane, P.O. Box 31220, Bethesda, Maryland 20824-1220; phone: 301-652-AOTA.

Brown Mackie College–Hopkinsville is authorized for operation as a postsecondary educational institution by the Tennessee Higher Education Commission (www.state.tn.us/thec).

The College is a nonresidential, smoke-free institution.

Academic Programs

Brown Mackie College–Hopkinsville provides higher education to traditional and nontraditional students through associate degree and diploma programs that can assist them in enhancing their career opportunities, broadening their perspectives through appropriate general education courses, thinking independently and critically, and improving problem-solving abilities.

Each College quarter comprises ten to twelve weeks. Programs are offered on a year-round basis, providing students with the ability to work uninterrupted toward their degrees. The College offers all programs in a unique One Course a Month format. This schedule allows students to focus studies on only one course for four weeks and has proven convenient for students with multiple obligations such as jobs and family.

Associate Degree Programs: Associate degree programs require a minimum of eight quarters to complete. The Associate of Applied Business degree is awarded in accounting technology, business management, criminal justice, and paralegal. The Associate of Applied Science degree is awarded in medical assisting, medical office management, and occupational therapy assistant.

Diploma Programs: The College also offers diploma programs in business, medical assistant, and medical coding and billing for healthcare.

Costs

Tuition for the 2010–11 academic year was $285 per credit hour with a general fee of $15 per credit hour. Tuition for the occupational therapy assistant program was $350 per credit hour, with a general fee of $15 per credit hour. The cost of textbooks and other instructional materials varied by program.

Financial Aid

Financial aid is available to those who qualify. The College maintains a full-time staff of financial aid professionals to assist qualified students in obtaining the financial assistance they require to meet their educational expenses. The College participates in several student aid programs. Forms of financial aid available through federal resources include Federal Pell Grants, Federal Supplemental Educational Opportunity Grants (FSEOG), the Federal Work-Study Program, Federal Stafford Student Loans (subsidized and unsubsidized), and the Federal PLUS Program. Students may apply for the College Access Program (CAP) grant. Eligible students may also apply for veterans' educational benefits. Students with physical or mental disabilities that are a handicap to employment may be eligible for training services through the State Vocational Rehabilitation Agency. For further information, students should contact the College's Student Financial Services Office.

Faculty

There are 4 full-time and approximately 20 adjunct instructors. The student-faculty ratio is 10:1.

Facilities and Resources

Brown Mackie College–Hopkinsville occupies a spacious building that has been specifically designed to provide a comfortable and effective environment for learning. The facility comprises approximately 17,100 square feet, including sixteen classrooms, two medical laboratories, an academic resource center, administrative and faculty offices, a bookstore, and a student lounge. Computer equipment for hands-on learning includes six networked laboratories. Medical equipment includes monocular and binocular microscopes, electrocardiograph, autoclave, centrifuge, and other equipment appropriate to hands-on laboratory and clinical instruction. Convenient parking is available to all students.

Location

The College is conveniently located at 4001 Fort Campbell Boulevard in Hopkinsville, Kentucky.

Admission Requirements

Each applicant for admission is assigned an Assistant Director of Admissions who directs the applicant through the steps of the admissions process, providing information on curriculum, policies, procedures, and services and assisting the applicant in setting necessary appointments and interviews.

To qualify for admission, each applicant must provide documentation of graduation from an accredited high school or from a state-approved secondary education curriculum or provide official documentation of high school graduation equivalency. All transcripts become the property of the College. Admission to the College is based upon the applicant meeting the stated requirements, a review of the applicant's previous education records, and a review of the applicant's career interests. If previous academic records indicate that the College's education and training programs would not benefit the applicant, the College reserves the right to advise the applicant not to enroll. Special requirements for enrollment into certain programs are discussed in the descriptions of those programs.

For the most recent information regarding admission requirements, please refer to the current academic catalog.

Application and Information

Applicants must complete and submit an application form, along with documentation of graduation from an accredited high school or state-approved secondary education curriculum or provide official documentation of high school graduation equivalency. For additional information, prospective students should contact:

Director of Admissions
Brown Mackie College–Hopkinsville
4001 Fort Campbell Boulevard
Hopkinsville, Kentucky 42240

Phone: 270-886-1302
       800-359-4753 (toll-free)
Fax: 270-886-3544
E-mail: bmchoadm@brownmackie.edu
Web site: http://www.brownmackie.edu/Hopkinsville

BROWN MACKIE COLLEGE–INDIANAPOLIS

INDIANAPOLIS, INDIANA

The College and Its Mission

Brown Mackie College–Indianapolis is one of over twenty-five locations in the Brown Mackie College family of schools (www.brownmackie.edu), which is dedicated to providing educational programs that prepare students to pursue entry-level positions in a competitive, rapidly changing workplace. Brown Mackie College schools offer bachelor's degree, associate degree, certificate, and diploma programs in health sciences, business, information technology, legal studies, and design to over 20,000 students in the Midwest, Southeast, Southwest, and Western United States.

Brown Mackie College–Indianapolis was founded in 2007 as a branch of Brown Mackie College–Findlay, Ohio.

Brown Mackie College–Indianapolis is accredited by the Accrediting Council for Independent Colleges and Schools (ACICS) to award bachelor's degrees, associate degrees, diplomas, and certificates. The Accrediting Council for Independent Colleges and Schools is listed as a nationally recognized accrediting agency by the United States Department of Education and is recognized by the Council for Higher Education Accreditation. ACICS can be contacted at 750 First Street NE, Suite 980, Washington, D.C. 20002; phone: 202-336-6780.

The occupational therapy assistant program is accredited by the Accreditation Council for Occupational Therapy Education (ACOTE) of the American Occupational Therapy Association (AOTA), located at 4720 Montgomery Lane, P.O. Box 31220, Bethesda, Maryland 20824; phone: 301-652-AOTA.

Brown Mackie College–Indianapolis is regulated by the Indiana Commission on Proprietary Education, 302 West Washington Street, Indianapolis, Indiana 46204; phone: 317-232-1320 or 800-227-5695 (toll-free). (Indiana advertising code: AC-0078).

Academic Programs

Brown Mackie College–Indianapolis provides higher education to traditional and nontraditional students through bachelor's degree, associate degree, diploma, and certificate programs that can assist them in enhancing their career opportunities, broadening their perspectives through appropriate general education courses, thinking independently and critically, and improving problem-solving abilities. The College strives to develop within its students the desire for lifelong and continued education.

Each College quarter comprises twelve weeks. Bachelor's degree programs require a minimum of sixteen quarters to complete. Associate degree programs require a minimum of eight quarters to complete. Programs are offered on a year-round basis, providing students with the ability to work uninterrupted toward their degrees. The College offers all programs in a unique One Course a Month format. This schedule allows students to focus studies on only one course for four weeks and has proven convenient for students with multiple obligations such as jobs and family.

Bachelor's Degree Programs: The Bachelor of Science degree is awarded in business administration, criminal justice, and legal studies.

Associate Degree Programs: The Associate of Science degree is awarded in business management, criminal justice, health care administration, medical assisting, and paralegal. The Associate of Applied Science degree is awarded in occupational therapy assistant.

Diploma Program: The College offers a diploma program in practical nursing.

Certificate Programs: The College offers certificate programs in business and medical assistant.

Costs

Tuition for most programs in the 2010–11 academic year was $303 per credit hour with a $15 per credit hour general fee. Tuition for the practical nursing diploma program was $350 per credit hour with a $25 per credit hour general fee applied to instructional costs for activities and services. For the occupational therapy assistant program, the tuition was $350 per credit hour with a $15 per credit hour general fee.

Financial Aid

Financial aid is available to those who qualify. The College maintains a full-time staff of financial aid professionals to assist qualified students in obtaining the financial assistance they require to meet their educational expenses. Available resources include federal and state aid, student loans from private lenders, and Federal Work-Study opportunities, both on and off college premises. Federal assistance programs are administered through the U.S. Department of Education, Office of Student Financial Assistance. Any U.S. citizen, national, or person in the United States for other than temporary reasons who is enrolled or accepted for enrollment may apply for these programs.

Each year, the College makes available scholarships of up to $1000 each to qualifying seniors from area high schools. No more than one scholarship is awarded per high school. In order to qualify, a senior must be graduating from a participating high school, have maintained a cumulative grade point average of at least 2.0, and submitted a brief essay. The student's extracurricular activities and community service are also considered. These scholarships are available only to students enrolling in one of the College's degree programs. Students awarded the scholarship must enroll at Brown Mackie College–Indianapolis between June and September immediately following their high school graduation. Applications for these scholarships can be obtained from the guidance departments of participating high schools. These applications must be completed and returned to the College by March 31.

Faculty

The College has 24 full-time instructors, 77 adjunct instructors, and 16 lab assistants, and a student-faculty ratio of 12:1. Faculty members provide tutoring and additional academic services to students as needed.

Facilities and Resources

Opened in January 2008, this modern facility offers more than 22,000 square feet of tastefully decorated classrooms, laboratories, and office space designed to the specifications of the College for its business, medical, and technical programs. Instructional equipment is comparable to industry-current technology used in business today. Modern classrooms for special instructional needs offer multimedia capabilities with surround sound and overhead projectors accessible through computer, DVD, or VHS. Internet access and instructional resources are available at the College's library. Experienced faculty members provide academic support and are committed to the academic and technical preparation of their students.

Location

Brown Mackie College–Indianapolis is located at 1200 North Meridian Street, Indianapolis, Indiana. The College is accessible by public transportation and provides ample parking at no cost.

Admission Requirements

Each applicant for admission is assigned an Assistant Director of Admissions, who directs the applicant through the steps of the admissions process, providing information on curriculum, policies, procedures, and services and assisting the applicant in setting necessary appointments and interviews.

To qualify for admission, each applicant must provide documentation of graduation from an accredited high school or from a state-approved secondary education curriculum or provide official documentation of high school graduation equivalency. All transcripts become the property of the College. Admission to the College is based on the applicant meeting the stated requirements, a review of the applicant's previous educational records, and a review of the applicant's career interests. If previous academic records indicate the College's education and training programs would not benefit the applicant, the College reserves the right to advise the applicant not to enroll. Special requirements for enrollment into certain programs are discussed in the descriptions of those programs.

For the most recent information regarding admission requirements, please refer to the current academic catalog.

Application and Information

Applicants must complete and submit an application form, along with documentation of graduation from an accredited high school or state-approved secondary education curriculum or official documentation of high school graduation equivalency.

For additional information, prospective students should contact:

Director of Admissions
Brown Mackie College–Indianapolis
1200 North Meridian Street, Suite 100
Indianapolis, Indiana 46204
Phone: 317-554-8301
      866-255-0279 (toll-free)
Fax: 317-632-4557
E mail: bmcindadm@brownmackie.edu
Web site: http://www.brownmackie.edu/Indianapolis

BROWN MACKIE COLLEGE–KANSAS CITY

LENEXA, KANSAS

The College and Its Mission

Brown Mackie College–Kansas City is one of over twenty-five locations in the Brown Mackie College family of schools (www.brownmackie.edu), which is dedicated to providing educational programs that prepare students to pursue entry-level positions in a competitive, rapidly changing workplace. Brown Mackie College schools offer bachelor's degree, associate degree, certificate, and diploma programs in health sciences, business, information technology, legal studies, and design to over 20,000 students in the Midwest, Southeast, Southwest, and Western United States.

The College was originally founded in Salina, Kansas, in July 1892 as the Kansas Wesleyan School of Business. In 1938, the College was incorporated as the Brown Mackie School of Business under the ownership of former Kansas Wesleyan instructors Perry E. Brown and A. B. Mackie. It became Brown Mackie College in January 1975.

Brown Mackie College in Lenexa, Kansas is a branch of Brown Mackie College in Salina, Kansas which accredited by the Higher Learning Commission and is a member of the North Central Association (NCA), 230 South LaSalle Street, Suite 7-500, Chicago, Illinois 60604-1413; phone: 800-621-7440 (toll free); www.ncahlc.org.

Brown Mackie College in Lenexa, Kansas is approved and authorized to grant the Associate of Applied Science (AAS) degree by the Kansas Board of Regents, 1000 Southwest Jackson Street, Suite 520, Topeka, Kansas 66612-1368.

The occupational therapy assistant program is accredited by the Accreditation Council for Occupational Therapy Education (ACOTE) of the American Occupational Therapy Association (AOTA), located at 4720 Montgomery Lane, P.O. Box 31220, Bethesda, Maryland 20824; phone: 301-652-AOTA.

Brown Mackie College–Kansas City is nonresidential, smoke free, and provides ample parking at no additional cost.

Academic Programs

Brown Mackie College–Kansas City provides higher education to traditional and nontraditional students through associate degree, diploma, and certificate programs that can assist them in enhancing their career opportunities, broadening their perspectives through appropriate general education courses, thinking independently and critically, and improving problem-solving abilities. The College strives to develop within its students the desire for lifelong and continued education.

In most programs, students can participate in day or evening classes, which begin every month. Programs are offered on a year-round basis, providing students with the ability to work uninterrupted toward completion of their programs. The College offers all programs in a unique One Course a Month

format. This schedule allows students to focus studies on only one course for four weeks and has proven convenient for students with multiple obligations such as jobs and family.

Associate Degree Programs: The Associate of Applied Science degree is awarded in accounting technology, architectural design and drafting technology, bioscience laboratory technology, business management, computer aided design and drafting technology, criminal justice, health and fitness training, health care administration, medical assisting, nursing, occupational therapy assistant, office management, paralegal, and veterinary technology.

Diploma Programs: The College also offers diploma programs in accounting, business, computer aided design and drafting technician, computer software applications, criminal justice, fitness trainer, medical assistant, and paralegal assistant.

Certificate Program: A certificate program is offered in practical nursing.

Costs

Tuition for programs in the 2010–11 academic year was $285 per credit hour and $15 per credit hour for general fees. Tuition for nursing programs was $325 per credit hour with general fees of $25 per credit hour. Tuition for the health and fitness training program was $295 per credit hour with general fees of $15 per credit hour. Tuition for the occupational therapy assistant program was $350 per credit hour with fees of $15 per credit hour. The cost of textbooks and other instructional materials varies by program.

Financial Aid

Financial aid is available to those who qualify. The College maintains a full-time staff of financial aid professionals to assist qualified students in obtaining financial assistance. The College participates in several student aid programs. Forms of financial aid available to qualified students through federal resources include Federal Pell Grants, Federal Supplemental Educational Opportunity Grants (FSEOG), Academic Competitiveness Grant, Federal Work-Study Program, Federal Perkins Loans, Federal Stafford Student Loans (subsidized and unsubsidized), Federal Direct Loans (subsidized and unsubsidized), and the Federal PLUS Program. Eligible students may apply for veterans' educational benefits. Students with physical or mental disabilities that are a handicap to employment may be eligible for training services through the state Vocational Rehabilitation Agency. For further information, students should contact the College's Student Financial Services Office.

Each year, the College makes available President's Scholarships of up to $1000 each to qualifying seniors from area high schools. No more than one scholarship is awarded per high school. In order to qualify, a senior must be graduating from a participating high school, have maintained a cumulative grade point average of at least 2.0, and submitted a brief essay. The student's extracurricular activities and community service are also considered. The President's Scholarship is available only to students enrolling in one of the College's degree programs. Students awarded the scholarship must enroll at Brown Mackie College–Kansas City between June and September immediately following their high school graduation. Applications for these scholarships can be obtained from the guidance departments of participating high schools. These applications must be completed and returned to the College by March 31.

Faculty

There are 23 full-time faculty members and 25 adjunct faculty members. The average class student-instructor ratio is 14:1.

Facilities and Resources

In addition to classrooms and computer labs, the College maintains a library of curriculum-related resources, technical and general education materials, academic and professional periodicals, and audiovisual resources. Internet access also is available for research. The College has a bookstore that stocks texts, courseware, and other educational supplies required for courses and a variety of personal, recreational, and gift items, including apparel, supplies, and general merchandise incorporating the College logo. Hours are posted at the bookstore entrance.

Location

Brown Mackie College–Kansas City is located at 9705 Lenexa Drive in Lenexa, Kansas, just off Interstate 35 at 95th Street in Johnson County. The Olathe course site is located at 450 North Rogers Road, Suite 175, in Olathe, Kansas, just off Interstate 35 and Santa Fe Street in Johnson County.

Admission Requirements

Each applicant for admission is assigned an Assistant Director of Admissions, who directs the applicant through the steps of the admissions process, providing information on curriculum, policies, procedures, and services and assisting the applicant in setting necessary appointments and interviews.

To qualify for admission, each applicant must provide documentation of graduation from an accredited high school or from a state-approved secondary education curriculum or provide official documentation of high school graduation equivalency. All transcripts become the property of the College. Admission to the College is based upon the applicant meeting the stated requirements, a review of the applicant's previous education records, and a review of the applicant's career interests. If previous academic records indicate that the College's education and training programs would not benefit the applicant, the College reserves the right to advise the applicant not to enroll. Special requirements for enrollment into certain programs are discussed in the descriptions of those programs.

For the most recent information regarding admission requirements, please refer to the current academic catalog.

Application and Information

Applicants must complete and submit an application form, along with documentation of graduation from an accredited high school or state-approved secondary education curriculum or official documentation of high school graduation equivalency. For additional information, prospective students should contact:

Director of Admissions
Brown Mackie College–Kansas City
9705 Lenexa Drive
Lenexa, Kansas 66215
Phone: 913-768-1900
       800-635-9101 (toll-free)
Fax: 913-495-9555
E-mail: bmckcadm@brownmackie.edu
Web site: http://www.brownmackie.edu/KansasCity

BROWN MACKIE COLLEGE–LOUISVILLE
LOUISVILLE, KENTUCKY

The College and Its Mission

Brown Mackie College–Louisville is one of over twenty-five locations in the Brown Mackie College family of schools (www.brownmackie.edu), which is dedicated to providing educational programs that prepare students to pursue entry-level positions in a competitive, rapidly changing workplace. Brown Mackie College schools offer bachelor's degree, associate degree, certificate, and diploma programs in health sciences, business, information technology, legal studies, and design to over 20,000 students in the Midwest, Southeast, Southwest, and Western United States.

Brown Mackie College–Louisville opened in 1972 as RETS Institute of Technology. The first RETS school was founded in 1935 in Detroit in response to the rapid growth of radio broadcasting and the need for qualified radio technicians. The RETS Institute changed its name to Brown Mackie College–Louisville in 2004.

Brown Mackie College–Louisville is accredited by the Accrediting Council for Independent Colleges and Schools (ACICS) to award bachelor's degrees, associate degrees, certificates, and diplomas. The Accrediting Council for Independent Colleges and Schools is listed as a nationally recognized accrediting agency by the United States Department of Education and is recognized by the Council for Higher Education Accreditation. ACICS can be contacted at 750 First Street NE, Suite 980, Washington, D.C. 20002-4241; phone: 202-336-6780.

Brown Mackie College–Louisville is licensed by the Kentucky Council on Postsecondary Education for all programs offered by the College. The council is located at 1024 Capital Center Drive, Suite 320 Frankfort, Kentucky 40601.

Brown Mackie College–Louisville is regulated by the Indiana Commission on Proprietary Education, 302 West Washington Street, Indianapolis, Indiana 46204; phone: 317-232-1320 or 800-227-5695 (toll-free). (Indiana advertising code: AC-0045).

The Brown Mackie College–Louisville's Associate of Applied Science degree in surgical technology is accredited by the Accrediting Bureau of Health Education Schools, 7777 Leesburg Pike, Suite 314N, Falls Church, Virginia 22043; phone: 703-917-9503.

The occupational therapy assistant program is accredited by the Accreditation Council for Occupational Therapy Education (ACOTE) of the American Occupational Therapy Association (AOTA), located at 4720 Montgomery Lane, P.O. Box 31220, Bethesda, Maryland 20824; phone: 301-652-AOTA.

The veterinary technology program is accredited as a program for educating veterinary technicians by the American Veterinary Medical Association (AVMA), 1931 North Meacham Road, Suite 100, Schaumburg, Illinois 60173.

Academic Programs

Brown Mackie College–Louisville provides higher education to traditional and nontraditional students through bachelor's degree, associate degree, and diploma programs that assist in enhancing their career opportunities, broadening their perspectives through appropriate general education courses, thinking independently and critically, and improving problem-solving abilities.

Each College quarter comprises twelve weeks. Bachelor's degree programs require a minimum of sixteen quarters to complete. Associate degree programs require a minimum of eight quarters to complete. Programs are offered on a year-round basis, providing students with the ability to work uninterrupted toward completion of their programs. The College offers all programs in a unique One Course a Month format. This allows students to focus studies on only one course for four weeks. This schedule has proven convenient for students with multiple obligations such as jobs and family.

Bachelor's Degree Programs: The Bachelor of Science degree is awarded in business administration, criminal justice, health care management, and legal studies.

Associate Degree Programs: The Associate of Applied Business degree is awarded in accounting technology, business management, computer networking and applications, criminal justice, graphic design, and paralegal. The Associate of Applied Science degree is awarded in biomedical equipment technology, electronics, health care administration, medical assisting, occupational therapy assistant, pharmacy technology, surgical technology, and veterinary technology.

Diploma Program: The College offers a diploma program in practical nursing.

Certificate Program: The College offers a certificate program in computer networking.

Costs

Tuition for most programs in the 2010–11 academic year was $285 per credit hour and the general fees were $15 per credit hour. The practical nursing diploma program was $350 per credit hour and the general fees were $25 per credit hour. The surgical technology program was $330 per credit hour and the general fees were $15 per credit hour. The occupational therapy program was $350 per credit hour, and the general fees were $15 per credit hour. The computer networking certificate program was $300 per credit hour and the general fees were $25 per credit hour. The length of the program determines total cost. The cost of textbooks and other instructional materials varies by program.

Financial Aid

Financial aid is available for those who qualify. The College maintains a full-time staff of financial aid professionals to assist qualified students in obtaining financial assistance. The College participates in several student aid programs. Forms of financial aid available through federal resources include the Federal Pell Grant Program, Federal Supplemental Educational Opportunity Grant (FSEOG) Program, Federal Work-Study Program, Federal Perkins Loan Program, Federal Stafford Student Loan Program (subsidized and unsubsidized), and the Federal PLUS Loan Program.

Each year, the College makes available President's Scholarships of $1000 each to qualifying seniors from area high schools. No more than one scholarship is awarded per high school. In order to qualify, a senior must have graduated from a participating high school, maintained a cumulative grade point average of at least 2.0, and submitted a brief essay. The student's extracurricular activities and community service are also considered. The President's Scholarship is available only to students enrolling in one of the College's degree programs. Students awarded the scholarship must enroll at Brown Mackie College–Louisville between June and September immediately following their high school graduation. Applications for these scholarships can be obtained from the guidance departments of participating high schools. These applications must be completed and returned to the College by March 31.

Faculty

There are 45 full-time and over 100 part-time faculty members at the College. The average student-faculty ratio is 20:1.

Facilities and Resources

Brown Mackie College–Louisville has more than 69,000 square feet of multipurpose classrooms, including networked computer laboratories, electronics laboratories, veterinary technology labs, medical labs, nursing labs, a resource center, and offices for administrative personnel as well as for student services such as admissions, student financial services, and career-services assistance. In 2009, 6,000 square feet were opened at the Louisville location. Included in this build-out were an occupational therapy lab, a criminal justice lab, additional classrooms, and faculty space. In 2010, 25,000 square feet opened at this location. This build-out included a biomedical equipment lab, additional classrooms, a career services center, and additional faculty/administration space.

The College is nonresidential; ample parking at no cost is available. The campus is a smoke-free facility.

Location

Brown Mackie College–Louisville is conveniently located at 3605 Fern Valley Road in Louisville, Kentucky. The College has a generous parking area and is easily accessible by public transportation.

Admission Requirements

Each applicant for admission is assigned an Assistant Director of Admissions who directs the applicant through the steps of the admissions process, providing information on curriculum, policies, procedures, and services and assisting the applicant in setting necessary appointments and interviews.

To qualify for admission, each applicant must provide documentation of graduation from an accredited high school or from a state-approved secondary education curriculum or provide official documentation of high school graduation equivalency. All transcripts become the property of the College. Admission to the College is based on the applicant meeting the stated requirements, a review of the applicant's previous educational records, and a review of the applicant's career interests. If previous academic records indicate the College's education and training programs would not benefit the applicant, the College reserves the right to advise the applicant not to enroll. Special requirements for enrollment into certain programs are discussed in the descriptions of those programs.

In addition to the College's general admission requirements, applicants enrolling in either the occupational therapy assistant program or the surgical technology program must document one of the following: a high school cumulative grade point average of at least 2.5, a score on the GED examination of at least 57 (557 if taken on or after January 15, 2002), or completion of 12 quarter-credit hours or 8 semester-credit hours of collegiate course work with a grade point average of at least 2.5. Credit hours may not include Professional Development (CF 1100), the Brown Mackie College–Louisville course. Students entering the program must also have completed a biology course with a grade of at least a C (or an average of at least 2.0 on a 4.0 scale).

In addition to the College's general admission requirements, applicants enrolling in the practical nursing program must document the following, which must be completed and a record of proof must appear in the student's file prior to the start of the nursing fundamentals course. No student will be admitted to a clinical agency unless all paperwork is completed. This paperwork includes records of (1) a complete physical, current to within six months of admission, (2) a two-step Mantoux test that is kept current throughout schooling, (3) a hepatitis B vaccination or signed refusal, (4) up-to-date immunizations, including tetanus and rubella, (5) a record of current CPR certification that is maintained throughout the student's clinical experience, and (6) hospitalization insurance or a signed waiver.

For the most recent information regarding admission requirements, prospective students should refer to the current academic catalog.

Application and Information

Applicants must complete and submit an application form along with documentation of graduation from an accredited high school or completion of state-approved secondary education curriculum or provide official documentation of high school graduation equivalency.

For additional information, prospective students should contact:

Director of Admissions
Brown Mackie College–Louisville
3605 Fern Valley Road
Louisville, Kentucky 40219
Phone: 502-968-7191
      800-999-7387 (toll-free)
Fax: 502-357-9956
E-mail: bmcloadm@brownmackie.edu
Web site: http://www.brownmackie.edu/Louisville

BROWN MACKIE COLLEGE–MERRILLVILLE

MERRILLVILLE, INDIANA

The College and Its Mission

Brown Mackie College–Merrillville is one of over twenty-five locations in the Brown Mackie College family of schools (www.brownmackie.edu), which is dedicated to providing educational programs that prepare students to pursue entry-level positions in a competitive, rapidly changing workplace. Brown Mackie College schools offer bachelor's degree, associate degree, certificate, and diploma programs in health sciences, business, information technology, legal studies, and design to over 20,000 students in the Midwest, Southeast, Southwest, and Western United States.

Founded in 1890 by A. N. Hirons as LaPorte Business College in LaPorte, Indiana, the institution later became known as Commonwealth Business College. In 1919, ownership was transferred to Grace and J. J. Moore, who successfully operated the College under the name of Reese School of Business for several decades. In 1975, the College came under the ownership of Steven C. Smith as Commonwealth Business College. A second location, now known as Brown Mackie College–Merrillville, was opened in 1984 in Merrillville, Indiana.

Brown Mackie College–Merrillville is accredited by the Accrediting Council for Independent Colleges and Schools (ACICS) to award bachelor's degrees, associate degrees, diplomas, and certificates. The Accrediting Council for Independent Colleges and Schools is listed as a nationally recognized accrediting agency by the United States Department of Education and is recognized by the Council for Higher Education Accreditation. ACICS can be contacted at 750 First Street NE, Suite 980, Washington, D.C. 20002; phone: 202-336-6780.

The College is licensed and regulated by the Indiana Commission on Proprietary Education, 302 West Washington Street, Indianapolis, Indiana 46204; phone: 317-232-1320 or 800-227-5695 (toll-free). (Indiana advertising code: AC-0138).

The Associate of Science degree in surgical technology is accredited by the Commission on Accreditation of Allied Health Education Programs (www.caahep.org) upon the recommendation of the Accreditation Review Committee on Education in Surgical Technology of the Commission on Accreditation of Allied Health Education Programs, 1361 Park Street, Clearwater, Florida 33756; phone: 727-210-2350.

The occupational therapy assistant Associate of Applied Science degree is accredited by the Accreditation Council for Occupational Therapy Education (ACOTE) of the American Occupational Therapy Association (AOTA), 4720 Montgomery Lane, P.O. Box 31220, Bethesda, Maryland 20824; phone: 301-652-AOTA.

The College is a nonresidential, smoke-free institution.

Academic Programs

Brown Mackie College–Merrillville provides higher education to traditional and nontraditional students through bachelor's degree, associate degree, diploma, and certificate programs that assist in enhancing their career opportunities, broadening their perspectives through appropriate general education courses, thinking independently and critically, and improving problem-solving abilities. The College strives to develop within its students the desire for lifelong and continued education.

Each College quarter comprises ten to twelve weeks. Bachelor's degree programs require a minimum of sixteen quarters to complete. Associate degree programs require a minimum of eight quarters to complete. Programs are offered on a year-round basis, providing students with the ability to work uninterrupted toward completion of their programs. The College offers all programs in a unique One Course a Month format. This allows students to focus on only one course for four weeks. This schedule has proven convenient for students with multiple obligations such as jobs and family.

Bachelor's Degree Programs: The Bachelor of Science degree is awarded in business administration, criminal justice, health care management, and legal studies.

Associate Degree Programs: The Associate of Science degree is awarded in accounting technology, administration in gerontology, business management, computer software technology, criminal justice, medical assisting, medical office management, paralegal, and surgical technology.

The Associate of Applied Science degree is awarded in biomedical equipment technology and occupational therapy assistant.

Diploma Program: A diploma program in practical nursing is offered.

Certificate Programs: The College offers certificate programs in accounting, business, computer software applications, criminal justice, medical assistant, and paralegal assistant.

Costs

Tuition for most programs in the 2010–11 academic year was $285 per credit hour and the fees were $15 per credit hour, with some exceptions. The practical nursing diploma program was $350 per credit hour and the fees were $25 per credit hour. For the surgical technology program, the tuition was $330 per credit hour and the fees were $15 per credit hour. For the occupational therapy assistant program the tuition was $350 per credit hour and the fees were $15 per credit hour. The length of the program determines total cost. Textbook fees vary according to program.

Financial Aid

Financial aid is available to those who qualify. The College maintains a full-time staff of financial aid professionals to assist qualified students in obtaining financial assistance. The College participates in several student aid programs. Forms of financial aid available through federal resources include the Federal Pell Grant Program, Federal Supplemental Educational Opportunity Grant (FSEOG) Program, Federal Work-Study Program, Federal Perkins Loan Program, Federal Stafford Student Loan Program (subsidized and unsubsidized), and the Federal PLUS Loan Program. Eligible students may apply for Indiana state awards, such as the Higher Education Award and Twenty-First Century Scholarships for high school students, the Core 40 awards, and veterans' educational benefits. Students with physical or mental disabilities that are a handicap to employment may be eligible for training services through the state's Bureau of Vocational Rehabilitation. For further information, students should contact the College's Student Financial Services Office.

Each year, the College makes available scholarships of $1000 each to qualifying seniors from area high schools. No more than one scholarship is awarded per high school. In order to qualify, a senior must be graduating from a participating high school, must be maintaining a cumulative grade point average of at least 2.0, and must submit a brief essay. The student's extracurricular activities and community service are also considered. These scholarships are available only to students enrolling in one of the College's degree programs. Students awarded the scholarship must enroll at Brown Mackie College–Merrillville between June and September immediately following their high school graduation. Applications for these scholarships can be obtained from the guidance departments of participating high schools. These applications must be completed and returned to the College by March 31.

Faculty

There are approximately 60 full-time and 25 part-time faculty members at the College, practitioners in their fields of expertise. The average student-faculty ratio is 17:1.

Facilities and Resources

Occupying 26,000 square feet, Brown Mackie College–Merrillville was opened to students in October 1998 in the Twin Towers complex of Merrillville and comprises several instructional rooms, including five computer labs with networked computers and four medical laboratories. The administrative offices, college library, and student lounge are all easily accessible to students. The College bookstore stocks texts, courseware, and other educational supplies required for courses at the College. Students also find a variety of personal, recreational, and gift items, including apparel, supplies, and general merchandise incorporating the College logo. Hours are posted at the bookstore entrance.

Location

Brown Mackie College–Merrillville is conveniently located in northwest Indiana at 1000 East 80th Place, Merrillville in the Twin Towers business complex just west of the intersection of U.S. Route 30 and Interstate 65. A spacious parking lot provides ample parking at no additional charge.

Admission Requirements

Each applicant for admission is assigned an Assistant Director of Admissions who directs the applicant through the steps of the admissions process, providing information on curriculum, policies, procedures, and services and assisting the applicant in setting necessary appointments and interviews.

To qualify for admission, each applicant must provide documentation of graduation from an accredited high school or completion of a state-approved secondary education curriculum or provide official documentation of high school graduation equivalency. All transcripts become the property of the College.

As part of the admission process, students are given an assessment of academic skills. Although the results of this assessment do not determine eligibility for admission, they provide the College with a means of determining the need for academic support as well as a means by which the College can evaluate the effectiveness of its educational programs. All new students are required to complete this assessment, which is readministered at the end of the student's program so results may be compared with those of the initial administration.

In addition to the College's general admission requirements, applicants enrolling in the practical nursing program must document the following, which must be completed, and a record of proof must appear in the student's file prior to the start of the nursing fundamentals course. No student will be admitted to a clinical agency unless all paperwork is completed. The paperwork is a requirement of all contracted agencies. This paperwork includes records of (1) a complete physical, current to within six months of admission, (2) a two-step Mantoux test that is kept current throughout schooling, (3) a hepatitis B vaccination or signed refusal, (4) up-to-date immunizations, including tetanus and rubella, (5) a record of current CPR certification that is maintained throughout the student's clinical experience, and (6) hospitalization insurance or a signed waiver.

For the most recent information regarding admission requirements, please refer to the current academic catalog.

Application and Information

Applicants must complete and submit an application form along with documentation of graduation from an accredited high school or completion of state-approved secondary education curriculum or provide official documentation of high school graduation equivalency.

For additional information, prospective students should contact:

Brown Mackie College–Merrillville
1000 East 80th Place, Suite 205M
Merrillville, Indiana 46410
Phone: 219-769-3321
      800-258-3321 (toll-free)
Fax: 219-738-1076
E-mail: bmcmeadm@brownmackie.edu
Web site: http://www.brownmackie.edu/Merrillville

BROWN MACKIE COLLEGE–MIAMI

MIAMI, FLORIDA

The College and Its Mission

Brown Mackie College–Miami is one of over twenty-five locations in the Brown Mackie College family of schools (www.brownmackie.edu), which is dedicated to providing educational programs that prepare students to pursue entry-level positions in a competitive, rapidly changing workplace. Brown Mackie College schools offer bachelor's degree, associate degree, certificate, and diploma programs in health sciences, business, information technology, legal studies, criminal justice, early childhood education, and design to over 20,000 students in the Midwest, Southeast, Southwest, and Western United States.

Brown Mackie College–Miami is accredited by the Accrediting Council for Independent Colleges and Schools (ACICS) to award bachelor's and associate degrees. The Accrediting Council for Independent Colleges and Schools is listed as a nationally recognized accrediting agency by the United States Department of Education and is recognized by the Council for Higher Education Accreditation. ACICS can be contacted at 750 First Street NE, Suite 980, Washington, D.C. 20002; phone: 202-336-6780.

The College is a nonresidential, smoke-free institution.

Academic Programs

Brown Mackie College–Miami provides higher education to traditional and nontraditional students through bachelor's degree and associate degree programs that assist them in enhancing their career opportunities, broadening their perspectives through appropriate general education courses, thinking independently and critically, and improving problem-solving abilities. The College strives to develop within its students the desire for lifelong and continued education.

Each College quarter comprises twelve weeks. Bachelor degree programs require a minimum of sixteen quarters to complete. Associate degree programs require a minimum of eight quarters to complete. Programs are offered on a year-round basis, providing students with the ability to work uninterrupted toward their degrees. The College offers all programs in a unique One Course a Month format. This allows students to focus studies on only one course for four weeks. This schedule has proven convenient for students with multiple obligations such as jobs and family.

Bachelor's Degree Programs: The Bachelor of Science degree is awarded in business administration, criminal justice, health care management, and information technology.

Associate Degree Programs: The Associate of Science degree is awarded in accounting technology, architectural design and drafting technology, biomedical equipment technology, business management, criminal justice, early childhood

education, health care administration, information technology, medical assisting, and paralegal.

Costs

Tuition in the 2010–11 academic year for all programs was $360 per credit hour; fees were $15 per credit hour. The cost of textbooks and other instructional materials varies by program.

Financial Aid

Financial aid is available for those who qualify. The College maintains a full-time staff of financial aid professionals to assist qualified students in obtaining financial assistance. The College participates in several student aid programs. Forms of financial aid available to qualified students through federal resources include the Federal Pell Grant Program, Federal Supplemental Educational Opportunity Grant (FSEOG) Program, Federal Work-Study Program, Federal Perkins Loan Program, Federal Stafford Student Loan Program (subsidized and unsubsidized), Federal PLUS loan program, and Florida State grant program. Eligible students may apply for veterans' educational benefits. Students with physical or mental disabilities that are a handicap to employment may be eligible for training services through the state Agency for Vocational Rehabilitation. For further information, students should contact the College Student Financial Services Office.

Each year, the College makes available President's Scholarships of $1000 each to qualifying seniors from area high schools. No more than one scholarship is awarded per high school. In order to qualify, a senior must be graduating from a participating high school, must be maintaining a cumulative grade point average of at least 2.0, and must submit a brief essay. The student's extracurricular activities and community service are also considered. The President's Scholarship is available only to students enrolling in one of the College's degree programs. Students awarded the scholarship must enroll at Brown Mackie College–Miami between June and September immediately following their high school graduation. Applications for these scholarships can be obtained from the guidance departments of participating high schools. These applications must be completed and returned to the College by March 31.

Faculty

There are 15 full-time and 27 adjunct faculty members at the College. The average student-faculty ratio is 20:1.

Facilities and Resources

Brown Mackie College–Miami is conveniently located at One Herald Plaza, Miami, Florida. The College occupies 50,000 square feet on the top floor of the Miami Herald building, which sits on beautiful Biscayne Bay and offers a clear view of the Miami and Miami Beach skylines. The College—owned and operated by Pittsburgh-based Education Management Corporation (EDMC)—offers hands-on experiences in its many labs, including a criminal justice lab featuring facial recognition software along with a multitude of forensic equipment. The computer networking lab, as well as multiple computer classrooms, offer students a modern and professional environment for study. Four medical labs are used to instruct clinical medical skills as well as biomedical equipment use and repair. Each student has access to the technology, tools, and facilities needed to complete projects in each subject area. Students are welcome to use the labs when they are not being used for scheduled classes.

The college features a comfortable student lounge as well as an on-site eatery available during all class shifts. The college bookstore offers retail items including textbooks, kits specific to programs of study, and college apparel. The on-site library offers multimedia resources including books, periodicals, and electronic resources specific to all academic programs offered. Course delivery at Brown Mackie College-Miami includes on-ground as well as blended courses.

Location

Brown Mackie College–Miami occupies space within the newly renovated One Herald Plaza in Miami, Florida. It is conveniently located adjacent to the Omni Metro Mover and bus stop, with access to Metro Rail and Florida's regional Tri-Rail system. Ample parking is also available.

Admission Requirements

Each applicant for admission is assigned an Assistant Director of Admissions, who directs the applicant through the steps of the admissions process, providing information on curriculum, policies, procedures, and services and assisting the applicant in setting necessary appointments and interviews. To qualify for admission, applicants must be a graduate of a public or private high school or a correspondence school or education center that is accredited by an agency that is recognized by the U.S. or State of Florida Department of Education or any of its approved agents. As part of the admissions process, applicants must sign a document attesting to graduation or completion and containing the information to obtain verification of such. Verification must be obtained within the first term. All transcripts become the property of the College. Admission to the College is based on the applicant meeting the stated requirements, a review of the applicant's previous educational records, and a review of the applicant's career interests. If previous academic records indicate the College's education and training programs would not benefit the applicant, the College reserves the right to advise the applicant not to enroll. Special requirements for enrollment into certain programs are discussed in the descriptions of those programs.

Students are given an assessment of academic skills during the first two weeks of class. Although the results of this assessment do not determine eligibility for admission, they provide the College with a means of determining the need for academic support as well as a means by which the College can evaluate the effectiveness of its educational programs. All new students are required to complete this assessment.

For the most recent information regarding admission requirements, please refer to the current academic catalog.

Application and Information

Applicants must complete and submit an application form.

Director of Admissions
Brown Mackie College–Miami
One Herald Plaza
Miami, Florida 33132-1418
Phone: 305-341-6600
          866-505-0335 (toll-free)
Fax: 305-373-8814
E-mail: bmmiaadm@brownmackie.edu
Web site: http://www.brownmackie.edu/Miami

BROWN MACKIE COLLEGE– MICHIGAN CITY

MICHIGAN CITY, INDIANA

The College and Its Mission

Brown Mackie College–Michigan City is one of over twenty-five locations in the Brown Mackie College family of schools (www.brownmackie.edu), which is dedicated to providing educational programs that prepare students to pursue entry-level positions in a competitive, rapidly changing workplace. Brown Mackie College schools offer bachelor's degree, associate degree, certificate, and diploma programs in health sciences, business, information technology, legal studies, and design to over 20,000 students in the Midwest, Southeast, Southwest, and Western United States.

Founded in 1890 by A. N. Hirons as LaPorte Business College in LaPorte, Indiana, the institution later became known as Commonwealth Business College. In 1919, ownership was transferred to Grace and J. J. Moore, who successfully operated the College under the name of Reese School of Business for several decades. In 1975, the College came under the ownership of Steven C. Smith as Commonwealth Business College. In 1997, the College relocated to its present site in Michigan City, Indiana.

The College was acquired by Education Management Corporation (EDMC) on September 2, 2003, and changed its name to Brown Mackie College–Michigan City in November 2004.

Brown Mackie College–Michigan City is accredited by the Accrediting Council for Independent Colleges and Schools (ACICS) to award bachelor's degrees, associate degrees, and certificates. The Accrediting Council for Independent Colleges and Schools is listed as a nationally recognized accrediting agency by the United States Department of Education and is recognized by the Council for Higher Education Accreditation. ACICS can be contacted at 750 First Street NE, Suite 980, Washington, D.C. 20002; phone: 202-336-6780.

The College is regulated by the Indiana Commission on Proprietary Education, 302 West Washington Street, Indianapolis, Indiana 46204; phone: 317-232-1320 or 800-227-5695 (toll-free). The Indiana advertising code for Brown Mackie College–Michigan City is AC-0138.

The College's medical assisting degree program is accredited by the Accrediting Bureau of Health Education Schools (ABHES), 7777 Leesburg Pike, Suite 314 North, Falls Church, Virginia 22043; phone: 703-917-9503.

The College's surgical technology program is accredited by the Commission on Accreditation of Allied Health Education Programs (CAAHEP), 1361 Park Street, Clearwater, Florida 33756; phone: 727-210-2350.

The College's veterinary technology degree program is accredited by the American Veterinary Medical Association's (AVMA) Committee on Veterinary Technician Education and Activities (CVTEA), 1931 North Meacham Road, Suite 100, Schaumberg, Illinois 60173; phone: 800-248-2862 (toll-free).

The College is a nonresidential, smoke-free institution.

Academic Programs

Brown Mackie College–Michigan City provides higher education to traditional and nontraditional students through bachelor's degree, associate degree, and certificate programs that assist in enhancing their career opportunities, broadening their perspectives through appropriate general education courses, thinking independently and critically, and improving problem-solving abilities. The College strives to develop within its students the desire for lifelong and continued education.

Each College quarter comprises twelve weeks. Bachelor's degree programs require a minimum of sixteen quarters to complete. Associate degree programs require a minimum of eight quarters to complete. Programs are offered on a year-round basis, providing students with the ability to work uninterrupted toward their degrees. The College offers all programs in a unique One Course a Month format. This allows students to focus studies on only one course for four weeks. This schedule has proven convenient for students with multiple obligations such as jobs and family.

Bachelor's Degree Programs: The Bachelor of Science degree is awarded in business administration, criminal justice, and legal studies.

Associate Degree Programs: The Associate of Science degree is awarded in accounting technology, business management, computer software technology, criminal justice, early childhood education, health and therapeutic massage, health care administration, medical assisting, medical office management, paralegal, surgical technology, and veterinary technology.

Certificate Programs: The College offers certificate programs in accounting, business, computer software applications, criminal justice, medical assistant, medical coding and billing, and paralegal assistant.

Costs

Tuition in the 2010–11 academic year was $285 per credit hour and fees were $15 per credit hour. For the surgical technology program, the tuition was $330 per credit hour and fees were $15 per credit hour. The cost of textbooks and other instructional materials varies according to the program.

Financial Aid

The College maintains a full-time staff of financial aid professionals to assist qualified students in obtaining financial assistance. The College participates in several student aid programs. Forms of financial aid available to qualified students through federal resources include the Federal Pell Grant Program, Federal Supplemental Educational Opportunity Grant (FSEOG) Program, Federal Work-Study Program, Federal Stafford Student Loan Program (subsidized and unsubsidized), and Federal PLUS loan program.

Eligible students may apply for Indiana state awards, such as the Higher Education Award and Twenty-First Century Scholarships for high school students, the Core 40 awards, and veterans' educational benefits. Students with physical or mental disabilities that are a handicap to employment may be eligible for training services through the state's Bureau of Vocational Rehabilitation. For further information, students should contact the College's Student Financial Services Office.

Each year, the College makes available scholarships of $1000 each to qualifying seniors from area high schools. No more than one scholarship is awarded per high school. In order to qualify, a senior must be graduating from a participating high school, must be maintaining a cumulative grade point average of at least 2.0, and must submit a brief essay. The student's extracurricular activities and community service are also considered. These scholarships are available only to students enrolling in one of the College's degree programs. Students awarded the scholarship must enroll at Brown Mackie College–Michigan City between June and September immediately following their high school graduation. Applications for these scholarships can be obtained from the guidance departments of participating high schools. These applications must be completed and returned to the College by March 31.

Faculty

There are 9 full-time and 31 part-time faculty members at the College. The average student-faculty ratio is 13:1. Each student is assigned a department chair.

Facilities and Resources

In 2002, the College underwent a major renovation that added 3,360 square feet for a total of 10,338 square feet of occupancy. An additional medical laboratory, a larger library, new classrooms, and a bookstore were added. All classrooms and the library are equipped with new technology, including multimedia projectors, surround sound audio systems, VCRs, and DVD players. Five of the ten new classrooms are equipped with networked computer systems. The two medical laboratories contain newly acquired medical equipment and instructional tools and supplies. Administrative offices are easily accessible to students. In 2008, a learning site was opened at 1623 S. Woodland Avenue in Michigan City. This site is approximately 6,500 square feet, and is conveniently located within a mile from the main campus.

Location

Brown Mackie College–Michigan City is conveniently located in northwest Indiana, at 325 East U.S. Highway 20, Michigan City, 1 mile north of Interstate 94, near the intersection of routes 20 and 421.

Admission Requirements

Each applicant for admission is assigned an Assistant Director of Admissions, who directs the applicant through the steps of the admissions process, providing information on curriculum, policies, procedures, and services, and assisting the applicant in setting necessary appointments and interviews.

To qualify for admission, each applicant must provide documentation of graduation from an accredited high school or completion of a state-approved secondary education curriculum or provide official documentation of high school graduation equivalency. All transcripts become the property of the College.

As part of the admission process, students are given an assessment of academic skills. Although the results of this assessment do not determine eligibility for admission, they provide the College with a means of determining the need for academic support, as well as a means by which the College can evaluate the effectiveness of its educational programs. All new students are required to complete this assessment.

For the most recent information regarding admission requirements, please refer to the current academic catalog.

Application and Information

Applicants must complete and submit an application form along with documentation of graduation from an accredited high school or completion of a state-approved secondary education curriculum or provide official documentation of high school graduation equivalency.

For additional information, prospective students should contact:

Director of Admissions
Brown Mackie College–Michigan City
325 East U.S. Highway 20
Michigan City, Indiana 46360
Phone: 219-877-3100
       800-519-2416 (toll-free)
Fax: 219-877-3110
E-mail: bmcmcadm@brownmackie.edu
Web site: http://www.brownmackie.edu/MichiganCity

BROWN MACKIE COLLEGE– NORTH CANTON

NORTH CANTON, OHIO

The College and Its Mission

Brown Mackie College–North Canton is one of over twenty-five locations in the Brown Mackie College family of schools (www.brownmackie.edu), which is dedicated to providing educational programs that prepare students to pursue entry-level positions in a competitive, rapidly changing workplace. Brown Mackie College schools offer bachelor's degree, associate degree, certificate, and diploma programs in health sciences, business, information technology, legal studies, and design to over 20,000 students in the Midwest, Southeast, Southwest, and Western United States.

The College opened in the 1980s as the National Electronics Institute. In 2002, the Southern Ohio College took ownership. The following year it became part of the Brown Mackie College family of schools.

Brown Mackie College–North Canton is accredited by the Accrediting Council for Independent Colleges and Schools (ACICS) to award associate degrees and diplomas. The Accrediting Council for Independent Colleges and Schools is listed as a nationally recognized accrediting agency by the U.S. Department of Education. Its accreditation of degree-granting institutions is recognized by the Council for Higher Education Accreditation. ACICS can be contacted at 750 First Street NE, Suite 980, Washington, D.C. 20002; phone: 202-336-6780.

The Brown Mackie College–North Canton Associate of Applied Science in surgical technology program is accredited by the Accrediting Bureau of Health Education Schools (http://www.abhes.org).

Brown Mackie College–North Canton's veterinary technology program has provisional programmatic accreditation granted by the American Veterinary Medical Association (AVMA) through the Committee on Veterinary Technician Education and Activities (CVTEA).

Brown Mackie College–North Canton is licensed by the Ohio State Board of Career Colleges and Schools, 35 East Gay Street, Suite 403, Columbus, Ohio 43215-3138. (Ohio registration #03-09-1688T).

The College is a nonresidential, smoke-free institution.

Academic Programs

Brown Mackie College–North Canton provides higher education to traditional and nontraditional students through associate degree and diploma programs that can assist students in enhancing their career opportunities, broadening their perspectives through appropriate general education courses, thinking independently and critically, and improving problem-solving abilities. The College strives to develop within its students the desire for lifelong and continued education.

Each College quarter comprises twelve weeks. Associate degree programs require a minimum of eight quarters to complete. Programs are offered on a year-round basis, providing students with the ability to work uninterrupted toward their degrees. The College offers all programs in a unique One Course a Month format. This schedule allows students to focus studies on only one course for four weeks and has proven convenient for students with multiple obligations such as jobs and family.

Associate Degree Programs: The Associate of Applied Business degree is awarded in accounting technology, business management, computer networking and applications, criminal justice, and paralegal. The Associate of Applied Science degree is awarded in computer-aided design and drafting technology, health care administration, medical assisting, pharmacy technology, surgical technology, and veterinary technology.

Diploma Programs: The College also offers diploma programs in accounting, business, computer aided design and drafting technician, criminal justice, medical assistant, paralegal assistant, and practical nursing.

Costs

Tuition for the 2010–11 academic year was $285 per credit hour and $15 per credit hour for general fees. The tuition for the surgical technology program was $330 per credit hour and $15 per credit hour for general fees. The tuition for the practical nursing program is $350 per credit hour and $25 per credit hour for general fees. The cost of textbooks and other instructional materials varies by program.

Financial Aid

Financial aid is available to those who qualify. The College maintains a full-time staff of financial aid professionals to assist qualified students in obtaining financial assistance. The College participates in several student aid programs. Forms of financial aid available through federal resources include the Federal Pell Grant Program, Federal Supplemental Educational Opportunity Grant (FSEOG) Program, Federal Work-Study Program, Federal Perkins Loan Program, Federal Stafford Student Loan Program (subsidized and unsubsidized), and the Federal PLUS Loan Program. Eligible students may also apply for state awards and veterans' educational benefits. Students with physical or mental disabilities that are a handicap to employment may be eligible for training services through the state Agency for Vocational Rehabilitation. For further information, students should contact the College's Student Financial Services Office.

Faculty

There are approximately 20 full-time and approximately 35 part-time faculty members. The average student-faculty ratio is approximately 19:1. Each student has a faculty and student adviser.

Facilities and Resources

The College comprises administrative offices, faculty and student lounges, a reception area, and spacious classrooms and laboratories. Instructional equipment includes personal computers, LANs, printers, and LCD projectors. The library provides support for the academic programs through volumes covering a broad range of subjects, as well as through Internet access. Vehicle parking is provided for both students and staff members.

Location

Brown Mackie College–North Canton is located at 4300 Munson Street, NW in Canton, Ohio. The school is easily accessible from I-77 and Route 687 and by the SARTA bus line.

Admission Requirements

Each applicant for admission is assigned an Assistant Director of Admissions, who directs the applicant through the steps of the admissions process, providing information on curriculum, policies, procedures, and services and assisting the applicant in setting necessary appointments and interviews. To qualify for admission, each applicant must provide documentation of graduation from an accredited high school or from a state-approved secondary education curriculum or provide official documentation of high school graduation equivalency. All transcripts become the property of the College. Admission to the College is based upon the applicant meeting the stated requirements, a review of the applicant's previous education records, and a review of the applicant's career interests. If previous academic records indicate that the College's education and training programs would not benefit the applicant, the College reserves the right to advise the applicant not to enroll. Special requirements for enrollment into certain programs are discussed in the descriptions of those programs.

For the most recent information regarding admission requirements, please refer to the current academic catalog.

Application and Information

Applicants must complete and submit an application form, along with documentation of graduation from an accredited high school or state-approved secondary education curriculum, or applicants must provide official documentation of high school graduation equivalency. For additional information, prospective students should contact:

Director of Admissions
Brown Mackie College–North Canton
4300 Munson Street NW
Canton, Ohio 44718-3674
Phone: 330-494-1214
Fax: 330-494-8112
E-mail: bmcncweb@brownmackie.edu
Web site: http://www.brownmackie.edu/North-Canton

BROWN MACKIE COLLEGE–NORTHERN KENTUCKY

FORT MITCHELL, KENTUCKY

The College and Its Mission

Brown Mackie College–Northern Kentucky is one of over twenty-five locations in the Brown Mackie College family of schools (www.brownmackie.edu), which is dedicated to providing educational programs that prepare students to pursue entry-level positions in a competitive, rapidly changing workplace. Brown Mackie College schools offer bachelor's degree, associate degree, certificate, and diploma programs in health sciences, business, information technology, legal studies, and design to more than 20,000 students in the Midwest, Southeast, Southwest, and Western United States.

The College was founded in Cincinnati, Ohio, in February 1927 as a traditional business college. In May 1981, the College opened a branch location in northern Kentucky, which moved in 1986 to its current location in Fort Mitchell.

Brown Mackie College–Northern Kentucky is accredited by the Accrediting Council for Independent Colleges and Schools (ACICS) to award bachelor's degrees, associate degrees, and diplomas. The Accrediting Council for Independent Colleges and Schools is listed as a nationally recognized accrediting agency by the United States Department of Education and is recognized by the Council for Higher Education Accreditation. ACICS can be contacted at 750 First Street NE, Suite 980, Washington, D.C. 20002; phone: 202-336-6780.

Brown Mackie College–Northern Kentucky is regulated by the Indiana Commission on Proprietary Education, 302 West Washington Street, Room E201, Indianapolis, Indiana 46204; phone: 317-232-1320 or 800-227-5695 (toll-free). (Indiana advertising code: AC-0150).

The College is licensed by the Ohio State Board of Career Colleges and Schools; 35 East Gay Street, Suite 403, Columbus, Ohio 43215; phone: 614-466-2752. (Ohio registration number: 06-03-1781T).

The occupational therapy assistant program is accredited by the Accreditation Council for Occupational Therapy Education (ACOTE) of the American Occupational Therapy Association (AOTA), located at 4720 Montgomery Lane, P.O. Box 31220, Bethesda, Maryland 20824; phone: 301-652-AOTA.

The surgical technology Associate of Science degree is accredited by the Commission on Accreditation of Allied Health Education Programs (www.caahep.org) upon the recommendation of the Accreditation Review Council on Education in Surgical Technology and Surgical Assisting (ARC/STSA).

Academic Programs

Brown Mackie College–Northern Kentucky provides higher education to traditional and nontraditional students through bachelor's degree, associate degree and diploma programs that assist them in enhancing their career opportunities, broadening their perspectives through appropriate general education courses, thinking independently and critically, and improving problem-solving abilities. The College strives to develop within its students the desire for lifelong and continued education.

Each College quarter comprises ten to twelve weeks. Bachelor's degree programs require a minimum of sixteen quarters to complete. Associate degree programs require a minimum of eight quarters to complete. Programs are offered on a year-round basis, providing students with the ability to work uninterrupted toward their degrees. The College offers all programs in a unique One Course a Month format. This allows students to focus studies on only one course for four weeks. This schedule has proven convenient for students with multiple obligations such as jobs and family.

Bachelor's Degree Programs: The Bachelor of Science degree is awarded in business administration, criminal justice, health care management, and legal studies.

Associate Degree Programs: The Associate of Applied Business degree is awarded in accounting technology, business management, computer software technology, criminal justice, health care administration, information technology, and paralegal.

The Associate of Applied Science degree is awarded in computer aided design and drafting technology, medical assisting, occupational therapy assistant, pharmacy technology, and surgical technology.

Diploma Programs: The College offers diploma programs in accounting, business, computer applications, computer software applications, medical assistant, and practical nursing.

Costs

Tuition for the 2010–11 academic year was $285 per credit hour and general fees were $15 per credit hour, with some exceptions. The practical nursing program tuition was $350 per credit hour and general fees were $25 per credit hour. The surgical technology tuition was $330 per credit hour. Tuition for the occupational therapy assistant program was $350 per credit hour and general fees were $15 per credit hour. The cost of textbooks and other instructional materials varies by program.

Financial Aid

Financial aid is available to those who qualify. The College maintains a full-time staff of financial aid professionals to assist qualified students in obtaining financial assistance. The College participates in several student aid programs. Forms of financial aid available through federal resources include Federal Pell Grants, Federal Supplemental Educational Opportunity Grants (FSEOG), Federal Work-Study Program awards, Federal Perkins Loans, Federal Stafford Student Loans (subsidized and unsubsidized), and Federal PLUS loans. Eligible students may apply for veterans' educational benefits. Students with physical or mental disabilities that are a handicap to employment may be eligible for training services through the state Vocational

Rehabilitation Agency. For further information, students should contact the College's Student Financial Services Office.

Each year, the College makes available President's Scholarships of $1000 each to qualifying seniors from area high schools. No more than one scholarship is awarded per high school. In order to qualify, a senior must have graduated from a participating high school, maintained a cumulative grade point average of at least 2.0, and submitted a brief essay. The student's extracurricular activities and community service are also considered. The President's Scholarship is available only to students enrolling in one of the College's degree programs. Students who receive the scholarship must enroll at Brown Mackie College–Northern Kentucky between June and September immediately following their high school graduation. Applications for these scholarships can be obtained from the guidance departments of participating high schools. These applications must be completed and returned to the College by March 31.

Faculty

There are 11 full-time and 30 adjunct faculty members. The student-faculty ratio is 15:1.

Facilities and Resources

Brown Mackie College–Northern Kentucky offers media presentation rooms for special instructional needs and a library that provides instructional resources and academic support for both faculty members and students.

The campus is nonresidential; public transportation and ample parking at no cost are available. The campus is a smoke-free facility.

Location

Brown Mackie College–Northern Kentucky is conveniently located at 309 Buttermilk Pike in Fort Mitchell, Kentucky. A spacious parking lot provides ample parking at no additional charge.

Admission Requirements

Each applicant for admission is assigned an Assistant Director of Admissions, who directs the applicant through the steps of the admissions process, providing information on curriculum, policies, procedures, and services and assisting the applicant in setting necessary appointments and interviews. To qualify for admission, each applicant must provide documentation of graduation from an accredited high school or from a state-approved secondary education curriculum or provide official documentation of high school graduation equivalency. All transcripts become the property of the College. Admission to the College is based upon the applicant meeting the stated requirements, a review of the applicant's previous education records, and a review of the applicant's career interests. If previous academic records indicate the College's education and training programs would not benefit the applicant, the College reserves the right to advise the applicant not to enroll. Special requirements for enrollment into certain programs are discussed in the descriptions of those programs.

In addition to the College's general admission requirements, applicants enrolling in the practical nursing program must document the following, which must be completed, and a record of proof must appear in the student's file prior to the start of the nursing fundamentals course. No student will be admitted to a clinical agency unless all paperwork is completed. The paperwork is a requirement of all contracted agencies. This paperwork includes records of (1) a complete physical, current to within six months of admission; (2) a two-step Mantoux test that is kept current throughout schooling; (3) a hepatitis B vaccination or signed refusal; (4) up-to-date immunizations, including tetanus and rubella; (5) a record of current CPR certification that is maintained throughout the student's clinical experience; and (6) hospitalization insurance or a signed waiver.

For the most recent information regarding admission requirements, prospective students should refer to the current academic catalog.

Application and Information

Applicants must complete and submit an application form, along with documentation of graduation from an accredited high school or state-approved secondary education curriculum or official documentation of high school graduation equivalency.

For additional information, prospective students should contact:

Director of Admissions
Brown Mackie College–Northern Kentucky
309 Buttermilk Pike
Fort Mitchell, Kentucky 41017
Phone: 859-341-5627
Fax: 859-341-6483
E-mail: bmcnkadm@brownmackie.edu
Web site: http://www.brownmackie.edu/NorthernKentucky

BROWN MACKIE COLLEGE–OKLAHOMA CITY

OKLAHOMA CITY, OKLAHOMA

The College and Its Mission

Brown Mackie College–Oklahoma City is one of over twenty-five locations in the Brown Mackie College family of schools (www.brownmackie.edu), which is dedicated to providing educational programs that prepare students to pursue entry-level positions in a competitive, rapidly changing workplace. Brown Mackie College schools offer bachelor's degree, associate degree, certificate, and diploma programs in health sciences, business, information technology, legal studies, and design to over 20,000 students in the Midwest, Southeast, Southwest, and Western United States.

Brown Mackie College–Oklahoma City is a branch campus of Brown Mackie College–Salina which is accredited by the Higher Learning Commission and a member of the North Central Association, 230 South LaSalle Street, Suite 7-500, Chicago, Illinois 60604-1413; phone: 800-621-7440 (toll-free); www.ncahlc.org.

This institution has been granted authority to operate in Oklahoma by the Oklahoma State Regents for Higher Education (OSRHE), 655 Research Parkway, Suite 200, Oklahoma City, Oklahoma 73101; phone: 405-225-9100.

The College is a nonresidential, smoke-free institution.

Academic Programs

Brown Mackie College–Oklahoma City provides higher education to traditional and nontraditional students through associate degree programs that can assist students in enhancing their career opportunities, broadening their perspectives through appropriate general education courses, thinking independently and critically, and improving problem-solving abilities. The College strives to develop within its students the desire for lifelong and continued education.

Each College quarter comprises twelve weeks. Associate degree programs require a minimum of eight quarters to complete. Programs are offered on a year-round basis, providing students with the ability to work uninterrupted toward their degrees. The College offers all programs in a unique One Course a Month format. This schedule allows students to focus studies on only one course for four weeks and has proven convenient for students with multiple obligations such as jobs and family.

Associate Degree Programs: The Associate of Applied Science degree is awarded in accounting technology, business management, health care administration, medical assisting, office management, and paralegal.

Costs

Tuition for the 2010–11 academic year was $285 per credit hour, and $15 per credit hour for general fees. The cost of textbooks and other instructional materials varies by program.

Financial Aid

Financial aid is available to those who qualify. The College maintains a full-time staff of financial aid professionals to assist qualified students in obtaining financial assistance. The College participates in several student aid programs. Forms of financial aid available through federal resources include the Federal Pell Grant Program, Federal Supplemental Educational Opportunity Grant (FSEOG) Program, Federal Work-Study Program, Federal Perkins Loan Program, Federal Stafford Student Loan Program (subsidized and unsubsidized), and the Federal PLUS Loan Program. Eligible students may also apply for state awards and veterans' educational benefits. Students with physical or mental disabilities that are a handicap to employment may be eligible for training services through the state Agency for Vocational Rehabilitation. For further information, students should contact the College's Student Financial Services Office.

Faculty

Classes at Brown Mackie College–Oklahoma City are scheduled to begin August 1, 2011. Faculty and student statistics were not available at time of publication.

Facilities and Resources

The College comprises administrative offices, faculty and student lounges, a reception area, and spacious classrooms and laboratories. Instructional equipment includes personal computers, LANs, printers, and transcribers. The library provides support for the academic programs through volumes covering a broad range of subjects, as well as through Internet access. Vehicle parking is provided for both students and staff members.

Location

Brown Mackie College–Oklahoma City is located at 7101 Northwest Expressway, Building 800, in Oklahoma City, Oklahoma.

Admission Requirements

Each applicant for admission is assigned an Assistant Director of Admissions who directs the applicant through the steps of the admissions process, providing information on curriculum, policies, procedures, and services and assisting the applicant in setting necessary appointments and interviews.

To qualify for admission, each applicant must provide documentation of graduation from an accredited high school or from a state-approved secondary education curriculum or provide official documentation of high school graduation equivalency. All transcripts become the property of the College. Admission to the College is based upon the applicant meeting the stated requirements, a review of the applicant's previous education records, and a review of the applicant's career interests. If previous academic records indicate that the College's education and training programs would not benefit the applicant, the College reserves the right to advise the applicant not to enroll. Special requirements for enrollment into certain programs are discussed in the descriptions of those programs.

For the most recent information regarding admission requirements, please refer to the current academic catalog.

Application and Information

Applicants must complete and submit an application form along with documentation of graduation from an accredited high school or state-approved secondary education curriculum, or applicants must provide official documentation of high school graduation equivalency.

For additional information, prospective students should contact:

Director of Admissions
Brown Mackie College–Oklahoma City
7101 Northwest Expressway, #800
Oklahoma City, Oklahoma 73132
Phone: 405-621-8000
         888-229-3280 (toll-free)
Fax: 405-621-8055
E-mail: bmcokcadm@brownmackie.edu
Web site: http://www.brownmackie.edu/Oklahoma-City

BROWN MACKIE COLLEGE–PHOENIX

PHOENIX, ARIZONA

The College and Its Mission

Brown Mackie College–Phoenix is one of over twenty-five locations in the Brown Mackie College family of schools (www.brownmackie.edu), which is dedicated to providing educational programs that prepare students to pursue entry-level positions in a competitive, rapidly changing workplace. Brown Mackie College schools offer bachelor's degree, associate degree, certificate, and diploma programs in health sciences, business, information technology, legal studies, and design to over 20,000 students in the Midwest, Southeast, Southwest, and Western United States.

Brown Mackie College–Phoenix was founded in 2009 as a branch of Brown Mackie College–Tucson, Arizona.

Brown Mackie College–Phoenix is accredited by the Accrediting Council for Independent Colleges and Schools (ACICS) to award bachelor's degrees, associate degrees, certificates, and diplomas. ACICS is listed as a nationally recognized accrediting agency by the United States Department of Education and is recognized by the Council for Higher Education Accreditation. ACICS can be contacted at 750 First Street NE, Suite 980, Washington, D.C. 20002; phone: 202-336-6780.

The occupational therapy assistant program is accredited by the Accreditation Council for Occupational Therapy Education (ACOTE) of the American Occupational Therapy Association (AOTA), located at 4720 Montgomery Lane, P.O. Box 31220, Bethesda, Maryland 20824; phone: 301-652-AOTA.

The surgical technology program is accredited by the Accrediting Bureau of Health Education Schools (ABHES), 7777 Leesburg Pike, Suite 314 North, Falls Church, Virginia 22043; phone: 703-917-9503.

This institution is licensed by the Arizona State Board for Private Postsecondary Education, 1400 West Washington Street, Room 2560, Phoenix, Arizona 85007; phone: 602-542-5709.

The College is a nonresidential, smoke-free institution.

Academic Programs

Brown Mackie College–Phoenix provides higher education to traditional and nontraditional students through bachelor's and associate degree programs that assist in enhancing their career opportunities, broadening their perspectives through appropriate general education courses, thinking independently and critically, and improving problem-solving abilities. The College strives to develop within its students the desire for lifelong and continued education.

Each College quarter comprises twelve weeks. Bachelor's degree programs require a minimum of sixteen quarters to complete. Associate degree programs require a minimum of eight quarters to complete. Programs are offered on a year-round basis, providing students with the ability to work uninterrupted toward completion of their programs. The College offers all programs in a unique One Course a Month format. This allows students to focus studies on only one course for four weeks. This schedule has proven convenient for students with multiple obligations such as jobs and family.

Bachelor's Degree Programs: The Bachelor of Science degree is awarded in business administration, criminal justice, health care management, and legal studies.

Associate Degree Programs: The Associate of Science degree is awarded in accounting technology, business management, criminal justice, health care administration, information technology, medical assisting, paralegal, and surgical technology.

The Associate of Applied Science degree is awarded in nursing and occupational therapy assistant.

Costs

Tuition for programs in the 2010–11 academic year was $285 per credit hour, with a $15 per credit hour general fee applied to instructional costs for activities and services. For the surgical technology program, the tuition was $330 per credit hour with a $15 per credit hour general fee applied to instructional costs for activities. For the occupational therapy assistant program, the tuition was $350 per credit hour with a $15 per credit hour general fee applied to instructional costs for activities. For the nursing program, the tuition was $390 per credit hour with a $25 per credit hour general fee applied to instructional costs for activities. The cost of textbooks and other instructional materials varies by program.

Financial Aid

Financial aid is available for those who qualify. The College maintains a full-time staff of financial aid professionals to assist qualified students in obtaining financial assistance. The College participates in several student aid programs. Forms of financial aid available to those who qualify through federal resources include the Federal Pell Grant Program, Federal Supplemental Educational Opportunity Grant (FSEOG) Program, Federal Work-Study Program, Federal Perkins Loan Program, Federal Stafford Student Loan Program (subsidized and unsubsidized), and the Federal PLUS Loan Program.

Each year, the College makes available President's Scholarships of $1000 each to qualifying seniors from area high schools. No more than one scholarship is awarded per high school. In order to qualify, a senior must be graduating from a participating high school, must be maintaining a cumulative grade point average of at least 2.0, and must submit a brief essay. The student's extracurricular activities and community service are also considered. The President's Scholarship is available only to students enrolling in one of the College's degree programs. Students awarded the scholarship must enroll at Brown Mackie College–Phoenix between June and September immediately following their high school graduation. Applications for these scholarships can be obtained from the guidance departments of participating high schools. These applications must be completed and returned to the College by March 31.

Faculty

Experienced faculty members provide academic support and are committed to the academic and technical preparation of their students. The College has both full- and part-time faculty members. The average student-faculty ratio is 14:1. Each student is assigned a program director as an adviser.

Facilities and Resources

Brown Mackie College–Phoenix has a variety of classrooms including computer labs housing the latest technology in the industry. High-speed access to the Internet and other online resources are available for students and faculty. Multimedia classrooms provide a learning environment equipped with overhead projectors, TVs, DVD/VCR players, computers, and sound systems.

Location

Brown Mackie College–Phoenix is conveniently located at 13430 North Black Canyon Highway, Suite 190 in Phoenix, Arizona. The College has a generous parking area and is easily accessible by public transportation.

Admission Requirements

Each applicant for admission is assigned an Assistant Director of Admissions who directs the applicant through the steps of the admissions process, providing information on curriculum, policies, procedures, and services and assisting the applicant in setting necessary appointments and interviews. To qualify for admission, each applicant must provide documentation of graduation from an accredited high school or from a state-approved secondary education curriculum or provide official documentation of high school graduation equivalency. All transcripts become the property of the College.

For the most recent information regarding admission requirements, please refer to the current academic catalog.

Application and Information

Applicants must complete and submit an application form, along with documentation of graduation from an accredited high school or state-approved secondary education curriculum or official documentation of high school graduation equivalency.

For additional information, prospective students should contact:

Director of Admissions
Brown Mackie College–Phoenix
13430 North Black Canyon Highway, Suite 190
Phoenix, Arizona 85029
Phone: 602-337-3044
       866-824-4793 (toll-free)
Fax: 480-375-2450
E-mail: bmcpxadmn@brownmackie.edu
Web site: http://www.brownmackie.edu/Phoenix

BROWN MACKIE COLLEGE– QUAD CITIES

BETTENDORF, IOWA

The College and Its Mission

Brown Mackie College–Quad Cities is one of over twenty-five locations in the Brown Mackie College family of schools (www.brownmackie.edu), which is dedicated to providing educational programs that prepare students to pursue entry-level positions in a competitive, rapidly changing workplace. Brown Mackie College schools offer bachelor's degree, associate degree, certificate, and diploma programs in health sciences, business, information technology, legal studies, and design to over 20,000 students in the Midwest, Southeast, Southwest, and Western United States.

Founded in 1890 by A. N. Hirons as LaPorte Business College in LaPorte, Indiana, the institution later became known as Commonwealth Business College. In 1919, ownership was transferred to Grace and J. J. Moore, who successfully operated the College for almost thirty years. Following World War II, Harley and Stephanie Reese operated the College under the name of Reese School of Business for several decades.

In 1975, the College came under the ownership of Steven C. Smith as Commonwealth Business College. A second location, now known as Brown Mackie College–Merrillville, was opened in 1984 in Merrillville, Indiana, and a third location was opened a year later in Davenport, Iowa. In 1987, the Davenport site relocated to Moline, Illinois. In September 2003, the College changed ownership again and the College's name was changed to Brown Mackie College–Moline in November 2004. In 2010, the College moved to its current location in Bettendorf, Iowa, and changed its name to Brown Mackie College–Quad Cities.

Brown Mackie College–Quad Cities is accredited by the Accrediting Council for Independent Colleges and Schools (ACICS) to award associate degrees and diplomas. ACICS is listed as a nationally recognized accrediting agency by the United States Department of Education and is recognized by the Council for Higher Education Accreditation. ACICS can be contacted at 750 First Street NE, Suite 980, Washington, D.C. 20002; phone: 202-336-6780.

The occupational therapy assistant program has applied for accreditation by the Accreditation Council for Occupational Therapy Education (ACOTE) of the American Occupational Therapy Association (AOTA), located at 4720 Montgomery Lane, P.O. Box 31220, Bethesda, Maryland 20824; phone: 301-652-AOTA.

Brown Mackie College–Quad Cities is approved and registered by the Iowa College Student Aid Commission (ICSAC) under the authority of Chapters 261 and 261B of the Iowa Code. ICSCA can be contacted at 200 10th Street, fourth floor, Des Moines, Iowa 50309-3609; phone: 877-272-4456 (toll-free); www.iowacollegeaid.gov.

Academic Programs

Brown Mackie College–Quad Cities provides higher education to traditional and nontraditional students through associate degree and diploma programs that can assist them in enhancing their career opportunities, broadening their perspectives through appropriate general education courses, thinking independently and critically, and improving problem-solving abilities. The College strives to develop within its students the desire for lifelong and continued education.

Each College quarter comprises twelve weeks. Programs are offered on a year-round basis, providing students with the ability to work uninterrupted toward the completion of their programs. The College offers all programs in a unique One Course a Month format. This schedule allows students to focus studies on only one course for four weeks and has proven convenient for students with multiple obligations such as jobs and family.

Associate Degree Programs: The Associate of Applied Science degree is awarded in accounting technology, business management, criminal justice, health care administration, information technology, medical assisting, occupational therapy assistant, and paralegal.

Diploma Programs: The College offers diploma programs in accounting, business, medical assistant, and medical coding and billing.

Costs

Tuition for the 2010–11 academic year was $285 per credit hour and $15 per credit hour for general fees. Tuition for the occupational therapy assistant program was $350 per credit hour and $15 per credit hour for general fees. Textbook costs vary by program.

Financial Aid

Financial aid is available to those who qualify. The College maintains a full-time staff of financial aid professionals to assist qualified students in obtaining the financial assistance they require to meet their educational expenses. The College participates in several student aid programs. Forms of financial aid available through federal resources include the Federal Pell Grant Program, Federal Supplemental Educational Opportunity Grant (FSEOG) Program, Federal Work-Study Program, Federal Perkins Loan Program, Federal Stafford Student Loan Program (subsidized and unsubsidized), and Federal PLUS loan program. Eligible students may apply for veterans' educational benefits. Students with physical or mental disabilities that are a handicap to employment may be eligible for training services through the state Agency for Vocational Rehabilitation. For further information, students should contact the College's Student Financial Services Office.

394   www.twitter.com/find_colleges

Each year, the College makes available scholarships of up to $1000 each to qualifying seniors from area high schools. Only one scholarship is awarded per high school. In order to qualify, a senior must be graduating from a participating high school, have maintained a cumulative grade point average of at least 2.0, and submitted a brief essay. The student's extracurricular activities and community service are also considered. These scholarships are available only to students enrolling in one of the College's diploma programs. Students awarded the scholarship must enroll at Brown Mackie College–Quad Cities between June and September immediately following their high school graduation. Applications for these scholarships can be obtained from the guidance departments of participating high schools. These applications must be completed and returned to the College by March 31.

Faculty

Brown Mackie College–Quad Cities has 2 full-time and 12 regular adjunct faculty members, with an average student-faculty ratio of 9:1.

Facilities and Resources

The College maintains a library of curriculum-related resources. Technical and general education materials, academic and professional periodicals, and audiovisual resources are available to both students and faculty members. Students have borrowing privileges at several local libraries. Internet access is available for research.

The College is a nonresidential, smoke-free institution.

Location

Brown Mackie College–Quad Cities is located at 2119 East Kimberly Road in Bettendorf, Iowa. The College is easily accessible by public transportation, and ample parking is available at no cost.

Admission Requirements

Each applicant for admission is assigned an Assistant Director of Admissions, who directs the applicant through the steps of the admissions process, providing information on curriculum, policies, procedures, and services and assisting the applicant in setting necessary appointments and interviews.

To qualify for admission, each applicant must provide documentation of graduation from an accredited high school or from a state-approved secondary education curriculum or provide official documentation of high school graduation equivalency. All transcripts become the property of the College. Admission to the College is based on the applicant meeting the above requirements, a review of the applicant's previous education records, and a review of the applicant's career interests. If previous academic records indicate that the College's education and training programs would not benefit the applicant, the College reserves the right to advise the applicant not to enroll. Special requirements for enrollment into certain programs are discussed in the descriptions of those programs.

Application and Information

Applicants must complete and submit an application form along with documentation of graduation from an accredited high school or state-approved secondary education curriculum, or applicants must provide official documentation of high school graduation equivalency. For further information, prospective students should contact:

Director of Admissions
Brown Mackie College–Quad Cities
2119 East Kimberly Road
Bettendorf, Iowa 52722

Phone: 563-344-1500
      888-420-1652 (toll-free)
Fax: 309-762-2374
E-mail: bmcmoadm@brownmackie.edu
Web site: http://www.brownmackie.edu/Quad-Cities

BROWN MACKIE COLLEGE–ST. LOUIS
FENTON, MISSOURI

The College and Its Mission

Brown Mackie College–St. Louis is one of over twenty-five locations in the Brown Mackie College family of schools (www.brownmackie.edu), which is dedicated to providing educational programs that prepare students to pursue entry-level positions in a competitive, rapidly changing workplace. Brown Mackie College schools offer bachelor's degree, associate degree, certificate, and diploma programs in health sciences, business, information technology, legal studies, and design to over 20,000 students in the Midwest, Southeast, Southwest, and Western United States.

Brown Mackie College was originally founded and approved by the Board of Trustees of Kansas Wesleyan College in Salina, Kansas on July 30, 1892. In 1938, the College was incorporated as the Brown Mackie School of Business under the ownership of Perry E. Brown and A. B. Mackie, former instructors at Kansas Wesleyan University in Salina, Kansas. Their last names formed the name of Brown Mackie. By January 1975, with improvements in curricula and higher degree-granting status, the Brown Mackie School of Business became Brown Mackie College.

Brown Mackie College–St. Louis is accredited by the Accrediting Council for Independent Colleges and Schools (ACICS) to award bachelor's degrees, associate degrees, and certificates. ACICS is listed as a nationally recognized accrediting agency by the United States Department of Education and is recognized by the Council for Higher Education Accreditation. ACICS can be contacted at 750 First Street NE, Suite 980, Washington, D.C. 20002; phone: 202-336-6780.

The occupational therapy assistant program has applied for accreditation by the Accreditation Council for Occupational Therapy Education (ACOTE) of the American Occupational Therapy Association (AOTA), located at 4720 Montgomery Lane, P.O. Box 31220, Bethesda, Maryland 20824; phone: 301-652-AOTA.

Academic Programs

Brown Mackie College–St. Louis provides higher education to traditional and nontraditional students through bachelor's and associate degree programs, and certificate programs, that assist in enhancing their career opportunities, broadening their perspectives through appropriate general education courses, thinking independently and critically, and improving problem-solving abilities. The College strives to develop within its students the desire for lifelong and continued education.

Each College quarter comprises twelve weeks. Bachelor's degree programs require a minimum of sixteen quarters to complete. Associate degree programs require a minimum of eight quarters to complete. Programs are offered on a year-round basis, providing students with the ability to work uninterrupted toward completion of their programs. The College offers all programs in a unique One Course a Month format. This allows students to focus studies on only one course for four weeks. This schedule has proven convenient for students with multiple obligations such as jobs and family.

Bachelor's Degree Programs: The Bachelor of Science degree is awarded in business administration, criminal justice, health care management, and legal studies.

Associate Degree Programs: The Associate of Applied Science degree is awarded in accounting technology, architectural design and drafting technology, business management, criminal justice, health care administration, information technology, medical assisting, nursing, occupational therapy assistant, office management, paralegal, pharmacy technology, surgical technology, and veterinary technology.

Certificate Programs: The College offers certificate programs in accounting, business, criminal justice, medical assistant, and paralegal assistant.

Costs

Tuition in the 2010–11 academic year for bachelor's and associate degrees and diploma programs was $260 per credit hour; fees were $15 per credit hour. Tuition for the surgical technology program was $310 per credit hour; fees were $15 per credit hour. Tuition for the occupational therapy assistant program was $325 per credit hour; fees were $15 per credit hour. The cost of textbooks and other instructional materials varies by program.

Financial Aid

Financial aid is available for those who qualify. The College maintains a full-time staff of financial aid professionals to assist qualified students in obtaining the financial assistance they require to meet their educational expenses. Available resources include federal and state aid, student loans from private lenders, and Federal Work-Study opportunities, both on and off college premises.

Each year, the College makes available scholarships of $1000 each to qualifying seniors from area high schools. No more than one scholarship is awarded per high school. In order to qualify, a senior must have graduated from a participating high school, maintained a cumulative grade point average of at least 2.0, and submitted a brief essay. The student's extracurricular activities and community service are also considered. These scholarships are available only to students enrolling in one of the College's degree programs. Students awarded the scholarship must enroll at Brown Mackie College–St. Louis between June and September immediately following their high school graduation. Applications for these scholarships can be obtained from the guidance departments of participating high schools. These applications must be completed and returned to the College by March 31.

Faculty

Experienced faculty members provide academic support and are committed to the academic and technical preparation of their students. The College has 3 full-time and 3 part-time instructors, with a student-faculty ratio of 20:1.

Facilities and Resources

A modern facility, Brown Mackie College–St. Louis offers more than 30,000 square feet of educational and administrative space. The College is equipped with multiple computer labs, housing over 200 computers. High-speed access to the Internet and other online resources are available for students and faculty. Multimedia classrooms are outfitted with overhead projectors, VCR/DVD players, and computers.

The campus is nonresidential. The College has a generous parking area and is easily accessible by public transportation. The campus is a smoke-free facility.

Location

Brown Mackie College–St. Louis is conveniently located at #2 Soccer Park Road in Fenton, Missouri.

Admission Requirements

Each applicant for admission is assigned an Assistant Director of Admissions who directs the applicant through the steps of the admissions process. They provide information on curriculum, policies, procedures, and services and assist the applicant in setting necessary appointments and interviews. To qualify for admission, each applicant must provide documentation of graduation from an accredited high school or from a state-approved secondary education curriculum, or provide official documentation of high school graduation equivalency. All transcripts become the property of the College. Admission to the College is based on the applicant meeting the stated requirements, a review of the applicant's previous educational records, and a review of the applicant's career interests. If previous academic records indicate the College's education and training programs would not benefit the applicant, the College reserves the right to advise the applicant not to enroll. Special requirements for enrollment into certain programs are discussed in the descriptions of those programs.

For the most recent information regarding admission requirements, prospective students should refer to the current academic catalog.

Application and Information

Applicants must complete and submit an application form, along with documentation of graduation from an accredited high school or state-approved secondary education curriculum or official documentation of high school graduation equivalency.

For additional information, prospective students should contact:

Director of Admissions
Brown Mackie College–St. Louis
#2 Soccer Park Road
Fenton, Missouri 63026
Phone: 636-651-3290
      888-874-4375 (toll-free)
Fax: 636-651-3349
E-mail: bmcstladm@brownmackie.edu
Web site: http://www.brownmackie.edu/StLouis

BROWN MACKIE COLLEGE–SALINA
SALINA, KANSAS

The College and Its Mission

Brown Mackie College–Salina is one of over twenty-five locations in the Brown Mackie College family of schools (www.brownmackie.edu), which is dedicated to providing educational programs that prepare students to pursue entry-level positions in a competitive, rapidly changing workplace. Brown Mackie College schools offer bachelor's degree, associate degree, certificate, and diploma programs in health sciences, business, information technology, legal studies, and design to over 20,000 students in the Midwest, Southeast, Southwest, and Western United States.

The College was originally founded in July 1892 as the Kansas Wesleyan School of Business. In 1938, the College was incorporated as the Brown Mackie School of Business under the ownership of former Kansas Wesleyan instructors Perry E. Brown and A. B. Mackie; it became Brown Mackie College in January 1975.

Brown Mackie College–Salina is accredited by the Higher Learning Commission and is a member of the North Central Association (NCA), 230 South LaSalle Street, Suite 7-500, Chicago, Illinois 60604-1413; phone 800-621-7440 (toll-free); www.ncahlc.org.

The occupational therapy assistant program is accredited by the Accreditation Council for Occupational Therapy Education (ACOTE) of the American Occupational Therapy Association (AOTA), located at 4720 Montgomery Lane, P.O. Box 31220, Bethesda, Maryland 20824-1220; phone: 301-652-AOTA.

Brown Mackie College–Salina's veterinary technology program has provisional programmatic accreditation granted by the American Veterinary Medical Association (AVMA) through the Committee on Veterinary Technician Education and Activities (CVTEA).

Brown Mackie College–Salina is approved and authorized to grant the Associate of Applied Science (A.A.S.) degree by the Kansas Board of Regents, 1000 Southwest Jackson Street, Suite 520, Topeka, Kansas 66612-1368.

Academic Programs

Brown Mackie College–Salina provides higher education to traditional and nontraditional students through associate degree, diploma, and certificate programs that can assist them in enhancing their career opportunities, broadening their perspectives through appropriate general education courses, thinking independently and critically, and improving problem-solving abilities. The College strives to develop within its students the desire for lifelong and continued education.

In most programs, students can participate in day or evening classes, which begin every month. Programs are offered on a year-round basis, providing students with the ability to work uninterrupted toward completion of their programs. The College offers all programs in a unique One Course a Month format. This schedule allows students to focus studies on only one course for four weeks and has proven convenient for students with multiple obligations such as jobs and family.

Associate Degree Programs: The Associate of Applied Science degree is awarded in accounting technology, architectural design and drafting technology, bioscience laboratory technology, business management, computer aided design and drafting technology, computer networking and applications, criminal justice, health and fitness training, health care administration, medical assisting, nursing, occupational therapy assistant, office management, paralegal, and veterinary technology. An associate degree in general studies is also offered to create a greater level of flexibility for students who may be unsure of their career choice, who want a more generalized education, or who want to transfer to a baccalaureate program.

Diploma Programs: The College also offers diploma programs in accounting, business, computer aided design and drafting technician, computer software applications, criminal justice, fitness trainer, medical assistant, and paralegal assistant.

Certificate Programs: Certificate programs are offered in computer networking and practical nursing.

Costs

Tuition for the 2010–11 academic year was $285 per credit hour and general fees were $15 per credit hour. Tuition for computer networking was $300 per credit hour and general fees were $25 per credit hour. Tuition for the nursing programs was $350 per credit hour and general fees were $25 per credit hour. Tuition for the occupational therapy assistant program was $350 per credit hour and general fees were $15 per credit hour. The cost of textbooks and other instructional materials varies by program.

Financial Aid

Financial aid is available to those who qualify. The College maintains a full-time staff of financial aid professionals to assist qualified students in obtaining financial assistance. The College participates in several student aid programs. Forms of financial aid that are available through federal resources include Federal Pell Grants, Federal Supplemental Educational Opportunity Grants (FSEOG), Academic Competitiveness Grant, Federal Work-Study Program awards, Federal Perkins Loans, Federal Stafford Student Loans (subsidized and unsubsidized), and Federal PLUS loans. Eligible students may apply for veterans' educational benefits. Students with physical or mental disabilities that are a handicap to employment may be eligible for training services through the state Vocational Rehabilitation Agency. For further information, students should contact the College's Student Financial Services Office.

Each year, the College makes available President's Scholarships of up to $1000 each to qualifying seniors from area high schools. No more than one scholarship is awarded per high school. In order to qualify, a senior must be graduating from a participating high school, have maintained a cumulative grade point average of at least 2.0, and submitted a brief essay. The student's extracurricular activities and community service are also considered. The President's Scholarship is available only to students enrolling in one of the College's degree programs. Students awarded the scholarship must enroll at Brown Mackie College–Salina between June and September immediately following their high school graduation. Applications for these scholarships can be obtained from the guidance departments of participating high schools. These applications must be completed and returned to the College by March 31.

The Merit Scholarship is a College-sponsored scholarship that may be awarded to students who demonstrate exceptional academic ability. To qualify for a Merit Scholarship, an applicant or student must have scored 21 or higher on the ACT or 900 or higher on the SAT. The maximum amount awarded by this scholarship to any student is $500.

Athletic scholarships may be awarded to students who participate in athletic programs that are sponsored by the College. Current sports are men's baseball, men's and women's basketball, and women's fast-pitch softball. Maximum awards for any applicant or student are determined by the College President. Further information is available from the Athletic Office. Recipients of athletic scholarships must achieve a cumulative grade point average of at least 2.0 by their graduation. Recipients who fail to maintain full-time status or the required grade point average forfeit their awards.

Faculty

There are 19 full-time and 19 adjunct faculty members. The average student-instructor ratio is 15:1.

Facilities and Resources

In addition to classrooms and computer labs, the College maintains a library of curriculum-related resources, technical and general education materials, academic and professional periodicals, and audiovisual resources. Internet access is also available for research. The College has a bookstore that stocks texts, courseware, and other educational supplies that are required for courses and a variety of personal, recreational, and gift items, including apparel, supplies, and general merchandise incorporating the College logo. Hours are posted at the bookstore entrance.

Location

Brown Mackie College–Salina is located at 2106 South Ninth Street in Salina, Kansas.

Admission Requirements

Each applicant for admission is assigned an Assistant Director of Admissions, who directs the applicant through the steps of the admissions process, providing information on curriculum, policies, procedures, and services and assisting the applicant in setting necessary appointments and interviews.

To qualify for admission, each applicant must provide documentation of graduation from an accredited high school or from a state-approved secondary education curriculum or provide official documentation of high school graduation equivalency. All transcripts become the property of the College. Admission to the College is based upon the applicant meeting the above requirements, a review of the applicant's previous education records, and a review of the applicant's career interests. If previous academic records indicate that the College's education and training programs would not benefit the applicant, the College reserves the right to advise the applicant not to enroll. Special requirements for enrollment into certain programs are discussed in the descriptions of those programs.

For the most recent information regarding admissions requirements, please refer to the most current academic catalog.

Application and Information

Applicants must complete and submit an application form, along with documentation of graduation from an accredited high school or state-approved secondary education curriculum or official documentation of high school graduation equivalency. For additional information, prospective students should contact:

Director of Admissions
Brown Mackie College–Salina
2106 South Ninth Street
Salina, Kansas 67401
Phone: 785-825-5422
         800-365-0433 (toll-free)
Fax: 785-827-7623
E-mail: bmcsaadm@brownmackie.edu
Web site: http://www.brownmackie.edu/Salina

BROWN MACKIE COLLEGE–SAN ANTONIO

SAN ANTONIO, TEXAS

The College and Its Mission

Brown Mackie College–San Antonio is one of over twenty-five locations in the Brown Mackie College family of schools (www.brownmackie.edu), which is dedicated to providing educational programs that prepare students to pursue entry-level positions in a competitive, rapidly changing workplace. Brown Mackie College schools offer bachelor's degree, associate degree, certificate, and diploma programs in health sciences, business, information technology, legal studies, and design to over 20,000 students in the Midwest, Southeast, Southwest, and Western United States.

Brown Mackie College was originally founded and approved by the Board of Trustees of Kansas Wesleyan College in Salina, Kansas on July 30, 1892. In 1938, the College was incorporated as the Brown Mackie School of Business under the ownership of Perry E. Brown and A. B. Mackie, former instructors at Kansas Wesleyan University in Salina, Kansas. Their last names formed the name of Brown Mackie. By January 1975, with improvements in curricula and higher degree-granting status, the Brown Mackie School of Business became Brown Mackie College.

Brown Mackie College–San Antonio is accredited by the Accrediting Council for Independent Colleges and Schools (ACICS) to award bachelor's and associate degrees. ACICS is listed as a nationally recognized accrediting agency by the United States Department of Education and is recognized by the Council for Higher Education Accreditation. ACICS can be contacted at 750 First Street NE, Suite 980, Washington, D.C. 20002; phone: 202-336-6780.

Academic Programs

Brown Mackie College–San Antonio provides higher education to traditional and nontraditional students through bachelor's degree and associate degree programs that assist in enhancing their career opportunities, broadening their perspectives through appropriate general education courses, thinking independently and critically, and improving problem-solving abilities. The College strives to develop within its students the desire for lifelong and continued education.

Each College quarter comprises twelve weeks. Bachelor's degree programs require a minimum of sixteen quarters to complete. Associate degree programs require a minimum of eight quarters to complete. Programs are offered on a year-round basis, providing students with the ability to work uninterrupted toward completion of their programs. The College offers all programs in a unique One Course a Month format. This allows students to focus studies on only one course for four weeks. This schedule has proven convenient for students with multiple obligations such as jobs and family.

Bachelor's Degree Programs: The Bachelor of Science degree is awarded in business administration, criminal justice, health care management, and legal studies.

Associate Degree Programs: The Associate of Science degree is awarded in accounting technology, architectural design and drafting technology, business management, criminal justice, health care administration, information technology, medical assisting, paralegal, pharmacy technology, and surgical technology.

Costs

Tuition in the 2010–11 academic year for most bachelor's and associate degree programs was $295 per credit hour; fees were $15 per credit hour. Tuition for the surgical technology program was $330 per credit hour; fees were $15 per credit hour. The cost of textbooks and other instructional materials varies by program.

Financial Aid

Financial aid is available for those who qualify. The College maintains a full-time staff of financial aid professionals to assist qualified students in obtaining the financial assistance they require to meet their educational expenses. Available resources include federal and state aid, student loans from private lenders, and Federal Work-Study opportunities, both on and off college premises.

Each year, the College makes available scholarships of $1000 each to qualifying seniors from area high schools. No more than one scholarship is awarded per high school. In order to qualify, a senior must have graduated from a participating high school, maintained a cumulative grade point average of at least 2.0, and submit a brief essay. The student's extracurricular activities and community service are also considered. These scholarships are available only to students enrolling in one of the College's degree programs. Students awarded the scholarship must enroll at Brown Mackie College–San Antonio between June and September immediately following their high school graduation. Applications for these scholarships can be obtained from the guidance departments of participating high schools. These applications must be completed and returned to the College by March 31.

Faculty

Experienced faculty members provide academic support and are committed to the academic and technical preparation of their students. The College has both full-time and part-time instructors, with a student-faculty ratio of 15:1.

Facilities and Resources

A modern facility, Brown Mackie College–San Antonio offers more than 35,000 square feet of educational and administrative space. The College is equipped with multiple computer labs, housing over 100 computers. High-speed access to the Internet and other online resources are available to students and faculty. Multimedia classrooms are outfitted with overhead projectors, VCR/DVD players, and computers.

The campus is nonresidential. The College has a generous parking area and is easily accessible by public transportation. The campus is a smoke-free facility.

Location

Brown Mackie College–San Antonio is conveniently located at 4715 Fredericksburg Road, in San Antonio, Texas.

Admission Requirements

Each applicant for admission is assigned an Assistant Director of Admissions who directs the applicant through the steps of the admissions process. They provide information on curriculum, policies, procedures, and services and assist the applicant in setting necessary appointments and interviews. To qualify for admission, each applicant must provide documentation of graduation from an accredited high school or from a state-approved secondary education curriculum or provide official documentation of high school graduation equivalency. All transcripts become the property of the College. Admission to the College is based on the applicant meeting the stated requirements, a review of the applicant's previous educational records, and a review of the applicant's career interests. If previous academic records indicate the College's education and training programs would not benefit the applicant, the College reserves the right to advise the applicant not to enroll. Special requirements for enrollment into certain programs are discussed in the descriptions of those programs.

For the most recent information regarding admission requirements, prospective students should refer to the current academic catalog.

Application and Information

Applicants must complete and submit an application form, along with documentation of graduation from an accredited high school or state-approved secondary education curriculum, or official documentation of high school graduation equivalency.

For additional information, prospective students should contact:

Director of Admissions
Brown Mackie College–San Antonio
4715 Fredericksburg Road, Suite 100
San Antonio, Texas 78229

Phone: 210-428-2210
      877-460-1714 (toll-free)
Fax: 210-428-2265
E-mail: bmsanadm@brownmackie.edu
Web site: http://www.brownmackie.edu/SanAntonio

BROWN MACKIE COLLEGE–SOUTH BEND

SOUTH BEND, INDIANA

The College and Its Mission

Brown Mackie College–South Bend is one of over twenty-five locations in the Brown Mackie College family of schools (www.brownmackie.edu), which is dedicated to providing educational programs that prepare students to pursue entry-level positions in a competitive, rapidly changing workplace. Brown Mackie College schools offer bachelor's degree, associate degree, certificate, and diploma programs in health sciences, business, information technology, legal studies, and design to over 20,000 students in the Midwest, Southeast, Southwest, and Western United States.

The College is one of the oldest institutions of its kind in the country and the oldest in the state of Indiana. Established in 1882 as the South Bend Commercial College, the school later changed its name to Michiana College. In 1930, the school was incorporated under the laws of the state of Indiana and was authorized to confer associate degrees and certificates in business. The College relocated to East Jefferson Boulevard in 1987. In September 2009, Brown Mackie College–South Bend officially opened a new 46,000-square-foot facility at 3454 Douglas Road in South Bend, Indiana.

Brown Mackie College–South Bend is accredited by the Accrediting Council for Independent Colleges and Schools (ACICS) to award bachelor's degrees, associate degrees, diplomas, and certificates. ACICS is listed as a nationally recognized accrediting agency by the United States Department of Education and is recognized by the Council for Higher Education Accreditation. ACICS can be contacted at 750 First Street NE, Suite 980, Washington, D.C. 20002; phone: 202-336-6780.

Brown Mackie College–South Bend is regulated by the Indiana Commission on Proprietary Education, 302 West Washington Street, Indianapolis, Indiana 46204; phone: 317-232-1320 or 800-227-5695 (toll-free). (Indiana advertising code for Brown Mackie–South Bend: AC-0110).

The Brown Mackie College–South Bend medical assisting Associate of Science degree program is accredited by the Commission on Accreditation of Allied Health Education Programs (www.caahep.org) upon the recommendation of the Curriculum Review Board of the American Association of Medical Assistants Endowment (AAMAE).

The occupational therapy assistant program is accredited by the Accreditation Council for Occupational Therapy Education (ACOTE) of the American Occupational Therapy Association (AOTA), located at 4720 Montgomery Lane, P.O. Box 31220, Bethesda, Maryland 20824-1220; phone: 301-652-AOTA.

The physical therapist assistant program at Brown Mackie College–South Bend is accredited by the Commission on Accreditation in Physical Therapy Education (CAPTE) of the American Physical Therapy Association (APTA), 1111 North Fairfax Street, Alexandria, Virginia 22314; phone: 703-706-3241.

The practical nursing program is accredited by the Indiana State Board of Nursing, 402 West Washington Street, Room W066, Indianapolis, Indiana 46204; phone: 317-234-2043.

The College is a nonresidential, smoke-free institution.

Academic Programs

Brown Mackie College–South Bend provides higher education to traditional and nontraditional students through bachelor's degree, associate degree, diploma, and certificate programs that assist in enhancing their career opportunities, broadening their perspectives through appropriate general education courses, thinking independently and critically, and improving problem-solving abilities.

Each College quarter comprises twelve weeks. Bachelor's degree programs require a minimum of sixteen quarters to complete. Associate degree programs require a minimum of eight quarters to complete. Programs are offered on a year-round basis, providing students with the ability to work uninterrupted toward completion of their programs. The College offers all programs in a unique One Course a Month format. This allows students to focus studies on only one course for four weeks. This schedule has proven convenient for students with multiple obligations such as jobs and family.

Bachelor's Degree Programs: The Bachelor of Science degree is awarded in business administration, criminal justice, health care management, and legal studies.

Associate Degree Programs: The Associate of Science degree is awarded in accounting technology, business management, computer software technology, criminal justice, health and therapeutic massage, health care administration, information technology, medical assisting, paralegal, and veterinary technology.

The Associate of Applied Science degree is awarded in occupational therapy assistant and physical therapist assistant.

Diploma Program: The College offers a diploma program in practical nursing.

Certificate Programs: The College offers certificate programs in accounting, business, computer software applications, criminal justice, medical assistant, and paralegal assistant.

Costs

Tuition for programs in the 2010–11 academic year was $285 per credit hour, with a $15 per credit hour general fee applied to instructional costs for activities and services. The cost of textbooks and other instructional materials varies by program. Tuition for the practical nursing program was $350 per credit hour, with a $25 per credit hour general fee applied to instructional costs for activities and services. Tuition for the physical therapist assistant program was $350 per credit hour. Tuition for the occupational therapy assistant program was $350 per credit hour.

Financial Aid

Financial aid is available for those who qualify. The College maintains a full-time staff of financial aid professionals to assist qualified students in obtaining financial assistance. The College participates in several student aid programs. Forms of financial aid available through federal resources include the Federal Pell Grant Program, Federal Supplemental Educational Opportunity Grant (FSEOG) Program, Federal Work-Study Program, Federal Perkins Loan Program, Federal Stafford Student Loan Program (subsidized and unsubsidized), and the Federal PLUS Loan Program.

Eligible students may apply for Indiana state awards, such as the Frank O'Bannon Grant Program (formerly the Indiana Higher Education Grant) and Twenty-First Century Scholars Program for high school students, the Core 40 awards, and veterans' educational benefits. Students with physical or mental disabilities that are a handicap may be eligible for training services through the state's Bureau of Vocational Rehabilitation. For further information, students should contact the College Student Financial Services Office.

Each year, the College makes available President's Scholarships of $1000 each to qualifying seniors from area high schools. No more than one scholarship is awarded per high school. In order to qualify, a senior must be graduating from a participating high school, must be maintaining a cumulative grade point average of at least 2.0, and must submit a brief essay. The student's extracurricular activities and community service are also considered. The President's Scholarship is available only to students enrolling in one of the College's degree programs. Students awarded the scholarship must enroll at Brown Mackie College–South Bend between June and September immediately following their high school graduation. Applications for these scholarships can be obtained from the guidance departments of participating high schools. These applications must be completed and returned to the College by March 31.

Faculty

There are 29 full-time and 46 part-time faculty members at the College. The average student-faculty ratio is 12:1. Each student is assigned a program director as an adviser.

Facilities and Resources

Brown Mackie College–South Bend's new location has a generous parking area and is easily accessible by public transportation. The College's smoke-free, three-story, 46,000-square-foot building offers a modern, professional environment for study. The facility offers "classrooms of the future," with instructor workstations and full multimedia capabilities that include surround sound and projection screens that can be accessed by computer, DVD, and VHS machines. The new facility includes medical, computer, and occupational and physical therapy labs, as well as a library and bookstore. The labs provide students with hands-on opportunities to apply knowledge and skills learned in the classroom. The veterinary technology lab is 2,600 square feet and includes surgery areas, treatment areas, and kennels.

Location

Brown Mackie College–South Bend is conveniently located at 3454 Douglas Road in South Bend, Indiana. The College has a generous parking area and is easily accessible by public transportation.

Admission Requirements

Each applicant for admission is assigned an Assistant Director of Admissions, who directs the applicant through the steps of the admissions process, providing information on curriculum, policies, procedures, and services, and assisting the applicant in setting necessary appointments and interviews. To qualify for admission, each applicant must provide documentation of graduation from an accredited high school or from a state-approved secondary education curriculum, or provide official documentation of high school graduation equivalency. All transcripts become the property of the College.

Admission to the College is based on the applicant meeting the stated requirements, a review of the applicant's previous educational records, and a review of the applicant's career interests. If previous academic records indicate the College's education and training programs would not benefit the applicant, the College reserves the right to advise the applicant not to enroll. Special requirements for enrollment into certain programs are discussed in the descriptions of those programs.

In addition to the College's general admission requirements, applicants enrolling in the occupational therapy assistant program will be required to complete COMPASS assessment before their first course is scheduled. COMPASS assessment scores will determine if the student will need transitional courses. If the student attains the minimum scores (reading 75, writing 60, and math 51) on all three sections, the student is scheduled in CF1100–Professional Development. If the student's score is below the minimum in any of the sections, the student is advised that they will be placed in transitional course(s). After successful completion of all the required transitional courses, the student will have one opportunity to retake the COMPASS assessment and achieve the minimum score(s). If the student does not successfully obtain the minimum scores in all three sections on the second attempt, the student will not be allowed to continue in the OTA program, but can be considered for another program at Brown Mackie College.

In addition to the general admission requirements, applicants to the physical therapist assistant program must document the following: a minimum high school cumulative grade point average of 3.0 on a 4.0 scale, or a minimum score of 600 on the GED examination (if taken on or after January 15, 2002) or 60 (if taken before January 15, 2002); a minimum of 12 quarter–credit hours or 9 semester–credit hours of consecutive collegiate course work with a minimum GPA of 3.0 on a 4.0 scale (these credit hours may be completed at Brown Mackie College); a biology course in high school or college with a minimum grade of a B (3.0 on a 4.0 scale); and 20 hours (total) of documented observation, volunteer, or employment hours in at least two different physical therapy settings with no less than 8 hours in one setting, completed within the past three years.

In addition to the College's general admission requirements, applicants enrolling in the practical nursing program must document the following: fulfillment of Brown Mackie College–South Bend general requirements; complete physical (must be current to within six months of admission); two-step Mantoux TB skin test (must be current throughout schooling); hepatitis B vaccination or signed refusal; up-to-date immunizations, including tetanus and rubella; record of current CPR certification (certification must be current throughout the clinical experience through health care provider certification or the American Heart Association); and hospitalization insurance or a signed waiver.

For the most recent information regarding admission requirements, please refer to the current academic catalog.

Application and Information

Applicants must complete and submit an application form along with documentation of graduation from an accredited high school or state-approved secondary education curriculum or official documentation of high school graduation equivalency.

For additional information, prospective students should contact:

Director of Admissions
Brown Mackie College–South Bend
3454 Douglas Road
South Bend, Indiana 46635
Phone: 574-237-0774
　　　　800-743-2447 (toll-free)
Fax: 574-237-3585
E-mail: bmcsbadm@brownmackie.edu
Web site: http://www.brownmackie.edu/SouthBend

BROWN MACKIE COLLEGE–TUCSON
TUCSON, ARIZONA

The College and Its Mission

Brown Mackie College–Tucson is one of over twenty-five locations in the Brown Mackie College family of schools (www.brownmackie.edu), which is dedicated to providing educational programs that prepare students to pursue entry-level positions in a competitive, rapidly changing workplace. Brown Mackie College schools offer bachelor's degree, associate degree, and diploma programs in health sciences, business, information technology, legal studies, and design to over 20,000 students in the Midwest, Southeast, Southwest, and Western United States.

Brown Mackie College was originally founded and approved by the Board of Trustees of Kansas Wesleyan College in Salina, Kansas on July 30, 1892. In 1938, the College was incorporated as the Brown Mackie School of Business under the ownership of Perry E. Brown and A. B. Mackie, former instructors at Kansas Wesleyan University in Salina, Kansas. Their last names formed the name of Brown Mackie. By January 1975, with improvements in curricula and higher degree-granting status, the Brown Mackie School of Business became Brown Mackie College.

Brown Mackie College entered the Arizona market in 2007 when it purchased a school that had been previously established in the Tucson area. That school had an established history in the community and was converted into what is now known as Brown Mackie College–Tucson. The historical timeline of Brown Mackie College–Tucson started in 1972 when Rockland West Corporation first formed a partnership with Lamson Business College. At that time the school was a career college that offered only short-term programs focusing on computer training and secretarial skills. In 1994 the College became accredited as a junior college and began offering associate degrees in academic subjects. The mission was then modified to include the goal of instilling in graduates an appreciation for lifelong learning through the general education courses that became a part of every program.

In 1996 the College applied for and received status as a senior college by the Accrediting Council for Independent Colleges and Schools. This gave the school the ability to offer course work leading to a Bachelor of Science degree in business administration. Since then the program offerings for bachelor's and associate degrees have expanded.

In 1986 the campus moved from 5001 East Speedway to the 4585 East Speedway location where it remains today. In 2008 two of the College's three buildings were remodeled which resulted in updated classrooms; networked computer laboratories; new medical, surgical technology, and forensics laboratories; a larger library; offices for student services such as academics, admissions, and student financial services; and a full-service college store. In 2009 the third building was remodeled to provide newer classrooms and a new career services department.

Brown Mackie College–Tucson is accredited by the Accrediting Council for Independent Colleges and Schools (ACICS) to award bachelor's degrees, associate degrees, and certificates. ACICS is listed as a nationally recognized accrediting agency by the United States Department of Education and is recognized by the Council for Higher Education Accreditation. ACICS can be contacted at 750 First Street NE, Suite 980, Washington, D.C. 20002; phone: 202-336-6780.

This institution is licensed by the Arizona State Board for Private Postsecondary Education, 1400 West Washington Street, Room 2560, Phoenix, Arizona 85007; phone: 620-542-5709.

The occupational therapy assistant program is accredited by the Accreditation Council for Occupational Therapy Education (ACOTE) of the American Occupational Therapy Association (AOTA), located at 4720 Montgomery Lane, P.O. Box 31220, Bethesda, Maryland 20824; phone: 301-652-AOTA.

The surgical technology program is accredited by the Accrediting Bureau of Health Education Schools (ABHES).

Academic Programs

Brown Mackie College–Tucson provides higher education to traditional and nontraditional students through bachelor's degree, associate degree, and diploma programs that assist in enhancing their career opportunities, broadening their perspectives through appropriate general education courses, thinking independently and critically, and improving problem-solving abilities. The College strives to develop within its students the desire for lifelong and continued education.

Each College quarter comprises twelve weeks. Bachelor's degree programs require a minimum of sixteen quarters to complete. Associate degree programs require a minimum of eight quarters to complete. Programs are offered on a year-round basis, providing students with the ability to work uninterrupted toward their degrees. The College offers all programs in a unique One Course a Month format. This allows students to focus studies on only one course for four weeks. This schedule has proven convenient for students with multiple obligations such as jobs and family.

Bachelor's Degree Programs: The Bachelor of Science degree is awarded in accounting, business administration, criminal justice, health care management, information technology, and legal studies.

Associate Degree Programs: The Associate of Science degree is awarded in accounting technology, business management, computer networking and security, criminal justice, early childhood education, graphic design, health care administration, information technology, medical assisting, paralegal, and surgical technology.

The Associate of Applied Science degree is awarded in biomedical equipment technology, health and fitness training, and occupational therapy assistant.

Diploma Program: A diploma is awarded in the fitness trainer program.

Costs

Tuition in the 2010–11 academic year for most bachelor's, associate, and diploma programs was $315 per credit hour; fees were $15 per credit hour. Tuition for the surgical technology program was $330 per credit hour; fees were $15 per credit hour. Tuition for the occupational therapy assistant program was $350 per credit hour; fees were $15 per credit hour. The cost of textbooks and other instructional expenses varies by program.

Financial Aid

Financial aid is available for those who qualify. The College maintains a full-time staff of financial aid professionals to assist qualified students in obtaining the financial assistance they require to meet their educational expenses. Available resources include federal and state aid, student loans from private lenders, and Federal Work-Study opportunities, both on and off college premises.

Each year, the College makes available scholarships of $1000 each to qualifying seniors from area high schools. No more than one scholarship is awarded per high school. In order to qualify, a senior must be graduating from a participating high school, must be maintaining a cumulative grade point average of at least 2.0, and must submit a brief essay. The student's extracurricular activities and community service are also considered. These scholarships are available only to students enrolling in one of the College's degree programs. Students awarded the scholarship must enroll at Brown Mackie College–Tucson between June and September immediately following their high school graduation. Applications for these scholarships can be obtained from the guidance departments of participating high schools. These applications must be completed and returned to the College by March 31.

Faculty

Experienced faculty members provide academic support and are committed to the academic and technical preparation of their students. The College has 15 full-time and 35 part-time instructors, with a student-faculty ratio of 12:1. Each student is assigned a faculty adviser.

Facilities and Resources

A modern facility, Brown Mackie College–Tucson offers more than 31,000 square feet of educational and administrative space. The College is equipped with multiple computer labs housing over 200 computers. High-speed access to the Internet and other online resources are available for students and faculty. Multimedia classrooms are outfitted with overhead projectors, VCR/DVD players, and computers. The campus is nonresidential; public transportation and parking at no cost are available.

Location

Brown Mackie College–Tucson is conveniently located at 4585 East Speedway Boulevard in Tucson, Arizona. The College has a generous parking area and is also easily accessible by public transportation.

Admission Requirements

Each applicant for admission is assigned an Assistant Director of Admissions who directs the applicant through the steps of the admissions process. They provide information on curriculum, policies, procedures, and services and assist the applicant in setting necessary appointments and interviews. To qualify for admission, each applicant must provide documentation of graduation from an accredited high school or from a state-approved secondary education curriculum, or provide official documentation of high school graduation equivalency. All transcripts become the property of the College. Admission to the College is based on the applicant meeting the stated requirements, a review of the applicant's previous educational records, and a review of the applicant's career interests. If previous academic records indicate the College's education and training programs would not benefit the applicant, the College reserves the right to advise the applicant not to enroll. Special requirements for enrollment into certain programs are discussed in the descriptions of those programs.

For the most recent information regarding admission requirements, please refer to the current academic catalog.

Application and Information

Applicants must complete and submit an application form, along with documentation of graduation from an accredited high school or state-approved secondary education curriculum or official documentation of high school graduation equivalency.

For additional information, prospective students should contact:

Senior Director of Admissions
Brown Mackie College–Tucson
4585 East Speedway Boulevard, Suite 204
Tucson, Arizona 85712
Phone: 520-319-3300
Fax: 520-325-0108
E-mail: bmctuadm@brownmackie.edu
Web site: http://www.brownmackie.edu/Tucson

BROWN MACKIE COLLEGE–TULSA

TULSA, OKLAHOMA

The College and Its Mission

Brown Mackie College–Tulsa is one of over twenty-five locations in the Brown Mackie College family of schools (www.brownmackie.edu), which is dedicated to providing educational programs that prepare students to pursue entry-level positions in a competitive, rapidly changing workplace. Brown Mackie College schools offer bachelor's degree, associate degree, certificate, and diploma programs in health sciences, business, information technology, legal studies, and design to over 20,000 students in the Midwest, Southeast, Southwest, and Western United States.

Brown Mackie College–Tulsa is accredited by the Accrediting Council for Independent Colleges and Schools (ACICS) to award bachelor's degrees, associate degrees, and diplomas. The Accrediting Council for Independent Colleges and Schools is listed as a nationally recognized accrediting agency by the United States Department of Education and is recognized by the Council for Higher Education Accreditation. ACICS can be contacted at 750 First Street NE, Suite 980, Washington, D.C. 20002; phone: 202-336-6780.

The occupational therapy assistant program has applied for accreditation by the Accreditation Council for Occupational Therapy Education (ACOTE) of the American Occupational Therapy Association (AOTA), located at 4720 Montgomery Lane, P.O. Box 31220, Bethesda, Maryland 20824; phone: 301-652-AOTA.

The institution is licensed by the Oklahoma Board of Private Vocational Schools (OBPVS), 3700 North Classen Boulevard, Suite 250, Oklahoma City, Oklahoma 73118; phone: 405-528-3370.

The institution has been granted authority to operate in Oklahoma by the Oklahoma State Regents for Higher Education (OSRHE), 655 Research Parkway, Suite 200, Oklahoma City, Oklahoma 73101; phone: 405-225-9100; www.okhighered.org.

The College is a nonresidential, smoke-free institution.

Academic Programs

Brown Mackie College–Tulsa provides higher education to traditional and nontraditional students through bachelor's and associate degree programs and diploma programs that can assist students in enhancing their career opportunities, broadening their perspectives through appropriate general education courses, thinking independently and critically, and improving problem-solving abilities. The College strives to develop within its students the desire for lifelong and continued education.

Each College quarter comprises twelve weeks. Bachelor's degree programs require a minimum of sixteen quarters to complete. Associate degree programs require a minimum of eight quarters to complete. Programs are offered on a year-round basis, providing students with the ability to work uninterrupted toward their degrees. The College offers all programs in a unique One Course a Month format. This schedule allows students to focus studies on only one course for four weeks and has proven convenient for students with multiple obligations such as jobs and family.

Bachelor's Degree Programs: The Bachelor of Science degree is awarded in business administration, criminal justice, health care management, and legal studies.

Associate Degree Programs: The Associate of Applied Science degree is awarded in accounting technology, business management, criminal justice, health care administration, information technology, medical assisting, occupational therapy assistant, office management, paralegal, and surgical technology.

Diploma Programs: The College also offers diploma programs in accounting, business, criminal justice, medical assistant, and paralegal assistant.

Costs

Tuition for the 2010–11 academic year was $285 per credit hour and $15 per credit hour for general fees. Tuition for the occupational therapy assistant program was $350 per credit hour and $15 per credit hour for general fees. Tuition for the surgical technology program was $330 per credit hour and $15 per credit hour for general fees. The cost of textbooks and other instructional materials varies by program.

Financial Aid

Financial aid is available to those who qualify. The College maintains a full-time staff of financial aid professionals to assist qualified students in obtaining financial assistance. The College participates in several student aid programs. Forms of financial aid available through federal resources include the Federal Pell Grant Program, Federal Supplemental Educational Opportunity Grant (FSEOG) Program, Federal Work-Study Program, Federal Perkins Loan Program, Federal Stafford Student Loan Program (subsidized and unsubsidized), and the Federal PLUS Loan Program. Eligible students may also apply for state awards and veterans' educational benefits. Students with physical or mental disabilities that are a handicap to employment may be eligible for training services through the state Agency for Vocational Rehabilitation. For further information, students should contact the College's Student Financial Services Office.

Faculty

There are 10 full-time and several adjunct faculty members. The average class size is 14 students. Each student has a faculty and student adviser.

Facilities and Resources

The College comprises administrative offices, a faculty and student lounge, a reception area, and spacious classrooms and laboratories. Instructional equipment includes personal computers, LANs, printers, and lab equipment. The library provides support for the academic programs through volumes covering a broad range of subjects, as well as through Internet access. Vehicle parking is provided for both students and staff members.

Location

Brown Mackie College–Tulsa is conveniently located at 4608 South Garnett Road, Suite 110 in Tulsa, Oklahoma. The College has a generous parking area and is easily accessible by public transportation.

Admission Requirements

Each applicant for admission is assigned an Assistant Director of Admissions who directs the applicant through the steps of the admissions process, providing information on curriculum, policies, procedures, and services and assisting the applicant in setting necessary appointments and interviews.

To qualify for admission, each applicant must provide documentation of graduation from an accredited high school or from a state-approved secondary education curriculum, or provide official documentation of high school graduation equivalency. All transcripts become the property of the College. Admission to the College is based upon the applicant meeting the stated requirements, a review of the applicant's previous education records, and a review of the applicant's career interests. If previous academic records indicate that the College's education and training programs would not benefit the applicant, the College reserves the right to advise the applicant not to enroll. Special requirements for enrollment into certain programs are discussed in the descriptions of those programs.

For the most recent information regarding admission requirements, please refer to the current academic catalog.

Application and Information

Applicants must complete and submit an application form along with documentation of graduation from an accredited high school or state-approved secondary education curriculum, or applicants must provide official documentation of high school graduation equivalency.

For additional information, prospective students should contact:

Senior Director of Admissions
Brown Mackie College–Tulsa
4608 South Garnett Road, Suite 110
Tulsa, Oklahoma 74146
Phone: 918-628-3700
      888-794-8411 (toll-free)
Fax: 918-828-9083
E-mail: bmctuladm@brownmackie.edu
Web site: http://www.brownmackie.edu/Tulsa

CAMDEN COUNTY COLLEGE

BLACKWOOD, NEW JERSEY

The College and Its Mission

Camden County College (CCC) is a fully-accredited comprehensive public community college in New Jersey. CCC provides accessible and affordable education. Since its inception in 1967, the College has grown to offer 100-plus associate degree and occupational certificate programs along with non-credit development courses and customized job training. The College also provides support services students need to transfer for further studies or to directly begin a career. The College has three locations: the main campus in Blackwood, the Camden city campus in the University District in Camden, and the William G. Rohrer Center in Cherry Hill, New Jersey.

The College is one of the largest community colleges in New Jersey and one of the most sophisticated in the nation. Recognized nationally as a leader in technology programs, the College is also regionally acknowledged as a vital resource for transfer education, customized training, and cultural events.

The main campus is situated on 320 sylvan acres near Philadelphia and New York, allowing students to take advantage of the cities for recreation, education, and work opportunities.

An $83-million capital initiative transforming many of the facilities and structural amenities on the main campus is under way. A new science building is under construction; roads, athletic fields, and parking are being upgraded. The College is easily accessible from Route 42 via Exit 7B which leads directly into the College's main entrance.

College housing is not available. If not commuting, students may reside at local apartment complexes that are within walking distance of the main campus.

Over twenty student clubs and service organizations, national honor societies, and other activities are available. The College also has a student newspaper, the *Campus Press*, and a radio station.

A variety of athletic activities are offered for the experienced competitor as well as the casual participant. Varsity teams for both men and women compete against other two-year college teams in the New Jersey Garden State Athletic Conference and Region XIX of the National Junior College Athletic Association. Men compete in soccer, golf, basketball, and baseball. Women compete in soccer, basketball, and softball. Students are encouraged to take advantage of College athletic facilities, including an all-weather, quarter-mile track; an athletic center with a weight and fitness room; basketball/volleyball courts, and various outdoor playing fields.

Academic Programs

Camden County College offers the following associate degrees: A.A., A.S., A.F.A., and A.A.S., as well as C.T. and C.A. certificates.

The College operates on a fifteen-week or thirteen-week semester and offers courses in arts, humanities, social sciences, business, computers, mathematics, health care, and science. Online and hybrid courses are offered. Summer sessions are five, seven, and eight weeks long; and online and weekend courses are offered as well. The College's academic calendar is accessible at www.camdencc.edu.

In general, approximately 60 credits are required to earn an associate degree and about 30 credits for a certificate. The total number of credits required varies by program.

Career programs (A.A.S.) include: Accounting; Addictions Counseling; Automotive Technology: (Apprentice, GM/ASEP and Toyota T-Ten); Biotechnology; Biotechnology: (Cell and Tissue Culture Option and Forensic Science Option); CADD: Computer Aided Drafting and Design; Computer Graphics; Computer Graphics: Game Design and Development; Computer Information Systems; Computer Information Systems: Personal Computer Option; Computer Integrated Manufacturing/Engineering Technology; Computer Systems Technology; Dental Assisting; Dental Hygiene ; Dietetic Technology; Engineering Technology: (Electrical Electronic Engineering; Electromechanical Engineering, and Mechanical Engineering); Finance; Fire Science Technology; Fire Science Technology: Administration Option; Health Information Technology; Health Science;

Health Science: (Certified Medical Assistant Option and Surgical Technology Option); Hospitality Technology; Management; Management: (Business Paraprofessional Management Option and Small Business Management Option); Marketing; Massage Therapy; Medical Laboratory Technology; Office Systems Technology Administrative Assistant; Office Systems Technology Administrative Assistant: Information Processing Option; Ophthalmic Science Technology; Paralegal Studies; Paramedic Sciences; Paramedic Sciences: Paramedic Educational Management Option; Photonics: (Laser/Electro-Optic Technology and Laser/Electro-Optic Technology Fiber Optic Option); Respiratory Therapy; Sign Language Interpreter Education; Technical Studies; Veterinary Technology; Video Imaging.

Transfer Programs (A.A./A.F.A./A.S.) include Applied and Fine Arts Option/Liberal Arts and Science (A.A.); Biology Option/Liberal Arts and Science (A.S.); Business Administration Option/Liberal Arts and Science (A.S.); Business Administration Option: Information Systems Track /Liberal Arts and Science (A.S.); Chemistry Option/Liberal Arts and Science (A.S.); Communications Option/Liberal Arts and Science (A.A.); Communications Option: (Photojournalism Track /Liberal Arts and Science (A.A.) and Public Relations/Advertising Track/Liberal Arts and Science (A.A.)); Computer Graphics Option/Liberal Arts and Science (A.A.); Computer Graphics Option: Electronic Publishing Track /Liberal Arts and Science (A.A.); Computer Science (A.A.); Computer Science (A.S.); Criminal Justice (A.S.); Dance Option/ Liberal Arts and Science (A.A.); Deaf Studies Option/Liberal Arts and Science (A.A.); Early Childhood Education Option/Liberal Arts and Science (A.A.); Elementary/Secondary Education (A.S.); Engineering Science (A.S.); English Option/Liberal Arts and Science (A.A.); Environmental Science Option/Liberal Arts and Science (A.S.); Food Science Option/Liberal Arts and Science (A.S.); Health and Exercise Science Option/Liberal Arts and Science (A.S.); History Option/ Liberal Arts and Science (A.A.); Human Services: (A.S.); Human Services: (Developmental Disabilities Option (A.S.) and Early Childhood Education Option (A.S.)); International Studies Option/ Liberal Arts and Science (A.A.); Language and Culture Option/Liberal Arts and Science (A.A.); Law, Government and Politics Option/Liberal Arts and Science (A.A.); Mathematics Option/Liberal Arts and Science (A.S.); Music Option/Liberal Arts and Science (A.A.); Nursing: Our Lady of Lourdes School of Nursing (A.S.); Nursing: Prenursing Option/Liberal Arts and Science (A.S.); Photography Option/Liberal Arts and Science (A.A.); Physics Option/Liberal Arts and Science (A.S.); Prepharmacy Option/Liberal Arts and Science (A.S.); Psychology Option/Liberal Arts and Science (A.A.); Speech Option/Liberal Arts and Science (A.A.); Sport Management (A.S.); Studio Art (AFA); Theatre Option/Liberal Arts and Science (A.A.).

Academic Certificate Programs (C.T.) offered are Computer Applications Programming; Computer Graphics; Computer Integrated Manufacturing Technology; Computer Programming; Computer Systems Technology; Dental Assisting; Developmental Disabilities; Medical Coding; Microsoft Office User Specialist; Office Assistant; Personal Computer Specialist; Photonics: Fiber Optic Technical Specialist; Practical Nursing; Social Services; Web Design Development.

Certificate of Achievement Programs (C.A.) include Addictions Counseling; Alternate Energy Engineering; Technology; Automotive General Technician; CADD: Computer Aided Drafting and Design; Computer Aided Manufacturing Technician; Computer Science; Computerized Accounting Specialist; Crime and Intelligence Analysis; Culinary; Educational Interpreter Training; Emergency and Disaster Management; Fine Art Techniques; Fire Science Technology: (Fire Administration and Fire Suppression); Food Services Management; Fundamentals of Policing; Hotel and Resort Management; Industrial Controls: Programmable Logic Controller; Instructional Aide Paraprofessional Core; Liberal Arts and Science; Linux/UNIX Administration; Management: Business Paraprofessional; Massage Therapy; Meeting and Event Planning; Multi-Skilled Technician; Music Recording; Nutrition Care Manager; Ophthalmic Medical Technician; Ophthalmic Science Apprentice; Paramedic Sciences; Personal Trainer; Real Estate Sales; Relational Database Management System Using ORACLE; Surgical Technology.

Off-Campus Programs

Camden County College has articulation agreements with regional four-year colleges and universities to offer bachelor's degree completion programs on the CCC campus. For more information, visit www.camdencc.edu.

Credit for Nontraditional Learning Experiences

CCC offers a number of opportunities including evaluating educational experiences approved by the American Council on Education and the Program on Non-Collegiate Sponsored Instruction and validating armed services training among others. Consult the College Catalog at www.camdencc.edu for more information.

Costs

For students entering in September 2011 tuition costs are $101 per credit for in-county residents, $105 per credit for out-of-county residents, and $180 per credit for international students. The general service fee per credit is $26, and the facility fee per credit is $2. Course fees vary depending on courses taken and hourly instruction fees vary depending on courses taken.

The cost of books and supplies is estimated to be $1450 for one year for a full-time student. The cost of books can be reduced by up to 50 percent of the cost of a new book by students who choose e-textbooks. Students also save by participating in book rentals and buybacks. Actual costs depend on the specific courses chosen.

Financial Aid

Financial aid comes in the form of scholarships, grants, loans and work study. Students are required to file a Free Application for Federal Student Aid (FAFSA) as soon as possible after January 1 of each year (the College's school code is 006865), as well as the College's authorization and certification form. Financial aid applications filed by May 1 and completed by June 1 of each year are given priority. Students must be admitted before an offer of financial aid can be made. Additional application information is available on www.camdencc.edu.

Faculty

The student-faculty ratio is 29:1. Faculty members are dedicated to teaching and supporting students throughout the academic year. In addition to the College's advisory staff, some faculty members may assist in providing academic advisement for their field of specialization. Full-time faculty members hold advanced degrees as do adjuncts.

Student Body Profile

Of the College's 23,379 credit students served in the financial year 2010, 74.5 percent are Camden county residents and 96 percent New Jersey residents. Approximately 54 percent of the students are Caucasian, 22 percent African American, 6 percent Asian, 8 percent Hispanic, and 1 percent American Indian/Alaskan native. The mean student age is 27.

Academic Facilities

The library is located on the Blackwood campus, and an e-library is located at the Cherry Hill location. Students in Camden city have access to the Rutgers University library and gym located near CCC in the city's University District. CCC offers open access computer labs, laser labs, automotive facility, ophthalmic facility, dental facility, and numerous other laboratories. The Otto R. Mauke Community Center houses a cyber café, student activities offices, cafeteria, and student lounge areas. The facility also contains student support offices including advising, Barnes and Noble bookstore, student employment, student transfer, and international student offices. The Papiano Gymnasium hosts a fitness center and variety of indoor and outdoor sports.

Location

The 320-acre main campus is located in Blackwood, New Jersey. The College is easily reached from the interstate highway system, is located a short distance from the PATCO high-speed train line service to and from Philadelphia and is available via NJ Transit buses. Lincoln Hall's Art Gallery, Dennis Flyer Memorial Theatre and Little Theatre and the Madison Connector Building's Civic Hall, home to the Center for Civic Leadership and Responsibility, are venues for College, county, and regional communities. The facilities host musical concerts, dance performances, theatrical presentations, lectures, workshops, community events, and a regional arts center. The conference center on the Camden city campus is used by businesses, community and government organizations.

Admission Requirements

The College has open enrollment. Students must be 18 years of age. A few selected programs have additional admission criteria. Prospective students should apply online at www.camdencc.edu. The Web site provides details about the enrollment process. There is no cost to apply to CCC.

Application and Information

Processing of applications for admission each year begins no later than February 15 for the fall semester and no later than October 1 for the spring semester. Rolling admission for a semester occurs through the last day of the semester.

Office of Admissions
Camden County College
P.O. Box 200
College Drive
Blackwood, New Jersey 08012

Phone: 856-227-7200
Web site: http://www.camdencc.edu

Connector Building contains light-filled atrium space for students to relax or purchase a beverage or snack at the Connector Café between classes. In addition to comfortable lounge areas, it houses the Center for Civic Leadership and Responsibility and two auditoriums.

COLLEGE OF THE DESERT
PALM SPRINGS, CALIFORNIA

The College and Its Mission

College of the Desert (COD) is a public community college that was founded in 1958. COD is fully accredited through the Western Association of Schools and Colleges (WASC) and offers a variety of certificate programs and associate degrees. The total student population is 12,000 and includes over 220 international students from over forty countries. College of the Desert focuses on preparing students to transfer to the many universities throughout the U.S. with special emphasis on the University of California and California State University systems. It also offers vocational degrees that prepare students with the skills they need for employment.

College of the Desert welcomes international students and offers services to help them succeed. COD's Intensive English Academy offers extensive English training. Admission is easier than at many other institutions, with just one application needed. A TOEFL scores of 32 (iBT) or 400 (paper) is required for direct admission to College of the Desert; the TOEFL is not required for study at the Intensive English Academy. The International Student Office provides specialized services for international students. Tuition and living expenses are reasonable, COD's transfer rate is strong, and the location offers both a comfortable environment and easy access to the major cities and attractions in Southern California.

Academic Programs

College of the Desert prepares students for successful transfer to the many public and private universities throughout the United States. The International Student Counselor can help students reach their transfer goals through individualized counseling, group workshops, and application assistance.

Students can choose from many associate degree and certificate programs in both the liberal arts and sciences. Certificate programs typically are one year in length while associate degree programs require two years of study. Majors include accounting, administration of justice, advanced transportation technologies, agribusiness, agriculture, air-conditioning/HVACR, alcohol/drug studies, anthropology, architectural technology, art, automotive alternate fuels, automotive technology, biology, building inspection technology, business administration, chemistry, communication, composition, computer information systems, computer science, construction management, culinary arts, digital design and production, early childhood education, economics, environmental horticulture, environmental sciences, fire technology, French, geography, general drafting, geology, golf management, history, hospitality management, Italian, journalism, liberal arts, literature, mass communication, mathematics, music, natural resources, nursing, philosophy, physical education, physics, plant science, political science, psychology, recreation, retail management, social science, sociology, Spanish, speech, theater arts, and turfgrass management.

College of the Desert operates on a semester schedule which includes the fall semester (late August–December) and spring semester (late January–May). The College also offers an optional summer session.

Special Programs and Services: COD's Intensive English Academy (IEA) is for students who want to learn English or improve their English before beginning college-level study. The IEA offers 30 hours per week of instruction in English for sixteen weeks. Eight-week programs are also available for those with only a limited time to study in the United States. Classes focus on grammar, reading, writing, listening, and speaking skills and are TOEFL prep–based. Classes are offered from beginner to advanced level. Students who complete the IEA advanced level will be admitted to College of the Desert without the TOEFL. Admission dates for the IEA are August, October, January, March, and June.

Off-Campus Programs

College of the Desert is part of the Southern California Foothill Consortium for Study Abroad. COD students are able to join the many study-abroad opportunities provided through this consortium while earning academic credit towards their degrees.

Costs

College of the Desert estimates annual tuition and living expenses for international students to be $15,000. This includes tuition of approximately $5260 per academic year (two semesters) and living expenses based on host family accommodations. Housing estimates are approximately $6000 per year for a host family providing rooming with meals. Off-campus apartment rental is available at an additional cost. Mandatory health insurance costs are approximately $800 per year. Miscellaneous costs such as textbooks and personal expenses are estimated at approximately $2940 per year. Students must pay for classes at the time of registration; housing expenses are paid on a monthly basis.

Annual tuition and living expenses for the Intensive English Academy are estimated at $18,000 for international students. Tuition is $1900 for the eight-week program, $3650 for the sixteen-week program, and $2350 for the eight-week summer accelerated program. Tuition fees include access to computer labs as well as various social activities offered throughout the program. Housing and miscellaneous expenses are the same as those for College of the Desert.

Financial Aid

Although financial aid is not available for international students, College of the Desert does offer scholarships for enrolled international students. COD offers approximately three to five merit-based scholarships each semester. Application requirements vary for each scholarship. International students enrolled at COD are allowed to work on campus; however, the College is not able to guarantee employment.

Faculty

College of the Desert is proud of its nationally recognized programs and the instructors who work to ensure students succeed and acquire the skills needed for their chosen field. All faculty members have a master's degree or Ph.D. and come from a variety of backgrounds and experiences. COD has approximately 110 full-time and 370 part-time faculty members on campus. Typical class size is 35 students.

The IEA program is taught by one full-time and five part-time faculty members. All IEA faculty members have a master's in English or TESOL. Typical class size is 10 students.

Student Body Profile

College of the Desert's student population is 12,000 with approximately 40 percent full-time and 60 percent part-time students. The College has a diverse population including Hispanic, Asian, African-American, European, and American Indian students. The 220 international students represent approximately forty countries around the world. Students' ages range from 18 to 80 but the average student is between 18 and 21. All students live off-campus as dormitories are not available. Students can enjoy a variety of social activities facilitated by the Student Life Office and are encouraged to participate in campus clubs, events, and student government.

Facilities and Resources

Student services at College of the Desert are very comprehensive and are focused on the diverse needs of the student population. Services include academic advising, athletics, a career center, computer centers with Wi-Fi access, counseling, a dining hall, foreign language labs, a library, math labs, social activities, student government, a transfer center, tutoring, and a writing center.

The International Student Office provides a variety of services dedicated to the needs of the international students at both COD and the IEA. This office provides assistance with application, airport arrival, housing, academic advising, personal counseling, immigration advising, orientation, social activities, scholarships, and university transfer assistance.

Location

College of the Desert located in Southern California, near the well-known resort city of Palm Springs. The small-town environment attracts a variety of national events including famous golf and tennis tournaments, the International Film Festival, and the Coachella Music and Arts Festival. COD is only a short drive from Los Angeles, San Diego, Disneyland, and the beautiful California beaches. COD offers students a safe environment in which to live and study.

At COD, students pursue their educational goals while enjoying lush landscapes, warm breezes, and a breathtaking panoramic view of the mountains. With only 15–20 days of rain each year and low humidity, students can enjoy many outdoor activities in the area. Hiking, tennis, golf, bicycle riding, shopping, and night life are just some of the options students can choose to pursue in their free time.

Admission Requirements

Admission to College of the Desert is quite simple. International students must submit the International Student Application which can be found at www.collegeofthedesert.edu/international. In addition, international students should submit certified copies of their high school/secondary school graduation certificate, bank information verifying required funding, and English proficiency including a 32 iBT TOEFL score or a 3.5 IELTS score. The College also has agreements with local ESL schools offering TOEFL waivers for completion of certain levels. Students who need assistance with housing should also submit the Housing Application.

As a community college, COD does not require a specific grade point average for admission; however, high school completion (or the equivalent) is required.

Admission to the Intensive English Academy is the same as the College; however, the IEA does not require a TOEFL score for admission.

College of the Desert is authorized to issue the I-20 to students who meet its admission requirements.

Application and Information

College of the Desert application deadlines are July 15 for the fall semester and December 15 for the spring semester.

Intensive English Academy application deadlines are approximately one month prior to the program start date.

International students can submit application materials to:

International Student Office
College of the Desert
43-500 Monterey Avenue
Palm Desert, California 92260

Phone: 760-776-7205
Fax: 760-862-1361
E-mail: cdelgado@collegeofthedesert.edu
Web site: http://www.collegeofthedesert.edu/international

Enjoying the view at College of the Desert.

FASHION INSTITUTE OF TECHNOLOGY
State University of New York
NEW YORK, NEW YORK

The College and Its Mission

The Fashion Institute of Technology (FIT) is New York's celebrated urban college for creative and business talent. A selective State University of New York (SUNY) college of art and design, business, and technology, FIT is a creative mix of innovative achievers, original thinkers, and industry pioneers. FIT balances a real-world-based curriculum and hands-on instruction with a rigorous liberal arts foundation. The college marries design and business, supports individual creativity in a collaborative environment, and encourages faculty members to match teaching expertise with professional experience. It offers a complete college experience with a vibrant student and residential life.

With an extraordinary location at the center of New York City—world capital of the arts, business, and media—FIT maintains close ties with the design, fashion, advertising, communications, and international commerce industries it serves. Academic departments consult with advisory boards of noted experts in their fields to ensure that the curriculum and classroom technology remain current with evolving industry practices. The college's faculty of successful professionals brings experience to the classroom, while field trips, guest lectures, and sponsored competitions introduce students to the opportunities and challenges of their disciplines.

FIT's mission is to produce well-rounded graduates—doers and thinkers who raise the professional bar to become the next generation of business pacesetters and creative icons.

FIT's four residence halls house 2,300 students in fully furnished single-, double-, triple-, and quad-occupancy rooms and suites. All students taking 12 or more credits are eligible for FIT housing, and students may apply for housing no matter where they live. Students have the option of either traditional or apartment-style accommodations. Various dining options and meal plans are available. Counselors and student staff members live in the halls, helping students adjust to college life and New York City.

FIT is accredited by the Middle States Association of Colleges and Schools, the National Association of Schools of Art and Design, and the Council for Interior Design Accreditation.

Academic Programs

FIT serves approximately 10,000 full-time, part-time, and evening/weekend students from the metropolitan area, New York State, across the country, and around the world, offering more than forty programs leading to the A.A.S., B.F.A., B.S., M.A., M.F.A., and M.P.S. degrees. Each undergraduate program includes a core of traditional liberal arts courses, providing students with a global perspective, critical-thinking skills, and the ability to communicate effectively. All degree programs are designed to prepare students for creative and business careers—the college's Career and Internship Center, which offers lifetime placement, reports a graduate employment rate of 90 percent—and to provide them with the prerequisite studies so they may go on to baccalaureate, master's, or doctoral degrees.

All students complete a two-year A.A.S. program in their major area of study and the liberal arts. They may then choose to either go on to a related, two-year B.F.A. or B.S. program or begin their careers with their A.A.S. degree, which qualifies them for entry positions in a range of creative and/or business professions.

Associate Degree Programs: For the A.A.S. degree, FIT offers eleven majors through its School of Art and Design and four through its Jay and Patty Baker School of Business and Technology. The fifteen A.A.S. degree programs are accessories design*, advertising and marketing communications*, communication design foundation*, fashion design*, fashion merchandising management* (with an online option), fine arts, illustration, interior design, jewelry design*, menswear, photography, production management: fashion and related industries, textile development and marketing*, textile/surface design*, and visual presentation and exhibition design. Programs with an asterisk (*) are also available in a one-year format for students with acceptable transferable credits.

Bachelor's Degree Programs: Most A.A.S. graduates opt to pursue a related, two-year baccalaureate-level program of study at the college. FIT offers twenty-four baccalaureate programs—thirteen B.F.A. programs through the School of Art and Design, ten B.S. programs through the Baker School of Business and Technology, and one B.S. program through the School of Liberal Arts. The thirteen B.F.A. degree programs are accessories design and fabrication, advertising design, computer animation and interactive media, fabric styling, fashion design (with specializations in children's wear, fashion design, intimate apparel, and knitting), fine arts, graphic design, illustration, interior design, packaging design, photography and the digital image, textile/surface design, and toy design. The eleven B.S. programs are advertising and marketing communications, cosmetics and fragrance marketing, direct and interactive marketing, entrepreneurship for the fashion and design industries, fashion merchandising management, home products development, international trade and marketing for the fashion industries, production management: fashion and related industries, technical design, textile development and marketing, and visual art management.

Liberal Arts Minor: The School of Liberal Arts offers FIT students the opportunity to minor in a variety of liberal arts areas in two forms: traditional subject-based minors and interdisciplinary minors unique to the FIT liberal arts curriculum. Selected minors include film and media, economics, Latin American studies, and sustainability.

Evening/Weekend Programs: FIT's School of Continuing Education and Professional Studies provides evening and weekend credit and noncredit classes to students and working professionals interested in pursuing a degree or certificate or furthering their knowledge of a particular industry, while balancing the demands of career or family. There are nine degree programs available through evening/weekend study: advertising and marketing communications (A.A.S. and B.S.), communication design foundation (A.A.S.), fashion design (A.A.S.), fashion merchandising management (A.A.S. and B.S.), graphic design (B.F.A.), illustration (B.F.A.), and international trade and marketing for the fashion industries (B.S.).

Honors Program: The Presidential Scholars honors program, available to academically exceptional students in all majors, offers special courses, projects, colloquia, and off-campus trips that broaden horizons and stimulate discourse. Presidential Scholars receive priority course registration and an annual merit stipend.

Internships: Internships are a required element of most programs and are available to all matriculated students. Nearly one third of internships result in job offers from the sponsoring organization; past sponsors include American Eagle, Bloomingdale's, Calvin Klein, Estée Lauder, Fairchild Publications, MTV, and Saatchi & Saatchi.

Precollege Programs: Precollege programs (Saturday and Sunday/Summer Live) are available to high school and middle school students during the fall, spring, and summer. More than sixty courses provide the chance to learn in an innovative environment, develop art and design portfolios, explore the business and technological sides of a wide range of creative careers, and discover natural talents and abilities.

Off-Campus Programs

The study-abroad experience lets students immerse themselves in diverse cultures and prepares them to live and work in a global community. Australia, China, England, France, and Mexico are some of the countries where FIT semester study-abroad courses are offered. Students can also study abroad during the winter or summer sessions, or for a semester or a full academic year concentrating in fashion design or fashion merchandising management in Italy.

Costs

As a SUNY college, FIT offers affordable tuition for both New York State residents and nonresidents. The 2010–11 associate-level tuition per semester for in-state residents was $1857; for nonresidents, $5571. Baccalaureate-level tuition per semester was $2584 for in-state residents and $6775 for nonresidents. Per-semester housing costs were $5685–$5850 for traditional residence hall accommodations with mandatory meal plan and $4825–$8760 for apartment-style accommodations. Meal plans ranged from $1555 to $1995 per semester. Textbook costs and other nominal fees, such as locker rental or laboratory use, vary per program. All costs are subject to change.

Financial Aid

FIT offers scholarships, grants, loans, and work-study employment for students with financial need. Nearly all full-time, matriculated undergraduate students who complete the financial aid application process receive some type of assistance. The college directly administers its own institutional grants and scholarships, which are provided by The Educational Foundation for the Fashion Industries. College-administered funding includes Federal Pell Grants, Federal Perkins Loans, Federal Supplemental Educational Opportunity Grants, Federal Work-Study Program awards, and the Federal Family Educational Loan Program, which includes student and parent loans. New York State residents who meet eligibility guidelines may also receive Tuition Assistance Program (TAP) and/or Educational Opportunity Program (EOP) grants. Financial aid applicants must file the Free Application for Federal Student Aid (FAFSA) and should also apply to all available outside sources of aid. Additional documentation may be requested by the Financial Aid Office. Applications for financial aid should be completed prior to February 15 for fall admission or prior to November 1 for spring admission.

Faculty

FIT's faculty is drawn from top professionals in academia, art, design, communications, and business, providing a curriculum rich in real-world experience and traditional educational values. Student-instructor interaction is encouraged, with a maximum class size of 25, and courses are structured to foster participation, independent thinking, and self-expression.

Student Body Profile

Fall 2010 enrollment was 10,386 with 8,261 students enrolled in degree programs. Fifty-five percent of degree-seeking students are enrolled in the School of Art and Design; 42 percent are in the Baker School of Business and Technology. The average age of the student population is 23. Forty-five percent of FIT's students are New York City residents, 23 percent are New York State (non–New York City) residents, and 32 percent are out-of-state residents or international students. The ethnic/racial makeup of the student body is approximately 0.16 percent American Indian or Alaskan, 11.56 percent Asian, 8.8 percent black, 16.52 percent Hispanic, 3.22 percent multiracial, 0.66 percent Native Hawaiian or Pacific Islander, and 59.08 percent white. There are 724 international students.

Student Activities

Participation in campus life is encouraged, and the college is home to more than seventy clubs, societies, athletic teams, major-related organizations, and hobby groups. Each organization is open to all students who have paid their activity fee.

Student Government: The Student Council, the governing body of the Student Association, grants all students the privileges and responsibilities of citizens in a self-governing college community. Faculty committees often include student representatives, and the president of the student government sits on FIT's Board of Trustees.

Athletics: FIT has intercollegiate teams in cross-country, half marathon, outdoor track, dance, table tennis, tennis, soccer, swimming and diving, and volleyball. Athletics and Recreation offers group fitness classes at no extra cost to students. Open gym activities allow students to participate in team and individual sports.

Events: Concerts, dances, field trips, films, flea markets, and other events are planned by the Student Association and Programming Board and various clubs. Student-run publications include a campus newspaper, a literary and art magazine, and the FIT yearbook.

Facilities and Resources

FIT's campus provides its students with classrooms, laboratories, and studios that reflect the most advanced educational and industry practices. The Fred P. Pomerantz Art and Design Center houses drawing, painting, photography, printmaking, and sculpture studios; display and exhibit design rooms; a model-making workshop; and a graphics printing service bureau. The Peter G. Scotese Computer-Aided Design and Communications facility provides the latest technology in computer graphics, photography, and the design of advertising, fashion, interiors, textiles, and toys. Other facilities include a professionally equipped fragrance-development laboratory, cutting and sewing labs, a design/research lighting laboratory, knitting lab, broadcasting studio, multimedia foreign languages laboratory, and twenty-three computer labs containing Mac and PC workstations in addition to several other labs with computers reserved for students in specific programs.

The Museum at FIT, New York City's only museum dedicated to fashion, contains one of the most important collections of fashion and textiles in the world. The museum operates year-round, and its exhibitions are free and open to the public. The Gladys Marcus Library provides more than 300,000 volumes of print, nonprint, and electronic materials. The periodicals collection includes over 500 current subscriptions, with a specialization in international design and trade publications; online resources include more than 90 searchable databases.

The David Dubinsky Student Center offers lounges, a game room, a student radio station, the Style Shop (a student-run boutique), a dining hall and full-service Starbucks, student government and club offices, comprehensive health services, two gyms, a fitness center, a dance studio, and a counseling center.

Location

Occupying an entire block in Manhattan's Chelsea neighborhood, FIT makes extensive use of the city's creative, commercial, and cultural resources, providing students unrivaled internship opportunities and professional connections. A wide range of cultural and entertainment options are available within a short walk of the campus, as is convenient access to several subway and bus routes and the city's major rail and bus transportation hubs.

Admission Requirements

Applicants for admission must be either candidates for or recipients of a high school diploma or a General Educational Development (GED) certificate. Admission is based on class rank, strength and performance in college-preparatory course work, and the student essay. A portfolio evaluation is required for art and design majors. Specific portfolio requirements are explained on FIT's Web site. SAT and ACT scores are required for placement in math and English classes and they are required for students applying to the Presidential Scholars honors program. Letters of recommendation are not required.

Transfer students must submit official transcripts for credit evaluation. Students may qualify for the one-year A.A.S. option if they hold a bachelor's degree or if they have a minimum of 30 transferable college credits, including 24 credits equivalent to FIT's liberal arts requirements.

Students seeking admission to a B.F.A. or B.S. program must hold an A.A.S. degree from FIT or an equivalent college degree and must meet the prerequisites for the specific major. Further requirements may include an interview with a departmental committee, review of academic standing, and portfolio review for applicants to B.F.A. programs. Any student who applies for baccalaureate-level transfer to FIT from a four-year program must have completed a minimum of 60 credits, including the requisite art or technical courses and the liberal arts requirements.

Application and Information

Students wishing to visit FIT are encouraged to attend a group information session and take a tour of FIT's campus. The visit schedule is available online at http://www.fitnyc.edu/visitfit. Candidates may apply online at http://www.fitnyc.edu/admissions. More information is available by contacting:

Admissions
Fashion Institute of Technology
227 West 27 Street, Room C139
New York, New York 10001-5992

Phone: 212-217-3760
      800-GO-TO-FIT (toll-free)
E-mail: fitinfo@fitnyc.edu
Web site: http://www.fitnyc.edu
      http://www.facebook.com/FashionInstituteofTechnology

FIDM/FASHION INSTITUTE OF DESIGN & MERCHANDISING

LOS ANGELES, CALIFORNIA

The Institute and Its Mission

FIDM/Fashion Institute of Design & Merchandising provides a dynamic and exciting community of learning in the fashion, graphics, interior design, digital media, and entertainment industries. Students can launch into one of thousands of exciting careers in as little as two years. FIDM offers two-year and four-year degree programs—Associate of Arts (A.A.), A.A. professional designation, A.A. advanced study, and Bachelor of Science.

FIDM offers a highly focused education that prepares students for the professional world. Students can choose from twenty specialized creative business and design majors. With a database of over 10,000 employer contacts and more than 1000 job postings each month, FIDM offers students and graduates ongoing career opportunities within the industries it serves. Since its inception, FIDM has graduated over 40,000 students in its forty-year history.

FIDM is accredited by the Accrediting Commission for Community and Junior Colleges of the Western Association of Schools and Colleges (WASC) and the National Association of Schools of Art and Design (NASAD).

Academic Programs

FIDM operates on a four-quarter academic calendar. Students can choose from twenty specialized creative business and design majors. New students may begin their studies at the start of any quarter throughout the year. A two-year Associate of Arts degree requires completion of 90 units. Advanced study programs are available to students who have previously completed an A.A. degree from FIDM. Professional designation programs are offered for students who want to enhance their previous education from another college or are interested in transferring to FIDM. For detailed information about FIDM majors please visit http://fidm.edu/majors/.

Bachelor of Science Degree Program: The Bachelor of Science in business management program prepares students who have received an A.A. degree from FIDM to enter the global industries of fashion, interior design, and entertainment.

Associate Degree Programs: FIDM offers Associate of Arts degrees in apparel industry management, beauty industry merchandising & marketing, digital media, fashion design, fashion knitwear design, graphic design, interior design, jewelry design, merchandise marketing (fashion merchandising or product development), textile design, and visual communications. All of these programs offer the highly specialized curriculum of a specific major combined with a core general education/liberal arts foundation.

Associate of Arts Advanced Study Programs: These programs develop specialized expertise in the student's unique area of study. They are open to students who possess extensive prior academic and professional experience within the discipline area. These areas include advanced fashion design, interior design specialties, film and TV costume design, footwear design, international manufacturing and product development, theater costume design, and visual communications. Completion requirements for these programs are 45 units. Some classes are offered online.

Transfer Arrangements: FIDM accepts course work from other accredited colleges if there is an equivalent course at FIDM and the grade is a C or better. FIDM courses at the 100, 200, and 300 levels are certified by FIDM to be baccalaureate level. FIDM maintains articulation agreements with selected colleges with the intent of enhancing a student's transfer opportunities. Students from other regionally accredited college programs have the opportunity to complement their previous college education by enrolling in FIDM's professional designation programs. FIDM offers professional designation programs in apparel industry management, fashion design, beauty industry management, digital media, graphic design, interior design, jewelry design, merchandise marketing (or product development), textile design, fashion knitwear design, and visual communications. Requirements for completion range from 45 to 66

units, depending on the field of study. For more information about FIDM transfer programs please visit http://fidm.edu/admissions/transfer-students/.

Internship and Co-op Programs: Internships are available within each of the various majors. Paid and volunteer positions provide work experience for students to gain practical application of classroom skills.

Special Programs and Services: FIDM's eLearning program ensures that a student's educational experience can take place anywhere in the world. The online courses are designed to replicate the experience of classes on campus. Students in the eLearning program are granted the same quality education as students on campus and have immediate access to valuable campus resources, including the FIDM library, career advisers, and instructors.

In response to student needs, FIDM has established an evening program in addition to the regular daytime courses. The program has been designed to accommodate the time requirements of working students. The entire evening program for the Associate of Arts degree can be completed in 2½ years.

FIDM offers English as a second language (ESL) for students requiring English development to complete their major field of study. The program is concurrent and within FIDM's existing college-level course work. These classes focus on the special needs of students in the areas of oral communication, reading comprehension, and English composition.

Community Programs: Community service programs are offered both independently and in cooperation with various community groups. General studies course credit may be awarded to participating students. Each FIDM campus identifies community projects that allow students to support local service agencies.

Off-Campus Programs

FIDM provides the opportunity for students to participate in academic study tours in Europe, Asia, and New York. These tours are specifically designed to broaden and enhance the specialized education offered at the Institute. Study tour participants may earn academic credit under faculty-supervised directed studies. Exchange programs are also available with Esmod, Paris; Instituto Artictico dell' Abbigliamento Marangoni, Milan; Accademia Internazionale d'Alta Mode e d'Arte del Costume Koefia, Rome; St. Martins School of Art, London; College of Distributive Trades, London; and Janette Klein Design School, Mexico City.

Credit for Nontraditional Learning Experiences

The Institute may give credit for demonstrated proficiency in areas related to college-level courses. Sources used to determine proficiency are the College-Level Examination Program (CLEP) and Credit for Academically Relevant Experience (CARE), an Institute-sponsored program.

Costs

For the 2010–11 academic year, tuition and fees started at $25,000, depending on the major selected by the student. Textbooks and supplies started at $2100 per year, depending on the major. First-year application fees start at $225 for California residents and range up to $525 for international students.

Financial Aid

There are several sources of financial funding available to the student, including federal financial aid and education loan programs, California state aid programs, institutional loan programs, and FIDM awards and scholarships. The FIDM Student Financial Services office and FIDM admissions advisers work with students and parents to help them find funding for an education at FIDM. For information on FIDM scholarships and financial aid please visit http://fidm.edu/admissions/tuition-financial-aid/scholarships.html.

Faculty

FIDM faculty members are selected as specialists in their fields. Many are actively employed in their respective fields of expertise. They bring daily exposure to their industry into the classroom for the benefit of the students. In pursuit of the best faculty members, consideration is given to both academic excellence as well as practical experience. FIDM has a 16:1 student-instructor ratio.

Student Body Profile

FIDM's ethnically and culturally diverse student body is one of the attractions to the Institute. Fifteen percent of the current student body are international students from more than thirty different countries. Twenty percent of the students are more than 25 years of age. More than 90 percent find career positions within one year of graduation.

Student Activities

The Student Activities Committee plans and coordinates social activities, cultural events, and community projects, including the ASID Student Chapter, International Club, Delta Epsilon Chi (DEX), Association of Manufacturing Students, Honor Society, and the Alumni Association. The students also produce their own trend newsletter, *The Mode*.

Facilities and Resources

Advisement/Counseling: Department chairs and other trained staff members assist students in selecting the correct sequence of courses to allow each student to complete degree requirements. The counseling department provides personal guidance and referral to outside counseling services as well as matching peer tutors to specific students' needs. Individual Development and Education Assistance (IDEA) centers at each campus provide students with additional educational assistance to supplement classroom instruction. Services are available in the areas of writing, mathematics, computer competency, study skills, research skills, and reading comprehension.

Career Planning/Placement Offices: Career planning and job placement are among the most important services offered by the college. Career assistance includes job search techniques, preparation for employment interviews, resume preparation, and job adjustment assistance. Services provided by the center include undergraduate placement, graduate placement, alumni placement, internships, and industry work/study programs. FIDM's full-time career services department and advisers provide support to help current students and graduates move toward their career goals. Employers post over 16,000 jobs a year on FIDM's Alumni Job Search site, available 24/7. Career advisers connect students to internships and directly to people in the industry. FIDM also offers job fairs, portfolio days, and networking days to allow students to meet alumni and industry leaders face-to-face.

Alumni Association: Students can expand their network instantly upon graduation. There are more than 40,000 FIDM grads and each of them is automatically granted a free lifetime membership in the Alumni Association, which keeps them well connected while providing up-to the minute alumni news and industry information. FIDM alumni chapter events are held in thirty-five locations around the United States, Europe, and Asia.

Library and Audiovisual Services FIDM's library goes beyond the traditional sources of information. The library houses a print and electronic collection of over 2.5 million titles encompassing all subject areas, with an emphasis on fashion, interior design, retailing, and costume. The library subscribes to over 160 international and national periodicals which offer the latest information on art, design, graphics, fashion, beauty, business, and current trends. The FIDM library also features an international video library, subscriptions to major predictive services, interior design workrooms, textile samples, a trimmings/findings collection, and access to the Internet. FIDM's Costume Museum houses more than 4,500 garments from the seventeenth century to present day. The collection includes items from the California Historical Society (First Families), the Hollywood Collection, and the Rudi Gernreich Collection.

State-of-the-art computer labs support and enhance the educational programs of the Institute. Specialized labs offer computerized cutting and marking, graphic and textile design, word processing, and database management.

Location

Established in 1969, FIDM is a private college that is proud to enroll more than 7,500 students a year. The main campus is in the heart of downtown Los Angeles near the famed California Mart and Garment District. This campus is adjacent to the beautiful Grand Hope Park. There are additional California branch campuses in San Francisco, San Diego, and Orange County. Take a virtual tour of the campuses and their locations at http://fidm.edu/visit-fidm/virtual-tour/.

Admission Requirements

The Institute provides educational opportunities to high school graduates or applicants that meet the Institute's Ability to Benefit (ATB) criteria to pursue a two-year Associate of Arts degree. In order to qualify for the professional designation programs students must meet the general education core requirements or have a U.S. accredited degree. All applicants must have an initial interview with an admissions representative. In addition, students must submit references and specific portfolio projects if applicable to the chosen major. The Institute is on the approved list of the U.S. Department of Justice for nonimmigrant students and is authorized to issue Certificates of Eligibility (Form I-20).

Application and Information

Applications are accepted on an ongoing basis. All prospective students should contact:Director of Admissions

FIDM/Fashion Institute of Design & Merchandising
919 South Grand Avenue
Los Angeles, California 90015
Phone: 800-624-1200 (toll-free)
Fax: 213-624-4799
Web site:　http://www.fidm.edu
　　　　　http://www.facebook.com/home.php#!/FIDMCollege
　　　　　http://twitter.com/#!/FIDM

FIDM Debut Show. Student designer: Kapasa Musonda.

FULL SAIL UNIVERSITY
WINTER PARK, FLORIDA

The College and Its Mission

Since 1979, Full Sail University, located outside of Orlando, Florida, has been an innovative educational leader for those pursuing careers in the entertainment industry. With over 34,500 alumni, graduate credits include work on OSCAR®-, Emmy®-, and GRAMMY®-winning projects; best-selling video games; and the top-grossing U.S. concert tours. Full Sail's 191-acre campus and online education platform proudly welcomes more than 12,400 students from fifty states and forty-nine countries.

The world of entertainment media is constantly innovating, and so is Full Sail University. All of the degree programs at Full Sail are built to reflect the needs of the entertainment media industry, so students can develop their skills working on real projects, using industry-standard workflows and processes—from conception and planning through production and delivery.

The Full Sail campus is equipped with industry-standard technology, and instructors and faculty members all have experience working in the fields they teach. Full Sail's accelerated degree programs not only get students out into the industry in half the time of traditional schools, but by using 40-hour weeks and 24-hour schedules, the programs prepare students for the entertainment field's tough deadlines and intense creative demands.

Full Sail does not offer on-campus housing, but students can find information from the Housing Department about affordable accommodations in the many apartment complexes near the school.

Full Sail University is accredited by the Accrediting Commission of Career Schools and Colleges (ACCSC), and is licensed by the Commission for Independent Education (CIEICU), Florida Department of Education.

Academic Programs

Full Sail University currently offers a total of thirty-three campus (http://www.fullsail.edu/degrees) and online degree (http://online.fullsail.edu/degrees) programs.

Through Full Sail's **Graphic Design** Associate degree program, students can learn what it takes to be an effective visual communicator. The program provides the specific skills and training needed to succeed in graphic and print design, as well as corporate branding, and students gain a thorough understanding of the principles and practices of the industry. Throughout the program, students build a portfolio that represents their unique design strengths and depth of experience. The associate degree program is offered on campus; the graphic design bachelor's degree is an online program.

For those interested in learning what that goes into creating high-quality audio tracks, Full Sail's **Recording Engineering** Associate degree program prepares students for entry-level careers in the recording arts. Students learn the fundamentals of recording, mixing, and mastering on equipment and software used in the industry, while studying core subjects such as music theory, electronics, and communications. Ultimately, students apply their new skills by conducting recording sessions with live musicians from start to finish.

The following are Full Sail's bachelor's degree programs:

Learn the tools and processes to bring amazing new worlds and characters to life. Full Sail's **Computer Animation** program instructs in the creation of 3-D computer graphics, emphasizing the techniques used throughout the entertainment media industry in feature-length films, visual effects, commercials, and video games. Students learn the entire animation process starting with storyboards and computer-generated models. These concepts are then fully developed into animation projects that culminate with the creation of the student's professional demo reel. This degree is offered on campus and online.

Creative writers are in high demand within the entertainment industry, and Full Sail's online **Creative Writing for Environment** program provides a challenging curriculum to help students perfect their writing and editorial skills by emphasizing visual storytelling, narrative structures, character development, scriptwriting, and storyboarding. Students write and workshop their writing in a variety of formats and genres including horror, science fiction, mystery, comedy, and suspense. This degree is offered online.

For students who envision designing the elements of tomorrow's media, Full Sail's **Digital Arts & Design** program delivers a comprehensive multimedia education that combines art and technology. Students receive a solid grounding in graphic design fundamentals and print work and then create projects in a multitude of digital and multimedia platforms. Students work with the latest industry software and leave the program with a cohesive demo reel to showcase their talent to prospective employers. This degree is offered on campus.

With the impact of viral videos, streaming-video options, and growth of independent films, applications of digital video and demand for high-quality projects are crucial. Full Sail's online **Digital Cinematography** program explores how these new technologies can create inspiring cinematic and commercial works. Students learn the creative process within the context of the film industry—from lighting, scripting, and HD video production to shooting in a variety of styles.

Full Sail's **Entertainment Business** program combines fundamental business courses with relevant industry insight. Students learn the basics of business management for music, television, and advertising. As they sharpen their writing skills, students also develop a deep understanding of the dynamics and economics of entertainment production. Students build their network by sharing ideas with peers and instructors who share the same passion for the industry. The final project is a complete business proposal unique to the student's interests. This degree is offered on campus and online.

The **Film** program teaches students the skills and provides the experience to pursue a career in the film, TV, and postproduction job markets. Students learn how to execute every role on a film set, from directing to cinematography to lighting and set design. Students make films using industry-standard cameras, equipment, and software on Full Sail's professional-level soundstages and backlot. This degree is offered on campus.

As gaming design technology evolves, Full Sail's **Game Art** program teaches students to develop specialized, realistic elements for breathtaking game experiences. The program's course work focuses on 3-D art and content creation, with a heavy emphasis on character development, shading and lighting, texturing, and modeling. Game Art students work with students in the Game Development program in a real-world production setting, creating a playable game from start to finish. This degree is offered on campus and online.

In the online **Game Design** program, students learn how to develop a game from concept to completion using the processes used by the world's top studios. The specialized curriculum teaches the elements of game development—from storytelling and narration to technology and production to leadership and project management. Using Full Sail's unique online platform, students can engage in the same interaction that exists between professional developers and artists.

The **Game Development** program teaches students about the game creation process from start to finish. Courses encompass preproduction and how to create game docs, programming and implementation, and game play and level design. Working in a production environment with a team of programmers, artists, and designers, students develop a playable video game. Students who complete the Entertainment Business degree program along with this degree earn a Master of Science degree. This degree is offered on campus.

The online **Internet Marketing** program explores the constantly evolving world of integrated marketing and its role in steering the online power of successful businesses in the 21st century. The curriculum prepares students for the changing field of online branding, e-commerce, search engine optimization (SEO), and the psychology of the online consumer. In the final capstone project, students create and produce their own Internet marketing campaign.

Growing technology options for mobile and Web-based applications have created an increased demand for skilled designers and developers. Full Sail's online **Mobile Development** program offers a cutting-edge curriculum with usability and design principles, software development and management, and application production for cell phones, iPads, Web sites, handheld games, and other devices.

Students learn what it takes to build a career in one of entertainment's most exciting industries through Full Sail's **Music Business** program. They learn fundamentals such as marketing, human relations, finance, and accounting, as well as unique music industry topics like artist development, music distribution, record label development, and the negotiation process. This degree is offered on campus and online.

The online **Music Production** program gives students the tools needed to pursue a career in writing, producing, and recording music for all types of media. Classes focus on the music-making process, from music composition and arranging to theory and ear training. Students use various software and hardware technologies and develop a digital portfolio showcasing their work.

For students who dream of being the production mastermind behind the next great recording, Full Sail's **Recording Arts** program lays the groundwork for this career. Students learn tracking and mixing techniques that can be applied to sound design and postproduction for film, television, video games, and multimedia applications in the same kind of recording studios and on the same kind of production gear used by today's professionals. This degree is offered on campus.

In the **Show Production** program, students master the techniques and equipment used in dynamic live productions while learning essential career skills. Students are immersed in the technology and tools at Full Sail Live—a custom-designed concert-venue environment—gaining the practical experience needed to hit the road with touring bands, run lights and sound at world-class performing arts halls, and take multimedia presentations to the next level. This degree is offered on campus.

The sports world is a business both on and off the field. Qualified professionals are needed to create new content, generate revenue, and establish fan branding within an evolving media landscape. Full Sail's online **Sports Marketing and Media** program covers concepts such as business principles, legal and ethical issues, public relations, and leadership. Students are prepared for positions where digital art and design, communication, distribution, game operations, and marketing all intersect.

Students can explore all aspects of Web site creation through Full Sail's on-campus and online **Web Design & Development** program. As the Internet emerges as the epicenter of communication, experienced professionals are needed to develop, implement, and maintain effective Web sites and databases. Students learn front-end design, back-end development, and client-side scripting development and deployment, and they are well-versed in coding formats like XHTML, CSS, and XML as well as Flash and ActionScript.

Costs

Tuition costs vary depending on the program, ranging from $30,380 to $77,500. The cost includes expenses such as textbooks, manuals, media, production materials, lab fees, technology fees, career-development assistance, and lifetime auditing. There is an additional fee for a computer and software; the primary component of this fee is Project LaunchBox, which provides students with a laptop computer and media creation software at a deep institutional discount.

Financial Aid

Each financial aid package is unique. Financial aid advisers work to ensure that students have the information they need to make decisions that will enable them to attend Full Sail. Since Full Sail is an accredited school, there are a number of packages consisting of grants and loans that are available to those who qualify and are tailored to each student's financial need.

Faculty

Full Sail's teachers are veterans of the industry and often work on professional projects as they teach, bringing to the classroom a wealth of techniques and tips learned from years of creating movies, music, games, and more.

Academic Facilities

As part of the University's commitment to provide students with facilities that mirror the experience of working in entertainment and media, Full Sail recently unveiled its latest on-campus expansion—a 2.2-acre project more than five years in the making, Full Sail Studios. It comprises the new Live Venue, a recording studio, a game production studio, an outdoor plaza courtyard, and an expansion to the school's on-campus film studio backlot.

Live Venue: This facility can accommodate live musical performances, monthly graduations, open-house events, multi-visual presentations, guest lectures, movie screenings, trade shows, and more.

Recording Studio: This new studio employs industry-current recording technology within a carefully crafted acoustical environment. Guests can view the recording process through oversized, acoustically treated windows that line the building's hallways.

Game Production Studio: This new game studio offers Game Development and Game Art students the perfect professional game studio environment to create and finish final projects. The studio has areas specifically designed for audio, graphics, and technical development.

Backlot and Courtyard: An illuminated archway leads to a production area complete with nineteen distinct scenic environments to accommodate students in the Film program. Amid the two newly constructed buildings is a spacious common area with seating areas and Wi-Fi to serve as a networking hub for students and faculty.

Location

Full Sail's college campus is situated in a beautiful area of central Florida in Winter Park. The school is 20 minutes from downtown Orlando, 35 minutes from Disney and Universal Studios, 1 hour from Cape Canaveral and the Atlantic beaches, and 2 hours from the Gulf of Mexico.

Admission Requirements

Admission requirements vary depending on the degree program. Associate and bachelor's degree applicants must submit a high school diploma or GED equivalent, with official high school transcripts and one recommendation letter. Acceptance to Full Sail's undergraduate degrees is not based on grade point average, SAT scores, or other standardized test scores.

Application and Information

For details concerning applications and deadlines, students should contact a Full Sail Admissions Representative.

Full Sail University
3300 University Boulevard
Winter Park, Florida 39792-7429

Phone: 407-679-6333
     800-226-7625 (toll-free)
E-mail: admissions@fullsail.com
Web site: http://www.fullsail.edu
     http://www.facebook.com/FullSailUniversity
     http://twitter.com/fullsailupdate

Full Sail Studios and Live Venue.

LANDMARK COLLEGE
PUTNEY, VERMONT

The College and Its Mission

Landmark College is one of only two accredited colleges in the country designed exclusively for students of average to superior intellectual potential with LD or AD/HD or other specific learning disabilities. Life-changing experiences are commonplace at Landmark College.

Landmark's beautiful campus offers all the resources students expect at a high-quality college, including an athletics center, a student center, a dining facility, a café, residence halls, and a Center for Academic Support. The College has also invested substantially in technology and offers a wireless network in all of its classrooms, along with LAN, telephone, and cable connections in all of the residence rooms. Notebook computers are required and are used in nearly every class session. The College's programs extensively integrate assistive technologies, such as Dragon Naturally Speaking, Kurzweil text-to-speech software, and Inspiration.

Landmark's faculty and staff members make it unique. The College's more than 80 full-time faculty members are all highly experienced in serving students with learning disabilities and attention deficit disorders. More than 100 staff members provide an array of support services that are unusually comprehensive for a student population of more than 490 students.

Academic Programs

Students can earn an associate degree in business administration, business studies, general studies, or liberal arts. Landmark College builds strong literacy, organizational, study, and other skills—positioning students to successfully pursue a baccalaureate or advanced degree and to be successful in their professional careers. More than 80 percent of Landmark College graduates go on to colleges or universities that grant four-year degrees.

With more than 80 faculty members and slightly more than 490 students, Landmark College's small classes and personalized instruction provide a uniquely challenging, yet supportive, academic program. Students at Landmark College learn how to learn.

The College's diverse curriculum includes English, communications, the humanities, math, science, foreign language, theater, video, music, art, physical education, and other classes taught in a multimodal, multimedia environment that is highly interactive. There is no "back of the room" in a Landmark College classroom, and all students participate in class discussions while building strong academic skills.

Landmark College has articulation agreements with a number of other colleges. These colleges have agreed to admit Landmark College graduates as juniors and transfer their credits if they attain a specific grade point average upon graduation from Landmark.

Through a carefully sequenced, integrated curriculum, students develop the confidence and independence needed to meet the demands of college work. When students graduate with an associate degree from Landmark College, they are ready to succeed in a four-year college, a technical or professional program, or the workforce.

Off-Campus Programs

The Landmark Study Abroad Program has developed programs with students' diverse learning styles in mind. Landmark College's faculty members design and teach experiential courses in their specific disciplines that fulfill Landmark core requirements while helping students gain confidence and independence in new academic structures. College faculty members accompany students abroad, providing them with the Landmark College academic experience in an international setting. The College offers summer credit programs in England, Ireland, Italy, and Spain; in January, a two-week program in Costa Rica is offered.

Costs

Landmark College's tuition for the 2010–11 academic year was $47,500. Room and board costs were $8500. Single rooms or suites are available at an added cost of between $1000 and $1500. A damage deposit of $300 is required.

Since admission to Landmark College requires a diagnosis of a learning disability or attention deficit disorder, in most cases, the entire cost of a Landmark College education may be tax deductible as a medical expense. For more information, parents are advised to consult a tax attorney.

Financial Aid

Landmark College participates in all major federal and state financial aid programs, including the Federal Pell Grant, Federal Family Education Loans, and work-study. Institutional scholarships are available. To apply for financial assistance, students should submit the Free Application for Federal Student Aid (FAFSA), the Landmark College Financial Aid Application, and federal tax returns.

Faculty

With the College's low student-faculty ratio, Landmark College faculty members are unusually accessible to students. There are more than 80 full-time faculty members, who provide classroom teaching, professional advising, and office hours to students. In addition, faculty members provide individualized instruction throughout the day and into the evening at the Charles Drake Center for Academic Support. Landmark College does not typically employ adjunct faculty members or student teaching assistants. Regular faculty members deliver all instruction and advising. Their depth of experience in serving students with learning differences ensures that students receive the individualized education that is most appropriate to their learning style.

Student Body Profile

Landmark College students come from thirty-eight states, two U.S. territories, and ten other countries. Approximately two thirds of the student body are men. Ninety-five percent of all students are residential students living on campus in one of twelve residence facilities. Representatives of multicultural groups make up approximately 14 percent of Landmark College students.

Student Activities

Landmark College closely integrates academics and student life. Academic deans, advisers, and faculty members work closely with student life deans and directors to provide a comprehensive program that serves the whole student. The goal is not simply to support academic success but also to guide and challenge students in their personal and social development. Each student has access to a comprehensive support team, including an academic adviser, classroom instructors, and a resident dean; an extensive program of athletics, adventure education, and activities; and a highly trained and experienced counseling department.

For a college its size, Landmark College has an extraordinary range of student-development resources, providing general educational, social, and recreational opportunities. Clubs at Landmark are active. In the past, they have included the Running Club, Monday Night Art, the Multicultural Awareness Club, the Gay/Lesbian/Bisexual/Transgender Alliance, the Mountain Biking Club, the Jazz Ensemble, *Impressions Literary Magazine,* the Coffee House Writers Group, the International Club, the Small Business Management Club, Choral Singing, the Weight Lifting Group, and the Spirituality Group.

Outdoor programs provide students with a diverse range of outdoor and experiential learning opportunities, including wilderness first-aid training, a ropes course, rock-climbing instruction, an indoor climbing wall, and a full inventory of camping equipment, cross-country skis, snowshoes, and mountain bikes. The College has an active intercollegiate and intramural athletics program that is supported by a well-equipped athletics center that opened in 2001.

Facilities and Resources

Landmark College's residence halls, academic buildings, athletics center, and student center provide a rich array of resources and educational, recreational, and social opportunities. The traditional brick campus, which was designed by noted architect Edward Durell Stone in the 1960s and entirely renovated beginning in the mid-1980s, includes such amenities as a 400-seat theater, an NCAA regulation basketball court, an exercise pool, three fitness centers, a tennis court, science laboratories, an infirmary, a Center for Academic Support, a bookstore, a café, a game room, an indoor climbing wall, and a ropes course.

Location

Located in scenic southeastern Vermont, Landmark College overlooks the Connecticut River Valley, with sweeping views of the mountains and valleys of southern Vermont and northern Massachusetts. Wilderness areas, national forests, ski areas, lakes and streams, and other natural attractions abound. Nearby Brattleboro, Vermont, and the five-college region in the Amherst, Massachusetts, area offer opportunities for culture, the arts, fine dining, and more. Putney is a picturesque Vermont village with several shops, stores, restaurants, a bakery/coffeehouse, a bookstore, and other resources.

The College is located just off Exit 4 on Interstate 91. The most convenient airport is Bradley International Airport in Hartford, Connecticut, which is about 1½ hours away by car. Metropolitan areas within a 4-hour driving radius include Boston, New York, and Providence.

Admission Requirements

Applicants to Landmark College must have a diagnosis of dyslexia, attention deficit disorder, or another specific learning disability. Diagnostic testing within the last three years is required, along with a diagnosis of a learning disability or

AD/HD. One of the Wechsler Scales (WAIS-III or WISC-III) administered within three years of application is required. Scores and subtest scores and their analysis are required to be submitted as well. Alternately, the Woodcock Johnson Cognitive Assessment may be substituted if administered within three years of application. Other criteria for admission include average to superior intellectual potential and high motivation to undertake the program.

The College offers rolling admission and enrolls students for fall and spring semesters. Students may begin in August (for the fall semester) or January (for the spring semester). The College offers credit-bearing courses each summer in addition to programs for students from other colleges, high school students, and students entering other colleges in the fall.

Application and Information

For more information, students should contact:

Office of Admissions
Landmark College
River Road South
Putney, Vermont 05346-0820

Phone: 802-387-6718
Fax: 802-387-6868
E-mail: admissions@landmark.edu
Web site: http://www.landmark.edu

Students on the campus of Landmark College.

MANOR COLLEGE
JENKINTOWN, PENNSYLVANIA

The College and Its Mission

Manor College is a private, coed Catholic college founded in 1947 by the Ukrainian Sisters of Saint Basil the Great. The College is characterized by its dedication to the education, growth, and self-actualization of the whole person through its personalized and nurturing atmosphere. Upon graduation, 50 percent of Manor's students are employed in their chosen fields; the remaining 50 percent of students transfer to four-year institutions to earn baccalaureate degrees.

There are approximately 900 full- and part-time students enrolled at Manor. Extracurricular activities include honor societies, men's and women's intercollegiate soccer and basketball, and women's volleyball, as well as the yearbook and special interest and cultural clubs. Manor provides free counseling and tutoring services through an on-campus learning center. Trained counselors are available to assist students on an individual and confidential basis for academic, career, and personal concerns. Upon entering Manor, students are assigned an academic adviser, who provides guidance and support throughout their Manor experience. Transfer counseling is available for students interested in pursuing a four-year degree.

The College's 35-acre campus includes a modern three-story dormitory, a library/administration building, and an academic building that also houses the bookstore, the dining hall, an auditorium/gymnasium, and a student lounge. The Ukrainian Heritage Studies Center and the Manor Dental Health Center are also located on the campus grounds. Manor is accredited by the Middle States Association of Colleges and Schools.

Academic Programs

Manor offers career-oriented, two-year associate degrees as well as transfer programs for pursuing a bachelor's degree. Internships provide theory with practice, enhancing employment opportunities. The liberal arts core ensures a common breadth of knowledge along with mobility and future advancement. Manor College offers ten programs with twenty majors/concentrations leading to associate degrees and transfer programs through its three divisions: Liberal Arts, Allied Health/Science/Mathematics, and Business.

The Liberal Arts Division offers **Associate in Arts** degrees in early childhood education, liberal arts, and psychology. In addition, the Liberal Arts Division provides a liberal arts transfer major as well as an elementary education transfer major, an early child-care major, and a concentration in communications.

The Allied Health/Science/Mathematics Division offers **Associate in Science** degrees in dental hygiene, expanded functions dental assisting, and veterinary technology. This division also includes allied health and science transfer programs for students who seek preprofessional programs in biotechnology, chiropractic, cytotechnology, general sciences, medical technology, nursing, occupational therapy, pharmacy, physical therapy, radiologic science, and veterinary technology.

The Business Division offers **Associate in Science** degrees in accounting, business administration, business administration/international business, business administration/management, business administration/marketing, information systems and technology, and paralegal studies. There are three certificate programs. There is a certificate program in paralegal studies for students who have a bachelor's degree, a legal nurse consultant certificate, and an expanded functions dental assisting certificate. Manor also offers selected courses through two modes of distance learning: online Web-based learning and teleconferencing.

The Office of Continuing Education serves adult learners by providing educational options for those who want to attend college on a part-time basis. The office also supports the needs of the community and business and industry by offering noncredit classes and workshops, as well as on- and off-site corporate training programs, throughout the year. Approved as an authorized provider by the International Association for Continuing Education and Training, the office also grants continuing education units (CEUs) for selected professional development courses each semester.

Off-Campus Programs

Externships are incorporated into various academic studies programs. Students earn credits as they gain practical experience under the supervision of professionals in a specific field of study. Externships are offered in the career-oriented programs of study and in some transfer programs. Manor's affiliation with several area hospitals, as well as Manor College's on-campus Dental Health Center, enables the allied health program student to fulfill clinical requirements at these sites. Students in other programs serve externships in law offices, courtrooms, day-care centers, businesses, and veterinary facilities. Manor has dual admissions, 2+2, and 2+3 articulation agreements with major allied health universities, hospitals, and local universities.

Credit for Nontraditional Learning Experiences

Manor College awards credit by examination for college-level learning through the College-Level Examination Program (CLEP). Manor administers exemption tests for courses not available through CLEP. Adults may also receive college credit for military experience and education through the Army/American Council on Education Registry Transcript System (AARTS), by submitting a transcript to Manor for evaluation of credits, and by requesting assessment of previous life and job experiences through nontraditional means.

Costs

Tuition for the 2011–12 academic year is $13,416 for full-time studies. Part-time study is $299 per credit hour. Students in certain allied health programs pay an additional $200 per year. On-campus room and board are available for men and women and cost $2986 per semester. There is an additional $400 fee for a private room per semester.

Financial Aid

Manor College offers need-based financial aid to eligible applicants in the form of grants, loans, and campus employment. Scholarships are awarded on the basis of academic promise. Approximately 85 percent of Manor's students receive some form of financial aid. Federally funded sources include the Federal Pell Grant, Federal Supplemental Educational Opportunity Grant, Federal Perkins Loan, Federal Stafford Student Loan, Federal PLUS loan, and Federal Work-Study Program. State-funded programs offered are the PHEAA State Grant and State Work-Study programs. The institutionally funded sources are the Manor Grant and the Resident Grant. Scholarships available for attendance at Manor include the following: Manor Presidential Scholarship; Joseph and Rose Wawriw Scholarships; Henry Lewandowski Memorial Scholarship; Elizabeth A. Stahlecker Memorial Scholarship; Mary Wolchonsky Scholarship; John Woloschuk Memorial Scholarship; Lorraine Osinski Keating Memorial Scholarship; Yuri and Jaroslava Rybak Scholarship; Dr. and Mrs. Volodymyr and Lydia Bazarko Scholarship; Heritage Foundation Scholarship of First Securities Federal Savings Bank; Father Chlystun Scholarship; Sesok Family Memorial Scholarship; Eileen Freedman Memorial Scholarship; Manor Allied Health, Science, and Math Division Scholarship; Business Division Scholarship; Liberal Arts Division Scholarship; Basilian Scholarships; Scholar Athlete Award; St. Basil Academy Scholarship; Wasyl and Jozefa Soroka Scholarships; and International Scholarships. Scholarship eligibility requirements vary; details are available from the Admissions Office.

Faculty

There are 24 full-time and 100 part-time faculty members at Manor. Forty-seven percent of the faculty members have master's degrees and 35 percent possess doctorates in their field. Faculty members spend three fourths of their time teaching and the remainder counseling and advising students. The overall faculty-student ratio is 1:13. Small class size allows for personal attention in an environment conducive to learning.

Student Body Profile

Of the approximately 900 full- and part-time students enrolled at Manor, 238 entered the College as full-time freshman students in fall 2009. Twenty percent of the recent freshman class lived in the on-campus residence hall. Twenty-nine percent of the recent freshman class were members of minority groups, including international students from Albania, Ecuador, Guatemala, Haiti, India, Korea, Pakistan, Philippines, Sierra Leone, Russia, Ukraine, and Uzbekistan.

Student Activities

Manor encourages students to develop leadership skills through active participation in all aspects of College life. A variety of options for extracurricular participation fall under the umbrella of Manor's student life department, including the Student Senate, athletic teams, and clubs. The Student Senate forms an important part of the College community. The Senate, representing the student population, responds to student interests and concerns and acts as a liaison between the administration and the student body. Other extracurricular activities include intercollegiate men's and women's basketball and soccer, and women's volleyball. Manor's sports teams compete in the National Junior College Athletic Association. Additional extracurricular activities include the honor societies, intramural sports, the yearbook, and various special interest and cultural clubs. Student services is also responsible for the campus ministry, the counseling center, the residence hall, and the on-campus security force.

Facilities and Resources

The Academic Building (also called Mother of Perpetual Help Hall) includes classrooms, lecture rooms, laboratories, the chapel, and the Offices of Student Services, Campus Ministry, and Counseling. The Academic Building is equipped with up-to-date facilities, including biology, chemistry, and clinical laboratories, as well as modern IBM-compatible microsystems network labs. The Learning Center provides professional and student tutors in all College subjects and conducts workshops in study and research skills. Courses in English as a second language are also offered at the center.

The Basileiad Library has the capacity for 60,000 books, journals, multimedia materials, and periodicals. The library offers study areas, a multimedia room, a special collections and rare book archive, and computer access. The current library collection contains 50,000 volumes, including a special law collection and a Ukrainian Language collection.

An on-campus community Manor Dental Health Center was established in 1979 as an adjunct to the Expanded Functions Dental Assisting (EFDA) Program. Located on the lower level of St. Josaphat Hall, the center provides students enrolled in the EFDA Program or the Dental Hygiene Program at Manor with training under the direct supervision of faculty dentists. Currently, more than 2,500 patients receive care, including the following services: general dentistry, oral hygiene, orthodontics, prosthodontics, endodontics, and cosmetic dentistry. Because Manor Dental Health Center is a teaching facility, the fees charged for services are lower than those charged by private practitioners. Community residents are welcome as patients.

The Ukrainian Heritage Studies Center, located on the campus, preserves and promotes Ukrainian heritage, arts, and culture through four areas: academic programs, a museum collection, a library, and archives. Special events, exhibits, workshops, and seminars are offered throughout the year. The center is open to the public for tours and educational presentations by appointment.

Location

Manor is located in Jenkintown, Pennsylvania, 15 miles north of Center City Philadelphia. Manor is accessible via public transportation and is located near the Pennsylvania Turnpike, Route 611, U.S. 1, and Route 232. Centers of cultural and historic interest are found in nearby Philadelphia, Valley Forge, and beautiful Bucks County. Manor's suburban campus is within walking distance of a large shopping mall, medical offices, and a township park.

Admission Requirements

Manor is open to qualified applicants of all races, creeds, and national origins. Candidates are required to have a high school diploma or its equivalent. Admission is based on the applicant's scholastic record, test scores, and interviews. The application procedure involves submission of a completed application form, a high school transcript, SAT or ACT scores (required for students less than 21 years old), an interview, and an essay. Transfer students must submit transcripts of all college work completed. International students must also submit results of the Test of English as a Foreign Language (TOEFL) or, for the Liberal Arts/ESL program, must have completed two years of English language study at the high school or college level in their native country.

Application and Information

Manor has a rolling admission policy. Students may apply for admission in either the fall or the spring semester. Interested students are invited to visit the campus and meet with the admissions staff, faculty members, program directors, and students. Open houses, career days and nights, and classroom visits are scheduled throughout the year. The Admissions Office is open Monday through Friday, 8:30 a.m. to 6 p.m. (Saturday hours are by appointment). Admissions staff members can schedule visits and answer questions concerning admission, careers, programs, special features, and student life. For application forms, program-of-study bulletins, and catalogs, students should write to:

Jeff Levine
Director of Admissions
Manor College
700 Fox Chase Road
Jenkintown, Pennsylvania 19046

Phone: 215-884-2216
E-mail: ftadmiss@manor.edu
Web site: http://www.manor.edu

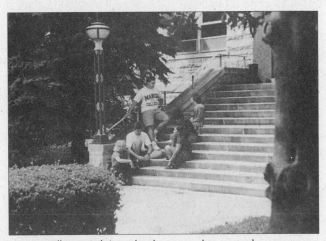

Manor College students relax between classes on the steps outside Mother of Perpetual Help Hall.

MIDDLE GEORGIA COLLEGE
COCHRAN, GEORGIA

The College and Its Mission

Founded in 1884, Middle Georgia College (MGC) is a public residential college in Cochran, Georgia, a city of 5,000 people about 40 miles south of Macon. The College is situated on 170 acres in this rural community. Sixty acres are developed with campus buildings and more than 100 acres are dedicated to woodlands and facilities for athletics and recreation.

The Dublin campus is located 30 miles to the east of the main residential campus. The Georgia Aviation campus is 20 miles away in Eastman and offers several aviation programs.

Middle Georgia College (MGC) is a state college offering associate degrees, limited bachelor's degrees, and certificates. The College is dedicated to providing a dynamic, learning-centered, caring, and technically advanced environment of excellence. As a multi-campus residential institution, the College pursues innovative opportunities to provide services to its traditional and nontraditional students primarily from rural areas of south central Georgia and maintains a recognized legacy of affordable higher education and community support services of the highest quality. The College also serves as the only higher education institution of aviation for the State of Georgia.

The College's historic main campus in Cochran offers academic programs of study through the baccalaureate degree for commuting and residential students. The Georgia Aviation campus in Eastman provides aviation specific technical education for the state while supporting the main campus' Bachelor of Science in Aviation Management degree program. The Dublin campus provides educational opportunities for central Georgia commuting students. In addition, MGC provides undergraduate education addressing the economic development needs of Georgia's heartland and the state's aviation industry.

To accomplish its mission, MGC commits to the following goals:

* Promoting a campuswide commitment to student learning that is embedded in course and program design, teaching, achievement, and student development activities

* Providing the highest-quality classroom and/or advanced distance learning instruction that enriches and challenges learners in all programs at all levels

* Creating a welcoming campus community that nurtures a culturally and ethnically diverse student body

* Offering programs of excellence leading to certificates and associate degrees to prepare students for immediate employment and/or acceptance to baccalaureate degree programs at Middle Georgia College or other colleges and universities

* Offering a signature aviation program that is the only public curriculum in Georgia leading to select baccalaureate degrees in aviation management as well as certificate and associate

programs in flight and aviation technology specialties that prepare students for immediate employment, careers, and further study in aviation

* Providing the Georgia Academy of Aviation, Mathematics, Engineering, and Sciences (GAMES) program that challenges gifted students to experience the rigors of higher education at an earlier entrance

* Providing the support resources, services, and learning activities that enhance student learning, facilitate student success, and promote personal enrichment

* Providing and supporting an adaptive, effective, and efficient human and physical infrastructure that maintains and supports the learning environment

Middle Georgia College is accredited by the Commission on Colleges of the Southern Association of Colleges and Schools to award associate and select baccalaureate degrees. Students attend MGC because of its family atmosphere, small class sizes, personal attention, and affordable tuition. To view a video about the College, prospective students should go online to http://www.youniversitytv.com/colleges/mgc.

Academic Programs

Associate Degree Programs: Middle Georgia College offers more than fifty programs that prepare students for transfer to another college or for placement on the workforce. The most popular fields of study are aviation, business administration, criminal justice, education, engineering, and nursing. Fifteen of MGC's associate degree program can be earned entirely online.

The career programs at the associate degree and certificate levels prepare students for employment immediately following graduation in nursing, aviation maintenance technology, aircraft structural technology, air traffic control, occupational therapy assistant, and surveying, among other careers.

Bachelor's Degree Programs: MGC offers three bachelor's degree programs: aviation management, early childhood/special education, and criminal justice.

Costs

In-state tuition and fees are $3100 per year. Out-of-state tuition and fees are $11,000 per year. Costs for housing and meals range from $7000 to $8000 per year, depending on the residence hall. Other fees, such as flight time, science labs, and books, may add to costs.

Financial Aid

Financial aid is available for those who qualify. The Free Application for Federal Student Aid (FAFSA) may be completed online at http://www.fafsa.ed.gov and must be submitted yearly.

The MGC Scholarship deadline is April 1 each year. Scholarship applications are available online at http://www.mgc.edu/FinancialAid/scholarships.cfm.

Faculty

The student-faculty ratio is 25:1. There are 134 faculty members, 37 percent of whom have terminal degrees. MGC faculty members teach their classes and provide time before and after class to help students. Teaching assistants or graduate assistants are not used at MGC.

Student Body Profile

Middle Georgia College has 3,500 students from 126 counties in Georgia, across the United States, and throughout the world. The student body is 54 percent women, 46 percent men, 56 percent Caucasian, and 40 percent African American. Thirty-three percent of the student body lives on campus in a residence hall.

Student Activities

There are more than thirty clubs and organizations, as well as many campus events including Homecoming, Spring Fling, Fall Festival, concerts, lectures, art shows, cultural programs, dances, and competitions. The Student Activities Center provides a place for students to hang out, shoot pool, or play ping pong, poker, or video games. There is also a robust intramural and activities program and a state-of-the-art wellness center.

Sports: Varsity sports include men's and women's basketball and soccer, men's baseball, and women's softball.

Facilities and Resources

The main campus contains numerous academic buildings, athletic facilities, residence halls, computer labs, a library, and a wellness and student center.

There are seven residence halls on MGC's main campus and one on the Georgia Aviation campus in Eastman. Students live in apartment-style halls, single suites, and double suites.

Location

The main campus is located in Cochran, Georgia, with campuses in Dublin and Eastman.

The Dublin campus has two classroom buildings serving the commuters in the surrounding area.

The Eastman campus is located at the Heart of Georgia Regional Airport, and the air traffic control tower is run by MGC students.

Admission Requirements

Applicants must have an academic core grade point average of 2.0 in order to be considered for admission. Starting with the spring semester 2012, students will also be required to submit SAT scores of at least 430 critical reading and 400 math; ACT scores of at least 17 English and 17 math; or COMPASS exam scores of at least 62 reading, 32 English, and 20 math.

Application and Information

Prospective student may apply to MGC online at http://www.mgc.edu by clicking on Admissions and selecting Apply Online.

For application forms and further information, students should contact:

Admissions Office
Middle Georgia College
1100 Second Street SE
Cochran, Georgia 31014

Phone: 877-642-2624 (toll-free)
E-mail: admissions@mgc.com
Web site: http://www.mgc.edu
        http://on.fb.me/middle_georgia_coll (Facebook)

MGC has an old-school look but is definitely not old school.

MOHAWK VALLEY COMMUNITY COLLEGE

UTICA AND ROME, NEW YORK

MVCC
MOHAWK VALLEY COMMUNITY COLLEGE

The College and Its Mission

Mission: Mohawk Valley Community College promotes student success and community involvement through a commitment to excellence and a spirit of service.

Vision: To transform lives by creating an innovative learning environment that meets the needs of the rapidly changing communities.

Statement of purpose: As a diverse institution with a global view, the College provides opportunities for affordable education, with support from Oneida County and the State of New York, and offers career, transfer, and transitional education and programs for personal and cultural enrichment; and supports community and economic development.

The College was founded in 1946 as the New York State Institute of Applied Arts and Sciences at Utica. One of five postsecondary institutions established on an experimental basis after World War II, the public institute offered programs leading to technical and semiprofessional employment in business and industry. After name changes in the 1950s, redefining its mission, the College moved to its current 80-acre campus location in Utica in 1960. In 1961, the College was renamed Mohawk Valley Community College. Today, the College offers a full range of academic programs.

The College is accredited by the Middle States Association of Colleges and Schools. Individual program accreditations are as follows: airframe and power plant technology by the Federal Aviation Administration (FAA); civil, electrical, and mechanical engineering technology and surveying technology by the Commission for Technology Accreditation of the Accreditation Board for Engineering and Technology, Inc. (ABET); nursing by the National League for Nursing Accrediting Commission (NLNAC); and respiratory care by the Commission on Accreditation of Allied Health Education Programs, in cooperation with the Committee on Accreditation for Respiratory Care.

Academic Programs

The College has been authorized to offer the following degrees and certificates: Associate in Arts (A.A.) degree, Associate in Science (A.S.) degree, Associate in Applied Science (A.A.S.) degree, Associate in Occupational Studies (A.O.S.) degree, and the MVCC Certificate.

The structure of academic programming at MVCC has two main purposes. Certificate, A.O.S., and A.A.S. programs emphasize the development of employable skills through a combination of classroom and laboratory instruction. Some programs also include internship experiences. A.A. and A.S. programs provide students with the liberal arts, science, mathematics, business, engineering, or computer course work necessary for transfer into the junior year of a preprofessional program at a four-year public or private college or university upon the completion of their associate degree.

The minimum number of credits needed to earn an associate degree is 62. The maximum credits required for a degree differ by program and degree type.

Opportunities for specialization include the honors program, independent study, internships, study abroad, and ROTC (Army and Air Force).

The College operates on a semester calendar. Fall classes begin before Labor Day and end before Christmas. Spring classes begin in mid-January and end in mid-May. The airframe and power plant certificate program follows a slightly different calendar, with opportunities for enrollment in August, December, and April.

Career and transfer programs are available. Majors offered include accounting (A.A.S.); administrative assistant (A.A.S.); air conditioning technology (A.O.S.); building management and maintenance (A.A.S.); business administration (A.S.); business management (A.A.S.); chemical dependency practitioner (A.A.S.); chemical technology (A.A.S.); civil engineering technology (A.A.S.); computer-aided drafting (A.O.S.); computer information systems (A.A.S.); computer science (A.S.); criminal justice (A.A.S.); culinary arts management (A.O.S.), also with baking and pastry emphasis; data processing, programming

and systems (A.A.S.); digital animation (A.A.S.); educational sign language interpretation (A.A.S.); electrical engineering technology (A.A.S.); electrical service technician (A.O.S.), with options in electrical maintenance and fiber optics; emergency medical services/paramedic (A.A.S.); engineering science (A.S.); environmental analysis–chemical technology (A.A.S.); financial services management (A.A.S.); fine arts (A.S.); fire protection technology (A.A.S., available to graduates of the Utica Fire Academy only); general studies (A.S.); general studies–childhood education (A.S.); graphic arts technology (A.A.S.); graphic design (A.A.S.); hotel technology–meeting services management (A.A.S.); human services (A.A.S.); illustration (A.A.S.); individual studies (A.A., A.A.S., A.S., and A.O.S.); international studies (A.A.); liberal arts–adolescence education (teacher transfer) (A.S.); liberal arts–childhood education (teacher transfer) (A.S.); liberal arts–humanities and social science (A.A.); liberal arts–psychology (A.S.); liberal arts–public policy (A.S.); liberal arts–theater (A.A.); manufacturing technology (A.O.S.); mathematics (A.S.); mechanical engineering technology (A.A.S.); mechanical technology–aircraft maintenance (A.A.S., requires an FAA-approved airframe and power plant license to enroll); media marketing and management (A.A.S.); medical assisting (A.A.S.); nursing (A.A.S.); nutrition and dietetics (A.S.); photography (A.A.S.); pre–environmental science (A.S.); programming and systems (A.A.S.); radiologic technology (A.S., transfer in only with appropriate radiology credentials); recreation and leisure services (A.A.S.); respiratory care (A.A.S.); restaurant management (A.A.S.); school facilities management (A.A.S., online); science (A.S.), with emphasis areas in biology, chemistry, physical education, physics, and sports medicine; semiconductor manufacturing technology (A.A.S.); surveying technology (A.A.S.); telecommunications technology–Verizon Next Step (A.A.S.); Web development and information design (A.A.S.); and welding technology (A.O.S.).

Certificate programs include administrative assistant; airframe and power plant technology; allied health care: medical claims management; carpentry and masonry; chef training; CNC machinist technology; coaching; computer-aided drafting; cybersecurity (online); electronic technician; English as a second language; finance; graphic communication; heating and air conditioning; individual studies: business and industry; industrial and commercial electricity; insurance; machinist technology; managerial accounting; media marketing and management; medical assistant; photography; refrigeration; school facilities management (online); small-business management; supervisory management; surgical technician; surveying; transportation management (online); and welding.

Credit for Nontraditional Learning Experiences

MVCC offers adult students the opportunity to earn credits through the CLEP examination, MVCC-administered examinations, life experience, and course work completed in a noncollegiate setting. The accumulated credit earned cannot exceed 75 percent of the student's degree program.

Costs

Tuition for New York State residents is $1700 per semester for full-time students and $120 per credit hour for part-time students; for out-of-state and international students, it is $3400 per semester for full-time students and $240 per credit hour for part-time students. The student activity fee is $110 per semester for full-time students and $5 per credit hour for part-time students, and the technology fee is $100 per semester full-time and $35 per semester part-time. Books and supplies range from $300 to $500 per semester, depending on the student's major. Residence hall occupants must purchase one of the available room and board packages each semester. Costs range from $3855 to $4745 per semester, depending on room type and meal plan chosen. The residence hall technology fee is $100 per semester for Internet and phone access. The residence hall social fee is $20 per semester. The residence hall orientation fee is $45 and covers new-resident orientation programming and meals.

Financial Aid

One of MVCC's major objectives is to make college affordable for all. Approximately 90 percent of MVCC students receive some form of state or federal financial aid. The College offers a comprehensive financial assistance program of scholarships, loans, and grants. Most of the financial assistance received by MVCC students is need based. Non–need-based scholarships include the Presidential Scholarship Program for the top 10 percent of Oneida County (the College's sponsoring county) graduates, two similar Exceptional Student Scholarships for those not from Oneida County, and the Sodexo/MVCC Meal Plan Scholarships, which consider exceptional citizenship. Students eligible for non–need-based scholarships are expected to apply for state and federal financial assistance as applicable.

Faculty

The full-time faculty members number 149, and the part-time faculty members number 130. Approximately 8 percent of all faculty members have doctoral degrees. The student-faculty ratio is approximately 20:1.

Student Body Profile

MVCC enrolls approximately 5,400 students each year. Enrollment is divided between the main campus in Utica, New York, and the branch campus in Rome, New York, with approximately 80 percent of the student population enrolled on the main campus.

The College is designed to be predominantly commuter based; 85 percent of the students live within 60 miles of the campus in central New York State. The College has added an additional residence hall on the main campus in Utica, increasing housing capacity to approximately 505 students.

The international student population is currently 80 students. Nineteen different countries are represented on campus.

The average age of students is about 22, with approximately 35 percent of the population being over the age of 25. Approximately 52 percent of the enrolled students are women. The racial/ethnic makeup of the campus is currently 80 percent white, non-Hispanic; 7 percent black, non-Hispanic; 1 percent American Indian/Alaskan native; 1 percent Asian/Pacific Islander; and 3 percent Hispanic. Of the total student body, 8 percent chose not to identify with any of the listed groups.

Enrolling students typically exhibit a 75 percent grade average in high school and a rank in the top 50 percent of their high school class.

Student Activities

The Student Activities program offers a wide variety of experiences for students through clubs, Student Congress, and other activities. On each campus, the staff assists students with the planning of events and programs. There are eighteen professional, curriculum-related clubs. In addition, there are more than forty service/interest clubs that provide students with the opportunity to participate in a wide range of social, cultural, theatrical, athletic, and international activities to broaden their experiences.

MVCC participates in Division III of the National Junior College Athletic Association. Men's teams include baseball, basketball, bowling, cross-country, golf, ice hockey, indoor track, lacrosse, soccer, tennis, and track and field. Women's teams include basketball, bowling, cross-country, golf, indoor track, lacrosse, softball, soccer, tennis, track and field, and volleyball.

Throughout the last decade, MVCC's athletic teams have an impressive record, winning more than 70 percent of their contests.

Facilities and Resources

The main campus in Utica is composed of three residence halls; the Alumni College Center, which includes dining facilities, a bookstore, and the health center; the Gymnasium; the Academic Building; the Science and Technology building; the Information Technology and Performing Arts Conference Center (open computer labs and a handicap-accessible, state-of-the-art theater), and Payne Hall (library, administrative offices, and a comprehensive Student Services Center). Construction is currenty under way for the Robert R. Jorgensen Athletic Center, which will add a 28,000-square-foot practice facility and a 5,000-square-foot fitness center.

The branch campus in Rome consists of the Rome Academic Building, including a bookstore and dining room facilities for the hospitality programs, and the John D. Plumley Science and Technology Complex that includes a library, classrooms, and labs.

The goal of MVCC's libraries is to link students to the information they need. With more than 86,000 volumes and over 500 periodical titles, MVCC offers a comprehensive collection to support the College's curricula; library holdings also include popular best-sellers and feature film collections. MVCC students as well as faculty and staff members may request materials outside the collection through the College's comprehensive interlibrary loan service. The online resources include catalogs and periodical indexes with full-text articles. Coin-operated photocopiers and microfilm reader/printers are also available.

Academic tutoring is available at no cost to students in the Learning Centers on both campuses. The centers offer instructional support in mathematics, writing, reading, study skills, life sciences, and computer and social sciences.

Location

The main campus is in Utica, New York, a small city of 60,000 people. The branch campus in Rome, New York, is located in a community of 30,000 people. The small-city atmosphere, coupled with a wide range of cultural activities, museums, access to the Adirondack Mountains, good public transportation, and sports venues, provides an excellent location for student growth and development.

Admission Requirements

The College is an open-admission, full-opportunity college. The College does not require applicants to complete standardized admissions tests such as the ACT or SAT.

Application and Information

Students can apply in a variety of ways. MVCC provides its own admission application (print and online versions); no processing fee is required. It is available from the Admissions Office or from selected high schools in central New York State. MVCC applications can be accessed on the College's Web site at www.mvcc.edu/apply. MVCC also participates in the SUNY application process. Students can use the SUNY application—hard copy or online version; SUNY processing fees apply.

For further information, interested students should contact:

Admissions Office
Mohawk Valley Community College
1101 Sherman Drive
Utica, New York 13501

Phone: 315-792-5354
Fax: 315-792-5527
E-mail: admissions@mvcc.edu (domestic)
        International.admissions@mvcc.edu (international)
Web site: http://www.mvcc.edu
          http://www.facebook.com/WeAreMVCC

Students walk by the Academic Building on the Utica campus at Mohawk Valley Community College.

VALLEY FORGE MILITARY COLLEGE

WAYNE, PENNSYLVANIA

The College and Its Mission

Valley Forge Military College—The Military College of Pennsylvania™ (VFMC) is a private, coeducational residential college that offers the freshman and sophomore years of college. The primary mission of the College is to prepare students for transfer to competitive four-year colleges and universities. Established in 1935, the College has a long tradition of fostering personal growth through a comprehensive system built on the five cornerstones that make Valley Forge unique: academic excellence, character development, leadership, personal motivation, and physical development for all students regardless of race, creed, or national origin. The diverse student body represents more than nineteen states and four countries. The College has an excellent transfer record, with 95 percent of cadets accepted to their first- or second-choice schools. More than 63 percent were admitted to the top-tier schools in the country.

Valley Forge Military College is the only college in the northeastern United States that offers qualified freshmen the opportunity to participate in an Early Commissioning Program, leading to a commission as a second lieutenant in the U.S. Army Reserves or Army National Guard at the end of their sophomore year. The U.S. Air Force Academy, the U.S. Coast Guard Academy, the U.S. Military Academy, and the U.S. Naval Academy have all sponsored cadets through their Foundation Scholarship Programs and other programs to attend Valley Forge Military College.

In October 2007, the Pennsylvania House of Representatives adopted a resolution introduced by then state Representative Bryan Lentz, designating Valley Forge Military College as the official military college of the commonwealth of Pennsylvania. For nearly two years, Valley Forge Military College has used the trademarked tagline "The Military College of Pennsylvania™," and now the designation is official. This in no way will change the name of the school; it will remain Valley Forge Military College. This resolution sets in stone what many local citizens, family members, and alumni already know—Valley Forge provides elite military education and training for future leaders in every aspect of society and is in a class of its own.

The College is accredited by the Middle States Association of Colleges and Schools and is approved by the Pennsylvania State Council of Education and the Commission on Higher Education of the Pennsylvania State Department of Education. The College is a member of the National Association of Independent Colleges and Universities, the Association of Independent Colleges/Universities of Pennsylvania, the Pennsylvania Association of Two-Year Colleges, and the Association of Military Colleges and Schools in the United States.

Academic Programs

All students are required to complete an academic program of 60 credits, including a core program of approximately 45 credits designed to establish the essential competencies that are necessary for continued intellectual development and to facilitate the transfer process. Included in the core program are one semester of computer science, two semesters of English, one semester of literature, two semesters of mathematics, one semester of science, and one semester of Western civilization. Qualified cadets must also complete a minimum of two semesters of military science. To satisfy the requirement for the associate degree, cadets must complete at least 15 additional credits in courses related to their selected area of concentration. Associate degrees are awarded upon satisfactory completion of the degree requirements with a quality point average of 2.0 or higher.

Associate Degree Programs: Valley Forge Military College offers concentrations in business, criminal justice, general studies, leadership, and liberal arts, leading to an Associate of Arts degree, as well as concentrations in general studies, life sciences, physical sciences, and pre-engineering, leading to an Associate of Science degree.

Transfer Arrangements: Transfer of academic credits and completion of the baccalaureate degree are facilitated by established relationships with a number of outstanding colleges and universities, including agreements with the neighboring institutions of Cabrini College, Eastern University, and Rosemont College.

Credit for Nontraditional Learning Experiences

Valley Forge Military College may give credit for demonstrated proficiency in areas related to college-level courses. Sources used to determine such proficiency are the College-Level Examination Program (CLEP), Advanced Placement (AP) examinations, Defense Activity for Nontraditional Education Support (DANTES), and the Office of Education Credit and Credentials of the American Council on Education (ACE). All such requests must be approved by the Office of the Dean.

Costs

The annual charge for 2011–12 is $40,265. This charge included haircuts, maintenance, room and board, tuition, uniforms, and other fees. Optional expenses may include fee-based courses, such as aviation, driver's education, membership in the cavalry troop or artillery battery, or scuba. A fee is charged for Health Center confinement over 24 hours' duration. For information on the payment plan, students should contact the Business Office.

Financial Aid

The College offers a combination of merit- and need-based scholarships and grants as well as endowed scholarships based on donor specifications to help VFMC cadets finance their education. The academic scholarships reward incoming and returning cadets for demonstrated academic excellence. Performance scholarships are awarded to eligible cadets who participate in the athletic teams, band, or choir. To qualify for federal, state, and VFMC grants, students must file the Free Application for Federal Student Aid (FAFSA) by the published priority deadlines. In addition, qualified cadets in the advanced ROTC commissioning program are eligible for two-year, full-tuition scholarships. These scholarships are supplemented by assistance for room and board provided by the College. The FAFSA is also required for ROTC scholarship applications.

Valley Forge Military College offers federal student aid to eligible cadets in the form of Federal Pell Grants, Federal Supplemental Educational Opportunity Grants (FSEOG), Federal Work-Study (FWS) Program positions, Federal Stafford Student Loans, and Parent Loans for Undergraduate Students (PLUS) through the Federal Family Education Loan Program. Applicants must file the FAFSA and the VFMC financial aid application for consideration for all student aid.

Faculty

There are 12 full-time and 11 part-time faculty members holding the academic rank of assistant professor, associate professor, instructor, or professor. These faculty members are selected for their professional ability and strong personal leadership qualities; 50 percent of the full-time staff members hold doctorates in their field. Faculty members perform additional duties as advisers and athletic coaches of extracurricular activities. The Military Science Department has 5 active-duty Army officers and 4 noncommissioned officers assigned as full-time faculty members for the ROTC program. The faculty-student ratio is approximately 1:12. Classes are small, and the classroom atmosphere contributes to a harmonious relationship between faculty members and the students.

Student Body Profile

The military structure of Valley Forge provides extraordinary opportunities for cadets to develop and exercise leadership abilities. The Corps of Cadets is a self-administering body organized in nine company units along military lines, with a cadet officer and noncommissioned officer organization for cadet control and administration. The College's cadets are appointed to major command positions in the Corps. The First Captain is generally a sophomore in the College. Cadet leadership and positive peer pressure within this structured setting result in a unique camaraderie among cadets. Cadets, through their student representatives, cooperate with the administration in enforcing regulations regarding student conduct. A Student Advisory Council represents the cadets in the school administration. The Dean's Council meets regularly to discuss aspects of academic life.

Student Activities

The proximity to many colleges and universities ensures a full schedule of local college-oriented events in addition to Valley Forge's own activities. Cadets are encouraged to become involved in community-service activities. The scholarship-supported Regimental Band has performed for U.S. presidents, royalty, and countless military and social events. The Regimental Chorus has performed at the Capitol Building in Washington, D.C.; New York's Carnegie Hall; and the Philadelphia Academy of Music. In addition, eligible students can participate in VFMC honor societies: Alpha Beta Gamma, Lambda Alpha Epsilon, or Phi Theta Kappa. Other available activities include Black Student Union, business and political clubs, flight training, French Club, participation in the local Radnor Fire Company, and Rotoract.

Sports: Athletics and physical well-being are important elements in a Valley Forge education. The aim of the program is to develop alertness, all-around fitness, character, competitive spirit, courage, esprit de corps, leadership, and genuine desire for physical and mental achievement. For students aspiring to compete at the Division I-A or Division I-AA level, Valley Forge's residential college football and basketball programs offer a distinctive opportunity that combines a strong academic transfer program with a highly successful athletic program that has habitually placed players at the national level. Continuing a legacy that began with its high school program, in only eight years, the College has placed 40 players on national-level teams in basketball and football. In the last seven years, the Valley Forge wrestling program has also produced 3 National Champions and 7 All-Americans in the National Collegiate Wrestling Association. Students may also compete at the collegiate level in men's and women's cross-country, men's and women's track and field, lacrosse, co-ed soccer, women's basketball, women's softball, women's volleyball, and tennis. Club and interscholastic teams are available in golf, and riflery.

Facilities and Resources

Campus buildings are equipped to meet student needs. A fiber-optic, Internet-capable computer network connects all campus classrooms, dormitory rooms, laboratories, and the library. All rooms are computer accessible and provide access to CadetNET, the institutional local area network. This network provides access to the library and the Internet. College classrooms are located in two buildings and contain biology, chemistry, and physics laboratories. A computer laboratory supports the computer science curriculum and student requirements through a local area network.

Library and Audiovisual Services: The May H. Baker Memorial Library is a learning resource center for independent study and research. The library has more than 100,000 volumes and audiovisual materials, microfilm, and periodicals and houses the Cadet Achievement Center. It provides online database access, membership in the Tri-State Library Consortium, and computer links to ACCESS Pennsylvania and other databases to support the College requirements.

Location

Valley Forge Military College is situated on a beautifully landscaped 100-acre campus in the Main Line community of Wayne, 15 miles west of Philadelphia and close to Valley Forge National Historic Park. Ample opportunities exist for cadets to enjoy cultural and entertainment resources and activities in the Philadelphia area.

Admission Requirements

Admission to the College is based upon review of an applicant's SAT or ACT scores, high school transcript, recommendations from a guidance counselor, and personal interview. Students may be accepted for midyear admission. Minimum requirements for admission on a nonprobation status are a high school diploma or equivalency diploma with a minimum 2.0 average, rank in the upper half of the class, and minimum combined SAT score of 850 or ACT score of 17. The College reviews the new SAT standards and scores on a case-by-case basis. An international student for whom English is a second language must have a minimum score of 550 on the paper-based version of the Test of English as a Foreign Language (TOEFL). Up to 20 percent of an entering class may be admitted on a conditional or probationary status, and individual entrance requirements may be waived by the Dean of the College for students who display a sincere commitment to pursuing a college degree.

Application and Information

Valley Forge Military College follows a program of rolling admissions. Applicants are notified of the admission decision as soon as their files are complete. A nonrefundable registration fee of $25 is required of all applicants.

For application forms and further information, students should contact:

College Admissions Officer
Valley Forge Military College
1001 Eagle Road
Wayne, Pennsylvania 19087
Phone: 800-234-VFMC (toll-free)
E-mail: admissions@vfmac.edu
Web site: http://college.vfmac.edu

On the campus of Valley Forge Military College.

Indexes

2010–11 Changes in Institutions

Following is an alphabetical listing of institutions that have recently closed, merged with other institutions, or changed their name or status. In the case of a name change, the former name appears first, followed by the new name.

Alexandria Technical College (Alexandria, MN): *name changed to Alexandria Technical and Community College.*

Apollo College (Spokane, WA): *name changed to Carrington College – Spokane.*

Apollo College–Boise (Boise, ID): *name changed to Carrington College – Boise.*

Apollo College–Phoenix (Phoenix, AZ): *name changed to Carrington College – Phoenix.*

Apollo College–Portland (Portland, OR): *name changed to Carrington College – Portland.*

Apollo College–Tri-City, Inc. (Mesa, AZ): *name changed to Carrington College – Mesa.*

Apollo College–Tucson, Inc. (Tucson, AZ): *name changed to Carrington College – Tucson.*

Apollo College–Westside, Inc. (Phoenix, AZ): *name changed to Carrington College – Phoenix Westside.*

ASA Institute, The College of Advanced Technology (Brooklyn, NY): *name changed to ASA The College For Excellence.*

ATA Career Education (Louisville, KY): *name changed to ATA College.*

ATI Career Training Center (Oakland Park, FL): *no longer degree granting.*

Aviation Institute of Maintenance–Virginia Beach (Virginia Beach, VA): *name changed to Aviation Institute of Maintenance–Chesapeake.*

Brigham Young University–Idaho (Rexburg, ID): *now classified as a 4-year college.*

California School of Culinary Arts (Pasadena, CA): *name changed to Le Cordon Bleu College of Culinary Arts in Los Angeles.*

Central Florida Community College (Ocala, FL): *name changed to College of Central Florida.*

College of Eastern Utah (Price, UT): *name changed to Utah State University–College of Eastern Utah.*

Concorde Career Institute (North Hollywood, CA): *name changed to Concorde Career College.*

Concorde Career Institute (Kansas City, MO): *name changed to Concorde Career College.*

Crimson Technical College (Inglewood, CA): *no longer degree granting.*

Denver Automotive and Diesel College (Denver, CO): *name changed to Lincoln Technical Institute.*

Doña Ana Branch Community College (Las Cruces, NM): *name changed to Doña Ana Community College.*

East Central Technical College (Fitzgerald, GA) : merged into a single entry for Wiregrass Georgia Technical College (Valdosta, GA).

ECPI Technical College (Raleigh, NC): *name changed to ECPI College of Technology and now classified as a 4-year college.*

ECPI Technical College (Richmond, VA): *name changed to ECPI College of Technology.*

Everest Institute (Long Beach, CA): *name changed to WyoTech Long Beach.*

Everest Institute (Cuyahoga Falls, OH): *name changed to Fortis College Cuyahoga Falls.*

Flint River Technical College (Thomaston, GA): *merged into a single entry for Southern Crescent Technical College (Griffin, GA).*

Florida Technical College (Jacksonville, FL): *closed.*

Gamla College (Brooklyn, NY): *no longer accredited by agency recognized by USDE or CHEA.*

Garrett College (McHenry, MD): *now classified as a 4-year college.*

Griffin Technical College (Griffin, GA): *name changed to Southern Crescent Technical College.*

Gulf Coast College (Tampa, FL): *name changed to Fortis College.*

Herzing College (Birmingham, AL): *name changed to Herzing University and now classified as a 4-year college.*

Herzing College (Winter Park, FL): *name changed to Herzing University and now classified as a 4-year college.*

Herzing College (Kenner, LA): *name changed to Herzing University and now classified as a 4-year college.*

Herzing College (Minneapolis, MN): *name changed to Herzing University.*

Lake City Community College (Lake City, FL): *name changed to Florida Gateway College.*

Medical Careers Institute (Newport News, VA): *merged into a single entry for ECPI College of Technology (Newport News, VA), which is classified as a 4-year college.*

Medical Careers Institute (Richmond, VA): *merged into a single entry for ECPI College of Technology (Richmond, VA).*

Medical Careers Institute (Virginia Beach, VA): *merged into a single entry for ECPI College of Technology (Virginia Beach, VA), which is classified as a 4-year college.*

MTI College of Business & Technology (Sacramento, CA): *name changed to MTI College.*

National Polytechnic College of Science (Wilmington, CA): *no longer enrolling new students.*

New England Culinary Institute at Essex (Essex Junction, VT): *closed and merged into a single entry for New England Culinary Institute (Montpelier, VT).*

New Hampshire Technical Institute (Concord, NH): *name changed to NHTI, Concord's Community College.*

Northland Community and Technical College–Thief River Falls (Thief River Falls, MN): *name changed to Northland Community and Technical College–Thief River Falls & East Grand Forks.*

Penn Foster Career School (Scranton, PA): *no longer degree granting.*

Pennsylvania Culinary Institute (Pittsburgh, PA): *name changed to Le Cordon Bleu Institute of Culinary Arts in Pittsburgh.*

Pensacola Junior College (Pensacola, FL): *name changed to Pensacola State College.*

Pierpont Community & Technical College of Fairmont State University (Fairmont, WV): *name changed to Pierpont Community & Technical College.*

The PJA School (Upper Darby, PA): *name changed to Prism Career Institute.*

Rockford Business College (Rockford, IL): *name changed to Rockford Career College.*

St. Cloud Technical College (St. Cloud, MN): *name changed to St. Cloud Technical & Community College.*

San Diego Golf Academy (Vista, CA): *name changed to Golf Academy of America.*

School of Communication Arts (Raleigh, NC): *name changed to Living Arts College.*

Springfield College in Illinois (Springfield, IL): *name changed to Benedictine University at Springfield.*

Taylor Business Institute (New York, NY): *closed.*

Utah Career College (West Jordan, UT): *name changed to Broadview University and now classified as a 4-year college.*

Utah Career College–Layton Campus (Layton, UT): *name changed to Broadview University-Layton and now classified as a 4-year college.*

Valdosta Technical College (Valdosta, GA): *name changed to Wiregrass Georgia Technical College.*

Western Career College (Emeryville, CA): *name changed to Carrington College of California – Emeryville.*

Western Career College (Fremont, CA): *closed.*

Western Career College (Pleasant Hill, CA): *name changed to Carrington College California – Pleasant Hill.*

Western Career College (Sacramento, CA): *name changed to Carrington College of California – Sacramento.*

Western Career College (San Jose, CA): *name changed to Carrington College California – San Jose.*

Western Career College (San Leandro, CA): *name changed to Carrington College California – San Leandro.*

Western Career College (Walnut Creek, CA): *name changed to Carrington College of California – Antioch.*

Western Culinary Institute (Portland, OR): *name changed to Le Cordon Bleu College of Culinary Arts in Portland.*

West Virginia Junior College (Bridgeport, WV): *name changed to West Virginia Junior College–Bridgeport.*

Associate Degree Programs at Two-Year Colleges

ACCOUNTING

Aiken Tech Coll (SC)
Albany Tech Coll (GA)
Alexandria Tech and Comm Coll (MN)
Allen Comm Coll (KS)
Amarillo Coll (TX)
Anoka-Ramsey Comm Coll (MN)
Anoka-Ramsey Comm Coll, Cambridge Campus (MN)
Arizona Western Coll (AZ)
ASA The Coll For Excellence (NY)
Athens Tech Coll (GA)
Atlanta Tech Coll (GA)
Augusta Tech Coll (GA)
Bainbridge Coll (GA)
Barton County Comm Coll (KS)
Beaufort County Comm Coll (NC)
Berkeley City Coll (CA)
Blackhawk Tech Coll (WI)
Bristol Comm Coll (MA)
Brown Mackie Coll–Tucson (AZ)
Bryant & Stratton Coll (WI)
Bucks County Comm Coll (PA)
Burlington County Coll (NJ)
Carroll Comm Coll (MD)
Casper Coll (WY)
Central Carolina Tech Coll (SC)
Central Georgia Tech Coll (GA)
Central Lakes Coll (MN)
Central New Mexico Comm Coll (NM)
Central Oregon Comm Coll (OR)
Central Wyoming Coll (WY)
Century Coll (MN)
Chandler-Gilbert Comm Coll (AZ)
Chattahoochee Tech Coll (GA)
Chipola Coll (FL)
Chippewa Valley Tech Coll (WI)
Cincinnati State Tech and Comm Coll (OH)
City Colls of Chicago, Harry S. Truman College (IL)
Clarendon Coll (TX)
Coll of Business and Technology (FL)
Colorado Mountain Coll (CO)
Colorado Mountain Coll, Alpine Campus (CO)
Colorado Mountain Coll, Timberline Campus (CO)
Columbus Tech Coll (GA)
Comm Coll of Philadelphia (PA)
Comm Coll of Rhode Island (RI)
Comm Coll of Vermont (VT)
Corning Comm Coll (NY)
Cowley County Comm Coll and Area Vocational–Tech School (KS)
Dakota Coll at Bottineau (ND)
Dakota County Tech Coll (MN)
Darton Coll (GA)
Daytona State Coll (FL)
De Anza Coll (CA)
DeKalb Tech Coll (GA)
Delaware Tech & Comm Coll, Jack F. Owens Campus (DE)
Delaware Tech & Comm Coll, Stanton/Wilmington Campus (DE)
Delaware Tech & Comm Coll, Terry Campus (DE)
Dodge City Comm Coll (KS)
Dutchess Comm Coll (NY)
Eastern Gateway Comm Coll (OH)
Eastfield Coll (TX)
East Los Angeles Coll (CA)

Edison State Comm Coll (OH)
El Centro Coll (TX)
Elgin Comm Coll (IL)
Fayetteville Tech Comm Coll (NC)
Florida State Coll at Jacksonville (FL)
Foothill Coll (CA)
Fox Valley Tech Coll (WI)
Frank Phillips Coll (TX)
Frederick Comm Coll (MD)
Fulton-Montgomery Comm Coll (NY)
GateWay Comm Coll (AZ)
Gateway Comm Coll (CT)
Georgia Highlands Coll (GA)
Georgia Northwestern Tech Coll (GA)
Golden West Coll (CA)
Gwinnett Tech Coll (GA)
Harford Comm Coll (MD)
Harper Coll (IL)
Harrison Coll, Anderson (IN)
Harrison Coll, Columbus (IN)
Harrison Coll, Indianapolis (IN)
Harrison Coll, Lafayette (IN)
Harrison Coll, Muncie (IN)
Harrison Coll (OH)
Hawkeye Comm Coll (IA)
Highland Comm Coll (IL)
Housatonic Comm Coll (CT)
Houston Comm Coll System (TX)
Howard Comm Coll (MD)
Illinois Eastern Comm Colls, Olney Central College (IL)
Indian River State Coll (FL)
Inver Hills Comm Coll (MN)
Ivy Tech Comm Coll–Lafayette (IN)
James Sprunt Comm Coll (NC)
Jamestown Business Coll (NY)
Johnston Comm Coll (NC)
John Wood Comm Coll (IL)
Kankakee Comm Coll (IL)
Kaskaskia Coll (IL)
Kent State U at Ashtabula (OH)
Kent State U at East Liverpool (OH)
Kent State U at Tuscarawas (OH)
Kilian Comm Coll (SD)
Kingsborough Comm Coll of the City U of New York (NY)
Lake Michigan Coll (MI)
Lake Region State Coll (ND)
Lake Superior Coll (MN)
Lamar Comm Coll (CO)
Lanier Tech Coll (GA)
Laramie County Comm Coll (WY)
Leeward Comm Coll (HI)
Lincoln Land Comm Coll (IL)
Linn-Benton Comm Coll (OR)
Lonestar Coll–Cy-Fair (TX)
Lonestar Coll–Kingwood (TX)
Lonestar Coll–North Harris (TX)
Lonestar Coll–Tomball (TX)
Long Island Business Inst (NY)
Los Angeles Harbor Coll (CA)
Lower Columbia Coll (WA)
Macomb Comm Coll (MI)
Manchester Comm Coll (CT)
Marion Tech Coll (OH)
Martin Comm Coll (NC)
Massachusetts Bay Comm Coll (MA)
McHenry County Coll (IL)
Mendocino Coll (CA)
Mesa Comm Coll (AZ)
Metropolitan Comm Coll–Business & Technology Campus (MO)

Metropolitan Comm Coll–Longview (MO)
Metropolitan Comm Coll–Maple Woods (MO)
Metropolitan Comm Coll–Penn Valley (MO)
Middle Georgia Tech Coll (GA)
Middlesex Comm Coll (CT)
Midlands Tech Coll (SC)
Minnesota State Coll–Southeast Tech (MN)
Minnesota State Comm and Tech Coll (MN)
Minnesota West Comm and Tech Coll (MN)
Missouri State U–West Plains (MO)
Mohave Comm Coll (AZ)
Monroe County Comm Coll (MI)
Montcalm Comm Coll (MI)
Montgomery County Comm Coll (PA)
Moraine Park Tech Coll (WI)
Morton Coll (IL)
Moultrie Tech Coll (GA)
Mountain View Coll (TX)
Muskegon Comm Coll (MI)
Nashua Comm Coll (NH)
Niagara County Comm Coll (NY)
Northeast Comm Coll (NE)
Northeast Iowa Comm Coll (IA)
Northern Essex Comm Coll (MA)
North Hennepin Comm Coll (MN)
North Iowa Area Comm Coll (IA)
Northland Comm and Tech Coll–Thief River Falls & East Grand Forks (MN)
Northwest Coll (WY)
Northwest Tech Coll (MN)
Norwalk Comm Coll (CT)
Ogeechee Tech Coll (GA)
Oklahoma City Comm Coll (OK)
Oklahoma State U, Oklahoma City (OK)
Onondaga Comm Coll (NY)
Orange Coast Coll (CA)
Palm Beach State Coll (FL)
Pennsylvania Highlands Comm Coll (PA)
Phoenix Coll (AZ)
Pima Comm Coll (AZ)
Potomac State Coll of West Virginia U (WV)
Pratt Comm Coll (KS)
Quinsigamond Comm Coll (MA)
Randolph Comm Coll (NC)
Rockingham Comm Coll (NC)
St. Cloud Tech & Comm Coll (MN)
St. Philip's Coll (TX)
Sandersville Tech Coll (GA)
Sandhills Comm Coll (NC)
San Diego City Coll (CA)
Santa Barbara City Coll (CA)
Santa Fe Comm Coll (NM)
Sauk Valley Comm Coll (IL)
Savannah Tech Coll (GA)
Scottsdale Comm Coll (AZ)
Seminole State Coll of Florida (FL)
Snow Coll (UT)
Solano Comm Coll (CA)
Southeastern Comm Coll (IA)
Southeastern Comm Coll (NC)
Southeast Tech Inst (SD)
Southern Crescent Tech Coll (GA)
South Georgia Tech Coll (GA)
South Suburban Coll (IL)
Southwest Georgia Tech Coll (GA)

Southwest Mississippi Comm Coll (MS)
Spartanburg Comm Coll (SC)
Spencerian Coll (KY)
Springfield Tech Comm Coll (MA)
Stark State Coll of Technology (OH)
Suffolk County Comm Coll (NY)
Terra State Comm Coll (OH)
Three Rivers Comm Coll (CT)
Trident Tech Coll (SC)
Trinity Valley Comm Coll (TX)
Tyler Jr Coll (TX)
U of Pittsburgh at Titusville (PA)
Vincennes U Jasper Campus (IN)
Waubonsee Comm Coll (IL)
Waukesha County Tech Coll (WI)
Wenatchee Valley Coll (WA)
Westchester Comm Coll (NY)
Western Iowa Tech Comm Coll (IA)
West Georgia Tech Coll (GA)
West Kentucky Comm and Tech Coll (KY)
White Mountains Comm Coll (NH)
Wilson Comm Coll (NC)
Wiregrass Georgia Tech Coll (GA)
Wisconsin Indianhead Tech Coll (WI)
Yakima Valley Comm Coll (WA)
Yavapai Coll (AZ)
YTI Career Inst–York (PA)

ACCOUNTING AND BUSINESS/MANAGEMENT

Bradford School (OH)
Bradford School (PA)
Fox Coll (IL)
Harrisburg Area Comm Coll (PA)
International Business Coll, Indianapolis (IN)
King's Coll (NC)
Lonestar Coll–Montgomery (TX)
Minneapolis Business Coll (MN)
Mitchell Tech Inst (SD)
Oakland Comm Coll (MI)
Spencerian Coll (KY)
Wood Tobe–Coburn School (NY)

ACCOUNTING AND COMPUTER SCIENCE

GateWay Comm Coll (AZ)

ACCOUNTING AND FINANCE

Jackson Comm Coll (MI)

ACCOUNTING RELATED

Dakota Coll at Bottineau (ND)
John Tyler Comm Coll (VA)
Mountain Empire Comm Coll (VA)
Raritan Valley Comm Coll (NJ)

ACCOUNTING TECHNOLOGY AND BOOKKEEPING

Alamance Comm Coll (NC)
Anoka-Ramsey Comm Coll (MN)
Anoka-Ramsey Comm Coll, Cambridge Campus (MN)
Austin Comm Coll (TX)
Bellingham Tech Coll (WA)
Big Bend Comm Coll (WA)
Borough of Manhattan Comm Coll of the City U of New York (NY)
Brown Mackie Coll–Akron (OH)
Brown Mackie Coll–Albuquerque (NM)

Brown Mackie Coll–Atlanta (GA)
Brown Mackie Coll–Boise (ID)
Brown Mackie Coll–Cincinnati (OH)
Brown Mackie Coll–Findlay (OH)
Brown Mackie Coll–Fort Wayne (IN)
Brown Mackie Coll–Greenville (SC)
Brown Mackie Coll–Hopkinsville (KY)
Brown Mackie Coll–Kansas City (KS)
Brown Mackie Coll–Louisville (KY)
Brown Mackie Coll–Merrillville (IN)
Brown Mackie Coll–Miami (FL)
Brown Mackie Coll–Michigan City (IN)
Brown Mackie Coll–North Canton (OH)
Brown Mackie Coll–Northern Kentucky (KY)
Brown Mackie Coll–Oklahoma City (OK)
Brown Mackie Coll–Phoenix (AZ)
Brown Mackie Coll–Quad Cities (IA)
Brown Mackie Coll–St. Louis (MO)
Brown Mackie Coll–Salina (KS)
Brown Mackie Coll–San Antonio (TX)
Brown Mackie Coll–South Bend (IN)
Brown Mackie Coll–Tucson (AZ)
Brown Mackie Coll–Tulsa (OK)
Cape Fear Comm Coll (NC)
Casper Coll (WY)
Catawba Valley Comm Coll (NC)
Cayuga County Comm Coll (NY)
Cecil Coll (MD)
Central Maine Comm Coll (ME)
Central Wyoming Coll (WY)
Chandler-Gilbert Comm Coll (AZ)
Clark Coll (WA)
Coll of Central Florida (FL)
Coll of Lake County (IL)
Coll of the Canyons (CA)
The Comm Coll of Baltimore County (MD)
Dakota Coll at Bottineau (ND)
Danville Area Comm Coll (IL)
Duluth Business U (MN)
Fiorello H. LaGuardia Comm Coll of the City U of New York (NY)
Front Range Comm Coll (CO)
Gadsden State Comm Coll (AL)
Gateway Comm and Tech Coll (KY)
GateWay Comm Coll (AZ)
Glendale Comm Coll (AZ)
Goodwin Coll (CT)
Grays Harbor Coll (WA)
Gulf Coast Comm Coll (FL)
Hagerstown Comm Coll (MD)
Harford Comm Coll (MD)
Harrisburg Area Comm Coll (PA)
H. Councill Trenholm State Tech Coll (AL)
Hillsborough Comm Coll (FL)
Holyoke Comm Coll (MA)
ITT Tech Inst, Norwood (OH)
ITT Tech Inst, Strongsville (OH)
ITT Tech Inst, Austin (TX)
ITT Tech Inst, Richardson (TX)
ITT Tech Inst, San Antonio (TX)
Ivy Tech Comm Coll–Bloomington (IN)
Ivy Tech Comm Coll–Central Indiana (IN)

Ivy Tech Comm Coll–Columbus (IN)
Ivy Tech Comm Coll–East Central (IN)
Ivy Tech Comm Coll–Kokomo (IN)
Ivy Tech Comm Coll–Lafayette (IN)
Ivy Tech Comm Coll–North Central (IN)
Ivy Tech Comm Coll–Northeast (IN)
Ivy Tech Comm Coll–Northwest (IN)
Ivy Tech Comm Coll–Richmond (IN)
Ivy Tech Comm Coll–Southeast (IN)
Ivy Tech Comm Coll–Southern Indiana (IN)
Ivy Tech Comm Coll–Southwest (IN)
Ivy Tech Comm Coll–Wabash Valley (IN)
Jefferson State Comm Coll (AL)
Johnston Comm Coll (NC)
Kent State U at Geauga (OH)
Kent State U at Trumbull (OH)
Kilgore Coll (TX)
Lake Region State Coll (ND)
Lawson State Comm Coll (AL)
Lehigh Carbon Comm Coll (PA)
Lower Columbia Coll (WA)
Lurleen B. Wallace Comm Coll (AL)
Metropolitan Comm Coll–Blue River (MO)
Metropolitan Comm Coll–Business & Technology Campus (MO)
Miami Dade Coll (FL)
Minnesota State Coll–Southeast Tech (MN)
Mohawk Valley Comm Coll (NY)
Montana State U–Great Falls Coll of Technology (MT)
Montgomery Coll (MD)
Montgomery County Comm Coll (PA)
Moraine Park Tech Coll (WI)
Northampton Comm Coll (PA)
North Iowa Area Comm Coll (IA)
North Seattle Comm Coll (WA)
Oakland Comm Coll (MI)
Olympic Coll (WA)
Onondaga Comm Coll (NY)
Owens Comm Coll, Toledo (OH)
Pensacola State Coll (FL)
Polk State Coll (FL)
Pueblo Comm Coll (CO)
Raritan Valley Comm Coll (NJ)
Rogue Comm Coll (OR)
Saint Charles Comm Coll (MO)
Salt Lake Comm Coll (UT)
San Juan Coll (NM)
Southern State Comm Coll (OH)
South Suburban Coll (IL)
Southwestern Michigan Coll (MI)
Tallahassee Comm Coll (FL)
Tompkins Cortland Comm Coll (NY)
Union County Coll (NJ)
The U of Montana–Helena Coll of Technology (MT)
Wenatchee Valley Coll (WA)
Westmoreland County Comm Coll (PA)

ACTING
Casper Coll (WY)
Central Wyoming Coll (WY)
KD Studio (TX)
Northampton Comm Coll (PA)
Santa Barbara City Coll (CA)

ADMINISTRATIVE ASSISTANT AND SECRETARIAL SCIENCE
Aiken Tech Coll (SC)
Alexandria Tech and Comm Coll (MN)
Allen Comm Coll (KS)
Altamaha Tech Coll (GA)
Amarillo Coll (TX)
Antelope Valley Coll (CA)
Arkansas State U–Mountain Home (AR)
Athens Tech Coll (GA)
Augusta Tech Coll (GA)
Austin Comm Coll (TX)
Bainbridge Coll (GA)
Barton County Comm Coll (KS)

Beaufort County Comm Coll (NC)
Blackhawk Tech Coll (WI)
Borough of Manhattan Comm Coll of the City U of New York (NY)
Bryant & Stratton Coll (WI)
Career Tech Coll (LA)
Carroll Comm Coll (MD)
Casper Coll (WY)
Central Carolina Tech Coll (SC)
Central Comm Coll–Columbus Campus (NE)
Central Comm Coll–Grand Island Campus (NE)
Central Comm Coll–Hastings Campus (NE)
Central Georgia Tech Coll (GA)
Central Lakes Coll (MN)
Central Maine Comm Coll (ME)
Central New Mexico Comm Coll (NM)
Central Oregon Comm Coll (OR)
Central Wyoming Coll (WY)
Century Coll (MN)
Chattahoochee Tech Coll (GA)
Chippewa Valley Tech Coll (WI)
Cincinnati State Tech and Comm Coll (OH)
Cleveland State Comm Coll (TN)
Clovis Comm Coll (NM)
Coll of Lake County (IL)
Coll of the Canyons (CA)
Collin County Comm Coll District (TX)
Columbus Tech Coll (GA)
The Comm Coll of Baltimore County (MD)
Comm Coll of Rhode Island (RI)
Comm Coll of Vermont (VT)
Corning Comm Coll (NY)
Cowley County Comm Coll and Area Vocational–Tech School (KS)
Crowder Coll (MO)
Dabney S. Lancaster Comm Coll (VA)
Dakota Coll at Bottineau (ND)
Darton Coll (GA)
Dawson Comm Coll (MT)
Daytona State Coll (FL)
De Anza Coll (CA)
DeKalb Tech Coll (GA)
Denmark Tech Coll (SC)
Dodge City Comm Coll (KS)
Doña Ana Comm Coll (NM)
Dutchess Comm Coll (NY)
Eastern Gateway Comm Coll (OH)
East Los Angeles Coll (CA)
Elaine P. Nunez Comm Coll (LA)
Elgin Comm Coll (IL)
Fiorello H. LaGuardia Comm Coll of the City U of New York (NY)
Florida State Coll at Jacksonville (FL)
Fox Coll (IL)
Fox Valley Tech Coll (WI)
Frank Phillips Coll (TX)
Fulton-Montgomery Comm Coll (NY)
Gadsden State Comm Coll (AL)
GateWay Comm Coll (AZ)
Glendale Comm Coll (AZ)
Golden West Coll (CA)
Grand Rapids Comm Coll (MI)
Gwinnett Tech Coll (GA)
Harper Coll (IL)
Harrisburg Area Comm Coll (PA)
Harrison Coll, Anderson (IN)
Harrison Coll, Columbus (IN)
Harrison Coll, Indianapolis (IN)
Harrison Coll, Lafayette (IN)
Harrison Coll, Muncie (IN)
Harrison Coll (OH)
H. Councill Trenholm State Tech Coll (AL)
Highland Comm Coll (IL)
Holyoke Comm Coll (MA)
Housatonic Comm Coll (CT)
Howard Comm Coll (MD)
Illinois Eastern Comm Colls, Frontier Community College (IL)
Illinois Eastern Comm Colls, Olney Central College (IL)
Illinois Eastern Comm Colls, Wabash Valley College (IL)
Indian River State Coll (FL)
Jackson Comm Coll (MI)
Jamestown Business Coll (NY)

Jefferson Coll (MO)
Jefferson State Comm Coll (AL)
Johnston Comm Coll (NC)
John Tyler Comm Coll (VA)
John Wood Comm Coll (IL)
J. Sargeant Reynolds Comm Coll (VA)
Kankakee Comm Coll (IL)
Kent State U at Ashtabula (OH)
Kent State U at Salem (OH)
Kent State U at Tuscarawas (OH)
Kingsborough Comm Coll of the City U of New York (NY)
Kirtland Comm Coll (MI)
Lake Michigan Coll (MI)
Lake Region State Coll (ND)
Lake Superior Coll (MN)
Lanier Tech Coll (GA)
Lawson State Comm Coll (AL)
Leeward Comm Coll (HI)
Lincoln Land Comm Coll (IL)
Linn-Benton Comm Coll (OR)
Lonestar Coll–Kingwood (TX)
Lonestar Coll–Montgomery (TX)
Lonestar Coll–North Harris (TX)
Lonestar Coll–Tomball (TX)
Los Angeles Harbor Coll (CA)
Lower Columbia Coll (WA)
Lurleen B. Wallace Comm Coll (AL)
Macomb Comm Coll (MI)
Manchester Comm Coll (CT)
Marion Tech Coll (OH)
Martin Comm Coll (NC)
McHenry County Coll (IL)
Mendocino Coll (CA)
Mesabi Range Comm and Tech Coll (MN)
Mesa Comm Coll (AZ)
Metropolitan Comm Coll–Blue River (MO)
Metropolitan Comm Coll–Longview (MO)
Metropolitan Comm Coll–Maple Woods (MO)
Metropolitan Comm Coll–Penn Valley (MO)
Miami Dade Coll (FL)
Middle Georgia Tech Coll (GA)
Middlesex Comm Coll (CT)
Midlands Tech Coll (SC)
Mid-Plains Comm Coll, North Platte (NE)
Minnesota State Coll–Southeast Tech (MN)
Minnesota State Comm and Tech Coll (MN)
Minnesota West Comm and Tech Coll (MN)
Mohawk Valley Comm Coll (NY)
Monroe County Comm Coll (MI)
Montcalm Comm Coll (MI)
Montgomery County Comm Coll (PA)
Moraine Park Tech Coll (WI)
Moraine Valley Comm Coll (IL)
Morton Coll (IL)
Moultrie Tech Coll (GA)
Muskegon Comm Coll (MI)
New Mexico State U–Alamogordo (NM)
Newport Business Inst, Williamsport (PA)
Niagara County Comm Coll (NY)
Northampton Comm Coll (PA)
Northeast Comm Coll (NE)
Northeast Iowa Comm Coll (IA)
Northern Essex Comm Coll (MA)
North Georgia Tech Coll (GA)
North Idaho Coll (ID)
North Iowa Area Comm Coll (IA)
Northland Comm and Tech Coll–Thief River Falls & East Grand Forks (MN)
North Seattle Comm Coll (WA)
Northwest Coll (WY)
Northwest-Shoals Comm Coll (AL)
Northwest Tech Coll (MN)
Norwalk Comm Coll (CT)
Ocean County Coll (NJ)
Ogeechee Tech Coll (GA)
Okefenokee Tech Coll (GA)
Olympic Coll (WA)
Orange Coast Coll (CA)
Palm Beach State Coll (FL)
Panola Coll (TX)
Paul D. Camp Comm Coll (VA)
Pima Comm Coll (AZ)

Potomac State Coll of West Virginia U (WV)
Pratt Comm Coll (KS)
Quinsigamond Comm Coll (MA)
Rainy River Comm Coll (MN)
Raritan Valley Comm Coll (NJ)
Reid State Tech Coll (AL)
St. Philip's Coll (TX)
Sandersville Tech Coll (GA)
Sandhills Comm Coll (NC)
San Diego City Coll (CA)
Santa Barbara City Coll (CA)
Santa Fe Comm Coll (NM)
Sauk Valley Comm Coll (IL)
Savannah Tech Coll (GA)
Scottsdale Comm Coll (AZ)
Seminole State Coll of Florida (FL)
Sheridan Coll (WY)
Snow Coll (UT)
Southeastern Comm Coll (IA)
Southeastern Tech Coll (GA)
Southern Crescent Tech Coll (GA)
South Georgia Tech Coll (GA)
Southside Virginia Comm Coll (VA)
Southwestern Coll of Business, Franklin (OH)
Southwest Georgia Tech Coll (GA)
Southwest Mississippi Comm Coll (MS)
Spartanburg Comm Coll (SC)
Springfield Tech Comm Coll (MA)
Stark State Coll of Technology (OH)
Tallahassee Comm Coll (FL)
Three Rivers Comm Coll (CT)
Tompkins Cortland Comm Coll (NY)
Trident Tech Coll (SC)
Tyler Jr Coll (TX)
U of Alaska Anchorage, Kodiak Coll (AK)
Vincennes U Jasper Campus (IN)
Waubonsee Comm Coll (IL)
Waukesha County Tech Coll (WI)
Wenatchee Valley Coll (WA)
Westchester Comm Coll (NY)
Western Iowa Tech Comm Coll (IA)
West Georgia Tech Coll (GA)
West Virginia Northern Comm Coll (WV)
White Mountains Comm Coll (NH)
Wiregrass Georgia Tech Coll (GA)
Wisconsin Indianhead Tech Coll (WI)
Yakima Valley Comm Coll (WA)
Yavapai Coll (AZ)

ADULT AND CONTINUING EDUCATION
Comm Care Coll (OK)

ADULT DEVELOPMENT AND AGING
Albany Tech Coll (GA)
Central Georgia Tech Coll (GA)
Comm Coll of Rhode Island (RI)
Dakota Coll at Bottineau (ND)
Fiorello H. LaGuardia Comm Coll of the City U of New York (NY)

ADVERTISING
Dakota Coll at Bottineau (ND)
Fashion Inst of Technology (NY)
Mohawk Valley Comm Coll (NY)
Muskegon Comm Coll (MI)
St. Cloud Tech & Comm Coll (MN)
Southwest Mississippi Comm Coll (MS)

AERONAUTICAL/AEROSPACE ENGINEERING TECHNOLOGY
Cincinnati State Tech and Comm Coll (OH)
Delaware Tech & Comm Coll, Jack F. Owens Campus (DE)
GateWay Comm Coll (AZ)

AERONAUTICS/AVIATION/ AEROSPACE SCIENCE AND TECHNOLOGY
The Comm Coll of Baltimore County (MD)
Hesston Coll (KS)
Lehigh Carbon Comm Coll (PA)
Miami Dade Coll (FL)

Northland Comm and Tech Coll–Thief River Falls & East Grand Forks (MN)
Orange Coast Coll (CA)

AEROSPACE, AERONAUTICAL AND ASTRONAUTICAL/SPACE ENGINEERING
Kilgore Coll (TX)

AFRICAN AMERICAN/BLACK STUDIES
Ilisagvik Coll (AK)
Owens Comm Coll, Toledo (OH)
San Diego City Coll (CA)
Santa Barbara City Coll (CA)
Solano Comm Coll (CA)

AFRICAN STUDIES
Solano Comm Coll (CA)

AGRIBUSINESS
Burlington County Coll (NJ)
Clarendon Coll (TX)
Crowder Coll (MO)
Eastern Arizona Coll (AZ)
Harrisburg Area Comm Coll (PA)
James Sprunt Comm Coll (NC)
Laramie County Comm Coll (WY)
Minnesota West Comm and Tech Coll (MN)
Northeast Comm Coll (NE)
Northeast Iowa Comm Coll (IA)
Northwest Coll (WY)
Ogeechee Tech Coll (GA)
Yavapai Coll (AZ)

AGRICULTURAL AND DOMESTIC ANIMAL SERVICES RELATED
Central Wyoming Coll (WY)

AGRICULTURAL AND FOOD PRODUCTS PROCESSING
Minnesota State Comm and Tech Coll (MN)
Minnesota West Comm and Tech Coll (MN)
Northeast Iowa Comm Coll (IA)

AGRICULTURAL BUSINESS AND MANAGEMENT
Arizona Western Coll (AZ)
Barton County Comm Coll (KS)
Casper Coll (WY)
Central Comm Coll–Columbus Campus (NE)
Central Comm Coll–Hastings Campus (NE)
Central Wyoming Coll (WY)
Danville Area Comm Coll (IL)
Dawson Comm Coll (MT)
Delaware Tech & Comm Coll, Jack F. Owens Campus (DE)
Delaware Tech & Comm Coll, Stanton/Wilmington Campus (DE)
Delaware Tech & Comm Coll, Terry Campus (DE)
Dodge City Comm Coll (KS)
Frank Phillips Coll (TX)
Highland Comm Coll (IL)
Illinois Eastern Comm Colls, Wabash Valley College (IL)
Indian River State Coll (FL)
Jefferson State Comm Coll (AL)
John Wood Comm Coll (IL)
J. Sargeant Reynolds Comm Coll (VA)
Lake Region State Coll (ND)
Lamar Comm Coll (CO)
Linn-Benton Comm Coll (OR)
Lonestar Coll–Cy-Fair (TX)
Mesa Comm Coll (AZ)
North Dakota State Coll of Science (ND)
Owens Comm Coll, Toledo (OH)
Potomac State Coll of West Virginia U (WV)
Pratt Comm Coll (KS)
Santa Rosa Jr Coll (CA)
Sheridan Coll (WY)
Snow Coll (UT)
Southeastern Comm Coll (IA)

Terra State Comm Coll (OH)
Yakima Valley Comm Coll (WA)
Yavapai Coll (AZ)

AGRICULTURAL BUSINESS AND MANAGEMENT RELATED
Chippewa Valley Tech Coll (WI)
Penn State Beaver (PA)
Penn State Brandywine (PA)
Penn State DuBois (PA)
Penn State Fayette, The Eberly Campus (PA)
Penn State Greater Allegheny (PA)
Penn State Hazleton (PA)
Penn State Lehigh Valley (PA)
Penn State Mont Alto (PA)
Penn State New Kensington (PA)
Penn State Schuylkill (PA)
Penn State Shenango (PA)
Penn State Wilkes-Barre (PA)
Penn State Worthington Scranton (PA)
Penn State York (PA)

AGRICULTURAL BUSINESS TECHNOLOGY
Laramie County Comm Coll (WY)

AGRICULTURAL COMMUNICATION/ JOURNALISM
Northwest Coll (WY)

AGRICULTURAL ECONOMICS
Clarendon Coll (TX)
Dodge City Comm Coll (KS)
North Iowa Area Comm Coll (IA)
Potomac State Coll of West Virginia U (WV)
Pratt Comm Coll (KS)

AGRICULTURAL/FARM SUPPLIES RETAILING AND WHOLESALING
Fox Valley Tech Coll (WI)
Hawkeye Comm Coll (IA)
Minnesota West Comm and Tech Coll (MN)
North Iowa Area Comm Coll (IA)
Western Iowa Tech Comm Coll (IA)

AGRICULTURAL MECHANICS AND EQUIPMENT TECHNOLOGY
Northeast Comm Coll (NE)

AGRICULTURAL MECHANIZATION
Dodge City Comm Coll (KS)
Fox Valley Tech Coll (WI)
Highland Comm Coll (IL)
Mesa Comm Coll (AZ)
Metropolitan Comm Coll–Longview (MO)
Northeast Comm Coll (NE)
Owens Comm Coll, Toledo (OH)
Potomac State Coll of West Virginia U (WV)
Pratt Comm Coll (KS)
Santa Rosa Jr Coll (CA)
Southwest Georgia Tech Coll (GA)
Wenatchee Valley Coll (WA)
Yakima Valley Comm Coll (WA)

AGRICULTURAL POWER MACHINERY OPERATION
Dawson Comm Coll (MT)
Hawkeye Comm Coll (IA)
Northeast Iowa Comm Coll (IA)

AGRICULTURAL PRODUCTION
Allen Comm Coll (KS)
Delaware Tech & Comm Coll, Jack F. Owens Campus (DE)
Illinois Eastern Comm Colls, Wabash Valley College (IL)
Laramie County Comm Coll (WY)
Lincoln Land Comm Coll (IL)
Minnesota West Comm and Tech Coll (MN)
Northeast Iowa Comm Coll (IA)
North Iowa Area Comm Coll (IA)
Northwest Coll (WY)

Southern State Comm Coll (OH)
Wenatchee Valley Coll (WA)

AGRICULTURAL PRODUCTION RELATED
Yakima Valley Comm Coll (WA)

AGRICULTURAL TEACHER EDUCATION
Linn-Benton Comm Coll (OR)
Northwest Coll (WY)
Potomac State Coll of West Virginia U (WV)
Pratt Comm Coll (KS)
Trinity Valley Comm Coll (TX)

AGRICULTURE
Arizona Western Coll (AZ)
Bainbridge Coll (GA)
Barton County Comm Coll (KS)
Casper Coll (WY)
Central New Mexico Comm Coll (NM)
Chipola Coll (FL)
Clarendon Coll (TX)
Cowley County Comm Coll and Area Vocational–Tech School (KS)
Crowder Coll (MO)
Dakota Coll at Bottineau (ND)
Darton Coll (GA)
Eastern Arizona Coll (AZ)
Georgia Highlands Coll (GA)
Kankakee Comm Coll (IL)
Kaskaskia Coll (IL)
Kilgore Coll (TX)
Lamar Comm Coll (CO)
Laramie County Comm Coll (WY)
Linn-Benton Comm Coll (OR)
Macomb Comm Coll (MI)
Mendocino Coll (CA)
Miami Dade Coll (FL)
Minnesota West Comm and Tech Coll (MN)
Missouri State U–West Plains (MO)
Northeast Comm Coll (NE)
North Idaho Coll (ID)
Owensboro Comm and Tech Coll (KY)
Potomac State Coll of West Virginia U (WV)
Pratt Comm Coll (KS)
Santa Rosa Jr Coll (CA)
Sheridan Coll (WY)
Snow Coll (UT)
Tyler Jr Coll (TX)
Yakima Valley Comm Coll (WA)
Yavapai Coll (AZ)

AGRICULTURE AND AGRICULTURE OPERATIONS RELATED
Northeast Comm Coll (NE)
Potomac State Coll of West Virginia U (WV)
Sheridan Coll (WY)

AGRONOMY AND CROP SCIENCE
Chipola Coll (FL)
Dodge City Comm Coll (KS)
Lamar Comm Coll (CO)
Mesa Comm Coll (AZ)
Minnesota West Comm and Tech Coll (MN)
Northeast Comm Coll (NE)
Potomac State Coll of West Virginia U (WV)
Southeastern Comm Coll (IA)
Yakima Valley Comm Coll (WA)

AIRCRAFT POWERPLANT TECHNOLOGY
Antelope Valley Coll (CA)
Florida State Coll at Jacksonville (FL)
Hallmark Inst of Aeronautics (TX)
Linn State Tech Coll (MO)
Pima Comm Coll (AZ)
St. Philip's Coll (TX)

AIRFRAME MECHANICS AND AIRCRAFT MAINTENANCE TECHNOLOGY
Amarillo Coll (TX)

Antelope Valley Coll (CA)
Florida State Coll at Jacksonville (FL)
Hallmark Coll of Technology (TX)
Hallmark Inst of Aeronautics (TX)
Ivy Tech Comm Coll–Wabash Valley (IN)
Lake Superior Coll (MN)
Lincoln Land Comm Coll (IL)
Linn State Tech Coll (MO)
Middle Georgia Tech Coll (GA)
Mohawk Valley Comm Coll (NY)
Nashua Comm Coll (NH)
Oklahoma City Comm Coll (OK)
St. Philip's Coll (TX)
Solano Comm Coll (CA)
Trident Tech Coll (SC)
The U of Montana–Helena Coll of Technology (MT)

AIRLINE PILOT AND FLIGHT CREW
Big Bend Comm Coll (WA)
Casper Coll (WY)
Central Oregon Comm Coll (OR)
Chandler-Gilbert Comm Coll (AZ)
Florida State Coll at Jacksonville (FL)
Fox Valley Tech Coll (WI)
Indian River State Coll (FL)
Inver Hills Comm Coll (MN)
Jackson Comm Coll (MI)
Lake Superior Coll (MN)
Lehigh Carbon Comm Coll (PA)
Miami Dade Coll (FL)
Mountain View Coll (TX)
New England Inst of Technology (RI)
Orange Coast Coll (CA)
Palm Beach State Coll (FL)
Salt Lake Comm Coll (UT)

AIR TRAFFIC CONTROL
Miami Dade Coll (FL)

ALLIED HEALTH AND MEDICAL ASSISTING SERVICES RELATED
Cincinnati State Tech and Comm Coll (OH)
North Seattle Comm Coll (WA)

ALLIED HEALTH DIAGNOSTIC, INTERVENTION, AND TREATMENT PROFESSIONS RELATED
Ivy Tech Comm Coll–Wabash Valley (IN)
Kent State U at Salem (OH)
Union County Coll (NJ)

ALTERNATIVE AND COMPLEMENTARY MEDICAL SUPPORT SERVICES RELATED
Anoka-Ramsey Comm Coll (MN)
Anoka-Ramsey Comm Coll, Cambridge Campus (MN)

ALTERNATIVE AND COMPLEMENTARY MEDICINE RELATED
American Coll of Healthcare Sciences (OR)
Quinsigamond Comm Coll (MA)

AMERICAN GOVERNMENT AND POLITICS
Oklahoma City Comm Coll (OK)

AMERICAN INDIAN/NATIVE AMERICAN STUDIES
Central Wyoming Coll (WY)
Ilisagvik Coll (AK)
Kilian Comm Coll (SD)
North Idaho Coll (ID)
Pima Comm Coll (AZ)
Santa Barbara City Coll (CA)

AMERICAN SIGN LANGUAGE (ASL)
Burlington County Coll (NJ)
Oklahoma State U, Oklahoma City (OK)
Union County Coll (NJ)

AMERICAN SIGN LANGUAGE RELATED
Union County Coll (NJ)

AMERICAN STUDIES
Bucks County Comm Coll (PA)
Foothill Coll (CA)
Miami Dade Coll (FL)

ANIMAL HEALTH
Front Range Comm Coll (CO)

ANIMAL/LIVESTOCK HUSBANDRY AND PRODUCTION
Frank Phillips Coll (TX)
Hawkeye Comm Coll (IA)
Pratt Comm Coll (KS)

ANIMAL SCIENCES
Alamance Comm Coll (NC)
Casper Coll (WY)
Dodge City Comm Coll (KS)
James Sprunt Comm Coll (NC)
John Wood Comm Coll (IL)
Lamar Comm Coll (CO)
Linn-Benton Comm Coll (OR)
Niagara County Comm Coll (NY)
Northeast Comm Coll (NE)
Northwest Coll (WY)
Potomac State Coll of West Virginia U (WV)
Pratt Comm Coll (KS)
Santa Rosa Jr Coll (CA)
Snow Coll (UT)
Trinity Valley Comm Coll (TX)
Yakima Valley Comm Coll (WA)

ANIMAL SCIENCES RELATED
Pensacola State Coll (FL)

ANIMAL TRAINING
Lamar Comm Coll (CO)

ANIMATION, INTERACTIVE TECHNOLOGY, VIDEO GRAPHICS AND SPECIAL EFFECTS
The Art Inst of Seattle (WA)
Austin Comm Coll (TX)
Burlington County Coll (NJ)
Coll of the Canyons (CA)
Collin County Comm Coll District (TX)
Front Range Comm Coll (CO)
Hagerstown Comm Coll (MD)
Houston Comm Coll System (TX)
Kent State U at Tuscarawas (OH)
Lehigh Carbon Comm Coll (PA)
Lonestar Coll–Cy-Fair (TX)
Lonestar Coll–Kingwood (TX)
Lonestar Coll–Montgomery (TX)
Lonestar Coll–North Harris (TX)
Lonestar Coll–Tomball (TX)
McHenry County Coll (IL)
Montgomery Coll (MD)
New England Inst of Technology (RI)
New Mexico State U–Alamogordo (NM)
Olympic Coll (WA)
Pima Comm Coll (AZ)
Pueblo Comm Coll (CO)
Raritan Valley Comm Coll (NJ)
Red Rocks Comm Coll (CO)
Southeast Tech Inst (SD)
Springfield Tech Comm Coll (MA)
Sullivan Coll of Technology and Design (KY)
Terra State Comm Coll (OH)
Union County Coll (NJ)

ANTHROPOLOGY
Austin Comm Coll (TX)
Barton County Comm Coll (KS)
Casper Coll (WY)
Darton Coll (GA)
Eastern Arizona Coll (AZ)
East Los Angeles Coll (CA)
Foothill Coll (CA)
Great Basin Coll (NV)
Indian River State Coll (FL)
Laramie County Comm Coll (WY)
Lonestar Coll–Cy-Fair (TX)
Lonestar Coll–Kingwood (TX)

Lonestar Coll–Montgomery (TX)
Lonestar Coll–North Harris (TX)
Miami Dade Coll (FL)
Muskegon Comm Coll (MI)
North Idaho Coll (ID)
Northwest Coll (WY)
Orange Coast Coll (CA)
Pima Comm Coll (AZ)
San Diego City Coll (CA)
Santa Barbara City Coll (CA)
Santa Rosa Jr Coll (CA)

APPAREL AND ACCESSORIES MARKETING
El Centro Coll (TX)
FIDM/The Fashion Inst of Design & Merchandising, Los Angeles Campus (CA)
FIDM/The Fashion Inst of Design & Merchandising, San Diego Campus (CA)
FIDM/The Fashion Inst of Design & Merchandising, San Francisco Campus (CA)

APPAREL AND TEXTILE MANUFACTURING
Fashion Inst of Technology (NY)
Westchester Comm Coll (NY)

APPAREL AND TEXTILES
Antelope Valley Coll (CA)
FIDM/The Fashion Inst of Design & Merchandising, Los Angeles Campus (CA)
FIDM/The Fashion Inst of Design & Merchandising, Orange County Campus (CA)
FIDM/The Fashion Inst of Design & Merchandising, San Francisco Campus (CA)
Indian River State Coll (FL)
Palm Beach State Coll (FL)

APPLIED HORTICULTURE/ HORTICULTURAL BUSINESS SERVICES RELATED
Chippewa Valley Tech Coll (WI)
Cincinnati State Tech and Comm Coll (OH)
Dakota Coll at Bottineau (ND)
Northeast Comm Coll (NE)

APPLIED HORTICULTURE/ HORTICULTURE OPERATIONS
Alamance Comm Coll (NC)
Catawba Valley Comm Coll (NC)
Central Comm Coll–Hastings Campus (NE)
Central Lakes Coll (MN)
Clark Coll (WA)
Dakota Coll at Bottineau (ND)
Delaware Tech & Comm Coll, Jack F. Owens Campus (DE)
Fayetteville Tech Comm Coll (NC)
Front Range Comm Coll (CO)
Harford Comm Coll (MD)
Hawkeye Comm Coll (IA)
Houston Comm Coll System (TX)
John Wood Comm Coll (IL)
Kankakee Comm Coll (IL)
Kent State U at Geauga (OH)
Kent State U at Salem (OH)
Lake Michigan Coll (MI)
McHenry County Coll (IL)
Montgomery Coll (MD)
Northeast Comm Coll (NE)
Santa Barbara City Coll (CA)
Southeast Tech Inst (SD)
Spartanburg Comm Coll (SC)
Westmoreland County Comm Coll (PA)

APPLIED MATHEMATICS
Muskegon Comm Coll (MI)

AQUACULTURE
Hillsborough Comm Coll (FL)
Yavapai Coll (AZ)

ARCHEOLOGY
Northwest Coll (WY)

ARCHITECTURAL DRAFTING AND CAD/CADD

Brown Mackie Coll–Albuquerque (NM)
Brown Mackie Coll–San Antonio (TX)
Carroll Comm Coll (MD)
Central New Mexico Comm Coll (NM)
Coll of Lake County (IL)
Coll of the Canyons (CA)
The Comm Coll of Baltimore County (MD)
Florida State Coll at Jacksonville (FL)
Glendale Comm Coll (AZ)
Harper Coll (IL)
Hawkeye Comm Coll (IA)
Indian River State Coll (FL)
Kaskaskia Coll (IL)
Lake Superior Coll (MN)
Lincoln Land Comm Coll (IL)
Macomb Comm Coll (MI)
Miami Dade Coll (FL)
Minnesota State Comm and Tech Coll (MN)
Montgomery Coll (MD)
Montgomery County Comm Coll (PA)
Northeast Comm Coll (NE)
North Seattle Comm Coll (WA)
Owens Comm Coll, Toledo (OH)
Phoenix Coll (AZ)
Pima Comm Coll (AZ)
Pittsburgh Tech Inst, Oakdale (PA)
St. Cloud Tech & Comm Coll (MN)
Santa Fe Comm Coll (NM)
South Suburban Coll (IL)
Sullivan Coll of Technology and Design (KY)
Waukesha County Tech Coll (WI)
Westmoreland County Comm Coll (PA)
Yavapai Coll (AZ)

ARCHITECTURAL ENGINEERING TECHNOLOGY

Amarillo Coll (TX)
Cape Fear Comm Coll (NC)
Catawba Valley Comm Coll (NC)
Central Maine Comm Coll (ME)
Cincinnati State Tech and Comm Coll (OH)
Comm Coll of Philadelphia (PA)
Daytona State Coll (FL)
Delaware Tech & Comm Coll, Jack F. Owens Campus (DE)
Delaware Tech & Comm Coll, Stanton/Wilmington Campus (DE)
Delaware Tech & Comm Coll, Terry Campus (DE)
Doña Ana Comm Coll (NM)
Dutchess Comm Coll (NY)
East Los Angeles Coll (CA)
Fayetteville Tech Comm Coll (NC)
Florida State Coll at Jacksonville (FL)
Front Range Comm Coll (CO)
Golden West Coll (CA)
Grand Rapids Comm Coll (MI)
Harper Coll (IL)
Harrisburg Area Comm Coll (PA)
Hillsborough Comm Coll (FL)
Honolulu Comm Coll (HI)
John Tyler Comm Coll (VA)
Los Angeles Harbor Coll (CA)
Miami Dade Coll (FL)
Midlands Tech Coll (SC)
Monroe County Comm Coll (MI)
New England Inst of Technology (RI)
Northampton Comm Coll (PA)
North Dakota State Coll of Science (ND)
Northland Comm and Tech Coll–Thief River Falls & East Grand Forks (MN)
Norwalk Comm Coll (CT)
Oakland Comm Coll (MI)
Oklahoma State U, Oklahoma City (OK)
Onondaga Comm Coll (NY)
Orange Coast Coll (CA)
Owens Comm Coll, Toledo (OH)

Penn State Fayette, The Eberly Campus (PA)
Penn State Worthington Scranton (PA)
Salt Lake Comm Coll (UT)
Sandhills Comm Coll (NC)
Seminole State Coll of Florida (FL)
Southeast Tech Inst (SD)
Stark State Coll of Technology (OH)
Sullivan Coll of Technology and Design (KY)
Terra State Comm Coll (OH)
Three Rivers Comm Coll (CT)
Wisconsin Indianhead Tech Coll (WI)

ARCHITECTURAL TECHNOLOGY

Arizona Western Coll (AZ)
John Tyler Comm Coll (VA)
Onondaga Comm Coll (NY)

ARCHITECTURE

Allen Comm Coll (KS)
Barton County Comm Coll (KS)
Clarendon Coll (TX)
Harrisburg Area Comm Coll (PA)
Howard Comm Coll (MD)
Kilgore Coll (TX)
Lonestar Coll–Cy-Fair (TX)
Lonestar Coll–Kingwood (TX)
Lonestar Coll–Montgomery (TX)
Lonestar Coll–North Harris (TX)
Santa Rosa Jr Coll (CA)
Sauk Valley Comm Coll (IL)

ARCHITECTURE RELATED

Santa Rosa Jr Coll (CA)
Sullivan Coll of Technology and Design (KY)

AREA STUDIES RELATED

Central Wyoming Coll (WY)

ARMY ROTC/MILITARY SCIENCE

Georgia Military Coll (GA)

ART

Allen Comm Coll (KS)
Amarillo Coll (TX)
Austin Comm Coll (TX)
Bainbridge Coll (GA)
Barton County Comm Coll (KS)
Berkeley City Coll (CA)
Bucks County Comm Coll (PA)
Burlington County Coll (NJ)
Carroll Comm Coll (MD)
Casper Coll (WY)
Cayuga County Comm Coll (NY)
Central New Mexico Comm Coll (NM)
Central Oregon Comm Coll (OR)
Central Wyoming Coll (WY)
Chipola Coll (FL)
Clarendon Coll (TX)
Coll of Lake County (IL)
Coll of the Canyons (CA)
Comm Coll of Philadelphia (PA)
Comm Coll of Rhode Island (RI)
Comm Coll of Vermont (VT)
Cowley County Comm Coll and Area Vocational–Tech School (KS)
Crowder Coll (MO)
Darton Coll (GA)
De Anza Coll (CA)
Dodge City Comm Coll (KS)
Douglas Education Center (PA)
Eastern Arizona Coll (AZ)
East Los Angeles Coll (CA)
Edison State Comm Coll (OH)
Foothill Coll (CA)
Frederick Comm Coll (MD)
Fulton-Montgomery Comm Coll (NY)
Georgia Highlands Coll (GA)
Golden West Coll (CA)
Grand Rapids Comm Coll (MI)
Great Basin Coll (NV)
Harper Coll (IL)
Harrisburg Area Comm Coll (PA)
Highland Comm Coll (IL)
Holyoke Comm Coll (MA)

Housatonic Comm Coll (CT)
Howard Comm Coll (MD)
Kilgore Coll (TX)
Kingsborough Comm Coll of the City U of New York (NY)
Kirtland Comm Coll (MI)
Lake Michigan Coll (MI)
Laramie County Comm Coll (WY)
Lehigh Carbon Comm Coll (PA)
Linn-Benton Comm Coll (OR)
Lonestar Coll–Cy-Fair (TX)
Lonestar Coll–Kingwood (TX)
Lonestar Coll–Montgomery (TX)
Lonestar Coll–North Harris (TX)
Lonestar Coll–Tomball (TX)
Mendocino Coll (CA)
Mesa Comm Coll (AZ)
Miami Dade Coll (FL)
Minnesota State Comm and Tech Coll (MN)
Mohave Comm Coll (AZ)
Mohawk Valley Comm Coll (NY)
Monroe County Comm Coll (MI)
Montgomery Coll (MD)
Montgomery County Comm Coll (PA)
Morton Coll (IL)
Muskegon Comm Coll (MI)
Northeast Comm Coll (NE)
North Idaho Coll (ID)
North Seattle Comm Coll (WA)
Northwest Coll (WY)
Norwalk Comm Coll (CT)
Oklahoma City Comm Coll (OK)
Oklahoma State U, Oklahoma City (OK)
Onondaga Comm Coll (NY)
Orange Coast Coll (CA)
Palm Beach State Coll (FL)
Phoenix Coll (AZ)
Pratt Comm Coll (KS)
Quinsigamond Comm Coll (MA)
Red Rocks Comm Coll (CO)
St. Philip's Coll (TX)
Sandhills Comm Coll (NC)
San Diego City Coll (CA)
Santa Fe Comm Coll (NM)
Santa Rosa Jr Coll (CA)
Sauk Valley Comm Coll (IL)
Sheridan Coll (WY)
Snow Coll (UT)
Solano Comm Coll (CA)
Suffolk County Comm Coll (NY)
Trinity Valley Comm Coll (TX)
Tyler Jr Coll (TX)

ART HISTORY, CRITICISM AND CONSERVATION

De Anza Coll (CA)
Foothill Coll (CA)
Muskegon Comm Coll (MI)
Palm Beach State Coll (FL)
Santa Barbara City Coll (CA)
Santa Fe Comm Coll (NM)
Santa Rosa Jr Coll (CA)
Terra State Comm Coll (OH)

ARTIFICIAL INTELLIGENCE

Metropolitan Comm Coll–Business & Technology Campus (MO)
San Diego City Coll (CA)
Southeastern Comm Coll (IA)
Sullivan Coll of Technology and Design (KY)

ART TEACHER EDUCATION

Casper Coll (WY)
Darton Coll (GA)
Eastern Arizona Coll (AZ)
Indian River State Coll (FL)
Muskegon Comm Coll (MI)
Pratt Comm Coll (KS)
Sandhills Comm Coll (NC)

ASIAN STUDIES

East Los Angeles Coll (CA)
Miami Dade Coll (FL)

ASTRONOMY

Lonestar Coll–Kingwood (TX)
Lonestar Coll–Montgomery (TX)
North Idaho Coll (ID)

ATHLETIC TRAINING

Allen Comm Coll (KS)

Barton County Comm Coll (KS)
Brown Mackie Coll–Fort Wayne (IN)
Brown Mackie Coll–Kansas City (KS)
Brown Mackie Coll–Salina (KS)
Brown Mackie Coll–Tucson (AZ)
Casper Coll (WY)
Central Wyoming Coll (WY)
Coll of the Canyons (CA)
Dodge City Comm Coll (KS)
Foothill Coll (CA)
Lake Michigan Coll (MI)
Northampton Comm Coll (PA)
North Idaho Coll (ID)
Northwest Coll (WY)
Orange Coast Coll (CA)
Pratt Comm Coll (KS)
Santa Barbara City Coll (CA)
Sauk Valley Comm Coll (IL)
Wenatchee Valley Coll (WA)

AUDIOLOGY AND SPEECH-LANGUAGE PATHOLOGY

Miami Dade Coll (FL)

AUDIOVISUAL COMMUNICATIONS TECHNOLOGIES RELATED

Brown Mackie Coll–Cincinnati (OH)
Lonestar Coll–Montgomery (TX)

AUTOBODY/COLLISION AND REPAIR TECHNOLOGY

Antelope Valley Coll (CA)
Bellingham Tech Coll (WA)
Casper Coll (WY)
Central Comm Coll–Hastings Campus (NE)
Century Coll (MN)
The Comm Coll of Baltimore County (MD)
Corning Comm Coll (NY)
Dakota County Tech Coll (MN)
Eastfield Coll (TX)
Florida State Coll at Jacksonville (FL)
Fox Valley Tech Coll (WI)
Hawkeye Comm Coll (IA)
H. Councill Trenholm State Tech Coll (AL)
Highland Comm Coll (IL)
Illinois Eastern Comm Colls, Olney Central College (IL)
Kaskaskia Coll (IL)
Kilgore Coll (TX)
Laramie County Comm Coll (WY)
Lincoln Land Comm Coll (IL)
Linn State Tech Coll (MO)
Mid-Plains Comm Coll, North Platte (NE)
Minnesota State Coll–Southeast Tech (MN)
Minnesota State Comm and Tech Coll (MN)
Montana State U–Great Falls Coll of Technology (MT)
Nashua Comm Coll (NH)
New England Inst of Technology (RI)
North Dakota State Coll of Science (ND)
Northeast Comm Coll (NE)
Northland Comm and Tech Coll–Thief River Falls & East Grand Forks (MN)
Pennco Tech (PA)
Pueblo Comm Coll (CO)
Randolph Comm Coll (NC)
St. Cloud Tech & Comm Coll (MN)
St. Philip's Coll (TX)
Salt Lake Comm Coll (UT)
San Juan Coll (NM)
Southeast Tech Inst (SD)
U of Arkansas Comm Coll at Morrilton (AR)
Waubonsee Comm Coll (IL)
Waukesha County Tech Coll (WI)
Western Iowa Tech Comm Coll (IA)

AUTOMATION ENGINEER TECHNOLOGY

Clovis Comm Coll (NM)

AUTOMOBILE/AUTOMOTIVE MECHANICS TECHNOLOGY

Aiken Tech Coll (SC)
Alamance Comm Coll (NC)
Amarillo Coll (TX)
Antelope Valley Coll (CA)
Austin Comm Coll (TX)
Barton County Comm Coll (KS)
Beaufort County Comm Coll (NC)
Bellingham Tech Coll (WA)
Big Bend Comm Coll (WA)
Blue Ridge Comm and Tech Coll (WV)
Cape Fear Comm Coll (NC)
Casper Coll (WY)
Catawba Valley Comm Coll (NC)
Central Comm Coll–Columbus Campus (NE)
Central Comm Coll–Grand Island Campus (NE)
Central Comm Coll–Hastings Campus (NE)
Central Maine Comm Coll (ME)
Central Oregon Comm Coll (OR)
Central Wyoming Coll (WY)
Century Coll (MN)
Chattahoochee Tech Coll (GA)
City Colls of Chicago, Harry S. Truman College (IL)
Clark Coll (WA)
Clovis Comm Coll (NM)
Coll of Central Florida (FL)
Coll of Lake County (IL)
Coll of the Canyons (CA)
Columbus Tech Coll (GA)
The Comm Coll of Baltimore County (MD)
Comm Coll of Philadelphia (PA)
Corning Comm Coll (NY)
Cowley County Comm Coll and Area Vocational–Tech School (KS)
Dakota County Tech Coll (MN)
Danville Area Comm Coll (IL)
Daytona State Coll (FL)
De Anza Coll (CA)
DeKalb Tech Coll (GA)
Delaware Tech & Comm Coll, Jack F. Owens Campus (DE)
Delaware Tech & Comm Coll, Stanton/Wilmington Campus (DE)
Denmark Tech Coll (SC)
Dodge City Comm Coll (KS)
Doña Ana Comm Coll (NM)
Eastern Arizona Coll (AZ)
Eastfield Coll (TX)
East Los Angeles Coll (CA)
Elgin Comm Coll (IL)
Fayetteville Tech Comm Coll (NC)
Florida State Coll at Jacksonville (FL)
Fox Valley Tech Coll (WI)
Front Range Comm Coll (CO)
Fulton-Montgomery Comm Coll (NY)
GateWay Comm Coll (AZ)
Gateway Comm Coll (CT)
Georgia Highlands Coll (GA)
Glendale Comm Coll (AZ)
Golden West Coll (CA)
Grand Rapids Comm Coll (MI)
Grays Harbor Coll (WA)
Gwinnett Tech Coll (GA)
Harrisburg Area Comm Coll (PA)
Hawkeye Comm Coll (IA)
Highland Comm Coll (IL)
Honolulu Comm Coll (HI)
Houston Comm Coll System (TX)
Illinois Eastern Comm Colls, Frontier Community College (IL)
Illinois Eastern Comm Colls, Olney Central College (IL)
Indian River State Coll (FL)
Ivy Tech Comm Coll–Central Indiana (IN)
Ivy Tech Comm Coll–Columbus (IN)
Ivy Tech Comm Coll–East Central (IN)
Ivy Tech Comm Coll–Kokomo (IN)
Ivy Tech Comm Coll–Lafayette (IN)
Ivy Tech Comm Coll–North Central (IN)
Ivy Tech Comm Coll–Northeast (IN)
Ivy Tech Comm Coll–Northwest (IN)

Ivy Tech Comm Coll–Richmond (IN)
Ivy Tech Comm Coll–Southern Indiana (IN)
Ivy Tech Comm Coll–Southwest (IN)
Ivy Tech Comm Coll–Wabash Valley (IN)
Jackson Comm Coll (MI)
Jefferson Coll (MO)
Kankakee Comm Coll (IL)
Kaskaskia Coll (IL)
Kent State U at Trumbull (OH)
Kilgore Coll (TX)
Kirtland Comm Coll (MI)
Lake Region State Coll (ND)
Lake Superior Coll (MN)
Laramie County Comm Coll (WY)
Leeward Comm Coll (HI)
Lincoln Land Comm Coll (IL)
Linn-Benton Comm Coll (OR)
Linn State Tech Coll (MO)
Lonestar Coll–Montgomery (TX)
Lonestar Coll–North Harris (TX)
Los Angeles Harbor Coll (CA)
Lower Columbia Coll (WA)
Macomb Comm Coll (MI)
Martin Comm Coll (NC)
McHenry County Coll (IL)
Mendocino Coll (CA)
Mesa Comm Coll (AZ)
Metropolitan Comm Coll–Longview (MO)
Midlands Tech Coll (SC)
Mid-Plains Comm Coll, North Platte (NE)
Minnesota West Comm and Tech Coll (MN)
Mohave Comm Coll (AZ)
Montcalm Comm Coll (MI)
Montgomery Coll (MD)
Moraine Park Tech Coll (WI)
Moraine Valley Comm Coll (IL)
Morton Coll (IL)
Muskegon Comm Coll (MI)
Nashua Comm Coll (NH)
New England Inst of Technology (RI)
Northampton Comm Coll (PA)
North Dakota State Coll of Science (ND)
Northeast Comm Coll (NE)
Northeast Iowa Comm Coll (IA)
North Idaho Coll (ID)
North Iowa Area Comm Coll (IA)
Northland Comm and Tech Coll–Thief River Falls & East Grand Forks (MN)
Northwest Tech Coll (MN)
Ogeechee Tech Coll (GA)
Oklahoma City Comm Coll (OK)
Oklahoma Tech Coll (OK)
Olympic Coll (WA)
Onondaga Comm Coll (NY)
Pensacola State Coll (FL)
Pima Comm Coll (AZ)
Pratt Comm Coll (KS)
Pueblo Comm Coll (CO)
Quinsigamond Comm Coll (MA)
Randolph Comm Coll (NC)
Rogue Comm Coll (OR)
St. Cloud Tech & Comm Coll (MN)
St. Philip's Coll (TX)
Sandhills Comm Coll (NC)
San Diego City Coll (CA)
San Juan Coll (NM)
Santa Barbara City Coll (CA)
Santa Rosa Jr Coll (CA)
Savannah Tech Coll (GA)
Seminole State Coll of Florida (FL)
Snow Coll (UT)
Solano Comm Coll (CA)
Southeastern Comm Coll (IA)
Southeast Tech Inst (SD)
Southern Crescent Tech Coll (GA)
Southwestern Michigan Coll (MI)
Southwest Mississippi Comm Coll (MS)
Spartanburg Comm Coll (SC)
Stark State Coll of Technology (OH)
State U of New York Coll of Technology at Alfred (NY)
Suffolk County Comm Coll (NY)
Trident Tech Coll (SC)
Trinity Valley Comm Coll (TX)
Tyler Jr Coll (TX)
Union County Coll (NJ)
U of Arkansas Comm Coll at Morrilton (AR)

The U of Montana–Helena Coll of Technology (MT)
Waubonsee Comm Coll (IL)
Waukesha County Tech Coll (WI)
Wenatchee Valley Coll (WA)
Western Iowa Tech Comm Coll (IA)
West Georgia Tech Coll (GA)
White Mountains Comm Coll (NH)
WyoTech, Fremont (CA)
Yakima Valley Comm Coll (WA)
Yavapai Coll (AZ)

AUTOMOTIVE ENGINEERING TECHNOLOGY

Burlington County Coll (NJ)
Central New Mexico Comm Coll (NM)
Cincinnati State Tech and Comm Coll (OH)
Corning Comm Coll (NY)
H. Councill Trenholm State Tech Coll (AL)
Lawson State Comm Coll (AL)
Macomb Comm Coll (MI)
Massachusetts Bay Comm Coll (MA)
Minnesota State Comm and Tech Coll (MN)
Montgomery County Comm Coll (PA)
Moraine Park Tech Coll (WI)
Owens Comm Coll, Toledo (OH)
Raritan Valley Comm Coll (NJ)
Springfield Tech Comm Coll (MA)
Terra State Comm Coll (OH)
WyoTech, Fremont (CA)

AVIATION/AIRWAY MANAGEMENT

Florida State Coll at Jacksonville (FL)
Inver Hills Comm Coll (MN)
Lake Superior Coll (MN)
Lincoln Land Comm Coll (IL)
Lonestar Coll–North Harris (TX)
Miami Dade Coll (FL)
Mountain View Coll (TX)
Northland Comm and Tech Coll–Thief River Falls & East Grand Forks (MN)

AVIONICS MAINTENANCE TECHNOLOGY

Antelope Valley Coll (CA)
Big Bend Comm Coll (WA)
Foothill Coll (CA)
Fox Valley Tech Coll (WI)
Gateway Comm Coll (CT)
Honolulu Comm Coll (HI)
Housatonic Comm Coll (CT)
Kankakee Comm Coll (IL)
Lake Region State Coll (ND)
Metropolitan Comm Coll–Maple Woods (MO)
Oklahoma City Comm Coll (OK)
Orange Coast Coll (CA)
Salt Lake Comm Coll (UT)
Solano Comm Coll (CA)
Three Rivers Comm Coll (CT)

BAKING AND PASTRY ARTS

The Art Inst of Seattle (WA)
Clark Coll (WA)
El Centro Coll (TX)
Elgin Comm Coll (IL)
Harrison Coll, Indianapolis (IN)
Montgomery County Comm Coll (PA)
The Restaurant School at Walnut Hill Coll (PA)
Westmoreland County Comm Coll (PA)
White Mountains Comm Coll (NH)

BANKING AND FINANCIAL SUPPORT SERVICES

Alamance Comm Coll (NC)
Alexandria Tech and Comm Coll (MN)
Allen Comm Coll (KS)
Austin Comm Coll (TX)
Barton County Comm Coll (KS)
Bristol Comm Coll (MA)
Catawba Valley Comm Coll (NC)
Central Georgia Tech Coll (GA)

Central New Mexico Comm Coll (NM)
Comm Coll of Rhode Island (RI)
Fayetteville Tech Comm Coll (NC)
Florida State Coll at Jacksonville (FL)
Fox Valley Tech Coll (WI)
Harper Coll (IL)
Harrisburg Area Comm Coll (PA)
Harrison Coll, Anderson (IN)
Harrison Coll, Columbus (IN)
Harrison Coll, Lafayette (IN)
Houston Comm Coll System (TX)
Indian River State Coll (FL)
Lanier Tech Coll (GA)
Mohawk Valley Comm Coll (NY)
Northeast Comm Coll (NE)
Ogeechee Tech Coll (GA)
Owens Comm Coll, Toledo (OH)
Pennsylvania Highlands Comm Coll (PA)
Phoenix Coll (AZ)
St. Cloud Tech & Comm Coll (MN)
Santa Fe Comm Coll (NM)
Seminole State Coll of Florida (FL)
Southeast Tech Inst (SD)
Terra State Comm Coll (OH)
Westmoreland County Comm Coll (PA)
Wiregrass Georgia Tech Coll (GA)

BARBERING

Oklahoma Tech Coll (OK)

BEHAVIORAL ASPECTS OF HEALTH

Darton Coll (GA)

BEHAVIORAL SCIENCES

Amarillo Coll (TX)
Ancilla Coll (IN)
Clarendon Coll (TX)
Colorado Mountain Coll (CO)
Colorado Mountain Coll, Alpine Campus (CO)
De Anza Coll (CA)
Dodge City Comm Coll (KS)
Fulton-Montgomery Comm Coll (NY)
Glendale Comm Coll (AZ)
Miami Dade Coll (FL)
Orange Coast Coll (CA)
San Diego City Coll (CA)
Santa Fe Comm Coll (NM)
Santa Rosa Jr Coll (CA)
Tyler Jr Coll (TX)
Vincennes U Jasper Campus (IN)

BIBLICAL STUDIES

Amarillo Coll (TX)
Hesston Coll (KS)

BILINGUAL AND MULTILINGUAL EDUCATION

Delaware Tech & Comm Coll, Terry Campus (DE)

BIOCHEMISTRY AND MOLECULAR BIOLOGY

Minnesota State Comm and Tech Coll (MN)

BIOENGINEERING AND BIOMEDICAL ENGINEERING

Anoka-Ramsey Comm Coll (MN)
Anoka-Ramsey Comm Coll, Cambridge Campus (MN)

BIOLOGICAL AND BIOMEDICAL SCIENCES RELATED

Darton Coll (GA)
Northeast Comm Coll (NE)

BIOLOGICAL AND PHYSICAL SCIENCES

Ancilla Coll (IN)
Burlington County Coll (NJ)
Central Oregon Comm Coll (OR)
Chipola Coll (FL)
City Colls of Chicago, Harry S. Truman College (IL)
Coll of Lake County (IL)
Coll of the Canyons (CA)
Colorado Mountain Coll (CO)

Colorado Mountain Coll, Alpine Campus (CO)
Comm Coll of Rhode Island (RI)
Corning Comm Coll (NY)
Dabney S. Lancaster Comm Coll (VA)
Dodge City Comm Coll (KS)
Dutchess Comm Coll (NY)
Elgin Comm Coll (IL)
Fulton-Montgomery Comm Coll (NY)
Georgia Highlands Coll (GA)
Golden West Coll (CA)
Highland Comm Coll (IL)
Howard Comm Coll (MD)
Illinois Eastern Comm Colls, Frontier Community College (IL)
Illinois Eastern Comm Colls, Lincoln Trail College (IL)
Illinois Eastern Comm Colls, Olney Central College (IL)
Illinois Eastern Comm Colls, Wabash Valley College (IL)
John Wood Comm Coll (IL)
J. Sargeant Reynolds Comm Coll (VA)
Kankakee Comm Coll (IL)
Kaskaskia Coll (IL)
Kilgore Coll (TX)
Kirtland Comm Coll (MI)
Lamar Comm Coll (CO)
Laramie County Comm Coll (WY)
Lincoln Land Comm Coll (IL)
Linn-Benton Comm Coll (OR)
Massachusetts Bay Comm Coll (MA)
McHenry County Coll (IL)
Metropolitan Comm Coll–Longview (MO)
Metropolitan Comm Coll–Maple Woods (MO)
Metropolitan Comm Coll–Penn Valley (MO)
Middlesex Comm Coll (CT)
Moraine Valley Comm Coll (IL)
Morton Coll (IL)
Niagara County Comm Coll (NY)
Northern Essex Comm Coll (MA)
North Idaho Coll (ID)
Penn State Beaver (PA)
Penn State DuBois (PA)
Penn State Fayette, The Eberly Campus (PA)
Penn State Greater Allegheny (PA)
Penn State New Kensington (PA)
Penn State Schuylkill (PA)
Penn State Shenango (PA)
Potomac State Coll of West Virginia U (WV)
Pratt Comm Coll (KS)
Rainy River Comm Coll (MN)
Sandhills Comm Coll (NC)
Sheridan Coll (WY)
Solano Comm Coll (CA)
Southside Virginia Comm Coll (VA)
South Suburban Coll (IL)
Southwest Mississippi Comm Coll (MS)
Suffolk County Comm Coll (NY)
Terra State Comm Coll (OH)
Trident Tech Coll (SC)
U of South Carolina Union (SC)
U of Wisconsin–Richland (WI)
Waubonsee Comm Coll (IL)

BIOLOGY/BIOLOGICAL SCIENCES

Allen Comm Coll (KS)
Amarillo Coll (TX)
Ancilla Coll (IN)
Anoka-Ramsey Comm Coll (MN)
Anoka-Ramsey Comm Coll, Cambridge Campus (MN)
Antelope Valley Coll (CA)
Arizona Western Coll (AZ)
Austin Comm Coll (TX)
Bainbridge Coll (GA)
Barton County Comm Coll (KS)
Bucks County Comm Coll (PA)
Burlington County Coll (NJ)
Carl Albert State Coll (OK)
Casper Coll (WY)
Cecil Coll (MD)
Central Oregon Comm Coll (OR)
Central Wyoming Coll (WY)
Clarendon Coll (TX)
Colorado Mountain Coll (CO)

Colorado Mountain Coll, Alpine Campus (CO)
Cowley County Comm Coll and Area Vocational–Tech School (KS)
Crowder Coll (MO)
Dakota Coll at Bottineau (ND)
Darton Coll (GA)
De Anza Coll (CA)
Delaware Tech & Comm Coll, Jack F. Owens Campus (DE)
Delaware Tech & Comm Coll, Stanton/Wilmington Campus (DE)
Dodge City Comm Coll (KS)
Eastern Arizona Coll (AZ)
East Los Angeles Coll (CA)
Fiorello H. LaGuardia Comm Coll of the City U of New York (NY)
Foothill Coll (CA)
Frank Phillips Coll (TX)
Frederick Comm Coll (MD)
Fulton-Montgomery Comm Coll (NY)
Georgia Military Coll (GA)
Golden West Coll (CA)
Harper Coll (IL)
Harrisburg Area Comm Coll (PA)
Indian River State Coll (FL)
Inver Hills Comm Coll (MN)
Kingsborough Comm Coll of the City U of New York (NY)
Lake Michigan Coll (MI)
Lamar Comm Coll (CO)
Laramie County Comm Coll (WY)
Lehigh Carbon Comm Coll (PA)
Linn-Benton Comm Coll (OR)
Lonestar Coll–Cy-Fair (TX)
Lonestar Coll–Kingwood (TX)
Lonestar Coll–Montgomery (TX)
Lonestar Coll–North Harris (TX)
Lonestar Coll–Tomball (TX)
Los Angeles Harbor Coll (CA)
Macomb Comm Coll (MI)
Mendocino Coll (CA)
Mesa Comm Coll (AZ)
Metropolitan Comm Coll–Longview (MO)
Metropolitan Comm Coll–Maple Woods (MO)
Metropolitan Comm Coll–Penn Valley (MO)
Miami Dade Coll (FL)
Minnesota State Comm and Tech Coll (MN)
Monroe County Comm Coll (MI)
Montgomery County Comm Coll (PA)
Northampton Comm Coll (PA)
Northeast Comm Coll (NE)
North Hennepin Comm Coll (MN)
North Idaho Coll (ID)
Northwest Coll (WY)
Oklahoma City Comm Coll (OK)
Orange Coast Coll (CA)
Owens Comm Coll, Toledo (OH)
Palm Beach State Coll (FL)
Potomac State Coll of West Virginia U (WV)
Pratt Comm Coll (KS)
Red Rocks Comm Coll (CO)
Saint Charles Comm Coll (MO)
St. Philip's Coll (TX)
Salt Lake Comm Coll (UT)
San Diego City Coll (CA)
San Juan Coll (NM)
Santa Barbara City Coll (CA)
Santa Fe Comm Coll (NM)
Santa Rosa Jr Coll (CA)
Sauk Valley Comm Coll (IL)
Sheridan Coll (WY)
Snow Coll (UT)
Solano Comm Coll (CA)
Southwest Mississippi Comm Coll (MS)
Springfield Tech Comm Coll (MA)
Suffolk County Comm Coll (NY)
Terra State Comm Coll (OH)
Trinity Valley Comm Coll (TX)
Tyler Jr Coll (TX)
Union County Coll (NJ)
Wenatchee Valley Coll (WA)

BIOLOGY/BIOTECHNOLOGY LABORATORY TECHNICIAN

Anoka-Ramsey Comm Coll (MN)
Anoka-Ramsey Comm Coll, Cambridge Campus (MN)

Athens Tech Coll (GA)
Austin Comm Coll (TX)
Berkeley City Coll (CA)
Collin County Comm Coll District (TX)
Delaware Tech & Comm Coll, Jack F. Owens Campus (DE)
Delaware Tech & Comm Coll, Stanton/Wilmington Campus (DE)
Foothill Coll (CA)
Hagerstown Comm Coll (MD)
Houston Comm Coll System (TX)
Lonestar Coll–Montgomery (TX)
Massachusetts Bay Comm Coll (MA)
Middlesex Comm Coll (CT)
Minnesota West Comm and Tech Coll (MN)
Montgomery Coll (MD)
Muskegon Comm Coll (MI)
Randolph Comm Coll (NC)
Salt Lake Comm Coll (UT)
Westmoreland County Comm Coll (PA)
Wilson Comm Coll (NC)

BIOMEDICAL TECHNOLOGY
Brown Mackie Coll–Cincinnati (OH)
Brown Mackie Coll–Fort Wayne (IN)
Brown Mackie Coll–Louisville (KY)
Brown Mackie Coll–Tucson (AZ)
Chattahoochee Tech Coll (GA)
Cincinnati State Tech and Comm Coll (OH)
Dakota County Tech Coll (MN)
Delaware Tech & Comm Coll, Terry Campus (DE)
Florida State Coll at Jacksonville (FL)
Gateway Comm Coll (CT)
Hillsborough Comm Coll (FL)
Howard Comm Coll (MD)
Miami Dade Coll (FL)
Minnesota State Coll–Southeast Tech (MN)
Muskegon Comm Coll (MI)
New Mexico State U–Alamogordo (NM)
North Seattle Comm Coll (WA)
Oklahoma City Comm Coll (OK)
Owens Comm Coll, Toledo (OH)
Penn State DuBois (PA)
Penn State Fayette, The Eberly Campus (PA)
Penn State Hazleton (PA)
Penn State New Kensington (PA)
Penn State Schuylkill (PA)
Penn State Shenango (PA)
Penn State York (PA)
St. Philip's Coll (TX)
Santa Barbara City Coll (CA)
Southeastern Comm Coll (IA)
Southeast Tech Inst (SD)
Stark State Coll of Technology (OH)
Western Iowa Tech Comm Coll (IA)

BIOTECHNOLOGY
Alamance Comm Coll (NC)
Augusta Tech Coll (GA)
Burlington County Coll (NJ)
Central New Mexico Comm Coll (NM)
Comm Coll of Rhode Island (RI)
El Centro Coll (TX)
GateWay Comm Coll (AZ)
Glendale Comm Coll (AZ)
Hillsborough Comm Coll (FL)
Howard Comm Coll (MD)
Ivy Tech Comm Coll–Central Indiana (IN)
Ivy Tech Comm Coll–Lafayette (IN)
Ivy Tech Comm Coll–North Central (IN)
Lehigh Carbon Comm Coll (PA)
Miami Dade Coll (FL)
Montgomery County Comm Coll (PA)
Northampton Comm Coll (PA)
Oklahoma City Comm Coll (OK)
Owens Comm Coll, Toledo (OH)
Raritan Valley Comm Coll (NJ)
Red Rocks Comm Coll (CO)
Santa Barbara City Coll (CA)

Springfield Tech Comm Coll (MA)
Tompkins Cortland Comm Coll (NY)

BLASTING
Moraine Park Tech Coll (WI)

BOILERMAKING
Ivy Tech Comm Coll–Southwest (IN)

BOTANY/PLANT BIOLOGY
North Idaho Coll (ID)
Palm Beach State Coll (FL)
Snow Coll (UT)

BROADCAST JOURNALISM
Amarillo Coll (TX)
Dodge City Comm Coll (KS)
Kingsborough Comm Coll of the City U of New York (NY)
Middlesex Comm Coll (CT)
Northwest Coll (WY)
Ocean County Coll (NJ)
Oklahoma City Comm Coll (OK)
Yakima Valley Comm Coll (WA)

BUILDING/CONSTRUCTION FINISHING, MANAGEMENT, AND INSPECTION RELATED
Central Comm Coll–Hastings Campus (NE)
Central New Mexico Comm Coll (NM)
The Comm Coll of Baltimore County (MD)
Fayetteville Tech Comm Coll (NC)
Frederick Comm Coll (MD)
Gwinnett Tech Coll (GA)
Inver Hills Comm Coll (MN)
Ivy Tech Comm Coll–Northwest (IN)
Lawson State Comm Coll (AL)
Mid-Plains Comm Coll, North Platte (NE)
Mohave Comm Coll (AZ)
Montgomery Coll (MD)
Northeast Comm Coll (NE)
Olympic Coll (WA)
Palm Beach State Coll (FL)
St. Philip's Coll (TX)
Salt Lake Comm Coll (UT)
Seminole State Coll of Florida (FL)
Snow Coll (UT)
Southeast Tech Inst (SD)
Springfield Tech Comm Coll (MA)

BUILDING/CONSTRUCTION SITE MANAGEMENT
Alexandria Tech and Comm Coll (MN)
Coll of the Canyons (CA)
The Comm Coll of Baltimore County (MD)
Hillsborough Comm Coll (FL)
Inver Hills Comm Coll (MN)
Lehigh Carbon Comm Coll (PA)
Metropolitan Comm Coll–Business & Technology Campus (MO)
Minnesota State Comm and Tech Coll (MN)
North Dakota State Coll of Science (ND)
North Hennepin Comm Coll (MN)

BUILDING CONSTRUCTION TECHNOLOGY
Sheridan Coll (WY)

BUILDING/HOME/CONSTRUCTION INSPECTION
Harrisburg Area Comm Coll (PA)
Inver Hills Comm Coll (MN)
McHenry County Coll (IL)
North Hennepin Comm Coll (MN)
Oklahoma State U, Oklahoma City (OK)
Orange Coast Coll (CA)
Phoenix Coll (AZ)
South Suburban Coll (IL)

BUILDING/PROPERTY MAINTENANCE
Bellingham Tech Coll (WA)
Cape Fear Comm Coll (NC)
Century Coll (MN)
Ivy Tech Comm Coll–Bloomington (IN)
Ivy Tech Comm Coll–Central Indiana (IN)
Ivy Tech Comm Coll–Columbus (IN)
Ivy Tech Comm Coll–East Central (IN)
Ivy Tech Comm Coll–Kokomo (IN)
Ivy Tech Comm Coll–Lafayette (IN)
Ivy Tech Comm Coll–North Central (IN)
Ivy Tech Comm Coll–Northeast (IN)
Ivy Tech Comm Coll–Northwest (IN)
Ivy Tech Comm Coll–Richmond (IN)
Ivy Tech Comm Coll–Southern Indiana (IN)
Ivy Tech Comm Coll–Southwest (IN)
Ivy Tech Comm Coll–Wabash Valley (IN)
Lincoln Land Comm Coll (IL)
Mohawk Valley Comm Coll (NY)
Pima Comm Coll (AZ)

BUSINESS ADMINISTRATION AND MANAGEMENT
Alamance Comm Coll (NC)
Alexandria Tech and Comm Coll (MN)
Allen Comm Coll (KS)
Amarillo Coll (TX)
Ancilla Coll (IN)
Anoka-Ramsey Comm Coll (MN)
Anoka-Ramsey Comm Coll, Cambridge Campus (MN)
Antelope Valley Coll (CA)
Arizona Western Coll (AZ)
Augusta Tech Coll (GA)
Austin Comm Coll (TX)
Bainbridge Coll (GA)
Barton County Comm Coll (KS)
Beaufort County Comm Coll (NC)
Berkeley City Coll (CA)
Blackhawk Tech Coll (WI)
Borough of Manhattan Comm Coll of the City U of New York (NY)
Bradford School (OH)
Bradford School (PA)
Bristol Comm Coll (MA)
Brown Mackie Coll–Akron (OH)
Brown Mackie Coll–Albuquerque (NM)
Brown Mackie Coll–Atlanta (GA)
Brown Mackie Coll–Boise (ID)
Brown Mackie Coll–Cincinnati (OH)
Brown Mackie Coll–Findlay (OH)
Brown Mackie Coll–Fort Wayne (IN)
Brown Mackie Coll–Greenville (SC)
Brown Mackie Coll–Hopkinsville (KY)
Brown Mackie Coll–Indianapolis (IN)
Brown Mackie Coll–Kansas City (KS)
Brown Mackie Coll–Louisville (KY)
Brown Mackie Coll–Merrillville (IN)
Brown Mackie Coll–Miami (FL)
Brown Mackie Coll–Michigan City (IN)
Brown Mackie Coll–North Canton (OH)
Brown Mackie Coll–Northern Kentucky (KY)
Brown Mackie Coll–Oklahoma City (OK)
Brown Mackie Coll–Phoenix (AZ)
Brown Mackie Coll–Quad Cities (IA)
Brown Mackie Coll–St. Louis (MO)
Brown Mackie Coll–Salina (KS)
Brown Mackie Coll–San Antonio (TX)
Brown Mackie Coll–South Bend (IN)
Brown Mackie Coll–Tucson (AZ)
Brown Mackie Coll–Tulsa (OK)
Bucks County Comm Coll (PA)

Burlington County Coll (NJ)
Cape Fear Comm Coll (NC)
Career Tech Coll (LA)
Carl Albert State Coll (OK)
Carroll Comm Coll (MD)
Casper Coll (WY)
Catawba Valley Comm Coll (NC)
Cayuga County Comm Coll (NY)
Cecil Coll (MD)
Central Carolina Tech Coll (SC)
Central Comm Coll–Columbus Campus (NE)
Central Comm Coll–Grand Island Campus (NE)
Central Comm Coll–Hastings Campus (NE)
Central Georgia Tech Coll (GA)
Central Lakes Coll (MN)
Central Maine Comm Coll (ME)
Central New Mexico Comm Coll (NM)
Central Oregon Comm Coll (OR)
Central Wyoming Coll (WY)
Century Coll (MN)
Chandler-Gilbert Comm Coll (AZ)
Chattahoochee Tech Coll (GA)
Chipola Coll (FL)
Chippewa Valley Tech Coll (WI)
Cincinnati State Tech and Comm Coll (OH)
City Colls of Chicago, Harry S. Truman College (IL)
Clarendon Coll (TX)
Clark Coll (WA)
Cleveland State Comm Coll (TN)
Clovis Comm Coll (NM)
Coll of Business and Technology (FL)
Coll of Lake County (IL)
Coll of the Canyons (CA)
Collin County Comm Coll District (TX)
Colorado Mountain Coll (CO)
Colorado Mountain Coll, Alpine Campus (CO)
The Comm Coll of Baltimore County (MD)
Comm Coll of Philadelphia (PA)
Comm Coll of Rhode Island (RI)
Comm Coll of Vermont (VT)
Corning Comm Coll (NY)
Cowley County Comm Coll and Area Vocational–Tech School (KS)
Crowder Coll (MO)
Dabney S. Lancaster Comm Coll (VA)
Dakota Coll at Bottineau (ND)
Dakota County Tech Coll (MN)
Darton Coll (GA)
Daytona State Coll (FL)
De Anza Coll (CA)
Delaware Tech & Comm Coll, Stanton/Wilmington Campus (DE)
Delaware Tech & Comm Coll, Terry Campus (DE)
Denmark Tech Coll (SC)
Dodge City Comm Coll (KS)
Doña Ana Comm Coll (NM)
Douglas Education Center (PA)
Duluth Business U (MN)
Dutchess Comm Coll (NY)
Dyersburg State Comm Coll (TN)
Eastern Arizona Coll (AZ)
Eastern Gateway Comm Coll (OH)
Eastfield Coll (TX)
East Los Angeles Coll (CA)
Edison State Comm Coll (OH)
El Centro Coll (TX)
Elgin Comm Coll (IL)
Fayetteville Tech Comm Coll (NC)
Fiorello H. LaGuardia Comm Coll of the City U of New York (NY)
Florida State Coll at Jacksonville (FL)
Foothill Coll (CA)
Fox Coll (IL)
Fox Valley Tech Coll (WI)
Frank Phillips Coll (TX)
Frederick Comm Coll (MD)
Fulton-Montgomery Comm Coll (NY)
Gateway Comm and Tech Coll (KY)
GateWay Comm Coll (AZ)
Gateway Comm Coll (CT)
Georgia Highlands Coll (GA)

Georgia Military Coll (GA)
Glendale Comm Coll (AZ)
Golden West Coll (CA)
Goodwin Coll (CT)
Grand Rapids Comm Coll (MI)
Grays Harbor Coll (WA)
Great Basin Coll (NV)
Gulf Coast Comm Coll (FL)
Gwinnett Tech Coll (GA)
Hagerstown Comm Coll (MD)
Harford Comm Coll (MD)
Harper Coll (IL)
Harrisburg Area Comm Coll (PA)
Harrison Coll, Anderson (IN)
Harrison Coll, Columbus (IN)
Harrison Coll, Indianapolis (IN)
Harrison Coll, Lafayette (IN)
Harrison Coll, Muncie (IN)
Harrison Coll (OH)
Hesston Coll (KS)
Highland Comm Coll (IL)
Hillsborough Comm Coll (FL)
Holyoke Comm Coll (MA)
Housatonic Comm Coll (CT)
Houston Comm Coll System (TX)
Howard Comm Coll (MD)
Ilisagvik Coll (AK)
Illinois Eastern Comm Colls, Wabash Valley College (IL)
Indian River State Coll (FL)
International Business Coll, Indianapolis (IN)
Inver Hills Comm Coll (MN)
ITT Tech Inst, Canton (MI)
ITT Tech Inst, Troy (MI)
ITT Tech Inst, Wyoming (MI)
ITT Tech Inst, Dayton (OH)
ITT Tech Inst, Hilliard (OH)
ITT Tech Inst, Norwood (OH)
ITT Tech Inst, Strongsville (OH)
ITT Tech Inst, Warrensville Heights (OH)
ITT Tech Inst, Youngstown (OH)
ITT Tech Inst, Green Bay (WI)
ITT Tech Inst, Greenfield (WI)
Ivy Tech Comm Coll–Bloomington (IN)
Ivy Tech Comm Coll–Central Indiana (IN)
Ivy Tech Comm Coll–Columbus (IN)
Ivy Tech Comm Coll–East Central (IN)
Ivy Tech Comm Coll–Kokomo (IN)
Ivy Tech Comm Coll–Lafayette (IN)
Ivy Tech Comm Coll–North Central (IN)
Ivy Tech Comm Coll–Northeast (IN)
Ivy Tech Comm Coll–Northwest (IN)
Ivy Tech Comm Coll–Richmond (IN)
Ivy Tech Comm Coll–Southeast (IN)
Ivy Tech Comm Coll–Southern Indiana (IN)
Ivy Tech Comm Coll–Southwest (IN)
Ivy Tech Comm Coll–Wabash Valley (IN)
Jackson Comm Coll (MI)
James Sprunt Comm Coll (NC)
Jamestown Business Coll (NY)
Jefferson Coll (MO)
Johnston Comm Coll (NC)
John Tyler Comm Coll (VA)
John Wood Comm Coll (IL)
J. Sargeant Reynolds Comm Coll (VA)
Kent State U at Ashtabula (OH)
Kent State U at East Liverpool (OH)
Kent State U at Geauga (OH)
Kent State U at Trumbull (OH)
Kent State U at Tuscarawas (OH)
Kilgore Coll (TX)
Kilian Comm Coll (SD)
Kingsborough Comm Coll of the City U of New York (NY)
King's Coll (NC)
Kirtland Comm Coll (MI)
Lake Michigan Coll (MI)
Lake Region State Coll (ND)
Lake-Sumter Comm Coll (FL)
Lake Superior Coll (MN)
Lamar Comm Coll (CO)
Laramie County Comm Coll (WY)
Lawson State Comm Coll (AL)

Leeward Comm Coll (HI)
Lehigh Carbon Comm Coll (PA)
Linn-Benton Comm Coll (OR)
Lonestar Coll–Cy-Fair (TX)
Lonestar Coll–Kingwood (TX)
Lonestar Coll–Montgomery (TX)
Lonestar Coll–North Harris (TX)
Lonestar Coll–Tomball (TX)
Long Island Business Inst (NY)
Los Angeles Harbor Coll (CA)
Lower Columbia Coll (WA)
Macomb Comm Coll (MI)
Manchester Comm Coll (CT)
Marion Tech Coll (OH)
Martin Comm Coll (NC)
Massachusetts Bay Comm Coll (MA)
McHenry County Coll (IL)
Mendocino Coll (CA)
Mesa Comm Coll (AZ)
Metropolitan Comm Coll–Blue River (MO)
Metropolitan Comm Coll–Business & Technology Campus (MO)
Metropolitan Comm Coll–Longview (MO)
Metropolitan Comm Coll–Maple Woods (MO)
Metropolitan Comm Coll–Penn Valley (MO)
Miami Dade Coll (FL)
Middlesex Comm Coll (CT)
Midlands Tech Coll (SC)
Mid-Plains Comm Coll, North Platte (NE)
Minneapolis Business Coll (MN)
Minnesota State Coll–Southeast Tech (MN)
Minnesota State Comm and Tech Coll (MN)
Minnesota West Comm and Tech Coll (MN)
Missouri State U–West Plains (MO)
Mohave Comm Coll (AZ)
Mohawk Valley Comm Coll (NY)
Monroe County Comm Coll (MI)
Montana State U–Great Falls Coll of Technology (MT)
Montcalm Comm Coll (MI)
Montgomery County Comm Coll (PA)
Moraine Park Tech Coll (WI)
Moraine Valley Comm Coll (IL)
Morton Coll (IL)
Motlow State Comm Coll (TN)
Mountain View Coll (TX)
MTI Coll, Sacramento (CA)
Muskegon Comm Coll (MI)
Nashua Comm Coll (NH)
New England Inst of Technology (RI)
Newport Business Inst, Williamsport (PA)
Niagara County Comm Coll (NY)
Northampton Comm Coll (PA)
Northeast Comm Coll (NE)
Northeast Iowa Comm Coll (IA)
Northern Essex Comm Coll (MA)
North Hennepin Comm Coll (MN)
North Idaho Coll (ID)
North Iowa Area Comm Coll (IA)
Northland Comm and Tech Coll–Thief River Falls & East Grand Forks (MN)
Northwest Coll (WY)
Northwest Tech Coll (MN)
Norwalk Comm Coll (CT)
Oakland Comm Coll (MI)
Ocean County Coll (NJ)
Oklahoma City Comm Coll (OK)
Oklahoma State U, Oklahoma City (OK)
Olympic Coll (WA)
Onondaga Comm Coll (NY)
Orange Coast Coll (CA)
Owensboro Comm and Tech Coll (KY)
Owens Comm Coll, Toledo (OH)
Pasco-Hernando Comm Coll (FL)
Paul D. Camp Comm Coll (VA)
Pensacola State Coll (FL)
Phoenix Coll (AZ)
Pima Comm Coll (AZ)
Pittsburgh Tech Inst, Oakdale (PA)
Polk State Coll (FL)
Potomac State Coll of West Virginia U (WV)
Pratt Comm Coll (KS)

Pueblo Comm Coll (CO)
Quinsigamond Comm Coll (MA)
Rainy River Comm Coll (MN)
Randolph Comm Coll (NC)
Raritan Valley Comm Coll (NJ)
Red Rocks Comm Coll (CO)
Rockingham Comm Coll (NC)
Rogue Comm Coll (OR)
St. Cloud Tech & Comm Coll (MN)
St. Philip's Coll (TX)
Salt Lake Comm Coll (UT)
Sandhills Comm Coll (NC)
San Diego City Coll (CA)
San Juan Coll (NM)
Santa Barbara City Coll (CA)
Santa Fe Comm Coll (NM)
Santa Rosa Jr Coll (CA)
Sauk Valley Comm Coll (IL)
Scottsdale Comm Coll (AZ)
Seminole State Coll of Florida (FL)
Snow Coll (UT)
Solano Comm Coll (CA)
Southeastern Comm Coll (IA)
Southeast Tech Inst (SD)
Southern Alberta Inst of Technology (AB, Canada)
Southern Crescent Tech Coll (GA)
Southside Virginia Comm Coll (VA)
Southwestern Coll of Business, Franklin (OH)
Southwestern Michigan Coll (MI)
Southwest Mississippi Comm Coll (MS)
Spartanburg Comm Coll (SC)
Spencerian Coll (KY)
Springfield Tech Comm Coll (MA)
Stark State Coll of Technology (OH)
State U of New York Coll of Technology at Alfred (NY)
Suffolk County Comm Coll (NY)
Tallahassee Comm Coll (FL)
Terra State Comm Coll (OH)
Three Rivers Comm Coll (CT)
Tompkins Cortland Comm Coll (NY)
Trident Tech Coll (SC)
Trinity Valley Comm Coll (TX)
Tyler Jr Coll (TX)
Union County Coll (NJ)
U of Alaska Anchorage, Kenai Peninsula Coll (AK)
U of Alaska Anchorage, Kodiak Coll (AK)
Vincennes U Jasper Campus (IN)
Volunteer State Comm Coll (TN)
Waubonsee Comm Coll (IL)
Wenatchee Valley Coll (WA)
Westchester Comm Coll (NY)
Western Iowa Tech Comm Coll (IA)
West Kentucky Comm and Tech Coll (KY)
Westmoreland County Comm Coll (PA)
White Mountains Comm Coll (NH)
Wilson Comm Coll (NC)
Wisconsin Indianhead Tech Coll (WI)
Wood Tobe–Coburn School (NY)
Yakima Valley Comm Coll (WA)
Yavapai Coll (AZ)
YTI Career Inst–York (PA)

BUSINESS ADMINISTRATION, MANAGEMENT AND OPERATIONS RELATED
Cecil Coll (MD)
Chandler-Gilbert Comm Coll (AZ)
Comm Care Coll (OK)
The Comm Coll of Baltimore County (MD)
GateWay Comm Coll (AZ)
Harrison Coll, Muncie (IN)
John Tyler Comm Coll (VA)
Mountain Empire Comm Coll (VA)
Southern Alberta Inst of Technology (AB, Canada)

BUSINESS AUTOMATION/ TECHNOLOGY/DATA ENTRY
ASA The Coll For Excellence (NY)
Casper Coll (WY)
Central Wyoming Coll (WY)
Clark Coll (WA)
Coll of Lake County (IL)
Collin County Comm Coll District (TX)
Crowder Coll (MO)
Dakota Coll at Bottineau (ND)

Danville Area Comm Coll (IL)
Delaware Tech & Comm Coll, Jack F. Owens Campus (DE)
Delaware Tech & Comm Coll, Stanton/Wilmington Campus (DE)
Delaware Tech & Comm Coll, Terry Campus (DE)
El Centro Coll (TX)
GateWay Comm Coll (AZ)
Hallmark Coll of Technology (TX)
Houston Comm Coll System (TX)
Illinois Eastern Comm Colls, Frontier Community College (IL)
Illinois Eastern Comm Colls, Lincoln Trail College (IL)
Illinois Eastern Comm Colls, Olney Central College (IL)
Illinois Eastern Comm Colls, Wabash Valley College (IL)
Ivy Tech Comm Coll–Bloomington (IN)
Ivy Tech Comm Coll–Central Indiana (IN)
Ivy Tech Comm Coll–Columbus (IN)
Ivy Tech Comm Coll–East Central (IN)
Ivy Tech Comm Coll–Kokomo (IN)
Ivy Tech Comm Coll–Lafayette (IN)
Ivy Tech Comm Coll–North Central (IN)
Ivy Tech Comm Coll–Northeast (IN)
Ivy Tech Comm Coll–Northwest (IN)
Ivy Tech Comm Coll–Richmond (IN)
Ivy Tech Comm Coll–Southeast (IN)
Ivy Tech Comm Coll–Southern Indiana (IN)
Ivy Tech Comm Coll–Southwest (IN)
Kaskaskia Coll (IL)
Lincoln Land Comm Coll (IL)
Macomb Comm Coll (MI)
Minnesota State Comm and Tech Coll (MN)
Mitchell Tech Inst (SD)
Northeast Iowa Comm Coll (IA)
Oakland Comm Coll (MI)
Panola Coll (TX)
The U of Montana–Helena Coll of Technology (MT)
Waubonsee Comm Coll (IL)
Western Iowa Tech Comm Coll (IA)

BUSINESS/COMMERCE
Allen Comm Coll (KS)
Anoka-Ramsey Comm Coll (MN)
Anoka-Ramsey Comm Coll, Cambridge Campus (MN)
Antelope Valley Coll (CA)
Arizona Western Coll (AZ)
Arkansas State U–Mountain Home (AR)
Austin Comm Coll (TX)
Berkeley City Coll (CA)
Bryant & Stratton Coll (WI)
Carl Albert State Coll (OK)
Cecil Coll (MD)
Central Wyoming Coll (WY)
Chandler-Gilbert Comm Coll (AZ)
Coll of Central Florida (FL)
Colorado Mountain Coll, Timberline Campus (CO)
The Comm Coll of Baltimore County (MD)
Comm Coll of Rhode Island (RI)
Dawson Comm Coll (MT)
DeKalb Tech Coll (GA)
Delaware Tech & Comm Coll, Jack F. Owens Campus (DE)
Delaware Tech & Comm Coll, Stanton/Wilmington Campus (DE)
Delaware Tech & Comm Coll, Terry Campus (DE)
Eastfield Coll (TX)
Elaine P. Nunez Comm Coll (LA)
El Centro Coll (TX)
Frank Phillips Coll (TX)
GateWay Comm Coll (AZ)
Glendale Comm Coll (AZ)
Goodwin Coll (CT)
Great Basin Coll (NV)
Hagerstown Comm Coll (MD)
Harford Comm Coll (MD)
Harrisburg Area Comm Coll (PA)
Inver Hills Comm Coll (MN)
Jefferson State Comm Coll (AL)
John Tyler Comm Coll (VA)

J. Sargeant Reynolds Comm Coll (VA)
Kankakee Comm Coll (IL)
Kaskaskia Coll (IL)
Kent State U at Salem (OH)
Kilgore Coll (TX)
Laramie County Comm Coll (WY)
Lincoln Land Comm Coll (IL)
Macomb Comm Coll (MI)
Massachusetts Bay Comm Coll (MA)
Mesabi Range Comm and Tech Coll (MN)
Metropolitan Comm Coll–Business & Technology Campus (MO)
Midlands Tech Coll (SC)
Minnesota West Comm and Tech Coll (MN)
Missouri State U–West Plains (MO)
Montgomery Coll (MD)
Montgomery County Comm Coll (PA)
Moraine Valley Comm Coll (IL)
New Mexico State U–Alamogordo (NM)
Northampton Comm Coll (PA)
North Dakota State Coll of Science (ND)
Northwest Coll (WY)
Ocean County Coll (NJ)
Onondaga Comm Coll (NY)
Owens Comm Coll, Toledo (OH)
Penn State Beaver (PA)
Penn State Brandywine (PA)
Penn State DuBois (PA)
Penn State Fayette, The Eberly Campus (PA)
Penn State Greater Allegheny (PA)
Penn State Hazleton (PA)
Penn State Lehigh Valley (PA)
Penn State Mont Alto (PA)
Penn State New Kensington (PA)
Penn State Schuylkill (PA)
Penn State Shenango (PA)
Penn State Wilkes-Barre (PA)
Penn State Worthington Scranton (PA)
Penn State York (PA)
Phoenix Coll (AZ)
Quinsigamond Comm Coll (MA)
Raritan Valley Comm Coll (NJ)
Rogue Comm Coll (OR)
Sheridan Coll (WY)
Southern State Comm Coll (OH)
Springfield Tech Comm Coll (MA)
Terra State Comm Coll (OH)
Union County Coll (NJ)
U of Arkansas Comm Coll at Morrilton (AR)
U of Pittsburgh at Titusville (PA)
West Virginia Northern Comm Coll (WV)

BUSINESS/CORPORATE COMMUNICATIONS
Cecil Coll (MD)
Houston Comm Coll System (TX)
Montgomery County Comm Coll (PA)
North Seattle Comm Coll (WA)

BUSINESS MACHINE REPAIR
De Anza Coll (CA)
Muskegon Comm Coll (MI)
Solano Comm Coll (CA)

BUSINESS, MANAGEMENT, AND MARKETING RELATED
Blue Ridge Comm and Tech Coll (WV)
Chandler-Gilbert Comm Coll (AZ)
Cincinnati State Tech and Comm Coll (OH)
Eastern Arizona Coll (AZ)
Heart of Georgia Tech Coll (GA)
Kankakee Comm Coll (IL)
Sandhills Comm Coll (NC)
Tompkins Cortland Comm Coll (NY)

BUSINESS/MANAGERIAL ECONOMICS
Potomac State Coll of West Virginia U (WV)

BUSINESS OPERATIONS SUPPORT AND SECRETARIAL SERVICES RELATED
Bristol Comm Coll (MA)
Eastern Arizona Coll (AZ)
Mountain Empire Comm Coll (VA)
Northeast Comm Coll (NE)

BUSINESS TEACHER EDUCATION
Allen Comm Coll (KS)
Amarillo Coll (TX)
Bainbridge Coll (GA)
Darton Coll (GA)
Eastern Arizona Coll (AZ)
Northern Essex Comm Coll (MA)
North Idaho Coll (ID)
Pratt Comm Coll (KS)
Snow Coll (UT)
Southwest Mississippi Comm Coll (MS)
Trinity Valley Comm Coll (TX)
Vincennes U Jasper Campus (IN)

CABINETMAKING AND MILLWORK
Central Georgia Tech Coll (GA)
GateWay Comm Coll (AZ)
Harrisburg Area Comm Coll (PA)
Ivy Tech Comm Coll–Bloomington (IN)
Ivy Tech Comm Coll–Central Indiana (IN)
Ivy Tech Comm Coll–Columbus (IN)
Ivy Tech Comm Coll–East Central (IN)
Ivy Tech Comm Coll–Kokomo (IN)
Ivy Tech Comm Coll–Lafayette (IN)
Ivy Tech Comm Coll–North Central (IN)
Ivy Tech Comm Coll–Northeast (IN)
Ivy Tech Comm Coll–Northwest (IN)
Ivy Tech Comm Coll–Richmond (IN)
Ivy Tech Comm Coll–Southern Indiana (IN)
Ivy Tech Comm Coll–Southwest (IN)
Ivy Tech Comm Coll–Wabash Valley (IN)
Macomb Comm Coll (MI)

CAD/CADD DRAFTING/DESIGN TECHNOLOGY
Brown Mackie Coll–Kansas City (KS)
Brown Mackie Coll–North Canton (OH)
Brown Mackie Coll–Northern Kentucky (KY)
Brown Mackie Coll–Salina (KS)
Central Oregon Comm Coll (OR)
Century Coll (MN)
Comm Coll of Vermont (VT)
Danville Area Comm Coll (IL)
Delaware Tech & Comm Coll, Stanton/Wilmington Campus (DE)
Front Range Comm Coll (CO)
Gateway Comm and Tech Coll (KY)
Glendale Comm Coll (AZ)
Harford Comm Coll (MD)
ITT Tech Inst, Bessemer (AL)
ITT Tech Inst, Madison (AL)
ITT Tech Inst, Mobile (AL)
ITT Tech Inst, Phoenix (AZ)
ITT Tech Inst, Tucson (AZ)
ITT Tech Inst (AR)
ITT Tech Inst, Anaheim (CA)
ITT Tech Inst, Lathrop (CA)
ITT Tech Inst, Oxnard (CA)
ITT Tech Inst, Rancho Cordova (CA)
ITT Tech Inst, San Bernardino (CA)
ITT Tech Inst, San Diego (CA)
ITT Tech Inst, San Dimas (CA)
ITT Tech Inst, Sylmar (CA)
ITT Tech Inst, Torrance (CA)
ITT Tech Inst, Aurora (CO)
ITT Tech Inst, Thornton (CO)
ITT Tech Inst, Fort Lauderdale (FL)
ITT Tech Inst, Fort Myers (FL)
ITT Tech Inst, Jacksonville (FL)
ITT Tech Inst, Lake Mary (FL)
ITT Tech Inst, Miami (FL)
ITT Tech Inst, Pinellas Park (FL)
ITT Tech Inst, Tallahassee (FL)
ITT Tech Inst, Tampa (FL)

ITT Tech Inst, Atlanta (GA)
ITT Tech Inst, Duluth (GA)
ITT Tech Inst, Kennesaw (GA)
ITT Tech Inst (ID)
ITT Tech Inst, Burr Ridge (IL)
ITT Tech Inst, Mount Prospect (IL)
ITT Tech Inst, Orland Park (IL)
ITT Tech Inst, Fort Wayne (IN)
ITT Tech Inst, Indianapolis (IN)
ITT Tech Inst, Merrillville (IN)
ITT Tech Inst, Newburgh (IN)
ITT Tech Inst, Cedar Rapids (IA)
ITT Tech Inst, Clive (IA)
ITT Tech Inst, Louisville (KY)
ITT Tech Inst, Baton Rouge (LA)
ITT Tech Inst, St. Rose (LA)
ITT Tech Inst (MD)
ITT Tech Inst, Norwood (MA)
ITT Tech Inst, Woburn (MA)
ITT Tech Inst, Canton (MI)
ITT Tech Inst, Swartz Creek (MI)
ITT Tech Inst, Troy (MI)
ITT Tech Inst, Wyoming (MI)
ITT Tech Inst, Eden Prairie (MN)
ITT Tech Inst, Arnold (MO)
ITT Tech Inst, Earth City (MO)
ITT Tech Inst, Kansas City (MO)
ITT Tech Inst (NE)
ITT Tech Inst, Henderson (NV)
ITT Tech Inst (NM)
ITT Tech Inst, Albany (NY)
ITT Tech Inst, Getzville (NY)
ITT Tech Inst, Liverpool (NY)
ITT Tech Inst, Charlotte (NC)
ITT Tech Inst, High Point (NC)
ITT Tech Inst, Morrisville (NC)
ITT Tech Inst, Akron (OH)
ITT Tech Inst, Columbus (OH)
ITT Tech Inst, Dayton (OH)
ITT Tech Inst, Hilliard (OH)
ITT Tech Inst, Maumee (OH)
ITT Tech Inst, Norwood (OH)
ITT Tech Inst, Strongsville (OH)
ITT Tech Inst, Warrensville Heights (OH)
ITT Tech Inst, Youngstown (OH)
ITT Tech Inst, Tulsa (OK)
ITT Tech Inst (OR)
ITT Tech Inst, Bensalem (PA)
ITT Tech Inst, Dunmore (PA)
ITT Tech Inst, Harrisburg (PA)
ITT Tech Inst, King of Prussia (PA)
ITT Tech Inst, Pittsburgh (PA)
ITT Tech Inst, Tarentum (PA)
ITT Tech Inst, Columbia (SC)
ITT Tech Inst, Greenville (SC)
ITT Tech Inst, Chattanooga (TN)
ITT Tech Inst, Cordova (TN)
ITT Tech Inst, Johnson City (TN)
ITT Tech Inst, Knoxville (TN)
ITT Tech Inst, Nashville (TN)
ITT Tech Inst, Arlington (TX)
ITT Tech Inst, Austin (TX)
ITT Tech Inst, DeSoto (TX)
ITT Tech Inst, Houston (TX)
ITT Tech Inst, Houston (TX)
ITT Tech Inst, Richardson (TX)
ITT Tech Inst, San Antonio (TX)
ITT Tech Inst, Webster (TX)
ITT Tech Inst (UT)
ITT Tech Inst, Chantilly (VA)
ITT Tech Inst, Norfolk (VA)
ITT Tech Inst, Richmond (VA)
ITT Tech Inst, Salem (VA)
ITT Tech Inst, Springfield (VA)
ITT Tech Inst, Everett (WA)
ITT Tech Inst, Seattle (WA)
ITT Tech Inst, Spokane Valley (WA)
ITT Tech Inst (WV)
ITT Tech Inst, Green Bay (WI)
ITT Tech Inst, Greenfield (WI)
ITT Tech Inst, Madison (WI)
Jefferson Coll (MO)
John Wood Comm Coll (IL)
Lake Superior Coll (MN)
Lonestar Coll–Montgomery (TX)
Lonestar Coll–North Harris (TX)
Minnesota State Coll–Southeast Tech (MN)
Montgomery County Comm Coll (PA)
Mountain Empire Comm Coll (VA)
Northampton Comm Coll (PA)
Northwest Coll (WY)
St. Philip's Coll (TX)
Sheridan Coll (WY)
South Suburban Coll (IL)

Sullivan Coll of Technology and Design (KY)
Waubonsee Comm Coll (IL)
YTI Career Inst–York (PA)

CANADIAN STUDIES
Owens Comm Coll, Toledo (OH)

CARDIOVASCULAR TECHNOLOGY
Augusta Tech Coll (GA)
Central Georgia Tech Coll (GA)
Darton Coll (GA)
Delaware Tech & Comm Coll, Stanton/Wilmington Campus (DE)
El Centro Coll (TX)
Harper Coll (IL)
Harrisburg Area Comm Coll (PA)
Houston Comm Coll System (TX)
Howard Comm Coll (MD)
Kirtland Comm Coll (MI)
Northland Comm and Tech Coll– Thief River Falls & East Grand Forks (MN)
Orange Coast Coll (CA)
Polk State Coll (FL)
St. Cloud Tech & Comm Coll (MN)
Southeast Tech Inst (SD)
Spencerian Coll (KY)

CARPENTRY
Alamance Comm Coll (NC)
Alexandria Tech and Comm Coll (MN)
Arizona Western Coll (AZ)
Austin Comm Coll (TX)
Central Georgia Tech Coll (GA)
Central Wyoming Coll (WY)
Elaine P. Nunez Comm Coll (LA)
Fulton-Montgomery Comm Coll (NY)
GateWay Comm Coll (AZ)
Grays Harbor Coll (WA)
Honolulu Comm Coll (HI)
Indian River State Coll (FL)
Ivy Tech Comm Coll–Central Indiana (IN)
Ivy Tech Comm Coll–East Central (IN)
Ivy Tech Comm Coll–Lafayette (IN)
Ivy Tech Comm Coll–North Central (IN)
Ivy Tech Comm Coll–Northwest (IN)
Ivy Tech Comm Coll–Southern Indiana (IN)
Ivy Tech Comm Coll–Southwest (IN)
Ivy Tech Comm Coll–Wabash Valley (IN)
John Wood Comm Coll (IL)
Kaskaskia Coll (IL)
Kirtland Comm Coll (MI)
Lake Superior Coll (MN)
Metropolitan Comm Coll–Business & Technology Campus (MO)
Minnesota State Coll–Southeast Tech (MN)
Minnesota State Comm and Tech Coll (MN)
Mitchell Tech Inst (SD)
Montana State U–Great Falls Coll of Technology (MT)
Moraine Park Tech Coll (WI)
New England Inst of Technology (RI)
North Idaho Coll (ID)
North Iowa Area Comm Coll (IA)
Northland Comm and Tech Coll– Thief River Falls & East Grand Forks (MN)
Oakland Comm Coll (MI)
St. Cloud Tech & Comm Coll (MN)
San Diego City Coll (CA)
San Juan Coll (NM)
Southwest Mississippi Comm Coll (MS)
Triangle Tech, Inc.–DuBois School (PA)
The U of Montana–Helena Coll of Technology (MT)
Wenatchee Valley Coll (WA)
Western Iowa Tech Comm Coll (IA)
The Williamson Free School of Mecha Trades (PA)

CERAMIC ARTS AND CERAMICS
De Anza Coll (CA)
Oakland Comm Coll (MI)
Palm Beach State Coll (FL)
Santa Fe Comm Coll (NM)

CHEMICAL ENGINEERING
Burlington County Coll (NJ)
Kilgore Coll (TX)
Muskegon Comm Coll (MI)

CHEMICAL TECHNOLOGY
Amarillo Coll (TX)
Cape Fear Comm Coll (NC)
Cincinnati State Tech and Comm Coll (OH)
Coll of Lake County (IL)
Comm Coll of Philadelphia (PA)
Comm Coll of Rhode Island (RI)
Corning Comm Coll (NY)
Delaware Tech & Comm Coll, Stanton/Wilmington Campus (DE)
Houston Comm Coll System (TX)
ITI Tech Coll (LA)
Lehigh Carbon Comm Coll (PA)
Massachusetts Bay Comm Coll (MA)
Mohawk Valley Comm Coll (NY)
Niagara County Comm Coll (NY)
Northampton Comm Coll (PA)
Raritan Valley Comm Coll (NJ)
Westmoreland County Comm Coll (PA)

CHEMISTRY
Allen Comm Coll (KS)
Amarillo Coll (TX)
Arizona Western Coll (AZ)
Austin Comm Coll (TX)
Bainbridge Coll (GA)
Barton County Comm Coll (KS)
Bucks County Comm Coll (PA)
Burlington County Coll (NJ)
Casper Coll (WY)
Clarendon Coll (TX)
Cowley County Comm Coll and Area Vocational–Tech School (KS)
Dakota Coll at Bottineau (ND)
Darton Coll (GA)
Dodge City Comm Coll (KS)
Eastern Arizona Coll (AZ)
East Los Angeles Coll (CA)
Foothill Coll (CA)
Frank Phillips Coll (TX)
Frederick Comm Coll (MD)
Great Basin Coll (NV)
Harper Coll (IL)
Harrisburg Area Comm Coll (PA)
Highland Comm Coll (IL)
Indian River State Coll (FL)
Kilgore Coll (TX)
Kingsborough Comm Coll of the City U of New York (NY)
Lake Michigan Coll (MI)
Laramie County Comm Coll (WY)
Linn-Benton Comm Coll (OR)
Lonestar Coll–Cy-Fair (TX)
Lonestar Coll–Kingwood (TX)
Lonestar Coll–Montgomery (TX)
Lonestar Coll–North Harris (TX)
Lonestar Coll–Tomball (TX)
Macomb Comm Coll (MI)
Mendocino Coll (CA)
Metropolitan Comm Coll–Longview (MO)
Metropolitan Comm Coll–Maple Woods (MO)
Metropolitan Comm Coll–Penn Valley (MO)
Miami Dade Coll (FL)
Northampton Comm Coll (PA)
Northeast Comm Coll (NE)
North Hennepin Comm Coll (MN)
North Idaho Coll (ID)
Northwest Coll (WY)
Oklahoma City Comm Coll (OK)
Orange Coast Coll (CA)
Owens Comm Coll, Toledo (OH)
Palm Beach State Coll (FL)
Potomac State Coll of West Virginia U (WV)
Pratt Comm Coll (KS)
Red Rocks Comm Coll (CO)

Saint Charles Comm Coll (MO)
St. Philip's Coll (TX)
Salt Lake Comm Coll (UT)
San Juan Coll (NM)
Santa Barbara City Coll (CA)
Santa Rosa Jr Coll (CA)
Sauk Valley Comm Coll (IL)
Snow Coll (UT)
Solano Comm Coll (CA)
Southwest Mississippi Comm Coll (MS)
Springfield Tech Comm Coll (MA)
Suffolk County Comm Coll (NY)
Terra State Comm Coll (OH)
Trinity Valley Comm Coll (TX)
Tyler Jr Coll (TX)
Union County Coll (NJ)
Wenatchee Valley Coll (WA)

CHEMISTRY TEACHER EDUCATION
The Comm Coll of Baltimore County (MD)
Harford Comm Coll (MD)
Montgomery Coll (MD)

CHILD-CARE AND SUPPORT SERVICES MANAGEMENT
Aiken Tech Coll (SC)
Alexandria Tech and Comm Coll (MN)
Antelope Valley Coll (CA)
Barton County Comm Coll (KS)
Carroll Comm Coll (MD)
Cayuga County Comm Coll (NY)
Cecil Coll (MD)
Central Carolina Tech Coll (SC)
Central Comm Coll–Columbus Campus (NE)
Central Comm Coll–Grand Island Campus (NE)
Central Comm Coll–Hastings Campus (NE)
Central Georgia Tech Coll (GA)
Central Lakes Coll (MN)
Central New Mexico Comm Coll (NM)
Central Oregon Comm Coll (OR)
Central Wyoming Coll (WY)
The Comm Coll of Baltimore County (MD)
Cowley County Comm Coll and Area Vocational–Tech School (KS)
Dakota Coll at Bottineau (ND)
Eastern Gateway Comm Coll (OH)
Eastfield Coll (TX)
Florida State Coll at Jacksonville (FL)
Gadsden State Comm Coll (AL)
Goodwin Coll (CT)
Grays Harbor Coll (WA)
Hagerstown Comm Coll (MD)
H. Councill Trenholm State Tech Coll (AL)
Highland Comm Coll (IL)
Hillsborough Comm Coll (FL)
Holyoke Comm Coll (MA)
Ivy Tech Comm Coll–Bloomington (IN)
Ivy Tech Comm Coll–Central Indiana (IN)
Ivy Tech Comm Coll–Columbus (IN)
Ivy Tech Comm Coll–East Central (IN)
Ivy Tech Comm Coll–Kokomo (IN)
Ivy Tech Comm Coll–Lafayette (IN)
Ivy Tech Comm Coll–North Central (IN)
Ivy Tech Comm Coll–Northeast (IN)
Ivy Tech Comm Coll–Northwest (IN)
Ivy Tech Comm Coll–Richmond (IN)
Ivy Tech Comm Coll–Southeast (IN)
Ivy Tech Comm Coll–Southern Indiana (IN)
Ivy Tech Comm Coll–Southwest (IN)
Ivy Tech Comm Coll–Wabash Valley (IN)
Jefferson Coll (MO)
Jefferson State Comm Coll (AL)
Kilgore Coll (TX)

Lake Region State Coll (ND)
Lawson State Comm Coll (AL)
Linn-Benton Comm Coll (OR)
Lurleen B. Wallace Comm Coll (AL)
Macomb Comm Coll (MI)
Massachusetts Bay Comm Coll (MA)
Minnesota State Coll–Southeast Tech (MN)
Minnesota West Comm and Tech Coll (MN)
Missouri State U–West Plains (MO)
Montcalm Comm Coll (MI)
Montgomery County Comm Coll (PA)
Northwest-Shoals Comm Coll (AL)
Northwest Tech Coll (MN)
Oakland Comm Coll (MI)
Orange Coast Coll (CA)
Phoenix Coll (AZ)
Rogue Comm Coll (OR)
St. Cloud Tech & Comm Coll (MN)
Santa Barbara City Coll (CA)
Southeast Tech Inst (SD)
Tompkins Cortland Comm Coll (NY)
Western Iowa Tech Comm Coll (IA)

CHILD-CARE PROVISION
Alexandria Tech and Comm Coll (MN)
Bucks County Comm Coll (PA)
Cincinnati State Tech and Comm Coll (OH)
City Colls of Chicago, Harry S. Truman College (IL)
Coll of Lake County (IL)
Coll of the Canyons (CA)
Collin County Comm Coll District (TX)
The Comm Coll of Baltimore County (MD)
Corning Comm Coll (NY)
Dakota Coll at Bottineau (ND)
Dakota County Tech Coll (MN)
Danville Area Comm Coll (IL)
Dawson Comm Coll (MT)
Eastern Arizona Coll (AZ)
Elaine P. Nunez Comm Coll (LA)
Elgin Comm Coll (IL)
Florida State Coll at Jacksonville (FL)
Gulf Coast Comm Coll (FL)
Harper Coll (IL)
Hawkeye Comm Coll (IA)
Highland Comm Coll (IL)
John Tyler Comm Coll (VA)
John Wood Comm Coll (IL)
Kaskaskia Coll (IL)
Kilgore Coll (TX)
Lake Region State Coll (ND)
Lake-Sumter Comm Coll (FL)
Lincoln Land Comm Coll (IL)
McHenry County Coll (IL)
Metropolitan Comm Coll–Penn Valley (MO)
Midlands Tech Coll (SC)
Montcalm Comm Coll (MI)
Montgomery Coll (MD)
Moraine Park Tech Coll (WI)
Moraine Valley Comm Coll (IL)
Northland Comm and Tech Coll– Thief River Falls & East Grand Forks (MN)
Orange Coast Coll (CA)
Pensacola State Coll (FL)
Raritan Valley Comm Coll (NJ)
Saint Charles Comm Coll (MO)
San Juan Coll (NM)
Southeast Tech Inst (SD)
South Suburban Coll (IL)
Trident Tech Coll (SC)
Waubonsee Comm Coll (IL)
Western Iowa Tech Comm Coll (IA)
Westmoreland County Comm Coll (PA)

CHILD DEVELOPMENT
Albany Tech Coll (GA)
Allen Comm Coll (KS)
Altamaha Tech Coll (GA)
Amarillo Coll (TX)
Antelope Valley Coll (CA)
Athens Tech Coll (GA)
Atlanta Tech Coll (GA)
Augusta Tech Coll (GA)

Austin Comm Coll (TX)
Carl Albert State Coll (OK)
Central Comm Coll–Grand Island Campus (NE)
Central Comm Coll–Hastings Campus (NE)
Central Georgia Tech Coll (GA)
Central Maine Comm Coll (ME)
Chattahoochee Tech Coll (GA)
Cleveland State Comm Coll (TN)
Collin County Comm Coll District (TX)
Columbus Tech Coll (GA)
Comm Coll of Vermont (VT)
Cowley County Comm Coll and Area Vocational–Tech School (KS)
Daytona State Coll (FL)
De Anza Coll (CA)
Dodge City Comm Coll (KS)
Dutchess Comm Coll (NY)
Dyersburg State Comm Coll (TN)
East Los Angeles Coll (CA)
Edison State Comm Coll (OH)
Foothill Coll (CA)
Frederick Comm Coll (MD)
Georgia Northwestern Tech Coll (GA)
Goodwin Coll (CT)
Heart of Georgia Tech Coll (GA)
Highland Comm Coll (IL)
Housatonic Comm Coll (CT)
Houston Comm Coll System (TX)
Howard Comm Coll (MD)
Illinois Eastern Comm Colls, Wabash Valley College (IL)
Indian River State Coll (FL)
Ivy Tech Comm Coll–Central Indiana (IN)
James Sprunt Comm Coll (NC)
Kankakee Comm Coll (IL)
Lanier Tech Coll (GA)
Mendocino Coll (CA)
Mesa Comm Coll (AZ)
Miami Dade Coll (FL)
Middle Georgia Tech Coll (GA)
Monroe County Comm Coll (MI)
Moultrie Tech Coll (GA)
Muskegon Comm Coll (MI)
Nashua Comm Coll (NH)
Northland Comm and Tech Coll–Thief River Falls & East Grand Forks (MN)
Northwest-Shoals Comm Coll (AL)
Ogeechee Tech Coll (GA)
Okefenokee Tech Coll (GA)
Oklahoma City Comm Coll (OK)
Polk State Coll (FL)
Pratt Comm Coll (KS)
Pueblo Comm Coll (CO)
Sandersville Tech Coll (GA)
Sandhills Comm Coll (NC)
Santa Rosa Jr Coll (CA)
Savannah Tech Coll (GA)
Seminole State Coll of Florida (FL)
Snow Coll (UT)
Southeastern Comm Coll (IA)
Southeastern Tech Coll (GA)
Southern Crescent Tech Coll (GA)
South Georgia Tech Coll (GA)
Southwest Georgia Tech Coll (GA)
Stark State Coll of Technology (OH)
Suffolk County Comm Coll (NY)
Trinity Valley Comm Coll (TX)
Tyler Jr Coll (TX)
U of Arkansas Comm Coll at Morrilton (AR)
Volunteer State Comm Coll (TN)
Westchester Comm Coll (NY)
West Georgia Tech Coll (GA)
Wiregrass Georgia Tech Coll (GA)
Yakima Valley Comm Coll (WA)

CHIROPRACTIC ASSISTANT

Barton County Comm Coll (KS)
Moraine Park Tech Coll (WI)

CINEMATOGRAPHY AND FILM/VIDEO PRODUCTION

Antelope Valley Coll (CA)
The Art Inst of New York City (NY)
The Art Inst of Ohio–Cincinnati (OH)
The Art Inst of Seattle (WA)
Bucks County Comm Coll (PA)
Cape Fear Comm Coll (NC)
Cincinnati State Tech and Comm Coll (OH)

Glendale Comm Coll (AZ)
Gulf Coast Comm Coll (FL)
Hillsborough Comm Coll (FL)
Houston Comm Coll System (TX)
New England Inst of Technology (RI)
Northwest Coll (WY)
Orange Coast Coll (CA)
Pensacola State Coll (FL)
Pima Comm Coll (AZ)
Raritan Valley Comm Coll (NJ)
Red Rocks Comm Coll (CO)
Santa Fe Comm Coll (NM)

CIVIL DRAFTING AND CAD/CADD

Delaware Tech & Comm Coll, Stanton/Wilmington Campus (DE)
North Seattle Comm Coll (WA)
Sullivan Coll of Technology and Design (KY)

CIVIL ENGINEERING

Fiorello H. LaGuardia Comm Coll of the City U of New York (NY)
Kilgore Coll (TX)
Saint Charles Comm Coll (MO)
Santa Rosa Jr Coll (CA)

CIVIL ENGINEERING TECHNOLOGY

Arizona Western Coll (AZ)
Bellingham Tech Coll (WA)
Chattahoochee Tech Coll (GA)
Chippewa Valley Tech Coll (WI)
Cincinnati State Tech and Comm Coll (OH)
Coll of Lake County (IL)
Delaware Tech & Comm Coll, Jack F. Owens Campus (DE)
Delaware Tech & Comm Coll, Terry Campus (DE)
Eastern Arizona Coll (AZ)
East Los Angeles Coll (CA)
Fayetteville Tech Comm Coll (NC)
Florida State Coll at Jacksonville (FL)
Gadsden State Comm Coll (AL)
Gulf Coast Comm Coll (FL)
Harrisburg Area Comm Coll (PA)
Hawkeye Comm Coll (IA)
Indian River State Coll (FL)
Lake Superior Coll (MN)
Linn-Benton Comm Coll (OR)
Linn State Tech Coll (MO)
Macomb Comm Coll (MI)
Miami Dade Coll (FL)
Midlands Tech Coll (SC)
Minnesota State Comm and Tech Coll (MN)
Mohawk Valley Comm Coll (NY)
Moraine Park Tech Coll (WI)
Moultrie Tech Coll (GA)
North Dakota State Coll of Science (ND)
Northern Essex Comm Coll (MA)
Oklahoma State U, Oklahoma City (OK)
Pensacola State Coll (FL)
Phoenix Coll (AZ)
Potomac State Coll of West Virginia U (WV)
Quinsigamond Comm Coll (MA)
St. Cloud Tech & Comm Coll (MN)
Sandhills Comm Coll (NC)
Seminole State Coll of Florida (FL)
Southeast Tech Inst (SD)
Springfield Tech Comm Coll (MA)
Stark State Coll of Technology (OH)
Suffolk County Comm Coll (NY)
Tallahassee Comm Coll (FL)
Three Rivers Comm Coll (CT)
Trident Tech Coll (SC)
Union County Coll (NJ)
Westchester Comm Coll (NY)
Yakima Valley Comm Coll (WA)

CLASSICS AND CLASSICAL LANGUAGES

Foothill Coll (CA)

CLINICAL LABORATORY SCIENCE/MEDICAL TECHNOLOGY

Amarillo Coll (TX)

Athens Tech Coll (GA)
Casper Coll (WY)
Chipola Coll (FL)
Darton Coll (GA)
Dodge City Comm Coll (KS)
GateWay Comm Coll (AZ)
Georgia Highlands Coll (GA)
Howard Comm Coll (MD)
Monroe County Comm Coll (MI)
North Idaho Coll (ID)
Orange Coast Coll (CA)
Spencerian Coll (KY)
Westchester Comm Coll (NY)

CLINICAL/MEDICAL LABORATORY ASSISTANT

Delaware Tech & Comm Coll, Jack F. Owens Campus (DE)
Minnesota State Comm and Tech Coll (MN)
Pima Comm Coll (AZ)
Wenatchee Valley Coll (WA)

CLINICAL/MEDICAL LABORATORY SCIENCE AND ALLIED PROFESSIONS RELATED

Houston Comm Coll System (TX)
Pima Comm Coll (AZ)
Southeast Tech Inst (SD)
Southwestern Coll of Business, Franklin (OH)

CLINICAL/MEDICAL LABORATORY TECHNOLOGY

Alamance Comm Coll (NC)
Alexandria Tech and Comm Coll (MN)
Austin Comm Coll (TX)
Barton County Comm Coll (KS)
Beaufort County Comm Coll (NC)
Blackhawk Tech Coll (WI)
Bristol Comm Coll (MA)
Central Comm Coll–Hastings Campus (NE)
Central Georgia Tech Coll (GA)
Central Maine Comm Coll (ME)
Central New Mexico Comm Coll (NM)
Chippewa Valley Tech Coll (WI)
Cincinnati State Tech and Comm Coll (OH)
Comm Coll of Philadelphia (PA)
Comm Coll of Rhode Island (RI)
DeKalb Tech Coll (GA)
Dutchess Comm Coll (NY)
Edison State Comm Coll (OH)
El Centro Coll (TX)
Elgin Comm Coll (IL)
Gadsden State Comm Coll (AL)
Harrisburg Area Comm Coll (PA)
Hawkeye Comm Coll (IA)
Housatonic Comm Coll (CT)
Houston Comm Coll System (TX)
Indian River State Coll (FL)
Ivy Tech Comm Coll–North Central (IN)
Ivy Tech Comm Coll–Wabash Valley (IN)
Jefferson State Comm Coll (AL)
John Wood Comm Coll (IL)
J. Sargeant Reynolds Comm Coll (VA)
Kankakee Comm Coll (IL)
Kaskaskia Coll (IL)
Kilgore Coll (TX)
Manchester Comm Coll (CT)
Marion Tech Coll (OH)
Miami Dade Coll (FL)
Midlands Tech Coll (SC)
Mid-Plains Comm Coll, North Platte (NE)
Minnesota State Comm and Tech Coll (MN)
Minnesota West Comm and Tech Coll (MN)
Mitchell Tech Inst (SD)
Montgomery County Comm Coll (PA)
Moraine Park Tech Coll (WI)
Northeast Iowa Comm Coll (IA)
North Hennepin Comm Coll (MN)
North Iowa Area Comm Coll (IA)
Okefenokee Tech Coll (GA)
Penn State Hazleton (PA)
Penn State Schuylkill (PA)
Phoenix Coll (AZ)

Pima Comm Coll (AZ)
St. Philip's Coll (TX)
Salt Lake Comm Coll (UT)
Sandhills Comm Coll (NC)
San Juan Coll (NM)
Southeast Tech Inst (SD)
Spartanburg Comm Coll (SC)
Springfield Tech Comm Coll (MA)
Stark State Coll of Technology (OH)
Trident Tech Coll (SC)
Tyler Jr Coll (TX)
Volunteer State Comm Coll (TN)
Wenatchee Valley Coll (WA)
Westchester Comm Coll (NY)
Western Iowa Tech Comm Coll (IA)

CLINICAL/MEDICAL SOCIAL WORK

Central Comm Coll–Grand Island Campus (NE)
Central Comm Coll–Hastings Campus (NE)
Dawson Comm Coll (MT)
Pima Comm Coll (AZ)

COMMERCIAL AND ADVERTISING ART

Alamance Comm Coll (NC)
Alexandria Tech and Comm Coll (MN)
Amarillo Coll (TX)
Antonelli Inst (PA)
Austin Comm Coll (TX)
Bryant & Stratton Coll (WI)
Bucks County Comm Coll (PA)
Burlington County Coll (NJ)
Catawba Valley Comm Coll (NC)
Central Comm Coll–Columbus Campus (NE)
Central Comm Coll–Hastings Campus (NE)
Central Lakes Coll (MN)
Cincinnati State Tech and Comm Coll (OH)
Clovis Comm Coll (NM)
Collin County Comm Coll District (TX)
Colorado Mountain Coll (CO)
The Comm Coll of Baltimore County (MD)
Dakota County Tech Coll (MN)
De Anza Coll (CA)
Delaware Tech & Comm Coll, Terry Campus (DE)
Duluth Business U (MN)
Dutchess Comm Coll (NY)
Eastern Arizona Coll (AZ)
Edison State Comm Coll (OH)
Fashion Inst of Technology (NY)
Fayetteville Tech Comm Coll (NC)
FIDM/The Fashion Inst of Design & Merchandising, Los Angeles Campus (CA)
FIDM/The Fashion Inst of Design & Merchandising, Orange County Campus (CA)
FIDM/The Fashion Inst of Design & Merchandising, San Diego Campus (CA)
FIDM/The Fashion Inst of Design & Merchandising, San Francisco Campus (CA)
Florida State Coll at Jacksonville (FL)
Fulton-Montgomery Comm Coll (NY)
Glendale Comm Coll (AZ)
Golden West Coll (CA)
Hagerstown Comm Coll (MD)
Highland Comm Coll (IL)
Honolulu Comm Coll (HI)
Housatonic Comm Coll (CT)
James Sprunt Comm Coll (NC)
Johnston Comm Coll (NC)
Kilgore Coll (TX)
Kingsborough Comm Coll of the City U of New York (NY)
Lake-Sumter Comm Coll (FL)
Linn-Benton Comm Coll (OR)
Macomb Comm Coll (MI)
Manchester Comm Coll (CT)
Metropolitan Comm Coll–Penn Valley (MO)
Miami Dade Coll (FL)
Middlesex Comm Coll (CT)
Midlands Tech Coll (SC)
Mid-Plains Comm Coll, North Platte (NE)

Mohawk Valley Comm Coll (NY)
Montgomery Coll (MD)
Montgomery County Comm Coll (PA)
Muskegon Comm Coll (MI)
Northern Essex Comm Coll (MA)
North Idaho Coll (ID)
Northwest Coll (WY)
Norwalk Comm Coll (CT)
Nossi Coll of Art (TN)
Oklahoma City Comm Coll (OK)
Orange Coast Coll (CA)
Owens Comm Coll, Toledo (OH)
Palm Beach State Coll (FL)
Pensacola State Coll (FL)
Phoenix Coll (AZ)
Pratt Comm Coll (KS)
Quinsigamond Comm Coll (MA)
Randolph Comm Coll (NC)
Saint Charles Comm Coll (MO)
San Diego City Coll (CA)
San Juan Coll (NM)
Santa Barbara City Coll (CA)
School of Advertising Art (OH)
Solano Comm Coll (CA)
Southeast Tech Inst (SD)
Springfield Tech Comm Coll (MA)
Terra State Comm Coll (OH)
Tompkins Cortland Comm Coll (NY)
Trident Tech Coll (SC)
Tyler Jr Coll (TX)
U of Arkansas Comm Coll at Morrilton (AR)
Wenatchee Valley Coll (WA)
Yavapai Coll (AZ)

COMMERCIAL PHOTOGRAPHY

Austin Comm Coll (TX)
Cecil Coll (MD)
Central Wyoming Coll (WY)
Fashion Inst of Technology (NY)
Fiorello H. LaGuardia Comm Coll of the City U of New York (NY)
Harford Comm Coll (MD)
Hawkeye Comm Coll (IA)
Houston Comm Coll System (TX)
Kilgore Coll (TX)
Mohawk Valley Comm Coll (NY)
Montgomery Coll (MD)
Northwest Coll (WY)
Nossi Coll of Art (TN)
Owens Comm Coll, Toledo (OH)
Phoenix Coll (AZ)
Randolph Comm Coll (NC)
Santa Fe Comm Coll (NM)
Springfield Tech Comm Coll (MA)

COMMUNICATION AND JOURNALISM RELATED

Cayuga County Comm Coll (NY)
Gadsden State Comm Coll (AL)
Sheridan Coll (WY)

COMMUNICATION AND MEDIA RELATED

Raritan Valley Comm Coll (NJ)

COMMUNICATION DISORDERS SCIENCES AND SERVICES RELATED

Bristol Comm Coll (MA)
Burlington County Coll (NJ)

COMMUNICATION SCIENCES AND DISORDERS

Red Rocks Comm Coll (CO)

COMMUNICATIONS SYSTEMS INSTALLATION AND REPAIR TECHNOLOGY

Bellingham Tech Coll (WA)
Bristol Comm Coll (MA)
Cayuga County Comm Coll (NY)
Central Maine Comm Coll (ME)
Mohawk Valley Comm Coll (NY)
North Seattle Comm Coll (WA)
Suffolk County Comm Coll (NY)

COMMUNICATIONS TECHNOLOGIES AND SUPPORT SERVICES RELATED

Harford Comm Coll (MD)
Montgomery Coll (MD)
Montgomery County Comm Coll (PA)

Ocean County Coll (NJ)

COMMUNICATIONS TECHNOLOGY

Athens Tech Coll (GA)
Daytona State Coll (FL)
Dodge City Comm Coll (KS)
ITT Tech Inst, Aurora (CO)
ITT Tech Inst, Thornton (CO)
ITT Tech Inst (ID)
ITT Tech Inst, Baton Rouge (LA)
ITT Tech Inst, St. Rose (LA)
ITT Tech Inst, Canton (MI)
ITT Tech Inst, Swartz Creek (MI)
ITT Tech Inst, Troy (MI)
ITT Tech Inst, Wyoming (MI)
ITT Tech Inst, Tulsa (OK)
ITT Tech Inst (UT)
ITT Tech Inst, Chantilly (VA)
ITT Tech Inst, Norfolk (VA)
ITT Tech Inst, Richmond (VA)
ITT Tech Inst, Salem (VA)
ITT Tech Inst, Springfield (VA)
ITT Tech Inst, Spokane Valley (WA)
Kent State U at Tuscarawas (OH)
Orange Coast Coll (CA)
Owens Comm Coll, Toledo (OH)
Pueblo Comm Coll (CO)

COMMUNITY HEALTH AND PREVENTIVE MEDICINE

Anoka-Ramsey Comm Coll (MN)
Anoka-Ramsey Comm Coll, Cambridge Campus (MN)

COMMUNITY HEALTH SERVICES COUNSELING

Kingsborough Comm Coll of the City U of New York (NY)
Oakland Comm Coll (MI)
Waubonsee Comm Coll (IL)

COMMUNITY ORGANIZATION AND ADVOCACY

Borough of Manhattan Comm Coll of the City U of New York (NY)
Cleveland State Comm Coll (TN)
Comm Coll of Vermont (VT)
Honolulu Comm Coll (HI)
Mohawk Valley Comm Coll (NY)
Quinsigamond Comm Coll (MA)
Tompkins Cortland Comm Coll (NY)
Volunteer State Comm Coll (TN)
Westchester Comm Coll (NY)

COMMUNITY PSYCHOLOGY

Dawson Comm Coll (MT)

COMPARATIVE LITERATURE

Foothill Coll (CA)
Miami Dade Coll (FL)
Oklahoma City Comm Coll (OK)
Palm Beach State Coll (FL)
Pratt Comm Coll (KS)

COMPUTER AND INFORMATION SCIENCES

Albany Tech Coll (GA)
Alexandria Tech and Comm Coll (MN)
Antelope Valley Coll (CA)
Arizona Western Coll (AZ)
Austin Comm Coll (TX)
Berkeley City Coll (CA)
Borough of Manhattan Comm Coll of the City U of New York (NY)
Bristol Comm Coll (MA)
Bucks County Comm Coll (PA)
Carl Albert State Coll (OK)
Carroll Comm Coll (MD)
Cayuga County Comm Coll (NY)
Cecil Coll (MD)
Central Comm Coll–Columbus Campus (NE)
Central Comm Coll–Grand Island Campus (NE)
Century Coll (MN)
Chandler-Gilbert Comm Coll (AZ)
Cincinnati State Tech and Comm Coll (OH)
Clarendon Coll (TX)
Clovis Comm Coll (NM)

Collin County Comm Coll District (TX)
The Comm Coll of Baltimore County (MD)
Comm Coll of Rhode Island (RI)
Comm Coll of Vermont (VT)
Corning Comm Coll (NY)
Cowley County Comm Coll and Area Vocational–Tech School (KS)
Dakota Coll at Bottineau (ND)
Darton Coll (GA)
Dawson Comm Coll (MT)
Delaware Tech & Comm Coll, Jack F. Owens Campus (DE)
Delaware Tech & Comm Coll, Stanton/Wilmington Campus (DE)
Delaware Tech & Comm Coll, Terry Campus (DE)
Denmark Tech Coll (SC)
Dutchess Comm Coll (NY)
Edison State Comm Coll (OH)
Florida State Coll at Jacksonville (FL)
Gadsden State Comm Coll (AL)
GateWay Comm Coll (AZ)
Glendale Comm Coll (AZ)
Hagerstown Comm Coll (MD)
Harford Comm Coll (MD)
Harper Coll (IL)
Harrisburg Area Comm Coll (PA)
Harrison Coll, Indianapolis (IN)
Hawkeye Comm Coll (IA)
H. Councill Trenholm State Tech Coll (AL)
Ivy Tech Comm Coll–Bloomington (IN)
Ivy Tech Comm Coll–Central Indiana (IN)
Ivy Tech Comm Coll–Columbus (IN)
Ivy Tech Comm Coll–East Central (IN)
Ivy Tech Comm Coll–Kokomo (IN)
Ivy Tech Comm Coll–Lafayette (IN)
Ivy Tech Comm Coll–North Central (IN)
Ivy Tech Comm Coll–Northeast (IN)
Ivy Tech Comm Coll–Northwest (IN)
Ivy Tech Comm Coll–Richmond (IN)
Ivy Tech Comm Coll–Southeast (IN)
Ivy Tech Comm Coll–Southern Indiana (IN)
Ivy Tech Comm Coll–Southwest (IN)
Ivy Tech Comm Coll–Wabash Valley (IN)
Jamestown Business Coll (NY)
Jefferson State Comm Coll (AL)
John Tyler Comm Coll (VA)
J. Sargeant Reynolds Comm Coll (VA)
Kilgore Coll (TX)
Kingsborough Comm Coll of the City U of New York (NY)
Lake Michigan Coll (MI)
Lake Region State Coll (ND)
Lake Superior Coll (MN)
Lawson State Comm Coll (AL)
Leeward Comm Coll (HI)
Lehigh Carbon Comm Coll (PA)
Linn-Benton Comm Coll (OR)
Lonestar Coll–Cy-Fair (TX)
Lonestar Coll–Kingwood (TX)
Lonestar Coll–North Harris (TX)
Lonestar Coll–Tomball (TX)
Lurleen B. Wallace Comm Coll (AL)
Massachusetts Bay Comm Coll (MA)
Metropolitan Comm Coll–Business & Technology Campus (MO)
Mid-Plains Comm Coll, North Platte (NE)
Mohawk Valley Comm Coll (NY)
Montgomery Coll (MD)
Montgomery County Comm Coll (PA)
Nashua Comm Coll (NH)
New England Inst of Technology (RI)
Northeast Comm Coll (NE)
Northern Essex Comm Coll (MA)
Northwest-Shoals Comm Coll (AL)

Ocean County Coll (NJ)
Owensboro Comm and Tech Coll (KY)
Penn State Schuylkill (PA)
Pennsylvania Highlands Comm Coll (PA)
Phoenix Coll (AZ)
Salt Lake Comm Coll (UT)
Santa Fe Comm Coll (NM)
Sheridan Coll (WY)
Spartanburg Comm Coll (SC)
Sullivan Coll of Technology and Design (KY)
Tallahassee Comm Coll (FL)
Terra State Comm Coll (OH)
Tompkins Cortland Comm Coll (NY)
Tyler Jr Coll (TX)
Westchester Comm Coll (NY)
West Kentucky Comm and Tech Coll (KY)
White Mountains Comm Coll (NH)

COMPUTER AND INFORMATION SCIENCES AND SUPPORT SERVICES RELATED

Career Tech Coll (LA)
Cayuga County Comm Coll (NY)
Chandler-Gilbert Comm Coll (AZ)
Colorado Mountain Coll (CO)
Dakota Coll at Bottineau (ND)
Darton Coll (GA)
Fiorello H. LaGuardia Comm Coll of the City U of New York (NY)
Florida State Coll at Jacksonville (FL)
Harrison Coll, Muncie (IN)
Highland Comm Coll (IL)
Inver Hills Comm Coll (MN)
Jackson Comm Coll (MI)
Linn-Benton Comm Coll (OR)
Metropolitan Comm Coll–Business & Technology Campus (MO)
Midlands Tech Coll (SC)
Mohawk Valley Comm Coll (NY)
Moraine Park Tech Coll (WI)
Northeast Comm Coll (NE)
North Idaho Coll (ID)
Northland Comm and Tech Coll–Thief River Falls & East Grand Forks (MN)
Oakland Comm Coll (MI)
Palm Beach State Coll (FL)
Pennsylvania Highlands Comm Coll (PA)
Pratt Comm Coll (KS)
Raritan Valley Comm Coll (NJ)
Seminole State Coll of Florida (FL)
Southeast Tech Inst (SD)
Southwestern Coll of Business, Franklin (OH)
Stark State Coll of Technology (OH)
Suffolk County Comm Coll (NY)
Sullivan Coll of Technology and Design (KY)
Tompkins Cortland Comm Coll (NY)
Union County Coll (NJ)
Waukesha County Tech Coll (WI)
Westchester Comm Coll (NY)
YTI Career Inst–York (PA)

COMPUTER AND INFORMATION SCIENCES RELATED

Berkeley City Coll (CA)
Bristol Comm Coll (MA)
Bucks County Comm Coll (PA)
Central Oregon Comm Coll (OR)
Chipola Coll (FL)
Corning Comm Coll (NY)
Dawson Comm Coll (MT)
Daytona State Coll (FL)
Eastfield Coll (TX)
Florida State Coll at Jacksonville (FL)
Gateway Comm Coll (CT)
Highland Comm Coll (IL)
Howard Comm Coll (MD)
Kent State U at East Liverpool (OH)
Lake-Sumter Comm Coll (FL)
Metropolitan Comm Coll–Blue River (MO)

Metropolitan Comm Coll–Business & Technology Campus (MO)
Metropolitan Comm Coll–Longview (MO)
Metropolitan Comm Coll–Maple Woods (MO)
Metropolitan Comm Coll–Penn Valley (MO)
Missouri State U–West Plains (MO)
Mohave Comm Coll (AZ)
Monroe County Comm Coll (MI)
North Idaho Coll (ID)
Northland Comm and Tech Coll–Thief River Falls & East Grand Forks (MN)
Pensacola State Coll (FL)
Potomac State Coll of West Virginia U (WV)
Sauk Valley Comm Coll (IL)
Seminole State Coll of Florida (FL)
Stark State Coll of Technology (OH)
Tyler Jr Coll (TX)
Westchester Comm Coll (NY)

COMPUTER AND INFORMATION SYSTEMS SECURITY

Alexandria Tech and Comm Coll (MN)
ASA The Coll For Excellence (NY)
Berkeley City Coll (CA)
Blackhawk Tech Coll (WI)
Brown Mackie Coll–Tucson (AZ)
Bryant & Stratton Coll (WI)
Century Coll (MN)
Chattahoochee Tech Coll (GA)
Collin County Comm Coll District (TX)
Cowley County Comm Coll and Area Vocational–Tech School (KS)
Edison State Comm Coll (OH)
El Centro Coll (TX)
Fayetteville Tech Comm Coll (NC)
Florida State Coll at Jacksonville (FL)
Frank Phillips Coll (TX)
Glendale Comm Coll (AZ)
Harford Comm Coll (MD)
Harrisburg Area Comm Coll (PA)
Lanier Tech Coll (GA)
Lehigh Carbon Comm Coll (PA)
Lonestar Coll–Montgomery (TX)
McHenry County Coll (IL)
Metropolitan Comm Coll–Business & Technology Campus (MO)
Minnesota State Comm and Tech Coll (MN)
Minnesota West Comm and Tech Coll (MN)
Montgomery Coll (MD)
Moraine Valley Comm Coll (IL)
Northampton Comm Coll (PA)
North Seattle Comm Coll (WA)
Norwalk Comm Coll (CT)
Oakland Comm Coll (MI)
St. Philip's Coll (TX)
Seminole State Coll of Florida (FL)
Sheridan Coll (WY)
Southeast Tech Inst (SD)
Southern Crescent Tech Coll (GA)
Springfield Tech Comm Coll (MA)
Sullivan Coll of Technology and Design (KY)
Westchester Comm Coll (NY)
Westmoreland County Comm Coll (PA)
Wilson Comm Coll (NC)
Wiregrass Georgia Tech Coll (GA)

COMPUTER ENGINEERING

New England Inst of Technology (RI)
Santa Barbara City Coll (CA)

COMPUTER ENGINEERING RELATED

Columbus Tech Coll (GA)
Daytona State Coll (FL)
Eastern Gateway Comm Coll (OH)
Gateway Comm Coll (CT)
Sandhills Comm Coll (NC)
Seminole State Coll of Florida (FL)
Stark State Coll of Technology (OH)

COMPUTER ENGINEERING TECHNOLOGY

Aiken Tech Coll (SC)
Amarillo Coll (TX)
Bucks County Comm Coll (PA)
Catawba Valley Comm Coll (NC)
Cincinnati State Tech and Comm Coll (OH)
Colorado Mountain Coll (CO)
Colorado Mountain Coll, Alpine Campus (CO)
Comm Coll of Rhode Island (RI)
DeKalb Tech Coll (GA)
Delaware Tech & Comm Coll, Stanton/Wilmington Campus (DE)
Delaware Tech & Comm Coll, Terry Campus (DE)
Doña Ana Comm Coll (NM)
Eastfield Coll (TX)
East Los Angeles Coll (CA)
Florida State Coll at Jacksonville (FL)
Fox Valley Tech Coll (WI)
Frederick Comm Coll (MD)
Fulton-Montgomery Comm Coll (NY)
Gateway Comm Coll (CT)
Grand Rapids Comm Coll (MI)
Houston Comm Coll System (TX)
Indian River State Coll (FL)
ITT Tech Inst, Bessemer (AL)
ITT Tech Inst, Madison (AL)
ITT Tech Inst, Mobile (AL)
ITT Tech Inst, Phoenix (AZ)
ITT Tech Inst, Tucson (AZ)
ITT Tech Inst (AR)
ITT Tech Inst, Anaheim (CA)
ITT Tech Inst, Lathrop (CA)
ITT Tech Inst, Oxnard (CA)
ITT Tech Inst, Rancho Cordova (CA)
ITT Tech Inst, San Bernardino (CA)
ITT Tech Inst, San Diego (CA)
ITT Tech Inst, San Dimas (CA)
ITT Tech Inst, Sylmar (CA)
ITT Tech Inst, Torrance (CA)
ITT Tech Inst, Aurora (CO)
ITT Tech Inst, Thornton (CO)
ITT Tech Inst, Fort Lauderdale (FL)
ITT Tech Inst, Fort Myers (FL)
ITT Tech Inst, Jacksonville (FL)
ITT Tech Inst, Lake Mary (FL)
ITT Tech Inst, Miami (FL)
ITT Tech Inst, Pinellas Park (FL)
ITT Tech Inst, Tallahassee (FL)
ITT Tech Inst, Tampa (FL)
ITT Tech Inst, Atlanta (GA)
ITT Tech Inst, Duluth (GA)
ITT Tech Inst, Kennesaw (GA)
ITT Tech Inst (ID)
ITT Tech Inst, Burr Ridge (IL)
ITT Tech Inst, Mount Prospect (IL)
ITT Tech Inst, Orland Park (IL)
ITT Tech Inst, Fort Wayne (IN)
ITT Tech Inst, Indianapolis (IN)
ITT Tech Inst, Merrillville (IN)
ITT Tech Inst, Newburgh (IN)
ITT Tech Inst, Cedar Rapids (IA)
ITT Tech Inst, Clive (IA)
ITT Tech Inst, Louisville (KY)
ITT Tech Inst, Baton Rouge (LA)
ITT Tech Inst, St. Rose (LA)
ITT Tech Inst (MD)
ITT Tech Inst, Norwood (MA)
ITT Tech Inst, Woburn (MA)
ITT Tech Inst, Canton (MI)
ITT Tech Inst, Swartz Creek (MI)
ITT Tech Inst, Troy (MI)
ITT Tech Inst, Wyoming (MI)
ITT Tech Inst, Eden Prairie (MN)
ITT Tech Inst, Arnold (MO)
ITT Tech Inst, Earth City (MO)
ITT Tech Inst, Kansas City (MO)
ITT Tech Inst (NE)
ITT Tech Inst, Henderson (NV)
ITT Tech Inst (NM)
ITT Tech Inst, Albany (NY)
ITT Tech Inst, Getzville (NY)
ITT Tech Inst, Liverpool (NY)
ITT Tech Inst, Charlotte (NC)
ITT Tech Inst, High Point (NC)
ITT Tech Inst, Morrisville (NC)
ITT Tech Inst, Akron (OH)
ITT Tech Inst, Columbus (OH)
ITT Tech Inst, Dayton (OH)
ITT Tech Inst, Hilliard (OH)

ITT Tech Inst, Maumee (OH)
ITT Tech Inst, Norwood (OH)
ITT Tech Inst, Strongsville (OH)
ITT Tech Inst, Warrensville Heights (OH)
ITT Tech Inst, Youngstown (OH)
ITT Tech Inst, Tulsa (OK)
ITT Tech Inst (OR)
ITT Tech Inst, Bensalem (PA)
ITT Tech Inst, Dunmore (PA)
ITT Tech Inst, Harrisburg (PA)
ITT Tech Inst, King of Prussia (PA)
ITT Tech Inst, Pittsburgh (PA)
ITT Tech Inst, Tarentum (PA)
ITT Tech Inst, Columbia (SC)
ITT Tech Inst, Greenville (SC)
ITT Tech Inst, Chattanooga (TN)
ITT Tech Inst, Cordova (TN)
ITT Tech Inst, Johnson City (TN)
ITT Tech Inst, Knoxville (TN)
ITT Tech Inst, Nashville (TN)
ITT Tech Inst, Arlington (TX)
ITT Tech Inst, Austin (TX)
ITT Tech Inst, DeSoto (TX)
ITT Tech Inst, Houston (TX)
ITT Tech Inst, Houston (TX)
ITT Tech Inst, Richardson (TX)
ITT Tech Inst, San Antonio (TX)
ITT Tech Inst, Webster (TX)
ITT Tech Inst (UT)
ITT Tech Inst, Chantilly (VA)
ITT Tech Inst, Norfolk (VA)
ITT Tech Inst, Richmond (VA)
ITT Tech Inst, Salem (VA)
ITT Tech Inst, Springfield (VA)
ITT Tech Inst, Everett (WA)
ITT Tech Inst, Seattle (WA)
ITT Tech Inst, Spokane Valley (WA)
ITT Tech Inst (WV)
ITT Tech Inst, Green Bay (WI)
ITT Tech Inst, Greenfield (WI)
ITT Tech Inst, Madison (WI)
Kent State U at Ashtabula (OH)
Kent State U at East Liverpool (OH)
Kent State U at Trumbull (OH)
Kent State U at Tuscarawas (OH)
Lehigh Carbon Comm Coll (PA)
Lonestar Coll–Kingwood (TX)
Los Angeles Harbor Coll (CA)
Massachusetts Bay Comm Coll (MA)
Miami Dade Coll (FL)
Minnesota State Comm and Tech Coll (MN)
Minnesota West Comm and Tech Coll (MN)
Monroe County Comm Coll (MI)
Nashua Comm Coll (NH)
Northern Essex Comm Coll (MA)
Oklahoma City Comm Coll (OK)
Onondaga Comm Coll (NY)
Orange Coast Coll (CA)
Owens Comm Coll, Toledo (OH)
Penn State New Kensington (PA)
Pima Comm Coll (AZ)
Potomac State Coll of West Virginia U (WV)
Quinsigamond Comm Coll (MA)
Sandhills Comm Coll (NC)
San Diego City Coll (CA)
Seminole State Coll of Florida (FL)
Springfield Tech Comm Coll (MA)
Sullivan Coll of Technology and Design (KY)
Three Rivers Comm Coll (CT)
Trident Tech Coll (SC)
Tyler Jr Coll (TX)
Westmoreland County Comm Coll (PA)
White Mountains Comm Coll (NH)
Yakima Valley Comm Coll (WA)

COMPUTER GRAPHICS

Antelope Valley Coll (CA)
Arizona Western Coll (AZ)
Berkeley City Coll (CA)
Burlington County Coll (NJ)
Carroll Comm Coll (MD)
Coll of Business and Technology (FL)
Corning Comm Coll (NY)
Cowley County Comm Coll and Area Vocational–Tech School (KS)
Creative Center (NE)
Daytona State Coll (FL)
De Anza Coll (CA)

Florida State Coll at Jacksonville (FL)
Gateway Comm Coll (CT)
Howard Comm Coll (MD)
Lonestar Coll–Kingwood (TX)
Mesabi Range Comm and Tech Coll (MN)
Metropolitan Comm Coll–Business & Technology Campus (MO)
Miami Dade Coll (FL)
Missouri State U–West Plains (MO)
Monroe County Comm Coll (MI)
Northern Essex Comm Coll (MA)
Northland Comm and Tech Coll–Thief River Falls & East Grand Forks (MN)
Orange Coast Coll (CA)
Phoenix Coll (AZ)
Pittsburgh Tech Inst, Oakdale (PA)
Quinsigamond Comm Coll (MA)
Seminole State Coll of Florida (FL)
Sullivan Coll of Technology and Design (KY)
Tallahassee Comm Coll (FL)
Trident Tech Coll (SC)
Tyler Jr Coll (TX)
Yakima Valley Comm Coll (WA)

COMPUTER HARDWARE ENGINEERING

Eastfield Coll (TX)
Florida State Coll at Jacksonville (FL)
Seminole State Coll of Florida (FL)
Stark State Coll of Technology (OH)
Sullivan Coll of Technology and Design (KY)

COMPUTER HARDWARE TECHNOLOGY

Comm Coll of Rhode Island (RI)
Lake Superior Coll (MN)
Oakland Comm Coll (MI)
Sullivan Coll of Technology and Design (KY)

COMPUTER/INFORMATION TECHNOLOGY SERVICES ADMINISTRATION RELATED

Barton County Comm Coll (KS)
Bucks County Comm Coll (PA)
Cleveland Inst of Electronics (OH)
Corning Comm Coll (NY)
Daytona State Coll (FL)
Dyersburg State Comm Coll (TN)
Eastfield Coll (TX)
El Centro Coll (TX)
Florida State Coll at Jacksonville (FL)
Hesston Coll (KS)
Hillsborough Comm Coll (FL)
Howard Comm Coll (MD)
Kent State U at Trumbull (OH)
Mesabi Range Comm and Tech Coll (MN)
Metropolitan Comm Coll–Business & Technology Campus (MO)
Oakland Comm Coll (MI)
Owensboro Comm and Tech Coll (KY)
Pennsylvania Highlands Comm Coll (PA)
Pueblo Comm Coll (CO)
Sandhills Comm Coll (NC)
Seminole State Coll of Florida (FL)
Southeast Tech Inst (SD)
Stark State Coll of Technology (OH)
Trident Tech Coll (SC)

COMPUTER INSTALLATION AND REPAIR TECHNOLOGY

Central Maine Comm Coll (ME)
Coll of Lake County (IL)
Fiorello H. LaGuardia Comm Coll of the City U of New York (NY)
Harrisburg Area Comm Coll (PA)
Kilgore Coll (TX)
Midlands Tech Coll (SC)
Montcalm Comm Coll (MI)
Northampton Comm Coll (PA)
Southeast Tech Inst (SD)
Sullivan Coll of Technology and Design (KY)
Waukesha County Tech Coll (WI)
Wisconsin Indianhead Tech Coll (WI)

COMPUTER NUMERICALLY CONTROLLED (CNC) MACHINIST TECHNOLOGY

Moraine Park Tech Coll (WI)

COMPUTER PROGRAMMING

Aiken Tech Coll (SC)
Altamaha Tech Coll (GA)
Amarillo Coll (TX)
Antelope Valley Coll (CA)
Athens Tech Coll (GA)
Atlanta Tech Coll (GA)
Augusta Tech Coll (GA)
Austin Comm Coll (TX)
Beaufort County Comm Coll (NC)
Bradford School (OH)
Bradford School (PA)
Bristol Comm Coll (MA)
Brown Mackie Coll–Hopkinsville (KY)
Bucks County Comm Coll (PA)
Casper Coll (WY)
Catawba Valley Comm Coll (NC)
Cecil Coll (MD)
Central Georgia Tech Coll (GA)
Chandler-Gilbert Comm Coll (AZ)
Chattahoochee Tech Coll (GA)
Chippewa Valley Tech Coll (WI)
Cincinnati State Tech and Comm Coll (OH)
Clark Coll (WA)
Collin County Comm Coll District (TX)
Comm Coll of Rhode Island (RI)
Corning Comm Coll (NY)
Dabney S. Lancaster Comm Coll (VA)
Dakota County Tech Coll (MN)
Danville Area Comm Coll (IL)
Daytona State Coll (FL)
De Anza Coll (CA)
DeKalb Tech Coll (GA)
Dodge City Comm Coll (KS)
Eastfield Coll (TX)
East Los Angeles Coll (CA)
Edison State Comm Coll (OH)
El Centro Coll (TX)
Fayetteville Tech Comm Coll (NC)
Fiorello H. LaGuardia Comm Coll of the City U of New York (NY)
Florida State Coll at Jacksonville (FL)
Fox Valley Tech Coll (WI)
Georgia Highlands Coll (GA)
Georgia Northwestern Tech Coll (GA)
Grand Rapids Comm Coll (MI)
Gwinnett Tech Coll (GA)
Harper Coll (IL)
Houston Comm Coll System (TX)
Indian River State Coll (FL)
International Business Coll, Indianapolis (IN)
Inver Hills Comm Coll (MN)
Johnston Comm Coll (NC)
Kilgore Coll (TX)
King's Coll (NC)
Lake Superior Coll (MN)
Lamar Comm Coll (CO)
Lanier Tech Coll (GA)
Laramie County Comm Coll (WY)
Lehigh Carbon Comm Coll (PA)
Lincoln Land Comm Coll (IL)
Linn State Tech Coll (MO)
Lonestar Coll–Montgomery (TX)
Lonestar Coll–Tomball (TX)
Macomb Comm Coll (MI)
Metropolitan Comm Coll–Business & Technology Campus (MO)
Metropolitan Comm Coll–Longview (MO)
Metropolitan Comm Coll–Maple Woods (MO)
Miami Dade Coll (FL)
Middlesex Comm Coll (CT)
Minneapolis Business Coll (MN)
Minnesota State Coll–Southeast Tech (MN)
Minnesota State Comm and Tech Coll (MN)
Mohawk Valley Comm Coll (NY)
Montgomery County Comm Coll (PA)
New England Inst of Technology (RI)
New Mexico State U–Alamogordo (NM)
Northampton Comm Coll (PA)

Northeast Comm Coll (NE)
Northern Essex Comm Coll (MA)
North Idaho Coll (ID)
Oakland Comm Coll (MI)
Olympic Coll (WA)
Orange Coast Coll (CA)
Palm Beach State Coll (FL)
Pennsylvania Highlands Comm Coll (PA)
Pittsburgh Tech Inst, Oakdale (PA)
Potomac State Coll of West Virginia U (WV)
Quinsigamond Comm Coll (MA)
St. Cloud Tech & Comm Coll (MN)
Sandhills Comm Coll (NC)
Santa Fe Comm Coll (NM)
Seminole State Coll of Florida (FL)
Solano Comm Coll (CA)
Southeastern Comm Coll (IA)
Southeast Tech Inst (SD)
Southern Crescent Tech Coll (GA)
Southwestern Michigan Coll (MI)
Stark State Coll of Technology (OH)
Suffolk County Comm Coll (NY)
Tallahassee Comm Coll (FL)
Terra State Comm Coll (OH)
Three Rivers Comm Coll (CT)
The U of Montana–Helena Coll of Technology (MT)
Vincennes U Jasper Campus (IN)
Waubonsee Comm Coll (IL)
Waukesha County Tech Coll (WI)
Westmoreland County Comm Coll (PA)
West Virginia Northern Comm Coll (WV)
Wiregrass Georgia Tech Coll (GA)
Wood Tobe–Coburn School (NY)

COMPUTER PROGRAMMING RELATED

Bucks County Comm Coll (PA)
Corning Comm Coll (NY)
Eastfield Coll (TX)
Florida State Coll at Jacksonville (FL)
Mesabi Range Comm and Tech Coll (MN)
Metropolitan Comm Coll–Business & Technology Campus (MO)
Moraine Park Tech Coll (WI)
Northern Essex Comm Coll (MA)
Pasco-Hernando Comm Coll (FL)
Pennsylvania Highlands Comm Coll (PA)
Seminole State Coll of Florida (FL)
Southeast Tech Inst (SD)
Southwest Mississippi Comm Coll (MS)
Stark State Coll of Technology (OH)
Tyler Jr Coll (TX)
Vincennes U Jasper Campus (IN)

COMPUTER PROGRAMMING (SPECIFIC APPLICATIONS)

Barton County Comm Coll (KS)
Brown Mackie Coll–Hopkinsville (KY)
Bucks County Comm Coll (PA)
Cecil Coll (MD)
Cincinnati State Tech and Comm Coll (OH)
Coll of Lake County (IL)
Comm Coll of Rhode Island (RI)
Cowley County Comm Coll and Area Vocational–Tech School (KS)
Danville Area Comm Coll (IL)
Daytona State Coll (FL)
Florida State Coll at Jacksonville (FL)
Gulf Coast Comm Coll (FL)
Harper Coll (IL)
Highland Comm Coll (IL)
Hillsborough Comm Coll (FL)
Holyoke Comm Coll (MA)
Houston Comm Coll System (TX)
Inver Hills Comm Coll (MN)
Kent State U at Salem (OH)
Lake Region State Coll (ND)
Lincoln Land Comm Coll (IL)
Linn-Benton Comm Coll (OR)
Macomb Comm Coll (MI)
Mesabi Range Comm and Tech Coll (MN)
Metropolitan Comm Coll–Business & Technology Campus (MO)
Missouri State U–West Plains (MO)

Mohave Comm Coll (AZ)
Monroe County Comm Coll (MI)
North Dakota State Coll of Science (ND)
Northeast Comm Coll (NE)
Northeast Iowa Comm Coll (IA)
Northern Essex Comm Coll (MA)
Orange Coast Coll (CA)
Owens Comm Coll, Toledo (OH)
Palm Beach State Coll (FL)
Pasco-Hernando Comm Coll (FL)
Pennsylvania Highlands Comm Coll (PA)
Pensacola State Coll (FL)
Potomac State Coll of West Virginia U (WV)
Quinsigamond Comm Coll (MA)
St. Cloud Tech & Comm Coll (MN)
Sandhills Comm Coll (NC)
Seminole State Coll of Florida (FL)
Southern State Comm Coll (OH)
Springfield Tech Comm Coll (MA)
Stark State Coll of Technology (OH)
Tallahassee Comm Coll (FL)
Trident Tech Coll (SC)

COMPUTER PROGRAMMING (VENDOR/PRODUCT CERTIFICATION)

Chandler-Gilbert Comm Coll (AZ)
Florida State Coll at Jacksonville (FL)
Inver Hills Comm Coll (MN)
Lake Region State Coll (ND)
Marion Tech Coll (OH)
Metropolitan Comm Coll–Business & Technology Campus (MO)
Raritan Valley Comm Coll (NJ)
Seminole State Coll of Florida (FL)
Stark State Coll of Technology (OH)
Sullivan Coll of Technology and Design (KY)

COMPUTER SCIENCE

Allen Comm Coll (KS)
Amarillo Coll (TX)
Anoka-Ramsey Comm Coll (MN)
Anoka-Ramsey Comm Coll, Cambridge Campus (MN)
Barton County Comm Coll (KS)
Borough of Manhattan Comm Coll of the City U of New York (NY)
Bristol Comm Coll (MA)
Bucks County Comm Coll (PA)
Burlington County Coll (NJ)
Central Oregon Comm Coll (OR)
Central Wyoming Coll (WY)
Century Coll (MN)
Chipola Coll (FL)
Coll of the Canyons (CA)
Comm Coll of Philadelphia (PA)
Comm Coll of Vermont (VT)
Corning Comm Coll (NY)
Cowley County Comm Coll and Area Vocational–Tech School (KS)
Darton Coll (GA)
Daytona State Coll (FL)
De Anza Coll (CA)
Dodge City Comm Coll (KS)
Dutchess Comm Coll (NY)
El Centro Coll (TX)
Fiorello H. LaGuardia Comm Coll of the City U of New York (NY)
Frederick Comm Coll (MD)
Fulton-Montgomery Comm Coll (NY)
Grand Rapids Comm Coll (MI)
Gwinnett Tech Coll (GA)
Harper Coll (IL)
Harrisburg Area Comm Coll (PA)
Highland Comm Coll (IL)
Howard Comm Coll (MD)
Indian River State Coll (FL)
Inver Hills Comm Coll (MN)
Kingsborough Comm Coll of the City U of New York (NY)
Lake Region State Coll (ND)
Lake-Sumter Comm Coll (FL)
Lamar Comm Coll (CO)
Lanier Tech Coll (GA)
Laramie County Comm Coll (WY)
Lonestar Coll–Cy-Fair (TX)
Lonestar Coll–Kingwood (TX)
Lonestar Coll–Montgomery (TX)
Lonestar Coll–North Harris (TX)
Lonestar Coll–Tomball (TX)

Massachusetts Bay Comm Coll (MA)
Metropolitan Comm Coll–Blue River (MO)
Metropolitan Comm Coll–Business & Technology Campus (MO)
Metropolitan Comm Coll–Longview (MO)
Metropolitan Comm Coll–Maple Woods (MO)
Metropolitan Comm Coll–Penn Valley (MO)
Miami Dade Coll (FL)
Minnesota West Comm and Tech Coll (MN)
Mitchell Tech Inst (SD)
Mohave Comm Coll (AZ)
Nashua Comm Coll (NH)
New England Inst of Technology (RI)
Niagara County Comm Coll (NY)
Northampton Comm Coll (PA)
Northeast Comm Coll (NE)
Northern Essex Comm Coll (MA)
North Hennepin Comm Coll (MN)
North Idaho Coll (ID)
Northland Comm and Tech Coll–Thief River Falls & East Grand Forks (MN)
Oklahoma City Comm Coll (OK)
Onondaga Comm Coll (NY)
Palm Beach State Coll (FL)
Potomac State Coll of West Virginia U (WV)
Red Rocks Comm Coll (CO)
Salt Lake Comm Coll (UT)
Santa Barbara City Coll (CA)
Santa Rosa Jr Coll (CA)
Snow Coll (UT)
Southwest Mississippi Comm Coll (MS)
Springfield Tech Comm Coll (MA)
Suffolk County Comm Coll (NY)
Trinity Valley Comm Coll (TX)
Tyler Jr Coll (TX)
Union County Coll (NJ)
Westchester Comm Coll (NY)
Yakima Valley Comm Coll (WA)

COMPUTER SOFTWARE AND MEDIA APPLICATIONS RELATED

Berkeley City Coll (CA)
Dakota Coll at Bottineau (ND)
Florida State Coll at Jacksonville (FL)
ITT Tech Inst, Bessemer (AL)
ITT Tech Inst, Tucson (AZ)
ITT Tech Inst, Thornton (CO)
ITT Tech Inst, Jacksonville (FL)
ITT Tech Inst, Lake Mary (FL)
ITT Tech Inst, Pinellas Park (FL)
ITT Tech Inst, Tallahassee (FL)
ITT Tech Inst, Tampa (FL)
ITT Tech Inst (ID)
ITT Tech Inst, Fort Wayne (IN)
ITT Tech Inst, Indianapolis (IN)
ITT Tech Inst, Newburgh (IN)
ITT Tech Inst, Louisville (KY)
ITT Tech Inst, Baton Rouge (LA)
ITT Tech Inst, St. Rose (LA)
ITT Tech Inst (MD)
ITT Tech Inst, Norwood (MA)
ITT Tech Inst, Woburn (MA)
ITT Tech Inst, Canton (MI)
ITT Tech Inst, Swartz Creek (MI)
ITT Tech Inst, Troy (MI)
ITT Tech Inst, Wyoming (MI)
ITT Tech Inst, Eden Prairie (MN)
ITT Tech Inst, Arnold (MO)
ITT Tech Inst, Earth City (MO)
ITT Tech Inst, Henderson (NV)
ITT Tech Inst (NM)
ITT Tech Inst, Albany (NY)
ITT Tech Inst, Getzville (NY)
ITT Tech Inst, Liverpool (NY)
ITT Tech Inst, Norwood (OH)
ITT Tech Inst, Strongsville (OH)
ITT Tech Inst, Youngstown (OH)
ITT Tech Inst (OR)
ITT Tech Inst, Harrisburg (PA)
ITT Tech Inst, Pittsburgh (PA)
ITT Tech Inst, Tarentum (PA)
ITT Tech Inst, Columbia (SC)
ITT Tech Inst, Greenville (SC)
ITT Tech Inst, Cordova (TN)

ITT Tech Inst, Knoxville (TN)
ITT Tech Inst, Nashville (TN)
ITT Tech Inst, Arlington (TX)
ITT Tech Inst, Richardson (TX)
ITT Tech Inst (UT)
ITT Tech Inst, Chantilly (VA)
ITT Tech Inst, Norfolk (VA)
ITT Tech Inst, Richmond (VA)
ITT Tech Inst, Springfield (VA)
ITT Tech Inst, Seattle (WA)
ITT Tech Inst, Green Bay (WI)
ITT Tech Inst, Greenfield (WI)
Marion Tech Coll (OH)
Mesabi Range Comm and Tech Coll (MN)
Metropolitan Comm Coll–Business & Technology Campus (MO)
Northland Comm and Tech Coll–Thief River Falls & East Grand Forks (MN)
Seminole State Coll of Florida (FL)
Stark State Coll of Technology (OH)

COMPUTER SOFTWARE ENGINEERING

Cleveland Inst of Electronics (OH)
Florida State Coll at Jacksonville (FL)
Seminole State Coll of Florida (FL)
Southeast Tech Inst (SD)
Stark State Coll of Technology (OH)

COMPUTER SOFTWARE TECHNOLOGY

Brown Mackie Coll–Fort Wayne (IN)
Brown Mackie Coll–Hopkinsville (KY)
Brown Mackie Coll–Merrillville (IN)
Brown Mackie Coll–Michigan City (IN)
Brown Mackie Coll–Northern Kentucky (KY)
Brown Mackie Coll–South Bend (IN)
ITT Tech Inst, Bessemer (AL)
ITT Tech Inst, Madison (AL)
ITT Tech Inst, Mobile (AL)
ITT Tech Inst, Phoenix (AZ)
ITT Tech Inst, Tucson (AZ)
ITT Tech Inst (AR)
ITT Tech Inst, Thornton (CO)
ITT Tech Inst, Jacksonville (FL)
ITT Tech Inst, Lake Mary (FL)
ITT Tech Inst, Pinellas Park (FL)
ITT Tech Inst, Tampa (FL)
ITT Tech Inst, Atlanta (GA)
ITT Tech Inst, Duluth (GA)
ITT Tech Inst, Kennesaw (GA)
ITT Tech Inst, Burr Ridge (IL)
ITT Tech Inst, Mount Prospect (IL)
ITT Tech Inst, Orland Park (IL)
ITT Tech Inst, Fort Wayne (IN)
ITT Tech Inst, Indianapolis (IN)
ITT Tech Inst, Newburgh (IN)
ITT Tech Inst, Cedar Rapids (IA)
ITT Tech Inst, Clive (IA)
ITT Tech Inst, Louisville (KY)
ITT Tech Inst, St. Rose (LA)
ITT Tech Inst, Canton (MI)
ITT Tech Inst, Swartz Creek (MI)
ITT Tech Inst, Troy (MI)
ITT Tech Inst, Wyoming (MI)
ITT Tech Inst, Eden Prairie (MN)
ITT Tech Inst, Arnold (MO)
ITT Tech Inst, Earth City (MO)
ITT Tech Inst, Kansas City (MO)
ITT Tech Inst (NE)
ITT Tech Inst, Henderson (NV)
ITT Tech Inst (NM)
ITT Tech Inst, Columbus (OH)
ITT Tech Inst, Dayton (OH)
ITT Tech Inst, Hilliard (OH)
ITT Tech Inst, Maumee (OH)
ITT Tech Inst, Norwood (OH)
ITT Tech Inst, Strongsville (OH)
ITT Tech Inst, Warrensville Heights (OH)
ITT Tech Inst, Youngstown (OH)
ITT Tech Inst, Tulsa (OK)
ITT Tech Inst (OR)
ITT Tech Inst, Greenville (SC)
ITT Tech Inst, Chattanooga (TN)
ITT Tech Inst, Cordova (TN)

ITT Tech Inst, Johnson City (TN)
ITT Tech Inst, Knoxville (TN)
ITT Tech Inst, Nashville (TN)
ITT Tech Inst, Arlington (TX)
ITT Tech Inst, Austin (TX)
ITT Tech Inst, DeSoto (TX)
ITT Tech Inst, Houston (TX)
ITT Tech Inst, Houston (TX)
ITT Tech Inst, Richardson (TX)
ITT Tech Inst, San Antonio (TX)
ITT Tech Inst, Webster (TX)
ITT Tech Inst (UT)
ITT Tech Inst, Richmond (VA)
ITT Tech Inst, Springfield (VA)
ITT Tech Inst, Everett (WA)
ITT Tech Inst, Seattle (WA)
ITT Tech Inst (WV)
ITT Tech Inst, Green Bay (WI)
ITT Tech Inst, Greenfield (WI)
ITT Tech Inst, Madison (WI)
Lonestar Coll–Montgomery (TX)
Miami Dade Coll (FL)
Rogue Comm Coll (OR)

COMPUTER SUPPORT SPECIALIST

Big Bend Comm Coll (WA)
Darton Coll (GA)
Southwestern Michigan Coll (MI)

COMPUTER SYSTEMS ANALYSIS

Amarillo Coll (TX)
Bristol Comm Coll (MA)
Central New Mexico Comm Coll (NM)
Chandler-Gilbert Comm Coll (AZ)
Florida State Coll at Jacksonville (FL)
Fox Valley Tech Coll (WI)
Glendale Comm Coll (AZ)
Hillsborough Comm Coll (FL)
Kirtland Comm Coll (MI)
Lehigh Carbon Comm Coll (PA)
Metropolitan Comm Coll–Business & Technology Campus (MO)
New England Inst of Technology (RI)
Oakland Comm Coll (MI)
Pensacola State Coll (FL)
Phoenix Coll (AZ)
Pima Comm Coll (AZ)
Quinsigamond Comm Coll (MA)
Waukesha County Tech Coll (WI)

COMPUTER SYSTEMS NETWORKING AND TELECOMMUNICATIONS

Aiken Tech Coll (SC)
Alexandria Tech and Comm Coll (MN)
Allen Comm Coll (KS)
Altamaha Tech Coll (GA)
Anoka-Ramsey Comm Coll (MN)
Anoka-Ramsey Comm Coll, Cambridge Campus (MN)
Athens Tech Coll (GA)
Augusta Tech Coll (GA)
Austin Comm Coll (TX)
Barton County Comm Coll (KS)
Bellingham Tech Coll (WA)
Blackhawk Tech Coll (WI)
Borough of Manhattan Comm Coll of the City U of New York (NY)
Brown Mackie Coll–Cincinnati (OH)
Brown Mackie Coll–Louisville (KY)
Brown Mackie Coll–North Canton (OH)
Brown Mackie Coll–Salina (KS)
Cape Fear Comm Coll (NC)
Catawba Valley Comm Coll (NC)
Central Georgia Tech Coll (GA)
Central Lakes Coll (MN)
Central Oregon Comm Coll (OR)
Century Coll (MN)
Chandler-Gilbert Comm Coll (AZ)
Chattahoochee Tech Coll (GA)
Chippewa Valley Tech Coll (WI)
City Colls of Chicago, Harry S. Truman College (IL)
Clark Coll (WA)
CollAmerica–Flagstaff (AZ)
Coll of Business and Technology (FL)
Coll of Lake County (IL)

Coll of the Canyons (CA)
Collin County Comm Coll District (TX)
Colorado Mountain Coll (CO)
Columbus Tech Coll (OH)
The Comm Coll of Baltimore County (MD)
Comm Coll of Rhode Island (RI)
Comm Coll of Vermont (VT)
Corning Comm Coll (NY)
Crowder Coll (MO)
Dakota County Tech Coll (MN)
Danville Area Comm Coll (IL)
Daytona State Coll (FL)
DeKalb Tech Coll (GA)
Delaware Tech & Comm Coll, Stanton/Wilmington Campus (DE)
Delaware Tech & Comm Coll, Terry Campus (DE)
Eastfield Coll (TX)
Edison State Comm Coll (OH)
Elgin Comm Coll (IL)
Fayetteville Tech Comm Coll (NC)
Florida State Coll at Jacksonville (FL)
Fox Valley Tech Coll (WI)
GateWay Comm Coll (AZ)
Glendale Comm Coll (AZ)
Gwinnett Tech Coll (GA)
Hallmark Coll of Technology (TX)
Harrisburg Area Comm Coll (PA)
Harrison Coll, Indianapolis (IN)
Hawkeye Comm Coll (IA)
Houston Comm Coll System (TX)
Howard Comm Coll (MD)
Inver Hills Comm Coll (MN)
Jefferson Coll (MO)
Kilgore Coll (TX)
Lake Region State Coll (ND)
Lake Superior Coll (MN)
Lanier Tech Coll (GA)
Lehigh Carbon Comm Coll (PA)
Lincoln Land Comm Coll (IL)
Linn State Tech Coll (MO)
Lonestar Coll–Montgomery (TX)
Marion Tech Coll (OH)
Mesabi Range Comm and Tech Coll (MN)
Metropolitan Comm Coll–Business & Technology Campus (MO)
Middle Georgia Tech Coll (GA)
Midlands Tech Coll (SC)
Minnesota State Coll–Southeast Tech (MN)
Minnesota State Comm and Tech Coll (MN)
Minnesota West Comm and Tech Coll (MN)
Montana State U–Great Falls Coll of Technology (MT)
Montgomery County Comm Coll (PA)
Moraine Park Tech Coll (WI)
Moultrie Tech Coll (GA)
Mountain View Coll (TX)
Northampton Comm Coll (PA)
Northern Essex Comm Coll (MA)
North Georgia Tech Coll (GA)
North Iowa Area Comm Coll (IA)
North Seattle Comm Coll (WA)
Northwest Tech Coll (MN)
Norwalk Comm Coll (CT)
Ogeechee Tech Coll (GA)
Okefenokee Tech Coll (GA)
Olympic Coll (WA)
Onondaga Comm Coll (NY)
Pasco-Hernando Comm Coll (FL)
Pima Comm Coll (AZ)
Potomac State Coll of West Virginia U (WV)
Pratt Comm Coll (KS)
Randolph Comm Coll (NC)
Raritan Valley Comm Coll (NJ)
St. Cloud Tech & Comm Coll (MN)
St. Philip's Coll (TX)
Sandersville Tech Coll (GA)
Savannah Tech Coll (GA)
Seminole State Coll of Florida (FL)
Southeastern Tech Coll (GA)
Southeast Tech Inst (SD)
Southern Crescent Tech Coll (GA)
South Georgia Tech Coll (GA)
Southwestern Michigan Coll (MI)
Southwest Georgia Tech Coll (GA)
Southwest Mississippi Comm Coll (MS)

Stark State Coll of Technology (OH)
Sullivan Coll of Technology and Design (KY)
Tallahassee Comm Coll (FL)
Terra State Comm Coll (OH)
Trident Tech Coll (SC)
Tyler Jr Coll (TX)
Vincennes U Jasper Campus (IN)
Waukesha County Tech Coll (WI)
Wenatchee Valley Coll (WA)
Westchester Comm Coll (NY)
West Georgia Tech Coll (GA)
Westmoreland County Comm Coll (PA)
Wilson Comm Coll (NC)
Wiregrass Georgia Tech Coll (GA)
Wisconsin Indianhead Tech Coll (WI)

COMPUTER TECHNOLOGY/ COMPUTER SYSTEMS TECHNOLOGY

Cape Fear Comm Coll (NC)
Central Lakes Coll (MN)
Central Wyoming Coll (WY)
Century Coll (MN)
Corning Comm Coll (NY)
Dakota Coll at Bottineau (ND)
Delaware Tech & Comm Coll, Jack F. Owens Campus (DE)
Delaware Tech & Comm Coll, Terry Campus (DE)
Gulf Coast Comm Coll (FL)
Harrison Coll, Indianapolis (IN)
Harrison Coll, Muncie (IN)
Hillsborough Comm Coll (FL)
Inver Hills Comm Coll (MN)
ITI Tech Coll (LA)
Kent State U at Trumbull (OH)
Lake-Sumter Comm Coll (FL)
Lake Superior Coll (MN)
Miami Dade Coll (FL)
Minnesota State Coll–Southeast Tech (MN)
Minnesota State Comm and Tech Coll (MN)
Minnesota West Comm and Tech Coll (MN)
Montgomery Coll (MD)
New England Inst of Technology (RI)
Oakland Comm Coll (MI)
Okefenokee Tech Coll (GA)
Pasco-Hernando Comm Coll (FL)
Paul D. Camp Comm Coll (VA)
Pittsburgh Tech Inst, Oakdale (PA)
Quinsigamond Comm Coll (MA)
St. Philip's Coll (TX)
Southeast Tech Inst (SD)
Southern State Comm Coll (OH)
Sullivan Coll of Technology and Design (KY)
U of Arkansas Comm Coll at Morrilton (AR)
West Virginia Jr Coll–Bridgeport (WV)

COMPUTER TYPOGRAPHY AND COMPOSITION EQUIPMENT OPERATION

Doña Ana Comm Coll (NM)
Fulton-Montgomery Comm Coll (NY)
Gateway Comm Coll (CT)
Housatonic Comm Coll (CT)
Indian River State Coll (FL)
Lamar Comm Coll (CO)
Lonestar Coll–Kingwood (TX)
Metropolitan Comm Coll–Longview (MO)
Northern Essex Comm Coll (MA)
Onondaga Comm Coll (NY)
Orange Coast Coll (CA)
Pratt Comm Coll (KS)

CONSERVATION BIOLOGY

Central Lakes Coll (MN)

CONSTRUCTION ENGINEERING TECHNOLOGY

Antelope Valley Coll (CA)
Burlington County Coll (NJ)
Central Comm Coll–Hastings Campus (NE)

Central Maine Comm Coll (ME)
Clark Coll (WA)
Coll of Lake County (IL)
Comm Coll of Philadelphia (PA)
Crowder Coll (MO)
Danville Area Comm Coll (IL)
De Anza Coll (CA)
Dodge City Comm Coll (KS)
Dutchess Comm Coll (NY)
Florida State Coll at Jacksonville (FL)
Fulton-Montgomery Comm Coll (NY)
Gulf Coast Comm Coll (FL)
Harrisburg Area Comm Coll (PA)
Houston Comm Coll System (TX)
Jefferson State Comm Coll (AL)
Lincoln Land Comm Coll (IL)
Macomb Comm Coll (MI)
Miami Dade Coll (FL)
Midlands Tech Coll (SC)
Mid-Plains Comm Coll, North Platte (NE)
New England Inst of Technology (RI)
North Dakota State Coll of Science (ND)
Norwalk Comm Coll (CT)
Oklahoma State U, Oklahoma City (OK)
Onondaga Comm Coll (NY)
Orange Coast Coll (CA)
Owens Comm Coll, Toledo (OH)
Pennsylvania Highlands Comm Coll (PA)
Pensacola State Coll (FL)
Raritan Valley Comm Coll (NJ)
Rogue Comm Coll (OR)
St. Philip's Coll (TX)
Santa Fe Comm Coll (NM)
Seminole State Coll of Florida (FL)
Snow Coll (UT)
Southeastern Comm Coll (IA)
South Suburban Coll (IL)
Southwest Mississippi Comm Coll (MS)
State U of New York Coll of Technology at Alfred (NY)
Suffolk County Comm Coll (NY)
Tallahassee Comm Coll (FL)
The Williamson Free School of Mecha Trades (PA)
Yavapai Coll (AZ)

CONSTRUCTION/HEAVY EQUIPMENT/EARTHMOVING EQUIPMENT OPERATION
GateWay Comm Coll (AZ)
Ivy Tech Comm Coll–Southwest (IN)
Ivy Tech Comm Coll–Wabash Valley (IN)

CONSTRUCTION MANAGEMENT
Casper Coll (WY)
Delaware Tech & Comm Coll, Jack F. Owens Campus (DE)
Delaware Tech & Comm Coll, Stanton/Wilmington Campus (DE)
Delaware Tech & Comm Coll, Terry Campus (DE)
Kankakee Comm Coll (IL)
Northampton Comm Coll (PA)
North Hennepin Comm Coll (MN)
Oakland Comm Coll (MI)
Oklahoma State U, Oklahoma City (OK)
Waubonsee Comm Coll (IL)

CONSTRUCTION TRADES
Casper Coll (WY)
Harrisburg Area Comm Coll (PA)
Ivy Tech Comm Coll–East Central (IN)
Ivy Tech Comm Coll–Northeast (IN)
Ivy Tech Comm Coll–Northwest (IN)
Ivy Tech Comm Coll–Richmond (IN)
Lamar Comm Coll (CO)
Lehigh Carbon Comm Coll (PA)
Northeast Iowa Comm Coll (IA)
Ogeechee Tech Coll (GA)
Oklahoma State U, Oklahoma City (OK)
Rogue Comm Coll (OR)

CONSTRUCTION TRADES RELATED
Arizona Western Coll (AZ)
Central Maine Comm Coll (ME)
Central New Mexico Comm Coll (NM)
Ivy Tech Comm Coll–East Central (IN)
Ivy Tech Comm Coll–Kokomo (IN)
Ivy Tech Comm Coll–Northeast (IN)
Ivy Tech Comm Coll–Richmond (IN)
Jackson Comm Coll (MI)
Mitchell Tech Inst (SD)
Tompkins Cortland Comm Coll (NY)

CONSUMER MERCHANDISING/RETAILING MANAGEMENT
Bucks County Comm Coll (PA)
Colorado Mountain Coll, Alpine Campus (CO)
Doña Ana Comm Coll (NM)
Dutchess Comm Coll (NY)
FIDM/The Fashion Inst of Design & Merchandising, Los Angeles Campus (CA)
FIDM/The Fashion Inst of Design & Merchandising, Orange County Campus (CA)
FIDM/The Fashion Inst of Design & Merchandising, San Diego Campus (CA)
FIDM/The Fashion Inst of Design & Merchandising, San Francisco Campus (CA)
Gateway Comm Coll (CT)
Golden West Coll (CA)
Howard Comm Coll (MD)
Indian River State Coll (FL)
Niagara County Comm Coll (NY)
Northland Comm and Tech Coll–Thief River Falls & East Grand Forks (MN)
Pennsylvania Highlands Comm Coll (PA)
Quinsigamond Comm Coll (MA)
Stark State Coll of Technology (OH)
Suffolk County Comm Coll (NY)
Three Rivers Comm Coll (CT)
Westchester Comm Coll (NY)

CONSUMER SERVICES AND ADVOCACY
San Diego City Coll (CA)

COOKING AND RELATED CULINARY ARTS
Bristol Comm Coll (MA)
Central Oregon Comm Coll (OR)
Leeward Comm Coll (HI)
Miami Dade Coll (FL)
Minnesota State Comm and Tech Coll (MN)

CORRECTIONS
Amarillo Coll (TX)
Antelope Valley Coll (CA)
Austin Comm Coll (TX)
Barton County Comm Coll (KS)
Bucks County Comm Coll (PA)
Cayuga County Comm Coll (NY)
Colorado Mountain Coll, Timberline Campus (CO)
Danville Area Comm Coll (IL)
De Anza Coll (CA)
Eastern Arizona Coll (AZ)
Eastern Gateway Comm Coll (OH)
Grand Rapids Comm Coll (MI)
Illinois Eastern Comm Colls, Frontier Community College (IL)
Illinois Eastern Comm Colls, Lincoln Trail College (IL)
Illinois Eastern Comm Colls, Olney Central College (IL)
Illinois Eastern Comm Colls, Wabash Valley College (IL)
Indian River State Coll (FL)
Jackson Comm Coll (MI)
Kilgore Coll (TX)
Kirtland Comm Coll (MI)
Lake Michigan Coll (MI)
Laramie County Comm Coll (WY)
Metropolitan Comm Coll–Longview (MO)
Metropolitan Comm Coll–Penn Valley (MO)
Montcalm Comm Coll (MI)
Moraine Park Tech Coll (WI)

Mountain Empire Comm Coll (VA)
Northeast Comm Coll (NE)
Oakland Comm Coll (MI)
Owens Comm Coll, Toledo (OH)
Polk State Coll (FL)
Raritan Valley Comm Coll (NJ)
Sauk Valley Comm Coll (IL)
Southern State Comm Coll (OH)
Three Rivers Comm Coll (CT)
Trinity Valley Comm Coll (TX)
Westchester Comm Coll (NY)
Wisconsin Indianhead Tech Coll (WI)

CORRECTIONS AND CRIMINAL JUSTICE RELATED
Albany Tech Coll (GA)
Career Tech Coll (LA)
Corning Comm Coll (NY)
Fayetteville Tech Comm Coll (NC)

COSMETOLOGY
Central New Mexico Comm Coll (NM)
Century Coll (MN)
Clary Sage Coll (OK)
Clovis Comm Coll (NM)
Cowley County Comm Coll and Area Vocational–Tech School (KS)
Dodge City Comm Coll (KS)
Douglas Education Center (PA)
Golden West Coll (CA)
Honolulu Comm Coll (HI)
Houston Comm Coll System (TX)
Indian River State Coll (FL)
Kirtland Comm Coll (MI)
Lamar Comm Coll (CO)
Lonestar Coll–Kingwood (TX)
Lonestar Coll–North Harris (TX)
Martin Comm Coll (NC)
Minnesota State Coll–Southeast Tech (MN)
Minnesota State Comm and Tech Coll (MN)
Montcalm Comm Coll (MI)
Northeast Iowa Comm Coll (IA)
Oakland Comm Coll (MI)
Olympic Coll (WA)
Pueblo Comm Coll (CO)
Randolph Comm Coll (NC)
Salt Lake Comm Coll (UT)
Sandhills Comm Coll (NC)
San Diego City Coll (CA)
San Juan Coll (NM)
Santa Barbara City Coll (CA)
Solano Comm Coll (CA)
Southeastern Comm Coll (IA)
Southwest Mississippi Comm Coll (MS)
Trinity Valley Comm Coll (TX)

COSMETOLOGY AND PERSONAL GROOMING ARTS RELATED
Bristol Comm Coll (MA)

COUNSELING PSYCHOLOGY
Kilian Comm Coll (SD)

COUNSELOR EDUCATION/SCHOOL COUNSELING AND GUIDANCE
East Los Angeles Coll (CA)
Pratt Comm Coll (KS)

COURT REPORTING
Gadsden State Comm Coll (AL)
GateWay Comm Coll (AZ)
Harrisburg Area Comm Coll (PA)
Houston Comm Coll System (TX)
Kilgore Coll (TX)
Long Island Business Inst (NY)
Miami Dade Coll (FL)
Midlands Tech Coll (SC)
Moraine Park Tech Coll (WI)
New York Career Inst (NY)
Oakland Comm Coll (MI)
Orleans Tech Inst (PA)
Pennsylvania Highlands Comm Coll (PA)
Prince Inst of Professional Studies (AL)
San Diego City Coll (CA)
South Suburban Coll (IL)
Stark State Coll of Technology (OH)

State U of New York Coll of Technology at Alfred (NY)
West Kentucky Comm and Tech Coll (KY)
Wisconsin Indianhead Tech Coll (WI)

CRAFTS, FOLK ART AND ARTISANRY
Harrisburg Area Comm Coll (PA)

CREATIVE WRITING
Austin Comm Coll (TX)
Berkeley City Coll (CA)
Foothill Coll (CA)
Kirtland Comm Coll (MI)
Owens Comm Coll, Toledo (OH)
Santa Fe Comm Coll (NM)
Tompkins Cortland Comm Coll (NY)

CRIMINALISTICS AND CRIMINAL SCIENCE
Central Lakes Coll (MN)
Century Coll (MN)
Harrisburg Area Comm Coll (PA)
Oakland Comm Coll (MI)

CRIMINAL JUSTICE/LAW ENFORCEMENT ADMINISTRATION
Aiken Tech Coll (SC)
Allen Comm Coll (KS)
Amarillo Coll (TX)
Antelope Valley Coll (CA)
Arizona Western Coll (AZ)
Arkansas State U–Mountain Home (AR)
ASA The Coll For Excellence (NY)
Athens Tech Coll (GA)
Bainbridge Coll (GA)
Beaufort County Comm Coll (NC)
Brown Mackie Coll–Akron (OH)
Brown Mackie Coll–Albuquerque (NM)
Brown Mackie Coll–Atlanta (GA)
Brown Mackie Coll–Boise (ID)
Brown Mackie Coll–Cincinnati (OH)
Brown Mackie Coll–Findlay (OH)
Brown Mackie Coll–Fort Wayne (IN)
Brown Mackie Coll–Greenville (SC)
Brown Mackie Coll–Hopkinsville (KY)
Brown Mackie Coll–Indianapolis (IN)
Brown Mackie Coll–Kansas City (KS)
Brown Mackie Coll–Louisville (KY)
Brown Mackie Coll–Merrillville (IN)
Brown Mackie Coll–Miami (FL)
Brown Mackie Coll–Michigan City (IN)
Brown Mackie Coll–North Canton (OH)
Brown Mackie Coll–Northern Kentucky (KY)
Brown Mackie Coll–Phoenix (AZ)
Brown Mackie Coll–St. Louis (MO)
Brown Mackie Coll–Salina (KS)
Brown Mackie Coll–San Antonio (TX)
Brown Mackie Coll–South Bend (IN)
Brown Mackie Coll–Tucson (AZ)
Brown Mackie Coll–Tulsa (OK)
Bryant & Stratton Coll (WI)
Bucks County Comm Coll (PA)
Casper Coll (WY)
Central Maine Comm Coll (ME)
Central Wyoming Coll (WY)
Colorado Mountain Coll (CO)
Colorado Mountain Coll, Timberline Campus (CO)
Comm Coll of Philadelphia (PA)
Comm Coll of Vermont (VT)
Corning Comm Coll (NY)
Cowley County Comm Coll and Area Vocational–Tech School (KS)
Dabney S. Lancaster Comm Coll (VA)
Darton Coll (GA)
Daytona State Coll (FL)
De Anza Coll (CA)
Delaware Tech & Comm Coll, Jack F. Owens Campus (DE)
Delaware Tech & Comm Coll, Stanton/Wilmington Campus (DE)

Delaware Tech & Comm Coll, Terry Campus (DE)
Denmark Tech Coll (SC)
Dodge City Comm Coll (KS)
Dutchess Comm Coll (NY)
Eastern Arizona Coll (AZ)
East Los Angeles Coll (CA)
Florida State Coll at Jacksonville (FL)
Frederick Comm Coll (MD)
Fulton-Montgomery Comm Coll (NY)
Gateway Comm and Tech Coll (KY)
Georgia Military Coll (GA)
Golden West Coll (CA)
Goodwin Coll (CT)
Grand Rapids Comm Coll (MI)
Gulf Coast Comm Coll (FL)
Harper Coll (IL)
Harrisburg Area Comm Coll (PA)
Harrison Coll, Anderson (IN)
Harrison Coll (OH)
Hillsborough Comm Coll (FL)
Housatonic Comm Coll (CT)
Howard Comm Coll (MD)
Indian River State Coll (FL)
ITT Tech Inst, Bessemer (AL)
ITT Tech Inst, Madison (AL)
ITT Tech Inst, Mobile (AL)
ITT Tech Inst, Phoenix (AZ)
ITT Tech Inst, Tucson (AZ)
ITT Tech Inst (AR)
ITT Tech Inst, Anaheim (CA)
ITT Tech Inst, Lathrop (CA)
ITT Tech Inst, Oxnard (CA)
ITT Tech Inst, Rancho Cordova (CA)
ITT Tech Inst, San Bernardino (CA)
ITT Tech Inst, San Diego (CA)
ITT Tech Inst, San Dimas (CA)
ITT Tech Inst, Sylmar (CA)
ITT Tech Inst, Torrance (CA)
ITT Tech Inst, Aurora (CO)
ITT Tech Inst, Thornton (CO)
ITT Tech Inst, Fort Lauderdale (FL)
ITT Tech Inst, Fort Myers (FL)
ITT Tech Inst, Jacksonville (FL)
ITT Tech Inst, Lake Mary (FL)
ITT Tech Inst, Miami (FL)
ITT Tech Inst, Pinellas Park (FL)
ITT Tech Inst, Tallahassee (FL)
ITT Tech Inst, Tampa (FL)
ITT Tech Inst, Atlanta (GA)
ITT Tech Inst, Duluth (GA)
ITT Tech Inst, Kennesaw (GA)
ITT Tech Inst (ID)
ITT Tech Inst, Burr Ridge (IL)
ITT Tech Inst, Mount Prospect (IL)
ITT Tech Inst, Orland Park (IL)
ITT Tech Inst, Fort Wayne (IN)
ITT Tech Inst, Indianapolis (IN)
ITT Tech Inst, Merrillville (IN)
ITT Tech Inst, Newburgh (IN)
ITT Tech Inst, Cedar Rapids (IA)
ITT Tech Inst, Clive (IA)
ITT Tech Inst, Louisville (KY)
ITT Tech Inst, Baton Rouge (LA)
ITT Tech Inst, St. Rose (LA)
ITT Tech Inst, Canton (MI)
ITT Tech Inst, Swartz Creek (MI)
ITT Tech Inst, Troy (MI)
ITT Tech Inst, Wyoming (MI)
ITT Tech Inst, Eden Prairie (MN)
ITT Tech Inst, Arnold (MO)
ITT Tech Inst, Earth City (MO)
ITT Tech Inst, Kansas City (MO)
ITT Tech Inst (NE)
ITT Tech Inst, Henderson (NV)
ITT Tech Inst (NM)
ITT Tech Inst, Columbus (OH)
ITT Tech Inst, Dayton (OH)
ITT Tech Inst, Hilliard (OH)
ITT Tech Inst, Maumee (OH)
ITT Tech Inst, Norwood (OH)
ITT Tech Inst, Strongsville (OH)
ITT Tech Inst, Warrensville Heights (OH)
ITT Tech Inst, Youngstown (OH)
ITT Tech Inst, Tulsa (OK)
ITT Tech Inst (OR)
ITT Tech Inst, Bensalem (PA)
ITT Tech Inst, Dunmore (PA)
ITT Tech Inst, Harrisburg (PA)
ITT Tech Inst, King of Prussia (PA)
ITT Tech Inst, Pittsburgh (PA)
ITT Tech Inst, Tarentum (PA)
ITT Tech Inst, Columbia (SC)
ITT Tech Inst, Greenville (SC)

ITT Tech Inst, Chattanooga (TN)
ITT Tech Inst, Cordova (TN)
ITT Tech Inst, Knoxville (TN)
ITT Tech Inst, Nashville (TN)
ITT Tech Inst (UT)
ITT Tech Inst, Chantilly (VA)
ITT Tech Inst, Norfolk (VA)
ITT Tech Inst, Richmond (VA)
ITT Tech Inst, Salem (VA)
ITT Tech Inst, Springfield (VA)
ITT Tech Inst, Everett (WA)
ITT Tech Inst, Seattle (WA)
ITT Tech Inst, Spokane Valley (WA)
ITT Tech Inst (WI)
ITT Tech Inst, Green Bay (WI)
ITT Tech Inst, Greenfield (WI)
ITT Tech Inst, Madison (WI)
Jackson Comm Coll (MI)
Jefferson Coll (MO)
John Tyler Comm Coll (VA)
Kankakee Comm Coll (IL)
Kaskaskia Coll (IL)
Kent State U at East Liverpool (OH)
Kilgore Coll (TX)
Kilian Comm Coll (SD)
Kirtland Comm Coll (MI)
Lake Michigan Coll (MI)
Lake-Sumter Comm Coll (FL)
Laramie County Comm Coll (WY)
Lehigh Carbon Comm Coll (PA)
Lonestar Coll–Cy-Fair (TX)
Lonestar Coll–Kingwood (TX)
Lonestar Coll–Montgomery (TX)
Lonestar Coll–North Harris (TX)
Lonestar Coll–Tomball (TX)
Lower Columbia Coll (WA)
Macomb Comm Coll (MI)
Manchester Comm Coll (CT)
Massachusetts Bay Comm Coll (MA)
Mendocino Coll (CA)
Mesa Comm Coll (AZ)
Metropolitan Comm Coll–Longview (MO)
Metropolitan Comm Coll–Maple Woods (MO)
Metropolitan Comm Coll–Penn Valley (MO)
Miami Dade Coll (FL)
Missouri State U–West Plains (MO)
Mohawk Valley Comm Coll (NY)
Montcalm Comm Coll (MI)
Mountain Empire Comm Coll (VA)
Muskegon Comm Coll (MI)
New England Inst of Technology (RI)
Niagara County Comm Coll (NY)
Northern Essex Comm Coll (MA)
North Hennepin Comm Coll (MN)
North Idaho Coll (ID)
Northland Comm and Tech Coll– Thief River Falls & East Grand Forks (MN)
Northwest Coll (WY)
Norwalk Comm Coll (CT)
Onondaga Comm Coll (NY)
Owens Comm Coll, Toledo (OH)
Palm Beach State Coll (FL)
Pasco-Hernando Comm Coll (FL)
Paul D. Camp Comm Coll (VA)
Pensacola State Coll (FL)
Polk State Coll (FL)
Pueblo Comm Coll (CO)
Quinsigamond Comm Coll (MA)
Raritan Valley Comm Coll (NJ)
Red Rocks Comm Coll (CO)
St. Philip's Coll (TX)
Salt Lake Comm Coll (UT)
Sandhills Comm Coll (NC)
Santa Barbara City Coll (CA)
Santa Rosa Jr Coll (CA)
Sauk Valley Comm Coll (IL)
Scottsdale Comm Coll (AZ)
Seminole State Coll of Florida (FL)
Snow Coll (UT)
Solano Comm Coll (CA)
Southeastern Comm Coll (IA)
Southern State Comm Coll (OH)
Southside Virginia Comm Coll (VA)
Southwestern Coll of Business, Franklin (OH)
Suffolk County Comm Coll (NY)
Tallahassee Comm Coll (FL)
Three Rivers Comm Coll (CT)
Tompkins Cortland Comm Coll (NY)
Trident Tech Coll (SC)

Trinity Valley Comm Coll (TX)
Tyler Jr Coll (TX)
Union County Coll (NJ)
U of Arkansas Comm Coll at Morrilton (AR)
Western Iowa Tech Comm Coll (IA)
West Kentucky Comm and Tech Coll (KY)
Yakima Valley Comm Coll (WA)

CRIMINAL JUSTICE/POLICE SCIENCE

Alexandria Tech and Comm Coll (MN)
Amarillo Coll (TX)
Antelope Valley Coll (CA)
Austin Comm Coll (TX)
Barton County Comm Coll (KS)
Beaufort County Comm Coll (NC)
Blackhawk Tech Coll (WI)
Borough of Manhattan Comm Coll of the City U of New York (NY)
Bucks County Comm Coll (PA)
Burlington County Coll (NJ)
Cape Fear Comm Coll (NC)
Carroll Comm Coll (MD)
Cayuga County Comm Coll (NY)
Cecil Coll (MD)
Central Lakes Coll (MN)
Century Coll (MN)
Chippewa Valley Tech Coll (WI)
Cincinnati State Tech and Comm Coll (OH)
Cleveland State Comm Coll (TN)
Clovis Comm Coll (NM)
Coll of Lake County (IL)
Coll of the Canyons (CA)
Collin County Comm Coll District (TX)
The Comm Coll of Baltimore County (MD)
Comm Coll of Rhode Island (RI)
Cowley County Comm Coll and Area Vocational–Tech School (KS)
Danville Area Comm Coll (IL)
Dawson Comm Coll (MT)
Daytona State Coll (FL)
De Anza Coll (CA)
Delaware Tech & Comm Coll, Jack F. Owens Campus (DE)
Delaware Tech & Comm Coll, Stanton/Wilmington Campus (DE)
Delaware Tech & Comm Coll, Terry Campus (DE)
Dyersburg State Comm Coll (TN)
Eastern Arizona Coll (AZ)
Eastern Gateway Comm Coll (OH)
East Los Angeles Coll (CA)
Edison State Comm Coll (OH)
Elgin Comm Coll (IL)
Florida State Coll at Jacksonville (FL)
Fox Valley Tech Coll (WI)
Gadsden State Comm Coll (AL)
Georgia Highlands Coll (GA)
Golden West Coll (CA)
Grand Rapids Comm Coll (MI)
Grays Harbor Coll (WA)
Hagerstown Comm Coll (MD)
Harford Comm Coll (MD)
Harrisburg Area Comm Coll (PA)
Hawkeye Comm Coll (IA)
Honolulu Comm Coll (HI)
Houston Comm Coll System (TX)
Illinois Eastern Comm Colls, Olney Central College (IL)
Indian River State Coll (FL)
Inver Hills Comm Coll (MN)
Jefferson Coll (MO)
Jefferson State Comm Coll (AL)
Johnston Comm Coll (NC)
John Wood Comm Coll (IL)
Kent State U at Ashtabula (OH)
Kent State U at Tuscarawas (OH)
Lake Region State Coll (ND)
Lawson State Comm Coll (AL)
Lincoln Land Comm Coll (IL)
Linn-Benton Comm Coll (OR)
Los Angeles Harbor Coll (CA)
Macomb Comm Coll (MI)
McHenry County Coll (IL)
Mendocino Coll (CA)
Metropolitan Comm Coll–Blue River (MO)

Metropolitan Comm Coll–Longview (MO)
Metropolitan Comm Coll–Maple Woods (MO)
Metropolitan Comm Coll–Penn Valley (MO)
Miami Dade Coll (FL)
Middlesex Comm Coll (CT)
Minnesota West Comm and Tech Coll (MN)
Missouri State U–West Plains (MO)
Mohave Comm Coll (AZ)
Monroe County Comm Coll (MI)
Montgomery Coll (MD)
Montgomery County Comm Coll (PA)
Moraine Valley Comm Coll (IL)
Morton Coll (IL)
Northeast Comm Coll (NE)
North Hennepin Comm Coll (MN)
North Idaho Coll (ID)
North Iowa Area Comm Coll (IA)
Northland Comm and Tech Coll– Thief River Falls & East Grand Forks (MN)
Northwest-Shoals Comm Coll (AL)
Oakland Comm Coll (MI)
Ocean County Coll (NJ)
Okefenokee Tech Coll (GA)
Oklahoma State U, Oklahoma City (OK)
Olympic Coll (WA)
Onondaga Comm Coll (NY)
Owensboro Comm and Tech Coll (KY)
Owens Comm Coll, Toledo (OH)
Palm Beach State Coll (FL)
Pima Comm Coll (AZ)
Quinsigamond Comm Coll (MA)
Raritan Valley Comm Coll (NJ)
Rockingham Comm Coll (NC)
Rogue Comm Coll (OR)
Saint Charles Comm Coll (MO)
Sandhills Comm Coll (NC)
San Juan Coll (NM)
Santa Fe Comm Coll (NM)
Sauk Valley Comm Coll (IL)
Southeast Tech Inst (SD)
Springfield Tech Comm Coll (MA)
Suffolk County Comm Coll (NY)
Terra State Comm Coll (OH)
Trinity Valley Comm Coll (TX)
Tyler Jr Coll (TX)
Union County Coll (NJ)
Vincennes U Jasper Campus (IN)
Volunteer State Comm Coll (TN)
Waubonsee Comm Coll (IL)
Waukesha County Tech Coll (WI)
Western Iowa Tech Comm Coll (IA)
West Virginia Northern Comm Coll (WV)
Wisconsin Indianhead Tech Coll (WI)
Yakima Valley Comm Coll (WA)
Yavapai Coll (AZ)

CRIMINAL JUSTICE/SAFETY

Alamance Comm Coll (NC)
Altamaha Tech Coll (GA)
Ancilla Coll (IN)
Augusta Tech Coll (GA)
Blue Ridge Comm and Tech Coll (WV)
Bristol Comm Coll (MA)
Catawba Valley Comm Coll (NC)
Central Carolina Tech Coll (SC)
Central Comm Coll–Columbus Campus (NE)
Central Comm Coll–Grand Island Campus (NE)
Central Comm Coll–Hastings Campus (NE)
Central Georgia Tech Coll (GA)
Central Lakes Coll (MN)
Central New Mexico Comm Coll (NM)
Century Coll (MN)
Chandler-Gilbert Comm Coll (AZ)
Chattahoochee Tech Coll (GA)
City Colls of Chicago, Harry S. Truman College (IL)
DeKalb Tech Coll (GA)
Dutchess Comm Coll (NY)
Eastfield Coll (TX)
Fayetteville Tech Comm Coll (NC)
Georgia Highlands Coll (GA)

Georgia Northwestern Tech Coll (GA)
Glendale Comm Coll (AZ)
Great Basin Coll (NV)
Harrison Coll, Indianapolis (IN)
Harrison Coll, Muncie (IN)
Heart of Georgia Tech Coll (GA)
Holyoke Comm Coll (MA)
Inver Hills Comm Coll (MN)
Ivy Tech Comm Coll–Bloomington (IN)
Ivy Tech Comm Coll–Central Indiana (IN)
Ivy Tech Comm Coll–East Central (IN)
Ivy Tech Comm Coll–Kokomo (IN)
Ivy Tech Comm Coll–North Central (IN)
Ivy Tech Comm Coll–Northwest (IN)
Ivy Tech Comm Coll–Southwest (IN)
Ivy Tech Comm Coll–Wabash Valley (IN)
James Sprunt Comm Coll (NC)
Kent State U at Trumbull (OH)
Lamar Comm Coll (CO)
Lanier Tech Coll (GA)
Lehigh Carbon Comm Coll (PA)
Linn-Benton Comm Coll (OR)
Midlands Tech Coll (SC)
Minnesota State Coll–Southeast Tech (MN)
Minnesota State Comm and Tech Coll (MN)
Monroe County Comm Coll (MI)
Moultrie Tech Coll (GA)
Mountain View Coll (TX)
New Mexico State U–Alamogordo (NM)
Northampton Comm Coll (PA)
North Georgia Tech Coll (GA)
North Hennepin Comm Coll (MN)
Phoenix Coll (AZ)
Pima Comm Coll (AZ)
Potomac State Coll of West Virginia U (WV)
Randolph Comm Coll (NC)
San Juan Coll (NM)
Santa Fe Comm Coll (NM)
Savannah Tech Coll (GA)
Sheridan Coll (WY)
Southeastern Tech Coll (GA)
Southern Crescent Tech Coll (GA)
South Georgia Tech Coll (GA)
South Suburban Coll (IL)
Southwest Georgia Tech Coll (GA)
West Georgia Tech Coll (GA)
Westmoreland County Comm Coll (PA)
White Mountains Comm Coll (NH)
Wilson Comm Coll (NC)
Wiregrass Georgia Tech Coll (GA)

CRIMINOLOGY

Northland Comm and Tech Coll– Thief River Falls & East Grand Forks (MN)

CRISIS/EMERGENCY/DISASTER MANAGEMENT

Casper Coll (WY)
Fayetteville Tech Comm Coll (NC)
Montgomery Coll (MD)

CRITICAL INCIDENT RESPONSE/SPECIAL POLICE OPERATIONS

Raritan Valley Comm Coll (NJ)

CROP PRODUCTION

Arizona Western Coll (AZ)
Barton County Comm Coll (KS)
Dakota Coll at Bottineau (ND)
Northeast Comm Coll (NE)
Northeast Iowa Comm Coll (IA)
Northwest Coll (WY)

CULINARY ARTS

Alamance Comm Coll (NC)
Albany Tech Coll (GA)
The Art Inst of Ohio–Cincinnati (OH)
The Art Inst of Seattle (WA)
Atlanta Tech Coll (GA)

Augusta Tech Coll (GA)
Austin Comm Coll (TX)
Bellingham Tech Coll (WA)
Blackhawk Tech Coll (WI)
Blue Ridge Comm and Tech Coll (WV)
Bradford School (OH)
Bucks County Comm Coll (PA)
Cape Fear Comm Coll (NC)
Central New Mexico Comm Coll (NM)
Central Wyoming Coll (WY)
Chattahoochee Tech Coll (GA)
Cincinnati State Tech and Comm Coll (OH)
Clark Coll (WA)
Collin County Comm Coll District (TX)
Columbus Culinary Inst at Bradford School (OH)
Comm Coll of Philadelphia (PA)
Culinary Inst of St. Louis at Hickey Coll (MO)
Daytona State Coll (FL)
Delaware Tech & Comm Coll, Stanton/Wilmington Campus (DE)
Delaware Tech & Comm Coll, Terry Campus (DE)
Elaine P. Nunez Comm Coll (LA)
El Centro Coll (TX)
Elgin Comm Coll (IL)
Fayetteville Tech Comm Coll (NC)
Florida State Coll at Jacksonville (FL)
Grand Rapids Comm Coll (MI)
Harrisburg Area Comm Coll (PA)
Harrison Coll, Indianapolis (IN)
H. Councill Trenholm State Tech Coll (AL)
Houston Comm Coll System (TX)
Indian River State Coll (FL)
Jefferson Coll (MO)
Kaskaskia Coll (IL)
Linn-Benton Comm Coll (OR)
Macomb Comm Coll (MI)
Miami Dade Coll (FL)
Mitchell Tech Inst (SD)
Mohave Comm Coll (AZ)
Monroe County Comm Coll (MI)
Montgomery County Comm Coll (PA)
Niagara County Comm Coll (NY)
Northampton Comm Coll (PA)
North Dakota State Coll of Science (ND)
Northeast Comm Coll (NE)
North Georgia Tech Coll (GA)
North Idaho Coll (ID)
Oakland Comm Coll (MI)
Ogeechee Tech Coll (GA)
Olympic Coll (WA)
Orange Coast Coll (CA)
Phoenix Coll (AZ)
The Restaurant School at Walnut Hill Coll (PA)
St. Philip's Coll (TX)
Salt Lake Comm Coll (UT)
Sandhills Comm Coll (NC)
Santa Fe Comm Coll (NM)
Santa Rosa Jr Coll (CA)
Savannah Tech Coll (GA)
Scottsdale Comm Coll (AZ)
Sheridan Coll (WY)
South Georgia Tech Coll (GA)
Suffolk County Comm Coll (NY)
Trident Tech Coll (SC)
Westchester Comm Coll (NY)
West Kentucky Comm and Tech Coll (KY)
Westmoreland County Comm Coll (PA)
West Virginia Northern Comm Coll (WV)
White Mountains Comm Coll (NH)

CULINARY ARTS RELATED

Bristol Comm Coll (MA)
Linn-Benton Comm Coll (OR)
Santa Barbara City Coll (CA)

CUSTOMER SERVICE MANAGEMENT

Alexandria Tech and Comm Coll (MN)
Catawba Valley Comm Coll (NC)

Central Oregon Comm Coll (OR)
Comm Coll of Rhode Island (RI)
Delaware Tech & Comm Coll, Stanton/Wilmington Campus (DE)

CUSTOMER SERVICE SUPPORT/CALL CENTER/ TELESERVICE OPERATION
Central Wyoming Coll (WY)
Delaware Tech & Comm Coll, Jack F. Owens Campus (DE)
Delaware Tech & Comm Coll, Stanton/Wilmington Campus (DE)
Union County Coll (NJ)

CYBER/COMPUTER FORENSICS AND COUNTERTERRORISM
Catawba Valley Comm Coll (NC)
Harper Coll (IL)

CYTOTECHNOLOGY
Barton County Comm Coll (KS)

DAIRY HUSBANDRY AND PRODUCTION
Linn-Benton Comm Coll (OR)
Northeast Iowa Comm Coll (IA)

DAIRY SCIENCE
Northeast Comm Coll (NE)

DANCE
Austin Comm Coll (TX)
Barton County Comm Coll (KS)
Casper Coll (WY)
Darton Coll (GA)
Kilgore Coll (TX)
Lonestar Coll–Cy-Fair (TX)
Lonestar Coll–North Harris (TX)
Lonestar Coll–Tomball (TX)
Miami Dade Coll (FL)
Northern Essex Comm Coll (MA)
Orange Coast Coll (CA)
Raritan Valley Comm Coll (NJ)
Santa Rosa Jr Coll (CA)
Snow Coll (UT)
Trinity Valley Comm Coll (TX)
Tyler Jr Coll (TX)
Westchester Comm Coll (NY)

DATA ENTRY/ MICROCOMPUTER APPLICATIONS
Arizona Western Coll (AZ)
Bellingham Tech Coll (WA)
Chandler-Gilbert Comm Coll (AZ)
Clark Coll (WA)
Comm Coll of Vermont (VT)
Eastern Arizona Coll (AZ)
Eastfield Coll (TX)
Elgin Comm Coll (IL)
Fiorello H. LaGuardia Comm Coll of the City U of New York (NY)
Florida State Coll at Jacksonville (FL)
Gateway Comm Coll (CT)
Glendale Comm Coll (AZ)
Howard Comm Coll (MD)
Lower Columbia Coll (WA)
Metropolitan Comm Coll–Business & Technology Campus (MO)
Montgomery Coll (MD)
Northland Comm and Tech Coll– Thief River Falls & East Grand Forks (MN)
Owensboro Comm and Tech Coll (KY)
Pratt Comm Coll (KS)
St. Philip's Coll (TX)
Seminole State Coll of Florida (FL)
Stark State Coll of Technology (OH)
Tyler Jr Coll (TX)

DATA ENTRY/ MICROCOMPUTER APPLICATIONS RELATED
Berkeley City Coll (CA)
Colorado Mountain Coll (CO)
Colorado Mountain Coll, Alpine Campus (CO)
Florida State Coll at Jacksonville (FL)

Metropolitan Comm Coll–Business & Technology Campus (MO)
Northland Comm and Tech Coll– Thief River Falls & East Grand Forks (MN)
Orange Coast Coll (CA)
Pratt Comm Coll (KS)
Seminole State Coll of Florida (FL)
Stark State Coll of Technology (OH)

DATA MODELING/ WAREHOUSING AND DATABASE ADMINISTRATION
Brown Mackie Coll–Akron (OH)
Brown Mackie Coll–Cincinnati (OH)
Chandler-Gilbert Comm Coll (AZ)
Florida State Coll at Jacksonville (FL)
Lake Superior Coll (MN)
Metropolitan Comm Coll–Business & Technology Campus (MO)
Moraine Park Tech Coll (WI)
Northland Comm and Tech Coll– Thief River Falls & East Grand Forks (MN)
Seminole State Coll of Florida (FL)

DATA PROCESSING AND DATA PROCESSING TECHNOLOGY
Aiken Tech Coll (SC)
Allen Comm Coll (KS)
Antelope Valley Coll (CA)
Bainbridge Coll (GA)
Bristol Comm Coll (MA)
Cecil Coll (MD)
Central Carolina Tech Coll (SC)
Central New Mexico Comm Coll (NM)
Dabney S. Lancaster Comm Coll (VA)
Danville Area Comm Coll (IL)
Dodge City Comm Coll (KS)
Eastern Gateway Comm Coll (OH)
Eastfield Coll (TX)
East Los Angeles Coll (CA)
El Centro Coll (TX)
Frederick Comm Coll (MD)
Fulton-Montgomery Comm Coll (NY)
Gateway Comm Coll (CT)
Great Basin Coll (NV)
Hallmark Coll of Technology (TX)
Highland Comm Coll (IL)
Housatonic Comm Coll (CT)
Jackson Comm Coll (MI)
Kingsborough Comm Coll of the City U of New York (NY)
Lamar Comm Coll (CO)
Los Angeles Harbor Coll (CA)
Mendocino Coll (CA)
Mesa Comm Coll (AZ)
Metropolitan Comm Coll–Business & Technology Campus (MO)
Metropolitan Comm Coll–Longview (MO)
Metropolitan Comm Coll–Maple Woods (MO)
Metropolitan Comm Coll–Penn Valley (MO)
Miami Dade Coll (FL)
Midlands Tech Coll (SC)
Monroe County Comm Coll (MI)
Montcalm Comm Coll (MI)
Morton Coll (IL)
Muskegon Comm Coll (MI)
Nashua Comm Coll (NH)
Northern Essex Comm Coll (MA)
Oakland Comm Coll (MI)
Orange Coast Coll (CA)
Palm Beach State Coll (FL)
Paul D. Camp Comm Coll (VA)
Polk State Coll (FL)
Potomac State Coll of West Virginia U (WV)
Quinsigamond Comm Coll (MA)
San Diego City Coll (CA)
San Juan Coll (NM)
Seminole State Coll of Florida (FL)
Spartanburg Comm Coll (SC)
Springfield Tech Comm Coll (MA)
Suffolk County Comm Coll (NY)
Tallahassee Comm Coll (FL)
Terra State Comm Coll (OH)
Three Rivers Comm Coll (CT)
Trinity Valley Comm Coll (TX)
Westchester Comm Coll (NY)

DENTAL ASSISTING
Athens Tech Coll (GA)
Bradford School (PA)
Central Comm Coll–Hastings Campus (NE)
Central Oregon Comm Coll (OR)
Central Wyoming Coll (WY)
Century Coll (MN)
Comm Care Coll (OK)
Dakota County Tech Coll (MN)
Eastern Gateway Comm Coll (OH)
Foothill Coll (CA)
H. Councill Trenholm State Tech Coll (AL)
International Business Coll, Indianapolis (IN)
Lake Michigan Coll (MI)
Midlands Tech Coll (SC)
Mid-Plains Comm Coll, North Platte (NE)
Minnesota State Comm and Tech Coll (MN)
Minnesota West Comm and Tech Coll (MN)
Mohave Comm Coll (AZ)
North Dakota State Coll of Science (ND)
Northern Essex Comm Coll (MA)
Northwest Tech Coll (MN)
Phoenix Coll (AZ)
Pueblo Comm Coll (CO)
Raritan Valley Comm Coll (NJ)
St. Cloud Tech & Comm Coll (MN)
Santa Fe Comm Coll (NM)
Union County Coll (NJ)

DENTAL HYGIENE
Amarillo Coll (TX)
Athens Tech Coll (GA)
Atlanta Tech Coll (GA)
Austin Comm Coll (TX)
Barton County Comm Coll (KS)
Bristol Comm Coll (MA)
Burlington County Coll (NJ)
Cape Fear Comm Coll (NC)
Catawba Valley Comm Coll (NC)
Central Comm Coll–Hastings Campus (NE)
Central Georgia Tech Coll (GA)
Century Coll (MN)
Chippewa Valley Tech Coll (WI)
Clark Coll (WA)
Coll of Lake County (IL)
Collin County Comm Coll District (TX)
Columbus Tech Coll (GA)
The Comm Coll of Baltimore County (MD)
Comm Coll of Philadelphia (PA)
Comm Coll of Rhode Island (RI)
Darton Coll (GA)
Daytona State Coll (FL)
Delaware Tech & Comm Coll, Stanton/Wilmington Campus (DE)
Fayetteville Tech Comm Coll (NC)
Florida State Coll at Jacksonville (FL)
Foothill Coll (CA)
Fox Valley Tech Coll (WI)
Georgia Highlands Coll (GA)
Grand Rapids Comm Coll (MI)
Gulf Coast Comm Coll (FL)
Harper Coll (IL)
Harrisburg Area Comm Coll (PA)
Hawkeye Comm Coll (IA)
Hillsborough Comm Coll (FL)
Indian River State Coll (FL)
Lake Superior Coll (MN)
Laramie County Comm Coll (WY)
Lonestar Coll–Kingwood (TX)
Miami Dade Coll (FL)
Middle Georgia Tech Coll (GA)
Midlands Tech Coll (SC)
Minnesota State Comm and Tech Coll (MN)
Mohave Comm Coll (AZ)
Montana State U–Great Falls Coll of Technology (MT)
Montgomery County Comm Coll (PA)
Northampton Comm Coll (PA)
North Dakota State Coll of Science (ND)
Oakland Comm Coll (MI)
Ogeechee Tech Coll (GA)
Orange Coast Coll (CA)
Owens Comm Coll, Toledo (OH)

Palm Beach State Coll (FL)
Pasco-Hernando Comm Coll (FL)
Pensacola State Coll (FL)
Phoenix Coll (AZ)
Pima Comm Coll (AZ)
Pima Medical Inst, Albuquerque (NM)
Pima Medical Inst, Seattle (WA)
Pueblo Comm Coll (CO)
Quinsigamond Comm Coll (MA)
Raritan Valley Comm Coll (NJ)
St. Cloud Tech & Comm Coll (MN)
Salt Lake Comm Coll (UT)
San Juan Coll (NM)
Santa Rosa Jr Coll (CA)
Sheridan Coll (WY)
Southeastern Tech Coll (GA)
Springfield Tech Comm Coll (MA)
Stark State Coll of Technology (OH)
Tallahassee Comm Coll (FL)
Trident Tech Coll (SC)
Tyler Jr Coll (TX)
Union County Coll (NJ)
Waukesha County Tech Coll (WI)
Western Iowa Tech Comm Coll (IA)
Westmoreland County Comm Coll (PA)
Yakima Valley Comm Coll (WA)

DENTAL LABORATORY TECHNOLOGY
J. Sargeant Reynolds Comm Coll (VA)
Pima Comm Coll (AZ)

DENTAL SERVICES AND ALLIED PROFESSIONS RELATED
Quinsigamond Comm Coll (MA)

DESIGN AND APPLIED ARTS RELATED
Howard Comm Coll (MD)
Kingsborough Comm Coll of the City U of New York (NY)
Mohawk Valley Comm Coll (NY)
Muskegon Comm Coll (MI)
Niagara County Comm Coll (NY)
Oklahoma City Comm Coll (OK)
Onondaga Comm Coll (NY)
Pratt Comm Coll (KS)
Raritan Valley Comm Coll (NJ)
Wenatchee Valley Coll (WA)
Westchester Comm Coll (NY)

DESIGN AND VISUAL COMMUNICATIONS
Blue Ridge Comm and Tech Coll (WV)
Bristol Comm Coll (MA)
Bryant & Stratton Coll (WI)
Creative Center (NE)
Douglas Education Center (PA)
Elgin Comm Coll (IL)
FIDM/The Fashion Inst of Design & Merchandising, Los Angeles Campus (CA)
FIDM/The Fashion Inst of Design & Merchandising, San Diego Campus (CA)
FIDM/The Fashion Inst of Design & Merchandising, San Francisco Campus (CA)
Florida State Coll at Jacksonville (FL)
Harford Comm Coll (MD)
Harrisburg Area Comm Coll (PA)
ITT Tech Inst, Bessemer (AL)
ITT Tech Inst, Madison (AL)
ITT Tech Inst, Mobile (AL)
ITT Tech Inst, Phoenix (AZ)
ITT Tech Inst, Tucson (AZ)
ITT Tech Inst (AR)
ITT Tech Inst, Anaheim (CA)
ITT Tech Inst, Lathrop (CA)
ITT Tech Inst, Oxnard (CA)
ITT Tech Inst, Rancho Cordova (CA)
ITT Tech Inst, San Bernardino (CA)
ITT Tech Inst, San Diego (CA)
ITT Tech Inst, San Dimas (CA)
ITT Tech Inst, Sylmar (CA)
ITT Tech Inst, Torrance (CA)
ITT Tech Inst, Aurora (CO)
ITT Tech Inst, Thornton (CO)
ITT Tech Inst, Fort Lauderdale (FL)
ITT Tech Inst, Jacksonville (FL)

ITT Tech Inst, Lake Mary (FL)
ITT Tech Inst, Miami (FL)
ITT Tech Inst, Pinellas Park (FL)
ITT Tech Inst, Tampa (FL)
ITT Tech Inst, Atlanta (GA)
ITT Tech Inst, Duluth (GA)
ITT Tech Inst, Kennesaw (GA)
ITT Tech Inst (ID)
ITT Tech Inst, Burr Ridge (IL)
ITT Tech Inst, Mount Prospect (IL)
ITT Tech Inst, Orland Park (IL)
ITT Tech Inst, Fort Wayne (IN)
ITT Tech Inst, Indianapolis (IN)
ITT Tech Inst, Newburgh (IN)
ITT Tech Inst, Louisville (KY)
ITT Tech Inst, Baton Rouge (LA)
ITT Tech Inst, St. Rose (LA)
ITT Tech Inst (MD)
ITT Tech Inst, Canton (MI)
ITT Tech Inst, Swartz Creek (MI)
ITT Tech Inst, Troy (MI)
ITT Tech Inst, Wyoming (MI)
ITT Tech Inst, Eden Prairie (MN)
ITT Tech Inst, Arnold (MO)
ITT Tech Inst, Earth City (MO)
ITT Tech Inst, Kansas City (MO)
ITT Tech Inst (NE)
ITT Tech Inst, Henderson (NV)
ITT Tech Inst (NM)
ITT Tech Inst, Albany (NY)
ITT Tech Inst, Getzville (NY)
ITT Tech Inst, Liverpool (NY)
ITT Tech Inst, Columbus (OH)
ITT Tech Inst, Dayton (OH)
ITT Tech Inst, Hilliard (OH)
ITT Tech Inst, Maumee (OH)
ITT Tech Inst, Norwood (OH)
ITT Tech Inst, Strongsville (OH)
ITT Tech Inst, Warrensville Heights (OH)
ITT Tech Inst, Youngstown (OH)
ITT Tech Inst, Tulsa (OK)
ITT Tech Inst (OR)
ITT Tech Inst, Columbia (SC)
ITT Tech Inst, Greenville (SC)
ITT Tech Inst, Chattanooga (TN)
ITT Tech Inst, Cordova (TN)
ITT Tech Inst, Knoxville (TN)
ITT Tech Inst, Nashville (TN)
ITT Tech Inst, Arlington (TX)
ITT Tech Inst, Austin (TX)
ITT Tech Inst, DeSoto (TX)
ITT Tech Inst, Houston (TX)
ITT Tech Inst, Houston (TX)
ITT Tech Inst, Richardson (TX)
ITT Tech Inst, San Antonio (TX)
ITT Tech Inst, Webster (TX)
ITT Tech Inst (UT)
ITT Tech Inst, Chantilly (VA)
ITT Tech Inst, Norfolk (VA)
ITT Tech Inst, Richmond (VA)
ITT Tech Inst, Springfield (VA)
ITT Tech Inst, Everett (WA)
ITT Tech Inst, Seattle (WA)
ITT Tech Inst, Spokane Valley (WA)
ITT Tech Inst (WV)
ITT Tech Inst, Green Bay (WI)
ITT Tech Inst, Greenfield (WI)
Ivy Tech Comm Coll–Central Indiana (IN)
Ivy Tech Comm Coll–Columbus (IN)
Ivy Tech Comm Coll–North Central (IN)
Ivy Tech Comm Coll–Southern Indiana (IN)
Ivy Tech Comm Coll–Southwest (IN)
Ivy Tech Comm Coll–Wabash Valley (IN)
Lonestar Coll–Cy-Fair (TX)
Lonestar Coll–Kingwood (TX)
Lonestar Coll–Montgomery (TX)
Lonestar Coll–North Harris (TX)
Oklahoma City Comm Coll (OK)
Pima Comm Coll (AZ)
Salt Lake Comm Coll (UT)
Santa Fe Comm Coll (NM)
Southeastern Tech Coll (GA)

DESKTOP PUBLISHING AND DIGITAL IMAGING DESIGN
Houston Comm Coll System (TX)
Leeward Comm Coll (HI)
Linn-Benton Comm Coll (OR)
New England Inst of Technology (RI)
Northeast Iowa Comm Coll (IA)
North Iowa Area Comm Coll (IA)

Northwest Coll (WY)
Owens Comm Coll, Toledo (OH)
Southeast Tech Inst (SD)
Sullivan Coll of Technology and Design (KY)
Terra State Comm Coll (OH)

DEVELOPMENTAL AND CHILD PSYCHOLOGY

Central Lakes Coll (MN)
Comm Coll of Vermont (VT)
De Anza Coll (CA)
East Los Angeles Coll (CA)
Fulton-Montgomery Comm Coll (NY)
Los Angeles Harbor Coll (CA)
Mendocino Coll (CA)
Muskegon Comm Coll (MI)
North Idaho Coll (ID)
San Diego City Coll (CA)
Trinity Valley Comm Coll (TX)

DIAGNOSTIC MEDICAL SONOGRAPHY AND ULTRASOUND TECHNOLOGY

Athens Tech Coll (GA)
Austin Comm Coll (TX)
Cape Fear Comm Coll (NC)
Central New Mexico Comm Coll (NM)
Chippewa Valley Tech Coll (WI)
Cincinnati State Tech and Comm Coll (OH)
Columbus Tech Coll (GA)
Comm Coll of Rhode Island (RI)
Darton Coll (GA)
Delaware Tech & Comm Coll, Jack F. Owens Campus (DE)
Delaware Tech & Comm Coll, Stanton/Wilmington Campus (DE)
El Centro Coll (TX)
Florida State Coll at Jacksonville (FL)
Foothill Coll (CA)
GateWay Comm Coll (AZ)
Gulf Coast Comm Coll (FL)
Harper Coll (IL)
Harrisburg Area Comm Coll (PA)
H. Councill Trenholm State Tech Coll (AL)
Hillsborough Comm Coll (FL)
Jackson Comm Coll (MI)
Laramie County Comm Coll (WY)
Lonestar Coll–Cy-Fair (TX)
Miami Dade Coll (FL)
Montgomery Coll (MD)
Northampton Comm Coll (PA)
Oakland Comm Coll (MI)
Owensboro Comm and Tech Coll (KY)
Owens Comm Coll, Toledo (OH)
Pensacola State Coll (FL)
Polk State Coll (FL)
Pueblo Comm Coll (CO)
St. Cloud Tech & Comm Coll (MN)
Southeast Tech Inst (SD)
Springfield Tech Comm Coll (MA)
Union County Coll (NJ)
West Kentucky Comm and Tech Coll (KY)

DIESEL MECHANICS TECHNOLOGY

Alexandria Tech and Comm Coll (MN)
Bellingham Tech Coll (WA)
Casper Coll (WY)
Central Comm Coll–Hastings Campus (NE)
Central Lakes Coll (MN)
Clark Coll (WA)
The Comm Coll of Baltimore County (MD)
Grays Harbor Coll (WA)
Great Basin Coll (NV)
Hawkeye Comm Coll (IA)
Illinois Eastern Comm Colls, Wabash Valley College (IL)
Johnston Comm Coll (NC)
Kilgore Coll (TX)
Laramie County Comm Coll (WY)
Linn-Benton Comm Coll (OR)
Lower Columbia Coll (WA)

Mid-Plains Comm Coll, North Platte (NE)
Minnesota State Comm and Tech Coll (MN)
Minnesota West Comm and Tech Coll (MN)
North Dakota State Coll of Science (ND)
Northeast Comm Coll (NE)
Oklahoma Tech Coll (OK)
Raritan Valley Comm Coll (NJ)
Rogue Comm Coll (OR)
St. Philip's Coll (TX)
Salt Lake Comm Coll (UT)
San Juan Coll (NM)
Santa Rosa Jr Coll (CA)
Sheridan Coll (WY)
Southeast Comm Inst (SD)
Southwest Mississippi Comm Coll (MS)
The U of Montana–Helena Coll of Technology (MT)
White Mountains Comm Coll (NH)

DIETETICS

Central Oregon Comm Coll (OR)
Cincinnati State Tech and Comm Coll (OH)
Dutchess Comm Coll (NY)
Florida State Coll at Jacksonville (FL)
Gateway Comm Coll (CT)
Harper Coll (IL)
Harrisburg Area Comm Coll (PA)
Miami Dade Coll (FL)
Orange Coast Coll (CA)
Owens Comm Coll, Toledo (OH)
Pensacola State Coll (FL)
Suffolk County Comm Coll (NY)
Westchester Comm Coll (NY)

DIETETICS AND CLINICAL NUTRITION SERVICES RELATED

Cowley County Comm Coll and Area Vocational–Tech School (KS)
Harrisburg Area Comm Coll (PA)

DIETETIC TECHNOLOGY

Brown Mackie Coll–Fort Wayne (IN)
Chandler-Gilbert Comm Coll (AZ)
Fiorello H. LaGuardia Comm Coll of the City U of New York (NY)
Harper Coll (IL)
Miami Dade Coll (FL)
Montana State U–Great Falls Coll of Technology (MT)
Westmoreland County Comm Coll (PA)

DIETITIAN ASSISTANT

Barton County Comm Coll (KS)
Chandler-Gilbert Comm Coll (AZ)
Florida State Coll at Jacksonville (FL)
Front Range Comm Coll (CO)
Hillsborough Comm Coll (FL)
Martin Comm Coll (NC)

DIGITAL COMMUNICATION AND MEDIA/MULTIMEDIA

Century Coll (MN)
Comm Coll of Vermont (VT)
Delaware Tech & Comm Coll, Terry Campus (DE)
Laramie County Comm Coll (WY)
Raritan Valley Comm Coll (NJ)
Sullivan Coll of Technology and Design (KY)
U of Alaska Anchorage, Kenai Peninsula Coll (AK)

DRAFTING AND DESIGN TECHNOLOGY

Albany Tech Coll (GA)
Allen Comm Coll (KS)
Amarillo Coll (TX)
Antelope Valley Coll (CA)
Austin Comm Coll (TX)
Bainbridge Coll (GA)
Beaufort County Comm Coll (NC)
Burlington County Coll (NJ)
Casper Coll (WY)

Cayuga County Comm Coll (NY)
Central Comm Coll–Columbus Campus (NE)
Central Comm Coll–Grand Island Campus (NE)
Central Comm Coll–Hastings Campus (NE)
Central Georgia Tech Coll (GA)
Central Oregon Comm Coll (OR)
Chattahoochee Tech Coll (GA)
Coll of Central Florida (FL)
Collin County Comm Coll District (TX)
Columbus Tech Coll (GA)
Comm Coll of Philadelphia (PA)
Corning Comm Coll (NY)
Cowley County Comm Coll and Area Vocational–Tech School (KS)
Crowder Coll (MO)
Dabney S. Lancaster Comm Coll (VA)
Daytona State Coll (FL)
DeKalb Tech Coll (GA)
Delaware Tech & Comm Coll, Jack F. Owens Campus (DE)
Delaware Tech & Comm Coll, Stanton/Wilmington Campus (DE)
Delaware Tech & Comm Coll, Terry Campus (DE)
Doña Ana Comm Coll (NM)
Eastern Arizona Coll (AZ)
Eastern Gateway Comm Coll (OH)
Eastfield Coll (TX)
East Los Angeles Coll (CA)
Florida State Coll at Jacksonville (FL)
Frederick Comm Coll (MD)
Gadsden State Comm Coll (AL)
Golden West Coll (CA)
Grand Rapids Comm Coll (MI)
Gulf Coast Comm Coll (FL)
Gwinnett Tech Coll (GA)
H. Councill Trenholm State Tech Coll (AL)
Highland Comm Coll (IL)
Honolulu Comm Coll (HI)
Houston Comm Coll System (TX)
Indian River State Coll (FL)
ITI Tech Coll (LA)
Ivy Tech Comm Coll–Central Indiana (IN)
Ivy Tech Comm Coll–Columbus (IN)
Ivy Tech Comm Coll–Kokomo (IN)
Ivy Tech Comm Coll–Lafayette (IN)
Ivy Tech Comm Coll–Northeast (IN)
Ivy Tech Comm Coll–Northwest (IN)
Kankakee Comm Coll (IL)
Kilgore Coll (TX)
Kirtland Comm Coll (MI)
Lake Michigan Coll (MI)
Lanier Tech Coll (GA)
Laramie County Comm Coll (WY)
Lawson State Comm Coll (AL)
Lehigh Carbon Comm Coll (PA)
Linn-Benton Comm Coll (OR)
Linn State Tech Coll (MO)
Lonestar Coll–North Harris (TX)
Los Angeles Harbor Coll (CA)
Lurleen B. Wallace Comm Coll (AL)
Macomb Comm Coll (MI)
Marion Tech Coll (OH)
Massachusetts Bay Comm Coll (MA)
Mesa Comm Coll (AZ)
Metropolitan Comm Coll–Business & Technology Campus (MO)
Miami Dade Coll (FL)
Middle Georgia Tech Coll (GA)
Mohave Comm Coll (AZ)
Mohawk Valley Comm Coll (NY)
Monroe County Comm Coll (MI)
Montcalm Comm Coll (MI)
Morton Coll (IL)
Mountain View Coll (TX)
Muskegon Comm Coll (MI)
Nashua Comm Coll (NH)
New England Inst of Technology (RI)
Niagara County Comm Coll (NY)
North Idaho Coll (ID)
Northland Comm and Tech Coll–Thief River Falls & East Grand Forks (MN)

Northwest-Shoals Comm Coll (AL)
Oakland Comm Coll (MI)
Oklahoma City Comm Coll (OK)
Oklahoma State U, Oklahoma City (OK)
Olympic Coll (WA)
Orange Coast Coll (CA)
Palm Beach State Coll (FL)
Pasco-Hernando Comm Coll (FL)
Pensacola State Coll (FL)
Saint Charles Comm Coll (MO)
Salt Lake Comm Coll (UT)
San Diego City Coll (CA)
San Juan Coll (NM)
Santa Barbara City Coll (CA)
Santa Fe Comm Coll (NM)
Seminole State Coll of Florida (FL)
Solano Comm Coll (CA)
Southeastern Comm Coll (IA)
Southern Crescent Tech Coll (GA)
Southern State Comm Coll (OH)
South Georgia Tech Coll (GA)
Southwestern Michigan Coll (MI)
Spartanburg Comm Coll (SC)
Stark State Coll of Technology (OH)
Suffolk County Comm Coll (NY)
Sullivan Coll of Technology and Design (KY)
Three Rivers Comm Coll (CT)
Triangle Tech, Inc.–DuBois School (PA)
Trinity Valley Comm Coll (TX)
U of Arkansas Comm Coll at Morrilton (AR)
Vincennes U Jasper Campus (IN)
Wiregrass Georgia Tech Coll (GA)

DRAFTING/DESIGN ENGINEERING TECHNOLOGIES RELATED

Blackhawk Tech Coll (WI)
Dabney S. Lancaster Comm Coll (VA)
De Anza Coll (CA)
Lonestar Coll–Montgomery (TX)
Macomb Comm Coll (MI)
Niagara County Comm Coll (NY)
Sullivan Coll of Technology and Design (KY)

DRAMA AND DANCE TEACHER EDUCATION

Darton Coll (GA)

DRAMATIC/THEATER ARTS

Allen Comm Coll (KS)
Amarillo Coll (TX)
American Academy of Dramatic Arts (CA)
Anoka-Ramsey Comm Coll (MN)
Anoka-Ramsey Comm Coll, Cambridge Campus (MN)
Arizona Western Coll (AZ)
Austin Comm Coll (TX)
Bainbridge Coll (GA)
Barton County Comm Coll (KS)
Bucks County Comm Coll (PA)
Burlington County Coll (NJ)
Central Wyoming Coll (WY)
Chandler-Gilbert Comm Coll (AZ)
Clarendon Coll (TX)
Coll of the Canyons (CA)
Colorado Mountain Coll (CO)
Comm Coll of Rhode Island (RI)
Cowley County Comm Coll and Area Vocational–Tech School (KS)
Crowder Coll (MO)
Darton Coll (GA)
De Anza Coll (CA)
Dodge City Comm Coll (KS)
Eastern Arizona Coll (AZ)
East Los Angeles Coll (CA)
Edison State Comm Coll (OH)
Fulton-Montgomery Comm Coll (NY)
Harrisburg Area Comm Coll (PA)
Highland Comm Coll (IL)
Howard Comm Coll (MD)
Indian River State Coll (FL)
Kilgore Coll (TX)
Kingsborough Comm Coll of the City U of New York (NY)
Lake Michigan Coll (MI)
Linn-Benton Comm Coll (OR)

Lonestar Coll–Cy-Fair (TX)
Lonestar Coll–Kingwood (TX)
Lonestar Coll–Montgomery (TX)
Lonestar Coll–North Harris (TX)
Lonestar Coll–Tomball (TX)
Manchester Comm Coll (CT)
Mendocino Coll (CA)
Miami Dade Coll (FL)
Mohawk Valley Comm Coll (NY)
Niagara County Comm Coll (NY)
Northeast Comm Coll (NE)
Northern Essex Comm Coll (MA)
North Idaho Coll (ID)
Oakland Comm Coll (MI)
Oklahoma City Comm Coll (OK)
Orange Coast Coll (CA)
Owens Comm Coll, Toledo (OH)
Palm Beach State Coll (FL)
Phoenix Coll (AZ)
Red Rocks Comm Coll (CO)
Saint Charles Comm Coll (MO)
St. Philip's Coll (TX)
San Diego City Coll (CA)
Santa Barbara City Coll (CA)
Santa Rosa Jr Coll (CA)
Sauk Valley Comm Coll (IL)
Scottsdale Comm Coll (AZ)
Sheridan Coll (WY)
Snow Coll (UT)
Suffolk County Comm Coll (NY)
Three Rivers Comm Coll (CT)
Trinity Valley Comm Coll (TX)
Tyler Jr Coll (TX)

DRAMATIC/THEATER ARTS AND STAGECRAFT RELATED

Bristol Comm Coll (MA)
St. Philip's Coll (TX)

DRAWING

De Anza Coll (CA)

EARLY CHILDHOOD EDUCATION

Aiken Tech Coll (SC)
Ancilla Coll (IN)
Arizona Western Coll (AZ)
Austin Comm Coll (TX)
Barton County Comm Coll (KS)
Big Bend Comm Coll (WA)
Blackhawk Tech Coll (WI)
Brown Mackie Coll–Akron (OH)
Brown Mackie Coll–Atlanta (GA)
Brown Mackie Coll–Cincinnati (OH)
Brown Mackie Coll–Findlay (OH)
Brown Mackie Coll–Louisville (KY)
Brown Mackie Coll–Miami (FL)
Brown Mackie Coll–Michigan City (IN)
Brown Mackie Coll–South Bend (IN)
Brown Mackie Coll–Tucson (AZ)
Cape Fear Comm Coll (NC)
Catawba Valley Comm Coll (NC)
Central Oregon Comm Coll (OR)
Central Wyoming Coll (WY)
Chippewa Valley Tech Coll (WI)
Clark Coll (WA)
Clovis Comm Coll (NM)
Coll of Central Florida (FL)
Collin County Comm Coll District (TX)
Colorado Mountain Coll, Timberline Campus (CO)
Comm Care Coll (OK)
The Comm Coll of Baltimore County (MD)
Comm Coll of Rhode Island (RI)
Comm Coll of Vermont (VT)
Delaware Tech & Comm Coll, Jack F. Owens Campus (DE)
Delaware Tech & Comm Coll, Stanton/Wilmington Campus (DE)
Delaware Tech & Comm Coll, Terry Campus (DE)
Fayetteville Tech Comm Coll (NC)
Fox Valley Tech Coll (WI)
Front Range Comm Coll (CO)
Gateway Comm and Tech Coll (KY)
Georgia Military Coll (GA)
Glendale Comm Coll (AZ)
Hagerstown Comm Coll (MD)
Harford Comm Coll (MD)
Harper Coll (IL)
Harrisburg Area Comm Coll (PA)

Ivy Tech Comm Coll–Bloomington (IN)
Ivy Tech Comm Coll–Central Indiana (IN)
Ivy Tech Comm Coll–Columbus (IN)
Ivy Tech Comm Coll–East Central (IN)
Ivy Tech Comm Coll–Kokomo (IN)
Ivy Tech Comm Coll–Lafayette (IN)
Ivy Tech Comm Coll–North Central (IN)
Ivy Tech Comm Coll–Northeast (IN)
Ivy Tech Comm Coll–Northwest (IN)
Ivy Tech Comm Coll–Richmond (IN)
Ivy Tech Comm Coll–Southeast (IN)
Ivy Tech Comm Coll–Southern Indiana (IN)
Ivy Tech Comm Coll–Southwest (IN)
Ivy Tech Comm Coll–Wabash Valley (IN)
Jackson Comm Coll (MI)
James Sprunt Comm Coll (NC)
Jefferson Coll (MO)
Johnston Comm Coll (NC)
Kent State U at Tuscarawas (OH)
Kingsborough Comm Coll of the City U of New York (NY)
Lake Michigan Coll (MI)
Lake-Sumter Comm Coll (FL)
Laramie County Comm Coll (WY)
Lehigh Carbon Comm Coll (PA)
Lower Columbia Coll (WA)
Montgomery Coll (MD)
Moraine Park Tech Coll (WI)
New Mexico State U–Alamogordo (NM)
Northampton Comm Coll (PA)
Northeast Comm Coll (NE)
North Iowa Area Comm Coll (IA)
North Seattle Comm Coll (WA)
Norwalk Comm Coll (CT)
Oklahoma State U, Oklahoma City (OK)
Olympic Coll (WA)
Owens Comm Coll, Toledo (OH)
Paul D. Camp Comm Coll (VA)
Pima Comm Coll (AZ)
Randolph Comm Coll (NC)
St. Philip's Coll (TX)
Sauk Valley Comm Coll (IL)
Sheridan Coll (WY)
Southwestern Michigan Coll (MI)
Southwest Mississippi Comm Coll (MS)
Springfield Tech Comm Coll (MA)
Tompkins Cortland Comm Coll (NY)
U of Alaska Anchorage, Kenai Peninsula Coll (AK)
Waukesha County Tech Coll (WI)
Wenatchee Valley Coll (WA)
Westmoreland County Comm Coll (PA)
White Mountains Comm Coll (NH)
Wilson Comm Coll (NC)
Wisconsin Indianhead Tech Coll (WI)

E-COMMERCE

Augusta Tech Coll (GA)
Catawba Valley Comm Coll (NC)
Central Georgia Tech Coll (GA)
Delaware Tech & Comm Coll, Jack F. Owens Campus (DE)
Delaware Tech & Comm Coll, Terry Campus (DE)
Eastfield Coll (TX)
Fayetteville Tech Comm Coll (NC)
Pasco-Hernando Comm Coll (FL)
St. Philip's Coll (TX)
Wiregrass Georgia Tech Coll (GA)

ECONOMICS

Allen Comm Coll (KS)
Austin Comm Coll (TX)
Barton County Comm Coll (KS)
Casper Coll (WY)
Clarendon Coll (TX)
Darton Coll (GA)
De Anza Coll (CA)
Foothill Coll (CA)
Georgia Highlands Coll (GA)
Indian River State Coll (FL)
Laramie County Comm Coll (WY)
Linn-Benton Comm Coll (OR)
Lonestar Coll–Cy-Fair (TX)
Lonestar Coll–Kingwood (TX)
Lonestar Coll–Montgomery (TX)

Lonestar Coll–North Harris (TX)
Lonestar Coll–Tomball (TX)
Miami Dade Coll (FL)
Muskegon Comm Coll (MI)
Oklahoma State U, Oklahoma City (OK)
Orange Coast Coll (CA)
Palm Beach State Coll (FL)
Potomac State Coll of West Virginia U (WV)
Red Rocks Comm Coll (CO)
Saint Charles Comm Coll (MO)
St. Philip's Coll (TX)
Salt Lake Comm Coll (UT)
Santa Barbara City Coll (CA)
Santa Rosa Jr Coll (CA)
Sauk Valley Comm Coll (IL)
Snow Coll (UT)
Terra State Comm Coll (OH)
Tyler Jr Coll (TX)
Wenatchee Valley Coll (WA)

EDUCATION

Bainbridge Coll (GA)
Bucks County Comm Coll (PA)
Burlington County Coll (NJ)
Cecil Coll (MD)
Central Oregon Comm Coll (OR)
Chipola Coll (FL)
Clarendon Coll (TX)
Clovis Comm Coll (NM)
The Comm Coll of Baltimore County (MD)
Comm Coll of Philadelphia (PA)
Comm Coll of Vermont (VT)
Cowley County Comm Coll and Area Vocational–Tech School (KS)
Crowder Coll (MO)
Dabney S. Lancaster Comm Coll (VA)
Dakota Coll at Bottineau (ND)
Dodge City Comm Coll (KS)
Eastfield Coll (TX)
Edison State Comm Coll (OH)
Elaine P. Nunez Comm Coll (LA)
Frederick Comm Coll (MD)
Georgia Military Coll (GA)
Hagerstown Comm Coll (MD)
Harford Comm Coll (MD)
Highland Comm Coll (IL)
Indian River State Coll (FL)
Inver Hills Comm Coll (MN)
Kent State U at Salem (OH)
Kilian Comm Coll (SD)
Kingsborough Comm Coll of the City U of New York (NY)
Laramie County Comm Coll (WY)
Lehigh Carbon Comm Coll (PA)
Linn-Benton Comm Coll (OR)
Lonestar Coll–Cy-Fair (TX)
Lonestar Coll–Kingwood (TX)
Lonestar Coll–Montgomery (TX)
Lonestar Coll–North Harris (TX)
Lonestar Coll–Tomball (TX)
Miami Dade Coll (FL)
Mohave Comm Coll (AZ)
Motlow State Comm Coll (TN)
Mountain View Coll (TX)
Muskegon Comm Coll (MI)
New Mexico State U–Alamogordo (NM)
Northeast Comm Coll (NE)
Northern Essex Comm Coll (MA)
North Idaho Coll (ID)
Owens Comm Coll, Toledo (OH)
Palm Beach State Coll (FL)
Paul D. Camp Comm Coll (VA)
Pensacola State Coll (FL)
Potomac State Coll of West Virginia U (WV)
Saint Charles Comm Coll (MO)
St. Philip's Coll (TX)
Santa Fe Comm Coll (NM)
Sauk Valley Comm Coll (IL)
Snow Coll (UT)
Southside Virginia Comm Coll (VA)
Southwest Mississippi Comm Coll (MS)
Terra State Comm Coll (OH)
Trinity Valley Comm Coll (TX)
Vincennes U Jasper Campus (IN)
Volunteer State Comm Coll (TN)
Wenatchee Valley Coll (WA)

EDUCATIONAL/INSTRUCTIONAL TECHNOLOGY

Collin County Comm Coll District (TX)
Ivy Tech Comm Coll–North Central (IN)

EDUCATIONAL LEADERSHIP AND ADMINISTRATION

Glendale Comm Coll (AZ)

EDUCATION (MULTIPLE LEVELS)

Carroll Comm Coll (MD)
Century Coll (MN)
Delaware Tech & Comm Coll, Jack F. Owens Campus (DE)
Delaware Tech & Comm Coll, Stanton/Wilmington Campus (DE)
Delaware Tech & Comm Coll, Terry Campus (DE)
Kirtland Comm Coll (MI)
Onondaga Comm Coll (NY)
Owens Comm Coll, Toledo (OH)
Pratt Comm Coll (KS)
U of Arkansas Comm Coll at Morrilton (AR)
Vincennes U Jasper Campus (IN)
Waubonsee Comm Coll (IL)
Westchester Comm Coll (NY)

EDUCATION RELATED

Corning Comm Coll (NY)
Miami Dade Coll (FL)
Yavapai Coll (AZ)

EDUCATION (SPECIFIC LEVELS AND METHODS) RELATED

Leeward Comm Coll (HI)

EDUCATION (SPECIFIC SUBJECT AREAS) RELATED

Saint Charles Comm Coll (MO)

ELECTRICAL AND ELECTRONIC ENGINEERING TECHNOLOGIES RELATED

Albany Tech Coll (GA)
Cincinnati State Tech and Comm Coll (OH)
J. Sargeant Reynolds Comm Coll (VA)
Lake Region State Coll (ND)
Miami Dade Coll (FL)
Minnesota State Comm and Tech Coll (MN)
Mohawk Valley Comm Coll (NY)
North Dakota State Coll of Science (ND)
Onondaga Comm Coll (NY)
Sheridan Coll (WY)
Sullivan Coll of Technology and Design (KY)
Terra State Comm Coll (OH)

ELECTRICAL AND ELECTRONICS ENGINEERING

Allen Comm Coll (KS)
Dutchess Comm Coll (NY)
Fiorello H. LaGuardia Comm Coll of the City U of New York (NY)
John Tyler Comm Coll (VA)
Lake Region State Coll (ND)

ELECTRICAL AND POWER TRANSMISSION INSTALLATION

Ivy Tech Comm Coll–Columbus (IN)
Minnesota West Comm and Tech Coll (MN)
Oklahoma State U, Oklahoma City (OK)
Orange Coast Coll (CA)
Polk State Coll (FL)
Rogue Comm Coll (OR)
St. Cloud Tech & Comm Coll (MN)

ELECTRICAL AND POWER TRANSMISSION INSTALLATION RELATED

Martin Comm Coll (NC)

Minnesota West Comm and Tech Coll (MN)

ELECTRICAL, ELECTRONIC AND COMMUNICATIONS ENGINEERING TECHNOLOGY

Aiken Tech Coll (SC)
Alamance Comm Coll (NC)
Allen Comm Coll (KS)
Amarillo Coll (TX)
Antelope Valley Coll (CA)
Athens Tech Coll (GA)
Augusta Tech Coll (GA)
Austin Comm Coll (TX)
Bainbridge Coll (GA)
Beaufort County Comm Coll (NC)
Brown Mackie Coll–Cincinnati (OH)
Brown Mackie Coll–Louisville (KY)
Burlington County Coll (NJ)
Cape Fear Comm Coll (NC)
Casper Coll (WY)
Catawba Valley Comm Coll (NC)
Cayuga County Comm Coll (NY)
Central Comm Coll–Columbus Campus (NE)
Central Comm Coll–Grand Island Campus (NE)
Central Comm Coll–Hastings Campus (NE)
Central Georgia Tech Coll (GA)
Central New Mexico Comm Coll (NM)
Central Oregon Comm Coll (OR)
Chattahoochee Tech Coll (GA)
Cincinnati State Tech and Comm Coll (OH)
Clark Coll (WA)
Cleveland Inst of Electronics (OH)
Coll of Lake County (IL)
Collin County Comm Coll District (TX)
Columbus Tech Coll (GA)
The Comm Coll of Baltimore County (MD)
Comm Coll of Rhode Island (RI)
Corning Comm Coll (NY)
Crowder Coll (MO)
Dabney S. Lancaster Comm Coll (VA)
Daytona State Coll (FL)
DeKalb Tech Coll (GA)
Delaware Tech & Comm Coll, Jack F. Owens Campus (DE)
Delaware Tech & Comm Coll, Stanton/Wilmington Campus (DE)
Delaware Tech & Comm Coll, Terry Campus (DE)
Dodge City Comm Coll (KS)
Doña Ana Comm Coll (NM)
Dutchess Comm Coll (NY)
Dyersburg State Comm Coll (TN)
Eastern Gateway Comm Coll (OH)
Eastfield Coll (TX)
East Los Angeles Coll (CA)
Edison State Comm Coll (OH)
Elgin Comm Coll (IL)
Fayetteville Tech Comm Coll (NC)
Florida State Coll at Jacksonville (FL)
Foothill Coll (CA)
Fox Valley Tech Coll (WI)
Frederick Comm Coll (MD)
Front Range Comm Coll (CO)
Fulton-Montgomery Comm Coll (NY)
Gadsden State Comm Coll (AL)
Gateway Comm Coll (CT)
Georgia Highlands Coll (GA)
Golden West Coll (CA)
Grand Rapids Comm Coll (MI)
Great Basin Coll (NV)
Gulf Coast Comm Coll (FL)
Gwinnett Tech Coll (GA)
Hallmark Inst of Technology (TX)
Harper Coll (IL)
Harrisburg Area Comm Coll (PA)
Hawkeye Comm Coll (IA)
Heart of Georgia Tech Coll (GA)
Highland Comm Coll (IL)
Hillsborough Comm Coll (FL)
Honolulu Comm Coll (HI)
Howard Comm Coll (MD)
Illinois Eastern Comm Colls, Wabash Valley College (IL)
Indian River State Coll (FL)
ITI Tech Coll (LA)

Ivy Tech Comm Coll–Bloomington (IN)
Ivy Tech Comm Coll–Central Indiana (IN)
Ivy Tech Comm Coll–Columbus (IN)
Ivy Tech Comm Coll–East Central (IN)
Ivy Tech Comm Coll–Kokomo (IN)
Ivy Tech Comm Coll–Lafayette (IN)
Ivy Tech Comm Coll–North Central (IN)
Ivy Tech Comm Coll–Northeast (IN)
Ivy Tech Comm Coll–Northwest (IN)
Ivy Tech Comm Coll–Richmond (IN)
Ivy Tech Comm Coll–Southeast (IN)
Ivy Tech Comm Coll–Southern Indiana (IN)
Ivy Tech Comm Coll–Southwest (IN)
Ivy Tech Comm Coll–Wabash Valley (IN)
Jackson Comm Coll (MI)
Johnston Comm Coll (NC)
Kankakee Comm Coll (IL)
Kaskaskia Coll (IL)
Kent State U at Ashtabula (OH)
Kent State U at Trumbull (OH)
Kent State U at Tuscarawas (OH)
Kilgore Coll (TX)
Kirtland Comm Coll (MI)
Lake-Sumter Comm Coll (FL)
Lake Superior Coll (MN)
Lanier Tech Coll (GA)
Lehigh Carbon Comm Coll (PA)
Lincoln Land Comm Coll (IL)
Linn State Tech Coll (MO)
Lonestar Coll–Cy-Fair (TX)
Lonestar Coll–North Harris (TX)
Lonestar Coll–Tomball (TX)
Los Angeles Harbor Coll (CA)
Macomb Comm Coll (MI)
Marion Tech Coll (OH)
McHenry County Coll (IL)
Mesa Comm Coll (AZ)
Metropolitan Comm Coll–Business & Technology Campus (MO)
Miami Dade Coll (FL)
Midlands Tech Coll (SC)
Minnesota State Coll–Southeast Tech (MN)
Minnesota State Comm and Tech Coll (MN)
Mitchell Tech Inst (SD)
Mohawk Valley Comm Coll (NY)
Monroe County Comm Coll (MI)
Montcalm Comm Coll (MI)
Montgomery County Comm Coll (PA)
Moultrie Tech Coll (GA)
Mountain Empire Comm Coll (VA)
Mountain View Coll (TX)
Muskegon Comm Coll (MI)
Nashua Comm Coll (NH)
New England Inst of Technology (RI)
New Mexico State U–Alamogordo (NM)
Northampton Comm Coll (PA)
Northeast Iowa Comm Coll (IA)
Northern Essex Comm Coll (MA)
North Idaho Coll (ID)
North Iowa Area Comm Coll (IA)
Northland Comm and Tech Coll–Thief River Falls & East Grand Forks (MN)
North Seattle Comm Coll (WA)
Oakland Comm Coll (MI)
Oklahoma City Comm Coll (OK)
Oklahoma State U, Oklahoma City (OK)
Olympic Coll (WA)
Onondaga Comm Coll (NY)
Orange Coast Coll (CA)
Owensboro Comm and Tech Coll (KY)
Owens Comm Coll, Toledo (OH)
Palm Beach State Coll (FL)
Penn State Brandywine (PA)
Penn State DuBois (PA)
Penn State Fayette, The Eberly Campus (PA)
Penn State Hazleton (PA)
Penn State New Kensington (PA)
Penn State Schuylkill (PA)
Penn State Shenango (PA)
Penn State Wilkes-Barre (PA)
Penn State Worthington Scranton (PA)

Penn State York (PA)
Pennsylvania Highlands Comm Coll (PA)
Pensacola State Coll (FL)
Pima Comm Coll (AZ)
Pittsburgh Tech Inst, Oakdale (PA)
Potomac State Coll of West Virginia U (WV)
Pueblo Comm Coll (CO)
Quinsigamond Comm Coll (MA)
Reid State Tech Coll (AL)
Rogue Comm Coll (OR)
St. Cloud Tech & Comm Coll (MN)
Salt Lake Comm Coll (UT)
San Diego City Coll (CA)
San Juan Coll (NM)
Santa Barbara City Coll (CA)
Santa Fe Comm Coll (NM)
Santa Rosa Jr Coll (CA)
Sauk Valley Comm Coll (IL)
Savannah Tech Coll (GA)
Scottsdale Comm Coll (AZ)
Seminole State Coll of Florida (FL)
Solano Comm Coll (CA)
Southeastern Comm Coll (IA)
Southeastern Tech Coll (GA)
Southeast Tech Inst (SD)
Southern Crescent Tech Coll (GA)
South Georgia Tech Coll (GA)
Southside Virginia Comm Coll (VA)
South Suburban Coll (IL)
Southwestern Michigan Coll (MI)
Southwest Mississippi Comm Coll (MS)
Spartanburg Comm Coll (SC)
Springfield Tech Comm Coll (MA)
Suffolk County Comm Coll (NY)
Sullivan Coll of Technology and Design (KY)
Terra State Comm Coll (OH)
Three Rivers Comm Coll (CT)
Tompkins Cortland Comm Coll (NY)
Triangle Tech, Inc.–DuBois School (PA)
Trident Tech Coll (SC)
Waubonsee Comm Coll (IL)
Waukesha County Tech Coll (WI)
Westchester Comm Coll (NY)
Western Iowa Tech Comm Coll (IA)
West Georgia Tech Coll (GA)
Westmoreland County Comm Coll (PA)
The Williamson Free School of Mecha Trades (PA)
Yakima Valley Comm Coll (WA)
YTI Career Inst–York (PA)

ELECTRICAL/ELECTRONICS DRAFTING AND CAD/CADD
Central New Mexico Comm Coll (NM)
Collin County Comm Coll District (TX)
Eastfield Coll (TX)
Waukesha County Tech Coll (WI)

ELECTRICAL/ELECTRONICS EQUIPMENT INSTALLATION AND REPAIR
Arizona Western Coll (AZ)
Cape Fear Comm Coll (NC)
Collin County Comm Coll District (TX)
Lake Region State Coll (ND)
Linn State Tech Coll (MO)
Macomb Comm Coll (MI)
Mesabi Range Comm and Tech Coll (MN)
New England Inst of Technology (RI)
Orange Coast Coll (CA)
Pittsburgh Tech Inst, Oakdale (PA)
St. Philip's Coll (TX)
Santa Barbara City Coll (CA)
Southeast Tech Inst (SD)
Sullivan Coll of Technology and Design (KY)

ELECTRICAL/ELECTRONICS MAINTENANCE AND REPAIR TECHNOLOGY RELATED
Mohawk Valley Comm Coll (NY)
Sullivan Coll of Technology and Design (KY)

ELECTRICIAN
Bellingham Tech Coll (WA)
Central Comm Coll–Hastings Campus (NE)
Clovis Comm Coll (NM)
Coll of Lake County (IL)
Dakota County Tech Coll (MN)
Fayetteville Tech Comm Coll (NC)
GateWay Comm Coll (AZ)
Gulf Coast Comm Coll (FL)
Harrisburg Area Comm Coll (PA)
H. Councill Trenholm State Tech Coll (AL)
Ivy Tech Comm Coll–Bloomington (IN)
Ivy Tech Comm Coll–Central Indiana (IN)
Ivy Tech Comm Coll–East Central (IN)
Ivy Tech Comm Coll–Kokomo (IN)
Ivy Tech Comm Coll–Lafayette (IN)
Ivy Tech Comm Coll–North Central (IN)
Ivy Tech Comm Coll–Northeast (IN)
Ivy Tech Comm Coll–Northwest (IN)
Ivy Tech Comm Coll–Richmond (IN)
Ivy Tech Comm Coll–Southern Indiana (IN)
Ivy Tech Comm Coll–Southwest (IN)
Ivy Tech Comm Coll–Wabash Valley (IN)
John Wood Comm Coll (IL)
Lake Superior Coll (MN)
Linn State Tech Coll (MO)
Lurleen B. Wallace Comm Coll (AL)
Minnesota West Comm and Tech Coll (MN)
Mitchell Tech Inst (SD)
Moraine Park Tech Coll (WI)
New Mexico State U–Alamogordo (NM)
Northampton Comm Coll (PA)
Northeast Comm Coll (NE)
Northeast Iowa Comm Coll (IA)
Northwest Coll (WY)
Oakland Comm Coll (MI)
Olympic Coll (WA)
Randolph Comm Coll (NC)
Waubonsee Comm Coll (IL)
West Kentucky Comm and Tech Coll (KY)
Wilson Comm Coll (NC)

ELECTROCARDIOGRAPH TECHNOLOGY
Delaware Tech & Comm Coll, Stanton/Wilmington Campus (DE)
Oklahoma State U, Oklahoma City (OK)

ELECTROMECHANICAL AND INSTRUMENTATION AND MAINTENANCE TECHNOLOGIES RELATED
Cape Fear Comm Coll (NC)
Catawba Valley Comm Coll (NC)
Cowley County Comm Coll and Area Vocational–Tech School (KS)
Gulf Coast Comm Coll (FL)
Randolph Comm Coll (NC)
Sullivan Coll of Technology and Design (KY)
Waukesha County Tech Coll (WI)

ELECTROMECHANICAL TECHNOLOGY
Blackhawk Tech Coll (WI)
Blue Ridge Comm and Tech Coll (WV)
Bristol Comm Coll (MA)
Central Maine Comm Coll (ME)
Chandler-Gilbert Comm Coll (AZ)
Chippewa Valley Tech Coll (WI)
Cincinnati State Tech and Comm Coll (OH)
Clarendon Coll (TX)
DeKalb Tech Coll (GA)
Delaware Tech & Comm Coll, Terry Campus (DE)
Dutchess Comm Coll (NY)

Edison State Comm Coll (OH)
Fox Valley Tech Coll (WI)
GateWay Comm Coll (AZ)
Hagerstown Comm Coll (MD)
Los Angeles Harbor Coll (CA)
Macomb Comm Coll (MI)
Martin Comm Coll (NC)
Montgomery County Comm Coll (PA)
Moraine Park Tech Coll (WI)
Muskegon Comm Coll (MI)
Nashua Comm Coll (NH)
Northampton Comm Coll (PA)
Northeast Comm Coll (NE)
Oakland Comm Coll (MI)
Owens Comm Coll, Toledo (OH)
Quinsigamond Comm Coll (MA)
Rockingham Comm Coll (NC)
St. Philip's Coll (TX)
Southeast Tech Inst (SD)
Springfield Tech Comm Coll (MA)
State U of New York Coll of Technology at Alfred (NY)
Union County Coll (NJ)

ELECTRONEURODIAGNOSTIC/ELECTRO-ENCEPHALOGRAPHIC TECHNOLOGY
Catawba Valley Comm Coll (NC)
Harford Comm Coll (MD)

ELEMENTARY EDUCATION
Allen Comm Coll (KS)
Amarillo Coll (TX)
Ancilla Coll (IN)
Arizona Western Coll (AZ)
Bainbridge Coll (GA)
Barton County Comm Coll (KS)
Carl Albert State Coll (OK)
Casper Coll (WY)
Cecil Coll (MD)
Central New Mexico Comm Coll (NM)
Central Wyoming Coll (WY)
Chandler-Gilbert Comm Coll (AZ)
Clarendon Coll (TX)
The Comm Coll of Baltimore County (MD)
Corning Comm Coll (NY)
Cowley County Comm Coll and Area Vocational–Tech School (KS)
Crowder Coll (MO)
Delaware Tech & Comm Coll, Jack F. Owens Campus (DE)
Delaware Tech & Comm Coll, Stanton/Wilmington Campus (DE)
Delaware Tech & Comm Coll, Terry Campus (DE)
Dodge City Comm Coll (KS)
Dutchess Comm Coll (NY)
Eastern Arizona Coll (AZ)
Fayetteville Tech Comm Coll (NC)
Frank Phillips Coll (TX)
Frederick Comm Coll (MD)
Fulton-Montgomery Comm Coll (NY)
GateWay Comm Coll (AZ)
Great Basin Coll (NV)
Hagerstown Comm Coll (MD)
Harford Comm Coll (MD)
Harper Coll (IL)
Howard Comm Coll (MD)
James Sprunt Comm Coll (NC)
Kankakee Comm Coll (IL)
Kilgore Coll (TX)
Kingsborough Comm Coll of the City U of New York (NY)
Lake Michigan Coll (MI)
Linn-Benton Comm Coll (OR)
Miami Dade Coll (FL)
Mohawk Valley Comm Coll (NY)
Monroe County Comm Coll (MI)
Montgomery Coll (MD)
Montgomery County Comm Coll (PA)
Muskegon Comm Coll (MI)
Northeast Comm Coll (NE)
Northern Essex Comm Coll (MA)
North Idaho Coll (ID)
Northwest Coll (WY)
Palm Beach State Coll (FL)
Phoenix Coll (AZ)
Pima Comm Coll (AZ)

Potomac State Coll of West Virginia U (WV)
Pratt Comm Coll (KS)
Red Rocks Comm Coll (CO)
San Juan Coll (NM)
Sauk Valley Comm Coll (IL)
Sheridan Coll (WY)
Snow Coll (UT)
Southwest Mississippi Comm Coll (MS)
Springfield Tech Comm Coll (MA)
Trinity Valley Comm Coll (TX)
Vincennes U Jasper Campus (IN)
Wilson Comm Coll (NC)

EMERGENCY CARE ATTENDANT (EMT AMBULANCE)
Barton County Comm Coll (KS)
Carroll Comm Coll (MD)
Clovis Comm Coll (NM)
Delaware Tech & Comm Coll, Stanton/Wilmington Campus (DE)
Southside Virginia Comm Coll (VA)
Waubonsee Comm Coll (IL)

EMERGENCY MEDICAL TECHNOLOGY (EMT PARAMEDIC)
Allen Comm Coll (KS)
Amarillo Coll (TX)
Arizona Western Coll (AZ)
Arkansas State U–Mountain Home (AR)
Athens Tech Coll (GA)
Augusta Tech Coll (GA)
Austin Comm Coll (TX)
Barton County Comm Coll (KS)
Blue Ridge Comm and Tech Coll (WV)
Borough of Manhattan Comm Coll of the City U of New York (NY)
Casper Coll (WY)
Catawba Valley Comm Coll (NC)
Cecil Coll (MD)
Central Oregon Comm Coll (OR)
Central Wyoming Coll (WY)
Century Coll (MN)
Chippewa Valley Tech Coll (WI)
Cincinnati State Tech and Comm Coll (OH)
Clark Coll (WA)
Coll of Central Florida (FL)
Collin County Comm Coll District (TX)
Columbus Tech Coll (GA)
The Comm Coll of Baltimore County (MD)
Corning Comm Coll (NY)
Cowley County Comm Coll and Area Vocational–Tech School (KS)
Darton Coll (GA)
Daytona State Coll (FL)
Delaware Tech & Comm Coll, Jack F. Owens Campus (DE)
Delaware Tech & Comm Coll, Stanton/Wilmington Campus (DE)
Delaware Tech & Comm Coll, Terry Campus (DE)
Doña Ana Comm Coll (NM)
Dutchess Comm Coll (NY)
Dyersburg State Comm Coll (TN)
Eastern Arizona Coll (AZ)
Eastern Gateway Comm Coll (OH)
East Los Angeles Coll (CA)
Elaine P. Nunez Comm Coll (LA)
El Centro Coll (TX)
Fayetteville Tech Comm Coll (NC)
Fiorello H. LaGuardia Comm Coll of the City U of New York (NY)
Florida State Coll at Jacksonville (FL)
Foothill Coll (CA)
Fox Valley Tech Coll (WI)
Frederick Comm Coll (MD)
Front Range Comm Coll (CO)
Gadsden State Comm Coll (AL)
Georgia Highlands Coll (GA)
Glendale Comm Coll (AZ)
Gulf Coast Comm Coll (FL)
Gwinnett Tech Coll (GA)
Hagerstown Comm Coll (MD)
Harper Coll (IL)

Harrisburg Area Comm Coll (PA)
H. Councill Trenholm State Tech Coll (AL)
Hillsborough Comm Coll (FL)
Houston Comm Coll System (TX)
Howard Comm Coll (MD)
Indian River State Coll (FL)
Inver Hills Comm Coll (MN)
Ivy Tech Comm Coll–Bloomington (IN)
Ivy Tech Comm Coll–Kokomo (IN)
Ivy Tech Comm Coll–North Central (IN)
Ivy Tech Comm Coll–Southwest (IN)
Ivy Tech Comm Coll–Wabash Valley (IN)
Jackson Comm Coll (MI)
Jefferson State Comm Coll (AL)
John Wood Comm Coll (IL)
J. Sargeant Reynolds Comm Coll (VA)
Kankakee Comm Coll (IL)
Kaskaskia Coll (IL)
Kent State U at Geauga (OH)
Kilgore Coll (TX)
Lake Michigan Coll (MI)
Lake-Sumter Comm Coll (FL)
Lamar Comm Coll (CO)
Laramie County Comm Coll (WY)
Lonestar Coll–Cy-Fair (TX)
Lonestar Coll–Montgomery (TX)
Lonestar Coll–North Harris (TX)
Lurleen B. Wallace Comm Coll (AL)
Macomb Comm Coll (MI)
McHenry County Coll (IL)
Metropolitan Comm Coll–Penn Valley (MO)
Miami Dade Coll (FL)
Mohave Comm Coll (AZ)
Mohawk Valley Comm Coll (NY)
Montana State U–Great Falls Coll of Technology (MT)
Montcalm Comm Coll (MI)
Moraine Park Tech Coll (WI)
Moraine Valley Comm Coll (IL)
Mountain Empire Comm Coll (VA)
North Dakota State Coll of Science (ND)
Northeast Comm Coll (NE)
Northeast Iowa Comm Coll (IA)
North Iowa Area Comm Coll (IA)
Northland Comm and Tech Coll–Thief River Falls & East Grand Forks (MN)
Oakland Comm Coll (MI)
Oklahoma City Comm Coll (OK)
Oklahoma State U, Oklahoma City (OK)
Orange Coast Coll (CA)
Pasco-Hernando Comm Coll (FL)
Pensacola State Coll (FL)
Polk State Coll (FL)
Pueblo Comm Coll (CO)
Quinsigamond Comm Coll (MA)
Rogue Comm Coll (OR)
Saint Charles Comm Coll (MO)
St. Cloud Tech & Comm Coll (MN)
San Diego City Coll (CA)
San Juan Coll (NM)
Santa Rosa Jr Coll (CA)
Scottsdale Comm Coll (AZ)
Seminole State Coll of Florida (FL)
Southeastern Comm Coll (IA)
Southern Crescent Tech Coll (GA)
Southern State Comm Coll (OH)
Southwestern Michigan Coll (MI)
Southwest Mississippi Comm Coll (MS)
Tallahassee Comm Coll (FL)
Trinity Valley Comm Coll (TX)
Tyler Jr Coll (TX)
Union County Coll (NJ)
U of Alaska Anchorage, Kenai Peninsula Coll (AK)
Westchester Comm Coll (NY)
Western Iowa Tech Comm Coll (IA)
Wisconsin Indianhead Tech Coll (WI)

ENERGY MANAGEMENT AND SYSTEMS TECHNOLOGY
Alexandria Tech and Comm Coll (MN)
Casper Coll (WY)
Century Coll (MN)

Dakota County Tech Coll (MN)
Delaware Tech & Comm Coll, Jack F. Owens Campus (DE)
Delaware Tech & Comm Coll, Stanton/Wilmington Campus (DE)
Delaware Tech & Comm Coll, Terry Campus (DE)
GateWay Comm Coll (AZ)
Illinois Eastern Comm Colls, Wabash Valley College (IL)
Laramie County Comm Coll (WY)
Macomb Comm Coll (MI)
Minnesota West Comm and Tech Coll (MN)
Mitchell Tech Inst (SD)
Montana State U–Great Falls Coll of Technology (MT)
Northeast Comm Coll (NE)
Northeast Iowa Comm Coll (IA)
Northwest Tech Coll (MN)
Pratt Comm Coll (KS)
Pueblo Comm Coll (CO)
The Williamson Free School of Mecha Trades (PA)
Wisconsin Indianhead Tech Coll (WI)

ENGINEERING

Allen Comm Coll (KS)
Amarillo Coll (TX)
Antelope Valley Coll (CA)
Arizona Western Coll (AZ)
Austin Comm Coll (TX)
Borough of Manhattan Comm Coll of the City U of New York (NY)
Bristol Comm Coll (MA)
Bucks County Comm Coll (PA)
Burlington County Coll (NJ)
Carl Albert State Coll (OK)
Casper Coll (WY)
Central Lakes Coll (MN)
Central New Mexico Comm Coll (NM)
Central Oregon Comm Coll (OR)
Central Wyoming Coll (WY)
Century Coll (MN)
Clarendon Coll (TX)
Coll of Lake County (IL)
The Comm Coll of Baltimore County (MD)
Comm Coll of Philadelphia (PA)
Comm Coll of Rhode Island (RI)
Danville Area Comm Coll (IL)
De Anza Coll (CA)
Dodge City Comm Coll (KS)
East Los Angeles Coll (CA)
Elgin Comm Coll (IL)
Frederick Comm Coll (MD)
Hagerstown Comm Coll (MD)
Harford Comm Coll (MD)
Harper Coll (IL)
Harrisburg Area Comm Coll (PA)
Highland Comm Coll (IL)
Holyoke Comm Coll (MA)
Howard Comm Coll (MD)
Indian River State Coll (FL)
Jefferson Coll (MO)
John Tyler Comm Coll (VA)
J. Sargeant Reynolds Comm Coll (VA)
Kankakee Comm Coll (IL)
Laramie County Comm Coll (WY)
Lehigh Carbon Comm Coll (PA)
Lincoln Land Comm Coll (IL)
Linn-Benton Comm Coll (OR)
Lonestar Coll–Cy-Fair (TX)
Lonestar Coll–Kingwood (TX)
Lonestar Coll–Montgomery (TX)
Lonestar Coll–North Harris (TX)
Lonestar Coll–Tomball (TX)
McHenry County Coll (IL)
Metropolitan Comm Coll–Business & Technology Campus (MO)
Metropolitan Comm Coll–Longview (MO)
Metropolitan Comm Coll–Penn Valley (MO)
Miami Dade Coll (FL)
Missouri State U–West Plains (MO)
Mohawk Valley Comm Coll (NY)
Montgomery Coll (MD)
Northampton Comm Coll (PA)
Northeast Comm Coll (NE)
North Hennepin Comm Coll (MN)
North Idaho Coll (ID)
Northwest Coll (WY)
Oakland Comm Coll (MI)

Ocean County Coll (NJ)
Orange Coast Coll (CA)
Owens Comm Coll, Toledo (OH)
Potomac State Coll of West Virginia U (WV)
Red Rocks Comm Coll (CO)
Saint Charles Comm Coll (MO)
Salt Lake Comm Coll (UT)
San Juan Coll (NM)
Santa Barbara City Coll (CA)
Santa Fe Comm Coll (NM)
Sheridan Coll (WY)
Southwest Mississippi Comm Coll (MS)
Springfield Tech Comm Coll (MA)
Suffolk County Comm Coll (NY)
Tallahassee Comm Coll (FL)
Terra State Comm Coll (OH)
Three Rivers Comm Coll (CT)
Tompkins Cortland Comm Coll (NY)
Tyler Jr Coll (TX)
Union County Coll (NJ)
Waubonsee Comm Coll (IL)

ENGINEERING/INDUSTRIAL MANAGEMENT

Delaware Tech & Comm Coll, Stanton/Wilmington Campus (DE)

ENGINEERING RELATED

Bristol Comm Coll (MA)
Macomb Comm Coll (MI)
Miami Dade Coll (FL)
Southeastern Comm Coll (IA)

ENGINEERING-RELATED TECHNOLOGIES

Gateway Comm Coll (CT)
Metropolitan Comm Coll–Business & Technology Campus (MO)

ENGINEERING SCIENCE

Bristol Comm Coll (MA)
Dutchess Comm Coll (NY)
Fiorello H. LaGuardia Comm Coll of the City U of New York (NY)
Fulton-Montgomery Comm Coll (NY)
Highland Comm Coll (IL)
Kingsborough Comm Coll of the City U of New York (NY)
Manchester Comm Coll (CT)
Middlesex Comm Coll (CT)
Montgomery County Comm Coll (PA)
Northern Essex Comm Coll (MA)
Norwalk Comm Coll (CT)
Onondaga Comm Coll (NY)
Raritan Valley Comm Coll (NJ)
Suffolk County Comm Coll (NY)
Three Rivers Comm Coll (CT)
Westchester Comm Coll (NY)

ENGINEERING TECHNOLOGIES AND ENGINEERING RELATED

Bristol Comm Coll (MA)
Burlington County Coll (NJ)
Carl Albert State Coll (OK)
The Comm Coll of Baltimore County (MD)
Comm Coll of Rhode Island (RI)
Harford Comm Coll (MD)
Harrisburg Area Comm Coll (PA)
J. Sargeant Reynolds Comm Coll (VA)
Montgomery County Comm Coll (PA)
North Dakota State Coll of Science (ND)
Ocean County Coll (NJ)
Raritan Valley Comm Coll (NJ)
Sullivan Coll of Technology and Design (KY)

ENGINEERING TECHNOLOGY

Allen Comm Coll (KS)
Antelope Valley Coll (CA)
Barton County Comm Coll (KS)
Collin County Comm Coll District (TX)
Comm Coll of Philadelphia (PA)
Cowley County Comm Coll and Area Vocational–Tech School (KS)

Darton Coll (GA)
De Anza Coll (CA)
DeKalb Tech Coll (GA)
Denmark Tech Coll (SC)
Dodge City Comm Coll (KS)
Florida State Coll at Jacksonville (FL)
Gateway Comm and Tech Coll (KY)
Gateway Comm Coll (CT)
Glendale Comm Coll (AZ)
Golden West Coll (CA)
Highland Comm Coll (IL)
Hillsborough Comm Coll (FL)
Honolulu Comm Coll (HI)
Indian River State Coll (FL)
Jefferson State Comm Coll (AL)
John Tyler Comm Coll (VA)
Kent State U at Ashtabula (OH)
Kent State U at Tuscarawas (OH)
Los Angeles Harbor Coll (CA)
Marion Tech Coll (OH)
Massachusetts Bay Comm Coll (MA)
Mesa Comm Coll (AZ)
Miami Dade Coll (FL)
Middlesex Comm Coll (CT)
Midlands Tech Coll (SC)
Muskegon Comm Coll (MI)
Nashua Comm Coll (NH)
Oklahoma State U, Oklahoma City (OK)
Pueblo Comm Coll (CO)
Salt Lake Comm Coll (UT)
San Diego City Coll (CA)
Santa Barbara City Coll (CA)
Southwestern Michigan Coll (MI)
Spartanburg Comm Coll (SC)
Sullivan Coll of Technology and Design (KY)
Three Rivers Comm Coll (CT)
Trident Tech Coll (SC)
Westchester Comm Coll (NY)

ENGINE MACHINIST

Northwest Tech Coll (MN)

ENGLISH

Amarillo Coll (TX)
Arizona Western Coll (AZ)
Bainbridge Coll (GA)
Barton County Comm Coll (KS)
Berkeley City Coll (CA)
Borough of Manhattan Comm Coll of the City U of New York (NY)
Burlington County Coll (NJ)
Carl Albert State Coll (OK)
Casper Coll (WY)
Central Wyoming Coll (WY)
Clarendon Coll (TX)
Coll of the Canyons (CA)
Colorado Mountain Coll (CO)
Colorado Mountain Coll, Alpine Campus (CO)
Darton Coll (GA)
De Anza Coll (CA)
Dodge City Comm Coll (KS)
Eastern Arizona Coll (AZ)
East Los Angeles Coll (CA)
Foothill Coll (CA)
Frank Phillips Coll (TX)
Frederick Comm Coll (MD)
Fulton-Montgomery Comm Coll (NY)
Georgia Highlands Coll (GA)
Great Basin Coll (NV)
Harper Coll (IL)
Indian River State Coll (FL)
Kilgore Coll (TX)
Lake Michigan Coll (MI)
Laramie County Comm Coll (WY)
Linn-Benton Comm Coll (OR)
Lonestar Coll–Cy-Fair (TX)
Lonestar Coll–Kingwood (TX)
Lonestar Coll–Montgomery (TX)
Lonestar Coll–North Harris (TX)
Lonestar Coll–Tomball (TX)
Mendocino Coll (CA)
Miami Dade Coll (FL)
Mohave Comm Coll (AZ)
Monroe County Comm Coll (MI)
Northeast Comm Coll (NE)
North Idaho Coll (ID)
Northwest Coll (WY)
Orange Coast Coll (CA)
Owens Comm Coll, Toledo (OH)
Palm Beach State Coll (FL)
Potomac State Coll of West Virginia U (WV)

Pratt Comm Coll (KS)
Raritan Valley Comm Coll (NJ)
Red Rocks Comm Coll (CO)
Saint Charles Comm Coll (MO)
St. Philip's Coll (TX)
Salt Lake Comm Coll (UT)
San Diego City Coll (CA)
Santa Barbara City Coll (CA)
Santa Rosa Jr Coll (CA)
Sauk Valley Comm Coll (IL)
Sheridan Coll (WY)
Solano Comm Coll (CA)
Southwest Mississippi Comm Coll (MS)
Suffolk County Comm Coll (NY)
Terra State Comm Coll (OH)
Trinity Valley Comm Coll (TX)

ENGLISH/LANGUAGE ARTS TEACHER EDUCATION

Darton Coll (GA)
Montgomery Coll (MD)

ENTREPRENEURIAL AND SMALL BUSINESS RELATED

Dakota Coll at Bottineau (ND)

ENTREPRENEURSHIP

Bristol Comm Coll (MA)
Casper Coll (WY)
Cincinnati State Tech and Comm Coll (OH)
Cowley County Comm Coll and Area Vocational–Tech School (KS)
Delaware Tech & Comm Coll, Jack F. Owens Campus (DE)
Delaware Tech & Comm Coll, Terry Campus (DE)
Eastern Arizona Coll (AZ)
Elgin Comm Coll (IL)
Goodwin Coll (CT)
Lamar Comm Coll (CO)
Laramie County Comm Coll (WY)
Missouri State U–West Plains (MO)
Mohawk Valley Comm Coll (NY)
Montana State U–Great Falls Coll of Technology (MT)
Montcalm Comm Coll (MI)
Northeast Comm Coll (NE)
North Iowa Area Comm Coll (IA)
Northland Comm and Tech Coll–Thief River Falls & East Grand Forks (MN)
Oakland Comm Coll (MI)
Randolph Comm Coll (NC)
Salt Lake Comm Coll (UT)
Santa Fe Comm Coll (NM)
Springfield Tech Comm Coll (MA)

ENVIRONMENTAL CONTROL TECHNOLOGIES RELATED

Central Carolina Tech Coll (SC)
Fox Valley Tech Coll (WI)
Hillsborough Comm Coll (FL)
Holyoke Comm Coll (MA)
Westchester Comm Coll (NY)

ENVIRONMENTAL DESIGN/ ARCHITECTURE

Scottsdale Comm Coll (AZ)

ENVIRONMENTAL ENGINEERING TECHNOLOGY

Austin Comm Coll (TX)
Cincinnati State Tech and Comm Coll (OH)
Collin County Comm Coll District (TX)
Crowder Coll (MO)
Dakota Coll at Bottineau (ND)
Georgia Northwestern Tech Coll (GA)
Kent State U at Trumbull (OH)
Massachusetts Bay Comm Coll (MA)
Metropolitan Comm Coll–Business & Technology Campus (MO)
Miami Dade Coll (FL)
Onondaga Comm Coll (NY)
Owens Comm Coll, Toledo (OH)
Pennsylvania Highlands Comm Coll (PA)
Salt Lake Comm Coll (UT)
San Diego City Coll (CA)

Sheridan Coll (WY)
Three Rivers Comm Coll (CT)

ENVIRONMENTAL/ ENVIRONMENTAL HEALTH ENGINEERING

Bristol Comm Coll (MA)
Central New Mexico Comm Coll (NM)
Central Wyoming Coll (WY)
Santa Barbara City Coll (CA)

ENVIRONMENTAL HEALTH

Amarillo Coll (TX)
Crowder Coll (MO)
North Idaho Coll (ID)

ENVIRONMENTAL SCIENCE

Anoka-Ramsey Comm Coll (MN)
Anoka-Ramsey Comm Coll, Cambridge Campus (MN)
Arizona Western Coll (AZ)
Burlington County Coll (NJ)
Casper Coll (WY)
Central Wyoming Coll (WY)
Clarendon Coll (TX)
Comm Coll of Vermont (VT)
Corning Comm Coll (NY)
Fiorello H. LaGuardia Comm Coll of the City U of New York (NY)
Harrisburg Area Comm Coll (PA)
Lake Michigan Coll (MI)
Montgomery County Comm Coll (PA)
Ocean County Coll (NJ)
St. Philip's Coll (TX)
Tyler Jr Coll (TX)

ENVIRONMENTAL STUDIES

Bucks County Comm Coll (PA)
Colorado Mountain Coll, Timberline Campus (CO)
Darton Coll (GA)
De Anza Coll (CA)
East Los Angeles Coll (CA)
Fulton-Montgomery Comm Coll (NY)
Goodwin Coll (CT)
Harford Comm Coll (MD)
Harper Coll (IL)
Harrisburg Area Comm Coll (PA)
Housatonic Comm Coll (CT)
Howard Comm Coll (MD)
Kent State U at Ashtabula (OH)
Kent State U at Tuscarawas (OH)
Middlesex Comm Coll (CT)
Minnesota State Comm and Tech Coll (MN)
Santa Barbara City Coll (CA)
Santa Fe Comm Coll (NM)
Santa Rosa Jr Coll (CA)
Stark State Coll of Technology (OH)
White Mountains Comm Coll (NH)

EQUESTRIAN STUDIES

Allen Comm Coll (KS)
Central Wyoming Coll (WY)
Dodge City Comm Coll (KS)
Lamar Comm Coll (CO)
Laramie County Comm Coll (WY)
Martin Comm Coll (NC)
Northwest Coll (WY)
Scottsdale Comm Coll (AZ)
Yavapai Coll (AZ)

ETHNIC, CULTURAL MINORITY, GENDER, AND GROUP STUDIES RELATED

New Mexico State U–Alamogordo (NM)
Santa Fe Comm Coll (NM)
Santa Rosa Jr Coll (CA)

EXECUTIVE ASSISTANT/ EXECUTIVE SECRETARY

Alamance Comm Coll (NC)
Bellingham Tech Coll (WA)
Cape Fear Comm Coll (NC)
Central New Mexico Comm Coll (NM)
Cincinnati State Tech and Comm Coll (OH)
Clark Coll (WA)
Clovis Comm Coll (NM)
Crowder Coll (MO)
Dakota Coll at Bottineau (ND)

Dakota County Tech Coll (MN)
Danville Area Comm Coll (IL)
Eastfield Coll (TX)
Edison State Comm Coll (OH)
El Centro Coll (TX)
Elgin Comm Coll (IL)
Gulf Coast Comm Coll (FL)
Hawkeye Comm Coll (IA)
Hillsborough Comm Coll (FL)
Ivy Tech Comm Coll–Bloomington (IN)
Ivy Tech Comm Coll–Central Indiana (IN)
Ivy Tech Comm Coll–Columbus (IN)
Ivy Tech Comm Coll–East Central (IN)
Ivy Tech Comm Coll–Kokomo (IN)
Ivy Tech Comm Coll–Lafayette (IN)
Ivy Tech Comm Coll–North Central (IN)
Ivy Tech Comm Coll–Northeast (IN)
Ivy Tech Comm Coll–Northwest (IN)
Ivy Tech Comm Coll–Richmond (IN)
Ivy Tech Comm Coll–Southeast (IN)
Ivy Tech Comm Coll–Southern Indiana (IN)
Ivy Tech Comm Coll–Southwest (IN)
Ivy Tech Comm Coll–Wabash Valley (IN)
Jackson Comm Coll (MI)
John Wood Comm Coll (IL)
Kaskaskia Coll (IL)
Kilgore Coll (TX)
Lake Region State Coll (ND)
Owensboro Comm and Tech Coll (KY)
Owens Comm Coll, Toledo (OH)
Pensacola State Coll (FL)
Quinsigamond Comm Coll (MA)
St. Cloud Tech & Comm Coll (MN)
Southern State Comm Coll (OH)
South Suburban Coll (IL)
Southwestern Michigan Coll (MI)
Springfield Tech Comm Coll (MA)
Terra State Comm Coll (OH)
The U of Montana–Helena Coll of Technology (MT)
Waubonsee Comm Coll (IL)
Western Iowa Tech Comm Coll (IA)
Westmoreland County Comm Coll (PA)
West Virginia Northern Comm Coll (WV)

FACILITIES PLANNING AND MANAGEMENT
Comm Coll of Philadelphia (PA)
Lonestar Coll–Kingwood (TX)

FAMILY AND COMMUNITY SERVICES
Glendale Comm Coll (AZ)
Phoenix Coll (AZ)
Snow Coll (UT)

FAMILY AND CONSUMER ECONOMICS RELATED
Orange Coast Coll (CA)
Yakima Valley Comm Coll (WA)

FAMILY AND CONSUMER SCIENCES/HOME ECONOMICS TEACHER EDUCATION
Antelope Valley Coll (CA)

FAMILY AND CONSUMER SCIENCES/HUMAN SCIENCES
Allen Comm Coll (KS)
Bainbridge Coll (GA)
East Los Angeles Coll (CA)
Indian River State Coll (FL)
Linn-Benton Comm Coll (OR)
Mesa Comm Coll (AZ)
Metropolitan Comm Coll–Penn Valley (MO)
Orange Coast Coll (CA)
Palm Beach State Coll (FL)
Phoenix Coll (AZ)
Pratt Comm Coll (KS)
Snow Coll (UT)

Solano Comm Coll (CA)
Tyler Jr Coll (TX)

FARM AND RANCH MANAGEMENT
Alexandria Tech and Comm Coll (MN)
Allen Comm Coll (KS)
Clarendon Coll (TX)
Crowder Coll (MO)
Dodge City Comm Coll (KS)
Frank Phillips Coll (TX)
Lamar Comm Coll (CO)
Northeast Comm Coll (NE)
Northland Comm and Tech Coll–Thief River Falls & East Grand Forks (MN)
Northwest Coll (WY)
Pratt Comm Coll (KS)
Snow Coll (UT)
Trinity Valley Comm Coll (TX)

FASHION AND FABRIC CONSULTING
Harper Coll (IL)
Santa Rosa Jr Coll (CA)

FASHION/APPAREL DESIGN
The Art Inst of New York City (NY)
The Art Inst of Seattle (WA)
Burlington County Coll (NJ)
Clary Sage Coll (OK)
El Centro Coll (TX)
Fashion Careers Coll (CA)
Fashion Inst of Technology (NY)
FIDM/The Fashion Inst of Design & Merchandising, Los Angeles Campus (CA)
FIDM/The Fashion Inst of Design & Merchandising, Orange County Campus (CA)
FIDM/The Fashion Inst of Design & Merchandising, San Diego Campus (CA)
FIDM/The Fashion Inst of Design & Merchandising, San Francisco Campus (CA)
Harper Coll (IL)
Honolulu Comm Coll (HI)
Houston Comm Coll System (TX)
Lehigh Carbon Comm Coll (PA)
Metropolitan Comm Coll–Penn Valley (MO)
Palm Beach State Coll (FL)
Phoenix Coll (AZ)
Santa Fe Comm Coll (NM)
Santa Rosa Jr Coll (CA)
Wade Coll (TX)
Wood Tobe–Coburn School (NY)

FASHION MERCHANDISING
Alexandria Tech and Comm Coll (MN)
The Art Inst of Ohio–Cincinnati (OH)
The Art Inst of Seattle (WA)
Blue Ridge Comm and Tech Coll (WV)
Doña Ana Comm Coll (NM)
Fashion Careers Coll (CA)
Fashion Inst of Technology (NY)
FIDM/The Fashion Inst of Design & Merchandising, Los Angeles Campus (CA)
FIDM/The Fashion Inst of Design & Merchandising, Orange County Campus (CA)
FIDM/The Fashion Inst of Design & Merchandising, San Diego Campus (CA)
FIDM/The Fashion Inst of Design & Merchandising, San Francisco Campus (CA)
Florida State Coll at Jacksonville (FL)
Gateway Comm Coll (CT)
Grand Rapids Comm Coll (MI)
Harper Coll (IL)
Harrison Coll, Indianapolis (IN)
Houston Comm Coll System (TX)
Howard Comm Coll (MD)
Indian River State Coll (FL)
Kilgore Coll (TX)
Kingsborough Comm Coll of the City U of New York (NY)

Lake Region State Coll (ND)
Mesa Comm Coll (AZ)
Metropolitan Comm Coll–Penn Valley (MO)
Minnesota State Comm and Tech Coll (MN)
Orange Coast Coll (CA)
Palm Beach State Coll (FL)
Phoenix Coll (AZ)
Pima Comm Coll (AZ)
San Diego City Coll (CA)
Santa Rosa Jr Coll (CA)
Scottsdale Comm Coll (AZ)
Solano Comm Coll (CA)
Southwest Mississippi Comm Coll (MS)
Trinity Valley Comm Coll (TX)
Wood Tobe–Coburn School (NY)

FASHION MODELING
Fashion Inst of Technology (NY)

FIBER, TEXTILE AND WEAVING ARTS
Antelope Valley Coll (CA)
FIDM/The Fashion Inst of Design & Merchandising, Orange County Campus (CA)
Mendocino Coll (CA)

FILM/CINEMA/VIDEO STUDIES
Carl Albert State Coll (OK)
De Anza Coll (CA)
Douglas Education Center (PA)
KD Studio (TX)
Orange Coast Coll (CA)
Santa Barbara City Coll (CA)
Santa Fe Comm Coll (NM)
Tallahassee Comm Coll (FL)
Yavapai Coll (AZ)

FILM/VIDEO AND PHOTOGRAPHIC ARTS RELATED
Westchester Comm Coll (NY)

FINANCE
Chipola Coll (FL)
Clarendon Coll (TX)
Comm Coll of Philadelphia (PA)
Dodge City Comm Coll (KS)
Doña Ana Comm Coll (NM)
East Los Angeles Coll (CA)
Frederick Comm Coll (MD)
Fulton-Montgomery Comm Coll (NY)
Harper Coll (IL)
Harrison Coll, Indianapolis (IN)
Harrison Coll, Muncie (IN)
Harrison Coll (OH)
Indian River State Coll (FL)
Kent State U at Ashtabula (OH)
Lonestar Coll–Cy-Fair (TX)
Lonestar Coll–Kingwood (TX)
Lonestar Coll–Montgomery (TX)
Lonestar Coll–North Harris (TX)
Lonestar Coll–Tomball (TX)
Macomb Comm Coll (MI)
Marion Tech Coll (OH)
Mendocino Coll (CA)
Mesa Comm Coll (AZ)
Miami Dade Coll (FL)
Monroe County Comm Coll (MI)
Morton Coll (IL)
Muskegon Comm Coll (MI)
Northern Essex Comm Coll (MA)
North Hennepin Comm Coll (MN)
Norwalk Comm Coll (CT)
Oklahoma City Comm Coll (OK)
Palm Beach State Coll (FL)
Polk State Coll (FL)
Salt Lake Comm Coll (UT)
San Diego City Coll (CA)
Santa Barbara City Coll (CA)
Scottsdale Comm Coll (AZ)
Seminole State Coll of Florida (FL)
Solano Comm Coll (CA)
Southeast Tech Inst (SD)
Southwest Mississippi Comm Coll (MS)
Springfield Tech Comm Coll (MA)
Stark State Coll of Technology (OH)
Tallahassee Comm Coll (FL)
Trinity Valley Comm Coll (TX)

Vincennes U Jasper Campus (IN)
Westchester Comm Coll (NY)
Wisconsin Indianhead Tech Coll (WI)

FINANCE AND FINANCIAL MANAGEMENT SERVICES RELATED
Bristol Comm Coll (MA)
Northeast Comm Coll (NE)

FINANCIAL PLANNING AND SERVICES
Barton County Comm Coll (KS)
Howard Comm Coll (MD)
Kilian Comm Coll (SD)
Minnesota State Comm and Tech Coll (MN)
Raritan Valley Comm Coll (NJ)
Waukesha County Tech Coll (WI)

FINE AND STUDIO ARTS MANAGEMENT
Owens Comm Coll, Toledo (OH)
Santa Fe Comm Coll (NM)

FINE ARTS RELATED
Carl Albert State Coll (OK)
Yavapai Coll (AZ)

FINE/STUDIO ARTS
Amarillo Coll (TX)
Anoka-Ramsey Comm Coll (MN)
Anoka-Ramsey Comm Coll, Cambridge Campus (MN)
Arizona Western Coll (AZ)
Berkeley City Coll (CA)
Bristol Comm Coll (MA)
Casper Coll (WY)
Chandler-Gilbert Comm Coll (AZ)
Clovis Comm Coll (NM)
Colorado Mountain Coll, Alpine Campus (CO)
Corning Comm Coll (NY)
Elgin Comm Coll (IL)
Fashion Inst of Technology (NY)
Foothill Coll (CA)
Fulton-Montgomery Comm Coll (NY)
Harper Coll (IL)
Inver Hills Comm Coll (MN)
Kankakee Comm Coll (IL)
Lake Superior Coll (MN)
Lincoln Land Comm Coll (IL)
Manchester Comm Coll (CT)
McHenry County Coll (IL)
Middlesex Comm Coll (CT)
Morton Coll (IL)
New Mexico State U–Alamogordo (NM)
Niagara County Comm Coll (NY)
Northampton Comm Coll (PA)
North Hennepin Comm Coll (MN)
Norwalk Comm Coll (CT)
Oklahoma City Comm Coll (OK)
Phoenix Coll (AZ)
Pratt Comm Coll (KS)
Raritan Valley Comm Coll (NJ)
Sandhills Comm Coll (NC)
Santa Barbara City Coll (CA)
South Suburban Coll (IL)
Springfield Tech Comm Coll (MA)
Terra State Comm Coll (OH)
Waubonsee Comm Coll (IL)
Westchester Comm Coll (NY)

FIRE PREVENTION AND SAFETY TECHNOLOGY
Antelope Valley Coll (CA)
Austin Comm Coll (TX)
Catawba Valley Comm Coll (NC)
Central New Mexico Comm Coll (NM)
Coll of Lake County (IL)
Coll of the Canyons (CA)
Collin County Comm Coll District (TX)
Delaware Tech & Comm Coll, Stanton/Wilmington Campus (DE)
Fayetteville Tech Comm Coll (NC)
Florida State Coll at Jacksonville (FL)
Fox Valley Tech Coll (WI)

Gulf Coast Comm Coll (FL)
Hillsborough Comm Coll (FL)
Houston Comm Coll System (TX)
Lake Superior Coll (MN)
Macomb Comm Coll (MI)
Montgomery Coll (MD)
Montgomery County Comm Coll (PA)
Moraine Valley Comm Coll (IL)
North Iowa Area Comm Coll (IA)
Northland Comm and Tech Coll–Thief River Falls & East Grand Forks (MN)
Ocean County Coll (NJ)
Oklahoma State U, Oklahoma City (OK)
Onondaga Comm Coll (NY)
Owens Comm Coll, Toledo (OH)
Pensacola State Coll (FL)
Rogue Comm Coll (OR)
Springfield Tech Comm Coll (MA)
Union County Coll (NJ)
Waukesha County Tech Coll (WI)
Westmoreland County Comm Coll (PA)
Wilson Comm Coll (NC)

FIRE SCIENCE/FIREFIGHTING
Amarillo Coll (TX)
Arizona Western Coll (AZ)
Augusta Tech Coll (GA)
Barton County Comm Coll (KS)
Blackhawk Tech Coll (WI)
Blue Ridge Comm and Tech Coll (WV)
Bristol Comm Coll (MA)
Burlington County Coll (NJ)
Casper Coll (WY)
Cecil Coll (MD)
Central Oregon Comm Coll (OR)
Central Wyoming Coll (WY)
Chattahoochee Tech Coll (GA)
Cincinnati State Tech and Comm Coll (OH)
Clovis Comm Coll (NM)
Coll of Central Florida (FL)
Collin County Comm Coll District (TX)
Comm Coll of Philadelphia (PA)
Comm Coll of Rhode Island (RI)
Corning Comm Coll (NY)
Crowder Coll (MO)
Danville Area Comm Coll (IL)
Daytona State Coll (FL)
Delaware Tech & Comm Coll, Stanton/Wilmington Campus (DE)
Dodge City Comm Coll (KS)
Doña Ana Comm Coll (NM)
East Los Angeles Coll (CA)
Florida State Coll at Jacksonville (FL)
Frederick Comm Coll (MD)
Gateway Comm and Tech Coll (KY)
Gateway Comm Coll (CT)
Georgia Northwestern Tech Coll (GA)
Glendale Comm Coll (AZ)
Harper Coll (IL)
Harrisburg Area Comm Coll (PA)
Honolulu Comm Coll (HI)
Indian River State Coll (FL)
John Wood Comm Coll (IL)
Lake-Sumter Comm Coll (FL)
Lanier Tech Coll (GA)
Laramie County Comm Coll (WY)
Lincoln Land Comm Coll (IL)
Lonestar Coll–Cy-Fair (TX)
Lonestar Coll–Montgomery (TX)
Los Angeles Harbor Coll (CA)
Lower Columbia Coll (WA)
McHenry County Coll (IL)
Mesa Comm Coll (AZ)
Metropolitan Comm Coll–Blue River (MO)
Miami Dade Coll (FL)
Mid-Plains Comm Coll, North Platte (NE)
Mohave Comm Coll (AZ)
Montana State U–Great Falls Coll of Technology (MT)
Moraine Valley Comm Coll (IL)
Northampton Comm Coll (PA)
Northeast Iowa Comm Coll (IA)
Norwalk Comm Coll (CT)
Oakland Comm Coll (MI)

Oklahoma State U, Oklahoma City (OK)
Olympic Coll (WA)
Owensboro Comm and Tech Coll (KY)
Owens Comm Coll, Toledo (OH)
Palm Beach State Coll (FL)
Phoenix Coll (AZ)
Pima Comm Coll (AZ)
Polk State Coll (FL)
Pueblo Comm Coll (CO)
Quinsigamond Comm Coll (MA)
Saint Charles Comm Coll (MO)
San Juan Coll (NM)
Santa Rosa Jr Coll (CA)
Savannah Tech Coll (GA)
Scottsdale Comm Coll (AZ)
Seminole State Coll of Florida (FL)
Solano Comm Coll (CA)
Southside Virginia Comm Coll (VA)
Southwestern Michigan Comm Coll (MI)
Springfield Tech Comm Coll (MA)
Stark State Coll of Technology (OH)
Three Rivers Comm Coll (CT)
Tyler Jr Coll (TX)
The U of Montana–Helena Coll of Technology (MT)
Volunteer State Comm Coll (TN)
Waubonsee Comm Coll (IL)
Wenatchee Valley Coll (WA)
Western Iowa Tech Comm Coll (IA)
West Georgia Tech Coll (GA)
West Kentucky Comm and Tech Coll (KY)
Westmoreland County Comm Coll (PA)
Wilson Comm Coll (NC)
Wiregrass Georgia Tech Coll (GA)
Yavapai Coll (AZ)

FIRE SERVICES ADMINISTRATION

Delaware Tech & Comm Coll, Stanton/Wilmington Campus (DE)
Jefferson State Comm Coll (AL)
Kirtland Comm Coll (MI)
Minnesota State Comm and Tech Coll (MN)
Mohawk Valley Comm Coll (NY)
Northampton Comm Coll (PA)
Quinsigamond Comm Coll (MA)

FISHING AND FISHERIES SCIENCES AND MANAGEMENT

Bellingham Tech Coll (WA)
Central Oregon Comm Coll (OR)
Dakota Coll at Bottineau (ND)
North Idaho Coll (ID)

FLORICULTURE/FLORISTRY MANAGEMENT

Dakota Coll at Bottineau (ND)
Danville Area Comm Coll (IL)
Santa Rosa Jr Coll (CA)
Westmoreland County Comm Coll (PA)

FOOD PREPARATION

Moraine Park Tech Coll (WI)

FOOD SCIENCE

Miami Dade Coll (FL)
Missouri State U–West Plains (MO)
Orange Coast Coll (CA)

FOOD SERVICE SYSTEMS ADMINISTRATION

Bucks County Comm Coll (PA)
Burlington County Coll (NJ)
Florida State Coll at Jacksonville (FL)
Harper Coll (IL)
Harrisburg Area Comm Coll (PA)
Mohawk Valley Comm Coll (NY)
Northeast Comm Coll (NE)
Phoenix Coll (AZ)
Santa Barbara City Coll (CA)

FOODS, NUTRITION, AND WELLNESS

Antelope Valley Coll (CA)
Carl Albert State Coll (OK)
Dutchess Comm Coll (NY)
Indian River State Coll (FL)
Orange Coast Coll (CA)

Palm Beach State Coll (FL)
Snow Coll (UT)

FOOD TECHNOLOGY AND PROCESSING

Honolulu Comm Coll (HI)
Orange Coast Coll (CA)
Stark State Coll of Technology (OH)
Westchester Comm Coll (NY)

FOREIGN LANGUAGES AND LITERATURES

Austin Comm Coll (TX)
Casper Coll (WY)
Central Oregon Comm Coll (OR)
Darton Coll (GA)
Eastern Arizona Coll (AZ)
Georgia Highlands Coll (GA)
Lake Michigan Coll (MI)
Linn-Benton Comm Coll (OR)
Lonestar Coll–Cy-Fair (TX)
Lonestar Coll–Kingwood (TX)
Lonestar Coll–Montgomery (TX)
Lonestar Coll–North Harris (TX)
Lonestar Coll–Tomball (TX)
Oklahoma City Comm Coll (OK)
Owens Comm Coll, Toledo (OH)
Saint Charles Comm Coll (MO)
Sheridan Coll (WY)

FORENSIC SCIENCE AND TECHNOLOGY

Arkansas State U–Mountain Home (AR)
Borough of Manhattan Comm Coll of the City U of New York (NY)
Carroll Comm Coll (MD)
Casper Coll (WY)
Catawba Valley Comm Coll (NC)
Comm Coll of Philadelphia (PA)
Cowley County Comm Coll and Area Vocational–Tech School (KS)
Darton Coll (GA)
Fayetteville Tech Comm Coll (NC)
Fox Valley Tech Coll (WI)
Macomb Comm Coll (MI)
Massachusetts Bay Comm Coll (MA)
Phoenix Coll (AZ)
Tompkins Cortland Comm Coll (NY)
U of Arkansas Comm Coll at Morrilton (AR)

FORESTRY

Allen Comm Coll (KS)
Bainbridge Coll (GA)
Barton County Comm Coll (KS)
Central Oregon Comm Coll (OR)
Darton Coll (GA)
Dodge City Comm Coll (KS)
Eastern Arizona Coll (AZ)
Georgia Highlands Coll (GA)
Grand Rapids Comm Coll (MI)
Indian River State Coll (FL)
Kilgore Coll (TX)
Miami Dade Coll (FL)
North Idaho Coll (ID)
Potomac State Coll of West Virginia U (WV)
Snow Coll (UT)

FOREST TECHNOLOGY

Albany Tech Coll (GA)
Central Oregon Comm Coll (OR)
Dabney S. Lancaster Comm Coll (VA)
Lurleen B. Wallace Comm Coll (AL)
Ogeechee Tech Coll (GA)
Okefenokee Tech Coll (GA)
Penn State Mont Alto (PA)
Pensacola State Coll (FL)
Potomac State Coll of West Virginia U (WV)
State U of New York Coll of Environmental Science & Forestry, Ranger School (NY)

FRENCH

Austin Comm Coll (TX)
Coll of the Canyons (CA)
East Los Angeles Coll (CA)
Indian River State Coll (FL)
Mendocino Coll (CA)
Miami Dade Coll (FL)
North Idaho Coll (ID)

Northwest Coll (WY)
Orange Coast Coll (CA)
Red Rocks Comm Coll (CO)
Saint Charles Comm Coll (MO)
Santa Barbara City Coll (CA)
Sauk Valley Comm Coll (IL)
Snow Coll (UT)
Solano Comm Coll (CA)

FUNERAL SERVICE AND MORTUARY SCIENCE

Allen Comm Coll (KS)
Amarillo Coll (TX)
Arkansas State U–Mountain Home (AR)
Barton County Comm Coll (KS)
The Comm Coll of Baltimore County (MD)
Fayetteville Tech Comm Coll (NC)
Fiorello H. LaGuardia Comm Coll of the City U of New York (NY)
Ivy Tech Comm Coll–Northwest (IN)
Jefferson State Comm Coll (AL)
John A. Gupton Coll (TN)
John Tyler Comm Coll (VA)
Miami Dade Coll (FL)
Monroe County Comm Coll (MI)
Northampton Comm Coll (PA)
Ogeechee Tech Coll (GA)
Randolph Comm Coll (NC)

FURNITURE DESIGN AND MANUFACTURING

Vincennes U Jasper Campus (IN)

GAME AND INTERACTIVE MEDIA DESIGN

Fayetteville Tech Comm Coll (NC)
Wilson Comm Coll (NC)

GENERAL STUDIES

Allen Comm Coll (KS)
Amarillo Coll (TX)
Ancilla Coll (IN)
Arizona Western Coll (AZ)
Austin Comm Coll (TX)
Barton County Comm Coll (KS)
Berkeley City Coll (CA)
Blue Ridge Comm and Tech Coll (WV)
Bristol Comm Coll (MA)
Brown Mackie Coll–Salina (KS)
Carroll Comm Coll (MD)
Casper Coll (WY)
Catawba Valley Comm Coll (NC)
Cecil Coll (MD)
Central New Mexico Comm Coll (NM)
Central Wyoming Coll (WY)
Chandler-Gilbert Comm Coll (AZ)
Cincinnati State Tech and Comm Coll (OH)
City Colls of Chicago, Harry S. Truman College (IL)
Clarendon Coll (TX)
Cleveland State Comm Coll (TN)
Clovis Comm Coll (NM)
Collin County Comm Coll District (TX)
Colorado Mountain Coll, Timberline Campus (CO)
Comm Coll of Rhode Island (RI)
Corning Comm Coll (NY)
Crowder Coll (MO)
Dakota Coll at Bottineau (ND)
Danville Area Comm Coll (IL)
Darton Coll (GA)
Elaine P. Nunez Comm Coll (LA)
Elgin Comm Coll (IL)
Frank Phillips Coll (TX)
Frederick Comm Coll (MD)
Front Range Comm Coll (CO)
Gadsden State Comm Coll (AL)
Gateway Comm and Tech Coll (KY)
GateWay Comm Coll (AZ)
Georgia Military Coll (GA)
Grays Harbor Coll (WA)
Harrisburg Area Comm Coll (PA)
Highland Comm Coll (IL)
Howard Comm Coll (MD)
Illinois Eastern Comm Colls, Frontier Community College (IL)
Illinois Eastern Comm Colls, Lincoln Trail College (IL)
Illinois Eastern Comm Colls, Olney Central College (IL)

Illinois Eastern Comm Colls, Wabash Valley College (IL)
Ivy Tech Comm Coll–Bloomington (IN)
Ivy Tech Comm Coll–Central Indiana (IN)
Ivy Tech Comm Coll–Columbus (IN)
Ivy Tech Comm Coll–East Central (IN)
Ivy Tech Comm Coll–Kokomo (IN)
Ivy Tech Comm Coll–Lafayette (IN)
Ivy Tech Comm Coll–North Central (IN)
Ivy Tech Comm Coll–Northeast (IN)
Ivy Tech Comm Coll–Northwest (IN)
Ivy Tech Comm Coll–Richmond (IN)
Ivy Tech Comm Coll–Southeast (IN)
Ivy Tech Comm Coll–Southern Indiana (IN)
Ivy Tech Comm Coll–Southwest (IN)
Ivy Tech Comm Coll–Wabash Valley (IN)
Jackson Comm Coll (MI)
James Sprunt Comm Coll (NC)
Jefferson State Comm Coll (AL)
John Tyler Comm Coll (VA)
John Wood Comm Coll (IL)
Kankakee Comm Coll (IL)
Kaskaskia Coll (IL)
Kilgore Coll (TX)
Kirtland Comm Coll (MI)
Lake Michigan Coll (MI)
Lawson State Comm Coll (AL)
Lehigh Carbon Comm Coll (PA)
Lincoln Land Comm Coll (IL)
Lurleen B. Wallace Comm Coll (AL)
Macomb Comm Coll (MI)
Manchester Comm Coll (CT)
Martin Comm Coll (NC)
Massachusetts Bay Comm Coll (MA)
McHenry County Coll (IL)
Miami Dade Coll (FL)
Missouri State U–West Plains (MO)
Montcalm Comm Coll (MI)
Motlow State Comm Coll (TN)
Nashua Comm Coll (NH)
New Mexico State U–Alamogordo (NM)
Niagara County Comm Coll (NY)
Northampton Comm Coll (PA)
Northeast Comm Coll (NE)
Northern Essex Comm Coll (MA)
Northwest Coll (WY)
Northwest-Shoals Comm Coll (AL)
Norwalk Comm Coll (CT)
Oakland Comm Coll (MI)
Ocean County Coll (NJ)
Oklahoma State U, Oklahoma City (OK)
Onondaga Comm Coll (NY)
Oregon Coast Comm Coll (OR)
Owens Comm Coll, Toledo (OH)
Panola Coll (TX)
Pennsylvania Highlands Comm Coll (PA)
Phoenix Coll (AZ)
Pima Comm Coll (AZ)
Pueblo Comm Coll (CO)
Quinsigamond Comm Coll (MA)
Red Rocks Comm Coll (CO)
Rogue Comm Coll (OR)
Saint Charles Comm Coll (MO)
Salt Lake Comm Coll (UT)
San Juan Coll (NM)
Santa Fe Comm Coll (NM)
Sheridan Coll (WY)
Southside Virginia Comm Coll (VA)
Southwestern Michigan Coll (MI)
Springfield Tech Comm Coll (MA)
Terra State Comm Coll (OH)
U of Arkansas Comm Coll at Morrilton (AR)
The U of Montana–Helena Coll of Technology (MT)
Volunteer State Comm Coll (TN)
Waubonsee Comm Coll (IL)
West Virginia Northern Comm Coll (WV)
White Mountains Comm Coll (NH)
Wilson Comm Coll (NC)

GEOGRAPHIC INFORMATION SCIENCE AND CARTOGRAPHY

Alexandria Tech and Comm Coll (MN)
Austin Comm Coll (TX)

Casper Coll (WY)
Harrisburg Area Comm Coll (PA)
Houston Comm Coll System (TX)
White Mountains Comm Coll (NH)

GEOGRAPHY

Allen Comm Coll (KS)
Austin Comm Coll (TX)
Cayuga County Comm Coll (NY)
The Comm Coll of Baltimore County (MD)
Darton Coll (GA)
East Los Angeles Coll (CA)
Holyoke Comm Coll (MA)
Lake Michigan Coll (MI)
Lonestar Coll–Cy-Fair (TX)
Lonestar Coll–Kingwood (TX)
Lonestar Coll–North Harris (TX)
Lonestar Coll–Tomball (TX)
Montgomery Coll (MD)
Orange Coast Coll (CA)
Pennsylvania Highlands Comm Coll (PA)
San Juan Coll (NM)
Santa Barbara City Coll (CA)
Snow Coll (UT)

GEOGRAPHY RELATED

Southern Alberta Inst of Technology (AB, Canada)

GEOLOGICAL AND EARTH SCIENCES/GEOSCIENCES RELATED

Burlington County Coll (NJ)

GEOLOGY/EARTH SCIENCE

Amarillo Coll (TX)
Arizona Western Coll (AZ)
Austin Comm Coll (TX)
Barton County Comm Coll (KS)
Casper Coll (WY)
Central Wyoming Coll (WY)
Colorado Mountain Coll, Alpine Campus (CO)
Eastern Arizona Coll (AZ)
East Los Angeles Coll (CA)
Georgia Highlands Coll (GA)
Grand Rapids Comm Coll (MI)
Great Basin Coll (NV)
Highland Comm Coll (IL)
Kilgore Coll (TX)
Lake Michigan Coll (MI)
Lonestar Coll–Cy-Fair (TX)
Lonestar Coll–Kingwood (TX)
Lonestar Coll–Montgomery (TX)
Lonestar Coll–North Harris (TX)
Lonestar Coll–Tomball (TX)
Miami Dade Coll (FL)
North Idaho Coll (ID)
Orange Coast Coll (CA)
Potomac State Coll of West Virginia U (WV)
Red Rocks Comm Coll (CO)
St. Philip's Coll (TX)
Salt Lake Comm Coll (UT)
San Juan Coll (NM)
Santa Barbara City Coll (CA)
Snow Coll (UT)
Trinity Valley Comm Coll (TX)
Tyler Jr Coll (TX)

GERMAN

Austin Comm Coll (TX)
Miami Dade Coll (FL)
North Idaho Coll (ID)
Orange Coast Coll (CA)
Red Rocks Comm Coll (CO)
Solano Comm Coll (CA)

GERONTOLOGY

Brown Mackie Coll–Merrillville (IN)
Fiorello H. LaGuardia Comm Coll of the City U of New York (NY)
Gateway Comm Coll (CT)
Midlands Tech Coll (SC)
Sandhills Comm Coll (NC)

GLAZIER

Metropolitan Comm Coll–Business & Technology Campus (MO)

GRAPHIC AND PRINTING EQUIPMENT OPERATION/ PRODUCTION

Burlington County Coll (NJ)

Central Comm Coll–Hastings
Campus (NE)
Central Maine Comm Coll (ME)
Eastfield Coll (TX)
Fox Valley Tech Coll (WI)
Fulton-Montgomery Comm Coll
(NY)
Golden West Coll (CA)
H. Councill Trenholm State Tech
Coll (AL)
Houston Comm Coll System (TX)
Macomb Comm Coll (MI)
Montgomery Coll (MD)
New England Inst of Technology
(RI)
Northwest Coll (WY)
San Diego City Coll (CA)
Southwestern Michigan Coll (MI)
Sullivan Coll of Technology and
Design (KY)

GRAPHIC COMMUNICATIONS
Clark Coll (WA)
Fox Valley Tech Coll (WI)
Hawkeye Comm Coll (IA)
Moraine Park Tech Coll (WI)
New England Inst of Technology
(RI)
Sullivan Coll of Technology and
Design (KY)
Waukesha County Tech Coll (WI)

GRAPHIC COMMUNICATIONS RELATED
Linn-Benton Comm Coll (OR)
Sullivan Coll of Technology and
Design (KY)

GRAPHIC DESIGN
The Art Inst of New York City (NY)
The Art Inst of Ohio–Cincinnati
(OH)
The Art Inst of Seattle (WA)
The Art Inst of York–Pennsylvania
(PA)
Barton County Comm Coll (KS)
Bradford School (OH)
Bradford School (PA)
Bristol Comm Coll (MA)
Brown Mackie Coll–Louisville (KY)
Burlington County Coll (NJ)
Casper Coll (WY)
Cecil Coll (MD)
Central Wyoming Coll (WY)
Coll of the Canyons (CA)
Comm Coll of Vermont (VT)
Dakota County Tech Coll (MN)
Douglas Education Center (PA)
Elgin Comm Coll (IL)
Fox Coll (IL)
Glendale Comm Coll (AZ)
Harrisburg Area Comm Coll (PA)
Highland Comm Coll (IL)
International Business Coll,
Indianapolis (IN)
Ivy Tech Comm Coll–Southwest
(IN)
Jackson Comm Coll (MI)
John Wood Comm Coll (IL)
Kankakee Comm Coll (IL)
King's Coll (NC)
Kirtland Comm Coll (MI)
Lake Michigan Coll (MI)
Lehigh Carbon Comm Coll (PA)
Lincoln Land Comm Coll (IL)
Minneapolis Business Coll (MN)
Minnesota State Comm and Tech
Coll (MN)
Montana State U–Great Falls Coll
of Technology (MT)
Moraine Park Tech Coll (WI)
Moraine Valley Comm Coll (IL)
New Mexico State U–Alamogordo
(NM)
Northampton Comm Coll (PA)
Northeast Comm Coll (NE)
North Hennepin Comm Coll (MN)
Norwalk Comm Coll (CT)
Oakland Comm Coll (MI)
Phoenix Coll (AZ)
Red Rocks Comm Coll (CO)
Salt Lake Comm Coll (UT)
Santa Rosa Jr Coll (CA)
Sullivan Coll of Technology and
Design (KY)
Wade Coll (TX)

Waubonsee Comm Coll (IL)
Waukesha County Tech Coll (WI)
Wood Tobe–Coburn School (NY)
Yavapai Coll (AZ)

GREENHOUSE MANAGEMENT
Century Coll (MN)
Dakota Coll at Bottineau (ND)

GUNSMITHING
Colorado School of Trades (CO)
Yavapai Coll (AZ)

HAIR STYLING AND HAIR DESIGN
Moraine Park Tech Coll (WI)

HAZARDOUS MATERIALS MANAGEMENT AND WASTE TECHNOLOGY
Barton County Comm Coll (KS)

HEALTH AIDE
Allen Comm Coll (KS)
Casper Coll (WY)
Northeast Comm Coll (NE)

HEALTH AIDES/ ATTENDANTS/ORDERLIES RELATED
Barton County Comm Coll (KS)
Moraine Valley Comm Coll (IL)

HEALTH AND MEDICAL ADMINISTRATIVE SERVICES RELATED
Barton County Comm Coll (KS)
GateWay Comm Coll (AZ)
Northeast Comm Coll (NE)
North Iowa Area Comm Coll (IA)
Pima Comm Coll (AZ)
Westmoreland County Comm Coll
(PA)

HEALTH AND PHYSICAL EDUCATION/FITNESS
Alexandria Tech and Comm Coll
(MN)
Allen Comm Coll (KS)
Antelope Valley Coll (CA)
Austin Comm Coll (TX)
Central Oregon Comm Coll (OR)
Clovis Comm Coll (NM)
Coll of the Canyons (CA)
Comm Care Coll (OK)
Corning Comm Coll (NY)
Dakota Coll at Bottineau (ND)
Darton Coll (GA)
Eastern Arizona Coll (AZ)
Holyoke Comm Coll (MA)
Houston Comm Coll System (TX)
Lake Michigan Coll (MI)
McHenry County Coll (IL)
Northeast Comm Coll (NE)
Northwest Coll (WY)
Raritan Valley Comm Coll (NJ)
San Juan Coll (NM)
Santa Fe Comm Coll (NM)
Sheridan Coll (WY)
Waubonsee Comm Coll (IL)

HEALTH AND PHYSICAL EDUCATION RELATED
Kingsborough Comm Coll of the
City U of New York (NY)
Santa Rosa Jr Coll (CA)

HEALTH/HEALTH-CARE ADMINISTRATION
Brown Mackie Coll–Akron (OH)
Brown Mackie Coll–Atlanta (GA)
Brown Mackie Coll–Boise (ID)
Brown Mackie Coll–Cincinnati (OH)
Brown Mackie Coll–Findlay (OH)
Brown Mackie Coll–Fort Wayne
(IN)
Brown Mackie Coll–Greenville (SC)
Brown Mackie Coll–Indianapolis
(IN)
Brown Mackie Coll–Kansas City
(KS)
Brown Mackie Coll–Louisville (KY)
Brown Mackie Coll–Miami (FL)

Brown Mackie Coll–Michigan City
(IN)
Brown Mackie Coll–North Canton
(OH)
Brown Mackie Coll–Northern
Kentucky (KY)
Brown Mackie Coll–Oklahoma City
(OK)
Brown Mackie Coll–St. Louis (MO)
Brown Mackie Coll–Salina (KS)
Brown Mackie Coll–San Antonio
(TX)
Brown Mackie Coll–South Bend
(IN)
Brown Mackie Coll–Tucson (AZ)
Comm Care Coll (OK)
GateWay Comm Coll (AZ)
Harrisburg Area Comm Coll (PA)
Inver Hills Comm Coll (MN)
North Idaho Coll (ID)
Oakland Comm Coll (MI)
Oklahoma State U, Oklahoma City
(OK)
Owens Comm Coll, Toledo (OH)
Pennsylvania Highlands Comm
Coll (PA)
Pensacola State Coll (FL)
Pima Comm Coll (AZ)
Pima Medical Inst, Mesa (AZ)
Pima Medical Inst, Tucson (AZ)
Pima Medical Inst (CA)
Pima Medical Inst, Denver (CO)
Pima Medical Inst (NV)
Pima Medical Inst, Albuquerque
(NM)
Pima Medical Inst, Seattle (WA)
Terra State Comm Coll (OH)
Tyler Jr Coll (TX)

HEALTH INFORMATION/ MEDICAL RECORDS ADMINISTRATION
Amarillo Coll (TX)
Barton County Comm Coll (KS)
Central New Mexico Comm Coll
(NM)
Comm Coll of Philadelphia (PA)
Darton Coll (GA)
Daytona State Coll (FL)
Dodge City Comm Coll (KS)
East Los Angeles Coll (CA)
Elaine P. Nunez Comm Coll (LA)
El Centro Coll (TX)
Florida State Coll at Jacksonville
(FL)
Hagerstown Comm Coll (MD)
Illinois Eastern Comm Colls,
Lincoln Trail College (IL)
Indian River State Coll (FL)
Lake-Sumter Comm Coll (FL)
Metropolitan Comm Coll–Penn
Valley (MO)
Miami Dade Coll (FL)
Northern Essex Comm Coll (MA)
Oklahoma City Comm Coll (OK)
Pensacola State Coll (FL)
Polk State Coll (FL)
Stark State Coll of Technology
(OH)
Terra State Comm Coll (OH)

HEALTH INFORMATION/ MEDICAL RECORDS TECHNOLOGY
ASA The Coll For Excellence (NY)
Atlanta Tech Coll (GA)
Austin Comm Coll (TX)
Borough of Manhattan Comm Coll
of the City U of New York (NY)
Burlington County Coll (NJ)
Carroll Comm Coll (MD)
Catawba Valley Comm Coll (NC)
Central Comm Coll–Hastings
Campus (NE)
Central Oregon Comm Coll (OR)
Chippewa Valley Tech Coll (WI)
Cincinnati State Tech and Comm
Coll (OH)
Coll of Central Florida (FL)
Collin County Comm Coll District
(TX)
Columbus Tech Coll (GA)
Danville Area Comm Coll (IL)
Darton Coll (GA)
Duluth Business U (MN)
Dyersburg State Comm Coll (TN)

Front Range Comm Coll (CO)
Harrison Coll, Anderson (IN)
Harrison Coll, Columbus (IN)
Harrison Coll, Lafayette (IN)
Harrison Coll, Muncie (IN)
Heart of Georgia Tech Coll (GA)
Highland Comm Coll (IL)
Houston Comm Coll System (TX)
ITT Tech Inst, Anaheim (CA)
ITT Tech Inst, Oxnard (CA)
ITT Tech Inst, San Bernardino (CA)
ITT Tech Inst, San Dimas (CA)
ITT Tech Inst, Sylmar (CA)
ITT Tech Inst, Torrance (CA)
ITT Tech Inst, Fort Lauderdale (FL)
ITT Tech Inst, Lake Mary (FL)
ITT Tech Inst, Miami (FL)
ITT Tech Inst, Tampa (FL)
ITT Tech Inst (ID)
ITT Tech Inst, Indianapolis (IN)
ITT Tech Inst (NM)
Kaskaskia Coll (IL)
Lehigh Carbon Comm Coll (PA)
Lonestar Coll–Cy-Fair (TX)
Lonestar Coll–Kingwood (TX)
Lonestar Coll–Montgomery (TX)
Lonestar Coll–North Harris (TX)
Lonestar Coll–Tomball (TX)
Midlands Tech Coll (SC)
Minnesota State Comm and Tech
Coll (MN)
Montana State U–Great Falls Coll
of Technology (MT)
Montgomery Coll (MD)
Moraine Park Tech Coll (WI)
Moraine Valley Comm Coll (IL)
North Dakota State Coll of Science
(ND)
Northeast Iowa Comm Coll (IA)
Ogeechee Tech Coll (GA)
Onondaga Comm Coll (NY)
Owens Comm Coll, Toledo (OH)
Panola Coll (TX)
Phoenix Coll (AZ)
Raritan Valley Comm Coll (NJ)
Saint Charles Comm Coll (MO)
St. Cloud Tech & Comm Coll (MN)
St. Philip's Coll (TX)
San Juan Coll (NM)
Santa Barbara City Coll (CA)
Southwestern Michigan Coll (MI)
Southwest Mississippi Comm Coll
(MS)
Tallahassee Comm Coll (FL)
Terra State Comm Coll (OH)
Tyler Jr Coll (TX)
Volunteer State Comm Coll (TN)
Waubonsee Comm Coll (IL)
West Georgia Tech Coll (GA)
West Virginia Northern Comm Coll
(WV)

HEALTH/MEDICAL PREPARATORY PROGRAMS RELATED
Darton Coll (GA)
Eastern Arizona Coll (AZ)
Miami Dade Coll (FL)
Northeast Comm Coll (NE)
Northwest Coll (WY)

HEALTH PROFESSIONS RELATED
Bucks County Comm Coll (PA)
Carl Albert State Coll (OK)
Carroll Comm Coll (MD)
Cincinnati State Tech and Comm
Coll (OH)
Comm Coll of Philadelphia (PA)
Gateway Comm and Tech Coll (KY)
Lanier Tech Coll (GA)
Mendocino Coll (CA)
Miami Dade Coll (FL)
Midlands Tech Coll (SC)
Oakland Comm Coll (MI)
Onondaga Comm Coll (NY)
Orange Coast Coll (CA)
Phillips Beth Israel School of
Nursing (NY)
Salt Lake Comm Coll (UT)
Southwest Mississippi Comm Coll
(MS)
Terra State Comm Coll (OH)
Volunteer State Comm Coll (TN)
Waycross Coll (GA)

HEALTH SERVICES ADMINISTRATION
Brown Mackie Coll–Phoenix (AZ)
Brown Mackie Coll–Tulsa (OK)
Harrisburg Area Comm Coll (PA)

HEALTH SERVICES/ALLIED HEALTH/HEALTH SCIENCES
Ancilla Coll (IN)
Arizona Western Coll (AZ)
Burlington County Coll (NJ)
Carl Albert State Coll (OK)
Cecil Coll (MD)
Central Wyoming Coll (WY)
Clarendon Coll (TX)
Dakota Coll at Bottineau (ND)
Georgia Military Coll (GA)
Goodwin Coll (CT)
Ilisagvik Coll (AK)
Northwest Coll (WY)
Raritan Valley Comm Coll (NJ)
Sheridan Coll (WY)

HEALTH TEACHER EDUCATION
Austin Comm Coll (TX)
Bainbridge Coll (GA)
Bucks County Comm Coll (PA)
Fulton-Montgomery Comm Coll
(NY)
Georgia Military Coll (GA)
Harper Coll (IL)
Howard Comm Coll (MD)
Kilgore Coll (TX)
Palm Beach State Coll (FL)
Pratt Comm Coll (KS)

HEALTH UNIT COORDINATOR/WARD CLERK
Southeast Tech Inst (SD)

HEATING, AIR CONDITIONING, VENTILATION AND REFRIGERATION MAINTENANCE TECHNOLOGY
Amarillo Coll (TX)
Antelope Valley Coll (CA)
Arizona Western Coll (AZ)
Bellingham Tech Coll (WA)
Blackhawk Tech Coll (WI)
Blue Ridge Comm and Tech Coll
(WV)
Central Comm Coll–Grand Island
Campus (NE)
Central Comm Coll–Hastings
Campus (NE)
Century Coll (MN)
Clovis Comm Coll (NM)
Coll of Business and Technology
(FL)
Coll of Lake County (IL)
Delaware Tech & Comm Coll, Jack
F. Owens Campus (DE)
Doña Ana Comm Coll (NM)
Eastfield Coll (TX)
Elaine P. Nunez Comm Coll (LA)
Elgin Comm Coll (IL)
Fayetteville Tech Comm Coll (NC)
GateWay Comm Coll (AZ)
Grand Rapids Comm Coll (MI)
Harper Coll (IL)
Harrisburg Area Comm Coll (PA)
Honolulu Comm Coll (HI)
Indian River State Coll (FL)
Ivy Tech Comm Coll–Bloomington
(IN)
Ivy Tech Comm Coll–Central
Indiana (IN)
Ivy Tech Comm Coll–Columbus
(IN)
Ivy Tech Comm Coll–East Central
(IN)
Ivy Tech Comm Coll–Kokomo (IN)
Ivy Tech Comm Coll–Lafayette (IN)
Ivy Tech Comm Coll–North Central
(IN)
Ivy Tech Comm Coll–Northeast (IN)
Ivy Tech Comm Coll–Northwest
(IN)
Ivy Tech Comm Coll–Richmond
(IN)

Ivy Tech Comm Coll–Southern Indiana (IN)
Ivy Tech Comm Coll–Southwest (IN)
Ivy Tech Comm Coll–Wabash Valley (IN)
Johnston Comm Coll (NC)
Kankakee Comm Coll (IL)
Kilgore Coll (TX)
Kirtland Comm Coll (MI)
Laramie County Comm Coll (WY)
Lehigh Carbon Comm Coll (PA)
Linn State Tech Coll (MO)
Lonestar Coll–Kingwood (TX)
Lonestar Coll–Montgomery (TX)
Lonestar Coll–North Harris (TX)
Macomb Comm Coll (MI)
Martin Comm Coll (NC)
Miami Dade Coll (FL)
Midlands Tech Coll (SC)
Mid-Plains Comm Coll, North Platte (NE)
Minnesota State Coll–Southeast Tech (MN)
Minnesota West Comm and Tech Coll (MN)
Mitchell Tech Inst (SD)
Mohave Comm Coll (AZ)
Moraine Park Tech Coll (WI)
Moraine Valley Comm Coll (IL)
Morton Coll (IL)
New England Inst of Technology (RI)
Northampton Comm Coll (PA)
North Dakota State Coll of Science (ND)
Northeast Comm Coll (NE)
North Idaho Coll (ID)
North Iowa Area Comm Coll (IA)
Northland Comm and Tech Coll–Thief River Falls & East Grand Forks (MN)
North Seattle Comm Coll (WA)
Orange Coast Coll (CA)
St. Cloud Tech & Comm Coll (MN)
St. Philip's Coll (TX)
Salt Lake Comm Coll (UT)
Sauk Valley Comm Coll (IL)
Southeast Tech Inst (SD)
Southwest Mississippi Comm Coll (MS)
Spartanburg Comm Coll (SC)
Trinity Valley Comm Coll (TX)
U of Arkansas Comm Coll at Morrilton (AR)
Waubonsee Comm Coll (IL)
Wenatchee Valley Coll (WA)
Westmoreland County Comm Coll (PA)
West Virginia Northern Comm Coll (WV)
Wilson Comm Coll (NC)

HEATING, VENTILATION, AIR CONDITIONING AND REFRIGERATION ENGINEERING TECHNOLOGY
Alamance Comm Coll (NC)
Austin Comm Coll (TX)
Chippewa Valley Tech Coll (WI)
Cincinnati State Tech and Comm Coll (OH)
DeKalb Tech Coll (GA)
Delaware Tech & Comm Coll, Stanton/Wilmington Campus (DE)
Front Range Comm Coll (CO)
Gadsden State Comm Coll (AL)
GateWay Comm Coll (AZ)
H. Councill Trenholm State Tech Coll (AL)
Jackson Comm Coll (MI)
Macomb Comm Coll (MI)
Martin Comm Coll (NC)
Miami Dade Coll (FL)
Minnesota State Comm and Tech Coll (MN)
Mohawk Valley Comm Coll (NY)
Moraine Park Tech Coll (WI)
North Dakota State Coll of Science (ND)
North Georgia Tech Coll (GA)
Oakland Comm Coll (MI)
Pennsylvania Highlands Comm Coll (PA)
Raritan Valley Comm Coll (NJ)
Savannah Tech Coll (GA)
Southern Crescent Tech Coll (GA)

South Georgia Tech Coll (GA)
Springfield Tech Comm Coll (MA)
Sullivan Coll of Technology and Design (KY)
Terra State Comm Coll (OH)
Wisconsin Indianhead Tech Coll (WI)

HEAVY EQUIPMENT MAINTENANCE TECHNOLOGY
Amarillo Coll (TX)
Beaufort County Comm Coll (NC)
Dakota County Tech Coll (MN)
Fox Valley Tech Coll (WI)
Highland Comm Coll (IL)
Linn State Tech Coll (MO)
Mesa Comm Coll (AZ)
Metropolitan Comm Coll–Longview (MO)
North Idaho Coll (ID)

HEAVY/INDUSTRIAL EQUIPMENT MAINTENANCE TECHNOLOGIES RELATED
Bellingham Tech Coll (WA)

HISPANIC-AMERICAN, PUERTO RICAN, AND MEXICAN-AMERICAN/ CHICANO STUDIES
Collin County Comm Coll District (TX)
East Los Angeles Coll (CA)
San Diego City Coll (CA)
Santa Barbara City Coll (CA)
Solano Comm Coll (CA)

HISTOLOGIC TECHNICIAN
Comm Coll of Rhode Island (RI)
Darton Coll (GA)
Houston Comm Coll System (TX)
Miami Dade Coll (FL)
Pima Comm Coll (AZ)

HISTOLOGIC TECHNOLOGY/ HISTOTECHNOLOGIST
Delaware Tech & Comm Coll, Stanton/Wilmington Campus (DE)
North Hennepin Comm Coll (MN)
Oakland Comm Coll (MI)
Phoenix Coll (AZ)

HISTORIC PRESERVATION AND CONSERVATION
Bucks County Comm Coll (PA)
Colorado Mountain Coll, Timberline Campus (CO)

HISTORY
Allen Comm Coll (KS)
Amarillo Coll (TX)
Ancilla Coll (IN)
Arizona Western Coll (AZ)
Austin Comm Coll (TX)
Bainbridge Coll (GA)
Barton County Comm Coll (KS)
Burlington County Coll (NJ)
Casper Coll (WY)
Clarendon Coll (TX)
Coll of the Canyons (CA)
Dakota Coll at Bottineau (ND)
Darton Coll (GA)
De Anza Coll (CA)
Dodge City Comm Coll (KS)
Eastern Arizona Coll (AZ)
East Los Angeles Coll (CA)
Foothill Coll (CA)
Frank Phillips Coll (TX)
Fulton-Montgomery Comm Coll (NY)
Georgia Highlands Coll (GA)
Georgia Military Coll (GA)
Great Basin Coll (NV)
Harper Coll (IL)
Highland Comm Coll (IL)
Indian River State Coll (FL)
Kilian Comm Coll (SD)
Lake Michigan Coll (MI)
Lamar Comm Coll (CO)
Laramie County Comm Coll (WY)
Lonestar Coll–Cy-Fair (TX)
Lonestar Coll–Kingwood (TX)
Lonestar Coll–Montgomery (TX)
Lonestar Coll–North Harris (TX)

Lonestar Coll–Tomball (TX)
Miami Dade Coll (FL)
Mohave Comm Coll (AZ)
Northern Essex Comm Coll (MA)
North Hennepin Comm Coll (MN)
North Idaho Coll (ID)
Northwest Coll (WY)
Oklahoma City Comm Coll (OK)
Oklahoma State U, Oklahoma City (OK)
Orange Coast Coll (CA)
Owens Comm Coll, Toledo (OH)
Palm Beach State Coll (FL)
Potomac State Coll of West Virginia U (WV)
Pratt Comm Coll (KS)
Red Rocks Comm Coll (CO)
Saint Charles Comm Coll (MO)
St. Philip's Coll (TX)
Salt Lake Comm Coll (UT)
Santa Barbara City Coll (CA)
Santa Rosa Jr Coll (CA)
Sauk Valley Comm Coll (IL)
Sheridan Coll (WY)
Snow Coll (UT)
Solano Comm Coll (CA)
Southwest Mississippi Comm Coll (MS)
Terra State Comm Coll (OH)
Trinity Valley Comm Coll (TX)
Wenatchee Valley Coll (WA)

HISTORY TEACHER EDUCATION
Darton Coll (GA)

HOME HEALTH AIDE/HOME ATTENDANT
Allen Comm Coll (KS)
Barton County Comm Coll (KS)

HOMELAND SECURITY
Goodwin Coll (CT)
Harper Coll (IL)
Long Island Business Inst (NY)

HOMELAND SECURITY, LAW ENFORCEMENT, FIREFIGHTING AND PROTECTIVE SERVICES RELATED
Barton County Comm Coll (KS)
Central Wyoming Coll (WY)
Century Coll (MN)
Georgia Military Coll (GA)
Glendale Comm Coll (AZ)
Goodwin Coll (CT)
J. Sargeant Reynolds Comm Coll (VA)
Laramie County Comm Coll (WY)
Miami Dade Coll (FL)
Onondaga Comm Coll (NY)
Pima Comm Coll (AZ)
Pittsburgh Tech Inst, Oakdale (PA)

HORSE HUSBANDRY/EQUINE SCIENCE AND MANAGEMENT
Cecil Coll (MD)
Clarendon Coll (TX)
Linn-Benton Comm Coll (OR)
Minnesota State Comm and Tech Coll (MN)
Santa Rosa Jr Coll (CA)
Yavapai Coll (AZ)

HORTICULTURAL SCIENCE
Central Lakes Coll (MN)
Century Coll (MN)
Chattahoochee Tech Coll (GA)
Columbus Tech Coll (GA)
Dakota Coll at Bottineau (ND)
Georgia Highlands Coll (GA)
Gwinnett Tech Coll (GA)
Kankakee Comm Coll (IL)
Lehigh Carbon Comm Coll (PA)
Linn-Benton Comm Coll (OR)
Mesa Comm Coll (AZ)
Miami Dade Coll (FL)
Missouri State U–West Plains (MO)
North Georgia Tech Coll (GA)
Oklahoma State U, Oklahoma City (OK)
Orange Coast Coll (CA)
Potomac State Coll of West Virginia U (WV)
Sheridan Coll (WY)

Southeast Tech Inst (SD)
Southern Crescent Tech Coll (GA)
South Georgia Tech Coll (GA)
Spartanburg Comm Coll (SC)
Trident Tech Coll (SC)
Trinity Valley Comm Coll (TX)
Tyler Jr Coll (TX)
The Williamson Free School of Mecha Trades (PA)

HOSPITAL AND HEALTH-CARE FACILITIES ADMINISTRATION
Allen Comm Coll (KS)
Minnesota West Comm and Tech Coll (MN)

HOSPITALITY ADMINISTRATION
Alexandria Tech and Comm Coll (MN)
Arizona Western Coll (AZ)
Austin Comm Coll (TX)
Bucks County Comm Coll (PA)
Burlington County Coll (NJ)
Casper Coll (WY)
Central New Mexico Comm Coll (NM)
Coll of the Canyons (CA)
Collin County Comm Coll District (TX)
Colorado Mountain Coll, Alpine Campus (CO)
Comm Coll of Vermont (VT)
Daytona State Coll (FL)
Doña Ana Comm Coll (NM)
Florida State Coll at Jacksonville (FL)
Fox Valley Tech Coll (WI)
Front Range Comm Coll (CO)
Gulf Coast Comm Coll (FL)
Harper Coll (IL)
Harrisburg Area Comm Coll (PA)
Hillsborough Comm Coll (FL)
Ivy Tech Comm Coll–East Central (IN)
Ivy Tech Comm Coll–North Central (IN)
Ivy Tech Comm Coll–Northeast (IN)
Ivy Tech Comm Coll–Northwest (IN)
Jefferson State Comm Coll (AL)
Lake Michigan Coll (MI)
Lonestar Coll–North Harris (TX)
Massachusetts Bay Comm Coll (MA)
Miami Dade Coll (FL)
Muskegon Comm Coll (MI)
Niagara County Comm Coll (NY)
North Idaho Coll (ID)
North Iowa Area Comm Coll (IA)
Olympic Coll (WA)
Onondaga Comm Coll (NY)
Pennsylvania Highlands Comm Coll (PA)
Pensacola State Coll (FL)
Pima Comm Coll (AZ)
Potomac State Coll of West Virginia U (WV)
Quinsigamond Comm Coll (MA)
San Diego City Coll (CA)
Scottsdale Comm Coll (AZ)
Sheridan Coll (WY)
Terra State Comm Coll (OH)
Three Rivers Comm Coll (CT)
Union County Coll (NJ)
Waukesha County Tech Coll (WI)
West Virginia Northern Comm Coll (WV)

HOSPITALITY ADMINISTRATION RELATED
Corning Comm Coll (NY)
Holyoke Comm Coll (MA)
Ivy Tech Comm Coll–Central Indiana (IN)
Ivy Tech Comm Coll–East Central (IN)
Ivy Tech Comm Coll–Northeast (IN)
Penn State Beaver (PA)

HOSPITALITY AND RECREATION MARKETING
Dakota Coll at Bottineau (ND)
Florida State Coll at Jacksonville (FL)
Montgomery County Comm Coll (PA)

Muskegon Comm Coll (MI)
Pueblo Comm Coll (CO)

HOTEL/MOTEL ADMINISTRATION
Albany Tech Coll (GA)
Athens Tech Coll (GA)
Atlanta Tech Coll (GA)
Bucks County Comm Coll (PA)
Cape Fear Comm Coll (NC)
Carl Albert State Coll (OK)
Central Comm Coll–Hastings Campus (NE)
Central Georgia Tech Coll (GA)
Central Oregon Comm Coll (OR)
Central Wyoming Coll (WY)
Cincinnati State Tech and Comm Coll (OH)
Coll of the Canyons (CA)
Colorado Mountain Coll, Alpine Campus (CO)
The Comm Coll of Baltimore County (MD)
Comm Coll of Philadelphia (PA)
Cowley County Comm Coll and Area Vocational–Tech School (KS)
Daytona State Coll (FL)
Delaware Tech & Comm Coll, Stanton/Wilmington Campus (DE)
Delaware Tech & Comm Coll, Terry Campus (DE)
Elgin Comm Coll (IL)
Florida State Coll at Jacksonville (FL)
Gateway Comm Coll (CT)
Georgia Highlands Coll (GA)
Gwinnett Tech Coll (GA)
Harrisburg Area Comm Coll (PA)
Houston Comm Coll System (TX)
Indian River State Coll (FL)
Manchester Comm Coll (CT)
Mohawk Valley Comm Coll (NY)
Montgomery Coll (MD)
Moraine Park Tech Coll (WI)
Muskegon Comm Coll (MI)
Northampton Comm Coll (PA)
Northern Essex Comm Coll (MA)
Norwalk Comm Coll (CT)
Oakland Comm Coll (MI)
Ogeechee Tech Coll (GA)
Orange Coast Coll (CA)
Palm Beach State Coll (FL)
Pittsburgh Tech Inst, Oakdale (PA)
Quinsigamond Comm Coll (MA)
The Restaurant School at Walnut Hill Coll (PA)
St. Philip's Coll (TX)
Sandhills Comm Coll (NC)
Santa Barbara City Coll (CA)
Savannah Tech Coll (GA)
Scottsdale Comm Coll (AZ)
Three Rivers Comm Coll (CT)
Tompkins Cortland Comm Coll (NY)
Trident Tech Coll (SC)
Union County Coll (NJ)
Yakima Valley Comm Coll (WA)

HOTEL, MOTEL, AND RESTAURANT MANAGEMENT
Fayetteville Tech Comm Coll (NC)

HOUSING AND HUMAN ENVIRONMENTS
Orange Coast Coll (CA)
Sullivan Coll of Technology and Design (KY)

HUMAN DEVELOPMENT AND FAMILY STUDIES
Georgia Military Coll (GA)
Orange Coast Coll (CA)
Penn State Brandywine (PA)
Penn State DuBois (PA)
Penn State Fayette, The Eberly Campus (PA)
Penn State Mont Alto (PA)
Penn State New Kensington (PA)
Penn State Schuylkill (PA)
Penn State Shenango (PA)
Penn State Worthington Scranton (PA)
Penn State York (PA)
Salt Lake Comm Coll (UT)

HUMAN DEVELOPMENT AND FAMILY STUDIES RELATED
Albany Tech Coll (GA)

HUMANITIES
Allen Comm Coll (KS)
Bristol Comm Coll (MA)
Bucks County Comm Coll (PA)
Cayuga County Comm Coll (NY)
Central Oregon Comm Coll (OR)
Coll of the Canyons (CA)
Colorado Mountain Coll (CO)
Colorado Mountain Coll, Alpine Campus (CO)
Corning Comm Coll (NY)
Dakota Coll at Bottineau (ND)
De Anza Coll (CA)
Dodge City Comm Coll (KS)
Dutchess Comm Coll (NY)
Fulton-Montgomery Comm Coll (NY)
Golden West Coll (CA)
Harper Coll (IL)
Housatonic Comm Coll (CT)
Indian River State Coll (FL)
Lake Michigan Coll (MI)
Laramie County Comm Coll (WY)
Lehigh Carbon Comm Coll (PA)
Lonestar Coll–Cy-Fair (TX)
Lonestar Coll–Kingwood (TX)
Lonestar Coll–Montgomery (TX)
Lonestar Coll–Tomball (TX)
Miami Dade Coll (FL)
Mohawk Valley Comm Coll (NY)
Montgomery County Comm Coll (PA)
Niagara County Comm Coll (NY)
Oklahoma City Comm Coll (OK)
Oklahoma State U, Oklahoma City (OK)
Onondaga Comm Coll (NY)
Orange Coast Coll (CA)
Pratt Comm Coll (KS)
Red Rocks Comm Coll (CO)
Salt Lake Comm Coll (UT)
Santa Fe Comm Coll (NM)
Santa Rosa Jr Coll (CA)
Snow Coll (UT)
Southwest Mississippi Comm Coll (MS)
Suffolk County Comm Coll (NY)
Terra State Comm Coll (OH)
Tompkins Cortland Comm Coll (NY)
Westchester Comm Coll (NY)

HUMAN RESOURCES MANAGEMENT
Anoka-Ramsey Comm Coll (MN)
Anoka-Ramsey Comm Coll, Cambridge Campus (MN)
Barton County Comm Coll (KS)
Clark Coll (WA)
Delaware Tech & Comm Coll, Terry Campus (DE)
Edison State Comm Coll (OH)
Fayetteville Tech Comm Coll (NC)
Fox Valley Tech Coll (WI)
Goodwin Coll (CT)
Harrison Coll, Anderson (IN)
Harrison Coll, Indianapolis (IN)
Harrison Coll, Lafayette (IN)
Harrison Coll, Muncie (IN)
Harrison Coll (OH)
Hawkeye Comm Coll (IA)
Lehigh Carbon Comm Coll (PA)
Minnesota State Comm and Tech Coll (MN)
Moraine Park Tech Coll (WI)
Moraine Valley Comm Coll (IL)
Waubonsee Comm Coll (IL)
Western Iowa Tech Comm Coll (IA)
Westmoreland County Comm Coll (PA)

HUMAN RESOURCES MANAGEMENT AND SERVICES RELATED
Barton County Comm Coll (KS)
Bryant & Stratton Coll (WI)

HUMAN SERVICES
Alexandria Tech and Comm Coll (MN)
Austin Comm Coll (TX)

Burlington County Coll (NJ)
Central Maine Comm Coll (ME)
Century Coll (MN)
Coll of Central Florida (FL)
Comm Coll of Philadelphia (PA)
Comm Coll of Vermont (VT)
Corning Comm Coll (NY)
Daytona State Coll (FL)
Delaware Tech & Comm Coll, Jack F. Owens Campus (DE)
Delaware Tech & Comm Coll, Stanton/Wilmington Campus (DE)
Delaware Tech & Comm Coll, Terry Campus (DE)
Denmark Tech Coll (SC)
Florida State Coll at Jacksonville (FL)
Frederick Comm Coll (MD)
Fulton-Montgomery Comm Coll (NY)
Gateway Comm Coll (CT)
Georgia Highlands Coll (GA)
Goodwin Coll (CT)
Grays Harbor Coll (WA)
Harper Coll (IL)
Harrisburg Area Comm Coll (PA)
Highland Comm Coll (IL)
Honolulu Comm Coll (HI)
Housatonic Comm Coll (CT)
Indian River State Coll (FL)
Inver Hills Comm Coll (MN)
Ivy Tech Comm Coll–Bloomington (IN)
Ivy Tech Comm Coll–Central Indiana (IN)
Ivy Tech Comm Coll–Columbus (IN)
Ivy Tech Comm Coll–East Central (IN)
Ivy Tech Comm Coll–Kokomo (IN)
Ivy Tech Comm Coll–Lafayette (IN)
Ivy Tech Comm Coll–North Central (IN)
Ivy Tech Comm Coll–Northeast (IN)
Ivy Tech Comm Coll–Northwest (IN)
Ivy Tech Comm Coll–Richmond (IN)
Ivy Tech Comm Coll–Southeast (IN)
Ivy Tech Comm Coll–Southern Indiana (IN)
Ivy Tech Comm Coll–Southwest (IN)
Ivy Tech Comm Coll–Wabash Valley (IN)
John Tyler Comm Coll (VA)
Kent State U at Ashtabula (OH)
Kingsborough Comm Coll of the City U of New York (NY)
Laramie County Comm Coll (WY)
Lehigh Carbon Comm Coll (PA)
Lonestar Coll–Kingwood (TX)
Lonestar Coll–Montgomery (TX)
Lonestar Coll–North Harris (TX)
Manchester Comm Coll (CT)
Marion Tech Coll (OH)
Massachusetts Bay Comm Coll (MA)
Mendocino Coll (CA)
Mesabi Range Comm and Tech Coll (MN)
Metropolitan Comm Coll–Longview (MO)
Miami Dade Coll (FL)
Middlesex Comm Coll (CT)
Minnesota West Comm and Tech Coll (MN)
Nashua Comm Coll (NH)
New Mexico State U–Alamogordo (NM)
Niagara County Comm Coll (NY)
Northern Essex Comm Coll (MA)
North Idaho Coll (ID)
Norwalk Comm Coll (CT)
Ocean County Coll (NJ)
Oklahoma State U, Oklahoma City (OK)
Owensboro Comm and Tech Coll (KY)
Pasco-Hernando Comm Coll (FL)
Pennsylvania Highlands Comm Coll (PA)
Pratt Comm Coll (KS)
Quinsigamond Comm Coll (MA)
Saint Charles Comm Coll (MO)

Sandhills Comm Coll (NC)
Santa Rosa Jr Coll (CA)
Sauk Valley Comm Coll (IL)
Southern State Comm Coll (OH)
Southside Virginia Comm Coll (VA)
Stark State Coll of Technology (OH)
Suffolk County Comm Coll (NY)
Three Rivers Comm Coll (CT)
Trident Tech Coll (SC)
Union County Coll (NJ)
U of Alaska Anchorage, Kenai Peninsula Coll (AK)
U of Pittsburgh at Titusville (PA)
Westmoreland County Comm Coll (PA)
White Mountains Comm Coll (NH)

HYDRAULICS AND FLUID POWER TECHNOLOGY
The Comm Coll of Baltimore County (MD)
Minnesota West Comm and Tech Coll (MN)
Owens Comm Coll, Toledo (OH)

HYDROLOGY AND WATER RESOURCES SCIENCE
Dodge City Comm Coll (KS)
Doña Ana Comm Coll (NM)
Indian River State Coll (FL)
Three Rivers Comm Coll (CT)

ILLUSTRATION
Creative Center (NE)
Douglas Education Center (PA)
Fashion Inst of Technology (NY)
Oklahoma State U, Oklahoma City (OK)

INDUSTRIAL AND PRODUCT DESIGN
The Art Inst of Seattle (WA)
Fiorello H. LaGuardia Comm Coll of the City U of New York (NY)
GateWay Comm Coll (AZ)
Kirtland Comm Coll (MI)
Orange Coast Coll (CA)

INDUSTRIAL ELECTRONICS TECHNOLOGY
Big Bend Comm Coll (WA)
Central Carolina Tech Coll (SC)
Central Lakes Coll (MN)
Danville Area Comm Coll (IL)
H. Councill Trenholm State Tech Coll (AL)
John Tyler Comm Coll (VA)
Lawson State Comm Coll (AL)
Lehigh Carbon Comm Coll (PA)
Lincoln Land Comm Coll (IL)
Lurleen B. Wallace Comm Coll (AL)
Midlands Tech Coll (SC)
Moraine Park Tech Coll (WI)
Moraine Valley Comm Coll (IL)
Northampton Comm Coll (PA)
Northland Comm and Tech Coll–Thief River Falls & East Grand Forks (MN)
Northwest-Shoals Comm Coll (AL)
Pima Comm Coll (AZ)
Randolph Comm Coll (NC)
Spartanburg Comm Coll (SC)
Sullivan Coll of Technology and Design (KY)
Wenatchee Valley Coll (WA)

INDUSTRIAL ENGINEERING
Blackhawk Tech Coll (WI)
Catawba Valley Comm Coll (NC)
Central Lakes Coll (MN)
Manchester Comm Coll (CT)
Montcalm Comm Coll (MI)
Santa Barbara City Coll (CA)

INDUSTRIAL MECHANICS AND MAINTENANCE TECHNOLOGY
Aiken Tech Coll (SC)
Alexandria Tech and Comm Coll (MN)
Bellingham Tech Coll (WA)
Big Bend Comm Coll (WA)
Casper Coll (WY)

Central Comm Coll–Hastings Campus (NE)
Clovis Comm Coll (NM)
Coll of Lake County (IL)
Danville Area Comm Coll (IL)
Gadsden State Comm Coll (AL)
Harrisburg Area Comm Coll (PA)
H. Councill Trenholm State Tech Coll (AL)
Illinois Eastern Comm Colls, Olney Central College (IL)
Ivy Tech Comm Coll–East Central (IN)
Kaskaskia Coll (IL)
Lower Columbia Coll (WA)
Macomb Comm Coll (MI)
Midlands Tech Coll (SC)
Minnesota State Coll–Southeast Tech (MN)
Moraine Park Tech Coll (WI)
Northeast Comm Coll (NE)
San Juan Coll (NM)
Southwestern Michigan Coll (MI)
Sullivan Coll of Technology and Design (KY)
Waubonsee Comm Coll (IL)
Western Iowa Tech Comm Coll (IA)
Westmoreland County Comm Coll (PA)

INDUSTRIAL PRODUCTION TECHNOLOGIES RELATED
Barton County Comm Coll (KS)
Bristol Comm Coll (MA)
Harford Comm Coll (MD)
Ivy Tech Comm Coll–Central Indiana (IN)
Ivy Tech Comm Coll–East Central (IN)
Ivy Tech Comm Coll–Lafayette (IN)
Ivy Tech Comm Coll–North Central (IN)
Ivy Tech Comm Coll–Northeast (IN)
Ivy Tech Comm Coll–Richmond (IN)
Ivy Tech Comm Coll–Southwest (IN)
Ivy Tech Comm Coll–Wabash Valley (IN)
Mohawk Valley Comm Coll (NY)
Moraine Park Tech Coll (WI)
Mountain Empire Comm Coll (VA)
Pima Comm Coll (AZ)
Southwestern Michigan Coll (MI)

INDUSTRIAL RADIOLOGIC TECHNOLOGY
Amarillo Coll (TX)
Comm Coll of Philadelphia (PA)
Cowley County Comm Coll and Area Vocational–Tech School (KS)
Daytona State Coll (FL)
Doña Ana Comm Coll (NM)
Eastern Gateway Comm Coll (OH)
Gateway Comm Coll (CT)
Indian River State Coll (FL)
Kankakee Comm Coll (IL)
Middlesex Comm Coll (CT)
Northern Essex Comm Coll (MA)
Orange Coast Coll (CA)
Palm Beach State Coll (FL)
Salt Lake Comm Coll (UT)
Sauk Valley Comm Coll (IL)
Southeastern Comm Coll (IA)
Tyler Jr Coll (TX)
Wenatchee Valley Coll (WA)
Yakima Valley Comm Coll (WA)

INDUSTRIAL SAFETY TECHNOLOGY
Northwest Tech Coll (MN)

INDUSTRIAL TECHNOLOGY
Albany Tech Coll (GA)
Allen Comm Coll (KS)
Arizona Western Coll (AZ)
Blackhawk Tech Coll (WI)
Central Comm Coll–Hastings Campus (NE)
Central Georgia Tech Coll (GA)
Central Oregon Comm Coll (OR)
Cleveland State Comm Coll (TN)
Columbus Tech Coll (GA)
Comm Coll of Vermont (VT)

Corning Comm Coll (NY)
Crowder Coll (MO)
Daytona State Coll (FL)
De Anza Coll (CA)
DeKalb Tech Coll (GA)
Dodge City Comm Coll (KS)
Eastern Gateway Comm Coll (OH)
Edison State Comm Coll (OH)
Elaine P. Nunez Comm Coll (LA)
FIDM/The Fashion Inst of Design & Merchandising, Orange County Campus (CA)
Frank Phillips Coll (TX)
Gateway Comm and Tech Coll (KY)
Gateway Comm Coll (CT)
Grand Rapids Comm Coll (MI)
Grays Harbor Coll (WA)
Great Basin Coll (NV)
Hagerstown Comm Coll (MD)
Illinois Eastern Comm Colls, Wabash Valley College (IL)
Ivy Tech Comm Coll–Bloomington (IN)
Ivy Tech Comm Coll–Central Indiana (IN)
Ivy Tech Comm Coll–Columbus (IN)
Ivy Tech Comm Coll–East Central (IN)
Ivy Tech Comm Coll–Kokomo (IN)
Ivy Tech Comm Coll–Lafayette (IN)
Ivy Tech Comm Coll–North Central (IN)
Ivy Tech Comm Coll–Northeast (IN)
Ivy Tech Comm Coll–Northwest (IN)
Ivy Tech Comm Coll–Richmond (IN)
Ivy Tech Comm Coll–Southeast (IN)
Ivy Tech Comm Coll–Southern Indiana (IN)
Ivy Tech Comm Coll–Southwest (IN)
Ivy Tech Comm Coll–Wabash Valley (IN)
J. Sargeant Reynolds Comm Coll (VA)
Kent State U at Ashtabula (OH)
Kent State U at Geauga (OH)
Kent State U at Salem (OH)
Kent State U at Trumbull (OH)
Kent State U at Tuscarawas (OH)
Kirtland Comm Coll (MI)
Lake Michigan Coll (MI)
Lanier Tech Coll (GA)
Linn-Benton Comm Coll (OR)
Lonestar Coll–Cy-Fair (TX)
Macomb Comm Coll (MI)
Manchester Comm Coll (CT)
Marion Tech Coll (OH)
Mesa Comm Coll (AZ)
Miami Dade Coll (FL)
Missouri State U–West Plains (MO)
Monroe County Comm Coll (MI)
Montcalm Comm Coll (MI)
Moraine Park Tech Coll (WI)
Mountain Empire Comm Coll (VA)
Muskegon Comm Coll (MI)
New England Inst of Technology (RI)
North Georgia Tech Coll (GA)
Northwest Tech Coll (MN)
Oakland Comm Coll (MI)
Olympic Coll (WA)
Owens Comm Coll, Toledo (OH)
Panola Coll (TX)
Paul D. Camp Comm Coll (VA)
Penn State York (PA)
Pennsylvania Highlands Comm Coll (PA)
Pima Comm Coll (AZ)
Saint Charles Comm Coll (MO)
San Diego City Coll (CA)
San Juan Coll (NM)
Santa Barbara City Coll (CA)
Savannah Tech Coll (GA)
Seminole State Coll of Florida (FL)
Southeast Tech Inst (SD)
Southern Crescent Tech Coll (GA)
South Georgia Tech Coll (GA)
Stark State Coll of Technology (OH)
Three Rivers Comm Coll (CT)
Trident Tech Coll (SC)
Vincennes U Jasper Campus (IN)
Waubonsee Comm Coll (IL)

West Georgia Tech Coll (GA)
Wilson Comm Coll (NC)
Yakima Valley Comm Coll (WA)

INFORMATION SCIENCE/STUDIES

Alamance Comm Coll (NC)
Allen Comm Coll (KS)
Altamaha Tech Coll (GA)
Amarillo Coll (TX)
Arkansas State U–Mountain Home (AR)
Athens Tech Coll (GA)
Augusta Tech Coll (GA)
Bainbridge Coll (GA)
Barton County Comm Coll (KS)
Beaufort County Comm Coll (NC)
Bristol Comm Coll (MA)
Bucks County Comm Coll (PA)
Cayuga County Comm Coll (NY)
Cecil Coll (MD)
Central Georgia Tech Coll (GA)
Central New Mexico Comm Coll (NM)
Chattahoochee Tech Coll (GA)
Cincinnati State Tech and Comm Coll (OH)
Columbus Tech Coll (GA)
Dabney S. Lancaster Comm Coll (VA)
Dakota Coll at Bottineau (ND)
De Anza Coll (CA)
DeKalb Tech Coll (GA)
Dodge City Comm Coll (KS)
Dutchess Comm Coll (NY)
Eastern Arizona Coll (AZ)
Elaine P. Nunez Comm Coll (LA)
El Centro Coll (TX)
Fayetteville Tech Comm Coll (NC)
Fiorello H. LaGuardia Comm Coll of the City U of New York (NY)
Florida State Coll at Jacksonville (FL)
Fulton-Montgomery Comm Coll (NY)
Georgia Highlands Coll (GA)
Georgia Northwestern Tech Coll (GA)
Grays Harbor Coll (WA)
Gwinnett Tech Coll (GA)
Howard Comm Coll (MD)
Indian River State Coll (FL)
Kankakee Comm Coll (IL)
Kaskaskia Coll (IL)
Kirtland Comm Coll (MI)
Lamar Comm Coll (CO)
Lanier Tech Coll (GA)
Lehigh Carbon Comm Coll (PA)
Lonestar Coll–Kingwood (TX)
Lonestar Coll–North Harris (TX)
Los Angeles Harbor Coll (CA)
Manchester Comm Coll (CT)
Martin Comm Coll (NC)
Massachusetts Bay Comm Coll (MA)
Mendocino Coll (CA)
Metropolitan Comm Coll–Blue River (MO)
Metropolitan Comm Coll–Business & Technology Campus (MO)
Miami Dade Coll (FL)
Middle Georgia Tech Coll (GA)
Montgomery County Comm Coll (PA)
Moultrie Tech Coll (GA)
Muskegon Comm Coll (MI)
Niagara County Comm Coll (NY)
Norwalk Comm Coll (CT)
Ogeechee Tech Coll (GA)
Okefenokee Tech Coll (GA)
Oklahoma State U, Oklahoma City (OK)
Orange Coast Coll (CA)
Panola Coll (TX)
Penn State DuBois (PA)
Penn State Hazleton (PA)
Penn State Lehigh Valley (PA)
Penn State New Kensington (PA)
Penn State Schuylkill (PA)
Polk State Coll (FL)
Quinsigamond Comm Coll (MA)
Salt Lake Comm Coll (UT)
Sandersville Tech Coll (GA)
Sandhills Comm Coll (NC)
Santa Barbara City Coll (CA)
Scottsdale Comm Coll (AZ)
Seminole State Coll of Florida (FL)
Sheridan Coll (WY)

Snow Coll (UT)
Southeastern Comm Coll (IA)
Southeastern Tech Coll (GA)
Southern Alberta Inst of Technology (AB, Canada)
South Georgia Tech Coll (GA)
Southside Virginia Comm Coll (VA)
Southwest Georgia Tech Coll (GA)
Suffolk County Comm Coll (NY)
Tompkins Cortland Comm Coll (NY)
Union County Coll (NJ)
Westchester Comm Coll (NY)
West Georgia Tech Coll (GA)
Yavapai Coll (AZ)

INFORMATION TECHNOLOGY

Atlanta Tech Coll (GA)
Blue Ridge Comm and Tech Coll (WV)
Brown Mackie Coll–Akron (OH)
Brown Mackie Coll–Albuquerque (NM)
Brown Mackie Coll–Boise (ID)
Brown Mackie Coll–Cincinnati (OH)
Brown Mackie Coll–Greenville (SC)
Brown Mackie Coll–Miami (FL)
Brown Mackie Coll–Northern Kentucky (KY)
Brown Mackie Coll–Phoenix (AZ)
Brown Mackie Coll–St. Louis (MO)
Brown Mackie Coll–San Antonio (TX)
Brown Mackie Coll–South Bend (IN)
Brown Mackie Coll–Tucson (AZ)
Brown Mackie Coll–Tulsa (OK)
Bucks County Comm Coll (PA)
Burlington County Coll (NJ)
Catawba Valley Comm Coll (NC)
Cecil Coll (MD)
Chandler-Gilbert Comm Coll (AZ)
City Colls of Chicago, Harry S. Truman College (IL)
Clovis Comm Coll (NM)
Coll of Central Florida (FL)
Comm Coll of Vermont (VT)
Corning Comm Coll (NY)
Dakota Coll at Bottineau (ND)
Daytona State Coll (FL)
Edison State Comm Coll (OH)
Fayetteville Tech Comm Coll (NC)
Florida State Coll at Jacksonville (FL)
Frederick Comm Coll (MD)
Gateway Comm and Tech Coll (KY)
Georgia Military Coll (GA)
Harrison Coll, Indianapolis (IN)
Harrison Coll, Muncie (IN)
Highland Comm Coll (IL)
Howard Comm Coll (MD)
Ilisagvik Coll (AK)
Illinois Eastern Comm Colls, Frontier Community College (IL)
ITI Tech Coll (LA)
James Sprunt Comm Coll (NC)
Jefferson Coll (MO)
Kent State U at Geauga (OH)
Kilian Comm Coll (SD)
Lake Region State Coll (ND)
Lonestar Coll–Cy-Fair (TX)
Lonestar Coll–Montgomery (TX)
Marion Tech Coll (OH)
McHenry County Coll (IL)
Mesabi Range Comm and Tech Coll (MN)
Metropolitan Comm Coll–Business & Technology Campus (MO)
Minnesota West Comm and Tech Coll (MN)
Missouri State U–West Plains (MO)
Mohave Comm Coll (AZ)
Monroe County Comm Coll (MI)
Montana State U–Great Falls Coll of Technology (MT)
New England Inst of Technology (RI)
New Mexico State U–Alamogordo (NM)
Northland Comm and Tech Coll–Thief River Falls & East Grand Forks (MN)
Norwalk Comm Coll (CT)
Oakland Comm Coll (MI)
Oklahoma State U, Oklahoma City (OK)
Owensboro Comm and Tech Coll (KY)
Owens Comm Coll, Toledo (OH)
Pasco-Hernando Comm Coll (FL)

Potomac State Coll of West Virginia U (WV)
Randolph Comm Coll (NC)
Raritan Valley Comm Coll (NJ)
Salt Lake Comm Coll (UT)
Santa Barbara City Coll (CA)
Savannah Tech Coll (GA)
Seminole State Coll of Florida (FL)
Southside Virginia Comm Coll (VA)
South Suburban Coll (IL)
Southwest Mississippi Comm Coll (MS)
Stark State Coll of Technology (OH)
Suffolk County Comm Coll (NY)
Sullivan Coll of Technology and Design (KY)
Tyler Jr Coll (TX)
Union County Coll (NJ)
West Virginia Northern Comm Coll (WV)
Wilson Comm Coll (NC)

INFORMATION TECHNOLOGY PROJECT MANAGEMENT

Clovis Comm Coll (NM)

INSTITUTIONAL FOOD WORKERS

James Sprunt Comm Coll (NC)
Santa Barbara City Coll (CA)

INSTRUMENTATION TECHNOLOGY

Amarillo Coll (TX)
Bellingham Tech Coll (WA)
Cape Fear Comm Coll (NC)
DeKalb Tech Coll (GA)
Florida State Coll at Jacksonville (FL)
Fox Valley Tech Coll (WI)
Houston Comm Coll System (TX)
ITI Tech Coll (LA)
Lower Columbia Coll (WA)
Mesabi Range Comm and Tech Coll (MN)
Moraine Valley Comm Coll (IL)
St. Cloud Tech & Comm Coll (MN)
Salt Lake Comm Coll (UT)
San Juan Coll (NM)
Yakima Valley Comm Coll (WA)

INSURANCE

Florida State Coll at Jacksonville (FL)
Mesa Comm Coll (AZ)
North Iowa Area Comm Coll (IA)
Oklahoma City Comm Coll (OK)
San Diego City Coll (CA)
Trinity Valley Comm Coll (TX)

INTERDISCIPLINARY STUDIES

Great Basin Coll (NV)
Lonestar Coll–Cy-Fair (TX)
Lonestar Coll–Kingwood (TX)
Lonestar Coll–Montgomery (TX)
Lonestar Coll–North Harris (TX)
Lonestar Coll–Tomball (TX)

INTERIOR DESIGN

Alexandria Tech and Comm Coll (MN)
Amarillo Coll (TX)
Antelope Valley Coll (CA)
The Art Inst of New York City (NY)
The Art Inst of Ohio–Cincinnati (OH)
The Art Inst of Seattle (WA)
The Art Inst of York–Pennsylvania (PA)
Cape Fear Comm Coll (NC)
Century Coll (MN)
Clary Sage Coll (OK)
Coll of the Canyons (CA)
Collin County Comm Coll District (TX)
Dakota County Tech Coll (MN)
Daytona State Coll (FL)
Delaware Tech & Comm Coll, Terry Campus (DE)
El Centro Coll (TX)
Fashion Inst of Technology (NY)
FIDM/The Fashion Inst of Design & Merchandising, Los Angeles Campus (CA)

FIDM/The Fashion Inst of Design & Merchandising, Orange County Campus (CA)
FIDM/The Fashion Inst of Design & Merchandising, San Diego Campus (CA)
FIDM/The Fashion Inst of Design & Merchandising, San Francisco Campus (CA)
Florida State Coll at Jacksonville (FL)
Fox Valley Tech Coll (WI)
Front Range Comm Coll (CO)
Gwinnett Tech Coll (GA)
Harford Comm Coll (MD)
Harper Coll (IL)
Hawkeye Comm Coll (IA)
Houston Comm Coll System (TX)
Indian River State Coll (FL)
Ivy Tech Comm Coll–North Central (IN)
Ivy Tech Comm Coll–Southwest (IN)
Lanier Tech Coll (GA)
Lehigh Carbon Comm Coll (PA)
Lonestar Coll–Kingwood (TX)
Mesa Comm Coll (AZ)
Miami Dade Coll (FL)
Montana State U–Great Falls Coll of Technology (MT)
Montgomery Coll (MD)
New England Inst of Technology (RI)
Northampton Comm Coll (PA)
Norwalk Comm Coll (CT)
Oakland Comm Coll (MI)
Ogeechee Tech Coll (GA)
Onondaga Comm Coll (NY)
Orange Coast Coll (CA)
Owens Comm Coll, Toledo (OH)
Palm Beach State Coll (FL)
Phoenix Coll (AZ)
Randolph Comm Coll (NC)
Raritan Valley Comm Coll (NJ)
San Diego City Coll (CA)
Santa Barbara City Coll (CA)
Santa Fe Comm Coll (NM)
Santa Rosa Jr Coll (CA)
Scottsdale Comm Coll (AZ)
Seminole State Coll of Florida (FL)
Suffolk County Comm Coll (NY)
Sullivan Coll of Technology and Design (KY)
Wade Coll (TX)
Waukesha County Tech Coll (WI)
Western Iowa Tech Comm Coll (IA)

INTERMEDIA/MULTIMEDIA

Bristol Comm Coll (MA)
Middlesex Comm Coll (CT)
Santa Fe Comm Coll (NM)

INTERNATIONAL BUSINESS/TRADE/COMMERCE

Austin Comm Coll (TX)
Central New Mexico Comm Coll (NM)
Cincinnati State Tech and Comm Coll (OH)
Comm Coll of Philadelphia (PA)
Foothill Coll (CA)
Frederick Comm Coll (MD)
Harper Coll (IL)
Houston Comm Coll System (TX)
Northeast Comm Coll (NE)
Oakland Comm Coll (MI)
Owens Comm Coll, Toledo (OH)
Raritan Valley Comm Coll (NJ)
Stark State Coll of Technology (OH)
Tompkins Cortland Comm Coll (NY)
Westchester Comm Coll (NY)

INTERNATIONAL/GLOBAL STUDIES

Burlington County Coll (NJ)
Central Wyoming Coll (WY)
Macomb Comm Coll (MI)
Salt Lake Comm Coll (UT)

INTERNATIONAL RELATIONS AND AFFAIRS

Casper Coll (WY)
De Anza Coll (CA)
Georgia Military Coll (GA)
Harrisburg Area Comm Coll (PA)
Massachusetts Bay Comm Coll (MA)

Miami Dade Coll (FL)
Northern Essex Comm Coll (MA)
Salt Lake Comm Coll (UT)
Santa Barbara City Coll (CA)

IRONWORKING

GateWay Comm Coll (AZ)
Ivy Tech Comm Coll–Lafayette (IN)
Ivy Tech Comm Coll–North Central (IN)
Ivy Tech Comm Coll–Northeast (IN)
Ivy Tech Comm Coll–Northwest (IN)
Ivy Tech Comm Coll–Southwest (IN)
Ivy Tech Comm Coll–Wabash Valley (IN)

ITALIAN

Miami Dade Coll (FL)

JAPANESE

Austin Comm Coll (TX)
East Los Angeles Coll (CA)
Snow Coll (UT)

JAZZ/JAZZ STUDIES

Comm Coll of Rhode Island (RI)

JOURNALISM

Allen Comm Coll (KS)
Amarillo Coll (TX)
Austin Comm Coll (TX)
Bainbridge Coll (GA)
Barton County Comm Coll (KS)
Bucks County Comm Coll (PA)
Burlington County Coll (NJ)
Carl Albert State Coll (OK)
Coll of the Canyons (CA)
Cowley County Comm Coll and Area Vocational–Tech School (KS)
Darton Coll (GA)
De Anza Coll (CA)
Dodge City Comm Coll (KS)
East Los Angeles Coll (CA)
Georgia Highlands Coll (GA)
Golden West Coll (CA)
Housatonic Comm Coll (CT)
Indian River State Coll (FL)
Kilgore Coll (TX)
Kingsborough Comm Coll of the City U of New York (NY)
Lonestar Coll–North Harris (TX)
Manchester Comm Coll (CT)
Miami Dade Coll (FL)
Monroe County Comm Coll (MI)
Northampton Comm Coll (PA)
Northeast Comm Coll (NE)
Northern Essex Comm Coll (MA)
North Idaho Coll (ID)
Northwest Coll (WY)
Orange Coast Coll (CA)
Palm Beach State Coll (FL)
Phoenix Coll (AZ)
Potomac State Coll of West Virginia U (WV)
San Diego City Coll (CA)
Solano Comm Coll (CA)
Suffolk County Comm Coll (NY)
Trinity Valley Comm Coll (TX)

JUVENILE CORRECTIONS

Danville Area Comm Coll (IL)
Kaskaskia Coll (IL)
Linn-Benton Comm Coll (OR)

KINDERGARTEN/PRESCHOOL EDUCATION

Alamance Comm Coll (NC)
Bainbridge Coll (GA)
Beaufort County Comm Coll (NC)
Bristol Comm Coll (MA)
Bucks County Comm Coll (PA)
Carroll Comm Coll (MD)
Casper Coll (WY)
Cecil Coll (MD)
Central Lakes Coll (MN)
Cleveland State Comm Coll (TN)
Collin County Comm Coll District (TX)
Comm Coll of Philadelphia (PA)
Comm Coll of Rhode Island (RI)
Daytona State Coll (FL)
Delaware Tech & Comm Coll, Jack F. Owens Campus (DE)

Delaware Tech & Comm Coll, Stanton/Wilmington Campus (DE)
Delaware Tech & Comm Coll, Terry Campus (DE)
Denmark Tech Coll (SC)
Dutchess Comm Coll (NY)
Elaine P. Nunez Comm Coll (LA)
Frederick Comm Coll (MD)
Fulton-Montgomery Comm Coll (NY)
Gateway Comm Coll (CT)
Georgia Highlands Coll (GA)
Great Basin Coll (NV)
Hesston Coll (KS)
Highland Comm Coll (IL)
Honolulu Comm Coll (HI)
Howard Comm Coll (MD)
Indian River State Coll (FL)
Johnston Comm Coll (NC)
Kent State U at Ashtabula (OH)
Manchester Comm Coll (CT)
Mendocino Coll (CA)
Metropolitan Comm Coll–Penn Valley (MO)
Miami Dade Coll (FL)
Nashua Comm Coll (NH)
Northern Essex Comm Coll (MA)
Northwest Coll (WY)
Orange Coast Coll (CA)
Owensboro Comm and Tech Coll (KY)
Palm Beach State Coll (FL)
Potomac State Coll of West Virginia U (WV)
Pratt Comm Coll (KS)
Quinsigamond Comm Coll (MA)
Raritan Valley Comm Coll (NJ)
Red Rocks Comm Coll (CO)
Sandhills Comm Coll (NC)
Santa Barbara City Coll (CA)
Santa Fe Comm Coll (NM)
Scottsdale Comm Coll (AZ)
Snow Coll (UT)
Solano Comm Coll (CA)
Southern State Comm Coll (OH)
Suffolk County Comm Coll (NY)
Tallahassee Comm Coll (FL)
Terra State Comm Coll (OH)
Three Rivers Comm Coll (CT)
Tompkins Cortland Comm Coll (NY)
Trinity Valley Comm Coll (TX)
Wenatchee Valley Coll (WA)
Yakima Valley Comm Coll (WA)

KINESIOLOGY AND EXERCISE SCIENCE

Barton County Comm Coll (KS)
Carroll Comm Coll (MD)
Central Oregon Comm Coll (OR)
Chandler-Gilbert Comm Coll (AZ)
Clarendon Coll (TX)
Dakota County Tech Coll (MN)
Delaware Tech & Comm Coll, Stanton/Wilmington Campus (DE)
Elgin Comm Coll (IL)
Glendale Comm Coll (AZ)
Lonestar Coll–Cy-Fair (TX)
Lonestar Coll–Kingwood (TX)
Lonestar Coll–Montgomery (TX)
Lonestar Coll–North Harris (TX)
Lonestar Coll–Tomball (TX)
Norwalk Comm Coll (CT)
Oakland Comm Coll (MI)
Orange Coast Coll (CA)
Raritan Valley Comm Coll (NJ)
St. Philip's Coll (TX)
Salt Lake Comm Coll (UT)
Santa Barbara City Coll (CA)
Sheridan Coll (WY)
South Suburban Coll (IL)

LABOR AND INDUSTRIAL RELATIONS

The Comm Coll of Baltimore County (MD)
Kingsborough Comm Coll of the City U of New York (NY)
San Diego City Coll (CA)

LANDSCAPE ARCHITECTURE

Foothill Coll (CA)
Oakland Comm Coll (MI)
Santa Rosa Jr Coll (CA)

LANDSCAPING AND GROUNDSKEEPING

Cape Fear Comm Coll (NC)
Century Coll (MN)
Cincinnati State Tech and Comm Coll (OH)
Clark Coll (WA)
Coll of Central Florida (FL)
Coll of Lake County (IL)
Coll of the Canyons (CA)
Dakota Coll at Bottineau (ND)
Dakota County Tech Coll (MN)
Danville Area Comm Coll (IL)
Harrisburg Area Comm Coll (PA)
Hillsborough Comm Coll (FL)
Johnston Comm Coll (NC)
Lake Michigan Coll (MI)
Lincoln Land Comm Coll (IL)
Miami Dade Coll (FL)
Oakland Comm Coll (MI)
Owens Comm Coll, Toledo (OH)
Pensacola State Coll (FL)
Sandhills Comm Coll (NC)
San Juan Coll (NM)
Santa Barbara City Coll (CA)
Springfield Tech Comm Coll (MA)
The Williamson Free School of Mecha Trades (PA)

LAND USE PLANNING AND MANAGEMENT

Colorado Mountain Coll, Timberline Campus (CO)
Lonestar Coll–Montgomery (TX)

LANGUAGE INTERPRETATION AND TRANSLATION

Allen Comm Coll (KS)
Century Coll (MN)
Indian River State Coll (FL)
Lonestar Coll–Cy-Fair (TX)
Lonestar Coll–North Harris (TX)
Oklahoma State U, Oklahoma City (OK)
Pima Comm Coll (AZ)
Terra State Comm Coll (OH)
Union County Coll (NJ)

LASER AND OPTICAL TECHNOLOGY

Amarillo Coll (TX)
Central New Mexico Comm Coll (NM)
Cincinnati State Tech and Comm Coll (OH)
Pima Comm Coll (AZ)
Springfield Tech Comm Coll (MA)
Three Rivers Comm Coll (CT)

LATIN

Austin Comm Coll (TX)

LATIN AMERICAN STUDIES

Miami Dade Coll (FL)
San Diego City Coll (CA)
Santa Rosa Jr Coll (CA)

LEGAL ADMINISTRATIVE ASSISTANT/SECRETARY

Alamance Comm Coll (NC)
Alexandria Tech and Comm Coll (MN)
Amarillo Coll (TX)
Arizona Western Coll (AZ)
Blackhawk Tech Coll (WI)
Bradford School (OH)
Bradford School (PA)
Career Tech Coll (LA)
Central Lakes Coll (MN)
Clark Coll (WA)
Clovis Comm Coll (NM)
Comm Coll of Rhode Island (RI)
Cowley County Comm Coll and Area Vocational–Tech School (KS)
Crowder Coll (MO)
Dabney S. Lancaster Comm Coll (VA)
Dakota County Tech Coll (MN)
DeKalb Tech Coll (GA)
Delaware Tech & Comm Coll, Jack F. Owens Campus (DE)
Delaware Tech & Comm Coll, Terry Campus (DE)

Dodge City Comm Coll (KS)
Eastern Gateway Comm Coll (OH)
Eastfield Coll (TX)
East Los Angeles Coll (CA)
Edison State Comm Coll (OH)
El Centro Coll (TX)
Elgin Comm Coll (IL)
Frederick Comm Coll (MD)
Fulton-Montgomery Comm Coll (NY)
Gateway Comm Coll (CT)
Golden West Coll (CA)
Grand Rapids Comm Coll (MI)
Harper Coll (IL)
Howard Comm Coll (MD)
International Business Coll, Indianapolis (IN)
Inver Hills Comm Coll (MN)
Jamestown Business Coll (NY)
Jefferson Coll (MO)
John Wood Comm Coll (IL)
Kent State U at Ashtabula (OH)
Kent State U at East Liverpool (OH)
King's Coll (NC)
Kirtland Comm Coll (MI)
Lake Michigan Coll (MI)
Lake Region State Coll (ND)
Lake Superior Coll (MN)
Lincoln Land Comm Coll (IL)
Linn-Benton Comm Coll (OR)
Lonestar Coll–North Harris (TX)
Los Angeles Harbor Coll (CA)
Lower Columbia Coll (WA)
Manchester Comm Coll (CT)
Metropolitan Comm Coll–Longview (MO)
Metropolitan Comm Coll–Maple Woods (MO)
Metropolitan Comm Coll–Penn Valley (MO)
Miami Dade Coll (FL)
Middlesex Comm Coll (CT)
Minneapolis Business Coll (MN)
Minnesota State Coll–Southeast Tech (MN)
Minnesota State Comm and Tech Coll (MN)
Monroe County Comm Coll (MI)
Moraine Park Tech Coll (WI)
Morton Coll (IL)
Muskegon Comm Coll (MI)
Newport Business Inst, Williamsport (PA)
Northampton Comm Coll (PA)
Northeast Comm Coll (NE)
North Idaho Coll (ID)
North Iowa Area Comm Coll (IA)
Olympic Coll (WA)
Orange Coast Coll (CA)
Palm Beach State Coll (FL)
St. Cloud Tech & Comm Coll (MN)
St. Philip's Coll (TX)
San Diego City Coll (CA)
Sauk Valley Comm Coll (IL)
Solano Comm Coll (CA)
Southwest Mississippi Comm Coll (MS)
Stark State Coll of Technology (OH)
Tallahassee Comm Coll (FL)
Three Rivers Comm Coll (CT)
Trinity Valley Comm Coll (TX)
Tyler Jr Coll (TX)
The U of Montana–Helena Coll of Technology (MT)
Vincennes U Jasper Campus (IN)
Wenatchee Valley Coll (WA)
Western Iowa Tech Comm Coll (IA)
Yakima Valley Comm Coll (WA)
Yavapai Coll (AZ)

LEGAL ASSISTANT/ PARALEGAL

Alexandria Tech and Comm Coll (MN)
Athens Tech Coll (GA)
Atlanta Tech Coll (GA)
Austin Comm Coll (TX)
Bellingham Tech Coll (WA)
Blue Ridge Comm and Tech Coll (WV)
Bradford School (OH)
Bradford School (PA)
Bristol Comm Coll (MA)
Brown Mackie Coll–Akron (OH)

Brown Mackie Coll–Albuquerque (NM)
Brown Mackie Coll–Atlanta (GA)
Brown Mackie Coll–Boise (ID)
Brown Mackie Coll–Cincinnati (OH)
Brown Mackie Coll–Findlay (OH)
Brown Mackie Coll–Fort Wayne (IN)
Brown Mackie Coll–Greenville (SC)
Brown Mackie Coll–Hopkinsville (KY)
Brown Mackie Coll–Indianapolis (IN)
Brown Mackie Coll–Kansas City (KS)
Brown Mackie Coll–Louisville (KY)
Brown Mackie Coll–Merrillville (IN)
Brown Mackie Coll–Miami (FL)
Brown Mackie Coll–Michigan City (IN)
Brown Mackie Coll–North Canton (OH)
Brown Mackie Coll–Northern Kentucky (KY)
Brown Mackie Coll–Oklahoma City (OK)
Brown Mackie Coll–Phoenix (AZ)
Brown Mackie Coll–St. Louis (MO)
Brown Mackie Coll–Salina (KS)
Brown Mackie Coll–San Antonio (TX)
Brown Mackie Coll–South Bend (IN)
Brown Mackie Coll–Tucson (AZ)
Brown Mackie Coll–Tulsa (OK)
Bryant & Stratton Coll (WI)
Bucks County Comm Coll (PA)
Burlington County Coll (NJ)
Cape Fear Comm Coll (NC)
Casper Coll (WY)
Central Carolina Tech Coll (SC)
Central Comm Coll–Grand Island Campus (NE)
Central Georgia Tech Coll (GA)
Central New Mexico Comm Coll (NM)
Chippewa Valley Tech Coll (WI)
Clark Coll (WA)
Clovis Comm Coll (NM)
Coll of the Canyons (CA)
Collin County Comm Coll District (TX)
Comm Care Coll (OK)
The Comm Coll of Baltimore County (MD)
Comm Coll of Philadelphia (PA)
Comm Coll of Rhode Island (RI)
Daytona State Coll (FL)
De Anza Coll (CA)
DeKalb Tech Coll (GA)
Doña Ana Comm Coll (NM)
Dutchess Comm Coll (NY)
Edison State Comm Coll (OH)
Elaine P. Nunez Comm Coll (LA)
El Centro Coll (TX)
Elgin Comm Coll (IL)
Fayetteville Tech Comm Coll (NC)
Fiorello H. LaGuardia Comm Coll of the City U of New York (NY)
Florida State Coll at Jacksonville (FL)
Frederick Comm Coll (MD)
Front Range Comm Coll (CO)
Gadsden State Comm Coll (AL)
Georgia Highlands Coll (GA)
Georgia Military Coll (GA)
Georgia Northwestern Tech Coll (GA)
Gulf Coast Comm Coll (FL)
Harford Comm Coll (MD)
Harper Coll (IL)
Harrisburg Area Comm Coll (PA)
Hillsborough Comm Coll (FL)
Houston Comm Coll System (TX)
Indian River State Coll (FL)
International Business Coll, Indianapolis (IN)
Inver Hills Comm Coll (MN)
ITT Tech Inst, Bessemer (AL)
ITT Tech Inst, Madison (AL)
ITT Tech Inst, Mobile (AL)
ITT Tech Inst, Phoenix (AZ)
ITT Tech Inst, Tucson (AZ)
ITT Tech Inst, AR (AR)
ITT Tech Inst, Anaheim (CA)
ITT Tech Inst, Lathrop (CA)
ITT Tech Inst, Oxnard (CA)

ITT Tech Inst, Rancho Cordova (CA)
ITT Tech Inst, San Bernardino (CA)
ITT Tech Inst, San Diego (CA)
ITT Tech Inst, San Dimas (CA)
ITT Tech Inst, Sylmar (CA)
ITT Tech Inst, Torrance (CA)
ITT Tech Inst, Aurora (CO)
ITT Tech Inst, Thornton (CO)
ITT Tech Inst, Fort Lauderdale (FL)
ITT Tech Inst, Fort Myers (FL)
ITT Tech Inst, Jacksonville (FL)
ITT Tech Inst, Lake Mary (FL)
ITT Tech Inst, Miami (FL)
ITT Tech Inst, Pinellas Park (FL)
ITT Tech Inst, Tampa (FL)
ITT Tech Inst, Atlanta (GA)
ITT Tech Inst, Duluth (GA)
ITT Tech Inst, Kennesaw (GA)
ITT Tech Inst (ID)
ITT Tech Inst, Burr Ridge (IL)
ITT Tech Inst, Mount Prospect (IL)
ITT Tech Inst, Orland Park (IL)
ITT Tech Inst, Fort Wayne (IN)
ITT Tech Inst, Indianapolis (IN)
ITT Tech Inst, Merrillville (IN)
ITT Tech Inst, Newburgh (IN)
ITT Tech Inst, Cedar Rapids (IA)
ITT Tech Inst, Clive (IA)
ITT Tech Inst, Louisville (KY)
ITT Tech Inst, Baton Rouge (LA)
ITT Tech Inst, St. Rose (LA)
ITT Tech Inst, Canton (MI)
ITT Tech Inst, Swartz Creek (MI)
ITT Tech Inst, Troy (MI)
ITT Tech Inst, Wyoming (MI)
ITT Tech Inst, Eden Prairie (MN)
ITT Tech Inst, Arnold (MO)
ITT Tech Inst, Earth City (MO)
ITT Tech Inst, Kansas City (MO)
ITT Tech Inst (NE)
ITT Tech Inst, Henderson (NV)
ITT Tech Inst (NM)
ITT Tech Inst, Akron (OH)
ITT Tech Inst, Columbus (OH)
ITT Tech Inst, Dayton (OH)
ITT Tech Inst, Hilliard (OH)
ITT Tech Inst, Maumee (OH)
ITT Tech Inst, Norwood (OH)
ITT Tech Inst, Strongsville (OH)
ITT Tech Inst, Warrensville Heights (OH)
ITT Tech Inst, Youngstown (OH)
ITT Tech Inst, Tulsa (OK)
ITT Tech Inst (OR)
ITT Tech Inst, Greenville (SC)
ITT Tech Inst, Chattanooga (TN)
ITT Tech Inst, Cordova (TN)
ITT Tech Inst, Johnson City (TN)
ITT Tech Inst, Knoxville (TN)
ITT Tech Inst, Nashville (TN)
ITT Tech Inst, Arlington (TX)
ITT Tech Inst, Austin (TX)
ITT Tech Inst, DeSoto (TX)
ITT Tech Inst, Houston (TX)
ITT Tech Inst, Houston (TX)
ITT Tech Inst, Richardson (TX)
ITT Tech Inst, San Antonio (TX)
ITT Tech Inst, Webster (TX)
ITT Tech Inst (UT)
ITT Tech Inst, Chantilly (VA)
ITT Tech Inst, Norfolk (VA)
ITT Tech Inst, Richmond (VA)
ITT Tech Inst, Salem (VA)
ITT Tech Inst, Springfield (VA)
ITT Tech Inst, Everett (WA)
ITT Tech Inst, Seattle (WA)
ITT Tech Inst, Spokane Valley (WA)
ITT Tech Inst (WV)
ITT Tech Inst, Green Bay (WI)
ITT Tech Inst, Greenfield (WI)
ITT Tech Inst, Madison (WI)
Ivy Tech Comm Coll–Bloomington (IN)
Ivy Tech Comm Coll–Central Indiana (IN)
Ivy Tech Comm Coll–Columbus (IN)
Ivy Tech Comm Coll–East Central (IN)
Ivy Tech Comm Coll–Kokomo (IN)
Ivy Tech Comm Coll–Lafayette (IN)
Ivy Tech Comm Coll–North Central (IN)
Ivy Tech Comm Coll–Northeast (IN)
Ivy Tech Comm Coll–Northwest (IN)

Ivy Tech Comm Coll–Richmond (IN)
Ivy Tech Comm Coll–Southeast (IN)
Ivy Tech Comm Coll–Southern Indiana (IN)
Ivy Tech Comm Coll–Southwest (IN)
Ivy Tech Comm Coll–Wabash Valley (IN)
Johnston Comm Coll (NC)
Kankakee Comm Coll (IL)
Kent State U at Trumbull (OH)
Kilgore Coll (TX)
King's Coll (NC)
Lake Region State Coll (ND)
Lake-Sumter Comm Coll (FL)
Lake Superior Coll (MN)
Laramie County Comm Coll (WY)
Lehigh Carbon Comm Coll (PA)
Macomb Comm Coll (MI)
Manchester Comm Coll (CT)
Marion Tech Coll (OH)
Massachusetts Bay Comm Coll (MA)
Metropolitan Comm Coll–Penn Valley (MO)
Miami Dade Coll (FL)
Midlands Tech Coll (SC)
Minneapolis Business Coll (MN)
Minnesota State Comm and Tech Coll (MN)
Missouri State U–West Plains (MO)
Mohave Comm Coll (AZ)
Montgomery Coll (MD)
Moraine Park Tech Coll (WI)
Mountain Empire Comm Coll (VA)
MTI Coll, Sacramento (CA)
Nashua Comm Coll (NH)
New Mexico State U–Alamogordo (NM)
New York Career Inst (NY)
Northampton Comm Coll (PA)
Northern Essex Comm Coll (MA)
North Hennepin Comm Coll (MN)
North Idaho Coll (ID)
Norwalk Comm Coll (CT)
Oakland Comm Coll (MI)
Ogeechee Tech Coll (GA)
Pasco-Hernando Comm Coll (FL)
Pensacola State Coll (FL)
Phoenix Coll (AZ)
Pima Comm Coll (AZ)
Raritan Valley Comm Coll (NJ)
Salt Lake Comm Coll (UT)
San Diego City Coll (CA)
San Juan Coll (NM)
Santa Fe Comm Coll (NM)
Seminole State Coll of Florida (FL)
Southern Crescent Tech Coll (GA)
South Georgia Tech Coll (GA)
South Suburban Coll (IL)
Suffolk County Comm Coll (NY)
Tallahassee Comm Coll (FL)
Tompkins Cortland Comm Coll (NY)
Trident Tech Coll (SC)
Union County Coll (NJ)
Volunteer State Comm Coll (TN)
Westchester Comm Coll (NY)
Westmoreland County Comm Coll (PA)
West Virginia Northern Comm Coll (WV)
Wilson Comm Coll (NC)
Yavapai Coll (AZ)

LEGAL STUDIES

Carroll Comm Coll (MD)
Foothill Coll (CA)
Harford Comm Coll (MD)
Lonestar Coll–North Harris (TX)
Macomb Comm Coll (MI)
Santa Barbara City Coll (CA)
Trident Tech Coll (SC)

LEGAL SUPPORT SERVICES RELATED

Clovis Comm Coll (NM)
Prince Inst of Professional Studies (AL)

LIBERAL ARTS AND SCIENCES AND HUMANITIES RELATED

Cascadia Comm Coll (WA)
Chandler-Gilbert Comm Coll (AZ)
Cleveland State Comm Coll (TN)
The Comm Coll of Baltimore County (MD)
Dakota Coll at Bottineau (ND)

Elaine P. Nunez Comm Coll (LA)
Fayetteville Tech Comm Coll (NC)
Front Range Comm Coll (CO)
Hagerstown Comm Coll (MD)
Harford Comm Coll (MD)
Holyoke Comm Coll (MA)
James Sprunt Comm Coll (NC)
Martin Comm Coll (NC)
Minnesota West Comm and Tech Coll (MN)
Mohawk Valley Comm Coll (NY)
Montana State U–Great Falls Coll of Technology (MT)
Montgomery Coll (MD)
New Mexico State U–Alamogordo (NM)
Northampton Comm Coll (PA)
Onondaga Comm Coll (NY)
Pueblo Comm Coll (CO)
Randolph Comm Coll (NC)
West Virginia Northern Comm Coll (WV)
Wilson Comm Coll (NC)

LIBERAL ARTS AND SCIENCES/ LIBERAL STUDIES

Aiken Tech Coll (SC)
Alamance Comm Coll (NC)
Alexandria Tech and Comm Coll (MN)
Amarillo Coll (TX)
Anoka-Ramsey Comm Coll (MN)
Anoka-Ramsey Comm Coll, Cambridge Campus (MN)
Antelope Valley Coll (CA)
Arkansas State U–Mountain Home (AR)
Bainbridge Coll (GA)
Barton County Comm Coll (KS)
Beaufort County Comm Coll (NC)
Berkeley City Coll (CA)
Big Bend Comm Coll (WA)
Borough of Manhattan Comm Coll of the City U of New York (NY)
Bristol Comm Coll (MA)
Bucks County Comm Coll (PA)
Burlington County Coll (NJ)
Cape Fear Comm Coll (NC)
Carroll Comm Coll (MD)
Cascadia Comm Coll (WA)
Casper Coll (WY)
Catawba Valley Comm Coll (NC)
Cayuga County Comm Coll (NY)
Cecil Coll (MD)
Central Carolina Tech Coll (SC)
Central Comm Coll–Columbus Campus (NE)
Central Comm Coll–Grand Island Campus (NE)
Central Comm Coll–Hastings Campus (NE)
Central Lakes Coll (MN)
Central Maine Comm Coll (ME)
Central New Mexico Comm Coll (NM)
Central Oregon Comm Coll (OR)
Century Coll (MN)
Chandler-Gilbert Comm Coll (AZ)
Chipola Coll (FL)
Cincinnati State Tech and Comm Coll (OH)
City Colls of Chicago, Harry S. Truman College (IL)
Clarendon Coll (TX)
Clark Coll (WA)
Cleveland State Comm Coll (TN)
Clovis Comm Coll (NM)
Coll of Central Florida (FL)
Coll of Lake County (IL)
Coll of the Canyons (CA)
Collin County Comm Coll District (TX)
Colorado Mountain Coll (CO)
Colorado Mountain Coll, Alpine Campus (CO)
Colorado Mountain Coll, Timberline Campus (CO)
The Comm Coll of Baltimore County (MD)
Comm Coll of Philadelphia (PA)
Comm Coll of Rhode Island (RI)
Comm Coll of Vermont (VT)
Corning Comm Coll (NY)
Cowley County Comm Coll and Area Vocational–Tech School (KS)
Crowder Coll (MO)

Dabney S. Lancaster Comm Coll (VA)
Dakota Coll at Bottineau (ND)
Danville Area Comm Coll (IL)
Dawson Comm Coll (MT)
De Anza Coll (CA)
Dodge City Comm Coll (KS)
Dutchess Comm Coll (NY)
Dyersburg State Comm Coll (TN)
Eastern Arizona Coll (AZ)
Eastfield Coll (TX)
East Los Angeles Coll (CA)
Edison State Comm Coll (OH)
Elaine P. Nunez Comm Coll (LA)
Elgin Comm Coll (IL)
Fayetteville Tech Comm Coll (NC)
Fiorello H. LaGuardia Comm Coll of the City U of New York (NY)
Florida State Coll at Jacksonville (FL)
Frank Phillips Coll (TX)
Frederick Comm Coll (MD)
Front Range Comm Coll (CO)
Fulton-Montgomery Comm Coll (NY)
Gadsden State Comm Coll (AL)
GateWay Comm Coll (AZ)
Gateway Comm Coll (CT)
Georgia Highlands Coll (GA)
Golden West Coll (CA)
Goodwin Coll (CT)
Grand Rapids Comm Coll (MI)
Grays Harbor Coll (WA)
Gulf Coast Comm Coll (FL)
Hagerstown Comm Coll (MD)
Harford Comm Coll (MD)
Harper Coll (IL)
Hawaii Tokai International Coll (HI)
Hawkeye Comm Coll (IA)
Hesston Coll (KS)
Highland Comm Coll (IL)
Hillsborough Comm Coll (FL)
Holyoke Comm Coll (MA)
Honolulu Comm Coll (HI)
Housatonic Comm Coll (CT)
Howard Comm Coll (MD)
Ilisagvik Coll (AK)
Illinois Eastern Comm Colls, Frontier Community College (IL)
Illinois Eastern Comm Colls, Lincoln Trail College (IL)
Illinois Eastern Comm Colls, Olney Central College (IL)
Illinois Eastern Comm Colls, Wabash Valley College (IL)
Indian River State Coll (FL)
Inver Hills Comm Coll (MN)
Ivy Tech Comm Coll–Bloomington (IN)
Ivy Tech Comm Coll–Central Indiana (IN)
Ivy Tech Comm Coll–Columbus (IN)
Ivy Tech Comm Coll–East Central (IN)
Ivy Tech Comm Coll–Kokomo (IN)
Ivy Tech Comm Coll–Lafayette (IN)
Ivy Tech Comm Coll–North Central (IN)
Ivy Tech Comm Coll–Northeast (IN)
Ivy Tech Comm Coll–Northwest (IN)
Ivy Tech Comm Coll–Richmond (IN)
Ivy Tech Comm Coll–Southeast (IN)
Ivy Tech Comm Coll–Southern Indiana (IN)
Ivy Tech Comm Coll–Southwest (IN)
Ivy Tech Comm Coll–Wabash Valley (IN)
Jackson Comm Coll (MI)
James Sprunt Comm Coll (NC)
Jefferson Coll (MO)
Jefferson State Comm Coll (AL)
Johnston Comm Coll (NC)
John Tyler Comm Coll (VA)
John Wood Comm Coll (IL)
J. Sargeant Reynolds Comm Coll (VA)
Kaskaskia Coll (IL)
Kent State U at Ashtabula (OH)
Kent State U at East Liverpool (OH)
Kent State U at Geauga (OH)
Kent State U at Salem (OH)
Kent State U at Trumbull (OH)
Kent State U at Tuscarawas (OH)
Kilian Comm Coll (SD)
Kingsborough Comm Coll of the City U of New York (NY)
Kirtland Comm Coll (MI)

Lake Michigan Coll (MI)
Lake Region State Coll (ND)
Lake-Sumter Comm Coll (FL)
Lake Superior Coll (MN)
Lamar Comm Coll (CO)
Lawson State Comm Coll (AL)
Leeward Comm Coll (HI)
Lehigh Carbon Comm Coll (PA)
Lincoln Land Comm Coll (IL)
Linn-Benton Comm Coll (OR)
Lonestar Coll–North Harris (TX)
Los Angeles Harbor Coll (CA)
Lower Columbia Coll (WA)
Lurleen B. Wallace Comm Coll (AL)
Macomb Comm Coll (MI)
Manchester Comm Coll (CT)
Martin Comm Coll (NC)
Massachusetts Bay Comm Coll (MA)
McHenry County Coll (IL)
Mendocino Coll (CA)
Mesabi Range Comm and Tech Coll (MN)
Mesa Comm Coll (AZ)
Metropolitan Comm Coll–Blue River (MO)
Metropolitan Comm Coll–Business & Technology Campus (MO)
Metropolitan Comm Coll–Longview (MO)
Metropolitan Comm Coll–Maple Woods (MO)
Metropolitan Comm Coll–Penn Valley (MO)
Middlesex Comm Coll (CT)
Midlands Tech Coll (SC)
Mid-Plains Comm Coll, North Platte (NE)
Minnesota State Comm and Tech Coll (MN)
Minnesota West Comm and Tech Coll (MN)
Mohave Comm Coll (AZ)
Mohawk Valley Comm Coll (NY)
Monroe County Comm Coll (MI)
Montcalm Comm Coll (MI)
Montgomery Coll (MD)
Montgomery County Comm Coll (PA)
Moraine Valley Comm Coll (IL)
Morton Coll (IL)
Motlow State Comm Coll (TN)
Mountain Empire Comm Coll (VA)
Mountain View Coll (TX)
Muskegon Comm Coll (MI)
Nashua Comm Coll (NH)
Niagara County Comm Coll (NY)
Northampton Comm Coll (PA)
North Dakota State Coll of Science (ND)
Northeast Comm Coll (NE)
Northeast Iowa Comm Coll (IA)
Northern Essex Comm Coll (MA)
North Hennepin Comm Coll (MN)
North Idaho Coll (ID)
North Iowa Area Comm Coll (IA)
Northland Comm and Tech Coll–Thief River Falls & East Grand Forks (MN)
North Seattle Comm Coll (WA)
Northwest Coll (WY)
Northwest-Shoals Comm Coll (AL)
Norwalk Comm Coll (CT)
Oakland Comm Coll (MI)
Ocean County Coll (NJ)
Oklahoma City Comm Coll (OK)
Orange Coast Coll (CA)
Oregon Coast Comm Coll (OR)
Owensboro Comm and Tech Coll (KY)
Palm Beach State Coll (FL)
Pasco-Hernando Comm Coll (FL)
Paul D. Camp Comm Coll (VA)
Penn State Beaver (PA)
Penn State Brandywine (PA)
Penn State DuBois (PA)
Penn State Fayette, The Eberly Campus (PA)
Penn State Greater Allegheny (PA)
Penn State Hazleton (PA)
Penn State Lehigh Valley (PA)
Penn State Mont Alto (PA)
Penn State New Kensington (PA)
Penn State Schuylkill (PA)
Penn State Shenango (PA)
Penn State Wilkes-Barre (PA)
Penn State Worthington Scranton (PA)

Penn State York (PA)
Pennsylvania Highlands Comm Coll (PA)
Pensacola State Coll (FL)
Phoenix Coll (AZ)
Pima Comm Coll (AZ)
Polk State Coll (FL)
Potomac State Coll of West Virginia U (WV)
Pratt Comm Coll (KS)
Pueblo Comm Coll (CO)
Quinsigamond Comm Coll (MA)
Rainy River Comm Coll (MN)
Randolph Comm Coll (NC)
Raritan Valley Comm Coll (NJ)
Red Rocks Comm Coll (CO)
Rockingham Comm Coll (NC)
Rogue Comm Coll (OR)
Saint Charles Comm Coll (MO)
St. Philip's Coll (TX)
Sandhills Comm Coll (NC)
San Diego City Coll (CA)
San Juan Coll (NM)
Santa Barbara City Coll (CA)
Sauk Valley Comm Coll (IL)
Seminole State Coll of Florida (FL)
Snow Coll (UT)
Solano Comm Coll (CA)
Southeastern Comm Coll (IA)
Southern State Comm Coll (OH)
Southside Virginia Comm Coll (VA)
South Suburban Coll (IL)
Southwestern Michigan Coll (MI)
Southwest Mississippi Comm Coll (MS)
Spartanburg Comm Coll (SC)
Springfield Tech Comm Coll (MA)
State U of New York Coll of Technology at Alfred (NY)
Suffolk County Comm Coll (NY)
Tallahassee Comm Coll (FL)
Terra State Comm Coll (OH)
Three Rivers Comm Coll (CT)
Tompkins Cortland Comm Coll (NY)
Trident Tech Coll (SC)
Trinity Valley Comm Coll (TX)
Tyler Jr Coll (TX)
Union County Coll (NJ)
U of Alaska Anchorage, Kenai Peninsula Coll (AK)
U of Alaska Anchorage, Kodiak Coll (AK)
U of Arkansas Comm Coll at Morrilton (AR)
U of Pittsburgh at Titusville (PA)
U of South Carolina Union (SC)
U of Wisconsin–Fox Valley (WI)
U of Wisconsin–Richland (WI)
U of Wisconsin–Sheboygan (WI)
U of Wisconsin–Waukesha (WI)
Vincennes U Jasper Campus (IN)
Volunteer State Comm Coll (TN)
Waubonsee Comm Coll (IL)
Waycross Coll (GA)
Wenatchee Valley Coll (WA)
Wentworth Military Academy and Coll (MO)
Westchester Comm Coll (NY)
Western Iowa Tech Comm Coll (IA)
Westmoreland County Comm Coll (PA)
West Virginia Northern Comm Coll (WV)
White Mountains Comm Coll (NH)
Wilson Comm Coll (NC)
Yakima Valley Comm Coll (WA)
Yavapai Coll (AZ)

LIBRARY AND ARCHIVES ASSISTING

Central Comm Coll–Hastings Campus (NE)
Clovis Comm Coll (NM)
Coll of the Canyons (CA)
Ivy Tech Comm Coll–Bloomington (IN)
Ivy Tech Comm Coll–Columbus (IN)
Ivy Tech Comm Coll–East Central (IN)
Ivy Tech Comm Coll–Kokomo (IN)
Ivy Tech Comm Coll–Lafayette (IN)
Ivy Tech Comm Coll–North Central (IN)
Ivy Tech Comm Coll–Northeast (IN)
Ivy Tech Comm Coll–Northwest (IN)
Ivy Tech Comm Coll–Richmond (IN)
Ivy Tech Comm Coll–Southeast (IN)

Ivy Tech Comm Coll–Southern Indiana (IN)
Ivy Tech Comm Coll–Southwest (IN)
Ivy Tech Comm Coll–Wabash Valley (IN)
Northeast Comm Coll (NE)
Oakland Comm Coll (MI)
Pueblo Comm Coll (CO)
Waubonsee Comm Coll (IL)

LIBRARY AND INFORMATION SCIENCE
Allen Comm Coll (KS)
Doña Ana Comm Coll (NM)
Indian River State Coll (FL)
Mesa Comm Coll (AZ)

LICENSED PRACTICAL/VOCATIONAL NURSE TRAINING
Alexandria Tech and Comm Coll (MN)
Amarillo Coll (TX)
Athens Tech Coll (GA)
ATS Inst of Technology (OH)
Bainbridge Coll (GA)
Barton County Comm Coll (KS)
Big Bend Comm Coll (WA)
Brown Mackie Coll–Kansas City (KS)
Brown Mackie Coll–Salina (KS)
Central Comm Coll–Columbus Campus (NE)
Central Comm Coll–Grand Island Campus (NE)
Central Maine Comm Coll (ME)
Central Oregon Comm Coll (OR)
Clovis Comm Coll (NM)
Colorado Mountain Coll (CO)
Comm Coll of Rhode Island (RI)
Dakota Coll at Bottineau (ND)
Darton Coll (GA)
De Anza Coll (CA)
Delaware Tech & Comm Coll, Jack F. Owens Campus (DE)
Dodge City Comm Coll (KS)
Eastern Gateway Comm Coll (OH)
El Centro Coll (TX)
Fiorello H. LaGuardia Comm Coll of the City U of New York (NY)
Grand Rapids Comm Coll (MI)
Howard Comm Coll (MD)
Indian River State Coll (FL)
Ivy Tech Comm Coll–Southeast (IN)
Jackson Comm Coll (MI)
Jefferson Coll (MO)
Jefferson State Comm Coll (AL)
Kirtland Comm Coll (MI)
Lake Region State Coll (ND)
Lamar Comm Coll (CO)
Lonestar Coll–Kingwood (TX)
Midlands Tech Coll (SC)
Mid-Plains Comm Coll, North Platte (NE)
Minnesota State Comm and Tech Coll (MN)
Montana State U–Great Falls Coll of Technology (MT)
Moraine Park Tech Coll (WI)
North Dakota State Coll of Science (ND)
Northeast Comm Coll (NE)
North Idaho Coll (ID)
North Iowa Area Comm Coll (IA)
Northland Comm and Tech Coll–Thief River Falls & East Grand Forks (MN)
North Seattle Comm Coll (WA)
Northwest Tech Coll (MN)
Owens Comm Coll, Toledo (OH)
Platt Coll, Oklahoma City (OK)
Saint Charles Comm Coll (MO)
St. Cloud Tech & Comm Coll (MN)
Sandhills Comm Coll (NC)
San Diego City Coll (CA)
Santa Barbara City Coll (CA)
Santa Rosa Jr Coll (CA)
Southeastern Comm Coll (IA)
Southeast Tech Inst (SD)
Southwest Mississippi Comm Coll (MS)
Trinity Valley Comm Coll (TX)
Tyler Jr Coll (TX)
Union County Coll (NJ)

The U of Montana–Helena Coll of Technology (MT)
Wenatchee Valley Coll (WA)

LINEWORKER
Chandler-Gilbert Comm Coll (AZ)
Dakota County Tech Coll (MN)
GateWay Comm Coll (AZ)
Harrisburg Area Comm Coll (PA)
Ivy Tech Comm Coll–Lafayette (IN)
Linn State Tech Coll (MO)
Minnesota State Comm and Tech Coll (MN)
Minnesota West Comm and Tech Coll (MN)
Mitchell Tech Inst (SD)
Moraine Park Tech Coll (WI)
Northeast Comm Coll (NE)
Raritan Valley Comm Coll (NJ)

LINGUISTICS
Foothill Coll (CA)

LIVESTOCK MANAGEMENT
Barton County Comm Coll (KS)
Northeast Comm Coll (NE)

LOGISTICS, MATERIALS, AND SUPPLY CHAIN MANAGEMENT
Arizona Western Coll (AZ)
Athens Tech Coll (GA)
Barton County Comm Coll (KS)
Cecil Coll (MD)
Central Comm Coll–Hastings Campus (NE)
Chattahoochee Tech Coll (GA)
Edison State Comm Coll (OH)
Georgia Military Coll (GA)
Houston Comm Coll System (TX)
Lehigh Carbon Comm Coll (PA)
Lonestar Coll–Cy-Fair (TX)
Randolph Comm Coll (NC)
Waubonsee Comm Coll (IL)

MACHINE SHOP TECHNOLOGY
Cape Fear Comm Coll (NC)
Coll of Lake County (IL)
Corning Comm Coll (NY)
Daytona State Coll (FL)
Eastern Arizona Coll (AZ)
Fayetteville Tech Comm Coll (NC)
Florida State Coll at Jacksonville (FL)
Ivy Tech Comm Coll–Central Indiana (IN)
Johnston Comm Coll (NC)
Metropolitan Comm Coll–Business & Technology Campus (MO)
Moraine Park Tech Coll (WI)
Orange Coast Coll (CA)
Pima Comm Coll (AZ)
Pueblo Comm Coll (CO)
Randolph Comm Coll (NC)
San Juan Coll (NM)
Southeast Tech Inst (SD)
West Kentucky Comm and Tech Coll (KY)
Westmoreland County Comm Coll (PA)

MACHINE TOOL TECHNOLOGY
Alamance Comm Coll (NC)
Alexandria Tech and Comm Coll (MN)
Altamaha Tech Coll (GA)
Amarillo Coll (TX)
Bellingham Tech Coll (WA)
Casper Coll (WY)
Central Comm Coll–Columbus Campus (NE)
Central Comm Coll–Hastings Campus (NE)
Central Lakes Coll (MN)
Central Maine Comm Coll (ME)
Clark Coll (WA)
Columbus Tech Coll (GA)
Corning Comm Coll (NY)
Cowley County Comm Coll and Area Vocational–Tech School (KS)
De Anza Coll (CA)
DeKalb Tech Coll (GA)

Elgin Comm Coll (IL)
Gwinnett Tech Coll (GA)
Hawkeye Comm Coll (IA)
H. Councill Trenholm State Tech Coll (AL)
Heart of Georgia Tech Coll (GA)
Illinois Eastern Comm Colls, Wabash Valley College (IL)
Ivy Tech Comm Coll–Bloomington (IN)
Ivy Tech Comm Coll–Central Indiana (IN)
Ivy Tech Comm Coll–Columbus (IN)
Ivy Tech Comm Coll–East Central (IN)
Ivy Tech Comm Coll–Kokomo (IN)
Ivy Tech Comm Coll–Lafayette (IN)
Ivy Tech Comm Coll–North Central (IN)
Ivy Tech Comm Coll–Northeast (IN)
Ivy Tech Comm Coll–Northwest (IN)
Ivy Tech Comm Coll–Richmond (IN)
Ivy Tech Comm Coll–Southern Indiana (IN)
Ivy Tech Comm Coll–Southwest (IN)
Ivy Tech Comm Coll–Wabash Valley (IN)
Johnston Comm Coll (NC)
Kankakee Comm Coll (IL)
Lake Michigan Coll (MI)
Lake Superior Coll (MN)
Linn-Benton Comm Coll (OR)
Linn State Tech Coll (MO)
Lower Columbia Coll (WA)
Macomb Comm Coll (MI)
Muskegon Comm Coll (MI)
Nashua Comm Coll (NH)
North Dakota State Coll of Science (ND)
Northern Essex Comm Coll (MA)
North Idaho Coll (ID)
Oakland Comm Coll (MI)
Orange Coast Coll (CA)
St. Cloud Tech & Comm Coll (MN)
San Diego City Coll (CA)
Sheridan Coll (WY)
Solano Comm Coll (CA)
Southeastern Comm Coll (IA)
Southeast Tech Inst (SD)
Southwestern Michigan Coll (MI)
Spartanburg Comm Coll (SC)
Trident Tech Coll (SC)
The U of Montana–Helena Coll of Technology (MT)
Western Iowa Tech Comm Coll (IA)
Westmoreland County Comm Coll (PA)
The Williamson Free School of Mecha Trades (PA)
Wiregrass Georgia Tech Coll (GA)

MANAGEMENT INFORMATION SYSTEMS
Bristol Comm Coll (MA)
Burlington County Coll (NJ)
Carl Albert State Coll (OK)
Carroll Comm Coll (MD)
Casper Coll (WY)
Cecil Coll (MD)
Central Oregon Comm Coll (OR)
Cincinnati State Tech and Comm Coll (OH)
Clovis Comm Coll (NM)
The Comm Coll of Baltimore County (MD)
Delaware Tech & Comm Coll, Jack F. Owens Campus (DE)
Delaware Tech & Comm Coll, Stanton/Wilmington Campus (DE)
Delaware Tech & Comm Coll, Terry Campus (DE)
GateWay Comm Coll (AZ)
Gwinnett Tech Coll (GA)
Hagerstown Comm Coll (MD)
Harford Comm Coll (MD)
Hillsborough Comm Coll (FL)
John Tyler Comm Coll (VA)
John Wood Comm Coll (IL)
J. Sargeant Reynolds Comm Coll (VA)
Kilgore Coll (TX)

Kirtland Comm Coll (MI)
Lake Region State Coll (ND)
Lake Superior Coll (MN)
Lamar Comm Coll (CO)
Linn State Tech Coll (MO)
Lonestar Coll–North Harris (TX)
Manchester Comm Coll (CT)
Martin Comm Coll (NC)
Miami Dade Coll (FL)
Moraine Valley Comm Coll (IL)
North Hennepin Comm Coll (MN)
Raritan Valley Comm Coll (NJ)
Tallahassee Comm Coll (FL)
Union County Coll (NJ)
U of Pittsburgh at Titusville (PA)
Vincennes U Jasper Campus (IN)
Yakima Valley Comm Coll (WA)

MANAGEMENT INFORMATION SYSTEMS AND SERVICES RELATED
Eastern Arizona Coll (AZ)
Gulf Coast Comm Coll (FL)
Harrisburg Area Comm Coll (PA)
Harrison Coll, Indianapolis (IN)
Harrison Coll, Muncie (IN)
Hillsborough Comm Coll (FL)
Martin Comm Coll (NC)
Metropolitan Comm Coll–Business & Technology Campus (MO)
Missouri State U–West Plains (MO)
Mohawk Valley Comm Coll (NY)
Montgomery Coll (MD)
Montgomery County Comm Coll (PA)
Pensacola State Coll (FL)

MANAGEMENT SCIENCE
Aiken Tech Coll (SC)
Blackhawk Tech Coll (WI)
Career Tech Coll (LA)
Delaware Tech & Comm Coll, Stanton/Wilmington Campus (DE)
Lonestar Coll–Cy-Fair (TX)

MANUFACTURING ENGINEERING
Bristol Comm Coll (MA)
Central Wyoming Coll (WY)
Kent State U at Trumbull (OH)
Lake Michigan Coll (MI)
New England Inst of Technology (RI)
Penn State Fayette, The Eberly Campus (PA)
Penn State Greater Allegheny (PA)
Penn State Hazleton (PA)
Penn State Wilkes-Barre (PA)
Penn State York (PA)

MANUFACTURING ENGINEERING TECHNOLOGY
Albany Tech Coll (GA)
Alexandria Tech and Comm Coll (MN)
Altamaha Tech Coll (GA)
Casper Coll (WY)
Central New Mexico Comm Coll (NM)
Central Oregon Comm Coll (OR)
Clark Coll (WA)
Coll of the Canyons (CA)
Dakota County Tech Coll (MN)
Danville Area Comm Coll (IL)
Delaware Tech & Comm Coll, Stanton/Wilmington Campus (DE)
Elgin Comm Coll (IL)
Fox Valley Tech Coll (WI)
Gadsden State Comm Coll (AL)
Gateway Comm and Tech Coll (KY)
GateWay Comm Coll (AZ)
Hawkeye Comm Coll (IA)
Houston Comm Coll System (TX)
Illinois Eastern Comm Colls, Wabash Valley College (IL)
John Wood Comm Coll (IL)
Lehigh Carbon Comm Coll (PA)
Linn State Tech Coll (MO)
Macomb Comm Coll (MI)
Minnesota State Comm and Tech Coll (MN)
Minnesota West Comm and Tech Coll (MN)

New England Inst of Technology (RI)
North Iowa Area Comm Coll (IA)
Northland Comm and Tech Coll–Thief River Falls & East Grand Forks (MN)
Northwest Tech Coll (MN)
Oakland Comm Coll (MI)
Owens Comm Coll, Toledo (OH)
Pensacola State Coll (FL)
Quinsigamond Comm Coll (MA)
Raritan Valley Comm Coll (NJ)
Rogue Comm Coll (OR)
Southern Crescent Tech Coll (GA)
South Georgia Tech Coll (GA)
Sullivan Coll of Technology and Design (KY)
Terra State Comm Coll (OH)
Union County Coll (NJ)
Waukesha County Tech Coll (WI)
Westmoreland County Comm Coll (PA)

MARINE BIOLOGY AND BIOLOGICAL OCEANOGRAPHY
Oregon Coast Comm Coll (OR)

MARINE MAINTENANCE AND SHIP REPAIR TECHNOLOGY
Alexandria Tech and Comm Coll (MN)
Cape Fear Comm Coll (NC)
Honolulu Comm Coll (HI)
Kingsborough Comm Coll of the City U of New York (NY)
Minnesota State Comm and Tech Coll (MN)
New England Inst of Technology (RI)
North Idaho Coll (ID)
Olympic Coll (WA)
Orange Coast Coll (CA)
Santa Barbara City Coll (CA)

MARINE SCIENCE/MERCHANT MARINE OFFICER
Indian River State Coll (FL)

MARKETING/MARKETING MANAGEMENT
Albany Tech Coll (GA)
Alexandria Tech and Comm Coll (MN)
Altamaha Tech Coll (GA)
Anoka-Ramsey Comm Coll (MN)
Anoka-Ramsey Comm Coll, Cambridge Campus (MN)
Antelope Valley Coll (CA)
Arizona Western Coll (AZ)
Athens Tech Coll (GA)
Atlanta Tech Coll (GA)
Augusta Tech Coll (GA)
Austin Comm Coll (TX)
Bainbridge Coll (GA)
Barton County Comm Coll (KS)
Bellingham Tech Coll (WA)
Blackhawk Tech Coll (WI)
Bristol Comm Coll (MA)
Bucks County Comm Coll (PA)
Casper Coll (WY)
Cecil Coll (MD)
Central Comm Coll–Columbus Campus (NE)
Central Georgia Tech Coll (GA)
Central Lakes Coll (MN)
Central Oregon Comm Coll (OR)
Century Coll (MN)
Chattahoochee Tech Coll (GA)
Chippewa Valley Tech Coll (WI)
Cincinnati State Tech and Comm Coll (OH)
Clarendon Coll (TX)
Coll of Central Florida (FL)
Colorado Mountain Coll, Alpine Campus (CO)
Comm Coll of Philadelphia (PA)
Comm Coll of Rhode Island (RI)
Cowley County Comm Coll and Area Vocational–Tech School (KS)
Dakota Coll at Bottineau (ND)
Dakota County Tech Coll (MN)
De Anza Coll (CA)
DeKalb Tech Coll (GA)

Delaware Tech & Comm Coll, Jack F. Owens Campus (DE)
Delaware Tech & Comm Coll, Stanton/Wilmington Campus (DE)
Delaware Tech & Comm Coll, Terry Campus (DE)
Dodge City Comm Coll (KS)
East Los Angeles Coll (CA)
Edison State Comm Coll (OH)
Elgin Comm Coll (IL)
Fayetteville Tech Comm Coll (NC)
FIDM/The Fashion Inst of Design & Merchandising, Orange County Campus (CA)
Florida State Coll at Jacksonville (FL)
Fox Valley Tech Coll (WI)
Frederick Comm Coll (MD)
GateWay Comm Coll (AZ)
Georgia Highlands Coll (GA)
Georgia Northwestern Tech Coll (GA)
Glendale Comm Coll (AZ)
Golden West Coll (CA)
Gwinnett Tech Coll (GA)
Harper Coll (IL)
Harrison Coll, Anderson (IN)
Harrison Coll, Columbus (IN)
Harrison Coll, Indianapolis (IN)
Harrison Coll, Lafayette (IN)
Harrison Coll, Muncie (IN)
Harrison Coll (OH)
Heart of Georgia Tech Coll (GA)
Highland Comm Coll (IL)
Houston Comm Coll System (TX)
Indian River State Coll (FL)
Jackson Comm Coll (MI)
Jamestown Business Coll (NY)
Kankakee Comm Coll (IL)
Kent State U at Ashtabula (OH)
Kingsborough Comm Coll of the City U of New York (NY)
Lake Michigan Coll (MI)
Lamar Comm Coll (CO)
Lanier Tech Coll (GA)
Lonestar Coll–Cy-Fair (TX)
Lonestar Coll–Kingwood (TX)
Lonestar Coll–Montgomery (TX)
Lonestar Coll–North Harris (TX)
Lonestar Coll–Tomball (TX)
Macomb Comm Coll (MI)
Manchester Comm Coll (CT)
Marion Tech Coll (OH)
Mesa Comm Coll (AZ)
Metropolitan Comm Coll–Longview (MO)
Metropolitan Comm Coll–Maple Woods (MO)
Metropolitan Comm Coll–Penn Valley (MO)
Miami Dade Coll (FL)
Middle Georgia Tech Coll (GA)
Middlesex Comm Coll (CT)
Minnesota State Comm and Tech Coll (MN)
Monroe County Comm Coll (MI)
Moraine Park Tech Coll (WI)
Morton Coll (IL)
Moultrie Tech Coll (GA)
Muskegon Comm Coll (MI)
Northampton Comm Coll (PA)
Northeast Comm Coll (NE)
Northern Essex Comm Coll (MA)
North Hennepin Comm Coll (MN)
Northland Comm and Tech Coll–Thief River Falls & East Grand Forks (MN)
Norwalk Comm Coll (CT)
Ogeechee Tech Coll (GA)
Orange Coast Coll (CA)
Palm Beach State Coll (FL)
Pasco-Hernando Comm Coll (FL)
Phoenix Coll (AZ)
Polk State Coll (FL)
Raritan Valley Comm Coll (NJ)
Rogue Comm Coll (OR)
Saint Charles Comm Coll (MO)
Salt Lake Comm Coll (UT)
San Diego City Coll (CA)
Santa Barbara City Coll (CA)
Sauk Valley Comm Coll (IL)
Savannah Tech Coll (GA)
Seminole State Coll of Florida (FL)
Solano Comm Coll (CA)
Southeastern Tech Coll (GA)
Southeast Tech Inst (SD)
Southern Crescent Tech Coll (GA)

South Georgia Tech Coll (GA)
Southwest Mississippi Comm Coll (MS)
Spartanburg Comm Coll (SC)
Springfield Tech Comm Coll (MA)
Stark State Coll of Technology (OH)
Suffolk County Comm Coll (NY)
Tallahassee Comm Coll (FL)
Terra State Comm Coll (OH)
Three Rivers Comm Coll (CT)
Trident Tech Coll (SC)
Trinity Valley Comm Coll (TX)
Union County Coll (NJ)
Waukesha County Tech Coll (WI)
Westchester Comm Coll (NY)
West Georgia Tech Coll (GA)
Westmoreland County Comm Coll (PA)
Wiregrass Georgia Tech Coll (GA)
Wisconsin Indianhead Tech Coll (WI)
Yakima Valley Comm Coll (WA)

MARKETING RELATED
Aiken Tech Coll (SC)
Dakota Coll at Bottineau (ND)

MARKETING RESEARCH
Lake Region State Coll (ND)

MASONRY
Alexandria Tech and Comm Coll (MN)
Dakota County Tech Coll (MN)
Florida State Coll at Jacksonville (FL)
Front Range Comm Coll (CO)
GateWay Comm Coll (AZ)
Ivy Tech Comm Coll–Central Indiana (IN)
Ivy Tech Comm Coll–Columbus (IN)
Ivy Tech Comm Coll–East Central (IN)
Ivy Tech Comm Coll–Lafayette (IN)
Ivy Tech Comm Coll–North Central (IN)
Ivy Tech Comm Coll–Northeast (IN)
Ivy Tech Comm Coll–Northwest (IN)
Ivy Tech Comm Coll–Southern Indiana (IN)
Ivy Tech Comm Coll–Southwest (IN)
Ivy Tech Comm Coll–Wabash Valley (IN)
Metropolitan Comm Coll–Business & Technology Campus (MO)

MASSAGE THERAPY
Arizona Western Coll (AZ)
Brown Mackie Coll–Michigan City (IN)
Brown Mackie Coll–South Bend (IN)
Career Tech Coll (LA)
Career Training Academy, Pittsburgh (PA)
Central Oregon Comm Coll (OR)
Chandler-Gilbert Comm Coll (AZ)
Comm Care Coll (OK)
Comm Coll of Rhode Island (RI)
Duluth Business U (MN)
Harford Comm Coll (MD)
Ivy Tech Comm Coll–Northeast (IN)
Minnesota State Coll–Southeast Tech (MN)
Northland Comm and Tech Coll–Thief River Falls & East Grand Forks (MN)
Oakland Comm Coll (MI)
Owens Comm Coll, Toledo (OH)
Phoenix Coll (AZ)
Pima Comm Coll (AZ)
Saint Charles Comm Coll (MO)
Sheridan Coll (WY)
Southwest Mississippi Comm Coll (MS)
Spencerian Coll (KY)
Springfield Tech Comm Coll (MA)
Waubonsee Comm Coll (IL)

MASS COMMUNICATION/ MEDIA
Amarillo Coll (TX)
Ancilla Coll (IN)
Arizona Western Coll (AZ)
Bucks County Comm Coll (PA)
Chipola Coll (FL)
Clarendon Coll (TX)

Crowder Coll (MO)
De Anza Coll (CA)
Dodge City Comm Coll (KS)
Dutchess Comm Coll (NY)
Frederick Comm Coll (MD)
Fulton-Montgomery Comm Coll (NY)
Georgia Military Coll (GA)
Grand Rapids Comm Coll (MI)
Harrisburg Area Comm Coll (PA)
Lake Michigan Coll (MI)
Laramie County Comm Coll (WY)
Miami Dade Coll (FL)
Middlesex Comm Coll (CT)
Monroe County Comm Coll (MI)
Niagara County Comm Coll (NY)
Northeast Comm Coll (NE)
North Idaho Coll (ID)
Northland Comm and Tech Coll–Thief River Falls & East Grand Forks (MN)
Oklahoma City Comm Coll (OK)
Orange Coast Coll (CA)
Palm Beach State Coll (FL)
Pratt Comm Coll (KS)
Red Rocks Comm Coll (CO)
Salt Lake Comm Coll (UT)
Snow Coll (UT)
Union County Coll (NJ)
Westchester Comm Coll (NY)

MATERIALS SCIENCE
Kent State U at Ashtabula (OH)
Northern Essex Comm Coll (MA)

MATHEMATICS
Allen Comm Coll (KS)
Amarillo Coll (TX)
Antelope Valley Coll (CA)
Arizona Western Coll (AZ)
Austin Comm Coll (TX)
Bainbridge Coll (GA)
Barton County Comm Coll (KS)
Borough of Manhattan Comm Coll of the City U of New York (NY)
Bucks County Comm Coll (PA)
Burlington County Coll (NJ)
Carl Albert State Coll (OK)
Casper Coll (WY)
Cecil Coll (MD)
Central Oregon Comm Coll (OR)
Central Wyoming Coll (WY)
Clarendon Coll (TX)
Coll of the Canyons (CA)
Colorado Mountain Coll (CO)
Colorado Mountain Coll, Alpine Campus (CO)
Corning Comm Coll (NY)
Crowder Coll (MO)
Dakota Coll at Bottineau (ND)
Darton Coll (GA)
De Anza Coll (CA)
Dodge City Comm Coll (KS)
Dutchess Comm Coll (NY)
Eastern Arizona Coll (AZ)
East Los Angeles Coll (CA)
Foothill Coll (CA)
Frank Phillips Coll (TX)
Frederick Comm Coll (MD)
Fulton-Montgomery Comm Coll (NY)
Golden West Coll (CA)
Great Basin Coll (NV)
Harper Coll (IL)
Harrisburg Area Comm Coll (PA)
Highland Comm Coll (IL)
Housatonic Comm Coll (CT)
Indian River State Coll (FL)
Kilgore Coll (TX)
Kingsborough Comm Coll of the City U of New York (NY)
Lake Michigan Coll (MI)
Lake-Sumter Comm Coll (FL)
Laramie County Comm Coll (WY)
Lehigh Carbon Comm Coll (PA)
Linn-Benton Comm Coll (OR)
Lonestar Coll–Cy-Fair (TX)
Lonestar Coll–Kingwood (TX)
Lonestar Coll–Montgomery (TX)
Lonestar Coll–North Harris (TX)
Lonestar Coll–Tomball (TX)
Macomb Comm Coll (MI)
Mendocino Coll (CA)
Mesa Comm Coll (AZ)
Miami Dade Coll (FL)
Mohave Comm Coll (AZ)
Monroe County Comm Coll (MI)

Montgomery County Comm Coll (PA)
Niagara County Comm Coll (NY)
Northampton Comm Coll (PA)
Northeast Comm Coll (NE)
North Hennepin Comm Coll (MN)
North Idaho Coll (ID)
Northwest Coll (WY)
Oklahoma City Comm Coll (OK)
Orange Coast Coll (CA)
Owens Comm Coll, Toledo (OH)
Palm Beach State Coll (FL)
Potomac State Coll of West Virginia U (WV)
Pratt Comm Coll (KS)
Red Rocks Comm Coll (CO)
Saint Charles Comm Coll (MO)
St. Philip's Coll (TX)
Sandhills Comm Coll (NC)
San Diego City Coll (CA)
San Juan Coll (NM)
Santa Barbara City Coll (CA)
Santa Rosa Jr Coll (CA)
Sauk Valley Comm Coll (IL)
Scottsdale Comm Coll (AZ)
Sheridan Coll (WY)
Snow Coll (UT)
Solano Comm Coll (CA)
Springfield Tech Comm Coll (MA)
Suffolk County Comm Coll (NY)
Terra State Comm Coll (OH)
Trinity Valley Comm Coll (TX)
Tyler Jr Coll (TX)
Union County Coll (NJ)
Wenatchee Valley Coll (WA)

MATHEMATICS AND COMPUTER SCIENCE
Crowder Coll (MO)

MATHEMATICS AND STATISTICS RELATED
Bristol Comm Coll (MA)

MATHEMATICS TEACHER EDUCATION
The Comm Coll of Baltimore County (MD)
Darton Coll (GA)
Delaware Tech & Comm Coll, Jack F. Owens Campus (DE)
Delaware Tech & Comm Coll, Stanton/Wilmington Campus (DE)
Delaware Tech & Comm Coll, Terry Campus (DE)
Frederick Comm Coll (MD)
Harford Comm Coll (MD)
Highland Comm Coll (IL)
Kankakee Comm Coll (IL)
Kaskaskia Coll (IL)
Montgomery Coll (MD)
Moraine Valley Comm Coll (IL)
Waubonsee Comm Coll (IL)

MECHANICAL DRAFTING AND CAD/CADD
Alexandria Tech and Comm Coll (MN)
Central Lakes Coll (MN)
City Colls of Chicago, Harry S. Truman College (IL)
Delaware Tech & Comm Coll, Jack F. Owens Campus (DE)
Edison State Comm Coll (OH)
Fox Valley Tech Coll (WI)
Lake Superior Coll (MN)
Macomb Comm Coll (MI)
Midlands Tech Coll (SC)
Minnesota State Comm and Tech Coll (MN)
Montgomery County Comm Coll (PA)
Moraine Park Tech Coll (WI)
North Iowa Area Comm Coll (IA)
North Seattle Comm Coll (WA)
Oakland Comm Coll (MI)
Pittsburgh Tech Inst, Oakdale (PA)
St. Cloud Tech & Comm Coll (MN)
Spartanburg Comm Coll (SC)
Sullivan Coll of Technology and Design (KY)
Waukesha County Tech Coll (WI)
Westmoreland County Comm Coll (PA)
Wisconsin Indianhead Tech Coll (WI)

MECHANICAL ENGINEERING
Bristol Comm Coll (MA)
Cayuga County Comm Coll (NY)
Fiorello H. LaGuardia Comm Coll of the City U of New York (NY)
Kilgore Coll (TX)
New England Inst of Technology (RI)
Saint Charles Comm Coll (MO)

MECHANICAL ENGINEERING/ MECHANICAL TECHNOLOGY
Alamance Comm Coll (NC)
Augusta Tech Coll (GA)
Beaufort County Comm Coll (NC)
Cape Fear Comm Coll (NC)
Cincinnati State Tech and Comm Coll (OH)
Coll of Lake County (IL)
Columbus Tech Coll (GA)
Comm Coll of Rhode Island (RI)
Corning Comm Coll (NY)
Danville Area Comm Coll (IL)
Delaware Tech & Comm Coll, Stanton/Wilmington Campus (DE)
Eastern Gateway Comm Coll (OH)
Edison State Comm Coll (OH)
Gadsden State Comm Coll (AL)
Gateway Comm Coll (CT)
Hagerstown Comm Coll (MD)
Harrisburg Area Comm Coll (PA)
Highland Comm Coll (IL)
Illinois Eastern Comm Colls, Lincoln Trail College (IL)
John Tyler Comm Coll (VA)
Kent State U at Ashtabula (OH)
Kent State U at Trumbull (OH)
Kent State U at Tuscarawas (OH)
Lehigh Carbon Comm Coll (PA)
Macomb Comm Coll (MI)
Marion Tech Coll (OH)
Massachusetts Bay Comm Coll (MA)
Midlands Tech Coll (SC)
Mohawk Valley Comm Coll (NY)
Montgomery County Comm Coll (PA)
Moraine Valley Comm Coll (IL)
Onondaga Comm Coll (NY)
Owens Comm Coll, Toledo (OH)
Penn State DuBois (PA)
Penn State Hazleton (PA)
Penn State New Kensington (PA)
Penn State Shenango (PA)
Penn State York (PA)
Potomac State Coll of West Virginia U (WV)
Sauk Valley Comm Coll (IL)
Southeastern Comm Coll (IA)
Southeast Tech Inst (SD)
Spartanburg Comm Coll (SC)
Springfield Tech Comm Coll (MA)
Stark State Coll of Technology (OH)
State U of New York Coll of Technology at Alfred (NY)
Sullivan Coll of Technology and Design (KY)
Terra State Comm Coll (OH)
Three Rivers Comm Coll (CT)
Trident Tech Coll (SC)
Union County Coll (NJ)
Westchester Comm Coll (NY)
Westmoreland County Comm Coll (PA)
Wilson Comm Coll (NC)

MECHANICAL ENGINEERING TECHNOLOGIES RELATED
John Tyler Comm Coll (VA)
Moraine Park Tech Coll (WI)
Terra State Comm Coll (OH)

MECHANIC AND REPAIR TECHNOLOGIES RELATED
Chandler-Gilbert Comm Coll (AZ)
Cincinnati State Tech and Comm Coll (OH)
Ivy Tech Comm Coll–Bloomington (IN)
Ivy Tech Comm Coll–Columbus (IN)
Ivy Tech Comm Coll–Kokomo (IN)
Ivy Tech Comm Coll–Lafayette (IN)
Ivy Tech Comm Coll–North Central (IN)
Ivy Tech Comm Coll–Northwest (IN)

Ivy Tech Comm Coll–Southwest (IN)
Macomb Comm Coll (MI)

MECHANICS AND REPAIR
Ivy Tech Comm Coll–Bloomington (IN)
Ivy Tech Comm Coll–Central Indiana (IN)
Ivy Tech Comm Coll–Columbus (IN)
Ivy Tech Comm Coll–Kokomo (IN)
Ivy Tech Comm Coll–Lafayette (IN)
Ivy Tech Comm Coll–North Central (IN)
Ivy Tech Comm Coll–Northeast (IN)
Ivy Tech Comm Coll–Northwest (IN)
Ivy Tech Comm Coll–Richmond (IN)
Ivy Tech Comm Coll–Southern Indiana (IN)
Ivy Tech Comm Coll–Southwest (IN)
Ivy Tech Comm Coll–Wabash Valley (IN)
Oakland Comm Coll (MI)
Rogue Comm Coll (OR)

MECHATRONICS, ROBOTICS, AND AUTOMATION ENGINEERING
Moraine Park Tech Coll (WI)

MEDICAL ADMINISTRATIVE ASSISTANT AND MEDICAL SECRETARY
Alamance Comm Coll (NC)
Alexandria Tech and Comm Coll (MN)
Amarillo Coll (TX)
Antelope Valley Coll (CA)
Barton County Comm Coll (KS)
Berkeley City Coll (CA)
Blackhawk Tech Coll (WI)
Bristol Comm Coll (MA)
Central Lakes Coll (MN)
Century Coll (MN)
Clark Coll (WA)
The Comm Coll of Baltimore County (MD)
Comm Coll of Philadelphia (PA)
Comm Coll of Rhode Island (RI)
Crowder Coll (MO)
Dabney S. Lancaster Comm Coll (VA)
Dakota Coll at Bottineau (ND)
Dakota County Tech Coll (MN)
Danville Area Comm Coll (IL)
Daytona State Coll (FL)
Dodge City Comm Coll (KS)
Eastern Gateway Comm Coll (OH)
East Los Angeles Coll (CA)
Edison State Comm Coll (OH)
Frederick Comm Coll (MD)
Fulton-Montgomery Comm Coll (NY)
Gateway Comm Coll (CT)
Goodwin Coll (CT)
Grand Rapids Comm Coll (MI)
Hallmark Coll of Technology (TX)
Harper Coll (IL)
Hawkeye Comm Coll (IA)
Howard Comm Coll (MD)
Illinois Eastern Comm Colls, Olney Central College (IL)
Indian River State Coll (FL)
Inver Hills Comm Coll (MN)
Jamestown Business Coll (NY)
Johnston Comm Coll (NC)
Kirtland Comm Coll (MI)
Lake Michigan Coll (MI)
Lake Region State Coll (ND)
Lake Superior Coll (MN)
Linn-Benton Comm Coll (OR)
Los Angeles Harbor Coll (CA)
Lower Columbia Coll (WA)
Manchester Comm Coll (CT)
Marion Tech Coll (OH)
Martin Comm Coll (NC)
Mesa Comm Coll (AZ)
Metropolitan Comm Coll–Longview (MO)
Metropolitan Comm Coll–Maple Woods (MO)

Metropolitan Comm Coll–Penn Valley (MO)
Middlesex Comm Coll (CT)
Minnesota State Coll–Southeast Tech (MN)
Minnesota State Comm and Tech Coll (MN)
Minnesota West Comm and Tech Coll (MN)
Monroe County Comm Coll (MI)
Montcalm Comm Coll (MI)
Morton Coll (IL)
Muskegon Comm Coll (MI)
Newport Business Inst, Williamsport (PA)
Northampton Comm Coll (PA)
Northeast Comm Coll (NE)
Northern Essex Comm Coll (MA)
North Idaho Coll (ID)
North Iowa Area Comm Coll (IA)
Northland Comm and Tech Coll–Thief River Falls & East Grand Forks (MN)
Northwest Tech Coll (MN)
Orange Coast Coll (CA)
Owens Comm Coll, Toledo (OH)
Polk State Coll (FL)
Potomac State Coll of West Virginia U (WV)
Rockingham Comm Coll (NC)
Saint Charles Comm Coll (MO)
St. Philip's Coll (TX)
Sandhills Comm Coll (NC)
Scottsdale Comm Coll (AZ)
Springfield Tech Comm Coll (MA)
Terra State Comm Coll (OH)
Trident Tech Coll (SC)
Tyler Jr Coll (TX)
The U of Montana–Helena Coll of Technology (MT)
Vincennes U Jasper Campus (IN)
Wenatchee Valley Coll (WA)
Western Iowa Tech Comm Coll (IA)
West Virginia Jr Coll–Bridgeport (WV)
Wisconsin Indianhead Tech Coll (WI)
Yakima Valley Comm Coll (WA)

MEDICAL/CLINICAL ASSISTANT
Alamance Comm Coll (NC)
ASA The Coll For Excellence (NY)
Barton County Comm Coll (KS)
Big Bend Comm Coll (WA)
Bradford School (OH)
Bradford School (PA)
Brown Mackie Coll–Akron (OH)
Brown Mackie Coll–Albuquerque (NM)
Brown Mackie Coll–Atlanta (GA)
Brown Mackie Coll–Boise (ID)
Brown Mackie Coll–Cincinnati (OH)
Brown Mackie Coll–Findlay (OH)
Brown Mackie Coll–Fort Wayne (IN)
Brown Mackie Coll–Greenville (SC)
Brown Mackie Coll–Hopkinsville (KY)
Brown Mackie Coll–Indianapolis (IN)
Brown Mackie Coll–Kansas City (KS)
Brown Mackie Coll–Louisville (KY)
Brown Mackie Coll–Merrillville (IN)
Brown Mackie Coll–Miami (FL)
Brown Mackie Coll–Michigan City (IN)
Brown Mackie Coll–North Canton (OH)
Brown Mackie Coll–Northern Kentucky (KY)
Brown Mackie Coll–Oklahoma City (OK)
Brown Mackie Coll–Phoenix (AZ)
Brown Mackie Coll–Quad Cities (IA)
Brown Mackie Coll–St. Louis (MO)
Brown Mackie Coll–Salina (KS)
Brown Mackie Coll–San Antonio (TX)
Brown Mackie Coll–South Bend (IN)
Brown Mackie Coll–Tucson (AZ)
Brown Mackie Coll–Tulsa (OK)
Bryant & Stratton Coll (WI)

Bucks County Comm Coll (PA)
Career Tech Coll (LA)
Career Training Academy, Pittsburgh (PA)
Central Comm Coll–Columbus Campus (NE)
Central Comm Coll–Grand Island Campus (NE)
Central Comm Coll–Hastings Campus (NE)
Central Maine Comm Coll (ME)
Central Oregon Comm Coll (OR)
Cincinnati State Tech and Comm Coll (OH)
Clark Coll (WA)
Clovis Comm Coll (NM)
Coll of Business and Technology (FL)
Comm Care Coll (OK)
Comm Coll of Philadelphia (PA)
Dakota Coll at Bottineau (ND)
Dakota County Tech Coll (MN)
De Anza Coll (CA)
DeKalb Tech Coll (GA)
Delaware Tech & Comm Coll, Jack F. Owens Campus (DE)
Delaware Tech & Comm Coll, Stanton/Wilmington Campus (DE)
Delaware Tech & Comm Coll, Terry Campus (DE)
Douglas Education Center (PA)
Duluth Business U (MN)
Dutchess Comm Coll (NY)
Eastern Gateway Comm Coll (OH)
East Los Angeles Coll (CA)
Edison State Comm Coll (OH)
El Centro Coll (TX)
Fox Coll (IL)
Goodwin Coll (CT)
Gwinnett Tech Coll (GA)
Hallmark Coll of Technology (TX)
Harford Comm Coll (MD)
Harper Coll (IL)
Harrisburg Area Comm Coll (PA)
Harrison Coll, Anderson (IN)
Harrison Coll, Columbus (IN)
Harrison Coll, Indianapolis (IN)
Harrison Coll, Lafayette (IN)
Harrison Coll, Muncie (IN)
Harrison Coll (OH)
H. Councill Trenholm State Tech Coll (AL)
Highland Comm Coll (IL)
International Business Coll, Indianapolis (IN)
Ivy Tech Comm Coll–Central Indiana (IN)
Ivy Tech Comm Coll–Columbus (IN)
Ivy Tech Comm Coll–East Central (IN)
Ivy Tech Comm Coll–Kokomo (IN)
Ivy Tech Comm Coll–Lafayette (IN)
Ivy Tech Comm Coll–North Central (IN)
Ivy Tech Comm Coll–Northeast (IN)
Ivy Tech Comm Coll–Northwest (IN)
Ivy Tech Comm Coll–Richmond (IN)
Ivy Tech Comm Coll–Southeast (IN)
Ivy Tech Comm Coll–Southern Indiana (IN)
Ivy Tech Comm Coll–Southwest (IN)
Ivy Tech Comm Coll–Wabash Valley (IN)
Jackson Comm Coll (MI)
James Sprunt Comm Coll (NC)
Johnston Comm Coll (NC)
King's Coll (NC)
Lehigh Carbon Comm Coll (PA)
Linn-Benton Comm Coll (OR)
Lower Columbia Coll (WA)
Macomb Comm Coll (MI)
Martin Comm Coll (NC)
Miami Dade Coll (FL)
Midlands Tech Coll (SC)
Minneapolis Business Coll (MN)
Minnesota West Comm and Tech Coll (MN)
Mitchell Tech Inst (SD)
Mohave Comm Coll (AZ)
Mohawk Valley Comm Coll (NY)

Montana State U–Great Falls Coll of Technology (MT)
Montgomery County Comm Coll (PA)
Moraine Park Tech Coll (WI)
New England Inst of Technology (RI)
Niagara County Comm Coll (NY)
North Iowa Area Comm Coll (IA)
North Seattle Comm Coll (WA)
Oakland Comm Coll (MI)
Olympic Coll (WA)
Orange Coast Coll (CA)
Phoenix Coll (AZ)
Randolph Comm Coll (NC)
Raritan Valley Comm Coll (NJ)
Salt Lake Comm Coll (UT)
Southeastern Comm Coll (IA)
Southern State Comm Coll (OH)
Southwestern Michigan Coll (MI)
Springfield Tech Comm Coll (MA)
Stark State Coll of Technology (OH)
Terra State Comm Coll (OH)
Wenatchee Valley Coll (WA)
West Virginia Jr Coll–Bridgeport (WV)
West Virginia Northern Comm Coll (WV)
Wood Tobe–Coburn School (NY)
YTI Career Inst–York (PA)

MEDICAL/HEALTH MANAGEMENT AND CLINICAL ASSISTANT
CollAmerica–Flagstaff (AZ)
Owens Comm Coll, Toledo (OH)
Pittsburgh Tech Inst, Oakdale (PA)
Terra State Comm Coll (OH)

MEDICAL INFORMATICS
The Comm Coll of Baltimore County (MD)

MEDICAL INSURANCE CODING
Alexandria Tech and Comm Coll (MN)
Barton County Comm Coll (KS)
Career Training Academy, Pittsburgh (PA)
Comm Care Coll (OK)
Cowley County Comm Coll and Area Vocational–Tech School (KS)
Dakota Coll at Bottineau (ND)
Goodwin Coll (CT)
Hallmark Coll of Technology (TX)
Harrison Coll, Anderson (IN)
Harrison Coll, Columbus (IN)
Harrison Coll, Lafayette (IN)
Minnesota West Comm and Tech Coll (MN)
Montana State U–Great Falls Coll of Technology (MT)
Moraine Park Tech Coll (WI)
Northeast Comm Coll (NE)
Springfield Tech Comm Coll (MA)
Terra State Comm Coll (OH)

MEDICAL INSURANCE/ MEDICAL BILLING
Goodwin Coll (CT)
Harrison Coll (OH)
Jackson Comm Coll (MI)
Southwest Mississippi Comm Coll (MS)
Spencerian Coll (KY)

MEDICAL OFFICE ASSISTANT
Barton County Comm Coll (KS)
Central Wyoming Coll (WY)
Dakota Coll at Bottineau (ND)
Front Range Comm Coll (CO)
Kankakee Comm Coll (IL)
Lincoln Land Comm Coll (IL)
Moraine Park Tech Coll (WI)
New York Career Inst (NY)
Pittsburgh Tech Inst, Oakdale (PA)
Quinsigamond Comm Coll (MA)
Sauk Valley Comm Coll (IL)
Terra State Comm Coll (OH)
White Mountains Comm Coll (NH)

MEDICAL OFFICE COMPUTER SPECIALIST
Lamar Comm Coll (CO)
Rogue Comm Coll (OR)

MEDICAL OFFICE MANAGEMENT
ASA The Coll For Excellence (NY)
Beaufort County Comm Coll (NC)
Big Bend Comm Coll (WA)
Brown Mackie Coll–Hopkinsville (KY)
Brown Mackie Coll–Merrillville (IN)
Brown Mackie Coll–Michigan City (IN)
Cape Fear Comm Coll (NC)
Career Tech Coll (LA)
Catawba Valley Comm Coll (NC)
Coll of Lake County (IL)
Columbus Tech Coll (GA)
Douglas Education Center (PA)
Elaine P. Nunez Comm Coll (LA)
Fayetteville Tech Comm Coll (NC)
Florida State Coll at Jacksonville (FL)
Fox Valley Tech Coll (WI)
Georgia Northwestern Tech Coll (GA)
Johnston Comm Coll (NC)
Kilian Comm Coll (SD)
Long Island Business Inst (NY)
Norwalk Comm Coll (CT)
Phoenix Coll (AZ)
Randolph Comm Coll (NC)
Spencerian Coll (KY)
Wilson Comm Coll (NC)

MEDICAL RADIOLOGIC TECHNOLOGY
Aiken Tech Coll (SC)
Albany Tech Coll (GA)
Athens Tech Coll (GA)
Augusta Tech Coll (GA)
Bellingham Tech Coll (WA)
Burlington County Coll (NJ)
Cape Fear Comm Coll (NC)
Carolinas Coll of Health Sciences (NC)
Catawba Valley Comm Coll (NC)
Central Georgia Tech Coll (GA)
Central New Mexico Comm Coll (NM)
Chattahoochee Tech Coll (GA)
Chippewa Valley Tech Coll (WI)
Coll of Lake County (IL)
Columbus Tech Coll (GA)
The Comm Coll of Baltimore County (MD)
El Centro Coll (TX)
Florida State Coll at Jacksonville (FL)
Foothill Coll (CA)
Gadsden State Comm Coll (AL)
GateWay Comm Coll (AZ)
Gulf Coast Comm Coll (FL)
Gwinnett Tech Coll (GA)
Hagerstown Comm Coll (MD)
Heart of Georgia Tech Coll (GA)
Hillsborough Comm Coll (FL)
Holyoke Comm Coll (MA)
Illinois Eastern Comm Colls, Olney Central College (IL)
Ivy Tech Comm Coll–Central Indiana (IN)
Ivy Tech Comm Coll–Columbus (IN)
Ivy Tech Comm Coll–East Central (IN)
Ivy Tech Comm Coll–Wabash Valley (IN)
Jackson Comm Coll (MI)
Johnston Comm Coll (NC)
Kent State U at Salem (OH)
Kilgore Coll (TX)
Lake Michigan Coll (MI)
Lanier Tech Coll (GA)
Lonestar Coll–Cy-Fair (TX)
Lonestar Coll–Kingwood (TX)
Lonestar Coll–Montgomery (TX)
Massachusetts Bay Comm Coll (MA)
Middle Georgia Tech Coll (GA)
Middlesex Comm Coll (CT)
Midlands Tech Coll (SC)
Mitchell Tech Inst (SD)
Mohawk Valley Comm Coll (NY)

Montgomery Coll (MD)
Montgomery County Comm Coll (PA)
Moraine Park Tech Coll (WI)
Niagara County Comm Coll (NY)
Northeast Comm Coll (NE)
Oakland Comm Coll (MI)
Owensboro Comm and Tech Coll (KY)
Owens Comm Coll, Toledo (OH)
Penn State New Kensington (PA)
Penn State Schuylkill (PA)
Pensacola State Coll (FL)
Pima Comm Coll (AZ)
Quinsigamond Comm Coll (MA)
St. Philip's Coll (TX)
Salt Lake Comm Coll (UT)
Santa Barbara City Coll (CA)
Southeastern Tech Coll (GA)
Southern Crescent Tech Coll (GA)
Southwest Georgia Tech Coll (GA)
Spartanburg Comm Coll (SC)
Spencerian Coll (KY)
Union County Coll (NJ)
Volunteer State Comm Coll (TN)
West Georgia Tech Coll (GA)
West Virginia Northern Comm Coll (WV)
Wiregrass Georgia Tech Coll (GA)

MEDICAL RECEPTION
Alexandria Tech and Comm Coll (MN)

MEDICAL STAFF SERVICES TECHNOLOGY
John Wood Comm Coll (IL)

MEDICAL TRANSCRIPTION
Alexandria Tech and Comm Coll (MN)
Barton County Comm Coll (KS)
Collin County Comm Coll District (TX)
Cowley County Comm Coll and Area Vocational–Tech School (KS)
Dakota Coll at Bottineau (ND)
El Centro Coll (TX)
Elgin Comm Coll (IL)
GateWay Comm Coll (AZ)
Jackson Comm Coll (MI)
Montana State U–Great Falls Coll of Technology (MT)
Moraine Park Tech Coll (WI)
Northern Essex Comm Coll (MA)
Oakland Comm Coll (MI)

MEDICATION AIDE
Barton County Comm Coll (KS)

MEDIUM/HEAVY VEHICLE AND TRUCK TECHNOLOGY
Dakota County Tech Coll (MN)
Edison State Comm Coll (OH)
Linn State Tech Coll (MO)
Northeast Comm Coll (NE)
Oakland Comm Coll (MI)
St. Cloud Tech & Comm Coll (MN)

MEETING AND EVENT PLANNING
Raritan Valley Comm Coll (NJ)

MENTAL AND SOCIAL HEALTH SERVICES AND ALLIED PROFESSIONS RELATED
John Tyler Comm Coll (VA)
J. Sargeant Reynolds Comm Coll (VA)
Waukesha County Tech Coll (WI)
Wisconsin Indianhead Tech Coll (WI)

MENTAL HEALTH COUNSELING
Comm Coll of Philadelphia (PA)
Comm Coll of Rhode Island (RI)
Dutchess Comm Coll (NY)
Gateway Comm Coll (CT)
Housatonic Comm Coll (CT)
Kingsborough Comm Coll of the City U of New York (NY)
Macomb Comm Coll (MI)

Middlesex Comm Coll (CT)
Northern Essex Comm Coll (MA)
Sandhills Comm Coll (NC)

MERCHANDISING
Bradford School (PA)
Northeast Comm Coll (NE)

MERCHANDISING, SALES, AND MARKETING OPERATIONS RELATED (GENERAL)
Minnesota State Comm and Tech Coll (MN)
Moraine Park Tech Coll (WI)
Southeast Tech Inst (SD)

MERCHANDISING, SALES, AND MARKETING OPERATIONS RELATED (SPECIALIZED)
Wade Coll (TX)

METAL AND JEWELRY ARTS
Fashion Inst of Technology (NY)
FIDM/The Fashion Inst of Design & Merchandising, Los Angeles Campus (CA)
Santa Fe Comm Coll (NM)

METAL FABRICATOR
Moraine Park Tech Coll (WI)

METALLURGICAL TECHNOLOGY
Kilgore Coll (TX)
Linn-Benton Comm Coll (OR)
Lonestar Coll–Cy-Fair (TX)
Macomb Comm Coll (MI)
Penn State DuBois (PA)
Penn State Fayette, The Eberly Campus (PA)
Penn State Hazleton (PA)
Penn State New Kensington (PA)
Penn State Schuylkill (PA)
Penn State Shenango (PA)
Penn State Wilkes-Barre (PA)
Penn State York (PA)

MIDDLE SCHOOL EDUCATION
Arkansas State U–Mountain Home (AR)
Austin Comm Coll (TX)
Collin County Comm Coll District (TX)
Darton Coll (GA)
Delaware Tech & Comm Coll, Jack F. Owens Campus (DE)
Delaware Tech & Comm Coll, Stanton/Wilmington Campus (DE)
Delaware Tech & Comm Coll, Terry Campus (DE)
Miami Dade Coll (FL)
Northampton Comm Coll (PA)
Panola Coll (TX)

MILITARY STUDIES
Barton County Comm Coll (KS)

MINING AND PETROLEUM TECHNOLOGIES RELATED
Pima Comm Coll (AZ)

MINING TECHNOLOGY
Casper Coll (WY)
Eastern Arizona Coll (AZ)
Illinois Eastern Comm Colls, Wabash Valley College (IL)
Sheridan Coll (WY)

MODERN LANGUAGES
Amarillo Coll (TX)
Barton County Comm Coll (KS)
Oklahoma City Comm Coll (OK)
San Diego City Coll (CA)
Tyler Jr Coll (TX)

MORTUARY SCIENCE AND EMBALMING
Lake Michigan Coll (MI)

MOTORCYCLE MAINTENANCE AND REPAIR TECHNOLOGY
Linn State Tech Coll (MO)

MULTI/INTERDISCIPLINARY STUDIES RELATED
Aiken Tech Coll (SC)
Alexandria Tech and Comm Coll (MN)
Anoka-Ramsey Comm Coll (MN)
Anoka-Ramsey Comm Coll, Cambridge Campus (MN)
Central Maine Comm Coll (ME)
Chippewa Valley Tech Coll (WI)
The Comm Coll of Baltimore County (MD)
Eastfield Coll (TX)
Fox Valley Tech Coll (WI)
Harford Comm Coll (MD)
Hawkeye Comm Coll (IA)
Inver Hills Comm Coll (MN)
Kilgore Coll (TX)
Lake Region State Coll (ND)
Laramie County Comm Coll (WY)
Linn-Benton Comm Coll (OR)
Midlands Tech Coll (SC)
Minnesota State Coll–Southeast Tech (MN)
Moraine Park Tech Coll (WI)
North Dakota State Coll of Science (ND)
North Hennepin Comm Coll (MN)
North Iowa Area Comm Coll (IA)
Northwest-Shoals Comm Coll (AL)
Panola Coll (TX)
Raritan Valley Comm Coll (NJ)
Sheridan Coll (WY)
Spartanburg Comm Coll (SC)
Waukesha County Tech Coll (WI)
Western Iowa Tech Comm Coll (IA)
West Virginia Northern Comm Coll (WV)
Wisconsin Indianhead Tech Coll (WI)

MUSEUM STUDIES
Casper Coll (WY)

MUSIC
Allen Comm Coll (KS)
Amarillo Coll (TX)
Anoka-Ramsey Comm Coll (MN)
Anoka-Ramsey Comm Coll, Cambridge Campus (MN)
Antelope Valley Coll (CA)
Arizona Western Coll (AZ)
Austin Comm Coll (TX)
Barton County Comm Coll (KS)
Bucks County Comm Coll (PA)
Burlington County Coll (NJ)
Carroll Comm Coll (MD)
Casper Coll (WY)
Central Wyoming Coll (WY)
Century Coll (MN)
Clarendon Coll (TX)
Coll of Lake County (IL)
Coll of the Canyons (CA)
Collin County Comm Coll District (TX)
Comm Coll of Philadelphia (PA)
Comm Coll of Rhode Island (RI)
Cowley County Comm Coll and Area Vocational–Tech School (KS)
Crowder Coll (MO)
Darton Coll (GA)
Dawson Comm Coll (MT)
De Anza Coll (CA)
Dodge City Comm Coll (KS)
Eastern Arizona Coll (AZ)
Eastfield Coll (TX)
East Los Angeles Coll (CA)
Elgin Comm Coll (IL)
Foothill Coll (CA)
Golden West Coll (CA)
Grand Rapids Comm Coll (MI)
Harper Coll (IL)
Holyoke Comm Coll (MA)
Howard Comm Coll (MD)
Indian River State Coll (FL)
Kilgore Coll (TX)
Kingsborough Comm Coll of the City U of New York (NY)
Lake Michigan Coll (MI)
Laramie County Comm Coll (WY)
Lincoln Land Comm Coll (IL)
Lonestar Coll–Cy-Fair (TX)
Lonestar Coll–Kingwood (TX)
Lonestar Coll–Montgomery (TX)
Lonestar Coll–North Harris (TX)
Lonestar Coll–Tomball (TX)

Manchester Comm Coll (CT)
McHenry County Coll (IL)
Mendocino Coll (CA)
Mesa Comm Coll (AZ)
Miami Dade Coll (FL)
Minnesota State Comm and Tech Coll (MN)
Morton Coll (IL)
Mountain View Coll (TX)
Niagara County Comm Coll (NY)
Northern Essex Comm Coll (MA)
North Idaho Coll (ID)
North Seattle Comm Coll (WA)
Northwest Coll (WY)
Oklahoma City Comm Coll (OK)
Onondaga Comm Coll (NY)
Orange Coast Coll (CA)
Palm Beach State Coll (FL)
Pima Comm Coll (AZ)
Pratt Comm Coll (KS)
Raritan Valley Comm Coll (NJ)
St. Philip's Coll (TX)
Salt Lake Comm Coll (UT)
Sandhills Comm Coll (NC)
San Diego City Coll (CA)
Santa Barbara City Coll (CA)
Sauk Valley Comm Coll (IL)
Sheridan Coll (WY)
Snow Coll (UT)
Solano Comm Coll (CA)
Southwest Mississippi Comm Coll (MS)
Suffolk County Comm Coll (NY)
Terra State Comm Coll (OH)
Trinity Valley Comm Coll (TX)
Wenatchee Valley Coll (WA)

MUSICAL INSTRUMENT FABRICATION AND REPAIR
Orange Coast Coll (CA)
Western Iowa Tech Comm Coll (IA)

MUSICAL THEATER
Casper Coll (WY)
KD Studio (TX)

MUSIC HISTORY, LITERATURE, AND THEORY
Owens Comm Coll, Toledo (OH)
Saint Charles Comm Coll (MO)
Snow Coll (UT)

MUSIC MANAGEMENT
Austin Comm Coll (TX)
Chandler-Gilbert Comm Coll (AZ)
Collin County Comm Coll District (TX)
Glendale Comm Coll (AZ)
Harrisburg Area Comm Coll (PA)
Houston Comm Coll System (TX)
Northeast Comm Coll (NE)
Orange Coast Coll (CA)
Owens Comm Coll, Toledo (OH)
Phoenix Coll (AZ)
Terra State Comm Coll (OH)

MUSIC PERFORMANCE
Casper Coll (WY)
Houston Comm Coll System (TX)
Macomb Comm Coll (MI)
Miami Dade Coll (FL)
Northeast Comm Coll (NE)
Oakland Comm Coll (MI)
Owens Comm Coll, Toledo (OH)
Red Rocks Comm Coll (CO)
Terra State Comm Coll (OH)

MUSIC RELATED
Carl Albert State Coll (OK)
Terra State Comm Coll (OH)

MUSIC TEACHER EDUCATION
Amarillo Coll (TX)
Casper Coll (WY)
Coll of Lake County (IL)
Darton Coll (GA)
Dodge City Comm Coll (KS)
Frederick Comm Coll (MD)
Highland Comm Coll (IL)
Miami Dade Coll (FL)
Northeast Comm Coll (NE)
North Idaho Coll (ID)
Sandhills Comm Coll (NC)
Snow Coll (UT)
Southwest Mississippi Comm Coll (MS)

Waubonsee Comm Coll (IL)
Wenatchee Valley Coll (WA)

MUSIC THEORY AND COMPOSITION
Houston Comm Coll System (TX)
Oakland Comm Coll (MI)

NAIL TECHNICIAN AND MANICURIST
Century Coll (MN)
Kirtland Comm Coll (MI)

NANOTECHNOLOGY
Chippewa Valley Tech Coll (WI)
Harper Coll (IL)
Lehigh Carbon Comm Coll (PA)

NATURAL RESOURCES/CONSERVATION
Central Lakes Coll (MN)
Central Oregon Comm Coll (OR)
Dakota Coll at Bottineau (ND)
Fox Valley Tech Coll (WI)
Fulton-Montgomery Comm Coll (NY)
Grays Harbor Coll (WA)
Mountain Empire Comm Coll (VA)
Niagara County Comm Coll (NY)
Olympic Coll (WA)
Santa Rosa Jr Coll (CA)
State U of New York Coll of Environmental Science & Forestry, Ranger School (NY)
Tompkins Cortland Comm Coll (NY)

NATURAL RESOURCES MANAGEMENT AND POLICY
Central Carolina Tech Coll (SC)
Coll of Lake County (IL)
Hawkeye Comm Coll (IA)
Northwest Coll (WY)
Santa Rosa Jr Coll (CA)

NATURAL SCIENCES
Amarillo Coll (TX)
Colorado Mountain Coll (CO)
Golden West Coll (CA)
Miami Dade Coll (FL)
Orange Coast Coll (CA)
Phoenix Coll (AZ)
U of Pittsburgh at Titusville (PA)

NETWORK AND SYSTEM ADMINISTRATION
Central Comm Coll–Grand Island Campus (NE)
Century Coll (MN)
Clovis Comm Coll (NM)
Dakota Coll at Bottineau (ND)
Eastfield Coll (TX)
Florida State Coll at Jacksonville (FL)
Houston Comm Coll System (TX)
Inver Hills Comm Coll (MN)
Kaskaskia Coll (IL)
Linn-Benton Comm Coll (OR)
Metropolitan Comm Coll–Business & Technology Campus (MO)
North Iowa Area Comm Coll (IA)
Northland Comm and Tech Coll–Thief River Falls & East Grand Forks (MN)
Owensboro Comm and Tech Coll (KY)
Palm Beach State Coll (FL)
Pennsylvania Highlands Comm Coll (PA)
Potomac State Coll of West Virginia U (WV)
Santa Barbara City Coll (CA)
Seminole State Coll of Florida (FL)
Southwest Mississippi Comm Coll (MS)
Springfield Tech Comm Coll (MA)
Sullivan Coll of Technology and Design (KY)
Tallahassee Comm Coll (FL)

NONPROFIT MANAGEMENT
Goodwin Coll (CT)
Miami Dade Coll (FL)

NUCLEAR ENGINEERING TECHNOLOGY

Delaware Tech & Comm Coll, Jack F. Owens Campus (DE)
Delaware Tech & Comm Coll, Stanton/Wilmington Campus (DE)

NUCLEAR MEDICAL TECHNOLOGY

Amarillo Coll (TX)
Darton Coll (GA)
Delaware Tech & Comm Coll, Stanton/Wilmington Campus (DE)
Fayetteville Tech Comm Coll (NC)
Frederick Comm Coll (MD)
GateWay Comm Coll (AZ)
Gateway Comm Coll (CT)
Harrisburg Area Comm Coll (PA)
Hillsborough Comm Coll (FL)
Houston Comm Coll System (TX)
Howard Comm Coll (MD)
Miami Dade Coll (FL)
Midlands Tech Coll (SC)
Oakland Comm Coll (MI)
Orange Coast Coll (CA)
Owens Comm Coll, Toledo (OH)
Southeast Tech Inst (SD)
Springfield Tech Comm Coll (MA)
Union County Coll (NJ)

NUCLEAR/NUCLEAR POWER TECHNOLOGY

Allen Comm Coll (KS)
Cape Fear Comm Coll (NC)
Florida State Coll at Jacksonville (FL)
Lake Michigan Coll (MI)
Linn State Tech Coll (MO)
Terra State Comm Coll (OH)
Three Rivers Comm Coll (CT)

NURSING ADMINISTRATION

South Suburban Coll (IL)

NURSING ASSISTANT/AIDE AND PATIENT CARE ASSISTANT/AIDE

Alexandria Tech and Comm Coll (MN)
Allen Comm Coll (KS)
Barton County Comm Coll (KS)
Century Coll (MN)
Elaine P. Nunez Comm Coll (LA)
Lake Region State Coll (ND)
Moraine Park Tech Coll (WI)
North Iowa Area Comm Coll (IA)
Sandhills Comm Coll (NC)
Southwest Mississippi Comm Coll (MS)
Western Iowa Tech Comm Coll (IA)

NUTRITION SCIENCES

Casper Coll (WY)
Mohawk Valley Comm Coll (NY)

OCCUPATIONAL HEALTH AND INDUSTRIAL HYGIENE

Niagara County Comm Coll (NY)

OCCUPATIONAL SAFETY AND HEALTH TECHNOLOGY

Central Maine Comm Coll (ME)
Central Wyoming Coll (WY)
The Comm Coll of Baltimore County (MD)
GateWay Comm Coll (AZ)
Honolulu Comm Coll (HI)
Ivy Tech Comm Coll–Central Indiana (IN)
Ivy Tech Comm Coll–Northeast (IN)
Ivy Tech Comm Coll–Northwest (IN)
Ivy Tech Comm Coll–Wabash Valley (IN)
Kilgore Coll (TX)
Lanier Tech Coll (GA)
Northwest Coll (WY)
Okefenokee Tech Coll (GA)
Oklahoma State U, Oklahoma City (OK)
San Diego City Coll (CA)

San Juan Coll (NM)
Southwest Mississippi Comm Coll (MS)
U of Alaska Anchorage, Kenai Peninsula Coll (AK)

OCCUPATIONAL THERAPIST ASSISTANT

Augusta Coll (GA)
Austin Comm Coll (TX)
Bristol Comm Coll (MA)
Brown Mackie Coll–Akron (OH)
Brown Mackie Coll–Albuquerque (NM)
Brown Mackie Coll–Atlanta (GA)
Brown Mackie Coll–Boise (ID)
Brown Mackie Coll–Findlay (OH)
Brown Mackie Coll–Fort Wayne (IN)
Brown Mackie Coll–Hopkinsville (KY)
Brown Mackie Coll–Indianapolis (IN)
Brown Mackie Coll–Kansas City (KS)
Brown Mackie Coll–Louisville (KY)
Brown Mackie Coll–Merrillville (IN)
Brown Mackie Coll–Northern Kentucky (KY)
Brown Mackie Coll–Phoenix (AZ)
Brown Mackie Coll–Salina (KS)
Brown Mackie Coll–South Bend (IN)
Brown Mackie Coll–Tucson (AZ)
Brown Mackie Coll–Tulsa (OK)
Cape Fear Comm Coll (NC)
Casper Coll (WY)
Cincinnati State Tech and Comm Coll (OH)
Comm Coll of Rhode Island (RI)
Darton Coll (GA)
Daytona State Coll (FL)
Delaware Tech & Comm Coll, Jack F. Owens Campus (DE)
Delaware Tech & Comm Coll, Stanton/Wilmington Campus (DE)
Fiorello H. LaGuardia Comm Coll of the City U of New York (NY)
Fox Valley Tech Coll (WI)
Goodwin Coll (CT)
H. Councill Trenholm State Tech Coll (AL)
Houston Comm Coll System (TX)
Ivy Tech Comm Coll–Central Indiana (IN)
J. Sargeant Reynolds Comm Coll (VA)
Kaskaskia Coll (IL)
Kilgore Coll (TX)
Lake Superior Coll (MN)
Lehigh Carbon Comm Coll (PA)
Lincoln Land Comm Coll (IL)
Macomb Comm Coll (MI)
Manchester Comm Coll (CT)
Midlands Tech Coll (SC)
New England Inst of Technology (RI)
North Dakota State Coll of Science (ND)
Northland Comm and Tech Coll– Thief River Falls & East Grand Forks (MN)
Oakland Comm Coll (MI)
Owens Comm Coll, Toledo (OH)
Panola Coll (TX)
Penn State DuBois (PA)
Penn State Mont Alto (PA)
Pima Medical Inst, Mesa (AZ)
Pima Medical Inst, Tucson (AZ)
Pima Medical Inst, Denver (CO)
Polk State Coll (FL)
Pueblo Comm Coll (CO)
Quinsigamond Comm Coll (MA)
Saint Charles Comm Coll (MO)
St. Philip's Coll (TX)
Salt Lake Comm Coll (UT)
South Suburban Coll (IL)
Springfield Tech Comm Coll (MA)
Western Iowa Tech Comm Coll (IA)
Wisconsin Indianhead Tech Coll (WI)

OCCUPATIONAL THERAPY

Amarillo Coll (TX)
Barton County Comm Coll (KS)

The Comm Coll of Baltimore County (MD)
Georgia Highlands Coll (GA)
Kent State U at East Liverpool (OH)
Lonestar Coll–Kingwood (TX)
Lonestar Coll–Tomball (TX)
Metropolitan Comm Coll–Penn Valley (MO)
Oklahoma City Comm Coll (OK)
Palm Beach State Coll (FL)
Sauk Valley Comm Coll (IL)
Stark State Coll of Technology (OH)
Trident Tech Coll (SC)
Yakima Valley Comm Coll (WA)

OFFICE MANAGEMENT

Alexandria Tech and Comm Coll (MN)
Arizona Western Coll (AZ)
Berkeley City Coll (CA)
Big Bend Comm Coll (WA)
Brown Mackie Coll–Akron (OH)
Brown Mackie Coll–Boise (ID)
Brown Mackie Coll–Cincinnati (OH)
Brown Mackie Coll–Findlay (OH)
Brown Mackie Coll–Fort Wayne (IN)
Brown Mackie Coll–Greenville (SC)
Brown Mackie Coll–Kansas City (KS)
Brown Mackie Coll–Oklahoma City (OK)
Brown Mackie Coll–St. Louis (MO)
Brown Mackie Coll–Salina (KS)
Brown Mackie Coll–Tulsa (OK)
Catawba Valley Comm Coll (NC)
Cincinnati State Tech and Comm Coll (OH)
Clovis Comm Coll (NM)
Coll of Central Florida (FL)
Dakota Coll at Bottineau (ND)
Delaware Tech & Comm Coll, Jack F. Owens Campus (DE)
Delaware Tech & Comm Coll, Stanton/Wilmington Campus (DE)
Delaware Tech & Comm Coll, Terry Campus (DE)
Fayetteville Tech Comm Coll (NC)
Florida State Coll at Jacksonville (FL)
Goodwin Coll (CT)
Grays Harbor Coll (WA)
Great Basin Coll (NV)
Howard Comm Coll (MD)
Ilisagvik Coll (AK)
Ivy Tech Comm Coll–Wabash Valley (IN)
Johnston Comm Coll (NC)
John Wood Comm Coll (IL)
Lake Region State Coll (ND)
Lake-Sumter Comm Coll (FL)
Northeast Comm Coll (NE)
Owens Comm Coll, Toledo (OH)
Randolph Comm Coll (NC)
South Suburban Coll (IL)
Wenatchee Valley Coll (WA)
Wilson Comm Coll (NC)

OFFICE OCCUPATIONS AND CLERICAL SERVICES

Alamance Comm Coll (NC)
Alexandria Tech and Comm Coll (MN)
Blue Ridge Comm and Tech Coll (WV)
Central Wyoming Coll (WY)
Century Coll (MN)
Clovis Comm Coll (NM)
Dakota Coll at Bottineau (ND)
Danville Area Comm Coll (IL)
Darton Coll (GA)
El Centro Coll (TX)
Florida State Coll at Jacksonville (FL)
Gateway Comm and Tech Coll (KY)
ITI Tech Coll (LA)
Lake Region State Coll (ND)
Lonestar Coll–Cy-Fair (TX)
Moraine Park Tech Coll (WI)
New Mexico State U–Alamogordo (NM)
Northeast Comm Coll (NE)
Southeast Tech Inst (SD)

The U of Montana–Helena Coll of Technology (MT)

OPERATIONS MANAGEMENT

Alexandria Tech and Comm Coll (MN)
Chippewa Valley Tech Coll (WI)
DeKalb Tech Coll (GA)
Fayetteville Tech Comm Coll (NC)
Fox Valley Tech Coll (WI)
Great Basin Coll (NV)
Hillsborough Comm Coll (FL)
Kilgore Coll (TX)
Lehigh Carbon Comm Coll (PA)
Macomb Comm Coll (MI)
McHenry County Coll (IL)
Moraine Park Tech Coll (WI)
Owens Comm Coll, Toledo (OH)
Pensacola State Coll (FL)
Stark State Coll of Technology (OH)
Terra State Comm Coll (OH)
Waukesha County Tech Coll (WI)
Wisconsin Indianhead Tech Coll (WI)

OPERATIONS RESEARCH

Delaware Tech & Comm Coll, Stanton/Wilmington Campus (DE)

OPHTHALMIC LABORATORY TECHNOLOGY

DeKalb Tech Coll (GA)
Middlesex Comm Coll (CT)

OPHTHALMIC TECHNOLOGY

Miami Dade Coll (FL)
Pima Medical Inst, Denver (CO)
Volunteer State Comm Coll (TN)

OPTICAL SCIENCES

Corning Comm Coll (NY)

OPTICIANRY

Comm Coll of Rhode Island (RI)
DeKalb Tech Coll (GA)
Hillsborough Comm Coll (FL)
Holyoke Comm Coll (MA)
Ogeechee Tech Coll (GA)
Raritan Valley Comm Coll (NJ)

OPTOMETRIC TECHNICIAN

Barton County Comm Coll (KS)
Hillsborough Comm Coll (FL)
J. Sargeant Reynolds Comm Coll (VA)
Raritan Valley Comm Coll (NJ)
Tyler Jr Coll (TX)

ORGANIZATIONAL BEHAVIOR

Chandler-Gilbert Comm Coll (AZ)
GateWay Comm Coll (AZ)

ORGANIZATIONAL LEADERSHIP

Olympic Coll (WA)

ORNAMENTAL HORTICULTURE

Antelope Valley Coll (CA)
Coll of Lake County (IL)
Dakota Coll at Bottineau (ND)
Foothill Coll (CA)
Golden West Coll (CA)
Gwinnett Tech Coll (GA)
Mendocino Coll (CA)
Mesa Comm Coll (AZ)
Miami Dade Coll (FL)
Orange Coast Coll (CA)
Santa Barbara City Coll (CA)
Solano Comm Coll (CA)

ORTHOTICS/PROSTHETICS

Century Coll (MN)

OUTDOOR EDUCATION

Corning Comm Coll (NY)

PAINTING AND WALL COVERING

GateWay Comm Coll (AZ)

Ivy Tech Comm Coll–Central Indiana (IN)
Ivy Tech Comm Coll–East Central (IN)
Ivy Tech Comm Coll–Lafayette (IN)
Ivy Tech Comm Coll–North Central (IN)
Ivy Tech Comm Coll–Northeast (IN)
Ivy Tech Comm Coll–Northwest (IN)
Ivy Tech Comm Coll–Southwest (IN)
Ivy Tech Comm Coll–Wabash Valley (IN)

PARKS, RECREATION AND LEISURE

Central New Mexico Comm Coll (NM)
Central Wyoming Coll (WY)
Coll of Central Florida (FL)
Coll of the Canyons (CA)
Colorado Mountain Coll, Timberline Campus (CO)
The Comm Coll of Baltimore County (MD)
Dakota Coll at Bottineau (ND)
Dutchess Comm Coll (NY)
Kingsborough Comm Coll of the City U of New York (NY)
Miami Dade Coll (FL)
Muskegon Comm Coll (MI)
Niagara County Comm Coll (NY)
Northern Essex Comm Coll (MA)
Northwest Coll (WY)
Norwalk Comm Coll (CT)
Onondaga Comm Coll (NY)
Phoenix Coll (AZ)
Red Rocks Comm Coll (CO)
San Diego City Coll (CA)
San Juan Coll (NM)
Santa Barbara City Coll (CA)
Santa Fe Comm Coll (NM)
Tallahassee Comm Coll (FL)
Wenatchee Valley Coll (WA)

PARKS, RECREATION AND LEISURE FACILITIES MANAGEMENT

Allen Comm Coll (KS)
Arizona Western Coll (AZ)
Augusta Tech Coll (GA)
Central Wyoming Coll (WY)
Chattahoochee Tech Coll (GA)
Colorado Mountain Coll, Alpine Campus (CO)
Colorado Mountain Coll, Timberline Campus (CO)
Dakota Coll at Bottineau (ND)
Mohawk Valley Comm Coll (NY)
Moraine Valley Comm Coll (IL)
North Georgia Tech Coll (GA)
Potomac State Coll of West Virginia U (WV)
Tompkins Cortland Comm Coll (NY)
YTI Career Inst–York (PA)

PARKS, RECREATION, LEISURE, AND FITNESS STUDIES RELATED

Cincinnati State Tech and Comm Coll (OH)
Dakota Coll at Bottineau (ND)
Tompkins Cortland Comm Coll (NY)

PASTORAL STUDIES/ COUNSELING

Hesston Coll (KS)

PATHOLOGIST ASSISTANT

Lake Region State Coll (ND)

PEACE STUDIES AND CONFLICT RESOLUTION

El Centro Coll (TX)

PERSONAL AND CULINARY SERVICES RELATED

GateWay Comm Coll (AZ)
Mohave Comm Coll (AZ)

PETROLEUM ENGINEERING
Kilgore Coll (TX)
Southern Alberta Inst of Technology (AB, Canada)

PETROLEUM TECHNOLOGY
Southwest Mississippi Comm Coll (MS)
U of Arkansas Comm Coll at Morrilton (AR)

PHARMACY
Barton County Comm Coll (KS)
Indian River State Coll (FL)

PHARMACY TECHNICIAN
Albany Tech Coll (GA)
ASA The Coll For Excellence (NY)
Augusta Tech Coll (GA)
Barton County Comm Coll (KS)
Brown Mackie Coll–Akron (OH)
Brown Mackie Coll–Albuquerque (NM)
Brown Mackie Coll–Atlanta (GA)
Brown Mackie Coll–Cincinnati (OH)
Brown Mackie Coll–Findlay (OH)
Brown Mackie Coll–Louisville (KY)
Brown Mackie Coll–North Canton (OH)
Brown Mackie Coll–Northern Kentucky (KY)
Brown Mackie Coll–St. Louis (MO)
Brown Mackie Coll–San Antonio (TX)
Casper Coll (WY)
Columbus Tech Coll (GA)
Comm Care Coll (OK)
Fayetteville Tech Comm Coll (NC)
Lonestar Coll–North Harris (TX)
Lonestar Coll–Tomball (TX)
Midlands Tech Coll (SC)
Minnesota State Comm and Tech Coll (MN)
Mohave Comm Coll (AZ)
Moraine Park Tech Coll (WI)
North Dakota State Coll of Science (ND)
Northland Comm and Tech Coll–Thief River Falls & East Grand Forks (MN)
North Seattle Comm Coll (WA)
Oakland Comm Coll (MI)
Pima Comm Coll (AZ)
Southern Crescent Tech Coll (GA)
West Georgia Tech Coll (GA)

PHILOSOPHY
Allen Comm Coll (KS)
Arizona Western Coll (AZ)
Austin Comm Coll (TX)
Barton County Comm Coll (KS)
Burlington County Coll (NJ)
Darton Coll (GA)
De Anza Coll (CA)
East Los Angeles Coll (CA)
Foothill Coll (CA)
Georgia Highlands Coll (GA)
Harper Coll (IL)
Indian River State Coll (FL)
Lake Michigan Coll (MI)
Lonestar Coll–Cy-Fair (TX)
Lonestar Coll–Kingwood (TX)
Lonestar Coll–Montgomery (TX)
Lonestar Coll–North Harris (TX)
Lonestar Coll–Tomball (TX)
Miami Dade Coll (FL)
Oklahoma City Comm Coll (OK)
Orange Coast Coll (CA)
Palm Beach State Coll (FL)
Red Rocks Comm Coll (CO)
Saint Charles Comm Coll (MO)
St. Philip's Coll (TX)
Santa Barbara City Coll (CA)
Santa Rosa Jr Coll (CA)
Snow Coll (UT)

PHLEBOTOMY TECHNOLOGY
Alexandria Tech and Comm Coll (MN)
Barton County Comm Coll (KS)
Casper Coll (WY)
Duluth Business U (MN)

PHOTOGRAPHIC AND FILM/VIDEO TECHNOLOGY
Catawba Valley Comm Coll (NC)

Central Lakes Coll (MN)
Daytona State Coll (FL)
Fiorello H. LaGuardia Comm Coll of the City U of New York (NY)
Miami Dade Coll (FL)
Oakland Comm Coll (MI)
Pensacola State Coll (FL)
Randolph Comm Coll (NC)
Salt Lake Comm Coll (UT)
Suffolk County Comm Coll (NY)
Westmoreland County Comm Coll (PA)

PHOTOGRAPHY
Amarillo Coll (TX)
Antelope Valley Coll (CA)
Antonelli Inst (PA)
The Art Inst of Seattle (WA)
Casper Coll (WY)
Cecil Coll (MD)
Coll of the Canyons (CA)
Colorado Mountain Coll (CO)
Comm Coll of Philadelphia (PA)
Dakota County Tech Coll (MN)
De Anza Coll (CA)
Delaware Tech & Comm Coll, Terry Campus (DE)
East Los Angeles Coll (CA)
Foothill Coll (CA)
Gwinnett Tech Coll (GA)
Harrisburg Area Comm Coll (PA)
Howard Comm Coll (MD)
Lonestar Coll–North Harris (TX)
Miami Dade Coll (FL)
Oakland Comm Coll (MI)
Onondaga Comm Coll (NY)
Orange Coast Coll (CA)
Palm Beach State Coll (FL)
San Diego City Coll (CA)
Santa Fe Comm Coll (NM)
Scottsdale Comm Coll (AZ)
Solano Comm Coll (CA)
Tompkins Cortland Comm Coll (NY)
Tyler Jr Coll (TX)

PHOTOJOURNALISM
Randolph Comm Coll (NC)

PHYSICAL AND BIOLOGICAL ANTHROPOLOGY
Cowley County Comm Coll and Area Vocational–Tech School (KS)

PHYSICAL EDUCATION TEACHING AND COACHING
Amarillo Coll (TX)
Barton County Comm Coll (KS)
Bucks County Comm Coll (PA)
Carl Albert State Coll (OK)
Casper Coll (WY)
Clarendon Coll (TX)
Crowder Coll (MO)
De Anza Coll (CA)
Dodge City Comm Coll (KS)
East Los Angeles Coll (CA)
Foothill Coll (CA)
Frederick Comm Coll (MD)
Fulton-Montgomery Comm Coll (NY)
Harper Coll (IL)
Indian River State Coll (FL)
Inver Hills Comm Coll (MN)
Kilgore Coll (TX)
Laramie County Comm Coll (WY)
Linn-Benton Comm Coll (OR)
Lonestar Coll–North Harris (TX)
Mendocino Coll (CA)
Miami Dade Coll (FL)
Montgomery County Comm Coll (PA)
Niagara County Comm Coll (NY)
Northern Essex Comm Coll (MA)
North Hennepin Comm Coll (MN)
North Iowa Area Comm Coll (IA)
Orange Coast Coll (CA)
Palm Beach State Coll (FL)
Potomac State Coll of West Virginia U (WV)
Pratt Comm Coll (KS)
Red Rocks Comm Coll (CO)
San Diego City Coll (CA)
Santa Barbara City Coll (CA)
Sauk Valley Comm Coll (IL)
Snow Coll (UT)
Solano Comm Coll (CA)

Southwest Mississippi Comm Coll (MS)
Trinity Valley Comm Coll (TX)
Tyler Jr Coll (TX)
Wenatchee Valley Coll (WA)

PHYSICAL SCIENCES
Amarillo Coll (TX)
Antelope Valley Coll (CA)
Austin Comm Coll (TX)
Barton County Comm Coll (KS)
Borough of Manhattan Comm Coll of the City U of New York (NY)
Carl Albert State Coll (OK)
Cecil Coll (MD)
Central Oregon Comm Coll (OR)
Central Wyoming Coll (WY)
Chandler-Gilbert Comm Coll (AZ)
Colorado Mountain Coll, Alpine Campus (CO)
Crowder Coll (MO)
Dakota Coll at Bottineau (ND)
Dodge City Comm Coll (KS)
Frederick Comm Coll (MD)
Fulton-Montgomery Comm Coll (NY)
GateWay Comm Coll (AZ)
Golden West Coll (CA)
Harper Coll (IL)
Harrisburg Area Comm Coll (PA)
Highland Comm Coll (IL)
Howard Comm Coll (MD)
Kent State U at Geauga (OH)
Lake Michigan Coll (MI)
Lehigh Carbon Comm Coll (PA)
Linn-Benton Comm Coll (OR)
Mendocino Coll (CA)
Miami Dade Coll (FL)
Montgomery County Comm Coll (PA)
North Idaho Coll (ID)
Palm Beach State Coll (FL)
Phoenix Coll (AZ)
Salt Lake Comm Coll (UT)
San Diego City Coll (CA)
San Juan Coll (NM)
Santa Fe Comm Coll (NM)
Snow Coll (UT)
Southwest Mississippi Comm Coll (MS)
Trinity Valley Comm Coll (TX)
Wenatchee Valley Coll (WA)

PHYSICAL SCIENCES RELATED
Dakota Coll at Bottineau (ND)

PHYSICAL THERAPY
Allen Comm Coll (KS)
Amarillo Coll (TX)
Athens Tech Coll (GA)
Barton County Comm Coll (KS)
Blackhawk Tech Coll (WI)
Central Oregon Comm Coll (OR)
Clarendon Coll (TX)
Daytona State Coll (FL)
De Anza Coll (CA)
Dodge City Comm Coll (KS)
Georgia Highlands Coll (GA)
Gwinnett Tech Coll (GA)
Housatonic Comm Coll (CT)
Indian River State Coll (FL)
Kent State U at Ashtabula (OH)
Kent State U at East Liverpool (OH)
Kilgore Coll (TX)
Kingsborough Comm Coll of the City U of New York (NY)
Lake Michigan Coll (MI)
Metropolitan Comm Coll–Penn Valley (MO)
Monroe County Comm Coll (MI)
Morton Coll (IL)
Oklahoma City Comm Coll (OK)
Palm Beach State Coll (FL)
Sauk Valley Comm Coll (IL)
Seminole State Coll of Florida (FL)
Stark State Coll of Technology (OH)
Suffolk County Comm Coll (NY)
Trident Tech Coll (SC)

PHYSICAL THERAPY TECHNOLOGY
Anoka-Ramsey Comm Coll (MN)
Austin Comm Coll (TX)
Barton County Comm Coll (KS)
Brown Mackie Coll–Fort Wayne (IN)
Brown Mackie Coll–South Bend (IN)
Carl Albert State Coll (OK)

Carroll Comm Coll (MD)
Chippewa Valley Tech Coll (WI)
Coll of Central Florida (FL)
Comm Coll of Rhode Island (RI)
Darton Coll (GA)
Delaware Tech & Comm Coll, Jack F. Owens Campus (DE)
Delaware Tech & Comm Coll, Stanton/Wilmington Campus (DE)
Dutchess Comm Coll (NY)
Edison State Comm Coll (OH)
Elgin Comm Coll (IL)
Fayetteville Tech Comm Coll (NC)
Fiorello H. LaGuardia Comm Coll of the City U of New York (NY)
Florida State Coll at Jacksonville (FL)
Fox Coll (IL)
GateWay Comm Coll (AZ)
Georgia Highlands Coll (GA)
Gulf Coast Comm Coll (FL)
Gwinnett Tech Coll (GA)
Houston Comm Coll System (TX)
Indian River State Coll (FL)
Ivy Tech Comm Coll–East Central (IN)
Jefferson State Comm Coll (AL)
Kankakee Comm Coll (IL)
Kaskaskia Coll (IL)
Kilgore Coll (TX)
Kingsborough Comm Coll of the City U of New York (NY)
Lake Superior Coll (MN)
Laramie County Comm Coll (WY)
Lehigh Carbon Comm Coll (PA)
Linn State Tech Coll (MO)
Lonestar Coll–Montgomery (TX)
Macomb Comm Coll (MI)
Manchester Comm Coll (CT)
Marion Tech Coll (OH)
Martin Comm Coll (NC)
Massachusetts Bay Comm Coll (MA)
Miami Dade Coll (FL)
Midlands Tech Coll (SC)
Mohave Comm Coll (AZ)
Montana State U–Great Falls Coll of Technology (MT)
Montgomery Coll (MD)
New England Inst of Technology (RI)
Niagara County Comm Coll (NY)
Northeast Comm Coll (NE)
North Iowa Area Comm Coll (IA)
Northland Comm and Tech Coll–Thief River Falls & East Grand Forks (MN)
Olympic Coll (WA)
Onondaga Comm Coll (NY)
Owens Comm Coll, Toledo (OH)
Pasco-Hernando Comm Coll (FL)
Penn State DuBois (PA)
Penn State Hazleton (PA)
Penn State Mont Alto (PA)
Penn State Shenango (PA)
Pensacola State Coll (FL)
Pima Medical Inst, Mesa (AZ)
Pima Medical Inst, Tucson (AZ)
Pima Medical Inst, Denver (CO)
Pima Medical Inst (NV)
Pima Medical Inst, Albuquerque (NM)
Pima Medical Inst, Seattle (WA)
Polk State Coll (FL)
Pueblo Comm Coll (CO)
Randolph Comm Coll (NC)
St. Philip's Coll (TX)
Salt Lake Comm Coll (UT)
San Juan Coll (NM)
Springfield Tech Comm Coll (MA)
Union County Coll (NJ)
U of Pittsburgh at Titusville (PA)
Volunteer State Comm Coll (TN)
Western Iowa Tech Comm Coll (IA)
West Kentucky Comm and Tech Coll (KY)

PHYSICIAN ASSISTANT
Barton County Comm Coll (KS)
The Comm Coll of Baltimore County (MD)
Foothill Coll (CA)
Georgia Highlands Coll (GA)
Lake Michigan Coll (MI)

PHYSICS
Allen Comm Coll (KS)

Amarillo Coll (TX)
Arizona Western Coll (AZ)
Austin Comm Coll (TX)
Barton County Comm Coll (KS)
Burlington County Coll (NJ)
Casper Coll (WY)
Cecil Coll (MD)
Darton Coll (GA)
De Anza Coll (CA)
Dodge City Comm Coll (KS)
Eastern Arizona Coll (AZ)
Foothill Coll (CA)
Frank Phillips Coll (TX)
Great Basin Coll (NV)
Highland Comm Coll (IL)
Indian River State Coll (FL)
Kilgore Coll (TX)
Kingsborough Comm Coll of the City U of New York (NY)
Lake Michigan Coll (MI)
Linn-Benton Comm Coll (OR)
Lonestar Coll–Cy-Fair (TX)
Lonestar Coll–Kingwood (TX)
Lonestar Coll–Montgomery (TX)
Lonestar Coll–North Harris (TX)
Lonestar Coll–Tomball (TX)
Los Angeles Harbor Coll (CA)
Miami Dade Coll (FL)
Northampton Comm Coll (PA)
Northeast Comm Coll (NE)
North Idaho Coll (ID)
Northwest Coll (WY)
Oklahoma City Comm Coll (OK)
Oklahoma State U, Oklahoma City (OK)
Orange Coast Coll (CA)
Red Rocks Comm Coll (CO)
Salt Lake Comm Coll (UT)
San Juan Coll (NM)
Santa Barbara City Coll (CA)
Santa Rosa Jr Coll (CA)
Sauk Valley Comm Coll (IL)
Snow Coll (UT)
Solano Comm Coll (CA)
Springfield Tech Comm Coll (MA)
Terra State Comm Coll (OH)
Tyler Jr Coll (TX)

PHYSICS TEACHER EDUCATION
The Comm Coll of Baltimore County (MD)
Harford Comm Coll (MD)
Montgomery Coll (MD)

PIPEFITTING AND SPRINKLER FITTING
GateWay Comm Coll (AZ)
Ivy Tech Comm Coll–Bloomington (IN)
Ivy Tech Comm Coll–Central Indiana (IN)
Ivy Tech Comm Coll–Columbus (IN)
Ivy Tech Comm Coll–East Central (IN)
Ivy Tech Comm Coll–Kokomo (IN)
Ivy Tech Comm Coll–Lafayette (IN)
Ivy Tech Comm Coll–North Central (IN)
Ivy Tech Comm Coll–Northeast (IN)
Ivy Tech Comm Coll–Northwest (IN)
Ivy Tech Comm Coll–Richmond (IN)
Ivy Tech Comm Coll–Southern Indiana (IN)
Ivy Tech Comm Coll–Southwest (IN)
Ivy Tech Comm Coll–Wabash Valley (IN)
Moraine Park Tech Coll (WI)
New England Inst of Technology (RI)
Oakland Comm Coll (MI)

PLANT NURSERY MANAGEMENT
Foothill Coll (CA)
Miami Dade Coll (FL)

PLASTICS AND POLYMER ENGINEERING TECHNOLOGY
Cincinnati State Tech and Comm Coll (OH)
Daytona State Coll (FL)
Grand Rapids Comm Coll (MI)
Kent State U at Tuscarawas (OH)
Macomb Comm Coll (MI)

Terra State Comm Coll (OH)
West Georgia Tech Coll (GA)

PLAYWRITING AND SCREENWRITING
Northwest Coll (WY)

PLUMBING TECHNOLOGY
Arizona Western Coll (AZ)
GateWay Comm Coll (AZ)
Macomb Comm Coll (MI)
Minnesota State Comm and Tech Coll (MN)
Minnesota West Comm and Tech Coll (MN)
Moraine Park Tech Coll (WI)
Northeast Iowa Comm Coll (IA)
Northland Comm and Tech Coll–Thief River Falls & East Grand Forks (MN)
Olympic Coll (WA)
St. Cloud Tech & Comm Coll (MN)

POLITICAL SCIENCE AND GOVERNMENT
Allen Comm Coll (KS)
Arizona Western Coll (AZ)
Austin Comm Coll (TX)
Bainbridge Coll (GA)
Barton County Comm Coll (KS)
Casper Coll (WY)
Darton Coll (GA)
De Anza Coll (CA)
Dodge City Comm Coll (KS)
Eastern Arizona Coll (AZ)
East Los Angeles Coll (CA)
Foothill Coll (CA)
Frederick Comm Coll (MD)
Georgia Highlands Coll (GA)
Highland Comm Coll (IL)
Indian River State Coll (FL)
Lake Michigan Coll (MI)
Laramie County Comm Coll (WY)
Lonestar Coll–Cy-Fair (TX)
Lonestar Coll–Kingwood (TX)
Lonestar Coll–Montgomery (TX)
Lonestar Coll–North Harris (TX)
Lonestar Coll–Tomball (TX)
Miami Dade Coll (FL)
Northern Essex Comm Coll (MA)
North Idaho Coll (ID)
Northwest Coll (WY)
Oklahoma City Comm Coll (OK)
Orange Coast Coll (CA)
Palm Beach State Coll (FL)
Pima Comm Coll (AZ)
Potomac State Coll of West Virginia U (WV)
Red Rocks Comm Coll (CO)
Saint Charles Comm Coll (MO)
St. Philip's Coll (TX)
Salt Lake Comm Coll (UT)
San Diego City Coll (CA)
Santa Barbara City Coll (CA)
Santa Rosa Jr Coll (CA)
Sauk Valley Comm Coll (IL)
Snow Coll (UT)
Solano Comm Coll (CA)
Trinity Valley Comm Coll (TX)
Tyler Jr Coll (TX)

POLYMER/PLASTICS ENGINEERING
Central Oregon Comm Coll (OR)

POLYSOMNOGRAPHY
Catawba Valley Comm Coll (NC)

PORTUGUESE
Miami Dade Coll (FL)

POULTRY SCIENCE
Crowder Coll (MO)
Delaware Tech & Comm Coll, Jack F. Owens Campus (DE)

PRECISION METAL WORKING RELATED
Oakland Comm Coll (MI)

PRECISION PRODUCTION RELATED
Lake Michigan Coll (MI)

Midlands Tech Coll (SC)
Saint Charles Comm Coll (MO)
Sheridan Coll (WY)
Waycross Coll (GA)

PRECISION PRODUCTION TRADES
Midlands Tech Coll (SC)
Owensboro Comm and Tech Coll (KY)
Santa Rosa Jr Coll (CA)

PRECISION SYSTEMS MAINTENANCE AND REPAIR TECHNOLOGIES RELATED
Mitchell Tech Inst (SD)

PRE-DENTISTRY STUDIES
Allen Comm Coll (KS)
Austin Comm Coll (TX)
Barton County Comm Coll (KS)
Casper Coll (WY)
Clarendon Coll (TX)
Darton Coll (GA)
Howard Comm Coll (MD)
Kilgore Coll (TX)
Lake Michigan Coll (MI)
Northeast Comm Coll (NE)
St. Philip's Coll (TX)
Sauk Valley Comm Coll (IL)

PRE-ENGINEERING
Amarillo Coll (TX)
Anoka-Ramsey Comm Coll (MN)
Anoka-Ramsey Comm Coll, Cambridge Campus (MN)
Barton County Comm Coll (KS)
Chipola Coll (FL)
Clovis Comm Coll (NM)
Coll of the Canyons (CA)
Colorado Mountain Coll, Alpine Campus (CO)
Comm Coll of Philadelphia (PA)
Corning Comm Coll (NY)
Cowley County Comm Coll and Area Vocational–Tech School (KS)
Crowder Coll (MO)
Darton Coll (GA)
De Anza Coll (CA)
Dodge City Comm Coll (KS)
East Los Angeles Coll (CA)
Edison State Comm Coll (OH)
Highland Comm Coll (IL)
Housatonic Comm Coll (CT)
Indian River State Coll (FL)
Lake Michigan Coll (MI)
Lamar Comm Coll (CO)
Linn-Benton Comm Coll (OR)
Lonestar Coll–North Harris (TX)
Los Angeles Harbor Coll (CA)
Macomb Comm Coll (MI)
Mesabi Range Comm and Tech Coll (MN)
Mesa Comm Coll (AZ)
Metropolitan Comm Coll–Longview (MO)
Metropolitan Comm Coll–Maple Woods (MO)
Miami Dade Coll (FL)
Middlesex Comm Coll (CT)
Monroe County Comm Coll (MI)
Northeast Comm Coll (NE)
North Hennepin Comm Coll (MN)
Oklahoma City Comm Coll (OK)
Oklahoma State U, Oklahoma City (OK)
Palm Beach State Coll (FL)
Polk State Coll (FL)
Potomac State Coll of West Virginia U (WV)
Pratt Comm Coll (KS)
Rainy River Comm Coll (MN)
Randolph Comm Coll (NC)
St. Philip's Coll (TX)
Sandhills Comm Coll (NC)
San Diego City Coll (CA)
Snow Coll (UT)
Three Rivers Comm Coll (CT)
Trinity Valley Comm Coll (TX)
Wenatchee Valley Comm Coll (WA)
Yakima Valley Comm Coll (WA)

PRE-LAW STUDIES
Allen Comm Coll (KS)

Barton County Comm Coll (KS)
Carl Albert State Coll (OK)
Casper Coll (WY)
Central Oregon Comm Coll (OR)
Central Wyoming Coll (WY)
Clarendon Coll (TX)
Darton Coll (GA)
Eastern Arizona Coll (AZ)
Kilgore Coll (TX)
Lake Michigan Coll (MI)
Laramie County Comm Coll (WY)
Northeast Comm Coll (NE)
St. Philip's Coll (TX)

PREMEDICAL STUDIES
Allen Comm Coll (KS)
Austin Comm Coll (TX)
Barton County Comm Coll (KS)
Casper Coll (WY)
Central Oregon Comm Coll (OR)
Clarendon Coll (TX)
Darton Coll (GA)
Eastern Arizona Coll (AZ)
Howard Comm Coll (MD)
Kilgore Coll (TX)
Lake Michigan Coll (MI)
Northeast Comm Coll (NE)
St. Philip's Coll (TX)
San Juan Coll (NM)
Sauk Valley Comm Coll (IL)
Springfield Tech Comm Coll (MA)

PRENURSING STUDIES
Arizona Western Coll (AZ)
Dakota Coll at Bottineau (ND)
Edison State Comm Coll (OH)
Georgia Military Coll (GA)
Northeast Comm Coll (NE)
Oklahoma State U, Oklahoma City (OK)
Randolph Comm Coll (NC)
St. Philip's Coll (TX)
Southwestern Michigan Coll (MI)

PRE-OCCUPATIONAL THERAPY
Casper Coll (WY)

PRE-OPTOMETRY
Casper Coll (WY)

PRE-PHARMACY STUDIES
Allen Comm Coll (KS)
Amarillo Coll (TX)
Austin Comm Coll (TX)
Casper Coll (WY)
Central Oregon Comm Coll (OR)
Darton Coll (GA)
Dodge City Comm Coll (KS)
Eastern Arizona Coll (AZ)
Howard Comm Coll (MD)
Kilgore Coll (TX)
Lake Michigan Coll (MI)
Laramie County Comm Coll (WY)
Northeast Comm Coll (NE)
Northwest Coll (WY)
St. Philip's Coll (TX)
Santa Rosa Jr Coll (CA)
Sauk Valley Comm Coll (IL)

PRE-PHYSICAL THERAPY
Casper Coll (WY)

PRE-VETERINARY STUDIES
Allen Comm Coll (KS)
Austin Comm Coll (TX)
Barton County Comm Coll (KS)
Casper Coll (WY)
Dakota Coll at Bottineau (ND)
Darton Coll (GA)
Howard Comm Coll (MD)
Kilgore Coll (TX)
Lake Michigan Coll (MI)
Northeast Comm Coll (NE)
Sauk Valley Comm Coll (IL)

PRINTING MANAGEMENT
Moraine Park Tech Coll (WI)

PRINTMAKING
De Anza Coll (CA)
Florida State Coll at Jacksonville (FL)

Santa Fe Comm Coll (NM)

PROFESSIONAL, TECHNICAL, BUSINESS, AND SCIENTIFIC WRITING
Austin Comm Coll (TX)
Cincinnati State Tech and Comm Coll (OH)
Coll of Lake County (IL)
De Anza Coll (CA)
Linn-Benton Comm Coll (OR)
Oklahoma State U, Oklahoma City (OK)
Southwestern Michigan Coll (MI)
Three Rivers Comm Coll (CT)

PSYCHIATRIC/MENTAL HEALTH SERVICES TECHNOLOGY
The Comm Coll of Baltimore County (MD)
Dutchess Comm Coll (NY)
Eastfield Coll (TX)
Fiorello H. LaGuardia Comm Coll of the City U of New York (NY)
Gulf Coast Comm Coll (FL)
Hagerstown Comm Coll (MD)
Harford Comm Coll (MD)
Hillsborough Comm Coll (FL)
Houston Comm Coll System (TX)
Ivy Tech Comm Coll–Bloomington (IN)
Ivy Tech Comm Coll–Central Indiana (IN)
Ivy Tech Comm Coll–Columbus (IN)
Ivy Tech Comm Coll–East Central (IN)
Ivy Tech Comm Coll–Kokomo (IN)
Ivy Tech Comm Coll–Lafayette (IN)
Ivy Tech Comm Coll–Northeast (IN)
Ivy Tech Comm Coll–Northwest (IN)
Ivy Tech Comm Coll–Richmond (IN)
Ivy Tech Comm Coll–Southeast (IN)
Ivy Tech Comm Coll–Southern Indiana (IN)
Ivy Tech Comm Coll–Southwest (IN)
Ivy Tech Comm Coll–Wabash Valley (IN)
Kingsborough Comm Coll of the City U of New York (NY)
Montgomery Coll (MD)
Montgomery County Comm Coll (PA)
North Dakota State Coll of Science (ND)

PSYCHOLOGY
Allen Comm Coll (KS)
Amarillo Coll (TX)
Austin Comm Coll (TX)
Bainbridge Coll (GA)
Barton County Comm Coll (KS)
Bucks County Comm Coll (PA)
Burlington County Coll (NJ)
Carroll Comm Coll (MD)
Casper Coll (WY)
Central Wyoming Coll (WY)
Chandler-Gilbert Comm Coll (AZ)
Clarendon Coll (TX)
Clovis Comm Coll (NM)
Coll of the Canyons (CA)
Colorado Mountain Coll (CO)
Crowder Coll (MO)
Dakota Coll at Bottineau (ND)
Darton Coll (GA)
De Anza Coll (CA)
Dodge City Comm Coll (KS)
Eastern Arizona Coll (AZ)
East Los Angeles Coll (CA)
Foothill Coll (CA)
Frank Phillips Coll (TX)
Frederick Comm Coll (MD)
Fulton-Montgomery Comm Coll (NY)
Georgia Highlands Coll (GA)
Georgia Military Coll (GA)
Great Basin Coll (NV)
Harper Coll (IL)
Harrisburg Area Comm Coll (PA)
Highland Comm Coll (IL)

Howard Comm Coll (MD)
Indian River State Coll (FL)
Kankakee Comm Coll (IL)
Kilgore Coll (TX)
Kilian Comm Coll (SD)
Lake Michigan Coll (MI)
Laramie County Comm Coll (WY)
Lehigh Carbon Comm Coll (PA)
Lonestar Coll–Cy-Fair (TX)
Lonestar Coll–Kingwood (TX)
Lonestar Coll–Montgomery (TX)
Lonestar Coll–North Harris (TX)
Mendocino Coll (CA)
Miami Dade Coll (FL)
Mohave Comm Coll (AZ)
Monroe County Comm Coll (MI)
Northeast Comm Coll (NE)
North Idaho Coll (ID)
Northwest Coll (WY)
Norwalk Comm Coll (CT)
Oklahoma City Comm Coll (OK)
Oklahoma State U, Oklahoma City (OK)
Owens Comm Coll, Toledo (OH)
Palm Beach State Coll (FL)
Potomac State Coll of West Virginia U (WV)
Pratt Comm Coll (KS)
Red Rocks Comm Coll (CO)
Saint Charles Comm Coll (MO)
St. Philip's Coll (TX)
Salt Lake Comm Coll (UT)
San Diego City Coll (CA)
San Juan Coll (NM)
Santa Barbara City Coll (CA)
Santa Fe Comm Coll (NM)
Santa Rosa Jr Coll (CA)
Sauk Valley Comm Coll (IL)
Sheridan Coll (WY)
Solano Comm Coll (CA)
Terra State Comm Coll (OH)
Trinity Valley Comm Coll (TX)
Tyler Jr Coll (TX)
Vincennes U Jasper Campus (IN)

PUBLIC ADMINISTRATION
Barton County Comm Coll (KS)
East Los Angeles Coll (CA)
Fayetteville Tech Comm Coll (NC)
Housatonic Comm Coll (CT)
Houston Comm Coll System (TX)
Laramie County Comm Coll (WY)
Miami Dade Coll (FL)
Mohawk Valley Comm Coll (NY)
Owens Comm Coll, Toledo (OH)
San Juan Coll (NM)
Scottsdale Comm Coll (AZ)
Solano Comm Coll (CA)
Tallahassee Comm Coll (FL)
Three Rivers Comm Coll (CT)
Westchester Comm Coll (NY)

PUBLIC ADMINISTRATION AND SOCIAL SERVICE PROFESSIONS RELATED
Cleveland State Comm Coll (TN)
J. Sargeant Reynolds Comm Coll (VA)
Oklahoma State U, Oklahoma City (OK)
Onondaga Comm Coll (NY)
Sauk Valley Comm Coll (IL)

PUBLIC HEALTH EDUCATION AND PROMOTION
Georgia Military Coll (GA)

PUBLIC HEALTH RELATED
Salt Lake Comm Coll (UT)

PUBLIC RELATIONS, ADVERTISING, AND APPLIED COMMUNICATION RELATED
Harper Coll (IL)

PUBLIC RELATIONS/IMAGE MANAGEMENT
Amarillo Coll (TX)
Cecil Coll (MD)
Crowder Coll (MO)
Glendale Comm Coll (AZ)

PURCHASING, PROCUREMENT/ ACQUISITIONS AND CONTRACTS MANAGEMENT

Cincinnati State Tech and Comm Coll (OH)
De Anza Coll (CA)

QUALITY CONTROL AND SAFETY TECHNOLOGIES RELATED

Blue Ridge Comm and Tech Coll (WV)
Ivy Tech Comm Coll–Lafayette (IN)
Ivy Tech Comm Coll–Wabash Valley (IN)
John Tyler Comm Coll (VA)
Macomb Comm Coll (MI)

QUALITY CONTROL TECHNOLOGY

Central Comm Coll–Columbus Campus (NE)
Central Comm Coll–Hastings Campus (NE)
Grand Rapids Comm Coll (MI)
Illinois Eastern Comm Colls, Frontier Community College (IL)
Illinois Eastern Comm Colls, Lincoln Trail College (IL)
Ivy Tech Comm Coll–Lafayette (IN)
Macomb Comm Coll (MI)
Mesa Comm Coll (AZ)
Metropolitan Comm Coll–Business & Technology Campus (MO)
Northampton Comm Coll (PA)
Owens Comm Coll, Toledo (OH)
Salt Lake Comm Coll (UT)

RADIATION PROTECTION/ HEALTH PHYSICS TECHNOLOGY

Aiken Tech Coll (SC)
Lonestar Coll–Cy-Fair (TX)
Lonestar Coll–Montgomery (TX)
Spartanburg Comm Coll (SC)

RADIO AND TELEVISION

Amarillo Coll (TX)
Austin Comm Coll (TX)
Bucks County Comm Coll (PA)
Central Wyoming Coll (WY)
Coll of the Canyons (CA)
Daytona State Coll (FL)
De Anza Coll (CA)
Dodge City Comm Coll (KS)
Foothill Coll (CA)
Golden West Coll (CA)
Gulf Coast Comm Coll (FL)
Illinois Eastern Comm Colls, Wabash Valley College (IL)
Miami Dade Coll (FL)
Northwest Coll (WY)
Onondaga Comm Coll (NY)
Pima Comm Coll (AZ)
San Diego City Coll (CA)

RADIO AND TELEVISION BROADCASTING TECHNOLOGY

Arizona Western Coll (AZ)
Borough of Manhattan Comm Coll of the City U of New York (NY)
Central Comm Coll–Hastings Campus (NE)
Houston Comm Coll System (TX)
Jefferson State Comm Coll (AL)
Leeward Comm Coll (HI)
Lehigh Carbon Comm Coll (PA)
Miami Dade Coll (FL)
New England Inst of Technology (RI)
Northampton Comm Coll (PA)
Northeast Comm Coll (NE)
Oakland Comm Coll (MI)
Salt Lake Comm Coll (UT)
Santa Fe Comm Coll (NM)
Springfield Tech Comm Coll (MA)
Tompkins Cortland Comm Coll (NY)
Waubonsee Comm Coll (IL)

RADIOLOGIC TECHNOLOGY/ SCIENCE

Amarillo Coll (TX)
Arizona Western Coll (AZ)

Austin Comm Coll (TX)
Barton County Comm Coll (KS)
Blackhawk Tech Coll (WI)
Career Tech Coll (LA)
Carl Albert State Coll (OK)
Carolinas Coll of Health Sciences (NC)
Casper Coll (WY)
Central Maine Medical Center Coll of Nursing and Health Professions (ME)
Central Oregon Comm Coll (OR)
Century Coll (MN)
Clark Coll (WA)
Comm Coll of Rhode Island (RI)
Danville Area Comm Coll (IL)
Delaware Tech & Comm Coll, Jack F. Owens Campus (DE)
Delaware Tech & Comm Coll, Stanton/Wilmington Campus (DE)
El Centro Coll (TX)
Elgin Comm Coll (IL)
Fayetteville Tech Comm Coll (NC)
Foothill Coll (CA)
GateWay Comm Coll (AZ)
Georgia Highlands Coll (GA)
Harper Coll (IL)
Harrisburg Area Comm Coll (PA)
H. Councill Trenholm State Tech Coll (AL)
Houston Comm Coll System (TX)
Jefferson State Comm Coll (AL)
John Wood Comm Coll (IL)
Kankakee Comm Coll (IL)
Kaskaskia Coll (IL)
Kilgore Coll (TX)
Lake Michigan Coll (MI)
Lake Superior Coll (MN)
Laramie County Comm Coll (WY)
Lincoln Land Comm Coll (IL)
Marion Tech Coll (OH)
Miami Dade Coll (FL)
Minnesota State Coll–Southeast Tech (MN)
Minnesota State Comm and Tech Coll (MN)
Minnesota West Comm and Tech Coll (MN)
Mitchell Tech Inst (SD)
Montana State U–Great Falls Coll of Technology (MT)
Moraine Valley Comm Coll (IL)
Northampton Comm Coll (PA)
Northeast Iowa Comm Coll (IA)
Northern Essex Comm Coll (MA)
Northland Comm and Tech Coll– Thief River Falls & East Grand Forks (MN)
Oklahoma State U, Oklahoma City (OK)
Owens Comm Coll, Toledo (OH)
Pasco-Hernando Comm Coll (FL)
Pima Comm Coll (AZ)
Pima Medical Inst, Mesa (AZ)
Pima Medical Inst, Tucson (AZ)
Pima Medical Inst (CA)
Pima Medical Inst, Denver (CO)
Pima Medical Inst (NV)
Pima Medical Inst, Albuquerque (NM)
Pima Medical Inst, Seattle (WA)
Polk State Coll (FL)
Pueblo Comm Coll (CO)
Randolph Comm Coll (NC)
St. Luke's Coll (IA)
Sandhills Comm Coll (NC)
South Suburban Coll (IL)
Spencerian Coll (KY)
Springfield Tech Comm Coll (MA)
Union County Coll (NJ)
Wenatchee Valley Coll (WA)
Westmoreland County Comm Coll (PA)

RADIOLOGIST ASSISTANT

Clovis Comm Coll (NM)

RADIO, TELEVISION, AND DIGITAL COMMUNICATION RELATED

Montgomery County Comm Coll (PA)
Northwest Coll (WY)

RANGE SCIENCE AND MANAGEMENT

Casper Coll (WY)
Central Wyoming Coll (WY)
Northwest Coll (WY)
Sheridan Coll (WY)
Snow Coll (UT)
Trinity Valley Comm Coll (TX)

REAL ESTATE

Amarillo Coll (TX)
Antelope Valley Coll (CA)
Austin Comm Coll (TX)
Bristol Comm Coll (MA)
Cincinnati State Tech and Comm Coll (OH)
Coll of the Canyons (CA)
Collin County Comm Coll District (TX)
Dakota County Tech Coll (MN)
De Anza Coll (CA)
Dodge City Comm Coll (KS)
Eastern Gateway Comm Coll (OH)
East Los Angeles Coll (CA)
Edison State Comm Coll (OH)
Florida State Coll at Jacksonville (FL)
Foothill Coll (CA)
Golden West Coll (CA)
Harrisburg Area Comm Coll (PA)
Houston Comm Coll System (TX)
Kent State U at Ashtabula (OH)
Los Angeles Harbor Coll (CA)
Mendocino Coll (CA)
Mesa Comm Coll (AZ)
Montgomery County Comm Coll (PA)
Morton Coll (IL)
Northeast Comm Coll (NE)
Northern Essex Comm Coll (MA)
North Seattle Comm Coll (WA)
Rainy River Comm Coll (MN)
San Diego City Coll (CA)
Santa Barbara City Coll (CA)
Scottsdale Comm Coll (AZ)
Southern State Comm Coll (OH)
Terra State Comm Coll (OH)
Trinity Valley Comm Coll (TX)
Westmoreland County Comm Coll (PA)

RECEPTIONIST

Alexandria Tech and Comm Coll (MN)
Bristol Comm Coll (MA)
Dakota Coll at Bottineau (ND)

RECORDING ARTS TECHNOLOGY

The Art Inst of Seattle (WA)
Collin County Comm Coll District (TX)
Comm Coll of Philadelphia (PA)
Glendale Comm Coll (AZ)
Lehigh Carbon Comm Coll (PA)
Miami Dade Coll (FL)
Montgomery County Comm Coll (PA)
New England Inst of Technology (RI)
Northeast Comm Coll (NE)
Phoenix Coll (AZ)
Springfield Tech Comm Coll (MA)
Union County Coll (NJ)

REGISTERED NURSING, NURSING ADMINISTRATION, NURSING RESEARCH AND CLINICAL NURSING RELATED

John Wood Comm Coll (IL)

REGISTERED NURSING/ REGISTERED NURSE

Aiken Tech Coll (SC)
Alamance Comm Coll (NC)
Alexandria Tech and Comm Coll (MN)
Amarillo Coll (TX)
Ancilla Coll (IN)
Anoka-Ramsey Comm Coll (MN)
Anoka-Ramsey Comm Coll, Cambridge Campus (MN)
Antelope Valley Coll (CA)
Athens Tech Coll (GA)
Austin Comm Coll (TX)
Bainbridge Coll (GA)

Barton County Comm Coll (KS)
Beaufort County Comm Coll (NC)
Bellingham Tech Coll (WA)
Big Bend Comm Coll (WA)
Blackhawk Tech Coll (WI)
Borough of Manhattan Comm Coll of the City U of New York (NY)
Bristol Comm Coll (MA)
Bucks County Comm Coll (PA)
Burlington County Coll (NJ)
Cape Fear Comm Coll (NC)
Carl Albert State Coll (OK)
Carolinas Coll of Health Sciences (NC)
Carroll Comm Coll (MD)
Casper Coll (WY)
Catawba Valley Comm Coll (NC)
Cayuga County Comm Coll (NY)
Cecil Coll (MD)
Central Carolina Tech Coll (SC)
Central Comm Coll–Grand Island Campus (NE)
Central Lakes Coll (MN)
Central Maine Comm Coll (ME)
Central Maine Medical Center Coll of Nursing and Health Professions (ME)
Central New Mexico Comm Coll (NM)
Central Oregon Comm Coll (OR)
Central Wyoming Coll (WY)
Century Coll (MN)
Chandler-Gilbert Comm Coll (AZ)
Chipola Coll (FL)
Chippewa Valley Tech Coll (WI)
Cincinnati State Tech and Comm Coll (OH)
City Colls of Chicago, Harry S. Truman College (IL)
Clarendon Coll (TX)
Clark Coll (WA)
Cleveland State Comm Coll (TN)
Clovis Comm Coll (NM)
Coll of Central Florida (FL)
Coll of Lake County (IL)
Coll of the Canyons (CA)
Collin County Comm Coll District (TX)
Colorado Mountain Coll (CO)
Columbus Tech Coll (GA)
Comm Coll of Philadelphia (PA)
Comm Coll of Rhode Island (RI)
Corning Comm Coll (NY)
Crowder Coll (MO)
Dabney S. Lancaster Comm Coll (VA)
Dakota Coll at Bottineau (ND)
Danville Area Comm Coll (IL)
Darton Coll (GA)
Daytona State Coll (FL)
De Anza Coll (CA)
Delaware Tech & Comm Coll, Jack F. Owens Campus (DE)
Delaware Tech & Comm Coll, Stanton/Wilmington Campus (DE)
Delaware Tech & Comm Coll, Terry Campus (DE)
Dodge City Comm Coll (KS)
Doña Ana Comm Coll (NM)
Dutchess Comm Coll (NY)
Dyersburg State Comm Coll (TN)
Eastern Arizona Coll (AZ)
East Los Angeles Coll (CA)
Edison State Comm Coll (OH)
El Centro Coll (TX)
Elgin Comm Coll (IL)
Fayetteville Tech Comm Coll (NC)
Fiorello H. LaGuardia Comm Coll of the City U of New York (NY)
Florida State Coll at Jacksonville (FL)
Fox Valley Tech Coll (WI)
Frederick Comm Coll (MD)
Front Range Comm Coll (CO)
Fulton-Montgomery Comm Coll (NY)
Gadsden State Comm Coll (AL)
Gateway Comm and Tech Coll (KY)
GateWay Comm Coll (AZ)
Gateway Comm Coll (CT)
Georgia Highlands Coll (GA)
Glendale Comm Coll (AZ)
Golden West Coll (CA)
Goodwin Coll (CT)
Grand Rapids Comm Coll (MI)
Grays Harbor Coll (WA)
Great Basin Coll (NV)

Gulf Coast Comm Coll (FL)
Hagerstown Comm Coll (MD)
Harford Comm Coll (MD)
Harper Coll (IL)
Harrisburg Area Comm Coll (PA)
Hawkeye Comm Coll (IA)
Hesston Coll (KS)
Highland Comm Coll (IL)
Hillsborough Comm Coll (FL)
Holyoke Comm Coll (MA)
Housatonic Comm Coll (CT)
Houston Comm Coll System (TX)
Howard Comm Coll (MD)
Illinois Eastern Comm Colls, Frontier Community College (IL)
Illinois Eastern Comm Colls, Olney Central College (IL)
Indian River State Coll (FL)
Inver Hills Comm Coll (MN)
ITT Tech Inst, Phoenix (AZ)
ITT Tech Inst, Fort Lauderdale (FL)
ITT Tech Inst, Jacksonville (FL)
ITT Tech Inst, Lake Mary (FL)
ITT Tech Inst, Tampa (FL)
ITT Tech Inst (ID)
ITT Tech Inst, Orland Park (IL)
ITT Tech Inst, Fort Wayne (IN)
ITT Tech Inst, Indianapolis (IN)
ITT Tech Inst, Merrillville (IN)
ITT Tech Inst, Newburgh (IN)
ITT Tech Inst, Louisville (KY)
ITT Tech Inst, Canton (MI)
ITT Tech Inst, Earth City (MO)
ITT Tech Inst (NE)
ITT Tech Inst, Henderson (NV)
ITT Tech Inst (NM)
ITT Tech Inst, Hilliard (OH)
ITT Tech Inst, Norwood (OH)
ITT Tech Inst, Tulsa (OK)
ITT Tech Inst (OR)
ITT Tech Inst, Norfolk (VA)
ITT Tech Inst (WV)
Ivy Tech Comm Coll–Bloomington (IN)
Ivy Tech Comm Coll–Central Indiana (IN)
Ivy Tech Comm Coll–East Central (IN)
Ivy Tech Comm Coll–Lafayette (IN)
Ivy Tech Comm Coll–North Central (IN)
Ivy Tech Comm Coll–Northwest (IN)
Ivy Tech Comm Coll–Richmond (IN)
Ivy Tech Comm Coll–Southeast (IN)
Ivy Tech Comm Coll–Southern Indiana (IN)
Ivy Tech Comm Coll–Southwest (IN)
Ivy Tech Comm Coll–Wabash Valley (IN)
Jackson Comm Coll (MI)
James Sprunt Comm Coll (NC)
Jefferson Coll (MO)
Jefferson State Comm Coll (AL)
Johnston Comm Coll (NC)
John Tyler Comm Coll (VA)
J. Sargeant Reynolds Comm Coll (VA)
Kankakee Comm Coll (IL)
Kaskaskia Coll (IL)
Kent State U at Ashtabula (OH)
Kent State U at East Liverpool (OH)
Kent State U at Tuscarawas (OH)
Kilgore Coll (TX)
Kingsborough Comm Coll of the City U of New York (NY)
Kirtland Comm Coll (MI)
Lake Michigan Coll (MI)
Lake-Sumter Comm Coll (FL)
Lake Superior Coll (MN)
Lamar Comm Coll (CO)
Laramie County Comm Coll (WY)
Lawson State Comm Coll (AL)
Lehigh Carbon Comm Coll (PA)
Lincoln Land Comm Coll (IL)
Linn-Benton Comm Coll (OR)
Lonestar Coll–Cy-Fair (TX)
Lonestar Coll–Kingwood (TX)
Lonestar Coll–Montgomery (TX)
Lonestar Coll–North Harris (TX)
Lonestar Coll–Tomball (TX)
Los Angeles Harbor Coll (CA)
Lower Columbia Coll (WA)
Lurleen B. Wallace Comm Coll (AL)
Macomb Comm Coll (MI)
Marion Tech Coll (OH)
Massachusetts Bay Comm Coll (MA)

McHenry County Coll (IL)
Mesa Comm Coll (AZ)
Metropolitan Comm Coll–Penn Valley (MO)
Miami Dade Coll (FL)
Midlands Tech Coll (SC)
Mid-Plains Comm Coll, North Platte (NE)
Minnesota State Coll–Southeast Tech (MN)
Minnesota State Comm and Tech Coll (MN)
Minnesota West Comm and Tech Coll (MN)
Missouri State U–West Plains (MO)
Mohave Comm Coll (AZ)
Mohawk Valley Comm Coll (NY)
Monroe County Comm Coll (MI)
Montcalm Comm Coll (MI)
Montgomery Coll (MD)
Montgomery County Comm Coll (PA)
Moraine Park Tech Coll (WI)
Moraine Valley Comm Coll (IL)
Morton Coll (IL)
Motlow State Comm Coll (TN)
Mountain Empire Comm Coll (VA)
Muskegon Comm Coll (MI)
New England Inst of Technology (RI)
New Mexico State U–Alamogordo (NM)
Niagara County Comm Coll (NY)
Northampton Comm Coll (PA)
Northeast Comm Coll (NE)
Northeast Iowa Comm Coll (IA)
Northern Essex Comm Coll (MA)
North Hennepin Comm Coll (MN)
North Idaho Coll (ID)
North Iowa Area Comm Coll (IA)
Northland Comm and Tech Coll–Thief River Falls & East Grand Forks (MN)
North Seattle Comm Coll (WA)
Northwest Coll (WY)
Northwest-Shoals Comm Coll (AL)
Northwest Tech Coll (MN)
Norwalk Comm Coll (CT)
Oakland Comm Coll (MI)
Ocean County Coll (NJ)
Oklahoma City Comm Coll (OK)
Oklahoma State U, Oklahoma City (OK)
Olympic Coll (WA)
Onondaga Comm Coll (NY)
Oregon Coast Comm Coll (OR)
Owensboro Comm and Tech Coll (KY)
Owens Comm Coll, Toledo (OH)
Palm Beach State Coll (FL)
Panola Coll (TX)
Pasco-Hernando Comm Coll (FL)
Paul D. Camp Comm Coll (VA)
Penn State Fayette, The Eberly Campus (PA)
Penn State Mont Alto (PA)
Penn State Worthington Scranton (PA)
Pensacola State Coll (FL)
Phillips Beth Israel School of Nursing (NY)
Phoenix Coll (AZ)
Pima Comm Coll (AZ)
Pima Medical Inst, Tucson (AZ)
Pima Medical Inst, Albuquerque (NM)
Polk State Coll (FL)
Pratt Comm Coll (KS)
Pueblo Comm Coll (CO)
Quinsigamond Comm Coll (MA)
Randolph Comm Coll (NC)
Raritan Valley Comm Coll (NJ)
Rockingham Comm Coll (NC)
Rogue Comm Coll (OR)
Saint Charles Comm Coll (MO)
St. Cloud Tech & Comm Coll (MN)
St. Joseph's Coll of Nursing (NY)
St. Luke's Coll (IA)
Salt Lake Comm Coll (UT)
Sandhills Comm Coll (NC)
San Diego City Coll (CA)
San Juan Coll (NM)
Santa Barbara City Coll (CA)
Santa Fe Comm Coll (NM)
Santa Rosa Jr Coll (CA)
Sauk Valley Comm Coll (IL)
Scottsdale Comm Coll (AZ)

Seminole State Coll of Florida (FL)
Sheridan Coll (WY)
Solano Comm Coll (CA)
Southeastern Comm Coll (IA)
Southern State Comm Coll (OH)
Southside Virginia Comm Coll (VA)
Southwestern Michigan Comm Coll (MI)
Southwest Georgia Tech Coll (GA)
Southwest Mississippi Comm Coll (MS)
Spartanburg Comm Coll (SC)
Spencerian Coll (KY)
Springfield Tech Comm Coll (MA)
Stark State Coll of Technology (OH)
Suffolk County Comm Coll (NY)
Tallahassee Comm Coll (FL)
Terra State Comm Coll (OH)
Three Rivers Comm Coll (CT)
Tompkins Cortland Comm Coll (NY)
Trident Tech Coll (SC)
Trinity Valley Comm Coll (TX)
Tyler Jr Coll (TX)
Union County Coll (NJ)
U of Arkansas Comm Coll at Morrilton (AR)
U of Pittsburgh at Titusville (PA)
Waubonsee Comm Coll (IL)
Waukesha County Tech Coll (WI)
Wenatchee Valley Coll (WA)
Westchester Comm Coll (NY)
Western Iowa Tech Comm Coll (IA)
West Kentucky Comm and Tech Coll (KY)
Westmoreland County Comm Coll (PA)
West Virginia Northern Comm Coll (WV)
White Mountains Comm Coll (NH)
Wilson Comm Coll (NC)
Wisconsin Indianhead Tech Coll (WI)
Yakima Valley Comm Coll (WA)
Yavapai Coll (AZ)

REHABILITATION AND THERAPEUTIC PROFESSIONS RELATED

Central Wyoming Coll (WY)
Union County Coll (NJ)

RELIGIOUS STUDIES

Allen Comm Coll (KS)
Amarillo Coll (TX)
Barton County Comm Coll (KS)
Cowley County Comm Coll and Area Vocational–Tech School (KS)
Kilgore Coll (TX)
Laramie County Comm Coll (WY)
Lonestar Coll–Cy-Fair (TX)
Lonestar Coll–Montgomery (TX)
Lonestar Coll–North Harris (TX)
Lonestar Coll–Tomball (TX)
Orange Coast Coll (CA)
Palm Beach State Coll (FL)
Trinity Valley Comm Coll (TX)

RESORT MANAGEMENT

Lehigh Carbon Comm Coll (PA)

RESPIRATORY CARE THERAPY

Amarillo Coll (TX)
Arkansas State U–Mountain Home (AR)
Athens Tech Coll (GA)
Augusta Tech Coll (GA)
Barton County Comm Coll (KS)
Burlington County Coll (NJ)
Casper Coll (WY)
Catawba Valley Comm Coll (NC)
Central New Mexico Comm Coll (NM)
Chippewa Valley Tech Coll (WI)
Cincinnati State Tech and Comm Coll (OH)
Collin County Comm Coll District (TX)
The Comm Coll of Baltimore County (MD)
Comm Coll of Philadelphia (PA)
Comm Coll of Rhode Island (RI)
Darton Coll (GA)
Daytona State Coll (FL)

Dodge City Comm Coll (KS)
Doña Ana Comm Coll (NM)
Eastern Gateway Comm Coll (OH)
East Los Angeles Coll (CA)
El Centro Coll (TX)
Fayetteville Tech Comm Coll (NC)
Florida State Coll at Jacksonville (FL)
Foothill Coll (CA)
Frederick Comm Coll (MD)
GateWay Comm Coll (AZ)
Georgia Highlands Coll (GA)
Goodwin Coll (CT)
Gulf Coast Comm Coll (FL)
Gwinnett Tech Coll (GA)
Harrisburg Area Comm Coll (PA)
Hawkeye Comm Coll (IA)
Hillsborough Comm Coll (FL)
Houston Comm Coll System (TX)
Indian River State Coll (FL)
Ivy Tech Comm Coll–Central Indiana (IN)
Ivy Tech Comm Coll–Lafayette (IN)
Ivy Tech Comm Coll–Northeast (IN)
Ivy Tech Comm Coll–Northwest (IN)
Ivy Tech Comm Coll–Southern Indiana (IN)
J. Sargeant Reynolds Comm Coll (VA)
Kankakee Comm Coll (IL)
Kaskaskia Coll (IL)
Lake Superior Coll (MN)
Lonestar Coll–Kingwood (TX)
Lonestar Coll–North Harris (TX)
Macomb Comm Coll (MI)
Manchester Comm Coll (CT)
Massachusetts Bay Comm Coll (MA)
Metropolitan Comm Coll–Penn Valley (MO)
Miami Dade Coll (FL)
Midlands Tech Coll (SC)
Mohawk Valley Comm Coll (NY)
Monroe County Comm Coll (MI)
Montana State U–Great Falls Coll of Technology (MT)
Moraine Park Tech Coll (WI)
Moraine Valley Comm Coll (IL)
Mountain Empire Comm Coll (VA)
Northeast Iowa Comm Coll (IA)
Northern Essex Comm Coll (MA)
Northland Comm and Tech Coll–Thief River Falls & East Grand Forks (MN)
Norwalk Comm Coll (CT)
Oakland Comm Coll (MI)
Oklahoma City Comm Coll (OK)
Onondaga Comm Coll (NY)
Orange Coast Coll (CA)
Pima Comm Coll (AZ)
Polk State Coll (FL)
Pueblo Comm Coll (CO)
Quinsigamond Comm Coll (MA)
Raritan Valley Comm Coll (NJ)
Rockingham Comm Coll (NC)
St. Luke's Coll (IA)
St. Philip's Coll (TX)
Sandhills Comm Coll (NC)
San Juan Coll (NM)
Santa Fe Comm Coll (NM)
Seminole State Coll of Florida (FL)
Southeastern Comm Coll (IA)
Southern State Comm Coll (OH)
Southside Virginia Comm Coll (VA)
Southwest Georgia Tech Coll (GA)
Spartanburg Comm Coll (SC)
Springfield Tech Comm Coll (MA)
Stark State Coll of Technology (OH)
Tallahassee Comm Coll (FL)
Trident Tech Coll (SC)
Tyler Jr Coll (TX)
Union County Coll (NJ)
Volunteer State Comm Coll (TN)
Westchester Comm Coll (NY)
West Kentucky Comm and Tech Coll (KY)
West Virginia Northern Comm Coll (WV)

RESPIRATORY THERAPY TECHNICIAN

Augusta Tech Coll (GA)
Borough of Manhattan Comm Coll of the City U of New York (NY)

Career Tech Coll (LA)
Columbus Tech Coll (GA)
Delaware Tech & Comm Coll, Jack F. Owens Campus (DE)
Delaware Tech & Comm Coll, Stanton/Wilmington Campus (DE)
Georgia Northwestern Tech Coll (GA)
Heart of Georgia Tech Coll (GA)
Miami Dade Coll (FL)
Missouri State U–West Plains (MO)
Northern Essex Comm Coll (MA)
Okefenokee Tech Coll (GA)
Pima Medical Inst, Mesa (AZ)
Pima Medical Inst, Tucson (AZ)
Pima Medical Inst (CA)
Pima Medical Inst, Denver (CO)
Pima Medical Inst (NV)
Pima Medical Inst, Albuquerque (NM)
Southeastern Tech Coll (GA)
Southern Crescent Tech Coll (GA)

RESTAURANT, CULINARY, AND CATERING MANAGEMENT

Central Comm Coll–Hastings Campus (NE)
Cincinnati State Tech and Comm Coll (OH)
Coll of Central Florida (FL)
Coll of Lake County (IL)
Coll of the Canyons (CA)
Delaware Tech & Comm Coll, Stanton/Wilmington Campus (DE)
Elgin Comm Coll (IL)
Fox Valley Tech Coll (WI)
Gulf Coast Comm Coll (FL)
Hillsborough Comm Coll (FL)
JNA Inst of Culinary Arts (PA)
John Wood Comm Coll (IL)
Linn-Benton Comm Coll (OR)
Mohawk Valley Comm Coll (NY)
Moraine Park Tech Coll (WI)
Moraine Valley Comm Coll (IL)
Orange Coast Coll (CA)
Pensacola State Coll (FL)
Pima Comm Coll (AZ)
Raritan Valley Comm Coll (NJ)
Waukesha County Tech Coll (WI)
Westmoreland County Comm Coll (PA)

RESTAURANT/FOOD SERVICES MANAGEMENT

Burlington County Coll (NJ)
Fiorello H. LaGuardia Comm Coll of the City U of New York (NY)
Hillsborough Comm Coll (FL)
Northampton Comm Coll (PA)
Norwalk Comm Coll (CT)
Oakland Comm Coll (MI)
Owens Comm Coll, Toledo (OH)
Quinsigamond Comm Coll (MA)
The Restaurant School at Walnut Hill Coll (PA)
St. Philip's Coll (TX)

RETAILING

Alamance Comm Coll (NC)
Burlington County Coll (NJ)
Casper Coll (WY)
Central Oregon Comm Coll (OR)
Clark Coll (WA)
Elgin Comm Coll (IL)
Florida State Coll at Jacksonville (FL)
Fox Coll (IL)
Harrisburg Area Comm Coll (PA)
Holyoke Comm Coll (MA)
Minnesota State Coll–Southeast Tech (MN)
Moraine Valley Comm Coll (IL)
Orange Coast Coll (CA)
Waubonsee Comm Coll (IL)
Waukesha County Tech Coll (WI)

RHETORIC AND COMPOSITION

Allen Comm Coll (KS)
Amarillo Coll (TX)
Austin Comm Coll (TX)
Bainbridge Coll (GA)

Carl Albert State Coll (OK)
Clarendon Coll (TX)
De Anza Coll (CA)
Dodge City Comm Coll (KS)
East Los Angeles Coll (CA)
Indian River State Coll (FL)
Kilgore Coll (TX)
Linn-Benton Comm Coll (OR)
Lonestar Coll–Cy-Fair (TX)
Lonestar Coll–Kingwood (TX)
Lonestar Coll–Montgomery (TX)
Lonestar Coll–North Harris (TX)
Lonestar Coll–Tomball (TX)
Mendocino Coll (CA)
Monroe County Comm Coll (MI)
Northeast Comm Coll (NE)
Pratt Comm Coll (KS)
St. Philip's Coll (TX)
San Diego City Coll (CA)
Sauk Valley Comm Coll (IL)
Trinity Valley Comm Coll (TX)

ROBOTICS TECHNOLOGY

Casper Coll (WY)
Central Lakes Coll (MN)
Daytona State Coll (FL)
Ivy Tech Comm Coll–Columbus (IN)
Ivy Tech Comm Coll–Lafayette (IN)
Ivy Tech Comm Coll–North Central (IN)
Ivy Tech Comm Coll–Northeast (IN)
Ivy Tech Comm Coll–Richmond (IN)
Ivy Tech Comm Coll–Southwest (IN)
Ivy Tech Comm Coll–Wabash Valley (IN)
Lonestar Coll–Montgomery (TX)
Macomb Comm Coll (MI)
Minnesota West Comm and Tech Coll (MN)
Oakland Comm Coll (MI)
Sullivan Coll of Technology and Design (KY)
Terra State Comm Coll (OH)

RUSSIAN

Austin Comm Coll (TX)

SALES, DISTRIBUTION, AND MARKETING OPERATIONS

Aiken Tech Coll (SC)
Burlington County Coll (NJ)
Central Carolina Tech Coll (SC)
Coll of the Canyons (CA)
Collin County Comm Coll District (TX)
Edison State Comm Coll (OH)
Gadsden State Comm Coll (AL)
Harper Coll (IL)
Harrisburg Area Comm Coll (PA)
Hawkeye Comm Coll (IA)
Lake Region State Coll (ND)
Midlands Tech Coll (SC)
Montgomery County Comm Coll (PA)
Northeast Iowa Comm Coll (IA)
North Iowa Area Comm Coll (IA)
Northwest Tech Coll (MN)
Owens Comm Coll, Toledo (OH)
St. Cloud Tech & Comm Coll (MN)
Santa Barbara City Coll (CA)
Spartanburg Comm Coll (SC)
Western Iowa Tech Comm Coll (IA)

SALON/BEAUTY SALON MANAGEMENT

Oakland Comm Coll (MI)

SCIENCE TEACHER EDUCATION

Darton Coll (GA)
Dutchess Comm Coll (NY)
Moraine Valley Comm Coll (IL)
Sandhills Comm Coll (NC)
Snow Coll (UT)

SCIENCE TECHNOLOGIES RELATED

Cascadia Comm Coll (WA)
Cincinnati State Tech and Comm Coll (OH)
Cleveland State Comm Coll (TN)

The Comm Coll of Baltimore County (MD)
Dakota Coll at Bottineau (ND)
Delaware Tech & Comm Coll, Stanton/Wilmington Campus (DE)
Front Range Comm Coll (CO)
Harford Comm Coll (MD)
North Dakota State Coll of Science (ND)
Pueblo Comm Coll (CO)
West Virginia Northern Comm Coll (WV)

SCULPTURE
De Anza Coll (CA)
Santa Fe Comm Coll (NM)

SECONDARY EDUCATION
Allen Comm Coll (KS)
Ancilla Coll (IN)
Arizona Western Coll (AZ)
Austin Comm Coll (TX)
Barton County Comm Coll (KS)
Carl Albert State Coll (OK)
Central Wyoming Coll (WY)
Clarendon Coll (TX)
Collin County Comm Coll District (TX)
Eastern Arizona Coll (AZ)
Frank Phillips Coll (TX)
Georgia Highlands Coll (GA)
Georgia Military Coll (GA)
Harrisburg Area Comm Coll (PA)
Howard Comm Coll (MD)
Kankakee Comm Coll (IL)
Lake Michigan Coll (MI)
Mohawk Valley Comm Coll (NY)
Montgomery County Comm Coll (PA)
Northampton Comm Coll (PA)
Northeast Comm Coll (NE)
Northwest Coll (WY)
Panola Coll (TX)
Red Rocks Comm Coll (CO)
San Juan Coll (NM)
Sauk Valley Comm Coll (IL)
Sheridan Coll (WY)
Springfield Tech Comm Coll (MA)

SECURITIES SERVICES ADMINISTRATION
Western Iowa Tech Comm Coll (IA)

SECURITY AND LOSS PREVENTION
Cincinnati State Tech and Comm Coll (OH)
Owens Comm Coll, Toledo (OH)
Union County Coll (NJ)

SELLING SKILLS AND SALES
Alexandria Tech and Comm Coll (MN)
Central Wyoming Coll (WY)
Clark Coll (WA)
Coll of Lake County (IL)
Danville Area Comm Coll (IL)
John Wood Comm Coll (IL)
Lake Superior Coll (MN)
McHenry County Coll (IL)
Minnesota State Coll–Southeast Tech (MN)
Orange Coast Coll (CA)
Santa Barbara City Coll (CA)

SHEET METAL TECHNOLOGY
GateWay Comm Coll (AZ)
Ivy Tech Comm Coll–Central Indiana (IN)
Ivy Tech Comm Coll–Lafayette (IN)
Ivy Tech Comm Coll–North Central (IN)
Ivy Tech Comm Coll–Northeast (IN)
Ivy Tech Comm Coll–Northwest (IN)
Ivy Tech Comm Coll–Southern Indiana (IN)
Ivy Tech Comm Coll–Southwest (IN)
Ivy Tech Comm Coll–Wabash Valley (IN)
Macomb Comm Coll (MI)
Oakland Comm Coll (MI)
Terra State Comm Coll (OH)

SIGN LANGUAGE INTERPRETATION AND TRANSLATION
Austin Comm Coll (TX)
Burlington County Coll (NJ)
Cincinnati State Tech and Comm Coll (OH)
Clovis Comm Coll (NM)
Coll of the Canyons (CA)
Collin County Comm Coll District (TX)
The Comm Coll of Baltimore County (MD)
Comm Coll of Philadelphia (PA)
Eastfield Coll (TX)
Florida State Coll at Jacksonville (FL)
Front Range Comm Coll (CO)
Golden West Coll (CA)
Houston Comm Coll System (TX)
Lake Region State Coll (ND)
Miami Dade Coll (FL)
Mohawk Valley Comm Coll (NY)
Montgomery Coll (MD)
Northern Essex Comm Coll (MA)
Oakland Comm Coll (MI)
Ocean County Coll (NJ)
Oklahoma State U, Oklahoma City (OK)
Phoenix Coll (AZ)
Pima Comm Coll (AZ)
Salt Lake Comm Coll (UT)
Santa Fe Comm Coll (NM)
Suffolk County Comm Coll (NY)
Tyler Jr Coll (TX)
Union County Coll (NJ)
Waubonsee Comm Coll (IL)
Wilson Comm Coll (NC)

SMALL BUSINESS ADMINISTRATION
Borough of Manhattan Comm Coll of the City U of New York (NY)
Bristol Comm Coll (MA)
Coll of the Canyons (CA)
Dakota Coll at Bottineau (ND)
Harper Coll (IL)
Harrisburg Area Comm Coll (PA)
Lake Region State Coll (ND)
Moraine Valley Comm Coll (IL)
North Hennepin Comm Coll (MN)
Raritan Valley Comm Coll (NJ)
South Suburban Coll (IL)
Springfield Tech Comm Coll (MA)
Waubonsee Comm Coll (IL)

SMALL ENGINE MECHANICS AND REPAIR TECHNOLOGY
Alexandria Tech and Comm Coll (MN)
Kirtland Comm Coll (MI)
Mitchell Tech Inst (SD)
North Dakota State Coll of Science (ND)

SOCIAL PSYCHOLOGY
Macomb Comm Coll (MI)

SOCIAL SCIENCES
Amarillo Coll (TX)
Arizona Western Coll (AZ)
Bristol Comm Coll (MA)
Bucks County Comm Coll (PA)
Burlington County Coll (NJ)
Carl Albert State Coll (OK)
Central Oregon Comm Coll (OR)
Central Wyoming Coll (WY)
Clarendon Coll (TX)
Coll of the Canyons (CA)
Colorado Mountain Coll (CO)
Colorado Mountain Coll, Alpine Campus (CO)
Comm Coll of Vermont (VT)
Corning Comm Coll (NY)
Dakota Coll at Bottineau (ND)
De Anza Coll (CA)
Dodge City Comm Coll (KS)
Dutchess Comm Coll (NY)
Foothill Coll (CA)
Fulton-Montgomery Comm Coll (NY)
Georgia Military Coll (GA)
Harrisburg Area Comm Coll (PA)
Housatonic Comm Coll (CT)
Howard Comm Coll (MD)
Indian River State Coll (FL)

J. Sargeant Reynolds Comm Coll (VA)
Kilgore Coll (TX)
Laramie County Comm Coll (WY)
Lehigh Carbon Comm Coll (PA)
Lonestar Coll–Cy-Fair (TX)
Lonestar Coll–Kingwood (TX)
Massachusetts Bay Comm Coll (MA)
Mendocino Coll (CA)
Miami Dade Coll (FL)
Montgomery County Comm Coll (PA)
Niagara County Comm Coll (NY)
Northeast Comm Coll (NE)
North Idaho Coll (ID)
Northwest Coll (WY)
Orange Coast Coll (CA)
Palm Beach State Coll (FL)
Pratt Comm Coll (KS)
San Diego City Coll (CA)
Santa Rosa Jr Coll (CA)
Sheridan Coll (WY)
Solano Comm Coll (CA)
Southwest Mississippi Comm Coll (MS)
State U of New York Coll of Technology at Alfred (NY)
Suffolk County Comm Coll (NY)
Terra State Comm Coll (OH)
Tyler Jr Coll (TX)
Vincennes U Jasper Campus (IN)
Westchester Comm Coll (NY)

SOCIAL STUDIES TEACHER EDUCATION
Casper Coll (WY)

SOCIAL WORK
Allen Comm Coll (KS)
Amarillo Coll (TX)
Austin Comm Coll (TX)
Barton County Comm Coll (KS)
Bristol Comm Coll (MA)
Bucks County Comm Coll (PA)
Casper Coll (WY)
Chandler-Gilbert Comm Coll (AZ)
Chipola Coll (FL)
Coll of Lake County (IL)
Comm Coll of Rhode Island (RI)
Cowley County Comm Coll and Area Vocational–Tech School (KS)
Darton Coll (GA)
Dodge City Comm Coll (KS)
Eastfield Coll (TX)
East Los Angeles Coll (CA)
Edison State Comm Coll (OH)
Elgin Comm Coll (IL)
Harrisburg Area Comm Coll (PA)
Holyoke Comm Coll (MA)
Illinois Eastern Comm Colls, Wabash Valley College (IL)
Indian River State Coll (FL)
Kilian Comm Coll (SD)
Lake Michigan Coll (MI)
Lawson State Comm Coll (AL)
Lonestar Coll–Montgomery (TX)
Manchester Comm Coll (CT)
Marion Tech Coll (OH)
Miami Dade Coll (FL)
Monroe County Comm Coll (MI)
Nashua Comm Coll (NH)
Northampton Comm Coll (PA)
Northeast Iowa Comm Coll (IA)
Owensboro Comm and Tech Coll (KY)
Owens Comm Coll, Toledo (OH)
Palm Beach State Coll (FL)
Potomac State Coll of West Virginia U (WV)
Pratt Comm Coll (KS)
Rogue Comm Coll (OR)
Saint Charles Comm Coll (MO)
St. Philip's Coll (TX)
Salt Lake Comm Coll (UT)
San Diego City Coll (CA)
San Juan Coll (NM)
Santa Fe Comm Coll (NM)
Sauk Valley Comm Coll (IL)
South Suburban Coll (IL)
Southwestern Michigan Coll (MI)
Terra State Comm Coll (OH)
Vincennes U Jasper Campus (IN)
Waubonsee Comm Coll (IL)
West Georgia Tech Coll (GA)
West Virginia Northern Comm Coll (WV)

SOCIAL WORK RELATED
Clarendon Coll (TX)

SOCIOLOGY
Allen Comm Coll (KS)
Austin Comm Coll (TX)
Bainbridge Coll (GA)
Barton County Comm Coll (KS)
Burlington County Coll (NJ)
Casper Coll (WY)
Clarendon Coll (TX)
Coll of the Canyons (CA)
Darton Coll (GA)
De Anza Coll (CA)
Eastern Arizona Coll (AZ)
East Los Angeles Coll (CA)
Foothill Coll (CA)
Frank Phillips Coll (TX)
Georgia Highlands Coll (GA)
Great Basin Coll (NV)
Highland Comm Coll (IL)
Indian River State Coll (FL)
Kilian Comm Coll (SD)
Lake Michigan Coll (MI)
Laramie County Comm Coll (WY)
Lonestar Coll–Cy-Fair (TX)
Lonestar Coll–Kingwood (TX)
Lonestar Coll–Montgomery (TX)
Lonestar Coll–North Harris (TX)
Lonestar Coll–Tomball (TX)
Miami Dade Coll (FL)
Mohave Comm Coll (AZ)
North Idaho Coll (ID)
Northwest Coll (WY)
Oklahoma City Comm Coll (OK)
Orange Coast Coll (CA)
Owens Comm Coll, Toledo (OH)
Pima Comm Coll (AZ)
Potomac State Coll of West Virginia U (WV)
Pratt Comm Coll (KS)
Red Rocks Comm Coll (CO)
Saint Charles Comm Coll (MO)
St. Philip's Coll (TX)
Salt Lake Comm Coll (UT)
San Diego City Coll (CA)
Santa Bárbara City Coll (CA)
Sauk Valley Comm Coll (IL)
Snow Coll (UT)
Trinity Valley Comm Coll (TX)
Vincennes U Jasper Campus (IN)
Wenatchee Valley Coll (WA)

SOCIOLOGY AND ANTHROPOLOGY
Harper Coll (IL)

SOIL SCIENCE AND AGRONOMY
Snow Coll (UT)

SOLAR ENERGY TECHNOLOGY
Arizona Western Coll (AZ)
San Juan Coll (NM)

SPANISH
Arizona Western Coll (AZ)
Austin Comm Coll (TX)
Berkeley City Coll (CA)
Coll of the Canyons (CA)
De Anza Coll (CA)
East Los Angeles Coll (CA)
Fiorello H. LaGuardia Comm Coll of the City U of New York (NY)
Foothill Coll (CA)
Indian River State Coll (FL)
Laramie County Comm Coll (WY)
Mendocino Coll (CA)
Miami Dade Coll (FL)
North Idaho Coll (ID)
Northwest Coll (WY)
Orange Coast Coll (CA)
Red Rocks Comm Coll (CO)
Saint Charles Comm Coll (MO)
St. Philip's Coll (TX)
Santa Barbara City Coll (CA)
Santa Fe Comm Coll (NM)
Sauk Valley Comm Coll (IL)
Snow Coll (UT)
Solano Comm Coll (CA)
Trinity Valley Comm Coll (TX)

SPANISH LANGUAGE TEACHER EDUCATION
The Comm Coll of Baltimore County (MD)

Frederick Comm Coll (MD)
Montgomery Coll (MD)

SPECIAL EDUCATION
Comm Coll of Rhode Island (RI)
Darton Coll (GA)
Highland Comm Coll (IL)
J. Sargeant Reynolds Comm Coll (VA)
Kankakee Comm Coll (IL)
Lehigh Carbon Comm Coll (PA)
Moraine Valley Comm Coll (IL)
San Juan Coll (NM)
Sauk Valley Comm Coll (IL)
Waubonsee Comm Coll (IL)
Wilson Comm Coll (NC)

SPECIAL EDUCATION–EARLY CHILDHOOD
Motlow State Comm Coll (TN)

SPECIAL EDUCATION–INDIVIDUALS WITH HEARING IMPAIRMENTS
Hillsborough Comm Coll (FL)

SPECIAL PRODUCTS MARKETING
Dutchess Comm Coll (NY)
El Centro Coll (TX)
Gateway Comm Coll (CT)
Indian River State Coll (FL)
Metropolitan Comm Coll–Penn Valley (MO)
Muskegon Comm Coll (MI)
Orange Coast Coll (CA)
Palm Beach State Coll (FL)
San Diego City Coll (CA)
Scottsdale Comm Coll (AZ)
Three Rivers Comm Coll (CT)
Yakima Valley Comm Coll (WA)

SPEECH COMMUNICATION AND RHETORIC
Barton County Comm Coll (KS)
Bristol Comm Coll (MA)
Casper Coll (WY)
Central Oregon Comm Coll (OR)
Collin County Comm Coll District (TX)
Dutchess Comm Coll (NY)
Eastfield Coll (TX)
Edison State Comm Coll (OH)
Fiorello H. LaGuardia Comm Coll of the City U of New York (NY)
Harper Coll (IL)
Laramie County Comm Coll (WY)
Lehigh Carbon Comm Coll (PA)
Lonestar Coll–Cy-Fair (TX)
Macomb Comm Coll (MI)
Manchester Comm Coll (CT)
Massachusetts Bay Comm Coll (MA)
Montgomery Coll (MD)
Montgomery County Comm Coll (PA)
Mountain View Coll (TX)
Northampton Comm Coll (PA)
Northwest Coll (WY)
Norwalk Comm Coll (CT)
Onondaga Comm Coll (NY)
Owens Comm Coll, Toledo (OH)
Red Rocks Comm Coll (CO)
Salt Lake Comm Coll (UT)
Santa Barbara City Coll (CA)
Sauk Valley Comm Coll (IL)
Tompkins Cortland Comm Coll (NY)
Tyler Jr Coll (TX)

SPEECH-LANGUAGE PATHOLOGY
Mitchell Tech Inst (SD)

SPEECH-LANGUAGE PATHOLOGY ASSISTANT
Fayetteville Tech Comm Coll (NC)

SPEECH TEACHER EDUCATION
Darton Coll (GA)
Highland Comm Coll (IL)
Pratt Comm Coll (KS)

SPORT AND FITNESS ADMINISTRATION/ MANAGEMENT

Barton County Comm Coll (KS)
Bucks County Comm Coll (PA)
Central Oregon Comm Coll (OR)
Century Coll (MN)
Clark Coll (WA)
Holyoke Comm Coll (MA)
Howard Comm Coll (MD)
Kingsborough Comm Coll of the City U of New York (NY)
Lake-Sumter Comm Coll (FL)
Lehigh Carbon Comm Coll (PA)
Niagara County Comm Coll (NY)
Northampton Comm Coll (PA)
North Iowa Area Comm Coll (IA)
Salt Lake Comm Coll (UT)
Springfield Tech Comm Coll (MA)
Tompkins Cortland Comm Coll (NY)
Union County Coll (NJ)

STATISTICS RELATED

Casper Coll (WY)

STRUCTURAL ENGINEERING

Bristol Comm Coll (MA)
Moraine Park Tech Coll (WI)

SUBSTANCE ABUSE/ ADDICTION COUNSELING

Amarillo Coll (TX)
Austin Comm Coll (TX)
Casper Coll (WY)
Central Oregon Comm Coll (OR)
Century Coll (MN)
Chippewa Valley Tech Coll (WI)
Clark Coll (WA)
Coll of Lake County (IL)
The Comm Coll of Baltimore County (MD)
Comm Coll of Rhode Island (RI)
Corning Comm Coll (NY)
Dawson Comm Coll (MT)
Delaware Tech & Comm Coll, Stanton/Wilmington Campus (DE)
Delaware Tech & Comm Coll, Terry Campus (DE)
Eastfield Coll (TX)
Florida State Coll at Jacksonville (FL)
Fox Valley Tech Coll (WI)
Gadsden State Comm Coll (AL)
Gateway Comm Coll (CT)
Harford Comm Coll (MD)
Housatonic Comm Coll (CT)
Howard Comm Coll (MD)
Kilian Comm Coll (SD)
Lower Columbia Coll (WA)
Mendocino Coll (CA)
Mesabi Range Comm and Tech Coll (MN)
Miami Dade Coll (FL)
Middlesex Comm Coll (CT)
Mohave Comm Coll (AZ)
Mohawk Valley Comm Coll (NY)
Moraine Park Tech Coll (WI)
Moraine Valley Comm Coll (IL)
Oklahoma State U, Oklahoma City (OK)
Olympic Coll (WA)
Sandhills Comm Coll (NC)
Southeastern Comm Coll (IA)
Suffolk County Comm Coll (NY)
Three Rivers Comm Coll (CT)
Tompkins Cortland Comm Coll (NY)
Tyler Jr Coll (TX)
Wenatchee Valley Coll (WA)
Westchester Comm Coll (NY)
Yakima Valley Comm Coll (WA)

SURGICAL TECHNOLOGY

Athens Tech Coll (GA)
Augusta Tech Coll (GA)
Austin Comm Coll (TX)
Bellingham Tech Coll (WA)
Brown Mackie Coll–Akron (OH)
Brown Mackie Coll–Atlanta (GA)
Brown Mackie Coll–Boise (ID)
Brown Mackie Coll–Cincinnati (OH)
Brown Mackie Coll–Findlay (OH)

Brown Mackie Coll–Fort Wayne (IN)
Brown Mackie Coll–Greenville (SC)
Brown Mackie Coll–Louisville (KY)
Brown Mackie Coll–Merrillville (IN)
Brown Mackie Coll–Michigan City (IN)
Brown Mackie Coll–North Canton (OH)
Brown Mackie Coll–Northern Kentucky (KY)
Brown Mackie Coll–Phoenix (AZ)
Brown Mackie Coll–St. Louis (MO)
Brown Mackie Coll–San Antonio (TX)
Brown Mackie Coll–Tucson (AZ)
Brown Mackie Coll–Tulsa (OK)
Cape Fear Comm Coll (NC)
Career Tech Coll (LA)
Central Carolina Tech Coll (SC)
Cincinnati State Tech and Comm Coll (OH)
Collin County Comm Coll District (TX)
Columbus Tech Coll (GA)
Comm Care Coll (OK)
DeKalb Tech Coll (GA)
El Centro Coll (TX)
Fayetteville Tech Comm Coll (NC)
Frederick Comm Coll (MD)
GateWay Comm Coll (AZ)
Georgia Northwestern Tech Coll (GA)
Harrisburg Area Comm Coll (PA)
Ivy Tech Comm Coll–Central Indiana (IN)
Ivy Tech Comm Coll–Columbus (IN)
Ivy Tech Comm Coll–East Central (IN)
Ivy Tech Comm Coll–Kokomo (IN)
Ivy Tech Comm Coll–Lafayette (IN)
Ivy Tech Comm Coll–Northwest (IN)
Ivy Tech Comm Coll–Southwest (IN)
Ivy Tech Comm Coll–Wabash Valley (IN)
Kilgore Coll (TX)
Kirtland Comm Coll (MI)
Lake Superior Coll (MN)
Lanier Tech Coll (GA)
Laramie County Comm Coll (WY)
Macomb Comm Coll (MI)
Manchester Comm Coll (CT)
Midlands Tech Coll (SC)
Mohave Comm Coll (AZ)
Montana State U–Great Falls Coll of Technology (MT)
Montgomery Coll (MD)
Montgomery County Comm Coll (PA)
Moraine Park Tech Coll (WI)
New England Inst of Technology (RI)
Niagara County Comm Coll (NY)
Northampton Comm Coll (PA)
Northeast Comm Coll (NE)
Northland Comm and Tech Coll– Thief River Falls & East Grand Forks (MN)
Oakland Comm Coll (MI)
Okefenokee Tech Coll (GA)
Oklahoma City Comm Coll (OK)
Owens Comm Coll, Toledo (OH)
Pittsburgh Tech Inst, Oakdale (PA)
St. Cloud Tech & Comm Coll (MN)
Sandhills Comm Coll (NC)
San Juan Coll (NM)
Savannah Tech Coll (GA)
Southeast Tech Inst (SD)
Southern Crescent Tech Coll (GA)
Southwest Georgia Tech Coll (GA)
Spencerian Coll (KY)
Springfield Tech Comm Coll (MA)
Trinity Valley Comm Coll (TX)
Tyler Jr Coll (TX)
Waukesha County Tech Coll (WI)
Western Iowa Tech Comm Coll (IA)
West Kentucky Comm and Tech Coll (KY)
West Virginia Northern Comm Coll (WV)
Wilson Comm Coll (NC)

SURVEYING ENGINEERING

Comm Coll of Rhode Island (RI)
Santa Rosa Jr Coll (CA)

SURVEYING TECHNOLOGY

Austin Comm Coll (TX)
Bellingham Tech Coll (WA)
Central New Mexico Comm Coll (NM)
Cincinnati State Tech and Comm Coll (OH)
Clark Coll (WA)
Coll of the Canyons (CA)
Delaware Tech & Comm Coll, Jack F. Owens Campus (DE)
Delaware Tech & Comm Coll, Stanton/Wilmington Campus (DE)
Fayetteville Tech Comm Coll (NC)
Indian River State Coll (FL)
Macomb Comm Coll (MI)
Mohawk Valley Comm Coll (NY)
Oklahoma State U, Oklahoma City (OK)
Owens Comm Coll, Toledo (OH)
Palm Beach State Coll (FL)
Penn State Wilkes-Barre (PA)
Phoenix Coll (AZ)
Salt Lake Comm Coll (UT)
Sandhills Comm Coll (NC)
Santa Fe Comm Coll (NM)
Sheridan Coll (WY)
Stark State Coll of Technology (OH)
State U of New York Coll of Environmental Science & Forestry, Ranger School (NY)
Tyler Jr Coll (TX)
U of Arkansas Comm Coll at Morrilton (AR)
White Mountains Comm Coll (NH)

SYSTEM, NETWORKING, AND LAN/WAN MANAGEMENT

Bradford School (OH)
Bradford School (PA)
Bryant & Stratton Coll (WI)
Coll of Business and Technology (FL)
Frank Phillips Coll (TX)
International Business Coll, Indianapolis (IN)
ITT Tech Inst, Bessemer (AL)
ITT Tech Inst, Madison (AL)
ITT Tech Inst, Mobile (AL)
ITT Tech Inst, Phoenix (AZ)
ITT Tech Inst, Tucson (AZ)
ITT Tech Inst (AR)
ITT Tech Inst, Anaheim (CA)
ITT Tech Inst, Lathrop (CA)
ITT Tech Inst, Oxnard (CA)
ITT Tech Inst, Rancho Cordova (CA)
ITT Tech Inst, San Bernardino (CA)
ITT Tech Inst, San Diego (CA)
ITT Tech Inst, San Dimas (CA)
ITT Tech Inst, Sylmar (CA)
ITT Tech Inst, Torrance (CA)
ITT Tech Inst, Aurora (CO)
ITT Tech Inst, Thornton (CO)
ITT Tech Inst, Fort Lauderdale (FL)
ITT Tech Inst, Fort Myers (FL)
ITT Tech Inst, Jacksonville (FL)
ITT Tech Inst, Lake Mary (FL)
ITT Tech Inst, Miami (FL)
ITT Tech Inst, Pinellas Park (FL)
ITT Tech Inst, Tallahassee (FL)
ITT Tech Inst, Tampa (FL)
ITT Tech Inst, Atlanta (GA)
ITT Tech Inst, Duluth (GA)
ITT Tech Inst, Kennesaw (GA)
ITT Tech Inst (ID)
ITT Tech Inst, Burr Ridge (IL)
ITT Tech Inst, Mount Prospect (IL)
ITT Tech Inst, Orland Park (IL)
ITT Tech Inst, Fort Wayne (IN)
ITT Tech Inst, Indianapolis (IN)
ITT Tech Inst, Merrillville (IN)
ITT Tech Inst, Newburgh (IN)
ITT Tech Inst, Cedar Rapids (IA)
ITT Tech Inst, Clive (IA)
ITT Tech Inst, Louisville (KY)
ITT Tech Inst, Baton Rouge (LA)
ITT Tech Inst, St. Rose (LA)
ITT Tech Inst (MD)
ITT Tech Inst, Norwood (MA)

ITT Tech Inst, Woburn (MA)
ITT Tech Inst, Canton (MI)
ITT Tech Inst, Swartz Creek (MI)
ITT Tech Inst, Troy (MI)
ITT Tech Inst, Wyoming (MI)
ITT Tech Inst, Eden Prairie (MN)
ITT Tech Inst, Arnold (MO)
ITT Tech Inst, Earth City (MO)
ITT Tech Inst, Kansas City (MO)
ITT Tech Inst (NE)
ITT Tech Inst, Henderson (NV)
ITT Tech Inst (NM)
ITT Tech Inst, Albany (NY)
ITT Tech Inst, Getzville (NY)
ITT Tech Inst, Liverpool (NY)
ITT Tech Inst, Charlotte (NC)
ITT Tech Inst, High Point (NC)
ITT Tech Inst, Morrisville (NC)
ITT Tech Inst, Akron (OH)
ITT Tech Inst, Columbus (OH)
ITT Tech Inst, Dayton (OH)
ITT Tech Inst, Hilliard (OH)
ITT Tech Inst, Maumee (OH)
ITT Tech Inst, Norwood (OH)
ITT Tech Inst, Strongsville (OH)
ITT Tech Inst, Warrensville Heights (OH)
ITT Tech Inst, Youngstown (OH)
ITT Tech Inst, Tulsa (OK)
ITT Tech Inst (OR)
ITT Tech Inst, Bensalem (PA)
ITT Tech Inst, Dunmore (PA)
ITT Tech Inst, Harrisburg (PA)
ITT Tech Inst, King of Prussia (PA)
ITT Tech Inst, Pittsburgh (PA)
ITT Tech Inst, Tarentum (PA)
ITT Tech Inst, Columbia (SC)
ITT Tech Inst, Greenville (SC)
ITT Tech Inst, Chattanooga (TN)
ITT Tech Inst, Cordova (TN)
ITT Tech Inst, Johnson City (TN)
ITT Tech Inst, Knoxville (TN)
ITT Tech Inst, Nashville (TN)
ITT Tech Inst, Arlington (TX)
ITT Tech Inst, Austin (TX)
ITT Tech Inst, DeSoto (TX)
ITT Tech Inst, Houston (TX)
ITT Tech Inst, Houston (TX)
ITT Tech Inst, Richardson (TX)
ITT Tech Inst, San Antonio (TX)
ITT Tech Inst, Webster (TX)
ITT Tech Inst (UT)
ITT Tech Inst, Chantilly (VA)
ITT Tech Inst, Norfolk (VA)
ITT Tech Inst, Richmond (VA)
ITT Tech Inst, Salem (VA)
ITT Tech Inst, Springfield (VA)
ITT Tech Inst, Everett (WA)
ITT Tech Inst, Seattle (WA)
ITT Tech Inst, Spokane Valley (WA)
ITT Tech Inst (WV)
ITT Tech Inst, Green Bay (WI)
ITT Tech Inst, Greenfield (WI)
ITT Tech Inst, Madison (WI)
King's Coll (NC)
Lonestar Coll–Montgomery (TX)
Lonestar Coll–Tomball (TX)
Metropolitan Comm Coll–Business & Technology Campus (MO)
Minneapolis Business Coll (MN)
Moraine Valley Comm Coll (IL)
MTI Coll, Sacramento (CA)
St. Philip's Coll (TX)
Waubonsee Comm Coll (IL)
Wood Tobe–Coburn School (NY)

SYSTEMS ENGINEERING

Kent State U at Trumbull (OH)

TEACHER ASSISTANT/AIDE

Alamance Comm Coll (NC)
Antelope Valley Coll (CA)
Borough of Manhattan Comm Coll of the City U of New York (NY)
Casper Coll (WY)
Central Maine Comm Coll (ME)
Central Wyoming Coll (WY)
Century Coll (MN)
Clovis Comm Coll (NM)
Comm Coll of Vermont (VT)
Dakota Coll at Bottineau (ND)
Danville Area Comm Coll (IL)
El Centro Coll (TX)
Fiorello H. LaGuardia Comm Coll of the City U of New York (NY)

Fulton-Montgomery Comm Coll (NY)
Highland Comm Coll (IL)
Illinois Eastern Comm Colls, Lincoln Trail College (IL)
Indian River State Coll (FL)
Kankakee Comm Coll (IL)
Kaskaskia Coll (IL)
Kingsborough Comm Coll of the City U of New York (NY)
Kirtland Comm Coll (MI)
Lehigh Carbon Comm Coll (PA)
Lincoln Land Comm Coll (IL)
Linn-Benton Comm Coll (OR)
Manchester Comm Coll (CT)
Mesa Comm Coll (AZ)
Miami Dade Coll (FL)
Montcalm Comm Coll (MI)
Montgomery County Comm Coll (PA)
Moraine Park Tech Coll (WI)
Moraine Valley Comm Coll (IL)
Northampton Comm Coll (PA)
Olympic Coll (WA)
Saint Charles Comm Coll (MO)
St. Cloud Tech & Comm Coll (MN)
St. Philip's Coll (TX)
Salt Lake Comm Coll (UT)
San Diego City Coll (CA)
Sheridan Coll (WY)
Southwestern Michigan Coll (MI)
Waubonsee Comm Coll (IL)
Waukesha County Tech Coll (WI)

TEACHING ASSISTANTS/ AIDES RELATED

Terra State Comm Coll (OH)

TECHNOLOGY/INDUSTRIAL ARTS TEACHER EDUCATION

Allen Comm Coll (KS)
Casper Coll (WY)
Central New Mexico Comm Coll (NM)
Cowley County Comm Coll and Area Vocational–Tech School (KS)
Eastern Arizona Coll (AZ)

TELECOMMUNICATIONS TECHNOLOGY

Amarillo Coll (TX)
Carl Albert State Coll (OK)
Cincinnati State Tech and Comm Coll (OH)
Clark Coll (WA)
Collin County Comm Coll District (TX)
Comm Coll of Rhode Island (RI)
DeKalb Tech Coll (GA)
Dutchess Comm Coll (NY)
Gadsden State Comm Coll (AL)
Howard Comm Coll (MD)
Illinois Eastern Comm Colls, Lincoln Trail College (IL)
Ivy Tech Comm Coll–North Central (IN)
Ivy Tech Comm Coll–Northwest (IN)
Lake Superior Coll (MN)
Marion Tech Coll (OH)
Miami Dade Coll (FL)
Minnesota State Comm and Tech Coll (MN)
Mitchell Tech Inst (SD)
Northern Essex Comm Coll (MA)
North Seattle Comm Coll (WA)
Penn State DuBois (PA)
Penn State Fayette, The Eberly Campus (PA)
Penn State Hazleton (PA)
Penn State New Kensington (PA)
Penn State Schuylkill (PA)
Penn State Shenango (PA)
Penn State Wilkes-Barre (PA)
Penn State York (PA)
Quinsigamond Comm Coll (MA)
Salt Lake Comm Coll (UT)
San Diego City Coll (CA)
Seminole State Coll of Florida (FL)
Solano Comm Coll (CA)
Springfield Tech Comm Coll (MA)
Trident Tech Coll (SC)
Union County Coll (NJ)
Waukesha County Tech Coll (WI)

THEATER DESIGN AND TECHNOLOGY

Carroll Comm Coll (MD)
Casper Coll (WY)
Central Wyoming Coll (WY)
Comm Coll of Rhode Island (RI)
Florida State Coll at Jacksonville (FL)
Harford Comm Coll (MD)
Howard Comm Coll (MD)
San Juan Coll (NM)
Santa Barbara City Coll (CA)
Southwestern Michigan Coll (MI)

THEATER/THEATER ARTS MANAGEMENT

Harper Coll (IL)

THERAPEUTIC RECREATION

Austin Comm Coll (TX)
Colorado Mountain Coll (CO)
Santa Barbara City Coll (CA)

TOOL AND DIE TECHNOLOGY

Gadsden State Comm Coll (AL)
Hawkeye Comm Coll (IA)
Ivy Tech Comm Coll–Bloomington (IN)
Ivy Tech Comm Coll–Central Indiana (IN)
Ivy Tech Comm Coll–Columbus (IN)
Ivy Tech Comm Coll–East Central (IN)
Ivy Tech Comm Coll–Kokomo (IN)
Ivy Tech Comm Coll–Lafayette (IN)
Ivy Tech Comm Coll–North Central (IN)
Ivy Tech Comm Coll–Northeast (IN)
Ivy Tech Comm Coll–Northwest (IN)
Ivy Tech Comm Coll–Richmond (IN)
Ivy Tech Comm Coll–Southern Indiana (IN)
Ivy Tech Comm Coll–Southwest (IN)
Ivy Tech Comm Coll–Wabash Valley (IN)
Macomb Comm Coll (MI)
Moraine Park Tech Coll (WI)
North Iowa Area Comm Coll (IA)
Oakland Comm Coll (MI)
Owens Comm Coll, Toledo (OH)
Southwestern Michigan Coll (MI)
Western Iowa Tech Comm Coll (IA)

TOURISM AND TRAVEL SERVICES MANAGEMENT

Albany Tech Coll (GA)
Amarillo Coll (TX)
Athens Tech Coll (GA)
Atlanta Tech Coll (GA)
Bradford School (OH)
Bradford School (PA)
Central Georgia Tech Coll (GA)
Dakota County Tech Coll (MN)
Daytona State Coll (FL)
Dutchess Comm Coll (NY)
Fiorello H. LaGuardia Comm Coll of the City U of New York (NY)
Fox Coll (IL)
Gwinnett Tech Coll (GA)
Harrisburg Area Comm Coll (PA)
Houston Comm Coll System (TX)
International Business Coll, Indianapolis (IN)
Kingsborough Comm Coll of the City U of New York (NY)
King's Coll (NC)
Miami Dade Coll (FL)
Minneapolis Business Coll (MN)
Moraine Valley Comm Coll (IL)
Northern Essex Comm Coll (MA)
Ogeechee Tech Coll (GA)
San Diego City Coll (CA)
Savannah Tech Coll (GA)
Three Rivers Comm Coll (CT)
Westmoreland County Comm Coll (PA)
Wood Tobe–Coburn School (NY)
Yakima Valley Comm Coll (WA)

TOURISM AND TRAVEL SERVICES MARKETING

Florida State Coll at Jacksonville (FL)

TRADE AND INDUSTRIAL TEACHER EDUCATION

Darton Coll (GA)
East Los Angeles Coll (CA)
Kilgore Coll (TX)
Pratt Comm Coll (KS)
Snow Coll (UT)
Southeastern Comm Coll (IA)
Wenatchee Valley Coll (WA)

TRANSPORTATION AND MATERIALS MOVING RELATED

Cecil Coll (MD)
Mid-Plains Comm Coll, North Platte (NE)
Muskegon Comm Coll (MI)
San Diego City Coll (CA)

TRANSPORTATION/MOBILITY MANAGEMENT

Cecil Coll (MD)
Hagerstown Comm Coll (MD)
Polk State Coll (FL)

TRUCK AND BUS DRIVER/COMMERCIAL VEHICLE OPERATION/INSTRUCTION

Alexandria Tech and Comm Coll (MN)
Central Comm Coll–Hastings Campus (NE)
Mohave Comm Coll (AZ)

TURF AND TURFGRASS MANAGEMENT

Catawba Valley Comm Coll (NC)
Cincinnati State Tech and Comm Coll (OH)
Coll of Lake County (IL)
Dakota Coll at Bottineau (ND)
Danville Area Comm Coll (IL)
Delaware Tech & Comm Coll, Jack F. Owens Campus (DE)
Houston Comm Coll System (TX)
Lake Michigan Coll (MI)
Linn State Tech Coll (MO)
North Georgia Tech Coll (GA)
Oklahoma State U, Oklahoma City (OK)
Sandhills Comm Coll (NC)
Sheridan Coll (WY)
Southeast Tech Inst (SD)
Western Iowa Tech Comm Coll (IA)
Westmoreland County Comm Coll (PA)
The Williamson Free School of Mecha Trades (PA)

URBAN FORESTRY

Dakota Coll at Bottineau (ND)

VEHICLE AND VEHICLE PARTS AND ACCESSORIES MARKETING

Central Comm Coll–Hastings Campus (NE)

VEHICLE MAINTENANCE AND REPAIR TECHNOLOGIES RELATED

Central Maine Comm Coll (ME)
Central New Mexico Comm Coll (NM)
J. Sargeant Reynolds Comm Coll (VA)
North Dakota State Coll of Science (ND)
Pennco Tech (PA)

VETERINARY/ANIMAL HEALTH TECHNOLOGY

Athens Tech Coll (GA)
Bradford School (OH)
Brown Mackie Coll–Akron (OH)
Brown Mackie Coll–Albuquerque (NM)
Brown Mackie Coll–Boise (ID)
Brown Mackie Coll–Cincinnati (OH)
Brown Mackie Coll–Findlay (OH)
Brown Mackie Coll–Kansas City (KS)
Brown Mackie Coll–Louisville (KY)
Brown Mackie Coll–Michigan City (IN)
Brown Mackie Coll–North Canton (OH)
Brown Mackie Coll–South Bend (IN)
Central Georgia Tech Coll (GA)
Central New Mexico Comm Coll (NM)
Coll of Central Florida (FL)
Colorado Mountain Coll (CO)
Comm Care Coll (OK)
The Comm Coll of Baltimore County (MD)
Delaware Tech & Comm Coll, Jack F. Owens Campus (DE)
Duluth Business U (MN)
Fiorello H. LaGuardia Comm Coll of the City U of New York (NY)
Foothill Coll (CA)
Fox Coll (IL)
Front Range Comm Coll (CO)
Gwinnett Tech Coll (GA)
Harrison Coll, Indianapolis (IN)
Hillsborough Comm Coll (FL)
Holyoke Comm Coll (MA)
International Business Coll, Indianapolis (IN)
Jefferson Coll (MO)
Jefferson State Comm Coll (AL)
Kaskaskia Coll (IL)
Kent State U at Tuscarawas (OH)
Lehigh Carbon Comm Coll (PA)
Lonestar Coll–Tomball (TX)
Macomb Comm Coll (MI)
Metropolitan Comm Coll–Maple Woods (MO)
Moraine Park Tech Coll (WI)
Northampton Comm Coll (PA)
Northeast Comm Coll (NE)
Northwest Coll (WY)
Oakland Comm Coll (MI)
Ogeechee Tech Coll (GA)
Oklahoma State U, Oklahoma City (OK)
Pima Comm Coll (AZ)
Pima Medical Inst, Tucson (AZ)
Pima Medical Inst (CA)
Pima Medical Inst (NV)
Pima Medical Inst, Seattle (WA)
San Juan Coll (NM)
Trident Tech Coll (SC)
Vet Tech Inst (PA)
Vet Tech Inst at Bradford School (OH)
Vet Tech Inst at Fox Coll (IL)
Vet Tech Inst at Hickey Coll (MO)
Vet Tech Inst at International Business Coll, Fort Wayne (IN)
Vet Tech Inst at International Business Coll, Indianapolis (IN)
Vet Tech Inst of Houston (TX)
Westchester Comm Coll (NY)
Yakima Valley Comm Coll (WA)

VISUAL AND PERFORMING ARTS

Amarillo Coll (TX)
Borough of Manhattan Comm Coll of the City U of New York (NY)
Bucks County Comm Coll (PA)
Chandler-Gilbert Comm Coll (AZ)
The Comm Coll of Baltimore County (MD)
Fiorello H. LaGuardia Comm Coll of the City U of New York (NY)
Frank Phillips Coll (TX)
Harford Comm Coll (MD)
Harrisburg Area Comm Coll (PA)
Lonestar Coll–Kingwood (TX)
Moraine Valley Comm Coll (IL)
Phoenix Coll (AZ)
Pima Comm Coll (AZ)

VISUAL AND PERFORMING ARTS RELATED

Florida State Coll at Jacksonville (FL)
John Tyler Comm Coll (VA)
J. Sargeant Reynolds Comm Coll (VA)
Kankakee Comm Coll (IL)
Northwest Coll (WY)

VITICULTURE AND ENOLOGY

Harrisburg Area Comm Coll (PA)
James Sprunt Comm Coll (NC)
Lake Michigan Coll (MI)

VOICE AND OPERA

Oakland Comm Coll (MI)
Snow Coll (UT)

WATCHMAKING AND JEWELRYMAKING

Austin Comm Coll (TX)
North Seattle Comm Coll (WA)

WATER QUALITY AND WASTEWATER TREATMENT MANAGEMENT AND RECYCLING TECHNOLOGY

Casper Coll (WY)
Coll of the Canyons (CA)
Delaware Tech & Comm Coll, Jack F. Owens Campus (DE)
Florida State Coll at Jacksonville (FL)
GateWay Comm Coll (AZ)
Linn-Benton Comm Coll (OR)
Moraine Park Tech Coll (WI)
Ogeechee Tech Coll (GA)
St. Cloud Tech & Comm Coll (MN)
Santa Fe Comm Coll (NM)

WEB/MULTIMEDIA MANAGEMENT AND WEBMASTER

Blackhawk Tech Coll (WI)
Casper Coll (WY)
Clark Coll (WA)
Clovis Comm Coll (NM)
Comm Coll of Rhode Island (RI)
Florida State Coll at Jacksonville (FL)
Fox Valley Tech Coll (WI)
ITT Tech Inst, Thornton (CO)
ITT Tech Inst, Jacksonville (FL)
ITT Tech Inst, Lake Mary (FL)
ITT Tech Inst, Pinellas Park (FL)
ITT Tech Inst, Tallahassee (FL)
ITT Tech Inst, Tampa (FL)
ITT Tech Inst (ID)
ITT Tech Inst, Baton Rouge (LA)
ITT Tech Inst, St. Rose (LA)
ITT Tech Inst, Norwood (MA)
ITT Tech Inst, Woburn (MA)
ITT Tech Inst, Canton (MI)
ITT Tech Inst, Swartz Creek (MI)
ITT Tech Inst, Troy (MI)
ITT Tech Inst, Wyoming (MI)
ITT Tech Inst, Arnold (MO)
ITT Tech Inst (NM)
ITT Tech Inst, Albany (NY)
ITT Tech Inst, Norwood (OH)
ITT Tech Inst, Strongsville (OH)
ITT Tech Inst (OR)
ITT Tech Inst, Tarentum (PA)
ITT Tech Inst, Columbia (SC)
ITT Tech Inst, Greenville (SC)
ITT Tech Inst (UT)
ITT Tech Inst, Chantilly (VA)
ITT Tech Inst, Norfolk (VA)
ITT Tech Inst, Richmond (VA)
ITT Tech Inst, Springfield (VA)
ITT Tech Inst, Everett (WA)
ITT Tech Inst, Seattle (WA)
ITT Tech Inst, Spokane Valley (WA)
Kilgore Coll (TX)
Kirtland Comm Coll (MI)
Lonestar Coll–Montgomery (TX)
Metropolitan Comm Coll–Business & Technology Campus (MO)
Monroe County Comm Coll (MI)
Moraine Valley Comm Coll (IL)
Northern Essex Comm Coll (MA)
Northland Comm and Tech Coll–Thief River Falls & East Grand Forks (MN)
Pennsylvania Highlands Comm Coll (PA)
Sandhills Comm Coll (NC)
Seminole State Coll of Florida (FL)
Sheridan Coll (WY)
Southwest Mississippi Comm Coll (MS)
Stark State Coll of Technology (OH)
Tompkins Cortland Comm Coll (NY)
Trident Tech Coll (SC)

West Virginia Jr Coll–Bridgeport (WV)

WEB PAGE, DIGITAL/MULTIMEDIA AND INFORMATION RESOURCES DESIGN

Alexandria Tech and Comm Coll (MN)
The Art Inst of New York City (NY)
The Art Inst of Ohio–Cincinnati (OH)
The Art Inst of Seattle (WA)
Berkeley City Coll (CA)
Borough of Manhattan Comm Coll of the City U of New York (NY)
Casper Coll (WY)
Cecil Coll (MD)
Central Georgia Tech Coll (GA)
Chattahoochee Tech Coll (GA)
Collin County Comm Coll District (TX)
Columbus Tech Coll (GA)
Dakota County Tech Coll (MN)
Edison State Comm Coll (OH)
El Centro Coll (TX)
Elgin Comm Coll (IL)
Florida State Coll at Jacksonville (FL)
GateWay Comm Coll (AZ)
Georgia Northwestern Tech Coll (GA)
Glendale Comm Coll (AZ)
Hagerstown Comm Coll (MD)
Harper Coll (IL)
Harrisburg Area Comm Coll (PA)
Hawkeye Comm Coll (IA)
Highland Comm Coll (IL)
ITT Tech Inst, Bessemer (AL)
ITT Tech Inst, Tucson (AZ)
ITT Tech Inst, Lathrop (CA)
ITT Tech Inst, Rancho Cordova (CA)
ITT Tech Inst, San Bernardino (CA)
ITT Tech Inst, San Diego (CA)
ITT Tech Inst, San Dimas (CA)
ITT Tech Inst, Sylmar (CA)
ITT Tech Inst, Thornton (CO)
ITT Tech Inst, Jacksonville (FL)
ITT Tech Inst, Lake Mary (FL)
ITT Tech Inst, Pinellas Park (FL)
ITT Tech Inst, Tampa (FL)
ITT Tech Inst, Duluth (GA)
ITT Tech Inst, Kennesaw (GA)
ITT Tech Inst (ID)
ITT Tech Inst, Mount Prospect (IL)
ITT Tech Inst, Orland Park (IL)
ITT Tech Inst, St. Rose (LA)
ITT Tech Inst (MD)
ITT Tech Inst, Norwood (MA)
ITT Tech Inst, Woburn (MA)
ITT Tech Inst, Canton (MI)
ITT Tech Inst, Swartz Creek (MI)
ITT Tech Inst, Troy (MI)
ITT Tech Inst, Wyoming (MI)
ITT Tech Inst, Eden Prairie (MN)
ITT Tech Inst, Arnold (MO)
ITT Tech Inst, Earth City (MO)
ITT Tech Inst (NE)
ITT Tech Inst, Henderson (NV)
ITT Tech Inst, Albany (NY)
ITT Tech Inst, Getzville (NY)
ITT Tech Inst, Liverpool (NY)
ITT Tech Inst, Charlotte (NC)
ITT Tech Inst, Hilliard (OH)
ITT Tech Inst, Norwood (OH)
ITT Tech Inst, Strongsville (OH)
ITT Tech Inst, Warrensville Heights (OH)
ITT Tech Inst (OR)
ITT Tech Inst, Bensalem (PA)
ITT Tech Inst, Harrisburg (PA)
ITT Tech Inst, King of Prussia (PA)
ITT Tech Inst, Pittsburgh (PA)
ITT Tech Inst, Tarentum (PA)
ITT Tech Inst, Columbia (SC)
ITT Tech Inst, Greenville (SC)
ITT Tech Inst, Cordova (TN)
ITT Tech Inst, Nashville (TN)
ITT Tech Inst, Austin (TX)
ITT Tech Inst, San Antonio (TX)
ITT Tech Inst (UT)
ITT Tech Inst, Chantilly (VA)
ITT Tech Inst, Norfolk (VA)
ITT Tech Inst, Richmond (VA)
ITT Tech Inst, Springfield (VA)
ITT Tech Inst, Everett (WA)
ITT Tech Inst, Seattle (WA)

Montgomery County Comm Coll (PA)

Lanier Tech Coll (GA)
Lehigh Carbon Comm Coll (PA)
Lonestar Coll–Montgomery (TX)
Mesabi Range Comm and Tech Coll (MN)
Metropolitan Comm Coll–Business & Technology Campus (MO)
Middle Georgia Tech Coll (GA)
Minnesota State Coll–Southeast Tech (MN)
Minnesota State Comm and Tech Coll (MN)
Monroe County Comm Coll (MI)
Montana State U–Great Falls Coll of Technology (MT)
Moraine Park Tech Coll (WI)
Motlow State Comm Coll (TN)
Moultrie Tech Coll (GA)
New England Inst of Technology (RI)
Niagara County Comm Coll (NY)
Northampton Comm Coll (PA)
Northern Essex Comm Coll (MA)
North Georgia Tech Coll (GA)
North Iowa Area Comm Coll (IA)
Northland Comm and Tech Coll–Thief River Falls & East Grand Forks (MN)
Norwalk Comm Coll (CT)
Oklahoma State U, Oklahoma City (OK)
Palm Beach State Coll (FL)
Pasco-Hernando Comm Coll (FL)
Phoenix Coll (AZ)
Pittsburgh Tech Inst, Oakdale (PA)
Pueblo Comm Coll (CO)
Quinsigamond Comm Coll (MA)
Raritan Valley Comm Coll (NJ)
St. Cloud Tech & Comm Coll (MN)
Seminole State Coll of Florida (FL)
Southeastern Tech Coll (GA)
Southern Crescent Tech Coll (GA)
Springfield Tech Comm Coll (MA)
Stark State Coll of Technology (OH)
Sullivan Coll of Technology and Design (KY)
Terra State Comm Coll (OH)
Trident Tech Coll (SC)
Volunteer State Comm Coll (TN)
Waubonsee Comm Coll (IL)
West Georgia Tech Coll (GA)

Westmoreland County Comm Coll (PA)
Wiregrass Georgia Tech Coll (GA)
Wisconsin Indianhead Tech Coll (WI)

WELDING TECHNOLOGY

Alamance Comm Coll (NC)
Alexandria Tech and Comm Coll (MN)
Antelope Valley Coll (CA)
Arizona Western Coll (AZ)
Austin Comm Coll (TX)
Bainbridge Coll (GA)
Beaufort County Comm Coll (NC)
Bellingham Tech Coll (WA)
Big Bend Comm Coll (WA)
Casper Coll (WY)
Central Comm Coll–Columbus Campus (NE)
Central Comm Coll–Grand Island Campus (NE)
Central Comm Coll–Hastings Campus (NE)
Central Lakes Coll (MN)
Central Wyoming Coll (WY)
Clark Coll (WA)
Clovis Comm Coll (NM)
Coll of the Canyons (CA)
Cowley County Comm Coll and Area Vocational–Tech School (KS)
Dawson Comm Coll (MT)
Dodge City Comm Coll (KS)
Doña Ana Comm Coll (NM)
Eastern Arizona Coll (AZ)
Elaine P. Nunez Comm Coll (LA)
Elgin Comm Coll (IL)
Fox Valley Tech Coll (WI)
Front Range Comm Coll (CO)
Grand Rapids Comm Coll (MI)
Grays Harbor Coll (WA)
Great Basin Coll (NV)
Honolulu Comm Coll (HI)
Jefferson Coll (MO)
Kankakee Comm Coll (IL)
Kilgore Coll (TX)
Kirtland Comm Coll (MI)
Lake Superior Coll (MN)
Linn-Benton Comm Coll (OR)
Linn State Tech Coll (MO)
Lonestar Coll–Cy-Fair (TX)
Lonestar Coll–Kingwood (TX)

Lonestar Coll–Montgomery (TX)
Lonestar Coll–North Harris (TX)
Lower Columbia Coll (WA)
Macomb Comm Coll (MI)
Mid-Plains Comm Coll, North Platte (NE)
Mohave Comm Coll (AZ)
Monroe County Comm Coll (MI)
Montana State U–Great Falls Coll of Technology (MT)
Montcalm Comm Coll (MI)
Moraine Park Tech Coll (WI)
Mountain View Coll (TX)
Muskegon Comm Coll (MI)
North Dakota State Coll of Science (ND)
Northeast Comm Coll (NE)
North Idaho Coll (ID)
North Iowa Area Comm Coll (IA)
Northland Comm and Tech Coll–Thief River Falls & East Grand Forks (MN)
Northwest Coll (WY)
Oakland Comm Coll (MI)
Oklahoma Tech Coll (OK)
Olympic Coll (WA)
Orange Coast Coll (CA)
Owens Comm Coll, Toledo (OH)
Pima Comm Coll (AZ)
Pratt Comm Coll (KS)
Pueblo Comm Coll (CO)
Rogue Comm Coll (OR)
St. Cloud Tech & Comm Coll (MN)
St. Philip's Coll (TX)
Salt Lake Comm Coll (UT)
San Diego City Coll (CA)
San Juan Coll (NM)
Sheridan Coll (WY)
Solano Comm Coll (CA)
Southeastern Comm Coll (IA)
Southwestern Michigan Coll (MI)
Southwest Mississippi Comm Coll (MS)
State U of New York Coll of Technology at Alfred (NY)
Terra State Comm Coll (OH)
Triangle Tech, Inc.–DuBois School (PA)
Trinity Valley Comm Coll (TX)
Tyler Jr Coll (TX)
The U of Montana–Helena Coll of Technology (MT)
Waubonsee Comm Coll (IL)

Westmoreland County Comm Coll (PA)

WELL DRILLING
Southwest Mississippi Comm Coll (MS)

WILDLAND/FOREST FIREFIGHTING AND INVESTIGATION
Fox Valley Tech Coll (WI)

WILDLIFE BIOLOGY
Dodge City Comm Coll (KS)
Eastern Arizona Coll (AZ)
North Idaho Coll (ID)
Pratt Comm Coll (KS)

WILDLIFE, FISH AND WILDLANDS SCIENCE AND MANAGEMENT
Barton County Comm Coll (KS)
Casper Coll (WY)
Dakota Coll at Bottineau (ND)
Front Range Comm Coll (CO)
Laramie County Comm Coll (WY)
North Idaho Coll (ID)
Ogeechee Tech Coll (GA)
Penn State DuBois (PA)
Potomac State Coll of West Virginia U (WV)

WOMEN'S STUDIES
Casper Coll (WY)
Foothill Coll (CA)
Northern Essex Comm Coll (MA)
Norwalk Comm Coll (CT)
Owens Comm Coll, Toledo (OH)
Santa Rosa Jr Coll (CA)
Suffolk County Comm Coll (NY)

WOOD SCIENCE AND WOOD PRODUCTS/PULP AND PAPER TECHNOLOGY
Allen Comm Coll (KS)
Dabney S. Lancaster Comm Coll (VA)
Ogeechee Tech Coll (GA)
Potomac State Coll of West Virginia U (WV)

WOODWORKING
Bucks County Comm Coll (PA)
Santa Fe Comm Coll (NM)

WOODWORKING RELATED
Oakland Comm Coll (MI)

WORD PROCESSING
Corning Comm Coll (NY)
Eastfield Coll (TX)
Florida State Coll at Jacksonville (FL)
Gateway Comm Coll (CT)
Metropolitan Comm Coll–Business & Technology Campus (MO)
Monroe County Comm Coll (MI)
Northland Comm and Tech Coll–Thief River Falls & East Grand Forks (MN)
Orange Coast Coll (CA)
Owensboro Comm and Tech Coll (KY)
Palm Beach State Coll (FL)
Pratt Comm Coll (KS)
Seminole State Coll of Florida (FL)
Stark State Coll of Technology (OH)
Tallahassee Comm Coll (FL)
Vincennes U Jasper Campus (IN)

WORK AND FAMILY STUDIES
Antelope Valley Coll (CA)
Arizona Western Coll (AZ)

WRITING
Allen Comm Coll (KS)
Austin Comm Coll (TX)
Berkeley City Coll (CA)

YOUTH SERVICES
Midlands Tech Coll (SC)

ZOOLOGY/ANIMAL BIOLOGY
Dakota Coll at Bottineau (ND)
North Idaho Coll (ID)
Palm Beach State Coll (FL)
Snow Coll (UT)

Associate Degree Programs at Four-Year Colleges

ACCOUNTING
AIB Coll of Business (IA)
American Public U System (WV)
Ashworth Coll (GA)
Baker Coll of Allen Park (MI)
Baker Coll of Auburn Hills (MI)
Baker Coll of Clinton Township (MI)
Baker Coll of Owosso (MI)
Boston U (MA)
Brookline Coll, Phoenix (AZ)
Brookline Coll (NM)
Bryant & Stratton Coll - Wauwatosa Campus (WI)
Calumet Coll of Saint Joseph (IN)
Central Pennsylvania Coll (PA)
Chestnut Hill Coll (PA)
Clarke U (IA)
Coll of Mount St. Joseph (OH)
Coll of St. Joseph (VT)
Coll of Saint Mary (NE)
Coll of Staten Island of the City U of New York (NY)
Dakota Wesleyan U (SD)
Davenport U, Grand Rapids (MI)
DeVry U Online (IL)
ECPI Coll of Technology, Virginia Beach (VA)
Elizabethtown Coll (PA)
Everest U, Lakeland (FL)
Everest U, Tampa (FL)
Everest U, Tampa (FL)
Fisher Coll (MA)
Florida National Coll (FL)
Franklin U (OH)
Goldey-Beacom Coll (DE)
Hawai`i Pacific U (HI)
Husson U (ME)
Immaculata U (PA)
Indiana Tech (IN)
Indiana U of Pennsylvania (PA)
Indiana Wesleyan U (IN)
Inter American U of Puerto Rico, Bayamón Campus (PR)
Inter American U of Puerto Rico, Guayama Campus (PR)
Inter American U of Puerto Rico, Metropolitan Campus (PR)
Inter American U of Puerto Rico, Ponce Campus (PR)
Johnson State Coll (VT)
Lake Superior State U (MI)
Lebanon Valley Coll (PA)
Liberty U (VA)
Maria Coll (NY)
Methodist U (NC)
Minnesota School of Business–Blaine (MN)
Missouri Southern State U (MO)
Mountain State U (WV)
Mount Aloysius Coll (PA)
Mount Marty Coll (SD)
Mount St. Mary's Coll (CA)
Muhlenberg Coll (PA)
Oklahoma Wesleyan U (OK)
Penn Foster Coll (AZ)
Point Park U (PA)
Regent U (VA)
Rogers State U (OK)
Saint Francis U (PA)
St. John's U (NY)
Saint Mary-of-the-Woods Coll (IN)
Shawnee State U (OH)
Southern Adventist U (TN)
Southwest Minnesota State U (MN)
State U of New York Coll of Technology at Delhi (NY)
Thiel Coll (PA)
Thomas More Coll (KY)
Tiffin U (OH)
Trine U (IN)
Union Coll (NE)
U of Cincinnati (OH)
The U of Findlay (OH)
U of Rio Grande (OH)
U of the Virgin Islands (VI)
The U of Toledo (OH)
Utah Valley U (UT)
Walsh U (OH)
Webber International U (FL)
Wilson Coll (PA)
Youngstown State U (OH)

ACCOUNTING AND BUSINESS/MANAGEMENT
AIB Coll of Business (IA)
Chestnut Hill Coll (PA)
International Business Coll, Fort Wayne (IN)
Kansas State U (KS)
Minnesota School of Business–Blaine (MN)
Young Harris Coll (GA)

ACCOUNTING AND COMPUTER SCIENCE
Lincoln U (MO)

ACCOUNTING AND FINANCE
AIB Coll of Business (IA)

ACCOUNTING RELATED
AIB Coll of Business (IA)
Franklin U (OH)
Montana State U Billings (MT)

ACCOUNTING TECHNOLOGY AND BOOKKEEPING
Baker Coll of Flint (MI)
DeVry U, Federal Way (WA)
Ferris State U (MI)
Gannon U (PA)
Lewis-Clark State Coll (ID)
Miami U (OH)
Montana State U Billings (MT)
Montana Tech of The U of Montana (MT)
New York City Coll of Technology of the City U of New York (NY)
New York Inst of Technology (NY)
Peirce Coll (PA)
Pennsylvania Coll of Technology (PA)
The U of Akron (OH)
U of Alaska Fairbanks (AK)
U of Cincinnati (OH)
U of Rio Grande (OH)

ADMINISTRATIVE ASSISTANT AND SECRETARIAL SCIENCE
Arkansas Tech U (AR)
Baker Coll of Auburn Hills (MI)
Baker Coll of Cadillac (MI)
Baker Coll of Clinton Township (MI)
Baker Coll of Jackson (MI)
Baker Coll of Muskegon (MI)
Baker Coll of Owosso (MI)
Ball State U (IN)
Baptist Bible Coll of Pennsylvania (PA)
Campbellsville U (KY)
Central Pennsylvania Coll (PA)
Clayton State U (GA)

Columbia Centro Universitario (PR)
Columbia Coll (PR)
Concordia Coll–New York (NY)
Dickinson State U (ND)
Dordt Coll (IA)
Faith Baptist Bible Coll and Theological Seminary (IA)
Florida National Coll (FL)
Free Will Baptist Bible Coll (TN)
Idaho State U (ID)
Inter American U of Puerto Rico, Bayamón Campus (PR)
Inter American U of Puerto Rico, San Germán Campus (PR)
Kuyper Coll (MI)
Lamar U (TX)
Lewis-Clark State Coll (ID)
Lincoln U (MO)
Maranatha Baptist Bible Coll (WI)
Miami U (OH)
Montana State U Billings (MT)
Montana Tech of The U of Montana (MT)
Mountain State U (WV)
Murray State U (KY)
New York Inst of Technology (NY)
Northern Michigan U (MI)
Ohio U–Chillicothe (OH)
Rider U (NJ)
Sul Ross State U (TX)
Tabor Coll (KS)
The U of Akron (OH)
U of Central Missouri (MO)
U of Rio Grande (OH)
U of the District of Columbia (DC)
The U of Toledo (OH)
Washburn U (KS)

ADULT AND CONTINUING EDUCATION
Fisher Coll (MA)

ADULT AND CONTINUING EDUCATION ADMINISTRATION
Concordia Coll–New York (NY)

ADULT DEVELOPMENT AND AGING
Madonna U (MI)
The U of Toledo (OH)

ADVERTISING
Fashion Inst of Technology (NY)
Inter American U of Puerto Rico, San Germán Campus (PR)
U of the District of Columbia (DC)
Xavier U (OH)

AERONAUTICAL/AEROSPACE ENGINEERING TECHNOLOGY
Purdue U (IN)
Vaughn Coll of Aeronautics and Technology (NY)

AERONAUTICS/AVIATION/AEROSPACE SCIENCE AND TECHNOLOGY
Embry-Riddle Aeronautical U–Worldwide (FL)
Indiana State U (IN)
Montana State U (MT)
Ohio U (OH)
Pacific Union Coll (CA)

U of Cincinnati (OH)
Vaughn Coll of Aeronautics and Technology (NY)
Walla Walla U (WA)

AFRICAN AMERICAN/BLACK STUDIES
U of Cincinnati (OH)

AGRIBUSINESS
Morehead State U (KY)
Southern Arkansas U–Magnolia (AR)
Southwest Minnesota State U (MN)
Vermont Tech Coll (VT)

AGRICULTURAL BUSINESS AND MANAGEMENT
Coll of Coastal Georgia (GA)
Dickinson State U (ND)
North Carolina State U (NC)

AGRICULTURAL BUSINESS AND MANAGEMENT RELATED
Penn State Abington (PA)
Penn State Altoona (PA)
Penn State Berks (PA)
Penn State Erie, The Behrend Coll (PA)
Penn State U Park (PA)

AGRICULTURAL PRODUCTION
Eastern New Mexico U (NM)
Western Kentucky U (KY)

AGRICULTURE
Dalton State Coll (GA)
North Carolina State U (NC)
Oklahoma Panhandle State U (OK)
South Dakota State U (SD)
Southern Utah U (UT)
U of Delaware (DE)
Young Harris Coll (GA)

AIRCRAFT POWERPLANT TECHNOLOGY
Embry-Riddle Aeronautical U–Daytona (FL)
Embry-Riddle Aeronautical U–Worldwide (FL)
Idaho State U (ID)
Pennsylvania Coll of Technology (PA)
U of Alaska Fairbanks (AK)

AIRFRAME MECHANICS AND AIRCRAFT MAINTENANCE TECHNOLOGY
Kansas State U (KS)
Northern Michigan U (MI)
St. Petersburg Coll (FL)
Thomas Edison State Coll (NJ)

AIRLINE PILOT AND FLIGHT CREW
Baker Coll of Flint (MI)
Baker Coll of Muskegon (MI)
Kansas State U (KS)
Lewis U (IL)
Santa Fe Coll (FL)
U of Alaska Fairbanks (AK)
Utah Valley U (UT)

AIR TRAFFIC CONTROL
LeTourneau U (TX)
Thomas Edison State Coll (NJ)

AIR TRANSPORTATION RELATED
Thomas Edison State Coll (NJ)

ALLIED HEALTH AND MEDICAL ASSISTING SERVICES RELATED
Florida National Coll (FL)
Jones Coll, Jacksonville (FL)
Stratford U, Falls Church (VA)
Thomas Edison State Coll (NJ)
Widener U (PA)
Young Harris Coll (GA)

ALLIED HEALTH DIAGNOSTIC, INTERVENTION, AND TREATMENT PROFESSIONS RELATED
Ball State U (IN)
Cameron U (OK)
Mercy Coll of Health Sciences (IA)
Pennsylvania Coll of Technology (PA)
Thomas Edison State Coll (NJ)

AMERICAN NATIVE/NATIVE AMERICAN LANGUAGES
Idaho State U (ID)
U of Alaska Fairbanks (AK)

AMERICAN SIGN LANGUAGE (ASL)
Bethel Coll (IN)
Idaho State U (ID)

ANIMAL/LIVESTOCK HUSBANDRY AND PRODUCTION
North Carolina State U (NC)
U of Connecticut (CT)

ANIMAL SCIENCES
Sul Ross State U (TX)
U of Connecticut (CT)
U of New Hampshire (NH)

ANIMAL SCIENCES RELATED
Santa Fe Coll (FL)

ANIMATION, INTERACTIVE TECHNOLOGY, VIDEO GRAPHICS AND SPECIAL EFFECTS
Mesa State Coll (CO)
National U (CA)

APPAREL AND TEXTILE MANUFACTURING
Fashion Inst of Technology (NY)

APPAREL AND TEXTILE MARKETING MANAGEMENT
U of the Incarnate Word (TX)

APPLIED HORTICULTURE/ HORTICULTURAL BUSINESS SERVICES RELATED
U of Massachusetts Amherst (MA)

APPLIED HORTICULTURE/ HORTICULTURE OPERATIONS
Pennsylvania Coll of Technology (PA)
Temple U (PA)
U of Connecticut (CT)
U of Maine at Augusta (ME)
U of New Hampshire (NH)

ARCHEOLOGY
Weber State U (UT)

ARCHITECTURAL DRAFTING AND CAD/CADD
Baker Coll of Flint (MI)
Baker Coll of Muskegon (MI)
Indiana U–Purdue U Indianapolis (IN)
New York City Coll of Technology of the City U of New York (NY)
Purdue U Calumet (IN)
Purdue U North Central (IN)
The U of Toledo (OH)
Western Kentucky U (KY)

ARCHITECTURAL ENGINEERING TECHNOLOGY
Baker Coll of Clinton Township (MI)
Baker Coll of Owosso (MI)
Baker Coll of Port Huron (MI)
Bluefield State Coll (WV)
Ferris State U (MI)
Indiana U–Purdue U Fort Wayne (IN)
Northern Kentucky U (KY)
Purdue U North Central (IN)
State U of New York Coll of Technology at Delhi (NY)
U of the District of Columbia (DC)
Vermont Tech Coll (VT)

ARCHITECTURAL TECHNOLOGY
Pennsylvania Coll of Technology (PA)
U of Maine at Augusta (ME)

ARCHITECTURE RELATED
Abilene Christian U (TX)

ARMY ROTC/MILITARY SCIENCE
Methodist U (NC)

ART
Coll of Coastal Georgia (GA)
Coll of Mount St. Joseph (OH)
Eastern New Mexico U (NM)
Felician Coll (NJ)
Hannibal-LaGrange U (MO)
Indiana Wesleyan U (IN)
Kent State U at Stark (OH)
Keystone Coll (PA)
Lourdes Coll (OH)
Methodist U (NC)
Northern Michigan U (MI)
Rivier Coll (NH)
State U of New York Empire State Coll (NY)
Union Coll (NE)
U of Rio Grande (OH)
The U of Toledo (OH)
Young Harris Coll (GA)

ART HISTORY, CRITICISM AND CONSERVATION
Clarke U (IA)
Thomas More Coll (KY)
U of Cincinnati (OH)

ARTIFICIAL INTELLIGENCE
Lamar U (TX)

ART TEACHER EDUCATION
Young Harris Coll (GA)

ASIAN STUDIES
U of Cincinnati (OH)

ASTRONOMY
Young Harris Coll (GA)

ATHLETIC TRAINING
Young Harris Coll (GA)

AUDIOLOGY AND SPEECH-LANGUAGE PATHOLOGY
U of Cincinnati (OH)

AUDIOVISUAL COMMUNICATIONS TECHNOLOGIES RELATED
AIB Coll of Business (IA)

AUTOBODY/COLLISION AND REPAIR TECHNOLOGY
Ferris State U (MI)
Idaho State U (ID)
Lewis-Clark State Coll (ID)
Montana State U Billings (MT)
Utah Valley U (UT)
Weber State U (UT)

AUTOMOBILE/AUTOMOTIVE MECHANICS TECHNOLOGY
Baker Coll of Flint (MI)
Dixie State Coll of Utah (UT)
Ferris State U (MI)
Idaho State U (ID)
Lamar U (TX)
Lewis-Clark State Coll (ID)
Mesa State Coll (CO)
Montana State U Billings (MT)
Montana Tech of The U of Montana (MT)
Northern Michigan U (MI)
Pennsylvania Coll of Technology (PA)
Pittsburg State U (KS)
Southern Adventist U (TN)
Southern Utah U (UT)
Utah Valley U (UT)
Walla Walla U (WA)

AUTOMOTIVE ENGINEERING TECHNOLOGY
Pennsylvania Coll of Technology (PA)
Santa Fe Coll (FL)
Vermont Tech Coll (VT)

AVIATION/AIRWAY MANAGEMENT
Mountain State U (WV)
Santa Fe Coll (FL)
U of the District of Columbia (DC)
Vaughn Coll of Aeronautics and Technology (NY)

AVIONICS MAINTENANCE TECHNOLOGY
Baker Coll of Flint (MI)
U of the District of Columbia (DC)
Vaughn Coll of Aeronautics and Technology (NY)

BAKING AND PASTRY ARTS
The Culinary Inst of America (NY)
Johnson & Wales U (FL)
Johnson & Wales U (RI)
Johnson & Wales U - Charlotte Campus (NC)
Kendall Coll (IL)
Pennsylvania Coll of Technology (PA)
Stratford U, Falls Church (VA)

BANKING AND FINANCIAL SUPPORT SERVICES
St. Petersburg Coll (FL)
Utah Valley U (UT)
Washburn U (KS)

BEHAVIORAL SCIENCES
Granite State Coll (NH)
Lewis-Clark State Coll (ID)
Methodist U (NC)

Oklahoma Wesleyan U (OK)
Utah Valley U (UT)

BIBLICAL STUDIES
Appalachian Bible Coll (WV)
Atlanta Christian Coll (GA)
Barclay Coll (KS)
Bethel Coll (IN)
Beulah Heights U (GA)
Boston Baptist Coll (MA)
Calvary Bible Coll and Theological Seminary (MO)
Carolina Christian Coll (NC)
Cincinnati Christian U (OH)
Clear Creek Baptist Bible Coll (KY)
Corban U (OR)
Covenant Coll (GA)
Dallas Baptist U (TX)
Emmaus Bible Coll (IA)
Faith Baptist Bible Coll and Theological Seminary (IA)
Free Will Baptist Bible Coll (TN)
Grace Coll (IN)
Heritage Christian U (AL)
Hillsdale Free Will Baptist Coll (OK)
Houghton Coll (NY)
John Brown U (AR)
Kuyper Coll (MI)
Lincoln Christian U (IL)
Maple Springs Baptist Bible Coll and Seminary (MD)
Mid-Atlantic Christian U (NC)
Simpson U (CA)
Southeastern Bible Coll (AL)
Southwestern Assemblies of God U (TX)
Trinity Coll of Florida (FL)
William Jessup U (CA)

BIOCHEMISTRY
Saint Joseph's Coll (IN)

BIOLOGICAL AND BIOMEDICAL SCIENCES RELATED
Alderson-Broaddus Coll (WV)

BIOLOGICAL AND PHYSICAL SCIENCES
Dalton State Coll (GA)
Ferris State U (MI)
Free Will Baptist Bible Coll (TN)
Jefferson Coll of Health Sciences (VA)
John Brown U (AR)
Ohio U–Zanesville (OH)
Penn State Altoona (PA)
Purdue U North Central (IN)
State U of New York Empire State Coll (NY)
Trine U (IN)
Valparaiso U (IN)
Young Harris Coll (GA)

BIOLOGY/BIOLOGICAL SCIENCES
Brewton-Parker Coll (GA)
Chestnut Hill Coll (PA)
Cleveland Chiropractic Coll– Kansas City Campus (KS)
Cleveland Chiropractic Coll–Los Angeles Campus (CA)
Coll of Coastal Georgia (GA)
Cumberland U (TN)
Dalton State Coll (GA)
Free Will Baptist Bible Coll (TN)
Immaculata U (PA)
Indiana U–Purdue U Fort Wayne (IN)
Indiana U South Bend (IN)
Indiana Wesleyan U (IN)
Lourdes Coll (OH)
Methodist U (NC)
Mount St. Mary's Coll (CA)
Oklahoma Wesleyan U (OK)
Presentation Coll (SD)
Purdue U North Central (IN)
Rogers State U (OK)
Shawnee State U (OH)
Thomas Edison State Coll (NJ)
Thomas More Coll (KY)
U of Cincinnati (OH)
U of New Hampshire at Manchester (NH)
U of Rio Grande (OH)

The U of Tampa (FL)
The U of Toledo (OH)
Utah Valley U (UT)
Wright State U (OH)
York Coll of Pennsylvania (PA)
Young Harris Coll (GA)

BIOLOGY/BIOTECHNOLOGY LABORATORY TECHNICIAN
Santa Fe Coll (FL)
U of the District of Columbia (DC)
Weber State U (UT)

BIOMEDICAL TECHNOLOGY
Baker Coll of Flint (MI)
ECPI Coll of Technology, Virginia Beach (VA)
Indiana U–Purdue U Indianapolis (IN)
Penn State Altoona (PA)
Penn State Berks (PA)
Penn State Erie, The Behrend Coll (PA)
Santa Fe Coll (FL)
Thomas Edison State Coll (NJ)
U of Arkansas for Medical Sciences (AR)

BIOTECHNOLOGY
Indiana U–Purdue U Indianapolis (IN)

BROADCAST JOURNALISM
Evangel U (MO)
Ohio U–Zanesville (OH)

BUILDING/CONSTRUCTION FINISHING, MANAGEMENT, AND INSPECTION RELATED
Baker Coll of Flint (MI)
John Brown U (AR)
Pratt Inst (NY)
State U of New York Coll of Technology at Delhi (NY)
Wentworth Inst of Technology (MA)

BUILDING/CONSTRUCTION SITE MANAGEMENT
Utah Valley U (UT)
Wentworth Inst of Technology (MA)

BUILDING/HOME/ CONSTRUCTION INSPECTION
Utah Valley U (UT)

BUILDING/PROPERTY MAINTENANCE
Southern Adventist U (TN)
Utah Valley U (UT)

BUSINESS ADMINISTRATION AND MANAGEMENT
AIB Coll of Business (IA)
American Public U System (WV)
Amridge U (AL)
Anderson U (IN)
Anna Maria Coll (MA)
Ashworth Coll (GA)
Austin Peay State U (TN)
Baker Coll of Allen Park (MI)
Baker Coll of Auburn Hills (MI)
Baker Coll of Flint (MI)
Baker Coll of Owosso (MI)
Ball State U (IN)
Benedictine Coll (KS)
Benedictine U (IL)
Bentley U (MA)
Bethel Coll (IN)
Brewton-Parker Coll (GA)
Brookline Coll, Phoenix (AZ)
Brookline Coll, Tucson (AZ)
Brookline Coll (NM)
Bryan Coll (TN)
Bryant & Stratton Coll - Wauwatosa Campus (WI)
Calumet Coll of Saint Joseph (IN)
Cameron U (OK)
Campbellsville U (KY)
Cazenovia Coll (NY)
Central Pennsylvania Coll (PA)
Chestnut Hill Coll (PA)
Clarion U of Pennsylvania (PA)
Cleary U (MI)

Coll of Coastal Georgia (GA)
Coll of Mount St. Joseph (OH)
Coll of St. Joseph (VT)
Coll of Saint Mary (NE)
Columbia Centro Universitario (PR)
Columbia Coll (PR)
Columbia Southern U (AL)
Concordia Coll–New York (NY)
Concord U (WV)
Corban U (OR)
Dakota State U (SD)
Dakota Wesleyan U (SD)
Dallas Baptist U (TX)
Dalton State Coll (GA)
Davenport U, Grand Rapids (MI)
DeVry U, North Brunswick (NJ)
Dixie State Coll of Utah (UT)
Edinboro U of Pennsylvania (PA)
Elizabethtown Coll (PA)
Everest U, Lakeland (FL)
Everest U, Tampa (FL)
Everest U, Tampa (FL)
Faulkner U (AL)
Ferris State U (MI)
Fisher Coll (MA)
Five Towns Coll (NY)
Florida Inst of Technology (FL)
Florida National Coll (FL)
Franklin U (OH)
Free Will Baptist Bible Coll (TN)
Friends U (KS)
Garrett Coll (MD)
Geneva Coll (PA)
Goldey-Beacom Coll (DE)
Grace Bible Coll (MI)
Hawai`i Pacific U (HI)
Herzing U (GA)
Husson U (ME)
Immaculata U (PA)
Indiana Tech (IN)
Indiana U of Pennsylvania (PA)
Indiana U–Purdue U Fort Wayne (IN)
Indiana Wesleyan U (IN)
Inter American U of Puerto Rico, Bayamón Campus (PR)
Inter American U of Puerto Rico, Guayama Campus (PR)
Inter American U of Puerto Rico, Metropolitan Campus (PR)
Inter American U of Puerto Rico, Ponce Campus (PR)
International Business Coll, Fort Wayne (IN)
Johnson State Coll (VT)
Jones Coll, Jacksonville (FL)
Jones International U (CO)
Kent State U (OH)
Kent State U at Stark (OH)
Keystone Coll (PA)
King's Coll (PA)
LA Coll International (CA)
Lake Superior State U (MI)
Lebanese American U (Lebanon)
Lebanon Valley Coll (PA)
Lincoln Memorial U (TN)
Lock Haven U of Pennsylvania (PA)
Long Island U, Brooklyn Campus (NY)
Madonna U (MI)
Maria Coll (NY)
Marietta Coll (OH)
Medgar Evers Coll of the City U of New York (NY)
Methodist U (NC)
MidAmerica Nazarene U (KS)
Midway Coll (KY)
Minnesota School of Business– Blaine (MN)
Missouri Baptist U (MO)
Montana State U Billings (MT)
Montreat Coll, Montreat (NC)
Mount Aloysius Coll (PA)
Mount Marty Coll (SD)
Muhlenberg Coll (PA)
Newbury Coll (MA)
Newman U (KS)
New Mexico Inst of Mining and Technology (NM)
Niagara U (NY)
Ohio U–Chillicothe (OH)
Oklahoma Panhandle State U (OK)
Oklahoma Wesleyan U (OK)
Peirce Coll (PA)
Penn Foster Coll (AZ)
Pennsylvania Coll of Technology (PA)

Pikeville Coll (KY)
Point Park U (PA)
Providence Coll (RI)
Regent U (VA)
Rider U (NJ)
Rivier Coll (NH)
Robert Morris U Illinois (IL)
Rogers State U (OK)
Rust Coll (MS)
Saint Francis U (PA)
St. John's U (NY)
Saint Joseph's U (PA)
St. Petersburg Coll (FL)
St. Thomas Aquinas Coll (NY)
Salve Regina U (RI)
Santa Fe Coll (FL)
Shawnee State U (OH)
Siena Heights U (MI)
Southern Adventist U (TN)
Southern California Inst of
    Technology (CA)
Southern Vermont Coll (VT)
Southwestern Assemblies of God U
    (TX)
Southwest Minnesota State U (MN)
Southwest U (LA)
State U of New York Coll of
    Technology at Delhi (NY)
State U of New York Empire State
    Coll (NY)
Stevens Inst of Business & Arts
    (MO)
Stratford U, Falls Church (VA)
Taylor U (IN)
Thomas Edison State Coll (NJ)
Thomas More Coll (KY)
Tiffin U (OH)
Trine U (IN)
Tulane U (LA)
Union Coll (NE)
The U of Akron (OH)
U of Alaska Fairbanks (AK)
U of Alaska Southeast (AK)
U of Arkansas–Fort Smith (AR)
U of Cincinnati (OH)
The U of Findlay (OH)
U of Maine at Augusta (ME)
U of Maine at Fort Kent (ME)
U of New Hampshire (NH)
U of New Hampshire at Manchester
    (NH)
U of Pennsylvania (PA)
U of Rio Grande (OH)
The U of Scranton (PA)
U of Sioux Falls (SD)
U of the Incarnate Word (TX)
U of the Virgin Islands (VI)
The U of Toledo (OH)
Upper Iowa U (IA)
Utah Valley U (UT)
Vermont Tech Coll (VT)
Villa Maria Coll of Buffalo (NY)
Walla Walla U (WA)
Walsh U (OH)
Wayland Baptist U (TX)
Waynesburg U (PA)
Webber International U (FL)
Western International U (AZ)
Western Kentucky U (KY)
Wilson Coll (PA)
Wright State U (OH)
Xavier U (OH)
York Coll of Pennsylvania (PA)
Young Harris Coll (GA)
Youngstown State U (OH)

BUSINESS ADMINISTRATION, MANAGEMENT AND OPERATIONS RELATED
AIB Coll of Business (IA)
Dixie State Coll of Utah (UT)
Embry-Riddle Aeronautical U–
    Worldwide (FL)
Mountain State U (WV)
U of Cincinnati (OH)

BUSINESS AND PERSONAL/ FINANCIAL SERVICES MARKETING
Dixie State Coll of Utah (UT)

BUSINESS AUTOMATION/ TECHNOLOGY/DATA ENTRY
Baker Coll of Clinton Township (MI)
ECPI Coll of Technology, Virginia
    Beach (VA)
Garrett Coll (MD)

Mesa State Coll (CO)
Montana State U Billings (MT)
Northern Michigan U (MI)
Skyline Coll (VA)
U of Rio Grande (OH)
The U of Toledo (OH)
Utah Valley U (UT)

BUSINESS/COMMERCE
Adams State Coll (CO)
AIB Coll of Business (IA)
Alvernia U (PA)
Andrew Jackson U (AL)
Baker Coll of Flint (MI)
Bryant & Stratton Coll - Wauwatosa
    Campus (WI)
Castleton State Coll (VT)
Coll of Staten Island of the City U of
    New York (NY)
Columbia Coll (MO)
Columbia Southern U (AL)
Crown Coll (MN)
Cumberland U (TN)
Dalton State Coll (GA)
Delaware Valley Coll (PA)
Ferris State U (MI)
Fisher Coll (MA)
Gannon U (PA)
Garrett Coll (MD)
Granite State Coll (NH)
Hillsdale Free Will Baptist Coll (OK)
Idaho State U (ID)
Indiana U East (IN)
Indiana U Kokomo (IN)
Indiana U Northwest (IN)
Indiana U South Bend (IN)
Indiana U Southeast (IN)
Keystone Coll (PA)
Limestone Coll (SC)
Mayville State U (ND)
Midway Coll (KY)
Missouri Southern State U (MO)
Montana State U Billings (MT)
Mount Vernon Nazarene U (OH)
New York U (NY)
Northern Kentucky U (KY)
Northern Michigan U (MI)
Northwestern State U of Louisiana
    (LA)
Penn State Abington (PA)
Penn State Altoona (PA)
Penn State Berks (PA)
Penn State Erie, The Behrend Coll
    (PA)
Penn State Harrisburg (PA)
Penn State U Park (PA)
Saint Leo U (FL)
Saint Mary-of-the-Woods Coll (IN)
Southern Arkansas U–Magnolia
    (AR)
Southern Nazarene U (OK)
Southern Wesleyan U (SC)
Southwestern Assemblies of God U
    (TX)
Spalding U (KY)
Thomas More Coll (KY)
Thomas U (GA)
Troy U (AL)
Tulane U (LA)
U of Bridgeport (CT)
U of Cincinnati (OH)
U of Massachusetts Lowell (MA)
U of New Hampshire (NH)
The U of Toledo (OH)
Wright State U (OH)
Youngstown State U (OH)

BUSINESS/CORPORATE COMMUNICATIONS
Chestnut Hill Coll (PA)

BUSINESS MACHINE REPAIR
Lamar U (TX)

BUSINESS, MANAGEMENT, AND MARKETING RELATED
Ball State U (IN)
Presentation Coll (SD)
Purdue U North Central (IN)
Sacred Heart U (CT)
Young Harris Coll (GA)

BUSINESS OPERATIONS SUPPORT AND SECRETARIAL SERVICES RELATED
Thomas Edison State Coll (NJ)

BUSINESS TEACHER EDUCATION
Wright State U (OH)

CABINETMAKING AND MILLWORK
Utah Valley U (UT)

CAD/CADD DRAFTING/DESIGN TECHNOLOGY
Ferris State U (MI)
Idaho State U (ID)
ITT Tech Inst, Tempe (AZ)
ITT Tech Inst, Clovis (CA)
ITT Tech Inst, Concord (CA)
ITT Tech Inst, Corona (CA)
ITT Tech Inst, South Bend (IN)
ITT Tech Inst (KS)
ITT Tech Inst, Lexington (KY)
ITT Tech Inst (MS)
ITT Tech Inst, Springfield (MO)
ITT Tech Inst, Charlotte (NC)
ITT Tech Inst, Oklahoma City (OK)
Montana Tech of The U of Montana
    (MT)
Northern Michigan U (MI)
Shawnee State U (OH)
U of Arkansas–Fort Smith (AR)

CARDIOVASCULAR TECHNOLOGY
Mercy Coll of Northwest Ohio (OH)
Molloy Coll (NY)
New York U (NY)
Santa Fe Coll (FL)
The U of Toledo (OH)

CARPENTRY
Idaho State U (ID)
Montana State U Billings (MT)
Montana Tech of The U of Montana
    (MT)
Southern Utah U (UT)
U of Alaska Fairbanks (AK)
U of Alaska Southeast (AK)

CHEMICAL ENGINEERING
U of New Haven (CT)
U of the District of Columbia (DC)

CHEMICAL TECHNOLOGY
Ball State U (IN)
Ferris State U (MI)
Indiana U–Purdue U Fort Wayne
    (IN)
Inter American U of Puerto Rico,
    Guayama Campus (PR)
Lawrence Technological U (MI)
Miami U (OH)
Millersville U of Pennsylvania (PA)
New York City Coll of Technology of
    the City U of New York (NY)
U of Cincinnati (OH)
U of Puerto Rico at Humacao (PR)
The U of Toledo (OH)
Weber State U (UT)

CHEMISTRY
Castleton State Coll (VT)
Chestnut Hill Coll (PA)
Clarke U (IA)
Coll of Coastal Georgia (GA)
Dalton State Coll (GA)
Immaculata U (PA)
Indiana U–Purdue U Indianapolis
    (IN)
Indiana U South Bend (IN)
Indiana Wesleyan U (IN)
Lake Superior State U (MI)
Lindsey Wilson Coll (KY)
Methodist U (NC)
Oklahoma Wesleyan U (OK)
Presentation Coll (SD)
Purdue U North Central (IN)
Southern Arkansas U–Magnolia
    (AR)
Thomas More Coll (KY)
U of Cincinnati (OH)
U of Rio Grande (OH)
The U of Tampa (FL)
U of the Incarnate Word (TX)
Utah Valley U (UT)
Wright State U (OH)
York Coll of Pennsylvania (PA)
Young Harris Coll (GA)

CHILD-CARE AND SUPPORT SERVICES MANAGEMENT
Bob Jones U (SC)
Cameron U (OK)
Chestnut Hill Coll (PA)
Eastern New Mexico U (NM)
Ferris State U (MI)
Henderson State U (AR)
Idaho State U (ID)
Mount Vernon Nazarene U (OH)
Nicholls State U (LA)
Purdue U Calumet (IN)
Rust Coll (MS)
Southeast Missouri State U (MO)
Weber State U (UT)
Youngstown State U (OH)

CHILD-CARE PROVISION
Mayville State U (ND)
Murray State U (KY)
Pennsylvania Coll of Technology
    (PA)
Saint Mary-of-the-Woods Coll (IN)
Santa Fe Coll (FL)
Trevecca Nazarene U (TN)

CHILD DEVELOPMENT
Arkansas Tech U (AR)
Evangel U (MO)
Kuyper Coll (MI)
Lamar U (TX)
Lewis-Clark State Coll (ID)
Madonna U (MI)
Northern Michigan U (MI)
Ohio U (OH)
Ohio U–Chillicothe (OH)
Southern Utah U (UT)
U of the District of Columbia (DC)
Youngstown State U (OH)

CHIROPRACTIC ASSISTANT
Palmer Coll of Chiropractic (IA)

CHRISTIAN STUDIES
Crown Coll (MN)
Dallas Baptist U (TX)
Huntington U (IN)
Regent U (VA)
Wayland Baptist U (TX)

CINEMATOGRAPHY AND FILM/ VIDEO PRODUCTION
Collins Coll (AZ)
Santa Fe Coll (FL)
U of Advancing Technology (AZ)

CITY/URBAN, COMMUNITY AND REGIONAL PLANNING
U of Cincinnati (OH)

CIVIL ENGINEERING TECHNOLOGY
Bluefield State Coll (WV)
Fairmont State U (WV)
Ferris State U (MI)
Idaho State U (ID)
Indiana U–Purdue U Fort Wayne
    (IN)
Indiana U–Purdue U Indianapolis
    (IN)
Montana Tech of The U of Montana
    (MT)
New York City Coll of Technology of
    the City U of New York (NY)
Penn Foster Coll (AZ)
Pennsylvania Coll of Technology
    (PA)
Point Park U (PA)
Purdue U Calumet (IN)
Purdue U North Central (IN)
U of New Hampshire (NH)
U of the District of Columbia (DC)
The U of Toledo (OH)
Vermont Tech Coll (VT)
Youngstown State U (OH)

CLINICAL LABORATORY SCIENCE/MEDICAL TECHNOLOGY
Arkansas State U (AR)
Dalton State Coll (GA)
Shawnee State U (OH)
Thomas Edison State Coll (NJ)
U of Arkansas for Medical Sciences
    (AR)

U of Cincinnati (OH)
The U of Toledo (OH)
Young Harris Coll (GA)

CLINICAL/MEDICAL LABORATORY ASSISTANT
U of Maine at Augusta (ME)

CLINICAL/MEDICAL LABORATORY SCIENCE AND ALLIED PROFESSIONS RELATED
Youngstown State U (OH)

CLINICAL/MEDICAL LABORATORY TECHNOLOGY
Baker Coll of Owosso (MI)
Boston U (MA)
Brookline Coll, Phoenix (AZ)
Brookline Coll, Tempe (AZ)
Brookline Coll, Tucson (AZ)
Coll of Coastal Georgia (GA)
Dalton State Coll (GA)
Ferris State U (MI)
Indiana U Northwest (IN)
Indiana U South Bend (IN)
Marshall U (WV)
Mount Aloysius Coll (PA)
Our Lady of the Lake Coll (LA)
St. Petersburg Coll (FL)
U of Maine at Presque Isle (ME)
U of Rio Grande (OH)
U of the District of Columbia (DC)
Youngstown State U (OH)

COMMERCIAL AND ADVERTISING ART
Baker Coll of Auburn Hills (MI)
Baker Coll of Clinton Township (MI)
Baker Coll of Muskegon (MI)
Baker Coll of Owosso (MI)
Baker Coll of Port Huron (MI)
Central Pennsylvania Coll (PA)
Collins Coll (AZ)
Fashion Inst of Technology (NY)
Ferris State U (MI)
Indiana U–Purdue U Fort Wayne
    (IN)
Mitchell Coll (CT)
New York City Coll of Technology of
    the City U of New York (NY)
Northern State U (SD)
Pennsylvania Coll of Technology
    (PA)
Pratt Inst (NY)
Robert Morris U Illinois (IL)
Santa Fe Coll (FL)
Suffolk U (MA)
U of Advancing Technology (AZ)
U of Cincinnati (OH)
U of New Haven (CT)
U of the District of Columbia (DC)
Utah Valley U (UT)
Villa Maria Coll of Buffalo (NY)
Virginia Intermont Coll (VA)

COMMERCIAL PHOTOGRAPHY
Fashion Inst of Technology (NY)
Paier Coll of Art, Inc. (CT)

COMMUNICATION
Thomas More Coll (KY)
Xavier U (OH)

COMMUNICATION AND JOURNALISM RELATED
Clarke U (IA)
Immaculata U (PA)
Keystone Coll (PA)
Madonna U (MI)
Tulane U (LA)
Valparaiso U (IN)
Young Harris Coll (GA)

COMMUNICATION AND MEDIA RELATED
Elizabethtown Coll (PA)
Keystone Coll (PA)
Lebanese American U (Lebanon)
Young Harris Coll (GA)

COMMUNICATION SCIENCES AND DISORDERS
Ohio U–Chillicothe (OH)

COMMUNICATIONS SYSTEMS INSTALLATION AND REPAIR TECHNOLOGY
Idaho State U (ID)

COMMUNICATIONS TECHNOLOGIES AND SUPPORT SERVICES RELATED
Southern Adventist U (TN)

COMMUNICATIONS TECHNOLOGY
AIB Coll of Business (IA)
East Stroudsburg U of Pennsylvania (PA)
ITT Tech Inst, Oklahoma City (OK)
Mesa State Coll (CO)
U of Puerto Rico at Humacao (PR)

COMMUNITY HEALTH AND PREVENTIVE MEDICINE
Utah Valley U (UT)

COMMUNITY ORGANIZATION AND ADVOCACY
State U of New York Empire State Coll (NY)
U of Alaska Fairbanks (AK)
The U of Findlay (OH)
U of New Hampshire (NH)

COMPUTER AND INFORMATION SCIENCES
American Public U System (WV)
Ashworth Coll (GA)
Baker Coll of Allen Park (MI)
Ball State U (IN)
Bethel Coll (IN)
Clarke U (IA)
Coll of Mount St. Joseph (OH)
Coll of Saint Mary (NE)
Columbia Coll (MO)
Dalton State Coll (GA)
Delaware Valley Coll (PA)
ECPI Coll of Technology, Virginia Beach (VA)
Edinboro U of Pennsylvania (PA)
Fisher Coll (MA)
Franklin U (OH)
Herzing U (GA)
Herzing U, Madison (WI)
Indiana Wesleyan U (IN)
Inter American U of Puerto Rico, Ponce Campus (PR)
Jones Coll, Jacksonville (FL)
King's Coll (PA)
Lewis-Clark State Coll (ID)
Lincoln U (MO)
Manchester Coll (IN)
Merrimack Coll (MA)
Midway Coll (KY)
Montana State U Billings (MT)
New York City Coll of Technology of the City U of New York (NY)
Penn Foster Coll (AZ)
Rogers State U (OK)
St. John's U (NY)
Skyline Coll (VA)
Troy U (AL)
Tulane U (LA)
U of Arkansas–Fort Smith (AR)
U of Cincinnati (OH)
U of Maine at Augusta (ME)
The U of Tampa (FL)
Utah Valley U (UT)
Washburn U (KS)
Webber International U (FL)

COMPUTER AND INFORMATION SCIENCES AND SUPPORT SERVICES RELATED
Cleary U (MI)
Florida National Coll (FL)
Husson U (ME)
Inter American U of Puerto Rico, Guayama Campus (PR)
Montana State U Billings (MT)
Utah Valley U (UT)

COMPUTER AND INFORMATION SCIENCES RELATED
Limestone Coll (SC)
Lindsey Wilson Coll (KY)
Madonna U (MI)

COMPUTER AND INFORMATION SYSTEMS SECURITY
Davenport U, Grand Rapids (MI)
ECPI Coll of Technology, Virginia Beach (VA)
Florida National Coll (FL)
St. John's U (NY)
Skyline Coll (VA)

COMPUTER ENGINEERING
Johnson & Wales U (RI)
The U of Scranton (PA)

COMPUTER ENGINEERING TECHNOLOGIES RELATED
Thomas Edison State Coll (NJ)

COMPUTER ENGINEERING TECHNOLOGY
Baker Coll of Owosso (MI)
Dalton State U (ID)
Indiana U–Purdue U Indianapolis (IN)
ITT Tech Inst, Tempe (AZ)
ITT Tech Inst, Clovis (CA)
ITT Tech Inst, Concord (CA)
ITT Tech Inst, Corona (CA)
ITT Tech Inst, South Bend (IN)
ITT Tech Inst (KS)
ITT Tech Inst, Lexington (KY)
ITT Tech Inst (MS)
ITT Tech Inst, Springfield (MO)
ITT Tech Inst, Charlotte (NC)
ITT Tech Inst, Oklahoma City (OK)
Lake Superior State U (MI)
Northern Michigan U (MI)
St. Petersburg Coll (FL)
U of Hartford (CT)
U of the District of Columbia (DC)
Vermont Tech Coll (VT)
Weber State U (UT)

COMPUTER GRAPHICS
Baker Coll of Cadillac (MI)
ECPI Coll of Technology, Virginia Beach (VA)
Florida National Coll (FL)
Indiana Tech (IN)
Mountain State U (WV)
U of Advancing Technology (AZ)

COMPUTER/INFORMATION TECHNOLOGY SERVICES ADMINISTRATION RELATED
Dalton State Coll (GA)
Keystone Coll (PA)
Limestone Coll (SC)
Maria Coll (NY)
Pennsylvania Coll of Technology (PA)
St. Petersburg Coll (FL)

COMPUTER INSTALLATION AND REPAIR TECHNOLOGY
Dalton State Coll (GA)
Inter American U of Puerto Rico, Bayamón Campus (PR)
U of Alaska Fairbanks (AK)

COMPUTER PROGRAMMING
Baker Coll of Muskegon (MI)
Baker Coll of Owosso (MI)
Baker Coll of Port Huron (MI)
Castleton State Coll (VT)
Coll of Staten Island of the City U of New York (NY)
Dakota State U (SD)
Delaware Valley Coll (PA)
ECPI Coll of Technology, Virginia Beach (VA)
Everest U, Lakeland (FL)
Everest U, Tampa (FL)
Florida National Coll (FL)
International Business Coll, Fort Wayne (IN)

Johnson & Wales U (RI)
Kent State U (OH)
Keystone Coll (PA)
Limestone Coll (SC)
Medgar Evers Coll of the City U of New York (NY)
Missouri Southern State U (MO)
Pennsylvania Coll of Technology (PA)
Purdue U Calumet (IN)
Saint Francis U (PA)
St. Petersburg Coll (FL)
Stratford U, Falls Church (VA)
U of Advancing Technology (AZ)
The U of Toledo (OH)
Walla Walla U (WA)
Youngstown State U (OH)

COMPUTER PROGRAMMING RELATED
American Public U System (WV)
Florida National Coll (FL)
Herzing U, Madison (WI)
Stratford U, Falls Church (VA)

COMPUTER PROGRAMMING (SPECIFIC APPLICATIONS)
Florida National Coll (FL)
Idaho State U (ID)
Indiana U East (IN)
Indiana U South Bend (IN)
Indiana U Southeast (IN)
Kent State U (OH)
The U of Toledo (OH)

COMPUTER PROGRAMMING (VENDOR/PRODUCT CERTIFICATION)
Peirce Coll (PA)

COMPUTER SCIENCE
Alderson-Broaddus Coll (WV)
Baker Coll of Allen Park (MI)
Baker Coll of Owosso (MI)
Boston U (MA)
Calumet Coll of Saint Joseph (IN)
Central Pennsylvania Coll (PA)
Coll of Coastal Georgia (GA)
Creighton U (NE)
Dalton State Coll (GA)
Everest U, Lakeland (FL)
Everest U, Tampa (FL)
Felician Coll (NJ)
Florida National Coll (FL)
Franklin U (OH)
Hawai`i Pacific U (HI)
Inter American U of Puerto Rico, Bayamón Campus (PR)
Inter American U of Puerto Rico, Ponce Campus (PR)
Lebanese American U (Lebanon)
Lyndon State Coll (VT)
Madonna U (MI)
Methodist U (NC)
Mountain State U (WV)
New York City Coll of Technology of the City U of New York (NY)
Southern California Inst of Technology (CA)
Thomas Edison State Coll (NJ)
The U of Findlay (OH)
U of Maine at Fort Kent (ME)
U of New Haven (CT)
U of Rio Grande (OH)
U of the Virgin Islands (VI)
Utah Valley U (UT)
Walsh U (OH)
Waynesburg U (PA)
Young Harris Coll (GA)

COMPUTER SOFTWARE AND MEDIA APPLICATIONS RELATED
Everest U, Tampa (FL)
International Academy of Design & Technology (FL)
ITT Tech Inst, Tempe (AZ)

COMPUTER SOFTWARE ENGINEERING
Vermont Tech Coll (VT)

COMPUTER SOFTWARE TECHNOLOGY
ITT Tech Inst, Tempe (AZ)
ITT Tech Inst, Clovis (CA)
ITT Tech Inst, Corona (CA)
ITT Tech Inst, South Bend (IN)
ITT Tech Inst (KS)
ITT Tech Inst, Lexington (KY)
ITT Tech Inst (MS)
ITT Tech Inst, Springfield (MO)
ITT Tech Inst, Oklahoma City (OK)

COMPUTER SYSTEMS ANALYSIS
Davenport U, Grand Rapids (MI)
Johnson & Wales U (RI)
Santa Fe Coll (FL)
U of Advancing Technology (AZ)
The U of Akron (OH)
The U of Toledo (OH)

COMPUTER SYSTEMS NETWORKING AND TELECOMMUNICATIONS
Baker Coll of Allen Park (MI)
Baker Coll of Flint (MI)
Clayton State U (GA)
DeVry Coll of New York (NY)
DeVry U, Phoenix (AZ)
DeVry U, Pomona (CA)
DeVry U, Westminster (CO)
DeVry U, Miramar (FL)
DeVry U, Orlando (FL)
DeVry U, Decatur (GA)
DeVry U, Chicago (IL)
DeVry U, Kansas City (MO)
DeVry U, North Brunswick (NJ)
DeVry U, Columbus (OH)
DeVry U, Fort Washington (PA)
DeVry U, Houston (TX)
DeVry U, Irving (TX)
DeVry U, Arlington (VA)
DeVry U, Federal Way (WA)
DeVry U Online (IL)
Florida National Coll (FL)
Herzing U, Madison (WI)
Idaho State U (ID)
Indiana Tech (IN)
Lincoln U (MO)
Montana Tech of The U of Montana (MT)
Pace U (NY)
Pennsylvania Coll of Technology (PA)
Robert Morris U Illinois (IL)
Stratford U, Falls Church (VA)
The U of Akron (OH)

COMPUTER TEACHER EDUCATION
Baker Coll of Flint (MI)

COMPUTER TECHNOLOGY/ COMPUTER SYSTEMS TECHNOLOGY
Collins Coll (AZ)
Dalton State Coll (GA)
Garrett Coll (MD)
New York City Coll of Technology of the City U of New York (NY)
Southeast Missouri State U (MO)
U of Cincinnati (OH)

COMPUTER TYPOGRAPHY AND COMPOSITION EQUIPMENT OPERATION
Baker Coll of Auburn Hills (MI)
Baker Coll of Cadillac (MI)
Baker Coll of Clinton Township (MI)
Baker Coll of Flint (MI)
Baker Coll of Jackson (MI)
Calumet Coll of Saint Joseph (IN)
U of Cincinnati (OH)
The U of Toledo (OH)

CONSTRUCTION ENGINEERING TECHNOLOGY
Baker Coll of Owosso (MI)
Coll of Staten Island of the City U of New York (NY)
Ferris State U (MI)
Lake Superior State U (MI)
Lawrence Technological U (MI)

New York City Coll of Technology of the City U of New York (NY)
Pennsylvania Coll of Technology (PA)
Santa Fe Coll (FL)
State U of New York Coll of Technology at Delhi (NY)
The U of Akron (OH)
The U of Toledo (OH)
Vermont Tech Coll (VT)

CONSTRUCTION MANAGEMENT
Ashworth Coll (GA)
U of Alaska Fairbanks (AK)
Vermont Tech Coll (VT)

CONSTRUCTION TRADES
Mesa State Coll (CO)
Northern Michigan U (MI)
Utah Valley U (UT)

CONSTRUCTION TRADES RELATED
John Brown U (AR)
Utah Valley U (UT)

CONSUMER MERCHANDISING/ RETAILING MANAGEMENT
Baker Coll of Owosso (MI)
Madonna U (MI)
The U of Toledo (OH)

COOKING AND RELATED CULINARY ARTS
Kendall Coll (IL)
Mesa State Coll (CO)

CORRECTIONS
Baker Coll of Muskegon (MI)
Garrett Coll (MD)
Lake Superior State U (MI)
Lamar U (TX)
Mount Aloysius Coll (PA)
U of the District of Columbia (DC)
The U of Toledo (OH)
Washburn U (KS)
Xavier U (OH)

CORRECTIONS ADMINISTRATION
John Jay Coll of Criminal Justice of the City U of New York (NY)

CORRECTIONS AND CRIMINAL JUSTICE RELATED
Corban U (OR)
Florida Inst of Technology (FL)

COSMETOLOGY
Lamar U (TX)

COUNSELING PSYCHOLOGY
Atlanta Christian Coll (GA)

COURT REPORTING
AIB Coll of Business (IA)

CREATIVE WRITING
U of Maine at Presque Isle (ME)

CRIMINAL JUSTICE/LAW ENFORCEMENT ADMINISTRATION
Anderson U (IN)
Arkansas State U (AR)
Ashworth Coll (GA)
Bemidji State U (MN)
Boise State U (ID)
Brookline Coll, Phoenix (AZ)
Brookline Coll, Tempe (AZ)
Brookline Coll, Tucson (AZ)
Brookline Coll (NM)
Bryant & Stratton Coll - Wauwatosa Campus (WI)
Calumet Coll of Saint Joseph (IN)
Campbellsville U (KY)
Castleton State Coll (VT)
Chestnut Hill Coll (PA)
Coll of Coastal Georgia (GA)
Coll of St. Joseph (VT)
Columbia Coll (MO)

Dalton State Coll (GA)
ECPI Coll of Technology, Virginia Beach (VA)
Everest U, Tampa (FL)
Everest U, Tampa (FL)
Faulkner U (AL)
Fisher Coll (MA)
Florida National Coll (FL)
Graceland U (IA)
Hannibal-LaGrange U (MO)
Hawai'i Pacific U (HI)
ITT Tech Inst, Tempe (AZ)
ITT Tech Inst, Clovis (CA)
ITT Tech Inst, Concord (CA)
ITT Tech Inst, Corona (CA)
ITT Tech Inst, South Bend (IN)
ITT Tech Inst (KS)
ITT Tech Inst, Lexington (KY)
ITT Tech Inst (MS)
ITT Tech Inst, Springfield (MO)
ITT Tech Inst, Oklahoma City (OK)
LA Coll International (CA)
Lake Superior State U (MI)
Lincoln U (MO)
Lock Haven U of Pennsylvania (PA)
MacMurray Coll (IL)
Mansfield U of Pennsylvania (PA)
Mesa State Coll (CO)
Methodist U (NC)
Northern Michigan U (MI)
Penn Foster Coll (AZ)
Regent U (VA)
Reinhardt U (GA)
St. John's U (NY)
St. Petersburg Coll (FL)
Santa Fe Coll (FL)
Skyline Coll (VA)
Southern Utah U (UT)
Southern Vermont Coll (VT)
Southwest U (LA)
Suffolk U (MA)
Thomas U (GA)
Tiffin U (OH)
Trine U (IN)
U of Arkansas at Pine Bluff (AR)
U of Arkansas–Fort Smith (AR)
The U of Findlay (OH)
U of Maine at Fort Kent (ME)
U of Maine at Presque Isle (ME)
Utah Valley U (UT)
Washburn U (KS)
Wayland Baptist U (TX)
York Coll of Pennsylvania (PA)
Young Harris Coll (GA)

CRIMINAL JUSTICE/POLICE SCIENCE
Arkansas State U (AR)
Armstrong Atlantic State U (GA)
Cameron U (OK)
Dalton State Coll (GA)
Ferris State U (MI)
Husson U (ME)
Idaho State U (ID)
John Jay Coll of Criminal Justice of the City U of New York (NY)
Lake Superior State U (MI)
MacMurray Coll (IL)
Miami U (OH)
Missouri Southern State U (MO)
Northern Kentucky U (KY)
Northwestern State U of Louisiana (LA)
Ohio U–Chillicothe (OH)
Oklahoma Panhandle State U (OK)
Rogers State U (OK)
The U of Akron (OH)
U of Arkansas at Pine Bluff (AR)
U of Louisiana at Monroe (LA)
U of New Haven (CT)
U of the District of Columbia (DC)
U of the Virgin Islands (VI)
The U of Toledo (OH)
Washburn U (KS)

CRIMINAL JUSTICE/SAFETY
Amridge U (AL)
Andrew Jackson U (AL)
Arkansas Tech U (AR)
Ball State U (IN)
Bethel Coll (IN)
Cazenovia Coll (NY)
Central Pennsylvania Coll (PA)
Columbia Southern U (AL)
Columbus State U (GA)
Dakota Wesleyan U (SD)
Dixie State Coll of Utah (UT)
Edinboro U of Pennsylvania (PA)

Everest U, Lakeland (FL)
Fisher Coll (MA)
Gannon U (PA)
Husson U (ME)
Idaho State U (ID)
Indiana Tech (IN)
Indiana U East (IN)
Indiana U Kokomo (IN)
Indiana U Northwest (IN)
Indiana U–Purdue U Indianapolis (IN)
Indiana U South Bend (IN)
Indiana Wesleyan U (IN)
Keystone Coll (PA)
King's Coll (PA)
Lourdes Coll (OH)
Madonna U (MI)
Manchester Coll (IN)
Minnesota School of Business–Blaine (MN)
Mountain State U (WV)
New Mexico State U (NM)
Northern Michigan U (MI)
Penn State Altoona (PA)
Pikeville Coll (KY)
Thomas Edison State Coll (NJ)
Thomas More Coll (KY)
U of Cincinnati (OH)
U of Maine at Augusta (ME)
The U of Scranton (PA)
Xavier U (OH)
Youngstown State U (OH)

CRIMINOLOGY
Dalton State Coll (GA)
Faulkner U (AL)
Indiana U of Pennsylvania (PA)
U of the District of Columbia (DC)

CROP PRODUCTION
North Carolina State U (NC)
U of Massachusetts Amherst (MA)

CULINARY ARTS
Baker Coll of Muskegon (MI)
Bob Jones U (SC)
The Culinary Inst of America (NY)
ECPI Coll of Technology, Virginia Beach (VA)
Idaho State U (ID)
Johnson & Wales U (CO)
Johnson & Wales U (FL)
Johnson & Wales U (RI)
Johnson & Wales U - Charlotte Campus (NC)
Kendall Coll (IL)
Keystone Coll (PA)
Mountain State U (WV)
Newbury Coll (MA)
Nicholls State U (LA)
Pennsylvania Coll of Technology (PA)
Robert Morris U Illinois (IL)
State U of New York Coll of Technology at Delhi (NY)
Stratford U, Falls Church (VA)
The U of Akron (OH)
U of Alaska Fairbanks (AK)
Utah Valley U (UT)

CULINARY ARTS RELATED
Delaware Valley Coll (PA)
Johnson & Wales U (CO)
Johnson & Wales U (FL)
Johnson & Wales U (RI)
Keystone Coll (PA)
New York Inst of Technology (NY)

DAIRY SCIENCE
Vermont Tech Coll (VT)

DANCE
Utah Valley U (UT)

DATA ENTRY/MICROCOMPUTER APPLICATIONS
Baker Coll of Allen Park (MI)
Florida National Coll (FL)
The U of Akron (OH)

DATA ENTRY/MICROCOMPUTER APPLICATIONS RELATED
Baker Coll of Allen Park (MI)
Florida National Coll (FL)

DATA PROCESSING AND DATA PROCESSING TECHNOLOGY
Baker Coll of Auburn Hills (MI)
Baker Coll of Cadillac (MI)
Baker Coll of Clinton Township (MI)
Baker Coll of Flint (MI)
Baker Coll of Jackson (MI)
Baker Coll of Muskegon (MI)
Baker Coll of Owosso (MI)
Baker Coll of Port Huron (MI)
Campbellsville U (KY)
Dordt Coll (IA)
Everest U, Lakeland (FL)
Florida National Coll (FL)
Lamar U (TX)
Miami U (OH)
Montana State U Billings (MT)
Mount Vernon Nazarene U (OH)
New York Inst of Technology (NY)
Northern State U (SD)
Pace U (NY)
Peirce Coll (PA)
U of Advancing Technology (AZ)
U of Cincinnati (OH)
The U of Toledo (OH)
Utah Valley U (UT)
Western Kentucky U (KY)
Youngstown State U (OH)

DENTAL ASSISTING
Boston U (MA)
ECPI Coll of Technology, Virginia Beach (VA)
Thomas Edison State Coll (NJ)
U of Alaska Fairbanks (AK)
U of Southern Indiana (IN)

DENTAL HYGIENE
Armstrong Atlantic State U (GA)
Baker Coll of Port Huron (MI)
Coll of Coastal Georgia (GA)
Dalton State Coll (GA)
Dixie State Coll of Utah (UT)
Ferris State U (MI)
Florida National Coll (FL)
Indiana U Northwest (IN)
Indiana U–Purdue U Fort Wayne (IN)
Indiana U–Purdue U Indianapolis (IN)
Indiana U South Bend (IN)
Lamar U (TX)
Missouri Southern State U (MO)
Mount Ida Coll (MA)
New York City Coll of Technology of the City U of New York (NY)
New York U (NY)
Pennsylvania Coll of Technology (PA)
St. Petersburg Coll (FL)
Santa Fe Coll (FL)
Shawnee State U (OH)
Southern Adventist U (TN)
Thomas Edison State Coll (NJ)
U of Alaska Fairbanks (AK)
U of Arkansas for Medical Sciences (AR)
U of Arkansas–Fort Smith (AR)
U of Bridgeport (CT)
U of Cincinnati (OH)
U of Maine at Augusta (ME)
U of New England (ME)
U of New Haven (CT)
Utah Valley U (UT)
Vermont Tech Coll (VT)
Western Kentucky U (KY)
West Liberty U (WV)
Youngstown State U (OH)

DENTAL LABORATORY TECHNOLOGY
Florida National Coll (FL)
Idaho State U (ID)
Indiana U–Purdue U Fort Wayne (IN)
New York City Coll of Technology of the City U of New York (NY)

DESIGN AND APPLIED ARTS RELATED
U of Maine at Presque Isle (ME)

DESIGN AND VISUAL COMMUNICATIONS
Collins Coll (AZ)

ITT Tech Inst, Tempe (AZ)
ITT Tech Inst, Clovis (CA)
ITT Tech Inst, Concord (CA)
ITT Tech Inst, South Bend (IN)
ITT Tech Inst (KS)
ITT Tech Inst, Lexington (KY)
ITT Tech Inst (MS)
ITT Tech Inst, Springfield (MO)
ITT Tech Inst, Oklahoma City (OK)
U of Advancing Technology (AZ)
U of Cincinnati (OH)
Utah Valley U (UT)

DESKTOP PUBLISHING AND DIGITAL IMAGING DESIGN
Ferris State U (MI)
Murray State U (KY)

DIAGNOSTIC MEDICAL SONOGRAPHY AND ULTRASOUND TECHNOLOGY
Arkansas State U (AR)
Baker Coll of Auburn Hills (MI)
Baker Coll of Owosso (MI)
Baker Coll of Port Huron (MI)
Ferris State U (MI)
Florida National Coll (FL)
Keystone Coll (PA)
Mercy Coll of Health Sciences (IA)
Mountain State U (WV)
St. Catherine U (MN)
Santa Fe Coll (FL)
U of Arkansas for Medical Sciences (AR)

DIESEL MECHANICS TECHNOLOGY
Idaho State U (ID)
Lewis-Clark State Coll (ID)
Montana State U Billings (MT)
Pennsylvania Coll of Technology (PA)
Utah Valley U (UT)
Vermont Tech Coll (VT)
Weber State U (UT)

DIETETICS
Life U (GA)

DIETETIC TECHNOLOGY
Youngstown State U (OH)

DIETITIAN ASSISTANT
Youngstown State U (OH)

DIGITAL COMMUNICATION AND MEDIA/MULTIMEDIA
Corcoran Coll of Art and Design (DC)
Indiana U–Purdue U Indianapolis (IN)
Vaughn Coll of Aeronautics and Technology (NY)

DIVINITY/MINISTRY
Amridge U (AL)
Atlantic Union Coll (MA)
Carson-Newman Coll (TN)
Christian Life Coll (IL)
Clear Creek Baptist Bible Coll (KY)
Faith Baptist Bible Coll and Theological Seminary (IA)
Great Lakes Christian Coll (MI)
Providence Coll (RI)
Southeastern Baptist Theological Seminary (NC)
Victory U (TN)

DRAFTING AND DESIGN TECHNOLOGY
Baker Coll of Auburn Hills (MI)
Baker Coll of Clinton Township (MI)
Baker Coll of Owosso (MI)
Baker Coll of Port Huron (MI)
Dalton State Coll (GA)
Herzing U, Madison (WI)
International Academy of Design & Technology (FL)
Johnson & Wales U (RI)
Kentucky State U (KY)
Lamar U (TX)
LeTourneau U (TX)
Lewis-Clark State Coll (ID)
Lincoln U (MO)
Montana State U (MT)

Montana State U Billings (MT)
Murray State U (KY)
Robert Morris U Illinois (IL)
Southern Utah U (UT)
The U of Akron (OH)
U of Rio Grande (OH)
The U of Toledo (OH)
Utah Valley U (UT)
Washburn U (KS)
Weber State U (UT)
Wright State U (OH)
Youngstown State U (OH)

DRAFTING/DESIGN ENGINEERING TECHNOLOGIES RELATED
Pennsylvania Coll of Technology (PA)
Thomas Edison State Coll (NJ)

DRAMATIC/THEATER ARTS
Adams State Coll (CO)
Clarke U (IA)
Methodist U (NC)
Thomas More Coll (KY)
Utah Valley U (UT)
Young Harris Coll (GA)

DRAMATIC/THEATER ARTS AND STAGECRAFT RELATED
Utah Valley U (UT)

DRAWING
Pratt Inst (NY)

EARLY CHILDHOOD EDUCATION
Adams State Coll (CO)
American Public U System (WV)
Ashworth Coll (GA)
Baker Coll of Allen Park (MI)
Baker Coll of Jackson (MI)
Baptist Bible Coll of Pennsylvania (PA)
Bethel Coll (IN)
Coll of Saint Mary (NE)
Dixie State Coll of Utah (UT)
Gannon U (PA)
Granite State Coll (NH)
Great Lakes Christian Coll (MI)
Indiana U–Purdue U Fort Wayne (IN)
Indiana U–Purdue U Indianapolis (IN)
Indiana U South Bend (IN)
Keystone Coll (PA)
Lake Superior State U (MI)
Lincoln U (MO)
Lindsey Wilson Coll (KY)
Manchester Coll (IN)
Maranatha Baptist Bible Coll (WI)
Mitchell Coll (CT)
Nova Southeastern U (FL)
Pacific Union Coll (CA)
Penn Foster Coll (AZ)
Point Park U (PA)
Rust Coll (MS)
St. Petersburg Coll (FL)
Southwestern Assemblies of God U (TX)
Taylor U (IN)
U of Alaska Fairbanks (AK)
U of Alaska Southeast (AK)
U of Arkansas–Fort Smith (AR)
U of Southern Indiana (IN)
U of the Virgin Islands (VI)
Utah Valley U (UT)
Washburn U (KS)
Washington Adventist U (MD)
Western Kentucky U (KY)
Xavier U (OH)
Young Harris Coll (GA)

ECONOMICS
Dalton State Coll (GA)
Hawai'i Pacific U (HI)
Immaculata U (PA)
Methodist U (NC)
State U of New York Empire State Coll (NY)
Thomas More Coll (KY)
The U of Tampa (FL)

EDUCATION
Baker Coll of Auburn Hills (MI)
Baker Coll of Cadillac (MI)

Cincinnati Christian U (OH)
Cumberland U (TN)
Dalton State Coll (GA)
Florida National Coll (FL)
Garrett Coll (MD)
Kent State U (OH)
Lamar U (TX)
Montana State U Billings (MT)
Montreat Coll, Montreat (NC)
Mount Olive Coll (NC)
National U (CA)
Saint Francis U (PA)
Southwestern Assemblies of God U (TX)
State U of New York Empire State Coll (NY)
U of Cincinnati (OH)
Villa Maria Coll of Buffalo (NY)
Young Harris Coll (GA)

EDUCATIONAL ADMINISTRATION AND SUPERVISION RELATED
The U of Montana Western (MT)

EDUCATIONAL/ INSTRUCTIONAL TECHNOLOGY
Cameron U (OK)

EDUCATION (MULTIPLE LEVELS)
Coll of Coastal Georgia (GA)

EDUCATION RELATED
The U of Akron (OH)

ELECTRICAL AND ELECTRONIC ENGINEERING TECHNOLOGIES RELATED
Lawrence Technological U (MI)
Northern Michigan U (MI)
Penn Foster Coll (AZ)
Point Park U (PA)
Thomas Edison State Coll (NJ)
Vaughn Coll of Aeronautics and Technology (NY)
Youngstown State U (OH)

ELECTRICAL AND ELECTRONICS ENGINEERING
Fairfield U (CT)
Merrimack Coll (MA)
Southern California Inst of Technology (CA)

ELECTRICAL AND POWER TRANSMISSION INSTALLATION
State U of New York Coll of Technology at Delhi (NY)
U of Alaska Southeast (AK)

ELECTRICAL, ELECTRONIC AND COMMUNICATIONS ENGINEERING TECHNOLOGY
Baker Coll of Cadillac (MI)
Baker Coll of Owosso (MI)
Bluefield State Coll (WV)
Cameron U (OK)
Columbia Coll (PR)
Dalton State Coll (GA)
DeVry Coll of New York (NY)
DeVry U, Phoenix (AZ)
DeVry U, Pomona (CA)
DeVry U, Westminster (CO)
DeVry U, Miramar (FL)
DeVry U, Orlando (FL)
DeVry U, Decatur (GA)
DeVry U, Chicago (IL)
DeVry U, Kansas City (MO)
DeVry U, North Brunswick (NJ)
DeVry U, Columbus (OH)
DeVry U, Fort Washington (PA)
DeVry U, Houston (TX)
DeVry U, Irving (TX)
DeVry U, Federal Way (WA)
DeVry U Online (IL)
ECPI Coll of Technology, Virginia Beach (VA)
Fairmont State U (WV)
Hamilton Tech Coll (IA)
Herzing U (GA)

Herzing U, Madison (WI)
Idaho State U (ID)
Indiana State U (IN)
Indiana U–Purdue U Fort Wayne (IN)
Indiana U–Purdue U Indianapolis (IN)
Inter American U of Puerto Rico, San Germán Campus (PR)
Kentucky State U (KY)
Lake Superior State U (MI)
Lamar U (TX)
Lawrence Technological U (MI)
New York City Coll of Technology of the City U of New York (NY)
Northern Michigan U (MI)
Northwestern State U of Louisiana (LA)
Penn Foster Coll (AZ)
Penn State Altoona (PA)
Penn State Berks (PA)
Penn State Erie, The Behrend Coll (PA)
Pennsylvania Coll of Technology (PA)
Pittsburg State U (KS)
Purdue U Calumet (IN)
Purdue U North Central (IN)
Skyline Coll (VA)
Southern Utah U (UT)
Thomas Edison State Coll (NJ)
The U of Akron (OH)
U of Hartford (CT)
U of Massachusetts Lowell (MA)
U of Puerto Rico at Humacao (PR)
U of the District of Columbia (DC)
The U of Toledo (OH)
Utah Valley U (UT)
Vermont Tech Coll (VT)
Youngstown State U (OH)

ELECTRICAL/ELECTRONICS EQUIPMENT INSTALLATION AND REPAIR
Lewis-Clark State Coll (ID)
U of Arkansas–Fort Smith (AR)

ELECTRICAL/ELECTRONICS MAINTENANCE AND REPAIR TECHNOLOGY RELATED
Pittsburg State U (KS)

ELECTRICIAN
Pennsylvania Coll of Technology (PA)

ELECTROMECHANICAL TECHNOLOGY
Idaho State U (ID)
John Brown U (AR)
New York City Coll of Technology of the City U of New York (NY)
Northern Michigan U (MI)
Purdue U Calumet (IN)
Shawnee State U (OH)
Utah Valley U (UT)

ELECTRONEURODIAGNOSTIC / ELECTROENCEPHALOGRAPHIC TECHNOLOGY
DeVry U, North Brunswick (NJ)

ELEMENTARY EDUCATION
Adams State Coll (CO)
Dalton State Coll (GA)
Ferris State U (MI)
Garrett Coll (MD)
Hillsdale Free Will Baptist Coll (OK)
Mountain State U (WV)
Mount St. Mary's Coll (CA)
New Mexico Highlands U (NM)
Rogers State U (OK)
U of Alaska Southeast (AK)
U of Cincinnati (OH)
Wilson Coll (PA)

EMERGENCY CARE ATTENDANT (EMT AMBULANCE)
Trinity Coll of Nursing and Health Sciences (IL)

EMERGENCY MEDICAL TECHNOLOGY (EMT PARAMEDIC)
Baker Coll of Cadillac (MI)
Baker Coll of Clinton Township (MI)
Baker Coll of Muskegon (MI)
Creighton U (NE)
Dixie State Coll of Utah (UT)
Idaho State U (ID)
Indiana U–Purdue U Indianapolis (IN)
Indiana U South Bend (IN)
Indiana U Southeast (IN)
Mercy Coll of Health Sciences (IA)
Mesa State Coll (CO)
Montana State U Billings (MT)
Mountain State U (WV)
Pacific Union Coll (CA)
Pennsylvania Coll of Technology (PA)
Rogers State U (OK)
St. Petersburg Coll (FL)
Santa Fe Coll (FL)
Shawnee State U (OH)
Spalding U (KY)
Trinity Coll of Nursing and Health Sciences (IL)
U of Arkansas for Medical Sciences (AR)
U of Cincinnati (OH)
U of Pittsburgh at Johnstown (PA)
U of Sioux Falls (SD)
The U of Toledo (OH)
Weber State U (UT)
Western Kentucky U (KY)
Youngstown State U (OH)

ENERGY MANAGEMENT AND SYSTEMS TECHNOLOGY
Baker Coll of Flint (MI)
Idaho State U (ID)
Montana State U Billings (MT)
U of Rio Grande (OH)

ENGINEERING
Coll of Staten Island of the City U of New York (NY)
Daniel Webster Coll (NH)
Dixie State Coll of Utah (UT)
Ferris State U (MI)
Geneva Coll (PA)
Lake Superior State U (MI)
Lindsey Wilson Coll (KY)
Mountain State U (WV)
Palm Beach Atlantic U (FL)
Purdue U North Central (IN)
Southern Adventist U (TN)
Union Coll (NE)
Utah Valley U (UT)
Washington Adventist U (MD)

ENGINEERING RELATED
McNally Smith Coll of Music (MN)

ENGINEERING-RELATED TECHNOLOGIES
U of Alaska Southeast (AK)

ENGINEERING SCIENCE
Daniel Webster Coll (NH)
State U of New York Coll of Technology at Delhi (NY)
U of Pittsburgh at Bradford (PA)

ENGINEERING TECHNOLOGIES AND ENGINEERING RELATED
Arkansas State U (AR)
Cameron U (OK)
McNally Smith Coll of Music (MN)
Missouri Southern State U (MO)
Rogers State U (OK)
State U of New York Maritime Coll (NY)
Thomas Edison State Coll (NJ)
Utah Valley U (UT)

ENGINEERING TECHNOLOGY
Austin Peay State U (TN)
ECPI Coll of Technology, Virginia Beach (VA)
Fairmont State U (WV)
John Brown U (AR)
Kansas State U (KS)

Lake Superior State U (MI)
Lincoln U (MO)
Miami U (OH)
Northern Kentucky U (KY)
St. Petersburg Coll (FL)
Skyline Coll (VA)
State U of New York Coll of Technology at Delhi (NY)
Wright State U (OH)
Youngstown State U (OH)

ENGLISH
Calumet Coll of Saint Joseph (IN)
Coll of Coastal Georgia (GA)
Dalton State Coll (GA)
Felician Coll (NJ)
Hannibal-LaGrange U (MO)
Hillsdale Free Will Baptist Coll (OK)
Immaculata U (PA)
Indiana U–Purdue U Fort Wayne (IN)
Indiana Wesleyan U (IN)
Lourdes Coll (OH)
Madonna U (MI)
Methodist U (NC)
Southwestern Assemblies of God U (TX)
Thomas More Coll (KY)
U of Cincinnati (OH)
The U of Tampa (FL)
Utah Valley U (UT)
Xavier U (OH)
Young Harris Coll (GA)

ENGLISH LANGUAGE AND LITERATURE RELATED
Presentation Coll (SD)

ENGLISH/LANGUAGE ARTS TEACHER EDUCATION
Edgewood Coll (WI)
John Brown U (AR)
Lyndon State Coll (VT)
Young Harris Coll (GA)

ENTREPRENEURSHIP
Baker Coll of Flint (MI)
Central Pennsylvania Coll (PA)
Peirce Coll (PA)
U of the District of Columbia (DC)

ENVIRONMENTAL CONTROL TECHNOLOGIES RELATED
Montana Tech of The U of Montana (MT)
Utah Valley U (UT)

ENVIRONMENTAL ENGINEERING TECHNOLOGY
Baker Coll of Flint (MI)
Baker Coll of Owosso (MI)
Baker Coll of Port Huron (MI)
New York City Coll of Technology of the City U of New York (NY)
Ohio U–Chillicothe (OH)
U of the District of Columbia (DC)
The U of Toledo (OH)

ENVIRONMENTAL SCIENCE
Florida Inst of Technology (FL)
Thomas Edison State Coll (NJ)
Young Harris Coll (GA)

ENVIRONMENTAL STUDIES
Columbia Coll (MO)
Dickinson State U (ND)
Mountain State U (WV)
Southern Vermont Coll (VT)
The U of Findlay (OH)
The U of Toledo (OH)

EQUESTRIAN STUDIES
Centenary Coll (NJ)
Midway Coll (KY)
Saint Mary-of-the-Woods Coll (IN)
The U of Findlay (OH)
U of Massachusetts Amherst (MA)
The U of Montana Western (MT)

EXECUTIVE ASSISTANT/ EXECUTIVE SECRETARY
Baker Coll of Allen Park (MI)
Baker Coll of Flint (MI)

Pacific Union Coll (CA)
Santa Fe Coll (FL)
U of Arkansas–Fort Smith (AR)
U of Cincinnati (OH)
Western Kentucky U (KY)

FAMILY AND COMMUNITY SERVICES
Baker Coll of Flint (MI)

FAMILY AND CONSUMER ECONOMICS RELATED
Dalton State Coll (GA)

FAMILY AND CONSUMER SCIENCES/HUMAN SCIENCES
Mount Vernon Nazarene U (OH)

FAMILY PSYCHOLOGY
Corban U (OR)

FASHION/APPAREL DESIGN
Fashion Inst of Technology (NY)
Fisher Coll (MA)
Parsons The New School for Design (NY)

FASHION MERCHANDISING
Fashion Inst of Technology (NY)
Fisher Coll (MA)
The Illinois Inst of Art–Tinley Park (IL)
Immaculata U (PA)
New York City Coll of Technology of the City U of New York (NY)
Parsons The New School for Design (NY)
Penn Foster Coll (AZ)
Stevens Inst of Business & Arts (MO)
U of Bridgeport (CT)
U of the District of Columbia (DC)
Weber State U (UT)

FASHION MODELING
Fashion Inst of Technology (NY)

FILM/CINEMA/VIDEO STUDIES
Burlington Coll (VT)

FINANCE
AIB Coll of Business (IA)
Ashworth Coll (GA)
Davenport U, Grand Rapids (MI)
Franklin U (OH)
Hawai'i Pacific U (HI)
Indiana Wesleyan U (IN)
Methodist U (NC)
Penn Foster Coll (AZ)
The U of Findlay (OH)
Walsh U (OH)
Youngstown State U (OH)

FINANCIAL PLANNING AND SERVICES
U of Maine at Augusta (ME)

FINE ARTS RELATED
Pennsylvania Coll of Technology (PA)
Saint Francis U (PA)

FINE/STUDIO ARTS
Adams State Coll (CO)
Corcoran Coll of Art and Design (DC)
Fashion Inst of Technology (NY)
Keystone Coll (PA)
Lindsey Wilson Coll (KY)
Madonna U (MI)
Merrimack Coll (MA)
New Mexico State U (NM)
Pratt Inst (NY)
Thomas More Coll (KY)
U of Maine at Augusta (ME)
U of New Hampshire at Manchester (NH)
Villa Maria Coll of Buffalo (NY)
York Coll of Pennsylvania (PA)

FIRE PREVENTION AND SAFETY TECHNOLOGY
Montana State U Billings (MT)
Santa Fe Coll (FL)
Thomas Edison State Coll (NJ)
The U of Akron (OH)
U of Nebraska–Lincoln (NE)
U of New Haven (CT)
The U of Toledo (OH)

FIRE PROTECTION RELATED
The U of Akron (OH)

FIRE SCIENCE/FIREFIGHTING
American Public U System (WV)
Idaho State U (ID)
Lake Superior State U (MI)
Lamar U (TX)
Lewis-Clark State Coll (ID)
Madonna U (MI)
Mountain State U (WV)
Providence Coll (RI)
St. Petersburg Coll (FL)
U of Alaska Fairbanks (AK)
U of Cincinnati (OH)
Utah Valley U (UT)
Vermont Tech Coll (VT)

FIRE SERVICES ADMINISTRATION
Columbia Coll (MO)
Columbia Southern U (AL)

FISHING AND FISHERIES SCIENCES AND MANAGEMENT
U of Alaska Southeast (AK)

FOOD PREPARATION
Keystone Coll (PA)

FOOD SCIENCE
Lamar U (TX)

FOOD SERVICE SYSTEMS ADMINISTRATION
Northern Michigan U (MI)
U of New Hampshire (NH)
U of New Haven (CT)

FOODS, NUTRITION, AND WELLNESS
Huntington Coll of Health Sciences (TN)
Madonna U (MI)
Southern Adventist U (TN)
U of Maine at Presque Isle (ME)

FOOD TECHNOLOGY AND PROCESSING
Arkansas State U (AR)
U of the District of Columbia (DC)
Washburn U (KS)

FOREIGN LANGUAGES AND LITERATURES
Coll of Coastal Georgia (GA)
Dalton State Coll (GA)
Southwestern Assemblies of God U (TX)

FOREIGN LANGUAGES RELATED
U of Alaska Fairbanks (AK)

FORENSIC SCIENCE AND TECHNOLOGY
Arkansas State U (AR)
St. Petersburg Coll (FL)
U of Arkansas–Fort Smith (AR)

FORESTRY
Coll of Coastal Georgia (GA)
Dalton State Coll (GA)
Keystone Coll (PA)
U of Maine at Fort Kent (ME)

FOREST TECHNOLOGY
Keystone Coll (PA)
Pennsylvania Coll of Technology (PA)
U of Maine at Fort Kent (ME)
U of New Hampshire (NH)

FRENCH
Chestnut Hill Coll (PA)
Idaho State U (ID)
Indiana U–Purdue U Fort Wayne (IN)
Methodist U (NC)
Thomas More Coll (KY)
U of Cincinnati (OH)
The U of Tampa (FL)
Xavier U (OH)
Young Harris Coll (GA)

FUNERAL SERVICE AND MORTUARY SCIENCE
Cincinnati Coll of Mortuary Science (OH)
Ferris State U (MI)
Mount Ida Coll (MA)
Point Park U (PA)
St. Petersburg Coll (FL)
U of the District of Columbia (DC)

GENERAL STUDIES
AIB Coll of Business (IA)
Alderson-Broaddus Coll (WV)
Alverno Coll (WI)
American Public U System (WV)
Anderson U (IN)
Arkansas State U (AR)
Arkansas Tech U (AR)
Asbury U (KY)
Atlanta Christian Coll (GA)
Averett U (VA)
Baptist Bible Coll of Pennsylvania (PA)
Barclay Coll (KS)
Belhaven U (MS)
Bob Jones U (SC)
Brewton-Parker Coll (GA)
Burlington Coll (VT)
Butler U (IN)
Calumet Coll of Saint Joseph (IN)
Cameron U (OK)
Castleton State Coll (VT)
Clearwater Christian Coll (FL)
Coll of Mount St. Joseph (OH)
Columbia Coll (MO)
Columbia Southern U (AL)
Concordia U, St. Paul (MN)
Dakota State U (SD)
Dalton State Coll (GA)
Dixie State Coll of Utah (UT)
Ferris State U (MI)
Fisher Coll (MA)
Friends U (KS)
Garrett Coll (MD)
Great Lakes Christian Coll (MI)
Hillsdale Free Will Baptist Coll (OK)
Idaho State U (ID)
Indiana Tech (IN)
Indiana U East (IN)
Indiana U Kokomo (IN)
Indiana U Northwest (IN)
Indiana U of Pennsylvania (PA)
Indiana U–Purdue U Fort Wayne (IN)
Indiana U–Purdue U Indianapolis (IN)
Indiana U South Bend (IN)
Indiana U Southeast (IN)
Indiana Wesleyan U (IN)
Johnson State Coll (VT)
La Salle U (PA)
Lawrence Technological U (MI)
Lebanon Valley Coll (PA)
Mercy Coll of Northwest Ohio (OH)
Miami U (OH)
Mid-Continent U (KY)
Monmouth U (NJ)
Montana State U Billings (MT)
Morehead State U (KY)
Mount Aloysius Coll (PA)
Mount Marty Coll (SD)
Mount Vernon Nazarene U (OH)
Newbury Coll (MA)
New Mexico Inst of Mining and Technology (NM)
New Mexico State U (NM)
Nicholls State U (LA)
Northern Michigan U (MI)
Northwest Christian U (OR)
Northwestern State U of Louisiana (LA)
Northwest U (WA)
Oak Hills Christian Coll (MN)
The Ohio State U at Lima (OH)
Oklahoma Panhandle State U (OK)
Our Lady of the Lake Coll (LA)

Pace U (NY)
Peirce Coll (PA)
Presentation Coll (SD)
Regent U (VA)
Shawnee State U (OH)
Siena Heights U (MI)
Silver Lake Coll (WI)
Simpson U (CA)
South Dakota School of Mines and Technology (SD)
South Dakota State U (SD)
Southeastern Louisiana U (LA)
Southern Adventist U (TN)
Southern Arkansas U–Magnolia (AR)
Southern Nazarene U (OK)
Southern Wesleyan U (SC)
Southwestern Assemblies of God U (TX)
State U of New York Coll of Technology at Delhi (NY)
Temple U (PA)
Tiffin U (OH)
Trevecca Nazarene U (TN)
Trinity Coll of Florida (FL)
Truett-McConnell Coll (GA)
U of Alaska Fairbanks (AK)
U of Alaska Southeast (AK)
U of Arkansas–Fort Smith (AR)
U of Bridgeport (CT)
U of Cincinnati (OH)
U of La Verne (CA)
U of Louisiana at Monroe (LA)
U of Maine at Fort Kent (ME)
U of Mobile (AL)
U of New Haven (CT)
U of North Florida (FL)
U of Rio Grande (OH)
The U of Toledo (OH)
U of Wisconsin–Superior (WI)
Utah State U (UT)
Utah Valley U (UT)
Viterbo U (WI)
Western Kentucky U (KY)
Wichita State U (KS)
Widener U (PA)
Winona State U (MN)
York Coll of Pennsylvania (PA)

GEOGRAPHIC INFORMATION SCIENCE AND CARTOGRAPHY
The U of Akron (OH)

GEOGRAPHY
Dalton State Coll (GA)
The U of Tampa (FL)
Wright State U (OH)

GEOGRAPHY RELATED
Adams State Coll (CO)

GEOLOGICAL AND EARTH SCIENCES/GEOSCIENCES RELATED
Utah Valley U (UT)

GEOLOGY/EARTH SCIENCE
Coll of Coastal Georgia (GA)
Dalton State Coll (GA)
Wright State U (OH)
Young Harris Coll (GA)

GERMAN
Indiana U–Purdue U Fort Wayne (IN)
Methodist U (NC)
Xavier U (OH)

GERONTOLOGY
Holy Cross Coll (IN)
Madonna U (MI)
Manchester Coll (IN)
Siena Heights U (MI)
Thomas More Coll (KY)
The U of Toledo (OH)

GRAPHIC AND PRINTING EQUIPMENT OPERATION/PRODUCTION
Dixie State Coll of Utah (UT)
Idaho State U (ID)
Lewis-Clark State Coll (ID)

GRAPHIC COMMUNICATIONS
Pennsylvania Coll of Technology (PA)
Walla Walla U (WA)

GRAPHIC DESIGN
Bryant & Stratton Coll - Wauwatosa Campus (WI)
Coll of Mount St. Joseph (OH)
Collins Coll (AZ)
Corcoran Coll of Art and Design (DC)
Ferris State U (MI)
The Illinois Inst of Art–Tinley Park (IL)
International Academy of Design & Technology (FL)
International Business Coll, Fort Wayne (IN)
Lebanese American U (Lebanon)
Madonna U (MI)
Mountain State U (WV)
Pacific Union Coll (CA)
Parsons The New School for Design (NY)
Penn Foster Coll (AZ)
Pratt Inst (NY)
Southern Adventist U (TN)
Union Coll (NE)
Villa Maria Coll of Buffalo (NY)

HAZARDOUS MATERIALS INFORMATION SYSTEMS TECHNOLOGY
American Public U System (WV)

HAZARDOUS MATERIALS MANAGEMENT AND WASTE TECHNOLOGY
Ohio U–Chillicothe (OH)

HEALTH AND MEDICAL ADMINISTRATIVE SERVICES RELATED
Kent State U (OH)

HEALTH AND PHYSICAL EDUCATION/FITNESS
Coll of Coastal Georgia (GA)
Robert Morris U Illinois (IL)
State U of New York Coll of Technology at Delhi (NY)
Utah Valley U (UT)

HEALTH AND PHYSICAL EDUCATION RELATED
Pennsylvania Coll of Technology (PA)
Thomas Edison State Coll (NJ)

HEALTH AND WELLNESS
Presentation Coll (SD)

HEALTH/HEALTH-CARE ADMINISTRATION
Baker Coll of Auburn Hills (MI)
Baker Coll of Flint (MI)
Brookline Coll, Phoenix (AZ)
Chestnut Hill Coll (PA)
ECPI Coll of Technology, Virginia Beach (VA)
Florida Inst of Technology (FL)
LA Coll International (CA)
Methodist U (NC)
Skyline Coll (VA)
The U of Scranton (PA)
Washburn U (KS)

HEALTH INFORMATION/MEDICAL RECORDS ADMINISTRATION
AIB Coll of Business (IA)
Baker Coll of Auburn Hills (MI)
Baker Coll of Cadillac (MI)
Baker Coll of Clinton Township (MI)
Baker Coll of Flint (MI)
Baker Coll of Jackson (MI)
Baker Coll of Port Huron (MI)
Boise State U (ID)
Dalton State Coll (GA)
Inter American U of Puerto Rico, San Germán Campus (PR)
Montana State U Billings (MT)
St. Petersburg Coll (FL)

Santa Fe Coll (FL)
U of Alaska Southeast (AK)

HEALTH INFORMATION/MEDICAL RECORDS TECHNOLOGY
Baker Coll of Flint (MI)
Baker Coll of Jackson (MI)
Brookline Coll, Phoenix (AZ)
Dakota State U (SD)
Davenport U, Grand Rapids (MI)
DeVry U, Pomona (CA)
DeVry U, Decatur (GA)
DeVry U, Chicago (IL)
DeVry U, North Brunswick (NJ)
DeVry U, Columbus (OH)
DeVry U, Fort Washington (PA)
DeVry U, Houston (TX)
DeVry U, Irving (TX)
DeVry U Online (IL)
Ferris State U (MI)
Fisher Coll (MA)
Idaho State U (ID)
Indiana U Northwest (IN)
Indiana U South Bend (IN)
Mercy Coll of Northwest Ohio (OH)
Molloy Coll (NY)
Northern Michigan U (MI)
Peirce Coll (PA)
Penn Foster Coll (AZ)
Pennsylvania Coll of Technology (PA)
St. Catherine U (MN)
Santa Fe Coll (FL)
U of Arkansas for Medical Sciences (AR)
Washburn U (KS)
Weber State U (UT)
Western Kentucky U (KY)

HEALTH/MEDICAL PREPARATORY PROGRAMS RELATED
Immaculata U (PA)
Ohio Valley U (WV)
Union Coll (NE)
U of Cincinnati (OH)

HEALTH PROFESSIONS RELATED
Arkansas Tech U (AR)
Fisher Coll (MA)
Lock Haven U of Pennsylvania (PA)
National U (CA)
Newman U (KS)
New York U (NY)
Northwest U (WA)
Ohio U–Chillicothe (OH)
Point Park U (PA)
Saint Mary's Coll of California (CA)
Union Coll (NE)
U of Alaska Southeast (AK)
U of Cincinnati (OH)
U of Hartford (CT)
Villa Maria Coll of Buffalo (NY)

HEALTH SERVICES ADMINISTRATION
Ashworth Coll (GA)
Florida National Coll (FL)

HEALTH SERVICES/ALLIED HEALTH/HEALTH SCIENCES
Ferris State U (MI)
Fisher Coll (MA)
Florida National Coll (FL)
Lindsey Wilson Coll (KY)
Pennsylvania Coll of Technology (PA)
U of Hartford (CT)
Victory U (TN)

HEALTH TEACHER EDUCATION
Young Harris Coll (GA)

HEATING, AIR CONDITIONING, VENTILATION AND REFRIGERATION MAINTENANCE TECHNOLOGY
Lamar U (TX)
Lewis-Clark State Coll (ID)
Montana State U Billings (MT)
Santa Fe Coll (FL)

State U of New York Coll of
Technology at Delhi (NY)
Utah Valley U (UT)

HEATING, VENTILATION, AIR CONDITIONING AND REFRIGERATION ENGINEERING TECHNOLOGY
Ferris State U (MI)
Northern Michigan U (MI)
Pennsylvania Coll of Technology (PA)
State U of New York Coll of Technology at Delhi (NY)
Utah Valley U (UT)

HEAVY EQUIPMENT MAINTENANCE TECHNOLOGY
Ferris State U (MI)
Pennsylvania Coll of Technology (PA)

HISTOLOGIC TECHNICIAN
Indiana U–Purdue U Indianapolis (IN)
Indiana U South Bend (IN)
Northern Michigan U (MI)
The U of Akron (OH)

HISTOLOGIC TECHNOLOGY/HISTOTECHNOLOGIST
Tarleton State U (TX)

HISTORY
American Public U System (WV)
Clarke U (IA)
Coll of Coastal Georgia (GA)
Corban U (OR)
Dalton State Coll (GA)
Indiana U–Purdue U Fort Wayne (IN)
Indiana Wesleyan U (IN)
John Brown U (AR)
Lindsey Wilson Coll (KY)
Lourdes Coll (OH)
Methodist U (NC)
Regent U (VA)
Rogers State U (OK)
State U of New York Empire State Coll (NY)
Thomas More Coll (KY)
U of Rio Grande (OH)
The U of Tampa (FL)
Utah Valley U (UT)
Wright State U (OH)
Xavier U (OH)
Young Harris Coll (GA)

HISTORY TEACHER EDUCATION
Young Harris Coll (GA)

HOMELAND SECURITY, LAW ENFORCEMENT, FIREFIGHTING AND PROTECTIVE SERVICES RELATED
Idaho State U (ID)
St. Petersburg Coll (FL)

HORTICULTURAL SCIENCE
Andrews U (MI)
State U of New York Coll of Technology at Delhi (NY)
U of Connecticut (CT)

HOSPITALITY ADMINISTRATION
AIB Coll of Business (IA)
American Public U System (WV)
Baker Coll of Flint (MI)
Baker Coll of Owosso (MI)
Florida National Coll (FL)
Lewis-Clark State Coll (ID)
Lexington Coll (IL)
New York City Coll of Technology of the City U of New York (NY)
St. Petersburg Coll (FL)
The U of Akron (OH)
U of Cincinnati (OH)
U of the District of Columbia (DC)
Utah Valley U (UT)

Webber International U (FL)
Western Kentucky U (KY)
Young Harris Coll (GA)
Youngstown State U (OH)

HOSPITALITY ADMINISTRATION RELATED
Indiana U–Purdue U Indianapolis (IN)
Penn State Berks (PA)
Purdue U (IN)
Purdue U Calumet (IN)
U of the District of Columbia (DC)

HOSPITALITY AND RECREATION MARKETING
State U of New York Coll of Technology at Delhi (NY)

HOTEL/MOTEL ADMINISTRATION
Baker Coll of Muskegon (MI)
Baker Coll of Owosso (MI)
Baker Coll of Port Huron (MI)
State U of New York Coll of Technology at Delhi (NY)
Stratford U, Falls Church (VA)
The U of Akron (OH)
U of the Virgin Islands (VI)

HUMAN DEVELOPMENT AND FAMILY STUDIES
Amridge U (AL)
Penn State Abington (PA)
Penn State Altoona (PA)
Penn State Berks (PA)
Penn State Erie, The Behrend Coll (PA)
Penn State U Park (PA)
State U of New York Empire State Coll (NY)

HUMAN DEVELOPMENT AND FAMILY STUDIES RELATED
The U of Toledo (OH)
Utah State U (UT)

HUMANITIES
Coll of the Humanities and Sciences, Harrison Middleton U (AZ)
Corban U (OR)
Faulkner U (AL)
Fisher Coll (MA)
Newbury Coll (MA)
Ohio U (OH)
Ohio U–Chillicothe (OH)
State U of New York Coll of Technology at Delhi (NY)
State U of New York Empire State Coll (NY)
Thomas More Coll (KY)
U of Alaska Southeast (AK)
The U of Findlay (OH)
Utah Valley U (UT)
Valparaiso U (IN)
Washburn U (KS)

HUMAN RESOURCES MANAGEMENT
Ashworth Coll (GA)
Baker Coll of Owosso (MI)
Chestnut Hill Coll (PA)
King's Coll (PA)
Montana State U Billings (MT)
Mountain State U (WV)
Penn Foster Coll (AZ)
Regent U (VA)
The U of Findlay (OH)

HUMAN RESOURCES MANAGEMENT AND SERVICES RELATED
Bryant & Stratton Coll - Wauwatosa Campus (WI)

HUMAN SERVICES
Baker Coll of Clinton Township (MI)
Baker Coll of Flint (MI)
Baker Coll of Muskegon (MI)
Beacon Coll (FL)
Bethel Coll (IN)
Cazenovia Coll (NY)

Chestnut Hill Coll (PA)
Coll of St. Joseph (VT)
Columbia Coll (MO)
Edinboro U of Pennsylvania (PA)
Elizabethtown Coll (PA)
Graceland U (IA)
Indiana U East (IN)
Mount Vernon Nazarene U (OH)
New York City Coll of Technology of the City U of New York (NY)
Southern Vermont Coll (VT)
State U of New York Empire State Coll (NY)
Thomas Edison State Coll (NJ)
U of Maine at Augusta (ME)
U of Maine at Fort Kent (ME)
The U of Scranton (PA)
Walsh U (OH)
Wayland Baptist U (TX)

HYDROLOGY AND WATER RESOURCES SCIENCE
Lake Superior State U (MI)
U of the District of Columbia (DC)

ILLUSTRATION
Fashion Inst of Technology (NY)
Pratt Inst (NY)

INDUSTRIAL AND ORGANIZATIONAL PSYCHOLOGY
Corban U (OR)

INDUSTRIAL ELECTRONICS TECHNOLOGY
Dalton State Coll (GA)
Ferris State U (MI)
Lewis-Clark State Coll (ID)
Penn Foster Coll (AZ)
Pennsylvania Coll of Technology (PA)

INDUSTRIAL ENGINEERING
Indiana Tech (IN)
The U of Toledo (OH)

INDUSTRIAL MECHANICS AND MAINTENANCE TECHNOLOGY
Dalton State Coll (GA)
Northern Michigan U (MI)
Pennsylvania Coll of Technology (PA)

INDUSTRIAL PRODUCTION TECHNOLOGIES RELATED
U of Alaska Fairbanks (AK)

INDUSTRIAL RADIOLOGIC TECHNOLOGY
Baker Coll of Owosso (MI)
Lamar U (TX)
Our Lady of the Lake Coll (LA)
U of the District of Columbia (DC)
Widener U (PA)

INDUSTRIAL TECHNOLOGY
Arkansas Tech U (AR)
Baker Coll of Muskegon (MI)
Dalton State Coll (GA)
Edinboro U of Pennsylvania (PA)
Indiana U–Purdue U Fort Wayne (IN)
Kansas State U (KS)
Kent State U (OH)
Millersville U of Pennsylvania (PA)
Murray State U (KY)
Oklahoma Panhandle State U (OK)
Purdue U Calumet (IN)
Purdue U North Central (IN)
St. Petersburg Coll (FL)
Southeastern Louisiana U (LA)
Southern Arkansas U–Magnolia (AR)
U of Arkansas at Pine Bluff (AR)
U of Rio Grande (OH)
The U of Toledo (OH)
Washburn U (KS)

INFORMATION SCIENCE/STUDIES
Baker Coll of Clinton Township (MI)

Baker Coll of Owosso (MI)
Beacon Coll (FL)
Calumet Coll of Saint Joseph (IN)
Campbellsville U (KY)
Dalton State Coll (GA)
Elizabethtown Coll (PA)
Everest U, Tampa (FL)
Faulkner U (AL)
Florida Inst of Technology (FL)
Goldey-Beacom Coll (DE)
Herzing U (GA)
Husson U (ME)
Immaculata U (PA)
Indiana U–Purdue U Fort Wayne (IN)
Johnson State Coll (VT)
Mansfield U of Pennsylvania (PA)
Newman U (KS)
Oklahoma Wesleyan U (OK)
Penn State Abington (PA)
Penn State Altoona (PA)
Penn State Berks (PA)
Penn State Erie, The Behrend Coll (PA)
Penn State U Park (PA)
Southern Utah U (UT)
Tulane U (LA)
Union Coll (NE)
U of Massachusetts Lowell (MA)
U of Pittsburgh at Bradford (PA)
The U of Scranton (PA)
The U of Toledo (OH)
Wright State U (OH)

INFORMATION TECHNOLOGY
AIB Coll of Business (IA)
Arkansas Tech U (AR)
Cameron U (OK)
Collins Coll (AZ)
Ferris State U (MI)
Franklin U (OH)
Keystone Coll (PA)
Minnesota School of Business–Blaine (MN)
Point Park U (PA)
Regent U (VA)
Thomas More Coll (KY)
Tiffin U (OH)
Trevecca Nazarene U (TN)
Vermont Tech Coll (VT)
Youngstown State U (OH)

INFORMATION TECHNOLOGY PROJECT MANAGEMENT
Pace U (NY)

INSTITUTIONAL FOOD WORKERS
Immaculata U (PA)
Kendall Coll (IL)

INSTRUMENTATION TECHNOLOGY
Idaho State U (ID)

INSURANCE
AIB Coll of Business (IA)

INTERDISCIPLINARY STUDIES
Kansas State U (KS)
Lesley U (MA)
State U of New York Empire State Coll (NY)
Suffolk U (MA)

INTERIOR ARCHITECTURE
U of New Haven (CT)
Villa Maria Coll of Buffalo (NY)

INTERIOR DESIGN
Baker Coll of Allen Park (MI)
Baker Coll of Auburn Hills (MI)
Baker Coll of Clinton Township (MI)
Baker Coll of Muskegon (MI)
Baker Coll of Owosso (MI)
Baker Coll of Port Huron (MI)
Coll of Mount St. Joseph (OH)
Fashion Inst of Technology (NY)
Indiana U–Purdue U Fort Wayne (IN)
Indiana U–Purdue U Indianapolis (IN)
International Academy of Design & Technology (FL)

Lebanese American U (Lebanon)
Montana State U (MT)
New York School of Interior Design (NY)
Parsons The New School for Design (NY)
Robert Morris U Illinois (IL)
Southern Utah U (UT)
Stevens Inst of Business & Arts (MO)
U of Cincinnati (OH)
Weber State U (UT)

INTERNATIONAL BUSINESS/TRADE/COMMERCE
AIB Coll of Business (IA)
Regent U (VA)
Utah Valley U (UT)
Young Harris Coll (GA)

INTERNATIONAL/GLOBAL STUDIES
Holy Cross Coll (IN)
Thomas More Coll (KY)

INTERNATIONAL RELATIONS AND AFFAIRS
American Public U System (WV)

JAZZ/JAZZ STUDIES
Five Towns Coll (NY)
Villa Maria Coll of Buffalo (NY)

JOURNALISM
Corban U (OR)
Dalton State Coll (GA)
Indiana U Southeast (IN)
Madonna U (MI)
Manchester Coll (IN)
Young Harris Coll (GA)

JOURNALISM RELATED
Adams State Coll (CO)

KINDERGARTEN/PRESCHOOL EDUCATION
Atlantic Union Coll (MA)
Baker Coll of Clinton Township (MI)
Baker Coll of Muskegon (MI)
Baker Coll of Owosso (MI)
Columbia Bible Coll (BC, Canada)
Fisher Coll (MA)
Keystone Coll (PA)
Maria Coll (NY)
Miami U (OH)
Mid-Atlantic Christian U (NC)
Mount Aloysius Coll (PA)
Mount St. Mary's Coll (CA)
Saint Mary-of-the-Woods Coll (IN)
Shawnee State U (OH)
U of Cincinnati (OH)
U of Rio Grande (OH)
Villa Maria Coll of Buffalo (NY)
Wilmington U (DE)

KINESIOLOGY AND EXERCISE SCIENCE
Southwestern Adventist U (TX)
Thomas More Coll (KY)

LABOR AND INDUSTRIAL RELATIONS
Rider U (NJ)
State U of New York Empire State Coll (NY)
Youngstown State U (OH)

LABOR STUDIES
Indiana U Kokomo (IN)
Indiana U Northwest (IN)
Indiana U–Purdue U Fort Wayne (IN)
Indiana U–Purdue U Indianapolis (IN)
Indiana U South Bend (IN)

LANDSCAPE ARCHITECTURE
Keystone Coll (PA)
State U of New York Coll of Technology at Delhi (NY)

LANDSCAPING AND GROUNDSKEEPING

North Carolina State U (NC)
Pennsylvania Coll of Technology (PA)
State U of New York Coll of Technology at Delhi (NY)
U of Massachusetts Amherst (MA)
Vermont Tech Coll (VT)

LASER AND OPTICAL TECHNOLOGY

Idaho State U (ID)

LAY MINISTRY

Maranatha Baptist Bible Coll (WI)
Nyack Coll (NY)
Southeastern Bible Coll (AL)

LEGAL ADMINISTRATIVE ASSISTANT/SECRETARY

Baker Coll of Auburn Hills (MI)
Baker Coll of Clinton Township (MI)
Baker Coll of Flint (MI)
Baker Coll of Jackson (MI)
Baker Coll of Muskegon (MI)
Baker Coll of Owosso (MI)
Baker Coll of Port Huron (MI)
Clarion U of Pennsylvania (PA)
Dordt Coll (IA)
Florida National Coll (FL)
International Business Coll, Fort Wayne (IN)
Lamar U (TX)
Lewis-Clark State Coll (ID)
Shawnee State U (OH)
U of Cincinnati (OH)
U of Rio Grande (OH)
U of the District of Columbia (DC)
The U of Toledo (OH)
Washburn U (KS)
Youngstown State U (OH)

LEGAL ASSISTANT/ PARALEGAL

American Public U System (WV)
Anna Maria Coll (MA)
Ashworth Coll (GA)
Brookline Coll, Phoenix (AZ)
Brookline Coll, Tucson (AZ)
Brookline Coll (NM)
Bryant & Stratton Coll - Wauwatosa Campus (WI)
Central Pennsylvania Coll (PA)
Clayton State U (GA)
Coll of Mount St. Joseph (OH)
Coll of Saint Mary (NE)
Davenport U, Grand Rapids (MI)
Everest U, Lakeland (FL)
Everest U, Tampa (FL)
Everest U, Tampa (FL)
Faulkner U (AL)
Ferris State U (MI)
Fisher Coll (MA)
Florida National Coll (FL)
Gannon U (PA)
Husson U (ME)
Idaho State U (ID)
International Business Coll, Fort Wayne (IN)
ITT Tech Inst, Tempe (AZ)
ITT Tech Inst, Clovis (CA)
ITT Tech Inst, Concord (CA)
ITT Tech Inst, Corona (CA)
ITT Tech Inst, South Bend (IN)
ITT Tech Inst (KS)
ITT Tech Inst, Lexington (KY)
ITT Tech Inst (MS)
ITT Tech Inst, Springfield (MO)
ITT Tech Inst, Oklahoma City (OK)
Jones Coll, Jacksonville (FL)
Lake Superior State U (MI)
Lewis-Clark State Coll (ID)
Madonna U (MI)
Maria Coll (NY)
Minnesota School of Business– Blaine (MN)
Mountain State U (WV)
Mount Aloysius Coll (PA)
Newman U (KS)
New York City Coll of Technology of the City U of New York (NY)
Peirce Coll (PA)
Penn Foster Coll (AZ)
Pennsylvania Coll of Technology (PA)
Robert Morris U Illinois (IL)

Saint Mary-of-the-Woods Coll (IN)
St. Petersburg Coll (FL)
Santa Fe Coll (FL)
Shawnee State U (OH)
Stevens Inst of Business & Arts (MO)
Suffolk U (MA)
Tulane U (LA)
The U of Akron (OH)
U of Alaska Fairbanks (AK)
U of Arkansas–Fort Smith (AR)
U of Cincinnati (OH)
U of Hartford (CT)
U of Louisville (KY)
The U of Toledo (OH)
Utah Valley U (UT)
Western Kentucky U (KY)
Widener U (PA)

LEGAL PROFESSIONS AND STUDIES RELATED

Florida National Coll (FL)

LEGAL STUDIES

Lake Superior State U (MI)
Maria Coll (NY)
St. John's U (NY)
U of Alaska Southeast (AK)
U of Hartford (CT)
U of New Haven (CT)

LIBERAL ARTS AND SCIENCES AND HUMANITIES RELATED

Adams State Coll (CO)
Ball State U (IN)
Ferris State U (MI)
Marymount Coll, Palos Verdes, California (CA)
Mesa State Coll (CO)
Mount Aloysius Coll (PA)
New York U (NY)
Nyack Coll (NY)
Pennsylvania Coll of Technology (PA)
Sacred Heart U (CT)
Taylor U (IN)
U of Hartford (CT)
U of Wisconsin–Green Bay (WI)
U of Wisconsin–La Crosse (WI)
Walsh U (OH)
Wayland Baptist U (TX)

LIBERAL ARTS AND SCIENCES/ LIBERAL STUDIES

Adams State Coll (CO)
Adelphi U (NY)
Alvernia U (PA)
Alverno Coll (WI)
Aquinas Coll (MI)
Aquinas Coll (TN)
Arkansas State U (AR)
Armstrong Atlantic State U (GA)
Ashland U (OH)
Austin Peay State U (TN)
Ball State U (IN)
Bard Coll (NY)
Bard Coll at Simon's Rock (MA)
Beacon Coll (FL)
Bemidji State U (MN)
Bethel Coll (IN)
Bethel U (MN)
Brenau U (GA)
Briar Cliff U (IA)
Bryan Coll (TN)
Bryn Athyn Coll of the New Church (PA)
Calumet Coll of Saint Joseph (IN)
Cazenovia Coll (NY)
Centenary Coll (NJ)
Christendom Coll (VA)
Clarion U of Pennsylvania (PA)
Clarke U (IA)
Clayton State U (GA)
Coll of Coastal Georgia (GA)
Coll of St. Joseph (VT)
Coll of Staten Island of the City U of New York (NY)
Columbia Coll (MO)
Columbus State U (GA)
Concordia Coll–New York (NY)
Concordia U (CA)
Cumberland U (TN)
Dallas Baptist U (TX)
Daniel Webster Coll (NH)
Dickinson State U (ND)
Dixie State Coll of Utah (UT)
Dominican Coll (NY)

Eastern New Mexico U (NM)
Edgewood Coll (WI)
Edinboro U of Pennsylvania (PA)
Emmanuel Coll (GA)
Emory U (GA)
Endicott Coll (MA)
Fairfield U (CT)
Fairleigh Dickinson U, Metropolitan Campus (NJ)
Faulkner U (AL)
Felician Coll (NJ)
Ferris State U (MI)
Fisher Coll (MA)
Five Towns Coll (NY)
Florida A&M U (FL)
Florida Atlantic U (FL)
Florida Coll (FL)
Florida Inst of Technology (FL)
Florida National Coll (FL)
Florida State U (FL)
Franklin Coll Switzerland (Switzerland)
Gannon U (PA)
Garrett Coll (MD)
Grace Bible Coll (MI)
Grand View U (IA)
Granite State Coll (NH)
Holy Cross Coll (IN)
Houghton Coll (NY)
Indiana State U (IN)
Indiana U Kokomo (IN)
Indiana U Northwest (IN)
Indiana U–Purdue U Indianapolis (IN)
Indiana U South Bend (IN)
Indiana U Southeast (IN)
John Brown U (AR)
Johnson State Coll (VT)
Kent State U (OH)
Kent State U at Stark (OH)
Kentucky State U (KY)
Keystone Coll (PA)
Kuyper Coll (MI)
Lake Superior State U (MI)
Lewis-Clark State Coll (ID)
Limestone Coll (SC)
Long Island U, Brooklyn Campus (NY)
Lourdes Coll (OH)
Maria Coll (NY)
Marymount Coll, Palos Verdes, California (CA)
Medaille Coll (NY)
Medgar Evers Coll of the City U of New York (NY)
Merrimack Coll (MA)
Mesa State Coll (CO)
Methodist U (NC)
MidAmerica Nazarene U (KS)
Midwestern State U (TX)
Minnesota State U Mankato (MN)
Minnesota State U Moorhead (MN)
Missouri Southern State U (MO)
Mitchell Coll (CT)
Molloy Coll (NY)
Montana State U Billings (MT)
Montreat Coll, Montreat (NC)
Mountain State U (WV)
Mount Aloysius Coll (PA)
Mount Marty Coll (SD)
Mount Olive Coll (NC)
Mount St. Mary's Coll (CA)
Neumann U (PA)
New England Coll (NH)
Newman U (KS)
New Saint Andrews Coll (ID)
New York City Coll of Technology of the City U of New York (NY)
New York U (NY)
Niagara U (NY)
Northern Kentucky U (KY)
Northern State U (SD)
Northwestern Coll (MN)
Nyack Coll (NY)
The Ohio State U at Marion (OH)
The Ohio State U–Mansfield Campus (OH)
The Ohio State U–Newark Campus (OH)
Ohio U (OH)
Ohio U–Chillicothe (OH)
Ohio Valley U (WV)
Oklahoma Wesleyan U (OK)
Penn State Abington (PA)
Penn State Altoona (PA)
Penn State Berks (PA)
Penn State Erie, The Behrend Coll (PA)

Penn State Harrisburg (PA)
Penn State U Park (PA)
Providence Coll (RI)
Quincy U (IL)
Reinhardt U (GA)
Rider U (NJ)
Rivier Coll (NH)
Rocky Mountain Coll (MT)
Rogers State U (OK)
St. Catherine U (MN)
St. John's U (NY)
Saint Joseph's U (PA)
Saint Leo U (FL)
St. Louis Christian Coll (MO)
Saint Mary-of-the-Woods Coll (IN)
St. Petersburg Coll (FL)
St. Thomas Aquinas Coll (NY)
Salve Regina U (RI)
Santa Fe Coll (FL)
Schreiner U (TX)
Southeastern Baptist Theological Seminary (NC)
Southern Polytechnic State U (GA)
Southern Vermont Coll (VT)
Spring Arbor U (MI)
Stephens Coll (MO)
Suffolk U (MA)
Tabor Coll (KS)
Thiel Coll (PA)
Thomas Edison State Coll (NJ)
Thomas More Coll (KY)
Thomas U (GA)
Trine U (IN)
Troy U (AL)
Truett-McConnell Coll (GA)
The U of Akron (OH)
U of Alaska Fairbanks (AK)
U of Alaska Southeast (AK)
U of Arkansas–Fort Smith (AR)
U of Cincinnati (OH)
U of Delaware (DE)
U of Hartford (CT)
U of La Verne (CA)
U of Maine at Augusta (ME)
U of Maine at Fort Kent (ME)
U of Maine at Presque Isle (ME)
U of New Hampshire at Manchester (NH)
U of North Florida (FL)
U of Pittsburgh at Bradford (PA)
U of Saint Mary (KS)
U of Sioux Falls (SD)
U of South Florida (FL)
U of the Incarnate Word (TX)
The U of Toledo (OH)
U of West Florida (FL)
U of Wisconsin–Eau Claire (WI)
U of Wisconsin–Platteville (WI)
U of Wisconsin–Stevens Point (WI)
U of Wisconsin–Superior (WI)
U of Wisconsin–Whitewater (WI)
Upper Iowa U (IA)
Valdosta State U (GA)
Villa Maria Coll of Buffalo (NY)
Washburn U (KS)
Waynesburg U (PA)
Western Connecticut State U (CT)
Western New England U (MA)
Wichita State U (KS)
Wilson Coll (PA)
Winona State U (MN)
Xavier U (OH)
Young Harris Coll (GA)
Youngstown State U (OH)

LIBRARY AND ARCHIVES ASSISTING

U of Maine at Augusta (ME)

LICENSED PRACTICAL/ VOCATIONAL NURSE TRAINING

Campbellsville U (KY)
Dickinson State U (ND)
ECPI Coll of Technology, Virginia Beach (VA)
Inter American U of Puerto Rico, Metropolitan Campus (PR)
Inter American U of Puerto Rico, Ponce Campus (PR)
Lamar U (TX)
Lewis-Clark State Coll (ID)
Maria Coll (NY)
Medgar Evers Coll of the City U of New York (NY)
Montana State U Billings (MT)
Ohio U–Chillicothe (OH)

Skyline Coll (VA)
U of the District of Columbia (DC)
Virginia State U (VA)

LINEWORKER

Pennsylvania Coll of Technology (PA)
Utah Valley U (UT)

LINGUISTICS

Oklahoma Wesleyan U (OK)

LOGISTICS, MATERIALS, AND SUPPLY CHAIN MANAGEMENT

The U of Akron (OH)
The U of Toledo (OH)

MACHINE SHOP TECHNOLOGY

Dalton State Coll (GA)
Missouri Southern State U (MO)

MACHINE TOOL TECHNOLOGY

Idaho State U (ID)
Lamar U (TX)
Mesa State Coll (CO)
Pennsylvania Coll of Technology (PA)
Weber State U (UT)

MANAGEMENT INFORMATION SYSTEMS

Amridge U (AL)
Arkansas State U (AR)
Cameron U (OK)
Columbia Centro Universitario (PR)
Columbia Coll (PR)
Garrett Coll (MD)
Husson U (ME)
Inter American U of Puerto Rico, Bayamon Campus (PR)
Johnson State Coll (VT)
Lake Superior State U (MI)
Liberty U (VA)
Lindsey Wilson Coll (KY)
Lock Haven U of Pennsylvania (PA)
Morehead State U (KY)
Ohio U–Chillicothe (OH)
Peirce Coll (PA)
Saint Joseph's Coll (IN)
Shawnee State U (OH)
Thiel Coll (PA)
U of Alaska Southeast (AK)
Wilson Coll (PA)
Wright State U (OH)

MANAGEMENT INFORMATION SYSTEMS AND SERVICES RELATED

Indiana U–Purdue U Indianapolis (IN)
Mount Aloysius Coll (PA)
Purdue U North Central (IN)
Santa Fe Coll (FL)

MANAGEMENT SCIENCE

Hawai'i Pacific U (HI)

MANUFACTURING ENGINEERING TECHNOLOGY

Lawrence Technological U (MI)
Lewis-Clark State Coll (ID)
Mesa State Coll (CO)
Morehead State U (KY)
Pennsylvania Coll of Technology (PA)
Thomas Edison State Coll (NJ)
The U of Akron (OH)
Wright State U (OH)

MARKETING/MARKETING MANAGEMENT

AIB Coll of Business (IA)
Ashworth Coll (GA)
Baker Coll of Allen Park (MI)
Baker Coll of Auburn Hills (MI)
Baker Coll of Cadillac (MI)
Baker Coll of Clinton Township (MI)
Baker Coll of Owosso (MI)
Central Pennsylvania Coll (PA)
Chestnut Hill Coll (PA)
Dalton State Coll (GA)
Daniel Webster Coll (NH)

Everest U, Lakeland (FL)
Florida Inst of Technology (FL)
Hawai`i Pacific U (HI)
Idaho State U (ID)
Miami U (OH)
Mount St. Mary's Coll (CA)
New York City Coll of Technology of
   the City U of New York (NY)
Peirce Coll (PA)
Penn Foster Coll (AZ)
Regent U (VA)
Southwest Minnesota State U (MN)
State U of New York Coll of
   Technology at Delhi (NY)
Tulane U (LA)
The U of Akron (OH)
Walsh U (OH)
Webber International U (FL)
Wright State U (OH)
Youngstown State U (OH)

MASONRY
Pennsylvania Coll of Technology
   (PA)

MASSAGE THERAPY
ECPI Coll of Technology, Virginia
   Beach (VA)
Idaho State U (ID)
Minnesota School of Business–
   Blaine (MN)

MASS COMMUNICATION/MEDIA
Adams State Coll (CO)
Inter American U of Puerto Rico,
   Bayamón Campus (PR)
Methodist U (NC)
Pennsylvania Coll of Technology
   (PA)
Southern Adventist U (TN)
Southwestern Assemblies of God U
   (TX)
U of Rio Grande (OH)
York Coll of Pennsylvania (PA)

MATHEMATICS
Clarke U (IA)
Coll of Coastal Georgia (GA)
Corban U (OR)
Creighton U (NE)
Dalton State Coll (GA)
Hawai`i Pacific U (HI)
Idaho State U (ID)
Indiana U–Purdue U Fort Wayne
   (IN)
Indiana Wesleyan U (IN)
Methodist U (NC)
Purdue U North Central (IN)
Shawnee State U (OH)
State U of New York Coll of
   Technology at Delhi (NY)
State U of New York Empire State
   Coll (NY)
Thomas Edison State Coll (NJ)
Thomas More Coll (KY)
Thomas U (GA)
Trine U (IN)
U of Rio Grande (OH)
The U of Tampa (FL)
Utah Valley U (UT)
Young Harris Coll (GA)

MATHEMATICS AND COMPUTER SCIENCE
Immaculata U (PA)

MATHEMATICS TEACHER EDUCATION
Corban U (OR)
Young Harris Coll (GA)

MECHANICAL DRAFTING AND CAD/CADD
Baker Coll of Flint (MI)
Cameron U (OK)
Indiana U–Purdue U Indianapolis
   (IN)
New York City Coll of Technology of
   the City U of New York (NY)
Purdue U Calumet (IN)

MECHANICAL ENGINEERING
Fairfield U (CT)
U of New Haven (CT)

MECHANICAL ENGINEERING/MECHANICAL TECHNOLOGY
Baker Coll of Flint (MI)
Bluefield State Coll (WV)
ECPI Coll of Technology, Virginia
   Beach (VA)
Fairmont State U (WV)
Ferris State U (MI)
Idaho State U (ID)
Indiana U–Purdue U Fort Wayne
   (IN)
Lake Superior State U (MI)
Lawrence Technological U (MI)
Miami U (OH)
New York City Coll of Technology of
   the City U of New York (NY)
Penn Foster Coll (AZ)
Penn State Altoona (PA)
Penn State Berks (PA)
Penn State Erie, The Behrend Coll
   (PA)
Point Park U (PA)
Thomas Edison State Coll (NJ)
The U of Akron (OH)
U of Rio Grande (OH)
U of the District of Columbia (DC)
The U of Toledo (OH)
Vermont Tech Coll (VT)
Youngstown State U (OH)

MECHANICAL ENGINEERING TECHNOLOGIES RELATED
Indiana U–Purdue U Indianapolis
   (IN)
Purdue U Calumet (IN)
Purdue U North Central (IN)
U of Massachusetts Lowell (MA)

MECHANIC AND REPAIR TECHNOLOGIES RELATED
Pennsylvania Coll of Technology
   (PA)
Thomas Edison State Coll (NJ)

MECHANICS AND REPAIR
Idaho State U (ID)
Lewis-Clark State Coll (ID)
Utah Valley U (UT)

MECHATRONICS, ROBOTICS, AND AUTOMATION ENGINEERING
Johnson & Wales U (RI)

MEDICAL ADMINISTRATIVE ASSISTANT AND MEDICAL SECRETARY
Baker Coll of Auburn Hills (MI)
Baker Coll of Cadillac (MI)
Baker Coll of Clinton Township (MI)
Baker Coll of Flint (MI)
Baker Coll of Jackson (MI)
Baker Coll of Muskegon (MI)
Baker Coll of Owosso (MI)
Baker Coll of Port Huron (MI)
Boise State U (ID)
Dickinson State U (ND)
Florida National Coll (FL)
Lamar U (TX)
Minnesota School of Business–
   Blaine (MN)
Montana State U Billings (MT)
Mountain State U (WV)
Pennsylvania Coll of Technology
   (PA)
U of Cincinnati (OH)
U of Rio Grande (OH)

MEDICAL/CLINICAL ASSISTANT
Arkansas Tech U (AR)
Baker Coll of Allen Park (MI)
Baker Coll of Auburn Hills (MI)
Baker Coll of Cadillac (MI)
Baker Coll of Clinton Township (MI)
Baker Coll of Flint (MI)
Baker Coll of Jackson (MI)
Baker Coll of Muskegon (MI)
Baker Coll of Owosso (MI)
Baker Coll of Port Huron (MI)

Central Pennsylvania Coll (PA)
Davenport U, Grand Rapids (MI)
ECPI Coll of Technology, Virginia
   Beach (VA)
Everest U, Tampa (FL)
Everest U, Tampa (FL)
Florida National Coll (FL)
Idaho State U (ID)
International Business Coll, Fort
   Wayne (IN)
Mercy Coll of Health Sciences (IA)
Montana State U Billings (MT)
Montana Tech of The U of Montana
   (MT)
Mountain State U (WV)
Mount Aloysius Coll (PA)
Ohio U–Chillicothe (OH)
Palmer Coll of Chiropractic (IA)
Penn Foster Coll (AZ)
Presentation Coll (SD)
Robert Morris U Illinois (IL)
Skyline Coll (VA)
The U of Akron (OH)
U of Alaska Fairbanks (AK)
U of Cincinnati (OH)
The U of Toledo (OH)
Youngstown State U (OH)

MEDICAL/HEALTH MANAGEMENT AND CLINICAL ASSISTANT
Florida National Coll (FL)
Lewis-Clark State Coll (ID)

MEDICAL INFORMATICS
Idaho State U (ID)
Montana Tech of The U of Montana
   (MT)

MEDICAL INSURANCE CODING
Baker Coll of Allen Park (MI)

MEDICAL INSURANCE/MEDICAL BILLING
Baker Coll of Allen Park (MI)
Everest U, Tampa (FL)
Everest U, Tampa (FL)

MEDICAL MICROBIOLOGY AND BACTERIOLOGY
Florida National Coll (FL)

MEDICAL OFFICE ASSISTANT
Bryant & Stratton Coll - Wauwatosa
   Campus (WI)
Lewis-Clark State Coll (ID)
Mercy Coll of Health Sciences (IA)

MEDICAL OFFICE COMPUTER SPECIALIST
Baker Coll of Allen Park (MI)

MEDICAL OFFICE MANAGEMENT
Dalton State Coll (GA)
Presentation Coll (SD)
The U of Akron (OH)

MEDICAL RADIOLOGIC TECHNOLOGY
Arkansas State U (AR)
Ball State U (IN)
Bluefield State Coll (WV)
Boise State U (ID)
Coll of Coastal Georgia (GA)
Ferris State U (MI)
Gannon U (PA)
Idaho State U (ID)
Inter American U of Puerto Rico,
   Ponce Campus (PR)
Inter American U of Puerto Rico,
   San Germán Campus (PR)
Keystone Coll (PA)
La Roche Coll (PA)
Mercy Coll of Health Sciences (IA)
Mercy Coll of Northwest Ohio (OH)
Missouri Southern State U (MO)
Morehead State U (KY)
Mount Aloysius Coll (PA)
Newman U (KS)
New York City Coll of Technology of
   the City U of New York (NY)

Northern Kentucky U (KY)
Pennsylvania Coll of Technology
   (PA)
St. Catherine U (MN)
Santa Fe Coll (FL)
Shawnee State U (OH)
Thomas Edison State Coll (NJ)
Trinity Coll of Nursing and Health
   Sciences (IL)
The U of Akron (OH)
U of Arkansas for Medical Sciences
   (AR)
U of Cincinnati (OH)
U of New Mexico (NM)

MEDICAL TRANSCRIPTION
Baker Coll of Flint (MI)
Baker Coll of Jackson (MI)
Dalton State Coll (GA)
U of Cincinnati (OH)

MEETING AND EVENT PLANNING
Cleary U (MI)

MENTAL AND SOCIAL HEALTH SERVICES AND ALLIED PROFESSIONS RELATED
U of Alaska Fairbanks (AK)
U of Maine at Augusta (ME)

MENTAL HEALTH COUNSELING
Lake Superior State U (MI)
The U of Toledo (OH)

MERCHANDISING
International Business Coll, Fort
   Wayne (IN)
The U of Akron (OH)

METAL AND JEWELRY ARTS
Fashion Inst of Technology (NY)

METALLURGICAL TECHNOLOGY
Penn State Altoona (PA)
Penn State Berks (PA)
Penn State Erie, The Behrend Coll
   (PA)

MIDDLE SCHOOL EDUCATION
Dalton State Coll (GA)
U of Cincinnati (OH)
Wright State U (OH)
Young Harris Coll (GA)

MILITARY HISTORY
American Public U System (WV)

MILITARY STUDIES
Hawai`i Pacific U (HI)

MILITARY TECHNOLOGIES AND APPLIED SCIENCES RELATED
Thomas Edison State Coll (NJ)

MINING AND PETROLEUM TECHNOLOGIES RELATED
U of the Virgin Islands (VI)

MINING TECHNOLOGY
Mountain State U (WV)

MISSIONARY STUDIES AND MISSIOLOGY
Corban U (OR)
Faith Baptist Bible Coll and
   Theological Seminary (IA)
Hillsdale Free Will Baptist Coll (OK)

MULTI/INTERDISCIPLINARY STUDIES RELATED
Arkansas Tech U (AR)
Cameron U (OK)
Miami U (OH)
Montana Tech of The U of Montana
   (MT)
Ohio U (OH)

Ohio U–Chillicothe (OH)
Pennsylvania Coll of Technology
   (PA)
Providence Coll (RI)
Thomas Edison State Coll (NJ)
U of Alaska Fairbanks (AK)
U of Arkansas–Fort Smith (AR)
U of Cincinnati (OH)
The U of Toledo (OH)
Utah Valley U (UT)

MUSIC
Alverno Coll (WI)
Clayton State U (GA)
Corban U (OR)
Five Towns Coll (NY)
Hannibal-LaGrange U (MO)
Hillsdale Free Will Baptist Coll (OK)
Methodist U (NC)
Mount Vernon Nazarene U (OH)
Musicians Inst (CA)
Pacific Union Coll (CA)
St. Petersburg Coll (FL)
Southwestern Assemblies of God U
   (TX)
Thomas Edison State Coll (NJ)
Thomas More Coll (KY)
U of Maine at Augusta (ME)
U of Rio Grande (OH)
Utah Valley U (UT)
Villa Maria Coll of Buffalo (NY)
York Coll of Pennsylvania (PA)
Young Harris Coll (GA)

MUSICAL THEATER
Young Harris Coll (GA)

MUSIC MANAGEMENT
Five Towns Coll (NY)
McNally Smith Coll of Music (MN)
Villa Maria Coll of Buffalo (NY)

MUSIC PERFORMANCE
Corban U (OR)
Inter American U of Puerto Rico,
   Metropolitan Campus (PR)
McNally Smith Coll of Music (MN)
Musicians Inst (CA)

MUSIC RELATED
Alverno Coll (WI)
Young Harris Coll (GA)

MUSIC TEACHER EDUCATION
Union Coll (NE)
Wright State U (OH)
Young Harris Coll (GA)

NATURAL RESOURCES/CONSERVATION
State U of New York Coll of
   Environmental Science and
   Forestry (NY)
Suffolk U (MA)

NATURAL RESOURCES MANAGEMENT AND POLICY
Lake Superior State U (MI)
U of Alaska Fairbanks (AK)

NATURAL SCIENCES
Alderson-Broaddus Coll (WV)
Indiana U East (IN)
Lourdes Coll (OH)
Madonna U (MI)
St. Petersburg Coll (FL)
U of Alaska Fairbanks (AK)
The U of Toledo (OH)
Washburn U (KS)
Young Harris Coll (GA)

NETWORK AND SYSTEM ADMINISTRATION
Florida National Coll (FL)
Peirce Coll (PA)
Pennsylvania Coll of Technology
   (PA)

NUCLEAR ENGINEERING TECHNOLOGY
Arkansas Tech U (AR)
Thomas Edison State Coll (NJ)

NUCLEAR MEDICAL TECHNOLOGY
Ball State U (IN)
Dalton State Coll (GA)
Ferris State U (MI)
Molloy Coll (NY)
Santa Fe Coll (FL)
Thomas Edison State Coll (NJ)
U of Cincinnati (OH)
The U of Findlay (OH)

NURSING SCIENCE
National U (CA)
Trinity Coll of Nursing and Health Sciences (IL)

NUTRITION SCIENCES
U of Cincinnati (OH)

OCCUPATIONAL SAFETY AND HEALTH TECHNOLOGY
Columbia Southern U (AL)
Fairmont State U (WV)
Indiana U Southeast (IN)
Lamar U (TX)
U of New Haven (CT)

OCCUPATIONAL THERAPIST ASSISTANT
Baker Coll of Muskegon (MI)
Inter American U of Puerto Rico, Ponce Campus (PR)
Jefferson Coll of Health Sciences (VA)
Maria Coll (NY)
Mountain State U (WV)
Newman U (KS)
Penn State Berks (PA)
Pennsylvania Coll of Technology (PA)
St. Catherine U (MN)
U of Louisiana at Monroe (LA)
U of Puerto Rico at Humacao (PR)
U of Southern Indiana (IN)
Washburn U (KS)

OCCUPATIONAL THERAPY
Coll of Coastal Georgia (GA)
Dalton State Coll (GA)
Keystone Coll (PA)
Shawnee State U (OH)
Southern Adventist U (TN)
Young Harris Coll (GA)

OFFICE MANAGEMENT
Baker Coll of Jackson (MI)
Dalton State Coll (GA)
Emmanuel Coll (GA)
Inter American U of Puerto Rico, Guayama Campus (PR)
Inter American U of Puerto Rico, Ponce Campus (PR)
Lake Superior State U (MI)
Miami U (OH)
Mount Vernon Nazarene U (OH)
Shawnee State U (OH)
Washburn U (KS)

OFFICE OCCUPATIONS AND CLERICAL SERVICES
Bob Jones U (SC)

OPERATIONS MANAGEMENT
Indiana U–Purdue U Fort Wayne (IN)
Indiana U–Purdue U Indianapolis (IN)
Purdue U North Central (IN)

OPTICAL SCIENCES
Indiana U of Pennsylvania (PA)

OPTICIANRY
New York City Coll of Technology of the City U of New York (NY)

OPTOMETRIC TECHNICIAN
Inter American U of Puerto Rico, Ponce Campus (PR)

ORGANIZATIONAL BEHAVIOR
Hawai`i Pacific U (HI)
Regent U (VA)
U of Cincinnati (OH)

ORGANIZATIONAL COMMUNICATION
Creighton U (NE)
Xavier U (OH)

ORGANIZATIONAL LEADERSHIP
AIB Coll of Business (IA)
Atlanta Christian Coll (GA)
Grace Coll (IN)
Huntington U (IN)

ORNAMENTAL HORTICULTURE
Ferris State U (MI)
Vermont Tech Coll (VT)

ORTHOTICS/PROSTHETICS
Baker Coll of Flint (MI)

OUTDOOR EDUCATION
Young Harris Coll (GA)

PAINTING
Pratt Inst (NY)

PARKS, RECREATION AND LEISURE
St. Petersburg Coll (FL)
State U of New York Coll of Technology at Delhi (NY)
U of Maine at Presque Isle (ME)
Young Harris Coll (GA)

PARKS, RECREATION AND LEISURE FACILITIES MANAGEMENT
Coll of Coastal Georgia (GA)
Indiana Tech (IN)
State U of New York Coll of Technology at Delhi (NY)
Webber International U (FL)

PARKS, RECREATION, LEISURE, AND FITNESS STUDIES RELATED
Indiana U Southeast (IN)
Southern Nazarene U (OK)

PASTORAL STUDIES/ COUNSELING
Indiana Wesleyan U (IN)
William Jessup U (CA)

PERCUSSION INSTRUMENTS
Five Towns Coll (NY)

PERSONAL AND CULINARY SERVICES RELATED
U of Cincinnati (OH)

PETROLEUM TECHNOLOGY
Montana State U Billings (MT)
Nicholls State U (LA)

PHARMACY TECHNICIAN
Baker Coll of Flint (MI)
Baker Coll of Jackson (MI)
Baker Coll of Muskegon (MI)
Everest U, Tampa (FL)
Everest U, Tampa (FL)
Madonna U (MI)
Robert Morris U Illinois (IL)

PHILOSOPHY
Coll of Coastal Georgia (GA)
Dalton State Coll (GA)
Methodist U (NC)
Thomas More Coll (KY)
U of Cincinnati (OH)
The U of Tampa (FL)
Utah Valley U (UT)
Young Harris Coll (GA)

PHOTOGRAPHIC AND FILM/ VIDEO TECHNOLOGY
St. John's U (NY)
U of Cincinnati (OH)
Villa Maria Coll of Buffalo (NY)

PHOTOGRAPHY
Albertus Magnus Coll (CT)

Corcoran Coll of Art and Design (DC)
International Academy of Design & Technology (FL)
Pacific Union Coll (CA)
St. Petersburg Coll (FL)
Thomas Edison State Coll (NJ)
U of Maine at Augusta (ME)

PHYSICAL EDUCATION TEACHING AND COACHING
Hillsdale Free Will Baptist Coll (OK)
Methodist U (NC)
U of Rio Grande (OH)
Young Harris Coll (GA)

PHYSICAL SCIENCES
Hillsdale Free Will Baptist Coll (OK)
New York City Coll of Technology of the City U of New York (NY)
U of Cincinnati (OH)
U of the District of Columbia (DC)
Utah Valley U (UT)

PHYSICAL THERAPY
Clarkson Coll (NE)
Coll of Coastal Georgia (GA)
Dalton State Coll (GA)
Southern Adventist U (TN)
Young Harris Coll (GA)

PHYSICAL THERAPY TECHNOLOGY
Arkansas State U (AR)
Arkansas Tech U (AR)
Baker Coll of Flint (MI)
Baker Coll of Muskegon (MI)
Brookline Coll, Phoenix (AZ)
Central Pennsylvania Coll (PA)
Dixie State Coll of Utah (UT)
ECPI Coll of Technology, Virginia Beach (VA)
Idaho State U (ID)
Inter American U of Puerto Rico, Ponce Campus (PR)
Jefferson Coll of Health Sciences (VA)
Louisiana Coll (LA)
Maria Coll (NY)
Mercy Coll of Health Sciences (IA)
Mountain State U (WV)
Mount Aloysius Coll (PA)
Our Lady of the Lake Coll (LA)
St. Catherine U (MN)
St. Petersburg Coll (FL)
Shawnee State U (OH)
Southern Illinois U Carbondale (IL)
U of Cincinnati (OH)
U of Evansville (IN)
U of Indianapolis (IN)
U of Puerto Rico at Humacao (PR)
Villa Maria Coll of Buffalo (NY)
Washburn U (KS)

PHYSICIAN ASSISTANT
Coll of Coastal Georgia (GA)
Dalton State Coll (GA)
Southern Adventist U (TN)

PHYSICS
Coll of Coastal Georgia (GA)
Dalton State Coll (GA)
Idaho State U (ID)
Purdue U North Central (IN)
Rogers State U (OK)
Thomas More Coll (KY)
U of the Virgin Islands (VI)
Utah Valley U (UT)
York Coll of Pennsylvania (PA)
Young Harris Coll (GA)

PIPEFITTING AND SPRINKLER FITTING
State U of New York Coll of Technology at Delhi (NY)

PLANT NURSERY MANAGEMENT
Pennsylvania Coll of Technology (PA)

PLANT PROTECTION AND INTEGRATED PEST MANAGEMENT
North Carolina State U (NC)

PLASTICS AND POLYMER ENGINEERING TECHNOLOGY
Ferris State U (MI)
Penn State Erie, The Behrend Coll (PA)
Pennsylvania Coll of Technology (PA)
Shawnee State U (OH)

POLITICAL SCIENCE AND GOVERNMENT
Adams State Coll (CO)
Coll of Coastal Georgia (GA)
Corban U (OR)
Dalton State Coll (GA)
Holy Cross Coll (IN)
Immaculata U (PA)
Indiana U–Purdue U Fort Wayne (IN)
Methodist U (NC)
Mount St. Mary's Coll (CA)
Thomas More Coll (KY)
U of Cincinnati (OH)
The U of Scranton (PA)
The U of Tampa (FL)
The U of Toledo (OH)
Xavier U (OH)
York Coll of Pennsylvania (PA)
Young Harris Coll (GA)

POLYSOMNOGRAPHY
Mercy Coll of Health Sciences (IA)

PRECISION METAL WORKING RELATED
Montana Tech of The U of Montana (MT)

PRE-DENTISTRY STUDIES
Coll of Coastal Georgia (GA)
Concordia U Wisconsin (WI)
U of Cincinnati (OH)
Young Harris Coll (GA)

PRE-ENGINEERING
Coll of Coastal Georgia (GA)
Dixie State Coll of Utah (UT)
Methodist U (NC)
Newman U (KS)
Niagara U (NY)
Northern State U (SD)
Siena Heights U (MI)
Southern Utah U (UT)
Young Harris Coll (GA)

PRE-LAW STUDIES
Calumet Coll of Saint Joseph (IN)
Ferris State U (MI)
Immaculata U (PA)
Northern Kentucky U (KY)
Peirce Coll (PA)
Thomas More Coll (KY)
U of Cincinnati (OH)
Wayland Baptist U (TX)
Young Harris Coll (GA)

PREMEDICAL STUDIES
Coll of Coastal Georgia (GA)
Concordia U Wisconsin (WI)
U of Cincinnati (OH)
Young Harris Coll (GA)

PRENURSING STUDIES
Anna Maria Coll (MA)
Concordia U Wisconsin (WI)
Keystone Coll (PA)
Lincoln Christian U (IL)
Reinhardt U (GA)
Tabor Coll (KS)

PRE-OPTOMETRY
Young Harris Coll (GA)

PRE-PHARMACY STUDIES
Coll of Coastal Georgia (GA)
Dalton State Coll (GA)
Emmanuel Coll (GA)
Ferris State U (MI)
Keystone Coll (PA)
Madonna U (MI)
U of Cincinnati (OH)
Young Harris Coll (GA)

PRE-VETERINARY STUDIES
Coll of Coastal Georgia (GA)

U of Cincinnati (OH)
Young Harris Coll (GA)

PROFESSIONAL, TECHNICAL, BUSINESS, AND SCIENTIFIC WRITING
Florida National Coll (FL)

PSYCHIATRIC/MENTAL HEALTH SERVICES TECHNOLOGY
Lake Superior State U (MI)
Pennsylvania Coll of Technology (PA)
The U of Toledo (OH)

PSYCHOLOGY
Ashworth Coll (GA)
Chestnut Hill Coll (PA)
Coll of Coastal Georgia (GA)
Corban U (OR)
Dalton State Coll (GA)
Eastern New Mexico U (NM)
Ferris State U (MI)
Fisher Coll (MA)
Hillsdale Free Will Baptist Coll (OK)
Indiana U–Purdue U Fort Wayne (IN)
Liberty U (VA)
Methodist U (NC)
Montana State U Billings (MT)
Muhlenberg Coll (PA)
Rogent U (VA)
Siena Heights U (MI)
Southwestern Assemblies of God U (TX)
Thomas More Coll (KY)
U of Cincinnati (OH)
U of Rio Grande (OH)
The U of Tampa (FL)
Utah Valley U (UT)
Wright State U (OH)
Xavier U (OH)
Young Harris Coll (GA)

PSYCHOLOGY RELATED
Mountain State U (WV)

PUBLIC ADMINISTRATION
Ferris State U (MI)
Florida National Coll (FL)
Indiana U Northwest (IN)
Indiana U–Purdue U Indianapolis (IN)
Indiana U South Bend (IN)
Point Park U (PA)
U of Maine at Augusta (ME)

PUBLIC ADMINISTRATION AND SOCIAL SERVICE PROFESSIONS RELATED
Point Park U (PA)
The U of Akron (OH)

PUBLIC HEALTH
American Public U System (WV)
U of Alaska Fairbanks (AK)
U of Alaska Southeast (AK)

PUBLIC HEALTH EDUCATION AND PROMOTION
U of Cincinnati (OH)

PUBLIC RELATIONS, ADVERTISING, AND APPLIED COMMUNICATION RELATED
John Brown U (AR)
Keystone Coll (PA)

PUBLIC RELATIONS/IMAGE MANAGEMENT
John Brown U (AR)
Xavier U (OH)

QUALITY CONTROL AND SAFETY TECHNOLOGIES RELATED
Lamar U (TX)
Madonna U (MI)

QUALITY CONTROL TECHNOLOGY
Baker Coll of Cadillac (MI)

Baker Coll of Flint (MI)
Baker Coll of Muskegon (MI)

**RADIATION PROTECTION/
HEALTH PHYSICS
TECHNOLOGY**
Indiana U South Bend (IN)
Indiana U Southeast (IN)
Thomas Edison State Coll (NJ)

RADIO AND TELEVISION
Lawrence Technological U (MI)
Northwestern Coll (MN)
Ohio U–Zanesville (OH)
Xavier U (OH)

**RADIO AND TELEVISION
BROADCASTING
TECHNOLOGY**
Lyndon State Coll (VT)
New York Inst of Technology (NY)
Southern Adventist U (TN)

**RADIOLOGIC TECHNOLOGY/
SCIENCE**
Allen Coll (IA)
Baker Coll of Clinton Township (MI)
Baker Coll of Muskegon (MI)
Champlain Coll (VT)
Clarkson Coll (NE)
Coll of St. Joseph (VT)
Dalton State Coll (GA)
Dixie State Coll of Utah (UT)
ECPI Coll of Technology, Virginia
　Beach (VA)
Fairleigh Dickinson U, Metropolitan
　Campus (NJ)
Florida National Coll (FL)
Holy Family U (PA)
Indiana U Kokomo (IN)
Indiana U Northwest (IN)
Indiana U–Purdue U Fort Wayne
　(IN)
Indiana U–Purdue U Indianapolis
　(IN)
Indiana U South Bend (IN)
Indiana U Southeast (IN)
Keystone Coll (PA)
Lewis-Clark State Coll (ID)
Mansfield U of Pennsylvania (PA)
Mesa State Coll (CO)
Montana Tech of The U of Montana
　(MT)
Mountain State U (WV)
Newman U (KS)
Northern Michigan U (MI)
Presentation Coll (SD)
Regis Coll (MA)
St. Petersburg Coll (FL)
Trinity Coll of Nursing and Health
　Sciences (IL)
U of Arkansas–Fort Smith (AR)
U of Rio Grande (OH)
Washburn U (KS)
Widener U (PA)
Xavier U (OH)

**RADIO, TELEVISION, AND
DIGITAL COMMUNICATION
RELATED**
Keystone Coll (PA)
Madonna U (MI)

REAL ESTATE
American Public U System (WV)
Lamar U (TX)
Miami U (OH)
Saint Francis U (PA)

RECEPTIONIST
Baker Coll of Allen Park (MI)

**RECORDING ARTS
TECHNOLOGY**
Five Towns Coll (NY)

**REGISTERED NURSING,
NURSING ADMINISTRATION,
NURSING RESEARCH AND
CLINICAL NURSING RELATED**
Anna Maria Coll (MA)

**REGISTERED NURSING/
REGISTERED NURSE**
Alcorn State U (MS)
Angelo State U (TX)
Anna Maria Coll (MA)
Aquinas Coll (TN)
Arkansas State U (AR)
Atlantic Union Coll (MA)
Baker Coll of Allen Park (MI)
Baker Coll of Auburn Hills (MI)
Baker Coll of Cadillac (MI)
Baker Coll of Clinton Township (MI)
Baker Coll of Flint (MI)
Baker Coll of Muskegon (MI)
Baker Coll of Owosso (MI)
Bethel Coll (IN)
Bluefield State Coll (WV)
Boise State U (ID)
Bryant & Stratton Coll - Wauwatosa
　Campus (WI)
Castleton State Coll (VT)
Clarion U of Pennsylvania (PA)
Coll of Coastal Georgia (GA)
Coll of Saint Mary (NE)
Coll of Staten Island of the City U of
　New York (NY)
Columbia Centro Universitario (PR)
Columbia Coll (MO)
Columbia Coll (PR)
Dalton State Coll (GA)
Dixie State Coll of Utah (UT)
ECPI Coll of Technology, Virginia
　Beach (VA)
Everest U, Tampa (FL)
Fairmont State U (WV)
Ferris State U (MI)
Florida National Coll (FL)
Freed-Hardeman U (TN)
Gardner-Webb U (NC)
Hannibal-LaGrange U (MO)
Idaho State U (ID)
Indiana U East (IN)
Indiana U Kokomo (IN)
Indiana U Northwest (IN)
Indiana U–Purdue U Indianapolis
　(IN)
Inter American U of Puerto Rico,
　Guayama Campus (PR)
Inter American U of Puerto Rico,
　Ponce Campus (PR)
Inter American U of Puerto Rico,
　San Germán Campus (PR)
ITT Tech Inst, South Bend (IN)
ITT Tech Inst (KS)
ITT Tech Inst, Oklahoma City (OK)
Judson Coll (AL)
Kent State U (OH)
Kentucky State U (KY)
Lamar U (TX)
La Roche Coll (PA)
Lincoln Memorial U (TN)
Lincoln U (MO)
Lock Haven U of Pennsylvania (PA)
Maria Coll (NY)
Marshall U (WV)
Mercy Coll of Health Sciences (IA)
Mercy Coll of Northwest Ohio (OH)
Mesa State Coll (CO)
Miami U (OH)
Midway Coll (KY)
Mississippi U for Women (MS)
Montana State U Billings (MT)
Montana Tech of The U of Montana
　(MT)
Morehead State U (KY)
Mount Aloysius Coll (PA)
Mount St. Mary's Coll (CA)
New York City Coll of Technology of
　the City U of New York (NY)
Northern Kentucky U (KY)
North Georgia Coll & State U (GA)
Northwestern State U of Louisiana
　(LA)
Ohio U (OH)
Our Lady of the Lake Coll (LA)
Pacific Union Coll (CA)
Penn State Altoona (PA)
Penn State Berks (PA)
Penn State Erie, The Behrend Coll
　(PA)
Pennsylvania Coll of Technology
　(PA)
Pikeville Coll (KY)
Presentation Coll (SD)
Purdue U North Central (IN)
Regis Coll (MA)
Reinhardt U (GA)

Rivier Coll (NH)
Robert Morris U Illinois (IL)
Rogers State U (OK)
St. Petersburg Coll (FL)
Santa Fe Coll (FL)
Shawnee State U (OH)
Southern Adventist U (TN)
Southern Arkansas U–Magnolia
　(AR)
Southern Vermont Coll (VT)
State U of New York Coll of
　Technology at Delhi (NY)
Sul Ross State U (TX)
Thomas U (GA)
Trinity Coll of Nursing and Health
　Sciences (IL)
Troy U (AL)
U of Arkansas–Fort Smith (AR)
U of Charleston (WV)
U of Cincinnati (OH)
U of Guam (GU)
U of Maine at Augusta (ME)
U of Mobile (AL)
U of New England (ME)
U of Pittsburgh at Bradford (PA)
U of Rio Grande (OH)
The U of South Dakota (SD)
U of the Virgin Islands (VI)
The U of Toledo (OH)
Utah Valley U (UT)
Vermont Tech Coll (VT)
Western Kentucky U (KY)
Young Harris Coll (GA)

**REHABILITATION AND
THERAPEUTIC PROFESSIONS
RELATED**
U of Cincinnati (OH)

RELIGIOUS EDUCATION
Apex School of Theology (NC)
Calvary Bible Coll and Theological
　Seminary (MO)
Cincinnati Christian U (OH)
Hillsdale Free Will Baptist Coll (OK)
Kuyper Coll (MI)
Methodist U (NC)

RELIGIOUS/SACRED MUSIC
Cincinnati Christian U (OH)
Corban U (OR)
Dallas Baptist U (TX)
Hillsdale Free Will Baptist Coll (OK)
Immaculata U (PA)
Indiana Wesleyan U (IN)
Mount Vernon Nazarene U (OH)

RELIGIOUS STUDIES
Atlantic Union Coll (MA)
Brewton-Parker Coll (GA)
Calumet Coll of Saint Joseph (IN)
Concordia Coll–New York (NY)
Corban U (OR)
Holy Apostles Coll and Seminary
　(CT)
Huntington U (IN)
Liberty U (VA)
Lourdes Coll (OH)
Madonna U (MI)
Missouri Baptist U (MO)
Mount Marty Coll (SD)
Mount Vernon Nazarene U (OH)
Northwest U (WA)
Presentation Coll (SD)
Southern Adventist U (TN)
Thomas More Coll (KY)
The U of Findlay (OH)
Xavier U (OH)
Young Harris Coll (GA)

RESPIRATORY CARE THERAPY
Boise State U (ID)
Coll of Coastal Georgia (GA)
Dakota State U (SD)
Dalton State Coll (GA)
Dixie State Coll of Utah (UT)
Ferris State U (MI)
Gannon U (PA)
Hannibal-LaGrange U (MO)
Idaho State U (ID)
Indiana U Northwest (IN)
Indiana U South Bend (IN)
Jefferson Coll of Health Sciences
　(VA)
Lamar U (TX)

Mansfield U of Pennsylvania (PA)
Molloy Coll (NY)
Morehead State U (KY)
Newman U (KS)
Northern Kentucky U (KY)
St. Petersburg Coll (FL)
Santa Fe Coll (FL)
Shawnee State U (OH)
Southern Adventist U (TN)
Thomas Edison State Coll (NJ)
Trinity Coll of Nursing and Health
　Sciences (IL)
The U of Akron (OH)
U of Arkansas for Medical Sciences
　(AR)
U of Cincinnati (OH)
U of Pittsburgh at Johnstown (PA)
U of Southern Indiana (IN)
U of the District of Columbia (DC)
The U of Toledo (OH)
Vermont Tech Coll (VT)
Washburn U (KS)
York Coll of Pennsylvania (PA)

**RESPIRATORY THERAPY
TECHNICIAN**
Florida National Coll (FL)
Northern Michigan U (MI)

**RESTAURANT, CULINARY,
AND CATERING
MANAGEMENT**
Arkansas Tech U (AR)
Bob Jones U (SC)
Ferris State U (MI)
St. Petersburg Coll (FL)
State U of New York Coll of
　Technology at Delhi (NY)

**RESTAURANT/FOOD
SERVICES MANAGEMENT**
Pennsylvania Coll of Technology
　(PA)
The U of Akron (OH)

RETAILING
Stevens Inst of Business & Arts
　(MO)

RETAIL MANAGEMENT
Penn Foster Coll (AZ)

**RHETORIC AND
COMPOSITION**
Dalton State Coll (GA)
Ferris State U (MI)

ROBOTICS TECHNOLOGY
Indiana U–Purdue U Indianapolis
　(IN)
Pennsylvania Coll of Technology
　(PA)
Purdue U (IN)
U of Rio Grande (OH)

RUSSIAN
Idaho State U (ID)

**SALES AND MARKETING/
MARKETING AND
DISTRIBUTION TEACHER
EDUCATION**
Wright State U (OH)

**SALES, DISTRIBUTION, AND
MARKETING OPERATIONS**
AIB Coll of Business (IA)
Baker Coll of Flint (MI)
Baker Coll of Jackson (MI)
Dalton State Coll (GA)
Minnesota School of Business–
　Blaine (MN)
The U of Findlay (OH)

**SCIENCE TEACHER
EDUCATION**
Wright State U (OH)

**SCIENCE TECHNOLOGIES
RELATED**
Madonna U (MI)
Maria Coll (NY)

Ohio Valley U (WV)
U of Alaska Fairbanks (AK)
U of Alaska Southeast (AK)
U of Cincinnati (OH)

SECONDARY EDUCATION
Dalton State Coll (GA)
Ferris State U (MI)
Mountain State U (WV)
Ohio U–Chillicothe (OH)
Rogers State U (OK)
U of Cincinnati (OH)
Utah Valley U (UT)
Young Harris Coll (GA)

**SECURITIES SERVICES
ADMINISTRATION**
Davenport U, Grand Rapids (MI)
Herzing U (GA)

**SECURITY AND LOSS
PREVENTION**
Ashworth Coll (GA)
John Jay Coll of Criminal Justice of
　the City U of New York (NY)

SELLING SKILLS AND SALES
Inter American U of Puerto Rico,
　San Germán Campus (PR)
The U of Akron (OH)

SHEET METAL TECHNOLOGY
Montana State U Billings (MT)

**SIGN LANGUAGE
INTERPRETATION AND
TRANSLATION**
Bethel Coll (IN)
Cincinnati Christian U (OH)
Mount Aloysius Coll (PA)
St. Catherine U (MN)
U of Louisville (KY)

**SMALL BUSINESS
ADMINISTRATION**
Lewis-Clark State Coll (ID)
The U of Akron (OH)

SOCIAL SCIENCES
Campbellsville U (KY)
Corban U (OR)
Divine Word Coll (IA)
Faulkner U (AL)
Fisher Coll (MA)
Hillsdale Free Will Baptist Coll (OK)
Long Island U, Brooklyn Campus
　(NY)
Ohio U–Zanesville (OH)
Shawnee State U (OH)
Southwestern Assemblies of God U
　(TX)
State U of New York Coll of
　Technology at Delhi (NY)
State U of New York Empire State
　Coll (NY)
Trine U (IN)
U of Cincinnati (OH)
The U of Findlay (OH)
U of Maine at Augusta (ME)
U of Sioux Falls (SD)
U of Southern Indiana (IN)
The U of Toledo (OH)
Valparaiso U (IN)
Wayland Baptist U (TX)

SOCIAL WORK
Dalton State Coll (GA)
Elizabethtown Coll (PA)
Ferris State U (MI)
Methodist U (NC)
Northern State U (SD)
Suffolk U (MA)
U of Cincinnati (OH)
U of Rio Grande (OH)
The U of Toledo (OH)
Wright State U (OH)
Youngstown State U (OH)

SOCIAL WORK RELATED
The U of Akron (OH)

SOCIOLOGY
Coll of Coastal Georgia (GA)

Dalton State Coll (GA)
Grand View U (IA)
Holy Cross Coll (IN)
Lourdes Coll (OH)
Marymount Manhattan Coll (NY)
Methodist U (NC)
Montana State U Billings (MT)
Thomas More Coll (KY)
U of Rio Grande (OH)
The U of Scranton (PA)
The U of Tampa (FL)
Wright State U (OH)
Xavier U (OH)
Young Harris Coll (GA)

SOLAR ENERGY TECHNOLOGY
Pennsylvania Coll of Technology
(PA)

SPANISH
Chestnut Hill Coll (PA)
Holy Cross Coll (IN)
Immaculata U (PA)
Indiana U–Purdue U Fort Wayne
(IN)
Methodist U (NC)
Thomas More Coll (KY)
U of Cincinnati (OH)
The U of Tampa (FL)
Xavier U (OH)
Young Harris Coll (GA)

SPECIAL EDUCATION
Edinboro U of Pennsylvania (PA)
Montana State U Billings (MT)
U of Cincinnati (OH)

SPECIAL EDUCATION RELATED
Minot State U (ND)

SPECIAL PRODUCTS MARKETING
Lamar U (TX)

SPEECH COMMUNICATION AND RHETORIC
Albertus Magnus Coll (CT)
American Public U System (WV)
Andrew Jackson U (AL)
Baker Coll of Jackson (MI)
Central Pennsylvania Coll (PA)
Coll of Mount St. Joseph (OH)
Corban U (OR)
Indiana Wesleyan U (IN)
John Brown U (AR)
Lyndon State Coll (VT)
Presentation Coll (SD)
Thomas Edison State Coll (NJ)
Trine U (IN)
Tulane U (LA)
U of Cincinnati (OH)
U of New Haven (CT)
U of Rio Grande (OH)
Utah Valley U (UT)
Wright State U (OH)

SPEECH-LANGUAGE PATHOLOGY
Baker Coll of Muskegon (MI)

SPORT AND FITNESS ADMINISTRATION/ MANAGEMENT
AIB Coll of Business (IA)
Garrett Coll (MD)
Lake Superior State U (MI)
Mount Vernon Nazarene U (OH)
U of Cincinnati (OH)

STRINGED INSTRUMENTS
Five Towns Coll (NY)

SUBSTANCE ABUSE/ ADDICTION COUNSELING
Indiana Wesleyan U (IN)
Newman U (KS)
St. Petersburg Coll (FL)
The U of Akron (OH)
The U of Toledo (OH)
Washburn U (KS)

SURGICAL TECHNOLOGY
Baker Coll of Clinton Township (MI)
Baker Coll of Flint (MI)
Baker Coll of Jackson (MI)
Baker Coll of Muskegon (MI)
ECPI Coll of Technology, Virginia
Beach (VA)
Everest U, Tampa (FL)
Lincoln U (MO)
Mercy Coll of Health Sciences (IA)
Montana State U Billings (MT)
Mount Aloysius Coll (PA)
Northern Michigan U (MI)
Our Lady of the Lake Coll (LA)
Pennsylvania Coll of Technology
(PA)
Presentation Coll (SD)
Robert Morris U Illinois (IL)
Trinity Coll of Nursing and Health
Sciences (IL)
The U of Akron (OH)
U of Arkansas for Medical Sciences
(AR)
U of Arkansas–Fort Smith (AR)
U of Cincinnati (OH)
U of Pittsburgh at Johnstown (PA)
Washburn U (KS)

SURVEYING TECHNOLOGY
Ferris State U (MI)
Pennsylvania Coll of Technology
(PA)
The U of Akron (OH)

SYSTEM, NETWORKING, AND LAN/WAN MANAGEMENT
Baker Coll of Auburn Hills (MI)
Dakota State U (SD)
Herzing U (GA)
International Business Coll, Fort
Wayne (IN)
ITT Tech Inst, Tempe (AZ)
ITT Tech Inst, Clovis (CA)
ITT Tech Inst, Concord (CA)
ITT Tech Inst, Corona (CA)
ITT Tech Inst, South Bend (IN)
ITT Tech Inst (KS)
ITT Tech Inst, Lexington (KY)
ITT Tech Inst (MS)
ITT Tech Inst, Springfield (MO)
ITT Tech Inst, Charlotte (NC)
ITT Tech Inst, Oklahoma City (OK)
Stratford U, Falls Church (VA)

TEACHER ASSISTANT/AIDE
Alverno Coll (WI)
Dordt Coll (IA)
Johnson Bible Coll (TN)
Lamar U (TX)
U of Alaska Fairbanks (AK)
Valparaiso U (IN)

TEACHING ASSISTANTS/AIDES RELATED
Trevecca Nazarene U (TN)

TECHNICAL TEACHER EDUCATION
New York Inst of Technology (NY)
Northern Kentucky U (KY)
Western Kentucky U (KY)

TELECOMMUNICATIONS TECHNOLOGY
ECPI Coll of Technology, Virginia
Beach (VA)
Inter American U of Puerto Rico,
Bayamón Campus (PR)
New York City Coll of Technology of
the City U of New York (NY)
Pace U (NY)
St. John's U (NY)
Skyline Coll (VA)

TERRORISM AND COUNTERTERRORISM OPERATIONS
American Public U System (WV)

THEATER DESIGN AND TECHNOLOGY
Johnson State Coll (VT)
U of Rio Grande (OH)

THEOLOGICAL AND MINISTERIAL STUDIES RELATED
California Christian Coll (CA)
Lincoln Christian U (IL)

THEOLOGY
Appalachian Bible Coll (WV)
Briar Cliff U (IA)
Creighton U (NE)
Immaculata U (PA)
Missouri Baptist U (MO)
Sacred Heart Major Seminary (MI)

THERAPEUTIC RECREATION
U of Southern Maine (ME)

TOOL AND DIE TECHNOLOGY
Ferris State U (MI)

TOURISM AND TRAVEL SERVICES MANAGEMENT
AIB Coll of Business (IA)
Baker Coll of Flint (MI)
Baker Coll of Muskegon (MI)
Fisher Coll (MA)
Florida National Coll (FL)
International Business Coll, Fort
Wayne (IN)
State U of New York Coll of
Technology at Delhi (NY)
Stevens Inst of Business & Arts
(MO)
The U of Akron (OH)

TOURISM PROMOTION
Florida National Coll (FL)

TRADE AND INDUSTRIAL TEACHER EDUCATION
Cincinnati Christian U (OH)
Murray State U (KY)

TRANSPORTATION AND MATERIALS MOVING RELATED
Baker Coll of Flint (MI)
The U of Toledo (OH)

TURF AND TURFGRASS MANAGEMENT
North Carolina State U (NC)
U of Massachusetts Amherst (MA)

URBAN STUDIES/AFFAIRS
Beulah Heights U (GA)
U of Cincinnati (OH)

VEHICLE AND VEHICLE PARTS AND ACCESSORIES MARKETING
Pennsylvania Coll of Technology
(PA)

VEHICLE MAINTENANCE AND REPAIR TECHNOLOGIES RELATED
Pennsylvania Coll of Technology
(PA)

VETERINARY/ANIMAL HEALTH TECHNOLOGY
Baker Coll of Cadillac (MI)
Baker Coll of Jackson (MI)
Baker Coll of Muskegon (MI)
Baker Coll of Port Huron (MI)
International Business Coll, Fort
Wayne (IN)
Lincoln Memorial U (TN)
Medaille Coll (NY)
Minnesota School of Business–
Blaine (MN)
Morehead State U (KY)
Mount Ida Coll (MA)
Northwestern State U of Louisiana
(LA)
Penn Foster Coll (AZ)
Purdue U (IN)
St. Petersburg Coll (FL)
State U of New York Coll of
Technology at Delhi (NY)
Sul Ross State U (TX)
Thomas Edison State Coll (NJ)
U of Cincinnati (OH)
U of Maine at Augusta (ME)
Vermont Tech Coll (VT)

VOICE AND OPERA
Five Towns Coll (NY)

WATER QUALITY AND WASTEWATER TREATMENT MANAGEMENT AND RECYCLING TECHNOLOGY
Lake Superior State U (MI)
Mesa State Coll (CO)
U of the District of Columbia (DC)
Western Kentucky U (KY)

WATER, WETLANDS, AND MARINE RESOURCES MANAGEMENT
Keystone Coll (PA)

WEB/MULTIMEDIA MANAGEMENT AND WEBMASTER
American Public U System (WV)
ECPI Coll of Technology, Virginia
Beach (VA)
Indiana Tech (IN)
Lewis-Clark State Coll (ID)
Montana Tech of The U of Montana
(MT)
Mountain State U (WV)
St. Petersburg Coll (FL)

WEB PAGE, DIGITAL/ MULTIMEDIA AND INFORMATION RESOURCES DESIGN
Baker Coll of Allen Park (MI)
DeVry U, Phoenix (AZ)
DeVry U, Pomona (CA)
DeVry U, Westminster (CO)
DeVry U, Miramar (FL)
DeVry U, Orlando (FL)
DeVry U, Decatur (GA)
DeVry U, Chicago (IL)
DeVry U, Kansas City (MO)
DeVry U, North Brunswick (NJ)
DeVry U, Columbus (OH)
DeVry U, Fort Washington (PA)
DeVry U, Houston (TX)
DeVry U, Irving (TX)
DeVry U, Arlington (VA)
DeVry U, Federal Way (WA)
DeVry U Online (IL)
Florida National Coll (FL)
Idaho State U (ID)
International Academy of Design &
Technology (FL)
ITT Tech Inst, Lexington (KY)
St. Petersburg Coll (FL)
Thomas More Coll (KY)
Utah Valley U (UT)

WELDING TECHNOLOGY
Ferris State U (MI)
Idaho State U (ID)
Lamar U (TX)
Lewis-Clark State Coll (ID)
Pennsylvania Coll of Technology
(PA)
State U of New York Coll of
Technology at Delhi (NY)
The U of Toledo (OH)

WILDLIFE, FISH AND WILDLANDS SCIENCE AND MANAGEMENT
Garrett Coll (MD)
Mountain State U (WV)

WOMEN'S MINISTRY'
Corban U (OR)

WOMEN'S STUDIES'
Fisher Coll (MA)
Indiana U–Purdue U Fort Wayne
(IN)

WOODWIND INSTRUMENTS
Five Towns Coll (NY)

WOODWORKING
Burlington Coll (VT)
State U of New York Coll of
Technology at Delhi (NY)

WORD PROCESSING
Baker Coll of Allen Park (MI)
Florida National Coll (FL)

WRITING
The U of Tampa (FL)

YOUTH MINISTRY
Calvary Bible Coll and Theological
Seminary (MO)
Corban U (OR)

Alphabetical Listing of Two-Year Colleges

Special Advertising Section

Thomas Jefferson University School of Population Health

University of Medicine & Dentistry of New Jersey

Saint Louis University

St. Mary's University

The Winston Preparatory Schools

Learn from a National Leader in
Population Health

Jefferson School of Population Health

- Master of Public Health (MPH); CEPH accredited

- PhD in Population Health Sciences

Online programs

- Master of Science in Health Policy (MS-HP)

- Master of Science in Healthcare Quality and Safety (MS-HQS)

- Master of Science in Chronic Care Management (MS-CCM)

- Certificates in Public Health, Health Policy, Healthcare Quality and Safety, Chronic Care Management

Population health – putting health and health care together

215-503-0174

www.jefferson.edu/population_health/ads.cfm

Jefferson
School of Population Health

THOMAS JEFFERSON UNIVERSITY

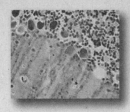

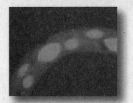
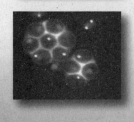

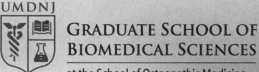
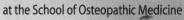

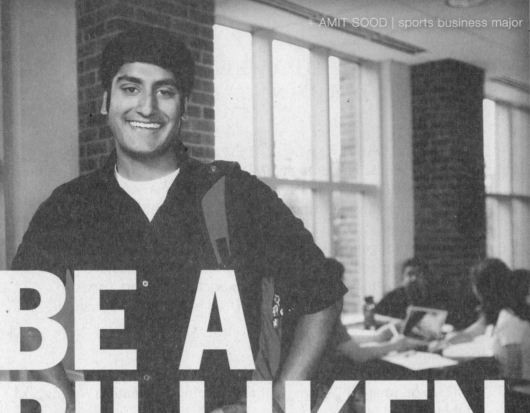
+ AMIT SOOD | sports business major

BE A BILLIKEN

Find out how the breadth and depth of the fully accredited undergraduate and graduate programs at Saint Louis University's **JOHN COOK SCHOOL OF BUSINESS** will give you the knowledge and tools necessary for success in today's global and highly technical business world.

—+ Visit **BeABilliken.com** for more information on our undergraduate business programs and to see what life is like as a Billiken.

To learn about our graduate business programs, attend an open house or visit **gradbiz.slu.edu.** +—————

SAINT LOUIS UNIVERSITY

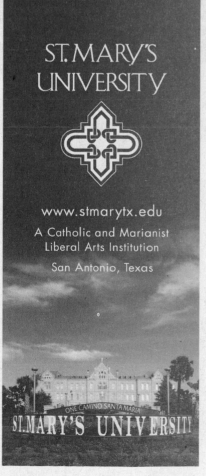

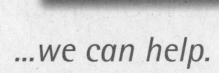

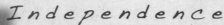